GW00598964

Air-Britain News

Civil Aircraft Registers of
The British Isles
2019

Sales Department:
Unit 1A, Munday Works Industrial Estate,
58-66 Morley Road, Tonbridge TN9 1RA
e-mail: sales@air-britain.co.uk
www.air-britain.co.uk/actbooks/catalog

Membership Enquiries:
1 Rose Cottages, 179 Penn Road,
Hazlemere, Bucks HP15 7NE
e-mail: membership@air-britain.co.uk

For full details of the books and magazines we publish,
and how to join Air-Britain, please visit us at www.air-britain.com

ISBN 978-0-85130-517-2

Printed by Bell & Bain Ltd,
Thornliebank, Glasgow G46 7UQ

COVER PHOTOGRAPHS:

Front: Comper Swift G-ACTF captured on a blue-sky day displaying at Old Warden on 2nd September 2018. (Andrew Goldsmith)

Rear: Top: Cirrus SR22T Platinum edition 2-RORO on arrival at Denham on 21st August 2018. (Brian G Nichols)

       Centre: British Airways Boeing 747-436 G-BYGC in BOAC anniversary retro colour scheme departing London-Heathrow on 23rd February 2019. (Laura Watts)

       Bottom: McDonnell Douglas MD-900 Explorer G-SASR operating as an Air Ambulance with Specialist Aviation Services in May 2018. (Barry Ambrose).

CIVIL AIRCRAFT REGISTERS OF THE BRITISH ISLES 2019

Air-Britain supports the fight against terrorism and the efforts of the Police
and other Authorities in protecting airports and airfields from criminal activity.

If you see anything suspicious do not hesitate to call the
Anti-Terrorist Hotline 0800 789321
or alert a Police Officer.

INTRODUCTION AND EDITORIAL

Welcome to the latest edition of the *Civil Aircraft Registers of the British Isles*. As usual the content is a collaborative effort: the UK Register data in SECTION 1 comes from the 'Database Team' which comprises **Peter Budden**, **Richard Cawsey**, **Don & Paul Hewins**, **Alan Johnson**, **Mel Kirby**, **Bernard Martin**, **Stuart McDiarmid**, **Dave Reid** and **Barrie Womersley**. The section is based on the weekly updates from the Civil Aviation Authority (CAA) records posted on the G-INFO database as provided by **Dave Reid**. **Barrie Womersley** maintains the list of bases in the UK while **Alan Johnson** inputs details of new registrations and cancellations, and also produces the monthly section for *Air-Britain News* and provides much additional info to the raw data provided by the CAA with the assistance of **Bernard Martin** who provides a huge amount of background knowledge of the UK Register and supporting data for both *Air-Britain News* and this publication. **Peter Budden** looks after those UK aircraft still extant, short-lived registrations that have come and gone in the period between the publication of last year's book and this one, and known reservations.

Richard Cawsey, in conjunction with the British Gliding Association, provides details of those gliders still operating under BGA auspices (SECTION 2), and of those registered on the main CAA register covered in SECTION 1, while **Lloyd Robinson**, who acts as Registrar for the organisation, has provided information on the AHUK (formerly BAPC) register (SECTION 3). **Don Hewins** updates the Republic of Ireland register (SECTION 4) as well as the Guernsey and Jersey registers (SECTIONS 6 & 7); while **Peter Budden** looks after the Isle of Man register (SECTION 5). Details of those Overseas-registered aircraft that are located in the UK & Ireland (SECTION 8) are provided by **Paul Hewins**.

The innovations we introduced last year to the layout of sections within the book appear to have been well received. SECTION 1 covers all those aircraft current on the UK register, as of 31 March 2019 (registrations are indicated in **bold**). Extant but not current airframes, known to exist since January 2014, are listed with non-bold registrations. Aircraft that have been registered and cancelled during the period since the last edition of this book are indicated with a star (★), and known reservations, mostly but not exclusively airliners, are indicated with brackets. Finally, those airframes held by musems but not actually current have a small (M) indication – the few that are still on the register are marked this way but also appear with bold registration. SECTION 2 covers Gliders including a decode of competition codes, plus the Irish glider register. SECTION 3 provides details of the Aviation Heritage UK (formerly British Aircraft Preservation Council) register, plus those of Ireland. SECTION 4 covers the Irish register, and SECTION 5 covers the current Isle of Man register as well as those registered and deleted during the year in both using the same coding as Section 1. The IoM register does not cover commercial aircraft in airline service but it does allow such aircraft to be registered between leases or when stored. SECTION 6 covers the Guernsey allocations, again with the same information while SECTION 7 addresses the Jersey register, both of which have the same exclusion on airliners in commercial service. SECTION 8 lists overseas registered aircraft based in the UK and Ireland along with a listing of those removed since the last edition while SECTION 9 provides a basic listing of aircraft held in museums and collections in the UK, plus a short International section which has been restricted to those aircraft that carry British civil registrations for reasons of space. Finally, SECTION 10 contains a selection of short appendices, with Overseas Registration Prefixes, the Military Serials Decode, 'B' Conditions Prefixes and a listing of aircraft carrying fictitious or no external markings.

There are tabs down the side of the page which we hope help readers navigate to the various sections in the book, and the movement of the index of each section – these now follow their relevant sections. For 2019, these have been redesigned into a three-column format and a certain amount of 'gardening' has been done to make them easier to use.

A fair percentage of the UK Register is devoted to amateur kit-built aircraft, microlights or hot air balloons. This is the area where the CAA devolves specific regulatory tasks to other bodies although overall responsibility for safety regulation remains with them. The devolved segment is a broad one and covers four large groups involved in recreational aviation. These are the British Balloon and Airship Club (BBAC) which governs balloon and airship activity, the Light Aircraft Association (LAA), which regulates amateur-built, vintage and other aircraft able to operate on a Permit to Fly, and the British Microlight Aircraft Association (BMAA) which regulates microlight activity; the fourth body, which is outside the subject of this book, is the British Parachute Association (BPA) which controls parachuting. As the majority of balloons and airships are produced commercially we are more concerned with the role of the BMAA and LAA. The BMAA is responsible for regulating those microlights which meet certain criteria – they must either have a wing that is flexible, and can move relative to the main body of the aircraft, or a fixed wing that is rigidly attached to the aircraft's body. Microlights operate on a Permit to Fly rather than a CofA and a growing number are classified as SSDR (Single Seat De-Regulated), which is an extension of the old Sub-115kg class. SSDR microlights must meet certain criteria as listed under the User Guide and in addition the aircraft and pilot must comply with the other requirements of the ANO (e.g. insurance, markings, licences, logbooks etc.) Some owners have permanently removed second seats to meet these requirements and the onus is now on them to determine the aircraft's airworthinesss; under the proposed new ANO – there will be no option to remain under a Permit to Fly reqime.

The LAA is responsible for the supervision of aircraft that are amateur-built by individuals, as opposed to commercial manufacturers. They operate on a Permit to Fly rather than a Certificate of Airworthiness (CofA). The LAA also regulates a significant number of microlight, vintage and classic aircraft, these being mainly types that do not qualify for an International Civil Aviation Organisation (ICAO) compliant CofA because of the demise of the manufacturer or other design authority. They have recently gained approval for dealing with jet engines.

Many amateur-built aircraft and microlights are now assembled by owners from kits of components supplied by commercial manufacturers to aid construction (the key is that 51% of the work over a minimum of 500 hours is performed by the 'builder'). To keep within the regulations it is important to avoid identifying an aircraft as a factory-built specimen as this would exclude it from the BMAA and LAA Permit system and require it to hold an ICAO compliant CofA. Thereby, both the BMAA and LAA have introduced their own dedicated plans numbering system designed to identify, specifically, those aircraft falling under their devolved regulatory powers. It is this BMAA and LAA reference which is used when a builder-owner seeks to register his aircraft with the CAA and it is this reference which is shown on the CAA's G-INFO database. Unfortunately for the aviation historian, this methodology has the effect of obscuring the real commercial construction (kit) number of the aircraft. Our unstinting thanks are due to those devoted members, notably Bernard Martin and Barry Taylor, who for a number of years have set out to establish and record the missing details by either developing commercial contacts or by physical examination of such aircraft. A look at SECTION 1 shows that there are still a number of new aircraft where little prime identity data is recorded and readers could assist in providing missing details if they find themselves in a legitimate position to ascertain them.

As explained in previous editions, many airlines now operate from multiple bases in the UK & overseas (e.g. easyJet and Ryanair) so all their fleet is shown at their nominal home-base but this is bracketed (this also applies to some executive aircraft & helicopter oprators). Some helicopters have a bracketed base where their 'helipad' is now known and the operators address is shown.

The Book Publication Committee is very grateful to all the following contributors this year. Our thanks go to Pete Bish, Dave Bougourd, Peter Budden, Ian Burnett, Mike Cain, Ian Callier, Richard Cawsey, Colman Corcoran, Terry Dann, Jeremy Day, Kevin Dupuy, Phil Dunnington, Don & Paul Hewins, Nigel Hitchman, Alan Johnson, Nigel & Phil Kemp, Mel Kirby, Bernard Martin, Stuart McDiarmid, Ken Parfitt, Dave Partington, Nigel Ponsford, Dave Reid, Bob Sauvary, Tony Smith, Martyn Steggalls, Barry V Taylor, Barrie Towey and to all the editors of other Air-Britain publications and those members who supply regular updates either direct or via various web-sites (and to anyone we may have inadvertently missed).

Any updates, corrections, amendments or additional information will appear in the monthly 'Around and About' section of *Air-Britain News* and can also be sent to the contact details below.

Sue Bushell
Editor, Civil Aircraft Registers of the British Isles
10 Crosslands
Fringford
Oxon OX27 8DF
Email: abneditor@air-britain.co.uk

A BRIEF HISTORICAL LOOK AT THE UK's CIVIL AIRCRAFT REGULATIONS

BACKGROUND

The Air Board was formed in May 1916 and established the Civil Aerial Transport Committee (CATC) a year later. The CATC's primary brief was to report on the measures necessary to develop aviation for civil and commercial purposes. Meantime the Air Force Bill received the Royal Assent in November 1917 leading to the creation of the Air Council and the Air Ministry. Although the Armistice was negotiated in November 1918, official restrictions on civil flying were not lifted as, technically, a state of war continued until the signing of the Peace Treaty in July 1919.

During the ensuing years, and largely instigated by de Havillands, there was considerable pressure on the Air Ministry to relax control of private aviation. In July 1933 the Secretary of State, Marquess of Londonderry appointed an independent committee under Lord Gorrell, chairman of the Royal Aeronautical Society. The Committee was charged 'To examine the requirements of the present air navigation regulations, with particular reference to those governing private flying in such matters as certificates of airworthiness; to consider whether, and in what respects, the present system of control by the Air Ministry should be modified by way of devolution or otherwise; to make recommendations in regard to these and any cognate questions which might remitted to them by the Secretary of State'. Initial investigations seemed to be directed towards opposing proposals for the UK to relinquish control to an international authority as discussed at a League of Nation's Disarmament Conference held at Geneva earlier that year. The UK Government had no desire to follow such thinking: although the country was in depression private flying continued to progress. In fact the early 1930s saw an expansion of private flying with an increase in licensed civil aerodromes including several new municipal airfields and, in addition, there was a steady growth in international and internal air services. But there was little increase in privately owned aeroplanes: in 1933 there were just 1055 aircraft on the Register of Aircraft, of which only 400 were so defined.

The report of the Gorrell Committee on 'Control of Private Flying' was issued in July 1934. The Committee was not unanimous in its findings: one member wanted control to remain with the Air Ministry whilst two others recommended immediate divorce in every aspect of civil aviation. Broadly the Committee agreed that airworthiness regulations and the system of checking design and construction should be handed to an independent body to be named 'The Air Registration Board'. The Air Ministry duly agreed that the new body would control the system of approved firms, airworthiness requirements, modification procedure, renewal of Certificates of Airworthiness, inspection certificates and supervision of competency of ground engineers. It was also agreed in principle that foreign C of As should have validity on a reciprocal basis. Although required for club aircraft the Air Council was prepared to make them optional for private flying and aerial work. Third party insurance became mandatory. Interestingly, gliders came under these general provisions.

In 1936 the Air Navigation Bill became law and provided for the formation of an Air Registration Board (ARB) based on the Gorrell Report proposal that the Certification of Airworthiness of civil aircraft should devolve upon a 'statutory autonomous board' formed from the British Corporation Register and Lloyds Register. The constituent groups were drawn from the Society of British Aircraft Constructors (SBAC), the two Insurance registers, commercial operators, and the Royal Aeronautical Society. The board was registered as a company on 26th February 1937. By 1939 the ARB's responsibilites had grown. The Register of Aircraft now contained 1,725 machines and some 75% were airworthy whilst several prototypes were flying under 'B' Conditions procedures, see Section 8 Part 3.

Despite the title the ARB had little to do with the issue of Certificates of Registration for civil aircraft. This was left to the Ministry of Civil Aviation which was created in 1944. In the mid 1950s this department merged with the Ministry of Transport to become the Ministry of Transport and Civil Aviation (MTCA). Responsibility passed through a series of departments before the CAA was born. In 1967 the Government set up a committee under the chairmanship of Sir Ronald Edwards to inquire into Britain's civil air transport. The committee's findings were published in 1969 and included a recommendation to establish a civil aviation authority. The Civil Aviation Act of 1971 created the new authority, as a public corporation, and it assumed full responsibilities on 1 April 1972. Thus, the Air Registration Board was embodied into the new CAA. Originally the CAA was established as an independent specialist aviation regulator and provider of air traffic services but following the separation of National Air Traffic Services from the CAA in 2001, the CAA now functions solely in the former role with all civil aviation regulatory functions (economic regulation, airspace policy, safety regulation and consumer protection) integrated within a single specialist body. It should be noted that the UK Government requires that the CAA's costs are met entirely from the charges on those whom it regulates. Unlike many other countries there is no direct Government funding of the CAA's work.

REGISTRATION OF AIRCRAFT

There were no international regulations controlling the registration of civil aircraft within the United Kingdom at the end of the First World War. Consequently the Air Ministry's Civil Air Department specified a system of temporary registration marks in May 1919 but this practice prevailed only until July of that year. Two temporary registers were established for (i) military aircraft sold for civil purposes and already bearing Service serials – existing aircraft would be allocated their serials as registration marks with the Service ring markings obliterated and (ii) new aircraft and those built from spares – they were allocated marks in a special Service sequence commencing at K100. Subsequently, a number of these aircraft were re-allocated registrations in the first permanent register which replaced the two temporary registers. This was inaugurated on 31st July 1919 and ran until 29th July 1928 when the registration G-EBZZ had been issued – see SECTION 1, Part 1. Meantime, the civil use of Airships and Balloons came under the supplementary air traffic regulations of the Air Navigation Act 1911-1919. and a separate lighter-than-air register series, G-FAAA to G-FAAZ, was established until the end of 1928.

With the growth of international civil aviation the Director-General of Civil Aviation decided to terminate the first series and he authorised a new sequence of registration marks commencing at G-AAAA including airships and balloons. This second permanent register was introduced retrospectively from 30th July 1928 and, in effect, continues today – see SECTION 1 Part 2. Registrations were usually allocated in alphabetical sequence until the late 1970s although there have been numerous sporadic exceptions to this rule throughout this time. The G-AAAA to G-AZZZ series was allocated by July 1972 and a new series G-BAAA onwards was used in the same month: this series became exhausted in June 2001. Notwithstanding this, and commencing in 1974, many registrations were issued ahead of the natural alphabetical sequence and came from all of the forthcoming G-Bxxx to G-Zxxx series, there had been previous examples like Accountant G-ATEL (August 1957), Concorde G-BSST (May 1968) and Harrier G-VSTO (June 1971). The advance G-Bxxx registrations were eventually subsumed within the proper sequence and we moved on to the G-Cxxx series which has been in regular use since June 2001 while the G-Dxxx series was populated by numerous gliders with effect from 2007.

Small parts of an original G-Cxxx series were allocated to Canadian civilian aircraft from 20th April 1920 until 31st December 1928 commencing with G-CAAA. Registration G-CAWI was the last to be issued although G-CAXP had been formally allocated earlier in May 1928, being ex G-EBXP. On 1st January 1929 Canada adopted the nationality marks CF, followed by a hyphen, and three registration marks running from AAA to ZZZ. Those aircraft registered previously with G-CAxx markings continued to display them until they were retired from service. In addition, two separate series of quasi-military markings were created for aircraft operated on Canadian Government Air Operations by the Royal Canadian Air Force (RCAF). Series G-CYAA to G-CYHD was used from 18th June 1920 to 11th June 1926 and G-CYUR to G-CYZZ, but not sequentially, from 15th March 1927 to 18th July 1931. The batch from G-CYHE to G-CYUQ were not allotted as the RCAF were using a numerical series for registration marks on aircraft in their use by this time and marks were being displayed in an abbreviated form, that is the last two letters only. Aircraft still wearing these marks were absorbed into the existent RCAF numerical series by 1939. Consequently, the Civil Aviation Authority has not allocated any further registrations from the G-CAxx range although nine advance registrations were issued between December 1977 and March 1999 and remain extant. These were not allocated previously although two were reserved in 1928.

In addition, two special registrations series have been used as shown below:

i) During 1979 and 1980 specific alpha-numeric registrations G-N81AC and G-N94AA to G-N94AE which were used for British Airways' Concordes,

ii) From 1981 until 1998 registration batches G-MBAA to G-MBZZ, G-MGAA to G-MGZZ, G-MJAA to G-MJZZ, G-MMAA to G-MNZZ, G-MTAA to G-MTZZ and G-MYAA to G-MZZZ which were allocated originally for microlight aircraft use. Subsequently, other aircraft can now be found within these batches.

A third series was established in January 1982 when registration blocks G-FYAA to G-FYZZ were confined to Minimum Lift Balloons. G-FYAA was allocated on 4th January 1982 and G-FYNC, the last, was allocated on 4th August 1986.

The CAA website explains the Availability and Reservation of UK Registration Marks and is recommended reading.

USER GUIDE

There are a number of purposes to this annual volume. The primary one is to list all aircraft on the current civil aircraft registers, giving full details of types and previous identities, registered ownership and/or operator, probable home base and certification of airworthiness status. This information reproduces, expands upon and amplifies the official country registers. However, we go well beyond that; included are all other known, but no longer currently registered, UK and Irish aircraft noted in a reasonably identifiable condition and which are displayed or on/for rebuild. Some of these are held for instructional, fire or spares use. The majority of these are located in the UK and Ireland but some are resident abroad. In addition we detail the extensive numbers of foreign registered aircraft now located in both the UK and Ireland, some of which may aspire to G-, M-, 2-, ZJ- or EI- registrations in due course. Finally, we include a comprehensive listing of all gliders in use throughout the area in order to present an all-inclusive guide of the civil aviation scene.

Secondly, on a more technical level, we cater for the aviation specialist and historian who wishes to know more about a particular aircraft by providing detailed information such as the reasons for that aircraft's non-airworthy state where known and if applicable. Also, it was our policy for many years to record engine details in the text, for example the modification of an airframe to receive a non-standard engine has to be approved by the CAA and is then recorded in their Register. When the first microlights appeared in 1981 there was little standardisation and, consequently, we recorded all engine information. Now the majority are produced commercially, either in whole or kit form, engine fitment is standard to type in many cases and so a default fit is shown in the Index sections. A similar situation exists for LAA and BMAA approved, and other miscellaneous imported, home-build types. We have reviewed the inclusion of optional engines and have limited the non-standard fits to significant ones such as Lycoming-powered Chipmunk glider-tugs.

A guide to the main text is as follows:

Registration Current UK registrations are set out in alphabetical order in SECTION 1. Aircraft no longer currently registered, but known to be recently extant, are shown in non-bold text. Those aircraft allocated and cancelled in the period since the last register are indicated thus: (★). Some known reservations are identified with bracketed registrations, and airframes held by museums are indicated thus (^{M}). A few aircraft, either real or static reproductions are identified in fictitious UK civil marks for display purposes and are identified in SECTION 10. Those marks which have been re-issued or reallotted, particularly either if the first holder or allottee did not use the marks or they were not allocated at the time, are shown with a suffix, for example (2), after the registration.

Type We adopt the official type description as set down by the manufacturer or designer. Where there is doubt, reference is made to the relevant editions of *Jane's All the World Aircraft*, *Airlife's World Aircraft*, *The General Aviation Handbook* and the *World Directory of Leisure Aviation*. Indication is given if the manufacturer is a successor company or a licence builder – although not always if it is merely a sub-contractor. Under this column, we show engine types if the engine is nonstandard for all LAA and BMAA approved and other home-build types and for those vintage and classic aircraft where engines do vary. In addition, and especially for the aforementioned types, we show the manufacturer. Final explanatory notes comment on the airframe's identity and the true position where it is at variance with official records. Numbers quoted in brackets for certain BMAA homebuilt types and their engines refer to detailed variants listed in their Homebuild Aircraft Data Sheets. These can be accessed at www.bmaa.org/techinfo.asp from which the HADS option can be selected and for each type listed the numbered variants can be displayed in full.

Construction Number Also often referred to as the 'Manufacturer's Serial Number (MSN)' the construction number (c/n) is quoted in all official registers. The c/n should be a constant traceable reference throughout an airframe's life by means of a unique identification plate or stamp contained somewhere on the airframe. Homebuilt and kit built examples may have a home-builder's personal reference number as well. Some aircraft have more than one build number, for example LAA and BMAA approved types. Both Associations use dedicated project number series for their approved designs and these are often accepted as 'construction numbers' in the absence of a more specific reference. The CAA records these as their prime identifier. However, most LAA and BMAA examples will also have Manufacturers' Plans or Kit numbers and we quote these as our prime reference where known. In these cases the LAA and BMAA project numbers are shown with the individual builder details. In the case of self-assembly main components often carry adhesive labels with individual kit numbers when packed by manufacturers, but during build these are often discarded and without any visible identity on a particular airframe, traceability is lost, unfortunately.

The Irish equivalent of the LAA is the Irish Light Aircraft Society and aircraft use a ILAS allocation as their construction number.

Production of early weightshift microlights were identfied with two separate construction numbers covering the Trike unit and the Sailwing respectively. As a rule the CAA only records the latter number although we record both numbers where known. Nonetheless, manufacturers Hornet, Mainair and Medway issued a composite construction number comprising of both units and this is generally adopted by the CAA. For example, Mainair Rapier G-BYBV is officially registered as c/n 1183-1198-7-W986 but only the first nine digits form the trike c/n.

Registration Date This is the date of the original registration for those particular marks, even when subsequently removed and restored.

Previous Identities These are set out in reverse order with the most recent identity first. Some of these may have been issued several times and are noted with a suffix as stated above. Registrations shown in parenthesis have been allotted but were never officially used to the best of our knowledge. The nationality of foreign military serials is indicated only where it may not be apparent. Manufacturers' test marks, also known as 'B Conditions' identities, are given where known.

Owner (Operator) This is the registered owner for current aircraft as recorded in CAA records. Where the operator is known to be different this is shown in parenthesis. Included under this heading come are details of the latest reported status, for example if the CofA is not current or the aircraft is known to be under repair plus details of any names and, in particular, any military colour schemes and marks worn. Some aircraft are shown as temporarily un-registered ('Temp unregd'); this is where the CAA has not received an application from a new owner following a sale. Usually the CAA gives a period of discretion and if no response is received the Certificate is cancelled and the aircraft is not permitted to fly. Such action usually stimulates the new owner to produce the relevant documentation.

(Unconfirmed) Base The information in this column is not guaranteed: there is no official information. Reports by members and other readers who visit airfields and strips are perused to compile this column. Aircraft change base frequently. Balloons are generally shown as being based at their owners' registered address unless we have further information. Bases for active flexwing aircraft can present a problem as trikes are often stored at owners' homes after flying whilst corresponding sailwings are pegged out at base airfields. When the location is uncertain the owner's hometown is shown in parenthesis.

Readers are reminded that the identification of a base, particularly if it is a private strip, is not an invitation to visit and in a number of cases visiting is actively discouraged because of previous abuses. We recognise the need for privacy in this area and consequently not all information held is published.

CERTIFICATES OF AIRWORTHINESS (CofA) STATUS

As a direct result of the European legislation UK-registered aircraft are divided into two groups: the specific aircraft are detailed in CAP747.

- *EASA aircraft*; that is, aircraft subject to regulation by EASA; and
- *Non-EASA aircraft*; that is, aircraft that remain subject to regulation by the CAA.

CofA Validity: Information is taken from data published by the CAA. The date indicates the currency of the aircraft's certificate and details of the coding suffix letters applied are set out below. In SECTION 1 the codings shown after the date of expiry indicate the CofA Certification category. The absence of a code letter means an aircraft holds a Private category CofA of either one- or three-year duration. Where a CofA has expired or lapsed and an aircraft has been reported since that date further details are shown.

As regular readers know, just because an aircraft has a current CofR does not necessarily mean that it is currently airworthy. Where a known accident has taken place a note is often included but, where a CofA is long-expired or not yet issued, and we have not received a recent report of status from members, we have introduced the No Flight Declaration shown in the CAA's G-INFO details. This indicates that, if an aircraft is not currently insured and the registered owner has made a declaration to the CAA that the aircraft will not be flown until evidence of insurance has been supplied to the CAA, the date of the declaration is displayed. Alternatively, we show an 'Insurance Evidence Verification' date, which indicates that if the CAA has requested details of the insurance on a particular aircraft, this date confirms when the details were verified as being in compliance with EC 785/2004. We hope this gives a clearer picture of the status of a particular aircraft when a CofA has lapsed.

Codes used are as follows:

E: EASA Standard CofA – this shows the expiry of the Airworthiness Review Certificate [EASA CofAs are non-expiring];

R: Restricted CofA – this now covers 'orphan' aircraft where the original design authority no longer exists but still come under EASA control;

C: CofA with Conditions

S: Standard – national legislation;

T: Transport – was issued to any Passenger aircraft operated for hire or reward, usually for either one or three years duration. No longer issued and very few aircraft remain in this category

P: Permit to Fly – originally introduced in December 1935, but then lapsed during the Second World War, this system was re-activated in 1950. It covers homebuilder, vintage and microlight aircraft. The major criterion for home-build aircraft set out by the LAA is that the aircraft must be amateur-built by its owner. A homebuilder must spend at least 500 hours in completing the project for it to qualify under the Permit scheme as homebuilt. Permits are issued by the CAA on the recommendation of the LAA. It is the 'prime document' and legalises flight of a Permit aircraft. The Permit is issued for the life of the aircraft but is only valid when certain conditions are fulfilled. The most fundamental of these is the Certificate of Validity (CofV) which is issued by the LAA following a satisfactory report concerning the annual inspection and test flying of the aircraft. The BMAA also operate a similar system on behalf of the CAA, the CofV requires a report every five years to ensure that aircraft have not 'put on weight' by adding equipment, moisture absorption etc. The BMAA issue a six-month 'Permit to Fly for Test' but this can be renewed/extended by the BMAA's Chief Technical Officer – they are not just for new build aircraft but also for test flying of modifications (different engines/different propellers/modified undercarriages etc).

W: EASA Permit to Fly

A: Aerial Work – this category normally indicates aerial advertising, mainly by hot air balloons, and a few banner-towing aircraft.

X: Non-expiring Exemptions were issued originally to early microlights and hot air balloons, only a few now remain.

None: A number of aircraft have now been declared to the BMAA as withdrawing from (or not requiring) the Permit to Fly scheme and they are now operating under the SSDR (Single Seat Deregulated) exemption granted by the CAA whereby the aircraft effectively becomes 'self-certified' by the pilot.

SSDR microlights must meet the following criteria:

1. Be designed to carry one person;
2. Have a maximum take off mass (which varies for a defined list of variations);
3. Has a stall speed or minimum flight speed in the landing configuration not exceeded 35 knots calibrated airspeed.

In addition the aircraft and pilot must comply with the other requirements of the ANO (e.g. insurance, markings, licences, logbooks etc.) Some owners have permanently removed second seats to meet these requirements and the onus is now on them to determine the aircraft's airworthinesss; under the proposed new ANO – there will be no option to remain under a Permit to Fly reqime. SSDRs have a note with details of insurance evidence [for those considered airworthy by the owner/pilot] or a No Fly date. There are also some gliders and balloons which do not require Airworthiness certification.

At the time of going to press, the situation regarding the UK's departure from the European Union ('Brexit') is not resolved, and its effects for aviation are not confirmed. However, the CAA has stated: "We would recognise EASA certificates, approvals and licences valid at the point of UK exit for use in the UK aviation system and on UK-registered aircraft for up to two years after the UK leaves the EU." It further states: "The UK's regulations on aircraft registration would not change. Therefore, Commonwealth citizens and nationals of any European Economic Area State would still be able to maintain an aircraft on the UK register."

GLOSSARY of TERMS and ABBREVIATIONS

AAC	Army Air Corps
AAIB	Air Accidents Investigation Branch
AB	Aktiebolaget (*Sweden: Joint Stock*)
ABAC	Association of British Aero Clubs and Centres
A/c	Aircraft
AC	Awaiting Certification
AERONCA	Aeronautical Corporation of America
AESL	Aero Engine Services Ltd
AGA	Army Gliding Association
AIA	Atelier Industriel de l'Aéronautique d'Alger
AIRCO	Aircraft Manufacturing Co
aka	also known as
AMD-BA	Avions Marcel Dassault-Breguet Aviation
ANEC	Air Navigation and Engineering Co
ANG	Air National Guard
ApS	Anpartsselskab (*Denmark: Limited Liability*)
APSS	Aviation Preservation Society of Scotland
ASS	Air Signallers School
AVIA	Azionara Vercellese Ind.Areo
BA	British Aircraft Manufacturing Co Ltd
BAC	British Aircraft Company
BAC	British Aircraft Corporation
BAT	British Aerial Transport Co Ltd
Belg.AF	Belgian Air Force
BoBMF	Battle of Britain Memorial Flight
BMAA	British Microlight Aircraft Association
Bol.AF	Bolivian Air Force
Burm.AF	Burmese Air Force
BV	Besloten Vennootschap (*Belgium: Private Limited Liability Company*)
BVBA	Besloten Vennootschap met Beperkte Aansprakelijkheid (*Netherlands: Private*)
CAARP	Coopérative des Ateliers Aéronautiques de la Région Parisienne
CAB	Constructions Aéronautiques de Béarn
CAB	Constructions Aéronautiques de Bourgogne
CAF	Canadian Air Force
CASA	Construcciones Aeronáuticas SA
CC	County Council
CCF	Canadian Car and Foundry
CEA	Centre Est Aviation
Chil.Army	Chilean Army
c/n	Construction number
Cobelavia	Compagnie Belge d'Aviation
CSS	Centralne Studium Samolotów
CZAL	Ceskoslovenske Zavody Automobilove a Letecke
Corp	Corporation
CofA	Certificate of Airworthiness
CofR	Certificate of Registration
ca	circa
c/s	Colour scheme
c/w	complete with
dbf	Destroyed by fire
DCAE	Defence College of Aeronautical Engineering
DEFRA	Department for Environment, Food and Rural Affairs
DEFTS	Defence Elementary Flying Training School
DF	Defence Force
DOSAAF	Dobrovol'noe Obshchestvo Sodeistviya Armii, Aviasii i Flotu
DTA	Delta Trikes Aviation

EASA	European Aviation Safety Agency
EKW	Eidgenössiche Konstruktions Werkstätte
EMBRAER	Empresa Brasileira de Aeronautica SA
EoN	Elliotts of Newbury Ltd
ERCO	Engineering and Research Corporation
ETPS	Empire Test Pilots' School
FAA	Fleet Air Arm
FAAM	Facility for Airborne Atmospheric Measurements
FLPH	Foot Launched Propelled Hang-glider
FTS	Flying Training School
f/f	First flight
Fr.AF	French Air Force (Armée de l'Air)
Fr.Army	French Army Aviation (Légère de l'Armée de Terre)
Fr.Navy	French Navy (Aéronautique Navale)
fsm	Full Scale Model
GAF	Government Aircraft Factory
GAF	German Air Force
GC	Gliding Club
German AAS	German Army Air Service
GmbH	Gesellschaft mit beschränkter Haftung (*Germany: Private Limited*)
HKG	Royal Hong Kong Auxiliary Air Force
IAA	Irish Aviation Authority
IAC	Integrated Aviation Consortium
IAC	Irish Air Corps
IAF	Indian Air Force
IAME	Ital-American Motor Engineering
IAR	Industria Aeronautica Romania
IAV	Intreprinderea de Avioane
ICA	Intreprinderea de Constructii Aeronautice-Brasov
ICAO	International Civil Aviation Organisation
IDF/AF	Israel Defense Forces/Air Force
IE	Insurance Evidence verification
IGA	Irish Gliding Association
III	Iniziative Industriali Italiane
IMCO	Intermountain Manufacturing Co
Int'l	International
IPTN	Industri Pesawat Terbang Nusantara
Ital.AF	Italian Air Force (Aeronautica Militare)
IWM	Imperial War Museum
Int'l	International
JAA	Joint Aviation Authority
JAR	Joint Aviation Regulations
KG	Kommanditgesellschaft (*Germany: Limited Partnership*)
KK	Kabushiki Kaisha (*Japan: Limited Company*)
LAA	Light Aircraft Association
LAK	Litovskaya Aviatsyonnaya Konstruktsiya
LET	Letecky Narodny Podnik
LLC	Limited Liability Corporation (*USA*)
LLP	Limited Liability Partnership (*UK*)
LVG	Luft-Verkehrs Gesellschaft
Lda	Limitada (*Portugal: Private Limited*)
Lsg	Leasing
Ltd	Limited (*UK*)
MBA	Micro Biplane Aviation
MBB	Messerschmitt-Bölkow-Blohm

Mex.AF	Mexican Air Force (Fuerza Aérea Mexicana)
Moz.PLAF	Mozambique People's Liberation Air Force
MPA	Man Powered Aircraft
N.SOL.O	General Partnership (*Slovenia: General Partnership*)
NEJSGA	Near East Joint Services Gliding Association
NF	No Flight declaration
NK	Not known
NV	Naamloze Vennootschap (*Belgium and Netherlands*)
ntu	Not taken up
n/w	nose-wheel
OGMA	Oficinas Gerais de Material Aeronautico
PAP	Propulsion Auxiliare Parapente
PFA	Popular Flying Association
PIK	Polytecknikkojen Ilmailukerho
PLAAF	People's Liberation Army Air Force (PRC)
PLC	Public Limited Company (*UK*)
Port AF	Portuguese Air Force (Força Aérea Portuguesa)
PRC	Peoples' Republic of China
PS	Plane Set
PT	Pesawat Terbang (*Indonesia*)
PWFU	Permanently Withdrawn from Use
PZL	Panstwowe Zaklady Lotnicze (State Aviation Works)
qv	Which see
R	Reservation
RAAF	Royal Australian Air Force
RAF	Royal Aircraft Factory
RAF	Royal Air Force
RAFC	RAF College
RAFGGA	RAF Germany Gliding Association
RAFGSA	RAF Gliding and Soaring Association
RCAF	Royal Canadian Air Force
RDAF	Royal Danish Air Force (Kongelije Flyvevåbnet)
Rep	Reproduction
RFC	Royal Flying Corps
RJAF	Royal Jordanian Air Force
RN	Royal Navy
RNAS	Royal Naval Air Service
RNAY	Royal Naval Aircraft Yard
RNGSA	RN Gliding and Soaring Association
R Neth.AF	Royal Netherlands Air Force (Koninklijke Luchtmaart)
R Neth.Navy	Royal Netherlands Navy (Koninklijke Marine)
RNZAF	Royal New Zealand Air Force
RoI	Republic of Ireland
RSAF	Royal Saudi Air Force
rts	Reduced to spares
SA	Société Anonyme (*France & Romania: Public Limited*)
SA	Sociedad Anónima (*Spain: Public Limited*)
SA	Spoika Akeyjna (*Poland: Private Limited*)
SAAC	Society of Amateur Aircraft Constructors
SAAF	South African Air Force
SArab AF	South Arabian Federation (South Yemen)
SAI	Skandinavsk Aero Industri
SAN	Société Aéronautique Normande
SAR	Search and Rescue

SAS	Société par Actions Simplifiées (*France: Joint Stock*)
SE	Scouting Experimental
SEAE	School of Electrical and Aeronautical Engineering
Sing.AF	Republic of Singapore Air Force
SIPA	Société Industrielle pour l'Aéronautique
SMA	Société de Motorisations Aéronautiques
SMD	Southern Microlight Developments
s/n	Serial Number
SNCAC	Société Nationale de Constructions Aéronautiques du Centre
SNCAN	Société Nationale de Constructions Aéronautiques du Nord
SOCATA	Société de Construction d'Avions de Tourisme et d'Affaires
SoS	Secretary of State
SpA	Società per Azioni (*Italy: Limited Liability*)
Span AF	Spanish Air Force (Ejército del Aire)
SPP	Strojirny Prvni Petilesky
Sp.zoo	Spółka z ograniczoną odpowiedzialnością (*Poland: Limited Liability*)
SRCM	Société de Recherches et de Constructions Mécaniques
Srl	Società a Responsabilità Limata (*Italy: Joint Stock*)
S.r.o	společnost s ručením omezeným (*Czech Republic: Limited Liability*)
Srs.	Series
SS	Special Shape (Balloon)
Swed.AF	Swedish Air Force (Flygvapnet)
Swed.Army	Swedish Army
Swed.Navy	Swedish Navy
SZD	Szybowcowy Zaklad Dowswiadczalny
TAD	Technical Aid and Demonstrator
TBA	To be advised
TEAM	Tennessee Engineering and Manufacturing
Turk.AF	Turkish Air Force (Turk Hava Kuvvetlei)
TWU	Tactical Weapons Unit
t/a	Trading as
tr	Trustee of
t/w	tail-wheel
UAS	University Air Squadron
ULM	Ultra-Léger Motorisé
USAAC	United States Army Air Corps
USAAS	United States Army Air Service
VTC	Vazduhoplovno Tehnicki Centar
VW	Volkswagen
WACO	Weaver Aircraft Corp
WFU	Withdrawn from Use
WGAF	West German Air Force
WSK	Wytwornia Sprzetu Komunikacy Jnego Okecie
Yug.AF	Yugoslav Air Force (Jugoslavensko Ratno zrakoplovstvo)

Air-Britain News

Air-Britain's monthly house magazine, averaging 200 pages per month is packed with indispensible information from around the world.

Sections include:

- **United Kingdom & Isle of Man Registers** – comprehensive review of all changes, including Additions, Cancellations, Changes of Ownership and Casualties.

- **Around and About** – Movements, base changes and other aviation happenings from around the UK and Ireland, plus reports of current and former UK-registered aircraft noted abroad.

- **U.S. Register** – covers all types except Airliners, Biz Jets and Biz Props (which have their own sections within the magazine). All additions, cancellations with fates where known, reservations and comprehensive details of 'dead' aircraft being purged from the US Register.

- **Overseas Registers** – Covers all registers other than the UK, Isle of Man, Channel Islands and US (with a handy prefix guide on the cover of each magazine). Regularly includes around 100 countries.

- **Derelict and Preserved** – News from museums and collections worldwide.

- **Display Diary** – Enables readers to share their experiences and logs of aircraft seen at UK & Ireland events, from major displays to very informal fly-ins. A chance to fill in those gaps in your logs and correct mis-sightings. We try to cover the more obscure airfields around the UK. Also notice of forthcoming events.

- **Hot Air Ballooning** – All known UK Balloon & Airship sightings, and reports on balloon meetings worldwide. Calendar covering all known forthcoming balloon events.

- **Military Aviation** – UK Military Movements covers the main active UK bases, utilising reports sent in from Air-Britain members plus recent unit movements. Overseas covers all other worldwide news.

- **Emergency Services** – News from Police Aviation News, including Police and all other emergency services.

- **Production** – Includes changes to Britten-Norman Islanders provided by B N I historians.

- **Biz Props** – production changes for Aero Commanders, King Airs, Cessna 400 series, MU-2s, Cheyennes, Merlins etc.

- **Biz Jets** – Gives as much detail as possible relating to the histories of purpose-built business jet aircraft (airliner types adapted for bizjet use are covered in Commercial Scene), from production line to final resting place. Records the many registration changes that occur around the world each month including ownership changes. Includes as many delivery flight details as possible for factory-new and exported aircraft, together with ferry flights from factory to completion centre for the larger types and base changes for all types when these can be identified.

- **Commercial Airline News** – Up to date coverage of airliner orders from airlines and leasing companies. News from the major civil aircraft manufacturers, in particular details of models being developed and tested. Fleet changes/disposals and leasing arrangements are an important part of the section and construction numbers, registrations and (where applicable) previous identities are shown. Also news of new routes, route frequency changes and changes of aircraft types used.

- **Commercial Scene** – Airline Production changes and orders for all Airliners – absolutely invaluable for keeping your files bang up to date.

**To request a complimentary copy of Air-Britain News,
please send an email to sales@air-britain.co.uk, mentioning BIR2019.**

For full information on how to subscribe go to www.air-britain.co.uk

---

SECTION 1 – UNITED KINGDOM

THE PERMANENT REGISTER

Information is updated to 1st March 2019.

Aircraft listed as registered on the official Civil Aviation Authority's Register website are marked in **bold**. Those that are extant and have been confirmed as such since 2013 but no longer current are displayed in roman (non-bold) text, and those which both joined and departed the register in the period since the publication of the 2018 edition of this volume are indicated with a star (★). Airframes held by museums and collections are indicated thus: (ᴹ).

The index for this section, covering only aircraft listed as registered, can be found on page 454.

Regn	Type Previous identity Owner/Cancellation details Prob Base	C/n	Regn date CofA expiry

G-EAAA – G-EAZZ

Regn	Type / details	C/n	Regn date / CofA expiry
G-EACNᴹ	BAT FK.23 Bantam K-123, F1654 Cancelled xx.xx.21 as PWFU As 'K-123' Originally registered as K-123 29.05.19 With Rijksmuseum, Amsterdam, Netherlands	FK23/15	22.07.1919
G-EACQᴹ	Avro 534 Baby VH-UCQ, G-AUCQ, G-EACQ, K-131 Sold 06.21 – to G-AUCQ – subsequently VH-UCQ As 'G-EACQ' With Queensland Museum, South Brisbane	534/1	29.05.1919
G-EAMLᴹ	Airco DH.6 C9449 Cancelled 19.09.19 – to South Africa Components only preserved as 'G-EAML' With South African Air Museum, Pretoria	xxxx	08.09.1919
G-EAOUᴹ	Vickers FB.27A Vimy IV (A5-1), G-EAOU, F8630 Cancelled xx.10.20 as PWFU As 'G-EAOU' At Adelaide Airport, SA	xxxx	23.10.1919 31.10.20
G-EAQMᴹ	Airco DH.9 F1278 Cancelled 08.02.21 as PWFU – to Australia As 'G-EAQM' Built by Waring & Gillow With Australian War Memorial, Canberra	xxxx	31.12.1919 01.01.21
G-EASD	Avro 504L S-AHAA, S-AAP, G-EASD, (RAF) G M New (Souldern, Bicester) Built by the Eastbourne Aviation Company Under restoration for Avro Heritage Museum, Woodford 2019 (NF 08.10.18)	E.5	26.03.20

G-EBAA – G-EBZZ

Regn	Type / details	C/n	Regn date / CofA expiry
G-EBHB	Avro 504K T W Harris RAF Henlow Built by Morgan & Co, Leighton Buzzard: reproduction Skysport Engineering; as 'E2977' in RAF c/s	E2977	17.07.23 02.05.19P
G-EBHX	de Havilland DH.53 Humming Bird No.8* Richard Shuttleworth Trustees(Old Warden) 'L'Oiseau-Mouche' *Competition No. – Lympne Trials 1923 Stored off site 03.18 (IE 01.05.15)	98	22.09.23 04.04.13P
G-EBIA	Royal Aircraft Factory SE.5A F904 'D7000', G-EBIA, F904 Richard Shuttleworth Trustees Old Warden Built by Wolseley Motors Ltd; as 'F904' in RFC 56 Sqdn c/s	654/2404	26.09.23 11.07.19P
G-EBIBᴹ	Royal Aircraft Factory SE.5A 'F939', G-EBIB, F937 Cancelled 01.12.46 by Sec of State Registered with c/n 688/2404 With Science Museum, South Kensington	687/2404	26.09.23 08.08.35
G-EBICᴹ	Royal Aircraft Factory.SE.5A 'B4563', 9208M, G-EBIC, F937 Cancelled xx.09.30 & 31.12.38 as PWFU As 'F938' Registered with c/n 687/2404 With RAF Museum, Hendon	688/2404	26.09.23 03.09.30
G-EBIR	de Havilland DH.51 Moth VP-KAA, (G-KAAA), G-EBIR Richard Shuttleworth Trustees Old Warden Aircraft Transport & Travel Ltd c/s	102	22.01.24 28.03.18P
G-EBJEᴹ	Avro 504K (9205M) Cancelled 01.12.34 as PWFU As 'E449' Includes components of Avro 548A G-EBKN ex E449 With RAF Museum, Hendon	927	xx.07.24 29.09.34
G-EBJGᴹ	Parnall Pixie III No.14**, No.17* Cancelled 01.12.46 by Sec of State *Competition No. – Lympne Trials 1924 **Competition No. – Lympne Trials 1926 Components only, with Midland Air Museum, Coventry	xxxx	xx.09.24 02.10.36
G-EBJO	Air Navigation and Engineering ANEC II No.7* Richard Shuttleworth Trustees Old Warden *Competition No. – Lympne Trials 1924	1	17.07.24 12.04.18P
G-EBKY	Sopwith Pup 'N5180', 'N5184', G-EBKY Richard Shuttleworth Trustees Old Warden Built by Sopwith Aviation Co Ltd as 'Dove'; as '9917' in RFC c/s to represent Beardmore built Pup	W/O 3004/14	27.03.25 20.08.18P
G-EBLV	de Havilland DH.60 Moth BAE Systems (Operations) Ltd Old Warden On loan to Richard Shuttleworth Trustees	188	22.06.25 03.06.19P
G-EBMBᴹ	Hawker Cygnet I No.14* Cancelled 30.11.61 *Competition No. – Lympne Trials 1924 With Royal Air Force Cosford Museum	1	29.07.25 30.11.61
G-EBNV	English Electric S.1 Wren (BAPC.11) G-EBNV, No.3* Richard Shuttleworth Trustees Old Warden '4' Composite – principally c/n 3 rebuilt by 1955/56 *Competition No. – Lympne Trials 1924 Noted 03.18 (IE 01.05.15)	3	09.04.26 05.06.15P
G-EBOVᴹ	Avro 581E Avian No 9* Cancelled 14.01.30 – to Australia Originally registered as Avro 581, to Avro 581A 1927 & later modified to Avro 581E *Competition No.– Lympne Trials 1926 With Queensland Museum, South Brisbane	5116	07.07.26 30.01.29
G-EBQPᴹ	de Havilland DH.53 Humming Bird J7326 P L Kirk & T G Pankhurst Salisbury Hall, London Colney Noted on long term restoration 10.18 as 'J-7326' in RAF c/s (NF 13.11.15)	114	??.04.27
G-EBWD	de Havilland DH.60X Moth Richard Shuttleworth Trustees Old Warden	552	02.03.28 09.04.19P
G-EBXUᴹ	de Havilland DH.60X Moth Cancelled 12.06.06 as EC-KCY As 'G-EBXU' With Fundación Infante de Orleans, Cuatro Vientos, Spain	627	02.05.28

G-EBYY[M] Cierva C.8L Mk.2 (Avro 617)   xxxx   21.06.28
           Cancelled xx.04.30 as PWFU   As 'G-EBYY'   13.07.29
           With Musée de l'Air et de l'Espace, Le Bourget, France

G-EBZM[M] Avro 594A Avian IIIA   R3/CN/160   xx.07.28
           Cancelled 01.12.46 by Sec of State   20.01.38
           Fitted with parts from G-ABEE
           On loan to the Manchester Museum of Science & Industry
           from The Aeroplane Collection, Hooton Park

G-AAAA – G-AAZZ

G-AAAH[M] de Havilland DH.60G Moth   804   30.08.28
           Cancelled xx.12.31   'Jason'   23.12.30
           Original build – note three BAPC replicas depicted
           as 'G-AAAH' also exist
           With Science Museum, South Kensington

G-AACN[M] Handley Page HP.39 Gugnunc   1   02.11.28
           K1908, G-AACN   Cancelled xx.12.30 – to K1908
           As 'G-AACN'
           With Science Museum, South Kensington

G-AADR (2) American Moth DH.60GM Gipsy Moth 138   02.06.86
           NC939M   E V Moffatt   Woodlow Farm, Bosbury 12.09.18P
           (IE 20.09.18)

G-AAEG   de Havilland DH.60G Gipsy Moth   1027   04.02.29
           D-EUPI, D-1599, G-AAEG   I B Grace
           (Sultan, Washington, USA)
           (NF 27.02.15)

G-AAHI   de Havilland DH.60G Gipsy Moth   1082   25.05.29
           A C Kuzyk, I C & N J W Reid tr N J W Reid
           Discretionary Settlement 2008   Breighton   10.08.19P
           Original fuselage used for rebuild of G-AAWO 1953

G-AAHY   de Havilland DH.60M Moth   1362   01.05.29
           HB-AFI, G-AAHY   D J Elliott (Headley, Thatcham)
           'Brooklands Flying Club'   06.09.19P

G-AAIN   Parnall Elf II   J.6   11.06.29
           Richard Shuttleworth Trustees   Old Warden   01.06.17P
           Undergoing refurbishment 03.18

G-AAJT   de Havilland DH.60G Gipsy Moth   1084   04.07.29
           NC947M, G-AAJT   M R Paul   Solent   01.07.19P

G-AALY   de Havilland DH.60G Gipsy Moth   1175   09.09.29
           F-AJKM, G-AALY   K M Fresson   Solent   15.05.05
           Composite & rebuilt from components (NF 28.02.18)

G-AAMX   Moth Corporation DH.60GM Moth   125   11.09.86
           NC926M   Cancelled 19.08.96 as PWFU   07.05.94
           RAF Stafford   In RAF Museum store 2018

G-AAMZ (2)[M] de Havilland DH.60G Moth   1293   13.07.87
           EC-ABX, EC-BAU, Spanish AF 30-52, EC-NAN,
           M-CNAN, MW-134
           Cancelled 04.09.98 – to N60MZ   As 'G-AAMZ'
           With Aviation Museum of Santa Paula, California

G-AANG (2) Bleriot Type XI   14   29.10.81
           BAPC.3   Richard Shuttleworth Trustees
           Old Warden   24.04.15P
           Built by 1910; no external markings; noted 03.18
           (IE 01.05.15)

G-AANH (2) Deperdussin Monoplane   43   29.10.81
           BAPC.4   Richard Shuttleworth Trustees
           Old Warden   27.06.19P
           Possibly c/n 143; no external markings

G-AANI (2) Blackburn 1912 Monoplane   9   29.10.81
           BAPC.5   Richard Shuttleworth Trustees
           Old Warden   26.07.19P
           No external markings

G-AANJ (2)[M] Luft-Verkehrs Gesellschaft C.VI 4503   29.10.81
           9239M, C7198, 18, '1594', C7198, 18
           Cancelled 11.12.03 as WFU   16.05.03
           As '7198:18' in German Air Force c/s
           Composite aircraft including parts from LVG 1594:
           captured 1916/17 & allotted RFC serial 'XG7'
           With Royal Air Force Cosford Museum

G-AANL (2) de Havilland DH.60M Moth   1446   26.06.87
           OY-DEH, R Danish AF S-357, S-107   R A Palmer   25.09.18P
           Sheardown Farm, Ibworth   'National Flying Services'
           Composite rebuild

G-AANM (2)[M] Bristol F 2b Fighter composite "67626"   16.07.87
           BAPC.166   Cancelled 14.12.10 as PWFU   25.06.07
           As 'D7889'   Built by British & Colonial Aero
           Co 1917
           With Canada Aviation Museum, Rockcliffe, Ontario

G-AANO (2) Moth Aircraft DH.60GMW Gipsy Moth 165   03.03.88
           N590N, NC590N   K F Crumplin   Henstridge
           Composite rebuild c.1991 (NF 10.02.17)

G-AAOK (2) Curtiss-Wright CW-12Q Travel Air 2026   18.11.81
           N370N, NC370N, NC352M
           Just Plane Trading Ltd   Top Farm, Croydon   27.08.19P

G-AAPZ   Desoutter I   D.25   ??.??.31
           Richard Shuttleworth Trustees   Old Warden   17.04.19P
           National Flying Services c/s; original CofR c12.29

G-AARO (2)[M] Arrow Sport A2-60   341   17.09.79
           N932S, NC932S   Cancelled 15.06.83 – to N280AS
           – subsequently N9325   As 'G-AARO'   18.02.83
           With National Air & Space Museum, Chantilly, Virginia

G-AATC   de Havilland DH.80A Puss Moth   2001   23.12.29
           ZK-ADU, VH-UON, G-AATC
           R A Palmer   Malshanger, Basingstoke
           On restoration 12.16 (NF 01.07.16)

G-AAUP   Klemm L25-1A   145   19.02.30
           J I Cooper (Old Warden)   'Clementine'   21.09.16P

G-AAWO   de Havilland DH.60G Gipsy Moth   1235   02.05.30
           A C Kuzyk, I C & N J W Reid tr I C Reid
           Discretionary Settlement 2009   Solent   31.07.19P
           Rebuilt 1953 with original fuselage of G-AAHI

G-AAXG   de Havilland DH.60M Moth   1542   02.08.34
           ZK-AEJ, (ZK-ADF), G-AAXG, F-AJZB, G-AAXG
           S H Kidston   Langham   'K5'   09.09.19P

G-AAYT   de Havilland DH.60G Gipsy Moth   1233   ??.05.30
           DR606, G-AAYT   P Groves   Solent
           (NF 30.11.18)

G-AAYX   Southern Martlet   202   14.05.30
           Richard Shuttleworth Trustees   Old Warden   02.04.19P

G-AAZG   de Havilland DH.60G Gipsy Moth   1253   23.05.30
           EC-AAE, EC-MMA, Spanish AF 30-94, M-CMMA,
           MW-133, G-AAZG
           E G & N S C English (Daventry & Henley-on-Thames) 07.07.14P
           Crashed Canons Ashby, Daventry 12.08.13 &
           extensively damaged

G-AAZP   de Havilland DH.80A Puss Moth   2047   04.06.30
           HL537, G-AAZP, SU-AAC, G-AAZP   R P Williams
           Folly Farm, Hungerford   'British Heritage'   13.08.19P

G-ABAA – G-ABZZ

G-ADAA[M] Avro 504K   xxxx   11.09.30
           9244M, 'H2311', G-ABAA   Cancelled 01.01.39   11.04.39
           On loan from RAF Museum to Manchester
           Museum of Sciences & Industry

G-ABAG   de Havilland DH.60G Gipsy Moth   1259   23.06.30
           A & P A Wood   Old Warden   28.08.19P

G-ABBB[M] Bristol 105A Bulldog IIA   7446   12.06.30
           'K2227', G-ABBB, R-11, G-ABBB
           Cancelled 22.09.61 as PWFU
           As 'K2227' in RAF 56 Sqdn c/s
           With RAF Museum, Hendon

G-ABDA   de Havilland DH.60G Gipsy Moth   1284   ??.07.30
           N60GD, N1284A, G-ABDA, 2595M, DG583, G-ABDA
           T A Bechtolsheimer   Turweston   19.05.19P

G-ABDW[M] de Havilland DH.80A Puss Moth   2051   23.08.30
           VH-UQB, G-ABDW   Cancelled xx.12.33 –
           to VH-UQB (1) – restored 25.03.77 & cancelled
           21.01.82 as PWFU   As 'VH-UQB'
           With National Museum of Flight Scotland,
           East Fortune

G-ABDX   de Havilland DH.60G Gipsy Moth   1294   01.08.30
           HB-UAS, G-ABDX   M D Souch   Hill Farm, Durley   27.09.17P

G-ABEV (2) de Havilland DH.60G Gipsy Moth   1823   10.03.77
           N4203E, G-ABEV (2), HB-OKI, CH-217
           S L G Darch   East Chinnock, Yeovil   15.05.09P
           (NF 02.03.16)

G-ABHE Aeronca C-2   A.100   02.12.30
        N S Chittenden (Trecangate Farm, Herodsfoot, Liskeard)
        Engine damaged 16.07.36, converted & flew as glider
        24.03.37 but no BGA Certificate issued). Damaged 1938 &
        components stored for rebuild to original configuration
        (SSDR microlight since 12.14) (IE 04.10.18)

G-ABJJ de Havilland DH.60G Gipsy Moth   1840   27.03.31
        CF-AAA, G-ABJJ, BK842, G-ABJJ B R Cox Coventry   18.06.19P

G-ABLK^M Avro 616 Avian V   R3/CN/523   27.01.31
        VH-UQG, G-ABLK Cancelled 01.09.31 – to VH-UQG (1):
        restored 01.08.32 – Cancelled 11.33
        Crashed south Reggane, Sahara 12.04.33
        With Queensland Museum, South Brisbane

G-ABLM^M Cierva C.24   710   22.04.31
        Cancelled as WFU 12.34   16.01.35
        On loan from Science Museum to de Havilland
        Aircraft Museum, London Colney

G-ABLS de Havilland DH.80A Puss Moth   2164   27.05.30
        T W Harris Duxford   25.05.16P
        On rebuild by Aircraft Restoration Company 12.18

G-ABMR^M Hawker Hart   H.H-1   28.05.31
        'J9933', G-ABMR
        Cancelled 02.02.59 – to J9933 & J9941   11.06.57
        As 'J9941' in RAF 57 Sqdn c/s
        With RAF Museum, Hendon

G-ABNT Civilian CAC.1 Coupe II   O.3   01.06.31
        Shipping & Airlines Ltd Biggin Hill   09.07.19P

G-ABNX Robinson Redwing 2   9   02.07.31
        C T Parry tr Redwing Syndicate Hill Farm, Durley 12.05.03P
        Noted 06.16 (NF 28.01.16)

G-ABOI Wheeler Slymph   AHW.1   17.07.31
        Cancelled 01.12.46 by Secretary of State
        Built by A H Wheeler On loan from A.H.Wheeler
        Dismantled components only
        With Midland Air Museum, Coventry

G-ABOX (2) Sopwith Pup   N5195   02.09.84
        N5195 A P & C M D St Cyrien AAC Middle Wallop   22.04.93P
        On loan to Museum of Army Flying as 'N5195'
        (NF 07.01.15)

G-ABSD de Havilland DH.60G Gipsy Moth   1883   21.11.31
        RAAF A7-96, VH-UTN, G-ABSD
        M E Vaisey (Hemel Hempstead)
        (NF 10.12.18)

G-ABUS Comper CLA.7 Swift   S32/4   27.02.32
        R C F Bailey (West Malling)
        (NF 20.10.15)

G-ABVE Arrow Active 2   2   19.03.32
        R A Fleming Breighton   27.04.18P

G-ABWD (2) de Havilland DH.83 Fox Moth   4009   16.07.32
        CH-344 M D Souch Hill Farm, Durley
        G-ABWD (1) sold as CH-344 08.32, crashed near
        Lyons, France 30.04.33 & damaged beyond repair
        (NF 24.12.18)

G-ABWP Spartan Arrow 1   78   ??.04.32
        R T Blain Redhill   12.11.19P

G-ABXL Granger Archaeopteryx   3A   03.06.32
        J R Granger (Beeston, Nottingham)
        Built by F & J Granger (NF 05.10.18)

G-ABYA de Havilland DH.60G Gipsy Moth   1906   ??.07.32
        M J Luck Gloucestershire   25.05.17E
        (IE 21.09.18)

G-ABZB (2) de Havilland DH.60G III Moth Major 5011   30.08.32
        SE-AEL, OY-DAK G M Turner Rendcomb   12.06.19P
        Original G-ABZB became SE-AIA: official p/i
        believed not correct: substantially based upon
        remains of c/n 5138 which relates to p/i

G-ACAA – G-ACZZ

G-ACBH^M Blackburn B.2   4700/3   01.12.32
        (2895M), G-ACBH Cancelled 14.07.42   27.11.41
        Fuselage only unrestored, in poor condition, bears
        traces of G-ADFO beneath current paintwork &
        appears to have replaced original fuselage
        With South Yorkshire Aircraft Museum, Doncaster

G-ACCB de Havilland DH.83 Fox Moth   4042   01.01.33
        E A Gautrey (Bedworth)
        (NF 29.01.16)

G-ACDA de Havilland DH.82A Tiger Moth   3175   06.02.33
        BB724, G-ACDA J Turnbull West Tisted
        'The De Havilland School of Flying'
        Composite rebuild   16.07.19P

G-ACDC de Havilland DH.82A Tiger Moth   3177   06.02.33
        BB726, G-ACDC
        The Tiger Club 1990 Ltd Damyns Hall, Upminster 23.10.19E
        Composite rebuild

G-ACDI de Havilland DH.82A Tiger Moth   3182   06.02.33
        BB742, G-ACDI Doublecube Aviation LLP
        Old Sarum   25.07.19E
        Composite rebuild

G-ACDJ de Havilland DH.82A Tiger Moth   3183   06.02.33
        BB729, G-ACDJ J A & R H Cooper Wickenby   18.08.07
        (NF 15.09.16)

G-ACEJ de Havilland DH.83 Fox Moth   4069   21.04.33
        K-F Grimminger Aalen-Elchingen, Germany
        'SMT Edinburgh'   01.08.19E

G-ACET de Havilland DH.84 Dragon   6021   21.04.33
        2779M, AW171, G-ACET G Cormack Cumbernauld
        (IE 26.04.17)

G-ACGL^M Comper CLA.7 Swift   S33/6   30.05.33
        WFU 22.03.40 & cancelled 01.12.46 in census '6'
        With Royal Air Force Cosford Museum

G-ACGR^M Percival Type D Gull Four IIA D.29   11.05.33
        Cancelled 07.12.34 – crashed Waterloo, Belgium 12.34 20.06.35
        As 'G-ACGR' Originally registered as P.1B
        With Koninklijk Leger Museum-Musée Royal de l'Armée,
        Brussels

G-ACGS de Havilland DH.85 Leopard Moth   7002   14.06.33
        ZK-AGS, (ZK-AGS), (HB-ODD), G-APKH, AX858,
        G-ACGS, PH-ALM, G-ACGS M J Miller Audley End
        (NF 21.06.16)

G-ACGZ de Havilland DH.60G III Moth Major 5030   30.05.33
        VT-AFW, G-ACGZ N H Lemon White Waltham   13.03.19P

G-ACIT de Havilland DH84 Dragon 1   6039   24.07.33
        Cancelled 26.04.02 as WFU   25.05.74
        Wroughton *In Science Museum store 2013*

G-ACLL de Havilland DH.85 Leopard Moth   7028   16.01.34
        AW165, G-ACLL D C M & V M Stiles (Andreas)   06.12.95P
        (NF 27.10.14)

G-ACMA de Havilland DH.85 Leopard Moth   7042   14.03.34
        BD148, G-ACMA P J Vacher Melhuish Farm, North
        Moreton   13.05.19P

G-ACMD (2) de Havilland DH.82A Tiger Moth 3195   20.01.88
        N182DH, EC-AGB, Spanish AF EE.1-104,
        30-104, 33-5 M J Bonnick Old Warden   25.07.19P
        Provenance doubtful: originally cancelled 15.01.65
        as broken up with remains sold 1969 as basis
        for N182DH

G-ACMN de Havilland DH.85 Leopard Moth   7050   ??.04.34
        X9381, G-ACMN K E & M R Slack Duxford   21.11.19E

G-ACNS de Havilland DH.60G III Moth Major 5068   ??.02.34
        ZS-???, G-ACNS C T Parry Malshanger, Basingstoke 21.05.12C
        Initial registration date believed to be 16.02.34;
        on rebuild 12.17 (NF 04.08.17)

G-ACOJ (2) de Havilland DH.85 Leopard Moth 7035   05.06.87
        F-AMXP C W Norman tr Norman Aeroplane Trust
        Rendcomb   20.04.19E
        Composite with wings from HB-OXO

G-ACOL (2) de Havilland DH.85 Leopard Moth 7045   21.12.83
        HB-OXO, CH-368 J Cresswell Batchley Farm, Hordle
        On rebuild 2017 using substantial parts of c/n 7086
        (VH-USM) (NF 09.11.17)

G-ACSP de Havilland DH.88 Comet   1994   21.08.34
        CS-AAJ, G-ACSP, E-1 D A, M L, P M & T M Jones Derby
        (IE 09.07.18)

G-ACSS de Havilland DH.88 Comet 1996 04.09.34
K5084, G-ACSS Richard Shuttleworth Trustees
Old Warden 'Grosvenor House' & '34' 16.08.19P
Four replicas exist as 'G-ACSS': (i) Mount Waverley,
Victoria, Australia; (ii) N88XD c/n T7 built 1993 @
Repeat Aircraft, Riverside CA, USA; (iii) BAPC.216; &
(iv) BAPC.257

G-ACTF Comper CLA.7 Swift S32/9 24.05.34
VT-ADO Richard Shuttleworth Trustees Old Warden 27.06.19P

G-ACUS (2) de Havilland DH.85 Leopard Moth 7082 17.11.77
HB-OXA, (G-ACUS) R A & V A Gammons
Old Warden 03.01.19E
Composite including parts ex HB-OXO c/n 7045

G-ACUUᴹ Cierva C.30A (Avro 671) 726 26.06.34
(G-AIXE), HM580, G-ACUU
Cancelled 14.11.88 as WFU As 'HM580:KX-K' 30.04.60
With Imperial War Museum, Duxford

G-ACUXᴹ Short S.16 Scion 1 S.776 26.06.34
VH-UUP Cancelled 02.38 – to VH-UUP (1) –
restored 25.03.77 – cancelled 05.01.82
Stripped frame stored
With Ulster Folk & Transport Museum, Holywood

G-ACVAᴹ Kay Gyroplane 33/1 1002 26.06.34
Cancelled 05.05.59
Built by Oddie Bradbury & Cull Ltd
With National Museum of Scotland, Edinburgh

G-ACWMᴹ Cierva C.30A (Avro 671) 715 24.07.34
(G-AHMK), AP506, G-ACWM
Cancelled 17.03.59 as WFU 13.07.40
On loan from E.D.ap Rees No marks carried
With The Helicopter Museum, Weston-super-Mare

G-ACWPᴹ Cierva C.30A (Avro 671) 728 24.07.34
AP507, G-ACWP Cancelled 01.06.40 as impressed 06.03.41
As 'AP507:KX-P' in RAF 529 Sqdn c/s
With Science Museum, South Kensington

G-ACXB (2) de Havilland DH.60G III Moth Major 5098 24.01.89
EC-ABY, EC-BAX, Spanish AF 30-53, EC-YAY
D F Hodgkinson (Meopham, Gravesend)
(NF 04.05.16)

G-ACXE British Klemm L 25c1 Swallow 21 29.10.34
J F Copeman tr ACXE Group (Bexhill-on-Sea)
(NF 09.02.18)

G-ACYKᴹ Spartan Cruiser III 101 02.05.35
Cancelled as destroyed 06.38 – crashed
Largs, Ayrshire 14.01.38 02.06.38
Fuselage only
With National Museum of Flight Scotland, East Fortune

G-ACYRᴹ de Havilland DH.89 Dragon Rapide 6261 15.10.34
Cancelled 10.03.59 by Sec of State 23.08.47
As 'G-ACYR' in Olley Air Services titles
With Museo de Aeronautica y Astronautica,
Cuatro Vientos, Spain

G-ADAA – G-ADZZ

G-ADAHᴹ de Havilland DH.89 Dragon Rapide 6278 30.01.35
Cancelled 18.02.59 as WFU 'Pioneer' 09.06.47
Allied Airways (Gandar Dower) titles
On loan from The Aeroplane Collection to
Manchester Museum of Sciences & Industry

G-ADEV (2) Avro 504K R3/LE/61400 18.04.84
G-ACNB, 'E3404'
Richard Shuttleworth Trustees Old Warden 19.08.19P
P/I unconfirmed but, if correct, is 3118M, BK892,
G-ADEV, H5199; as 'E3273' in RAF 77 Sqdn c/s to
represent night fighter

G-ADGP Miles M.2L Hawk Speed Six 160 20.05.35
(N.....), G-ADGP The Richard Ormonde Shuttleworth
Remembrance Trust Old Warden '8' 17.07.19P
Built by Phillips & Powis Aircraft Ltd

G-ADGT de Havilland DH.82A Tiger Moth 3338 23.05.35
BB697, G-ADGT Finest Hour Warbirds Ltd Bicester 25.08.12C
Carries 'BB697' on tail (NF 14.08.18)

G-ADGV de Havilland DH.82A Tiger Moth 3340 23.05.35
(D-E...), G-ADGV, (G-BACW), BB694, G-ADGV
M van Dijk & M R van der Straaten
Breda Int'l, Netherlands 25.11.15E
Operated by Vliegend Museum

G-ADHD (2) de Havilland DH.60G III Moth Major 5105 17.02.88
EC-..., Spanish AF 34-5, EC-W32
M E Vaisey (Hemel Hempstead)
Rebuild of ex Spanish components from USA
(NF 14.10.14)

G-ADIA de Havilland DH.82A Tiger Moth 3368 13.08.35
BB747, G-ADIA
S J Beaty Wold Lodge, Finedon 'Jock' 15.03.19P

G-ADJJ de Havilland DH.82A Tiger Moth 3386 29.08.35
BB819, G-ADJJ
J M Preston Watchford Farm, Yarcombe 26.04.19E

G-ADKC de Havilland DH.87B Hornet Moth 8064 27.03.36
X9445, G-ADKC C G & S Winch Solent 03.06.19P

G-ADKK de Havilland DH.87B Hornet Moth 8033 09.11.35
W5749, G-ADKK
S W Barratt & A J Herbert Old Warden 23.10.19P

G-ADKL de Havilland DH.87B Hornet Moth 8035 ??.11.35
F-BCJO, G-ADKL, W5750, G-ADKL
J S & P R Johnson Lavenham 16.07.19P

G-ADKM de Havilland DH.87B Hornet Moth 8037 12.11.35
W5751, G-ADKM J M O Miller Old Buckenham 06.09.17P
(IE 29.06.18)

G-ADLY de Havilland DH.87B Hornet Moth 8020 05.10.35
W9388, G-ADLY Treetops Aircraft LLP
Goodwood 'Leicestershire Foxhound II' 26.03.19E

G-ADMF British Aircraft L.25c Swallow II 406 13.01.38
EI-AFF, G-ADMF D A Edwards Shobdon
(IE 30.07.18)

G-ADMT de Havilland DH.87B Hornet Moth 8093 08.05.36
J A Jennings Felthorpe 'Curlew' 07.02.20P

G-ADMWᴹ Miles M.2H Hawk Major 177 30.07.35
8379M, G-ADMW, DG590, G-ADMW
Cancelled 16.09.86 by CAA 30.07.65
Built by Phillips & Powis Aircraft Ltd
With Montrose Air Station Heritage Centre

G-ADND de Havilland DH.87B Hornet Moth 8097 04.08.36
W9385, G-ADND D M & S M Weston Oaksey Park 30.05.19P
As 'W9385:YG-L' & '3' in RAF upper camouflage
& lower yellow c/s

G-ADNE de Havilland DH.87B Hornet Moth 8089 10.03.36
X9325, G-ADNE
R Felix tr G-ADNE Group Oaksey Park 'Ariadne' 11.05.19E

G-ADNL Miles M.5 Sparrowhawk 239 12.08.35
D Shew Hill Farm, Durley
Built by Phillips & Powis Aircraft Ltd; reconstructed
c.1953 as M.77 Sparrowjet (NF 09.07.18)

G-ADNZ (2) de Havilland DH.82A Tiger Moth 85614 10.10.74
6948M, DE673 D C Wall Tibenham 29.03.19P
As 'DE673' in RAF yellow c/s

G-ADOTᴹ de Havilland DH.87B Hornet Moth 8027 06.10.35
X9326, G-ADOT Cancelled 18.09.63 as WFU 15.10.59
With de Havilland Aircraft Museum, London Colney

G-ADPC de Havilland DH.82A Tiger Moth 3393 24.09.35
BB852, G-ADPC P D & S E Ford Derby 21.07.19E

G-ADPJ BAC Drone 2 7 21.08.35
M J Aubrey Llanfyrnach
Displayed Classic Ultralight Heritage (NF 08.08.18)

G-ADPRᴹ Percival Type D Gull Six D.55 29.08.35
AX866, G-ADPR Cancelled 17.07.40 as impressed
– to AX866, restored 15.08.46: cancelled 14.03 95
to ZK-DPR 01.08.95 As 'G-ADPR'
At Jean Batten Memorial, Auckland, New Zealand

G-ADPS British Aircraft L.25c Swallow II 410 04.09.35
J F Hopkins Watchford Farm, Yarcombe 26.09.17P

G-ADRA (2) Pietenpol Air Camper PFA 1514 10.04.78
A J Mason Bicester 'Edna May' 19.07.19P
Built by A J Mason

G-ADRR (2) Aeronca C.3   A733   06.09.88
N17423, NC17423   C J & M A Essex   Old Warden   13.11.19P
*Official c/n A734 is incorrect: c/n A733 confirmed
by original FAA documentation*

G-ADUR de Havilland DH.87B Hornet Moth   8085   10.03.36
(VH-...), G-ADUR, N9026Y, G-ADUR
C J & P R Harvey   Old Buckenham   19.05.19P

G-ADWJ de Havilland DH.82A Tiger Moth   3450   09.12.35
BB803, G-ADWJ   K F Crumplin   Henstridge   25.06.16E
*Operated by Tiger Moth Training; as 'BB803:75' in
RAF camouflage c/s*

G-ADWOᴹ de Havilland DH.82A Tiger Moth   3455   09.12.35
BB807, G-ADWO   Cancelled 15.09.58 as destroyed
*As 'BB807'
Restored 03.51 & overhauled with fuselage of BB860
(ex G-ADXT): damaged landing Christchurch 31.07.58
& WFU: fuselage,.parts ex G-AOAC & parts ex G-AOJJ
used in composite rebuild 1987/90: completed to static
condition 1990)
With Solent Sky, Southampton*

G-ADWT Miles M.2W Hawk Trainer   215   18.11.35
CF-NXT, G-ADWT, NF750, G-ADWT
K-F Grimminger   Aalen-Elchingen, Germany   28.09.15P
Built by Phillps & Powis Aircraft Ltd (IE 29.11.18)

G-ADXS   Mignet HM.14 Pou-du-Ciel   CLS.1   18.11.35
Cancelled 01.12.36 as WFU
*Breighton   On display 12.16
'The Fleeing Fly'   Built by C L Storey*

G-ADYS Aeronca C.3   A-600   ??.01.36
E P & P A Gliddon   Newgate Foot Farm, Saltergate   21.05.19P
Carries 'London Air Park Flying Club, Hanworth' on tail

G-AEAA – G-AEZZ

G-AEBB Mignet HM.14 Pou-Du-Ciel   KWO.1   24.01.36
Richard Shuttleworth Trustees   Old Warden
Built by K W Owen; noted 03.18 (IE 01.05.15)

G-AEBJ Blackburn B.2 Srs 1   6300/8   04.02.36
BAE Systems (Operations) Ltd   Old Warden   19.09.19P
On loan to Richard Shuttleworth Trustees

G-AEDB BAC Drone 2   13   18.03.36
(BGA 2731), G-AEDB
M J & S Honeychurch   (Charlton, Pewsey)
*Composite build including wings of G-AEJH &
tail of G-AEEN (NF 18.04.16)*

G-AEDU (2) de Havilland DH.90A Dragonfly   7526   04.06.79
N190DH, G-AEDU, ZS-CTR, CR-AAB
GAEDU Ltd   Biggin Hill   20.04.19E

G-AEEG Miles M.3A Falcon Major   216   14.03.36
SE-AFN, Swedish AF 913, SE-AFN, G-AEEG, U-20
Shipping & Airlines Ltd   Biggin Hill   09.04.19P
*Built by Phillips & Powis Aircraft Ltd;
carries 'SE-AFN' on rudder*

G-AEEHᴹ Mignet HM.14 Pou-Du-Ciel   EGD.1   13.03.36
WFU 15.05.38 & cancelled 08.46 in census 15.05.38
*Built by E G Davis
With Royal Air Force Cosford Museum*

G-AEFG Mignet HM.14 Pou-du-Ciel   JN.1   27.03.36
Cancelled in 31.03.38 census
Selby   Allocated BAPC.75 & noted 01.12   Built by J Nolan

G-AEFT Aeronca C.3   A-610   17.04.36
N S Chittenden   Woodlands Barton Farm, Roche   14.06.19P

G-AEGVᴹ Mignet HM.14 Pou-Du-Ciel   EMAC.1   22.04.36
Cancelled 12.37 – WFU 26.05.37   26.05.37
*Built by East Midlands Aviation Company
With Midland Air Museum, Coventry*

G-AEHMᴹ Mignet HM.14 Pou-du-Ciel   HJD1   30.04.36
Cancelled 04.03.39   'Blue Finch'
*Built by H J Dolman
With M Shed, Bristol*

G-AEJZᴹ Mignet HM.14 Pou-du-Ciel   TLC.1   09.06.36
G-AEJZ   Cancelled 31.12.38 in census
*As 'G-AEJZ'   Allocated 'BAPC.120'   Built by T L Crosland
With South Yorkshire Aircraft Museum, Doncaster*

G-AEKRᴹ Mignet HM.14 Pou-Du-Ciel   CAC.1   26.06.36
Cancelled 31.07.38 as PWFU   22.06.37
*Built by E Claybourne & Co   Stored Doncaster
1938/1960: dbf RAF Finningley 04.09.70: rebuilt &
allocated 'G-AEKR' (BAPC.121)
With Museum & Art Gallery, Doncaster*

G-AEKVᴹ Kronfeld Drone   30   13.01.37
BGA 2510, G-AEKV   Cancelled 14.01.99 as PWFU   06.10.60
*With Brooklands Museum, Weybridge, on loan to
The Glider Heritage Centre, Lasham*

G-AEKW Miles M.12 Mohawk   298   04.07.36
HM503, G-AEKW, U-08, G-AEKW
Cancelled 08.11.41 by Sec of State – restored 05.46,
cancelled 01.01.50 as destroyed   01.03.50
In RAF Museum store 2018

G-AELO de Havilland DH.87B Hornet Moth   8105   30.07.36
AW118, G-AELO   M J Miller   Audley End   04.12.18P

G-AENP (2) Hawker Afghan Hind   41H/81902   29.10.81
(BAPC.78), R Afghan AF
Richard Shuttleworth Trustees   Old Warden   26.06.16P
As 'K5414:XV' in RAF 15 Sqdn silver c/s; noted 03.18

G-AEOA de Havilland DH.80A Puss Moth   2184   01.10.36
ES921, G-AEOA, YU-PAX, UN-PAX
A & P A Wood   (Halstead & Dunmow)   27.06.95P
(NF 04.09.14)

G-AEOF (2) Rearwin 8500 Sportster   462   01.12.81
N15863, NC15863
Just Plane Trading Ltd   Top Farm, Croydon   24.05.19P

G-AEPH Bristol F.2b Fighter   7575   13.11.36
D8096, G-AEPH, D8096
Richard Shuttleworth Trustees   Old Warden   13.04.19P
Original c/n 3746; rebuilt c.1931; as 'D8096:D' in RAF c/s

G-AERDᴹ Percival Type D Gull Six   D.65   16.09.77
HB-OFU   Cancelled 28.11.86 – to Australia
*As 'G-AERD'
With National Museum of Australia, Canberra*

G-AERV Miles M.11A Whitney Straight   307   30.12.36
EM999, G-AERV   P W Bishop   White Waltham   03.10.18P

G-AESB (2) Aeronca C.3   A638   05.08.88
N15742, NC15742
R J M Turnbull   Rydinghurst Farm, Cranleigh
(NF 10.04.18)

G-AESE de Havilland DH.87B Hornet Moth   8108   13.01.37
W5775, G-AESE   B R Cox   Coventry   'Sheena'   08.06.16E
*Ground looped, port u/c collapsed Coventry 30.07.16
& substantially damaged*

G-AESZ Chilton DW.1   DW1/1   ??.01.37
R E Nerou   Old Warden   '29'   29.08.18P
On loan to Richard Shuttleworth Trustees

G-AETAᴹ Caudron G.III   7487   29.01.37
OO-ELA, O-BELA, (9203M)
Cancelled xx.08.38 as PWFU   As '3066' in RNAS c/s
*Also registered as c/n 5019 or 5021
With RAF Museum, Hendon*

G-AETG Aeronca 100   AB110   ??.02.37
J J Teagle tr J Teagle & Partners   (Overton, Basingstoke)
(NF 21.05.18)

G-AEUJ Miles M.11A Whitney Straight   313   19.02.37
R E Mitchell   Sleap
Built by Phillip & Powis Aircraft Ltd (NF 13.10.17)

G-AEVS Aeronca 100   AB114   ??.03.37
R A Fleming   Breighton   'Jeeves'   16.06.19P
Composite build including parts of original G-AEXD

G-AEVZᴹ British Aircraft L.25c Swallow II   475   19.03.37
Cancelled 07.09.01 to EC-IMP   As 'G-AEVZ'   15.06.01
With Fundación Infante de Orleans, Cuatro Vientos, Spain

G-AEXD Aeronca 100   AB124   01.04.37
M A & N Mills   Sywell
*Comprises parts of G-AESP after rebuild 1958;
active 04.15 (IE 20.01.15)*

G-AEXF Percival Type E Mew Gull   E.22   18.05.37
ZS-AHM   Richard Shuttleworth Trustees   Old Warden   01.05.19P
*Re-Built by T M Storey – project PFA 13-10020 (1972-1978)
another replica at Thorpe Camp, Woodhall Spa as 'G-AEXF'*

| G-AEXT | Dart Kitten II | 123 | ??.04.37 |

G-AEXT | Dart Kitten II | 123 | ??.04.37
R A Fleming   Breighton | | | 13.05.19P

G-AEXZ | Taylor J-2 Cub | 997 | 05.02.38
J R & M Dowson   (Arnesby, Leicester)
Built by Taylor Aircraft Co Inc (NF 25.09.14)

G-AEZF | Short S.16 Scion | PA.1008 | 18.06.37
M-5   Cancelled xx.05.54 as WFU
Rochester   For long term static rebuild 06.16,
by Medway Aircraft Preservation Society)

G-AEZJ | Percival Type K Vega Gull | K.65 | 02.07.37
SE-ALA, D-IXWD, PH-ATH, G-AEZJ
Comanche Warbirds Ltd   Biggin Hill | | | 30.01.19E

G-AFAA – G-AFZZ

G-AFAX[M] | British Aircraft Eagle 2 | 138 | 29.07.37
VH-ACN (1), G-AFAX   Cancelled 10.06.08 – to EC-KVR | | | 15.05.08
As 'G-AFAX'
With Fundación Infante de Orleans, Cuatro Vientos, Spain

G-AFBS[M] | Miles M.14A Hawk Trainer 3 | 539 | 17.09.37
(G-AKKU), BB661, G-AFBS   Cancelled 22.12.95 by CAA | | | 25.02.63
With Imperial War Museum, Duxford

G-AFCL | British Aircraft L.25c Swallow II | 462 | 03.11.37
D & J Cresswell   Batchley Farm, Hordle | | | 02.11.17P

G-AFDO (2) | Piper J-3C-65 Cub | 2593 | 07.06.88
N21697, NC21697   R J Wald   (Llwynhendy, Llanelli)
'Butter Cub' | | | 27.09.19P
Fuselage No.2633

G-AFEL (2) | Monocoupe 90A | A782 | 07.06.82
N19432, NC194323
M Rieser   Straubing-Wallmühle, Bayern, Germany | | | 28.09.19P

G-AFFD | Percival Type Q Six | Q21 | 12.02.38
(G-AIEY), X9407, G-AFFD
R H Ford tr G-AFFD Restoration Group   Seething
As 'X4907' in RAF c/s (NF 17.01.13)

G-AFFH | Taylor J-2 Cub | 1166 | 26.03.38
EC-ALA, G-AFFH   M J Honeychurch   (Charlton, Pewsey)
Built by Taylor Aircraft Co Inc (NF 13.02.18)

G-AFGD | British Aircraft L.25c Swallow II | 469 | 04.04.38
BK897, G-AFGD
D A Edwards tr South Wales Swallow Group   Shobdon | | | 10.07.14P
Carries 'BK897' on rear fuselage (IE 24.07.17)

G-AFGE | British Aircraft L.25c Swallow II | 470 | 04.04.38
BK894, G-AFGE
A A M & C W N Huke   Manor Farm, Dinton | | | 08.08.18P
(IE 14.08.18)

G-AFGH | Chilton DW.1 | DW1/2 | 20.03.38
G L & M L Joseph   Denford Manor, Hungerford
(NF 25.09.14)

G-AFGI | Chilton DW.1 | DW1/3 | 30.03.38
K A A McDonald   White Waltham | | | 28.01.19P

G-AFGM (2) | Piper J-4A Cub Coupe | 4-943 | 30.12.81
N26895, NC26895   P H Wilkinson   Falgunzeon | | | 24.08.19P

G-AFGZ | de Havilland DH.82A Tiger Moth | 3700 | 09.05.38
G-AMHI, BB759, G-AFGZ   M R Paul   Solent | | | 14.06.18P

G-AFHA (2) | Moss MA.1 | MA 1/2 | 27.02.67
K Miller   (Coventry)
Small components stored (NF 09.09.14)

G-AFIN | Chrislea LC.1 Airguard | LC1 | 07.07.38
BAPC.203   T W J Carnall   Dunkeswell
(NF 27.02.18)

G-AFIR | Phoenix Luton LA-4A Minor | JSS2 | 07.07.38
Parasol Aircraft Company Ltd
(Priors Byne Farm, Partridge Green)
Built by J S Squires; on rebuild 01.16 (NF 21.04.16)

G-AFIU[M] | Parker CA.4 Parasol (Luton Minor). | CA-4 | 19.10.82
Cancelled 31.03.99 by CAA
Built by C.F. Parker at Codsall, Staffordshire in 1937
Under restoration with wings & tail ex G-ATWS
With The Aeroplane Collection, Hooton Park

G-AFJA | Taylor-Watkinson Dingbat | DB100 | 02.08.38
Cancelled 01.12.14 by CAA | | | 20.06.75
Walkeridge Farm, Overton   On rebuild 06.16

G-AFJB | Foster-Wikner GM.1 Wicko | 5 | 15.08.38
DR613, G-AFJB
J Dible   Roughay Farm, Lower Upham | | | 04.09.18P

G-AFJR[M] | Tipsy Trainer 1 | 2 | 20.08.38
Cancelled 12.04.89 as TWFU | | | 10.09.64
As 'G-AFJR'   Converted to Belfair
With Koninklijk Leger Museum-Musée Royal de l'Armée,
Brussels

G-AFJU | Miles M.17 Monarch | 789 | 25.08.38
X9306, G-AFJU   P W Bishop   Rotary Farm, Hatch
Built by Phillips & Powis Aircraft Ltd; on rebuild 05.15
(IE 28.02.18)

G-AFJV (2) | Moss MA.2 | MA 2/2 | 27.02.67
K Miller   (Coventry)
Small components stored (NF 09.09.14)

G-AFLW | Miles M-17 Monarch | 792 | 02.11.38
Cancelled 03.05.01 by CAA | | | 30.07.98
White Waltham   Stored 02.14

G-AFNG | de Havilland DH.94 Moth Minor | 94014 | 02.05.39
AW112, G-AFNG   Cancelled 14.03.11 as sold in France | | | 21.10.98
Orbigny, France   Stored for rebuild 07.17

G-AFNI | de Havilland DH.94 Moth Minor | 94035 | 11.05.39
W7972, G-AFNI
J Jennings   (Oak Farm, Bylaugh, Dereham)
(NF 22.10.18)

G-AFOB | de Havilland DH.94 Moth Minor | 94018 | 16.05.39
X5117, G-AFOB
K Cantwell   (Oak Farm, Bylaugh, Dereham) | | | 11.05.93P
(NF 22.10.18)

G-AFOJ | de Havilland DH.94 Moth Minor | 9407 | 21.07.39
E-1, E-0236, G-AFOJ
A H Soper   Jenkin's Farm, Navestock
(NF 10.12.15)

G-AFPN | de Havilland DH.94 Moth Minor | 94044 | 23.05.39
X9297, G-AFPN
A A A Maitland tr The Moth Minor Group   Shobdon | | | 18.08.19P
Official c/n 94016 is incorrect

G-AFRV[M] | Tipsy Trainer I | 10 | 15.07.39
Cancelled 10.02.87 by CAA   As 'G-AFRV'
With Koninklijk Leger Museum-Musée Royal de l'Armée,
Brussels

G-AFRZ | Miles M.17 Monarch | 793 | 24.03.39
G-AIDE, W6463, G-AFRZ   R E Mitchell   Sleap
Built by Phillips & Powis Aircraft Ltd (NF 13.10.17)

G-AFSC | Tipsy Trainer 1 | 11 | 15.07.39
D M Forshaw   High Cross, Ware | | | 14.08.15P
(IE 06.03.18)

G-AFSV | Chilton DW.1A | DW1A/1 | 05.04.39
R E Nerou   (Coventry)
(NF 03.12.14)

G-AFTA | Hawker Tomtit | 30380 | 26.04.39
K1786, G-AFTA, K1786
Richard Shuttleworth Trustees   Old Warden | | | 03.07.18P
As 'K1786' in RAF silver c/s

G-AFTN[M] | Taylorcraft Plus C2 | 102 | 02.05.39
HL535, G-AFTN   Cancelled 13.01.99 by CAA | | | 01.11.57
With Snibston Discovery Park, Coalville

G-AFUP (2) | Luscombe 8A | 1246 | 07.06.88
N25370, NC25370   R Dispain   (Fordingbridge) | | | 12.03.97P
(NF 23.09.14)

G-AFWH (2) | Piper J-4A Cub Coupe | 4-1341 | 14.01.82
N33093, NC33093
R D W Norton & C W Stearn   (Ely) | | | 02.07.01P
(NF 30.07.18)

G-AFWI | de Havilland DH.82A Tiger Moth | 82187 | 19.07.39
BB814, G-AFWI   J N Bailey   Crowfield | | | 22.11.18P

G-AFWT | Tipsy Trainer 1 | 13 | 01.08.39
N Parkhouse   Chelworth House, Chelwood Gate | | | 05.11.16P
(NF 02.11.18)

G-AFYD (2) | Luscombe 8F Silvaire | 1044 | 29.07.75
N25120, NC25120
J D Iliffe   Haw Farm, Hampstead Norreys | | | 15.09.18E
(NF 12.11.18)

G-AFYO (2)	Stinson HW-75 Voyager	7039	25.04.77
	F-BGQP, NC22586		
	M Lodge Westfield Farm, Hailsham		19.06.19P
	P/i French Army '22586' not confirmed		
G-AFZA (2)	Piper J-4A Cub Coupe	4-873	27.06.84
	N26198, NC26198		
	R A Benson Trenchard Farm, Eggesford		02.12.02P
	(NF 14.01.16)		
G-AFZE	Heath Parasol	P.A.1	25.08.39
	C J Essex (Coventry)		
	Built by R H Parker (NF 29.09.17)		
G-AFZK (2)	Luscombe 8A	1042	24.10.88
	N25118, NC25118		
	M G Byrnes Brittas House, RoI		15.06.09P
	(NF 19.05.16)		
G-AFZL (2)	Porterfield CP-50	581	18.03.82
	N25401, NC25401		
	P G Lucas & S H Sharpe White Waltham		29.01.19P

G-AGAA – G-AGZZ

G-AGAT (2)	Piper J-3F-50 Cub	4062	17.07.87
	N26126, NC26126		
	A S Bathgate Castleton Farm, Gorebridge		27.06.17P
	(IE 30.06.17)		
G-AGBN[M]	General Aircraft GAL.42 Cygnet 2	111	04.10.40
	ES915, G-AGBN Cancelled 08.07.41 by Sec of State:		
	restored 11.02.46, cancelled 15.11.88 as WFU		28.11.80
	With National Museum of Flight Scotland, East Fortune		
G-AGEG (2)	de Havilland DH.82A Tiger Moth	82710	16.08.82
	N9146, D-EDIL, R Netherlands AF A-32,		
	PH-UFK, R Netherlands AF A-32, R4769		
	C W Norman tr Norman Aeroplane Trust		
	Rendcomb		09.04.19P
G-AGHY (2)	de Havilland DH.82A Tiger Moth	82292	17.02.88
	N9181 P Groves tr G-AGHY Group Solent		19.07.19P
G-AGIV (2)	Piper J-3C-65 Cub (*L-4J-PI*)	12676	13.08.82
	OO-AFI, OO-GBA, 44-80380		
	C E Davis tr J3 Cub Group Compton Abbas		16.05.19P
	(Fuselage No.12506)		
G-AGJG	de Havilland DH.89A Dragon Rapide	6517	25.10.43
	X7344 D J T & M J Miller Duxford		
	'Scottish Airways' in WW2 camouflage scheme		01.05.19E
G-AGLK	Auster 5D	1137	25.08.44
	RT475 D K Chambers & M A Farrelly		
	Welshpool *Carries 'Goldhawk' & 'Hawk' logo on tail*		15.07.14P
	Built by Taylorcraft Aeroplanes (England) Ltd (NF 22.05.18)		
G-AGMI (2)	Luscombe 8E Silvaire Deluxe	1569	15.11.88
	N28827, NC28827 D Campbell & R Travis		
	tr Oscar Flying Group Kittyhawk Farm, Ripe		12.06.19P
G-AGNJ (2)	de Havilland DH.82A Tiger Moth	660	21.02.89
	VP-YOJ, ZS-BGF, SAAF 2366		
	A J, P B & P J Borsberry (Kidmore End, Reading)		
	Built by de Havilland Aircraft Proprietary Ltd, Australia		
	(NF 04.02.16)		
G-AGNV[M]	Avro 685 York C.1	1223	20.08.45
	'MW100', 'LV633', G-AGNV, TS798		
	Cancelled 07.05.65 as PWFU *As 'TS798'*		06.03.65
	With Royal Air Force Cosford Museum		
G-AGOH[M]	Auster J/1 Autocrat	1442	08.10.45
	Cancelled 07.08.08 as PWFU		24.08.95
	With Snibston Discovery Park, Coalville		
G-AGOS	Reid & Sigrist RS.4 Desford Trainer	03	01.05.45
	VZ728, G-AGOS		
	Leicestershire County Council Spanhoe		
	As 'VZ728' in RAF c/s; noted 02.18 (IE 14.07.15)		
G-AGOY	Miles M.38 Messenger 3	4690	05.06.45
	EI-AGE, G-AGOY, HB-EIP, G-AGOY, U-0247		
	S A Blanchard (Cottingham)		
	On rebuild 02.18 (NF 15.11.18)		
G-AGPG[M]	Avro C19 Series 2	1212	15.06.45
	Cancelled 05.11.75 as WFU		13.02.71
	At Avro Heritage Museum, Woodford; front fuselage only		

G-AGPK (2)	de Havilland DH.82A Tiger Moth	86566	27.10.88
	N657DH, F-BGDN, French AF, PG657		
	T K Butcher Clacton-on-Sea		12.05.19E
	Built by Morris Motors Ltd; fitted with wings, tailplane,		
	fin & rudder 2002 ex G-ANLH; as 'PG657' in RAF c/s		
G-AGRU[M]	Vickers 657 Viking 1	112	08.05.46
	VP-TAX, G-AGRU		
	Cancelled 08.12.46, 16.06.48 & 09.06.64 as sold *'Vagrant'*		
	BEA titles		09.01.64
	With Brooklands Museum, Weybridge		
G-AGRW[M]	Vickers 639 Viking 1	115	08.05.46
	XF640, G-AGRW Cancelled 19.02.68 as PWFU		09.07.68
	(Originally registered as Vickers 498 Viking 1A		
	Austrian Airlines titles		
	With Austrian Aviation Museum, Bad Voslau		
G-AGSH	de Havilland DH.89A Dragon Rapide 6	6884	25.07.45
	EI-AJO, G-AGSH, NR808		
	P H Meeson Old Warden *'Jemma Meeson'*		02.05.19E
	Built by Brush Coachworks Ltd; on loan to Richard		
	Shuttleworth Trustees; British European Airways c/s		
G-AGTM	de Havilland DH.89A Dragon Rapide 6	6746	19.09.45
	JY-ACL, OD-ABP, G-AGTM, NF875		
	B R Cox Coventry *'Sybille'*		19.05.15E
	Built by Brush Coachworks Ltd (NF 30.09.16)		
G-AGTO	Auster 5J1 Autocrat	1822	02.10.45
	M J Barnett & D J T Miller Audley End		29.08.19P
G-AGTT	Auster 5J1 Autocrat	1826	02.10.45
	Parasol Aircraft Company Ltd (Barcombe, Lewes)		
	(NF 30.11.17)		
G-AGVG	Auster 5J1 Autocrat	1858	07.12.45
	P J & S J Benest Little Farm, Hamstead Marshall		25.07.19P
	Built by Taylorcraft Aeroplanes (England) Ltd;		
	modified tail surfaces		
G-AGXN	Auster J1N Alpha	1963	22.01.46
	J J Teagle tr Gentleman's Aerial Touring Carriage Group		
	Popham		10.06.19P
G-AGXU	Auster J1N Alpha	1969	24.01.46
	L J Kingscott (Oaksey, Malmesbury)		13.08.06
	(NF 06.03.15)		
G-AGXV	Auster 5J1 Autocrat	1970	01.02.46
	M J Barnett Little Gransden *'Pamela IV'*		13.11.14P
	(NF 12.10.18)		
G-AGYD	Auster J1N Alpha	1985	04.02.46
	P R Hodson Little Gransden		
	(NF 12.10.18)		
G-AGYH	Auster J1N Alpha	1989	04.02.46
	I M Staves (Northallerton)		
	(NF 23.03.18)		
G-AGYT	Auster J1N Alpha	1862	18.01.46
	P J Barrett (Lightwater)		
	(NF 23.03.16)		
G-AGYU	de Havilland DH.82A Tiger Moth	85265	10.01.46
	DE208 S A Firth Forwood Farm, Treswell		14.05.19P
	Built by Morris Motors Ltd; as 'DE208' in RAF c/s		
G-AGYY (2)	Ryan ST3KR (*PT-21-RY*)	1167	15.06.83
	N56792, 41-1967		
	H de Vries Hoogeveen, Netherlands		31.10.19P
	As '27' in USAAC c/s		
G-AGZZ (2)	de Havilland DH.82A Tiger Moth	T256	14.05.82
	N3862, VH-BTU, VH-RNM, VH-BMY, RAAF A17-503		
	C R Davies Allensmore		17.09.19P
	Built by de Havilland Aircraft Proprietary Ltd, Australia		

G-AHAA – G-AHZZ

G-AHAA	Miles M.28 Mercury 6	6268	26.01.46
	OY-ALW, D-EHAB, G-AHAA		
	S A Blanchard North Coates		
	(IE 01.10.18)		
G-AHAG	de Havilland DH.89A Dragon Rapide 6	6926	31.01.46
	RL944 Scillonia Airways Ltd Membury *'Bryher'*		29.05.19E
	Built by Brush Coachworks Ltd		
G-AHAL	Auster J1N Alpha	1870	31.01.46
	J W Frecklington & R Merewood t/a Wickenby Aviation		
	Wickenby		29.10.19P

G-AHAM	Auster 5J1 Autocrat	1885	21.01.46
	Intema Engineering BVBA Hasselt-Kiewit, Belgium		04.06.19P
G-AHAN (2)	de Havilland DH.82A Tiger Moth	86553	31.05.85
	N90406, F-BGDG, French AF, PG644		
	J J Kershaw tr G-AHAN Flying Group Bicester		26.10.18P
	Built by Morris Motors Ltd		
G-AHAO	Auster 5J1 Autocrat	1886	07.02.46
	SE-BYU, G-AHAO		
	R Callaway-Lewis (South Mundham, Chichester)		31.05.19P
G-AHAP	Auster 5J1 Autocrat	1887	08.02.46
	W D Hill Fenland		
	(NF 18.03.18)		
G-AHAU	Auster 5J1/160 Autocrat	1850	11.02.46
	(HB-EOL) D Smith tr Andreas Auster Group Andreas		23.05.19P
	Built by Taylorcraft Aeroplanes (England) Ltd;		
	Built by-up fin & fuselage fillet		
G-AHBL	de Havilland DH.87B Hornet Moth	8135	06.02.46
	P6786, CF-BFN Shipping & Airlines Ltd Biggin Hill		24.01.19E
G-AHBM	de Havilland DH.87B Hornet Moth	8126	06.02.46
	P6785, CF-BFJ, (CF-BFO), CF-BFJ		
	E P & P A Gliddon Newgate Foot Farm, Saltergate		23.06.19P
G-AHCL	Auster J1N Alpha	1977	13.05.46
	G-OJVC, G-AHCL		
	N Musgrave RAF Mona *'Patience'*		17.07.19P
	Originally registered as J1 Autocrat		
G-AHCR	Gould-Taylorcraft Plus D Special	211	15.04.46
	LB352 S F Griggs Dunkeswell		09.02.18P
	Built by Taylorcraft Aeroplanes (England) Ltd;		
	as 'LB352' in RAF c/s		
G-AHEC (2)	Luscombe 8A	3428	28.10.88
	N72001, NC72001		
	A F Wankowski (Wolves Hall, Tendering)		14.07.05P
	On rebuild 2017 (NF 03.11.15)		
G-AHED	de Havilland DH.89A Dragon Rapide 6	6944	27.02.46
	RL962 Cancelled 03.03.69 as PWFU		17.04.68
	RAF Stafford *In RAF Museum store 2018*		
G-AHGW	Taylorcraft Plus D	222	02.09.46
	LB375 R Ellingworth & N A Preston Spanhoe		03.05.96P
	On rebuild 10.17 as 'LB375' (NF 29.06.17)		
G-AHGZ	Taylorcraft Plus D	214	24.04.46
	LB367 P H B Cole Craysmarsh Farm, Melksham		01.09.19P
	As 'LB367' in RAF c/s		
G-AHHH	Auster J1N Alpha	2011	11.05.46
	F-BAVR, G-AHHH		
	G J Molloy & K Moore Sleap *'Ginger'*		05.06.19P
G-AHHK	Auster J/1 Autocrat	2014	11.05.46
	Cancelled 03.04.89 by CAA		22.03.70
	Carr Farm, Thorney, Newark *Frame only 02.15*		
G-AHHPM	Auster J/1N Alpha	2019	11.05.46
	G-SIME, G-AHHP Cancelled 22.02.99 by CAA		08.03.86
	Reported with South Yorkshire Aircraft Museum,		
	Doncaster Frame only		
G-AHHT	Auster J1N Alpha	2022	11.05.46
	N J Hudson & P T Sinclair tr South Downs Auster Group		
	Durleighmarsh Farm, Rogate		08.09.19P
G-AHHXM	Taylorcraft Plus D	173	20.05.46
	OY-DSZ, D-ELUV, D-ELUS, G-AHHX, LB314		
	Cancelled 04.10.56 as sold Germany *As 'LB314'*		
	Built by Auster Aircraft Ltd		
	With South Yorkshire Aircraft Museum, Doncaster		
G-AHIP (2)	Piper J-3C-65 Cub (*L-4H-PI*)	12008	03.07.85
	OO-GEJ, OO-ALY, 44-79826		
	A D Pearce Eastbach Spence, English Bicknor		07.08.19P
	Fuselage No.11950 – but see G-AJAD;		
	as '479712:8-R' in USAF c/s		
G-AHIZ	de Havilland DH.82A Tiger Moth	xxxx	23.04.46
	PG624 CFG Flying Ltd Cambridge		02.07.19E
	Built by Morris Motors Ltd; official c/n '4610' is incorrect		
G-AHKOM	Taylorcraft Plus D	228	24.04.46
	LB381 Cancelled 10.03.56 – to D-ECOD		
	– subsequently OY-DSH As 'LB381'		
	With Dansk Veteranflysamling, Stauning, Denmark		

G-AHKX	Avro C19 Series 2	1333	18.05.46
	BAE Systems (Operations) Ltd Old Warden		
	'RAF Coningsby'		
	On loan to Richard Shuttleworth Trustees;		
	as 'TX176' in RAF c/s		
G-AHKYM	Miles M.18 Series 2	4426	26.04.46
	HM545, U-0224, U-8 Cancelled 19.03.92 as WFU		20.09.89
	With National Museum of Flight Scotland, East Fortune		
G-AHLK	Auster 3	700	01.05.46
	NJ889 J H Powell-Tuck Preston Court, Ledbury		16.10.18P
	Built by Taylorcraft Aeroplanes (England) Ltd;		
	as 'NJ889' in RAF c/s		
G-AHLT	de Havilland DH.82A Tiger Moth	82247	02.05.46
	N9128 M P Waring Solent		29.10.19E
G-AHMJM	Cierva C.30A (*Avro 671*) (Rota I)	R3/CA/43	08.05.46
	K4235 Cancelled 09.02.50 as WFU – restored 08.04.93,		
	cancelled 12.11.98 – to USA *As 'K4235'*		
	Official c/n 774 incorrect & was Danish Avro 621		
	With Fantasy of Flight, Polk City, Florida		
G-AHMN	de Havilland DH.82A Tiger Moth	82223	08.05.46
	N6985 A D Barton Newquay Cornwall		27.05.02
	(NF 19.03.18)		
G-AHNR (2)	Taylorcraft BC-12D	7204	15.11.88
	N43545, NC43545 T M Buick Deanland		08.08.14P
	(NF 13.01.16)		
G-AHOO (2)	de Havilland DH.82A Tiger Moth	86150	06.06.85
	6940M, EM967		
	J T Milsom France Farm, Rushall		28.08.19P
	Built by Morris Motors Ltd		
G-AHPZ	de Havilland DH.82A Tiger Moth	83794	22.05.46
	EI-AFJ, G-AHPZ, T7280 N J Wareing Solent		09.07.19P
G-AHRIM	de Havilland DH.104 Dove 1B	04008	11.07.46
	4X-ARI, G-AHRI Cancelled 18.05.72 as WFU		
	With Newark Air Museum, Winthorpe		
G-AHSA	Avro 621 Tutor	K3215	21.06.46
	K3215, G-AHSA, K3215		
	Richard Shuttleworth Trustees Old Warden		09.10.18P
	As 'K 3241' in RAF CFS Aerobatic Team c/s		
G-AHSD	Taylorcraft Plus D	182	01.07.46
	LB323 K B Owen Spanhoe		
	As 'LB323' in AAC c/s; on rebuild 10.17 (IE 30.05.18)		
G-AHSO	Auster J/1N Alpha	2123	08.08.46
	Cancelled 06.04.09 by CAA		06.04.95
	Northfield Farm, Mavis Enderby		
	Stored for spares use 08.13		
G-AHSP	Auster 5J1 Autocrat	2134	08.08.46
	F-BGRO, G-AHSP R M Weeks Earls Colne		15.08.19P
G-AHSS	Auster J1N Alpha	2136	08.08.46
	G W Tomkins Spanhoe *'Sunday Sierra'*		29.03.17P
G-AHTE	Percival Proctor V	AE58	26.06.46
	D K Tregilgas Great Oakley		
	(NF 10.05.18)		
G-AHTWM	Airspeed AS.40 Oxford 1	3083	06.06.46
	V3388 Cancelled 03.04.89 by CAA *As 'V3388'*		15.12.60
	With Imperial War Museum, Duxford		
G-AHUF (2)	de Havilland DH.82A Tiger Moth	86221	26.02.85
	A2123, NL750 S A Crossland tr Eaglescott		
	Tiger Moth Group Eaglescott		24.04.19E
	Built by Morris Motors Ltd; as 'T-7997' in RAF c/s		
G-AHUG	Taylorcraft Plus D	153	05.06.46
	LB282 N C Dickinson Wycombe Air Park		
	Fuselage frame noted 07.16 (NF 03.12.15)		
G-AHUIM	Miles M.38 Messenger 2A	6335	19.07.46
	Cancelled 21.11.73 as PWFU		04.09.60
	Comprises cockpit section, engine cowls, outer wings		
	& rear fuselage stringers ex G-AHUI, fins, rudders,		
	forward part of rear fuselage ex G-AJFF & rear fuselage		
	ex EI-AGB (ex G-AHFP)		
	With The Aeroplane Collection, Hooton Park		
G-AHUJ	Miles M.14A Hawk Trainer 3	1900	06.06.46
	R1914 F Baldanza Gloucestershire		18.04.19P
G-AHUN (2)	Globe GC-1B Swift	3536	24.07.86
	EC-AJK, OO-KAY, NC77764		
	R J Hamlett North Weald		04.08.95P
	On rebuild 07.18 (NF 29.06.16)		

G-AHUV	de Havilland DH.82A Tiger Moth	3894	24.06.46
	N6593 A D Gordon Lude Farm, Blair Atholl		09.08.19P
G-AHVU	de Havilland DH.82A Tiger Moth	84728	14.08.46
	T6313		
	Vintage Aircraft Factory Ltd Newquay Cornwall		29.01.15E
	On rebuild 05.17 (NF 06.12.18)		
G-AHVV	de Havilland DH.82A Tiger Moth	86123	24.06.46
	EM929 M Arter Eaglescott		04.06.16E
	Built by Morris Motors Ltd (IE 23.10.18)		
G-AHWJ	Taylorcraft Plus D	165	20.06.46
	LB294 Cancelled 11.11.11 as PWFU		30.06.71
	Worthing Displayed Saywell Int'l HQ as 'LB294'		
G-AHXW^M	de Havilland DH.89A Dragon Rapide	6782	11.07.46
	N683DH, G-AHXW, NR683		
	Cancelled 16.03.71 – to N683DH		
	Built Brush Coachworks Ltd; at Historic Flight Foundation,		
	Paine Field; as 'G-AHXW'		

G-AIAA – G-AIZZ

G-AIBE^M	Fairey Fulmar 2	F.3707	29.07.46
	N1854, G-AIBE, N1854 Cancelled 30.04.59 – to N1854		06.07.59
	As 'N1854'		
	With Fleet Air Arm Museum, RNAS Yeovilton		
G-AIBH	Auster J1N Alpha	2113	19.08.46
	M J Bonnick Rectory Farm, Abbotsley		18.06.19E
G-AIBM	Auster 5J1 Autocrat	2148	02.09.46
	R Greatrex Colthrop Manor Farm, Thatcham		29.08.19P
G-AIBR	Auster J1N Alpha	2151	02.09.46
	P R Hodson Northrepps		23.08.19P
G-AIBW	Auster J1N Alpha	2158	02.09.46
	C R Sunter Breighton		03.04.19P
G-AIBX	Auster 5J1 Autocrat	2159	02.09.46
	B H Beeston tr Wasp Flying Group Little Gransden		11.05.18P
G-AIBY	Auster 5J1 Autocrat	2160	02.09.46
	D Morris Sherburn-in-Elmet		
	(NF 20.03.18)		
G-AICX (2)	Luscombe 8A	2568	27.01.88
	N71141, NC71141 C C & J M Lovell		
	Stonefield Park, Chilbolton 'Easy Grace'		10.09.19P
G-AIDL	de Havilland DH.89A Dragon Rapide 6	6968	23.08.46
	TX310 Cirrus Aviation Ltd Clacton-on-Sea		10.09.19E
	Built by Brush Coachworks Ltd; operated by Classic Wings;		
	as 'TX310' in RAF c/s. Noted 02.19		
G-AIDN	Supermarine 502 Spitfire T.8	6S/729058	22.08.46
	N58JE, G-AIDN, N32, MT818		
	Biggin Hill Heritage Hangar Ltd Biggin Hill		04.04.19P
	As 'MT818' in RAF c/s		
G-AIDS	de Havilland DH.82A Tiger Moth	84546	22.08.46
	T6055 T W J Dann & K D Pogmore		
	Benson's Farm, Laindon 'The Sorcerer'		09.09.19P
G-AIEK	Miles M.38 Messenger 2A	6339	27.08.46
	U-9 M Hales North Coates		22.09.14E
	As 'RG333' in RAF 2 TAF Communication Sqdn c/s		
	(IE 04.07.18)		
G-AIFZ	Auster J1N Alpha	2182	02.11.46
	M D Anstey Rushett Farm, Chessington		26.05.19P
G-AIGD	Auster 5J1 Autocrat	2186	02.11.46
	R M D Saw Bodmin		27.02.19P
G-AIGF	Auster J1N Alpha	2188	05.11.46
	D W Mathie Brook Farm, Burgate, Diss		03.04.19P
G-AIGP	Auster J/1 Autocrat	2165	12.10.46
	Cancelled 30.10.73 as WFU		19.06.72
	Northfield Farm, Mavis Enderby		
	Stored for spares use 08.13		
G-AIGT	Auster J1N Alpha	2176	12.10.46
	M J Miller Audley End		
	(NF 22.10.18)		
G-AIIH	Piper J-3C-65 Cub (L-4H-PI)	11945	14.09.46
	44-79649 N G Busschau & M S Pettit		
	Oaklands Farm, Stonesfield		19.12.06P
	As '44-79649:69-K' in USAAF c/s (NF 18.06.15)		

G-AIJK^M	Auster V J/4 Archer	2067	13.11.46
	Cancelled 08.08.68 as WFU		24.08.68
	Stored stripped of fabric		
	With Snibston Discovery Park, Coalville		
G-AIJM	Auster 5J4	2069	13.11.46
	EI-BEU, G-AIJM N Huxtable Wycombe Air Park		
	Stored dismantled 06.18 (NF 31.07.15)		
G-AIJS	Auster 5J4	2074	13.11.46
	R J Lane (Dannemois, France)		
	(NF 27.11.18)		
G-AIJT	Auster 5J4/100	2075	13.11.46
	J L Thorogood tr Aberdeen Auster Flying Group		
	Pittrichie Farm, Whiterashes		22.06.18P
	(IE 05.10.18)		
G-AIKE	Auster 5	1097	15.11.46
	NJ728 Stearman Services Ltd Dunkeswell		11.04.19E
	Built by Taylorcraft Aeroplanes (England) Ltd;		
	frame No.TAY 2450; as 'NJ728' in RAF c/s		
G-AIKR^M	Airspeed AS.65 Consul	4338	25.09.46
	PK286 Cancelled 10.05.65 as WFU		14.05.65
	With Air Force Museum of New Zealand, Christchurch		
G-AIPR	Auster 5J4	2084	09.01.47
	M A & N Mills (Maidenhead)		27.09.07P
	On rebuild 07.13 (NF 19.01.15)		
G-AIPV	Auster 5J1 Autocrat	2203	09.01.47
	W P Miller Northfield Farm, Mavis Enderby		
	'Buttercup'		07.02.05
	(NF 29.10.15)		
G-AIRC	Auster 5J1 Autocrat	2215	13.01.47
	C & K Jones & C Morris Conor Airpark, Kilkenny, RoI		24.02.18P
G-AIRK	de Havilland DH.82A Tiger Moth	82336	22.10.46
	N9241 J S & P R Johnson Lavenham		01.08.07
	(NF 30.10.14)		
G-AISA	Tipsy Trainer 1	17	24.04.47
	J Pollard Old Warden		19.06.19P
G-AISC	Tipsy Trainer 1	19	24.04.47
	D R Shepherd tr Wagtail Flying Group (Prestwick)		
	(NF 24.09.18)		
G-AISS (2)	Piper J-3C-65 Cub (L-4H-PI)	12077	03.09.85
	D-ECAV, SL-AAA, 44-79781		
	F M Watson & K W Wood Insch		25.06.97P
	Fuselage No.11904; noted 10.16 (NF 24.05.18)		
G-AIST	Supermarine 300 Spitfire IA	WASP/20/2	25.10.46
	AR213 Spitfire The One Ltd Duxford		04.06.19P
	Built by Westland Aircraft Ltd: modified Heston Aircraft		
	Company as c/n HA1 6S/5 139; as 'P7308:XR-D' in RAF c/s		
G-AISU^M	Vickers Supermarine 349 Spitfire LF.VB	CBAF.1061	25.10.46
	AB910 Cancelled 22.08.55 as transferred to Military Marks		
	'Peter John 1' As 'AB910:SH-F' in RAF 64 Sqdn c/s		
	With Battle of Britain Memorial Flight, RAF Coningsby		
G-AISX	Piper J-3C-85 Cub (L-4H-PI)	11663	08.10.46
	43-30372 N P Wedi tr Cubfly Wycombe Air Park		10.07.19P
	Fuselage No.11489: possibly rebuilt with airframe		
	ex EC-AQZ; as '330372' in USAAF c/s		
G-AITB^M	Airspeed AS.40 Oxford 1	xxxx	01.11.46
	MP425 Cancelled 31.10.61 as PWFU		24.05.61
	As 'MP425:G' in RAF 1536 (BAT) Flt c/s		
	With RAF Museum, Hendon		
G-AITF^M	Airspeed AS.40 Oxford 1	xxxx	01.11.46
	ED290 Cancelled 31.10.61 as PWFU As 'G-AITF'		08.06.60
	With South African Air Museum, Pretoria		
G-AIUA	Miles M.14A Hawk Trainer 3	2035	11.11.46
	T9768 D S Hunt (Balcombe, Crawley)		
	Wings ex G-ANWO fitted 1960s & original centre section		
	used to rebuild G-AKPF; displayed Wings Museum		
	(NF 12.01.16)		
G-AIVG^M	Vickers 610 Viking 1B	220	18.11.46
	Cancelled as destroyed after crash at Le Bourget		
	on 13.10.53		12.02.54
	Basle Airport, Switzerland		
	Dismantled on slow rebuild 02.17		
G-AIXA^M	Taylorcraft Plus D	134	13.01.47
	LB264 Cancelled 13.12.02 by CAA (As 'LB264')		21.02.02
	With RAF Museum, Hendon		

G-AIXJ	de Havilland DH.82A Tiger Moth	85434	28.11.46
	DE426 D Green (Sutton Farm, Sutton, Pulborough)		02.08.19P
	Built by Morris Motors Ltd – rebuilt by Newbury Aeroplane		
	Company c.1991 with probable composite airframe		
G-AIXN	Mráz M-1C Sokol	112	22.04.47
	OK-BHA Sokol Flying Group Ltd Turweston		25.02.19P
G-AIYG (2)	SNCAN Stampe SV.4B	21	31.08.89
	OO-CKZ, F-BCKZ, French AF		
	J E Henny Antwerp-Duerne, Belgium		02.05.19E
G-AIYR	de Havilland DH.89A Dragon Rapide 6	6676	11.12.46
	HG691 Spectrum Leisure Ltd Duxford		01.05.19E
	Built by Brush Coachworks Ltd; as 'HG691' in RAF c/s;		
	operated by Classic Wings		
G-AIYS	de Havilland DH.85 Leopard Moth	7089	16.12.46
	YI-ABI, SU-ABM M R Paul Solent		08.05.19P
G-AIZE[M]	Fairchild F.24W-41A Argus II (UC-61A-FA)	565	18.12.46
	N9996F, G-AIZE, 43-14601		
	Cancelled 06.04.73 as PWFU		06.08.66
	As 'FS628' in South East Asia Command (SEAC) c/s		
	With Royal Air Force Cosford Museum		
G-AIZG[M]	Vickers Supermarine 236 Walrus 1	6S/21840	20.12.46
	EI-ACC, Irish Air Corp N-18, L2301		
	Cancelled 05.01.49 as Reduced to Spares *As 'L2301'*		
	With Fleet Air Arm Museum, RNAS Yeovilton		
G-AIZU	Auster 5J1 Autocrat	2228	31.01.47
	C J & J G B Morley Popham		01.07.19P

G-AJAA – G-AJZZ

G-AJAD (2)	Piper J-3C-65 Cub (L-4H-PI)	11700	26.06.84
	OO-GEJ, 44-79712		
	C R Shipley Avon Farm, Saltford		27.04.18P
	Fuselage No.11835 & registered with c/n 11700:		
	airframe has original fuselage of OO-GEJ discarded		
	in rebuild in 1970s: OO-GEJ rebuilt with Fuselage		
	No.11950 ex OO-ALY ex 44-79826 (now		
	G-AHIP). OO-ALY rebuilt from c/n 11700 ex OO-TON		
	(ex 43-30409) (IE 06.07.18)		
G-AJAE	Auster J1N Alpha	2237	04.02.47
	D F Keller Andernos-les-Bains, France		27.09.18P
	Force landed 24.06.18 Levignac-de-Guyenne,		
	France & extensively damaged		
G-AJAJ	Auster J1N Alpha	2243	04.02.47
	N K Geddes South Barnbeth Farm, Bridge of Weir		12.06.15P
	(IE 04.03.17)		
G-AJAM	Auster 5J2 Arrow	2371	08.02.47
	D A Porter Griffins Farm, Temple Bruer		11.11.19P
G-AJAP (2)	Luscombe 8A	2305	26.01.89
	N45778, NC45778		
	M Flint Boughton (South), Downham Market		14.08.18P
	Carries 'NC45778' on tail		
G-AJAS	Auster J1N Alpha	2319	14.03.47
	P Ferguson & T Garner Spanhoe		23.04.19P
G-AJBJ	de Havilland DH.89A Dragon Rapide	6765	20.01.47
	NF894 Cancelled 16.12.91 by CAA		14.09.61
	Ley Farm, Chirk *Noted without marks 09.17*		
G-AJCL (2)	de Havilland DH.89A Dragon Rapide	6722	07.09.48
	NF851 Cancelled 24.05.71 as destroyed		
	Ley Farm, Chirk *Noted without marks 09.17*		
G-AJCP (2)	Druine D.31 Turbulent	PFA 512	09.02.59
	B R Pearson tr Turbulent Group Eaglescott		
	Built by Rollason Aircraft and Engines Ltd – project PFA 512		
	(NF 28.10.15)		
G-AJDW	Auster 5 J/1 Autocrat	2320	14.03.47
	Cancelled 20.11.96 by CAA		17.11.77
	Northfield Farm, Mavis Enderby		
	Stored for spares use 08.13		
G-AJDY	Auster J1N Alpha	2322	14.03.47
	W Bayman Ranston Farm, Iwerne Courtney		30.09.16P
	As 'MT182' in RAF camouflage c/s with invasion stripes		
	(IE 20.03.17)		
G-AJEB[M]	Auster J/1N Alpha	2325	14.03.47
	Cancelled 09.06.81 as PWFU		27.03.69
	With The Aeroplane Collection, Hooton Park		

G-AJEE	Auster 5J1 Autocrat	2309	14.03.47
	A C Whitehead Manchester Barton 'Echo Echo'		10.04.19P
G-AJEH	Auster J1N Alpha	2312	14.03.47
	P & T J Harrison (Barcombe, Lewes)		
	(NF 20.11.15)		
G-AJEI	Auster J1N Alpha	2313	14.03.47
	J Siddall Sandcroft Farm, Messingham		09.07.19P
	Originally registered as Auster J/1 Autocrat; composite		
	rebuild 1976 with fuselage of F-BFUT c/n 3357		
G-AJEM	Auster 5J1 Autocrat	2317	14.03.47
	F-BFPB, G-AJEM		
	A L Aish Lodge Farm, Higher Durston		19.08.19P
G-AJES (2)	Piper J-3C-65 Cub (L-4H-PI)	11776	21.09.84
	OO-ACB, 43-30485 D E Jarvis Shifnal		10.07.19P
	Fuselage No.11602; as '330485:C-44' in USAAC c/s		
G-AJGJ[M]	Auster 5	1147	31.01.47
	RT486 E J Downing & D Gotts tr Auster RT486		
	Flying Group (Old Sarum)		16.05.18P
	Built by Taylorcraft Aeroplanes (England) Ltd;		
	at RAF Manston History Museum		
	as 'RT486:PF-A' in RAF c/s		
G-AJHS	de Havilland DH.82A Tiger Moth	82121	12.02.47
	N6866 J M Voeten & R A Zwarts tr Flying Wires		
	Breda Int'l, Netherlands		21.09.19E
	Operated by Vliegend Museum Seppe		
G-AJIH	Auster 5J1 Autocrat	2318	02.04.47
	S Alexander Gloucestershire		14.08.15P
	As 'TJ518' in RAF c/s (NF 18.05.18)		
G-AJIS	Auster J1N Alpha	2336	30.04.47
	J J Hill Baxby Manor, Husthwaite		27.10.17P
	(IE 07.12.18)		
G-AJIT	Auster Kingsland	2337	30.04.47
	S J Farrant (Hydestile, Godalming)		22.06.15P
	Landed heavily Netherthorpe 10.09.14 &		
	substantially damaged (NF 23.06.15)		
G-AJIU	Auster 5J1 Autocrat	2338	30.04.47
	M D Greenhalgh Netherthorpe		20.06.03
	Stored 07.16 (NF 12.01.11)		
G-AJIW	Auster J1N Alpha	2340	30.04.47
	R J Guess Shacklewell Lodge Farm, Empingham		28.04.18P
G-AJIX	Auster 5J1 Autocrat	2341	30.04.47
	VH-SAD, VH-AQO, VH-AQN, G-AJIX		
	S G Rule (Witchford, Ely)		
	(NF 27.02.17)		
G-AJJP[M]	Fairey FB.2 Jet Gyrodyne	9420 & FB.2	01.03.47
	Cancelled 09.11.50: to RAF as XD759		
	As 'XJ389' On loan from RAF Museum		
	With Museum of Berkshire Aviation, Woodley		
G-AJJS (2)	Cessna 120	13047	07.01.87
	8R-GBO, VP-GBO, VP-TBO, N1106M, YV-T-CTA,		
	NC2786N G A Robson Wickenby		25.10.19P
	Rebuilt 1994 with new airframe?		
G-AJJT (2)	Cessna 120	12881	27.01.88
	N2621N, NC2621N		
	J S Robson tr Juliet Tango Group Compton Abbas		22.05.19P
G-AJJU (2)	Luscombe 8E Silvaire Deluxe	2295	10.01.89
	N45768, NC45768		
	M F A Hudson Old Sarum 'Juliet Uniform'		08.05.19P
G-AJKB	Luscombe 8E Silvaire Deluxe	3058	04.01.89
	N71631, NC71631		
	T G Carter Manchester Barton 'Lusky'		05.12.19P
G-AJOC[M]	Miles M.38 Messenger 2A	6370	23.04.47
	Cancelled 05.01.82 as WFU		18.05.72
	Rear fuselage – stored		
	With Ulster Folk & Transport Museum, Holywood		
G-AJOE	Miles M.38 Messenger 2A	6367	28.04.47
	P W Bishop Turweston		04.06.18E
G-AJON (2)	Aeronca 7AC Champion	7AC-2633	03.01.86
	OO-TWH		
	T W J Carnall tr Mudsville Flyers Dunkeswell		10.05.08P
	Frame stored 07.18 (NF 07.12.18)		
G-AJOZ[M]	Fairchild 24W-41A Argus 1 (UC-61-FA) 347		21.04.4
	FK387, 42-32142 Cancelled 27.02.67 as PWFU		15.12.63
	Crashed Rennes, France 16.08.62		
	With Yorkshire Air Museum, Elvington		

G

G-AJPI Fairchild 24R-46A Argus III (*UC-61A-FA*) 851 26.04.47
HB614, 43-14887 R Sijben (Heel, Netherlands) 27.06.10E
As '314887' in USAAF c/s (NF 22.12.15)

G-AJRB Auster 5J1 Autocrat 2350 12.05.47
Southern Alps Ltd Romney Street Farm, Sevenoaks 09.05.19P

G-AJREᴹ Auster V J/1 Autocrat 2603 12.05.47
Cancelled 16.11.12 by CAA *'Gulf Aviation'* 04.06.12
With Sharjah Aviation Museum, Sharjah, UAE

G-AJRHᴹ Auster J/1N Alpha 2606 12.05.47
Cancelled 18.01.99 by CAA 05.06.69
With Charnwood Museum, Loughborough

G-AJRS Miles M.14A Hawk Trainer 3 1750 30.04.47
P6382, G-AJDR, G-AJRS, P6382
Richard Shuttleworth Trustees Old Warden 27.06.19P
Composite aircraft & flew as 'G-AJDR' from 01.54 to 03.71;
as 'P6382:C' in RAF 16 EFTS c/s c/s with camouflaged
surfaces

G-AJSNᴹ Fairchild F.24W-41A Argus 2 849 08.05.47
HB612, 43-14885 Cancelled 12.03.73 as PWFU 09.05.69
With Ulster Aviation Society, Lisburn

G-AJTW de Havilland DH.82A Tiger Moth 82203 21.05.47
N6965 J A Barker Tibenham *'Rosemary B'* 09.09.00
As 'N6965:FL-J' in RAF c/s (NF 23.02.16)

G-AJUE Auster 5J1 Autocrat 2616 05.06.47
P H B Cole Craysmarsh Farm, Melksham 14.08.19P

G-AJUL Auster J1N Alpha 2624 18.06.47
A J Martin (Sible Hedingham, Halstead)
(NF 19.04.18)

G-AJVE de Havilland DH.82A Tiger Moth 85814 28.05.47
DE943 R A Gammons RAF Henlow 08.08.19P
Composite rebuild 1981 including substantial parts
of G-APGL c/n 86460 ex NM140

G-AJVH Fairey Swordfish II xxxx 28.05.47
LS326 Cancelled 30.04.59 by CAA
RNAS Yeovilton As 'LS326:L2' in RN 836 Sqn c/s
with Royal Navy Historic Flight 'City of Liverpool'

G-AJWB Miles M.38 Messenger 2A 6699 17.06.47
P W Bishop Turweston 18.06.19E

G-AJXC Auster 5 1409 11.06.47
TJ343 R D Helliar-Symons, K A & S E W Williams
White Waltham 28.03.19P
Built by Taylorcraft Aeroplanes (England) Ltd;
as 'TJ343' in RAF c/s

G-AJXV Auster 4 1065 08.09.47
F-BEEJ, G-AJXV, NJ695
P C J Farries Carr Fm, Thorney, Newark *'Little Lulu'* 10.10.19P
Built by Taylorcraft Aeroplanes (England) Ltd;
as 'NJ695' in RAF c/s

G-AJXY Auster 4 792 04.05.48
MT243 A G Barrell tr X-Ray Yankee Group
(Bedfield, Woodbridge)
Built by Taylorcraft Aeroplanes (England) Ltd (NF 10.12.15)

G-AJYB Auster J1N Alpha 847 03.02.49
MS974 P J Shotbolt Manor Farm, Braceborough 28.08.19P
Built by Taylorcraft Aeroplanes (England) Ltd

G-AKAA – G-AKZZ

G-AKAT Miles M.14A Hawk Trainer 3 2005 02.07.47
F-AZOR, G-AKAT, T9738 R A Fleming Breighton 11.05.19P
As 'T9738' in RAF c/s

G-AKBO Miles M.38 Messenger 2A 6378 15.07.47
N P Lee Breighton 22.05.19P

G-AKDF Miles M.38 Messenger 2A 6706 16.08.47
C W P Turner (Snitterfield, Stratford-upon-Avon)
(NF 15.10.15)

G-AKDK Miles M.65 Gemini 1A 6469 22.08.47
C W P Turner (Snitterfield, Stratford-upon-Avon)
(NF 19.10.15)

G-AKDN de Havilland DHC-1A Chipmunk 10 11 14.08.47
K A Large & J Morley Durham Tees Valley 07.11.16E
Operated by Flying Fox Aviation (IE 01.10.18)

G-AKDWᴹ de Havilland DH.89A Dragon Rapide 6897 25.08.47
F-BCDB, G-AKDW, YI-ABD, NR833
de Havilland Aircraft Museum Trust Ltd
Salisbury Hall, London Colney
Built by Brush Coachworks Ltd; on rebuild 10.18
(NF 04.10.16)

G-AKELᴹ Miles M.65 Gemini 1A 6484 08.09.47
Cancelled 30.05.84 as WFU 29.04.72
Centre section – stored
With Ulster Folk & Transport Museum, Holywood

G-AKEN Miles M.65 Gemini 1A 6486 08.09.47
VH-GBB, VH-BTP, G-AKEN
C W P Turner (Snitterfield, Stratford-upon-Avon)
(NF 08.10.18)

G-AKEX Percival P.34 Proctor III H549 26.08.47
SE-BTR, G-AKEX, LZ791 M Biddulph Great Oakley
Built by F Hills and Sons Ltd (NF 02.09.15)

G-AKHP Miles M.65 Gemini 1A 6519 03.10.47
S A Blanchard Beverley (Linley Hill) 30.04.19P

G-AKHU Miles M.65 Gemini 1A 6522 18.10.47
VH-BOB, (VH-DFP), VH-WEK, VH-WEJ, VH-BMV, G-AKHU
C W P Turner (Snitterfield, Stratford-upon-Avon)
(NF 08.10.18)

G-AKIB (2) Piper J-3C-90 Cub (*L-4H-PI*) 12311 18.04.84
OO-RAY, 44-80015
R Horner Westacott Farm, Coldridge 02.04.19P
Fuselage No.12139; as '480015:44-M' in USAAC c/s

G-AKIF de Havilland DH.89A Dragon Rapide 6838 24.09.47
LN-BEZ, G-AKIF, NR750
Airborne Taxi Services Ltd Duxford 17.03.19E
Operated by Classic Wings

G-AKIN Miles M.38 Messenger 2A 6728 19.09.47
R M Kimbell tr Sywell Messenger Trust Sywell 06.08.19P

G-AKISᴹ Miles M.38 Messenger 2A 6725 19.09.47
Cancelled 24.02.70 as WFU As 'G-AKIS' 05.08.70
With Koninklijk Leger Museum-Musée Royal de l'Armée,
Brussels

G-AKIU Percival Proctor V AE129 20.02.48
G G L James Sleap 30.06.17E
Cleared to fly 01.02.19 (IE 03.07.18)

G-AKKB Miles M.65 Gemini 1A 6537 28.10.47
D R Gray Liverpool John Lennon 16.07.19P

G-AKKH Miles M.65 Gemini 1A 6479 23.07.48
OO-CDO P J Hebdon Coventry 06.04.18P
Official p/i OO-CDP (c/n 6480) is incorrect

G-AKKYᴹ Miles M.14A Hawk Trainer 3 2078 23.06.48
T9841 Cancelled 12.04.73 as WFU 06.11.64
Also allocated BAPC.44 to reflect rebuild status from
various parts As 'L6906'
With Museum of Berkshire Aviation, Woodley

G-AKLWᴹ Short SA.6 Sealand 1 SH.1571 26.11.47
(USA), R Saudi AF, SU-AHY, G-AKLW
Cancelled 23.08.51 – to Egypt & SU-AHY
On display & under restoration
With Ulster Folk & Transport Museum, Holywood

G-AKNPᴹ Short S.45 Solent 3 S.1295 02.12.47
NJ203 Cancelled 20.03.51 – to VH-TOB
– subsequently N9946F
As 'G-AKNP' in BOAC titles 'City of Cardiff'
With Western Aerospace Museum, Oakland, California

G-AKNVᴹ de Havilland DH.89A Dragon Rapide 6458 02.12.47
G-AKNV, EI-AGK, G-AKNV, R5922
Cancelled 27.09.55 – to OO-AFG & OO-CNP
As 'G-AKNV' in Lancashire Aircraft Corporation c/s
With Koninklijk Leger Museum-Musée Royal de l'Armée,
Brussels

G-AKOE de Havilland DH.89A Dragon Rapide 4 6601 03.12.47
X7484 Cancelled 18.06.02 by CAA 25.07.82
Ley Farm, Chirk *Noted 09.17*

G-AKOWᴹ Taylorcraft J Auster 5 1579 23.12.47
PH-NAD (2), PH-NEG, G-AKOW, TJ569
Cancelled 05.08.87 as WFU As 'TJ569' 26.06.82
Registered as c/n TJ569A after rebuild in Holland
With Museum of Army Flying, AAC Middle Wallop

G-AKPF	Miles M.14A Hawk Trainer 3	2228	27.01.48
	V1075 D S Bramwell Old Warden		16.04.19P
	Composite rebuilt (i) 1955 [centre-section ex G-AIUA,		
	fuselage ex G-ANLT & wings ex G-AHYL], (ii) 1970/8		
	[10% fuselage ex G-AKPF & tail unit ex G-ANLT];		
	as 'N3788' in RAF c/s		

G-AKPI	Auster 5	1088	27.01.48
	NJ703 M D Grinstead Boston		
	As 'NJ703' in RAF c/s (NF 06.07.17)		

G-AKRP	de Havilland DH.89A Dragon Rapide 4	6940	26.01.48
	CN-TTO, (F-DAFS), G-AKRP, RL958		
	B R Pearson tr Eaglescott Dominie Group Coventry		
	'Northamptonshire Rose'		06.01.08S
	(NF 30.07.18)		

G-AKSY	Auster 5	1567	10.02.48
	F-BGOO, G-AKSY, TJ534 S J Farrant West Tisted		04.06.19P
	Built by Taylorcraft Aeroplanes (England) Ltd; as 'TJ534'		
	in AAC camouflage c/s & invasion stripes on wings		

G-AKSZ	Auster 5D	1503	10.02.48
	F-BGPQ, G-AKSZ, TJ457		
	D K Chambers & M A Farrelly Welshpool		18.06.18P
	Built by Taylorcraft Aeroplanes (England) Ltd;		
	large fin & rudder		

G-AKTH (2)	Piper J-3C-65 Cub (L-4J-PI)	13211	14.07.86
	OO-AGL, PH-UCR, 45-4471		
	G W S Turner Goodwood		08.05.16P
	Frame No.13041?; official c/n 13047 is incorrect		
	(NF 05.10.18)		

G-AKTI (2)	Luscombe 8A	4101	27.05.87
	N1374K, NC1374K C Chambers Aughrim, Kilkeel		23.07.19P

G-AKTK (2)	Aeronca 11BC Chief	11AC-1017	13.03.89
	N9379E, NC9379E		
	A C Batchelar Swanborough Farm, Lewes		11.11.19P

G-AKTO (2)	Aeronca 7BCM Champion	7AC-940	19.05.88
	N8515X, N82311, NC82311		
	R M Davies Plaistows Farm, St Albans		30.06.14P
	Modified ex 7AC standard 1950 (NF 09.10.15)		

G-AKTP (2)	Piper PA-17 Vagabond	17-82	24.06.88
	N4683H, NC4683H		
	P J B Lewis tr Golf Tango Papa Group Swansea		05.08.03P
	(NF 21.02.18)		

G-AKTR (2)	Aeronca 7AC Champion	7AC-3017	19.06.89
	N58312, NC58312 E Gordon Breighton 'Eddie'		27.09.18P

G-AKTS (2)	Cessna 120	11875	26.05.88
	N77434, NC77434 M Isterling Insch		26.05.19P

G-AKTT (2)	Luscombe 8A	3279	21.07.88
	N71852, NC71852 S J Charters		
	(Eddsfield, Octon Lodge Farm, Thwing)		23.06.92P
	(NF 25.04.16)		

G-AKUE (2)	de Havilland DH.82A Tiger Moth	P68	12.02.86
	ZS-FZL, CR-AGM, Port.AF ????		
	D F Hodgkinson Redhill		12.07.19E
	Built by OGMA		

G-AKUF (2)	Luscombe 8F Silvaire	4794	01.08.88
	N2067K, NC2067K		
	M O Loxton Parsonage Farm, Eastchurch		07.08.03P
	(NF 22.10.18)		

G-AKUH (2)	Luscombe 8E Silvaire Deluxe	4644	24.10.88
	G-GIST, G-AKUH, N1917K, NC1917K		
	A G Palmer Wellesbourne Mountford 'Lucy Too'		02.12.19P

G-AKUJ (2)	Luscombe 8E Silvaire Deluxe	5282	04.08.88
	N2555K, NC2555K		
	P R Bentley South Longwood Farm, Owslebury		07.08.19P

G-AKUK (2)	Luscombe 8A	5793	28.10.88
	N1166B, NC1166B		
	O R Watts South Longwood Farm, Owslebury		17.09.10P
	(NF 28.04.15)		

G-AKUL (2)	Luscombe 8A	4189	09.02.89
	N1462K, NC1462K K R H Wingate Dunkeswell		
	(NF 21.12.15)		

G-AKUM (2)	Luscombe 8F Silvaire	6452	17.02.88
	N2025B D A Young North Weald		15.11.19P

G-AKUN (2)	Piper J-3C-85 Cub	6914	13.01.89
	N38304, NC38304		
	W R Savin Coldharbour Farm, Willingham		10.11.11P
	(NF 10.04.18)		

G-AKUO (2)	Aeronca 11AC Chief	11AC-1376	16.01.89
	N9730E, NC9730E		
	A G Collicott & C V Dadswell Goodwood		25.04.18P

G-AKUP (2)	Luscombe 8E Silvaire Deluxe	5501	09.05.89
	N2774K, NC2774K D A Young North Weald		
	Dismantled for rebuild 07.18 (NF 18.10.18)		

G-AKUR (2)	Cessna 140	13819	26.01.89
	N1647V, NC1647V C G Applegarth Goodwood		21.09.95
	(NF 25.04.16)		

G-AKUW	Chrislea CH.3 Series 2 Super Ace	105	08.03.48
	R J S G Clark RAF Barkston Heath		18.01.18P
	(IE 06.03.18)		

G-AKVF	Chrislea CH.3 Series 2 Super Ace	114	08.03.48
	AP-ADT, G-AKVF Cancelled 15.05.18 by CAA		31.05.13
	Coventry Stored 08.18		

G-AKVM (2)	Cessna 120	13431	10.01.89
	N3173N, NC3173N P A Espin Wickenby		29.06.18P

G-AKVN (2)	Aeronca 11AC Chief	11AC-469	13.01.89
	N3742B, N86047, NC86047		
	P A Jackson Priory Farm, Tibenham		15.05.19P
	Carries '3742B' on fin		

G-AKVO (2)	Taylorcraft BC-12D	9845	10.01.89
	N44045, NC44045		
	R D Leigh tr G-AKVO Flying Group Darley Moor		03.07.19P

G-AKVP (2)	Luscombe 8A	5549	21.07.48
	N2822K, NC2822K		
	J M Edis Charity Farm, Baxterley		05.08.19P

G-AKVR	Chrislea CH.3 Series 4 Skyjeep	125	08.03.48
	VH-OLD, VH-RCD, VH-BRP, G-AKVR		
	R B Webber Trenchard Farm, Eggesford		03.05.19P

G-AKVZ	Miles M.38 Messenger 4B	6352	25.06.48
	RH427 Shipping & Airlines Ltd Biggin Hill		21.05.16E
	(IE 20.07.17)		

G-AKWS	Auster 5A-160	1237	01.04.48
	RT610 M C Hayes Woonton		10.06.13P
	Built by Taylorcraft Aeroplanes (England) Ltd;		
	as 'RT610' in AAC c/s (NF 28.09.17)		

G-AKXP	Auster 5	1017	13.04.48
	NJ633 M J Nicholson Old Sarum		21.02.17P
	Built by Taylorcraft Aeroplanes (England) Ltd;		
	as 'NJ633' in RAF c/s (IE 23.10.17)		

G-AKXS	de Havilland DH.82A Tiger Moth	83512	13.04.48
	T7105 G J & J Eagles Oaksey Park		21.03.03
	(NF 22.05.18)		

G-AKZN	Percival P.34A Proctor III	K.386	24.05.48
	8380M, Z7197 Cancelled 27.09.63 as WFU		29.11.63
	RAF Stafford *In RAF Museum store 2018 as 'Z7197'*		

G-ALAA – G-ALZZ

G-ALAH	Miles M.38 Messenger 4A	RH377	28.05.48
	RH377 C W P Turner (Snitterfield, Stratford-upon-Avon)		
	(NF 08.10.18)		

G-ALAR	Miles M.38 Messenger 4A	–	28.05.48
	VP-KJL, G-ALAR, RH371		
	C W P Turner (Snitterfield, Stratford-upon-Avon)		
	(NF 08.10.18)		

G-ALBD	de Havilland DH.82A Tiger Moth	84130	27.05.48
	T7748 D Shew Hill Farm, Durley		
	Stored 06.16 (NF 09.07.18)		

G-ALBJ	Auster 5	1831	03.06.48
	TW501 B M Vigor Dunkeswell		07.08.19P
	Built by Taylorcraft Aeroplanes (England) Ltd;		
	as 'TW501' in AAC silver with yellow bands c/s		

G-ALBK	Auster 5	1273	03.06.48
	RT644 J S & J S Allison		
	Ventfield Farm, Horton-cum-Studley 'Beauty'		01.01.19P
	Built by Taylorcraft Aeroplanes (England) Ltd		

G-ALBN^M Bristol 173 Mk.1   12871   29.07.48
          7648M, XF785 Cancelled 21.07.60   22.09.54
          To RAF & as 'XF785'
          With Aerospace Bristol

G-ALCK^M Percival Proctor III   H.536   18.06.48
          LZ766 Cancelled 19.08.65 as PWFU As 'LZ766'   19.06.63
          With Imperial War Museum, Duxford

G-ALCU^M de Havilland DH.104 Dove 2B   04022   03.08.48
          VT-CEH Cancelled 08.09.78 as WFU   16.03.73
          As 'G-ALVD' in 'Dunlop Aviation Division' c/s
          With Midland Air Museum, Coventry

G-ALDG^M Handley Page HP.81 Hermes IV   HP.81/8   27.10.49
          Cancelled 12.10.68 as WFU 'Horsa'   09.01.63
          BOAC c/s Fuselage only
          With Duxford Aviation Society

G-ALEH (2) Piper PA-17 Vagabond   17-87   17.08.81
          N4689H, NC4689H
          A J Coker Maypole Farm, Chislet   06.12.18P

G-ALFA   Auster 5   1236   20.10.48
          RT607 A E Jones RAF Barkston Heath   29.10.19P
          Built by Taylorcraft Aeroplanes (England) Ltd;
          P/i not confirmed (i) c/n 1236 sold 04.48 as 'HB-EOC'
          & (ii) also reported as c/n 826 (ex MS958)

G-ALFU^M de Havilland DH.104 Dove 6   04234   14.12.48
          Cancelled 14.11.72 as WFU   04.06.71
          With Duxford Aviation Society

G-ALGA (2) Piper PA-15 Vagabond   15-348   03.12.86
          N4575H, NC4575H S T Gilbert Enstone   13.02.18P
          (IE 22.02.18)

G-ALGT   Supermarine 379 Spitfire F.XIVc   6S-432263   09.02.49
          RM689, 'RM619', G-ALGT, RM689
          Rolls-Royce PLC East Midlands   31.07.92P
          Crashed Woodford 27.06.92 & substantially damaged;
          fuselage used as simulator 2018 (NF 16.09.15)

G-ALIJ   Piper PA-17 Vagabond   17-166   13.02.87
          N4866H
          D Crouchman tr Hampshire Flying Group Popham   03.07.19P

G-ALIW (2) de Havilland DH.82A Tiger Moth   82901   17.08.81
          N27WB, ZK-ATI, RNZAF NZ899, R5006
          F R Curry (St Helier, Jersey)   01.08.19P

G-ALJF   Percival P.34 Proctor III   K.427   03.03.49
          Z7252 J F Moore Biggin Hill   09.09.13C
          Crash landed into trees Rolvenden 24.07.12 &
          substantially damaged (NF 18.09.16)

G-ALJL   de Havilland DH.82A Tiger Moth   84726   07.03.49
          T6311 T A Kinnaird White Waltham   27.08.19P
          Built by Morris Motors Ltd

G-ALJR^M Abbott-Baynes Scud III   2   16.03.49
          BGA 283/ACF, G-ALJR, BGA 283
          The Gliding Heritage Centre Lasham
          (NF 30.09.16)

G-ALLF   Slingsby T.30A Prefect   548   29.03.49
          BGA 599, PH-1, BGA 599, G-ALLF, BGA 599
          The Gliding Heritage Centre Lasham 'ARK'
          (NF 04.09.14)

G-ALMA   Piper J-3C-65 Cub   12214   25.04.49
          G-BBXS, N9865F, G-ALMA, 44-79918
          M J Butler Spanhoe   14.09.00P
          Stored for rebuild project 2018 (IE 30.05.18)

G-ALNA   de Havilland DH.82A Tiger Moth   85061   11.04.49
          T6774 S E Ford Derby   12.11.16E
          As 'EM973' in RAF c/s (IE 17.09.18)

G-ALND   de Havilland DH.82A Tiger Moth   82308   12.04.49
          N9191 D Shew Hill Farm, Durley
          On rebuild 07.16 (NF 12.11.15)

G-ALNV   Auster 5   1216   21.04.49
          RT578 Cancelled 01.05.59 as PWFU   04.07.50
          Carr Farm, Thorney, Newark Frame only 02.15

G-ALRD^M Scott Viking 1   6
          G-ALRD, BGA 416 As ' AHU'
          With The Gliding Heritage Centre, Lasham

G-ALRU^M EoN Baby   EoN/B/004   25.05.49
          BGA 628 Cancelled 10.01.64 as Marks WFU As 'ASR'
          Donated by R Kent
          With The Gliding Heritage Centre, Lasham

G-ALRX^M Bristol 175 Britannia Series 101   12874   25.06.51
          Cancelled 05.04.54 as PWFU
          Stored Filton for display Bristol Aero Collection Trust
          Front fuselage only

G-ALSP^M Bristol 171 Sycamore HR12   12900   17.11.50
          Cancelled 26.03.52 – to RAF as WV783
          As 'WV783' in CFS c/s
          With RAF Museum, Hendon

G-ALSS^M Bristol 171 Sycamore 3   12887   09.06.49
          Cancelled 17.11.50 – to RAF & as WA576
          With Dumfries & Galloway Aviation Museum, Dumfries

G-ALST^M Bristol 171 Sycamore 3   12888   09.06.49
          Cancelled 17.11.50 – to RAF As 'WA577'
          With North East Land Sea and Air Museum, Usworth

G-ALSW^M Bristol 171 Sycamore 3   12891   17.11.50
          Cancelled 26.03.52 – to RAF as WT933 As 'WT933'
          With Newark Air Museum, Winthorpe

G-ALSX^M Bristol 171 Sycamore 3   12892   17.11.50
          G-48-1, G-ALSX, VR-TBS, G-ALSX
          Cancelled 31.01.66 as WFU   24.09.65
          On loan from E.D.ap Rees
          With The Helicopter Museum, Weston-super-Mare

G-ALTD^M Bristol 171 Sycamore HR12   12898   17.11.50
          WV781 Cancelled 26.03.52 – to RAF as WV781
          As 'WV781' Forward fuselage only
          With Caernarfon Airworld Museum

G-ALTO (2) Cessna 140   14253   19.01.82
          N2040V M L, P M & T M Jones Derby   02.06.19E

G-ALUC   de Havilland DH.82A Tiger Moth   83094   28.06.49
          R5219
          Tiger Moth Experience Ltd Sherburn-in-Elmet   30.10.19E

G-ALWB   de Havilland DHC-1 Chipmunk 22A   C1/0100   28.12.49
          OE-ABC, G-ALWB D J & P A D Neville RAF Henlow   18.06.19P

G-ALWC^M Douglas C-47A-25-DK Dakota   13590   10.01.50
          KG723, 42-93654 Cancelled 11.82 – to (F-GBOL) –
          cancelled 29.02.84 by CAA, restored 01.05.84,
          cancelled 03.04.89 by CAA As 'G-ALWC'   06.02.83
          With Ailes Anciennes Toulouse, Blagnac, France

G-ALWF^M Vickers 701 Viscount   5   02.01.50
          Cancelled 18.04.72 as WFU 'Sir John Franklin'   16.04.72
          BEA c/s
          With Duxford Aviation Society

G-ALWS   de Havilland DH.82A Tiger Moth   82415   24.01.50
          N9328 J G Norris Henstridge   13.06.18E
          Officially registered with c/n 82413; operated by Tiger Moth
          Training; as 'N-9328:69' in RAF camouflage c/s

G-ALWW   de Havilland DH.82A Tiger Moth   86366   24.01.50
          NL923 D E Findon Bidford   02.04.19E
          Built by Morris Motors Ltd

G-ALXT   de Havilland DH.89A Dragon Rapide 6736   24.01.50
          4R-AAI, CY-AAI, G-ALXT, NF865
          Cancelled 05.07.51 to CY-AAI
          Wroughton Railway Air Service titles 'Star of Scotia'
          In Science Museum store 2013

G-ALXZ   Auster 5-150   1082   01.02.50
          D-EGOF, PH-NER, G-ALXZ, NJ689
          P J Tyler Breighton   31.07.17P
          Built by Taylorcraft Aeroplanes (England) Ltd;
          frame No.TAY24070; extended fin; as 'NJ689'
          in RAF desert camo c/s (IE 16.07.18)

G-ALYB^M Taylorcraft J Auster 5   1173   03.02.50
          RT520 Cancelled 29.02.84 by CAA   26.05.63
          Fuselage only
          With South Yorkshire Aircraft Museum, Doncaster

G-ALYG^M Taylorcraft J Auster 5D   835   14.03.50
          MS968 (?) Cancelled 15.10.14 by CAA
          Built by Taylorcraft Aeroplanes (England) Ltd
          Frame only
          With Boscombe Down Aviation Centre, Old Sarum

G-ALZE^M Britten-Norman BN-1F   1   16.03.50
          Cancelled 08.06.89 as WFU
          With Solent Sky, Southampton

G

G-ALZO (2)^M Airspeed AS.57 Ambassador 2   5226   05.04.50
RJordan AF 108, G-ALZO, (G-AMAD)
Cancelled 10.09.81 as WFU   14.05.71
Dan Air c/s
With Duxford Aviation Society

G-AMAA – G-AMZZ

G-AMAU^M Hawker Hurricane IIc   xxxx   01.05.50
PZ865 Cancelled 19.12.72 as transferred to Military Marks
As 'PZ865:JX-E' in RAF 1 Sqdn c/s
12,780th & final Hurricane built by)
With Battle of Britain Memorial Flight, RAF Coningsby

G-AMAW Luton LA-4 Minor   JRC-01   29.04.50
The Real Aeroplane Company Ltd   Breighton
Built by J R Coates – aka Swalesong SA.I with c/n SA.I;
stored 09.17 (NF 30.10.18)

G-AMBB de Havilland DH.82A Tiger Moth   85070   01.05.50
T6801 J Eagles Oaksey Park
Composite rebuild – some parts to 'G-MAZY'?
(NF 04.07.18)

G-AMCA^M Douglas C-47B-30DK Dakota 3   16218 & 32966   01.06.50
KN487, 44-76634 Cancelled 16.10.03 as WFU   10.12.00
Unmarked & damaged Valkenburg, Zuid-Holland 12.13
With Aviodrome Museum, Lelystad, Netherlands

G-AMCK de Havilland DH.82A Tiger Moth   84641   15.06.50
N65N, C-GBBF, SLN-05, D-EGXY, HB-UAC, G-AMCK,
T6193 M R Masters Solent*'The Liver Bird'*   31.05.16E
Forced landed on approach to Branscombe 13.05.16 &
substantially damaged; on rebuild 08.16 (NF 14.09.16)

G-AMCM de Havilland DH.82A Tiger Moth   85295   14.12.50
DE249 J I Cooper Denford Manor, Hungerford
Registered with c/n '89259' (NF 21.10.14)

G-AMDA^M Avro 652A Anson 1   xxxx   20.07.50
N4877 Cancelled 09.09.81 by CAA   *As 'N4877:MK-V'*   04.12.62
With Imperial War Museum, Duxford

G-AMDD^M de Havilland DH.104 Dove 6   04292   08.08.50
Cancelled 26.09.68 – to VQ-ZJC – subsequently
3D-AAI, VP-YKF & IAC 176 *As 'VP-YKF'*
Originally registered as Series 2, then Series 2B
With Meath Aero Museum at Ashbourne, RoI

G-AMEN (2) Piper PA-18 Super Cub 95 (L-18C-PI) 18-1998   29.12.81
(G-BJTR), I-EIAM/E.I.71, Ital Mil MM52-2398,
52-2398 W Cook & A Lovejoy tr The G-AMEN
Flying Group Popham   16.05.19P
Fuselage No.18-1963; rebuilt in Italy as
c/n OMA.71-08

G-AMHF de Havilland DH.82A Tiger Moth   83026   06.02.51
R5144 A J West Long Last Farm, Pavenham   07.06.19P
Rebuilt with components ex G-BABA
c/n 86584 ex F-BGDT/PG687

G-AMHJ^M Douglas C-47A-35-DL Dakota   13468   06.02.47
SU-AZI, G-AMHJ, ZS-BRW, KG651, 42-108962
Cancelled 23.01.03 as PWFU   *As 'KG651'*   05.12.00
With Metheringham Airfield Visitor Centre, Martin Moor

G-AMIV de Havilland DH.82A Tiger Moth   83105   09.04.51
D-EDHA, G-AMIV, R5246
RAF Station Czechoslovakia SRO
(Podhorany u Ronova, Czech Republic)   08.05.14C
(IE 07.02.19)

G-AMKU Auster 5J1S Autocrat   2721   10.07.51
ST-ABD, SN-ABD, G-AMKU
P G Lipman Romney Street Farm, Sevenoaks   17.06.19P

G-AMLF^M de Havilland DH.82A Tiger Moth   86572   18.08.51
PG675 Cancelled 21.07.71 – to N675LF *As 'G-ADGV'*
With Aviation Museum of Santa Paula, California

G-AMLZ^M Percival P.50 Prince 6E   P 46   23.11.51
(VR-TBN) Cancelled 09.10.84 as WFU   18.06.71
With Wirral Aviation Society, Liverpool-John Lennon

G-AMMS Auster J5K Aiglet Trainer   2745   11.10.51
G P J Rowden Dunkeswell   12.07.19P

G-AMNN de Havilland DH.82A Tiger Moth   86457   24.12.51
NM137 I J Perry Brighton City   30.04.19E
Composite rebuild with unidentified airframe: original
G-AMNN possibly absorbed into G-BPAJ qv

G-AMOG (2)^M Vickers 701 Viscount   7   23.05.52
(G-AMNZ) Cancelled 17.05.76 as WFU   14.06.77
'RMA Robert Falcon Scott'   BEA titles
With National Museum of Flight Scotland, East Fortune

G-AMPG (2) Piper PA-12 Super Cruiser   12-985   25.03.85
N2647M, NC2647 D J Harrison Tatenhill   22.06.16P
Hoerner wing-tips

G-AMPI (2) SNCAN Stampe SV.4C   213   13.02.84
N6RA, F-BCFX
Ardmore Aviation Services Ltd   Duxford   11.02.19P

G-AMPO^M Douglas C-47B-30DK Dakota 3   16437 & 33185   25.02.52
LN-RTO, KN566, 44-76853
Cancelled 18.10.01 as WFU   *As 'FZ626:YS-DH'*   29.03.97
Registered with c/ns 16438 & 33186
At RAF Brize Norton

G-AMPY Douglas C-47B-15-DK   15124/26569   08.03.52
(EI-BKJ), G-AMPY, N15751, G-AMPY, TF-FIO, G-AMPY,
JY-ABE, G-AMPY, KK116, 43-49308
RVL Aviation Ltd East Midlands   09.07.16E
Built by 1943 as DC-3C-R-1830-90C & converted as
Dakota C.4 with RAF as KK116; as 'KK116' in RAF c/s;
active 02.18

G-AMRA Douglas C-47B-15-DK   15290/26735   08.03.52
XE280, G-AMRA, KK151, 43-49474
Forderverein Rosinenbomber E.V.
Berlin-Schonefeld, Germany   25.09.13E
Noted as 'D-CXXX' 06.16

G-AMRF Auster J5F Aiglet Trainer   2716   20.03.52
VT-DHA, G-AMRF D A Hill Fenland   31.03.07
(NF 05.04.16)

G-AMRK Gloster Gladiator I   L8032   16.05.52
L8032, 'K8032', G-AMRK, L8032
Richard Shuttleworth Trustees Old Warden   28.06.19P
As 'K7985 'in RAF 73 Sqdn silver c/s

G-AMSG SIPA 903   77   25.11.81
OO-VBL, F-BGHB
S W Markham Valentine Farm, Odiham   03.07.19P

G-AMTA Auster J5F Aiglet Trainer   2780   24.05.52
J D Manson Nottingham City   18.11.19P

G-AMTF de Havilland DH.82A Tiger Moth   84207   11.06.52
OO-TMW, G-AMTF, ZK-AVE, G-AMTF, T7842
H A D Monro Headcorn   06.01.18E
As 'T-7842' in RAF c/s

G-AMTK de Havilland DH.82A Tiger Moth   3982   18.06.52
N6709 S W McKay & M E Vaisey
(Berkhamsted & Hemel Hempstead)
(NF 10.12.18)

G-AMTM Auster J1 Autocrat   3101   03.07.52
G-AJUJ R J Stobo Oaklands Farm, Stonesfield   29.09.12P
Auster rebuild – originally c/n 2622 (NF 24.07.17)

G-AMTP^M de Havilland DH.82A Tiger Moth   84875   17.07.52
T6534Cancelled 29.08.52 – to OO-ETP *As 'T6534'*
With Koninklijk Leger Museum-Musée Royal de l'Armée,
Brussels

G-AMTV de Havilland DH.82A Tiger Moth   3858   05.08.52
OO-SOE, G-AMTV, N6545 E Scurr Sywell   14.05.19E

G-AMUF de Havilland DHC-1 Chipmunk 21   C1/0832   02.09.52
The Redhill Tailwheel Flying Club Ltd Redhill   02.05.19E

G-AMUI Auster J5F Aiglet Trainer   2790   29.08.52
R B Webber Trenchard Farm, Eggesford
(NF 24.07.18)

G-AMUW^M Phoenix Luton LA-4A Minor   WP.1   22.09.52
Cancelled 13.04.73.as PWFU
Built by W Petrie Identity unconfirmed: appears
sold to J.Smith.who modified & incorporated fuselage
into unfinished project
With Scalloway Museum, Lerwick

G-AMVD Auster 5   1565   06.10.52
F-BGTF, G-AMVD, TJ565
M Hammond Airfield Farm, Hardwick   08.08.18P
Built by Taylorcraft Aeroplanes (England) Ltd; as 'TJ565' in
RAF camouflage & D-Day stripes c/s plus 652 Sqdn crest

G-AMVP Tipsy Junior   J111   23.10.52
OO-ULA R A Fleming Breighton   10.10.18P

G-AMVS de Havilland DH.82A Tiger Moth   82784   12.11.52
OO-SOJ, G-AMVS, R4852   D Shew   Hill Farm, Durley
On rebuild 07.16 (NF 12.11.15)

G-AMWI^M Bristol 171 Sycamore 4   13070   01.12.52
Cancelled 1958 – to RN as XN635 – subsequently
VH-BAW   *As 'XR592'*
With Camden Museum of Aviation, NSW

G-AMXA^M de Havilland DH.106 Comet C.2R   06023   08.01.53
Cancelled 02.03.55. – to RAF as XK655
Cockpit only   'BOAC'
With Al Mahatta Museum, Sharjah, UAE

G-AMXR^M de Havilland DH.104 Dove 6   04379   21.01.53
D-CFSB, G-AMXR, N4280V
Cancelled 22.07.54 – to D-CFSB 07.54
Subsequently as & as 'D-IFSB' (1)
With Historical Aviation Centre, Morgansfield, Fishburn

G-AMXX^M de Havilland DH.104 Dove 2A   04406   22.01.53
Cancelled 21.10.54 – to RN as Sea Devon C.20
XJ348 – restored 06.01.82 as G-NAVY: cancelled
2.07.91 as WFU   *As 'XJ348'*
With Flugausstellung-Hermeskeil, Trier, Germany

G-AMYD Auster J5L Aiglet Trainer   2773   13.02.53
R D Thomasson   Strubby   08.06.19P

G-AMYJ^M Douglas C-47B-25DK Dakota 6   15968 & 32716   23.02.53
SU-AZF, G-AMYJ, XF747, G-AMYJ, KN353,
44-76384   Cancelled 12.12.01 as WFU   04.04.97
As 'KN353' in taxiable condition
With Yorkshire Air Museum, Elvington

G-AMZI Auster J5F Aiglet Trainer   3104   04.05.53
J F Moore   Biggin Hill   30.09.16E
(IE 21.09.18)

G-AMZT Auster J5F Aiglet Trainer   3107   28.05.53
R B Webber   Trenchard Farm, Eggesford   02.08.19P

G-ANAA – G-ANZZ

G-ANAF Douglas C-47B-35-DK   33436   17.06.53
N170GP, G-ANAF, KP220, 44-77104
RVL Aviation Ltd   East Midlands   09.05.17E
Became Dakota C.3 as KP220

G-ANAV de Havilland DH.106 Comet 1A   06013   15.08.53
CF-CUM   Cancelled 01.07.55 as WFU
Wroughton   *Broken up RAE Farnborough 1955*
Nose section in Science Museum store 2013

G-ANBY de Havilland DH.82A Tiger Moth   86042   02.09.53
EM840   Cancelled 30.04.59 as PWFU
Middle Wallop
Composite airframe, on rebuild 04.14 as 'EM840'

G-ANBZ de Havilland DH.82A Tiger Moth   85621   02.09.53
D-ELYG, SL-AAF, G-ANBZ, DE680
D Shew   Hill Farm, Durley
(NF 07.04.16)

G-ANCF^M Bristol 175 Britannia Series 308F   12922   03.01.58
5Y-AZP, G-ANCF, LV-GJB, LV-PPJ, (G-ANCF),
G-14-1, G-18-4, G-ANCF, (N6597C)
Cancelled 21.02.84 as WFU   12.01.81
Originally registered as Series 305
Displayed Wirral Aviation Society, Liverpool Crown Plaza
Hotel, Liverpool-John Lennon Airport   Fuselage only
With Britannia Aircraft Preservation Trust

G-ANCS de Havilland DH.82A Tiger Moth   82824   12.09.53
R4907   C M Edwards & E A Higgins   Rochester   05.07.19E

G-ANDE de Havilland DH.82A Tiger Moth   85957   23.09.53
G-YVFS, G-ANDE, EM726   K M Perkins   Headcorn   29.03.10S
Built by Morris Motors Ltd; as 'EM726:FY' in RAF c/s
(NF 18.04.18)

G-ANDM de Havilland DH.82A Tiger Moth   3946   23.09.53
EI-AGP, G-ANDM, EI-AGP, G-ANDM, (G-ANDI), N6642
N J Stagg   (Iron Acton, Bristol)   15.07.19P

G-ANDP de Havilland DH.82A Tiger Moth   82868   22.09.53
D-EBEC, N9920F, G-ANDP, R4960
J McCullough   Newtownards   25.10.19P

G-ANEH de Havilland DH.82A Tiger Moth   82067   29.09.53
N6797   G J Wells   Wycombe Air Park   24.08.18P
As 'N-6797' in RAF yellow c/s

G-ANEJ^M de Havilland DH.82A Tiger Moth   85592   01.10.53
DE638   Cancelled 10.09.73 as PWFU –
DBR landing Owstwich, Yorkshire 15.05.65 –
to R.Malaysian AF 02.89   *As 'T7245'*   01.02.66
With Muzium Tentera Udara Diraja Malaysia,
Kuala Lumpur, Malyasia

G-ANEL de Havilland DH.82A Tiger Moth   82333   01.10.53
N9238   Totalsure Ltd   Langham   13.08.19E

G-ANEM de Havilland DH.82A Tiger Moth   82943   01.10.53
EI-AGN, G-ANEM, R5042
P J Benest   Little Farm, Hamstead Marshall   24.10.19P

G-ANEN de Havilland DH.82A Tiger Moth   85418   02.10.53
OO-ACG, G-ANEN, DE410
D B Wildridge tr G-ANEN Group   Bicester   20.03.19P

G-ANEW de Havilland DH.82A Tiger Moth   86458   06.10.53
NM138   K F Crumplin   Henstridge   07.07.18E
Built by Morris Motors Ltd; operated by Tiger Moth
Training; as 'NM-138:41' in RAF camouflage c/s

G-ANEZ de Havilland DH.82A Tiger Moth   84218   20.10.53
T7849   C D J Bland   Yafford House, Yafford   25.10.19P

G-ANFC de Havilland DH.82A Tiger Moth   85385   13.10.53
DE363   G Pierce   Ley Farm, Chirk   09.10.03
Built by Morris Motors Ltd (NF 29.06.18)

G-ANFH^M Westland WS.55 Whirlwind Series 1   WA.15   27.10.53
Cancelled 02.09.77 as WFU   17.07.71
On loan from E.D.ap Rees   No marks carried
With The Helicopter Museum, Weston-super-Mare

G-ANFI de Havilland DH.82A Tiger Moth   85577   16.10.53
DE623   G P Graham   Cardiff   11.07.19P
Built by Morris Motors Ltd; as 'DE623' in RAF yellow c/s
Another Tiger Moth as 'DE623' (ex D-EDON) is displayed
@ Auto und Technik Museum, Sinsheim, Germany

G-ANFL de Havilland DH.82A Tiger Moth   84617   22.10.53
T6169   Felthorpe Tiger Group Ltd   Felthorpe   02.05.19P
Built by Morris Motors Ltd

G-ANFM de Havilland DH.82A Tiger Moth   83604   22.10.53
T5888   A J Coker & J Towell tr Reading Flying Group
White Waltham   08.08.19P
Built by Morris Motors Ltd

G-ANFP de Havilland DH.82A Tiger Moth   82530   28.10.53
N9503   R Santus   Podhorany, Slovak Republic   05.05.19E
As 'N9503:39' in RAF camouflage c/s

G-ANFU^M Taylorcraft J Auster 5   1748   31.10.53
TW385   Cancelled 03.08.76 as WFU   17.02.71
As 'NJ719' with starboard wing ex G-AKPH
On rebuild with frame of un-identified Auster 05.93
With North East Land Sea and Air Museum, Usworth

G-ANFV de Havilland DH.82A Tiger Moth   85904   01.12.53
DF155   Avalon Ventures Ltd   Clacton-on-Sea
Built by Morris Motors Ltd; stored awaiting rebuild 02.19
(NF 15.08.18)

G-ANFW^M de Havilland DH.82A Tiger Moth   85660   05.11.53
DE730   Cancelled 10.03.00 by CAA   21.07.01
As 'G-ANFW'   Built by Morris Motors
Registered with Fuselage No.3737
With Malta Aviation Museum Foundation, Ta'Qali, Malta

G-ANHI de Havilland DH.82A Tiger Moth   83002   04.12.53
R5120   A D Barton   Newquay Cornwall
On rebuild 05.17 (NF 23.04.17)

G-ANHK de Havilland DH.82A Tiger Moth   82442   04.12.53
F-BHIM, G-ANHK, N9372
T A Jackson   Netherthorpe   25.05.18E

G-ANHR Auster 5   759   05.12.53
MT192   H L Swallow   Hibaldstow   20.07.86
Built by Taylorcraft Aeroplanes (England) Ltd;
frame stored in hangar rafters 04.12 (NF 26.02.16)

G-ANHS Auster 4   737   05.12.53
MT197   R Ellingworth & C Tyers   Spanhoe   18.12.19P
Built by Taylorcraft Aeroplanes (England) Ltd;
as 'MT197' in RAF c/s

G-ANHW Auster 5D   1396   05.12.53
TJ320   Cancelled 15.12.71 as WFU   09.03.70
Carr Farm, Thorney , Newark   *Fuselage only 02.15*

G-ANHX Auster 5D   2064   05.12.53
TW519 T Taylor RNAS Yeovilton   28.02.19P
Built by Taylorcraft Aeroplanes (England) Ltd;
as 'TW519:ROA-V' in AAC camouflage c/s

G-ANIE Auster 5   1809   05.12.53
TW467 R T Ingram Hardwick   13.05.19P
Built by Taylorcraft Aeroplanes (England) Ltd;
as 'TW467' in camouflage c/s with invasion stripes

G-ANIJ Auster 5D   1680   05.12.53
TJ672 G M Rundle (Overton, Basingstoke)
Built by Taylorcraft Aeroplanes (England) Ltd; as
'TJ672: DT-S' in RAF c/s (NF 10.11.14)

G-ANIS[M] Taylorcraft Auster 5   1429   05.12.53
TJ375 Cancelled 08.10.81 by CAA   19.09.76
With South East Aviation Enthusiasts Group, Dromod, Rol

G-ANIX (2)[M] de Havilland DH.82 Tiger Moth   84764   03.12.53
D-EFTF (2), G-ANIX (2), (G-ANIV), T6390
Cancelled 30.06.00 - to Germany *As 'T6390'*
Composite rebuild of unidentified Tiger Moth
1990/92 which used paperwork of D-ELOM,
former G-ANIX ex T6390
With Sammlung Koch – Historische Flugzeug,
Grossenhein, Germany

G-ANJA de Havilland DH.82A Tiger Moth   82459   07.12.53
N9389 A D Hodgkinson (Doddington, March)   17.01.09S
As 'N-9389' in RAF c/s (NF 01.04.16)

G-ANJD de Havilland DH.82A Tiger Moth   84652   08.12.53
T6226 D O Lewis Old Warden   10.05.19P
Built by Morris Motors Ltd

G-ANJI de Havilland DH.82A Tiger Moth   85099   12.12.53
C-GIZA, N548DH, F-BHIQ, G-ANJI, T6830
A Watt Insch
In Australian Army c/s as 'A17-376' (NF 17.09.18)

G-ANJK de Havilland DH.82A Tiger Moth   84557   12.12.53
T6066 H M M Haines (Norton Fitzwarren, Taunton)
Frame on rebuild 04.17 (NF 03.10.18)

G-ANJV[M] Westland WS-55 Whirlwind Series 3 WA.24   14.12.53
VR-BET, G-ANJV Cancelled 08.01.74 on sale in Bermuda
On loan from E.D.ap Rees No marks carried
With The Helicopter Museum, Weston-super-Mare

G-ANKK de Havilland DH.82A Tiger Moth   83590   24.12.53
T5854 P A Cambridge tr Halfpenny Green Tiger Group
Charity Farm, Baxterley   16.12.11C
As 'T-5854' in RAF c/s (NF 04.08.15)

G-ANKT de Havilland DH.82A Tiger Moth   85087   24.12.53
T6818 Richard Shuttleworth Trustees Old Warden 31.08.19P
As 'K-2585' in RAF CFS red & silver c/s

G-ANKV de Havilland DH.82A Tiger Moth   84166   30.12.53
T7793 J A Cooper Wickenby
Original not converted & presumed scrapped by late 1950s:
'T7793' rebuilt from components pre 1994 (NF 11.07.16)

G-ANKZ de Havilland DH.82A Tiger Moth   3803   30.12.53
(N.....), F-BHIO, G-ANKZ, N6466 T D Le Mesurier
tr G-ANKZ Tiger Moth Compton Abbas   17.07.18P
As 'N-6466' in RAF yellow c/s; noted less engine 09.18
(IE 09.08.18)

G-ANLD de Havilland DH.82A Tiger Moth   85990   30.12.53
OO-DPA, G-ANLD, EM773
Lord A J D Douglas-Hamilton Goodwood   17.12.19P

G-ANLS de Havilland DH.82A Tiger Moth   85862   07.01.54
DF113 P A Gliddon Solent   19.08.19P
Built by Morris Motors Ltd

G-ANLW Westland S.51 Widgeon Series 2 WA/H/133   23.03.54
"MD499", G-ANLW Cancelled 15.11.02 as PWFU   27.05.81
Sywell *Stored 09.18*

G-ANMO de Havilland DH.82A Tiger Moth   3255   22.01.54
F-BHIU, G-ANMO, K4259 K M Perkins Headcorn   28.04.19E
Operated by Aero Legends; as 'K-4259:71' in
RAF silver with yellow bands c/s

G-ANMY de Havilland DH.82A Tiger Moth   85466   22.01.54
OO-SOL, 'OO-SOC', G-ANMY, DE470
A R & M A Baxter (Newthorpe, Nottingham)   03.06.17P
Built by Morris Motors Ltd; as 'DE-470:16' in RAF silver c/s
with yellow bands: 'G-ANMY' on rear fuselage; damaged
on take off Brimpton 05.06.16

G-ANNG de Havilland DH.82A Tiger Moth   85504   22.01.54
DE524 Doublecube Aviation LLP Old Sarum   08.06.19E
Built by Morris Motors Ltd

G-ANNI de Havilland DH.82A Tiger Moth   85162   22.01.54
T6953 C E, M E & O C Ponsford West Tisted   13.05.19E
As 'T-6953' in RAF red & silver c/s

G-ANNK de Havilland DH.82A Tiger Moth   83804   22.01.54
F-BFDO, G-ANNK, T7290 J Y Kaye Audley End   23.04.19P
Built by Morris Motors Ltd; as 'T-7290:14' in RAF c/s

G-ANNN de Havilland DH.82A Tiger Moth   84073   02.02.54
T5968 Cancelled 06.11.00 as PWFU
Thorpe Camp, Tattershall Thorpe
Parts stored at visitor's centre 06.16

G-ANOD de Havilland DH.82A Tiger Moth   84588   16.02.54
T6121 P G Watson (Chalkhouse Green, Reading)
Built by Morris Motors Ltd (NF 12.01.16)

G-ANOH de Havilland DH.82A Tiger Moth   86040   22.02.54
EM838
N Parkhouse Chelworth House, Chelwood Gate   17.05.19P
Built by Morris Motors Ltd

G-ANOK SAAB 91C Safir   91-311   22.04.54
(SE-CEH) N C Stone Selby House Farm, Stanton
(NF 21.06.16)

G-ANOM de Havilland DH.82A Tiger Moth   82086   02.03.54
N6837 W J Pitts Sywell   03.05.19P

G-ANON de Havilland DH.82A Tiger Moth   84270   04.03.54
T7909 M Kelly Sherburn-in-Elmet   04.09.18P
Built by Morris Motors Ltd; as 'T7909' in RAF c/s

G-ANOO de Havilland DH.82A Tiger Moth   85409   11.03.54
DE401 R K Packman Compton Abbas   30.07.19P
Built by Morris Motors Ltd

G-ANOV[M] de Havilland DH.104 Dove 6   04445   11.03.54
G-5-16 Cancelled 06.07.81 as WFU   31.05.75
Civil Aviation Authority titles
With National Museum of Flight Scotland, East Fortune

G-ANOW[M] de Havilland DHC-1 Chipmunk 21   C1/0972   08.03.54
Cancelled 19.07.68 – to CX-BGH
As 'G-ANOW' 'Urutau'
With Museo Aeronautico, Montevideo, Uruguay

G-ANPE de Havilland DH.82A Tiger Moth   83738   27.03.54
G-IESH, G-ANPE, F-BHAT, G-ANPE, T7397
T K Butcher Clacton-on-Sea   09.08.12C
Built by Morris Motors Ltd; stored dismantled 10.15
(NF 03.09.18)

G-ANPK de Havilland DH.82A Tiger Moth   3571   05.04.54
L6936 A D Hodgkinson (Doddington, March)   10.07.97
(NF 18.01.19)

G-ANPP Percival P.34 Proctor III   H.264   08.04.54
HM354 Cancelled 03.04.89 by CAA   05.05.69
Great Oakley
Partially restored frame and wings stored 12.15

G-ANRF de Havilland DH.82A Tiger Moth   83748   24.05.54
T5850 C D Cyster Fife   17.07.15P
Built by Morris Motors Ltd (NF 28.07.17)

G-ANRM de Havilland DH.82A Tiger Moth   85861   08.06.54
DF112 Spectrum Leisure Ltd Clacton-on-Sea   20.05.19E
Built by Morris Motors Ltd; operated by Classic Wings
as 'DF112' in RAF c/s; on rebuild 02.19

G-ANRN de Havilland DH.82A Tiger Moth   83133   24.05.54
T5368 J J V Elwes Ranston Farm, Iwerne Courtney 12.06.18P

G-ANRP Auster 5   1789   21.05.54
TW439 C L Petty Breighton   09.11.18P
Built by Taylorcraft Aeroplanes (England) Ltd;
as 'TW439' in RAF c/s

G-ANRX[M] de Havilland DH.82A Tiger Moth   3863   25.05.54
N6550 Cancelled 08.06.67 as WFU 'Border City'   20.06.61
With de Havilland Aircraft Museum, London Colney

G-ANSG[M] de Havilland DH.82A Tiger Moth   85569   02.06.54
DE615 Cancelled 19.09.57 as destroyed – crashed
near Caen, France 15.06.57 *As 'G-ANSG'*
With Amicale Jean-Baptiste Salis, La Ferté-Alais, France

G-ANSM de Havilland DH.82A Tiger Moth   82909   03.06.54
R5014 P D G Grist t/a Douglas Aviation Sibson   16.06.17E
Built by Morris Motors Ltd (IE 06.07.18)

G-ANSO[M] Gloster Meteor T.7 G5/1525 12.06.54
G-7-1 Cancelled 11.08.59 - to SE-DCC *As 'WS774:4'*
Originally built & registered 19.06.50, as
Meteor F.8 G-AMCJ (G5/1210): to R.Danish AF 490,
Egyptian AF 1424, then rebuilt as G-ANSO
With Svedinos Bil Och Flygmuseum, Halmstad, Sweden

G-ANTE de Havilland DH.82A Tiger Moth 84891 20.09.54
T6562 I L Cheese (Chilton, Didcot)
'Brooklands Aviation Ltd, Sywell' 04.07.19P
Built by Morris Motors Ltd

G-ANTK[M] Avro 685 York C.1 xxxx 23.07.54
MW232 Cancelled 29.10.64 as WFU 29.10.64
Dan Air c/s
With Duxford Aviation Society

G-ANUO[M] de Havilland DH.114 Heron 2D 14062 27.09.54
Cancelled 09.08.96 as WFU 12.09.86
As 'G-AOXL' in Morton Air Services c/s: original G-AOXL
Flyhistorick Museum Sola, Stavangar-Lufthavn
With Croydon Airport Visitor Centre

G-ANUW[M] de Havilland DH.104 Dove 6 04458 16.05.55
Cancelled 05,06,96 as PWFU 22.07.81
With East Midlands Aeropark, East Midlands

G-ANVU[M] de Havilland DH.104 Dove 1B 04082 12.11.54
VR-NAP Cancelled 20.06.85 by CAA: restored
15.04.86: cancelled 16.09.86 to Sweden *As 'G-ANVU'* 14.09.77
Originally registered as Series 1
With Flygvapenmuseum, Malmslätt, Linköping, Sweden

G-ANVY Percival Proctor IV H772 23.11.54
SE-CEA, G-ANVY, RM169 J W Tregilgas Great Oakley
(*NF 10.07.15*)

G-ANWB de Havilland DHC-1 Chipmunk 21 C1/0987 15.02.55
G-5-17 G Briggs Blackpool 05.10.17E

G-ANXB[M] de Havilland DH.114 Heron 1B 14048 03.12.54
G-5-14 Cancelled 02.11.81 as PWFU 25.03.79
'Sir James Young Simpson' BEA Scottish Airways c/s
With Newark Air Museum, Winthorpe

G-ANXC Auster J5R Alpine 3135 04.12.54
5Y-UBD, VP-UBD, G-ANXC, (AP-AHG), G-ANXC
R B Webber tr Alpine Group Trenchard Farm, Eggesford 24.08.16P
(*IE 07.12.18*)

G-ANXR Percival Proctor IV H 803 14.12.54
RM221 N H T Cottrell Headcorn 26.06.18E
Built by F Hills and Sons Ltd; as 'RM221' in RAF c/s

G-ANZT Thruxton Jackaroo 84176 04.03.55
T7798 D J & P A D Neville RAF Henlow 13.06.19P
Originally built as DH.82A Tiger Moth

G-ANZU de Havilland DH.82A Tiger Moth 3583 09.03.55
L6938 M I Lodge Walton Wood Farm, Thorpe Audlin
(*NF 02.12.15*)

G-ANZZ de Havilland DH.82A Tiger Moth 85834 14.03.55
DE974 T K Butcher Clacton-on-Sea 19.07.19E
Built by Morris Motors Ltd; as 'DE974' in RAF c/s

G-AOAA – G-AOZZ

G-AOAA de Havilland DH.82A Tiger Moth 85908 14.03.55
DF159 R C P Brookhouse Old Buckenham
Built by Morris Motors Ltd (IE 22.07.18)

G-AOAI[M] Blackburn Beverley C.1 1002 15.03.55
XB259 Cancelled 30.03.55 to Military marks
As 'XB259'
With Fort Paull Armouries, Paull

G-AOBG Somers-Kendall SK-1 1 30.03.55
P W Bishop Rotary Farm, Hatch
Fuselage stored 04.15 (IE 28.02.18)

G-AOBH de Havilland DH.82A Tiger Moth 84350 31.03.55
T7997 P Nutley Eaglescott 28.06.13C
Built by Morris Motors Ltd; officially registered with
c/n 83818 ex T7997; as 'NL750' in RAF c/s (NF 21.12.16)

G-AOBJ de Havilland DH.82A Tiger Moth 85830 07.05.55
N10RM, D-EBIG, G-AOBY, DE970
A D Hodgkinson (Doddington, March) 07.05.98
(*NF 01.04.16*)

G-AOBU Hunting Percival P.84 Jet Provost T.1 P84/6 02.05.55
XM129, G-AOBU, G-42-1 T J Manna North Weald 13.03.07P
As 'XD693:Z-Q' in RAF 2 FTS c/s; in open storage 07.18
(*NF 15.06.15*)

G-AOBX de Havilland DH.82A Tiger Moth 83653 26.04.55
T7187 S Bohill-Smith tr David Ross Flying Group
White Waltham 24.07.19P
Built by Morris Motors Ltd

G-AOCP Auster 5 1800 25.05.56
TW462 Cancelled 22.06.68 as WFU 22.06.68
Carr Farm, Thorney, Newark *Frame only 02.15*

G-AOCR (2) Auster 5D 1060 25.05.56
EI-AJS, G-AOCR, NJ673 D A Hill Fenland
Built by Taylorcraft Aeroplanes (England) Ltd;
as 'NJ673' in RAF c/s (NF 05.04.16)

G-AOCU (2) Auster 5 986 08.06.56
MT349 S J Ball Tatenhill 29.07.19P
Built by Taylorcraft Aeroplanes (England) Ltd

G-AODA[M] Westland WS-55 Whirlwind Series 3 WA.113 13.05.55
9Y-TDA, EP-HAC, G-AODA Cancelled 23.09.93 by CAA 23.08.91
'Dorado' Bristow Helicopters c/s
With The Helicopter Museum, Weston-super-Mare

G-AODR de Havilland DH.82A Tiger Moth 86251 04.08.55
G-ISIS, G-AODR, NL779
T Groves tr G-AODR Group (Lee-on-the-Solent)
Built by Morris Motors Ltd (NF 06.06.18)

G-AODT de Havilland DH.82A Tiger Moth 83109 04.08.55
R5250 R A Harrowven Tibenham 08.07.19P

G-AOEH Aeronca 7AC Champion 7AC-2144 08.09.55
N79854, OO-TWF
A Gregori Nethershields Farm, Chapelton 19.07.10P
(*NF 25.08.17*)

G-AOEI de Havilland DH.82A Tiger Moth 82196 14.09.55
N6946 CFG Flying Ltd Cambridge 25.04.19E
Registered with fuselage no.MCO/DH3409 which
corresponds to DE298 [c/n 85332]: probably composite
airframe

G-AOEL[M] de Havilland DH.82A Tiger Moth 82537 27.09.55
N9510 Cancelled 21.01.82 as WFU 18.07.72
With National Museum of Scotland, Edinburgh

G-AOES de Havilland DH.82A Tiger Moth 84547 06.10.55
T6056 P D & S E Ford Derby 15.06.02
Built by Morris Motors Ltd 1941; reported on rebuild with
Airspeed Aviation (NF 19.05.15)

G-AOET de Havilland DH.82A Tiger Moth 85650 07.10.55
DE720 P H Meeson AAC Middle Wallop 01.06.13C
Built by Morris Motors Ltd (IE 31.01.18)

G-AOEX Thruxton Jackaroo 86483 10.10.55
NM175 A T Christian Walkeridge Farm, Overton
Originally built as DH.82A Tiger Moth (IE 07.01.19)

G-AOFE de Havilland DHC-1 Chipmunk 22A C1/0150 13.09.56
WB702 W J Quinn Goodwood 04.03.19P
As 'WB702' in RAF c/s

G-AOFJ Auster Alpha 5 3401 03.10.56
Cancelled 29.03.12 by CAA 09.12.10
Lodge Farm, Burston *Stored dismantled 10.13*

G-AOFM[M] Auster J/5P Autocar 3178 08.07.97
Cancelled 28.11.06 to Australia 13.05.08
VH-marks NTU
With Darwin Aviation Museum, Darwin, NT

G-AOFS Auster J5L Aiglet Trainer 3143 28.10.55
EI-ALN, G-AOFS P N A Whitehead Leicester 19.12.18P

G-AOGA[M] Miles M.75 Aries 1 75/1007 09.11.55
EI-ANB, G-AOGA Cancelled 18.05.63 – to EI-ANB
– restored 10.09.63– cancelled 30.05.84 as PWFU 10.10.69
Stored off site
With South East Aviation Enthusiasts Group, Dromod, RoI

G-AOGE Percival P.34 Proctor III H.210 24.11.55
BV651 Cancelled 19.01.99 by CAA 21.05.84
Biggin Hill *Stored for rebuild 08.16*

G-AOGI de Havilland DH.82A Tiger Moth 85922 14.12.55
(N....), OO-SOA, G-AOGI, DF186
A E Taylor (Friskney, Boston)
Built by Morris Motors Ltd (NF 28.06.18)

G-AOGR	de Havilland DH.82A Tiger Moth	84566	20.01.56
	XL714, G-AOGR, T6099		
	R J S G Clark Griffins Farm, Temple Bruer		28.08.19P
	Built by Morris Motors Ltd; as 'XL714' in RAF		
	camouflage upper & yellow lower c/s		

G-AOGV	Auster J5R Alpine	3302	02.02.56
	R E Heading (Thorney, Peterborough)		
	Noted dismantled 05.15 (NF 27.10.15)		

G-AOHY	de Havilland DH.82A Tiger Moth	3850	23.02.56
	N6537 S W Turley Wickenby		24.11.16E
	As 'N6537' in RAF c/s		
	Failed to climb on take-off Wickenby 17.07.16,		
	overturned & extensively damaged		

G-AOHZ	Auster J5P Autocar	3252	28.02.56
	R W Eaton & A J Kay (Chesterfield)		25.09.03
	(NF 08.01.18)		

G-AOIE[M]	Douglas DC-7C	45115	27.08.56
	PH-SAX, G-AOIE Cancelled 10.04.67 – to PH-SAX		
	– restored 18.11.69: cancelled 01.05.81 as WFU		
	Scrapped 10.97: forward fuselage only		
	With South East Aviation Enthusiasts Group, Dromod, RoI		

G-AOIM	de Havilland DH.82A Tiger Moth	83536	27.08.56
	T7109 R C P Brookhouse Bicester		22.03.19E
	Built by Morris Motors Ltd; as 'T7109' in RAF c/s		

G-AOIR	Thruxton Jackaroo	82882	13.01.56
	R4972 K M Perkins Sywell		21.07.19E
	Originally built as DH.82A Tiger Moth;		
	operated by Aero Legends		

G-AOIS	de Havilland DH.82A Tiger Moth	83034	13.01.56
	R5172 B S Floodgate & R J Moore Sywell		14.05.19E
	As 'R5172:FIJE' in RAF yellow c/s		

G-AOJH	de Havilland DH.83C Fox Moth	FM42	29.03.56
	AP-ABO Connect Properties Ltd Rendcomb		23.10.18P
	Built by de Havilland Aircraft of Canada Ltd		

G-AOJJ	de Havilland DH.82A Tiger Moth	85877	05.04.56
	DF128 E Lay & T J Pegram tr JJ Flying Group		
	White Waltham		05.09.19P
	Built by Morris Motors Ltd; as 'DF-128:RCO-U'		
	in RAF yellow c/s		

G-AOJK	de Havilland DH.82A Tiger Moth	82813	05.04.56
	R4896 P L Green Andrewsfield		09.04.19P

G-AOJR	de Havilland DHC-1 Chipmunk 22	C1/0205	09.04.56
	SE-BBS, OY-DFB, D-EGIM, G-AOJR, D-EGIM,		
	G-AOJR, WB756		
	J G H Caubergs & N Marien Namur-Suarlee, Belgium		31.07.19E

G-AOJT[M]	de Havilland DH.106 Comet 1XB	06020	11.05.56
	F-BGNX Cancelled 09.07.56 as WFU		05.07.56
	Fuselage only, in green primer: no marks carried		
	With de Havilland Aircraft Museum, London Colney		

G-AOKL	Percival P.40 Prentice T.1	PAC-208	13.04.56
	VS610 N J Butler Fordoun		
	(NF 11.10.17)		

G-AOKO[M]	Percival P.40 Prentice 1	PAC-234	13.04.56
	VS621 Cancelled 09.10.84 as WFU *Stored*		23.10.72
	With South Yorkshire Aircraft Museum, Doncaster		

G-AOKZ[M]	Percival P.40 Prentice 1	PAC-238	20.04.56
	VS623 Cancelled 04.10.61 as PWFU		
	Became instructional airframe		
	As 'VS623' with wings from G-AONB – no wheel spats		
	With Midland Air Museum, Coventry		

G-AOLK	Percival P.40 Prentice 1	PAC/225	25.04.56
	VS618 Cancelled 09.02.10 by CAA		17.09.10
	RAF Stafford *In RAF Museum store 2018 as 'VS618'*		

G-AOLU	Percival P.40 Prentice T.1	B3/1A/PAC/283	25.04.56
	EI-ASP, G-AOLU, VS356 N J Butler Fordoun		
	Both officially registered p/i (VS356) & c/n (5830/3)		
	are not correct; on rebuild 07.17 (NF 28.06.18)		

G-AORG	de Havilland DH.114 Sea Heron C.1	14101	01.05.56
	XR441, G-AORG, G-5-16		
	Duchess of Brittany (Jersey) Ltd Jersey		
	'Jersey Airlines' & 'Duchess of Brittany'		24.07.19E

G-AORW	de Havilland DHC-1 Chipmunk 22A	C1/0130	28.05.56
	WB682 S Maric Glasgow Prestwick		07.05.15E
	Blown over 04.12.13 Glasgow Prestwick &		
	substantially damaged; on rebuild 05.18 using		
	spares ex G-BDEU (NF 15.11.16)		

G-AOSK	de Havilland DHC-1 Chipmunk 22A	C1/0178	26.06.56
	WB726 P McMillan Turweston		03.12.18P
	As 'WB726:E' in RAF Cambridge UAS c/s		

G-AOSU	de Havilland DHC-1 Chipmunk 22	C1/0217	28.06.56
	WB766 Cancelled 25.05.05 by CAA		28.06.06
	Tatabanya, Hungary *Displayed 09.18*		

G-AOSY	de Havilland DHC-1 Chipmunk 22	C1/0037	29.06.56
	WB585 P Wood tr Chippy Sierra Yankee Group		
	Audley End		15.04.19E
	As 'WB585:M in RAF red & white c/s		

G-AOTD	de Havilland DHC-1 Chipmunk 22	C1/0040	30.06.56
	WB588 S Piech Old Sarum		01.05.19P
	As 'WB588:D' in RAF silver & yellow bands c/s		

G-AOTF	de Havilland DHC-1 Chipmunk 23	C1/0015	02.07.56
	WB563 A C Darby RAF Halton		26.03.15E
	Lycoming O-360-A4A (IE 30.11.15)		

G-AOTI[M]	de Havilland DH.114 Heron 2D	14107	25.07.56
	G-5-19 Cancelled 17.10.95 as WFU 'Rolls-Royce'		24.06.87
	With de Havilland Aircraft Museum, London Colney		

G-AOTK	Druine D.53 Turbi	1	01.11.56
	J S & P R Johnson Lavenham		28.03.19P
	Built by TK Flying Group – project PFA 230		

G-AOTR	de Havilland DHC-1 Chipmunk 22	C1/0045	12.07.56
	HB-TUH, D-EGOG, G-AOTR, WB604		
	S J Sykes Compton Abbas		11.07.19E

G-AOTY	de Havilland DHC-1 Chipmunk 22A	C1/0522	12.07.56
	WG472 Retro Track & Air (UK) Ltd (Cam, Dursley)		02.11.18P
	As 'WG472' in RAF c/s		

G-AOUJ[M]	Fairey Ultralight Helicopter	F.9424	01.08.56
	XJ928 Cancelled 26.2.69 as Destroyed		29.03.59
	On loan from E.D.ap Rees		
	With The Helicopter Museum, Weston-super-Mare		

G-AOUO[M]	de Havilland DHC-1 Chipmunk 22	C1/0179	10.08.56
	WB730 The Royal Air Force Gliding & Soaring		
	Association Hooton Park		03.04.14E
	Displayed Aeroplane Collection, less engine 12.18		
	(NF 25.06.15)		

G-AOUP	de Havilland DHC-1 Chipmunk 22	C1/0180	10.08.56
	WB731 A R Harding (Milden, Ipswich)		13.06.17P
	(IE 08.02.19)		

G-AOUR[M]	de Havilland DH.82A Tiger Moth	86341	14.08.56
	NL898 Cancelled 08.07.65 as PWFU		19.11.66
	With Ulster Folk & Transport Museum, Holywood		

G-AOVF[M]	Bristol 175 Britannia Series 312F	13237	13.02.57
	9Q-CAZ, G-AOVF Cancelled 21.11.84 as PWFU		14. 12.77
	'Schedar' As '497' in RAF Air Support Command c/s)		
	With Royal Air Force Cosford Museum		

G-AOVT[M]	Bristol 175 Britannia 312	3427	23.06.58
	Cancelled 21.09.81 as WFU		11.03.75
	Monarch c/s		
	With Duxford Aviation Society		

G-AOVW	Auster 5	894	16.11.59
	MT119 B Marriott Hanbeck Farm, Wilsford		24.05.19P
	Built by Taylorcraft Aeroplanes (England) Ltd		

G-AOXG[M]	de Havilland DH.82A Tiger Moth	83805	03.10.56
	XL717, G-AOXG, T7291 Cancelled 31.10.56: sold as XL717		
	As 'G-ABUL'		
	With Fleet Air Arm Museum, RNAS Yeovilton		

G-AOXN	de Havilland DH.82A Tiger Moth	85958	31.10.56
	EM727 S L G Darch East Chinnock, Yeovil		21.12.01
	Built by Morris Motors Ltd (NF 24.05.18)		

G-AOZE[M]	Westland S.51 Series 2 Widgeon	WA/H/141	11.01.57
	5N-ABW, G-AOZE Cancelled 20.06.62 on sale in Nigeria		
	On loan from E.D.ap Rees		
	With The Helicopter Museum, Weston-super-Mare		

G-AOZH	de Havilland DH.82A Tiger Moth	86449	18.01.57
	NM129 The Frensham Tiger Company Ltd		
	Wishanger Farm, Churt		21.09.19P
	Built by Morris Motors Ltd; 'K2572' in RAF c/s		

G-AOZL	Auster J5Q Alpine	3202	05.02.57
	R M Weeks Graveley Hall Farm, Graveley		
	(NF 05.02.16)		

G-AOZP	de Havilland DHC-1 Chipmunk 22A	C1/0183	14.02.57
	WB734 S J Davies Retford Gamston		22.11.19P

G-APAA – G-APZZ

G-APAF Auster 5 3404 25.03.57
G-CMAL, G-APAF J J J Mostyn (AAC Netheravon) 11.06.19P
As 'TW511' in AAC c/s

G-APAH Auster 5 3402 29.03.57
T J Goodwin Lodge Farm, St Osyth 15.01.19P

G-APAL de Havilland DH.82A Tiger Moth 82102 03.04.57
N6847 P J Shotbolt Manor Farm, Braceborough 26.07.19P
As 'N6847' in RAF yellow c/s

G-APAM de Havilland DH.82A Tiger Moth 3874 03.04.57
N6580 R P Williams tr Myth Group
Folly Farm, Hungerford 'Myth' 23.10.19P

G-APAO de Havilland DH.82A Tiger Moth 82845 03.04.57
R4922 H J Maguire Clacton-on-Sea 16.05.19E
As 'R4922' in RAF c/s

G-APAP de Havilland DH.82A Tiger Moth 83018 03.04.57
R5136 S E Ford Darley Moor 31.10.18E
As 'R-5136' in RAF upper camouflage & lower yellow c/s

G-APAS^M de Havilland DH.106 Comet 1A 06022 23.05.57
8351M, XM823, G-APAS, G-5-23, F-BGNZ
Cancelled 22.10.58 – to Military use *BOAC titles*
With Royal Air Force Cosford Museum

G-APBE Auster 5 3403 07.05.57
E G & G R Woods Haw Farm, Hampstead Norreys 01.11.18P

G-APBI de Havilland DH.82A Tiger Moth 86097 16.05.57
EM903 C J Zeal (Twyford, Reading)
Built by Morris Motors Ltd (NF 18.01.16)

G-APBO Druine D.53 Turbi PFA 229 03.06.57
R C Hibberd Coate, Devizes 06.12.19P
Built by F Roche – project PFA 229

G-APBW Auster 5A Alpha 3405 23.05.57
N Huxtable Cheddington 20.12.18P

G-APCB Auster J5Q Alpine 3204 05.06.57
A A Beswick Thruxton 25.08.10P
(NF 25.11.16)

G-APCC de Havilland DH.82A Tiger Moth 86549 11.06.57
PG640 L J Rice Quebec Farm, Knook 18.06.16E
(IE 20.09.18)

G-APDB^M de Havilland DH.106 Comet 4 6403 02.05.57
9M-AOB, G-APDB Cancelled 18.02.74 as WFU 07.10.74
BOAC c/s
With Duxford Aviation Society

G-APEP^M Vickers 953C Vanguard Merchantman 719 09.09.57
Cancelled 28.02.97 as WFU 'Superb' 01.10.98
Hunting Cargo Airlines titles
With Brooklands Museum, Weybridge

G-APFA Druine D.52 Turbi PFA 232 05.02.57
T W J Carnall Dunkeswell 22.09.92P
Built by Britten-Norman Ltd – project PFA 232;
on rebuild 03.18 (NF 12.02.18)

G-APFU de Havilland DH.82A Tiger Moth 86081 28.08.57
EM879 C L Griffiths Henstridge 06.09.19P

G-APFV (2) Piper PA-23-160 Apache 23-1686 11.12.59
G-MOLY, EI-BAW, G-APFV, EI-ALK, N10F
J L Thorogood Pittrichie Farm, Whiterashes 01.06.19E

G-APHV^M Avro 652A Anson C.19 Series 2 xxxx 19.09.57
VM360 Cancelled 21.01.82 as PWFU *As 'VM360'* 15.06.73
With National Museum of Flight Scotland, East Fortune

G-APIE Tipsy Belfair 535 22.10.57
(OO-TIE) D Beale Fenland 15.04.19P

G-APIK Auster J1N Alpha 3375 11.11.57
K D Jones tr Deadwood Flying Group
Preston Court, Ledbury 29.08.19P

G-APIM^M Vickers 806 Viscount 412 19.11.57
Cancelled 01.03.91 as PWFU 'Viscount Stephen Piercey' 19.07.88
DBR 11.01.88 when struck by Short SD.3-30 G-BHWT
British Air Ferries titles
With Brooklands Museum, Weybridge

G-APIT^M Percival P.40 Prentice T.1 PAC-016 28.11.57
VR192 Cancelled 06.11.79 as PWFU
With Romney Marsh Wartime Collection, Romney Marsh

G-APIY^M Percival P.40 Prentice 1 PAC-075 28.11.57
VR249 Cancelled 19.04.73 18.03.67
As 'VR249:FA-EL' in RAFC c/s WFU 18.3.67
With Newark Air Museum, Winthorpe

G-APIZ Druine D.31 Turbulent PFA 478 22.11.57
R G Meredith Fowle Hall Farm, Laddingford '31' 04.10.19P
Built by Rollason Aircraft and Engines Ltd
– project PFA 478

G-APJB Percival P.40 Prentice T.1 PAC-086 28.11.57
VR259 K M Perkins Headcorn 09.05.19E
As 'VR259:M' in RAF 2 Air Signallers School c/s

G-APJJ (2)^M Fairey Ultralight Helicopter F.9428 04.12.57
Cancelled 02.03.73 as WFU 01.04.59
'Royal Navy' c/s
With Midland Air Museum, Coventry

G-APJZ Auster J1N Alpha 3382 03.01.58
5N-ACY, (VR-NDR), G-APJZ
P G Lipman Romney Street Farm, Sevenoaks
(NF 12.11.18)

G-APLG^M Auster J/5L Aiglet Trainer 3148 04.03.58
Cancelled 11.02.99 by CAA 26.10.68
With Solway Aviation Museum, Carlisle Lake District

G-APLO de Havilland DHC-1 Chipmunk 22 C1/0144 01.05.58
EI-AHU, WB696
P M Luijken Midden Zeeland, Netherlands 03.05.18E

G-APLU de Havilland DH.82A Tiger Moth 85094 02.04.58
VR-AAY, F-OBKK, G-APLU, T6825
M E Vaisey Rush Green 06.06.19E
Built by Morris Motors Ltd

G-APMH Auster J1U Workmaster 3502 15.04.58
F-OBOA, G-APMH M R P Thorogood Insch 11.11.19P

G-APMX de Havilland DH.82A Tiger Moth 85645 09.05.58
DE715 T A P Hubbard tr Foley Farm Flying Group
Redwood Cottage, Meon 05.09.19P
Built by Morris Motors Ltd

G-APMY^M Piper PA-23-160 Apache 23-1258 15.05.58
EI-AJT Cancelled 25.11.81 as PWFU 01.11.81
United Steel c/s
With South Yorkshire Aircraft Museum, Doncaster

G-APNJ^M Cessna 310 35335 02.06.58
EI-AJY, N3635D Cancelled 05.12.83 as WFU 28.11.74
With Newark Air Museum, Winthorpe

G-APNT Phoenix Currie Wot HAC-3 18.06.58
S Slater Turweston 'Airymouse' 26.03.19P
Built by Hampshire Aero Club; official c/n, P6399, is
corruption of original Certificate of Registration No.R6399/1

G-APNV^M Saunders-Roe P.531-1 S2/5268 24.06.58
Cancelled 01.10.59 – to XN332 10.59 *As 'XN332:759'*
With Fleet Air Arm Museum, RNAS Yeovilton

G-APNZ Druine D.31 Turbulent PFA 482 17.04.58
Turbulent G-APNZ Preservation Society Derby 13.12.95P
Built by Rollason Aircraft and Engines Ltd – project PFA 482
(IE 09.06.18)

G-APOI^M Saunders-Roe Skeeter Srs.8 S2/5081 29. 07.58
Cancelled 14.04.10 by CAA 02.08.00
With Solent Sky, Southampton

G-APPA de Havilland DHC-1 Chipmunk 22 C1/0792 11.09.58
N5073E, G-APPA, WP917
M B Phillips (Newton St Cyres, Exeter)
(NF 07.08.17)

G-APPL Percival P.40 Prentice T.1 PAC-013 07.10.58
VR189 S J Saggers Biggin Hill 27.04.17E
(IE 20.09.18)

G-APPM de Havilland DHC-1 Chipmunk 22 C1/0159 14.10.58
WB711 E H W Moore Jersey 01.08.18P
As 'WB711' in RAF white & red c/s

G-APPN^M de Havilland DH.82A Tiger Moth 83839 17.10.58
T7328 Cancelled 15.07.08 – to Spain *As 'T7328'*
With Fundacio Parc Aeronautic De Catalunya,
Sabadell, Spain

G-APRL^M Armstrong-Whitworth 650 Argosy Series 101 AW.6652 02.01.59
N890U, N602Z, N6507R, G-APRL
Cancelled 19.11.87 as WFU 'Edna' 23.03.87
Elan titles
With Midland Air Museum, Coventry

G-APRO Auster 6A   –   21.01.59
        N370WJ, G-APRO, WJ370
        H Wankowska & A F Wankowski   Crowfield   28.03.19P
        Carries 'NX 370WJ' on rudder

G-APRS Scottish Aviation Twin Pioneer 3   561   09.01.59
        G-BCWF, XT610, G-APRS, (PI-C430)
        Cancelled 06.12.17 as WFU   15.07.08
        Mains Farm, Thornhill
        Used as accommodation at glamping site 06.18

G-APRT^M Taylor JT.1 Monoplane   PFA 537   15.01.59
        Cancelled 16.04.12 as WFU   31.07.12
        Built by J Taylor as project PFA537
        With Newark Air Museum, Winthorpe

G-APSA Douglas DC-6A   45497   12.02.59
        4W-ABQ, HZ-ADA, G-APSA, CF-MCK
        G-APSA Ltd   Coventry   23.05.09
        British Eagle c/s (NF 14.02.17)

G-APSO de Havilland DH.104 Dove 5   04505   16.02.59
        (N1046T), G-APSO   Cancelled 02.05.01 as WFU   08.07.78
        Calcutt, Swindon
        Forward fuselage at Kingshill Recycling Centre, 04.13

G-APSR Auster J1U Workmaster   3499   22.04.59
        OO-HXA, G-APSR, VP-JCD, G-APSR, (F-OBHR)
        D & K Aero Services Ltd
        Sint-Truiden, Limburg, Belgium   20.07.17E

G-APTR Auster J1N Alpha   3392   15.04.59
        C R Shipley   Avon Farm, Saltford   02.08.11P
        (IE 06.06.18)

G-APTU Auster 5   3413   20.04.59
        A J & J M Davis tr G-APTU Flying Group Leicester 08.06.98
        (NF 06.02.18)

G-APTW^M Westland S-51 Series 2 Widgeon   WA/H/150   27.04.59
        Cancelled 24.08.77 as WFU   26.09.75
        With North East Land Sea and Air Museum, Usworth

G-APTY Beech G35 Bonanza   D-4789   04.06.59
        EI-AJG   G E Brennand   Blackpool   02.08.19E

G-APTZ Druine D.31 Turbulent   PFA 508   18.03.59
        J T Britcher   Damyns Hall, Upminster   18.06.08P
        Built by Rollason Aircraft and Engines Ltd – project PFA 508
        (NF 13.07.18)

G-APUD^M Bensen B-7Mc   KHW.1   11.05.59
        Cancelled 27.02.70 as WFU   27.09.60
        Built by K. H. Wallis
        On loan from The Aeroplane Collection to
        Manchester Museum of Sciences & Industry

G-APUE Orlican L-40 Meta-Sokol   150708   02.06.59
        OK-NMB   I Tvrdik   (Rudna, Czech Republic)   08.03.19E

G-APUG^M Phoenix Luton LA5 Major   PAL.1203   13.05.59
        Cancelled 05.08.87 as PWFU
        Built by L D Blyth
        With Norfolk & Suffolk Aviation Museum, Flixton

G-APUP^M Sopwith Pup replica   B.5292   13.02.59
        9213M, G-APUP, N5182   Cancelled 04.10.84 by CAA 28.06.78
        As 'N5182'
        Built by K C D St Cyrien – project PFA 1582
        With Royal Air Force Cosford Museum

G-APUR Piper PA-22-160 Tri-Pacer   22-6711   03.07.59
        S T A Hutchinson   Newtownards   09.08.19E

G-APUW Auster J5V Series 160 Autocar   3273   23.06.59
        E S E & P B Hibbard   Tibenham   01.08.19P

G-APUY Druine D.31 Turbulent   PFA 509   24.06.59
        C Jones   (Hazel Grove, Stockport)
        Built by K F W Turner – project PFA 509 (IE 30.04.15)

G-APVG Auster J5L Aiglet Trainer   3306   10.07.59
        (ZK-BQK)   R E Tyers   Spanhoe   'Shell' logo on tail 09.07.18P
        C/n 3306 originally allocated 05.56
        as J/5R Alpine ZK-BQK

G-APVN Druine D.31 Turbulent   PFA 511   24.07.59
        R Sherwin   Swanborough Farm, Lewes   24.06.94P
        Built by J P Knight – project PFA 511; stored 07.15
        (NF 02.12.15)

G-APVS Cessna 170B   26156   07.08.59
        N2512C   N Simpson   East Kirkby   21.05.19E

G-APVT de Havilland DH.82A Tiger Moth   3250   07.08.59
        K4254   M C Boddington   Sywell
        (NF 21.07.17)

G-APVU Orlican L-40 Meta-Sokol   150706   21.08.59
        OK-NMI   M J & S E Aherne   (Oswaldkirk, York)
        (NF 16.01.15)

G-APVV^M Mooney M.20A   1474   30.07.59
        N8164E   Cancelled 30.04.89 by CAA   19.09.81
        Crashed Barton 11.01.81
        With Newark Air Museum, Winthorpe

G-APVZ Druine D.31 Turbulent   PFA 545   23.07.59
        The Tiger Club 1990 Ltd   Damyns Hall, Upminster 06.05.19P
        Built by Rollason Aircraft and Engines Ltd – project PFA 545

G-APWA^M Handley Page HPR.7 Dart Herald 100   149   28.09.59
        PP-SDM, G-APWA, PP-SDM, PP-ASV, G-APWA
        Cancelled 29.01.87 as WFU   06.04.82
        BEA titles
        With Museum of Berkshire Aviation, Woodley

G-APWJ^M Handley Page HPR.7 Dart Herald 201   158   28.09.59
        Cancelled 10.07.85 as WFU   21.12.85
        Air UK c/s
        With Duxford Aviation Society

G-APWK^M Westland S.51 Series 2 Widgeon   WA/H/152   26.08.59
        Cancelled 10.09.73 by CAA   22.05.70
        Forward fuselage only
        With 'Carpetbagger' Aviation Museum, Harrington

G-APWL EoN AP.10 460 Standard Series.1A   EoN/S/001   02.09.59
        BGA 1172/BRK, G-APWL, RAFGSA268, G-APWL
        Cancelled 18.02.10 by CAA   26.04.00
        Oxford   *Displayed at Airplan Flight Equipment*

G-APWN^M Westland WS-55 Whirlwind 3   WA.298   08.09.59
        VR-BER, G-APWN, 5N-AGI, G-APWN
        Cancelled 25.06.81 as WFU   'Skerries'   17.05.78
        Bristow Helicopters titles
        With Midland Air Museum, Coventry

G-APWU^M Thurston Tawney Owl   TA1-1   23.09.59
        Cancelled 15.09.86 by CAA
        Believed with Historical Aviation Centre, Morgansfield, Fishburn

G-APWY Piaggio P.166   362   16.12.59
        Cancelled 20.10.00 by CAA   14.03.81
        Wroughton   *In Science Museum store 2013*

G-APXJ Piper PA-24-250 Comanche   24-291   11.12.59
        VR-NDA, N10F   T Wildsmith   Netherthorpe   04.10.19E

G-APXR Piper PA-22-160 Tri-Pacer   22-7172   29.01.60
        N10F   A Troughton   Armagh Field, Woodview   31.03.11E
        (NF 19.02.19)

G-APXT Piper PA-22-150 Caribbean   22-3854   16.02.60
        N4545A   A D A Smith   White Waltham   01.08.18E
        Converted to PA-20 Pacer configuration (IE 05.09.18)

G-APXU Piper PA-22-150 Tri-Pacer   22-474   10.02.60
        N1723A   C J Cauwood   Spanhoe
        'The Mighty Tri Pacer'   12.12.18E

G-APXX^M de Havilland DHA.3 Drover 2   5014   15.12.61
        VH-EAZ, VH-EAS, G-APXX
        Cancelled 26.11.73 as PWFU   *As 'VH-FDT'*
        With South Wales Aircraft Museum, St Athan

G-APYB Tipsy Nipper T.66 Series 3   T66/S/39   28.01.60
        B O Smith   Turners Arms Farm, Yearby   12.06.96P
        Built by Avions Fairey SA; on rebuild 04.13 (NF 21.01.16)

G-APYD de Havilland DH.106 Comet 4B   6438   21.01.60
        SX-DAL, G-APYD   Cancelled 23.11.79 as WFU   03.08.79
        Wroughton   *Dan-Air titles*
        In Science Museum store 2013

G-APYG de Havilland DHC-1 Chipmunk 22   C1/0060   11.11.60
        OH-HCB, WB619   J M & P A Doyle   Compton Abbas 26.03.19P

G-APYT Champion 7FC Tri-Traveler   387   09.05.60
        N F O'Neill   Newtownards   26.04.19P
        Tailwheel u/c

G-APYW Piper PA-22-150 Tri-Pacer   22-4994   03.03.60
        N7131D   Cancelled 12.07.93 by CAA   06.07.88
        Midden Zeeland, Netherlands   *On long term rebuild 04.15*

G-APZJ Piper PA-18-150 Super Cub   18-7233   29.01.60
        N10F   S G Jones   Membury   28.07.19E
        Rebuilt 1986 with fuselage frame ex G-ATRH (18-7830)

G-APZL Piper PA-22-160 Tri-Pacer   22-7054   27.01.60
EI-ALF, N10F   B Robins   (Catcott, Bridgwater)   14.05.99
(NF 29.05.18)

G-ARAA – G-ARZZ

G-ARAD[M] Phoenix Luton LA-5A Major   PAL/1204   29.04.60
Cancelled 16.10.02 as WFU – completed but not flown
Built by W T Spoat – project PFA 836
With North East Land Sea and Air Museum, Usworth

G-ARAM Piper PA-18-150 Super Cub   18-7312   17.05.60
N10F   Skymax (Aviation) Ltd   Sywell   22.06.02
Fuselage stored 08.16 (IE 14.11.18)

G-ARAN Piper PA-18-150 Super Cub   18-7307   28.04.60
N10F   J P Dehnel tr G-ARAN Group   Leicester   24.02.19E

G-ARAP Champion 7FC Tri-Traveler   394   12.09.60
J J McGonagle   Bellarena
Noted 04.16 (NF 26.01.15)

G-ARAS Champion 7FC Tri-Traveler   396   12.09.60
G J Taylor tr Alpha Sierra Flying Group
Yeatsall Farm, Abbots Bromley   22.06.01P
(NF 12.06.18)

G-ARAW Cessna 182C Skylane   52843   18.05.60
N8943T   A J Holmes & R L McLean   Rufforth   07.10.19E

G-ARAX Piper PA-22-150 Tri-Pacer   22-3830   22.04.60
N4523A   C W Carnall   Derby   03.10.11E
Official type data 'PA-22-150 Caribbean' is incorrect
(NF 03.11.14)

G-ARAZ de Havilland DH.82A Tiger Moth   82867   05.03.60
R4959   Avalon Ventures Ltd   Clacton-on-Sea   12.07.19P
As 'R-4959:59' in RAF yellow & camouflage c/s

G-ARBE de Havilland DH.104 Dove 8   04517   06.05.60
M Whale   (Swindon)   03.10.02
(NF 16.01.15)

G-ARBG Tipsy Nipper T.66 Series 2   ABAC1   11.05.60
D Shrimpton   Watchford Farm, Yarcombe   08.02.19P
Originally built by Avions Fairey SA as c/n T66.57

G-ARBM Auster 5J1B Aiglet   2792   08.06.60
EI-AMO, G-ARBM, VP-SZZ, VP-KKR
A D Hodgkinson   (Doddington, March)   06.06.03
(NF 02.02.15)

G-ARBS Piper PA-22-160 Tri-Pacer   22-6858   24.08.60
N2868Z   S D Rowell   Fenland   *'Greta'*   05.11.18E
Converted to PA-20 Pacer configuration (IE 12.11.18)

G-ARBZ Druine D.31 Turbulent   PFA 553   06.05.60
R Vary tr G-ARBZ Group   (Guildford)   18.06.19P
Built by Rollason Aircraft and Engines Ltd – project PFA 553

G-ARCF Piper PA-22-150 Tri-Pacer   22-4563   28.06.60
N5902D   M J Speakman   North Coates   12.07.18E
Officially type 'PA-22-150 Caribbean' is incorrect
(IE 04.10.18)

G-ARCS Auster D6 Series 180   3703   04.07.60
L I Bailey   Watling Lodge, Norton   22.08.19P

G-ARCT Piper PA-18 Super Cub 95   18-7375   06.07.60
EI-AVE, G-ARCT, EI-AVE, G-ARCT, N10F
P Morgan   Navan, RoI   16.12.19E

G-ARCV Cessna 175A Skylark   56757   07.11.60
N8057T   C Campbell & R Francis   (Leeds & Odiham)   03.09.05
(NF 20.03.17)

G-ARCW Piper PA-23 Apache   23-796   07.07.60
N2187P   F W Ellis   Water Leisure Park, Skegness   24.08.07
Modified to PA-23-160 standard (NF 04.01.19)

G-ARCX[M] Gloster Meteor NF.14   AW.2163   8.09.60
WM261   WFU 02.69 – cancelled 25.10.73 as WFU   20.02.69
Built by Armstrong-Whitworth Aircraft
With National Museum of Flight Scotland, East Fortune

G-ARDB Piper PA-24-250 Comanche   24-2166   15.08.60
PH-RON, G-ARDB, N7019P
P Crook   Exeter Int'l   30.04.19E

G-ARDD Scintex CP.301-C1 Emeraude   549   04.07.60
D Hurst & P J Huxley   Headcorn   12.12.18P
Built by Société Scintex; rebuilt by EMK Aeroplanes Ltd
as c/n EMK.004

G-ARDE[M] de Havilland DH.104 Dove 6   04469   15.11.60
I-TONY   Cancelled 30.05.01 by CAA   25.08.91
As 'G-AJPR' in 'Gulf Aviation' c/s
With Al Mahatta Museum, Sharjah, UAE

G-ARDJ Auster D6 Series 180   3704   15.07.60
P N A Whitehead   Leicester
(NF 24.05.18)

G-ARDO Jodel D.112J   146   22.08.60
F-PBTE, F-BBTE, F-WBTE
W R Prescott   (Rostrevor, Newry)   30.05.07P
Built by Etablissement Couesnon; composite with fuselage
of G-AYEO ex F-BIGG [c/n 684] c.1974 (NF 04.08.18)

G-ARDS Piper PA-22-150 Caribbean   22-7154   04.09.60
N3214Z   S A Rennison   Sherburn-in-Elmet   12.04.18E

G-ARDY Tipsy Nipper T.66 Series 2   55   10.08.60
J K Davies   (Eccleston, Chester)   12.12.00P
Built by Avions Fairey SA (IE 28.01.18)

G-ARDZ Jodel D.140A Mousquetaire   49   10.11.60
C M Connally tr G-ARDZ Flying Group
White Waltham   10.04.19P
Built by Société Aéronautique Normande

G-AREA[M] de Havilland DH.104 Dove 8   04520   03.08.60
Cancelled 19.09.00 by CAA   18.09.87
British Aerospace c/s
With de Havilland Aircraft Museum, London Colney

G-AREH de Havilland DH.82A Tiger Moth   85287   04.07.60
(G-APYV), 6746M, DE241   A J Hastings & A Mustard   Fife
Built by Morris Motors Ltd (NF 18.10.16)

G-AREI Auster 3   518   14.12.60
9M-ALB, VR-RBM, VR-SCJ, MT438
R B Webber   Trenchard Farm, Eggesford   *'Akyab'*   12.07.19P
Built by Taylorcraft Aeroplanes (England) Ltd;
as 'MT438' in SEAC c/s

G-AREL Piper PA-22-150 Caribbean   22-7284   14.09.60
N3344Z   R Gibson tr The Caribbean Flying Club
White Waltham   22.03.19E

G-AREO Piper PA-18-150 Super Cub   18-7407   24.08.60
N10F   E P Parkin   Derby   02.04.19E

G-ARET Piper PA-22-160 Tri-Pacer   22-7590   02.09.60
N10F   L A Runnalls   Enstone
NF 09.02.18

G-AREX Aeronca 15AC Sedan   15AC-61   12.09.60
CF-FNM
R J M Turnbull   Rydinghurst Farm, Cranleigh   21.05.19E

G-AREZ Druine D.31 Turbulent   PFA 561   22.09.60
R E Garforth   Southend   15.01.20P
Built by Rollason Aircraft and Engines Ltd – project PFA 561

G-ARFB Piper PA-22-150 Caribbean   22-7518   08.09.60
N3625Z   G Harvey   Derby   19.06.16E
Stored 02.18 (IE 21.11.16)

G-ARFD Piper PA-22-160 Tri-Pacer   22-7565   08.09.60
N3667Z   T J Alderdice   Mullaghglass   23.04.19E

G-ARFI Cessna 150A   15059100   01.02.61
N41836, G-ARFI, N7000X
N M G Pearson   Henstridge   30.04.16E
Noted 09.18 (NF 31.10.17)

G-ARFO Cessna 150A   15059174   23.03.61
N7074X   P M Fawley   Thruxton   28.10.19E

G-ARFT Jodel DR.1050 Ambassadeur   170   27.10.60
R Shaw   (Sowerby Bridge)
Built by Société Aéronautique Normande (NF 20.03.18)

G-ARFV Tipsy Nipper T.66 Series 2   44   05.10.60
J J Austin   Croft Farm, Croft-on-Tees   27.04.17P
Built by Avions Fairey SA

G-ARGB Auster 6A Tugmaster   2593   12.10.60
VF635   Cancelled 21.06.74 as WFU   21.06.74
Carr Farm, Thorney, Newark   *Dismantled 02.15*

G-ARGO Piper PA-22-108 Colt   22-8034   18.01.61
M Magrabi   Bournemouth   29.03.18E

G-ARGV Piper PA-18-150 Super Cub   18-7559   20.12.60
N10F   Wolds Gliding Club Ltd   Pocklington   23.05.19E

G-ARGZ Druine D.31 Turbulent   PFA 562   07.11.60
The Tiger Club 1990 Ltd   Damyns Hall, Upminster   10.05.19P
Built by Rollason Aircraft and Engines Ltd – project PFA 562

G-ARHB	Forney F-1A Aircoupe	5733	17.04.61
	R E Dagless Holly Hill Farm, Guist		29.09.18E
	Built by Air Products Inc		
G-ARHC	Forney F-1A Aircoupe	5734	26.05.61
	E G Girardey Wellcross Farm, Slinfold		13.05.19E
	Built by Air Products Inc		
G-ARHF	Forney F-1A Aircoupe	5737	26.05.61
	Cancelled 10.11.95 by CAA		
	Northrepps *Stored 01.17*		
G-ARHM	Auster 6A	2515	05.01.61
	VF557 R C P Brookhouse Headcorn		14.10.19P
	As 'VF557:H' in RAF 6 Sqdn c/s		
G-ARHR	Piper PA-22-150 Caribbean	22-7576	10.01.61
	N3707Z A R Wyatt Sandown		11.04.19E
G-ARHXᴹ	de Havilland DH.104 Dove 8	04513	11.01.61
	Cancelled 06.12.78 as PWFU		08.09.78
	With North East Land Sea and Air Museum, Usworth		
G-ARHZ	Druine D.62A Condor	RAE/602	13.12.60
	B R Hunter Sandcroft Farm, Messingham		12.11.19P
	Built by Rollason Aircraft and Engines Ltd – project PFA 247		
G-ARID	Cessna 172B Skyhawk	17248209	02.02.61
	N7709X Secint Air Support Ltd (Leamington Spa)		27.11.18E
G-ARIF	Ord-Hume O-H 7 Minor Coupe	O-H/7	22.08.60
	M J Aubrey Llanfyrnach		
	Built by A W J G Ord-Hume ex modified Luton LA-4C Minor;		
	displayed Classic Ultralight Heritage (NF 08.08.18)		
G-ARIH	Auster 6A	2463	23.01.61
	TW591 D Potuznik (Potsdam, Germany)		14.12.18P
	As 'TW591:N' in RAF 664 (AOP) Sqdn c/s		
G-ARIK	Piper PA-22-150 Caribbean	22-7570	26.01.61
	N3701Z A Taylor Manor Farm, Binham		24.06.19E
G-ARIL	Piper PA-22-150 Caribbean	22-7574	26.01.61
	N3705Z S Eustathiou Spanhoe		23.08.14E
	On rebuild 10.17 (IE 09.10.17)		
G-ARIM	Druine D.31 Turbulent	PFA 510	27.02.61
	S R P Harper & J C Holland tr India Mike Group		
	Kiln Farm, Hungerford		20.11.18P
	Built by A Schima – project PFA 510		
G-ARJB	de Havilland DH.104 Dove 8	04518	29.09.60
	M Whale (Swindon) *'JCB' & 'Exporter'*		
	(NF 16.01.15)		
G-ARJS	Piper PA-23-160 Apache G	23-1977	03.03.61
	N10F Bencray Ltd Blackpool		16.11.11E
	(NF 04.10.18)		
G-ARJT	Piper PA-23-160 Apache G	23-1981	03.03.61
	N10F J H Ashcroft Netherthorpe		18.08.07
	(NF 29.10.18)		
G-ARJU	Piper PA-23-160 Apache G	23-1984	03.03.61
	N10F F W & I F Ellis Water Leisure Park, Skegness		08.10.15E
	(IE 21.05.18)		
G-ARKD	Commonwealth CAC-18 Mustang 22	1330	24.02.61
	VH-BVM, RAAF A68-5		
	Classic Flying Machine Collection Ltd Mendlesham		
	(NF 04.04.16)		
G-ARKG	Auster J5G Cirrus Autocar	3061	22.02.61
	AP-AHJ, VP-KKN A G Boon & C L Towell		
	Ranksborough Farm, Langham		24.08.19P
	As 'RAN A11-301':'NAVY 931' in RAN silver c/s;		
	carries 'Skippy' & 'NW' on tail		
G-ARKJ	Beech N35 Bonanza	D-6736	05.05.61
	G D E Macdonald Lasham		06.07.19E
G-ARKK	Piper PA-22-108 Colt	22-8290	12.04.61
	R D Welfare Stoneacre Farm, Farthing Corner		07.05.19E
G-ARKM	Piper PA-22-108 Colt	22-8313	12.04.61
	S Hutton & G J Prisk Perranporth		02.07.19E
G-ARKP	Piper PA-22-108 Colt	22-8364	19.05.61
	I J Mitchell & D S White Headcorn		04.08.19E
G-ARKS	Piper PA-22-108 Colt	22-8422	07.06.61
	A J Silvester Wolverhampton Halfpenny Green		05.03.19E

G-ARKUᴹ	de Havilland DH.114 Heron 2	14072	17.03.61
	VR-NAQ Cancelled 28.03.61 – to RN as XR445 –		
	restored 20.04.90 as G-ODLG (2), to (VH-NJP),		
	restored 31.08.93, cancelled 08.09.93 – to VH-NJP		
	As 'G-ANFE' in 'Gulf Aviation c/s		
	With Al Mahatta Museum, Sharjah, UAE		
G-ARLG	Auster D4/108	3606	04.04.61
	R D Helliar-Symons tr Auster D4 Group		
	Bourne Park, Hurstbourne Tarrant		13.07.18P
	(IE 17.09.18)		
G-ARLK	Piper PA-24-250 Comanche	24-2433	25.05.61
	EI-ALW, G-ARLK, N10F R P Jackson Headcorn		27.11.19E
G-ARLPᴾᴹ	Beagle A.61 Terrier 1	3724	11.04.61
	VX123 Cancelled 09.07.18 as PWFU 31.10.91		
	Officially quoted with c/n 2573 (VF631) which became		
	G-ARLM (2) then G-ASDK; frame on display) at Norfolk		
	& Suffolk Museum. Flixton		
G-ARLR	Beagle A.61 Terrier 2	B.601	11.04.61
	VW996 M Palfreman Bagby		09.09.01
	Stored 02.18 (NF 08.12.14)		
G-ARLZ	Druine D.31A Turbulent	RAE/578	07.04.61
	A D Wilson Little Gransden		11.09.19P
	Built by Rollason Aircraft and Engines Ltd		
G-ARMC	de Havilland DHC-1 Chipmunk 22A	C1/0151	26.04.61
	WB703 J T H Henderson tr John Henderson		
	Childrens Trust White Waltham		21.07.19P
	As 'WB703' in RAF c/s		
G-ARMD	de Havilland DHC-1 Chipmunk 22A	C1/0237	26.04.61
	WD297 Cancelled 26.06.15 by CAA		05.06.76
	Prestwick *Stored for rebuild 06.18*		
G-ARMF	de Havilland DHC-1 Chipmunk 22A	C1/0394	26.04.61
	WG322 M Harvey (Nazeing, Waltham Abbey)		12.10.98
	As 'WG322:H' in RAF c/s (NF 19.04.17)		
G-ARMG	de Havilland DHC-1 Chipmunk 22A	C1/0575	26.04.61
	WK558 L J Irvine Turweston		17.08.18P
	As 'WK558:DH' in RAF c/s		
G-ARMN	Cessna 175B Skylark	17556994	18.08.61
	N8294T Brimpton Aviation Group Ltd Brimpton		04.01.19E
G-ARMO	Cessna 172B Skyhawk	172-48560	12.06.61
	N8060X R D Leigh Tatenhill		25.04.19E
G-ARMR	Cessna 172B Skyhawk	172-48566	12.06.61
	N8066X T W Gilbert Enstone		27.06.15E
	Nose u/c collapsed landing Sandown 07.06.15;		
	noted 07.16 (NF 16.09.15)		
G-ARMZ	Druine D.31 Turbulent	PFA 565	02.05.61
	The Tiger Club 1990 Ltd Damyns Hall, Upminster		19.04.19P
	Built by Rollason Aircraft and Engines Ltd – project PFA 565		
G-ARNB	Auster J5G Cirrus Autocar	3169	18.05.61
	AP-AHL, VP-KNL		
	R F Tolhurst (Payden Street Farm, Lenham)		
	(NF 20.02.18)		
G-ARNE	Piper PA-22-108 Colt	22-8502	15.06.61
	R Carter tr The Shiny Colt Group Old Buckenham		07.05.19E
G-ARNG	Piper PA-22-108 Colt	22-8547	26.06.61
	D Lamb Hunsdon *'Awful Red'*		20.01.19E
G-ARNI	Piper PA-22-108 Colt	22-8575	26.07.61
	Cancelled 24.01.03 by CAA		15.06.98
	Headcorn *Frame stored 08.18*		
G-ARNJ	Piper PA-22-108 Colt	22-8587	03.08.61
	R A Keech Sleap *'Winnie May'*		26.01.19E
G-ARNK	Piper PA-22-108 Colt	22-8622	05.09.61
	S J Smith Leicester		09.11.17E
	Tailwheel conversion		
G-ARNL	Piper PA-22-108 Colt	22-8625	03.08.61
	M R Harrison (Stratford-upon-Avon)		20.07.18E
	(IE 06.08.18)		
G-ARNN	Globe GC-1B Swift	1272	11.05.61
	VP-YMJ, VP-RDA, ZS-BMX, NC3279K		
	Cancelled 26.01.11 by CAA		11.07.74
	Spanhoe Lodge *Fuselage stored 02.18*		
G-ARNO	Beagle A.61 Terrier 1	3722	08.05.61
	VX113 M C R Wills Southend		04.10.16P
	Official p/i shown as VX115l as 'VX113:36' in AAC		
	camouflage c/s; noted 02.19		

G-ARNP   Beagle A.109 Airedale   B.503   10.05.61
M & S W Isbister   North Weald   30.04.19P
Originally registered with c/n A.109-P1

G-ARNY   Jodel D.117   595   13.06.61
F-BHXQ   P Jenkins tr G-ARNY Flying Group
Knockbain Farm, Dingwall   26.04.19P
Built by Société Aéronautique Normande

G-ARNZ   Druine D.31 Turbulent   PFA 579   28.06.61
The Tiger Club 1990 Ltd   Damyns Hall, Upminster   31.07.19P
Built by Rollason Aircraft and Engines Ltd – project PFA 579

G-AROA   Cessna 172B Skyhawk   48628   19.09.61
N8128X   C Blois tr Phoenix Flying Group   Beccles   26.01.19E

G-AROJ   Beagle A.109 Airedale   B.508   17.05.61
HB-EUC, G-AROJ   Cancelled 21.01.80 as WFU   08.01.76
Carr Farm, Thorney, Newark   *Dismantled 02.15*

G-ARON   Piper PA-22-108 Colt   22-8822   23.11.61
Secint Aerospace Ltd   Coventry   23.09.17E
(IE 02.04.18)

G-AROW   Jodel D.140B Mousquetaire II   71   13.09.61
J P M & P White   (Belfast & Fethard, Co Tipperary, RoI)   19.05.19P
Built by Société Aéronautique Normande

G-AROY   Boeing Stearman A75N1 Kaydet *(PT-17)* 75-4775   06.06.61
N56418, 42-16612
J S Mann   Great Ashfield, Bury St Edmunds   19.12.18E

G-ARPO (2)ᴹ   de Havilland DH.121 Trident 1C   2116   23.03.64
(G-ARPP)   Cancelled 06.01.05 as PWFU   12.01.86
With North East Land Sea and Air Museum, Usworth

G-ARRD   Jodel DR.1051 Ambassadeur   274   20.07.61
R J Arnold   (RAF Wyton)   05.12.17P
Built by Société Aéronautique Normande (IE 01.02.18)

G-ARRE   Jodel DR.1050 Ambassadeur   275   20.07.61
R Weininger   (West Haddon, Northampton)   16.08.18P
Built by Société Aéronautique Normande

G-ARRI   Cessna 175B Skylark   17557001   05.10.61
N8301T   R J Bentley   (Nenagh, Co Tipperary, RoI)   19.09.14E
(NF 19.09.16)

G-ARRL   Auster J1N Alpha   2115   13.06.61
VP-KFK, VP-KPF, VP-KFK, VP-UAK
A C Ladd   Romney Street Farm, Sevenoaks   25.09.18P

G-ARRMᴹ   Beagle B.206X   B.001   23.06.61
Cancelled 09.04.74 as PWFU   23.12.64
Originally registered as Beagle B.206 Series 1
(c/n B2/1010) & re-designated 09.61
On loan to Farnborough Air Sciences Trust
from Brooklands Museum

G-ARRO   Beagle A.109 Airedale   B.507   16.06.61
EI-AYL, G-ARRO, (EI-AVP), G-ARRO
M & S W Isbister   Spanhoe
Originally registered as c/n A 109-P5; stored
dismantled 08.15 less marks (NF 15.09.14)

G-ARRS   Piel CP.301A Emeraude   226   29.06.61
F-BIMA   J F Sully   Sturgate   29.08.18P
Built by Société Menavia (IE 05.08.18)

G-ARRT   Wallis WA-116/Mc   2   28.06.61
Cancelled 03.08.16 as PWFU   26.05.83
Old Warden   *Stored 10.16, displayed Sywell 09.18*

G-ARRU   Druine D.31 Turbulent   PFA 502   28.06.61
D G Huck   (Harborough Magna, Rugby)   27.02.97P
Built by J O'Connor – project PFA 502 (NF 14.05.18)

G-ARRX   Auster 6A   2281   04.07.61
VF512   J E D Mackie   Popham   *'Peggy Too'*   15.05.19P
As 'VF512:PF-M' in RAF 43 OTU silver with
yellow bands c/s

G-ARRY   Jodel D.140B Mousquetaire II   72   13.09.61
C Thomas   Bodmin   20.10.14P
Built by Société Aéronautique Normande (IE 14.08.18)

G-ARRZ   Druine D.31 Turbulent   PFA 580   21.08.61
T A Stambach   RAF Henlow
Built by Rollason Aircraft and Engines Ltd – project PFA 580;
crashed 21.07.90 & wreck stored (NF 10.11.15)

G-ARSG   Avro Triplane Type IV replica   TRI.1   29.10.81
(BAPC.1)   Richard Shuttleworth Trustees
Old Warden   *'12'*   26.09.18P
Built by Hampshire Aero Club

G-ARSLᴹ   Beagle A.61 Terrier 2   2539   13.07.61
VF581   Cancelled 04.08.14 as PWFU   20.05.14
As 'VF581:G' in AAC c/s
With National Museum of Flight Scotland, East Fortune

G-ARSX   Piper PA-22-160 Tri-Pacer   22-6712   08.08.61
N2907Z   Cancelled 12.02.02 as PWFU
Newtownards   *Spares use 02.14*

G-ARTH   Piper PA-12 Super Cruiser   12-3278   22.09.61
EI-ADO   G R Trotter   Popham   30.04.19P

G-ARTJ   Bensen B.8M   07   22.09.61
Cancelled 06.06.75 as WFU
Rufforth East   *Displayed at The Gyrocopter*
Experience, 06.13 & NEC Birmingham 12.13

G-ARTL   de Havilland DH.82A Tiger Moth   '83795'   22.09.61
'T7281'   F G Clacherty   Great Fryup Dale, Egton   30.05.19P
P/i not confirmed – if correct the c/n is 83795;
as 'T7281' in RAF c/s

G-ARTM   Beagle A.61 Terrier 1   3723   09.10.61
WE536   Cancelled 12.09.73 as WFU   13.11.71
Carr Farm, Thorney, Newar   *Dismantled 07.16*

G-ARTZ (1)ᴹ   McCandless M.2   M2-1   xx.10.61
Replaced by G-ARTZ (2) – see below   *(Stored)*
With Ulster Folk & Transport Museum, Holywood

G-ARTZ (2)   McCandless M.4 Gyroplane   M4-1   24.10.61
W R Partridge   Tregolds Farm, St Merryn
Noted 04.16 (NF 23.01.10)

G-ARUE (2)ᴹ   de Havilland DH.104 Dove 7   04530   07.10.80
Irish Air Corps 194, (G-ARUE)
Cancelled 17.07.86 by CAA – to D-IKER
No marks carried
With Auto und Technik Museum, Sinsheim, Germany

G-ARUG   Auster J5G Cirrus Autocar   3272   02.01.62
D P H Hulme   Biggin Hill   19.02.20P
Built by Beagle-Auster Aircraft Ltd

G-ARUI   Beagle A.61 Terrier 1   2529   09.03.62
VF571   T W J Dann   Stow Maries   09.05.19P

G-ARUL   LeVier Cosmic Wind   103   28.11.61
N22C   P G Kynsey   Duxford   04.07.19P
Built by Tony LeVier Associates Inc: rebuilt 1973
as project PFA 1511

G-ARUO   Piper PA-24 Comanche   24-2427   16.01.62
N7251P   Cancelled 18.07.00 by CAA   22.08.00
Farley Farm, Farley Chamberlayne   *Stored derelict 12.17*

G-ARUV   Piel CP.301-1 Emeraude   xxxx   02.02.62
Cancelled 18.04.16 as TWFU   11.05.13
Bodmin   *Built M N Harrison – project PFA 700*
On rebuild 10.17

G-ARUY   Auster J1N Alpha   3394   02.02.62
D K Tregilgas   Great Oakley   15.10.19P

G-ARVFᴹ   Vickers VC-10-1101   808   16.01.63
Cancelled 11.04.83 as WFU   *As 'G-ARVF' in UAE titles*   23.07.83
With Flugausstellung Hermeskeil, Trier, Germany

G-ARVN (2)ᴹ   Servotec CR LTH1 Grasshopper 1   116.02.63
Cancelled 14.03.77 as WFU   18.05.63
On loan from E.D.ap Rees
With The Helicopter Museum, Weston-super-Mare

G-ARVO   Piper PA-18 Super Cub 95   18-7252   18.01.83
D-ENFI, N3376Z
M P & S T Barnard   Hinton-in-the-Hedges   26.06.19E

G-ARVT   Piper PA-28-160 Cherokee   28-379   23.01.62
S Hynd   Glasgow   12.07.19E
Operated by Glasgow Flying Club

G-ARVU   Piper PA-28-160 Cherokee   28-410   30.03.62
PH-ONY, G-ARVU
T W Mitchell tr VU Flying Group   Elmsett   05.12.18E

G-ARVV   Piper PA-28-160 Cherokee   28-451   11.07.62
G E Hopkins   Shobdon   17.03.09E
Stored 09.14 (NF 07.08.15)

G-ARVZ   Druine D.62B Condor   RAE/606   06.12.61
A A M Huke   Manor Farm, Dinton   30.07.19P
Built by Rollason Aircraft and Engines Ltd

G-ARWB   de Havilland DHC-1 Chipmunk 22A   C1/0621   02.01.62
WK611   P S Oglesby tr Thruxton Chipmunk
Flying Group   Thruxton   28.06.19P
As 'WK611' in RAF silver with yellow bands c/s

G-ARWR	Cessna 172C Skyhawk	172-49172	13.04.62
	N1472Y M McCann tr Devanha Flying Group Insch		09.05.19E
G-ARWS	Cessna 175C Skylark	17557102	12.04.62
	N8502X M D Fage Tatenhill		25.05.19E
G-ARXB	Beagle A.109 Airedale	B.509	05.02.62
	EI-BBK, G-ARXB, EI-ATE, G-ARXB		
	M & S W Isbister Spanhoe		
	Originally registered with c/n A 109-2;		
	stored dismantled 08.15 less marks (NF 15.09.14)		
G-ARXC	Beagle A.109 Airedale	B.510	09.04.62
	EI-ATD, G-ARXC Cancelled 12.04.89 as PWFU		27.06.76
	Carr Farm, Thorney, Newark *Dismantled 02.15*		
G-ARXD	Beagle A.109 Airedale	B.511	09.04.62
	D Howden (Tullochvenus Farm, Lumphanan, Banchory)		
	Originally registered with c/n A 109-4 (NF 10.04.18)		
G-ARXG	Piper PA-24-250 Comanche	24-3154	21.02.62
	N10F R F Corstin Dunsfold		08.09.19E
G-ARXH[M]	Bell 47G	40	13.02.62
	N120B, NC120B		
	T B Searle (Southfields Farm, Husbands Bosworth)		
	Displayed Armourgeddon Military Vehicle Museum 08.17		
	(NF 14.03.18)		
G-ARXN	Tipsy Nipper T.66 Series 2	77	03.07.62
	J F Bakewell Jericho Farm, Lambley		19.08.80E
	(IE 25.09.18)		
G-ARXP	Phoenix Luton LA-4A Minor	PAL 1119	23.02.62
	R M Weeks Benson's Farm, Laindon		17.10.95P
	Built by W C Hymas – project PFA 816; fuselage only		
	01.14: wings at owner's home (NF 05.02.16)		
G-ARXT	Jodel DR.1050 Ambassadeur	355	14.03.62
	B F Enock tr CJM Flying Group		
	Wellesbourne Mountford		08.05.19P
	Built by Société Aéronautique Normande		
G-ARXU	Auster 6A	2295	05.03.62
	VF526 S D & S P Allen Strubby		29.11.19P
	Built by Taylorcraft Aeroplanes (England) Ltd;		
	as 'VF526:T' in AAC c/s		
G-ARYB[M]	de Havilland DH.125 Series 1	25002	01.03.62
	Cancelled 04.03.69		22.01.68
	Mounted wingless on plinths		
	With Midland Air Museum, Coventry		
G-ARYC[M]	de Havilland DH.125 Series 1	25003	01.03.62
	Cancelled 31.03.76 as WFU		01.08.73
	'Rolls-Royce – Bristol Engine Division' titles		
	(starboard) & 'Bristol Siddeley' titles (port)		
	With de Havilland Aircraft Museum, London Colney		
G-ARYD[M]	Auster AOP.6	xxxx	08.03.62
	WJ358 Cancelled 05.08.87 as WFU *As 'WJ358'*		
	Conversion abandoned 09.63		
	With Museum of Army Flying, AAC Middle Wallop		
G-ARYH	Piper PA-22-160 Tri-Pacer	22-7039	09.03.62
	N3102Z Cancelled 10.03.17 by CAA		08.11.16
	(Fenland) For sale as rebuild project 10.16		
G-ARYI	Cessna 172C Skyhawk	49260	13.07.62
	N1560Y Cancelled 19.11.10 by CAA		10.08.03
	Enstone *Open store 11.18*		
G-ARYK	Cessna 172C Skyhawk	172-49288	13.07.62
	N1588Y Full Sutton Flying Centre Ltd Full Sutton		10.12.18E
G-ARYR	Piper PA-28-180 Cherokee B	28-770	12.07.62
	J Sutherley tr G-ARYR Flight Group Denham		14.02.19E
G-ARYS	Cessna 172C Skyhawk	172-49291	13.07.62
	N1591Y N E Binner tr GARYS Group Full Sutton		10.05.19E
G-ARYV	Piper PA-24-250 Comanche	24-2516	17.04.62
	N7337P D C Hanss Cranfield		02.08.19E
G-ARYZ[M]	Beagle A.109 Airedale	B.512	09.04.62
	Cancelled 16.09.15 as PWFU		26.02.01
	With South Yorkshire Aircraft Museum, Doncaster		
G-ARZB[M]	Wallis WA-116 Series 1 Agile	B.203	18.04.62
	XR943, G-ARZB Cancelled 03.08.16 as PWFU		29.06.93
	'Little Nellie'		
	Built by Beagle-Miles Aircraft Ltd as Beagle-Wallis WA.116 Srs 1		
	With Shuttleworth Collection, Old Warden		
G-ARZS	Beagle A.109 Airedale	B.515	11.05.62
	EI-BAL, G-ARZS M & S W Isbister Spanhoe		
	Stored dismantled 08.15 less marks (NF 15.09.14)		
G-ARZW	Phoenix Currie Wot	1	25.05.62
	B R Pearson Eaglescott		
	Built by J H B Urmston; on rebuild as Pfalz D VII		
	scale replica 2018? (NF 30.10.18)		

G-ASAA – G-ASZZ

G-ASAA	Phoenix Luton LA-4A Minor	O-H/4	19.04.62
	M J Aubrey Llanfyrnach		07.06.01P
	Built by A W G Ord-Hume; displayed Classic Ultralight		
	Heritage (NF 04.11.15)		
G-ASAI	Beagle A.109 Airedale	B.516	26.06.62
	K R Howden (Lumphanan, Banchory)		
	(NF 30.11.18)		
G-ASAJ	Beagle A.61 Terrier 2	B.605	26.06.62
	WE569 T Bailey Croft Farm, Defford		07.11.19P
	Initially allocated c/n 3732; as 'WE569' [Auster T7]		
	in AAC silver with yellow training bands c/s		
G-ASAL (2)	Scottish Aviation Bulldog Srs 120/124	BH120/239	05.09.73
	(G-BBHF), G-31-17		
	Pioneer Flying Company Ltd Glasgow Prestwick		04.05.19P
G-ASAT[M]	Morane Saulnier MS.880B Rallye Club	178	21.06.62
	Cancelled 18.01.11 as PWFU		02.08.08
	With City of Norwich Aviation Museum		
G-ASAU	SOCATA MS.880B Rallye Club	179	21.06.62
	D M Evans tr Juliet Tango Group Welshpool		14.05.19E
G-ASAX	Beagle A.61 Terrier 2	B.609	12.06.62
	TW533 A D Hodgkinson (Doddington, March)		01.09.96
	Converted from Auster AOP.6 c/n 1911 (NF 11.01.19)		
G-ASAZ	Hiller UH-12E-4	2070	18.06.62
	N5372V		
	R C Hields t/a Hields Aviation Sherburn-in-Elmet		05.09.16E
	Stored 09.18		
G-ASBA	Phoenix Currie Wot	AE-1	16.08.62
	K Higbee (Dymchurch, Romney Marsh)		17.05.19P
	Built by A Etherbridge – project PFA 3005		
G-ASBH	Beagle A.109 Airedale	B.519	26.06.62
	D T Smollett Bratton Clovelly, Okehampton		19.02.99
	(NF 19.06.18)		
G-ASBY	Beagle A.109 Airedale	B.523	23.07.62
	Cancelled 20.04.10 by CAA		22.03.80
	Ashford, Kent		
	Advertised for sale 12.13 from "London" area		
G-ASCC	Beagle E3	B701	23.07.62
	(G-25-13), XP254		
	R Warner Westside Farm, Whittlesford		12.11.19P
	Conversion of Auster AOP.11 (c/n B5/10/162);		
	as 'XP254' in AAC c/s		
G-ASCD[M]	Beagle A.61 Terrier 2	B.615	23.07.62
	PH-SFT, (PH-SCD), G-ASCD, VW993		
	Cancelled 05.10.89 as WFU *As 'VW993'*		26.09.71
	With Yorkshire Air Museum, Elvington		
G-ASCF[M]	Beagle A.61 Terrier 2	B.617	23.07.62
	WE548 Cancelled 10.04.67 – to SE-ELO *As 'RT514'*		
	With Forsvarsmuseet Flysamlingen, Gardemoen, Norway		
G-ASCH	Beagle A.61 Terrier 2	B.619	01.08.62
	VF565 D S Wilkinson Oaksey Park		05.08.19P
G-ASCM	Isaacs Fury II	1	01.08.62
	R F Redknap Enstone		12.04.18P
	Built by J O Isaacs – project PFA 2002/1B (Membership no);		
	as 'K2050' in pre-war RAF c/s		
G-ASCT[M]	Bensen B.7Mc	DC.3	14.08.62
	Cancelled 20.09.73 as PWFU		11.11.66
	Built by D.Campbell		
	With The Helicopter Museum, Weston-super-Mare		
G-ASCZ	Piel CP.301A Emeraude	233	01.10.62
	F-BIMG P Johnson Goodwood		08.05.19P
	Built by Société Menavia		
G-ASDK	Beagle A.61 Terrier 2	B.702	26.10.62
	G-ARLM, G-ARLP (1), VF631		
	J L Swallow Hibaldstow		04.11.10P
	Converted from Auster AOP.6 c/n 2573; on rebuild 08.13		
	(NF 14.11.17)		

G-ASDL[M]	Beagle A.61 Terrier 2	B.703	26.10.62
	G-ARLN (2), WE558 Cancelled 17.08.04 as destroyed		30.05.00
	Also c/ns 3727 (1) & B.632 (1)		
	With East Midlands Aeropark, East Midlands		
G-ASDY	Wallis WA-116/F	B.204	09.11.62
	XR944, G-ARZC Cancelled 03.08.16 as PWFU		28.10.97
	Old Warden Stored 10.16		
G-ASEA	Phoenix Luton LA-4A Minor	PAL 1154	14.11.62
	B W Faulkner Twentyways Farm, Ramsdean		
	Built by M Fawkes & G P Smith (IE 12.10.15)		
G-ASEB	Phoenix Luton LA-4A Minor	PAL 1149	26.11.62
	S R P Harper Kiln Farm, Hungerford		25.04.19P
	Built by J A Anning		
G-ASEJ	Piper PA-28-180 Cherokee B	28-1049	10.01.63
	EI-BBC, G-ASEJ		
	N G Pittman tr Perranporth Pilots Group Perranporth		
	(IE 22.01.19)		
G-ASEO	Piper PA-24-250 Comanche	24-3367	23.01.63
	(G-ASDX), N10F M Scott Solent		06.03.16E
	(NF 30.05.18)		
G-ASEP	Piper PA-23-235 Apache	27-541	28.01.63
	J R & R J Sharpe Napps Field, Billericay		
	'Shock Models – www.Shockmodels.co.uk'		28.06.19E
	Official type data 'PA-23-235 Aztec' is incorrect;		
	badged 'Apache 235'		
G-ASEU	Druine D.62A Condor	RAE/607	12.02.63
	R A S Sutherland (Edderton, Tain)		20.07.15P
	Built by Rollason Aircraft and Engines Ltd; stalled on		
	downwind leg Insch 18.04.15 & extensively damaged		
	(NF 24.08.15)		
G-ASFA	Cessna 172D Skyhawk	17250182	21.02.63
	N2582U D Austin Elstree		20.07.16E
	Noted 07.18 (IE 15.08.16)		
G-ASFD	SPP Morava L-200A	170808	26.02.63
	OK-PHH M Emery (Redhill RH1)		
	(NF 10.12.18)		
G-ASFL	Piper PA-28-180 Cherokee B	28-1170	07.03.63
	M J Phillips tr G-ASFL Group Old Sarum		14.03.19E
G-ASFR	Bölkow BÖ.208C Junior	522	12.03.63
	D-EGMO S T Dauncey Turners Arms Farm, Yearby		
	(NF 28.02.18)		
G-ASFX	Druine D.31 Turbulent	PFA 513	18.03.63
	E F Clapham & T A Wilcox (Oldbury-on-Severn & Yate)		28.08.19P
	Built by E F Clapham – project PFA 513		
G-ASGC[M]	Vickers Super VC-10 Series 1151	853	11.04.63
	Cancelled 22.04.80 s WFU		20.04.80
	BOAC-Cunard c/s		
	With Duxford Aviation Society		
G-ASHS	SNCAN Stampe SV.4C(G)	265	23.04.63
	F-BCFN J W Beaty Sibson		09.05.19P
	Original fuselage used in rebuild of G-AWEF ca 1980:		
	rebuilt 1984 with fuselage of G-AZIR c/n 452 ex F-BCXR		
G-ASHT	Druine D.31 Turbulent	PFA 1610	23.04.63
	C W N Huke Manor Farm, Dinton		28.09.17P
	Built by Rollason Aircraft and Engines Ltd –		
	project PFA 1610		
G-ASHU	Piper PA-15 Vagabond	15-46	01.05.63
	N4164H, NC4164H T J Ventham tr The Calybe Flying		
	Group Farley Farm, Farley Chamberlayne *'Calybe'*		12.09.19P
G-ASHV	Piper PA-23-250 Aztec B	27-2347	01.05.63
	N10F Cancelled 20.06.88 as PWFU		22.07.85
	Alderney On Airport Fire Service fire dump 2016		
G-ASHX	Piper PA-28-180 Cherokee B	28-1266	03.05.63
	N7382W Powertheme Ltd Manchester Barton		23.03.19E
G-ASII	Piper PA-28-180 Cherokee B	28-1264	21.05.63
	T N & T R Hart & R W S Matthews Dunkeswell		25.05.19E
G-ASIJ	Piper PA-28-180 Cherokee B	28-1333	21.05.63
	N7445W A Wilson North Weald		14.04.19E
G-ASIL	Piper PA-28-180 Cherokee B	28-1350	21.05.63
	N7461W M J Pink Henstridge		15.05.19E
G-ASIP	Auster 6A Tugmaster	2549	22.05.63
	VF608 Cancelled 31.03.82 by CAA		19.07.73
	Hoogeveen, Netherlands *On rebuild 01.18*		

G-ASIS	Jodel D.112	1166	24.02.81
	EI-CKX, G-ASIS, F-BKNR		
	W R Prescott Derryogue, Kilkeel		30.09.19P
	Built by Société Wassmer Aviation		
G-ASIT	Cessna 180	32567	24.05.63
	N7670A W J D Tollett Turweston		26.06.19E
G-ASIX[M]	Vickers VC-10 Series 1103	820	29.05.63
	Cancelled 06.10.72 – to A4O-AB *As 'A4O-AB'*		
	With Brooklands Museum, Weybridge		
G-ASIY	Piper PA-25-235 Pawnee	25-2446	30.05.63
	Kent Gliding Club Ltd Challock		16.02.18E
G-ASJL	Beech H35 Bonanza	D-5132	14.06.63
	N5582D R L Dargue Fairoaks		04.05.19E
G-ASJV	Supermarine 361 Spitfire LF.IXb	CBAF 5562	03.07.63
	OO-ARA, Belgian AF SM-41, Fokker B-13,		
	R Netherlands AF H-68, AF H-105, MH434		
	Merlin Aviation Ltd Duxford		03.05.19P
	Operated by The Old Flying Machine Company;		
	as 'MH434:ZD-B' in RAF c/s		
G-ASJZ	Jodel D.117A	826	05.07.63
	F-BITD B Russel Roughay Farm, Lower Upham		21.02.19P
	Built by Société Aéronautique Normande		
G-ASKB[M]	de Havilland DH.98 Mosquito TT.35		
	With EAA AirVenture Museum, Oshkosh, Wisconsin		
	on loan from Fantasy of Flight, Polk City, Florida		
G-ASKC[M]	de Havilland DH.98 Mosquito TT.35	xxxx	08.07.63
	TA719 Cancelled 03.09.64 as PWFU *As 'TA719:6 T'*		18.01.64
	With Imperial War Museum, Duxford		
G-ASKK[M]	Handley Page HPR.7 Dart Herald 211	161	17.07.63
	PP-ASU, G-ASKK, PI-C910, CF-MCK		
	Cancelled 29.04.85 as WFU		19.05.85
	With City of Norwich Aviation Museum		
G-ASKL	Jodel D.150 Mascaret	27	18.07.63
	J M Graty Nuthampstead		06.11.18P
	Built by Société Aéronautique Normande		
G-ASKP	de Havilland DH.82A Tiger Moth	3889	22.07.63
	N6588 The Tiger Club 1990 Ltd		
	Damyns Hall, Upminster		27.09.19E
G-ASKT	Piper PA-28-180 Cherokee B	28-1410	24.07.63
	N7497W T A Herbert Biggin Hill		11.07.19E
G-ASLR	Agusta Bell 47J-2 Ranger	2057	03.09.63
	Cancelled 28.02.97 as PWFU		07.03.96
	Las Chafiras, Tenerife, Spain		
	On display at car wash 06.18		
G-ASLV	Piper PA-28-235 Cherokee	28-10048	11.09.63
	S W Goodswen Mahon, Spain		07.08.19E
	Official type data 'PA-28-235 Cherokee Pathfinder'		
	is incorrect		
G-ASMA	Piper PA-39 Twin Comanche C/R	30-143	17.09.63
	N10F K Cooper Farley Farm, Farley Chamberlayne		21.08.17E
	Official type data 'PA-30 Twin Comanche' is incorrect		
	(IE 01.06.18)		
G-ASME	Bensen B.8M	12	24.09.63
	Cancelled 13.01.14 by CAA		19.08.12
	North Coates *Stored 01.19*		
G-ASMF	Beech D95A Travel Air	TD-565	26.09.63
	Cancelled 24.02.15 by CAA		11.08.06
	(Owner's home) *Departed White Waltham by road 12.17*		
G-ASMJ	Cessna F172E	F172-0029	25.10.63
	Aeroscene Ltd Sherburn-in-Elmet		19.06.19E
	Built by Reims Aviation SA; Wichita c/n 17250584		
G-ASML	Phoenix Luton LA-4A Minor	PAL 1148	28.10.63
	O D Lewis North Coates		04.06.19P
	Built by R M Kirby – project PFA 802		
G-ASMM	Druine D.31 Turbulent	PFA 1611	31.10.63
	K J Butler Goodwood *'Mouche Miel'*		24.06.16P
	Built by Rollason Aircraft and Engines Ltd –		
	project PFA 1611		
G-ASMS	Cessna 150A	15059204	18.11.63
	N7104X M & W Long Wickenby		05.04.19E
G-ASMT	Fairtravel Linnet 2	004	20.11.63
	P Harrison Swanborough Farm, Lewes		17.07.08P
	(IE 04.11.14)		

G-ASMV	Scintex CP.1310-C3 Super Emeraude	919	22.11.63
	D G Hammersley Tatenhill		07.11.94
	(IE 10.08.18)		

G-ASMW	Cessna 150D	15060247	26.11.63
	N4247U D C & M Bonsall t/a Dukeries Aviation		
	Breighton		06.09.19E

G-ASMY	Piper PA-23-160 Apache H	23-2032	03.12.63
	N4309Y R D Forster Beccles		25.11.95
	Stored 01.18 (NF 07.03.16)		

G-ASMZ	Beagle A.61 Terrier 2	B.629	04.12.63
	G-35-11, VF516 J & R Pike & S Woodgate Eshott		12.12.19P
	Conversion of Auster AOP.10 c/n 2285;		
	as 'VF516' in RAF c/s		

G-ASNC	Beagle D5/180 Husky	3678	09.12.63
	Peterborough & Spalding Gliding Club Ltd Crowland		02.07.19P

G-ASNI	Scintex CP.1310-C3 Super Emeraude	925	20.12.63
	Douglas Electronics Industries Ltd Wickenby		28.03.16P

G-ASNK	Cessna 205	205-0400	27.12.63
	N8400Z Justgold Ltd Blackpool		29.06.06
	(NF 04.10.18)		

G-ASNW	Cessna F172E	F172-0031	13.01.64
	D R Hayward tr G-ASNW Group Draycott		14.12.18E
	Built by Reims Aviation SA; Wichita c/n 17250613		

G-ASNY[M]	Campbell-Bensen B.8M	RCA/203	15.01.64
	Cancelled 17.12.91 by CAA		16.03.70
	With Newark Air Museum, Winthorpe		

G-ASOH	Beech 95-B55A Baron	TC-656	31.01.64
	G Davis & C Middlemiss Biggin Hill		20.10.14E
	(IE 18.03.16)		

G-ASOI	Beagle A.61 Terrier 2	B.627	31.01.64
	G-35-11, WJ404 G D B Delmege Bidford		30.09.16P
	As 'WJ404' in Army Air Corps c/s		

G-ASOK	Cessna F172E	F172-0057	31.01.64
	D W Disney Derby		17.01.19E
	Built by Reims Aviation SA		

G-ASOM	Beagle A.61 Terrier 2	B.622	03.02.64
	G-JETS, G-ASOM, G-35-11, VF505		
	D Humphries & W Parsons tr GASOM.org		
	Old Hay Farm, Paddock Wood		11.07.19P

G-ASPF	Jodel D.120 Paris-Nice	02	26.02.64
	F-BFNP G W Street Pittrichie Farm, Whiterashes		07.06.19P
	Built by Société des Etablissements Benjamin Wassmer		

G-ASPP	Bristol Boxkite replica	BOX.1	29.10.81
	(BAPC.2) Richard Shuttleworth Trustees		
	Old Warden		30.08.19P
	Built by F G Miles Group for 'Those Magnificent Men in		
	Their Flying Machines' film; no external markings		

G-ASPS	Piper J-3C-90 Cub	22809	02.03.64
	N3571N, NC3571N S Slater Bicester		16.07.18P
	Fuselage No.21971		

G-ASPV (2)	de Havilland DH.82A Tiger Moth	84167	05.03.64
	T7794 Oldstead Aero LLP (Easingwold, York)		27.02.19P
	Built by Morris Motors Ltd; original G-ASPV – sold		
	Norway 07.75 & rebuilt with c/n 85738 ex G-ANSE		
	& became LN-MAX then LN-BDO; as 'T7794' in RAF		
	c/s; logbooks & unidentified components used in rebuild		
	c.1975 as G-ASPV (2): possible provenance to either		
	G-ANDW or G-ANOM		

G-ASRC	Druine D.62C Condor	RAE/609	11.03.64
	A C Bell (Mapperley, Nottingham)		14.03.19P
	Built by Rollason Aircraft and Engines Ltd		

G-ASRF[M]	Gowland GWG.2 Jenny Wren	GWG.2	18.03.64
	Cancelled 11.12.96 by CAA		04.06.71
	Built by G W Gowland – project PFA 1300 using		
	modified Luton Minor wings ex G-AGEP		
	With Norfolk & Suffolk Aviation Museum, Flixton		

G-ASRK	Beagle A.109 Airedale	B.538	26.03.64
	M Wilson Headcorn 'Biopathica'		07.07.17P
	(IE 02.01.18)		

G-ASRO	Piper PA-30 Twin Comanche	30-395	31.03.64
	N10F D W Blake tr Five Star Flying Group Tatenhill		04.04.19E

G-ASRT	Jodel D.150 Mascaret	45	06.04.64
	P Turton Ash House Farm, Winsford		03.06.94P
	Built by Société Aéronautique Normande (NF 04.09.14)		

G-ASRW	Piper PA-28-180 Cherokee B	28-1606	21.04.64
	N11C G N Smith Thorpe Abbotts		14.05.19E

G-ASSF	Cessna 182G Skylane	18255593	05.05.64
	N2493R Cancelled 12.07.11 as PWFU		10.04.08
	Derby *Wreck open store 10.13*		

G-ASSM[M]	Hawker Siddeley HS.125 Series 1/522	25010	05.05.64
	5N-AMK, G-ASSM Cancelled 28.05.80 as sold in Nigeria		
	With Science Museum, South Kensington		

G-ASSP	Piper PA-30 Twin Comanche	30-458	07.05.64
	N10F P H Tavener Annemasse, France		22.12.07E
	(NF 08.08.18)		

G-ASSS	Cessna 172E Skyhawk	17251467	07.05.64
	N5567T P R March & P Turner tr Triple Sierra		
	Flying Group Gloucestershire		01.08.19E

G-ASSV	Kensinger KF	02	11.05.64
	N23S C I Jefferson Priory Farm, Tibenham		
	Built by N Kensinger – project PFA 168-13923;		
	stored dismantled 10.16 in trailer (NF 15.03.18)		

G-ASSW	Piper PA-28-140 Cherokee	28-20055	11.05.64
	N11C Merseyflight Ltd Liverpool John Lennon		20.05.19E

G-ASSY	Druine D.31 Turbulent	PFA 586	12.05.64
	C M Bracewell (Coldridge, Crediton)		
	Built by F J Parker – project PFA 586 (NF 16.08.17)		

G-ASTG	Nord 1002 Pingouin II	183	21.05.64
	F-BGKI, French AF 183		
	R J Fray Furze Farm, Haddon		24.07.19P
	As 'BG-KM' in Luftwaffe c/s		

G-ASTI	Auster 6A Tugmaster	3745	27.05.64
	WJ359 S J Partridge (Punnetts Town, Heathfield)		04.10.19P
	Built by Taylorcraft Aeroplanes (England) Ltd		

G-ASTL[M]	Fairey Firefly 1	F.5607	01.06.64
	SE-BRD, Z2033 Cancelled 03.02.82 as PWFU		
	'Evelyn Tentions'		
	As 'Z2033: N:275' in 1771 Sqdn SEAC c/s)		
	With Fleet Air Arm Museum, RNAS Yeovilton		

G-ASTP[M]	Hiller UH-12C	1045	04.06.64
	N9750C Cancelled 24.01.90 by CAA		03.07.82
	With The Helicopter Museum, Weston-super-Mare		

G-ASUB	Mooney M.20E Super 21	397	24.04.64
	N7158U S C Coulbeck North Coates		05.10.19E
	Official p/i 'N715BU' is incorrect		

G-ASUD	Piper PA-28-180 Cherokee B	28-1654	29.06.64
	N7673W M B Yeulett tr G-ASUD Group		
	Andrewsfield		10.05.19E

G-ASUE	Cessna 150D	15060718	30.06.64
	N6018T D Huckle (Ware)		
	(NF 17.09.18)		

G-ASUG[M]	Beech E18S-9700	BA-111	03.07.64
	N575C, N555CB, N24R Cancelled 12.05.75 as PWFU		23.07.75
	Loganair c/s		
	With National Museum of Flight Scotland, East Fortune		

G-ASUI	Beagle A.61 Terrier 2	B.641	06.07.64
	VF628 Cancelled 30.04.15 by CAA		11.01.10
	Lodge Farm, Durston *Stored 06.17*		

G-ASUP	Cessna F172E	F172-0071	22.07.64
	S A Williams St Athan		06.12.19E
	Built by Reims Aviation SA		

G-ASUS	Jurca MJ.2E Tempête	67	28.07.64
	R E Hughes & D J Millin Dunkeswell '67'		01.09.15P
	Built by D G Jones – project PFA 2001 (NF 23.05.18)		

G-ASVG	Piel CP.301B Emeraude	109	07.08.64
	F-BILV R B M Etherington Dunkeswell 'Emma II'		30.11.18P
	Built by Ateliers Aeronautique Rousseau;		
	carries 'F-BILV' on tail		

G-ASVM	Cessna F172E	F172-0077	11.08.64
	M Tobutt Gloucestershire		10.04.19E
	Built by Reims Aviation SA		

G-ASVO[M]	Handley Page HPR.7 Dart Herald 214	185	13.08.64
	PP-SDG, G-ASVO, G-8-3 Cancelled 25.09.01 by CAA		14.01.00
	WFU after collision Hurn 08.04.97 front fuselage only		
	With Morayvia Sci-Tech Experience Project, Kinloss		

G-ASVZ	Piper PA-28-140 Cherokee	28-20357	24.08.64
	N11C Scillonian Marine Consultants Ltd		
	St Mary's, Isles of Scilly		09.03.19E

G-ASWF	Beagle A.109 Airedale	B.537	26.08.64	
	Cancelled 03.02.89 by CAA		24.07.83	
	Spanhoe *Open store derelict 09.15*			
G-ASWH	Phoenix-Luton LA5A Minor	PAL1225	31.08.64	
	Cancelled 09.05.01 by CAA		22.06.78	
	Hill Farm, Durley *Stored for sale 11.17*			
G-ASWJ[M]	Beagle B.206C Series 1	B.009	09.09.64	
	8449M Cancelled 09.09.75 as WFU			
	With Midland Air Museum, Coventry			
G-ASWW	Piper PA-30 Twin Comanche	30-556	01.10.64	
	N7531Y, N10F Cancelled 12.08.09 as PWFU		06.11.07	
	Eshott *Fuselage stored 05.13*			
G-ASWX	Piper PA-28-180 Cherokee C	28-1932	01.10.64	
	N11C Gasworks Flying Group Ltd Old Warden		09.02.19E	
G-ASXC	SIPA 903	8	06.10.64	
	G-DWEL, G-ASXC, F-BEYK			
	T M Buick Swanborough Farm, Lewes		20.03.16P	
	(NF 03.06.16)			
G-ASXD	Brantly B.2B	435	07.10.64	
	S Crossland tr Brantly G-ASXD Group Eaglescott		02.07.05	
	Noted 05.16 (NF 07.01.16)			
G-ASXJ	Phoenix-Luton LA4A Minor	xxxx	14.10.64	
	Cancelled 24.02.12 by CAA		17.12.08	
	Long Marston *Built by P D Lea & E A Linguard –*			
	project PFA 801 Stored 07.12			
G-ASXS	Jodel DR.1050 Ambassadeur	133	19.10.64	
	F-BJNG C P Wilkinson Finmere		08.10.19P	
	Built by Société Aéronautique Normande			
G-ASXU	Jodel D.120A Paris-Nice	196	19.10.64	
	F-BKAG M Ferid tr G-ASXU Group			
	Stoneacre Farm, Farthing Corner		31.05.19P	
	Built by Société des Etablissements Benjamin Wassmer			
G-ASXX[M]	Avro 683 Lancaster B.VII	NX611	22.10.64	
	(8375M)m G-ASXX, French Navy WU-15, NX611			
	H C Panton tr Panton Family Trust East Kirkby			
	As 'NX611:DX-F' in RAF 630 Sqdn c/s 'City of Sheffield'			
	(starboard) & 'NX611:LE-H' in 57 Sqdn c/s 'Just Jane' (port)			
	(NF 29.09.16)			
G-ASYD[M]	BAC One Eleven 475AM	BAC.053	09.11.64	
	Cancelled 25.07.94 as WFU		13.07.94	
	Originally registered as Series 400AM: converted to			
	prototype Series 500 in 1967 & Series 475EM in 1970			
	With Brooklands Museum, Weybridge			
G-ASYG	Beagle A.61 Terrier 2	B.637	03.11.64	
	VX927 D & R L McDonald Trencin, Slovak Republic		18.07.18E	
	Rebuilt to Auster T.7 standard; as 'VX927' in AAC c/s			
G-ASYJ	Beech D95A TravelAir	TD-595	06.11.64	
	N8675Q Crosby Aviation (Jersey) Ltd Jersey		09.12.14E	
	(IE 24.08.16)			
G-ASYK	Piper PA-30-160 Twin Comanche	30-573	06.11.64	
	N7543Y Cancelled 30.10.96 as PWFU		28.07.97	
	Farley Farm, Farley Chamberlayne *Derelict 12.17*			
G-ASYP	Cessna 150E	15060794	23.11.64	
	N6094T R J Brown tr Henlow Flying Group			
	RAF Henlow		08.02.19E	
G-ASZB	Cessna 150E	15061113	16.12.64	
	N3013J Akki Aviation Services Ltd Turweston		30.05.19E	
G-ASZD	Bölkow BÖ.208A2 Junior	563	16.12.64	
	D-ENKI S L Wilkes Cambridge		21.10.18P	
G-ASZE[M]	Beagle A.61 Terrier 2	B.636	17.12.64	
	VF552 J Koch t/a Historische Flugzeuge			
	(Grossenhein, Germany)		28.08.19P	
	Conversion of Auster AOP.6 c/n 2510			
G-ASZR	Fairtravel Linnet 2	005	05.01.65	
	R Hodgson Swanborough Farm, Lewes		29.10.19P	
G-ASZU	Cessna 150E	15061152	13.01.65	
	N3052J IAE Ltd Cranfield		04.05.19E	
G-ASZV	Tipsy Nipper T.66 Series 2	T66/5/45	14.01.65	
	5N-ADE, 5N-ADY, VR-NDD			
	A M E Vervaeke (Hulste, Belgium)		02.07.15P	
	Built by Avions Fairey SA (NF 24.10.18)			
G-ASZX	Beagle A.61 Terrier 1	B.3742	18.01.65	
	(SE-ELO), WJ368			
	R B Webber Trenchard Farm, Eggesford		08.07.19P	
	As 'WJ368' in AAC camouflage c/s			

G-ATAA – G-ATZZ

G-ATAG	Jodel DR.1050 Ambassadeur	226	25.01.65	
	F-BKGG T M Gamble Wishanger Farm, Frensham		04.10.02	
	Built by Centre-Est Aéronautique (NF 30.05.18)			
G-ATAS	Piper PA-28-180 Cherokee C	28-2137	04.02.65	
	N11C B J Portus tr G-ATAS Group Andrewsfield		04.11.18E	
G-ATAU	Druine D.62B Condor	RAE/610	10.02.65	
	M C Burlock Brimpton		24.09.19P	
	Built by Rollason Aircraft and Engines Ltd			
G-ATAV	Druine D.62C Condor	RAE/611	10.02.65	
	C D Swift Damyns Hall, Upminster		11.08.17P	
	Built by Rollason Aircraft and Engines Ltd (IE 04.10.18)			
G-ATBG	Nord 1002 Pingouin II	121	24.02.65	
	F-BGVX, F-OTAN-5, French Army			
	Ardmore Aviation Services Ltd Duxford		08.07.19P	
	As 'NJ+C11' in Luftwaffe c/s			
G-ATBH	SPP Aero 145	20-015	24.02.65	
	P D Aviram Redhill			
	(IE 30.10.18)			
G-ATBJ	Sikorsky S-61N	61269	12.03.65	
	N10043? British International Helicopter Services Ltd			
	RAF Mount Pleasant, Falkland Islands		01.03.18E	
G-ATBL	de Havilland DH.60G Gipsy Moth	1917	02.03.65	
	HB-OBA, CH-353 Comanche Warbirds Ltd Duxford		07.08.18P	
G-ATBP	Alpavia Fournier RF3	59	11.03.65	
	D McNicholl Easter Farm, Fearn		12.08.18E	
G-ATBS	Druine D.31 Turbulent	PFA 1620	16.03.65	
	C J L Wolf Welshpool *'Fly Baby Fly'*		13.03.18P	
	Built by C R Shilling – project PFA 1620			
G-ATBU	Beagle A.61 Terrier 2	B.635	17.03.65	
	VF611 T Jarvis Hinton-in-the-Hedges			
	20.06.19P			
	Conversion of Auster AOP.6 c/n 2552			
G-ATBX	Piper PA-20-135 Pacer	20-904	19.03.65	
	VP-KRX, VR-TCH, VP-KKE			
	G D & P M Thomson Wellesbourne Mountford		24.05.15E	
	(IE 29.05.15)			
G-ATBZ[M]	Westland WS-58 Wessex 60 Series 1	WA.461	22.03.65	
	Cancelled as TWFU 23.11.82 – WFU 5.12.81 –			
	to G-17-4		15.12.81	
	With The Helicopter Museum, Weston-super-Mare			
G-ATCC	Beagle A.109 Airedale	B.542	25.03.65	
	North East Flight Training Ltd Longside		26.11.19P	
G-ATCD	Beagle D5/180 Husky	3683	25.03.65	
	D J O'Gorman Enstone		10.05.18P	
G-ATCE	Cessna U206	U2060380	25.03.65	
	N2180F Fly High Icarius (Tallard, France)		02.08.08E	
	(NF 07.02.17)			
G-ATCJ	Phoenix Luton LA-4A Minor	PAL 1163	05.04.65	
	A R Hutton Perth		15.09.09P	
	Built by R M Sharphouse – project PFA 812 (IE 06.08.18)			
G-ATCL	Victa Airtourer 100	93	05.04.65	
	A D Goodall Oaksey Park		25.07.05	
	Stored outside 01.19, poor condition (NF 20.10.15)			
G-ATCN	Phoenix Luton LA-4A Minor	PAL 1118	07.04.65	
	The Real Aeroplane Company Ltd Breighton		23.08.19P	
	Built by D G Peacock			
G-ATCX	Cessna 182H Skylane	18255848	26.04.65	
	N3448S K Sheppard Hinton-in-the-Hedges		01.02.19E	
G-ATDA	Piper PA-28-160 Cherokee	28-206	27.04.65	
	EI-AME, (G-ARUV) Henstridge Airfield Ltd Henstridge		02.08.18E	
G-ATDB	SNCAN 1101 Noralpha	186	27.04.65	
	F-OTAN-6, French Mil Cancelled 11.10.00 as PWFU		22.11.78	
	Prestwick *Stored 08.06*			
G-ATDN	Beagle A.61 Terrier 2	B.638	07.05.65	
	TW641 S J Saggers Headcorn		30.09.16E	
	Conversion of Auster AOP.6 c/n 2499			
	As 'TW641' in AAC c/s (IE 20.09.18)			
G-ATDO	Bölkow BÖ.208C Junior	576	10.05.65	
	D-EGZU P Thompson Crosland Moor		06.12.18P	
G-ATEF	Cessna 150E	15061378	25.05.65	
	N3978U B M Scott tr Swans Aviation Blackbushe		23.11.18E	

G-ATEM	Piper PA-28-180 Cherokee C	28-2329	26.05.65
	N11C G D Wyles Berry Farm, Bovingdon		02.08.19E
G-ATEV	Jodel DR.1050 Ambassadeur	18	31.05.65
	F-BJHL J L Altrip & J C Carter		
	(Cambridge & Gerrards Cross)		13.08.71P
	Built by Centre-Est Aéronautique (NF 04.12.18)		
G-ATEW	Piper PA-30 Twin Comanche	30-719	03.06.65
	N7640Y J M Charlton Cannes-Mandelieu, France		10.10.19E
G-ATEX	Victa Airtourer 100	110	03.06.65
	(VH-MTU) S Turner Southend		07.03.17E
	Noted 02.19 (IE 01.06.18)		
G-ATEZ	Piper PA-28-140 Cherokee	28-21044	08.06.65
	N11C EFI Aviation Ltd Old Buckenham		06.09.16E
G-ATFD	Jodel DR.1050 Ambassadeur	311	14.06.65
	F-BKIM K D Hills Barton Ashes, Crawley Down		13.03.19P
	Built by Centre-Est Aéronautique		
G-ATFG[M]	Brantly B.2B	448	16.06.65
	Cancelled 25.09.87 as WFU		25.03.85
	Composite with parts from G-ASLO & G-AXSR		
	With The Helicopter Museum, Weston-super-Mare		
G-ATFM	Sikorsky S-61N Mk.II	61270	21.06.65
	CF-OKY, N10052? British International Helicopter		
	Services Ltd Newquay Cornwall		01.10.19E
G-ATFR	Piper PA-25 Pawnee	25-135	28.06.65
	OY-ADJ, N10F Cancelled 20.03.18 by CAA 25.08.17		
	Kettering *Displayed at Kestrel Caravans 05.18*		
G-ATFY	Cessna F172G	F172-0199	08.07.65
	J M Vinall Rayne Hall Farm, Rayne		06.07.19E
	Built by Reims Aviation SA		
G-ATGN[M]	Thorn K-800 Coal Gas Balloon	2	12.07.65
	Cancelled 23.06.81 as WFU		
	Built by J Thorn		
	With British Balloon Museum & Library, Newbury		
G-ATGY	Gardan GY-80-160 Horizon	121	20.07.65
	D H Mackay Enstone		03.05.19R
	Built by Sud Aviation		
G-ATHD	de Havilland DHC-1 Chipmunk 22	C1/0837	26.07.65
	WP971, G-ATHD, WP971 O L Cubitt & P G Lucas		
	tr Spartan Flying Group Denham		10.04.19P
	As 'WP971' in RAF silver c/s with blue training bands		
	& CFS insignia		
G-ATHK	Aeronca 7AC Champion	7AC-971	02.08.65
	N82339, NC82339		
	T C Barron Calcot Peak Farm, Calcot		17.06.19P
G-ATHM	Wallis WA-116/F	211	03.08.65
	4R-ACK, G-ATHM Cancelled 03.08.16 as PWFU		29.05.93
	Old Warden *Stored 10.16*		
G-ATHR	Piper PA-28-180 Cherokee C	28-2343	11.08.65
	EI-AOT, N11C Azure Flying Club Ltd Cranfield		21.07.19E
	Operated by Thomsonfly Flying Club		
G-ATHT	Victa Airtourer 115	120	16.08.65
	D L Haines tr Cotswold Flying Group Gloucestershire		24.09.16E
	(IE 24.05.17)		
G-ATHU	Beagle A.61 Terrier 1	AUS/127/FM	16.08.65
	7435M, WE539 J A L Irwin Park Farm, Eaton Bray		11.07.19P
G-ATHV	Cessna 150F	15062019	16.08.65
	N8719S R C Benyon & S Doyle		
	Woolston Moss, Warrington		02.04.19E
G-ATHZ	Cessna 150F	15061586	20.08.65
	(EI-AOP), N6286R R D Forster Beccles		27.03.98
	Stored 01.18 (NF 07.03.16)		
G-ATIC	Jodel DR.1050 Ambassadeur	006	23.08.65
	F-BJCJ T A Major, Trevissick Farm, Porthtowan		15.10.19P
	Built by Société Aéronautique Normande		
G-ATIN	Jodel D.117	437	08.09.65
	F-BHNV C E C & C M Hives RAF Waddington		04.09.19P
	Built by Société Aéronautique Normande		
G-ATIR	SNCAN Stampe SV.4C	1047	09.09.65
	F-BNMC, G-ATIR, F-BMKQ, French Navy 1047,		
	F-BCDM, French Navy 1047		
	A Trueman Little Gransden 'Lizzy t'		21.05.19P
	Built by Atelier industriel de l'Aéronautique		
G-ATIS	Piper PA-28-160 Cherokee C	28-2713	09.09.65
	N11C A Lonsdale (Stockton-on-Tees)		13.11.19E

G-ATIZ	Jodel D.117	636	15.09.65
	F-BIBR R A Smith Tower Farm, Wollaston		17.07.17P
	Built by Société Aéronautique Normande (IE 01.05.18)		
G-ATJA	Jodel DR.1050 Ambassadeur	378	15.09.65
	F-BKHL P Kellett & S L Lewis tr Bicester Flying Group		
	Lower Upham Farm, Chiseldon		19.02.19P
	Built by Société Aéronautique Normande		
G-ATJC	Victa Airtourer 100	125	16.09.65
	Aviation West Ltd Easterton		21.03.13E
	(NF 08.08.18)		
G-ATJG	Piper PA-28-140 Cherokee	28-21299	20.09.65
	D & J Albon Goodwood		31.03.14E
	Stored 07.16 (NF 04.08.18)		
G-ATJL	Piper PA-24-260 Comanche	24-4203	23.09.65
	N8752P, N10F S J Ollier Tatenhill		07.11.19E
G-ATJN	Jodel D.119	863	23.09.65
	F-PINZ L Jackson tr Real Hart Flying Group		
	Wickenby		24.08.19P
	Built by Etablissement Dormois		
G-ATJV	Piper PA-32-260 Cherokee Six	32-103	07.10.65
	TF-GOS, G-ATJV, N11C Wingglider Ltd Hibaldstow		30.10.19E
G-ATKH	Phoenix Luton LA-4A Minor	PFA 809	25.10.65
	H E Jenner (Matfield, Tonbridge)		04.08.06P
	Built by E B W Woodhall – project PFA 809 (NF 18.10.18)		
G-ATKI	Piper J-3C-65 Cub	17545	25.10.65
	N70536, NC70536 M A Sims		
	Lower Upham Farm, Chiseldon		11.04.19P
G-ATKT	Cessna F172G	F172-0206	09.11.65
	R J D Blois Hill Farm, Yoxford		11.02.19E
	Built by Reims Aviation SA		
G-ATKX	Jodel D.140C Mousquetaire III	163	19.11.65
	P J Petitt tr Kilo X-Ray Syndicate Redhill		25.05.19P
	Built by Société Aéronautique Normande		
G-ATLA	Cessna 182J Skylane	18256923	24.11.65
	N2823F J T & J W Whicher Henstridge		26.07.19E
G-ATLB	Jodel DR.1050-M Excellence	78	29.11.65
	F-BIVG P J Nightingale tr Le Syndicate du Petit Oiseau		
	Great Oakley		09.05.19P
	Built by Société Aéronautique Normande		
G-ATLH	Fewsdale Tigercraft Gyroplane	FT 5	06.12.65
	Cancelled 10.02.82 as WFU		
	(Not Known) *Displayed Sywell 09.17*		
G-ATLM	Cessna F172G	F172-0252	06.12.65
	M Wilson Sandtoft		17.09.16E
	Built by Reims Aviation SA		
G-ATLP	Bensen B.8M	17	09.12.65
	R F G Moyle Tregolds Farm, St Merryn		19.05.97P
	Built by C D Julian; stored 04.16 (NF 31.10.18)		
G-ATLT	Cessna U206A	U2060523	13.12.65
	N4823F Skydive Jersey Ltd Jersey		16.08.19E
G-ATLV	Jodel D.120 Paris-Nice	224	15.12.65
	F-BKNQ H T & I A Robinson Breighton		10.05.19P
	Built by Société des Etablissements Benjamin Wassmer		
G-ATMC	Cessna F150F	F150-0020	28.12.65
	M Biddulph Elmsett		18.05.19E
	Built by Reims Aviation SA; Wichita c/n 15062849		
G-ATMH	Beagle D5/180 Husky	3684	03.01.66
	J L Thorogood (Leslie, Insch)		08.07.14P
	Fuselage on rebuild Leicester & wings on repair		
	Southend 02.19 (NF 23.02.18)		
G-ATMM	Cessna F150F	F150-0016	06.01.66
	(N....), G-ATMM R D Forster Beccles		07.07.18E
	Built by Reims Aviation SA, Wichita c/n 15062775		
G-ATMN (2)	Cessna F150F	F150-0060	06.01.66
	(G-ATNE) Cancelled 21.10.04 as WFU		02.07.84
	Not known *Built by Reims Aviation SA;*		
	Wichita c/n 15063526; used by Mission		
	Aviation Fellowship as travelling exhibit 10.17		
G-ATNB	Piper PA-28-180 Cherokee C	28-3057	20.01.66
	N11C C K Delgahawattegedara Great Oakley		02.10.19E
G-ATNE	Cessna F150F	F150-0042	20.01.66
	Cirrus Aircraft UK Ltd & T & T Wright Sywell		17.05.19E
	Built by Reims Aviation SA; Wichita c/n 15063252		

G-ATNL	Cessna F150F	F150-0066	25.01.66	
	J P Nugent t/a Wicklow Wings	Newcastle, RoI		
	Built by Reims Aviation SA; Wichita c/n 15063652 (IE 12.06.16)			
G-ATNV	Piper PA-24-260 Comanche	24-4350	28.01.66	
	N8896P K Powell Kings Farm, Thurrock		10.11.18E	
G-ATOH	Druine D.62B Condor	RAE/612	03.02.66	
	J Cooke tr Three Spires Flying Group			
	Shenstone Hall Farm, Shenstone		17.08.19P	
	Built by Rollason Aircraft and Engines Ltd			
G-ATOI	Piper PA-28-140 Cherokee	28-21556	03.02.66	
	N11C Rayham Ltd Biggin Hill		07.02.19E	
G-ATOJ	Piper PA-28-140 Cherokee	28-21584	03.02.66	
	N11C British Northwest Airlines Ltd Blackpool		03.03.11E	
	Noted on fire dump 03.16 (NF 15.12.15)			
G-ATOK	Piper PA-28-140 Cherokee	28-21612	03.02.66	
	N11C A Allan & C A Roberts tr ILC Flying Group			
	White Waltham		19.06.18E	
G-ATON	Piper PA-28-140 Cherokee	28-21654	03.02.66	
	N11C T C J Bridgwater tr Stirling Flying Syndicate			
	Shobdon		03.05.19E	
G-ATOO	Piper PA-28-140 Cherokee	28-21668	03.02.66	
	N11C A Pattinson t/a Caralair Aviation Blackpool		10.05.19E	
G-ATOP	Piper PA-28-140 Cherokee	28-21682	03.02.66	
	N11C P R Coombs tr Aero 80 Flying Group Popham		05.09.19E	
G-ATOR	Piper PA-28-140 Cherokee	28-21696	03.02.66	
	N11C E M Taylor tr G-ATOR Flying Group			
	(Amesbury)		27.07.19E	
G-ATOT	Piper PA-28-180 Cherokee C	28-3061	03.02.66	
	N11C Sirius Aviation Ltd Jersey		12.01.19E	
G-ATOU	Mooney M.20E Super 21	961	03.02.66	
	N5946Q DbProf Doo Skofijica, Slovenia		12.10.18E	
G-ATOYᴹ	Piper PA-24-260 Comanche B	24-4346	07.02.66	
	N8893P Crashed 06.03.79 near Elstree – cancelled			
	14.05.79 as destroyed *'Myth Too' Fuselage only*			
	With National Museum of Flight Scotland, East Fortune			
G-ATPD	Hawker Siddeley HS.125 Series 1B/522	25085	11.02.66	
	5N-AGU, G-ATPD Cancelled 02.12.03 as WFU		14.10.98	
	Bournemouth *Derelict on fire dump 03.19*			
G-ATPT	Cessna 182J Skylane	18257056	22.02.66	
	N2956F C Beer tr Papa Tango Group Elstree		17.10.18E	
G-ATPV	Gardan GY-20 Minicab	JB-01	22.02.66	
	F-PJKA P T Stephenson Full Sutton		29.03.19P	
	Rebuilt by J Barritault-Bauge, ex GY-20 F-PHUC c/n A 155			
G-ATRG	Piper PA-18-150 Super Cub	18-7764	01.03.66	
	5B-CAB, N4985Z Dorset Gliding Club Ltd			
	Eyres Field		31.05.19E	
G-ATRI	Bolkow Bo.208C Junior	602	03.03.66	
	D-ECGY Cancelled 31.03.11 as PWFU		08.10.11	
	Pilmuir Farm, Fife *Used as children's play thing 01.15*			
G-ATRK	Cessna F150F	F150-0049	04.03.66	
	(G-ATNC) Falcon Aviation Ltd			
	Bourne Park, Hurstbourne Tarrant		08.01.17E	
	Built by Reims Aviation SA; Wichita c/n 15063381 (NF 25.04.18)			
G-ATRM	Cessna F150F	F150-0053	04.03.66	
	(G-ATNJ) North East Aviation Ltd Eshott		20.12.19E	
	Built by Reims Aviation SA; Wichita c/n 15063454			
G-ATRP	Piper PA-28-140 Cherokee	28-21885	04.03.66	
	N11C Cancelled 10.11.86 as WFU		20.09.84	
	Southend *Wreck stored dismantled 01.19*			
G-ATRW	Piper PA-32-260 Cherokee Six	32-360	08.03.66	
	N11C Moxley Architects Ltd & J Pringle			
	t/a Pringle Brandon Architects Biggin Hill		13.10.16E	
G-ATRX	Piper PA-32-260 Cherokee Six	32-390	08.03.66	
	N11C S P Vincent Wolverhampton Halfpenny Green		26.11.19E	
G-ATSI	Bölkow BÖ.208C Junior	605	14.03.66	
	D-EFNU M Wright tr GATSI Bolkow Group Tilstock		29.08.19E	
G-ATSL	Cessna F172G	F172-0260	16.03.66	
	Aircraft Engineers Ltd Glasgow Prestwick		05.12.19E	
	Built by Reims Aviation SA			
G-ATSR	Beech M35 Bonanza	D-6236	29.03.66	
	EI-ALL V S E Norman Rendcomb		15.07.19E	
G-ATSY	Wassmer WA.41 Super Baladou IV	117	12.04.66	
	Cancelled 06.03.15 as PWFU		23.11.91	
	Crofton On Tees *In paintball park 03.18*			
G-ATSZ	Piper PA-30 Twin Comanche B	30-1002	13.04.66	
	EI-BPS, G-ATSZ, (AN-...), G-ATSZ, (EI-BBS),			
	G-ATSZ, N7912Y Sierra Zulu Aviation Ltd Cambridge	04.04.19E	
G-ATTB	Beagle Wallis WA-116/F	214	19.04.66	
	Aerial Media Ltd Old Buckenham		29.07.09P	
	Originally built Wallis Autogyros Ltd as Wallis WA.116			
	Series 1; rebuilt from damaged G-ARZC			
	As 'XR944' in RAF c/s (NF 26.11.14)			
G-ATTI	Piper PA-28-140 Cherokee	28-21951	24.04.66	
	N11C A J Tobias Brighton City		16.10.19E	
G-ATTK	Piper PA-28-140 Cherokee	28-21959	25.04.66	
	N11C D J E Fairburn tr G-ATTK Flying Group			
	Southend		21.10.19E	
G-ATTN	Piccard HAB (62,000 cu ft)	15 & 1352	27.04.66	
	Cancelled 05.12.77 as PWFU			
	Wroughton *Envelope & basket stored 06.94*			
	'The Red Dragon' In Science Museum store 2013			
G-ATTR	Bölkow BÖ.208C Junior	612	28.04.66	
	D-EHEH S Luck Audley End		23.05.19E	
G-ATTUᴹ	Piper PA-28-140 Cherokee	28-21987	02.05.66	
	Cancelled 04.09.92 as PWFU		04.10.93	
	Geneva, Switzerland *Preserved 06.18*			
G-ATTV	Piper PA-28-140 Cherokee	28-21991	02.05.66	
	N11C J Roome tr G-ATTV Group North Weald		22.04.19E	
G-ATTX	Piper PA-28-180 Cherokee C	28-3390	02.05.66	
	PH-VDP, (G-ATTX), N11C			
	I M Hallifax tr GATTX Flying Group Earls Colne		04.05.19E	
G-ATUB	Piper PA-28-140 Cherokee	28-21971	02.05.66	
	N11C J P Nugent t/a Wicklow Wings			
	Newcastle, RoI		13.07.17E	
	(IE 09.08.17)			
G-ATUF	Cessna F150F	F150-0040	04.05.66	
	I Burnett Humberside *'Honeysuckle'*		26.09.18E	
	Built by Reims Aviation SA; Wichita c/n 15063229			
G-ATUG	Druine D.62B Condor	RAE/614	04.05.66	
	D L R J Keeping (St Austell)		27.03.19P	
	Built by Rollason Aircraft and Engines Ltd			
G-ATUH	Tipsy Nipper T.66 Series 1	6	04.05.66	
	OO-NIF H Abraham (Zurich, Switzerland)		26.06.17P	
	Built by Avions Fairey SA			
G-ATUI	Bölkow BÖ.208C Junior	611	04.05.66	
	D-EHEF G J Ball Thruxton		11.04.19E	
G-ATVF	de Havilland DHC-1 Chipmunk 22	C1/0265	25.05.66	
	WD327 P A Moslin tr ATVF Syndicate			
	(Ashbourne, Derby)		14.06.19P	
	Lycoming O-360-A4A			
G-ATVK	Piper PA-28-140 Cherokee	28-22006	27.05.66	
	N11C J Turner White Waltham		25.03.19E	
G-ATVO	Piper PA-28-140 Cherokee	28-22020	27.05.66	
	N11C Perryair Ltd (Brighton City)		04.01.18E	
	Ditched into sea Widewater Beach, Lancing 30.03.17,			
	recovered & beached (IE 06.01.18)			
G-ATVPᴹ	Vickers FB.5 Gunbus replica	VAFA-01 & FB.5	31.05.66	
	Cancelled 27.02.69 as WFU *As '2345' in RFC c/s*		06.05.69	
	Built by Vintage Aircraft & Flying Association			
	With RAF Museum, Hendon			
G-ATVW	Druine D.62B Condor	RAE/615	07.06.66	
	A G & B N Stevens St Mary's, Isles of Scilly		25.07.19P	
	Built by Rollason Aircraft and Engines Ltd			
G-ATVX	Bölkow BÖ.208C Junior	615	09.06.66	
	D-EHER R A Lowe & G W Mair tr Moray Firth			
	Flying Group Inverness		20.09.19P	
G-ATWA	Jodel DR.1050 Ambassadeur	296	10.06.66	
	F-BKHA T Coggins tr One Twenty Group			
	(Markfield, Leeds)		12.10.18P	
	Built by Société Aéronautique Normande			
G-ATWB	Jodel D.117	423	10.06.66	
	F-BHNH D P Ash tr Andrewsfield Whisky Bravo Group			
	Andrewsfield		06.08.19P	
	Built by Société Aéronautique Normande			

G-ATWJ Cessna F172F   F172-0095   21.06.66
EI-ANS   Shenley Farms (Aviation) Ltd   Headcorn   04.10.19E
Built by Reims Aviation SA; operated by Weald Air Services Ltd

G-ATXA Piper PA-22-150 Caribbean   22-3730   08.07.66
N4403A   I C Mills   Sherburn-in-Elmet
Converted to PA-20 Pacer configuration

G-ATXD Piper PA-30 Twin Comanche B   30-1166   12.07.66
N8053Y   M Bagshaw   Blackbushe   07.02.19E

G-ATXH[M]   Handley Page HP.137 Jetstream 200   198   15.07.66
Cancelled 22.04.71 as PWFU   *At South Yorkshire
Aircraft Museum, Doncaster; cockpit only*

G-ATXL[M]   Avro 504K replica   HAC-1   19.07.66
Cancelled 06.08.71 – to N2929   *As 'E2939'*
Built by Hampshire Aero Club
With Rheinbeck Aerodrome Museum, New York

G-ATXM   Piper PA-28-180 Cherokee   28-2759   19.07.66
N8809J   Cancelled 25.06.08 by CAA   12.10.02
Southend   *For Aircraft Maintenance Apprenticeship
Training Facility 01.13*

G-ATXN Mitchell-Procter Kittiwake I   1   19.07.66
R G Day   Biggin Hill   16.06.10P
Built by R Procter – project PFA 1306 (NF 23.05.16)

G-ATXO SIPA 903   41   19.07.66
F-BGAP   C H Morris   Deanland   27.06.19P

G-ATXR[M]   Abingdon Spherical Free HAB   AFB-1   22.07.66
Cancelled 14.07.86 by CAA   01.09.76
*Built by RAF Abingdon Free Balloon Club   Basket only
With British Balloon Museum & Library, Newbury*

G-ATXX[M]   McCandless M.4   M4-3   27.07.66
Cancelled 09.09.70 as WFU
With Ulster Folk & Transport Museum, Holywood

G-ATXZ Bölkow BÖ.208C Junior   624   28.07.66
D-ELNE   M J Beardmore
Manor Farm, Drayton St Leonard   11.10.19P

G-ATYM Cessna F150G   F150-0074   15.08.66
P W Fisher tr GYM Group   Wick John O'Groats   04.09.19E
Built by Reims Aviation SA

G-ATYS Piper PA-28-180 Cherokee C   28-3296   19.08.66
N9226J   A J Hardy tr Cherokee Challenge Syndicate
Wycombe Air Park   30.08.19E

G-ATZM Piper J-3C-90 Cub Special   20868   26.09.66
N2092M, NC2092M   N D Marshall   RAF Halton   03.05.19P
Fuselage No.21310

G-ATZS Wassmer WA.41 Super Baladou IV   128   30.09.66
I R Siddell   Headcorn   11.05.18R
(IE 17.09.18)

G-ATZZ Cessna F150G   F150-0136   14.10.66
G-DENB, G-ATZZ, (G-RTHI), G-ATZZ
J P Nugent   Newcastle, RoI   19.10.18E
Built by Reims Aviation SA (NF 21.02.19)

G-AVAA – G-AVZZ

G-AVAA[M]   Cessna F150G   F150-0164   14.10.66
Cancelled 16.04.96 by CAA   05.07.96
*Built by Reims Aviation SA   Fuselage only
With South Yorkshire Aircraft Museum, Doncaster*

G-AVAV Supermarine 509 Spitfire Tr.9   CBAF 7269   08.11.66
D-FMKN, N8R, G-AVAV, Irish Air Corps 159, G-15-172,
MJ772   Warbird Experiences Ltd   Biggin Hill
On restoration 01.19 as 'MJ772' (NF 01.02.16)

G-AVAW Druine D.62C Condor   RAE/617   10.11.66
S Banyard tr Condor Aircraft Group   Tibenham   27.08.19P
Built by Rollason Aircraft and Engines Ltd

G-AVAX   Piper PA-28-180 Cherokee C   28-3798   11.11.66
N11C   Cancelled 11.11.13 by CAA   14.09.13
Fairoaks   *Stored 11.13*

G-AVBG Piper PA-28-180 Cherokee C   28-3801   11.11.66
N11C   M C Plomer-Roberts   Wellesbourne Mountford   12.09.19E

G-AVBH Piper PA-28-180 Cherokee C   28-3802   11.11.66
N11C   Tenterfield (Holdings) Ltd
New Lane Farm, North Elmham   18.05.19E

G-AVBR Piper PA-28-180 Cherokee C   28-3931   14.11.66
F-BOSO, G-AVBR, N9679J
G Cormack   Easter Poldar Farm, Thornhill
(IE 18.03.19)

G-AVBS Piper PA-28-180 Cherokee C   28-3938   14.11.66
N11C   J K Shipley tr Bravo Sierra Flying Group
Newquay Cornwall   25.08.19E

G-AVBT Piper PA-28-180 Cherokee C   28-3945   14.11.66
N11C   W T D Gillam   Henstridge   15.05.19E

G-AVCM Piper PA-24-260 Comanche B   24-4520   05.12.66
N9054P   R F Smith   Stapleford   07.11.19E
Official p/i 'N3492F' is incorrect

G-AVCN   Britten Norman BN-2A-8 Islander   3   06.12.66
N290VL, F-OGHG, G-AVCN   Cancelled 09.06.15 as PWFU
East Wight, IOW   *On rebuild to static configuration 03.16*

G-AVCS   Beagle A.61 Terrier   –   12.12.66
WJ363   Cancelled 03.04.89 by CAA
Lisburn   *Originally regd as Auster 7 but actually an
Auster 10; stored dismantled 12.13*

G-AVCV Cessna 182J Skylane   18257492   15.12.66
N3492F   R J Hendry   Dunkeswell   07.05.19E

G-AVDA Cessna 182K Skylane   18257959   16.12.66
N2759Q   F W & I F Ellis   Water Leisure Park, Skegness   05.03.19E

G-AVDF Beagle B.121 Pup Series 1   B121-001   28.12.66
D I Collings   Turweston
On rebuild 02.17 (NF 17.01.17)

G-AVDG   Wallis WA-116 Series1 Agile   215   28.12.66
Cancelled 03.08.16 as PWFU   29.05.92
Old Warden   *Stored 10.16*

G-AVDH   Wallis WA-116 Series1 Agile   216   28.12.66
Cancelled 19.02.69 as PWFU
Reymerston Hall, Norwich   *Major surviving
parts for rebuild of G-AXAS & rest rebuilt 2008
to represent 'G-ARZB'*

G-AVDT Aeronca 7AC Champion   7AC-6932   05.01.67
N3594E, NC3594E   D & N Cheney
Gransha, Rathfriland   09.07.19P

G-AVDV Piper PA-22-150 Caribbean   22-3752   05.01.67
N4423A   L Beardmore & R W Taberner   Derby   25.08.17E
*Converted to PA-20 Pacer configuration
Badged 'Super Pacer' (IE 02.07.18)*

G-AVEF Jodel D.150 Mascaret   16   19.01.67
F-BLDK   C E Bellhouse   Pent Farm, Postling   19.12.18E
Built by Société Aéronautique Normande

G-AVEH SIAI Marchetti S.205-20/R   346   20.01.67
S W Brown   Fenland   29.11.18E

G-AVEM Cessna F150G   F150-0198   23.01.67
N J A Rutherford   (Dockenfield, Farnham)   11.01.19E
Built by Reims Aviation SA

G-AVEN Cessna F150G   F150-0202   23.01.67
M Ali   Little Staughton   08.12.17E
Built by Reims Aviation SA; stored 05.18 (NF 18.09.18)

G-AVEO Cessna F150G   F150-0204   23.01.67
G-DENA, G-AVEO, EI-BOI, G-AVEO
C P Dawes tr G-AVEO Flying Group   Darley Moor   24.11.18E
Built by Reims Aviation SA

G-AVER Cessna F150G   F150-0206   23.01.67
Upperstack Ltd t/a LAC Flying School
Manchester Barton   31.03.19E
Built by Reims Aviation SA

G-AVEU Wassmer WA.41 Super Baladou IV   136   27.01.67
J Reed & C P Taylor tr The Baladou Flying Group
Old Warden   17.03.19R

G-AVEX Druine D.62 Condor   RAE/616   31.01.67
R Manning   Netherthorpe   06.08.19P
Built by Rollason Aircraft and Engines Ltd

G-AVEY Phoenix Currie Super Wot   SE.100   31.01.67
F R Donaldson   Hinton-in-the-Hedges   03.07.07P
*Built by K Sedgwick – project PFA 3006
Carries '2-B-7' in pseudo-WW2 early USN c/s (NF 15.03.16)*

G-AVFB[M]   Hawker Siddeley HS.121 Trident 2E   2141   01.02.67
5B-DAC, G-AVFB   Cancelled 19.06.72 to Cyprus –
restored 12.05.77, cancelled 09.07.82 as PWFU   30.09.82
*BEA c/s
With Duxford Aviation Society*

G

G-AVFE	HS.121 Trident 2E	2144	01.02.67	

Cancelled 20.03.85 as WFU
Belfast Int'l   *Used by fire department for training 12.13*

G-AVFHᴹ Hawker Siddeley HS.121 Trident 2E   2147   01.02.67
Cancelled 12.05.82   18.05.83
WFU 24.10.81   'BEA' c/s: forward fuselage section only
With de Havilland Aircraft Museum, London Colney

G-AVFR Piper PA-28-140 Cherokee   28-22747   01.02.67
N11C   C Holden & S Powell   Husbands Bosworth   12.01.16E
Fuselage behind hangar 07.16 (IE 20.09.18)

G-AVFU Piper PA-32-300 Cherokee Six   32-40182   01.02.67
N11C   Tertium Treuboden Immobilien GmbH
(Hannover-Herrenhausen, Germany)   04.06.19E

G-AVFX Piper PA-28-140 Cherokee   28-22757   01.02.67
N11C   A E & R A Fielding   Strathallan   11.05.19E

G-AVFZ Piper PA-28-140 Cherokee   28-22767   01.02.67
N11C   D S Vennard tr G-AVFZ Group   Henstridge   26.07.19E

G-AVGA Piper PA-24-260 Comanche B   24-4489   31.01.67
N9027P   G M Moir   Derby   01.06.19E

G-AVGC Piper PA-28-140 Cherokee   28-22777   31.01.67
N11C   L McIlwain   Letterkenny, RoI   12.01.19E

G-AVGE Piper PA-28-140 Cherokee   28-22787   31.01.67
N11C   D Marrani & P Ruderham   Jersey   09.12.19E

G-AVGI   Piper PA-28-140 Cherokee   28-22822   31.01.67
N11C   Cancelled 19.04.13 as PWFU   22.05.13
Croft Farm, Defford   *Wings dumped 03.14*

G-AVGJ Jodel DR.1050 Sicile   265   31.01.67
F-BJYJ   I B Melville   (Thame)
Built by Société Aéronautique Normande (IE 03.04.18)

G-AVGU   Cessna F150G   F150-0199   08.02.67
Cancelled 11.09.14 as PWFU   15.06.12
Cranfield   *Built by Reims Aviation SA; stored 07.15*

G-AVGZ Jodel DR.1050 Sicile   341   14.02.67
F-BKPR   A F & S Williams   Dunkeswell   06.02.19P
Built by Centre-Est Aéronautique

G-AVHE**ᴹ** Vickers 812 Viscount   363   20.02.67
(G-AVGY), N251V   Cancelled 14.02.73 as destroyed
WFU 30.03.70 & broken up 08.72: forward fuselage
only as 'G-AVHE'
With Albatros Flugmuseum, Stuttgart, Germany

G-AVHH Cessna F172H   F172-0337   20.02.67
Alpha Victor Ltd   Old Buckenham   24.11.18E
Built by Reims Aviation SA

G-AVHL Jodel DR.105A Ambassadeur   90   23.02.67
F-BIVY   J W Baker tr Seething Jodel Group   Seething   15.07.19P
Built by Société Aéronautique Normande

G-AVHM Cessna F150G   F150-0181   24.02.67
R D Forster   Beccles   29.01.19E
Built by Reims Aviation SA; rebuilt 1997 with wings
ex G-ATRL qv

G-AVHT**ᴹ** Beagle E.3   xxxx   01.03.67
WZ711   Cancelled 23.02.18 as PWFU   01.07.16
Fuselage as 'WZ711' in camouflage c/s
With South Yorkshire Aircraft Museum, Doncaster

G-AVHY Sportavia-Putzer Fournier RF4D   4009   10.03.67
I K G Mitchell   (Halesland)   02.06.11P
(NF 16.02.15)

G-AVIB Cessna F150G   F150-0180   10.03.67
K W Wood   Insch   18.12.17E
Built by Reims Aviation SA (IE 04.01.18)

G-AVIC Cessna F172H   F172-0320   10.03.67
N17011   Leeside Flying Ltd   Cork, RoI   30.01.19E
Built by Reims Aviation SA

G-AVID   Cessna 182K   18257734   10.03.67
N2534Q   Cancelled 25.02.10 as PWFU   18.04.06
Fern, Angus   *Ex para drop trainer, stored in field 04.18*

G-AVIL Alon A-2 Aircoupe   A-5   14.03.67
N5471E   G D J Wilson   Trenchard Farm, Eggesford   07.08.19E

G-AVIN SOCATA MS.880B Rallye Club   884   14.03.67
R A C Stephens   Dunsfold   22.08.18E

G-AVIP Brantly B.2B   471   14.03.67
B R Pearson tr Eaglescott Brantly Group   Eaglescott   19.07.15E
(NF 16.08.17)

G-AVIS Cessna F172H   F172-0413   14.03.67
J P A Freeman   Headcorn   28.09.18E
Built by Reims Aviation SA

G-AVIT Cessna F150G   F150-0217   14.03.67
P Cottrell   Wellesbourne Mountford   24.05.19E
Built by Reims Aviation SA

G-AVJF Cessna F172H   F172-0393   31.03.67
D T A & J A Rees   Haverfordwest   05.09.19E
Built by Reims Aviation SA

G-AVJG   Cessna 337B Super Skymaster   3370715   31.03.67
N2415S   Cancelled 30.07.96 by CAA   31.05.82
Galbally, ROI   *Stored dismantled 12.13*

G-AVJJ Piper PA-30 Twin Comanche B   30-1420   07.04.67
N8285Y   A H Manser   Gloucestershire   17.04.19E

G-AVJK Jodel DR.1050-M Excellence   453   07.04.67
F-BLJH   D A Sutton tr Juliet Kilo Syndicate
Sackville Lodge Farm, Riseley   08.07.19P
Built by Société Aéronautique Normande; originally built as
DR.1051 & converted to DR.1050-M c.1967

G-AVJOᴹ Fokker E.III replica   PPS/FOK/6   12.04.67
Bianchi Aviation Film Services Ltd   Stow Maries   24.04.17P
Built by Personal Plane Services Ltd
As '107/15' in German Air Service c/s

G-AVJV   Wallis WA-117 Series 1   K/402/X   12.04.67
Cancelled 03.08.16 as PWFU   21.04.89
Old Warden   *Stored 10.16*

G-AVJW   Wallis WA-118/M Meteorite   K/502/X   12.04.67
Cancelled 03.08.16 as PWFU   21.04.83
Old Warden   *Stored 10.16*

G-AVKB Brochet MB.50 Pipistrelle   02   17.04.67
F-PFAL   R E Garforth   (Hockley)   30.10.96P
(NF 24.10.16)

G-AVKD Sportavia-Putzer Fournier RF4D   4024   19.04.67
R E Cross tr Lasham R F 4 Group   Lasham   07.06.19P

G-AVKE**ᴹ** Gadfly HDW-1   HDW-1   19.04.67
Cancelled 12.10.81 as WFU
On loan from E.D.ap Rees
With The Helicopter Museum, Weston-super-Mare

G-AVKG Cessna F172H   F172-0345   21.04.67
A J Austen   Oaksey Park   07.09.18E
Built by Reims Aviation SA; rebuilt 1986 with
fuselage of G-AVDC (c/n F172-0382)

G-AVKI Nipper T.66 RA.45 Series 3   S102   24.04.67
T C R Trudgill   RAF Henlow   17.05.18P
Originally built by Avions Fairey SA c/n T66/31: rebuilt
by Slingsby Sailplanes Ltd as c/n 1587 for Nipper Aircraft Ltd

G-AVKK Nipper T.66 RA.45 Series 3   S104   24.04.67
EI-BJH, G-AVKK   C Watson   Newtownards   06.04.19P
Originally built by Avions Fairey SA c/n T66/74; rebuilt
by Slingsby Sailplanes Ltd as c/n 1588 for Nipper Aircraft Ltd

G-AVKL   Piper PA-30 Twin Comanche B   30-1418   25.04.67
OY-DHL, G-AVKL, N8284Y   Cancelled 28.09.07 as WFU   27.06.08
Brighton City
Instructional airframe at Northbrook College 09.16

G-AVKP Beagle A.109 Airedale   B.540   26.04.67
SE-EGA   D R Williams   (Child's Ercall)   26.09.03
(NF 20.10.15)

G-AVKR Bölkow BÖ.208C Junior   648   28.04.67
D-EGRA   L Hawkins
Farley Farm, Farley Chamberlayne   03.09.09E
Stored 06.16 (NF 28.07.15)

G-AVLB Piper PA-28-140 Cherokee   28-23158   08.05.67
N11C   M Wilson   Little Gransden   29.01.19E

G-AVLC Piper PA-28-140 Cherokee   28-23178   08.05.67
N11C   R G Allgood & P G Evans   Shipdham   28.05.19E

G-AVLE Piper PA-28-140 Cherokee   28-23223   08.05.67
N11C   G E Wright   Jericho Farm, Lambley   27.04.12E
(NF 18.05.18)

G-AVLF Piper PA-28-140 Cherokee   28-23268   08.05.67
N11C   S Owen tr Woodbine Group   White Waltham   09.08.18E

G-AVLG Piper PA-28-140 Cherokee   28-23358   08.05.67
N11C   R J Everett   Bentwaters   08.08.11E
(NF 13.11.18)

G-AVLI   Piper PA-28-140 Cherokee   28-23388   08.05.67
N11C   I R Richmond & D Westcott
tr Lima India Aviation Group   North Weald   26.04.19E

G-AVLJ   Piper PA-28-140 Cherokee   28-23393   08.05.67
9H-AAZ, G-AVLJ, N11C
Cherokee Aviation Holdings (Jersey) Ltd   Jersey   20.08.19E

G-AVLM   Beagle B.121 Pup Series 3   B121-003   08.05.67
D A & T M Jones   Derby   29.04.69
(NF 09.07.18)

G-AVLN   Beagle B.121 Pup Series 2   B121-004   08.05.67
A Swietochowska tr Dogs Flying Group   Sywell   29.04.19R

G-AVLO   Bölkow BÖ.208C Junior   650   08.05.67
D-EGUC   E C Murgatroyd
Sackville Lodge Farm, Riseley   28.06.19P

G-AVLT   Piper PA-28-140 Cherokee   28-23328   09.05.67
G-KELC, G-AVLT, N11C   R F Redknap   Enstone   01.03.19E

G-AVLY   Jodel D.120A Paris-Nice   331   11.05.67
S M S Smith   Halwell   10.05.19P
Built by Société Wassmer Aviation

G-AVMB   Druine D.62B Condor   RAE/621   12.05.67
F Baldanza   *'Spirit of Silver City'*   Gloucestershire   24.05.19P
Built by Rollason Aircraft and Engines Ltd

G-AVMD   Cessna 150G   15065504   16.05.67
N2404J   York Aircraft Leasing Ltd   Breighton   24.05.19E

G-AVMF   Cessna F150G   F150-0203   17.05.67
J F Marsh   Newton Hall Farm, Newton   30.06.19E
Built by Reims Aviation SA

G-AVMJ   BAC One-Eleven 510ED   BAC.138   11.05.67
Cancelled 11.05.01 by CAA   17.11.94
Trensham College, Kettering
Fuselage used as cabin trainer 10.13

G-AVMO[M]   BAC One Eleven 510ED   BAC.143   11.05.67
Cancelled 12.07.93 as WFU   *'Lothian Region'*   03.02.95
British Airways titles
With National Museum of Flight Scotland, East Fortune

G-AVMT   BAC One-Eleven 510ED   BAC.147   11.05.67
Cancelled 17.12.04 as WFU   05.12.03
Cardiff   *Used as fire trainer 01.15*

G-AVMU[M]   BAC One Eleven 510ED   BAC.148   11.05.67
Cancelled 12.07.93 as WFU   *'County of Dorset'*   08.01.95
British Airways c/s
With Duxford Aviation Society

G-AVNC   Cessna F150G   F150-0200   18.05.67
J Turner   Popham   24.05.04
Built by Reims Aviation SA (NF 02.03.18)

G-AVNE[M]   Westland WS-58 Wessex 60 Series 1   WA.561   15.05.67
G-17-3, G-AVNE, 5N-AJL, G-AVNE, 9M-ASS, VH-BHC,
PK-HBQ, G-AVNE, (G-AVMC)
Cancelled 23.11.82 as TWFU   *As 'G-AVNE' & 'G-17-3'*   07.02.83
With The Helicopter Museum, Weston-super-Mare

G-AVNN   Piper PA-28-180 Cherokee C   28-4049   26.05.67
N11C   J Acres tr G-AVNN Flying Group   Eaglescott   11.05.19E

G-AVNO   Piper PA-28-180 Cherokee C   28-4105   26.05.67
N11C   A F Cornell tr November Oscar Flying Group
Southend   28.11.19E

G-AVNS   Piper PA-28-180 Cherokee C   28-4129   26.05.67
N11C   Fly (Fu Lai) Aviation Ltd   Rochester   10.12.18E

G-AVNU   Piper PA-28-180 Cherokee C   28-4153   26.05.67
N11C   O Durrani   Lydd   12.04.19E

G-AVNW   Piper PA-28-180 Cherokee C   28-4210   26.05.67
N11C   Len Smith's (Aviation) Ltd   Popham   *'63'*   29.08.19E

G-AVNY   Sportavia-Putzer Fournier RF4D   4029   26.05.67
G-IVEL, G-AVNY   J B Giddins
Hinton-in-the-Hedges   03.11.19E

G-AVNZ   Sportavia-Putzer Fournier RF4D   4030   26.05.67
C D Pidler   Watchford Farm, Yarcombe   21.09.19E

G-AVOA   Jodel DR.1050 Ambassadeur   195   31.05.67
F-BJYY   D A Willies   Old Manor Farm, Anwick   19.06.19P
Built by Société Aéronautique Normande

G-AVOD   Beagle D5/180 Husky   3688   06.06.67
PAW Flying Services Ltd   East Winch   04.09.92
Frame stored 07.13 (NF 30.11.17)

G-AVOH   Druine D.62B Condor   RAE/622   06.06.67
G Coleman tr Condor Group   Hinton-in-the-Hedges   29.10.19P
Built by Rollason Aircraft and Engines Ltd

G-AVOM   Robin DR.221 Dauphin   65   06.06.67
P M Long tr Avon Flying Group   Bidford   02.05.19E
Built by Centre-Est Aéronautique

G-AVOO   Piper PA-18-150 Super Cub   18-8511   07.06.67
N10F   Dublin Gliding Club Ltd
Gowran Grange, RoI   *'Terry Mac'*   23.07.18E

G-AVOU   Slingsby T.56 SE.5A replica   1591   08.06.67
N908AC, EI-ARI, G-AVOU
N C Ravine tr Sywell SE5 Group   Sywell
Originally built by as Slingsby T.56 Currie Wot (SE5 Replica)
On rebuild 08.16 as 'A4850' (NF 01.07.15)

G-AVOZ   Piper PA-28-180 Cherokee C   28-3711   13.06.67
N9574J   R Flavell tr Oscar Zulu Flying Group
Wycombe Air Park   06.02.19E

G-AVPC[M]   Druine D.31 Turbulent   PFA 544   15.06.67
Cancelled 13.09.02 as PWFU   28.09.99
Built by J Sharp – project PFA 544
With National Museum of Flight Scotland, East Fortune

G-AVPD   Jodel D.9 Bébé   MAC1 & 521   15.06.67
S W McKay   (Berkhamsted)
Built by S W McKay – project PFA 927 (NF 09.04.18)

G-AVPH   Cessna F150G   F1500197   20.06.67
Cancelled 26.03.02 by CAA   09.04.86
Ellough, Beccles   *Built by Reims Aviation SA*
Fuselage stored 01.18

G-AVPI   Cessna F172H   F172-0409   20.06.67
D R Larder   (Willoughby, Alford)   30.05.03
Built by Reims Aviation SA (NF 06.07.18)

G-AVPJ   de Havilland DH.82A Tiger Moth   86326   20.06.67
NL879   C C Silk   Bericote Farm, Blackdown   24.05.19P
Built by Morris Motors Ltd

G-AVPM   Jodel D.117   593   20.06.67
F-BHXO   L B Clark   Breighton   24.05.13P
Built by Société Aéronautique Normande (NF 03.02.15)

G-AVPO   Hindustan HAL-26 Pushpak   PK-127   31.03.83
9M-AOZ, VT-DWL   B Johns   Bidford   19.07.19P

G-AVPS   Piper PA-30-160 Twin Comanche B   30-1548   27.06.67
N8393Y   Cancelled 06.07.05 by CAA   11.11.05
Farley Farm, Farley Chamberlayne   *Stored 12.17*

G-AVPV   Piper PA-28-180 Cherokee C   28-2705   27.06.67
9J-RBP, N11C   K A Passmore
Rayne Hall Farm, Rayne   08.03.03
(NF 03.12.18)

G-AVPY   Piper PA-25-235 Pawnee C   25-4330   07.07.67
N4636Y, N10F   Southdown Gliding Club Ltd
Parham Park   05.08.19E

G-AVRK   Piper PA-28-180 Cherokee C   28-4041   11.07.67
N11C   Scenic Air Tours North East Ltd
Durham Tees Valley   17.05.19E

G-AVRS   Gardan GY-80-180 Horizon   224   14.07.67
N M Robbins   Sandford Hall, Knockin   26.10.19R
Built by Sud Aviation

G-AVRU   Piper PA-28-180 Cherokee C   28-4025   17.07.67
N11C   D M Barnett tr Lanpro   North Weald   14.07.19E

G-AVRW   Gardan GY-20 Minicab   OH.1549   18.07.67
D J Smith tr Kestrel Flying Group
Glebe Farm, Hougham   02.10.19P
Built by R Hart to JB.01 Minicab standard
– project PFA 1800

G-AVRZ   Piper PA-28-180 Cherokee C   28-4137   24.07.67
N11C   K B Dupuy tr RZ Group   Southend   13.02.20E

G-AVSA   Piper PA-28-180 Cherokee C   28-4184   24.07.67
N11C   D M Edes & D H Munro tr Easter Flying Group
Easter Farm, Fearn   20.09.19E

G-AVSB   Piper PA-28-180 Cherokee C   28-4191   24.07.67
N11C   G Cormack   Cumbernauld   09.08.19E

G-AVSC   Piper PA-28-180 Cherokee C   28-4193   24.07.67
N11C   M White tr G-AVSC Group   Dunkeswell   11.10.19E

G-AVSD   Piper PA-28-180 Cherokee C   28-4195   24.07.67
N11C   C B D Owen   Haverfordwest   16.07.19E

G-AVSE	Piper PA-28-180 Cherokee C	28-4196	24.07.67
	N11C F Glendon Kilrush, RoI		29.06.19E
G-AVSF	Piper PA-28-180 Cherokee C	28-4197	24.07.67
	N11C S E Pick & D A Rham tr Monday Club		
	Blackbushe		01.10.19E
G-AVSI	Piper PA-28-140 Cherokee	28-23148	24.07.67
	N11C C M Royle tr G-AVSI Flying Group		
	White Waltham		27.04.19E
G-AVSP	Piper PA-28-180 Cherokee C	28-3952	08.08.67
	N11C, (PJ-ACT) C & J Willis Biggin Hill		01.09.19E
G-AVSR	Beagle D5/180 Husky	3689	08.08.67
	S D J Holwill Dunkeswell		09.04.19P
G-AVTC	Nipper T.66 RA.45 Series 3	S106	09.08.67
	J Crawford (Headington, Oxford)		25.02.10P
	Built by Slingsby Aircraft Co Ltd as c/n 1583		
	for Nipper Aircraft Ltd (IE 27.11.15)		
G-AVTL[M]	Brighton Ax7-65 HAB	01	17.08.67
	Cancelled 11.09.81 as WFU		
	Built by Hot-Air Group & originally regd as Hot-Air Group		
	¼ Free Balloon with c/n 1		
	With British Balloon Museum & Library, Newbury		
G-AVTP	Cessna F172H	F172-0458	17.08.67
	J Davies Netherthorpe		19.07.19E
	Built by Reims Aviation SA; carries 'Skyhawk' on tail		
G-AVTT[M]	Ercoupe 415D	4399	21.08.67
	SE-BFZ Cancelled 12.04.02 as TWFU		20.01.86
	With South Yorkshire Aircraft Museum, Doncaster		
G-AVUG	Cessna F150H	F150-0234	11.09.67
	V J Larkin tr Skyways Flying Group Netherthorpe		15.11.19E
	Built by Reims Aviation SA		
G-AVUH	Cessna F150H	F150-0244	11.09.67
	A G McLaren Strubby		07.10.19E
	Built by Reims Aviation SA		
G-AVUO	Phoenix Luton LA-4A Minor	PAL 1313	21.09.67
	M E Vaisey (Hemel Hempstead)		
	Built by C P Butterfield; not completed & parts used		
	in construction of G-AXKH qv (NF 10.12.18)		
G-AVUS	Piper PA-28-140 Cherokee	28-24065	25.09.67
	(G-AVUT), N11C P K Pemberton Blackpool		19.12.18E
G-AVUT	Piper PA-28-140 Cherokee	28-24085	25.09.67
	(G-AVUU), N11C Bencray Ltd Blackpool		19.08.14E
	(NF 04.10.18)		
G-AVUU	Piper PA-28-140 Cherokee	28-24100	25.09.67
	(G-AVUS), N11C Cancelled 18.04.12 as PWFU		11.05.09
	Marsh Barton, Exeter		
	Stored Exeter Surplus, Bankers Yard 12.14		
G-AVUZ	Piper PA-32-180 Cherokee Six	32-40302	29.09.67
	N11C Ceesix Ltd Jersey		18.04.19E
G-AVVC	Cessna F172H	F172-0443	29.09.67
	M Grover tr Victor Charlie Flying Group		
	Durham Tees Valley		04.02.19E
	Built by Reims Aviation SA		
G-AVVO[M]	Avro 652A Anson 19 Series 2	34219	06.10.67
	VL348 Cancelled 16.09.72 by CAA As 'VL348'		06.10.67
	With Newark Air Museum, Winthorpe		
G-AVWA	Piper PA-28-140 Cherokee	28-23660	19.10.67
	N11C SFG Ltd Old Buckenham		06.03.19E
G-AVWD	Piper PA-28-140 Cherokee	28-23700	19.10.67
	N11C M Howells Woolston Moss, Warrington		12.09.19E
G-AVWI	Piper PA-28-140 Cherokee	28-23800	19.10.67
	N11C L M Middleton Cranfield		24.09.19E
G-AVWL	Piper PA-28-140 Cherokee	28-24000	19.10.67
	N11C D H Kirkwood tr G-AVWL Group		
	Durham Tees Valley		06.11.18E
G-AVWM	Piper PA-28-140 Cherokee	28-24005	19.10.67
	P E Preston tr G-AVWM Group Southend		24.07.19E
	Operated by Southend Flying Club		
G-AVWO	Piper PA-28R-180 Cherokee Arrow	28R-30205	19.10.67
	N11C S S Bamrah Biggin Hill 'Lovely Girl'		27.03.19E
G-AVWR	Piper PA-28R-180 Cherokee Arrow	28R-30242	19.10.67
	N11C R W Scarr tr G-AVWR Flying Group		
	Dunkeswell		23.07.19E

G-AVWT	Piper PA-28R-180 Cherokee Arrow	28R-30362	19.10.67
	N11C A C Brett tr Whiskey Tango Flying Group		
	Cambridge		14.08.19E
G-AVWU	Piper PA-28R-180 Cherokee Arrow	28R-30380	19.10.67
	N11C M Ali & S Din Cranfield		07.02.19E
G-AVWV	Piper PA-28R-180 Cherokee Arrow	28R-30404	19.10.67
	N11C R V Thornton Perth		18.10.19E
G-AVWY	Sportavia-Putzer Fournier RF4D	4031	26.10.67
	S A W Becker Goodwood		19.09.19P
G-AVXA	Piper PA-25-235 Pawnee C	25-4244	26.10.67
	N4576Y The South Wales Gliding Club Ltd Usk		19.07.19E
	Rebuilt using new frame – c/n unknown		
G-AVXD	Nipper T.66 RA.45 Series 3	S109	26.10.67
	J A Brompton Eddsfield, Octon Lodge Farm, Thwing		06.08.19P
	Built by Slingsby Aircraft Co Ltd as c/n 1606		
	for Nipper Aircraft Ltd		
G-AVXF	Piper PA-28R-180 Cherokee Arrow	28R-30044	26.10.67
	N11C A D C McNeile tr GAVXF Group North Weald		17.04.19E
G-AVXW	Druine D.62B Condor	RAE/625	03.11.67
	C W A Holliday Breighton		25.02.19P
	Built by Rollason Aircraft and Engines Ltd		
G-AVXY	Auster AOP.9	'AUS/120'	07.11.67
	XK417 G J Siddall Sandcroft Farm, Messingham		09.07.00P
	Officially registered as Frame no. AUS/120 &		
	probably AUS.10/92; on rebuild as 'XK417'		
	(NF 31.10.14) (		
G-AVYK	Beagle A.61 Terrier 3	B.642	20.11.67
	WJ357 R Burgun		
	Riding Bank Farm, Melbourne, Derby		28.08.93
	(NF 15.05.18)		
G-AVYL	Piper PA-28-180 Cherokee D	28-4622	24.11.67
	N11C Cotswold Aero Maintenance Ltd Cotswold		25.07.19E
G-AVYM	Piper PA-28-180 Cherokee D	28-4638	24.11.67
	N11C Camborne Insurance Services Ltd		
	Newquay Cornwall		28.11.18E
G-AVYP	Piper PA-28-140 Cherokee	28-24211	24.11.67
	Cancelled 03.07.03 by CAA		17.12.94
	Belfast Int'l *Stored dismantled 12.13*		
G-AVYR	Piper PA-28-140 Cherokee	28-24226	24.11.67
	Cancelled 18.09.13 as PWFU		31.10.12
	Fareham College *Inst frame at CEMAST 01.19*		
G-AVYS	Piper PA-28R-180 Cherokee Arrow	28R-30456	24.11.67
	N11C A N Harris Oxford		08.09.18E
G-AVYT	Piper PA-28R-180 Cherokee Arrow	28R-30472	24.11.67
	N11C M Bonsall Retford Gamston		24.04.19E
G-AVZB	LET Z-37 Cmelak	04-08	30.11.67
	OK-WKQ Cancelled 21.12.88 as WFU		05.04.84
	Wroughton *In Science Museum store 2013*		
G-AVZP	Beagle B.121 Pup Series 1	B121-008	19.12.67
	T A White Bagby		30.07.19R
G-AVZU	Cessna F150H	F150-0283	29.12.67
	R D Forster Beccles		30.07.17E
	Built by Reims Aviation SA; carries 'Rain Air (Beccles)'		
	on fin' stored 01.18 (NF 13.11.18)		
G-AVZV	Cessna F172H	F172-0511	29.12.67
	S E Waddy Shacklewell Lodge Farm, Empingham		26.10.18E
	Built by Reims Aviation SA		
G-AVZW	EAA Biplane Model B	PFA 1314	29.12.67
	C Edmondson Brimpton		17.07.19P
	Built by R G Maidment – project PFA 1314		

G-AWAA – G-AWZZ

G-AWAC	Gardan GY-80-180 Horizon	234	29.12.67
	P B Hodgson Enstone		11.06.04
	Built by Sud Aviation (NF 22.08.18)		
G-AWAJ	Beech D55 Baron	TE-536	01.01.68
	B F Whitworth Blackpool		26.06.18E
G-AWAU	Vickers FB.27A Vimy Replica	VAFA-02	08.01.68
	"H651" Cancelled 19.07.73 as PWFU		04.08.69
	RAF Stafford *In RAF Museum store 2018 as 'F8614'*		

G-AWAWᴹ Cessna F150F · F150-0037 · 05.01.68
OY-DKJ　Cancelled 16.05.90 as WFU · 08.06.92
Built by Reims Aviation SA, Wichita c/n 15063167
With Science Museum, South Kensington

G-AWAX　Cessna 150D · 15060153 · 05.01.68
OY-TRJ, N4153U　PropsnBlades BVBA
Sint-Truiden, Limburg, Belgium · 30.10.19E
Tailwheel conversion

G-AWAZ　Piper PA-28R-180 Cherokee Arrow · 28R-30512 · 08.01.68
N11C　D A C Clissett & R A Mailer　Stapleford · 17.04.19E

G-AWBA　Piper PA-28R-180 Cherokee Arrow · 28R-30528 · 08.06.68
N11C　Cancelled 02.03.12 as destroyed · 29.03.11
Fenland　*Stored for spares 04.15*

G-AWBB　Piper PA-28R-180 Cherokee Arrow · 28R-30552 · 08.01.68
N11C　P J Young　Neat's Ling Farm, Ringstead · 05.01.19E

G-AWBC　Piper PA-28R-180 Cherokee Arrow · 28R-30572 · 08.01.68
N11C　Anglo Property Services Ltd　Bournemouth · 09.05.19E

G-AWBG　Piper PA-28-140 Cherokee · 28-24286 · 08.01.68
N11C　I Herdis　Perth · 02.10.19E

G-AWBH　Piper PA-28-140 Cherokee · 28-24306 · 08.01.68
Cancelled 16.03.10 as PWFU · 31.12.04
Chopwell, Tyne & Wear
Stored dismantled at private house 07.15

G-AWBM　Druine D.31A Turbulent · PFA 1647 · 17.01.68
J J B Leasor　Eaglescott · 30.04.15P
Built by J R D Bygrave – project PFA 1647 (IE 28.01.18)

G-AWBS　Piper PA-28-140 Cherokee · 28-24331 · 22.01.68
N11C　R A Ballard　RAF Henlow · 21.02.19E

G-AWBUᴹ Morane Saulnier Type N replica · PPS/REP/7 · 22.01.68
Bianchi Aviation Film Services Ltd　Stow Maries · 28.04.04P
Built by D E Bianchi
As 'MS824' in French AF c/s (NF 05.11.18)

G-AWBX　Cessna F150H · F150-0286 · 22.01.68
R Nightingale　Dunkeswell · 02.05.13E
Built by Reims Aviation SA; stored 05.16 less marks
& white overall (NF 19.02.18)

G-AWCN　Reims FR172E Rocket · FR17200020 · 25.01.68
M Elsey　Bodmin · 07.12.18E

G-AWCP　Cessna F150H · F150-0354 · 29.01.68
C E Mason　Shobdon · 02.05.19E
Built by Reims Aviation SA; tailwheel conversion

G-AWCRᴹ Piccard Ax6 HAB · 6204 · 29.01.68
Cancelled 24.05.78 as WFU
With British Balloon Museum & Library, Newbury

G-AWDA　Nipper T.66 RA.45 Series 3 · S117 · 07.02.68
H Abraham　(Zurich, Switzerland) · 11.11.19P
Built by Slingsby Aircraft Co Ltd as c/n 1624
for Nipper Aircraft Ltd

G-AWDO　Druine D.31 Turbulent · PFA 1649 · 21.02.68
R N Crosland　Deanland · 18.05.19P
Built by R Watling-Greenwood – project PFA 1649

G-AWDR　Reims FR172E Rocket · FR17200004 · 21.02.68
B A Wallace　Nuthampstead · 20.06.19E

G-AWDU　Brantly B.2B · 481 · 23.02.68
N J M Freeman　(Menith Wood, Worcester) · 03.01.14E
(IE 20.12.16)

G-AWDW　Campbell-Bensen CB.8MS · DS1330 · 26.02.68
M R Langton　(Taplow. Maidenhead)
Built by D J C Summerfield (NF 10.04.18)

G-AWEA　Beagle B.121 Pup Series 1 · B121-012 · 28.02.68
OO-WEA, G-AWEA　T S Walker　Derby · 15.02.19R

G-AWEF　SNCAN Stampe SV.4C(G) · 549 · 29.03.68
F-BDCT　R A F Buchanan　Headcorn · 26.03.19E
Rebuilt with original fuselage ex G-ASHS (265) qv

G-AWEI　Druine D.62B Condor · RAE/628 · 06.03.68
P A Gange　Barton Ashes, Crawley Down · 26.02.19P
Built by Rollason Aircraft and Engines Ltd

G-AWEK　Sportavia-Putzer Fournier RF4D · 4071 · 06.03.68
A F & M P J Hill　Brighton City · 01.12.19P
Fitted with wing ex G-BIIF 2009

G-AWEL　Sportavia-Putzer Fournier RF4D · 4077 · 07.03.68
A B Clymo　Wolverhampton Halfpenny Green · 29.11.17P
(IE 17.09.18)

G-AWEP　Gardan GY-20 Minicab · PFA 1801 · 12.03.68
R K Thomas　Whaley Farm, New York · 05.02.14P
Built by F S Jackson to JB.01 Minicab standard
– project PFA 1801; overturned on landing Sittles Farm
06.07.13 (NF 11.05.15)

G-AWES　Cessna 150H · 15068626 · 20.03.68
N22933　R J Wills　Elstree · 27.07.19E

G-AWEV　Piper PA-28-140 Cherokee · 28-24460 · 21.03.68
N11C　W J Layzell　Old Buckenham · 01.01.10E
(NF 23.03.16)

G-AWEX　Piper PA-28-140 Cherokee · 28-24472 · 21.03.68
N11C　J W McLeavy　Beverley (Linley Hill) · 12.09.19E

G-AWEZ　Piper PA-28R-180 Cherokee Arrow · 28R-30592 · 21.03.68
N11C　Cancelled 30.11.17 as PWFU · 11.03.18
Stapleford　*Stored 05.18*

G-AWFB　Piper PA-28R-180 Cherokee Arrow · 28R-30689 · 21.03.68
N11C　J C Luke　Gloucestershire · 05.04.17E
(IE 04.10.18)

G-AWFC　Piper PA-28R-180 Cherokee Arrow · 28R-30670 · 21.03.68
N11C　A Simpson　Cumbernauld · 18.02.19E

G-AWFD　Piper PA-28R-180 Cherokee Arrow · 28R-30669 · 21.03.68
N11C　C G Sims　Enstone · 05.08.19E

G-AWFF　Cessna F150H · F150-0280 · 25.03.68
R A Marven　Coleman Green, St Albans · 16.05.19E
Built by Reims Aviation SA

G-AWFJ　Piper PA-28R-180 Cherokee Arrow · 28R-30688 · 26.03.68
N11C　Airways Aero Associations Ltd
Wycombe Air Park · 03.01.20E

G-AWFN　Druine D.62B Condor · RAE/629 · 27.03.68
C C Bland　Spanhoe · 12.10.18P
Built by Rollason Aircraft and Engines Ltd

G-AWFO　Druine D.62B Condor · RAE/630 · 27.03.68
R E & T A Major　Trevissick Farm, Porthtowan · 14.11.19P
Built by Rollason Aircraft and Engines Ltd

G-AWFP　Druine D.62B Condor · RAE/631 · 27.03.68
S J Westley　Cranfield · 30.09.16P
Built by Rollason Aircraft and Engines Ltd (NF 07.09.17)

G-AWFS　Piper PA-25-235 Pawnee C · 25-4368 · 29.03.68
N4648Y　Cancelled 15.02.74 as destroyed
Enstone
Believed to be bare metal frame in open store 08.17

G-AWFT　Jodel D.9 Bébé · PFA 932 · 29.03.68
W H Cole　Spilsted Farm, Sedlescombe
Built by W H Cole – project PFA 932 (NF 17.04.18)

G-AWFW　Jodel D.117 · 599 · 02.04.68
PH-VRE, F-BHXU　J Pool
Low Hill Farm, North Moor, Messingham · 30.08.14P
Built by Société Aéronautique Normande (NF 12.04.18)

G-AWFZ　Beech 19A Musketeer Sport · MB-323 · 03.04.68
N2811B　R E Crowe　Cranfield · 20.12.18E

G-AWGK　Cessna F150H · F150-0347 · 08.04.68
G E Allen　Sturgate · 05.07.18E
Built by Reims Aviation SA

G-AWGN　Sportavia-Putzer Fournier RF4D · 4084 · 09.04.68
R J Grimstead　Shipbourne Farm, Wisborough Green · 21.08.19P

G-AWGZ　Taylor JT.1 Monoplane · M1 · 17.04.68
A D Szymanski　Eshott · 10.05.19P
Built by J Morris – project PFA 1406

G-AWHBᴹ CASA 2111D (Heinkel 111H-16) · 049 · 14.05.68
Spanish AF B2I-57　Cancelled 11.09.74 as WFU,
restored 16.10.89 – cancelled 27.04.01 – to USA
As 'G-AWHB'
Officially quoted as c/n 167 ex Spanish AF B2I-37
With Flying Heritage and Combat Armor Museum,
Seattle, Washington

G-AWHC　Hispano HA.1112-M4L Buchón · 40/2 · 14.05.68
N1109G, G-AWHC, Spanish AF C4K-112
Air Leasing Ltd　Sywell · 17.12.18P
Built by Hispano Aviación
As '11 Red' in Luftwaffe c/s

G-AWHH　Hispano HA.1112-M1L Buchón · 145 · 14.05.68
N6036, G-AWHH, Spanish AF C4K-105
Anglia Aircraft Restorations Ltd　Duxford · 07.07.19P
Built by Hispano Aviación
As 'White 9' in Luftwaffe c/s

G-AWHK Hispano HA.1112-M1L Buchón   172   14.05.68
G-BWUE, N9938, G-AWHK, Spanish AF C4K-102
Historic Flying Ltd   Duxford   21.06.19P
Built by Hispano Aviación; contains fuselage of
Spanish AF C4K-154 c/n 223 during rebuild as G-BWUE
As 'Yellow 10' in Luftwaffe c/s

G-AWHM Hispano HA.1112-M1L Buchón   187   14.05.68
N90604, G-AWHM, Spanish AF C4K-99
Air Leasing Ltd   Sywell   16.05.19P
Built by Hispano Aviación
As '7 Yellow' in Luftwaffe c/s

G-AWHR Hispano HA.1112-M1L Buchón   220   14.05.68
N4109G, G-AWHR, Spanish AF C4K-152
Air Leasing Ltd   Sywell
Built by Hispano Aviación; on restoration 09.18 (NF 07.09.18)

G-AWHX Rollason Beta B.2   RAE/04   17.04.68
(G-ATEE)   T Jarvis   Hinton-in-the-Hedges
Built by Rollason Aircraft and Engines Ltd; includes
parts ex unfinished Phoenix Luton Beta Srs.1
G-ATEE project PFA 247 (NF 27.02.18)

G-AWHY Falconar F-11-3   PFA 1322   17.04.68
G-BDPB, (G-AWHY)
K J Butler tr Why Fly Group   Goodwood   03.05.19P
Built by A E Pritchard & A E Riley-Gale – project PFA 1322

G-AWIF Brookland Mosquito   LC-1   17.04.68
Cancelled 27.11.18 by CAA   07.01.82
Durham Tees Valley   On display 08.18

G-AWII Supermarine 349 Spitfire LF.Vc   WASP/20/223 25.04.68
AR501   Richard Shuttleworth Trustees   Old Warden   17.05.19P
Built by Westland Aircraft Ltd
As 'AR501:DU-E' in RAF 312 Sqdn c/s

G-AWIJ[M] Vickers Supermarine 329 Spitfire IIA   CBAF.14   25.04.68
P7350   Cancelled 29.02.84 to MOD
As 'P7350:XT-D' in RAF 41 Sqdn c/s
With Battle of Britain Memorial Flight, RAF Coningsby

G-AWIR Bushby-Long Midget Mustang   PFA 1315   30.04.68
R Ellingworth   Leicester   13.11.19P
Built by A F Jarman & Co Ltd – project PFA 1315

G-AWIT Piper PA-28-180 Cherokee D   28-4987   30.04.68
N11C   Gawit Ltd   Andreas   16.06.18E

G-AWIV Storey TSR.3   1325   30.04.68
J A Wardlow   Wickenby   18.06.08P
Built by J M Storey – project PFA 1325, officially
registered as c/n '1325'; on rebuild 07.18 (NF 15.04.16)

G-AWIW SNCAN Stampe SV.4B   532   02.05.68
F-BDCC   R E Mitchell   Sleap
(NF 13.10.17)

G-AWJB[M] Brighton MAB-65 HAB   MAB-3   03.05.68
Cancelled 04.12.70 on sale to Italy (ntu)
– subsequently HB-BOU (1) 02.73   As 'HB-BOU'
With British Balloon Museum & Library, Newbury

G-AWJE Nipper T.66 RA.45 Series 3   S121   08.05.68
K G G Howe   Brighton   28.08.17P
Built by Slingsby Aircraft Co Ltd as c/n 1628
for Nipper Aircraft Ltd (IE 30.09.17)

G-AWJV[M] de Havilland DH.98 Mosquito TT.35   xxxx   21.05.68
TA634   Cancelled 19.10.70 as WFU
As 'TA634:8K-K' in RAF 571 Sqdn c/s
With de Havilland Aircraft Museum, London Colney

G-AWJX Moravan Zlin Z-526 Trener Master 1049   22.05.68
M Baer   Luxters Farm, Hambleden   26.05.19E

G-AWKD Piper PA-17 Vagabond   17-192   27.05.68
F-BFMZ, N4892H   D Legg tr Kilo Delta Flying Group
Enstone   10.10.19P

G-AWKO Beagle B.121 Pup Series 1   B121-019   11.06.68
J Martin   North Weald   05.10.19R

G-AWKX Beech A65 Queen Air   LC-303   21.06.68
Cancelled 19.12.90 as PWFU   25.10.89
Brighton City   *Front fuselage used as instructional*
airframe at Northbrook College 10.14

G-AWLF Cessna F172H   F172-0536   27.06.68
C Robb   (Nutts Corner, Crumlin)   05.01.07
Built by Reims Aviation SA (NF 20.09.18)

G-AWLG SIPA 903   82   27.06.68
F-BGHG   S W Markham   Valentine Farm, Odiham
(NF 09.06.18)

G-AWLI Piper PA-22-150 Tri-Pacer   22-5083   01.07.68
N7256D   D Mack & A P S Maynard
tr North Hangar Group   Brighton City   23.04.19E
Official type data 'PA-22-150 Caribbean' is incorrect

G-AWLO Boeing Stearman E75 Kaydet (PT-13D)   75-5563   09.07.68
5Y-KRR, VP-KRR, 42-17400
N D Pickard   Little Gransden   13.08.19E
Operated by Sky High Advertising Ltd

G-AWLP Mooney M.20F Executive   680200   09.07.68
I C Lomax   Retford Gamston   07.07.00
(NF 20.03.18)

G-AWLR Nipper T.66 RA.45 Series 3   S125   09.07.68
T D Reid   Newtownards   16.05.05P
Built by Slingsby Aircraft Co Ltd as c/n 1662
for Nipper Aircraft Ltd (NF 15.03.18)

G-AWLS Nipper T.66 RA.45 Series 3   S126   09.07.68
G A Dunster & B Gallacher   (Loughton)
Built by Slingsby Aircraft Co Ltd as c/n 1663
for Nipper Aircraft Ltd (IE 06.03.15)

G-AWLX Auster 5J2 Arrow   2378   10.07.68
F-BGJQ, OO-ABZ   A E Taylor   (Friskney, Boston)
(NF 28.06.18)

G-AWLZ Sportavia-Putzer Fournier RF4D   4099   12.07.68
D M Bland tr Nympsfield RF4 Group   Gloucestershire   18.06.19P

G-AWMD Jodel D.11   PFA 904   19.07.68
J R Cooper   Rhigos   22.08.19P
Built by F H French – project PFA 904

G-AWMF Piper PA-18-150 Super Cub   18-8674   23.07.68
N4356Z   Booker Gliding Club Ltd   Wycombe Air Park   03.03.14E
Suffered loss of engine power on take-off at Wycombe
Air Park 18.05.13 & extensively damaged (NF 19.01.17)

G-AWMN Phoenix Luton LA-4A Minor   PFA 827   30.07.68
S Penfold   Waits Farm, Belchamp Walter   21.04.16P
Built by R Wilks – project PFA 827 (IE 04.10.18)

G-AWMO[M] Omega O-84 HAB   01   31.07.68
Cancelled 13.05.69 to OY-BOB
Built by Omega Aerostatics Ltd   As 'OY-BOB'
With British Balloon Museum & Library, Newbury

G-AWMR Druine D.31 Turbulent   43   01.08.68
B E Holz   (Berlin, Germany)   'Demelza'   10.04.18P
Built by S J Hargreaves – project PFA 1661
(IE 30.05.18)

G-AWMT Cessna F150H   F150-0360   01.08.68
Strategic Synergies Ltd   Inverness   05.08.16E
Built by Reims Aviation SA

G-AWNT Britten-Norman BN-2A Islander   32   02.08.68
Precision Terrain Surveys Ltd   Solent   07.09.18E

G-AWOE Aero Commander 680E   680E-753-41 05.06.68
N3844C   Cancelled 21.12.15 by CAA   22.06.10
Elstree   *In open stored 02.19*

G-AWOH Piper PA-17 Vagabond   17-191   06.08.68
F-BFMY, N4891H   K Downes & A Lovejoy
New Barn Farm, Crawley   24.07.03P
On rebuild 10.16 (NF 10.10.14)

G-AWOK[M] Sussex Gas Balloon   SARD.1   07.08.68
Cancelled 29.02.84 as WFU   *Withdrawn 1970*
Built by University of Sussex Ballooning Society
With British Balloon Museum & Library, Newbury

G-AWON[M] English Electric Lightning F.53   95291   09.08.68
G-27-56   Cancelled 09.68 – to R.Saudi AF 04.69
as 53-686 subsequently R Saudi AF 201, 203 &
1305   As '53-686'
With City of Norwich Aviation Museum

G-AWOT Cessna F150H   F150-0389   14.08.68
North East Aviation Ltd   Eshott   15.07.19E
Built by Reims Aviation SA

G-AWOU Cessna 170B   25829   16.08.68
VQ-ZJA, ZS-CKY, CR-ADU, N3185A
S Billington   Ashcroft   17.05.19E

G-AWPH Percival P.56 Provost T.1   PAC/F/003   06.09.68
WV420   J A D Bradshaw
Hopkiln Farm, Three Mile Cross   16.11.18P

G-AWPJ Cessna F150H F150-0376 09.09.68
Global Aviation Ltd Humberside 17.01.19E
Built by Reims Aviation SA; operated by
Humberside Flying Club

G-AWPN Shield Xyla 2 13.09.68
J P Gilbert Stow Maries 19.08.19P
Built by G W Shield – project PFA 1320

G-AWPU Cessna F150J F150-0411 18.09.68
Westair Flying Services Ltd Blackpool 06.11.18E
Built by Reims Aviation SA

G-AWPW Piper PA-12 Super Cruiser 12-3947 23.09.68
N78572, NC78572 AK Leasing (Jersey) Ltd Jersey 26.12.18E

G-AWPY^M Campbell-Bensen B.8M CA.314 20.09.68
Cancelled 19.03.09 by CAA
Mocked-up as 'Little Nellie' with 'G-ARZB' on tail
With Miami Auto Museum, Florida

G-AWPZ Andreasson BA-4B 1 24.09.68
SE-XBS J M Vening Goodwood 10.05.19P
Built by B Andreasson; Malmö Flygindustri (MFI)
c/n plate on rear fuselage (port) shows c/n 01

G-AWRP^M Servotec CR.LTH.1 Grasshopper II GB.1 14.10.68
Cancelled 05.12.83 as WFU 12.05.72
With The Helicopter Museum, Weston-super-Mare

G-AWRS^M Avro 652A Anson C.19 Series 2 '33785' 14.10.68
TX213 Cancelled 30.05.84 as PWFU As 'TX213' 10.08.73
With North East Land Sea and Air Museum, Usworth

G-AWRY Percival P.56 Provost T.1 PAC/F/339 29.10.81
XF836, 8043M A J House
(Hopgoods Green, Bucklebury, Reading)
As 'XF836' in RAF c/s (NF 20.03.18)

G-AWSA^M Avro 652A Anson C.19/2 '293483' 21.10.68
(N5054), G-AWSA, VL349
Cancelled 18.08.69 as sold in US – not delivered
As 'VL349:V7-Q'
With Norfolk & Suffolk Aviation Museum, Flixton

G-AWSH Moravan Zlin Z-526 Trener Master 1052 23.11.68
OK-XRH, G-AWSH P A Colman
Luxters Farm, Hambleden 01.08.19E

G-AWSL Piper PA-28-180 Cherokee D 28-4907 30.10.68
N11C A H & A H Brown Kings Farm, Thurrock 16.01.19E

G-AWSM Piper PA-28-235 Cherokee C 28-11125 30.10.68
N11C Aviation Projects Ltd Brighton City 01.11.18E
Official type data 'PA-28-235 Cherokee Pathfinder'
is incorrect

G-AWSN Druine D.62B Condor RAE/632 31.10.68
P C Hazlehurst tr The Condor Club Bellarena 19.07.19P
Built by Rollason Aircraft and Engines Ltd

G-AWSP Druine D.62B Condor RAE/634 31.10.68
M C Burlock Brimpton 08.07.19P
Built by Rollason Aircraft and Engines Ltd

G-AWSS Druine D.62B Condor RAE/636 31.10.68
N J Butler (Laurencekirk) 19.10.94P
Built by Rollason Aircraft and Engines Ltd (NF 11.10.17)

G-AWST Druine D.62B Condor RAE/637 31.10.68
J E Hobbs Sandown 08.10.19P
Built by Rollason Aircraft and Engines Ltd

G-AWSV^M Saro Skeeter AOP.12 S2/5107 31.10.68
XM553 Cancelled 23.05.95 as WFU As 'XM553' 22.02.95
With Yorkshire Air Museum, Elvington

G-AWSW Beagle D5/180 Husky 3690 01.01.68
XW635, G-AWSW C Tyers t/a Windmill Aviation
Spanhoe 02.07.19P
As 'XW635' in RAF white & red c/s

G-AWTJ Cessna F150J F1500419 08.11.68
Cancelled 18.05.10 by CAA 08.12.04
Elstree *In open store dismantled 02.19*

G-AWTL Piper PA-28-180 Cherokee D 28-5068 12.11.68
N11C Ravenair Aircraft Ltd Liverpool John Lennon 27.07.17E

G-AWTP Schleicher Ka 6E 4123 12.11.68
BGA 3426/FPV, N29JG, G-AWTP, RAFGSA 29
S A Smith Wycombe Air Park 'FPV' 11.09.19E

G-AWTS Beech 19A Musketeer Sport MB-412 14.11.68
OO-BGN, G-AWTS, N2763B
Golf Tango Sierra Ltd Swansea 13.02.15E
(IE 02.06.17)

G-AWTV Beech 19A Musketeer Sport MB-424 14.11.68
N2770B J Whittaker Welshpool 11.08.17E

G-AWTX Cessna F150J F150-0404 18.11.68
R D Forster Beccles 02.07.19E
Built by Reims Aviation SA; carries 'Rain Air (Beccles)'
on fin

G-AWUB Gardan GY-201 Minicab A205 22.11.68
F-PERX R A Hand RAF Barkston Heath 21.08.19P
Built by Aeronautique Havraise

G-AWUE Jodel DR.1050 Ambassadeur 299 22.11.68
F-BKHE F M Watson & K W Wood Insch 02.04.19P
Built by Société Aéronautique Normande

G-AWUJ Cessna F150H F150-0332 25.11.68
Hardman Aviation Ltd Blackbushe 14.03.19E
Built by Reims Aviation SA

G-AWUL Cessna F150H F150-0346 25.11.68
A J Baron Ventfield Farm, Horton-cum-Studley 19.05.19E
Built by Reims Aviation SA

G-AWUN Cessna F150H F150-0377 25.11.68
I Crookham tr G-AWUN Group Beverley (Linley Hill) 12.08.19E
Built by Reims Aviation SA

G-AWUP Cessna F150H F1500381 25.11.68
Cancelled 09.01.89 by CAA
Middletown, Co Armagh *Built by Reims Aviation SA*
Fuselage stored unmarked 10.13

G-AWUS Cessna F150J F1500394 25.11.68
Cancelled 04.07.94 by CAA 26.06.87
Nethershields Farm, Chapleton
Built by Reims Aviation SA; stored 08.16

G-AWUT Cessna F150J F150-0405 25.11.68
Aerospace Resources Ltd Redhill 24.04.19E
Built by Reims Aviation SA

G-AWUU Cessna F150J F150-0408 25.11.68
EI-BRA, G-AWUU D P Jones Top Farm, Croydon 06.09.19E
Built by Reims Aviation SA

G-AWUX Cessna F172H F1720577 25.11.68
Cancelled 30.04.18 as destroyed 18.06.17
Perranporth *Built by Reims Aviation SA*
Wreck for sale 04.18

G-AWUZ Cessna F172H F172-0587 25.11.68
J C McKenna tr Five Percent Flying Group
Brighton City 06.06.19E
Built by Reims Aviation SA

G-AWVA Cessna F172H F172-0597 25.11.68
Barton Air Ltd Manchester Barton 21.02.19E
Built by Reims Aviation SA

G-AWVC Beagle B.121 Pup Series 1 B121-026 27.11.68
(OE-CUP) P I Meaby Wellesbourne Mountford 31.01.16R

G-AWVE Jodel DR.1050-M1 Sicile Record 612 27.11.68
F-BMPQ E A Taylor (Southend-on-Sea) 18.05.00
Built by Centre-Est Aéronautique (NF 08.02.16)

G-AWVG AESL Airtourer T2 (115) 513 29.11.68
OO-WIC, G-AWVG C J Scholfield Top Farm, Croydon 17.01.19E
Assembled Glos Air Ltd

G-AWVJ Handley Page 137 Jetstream 1 206 29.11.68
(N1036S), G-AWVJ Cancelled 22.05.69 – sold to N1036S
Brighton City *(NTU & restored 07.73 as 'XX475';*
instructional airframe at Northbrook College 08.14

G-AWVN Aeronca 7AC Champion 7AC-6005 04.12.68
N2426E, NC2426E
P K Brown tr Champ Flying Group Rush Green 15.02.19P

G-AWVZ Jodel D.112 898 12.12.68
F-PKVL D C Stokes
Lower Withial Farm, East Pennard 14.09.19P
Built by J Coupe

G-AWWE Beagle B.121 Pup Series 2 B121-032 12.12.68
G-35-032 C H Boylan & A F Hayes tr Pup Flyers
Coventry 17.09.19R

G-AWWI Jodel D.117 728 13.12.68
F-BIDU J Pool
Low Hill Farm, North Moor, Messingham 27.08.13P
Built by Société Aéronautique Normande (IE 21.12.17)

G-AWWN Jodel DR.1050 Sicile 398 08.01.69
F-BLJA M A Baker Stows Farm, Tillingham 10.04.19P
Built by Société Aéronautique Normande

G-AWWO	Jodel DR.1050 Ambassadeur	552		08.01.69
	F-BLOI W G Brooks Bowden Farm, Burbage			
	'Metisse'			20.04.19P
	Built by Centre-Est Aéronautique			
G-AWWP	Aerosport Woody Pusher Mk.3	WA 163		07.01.69
	M S & R D Bird Glebe Farm, Stockton			
	Built by Woods Aeroplanes – project PFA 1323;			
	stored 05.17 (NF 03.04.18)			
G-AWWU	Reims FR172F Rocket	FR17200111		15.01.69
	V A Aldea & S Sabau			
	(Timisoara, Timis & Vladimirescu, Arad, Romania)			02.04.19E
G-AWXR	Piper PA-28-180 Cherokee D	28-5171		24.01.69
	N11C Aero Clube da Costa Verde			
	Espinho, Porto, Portugal			24.09.16E
G-AWXS	Piper PA-28-180 Cherokee D	28-5283		24.01.69
	N11C J E Rowley Hawarden			20.01.13E
	(NF 01.03.17)			
G-AWXZ	SNCAN Stampe SV.4C	360		30.01.69
	F-BHMZ, French Army, F-BCOI			
	Bianchi Aviation Film Services Ltd Turweston			08.08.14C
	(IE 25.08.15)			
G-AWYI	Royal Aircraft Factory BE.2c replica	001		05.02.69
	N1914B, G-AWYI			
	M C Boddington & S Slater Sywell			10.08.19P
	Built by C Boddington			
	As '687' in Royal Flying Corps c/s			
G-AWYJ	Beagle B.121 Pup Series 2	B121-038		10.02.69
	G-35-038 H C Taylor Popham			11.10.18R
G-AWYL	Robin DR.253B Regent	143		11.02.69
	T C van Lonkhuyzen Navan, RoI			24.09.18E
	Built by Centre-Est Aéronautique			
G-AWYO	Beagle B.121 Pup Series 1	B121-041		11.02.69
	G-35-041 B R C Wild Popham			07.08.19R
G-AWYV	BAC One-Eleven 501EX	BAC.178		11.02.69
	Cancelled 17.02.04 as PWFU 24.06.04			
	Alton Garden Centre *Front fuselage preserved as*			
	'The Departure Lounge Café' 03.15			
G-AWYYᴹ	Slingsby T.57 Sopwith Camel F.1 replica	1701		14.02.69
	'C1701', N1917H, G-AWYY			
	Cancelled 25.11.91 as WFU			01.09.85P
	As 'B6401'			
G-AWZJᴹ	Hawker Siddeley HS.121 Trident 3B Series 101	2311		14.01.69
	Cancelled 07.03.86 as WFU			12.09.86
	Front fuselage only			
	With Dumfries & Galloway Aviation Museum, Dumfries			
G-AWZKᴹ	Hawker Siddeley HS.121 Trident 3B Series 101	2312		14.01.69
	Cancelled 29.05.90 as WFU			14.10.86
	BEA Quarter Union Jack titles			
	With Runway Visitor Park, Manchester Airport			
G-AWZM	Hawker Siddeley HS.121 Trident 3B Series 101	2314		14.01.69
	Cancelled 18.03.86 as WFU			13.12.85
	Wroughton *WFU 13.12.85; British Airways titles*			
	In Science Museum store 2013			
G-AWZS	Hawker Siddeley HS.121 Trident 3B Series 101	2319		14.01.69
	Cancelled 18.03.86 as WFU			09.09.86
	Durham Tees Valley *In poor condition as fire trainer 04.17*			

G-AXAA – G-AXZZ

G-AXAB	Piper PA-28-140 Cherokee	28-20238		17.02.69
	EI-AOA, N6206W Bencray Ltd Blackpool			21.09.12E
	Operated by Blackpool and Fylde Aero Club (NF 04.10.18)			
G-AXAN	de Havilland DH.82A Tiger Moth	85951		21.02.69
	F-BDMM, French AF, EM720 A J Harrison Duxford			02.03.19E
	Built by Morris Motors Ltd			
	As 'EM720' in RAF c/s			
G-AXAS	Wallis WA-116/T/Mc	217		25.02.69
	Cancelled 03.08.16 as PWFU			16.07.13
	Old Warden *Stored 10.16*			
G-AXAT	Jodel D.117A	836		26.02.69
	F-BITJ D A White Kittyhawk Farm, Ripe			26.06.19P
	Built by Société Aéronautique Normande			
G-AXBG	Bensen B.8M	RC1		12.03.69
	G Mowll (Llanrug, Caernarfon)			
	Built by R Curtis (NF 03.09.15)			
G-AXBJ	Cessna F172H	F172-0573		12.03.69
	Central Horizon Partnership LLP Cumbernauld			08.05.19E
	Built by Reims Aviation SA			
G-AXBW	de Havilland DH.82A Tiger Moth	83595		12.03.69
	6854M, T5879 WJE Associates Ltd (Crowthorne)			04.05.18P
	As 'T-5879:RUC-W' in RAF Cambridge UAS silver c/s,			
	with yellow bands (NF 02.10.18)			
G-AXBZ	de Havilland DH.82A Tiger Moth	86552		14.03.69
	F-BGDF, French AF, PG643			
	W J de J Cleyndert Hill Farm, Durley			02.03.19P
	Built by Morris Motors Ltd; silver c/s with RAF fin flash			
G-AXCA	Piper PA-28R-200 Cherokee Arrow	28R-35053		18.03.69
	N11C A J Bale tr The Charlie Alpha Group			
	North Weald			22.05.19E
G-AXCG	Jodel D.117	510		19.03.69
	PH-VRA, F-BHXI D J Millin Dunkeswell			14.01.19P
	Built by Société Aéronautique Normande			
G-AXCI	Bensen B8M	CEW.1		20.03.69
	Cancelled 07.02.74 as WFU			
	(Bristol) *For sale from Bristol area 04.17*			
G-AXCY	Jodel D.117A	499		31.03.69
	F-BHXB S Marom Compton Abbas			
	'La Dame en Rouge'			22.07.19P
	Built by Société Aéronautique Normande			
G-AXDC	Piper PA-23-250 Aztec D	27.4169		08.04.69
	N6829Y Cancelled 29.11.10 by CAA			24.08.98
	(Stansted Abbots) *Advertised for sale 10.14*			
G-AXDI	Cessna F172H	F172-0574		14.04.69
	J R & M F Leusby Rochester			02.05.19E
	Built by Reims Aviation SA			
G-AXDK	Robin DR.315 Petit Prince	378		16.04.69
	D W Wiseman Blackpool			23.08.18E
	Built by Centre-Est Aéronautique			
G-AXDNᴹ	BAC Concorde	01		16.04.69
	Cancelled 10.11.86 as WFU			30.09.77
	Officially registered with Bristol c/n 13522			
	With Duxford Aviation Society			
G-AXDV	Beagle B.121 Pup Series 1	B121-049		18.04.69
	S R Hopkins Shobdon			07.08.19R
G-AXED	Piper PA-25-235 Pawnee B	25-3586		24.04.69
	OH-PIM, OH-CPY, N7540Z			
	Wolds Gliding Club Ltd Pocklington			04.06.18E
G-AXEHᴹ	Beagle Bulldog Series 125	B.125-001		25.04.69
	Cancelled 15.01.77 as WFU *Stored*			15.01.77
	Originally registered as Beagle B.125 Bulldog 1			
	With National Museum of Flight Scotland, East Fortune			
G-AXEI	Ward P 45 Gnome	P-45		25.04.69
	Cancelled 30.05.84 as WFU			
	Breighton *Built by M Ward; noted 12.16*			
G-AXEO	Scheibe SF25B Falke	4645		01.05.69
	D-KEBC P F Moffatt Milfield			28.06.07
	(NF 14.12.18)			
G-AXEV	Beagle B.121 Pup Series 2	B121-070		06.05.69
	D G Benson & D S Russell Gloucestershire			14.08.19R
G-AXFMᴹ	Servotec CR.LTH.1 Grasshopper II	GB.2		19.05.69
	Cancelled 05.12.83 as WFU			
	Completed as Ground-Running Rig			
	With The Helicopter Museum, Weston-super-Mare			
G-AXFN	Jodel D.119	980		19.05.69
	F-PHBU D W Garbe (Bath)			25.11.17P
	Built by M Ganu; force landed after take off from			
	Netherthorpe 06.05.17 & extensively damaged (NF 26.07.18)			
G-AXGE	SOCATA MS.880B Rallye Club	1353		23.05.69
	T R Scorer Compton Abbas			04.06.19E
G-AXGG	Cessna F150J	F150-0440		28.05.69
	A J Simpson Kilrush, RoI			30.10.19E
	Built by Reims Aviation SA			
G-AXGP	Piper J-3C-90 Cub (L-4J-PI)	12544		02.06.69
	F-BGPS, F-BDTM, 44-80248			
	A P Acres (Crawley Down, Crawley)			03.12.19P
	Fuselage No.12374; reported as c/n 9542 ex 43-28251			
	As '3681' in USAF c/s			
G-AXGR	Phoenix Luton LA-4A Minor	PAL 1125		02.06.69
	B A Schlussler Black Springs Farm, Castle Bytham			23.09.06P
	Built by R Spall (NF 09.10.18)			

G-AXGS Druine D.62B Condor   RAE/638   03.06.69
J Houlston tr SAS Flying Group   Compton Abbas   22.05.19P
Built by Rollason Aircraft and Engines Ltd

G-AXGV Druine D.62B Condor   RAE/641   03.06.69
R C Weston tr AXGV Group   (Knockholt, Sevenoaks)   20.02.19P
Built by Rollason Aircraft and Engines Ltd

G-AXGZ Druine D.62B Condor   RAE/643   03.06.69
G E Horder   Thruxton   23.09.19P
Built by Rollason Aircraft and Engines Ltd

G-AXHO Beagle B.121 Pup Series 2   B121-077   09.06.69
L H Grundy   Kings Farm, Thurrock   27.11.19R

G-AXHP Piper J-3C-65 Cub (*L-4J-PI*)   12932   09.06.69
F-BETT, NC74121, 44-80636   Witham (Specialist Vehicles)
Ltd   Ponton Heath Farm, Great Ponton   06.11.19P
Fuselage No.12762; Registered with c/n 'AF36506'
which is USAAC contract number
As '480636:A-58' in USAAC c/s

G-AXHR Piper J-3C-65 Cub (*L-4H-PI*)   10892   09.06.69
F-BETI, 43-29601   D J Dash   Great Oakley
'Ted's Mustang'   31.01.19P
As '329601:D-44' in USAAF olive drab &
invasion stripes c/s

G-AXHV Jodel D.117A   695   09.06.69
F-BIDF   J S Ponsford tr Derwent Flying Group
Tatenhill   22.08.19P
Built by Société Aéronautique Normande

G-AXIA Beagle B.121 Pup Series 1   B121-078   17.06.69
C K Parsons   Cotswold   'College of Aeronautics'   25.03.19R

G-AXIE Beagle B.121 Pup Series 2   B121-087   17.06.69
J P Thomas   Elstree   31.05.19R

G-AXIG[M] Scottish Aviation Bulldog Series 100/104   BH120/002   24.06.69
Cancelled 21.04.11 as PWFU   12.11.11
With National Museum of Scotland, Edinburgh

G-AXIO Piper PA-28-140 Cherokee B   28-25764   26.06.69
N11C   R Wallace   Denham   13.11.19E

G-AXIR Piper PA-28-140 Cherokee B   28-25795   26.06.69
N11C   J L Sparks   St Athan   12.02.19E
Operated by Horizon Flight Training

G-AXIX AESL Airtourer T4 (150)   A527   03.07.69
J C Wood   Shobdon   14.02.19E
Assembled Glos Air Ltd

G-AXJB Omega 84   04   09.07.69
Semajan Ltd t/a Southern Balloon Group
Saint-Michel, Gers, France
Initially flown as G-AXDT; noted inflated 05.16 (NF 25.03.15)

G-AXJH Beagle B.121 Pup Series 2   B121-089   11.07.69
D Collings tr Henry Flying Group   Popham   28.02.19R

G-AXJI Beagle B.121 Pup Series 2   B121-090   11.07.69
P L Parsons   Fenland   24.06.19R

G-AXJJ Beagle B.121 Pup Series 2   B121-091   11.07.69
D A, M L, P M & T M Jones   Derby   17.10.19R

G-AXJO Beagle B.121 Pup Series 2   B121-094   11.07.69
J A D Bradshaw   Hopkiln Farm, Three Mile Cross   17.09.15R
(NF 09.04.18)

G-AXJR Scheibe SF25B Falke   4652   04.07.69
D-KICD   R I Hey tr The Falke Syndicate   Nympsfield 19.10.18E

G-AXJV Piper PA-28-140 Cherokee B   28-25572   14.07.69
N11C   L J Tickell tr Seahawk Flying Group
RNAS Culdrose   03.05.19E

G-AXJX Piper PA-28-140 Cherokee B   28-25990   14.07.69
N11C   Horizon Aviation Ltd   Cotswold   04.10.19E

G-AXKH Phoenix Luton LA-4A Minor   PAL 1316   21.07.69
M E Vaisey   (Hemel Hempstead)
Built by M E Vaisey – project PFA 823 (NF 14.10.14)

G-AXKJ Jodel D.9 Bébé   SAS.002   22.07.69
K D Doyle   (Broadstairs)   08.01.19P
Built by Southdown Aero Services Ltd
– project PFA 941: originally project PFA 928B

G-AXKO Westland-Bell 47G-4A   WA720   22.07.69
G-17-5   M Gallagher   (Ballinamore, Co Leitrim, Rol) 04.12.18E

G-AXKS[M] Westland-Bell 47G-4A   WA.723   22.07.69
G-17-8   Cancelled 22.04.82 as WFU   21.09.82
With Museum of Army Flying, AAC Middle Wallop

G-AXKX Westland-Bell 47G-4A   WA728   22.07.69
G-17-13   R A Dale   (Ontario, Canada)   16.09.19E

G-AXLI Nipper T.66 RA.45 Series 3   S131   25.07.69
P R Howson   (Trowbridge)   03.09.19P
Built by Slingsby Aircraft Co Ltd as c/n 1701 for
Nipper Aircraft Ltd; force landed near Farleigh, Bath
11.01.19 & substantially damaged

G-AXLJ Nipper T.66 RA.45 Series 3   S132/1708   24.07.69
OO-WBR, HB-SPN, G-AXLJ
R J Hodder   Eastfield Farm, Manby
Built by Slingsby Aircraft Co Ltd (NF 11.08.15)

G-AXLS Jodel DR.105A Ambassadeur   86   31.07.69
F-BIVR   J J Boon tr Axle Flying Club   Popham   03.06.19P
Built by Société Aéronautique Normande

G-AXLZ Piper PA-18 Super Cub 95 (*L-18C-PI*)   18-2052   31.07.69
PH-NLB, R Netherland AF R-45, 8A-45, 52-2452
Perryair Ltd   (Brighton City)   13.06.16E
Fuselage No.18-2065; crashed on take-off Brighton
City 18.07.16 & substantially damaged; fuselage
removed, wings hangared (NF 08.11.17)

G-AXMA Piper PA-24 Comanche   24-3467   05.08.69
N8214P   B C Faulkner   Thruxton   25.05.19E

G-AXMT Bücker Bü.133C Jungmeister   46   19.08.69
D-EIBU, G-AXMT, N133SJ, G-AXMT, HB-MIY,
Swiss AF U-99   R A Fleming & A J E Smith   Breighton 05.06.19P
Built by AG Fur Dornier-Flugzeuge
In Swiss A/F c/s as 'U-99'

G-AXMW Beagle B.121 Pup Series 1   B121-101   19.08.69
DJP Engineering (Knebworth) Ltd   Audley End   27.12.17R

G-AXMX Beagle B.121 Pup Series 2   B121-103   19.08.69
VH-UPT, G-AXMX, G-35-103
G Van Aston tr Bob The Beagle Group   Hawarden   06.03.18R

G-AXNJ Jodel D.120 Paris-Nice   52   29.08.69
F-BHYO   J Pool   Mount Airey Farm, South Cave   14.01.19P
Built by Société des Etablissements Benjamin Wassmer

G-AXNN Beagle B.121 Pup Series 2   B121-104   03.06.69
A C Bloom tr November November Flying Group
Brighton City   17.09.18R

G-AXNP Beagle B.121 Pup Series 2   B121-106   03.09.69
J W Ellis & R J Hemmings   Sleap   05.11.18R

G-AXNR Beagle B.121 Pup Series 2   B121-108   03.09.69
J C Taylor tr AXNR Group   Audley End   10.06.19R

G-AXNS Beagle B.121 Pup Series 2   B121-110   03.09.69
D Beckwith & D Long tr Derwent Aero Group
Retford Gamston   16.01.19R

G-AXNW SNCAN Stampe SV.4C   381   11.09.69
F-BFZX, French AF   R S Grace   Sywell   15.10.19P

G-AXNZ Pitts S-1C   EBX2   16.09.69
D J Harvey tr November Zulu Group   Blackpool   31.01.19P
Built by W Berry & A Etheridge – project PFA 1383

G-AXOH SOCATA MS.894A Rallye Minerva 220   11062   17.09.69
D-EAGU   L C Clark   Roughay Farm, Lower Upham   12.06.19E

G-AXOJ Beagle B.121 Pup Series 2   B121-109   24.09.69
G-35-109   T J Martin tr Pup Flying Group   Rochester 12.09.19R

G-AXOT SOCATA MS.893A Rallye Commodore 180   11433   03.10.69
P Evans   Manor Farm, Dalscote   13.03.19E

G-AXOZ Beagle B.121 Pup Series 1   B121-115   07.10.69
N70290, G-AXOZ, G-35-115   E G Williams   Bagby   13.07.19R

G-AXPA Beagle B.121 Pup Series 1   B121-116   07.10.69
D-EATL, G-AXPA, G-35-116
C B Copsey   Rayne Hall Farm, Rayne   23.06.17R
(IE 28.07.17)

G-AXPC Beagle B.121 Pup Series 1   B121-119   07.10.69
PH-VRS, G-AXPC   T A White   Bagby   01.05.19R

G-AXPF Reims/Cessna F150K   F15000543   14.10.69
T W Gilbert   Enstone   22.04.02
Stored externally 09.15 less rudder & tailplane (NF 20.03.18)

G-AXPG Mignet HM.293   PFA 1333   14.10.69
W H Cole   Spilsted Farm, Sedlescombe
Built by W H Cole – project PFA 1333 (NF 30.05.18)

G-AXPN Beagle B.121 Pup Series 2   B121-123   20.10.69
G-35-123   R J Burgess & P Wood   Audley End   27.08.19E

G-AXPZ	Campbell Cricket	CA-320	03.11.69
	W R Partridge Tregolds Farm, St Merryn		24.07.09P
	(NF 09.03.11)		
G-AXRA[M]	Campbell Cricket	CA 321A	15.07.70
	Cancelled 25.10.90 by CAA		
	With The Helicopter Museum, Weston-super-Mare		
G-AXRC	Campbell Cricket	CA-323	03.11.69
	L R Morris (Kilkeel, Newry)		
	(NF 13.11.15)		
G-AXRP	SNCAN Stampe SV.4C	554	07.11.69
	G-BLOL, G-AXRP, F-BDCZ C C & C D Manning		
	(Bledlow, Princes Risborough)		05.09.18P
	Registered 12.02.85 as G-BLOL for rebuild but restored		
	as G-AXRP; official immediate p/i F-BDCZ is incorrect		
G-AXRR	Auster AOP.9	AUS/178	07.11.69
	XR241, G-AXRR, XR241 R B Webber		
	Trenchard Farm, Eggesford		31.05.19P
	Frame No.AUS/178		
	As 'XR241' in AAC camouflage c/s		
G-AXSC	Beagle B.121 Pup Series 1	B121-138	13.11.69
	G-35-138 M P Whitley Derby		28.04.07
	(NF 01.10.18)		
G-AXSD	Beagle B121 Pup	B121-139	13.11.69
	G-35-139 Cancelled 02.02.11 by CAA		10.05.08
	Langtoft, Yorkshire *On rebuild 01.18*		
G-AXSG	Piper PA-28-180 Cherokee E	28-5605	17.11.69
	N11C Seagull Aviation Ltd Perranporth		13.02.19E
G-AXSI	Reims/Cessna F172H	F17200687	19.11.69
	G-SNIP, G-AXSI R Lattanzi		
	(Monte Falco, Perugia, Italy)		24.10.19E
G-AXSM	Jodel DR.1051 Sicile	512	20.11.69
	F-BLRH M S & T R G Barnby Iden		10.04.19P
	Built by Centre-Est Aéronautique		
G-AXSW	Reims/Cessna FA150K Aerobat	FA1500003	25.11.69
	R J Whyham Blackpool		07.11.19E
G-AXSZ	Piper PA-28-140 Cherokee B	28-26188	26.11.69
	N11C D A Cowan tr White Wings Flying Group		
	White Waltham		04.01.19E
G-AXTA	Piper PA-28-140 Cherokee B	28-26301	26.11.69
	N11C P J Farrell tr G-AXTA Aircraft Group		
	Brighton City		24.03.19E
G-AXTC	Piper PA-28-140 Cherokee B	28-26265	26.11.69
	N11C W J Knott tr G-AXTC Group North Coates		28.03.19E
G-AXTJ	Piper PA-28-140 Cherokee B	28-26241	26.03.19
	N11C J P Nugent Newcastle, RoI		10.06.19E
G-AXTL	Piper PA-28-140 Cherokee B	28-26247	26.11.69
	N11C Bristol & Wessex Aeroplane Club Ltd Bristol		04.05.19E
G-AXTO	Piper PA-24-260 Comanche C	24-4900	28.11.69
	N9449P, N9705N D L Edwards		
	Dunkeswell *'Betsy Baby'*		02.04.19E
	Official p/i N9449 is incomplete		
G-AXUA	Beagle B.121 Pup Series 1	B121-150	04.12.69
	G-35-150 P Wood (Wendens Ambo, Saffron Walden)		05.06.08
	(NF 12.11.18)		
G-AXUB	Britten-Norman BN-2A Islander	121	04.12.69
	5N-AIJ, G-AXUB, N859JA, G-51-47		
	Headcorn Parachute Club Ltd Headcorn		28.08.19E
G-AXUC	Piper PA-12 Super Cruiser	12-621	05.12.69
	5Y-KFR, VP-KFR, ZS-BIN		
	Weald Air Services Ltd Headcorn		20.08.18E
G-AXUF	Reims/Cessna FA150K Aerobat	FA1500043	09.12.69
	K A O'Connor Dublin Weston, RoI		16.07.16E
	(NF 10.01.18)		
G-AXUJ	Auster 5J1 Autocrat	1957	11.12.69
	G-OSTA, G-AXUJ, PH-OTO		
	P J Gill Sandcroft Farm, Messingham		02.04.19P
G-AXUK	Jodel DR.1050 Ambassadeur	292	11.12.69
	F-BJYU G J Keegan tr Downland Flying Group (2Kl)		
	Deanland		12.04.19P
	Built by Société Aéronautique Normande		
G-AXVB	Reims/Cessna F172H	F17200703	22.12.69
	M Lazar (Reghin, Mures, Romania)		19.06.18E

G-AXVL[M]	Campbell Cricket	CA/328	01.01.70
	Cancelled 25.06.70 to Kuwait *As 'G-AXVL'*		
	Believed with Military Museum, Damascus, Syria		
G-AXVM	Campbell Cricket	CA-329	01.01.70
	D M Organ Gloucestershire		14.06.19P
G-AXVN	McCandless M.4-6 Gyroplane	M4-6	05.01.70
	W R Partridge (Tregolds Farm, St Merryn)		
	(NF 12.03.12)		
G-AXVU[M]	Omega 84 HAB	09	07.01.70
	Cancelled 22.08.89 as WFU		28.04.77
	With British Balloon Museum & Library, Newbury		
G-AXVV	Piper J3C-65	10863	07.01.70
	F-BBQB, 43-29572 Cancelled 12.04.99 by CAA		16.06.73
	Rathcoole, RoI *Stored 06.16*		
G-AXWA	Auster AOP.9	B5/10/133	13.01.70
	XN437 C M Edwards (Welling)		
	(NF 10.04.18)		
G-AXWT	Jodel D.11	PFA 911	26.01.70
	C S Jackson (Handcross, Haywards Heath)		02.06.00P
	Built by C King & R C Owen – project PFA 911		
	(NF 20.11.15)		
G-AXWV	Robin DR.253 Regent	104	02.02.70
	F-OCKL R Friedlander & D C Ray		
	Manor Farm, Grateley		29.10.18E
	Built by Centre-Est Aéronautique		
G-AXWZ	Piper PA-28R-200 Cherokee Arrow	28R-35605	03.02.70
	N11C R Silcock tr Whisky Zulu Group Andrewsfield		21.02.19E
G-AXXC	Piel CP.301B Emeraude	117	04.02.70
	F-BJAT M Breen & D Carr (Cuffesgrange, Kilkenny)		02.01.19P
	Built by Ateliers Aeronautique Rousseau		
G-AXXP[M]	Bradshaw 76 (Ax7) HAB	RB.001	20.02.70
	Cancelled 09.09.81 WFU 02.77		
	Built by R F D Bradshaw		
	With British Balloon Museum & Library, Newbury		
G-AXXV	de Havilland DH.82A Tiger Moth	85852	24.02.70
	F-BGJI, French AF, DE992		
	Fly Tiger Moth Ltd White Waltham		29.08.19P
	Built by Morris Motors Ltd		
	As 'DE-992' in RAF camouflage c/s		
G-AXXW	Jodel D.11/	632	26.02.70
	F-BIBN R K G Delve Turweston		21.11.14P
	Built by Société Aéronautique Normande;		
	stored engineless 06.17 (IE 15.11.18)		
G-AXYK	Taylor JT.1 Monoplane	PFA 1409	02.03.70
	G V Wright Shobdon		09.08.19P
	Built by C Oakins – project PFA 1409		
G-AXYU	Jodel D.9 Bébé	547	05.03.70
	EI-BVE, G-AXYU P Turton (Holmes Chapel, Crewe)		13.09.01P
	Built by J A Littlechild (NF 14.12.18)		
G-AXYY	WHE Airbuggy	1004	10.03.70
	Cancelled 11.02.97 by CAA		08.11.87
	(Rye) *For sale as rebuild project 06.16*		
G-AXZD	Piper PA-28-180 Cherokee E	28-5609	12.03.70
	N11C Sirius Aviation Ltd Wycombe Air Park		15.03.19E
G-AXZH	Glasflügel Standard Libelle	82	12.03.70
	BGA 2247/DNL, RAFGSA 742, RAFGSA 16, G-AXZH		
	M C Gregorie Gransden Lodge *'123'*		06.05.18E
G-AXZK	Britten-Norman BN-2A-26 Islander	153	01.03.70
	V2-LAD, VP-LAD, G-AXZK, G-51-153		16.04.06
	Cancelled 25.02.11 by CAA		
	Bembridge *Fuselage stored 01.16*		
G-AXZM	Nipper T.66 RA.45 Series 3	1709	16.03.70
	G R Harlow (Hamsterley Mill, Rowlands Gill)		
	Built by Slingsby Aircraft Co Ltd (for Nipper Aircraft		
	Ltd; rebuild by S J Booth & A Young – project PFA 1378		
	(NF 10.07.18)		
G-AXZO	Cessna 180	31137	17.03.70
	N3639C B C Faulkner Thruxton		07.01.14E
	(NF 21.02.17)		
G-AXZP	Piper PA-E23-250 Aztec D	27-4464	17.03.70
	N13819 D M Harbottle Biggin Hill		19.05.18E
G-AXZT	Jodel D.117A	607	17.03.70
	F-BIBD P Guest (Leeds)		16.05.19P
	Built by Société Aéronautique Normande		

G-AXZU Cessna 182N Skylane 18260104 19.03.70
N92233 W Gollan Errol 05.12.19E

G-AYAA – G-AYZZ

G-AYAB Piper PA-28-180 Cherokee E 28-5804 24.03.70
N11C L Kretschmann (Erfurt, Germany) 19.10.18E

G-AYAC Piper PA-28R-200 Cherokee Arrow 28R-35606 24.03.70
N11C P J Spencer tr Fersfield Flying Group
Knettishall 05.04.19E

G-AYAJ^M Cameron O-84 HAB 11 31.03.70
Cancelled 01.02.90 as PWFU
Built by D A Cameron
With British Balloon Museum & Library, Newbury

G-AYAL^M Omega 56 HAB 10 02.04.70
Cancelled 18.10.84 by CAA 25.08.76
With British Balloon Museum & Library, Newbury

G-AYAN Cadet III Motor Glider 003 06.04.70
BGA 1224, RAFGSA.223 R Moyse Lasham
'Vintage Gliding Club' 07.11.18P
Rebuilt by P J Martin & D R Wilkinson – project
PFA 1385 from Slingsby T 31B (Frame no.
'SSK/F/C/776')

G-AYAR Piper PA-28-180 Cherokee E 28-5797 08.04.70
N11C P McKay Enstone 13.06.19E

G-AYAT Piper PA-28-180 Cherokee E 28-5801 08.04.70
N11C A Goodchild tr G-AYAT Flying Group Seething 28.07.19E

G-AYAW Piper PA-28-180 Cherokee E 28-5805 14.04.70
N11C S J Hornsby & R Jones
tr North East Flyers Group Eshott 15.07.19E

G-AYBG Scheibe SF25B Falke 4696 13.04.70
(D-KECJ) J E & S L Hoy t/a Anglia Sailplanes
(Dickleburgh, Diss) 04.04.97
(NF 19.07.16)

G-AYBP Jodel D.112 1131 16.04.70
F-PMEK A Gregori Strathaven 06.09.18P
Built by Aero Club du Rousillon

G-AYBR Jodel D.112 1259 16.04.70
F-BMIG I S Parker (Burnham-on-Crouch) 21.08.14P
Built by Société Wassmer Aviation (NF 21.04.16)

G-AYBX^M Campbell Cricket CA/331 20.04.70
Cancelled 01.09.70 – to Kuwait *As 'G-AYBX'*
With Military Museum, Alexandria, Egypt

G-AYCC Campbell Cricket CA-336 20.04.70
G W Auld (Erskine) 02.10.19P

G-AYCE Scintex CP.301-C Emeraude 530 20.04.70
F-BJFH A C Beech New Farm, Felton 28.01.19P
Built by Scintex Scintex

G-AYCF Reims/Cessna FA150K Aerobat FA150055 22.04.70
C G Applegarth Goodwood 15.07.19E

G-AYCG SNCAN Stampe SV.4C 59 24.04.70
F-BOHF, F-BBAE, French AF
G W Lynch Old Buckenham 19.12.14E
(NF 05.02.18)

G-AYCK SNCAN Stampe SV.4C(G) 1139 28.04.70
G-BUNT, G-AYCK, F-BANE, French Navy 1139
A A M & C W N Huke Manor Farm, Dinton 04.05.19P
Buit Atelier Industriel de l'Aéronautique d'Alger

G-AYCO Robin DR.360 Chevalier 362 29.04.70
F-BRFI R H Underwood Stow Maries 17.01.19E
Built by Centre-Est Aéronautique

G-AYCP Jodel D.112 67 30.04.70
F-BGKO J D Bradley Breighton 10.08.19P
Built by Société Aéronautique Normande

G-AYCT Reims/Cessna F172H F17200724 01.05.70
J R Benson Full Sutton 08.06.19E

G-AYDI de Havilland DH.82A Tiger Moth 85910 07.05.70
F-BDOE, French AF, DF174
E G & G R Woods Haw Farm, Hampstead Norreys 22.05.19P

G-AYDR SNCAN Stampe SV.4C 307 13.05.70
F-BCLG D J Ashley Dolafallen Farm, LLanwrthwl
(NF 11.10.17)

G-AYDV Coates Swalesong SA.II Series 1 PFA 1353 18.05.70
The Real Aeroplane Company Ltd Breighton 08.08.07P
Built by J R Coates – project PFA 1353;
on rebuild 12.16 (NF 30.10.18)

G-AYDX Beagle A.61 Terrier 2 B.647 20.05.70
VX121 T S Lee Spanhoe 30.03.19P

G-AYDY Phoenix Luton LA-4A Minor PAL 1302 21.05.70
J Dible (Stillorgan, Dublin, RoI) 07.01.16P
Built by L J E Goldfinch – project PFA 817 (IE 09.07.18)

G-AYDZ Robin DR.200 1 21.05.70
F-BLKV, F-WLKV C H Boyles tr Zero One Group
Enstone 19.12.18E
Built by Centre-Est Aéronautique

G-AYEB Jodel D.112 586 26.05.70
F-BIQR S A King & C Marshall tr Echo Bravo
Partnership Griffins Farm, Temple Bruer 28.08.19P
Built by Société des Etablissements Benjamin Wassmer

G-AYEE Piper PA-28-180 Cherokee E 28-5813 28.05.70
N11C Aliter Professional Ltd Alderney 24.07.19E

G-AYEF Piper PA-28-180 Cherokee E 28-5815 28.05.70
N11C C J Harris tr Pegasus Flying Group
Manchester Barton 31.05.19E

G-AYEG Falconar F-9 PFA 1321 29.05.70
R J Ripley Sackville Lodge Farm, Riseley 25.06.10P
Built by G R Gladstone – project PFA 1321 (IE 14.12.18)

G-AYEH Jodel DR.1050 Ambassadeur 455 08.06.70
F-BLJB T J N H Palmer Hill Farm, Nayland
'Jemima' 16.06.19P
Built by Société Aéronautique Normande

G-AYEJ Jodel DR.1050 Ambassadeur 253 01.06.70
F-BJYG J R M Hore tr The Bluebird Flying Group
Enstone 18.03.19P
Built by Société Aéronautique Normande

G-AYEN Piper J-3C-65 Cub (L-4H-PI) 9696 04.06.70
F-BGQD, (F-BGQA), French AF, 44-79888
C F Morris & P J Warde Grove Farm, Raveningham 06.08.18P
Fuselage No.12012: official identity s/n '43835' but,
probably, fuselages exchanged with F-BGQA during
conversion 1952/53

G-AYEO Dormois Jodel D.112 684 04.06.70
F-BIGG Cancelled 05.11.74 as PWFU
Manston *On rebuild 12.13*

G-AYEU Gyroflight Hornet 12 08.06.70
Cancelled 04.10.84 as WFU
(Falmouth) *Stored 06.16*

G-AYEW Jodel DR.1050 Sicile 443 11.06.70
F-BLMJ J R Hope Dunkeswell 23.06.19P
Built by Centre-Est Aéronautique

G-AYEY Cessna F150K F1500553 15.06.70
Cancelled 02.03.99 by CAA 14.10.89
Fareham College *Built by Reims Aviation SA*
Instructional frame at CEMAST 01.19

G-AYFA Scottish Aviation Twin Pioneer 3 538 15.06.70
Cancelled 16.05.91 as PWFU 24.05.82
Front fuselage only
With Dumfries & Galloway Aviation Museum, Dumfries

G-AYFC Druine D.62B Condor RAE/644 19.06.70
A R Chadwick Breighton 10.06.19P
Built by Rollason Aircraft and Engines Ltd

G-AYFD Druine D.62B Condor RAE/645 19.06.70
B G Manning Little Down Farm, Milson '94' 08.08.19P
Built by Rollason Aircraft and Engines Ltd

G-AYFE Druine D.62C Condor RAE/646 19.06.70
M Soulsby Selby House Farm, Stanton 04.06.19P
Built by Rollason Aircraft and Engines Ltd

G-AYFF Druine D.62B Condor RAE/647 19.06.70
H Stuart Morgansfield, Fishburn 22.12.19P
Built by Rollason Aircraft and Engines Ltd

G-AYFV Andreasson BA-4B 002 26.06.70
N J W Reid Solent 29.10.19P
Built by Crosby Aviation Ltd – project PFA 1359

G-AYGA Jodel D.117 436 30.06.70
F-BHNU J W Bowes Oxenhope 28.08.19P
Built by Société Aéronautique Normande

G-AYGB	Cessna 310Q	310Q-0111	02.07.70
	N7611Q Cancelled 23.06.94 by CAA		23.10.87
	Perth *Instructional frame 07.16*		
G-AYGC	Reims/Cessna F150K	F15000556	02.07.70
	J R Grainger tr Alpha Aviation Group		
	Manchester Barton		20.12.18E
G-AYGD	Jodel DR.1051 Sicile	515	03.07.70
	F-BLRE J F M Bartlett & J P Liber Oaksey Park		17.10.19P
	Built by Centre-Est Aéronautique		
G-AYGE	SNCAN Stampe SV.4C	242	06.07.70
	F-BCGM P Anderson Headcorn		21.05.19P
G-AYGG	Jodel D.120 Paris-Nice	184	10.07.70
	F-BJPH J M Dean Stoneacre Farm, Farthing Corner		24.03.19P
	Built by Société des Etablissements Benjamin Wassmer		
G-AYGX	Reims FR172G Rocket	FR17200208	15.07.70
	D A G Fraser New Farm, Felton *'Lady Dorothy'*		27.08.19E
G-AYHA	American AA-1 Yankee	AA1-0396	21.07.70
	N6196L G J Fricker & N T Oakman Duxford		27.09.19E
G-AYHS[M]	BAC 167 Strikemaster Mk.84	EEP/JP/1934	22.07.70
	N72445, XB-GKO, N21463, G-27-143, G-AYHS,		
	G-27-143		
	Cancelled 28.09.70 – to Singapore AF as 314 *As 'XR366'*		
	Plane Set 151		
	With Olympia Flight Museum, Olympia, Washington		
G-AYHX	Jodel D.117A	903	23.07.70
	F-BIVE L E Cowling Oxenhope		04.02.19P
	Built by Société Aéronautique Normande		
G-AYIA	Hughes 369HS *(500)*	990120S	29.07.70
	G D E Bilton (Monaco, Principality of Monaco)		16.07.88
	Badly damaged in south of France 01.06.88; sold in		
	New Zealand for spares 08.97)		
G-AYIG	Piper PA-28-140 Cherokee C	28-26878	31.07.70
	N11C J L Sparks St Athan		14.05.19E
G-AYII	Piper PA-28R-200 Cherokee Arrow	28R-35736	04.08.70
	N11C N P Wilson (Basingstoke)		11.05.19E
G-AYIJ	SNCAN Stampe SV.4B	376	04.08.70
	F-BCOM J H D Newman tr India Juliet Stampe Group		
	Headcorn		01.10.19E
G-AYJA	Jodel DR.1050 Ambassadeur	150	08.09.70
	F-BJJJ D M Blair RAF Mona		31.07.19P
	Built by Société Aéronautique Normande		
G-AYJB	SNCAN Stampe SV.4C(G)	560	08.09.70
	F-BDDF F J M & J P Esson Bere Farm, Warnford		
	'Odette'		14.11.19P
G-AYJD	Alpavia Fournier RF3	11	08.09.70
	F-BLXA M J Millar tr Juliet Delta Group Ringmer		19.04.19P
G-AYJP	Piper PA-28-140 Cherokee C	28-26403	15.09.70
	N11C Demero Ltd & Livingstone Skies Ltd		
	Hinton-in-the-Hedges		12.11.19E
G-AYJR	Piper PA-28-140 Cherokee C	28-26694	15.09.70
	N11C Turweston Flying School Ltd Turweston		20.05.19E
G-AYJY	Isaacs Fury II	PFA 1373	23.09.70
	G E Croft (Brant Broughton, Lincoln)		21.12.18P
	Built by A V Francis – project PFA 1373		
	As 'K2065' in RAF c/s		
G-AYKD	Jodel DR.1050 Ambassadeur	351	30.09.70
	F-BKHR K L & L S Johnson Lodge Farm, St Osyth		03.12.19P
	Built by Société Aéronautique Normande		
G-AYKG	Socata ST-10 Diplomate	117	30.09.70
	Cancelled 27.06.75 as PWFU		
	Turney Hill *Displayed at Tulleys Farm, 10.18*		
G-AYKJ	Jodel D.117A	730	06.10.70
	F-BIDX R J Hughes (Hepworth, Diss)		20.06.19P
	Built by Société Aéronautique Normande		
G-AYKK	Jodel D.117	378	06.10.70
	F-BHGM J M Whitham Crosland Moor		22.05.85P
	Built by Société Aéronautique Normande;		
	on rebuild 11.18 (NF 07.10.18)		
G-AYKS	Leopoldoff L.7 Colibri	125	08.10.70
	F-PCZX, F-APZQ W B Cooper		
	Walkeridge Farm, Overton		24.10.19P
G-AYKT	Jodel D.117	507	09.10.70
	F-BGYY, F-OAYY D I Walker Popham		19.04.19P
	Built by Société Aéronautique Normande		

G-AYKW	Piper PA-28-140 Cherokee C	28-26931	12.10.70
	N11C N Fallow tr Kilo Whiskey Group		
	Morgansfield, Fishburn		10.12.18E
G-AYKZ	SAI Kramme KZ-VIII	202	13.10.70
	HB-EPB, OY-ACB R E Mitchell Sleap		17.07.81P
	(NF 13.10.17)		
G-AYLA	AESL Airtourer T2 (115)	524	12.10.70
	C P L Jenkins Little Gransden		23.09.18E
	Assembled Glos Air Ltd		
G-AYLC	Jodel DR.1051 Sicile	536	12.10.70
	F-BLZG M R Coreth tr G-AYLC Flying Group		
	Wing Farm, Longbridge Deverill		15.06.19P
	Built by Centre-Est Aéronautique		
G-AYLF	Jodel DR.1051 Sicile	547	14.10.70
	F-BLZQ R Twigg RAF Wyton		29.11.19P
	Built by Centre-Est Aéronautique: official record as built		
	by Société Aéronautique Normande is incorrect		
G-AYLL	Jodel DR.1050 Ambassadeur	11	27.10.70
	F-BJHK G Bell Breighton		14.11.14P
	Built by Centre-Est Aéronautique (NF 08.08.17)		
G-AYLP	American AA-1 Yankee	AA1-0445	21.10.70
	EI-AVV, G-AYLP D Nairn Henstridge		15.06.11E
	In open store less engine 09.18 (NF 21.12.16)		
G-AYME	Sportavia-Putzer Fournier RF5	5089	06.11.70
	C A Foss tr Romeo Foxtrot Group Parham Park		11.08.18P
	(IE 04.10.18)		
G-AYMK	Piper PA-28-140 Cherokee C	28-26772	17.11.70
	N11C, (PT-DPU) B Hutchinson & R Quinn Blackpool		01.04.19E
G-AYMO[M]	Piper PA-23-250 Aztec C	27-2995	18.11.70
	5Y-ACX, N5845Y, (N5844Y)		
	Cancelled 27.11.03 as PWFU		19.09.13
	With City of Norwich Aviation Museum		
G-AYMP	Phoenix Currie Wot Special	PFA 3014	08.11.70
	R C Hibberd (Coate, Devizes)		04.10.94P
	Built by E H Gould – project PFA 3014 (IE 21.11.16)		
G-AYMR	Lederlin 380L Ladybug	EAA/55189	19.11.70
	P J Brayshaw Haddock Stone Farm, Markington		
	Built by J S Brayshaw – project PFA 1513 (NF 08.01.15)		
G-AYMU	Jodel D.112	1015	23.11.70
	F-BJPB M R Baker (Eastbourne)		05.06.92P
	(uilt by Société des Etablissements Benjamin Wassmer		
	(NF 07.10.18)		
G-AYMV	Western 20	002	23.11.70
	R G Turnbull Glasbury, Hereford *'Tinkerbelle'*		
	(NF 11.06.18)		
G-AYNA	Phoenix Currie Wot	PFA 3016	25.11.70
	D R Partridge Damyns Hall, Upminster		15.06.16P
	Built by R W Hart – project PFA 3016		
G-AYNF	Piper PA-28-140 Cherokee C	28-26778	03.12.70
	N11C, (PT-DPV) BW Aviation Ltd		
	Wellesbourne Mountford		21.12.18E
G-AYNJ	Piper PA-28-140 Cherokee C	28-26810	03.12.70
	N11C S Doherty East Midlands		25.02.20E
G-AYNN	Cessna 185B Skywagon	185-0518	11.12.70
	8R-GCC, VP-GCC, N2518Z Bencray Ltd Blackpool		25.09.16E
	(NF 04.10.18)		
G-AYNP[M]	Westland WS.55 Whirlwind HAR10	WA.71	14.12.70
	G-AYNP, ZS-HCY, G-AYNP, XG576		
	Cancelled 22.02.94 by CAA *As 'XG576:CU-570'*		27.10.85
	With Sammler und Hobbywelt Sammlung, Buseck, Germany		
G-AYOW	Cessna 182N Skylane	18260481	06.01.71
	N8941G R Warner Cambridge		13.08.19E
G-AYOZ	Reims/Cessna FA150L Aerobat	FA1500085	07.01.71
	P J Worrall Fenland		01.07.18E
G-AYPE	MBB Bölkow BÖ.209 Monsun 160RV	123	11.01.71
	D-EFJA Papa Echo Ltd Biggin Hill		05.12.19E
G-AYPG	Reims/Cessna F177RG Cardinal RG	F177RG0007	11.01.71
	D P McDermott Haverfordwest		07.08.19E
	Wichita c/n 177RG0102		
G-AYPH	Reims/Cessna F177RG Cardinal RG	F177RG0018	11.01.71
	M L & T M Jones Derby		27.05.07
	Wichita c/n 177RG0146; stored 05.17 (NF 10.04.18)		

G-AYPJ	Piper PA-28-180 Cherokee E	28-5821	12.01.71
	N11C R B Petrie Caernarfon		01.10.04
	(NF 18.05.18)		
G-AYPM	Piper PA-18 Super Cub 95 *(L-18C-PI)*	18-1373	13.01.71
	French Army 18-1373, 51-15373		
	A N R Houghton & J C Tempest		
	Ranksborough Farm, Langham		19.09.19P
	Fuselage No.18-1282		
	As '115373:A-373' in US Army c/s		
G-AYPO	Piper PA-18 Super Cub *(L-18C-PI)*	18-1615	13.01.71
	French Army 18-1615, 51-15615		
	A W Knowles Bodmin		25.07.19E
	Fuselage No.18-1325; rebuilt 1984 using OO-TSJ		
	c/n 18-1398 ex LN-TSJ, OO-HMH, 51-15398		
G-AYPS	Piper PA-18 Super Cub 95 *(L-18C-PI)*	18-2092	13.01.71
	French Army 18-2092, 52-2492		
	D Racionzer & P Wayman Inverness		26.06.19P
G-AYPU	Piper PA-28R-200 Cherokee Arrow B	28R-7135005	13.01.71
	N11C Monalto Investments Ltd Jersey		14.05.19E
G-AYPV	Piper PA-28-140 Cherokee D	28-7125039	13.01.71
	N11C The Ashley Gardner Flying Club Ltd		
	Isle of Man		29.06.19E
G-AYPZ	Campbell Cricket	CA-343	13.01.71
	A Melody (Uxbridge)		21.04.04P
	(NF 25.08.17)		
G-AYRC	Campbell Cricket		13.01.71
	(VP-Bxx), G-AYRC B L Johnson		
	(Stanwick, Wellingborough)		
	(NF 19.02.18)		
G-AYRG	Reims/Cessna F172K	F17200761	14.01.71
	I G Harrison Netherthorpe		28.03.19E
G-AYRH	GEMS MS892A Rallye Commodore 150	10558	14.01.71
	F-BNBX Cancelled 07.02.12 as TWFU		12.01.03
	Haverfordwest *Stored 07.13*		
G-AYRI	Piper PA-28R-200 Cherokee Arrow B	28R-7135004	15.01.71
	N11C J C Houdret White Waltham		04.01.19E
	Official type data 'PA-28R-200 Cherokee Arrow II'		
	is incorrect		
G-AYRL	Sportavia-Putzer SFS31 Milan	6606	19.01.71
	K M Fresson & A Hoskins (Storrington, Pulborough)		
	(NF 16.01.18)		
G-AYRM	Piper PA-28-140 Cherokee D	28-7125049	19.01.71
	N11C M J Luck Gloucestershire		15.10.07E
	(NF 11.10.16)		
G-AYRO	Reims/Cessna FA150L Aerobat	FA1500102	21.01.71
	AJW Construction Ltd Bournemouth		25.02.18E
	Stored 02.19		
G-AYRS	Jodel D.120 Paris-Nice	255	22.01.71
	F-BMAV L R H d'Eath Knettishall		13.06.19P
	Built by Société Wassmer Aviation		
G-AYRT	Reims/Cessna F172K	F17200777	22.01.71
	S Macfarlane Sherburn-in-Elmet		05.07.19E
G-AYSB	Piper PA-30 Twin Comanche C	30-1916	01.02.71
	N8760Y Charles Lock (1963) Ltd Stapleford		28.08.18E
G-AYSH	Taylor JT.1 Monoplane	PFA 1413	10.02.71
	C J Lodge Retreat Farm, Little Baddow		07.07.19P
	Built by C J Lodge – project PFA 1413		
G-AYSK	Phoenix Luton LA-4A Minor	PFA 832	17.02.71
	P A Gasson (Hersden, Canterbury)		24.05.05P
	Built by L Plant – project PFA 832 (NF 18.10.18)		
G-AYSX	Reims/Cessna F177RG Cardinal RG	F177RG0024	17.02.71
	M Clarke Stapleford		23.09.19E
	Wichita c/n 177RG0175		
G-AYSY	Reims/Cessna F177RG Cardinal RG	F177RG0026	17.02.71
	S A Tuer Bagby		06.11.19E
	Wichita c/n 177RG0180; for sale with		
	Flying Fox Aviation 11.18		
G-AYTAᴹ	SOCATA MS.880B Rallye Club	1789	19.02.71
	Cancelled 12.05.93 as WFU		07.11.88
	With Manchester Museum of Sciences & Industry		
G-AYTR	Piel CP.301A Emeraude	229	03.03.71
	F-BIMD M A Smith Eshott		26.10.18P
	Built by Société Menavia		
G-AYTT	Phoenix PM-3 Duet	PFA 841	04.03.71
	J K Houlgrave & R B Webber		
	Trenchard Farm, Eggesford		02.07.14P
	Built by A J Knowles – project PFA 841; officially		
	registered as 'Luton Minor III Duet' (IE 07.12.18)		
G-AYTV	Jurca MJ.2D Tempête	PFA 2002	10.03.71
	C W Kirk Jericho Farm, Lambley		29.09.14P
	Built by A Baggallay – project PFA 2002 (NF 06.04.17)		
G-AYUB	Robin DR.253B Regent	185	15.03.71
	P J Coward, EES Aviation Services Ltd &		
	Forbes Insurance Ltd Rothwell Lodge Farm, Kettering		27.02.19E
	Built by Centre-Est Aéronautique		
G-AYUH	Piper PA-28-180 Cherokee F	28-7105042	17.03.71
	N11C Broadland Flying Group Ltd Old Buckenham		25.03.19E
G-AYUJ	Evans VP-1 Series 2	PFA 1538	17.03.71
	T N Howard Barton Ashes, Crawley Down		
	'Unforgettable Juliet'		18.09.17P
	Built by J A Wills – project PFA 1538; made heavy		
	landing Barton Ashes, Crawley Down 13.07.17		
G-AYUM	Slingsby T61A Falke	1730	19.03.71
	M H Simms & N A Stone Shipdham		10.06.02
	(NF 08.09.14)		
G-AYUN	Slingsby T61A Falke	1731	19.03.71
	R J Watts tr G-AYUN Group Rattlesden		15.06.08E
	Stored 07.15 (NF 10.09.18)		
G-AYUP	Slingsby T61A Falke	1735	19.03.71
	XW983, G-AYUP P R Williams (Stow on the Wold)		15.07.96
	(NF 12.12.18)		
G-AYUR	Slingsby T61A Falke	1736	19.03.71
	C O'Mahoney (London SW11)		30.10.18E
G-AYUS	Taylor JT.1 Monoplane	PFA 1412	19.03.71
	J G W Newton (Seaford)		12.09.19P
	Built by D G J Barker – project PFA 1412		
G-AYUT	Jodel DR.1050 Ambassadeur	479	22.03.71
	F-BLJZ G Bell & S P Garton Breighton		23.04.19P
	Built by Société Aéronautique Normande		
G-AYUV	Reims/Cessna F172H	F17200752	26.03.71
	Justgold Ltd Blackpool		31.07.15E
	(NF 04.10.18)		
G-AYVO	Wallis WA-120 Series 1	K/602/X	06.04.71
	Cancelled 03.08.16 as PWFU		31.12.75
	Old Warden *Stored 10.16, displayed Sywell 09.18*		
G-AYVP	Aerosport Woody Pusher	181	06.04.71
	J R Wraight (Chatham)		
	Built by J R Wraight – project PFA 1344 (NF 14.10.16)		
G-AYWD	Cessna 182N Skylane	18260468	15.04.71
	N8928G S I Zarb tr Wild Dreams Group Leicester		21.01.19E
G-AYWH	Jodel D.117A	844	16.04.71
	F-BIVO D Kynaston Coldharbour Farm, Willingham		01.10.19P
	Built by Société Aéronautique Normande		
G-AYWM	AESL Airtourer T5 (Super 150)	A534	16.04.71
	M E Eavers tr Star Flying Group Gloucestershire		09.09.18E
G-AYWT	SNCAN Stampe SV.4C(G)	1111	21.04.71
	F-BLEY, F-BAGL S T Carrel White Waltham		11.12.18E
	Built Atelier Industriel de l'Aéronautique		
G-AYXP	Jodel D.117A	693	27.04.71
	F-BIDD G N Davies Shobdon		12.08.19P
	Built by Société Aéronautique Normande		
G-AYXS	SIAI Marchetti S.205-18/R	4-165	28.04.71
	OY-DNG M Llewellyn & B Vincent Top Farm, Croydon		21.08.15E
G-AYXTᴹ	Westland WS-55 Whirlwind HAS.7 (Series.2)	WA.167	28.04.71
	XK940 Cancelled 08.08.00 by CAA *As 'XK940'*		04.02.99
	With The Helicopter Museum, Weston-super-Mare		
G-AYXU	Champion 7KCAB Citabria	232-70	28.04.71
	N7587F E V Moffatt & J S Peplow		
	Woodlow Farm, Bosbury		28.03.18E
G-AYXV	Cessna FA150L	0117	29.04.71
	Cancelled 24.09.79 as WFU		
	Netherfield Farm, Chapleton		
	Built by Reims Aviation SA; stored 08.16		
G-AYXW	Evans VP1	xxxx	30.04.71
	Cancelled 07.06.02 by CAA		15.08.11
	Morgansfield, Fishburn *Built by J S Penny –*		
	project PFA/1544; stored 12.14		

G-AYYO Jodel DR.1050-M1 Sicile Record 622 11.05.71
EI-BAI, G-AYYO, F-BMPZ S A Daniels
tr Bustard Jodel Group MoD Boscombe Down 06.12.18P
Built by Centre-Est Aéronautique

G-AYYT Jodel DR.1050-M1 Sicile Record 587 13.05.71
F-BMGU O Prince Brighton 25.09.19P
Built by Centre-Est Aéronautique

G-AYYU Beech C23 Sundowner 180 M-1353 14.05.71
D M Powell Sturgate 22.12.18E

G-AYZH Taylor JT.2 Titch PFA 060-1316 21.05.71
T Jarvis Hinton-in-the-Hedges 'CATCH 22' 20.06.19P
Built by T D Gardner – project PFA 1316
– amended to PFA 060-1316

G-AYZI SNCAN Stampe SV.4C 15 24.05.71
(EI-…), G-AYZI, F-BBAA, French AF
R J & R J Anderson Tibenham 11.07.19P

G-AYZJᴹ Westland WS-55 Whirlwind HAS.7 WA.263 24.05.71
XM685 Cancelled 29.12.80 as WFU
As 'XM685:PO-513' Also c/n WAG/34
With Newark Air Museum, Winthorpe

G-AYZK Jodel DR.1050-M1 Sicile Record 590 24.05.71
F-BMGY G J McDill Westmoor Farm, Thirsk 08.10.06
Built by Centre-Est Aéronautique (IE 01.02.18)

G-AYZS Druine D.62B Condor RAE/650 04.06.71
P S Bates (Weldon, Corby) 06.08.19P
Built by Rollason Aircraft and Engines

G-AYZU Slingsby T61A Falke 1740 04.06.71
S Borthwick (Larbert) 10.06.07
(NF 23.08.16)

G-AYZW Slingsby T61A Falke 1743 04.06.71
I D Walton tr G-ZW Group Lleweni Parc 21.11.18E

G-AZAA – G-AZZZ

G-AZAB Piper PA-30 Twin Comanche B 30-1475 08.06.71
5H-MNM, 5Y-AGB M Nelson Sibson 15.11.19E

G-AZAJ Piper PA-28R-200 Cherokee Arrow B 28R-7135116 18.06.71
N11C P Woulfe Stapleford 18.07.19E
Official type data 'PA-28R-200 Cherokee Arrow II'
is incorrect

G-AZAUᴹ Servotec CR.LTH.1 Grasshopper II GB.3 21.06.71
Cancelled 05.12.83 as WFU *Incomplete Rig*
With The Helicopter Museum, Weston-super-Mare

G-AZAZᴹ Bensen B.8M RNEC.1 02.07.71
Cancelled 19.09.75 as WFU
Built by T E Davies
With Fleet Air Arm Museum, RNAS Yeovilton

G-AZBB MBB Bölkow BÖ.209 Monsun 160FV 137 01.07.71
D-EFJO J A Webb Farley Farm, Farley Chamberlayne 03.05.08
Stored 06.16 (NF 16.06.15)

G-AZBE AESL Airtourer T5 (Super 150) A535 05.07.71
B J Edmondson tr 607 Group
Shotton Colliery, Peterlee 19.05.17E
Active 09.18 (IE 03.08.18)

G-AZBHᴹ Cameron O-84 HAB 23 08.07.71
Cancelled 30.08.85 as WFU 31.03.85
With British Balloon Museum & Library, Newbury

G-AZBI Jodel D.150 Mascaret 43 12.07.71
F-BMFB R J Wald (Llwynhendy, Llanelli) 25.04.19P
Built by Société Aéronautique Normande

G-AZBL Jodel D.9 Bébé PFA 938 12.07.71
P A Gasson (Hersden, Canterbury)
Built by D S Morgans – project PFA 938 (NF 20.11.15)

G-AZBN Noorduyn AT-16-ND Harvard IIB 14A-1431 13.07.71
PH-HON, R Netherlands AF B-97, FT391, 43-13132
Swaygate Ltd Goodwood 13.11.19P
As 'FT391' in RAF c/s

G-AZBT Western 0-65 HAB 005 15.07.71
Cancelled 19.05.93 by CAA 09.04.76
Not Known *Inflated Pidley 05.16 'Hermes'*

G-AZBU Auster AOP.9 'AUS/183' 15.07.71
7862M, XR246 K Brooks tr Auster Nine Group
Coles Farm, Gaddesby 18.04.19P
Officially registered with Frame no. AUS/183
As 'XR246' in RAE c/s

G-AZCB SNCAN Stampe SV.4C(G) 140 21.07.71
F-BBCR M J Coward Brighton City 02.11.18E

G-AZCE Pitts S-1C 373H 26.07.71
R J Oulton (Tutshill, Chepstow)
Built by R J Oulton – project PFA 1527 (NF 02.03.18)

G-AZCK Beagle B.121 Pup Series 2 B121-153 30.07.71
P Crone Carlisle Lake District 22.04.18R

G-AZCL Beagle B.121 Pup Series 2 B121-154 30.07.71
J M Henry & Flew LLP Bournemouth 24.07.18R

G-AZCMᴹ Beagle B.121 Pup Series.150 B121-155 30.07.71
G-35-155 Cancelled 04.05.72 to HB-NAV
As 'HB-NAV:A' On loan from W Fern
With South Yorkshire Aircraft Museum, Doncaster

G-AZCN Beagle B.121 Pup Series 2 B121-156 30.07.71
HB-NAY, G-AZCN
E J Spencer tr Snoopy Flying Group Derby 21.08.18R

G-AZCP Beagle B.121 Pup Series 1 B121-158 30.07.71
(D-EKWA), G-AZCP K N St Aubyn Lydd 09.05.18R

G-AZCT Beagle B.121 Pup Series 1 B121-161 30.07.71
J C Metcalf Shacklewell Lodge Farm, Empingham 22.01.18R

G-AZCU Beagle B.121 Pup Series 1 B121-162 30.07.71
D W Locke Popham 23.05.19R

G-AZCV Beagle B.121 Pup Series 2 B121-163 30.07.71
HB-NAR, G-AZCV N R W Long Henstridge
'Great Circle Design' 25.07.18R

G-AZCZ Beagle B.121 Pup Series 2 B121-167 30.07.71
L Northover Cardiff 27.11.18R

G-AZDD MBB Bölkow BÖ.209 Monsun 150FF 143 03.08.71
D-EBJC C E Evans & J D Hall
tr Double Delta Flying Group Rochester 28.03.19E

G-AZDE Piper PA-28R-200 Cherokee Arrow B 28R-7135141 03.08.71
N11C Insight Aviation Group Ltd Bournemouth 20.04.08E
(NF 06.06.18)

G-AZDG Beagle B.121 Pup Series 2 B121-145 17.06.85
(G-BLYM), HB-NAM, (VH-EPT), G-35-145
P J Beeson Andrewsfield 21.03.18R

G-AZDJ Piper PA-32-300 Cherokee Six D 32-7140068 23.08.71
OY-AJK, G-AZDJ, N5273S Delta Juliet Ltd Cardiff 05.07.19E

G-AZDY de Havilland DH.82A Tiger Moth 86559 25.08.71
F-BGDJ, French AF, PG650
B A Mills Armshold Farm, Great Eversden 18.08.97
Built by Morris Motors Ltd (NF 13.10.15)

G-AZEF Jodel D.120 Paris-Nice 321 01.09.71
F-BNZS P W Armstrong tr G-AZEF Group
Griffins Farm, Temple Bruer 20.07.19P
Built by Société Wassmer Aviation

G-AZEG Piper PA-28-140 Cherokee D 28-7125530 01.09.71
N11C S Kennaugh Isle of Man 08.08.19E

G-AZERᴹ Cameron O-42 (Ax5) HAB 26 09.09.71
Cancelled 25.03.92 by CAA 15.05.81
With British Balloon Museum & Library, Newbury

G-AZEV Beagle B.121 Pup Series 2 B121-131 15.09.71
VH-EPM, G-35-131 A P Amor Popham 15.08.19R

G-AZEW Beagle B.121 Pup Series 2 B121-132 15.09.71
VH-EPN, G-35-132 D Ridley Deanland 07.09.18R

G-AZEY Beagle B.121 Pup Series 2 B121-136 15.09.71
HB-NAK, G-AZEY, VH-EPP, G-35-136
A H Cameron Popham 07.08.19R

G-AZFA Beagle B.121 Pup Series 2 B121-143 15.09.71
VH-EPR. G-35-143 M R Badminton Bagby 06.03.19R

G-AZFC Piper PA-28-140 Cherokee D 28-7125486 16.09.71
N11C M J Berry tr WLS Flying Group
White Waltham 24.05.19E

G-AZFI Piper PA-28R-200 Cherokee Arrow B 28R-7135160 21.09.71
N11C GAZFI Ltd Sherburn-in-Elmet 22.05.19E
Official type data 'PA-28R-200 Cherokee Arrow II'
is incorrect

G-AZFM Piper PA-28R-200 Cherokee Arrow B   28R-7135218   24.09.71
N11C   PL Photography Ltd   Cardiff   28.02.19E
Official data type 'PA-28R-200 Cherokee Arrow II'
is incorrect

G-AZGA Jodel D.120 Paris-Nice   144   30.09.71
F-BIXV   N J Owen & P Turton
Ash House Farm, Winsford   18.04.14P
Built by Société des Etablissements Benjamin Wassmer
(IE 27.02.17)

G-AZGC SNCAN Stampe SV.4C   120   04.10.71
F-BCGE   D J Ashley   Dolafallen Farm, Llanwrthwl
(NF 11.10.17)

G-AZGE SNCAN Stampe SV.4C   576   06.10.71
F-BDDV   D Capon & M Flint   Old Buckenham   01.12.15E
(NF 14.11.18)

G-AZGF Beagle B.121 Pup Series 2   B121-076   06.10.71
PH-KUF, G-35-076   G Van Aston & J W Ellis   Sleap   02.05.98
(NF 12.08.14)

G-AZGL SOCATA MS.894A Rallye Minerva 220   11929   07.10.71
The Cambridge Aero Club Ltd   Cambridge   23.02.19E

G-AZGY Piel CP.301B Emeraude   122   12.10.71
F-BRAA   R H Braithwaite   RAF Henlow   20.07.19P
Built by Ateliers Aeronautique Rousseau

G-AZGZ de Havilland DH.82A Tiger Moth   86489   13.10.71
F-BGCF, French AF, NM181   R J King   RAF Henlow   27.07.19P
Built by Morris Motors Ltd
As 'NM181' in RAF camouflage & yellow c/s

G-AZHB Robin HR.100/200B Royal   118   14.10.71
J P Armitage   Sandown   25.04.19E

G-AZHC Jodel D.112   585   18.10.71
F-BIQQ   T P Hope tr Aerodel Flying Group   Breighton   11.09.19P
Built by Société des Etablissements Benjamin Wassmer

G-AZHD Slingsby T61A Falke   1753   18.10.71
R J Shallcrass   Challock   04.09.15E

G-AZHH K & S SA.102.5 Cavalier   PFA 1393   20.10.71
M W Place   Full Sutton   05.06.19P
Built by D Buckle – project PFA 1393

G-AZHI AESL Airtourer T5 (Super 150)   A540   20.10.71
Flying Grasshoppers Ltd   Rochester   24.05.19E

G-AZHJ   SA Twin Pioneer Series 3   577   20.10.71
G-31-16, XP295   Cancelled 23.07.97 as TWFU   23.08.90
Compton Verney   Spares use 12.16

G-AZHK Robin HR.100/200B Royal   113   22.10.71
G-ILEG, G-AZHK   A Johnston tr The Bield Flying Group
Inverness   28.10.19E

G-AZHT AESL Airtourer 115   525   29.10.71
Aviation West Ltd   Nethershiclds Farm, Chapelton
Stored 08.16 (NF 08.08.18)

G-AZHU Phoenix Luton LA-4A Minor   PFA 839   01.11.71
J Owen   Hill Farm, Nayland   18.10.18P
Built by A E Morris – project PFA 839

G-AZHX Scottish Aviation Bulldog Srs 120/121   BH100/126   04.11.71
G-DOGE, G-AZHX, SE-LNO, Swedish Army 61022,
G-AZHX   T W Harris   Holmbeck Farm, Burcott   22.06.18E

G-AZIB SOCATA ST-10 Diplomate   141   04.11.71
W B Bateson   Blackpool   17.02.07
(NF 04.10.18)

G-AZII Jodel D.117A   848   12.11.71
F-BNDO, F-OBFO   D H G Cotter   Full Sutton   22.08.19P
Built by Société Aéronautique Normande

G-AZIJ Robin DR.360 Chevalier   634   15.11.71
L J Brian tr India Juliet Flying Group   Fenland   03.01.19E

G-AZILᴹ Slingsby T61A Falke   1756   16.11.71
M A Savage   Dumfries   13.10.14E
To Dumfries & Galloway Aviation Museum 02.19
(NF 09.02.18)

G-AZIP Cameron O-65   29   24.11.71
P G Dunnington tr Dante Balloon Group
Newtown, Hungerford   'BOAC Speedbird'   05.05.81A
(IE 10.04.18)

G-AZJC Sportavia-Putzer Fournier RF5   5108   30.11.71
D M Bland tr Seighford RF5 Group   Seighford   03.09.19P

G-AZJE Gardan GY-20 Minicab   JBE1   01.12.71
J Evans   Niton Undercliff, Ventnor
Built by J B Evans to JB.01 Minicab standard
– project PFA 1806 (NF 18.09.18)

G-AZJIᴹ Western O-65 HAB   007   02.12.71
Cancelled 19.05.93 by CAA
With British Balloon Museum & Library,
Newbury

G-AZJN Robin DR.300-140 Major   642   06.12.71
A A Annaev tr Wight Eagle Flying Group   Sandown   24.04.19E

G-AZJV Reims/Cessna F172L   F17200810   08.12.71
M W Smith tr GAZJV Flying Group   Exeter Int'l   23.03.19E

G-AZKE SOCATA MS.880B Rallye Club   1950   08.12.71
(LX-SDT)   Profit Invest Sp Zoo   (Wroclaw, Poland)   22.11.18E

G-AZKK Cameron O-56 HAB   32   13.12.71
Cancelled 12.02.10 as PWFU   23.12.82
Not Known   *Inflated Donnington Grove Club 01.19*

G-AZKP Jodel D.117   419   20.12.71
F-BHND   J Pool   (Barton-upon-Humber)   05.08.14P
Built by Société Aéronautique Normande

G-AZKR Piper PA-24 Comanche   24-2192   23.12.71
N7044P   S J McGovern   (Carlton Miniott, Thirsk)   17.03.17E
(IE 14.05.18)

G-AZKS American AA-1 Yankee   AA1-0334   23.12.71
N6134L   I R Matterface   Bournemouth   01.06.10E
Stored dismantled 10.14 (NF 17.04.15)

G-AZKW Reims/Cessna F172L   F17200836   23.12.71
G W Brown   Priors Farm, Peasemore   10.10.19E

G-AZKZ Reims/Cessna F172L   F17200814   23.12.71
R D Forster   Beccles   29.01.19E

G-AZLE Boeing Stearman A75N1 Kaydet (N2S-5)   75-8543   29.12.71
CF-XRD, N5619N, USN 43449
DH Heritage Flights Ltd   Compton Abbas   21.02.19E
As '1102:102' in US Navy c/s

G-AZLF Jodel D.120 Paris-Nice   230   30.12.71
F-BLFL   D C O'Dwyer   Maypole Farm, Chislet   27.06.18P
Built by Société Wassmer Aviation

G-AZLN Piper PA-28-180 Cherokee F   28-7105210   03.01.72
N11C   Enstone Sales & Services Ltd & J Logan
Enstone   27.11.18E

G-AZLPᴹ Vickers 813 Viscount   346   04.01.72
(ZS-SBT), ZS-CDT   Cancelled 19.12.86 as PWFU   03.04.82
Fuselage only
With North East Land Sea and Air Museum, Usworth

G-AZLS Vickers 813 Viscount   348   04.01.72
ZS-CDV, (ZS-SBV), ZS-CDV
Cancelled 19.12.86 as PWF   09.06.83 U
Durham Tess Valley   *On fire dump 04.17*

G-AZLV Cessna 172K Skyhawk   17257908   10.01.72
4X-ALM, N79138   A W Robson tr G-AZLV Flying Group
RAF Waddington   16.02.19E

G-AZLY Reims/Cessna F150L   F15000771   10.01.72
H Mackintosh   Old Hay Farm, Paddock Wood   04.10.16E

G-AZMC Slingsby T61A Falke   1757   12.01.72
P J R White   Enstone   10.09.13E
(NF 02.03.16)

G-AZMD Slingsby T61C Falke   1758   12.01.72
H Abraham   (Frome)   09.10.17E
(NF 15.02.18)

G-AZMJ American AA-5 Traveler   AA5-0019   27.01.72
W R Partridge   Tregolds Farm, St Merryn   28.09.17E
(IE 22.11.18)

G-AZMX   Piper PA-28-140 Cherokee   28-24777   07.02.71
SE-FLL, LN-LMK (3)   Cancelled 09.01.84 as PWFU   24.01.83
Ley Farm, Chirk   *Open store 09.17*

G-AZMZ SOCATA MS.893A Rallye Commodore 180   11927   08.02.72
J Palethorpe   Wolverhampton Halfpenny Green   05.08.19E

G-AZNAᴹ   Vickers 813 Viscount   350   08.02.72
(G-AZLU), ZS-CDX, (ZS-SBX), ZS-CDX
Cancelled 17.06.92 by CAA   *As 'G-AZNA'*   24. 08.90
At Kokorico Night Club, Eeklo-Gent, Belgium

G-AZNK SNCAN Stampe SV.4A   290   15.02.72
F-BKXF, F-BCGZ   I Noakes   (Uckfield)   'Globird'   09.09.10E
(NF 28.07.18)

G-AZNL	Piper PA-28R-200 Cherokee Arrow II	28R-7235006	16.02.72
	N11C B P Liversidge Elmsett		02.08.19E
G-AZNO	Cessna 182P Skylane	18261005	18.02.72
	N7365Q N A Baxter Sandtoft		31.05.19E
G-AZNT	Cameron O-84	34	21.02.72
	P Glydon Knowle, Bristol		05.06.85A
	(NF 13.11.18)		
G-AZOA	MBB Bölkow BÖ.209 Monsun 150FF	183	21.02.72
	D-EAAY M W Hurst Sleap		22.08.19E
G-AZOB	MBB Bölkow BÖ.209 Monsun 150FF	184	21.02.72
	D-EAAZ J A Webb Farley Farm, Farley Chamberlayne		
	Noted as derelict fuselage 04.15 (NF 16.06.15)		
G-AZOE	AESL Airtourer T2 (115)	528	21.02.72
	R Smith Stornoway		07.04.17E
	(IE 01.05.18)		
G-AZOF	AESL Airtourer T5 (Super 150)	A549	21.02.72
	C Goldsmith St Athan		22.05.19
G-AZOG	Piper PA-28R-200 Cherokee Arrow II	28R-7235009	21.02.72
	N11C S J Lowe Southend		02.03.19E
	Operated by Southend Flying Club		
G-AZOL	Piper PA-34-200 Seneca	34-7250075	28.02.72
	N4348T Stapleford Flying Club Ltd Stapleford		16.09.19E
G-AZOO[M]	Western O-65 HAB	015	01.03.72
	Cancelled 17.04.09 by CAA		06.06.77
	With British Balloon Museum & Library, Newbury		
G-AZOU	Jodel DR.1050 Sicile	354	07.03.72
	F-BJYX D Elliott & D Holl tr Horsham Flying Group		
	Wellcross Farm, Slinfold		09.07.19P
	Built by Société Aéronautique Normande		
G-AZOZ	Reims/Cessna FRA150L Aerobat	FRA1500136	07.03.72
	A Mitchell Earls Colne		17.04.18E
G-AZPA	Piper PA-25-235 Pawnee C	25-5223	07.03.72
	N8797L, N9749N Black Mountains Gliding Club		
	Talgarth		07.03.19E
G-AZPC	Slingsby T61C Falke	1767	07.03.72
	D Heslop & J M Kimberley Wormingford		22.10.18E
G-AZPF	Sportavia-Putzer Fournier RF5	5001	10.03.72
	D-KOLT E C Mort Manchester Barton		09.08.17P
G-AZPH[M]	Pitts S.1S	S1S-001-C	13.03.72
	N11CB Cancelled 08.01.97 as WFU *'Neil Williams'*		04.09.91
	Ground-looped landing Little Snoring 10.05.91		
	With Science Museum, South Kensington		
G-AZPX	Western O-31	011	20.03.72
	Zebedee Balloon Service Ltd Newtown, Hungerford		
	(IE 18.05.18)		
G-AZRA	MBB Bölkow BÖ.209 Monsun 150FF	192	21.03.72
	D-EAIH Alpha Flying Ltd White Waltham		15.02.19E
G-AZRH	Piper PA-28-140 Cherokee D	28-7125585	23.03.72
	N11C H B Carter tr Trust Flying Group Jersey		06.08.19E
G-AZRI	Payne Free Balloon	GFP1	21.03.72
	C A Butter & J J T Cooke		
	Marsh Benham & Urgup Nevsehir, Turkey		
	Built by G F Payne (IE 13.04.15)		
G-AZRK	Sportavia-Putzer Fournier RF5	5112	23.03.72
	A B Clymo & J F Rogers Shenington		26.11.18P
G-AZRL	Piper PA-18 Super Cub 95 (*L-18C-PI*)	18-1331	23.03.72
	OO-SBR, OO-HML, French Army 18-1331, 51-15331		
	P Cooper, I Laws & R D Potter Andrewsfield		13.05.18E
	Fuselage No.18-1213		
G-AZRM	Sportavia-Putzer Fournier RF5	5111	24.03.72
	M J Millar tr Romeo Mike Group Ringmer		13.08.18P
G-AZRN	Cameron O-84	28	28.03.72
	C J Desmet Brussels, Belgium		04.07.81A
	(NF 21.01.16)		
G-AZRS	Piper PA-22-150 Tri-Pacer	22-5141	28.03.72
	XT-AAH, F-OCGZ, French Army 22-5141, 'FMKAC', N10F		
	R H Hulls Manstage Farm, Boadbury *'Sandpiper'*		27.09.12E
	Official type data 'PA-22-150 Caribbean' is incorrect;		
	stored 01.15 (NF 31.05.18)		
G-AZRX	Sud-Aviation Gardan GY-80-160 Horizon	14	04.04.72
	F-BLIJ Cancelled 21.10.91 by CAA		20.02.92
	Southend-on-Sea *Displayed on golf course at*		
	Adventure Island, Southend Seafront, 01.19		

G-AZRZ	Cessna U206F	U20601803	04.04.72
	N9603G Cornish Parachute Club Ltd Perranporth		30.07.19E
G-AZSA	SNCAN Stampe SV.4B	1203	05.04.72
	V-61 M R Dolman (Cliddesden, Basingstoke)		02.12.10C
	Built by Société Stampe et Renard;		
	official c/n '64' is incorrect (NF 29.11.17)		
G-AZSC	Noorduyn AT-16-ND Harvard IIB	14A-1363	07.04.72
	PH-SKK, R Netherlands AF B-19, FT323, 43-13064		
	Goodwood Road Racing Company Ltd Goodwood		23.07.19E
	As '43:SC' in USAAF c/s		
G-AZSF	Piper PA-28R-200 Cherokee Arrow II	28R-7235048	10.04.72
	N11C Smart People Dont Buy Ltd		
	Doncaster Sheffield		15.07.19E
	Operated by Aero Flight Training		
G-AZSP[M]	Cameron O-84 HAB	43	18.04.72
	Cancelled 11.01.82 as WFU		22.03.82
	With British Balloon Museum & Library, Newbury		
G-AZTA	MBB Bölkow BÖ.209 Monsun 150FF	190	25.04.72
	D-EAIF E C Dugard & P A Grant Brighton City		21.06.19E
G-AZTF	Reims/Cessna F177RG Cardinal RG	F177RG0054	28.04.72
	R Burgun Derby		19.07.19E
G-AZTM	AESL Airtourer T2 (115)	530	28.04.72
	B J Edmondson tr Victa Restoration Group		
	Shotton Colliery, Peterlee		
	(NF 14.10.15)		
G-AZTS	Reims/Cessna F172L	F17200866	28.04.72
	Eastern Air Executive Ltd Sturgate		22.06.18E
G-AZTV	Stolp SA.500 Starlet	SSM 2	19.05.72
	G G Rowland Old Sarum		07.02.12P
	Built by S S Miles – project PFA 1584 (IE 16.12.18)		
G-AZUM	Reims/Cessna F172L	F17200863	11.05.72
	J A Latham tr Fowlmere Fliers Fowlmere		31.05.19E
G-AZUV[M]	Cameron O-65 HAB	41	12.05.72
	Cancelled 06.01.82 by CAA		23.06.83
	With British Balloon Museum & Library, Newbury		
G-AZUW[M]	Cameron A-140 HAB	45	12.05.72
	Cancelled 07.06.73 – to F-WTVO – subsequently		
	F-BTVO & 5Y-SIL *As '5Y-SIL'*		
	With British Balloon Museum & Library, Newbury		
G-AZUY	Cessna 310L	310L0012	15.05.72
	SE-FEC, LN-LMH, N2212F W B Bateson Blackpool		05.11.05
	(NF 04.10.18)		
G-AZUZ	Reims/Cessna FRA150L Aerobat	FRA1500146	16.05.72
	J T Bonsall & D J Parker Netherthorpe		08.02.19E
G-AZVA	MBB Bölkow BÖ.209 Monsun 150FF	177	16.05.72
	(D-EAAQ) M P Brinkmann		
	Bonn-Hangelar, Nordrhein-Westphalen, Germany		15.12.18E
G-AZVB	MBB Bölkow BÖ.209 Monsun 150FF	178	16.05.72
	(D-EAAS) R K Galbally & E W Russell Earls Colne		02.12.19E
G-AZVG	American AA-5 Traveler	AA5-0075	16.05.72
	E Dohrn Solent		26.12.18E
G-AZVI	SOCATA MS.892A Rallye Commodore 150	12039	06.05.72
	G C Jarvis Henstridge		20.08.16E
	Noted 09.18 (IE 07.08.18)		
G-AZVJ	Piper PA-34-200 Seneca	34-7250125	16.05.72
	N4529T Cancelled 09.02.09 as PWFU		21.08.03
	Headcorn *Open store derelict 10.16*		
G-AZVL	Jodel D.119	794	19.05.72
	F-BILB J C Metcalf Spanhoe		09.09.18P
	Built by Etablissement Valladeau		
G-AZVP	Reims/Cessna F177RG Cardinal RG	F177RG0057	22.05.72
	R Onger (Ostrava-Hulvaky, Czech Republic)		26.05.16E
G-AZVT[M]	Cameron O-84 HAB	40	30.05.72
	Cancelled 04.08.98 by CAA		02.06.78
	With British Balloon Museum & Library, Newbury		
G-AZWB	Piper PA-28-140 Cherokee E	28-7225244	05.06.72
	N11C P Alexander tr G-AZWB Flying Group		
	Oaksey Park		09.05.19E
G-AZWF	Jodel DR.1050 Ambassadeur	130	07.06.72
	F-BJJT J A D Reedie tr Cawdor Flying Group		
	Inverness		21.07.17P
	Built by Société Aéronautique Normande;		
	composite rebuild c.1975-81 included fuselage		
	of SAN DR.1050M F-BLJX c/n 492 (IE 03.12.18)		

G-AZWS	Piper PA-28R-180 Cherokee Arrow	28R-30749	08.06.72
	N4993J K M Turner Cotswold		16.08.19E
G-AZWT	Westland Lysander IIIA	Y1536	09.06.72
	RCAF 1582, V9552 Richard Shuttleworth Trustees		
	Old Warden		13.04.19P
	As 'V9367:MA-B' in (black) RAF 161 Sqdn c/s		
G-AZWY	Piper PA-24-260 Comanche C	24-4806	16.06.72
	N9310P H M Donnan (Troon)		20.05.19E
G-AZXBM	Cameron O-65	48	20.06.72
	Cancelled by CAA 05.07.18		06.05.81
	With British Balloon Museum & Library, Newbury		
G-AZXD	Reims/Cessna F172L	F17200878	20.06.72
	A M Dinnie Wycombe Air Park		19.10.18E
G-AZYA	Gardan GY-80-160 Horizon	57	07.07.72
	F-BLPT R G Whyte (Kilsby, Rugby)		04.06.08E
	Built by Sud Aviation (NF 04.12.18)		
G-AZYBM	Bell 47H-1	1538	04.07.72
	LN-OQG, SE-HBE, OO-SHW		
	Cancelled 22.04.85 as Destroyed *As 'OO-SHW'*		08.09.84
	On loan from E.D.ap Rees		
	With The Helicopter Museum, Weston-super-Mare		
G-AZYD	SOCATA MS.893A Rallye Commodore 180	10645	30.06.72
	F-BNSE Staffordshire Gliding Club Ltd		
	Kings Farm, Thurrock		07.12.15E
	Built by Gérance des Etablissements Morane-Saulnier		
	(GEMS); stored 10.17 (IE 12.02.16)		
G-AZYF	Piper PA-28-180 Cherokee B	28-5227	23.06.72
	N7813Mm, G-AZYF, 5Y-AJK, N7813N		
	SI Aviation Services Ltd (Parsons Green, St Ives)		01.11.19E
G-AZYLM	Portslade Free HAB	MK 17	10.07.72
	Cancelled 25.04.85 as PWFU		
	Built by Portslade School		
	With British Balloon Museum & Library, Newbury		
G-AZYS	Scintex CP.301-C1 Emeraude	568	07.07.72
	F-BJAY D G Drew & C G Ferguson		
	Jericho Farm, Lambley		20.07.18P
	Built by Société Menavia (IE 04.10.18)		
G-AZYU	Piper PA-23-250 Aztec E	27-4601	13.07.72
	N13983 M E & M H Cromati & F & N P Samuelson		
	Sandown		08.06.19E
G-AZYY	Slingsby T61A Falke	1770	12.07.72
	T A Smith (Saltburn-by-Sea)		27.11.18P
G-AZYZ	Wassmer WA.51A Pacific	30	14.07.72
	F-OCSE W A Stewart (Dounby, Orkney)		04.09.13P
	(NF 08.05.18)		
G-AZZO	Piper PA-28-140 Cherokee	28-22887	18.07.72
	N4471J Cancelled 08.08.12 by CAA		06.08.03
	Stapleford *Stored 10.13*		
G-AZZR	Reims/Cessna F150L	F15000690	24.07.72
	LN-LJX D Petrie Perth		19.10.19E
G-AZZV	Reims/Cessna F172L	F17200883	18.07.72
	R Wyse tr ZV Flying Group Trevethoe Farm, Lelant		07.07.19E
G-AZZX	Cessna FRA150L Aerobat	FRA1500152	27.07.72
	Cancelled 09.05.01 by CAA		16.08.88
	Plaistows Farm, St Albans *Built by Reims Aviation SA*		
	Noted 07.16		
G-AZZZ	de Havilland DH.82A Tiger Moth	86311	27.07.72
	F-BGJE, French AF, NL864		
	S W McKay RAF Henlow		30.05.19E
	Built by Morris Motors Ltd		

G-BAAA – G-BAZZ

G-BAAD	Evans VP-1	PFA 1540	27.07.72
	C S Whitwell tr The Breighton VP-1 Group Breighton		20.09.11P
	Built by R W Husband – project PFA 1540;		
	on rebuild 12.16) (NF 02.05.14)		
G-BAAF	Manning-Flanders MF.1 replica	PPS/REP/8	27.07.72
	Bianchi Aviation Film Services Ltd (Stow Maries)		06.08.96E
	Built by Personal Plane Services Ltd;		
	no external markings (NF 06.11.18)		
G-BAAI	SOCATA MS.893A Rallye Commodore 180	10705	31.07.72
	F-BOVG R D Taylor Thruxton		11.09.00
	Noted 04.18 (NF 09.05.18)		

G-BAAW	Jodel D.119	366	11.08.72
	F-BHMY P J Newson tr Alpha Whiskey Flying Group		
	Monewden		29.06.19P
	Built by Etablissement Valladeau		
G-BABC	Reims/Cessna F150L	F15000831	15.08.72
	P Tribble RAF Henlow		09.11.18E
G-BABD	Reims/Cessna FRA150L Aerobat	FRA1500153	03.08.72
	R Warner (Whittlesford)		23.07.14E
	(NF 04.12.15)		
G-BABE	Taylor JT.2 Titch	PEB.01	03.08.72
	E R White (Aston, Sheffield)		14.11.14P
	Built by P E Barker – project PFA 1394 (NF 12.10.16)		
G-BABG	Piper PA-28-180 Cherokee C	28-2031	15.08.72
	PH-APU, N7978W R Nightingale Bristol		22.08.19E
G-BABK	Piper PA-34-200 Seneca	34-7250219	18.08.72
	PH-DMN, G-BABK, N5203T		
	Stapleford Flying Club Ltd Stapleford		18.11.19E
G-BABYM	Taylor JT.2 Titch	JRB-2	21.08.72
	Cancelled 04.12.96 by CAA		10.10.91
	Built by J Bygraves – project PFA 3204		
	With Norfolk & Suffolk Aviation Museum, Flixton		
G-BACB	Piper PA-34-200 Seneca	34-7250251	25.08.72
	N5354T Milbrooke Motors Ltd North Weald		15.11.19E
G-BACE	Sportavia-Putzer Fournier RF5	5102	25.08.72
	(PT-DVZ), D-KCID		
	N P Harrison tr G-BACE Fournier Group Dunkeswell		05.07.19E
G-BACJ	Jodel D.120 Paris-Nice	315	01.09.72
	F-BNZC J M Allan tr Wearside Flying Association		
	Morgansfield, Fishburn		26.11.18P
	Built by Société Wassmer Aviation		
G-BACL	Jodel D.150 Mascaret	31	04.09.72
	F-BSTY, CN-TYY P I Morgans Haverfordwest		06.07.17P
	Built by Société Aéronautique Normande		
G-BACN	Reims/Cessna FRA150L Aerobat	FRA1500161	04.09.72
	F Bundy Bodmin		16.11.19E
G-BACO	Reims/Cessna FRA150L Aerobat	FRA1500163	04.09.72
	R Haverson Old Buckenham		23.05.19E
G-BADC	Rollason Beta B.2A	xxxx	07.09.72
	A P Grimley Woolston Moss, Warrington		20.06.19P
	Built by H M Mackenzie – project PFA 002-10140; originally		
	registered to J J Feely with c/n JJF.1 (project PFA 1384)		
G-BADH	Slingsby T61A Falke	1774	06.09.72
	M J Lake Palukyns, Lithuania		07.09.18E
G-BADJ	Piper PA-E23-250 Aztec E	27-4841	11.09.72
	N14279 K A W Ashcroft (Eaton Socon)		02.08.08E
	(NF 06.04.17)		
G-BADM	Druine D.62B Condor	xxxx	08.09.72
	D J Wilson tr Delta Mike Condor Group		
	Compton Abbas		03.06.19P
	Built by M Harris & K Worksworth – project		
	PFA 049-11442 using uncompleted Rollason-built frame		
G-BADU	Cameron O-56 HAB	47	18.09.72
	Cancelled 19.05.93 by CAA		29.03.78
	Not Known *Inflated Pidley 04.18*		
G-BADV	Brochet MB.50 Pipistrelle	78	13.09.72
	F-PBRJ W B Cooper (Micheldever, Winchester)		
	Built by A Bouriquat; on rebuild 2017 (NF 10.04.18)		
G-BADW	Pitts S-2A	2035	21.09.72
	R E Mitchell Sleap		16.09.95
	Built by Aerotek Inc (NF 13.10.17)		
G-BADZ	Pitts S-2A	2038	21.09.72
	R F Warner Oaksey Park		23.04.19E
	Built by Aerotek Inc		
G-BAEB	Robin DR.400-160 Chevalier	733	19.09.72
	G D Jones (Ramsey, Isle of Man)		20.04.12E
	(NF 13.03.18)		
G-BAEE	Jodel DR.1050-M1 Sicile Record	579	29.09.72
	F-BMGN R Little Jackrells Farm, Southwater		15.07.19P
	Built by Centre-Est Aéronautique		
G-BAEM	Robin DR.400-120 Petit Prince	728	25.09.72
	M A Webb White Waltham		05.06.19E
G-BAEN	Robin DR.400-180 Régent	736	25.09.72
	A Aveling tr Regent Aero Lasham		27.11.19E

G-BAEO	Reims/Cessna F172M	F17200911	14.09.72
	Sherburn Engineering Ltd Sherburn-in-Elmet		12.04.19E
	Rebuilt with original fuselage & parts ex G-YTWO		
G-BAEP	Reims/Cessna FRA150L Aerobat	FRA1500170	14.09.72
	Peterborough Flying School Ltd Sibson		15.11.19E
G-BAER	LeVier Cosmic Wind	106	14.09.72
	A G Truman Lasham		18.09.06P
	Built by R S Voice – project PFA 1571 (NF 17.12.18)		
G-BAET	Piper J-3C-65 Cub (*L-4H*)	11605	26.09.72
	OO-AJI, 43-30314 C J Rees Valley Farm, Winwick		10.11.05P
	Fuselage No.11430		
	As '330314' in USAAF c/s (IE 22.11.18)		
G-BAEV	Reims/Cessna FRA150L Aerobat	FRA1500173	27.09.72
	Hull Aero Club Ltd Beverley (Linley Hill)		18.05.14E
	Undercarriage collapsed landing Beverley (Linley Hill)		
	26.09.15 & substantially damaged; noted behind hangars		
	05.16) (IE 23.10.15)		
G-BAEW	Reims/Cessna F172M	F17200914	27.09.72
	N12798 London Denham Aviation Ltd Denham		09.04.94
	(NF 06.12.17)		
G-BAEY	Reims/Cessna F172M	F17200915	28.09.72
	High Level Photography Ltd Gloucestershire		10.06.19E
G-BAEZ	Reims/Cessna FRA150L Aerobat	FRA1500169	28.09.72
	Donair Flying Club Ltd East Midlands		03.04.13E
	(NF 03.06.16)		
G-BAFA	American AA-5 Traveler	AA5-0201	06.10.72
	N6136A C F Mackley Sleap		31.08.01
	(NF 18.01.16)		
G-BAFG	de Havilland DH.82A Tiger Moth	85995	13.10.72
	F-BGEL, French AF, EM778		
	Tiger Moth Experience Ltd Sherburn-in-Elmet		22.01.19E
	Built by Morris Motors Ltd		
G-BAFL	Cessna 182P Skylane	18261469	15.08.72
	N21180 R B Hopkinson & A S Pike		
	Wellesbourne Mountford		09.04.19E
G-BAFT	Piper PA-18-150 Super Cub	18-5340	03.08.72
	(D-E...), French Army 18-5340, N10F		
	J F Hammond (Market Rasen)		23.07.19E
G-BAFU	Piper PA-28-140 Cherokee	28-20759	11.10.72
	PH-NLS C E Taylor Dunkeswell		09.12.19E
G-BAFV	Piper PA-18 Super Cub 95 (*L-18C-PI*)	18-2045	24.10.72
	PH-WJK, R Netherlands AF R-40, 8A-40, 52-2445		
	S J & T F Thorpe Coldharbour Farm, Willingham		26.07.19E
	Fuselage No.18-2055		
G-BAFW	Piper PA-28-140 Cherokee	28-21050	24.10.72
	PH-NLT A J Peters Derby		04.06.11E
	Stored 05.17 (IE 04.10.18)		
G-BAFX	Robin DR.400-140 Earl	739	30.10.72
	M C R Sims t/a MCRS Aviation Goodwood		22.08.19E
G-BAGB	SIAI Marchetti SF.260	107	20.10.72
	(D-E...), LN-BIV V Balzer Airport Baden-Baden, Germany		
	03.11.19E		
G-BAGC	Robin DR.400-140 Earl	737	13.10.72
	J R Roberts Rufforth		05.04.19E
G-BAGF	Jodel D.92 Bébé	59	13.11.72
	F-PHFC J Hoskins Earls Colne		
	Built by Aéro-club de Basse Moselle (NF 06.05.16)		
G-BAGG (2)	Piper PA-32-300 Cherokee Six	32-7340186	07.12.73
	N9562N Aero Rentals Ltd Earls Colne		16.12.18E
G-BAGN	Reims/Cessna F177RG Cardinal RG	F177RG0068	24.10.72
	F T Marty (Le Bugue, France)		28.10.18E
G-BAGR	Robin DR.400-140 Earl	753	30.10.72
	J D Last Caernarfon		01.04.19E
G-BAGS	Robin DR.400-120 Dauphin 2+2	760	30.10.72
	M Whale (Swindon)		16.01.03
	(NF 16.01.15)		
G-BAGT	Helio H.295 Super Courier	1288	31.10.72
	CR-LJG D C Hanss Spanhoe		01.06.18E
	As '66-374:EO' in Vietnam War camouflage c/s of		
	5th Special Operations Squadron, USAF (IE 18.11.18)		
G-BAGX	Piper PA-28-140 Cherokee	28-23633	30.10.72
	N3574K I Lwanga Denham		02.01.19E
G-BAGY	Cameron O-84	54	17.10.72
	P G Dunnington tr Dante Balloon Group		
	Newtown, Hungerford		16.06.81A
	(IE 10.04.18)		
G-BAHD	Cessna 182P Skylane	18261501	25.10.72
	N21228 Cancelled 27.08.15 as destroyed		04.09.15
	Alchester *Cockpit for sale as simulator 06.17*		
G-BAHF	Piper PA-28-140 Cherokee Fliteliner	28-7125215	30.10.72
	N431FL Warwickshire Aviation Ltd		
	Wellesbourne Mountford		20.08.19E
G-BAHH	Wallis WA-121/Mc	K701X	07.11.72
	Cancelled 03.08.16 as PWFU		14.02.06
	Old Warden *Stored 10.16*		
G-BAHI	Cessna F150H	F150-0330	06.11.72
	PH-EHA M Player t/a MJP Aviation & Sales		
	Shannon, RoI		14.12.07E
	Built by Reims Aviation SA; fuselage displayed Atlantic		
	AirVenture Shannon Aviation Museum 05.16 (NF 12.12.14)		
G-BAHJ	Piper PA-24-250 Comanche	24-1863	06.11.72
	PH-RED, N6735P K Cooper		
	Wolverhampton Halfpenny Green		18.12.18E
G-BAHL	Robin DR.400-160 Chevalier	704	08.11.72
	F-OCSR J B McVeighty Breighton		16.05.11E
	Noted 12.16 (NF 17.02.15)		
G-BAHP	Volmer VJ.22 Sportsman	PFA 1313	09.11.72
	G K Holloway tr Seaplane Group Aboyne		18.10.93P
	Built by J P Crawford – project PFA 1313 (NF 20.02.18)		
G-BAHS	Piper PA-28R-200 Cherokee Arrow II	28R-7335017	09.11.72
	N15147 A R N Morris Shobdon		20.10.16E
G-BAHX	Cessna 182P Skylane	18261588	16.11.72
	N21363 M D J Moore Eaglescott		23.09.14E
	Stored 09.17 (IE 11.11.16)		
G-BAIG	Piper PA-34-200 Seneca	34-7250243	21.11.72
	OY-BSU, G-BAIG, N5257T Mid-Anglia Flight Centre		
	Ltd t/a Mid-Anglia School of Flying Little Staughton		07.05.19E
G-BAIH	Piper PA-28R-200 Cherokee Arrow II	28R-7335011	21.11.72
	N11C M G West Cotswold		09.08.19E
G-BAIK	Reims/Cessna F150L	F15000903	22.11.72
	D A & T M Jones Derby		18.04.13E
	(NF 24.08.18)		
G-BAIR	Thunder Ax-7-77 HAB	003	27.11.72
	Cancelled 26.02.90 by CAA		
	Not Known *Inflated Pidley 05.16*		
G-BAIS	Reims/Cessna F177RG Cardinal RG	F177RG0069	13.11.72
	R M Graham & E P Howard tr Cardinal Syndicate		
	Seething		15.02.19E
G-BAIW	Reims/Cessna F172M	F17200928	14.11.72
	Jindalee Ltd Perranporth		28.08.19E
G-BAIZ	Slingsby T61A Falke	1776	27.11.72
	R G Sangster tr Falke Syndicate Hinton-in-the-Hedges		20.11.10E
	(NF 16.08.17)		
G-BAJA	Reims/Cessna F177RG Cardinal RG	F177RG0078	29.11.72
	Aviation Facilities Rotterdam BV		
	Lelystad, Netherlands		06.05.19E
G-BAJB	Reims/Cessna F177RG Cardinal RG	F177RG0080	29.11.72
	J D Loveridge Guernsey		31.10.19E
G-BAJE	Cessna 177 Cardinal	17700812	30.11.72
	N29322 C Quist Lelystad, Netherlands		07.01.19E
G-BAJN	American AA-5 Traveler	AA5-0259	29.11.72
	John Wong Aviation Ltd Cranfield		27.06.19E
G-BAJO	American AA-5 Traveler	AA5-0260	29.11.72
	Montgomery Aviation Ltd Welshpool		19.12.19E
G-BAJR	Piper PA-28-180 Cherokee Challenger	28-7305008	01.12.72
	N11C A C Sturgeon Old Warden		09.10.18E
	Official type data 'PA-28-180 Cherokee' is incorrect		
	Ditched off Whitesands Beach, Pembroke 04.09.18		
G-BAJV	K&S SA.102.5 Cavalier	xxxx	08.12.72
	Cancelled 08.12.81 as WFU		
	Leicester College *Built by AJ Starkey – project*		
	PFA 01-10002; being completed 12.16 by students		
G-BAJZ	Robin DR.400-120 Dauphin 2+2	759	04.12.72
	Prestwick Flying Club Ltd Glasgow Prestwick		10.04.19E

G-BAKD Piper PA-34-200 Seneca 34-7350013 28.11.72
N1378T Cancelled 17.11.11 as PWFU 30.12.07
Headcorn *Open store derelict 10.16*

G-BAKH Piper PA-28-140 Cherokee F 28-7325014 12.12.72
N11C British Northwest Airlines Ltd
(Manchester Barton) 16.11.17E
Crashed near M62 after take-off Manchester Barton
09.09.17 & substantially damaged

G-BAKJ Piper PA-30 Twin Comanche B 30-1232 13.12.72
TJ-AAI, TJ-ADH, N8122Y E R & P M Jones Derby 08.05.18E

G-BAKM Robin DR.400-140 Earl 755 15.12.72
D V Pieri Kirkbride 27.09.19E

G-BAKN SNCAN Stampe SV.4C 348 15.12.72
F-BCOY M Holloway Watchford Farm, Yarcombe 18.07.19P

G-BAKR Jodel D.117 814 27.12.72
F-BIOV J Jennings
Stoneacre Farm, Farthing Corner 02.05.19P
Built by Société Aéronautique Normande

G-BAKV Piper PA-18-150 Super Cub 18-8993 22.12.72
N9744N W J Murray Thruxton 17.08.07
(NF 04.12.18)

G-BAKW Beagle B.121 Pup Series 2 B121-175 15.12.72
M J Evans & R A Swetman tr Cunning Stunts
Flying Group Redhill 13.04.19R

G-BALD Cameron O-84 58 02.01.73
C A Gould Ipswich 07.06.06
(NF 23.12.14)

G-BALF Robin DR.400-140 Earl 772 05.01.73
D A & G Wasey Oaksey Park 01.08.19E

G-BALG Robin DR.400-180 Régent 771 05.01.73
S G Jones Membury 25.05.12E
(IE 20.02.18)

G-BALH Robin DR.400-140B Major 80 766 05.01.73
C Johnson tr G-BALH Flying Group Fenland 16.04.19E

G-BALJ Robin DR.400-180 Régent 767 05.01.73
D A Batt & D de L Rowe tr G-BALJ Flying Group
Fridd Farm, Bethersden 19.10.18E

G-BALK SNCAN Stampe SV-4C 387 03.01.73
F-BBAN, Fr.Mil Cancelled 04.12.96 by CAA
Insch *Frame stored 10.16*

G-BALN Cessna T310Q 310Q0684 08.01.73
N7980Q O'Brien Properties Ltd Brighton City 20.07.12E
(NF 05.11.18)

G-BALS (2) Tipsy Nipper T.66 Series 3 xxxx 22.08.77
N C Spooner (Ardleigh, Colchester)
Built by L W Shaw – project PFA 025-10052; originally
registered to K&S Cavalier 102.5 – project PFA 1598
(NF 20.04.16)

G-BAMB Slingsby T61C Falke 1778 09.01.73
H J Bradley Rufforth 23.07.18E

G-BAMC Reims/Cessna F150L F15000892 12.01.73
R W Marchant & K Meredith Strubby 30.07.19E

G-BAMG Avions Lobet Ganagobie xxxx 11.01.73
Cancelled 05.08.91 by CAA
Middlesbrough *Built by J D Brompton – project*
PFA 1336; used for design study at Teesside
University of Science

G-BAMH[M] Westland S-55 Whirlwind Series 3 WA.83 10.01.73
VR-BEP, G-BAMH, XG588
Cancelled 31.10.73 – to VR-BEP 10.73
As 'XG588' in SAR c/s
With East Midlands Aeropark, East Midlands

G-BAMK[M] Cameron D-96 HA Airship 72 11.01.73
Cancelled 16.08.00 by CAA 24.04.90
With British Balloon Museum & Library, Newbury

G-BAML[M] Bell 206B JetRanger 36 05.01.73
N7844S Cancelled 07.07.03 as Destroyed *Stored* 01.06.00
With South Yorkshire Aircraft Museum, Doncaster

G-BAMM Piper PA-28-235 Cherokee 28-10642 16.01.73
SE-EOA Cancelled 09.04.08 as destroyed 04.04.08
Sandown *Noted 12.13*

G-BAMR Piper PA-16 Clipper 16-392 12.01.73
F-BFMS, CU-P339 R H Royce RAF Barkston Heath 17.12.18E

G-BAMU Robin DR.400-160 Chevalier 778 15.01.73
N P Tyne tr Alternative Flying Group Sywell 14.11.19E

G-BAMV Robin DR.400-180 Régent 777 15.01.73
K Jones (Broad Hinton, Swindon) 08.05.12E
(NF 27.04.15)

G-BAMY Piper PA-28R-200 Cherokee Arrow II 28R-7335015 09.01.73
N11C Flying Pig UK Ltd Lydd 19.03.19E

G-BANA Robin DR.221 Dauphin 73 22.01.73
F-BOZR G T Pryor Tibenham 28.10.19E
Built by Centre-Est Aéronautique

G-BANB Robin DR.400-180 Régent 776 22.01.73
M Ingvardsen (Tenby) 25.08.18E

G-BANC Gardan GY-201 Minicab A203 22.01.73
F-PCZV, F-BCZV C R Shipley Avon Farm, Saltford 31.05.02P
Built by M Ducreuzet (NF 04.04.16)

G-BANF Phoenix Luton LA-4A Minor PFA 838 22.01.73
N F O'Neill (Belfast) 05.06.92P
Built by D W Bosworth – project PFA 838 (NF 05.04.18)

G-BANU Jodel D.120 Paris-Nice 247 31.01.73
F-BLNZ C H Kilner
Shacklewell Lodge Farm, Empingham 31.08.19P
Built by Société Wassmer Aviation

G-BANV Phoenix Currie Wot PFA 3010 25.01.73
A A M & C W N Huke Manor Farm, Dinton
Built by C Turner – project PFA 3010 (NF 07.03.17)

G-BANW Scintex CP.1330 Super Emeraude 941 30.01.73
PH-VRF A Berry Popham 31.07.15P
Built by Société Scintex (NF 18.12.18)

G-BANX Reims/Cessna F172M F17200941 31.01.73
Oakfleet 2000 Ltd Biggin Hill 02.05.19E

G-BAOB Cessna F172M Skyhawk F17200949 02.02.73
Cancelled 17.12.10 by CAA 12.05.07
Andrewsfield *Built by Reims Aviation SA*
Noted in open store 03.19

G-BAOJ SOCATA MS.880B Rallye Club 2252 06.02.73
G Jones (Llanfairfechan) 24.05.08E
Reported as dismantled & roaded to Bedfordshire
post 2016 (IE 22.04.16)

G-BAOP Cessna FRA150L Aerobat FRA1500190 05.02.73
Cancelled 01.05.14 as WFU 11.04.02
Ellough, Beccles *Built by Reims Aviation SA*
Fuselage stored 01.18

G-BAOU Grumman American AA-5 Traveler AA5-0298 08.02.73
R C Mark Shobdon 27.06.14E
(NF 20.10.15)

G-BAPB de Havilland DHC-1 Chipmunk 22A C1/0001 26.02.73
WB549 R C P Brookhouse Old Buckenham 13.10.14E
Noted as 'WB549' on maintenance Audley End 11.18
(IE 28.01.16)

G-BAPI Reims/Cessna FRA150L Aerobat FRA1500195 08.02.73
L J Brian tr BAPI Group Fenland 19.08.09W
(IE 22.11.18)

G-BAPJ Reims/Cessna FRA150L Aerobat FRA1500196 08.02.73
T White Liverpool John Lennon 21.10.18E

G-BAPL Piper PA-23-250 Aztec E 27-7304966 12.02.73
N14377 Donington Aviation Ltd East Midlands 07.10.07E
(NF 30.08.18)

G-BAPP Evans VP-1 Series 2 PFA 1580 13.02.73
I Pearson (Falmouth) 18.08.13P
Built by M Crow & M J Drybanski – project PFA 1580;
stored 07.16 (NF 27.07.18)

G-BAPR Jodel D.11 F5295 14.02.73
W Hinchcliffe Dalkeith Farm, Winwick 17.04.06P
Built by Crantech Flying Group – project PFA 914
(using Falconar plans) (NF 14.06.16)

G-BAPS[M] Campbell Cougar Gyroplane CA/6000 14.02.73
Cancelled 21.01.87 by CAA 20.05.74
On loan from A.M.W.Curzon-Howe-Herrick
With The Helicopter Museum, Weston-super-Mare

G-BAPV Robin DR.400-160 Chevalier 742 19.02.73
F-OCSR, N6428Y Cancelled 23.03.12 by CAA 22.08.03
Kirkbride *On rebuild at 06.16*

G-BAPW Piper PA-28R-180 Cherokee Arrow 28R-30697 21.02.73
5Y-AIR, N4951J J L Shields Earls Colne 18.01.19E

G-BAPX	Robin DR.400-160 Chevalier	789	21.02.73
	T Farnell & J M Gibbon tr White Rose Aviators		
	Sherburn-in-Elmet		23.04.19E
G-BAPY	Robin HR.100/210 Safari	153	21.02.73
	D G Doyle Headcorn		16.06.18E
G-BARC	Reims FR172J Rocket	FR17200356	05.03.73
	(D-EEDK) A R Chipp tr Severn Valley Aviation Group		
	Croft Farm, Defford		03.06.19E
G-BARF	Jodel D.112	1019	05.03.73
	F-BJPF R N Jones Shobdon		21.05.19P
	Built by Société des Etablissements Benjamin Wassmer		
G-BARH	Beech C23 Sundowner 180	M-1473	02.03.73
	A G Partoon (Knowle, Solihull)		04.10.18E
G-BARN	Taylor JT.2 Titch	RN.1	05.03.73
	R G W Newton Westfield Farm, Hailsham		21.06.19P
	Built by R G W Newton – project PFA 060-11136		
G-BARS	de Havilland DHC-1 Chipmunk 22	C1/0557	26.02.73
	WK520 J Beattie & R M Scarre RNAS Yeovilton		19.06.19P
	As '1377' in Portuguese AF c/s		
G-BARV	Cessna 310Q	310Q0774	07.03.73
	Cancelled 14.11.11 as PWFU		18.08.09
	Full Sutton *Spares use 04.16*		
G-BARZ	Scheibe SF28A Tandem Falke	5724	08.03.73
	(D-KAUK) K Kiely RAF Linton-on-Ouse		11.01.19E
G-BASH	Grumman American AA-5 Traveler	AA5-0319	12.03.73
	EI-AWV, G-BASH, N5419L		
	C Sellen tr BASH Flying Group Popham		18.12.19E
G-BASJ	Piper PA-28-180 Cherokee Challenger	28-7305136	13.03.73
	N11C Bristol Aero Club Gloucestershire		21.01.19E
	Official type data 'PA-28-180 Cherokee' is incorrect		
G-BASN	Beech C23 Sundowner 180	M-1476	13.03.73
	J Cheetham tr Beech G-BASN Group Syndicate		
	Bournemouth		19.03.19E
G-BASO	Lake LA-4-180 Amphibian	358	16.03.73
	N2025L Ulster Seaplane Association Ltd Causeway		19.06.06
	Built by Consolidated Aeronautics Inc; noted 03.16		
	(NF 04.05.18)		
G-BASP	Beagle B.121 Pup Series 1	B121-149	14.03.73
	SE-FOC, G-35-140 B J Coutts Sibson		18.10.18R
G-BATV	Piper PA-28-180 Cherokee F	28-7105022	26.03.73
	N5168S A C Hogben tr Scoreby Flying Group		
	Full Sutton		05.03.19E
G-BATW	Piper PA-28-140 Cherokee Fliteliner	28-7225587	26.03.73
	N742FL Cancelled 18.11.16 by CAA		24.10.14
	Perth College *Instructional use 10.16*		
G-BAUC	Piper PA-25-235 Pawnee C	25-5243	26.03.73
	N8761L Southdown Gliding Club Ltd Parham Park		18.07.19E
G-BAUH	Jodel D.112	870	29.03.73
	F-BILO D & G A Shepherd tr G-BAUH Flying Group		
	Seething		30.04.19P
	Built by Etablissement Dormois		
G-BAUI	Piper PA-23-250 Aztec D	27-4335	29.03.73
	LN-RTS Cancelled 26.01.89 by CAA		05.12.88
	Gloucestershire *Open store 02.19*		
G-BAUJ	Piper PA-23-250 Aztec E	27-7304986	29.03.73
	N14390 Cancelled 31.10.02 by CAA		25.07.94
	Cranfield *Open store 12.15, advertised for sale on eBay*		
G-BAVB	Reims/Cessna F172M	F17200965	10.04.73
	D G Smith Rochester		15.11.19E
G-BAVH	de Havilland DHC-1 Chipmunk 22	C1/0841	10.04.73
	WP975 G D E MacDonald tr G-BAVH Syndicate		
	Lasham		16.08.19E
G-BAVL	Piper PA-23-250 Aztec E	27-4671	10.04.73
	N14063 A V & S P Chilcott Durham Tees Valley		06.09.19E
G-BAVO	Boeing Stearman A75N1 Kaydet	'3250-1405'	13.04.73
	4X-AIH R C McCarthy Enstone		30.11.17E
	Original p/i unknown: registered with part no		
	'c/n 3250-1405'; as '26' in USAAC c/s		
G-BAVR	Grumman American AA-5 Traveler	AA5-0348	12.04.73
	M Reusche (Offingen, Germany)		15.11.19E
G-BAVUᴹ	Cameron A-105 HAB	66	11.04.73
	Cancelled 06.12.01 by CAA		05.10.84
	With British Balloon Museum & Library, Newbury		

G-BAWG	Piper PA-28R-200 Cherokee Arrow II	28R-7335133	18.04.73
	N11C Solent Air Ltd Goodwood		01.04.19E
G-BAWK	Piper PA-28-140 Cherokee F	28-7325243	24.04.73
	J P Nugent Newcastle, RoI		28.12.18E
G-BAXE	Hughes 269A-1 (300)	1130313	02.05.73
	N8931F Reeve Newfields Ltd		
	(Long Itchington, Southam)		21.12.93
	(NF 03.11.15)		
G-BAXFᴹ	Cameron O-77 HAB	74	03.05.73
	Cancelled 05.09.95 by CAA		20.07.86
	With British Balloon Museum & Library, Newbury		
G-BAXKᴹ	Thunder Ax7-77 HAB	005	09.05.73
	Cancelled 07.09.01 as WFU		02.07.91
	With British Balloon Museum & Library, Newbury		
G-BAXS	Bell 47G-5	7908	11.05.73
	5B-CFB, G-BAXS, N4098G C R Johnson		
	Top o' th' Close Farm, Upper Cumberworth		05.07.19E
G-BAXU	Reims/Cessna F150L	F15000959	14.05.73
	Peterborough Flying School Ltd Sibson		08.02.19E
G-BAXV	Reims/Cessna F150L	F15000966	14.05.73
	G E Fox Blackpool		24.07.19E
G-BAXX	Cessna F150L	F15000960	14.05.73
	Cancelled 08.10.80 as destroyed		01.12.79
	Kesgrave *Built by Reims Aviation SA*		
	At Suffolk Aviation Heritage Museum 06.18		
G-BAXY	Reims/Cessna F172M	F17200905	15.05.73
	N10636 The Light Aircraft Company Ltd		
	Little Snoring		07.02.19E
G-BAXZ	Piper PA-28-140 Cherokee C	28-26760	15.05.73
	PH-NLX, N11C T C Elkins & T D Kaby		
	tr G-BAXZ (87) Syndicate Turweston		24.04.19E
G-BAYL	SNCAN Nord 1203 Norecrin VI	161	18.05.73
	F-BEQV Cancelled 14.11.91 by CAA		
	Ley Farm, Chirk *Dumped 09.17*		
G-BAYO	Cessna 150L	15074435	18.05.73
	N19471 D T A & J A Rees Haverfordwest		25.09.19E
G-BAYP	Cessna 150L	15074017	18.05.73
	N18651 D I Thomas tr Yankee Papa Flying Group		
	Popham		07.03.19E
G-BAYR	Robin HR.100/210 Safari	164	18.05.73
	D G Doyle Rochester		24.05.15E
	(NF 04.08.16)		
G-BAYV	SNCAN Nord 1101 Noralpha	193	22.05.73
	F-BLTN, French AF Cancelled 28.04.83 as WFU		02.08.75
	Newquay *Noted 03.16, painted as '3 Red'*		
G-BAZC	Robin DR.400-160 Chevalier	824	29.05.73
	S G Jones Membury		
	(NF 10.11.17)		
G-BAZM	Jodel D.11	1416	31.05.73
	C W Baylis tr Watchford Jodel Group		
	Watchford Farm, Yarcombe		30.05.19P
	Built by Bingley Flying Group – project PFA 915;		
	badged as 'D 113'		
G-BAZS	Reims/Cessna F150L	F15000954	01.06.73
	Full Sutton Flying Centre Ltd Full Sutton		22.10.19E

G-BBAA – G-BBZZ

G-BBAW	Robin HR.100/210 Safari	167	12.06.73
	F A Purvis Eshott		19.12.18E
G-BBAX	Robin DR.400-140 Earl	835	12.06.73
	G J Bissex & P H Garbutt Norton Malreward		19.10.19E
G-BBAY	Robin DR.400-140 Earl	841	12.06.73
	S R Evans Top Farm, Croydon		19.10.19E
G-BBBB	Taylor JT.1 Monoplane	SAM/01	04.06.73
	M C Arnold Sturgate		09.01.19P
	Built by S A MacConnacher – project PFA 1422		
G-BBBC	Reims/Cessna F150L	F15000864	14.06.73
	N10635 S Collins & C A Widdowson Full Sutton		29.04.14E
	(NF 25.02.17)		
G-BBBI	Grumman American AA-5 Traveler	AA5-0392	15.06.73
	R Madden Glasgow Prestwick		29.06.16E
	(IE 07.08.18)		

G-BBBN Piper PA-28-180 Cherokee Challenger 28-7305365 20.06.73
N11C Estuary Aviation Ltd Southend 17.12.19E
Official type data 'PA-28-180 Cherokee' is incorrect

G-BBBO Sipa 903 67 16.01.74
F-BGBQ Cancelled 03.06.11 by CAA 09.09.09
Dirleton, Archerfield *On rebuild 06.14*

G-BBBVᴹ Handley Page HP.137 Jetstream 234 26.06.73
N14234, N102SC, N1BE, (N200SE), G-BBBV, G-8-12
Cancelled 21.08.74 – to (N200SE) 08.74 *As 'N14234'*
Fuselage used by BAe as Jetstream 31 mock-up
With National Museum of Flight Scotland, East Fortune

G-BBBW Clutton FRED Series II DLW.1 26.06.73
M Palfreman (Aiskew, Bedale) 19.06.08P
Built by D Webster – project PFA 1551 (NF 08.12.04)

G-BBBY Piper PA-28-140 Cherokee Cruiser 28-7325533 28.06.73
N9501N I M Ashpole tr Ledbury Flying Group
(Bridstow, Ross-on-Wye) 21.06.19E

G-BBCB Western O-65 HAB 018 29.06.73
Cancelled 14.12.16 by CAA
Not Known *Inflated Pidley 04.18*

G-BBCH Robin DR.400 2+2 850 04.07.73
A V Harmer Hardwick 10.04.14E
Airframe noted 04.16 (NF 18.02.18)

G-BBCKᴹ Cameron O-77 HAB 76 04.07.73
Cancelled 27.01.09 as PWFU 15.06.89
With British Balloon Museum & Library, Newbury

G-BBCN Robin HR.100/210 Safari 168 11.07.73
J C King Thruxton 26.09.19E

G-BBCS Robin DR.400-140B Major 80 851 12.07.73
M J Medland Spanhoe 02.03.19E

G-BBCY Phoenix Luton LA-4A Minor PFA 825 17.07.73
A W McBlain Kilkerran 29.09.11P
Built by C H Difford – project PFA 825
(initially regd with c/n LA4A) (IE 14.08.18)

G-BBCZ Grumman American AA-5 Traveler AA5-0382 18.07.73
A J Gomes Redhill 20.08.11E
Damaged by flood 12.13; in open store 01.16
(NF 22.08.16)

G-BBDC Piper PA-28-140 Cherokee Cruiser 28-7325437 18.07.73
N Wright Blackpool 14.08.19E

G-BBDE Piper PA-28R-200 Cherokee Arrow II 28R-7335250 18.07.73
(EI-...), G-BBDE, N11C
R L Coleman, J Kemp & P Knott Elstree 02.08.19E

G-BBDGᴹ BAC Concorde Type 1 Variant 100 13523 & 100-02 07.08.73
Cancelled 10.08.84 as PWFU xx.03.82
With Brooklands Museum, Weybridge

G-BBDH Reims/Cessna F172M F17200990 19.07.73
J D Woodward Henstridge 11.10.19E

G-BBDL Grumman American AA-5 Traveler AA5-0406 18.07.73
M Kadir Wolverhampton Halfpenny Green 31.07.19E

G-BBDM Grumman American AA-5 Traveler AA5-0407 18.07.73
A W Harris tr Jackaroo Aviation Group Thruxton 03.04.19E

G-BBDO Piper PA-23-250 Aztec E 27-7305120 24.07.73
N40361 J W Anstee tr G-BBDO Flying Group
Henstridge 04.06.16E
Noted 09.18 (IE 13.02.18)

G-BBDP Robin DR.400-160 Chevalier 853 25.07.73
Robin Lance Aviation Associates Ltd Rochester 03.08.17E
(NF 16.08.18)

G-BBDT Cessna 150H 15068839 26.07.73
N23272 J Brookes tr Delta Tango Group Full Sutton 11.10.19E

G-BBDV SIPA 903 7 30.07.73
F-BEYY J Owen Great Oakley 08.07.19P
Originally ex F-BEYJ c/n 7; rebuilt 1978 ex F-BEYY c/n 21

G-BBEA Phoenix Luton LA-4A Minor PFA 843 30.07.73
D S Evans (Gwinear, Hayle) 09.05.11P
Built by G J Hewitt – project PFA 843; initially
registered to S A Knight with c/n SAK.1 (NF 30.04.18)

G-BBEB Piper PA-28R-200 Cherokee Arrow II 28R-7335292 31.07.73
N9514N G A Dunster & A Taplin tr March Flying Group
Stapleford 15.05.19E

G-BBEDᴹ Socata MS.894A Rallye Minerva 220 12097 30.07.73
Cancelled 23.06.09 by CAA 13.09.87
With East Midlands Aeropark, East Midlands

G-BBEN Bellanca 7GCBC Citabria 496-73 07.08.73
(D-EAUT), N36416 C A G Schofield
Green Meadows, Harpsden 10.05.02
(NF 23.04.18)

G-BBEV Piper PA-28-140 Cherokee D 28-7125340 08.08.73
LN-MTM Cancelled 16.05.07 as PWFU 09.09.01
Blackpool *Fuselage on fire dump 03.16*

G-BBEX Cessna 185A Skywagon 185-0491 07.08.73
EI-CMC, G-BBEX, 4X-ALD, N99992, N1691Z 27.02.08
Cancelled 04.01.11 by CAA
Kaposvar, Hungary *Stored 10.16*

G-BBFD Piper PA-28R-200 Cherokee Arrow II 28R-7335342 08.08.73
N9517N C H Rose tr G-BBFD Flying Group
White Waltham 12.01.19E

G-BBFL Gardan GY-201 Minicab 21 17.08.73
F-BHCQ R Smith Griffins Farm, Temple Bruer 18.10.19P
Built by SRCM (Societe de Recherches et de
Constructions Mecanique)

G-BBFSᴹ Vandem-Bemden K-460 Gas Balloon 75 10.08.73
OO-BGX Cancelled 19.05.93 by CAA
Built by F Vandem-Bemden – project VDB-16
With British Balloon Museum & Library, Newbury

G-BBFV Piper PA-32-260 Cherokee Six 32-778 13.08.73
5Y-ADF A M W Driskell Rochester 20.09.19E

G-BBGI Fuji FA.200-160 Aero Subaru FA200-228 21.08.73
A & P West Bournemouth 30.06.17E

G-BBGN Cameron A-375 HAB 90 23.08.73
Cancelled 22.08.89 as WFU
Wroughton *In Science Museum store 2013*

G-BBGR Cameron O-65 HAB 85 20.08.73
Cancelled 19.12.08 as PWFU 26.05.81
Not Known *Inflated Pidley 05.16*

G-BBGZ Cambridge HABA 42 HAB CHABA 42 31.08.73
Cancelled 26.10.10 as PWFU
Not Known *Inflated Donnington Grove Club 01.19*

G-BBHF Piper PA-23-250 Aztec E 27-7305166 05.09.73
N40453 Eastern Air Executive Ltd Sturgate 26.09.18E
(IE 23.10.18)

G-BBHJ Piper J-3C-65 Cub 16378 07.09.73
OO-GEC M L Joseph tr Wellcross Flying Group
Wellcross Farm, Slinfold 02.07.19P
Fuselage No.16037

G-BBHK Noorduyn AT-16-ND Harvard IIB 14-787 07.09.73
PH-PPS, (PH-HTC), R Netherlands AF B-158, FH153,
42-12540 M Kubrak Konstancin-Obory,
Województwo Mazowieckie, Poland 09.05.19P
As 'FH153:58' in RCAF c/s

G-BBHY Piper PA-28-180 Cherokee Challenger 28-7305474 07.09.73
EI-BBS, G-BBHY, N9508N
G K Clarkson Haverfordwest 18.10.18E
Official type data 'PA-28-180 Cherokee' is incorrect

G-BBIF Piper PA-23-250 Aztec E 27-7305234 10.09.73
N9736N Marshall of Cambridge Aerospace Ltd
Cambridge 12.06.19E

G-BBIL Piper PA-28-140 Cherokee 28-22567 13.09.73
SE-FAR, N4219J B W Hewison tr Saxondale Group
North Weald 27.08.19E

G-BBIO Robin HR.100/210 Safari 178 14.09.73
R P Caley Beverley (Linley Hill) 02.12.16E

G-BBIX Piper PA-28-140 Cherokee E 28-7225442 17.09.73
LN-AEN F A Griffiths tr Sterling Aviation
White Waltham 10.12.19E

G-BBJB Thunder Ax7-77 HAB 009 17.09.73
Cancelled 28.04.93 as PWFU
Not Known *Inflated Pidley 04.14*

G-BBJI Isaacs Spitfire 2 18.09.73
S Vince tr G-BBJI Group Felthorpe 26.06.07P
Built by J O Isaacs – project PFA 027-10055 (NF 22.06.16)

G-BBJU Robin DR.400-140 Earl 874 19.09.73
P F Moderate Headcorn 12.06.19E

G-BBJV Reims/Cessna F177RG Cardinal RG F177RG0098 20.09.73
P R Powell Bournemouth 29.10.19E

G-BBJX Reims/Cessna F150L F15001017 20.09.73
York Aircraft Leasing Ltd Breighton 14.03.19E

G-BBJY	Reims/Cessna F172M	F17201075	20.09.73
	D G Wright Derby		30.06.11E
	(NF 20.12.18)		
G-BBJZ	Reims/Cessna F172M	F17201035	20.09.73
	J Heffernan Monaco, Monaco		31.05.19E
G-BBKA	Reims/Cessna F150L	F15001029	20.09.73
	Aviolease Ltd Doncaster Sheffield		10.12.19E
	Operated by Yorkshire Aero Club		
G-BBKB	Reims/Cessna F150L	F15001030	20.09.73
	Justgold Ltd Blackpool		30.05.15E
	(NF 04.10.18)		
G-BBKG	Reims FR172J Rocket	FR17200465	20.09.73
	R Wright Coventry		27.06.19E
G-BBKI	Reims/Cessna F172M	F17201069	20.09.73
	C W Burman East Winch		14.08.19E
G-BBKL	Piel CP.301A Emeraude	237	21.09.73
	F-BIMK P J Swain Sandford Hall, Knockin		30.11.18P
	Built by Société Menavia		
G-BBKX	Piper PA-28-180 Cherokee Challenger	28-7305581	26.09.73
	N9550N Royal Aircraft Establishment Aero Club Ltd		
	Farnborough		28.02.19E
	Official type data 'PA-28-180 Cherokee' is incorrect		
G-BBKY	Reims/Cessna F150L	F15000991	26.09.73
	F W Astbury Netherthorpe		03.07.19E
G-BBKZ	Cessna 172M Skyhawk	17261495	27.09.73
	N20694 R S Thomson tr KZ Flying Group Exeter Int'l		18.05.19E
G-BBLH	Piper J-3C-65 Cub (*L-4B-PI*)	10549	24.09.73
	F-BFQY, French Army, 43-1145		
	Shipping & Airlines Ltd Biggin Hill		06.07.19E
	Fuselage No.9838		
	As '31145:G-26' in 183rd Field Battalion USAAC c/s		
G-BBLLᴹ	Cameron O-84 HAB	84	02.10.73
	Cancelled 19.05.93 by CAA		25.05.81
	With British Balloon Museum & Library, Newbury		
G-BBLS	Grumman American AA-5 Traveler	AA5-0440	08.10.73
	EI-AYM, G-BBLS A Grant Perth		07.08.19E
G-BBLU	Piper PA-34-200 Seneca	34-7350271	08.10.73
	N55984 R H R Rue Turweston		29.06.16E
	In open store 2017		
G-BBMB	Robin DR.400-180 Régent	848	27.09.73
	5Y-ASB N Clark & K Wade Eshott		20.09.19E
G-BBMH	EAA Biplane Sport Model P1	PFA 1348	11.10.73
	M V Batin tr G-BBMH Flying Group Bembridge		20.03.19P
	Built by K Dawson – project PFA 1348		
G-BBMN	de Havilland DHC-1 Chipmunk 22	C1/0300	12.10.73
	WD359 S Baker (Cranleigh) '3'		25.02.19P
G-BBMO	de Havilland DHC-1 Chipmunk 22	C1/0550	12.10.73
	WK514 T de la Fosse & S N D Turner		
	tr Mike Oscar Group Wellesbourne Mountford		07.05.10P
	As 'WK514' in RAF c/s		
G-BBMR	de Havilland DHC-1 Chipmunk 22	C1/0213	12.10.73
	WB763 M D Whalley tr G-BBMR Syndicate Turweston		
	As 'WB763:K' in RAF c/s; on rebuild 09.18 (NF 14.06.18)		
G-BBMT	de Havilland DHC-1 Chipmunk 22	C1/0712	12.10.73
	WP831 J Evans & D Withers tr MT Group Leicester		07.08.19P
	Carries 'WP831' on rear fuselage		
G-BBMV	de Havilland DHC-1 Chipmunk 22	C1/0432	12.10.73
	WG348 Boultbee Classic LLP Goodwood		06.05.19E
	As 'WG348' in RAF c/s		
G-BBMW	de Havilland DHC-1 Chipmunk 22	C1/0641	12.10.73
	WK628 G Fielder & A Wilson		
	Wellcross Farm, Slinfold		20.09.18E
	As 'WK628' in RAF silver & yellow bands c/s		
G-BBMZ	de Havilland DHC-1 Chipmunk 22	C1/0563	12.10.73
	WK548 W N Gibson tr G-BBMZ Chipmunk Syndicate		
	Wycombe Air Park		25.05.19P
G-BBNA	de Havilland DHC-1 Chipmunk 22	C1/0491	12.10.73
	WG417 Coventry Gliding Club Ltd		
	Husbands Bosworth		30.06.19P
	Lycoming O-360-A4M		
G-BBNCᴹ	de Havilland DHC-1 Chipmunk T.10	C1/0682	12.10.73
	WP790 Cancelled 23.09.74 as WFU		
	As 'WP790:T' with incomplete Birmingham UAS markings		
	With de Havilland Aircraft Museum, London Colney		

G-BBND	de Havilland DHC-1 Chipmunk 22	C1/0225	12.10.73
	WD286 D Fradley & W Norton tr Bernoulli Syndicate		
	Old Warden		14.06.19P
	As 'WD286' in RAF silver & yellow bands c/s		
G-BBNI	Piper PA-34-200 Seneca	34-7350312	16.10.73
	N56286 D H G Penney Fenland		13.07.13E
	(NF 02.03.16)		
G-BBNJ	Reims/Cessna F150L	F15001038	16.10.73
	K Rowell Sherburn-in-Elmet		14.02.19E
G-BBNT	Piper PA-31-350 Chieftain	31-7305107	22.10.73
	EI-CNM, N1201H, G-BBNT, N74958		
	Atlantic Bridge Aviation Ltd Lydd		17.09.19E
	Operated by Lyddair Ltd		
G-BBNZ	Reims/Cessna F172M	F17201054	23.10.73
	CG Aviation Ltd Perth		06.09.19E
G-BBOA	Reims/Cessna F172M	F17201066	23.10.73
	Cirrus Aviation Ltd Clacton-on-Sea		06.08.19E
G-BBOH	Craft-Pitts S-1S	AJEP-P-SI-S-1	25.10.73
	P H Meeson (London SW1)		16.05.08P
	Built by Pitts Aviation Enterprises Inc		
	– project PFA 1570 (IE 31.01.18)		
G-BBOL	Piper PA-18-150 Super Cub	18-7561	26.10.73
	D-EMFE, N3821Z N Moore Aston Down		18.07.10E
	Stored 02.18 (NF 16.12.16)		
G-BBOR	Bell 206B-2 JetRanger II	1197	30.10.73
	(SE-...), G-BBOR G B D Budworth		
	Bylaugh Hall, Bylaugh		30.09.19E
G-BBOXᴹ	Thunder Ax7-77 HAB	011	24.10.73
	Cancelled 19.01.10 as WFU		23.12.82
	With British Balloon Museum & Library, Newbury		
G-BBPP	Piper PA-28-180 Cherokee Archer	28-7405007	30.10.73
	G-WACP, G-BBPP, N9559N		
	A D R Northeast RAF Benson		25.02.19E
G-BBPS	Jodel D.117	597	30.10.73
	F-BHXS V F Flett Shempston Farm, Lossiemouth		28.08.18P
	Built by Société Aéronautique Normande;		
	force landed near Shempston Farm, Lossiemouth		
	25.02.18 & substantially damaged		
G-BBRA	Piper PA-23-250 Aztec E	27-7305197	12.11.73
	N40479 Sulafat OU (Tallinn, Estonia)		07.05.19E
G-BBRB	de Havilland DH.82A Tiger Moth	85934	21.11.73
	OO-EVB, Belgian AF T-8, ETA-8, DF198		
	R Barham (West Wickham)		
	(NF 15.03.16)		
G-BBRC	Fuji FA.200-180 Aero Subaru	FA200-235	08.11.73
	G-BBRC Ltd Blackbushe		25.06.19E
G-BBRI	Bell 47G-5A	25158	08.11.73
	N18092 Alan Mann Aviation Group Ltd		
	(Isfield, Uckfield)		28.07.02
	Composite following several major rebuilds (NF 29.04.15)		
G-BBRN	Mitchell-Procter Kittiwake I	PFA 1352	20.11.73
	XW784 H M Price (Upavon, Pewsey)		15.03.08P
	Built by Air Engineering, HMS Daedalus –		
	project 02/PFA 1352		
	As 'XW784:VL' in RN c/s (NF 14.07.15)		
G-BBRX	SIAI Marchetti S.205-18/F	342	13.11.73
	LN-VYH, OO-HAQ Cancelled 25.08.10 as destroyed		15.06.10
	Fenland *Stored for spares use 08.16*		
G-BBRZ	Grumman American AA-5 Traveler	AA5-0471	15.11.73
	(EI-AYV), G-BBRZ B McIntyre Causeway		15.08.19E
	Official p/i 'N11C' is incorrect		
G-BBSA	Grumman American AA-5 Traveler	AA5-0472	15.11.73
	Usworth 84 Flying Associates Ltd Durham Tees Valley		26.04.19E
G-BBSC	Beech B.24R Sierra 200	MC-217	15.11.73
	Cancelled 27.07.01 by CAA		03.06.99
	Ballymoney *Wreck stored 2013*		
G-BBSS	de Havilland DHC-1 Chipmunk 22	C1/0520	21.11.73
	WG470 Coventry Gliding Club Ltd		
	Husbands Bosworth		14.03.19P
	Lycoming O-360-A4A		
G-BBTB	Reims/Cessna FRA150L Aerobat	FRA1500224	26.11.73
	S E Waddy Shacklewell Lodge Farm, Empingham		13.09.19E

G-BBTG	Reims/Cessna F172M	F17201097	26.11.73	
	C Walton Ltd t/a Jetstream Aero Bruntingthorpe		29.10.14E	
	(IE 18.09.15)			
G-BBTH	Reims/Cessna F172M	F17201089	26.11.73	
	Ormand Flying Club Ltd Birr, RoI		22.10.19E	
G-BBTJ	Piper PA-23-250 Aztec E	27-7305131	27.11.73	
	N40369 Cancelled 07.06.18 as PWFU		08.09.10	
	Not Known *Left Wickenby by road 2016 for static use*			
G-BBTY	Beech C23 Sundowner 180	M-1525	29.11.73	
	D J Sanders tr G-BBTY Group St Athan		09.12.19E	
G-BBUJ	Cessna 421B Golden Eagle	421B0335	07.12.73	
	(CS-...), G-BBUJ, OY-RYD			
	Aero VIP Companhia de Transportes & Servicos Aereos SA			
	Portimão, Portugal		18.05.00	
	(NF 25.06.15)			
G-BBUT	Western O-65	020	11.12.73	
	R G Turnbull Glasbury, Hereford			
	(NF 11.06.18)			
G-BBUU	Piper J-3C-65 Cub (*L-4A-PI*)	10529	14.01.74	
	F-BBSQ, F-OAEZ, French AF, 43-29238			
	C Stokes Hulcote Farm, Hulcote		11.05.19P	
	Fuselage No.10354			
G-BBVFᴹ	Scottish Aviation Twin Pioneer 3	558	17.12.73	
	7978M, XM961 Cancelled 08.08.83		14.05.82	
	With National Museum of Flight Scotland, East Fortune			
G-BBVO	Isaacs Fury II	DBW.1	20.12.73	
	S Vince Felthorpe		08.03.18P	
	Built by D Silsbury – project PFA 011-10091;			
	initially regd to D B Wilson with c/n DBW.1			
	As 'K5682:6 in RAF c/s			
G-BBXB	Reims/Cessna FRA150L Aerobat	FRA1500236	16.01.74	
	D C & M Somerville Beverley (Linley Hill)		27.06.19E	
G-BBXK	Piper PA-34-200 Seneca	34-7450056	21.01.74	
	G-FBPL, G-BBXK, N54366 A Elliott Blackpool		07.04.08E	
	Noted 11.16 (NF 25.11.16)			
G-BBXW	Piper PA-28-151 Cherokee Warrior	28-7415050	21.01.74	
	PH-CPL, G-BBXW, N9599N			
	Bristol Aero Club Gloucestershire		30.01.19E	
G-BBXY	Bellanca 7GCBC Citabria	614-74	01.02.74	
	N57639 S A Windus Truleigh Manor Farm, Edburton		12.03.08E	
	(NF 10.11.14)			
G-BBYB	Piper PA-18 Super Cub 95 (*L-18C-PI*)	18-1627	04.02.74	
	PH-TMA, (D-ENCH), French Army 18-1627, 51-15627			
	Perryair Ltd Brighton City		06.07.19E	
	Fuselage No.18-1628			
G-BBYH	Cessna 182P Skylane	18262814	06.02.74	
	N52744 Ramco (UK) Ltd			
	Poplar Farm, Croft, Skegness		03.05.19E	
G-BBYP	Piper PA-28-140 Cherokee F	28-7425158	19.02.74	
	N9620N P J Terry Solent *'Blue Angel'*		02.05.19E	
G-BBYUᴹ	Cameron O-56 HAB	96	19.02.74	
	Cancelled 09.08.89 as WFU		28.02.82	
	With British Balloon Museum & Library, Newbury			
G-BBZH	Piper PA-28R-200 Cherokee Arrow	28R-7435102	22.02.74	
	N9608N S I Tugwell Rayne Hall Farm, Rayne		30.03.16E	
	(IE 30.01.17)			
G-BBZN	Fuji FA.200-180 Aero Subaru	FA200-230	26.02.74	
	D Kynaston, P D Wedd & J S V Westwood Cambridge		23.04.19E	
G-BBZV	Piper PA-28R-200 Cherokee Arrow II	28R-7435105	11.03.74	
	N9609N P B Mellor Cambridge		29.01.19E	

G-BCAA – G-BCZZ

G-BCAH	de Havilland DHC-1 Chipmunk 22	C1/0372	06.05.74	
	WG316 Century Aviation Ltd Tatenhill		19.03.19P	
	As 'WG316:22' in RAF white & red c/s			
	with badge of 2 FTS			
G-BCARᴹ	Thunder Ax7-77 HAB	019	05.03.74	
	Cancelled 02.04.92 by CAA			
	With British Balloon Museum & Library, Newbury			
G-BCAS	Thunder Ax7-77 HAB	018	05.03.74	
	Cancelled 20.11.01 by CAA		09.04.91	
	Not known *Inflated Pidley 04.18*			
-BCAZ	Piper PA-12 Super Cruiser	12-2312	12.03.74	
	5Y-KGK, VP-KGK, ZS-BYJ, ZS-BPH			
	J Forshaw (Thames Ditton)		01.06.18E	
G-BCBG	Piper PA-23-250 Aztec E	27-7305224	13.03.74	
	VP-BBN, VR-BBN, (VR-BDM), G-BCBG, N40494			
	F Kusserow tr Pilots without Limits			
	Mannheim City, Germany		28.06.19E	
G-BCBH	Fairchild 24R-46A Argus III (*UC-61K-FA*)	975	13.03.74	
	(VH-AAQ), G-BCBH, ZS-AXH, HB737, 43-15011			
	H Mackintosh Spanhoe		14.02.19P	
	As 'HB737' in RAF c/s			
G-BCBJ	Piper PA-25-235 Pawnee C	25-2380/R	18.03.74	
	Deeside Gliding Club (Aberdeenshire) Ltd Aboyne		23.08.19E	
	Rebuild of G-ASLA [25-2380]			
G-BCBL	Fairchild 24R-46A Argus III (*UC-61K-FA*)	989	19.03.74	
	OO-EKE, D-EKEQ, HB-AEC, HB751, 43-15025			
	F J Cox Gorrell Farm, Woolsery			
	As 'HB751' in RAF c/s (NF 08.11.13)			
G-BCBR	Wittman W.8 Tailwind	TW3-380	20.03.74	
	D P Jones Top Farm, Croydon		12.06.14P	
	Built by AJEP Developments (NF 15.03.16)			
G-BCBX	Reims/Cessna F150L	F15001001	25.03.74	
	F-BUEO P Lodge & J G McVey			
	Liverpool John Lennon		22.07.19E	
G-BCCE	Piper PA-23-250 Aztec E	27-7405282	03.04.74	
	N40544 Golf Charlie Echo Ltd Brighton City		28.02.19E	
	Operated by The Flying Hut			
G-BCCF	Piper PA-28-180 Cherokee Archer	28-7405069	03.04.74	
	N9632N J Ormerod tr Charlie Foxtrot Aviation			
	Liverpool John Lennon		12.04.19E	
G-BCCK	Grumman American AA-5 Traveler	AA5-0547	08.04.74	
	Prospect Air Ltd Hawarden		18.09.19E	
G-BCCR	Piel CP.301A Emeraude	xxxx	08.04.74	
	Cancelled 08.01.16 as PWFU		29.07.15	
	Barton Ashes *Built by Korist Flying Group –*			
	project PFA 712; for sale as rebuild project 10.18			
G-BCCX	de Havilland DHC-1 Chipmunk 22	C1/0531	17.04.74	
	WG481 Charlie X-Ray Syndicate Ltd RAF Odiham		03.08.19P	
G-BCCY	Robin HR.200-100 Club	37	18.04.74	
	B A Mills (Little Eversden)		30.04.19E	
G-BCDK (2)	Partenavia P68B	32	04.07.75	
	A6-ALN, G-BCDK Amazon'Air Services			
	(Acqui Terme, Piedmont, Italy)		28.04.16E	
	(IE 24.06.16)			
G-BCDL	Cameron O-42	115	24.04.74	
	B O & D P Turner Leigh upon Mendip, Radstock		13.07.83A	
	(NF 08.02.16)			
G-BCDY	Reims/Cessna FRA150L Aerobat	FRA1500237	07.05.74	
	Leased Flight Ltd Brighton City		04.12.19E	
G-BCEE	Grumman American AA-5 Traveler	AA5-0571	07.05.74	
	P J Marchant RAF Henlow		22.11.19E	
G-BCEF	Grumman-American AA-5 Traveler	AA5-0572	07.05.74	
	Cancelled 12.02.15 by CAA		10.08.11	
	Stapleford *Stored 03.16*			
G-BCEN	Fairey B-N BN-2A-26 Islander	403	06.05.74	
	4X-AYG, SX-BFB, 4X-AYG, N90JA, G-BCEN			
	Britten-Norman Ltd Solent		29.10.19E	
G-BCEP	Grumman American AA-5 Traveler	AA5-0576	07.05.74	
	C M James tr Sandown Aircraft Group G-Bcep			
	Bembridge		12.04.19E	
G-BCER	Gardan GY-201 Minicab	8	08.05.74	
	F-BGJP A & J A Stewart (Monifieth, Dundee)		24.07.19P	
	Built by Constructions Aeronautique de Bearn			
G-BCEU	Cameron O-42	111	09.05.74	
	P Glydon Knowle, Bristol		31.05.85A	
	Active 09.18 (NF 09.10.18)			
G-BCEY	de Havilland DHC-1 Chipmunk 22	C1/0515	14.05.74	
	WG465 M H Gush & N S M Rendall			
	tr Gopher Flying Group White Waltham		17.10.19P	
	As 'WG465' in RAF silver & yellow bands c/s			
G-BCFCᴹ	Cameron 0-65 HAB	116	15.05.74	
	Cancelled 06.12.01 by CAA		20.03.88	
	With British Balloon Museum & Library, Newbury			

G-BCFD[M]	West Ax3-15 HAB	JW.1	16.05.74
	Cancelled 30.01.87 by CAA		
	Built by J West		
	With British Balloon Museum & Library, Newbury		
G-BCFE[M]	Byrne Odyssey 4000 MLB	AJB-2	20.05.74
	Cancelled 19.09.85 as WFU		
	Built by A J Byrne		
	With British Balloon Museum & Library, Newbury		
G-BCFN[M]	Cameron O-65	109	08.07.91
	Cancelled 24.01.19 as PWFU		15.05.77
	Displayed at National Museum of Flight Scotland,		
	East Fortune		
G-BCFO	Piper PA-18-150 Super Cub	18-5335	29.05.74
	G-MUDI, G-BCFO, (D-EIOZ), French Army 18-5335, N10F		
	D J Ashley Dolafallen Farm, Llanwrthwl		21.06.19E
G-BCFR	Reims/Cessna FRA150L Aerobat	FRA1500244	30.05.74
	M Ball tr Foxtrot Romeo Group Earls Colne		02.05.19E
G-BCFW	SAAB 91D Safir	91-437	29.05.74
	PH-RLZ D R Williams (Standford Bridge, Newport)		24.07.06
	(NF 06.03.18)		
G-BCGB	Bensen B.8	PCL-14	03.06.74
	A Melody (Uxbridge)		14.09.14P
	Built by P C Lovegrove (NF 24.08.17)		
G-BCGC	de Havilland DHC-1 Chipmunk 22	C1/0776	13.03.74
	WP903 S G Smith tr Henlow Chipmunk Group		
	RAF Henlow		25.09.19P
	As 'WP903' in RAF Queen's Flight (red) c/s		
G-BCGH	SNCAN NC.854S	122	10.06.74
	F-BAFG P L Lovegrove (Ferndown)		03.06.14P
	(IE 27.09.18)		
G-BCGI	Piper PA-28-140 Cherokee Cruiser	28-7425283	10.06.74
	N9573N D H G Penney Sandtoft		06.12.19E
G-BCGJ	Piper PA-28-140 Cherokee Cruiser	28-7425286	10.06.74
	N9574N Demero Ltd & Livingstone Skies Ltd		
	Hinton-in-the-Hedges		12.03.19E
G-BCGM	Jodel D.120 Paris-Nice	50	15.07.74
	F-BHQM, F-BHYM S E Wilks Husbands Bosworth		24.05.19P
	Built by Société des Etablissements Benjamin Wassmer		
G-BCGN	Piper PA-28-140 Cherokee F	28-7425323	10.06.74
	N9595N C F Hessey Oxford		31.01.19E
G-BCGP[M]	Gazebo Ax6-65 HAB	1	13.06.74
	Cancelled 18.12.79 as WFU		
	With British Balloon Museum & Library, Newbury		
G-BCGS	Piper PA-28R-200 Cherokee Arrow II	28R-7235133	13.06.74
	N4893T Leased Flight Ltd Brighton City		24.09.19E
G-BCGW	Jodel D.11	CC001	14.06.74
	G H Chittenden (London NW7)		
	Built by G H & M D Chittenden – project PFA 912;		
	originally s/n EAA/61554 (NF 22.10.14)		
G-BCHL	de Havilland DHC-1 Chipmunk 22A	C1/0680	20.06.74
	WP788 Shropshire Soaring Ltd Sleap		25.04.19P
	As 'WP788' in RAF c/s		
G-BCHP	Scintex CP.1310-C3 Super Emeraude	902	24.06.74
	G-JOSI, G-BCHP, F-BJVQ		
	P Durdey (Chew Magna, Bristol)		12.11.18P
G-BCHT	Schleicher ASK 16	16021	25.06.74
	(BGA 1996), D-KAMY		
	D E Cadisch tr Dunstable K16 Group Dunstable Downs		26.08.19E
G-BCHX	Scheibe SF23A Sterling	2013	28.06.74
	D-EGIZ Cancelled 22.03.02 by PWFU		29.06.83
	Rufforth *Frame suspended from roof 02.19*		
G-BCIH	de Havilland DHC-1 Chipmunk 22	C1/0304	03.07.74
	WD363 P J Richie MoD Netheravon		24.04.19P
	As 'WD363:5' in RAF c/s		
G-BCIN	Thunder Ax7-77 HAB	030	05.07.74
	Cancelled 12.02.09 by CAA		05.05.84
	Not Known *Inflated Donnington Grove Club 01.19*		
G-BCIR	Piper PA-28-151 Cherokee Warrior	28-7415401	09.07.74
	N9587N Aerobility Blackbushe		16.05.19E
G-BCJH	Mooney M20F Executive	670126	11.07.74
	N9549M Cancelled 26.09.00 by CAA		30.06.91
	Bourn *Noted derelict 06.13*		

G-BCJM	Piper PA-28-140 Cherokee F	28-7425321	17.07.74
	N9592N P Lodge & J G McVey		
	Liverpool John Lennon		07.06.19E
G-BCJN	Piper PA-28-140 Cherokee Cruiser	28-7425350	17.07.74
	N9618N Bristol & Wessex Aeroplane Club Ltd Bristol		21.03.19E
G-BCJO	Piper PA-28R-200 Cherokee Arrow II	28R-7435272	17.07.74
	N9640N R Ross Gloucestershire		27.07.18E
G-BCJP	Piper PA-28-140 Cherokee	28-24187	15.08.74
	N1766J S Turton Eaglescott		09.09.19E
G-BCKN	de Havilland DHC-1 Chipmunk 22	C1/0707	05.08.74
	WP811 M D Cowburn Husbands Bosworth		22.05.18P
	On maintenance 11.18 @ Audley End as		
	'WP811' in RAF c/s		
G-BCKS	Fuji FA.200-180AO Aero Subaru	FA200-250	02.08.74
	G J Ward Dunkeswell		11.07.19E
G-BCKT	Fuji FA.200-180 Aero Subaru	FA200-251	02.08.74
	A G Dobson Hawarden		11.11.19E
G-BCKU	Reims/Cessna FRA150L Aerobat	FRA1500256	01.08.74
	Forge Consulting Ltd Abbeyshrule, RoI		06.06.19E
G-BCKV	Reims/Cessna FRA150L Aerobat	FRA1500251	01.08.74
	M Bonsall Netherthorpe		03.05.19E
G-BCLI	Grumman American AA-5 Traveler	AA5-0643	12.08.74
	S J Oak tr G-BCLI Group Henstridge		24.01.20E
	(IE 16.12.18)		
G-BCLS	Cessna 170B	20946	23.08.74
	N8094A M J Whiteman-Haywood		
	Brant Farm, Bewdley		06.07.14E
	(IE 04.07.18)		
G-BCLU	Jodel D.117	506	28.08.74
	F-BHXG R A Stocks (Drighlington, Bradford)		18.07.19P
	Built by Société Aéronautique Normande		
G-BCLW[M]	Grumman American AA1B Trainer	AA1B-0463	29.08.74
	Cancelled 03.08.17 as PWFU		09.06.13
	At South Yorkshire Aircraft Museum, Doncaster		
G-BCMD	Piper PA-18 Super Cub 95 (*L-18C-PI*)	18-2055	04.09.74
	OO-SPF, R Netherlands AF R70, 52-2455		
	P Stephenson Great Oakley		31.07.15E
	Fuselage No.18-2071		
G-BCMJ	K & S SA.102.5 Cavalier	PFA 001-1546	09.09.74
	N F Andrews (Oakham)		
	Built by M Johnson – project PFA 001-1546;		
	original c/n MJ.1; tailwheel u/c (NF 09.07.18)		
G-BCMT	Isaacs Fury II	PFA 1522	09.09.74
	R W Burrows (Watton, Thetford)		
	Built by M H Turner – project PFA 1522 (NF 02.11.18)		
G-BCNC	Gardan GY-201 Minicab	A202	09.09.74
	F-BICF J R Wraight (Chatham)		
	Built by Nouvelle Soc Cometal (NF 14.10.16)		
G-BCNP	Cameron O-77	117	16.09.74
	P Spellward Bristol BS9		28.07.00A
	(NF 13.12.16)		
G-BCNX	Piper J-3C-65 Cub (*L-4H-PI*)	11831	17.09.74
	F-BEGM, French AF, 43-29877		
	C M L Edwards Monewden		13.05.19P
	Fuselage No.10993		
G-BCOB	Piper J-3C-65 Cub (*L-4H-PI*)	10696	19.09.74
	F-BCPV, 43-29405 C Marklew-Brown Bicester		26.06.19P
	Fuselage No.10521; as '329405:23-A' in USAAF c/s		
G-BCOH[M]	Avro 683 Lancaster Mk.10 AR	277	24.09.74
	CF-TQC, RCAF KB976 Cancelled 23.02.93		
	As 'G-BCOH' Built by Victory Aircraft, Canada		
	With Fantasy of Flight, Polk City, Florida		
G-BCOI	de Havilland DHC-1 Chipmunk 22	C1/0759	24.09.74
	WP870 M J Diggins Rayne Hall Farm, Rayne		22.11.18P
	As 'WP870:12' in RAF grey c/s		
G-BCOJ	Cameron O-56 HAB	124	25.09.74
	Cancelled 17.12.09 as PWFU		12.07.87
	Not known *Inflated Pidley 05.16*		

G-BCOM	Piper J-3C-90 Cub (*L-4A-PI*) 10478	27.09.74	
	F-BDTP, F-BFQP, OO-ADI, 43-29187		
	A D Reohorn tr BCOM Flying group Brighton City		
	'Dougal'	08.07.02P	
	Fuselage No.10303; officially registered as c/n 12040		
	which is the correct identity of G-BGPD: fuselages		
	probably exchanged in France (NF 18.06.18)		

G-BCOO   de Havilland DHC-1 Chipmunk 22   C1/0209   10.10.74
WB760   M A Petrie tr Double Oscar Chipmunk Group
Hawarden   25.05.17E
(IE 16.04.18)

G-BCOR   SOCATA Rallye 100ST   2544   07.01.75
F-OCZK   T J Horsley tr Oscar Romeo Group
Andrewsfield   20.04.19E

G-BCOU   de Havilland DHC-1 Chipmunk 22   C1/0559   10.10.74
WK522   P J Loweth tr The Loweth Flying Group
Duxford   *'Thunderbird 5'*   25.11.19E
As 'WK522' in RAF c/s

G-BCOY   de Havilland DHC-1 Chipmunk 22   C1/0212   10.10.74
WB762   Coventry Gliding Club Ltd
Husbands Bosworth   25.02.19P
Lycoming O-360-A4M

G-BCPD   Gardan GY-201 Minicab   18   24.10.74
F-BGKN   P R Cozens   Hinton-in-the-Hedges   20.06.19P
Built by Constructions Aéronautiques du Béarn

G-BCPG   Piper PA-28R-200 Cherokee Arrow   28R-35705   16.10.74
N4985S   A J B Borak & E J Burgham
Durham Tees Valley   15.08.19E
Official type data 'PA-28R-200 Cherokee Arrow II'
is incorrect; operated by Flying Fox Aviation

G-BCPH   Piper J-3C-65 Cub (*L-4H-PI*)   11225   13.12.74
F-BCZA, French AF, 43-29934
G Earl   Landmead Farm, Garford   19.10.12P
Fuselage No.11050; as '329934:B-72' in USAAF c/s
(IE 25.04.15)

G-BCPJ   Piper J-3C-65 Cub (*L-4J-PI*)   13206   05.11.74
F-BDTJ, 45-4466   J W Widdows   Jersey   10.05.13P
Fuselage No.13036 (IE 21.05.18)

G-BCPKᴹ   Cessna F172M Skyhawk II   F17201194   21.10.74
(D-ELOB)   Cancelled 18.08.14 as WFU   12.01.01
Usworth   *Built by Reims Aviation SA*
Displayed at NE Land Air & Sea Museum

G-BCPN   Grumman American AA-5 Traveler   AA5-0665   21.10.74
N6155A   J R Walker tr G-BCPN Group
Nottingham City   14.03.19E

G-BCPU   de Havilland DHC-1 Chipmunk 22   C1/0839   24.10.74
WP973   P Green   White Waltham   01.02.19E
As 'WP973' in RAF silver c/s with insignia of 10 AEF

G-BCPXᴹ   Szep HFC.125   AS.001   24.10.74
Cancelled 11.01.00 as PWFU   *As 'G-BCPX'*   20.09.97
Built a Szep – project PFA 012-10019
With Kozlekedesi Muzeum, Budapest, Hungary

G-BCRB   Reims/Cessna F172M   F17201259   29.10.74
Wingtask 1995 Ltd   Seething   22.07.19E

G-BCRL   Piper PA-28-151 Cherokee Warrior   28-7415689   05.11.74
N9564N   E T Hawkins & N Smithson
tr Romeo Lima Flying Club   Humberside   06.12.19E

G-BCRR   Grumman American AA-5B Tiger   AA5B-0006   07.11.74
S Waite   Sherburn-in-Elmet   01.09.19E

G-BCRX   de Havilland DHC-1 Chipmunk 22   C1/0232   22.11.74
WD292   M I Robinson & P J Tuplin   White Waltham   30.07.19P
As 'WD292' in RAF silver & yellow bands c/s

G-BCSA   de Havilland DHC-1 Chipmunk 22   C1/0691   25.11.74
WP799   Shenington Gliding Club   Shenington   11.01.19P
Lycoming O-360-A4A

G-BCSL   de Havilland DHC-1 Chipmunk 22   C1/0524   26.11.74
WG474   De Havilland & Partners Ltd   Derby   27.06.17E
(IE 17.12.18)

G-BCTF   Piper PA-28-151 Cherokee Warrior   28-7515033   11.12.74
N9585N   I J Hiatt   Little Staughton   07.06.16E
Rebuilt 1989 & 1990 using major components
ex G-BFXZ; stored 02.18) (NF 07.11.16)

G-BCTI   Schleicher ASK 16   16029   23.12.74
D-KIWA   J G Batch tr Tango India Syndicate
Hinton-in-the-Hedges   11.10.17E
(IE 19.04.18)

G-BCTK   Reims FR172J Rocket   FR17200546   23.12.74
M G E Morton   Bere Farm, Warnford   23.05.19E

G-BCUB   Piper J-3C-65 Cub (*L-4J-PI*)   13370   13.12.74
F-BFBU, 45-4630   S L Goldspink   Old Warden   13.06.01P
Officially c/n '13186' is incorrect: relates to
G-BDOL (qv) – frames switched during
Lippert Reed conversion (NF 27.11.18)

G-BCUF   Reims/Cessna F172M   F17201279   03.01.75
R N Howell t/a Howell Plant Hire & Construction
The Hall, Sutton on Sea   14.10.19E

G-BCUH   Reims/Cessna F150M   F15001195   07.01.75
S Newman tr G-BCUH Group   Elstree   27.03.19E

G-BCUJ   Reims/Cessna F150M   F15001176   09.01.75
C G Dodds   Andrewsfield   19.02.19E

G-BCUO   Scottish Aviation Bulldog Srs 120/122   BH120/371   09.01.75
Ghana AF G-107, G-BCUO
Cranfield University   Cranfield   06.09.19E

G-BCUS   Scottish Aviation Bulldog Srs 120/122   BH120/373   09.01.75
Ghana AF G-109, G-BCUS   R G Hayes tr Falcon Group
Oaksey Park   *'121' & 'Skysport'*   02.08.19E

G-BCUV   Scottish Aviation Bulldog Srs 120/122   BH120/376   09.01.75
Ghana AF G-112, G-BCUV   Flew LLP   Bournemouth   05.08.14E
Exemption to carry 'XX704' in RAF c/s;
stored less marks 06.17 (IE 23.01.18)

G-BCUW   Cessna F177RG Cardinal RG   F177RG0119   10.01.75
SE-GKL   Cancelled 18.08.04 by CAA   12.05.00
Hulcote Farm   *Built by Reims Aviation SA*
Stored 03.13

G-BCUY   Reims/Cessna FRA150M Aerobat   FRA1500269   14.01.75
J C Carpenter   Clipgate Farm, Denton   27.03.19E

G-BCVB   Piper PA-17 Vagabond   17-190   22.01.75
F-BFMT, N4890H   A T Nowak   Popham   24.07.17P

G-BCVC   SOCATA Rallye 100ST   2548   16.01.75
F-OCZO   W Haddow   Glasgow Prestwick   30.07.16E
Stored 05.18 (NF 04.09.15)

G-BCVF   Practavia Pilot Sprite 115   GBC.1   27.01.75
A C Barber   Spanhoe   21.11.18P
Built by G B Castle – project PFA 1362

G-BCVG   Reims/Cessna FRA150L Aerobat   FRA1500245   16.01.75
(I-AFAD)   I G Cooper tr G-BCVG Flying Group
Compton Abbas   14.08.19E

G-BCVH   Reims/Cessna FRA150L Aerobat   FRA1500258   16.01.75
C Quist   Hilversum, Netherlands   28.10.19E

G-BCVJ   Reims/Cessna F172M   F17201305   16.01.75
Rothland Ltd   RAF Woodvale   05.07.19E

G-BCVY   Piper PA-34-200T Seneca II   34-7570022   28.01.75
N32447   Topex Ltd   Cardiff   10.07.18E

G-BCWB   Cessna 182P Skylane   18263566   29.01.75
N5848J   A J Mew & M F Oliver   White Waltham   12.08.19E

G-BCWH   Practavia Pilot Sprite 115   PFA 1366   03.02.75
A T Fines   Shipdham   28.08.19P
Built by K B Parkinson & R Tasker – project PFA 1366

G-BCWK   Alpavia Fournier RF3   24   07.02.75
F-BMDD   T J Hartwell   Sackville Lodge Farm, Riseley
(NF 30.10.18)

G-BCWLᴹ   Westland Lysander IIIA   1244   09.09.75
RCAF   Cancelled 03.06.99 - to USA   *As 'V9281'*
Built by National Steel Car Corporation Ltd
Composite – main airframe possibly RCAF 2403,
parts from RCAF 2341, 2349, 2391
With Fantasy of Flight, Polk City, Florida

G-BCXE   Robin DR.400 2+2   1015   19.02.75
Weald Air Services Ltd   Headcorn   01.09.19E

G-BCXJ   Piper J-3C-65 Cub (*L-4J-PI*)   13048   21.02.75
F-BFFH, OO-SWA, 44-80752   A J Blackford
Craysmarsh Farm, Melksham   *'Juliet'*   25.04.19P
Fuselage No.12878; as '480752:E-39' in USAAC c/s

G-BCXN de Havilland DHC-1 Chipmunk 22 C1/0692 07.03.75
WP800 J A Moolenschot (Sunbury-on-Thames) 21.11.19P
As 'WP800:2' in RAF silver & yellow training bands,
red cheat line c/s, 'Southampton UAS' badge

G-BCXO MBB Bolkow Bo.105DD S.80 27.02.75
'G-BOND', D-HDCE Cancelled 04.03.92 as WFU 23.05.94
Land End *Original pod, c/n S.80 replaced 1992,*
rebuilt & displayed as 'G-CDBS'

G-BCYH Cadet III Motor Glider 2 10.03.75
BGA 1158, RAFGSA 264, XA297
R O Johnson tr G-BCYH Group
(Leighton Bromswold, Huntingdon) 31.10.19P
Built by D C Pattison – project PFA 1568; converted ex Slingsby
T.31B c/n 839

G-BCYKᴹ Avro (Canada) CF-100 Canuck Mk.IV xxxx 18.03.75
RCAF 18393 Cancelled 15.09.81 as WFU
As '18393' in RCAF c/s
With Imperial War Museum, Duxford

G-BCYM de Havilland DHC-1 Chipmunk 22 C1/0598 13.03.75
WK577 D J Fry tr G-BCYM Group Oaksey Park 11.03.19P
As 'WK577' in RAF c/s

G-BCYR Reims/Cessna F172M F17201288 20.03.75
D M Lockley Plockton 25.01.19E

G-BCZH de Havilland DHC-1 Chipmunk 22 C1/0635 19.03.75
WK622 J A Simms Breighton
On rebuild 01.13 (NF 19.02.19)

G-BCZO Cameron O-77 HAB 158 27.03.75
Cancelled 02.04.12 as PWFU 11.10.86
Not known *Inflated Pidley 05.16*

G-BDAA – G-BDZZ

G-BDACᴹ Cameron 0-77 HAB 146 02.04.75
Cancelled 14.11.95 by CAA *Inflated 04.14*
With British Balloon Museum & Library, Newbury

G-BDAD Taylor JT.1 Monoplane PFA 1453 02.04.75
R Pike & S Woodgate Eshott 22.06.17P
Built by J F Bakewell – project PFA 1453

G-BDAG Taylor JT.1 Monoplane PFA 1430 01.04.75
R C Bunce & R L Soutar Longside 18.11.19P
Built by R S Basinger – project PFA 1430

G-BDAI Reims/Cessna FRA150M Aerobat FRA1500266 21.04.75
S J Brenchley Solent 25.10.19E

G-BDAK Rockwell Commander 112A 252 10.04.75
N1252J M C Wilson Top Farm, Croydon 07.06.19E

G-BDAM Noorduyn AT-16-ND Harvard IIB 14-726 10.04.75
C-GFLR, G-BDAM, LN-MAA, Swedish AF 16047,
FE992, 42-12479 Black Star Aviation Ltd Duxford 20.11.19E
As 'FE992:ER-992' in RCAF c/s

G-BDAO SIPA S91 2 10.04.75
F-BEPT S B Churchill
Eastbach Spence, English Bicknor 17.01.19P

G-BDAP Wittman W.8 Tailwind 0387 09.04.75
D G Kelly Easterton 24.01.18P
Built by A & J Whiting – project PFA 3507

G-BDAR Evans VP-1 Series 2 PFA 1537 10.04.75
P W Cooper & A J Gillson Seighford
Built by M J Dunmore & S C Foggin
– project PFA 1537 (NF 17.10.18)

G-BDAY Thunder Ax5-42 Series 1 042 08.04.75
J F Till Welburn, York 20.06.18E
(IE 06.12.18)

G-BDBD Wittman W.8 Tailwind 133 25.04.75
N1198S P A Hall Turweston 22.02.12P
Built by Hamilton Tool Company (NF 13.11.17)

G-BDBF Clutton FRED Series II xxxx 15.04.75
G E & R E Collins (Derby) 18.03.98P
Built by W T Morrell – project PFA 1528;
on rebuild 06.13 (NF 17.09.14)

G-BDBI Cameron O-77 162 15.04.75
C Jones Sonning Common, Reading 11.07.87A
Noted tethered 01.19 (NF 12.04.18)

G-BDBSᴹ Short SD.3-30 UTT SH.1935 & SH.3001 21.04.75
G-14-3001
Cancelled 01.07.93 as WFU 26.09.92
Airframe originally laid down as SC.7 Skyvan c/n SH.1935;
displayed at Ulster Aviation Society, Long Kesh

G-BDBU Reims/Cessna F150M F15001174 30.04.75
G E Fox Bagby 03.12.16E

G-BDBV Jodel D.11A V3 23.04.75
D-EGIB S Pavey tr Seething Jodel Group Seething 08.07.19P
Built by W Wolfrum

G-BDCCᴹ de Havilland DHC-1 Chipmunk 22 C1/0258 25.04.75
WD321 Cancelled 08.04.04 as PWFU
With Boscombe Down Aviation Centre, Old Sarum

G-BDCD Piper J-3C-65 Cub (*L-4J-PI*) 12429 28.04.75
OO-AVS, 44-80133 S Willard tr Cubby Cub Group
Frieslands Farm, Washington 26.06.15P
Fuselage No.12257; as '480133:B-44' in US Army c/s

G-BDCI Piel CP.301A Emeraude 503 25.04.75
F-BIRC M T Slater Sackville Lodge Farm, Riseley 14.06.19P
Built by Société Menavia

G-BDCO Beagle B.121 Pup Series 1 B121-171 06.05.75
(N.....), G-BDCO M R Badminton (Eshott) 28.07.97
Official p/i 'N1931G' is incorrect; relates to
Cessna 421B G-BDCS (NF 28.10.15)

G-BDDF Jodel D.120 Paris-Nice 97 20.05.75
F-BIKZ J V Thompson Breighton 10.11.03P
Built by Société des Etablissements Benjamin Wassmer;
on rebuild 12.16 (NF 29.03.18)

G-BDDG Jodel D.112 855 20.05.75
F-BILM D G Palmer Sturgate 28.07.04P
Built by Etablissement Dormois (NF 05.04.16)

G-BDDS Piper PA-25-260 Pawnee C 25-4757 22.05.75
CS-AIU, N10F Black Mountains Gliding Club Talgarth 15.04.12E
(IE 21.05.18)

G-BDDX Whittaker MW2B Excalibur 001 28.05.75
Cancelled 23.06.83 as PWFU
Newton Abbot *Built by M W Whittaker – project*
PFA 041-10106 Displayed Trago Mills
Shopping Centre 03.16

G-BDEH Jodel D.120A Paris-Nice 239 02.06.75
F-BLNE N J Cronin Garston Farm, Marshfield 13.07.19P
Built by Société Wassmer Aviation

G-BDEI Jodel D.9 Bébé 585 02.06.75
J R M Hore tr The Noddy Flying Group
White Waltham *'Noddy'* 26.04.16P
Built by L T Dix – project PFA 936 (NF 27.06.16)

G-BDEU de Havilland DHC-1 Chipmunk 22 C1/0704 17.06.75
WP808 Cancelled 08.05.14 as destroyed 27.01.13
Prestwick *Dumped stripped of spares 04.18*

G-BDEX Reims/Cessna FRA150M Aerobat FRA1500279 12.06.75
A P F Tucker (Northam, Bideford) 30.07.06
(NF 15.09.15)

G-BDEY Piper J-3C-65 Cub (*L-4J-PI*) 12538 17.06.75
OO-AAT, OO-GAC, 44-80242
A V Williams (London SW6) 19.04.19P
Official c/n 12366 is Frame No.

G-BDFB Phoenix Currie Wot xxxx 20.06.75
J Jennings Felthorpe 07.10.19P
Built by D F Faulkner-Bryant & J Jennings
– project PFA 3008

G-BDFH Auster AOP.9 B5/10/176 24.06.75
XR240 R B Webber Trenchard Farm, Eggesford 28.05.15P
Officially registered with Frame No. AUS/177;
as 'XR240' in AAC c/s (IE 07.12.18)

G-BDFJ Cessna F150M 1501182 25.06.75
Cancelled 03.03.11 by CAA 13.07.02
Shacklewell Lodge, Empringham
Built by Reims Aviation SA; stored 04.18

G-BDFR Fuji FA.200-160 Aero Subaru FA200-262 07.07.75
C B Mellor Sherburn-in-Elmet 01.08.19E

G-BDFUᴹ PMPS Dragonfly MPA Mk.1 01 14.07.75
Cancelled 05.12.83 as WFU
Built by Prestwick MPA Group
On loan from R.Churcher & R.J.Hardy Stored
With National Museum of Flight Scotland, East Fortune

G-BDFW	Rockwell Commander 112A	308	18.06.75
	N1308J Cancelled 05.04.11 by CAA		22.11.08
	Blackbushe *Noted 06.16*		
G-BDFX	Auster 5	2060	09.07.75
	F-BGXG, TW517 A D Pearce		
	Eastbach Spence, English Bicknor		
	Built by Taylorcraft Aeroplanes (England) Ltd (NF 10.07.17)		
G-BDFY	Grumman American AA-5 Traveler	AA5-0806	10.07.75
	G Robertson tr The Grumman Group Kirknewton		12.09.19E
	Operated by Edinburgh Flying Club		
G-BDGB	Gardan GY-20 Minicab (JB.01 standard)	PFA 1819	23.06.75
	T W Slater School Road, Hinderclay		11.04.18P
	Built by D G Burden – project PFA 1819		
G-BDGM	Piper PA-28-151 Cherokee Warrior	28-7415165	30.07.75
	N41307 W Ali Lydd		21.11.19E
G-BDGY	Piper PA-28-140 Cherokee	28-23613	05.08.75
	N3536K J Eagles Oaksey Park		02.09.02
	Stored dismantled 09.16 (NF 18.05.18)		
G-BDHJ	Pazmany PL-1 Laminar	PFA 3604	05.08.75
	Cancelled 11.05.01 by CAA		05.11.97
	Sleap *Stored 01.18*		
G-BDHK	Piper J-3C-65 Cub (*L-4A-PI*)	8969	24.07.75
	F-PHFZ, 42-38400 S Pritchard tr Knight Flying Group		
	Eastbach Spence, English Bicknor		05.06.19P
	Fuselage No.9068; official c/n shown '261' has		
	p/i 42-36414 which corresponds to c/n 8538 (N75366);		
	as '329417' in USAAC c/s		
G-BDIE	Rockwell Commander 112A	342	14.08.75
	N1342J R J Adams & J McAleer Turweston		17.12.19E
G-BDIG	Cessna 182P Skylane II	18263938	26.08.75
	N9877E A Horton & J Lee Headcorn		15.05.19E
	Assembled Reims Aviation with c/n 0020		
G-BDIHᴹ	Jodel D.117	812	22.08.75
	F-BIOT T A S Rayner		
	(Congalton Gardens, East Lothian)		12.08.17P
	Built by Société Aéronautique Normande; damaged		
	Bedlands Gate 03.06.17; used for spares in rebuild		
	of G-BYBE 2019 (NF 21.11.17)		
G-BDIN	Scottish Aviation Bulldog Srs 100/125	BH120/377	20.08.75
	Jordanian A/F 408, JY-BAI, G-BDIN		
	Cancelled 01.08.07 as PWFU		04.07.76
	Aeroventure, Doncaster Spare use 03.13		
G-BDIWᴹ	de Havilland DH.106 Comet 4C	6470	01.09.75
	XR398 Cancelled 23.02.81 to Germany		08.06.81
	As 'G-BDIW' in Dan-Air titles		
	With Flugausstellung Hermeskeil, Trier, Germany		
G-BDIXᴹ	de Havilland DH.106 Comet 4C	6471	01.09.75
	XR399 Cancelled 02.09.91 by CAA *Dan-Air titles*		11.10.81
	With National Museum of Flight Scotland, East Fortune		
G-BDJD	Jodel D.112	PFA 910	03.09.75
	The Real Aeroplane Company Ltd Garton *'Marianne'*		02.07.17P
	Built by J V Derrick – project PFA 910		
G-BDJG	Phoenix Luton LA-4A Minor	PFA 828	03.09.75
	I K G Mitchell tr Luton Minor Group Dunkeswell		
	'Piglet'		02.04.18P
	Built by D J Gaskin – project PFA 828		
G-BDJP	Piper J-3C-90 Cub	22992	11.12.75
	OO-SKZ, PH-NCV, NC3908K S T Gilbert Enstone		18.05.03
	Fuselage No.21017 (NF 22.02.18)		
G-BDJR	SNCAC NC.858	2	30.09.75
	F-BFIY P L Lovegrove New Barn Farm, Crawley		23.05.92P
	On rebuild 10.16 (NF 16.01.15)		
G-BDKC	Cessna A185F Skywagon	185-02569	30.09.75
	N1854R G Duncan tr Lude & Invergarry Farm		
	Partnership Lude Farm, Blair Atholl		19.05.19E
G-BDKD	Enstrom F-28A	319	30.09.75
	P J Price (Hoghton, Preston)		22.12.16E
	(NF 04.01.19)		
G-BDKH	Piel CP.301A Emeraude	241	15.10.75
	F-BIMN R K GriggsMEast Fortune		18.06.19P
	Built by Société Menavia		
G-BDKM	SIPA 903	98	17.11.75
	F-BGHX S W Markham Valentine Farm, Odiham		09.08.11P
	(IE 07.08.18)		

G-BDKU	Taylor JT1 Monoplane	xxxx	22.10.75
	Cancelled 21.10.02 by CAA		05.08.03
	Birchwood House, North Driffield		
	Built by N T Whisler – project PFA 1456		
	For sale as rebuild project 02.19		
G-BDKW	Rockwell Commander 112A	106	03.11.75
	N1277J, ZS-MIB, N1106J N J Taaffe		
	Ranksborough Farm, Langham		30.03.19E
G-BDLO	Grumman American AA-5A Cheetah	AA5A-0026	03.11.75
	N6154A D Kryl Bournemouth		02.08.19E
G-BDLT	Rockwell Commander 112A	363	04.11.75
	N1363J I Parkinson Eshott		25.05.19E
G-BDLY	K & S SA.102.5 Cavalier	xxxx	14.11.75
	P R Stevens Thruxton		02.06.04P
	Built by B S Reeve – project PFA 001-10011		
	(NF 20.03.18)		
G-BDMS	Piper J-3C-65 Cub (*L-4J-PI*)	13049	04.11.75
	F-BEGZ, 44-80753 A T H Martin Old Sarum		24.04.19P
	As 'FR886' in RAF camouflage c/s		
G-BDMW	Jodel DR.100A Ambassadeur	79	02.12.75
	F-BIVM Vectis Gliding Club Ltd Bembridge		22.10.19P
	Built by Société Aéronautique Normande		
G-BDNC	Taylor JT.1 Monoplane	PFA 1454	08.12.75
	R Pike & S Woodgate Eshott		15.07.16P
	Built by N J Cole – project PFA 1454 (NF 23.05.18)		
G-BDNG	Taylor JT.1 Monoplane	PFA 1405	12.12.75
	E C & P King Eastbach Spence, English Bicknor		21.05.19P
	Built by D J Phillips – project PFA 1405		
G-BDNT	Jodel D.92 Bébé	397	02.01.76
	F-PINL R J Stobo Oaklands Farm, Stonesfield		15.02.12P
	Built by J Siry (NF 21.07.17)		
G-BDNU	Reims/Cessna F172M	F17201405	02.01.76
	E Crespen tr EMC Flyers Elstree		28.08.19E
G-BDNW	Grumman American AA-1B Trainer	AA1B-0588	08.01.76
	N A Baxter (Goxhill, Barrow)		27.11.12E
	(NF 07.03.17)		
G-BDNX	Grumman American AA-1B Trainer	AA1B-0590	08.01.76
	N Clark Old Sarum		27.07.16E
	(IE 20.12.16)		
G-BDOD	Reims/Cessna F150M	F15001266	20.01.76
	P R Green tr OD Group RAF Benson		18.06.19E
G-BDOG	Dukeries Bulldog 200	200/381	18.12.75
	D C Bonsall Netherthorpe *'Phoenix Flying Group'*		10.05.19P
	Built by Scottish Aviation Ltd		
G-BDOL	Piper J-3C-65 Cub (*L-4J-PI*)	13186	18.12.75
	F-BCPC, 45-4446 L R Balthazor Coventry		21.11.18P
	Fuselage No.13016; official c/n '13370' is incorrect:		
	airframes switched on UK conversion – holds c/n &		
	USAAC plates relating to c/n 13370 (G-BCUB (qv);		
	as '454630:LI-7' in USAF c/s		
G-BDOT	Fairey Britten-Norman BN-2A MkIII-2 Trislander		
		1025	21.01.76
	ZK-SFF, N900TA, N903GD, N3850K, VH-BPB, G-BDOT		
	Cancelled 28.04.09 sold in Philippines		03.03.09
	Manila, Philippines *Stored 02.13*		
G-BDPA	Piper PA-28-151 Cherokee Warrior	28-7615033	26.01.76
	N9630N J H Sandham t/a JH Sandham Aviation		
	Carlisle Lake District		17.12.19E
G-BDPJ	Piper PA-25-235 Pawnee B	25-3665	02.02.76
	(PH-VBF), G-BDPJ, SE-EPZ		
	G C Westgate t/a GliderFX Parham Park		09.05.19E
G-BDPK	Cameron O-56 HAB	191	04.02.76
	Cancelled 26.11.10 as PWFU		29.12.88
	Not Known *Inflated Amersfoort, 10.16 'Manpower'*		
G-BDRD	Reims/Cessna FRA150M Aerobat	FRA1500289	09.02.76
	CBM Associates Consulting Ltd Beverley (Linley Hill)		13.06.19E
G-BDRG	Taylor JT.2 Titch	xxxx	19.12.78
	D R Gray (Wilmslow)		
	Built by D R Gray – project PFA 060-10295 (NF 18.05.18)		
G-BDRL	Stits SA-3A Playboy	P-689	12.02.76
	N730GF Cancelled 11.05.01 by CAA		17.06.98
	Urney, Strabane *Stored 12.13*		

G-BDSA	Clutton FRED Series 2	LAS-1803	23.02.76
	EI-BFS, G-BDSA Cancelled 29.09.00 by CAA		
	Ballymoney *Built by R A Yates – project*		
	PFA 29-10141; stored 12.13		
G-BDSB	Piper PA-28-181 Archer II	28-7690107	23.02.76
	N8221C Testfair Ltd Fairoaks		06.02.19E
G-BDSF	Cameron O-56	209	01.03.76
	J H Greensides Burton Pidsea, Hull *'Energis'*		29.11.09E
	(NF 29.11.16)		
G-BDSH	Piper PA-28-140 Cherokee Cruiser	28-7625063	01.03.76
	N9638N D Jones tr The Wright Brothers Flying Group		
	Nottingham City		24.09.19E
G-BDSK	Cameron O-65	166	03.03.76
	Semajan Ltd t/a Southern Balloon Group		
	Newbury *'Carousel II'*		15.09.09E
	Stored with The British Balloon Museum		
	& Library 01.17 (NF 16.03.16)		
G-BDSM	Slingsby T.31 Motor Cadet III	2464/3B	05.03.76
	F C J Wevers (Amersfoort, Netherlands)		22.05.02P
	Built by J A L Parton – project PFA 042-10507;		
	rebuilt by D W Savage (NF 13.03.18)		
G-BDTB	Evans VP-1 Series 2	PFA 7009	15.03.76
	C J Riley Sturgate		29.10.04P
	Built by T E Boyes – project PFA 7009 (NF 04.07.18)		
G-BDTL	Evans VP-1 Series 2	PFA 7012	17.03.76
	S A Daniels MoD Boscombe Down		06.08.18P
	Built by A K Lang – project PFA 7012		
G-BDTO	Fairey B-N BN-2A Mk.III-2 Trislander	1027	16.03.76
	G-RBSI, G-OTSB, G-BDTO, 8P-ASC, G-BDTO,		
	(C-GYOX), G-BDTO Cancelled 10.02.17 as PWFU		31.03.16
	Guernsey *On Airport Fire Service fire dump 05.17*		
G-BDTT[M]	Bede BD-5	3795	17.03.76
	Cancelled 02.02.87 by CAA		
	Built by TT Group – project.PFA 014-10084		
	With Solway Aviation Museum, Carlisle Lake District		
G-BDTU	Van Den Bemden Omega III	AFB4	16.03.76
	R G Turnbull Glasbury, Hereford		
	Tethered Gas Balloon; built by A Van den Bemden		
	(AFB c/n = Abingdon Free Balloon) (NF 11.06.18)		
G-BDTV	Mooney M.20F Executive	22-1307	16.03.76
	N6934V F Laufenstein tr Hallergemeinschaft G-BDTV		
	(Essen, Germany)		11.02.19E
G-BDTX	Reims/Cessna F150M	F15001275	19.03.76
	F W & I F Ellis Water Leisure Park, Skegness		20.06.19E
G-BDUI	Cameron V-56	218	19.03.76
	D J W Johnson Alton		06.07.91A
	(NF 08.05.17)		
G-BDUL	Evans VP-1 Series 2	xxxx	25.03.76
	J C Lindsay Retreat Farm, Little Baddow		26.09.19P
	Built by C Goodman – project PFA 1557		
G-BDUM	Reims/Cessna F150M	F15001301	29.03.76
	F-BXZB B J Colburn & P Robichaud Henstridge		06.12.19E
G-BDUN	Piper PA-34-200T Seneca II	34-7570163	29.03.76
	(EI-BLR), G-BDUN, SE-GIA R Paris Alderney		01.07.17E
	Stored with advanced corrosion 09.16		
G-BDUO	Reims/Cessna F150M	F15001304	29.03.76
	S J Anderson & B A Nicholson		
	Wolverhampton Halfpenny Green		12.06.19E
G-BDUP[M]	Bristol 175 Britannia Series 253	13508	31.03.76
	EL-WXA, CU-T120, G-BDUP, XM496		
	Cancelled 09.08.84 to CU-T120 *As 'XM496' in RAF c/s*		
	With Bristol Britannia XM496 Preservation Society, Cotswold		
G-BDUY	Robin DR.400-140B Major 80	1120	05.04.76
	I A Anderson Ardiffery Mains Farm, Hatton		11.04.19E
G-BDUZ	Cameron V-56	213	30.03.76
	P J Bish t/a Zebedee Balloon Service		
	Newtown, Hungerford		29.11.09E
	(NF 18.05.18)		
G-BDVA	Piper PA-17 Vagabond	17-206	23.04.76
	CN-TVY, F-BFFE I M Callier		
	Berry Grove Farm, West Liss		13.07.19P
G-BDVB	Piper PA-15 Vagabond	15-229	23.04.76
	F-BHHE, SL-AAY, F-BETG B P Gardner Popham		09.08.19P
	Officially registered as 'PA-17'		

G-BDVC	Piper PA-17 Vagabond	17-140	29.09.76
	F-BFBL C R & R J Whitcombe (Liss)		23.09.19P
G-BDVG[M]	Thunder Ax6-56A HAB	067	02.04.76
	Cancelled 03.04.92 by CAA		26.05.95
	With British Balloon Museum & Library, Newbury		
G-BDWA	SOCATA Rallye 150ST	2695	20.04.76
	Cancelled 12.02.09 by CAA		07.06.01
	Craigavon, Bannfoot *Noted 12.13*		
G-BDWE	Flaglor Sky Scooter	KF-S-66	12.04.76
	P King Eastbach Spence, English Bicknor		04.09.12P
	Built by D W Evernden – project PFA 1332;		
	noted 04.16 (NF 31.08.18)		
G-BDWJ	Replica Plans SE.5A	xxxx	27.04.76
	'C1904', 'F8010' D W Linney		
	Middlegate Farm, Pitney		15.08.19P
	Built by M L Beach – project PFA 020-10034;		
	as 'F8010:Z' in RAF c/s		
G-BDWM	Bonsall DB-1 Mustang replica	xxxx	03.05.76
	D C Bonsall Sherburn-in-Elmet *'Rosie'*		09.05.19P
	Built by D C Bonsall – project PFA 073-10200;		
	as '414673/LH-I' in USAAF c/s		
G-BDWO[M]	Howes Ax6 HAB	RBH-2	05.05.76
	Cancelled 08.12.14 *'Griffin' Inflated 05.10*		
	Built by R B & C Howes		
	With British Balloon Museum & Library, Newbury		
G-BDWY	Piper PA-28-140 Cherokee E	28-7225378	14.05.76
	PH-NSC, N11C N Donohue Little Snoring		02.09.16E
G-BDXJ	Boeing 747-236B	21831	02.05.80
	N1792B Cancelled 12.01.11 as PWFU		18.11.07
	Dunsfold *Open store 06.17 as 'N88892'*		
G-BDXX	SNCAN NC.858S	110	17.05.76
	F-BEZQ K M Davis (Thornwood, Epping)		03.07.96P
	On rebuild 07.18 (NF 20.01.16)		
G-BDYG[M]	Percival P.56 Provost T.1	PAC/F/056	25.05.76
	7696M, WV493 Cancelled 04.11.91 by CAA		28.11.80
	As 'WV493:29 A-P'		
	With National Museum of Flight Scotland, East Fortune		
G-BDYH	Cameron V-56 HAB	233	24.05.76
	Cancelled 21.12.09 as PWFU		25.11.90
	Not Known *Inflated Pidley 04.18*		
G-BDZA	Scheibe SF25E Super Falke	4320	01.06.76
	(D-KECW) N A White tr Hereward Flying Group		
	Crowland		30.07.19E
G-BDZD	Reims/Cessna F172M	F17201478	01.06.76
	M Watkinson Dunkeswell		13.09.19E
G-BDZG	Slingsby T59H Kestrel 22	1868	03.06.76
	BGA 2481/DYG, G-BDZG R E Gretton Crowland *'592'*		
	(IE 17.09.17)		

G-BEAA – G-BEZZ

G-BEAB	Jodel DR.1051 Sicile	228	18.08.76
	F-BKGH R C Hibberd Coate, Devizes		13.07.07
	Built by Société Aéronautique Normande; stored 10.15		
	(IE 28.11.15)		
G-BEAC	Piper PA-28-140 Cherokee	28-21963	04.06.76
	4X-AND A Bagley-Murray & R Murray Humberside		14.08.19E
G-BEAH	Auster 5J2 Arrow	2366	28.06.76
	F-BFUV, F-BFVV, OO-ABS		
	J G Parish tr Bedwell Hey Flying Group		
	Bedwell Hey Farm, Little Thetford, Ely *'Llewellyn'*		16.05.19P
G-BEBC[M]	Westland WS-55 Whirlwind HAR.10	WA.371	25.06.76
	8463M, XP355 Cancelled 05.12.83 as WFU		
	As 'XP355:A'		
	With City of Norwich Aviation Museum		
G-BEBN	Cessna 177B Cardinal	17701631	01.07.76
	4X-CEW, N34084 S K Gheyi Norwich Int'l		09.02.19E
G-BEBR	Gardan GY-201 Minicab	xxxx	05.07.76
	A R Hawes Monewden		31.03.16P
	Built by A S Jones – project PFA 1824;		
	originally project PFA 1670		

G

G-BEBS	Andreasson BA-4B	HA/01	07.07.76
	T D Wood Garston Farm, Marshfield		17.09.15P
	Built by D M Fenton (t/a Hornet Aviation)		
	– project PFA 038-10157		
G-BEBU	Rockwell Commander 112A	272	08.07.76
	N1272J I Hunt Cardiff		19.06.04
	(NF 16.12.15)		
G-BEBZ	Piper PA-28-151 Cherokee Warrior	28-7615328	14.07.76
	N6193J P E Taylor Jersey		14.06.19E
G-BECB	SOCATA Rallye 100ST	2783	14.07.76
	D H Tonkin Tregolds Farm, St Merryn		27.09.19E
G-BECEᴹ	Aerospace Developments AD500		
	Series B.1 Airship (Hot Air)		14.07.76
	Cancelled 30.05.84 by CAA		01.04.79
	Damaged in gales Cardington 09.03.79:		
	gondola only stored		
	With South Yorkshire Aircraft Museum, Doncaster		
G-BECF	Scheibe SF25A Motorfalke	4555	14.07.76
	OO-WIZ, (D-KARA) Cancelled 26.10.09 as TWFU		01.03.94
	Upper Hale, Farnham *Stored at private address 01.15*		
G-BECK	Cameron V-56	136	27.07.76
	A M & N H Ponsford Leeds		09.05.06A
	(NF 21.01.19)		
G-BECN	Piper J-3C-65 Cub (*L-4J-PI*)	12776	27.07.76
	F-BCPS, 44-80480 G Denney tr CN Cub Group		
	Audley End *'Miss Monica'*		31.07.19E
	As '480480:44-E' in USAAC c/s		
G-BECS	Thunder Ax6-56A HAB	074	04.08.76
	Cancelled 24.08.10 as PWFU		05.06.08
	Not Known *Inflated Ashton Court 08.18*		
G-BECT	CASA 1-131E Jungmann Series 2000	3974	03.08.76
	Spanish AF E3B-338 I R Hannah Deanland		18.06.19P
	As 'A-57' in Swiss AF c/s		
G-BECW	CASA 1-131E Jungmann Series 2000	2037	03.08.76
	Spanish AF E3B-423		
	C M Rampton Pent Farm, Postling		04.11.06P
	Earlier rebuild incorporated parts of G-BECY		
	ex E3B-459 (IE 07.01.19)		
G-BECZ	Mudry CAP 10B	68	26.07.76
	F-BXHK The London Aerobatic Company Ltd		
	Seething		02.06.07
	(IE 29.10.18)		
G-BEDA	CASA 1-131E Jungmann Series 2000	2099	03.08.76
	Spanish AF E3B-504		
	T Callier Grove Farm, Raveningham		11.12.19P
G-BEDB	SNCAN Nord 1203 Norecrin II	117	05.08.76
	F-BEOB Cancelled 14.11.91 by CAA		11.06.80
	Ley Farm, Chirk *Noted on rebuild 09.17*		
G-BEDF	Boeing B-17G-105-VE Fortress	8693	05.08.76
	N17TE, F-BGSR, 44-85784		
	B17 Preservation Ltd Duxford *'Sally B'*		29.04.19P
	As '124485:DF-A' in USAAC c/s		
G-BEDG	Rockwell Commander 112A	482	05.08.76
	N1219J G-BEDG Ltd Fairoaks		18.02.19E
G-BEDJ	Piper J-3C-65 Cub (*L-4J-PI*)	12890	05.08.76
	F-BDTC, 44-80594 R L Earl White Waltham		16.10.19P
	Fuselage No.12720		
G-BEDVᴹ	Vickers 668 Varsity T.1	xxxx	26.07.76
	WJ945 Cancelled 15.06.89 by CAA As 'WJ945:21'		15.10.87
	With Cornwall Aviation Heritage Centre, Newquay Cornwall		
G-BEEEᴹ	Thunder Ax6-56A HAB	070	20.08.76
	Cancelled 19.05.93 by CAA		11.05.84
	With British Balloon Museum & Library, Newbury		
G-BEEH	Cameron V-56	250	24.08.76
	Sade Balloons Ltd London NW8 *'Tywi'*		05.11.10E
	(IE 22.10.16)		
G-BEEI	Cameron N-77	249	24.08.76
	A P Griffiths Rushden		02.08.19E
G-BEER	Isaacs Fury II	PFA 1588	31.08.76
	C E Styles Damyns Hall, Upminster		25.09.19P
	Built by M J Clark – project PFA 1588;		
	as 'K2075' in RAF 43 Sqdn c/s		
G-BEFA	Piper PA-28-151 Cherokee Warrior	28-7615416	08.09.76
	N6978J M Lawrynowicz Wycombe Air Park		06.12.18E
	(IE 03.01.19)		

G-BEFV	Evans VP-2	V2-2390 & YA-3	05.10.76
	Cancelled 06.12.95 by CAA		
	Stonehouse, Gloucester		
	Built by M S Gaunt – project PFA 063-10203		
	Displayed 12.17, Tile Trader Ryeford Industrial Estate		
G-BEGG	Scheibe SF25E Super Falke	4326	15.10.76
	(D-KDFB) J L Cowan tr G-BEGG Motorfalke		
	Hinton-in-the-Hedges		18.04.19E
G-BEHH	Piper PA-32R-300 Cherokee Lance	32R-7680323	29.10.76
	N6172J K Swallow Sherburn-in-Elmet		06.09.19E
G-BEHU	Piper PA-34-200T Seneca II	34-7670265	03.11.76
	N6175J Heli Air Ltd Wellesbourne Mountford		03.07.18E
G-BEHV	Reims/Cessna F172N	F17201541	03.11.76
	Leading Edge Flight Training Ltd Glasgow		10.01.19E
G-BEHXᴹ	Evans VP-2	V2 2338	08.11.76
	Cancelled 16.12.02 as PWFU		
	Built by G S Adams – project PFA 7222		
	With Ulster Aviation Society, Lisburn		
G-BEIF	Cameron O-65	259	17.11.76
	C Vening Chichester Marina, Chichester *'Solitaire'*		25.10.10E
	(NF 28.02.18)		
G-BEIG	Reims/Cessna F150M	F15001361	18.11.76
	R D Forster Beccles		01.11.17E
	Stored 01.18		
G-BEII	Piper PA-25-235 Pawnee D	25-7656059	16.11.76
	N54918 The Burn Gliding Club Ltd Burn		21.06.19E
G-BEIP	Piper PA-28-181 Archer II	28-7790158	22.11.76
	N6628F A Reckermann (Bochum, Germany)		06.11.19E
G-BEIS	Evans VP-1	PFA 7029	25.11.76
	D L Haines Gloucestershire		
	Built by D J Park – project PFA 7029 (NF 29.01.16)		
G-BEJA	Thunder Ax-6-56A HAB	098	31.12.76
	Cancelled 27.02.90 by CAA		27.05.92
	Not Known *Inflated Pidley 05.16*		
G-BEJDᴹ	Avro 748 Series 1/105	1543	17.12.76
	LV-HHE, LV-PUF Cancelled 08.04.10 as PWFU		29.03.06
	With Wirral Aviation Society, Liverpool-John Lennon		
G-BEJK	Cameron S-31	256	01.12.76
	A M & N H Ponsford t/a Rango Balloon & Kite Company		
	Leeds *'Esso'*		
	(NF 17.05.18)		
G-BEKM	Evans VP-1	PFA 7025	10.01.77
	G J McDill Westmoor Farm, Thirsk		23.03.95P
	Built by G J McDill – project PFA 7025 (NF 28.01.16)		
G-BEKN	Reims/Cessna FRA150M Aerobat	FRA1500318	12.01.77
	Peterborough Flying School Ltd Sibson		11.01.19E
G-BEKO	Reims/Cessna F182Q Skylane II	F18200037	12.01.77
	F J & G J Leese Sherburn-in-Elmet		21.03.19E
G-BELT	Cessna F150J	F150-0409X	26.01.77
	R J Whyham Blackpool		21.09.15E
	Built by Reims Aviation SA; rebuilt, ex G-ATND		
	& G-AWUV (NF 18.04.17)		
G-BEMB	Reims/Cessna F172M	F17201487	27.01.77
	Stocklaunch Ltd Goodwood		23.04.19E
G-BEMW	Piper PA-28-181 Archer II	28-7790243	09.02.77
	N9566N Touch & Go Ltd White Waltham		25.05.19E
G-BEMY	Reims/Cessna FRA150M Aerobat	FRA1500315	09.02.77
	J R Power Kilrush, RoI		26.04.19E
G-BEND	Cameron V-56	260	14.02.77
	P J Bish tr Dante Balloon Group		
	Newtown, Hungerford *'Le Billet'*		01.01.94A
	(IE 10.04.18)		
G-BENJ	Rockwell Commander 112B	522	07.03.77
	N1391J J D Harries tr Benj Flying Group		
	Top Farm, Croydon		21.01.20E
G-BEOE	Reims/Cessna FRA150M Aerobat	FRA1500322	21.03.77
	W J Henderson Eshott		15.07.19E
G-BEOH	Piper PA-28R-201T Turbo Cherokee Arrow III		
		28R-7703038	11.03.77
	N1905H S J Goodburn tr Gloucestershire Flying Club		
	Gloucestershire		03.07.18E
G-BEOI	Piper PA-18-150 Super Cub	18-7709028	11.03.77
	N54976 Southdown Gliding Club Ltd Parham Park		18.04.19E

G-BEOK	Reims/Cessna F150M	F15001366	14.03.77
	M P O'Connor (Redcar)		26.09.19E
G-BEOL	Short SC.7 Skyvan 3 Variant 100	SH.1954	16.03.77
	ZS-OIO, JA8803 (2), G-BEOL, G-14-122		
	Liberty Aviation Ltd Kortrijk-Wevelgem Int'l, Belgium		09.07.19E
	As 'Austrian Air Force 5S-TC'		
G-BEOX[M]	Lockheed 414 Hudson IIIA (A-29A-LO) 414-6464		25.03.77
	VH-AGJ, VH-SMM, R.Australian AF A16-199, FH174,		
	41-36975 Cancelled 22.12.81 as WFU		
	As 'A16-199: SF-R'		
	With RAF Museum, Hendon		
G-BEOY	Reims/Cessna FRA150L Aerobat	FRA1500150	30.03.77
	F-BTFS J N Ponsford Goodwood		24.07.19E
G-BEOZ[M]	Armstrong-Whitworth AW.650 Argosy 101 6660		28.03.77
	N895U, N6502R, G-1-7 Cancelled 19.11.87 as WFU		28.05.86
	'Fat Albert' Elan titles		
	With East Midlands Aeropark, East Midlands		
G-BEPO[M]	Cameron N-77 HAB	279	01.04.77
	Cancelled 14.05.98 as WFU		27.06.94
	With British Balloon Museum & Library, Newbury		
G-BEPV	Fokker S11-1 Instructor	6274	13.04.77
	PH-ANK, R Netherlands Navy 174, R Netherlands AF E-31		
	M & S W Isbister & C Tyers Spanhoe		
	'Kon.Marine' & 'S11-174'		05.11.19P
	As '174:K' in Royal Netherlands Navy yellow c/s		
G-BEPY	Rockwell Commander 112B	524	20.04.77
	N1399J T L Rippon Sywell		14.06.19E
G-BEPZ[M]	Cameron D-96 HA Airship	300	13.04.77
	Cancelled 28.04.94 as WFU		12.02.90
	Damaged Warren Farm, Savernake Forest 08.01.94		
	& DBR during recovery		
	With British Balloon Museum & Library, Newbury		
G-BERA	SOCATA Rallye 150ST	2821	13.04.77
	F-ODEX A C Stamp Redhill		09.01.20E
G-BERI	Rockwell Commander 114	14234	06.05.77
	N4909W M J Metham & L J Turner tr G-BERI Group		
	Thruxton		02.08.18E
G-BERN	Saffery S.330	4	19.04.77
	B Martin Somersham, Huntingdon 'Beeze I'		
	Extant 02.18		
G-BERT	Cameron V-56	273	19.04.77
	E C Barker (Penne, Midi-Pyrénées, France) 'Bert'		28.12.16E
G-BERW	Rockwell Commander 114	14214	06.05.77
	N4884W Cancelled 27.07.07 as PWFU		05.05.07
	Henstridge Noted 04.14		
G-BERY	Grumman American AA-1B Trainer	AA1B-0193	27.10.77
	N9693L P B Anderson North Weald '79'		10.05.19E
G-BESY[M]	BAC 167 Strikemaster Mk.88A	xxxx	26.04.77
	Saudi AF 1133, G-27-299 Cancelled 18.04.83 by CAA		
	– to Saudi AF as 1133 As '1133' in Saudi AF c/s		
	Plane Set 364		
	With Imperial War Museum, Duxford		
G-BETD	Robin HR.200-100 Club	20	28.04.77
	PH-SRL C L Wilsher Sywell		05.12.19E
	Built by Avions Pierre Robin		
G-BETE	Rollason Beta B.2A	xxxx	26.04.77
	T M Jones Derby		
	Built by T Jones – project PFA 002-10169;		
	incorporates parts ex project PFA 1304 (IE 09.07.18)		
G-BETF[M]	Cameron Champion 35 SS HAB	280	17.05.77
	Cancelled 24.01.92 as WFU		06.04.84
	Champion Spark Plug		
	With British Balloon Museum & Library, Newbury		
G-BETH[M]	Thunder Ax6-56A HAB	113	27.05.77
	Cancelled 11.05.93 as WFU		31.05.78
	With British Balloon Museum & Library, Newbury		
G-BETM	Piper PA-25-235 Pawnee D	25-7656066	05.05.77
	N54927 Yorkshire Gliding Club (Proprietary) Ltd		
	Sutton Bank		18.07.19E
G-BETO	Morane-Saulnier MS.885 Super Rallye 34		18.05.77
	F-BKED Cancelled 27.10.06 as PWFU		11.12.04
	Farley Farm, Farley Chamberlayne Stored 03.13		

G-BEUA	Piper PA-18-150 Super Cub	18-8212	21.06.77
	D-ECSY, N4146Z London Gliding Club Proprietary Ltd		
	Dunstable Downs		29.01.11E
	(IE 08.04.18)		
G-BEUD	Robin HR.100/285 Tiara	534	08.06.77
	F-BXRC D A Gathercole & A J Verlander Spanhoe		01.12.18E
G-BEUI	Piper J-3C-65 Cub (L-4H-PI)	12174	19.05.77
	F-BFEC, F-OAJF, French AF, 44-79878		
	Lytham St Annes Spitfire Display Team Ltd Blackpool		17.05.19P
	Fuselage No.12002; official c/n '43-29245' conflicts		
	with G-KIRK; as '479878:MF-D' in US Army c/s		
G-BEUM	Taylor JT.1 Monoplane	PFA 1438	08.06.77
	Condor Aviation International Ltd		
	Birchwood Lodge, North Duffield		28.07.04P
	Built by Speedwell Sailplanes (NF 22.12.15)		
G-BEUP	Robin DR.400-180 Régent	1228	19.05.77
	M C R Sims t/a MCRS Aviation Goodwood		10.04.18E
G-BEUU	Piper PA-18 Super Cub 95 (L-18C-PI) 18-1551		27.06.77
	F-BOUU, French Army 18-1551, 51-15551		
	C Gartland Felthorpe		25.10.19P
	Fuselage No.18-1523		
G-BEUV	Thunder Ax6-56A HAB	115	27.05.77
	Cancelled 20.05.93 by CAA		19.12.81
	Not Known Inflated Ashton Court 08.18 'Webbs'		
G-BEUX	Reims/Cessna F172N	F17201596	30.05.77
	Zentelligence Ltd Maypole Farm, Chislet		08.02.19E
G-BEUY	Cameron N-31	283	31.05.77
	J J Daly Halfway House, Waterford, RoI		02.08.19E
G-BEVB	SOCATA Rallye 150ST	2860	02.06.77
	L Clarke City of Derry		11.08.19E
G-BEVC	SOCATA Rallye 150ST	2861	02.06.77
	M Jennings & M P Whitley tr Wolds Flyers Syndicate		
	Bagby		17.07.19E
	Stored 02.18		
G-BEVG	Piper PA-34-200T Seneca II	34-7570060	31.05.77
	(D-Gxxx), G-BEVG, VQ-SAM, N32854		
	AWA Aeronautical Web Academy LDA		
	(Prior Velho, Portugal)		20.01.17E
	(IE 06.12.18)		
G-BEVI (3)[M]	Thunder Ax7-77A HAB	125	30.05.77
	Cancelled 08.01.92 as WFU		
	With British Balloon Museum & Library, Newbury		
G-BEVO	Sportavia-Putzer Fournier RF5	5107	27.06.77
	5N-AIX, D-KAAZ M Hill		
	(Ettington, Stratford-upon-Avon)		15.05.18P
	(IE 05.09.18)		
G-BEVS	Taylor JT.1 Monoplane	PFA 1429	08.06.77
	D Hunter Orange Grove Barn, Chavenage Green		23.04.19P
	Built by D Hunter – project PFA 1429		
G-BEVT	Fairey B-N BN-2A Mk.III-2 Trislander	1057	10.06.77
	Aurigny Air Services Ltd Duxford		13.07.17E
	Displayed externally 2019		
G-BEWN	de Havilland DH.82A Tiger Moth	T305	16.06.77
	VH-WAL, RAAF A17-529		
	H D Labouchere Langham		30.04.19P
	Built by de Havilland Aircraft Proprietary Ltd,		
	Australia as c/n 952		
G-BEWO	Moravan Zlin Z-326 Trener Master	915	23.11.77
	CS-ALU T Cooper Goodwood		24.03.19E
G-BEWP	Cessna F150M Commuter	F1501426	13.06.77
	Cancelled 06.12.83 as destroyed		
	Perth Built by Reims Aviation SA		
	Instructional frame 07.16		
G-BEWR	Reims/Cessna F172N	F17201613	13.06.77
	Aerotech Solent Ltd Solent		11.04.19E
G-BEWX	Piper PA-28R-201 Arrow III	28R-7737070	23.06.77
	N5723V P J Collins & T M Freeman		
	tr Three Greens Arrow Group Headcorn		08.03.19E
G-BEWY	Bell 206B JetRanger	348	27.06.77
	G-CULL, EI-BXQ, G-BEWY, 9Y-TDF		
	Polo Aviation Ltd Urchinwood Manor, Congresbury		20.10.17E
G-BEXJ	Britten-Norman BN-2A-26 Islander	2020	30.06.77
	D-IORF, N100DA, N60PA. G-BEXJ, N412JA,		
	G-51-2020, G-BEXJ		
	Channel Islands Air Search Ltd Guernsey		28.02.19E

G-BEXN	Grumman American AA-1C Lynx	AA1C-0045	07.09.77
	N6147A G S Page Earls Colne *'0045' & 'XN'*		01.06.18E
G-BEXO	Piper PA-23-160 Apache	23-213	04.07.77
	OO-APH, N1176P Cancelled 04.02.09 by CAA		13.08.03
	Stapleford *Open store 03.16*		
G-BEXW	Piper PA-28-181 Archer II	28-7790521	11.07.77
	N38122 S S Bamrah t/a Jet World Biggin Hill		14.12.13E
	(IE 23.11.18)		
G-BEXX	Cameron V-56 HAB	274	29.06.77
	Cancelled 12.06.15 as PWFU		02.07.86
	Not Known *Inflated Pidley 05.16*		
G-BEYA	Enstrom 280C Shark	1104	15.08.77
	D W C Holmes (Langley Mill, Nottingham)		10.09.19E
G-BEYBᴹ	Fairey Flycatcher replica	WA/3	11.07.77
	Cancelled 12.07.96 as WFU *As 'S1287:5' in FAA c/s*		
	Built by Westward Airways (Lands End) Ltd		
	With Fleet Air Arm Museum, RNAS Yeovilton		
G-BEYL	Piper PA-28-180 Cherokee Archer	28-7405098	06.09.77
	PH-SDW, N9518N		
	D W Gerrard tr Yankee Lima Group Henstridge		16.05.19E
G-BEYT	Piper PA-28-140 Cherokee	28-20330	19.07.77
	D-EBWO, N6280W J N Plange Beverley (Linley Hill)		13.08.15E
G-BEYV	Cessna T210M Turbo Centurion II	21061583	19.07.77
	N732KX P Middleton Kings Farm, Thurrock		28.03.19E
G-BEYZ	Jodel DR.1050-M1 Sicile Record	588	22.07.77
	F-BMGV W H Bliss Loadman Farm, Hexham		30.09.19P
	Built by Centre-Est Aéronautique		
G-BEZC	Grumman American AA-5 Traveler	AA5-0493	29.07.77
	F-BUYN, (N7193L) A T Paton tr Easter Flying Group		
	Easter Farm, Fearn		23.10.19E
G-BEZE	Rutan VariEze	xxxx	26.07.77
	S K Cockburn (Stanford-le-Hope)		02.06.04P
	Built by J Berry – project PFA 074-10207 (NF 09.04.18)		
G-BEZF	Grumman American AA-5 Traveler	AA5-0538	29.07.77
	F-BVJP D L Keverne tr Assets of the		
	G-BEZL Flying Group Turweston		05.03.19E
G-BEZG	Grumman American AA-5 Traveler	AA5-0561	29.07.77
	F-BVRJ M D R Harling Shobdon		25.06.19E
G-BEZH	Grumman American AA-5 Traveler	AA5-0566	29.07.77
	F-BVRK, N9566L P Middlebrooke tr The ZH Group		
	Nottingham City		07.09.19E
	Damaged on landing Nottingham City 30.01.19		
G-BEZI	Grumman American AA-5 Traveler	AA5-0567	29.07.77
	F-BVRL, N9567L C, J & L Campbell Breighton		07.02.17E
	(IE 03.04.18)		
G-BEZK (2)	Cessna F172H	F172-0462	17.08.77
	D-EBUD, D-ENHC, R Canadian AF SLN-07, N20462		
	S Jones Beccles		21.07.18E
	Built by Reims Aviation SA		
G-BEZL	Piper PA-31 Navajo C	31-7712054	01.08.77
	SE-GPA 2 Excel Aviation Ltd Sywell		11.08.19E
G-BEZO	Reims/Cessna F172M	F17201392	24.08.77
	Staverton Flying School @ Skypark Ltd		
	Gloucestershire		26.04.19E
G-BEZP	Piper PA-32-300 Cherokee Six	32-7740087	19.08.77
	N38572 T P McCormack & J K Zealley		
	White Waltham		21.11.19E
G-BEZR	Cessna F172M Skyhawk II	F17201395	24.08.77
	Cancelled 30.03.16 as destroyed		06.05.16
	Bournemouth *Built by Reims Aviation SA*		
	On rebuild 10.16		
G-BEZS	Cessna FR172J Rocket	F1720562	11.08.77
	Cancelled 16.03.95 as PWFU		22.09.79
	(St Albans) *Built by Reims Aviation SA*		
	Derelict fuselage stored 10.16		
G-BEZV	Reims/Cessna F172M	F17201474	24.08.77
	(I-CCAY) Alexander Air Ltd Aberdeen Int'l		18.04.19E
G-BEZY	Rutan VariEze	xxxx	26.07.77
	J P Kynaston Holmbeck Farm, Burcott		18.05.96P
	Built by R J Jones – project PFA 074-10225 (NF 10.11.17)		
G-BEZZ	Jodel D.112	397	12.08.77
	F-BHMC K R Nestor tr G-BEZZ Group		
	Manchester Barton		02.12.19P
	Built by Passot Aviation		

G-BFAA – G-BFZZ

G-BFAA	Sud-Aviation Garden GY-80-160 Horizon	78	20.10.77
	F-BLVY Cancelled 06.01.12 as PWFU		
	Enstone *Stored 08.17*		
G-BFABᴹ	Cameron N-56 HAB	297	15.08.77
	Cancelled 21.04.92 by CAA		10.08.92
	With British Balloon Museum & Library, Newbury		
G-BFAF	Aeronca 7BCM Champion (*L-16A-AE*)	7BCM-11	15.08.77
	N797US, N2552B, 47-797 D A Crompton		
	(Church Lawton, Stoke-on-Trent)		17.05.19P
	As '47-797:A-797' in US Army c/s		
G-BFAI	Rockwell Commander 114	14304	17.08.77
	N4984W Cancelled 28.06.17 as PWFU		02.06.15
	Kings Farm, Thurrock *Open store. derelict 06.17*		
G-BFAP	SIAI Marchetti S.205-20/R	4-213	01.09.77
	I-ALEN N C du Piesanie		
	Watchford Farm, Yarcombe		08.03.19E
G-BFAS	Evans VP-1 Series 2	PFA 7033	15.08.77
	A I Sutherland Fearn		07.12.16P
	Built by A I Sutherland – project PFA 7033		
G-BFAW	de Havilland DHC-1 Chipmunk 22	C1/0733	31.08.77
	8342M, WP848 M L J Goff Old Buckenham		08.10.19P
	As 'WP848' in RAF c/s		
G-BFAX	de Havilland DHC-1 Chipmunk 22	C1/0496	31.08.77
	8394M, WG422 S R Symonds Derby		03.08.17P
	As 'WG422:16' in RAF c/s		
G-BFBA	Jodel DR.100A Ambassadeur	88	12.09.77
	F-BIVU R E Nicholson		
	(Cat and Fiddle Park, Clyst St. Mary)		11.05.17P
	Built by Société Aéronautique Normande		
G-BFBB	Piper PA-23-250 Aztec E	27-7405294	01.09.77
	SE-GBI Cancelled 06.04.17 as PWFU		04.08.10
	Elstree *Open store 02.19*		
G-BFBE	Robin HR.200-100 Club	12	09.09.77
	PH-SRK A C Pearson Rochester		26.05.19E
G-BFBM	Saffery S.330	7	01.09.77
	B Martin Somersham, Huntingdon *'Beeze II'*		
	Extant 02.18		
G-BFBR	Piper PA-28-161 Cherokee Warrior II	28-7716277	15.09.77
	N38845 Flying at Lee on Solent Ltd		
	t/a Phoenix Aviation Solent		23.05.19E
G-BFBY	Piper J-3C-65 Cub (*L-4H-PI*)	10998	29.09.77
	F-BDTG, 43-29707 M Shaw Old Buckenham		
	'you can run but you can't hide'		03.07.19P
	As '329707:44-S' in US Army Air Corps c/s		
G-BFCT	Cessna TU206F	U20603202	15.09.77
	(LN-TVF), N8341Q D I Schellingerhout		
	Mount Airey Farm, South Cave		17.05.19E
	Badged 'Stationair II'		
G-BFCZᴹ	Sopwith Camel F.1 replica	WA/2	12.10.77
	Cancelled 23.01.03 as WFU *As 'B7270'*		23.02.89
	Built by Westward Airways (Lands End) Ltd		
	With Brooklands Museum, Weybridge		
G-BFDC	de Havilland DHC-1 Chipmunk 22	C1/0525	15.11.77
	7989M, WG475 N F O'Neill Newtownards		17.06.19P
G-BFDE	Sopwith Tabloid Scout Replica	168	22.09.77
	Cancelled 08.12.86 as PWFU		04.06.83
	RAF Stafford *Built by D M Cashmore*		
	– project PFA 067-10186		
	In RAF Museum store 2018 as '168'		
G-BFDI	Piper PA-28-181 Archer II	28-7790382	05.10.77
	N2205Q Truman Aviation Ltd Nottingham City		13.11.19E
G-BFDK	Piper PA-28-161 Warrior II	28-7816010	23.09.77
	N40061 S T Gilbert Elstree		07.04.19E
	Operated by Stars Fly		
G-BFDL	Piper J-3C-65 Cub (*L-4J-PI*)	13277	30.11.77
	HB-OIF, 45-4537 B A Nicholson Fordoun		27.06.18P
	Fuselage No.13107; as '454537:J-04' in USAAC c/s		
G-BFDO	Piper PA-28R-201T Turbo Cherokee Arrow III		
		28R-7703212	03.10.77
	N38396 D J Blackburn & J Driver Elstree		10.04.19E

G-BFEB Jodel D.150 Mascaret 34 14.10.77
F-BMJR, OO-LDY, F-BLDX
M E Doig tr G-BFEB Syndicate Portmoak 14.11.19P
Built by Société Aéronautique Normande

G-BFEF Agusta-Bell 47G-3B1 Sioux AH.1 1541 11.10.77
XT132 I F Vaughan Guernsey 05.07.19E

G-BFEH Jodel D.117A 828 05.10.77
F-BITG M D Mold Watchford Farm, Yarcombe 19.11.19P
Built by Société Aéronautique Normande

G-BFEK Reims/Cessna F152 II F15201442 11.10.77
Staverton Flying School @ Skypark Ltd Gloucestershire 08.03.19E

G-BFEV Piper PA-25-235 Pawnee D 25-7756060 20.10.77
N82547 Yorkshire Gliding Club (Proprietary) Ltd
Sutton Bank 13.02.19E

G-BFFB Evans VP-2 V2-2289 27.10.77
Cancelled 02.09.91 by CAA
Mount Airey, South Cave *Built by D Bradley –*
project PFA 063-10159; stored 07.15

G-BFFE Reims/Cessna F152 II F15201454 27.10.77
A J Hastings Glasgow Prestwick 29.04.10E
Stored 05.18 (NF 03.11.16)

G-BFFP Piper PA-18-150 Super Cub 18-8187 09.11.77
PH-OTC, N10F East Sussex Gliding Club Ltd
Ringmer 30.08.19E
Fuselage No.18-8402

G-BFFW Reims/Cessna F152 II F15201447 14.11.77
Stapleford Flying Club Ltd Stapleford 03.12.19E

G-BFGD Reims/Cessna F172N F17201545 14.11.77
F-WZDT J L Tobias tr Wannabe Flyers Popham 31.01.20E

G-BFGG Reims/Cessna FRA150M Aerobat FRA1500321 14.11.77
F-WZDS G Oliver Retford Gamston 13.11.19E

G-BFGH Reims/Cessna F337G Super Skymaster F33700081 14.11.77
S Findlay (Lower Mains, Dollar) 23.07.18E
Wichita c/n 33701754

G-BFGK Jodel D.117 644 27.06.78
F-BIBT A D Eastwood
Stoneacre Farm, Farthing Corner 22.10.19P
Built by Société Aéronautique Normande

G-BFGL Reims/Cessna FA152 Aerobat FA1520339 14.11.77
E-Plane Ltd Fenland 17.02.19E

G-BFGS SOCATA MS.893E Rallye 180GT 12571 31.08.76
F-BXYK, French AF 12571, F-SCAZ, "41-AZ"
Cancelled 24.01.12 as PWFU 23.12.11
Picton, Yarm *In Battlezone paintball park 06.18*

G-BFGZ Reims/Cessna FRA150M Aerobat FRA1500329 28.11.77
C M Barnes Hardwick 05.03.19E

G-BFHH de Havilland DH.82A Tiger Moth 85933 25.11.77
F-BDOH, French AF, DF197 P & T J Harrison
(Barcombe, Lewes) 26.05.07
Built by Morris Motors Ltd (NF 26.06.17)

G-BFHI Piper J-3C-65 Cub (L-4J-PI) 12532 25.11.77
F-BFBT, 44-80236 N Glass & A J Richardson
(Craigavon) 28.05.04P
(NF 01.03.16)

G-BFHR Robin DR.220 2+2 30 01.12.77
F-BOCX B Carter Thruxton 28.06.19E
Built by Centre-Est Aéronautique

G-BFHU Reims/Cessna F152 II F15201461 07.12.77
M Bonsall Netherthorpe 14.10.19E

G-BFHX Evans VP-1 xxxx 02.12.77
D A Milstead (West Chiltington, Pulborough) 07.04.99P
Built by D F Gibson – project PFA 062-10283
(NF 16.08.17)

G-BFIB Piper PA-31 Turbo Navajo 31-684 21.12.77
LN-NPE, OY-DVH, LN-RTJ
2 Excel Aviation Ltd Sywell 03.04.19E

G-BFID Taylor JT.2 Titch xxxx 13.12.77
D J Howell Wolverhampton Halfpenny Green 29.08.19P
Built by W F Adams – project PFA 060-10311

G-BFIE Reims/Cessna FRA150M Aerobat FRA1500331 12.01.78
J P A Freeman Headcorn 13.05.18E
(IE 11.12.18)

G-BFIG Reims/Cessna FR172K Hawk XP FR17200615 12.01.78
K Rogan Dublin Weston, RoI 26.09.19E

G-BFIN Grumman American AA-5A Cheetah AA5A-0520 22.03.78
N6145A Aircraft Engineers Ltd Glasgow Prestwick 20.08.18E

G-BFIPM Wallbro Monoplane 1909 replica WA-1 16.12.77
Cancelled 28.03.01 as TWFU
Built by K H Wallis No marks carried
With Shuttleworth Collection, Old Warden

G-BFIT Thunder Ax6-56Z 136 20.12.77
J A G Tyson Painswick, Stroud 'Folly' 03.05.91A
(NF 20.03.18)

G-BFIU Reims/Cessna FR172K Hawk XP FR17200591 12.01.78
N96098 A R Greenly (Navenby, Lincoln) 11.04.19E

G-BFIV Reims/Cessna F177RG Cardinal RG F177RG0161 12.01.78
N96106 C Fisher & M L Miller Henstridge 28.05.19E

G-BFIX Thunder Ax7-77A 133 09.12.77
S J Owen Standish, Wigan 'Animal Magic' 23.01.79
(NF 24.07.15)

G-BFIY Reims/Cessna F150M F15001381 11.01.78
OE-CMT Blackbushe Flying Club Ltd Blackbushe 10.05.19E

G-BFJR Reims/Cessna F337G Super Skymaster F33700082 04.01.78
N46297, (N53658) City North Ltd (Romsey) 22.10.09E
Wichita c/n 33701761 (IE 03.05.18)

G-BFJZ Robin DR.400-140B Major 80 1290 20.01.78
Weald Air Services Ltd Headcorn 16.05.19E

G-BFKB Reims/Cessna F172N F17201601 16.01.78
PH-AXO C Chapman & H Dobson
tr Shropshire Flying Group Sleap 17.06.19E

G-BFKF Cessna FA152 Aerobat FA1520337 26.01.78
Cancelled 06.10.17 as PWFU 15.08.14
Conington *Built by Reims Aviation SA*
Stored dismantled 06.18

G-BFKL Cameron N-56 369 23.01.78
Merrythought Ltd Telford 'Merrythought Toys' 17.07.92A
Noted 05.16 (NF 02.11.15)

G-BFLPM Amethyst Ax6-56 001 20.02.78
Cancelled by CAA 22.11.01 17.10.09
With British Balloon Museum & Library, Newbury

G-BFLU Reims/Cessna F152 II F15201433 15.02.78
Swiftair Maintenance Ltd Elstree 09.07.19E
Operated by Flight Training London Ltd

G-BFLX Grumman American AA-5A Cheetah AA5A-0524 14.03.78
N6147A A M Verdon
Farley Farm, Farley Chamberlayne 17.07.19E

G-BFLZ Beech 95-A55 Baron TC-220 16.03.78
PH-ILE, HB-GOV D Pye Blackpool 27.08.09E
(NF 15.01.19)

G-BFMF Cassutt Racer IIIM xxxx 17.02.78
T D Gardner Wolverhampton Halfpenny Green '53' 21.05.19P
Built by P H Lewis – project PFA 034-10147

G-BFMG Piper PA-28-161 Cherokee Warrior II 28-7716160 11.05.78
N3506Q Andrewsfield Aviation Ltd Andrewsfield 20.12.19E

G-BFMH Cessna 177B Cardinal 17702034 18.04.78
N34836 Aerofoil Aviation Ltd Leeds Bradford 26.04.19E

G-BFMK Reims/Cessna FA152 Aerobat FA1520344 06.03.78
The Leicestershire Aero Club Ltd Leicester 16.03.19E

G-BFMR Piper PA-20 Pacer 20-130 20.02.78
N7025K J Knight (Shadoxhurst, Ashford) 06.03.06
(NF 02.08.18)

G-BFMX Reims/Cessna F172N F17201732 24.08.78
M Rowe Pent Farm, Postling 22.01.19E

G-BFNG Jodel D.112 1321 06.03.78
F-BNHI P H Jeffcote tr NG Group Leicester 28.06.19P
Built by Société Wassmer Aviation

G-BFNI Piper PA-28-161 Warrior II 28-7816215 08.03.78
N9505N P R J Welch t/a Lion Services Hawarden 13.01.20E

G-BFNK Piper PA-28-161 Warrior II 28-7816282 08.03.78
N9527N Parachuting Aircraft Ltd Old Sarum 21.11.19E

G-BFNM Globe GC-1B Swift 2205 15.06.78
N78205, NC78205 M J Butler Pocklington 10.05.19P

G-BFOE Reims/Cessna F152 II F15201475 23.03.78
Redhill Air Services Ltd
Wolverhampton Halfpenny Green 29.01.20E

G-BFOF	Reims/Cessna F152 II	F15201448	09.03.78
	Ionian Aviation Ltd (Petrich, Bulgaria)		09.11.19E
G-BFOG	Cessna 150M	15076223	13.03.78
	N66706 J P Nugent t/a Wicklow Wings Newcastle, RoI		
G-BFOJ	American AA-1 Yankee	AA1-0395	04.04.78
	OH-AYB, (LN-KAJ), (N6195L)		
	J J N Carpenter Bournemouth		08.11.19E
G-BFOP	Jodel D.120 Paris-Nice	32	23.03.78
	F-BHTX J K Cook & E Leggoe Bournemouth *'Jean'*		20.12.17P
	Built by Société des Etablissements Benjamin Wassmer		
G-BFOU	Taylor JT.1 Monoplane	xxxx	17.03.78
	G Bee (Stockton-on-Tees)		
	Built by I N M Cameron – project PFA 055-10333		
	(NF 26.01.16)		
G-BFOV	Reims/Cessna F172N	F17201675	18.05.78
	M C Walker Brighton City		21.10.19E
G-BFOZᴹ	Thunder Ax6-56 Plug HAB	144	20.03.78
	Cancelled 16.04.92 by CAA Inflated 04.14		10.09.89
	With British Balloon Museum & Library, Newbury		
G-BFPA	Scheibe SF25B Falke	46179	29.03.78
	D-KAGM W J Grieve Balado		04.05.19E
	(IE 21.09.17)		
G-BFPH	Reims/Cessna F172K	F17200802	23.03.78
	PH-VHN T Marriott tr Linc-Air Flying Group		
	Retford Gamston		23.08.19E
G-BFPO	Rockwell Commander 112B	530	10.05.78
	N1412J Doerr International Ltd Sywell		01.08.19E
G-BFPP	Bell 47J-2 Ranger	2851	23.05.78
	F-BJAN, TR-LKD, F-OCBU M R Masters Solent		11.11.99
	(NF 06.03.17)		
G-BFPR	Piper PA-25-235 Pawnee D	25-7856007	04.04.78
	SE-KGY, I-TOZU, G-BFPR, N82591		
	The Windrushers Gliding Club Ltd Bicester		17.04.19E
	Lycoming O-540-G1A5		
G-BFPS	Piper PA-25-235 Pawnee D	25-7856013	04.04.78
	N82598 C A M M Neidt (Roosendaal, Netherlands)		25.04.19E
G-BFPZ	Reims/Cessna F177RG Cardinal RG	F177RG0079	03.04.78
	N56PZ, G-BFPZ, PH-AUK, D-EGBM, (OO-DVE)		
	G E Thompson (Barton-upon-Humber)		29.03.11E
	(NF 29.11.18)		
G-BFRI	Sikorsky S-61N Mk.II	61809	26.05.78
	British International Helicopter Services Ltd		
	RAF Mount Pleasant, Falkland Islands		16.01.19E
G-BFRR	Reims/Cessna FRA150M Aerobat	FRA1500326	19.04.78
	LN-ALO S Cosgrove tr Romeo Romeo Flying Club		
	Tatenhill		11.11.19E
G-BFRS	Reims/Cessna F172N	F17201555	19.04.78
	LN-ALP Aerocomm Ltd Kings Farm, Thurrock		23.08.19E
G-BFRV	Reims/Cessna FA152 Aerobat	FA1520345	17.04.78
	Cristal Air Ltd Brighton City		06.10.19E
G-BFRY	Piper PA-25-260 Pawnee B	25-7405789	23.05.78
	SE-GIB Yorkshire Gliding Club (Proprietary) Ltd		
	Sutton Bank		10.07.15E
	Noted 01.17 (IE 26.04.18)		
G-BFSA	Reims/Cessna F182Q Skylane II	F18200074	17.04.78
	F-WZDG R Fernandes tr Delta Lima Flying Group		
	Retford Gamston		05.09.19E
G-BFSC	Piper PA-25-235 Pawnee D	25-7656068	02.06.78
	N82302 Essex Gliding Club Ltd Ridgewell		27.04.19E
	Official p/i 'N9503N' is incorrect		
G-BFSD	Piper PA-25-235 Pawnee D	25-7656084	02.06.78
	N82338 Deeside Gliding Club (Aberdeenshire) Ltd		
	Aboyne		07.01.20E
G-BFSK	Piper PA-23-160 Apache	23-576	14.04.78
	OO-NVC, OO-HVL, OO-PIP		
	Cancelled 05.12.83 as WFU		
	Croughton *Submerged in gravel pit for diving school 12.13*		
-BFSS	Reims FR172G Rocket	FR17200167	07.07.78
	OH-CDY Albedale Farms Ltd Manor Farm, Grateley		16.01.20E
G-BFSY	Piper PA-28-181 Archer II	28-7890200	19.04.78
	N9503N A S Domone tr Downland Aviation		
	Goodwood		05.02.20E
G-BFSZ	Piper PA-28-161 Warrior II	28-7816468	19.04.78
	G-KBPI, G-BFSZ, N9556N R J Whyham Blackpool		
	(NF 22.10.15)		
G-BFTC	Piper PA-28R-201T Turbo Arrow III	28R-7803197	19.04.78
	N3868M D Petty tr Top Cat Flying Group		
	Sherburn-in-Elmet		05.04.19E
	Official type data 'PA-28R-201T Turbo		
	Cherokee Arrow III' is incorrect		
G-BFTF	Grumman American AA-5B Tiger	AA5B-0879	07.09.78
	FC Burrow Ltd Sherburn-in-Elmet		01.10.19E
G-BFTG	Grumman American AA-5B Tiger	AA5B-0777	15.05.78
	D Hepburn & G R Montgomery Perth		24.11.16E
G-BFTH	Reims/Cessna F172N	F17201671	03.05.78
	T W Oakley Eddsfield, Octon Lodge Farm, Thwing		15.05.19E
G-BFTZᴹ	SOCATA MS.880B Rallye Club	1269	02.06.78
	F-BPAX Cancelled 14.11.91 by CAA *'Kathy S'*		19.09.81
	On loan from The Aeroplane Collection		
	With Newark Air Museum, Winthorpe		
G-BFUB	Piper PA-32RT-300 Lance II	32R-7885052	18.05.78
	N9509C J Lowndes		
	Wolverhampton Halfpenny Green		28.06.19E
	Official type data 'PA-32R-300 Cherokee Lance II'		
	is incorrect		
G-BFUD	Scheibe SF25E Super Falke	4313	19.05.78
	D-KLDC J S Halford tr SF25E Syndicate Eyres Field		09.09.19E
G-BFUZ	Cameron V-77 HAB	398	24.05.78
	Cancelled 25.02.13 as PWFU		18.04.10
	Not Known *Inflated Pidley 04.18*		
G-BFVG	Piper PA-28-181 Archer II	28-7890408	01.06.78
	N31746, N9558N C J P Mrziglod		
	(Eppelborn, Germany)		16.11.16E
G-BFVH	AirCo DH.2 replica	WA4	01.06.78
	S W Turley RAF Scampton		05.03.19P
	Built by Westward Airways (Lands End) Ltd;		
	also allocated BAPC 112; as '5964' in RFC c/s		
	(represents 24 Sqdn a/c of Major L G Hawker VC)		
G-BFVS	Grumman American AA-5B Tiger	AA5B-0784	11.08.78
	N28736 T R Chapman & M R Place		
	tr G-BFVS Flying Group Denham		24.04.19E
G-BFVU	Cessna 150L	15074684	10.08.78
	N75189 A N Mole Crowfield		02.08.19E
G-BFWB	Piper PA-28-161 Warrior II	28-7816584	22.06.78
	N31752 Mid-Anglia Flight Centre Ltd		
	t/a Mid-Anglia School of Flying Cambridge		22.02.19E
G-BFWD	Phoenix Currie Wot	PFA 3009	22.06.78
	A Foan Dunkeswell		03.02.20P
	Built by F E Nuthall – project PFA 3009;		
	as 'C3009:B' in RAF c/s & in SE5A configuration		
G-BFWK	Piper PA-28-161 Warrior II	28-7816610	23.06.78
	N9589N Cancelled 26.05.98 as PWFU		08.12.99
	Londonderry *Fuselage at Oakfire Paintball park 10.13*		
G-BFXF	Andreasson BA-4B	AAB-001	10.07.78
	P N Birch (Trunch, North Walsham)		30.08.07P
	Built by A Brown – project PFA 038-10351 (NF 07.01.19)		
G-BFXG	Druine D.31 Turbulent	PFA 1663	10.07.78
	R J Stobo tr XG Group Oaklands Farm, Stonesfield		
	Built by S Griffin, E J I Musty & M J Whatley		
	– project PFA 1663 (NF 28.06.16)		
G-BFXK	Piper PA-28-140 Cherokee F	28-7325387	01.08.78
	PH-NSK G-BFXK Owners Ltd Rochester		26.11.18E
	(IE 03.01.19)		
G-BFXR	Jodel D.112	247	27.07.78
	F-BFTM R G Marshall (Scholes, Holmfirth)		01.09.11P
	Built by Société des Etablissements Benjamin Wassmer		
	(NF 27.10.16)		
G-BFXS	Rockwell Commander 114	14271	03.08.78
	N4949W Romeo Whiskey Ltd Old Buckenham		14.04.19E
G-BFXW	Grumman American AA-5B Tiger	AA5B-0940	21.02.79
	A M & J D Arnold (Folkestone)		09.04.19E
G-BFXX	Gulfstream American AA-5B Tiger	AA5B-0917	03.10.78
	W R Gibson North Weald		12.02.19E
G-BFYA	MBB Bölkow BÖ.105DB	S.321	31.10.78
	D-HJET Wessex Aviation Ltd Biggin Hill		25.05.09E
	Stored 05.15 (NF 09.06.15)		

G-BFYI	Westland-Bell 47G-3B-1	WAN-17	24.01.79	
	XT167 K P Mayes Stone House, Goathland		06.12.14E	
	(NF 09.12.16)			
G-BFYK	Cameron V-77	433	16.08.78	
	EI-BAY, G-BFYK L E Jones Worcester		21.09.09E	
	(NF 29.03.16)			
G-BFYL	Evans VP-2	xxxx	15.08.78	
	F C Handy (Wolverhampton)		17.12.98P	
	Built by A G Wilford – project PFA 063-10146			
	(NF 21.06.16)			
G-BFYO[M]	SPAD XIII replica	0035	16.11.78	
	'53398', D-EOWM Cancelled 14.10.86 as WFU		21.06.82	
	As '54513:1' in 3rd Escadrille French AF c/s			
	Built by Williams Flugzeugbau			
	With American Air Museum, Duxford			
G-BFYW	Slingsby T65A Vega 17L	1888	01.09.78	
	BGA 2592 D A Blunden Parham Park 'FYW'		13.01.19E	
G-BFZA	Alpavia Fournier RF3	5	14.09.78	
	F-BLEL T J Hartwell Sackville Lodge Farm, Riseley			
	Carries 'F-BLEL' on fuselage roof (NF 30.10.18)			
G-BFZB	Piper J-3C-65 Cub (*L-4J-PI*)	13019	21.09.78	
	D-ECEL, HB-OSP, 44-80723			
	M S Pettit Oaklands Farm, Stonesfield		29.05.19P	
	Fuselage No.12849; as '480723:E5-J' in USAF c/s			
G-BFZD	Reims/Cessna FR182 Skylane RG II	FR18200010	09.10.78	
	A R Harris Sleap		04.02.19E	
G-BFZH	Piper PA-28R-200 Cherokee Arrow	28R-35307	25.10.78	
	OY-BDB Aircraft Engineers Ltd Glasgow Prestwick		17.04.19E	
G-BFZM	Rockwell Commander 112TC-A	13191	09.10.78	
	N4661W J A Hart & R J Lamplough Bournemouth		21.08.09E	
	Open store Bournemouth 02.19 (NF 24.11.15)			
G-BFZO	Grumman American AA-5A Cheetah	AA5A-0697	01.11.78	
	R D Billins tr G-BFZO Flying Group Cranfield		08.06.19E	
G-BFZR[M]	Gulfstream AA-5B Tiger	AA5B-097	30.04.04	
	EI-BJS Cancelled 03.11.05 by CAA *As 'GO-CSE'*		24.05.07	
	With Bournemouth Aviation Museum, Bournemouth			

G-BGAA – G-BGZZ

G-BGAA	Cessna 152 II	15281894	18.07.78	
	N67529 PJC (Leasing) Ltd Stapleford		05.06.19E	
G-BGAB	Reims/Cessna F152 II	F15201531	13.10.78	
	TG Aviation Ltd Lydd		29.04.19E	
	Operated by Thanet Flying Club			
G-BGAE	Reims/Cessna F152 II	F15201540	08.11.78	
	Aerolease Ltd Conington		21.03.19E	
G-BGAF	Cessna FA152 Aerobat	FA1520349	13.10.78	
	Cancelled 28.03.17 as destroyed		25.06.14	
	Southend *Built by Reims Aviation SA*			
	Wreck in open store 01.19			
G-BGAH	Clutton FRED Srs 2	xxxx	15.02.78	
	Cancelled 02.09.91 by CAA			
	Tibenham *Built by G A Harris – project*			
	PFA 029-10324; stored 05.17			
G-BGAJ	Reims/Cessna F182Q Skylane II	F18200096	13.10.78	
	B & C K Blumberg Alderney		20.06.19E	
G-BGAS[M]	Colting Ax8-105A HAB	001	27.06.78	
	Cancelled 23.12.81 as destroyed		12.09.82	
	Destroyed Flims, Switzerland 20.09.80; basket only			
	With British Balloon Museum & Library, Newbury			
G-BGAX	Piper PA-28-140 Cherokee F	28-7325409	20.10.78	
	PH-NSH B L Newbold tr G-BGAX Group			
	Sherburn-in-Elmet		04.04.19E	
G-BGAY	Cameron O-77 HAB	446	04.12.78	
	Cancelled 04.08.98 by CAA		16.12.91	
	Hungerford *Inflated Pidley 05.16*			
G-BGAZ	Cameron V-77	439	20.10.78	
	C J Madigan & D H McGibbon			
	Bristol BS3 *'Cameron Balloons'*		26.07.19E	
	Envelope rebuilt – details not known			
G-BGBA	Robin R2100A Club	133	02.05.78	
	F-OCBJ Cancelled 09.04.14 as PWFU		23.10.12	
	Gloucestershire *Fuselage stored 07.15,*			
	wings to G-OCAC 03.12			

G-BGBE	Jodel DR.1050 Ambassadeur	260	29.11.78	
	F-BJYT B & J A Mawby Holmbeck Farm, Burcott		27.08.19P	
	Built by Centre-Est Aéronautique			
G-BGBF	Druine D.31A Turbulent	PFA 1658	24.10.78	
	T A Stambach RAF Henlow		25.03.04P	
	Built by L Davies – project PFA 1658; dismantled 07.18			
	(NF 10.11.15)			
G-BGBG	Piper PA-28-181 Archer II	28-7990012	02.11.78	
	N39730 Harlow Printing Ltd Carlisle Lake District		16.12.19E	
G-BGBI	Reims/Cessna F150L	F15000688	28.11.78	
	PH-LUA P M Cobban & T J Gilpin tr BI Flying Group			
	Bourn		18.04.19E	
G-BGBK	Piper PA-38-112 Tomahawk	38-78A0433	02.11.78	
	N9738N Smart People Dont Buy Ltd Nottingham City		26.08.19E	
G-BGBV	Slingsby T65A Vega	1890	25.10.78	
	BGA 2800/EMS, G-BGBV M P Day Tibenham 'T65'		13.06.19E	
G-BGBW	Piper PA-38-112 Tomahawk	38-78A0670	08.11.78	
	N9710N Smart People Dont Buy Ltd Nottingham City		20.05.19E	
G-BGCB	Slingsby T65A Vega	1892	20.11.78	
	BGA 2794/EML, G-BGCB F J Bradley & G Wright			
	Skelling Farm, Skirwith 'EML'		05.04.19E	
G-BGCM	Gulfstream American AA-5A Cheetah	AA5A-0835	23.03.78	
	R W Walker Beverley (Linley Hill)		16.04.19E	
G-BGCO	Piper PA-44-180 Seminole	44-7995128	20.12.78	
	N2103D BAE Systems (Operations) Ltd Warton		07.03.19E	
G-BGCU	Slingsby T65A Vega	1893	28.11.78	
	BGA 2611/EDV, G-BGCU P Hadfield Rhigos		30.07.14E	
	(NF 07.08.18)			
G-BGCY	Taylor JT.1 Monoplane	xxxx	23.11.78	
	M R Punter (St Issey, Wadebridge)		14.03.17P	
	Built by M T Taylor – project PFA 055-10370			
	(IE 02.07.17)			
G-BGEF	Jodel D.112	1309	07.12.78	
	F-BMYL G G Johnson Water Leisure Park, Skegness		12.09.96P	
	Built by Société Wassmer Aviation (NF 30.08.18)			
G-BGEH	Monnett Sonerai II	xxxx	01.12.78	
	E C Murgatroyd (Bromham, Bedford)		16.08.96P	
	Built by R E Finlay – project PFA 015-10254;			
	noted 03.17 (NF 12.04.16)			
G-BGEI	Oldfield Baby Lakes	xxxx	01.12.78	
	D H Greenwood Woolston Moss, Warrington		30.04.19P	
	Built by D H Greenwood – project PFA 010-10016,			
	incorporating fuselage ex project PFA 1576			
	Note G-BGLS (as 'G-BGEI') in showroom roof at Chariots			
	Specialist Cars, Kettering 2018)			
G-BGES	Phoenix Currie Super Wot	'10291'	30.11.78	
	N M Bloom Abbots Hill Farm, Hemel Hempstead		13.05.19P	
	Originally registered to J R Roberts as c/n JR.1;			
	c/n changed to '10291' (project PFA 058-10291)			
G-BGFF	Clutton FRED Series II	xxxx	18.12.78	
	P C Appleton & I Pearson (Falmouth)		04.03.09P	
	Built by G R G Smith – project PFA 029-10261;			
	stored 07.16 (NF 07.02.19)			
G-BGFG	Gulfstream American AA-5A Cheetah	AA5A-0687	25.01.79	
	N6158A A J Williams (Grantham)		30.05.10E	
	(NF 14.05.18)			
G-BGFJ	Jodel D.9 Bébé	PFA 1324	11.12.78	
	R J Stobo Oaklands Farm, Stonesfield		12.06.19P	
	Built by C M Fitton – project PFA 1324;			
	originally allocated as Type Falconar F4			
G-BGFX	Reims/Cessna F152 II	F15201555	28.12.78	
	Redhill Air Services Ltd Redhill		21.07.19E	
G-BGGA	Bellanca 7GCBC Citabria 150S	1104-79	05.02.79	
	P C Woolley Cadwell Park, Louth		21.09.19E	
G-BGGB	Bellanca 7GCBC Citabria 150S	1105-79	07.02.79	
	D A Payne City of Derry		04.04.19E	
G-BGGC	Bellanca 7GCBC Citabria 150S	1106-79	05.02.79	
	P F H de Coninck Dunkerque, France		07.03.19E	
G-BGGD	Bellanca 8GCBC Scout	284-78	05.02.79	
	Bidford Gliding & Flying Club Ltd Bidford		05.08.19E	
G-BGGE	Piper PA-38-112 Tomahawk	38-79A0161	10.01.79	
	N9673N Smart People Dont Buy Ltd Nottingham City		12.04.19E	

G

G-BGGI	Piper PA-38-112 Tomahawk	38-79A0165	10.01.79
	N9675N Smart People Dont Buy Ltd Nottingham City		17.06.19E
G-BGGM	Piper PA-38-112 Tomahawk	38-79A0170	10.01.79
	N9698N G E Fox Bagby		04.09.19E
G-BGGO	Reims/Cessna F152 II	F15201569	08.03.79
	East Midlands Flying School Ltd East Midlands		07.09.19E
G-BGGP	Reims/Cessna F152 II	F15201580	08.03.79
	East Midlands Flying School Ltd East Midlands		05.04.17E
	(NF 30.04.18)		
G-BGGU	Wallis WA-116/S	702	28.12.78
	Cancelled 03.08.16 as PWFU		
	Old Warden *Stored 10.16*		
G-BGGW	Wallis WA-122/R-R	704	28.12.78
	Cancelled 03.08.16 as PWFU		06.07.13
	Old Warden *Stored 10.16*		
G-BGHF[M]	Westland WG.30 Series 100-60	WA.001.P	04.01.79
	Cancelled 29.03.89 as WFU		01.08.86
	With The Helicopter Museum, Weston-super-Mare		
G-BGHJ	Reims/Cessna F172N	F17201777	15.01.79
	EI-BVF, G-BGHJ Airplane Ltd Humberside		12.08.19E
G-BGHM	Robin R1180T Aiglon	227	19.02.79
	P Price Blackpool		11.06.19E
G-BGHS	Cameron N-31	501	15.01.79
	G Gray East Worldham, Alton *'Champion'*		29.05.19E
G-BGHT	Falconar F-12	xxxx	17.01.79
	C R Coates (Sneaton Thorpe, Whitby)		
	Built by T K Baillie – project PFA 022-10040		
	(NF 15.02.16)		
G-BGHU	North American T-6G-NF Texan	182-729	22.01.79
	Port AF 707, French AF 115042, 51-15042		
	C E Bellhouse Pent Farm, Postling *'Carly'*		14.06.19E
	As '115042:TA-042' in USAF c/s		
G-BGHY	Taylor JT.1 Monoplane	PFA 1455	12.01.79
	J H Mangan Little Snoring		09.12.15P
	Built by J Prowse – project PFA 1455 (IE 28.01.18)		
G-BGIB (2)	Cessna 152 II	15282161	03.07.79
	N68169 Redhill Air Services Ltd Fairoaks		13.01.19E
	Operated by Fairoaks Flight Centre		
G-BGIG	Piper PA-38-112 Tomahawk	38-78A0773	23.01.79
	N2607A Leading Edge Flight Training Ltd Glasgow		19.11.19E
G-BGIU	Cessna F172H	F172-0620	26.02.79
	PH-VIT S J Windle Exeter Int'l		03.01.18E
	Built by Reims Aviation SA		
G-BGIY	Reims/Cessna F172N	F17201824	31.01.79
	Leading Edge Flight Training Ltd Glasgow		19.10.19E
	Operated by Glasgow Flying Club		
G-BGKE[M]	BAC One Eleven 539GL	BAC.263	30.01.80
	Cancelled 01.03.94 – to MoD as ZH763 *As 'ZH763'*		25.02.92
	With Cornwall Aviation Heritage Centre, Newquay Cornwall		
G-BGKO	Gardan GY-20 Minicab	1827	14.02.79
	Condor Aviation International Ltd		
	Birchwood Lodge, North Duffield		
	Built by R B Webber – project PFA 1827;		
	stored dismantled late 2016 (NF 22.12.15)		
G-BGKP	MBB Bolkow Bo105D	S.212	01.08.79
	Cancelled 10.07.86 as destroyed		
	Thruxton *Travelling exhibit for Hampshire*		
	Air Ambulance 12.15		
G-BGKS	Piper PA-28-161 Warrior II	28-7916221	12.02.79
	N9562N Fly With The Best Ltd Dundee		04.06.19E
	Operated by Tayside Aviation		
G-BGKT	Auster AOP.9	B5/10/137	28.12.78
	XN441 G T Gimblett tr Kilo Tango Group		
	(Goscott Farm, Week St Mary)		21.08.19P
	Officially registered with Frame number AUS/137;		
	as 'XN441' in AAC c/s		
G-BGKU	Piper PA-28R-201 Arrow III	28R-7837237	08.03.79
	N31585 Aerolease Ltd Conington		21.06.19E
	Official type data 'PA-28R-201 Cherokee Arrow III'		
	is incorrect		
G-BGKV	Piper PA-28R-201 Arrow III	28R-7737156	21.05.79
	N44985 R N Mayle Brighton City		12.05.19E
G-BGKY	Piper PA-38-112 Tomahawk	38-78A0737	02.03.79
	N9732N APB Leasing Ltd Swansea		02.02.19E

G-BGKZ	Auster J5F Aiglet Trainer	2776	15.12.78
	F-BGKZ R B Webber Trenchard Farm, Eggesford		25.02.95
	(NF 28.10.15)		
G-BGLA	Piper PA-38-112 Tomahawk	38-78A0741	09.03.79
	N9699N J T Mountain		
	(Bourne Park, Hurstbourne Tarrant)		09.06.10E
	(NF 05.02.16)		
G-BGLB	Bede BD.5B	3796	02.03.79
	Cancelled 21.11.91 by CAA		04.08.81
	Wroughton *Built by W Sawney – project PFA 14-10085*		
	In Science Museum store 2013		
G-BGLF	Evans VP-1 Series 2	xxxx	28.02.79
	B A Schlussler Black Springs Farm, Castle Bytham		30.05.19P
	Built by R A Abrahams – project PFA 062-10388		
G-BGLG	Cessna 152 II	15282092	11.04.79
	N67909 Cloud Global Ltd Perth		30.10.19E
G-BGLK	Monnett Sonerai IIL	xxxx	24.02.78
	Cancelled 09.07.13 by CAA		01.06.05
	North Weald *Built by G L Kemp*		
	– project PFA 015-10304; stored 05.18		
G-BGLO	Reims/Cessna F172N	F17201900	08.03.79
	D K Fung Kings Farm, Thurrock		
	(IE 29.08.18)		
G-BGLS	Oldfield Baby Lakes	xxxx	11.12.78
	Cancelled 12.12.11 by CAA		
	Kettering *Built by D S Morgan – project*		
	PFA 010-10237; suspended from ceiling Chariots		
	Specialist Cars as 'G-BGEI'		
-BGLZ	Stits SA-3A Playboy	71-100	19.06.79
	N9996 W Hinchcliffe Dalkeith Farm, Winwick		18.04.19P
	Built by D J Stadler		
G-BGME	SIPA 903	96	01.01.81
	G-BCML, 'G-BCHU', F-BGHU M Emery Redhill		17.06.94P
	(NF 10.12.18)		
G-BGMJ	Gardan GY-201 Minicab	12	19.06.78
	F-BGMJ A W Wakefield tr G-BGMJ Group Sibson		04.07.19P
	Built by Constructions Aéronautique de Bearn		
G-BGMP	Cessna F172G	F172-0240	26.03.79
	PH-BNV B M O'Brien Headcorn		27.04.19E
	Built by Reims Aviation SA		
G-BGMR	Gardan GY-20 Minicab	xxxx	12.03.79
	P A Hall Turweston		14.07.15P
	Built by A B Holloway to JB.01 Minicab standard		
	– project PFA 056-10153; on rebuild 01.16 (IE 04.10.16)		
G-BGMS	Taylor JT.2 Titch	MS1	20.10.78
	M A J Spice (Middlewich)		
	Built by M A J Spice – project PFA 060-10400		
	(NF 01.02.16)		
G-BGMT	SOCATA Rallye 235E Gabier	13126	14.09.78
	M Faulkner & C G Wheeler Morgansfield, Fishburn		30.05.19E
G-BGMV	Scheibe SF25B Falke	4648	15.05.79
	D-KEBG Cancelled 14.07.15 as PWFU		16.11.01
	Grange Farm, North Lopham *Stored 02.17*		
G-BGND	Reims/Cessna F172N	F17201576	03.03.78
	PH-AYI, (F-GAQA) A J M Freeman Andrewsfield		21.12.19E
G-BGNT	Reims/Cessna F152 II	F15201644	23.10.79
	Aerolease Ltd Conington		01.02.19E
G-BGNV	Gulfstream American GA-7 Cougar	GA7-0078	20.04.79
	N790GA D D Saint Norton Malreward		13.10.19E
G-BGOG	Piper PA-28-161 Warrior II	28-7916350	08.06.79
	N9639N W D Moore & F J Morris Turweston		25.01.20E
G-BGOI	Cameron O-56 HAB	526	04.04.79
	Cancelled 14.01.11 by CAA		
	Not Known *Inflated Bath 12.18*		
G-BGOL	Piper PA-28R-201T Turbo Arrow III	28R-7803335	11.04.79
	N36705 R G Jackson Bournemouth		16.05.19E
	Official type data 'PA-28R-201T Turbo Cherokee		
	Arrow III' is incorrect		
G-BGON	Gulfstream American GA-7 Cougar	GA7-0095	24.04.79
	N9527Z D J Derby & J Prus-Wisniewski		
	Wolverhampton Halfpenny Green		03.05.19E
G-BGOO[M]	Colt Flame 56 Flame HAB	039	27.04.79
	Cancelled 19.05.93 by CAA		
	With British Balloon Museum & Library, Newbury		

G-BGOR	North American AT-6D Harvard III	88-14863	28.03.79
	FAP1508, SAAF 7504, EX935, 41-33908		
	M W Levy & A P Wilson North Weald		04.07.15P
	Also reported as c/n 88-14880;		
	as '14863' in USAAF c/s (IE 06.07.18)		
G-BGPB	CCF T-6 Harvard Mk.4 (*T-6J-CCF Texan*) CCF4-538		04.04.79
	Portuguese AF 1747, West German AF BF+050,		
	AA+050, 53-4619		
	Aircraft Spares & Materials Ltd Duxford		18.04.19E
	Built by Canadian Car & Foundry Co;		
	as '1747' in Portuguese AF c/s		
G-BGPD	Piper J-3C-65 Cub (*L-4H-PI*)	12040	18.04.79
	F-BFQP, F-BDTP, 44-79744		
	P R Whiteman Marsh Hill Farm, Aylesbury		21.06.19P
	Fuselage No.11867; official c/n '10478' (ex 43-29187,		
	OO-ADI, F-BFQP) is incorrect; presumably		
	fuselages exchanged in France – see G-BCOM;		
	as '479744:49-M' in USAAF c/s		
G-BGPFᴹ	Thunder Ax6-56Z HAB	206	13.07.79
	Cancelled 21.11.89 as WFU		27.06.82
	With British Balloon Museum & Library, Newbury		
G-BGPH	Gulfstream American AA-5B Tiger	AA5B-1248	14.08.79
	(G-BGRU) Shipping & Airlines Ltd Biggin Hill		11.03.19E
G-BGPI	Plumb BGP-1	xxxx	26.06.78
	B G Plumb Hinton-in-the-Hedges		22.01.19P
	Built by B G Plumb – project PFA 083-10359		
G-BGPJ	Piper PA-28-161 Warrior II	28-7916288	24.04.79
	N9602N West Lancs Warrior Co Ltd RAF Woodvale		03.04.19E
G-BGPL	Piper PA-28-161 Warrior II	28-7916289	20.04.79
	N9603N Aviation Advice & Consulting Ltd		
	Wellesbourne Mountford		22.10.19E
G-BGPM	Evans VP-2	xxxx	17.04.79
	Condor Aviation International Ltd		
	Mount Airey Farm, South Cave		
	Built by T Painter – project PFA 063-10335;		
	wings stored late 2016 (NF 20.10.15)		
G-BGPN	Piper PA-18-150 Super Cub	18-7909044	12.04.79
	N9750N A R Darke Baynards Park, Cranleigh		07.05.18E
	(IE 02.02.19)		
G-BGRE	Beech 200 Super King Air	BB-568	08.05.79
	Killinchy Aerospace Holdings Ltd Chalgrove		16.10.18E
G-BGRI	Jodel DR.1050 Sicile	540	27.04.79
	F-BLZJ R G Hallam Sleap		25.06.19P
	Built by Centre-Est Aéronautique		
G-BGRM	Piper PA-38-112 Tomahawk	38-79A1067	01.08.79
	N9673N V Baltzopoulos Sleap		20.05.19E
G-BGRO	Reims/Cessna F172M	F17201129	04.05.78
	PH-KAB A N Pirie t/a Cammo Aviation Kirknewton		14.01.19E
G-BGRR	Piper PA-38-112 Tomahawk	38-78A0336	08.05.79
	OO-FLT, N9685N S P Vincent		
	Wolverhampton Halfpenny Green		03.05.19E
G-BGRT	Steen Skybolt	xxxx	12.09.78
	F Ager St Johann in Tirol, Austria		06.04.19P
	Built by R C Teverson – project PFA 064-10171		
G-BGRX	Piper PA-38-112 Tomahawk	38-79A0609	11.05.79
	N9662N N M Robinson Bournemouth		15.04.16E
	(NF 10.10.17)		
G-BGSA	SOCATA MS.892E Rallye 150GT	12838	29.05.79
	F-GAKC B Huda & P W Osborne Jersey		27.04.17E
	(IE 17.05.18)		
G-BGSBᴹ	Hunting-Percival P.56 Provost T.1	PAC/F/057	21.05.79
	7922M, WV494		
	Cancelled 11.12.87 – to Oman AF 1982 *As 'XF868'*		
	Also c/n P56/57: official c/n quoted as 886391		
	With Sultanate of Oman Armed Forces Museum, Muscat		
G-BGSH	Piper PA-38-112 Tomahawk	38-79A0562	11.05.79
	N9719N Cancelled 31.07.17 as PWFU		17.07.16
	Liverpool *Stored 10.18*		
G-BGSJ	Piper J-3C-65 Cub (*L-4A-PI*)	8781	21.05.79
	F-BGXJ, French AF, 42-36657		
	M A V Gatehouse Dunkeswell		05.06.19P
	Fuselage No.8917; as '236657:D-72' in USAAC c/s		

G-BGSV	Reims/Cessna F172N	F17201830	01.08.79
	Southwell Air Services Ltd (Beverley (Linley Hill))		21.03.19E
	Crashed Watton Beck, Wilfholme 10.10.18		
	& substantially damaged		
G-BGSW	Beech F33 Bonanza	CD-1253	30.05.79
	OH-BDD J J Noakes Bournemouth		28.07.17E
	Stored 02.19		
G-BGSY	Gulfstream American GA-7 Cougar	GA7-0096	04.06.79
	P J K Luthaus Marl-Loemuhle, Germany		31.10.19E
G-BGTC	Auster AOP.9	'AUS/168'	12.10.79
	XP282 J R Davison (Haltham, Horncastle)		09.06.97
	Officially registered with Frame no.AUS/168;		
	on rebuild 05.18 (NF 19.03.18)		
G-BGTF	Piper PA-44-180 Seminole	44-7995287	20.06.79
	G-OPTC, EI-SKD, G-BGTF, N2131Y		
	N A Baxter Sandtoft		06.11.19E
G-BGTI	Piper J-3C-65 Cub (*L-4J-PI*)	12940	17.05.79
	F-BFFL, 44-80644 A P Broad		
	Brandy Wharf, Waddingham		24.10.19P
	Fuselage No.12770		
G-BGUB (2)	Piper PA-32-300 Cherokee Six	32-7940252	29.11.79
	N2387U D P & E A Morris Little Gransden		18.11.19E
G-BGVB	Robin DR.315 Petit Prince	308	20.07.79
	F-BPOP K Hartmann Neustadt, Germany		06.12.19E
	Built by Centre-Est Aéronautique		
G-BGVE	Scintex CP.1310-C3 Super Emeraude	931	08.06.79
	F-BMJE R Whitwell Sturgate		04.08.15P
	(NF 11.01.17)		
G-BGVH	Beech 76 Duchess	ME-260	08.06.79
	M D Darragh Exeter Int'l		05.12.20E
G-BGVN	Piper PA-28RT-201 Arrow IV	28R-7918168	22.06.79
	N2846U John Wailing Ltd Fairoaks		06.11.19E
G-BGVS	Reims/Cessna F172M	F17200992	03.05.79
	PH-HVS, (PH-LUK) Enterprise Purchasing Ltd		
	Fairoaks		31.08.19E
G-BGVY	Gulfstream American AA-5B Tiger	AA5B-1080	21.08.79
	(G-BGVU), (F-GBOO)		
	C Woodhouse tr G-BGVY Co-Ownership Headcorn		02.01.20E
G-BGVZ	Piper PA-28-181 Archer II	28-7990528	12.07.79
	N2886A M & W A Walsh RAF Woodvale		15.06.17E
	(IE 01.06.18)		
G-BGWC	Robin DR.400-180 Régent	1420	26.06.79
	G C Bremner & R J Guess		
	Shacklewell Lodge Farm, Empingham		13.12.19E
G-BGWM	Piper PA-28-181 Archer II	28-7990458	29.06.79
	N2817Y Thames Valley Flying Club Ltd		
	Wycombe Air Park		12.04.19E
G-BGWO	Jodel D.112	227	22.06.79
	F-BHGQ J Smart tr G-BGWO Group		
	Watchford Farm, Yarcombe		26.08.19P
	Built by Etablissement Valladeau		
G-BGWV	Aeronca 7AC Champion	7AC-4082	23.08.79
	OO-GRI, OO-TWR Cancelled 09.01.13 as TWFU		
	Netherfields Farm, Chapleton *Spares use 08.16*		
G-BGWZᴹ	Eclipse Super Eagle	ESE.007	29.06.79
	Cancelled 05.12.83 as WFU *No marks carried*		
	With Fleet Air Arm Museum, RNAS Yeovilton		
G-BGXA	Piper J-3C-65 Cub (*L-4H-PI*)	10762	01.03.78
	F-BGXA, French AF, 43-29471 P King		
	Eastbach Spence, English Bicknor		04.09.12P
	Fuselage No.10587; as '329471:F-44' in USAAC c/s;		
	noted 04.16 (NF 31.08.18)		
G-BGXBᴹ	Piper PA-38-112 Tomahawk	38-79A1007	02.07.79
	N9728N Cancelled 22.02.10 as PWFU		10.03.01
	With National Museum of Flight Scotland, East Fortune		
G-BGXC	SOCATA TB-10 Tobago	35	19.10.79
	M H & S H Cundey Redhill		23.09.19E
G-BGXD	SOCATA TB-10 Tobago	39	19.10.79
	Whitewest Ltd Blackpool		01.11.19E
G-BGXR	Robin HR.200-100 Club	53	01.10.79
	F-BVYH J R Cross Yeatsall Farm, Abbots Bromley		02.10.19E
G-BGXS	Piper PA-28-236 Dakota	28-7911198	12.07.79
	N2836Z M Holland tr G-BGXS Group		
	Retford Gamston		10.04.19E

G-BGXT	SOCATA TB-10 Tobago	40	03.10.79
	J L Alexander Haverfordwest		23.05.19E
G-BGYH	Piper PA-28-161 Warrior II	28-7916313	17.07.79
	N209LG, N580X, G-BGYH, N9619N		
	Tayside Aviation Ltd Dundee		02.02.19E
	Operated by Tayside Aviation		
G-BGYN	Piper PA-18-150 Super Cub	18-7709137	19.07.79
	N62747 D B & J R Dunford		
	South Longwood Farm, Owslebury		13.03.19E
G-BGYT^M	Embraer EMB-110P1 Bandeirante	110-234	11.10.79
	N104VA, G-BGYT, PT-SAA Cancelled 26.09.06 by CAA		12.01.06
	Manx c/s		
	With Manx Aviation and Military Museum, Ronaldsway		
G-BGZJ	Piper PA-38-112 Tomahawk	38-79A0999	07.09.79
	Cancelled 25.02.97 by CAA		14.06.92
	Thruxton *On fire dump 12.15*		

G-BHAA – G-BHZZ

G-BHAA	Cessna 152 II	15281330	12.02.79
	N49809 Herefordshire Aero Club Ltd Shobdon		22.11.19E
G-BHAD	Cessna A152 Aerobat	A1520807	12.02.79
	N7390L Cirrus Aviation Ltd Clacton-on-Sea		19.05.19E
G-BHAI	Reims/Cessna F152 II	F15201625	14.08.79
	(D-EJAY) ACS Aviation Ltd Perth		28.02.19E
G-BHAJ	Robin DR.400-160 Major	1430	22.08.79
	Rowantask Ltd Headcorn		13.06.19E
G-BHAR	Westland-Bell 47G-3B1	WA353	07.08.79
	XT194 Cancelled 13.02.13 by CAA		08.09.11
	Tain, Highlands *On rebuild with Heli Highlands 04.18*		
	Line no. WAN-44		
G-BHAV	Reims/Cessna F152 II	F15201633	15.08.79
	M L & T M Jones Derby		06.12.13E
	(IE 09.07.18)		
G-BHBA	Campbell Cricket	SMI-1	15.08.79
	S N McGovern (Aylesbury)		27.11.10P
	Built by S M Irwin (NF 03.03.17)		
G-BHBE	Westland-Bell Soloy 47G-3B-1	WAP-136	29.10.79
	XT510 TR Smith (Agricultural Machinery) Ltd		
	New Lane Farm, North Elmham		21.12.01
	(NF 24.05.16)		
G-BHBG	Piper PA-32R-300 Cherokee Lance	32R-7780515	18.09.79
	N408RC, N9590N D Moorman Rochester		13.04.19E
G-BHBT	Marquart MA.5 Charger	xxxx	03.09.79
	D M Stevens tr Bravo Tango Group Goodwood		09.01.20P
	Built by R G Maidment – project PFA 068-10190		
G-BHCC	Cessna 172M Skyhawk II	17266711	26.10.79
	(G-BGLY), N80713 Staverton Flying School		
	@ Skypark Ltd Gloucestershire		20.05.19E
G-BHCE	Jodel D.117A	381	01.10.79
	F-BHME D R W Muir tr Charlie Echo Group Sleap		10.06.19P
	Built by Société Aéronautique Normande as D.112;		
	converted to D.117A during rebuild c.1985		
G-BHCM	Cessna F172H	F172-0468	25.09.79
	SE-FBD J Dominic Denham		10.04.19E
	Built by Reims Aviation SA		
G-BHCP	Reims/Cessna F152 II	F15201640	31.10.79
	Eastern Air Executive Ltd Sturgate		14.02.19E
G-BHCZ	Piper PA-38-112 Tomahawk	38-78A0321	26.09.79
	N214MD J E Abbott Goodwood		08.11.19E
G-BHDD^M	Vickers 668 Varsity T.1	xxxx	18.10.79
	WL626 Cancelled 21.11.09 as PWFU		
	With East Midlands Aeropark, East Midlands		
G-BHDE	SOCATA TB-10 Tobago	58	02.01.80
	J C Parker & P A Parry Turweston		12.02.19E
G-BHDK^M	Boeing TB-29A-45-BN Superfortress	11225	27.09.79
	44-61748 Cancelled 29.02.84 as WFU		
	As '461748:Y' in USAF c/s 'Hawg Wild'		
	With American Air Museum, Duxford		
G-BHDM	Reims/Cessna F152 II	F15201684	15.10.79
	A D R Northeast Wycombe Air Park		26.04.19E
G-BHDP	Reims/Cessna F182Q Skylane II	F18200131	15.10.79
	Zone Travel Ltd Wycombe Air Park		23.08.19E

G-BHDR	Cessna F152 II	F15201680	15.10.79
	Cancelled 13.12.10 by CAA		29.07.07
	RAF Leuchars *Built by Reims Aviation SA*		
	Rebuilt 2003/4 using parts of G-BPGM;		
	wreck dumped 05.14		
G-BHDS	Reims/Cessna F152 II	F15201682	15.10.79
	Redmosaic Formacao de Technicos de Aeronaves		
	Unipessoal Lda Cascais, Portugal		05.02.19E
G-BHDV	Cameron V-77	585	01.02.80
	P Glydon tr G-BHDV Group Knowle, Bristol		12.05.16E
	(IE 11.04.18)		
G-BHDX	Reims/Cessna F172N	F17201889	05.10.79
	P C & P T Appleton Bodmin		18.09.19E
G-BHDZ	Reims/Cessna F172N	F17201911	03.12.79
	H Mackintosh Spanhoe		08.08.19E
G-BHED	Reims/Cessna FA152 Aerobat	FA1520359	03.12.79
	Skytrek Flying School Ltd Rochester		17.12.19E
G-BHEG	Jodel D.150 Mascaret	46	03.07.80
	PH-ULS, OO-SET M Kolev Manchester Barton		30.04.19P
	Built by Société Aéronautique Normande		
G-BHEK	Scintex CP.1315-C3 Super Emeraude	923	11.10.79
	F-BJMU D B Winstanley Woolston Moss, Warrington		23.08.19P
	Built by Société Scintex		
G-BHEL	Jodel D.117	735	08.10.79
	F-BIOA D W & S J McAllister Bagby		22.03.19P
	Built by Société Aéronautique Normande		
G-BHEN	Reims/Cessna FA152 Aerobat	FA1520363	03.01.80
	The Leicestershire Aero Club Ltd Leicester		10.02.20E
G-BHEU	Thunder Ax7-65	238	16.10.79
	L J Wigfield Rode, Frome		01.12.19E
G-BHEV	Piper PA-28R-200 Cherokee Arrow II	28R-7435159	23.10.79
	PH-BOY, N41244 P Hardy tr 7-Up Group		
	Retford Gamston		17.05.19E
G-BHFC	Reims/Cessna F152 II	F15201436	07.04.78
	J H Sandham t/a JH Sandham Aviation		
	Carlisle Lake District		14.09.16E
	(IE 07.02.19)		
G-BHFE	Piper PA-44-180 Seminole	44-7995324	02.10.79
	Abu Dhabi AF 0052, G-BHFE, N2383U		
	Transport Command Ltd Brighton City		14.02.14E
	(NF 27.09.16)		
G-BHFG	SNCAN Stampe SV.4C	45	31.10.79
	F-BJDN, French Navy 45, French AF		
	G W Lynch Old Buckenham		17.04.08
	(NF 05.02.18)		
G-BHFH	Piper PA-34-200T Seneca II	34-7970482	23.10.79
	N8075Q Andrews Professional Colour Laboratories Ltd		
	Headcorn		26.09.19E
G-BHFI	Reims/Cessna F152 II	F15201685	22.10.79
	W M Brown & S J Donno tr BAe (Warton) Flying Club		
	Blackpool		19.06.19E
G-BHFJ	Piper PA-28RT-201T Turbo Arrow IV	28R-7931298	22.10.79
	N8072R S A Cook & A D R Northeast		
	Wycombe Air Park		02.10.19E
G-BHFK	Piper PA-28-151 Cherokee Warrior	28-7615088	12.12.79
	N8325C M F Forster tr G-BHFK Flying Group		
	Cranfield		02.08.19E
G-BHGC	Piper PA-18-150 Super Cub	18-8793	03.04.79
	PH-NKH, N4447Z		
	C R Dacey Wellcross Farm, Slinfold		31.07.19E
G-BHGF	Cameron V-56	574	05.11.79
	P Spellward Bristol BS9 *'Biggles'*		01.06.16E
	(IE 03.02.17)		
G-BHGJ	Jodel D.120 Paris-Nice	336	15.01.80
	F-BOYB M Devlin tr Golf Juliet Enstone		12.07.18P
	Built by Société Wassmer Aviation (IE 17.08.18)		
G-BHGO	Piper PA-32-260 Cherokee Six	32-7800007	16.11.79
	PH-BGP, N9656C Woodpecker Air.Com Ltd		
	(Bedwas, Caerphilly)		29.08.19E
G-BHGP	Socata TB-10 Tobago	100	17.01.80
	Cancelled 21.03.07 as TWFU		29.05.05
	Stapleford *Noted derelict 02.16*		

G-BHGY	Piper PA-28R-200 Cherokee Arrow II	28R-7435086	23.11.79	
	PH-NSL, N57365 Truman Aviation Ltd			
	Nottingham City		16.05.19E	
G-BHHE	Jodel DR.1051-M1 Sicile Record	628	26.04.80	
	F-BMZC D F Hurn Sandown		01.10.19P	
	Built by Centre-Est Aéronautique			
G-BHHG	Reims/Cessna F152 II	F15201725	04.03.80	
	TG Aviation Ltd Lydd		10.01.20E	
	Operated by Thanet Flying Club			
G-BHHH	Thunder Ax7-65 Bolt	245	05.12.79	
	J M J Roberts North Weald, Epping		19.07.19E	
G-BHHK^M	Cameron N-77 HAB	547	05.12.79	
	Cancelled 25.03.09 as WFU		07.12.87	
	With British Balloon Museum & Library, Newbury			
G-BHHN	Cameron V-77	549	29.11.79	
	P C Gooch Alresford *'Valley Crusader'*		02.03.19E	
G-BHIA	Cessna F152 II	1712	03.01.80	
	Cancelled 23.07.92 as PWFU		04.05.86	
	Dublin Weston *Built by Reims Aviation SA*			
	Fuselage on fire dump 05.14			
G-BHIB	Reims/Cessna F182Q Skylane II	F18200134	18.12.79	
	M S Williams Husbands Bosworth		06.02.20E	
G-BHIC	Cessna F182Q Skylane II	F18200135	18.12.79	
	Cancelled 04.05.07 as destroyed		03.08.08	
	Edinburgh *Built by Reims Aviation SA*			
	On fire dump 09.16			
G-BHII	Cameron V-77	548	10.12.79	
	R V Brown Maidenhead *'Tosca'*		02.09.96A	
	(NF 20.08.18)			
G-BHIJ	Eiriavion PIK-20E	20241	09.01.80	
	I P Freestone & P J Shout Saltby		14.06.19E	
G-BHIN	Reims/Cessna F152 II	F15201715	28.01.80	
	Sussex Flying Club Ltd Brighton City		03.12.19E	
G-BHIS	Thunder Ax7-65 Bolt	254	26.11.79	
	J R Wilson tr Hedge Hoppers Balloon Group			
	Oxford OX2 *'Yo-Yo'*		30.10.09E	
	(IE 03.02.17)			
G-BHIY	Reims/Cessna F150K	F15000627	18.12.79	
	F-BRXR N J Butler (Laurencekirk)		20.05.16E	
	Damaged in gales 2016 (NF 07.06.17)			
G-BHJF	SOCATA TB-10 Tobago	83	02.01.80	
	J L Sparks St Athan		22.07.19E	
	Operated by Horizon Flight Training			
G-BHJI	Mooney M.20J Mooney 201	24-0925	11.02.80	
	N3753H Otomed APS Aarhus, Denmark		22.02.19E	
G-BHJK	Maule M-5-235C Lunar Rocket	7296C	25.02.80	
	N56359 M K H Bell Fife		23.06.08E	
	Noted 07.17 (NF 16.01.19)			
G-BHJN	Sportavia-Putzer Fournier RF4D	4021	03.01.80	
	F-BORH R G Wilkens tr RF4 Group Enstone		14.03.19P	
G-BHJO	Piper PA-28-161 Warrior II	28-7816213	04.01.80	
	OO-FLD, N9507N, N6034H			
	SC Airlease Ltd Dundee		03.02.20E	
	Operated by Tayside Aviation			
G-BHJS	Partenavia P68B	172	28.12.79	
	I-KLUB Flew LLP Bournemouth		29.10.19E	
G-BHJU	Robin DR.400 2+2	1288	09.01.80	
	D-ECDK J R Barlow & J E Morris tr Ageless Aeronauts			
	Lydd		16.05.19E	
G-BHKE	Bensen B 8MS	VW.1	07.01.80	
	Cancelled 03.02.04 by CAA			
	Kirkbride *Built by V C Whitehead – project*			
	PFA G/01-1009; stored for sale 05.18			
G-BHKN^M	Colt 14A Cloudhopper HAB	068	17.01.80	
	Cancelled 05.12.89 as WFU			
	Officially regd as Colt 12A			
	With British Balloon Museum & Library, Newbury			
G-BHKR^M	Colt 14A Cloudhopper HAB	071	17.01.80	
	Cancelled 05.12.89 as WFU			
	Officially regd as Colt 12A			
	With British Balloon Museum & Library, Newbury			
G-BHKT	Jodel D.112	1265	10.01.80	
	F-BMIQ G Dawes Clipgate Farm, Denton		28.08.18P	
	Built by Société Wassmer Aviation (IE 03.01.19)			

G-BHLE	Robin DR.400-180 Régent	1466	25.01.80	
	A V Harmer Hardwick		13.04.19E	
G-BHLH	Robin DR.400-180 Régent	1320	11.02.80	
	F-GBIG R Turner tr G-BHLH Group			
	Wycombe Air Park		28.01.20E	
G-BHLJ	Saffery-Rigg S.200 Skyliner	1AR/01	23.01.80	
	I A Rigg Pendlebury, Swinton			
	Built by C Saffrey; noted 05.16			
G-BHLW	Cessna 120	10210	24.03.80	
	N73005, NC73005 I J F Macdonald			
	tr Moray Flying Group Easterton *'Sky Ranger'*		11.06.19P	
G-BHLX	Grumman American AA-5B Tiger	AA5B-0573	01.02.80	
	OY-GAR M D McPherson Holmbeck Farm, Burcott		04.10.19E	
G-BHMA	SIPA 903	61	13.03.80	
	OO-FAE, F-BGBK H J Taggart			
	(Clonard, Enfield, Co Meath, RoI)		24.07.12P	
	(NF 16.02.18)			
G-BHMG	Reims/Cessna FA152 Aerobat	FA1520368	10.06.80	
	North Weald Flying Group Ltd North Weald		27.11.19E	
G-BHMJ	Avenger T.200-2112	2	29.01.80	
	R Light Stockport			
	Built by R Light; noted 05.16			
G-BHMK	Avenger T.200-2112	3	29.01.80	
	P Kinder Stockport *'Lord Anthony II'*			
	Built by P Kinder			
G-BHMO	Piper PA-20 Pacer	20-89	16.04.80	
	F-BDRO Cancelled 01.04.97 by CAA		01.09.90	
	Grimsby *Stored 01.18 at North East Lincs Reclamation*			
G-BHMT	Evans VP-1	PFA 062-10473	18.02.80	
	J Hoskins (Didcot)		14.10.09P	
	Built by P E J Sturgeon – project PFA 062-10473			
	(NF 18.11.16)			
G-BHMY^M	Fokker F.27 Friendship 600	10196	06.05.80	
	F-GBDK (2), (F-GBRV), PK-PFS, JA8606, PH-FDL			
	Cancelled 22.03.03 as PWFU		22.05.99	
	Donated by KLM (UK) Ltd – less engines			
	With City of Norwich Aviation Museum			
G-BHNC	Cameron O-65	588	07.02.80	
	D Bareford & C Charley			
	Kidderminster & Loughborough *'Hot 'n' Cold'*		23.06.19E	
G-BHNK	Jodel D.120A Paris-Nice	243	26.03.80	
	F-BLNK G J Prisk Trevissick Farm, Porthtowan		25.05.19P	
	Built by Société des Etablissements Benjamin Wassmer			
G-BHNO	Piper PA-28-181 Archer II	28-8090211	07.02.80	
	N81413 HJK Asset Management Ltd			
	Wolverhampton Halfpenny Green		05.04.19E	
G-BHNP	Eiriavion PIK-20E	20253	29.02.80	
	D A Sutton Sackville Lodge Farm, Riseley		26.05.19E	
G-BHNV	Westland-Bell 47G-3B-1	WA/700	11.03.80	
	F-GHNM, G-BHNV, XW180 S W Hutchinson			
	Trenholme Farm, Ingleby Arncliffe			
	Official c/n 'WAT-222' is incorrect (NF 22.10.16)			
G-BHNX	Jodel D.117	493	07.09.78	
	F-BHNX M J A Trudgill RAF Henlow			
	Built by Société Aéronautique Normande;			
	on rebuild 07.18 (NF 09.02.16)			
G-BHOA	Robin DR.400-160 Major	1478	27.01.80	
	T L Trott Rochester		01.09.19E	
G-BHOL	Jodel DR.1050 Ambassadeur	35	06.02.80	
	F-BJQL S J Pearson Rochester		09.03.11C	
	Built by Centre-Est Aéronautique; stored 08.17			
	(IE 28.05.15)			
G-BHOM	Piper PA-18 Super Cub 95 (L-18C-PI)	18-1391	07.03.80	
	OO-PIU, OO-HMT, French Army 51-15391 (c/s FMAKD)			
	D R & R M Lee Shobdon		24.04.19P	
	Fuselage No.18-1272; as '181391:AN-R' in			
	French Army c/s			
G-BHOR	Piper PA-28-161 Warrior II	28-8016331	12.06.80	
	N82162 R K Seaward tr Oscar Romeo Flying Group			
	Biggin Hill		09.08.19E	
G-BHOT	Cameron V-65	777	15.09.81	
	J A Baker tr Dante Balloon Group			
	Ruscombe, Reading *'British Airways'*		08.08.99A	
	(IE 10.04.18)			

G-BHOZ SOCATA TB-9 Tampico 84 11.03.80
A W Hill   (Holme, Newark) 30.07.19E

G-BHPK Piper J-3C-65 Cub (*L-4A-Pl*) 8979 26.02.80
F-BEPK, French Army, 42-38410
L B Smith tr L4 Group   Priory Farm, Tibenham 10.02.20P
*Fuselage No.9098; official c/n '12161' is incorrect
& applies to F-BFYU (s/n 44-7986);
as '238410:44-A' in USAAF c/s*

G-BHPL CASA 1-131E Jungmann Series 1000 1058 17.07.80
Spanish AF E3B-350   A Burroughes   Henstridge 04.06.19P
As 'DG+BE' in Luftwaffe c/s

G-BHPS Jodel D.120A Paris-Nice 148 11.06.80
F-BIXI   M Conrad & M C Hayes
tr Papa Sierra Syndicate   North Weald 19.08.19P
Built by Société des Etablissements Benjamin Wassmer

G-BHPZ Cessna 172N Skyhawk II 17272017 26.03.80
N6411E   O'Brien Properties Ltd   Redhill 13.06.19E

G-BHRC Piper PA-28-161 Warrior II 28-7916430 03.04.80
N9527N   The Sherwood Flying Club Ltd
Nottingham City 30.01.20E

G-BHRH Reims/Cessna FA150K Aerobat FA1500056 24.03.80
PH-ECB, D-ECBL, (D-EKKW)   Merlin Flying Club Ltd
Tatenhill 14.06.19E

G-BHRK Colt Saucepan-56 22.08.80
D P Busby   Broughton, Kettering   'AMC' 14.05.86A
*Saucepan special shape; noted tethered 01.19
(NF 23.08.18)*

G-BHRO Rockwell Commander 112A 364 20.03.80
N1364J   M G Cookson   North Weald 06.02.19E

G-BHRR Piel CP.301A Emeraude 270 28.03.80
F-BISK   B Mills   Rochester 06.09.19P
Built by Société Menavia

G-BHRW Robin DR.221 Dauphin 93 10.07.80
F-BPCP   Cancelled 07.06.17 as PWFU 10.08.17
North Coates   *Wreck stored 03.19*

G-BHSB Cessna 172N Skyhawk II 17272977 25.06.80
(N1225F)   J W Cope & M P Wimsey   Strubby 24.05.19E

G-BHSD Scheibe SF25E Super Falke 4357 21.07.80
D-KDGG   K E Ballington   Kirton in Lindsey 11.03.17E

G-BHSE Rockwell Commander 114 14161 15.05.80
N4831W, AN-BRL, (N4831W)
Flight Software Services Ltd & LX Avionics Ltd
(Bretby, Burton-on-Trent) 06.06.19E

G-BHSL CASA 1-131-E3B Jungmann 1117 18.06.80
Spanish AF E3B-236   A F Kutz
(Baienfurt, Baden-Württemberg) 19.07.96P
Carries 'KG+GB' in Luftwaffe c/s (NF 30.11.18)

G-BHSN^M Cameron N-56 HAB 595 10.04.80
Cancelled 14.08.15 by CAA 09.07.05
With British Balloon Museum & Library, Newbury

G-BHSY Jodel DR.1050 Sicile 546 06.05.80
F-BLZO   T R Allebone tr Sierra Yankee Flying Group
Easton Maudit 04.08.14P
Built by Centre-Est Aéronautique (IE 04.07.18)

G-BHTA Piper PA-28-236 Dakota 28-8011102 22.04.80
N8197H   Dakota Ltd   Jersey 09.04.19E

G-BHTC Jodel DR.1051-M1 Sicile Record 581 01.05.80
F-BMGR   B J Rawlings
Clutton Hill Farm, High Littleton 15.02.19P
Built by Centre-Est Aéronautique

G-BHTG Thunder Ax6-56 Bolt 273 18.04.80
The British Balloon Museum & Library Ltd
Wellingborough 16.04.16E
(NF 09.02.18)

G-BHUB^M Douglas C-47A-85-DL Skytrain 19975 30.04.80
'G-AGIV', 'FD988', 'KG418',Spanish AF T3-29,
N51V, N9985F, SE-BBH, 43-15509
Cancelled 19.10.81 as WFU
*As '315509:W7-S' in USAAF c/s
With American Air Museum, Duxford*

G-BHUE Jodel DR.1050 Ambassadeur 185 21.04.80
F-BERM, F-OBRM   M J Harris
(Lower Broadheath, Worcester)
Built by Société Aéronautique Normande (NF 14.03.18)

G-BHUG Cessna 172N Skyhawk II 17272985 24.06.80
N1283F   L Marriott & R Wainwright tr G-BHUG Group
Dunkeswell 29.04.19E

G-BHUI Cessna 152 II 15283144 27.05.80
N46932   South Warwickshire School of Flying Ltd
Wellesbourne Mountford 03.10.19E

G-BHUJ Cessna 172N Skyhawk II 17271932 27.05.80
N5752E   Cancelled 11.07.16 by CAA 01.10.16
Southend   *Wreck in open store 01.19*

G-BHUM de Havilland DH.82A Tiger Moth 85453 09.06.80
VT-DGA, VT-DDN, RIAF, SAAF 4622, DE457
S G Towers   Green Farm, Beckwithshaw 04.05.19P

G-BHUO Evans VP-2 xxxx 12.05.80
Cancelled 28.08.00 by CAA 21.12.94
Yearby, Co Durham   *Built by R A Povall
– project PFA 063-10552; stored 04.15*

G-BHUU Piper PA-25-235 Pawnee D 25-8056035 28.05.80
N2440Q   Booker Gliding Club Ltd   Wycombe Air Park 15.06.19E
Modified to PA-25-260 standard

G-BHVB Piper PA-28-161 Warrior II 28-8016260 16.05.80
N9638N   A S Bamrah t/a Falcon Flying Services
Biggin Hill 09.09.07
*Fuselage stored externally 01.17 in green primer
less marks (IE 23.01.18)*

G-BHVF Jodel D.150 Mascaret 11 28.10.80
F-BLDF   D J Gibson tr Groupe Ariel   Henstridge 16.05.19P
Built by Société Aéronautique Normande

G-BHVP Cessna 182Q Skylane II 18267071 15.12.80
N97374   G S Chapman tr G-BHVP Flying Group
Little Gransden 04.07.19E

G-BHVR Cessna 172N Skyhawk II 17270196 27.05.80
N738SG   B Marlow tr Victor Romeo Group   Elstree 11.12.18E

G-BHVV Piper J-3C-65 Cub (*L-4A-Pl*) 8953 27.06.80
F-BGXF, French Army, 42-38384
T Kattinger   (Sutton, Sandy) 15.10.10P
*Fuselage No.9048; official c/n '10291' is incorrect
& became F-BEGF (s/n 43-1430): frames probably
exchanged in 1953 rebuild); as '42-38384' in USMC c/s
(IE 01.11.18)*

G-BHWA Reims/Cessna F152 II F15201775 28.03.80
DSFT Ltd   Doncaster Sheffield 08.08.19E

G-BHWB Reims/Cessna F152 II F15201776 14.04.80
(G-BHWA)   CM Aviation Ltd   Wickenby 27.11.19E

G-BHWY Piper PA-28R-200 Cherokee Arrow II 28R-7435059 17.06.80
N56904   R B Cheek tr Kilo Foxtrot Group   Sandown 19.04.19E

G-BHWZ Piper PA-28-181 Archer II 28-7890299 08.04.80
N3379M   M A Abbott   (Chichester) 03.12.19E

G-BHXA Scottish Aviation Bulldog Srs 120/1210 BH120/407 09.06.80
Botswana DF OD1, G-BHXA   Airplan Flight Equipment
Ltd   Blackbushe   'Deltair Aviation' 28.04.17E
Built by British Aerospace (IE 09.07.18)

G-BHXB Scottish Aviation Bulldog Srs 120/1210 BH120/408 04.03.91
G-JWCM, G-BHXB, Botswana DF OD2, G-BHXB
S D Wright tr XB Group   Eshott 06.11.19P
Built by British Aerospace

G-BHXD Jodel D.120 Paris-Nice 258 03.07.80
F-BMIA   R E Guscott   Upfield Farm, Whitson 22.03.17P
Built by Société Wassmer Aviation (IE 30.07.18)

G-BHXS Jodel D.120 Paris-Nice 133 27.08.80
F-BIXS   R I Walker tr Plymouth Jodel Group   Bodmin 26.11.19P
Built by Société des Etablissements Benjamin Wassmer

G-BHXY Piper J-3C-65 Cub (*L-4H-Pl*) 11905 01.07.80
D-EAXY, F-BFQX, 44-79609   F W Rogers
Bealbury, St Mellion 23.08.19P
Fuselage No.11733; as '44-79609:44-S in USAAF c/s

G-BHYA Cessna R182 Skylane RG II R18200532 10.07.80
N1717R   J Jarier   (La Mole, Provence-Alpes, France) 19.07.18E

G-BHYC Cessna 172RG Cutlass II 172RG0404 24.06.80
(N4868V)   V Hutchinson tr BHM Aviation   City of Derry 21.08.19E

G-BHYD Cessna R172K Hawk XP R1722734 11.12.80
N736RS   A J House   Brimpton 06.02.20E

G-BHYI SNCAN Stampe SV.4A 18 11.07.80
F-BAAF, French AF   D Hicklin   Lavenham 25.07.19
(IE 06.07.18)

G-BHYP	Reims/Cessna F172M	F17201108	30.06.80
	OY-BFR Avior Ltd Oxford		26.03.19E
G-BHYR	Reims/Cessna F172M	F17200922	30.06.80
	OY-DZH, SE-FZH, (OH-CFQ)		
	R G Forster tr G-BHYR Group Stapleford		04.07.19E
G-BHYV	Evans VP-1	LC2(PFA 1598)	02.07.80
	J L Van Wijk Zandhoven, Belgium		
	Built by L Chiappi – project PFA 1569 NF 05.02.19)		
G-BHZE	Piper PA-28-181 Archer II	28-7890291	04.11.80
	OO-FLR, (OO-HCM), N3053M		
	J A L Brown tr Dave Flying Group Brighton City		12.03.19E
G-BHZH	Reims/Cessna F152 II	F15201786	25.07.80
	Plymouth Flying School Ltd t/a FlyNQY Pilot Training		
	Newquay Cornwall		05.09.19E
G-BHZK	Gulfstream American AA-5B Tiger	AA5B-0743	08.09.80
	N28670 D T Rooke tr ZK Group Elstree		29.05.19E
G-BHZO	Gulfstream American AA-5A Cheetah	AA5A-0692	21.07.80
	N26750 J Linehan tr PG Air Headcorn		06.03.19E
G-BHZR	Scottish Aviation Bulldog Srs 120/1210	BH120/410	23.07.80
	Botswana DF OD4, G-BHZR		
	J G McTaggart Archerfield *'Winston'*		14.02.19P
	Built by British Aerospace		
G-BHZS	Scottish Aviation Bulldog Series 120/1210	BH120/411	23.07.80
	Botswana DF OD5, G-BHZS		
	Cancelled 19.12.12 by CAA		20.02.06
	Derby *Open store 05.17*		
G-BHZT	Scottish Aviation Bulldog Srs 120/1210	BH120/412	23.07.80
	Botswana DF OD6, G-BHZT D M Curties Cotswold		24.04.19E
	Built by British Aerospace		
G-BHZU	Piper J-3C-65 Cub (*L-4B-PI*)	9775	17.07.80
	F-BETO, (F-BFKH), 43-914 P F Durnford Sandtoft		22.05.19P
	Fuselage No.9606; fitted to F-BETO during 1961		
	rebuild replacing ex 45-4424 (c/n 13164);		
	as '3914' in USAAF c/s		
G-BHZV	Jodel D.120A Paris-Nice	278	23.07.80
	F-BMON J Gunson tr G-BHZV Group		
	Brook Farm, Pilling		25.06.19P
	Built by Société Wassmer Aviation		

G-BIAA – G-BIZZ

G-BIAC	SOCATA Rallye 235E Gabier	13323	17.07.80
	B Brou Maypole Farm, Chislet		08.08.19E
G-BIAH	Jodel D.112	1218	20.08.80
	F-BMAH K J Steele Old Sarum		25.10.17P
	Built by Société Wassmer Aviation		
G-BIAI	Wallingford WMB.2 Windtracker	8	01.07.80
	I Chadwick Caterham *'Amanda I'*		
G-BIAP	Piper PA-16 Clipper	16-732	25.06.80
	F-BBGM, F-OAGS P J Bish Draycott		14.05.19E
	Fuselage No.16-733		
G-BIAR	Rigg Skyliner II	IAR/02	09.07.80
	I A Rigg Pendlebury, Swinton		
	Noted 05.16		
G-BIAT[M]	Sopwith Pup replica	001	03.12.82
	Cancelled 09.08.89 - to Australia – NTU *As 'N6460'*		
	Built by Skysport Engineering Ltd		
	With Air Force Museum of New Zealand, Christchurch		
G-BIAU[M]	Sopwith Pup replica	EMK 002	04.01.83
	Cancelled 10.03.97 as WFU *As 'N6452' in RNAS c/s*		13.09.89P
	Built by Skysport Engineering		
	With Fleet Air Arm Museum, RNAS Yeovilton		
G-BIAX	Taylor JT.2 Titch	PFA 3228	30.07.80
	C S Hales & P J Hebdon Shenington		11.05.04P
	Built by J T Everest & G F Rowley		
	– project PFA 3228 (NF 27.04.17)		
G-BIAY	Grumman American AA-5 Traveler	AA5-0423	26.08.80
	(D-E), G-BIAY, OY-GAD, N7123L		
	A Dilcher tr G-BIAY Group (Erlangen, Germany)		15.05.19E

G-BIAZ[M]	Cameron AT-165 HAB	400	07.02.78
	Cancelled 27.05.80 as destroyed		03.04.80
	Used for 1978 Atlantic attempt: hot air envelope		
	destroyed Trubenbuch, Austria 14.01.80: inner		
	helium cell envelope only with British Balloon		
	Museum & Library, Newbury; basket only with		
	Anderson-Abruzzo Int'l Balloon Museum,		
	Albuquerque, New Mexico		
G-BIBA	SOCATA TB-9 Tampico	149	17.07.80
	TB Aviation Ltd Denham		06.06.19E
G-BIBB	Mooney M.20C Mark 21	2803	22.07.80
	OH-MOD Cancelled 16.12.10 by CAA		23.06.08
	Henstridge *Stored dismantled unmarked 04.14*		
G-BIBG	Sikorsky S-76A II +	760083	18.08.80
	5N-BCE Cancelled 08.12.09 as PWFU		18.08.09
	Cotswold *Noted Lufthansa Resource Technical*		
	Training 11.16		
G-BIBO	Cameron V-65	667	07.08.80
	D M Hoddinott Bristol BS8		12.06.17E
	(IE 04.08.17)		
G-BIBS	Cameron P-20	671	14.08.80
	Cameron Balloons Ltd Bristol BS3		
	(NF 05.02.18)		
G-BIBT	Gulfstream American AA-5B Tiger	AA5B-1047	08.09.80
	N4518V Bravo Tango Ltd Swansea		24.09.19E
G-BIBX	Wallingford WMB.2 Windtracker	9	18.08.80
	I A Rigg Pendlebury, Swinton		
	Noted 05.16		
G-BICD	Auster 5	735	20.08.80
	F-BFXH, MT166 T R Parsons Eagle Moor, Grantham		16.08.19P
	As 'MT166' in RAF c/s		
G-BICE	North American AT-6C-1-NT Texan IIA	88-9755	03.09.80
	Portuguese AF 1545, SAAF 7084, EX302, 41-33275		
	C M L Edwards Great Oakley		22.10.15P
	As '41-33275:CE' in USAAF c/s (IE 31.03.17)		
G-BICG	Reims/Cessna F152 II	F15201796	03.09.80
	M A Khan Elstree		16.04.19E
	Operated by MAK Aviation		
G-BICM	Colt 56A	095	01.09.80
	M R Stokoe Tatsfield, Westerham *'Ladybird'*		23.01.20E
G-BICP	Robin DR.360 Chevalier	610	02.10.80
	F-BSPH J B McVeighty (Huntington, York)		28.07.08E
	(NF 28.01.19)		
G-BICR	Jodel D.120A Paris-Nice	135	05.09.80
	F-BIXR M B Blackmore & T W J Carnall		
	Dunkeswell		04.01.14P
	Built by Société des Etablissements Benjamin Wassmer		
	(NF 27.02.18)		
G-BICS	Robin R2100A Club	128	04.12.80
	F-GBAC Cancelled 31.07.18 as PWFU		16.09.17
	Spalding *For sale as rebuild project 08.18*		
G-BICU	Cameron V-56	680	09.09.80
	G A Chadwick t/a Black Pearl Balloons Caterham		18.04.11E
	(IE 31.05.18)		
G-BICW	Piper PA-28-161 Warrior II	28-7916309	08.10.80
	N2091N S Morley tr Charlie Whisky Flying Group		
	Blackbushe		11.05.19E
G-BICY	Piper PA-23-160 Apache	23-1640	26.09.80
	OO-AOL, 5N-ACL, VR-NDF, PH-ACL, N4010P		
	Cancelled 01.08.06 as PWFU		15.07.07
	Caterham *Spares use 04.18*		
G-BIDD	Evans VP-1	PFA 062-10974	27.10.78
	J Hodgkinson (Hill Farm, Nayland)		02.12.00P
	Built by J Wedgebury – project PFA 062-10167		
	(NF 14.12.15)		
G-BIDG	Jodel D.150 Mascaret	08	11.09.80
	F-BLDG D R Gray Woolston Moss, Warrington		24.04.18P
	Built by Société Aéronautique Normande (IE 30.05.18)		
G-BIDH	Cessna 152 II	15280546	12.09.80
	G-DONA, G-BIDH, N25234 Hull Aero Club Ltd		
	(Beverley (Linley Hill))		30.01.18E
	Veered off runway landing Beverley (Linley Hill)		
	27.08.17 & substantially damaged; under repair 12.17		

G-BIDI   Piper PA-28R-201 Arrow III   28R-7837135   11.11.80
N3759M   S Jameson   (Wem, Shrewsbury)   17.10.19E
Official type data 'PA-28R-201 Cherokee Arrow III'
is incorrect

G-BIDJ   Piper PA-18A-150 Super Cub   18-6007   22.09.80
PH-MAY, N7798D   S M Hart   High Cross, Ware   16.05.19E
Fuselage No.18-6089

G-BIDK   Piper PA-18-150 Super Cub (*L-21A-PI*)   18-6591   22.09.80
PH-MAI, R Netherlands AF R-211, 51-15679, N7194K
Y Leysen   White Waltham   17.05.19E
Composite – original fuselage no.18-6714 (c/n 18-6591)
ex LN-TVB, N9285D; rebuilt 1976 with fuselage
no.18-503 (c/n 18-565) ex RNeth AF R-211

G-BIDO   Piel CP.301A Emeraude   327   25.03.81
F-POIO   A R Plumb   (Mumbles, Swansea)   01.09.11P
Built by Piel Aviation (NF 17.10.18)

G-BIDV^M   Colt 17A Cloudhopper HAB   789   29.01.79
Cancelled 20.05.93 by CAA   19.12.89
Originally Colt 14A c/n 034
With British Balloon Museum & Library, Newbury

G-BIDW^M   Sopwith 1½ Strutter replica   WA/5   24.09.80
'9382'   Cancelled 04.02.87 by CAA   29.12.80
As 'A8226' in RFC 45 Sqdn c/s
Built by Westward Airways (Lands End) Ltd
With Royal Air Force Cosford Museum

G-BIDX   Jodel D.112   876   19.09.80
F-BIQY   P Turton   Ash House Farm, Winsford   05.09.05P
Built by Société des Etablissements Benjamin Wassmer
(NF 14.12.18)

G-BIEN   Jodel D.120A Paris-Nice   218   03.06.81
F-BKNK   M J Sharp   RAF Barkston Heath   19.05.06P
Built by Société Wassmer Aviation (NF 01.04.17)

G-BIEO   Jodel D.112   1296   19.03.82
F-BMOK   R S & S C Solley   Garlinge Farm, Ripple   12.04.19P
Built by Société Wassmer Aviation

G-BIES   Maule M-5-235C Lunar Rocket   7334C   24.07.81
N56394   William Procter Ltd   Stows Farm, Tillingham   26.01.19E

G-BIET   Cameron O-77   674   30.09.80
G M Westley   Byworth, Petworth   11.01.02A
(NF 17.11.15)

G-BIEY   Piper PA-28-151 Cherokee Warrior   28-7715213   10.11.80
PH-KDH, OO-HCB, N9540N   M J Isaac   Full Sutton   03.02.20E

G-BIFB   Piper PA-28-150 Cherokee C   28-1968   06.10.80
4X-AEC   D H G Penney   Sandtoft   29.05.09E
On rebuild 10.16 (NF 21.03.16)

G-BIFO   Evans VP-1 Series 2   xxxx   29.09.80
G W Hancox   Priory Farm, Tibenham
'The Bear In The Air'   04.02.20P
Built by P Raggett – project PFA 062-10411

G-BIFP   Colt 56C   097   14.10.80
J W Adkins   Market Harborough
(IE 12.06.15)

G-BIFY   Reims/Cessna F150L   F15000829   09.10.80
PH-CEZ   North Weald Flying Group Ltd   North Weald   13.11.19E

G-BIGB   Bell 212   30853   14.10.88
N362EH, G-UHUK, N362EH, XA-TRX, N362EH, N212AH,
C-FPKV, N212AH, C-GVIM, G-BIGB, ZS-HHU, G-BIGB,
EI-BRE, G-BIGB, ZS-HHU, A2-ACJ, ZS-HHU, N16831
SJ Contracting Services Ltd t/a Heli-Lift Services
(Beckley, Oxford)   08.01.20E

G-BIGF^M   Thunder Ax7-77 Bolt HAB   295   10.02.81
Cancelled 06.11.01 as PWFU   06.09.91
With British Balloon Museum & Library, Newbury

G-BIGJ   Reims/Cessna F172M   F17200936   02.12.80
PH-SKT   Cirrus Aviation Ltd   Clacton-on-Sea   09.06.16E
Blown over during storm at Clacton-on-Sea 28.03.16
(NF 06.02.18)

G-BIGK   Taylorcraft BC-12D   8302   29.10.80
N96002, NC96002   R A Benson
Trenchard Farm, Eggesford   07.10.19P
Carries 'NC96002' on rear fuselage

G-BIGL   Cameron O-65   690   22.10.80
P L & S V Mossman   Llanishen, Chepstow   08.05.17E
(IE 07.01.19)

G-BIGP^M   Bensen B.8M   xxxx   14.10.80
Cancelled 27.11.08 as PWFU   20.10.97
Built by R H S Cooper – project.PFA G/01-1005
With The Helicopter Museum, Weston-super-Mare

G-BIGR   Avenger T.200-2112   4   06.10.80
R Light   Stockport
Built by R Light

G-BIGT^M   Colt 77A HAB   078   28.02.80
Cancelled 04.02.87 by CAA   20.02.83
With British Balloon Museum & Library, Newbury

G-BIGX   Bensen B.8M   JRM-2   05.11.80
W C Turner   (Malvern)
Built by J R Martin (NF 21.07.15)

G-BIHD   Robin DR.400-160 Chevalier   1510   29.10.80
R C Boll   (Kevelaer, Germany)   21.06.19E

G-BIHF   Replica Plans SE.5A   xxxx   27.10.80
C J Zeal   White Waltham   'Lady Di'   06.09.11P
Built by K J Garrett – project PFA 020-10548;
as 'F-943' in RFC 92 Sqdn c/s (NF 18.01.16)

G-BIHI   Cessna 172M Skyhawk II   17266854   18.11.80
(G-BIHA), N1125U   D H G Penney   (Tunbridge Wells)   15.02.15E
Nosewheel collapsed landing Fenland 18.09.14
(NF 26.11.15)

G-BIHO   de Havilland DHC-6-310 Twin Otter   738   09.01.81
A6-ADB, G-BIHO   Isles of Scilly Skybus Ltd
Land's End   18.04.19E

G-BIHT   Piper PA-17 Vagabond   17-41   09.01.81
N138N, N8N, N4626H, NC4626H   N F Andrews
Black Springs Farm, Castle Bytham   09.10.19P

G-BIHU   Saffery S.200   25   05.11.80
B L King   Weedon, Northampton
Built by Cupro Sapphire Ltd

G-BIHX   Bensen B.8MR   xxxx   12.11.80
P P Willmott   (Waltham, Grimsby)   08.07.12P
Built by P P Willmott – project PFA G/01-1003
(NF 17.01.19)

G-BIIA   Alpavia Fournier RF3   51   14.11.80
F-BMTA   C H Dennis   Dunkeswell   17.06.19E

G-BIID   Piper PA-18 Super Cub 95 (*L-18C-PI*)   18-1606   05.01.81
OO-LPA, OO-HMK, French Army 18-1606, 51-15606
D A Lacey   Cumbernauld   30.03.19P
Fuselage No.18-1558

G-BIIF   Fournier RF4D   4047   25.11.80
G-BVET, F-BOXG   K M Fresson   Solent   18.03.93A
(NF 28.02.18)

G-BIIK   SOCATA MS.883 Rallye 115   1552   28.11.80
F-BSAP   A C Bloomberg   (Wheathampstead)   14.03.19E

G-BIIO   Pilatus B-N BN-2T Islander   2102   01.12.80
F-HDEV, LX-KEV, LX-III, V2-LDF, (OB-T-1282),
V2-LDF, VP-LMF, N660J, G-BIIO
Islander Aircraft Ltd   Cumbernauld   16.09.17E
(IE 02.08.18)

G-BIIT   Piper PA-28-161 Warrior II   28-8116052   01.12.80
N82744   Tayside Aviation Ltd   Dundee   09.05.19E

G-BIIZ   Great Lakes 2T-1A Sport Trainer   57   01.04.81
N603K, NC603K   Airborne Adventures Ltd   Blackpool   04.02.99S
On rebuild 02.16 (IE 04.04.16)

G-BIJB   Piper PA-18-150 Super Cub   18-8009001   18.08.80
N23923, N2573H   James Aero Ltd   Stapleford   05.10.19E
Operated by Stapleford Flying Club

G-BIJD   Bölkow BÖ.208C Junior   636   09.12.80
PH-KAE, (PH-DYM), OO-SIS, (D-EGFA)
J D Day   Derby   21.04.19E

G-BIJE   Piper J-3C-65 Cub (*L-4A-PI*)   8367   05.05.81
F-BIGN, French Army, 42-15248
R L Hayward & A G Scott   (Cardiff & Trostrey, Usk)
Fuselage No.8504; originally registered with c/n 8865
(NF 04.02.16)

G-BIJS   Phoenix Luton LA-4A Minor   PFA 835   18.05.78
C C & J M Lovell   Stonefield Park, Chilbolton   14.11.95P
Built by I J Smith – project PFA 835; Phoenix
plans no PAL 1348 not confirmed (NF 28.01.19)

G-BIJU	Piel CP.301A Emeraude	221	10.06.80
	G-BHTX, F-BIJU W A Baumann tr Eastern		
	Taildraggers Flying Club Hardwick		29.11.19P
	Built by Société Menavia		
G-BIJV	Reims/Cessna F152 II	F15201813	22.12.80
	A S Bamrah t/a Falcon Flying Services Blackbushe		09.07.19E
G-BIJW	Reims/Cessna F152 II	F15201820	22.12.80
	A S Bamrah t/a Falcon Flying Services RAF Henlow		27.05.19E
G-BIKE	Piper PA-28R-200 Cherokee Arrow II	28R-7335173	18.04.80
	OY-DVT, N55047 R Taylor Rochester		20.06.19E
G-BIKT	Boeing 757-236	23398	01.11.85
	D-ALEG, OO-DPO, G-BIKT		
	DHL Air Ltd East Midlands		03.11.05
	Line No: 77 (IE 08.11.18)		
G-BIKX	Boeing 757-236(SF)	23493	14.03.86
	D-ALEI, OO-DPJ, G-BIKX		
	DHL Air Ltd East Midlands		05.11.18E
	Line No: 90		
G-BILB	Wallingford WMB.2 Windtracker	14	22.01.81
	B L King Weedon, Northampton		
G-BILE	Morris Scruggs BL-2B	81231	13.03.81
	P D Ridout Botley		
G-BILG	Morris Scruggs BL-2B	81232	13.03.81
	P D Ridout Botley		
G-BILH	Slingsby T65C Sport Vega	1942	03.02.81
	BGA 2700/EHN, G-BILH, BGA 2700/EHN		
	P Woodcock Burn *'EHN'*		23.04.15E
	(NF 30.01.17)		
G-BILI	Piper J-3C-65 Cub (L-4J-PI)	13207	14.01.81
	F-BDTB, 45-4467		
	Historic & Classic Aircraft Sales Wycombe Air Park		23.07.19P
	Fuselage No.13044; as '454467:J-44' in US Army c/s		
G-BILK	Cessna FA152 Aerobat	FA1520372	09.01.81
	Cancelled 10.08.01 as destroyed		13.05.02
	Thruxton *Built by Reims Aviation SA*		
	On fire dump 01.16		
G-BILR	Cessna 152 II	15284822	19.03.81
	N4822P APB Leasing Ltd Sleap		08.05.19E
G-BILS	Cessna 152 II	15284857	03.06.81
	N4954P Mona Aviation Ltd t/a Mona Flying Club		
	RAF Mona		23.09.19E
G-BILU	Cessna 172RG Cutlass II	172RG0564	29.01.81
	N5540V Full Sutton Flying Centre Ltd Full Sutton		26.04.19E
G-BILZ	Taylor JT.1 Monoplane	xxxx	15.12.80
	A Petherbridge North Coates		
	Built by G Beaumont – project PFA 055-10124;		
	wings only noted 01.19 (NF 06.06.18)		
G-BIMK	Tiger T200 Series 1	7/MKB-01	22.12.80
	M K Baron Woodley, Stockport		
	Built by M K Baron		
G-BIMM	Piper PA-18-150 Super Cub (L-21B-PI)	18-3868	08.01.81
	PH-VHO, R Netherlands AF R-178, 54-2468		
	Spectrum Leisure Ltd Clacton-on-Sea		26.01.20E
	Fuselage No.18-3881		
G-BIMN	Steen Skybolt	xxxx	31.12.80
	R J Thomas Hamilton Farm, Bilsington		27.07.19P
	Built by C R Williamson – project PFA 064-10329		
G-BIMT	Reims/Cessna FA152 Aerobat	FA1520361	09.01.81
	N8062L Staverton Flying School @ Skypark Ltd		
	Gloucestershire		17.05.19E
G-BIMX	Rutan VariEze	xxxx	06.01.81
	D G Crew Biggin Hill		02.04.15P
	Built by A S Knowles – project PFA 074-10544		
	(IE 25.04.15)		
G-BIMZ	Beech 76 Duchess	ME-169	20.03.81
	N6021K D C S Gunning Fowlmere		10.05.19E
G-BINL	Morris Scruggs BL-2B	81216	05.02.81
	P D Ridout Eastleigh		
G-BINM	Morris Scruggs BL-2B	81217	05.02.81
	P D Ridout Eastleigh		
G-BINR	Unicorn UE-1A	81004	20.01.81
	I Chadwick t/a Unicorn Group Caterham *'Lady Diana'*		
	(NF 13.01.11)		

G-BINS	Unicorn UE-2A	80002	22.12.80
	I Chadwick t/a Unicorn Group Caterham *'Caroline'*		
	(NF 13.01.11)		
G-BINT	Unicorn UE-1A	80001	22.12.80
	D E Bint Downham Market		
G-BINX	Morris Scruggs BL-2B	81219	05.02.81
	P D Ridout Eastleigh		
G-BINY	Morton Oriental Air-Bag	OAB-001	22.01.81
	J L Morton Wokingham		
G-BIOA	Hughes 369D (*500*)	1200880D	09.02.81
	OO-HFS, LX-HLE, OO-HFS, G-BIOA AH Helicopter		
	Services Ltd Knowle House Cottage, Lustleigh		24.06.19E
G-BIOB	Reims/Cessna F172P	F17202042	23.01.81
	High Level Photography Ltd Fairoaks		10.07.19E
G-BIOC	Reims/Cessna F150L	F15000848	03.02.81
	F-BUEC G W T Farrington St Mary's, Isles of Scilly		14.02.20E
G-BIOI	Jodel DR.1050-M Excellence	477	21.01.81
	F-BLJQ A A Alderdice Aughrim, Kilkeel		07.06.19P
	Built by Société Aéronautique Normande		
G-BIOJ	Rockwell Commander 112TC-A	13192	22.01.82
	N4662W Cancelled 03.04.14 by CAA		13.12.02
	Caterham *Spares use 04.18*		
G-BIOK	Reims/Cessna F152 II	F15201810	02.02.81
	N Foster Carlisle Lake District		02.12.19E
G-BIOU	Jodel D.117A	813	09.08.78
	F-BIOU M R Routh Dunkeswell		23.04.19P
	Built by Société Aéronautique Normande		
G-BIPA	Grumman American AA-5B Tiger	AA5B-0200	24.03.81
	OY-GAM Tri-Star Developments Ltd		
	(Douglas, Isle of Man)		25.11.10E
	(NF 24.06.16)		
G-BIPH	Morris Scruggs BL-2B	81224	10.02.81
	C M Dewsnap Owlsmoor, Sandhurst		
G-BIPI	Everett Gyroplane	001	30.04.81
	J G Farina (Alveley, Bridgnorth)		19.06.01P
	(NF 04.10.17)		
G-BIPN	Alpavia Fournier RF3	35	26.02.81
	F-BMDN M C Desmond tr G-BIPN Group		
	Cranwell North		01.05.19P
G-BIPT	Jodel D.112	1254	11.03.81
	F-BMIB C R Davies Allensmore		26.06.19P
	Built by Société Wassmer Aviation		
G-BIPV	Gulfstream American AA-5B Tiger	AA5B-0981	10.03.81
	N28266 Echo Echo Ltd Bournemouth		21.06.19E
G-BIPW	Avenger T.200-2112	10	24.02.81
	B L King Weedon, Northampton		
G-BIRB	SOCATA MS.880B Rallye 100T	2460	30.08.81
	F-BVAO Cancelled 13.07.92 by CAA		16.09.90
	Shanklin, Isle Of Wight		
	Displayed 'Jungle Jim's Theme Park' 08.18 in zebra c/s		
G-BIRD	Pitts S-1D	707H	03.11.77
	N E Smith (Mannings Heath, Horsham)		04.12.14P
	Built by R N York – project PFA 1596 (IE 18.03.16)		
G-BIRE	Colt 56 Satzenbrau Bottle	323	04.03.81
	D M Hoddinott Bristol BS8 *'Satzenbrau'*		24.05.08
	(IE 04.08.17)		
G-BIRI	CASA 1-131E Jungmann Series 1000	1074	14.04.81
	Spanish AF E3B-113 D Watt (Yaxley, Peterborough)		16.06.11P
	(NF 18.08.16)		
G-BIRL	Avenger T.200-2112	8	10.03.81
	R Light Stockport		
	Built by R Light		
G-BIRP	Ridout Arena Mk.17 Skyship	1	13.03.81
	A S Ridout Eastleigh		
	Built by P D Ridout		
G-BIRT	Robin R1180TD Aiglon	276	25.03.81
	OO-FIS W d Hall Gutchpool Farm, Gillingham		30.04.19E
G-BIRW[M]	Morane-Saulnier MS.505 Criquet	695/28	10.04.81
	OO-FIS, F-BDQS, French AF 695		
	Cancelled 15.11.88 as WFU		03.06.83
	As 'FI+S' in Luftwaffe c/s		
	With National Museum of Flight Scotland, East Fortune		

G-BISG	Clutton FRED Series III	RAC 01-224	13.03.81
	T Littlefair (Pennington, Lymington) *'Fuzz Bee'*		
	Built by R A Coombe – project PFA 029-10675		
	(NF 04.04.18)		
G-BISH	Cameron V-65	707	16.03.81
	P J Bish Newtown, Hungerford *'Tsaritsa'*		15.06.19E
G-BISL	Morris Scruggs BL-2B	81233	13.03.81
	P D Ridout Eastleigh		
	Built by D Morris		
G-BISM	Morris Scruggs BL-2C	81234	13.03.81
	P D Ridout Eastleigh		
	Built by D Morris		
G-BISS	Morris Scruggs BL-2C	81235	13.03.81
	P D Ridout Eastleigh		
	Built by D Morris		
G-BIST	Morris Scruggs BL-2C	81236	13.03.81
	P D Ridout Eastleigh		
	Built by D Morris		
G-BISX	Colt 56A	324	18.03.81
	C D Steel St Boswells, Melrose		18.08.99A
	(NF 05.04.16)		
G-BITA	Piper PA-18-150 Super Cub	18-8109037	24.03.81
	N82585 P T Shaw Rush Green		19.01.19E
G-BITE	SOCATA TB-10 Tobago	193	07.05.81
	N A Baxter Sandtoft		09.05.19E
G-BITF	Reims/Cessna F152 II	F15201822	27.03.81
	J Parker tr GBITF Owners Fife		14.09.19E
G-BITH	Reims/Cessna F152 II	F15201825	27.03.81
	G-TFSA, G-BITH J R Hyde Derby		23.07.16E
	Stored 05.17 (IE 23.10.17)		
G-BITK	Clutton FRED Series II	xxxx	23.03.81
	I Pearson (Falmouth)		
	Built by B J Miles – project PFA 029-10369;		
	stored 07.16 (NF 27.07.18)		
G-BITO	Jodel D.112D	1200	20.03.81
	F-BIUO A Dunbar Ashcroft		05.09.02P
	Built by Etablissement Valladeau (NF 06.08.18)		
G-BITY	Bell FD.31T	2604	25.03.81
	A J Bell Bognor Regis		
G-BIUL	Cameron Bellows 60SS HAB	703	27.03.81
	Cancelled 26.06.98 as PWFU		12.05.91
	Abingdon *Inflated Pidley 05.16*		
	Expansion Joint special shape		
G-BIUP	SNCAN NC.854S	54	04.06.81
	(G-AMPE), G-BIUP, F-BFSC S A Richardson		
	Griffins Farm, Temple Bruer		26.03.19P
G-BIUY	Piper PA-28-181 Archer II	28-8190133	03.04.81
	N8318X Redhill Air Services Ltd Fairoaks		17.03.19E
G-BIVA	Robin R2112 Alpha	137	06.05.81
	F-GBAZ A J Hopper tr Victor Alpha Group		
	Pent Farm, Postling		23.05.19E
G-BIVB	Jodel D.112	1009	18.09.81
	(G-BIVC), F-BJII D V Magee Dunkeswell		13.02.19P
	Built by Société des Etablissements Benjamin Wassmer		
G-BIVC	Jodel D.112	1219	01.06.81
	F-BMAI T D Wood (Yate, Bristol)		13.07.00P
	Built by Société Wassmer Aviation (NF 25.10.16)		
G-BIVF	Scintex CP.301-C3 Emeraude	594	04.11.81
	F-BJVN E Stephenson Eshott *'Emma'*		18.10.19P
	Built by Société Menavia		
G-BIVK	Bensen B.8MV	xxxx	10.04.81
	M J Atyeo (Bridport) *'Skyrider'*		19.11.03P
	Built by J G Toy – project PFA G/01-1008;		
	officially registered as B.8M (NF 27.01.15)		
G-BIVV	Gulfstream American AA-5A Cheetah	AA5A-0857	26.05.81
	Cancelled 03.10.08 by CAA		18.07.05
	North Weald *On airport fire dump 06.15*		
G-BIWA	Ridout Stevendon Skyreacher	102	08.06.81
	S D Barnes Eastleigh		
G-BIWB	Morris Scruggs RS.5000	81541	08.06.81
	P D Ridout Eastleigh		
G-BIWC	Morris Scruggs RS.5000	81546	26.06.81
	P D Ridout Eastleigh *'Waterloo'*		

G-BIWF	Ridout Warren Windcatcher	13	03.07.81
	P D Ridout Eastleigh		
G-BIWG	Ridout Zelenski Mk.2	Z.401	03.07.81
	P D Ridout Eastleigh		
	Official c/n '2401' is incorrect		
G-BIWJ	Unicorn UE-1A	81014	14.07.81
	B L King Weedon, Northampton		
	Built by Unicorn Group		
G-BIWN	Jodel D.112	1314	05.06.81
	F-BNCN J Steele (Ballymena)		01.01.20P
	Built by Société Wassmer Aviation		
G-BIWR	Mooney M.20F Executive	22-1339	01.06.81
	N6972V M Broady Sleap		28.02.19E
G-BIXA	SOCATA TB-9 Tampico	205	07.05.81
	W Maxwell Perth		28.11.19E
G-BIXB	SOCATA TB-9 Tampico	208	07.05.81
	B G Adams Shobdon		22.05.19E
G-BIXL	North American P-51D-20-NA Mustang	38675	03.07.81
	Israel DF AF2343?, Swedish AF 26116, 44-72216		
	R W Tyrrell Duxford *'Miss Helen'*		25.04.19P
	As '472216:HO-M' in 487thFS/352ndFG USAF c/s		
G-BIXN	Boeing Stearman A75N1 Kaydet (*PT-17*) 75-2248		15.06.81
	N51132, 41-8689 V S E Norman Rendcomb		
	Bare frame stored 2017 (NF 13.03.18)		
G-BIXW	Colt 56B	348	18.05.81
	N A P Bates Ross-on-Wye *'Spam'*		17.08.97
	(NF 26.04.16)		
G-BIXX	Pearson Series 2	327	08.05.81
	D Pearson Solihull		
G-BIXZ	Grob G109	6019	14.05.81
	D-KGRO C Beck (Harrogate)		07.04.14E
	(NF 11.05.18)		
G-BIYI	Cameron V-65	722	21.05.81
	R J Mitchener & P F Smart Andover & Basingstoke		
	'Pennyhill Park Hotel'		08.07.10E
	Noted 01.19 (IE 16.02.18)		
G-BIYJ	Piper PA-18 Super Cub 95 (*L-18C-PI*) 18-1000		05.06.81
	Italian AF MM51-1530, I-EIST, Italian AF MM51-15303,		
	51-15303 N J Butler Fordoun		06.06.17P
	Struck combine harvester, overturned Lundin Links,		
	Fife 18.07.17 & substantially damaged; for potential		
	rebuild 10.17 (NF 30.11.17)		
G-BIYK	Isaacs Fury II	xxxx	20.05.81
	M J Sharp RAF Barkston Heath		05.05.11P
	Built by R S Martins – project PFA 011-10418		
	(NF 24.09.18)		
G-BIYR	Piper PA-18-150 Super Cub (*L-21B-PI*) 18-3841		26.05.81
	(G-BIYB), PH-GER, R Netherlands AF R-151, 5G-96,		
	54-2441 B H & M J Fairclough tr Delta Foxtrot		
	Flying Group Watchford Farm, Yarcombe		26.05.19E
	Fuselage No.18-3843; as 'R-151' in R Netherlands AF c/s		
G-BIYU	Fokker S11-1 Instructor	6206	13.05.81
	(PH-HOM), R Netherlands AF E-15		
	A Eckersley tr Fokker Syndicate RAF Linton-on-Ouse		06.09.17P
	As 'E-15' in R Netherlands AF c/s; stored 10.18		
	(IE 18.08.18)		
G-BIYW	Jodel D.112	1209	25.05.81
	F-BLNR R C Hibberd Coate, Devizes		26.03.19P
	Built by Société Wassmer Aviation		
G-BIYX	Piper PA-28-140 Cherokee Cruiser	28-7625064	19.06.81
	OY-BLD W B Bateson Blackpool		16.06.18E
	(NF 04.10.18)		
G-BIYY	Piper PA-18 Super Cub 95 (*L-18C-PI*) 18-1979		02.06.81
	Italian AF MM52-2379, I-EIGA, Italian AF MM52-2379,		
	52-2379 A E Taylor Fenland		27.02.18E
	Fuselage No.18-1914 (NF 29.11.18)		
G-BIZE	SOCATA TB-9 Tampico	209	15.06.81
	9H-ABJ, G-BIZE Just Plane Trading Ltd		
	Top Farm, Croydon		09.08.19E
G-BIZF	Reims/Cessna F172P	F17202070	16.06.81
	R S Bentley Main Hall Farm, Conington		16.10.19E
G-BIZG	Reims/Cessna F152 II	F15201873	16.06.81
	M A Judge t/a Aerogroup 78 Netherthorpe		24.09.19E

G-BIZK	Nord 3202-B1		78	22.11.85
	N2255E, French Army A I Milne			
	Great Friars' Thornes Farm, Swaffham			19.09.19P
	As '78' in French ALAT yellow c/s			
G-BIZM	Nord 3202B		91	22.11.85
	N2256K, French Army Global Aviation Ltd			
	Humberside			28.03.19P
G-BIZO	Piper PA-28R-200 Cherokee Arrow II	28R-7535339		16.06.81
	OY-DLH, N1578X Bristol Flying Club Ltd Bristol			12.04.19E
G-BIZR	SOCATA TB-9 Tampico		210	15.06.81
	G-BSEC, G-BIZR R A Danby Bournemouth			29.06.19E
G-BIZV	Piper PA-18 Super Cub 95		18-2001	12.06.81
	I-EIDE/E.I.74, Italian Mil MM52-2401, 52-2401			
	J P Nugent Newcastle, RoI			27.07.15P
	As '18-2001' in US Army c/s			
G-BIZY	Jodel D.112		1120	13.07.81
	F-BKJL T R Fray Ranksborough Farm, Langham			24.11.19P
	Built by Société Wassmer Aviation			

G-BJAA – G-BJZZ

G-BJAD[M]	Clutton FRED Series II		CA.1	11.06.81
	Cancelled 13.03.09 by CAA			
	Built by C Allison – project PFA 29-10586			
	With Newark Air Museum, Winthorpe			
G-BJAE	Starck AS.80 Holiday		04	17.06.81
	F-PGGA, F-WGGA D J & S A E Phillips			
	(Leamington Spa)			08.08.92P
	Built by J R Lavadoux (NF 15.01.19)			
G-BJAF	Piper J-3C-65 Cub (*L-4A-PI*)		8437	23.06.81
	D-EJAF, HB-OAD, 42-15318 P J Cottle			
	Craysmarsh Farm, Melksham			10.08.19P
	Fuselage No.8540			
G-BJAG	Piper PA-28-181 Archer II	28-7990353		23.06.81
	PH-LDB, (PH-BEG), (OO-FLM), N2244W			
	C R Chubb Lydd			03.02.19E
G-BJAJ	Gulfstream American AA-5B Tiger	AA5B-1177		02.07.81
	N4532V A J Byrne tr Draycott Tiger Club Draycott			17.12.19E
G-BJAL	CASA 1-131E Jungmann Series 1000	1028		11.09.78
	Spanish AF E3B-114 S B J Chandler tr G-BJAL Group			
	Breighton			29.06.19P
	Spanish AF serial no. conflicts with G-BUCC			
G-BJAO	Montgomerie-Bensen B.8MR	GLS-01		28.08.81
	A P Lay Henstridge			02.04.01P
	Built by A Gault – project PFA G/01-1001 (NF 14.10.16)			
G-BJAP	de Havilland DH.82A Tiger Moth replica	0482		15.06.81
	K Knight (Storridge, Malvern)			05.05.17P
	Built by J A Pothecary – project PFA 157-12897;			
	composite rebuild; on rebuild 09.17; as 'K2587'			
	in pre-war RAF 32 Sqdn:CFS c/s (IE 10.12.18)			
G-BJAS	Rango NA-9		TL-19	22.06.81
	A Lindsay Twickenham			
G-BJAW	Cameron V-65 HAB		745	19.06.81
	Cancelled 02.02.10 as PWFU			16.04.86
	Not Known Inflated Pidley 05.16			
G-BJAY	Piper J-3C-65 Cub (*L-4H-PI*)		12086	01.11.78
	F-BFBN, OO-EAC, 44-79790 D W Finlay			
	(Levignac de Guyenne, Lot-et-Garonne, France)			24.10.19P
	Fuselage No.11914; as '44-79790' in USAAF c/s			
G-BJBK	Piper PA-18 Super Cub 95 (*L-18C-PI*)		18-1431	21.08.81
	F-BOME, French Army 51-15431			
	M S Bird New Barn Farm, Crawley			09.07.10P
	Fuselage No.18-1370; on rebuild 06.17 (IE 10.04.18)			
G-BJBM[M]	Monnett Sonerai I		xxxx	02.07.81
	I Pearson Newquay Cornwall *'The Answer'*			25.09.12P
	Built by Lyster Aviation Ltd – project PFA 015-10022;			
	on display Cornwall Aviation Heritage Centre (IE 27.07.18)			
G-BJBO	Robin DR.250/160 Capitaine		40	24.08.81
	F-BNJG J A Hobby tr Wiltshire Flying Group			
	Oaksey Park			17.08.19E
	Built by Centre-Est Aéronautique			
G-BJBW	Piper PA-28-161 Warrior II	28-8116280		22.02.81
	N2913Z C Greenland & T G Phillips tr 152 Group			
	Popham			07.05.19E

G-BJBX	Piper PA-28-161 Warrior II	28-8116269		17.07.81
	N8414H Cancelled 11.10.10 by CAA			15.06.10
	Full Sutton *Spares use 04.16*			
G-BJCA	Piper PA-28-161 Warrior II	28-7916473		30.07.81
	N2846D Falcon Flying Services Ltd Brighton City			09.12.19E
G-BJCF	Scintex CP.1310-C3 Super Emeraude	936		19.11.81
	F-BMJH R N R Bellamy Bodmin			26.01.18P
G-BJCI	Piper PA-18-150 Super Cub		18-6658	10.09.81
	N9388D The Borders (Milfield) Gliding Club Ltd			
	Milfield			17.05.19E
G-BJCW	Piper PA-32R-301 Saratoga SP	32R-8113094		06.08.81
	N2866U Golf Charlie Whisky Ltd Fairoaks			16.05.19E
G-BJDE	Reims/Cessna F172M	F17200984		25.08.81
	OO-MSS, D-EGBR S Bridgeman & M Rowntree			
	Sandown			29.03.19E
G-BJDF	SOCATA MS.880B Rallye 100T	3000		21.09.81
	F-GAKP C J D S Prado Santarém, Ribatejo, Portugal			07.07.13E
	(NF 21.07.16)			
G-BJDK	Ridout European E.157	S2		17.08.81
	E Osborn t/a Aeroprint Tours Eastleigh			
	Built by P D Ridout			
G-BJDO	Gulfstream American AA-5A Cheetah	AA5A-0823		03.08.81
	N26936 Cancelled 27.10.08 by CAA			11.04.03
	Farley Farm, Farley Chamberlayne *Stored 12.17*			
G-BJDW	Reims/Cessna F172M	F17201417		10.08.81
	PH-JBE Hardman Aviation Ltd Blackbushe			12.04.19E
G-BJEC	Pilatus B-N BN-2T Islander	2118		02.06.04
	ZH537, G-SELX, G-BJEC, UAE AF 318, 411, G-BJEC			
	Islander Aircraft Ltd Cumbernauld			22.03.19E
	Originally registered as Pilatus B-N BN-2B Islander			
G-BJED	Pilatus B-N BN-2T Islander	2119		28.07.81
	G-MAFF, G-BJED Islander Aircraft Ltd			
	(Cumbernauld)			28.03.19E
	Originally registered as Pilatus B-N BN-2B Islander			
G-BJEF	Pilatus B-N BN-2T Islander	2121		28.07.81
	C9-TAK, G-BJEF Islander Aircraft Ltd			
	(Cumbernauld)			07.04.14
	Originally registered as Pilatus B-N BN-2B Islander			
	(IE 14.09.15)			
G-BJEI	Piper PA-18 Super Cub 95 (*L-18C-PI*)	18-1988		27.07.81
	I-EILO/E.I.66, Ital Mil M52-2388, 52-2388			
	E M Cox Belle Vue Farm, Yarnscombe			26.11.18P
	Fuselage No.18-1938			
G-BJEJ	Pilatus B-N BN-2T Islander	2124		28.07.81
	C9-TAJ, G-BJEJ Islander Aircraft Ltd (Cumbernauld)			11.03.08
	Originally registered as Pilatus B-N BN-2B Islander			
	(NF 22.12.15)			
G-BJEL	SNCAN NC.854S	113		07.08.81
	F-BEZT C A James Rookery Farm, Doynton *'Jessie'*			30.09.19P
G-BJEV	Aeronca 11AC Chief	11AC-270		12.08.81
	N85897, NC85897 M B Blackmore Dunkeswell			19.09.19P
	As '897:E' in US Navy c/s			
G-BJEX	Bölkow BÖ.208C Junior	690		27.08.81
	F-BRHY, D-EEAM G D H Crawford			
	(Rotherfield Greys, Henley-on-Thames)			
	Built by Waggon und Maschinenbau AG (NF 17.04.18)			
G-BJFC	Ridout European E.8	S1		17.08.81
	P D Ridout Eastleigh			
	Built by P D Ridout			
G-BJFE	Piper PA-18 Super Cub 95 (*L-18C-PI*)	18-2022		17.08.81
	I-EISU/E.I.91, Italian Mil MM52-2422, 52-2422			
	P H Wilmot-Allistone Watchford Farm, Yarcombe			22.08.07P
	(NF 18.02.15)			
G-BJFM	Jodel D.120 Paris-Nice	227		08.10.81
	F-BLFM J V George Popham			02.09.19P
	(uilt by Société Wassmer Aviation			
G-BJGM	Unicorn UE-1A	81015		21.08.81
	D Eaves & P D Ridout Southampton & Eastleigh			
	'Capricorn'			
	Built by Unicorn Group			
G-BJGY	Reims/Cessna F172P	F17202128		13.10.81
	K & S Martin Gunton Park, Suffield			19.06.10E
G-BJHB	Mooney M.20J Mooney 201	24-1190		23.12.81
	N1145G Zitair Flying Club Ltd Wycombe Air Park			22.07.19E

G-BJHK	EAA Acrosport	xxxx	20.03.80	

G-BJHK EAA Acrosport xxxx 20.03.80
M R Holden Windsor Farm, Hagworthingham 31.08.04P
Built by J H Kimber – project PFA 072-10470;
stored 05.16 (NF 18.10.18)

G-BJHS^M Short S.25 Sandringham SH.55C 11.09.81
(EI-BYI), G-BJHS, N158J, VH-BRF, RNZAF NZ4108, ML814
Cancelled 12.08.93 - to N814ML
Carries 'N814ML, G-BJHS & ML814'
Sunderland GR.3 conversion as c/n SH974)
With Fantasy of Flight, Polk City, Florida

G-BJHV^M Voisin Scale replica MPS-1 01.09.81
Cancelled 04.07.91 by CAA
Built by M P Sayer On loan from M.P.Sayer
With Brooklands Museum, Weybridge

G-BJIA Allport Hot Air Free 1 02.09.81
D J Allport Bourne
Built by D J Allport

G-BJIC Eaves Dodo 1A 3 04.09.81
P D Ridout Eastleigh
Built by D Eaves

G-BJID Osprey Lizzieliner 1B 28 04.09.81
P D Ridout Eastleigh
Built by A P Chown

G-BJIG Slingsby T67A 1992 16.09.81
A D Hodgkinson Dunkeswell 15.05.04
Noted 03.18 (NF 11.01.19)

G-BJIV Piper PA-18-150 Super Cub 18-8262 17.09.81
N5972Z B F Walker (Cam, Dursley) 14.06.19E

G-BJKX Cessna F152 II F15201881 22.09.81
Cancelled 19.01.89 as PWFU 01.07.91
Mullinger, RoI *Built by Reims Aviation SA*
For sale as rebuild project 11.15

G-BJLC Monnett Sonerai IIL 942L 18.09.81
P D Yeo Henstridge 11.05.98P
Built by J P Whitham – project PFA 015-10634 (NF 12.12.18)

G-BJLF Unicorn UE-1C 81018 21.09.81
I Chadwick t/a Unicorn Group Caterham
Built by Unicorn Group (NF 10.01.11)

G-BJLG Unicorn UE-1B 81017 21.09.81
I Chadwick t/a Unicorn Group Caterham
Built by Unicorn Group (NF 13.01.11)

G-BJLX Cremer Cracker 711 24.09.81
P W May Wilmslow
Built by P A Cremer

G-BJLY Cremer Cracker 709 24.09.81
P Cannon Luton LU4
Built by P A Cremer

G-BJML Cessna 120 10766 05.10.81
N76349, NC76349 R A Smith
Wellcross Farm, Slinfold 29.06.19P

G-BJMM^M Cremer MLB 717 29.09.81
Cancelled 18.10.88 as PWFU
With South East Aviation Enthusiasts Group, Dromod, RoI

G-BJMR Cessna 310R II 310R1624 16.07.79
N2631Z J H Sandham t/a JH Sandham Aviation
Carlisle Lake District 22.06.18E
(IE 07.02.19)

G-BJMW Thunder Ax8-105 369 14.10.81
G M Westley Byworth, Petworth 11.01.02A
(NF 17.11.15)

G-BJMX Ridout Jarre JR-3 81601 06.10.81
P D Ridout Eastleigh
Built by P D Ridout

G-BJMZ Ridout European EA-8A S5 06.10.81
P D Ridout Eastleigh
Built by P D Ridout

G-BJNA Ridout Arena Mk.117P 202 06.10.81
P D Ridout Eastleigh
Built by P D Ridout

G-BJND Osprey Mk.1E AKC-53 07.10.81
A Billington & D Whitmore (Liverpool L38 & Wigan)
Built by A P Chown

G-BJNG Slingsby T67A 1993 16.10.81
D F Hodgkinson Dunkeswell 23.07.01
Noted 03.18 (NF 05.05.18)

G-BJNH Osprey Mk.1E AKC-57 08.10.81
D A Kirk Manchester M22
Built by A P Chown

G-BJNY Aeronca 11CC Super Chief 11CC-264 28.10.81
CN-TYZ, F-OAEE D M & P I Morgans
Furze Hill Farm, Rosemarket
(NF 16.11.18)

G-BJNZ Piper PA-23-250 Aztec F 27-7954099 05.10.81
G-FANZ, N6905A, C-GTJG J A D Richardson
Wellesbourne Mountford 27.07.19E

G-BJOB Jodel D.140C Mousquetaire III 118 02.11.81
F-BMBD T W M Beck & M J Smith
Butlers Ghyll Farm, Southwater 23.05.19P
Built by Société Aéronautique Normande

G-BJOD Hollman Sportster HA-2M HP81-01 26.10.81
Cancelled 19.06.91 by CAA
Ashley Farm, Binfield *Built by H J Goddard &*
W O'Riordan; stored 06.17

G-BJOE Jodel D.120A Paris-Nice 177 12.11.81
F-BJIU D R Gibby Haverfordwest 09.08.19P
Built by Société des Etablissements Benjamin Wassmer

G-BJOH Pilatus B-N BN-2T Islander 2034 29.10.81
ZF573, G-SRAY, G-OPBN, G-BJOH
Islander Aircraft Ltd Cumbernauld 25.02.20E

G-BJOT Jodel D.117 688 12.11.81
F-BJCO, CN-TVH, F-DABU R A Kilbride Full Sutton 15.07.19P
Built by Société Aéronautique Normande

G-BJOV Reims/Cessna F150K F15000558 04.02.82
PH-VSD P Anderson tr G-BJOV Flying Group
Rochester *'101'* 30.08.19E

G-BJPI Bede BD-5G 1 30.10.81
M D McQueen (Beckenham)
Built by M D McQueen – project PFA 014-10218
(NF 15.09.18)

G-BJPL Osprey Mk.4A AKC-39 13.10.81
M Vincent St Helier JE2
Built by A P Chown

G-BJRA Osprey Mk.4B AKC-87 23.10.81
E Osborn t/a Aeroprint Tours Eastleigh
Built by A P Chown

G-BJRG Osprey Mk.4B AKC-95 26.10.81
A E de Gruchy St Brelade JE3
Built by A P Chown

G-BJRH Rango NA-36/AX3 NHP-23 04.11.81
N H Ponsford t/a Rango Balloon & Kite Company Leeds

G-BJRP Cremer Cracker 15-712PAC 29.10.81
M D Williams Houghton Regis, Dunstable
Built by P A Cremer

G-BJRR Cremer Cracker 15-715PAC 29.10.81
M D Williams Houghton Regis, Dunstable
Built by P A Cremer

G-BJRV Cremer Cracker 15-713PAC 29.10.81
M D Williams Houghton Regis, Dunstable
Built by P A Cremer

G-BJSS Allport Hot Air Free 2 09.11.81
D J Allport Bourne
Built by D J Allport

G-BJST CCF T-6 Harvard Mk.4 CCF4-292 21.12.81
Italian AF MM53-795, (51-17110)
G J Fricker tr G-BJST Group Duxford *'Wacky Wabbit'* 20.01.20E
Built by Canadian Car & Foundry Co;
as 'AJ841' in RAF desert c/s

G-BJSV Piper PA-28-161 Warrior II 28-8016229 25.11.81
PH-VZL, (OO-HLM), N35787
Flevo Aviation BV Lelystad, Netherlands 09.06.19E

G-BJSW Thunder Ax7-65Z 378 16.11.81
J Edwards Northampton *'Sandicliffe Ford'* 27.09.09E
Noted 05.16 (IE 13.01.16)

G-BJSZ Piper J-3C-65 Cub (L-4H-PI) 12047 20.11.81
D-EHID, (D-ECAX), (D-EKAB), PH-NBP, 44-79751
S T Gilbert Enstone 28.03.19P

G-BJTB Cessna A150M Aerobat A1500627 28.10.82
(G-BIVN), N9818J Cirrus Aviation Ltd Clacton-on-Sea 27.11.07E
Stored dismantled 03.15 (NF 22.10.18)

G-BJTF	Kirk Skyrider Mk.1	KSR-01	18.11.81
	D A Kirk Manchester M22		
G-BJTN	Osprey Mk.4B	ASC-112	23.11.81
	M Vincent St Helier JE2		
	Built by Solent Balloon Group		
G-BJTP	Piper PA-18 Super Cub 95 (*L-18C-PI*)	18-999	26.11.81
	Italian Army EI-51, I-EICO:EI-51, Italian Army MM51-15302,		
	51-15302 G J Molloy (Bomere Heath, Shrewsbury)		
	'Sittin' Duck'		08.11.13P
	As 'MM51-15302:EI-51' in Italian Army c/s (NF 26.10.16)		
G-BJTY	Osprey Mk.4B	ASC-115	23.11.81
	A E de Gruchy St Brelade JE3		
	Built by Solent Balloon Group		
G-BJUB	Wild BVS Special 01	VS/PW 01	25.11.81
	P G Wild Beverley		
G-BJUD	Robin DR.400-180R Remorqueur	870	27.11.81
	PH-SRM Lasham Gliding Society Ltd Lasham		22.02.19E
	Rebuilt using new fuselage; original scrapped		
	Membury 11.88		
G-BJUE	Osprey Mk.4B	ASC-114	23.11.81
	M Vincent St Helier JE2		
	Built by Solent Balloon Group		
G-BJUR	Piper PA-38-112 Tomahawk	38-79A0915	05.02.82
	N9722N Smart People Dont Buy Ltd Cardiff		20.04.16E
	(IE 06.04.17)		
G-BJUS	Piper PA-38-112 Tomahawk	38-80A0065	10.12.81
	N9690N J D Williams Elstree		09.05.19E
	Operated by Fly Elstree		
G-BJUU	Osprey Mk.4B	ASC-113	23.11.81
	M Vincent St Helier JE2		
	Built by Solent Balloon Group		
G-BJUV	Cameron V-20	792	09.12.81
	P Spellward Bristol BS9 *'Busy Bee'*		
	(IE 22.08.16)		
G-BJVC	Evans VP-2	xxxx	17.02.82
	Cancelled 13.02.15 by CAA		19.06.91
	Shenington *Built by R G Fenn*		
	– project PFA 063-10599; stored 02.15		
G-BJVH	Reims/Cessna F182Q Skylane II	F18200106	21.12.81
	D-EJMO, PH-AXU (2) R Beggs Isle of Man		03.04.19E
G-BJVJ	Reims/Cessna F152 II	F15201906	06.01.82
	Wilkins & Wilkins (Special Auctions) Ltd		
	t/a Henlow Flying Club RAF Henlow		28.11.19E
G-BJVK	Grob G109	6074	11.03.82
	J M & J R Kimberley Wolves Hall, Tendering		22.05.92
	(NF 05.12.17)		
G-BJVM	Cessna 172N Skyhawk II	17269374	14.12.81
	N737FA R D Forster Beccles		02.11.17E
	Stored 01.18		
G-BJVS	Scintex CP.1310-C3 Super Emeraude	903	05.01.79
	F-BJVS D Barrow Breighton		28.08.18P
	(IE 01.10.18)		
G-BJVU	Thunder Ax6-56 Bolt	397	31.12.81
	N R Beckwith Skewsby, York		14.01.19E
G-BJWI	Reims/Cessna F172P	F17202172	14.05.82
	Falcon Flying Services Ltd Fairoaks		06.10.19E
G-BJWT	Wittman W.10 Tailwind	xxxx	05.01.82
	R F Lea Dunkeswell		04.02.19P
	Built by J F Bakewell – project PFA 031-10688		
G-BJWV	Colt 17A Cloudhopper	391	22.01.82
	D T Mayes Leamington Spa *'Bryant Homes'*		26.03.97A
	(NF 16.09.15)		
G-BJWW	Reims/Cessna F172P	F17202148	01.02.82
	(D-EFTV) D Westoby Isle of Man		13.10.19E
	Operated by Isle of Man Flight Training		
G-BJWX	Piper PA-18 Super Cub 95 (*L-18C-PI*)	18-1985	23.02.82
	Ital.AF EI-64, I-EIME/E.I.64, Ital Mil MM52-2385, 52-2385		
	R A G Lucas Goodwood		23.04.19P
G-BJWY[M]	Sikorsky S-55 (HRS.2) Whirlwind HAR.21 55289		25.01.82
	A2576, WV198, US Navy 130191		
	Cancelled 23.02.94 by CAA *Displayed at Cornwall*		
	Aviation Heritage Centre, Newquay as 'WV198:K'		

G-BJWZ	Piper PA-18 Super Cub 95 (*L-18C-PI*)	18-1361	18.01.82
	OO-HMO, French Army 18-1361, 51-15361		
	R K Seaward tr G-BJWZ Syndicate Redhill		22.05.19P
	Fuselage No.18-1262		
G-BJXA	Slingsby T67A	1994	08.02.82
	G-GFAA, G-BJXA P K Pemberton Blackpool		21.09.19E
G-BJXB	Slingsby T67A	1995	08.02.82
	D Pegley (Wisborough Green, Billingshurst)		24.02.17E
G-BJXK	Sportavia-Putzer Fournier RF5	5054	03.02.82
	D-KINB S J Jenkins tr RF5 Syndicate Usk		20.10.19E
G-BJXP[M]	Colt 56B HAB	393	29.03.82
	Cancelled 29.01.14 as PWFU		09.09.00
	With British Balloon Museum & Library, Newbury		
G-BJXR	Auster AOP.9	xxxx	02.02.82
	XR267 I Churm & J Hanson Tatenhill		08.10.19P
	Built by Beagle-Auster Aircraft Ltd; officially registered		
	with Frame no.[AUS/] 184; as 'XR267' in AAC c/s		
G-BJXX	Piper PA-23-250 Aztec E	27-4692	07.04.82
	F-BTCM, N14094 V Bojovic (Belgrade, Serbia)		23.06.01
	Noted Belgrade Aviation Academy 02.17		
	as instructional airframe		
G-BJXZ	Cessna 172N Skyhawk II	17273039	24.03.82
	PH-CAA, N1949F T M Jones Derby		02.08.19E
G-BJYD	Reims/Cessna F152 II	F15201915	25.03.82
	N J James Welshpool		19.04.19E
G-BJYF	Colt 56A	401	01.03.82
	S Seguineau Valbonne, France *'Fanta'*		03.07.19E
G-BJYK	Jodel D.120A Paris-Nice	185	11.05.82
	(G-BJWK), F-BJPK M W Bodger		
	Yeatsall Farm, Abbots Bromley		10.08.18P
	Built by Société des Etablissements Benjamin Wassmer		
	(NF 18.02.19)		
G-BJYT	Pilatus B-N BN-2T Islander	2139	02.03.82
	F HFIT, ES PNW, G-WOTG, G-BJYT		
	Islander Aircraft Ltd Cumbernauld		09.01.19E
G-BJZB	Evans VP-2	xxxx	10.03.82
	T Turner tr VW Flyers Audley End		15.01.03P
	Built by A Graham – project PFA 063-10633		
	(NF 15.03.17)		
G-BJZC[M]	Thunder Ax7-65Z HAB	416	05.03.82
	Cancelled 08.07.98 as PWFU *'Greenpeace'*		17.06.94
	With Norfolk & Suffolk Aviation Museum, Flixton		
G-BJZN	Slingsby T67A	1997	31.03.82
	A R T Marsland tr ZN Group Breighton *'Annie'*		24.01.19E
G-BJZR	Colt 42A	402	18.03.82
	A F Selby tr Selfish Balloon Group		
	Woodhouse Eaves, Loughborough *'Selfish'*		28.09.13E
	(NF 30.06.16)		

G-BKAA – G-BKZZ

G-BKAE	Jodel D.120 Paris-Nice	200	05.05.82
	F-BKCE P Dixon tr Bumble Bee Group		
	Shacklewell Lodge Farm, Empingham		19.12.19P
	Built by Société des Etablissements Benjamin Wassmer		
G-BKAF	Clutton FRED Series II	xxxx	23.03.82
	N Glass (Gilford, Craigavon)		30.05.97P
	Built by L G Millen – project PFA 029-10337 (NF 07.04.16)		
G-BKAM	Slingsby T67M-160 Firefly	1999	26.04.82
	R C P Brookhouse RAF Benson		15.04.19E
G-BKAO	Jodel D.112	249	22.03.82
	F-BFTO H G Mayes & A J Wright		
	(Coalville & Scarborough) *'The Amy Louise'*		17.10.18P
	Built by Société des Etablissements Benjamin Wassmer		
	(IE 01.02.18)		
G-BKAS	Piper PA-38-112 Tomahawk	38-79A1075	16.04.82
	N24291, N9670N Cancelled 06.11.17 by CAA		23.05.13
	Littles Staughton *Stored dismantled 01.18*		
G-BKAY	Rockwell Commander 114	14411	28.09.81
	SE-GSN D L Bunning Dunkeswell		22.08.19E
G-BKAZ	Cessna 152 II	15282832	27.04.82
	N89705 Cloud Global Ltd Perth		03.06.19E

G-BKBB[M] Hawker Fury replica   WA/6   02.04.82
OO-HFU, OO-XFU   Cancelled 25.01.91 – to OO-XFU
subsequently OO-HFU, restored 04.11.96, cancelled
22.04.09 – to N31FY   *As 'K1930*   03.06.04
Built by Westward Airways (Lands End) Ltd
With Military Aviation Museum, Virginia Beach, Virginia

G-BKBD Thunder Ax3 Maxi Sky Chariot   418   05.04.82
A B Court   Morda, Oswestry
(IE 25.07.18)

G-BKBF SOCATA MS.894A Rallye Minerva 220   11622   08.09.82
F-BSKZ   R Wyse tr BKBF Flying Group   Draycott   03.07.15E
(NF 30.08.18)

G-BKBK SNCAN Stampe SV.4A   318   30.03.82
EI-CJR, G-BKBK, OO-CLR, F-BCLR
D J Pearson   Wolverhampton Halfpenny Green   23.06.94
(NF 21.06.17)

G-BKBP Bellanca 7GCBC Citabria   465-73   01.06.82
N8693   J R & M G Jefferies t/a HG Jefferies & Son
Little Gransden   09.11.15E
(NF 16.05.18)

G-BKBR (2)[M]   Cameron Chateau 84SS HAB   743   11.05.82
Cancelled 29.04.93 as WFU
Forbes Chateau de Balleroy shape
With Musée des Ballons, Chateau de Balleroy,
France

G-BKBS Bensen B.8MV   xxxx   14.04.82
A R Hawes   Monewden   21.03.11P
Built by G Dawe – project PFA G/01-1027 (NF 29.11.18)

G-BKBV SOCATA TB-10 Tobago   288   04.06.82
F-BNGO   F T J Alstormer & H Buchner tr G-BKBV Group
(Frankenthal & Dieberg, Germany)   *'Cocoa'*   12.04.19E

G-BKBW SOCATA TB-10 Tobago   289   04.06.82
N Harradine & D Stevenson tr Merlin Aviation   Bristol   12.02.20E

G-BKCC Piper PA-28-180 Cherokee Archer   28-7405099   13.05.82
OY-BGY   DR Flying Club Ltd   Gloucestershire   06.02.19E

G-BKCE Reims/Cessna F172P   F17202135   26.04.82
N9687R   The Leicestershire Aero Club Ltd   Leicester   28.06.19E

G-BKCI Brügger MB.2 Colibri   xxxx   22.04.82
M R Walters   Derby   01.10.19P
Built by E R Newall & M R Walters
– project PFA 043-10692

G-BKCJ Oldfield Baby Lakes   xxxx   12.05.82
B L R J Keeping   Davidstow Moor   26.01.99P
Built by S V Roberts – project PFA 010-10714
(NF 05.08.16)

G-BKCN Phoenix Currie Wot   PFA 3018   27.04.82
N A A Pogmore   (Sherburn-in-Elmet, Leeds)   22.11.08P
Built by S E O Tomlinson – project PFA 3018
(NF 22.03.18)

G-BKCV EAA Acrosport II   430   05.05.82
R J Bower   Maypole Farm, Chislet   *'Aerotation'*   02.07.19P
Built by M J Clark – project PFA 072A-10776

G-BKCW Jodel D.120A Paris-Nice   285   01.06.82
(G-BKCP), F-BMYF
I C Waddell tr Dundee Flying Group   Perth   29.11.18P
Built by Société Wassmer Aviation

G-BKCX Mudry CAP 10B   149   28.07.82
G N Davies   (Shobdon)   02.09.19E

G-BKCZ Jodel D.120A Paris-Nice   207   23.04.82
F-BKCZ   I K Ratcliffe   Deanland   15.10.19P
Built by Société Wassmer Aviation

G-BKDH Robin DR.400-120 Petit Prince   1582   25.05.82
PH-CAB   Marine & Aviation Ltd   Solent   13.02.19E

G-BKDJ Robin DR.400-120 Petit Prince   1584   25.05.82
PH-CAC   I C Colwell & S Pritchard   Gloucestershire   22.03.19E

G-BKDP Clutton FRED Series III   xxxx   24.05.82
M Whittaker   (Essington, Wolverhampton)
Built by M Whittaker – project PFA 029-10650
(NF 17.02.16)

G-BKDR Pitts S-1S   xxxx   14.06.82
L E Richardson   Oaksey Park   05.02.19P
Built by Maypole Engineering Ltd
– project PFA 009-10654

G-BKDT[M] Royal Aircraft Factory SE.5a replica   278   26.05.82
Cancelled 11.07.91 by CAA   *As 'F943:S'*
Built by J A Tetley – project PFA 080-10325
Note 'F-943' carried also by G-BIHF
With Yorkshire Air Museum, Elvington

G-BKDX Jodel DR.1050 Ambassadeur   55   01.06.82
F-BITX   D G T & R J Ward   (Brinsley, Nottingham)   07.07.17P
Built by Société Aéronautique Normande;
damaged landing Netherthorpe 13.11.16 (IE 07.08.18)

G-BKER Replica Plans SE.5A   xxxx   15.06.82
N K Geddes   South Barnbeth Farm, Bridge of Weir   07.09.18P
Built by N K Geddes – project PFA 020-10641;
as 'F5447:N' in RAF c/s (IE 07.12.18)

G-BKES[M] Cameron Bottle 57 SS HAB   846   25.06.82
Cancelled 01.05.90 by CAA   13.05.87
Robinsons Barley Water Bottle
With British Balloon Museum & Library, Newbury

G-BKET Piper PA-18 Super Cub 95 (*L-18C-PI*)   18-1990   17.06.82
Italian Army EI-67, I-EIBI:EI-67, Italian Army MM52-2390,
52-2390   N J F Campbell   Inverness   27.09.19P

G-BKEV Reims/Cessna F172M   F17201443   08.07.82
PH-WLH, OO-CNE   G Henn tr Derby Arrows   Derby   20.12.19E

G-BKEW Bell 206B-3 JetRanger III   3010   08.07.82
D-HDAD   G Birchmore, R J Palmer & R Toghill
Gloucestershire   28.04.19E

G-BKFC Reims/Cessna F152 II   F15201443   01.09.82
OO-AWB   C Walton Ltd   Bruntingthorpe   28.02.19E

G-BKFF[M] Westland WG.30 Series.100   006   22.06.82
G-17-30   Cancelled 06.12.82   *To & as 'N5840T'*
With The Helicopter Museum, Weston-super-Mare

G-BKFG Thunder Ax3 Maxi Sky Chariot   431   28.06.82
S G Whatley   Bristol BS3
(IE 14.09.16)

G-BKFI Evans VP-1 Series 2   xxxx   24.06.82
A S Watts   Newquay Cornwall   28.01.17P
Built by R F A Lavergne – project PFA 062-10491;
stored 05.17

G-BKFK Isaacs Fury II   xxxx   25.06.82
R S & S C Solley   Garlinge Farm, Ripple   21.06.19P
Built by G C Jones – project PFA 011-10038

G-BKFR Piel CP.301C Emeraude   519   30.06.82
F-BUUR, F-BJFF   M J Gale tr Devonshire Flying Group
Trenchard Farm, Eggesford   20.12.19P
Built by Société Menavia

G-BKFW Percival P.56 Provost T.1   PAC/F/303   21.09.82
XF597   J E M Atkinson   Audley End   27.07.07P
As 'XF597:AH' in RAF College c/s;
on rebuild 11.18 (NF 20.09.18)

G-BKGA SOCATA MS.892E Rallye 150GT   13287   15.07.82
F-GBXJ   C J Spradbery   Coventry   01.10.19E

G-BKGB Jodel D.120 Paris-Nice   267   21.06.82
F-BMOB   B A Ridgway   Rhigos   20.03.19P
Built by Société Wassmer Aviation

G-BKGC Maule M-6-235C Super Rocket   7413C   23.07.82
N56465   K V Marks   Lydd   19.02.19E

G-BKGD[M] Westland WG.30 Series 100   002   15.07.82
G-BKBJ   Cancelled 15.04.93 as PWFU
With The Helicopter Museum, Weston-super-Mare

G-BKGL Beech 3TM (D18S)   CA-164   14.07.82
CF-QPD, RCAF 5193, RCAF 1564
A N R Houghton   Leicester   18.07.19E
Beech c/n A-764; as '1164:64' in USAAC c/s

G-BKGM Beech 3NM (D18S)   CA-203   14.07.82
N5063N, G-BKGM, CF-SUQ, RCAF 2324
Bristol Airways Ltd   Carson City, Nevada, USA   28.10.19E
Beech c/n A-853

G-BKGT SOCATA Rallye 110ST Galopin   3361   23.07.82
Cancelled 17.11.11 as PWFU   14.02.09
Treswell, Notts   Spares use for G-BYPN 08.14

G-BKGW Reims/Cessna F152 II   F15201878   11.08.82
N9071N   The Leicestershire Aero Club Ltd   Leicester   26.04.19E

G-BKHD Oldfield Baby Lakes   8133-F-802B   05.08.82
P J Tanulak   (Myddle, Shrewsbury)   11.04.96P
Built by P J Tanulak – project PFA 010-10718
(NF 04.01.19)

G-BKHG Piper J-3C-65 Cub (*L-4H-PI*) 12062 13.09.82
F-BCPT, NC79807, 44-79766 T W Harris
Holmbeck Farm, Burcott *'Puddle Jumper'* 25.07.19P
As '479766:63-D' in USAAC HQ 9th Army c/s

G-BKHW Stoddard-Hamilton Glasair RG 357 27.08.82
D W Rees Wolverhampton Halfpenny Green 15.02.17P
Built by N Clayton – project PFA 149-11312

G-BKHY Taylor JT.1 Monoplane PFA 1416 08.09.82
B C J O'Neill Benson's Farm, Laindon 12.08.16P
Built by J Hall – project PFA 1416 (IE 12.11.18)

G-BKIE Shorts SD-3-30 Variant 100 SH.3005 15.09.82
G-SLUG, G-BKIE, G-METP, G-METO, G-BKIE,
C-GTAS, G-14-3005 Cancelled 16.09.97 as PWFU 22.08.93
Durham Tees Valley *On airport fire dump 04.17*

G-BKIF Fournier RF6B-100 3 08.10.82
F-GADR M J Pamphilon Gloucestershire 09.03.19E

G-BKII Reims/Cessna F172M F17201370 08.10.82
PH-PLO, (D-EGIA) Sealand Aerial Photography Ltd
Goodwood 06.03.19E

G-BKIJ Reims/Cessna F172M F17200920 15.10.82
PH-TGZ Cirrus Aviation Ltd Clacton-on-Sea 30.07.19E

G-BKIR Jodel D.117 737 30.09.82
F-BIOC D M Hardaker New House Farm, Birds Edge 28.08.92P
Built by Société Aéronautique Normande (NF 08.04.16)

G-BKIS SOCATA TB-10 Tobago 329 22.09.82
D Hoare Thruxton 20.08.19E

G-BKIT SOCATA TB-9 Tampico 330 22.09.82
P J Dunglinson Bristol 15.07.19E

G-BKIU Colt 17A Cloudhopper 420 29.09.82
S R J Pooley Elstree 30.08.09E
(NF 15.09.15)

G-BKIX Cameron V-31 Air Chair 863 23.09.82
(G-BKGJ) K J & M E Gregory Hascot Hill, Stowmarket 17.02.16E
(IE 04.05.16)

G-BKIZ Cameron V-31 Air Chair 842 01.02.83
A P S Cox Basingstoke 10.09.09E
(NF 10.12.15)

G-BKJB Piper PA-18-135 Super Cub (*L-21A-PI*) 18-574 01.08.83
PH-GAI, R Netherlands AF R-204, 51-15657, N1003A
K E Burnham Coventry 25.01.19E
Fuselage No.18-522

G-BKJS Jodel D.120A Paris-Nice 191 04.10.82
F-BJPS T J Nicholson Maypole Farm, Chislet 02.10.18P
Built by Société des Etablissements Benjamin Wassmer
(IE 01.02.19)

G-BKJT^M Cameron O-65 148 22.11.82
Cancelled by CAA 19.05.93 03.01.87
With British Balloon Museum & Library, Newbury

G-BKJW Piper PA-23-250 Aztec E 27-4716 03.11.78
N14153 Alan Williams Entertainments Ltd Southend 16.06.18E
Noted 02.19

G-BKKI Westland WG.30 Series.100 003 01.11.82
Cancelled 08.01.91 as PWFU 28.06.85
Yeovil *Noted 12.13*

G-BKKN Cessna 182R Skylane II 18267801 30.11.82
N6218N R A Marven Coleman Green, St Albans 30.08.19E

G-BKKO Cessna 182R Skylane II 18267852 30.11.82
N4907H M A Smith Sherburn-in-Elmet 17.10.19E

G-BKKP Cessna 182R Skylane II 18267968 30.11.82
N679LS, TC-MTR, N9600H D Jaffa North Weald 13.02.20E

G-BKKZ Pitts S-1S xxxx 10.11.82
(G-BIVW) P G Gabriele Morgansfield, Fishburn 29.03.17P
Built by J A Coutts – project PFA 009-10525
(NF 16.11.18)

G-BKLJ Westland Scout AH.1 F9618 06.07.83
5X-UUX, G-17-2 Cancelled 07.02.91 by CAA
Knutsford, Cheshire *Displayed 06.15 at Oliver Valves,*
as '5X-UUX' in Uganda Police c/s

G-BKLO Reims/Cessna F172M F17201380 22.03.83
PH-BET, D-EFMS Stapleford Flying Club Ltd
Stapleford 11.06.19E

G-BKLZ^M Vinten Wallis WA-116MC UMA-01 08.12.82
Cancelled 08.06.89 as destroyed 16.12.83
As 'G-55-2' Vinten VJ-22 Autogyro
With Flugausstellung Hermeskeil, Trier, Germany

G-BKMA Mooney M.20J Mooney 201 24-1316 13.12.82
N1170N N M McGovern tr Foxtrot Whiskey Aviation
Cambridge 13.12.19E

G-BKMB Mooney M.20J Mooney 201 24-1307 15.12.82
N1168P W A Cook tr G-BKMB Flying Group
Sherburn-in-Elmet 23.05.19E

G-BKMG Handley Page 0/400 replica TPG-1 08.12.82
A Baggallay tr The Paralyser Group (Letchworth)
Built by Paralyser Group; project is to construct
forward nose section only (NF 10.09.12)

G-BKMR^M Thunder Ax3 Maxi Sky Chariot HAB 497 12.01.83
Cancelled 23.04.98 as WFU *Inflated 04.14* 31.08.90
With British Balloon Museum & Library, Newbury

G-BKMT Piper PA-32R-301 Saratoga SP 32R-8213013 04.02.83
N8005Z P Ashworth Swansea 05.07.19E

G-BKMW^M Short SD3-30-200 Sherpa SH.3094 13.12.82
Cancelled 14.11.96 as PWFU 14.09.90
With Ulster Folk & Transport Museum, Holywood

G-BKNI Gardan GY-80-160D Horizon 249 28.01.83
F-BRJN Cancelled 14.01.10 as PWFU 13.05.02
Bourn *Open store 06.13*

G-BKNN^M Cameron Minar-E-Pakistan HAB 900 07.02.82
Cancelled 29.04.93 as WFU
240ft Moslem National Monument shape
With Musée des Ballons, Chateau de Balleroy, France

G-BKNO Monnett Sonerai IIL 792 11.03.83
S Hardy Park Farm, Eaton Bray 15.06.99P
Built by K Bailey & S Tattersfield
– project PFA 015-10528 (IE 24.07.15)

G-BKNZ Piel CP.301A Emeraude 296 21.01.83
F-BISZ A K Halvorsen (Prestbury, Macclesfield) 02.10.19P
Built by Société Menavia

G-BKOA SOCATA MS.893E Rallye 180GT 12432 02.03.83
F-BOFB, F-ODAT, F-BVAT M Jarrett Bodmin 31.10.05
(NF 23.11.18)

G-BKOB Moravan Zlin Z-326 Trener Master 757 28.09.81
F-BKOB A L Rae Trenchard Farm, Eggesford 24.05.19E

G-BKOK Pilatus B-N BN-2B-26 Islander 2174 27.01.83
OY-CFV, G-BKOK Cormack (Aircraft Services) Ltd
(Cumbernauld)
(NF 16.09.15)

G-BKOR^M Barnes 77 Firefly F7-046 01.07.83
Cancelled by CAA 15.05.98 17.10.09
With British Balloon Museum & Library, Newbury

G-BKOT Wassmer WA.81 Piranha 813 17.02.87
F-GAIP B J Griffiths (Tatenhill, Burton-on-Trent)
(NF 26.09.17)

G-BKOU Hunting Percival P.84 Jet Provost T.3 PAC/W/13901 17.02.83
XN637 G-BKOU/2 Ltd North Weald
'Where Eagles Share' 27.07.19P
As 'XN637' in RAF blue & red c/s

G-BKPA Hoffmann H36 Dimona 3522 16.06.83
R S Skinner Tatenhill 18.08.19E

G-BKPB Aerosport Scamp xxxx 23.02.83
J M Brightwell (Derby) 08.08.07P
Built by R Scroby – project PFA 117-10736 (NF 02.03.18)

G-BKPC Cessna A185F Skywagon
(*A185F AGcarryall*) 18503809 10.07.80
N4599E P C Hambilton & C Taylor
(Chorley & Preston) 10.11.07E
Badly damaged Manchester Barton 06.03.05;
wreck taken to Bank End Farm, Cockerham,
broken up & removed by 12.14 (NF 02.11.18)

G-BKPD Viking Dragonfly xxxx 11.03.83
E P Browne & G J Sargent
(Saffron Walden & Newmarket) 20.01.00P
Built by P E J Sturgeon – project PFA 139-10897
(NF 03.11.15)

G-BKPG^M Luscombe P3 Rattler Strike 003 07.03.83
Cancelled 31.07.91 by CAA
With Newark Air Museum, Winthorpe

G

G-BKPS	Grumman American AA-5B Tiger	AA5B-0007	07.03.83
	OO-SAS, OO-HAO, (OO-WAY), N1507R		
	A E T Clarke Rochester		15.11.19E
G-BKPX	Jodel D.120A Paris-Nice	240	17.01.84
	F-BLNG S H Barr (Aghadowey, Coleraine)		15.05.19P
	Built by Société Wassmer Aviation		
G-BKPY^M	SAAB 91B/2 Safir	91321	23.03.83
	R NorAF 56321 Cancelled 08.02.02 as WFU		
	As '56321' in R.NorAF c/s		
	With Newark Air Museum, Winthorpe		
G-BKPZ	Pitts S-1T	xxxx	04.03.83
	D A Slater Dunkeswell		17.05.19P
	Built by G C Masterton – project PFA 009-10852		
G-BKRA	North American T-6G-NH Texan	51-15227	19.08.83
	Ital.AF MM53664, Ital.AF RM-9, 51-15227		
	First Air Ltd Haverfordwest		13.08.16E
	As '115227' in US Navy c/s (NF 24.01.18)		
G-BKRF	Piper PA-18 Super Cub 95 (*L-18C-PI*)	18-1525	07.11.83
	F-BOUI, French Army, 51-15525		
	T F F Van Erck Antwerp-Duerne, Belgium		20.11.13P
	Fuselage No.18-1502 (NF 28.02.18)		
G-BKRG^M	Beech C-45G-BH	AF-222	05.05.83
	N75WB, N9072Z, 51-11665 Cancelled 27.04.98 as WFU		
	As 'G-BKRG' Registered as C-45H		
	With Aviodrome Museum, Lelystad, Netherlands		
G-BKRH	Brügger MB.2 Colibri	142	15.03.83
	T C Darters Valley Farm, Winwick		09.06.19P
	Built by M R Benwell – project PFA 043-10150		
G-BKRK	SNCAN Stampe SV.4C	57	30.03.83
	French Navy 57 J R Bisset tr Strathgadie		
	Stampe Group (Birnie, Elgin)		28.06.98
	(NF 08.03.18)		
G-BKRL^M	Chichester-Miles Leopard	001	21.03.83
	Cancelled 25.01.99 as WFU		14.12.91
	With Bournemouth Aviation Museum, Bournemouth		
G-BKRN	Beech D18S (Expeditor 3N)	CA-75	14.04.83
	CF-DTN, RCAF 1500, 43-35943 A A Marshall &		
	P L Turland Bruntingthorpe *'Naval Encounter'* & *'943'*		
	As '43-35943' in US Navy c/s (NF 18.03.16)		
G-BKRU	Crossley Racer	xxxx	30.03.83
	S Alexander Shobdon		
	Built by M S Crosskey – project PFA 131-10797		
	(NF 18.05.18)		
G-BKSC	Saro Skeeter AOP.12	S2/7076	23.05.83
	XN351 Cancelled 11.10.00 by CAA		08.11.84
	(Norwich) *Stored at private address as 'XN351'*		
	in Army c/s 03.16		
G-BKSE	QAC Quickie 1	xxxx	06.04.83
	M D Burns (Kirkintilloch, Glasgow)		
	Built by M D Burns, H Ibbott & C G Taylor		
	– project PFA 094-10784 (NF 30.10.15)		
G-BKST	Rutan VariEze	12718-001	20.04.83
	R Towle (Humshaugh, Hexham)		
	Built by R Towle (NF 14.12.18)		
G-BKTA	Piper PA-18 Super Cub 95 (*L-18C-PI*)	18-3223	10.05.83
	OO-HBA, Belgian AF OL-L49, L-149, 53-4823		
	M J Dyson Antrobus, Northwich		29.04.19P
	Fuselage No.18-3246		
G-BKTH	Hawker Sea Hurricane IB	CCF/41H/4013	24.05.83
	Z7015 Richard Shuttleworth Trustees Old Warden		19.05.19P
	Built by Canadian Car & Foundry Co;		
	as 'Z7015:7-L' in RN 880 Sqdn c/s		
G-BKTM	PZL-Bielsko SZD-45A Ogar	B-656	31.05.83
	S Pollard tr Hinton Ogar Group Hinton-in-the-Hedges		25.06.19E
G-BKTR	Cameron V-77 HAB	951	06.06.83
	Cancelled 09.06.11 as PWFU		25.09.09
	Not Known *Inflated Pidley 05.16*		
G-BKTZ	Slingsby T67M Firefly	2004	26.08.83
	G-SFTV Formation Flying Ltd Breighton		14.07.19E
G-BKUE	SOCATA TB-9 Tampico	369	31.05.83
	F-BNGX R N Swinney tr Fife TB9ers Fife		02.05.19E
G-BKUI	Druine D.31 Turbulent	xxxx	28.06.83
	E Shouler Beeches Farm, South Scarle		
	Built by A Onoufriou – project PFA 048-10789		
	(NF 12.11.15)		

G-BKUR	Piel CP.301A Emeraude	280	19.10.83
	(G-BKBX), F-BMLX, F-OBLY T Harvey		
	Sorbie Farm, Kingsmuir		16.07.19P
	Built by Société Menavia		
G-BKVC	SOCATA TB-9 Tampico	372	04.07.83
	F-BNGQ A I Eskander & S J Fawley		
	(Rochdale & Oldham)		18.04.19E
G-BKVF	Clutton FRED Series III	247	29.07.83
	I Pearson Newquay Cornwall		
	Built by N E Johnson – project PFA 029-10791; displayed		
	in Cornwall Aviation Heritage Centre (NF 18.03.16)		
G-BKVG	Scheibe SF25E Super Falke	4362	25.08.83
	(D-KNAE) G-BKVG Ltd North Hill		18.02.20E
G-BKVK	Auster AOP.9	'AUS/10/2'	08.08.83
	WZ662 J A Keen & M Walker Liverpool John Lennon		02.08.18P
	Officially registered with Frame no.AUS/10/2;		
	as 'WZ662:ARMY' in AAC camouflage c/s &		
	dayglo areas under wings		
G-BKVL	Robin DR.400-160 Chevalier	1625	26.07.83
	T Renton Andreas		21.05.19E
G-BKVM	Piper PA-18-150 Super Cub (*L-21A-PI*)	18-849	26.08.83
	PH-KAZ, R Netherlands AF R-214, 51-15684		
	M C Curtis Dunkeswell *'Spirit of Goxhill'*		11.12.18E
	Fuselage No.18-824; as '115684:849' in US Army c/s		
G-BKVO	Pietenpol AirCamper	xxxx	08.08.83
	Cancelled 11.02.13 by CAA		02.09.11
	Lodge Farm, Durston *Built by M J Honeychurch*		
	– project PFA 047-10799; stored dismantled 10.13		
G-BKVP	Pitts S-1D	002	19.08.83
	S A Smith Wick John O'Groats		20.02.20P
	Built by P J Leggo – project PFA 009-10800		
G-BKVY	Airtour B-31	AH001	09.08.83
	T J Hilditch tr Cloud Nine Balloon Group		
	Southwick, Brighton		
	(IE 09.07.18)		
G-BKWD	Taylor JT.2 Titch	xxxx	17.08.83
	J F Sully Sturgate		18.09.19P
	Built by E H Booker – project PFA 060-10232;		
	originally allocated as project PFA 060-10143		
G-BKWR	Cameron V-65	970	26.08.83
	Window on the World Ltd London SW4		18.01.07A
	(IE 20.02.18)		
G-BKXA	Robin R2100A Club	114	24.11.83
	F-GAOS M Wilson Little Gransden		22.10.99
	Noted 08.15 (NF 15.03.16)		
G-BKXD	Aerospatiale SA365N Dauphin 2	6088	07.09.83
	F-WMHD Cancelled 08.04.13 as PWFU		17.12.10
	Rzeszow, Poland *At Zespol Szkol Mechaniczynch 07.15*		
G-BKXF	Piper PA-28R-200 Cherokee Arrow II	28R-7335351	10.11.83
	OY-DZN, N56092 G Booth Sturgate		30.09.19E
G-BKXJ	Rutan VariEze	xxxx	29.09.83
	G-TIMB, G-BKXJ K O Miller (Gamlingay, Sandy)		15.08.07P
	Built by B Wronski – project PFA 074-10795 (NF 31.07.18)		
G-BKXM	Colt 17A Cloudhopper	531	03.10.83
	R G Turnbull Glasbury, Hereford		19.08.09E
	(NF 21.10.16)		
G-BKXO	Rutan Long-EZ	xxxx	24.10.83
	L T O'Connor & R L Soutar Inverness		13.03.19P
	Built by P Wareham – project PFA 074A-10580		
G-BKXP	Auster AOP.6	2830	12.10.83
	Belg.AF A-14, VT987 D K Chambers & M A Farrelly		
	Welshpool		
	Frame No.TAY841BJ (NF 24.01.19)		
G-BKXR	Druine D.31A Turbulent	303	01.11.83
	OY-AMW S Crossland tr GBKXR Turbulent Group		
	Eaglescott		12.08.15P
	Built by H Husted (NF 14.02.19)		
G-BKXX^M	Cameron V-65	1000	01.09.83
	Cancelled 28.11.01 as PWFU		
	At History of Ballooning, Sint Niklaas		
G-BKZF	Cameron V-56 HAB	246	14.11.83
	F-BXUK Cancelled 28.05.14 by PWFU		18.03.97
	Not Known *Inflated Amersfoort, 10.16*		

G-BKZM	Isaacs Fury	PFA 011-10742	27.09.83
	L C Wells Griffins Farm, Temple Bruer		
	Built by J Evans & R J Smith – project PFA 011-10742		
	stored 07.13 as 'K2060' (NF 02.07.15)		
G-BKZT	Clutton FRED Series II	xxxx	20.10.83
	U Chakravorty Clipgate Farm, Denton		02.07.02P
	Built by A E Morris – project PFA 29-10715 (NF 10.07.18)		
G-BKZV	Bede BD-4	380	31.08.84
	ZS-UAB Cancelled 20.08.16 by PWFU		17.07.15
	Nottingham City *Wreck stored 12.16*		

G-BLAA – G-BLZZ

G-BLAC	Reims/Cessna FA152 Aerobat	FA1520370	25.03.80
	W Ali Cranfield		05.12.19E
G-BLAF	Stolp SA.900 V-Star	xxxx	13.09.83
	A T Lane Sibson		27.03.19P
	Built by J E Malloy – project PFA 106-10651		
G-BLAG	Pitts S-1D	xxxx	22.02.10
	G-IIIP, G-BLAG Cirrus Aircraft UK Ltd Sywell		14.06.19E
	Built by B Bray – project PFA 009-10195		
G-BLAI	Monnett Sonerai IIL	PFA 015-10573	06.12.83
	T Simpson (Kirkcaldy)		12.01.99P
	Built by T Simpson – project PFA 015-10573;		
	official c/n 'PFA 015-10583' is incorrect (NF 23.03.18)		
G-BLAM	Robin DR.360 Chevalier	345	06.02.84
	F-BRCM J S Dalton Rochester		02.11.18E
	Built by Centre-Est Aéronautique		
G-BLAT	Jodel D.150 Mascaret	56	30.01.84
	F-BNID N T Coote & I R Willis tr G-BLAT Flying Group		
	Perth		22.03.13P
	Built by Société Aéronautique Normande;		
	on rebuild 07.16 (NF 14.08.17)		
G-BLCH	Colt 65D	392b	14.11.83
	G-BJHT (1) R S Breakwell Billingsley, Bridgnorth		
	Rebuilt by Sackville Balloons with c/n 392b (NF 27.10.15)		
G-BLCI	EAA Acrosport P	P10A	29.02.84
	N6AS M R Holden (Hagworthingham, Spilsby)		16.06.97P
	(NF 18.10.18)		
G-BLCT	Robin DR.220 2+2	23	22.12.83
	F-BOCQ F N P Maurin Rayne Hall Farm, Rayne		20.12.19E
	Built by Centre-Est Aéronautique		
G-BLCU	Scheibe SF25B Falke	4699	30.12.83
	D-KECC J D Johnson tr Charlie Uniform Syndicate		
	Rufforth		06.07.18E
	(IE 20.07.18)		
G-BLCY	Thunder Ax7-65Z	487	13.01.84
	M A Stelling South Queensferry		17.06.19E
G-BLDB	Taylor JT.1 Monoplane	xxxx	28.12.83
	J Hefford Old Warden		20.11.12P
	Built by C J Bush – project PFA 055-10506 (IE 07.06.18)		
G-BLDC	K & S Jungster 1	xxxx	29.12.83
	Cancelled 06.03.99 by CAA		
	Longside, Peterhead *Built by C A Lacock*		
	– project PFA 044-10701; stored part built 08.18		
G-BLDD	Wag Aero CUBy AcroTrainer	xxxx	29.12.83
	Cancelled 12.01.18 as destroyed		02.08.11
	Mount Airey Farm *Built by C A Lacock*		
	– project PFA 108-10653; frame stored 06.18		
G-BLDG	Piper PA-25-235 Pawnee	25-4501	09.01.84
	SE-FLB, LN-VYM York Gliding Centre Ltd Rufforth		04.09.15E
	Originally registered as 'Piper PA-25 Series 260C';		
	noted dismantled 10.17 (NF 21.10.16)		
G-BLDK	Robinson R22	0139	17.01.84
	C-GSGU Flight Academy (Gyrocopters) Ltd		
	Manchester Barton		20.10.17E
G-BLDN	Rand Robinson KR-2	xxxx	12.01.84
	P R Diffey Cark		21.05.10P
	Built by R Y Kendal – project PFA 129-10913		
	(NF 15.08.18)		
G-BLDV	Pilatus B-N BN-2B-26 Islander	2179	13.01.84
	D-INEY, G-BLDV Loganair Ltd Kirkwall		16.07.19E

G-BLES	Stolp SA.750 Acroduster Too	197	08.12.83
	R K Woodland Henstridge		16.07.19P
	Built by W G Hosie – project PFA 089-10428		
G-BLFE[M]	Cameron Sphinx 72SS HAB	1011	22.02.84
	Cancelled 29.04.93 as WFU		
	Egyptian Sphinx shape		
	With Musée des Ballons, Chateau de Balleroy, France		
G-BLFI	Piper PA-28-181 Archer II	28-8490034	22.02.84
	N4333Z Fly Elstree Ltd Elstree		01.09.19E
	Operated by Fly Elstree		
G-BLFZ	Piper PA-31 Navajo C	31-7912106	21.03.84
	PH-RWS, (PH-ASV), N3538W		14.11.10
	Cancelled 27.01.17 by CAA		
	White Waltham *Used for filming 08.18 as 'N247CK'*		
G-BLGH	Robin DR.300-180R Remorqueur	570	10.04.84
	D-EAFL Booker Gliding Club Ltd Wycombe Air Park		24.07.19E
G-BLGO	Bensen B.8MV	RB-01	18.06.84
	Cancelled 11.06.02 by CAA		15.08.87
	St Merryn, Cornwall *Stored 01.14*		
G-BLGS	SOCATA Rallye 180T Galerien	3206	07.07.78
	A Waters t/a London Light Aircraft Dunstable Downs		21.05.99
	For spares use 06.17 (NF 09.02.18)		
G-BLGV	Bell 206B-2 JetRanger II	982	02.05.84
	5B-JSB, C-FDYL, CF-DYL Heliflight (UK) Ltd		
	Gloucestershire		19.08.19E
	Operated by HH Helicopters Ltd t/a Cotswold Helicopters		
G-BLGX	Thunder Ax7-65 HAB	551	16.04.84
	Cancelled 19.05.93 by CAA		
	Not Known *Inflated Amersfoort, 10.16*		
	'45 Old Scotch Whisky'		
G-BLHH	Robin DR.315 Petit Prince	324	03.07.84
	F-BPRH S J Luck Tower Farm, Wollaston		10.07.19E
	Built by Centre-Est Aéronautique		
G-BLHJ	Reims/Cessna F172P	F17202182	26.03.84
	J H Sandham t/a JH Sandham Aviation Oban		30.06.17E
	Stored 08.18 (IE 07.02.19)		
G-BLHM (2)	Piper PA-18 Super Cub 95 (L-18C-PI)	18-3120	23.07.84
	LX-AIM, D-EOAB, Belgian AF OL-L46, L-46, 53-4720		
	A G Edwards Pennant Uchaf Farm, Llandegla		08.08.19P
	Fuselage No.18-3088		
G-BLHR	Gulfstream American GA-7 Cougar	GA7-0109	12.04.84
	OO-RTI, (OO-HRC), N751G		
	R Ellingworth & H Mackintosh Spanhoe		17.11.18E
G-BLHS	Bellanca 7ECA Citabria 115	1342-80	12.04.84
	OO-RTQ Devon & Somerset Flight Training Ltd		
	Dunkeswell		12.07.19E
G-BLHW	Varga 2150A Kachina	VAC 161-80	17.04.84
	J B Webb (Letchworth)		31.10.19E
G-BLID[M]	de Havilland DH.112 Venom FB.50	815	13.07.84
	J-1605 Cancelled 15.12.09 by CAA		
	As 'J-1605' Built by F + W Emmen		
	With Gatwick Aviation Museum, Charlwood		
G-BLIK	Wallis WA-116/F/S	K218X	30.04.84
	Cancelled 03.08.16 as PWFU		30.06.13
	Old Warden *Stored 10.16*		
G-BLIO[M]	Cameron R-42 Gas/HAB	1015	17.04.84
	Cancelled 24.01.90 as destroyed		17.05.84
	With British Balloon Museum & Library, Newbury		
G-BLIT	Thorp T-18C	xxxx	24.04.84
	R M Weeks Earls Colne		11.07.19P
	Built by A J Waller – project PFA 076-10550		
G-BLIW	Percival P.56 Provost T.51	PAC/F/125	12.06.85
	IAC.177 A D M & K B Edie Brighton City		16.05.05P
	As 'WV514:CN in RAF c/s (NF 05.01.12)		
G-BLIX	Saro Skeeter AOP.12	S2/5094	03.05.84
	PH-HOF, (PH-SRE), XL809 K M Scholes		
	(Clapham, Bedford)		02.06.06
	As 'XL809' in RAF c/s (NF 14.10.15)		
G-BLIY	SOCATA MS.892A Rallye Commodore 150	11639	09.05.84
	F-BSCX Cancelled 24.07.13 by CAA		24.02.12
	Womersley *Submerged at Blue Lagoon Diving*		
	& Leisure Centre 08.18		
G-BLJM	Beech 95-B55 Baron	TC-1997	03.03.78
	SE-GRT A H G Herbst Worms, Germany		29.12.19E

G-BLJO Reims/Cessna F152 II   F15201627   21.06.84
OY-BNB   Redhill Air Services Ltd   Rougham   13.01.20E
Operated by Skyward Air Training

G-BLKAᴹ de Havilland DH.112 Venom FB.Mk.54 (FB.4)
(G-VENM (1)), Swiss AF J-1790   960   13.07.84
Cancelled 13.10.00 by CAA   *As 'J-1790' in Swiss A/F c/s*   14.07.95
Built by F + W   Officially registered as c/n 431
With Historical Aviation Centre, Morgansfield, Fishburn

G-BLKM Jodel DR.1051 Sicile   519   26.06.84
F-BLRO   F H Lissimore tr Kilo Mike Group   Biggin Hill   13.05.19P
Built by Centre-Est Aéronautique

G-BLKUᴹ Colt Flame 56 SS HAB   572   17.07.84
Cancelled 01.05.92 as WFU   29.04.91
Unmarked, basket & envelope
On loan from British Balloon Museum & Library
to Manchester Museum of Sciences & Industry

G-BLKZ Pilatus P.2-05   600-45   30.07.84
Swiss AF U-125, A-125   Cancelled 22.08.08 as PWFU   19.02.08
Newquay Cornwall   *Official c/n is '45'*
Used as travelling exhibit 10.15 as 'A-125' in Swiss AF c/s

G-BLLA Bensen B.8M   xxxx   27.06.84
K T Donaghey   (Fintona, Omagh)   19.10.18P
Built by K T Donaghey – project PFA G/01-1055

G-BLLB Bensen B.8MR   xxxx   04.09.84
D H Moss   Henstridge   14.06.01P
Built by D H Moss – project PFA G/01A-1059
(NF 02.05.18)

G-BLLD Cameron O-77   1060   16.07.84
G Birchall   Burscough, Ormskirk   24.08.07A
(NF 06.12.18)

G-BLLH Robin DR.220 2+2   131   17.07.84
F-BROM   J K Houlgrave   Trenchard Farm, Eggesford   06.06.14E
Built by Centre-Est Aéronautique (IE 14.02.19)

G-BLLO Piper PA-18 Super Cub 95   18-3099   11.07.84
D-EAUB, Belgian AF OL-L25, L-25, 53-4699
M F Watts   Retford Gamston   10.04.19P
Fuselage No.18-3058

G-BLLP Slingsby T67B Firefly   2008   19.07.84
Air Navigation & Trading Company Ltd   Blackpool   04.12.00
(NF 29.03.16)

G-BLLR Slingsby T67C Firefly   2011   19.07.84
R L Brinklow   Oaksey Park   17.03.08E
Built by as T.67B & modified to T.67C Firefly
standard (NF 08.01.15)

G-BLLS Slingsby T67B Firefly   2013   13.07.84
T Wolfshohl   (Erfstadt, Germany)   17.05.19E

G-BLLW Colt 56B   578   11.09.84
C J Dunkley   Wendover, Aylesbury   *'Angel Clare'*   02.01.20E

G-BLLZ Rutan Long-EZ   xxxx   16.07.84
R S Stoddart-Stones   (Woldingham, Caterham)   22.06.94P
Built by E F Braddon, D G Machin, G E Relf &
D C Shepherd – project PFA 074A-10830 (NF 23.08.16)

G-BLMA Moravan Zlin Z-526 Trener Master   922   23.03.84
F-BORS   G P Northcott   Lydd   21.03.20E

(G-BLMC)ᴹ Avro 698 Vulcan B.2A   xxxx   R
XM575   Reservation 08.84 not taken up   *As 'XM575'*
With East Midlands Aeropark, East Midlands

G-BLMG Grob G109B   6322   27.09.84
K R Buckner tr G-BLMG Group   Bicester   13.10.19E

G-BLMI Piper PA-18 Super Cub 95 *(L-18C-PI)*   18-2066   05.06.84
D-ENWI, R Netherlands AF R-55, 52-2466
T F F Van Erck   Antwerp-Duerne, Belgium   04.01.11P
Fuselage No.18-2086; as '52-2466: R-55' in
R Netherlands AF c/s (NF 10.03.16)

G-BLMN Rutan Long-EZ   xxxx   03.07.84
K W Taylor   Old Buckenham   22.10.19P
Built by N J & R A Farrington – project PFA 074A-10648

G-BLMP Piper PA-17 Vagabond   17-193   15.05.84
F-BFMR, N4893H   C W Thirtle   Bodmin   09.04.19P

G-BLMR Piper PA-18 Super Cub *(L-18C-PI)*   18-2057   29.05.84
PH-NLD, R Netherlands AF R-72, 52-2457
M Vickers   Brighton City   08.01.20E
Fuselage No.18-2070

G-BLMT Piper PA-18-135 Super Cub   18-2706   12.09.84
D-ELGH, N8558C   I S Runnalls   Enstone   11.02.17E
Fuselage No.18-2724 (IE 27.04.17)

G-BLMW Nipper T.66 RA.45 Series 3   xxxx   31.08.84
S L Millar   Crowland   28.01.20P
Built by S L Millar – project PFA 025-11020

G-BLNI Pilatus B-N BN-2B-26 Islander   2188   03.09.84
VP-FBI, G-BLNI   Islander Aircraft Ltd   Cumbernauld
(IE 26.04.17)

G-BLNO Clutton FRED Series III   xxxx   17.10.84
L W Smith   (Sale)
Built by L W Smith – project PFA 029-10559 (NF 20.11.18)

G-BLOR Piper PA-30 Twin Comanche   30-59   19.07.85
HB-LAE, N7097Y, N10F   M C Jordan
Watchford Farm, Yarcombe   23.05.19E

G-BLOS Cessna 185A Skywagon   185-0359   17.09.84
LN-BDS, N4159Y   J R Chapman & G P Harrington
Compton Abbas   21.02.19E

G-BLOT Colt 56B   424   11.09.84
P Dickinson   St Martins, Oswestry   *'Pathfinder'*   17.07.96A
(NF 21.03.18)

G-BLPB Turner TSW-2 Hot Two Wot   xxxx   19.10.84
I R Nash tr Papa Bravo Group
Lower Upham Farm, Chiseldon   04.09.19P
Built by K M Thomas & J R Woolford
– project PFA 046-10606

G-BLPE Piper PA-18 Super Cub *(L-18C-PI)*   18-3084   28.09.84
D-ECBE, Belgian Army L-10, 53-4684
A A Haig-Thomas   Sandown   11.04.19P
C/n quoted also as 18-3083

G-BLPF Reims FR172G Rocket   FR17200187   29.01.85
N4594Q, D-EEFL   S Culpin   Fenland   14.04.19E

G-BLPG Auster J1N Alpha   3395   21.05.82
G-AZIH   S J Heighway   Dunkeswell   19.04.19P
As '16693:693' in RCAF yellow c/s

G-BLPP Cameron V-77   432   19.09.78
G B Davies   Thorney, Peterborough   11.05.19E

G-BLRC Piper PA-18-135 Super Cub   18-3602   27.11.84
OO-DKC, PH-DKC, R Netherlands AF R-112, 54-2402
S Hornung tr Supercub Group   Seething   27.03.19E
Fuselage No.18-3790 (?); possibly used on rebuild
of OO-POU ex D-EHRY (c/n 18-7860) c.1984

G-BLRF Slingsby T67C Firefly   2014   30.11.84
R C Nicholls   Wellesbourne Mountford   13.02.19E

G-BLRL Scintex CP.301-C1 Emeraude   552   05.11.84
(G-BLNP), F-BJFT   A M Smith
Low Hill Farm, North Moor, Messingham   25.03.19P
Built by Société Scintex

G-BLRWᴹ Cameron Elephant 77SS HAB   1074   14.12.84
Cancelled 14.11.02 by CAA   01.10.00
'Great Sky Elephant'
With Musée des Ballons, Chateau de Balleroy, France

G-BLTC Druine D.31A Turbulent   xxxx   18.12.84
S J Butler   RAF Henlow   24.04.19P
Built by A W Burton & G P Smith
– project PFA 048-10964

G-BLTM Robin HR.200-100 Club   96   21.11.84
F-GAEC   Troughton Engineering Aircraft
Maintenance Ltd   (Newry)   16.12.14E
(NF 25.02.19)

G-BLTN Thunder Ax7-65   621   04.01.85
V Michel   London SE27   22.06.18E
(IE 03.01.19)

G-BLTR Scheibe SF25B Falke   4823   23.01.85
D-KHEC   V Mallon   (Geldern, Germany)   01.04.94
Built by Sportavia-Pützer GmbH & Co. KG (NF 12.12.17)

G-BLTS Rutan Long-EZ   xxxx   14.01.85
R W Cutler   (Thorverton, Exeter)
Built by R W Cutler – project PFA 074A-10741
(NF 04.07.18)

G-BLTT Slingsby T.67B Firefly   2023   16.01.85
Cancelled 28.07.04 by CAA   05.08.00
Haverfordwest   *Wreck dumped 07.15*

G-BLTW Slingsby T67B Firefly 2026 16.01.85
R L Brinklow Pent Farm, Postling 15.09.06
Stored dismantled 08.14 (NF 08.01.15)

G-BLUE Colt 77A 11 03.10.95
D P Busby Broughton, Kettering 20.09.99A
Built by Colting Balloon Company; originally
registered 02.05.78 as 'Colting Ax-77' (NF 02.08.17)

G-BLUJ Cameron V-56 1150 17.04.85
F R Battersby Worsley, Manchester 04.12.18E

G-BLUV Grob G109B 6336 01.02.85
T Asplin & J Brooks tr 109 Flying Group North Weald 24.09.19E

G-BLUX Slingsby T67M-200 Firefly 2027 31.01.85
G-7-145, G-BLUX, G-7-113 R L Brinklow
t/a Richard Brinklow Aviation Pent Farm, Postling 27.04.07
Stored dismantled 08.14

G-BLUZ de Havilland DH.82 Queen Bee 1435 09.04.85
LF858 P Finch & J Flynn tr The Bee Keepers Group
RAF Henlow 27.07.19P
Correct type is 'DH.82 Queen Bee';
as 'LF858' in RAF camouflage c/s

G-BLVA Airtour AH-31 004 12.02.86
S Church & D L Peltan Almondsbury & Bristol BS32
Active 08.17 (IE 07.06.18)

G-BLVB Airtour AH-56 005 12.02.86
Z Daly Halfway House, Waterford, RoI
(IE 06.02.19)

G-BLVI Slingsby T67M Firefly II 2017 01.02.85
(PH-KIF), G-BLVI M L Scott Bagby 09.06.18E

G-BLVK Mudry CAP 10B 141 01.03.85
JY-GSR R W H Cole (Churchill Farm, Sedlescombe) 27.05.11E
(NF 03.06.16)

G-BLVL Piper PA-28-161 Warrior II 28-8416109 11.02.85
N43677 TG Aviation Ltd Lydd 07.12.19E

G-BLVS Cessna 150M 15076869 19.02.85
EI-BLS, N45356 D H G Penney Sandtoft 14.12.07E
Noted 04.18 (NF 29.06.15)

G-BLVW Cessna F172H F172-0422 16.05.85
D-ENQU R Holloway Stapleford 10.07.00
Built by Reims Aviation SA (NF 18.09.18)

G-BLWB[M] Thunder Ax6-56 Srs.1 HAB 645 22.02.85
Cancelled 28.11.01 as WFU 10.11.99
With British Balloon Museum & Library, Newbury

G-BLWD Piper PA-34-200T Seneca II 34-8070334 14.03.85
ZS-KKV, ZS-XAT, N8253E Bencray Ltd Blackpool 07.05.05
(NF 04.10.18)

G-BLWM[M] Bristol 20 M.1C replica xxxx 12.03.85
'C4912' Cancelled 12.05.88 by CAA 12.08.87
As 'C4994' in RFC c/s Built by D M Cashmore
– project PFA 112-10862)
With Royal Air Force Cosford Museum

G-BLWP Piper PA-38-112 Tomahawk 38-78A0367 07.06.85
OY-BTW APB Leasing Ltd Sleap 20.05.17E
(NF 21.01.19)

G-BLWT Evans VP-1 Series 2 xxxx 27.03.85
M W Olliver Ranston Farm, Iwerne Courtney 10.04.12P
Built by G B O'Neill – project PFA 062-10639;
noted 04.14 (NF 23.01.18)

G-BLWV Cessna F152 II F15201843 25.02.85
EI-BIN Cancelled 18.06.10 as PWFU 14.07.10
Redhill *Built by Reims Aviation SA*
Wreck in open store 12.16

G-BLWW Aerocar Mini-Imp Model C xxxx 01.03.85
Cancelled 13.10.00 by CAA 04.06.87
Sleap *Built by W E Wilks – project PFA 136-10880*
Stored 02.18

G-BLWY Robin R2160 Alpha Sport 176 15.04.85
F-GCUV, SE-GXE Pure Aviation Support Services Ltd
Gloucestershire 08.01.20E

G-BLXA SOCATA TB-20 Trinidad 284 11.04.85
SE-IMO, F-ODOH A Durose Tatenhill 24.03.19E

G-BLXG Colt 21A Cloudhopper 605 02.05.85
D P Busby Broughton, Kettering 16.05.19E

G-BLXH Alpavia Fournier RF3 39 25.03.85
F-BMDQ R J Cronk tr G-BLXH group
Hinton-in-the-Hedges 08.08.19P

(G-BLXI (1))[M] Blériot Type XI replica EMK 010 03.85R
NTU – to BAPC.132
Built by L.D.Goldsmith 1976 – project PFA 088-10864
from original components: rebuilt by Skysport
Engineering 1982 Possibly same a/c as BAPC.189
No marks carried
With Musée de L'Automobiliste, Cannes

G-BLXI (2) Scintex CP.1310-C3 Super Emeraude 937 01.04.85
F-BMJI W D Garlick Brock Farm, Billericay 19.07.19P

G-BLXO Jodel D.150 Mascaret 10 09.05.85
F-BLDB M T Parsonage Bagby 06.12.19P
Built by Société Aéronautique Normande

G-BLXS Aérospatiale AS.332L Super Puma 2157 14.05.85
VH-BZB, LN-OND, G-BLXS
Airbus Helicopters Leasing Services Ltd (Dublin, RoI)
(IE 16.11.18)

G-BLXT Eberhardt SE.5E - 06.10.89
N4488, AS22-296 USAAS Flying A Services Ltd Sywell 15.09.16P
Built by Eberhart Steel Products Company;
as 'A.S.22-296' in US Army Air Service c/s (NF 02.10.18)

G-BLYD SOCATA TB-20 Trinidad 518 01.05.85
S Picco (Nimis, Udine, Italy) 10.03.19E

G-BLYJ Cameron V-77 HAB 0408 01.05.85
Cancelled 07.05.93 as destroyed
Not Known *Inflated Pidley 04.14*

G-BLYP Robin R3000/120 109 15.05.85
Cancelled 01.12.14 as PWFU 05.05.01
Headcorn *Stored dismantled 06.16*

G-BLZA Scheibe SF25B Falke 4684 22.05.85
D-KBAJ G W L Howarth tr Zulu Alpha Syndicate
RAF Halton 22.05.15E
(IE 31.01.19)

G-BLZF Thunder Ax7-77 HAB 660 03.06.85
Cancelled 30.03.09 as PWFU 10.09.03
Not Known *Inflated Pidley 05.16*

G-BLZH Reims/Cessna F152 II F15201965 21.06.85
P d'Costa Wolverhampton Halfpenny Green 17.12.15E
(NF 16.08.17)

G-BLZJ Aérospatiale AS.332L Super Puma 2123 13.06.85
LN-OMI, G-BLZJ, LN-OMI, G-PUMJ, LN-OMI,
G-BLZJ, LN-OMI, G-BLZJ, LN-OMI
Airbus Helicopters Marseille, France 15.04.15E
Used for spares 03.15 (NF 05.05.15)

G-BLZP Reims/Cessna F152 II F15201959 10.07.85
East Midlands Flying School Ltd East Midlands 08.06.19E

G-BMAA – G-BMZZ

G-BMAD Cameron V-77 1166 10.06.85
M A Stelling South Queensferry 'Nautilus' 29.09.99A
'Skull & Crossbones' artwork (NF 27.01.16)

G-BMAO Taylor JT.1 Monoplane PFA 1411 29.07.85
N D Plumb Hinton-in-the-Hedges 25.02.20P
Built by V A Wordsworth – project PFA 1411

G-BMAX Clutton FRED Series II xxxx 20.12.78
D A Arkley (Littley Green, Chelmsford) 24.08.99P
Built by D A Arkley & P Cawkwell
– project PFA 029-10322 (NF 29.04.16)

G-BMAY Piper PA-18-135 Super Cub (L-21B-PI) 18-3925 03.07.85
OO-LWB, I-EIJZ/E.I.229, Ital Mil MM54-2525, 54-2525
R W Davies Little Engeham Farm, Woodchurch 16.04.19E
Fuselage No.18-3961

G-BMBB Reims/Cessna F150L F15001136 02.08.85
OO-LWM, PH-GAA G E Fox Bagby 20.09.17E

G-BMBJ Schempp-Hirth Janus CM 20 09.09.85
(G-BLZL) M Critchlow tr BJ Flying Group Keevil 'BJ' 22.04.19E

G-BMBZ Scheibe SF25E Super Falke 4322 17.07.85
D-KEFQ K E Ballington (Ashby-de-la-Zouch) 26.09.08E
Noted dismantled 06.17 (NF 22.10.14)

G-BMCC	Thunder Ax7-77	705	12.07.85
	D P Busby Broughton, Kettering *'Charlie Charlie'*		23.02.99A
	(NF 04.08.16)		
G-BMCD	Cameron V-65	1234	26.06.85
	R Lillyman Irchester, Wellingborough		08.09.09E
	(NF 07.08.15)		
G-BMCG	Grob G109B	6362	25.07.85
	(Egypt AF 673) D K R Draper Goodwood		11.02.20E
G-BMCI	Reims/Cessna F172H	F17200683	19.08.85
	OO-WID A B Davis Fife		19.01.20E
G-BMCN	Reims/Cessna F152 II	F15201471	07.08.85
	D-ELDM G Price t/a Skytrek Air Services Rochester		11.09.19E
G-BMCS	Piper PA-22-135 Tri-Pacer	22-1969	06.09.85
	5Y-KMH, VP-KMH, ZS-DJI		
	M P Brigden-Gwinnutt Enstone		26.09.18E
G-BMCV	Reims/Cessna F152 II	F15201963	02.10.85
	M Bonsall Netherthorpe		02.07.19E
G-BMCX	Aérospatiale AS.332L Super Puma	2164	07.10.85
	Airbus Helicopters Marseille, France		25.04.15E
	(NF 05.05.15)		
G-BMDB^M	Replica Plans SE.5A	xxxx	12.08.85
	D E Blaxland Stow Maries		11.06.19P
	Built by D Biggs – project PFA 020-10931;		
	as 'F235:B' in RAF c/s		
G-BMDD	Cadet Motor Glider	xxxx	08.08.85
	A R Hutton (Stanley, Perth)		
	Built by D H Johnstone – project PFA 042-11070		
	(NF 17.12.18)		
G-BMDE	Pietenpol Air Camper	xxxx	12.08.85
	P B Childs Middlegate Farm, Pitney		16.07.19P
	Built by D Silsbury – project PFA 047-10989		
G-BMDJ	Price Ax7-77S	003	01.08.85
	R A Benham Aston-on-Trent, Derby		
	Built by T P Price – c/n TPB.1 and registered		
	as Price TPB.1 (NF 30.01.19)		
G-BMDP	Partenavia P64B Oscar 200	08	20.08.85
	HB-EPQ J L Sparks St Athan		21.09.10E
	(NF 05.02.18)		
G-BMDS	Jodel D.120 Paris-Nice	281	12.08.85
	F-BMOS A James Haw Farm, Hampstead Norreys		27.09.11P
	Built by Société Wassmer Aviation; on rebuild 12.16		
	(NF 21.03.18)		
G-BMEA	Piper PA-18 Super Cub 95 (*L-18C-PI*)	18-3204	27.08.85
	(D-ECZF), Belgian AF OL-L07, Belg.AF L-130, 53-4804		
	M J Butler Spanhoe		02.03.20P
	Fuselage no.18-3216; reported as fuselage no.		
	18-3206 ex OL-L20, L-120, 53-4794 (c/n 18-3194)		
G-BMEB	Rotorway Scorpion 145	2896	10.12.85
	VR-HJB Cancelled 28.04.05 by CAA		10.12.85
	Cloughmills, Co Antrim *Built by Hong Kong*		
	Aircraft Engineering Co Ltd; stored as VR-HJB 12.13		
G-BMEH	Jodel D.150 Super Mascaret	62	15.08.85
	C J & R J Lewis Garston Farm, Marshfield		
	'Noir Coupar'		21.05.08P
	Built by E J Horsfall – project PFA 151-11047; rebuild		
	of Jodel D.150 Mascaret (SAN c/n 62) (NF 21.02.19)		
G-BMET	Taylor JT.1 Monoplane	xxxx	04.09.85
	M K A Blyth Little Gransden		18.09.17P
	Built by M Blythe – project PFA 1465 (IE 22.11.18)		
G-BMEU	Isaacs Fury II	xxxx	11.09.85
	I G Harrison Netherthorpe		
	Built by G R G Smith – project PFA 011-10179;		
	as 'S1615' in RAF c/s (IE 11.01.19)		
G-BMEW^M	Lockheed 18-56 Lodestar (*C-60A-5-LO*) 18-2444		30.09.85
	OH-SIR, (N283M), OH-MAP, N283M, N9223R, N105G,		
	N69898 ,NC69898, 42-55983		
	Cancelled 15.07.86 – to Canada		
	As 'G-AGIH' Gulfstar conversion c.4.59		
	With Forsvarsmuseet Flysamlingen, Gardemoen, Norway		
G-BMEX	Cessna A150K Aerobat	A1500169	18.09.85
	N8469M Cotswold Flying School Ltd Draycott		19.06.19E
G-BMEZ^M	Cameron DP-70 HA Airship	1130	18.09.85
	Cancelled 20.06.91 as sold as EC-FUS – 04.05.89		
	Originally regd as D-50 Envelope only		
	With British Balloon Museum & Library, Newbury		

G-BMFD	Piper PA-23-250 Aztec F	27-7954080	06.09.79
	G-BGYY, N6834A, N9741N		
	Giles Aviation Ltd Headcorn		27.06.19E
G-BMFI	PZL-Bielsko SZD-45A Ogar	B-657	23.09.85
	S L Morrey Andreas		30.05.08E
	(IE 27.05.15)		
G-BMFN	QAC Quickie Tri-Q 200	PFA 094A1-11062	27.09.85
	R F Thomson (Weston-super-Mare)		01.05.02P
	(NF 18.02.16)		
G-BMFP	Piper PA-28-161 Warrior II	28-7916243	01.11.85
	N3032L Aerobility Blackbushe		02.08.19E
G-BMFY	Grob G109B	6401	08.10.85
	P J Shearer Lamb Holm Farm, Holm		10.05.19E
G-BMFZ	Cessna F152 II	F15201953	03.12.85
	Cancelled 13.12.10 by CAA		27.05.10
	Bodmin *Built by Reims Aviation SA; dismantled 10.17*		
G-BMGB	Piper PA-28R-200 Cherokee Arrow II	28R-7335099	08.11.85
	N15864 M J Gregory tr G-BMGB Group Cotswold		22.02.19E
G-BMGC	Fairey Swordfish II	xxxx	23.10.85
	RCN 5856, W5686 Cancelled 02.09.91 by CAA		
	RNAS Yeovilton		
	Built by Blackburn Aeroplane & Motor Company		
	Ltd; as 'W5856:A2A' in RN 810Sqn c/s with		
	Royal Navy Historic Flight 'City of Leeds'		
G-BMGG	Cessna 152 II	15279592	10.10.85
	OO-ADB, PH-ADB, D-EHUG, F-GBLM, N757AT		
	J R Flieger (Warsaw, Poland)		12.04.19E
G-BMGR	Grob G109B	6396	27.11.85
	M Clarke tr G-BMGR Group Lasham		27.04.19E
G-BMHA	Rutan Long-EZ	xxxx	18.10.85
	S F Elvins (Bristol BS16)		
	Built by S F Elvins – project PFA 074A-10973;		
	for sale 02.19 (NF 18.10.18)		
G-BMHJ	Thunder Ax7-65 HAB	743	02.01.86
	Cancelled 08.12.11 as PWFU		19.05.92
	Not Known *Inflated Pidley 04.18*		
G-BMHL	Wittman W.8 Tailwind	xxxx	28.11.85
	S J Moody Shenstone Hall Farm, Shenstone		07.10.19P
	Built by T G Hoult – project PFA 031-10503		
G-BMHS	Reims/Cessna F172M	F17200964	07.04.86
	PH-WAB G Campbell Sibson		30.07.19E
G-BMHT	Piper PA-28RT-201T Turbo Arrow IV	28R-8231010	18.11.85
	ZS-LCJ, N8462Y P A Lamming & G Lungley		
	tr G-BMHT Flying Group Sherburn-in-Elmet		18.04.19E
G-BMID	Jodel D.120 Paris-Nice	259	18.08.81
	F-BMID T W Nicholas tr G-BMID Flying Group Sleap		15.02.20P
	Built by Société Wassmer Aviation		
G-BMIG	Cessna 172N Skyhawk II	17272347	13.05.86
	ZS-KGI, (N48630) R B Singleton-McGuire		
	Water Leisure Park, Skegness		15.06.19E
G-BMIM	Rutan Long-EZ	8102-160	12.12.85
	OY-CMT, OY-8102 V E Jones Solent		25.05.17P
	Built by K A I Christensen (NF 29.10.18)		
G-BMIO	Stoddard-Hamilton Glasair RG	xxxx	25.11.85
	P Bint & L McMahon tr G-BMIO Group Cotswold		29.11.19P
	Built by A H Carrington – project PFA 149-11016		
G-BMIP	Jodel D.112	1264	07.12.78
	F-BMIP F J E Brownsill (Fairford)		07.05.19P
	Built by Société Wassmer Aviation		
G-BMIR (2)	Westland Wasp HAS.1	F9670	24.01.86
	XT788 Cancelled 22.12.95 by CAA		
	Storwood, Pocklington		
	Stored as 'XT788:474' 11.17 at Melbourne Autos		
G-BMIV	Piper PA-28R-201T Turbo Cherokee Arrow III		
		28R-7703154	07.01.86
	ZS-JZW, N5816V Firmbeam Ltd		
	(Westham, Pevensey)		01.02.19E
G-BMIW	Piper PA-28-181 Archer II	28-8190093	06.12.85
	ZS-KTJ, N8301J Oldbus Ltd Brighton City		18.01.20E
G-BMIX	SOCATA TB-20 Trinidad	579	05.12.85
	EI-BSV, G-BMIX G Hance tr Falcon Flying Group		
	Aberdeen Int'l		07.03.19E

G-BMIY Oldfield Baby Great Lakes xxxx 03.12.85
G-NOME J B Scott (Thornton-Cleveleys)
*Built by D M Brown, K B Parkinson & J B Scott
– project PFA 010-10194 (NF 15.03.16)*

G-BMIZ Robinson R22 Beta 0505 11.11.85
OO-VCE, OO-XCE, G-BMIZ, N2270B
Heli Air Ltd Wellesbourne Mountford 25.09.19E

G-BMJA Piper PA-32R-301 Saratoga SP 32R-8113019 23.12.85
ZS-KTH, N8309E J Cottrell Goodwood 05.12.19E

G-BMJB Cessna 152 II 15280030 03.02.86
N757VD A J Gomes Redhill 16.06.00
(NF 23.09.16)

G-BMJD Cessna 152 II 15279755 21.11.85
N757HP Donair Flying Club Ltd East Midlands 10.10.19E

G-BMJJ Cameron Watch-75 1207 28.11.85
HB-BHB, G-BMJJ D P Busby Broughton, Kettering
'Swatch' 09.08.18E
Watch special shape

G-BMJL Rockwell Commander 114 14006 08.01.86
A2-JRI, ZS-JRI, N1906J D J & S M Hawkins
(London SW5) 09.09.19E

G-BMJM Evans VP-1 Series 2 xxxx 21.11.85
C J Clarke Bidford 22.05.19P
Built by J A Mawby – project PFA 062-10763

G-BMJN Cameron O-65 1212 06.12.85
P M Traviss Low Worsall, Yarm 'F'red' 11.05.08A
(NF 22.10.18)

G-BMJO Piper PA-34-220T Seneca III 34-8533036 05.12.85
N6919K, N9565N Fastnet Jet Alliance Ltd Cork, RoI 27.02.18E

G-BMJX Wallis WA-116/X Series 1 K219X 31.12.85
Cancelled 03.08.16 as PWFU 01.04.89
Old Warden *Stored 10.16*

G-BMJY SPP Yakovlev Yak C-18A '627' 21.01.86
FAD 627 W A E Moore Draycott 15.08.19P
*P/i is Fuerza Aerea Dominicana 627;
as '07' (yellow) in Russian AF c/s*

G-BMJZ Cameron N-90 HAB 1219 16.12.85
Cancelled 13.11.09 as PWFU 31.03.94
Not Known *Inflated Bath 01.19*

G-BMKB Piper PA-18-135 Super Cub (L-21B-PI) 18-3817 11.12.85
OO-DKB, PH-DKB, (PH-GRP), R Netherlands AF R-127,
54-2417 Cubair Flight Training Ltd Redhill 21.03.19E
Fuselage No.18-3818

G-BMKC Piper J-3C-65 Cub (L-4H-PI) 11145 02.01.86
F-BFBA, 43-29854
P R Monk Biggin Hill 'Little Rockette Jnr' 30.05.19P
*Fuselage No.10970; as '329854:44-R' in
533rd BS/381st Bomb Group USAAF c/s*

G-BMKF Robin DR.221 Dauphin 96 03.02.86
F-BPCS L J & S T Gilbert Enstone 22.03.09E
Built by Centre-Est Aéronautique (NF 15.08.18)

G-BMKG Piper PA-38-112 Tomahawk II 38-82A0050 03.02.86
ZS-LGC, N91544 Cancelled 05.02.18 as destroyed 17.01.13
East Linton *Stored private site 05.18*

G-BMKJ Cameron V-77 1235 02.01.86
Zebedee Balloon Service Ltd Hungerford 10.05.09E
(NF 17.04.15)

G-BMKK Piper PA-28R-200 Cherokee Arrow II 28R-7535265 16.01.86
ZS-JNY, N9537N P M Murray Eshott 17.01.13E
Stored dismantled 09.18 (NF 25.05.16)

G-BMKP Cameron V-77 724 10.01.86
(G-BMFX) R Bayly Clutton, Bristol 07.08.93A
(NF 04.04.16)

G-BMKR Piper PA-28-161 Warrior II 28-7916220 14.06.84
G-BGKR, N9561N Steve Batchelor Ltd Solent 21.06.19E

G-BMKV Thunder Ax7-77 772 21.01.86
Zebedee Balloon Service Ltd Newtown, Hungerford 17.06.19E

G-BMKY Cameron O-65 1246 04.03.86
A R Rich Hyde 'Orion' 03.05.10E
(IE 06.08.15)

G-BMLJ Cameron N-77 1263 07.03.86
C J Dunkley t/a Wendover Trailers
Wendover, Aylesbury 'Blackpool Pleasure Beach' 11.02.12E
Inflated 05.16 (NF 17.04.14)

G-BMLK Grob G109B 6424 24.02.86
R W Bowhill tr Brams Syndicate Rufforth 01.08.19E

G-BMLL Grob G109B 6420 13.03.86
M D Peters tr GBMLL Flying Group Dunstable Downs 10.08.19E

G-BMLS Piper PA-28R-201 Arrow III 28R-7737167 11.02.86
N47496 R M Shorter Wycombe Air Park 16.04.19E
*Official type data 'PA-28R-201 Cherokee Arrow III'
is incorrect*

G-BMLT Pietenpol Air Camper xxxx 28.01.86
W E R Jenkins Strubby 05.07.19P
Built by R A & F Hawke – project PFA 047-10949

G-BMLX Reims/Cessna F150L F15000700 21.03.86
PH-VOV J P A Freeman Headcorn 17.04.19E

G-BMMF Clutton FRED Series II xxxx 20.02.86
R C Thomas (Boverton, Llantwit Major)
'Thank you Girl' 18.07.03P
*Built by J M Jones – project PFA 029-10296
(NF 10.01.18)*

G-BMMI Pazmany PL-4A xxxx 06.02.86
P I Morgans (Rosemarket, Milford Haven) 18.07.03P
*Built by M L Martin – project PFA 017-10149
(NF 16.11.18)*

G-BMMJ Issoire PIK-30 720 13.06.86
4X-GMM, G-BMMJ I B Kennedy tr LRU Group
(Cardiff CF23) 06.03.20R

G-BMMK Cessna 182P Skylane II 18264117 24.03.86
OO-AVU, N6129F J W Hardy tr Lambley Flying Group
Jericho Farm, Lambley 18.09.19E
Assembled Reims Aviation with c/n 0038

G-BMMM Cessna 152 II 15284793 10.09.86
N4652F Falcon Flying Services Ltd Biggin Hill 14.04.19E

G-BMMP Grob G109B 6432 27.06.86
G-BMMP Ltd Sleap 20.08.19E

G-BMMV ICA-Brasov IS-28M2A 57 10.03.86
C D King & C I Roberts Trenchard Farm, Eggesford 07.11.17E

G-BMMW Thunder Ax7-77 782 10.03.86
P A George Littlemore, Oxford 'Ethos' 03.06.96A
(IE 05.06.17)

G-BMOE Piper PA-28R-200 Cherokee Arrow II 28R-7635226 20.05.86
PH-PCB, OO-HAS, N9221K SC Airlease Ltd
(South Shields) 01.12.19E

G-BMOF Cessna U206G U20603658 17.04.86
N7427N Wild Geese Parachute Ltd
McMaster's Farm, Movenis 15.04.19E

G-BMOH Cameron N-77 1270 02.04.86
I M Taylor Brambridge, Eastleigh 'Ellen Gee' 02.03.19E

G-BMOJ Cameron O-56A HAB 1275 04.04.86
Cancelled 06.11.01 as PWFU 27.07.89
Aylmerton, Norfolk *To M Burdett 10.18*

G-BMOK ARV ARV-1 Super 2 011 14.04.86
R E Griffiths Middle Stoke, Isle of Grain 28.09.19P

G-BMOO Clutton FRED Series II xxxx 11.04.86
Cancelled 22.02.99 by CAA 08.08.91
Barwell *Built by N Purriant – project PFA 029-10770
Static, used as Webster Whirlwind radial test bed 09.17*

G-BMPC Piper PA-28-181 Archer II 28-7790436 23.04.86
LN-NAT C J & R J Barnes East Midlands 10.11.19E

G-BMPD Cameron V-65 HAB 1200 04.06.86
Cancelled 31.07.18 by CAA 30.07.10
Not Known *Inflated Pidley 04.18*

G-BMPL Optica OA.7 Optica 016 14.04.86
J K Edgley Thruxton 02.08.97
(NF 28.01.19)

G-BMPR Piper PA-28R-201 Arrow III 28R-7837175 22.04.86
ZS-LMF, N417GH T J Brammer t/a Sterling Aviation
Biggin Hill 05.04.19E
*Official type data 'PA-28R-20 Cherokee Arrow III'
is incorrect*

G-BMPS Strojnik S-2A 045 18.04.86
G J Green (Darley Bridge, Matlock)
Built by T J Gardiner (NF 29.02.16)

G-BMPY de Havilland DH.82A Tiger Moth 82619 25.04.86
ZS-CNR, SAAF?? N M Eisenstein
Sandford Hall, Knockin 18.04.18P

G-BMRA Boeing 757-236(SF) 23710 02.03.87
DHL Air Ltd East Midlands 02.08.19E
Line No: 123

G-BMRB Boeing 757-236(SF) 23975 25.09.87
DHL Air Ltd East Midlands 29.09.19E
Line No: 145

G-BMRD Boeing 757-236(SF) 24073 02.12.87
(N.....), G-BMRD DHL Air Ltd East Midlands 03.03.19E
Line No: 166

G-BMRF Boeing 757-236(SF) 24101 13.05.88
DHL Air Ltd East Midlands 17.05.19E
Line No: 175

G-BMRI Boeing 757-236(SF) 24267 17.02.89
VT-BDK, OO-DPL, G-BMRI DHL Air Ltd
East Midlands 17.12.19E
Line No: 211

G-BMRJ Boeing 757-236(SF) 24268 06.03.89
DHL Air Ltd East Midlands 13.03.19E
Line No: 214

G-BMSA Stinson HW-75 Voyager 7040 26.03.86
G-MIRM, G-BMSA, G-BCUM, F-BGQO, NC21189
P Fraser-Bennison Kittyhawk Farm, Ripe *'Iron Eagle'* 31.08.18P

G-BMSB Supermarine 509 Spitfire Tr.9 CBAF 7722 03.05.78
G-ASOZ, IAC158, G-15-171, MJ627
Warbird Experiences Ltd Biggin Hill 16.02.20P
As 'MJ627:9G-Q' in RAF 441 Sqdn c/s

G-BMSC Evans VP-2 V2-482MSC 25.08.82
R S Acreman (Pooll Farm, Levedale, Stafford) 29.04.05P
Built by Youth Opportunity Project
– project PFA 63-10785 (NF 20.07.17)

G-BMSD Piper PA-28-181 Archer II 28-7690070 02.07.86
EC-CVH, N9646N R E Parsons Norwich Int'l 09.12.19E

G-BMSE Valentin Taifun 17E 1082 20.05.86
D-KHVA (17) D O'Donnell Aboyne 24.02.19E

G-BMSG Saab 32A Lansen 32028 22.07.86
Fv32028 Cancelled 20.06.14 by CAA
Willenhall, West Midlands
Nose stored in scrapyard 05.14

G-BMSL Clutton FRED Series III xxxx 19.05.86
(N.....), G-BMSL G Smith (Fancy Farm, Dunkeswell) 14.09.15P
Built by A C Coombe – project PFA 29-11142
(IE 17.09.17)

G-BMTA Cessna 152 II 15282864 27.08.86
N89776 ACS Aviation Ltd Perth 09.08.19E

G-BMTB Cessna 152 II 15280672 19.08.86
N25457 Stapleford Flying Club Ltd Stapleford 04.09.19E

G-BMTJ Cessna 152 II 15285010 19.06.86
N6389P The Pilot Centre Ltd Denham 16.06.19E

G-BMTU Pitts S-1E xxxx 04.06.86
N A A Pogmore Sherburn-in-Elmet 16.08.17P
Built by O R Howe – project PFA 009-10801
(NF 23.01.19)

G-BMTX Cameron V-77 733 19.06.86
J M Langley Ebley, Stroud *'Boondoggle'* 07.09.09E
(NF 15.09.16)

G-BMUG Rutan Long-EZ xxxx 17.06.86
A G Sayers RAF Barkston Heath 26.11.19P
Built by P Richardson – project PFA 074A-10987

G-BMUN[M] Cameron Harley 78SS HAB 1188 10.06.86
Cancelled 12.11.01 as WFU 23.05.99
Harley Davidson Motorcycle shape
With Musée des Ballons, Chateau de Balleroy, France

G-BMUO Cessna A152 Aerobat A1520788 04.06.86
4X-ALJ, N7328L Redhill Air Services Ltd Redhill 07.11.19E

G-BMUT Piper PA-34-200T Seneca II 34-7570320 23.01.87
EC-CUH, N3935X M Iqbal Cranfield 22.12.09E
Stored derelict 08.17 (IE 13.11.18)

G-BMUU Thunder Ax7-77 827 01.08.86
A R Hill Hawkhurst, Cranbrook *'Fiesta'* 05.06.16E

G-BMUZ Piper PA-28-161 Warrior II 28-8016329 24.07.86
EC-DMA, N9559N Redhill Air Services Ltd Redhill 21.01.19E

G-BMVA Scheibe SF.25B Falke 46223 28.07.86
RAFGGA 512, D-KAEN Cancelled 16.04.14 as PWFU 05.06.08
Roudham, Thetford *In Combat Paintball Park 07.18*

G-BMVB Reims/Cessna F152 II F15201974 10.09.86
W Ali Southend 08.11.18E
Noted 02.19

G-BMVL Piper PA-38-112 Tomahawk 38-79A0033 05.09.86
N2391B FlightpathBlackpool Ltd Blackpool 01.05.19E
Overturned on landing Caernarfon 12.05.18 &
substantially damaged

G-BMVM Piper PA-38-112 Tomahawk 38-79A0025 05.09.86
N2359B Cancelled 18.08.17 as destroyed 23.03.17
Liverpool *Stored, to be a simulator 09.17*

G-BMVT Thunder Ax7-77A HAB 102 15.07.86
SE-ZYY Cancelled 04.09.14 as PWFU
Not Known *Inflated Pidley 04.18*

G-BMVU Monnett Moni xxxx 14.08.86
T McKinley Bembridge 08.06.12P
Built by S R Lee – project PFA 142-10948 (NF 14.09.18)

G-BMWF ARV ARV-1 Super 2 013 01.07.86
D L Aspinall Oban 09.08.19P

G-BMWN[M] Cameron Temple 80SS HAB 1211 09.07.86
Cancelled 14.11.02 by CAA *'Temple'* 17.06.96
With Musée des Ballons, Chateau de Balleroy, France

G-BMWR Rockwell Commander 112A 365 23.09.86
N1365J T A Stoate Blackbushe 07.10.18E

G-BMWU Cameron N-42 1346 22.12.88
I Chadwick Caterham *'Helix'* 28.06.18E

G-BMXA Cessna 152 II 15280125 14.07.86
N757ZC ACS Aviation Ltd Doncaster Sheffield 29.05.19E
Operated by Leading Edge Flight Training

G-BMXB Cessna 152 II 15280996 14.07.86
N48840 Devon & Somerset Flight Training Ltd
Dunkeswell 23.08.19E

G-BMXC Cessna 152 II 15280416 14.07.86
N24858 MK Aero Support Ltd North Weald 23.05.19E

G-BMYA Colt 56A HAB 864 13.08.86
Cancelled 29.04.97 as PWFU 02.12.92
Abingdon *Stored 2014 'British Gas'*

G-BMYG Reims/Cessna FA152 Aerobat FA1520365 23.10.86
OO-JCA, (OO-JCC), PH-AXG
Central Horizon Partnership LLP Cumbernauld 03.09.19E
Operated by Phoenix Flight Training

G-BMYI Grumman American AA-5 Traveler AA5-0568 01.09.86
EI-BJF, F-BVRM, N9568L
S C & W C Westran Brighton City 16.10.08E
Noted 02.16 (NF 08.02.19)

G-BMYN Colt 77A HAB 873 02.09.86
Cancelled 03.11.10 as PWFU 24.03.07
Not Known *Inflated Pidley 05.16*

G-BMYP[M] Fairey Gannet AEW.3 F.9461 19.09.86
8610M, XL502 Cancelled 22.02.05 by CAA
As 'XL502' in 849 Sqdn:'B' Flight RN c/s
Built by Westland Aircraft Ltd
With Yorkshire Air Museum, Elvington

G-BMYS Thunder Ax7-77Z HAB 887 03.11.86
Cancelled 02.06.10 as PWFU 01.06.01
Not Known *Inflated Amersfoort, 10.16*

G-BMYU Jodel D.120 Paris-Nice 289 23.06.86
F-BMYU J A Northen Breighton 01.09.19P
Built by Société Wassmer Aviation

G-BMZF[M] WSK-Mielec LIM-2 (MiG-15bis) 1B-01420 18.12.86
Polish AF 01420 Cancelled 23.02.90 as WFU
North Korean c/s
With Fleet Air Arm Museum, RNAS Yeovilton

G-BMZN Everett Gyroplane Series 1 008 13.11.86
P A Gardner (Condover, Shrewsbury) 14.01.20P

G-BMZP Everett Gyroplane Series 1 010 14.11.86
Cancelled 25.03.08 by CAA 10.04.02
Birchwood House, North Driffield
Stored 01.14, roaded out 12.16

G-BMZS Everett Gyroplane Series 1 012 13.11.86
R F G Moyle Tregolds Farm, St Merryn 31.07.18P
(IE 31.08.18)

G-BMZW	Bensen B.8MR	xxxx	16.10.86
	P D Widdicombe (Huntington, York)		25.08.99P
	Built by P D Widdicombe – project PFA G/01-1021		
	(NF 27.09.16)		
G-BMZX	Wolf W-11 Boredom Fighter	xxxx	31.10.86
	N Wright Popham		28.08.14P
	Built by J J Penney – project PFA 146-11042;		
	as '7' in USAAC c/s (IE 05.09.18)		

G-BNAA – G-BNZZ

G-BNAI	Wolf W-11 Boredom Fighter	xxxx	31.10.86
	C M Bunn Haverfordwest		28.04.19P
	Built by P J Gronow – project PFA 146-11083;		
	as '5:146-11083' in USAAC c/s to represent replica Spad		
G-BNAJ	Cessna 152 II	15282527	03.11.86
	C-GZWF, (N69173) Galair Ltd Biggin Hill		06.03.13E
	Noted dismantled 12.16 (NF 20.04.16)		
G-BNAN	Cameron V-65	1333	28.10.86
	A M & N H Ponsford t/a Rango Balloon & Kite Company		
	Leeds *'Actually'*		07.07.01A
	(NF 21.01.19)		
G-BNAW	Cameron V-65	1366	24.10.86
	A & P A Walker Haske Barton, Crediton		
	'Hippo-Thermia'		08.07.15E
	(NF 20.11.18)		
G-BNBU	Bensen B.8MV	xxxx	16.06.99
	B A Lyford (Paignton)		
	Built by D T Murchie – project PFA G/01-1070		
	(NF 04.10.16)		
G-BNCB	Cameron V-77	1401	02.12.86
	E K Read Timperley, Altrincham		
	'The Phoenix Tyre & Battery Co Ltd'		28.03.17E
G-BNCR	Piper PA-28-161 Warrior II	28-8016111	10.12.86
	G-PDMT, ZS-LGW, N8103D		
	Airways Aero Associations Ltd Wycombe Air Park		21.02.19E
	Operated by British Airways Flying Club; Union Flag c/s		
G-BNCS	Cessna 180	30022	07.01.87
	OO-SPA, D-ENUX, N2822A		
	C Elwell Transport (Repairs) Ltd Tatenhill		17.02.95
	(NF 26.04.16)		
G-BNDG	Wallis WA-201 Series 1	K220X	22.01.87
	Cancelled 03.08.16 as PWFU		03.03.88
	Old Warden *Stored 10.16*		
G-BNDP	Brügger MB.2 Colibri	xxxx	08.01.87
	J M Boden Griffins Farm, Temple Bruer		18.03.17P
	Built by M Black – project PFA 043-10956 (NF 12.06.17)		
G-BNDR	SOCATA TB-10 Tobago	740	12.02.87
	J Segonne Lyon-Bron, France		14.04.19E
G-BNDT	Brügger MB.2 Colibri	xxxx	08.01.87
	G D Gunby Monewden		05.06.18P
	Built by A Szep – project PFA 043-10981		
G-BNDWᴹ	de Havilland DH.82A Tiger Moth	3942	10.12.86
	N6638 Cancelled 19.07.12 by CAA		
	Caernarfon *Stored 08.15 as 'N5137' in RAF c/s*		
G-BNEE	Piper PA-28R-201 Arrow III	28R-7837084	28.01.87
	N630DJ, N9518N C I Jarvis tr Britannic		
	Management Aviation White Waltham		20.04.19E
	Official type data 'PA28R-201 Cherokee Arrow III'		
	is incorrect		
G-BNEL	Piper PA-28-161 Warrior II	28-7916314	27.04.87
	N2246U NM Flight Services Ltd Redhill		23.06.19E
G-BNEO	Cameron V-77	1408	09.02.87
	J G O'Connell Pattiswick, Braintree *'Rowtate'*		02.11.00
	(NF 18.12.18)		
G-BNFG	Cameron O-77 HAB	1416	05.03.87
	Cancelled 18.08.16 as PWFU		13.01.94
	Not Known *Inflated Pidley 04.18*		
G-BNFKᴹ	Cameron Egg 89SS HAB	1436	20.02.87
	Cancelled 14.11.02 by CAA *'Faberge Easter Egg'*		15.07.02
	Fabergé Rosebud Egg shape		
	With Musée des Ballons, Chateau de Balleroy, France		
G-BNFO	Cameron V-77 HAB	816	05.03.87
	Cancelled 08.08.14 by CAA		07.08.11
	Not Known *Inflated Pidley 04.18*		

G-BNFP	Cameron O-84	1474	29.04.87
	M Clarke Egham *'Dragonfly'*		25.07.19E
G-BNFR	Cessna 152 II	15282035	08.04.87
	N67817 A Jahanfar Andrewsfield		11.05.19E
G-BNFV	Robin DR.400-120 Petit Prince	1767	04.03.87
	J P A Freeman Headcorn		19.02.20E
G-BNGE	Auster AOP.6	1925	18.03.87
	7704M, TW536 K A Hale MoD Netheravon		27.04.19P
	As 'TW536' in AAC camouflage c/s		
G-BNGJ	Cameron V-77	1487	18.03.87
	S W K Smeeton Ely *'Latham Timber'*		18.10.13E
	(IE 03.01.19)		
G-BNGO	Thunder Ax7-77	971	26.03.87
	J S Finlan tr G-BNGO Group		
	Taupiri, Waikato, New Zealand *'Thunderbird'*		16.04.06
	(NF 20.07.18)		
G-BNGT	Piper PA-28-181 Archer II	28-8590036	29.04.87
	N149AV, N9559N A Soojeri Glasgow Prestwick		11.12.18E
G-BNGV	ARV ARV-1 Super 2	021	04.06.87
	N A Onions Andrewsfield		28.04.06
	(NF 21.01.19)		
G-BNGW	ARV ARV-1 Super 2	022	04.06.87
	Southern Gas Turbines Ltd Goodwood		14.10.11P
	Noted 06.14 (IE 25.06.18)		
G-BNGY	ARV ARV-1 Super 2	019	09.06.87
	(G-BMWL) J & P Morris Shobdon		31.07.19P
G-BNHB	ARV ARV-1 Super 2	026	13.07.87
	N A Onions & L J Russell Andrewsfield		18.07.17P
	(IE 30.05.18)		
G-BNHG	Piper PA-38-112 Tomahawk II	38-82A0030	23.03.87
	N91435 Cancelled 27.09.17 as PWFU		27.06.17
	Inverness *Instructional use 09.17*		
G-BNHJ	Cessna 152 II	15281249	04.06.87
	N49418 The Pilot Centre Ltd Denham		22.12.19E
G-BNHK	Cessna 152 II	15285355	30.03.87
	N80161 G W Andrew tr Wayfarers Flying Group Derby		20.08.19E
G-BNHL	Colt Beer Glass	1042	24.03.87
	M R Stokoe Tatsfield, Westerham *'Gatzweilers Alt'*		15.02.19E
G-BNHNᴹ	Colt Ariel Bottle SS HAB	1045	30.03.87
	Cancelled 24.01.92 as WFU		05.05.89
	With British Balloon Museum & Library, Newbury		
G-BNHT	Alpavia Fournier RF3	80	13.04.87
	(D-KITX), G-BNHT, F-BMTO J Farquhar & I Hardy		
	tr G-BNHT Group Husbands Bosworth		25.06.19P
G-BNID	Cessna 152 II	15284931	24.04.87
	N5378P MK Aero Support Ltd Andrewsfield		21.06.15E
	(IE 20.11.16)		
G-BNIK	Robin HR.200-120 Club	43	15.04.87
	LX-AIK, LX-PAA M Wennington tr G-BNIK Group		
	Leicester		11.04.19E
G-BNIN	Cameron V-77	1079	15.04.87
	G-RRSG, (G-BLRO) J L & T J Hilditch		
	t/a Cloud Nine Balloon Group Hertford		18.05.09E
	Stored Hertfordshire Balloon Collection (NF 22.12.15)		
G-BNIO	Luscombe 8A	2120	15.04.87
	N45593, NC45593 R C Dyer & M Richardson		
	Landmead Farm, Garford		16.04.19P
G-BNIP	Luscombe 8A	3547	15.04.87
	N77820, NC77820 E L Watts		
	Roughay Farm, Lower Upham		06.03.19P
G-BNIU	Cameron O-77	1499	28.04.87
	M E Dubois Vineuil, Loir-et-Cher, France		
	'Mitchell Air Power'		02.03.15E
	(NF 02.08.17)		
G-BNIV	Cessna 152 II	15284866	24.04.87
	N4972P Smart People Dont Buy Ltd		
	Wellesbourne Mountford		23.10.19E
G-BNIW	Boeing Stearman A75L300 *(PT-17)*	75-1526	22.04.87
	N49291, 41-7967 Skymax (Aviation) Ltd Headcorn		28.07.16E
	(NF 14.11.18)		
G-BNJB	Cessna 152 II	15284865	27.04.87
	N4970P Aerolease Ltd Conington		21.03.19E

G-BNJC Cessna 152 II 15283588 27.04.87
N4705B Stapleford Flying Club Ltd Stapleford 18.07.19E

G-BNJH Cessna 152 II 15285401 21.07.87
C-GORA, (N93101) ACS Aviation Ltd Perth 14.09.19E

G-BNJT Piper PA-28-161 Warrior II 28-8116184 11.06.87
N8360T M Jones tr Hawarden Flying Group
Hawarden 11.03.19E

G-BNJUM Cameron Bust 80SS HAB 1324 13.05.87
Cancelled 01.5.03 as WFU *'Ludwig von Beethoven'* 19.01.03
With Musée des Ballons, Chateau de Balleroy, France

G-BNKC Cessna 152 II 15281036 26.05.87
N48894 Herefordshire Aero Club Ltd Shobdon 13.11.19E

G-BNKD Cessna 172N Skyhawk II 17272329 19.05.87
N4681D R Nightingale Bristol 28.02.19E

G-BNKE Cessna 172N Skyhawk II 17273886 20.05.87
N6534J I Gordon tr Kilo Echo Flying Group Derby 27.04.19E

G-BNKH Piper PA-38-112 Tomahawk II 38-81A0078 14.05.87
N25874 M C R Sims Goodwood 15.09.19E

G-BNKI Cessna 152 II 15281765 19.05.87
N67337 The Royal Air Force Halton Aeroplane Club Ltd
RAF Halton 24.05.19E

G-BNKP Cessna 152 II 15281286 18.05.87
N49460 Spectrum Leisure Ltd Clacton-on-Sea 16.04.19E

G-BNKR Cessna 152 II 15281284 18.05.87
N49458 Airways Aero Associations Ltd
Wycombe Air Park 08.08.19E

G-BNKS Cessna 152 II 15283186 18.05.87
N47202 APB Leasing Ltd Sleap 11.07.19E

G-BNKT Cameron O-77 1356 13.02.87
A A Brown Worplesdon, Guildford *'Katie II'* 30.12.19E

G-BNKV Cessna 152 II 15283079 18.05.87
N46604 Cristal Air Ltd Redhill 03.02.19E

G-BNLN Boeing 747-436 24056 26.07.90
British Airways PLC London Heathrow 01.07.19E
Line No: 802

G-BNLP Boeing 747-436 24058 17.12.90
British Airways PLC St Athan 10.09.19E
Line No: 828; noted 12.18 for part-out/scrapping

G-BNLY (3) Boeing 747-436 27090 10.02.93
N60659 British Airways PLC London Heathrow 16.02.19E
Line No: 959

G-BNMB Piper PA-28-151 Cherokee Warrior 28-7615369 06.10.87
N6826J Aviation Advice & Consulting Ltd
Wellesbourne Mountford 13.03.19E

G-BNMC Cessna 152 15282564 29.05.87
N69218 Cancelled 19.09.09 by CAA 10.08.03
Derby *Stored 06.14*

G-BNMD Cessna 152 II 15283786 28.05.87
N5170B T M Jones Derby 28.07.01
(IE 09.07.18)

G-BNME Cessna 152 II 15284888 25.09.87
N5159P M Bonsall Netherthorpe 28.01.20E

G-BNMF Cessna 152 15285563 21.07.87
N93858 Redhill Air Services Ltd Rougham 07.02.20E
Operated by Skyward Flight Training

G-BNMH Pietenpol Air Camper NH-1-001 02.06.87
N M Hitchman (Adderbury, Banbury)
Built by N M Hitchman; wings & tailplane stored 2016
(NF 23.11.16)

G-BNMI Colt Black Knight SS HAB 1096 01.06.87
Cancelled 04.11.03 as PWFU 26.09.91
Not Known *Inflated Pidley 05.16*

G-BNML Rand Robinson KR-2 xxxx 23.06.87
P J Brookman (Markfield) 18.12.13P
Built by R J Smyth – project PFA 129-11240
(NF 28.11.16)

G-BNMO Cessna TR182 Turbo Skylane RG II R18200956 03.07.87
N738RK Smiemans Beheer BV Goodwood 21.05.19E

G-BNMX Thunder Ax7-77 1003 15.06.87
P Coman Taverham, Norwich 29.06.19E

G-BNNAM Stolp Starduster Too 1462 29.06.87
N8SD Cancelled 11.07.17 as destroyed 30.04.18
Built by T C Maxwell Fuselage only
With South Yorkshire Aircraft Museum, Doncaster;
front fuselage used as travelling exhibit 06.18

G-BNNE Cameron N-77 1413 15.06.87
R D Allen, L P Hooper & M J Streat Bristol & Oswestry 26.05.19E

G-BNNIM Boeing 727-276 ADV 20950 10.12.86
VH-TBK Cancelled 04.08.03 as PWFU *As 'G-BNNI'*
Displayed premises '727 communication A/S'
near motorway E45
At Stilling, Arhus, Denmark

G-BNNO Piper PA-28-161 Warrior II 28-8116099 15.06.87
N8307X Tor Financial Consulting Ltd Norwich Int'l 29.08.19E

G-BNNRM Cessna 152 II 15285146 15.06.87
N40SX, N40SU, N6121Q Cancelled 08.09.11 as PWFU 15.11.08
Fuselage only
With Solway Aviation Museum, Carlisle Lake District;
used as children's plaything 11.17

G-BNNT Piper PA-28-151 Cherokee Warrior 28-7615056 12.06.87
N7624C S T Gilbert Enstone 19.09.19E

G-BNNU Piper PA-38-112 Tomahawk II 38-81A0037 12.06.87
N25650 P Lodge & J G McVey
Liverpool John Lennon 27.07.19E

G-BNNX Piper PA-28R-201T Turbo Cherokee Arrow III
28R-7703009 14.07.87
N9005F Professional Flying Ltd Bristol 06.09.19E

G-BNNY Piper PA-28-161 Warrior II 28-8016084 01.09.87
N8092M A S Bamrah t/a Falcon Flying Services
Biggin Hill 08.01.20E

G-BNNZ Piper PA-28-161 Warrior II 28-8016177 24.07.87
N8135Y Falcon Flying Services Ltd RAF Henlow 03.05.19E
Operated by Henlow Flying Club

G-BNOB Wittman W.8 Tailwind xxxx 13.07.87
D G Hammersley Yeatsall Farm, Abbots Bromley
'Imogen' 14.05.02P
Built by D G Hammersley – project PFA 3502
(NF 03.08.16)

G-BNOF Piper PA-28-161 Warrior II 2816014 26.06.87
N9122B Tayside Aviation Ltd Dundee 11.11.19E

G-BNOH Piper PA-28-161 Warrior II 2816016 26.06.87
N9122L Sherburn Aero Club Ltd Sherburn-in-Elmet 11.02.20E

G-BNOJ Piper PA-28-161 Warrior II 2816018 26.06.87
N9122R W M Brown & G A J Henderson
tr BAe (Warton) Flying Club Blackpool 15.06.19E

G-BNOM Piper PA-28-161 Warrior II 2816024 26.06.87
J H Sandham t/a JH Sandham Aviation
Carlisle Lake District 31.07.19E

G-BNON Piper PA-28-161 Warrior II 2816025 26.06.87
Tayside Aviation Ltd Glasgow 25.03.19E

G-BNOP Piper PA-28-161 Warrior II 2816027 26.06.87
S J Donno & G A J Henderson
tr BAe (Warton) Flying Club Blackpool 16.09.19E

G-BNPE Cameron N-77 1519 25.08.87
(G-BNPX) R N Simpkins Mangotsfield, Bristol
'Skint Garden Denters' 05.05.10E
(IE 06.11.17)

G-BNPF Cadet III Motor Glider 826 03.11.87
XA284 S Luck, P Norman & D R Winder
Audley End *'Noddy'* 10.01.20P
Built by S Luck, P Norman & D R Winder
– project PFA 042-11122; rebuilt ex Slingsby
T31M XA284 & wings ex XE791

G-BNPH Percival P.66 Pembroke C.1 P66/41 30.06.87
WV740 M A Stott St Athan 09.01.19P
Officially registered with c/n 'PAC66/027';
as 'WV740' in RAF 60 Sqdn c/s

G-BNPM Piper PA-38-112 Tomahawk 38-79A0374 28.07.87
N2561D D & L K Britten North Weald 22.02.20E

G-BNPO Piper PA-28-181 Archer II 28-7890123 28.07.87
N47720 S J Waddy
Shacklewell Lodge Farm, Empingham 13.09.19E

G-BNPU Hunting-Percival P66 Pembroke C.1 P66/87 30.06.87
XL929 Cancelled 11.08.88 as PWFU
Compton Verney *Spares use 12.16*

G-BNPV Bowers Fly Baby 1A/1B xxxx 02.07.87
A Berry (Virginia Water) 14.04.19P
Built by J G Day – project PFA 16-11120; as '1801/18'
in German Army Air Service c/s to represent Junkers CL1

G-BNPY Cessna 152 II 15280249 30.06.87
N24388 G Tennant Retford Gamston 19.08.19E

G-BNRA SOCATA TB-10 Tobago 772 15.07.87
R L H Walker tr Double D Airgroup Nottingham City
'Triple One' 11.06.19E

G-BNRG Piper PA-28-161 Warrior II 28-8116217 07.07.87
N83810 Glenn Aviation Ltd RAF Brize Norton 04.04.19E
Operated by Brize Norton Flying Club

G-BNRL Cessna 152 II 15284250 13.07.87
N5084L Andrewsfield Aviation Ltd Andrewsfield 26.07.19E

G-BNRP Piper PA-28-181 Archer II 28-7790528 25.11.87
N984BT PA-28 Warrior Ltd RAF Cosford 02.02.19E

G-BNRR Cessna 172P Skyhawk II 17274013 13.07.87
N5213K C Surman t/a Wentworth Productions
Elstree *'U.S. Air Force'* & *'74013'* 31.10.19E

G-BNRW Colt 69A 1101 27.08.87
D Charles Westgate, Driffield 20.11.17E

G-BNRX Piper PA-34-200T Seneca II 34-7970336 25.11.87
N2898A Sky Zone Services Aereos Lda
Cascais, Portugal 11.03.19E

G-BNRY Cessna 182Q Skylane II 18265629 20.07.87
N735RR K F & S J Farey White Waltham 03.08.19E

G-BNSG Piper PA-28R-201 Arrow III 28R-7837205 30.07.87
N9516C Odhams Air Services Ltd Andrewsfield 28.06.19E
Official type data 'PA-28R-201 Cherokee Arrow III'
is incorrect

G-BNSL Piper PA-38-112 Tomahawk II 38-81A0086 21.07.87
N25956 P Lodge & J G McVey Liverpool John Lennon 12.12.19E

G-BNSM Cessna 152 II 15285342 23.07.87
N68948 Cornwall Flying Club Ltd Bodmin 21.05.19E

G-BNSN Cessna 152 II 15285776 21.07.87
N94738 The Pilot Centre Ltd Denham 23.03.19E

G-BNSR Slingsby T67M Firefly II 2047 20.08.87
E Whitehead tr Slingsby SR Group Redhill 25.06.19E

G-BNST Cessna 172N Skyhawk II 17273661 21.09.87
N4670J J Revill t/a CSG Bodyshop Netherthorpe 27.09.19E

G-BNSU Cessna 152 II 15281245 02.12.87
N49410 Inewvation LDA
(Santo Estavao, Tavira, Portugal) 06.10.18E
(IE 03.01.19)

G-BNSY Piper PA-28-161 Warrior II 28-8016017 18.08.87
N4512M Fast Aviation Ltd Bournemouth 06.11.09E
(NF 24.10.18)

G-BNSZ Piper PA-28-161 Warrior II 28-8116315 20.08.87
N8433B O G Hogan Wolverhampton Halfpenny Green 06.07.19E

G-BNTD Piper PA-28-161 Cherokee Warrior II 28-7716235 05.08.87
N38490, N9539N DSFT Ltd Doncaster Sheffield 21.06.19E
Operated by Doncaster Sheffield Flight Training

G-BNTP Cessna 172N Skyhawk II 17272030 04.09.87
N6531E Westnet Ltd Manchester Barton 18.02.20E

G-BNUC Cameron O-77 HAB 1575 18.08.87
Cancelled 13.05.10 by CAA
Not known *Inflated Pidley 05.16*

G-BNUL Cessna 152 II 15284486 02.10.87
N4852M A D R Northeast Wycombe Air Park 16.05.19E

G-BNUN Beech 58PA Baron TJ-256 19.08.87
N6732Y SMB Aviation Ltd East Midlands 01.05.19E

G-BNUO Beech 76 Duchess ME-250 29.09.87
N6635Y Professional Flight Simulation Ltd
Bournemouth 29.06.19E

G-BNUT Cessna 152 II 15279458 26.08.87
N714VC Stapleford Flying Club Ltd Stapleford 31.05.19E

G-BNUY Piper PA-38-112 Tomahawk II 38-81A0093 10.09.87
N26006 D C Storey (Hamnavoe, Shetland) 17.08.03
(NF 17.12.18)

G-BNVB Grumman American AA-5A Cheetah AA5A-0758 28.08.87
N26843 M E Hicks St Mary's, Isles of Scilly 07.06.19E

G-BNVE Piper PA-28-181 Archer II 28-8490046 28.08.87
N4338D M C Plomer-Roberts
Wellesbourne Mountford 10.03.19E

G-BNVT Piper PA-28R-201T Turbo Cherokee Arrow III
28R-7703157 26.01.88
N5863V C M Murphy tr Victor Tango Group
Glasgow Prestwick 16.05.19E

G-BNXE Piper PA-28-161 Warrior II 28-8116034 24.09.87
N8262D M S Brown Gloucestershire 15.04.19E

G-BNXL Glaser-Dirks DG-400 4-216 02.10.87
J Mjels Sutton Bank *'L11'* 14.05.19E

G-BNXM Piper PA-18 Super Cub 95 (L-21B-PI) 18-4019 23.11.87
I-EIVC:EI-276, Italian Army MM54-2619, 54-2619
K A A McDonald & N G Rhind
Jenkin's Farm, Navestock 11.09.18P
Rebuilt with Italian fuselage No.0006;
as '26359:32' in US Navy c/s

G-BNXU Piper PA-28-161 Warrior II 28-7916129 23.09.87
N2082C J Barnett tr Friendly Warrior Group
Newtownards 15.06.19E

G-BNXV Piper PA-38-112 Tomahawk 38-79A0826 10.12.87
N2399N W B Bateson Blackpool 20.08.15E
(NF 04.10.18)

G-BNXZ Thunder Ax7-77 1105 13.10.87
A S Dear, R B Green & W S Templeton tr Hale Hot Air
Balloon Group Warminster & Fordingbridge
'Dragonfly' 30.08.11E
(NF 21.08.13)

G-BNYD Bell 206B-2 JetRanger II 1911 01.10.87
N3254P, C-GTWM, N49712 Heli Consultants Ltd
(Canterbury) 26.07.18E
Stored 10.18 (IE 14.02.18)

G-BNYL Cessna 152 II 15280671 06.10.87
N25454 V J Freeman Headcorn 29.01.20E

G-BNYM Cessna 172N Skyhawk II 17273854 13.11.87
N6089J D J Skinner tr Kestrel Syndicate
MoD Netheravon 29.03.19E

G-BNYO Beech 76 Duchess ME-78 28.10.87
N2010P Skies Airline Training AB Nyköping, Sweden 23.04.19E

G-BNYP Piper PA-28-181 Archer II 28-8490027 19.10.87
N4330K D H Nash (Kensworth, Dunstable) 06.03.19E
Operated by Sandra's Flying Group

G-BNYZ SNCAN Stampe SV.4E 200 10.12.87
F-BFZR, French Navy 200
Bianchi Aviation Film Services Ltd Turweston 28.07.19E
Reported as ex N180SV (c/n '200-53') or
ex Belgian V-53 (c/n 1195)

G-BNZB Piper PA-28-161 Warrior II 28-7916521 18.11.87
N2900U Falcon Flying Services Ltd Biggin Hill 13.03.20E

G-BNZC de Havilland DHC-1 Chipmunk 22 C1/0778 11.11.87
G-ROYS, 7438M, WP905
Richard Shuttleworth Trustees Old Warden 01.10.19P
As 'RCAF 671' in RCAF yellow c/s

G-BNZK Thunder Ax7-77 1104 10.11.87
T D Marsden Limber, Grimsby *'Shropshire Lass'* 28.05.97A
(NF 04.04.18)

G-BNZL RotorWay Scorpion 133 2839 02.11.87
J R Wraight (Chatham)
Built by J Evans (NF 14.10.16)

G-BNZM Cessna T210N Turbo Centurion II 21063640 09.11.87
N4828C A J M Freeman North Weald 02.04.19E

G-BNZN Cameron N-56 1471 09.11.87
SE-ZFA, G-BNZN P Lesser Partille, Sweden
'Cameron Balloons' 04.07.18E

G-BNZO RotorWay Exec RW152/3535 09.11.87
J S David Street Farm, Takeley 10.12.18P
Built by M J Wiltshire

G-BNZRM Clutton-Tabenor FRED Srs.II xxxx 10.11.87
Cancelled 11.08.10 as PWFU
Built by R M Waugh – project PFA/29-10727
With Ulster Aviation Society, Lisburn

G-BNZZ Piper PA-28-161 Warrior II 28-8216184 17.11.87
N8253Z Providence Aviation Ltd
Wellesbourne Mountford 25.01.18E

G-BOAA – G-BOZZ

G-BOAA^M BAC Concorde Type 1 Variant 102   206 & 100-006   03.04.74
G-N94AA, G-BOAA   Cancelled 04.05.04 as WFU   24.02.01
With National Museum of Flight Scotland, East Fortune

G-BOAB BAC Concorde Type 1 Variant 102   208 & 100-008   03.04.74
G-N94AB, G-BOAB   Cancelled 04.05.04 as WFU   19.09.01
Heathrow   *Preserved by British A/W Engineering*

G-BOAC^M BAC Concorde Type 1 Variant 102   204 & 100-004   03.04.74
G-N81AC, G-BOAC   Cancelled 04.05.04 as WFU   16.05.05
With Runway Visitor Park, Manchester Airport

G-BOAD^M BAC Concorde Type 1 Variant 102   210 & 100-010   09.05.75
G-N94AD, G-BOAD   Cancelled 04.05.04 as WFU   03.12.04
As 'G-BOAD'
With Intrepid Air & Space Museum, New York

G-BOAE^M BAC Concorde Type 1 Variant 102   212 & 100-012   09.05.75
G-N94AE, G-BOAE   Cancelled 04.05.04 as WFU   18.07.05
With Concorde Experience Museum, Seawell, Barbados

G-BOAF^M BAC Concorde Type 1 Variant 102   216 & 100-016   12.06.80
G-N94AF, G-BFKX   Cancelled 04.05.04 as WFU   11.06.04
With Aerospace Bristol

G-BOAG^M BAC Concorde Type 1 Variant 102   214 & 100-014   09.02.81
G-BFKW   Cancelled 04.05.04 as WFU   As 'G-BOAG'   03.04.05
With Museum of Flight, Seattle, Washington

G-BOAH Piper PA-28-161 Warrior II   28-8416030   21.01.88
N43401, N9554N   Aircraft Engineers Ltd
Glasgow Prestwick   07.05.19E

G-BOAI Cessna 152 II   15279830   08.01.88
C-GSJH, N757LS   Aviation Spirit Ltd
Wolverhampton Halfpenny Green   24.10.18E

G-BOAL Cameron V-65   1600   05.11.87
A M & N H Ponsford   Leeds   'No Name Balloon'   07.02.02A
(NF 21.01.19)

G-BOAU Cameron V-77   1606   10.12.87
G T Barstow   Llandrindod Wells   21.10.09E
(NF 14.02.17)

G-BOBA Piper PA-28R-201 Arrow III   28R-7837232   04.01.88
N31249   SC Airlease Ltd   (South Shields)   17.06.19E
Official type data 'PA-28R-201 Cherokee Arrow III'
is incorrect

G-BOBR Cameron N-77   1623   10.12.87
I R F Worsman   Dundee   24.04.06A
(NF 11.09.17)

G-BOBT Stolp SA.300 Starduster Too   CJ-01   15.12.87
N690CM   S C A Lever tr G-BOBT Group
White Waltham   18.02.19P
Built by C J Anderson

G-BOBV Reims/Cessna F150M   F15001415   14.12.87
EI-BCV   M L Brown & P L Hill   Leicester   27.02.19E

G-BOBY Monnett Sonerai II   xxxx   26.10.78
R G Hallam   (Nether Alderley, Macclesfield)
Built by R G Hallam – project PFA 015-10223;
rebuilt in low-wing configuration (IE 15.11.18)

G-BOCB^M Hawker Siddeley HS125 Series 1B/522   25106   14.09.87
G-OMCA, G-DJMJ, G-AWUF, 5N-ALY, G-AWUF, HZ-BIN
Cancelled 22.02.95 as PWFU   16.10.90
Port Talbot, Wales   *For sale from Port Talbot area 06.18*

G-BOCI Cessna 140A   15497   17.11.87
N5366C   J B Bonnell tr Charlie India Aviators   Popham   19.07.19E

G-BOCK Sopwith Triplane replica   NAW-1   26.01.88
Richard Shuttleworth Trustees   Old Warden   'Dixie II'   12.04.19P
Built by Northern Aeroplane Workshops; uses
Sopwith Triplane c/n 153 plate to reflect late
production example; as 'N6290' in RNAS 8 Sqdn c/s

G-BOCL Slingsby T67C Firefly   2035   05.01.88
Richard Brinklow Aviation Ltd   Pent Farm, Postling   26.02.07
Stored dismantled 08.14 (NF 16.10.18)

G-BOCM Slingsby T67C Firefly   2036   05.01.88
Richard Brinklow Aviation Ltd   Leicester   22.07.10E
Stored less engine 10.17 (NF 18.10.18)

G-BOCN Robinson R22 Beta   0726   08.01.88
N....., G-BOCN   HQ Aviation Ltd   (Denham)   17.02.17E

G-BOCU Piper PA-34-220T Seneca III   3433114   26.02.88
EC-JDA, G-BOCU   Advanced Aircraft Leasing
(Teesside) Ltd   Durham Tees Valley   04.06.19E

G-BODB Piper PA-28-161 Warrior II   2816042   23.02.88
N9606N   Sherburn Aero Club Ltd   Sherburn-in-Elmet   06.12.19E

G-BODD Piper PA-28-161 Warrior II   2816040   23.02.88
N9604N   CG Aviation Ltd   Perth   19.11.10E
Operated by ACS Flight Training

G-BODE Piper PA-28-161 Warrior II   2816039   23.02.88
N9603N   Sherburn Aero Club Ltd   Sherburn-in-Elmet   20.01.20E

G-BODI Stoddard-Hamilton Glasair III RG   3088   14.04.89
(HB-...), G-BODI   A P Durston
(West Chiltington, Pulborough)   18.05.09P
Built by Jackson Barr Ltd (NF 15.10.15)

G-BODO Cessna 152 II   15282404   29.01.88
N68923   Enstone Sales & Services Ltd   Enstone   04.03.20E

G-BODR Piper PA-28-161 Warrior II   28-8116318   05.01.88
N8436B   Airways Aero Associations Ltd
Wycombe Air Park   20.11.19E
Operated by British Airways Flying Club; Union Flag c/s

G-BODS Piper PA-38-112 Tomahawk   38-79A0410   03.02.88
N2379F   T W Gilbert   Enstone   30.03.15E
Struck hedge landing Hinton-in-the-Hedges 05.06.14
& extensively damaged; noted dismantled 01.16
(NF 22.10.18)

G-BODT Jodel D.18   173   14.01.88
A H McGirr tr The Jodel Syndicate   Perth   16.10.19P
Built by R A Jarvis – project PFA 169-11290

G-BODU Scheibe SF25C Falke 2000   44434   19.01.88
D-KIAA   Hertfordshire County Scout Council
Gransden Lodge   11.05.19E

G-BODW^M Bell 206B Jet Ranger II   784   18.12.89
N2951W, N2951N, G-BODW
Cancelled 05.04.94 as Destroyed   02.05.94
Hulk only
With The Helicopter Museum, Weston-super-Mare

G-BODX Beech 76 Duchess   ME-309   26.02.88
N67094   Cancelled 22.10.09 as PWFU   03.09.09
Wickford, Essex   *In Wickford Action paintball park 04.16*

G-BODY Cessna 310R II   310R1503   17.12.87
N4897A   Reconnaissance Ventures Ltd t/a RVL Group
East Midlands   11.05.19E

G-BODZ Robinson R22 Beta   0729   08.01.88
Langley Aviation Ltd   Retford Gamston   22.05.19E

G-BOEE Piper PA-28-181 Archer II   28-7690359   20.01.88
N6168J   G M & J C Brinkley
Standalone Farm, Meppershall   05.12.19E

G-BOEH Robin DR.340 Major   434   04.01.88
F-BRVN   B W Griffiths   (Manselton, Swansea)   09.07.19E

G-BOEK Cameron V-77   1658   25.01.88
R I M Kerr, P McCheyne & R S McLean
Bristol   'Secret Leader'   01.07.19E

G-BOEM Pitts S-2A   2255   17.02.88
N31525   M Murphy   Leicester   24.05.19E
Built by Aerotek Inc

G-BOEN Cessna 172M Skyhawk   17261325   12.02.88
N20482   R Kolozsi   (Bratislava, Slovak Republic)   16.04.11E
(IE 16.05.18)

G-BOER Piper PA-28-161 Warrior II   28-8116094   21.01.88
N83030   E Fox   Bagby   20.07.19E

G-BOET Piper PA-28RT-201 Arrow IV   28R-8018020   28.01.88
G-IBEC, G-BOET, N8116V   B C Chambers   Jersey   06.01.20E

G-BOEW Robinson R22 Beta   0750   27.01.88
Cancelled 27.06.08 as PWFU   13.04.06
Newcastle Int'l   Noted 02.14

G-BOEX Robinson R22 Beta   0751   27.01.88
Cancelled 11.10.02 as PWFU   12.03.03
Adventure Island, Southend-on-Sea seafront
Stored on top of pay booth 01.19 – identity not confirmed

G-BOFC Beech 76 Duchess   ME-217   28.01.88
N6628M   Odhams Air Services Ltd   Andrewsfield   24.04.19E

G-BOFE Piper PA-34-200T Seneca II   34-7870381   22.02.88
SP-NIT, G-BOFE, N39493
Atlantic Flight Training Academy Ltd   Cork, RoI   11.12.19E

G-BOFL Cessna 152 II   15284101   28.01.88
N5457H   S A Abid   Little Staughton   30.11.11E
Stored dismantled 02.18 (IE 31.07.17)

G-BOFM Cessna 152 II 15284730 28.01.88
N6445M Cancelled 26.02.13 by CAA 28.09.11
Little Staughton *Stored 01.18*

G-BOFW Cessna A150M Aerobat A1500612 15.02.88
N9803Q P J Wagstaff tr Golf Fox Whisky Group
Elstree 07.05.19E

G-BOFY Piper PA-28-140 Cherokee Cruiser 28-7425374 03.02.88
N43521 R A Brown (Clowne, Chesterfield) 29.07.09E
(IE 06.02.19)

G-BOFZ Piper PA-28-161 Warrior II 28-7816255 10.02.88
N2189M NAL Asset Management Ltd Dunkeswell 23.12.19E

G-BOGI Robin DR.400-180 Régent 1821 15.02.88
T Davis Rochester 15.10.19E

G-BOGK ARV ARV-1 Super 2 xxxx 10.02.88
M K Field Sleap 22.03.13P
Built by Monewden Flying Group
– project PFA 152-11138 (IE 05.02.19)

G-BOGLᴹ Thunder Ax7-77 HAB 953 08.04.88
Cancelled 06.12.95 as sold in Germany as D-OUYO
Inflated 04.14
With British Balloon Museum & Library, Newbury

G-BOGM Piper PA-28RT-201T Turbo Arrow IV 28R-8031077 10.02.88
N8173C M Sarsango Bournemouth 19.08.19E

G-BOGO Piper PA-32R-301T Turbo Saratoga SP 32R-8029064 06.04.88
N8165W GIF International Services KFT
(Budapest, Hungary) 25.07.18E
(NF 28.08.18)

G-BOGRᴹ Colt 180A HAB 1183 11.05.88
Cancelled 28.04.97 as WFU 13.03.92
With British Balloon Museum & Library, Newbury

G-BOGT Colt 77A HAB 1212 21.03.88
Cancelled 09.05.97 as PWFU 02.12.94
Not Known *Inflated Pidley 04.18 'British Gas'*

G-BOGY Cameron V-77 HAB 1650 15.02.88
Cancelled 21.07.15 as PWFU 26.04.13
Hungerford *Stored 12.16*

G-BOHA Piper PA-28-161 Warrior II 28-7816352 16.03.88
N3526M Flying at Lee on Solent Ltd
t/a Phoenix Aviation Solent 07.03.19E

G-BOHD Colt 77A 1214 04.03.88
D B Court Ormskirk *'Mercedes-Benz'* 05.08.02
(NF 13.04.16)

G-BOHH Cessna 172N Skyhawk II 17273906 19.02.88
N131FR, N7333J Staverton Flying School @ Skypark Ltd
Gloucestershire 17.05.19E

G-BOHI Cessna 152 II 15281241 29.02.88
N49406 Cirrus Aviation Ltd Clacton-on-Sea 13.07.19E

G-BOHJ Cessna 152 II 15280558 29.02.88
N25259 M Power Wickenby 16.01.20E

G-BOHM Piper PA-28-180 Cherokee Challenger 28-7305287 18.02.88
N55000 B F Keogh & R A Scott Cotswold 09.05.19E
Official type data 'PA-28-180 Cherokee' is incorrect

G-BOHO Piper PA-28-161 Warrior II 28-8016196 25.02.88
N747RH, N9560N D C Curgenven &
H M Sherriff tr Egressus Flying Group Duxford 19.01.20E

G-BOHR Piper PA-28-151 Cherokee Warrior 28-7515245 29.02.88
C-GNFE R M E Garforth Southend 06.03.19E

G-BOHV Wittman W.8 Tailwind 621 03.03.88
D H Greenwood Woolston Moss, Warrington 22.05.19P
Built by R A Povall – project PFA 031-11151

G-BOHW Van's RV-4 xxxx 16.06.88
E C Murgatroyd Sackville Lodge Farm, Riseley 01.10.19P
Built by R W H Cole – project PFA 181-11309

G-BOIB Wittman W.10 Tailwind xxxx 03.03.88
C R Nash (Gomeldon, Salisbury) 31.07.14P
Built by P H Lewis – project PFA 031-10551; ran into
hedge on take off from strip near Winchester
21.04.14 & substantially damaged (NF 28.07.16)

G-BOIC Piper PA-28R-201T Turbo Arrow III 28R-7803123 07.04.88
N2336M S P Donoghue Stapleford 23.05.19E
Official type data 'PA-28R-201T Turbo Cherokee
Arrow III' is incorrect

G-BOID Bellanca 7ECA Citabria 1092-75 03.03.88
N8676V D Mallinson Sherburn-in-Elmet 18.04.19E

G-BOIG Piper PA-28-161 Warrior II 28-8516027 01.03.88
N4390B, N9519N R Flanagan tr GFT Warrior Group
Retford Gamston 22.11.19E

G-BOIK Air Command 503 Commander xxxx 08.03.88
F G Shepherd (Leadgate, Alston)
Built by G R Horner – project PFA G/04-1090 (NF 16.01.15)

G-BOIL Cessna 172N Skyhawk II 17271301 02.03.88
N23FL, N23ER, (N2494E) Upperstack Ltd
t/a LAC Flying School Manchester Barton 01.11.19E
Operated by Lancashire Aero Club

G-BOIO Cessna 152 II 15280260 07.03.88
N24445 J H Sandham t/a JH Sandham Aviation
Carlisle Lake District 07.10.18E
(IE 07.02.19)

G-BOIR Cessna 152 II 15283272 07.03.88
N48041 APB Leasing Ltd Sleap 10.05.19E

G-BOIT SOCATA TB-10 Tobago 810 10.03.88
Naval Aviation Ltd RNAS Yeovilton *'Fly Navy'* 25.09.19E

G-BOIV Cessna 150M 15078620 22.03.88
N704HH M J Page tr India Victor Group Seething 18.01.20E

G-BOIX Cessna 172N Skyhawk II 17271206 09.03.88
C-GMMX, N2253E J W N Sharpe Bristol 27.03.19E

G-BOIY Cessna 172N Skyhawk II 17267738 09.03.88
N73901 S Smith Newcastle, RoI 12.04.19E

G-BOIZ Piper PA-34-200T Seneca II 34-8070014 25.02.88
N81081 K J Nicpon tr OCTN Trust
(Bishops Waltham, Southampton) 14.10.12E
(NF 27.03.14)

G-BOJB Cameron V-77 1615 11.03.88
S R Skinner Thame 27.10.18E

G-BOJI Piper PA-28RT-201 Arrow IV 28R-7918221 31.03.88
N2919X M J Berry & V Franklin tr Arrow Two Group
Blackbushe 01.03.20E

G-BOJM Piper PA-28-181 Archer II 28-8090244 21.03.88
N8155L R P Emms Retford Gamston 12.06.19E

G-BOJS Cessna 172P Skyhawk II 17274582 29.03.88
N52699 Paul's Planes Ltd Denham 15.12.19E

G-BOJW Piper PA-28-161 Cherokee Warrior II 28-7716038 28.03.88
N1668H Flying at Lee on Solent Ltd
t/a Phoenix Aviation Solent 16.01.20E

G-BOJZ Piper PA-28-161 Warrior II 28-7916223 28.03.88
N2113J Scenic Air Tours North East Ltd
Durham Tees Valley 04.04.19E
Operated by Scenic Airtours

G-BOKA Piper PA-28-201T Turbo Dakota 28-7921076 15.03.88
N2860S CBG Aviation Ltd Fairoaks 16.05.19E

G-BOKB Piper PA-28-161 Warrior II 28-8216077 29.03.88
N8013Y Flying Time Ltd Brighton City 07.12.19E

G-BOKH Whittaker MW7 xxxx 21.03.88
(G-MTWT) I Pearson (Falmouth) 11.06.11P
Built by M Whittaker – project PFA 171-11231;
stored 07.16 (NF 27.07.18)

G-BOKJ Whittaker MW.7 xxxx 21.03.88
(G-MTWV) Cancelled 17.05.01 as PWFU 04.06.97
(Falmouth) *Built by M N Gauntlett*
– project PFA 171-11281; for sale 06.16

G-BOKW Bölkow BÖ.208C Junior 689 06.01.88
G-BITT, F-BRHX, (D-EEAL)
A Petherbridge tr The Bat Group North Coates 17.11.19P

G-BOKX Piper PA-28-161 Warrior II 28-7816680 28.03.88
N39709 Turweston Flying Club Ltd Turweston 13.10.19E

G-BOKY Cessna 152 II 15285298 06.04.88
N67409 D F F & J E Poore (St Leonards, Ringwood) 31.07.11E
(NF 09.07.18)

G-BOLB Taylorcraft BC-12-65 3165 17.05.88
N36211, NC36211 C E Tudor Leicester
'Spirit Of California' 07.08.19P

G-BOLC Fournier RF6B-100 1 28.03.88
F-BVKS I K G Mitchell tr Devon & Somerset RF Group
Dunkeswell 02.05.17E
(NF 20.10.17)

G-BOLD	Piper PA-38-112 Tomahawk	38-78A0180	08.07.88	
	N9740T B R Pearson tr G-BOLD Group Eaglescott	16.03.09E	
	Noted 12.17 (NF 30.07.18)		
G-BOLE	Piper PA-38-112 Tomahawk	38-78A0475	13.07.88	
	N2506E Smart People Dont Buy Ltd		
	Doncaster Sheffield	16.08.19E	
	Operated by Aero Flight Training		
G-BOLG	Bellanca 7KCAB Citabria	517-75	25.11.88	
	N8706V B R Pearson tr Aerotug Eaglescott	03.05.19E	
G-BOLI	Cessna 172P Skyhawk II	17275484	30.03.88	
	N63794 W White tr BOLI Flying Club Denham	16.08.19E	
G-BOLL	Lake LA-4-200 Skimmer	295	04.05.88	
	(F-GRMX), G-BOLL, EI-ANR, N1133L		
	M C Holmes Causeway	29.08.18E	
G-BOLN	Colt 21A Cloudhopper	1226	04.05.88	
	G Everett Sandway, Maidstone	26.09.09E	
	(IE 06.03.18)		
G-BOLO	Bell 206B-2 JetRanger II	1522	02.11.87	
	N59409 Hargreaves Leasing Ltd		
	(Rustington, Littlehampton)	11.06.19E	
	Operated by Blades Helicopters		
G-BOLP	Colt 21A Cloudhopper HAB	1227	04.05.88	
	Cancelled 11.12.13 by CAA	11.10.09	
	(Portugal) *To Roger Guild 2013*		
G-BOLR	Colt 21A Cloudhopper	1228	03.05.88	
	C J Sanger-Davies Hawarden, Deeside	02.02.18E	
G-BOLS	Clutton FRED Series II	xxxx	06.04.88	
	I F Vaughan (St Martin, Guernsey) *'The Ruptured Uck'*		
	Built by R J Goodburn – project PFA 029-10676		
	(NF 29.06.18)		
G-BOLT	Rockwell Commander 114	14428	16.10.78	
	N5883N N N Drew (Great Witley, Worcester)	17.08.19E	
G-BOLU	Robin R3000/120	106	14.04.88	
	F-GFAO, SE-IMS J M Smith & P J R White Enstone	05.08.19E	
G-BOLV	Cessna 152 II	15280492	08.04.88	
	N24983 A J Gomes Redhill	06.10.19E	
G-BOLW	Cessna 152 II	15280589	09.06.88	
	N25316 P E Preston tr G-BOLW Group Southend	21.09.19E	
	Operated by Southend Flying Club		
G-BOLY	Cessna 172N Skyhawk II	17269004	31.03.88	
	N734PJ M J Crack tr Lima Yankee Flying Group		
	Andrewsfield	16.10.19E	
G-BOMB	Cassutt Racer IIIM	xxxx	18.12.78	
	Air Race CC Ltd (Waltham Abbey) *'Attack' & '11'*	28.10.19P	
	Built by D Ford – project PFA 034-10386		
G-BOMO	Piper PA-38-112 Tomahawk II	38-81A0161	08.04.88	
	N91324 APB Leasing Ltd Swansea	11.08.19E	
G-BOMP	Piper PA-28-181 Archer II	28-7790249	08.04.88	
	N8482F A Flinn Sandtoft	29.08.19E	
G-BOMS	Cessna 172N Skyhawk II	17269448	11.04.88	
	N737JG Penchant Ltd Coventry	19.05.19E	
G-BOMU	Piper PA-28-181 Archer II	28-7790318	08.04.88	
	N1631H R J Houghton Blackbushe	07.11.19E	
G-BOMY	Piper PA-28-161 Warrior II	28-8216049	28.06.88	
	N8457S Sunrise Global Asset Management Ltd		
	Wycombe Air Park	28.03.19E	
G-BOMZ	Piper PA-38-112 Tomahawk	38-78A0635	30.06.88	
	N2315A I C Barlow & I Cummins		
	tr BOMZ Aviation Wycombe Air Park	14.11.19E	
G-BONC	Piper PA-28RT-201 Arrow IV	28R-7918007	13.05.88	
	C-GXYX, N3069K SC Airlease Ltd Dundee	13.11.19E	
G-BONG	Enstrom F-28A-UK	154	22.04.88	
	N9604 G E Heritage Breach Oak Farm, Corley	20.09.17E	
	(IE 02.10.17)		
G-BONP	CFM Streak Shadow	108 & SS-01P	04.05.88	
	G J Chater Landmead Farm, Garford	26.06.19P	
	Built by CFM Metal-Fax – project PFA 161-11344		
G-BONR	Cessna 172N Skyhawk II	17268164	18.04.88	
	C-GYGK, (N733BH) D I Craik Biggin Hill	06.09.19E	
G-BONS	Cessna 172N Skyhawk II	17268345	18.04.88	
	C-GIUF R W Marchant & K Meredith		
	Little Engeham Farm, Woodchurch	17.09.11E	
	(NF 19.02.19)		

G-BONT	Slingsby T67M Firefly II	2054	03.05.88	
	G-UCRM, G-BONT Vigilant Aviation Ltd		
	(Saffron Walden)	04.03.19E	
G-BONU	Slingsby T67B Firefly	2037	03.05.88	
	R L Brinklow Pent Farm, Postling	29.06.00	
	Stored dismantled 08.14 (NF 08.01.15)		
G-BONW	Cessna 152 II	15280401	15.04.88	
	OY-CPL, N24825 Upperstack Ltd		
	t/a LAC Flying School Manchester Barton	07.09.19E	
G-BONY	Denney Kitfox Model 1	166	11.05.88	
	R Dunn Lower Manor Farm, Chickerell *'Foxy Lady'*	01.10.15P	
	Built by J S Penny – project PFA 172-11351;		
	badged 'Mk.2' (IE 04.10.18)		
G-BONZ	Beech V35B Bonanza	D-10282	06.04.88	
	N6661D R H Townsend (Wisbech St Mary)	21.02.20E	
G-BOOB	Cameron N-65	515	12.11.79	
	P J Hooper Southville, Bristol *'Cracker'*	23.07.15E	
	(NF 25.02.19)		
G-BOOC	Piper PA-18-150 Super Cub	18-8279	29.04.88	
	SE-EPC S A C Whitcombe Redwood Cottage, Meon	20.02.20E	
G-BOOD	Slingsby T.31 Motor Cadet III	xxxx	04.05.88	
	XE810 D G Bilcliffe (Evie, Orkney)	07.11.17P	
	Built by P J Titherington – project PFA 042-11264;		
	rebuilt from c/n 923 (IE 07.12.16)		
G-BOOE	Gulfstream American GA-7 Cougar	GA7-0093	07.06.88	
	N718G S J Olechnowicz Retford Gamston	28.01.20E	
G-BOOF	Piper PA-28-181 Archer II	28-7890084	16.06.88	
	N47510 Blackbushe Flying Club Ltd Blackbushe	05.02.20E	
G-BOOG	Piper PA-28RT-201T Turbo Arrow IV	28R-8331036	06.05.88	
	N4303K S J Brenchley Solent	09.05.18E	
	Official type 'PA-28RT-201T Turbo Cherokee		
	Arrow IV' is incorrect (NF 14.08.18)		
G-BOOH	Jodel D.112	481	16.05.88	
	F-BHVK T K Duffy Monewden	05.06.19P	
	Built by Etablissement Valladeau		
G-BOOL	Cessna 172N Skyhawk II	17272486	27.04.88	
	C-GJSY, N5271D A van Rooijen		
	Grimbergen, Belgium	20.06.19E	
G-BOOW	Aerosport Scamp	xxxx	10.05.88	
	D A Weldon Newcastle, RoI	12.01.20P	
	Built by C Tyers – project PFA 117-10709		
G-BOOX	Rutan Long-EZ	xxxx	03.05.88	
	I R Wilde Deenethorpe	25.10.19P	
	Built by I R Thomas & I R Wilde		
	– project PFA 74A-10844		
G-BOOZ	Cameron N-77	904	21.06.83	
	(G-BKSJ) J E F Kettlety Littleton Drew, Chippenham	09.05.15E	
	(NF 09.09.16)		
G-BOPA	Piper PA-28-181 Archer II	28-8490024	28.04.88	
	N43299 Flyco Ltd Denham	26.09.18E	
G-BOPC	Piper PA-28-161 Warrior II	28-8216006	06.05.88	
	N2124X Aeros Leasing Ltd Cardiff	26.09.19E	
G-BOPD	Bede BD-4	632	25.05.88	
	N632DH S T Dauncey Turners Arms Farm, Yearby	14.07.19P	
	Built by D E Hewes		
G-BOPH	Cessna TR182 Turbo Skylane RG II	R18201031	11.05.88	
	N756BJ J M Mitchell Derby	07.03.19E	
G-BOPO	FLS OA.7 Optica Series 301	021	17.05.88	
	EC-FVM, EC-435, G-BOPO J K Edgley Thruxton	18.06.17P	
G-BOPR	FLS OA.7 Optica Series 301	023	17.05.88	
	Aeroelvira Ltd Thruxton		
	(NF 28.03.18)		
G-BOPU	Grob G115	8059	10.05.88	
	J L Sparks St Athan	22.05.19E	
	Operated by Horizon Flight Training		
G-BORB	Cameron V-77	1348	24.08.88	
	M H Wolff London SW3	19.12.18E	
G-BORE	Colt 77A	642	24.05.88	
	C J Medcalf Enfield *'My Little Secret'*	20.04.11E	
	(NF 10.09.18)		

G-BORG	Campbell Cricket replica	xxxx	08.06.88
	R L Gilmore (Cressage, Shrewsbury)		25.04.05P
	Built by N G Bailey – project PFA G/03-1085		
	(NF 12.11.18)		
G-BORH	Piper PA-34-200T Seneca II	34-8070352	07.06.88
	N8261V Cancelled 21.02.11 by CAA		21.03.08
	Elstree *Open store 02.19*		
G-BORK	Piper PA-28-161 Warrior II	28-8116095	08.06.88
	G-IIIC, G-BORK, N83036 Turweston Flying Club Ltd		
	Turweston		30.04.19E
G-BORL	Piper PA-28-161 Warrior II	28-7816256	28.09.88
	N2190M Westair Flying Services Ltd Blackpool		10.04.19E
G-BORN	Cameron N-77	1777	13.05.88
	I Chadwick Caterham *'Ian'*		27.06.14E
	(IE 31.05.18)		
G-BORW	Cessna 172P Skyhawk II	17274301	23.08.88
	N51357 Briter Aviation Services Ltd Coventry		07.02.20E
G-BORY	Cessna 150L	15072292	27.05.88
	N6792G D H G Penney Sandtoft		21.07.09E
	Noted 04.18 (NF 13.03.18)		
G-BOSE	Piper PA-28-181 Archer II	28-8590007	17.05.88
	N143AV R Pawsey & P Pichon tr G-BOSE Group		
	White Waltham		01.06.19E
G-BOSJ	Nord 3400	124	26.05.88
	N9048P, French Army 'MOO' A I Milne		
	Great Friars' Thornes Farm, Swaffham		01.11.94
	As '124' in French AF c/s (NF 25.01.16)		
G-BOSM	Robin DR.253B Regent	168	24.05.88
	F-BSBH A G Stevens Mount Airey Farm, South Cave		11.09.18E
	Built by Centre-Est Aéronautique		
G-BOSN	Aérospatiale AS.355F1 Ecureuil 2	5266	22.08.88
	N2109L, 5N-AYL, G-BOSN, 5N-AYL		
	Helicopter & Pilot Services Ltd Wycombe Air Park		25.03.19E
G-BOSO	Cessna A152 Aerobat	A1520975	25.05.88
	N761PD Redhill Air Services Ltd Redhill		12.10.17E
	(IE 22.03.18)		
G-BOSU	Piper PA-28-140 Cherokee Cruiser	28-7325449	19.07.88
	N55635 Cancelled 12.07.07 as PWFU		08.06.01
	Lost Island, World of Golf, Sidcup		
	Unmarked with zebra stripes 06.13		
G-BOTD	Cameron O-105	1611	06.06.88
	J Taylor Huddlesford, Lichfield		18.05.19E
G-BOTF	Piper PA-28-151 Cherokee Warrior	28-7515436	08.06.88
	C-GGIF P E Preston tr G-BOTF Group Southend		24.11.19E
	Operated by Southend Flying Club		
G-BOTG	Cessna 152 II	15283035	09.06.88
	N46343 Donington Aviation Ltd East Midlands		20.02.20E
G-BOTH	Cessna 182Q Skylane II	18267558	09.06.88
	N202PS, N114SP, N5172N P G Guilbert Guernsey		30.11.19E
G-BOTI	Piper PA-28-161 Warrior II	28-7515251	09.06.88
	C-GNFF A S Bamrah t/a Falcon Flying Services		
	Biggin Hill		03.12.19E
	Originally built as PA-28-151 Cherokee Warrior		
G-BOTK	Cameron O-105	1765	09.06.88
	N Woodham Fawley, Southampton		06.03.11E
	(NF 13.09.16)		
G-BOTL[M]	Colt 42A SS HAB	466	23.11.82
	Cancelled 21.11.89 as WFU		
	With British Balloon Museum & Library, Newbury		
G-BOTN	Piper PA-28-161 Warrior II	28-7916261	09.06.88
	N2173N Flying Time Ltd Brighton City		24.09.19E
G-BOTO	Bellanca 7ECA Citabria	939-73	09.06.88
	N57398 A K Hulme Andrewsfield		31.08.18E
G-BOTP	Cessna 150J	15070736	02.08.88
	N61017 R F Finnis & C P Williams Thruxton		02.07.19E
G-BOTU	Piper J-3C-65 Cub	19045	08.07.88
	N98803, NC98803 T L Giles Browns Farm, Hitcham		02.04.19P
G-BOTV	Piper PA-32RT-300 Lance II	32R-7885153	07.06.88
	N36039 Robin Lance Aviation Associates Ltd		
	Rochester		21.05.15E
	Official type 'PA-32R-300 Cherokee Lance II'		
	is incorrect (NF 16.08.18)		

G-BOTW	Cameron V-77	1761	14.06.88
	M R Jeynes Redditch		27.10.10E
	(NF 24.04.18)		
G-BOUE	Cessna 172N Skyhawk II	17273235	08.08.88
	N6535F G N R Bradley tr Swift Group		
	Retford Gamston		17.02.20E
G-BOUJ	Cessna 150M	15076373	25.08.88
	N3058V L J R Huntington tr The UJ Flying Group		
	Holmbeck Farm, Burcott		30.11.17E
G-BOUK	Piper PA-34-200T Seneca II	34-7570124	31.08.88
	N33476 C J & R J Barnes East Midlands		10.11.19E
G-BOUM	Piper PA-34-200T Seneca II	34-7670136	03.08.88
	N8401C Sky Zone Services Aereos Lda		
	(São Domingos de Rana, Cascais, Portugal)		01.04.18E
	(IE 04.07.18)		
G-BOUT	Colomban MC-12 Cri-Cri	12-0135	14.06.88
	N120JN C K Farley Eaglescott		
	Built by J A Nelson; on rebuild 2017 (NF 17.10.14)		
G-BOUV	Montgomerie-Bensen B.8MR	xxxx	23.06.88
	L R Phillips (Shafton, Barnsley)		13.06.03P
	Built by P Wilkinson – project PFA G/01-1092		
	(NF 30.10.18)		
G-BOVB	Piper PA-15 Vagabond	15-180	23.06.88
	N4396H, NC4396H J R Kimberley		
	(Lawford, Manningtree)		18.05.05P
	(NF 29.06.18)		
G-BOVK	Piper PA-28-161 Warrior II	28-8516061	07.09.88
	N69168 Tayside Aviation Ltd Dundee		08.04.19E
G-BOVS	Cessna 150M	15078663	21.07.88
	N704KC Cancelled 01.09.05 as destroyed		
	Cotswold *Wreck dumped 05.14*		
G-BOVU	Stoddard-Hamilton Glasair III	3090	16.09.88
	E Andersen Solent		29.08.18P
	Built by A H Carrington		
G-BOWB	Cameron V-77	1767	13.07.88
	R A Benham Aston-on-Trent, Derby		
	'Richard's Rainbow'		09.05.19E
G-BOWK	Cameron N-90 HAB	1764	01.08.88
	Cancelled 08.11.01 as PWFU		
	Not Known *Inflated Pidley, 05.16*		
G-BOWM	Cameron V-56	1781	26.07.88
	R S Breakwell Billingsley, Bridgnorth		14.08.16E
G-BOWN	Piper PA-12 Super Cruiser	12-1912	26.07.88
	N3661N, NC3661N T L Giles Browns Farm, Hitcham		26.09.19P
G-BOWO	Cessna R182 Skylane RG II	R18200146	20.07.88
	(G-BOTR), N2301C P E Crees Rhosgoch		07.06.19E
G-BOWP	Jodel D.120A Paris-Nice	319	26.07.88
	F-BNZM T E CumminsmFull Sutton		05.06.19P
	Built by Société Wassmer Aviation		
G-BOWV	Cameron V-65	1800	24.08.88
	R A Harris Streatham Rise, Exeter *'Sigmund'*		02.03.20E
G-BOWY	Piper PA-28RT-201T Turbo Arrow IV	28R-8131114	08.08.88
	N404EL, N83648 D R D Lassiter, S G Moreley		
	& B Moseley Blackbushe		21.02.18E
	(NF 24.10.18)		
G-BOWZ	Bensen B.80V	xxxx	27.07.88
	U-B40, B-BOWZ A J Gascoigne		
	(Mansfield Woodhouse, Mansfield)		29.10.08P
	Built by W M Day – project PFA G/01-1060 (NF 07.08.18)		
G-BOXA	Piper PA-28-161 Warrior II	2816075	01.11.88
	N9149Q Westwings International Ltd (Swindon)		01.01.19E
G-BOXB	Piper PA-28-161 Warrior II	2816064	12.08.88
	N9142H Cancelled 26.08.03 by CAA		06.02.03
	Cotswold *Cockpit stored 01.18*		
G-BOXC	Piper PA-28-161 Warrior II	2816063	12.08.88
	N9142D M A Lee Durham Tees Valley		05.03.19E
	Operated by Eden Flight Training		
G-BOXG	Cameron O-77	1792	26.08.88
	Associazione Sportiva Dilettantistica Exper1ence		
	Torgiano, Perugia, Italy		31.07.19E
G-BOXH	Pitts S-1S	MP4	29.07.88
	N8LA S A Wilson (Dromara, Dromore)		20.06.19P

G

G-BOXJ	Piper J-3C-90 Cub (*L-4H-PI*)	12193	01.08.88
	OO-ADJ, 44-79897		
	A Bendkowski Rochester *'Jumping Jimmy'*		14.08.19P
	Fuselage No.12021; as '479897:JD' in USAF c/s		
G-BOXR	Grumman American GA-7 Cougar	GA7-0059	19.10.88
	N772GA London School of Flying Ltd Elstree		17.06.19E
	C/n plate shows manufacturer 'Gulfstream American'		
G-BOXT	Hughes 269C (*300*)	1040367	01.08.88
	SE-HMR, PH-JOH, D-HBOL		
	Jetscape Leisure Ltd Gloucestershire		22.12.17E
G-BOXV	Pitts S-1S	7-0433	08.08.88
	N27822 C Waddington Shobdon		20.11.18P
	Built by J R Castrillo		
G-BOXW	Cassutt Racer IIIM	xxxx	11.08.88
	D I Johnson (Leigh-on-Sea)		
	Built by D I Johnson – project PFA 34-11317		
	(NF 11.02.19)		
G-BOXY	Piper PA-28-181 Archer II	28-7990175	29.07.88
	N3073D Cancelled 22.10.02 as destroyed		11.04.04
	(Filton) *Cockpit used as simulator, 10.16*		
	by 2152 Sqn ATC		
G-BOYB	Cessna A152 Aerobat	A1520928	29.07.88
	N761AW Fly Elstree Ltd Elstree		13.09.19E
G-BOYC	Robinson R22 Beta	0837	22.08.88
	M D Thorpe t/a Yorkshire Helicopters Leeds Heliport		02.10.17E
	(NF 28.01.19)		
G-BOYF	Sikorsky S-76B	760343	15.09.88
	Darley Stud Management Company Ltd		
	London Stansted		24.11.19E
	Operated by Air Harrods		
G-BOYH	Piper PA-28-161 Warrior II	28-7715290	08.08.88
	N8795F R Nightingale Bristol		15.05.19E
	Originally built as PA-28-151 Cherokee Warrior		
G-BOYI	Piper PA-28-161 Warrior II	28-7816183	08.08.88
	N9032K Aviation Advice & Consulting Ltd Dundee		02.02.20E
	Operated by Tayside Aviation		
G-BOYL	Cessna 152 II	15284379	11.08.88
	N6232L Redhill Air Services Ltd Redhill		16.04.19E
G-BOYM	Cameron O-84	1796	25.08.88
	M P Ryan West Ilsley, Newbury *'Frontline'*		21.09.09E
	(NF 22.11.16)		
G-BOYO	Cameron V-20	1843	27.09.88
	J L Hilditch & T Ward Brighton & Nottingham		
	'Ross Balloon Rides'		
	(IE 09.07.18)		
G-BOYR	Cessna FA337G Super Skymaster	F33700070	09.09.88
	PH-RPE Cancelled 07.04.98, sold in Russia		17.07.98
	Mount Rule Farm, IoM *Built by Reims Aviation SA*		
	Wichita c/n 33701589; stored 01.14		
G-BOYV	Piper PA-28R-201T Turbo Cherokee Arrow III		
		28R-7703014	01.09.88
	N1143H P Lodge Liverpool John Lennon		18.06.19E
G-BOYX	Robinson R22 Beta	0862	25.08.88
	N90813 R Towle (Humshaugh, Hexham)		
	(NF 14.12.18)		
G-BOZI	Piper PA-28-161 Warrior II	28-8116120	14.07.88
	(G-BOSZ), N8318A Aerolease Ltd Conington		14.11.19E
G-BOZO	Gulfstream American AA-5B Tiger	AA5B-1282	12.08.88
	N4536Q J Le Moignan Guernsey		25.09.17E
	(IE 20.07.18)		
G-BOZR	Cessna 152 II	15284614	07.09.88
	N6083M Adam Russell Ltd (Ilford)		11.09.19E
G-BOZS	Pitts S-1C	221H	31.08.88
	N10EZ S D Blakey Bidford		15.05.14P
	Built by W A Orr (NF 09.07.18)		
G-BOZU	Aero Dynamics Sparrow Hawk Mk II	xxxx	12.12.88
	Cancelled 09.06.10 as PWFU		
	Bere Regis *Built by R V Phillimore – project*		
	PFA 184-11371; displayed at Skirmish paintball)		
G-BOZV	Robin DR.340 Major	416	09.08.88
	F-BRTS S D Kent & C J Turner		
	Garston Farm, Marshfield		10.01.20E

G-BOZW	Bensen B.8MR	xxxx	01.09.88
	M E Wills (Lytchett Matravers, Poole)		09.08.19P
	Built by M E Wills – project PFA G/01-1096		
G-BOZY	Cameron RTW-120	1770	01.09.88
	Magical Adventures Ltd West Bloomfield, MI, USA		21.04.97
	(NF 03.06.15)		
G-BOZZ	Gulfstream American AA-5B Tiger	AA5B-1155	22.08.88
	N4530N H Feldberg (Hagen, Germany)		25.10.19E

G-BPAA – G-BPZZ

G-BPAA	Smith Acro Advanced	xxxx	26.08.88
	B O & F A Smith Turners Arms Farm, Yearby		20.07.17P
	Built by B O Smith – project PFA 200-11528		
	(IE 14.08.18)		
G-BPAB	Cessna 150M	15077244	21.09.88
	N63335 A Carter		
	Rayne Hall Farm, Rayne		26.02.20E
G-BPAF	Piper PA-28-161 Cherokee Warrior II	28-7716142	06.09.88
	N3199Q S T & T W Gilbert Cotswold		09.10.19E
	Operated by Freedom Aviation/Kemble Aero Club		
G-BPAJ	de Havilland DH.82A Tiger Moth	83472	05.11.80
	G-AOIX, T7087 J M Hodgson & J D Smith		
	Brookfield Farm, Great Stukeley		10.08.19P
	Built by Morris Motors Ltd; possible composite		
	rebuild from original G-AMNN qv		
G-BPAL	de Havilland DHC-1 Chipmunk 22	C1/0437	29.10.86
	G-BCYE, WG350 K F & P Tomsett Portimão, Portugal		13.09.19E
	As 'WG350' in RAF c/s		
G-BPAW	Cessna 150M	15077923	05.09.88
	N8348U P D Sims tr G-BPAW Group Popham		25.02.20E
G-BPAY	Piper PA-28-181 Archer II	28-8090191	12.09.88
	N3568X White Waltham Airfield Ltd White Waltham		18.08.19E
G-BPBI	Cessna 152 II	15280368	16.09.88
	N24772 Cancelled 11.02.91 as PWFU		11.07.92
	Dublin Weston *On fire dump 05.14*		
G-BPBJ	Cessna 152 II	15283639	09.09.88
	N4793B P G Haines & W Shaw		
	Whaley Farm, New York		10.11.19E
G-BPBK	Cessna 152 II	15283417	09.09.88
	N49095 Swiftair Maintenance Ltd Doncaster Sheffield		20.08.19E
	Operated by Yorkshire Aero Club		
G-BPBM	Piper PA-28-161 Warrior II	28-7916272	12.09.88
	N3050N Redhill Air Services Ltd Nottingham City		24.03.19E
G-BPBO	Piper PA-28RT-201T Turbo Arrow IV	28R-8131195	28.09.88
	N8431H G N Broom & T R Lister Conington		08.07.19E
G-BPBP	Brügger MB.2 Colibri	xxxx	06.02.78
	D A Preston Cark		12.02.20P
	Built by B Perkins – project PFA 43-10246		
G-BPCA	Pilatus B-N BN-2B-26 Islander	2198	28.01.88
	G-BLNX Loganair Ltd Kirkwall		16.02.20E
G-BPCF	Piper J-3C-65 Cub	4532	12.05.89
	N140DC, N28033, NC28033 B M O'Brien Headcorn		21.05.19P
	Lippert Reed clipped-wing conversion – s/n SA811SW		
G-BPCI	Cessna R172K Hawk XP	R1722360	03.01.89
	N9976V N A Bairsto		
	Shacklewell Lodge Farm, Empingham		24.04.19E
G-BPCK	Piper PA-28-161 Warrior II	28-8016279	26.09.88
	N8529N, C-GMEI, N9519N		
	Compton Abbas Airfield Ltd Compton Abbas		
	'Compton Abbas Flying School & Restaurant'		07.05.19E
G-BPCL	Scottish Aviation Bulldog Srs 120/128	BH120/393	20.09.88
	HKG-6, G-31-19 Isohigh Ltd t/a 121 Group		
	North Weald		10.03.19E
	As 'HKG-6' in Royal Hong Kong AAF c/s		
G-BPCR	Mooney M.20K Mooney 231	25-0532	23.09.88
	N98433 R & T Harris Biggin Hill		27.06.18E
G-BPCV	Montgomerie-Bensen B.8MR	xxxx	11.10.88
	Cancelled 18.10.10 by CAA		25.07.91
	Rayne Hill Farm, Braintree *Built by J Fisher*		
	– project PFA G/01-1088; stored 12.15		
G-BPDE	Colt 56A HAB	1296	26.10.88
	Cancelled 13.12.01 by CAA		25.06.97
	Not Known *Inflated Amersfoort, 10.16*		

G-BPDJ Chris Tena Mini Coupe 275 04.10.88
N13877 R B McComish Bow, Totnes
Built by F H Walker; used as travelling exhibit for
Royal British Legion fundraising 2018 (NF 20.11.18)

G-BPDM CASA 1-131E Jungmann Series 2000 2058 24.10.88
Spanish AF E3B-369 J D Haslam
(Scruton, Northallerton) 22.06.96P
(NF 13.11.15)

G-BPDT Piper PA-28-161 Warrior II 28-8416004 22.12.88
N4317Z Westwings International Ltd (Swindon) 26.02.19E

G-BPDV Pitts S-1S 27P 15.09.88
N330VE J Vize tr G-BPDV Syndicate Leicester 27.06.19P
Built by C H Pitts

G-BPEL Piper PA-28-151 Cherokee Warrior 28-7415172 10.10.88
C-FEYM Cancelled 28.02.02 as WFU 08.02.92
Southend *Wreck stored dismantled 01.19*

G-BPEM Cessna 150K 15071707 24.10.88
N6207G D Wright Full Sutton 03.05.19E

G-BPEO Cessna 152 II 15283775 10.10.88
C-GQVO, (N5147B) Swiftair Maintenance Ltd
Wellesbourne Mountford 08.04.19E

G-BPES Piper PA-38-112 Tomahawk II 38-81A0064 02.11.88
N25728 Smart People Dont Buy Ltd Coventry 06.02.20E

G-BPEZ Colt 77A 1324 14.10.88
J W Adkins Market Harborough
'Thunder & Colt Balloons' 08.10.13E
Noted 05.16 (NF 22.09.15)

G-BPFD Jodel D.112 312 03.11.88
F-PHJT M & S Mills Plashes Farm, Bednall 15.08.19P
Built by Aero Club de L'Orne

G-BPFH Piper PA-28-161 Warrior II 28-8116201 03.11.88
N83723 Aircraft Engineers Ltd Glasgow Prestwick 02.10.15E
Stored 05.18 (NF 16.09.17)

G-BPFI Piper PA-28-181 Archer II 28-8090113 05.01.89
N8103G S D Hodgson & S Pegg Tatenhill 13.12.19E

G-BPFJ Cameron Club 90 SS HAB 1834 14.11.88
Cancelled 09.05.97 as WFU 10.12.93
Not Known *Inflated Pidley 04.14*
Budweiser Beer Can special shape

G-BPFL Davis DA-2A 051 27.10.88
N72RJ P E Barker RAF Benson 09.08.19P
Built by A Tribling

G-BPFM Aeronca 7AC Champion 7AC-4751 13.10.88
N1193E, NC1193E C C Burton Bodmin 03.04.19P

G-BPFZ Cessna 152 II 15285741 27.10.88
N94594 Devon & Somerset Flight Training Ltd
Dunkeswell 03.04.15E

G-BPGD Cameron V-65 4969 09.09.88
Gone With The Wind Ltd Bristol BS8 *'Silver Lining'* 07.03.19E
Original c/n 2000; rebuilt with new envelope
c/n 4969 c.08.01

G-BPGE Cessna U206C U2061013 07.11.88
N29017 K Brady tr Scottish Parachute Club
Strathallan 06.09.19E

G-BPGH EAA Acrosport II 422 14.11.88
N12JE R Clark & A C May Guernsey 11.09.12P
Built by J Ellenbaas (NF 24.02.16)

G-BPGK Aeronca 7AC Champion 7AC-7187 07.02.89
N4409E P J Clegg Newcastle, RoI *'Takeoff Time'* 30.07.18P

G-BPGU Piper PA-28-181 Archer II 28-8490025 26.10.88
N4330B G Underwood Nottingham City 12.03.19E

G-BPGZ Cessna 150G 15064912 14.11.88
N3612J J B Scott Blackpool 20.05.19E

G-BPHD Cameron N-42 HAB 1863 21.02.89
Cancelled 15.11.10 as TWFU 09.06.02
Not Known *Inflated Pidley 05.16*

G-BPHG Robin DR.400-180 Régent 1887 29.11.88
A R Paul Turweston 18.12.19E

G-BPHH Cameron V-77 1840 02.12.88
C D Aindow Horsmonden, Tonbridge 08.04.17E

G-BPHI Piper PA-38-112 Tomahawk 38-79A0002 22.11.88
N2535H M Fox t/a Flying Fox Aviation Bagby 24.11.13E
In open store 07.15 (NF 07.02.18)

G-BPHO Taylorcraft BC-12D 8497 10.01.89
N96197, NC96197 S Newlands & C O'Connell
tr Taylorcraft Flying Group (Malahide, Co Dublin
& Robinstown, Co Meath, RoI) *'Spirit of Missouri'* 22.11.19P

G-BPHP Taylorcraft BC-12-65 2799 12.12.88
N33948, NC33948 J M Brightwell Derby 09.08.11P
(NF 15.12.17)

G-BPHR de Havilland DH.82A Tiger Moth 045 03.01.89
N48DH, VH-BLX, RAAF A17-48
N Parry tr A17-48 Group Lotmead Farm, Wanborough 19.07.19P
Built by de Havilland Aircraft Proprietary Ltd,
Bankstown, Australia; as 'A17-48' in RAAF yellow c/s
with code '48' on cowling

G-BPHU Thunder Ax7-77 1365 19.12.88
R P Waite Newborough, Burton-on-Trent 26.05.17E

G-BPHZ Morane Saulnier MS.500 Criquet 53 17.04.89
F-BJQC, French Army Aero Vintage Ltd
(Wheel Park Farm, Westfield) 29.04.09P
Built as Type MS.505; converted to Type MS.500
standard 2018 (NF 06.12.18)

G-BPIF Bensen-Parsons Two-Place Gyroplane UK01 19.12.88
B J L P & W J A L de Saar (Destelbergen, Belgium) 28.03.96P
Built by W Parsons (NF 09.02.19)

G-BPII Denney Kitfox Model 1 213 15.12.88
K Bell tr Dolphin Flying Group (Prestwick) 21.12.16P
Built by R Derbyshire – project PFA 172-11496

G-BPIR Scheibe SF25E Super Falke 4332 15.12.88
N25SF, (D-KDFX) A P Askwith Rhosgoch 23.04.19E

G-BPIU Piper PA-28-161 Warrior II 28-7916303 28.12.88
N3028T T S Rafter tr Golf India Uniform Group
Fairoaks 03.04.19E

G-BPIV Bristol 149 Blenheim IV 10201 15.02.89
'Z5722', RCAF 10201 Blenheim (Duxford) Ltd Duxford 21.01.20P
Built by Fairchild Aircraft Ltd as Bolingbroke IVT;
rebuilt 2014 with Mk.I nose section;
as 'L6739:YP-Q' in RAF c/s; comprises Bolingbroke
fuselage ex RCAF 10201 & wings ex RCAF 9073

G-BPIZ Gulfstream American AA-5B Tiger AA5B-1154 14.02.89
N4530L N R F McNally Goodwood 21.08.19E

G-BPJG Piper PA-18-150 Super Cub 18-8350 04.01.89
SE-EZG, N4172Z N P Shields Enstone 23.12.18E

G-BPJS Piper PA-28-161 Cadet 2841025 12.01.89
EC-IBG, G-BPJS, N9154Z Redhill Air Services Ltd
Redhill 29.04.16E
(IE 22.03.18)

G-BPJW Cessna A150K Aerobat A1500127 04.01.89
CF-AJX, CF-AJX, N8427M G Duck
Beverley (Linley Hill) 30.08.13E
(IE 16.02.16)

G-BPKF Grob G115 8075 03.01.89
Swiftair Maintenance Ltd Coventry 27.01.20E

G-BPKK Denney Kitfox Model 1 xxxx 19.12.88
F McDonagh Full Sutton *'Judith'* 04.11.19P
Built by R W Holmes – project PFA 172-11411

G-BPKM Piper PA-28-161 Warrior II 28-7916341 06.01.89
PH-CKO, N2140X, N9630N Pure Aviation Support
Services Ltd Aberdeen Int'l 13.03.19E
Operated by Alexander Air Flight Training

G-BPKN^M Colt AS-80 Mk.II HA Airship 1297 11.01.89
Cancelled 07.01.91 by CAA 14.03.91
With British Balloon Museum & Library, Newbury

G-BPKT Piper J-5A Cub Cruiser 5-624 14.03.89
EI-CGV, G-BPKT, N35372, NC35372
A J Greenslade (Plymouth) 25.02.92P
As '5-624KT:Airship Squadron 32' in USN c/s
(NF 12.11.14)

G-BPLD^M Thunder & Colt AS-261 HA Airship 1380 25.01.89
Cancelled 13.06.89 – to F-WGGM, F-GHRI 05.91
to & *as F-WGGM*
With British Balloon Museum & Library, Newbury

G-BPLF Cameron V-77 HAB 1903 16.01.89
Cancelled 22.09.04 by CAA 05.06.01
Not Known *Inflated Tibenham 01.19*

G

G-BPLM	SNCAN Stampe SV.4C	1004	08.02.89
	F-BHET, French Army, F-BDKC		
	C J Jesson Headcorn		18.10.18E
	Built by Atelier industriel de l'Aéronautique		
G-BPLT^M	Bristol 20 M.1C replica	AJD-1	18.01.89
	Cancelled 22.06.89 – to CC-DMA		
	As 'C4988' Built by AJD Engineering Ltd Stored 2016		
	With Museo Nacional de Aeronautica de Chile, Los Cerillos		
G-BPLV	Cameron V-77	1822	23.01.89
	O LeClercq Etigny, Bourgogne-Franche-Comté, France	15.09.16E
G-BPLZ	Hughes 369HS (500)	910342S	15.02.89
	N126CM M A & R J Fawcett (Leeds LS12)	20.03.17E
	(IE 19.07.18)		
G-BPME	Cessna 152 II	15285585	24.01.89
	N94021 London School of Flying Ltd Elstree	27.03.19E
	Operated by Flight Training London Ltd		
G-BPMF	Piper PA-28-161 Warrior II	28-7515050	02.02.89
	C-GOXL A Hill & P A Lewis tr Mike Foxtrot Group		
	Walney Island	12.07.19E
	Originally built as PA-28-151 Cherokee Warrior		
G-BPML	Cessna 172M Skyhawk II	17267102	17.11.89
	N1435U N A Bilton Priory Farm, Tibenham	15.12.19E
G-BPMM	Champion 7ECA Citabria	498	22.03.89
	N5132T J McCullough Newtownards	25.10.19P
G-BPMU	Nord 3202B	70	26.01.89
	(G-BIZJ), N22546, French Army		
	E C Murgatroyd (Bromham, Bedford)		
	(NF 12.04.16)		
G-BPMW	QAC Quickie Q.2	xxxx	13.03.89
	G-OICI, G-OGKN P M Wright (Ipswich)		
	Built by R Davidson-Outbridge		
	– project PFA 094A-10790 (NF 16.11.18)		
G-BPMP^M	Douglas C-47A-50-DL Dakota	10073	02.02.89
	N54607, (N9842A), N54607, R Moroccan AF		
	20669/CNALM, CN-CCL, F-BEFA, 42-24211		
	Cancelled as WFU 18.04.95		
	Front fuselage only, unmarked		
	At Luchtvaart Hobby Shop, Aalsmeerderburg, Netherlands		
G-BPNI	Robinson R22 Beta	0948	06.02.89
	G J Collins (Lanark)		06.05.17E
	Rolled after touch-down West Calder 26.06.16		
	& substantially damaged		
G-BPNO	Moravan Zlin Z-526 Trener Master	930	18.02.86
	F-BPNO E Bunnage-Flavell Solent	07.06.19E
G-BPOB	Sopwith F.1 Camel replica	TM-10	14.03.89
	N8997 Bianchi Aviation Film Services Ltd Turweston	02.07.19P
	Built by Tallmantz Aviation Inc; as 'N6377' in RN c/s		
G-BPOM	Piper PA-28-161 Warrior II	28-8416118	15.02.89
	N4373Q, N9619N C Dale tr POM Flying Group		
	Humberside	23.10.19E
G-BPOS	Cessna 150M	15075905	21.02.89
	N66187 Hull Aero Club Ltd Beverley (Linley Hill)	19.04.19E
G-BPOT	Piper PA-28-181 Archer II	28-7790267	07.02.89
	N8807F P S Simpson Brighton City	25.03.20E
G-BPOU	Luscombe 8A	4159	14.02.89
	N1432K, NC1432K J L Grayer Kittyhawk Farm, Ripe	29.08.19P
G-BPOV^M	Cameron Magazine 90SS HAB	1890	10.03.89
	Cancelled 14.11.02 by CAA 'Forbes Capitalist Tool'	05.07.01
	Forbes Magazine shape		
	With Musée des Ballons, Chateau de Balleroy, France		
G-BPPE	Piper PA-38-112 Tomahawk	38-79A0189	15.02.89
	N2445C First Air Ltd Haverfordwest	05.08.16E
	Rebuilt with parts ex G-BNPL post 1995 (NF 24.01.18)		
G-BPPF	Piper PA-38-112 Tomahawk	38-79A0578	15.02.89
	N2329K D J Bellamy tr Bristol Strut Flying Group		
	Cotswold	20.05.19E
G-BPPK	Piper PA-28-151 Cherokee Warrior	28-7615054	10.03.89
	N7592C Damarah Ltd Biggin Hill	23.08.19E
	Operated by Falcon Flying Services		
G-BPPO	Luscombe 8A	2541	15.02.89
	N3519M, N71114, NC71114		
	P Dyer Oakside Farm, Ringmer		16.07.19P

G-BPPP	Cameron V-77	1700	29.02.88
	R J Michener tr Sarnia Balloon Group Andover		
	'Thruppence'		28.06.97A
	(IE 17.07.18)		
G-BPPZ	Taylorcraft BC-12D	7988	22.03.89
	N28286, NC28286 G C Smith Popham '37'	12.07.19P
G-BPRC	Cameron Elephant-77	1871	21.02.89
	A Schneider Südlohn, North Rhine-Westphalia,		
	Germany 'Auf zum Forellenhof nach Borken'	27.03.08A
	(IE 19.06.18)		
G-BPRD	Pitts S-1C	ZZ1	21.02.89
	N10ZZ M W Bodger Yeatsall Farm, Abbots Bromley	17.09.15P
	Built by P C Serkland (NF 16.01.17)		
G-BPRI	Aérospatiale AS.355F1 Ecureuil 2	5181	22.02.89
	G-TVPA, G-BPRI, N364E MW Helicopters Ltd		
	Stapleford	12.02.19E
	Operated by Excel Charter Ltd		
G-BPRJ	Aérospatiale AS.355F1 Ecureuil 2	5201	22.02.89
	N368E PLM Dollar Group Ltd Dalcross Heliport	06.12.19E
	Uses callsign 'Osprey 61'		
G-BPRL	Aérospatiale AS.355F1 Ecureuil 2	5154	22.02.89
	N362E MW Helicopters Ltd Stapleford	02.11.14E
	Operated by Excel Charter Ltd (IE 23.09.15)		
G-BPRM	Reims/Cessna F172L	F17200825	20.04.88
	G-AZKG BJ Aviation Ltd Welshpool	28.01.20E
G-BPRO	Cessna A150K Aerobat	A1500221	01.03.89
	N221AR, VP-LAQ, 8P-LAC, N5921J		
	Cancelled 23.11.00 by CAA		24.03.99
	Great Yarmouth		
	Displayed 10.16 at Louis The Lion Adventure Park		
G-BPRV	Piper PA-28-161 Warrior II	28-8316039	24.02.89
	N4292G Cancelled 20.06.97 as destroyed		15.08.98
	Dunkeswell Cockpit stored 01.18		
G-BPRX	Aeronca 11AC Chief	11AC-94	03.03.89
	N86288, NC86288 A F Kutz		
	(Baienfurt, Baden-Württemberg, Germany)		04.10.19P
G-BPRY	Piper PA-28-161 Warrior II	28-8416120	02.03.89
	N4373Y, N9621N White Wings Aviation Ltd		
	East Midlands '17'		29.03.19E
G-BPSH	Cameron V-77 HAB	1837	21.02.89
	Cancelled 26.01.16 as PWFU		05.04.97
	Not Known Inflated Pidley 05.16		
G-BPSL	Cessna 177 Cardinal	17701138	03.03.89
	N659SR Cancelled 20.01.16 as PWFU		21.07.15
	Kings Farm, Thurrock Stored 05.17		
G-BPSO	Cameron N-90	1959	10.03.89
	J Oberprieler Mauern, Bavaria, Germany		24.08.14E
	(NF 18.01.16)		
G-BPSP^M	Cameron Ship 90SS HAB	1848	10.03.89
	Cancelled 14.11.02 by CAA 'Santa Maria'	17.06.94
	Columbus Santa Maria shape		
	With Musée des Ballons, Chateau de Balleroy, France		
G-BPSR	Cameron V-77	1962	10.03.89
	K J A Maxwell Uckfield 'Norma Jean'	11.05.05
	(NF 15.06.18)		
G-BPTA	Stinson 108-2 Voyager	108-3429	22.03.89
	N429C, NC429C M L Ryan Garston Farm, Marshfield	11.03.18E
	Built by Consolidated Vultee Aircraft Corporation		
	(IE 01.06.18)		
G-BPTD	Cameron V-77	2001	14.03.89
	J Lippett Coat, Martock		31.05.04A
	(NF 14.04.16)		
G-BPTE	Piper PA-28-181 Archer II	28-7690178	09.03.89
	N8553E A J Gomes Biggin Hill	07.09.19E
G-BPTG	Rockwell Commander 112TC	13067	31.03.89
	N4577W B Ogunyemi Perth	28.05.19E
G-BPTI	SOCATA TB-20 Trinidad	414	21.04.89
	N41BM N Davis Blackbushe	17.07.19E
G-BPTL	Cessna 172N Skyhawk II	17268652	22.03.89
	N733YJ M J Spittal Fenland	20.10.19E
G-BPTS	CASA 1-131E Jungmann Series 2000	E3B-153	23.05.89
	Spanish AF E3B-153, '781-75' E P Parkin Derby	25.09.18P
	As 'E3B-153:781-75' in Spanish AF c/s (IE 01.03.19)		

G-BPTU	Cessna 152 II	15282955	22.03.89
	N45946 Cancelled 13.10.14 by CAA		21.10.06
	Little Staughton *Stored dismantled 01.18*		

G-BPTV	Bensen B.8	xxxx	30.03.89
	C Munro (Trawden, Colne)		
	Built by L Chiappi – project PFA G/01-1058		
	(NF 06.11.18)		

G-BPTZ	Robinson R22 Beta	0958	22.03.89
	Kuki Helicopter Sales Ltd & S J Nicholls		
	Retford Gamston		12.01.18E

G-BPUA	EAA Biplane	SAAC-O2	30.03.89
	EI-BBF T M Leitan & N C Scanlan Enstone		18.10.19P
	Built by B B Feeley – project SAAC-02		

G-BPUB	Cameron V-31 Air Chair	1114	15.03.89
	M T Evans Radstock		02.10.16E
	(IE 07.06.18)		

G-BPUL	Piper PA-18A-150 Super Cub (*L-18C-PI*)	18-2517	12.04.89
	OO-LUL, PH-NEV B M Reed tr Vintage Tug Group		
	Lasham		22.04.19E
	Fuselage No. may be in 18-25xx series		

G-BPUM	Cessna R182 Skylane RG II	R18200915	02.05.89
	N738DZ R C Chapman Marley Hall, Ledbury		02.08.19E

G-BPUP	Whittaker MW7	171-11-473	02.08.89
	J H Beard (Buckfast, Buckfastleigh)		
	Built by J H Beard – project PFA 171-11473		
	(NF 31.05.16)		

G-BPUR	Piper J-3L-65 Cub	4708	14.06.89
	N30228, NC30228 G R J Caunter Popham		14.05.19P
	Fuselage No.4764; as '379994:J-52' in USAAF c/s		

G-BPUU	Cessna 140	13722	31.03.89
	N4251N, NC4251N D R Speight Full Sutton		05.03.15E
	(IE 25.04.15)		

G-BPUY	Cessna 150K	15071427	25.04.89
	N8386U Cancelled 22.12.95 by CAA		
	Plaistows Farm, St Albans *Noted 06.16*		

G-BPVA	Cessna 172F Skyhawk	17252286	13.04.89
	N8386U P Makin & M Stafford tr South Lancashire		
	Flyers Group Manchester Barton		13.10.19E

G-BPVE^M	Bleriot Type XI 1909 replica	1	20.06.89
	N1197 Bianchi Aviation Film Services Ltd		
	Stow Maries		29.06.01P
	Built by H Troutman; as '10' (NF 05.11.18)		

G-BPVH	Cub Aircraft J-3 Prospector	178C	07.04.89
	CF-DRY D E Cooper-Maguire		
	Frieslands Farm, Washington		18.08.05P
	Built by Cub Aircraft Corp, Hamilton, Ontario, Canada;		
	official type 'Piper J3C-65 Cub' is incorrect (NF 16.10.15)		

G-BPVI	Piper PA-32R-301 Saratoga SP	3213021	24.04.89
	N91685 M T Coppen Goodwood		26.02.19E

G-BPVK	Varga 2150A Kachina	VAC-85-77	04.05.89
	N4626V M W Olliver Ranston Farm, Iwerne Courtney		28.07.19P

G-BPVN	Piper PA-32R-301T Turbo Saratoga SP	32R-8029073	14.04.89
	N8178W O Green Gloucestershire		03.02.20E

G-BPVO	Cassutt Racer IIIM	DG1	13.04.89
	N19DD J B Wilshaw Priory Farm, Tibenham		
	'VooDoo' & '2'		21.05.18P
	Built by D Giorgi		

G-BPVW	CASA 1-131E Jungmann Series 2000	2133	17.05.89
	Spanish AF E3B-559 C & J Labeij Goodwood		18.06.09P
	(IE 27.07.15)		

G-BPVZ	Luscombe 8E Silvaire Deluxe	5565	09.05.89
	N2838K, NC2838K S M Thomas & A P Wilkie		
	Morgansfield, Fishburn		30.10.19P

G-BPWC	Cameron V-77 HAB	1986	12.04.89
	Cancelled 25.07.17 as PWFU		19.07.17
	Not Known *Inflated Ragley Hall 05.18 'Hot Flush'*		

G-BPWE	Piper PA-28-161 Warrior II	28-8116143	02.05.89
	N8330P Warrior BPWE Ltd Stapleford		19.03.20E

G-BPWG	Cessna 150M	15076707	10.04.89
	(G-BPTK), N45029 W Spicer tr GB Pilots		
	Wilsford Group Hanbeck Farm, Wilsford		15.05.19E

G-BPWK	Sportavia-Putzer RF5B Sperber	51036	17.04.89
	N56JM, (D-KEAR) K J Burns tr G-BPWK Group		
	Husbands Bosworth		04.07.16P
	Overran runway landing Usk 03.06.16 & damaged		
	(NF 19.10.16)		

G-BPWL	Piper PA-25-235 Pawnee	25-2304	14.04.89
	N6690Z, G-BPWL, N6690Z M H Simms		
	(Shipham, Thetford)		08.07.11E
	(NF 15.02.19)		

G-BPWM	Cessna 150L	15072820	17.04.89
	N1520Q P d'A Button Old Sarum		27.01.19E

G-BPWN	Cessna 150L	15074325	17.04.89
	N19308 R J Grantham (Radstock, Bath)		02.02.20E

G-BPWR	Cessna R172K Hawk XP	R1722953	21.04.89
	N758AZ D T A & J A Rees Haverfordwest		20.06.19E

G-BPWS	Cessna 172P Skyhawk II	17274306	21.04.89
	N51387 Chartstone Ltd Redhill		14.03.20E

G-BPXA	Piper PA-28-181 Archer II	28-8390064	12.05.89
	N4305T R Carr & G P Robinson		
	tr Cherokee Flying Group Netherthorpe		26.04.19E

G-BPXE	Enstrom 280C Shark	1089	21.04.89
	N379KH, C-GMLH, N660H A M Healy		
	Hampden Manor, Little Hampden		06.11.19E

G-BPXJ	Piper PA-28RT-201T Turbo Arrow IV	28R-8231023	21.04.89
	N8061U E Swift Newcastle, RoI		11.06.18E

G-BPXX	Piper PA-34-200T Seneca II	34-7970069	21.04.89
	N923SM, N9556N M Magrabi Bournemouth		22.12.17E
	(NF 25.06.18)		

G-BPYJ	Wittman W.8 Tailwind	xxxx	12.05.89
	J P & Y Mills Ashcroft		17.08.19P
	Built by J Dixon – project PFA 031-11028		

G-BPYK	Thunder Ax7-77	1166	15.05.89
	P J Waller Wymondham		29.06.19E

G-BPYL	Hughes 369D (*500*)	1000796D	10.05.89
	N65AM, G-BPYL, HB-XKT Morcorp (BVI) Ltd		
	Little Park Farm, Somerton		23.12.15E
	(IE 03.08.17)		

G-BPYN	Piper J-3C-65 Cub (*L-4H-PI*)	11422	14.03.79
	F-BFYN, HB-OFN, 43-30131		
	D W Stubbs tr Aquila Group White Waltham		18.09.19P

G-BPYR	Piper PA-31 Navajo C	31-7812032	15.05.89
	G-ECMA, N27493 2 Excel Aviation Ltd Sywell		04.01.20E

G-BPYT	Cameron V-77	1984	09.05.89
	M H Redman Stalbridge, Sturminster Newton		
	(NF 08.02.19)		

G-BPYV	Cameron V-77 HAB	1992	17.05.89
	Cancelled 15.10.12 as PWFU		06.05.11
	Not Known *Inflated Longleat 09.18*		
	'Spa Vehicle Electrics'		

G-BPZB	Cessna 120	8898	25.05.89
	N89853, NC89853 J F Corkin tr Cessna 120 Group		
	Redhill		06.11.19P

G-BPZC	Luscombe 8A	4322	06.06.89
	N1595K, NC1595K C C & J M Lovell		
	(Kingsclere, Newbury)		
	(NF 22.10.15)		

G-BPZD	SNCAN NC.858S	97	26.01.79
	F-BEZD G Richards tr Zulu Delta Syndicate		
	Acton Farm, Wittersham		21.06.19P

G-BPZE	Luscombe 8E Silvaire Deluxe	3904	06.06.89
	N1177K, NC1177K M A Watts		
	Roughay Farm, Lower Upham		02.05.08P
	(NF 30.01.19)		

G-BPZM	Piper PA-28RT-201 Arrow IV	28R-7918238	12.05.89
	G-ROYW, G-CRTI, SE-ICY M D Darragh Exeter Int'l		27.10.18E

G-BPZY	Pitts S-1C	RN-1	15.05.89
	N1159 J S Mitchell White Waltham		08.05.19P
	Built by R N Newbauer		

G-BRAA – G-BRZZ

G-BRAA (2) Pitts S-1C 101-GM 12.05.89
N14T D A Whitmore tr Haverfordwest Pitts
Haverfordwest 03.12.19P
Built by G R Miller

G-BRAJ Cameron V-77 HAB 1876 25.05.89
Cancelled 17.12.04 by CAA
Northampton *Inflated Pidley 04.18*

G-BRAK Cessna 172N Skyhawk II 17273795 23.06.88
C-GBPN, (N5438J) Falcon Flying Services Ltd
Biggin Hill 27.10.19E

G-BRAM[M] Mikoyan MiG-21PF xxxx 22.05.89
Hungarian AF 503 Cancelled 16.04.99 by CAA
As '503' in Hungarian Air Force c/s
With Royal Air Force Cosford Museum

G-BRAP Thermal Aircraft 104 001 07.08.98
J Yarrow Wendover, Aylesbury
Built by J Yarrow (IE 23.04.18)

G-BRAR Aeronca 7AC Champion 7AC-6564 14.06.89
N2978E, NC2978E R B Armitage
Maypole Farm, Chislet 16.12.19P

G-BRBA Piper PA-28-161 Warrior II 28-7916109 25.05.89
N2090B Over the Air Group Ltd (Naburn, York) 11.02.20E

G-BRBC North American T-6G-NH Texan 182-156 04.09.92
Ital.AF MM54099, 51-14470 A P Murphy
(Little Canfield, Dunmow)
(NF 07.11.18)

G-BRBD Piper PA-28-151 Cherokee Warrior 28-7415315 28.06.89
N41702 Compton Abbas Airfield Ltd
Compton Abbas *'Shaftesbury Belle'* 26.09.19E

G-BRBE Piper PA-28-161 Warrior II 28-7916437 13.06.89
N2815D Jesterhoudt Holding BV
Lelystad, Netherlands 20.01.12E
(NF 08.05.18)

G-BRBG Piper PA-28-180 Cherokee Archer 28-7505248 12.06.89
N3927X P M Carter Great Massingham 18.12.19E

G-BRBH Cessna 150H 15069283 13.06.89
N50410 Horizon Aircraft Engineering Ltd
St Athan 03.01.20E

G-BRBI Cessna 172N Skyhawk II 17269613 07.07.89
N737RJ N A J Robinson tr Skyhawk Flying Group
Popham 19.11.19E

G-BRBJ Cessna 172M Skyhawk II 17267492 26.05.89
N73476 J H Sandham t/a JH Sandham Aviation
Carlisle Lake District 12.01.02
(NF 28.11.17)

G-BRBK Robin DR.400-180 Régent 1915 31.05.89
A D Friday Lydd 15.02.19E

G-BRBL Robin DR.400-180 Régent 1920 05.07.89
R J Kelly & U A Schliessler Wycombe Air Park 20.04.19E

G-BRBM Robin DR.400-180 Régent 1921 05.07.89
R W Davies Little Engeham Farm, Woodchurch 17.04.19E

G-BRBN Pitts S-1S 3 14.07.89
N81BG A George tr G-BRBN Flying Group
Gloucestershire 07.11.18P
Built by W L Garner

G-BRBO Cameron V-77 1877 30.05.89
D Joly London W1 *'Patches'* 19.07.18E

G-BRBP Cessna 152 II 15284915 14.06.89
N5324P The Pilot Centre Ltd Denham 28.01.20E

G-BRBV Piper J-4A Cub Coupe 4-1080 13.06.89
N27860, NC27860 P Clarke (Shipston-on-Stour) 14.01.20P

G-BRBW Piper PA-28-140 Cherokee Cruiser 28-7425153 03.07.89
N40737 Air Navigation & Trading Company Ltd
Blackpool 06.10.19E

G-BRBX Piper PA-28-181 Archer II 28-7690185 20.07.89
N8674E A R Dent & K Foster
tr Trent 199 Flying Group Tatenhill 03.05.19E

G-BRCA Jodel D.112 1203 11.07.89
F-BLIU R C Jordan Marsh Hill Farm, Aylesbury 01.04.19P
Built by Etablissement Valladeau

G-BRCD Cessna A152 Aerobat A1520796 08.06.89
N7377L D J Hockings Spilsted Farm, Sedlescombe 14.09.07
On rebuild 11.17 (NF 04.04.16)

G-BRCE Pitts S-1C 1001 22.06.89
N4611G M P & S T Barnard
(Stony Stratford, Milton Keynes) 25.11.97P
Built by Blake & Davis (NF 04.11.15)

G-BRCJ Cameron H-20 2028 13.06.89
(OO-BXV), G-BRCJ P A Sweatman Coventry CV5 09.10.13E
(IE 12.06.15)

G-BRCM Cessna 172L Skyhawk 17259960 19.06.89
N3860Q D C C Handley & D A Williams
Little Staughton 17.09.08E
On rebuild 06.13 (IE 13.06.16)

G-BRCO Cameron H-20 HAB 2030 19.06.89
Cancelled 09.10.14 as PWFU 10.01.03
Not Known *Inflated Pidley 05.16*

G-BRCT Denney Kitfox Model 2 xxxx 23.06.89
P R Dalton (Great Longstone, Bakewell) 04.06.19P
Built by M L Roberts – project PFA 172-11521

G-BRCV Aeronca 7AC Champion 7AC-282 19.09.89
N81661, NC81661 J Davies Haverfordwest 07.06.18P
(IE 17.09.18)

G-BRCW Aeronca 11BC Chief 11AC-386 16.10.89
N85964, NC85964 R B Griffin
Little Trostrey Farm, Kemeys Commander 27.11.19P
Official c/n '11AC-366' is incorrect

G-BRDB Zenair CH701 xxxx 11.07.89
Cancelled 04.03.10 as destroyed 24.10.10
Zoersel-Oostmalle. Antwerp
Built by D L Bowtell – project PFA 187-11412
On rebuild 07.12

G-BRDD Mudry CAP 10B 224 03.08.88
T A Smith Tibenham 10.07.19E

G-BRDF Piper PA-28-161 Cherokee Warrior II 28-7716085 26.06.89
N1139Q White Waltham Airfield Ltd
White Waltham 28.08.19E
Operated by West London Aero Services

G-BRDG Piper PA-28-161 Warrior II 28-7816047 26.06.89
N44934 A S Bamrah t/a Falcon Flying Services
Biggin Hill 28.06.19E

G-BRDJ Luscombe 8F Silvaire 3411 28.06.89
N71984, NC71984 D Ratcliffe tr G-BRDJ Group
Popham 18.07.19P
Official type data 'Luscombe 8F' is incorrect

G-BRDM Piper PA-28-161 Cherokee Warrior II 28-7716004 26.06.89
N8464F White Waltham Airfield Ltd White Waltham 07.09.19E
Operated by West London Aero Services

G-BRDO Cessna 177B Cardinal 17702166 13.07.89
N35030 K Khan & D Malloch tr Cardinal Aviation
Durham Tees Valley 08.08.19E

G-BRDV[M] Viking Spitfire prototype replica HD36/001 03.07.89
Cancelled 19.05.00 as WFU 18.02.95
As 'K5054' in RAF c/s
Built by Viking Wood Products – project PFA 130-10796
On loan from Replica Spitfire Ltd to Kent
Battle of Britain Museum, Hawkinge

G-BRDW Piper PA-24 Comanche 24-1733 12.03.90
N6612P I P Gibson (Esher) 19.08.19E

G-BREA Bensen B.8MR xxxx 06.07.89
D J Martin (Glazebury, Warrington) 30.11.11P
Built by R Firth – project PFA G/01-1006 (NF 17.11.14)

G-BREB Piper J-3C-65 Cub 7705 03.07.89
N41094, NC41094 J R Wraight Pent Farm, Postling 04.06.19P

G-BREM Air Command 532 Elite 0614 20.07.89
Cancelled 16.11.01 by CAA 25.03.91
Garyvard, Isle of Lewis *Built by P Leach &*
D Gunning – project PFA G/04-1139
Stored dismantled 06.14

G-BRER Aeronca 7AC Champion 7AC-6758 12.07.89
N3157E, NC3157E M Hough Bodmin 16.03.16P
(IE 20.09.18)

G-BREU Montgomerie-Bensen B.8MR xxxx 20.07.89
J S Firth Sherburn-in-Elmet 19.04.19P
Built by M Hayward – project PFA G/01A-1137

G-BREX	Cameron O-84	2019	14.07.89
	R T Gourley Maghera		29.05.19E
G-BREY	Taylorcraft BC-12D	7299	14.07.89
	N43640, NC43640 R A C Lees tr BREY Group		
	Leicester		21.05.19P
G-BREZ	Cessna 172M Skyhawk	17266742	14.07.89
	EI-CHS, G-BREZ, N80775 R G Rutty Dunkeswell		01.08.19E
G-BRFB	Rutan Long-EZ	xxxx	14.07.89
	N M Robbins	Sleap	17.11.19P
	Built by R A Gardiner – project PFA 074A-10646		
G-BRFCM	Percival P.57 Sea Prince T.1	P57-71	10.09.80
	N7SY, G-BRFC, WP321 M A Stott St Athan		
	Displayed South Wales Aircraft Museum as 'WP321'		
	(NF 19.07.16)		
G-BRFF	Colt 90A HAB	1548	14.07.89
	Cancelled 13.12.01 by CAA		17.07.97
	Not Known Inflated Donnington Grove Club 01.19		
	'Zycomm'		
G-BRFH	Colt 90A HAB	1543	14.07.89
	Cancelled 09.11.01 as PWFU		14.03.97
	Not Known Inflated Pidley 05.16		
G-BRFI	Aeronca 7DC Champion	7AC-4609	01.08.89
	N1058E, NC1058E S J Ball (Overseal, Swadlincote)		
	(NF 07.07.15)		
G-BRFJ	Aeronca 11AC Chief	11AC-796	28.07.89
	N9163E, NC9163E J M Mooney		
	Loch View House, Limerigg		11.09.02P
	(NF 01.03.16)		
G-BRFM	Piper PA-28-161 Warrior II	28-7916279	17.10.89
	N2234P Swiftair Maintenance Ltd Coventry		26.06.19E
G-BRFW	Montgomerie-Bensen B.8 Two-Seat	xxxx	20.07.89
	A J Barker Sorbie Farm, Kingsmuir		07.09.06P
	Built by J M Montgomerie – project PFA G/01-1073		
	(NF 28.03.18)		
G-BRFX	Pazmany PL-4A	xxxx	14.07.89
	D E Hills (Ipswich)		
	Built by D E Hills – project PFA 017-10079 (NF 22.10.18)		
G-BRGD	Cameron O-84	2043	20.07.89
	P A Davies Loxton, Axbridge		02.05.19E
G-BRGF	Luscombe 8E Silvaire Deluxe	5475	20.07.89
	N23FP, N944BL, N2748K, NC2748K		
	J A Coutts (Nuttree Farm, Redenhall)		31.07.17P
	(NF 08.12.17)		
	Hit crop, overturned landing Old Buckenham		
	11.06.17 & substantially damaged		
G-BRGI	Piper PA-28-180 Cherokee E	28-5827	24.07.89
	N77VG, N11VG R A Buckfield Rochester		29.08.19E
G-BRGT	Piper PA-32-260 Cherokee Six	32-658	07.11.89
	N3744W T J W Hood & A A Mattacks Biggin Hill		25.05.18E
G-BRGW	Gardan GY-20 Minicab	PFA 1823	13.11.78
	R G White (Bossington Farm, Bossington)		13.01.20P
	Built by R G White – project PFA 1823;		
	constructed to JB.01 Minicab standard		
G-BRHA	Piper PA-32RT-300 Lance II	32R-7985076	27.07.89
	N2093P P Mackinnon tr Lance G-BRHA Group		
	Earls Colne		29.11.19E
G-BRHG	Colt 90A HAB	1568	11.09.89
	Cancelled 31.08.12 as PWFU		17.08.04
	Not Known Inflated Longleat 09.18		
G-BRHLM	Montgomerie-Bensen B 8MR	xxxx	07.08.89
	Cancelled 19.10.10 as PWFU		26.08.03
	Built by N D Marshall – project PFA G/01A-1123		
	With Solway Aviation Museum, Carlisle Lake District		
G-BRHO	Piper PA-34-200 Seneca	34-7350037	20.09.89
	N15222 Transair (CI) Ltd Guernsey		24.03.16E
G-BRHP	Aeronca O-58B Grasshopper	058B8533	02.08.89
	N58JR, N46536, 43-1923 R B McComish Bow, Totnes		30.05.19P
	Type is L-3C-AE if US Army s/n '43-1923' is correct;		
	as '3-1923' in USAAC c/s		
G-BRHR	Piper PA-38-112 Tomahawk	38-79A0969	21.08.89
	N2377P Tango Romeo Aviation Ltd Elstree		23.10.19E
G-BRHX	Luscombe 8E Silvaire Deluxe	5114	08.08.89
	N176M, N2387K, NC2387K R N R Bellamy Bodmin		17.02.20P

G-BRHY	Luscombe 8E Silvaire Deluxe	5138	08.08.89
	N2411K, NC2411K R A Keech Sleap		03.07.19P
G-BRIA	Cessna 310L	310L0010	04.08.89
	N2210F Cancelled 17.12.10 by CAA		26.09.08
	Cotswold Fuselage stored 12.18		
G-BRIH	Taylorcraft BC-12D	7421	24.08.89
	N43762, NC43762 M J Medland		
	Hinton-in-the-Hedges		17.04.08P
	Stored 04.15 (NF 02.03.16)		
G-BRIJ	Taylorcraft F-19	F-119	23.08.89
	N3863T E N L Troffigue Compton Abbas		12.06.01P
	Noted less wings & engine 09.18 (NF 10.01.18)		
G-BRIK	Nipper T.66 RA.45 Series 3	xxxx	26.04.77
	G Kingaby Clipgate Farm, Denton		10.10.19P
	Built by C W R Piper – project PFA 025-1017;		
	construction was rebuild of G-AVKH		
G-BRIL	Piper J-5A Cub Cruiser	5-572	02.08.89
	N35183, NC35183 D J Bone		
	Spite Hall Farm, Pinchinthorpe		09.04.19P
G-BRIV	SOCATA TB-9 Tampico Club	939	24.08.89
	S J Taft Strubby		11.10.17E
	(IE 22.11.18)		
G-BRIY	Taylorcraft DF-65	6183	01.02.90
	N59687, NC59687, 42-58678 S R Potts		
	Selby House Farm, Stanton		10.07.98P
	Built as Taylorcraft TG-6 glider (NF 26.03.18)		
G-BRJA	Luscombe 8A	3744	12.09.89
	N1017K, NC1017K A D Keen Halwell		26.04.12P
	(IE 18.09.17)		
G-BRJC	Cessna 120	xxxx	21.08.89
	N1833N, NC1833N J Hodgson Breighton		27.02.20P
	Rebuilt with unidentified replacement fuselage		
	2017; original fuselage c/n 12077 to South Yorkshire		
	Air Museum 2017		
G-BRJC (1)M	Cessna 120	12077	
	Original fuselage only		
	With South Yorkshire Aircraft Museum, Doncaster		
G-BRJK	Luscombe 8A	4205	21.08.89
	N1478K, NC1478K R C Dyer & M Richardson		
	(Salisbury & Epsom)		17.08.17P
G-BRJL	Piper PA-15 Vagabond	15-157	21.08.89
	N4370H, NC4370N A R Williams		
	Garston Farm, Marshfield		21.12.19P
G-BRJN	Pitts S-1C	1-MA	23.08.89
	N6A W Chapel Sherburn-in-Elmet		28.06.19P
	Built by M G Acker		
G-BRJV	Piper PA-28-161 Cadet	2841167	24.08.89
	N9185G Redhill Air Services Ltd Redhill		07.02.20E
G-BRJX	Rand Robinson KR-2	xxxx	22.08.89
	J R Bell (Parcllyn, Cardigan)		15.04.97P
	Built by C Willcocks – project PFA 129-11386		
	(NF 30.08.18)		
G-BRJY	Rand Robinson KR-2	xxxx	22.08.89
	R E Taylor (Bonar Bridge, Ardgay)		23.05.96P
	Built by J M Scott – project PFA 129-11308		
	(NF 09.03.18)		
G-BRKC	Auster 5J1 Autocrat	2749	31.08.89
	F-BFYT J W Conlon Bury Farm, High Easter		01.08.19P
G-BRKH	Piper PA-28-236 Dakota	28-7911003	30.08.89
	N21444 T A White White Waltham		06.04.19E
G-BRKL	Cameron H-34	2075	29.08.89
	R M Powell Upper Timsbury, Romsey		21.01.19E
G-BRKW	Cameron V-77	2093	01.09.89
	T J Parker Asheldham, Southminster		11.12.09E
	(NF 08.03.18)		
G-BRKX	Air Command 532 Elite	0619	08.09.89
	Cancelled 28.02.02 by CAA		10.12.90
	Garyvard, Isle of Lewis 'Cloud Steamer'		
	Built by K Davis – project PFA G/04-1150; for sale 12.17		
G-BRKY	Viking Dragonfly Mk II	xxxx	07.09.89
	Polar Bear Services Ltd (Reading)		08.06.94P
	Built by G D Price – project PFA 139-11117 (NF 20.01.17)		

G-BRLB	Air Command 532 Elite	0622	04.09.89
	F G Shepherd (Leadgate, Alston)		
	Built by H R Bethune (NF 16.01.15)		

G-BRLF	Campbell Cricket replica	xxxx	06.09.89
	J L G McLane (Gilling East, York)		11.09.13P
	Built by D Wood – project PFA G/03-1077 (NF 21.03.18)		

| G-BRLG | Piper PA-28RT-201T Turbo Arrow IV | 28R-8431027 | 12.09.89 |
| | N4379P, N9600N N R Quirk Liverpool John Lennon | | 22.02.19E |

G-BRLI	Piper J-5A Cub Cruiser	5-822	23.08.89
	N35951, NC35951 D J M Eardley		
	(Crissay-sur-Manse, Indre-et-Loire, France)		03.01.20P

G-BRLL	Cameron A-105	2032	07.09.89
	P A Sweatman Coventry CV5		04.04.06
	(NF 26.06.15)		

G-BRLO	Piper PA-38-112 Tomahawk	38-78A0621	26.10.89
	N2397K, N9680N A J Gomes Biggin Hill		15.06.16E
	(NF 28.08.18)		

G-BRLP	Piper PA-38-112 Tomahawk	38-78A0011	04.10.89
	N9301T Highland Aviation Training Ltd Inverness		07.07.19E
	Operated by Highland Flying Club		

| G-BRLR | Cessna 150G | 15064822 | 04.10.89 |
| | N4772X T Adams & D Bull Eshott | | 15.01.20E |

G-BRLS	Thunder Ax7-77	1603	29.09.89
	J R Palmer Wisborough Green, Billingshurst		29.04.15E
	(NF 10.08.17)		

G-BRMAᴹ	Westland-Sikorsky S-51 Dragonfly HR.5	WA/H/50	15.06.78
	WG719 Cancelled 30.03.89 as WFU *As 'WG719'*		
	On loan from E.D.ap Rees		
	With The Helicopter Museum, Weston-super-Mare		

G-BRMBᴹ	Bristol 192 Belvedere HC.1	13347	15.06.78
	7997M, XG452 Cancelled 03.07.96 as WFU		
	As 'XG452' On loan from E.D.ap Rees		
	With The Helicopter Museum, Weston-super-Mare		

G-BRME	Piper PA-28-181 Archer II	28-7790105	14.09.89
	OY-BTA S S Bamrah Biggin Hill		20.07.19E
	Operated by Henlow Aero Club		

| G-BRMT | Cameron V-31 Air Chair | 2038 | 31.08.89 |
| | B M Reed Antigny, Vienne, France | | 25.07.18E |

| G-BRMU | Cameron V-77 | 2109 | 19.09.89 |
| | P Spellward Bristol BS9 | | 30.06.18E |

G-BRMV	Cameron O-77	11487	25.09.89
	P D Griffiths Blackfield, Southampton *'Viscount'*		21.08.18E
	Original envelope c/n 2103 replaced by c/n 11487 c.2011		

G-BRNC	Cessna 150M	15078833	29.09.89
	N704SG R Price & S Silvester tr G-BRNC Group		
	Sandtoft		05.12.19E

G-BRND	Cessna 152 II	15283776	07.11.89
	N5148B M L & T M Jones Derby		20.03.19E
	Operated by Derby Aero Club		

G-BRNE	Cessna 152 II	15284248	04.10.89
	N5082L Redhill Air Services Ltd Redhill		15.02.10E
	Bounced & porpoised landing Redhill 13.06.09 & nose		
	gear collapsed; noted dumped 01.16 (NF 23.09.16)		

| G-BRNK | Cessna 152 II | 15280479 | 22.09.89 |
| | N24969 D C & M Bonsall Leicester | | 15.01.20E |

G-BRNMᴹ	Chichester-Miles Leopard	002	17.10.89
	Cancelled 31.01.05 as WFU		
	With Midland Air Museum, Coventry		

| G-BRNN | Cessna 152 II | 15284735 | 22.09.89 |
| | N6452M Eastern Air Executive Ltd Sturgate | | 20.09.19E |

| G-BRNT | Robin DR.400-180 Régent | 1935 | 03.10.89 |
| | C E, M E & O C Ponsford Goodwood *'Dolly'* | | 19.03.19E |

G-BRNU	Robin DR.400-180 Régent	1937	31.10.89
	November Uniform Travel Syndicate Ltd		
	White Waltham		16.06.19E

G-BRNW	Cameron V-77	2138	02.10.89
	N Robertson & G Smith Bristol & Walton-on-Thames		
	'Mr Blue Sky'		04.08.06A
	(NF 02.08.18)		

G-BRNX	Piper PA-22-150 Tri-Pacer	22-2945	03.10.89
	N2610P S N Askey Lower Upham Farm, Chiseldon		28.01.19E
	Official type 'PA-22-150 Caribbean' is incorrect		

| G-BROE | Cameron N-65 | 2098 | 05.10.89 |
| | A I Attwood Aylesbury | | 22.08.19E |

| G-BROG | Cameron V-65 | 2121 | 06.09.89 |
| | R Kunert Finchampstead, Wokingham | | 30.04.18E |

G-BROJ	Colt 31A	1468	06.10.89
	N J Langley Henbury, Bristol *'Fly Virgin'*,		
	'Pocari Sweat' & *'Nature Made Vitamins'*		22.03.19E
	Built by Thunder & Colt Ltd		

| G-BROO | Luscombe 8E Silvaire Deluxe | 6154 | 28.09.89 |
| | N75297, N1527B, NC1527B P R Bush Haverfordwest | | 26.04.19P |

G-BROP	Van's RV-4	3	25.10.89
	G-NADZ, G-BROP, N19AT N Huxtable & K Keen		
	Wycombe Air Park		07.05.14P
	Built by A E Tolle (NF 18.01.18)		

G-BROR	Piper J-3C-65 Cub (*L-4H-PI*)	10885	07.12.89
	F-BHMQ, 43-29594 J H Bailey & P Goring		
	tr White Hart Flying Group Sturgate		04.08.19P

| G-BROX | Robinson R22 Beta | 1127 | 13.10.89 |
| | N8061V Phoenix Helicopter Academy Ltd Blackbushe | | 13.10.19E |

| G-BROY | Cameron O-90 | 2173 | 06.09.89 |
| | R Rebosio Novate Milanese, Milan, Italy | | 30.01.19E |

G-BROZ	Piper PA-18-150 Super Cub	18-6754	20.09.89
	HB-ORC, N9572D P G Kynsey		
	Fowle Hall Farm, Laddingford		12.03.19E

| G-BRPE | Cessna 120 | 13326 | 11.10.89 |
| | N3068N, NC3068N C G Applegarth Goodwood | | 18.06.18P |

G-BRPF	Cessna 120	9902	11.10.89
	N72723, NC72723 M A Potter		
	Belle Vue Farm, Yarnscombe		27.02.19P

G-BRPG	Cessna 120	9882	11.10.89
	N72703, NC72703 I C Lomax (Thirtlebury, Hull)		29.08.94P
	(NF 20.03.18)		

| G-BRPH | Cessna 120 | 12137 | 11.10.89 |
| | N1893N, NC1893N R Kelvey Tibenham | | 06.08.19P |

G-BRPJ	Cameron N-90 HAB	2071	11.09.89
	Cancelled 29.09.10 as PWFU		10.03.99
	Hungerford *Stored 12.16*		

G-BRPK	Piper PA-28-140 Cherokee F	28-7325070	17.11.89
	N15449 S H Cassia tr G-BRPK Group		
	(Cottered, Buntingford)		29.04.19E

G-BRPL	Piper PA-28-140 Cherokee Cruiser	28-7325160	13.10.89
	N15771 British Northwest Airlines Ltd Blackpool		06.11.05
	On fire dump 03.16 (NF 15.12.15)		

G-BRPM	Tipsy Nipper T.66 Series 3B	xxxx	04.03.85
	J H H Turner Kildalloig, Campbeltown		
	Built by R Morris – project PFA 025-11038 (NF 26.04.18)		

G-BRPP	Gyroflight Brookland Hornet	DC-1	16.10.89
	B J L P & W J A L de Saar (Destelbergen, Belgium)		19.08.93P
	(NF 08.02.19)		

G-BRPR	Aeronca O-58B Grasshopper	058B8823	17.10.89
	N49880, 43-1952 A F Kutz		
	Baienfurt, Baden-Württemberg		28.06.12P
	If p/i is '43-1952' is correct the type is L-3C-AE;		
	as '31952' in USAAC c/s (NF 04.04.18)		

| G-BRPS | Cessna 177B Cardinal | 17702101 | 23.10.89 |
| | N34935 W Parent Grimbergen, Belgium | | 11.04.19E |

G-BRPT	Rans S-10 Sakota	0589.052	18.10.89
	J A Harris Henstridge		19.02.16P
	Built by J G Beesley – project PFA 194-11554		

G-BRPU	Beech 76 Duchess	ME-140	17.10.89
	N6007Z Cancelled 29.06.12 as PWFU		10.08.12
	Bournemouth *Fuselage stored 09.18*		

| G-BRPV | Cessna 152 II | 15285228 | 06.11.89 |
| | N6311Q Eastern Air Executive Ltd Sturgate | | 13.06.19E |

G-BRPX	Taylorcraft BC-12D	6462	12.12.89
	N39208, NC39208 G Talkes tr G-BRPX Group		
	Leicester		08.03.19P

| G-BRPY | Piper PA-15 Vagabond | 15-141 | 23.10.89 |
| | N4356H, NC4356H C S Whitwell Breighton | | 13.06.19E |

G-BRPZ	Luscombe 8A	911	13.12.89
	N22089, NC22089 C A Flint		
	(Walpole St Peter, Wisbech)		08.12.09P
	(NF 02.03.18)		

G-BRRA Supermarine 361 Spitfire IX   CBAF.IX.1875   10.10.89
CF-FLC, G-BRRA, Belgian AF SM29, Fokker B-1,
R Netherlands AF H-59, H-119, MK912
Peter Monk Ltd   Biggin Hill   26.09.15P
Crashed after take off Biggin Hill 01.08.15 &
substantially damaged; for restoration 01.19;
as 'MK912:SH-L' in RAF c/s (NF 17.06.16)

G-BRRB Luscombe 8E Silvaire Deluxe   2611   23.10.89
N71184, NC71184   CAV Aircraft Services Ltd   (Solent)   14.05.00P
(NF 26.08.16)

G-BRRF Cameron O-77   2101   24.10.89
G J & K P Storey   Sawbridgeworth   *'Come Fly With Us'*   13.09.10E
Inflated 05.16 (IE 16.08.16)

G-BRRK Cessna 182Q Skylane II   18266160   30.10.89
N759PW   Werewolf Aviation Ltd   Elstree   14.09.19E

G-BRRP Pitts S-1S   7-0332   01.11.89
G-WAZZ, G-BRRP, N5TD   T Q Short   Gloucestershire   11.04.17P
Built by T H Decarlo (IE 12.11.18)

G-BRRR Cameron V-77   2070   13.10.89
G J & K P Storey   Sawbridgeworth
'Kent & Sussex Tree Surgeons'   24.04.19P

G-BRRU Colt 90A   1591   01.11.89
Reach for the Sky Ltd   Worplesdon, Guildford   05.09.19E

G-BRSD (2) Cameron V-77   2174   08.11.89
M E Granger   Castle Bytham, Grantham   02.04.13E
(NF 28.09.15)

G-BRSF (2) Supermarine 361 Spitfire HF.IXc   CBAF IX 3279   02.11.89
South African AF 563, RR232
M B Phillips   Goodwood   16.08.19P
Composite includes tail ex JF629 (Mk.VIII), wings
ex R Thai AF U14-6:93 (Mk.XIV) & parts ex RM873;
as 'RR232' in RAF c/s; operated by Boultbee Flight Academy

G-BRSO CFM Streak Shadow   K 133-SA   16.11.89
I Pearson   Perranporth
Built by P H Slade – project PFA 161A-11601
(SSDR microlight since 07.14) (IE 16.12.18)

G-BRSP MODAC (Air Command) 503   xxxx   13.11.89
G M Hobman   (York)   29.06.11P
Built by D R G Griffith – project PFA G/04-1158
(NF 09.07.18)

G-BRSW Luscombe 8A   3249   15.11.89
N71822, NC71822   P H Needham
tr Bloody Mary Aviation   Fenland   *'Bloody Mary'*   25.02.20P

G-BRSX Piper PA-15 Vagabond   15-117   27.10.89
N4334H, NC4334H   G J Slater tr Sierra Xray Group
Clench Common   23.04.19P

G-BRSY Hatz CB-1   6   15.11.89
N2257J   J J Reilly   (Mullinahone, Thurles, Rol)   24.10.18P
Built by M Ondrus

G-BRTD Cessna 152 II   15280023   11.01.90
N757UW   C Greenland & T G Phillips tr 152 Group
Popham   25.04.19E

G-BRTJ Cessna 150F   15061749   22.11.89
N8149S   T O'Driscoll   Newcastle, Rol   12.04.19E

G-BRTL Hughes 369E (500)   0356E   05.01.90
(F-GHLF)   Road Tech Computer Systems Ltd
Stoke Goldington   04.02.20E

G-BRTP Cessna 152 II   15281275   28.11.89
N49448   R Lee   Mount Airey Farm, South Cave   20.09.19E

G-BRTT Schweizer 269C (300)   S 1411   29.11.89
Technical Exponents Ltd   Bennett's Field, Denham   09.01.19E

G-BRTW Glaser-Dirks DG-400   4-259   22.12.89
I J Carruthers   Feshiebridge   07.07.18E
(IE 13.02.19)

G-BRTX Piper PA-28-151 Cherokee Warrior   28-7615085   27.12.89
N8307C   T Mahmood   Cranfield   06.11.19E

G-BRUA Cessna 152 II   15281212   11.01.90
N49267   Cancelled 21.11.05 as PWFU   05.11.05
Exeter Int'l   *Wreck in Iscavia hangar 06.16*

G-BRUB Piper PA-28-161 Warrior II   28-8116177   27.12.89
N8351Y   Flytrek Ltd   Compton Abbas   22.03.19E

G-BRUD Piper PA-28-181 Archer II   28-8390010   09.02.90
N8300S   A S Bamrah t/a Falcon Flying Services
Biggin Hill   23.11.19E

G-BRUG Luscombe 8E Silvaire Deluxe   4462   15.12.89
N1735K, NC1735K
N W Barratt   Ranston Farm, Iwerne Courtney   28.05.19P

G-BRUJ Boeing Stearman A75N1 Kaydet (PT-17) 75-4299   06.04.90
N55557, 42-16136
R L McDonald   (Trencin, Slovak Republic)   12.09.18
As '6136:205' in USN c/s

G-BRUM Cessna A152 Aerobat   A1520870   12.03.86
N4693A   A J Gomes   Redhill   15.06.08E
Noted dumped 01.16 (IE 22.03.18)

G-BRUN Cessna 120   9294   29.08.89
G-BRDH, N72127, NC72127
I C Mills   Sherburn-in-Elmet   19.12.19P

G-BRUO Taylor JT.1 Monoplane   xxxx   15.12.89
S T S Bygrave   Exeter Int'l   24.04.14P
Built by P C Cardno – project PFA 55-10859
(IE 03.11.15)

G-BRUV Cameron V-77   2100   16.08.89
R F & T W Benbrook   *'biG-BRUVver'*
Romford & Braintree   22.08.19E

G-BRUX Piper PA-44-180 Seminole   44-7995151   08.03.79
N2245E   M Ali   Cranfield   02.10.19E

G-BRVB Stolp SA.300 Starduster Too   409   21.12.89
N33MH   J R L Sudupe   (Meco, Madrid, Spain)   30.09.19P
Built by M Hoover

G-BRVE Beech D17S Traveller   6701   12.03.90
N1193V, NC1193V, USN 32874, FT475,
44-67724, (USN 23689)   Patina Ltd   Duxford   29.06.15E
Operated by The Fighter Collection; noted 07.18
with inhibited engine (IE 02.07.15)

G-BRVF Colt 77A   1651   19.12.89
J W Adkins   Market Harborough   10.05.19E

G-BRVG North American SNJ-7C Texan   88-17676   24.01.90
N830X, N4134A, USN 90678, (42-85895)
D J Gilmour   Rochester   30.06.17E
As '27:VS-932' in US Navy c/s

G-BRVH Smyth Model S Sidewinder   xxxx   19.12.89
B D Deleporte   Abbeville-Buigny-Saint Maclou, France   10.05.02P
Built by I S Bellamy – project PFA 92-11251
(NF 10.04.15)

G-BRVI Robinson R22 Beta   1240   27.12.89
M D Thorpe t/a Yorkshire Helicopters   Leeds Heliport   05.01.19E

G-BRVJ Cadet III Motor Glider   701   24.01.90
BGA 3360, WT906   B Outhwaite
Turners Arms Farm, Yearby   31.10.18P
Built by D F Micklethwaite & J R Paskins
– project PFA 42-11382: converted ex Slingsby
T31B WT906 (c/n 701)

G-BRVL Pitts S-1C   559H   10.01.90
N2NW   M F Pocock   Leicester   21.06.19P
Built by N Williams

G-BRVO Aérospatiale AS.350B Ecureuil   2315   03.01.90
Rotorhire LLP   Parsonage Farm, Eastchurch   09.06.19E

G-BRVR Barnett Rotorcraft J4B   216-2   20.02.90
Cancelled 21.04.09 as PWFU   04.04.89
Co.Donegal, Rol   *On display, at The Bog Hotel 03.16*

G-BRVZ Jodel D.117   433   22.12.89
F-BHNR   L Holland   Yeatsall Farm, Abbots Bromley   12.06.18P
Built by Société Aéronautique Normande

G-BRWA Aeronca 7AC Champion   7AC-351   20.03.90
N81730, NC81730   S J Donno   Blackpool   11.05.17P
(IE 07.08.18)

G-BRWC Cessna 152 II   15281918   19.01.90
TF-GMT, N67569   Cancelled 16.02.99 as PWFU   15.05.93
Derby   *Derelict in open store 10.13*

G-BRWP CFM Streak Shadow   K 122   17.01.90
D Brunton & T Macdonald   Eshott
Built by D F Gaughan – project PFA 161A-11596
(SSDR mcrolight since 01.16) (IE 22.01.16)

G-BRWR Aeronca 11AC Chief   11AC-1319   17.01.90
N9676E, NC9676E   A W Crutcher   Cardiff   24.07.19P

G-BRWT Scheibe SF25C Falke 2000   44480   11.01.90
D-KIAY   Booker Gliding Club Ltd   Wycombe Air Park   01.06.19E

G-BRWU Phoenix Luton LA-4A Minor   PFA 1141   18.01.90
R A Benson   Trenchard Farm, Eggesford   08.08.18P
Built by P K Pike & R B Webber – project PFA 1141
(IE 04.10.18)

G-BRWV Brügger MB.2 Colibri   xxxx   18.01.90
M P Wakem   Welshpool   25.02.20P
Built by S J McCollom – project PFA 43-11027

G-BRWZᴹ Cameron Macaw 90SS HAB   2206   29.01.90
Cancelled 04.11.02 by CAA   10.06.09
With Musée des Ballons, Chateau de Balleroy, France

G-BRXA Cameron O-120   2217   19.01.90
R J Mansfield   Bowness-on-Windermere   16.04.12E
(NF 27.07.17)

G-BRXD Piper PA-28-181 Archer II   28-8290126   19.02.90
D-EHWN, N9690N, N8203E   Xraydelta Ltd   Welshpool   04.04.19E

G-BRXE Taylorcraft BC-12D   9459   25.01.90
N95059, NC95059   W J Durrad & B T Morgan
Eastbach Spence, English Bicknor   *'Flying Fishes'*   29.06.19P

G-BRXF Aeronca 11AC Chief   11AC-1033   25.01.90
N9396E, NC9396E
C G Nice tr Aeronca Flying Group   Andrewsfield   22.06.19P

G-BRXG Aeronca 7AC Champion   7AC-3910   01.03.90
N85178, NC85178
J W Day tr X-Ray Golf Flying Group   Elmsett   27.06.19P

G-BRXH Cessna 120   10462   25.01.90
N76068, NC76068   A C Garside tr BRXH Group
Headcorn   10.04.19P

G-BRXL Aeronca 11AC Chief   11AC-1629   31.01.90
N3254E, NC3254E   P L Green   Andrewsfield
'Fat Bullet'   24.11.16P
As '42-78044' in US Army AC c/s (IE 25.08.17)

G-BRXP SNCAN Stampe SV.4C   678   02.02.90
N33528, F-BGGU, French AF 678, (F-BDNX)
T Brown   Headcorn   *'SFASA Saint-Yan'*   14.08.19P

G-BRXS Howard Special T-Minus   REC-1   14.02.90
N2278C   F A Bakir   (Sale)   12.04.08P
Built by C Howard from modified Taylorcraft BC
(NF 07.10.15)

G-BRXU Aérospatiale AS.332L Super Puma   2092   06.03.90
5N-BGO, G-BRXU, VH-BHV, G-BRXU, HC-BMZ
Airbus Helicopters   Marseille, France   19.12.15E
(IE 06.03.19)

G-BRXW Piper PA-24-260 Comanche   24-4069   16.02.90
N8621P   C Roberts-York   (Woking)   21.02.19E

G-BRXY Pietenpol Air Camper   xxxx   07.02.90
P S Ganczakowski   Little Gransden   14.08.19P
Built by A E Morris – project PFA 047-11416

G-BRZA Cameron O-77   2231   07.02.90
N M Benjamin & S J Nichols   Guildford & Aldershot
'Wycombe Insurance'   14.04.19E
Originally registered with c/n 2237 which became
G-BSCA

G-BRZCᴹ Cameron N-90 HAB   2227   08.02.90
Cancelled 29.04.97 as WFU   02.12.92
With British Balloon Museum & Library, Newbury

G-BRZD HAPI Cygnet SF-2A   xxxx   08.02.90
P D Begley   (Bancroft Park, Milton Keynes)   02.05.19P
Built by L G Millen – project PFA 182-11443

G-BRZF Enstrom 280C Shark   1163   12.03.90
G-IDUP, G-BRZF, N5687D   M Richardson
(West Hallam, Ilkeston)   22.09.14E
(NF 18.09.17)

G-BRZK Stinson 108-2 Voyager   108-2846   17.04.90
N9846K, NC9846K   D A Gathercole   Spanhoe   18.02.13C
Built by Consolidated Vultee Aircraft; on rebuild 10.17
(NF 09.07.15)

G-BRZL Pitts S-1D   01   26.02.90
N899RN   T R G Barnby   (Fairlight, Hastings)   02.08.96P
Built by R C Nelson (NF 16.01.19)

G-BRZW Rans S-10 Sakota   0789.058   21.02.90
D L Davies   (Holywell)   06.08.98P
Built by D L Davies – project PFA 194-11932
(NF 03.01.19)

G-BRZX Pitts S-1S   711-H   22.02.90
N272H   A J Millson tr Zulu Xray Group   Andrewsfield   25.08.19P
Built by M M Lotero

G-BSAA – G-BSZZ

G-BSAH Pilatus B-N BN-2T Islander   2235   26.02.90
ZH536, G-BSAH   Islander Aircraft Ltd   Cumbernauld   23.10.19E

G-BSAI Stoddard-Hamilton Glasair III   3102   31.01.90
K J & P J Whitehead   Wycombe Air Park   25.07.18P
Built by K J Whitehead

G-BSAJ CASA 1-131E Jungmann Series 2000   2209   23.01.90
Spanish AF E3B-209   P G Kynsey   Duxford   15.07.19P

G-BSAK Colt 21A Sky Chariot   1696   26.02.90
M D Mitchell   Longue Jumelles, Maine-et-Loire, France   21.09.18E

G-BSAV Thunder Ax7-77   1555   26.02.90
C A & I G Lloyd   Castle Donington, Derby
'Burnt Savings'   22.06.03A
(NF 01.02.16)

G-BSAW Piper PA-28-161 Warrior II   28-8216152   27.02.90
N8203C, YV-2265P, N8203C   Compton Abbas Airfield Ltd
Compton Abbas   *'Compton Abbas Airfield'*   20.03.19E
Operated by Abbas Air

G-BSAZ Denney Kitfox Model 2   xxxx   05.03.90
(G-BRVW)   A J Lloyd   Shobdon   26.06.97P
Built by P E Hinkley – project PFA 172-11664;
frame noted 06.15 (NF 22.08.16)

G-BSBA Piper PA-28-161 Warrior II   28-8016041   01.03.90
N2574U   Falcon Flying Services Ltd   Fairoaks   28.05.19E
Operated by London Transport Flying Club

G-BSBG CCF T-6 Harvard Mk.4 *(T-6J-CCF Texan)*   CCF4-483   05.03.90
Mozambique PLAF 1753, Portuguese AF 1753,
West German AF BF+053, AA+053, 52-8562
A P St John   Liverpool John Lennon   27.06.19P
Built by Canadian Car & Foundry Co;
as '28562:TA-562' in USAF c/s

G-BSBH Short SD.3-30 Variant 100   SH3000   06.07.74
Cancelled 08.12.88 as PWFU
Portadown, Co Armagh   *Fuselage in scrapyard 11.13*

G-BSBR Cameron V-77   2247   26.02.90
R P Wade   Shevington, Wigan   *'Honey'*   26.09.10E
(NF 22.10.16)

G-BSBT Piper J-3C-65 Cub   17712   09.03.90
N70694, NC70694   A R Elliott   Forge Farm, Headley   28.03.19P

G-BSBV Rans S-10 Sakota   1089.064   09.03.90
S Bain   (Rowardennan, Glasgow)   22.04.11P
Built by J Whiting – project PFA 194-11769
(NF 28.06.18)

G-BSCC Colt 105A   1006   15.03.90
A F Selby   Woodhouse Eaves, Loughborough   09.08.12E
Built by Thunder & Colt Ltd (NF 23.10.15)

G-BSCE Robinson R22 Beta   1245   15.03.90
Kuki Helicopter Sales Ltd   Retford Gamston   20.06.18E

G-BSCG Denney Kitfox Model 2   xxxx   23.04.90
D J Couzens   (Moortown, Market Rasen)   21.06.14P
Built by A C & T G Pinkstone – project PFA 172-11620;
stalled on take off Blackshawhead 13.06.14 &
substantially damaged (NF 28.01.19)

G-BSCI Colt 77A   1683   16.03.90
S C Kinsey   Ebberley, Torrington   27.09.09E
(NF 07.07.16)

G-BSCK Cameron H-24   2263   16.03.90
J D Shapland   St Eval, Wadebridge   *'Monacle'*   18.12.06
(NF 05.09.18)

G-BSCM Denney Kitfox Mk2   xxxx   28.03.90
G-MSCM, G-BSCM   H D Colliver
Landmead Farm, Garford   08.07.03P
Built by M Richardson – project PFA 172-11745
(NF 13.02.19)

G-BSCN SOCATA TB-20 Trinidad   1070   27.03.90
D-EGTC, G-BSCN   T W Gilbert   Enstone   31.07.19E

G-BSCO Thunder Ax7-77   1635   06.03.90
F J Whalley   Cleish, Kinross   *'Bluebell'*   10.12.18E

G-BSCP	Cessna 152 II	15283289	20.03.90
	N48135 The Moray Flying Club (1990)		
	Kinloss Barracks, Kinloss		16.10.19E
G-BSCS	Piper PA-28-181 Archer II	28-7890064	03.04.90
	N47392 A C Renouf Jersey		11.07.19E
	Operated by Jersey Aero Club		
G-BSCV	Piper PA-28-161 Warrior II	28-7816135	22.03.90
	C-GQXW R J L Beynon tr Southwood Flying Group		
	Earls Colne		18.02.20E
G-BSCW	Taylorcraft BC-65	1798	22.03.90
	N24461, NC24461 G Johnson		
	Shotton Colliery, Peterlee		01.10.18P
	Carries 'NC24461' on tail		
G-BSCY	Piper PA-28-161 Warrior II	28-7515046	22.03.90
	C-GOBE M C Plomer-Roberts		
	Wellesbourne Mountford		12.06.19E
	Originally built as PA-28-151 Cherokee Warrior		
G-BSCZ	Cessna 152 II	15282199	22.03.90
	N68226 The Royal Air Force Halton Aeroplane Club Ltd		
	RAF Halton		04.12.19E
G-BSDA	Taylorcraft BC-12D	7316	15.11.90
	N43657, NC43657 A D Pearce		
	Eastbach Spence, English Bicknor		14.09.12P
	(NF 21.11.17)		
G-BSDD	Denney Kitfox Model 2	xxxx	28.03.90
	C Morris (Lytham St Annes)		01.05.19P
	Built by J Cook & M Richardson – project PFA 172-11797		
G-BSDH	Robin DR.400-180 Régent	1980	18.04.90
	S M Turner tr G-BSDH Group Sywell		21.05.19E
G-BSDK	Piper J-5A Cub Cruiser	5-175	28.03.90
	N30337, NC30337 M Bergin tr Ballyboughal		
	J5 Flying Group Ballyboughal, RoI		16.08.19P
G-BSDN	Piper PA-34-200T Seneca II	34-7970335	02.04.90
	N2893A S J Green Wolverhampton Halfpenny Green		
	'www.hgfc.co.uk'		11.10.11E
	Stored 03.16 less engine (NF 29.03.16)		
G-BSDO	Cessna 152 II	15281657	23.05.90
	N65894 Cloud Global Ltd Perth		07.11.19E
G-BSDP	Cessna 152 II	15280268	11.06.90
	N24468 Paul's Planes Ltd Denham		05.04.19E
G-BSDS	Boeing Stearman A75 Kaydet (PT-13A)	75-118	06.04.90
	N57852, 38-470 L W Scattergood		
	Biel-Kappelen, Bern, Switzerland		14.06.19
	As '118' in US Army Air Corps c/s		
G-BSDW	Cessna 182P Skylane II	18264688	09.04.90
	N9125M Clipper Data Ltd Bodmin		18.12.19E
G-BSDX	Cameron V-77	541	30.03.90
	(G-BGWA), G-SNOW (1) G P & S J Allen Abingdon		16.10.09E
	Officially registered with c/n 2050: canopy fitted		
	to G-SNOW & rebuilt with G-SNOW's original		
	canopy c/n 541 (NF 30.03.16)		
G-BSDZ	Enstrom 280FX Shark	2051	03.04.90
	OO-MHV, (OO-JMH), G-ODSC, G-BSDZ		
	C D Meek Brighton City		18.12.19E
G-BSEA	Thunder Ax7-77	1524	03.04.90
	B T Lewis Headington, Oxford		15.02.20E
G-BSED	Piper PA-20 Pacer	22-6377	07.06.90
	N9404D M D N Fisher Croft Farm, Defford		22.10.19
	Built as Piper PA-22-160 Tri-Pacer; converted to		
	PA-20 Pacer configuration 2010		
G-BSEE	Rans S-9 Chaos	xxxx	02.03.90
	A R Hawes Hill Farm, Nayland		07.03.20E
	Built by P M Semler – project PFA 196-11635		
G-BSEF	Piper PA-28-180 Cherokee C	28-1846	18.04.90
	N7831W I D Wakeling		
	(Kewstoke, Weston-super-Mare)		02.11.06
	(NF 30.04.18)		
G-BSEH	Cameron V-77	2167	03.04.90
	OE-SNI, HB-QML, D-OMAG, D-OSEH(1), G-BSEH		
	L M P Vernackt Izegem, Belgium		19.06.19E
G-BSEJ	Cessna 150M	15076261	04.05.90
	N66767 J R Nicholas Haverfordwest		27.07.19E
G-BSEL	Slingsby T61G Falke	1986	31.03.80
	D G Holley Bicester		28.06.17E
	(IE 04.10.18)		
G-BSER	Piper PA-28-160 Cherokee B	28-790	19.04.90
	N5665W Yorkair Ltd Bagby		16.09.19E
G-BSEU	Piper PA-28-181 Archer II	28-7890108	01.05.90
	N47639 Herefordshire Aero Club Ltd Shobdon		01.05.19E
G-BSEV	Cameron O-77	2271	20.04.90
	P B Kenington Devauden, Chepstow 'Donor Card'		07.05.19E
G-BSEY	Beech A36 Bonanza	E-1873	17.05.90
	N1809F P Malam-Wilson Coventry		23.03.19E
G-BSFA	Aero Designs Pulsar	176	18.04.90
	P F Lorriman (High Halstow, Rochester)		08.06.06P
	Built by S A Gill – project PFA 202-11754; tricycle u/c		
	(NF 23.11.18)		
G-BSFD	Piper J-3C-65 Cub	16037	25.05.90
	N88419, NC88419 P E S Latham Sleap 'Naomi'		11.07.19P
	As '16037' in US Army c/s		
G-BSFE	Piper PA-38-112 Tomahawk II	38-82A0033	26.04.90
	N91452 Leading Edge Flight Training Ltd		
	Glasgow Prestwick		17.06.19E
G-BSFF	Robin DR.400-180R Remorqueur	1295	20.04.90
	D-ELMM Lasham Gliding Society Ltd Lasham		04.07.19E
G-BSFP	Cessna 152	15285548	09.05.90
	N93764 The Pilot Centre Ltd Denham		18.08.19E
G-BSFR	Cessna 152 II	15282268	09.05.90
	N68341 Galair Ltd Biggin Hill		15.02.20E
G-BSFW	Piper PA-15 Vagabond	15-273	26.04.90
	N4484H, NC4484H J R Kimberley		
	Wolves Hall, Tendering		21.12.05P
	(NF 29.06.18)		
G-BSFX	Denney Kitfox Model 2	506	23.04.90
	F Colman Causey Park, Morpeth		13.06.19P
	Built by D A McFadyean – project PFA 172-11723		
G-BSGD	Piper PA-28-180 Cherokee E	28-5691	04.05.90
	N3463R R J Cleverley Draycott		11.07.19E
G-BSGF	Robinson R22 Beta	1383	01.05.90
	Heliyorks Ltd Humberside		13.02.20E
G-BSGG	Denney Kitfox Model 2	xxxx	01.05.90
	S E Lyden (Terrington St Clement, King's Lynn)		22.12.17P
	Built by C G Richardson – project PFA 172-11666		
G-BSGH	Airtour AH-56B	014	01.05.90
	A R Hardwick Shefford 'Reach for the Sky'		
	(NF 01.07.15)		
G-BSGJ	Monnett Sonerai II	300	01.05.90
	N34WH J L Loweth Audley End		
	Built by W Hossink; on rebuild 12.14 (NF 07.08.15)		
G-BSGK	Piper PA-34-200T Seneca II	34-7870331	22.05.90
	N36450 Cancelled 12.10.12 as PWFU		18.11.09
	Gloucestershire Stored 09.14		
G-BSGP	Cameron N-65 HAB	2293	01.05.90
	Cancelled 29.11.15 as PWFU		17.06.09
	Hungerford Stored 07.16		
G-BSGS	Rans S-10 Sakota	1289.076	09.05.90
	M R Parr Kirkbride		22.07.19E
	Built by R Handley – project PFA 194-11724		
G-BSGT	Cessna T210N Turbo Centurion II	21063361	21.05.90
	LX-ATL, D-EOGB, N5308A E A T Brenninkmeyer		
	Biggin Hill		04.02.20E
	Reims-assembled with c/n F2100020		
G-BSGV	Rotorway Exec	3823	08.05.90
	Cancelled 07.04.95 by CAA		
	Wokingham On display at A1 Motorspares 01.18		
G-BSHA	Piper PA-34-200T Seneca II	34-7670216	02.05.90
	N9707K Justgold Ltd Blackpool		19.12.09E
	(NF 04.10.18)		
G-BSHC	Colt 69A	1668	08.05.90
	Magical Adventures Ltd West Bloomfield, MI, USA		29.09.09E
	(NF 03.06.15)		
G-BSHH	Luscombe 8E Silvaire Deluxe	3981	11.05.90
	N1254K, NC1254K CAV Aircraft Services Ltd Solent	26.09.17P
	Overturned on takeoff Porthtowan 08.07.17		
	& substantially damaged (NF 08.01.18)		

G-BSHO	Cameron V-77	2313	16.05.90
	D J Duckworth & J C Stewart Bristol & Chesham		09.07.19E
G-BSHP	Piper PA-28-161 Warrior II	28-8616002	31.05.90
	N190X, G-BSHP, N9107Y		
	NAL Asset Management Ltd Durham Tees Valley		29.10.19E
G-BSHY	EAA Acrosport	xxxx	17.04.90
	Cancelled 28.03.18 as destroyed		20.12.05
	Eastfield Farm, Manby *Built by T Butterworth*		
	& R J Hodder – project PFA 072-10928; stored 06.18		
G-BSIC	Cameron V-77	2322	17.05.90
	R Parr Chatteris PE16		11.05.19E
G-BSIF	Denney Kitfox Model 2	xxxx	05.07.90
	S M Dougan Popham		15.08.14P
	Built by R M Kimbell & M H Wylde – project		
	PFA 172-11889; noted 06.15 (IE 25.04.15)		
G-BSIG	Colt 21A Cloudhopper	1322	18.05.90
	C J Dunkley Wendover, Aylesbury		27.03.15E
	(IE 22.05.18)		
G-BSIH	Rutan Long-EZ	1200-1	31.05.90
	W S Allen Gloucestershire		
	Built by W S Allen – project PFA 074A-11492		
	(NF 02.08.18)		
G-BSII	Piper PA-34-200T Seneca II	34-8070336	16.05.90
	N8253N R Knowles		
	Wolverhampton Halfpenny Green		27.07.18E
	(NF 20.02.19)		
G-BSIJ	Cameron V-77	2164	23.05.90
	G B Davies Thorney, Peterborough		29.06.19E
G-BSIM	Piper PA-28-181 Archer II	28-8690017	22.05.90
	N9092Y A S Bamrah Biggin Hill		20.05.19E
G-BSIO	Cameron Furness Building-56	2310	25.05.90
	R E Jones Lytham St Annes		
	'Pinkie' & 'Furness Building Society'		02.06.14E
	(NF 12.10.17)		
G-BSIY	Schleicher ASK 14	14005	04.06.90
	5Y-AID, D-KOIC P W Andrews Husbands Bosworth		19.04.19E
G-BSJX	Piper PA-28-161 Warrior II	28-8216084	30.05.90
	N8036N Andrewsfield Aviation Ltd Andrewsfield		16.08.19E
G-BSJZ	Cessna 150J	15070485	07.05.91
	N60661 J M Vinall (Dunmow)		20.11.09E
	(NF 20.07.18)		
G-BSKA	Cessna 150M	15076137	31.07.90
	N66588 GS Aviation (Europe) Ltd Clench Common		17.01.20E
G-BSKG	Maule MX-7-180 Super Rocket	11072C	07.06.90
	A J Lewis Brookend, Woolaston		10.05.19E
G-BSKW	Piper PA-28-181 Archer II	2890138	01.06.90
	N91940 R J Whyham Blackpool		23.09.19E
G-BSLA	Robin DR.400-180 Régent	1997	22.06.90
	A B McCoig tr Robin Lima Alpha Group		
	(Cheam, Sutton)		17.04.19E
G-BSLH	CASA 1-131E Jungmann Series 2000	2222	27.07.90
	Spanish AF E3B-622 M A Warden		
	Biel-Kappelen, Bern, Switzerland		12.08.19P
	Built by Bucker Prado SL, Albacete, Spain		
G-BSLK	Piper PA-28-161 Warrior II	28-7916018	15.06.90
	N20849 M C Plomer-Roberts		
	Wellesbourne Mountford		20.08.19E
G-BSLM	Piper PA-28-160 Cherokee	28-308	22.06.90
	N5262W Fly (Fu Lai) Aviation Ltd Bournemouth		04.09.19E
G-BSLT	Piper PA-28-161 Warrior II	28-8016303	19.06.90
	N81817 CG Aviation Ltd Perth		20.07.19E
	Operated by ACS Flight Training		
G-BSLU	Piper PA-28-140 Cherokee	28-24733	19.06.90
	OY-PJL, OH-PJL, SE-FFA		
	Merseyflight Ltd t/a Merseyflight Air Training School		
	Liverpool John Lennon		09.07.19E
G-BSLV	Enstrom 280FX Shark	2054	26.06.90
	D-HHAS, G-BSLV B M B Roumier		
	(Saint-Viâtre, Loir-et-Cher, France)		10.07.19E
G-BSLW	Bellanca 7ECA Citabria	431-66	16.07.90
	N9696S P W Carlton & D F P Finan		
	Morgansfield, Fishburn		06.09.03
	On rebuild 12.17 (NF 21.06.18)		

G-BSLX	WAR Focke-Wulf FW190 replica	24	19.06.90
	N698WW S Freeman Hardwick		06.11.13D
	Built by W Wilson; as '4+1' in Luftwaffe c/s (NF 26.07.17)		
G-BSME	Bölkow BÖ.208C Junior	596	25.06.90
	D-ECGA D J Hampson Goodwood		07.05.19E
G-BSMF[M]	Avro 652A Anson C.19	xxxx	05.09.90
	TX183 Cancelled 23.04.01 as sold to UAE		
	As 'G-AKVW' in 'Gulf Aviation' c/s		
	With Al Mahatta Museum, Sharjah, UAE		
G-BSMM	Colt 31A Sky Chariot	1779	27.06.90
	P Spellward Bristol		04.10.18E
	Built by Thunder & Colt Ltd		
G-BSMN	CFM Streak Shadow	K.137-SA	26.06.90
	D R C Pugh (Trefeglws, Caersws)		26.07.19P
	Built by K Daniels – project PFA 161A-11656		
G-BSMT	Rans S-10 Sakota	1289.077	29.06.90
	T D Wood Garston Farm, Marshfield		21.09.16P
	Built by N Woodworth – project PFA 194-11793		
	(IE 28.01.18)		
G-BSMV	Piper PA-17 Vagabond	17-94	29.06.90
	N4696H, NC4696H A Cheriton		
	Wellesbourne Mountford *'Sophie'*		06.08.19P
	Carries 'N4696H' on rudder		
G-BSMX[M]	Bensen B.8MR	xxxx	03.07.90
	Cancelled 17.05.10 as PWFU		
	Built by J S E R McGregor – project PFA G/01-1171		
	With Caernarfon Airworld Museum		
G-BSNE	Luscombe 8E Silvaire Deluxe	5757	02.11.90
	N1130B, NC1130B O R Watts		
	South Longwood Farm, Owslebury		24.11.16P
	Carries 'B's Neez' on tail (NF 06.03.17)		
G-BSNF	Piper J-3C-65 Cub	3070	17.08.90
	N23317, NC23317 D A Hammant		
	(Ludford, Market Rasen)		17.09.19P
	Fuselage No.3116; Lippert Reed conversion		
G-BSNG	Cessna 172N Skyhawk II	17270192	19.07.90
	N738SB A J & P C Macdonald Oban		04.08.19E
G-BSNT	Luscombe 8A	1679	16.07.90
	N37018, NC37018 H E Simons Fairoaks		09.04.14P
	Built by as Model 8C (NF 28.02.19)		
G-BSNU	Colt 105A	1811	23.07.90
	M P Rich tr Gone Ballooning Warmley, Bristol		
	'Sun Rise'		18.04.18E
	Built by Thunder & Colt Ltd (IE 04.05.18)		
G-BSNX	Piper PA-28-181 Archer II	28-7990311	19.07.90
	N3028S Redhill Air Services Ltd Rougham		25.08.19E
	Operated by Skyward Flight Training		
G-BSOE	Luscombe 8A	4331	22.08.90
	N1604K, NC1604K R G Downhill (St Ives, Ringwood)		
	C/n indicates Model 8E (NF 29.07.16)		
G-BSOF	Colt 25A Sky Chariot Mk.II	1820	27.07.90
	J M Bailey Pill, Bristol *'Thunder & Colt Sky Chariot'*		18.05.09E
	Built by Thunder & Colt Ltd (NF 04.08.15)		
G-BSOG	Cessna 172M Skyhawk II	17263636	16.07.90
	N1508V D G C Ettridge tr Gloster Aero Group		
	Gloucestershire		15.08.19E
G-BSOJ	Thunder Ax7-77	1818	31.07.90
	JA-..., G-BSOJ R J S Jones Enville, Stourbridge		13.07.09E
	Built by Thunder & Colt Ltd (NF 20.05.16)		
G-BSOK	Piper PA-28-161 Warrior II	28-7816191	19.07.90
	N9749K G E Fox Bagby		09.09.13E
	Stored 10.16 less marks (NF 11.12.15)		
G-BSOM	Glaser-Dirks DG-400	4-126	12.07.90
	LN-GMC, D-KGDG P Ryland Tibenham *'OM'*		29.05.19E
G-BSON	Green S-25	001	07.06.90
	J J Green Newbury		
	Built by J J Green; manufactured using fabric ex fire		
	damaged Cameron N-850 PH-EEN; noted tethered 01.19		
	(NF 03.09.18)		
G-BSOO	Cessna 172F Skyhawk	17252431	19.07.90
	N8531U R E Pozerskis tr The Oscar Oscar Group		
	Bruntingthorpe		01.11.19E

G-BSOR CFM Streak Shadow   K.131-SA   23.10.89
A Parr   Deanland   03.06.14P
Built by J P Sorensen – project PFA 161A-11602
(IE 25.02.19)

G-BSOU Piper PA-38-112 Tomahawk II   38-81A0130   23.07.90
N23373   Leading Edge Flight Training Ltd   Glasgow   05.09.19E

G-BSOX Luscombe 8E Silvaire Deluxe   2318   07.08.90
N45791, NC45791 R Dauncey Brighton City
'Bobby Sox'   19.01.18P
(IE 07.08.18)

G-BSOZ Piper PA-28-161 Warrior II   28-7916080   14.08.90
N30220   Pactum Company Ltd Elstree   23.01.19E

G-BSPA QAC Quickie Q.2   2227   16.08.90
N227T   B K Glover & G V McKirdy Enstone   25.05.06P
Built by C C & M A Wilde (NF 11.04.18)

G-BSPC Jodel D.140C Mousquetaire III   150   02.11.81
F-BMFN   B E Cotton (Florida, USA)
Built by Société Aéronautique Normande;
on rebuild 05.18 (NF 23.05.16)

G-BSPE Reims/Cessna F172P   F17202073   31.12.80
G E Fox   Bagby   11.11.19E

G-BSPG Piper PA-34-200T Seneca II   34-8070168   08.08.90
N8176S   Andrews Professional Colour
Laboratories Ltd Headcorn   25.09.19E

G-BSPJ Campbell Cricket replica   xxxx   03.08.90
Cancelled 30.07.10 by CAA   08.01.04
Lisbellaw, Co Fermagh *Built by P Barlow, C Jones
& A Scott – project PFA G/01-1061; stored 03.16*

G-BSPK Cessna 195A   7691   14.08.90
N1079D   A G & D L Bompas Biggin Hill   08.01.20

G-BSPL CFM Streak Shadow   K140-SA   26.07.90
G L Turner   Pittrichie Farm, Whiterashes   17.07.19P
Built by CFM Metal-Fax

G-BSPM Piper PA-28-161 Warrior II   28-8116046   27.07.90
N82679   Cancelled 11.07.11 as PWFU   23.01.11
Wickford, Essex *In Wickford Action paintball park 06.14*

G-BSPN Piper PA-28R-201T Turbo Cherokee Arrow III
                                            28R-7703171   31.07.90
N5965V   J A Crew & J Gisbourne Bidford   04.04.19E

G-BSRH Pitts S-1C   LS-2   07.08.90
N4111   T L & T W Davis Popham   21.06.19P
Built by L Smith; 'Formerly N4111' on rudder

G-BSRI Neico Lancair 235   xxxx   09.08.90
P M Harrison Strubby   01.01.20P
Built by G Lewis – project PFA 191-11467; tricycle u/c

G-BSRK ARV ARV-1 Super 2   007   08.08.90
ZK-FSQ   J Svensen (Barmouth)   10.12.19P

G-BSRL Campbell Cricket replica   xxxx   08.08.90
M Brudnicki (Greenford)   29.08.18P
*Built by I Rosewall – project PFA G/03-1325
using Everett Gyroplane Series 2 c/n 0022*

G-BSRP RotorWay Exec   3824   15.08.90
R J Baker   (Tardebigge, Bromsgrove)   01.05.08P
Built by J P Dennison (NF 20.08.18)

G-BSRR Cessna 182Q Skylane II   18266915   25.07.90
N96961   C M Moore Turweston   01.04.19E

G-BSRT Denney Kitfox Model 2   xxxx   09.08.90
S J Walker (Poole)   31.08.15P
Built by L R James – project PFA 172-11873

G-BSRX CFM Streak Shadow   K 148-SA   15.08.90
I P Freestone   Husbands Bosworth   26.10.16P
Built by C Penman – project PFA 206-11870
(IE 06.05.18)

G-BSSA Luscombe 8E Silvaire Deluxe   4176   15.08.90
N1449K, NC1449K   K R Old tr Luscombe Flying Group
White Waltham   17.05.19P

G-BSSB Cessna 150L   15074147   15.08.90
N19076   D T A Rees Haverfordwest   05.10.19E

G-BSSC Piper PA-28-161 Warrior II   28-8216176   15.08.90
N81993, N9529N, N8234B   D Clarke
t/a Sky Blue Flight Training   Great Massingham   25.03.19E

G-BSSF Denney Kitfox Model 2   xxxx   15.08.90
F W Astbury   Netherthorpe   09.10.08P
Built by D M Orrock – project PFA 172-11796
(NF 17.05.16)

G-BSSI Rans S-6-116N Coyote II   0190.112   17.08.90
(G-MWJA)   D Brunton Eshott   07.01.20P
Built by D A Farnworth – project PFA 204-11782

G-BSSK QAC Quickie Q.2   xxxx   05.09.90
R Greatrex   (Crowthorne)   23.09.99P
Built by D G Greatrex – project PFA 094A-11354
(NF 06.12.18)

G-BSSP Robin DR.400-180R Remorqueur   2015   24.09.90
Soaring (Oxford) Ltd   RAF Syerston   05.02.20E
Operated by Air Cadets Gliding School

G-BSST[M] BAC Concorde 002   002
06.05.68 Cancelled 21.01.87 as WFU – WFU 04.03.76   31.10.74P
Officially registered with Bristol c/n 13520
On loan from Science Museum to
Fleet Air Arm Museum, RNAS Yeovilton

G-BSSY Polikarpov Po-2   0094   06.11.90
N588NB, G-BSSY, YU-CLJ
Richard Shuttleworth Trustees   Old Warden   14.04.19P
*Probably Soviet-Built by Po-2 & ex Yugoslav AF (JRV)
0094; as '28' in Russian Air Force camouflage c/s*

G-BSTC Aeronca 11AC Chief   11AC-1660   15.10.90
N3289E, NC3289E   E Gordon   (Silsden, Keighley)   26.06.93P
For use as spares for G-AKTR (NF 31.01.19)

G-BSTE Aérospatiale AS.355F2 Ecureuil 2 5453   29.08.90
Oscar Mayer Ltd   Redhill   29.01.19E

G-BSTH Piper PA-25-235 Pawnee C   25-5009   25.09.90
N8599L   L G Appelbeck East Winch   08.06.15
(NF 07.09.18)

G-BSTI Piper J-3C-65 Cub   19144   31.08.90
N6007H, NC6007H   S P Reeve (Haslemere)   04.04.19P
Fuselage No.19073

G-BSTK Thunder Ax8-90   1838   17.09.90
M Williams Wadhurst   28.01.08
Built by Thunder & Colt Ltd (NF 12.11.18)

G-BSTL Rand Robinson KR-2   xxxx   06.09.90
N Brauns & C S Hales Shenington   08.05.14P
Built by C S Hales – project PFA 129-11863
(NF 27.11.16)

G-BSTM Cessna 172L Skyhawk   17260143   25.09.90
N4243Q   T G Scotcher tr G-BSTM Group   Duxford   24.07.19E

G-BSTO Cessna 152 II   15282133   04.09.90
N68005   M A Stott   Exeter Int'l   20.01.20E

G-BSTP Cessna 152 II   15282925   04.09.90
N89953   LAC Aircraft Ltd   Lydd   30.06.19E

G-BSTR Grumman American AA-5 Traveler   AA5-0688   08.10.90
OO-ALR, OO-HAN, (OO-WAZ)
J C M Alty   Wellesbourne Mountford   09.04.19E

G-BSTT Rans S-6 Coyote II   0190.115   05.09.90
D G Palmer   Easter Nether Cabra Farm, Fetterangus   02.12.02P
Built by M W Holmes – project PFA 204-11880
(NF 04.09.15)

G-BSTV Piper PA-32-300 Cherokee Six   32-40378   13.09.90
N4069R   Cancelled 10.05.10 by CAA   19.05.99
Willey Park Farm, Caterham   *Noted 06.13*

G-BSTX Luscombe 8A   3301   10.09.90
EI-CDZ, G-BSTX, N71874, NC71874
R J Bentley   Mullinghar, RoI   26.05.10P
(NF 10.10.17)

G-BSTZ Piper PA-28-140 Cherokee Cruiser 28-7725153   02.10.90
N1674H   Air Navigation & Trading Company Ltd
Blackpool   08.03.19E

G-BSUA Rans S-6 Coyote II   0190.109   29.10.90
A J Todd   Hallyards Farm, Bucknall   07.04.10P
*Built by P S Dopson – project PFA 204-11910;
stored 07.16 (NF 30.09.15)*

G-BSUB Colt 77A   1801   30.10.90
E Stephens   Usk   11.08.13E
(NF 14.12.15)

G-BSUD Luscombe 8A   1745   14.09.90
N37084, NC37084   M J Negus tr Luscombe Quartet
Stoneacre Farm, Farthing Corner   22.05.19P

G-BSUH	Cessna 140	8092	15.10.90
	N89088, NC89088 Cancelled 28.04.95 by CAA		02.05.94
	Limetree, RoI *On rebuild 06.16*		
G-BSUK	Colt 77A	1374	21.09.90
	T Knight Ightfield, Whitchurch		16.09.16E
G-BSUO	Scheibe SF25C Falke 2000	44501	06.12.90
	D-KIOK A Mutch tr Portmoak Falke Syndicate		
	Portmoak		08.11.19E
G-BSUT	Rans S-6-ESA Coyote II	0990.138	02.10.90
	Cancelled 21.01.08 by CAA		08.02.07
	Eccleston, Chorley *Built by P Clegg – project*		
	PFA 204-11897; tri-cycle u/c; stored 10.12		
G-BSUV	Cameron O-77	2407	26.09.90
	I R F Worsman Dundee		30.12.19E
G-BSUX	Carlson Sparrow II	xxxx	05.10.90
	K Redfearn Croft Farm, Croft-on-Tees		21.10.14P
	Built by J Stephnson – project PFA 209-11794;		
	on rebuild 08.15 (NF 19.11.18)		
G-BSUZ	Denney Kitfox Model 2	745	10.09.90
	J D Randall (Purley-on-Thames, Reading)		05.06.17P
	Built by E T Wicks – project PFA 172-11875;		
	bounced landing Lower Wasing Farm, Brimpton		
	12.09.18 & substantially damaged		
G-BSVB	Piper PA-28-181 Archer II	2890098	10.09.90
	N9155S Veebee Aviation Ltd North Weald		21.01.20E
G-BSVE	Binder CP.301S Smaragd	113	27.09.90
	HB-SED R E Perry tr Smaragd Flying Group		
	Halesland		21.06.19P
G-BSVG	Piper PA-28-161 Warrior II	28-8516013	02.10.90
	C-GZAV Airways Aero Associations Ltd		
	Wycombe Air Park		05.12.19E
	Operated by British Airways Flying Club; Union Flag c/s		
G-BSVH	Piper J-3C-65 Cub	15360	02.10.90
	N87702, NC87702 G J Digby		
	Jenkin's Farm, Navestock		07.08.19P
	Fuselage No.15003		
G-BSVK	Denney Kitfox Model 2	xxxx	02.10.90
	H D Colliver (Grove, Wantage)		05.04.94P
	Built by K P Wordsworth – project PFA 172-11731		
	(IE 12.08.18)		
G-BSVM	Piper PA-28-161 Warrior II	28-8116173	07.11.90
	N8351N EFG (Flying Services) Ltd Biggin Hill		15.02.19E
G-BSVN	Thorp T-18	107	17.09.90
	N4881 M D Moaby Conington		19.06.18P
	Built by M R Miller		
G-BSVP	Piper PA-23-250 Aztec F	27-7754115	09.02.78
	N959JB, G-BSVP, N63787 S G Spier Elstree		25.02.20E
G-BSVR	Schweizer 269C (*300*)	S 1236	14.11.90
	OO-JWW, D-HLEB M K E Askham		
	The Rectory Farm, Low Catton		05.10.19E
G-BSVS	Robin DR.400-100 Cadet	2017	22.10.90
	D M Chalmers Upper Harford Farm,		
	Bourton-on-the-Water		12.04.19E
G-BSWB	Rans S-10 Sakota	0489.046	08.10.90
	F A Hewitt Garston Farm, Marshfield		01.06.19P
	Built by F A Hewitt – project PFA 194-11560		
G-BSWC	Boeing Stearman E75 Kaydet (*PT-13D*)	75-5560	16.11.90
	N17112, N5021V, 42-17397 D A Jack Thruxton		24.07.19E
	As '112' in USAAC c/s		
G-BSWF	Piper PA-16 Clipper	16-475	12.10.90
	N5865H GW Evans Ltd Pent Farm, Postling		26.05.19
G-BSWG	Piper PA-17 Vagabond	15-99	08.10.90
	N4316H, NC4316H M J Benham Headcorn		02.10.19P
G-BSWH	Cessna 152 II	15281365	15.10.90
	N49861 Airspeed Aviation Ltd Derby		14.03.02
	(IE 06.07.18)		
G-BSWL	Slingsby T61F Venture T.2	1974	15.10.90
	EI-CCQ, G-BSWL, ZA655 R J Bastin tr G-BSWL Group		
	Kirton in Lindsey		21.06.19E
G-BSWM	Slingsby T61F Venture T.2	1965	12.10.90
	ZA629 B C Irwin tr Venture Gliding Group Bellarena		10.06.19E
G-BSWR	Pilatus B-N BN-2T Islander	2245	22.10.90
	Police Service of Northern Ireland Belfast Int'l		08.07.19
	Operated by PNSI Air Support Unit as callsign 'Scout 2'		

G-BSWV	Cameron N-77	2369	22.10.90
	S Charlish Newtown, Hungerford *'Leicester Mercury'*		30.09.09E
	(NF 01.05.18)		
G-BSXA	Piper PA-28-161 Warrior II	28-8416121	11.12.90
	N4373Z, N9622N A S Bamrah		
	t/a Falcon Flying Services Biggin Hill		03.08.19E
G-BSXB	Piper PA-28-161 Warrior II	28-8416125	04.12.90
	N4374D, N9626N S R Mendes Redhill		11.06.18E
G-BSXC	Piper PA-28-161 Warrior II	28-8416126	04.12.90
	N4374F, N9627N Shoreham Flying Club Ltd		
	Brighton City		06.02.20E
G-BSXD	Soko P-2 Kraguj	030	22.10.90
	Yug.AF 30146 Airfield Aviation Ltd		
	Morgansfield, Fishburn		19.07.18P
	As '30146:146' in Yugoslav Air Force c/s (IE 26.09.18)		
G-BSXI	Mooney M.20E Super 21	700056	31.10.90
	N6766V D H G Penney Fenland		09.06.11E
	(NF 29.06.15)		
G-BSXM	Cameron V-77	2446	05.11.90
	C A Oxby Bowes, Barnard Castle *'Oxby'*		01.10.06A
	(NF 04.12.18)		
G-BSXN	Robinson R22 Beta	1611	14.11.90
	Cancelled 22.09.04 as destroyed		11.06.06
	Newcastle Int'l *Noted 02.14*		
G-BSXT	Piper J-5A Cub Cruiser	5-498	08.11.90
	EI-AXT, G-BSXT, N33409, NC33409		
	G V Crowe tr Great American Flyers Felthorpe		23.08.13P
	As '42-5772' in US Army c/s (IE 31.07.18)		
G-BSYF	Luscombe 8E Silvaire Deluxe	3455	12.11.90
	N72028, NC72028 V R Leggott		
	Coldharbour Farm, Willingham		11.07.19E
	Originally built as Luscombe 8A: rebuilt as Model 8E c.2002		
G-BSYG	Piper PA-12 Super Cruiser	12-2106	12.11.90
	N3228M, NC3228M E R Newall tr Fat Cub Group		
	Breighton		06.05.19P
G-BSYH	Luscombe 8A	2842	13.11.90
	N71415, NC71415 N R Osborne Perth		13.01.20P
G-BSYJ	Cameron N-77 HAB	2441	13.11.90
	Cancelled 12.12.01 as PWFU		16.12.99
	Not Known *Inflated Pidley 05.16*		
G-BSYO	Piper J-3C-65 Cub (*L-4B-PI*)	12809	19.02.91
	(G-BSMJ), (G-BRHE), EC-AIY, HB-ODO, HB-OUA,		
	44-80513 C R Reynolds Pent Farm, Postling		05.09.19P
	Fuselage No.12639; official c/n '10244' is not		
	correct & relates to HB-OVG (ex F-BFYF & 43-1383);		
	as 'XC' in French Army c/s		
G-BSYU	Robin DR.400-180 Régent	2027	26.11.90
	P D Smoothy Hinton-in-the-Hedges		30.04.19E
G-BSYV	Cessna 150M	15078371	16.11.90
	N9423U E-Plane Ltd Sandtoft		03.05.19E
G-BSYY	Piper PA-28-161 Warrior II	2816009	26.11.90
	N440X, G-BSYY, N9100X Aerobility Blackbushe		28.04.19E
G-BSYZ	Piper PA-28-161 Warrior II	28-8516051	22.11.90
	N6908H F C P Hood Longside *'Knight of the Thistle'*		21.11.19E
	Operated by North East Flight Training		
G-BSZB	Stolp SA.300 Starduster Too	545	03.12.90
	N5495M P J B Lewis Swansea		05.07.19P
	Built by J W Matthews		
G-BSZF	Robin DR.250/160 Capitaine	32	29.11.90
	F-BNJB J B Randle Church Farm, Piltdown		29.07.19E
	Built by Centre-Est Aéronautique		
G-BSZI	Cessna 152 II	15285856	17.12.90
	N95139 Cancelled 20.06.13 by CAA		28.08.10
	Urney, Strabane *Wreck stored 12.13*		
G-BSZJ	Piper PA-28-181 Archer II	28-8190216	06.12.90
	N8373Z R D Fuller & M L A Pudney		
	West Newlands Farm, St Lawrence *'21'*		24.06.19E
G-BSZM	Montgomerie-Bensen B.8MR	xxxx	30.11.90
	P C W Raine Walkeridge Farm, Overton		02.12.19P
	Built by J H H Turner – project PFA G/01-1193		
G-BSZO	Cessna 152 II	15280221	30.11.90
	N24334 A Jahanfar tr G-BSZO Group Southend		19.07.19E
	Operated by Southend Flying Club		

G-BSZT Piper PA-28-161 Warrior II   28-8116027   31.12.90
N8260D   Golf Charlie Echo Ltd   Brighton City   16.04.19E
Operated by The Flying Hut

G-BSZV Cessna 150F   15062304   03.12.90
N3504L   C A Davis   Old Sarum   30.08.19E

G-BSZW Cessna 152 II   15281072   03.12.90
N48958   S T & T W Gilbert   Elstree   28.02.20E
Operated by Stars Fly

G-BTAA – G-BTZZ

G-BTAK EAA Acrosport II   1468   27.12.90
N440X   A D Friday   Headcorn   06.11.19P
Built by A P Savage

G-BTAL Reims/Cessna F152 II   F15201444   07.04.78
Herefordshire Aero Club Ltd   Shobdon   22.05.19E

G-BTAM Piper PA-28-181 Archer II   2890093   10.01.91
RA-01765, G-BTAM, N9153D
The Ashley Gardner Flying Club Ltd   Isle of Man   01.03.19E

G-BTAW Piper PA-28-161 Warrior II   28-8616031   14.12.90
N9259T   T J Parish tr Piper Flying Group
Newcastle Int'l   16.12.19E

G-BTAZ[M] Evans VP-2   xxxx   13.12.90
Cancelled 12.03.09 by CAA
Built by G S Poulter – project PFA 063-11474
With City of Norwich Aviation Museum

G-BTBA Robinson R22 Beta   1717   18.03.91
Solent Helicopters Ltd t/a Elite Helicopters   Goodwood   23.11.19E

G-BTBC Piper PA-28-161 Warrior II   28-7916414   19.12.90
HA-WRB, G-BTBC, N28755   M A Khan   Elstree   20.07.19E
Operated by MAK Aviation

G-BTBG Denney Kitfox Model 2   xxxx   18.12.90
A S Cadney   (Leamington Spa)   04.09.18P
Built by J Catley – project PFA 172-11845 (IE 16.12.18)

G-BTBH Ryan ST3KR (PT-22-RY)   2063   18.02.91
N854, N50993, 41-20854   R C Piper   Goodwood   13.06.13P
On maintenance 11.18 @ Audley End;
as '854' in US Army Air Corp c/s (IE 10.08.15)

G-BTBJ Cessna 190   16046   02.10.91
F-AZRE, G-BTBJ, N4461C   P W Moorcroft   Derby   02.05.16E
(IE 21.08.17)

G-BTBL Montgomerie-Bensen B.8MR   xxxx   21.12.90
N H Collins t/a AES Radionic Surveillance Systems
(Alrewas, Burton-on-Trent)   02.09.01P
Built by J M Montgomerie – project PFA G/01A-1183
(NF 31.07.18)

G-BTBU Piper PA-18-150 Super Cub   18-7509010   03.01.91
N9665P   S D Edwards   Redhill   17.06.14E
(NF 25.09.15)

G-BTBV Cessna 140   12727   02.04.91
N2474N   U Reichenbach   (Thun, Switzerland)   02.05.19E

G-BTBW Cessna 120   14220   24.01.91
N2009V, NC2009V   K U Platzer
Tannheim, Germany   '40'   09.11.18E

G-BTBY Piper PA-17 Vagabond   17-195   04.01.91
N4894H   F M Ward   Manor House Farm, Dishforth   22.05.19P

G-BTCB Air Command 582 Sport   0634   09.01.91
G Scurrah   (Duddon Bridge, Millom)
Built by G Scurrah – project PFA G/04-1198 (NF 05.09.16)

G-BTCE Cessna 152 II   15281376   09.01.91
N49876   S T Gilbert   Enstone   11.01.19E
Tailwheel conversion

G-BTCH Luscombe 8E Silvaire Deluxe   6403   11.02.91
N1976B   M W Orr   Compton Abbas   21.06.19P

G-BTCI Piper PA-17 Vagabond   17-136   11.01.91
N4839H, NC4839H   T R Whittome   (Inverness)   09.08.05P
Stored 04.12 for rebuild (NF 10.03.15)

G-BTCJ Luscombe 8E Silvaire Deluxe   1869   16.01.91
N41908, NC41908   D Snook   (Salisbury)   06.05.12P
(NF 05.07.17)

G-BTCZ Cameron Chateau-84   2246   18.01.91
Balleroy Developpement SAS   Balleroy,
Basse-Normandie, France   'Chateau II'   17.07.17E
Forbes Chateau de Balleroy special shape

G-BTDA Slingsby T61F Venture T.2   1870   17.04.91
XZ550   S W Naylor tr G-BTDA Group   Easterton   18.04.17E
(IE 30.01.19)

G-BTDC Denney Kitfox Model 2   xxxx   11.01.91
R Palmer   (Cosby)   12.10.19P
Built by D Collinson & O Smith – project PFA 172-11483

G-BTDD CFM Streak Shadow   K 127-SA   14.01.91
R J Creasey tr The Adventurous SSDR Group
Plaistows Farm, St Albans
Built by S J Evans – project PFA 161A-11622
(SSDR microlight since 04.16) (IE 19.04.16)

G-BTDE Cessna C-165 Airmaster   551   18.01.91
N21911, NC21911   R H Screen   Popham   06.03.20

G-BTDF Luscombe 8F Silvaire   2205   17.04.91
N45678, NC45678   G Johnson   (North Shields)   19.08.93P
(NF 02.03.18)

G-BTDN Denney Kitfox Model 2   688   22.01.91
D Rudd   (Eastleigh)   20.09.19P
Built by A B Butler – project PFA 172-11826

G-BTDR Aero Designs Pulsar   xxxx   24.01.91
A & P Kingsley-Dobson   Redhill   10.05.19P
Built by R M Hughes & T Packe – project PFA 202-11962

G-BTDT CASA 1-131E Jungmann Series 2000   2131   05.02.91
Spanish AF E3B.505   C Butler & G G Ferriman
Netherthorpe   08.08.19P

G-BTDV Piper PA-28-161 Warrior II   28-7816355   25.02.91
N3548M   Falcon Flying Services Ltd   Biggin Hill   05.03.20E

G-BTDW Cessna 152 II   15279864   25.02.91
N757NC   J H Sandham t/a JH Sandham Aviation   Oban   12.02.20E

G-BTDY Piper PA-18-150 Super Cub   18-8109007   28.01.91
N24570   N J Butler   Fordoun   23.07.94
(NF 01.02.19)

G-BTDZ CASA 1-131E Jungmann Series 2000   2104   05.02.91
Spanish AF E3B-524   M & R J Pickin   Headcorn   27.03.19P
C/n conflicts with G-JGMN (qv)

G-BTEI Everett Campbell Cricket   023   31.01.91
Cancelled 23.05.01 by CAA   21.12.98
Lisbellaw, Co Fermagh   Stored 02.16

G-BTEL CFM Streak Shadow   K 125-SA   31.01.91
J E Eatwell   MoD Boscombe Down   01.02.20P
Built by J E Eatwell – project PFA 206-11667

G-BTES Cessna 150H   15068371   29.04.91
N22575   J Taylor   Biggin Hill   13.11.19E

G-BTET Piper J-3C-65 Cub   18296   05.02.91
N98141, NC98141
P Fowler tr City of Oxford Flying Group   Enstone   04.12.13P
Fuselage frame noted 09.18 (NF 20.06.16)

G-BTEU Aerospatiale SA.365N2 Dauphin 2   6392   11.02.91
Cancelled 11.06.15 as PWFU   18.05.15
Newton Arcliffe   *Used as cabin trainer by*
Great North Air Ambulance 11.17

G-BTEW Cessna 120   10238   29.04.91
C-FELE   A I & J H Milne
Great Friars' Thornes Farm, Swaffham   29.06.19

G-BTFC Reims/Cessna F152 II   F15201668   23.05.79
Aircraft Engineers Ltd   Glasgow Prestwick   21.06.19E

G-BTFE Parsons Gyroplane Model 1   38   13.02.91
A Corleanca   (Ferryhill)   27.10.01P
Built by I Brewster (NF 26.07.16)

G-BTFG Boeing Stearman A75N1 Kaydet (N2S-4) 75-3441   20.02.91
N4467N, USN 30010   TG Aviation Ltd
Pent Farm, Postling   06.07.19
As '441' in US Navy red & white c/s

G-BTFJ Piper PA-15 Vagabond   15-159   13.02.91
N4373H, NC4373H   R Ellingworth & N A Preston
Sibson   'Bluebell'   06.03.20E

G-BTFL Aeronca 11AC Chief   11AC-1727   18.02.91
N3403E, NC3403E   J G Vaughan tr BTFL Group
Eastbach Spence, English Bicknor   05.06.19P

G-BTFO Piper PA-28-161 Warrior II   28-7816580   12.03.91
N31728   Flyfar Ltd   RAF Woodvale   22.02.20E

G-BTFP Piper PA-38-112 Tomahawk   38-78A0340   17.04.91
N6201A   M A Lee   Durham Tees Valley   02.12.19E

G-BTFT	Beech 58 Baron	TH-979	14.03.91
	N2036W Fastwing Air Charter Ltd Compton Abbas		12.08.19E
G-BTFU	Cameron N-90	2391	28.02.91
	A C K Rawson & J J Rudoni t/a Wickers World		
	Hot Air Balloon Company Stafford *'Maltesers II'*		28.10.10E
	(IE 17.07.18)		
G-BTFV	Whittaker MW7	xxxx	08.02.91
	P A Gasson (Hersden, Canterbury)		11.12.12P
	Built by S J Luck – project PFA 171-11722 (NF 13.11.18)		
G-BTGD	Rand Robinson KR-2	xxxx	22.02.91
	S R Winter (Myddfai, Llandovery)		02.08.08P
	Built by D W Mullin – project PFA 129-11150 (NF 18.04.18)		
G-BTGI	Rearwin 175 Skyranger	1517	26.02.91
	N32308, NC32308 J M Fforde (Clyro, Hereford)		11.07.18P
G-BTGJ	Smith DSA-1 Miniplane	NM.II	25.03.91
	N1471 D J Howell Wolverhampton Halfpenny Green		08.10.19P
	Built by S J Malovic		
G-BTGL	Avid Speed Wing	xxxx	27.02.91
	J St Clair-Quentin (Adriers, Nouvelle-Aquitaine)		04.07.13P
	Built by A J Maxwell – project PFA 189-11885		
	(NF 17.11.16)		
G-BTGM	Aeronca 7AC Champion	7AC-3665	11.03.91
	N84943, NC84943 A R Hausler tr Heligan Champ		
	Group Shempston Farm, Lossiemouth		06.11.18P
	(IE 09.02.19)		
G-BTGO	Piper PA-28-140 Cherokee D	28-7125613	20.02.91
	N1998T Demero Ltd & Livingstone Skies Ltd Oxford		21.10.19E
G-BTGR	Cessna 152 II	15284447	28.02.91
	N6581L A J Gomes Brighton City		25.07.00
	(NF 07.04.16)		
G-BTGS (2)	Stolp SA.300 Starduster Too	EAA/50553	30.09.87
	G-AYMA G N Elliott tr Mr GN Elliott & Partners		
	Goodwood		13.06.18P
	Built by P J Leggo – project PFA 035-10076;		
	project originally allocated to T G Solomon		
G-BTGT	CFM Streak Shadow	K 164-SA	01.03.91
	(G-MWPY) J Heunis (Chieveley, Newbury)		01.04.13P
	Built by M Allison – project PFA 206-11964 (NF 27.02.19)		
G-BTGV	Piper PA-34-200T Seneca II	34-7970077	26.03.91
	N3004H Cancelled 13.07.11 as PWFU		16.08.11
	Oxford *On fire dump 10.13*		
G-BTGW	Cessna 152 II	15279812	05.03.91
	N757KY Stapleford Flying Club Ltd Stapleford		10.07.19E
G-BTGX	Cessna 152 II	15284950	05.03.91
	N5462P Stapleford Flying Club Ltd Stapleford		16.08.19E
G-BTGY	Piper PA-28-161 Warrior II	28-8216199	05.03.91
	N209FT, N9574N Stapleford Flying Club Ltd		
	Stapleford		13.06.19E
G-BTGZ	Piper PA-28-181 Archer II	28-7890160	08.04.91
	N47956 Nick Deyong Ltd Elstree		08.02.20E
G-BTHE	Cessna 150L	15075340	07.03.91
	N11348 General Technics Ltd		
	(Sulhampstead, Reading)		03.05.19E
G-BTHF	Cameron V-90	2543	07.03.91
	N J & S J Langley Henbury, Bristol		31.03.20E
G-BTHK	Thunder Ax7-77	1906	11.03.91
	M S Trend Wateringbury, Maidstone		25.06.06A
	(NF 13.11.18)		
G-BTHP	Thorp T.211	101	13.06.91
	M J Newton Manchester Barton		05.06.12P
	(NF 10.08.15)		
G-BTHX	Colt 105A	1939	18.03.91
	I J Wadey Storrington, Pulborough		02.05.16E
	Built by Thunder & Colt Ltd		
G-BTHY	Bell 206B-3 JetRanger III	2290	20.03.91
	N6606M, VH-BIQ, ZK-HBQ, DQ-FEN, ZK-HLU		
	Suffolk Helicopters Ltd Ransomes Europark, Ipswich		29.11.19E
G-BTIE	SOCATA TB-10 Tobago	187	30.03.81
	D J & S N Taplin Redhill		11.11.09E
	(NF 10.11.17)		
G-BTIF	Denney Kitfox Model 3	684	27.02.91
	D S Lally (Anderton, Chorley)		31.05.12P
	Built by J Scott & C R Thompson		
	– project PFA 172-11862 (NF 30.06.15)		

G-BTIG	Montgomerie-Bensen B.8MR	xxxx	21.03.91
	G H Leeming RAF Mona		11.07.17P
	Built by N Beales & D Beevers – project PFA G/01-1093		
G-BTII	Gulfstream American AA-5B Tiger	AA5B-1256	05.06.91
	N4560S D R Farrar tr G-BTII Group		
	Sherburn-in-Elmet *'George Frederick'*		05.04.19E
G-BTIJ	Luscombe 8E Silvaire Deluxe	5194	03.04.91
	N2467K, NC2467K S J M Hornsby		
	Ranston Farm, Iwerne Courtney		13.12.19P
G-BTIL	Piper PA-38-112 Tomahawk	38-80A0004	26.03.91
	N24730 B R Pearson Eaglescott		
	Stored 12.17 as 'N24730' (NF 30.10.18)		
G-BTIM	Piper PA-28-161 Cadet	2841159	24.08.89
	N9185D, (SE-KIO) White Waltham Airfield Ltd		
	White Waltham		14.02.20E
G-BTIN	Cessna 150C	150-59905	26.03.91
	N7805Z Cancelled 10.05.01 as PWFU		06.10.01
	Perth (City Centre)		
	As instructional airframe Perth College 07.16		
G-BTIV	Piper PA-28-161 Warrior II	28-8116044	10.05.91
	N82697 B R Pearson tr Warrior Group Eaglescott		24.07.06
	(NF 26.09.18)		
G-BTJA	Luscombe 8E Silvaire Deluxe	5037	04.04.91
	N2310K, NC2310K N C Wildey (Chapel-en-le-Frith)		18.07.19P
G-BTJB	Luscombe 8E Silvaire Deluxe	6194	04.04.91
	N1567B, NC1567B M O Loxton		
	Parsonage Farm, Eastchurch		23.07.19E
G-BTJC	Luscombe 8F Silvaire	6589	04.04.91
	N2162B M Colson Glebe Farm, Stockton		20.01.19E
G-BTJD	Thunder Ax8-90 Series 2	1865	28.03.91
	L J Whitelock Bristol		19.06.17E
	Inflated Bath 12.18 (NF 08.06.18)		
G-BTJL	Piper PA-38-112 Tomahawk	38-79A0863	03.04.91
	N2477N A5E Ltd Bournemouth		14.05.15E
	Fuselage noted 06.17 (NF 27.08.18)		
G-BTJO	Thunder Ax9-140	1948	03.04.91
	G P Lane (Little Horwood, Milton Keynes)		08.04.92
	(NF 08.04.16)		
G-BTJS	Montgomerie-Bensen B.8MR	xxxx	08.04.91
	B F Pearson (Eakring, Newark)		13.03.10P
	Built by J M P Annand – project PFA G/01-1083		
	(NF 10.05.16)		
G-BTJX	Rans S-10 Sakota	0790.114	09.04.91
	J A Harris (Bourton, Gillingham)		15.09.04P
	Built by M Goacher – project PFA 194-12014		
	(NF 05.04.18)		
G-BTKA	Piper J-5A Cub Cruiser	5-954	11.04.91
	N38403, NC38403 Turweston Flying Club Ltd		
	Turweston		22.09.19P
G-BTKB	Murphy Renegade 912	xxxx	11.04.91
	J & P Calvert Newton-on-Rawcliffe		04.03.20P
	Built by G S Blundell – project PFA 188-11876		
G-BTKD	Denney Kitfox Model 4	853	15.04.91
	R A Hills (Hazelby Bryan, Sturminster Newton)		03.10.19P
	Built by J F White – project PFA 172-11941;		
	c/n may be 653 which is also attributed to N653CP		
G-BTKL	MBB Bölkow BÖ.105DB-4	S.422	02.05.91
	D-HDMU, Swedish Army 09076, D-HDMU		
	Helicom Ltd Cuneo Int'l, Italy		16.07.19E
G-BTKP	CFM Streak Shadow	K 174	24.04.91
	M J Mawle & P F Morgan (Swindon & Taunton)		28.05.19P
	Built by K S Woodward – project PFA 206-12036		
G-BTKT	Piper PA-28-161 Warrior II	28-8216218	09.05.91
	N429FT, N9606N Falcon Flying Services Ltd		
	Biggin Hill		16.04.19E
G-BTKV	Piper PA-22-160 Tri-Pacer	22-7157	25.04.91
	N3216Z R A Moore Gransha, Rathfriland		05.01.18
	(IE 02.07.18)		
G-BTKW	Cameron O-105	2566	25.04.91
	L J Whitelock Bristol		09.03.01A
	(NF 23.08.17)		
G-BTKX	Piper PA-28-181 Archer II	28-7890146	14.05.91
	N47866 R M Pannell Eaglescott		19.07.19E

G-BTLB	Wassmer WA.52 Europa	42	17.04.89
	F-BTLB D Crouchman tr Hampshire Flying Group		
	Popham		10.05.19E
G-BTLG	Piper PA-28R-200 Cherokee Arrow	28R-35811	29.04.91
	N5045S S A Thomas RNAS Yeovilton		13.04.19E
G-BTLL	Pilatus P.3-03	323-5	18.04.91
	Swiss AF A-806 R E Dagless Holly Hill Farm, Guist	23.06.94P	
	As 'A-806' in Swiss Air Force c/s (IE 10.07.18)		
G-BTLP	Grumman American AA-1C Lynx	AA1C-0109	13.05.91
	N9732U Partlease Ltd Stapleford '28'		04.07.19E
	Operated by Stapleford Flying Club		
G-BTMA	Cessna 172N Skyhawk II	17273711	02.05.91
	N5136J R F Wondrak Enstone		12.02.20E
G-BTMH	Colt 90A HAB	1963	14.05.91
	Cancelled 22.11.06 as PWFU		19.08.01
	Not Known Inflated Pidley 05.16		
G-BTMK	Cessna R172K Hawk XP	R1722787	10.06.91
	N736TZ K E Alford Clutton Hill Farm, High Littleton	10.10.19E	
G-BTML	Cameron Rupert Bear-90	2533	16.05.91
	S C Kinsey Ebberley, Torrington		08.05.97A
	Active 08.18 (NF 18.09.18)		
G-BTMO	Colt 69A	2004	20.05.91
	Cameron Balloons Ltd Bristol		
	Built by Thunder & Colt Ltd (NF 05.02.18)		
G-BTMP	Campbell Cricket replica	xxxx	20.05.91
	P A Gardner (Condover, Shrewsbury)		06.09.17P
	Built by D G Hill – project PFA G/03-1226		
	(NF 20.06.18)		
G-BTMR	Cessna 172M Skyhawk II	17264985	20.05.91
	N64047 Hull Aero Club Ltd Beverley (Linley Hill)	23.08.19E	
G-BTMV	Everett Gyroplane Series 2	025	21.05.91
	L Armes (Pitsea, Basildon)		
	(NF 12.11.18)		
G-BTNA	Robinson R22 Beta	1800	23.05.91
	N40820 HQ Aviation Ltd Denham		14.02.19E
G-BTNC	Aérospatiale AS.365N2 Dauphin 2	6409	21.06.91
	Multiflight Ltd Leeds Bradford		19.05.19E
G-BTNE	Piper PA-28-161 Warrior II	28-8116212	22.07.91
	N8379H Cancelled 30.05.13 as destroyed		09.08.13
	Wellesbourne Mountford Wreck dumped 05.13		
G-BTNH	Piper PA-28-161 Warrior II	28-8216202	28.05.91
	G-DENH, G-BTNH, N253FT, N9577N		
	A S Bamrah t/a Falcon Flying Services Fairoaks	09.10.19E	
G-BTNO	Aeronca 7AC Champion	7AC-3132	31.05.91
	N84441, NC84441 J M Farquhar		
	Shempston Farm, Lossiemouth 'Karen Anne'		05.09.19P
G-BTNR	Denney Kitfox Model 3	921	31.05.91
	J Beirne tr High Notions Flying Group		
	Limetree, Portarlington, RoI		02.10.12P
	Built by J W G Ellis – project PFA 172-12035;		
	stored 05.17 (NF 27.07.18)		
G-BTNT	Piper PA-28-151 Cherokee Warrior	28-7615401	31.05.91
	N6929J Azure Flying Club Ltd Cranfield		19.04.19E
G-BTNV	Piper PA-28-161 Warrior II	28-7816590	20.06.91
	N31878 B Somerville & P A Teasdale		
	Manchester Barton		13.10.19E
G-BTNW	Rans S-6-ESA Coyote II	0391.174	03.06.91
	A J S Crowley tr Coyote Ugly Group Otherton		04.05.19P
	Built by A Barbone – project PFA 204-12077		
G-BTOG	de Havilland DH.82A Tiger Moth	86500	05.09.91
	F-BGCJ, French AF, NM192		
	S W Barratt tr TOG Group Audley End		
	Built by Morris Motors Ltd; on rebuild 11.18 (NF 30.07.18)		
G-BTOI	Cameron N-77	2588	20.06.91
	Zebedee Balloon Service Ltd Newtown, Hungerford	13.07.19E	
G-BTOL	Denney Kitfox Model 3	919	26.06.91
	P J Gibbs Woodlands Barton Farm, Roche		31.07.18P
	Built by C R Phillips – project PFA 172-12052		
	(IE 04.10.18)		
G-BTON	Piper PA-28-140 Cherokee Cruiser	28-7425343	15.07.91
	N43193 R Nightingale Dunkeswell		03.01.15E
	(IE 13.07.15)		

G-BTOO	Pitts S-1C	5215-24A	12.06.91
	N37H T L Davis Popham		11.06.16P
	Built by E Lawrence		
G-BTOP	Cameron V-77	2484	14.06.91
	J J Winter Michaelston-y-Fedw, Cardiff 'Big Top'		
	(NF 14.03.18)		
G-BTOT	Piper PA-15 Vagabond	15-60	22.05.91
	N4176H, NC4176H J E D Rogerson		
	tr Vagabond Flying Group Morgansfield, Fishburn	08.02.20P	
G-BTOU	Cameron O-120	2606	02.07.91
	J J Daly Halfway House, Waterford, RoI		23.07.13E
	(NF 29.10.16)		
G-BTOW	SOCATA Rallye 180T Galerien	3360	09.11.82
	F-BNGZ M Jarrett Manor Farm, Glatton		07.06.17E
	(IE 07.06.18)		
G-BTOZ	Thunder Ax9-120 Series 2	2008	28.06.91
	H G Davies Woodmancote, Cheltenham		18.06.14E
	(NF 06.10.17)		
G-BTPT	Cameron N-77	2575	10.06.91
	H J Andrews Rowledge, Farnham		01.07.09E
	(NF 20.11.15)		
G-BTPV	Colt 90A	1956	14.06.91
	J S Russon & C J Wootton Cheadle Hulme & Ormskirk		
	'Mondial Assistance'		05.06.19E
	Built by Thunder & Colt Ltd		
G-BTPX	Thunder Ax8-90 Series 1	1873	18.06.91
	B J Ross Fareham		16.07.18E
	Built by Cameron Balloons Ltd		
G-BTRC	Avid Speed Wing	913	02.07.91
	H Bishop (East Grinstead)		21.11.17P
	Built by A A Craig – project PFA 189-12076		
G-BTRF	Aero Designs Pulsar	xxxx	04.07.91
	P F Crosby & C Smith Spilsted Farm, Sedlescombe	19.10.19P	
	Built by C Smith – project PFA 202-12051; tricycle u/c		
G-BTRG	Aeronca 65C	C4149	04.07.91
	N22466, NC22466 Condor Aviation International Ltd		
	Birchwood Lodge, North Duffield		24.04.19P
G-BTRI	Aeronca 11CC Super Chief	11CC-246	04.07.91
	N4540E, NC4540E H Wankowska & A F Wankowski		
	Crowfield		27.06.19P
G-BTRK	Piper PA-28-161 Warrior II	28-8216206	08.07.91
	N297FT, N9594N Stapleford Flying Club Ltd		
	Stapleford		08.10.19E
G-BTRL	Cameron N-105	2622	05.07.91
	J Lippett Coat, Martock 'Harrods'		24.08.02
	(NF 14.04.16)		
G-BTRR	Thunder Ax7-77	1905	12.07.91
	P J Wentworth Stanford in the Vale, Faringdon		03.09.13E
	(NF 30.11.16)		
G-BTRS	Piper PA-28-161 Warrior II	28-8116004	12.07.91
	N8248V D Kaye & L Millward tr Airwise Flying Group		
	Manchester Barton		22.02.20E
G-BTRT	Piper PA-28R-200 Cherokee Arrow II	28R-7535270	24.07.91
	N1189X C D Barden & S R Williams		
	tr Romeo Tango Group Manchester Barton	16.08.19E	
G-BTRU	Robin DR.400-180 Régent	2089	12.07.91
	R H Mackay Easterton		10.04.19E
G-BTRW	Slingsby T61F Venture T.2	1968	05.07.91
	ZA632 P Asbridge Lleweni Parc		31.05.17E
	(NF 10.05.18)		
G-BTRY	Piper PA-28-161 Warrior II	28-8116190	18.07.91
	N8363L C S Jennings (Much Marcle, Ledbury)		08.03.19E
G-BTRZ	Jodel D.18	148	16.07.91
	A P Aspinall Little Gransden		27.08.19P
	Built by R Collin – project PFA 169-11271		
G-BTSC[M]	Evans VP-2	xxxx	20.10.78
	I Pearson Newquay Cornwall		13.02.96P
	Built by D J Kearn & Truro School – project		
	PFA 063-10342; on display Cornwall Aviation		
	Heritage Centre 08.18 (IE 05.07.17)		
G-BTSJ	Piper PA-28-161 Warrior II	28-7816473	23.07.91
	N9417C Coastal Air (SW) Ltd Newquay Cornwall		19.01.20E
	Operated by Flynqy		

G-BTSN	Cessna 150G	15065106	30.08.91
	N3806J Cancelled 04.06.18 by CAA		16.12.14
	Newcastle, ROI *Stored dismantled 08.18*		
G-BTSP	Piper J-3C-65 Cub	7647	30.08.91
	N41013, NC41013 D J Pilkington Blackpool		20.09.18P
G-BTSR	Aeronca 11AC Chief	11AC-785	30.08.91
	N9152E, NC9152E J M O Miller (Weybread, Ipswich)		15.03.19P
G-BTSV	Denney Kitfox Model 3	xxxx	24.07.91
	R J Folwell Wishanger Farm, Frensham		04.06.14P
	Built by D J Sharland – project PFA 172-11920		
	(NF 27.04.18)		
G-BTSX	Thunder Ax7-77	2027	24.07.91
	A J Gregory Calcot, Cheltenham		04.04.19E
G-BTSY	English Electric Lightning F.6	95207	25.07.91
	XR724 Cancelled 26.05.92 as TWFU		
	Binbrook *Stored as 'XR724'*		
G-BTSZ	Cessna 177A Cardinal	17701198	30.07.91
	N30332 Henlow Aviation Ltd RAF Henlow		01.10.19E
G-BTTD	Montgomerie-Bensen B.8MR	xxxx	31.07.91
	A J P Herculson (Fakenham)		28.04.05P
	Built by K J Parker – project PFA G/01-1204 (NF 14.07.16)		
G-BTTR	Pitts S-2A	2208	16.08.91
	N38MP D Hall tr Yellowbird Adventures Syndicate		
	White Waltham		19.04.19E
	Built by Aerotek Inc		
G-BTTS	Colt 77A HAB	1861	16.08.91
	Cancelled 13.08.10 as PWFU		04.05.08
	Not Known *Inflated Pidley 05.16*		
G-BTTW	Thunder Ax7-77	2016	27.08.91
	T D Gibbs Petworth		07.06.19E
G-BTTY	Denney Kitfox Model 2	xxxx	29.07.91
	B J Clews & L W Whittington Bodmin		22.05.19P
	Built by K J Fleming – project PFA 172-11823		
G-BTTZ	Slingsby T61F Venture T.2	1961	30.07.91
	ZA625 M G Reynolds tr Upwood Motorglider Group		
	(Bourn)		26.07.19
G-BTUA	Slingsby T61F Venture T.2	1985	20.08.91
	ZA666 Shenington Gliding Club Shenington		17.01.20E
G-BTUB	Yakovlev Yak C-11	172623	29.08.91
	(France), Egypt AF 543 G G L James Sleap		18.06.19P
	Built by Strojírny první petilesky (SPP)		
	carries Soviet AF c/s less serial		
G-BTUG	SOCATA Rallye 180T Galerien	3208	10.07.78
	L C Clark & D Moore Sandhill Farm, Shrivenham		11.04.18E
	(03.05.19E)		
G-BTUH	Cameron N-65	1452	28.08.91
	J S Russon Cheadle Hulme, Cheadle *'Zanussi'*		10.04.16E
	(NF 05.02.19)		
G-BTUK	Pitts S-2A	2260	02.09.91
	N5300J S H Elkington Wickenby		21.12.19E
	Built by Aerotek Inc		
G-BTUM	Piper J-3C-65 Cub	19516	06.09.91
	N6335H, NC6335H I M Mackay tr G-BTUM Syndicate		
	White Waltham *'Jingle-Belle'*		21.08.19P
	Fuselage No.19586		
G-BTUC^M	Embraer EMB-312 Tucano	312007	19.06.86
	G-14-007, PP-ZTC Cancelled 20.12.96 as WFU		11.09.93
	With Ulster Aviation Society, Lisburn		
G-BTUR	Piper PA-18 Super Cub 95 (L-18C-PI)	18-3205	11.09.91
	OO-LVM, Belg.AF OL-L08, Belg.AF L-131, 53-4805		
	P S Gilmour RAF Leuchars		14.12.19
	Fuselage No.18-3218		
G-BTUS	Whittaker MW7	xxxx	05.09.91
	C T Bailey Lotmead Farm, Wanborough		20.06.06P
	Built by J F Bakewell – project PFA 171-11999		
	(NF 31.07.18)		
G-BTUW	Piper PA-28-151 Cherokee Warrior	28-7415066	12.09.91
	N54458 T S Kemp Enstone		02.01.20E
G-BTUZ	American General AG-5B Tiger	10075	03.10.91
	N11939 Meadowland Aviation LLP Sleap		21.04.19E
G-BTVA	Thunder Ax7-77	2009	16.09.91
	M Mansfield Sawtry, Huntingdon		07.07.18E
	(IE 09.07.18)		

G-BTVC	Denney Kitfox Model 2	xxxx	23.09.91
	G C Jiggins Longacre Farm, Sandy		02.01.15P
	Built by R Swinden – project PFA 172-11784		
	(IE 04.10.18)		
G-BTVE	Hawker Demon I	K8203	18.09.91
	2292M, K8203 Demon Displays Ltd Old Warden		04.09.18P
	Built by Boulton Paul Aircraft Ltd;		
	as 'K8203' in RAF 64 Sqdn silver c/s		
G-BTVV^M	Reims/Cessna F337G Super Skymaster	F33700058	25.09.91
	PH-RPD, N1876M Cancelled 19.02.14 as PWFU		12.01.03
	With Aviation Museum at Atlantic AirVenture, Shannon		
G-BTVW	Cessna 152 II	15279631	23.09.91
	N757CK Madalena Cruel Lda		
	Santarém, Ribatejo, Portugal		05.02.20E
G-BTVX	Cessna 152 II	15283375	23.09.91
	N48786 S J Nicholls Retford Gamston		03.04.19E
G-BTWB	Denney Kitfox Model 3	920	21.08.91
	(G-BTTM) C J Scott (Edinburgh EH1)		08.02.19P
	Built by J E Tootell – project PFA 172-12278		
G-BTWC	Slingsby T61F Venture T.2	1975	23.09.91
	ZA656 G W Beard tr 621 Venture Syndicate		
	Nympsfield		18.07.19E
	As 'ZA656' in RAF c/s		
G-BTWD	Slingsby T61F Venture T.2	1976	23.09.91
	ZA657 York Gliding Centre Ltd t/a York Gliding Centre		
	Rufforth		12.11.17E
G-BTWE	Slingsby T61F Venture T.2	1980	23.09.91
	ZA661 P Lazenby tr Aston Down G-BTWE Syndicate		
	Aston Down		29.07.19E
G-BTWF	de Havilland DHC-1 Chipmunk 22	C1/0564	30.09.91
	WK549 J A Simms Breighton *'City of York'*		19.05.17P
	As 'WK549' in RAF c/s (IE 08.12.17)		
G-BTWI	EAA Acrosport	230	02.10.91
	N10JW J O'Connell Top Farm, Croydon *'The Hatiron'*		29.11.19P
	Built by J N Wharton		
G-BTWL	Wag-Aero CUBy Sport Trainer	xxxx	03.10.91
	F E Tofield (Billinghay, Lincoln) *'Harry Ferguson'*		28.03.17P
	Built by Penair – project PFA 108-10893 (NF 18.01.19)		
G-BTWY	Aero Designs Pulsar	xxxx	15.10.91
	R Bishop Spilsted Farm, Sedlescombe		26.07.19P
	Built by A K Pirie & J J Pridal – project		
	PFA 202-12040; tailwheel u/c		
G-BTWZ	Rans S-10 Sakota	0990.117	15.10.91
	J T Phipps North Weald		23.03.18P
	Built by D G Hey – project PFA 194-12117; noted 07.18		
G-BTXD (2)	Rans S-6-ESA Coyote II	0591.191	22.10.91
	A I Sutherland Kylarrick House, Edderton		08.02.19P
	Built by M Isterling – project PFA 204-12104;		
	tailwheel u/c		
G-BTXF	Cameron V-90	2692	02.10.91
	G Thomason Satterthwaite, Ulverston		03.03.03
	(NF 28.02.18)		
G-BTXI	Noorduyn AT-16-ND Harvard IIB	14-429	05.10.91
	Swedish AF 16105, RCAF FE695, FE695, 42-892		
	Patina Ltd Duxford		30.06.19P
	Operated by The Fighter Collection;		
	as 'FE695:94' in RAF c/s		
G-BTXK	Thunder Ax7-65	1910	28.10.91
	ZS-HYP, G-BTXK A F Selby		
	Woodhouse Eaves, Loughborough		31.07.19E
G-BTXM	Colt 21A Cloudhopper	2082	29.10.91
	H J Andrews Rowledge, Farnham		30.08.09E
	(NF 20.11.15)		
G-BTXX	Bellanca 8KCAB Decathlon	595-80	01.10.91
	OY-CYC, SE-IEP, N5063G Tatenhill Aviation Ltd		
	Tatenhill		20.05.19E
G-BTXZ	Zenair CH.250 Zenith	xxxx	24.10.91
	J E Glendinning tr G-BTXZ Group		
	Hinton-in-the-Hedges		07.06.19P
	Built by B F Arnall – project PFA 113-12170		
G-BTYC	Cessna 150L	15075767	04.11.91
	N66002 Z Stevens Leicester		21.05.19E
G-BTYI	Piper PA-28-181 Archer II	28-8190078	15.11.91
	N8287T S W Hedges Coventry		30.03.19E

G-BTYT	Cessna 152 II	15280455	25.11.91
	N24931 Cristal Air Ltd Brighton City		22.02.19E
G-BTYXM	Cessna 140	11004	27.11.91
	N76568, NC76568		
	Cancelled 17.01.13 by CAA as TWFU *Fuselage only*	23.02.98
	With South Yorkshire Aircraft Museum, Doncaster	
G-BTYY	Curtiss Robertson C-2 Robin	475	08.10.91
	N348K, NC348K R W Hatton Goodwood		01.09.97P
	(NF 26.09.17)	
G-BTZA	Beech F33A Bonanza	CE-957	22.11.91
	PH-BNT H Mendelssohn tr G-BTZA Group	
	Kirknewton		01.07.19E
G-BTZB	Yakovlev Yak-50	801810	27.11.91
	DOSAAF 77 Airborne Services Ltd Henstridge		09.11.19P
	As Soviet AF '18'	
G-BTZD	Yakovlev Yak-1	8188	10.12.91
	1342, (Soviet AF) Historic Aircraft Collection Ltd	
	(Wheel Park Farm, Westfield)	
	(NF 09.08.18)	
G-BTZP	SOCATA TB-9 Tampico Club	1421	18.12.91
	M W Orr Little Staughton		18.06.08E
	Stored 02.18 (NF 31.01.19)	
G-BTZS	Colt 77B	2088	18.12.91
	P T R Ollivere Eastbourne		27.05.04
	Built by Thunder & Colt Ltd (NF 19.07.18)	
G-BTZU	Cameron C-60	2734	20.12.91
	S A Simington Eccles, Norwich		11.07.19E
G-BTZV	Cameron V-77	2410	20.12.91
	J W Tyrrell Stourport-on-Severn		19.08.15E
	(NF 20.02.17)	
G-BTZX	Piper J-3C-65 Cub	18871	27.02.92
	N98648, NC98648 G V Wright tr ZX Cub Group	
	Bidford		16.01.19
G-BTZY	Colt 56A	2084	17.10.91
	R J Maud Zaandam, Netherlands		18.05.19E
	Built by Thunder & Colt Ltd	
G-BTZZ	CFM Streak Shadow	K 169-SA	23.12.91
	T Garnham Priory Farm, Tibenham		01.06.19P
	Built by D R Stennett – project PFA 206-12155	

G-BUAA – G-BUZZ

G-BUAB	Aeronca 11AC Chief	11AC-1759	17.01.92
	N3458E, NC3458E P King	
	Eastbach Spence, English Bicknor		10.09.19P
G-BUAG	Jodel D.18	xxxx	03.01.92
	R W Buckley (Tunley, Bath)		01.07.03P
	Built by A L Silcox – project PFA 169-11651	
	(NF 07.08.18)	
G-BUAI	Everett Gyroplane Series 3	030	06.01.92
	D Stevenson Mendlesham		09.04.04P
	(NF 06.11.18)	
G-BUAM	Cameron V-77	2470	10.01.92
	S W K Smeeton Ely *'J&E Page Flowers'*		31.10.19E
G-BUAO	Luscombe 8A	4089	15.01.92
	N1362K, NC1362K C R Carroll & M R Cross	
	tr G-BUAO Group (South Longwood Farm, Owslebury)	11.08.04P
	Damaged landing 09.04.04 Lower Upham,	
	Ogbourne St George (IE 05.02.19)	
G-BUAR	Supermarine 358 Seafire III	xxxx	21.01.92
	French Navy 12F.2, French Navy IF9, PP972	
	Flying A Services Ltd Sywell		02.07.18P
	Built by Westland Aircraft Ltd; as 'PP972:II-5'	
	in RN 880 Sqdn c/s (NF 02.10.18)	
G-BUAV	Cameron O-105	2767	27.01.92
	O & T Dorrell Ashbourne & Derby		26.03.15E
	(NF 27.09.18)	
G-BUBG	Pilatus B-N BN-2T Islander	2264	14.02.92
	VT-SKI, G-JSPC, G-BUBG G Cormack Cumbernauld	13.02.06
	(NF 03.03.17)	
G-BUBLM	Thunder Ax8-105 HAB	1147	10.12.87
	Cancelled 16.06.98 as WFU		16.09.91
	With British Balloon Museum & Library, Newbury	

G-BUBN	Pilatus B-N BN-2B-26 Islander	2270	14.02.92
	Isles of Scilly Skybus Ltd Land's End		18.02.20E
G-BUBP	Pilatus B-N BN-2B-26 Islander	2272	14.02.92
	D-ILFC, JA5321, G-BUBP	
	Isles of Scilly Skybus Ltd Land's End		21.08.19E
G-BUBS	Lindstrand LBL 77B	144	10.10.94
	M Saveri Narni, Terni, Italy *'Bubbles'*		09.04.19E
G-BUBT	Stoddard-Hamilton Glasair IIS RG	xxxx	06.02.92
	I-GLSR, G-BUBT T White Liverpool John Lennon	17.10.19P
	Built by M D Evans – project PFA 149-11633	
G-BUBY	Thunder Ax8-105 Series 2	2115	03.02.92
	D W Torrington Selby *'Jorvik Viking Centre'*		14.05.19E
G-BUCA	Cessna A150K Aerobat	A1500220	14.06.89
	N5920J R J Whyham Blackpool		07.12.16E
G-BUCC	CASA 1-131E Jungmann Series 1000	1109	11.09.78
	G-BUEM, G-BUCC, Spanish AF E3B-114	
	R N Crosland Deanland		27.04.19P
	Spanish AF serial conflicts with G-BJAL;	
	as 'BU+CC: w/nr.1109' in Luftwaffe c/s	
G-BUCG	Schleicher ASW 20L TOP	20396	19.02.92
	BGA 3140, I-FEEL W B Andrews	
	Davidstow Moor *'344'*		03.08.19E
G-BUCH	Stinson V-77 Reliant (AT-19)	77-381	21.02.92
	N9570H, FB531 Sopwith Court Ltd White Waltham	19.09.19
G-BUCK	CASA 1-131E Jungmann Series 1000	1113	11.09.78
	Spanish AF E3B-322 D M Byass tr Jungmann	
	Flying Group White Waltham		04.12.15P
	(NF 30.01.19)	
G-BUCM	Hawker Sea Fury FB.11	VX653	26.02.92
	VX653 Patina Ltd Duxford	
	On restoration & unmarked 07.18 (NF 14.10.15)	
G-BUCO	Pietenpol Air Camper	xxxx	10.02.92
	A James Haw Farm, Hampstead Norreys		13.08.19P
	Built by A James – project PFA 047-11829	
G-BUCS	Cessna 150F	15062368	25.08.89
	N3568L Cancelled 03.02.99 as PWFU		01.04.04
	Lydd *Stored dismantled 08.14*	
G-BUCT	Cessna 150L	15075326	14.06.89
	N11320 Air Navigation & Trading Company Ltd	
	Blackpool		05.12.19E
G-BUDA	Slingsby T61F Venture T.2	1963	18.02.92
	ZA627 P A Moslin tr G-BUDA Syndicate	
	(Ashbourne)		30.06.18E
	(IE 19.12.18)	
G-BUDC	Slingsby T61F Venture T.2	1971	18.02.92
	ZA652 G M Hall Enstone		03.04.18E
	As 'ZA652' in RAF c/s	
G-BUDE	Piper PA-20 Pacer	22-980	09.04.92
	N1144C P Robinson	
	Upper Harford Farm, Bourton-on-the-Water		05.11.19
	Built as PA-22-135 Tri-Pacer'	
G-BUDFM	Rand Robinson KR-2	xxxx	26.02.92
	Cancelled 16.07.12 as PWFU		03.12.03
	Built by J B McNab – project PFA 129-11155	
	With Boxted Airfield Historical Group Museum, Boxted	
G-BUDI	Aero Designs Pulsar	xxxx	25.02.92
	R W L Oliver Fairoaks		04.06.19P
	Built by R W L Oliver – project PFA 202-12185	
G-BUDK	Thunder Ax7-77	2076	02.03.92
	W Evans Bangor Isycoed, Wrexham		09.09.09E
	(NF 27.07.15)	
G-BUDL	Auster 3	458	05.03.92
	PH-POL, R Netherlands AF 8A-2, R-17, NX534	
	I R Leek Spanhoe		07.03.20P
	Built by Taylorcraft Aeroplanes (England) Ltd;	
	officially registered as '5810' (Frame No.TAY 5810);	
	as 'NX534' in RAF camouflage c/s	
G-BUDN	Cameron Shoe-90	2761	06.03.92
	Magical Adventures Ltd West Bloomfield, MI, USA	
	'Converse Allstar Boot'		29.09.09E
	(NF 03.06.15)	
G-BUDO	PZL-110 Koliber 150	03900045	12.03.92
	(D-EIVT) A S Vine Haverfordwest		27.07.06
	(NF 07.08.18)	

G

G-BUDR	Denney Kitfox Model 3	1086	16.03.92
	J M Pipping (Moorlinch, Bridgwater)		28.08.19P
	Built by D Silsbury – project PFA 172-12107;		
	flies from Westonzoyland'		
G-BUDS	Rand Robinson KR-2	xxxx	31.12.85
	B E Wagenhauser (Farleigh Hungerford, Bath)		
	Built by D W Munday – project PFA 129-10937		
	(IE 14.03.19)		
G-BUDT	Slingsby T61F Venture T.2	1883	30.03.92
	XZ563 R Birch tr G-BUDT Group Aston Down		23.08.12E
	On rebuild 01.19 (IE 10.03.17)		
G-BUDW	Brügger MB.2 Colibri	xxxx	19.03.92
	G-GODS S P Barrett Northfield Farm, Mavis Enderby		21.07.19P
	Built by J M Hoblyn – project PFA 043-10644		
G-BUEC	Van's RV-6	21015	17.03.92
	A H Harper High Ham, Langport		11.07.19P
	Built by R D Harper & D W Richardson		
	– project PFA 181A-11884		
G-BUED	Slingsby T61F Venture T.2	1979	12.03.92
	ZA660 F B Rutterford tr Venture Syndicate Challock		24.03.20P
G-BUEF	Cessna 152 II	15280862	17.03.92
	N25928 A L Brown t/a Channel Aviation Bourn		25.05.19E
G-BUEG	Cessna 152 II	15280347	17.03.92
	N24736 P Rudd Rochester		06.10.18E
G-BUEI	Thunder Ax8-105	2172	23.03.92
	P J Hooper Southville, Bristol		03.04.19E
G-BUEK	Slingsby T61F Venture T.2	1879	30.03.92
	XZ559 P Baldwin & G E Draycott tr G-BUEK Group		
	Shipdham		01.07.19E
G-BUEN	Magni M14 Scout	VPM14UK101	19.03.92
	C R Gordon Kame Steading, Craigrothie		15.10.19P
G-BUEP	Maule MXT-7-180 Super Rocket	14023C	24.03.92
	N J B Bennett Henstridge		25.03.19E
G-BUET	Colt Flying Drinks Can SS HAB	2162	30.03.92
	Cancelled 29.04.97 as PWFU		10.12.93
	Not Known *Inflated Pidley 04.14*		
	Budweiser Beer Can special shape		
G-BUEU	Colt 21A Cloudhopper HAB	2163	30.03.92
	Cancelled 29.04.97 as WFU		02.12.94
	Not Known *Inflated Pidley 04.18*		
G-BUEW	Rans S-6 Coyote II	0190-111	01.04.92
	G-MWYF, (EI-CEL) C Cheeseman Bodmin		03.07.17P
	Built by D J O'Gorman – project PFA 204-12021;		
	tricycle u/c; made heavy landing Davidstow Moor		
	30.08.16 & damaged		
G-BUEZᴹ	Hawker Hunter F.6A	S4/U/3275	03.04.92
	XF375 Cancelled 28.08.01 as PWFU		
	As 'XF375:6' in ETPS c/s		
	Built by Armstrong-Whitworth Aircraft Ltd		
	With Boscombe Down Aviation Centre, Old Sarum		
G-BUFF	Jodel D112	1302	09.08.78
	F-BMYD Cancelled 29.08.91 by CAA		
	Watchford Farm *For sale as rebuild project 01.17*		
G-BUFG	Slingsby T61F Venture T.2	1977	03.04.92
	ZA658 G W Withers Kirton in Lindsey		03.02.19E
	(IE 18.03.19)		
G-BUFH	Piper PA-28-161 Warrior II	28-8416076	15.04.92
	N43520 County Connections Ltd		
	t/a Solent School of Flying Bournemouth		06.07.19E
G-BUFN	Slingsby T61F Venture T.2	1967	08.04.92
	ZA631 Cancelled 12.01.12 as destroyed		19.08.01
	Rufforth *Stored for rebuild 10.16*		
G-BUFR	Slingsby T61F Venture T.2	1880	09.04.92
	XZ560 Buckminster Gliding Club Ltd Saltby		05.02.19E
G-BUFV	Avid Speed Wing Mk.4	xxxx	15.04.92
	Cancelled 18.04.12 as PWFU		16.09.05
	Toomebridge *Built by S C Ord – project*		
	PFA 189-12192; wreck stored 12.13		
G-BUFY	Piper PA-28-161 Warrior II	28-8016211	14.04.92
	N130CT, N8TS, N3571K Bickertons Aerodromes Ltd		
	Denham		01.07.19E
	Operated by The Pilots Centre		
G-BUGJ	Robin DR.400-180 Régent	2137	28.04.92
	W E R Jenkins (Martin, Lincoln)		16.08.19E

G-BUGL	Slingsby T61F Venture T.2	1966	29.04.92
	ZA630 S L Hoy Tibenham		27.01.16E
	Carries 'ZA630' on tail		
G-BUGM	CFM Streak Shadow	K 176-SA	29.04.92
	M A Avossa (Leicester)		15.06.12P
	Built by W J de Gier – project PFA 206-12069		
	(NF 10.08.16)		
G-BUGP	Cameron V-77	2278	10.03.92
	OO-BEE R Churcher Chilham, Canterbury		12.07.13E
	(NF 28.01.19)		
G-BUGS	Cameron V-77	2482	14.04.92
	S J Dymond Tidworth *'Bugs Bunny'*		14.09.01
	(NF 13.03.18)		
G-BUGT	Slingsby T61F Venture T.2	1871	22.04.92
	XZ551 York Gliding Centre (Operations) Ltd Rufforth		17.07.19E
G-BUGV	Slingsby T61F Venture T.2	1884	28.04.92
	XZ564 T D Fielder tr The Venture Flying Group		
	at Enstone Enstone		11.09.19E
	Rebuilt by McLean Aviation with fuselage		
	ex PH-940 (1872); original fuselage stored 10.16		
G-BUGW	Slingsby T61F Venture T.2	1962	22.04.92
	ZA626 G M Wiseman Old Sarum		24.03.16E
	(NF 16.10.18)		
G-BUGY	Cameron V-90	2800	09.04.92
	I J Culley tr Dante Balloon Group Newtown, Hungerford		15.06.19E
G-BUGZ	Slingsby T61F Venture T.2	1981	22.04.92
	ZA662 R W Spiller tr Dishforth Flying Group Bagby		18.07.19E
G-BUHA	Slingsby T61F Venture T.2	1970	29.04.92
	ZA634 C D Hayball tr Saltby Flying Group Saltby		03.09.18E
	As 'ZA634:C' in RAF c/s (IE 18.03.19)		
G-BUHM	Cameron V-77	2481	07.05.92
	P T Lickorish Shenley Church End, Milton Keynes		09.08.09E
	Noted 05.16 (NF 08.08.18)		
G-BUHO	Cessna 140	14402	01.05.92
	N2173V W B Bateson (Tain)		26.10.14E
	Original fuselage displayed South Yorkshire		
	Air Museum 2017 (NF 04.10.18)		
G-BUHR	Slingsby T61F Venture T.2	1874	08.05.92
	XZ554 The Northumbria Gliding Club Ltd Currock Hill		01.08.19E
G-BUHS	Stoddard-Hamilton Glasair TD	149	08.05.92
	C-GYMB T F Horrocks (Halkirk)		19.10.12P
	Built by F L Binder (NF 08.05.18)		
G-BUHU	Cameron N-105	2785	13.05.92
	M Rate Northampton *'Land Rover'*		23.06.18E
G-BUHZ	Cessna 120	14950	01.05.92
	N3676V P R Hughes tr The Cessna 140 Group		
	RAF Henlow		29.04.19P
G-BUIF	Piper PA-28-161 Warrior II	28-7916406	29.05.92
	N28375 Redhill Air Services Ltd Redhill		31.07.19E
G-BUIG	Campbell Cricket replica	xxxx	27.05.92
	R H Braithwaite RAF Henlow		24.10.18P
	Built by T A Holmes – project PFA G/03-1173		
G-BUIH	Slingsby T61F Venture T.2	1876	29.05.92
	XZ556 M S Johnson tr The Falcon Gliding Group		
	Wellesbourne Mountford		14.01.20P
G-BUIJ	Piper PA-28-161 Warrior II	28-8116210	03.06.92
	N83784 D J & S N Taplin Redhill		19.05.19E
G-BUIK	Piper PA-28-161 Warrior II	28-7916469	02.06.92
	N2845P D S Lawer North Weald *'111'*		19.04.19E
G-BUIL	CFM Streak Shadow	K 182-SA	08.05.92
	A A Castleton (Pensford, Bristol)		13.08.13P
	Built by P N Bevan & L M Poor – project PFA 206-12121		
	(NF 01.03.19)		
G-BUIN	Thunder Ax7-77	1882	05.06.92
	P C Johnson Hucclecote, Gloucester		04.06.15E
	(NF 26.09.16)		
G-BUIP	Denney Kitfox Model 2	xxxx	08.06.92
	S Porter Causeway		24.09.18P
	Built by G D Lean – project PFA 172-11874		
G-BUIZ	Cameron N-90	2850	12.06.92
	G A Boyle Haverill *'Hutchinson Telecoms'*		11.02.20E
	Telecoms special shape		

G-BUJA	Slingsby T61F Venture T.2	1972	22.05.92
	ZA653 Wolds Gliding Club Ltd Pocklington		13.09.19E

G-BUJB	Slingsby T61F Venture T.2	1978	21.05.92
	ZA659 O F Vaughan tr Falke Syndicate Shobdon		11.02.19E

G-BUJE	Cessna 177B Cardinal	17701920	10.06.92
	N34646 E Smith tr FG93 Group Compton Abbas		21.08.19E

G-BUJH	Colt 77B	2207	23.06.92
	B Fisher Guildford		23.07.16E
	Built by Thunder & Colt Ltd		

G-BUJI	Slingsby T61F Venture T.2	1882	22.05.92
	XZ562 R J Hale tr Solent Venture Syndicate Solent		13.06.19E

G-BUJJ	Avid Speed Wing	213	20.10.92
	N614JD P P Trangmar Deanland		24.04.18P
	Built by M Cox; landed heavily Breighton 11.05.17		
	& substantially damaged (IE 30.05.18)		

G-BUJM	Cessna 120	11784	19.06.92
	N77343, NC77343 K G Grayson Tatenhill		02.06.19

G-BUJN	Cessna 172N Skyhawk II	17272713	19.06.92
	N6315D Warwickshire Aviation Ltd		
	Wellesbourne Mountford		11.07.19E

G-BUJO	Piper PA-28-161 Cherokee Warrior II	28-7716077	19.06.92
	N1014Q A S Bamrah t/a Falcon Flying Services		
	Biggin Hill		16.08.19E
	Operated by Alouette Flying Club		

G-BUJP	Piper PA-28-161 Warrior II	28-7916047	19.06.92
	N21624 Flying at Lee on Solent Ltd		
	t/a Phoenix Aviation Solent		03.04.19E

G-BUJV	Avid Speed Wing Mk.4	xxxx	03.07.92
	C Thomas (Colan, Newquay)		28.07.94P
	Built by D N Anderson – project PFA 189-12250		
	(NF 21.03.16)		

G-BUJW[M]	Thunder Ax8-90 HAB	2208	06.07.92
	Cancelled 19.11.13 as PWFU		
	With British Balloon Museum & Library, Newbury		

G-BUJX	Slingsby T61F Venture T.2	1873	07.07.92
	XZ553 York Gliding Centre Ltd Rufforth		04.09.14E
	(NF 07.04.17)		

G-BUJZ	RotorWay Exec 90	5119/6973	09.07.92
	Cancelled 21.02.19 by CAA		07.09.07
	Street Farm, Takeley *Stored part rebuilt 10.18*		

G-BUKB	Rans S-10 Sakota	0790.112	13.07.92
	M K Blatch (Faringdon)		18.04.07P
	Built by M K Blatch – project PFA 194-12078		
	(IE 21.12.18)		

G-BUKF	Denney Kitfox Model 4	xxxx	02.06.92
	A G V McClintock tr Kilo Foxtrot Group East Fortune		21.06.19P
	Built by M R Crosland – project PFA 172A-12247		

G-BUKH	Druine D.31 Turbulent	xxxx	14.08.92
	G Haye Strathaven		23.08.19P
	Built by J S Smith – project PFA 048-11419		

G-BUKI	Thunder Ax7-77	2239	08.07.92
	Airxcite Ltd t/a Virgin Balloon Flights		
	Stafford Park, Telford *'Virgin'*		24.06.11E
	(NF 19.10.18)		

G-BUKK	Bücker Bü.133C Jungmeister	27	15.11.89
	N44DD, HB-MKG, Swiss AF U-80		
	B R Cox Coventry		12.10.18P
	Built by Dornier-Werke AG; as 'U-80:RV' in Swiss AF c/s		

G-BUKO	Cessna 120	13089	15.07.92
	N2828N, NC2828N P Kelsey tr Peregrine Flying Group		
	Tatenhill		18.11.19P

G-BUKP	Denney Kitfox Model 2	xxxx	22.07.92
	K C Smith (Lowestoft)		09.04.15P
	Built by T D Reid – project PFA 172-12301 (NF 19.09.18)		

G-BUKR	SOCATA MS.880B Rallye 100T	2923	27.07.92
	LN-BIY G R Russell tr G-BUKR Flying Group		
	Middle Pymore Farm, Bridport		09.07.19E

G-BUKU	Luscombe 8E Silvaire Deluxe	4720	30.07.92
	N1993K, NC1993K D J Warren tr Silvaire Flying Group		
	Old Hay Farm, Paddock Wood		29.06.19P

G-BUKZ	Evans VP-2	xxxx	05.08.92
	P R Farnell (Malton)		
	Built by P R Farnell – project PFA 063-10761 (NF 09.02.18)		

G-BULB	Thunder Ax7-77	1968	03.07.92
	A Lutz Newnham		03.03.14E
	Built by Thunder & Colt Ltd (NF 03.11.17)		

G-BULC	Avid Speed Wing Mk.4	1055	06.07.92
	P P Trangmar (Hailsham)		06.12.19P
	Built by C Nice – project PFA 189-12202		

G-BULG	Van's RV-4	JRV4-1	28.07.92
	C-FELJ V D Long Fir Grove, Wreningham		13.05.19P
	Built by L Johnson		

G-BULJ	CFM Streak Shadow	K 191-SA	10.08.92
	D R Stansfield Bagby		28.06.19P
	Built by C C Brown – project PFA 206-12199		

G-BULL	Scottish Aviation Bulldog Srs 120/128	BH120/392	20.09.88
	HKG-5, G-31-18 Bulldog Aeros Ltd Cotswold		04.04.19E
	As 'HKG-5' in Royal Hong Kong AAF c/s		

G-BULN	Colt 210A	2265	13.08.92
	H G Davies Woodmancote, Cheltenham		09.08.09E
	Built by Thunder & Colt Ltd (NF 04.01.19)		

G-BULO	Luscombe 8F Silvaire	4216	13.08.92
	N1489K, NC1489K B W Foulds		
	Yeatsall Farm, Abbots Bromley		23.11.18P

G-BULR	Piper PA-28-140 Cherokee B	28-25230	08.07.92
	HB-OHP, N7320F D H G Penney Sandtoft		04.07.08E
	Fuselage dumped 04.17 outside hangar (NF 01.06.15)		

G-BULT	Everett Gyroplane Series 1	xxxx	20.08.92
	A T Pocklington (Birchanger, Bishop's Stortford)		26.05.05P
	Built by A T Pocklington – project PFA G/03A-1213		
	(NF 19.01.16)		

G-BULY	Avid Flyer	xxxx	12.08.92
	C Coleman (Godalming)		16.09.14P
	Built by M O Breen – project PFA 189-12309		
	(NF 21.09.17)		

G-BULZ	Denney Kitfox Model 2	xxxx	31.07.92
	T G F Trenchard		
	Newton Peveril Farm, Sturminster Marshall		16.10.18P
	Built by D J Dumulo – project PFA 172-11546		

G-BUMP	Piper PA-28-181 Archer II	28-7790437	17.01.79
	PH-MVA, OO-HCH, N3105Q M J Green & D Major		
	Humberside		16.01.20E

G-BUNB	Slingsby T61F Venture T.2	1969	25.08.92
	ZA633 R M Peach tr Wessex Ventures 2016		
	Kingston Deverill		06.08.19E

G-BUNC	PZL-104 Wilga 35A	129444	02.09.92
	SP-TWP R F Goodman Husbands Bosworth		10.09.19E

G-BUNG	Cameron N-77	2905	02.09.92
	A Kaye Irchester, Wellingborough *'Bungle'*		20.06.10E
	(NF 06.10.17)		

G-BUNI	Cameron Bunny 90SS HAB	2897	23.09.92
	Cancelled 11.03.03 as destroyed		29.10.99
	Not Known *Inflated Pidley 04.14 'Cadburys Caramel'*		

G-BUNO	Neico Lancair 320	249	11.09.92
	J Softley (Newbury)		
	Built by J Softley – project PFA 191-12332 (NF 06.12.18)		

G-BUOA	Whittaker MW6-S Fatboy Flyer	xxxx	25.09.92
	H N Graham (Lisbellaw, Enniskillen)		04.10.06P
	Built by D A Izod – project PFA 164-11959;		
	stored 2016 (NF 30.07.18)		

G-BUOB	CFM Streak Shadow	K 186-SA	29.09.92
	J M Hunter (Masnuy St Jean, Belgium)		30.05.19P
	Built by A M Simmons – project PFA 206-12156		

G-BUOD	Replica Plans SE.5A	xxxx	05.10.92
	M D Waldron Croft Farm, Defford		20.04.19P
	Built by M D Waldron – project PFA 020-10474;		
	as 'B595:W' in RFC 56 Sqdn c/s		

G-BUOF	Druine D.62B Condor	xxxx	06.10.92
	D W Collins Henstridge		23.03.19P
	Built by K Jones – project PFA 49-11236		

G-BUOL	Denney Kitfox Model 3	xxxx	12.10.92
	P Dennington Eshott		27.09.16P
	Built by J G D Barbour – project PFA 172-12142		
	(IE 06.08.18)		

G-BUON	Avid Aerobat	xxxx	13.10.92
	T P Beare (Ashwater, Beaworthy)		22.09.17P
	Built by I A J Lappin – project PFA 189-12160		
	(IE 07.08.18)		

G

G-BUOS	Supermarine 394 Spitfire FR.XVIIIe	6S-672224	19.10.92
	SE-BIN, G-BUOS, Israel AF HS687, SM845		
	Spitfire Ltd Humberside		11.01.20P
	As 'SM845:R' in RAF overall silver c/s		
G-BUOW	Aero Designs Pulsar XP	xxxx	22.10.92
	T J Hartwell Sackville Lodge Farm, Riseley		08.06.95P
	Built by D F Gaughan – project PFA 202-12206		
	(NF 30.10.18)		
G-BUPA	Rutan Long-EZ	750	22.09.92
	N72SD N G Henry (Oxford)		27.04.06P
	Built by D Moore (NF 17.04.15)		
G-BUPB	Stolp SA.300 Starduster Too	RH100	03.11.92
	N8035E J R Edwards & J W Widdows Enstone		05.08.14P
	Built by R Harte (NF 08.06.18)		
G-BUPC	Rollason Beta B.2	xxxx	29.10.92
	C A Rolph (Storrington, Pulborough)		03.06.03P
	Built by C A Rolph – project PFA 002-12369		
	(NF 19.01.16)		
G-BUPF	Bensen B.8MR	xxxx	05.11.92
	P W Hewitt-Dean Draycott		23.01.19P
	Built by G M Hobman – project PFA G/01-1209		
G-BUPH	Colt 25A	2023	10.11.92
	LY-BUP, G-BUPH M E White Abbeyview, Trim, RoI		19.09.19E
G-BUPJ	Fournier RF4D	4119	10.11.92
	N7752 Cancelled 28.10.10 as PWFU		
	Ranksborough Farm, Langham		
	Stored for sale as rebuild project 10.18		
G-BUPM	Magni M16 Tandem Trainer	VPM16UK102	16.10.92
	A Kitson RAF Mona		18.07.08P
	(NF 14.10.15)		
G-BUPP	Cameron V-42	2789	21.07.92
	C L Schoeman Basildon		13.05.04A
	(NF 19.01.16)		
G-BUPR	Jodel D.18	159	23.11.92
	R W Burrows Priory Farm, Tibenham		19.07.19P
	Built by R W Burrows – project PFA 169-11289		
G-BUPU	Thunder Ax7-77	2305	25.11.92
	R C Barkworth & D G Maguire Allens Park, CO, USA		26.03.01
	(NF 19.02.19)		
G-BUPV	Great Lakes 2T-1A Sport Trainer	126	26.11.92
	N865K, NC865K R J Fray Furze Farm, Haddon		03.10.17P
	(IE 02.04.18)		
G-BUPW	Denney Kitfox Model 3	xxxx	22.10.92
	S G Metcalfe Bleaze Hall, Old Hutton, Kendal		24.06.16P
	Built by D Sweet – project PFA 172-12281		
G-BURE	Jodel D.9 Bebe	xxxx	30.11.92
	Cancelled 06.07.15 as WFU		
	Prestwick Built by C R Kingsford & P B Shilling		
	– project PFA 944; under construction 08.17		
G-BURH	Cessna 150E	15061225	02.12.92
	EI-AOO, G-BURH, EI-AOO, N3525J		
	C Sheridan (Collon, Co Louth, RoI)		07.11.19E
G-BURI	Enstrom F-28C	433	11.12.92
	N51743 D W C Holmes (Langley Mill, Nottingham)		19.12.19E
G-BURL	Colt 105A	2297	18.11.92
	J E Rose Abingdon *'Isis'*		09.06.06
	Built by Thunder & Colt Ltd (NF 22.01.19)		
G-BURP	RotorWay Exec 90	5116	08.10.92
	N K Newman Hawarden		13.09.96P
	Built by A G A Edwards; stored 08.15 (NF 06.02.14)		
G-BURR	Auster AOP.9	B5/10/32	28.09.92
	7851M, WZ706 P J Gill t/a Annic Aviation		
	Darley Moor *'Army'*		26.03.19P
	As 'WZ706' in AAC camouflage c/s & dayglo areas		
G-BURZ	Hawker Nimrod II	41H-59890	22.12.91
	K3661 Historic Aircraft Collection Ltd Duxford		25.05.19P
	As 'K3661:562' in RAF 802 Sqdn c/s		
G-BUSN	RotorWay Exec 90	5141	06.01.93
	J P McEnroe Street Farm, Takeley		25.04.16P
	(IE 24.06.16)		
G-BUSR	Aero Designs Pulsar	xxxx	15.12.92
	S S Bateman & R A Watts Cheddington		21.06.19P
	Built by S S Bateman & R A Watts		
	– project PFA 202-12356; tailwheel u/c		

G-BUSS	Cameron Bus-90	1685	11.03.88
	Magical Adventures Ltd West Bloomfield, MI, USA		
	'National Express'		31.01.96
	(NF 03.06.15)		
G-BUSV	Colt 105A	2324	12.01.93
	H C J Williams Langford, Bristol		18.05.18E
	Built by Thunder & Colt Ltd (IE 17.09.18)		
G-BUSW	Rockwell Commander 114	14079	18.01.93
	N4749W M J P Lynch Wellesbourne Mountford		14.12.15E
	(IE 08.12.17)		
G-BUTB	CFM Streak Shadow	K 190	20.01.93
	H O Maclean Oban		15.05.19P
	Built by F A H Ashmead – project PFA 206-12243		
G-BUTD	Van's RV-6	xxxx	21.01.93
	B S Carpenter Eastfield Farm, Manby		14.08.19P
	Built by N Reddish – project PFA 181-12152		
G-BUTE	Anderson EA-1 Kingfisher Amphibian	xxxx	15.08.91
	G-BRCK Cancelled 23.01.14 by CAA		15.10.99
	Cumbernauld Built by T Crawford		
	– project PFA 132-10798; stored 2013		
G-BUTF	Aeronca 11AC Chief	11AC-1578	21.01.93
	N3231E, NC3231E A W Crutcher Cardiff		26.06.12P
	(NF 05.07.18)		
G-BUTG	Zenair CH.601HD Zodiac	xxxx	22.01.93
	A Brown Hunsdon		07.12.18P
	Built by J M Scott – project PFA 162-12225		
G-BUTH	Robin DR.220 2+2	6	10.02.93
	F-BNVK P J Gristwood tr Phoenix Flying Group		
	Dunkeswell		08.10.19E
	Built by Centre-Est Aéronautique		
G-BUTJ	Cameron O-77	2991	25.01.93
	C & P Collins Clifton, Preston *'Purple Haze'*		15.05.17E
G-BUTK	Murphy Rebel	xxxx	25.01.93
	A J Gibson Watchford Farm, Yarcombe		17.09.18P
	Built by D Webb – project PFA 232-12091		
G-BUTM	Rans S-6-116 Coyote II	0792.323	22.01.93
	J C Holland Kiln Farm, Hungerford		23.08.19P
	Built by M Rudd – project PFA 204A-12414;		
	tailwheel u/c		
G-BUTT	Reims/Cessna FA150K Aerobat	FA1500029	18.08.86
	G-AXSJ Fis Ato Europe SL		
	(Vejer, Costa de la Luz, Spain)		23.02.20E
G-BUTX	Bücker Bü.133C Jungmeister	xxxx	03.02.93
	Spanish AF ES.1-4, Spanish AF 35-4		
	S R Stead White Waltham		12.04.19P
	Officially c/n 'ES.1-4' but possibly CASA-built		
	I-133L c/n 1010		
G-BUTY	Brügger MB.2 Colibri	xxxx	30.11.92
	R M Lawday (Milford, Derby)		
	Built by R M Lawday – project PFA 043-12387		
	(NF 08.03.16)		
G-BUTZ	Piper PA-28-180 Cherokee C	28-3107	23.04.93
	G-DARL, 4R-ARL, 4R-ONE, SE-EYD		
	D M Cansdale & N T W Pooley tr G-BUTZ Flying Group		
	(Bury St Edmunds)		15.10.19E
G-BUUA	Slingsby T67M Firefly II	2111	17.03.93
	Heartland Aviation Ltd Brighton City		27.07.19E
G-BUUC	Slingsby T67M Firefly II	2113	17.03.93
	Swiftair Maintenance Ltd Leicester		22.11.19E
G-BUUE	Slingsby T67M Firefly II	2115	17.03.93
	J R Bratty Nottingham City		29.10.19E
G-BUUF	Slingsby T67M Firefly II	2116	17.03.93
	Nautx Aviation Ltd Dunkeswell		07.02.19E
G-BUUI	Slingsby T67M Firefly II	2119	17.03.93
	Bustard Flying Club Ltd MoD Boscombe Down		17.12.19E
G-BUUJ	Slingsby T67M Firefly II	2120	17.03.93
	R M Rennoldson tr Blue Skies Flying Group		
	Full Sutton		01.03.20E
G-BUUK	Slingsby T67M Firefly II	2121	17.03.93
	Avalanche Aviation Ltd Sleap		19.03.20E
G-BUUL	Slingsby T67M Firefly II	2122	17.03.93
	F-HVAI, HA-WAI, G-BUUL Air Ministry Aviation Ltd		
	Wolverhampton Halfpenny Green		11.07.18E

G-BUUO	Cameron N-90 HAB	2994	09.02.93
	Cancelled 11.01.10 as PWFU		19.06.03
	Not Known *Inflated Bath 12.18*		

G-BUUU[M]	Cameron Bottle 77 SS HAB	2980	11.02.93
	Cancelled 22.10.01 by CAA		04.03.94
	Bells Whiskey Bottle		
	With British Balloon Museum & Library, Newbury		

| G-BUUX | Piper PA-28-180 Cherokee D | 28-5128 | 17.02.93 |
| | OY-BCW   M A Judge t/a Aerogroup 78   Netherthorpe | | 19.02.20E |

G-BUVA	Piper PA-22-135 Tri-Pacer	22-1301	12.02.93
	N8626C C B Reynolds tr Oaksey VA Group		
	Oaksey Park		09.11.19

G-BUVB	Colt 77A	2041	22.02.93
	L B Humphrey Horsted Keynes, Haywards Heath		03.07.19E
	Built by Thunder & Colt Ltd		

G-BUVM	Robin DR.250/160 Capitaine	54	11.03.93
	OO-NJR, F-BNJR G Mills tr G-BUVM Group		
	Crosland Moor		04.04.19E
	Built by Centre-Est Aéronautique		

G-BUVN	CASA 1-131E Jungmann Series 2000	2092	12.03.93
	EC-333, Spanish AF E3B-487		
	W V Egmond Hoogeveen, Netherlands		08.08.19P
	As 'BI:005' in R Netherlands AF c/s		

G-BUVO	Reims/Cessna F182P Skylane II	F18200022	10.03.93
	G-WTFA, PH-VDH, D-EJCL P N Stapleton		
	tr Romeo Mike Flying Group Newquay Cornwall		18.04.19E

| G-BUVR | Christen A-1 Husky | 1162 | 12.03.93 |
| | E M Smiley-Jones   Leicester | | 19.09.19E |

G-BUVT	Colt 77A	2382	12.03.93
	N A Carr Leicester		30.07.15E
	Built by Thunder & Colt Ltd (NF 19.01.17)		

G-BUVW	Cameron N-90	3020	19.03.93
	L J Whitelock Bristol *'Bristol Balloon Fiesta'*		28.02.11E
	(NF 24.08.17)		

G-BUVX	CFM Streak Shadow SA	K 214-SA	22.03.93
	Light Aircraft Holdings Ltd (Bradford BD2)		
	'up up and away…'		10.05.18P
	Built by G K R Linney – project PFA 206-12410		
	(IE 10.10.18)		

G-BUWE	Replica Plans SE.5A	xxxx	25.03.93
	Airpark Flight Centre Ltd Coventry		04.07.13P
	Built by D Biggs – project PFA 020-11816;		
	as 'C9533:M' in RFC c/s (IE 14.07.16)		

| G-BUWF | Cameron N-105 | 3036 | 26.03.93 |
| | R E Jones   Lytham St Annes | | 15.05.17E |

G-BUWH	Parsons Two-Place Gyroplane	xxxx	01.04.93
	R V Brunskill (Wallsend)		22.08.95P
	Built by R V Brunskill – project PFA G/08-1215		
	(NF 07.03.16)		

| G-BUWI | Lindstrand LBL 77A | 023 | 05.04.93 |
| | G A Chadwick   Caterham | | 01.08.19E |

G-BUWK	Rans S-6-116N Coyote II	1292.410	07.04.93
	R Warriner Bradley's Lawn, Heathfield		03.06.19P
	Built by R Warriner – project PFA 204A-12448;		
	tricycle u/c		

G-BUWL	Piper J-4A Cub Coupe	4-1047	08.04.93
	N27828, NC27828 M L Ryan Garston Farm, Marshfield		
	(NF 19.01.16)		

G-BUWR	CFM Streak Shadow	K 177-SA	26.04.93
	T Harvey Grove Farm, Raveningham		18.07.19P
	Built by T Harvey – project PFA 206-12068		

G-BUWS	Denney Kitfox Model 2	xxxx	26.04.93
	J E Brewis (Surby, Port Erin, Isle of Man)		
	Built by J E Brewis – project PFA 172-11831		
	(NF 03.06.16)		

G-BUWT	Rand Robinson KR-2	xxxx	05.04.93
	G Bailey-Woods (Ulverston)		
	Built by C M Coombe – project PFA 129-10952		
	(NF 06.08.18)		

| G-BUWU | Cameron V-77 | 3053 | 27.04.93 |
| | T R Dews   Hill Deverill, Warminster   *'Fairways'* | | 11.10.19E |

G-BUXC	CFM Streak Shadow SA-M	K 188	20.04.93
	N R Beale Deppers Bridge, Southam		
	Built by T Hosier – project PFA 206-12177		
	(SSDR microlight since 09.14) (IE 20.01.17)		

G-BUXI	Steen Skybolt	xxxx	16.03.93
	M S Rogerson tr Leipzig Aviators Group White Waltham		30.09.19P
	Built by M Frankland – project PFA 064-10755		

G-BUXK	Pietenpol Air Camper	xxxx	12.05.93
	B M D Nelson Finmere		31.08.07P
	Built by G R G Smith – project PFA 047-11901		
	(NF 09.12.18)		

G-BUXL	Taylor JT.1 Monoplane	xxxx	12.05.93
	P J Hebdon Shenington		28.10.19P
	Built by M W Elliott – project PFA 055-11819		

G-BUXN	Beech C23 Sundowner 180	M-1752	13.05.93
	N9256S Cancelled 14.03.16 as PWFU		31.03.14
	Bournemouth *Open store 02.19*		

G-BUXX	Piper PA-17 Vagabond	17-28	31.03.93
	N4611H, NC4611H		
	R Reid tr G-BUXX Group (Langham, Oakham)		29.02.20P

G-BUXY	Piper PA-25-235 Pawnee	25-2705	18.03.93
	C-GZCR, N6959Z The Bath, Wilts & North Dorset		
	Gliding Club Ltd Kingston Deverill		24.01.20E

G-BUYB	Aero Designs Pulsar	xxxx	28.05.93
	A R Thorpe Solent		13.09.19P
	Built by A P Fenn – project PFA 202-12193;		
	tailwheel u/c		

| G-BUYC | Cameron C-80 | 3095 | 28.05.93 |
| | R P Cross   Ramsbury, Marlborough   *'Windrush'* | | 23.05.19E |

G-BUYD	Thunder Ax-8-90 HAB	2422	28.05.93
	Cancelled 11.06.15 as PWFU		08.06.15
	Not Known *Inflated Pidley 05.16*		

G-BUYE	Aeronca 7AC Champion	7AC-4327	30.04.93
	N85584, NC85584 A A Gillon		
	(Midsomer Norton, Radstock)		16.11.96P
	(NF 07.02.18)		

G-BUYF	American Aircraft Falcon XP	600179	13.05.93
	N512AA M J Hadland Rossall Field, Cockerham		31.10.19P
	Built by R W Harris		

G-BUYK	Denney Kitfox Model 4	xxxx	01.06.93
	M S Shelton Hill Farm, Nayland		09.05.19P
	Built by R D L Mayes – project PFA 172A-12214		

G-BUYL	Rotary Air Force RAF 2000	H2-92-361	02.06.93
	C-FPFN M H J Goldring Tregolds Farm, St Merryn		21.10.19P
	Built by D A Lafleur; rebuilt by Newtonair		
	using parts ex G-TXSE		

G-BUYO	Colt 77A	2398	04.06.93
	D A B Ackermann		
	Grafenhausen, Baden Wurttemberg, Germany		24.03.19E
	Built by Thunder & Colt Ltd		

| G-BUYS | Robin DR.400-180 Régent | 2197 | 21.06.93 |
| | P R Currer tr G-BUYS Flying Group   Nuthampstead | | 17.04.20E |

G-BUYU	Bowers Fly Baby 1A	xxxx	07.06.93
	R C Piper Popham		16.04.18P
	Built by J A Nugent – project PFA 016-12222;		
	as '1803/18' in German Army Air Service c/s		
	as 'Junkers CL1'		

G-BUYY	Piper PA-28-180 Cherokee B	28-1028	18.03.93
	C-FXDP, CF-XDP, N7214W		
	A J Hedges & C E Yates tr G-BUYY Group Henstridge		09.05.16E

G-BUZA	Denney Kitfox Model 3	1178	10.06.93
	G O Newell (Pwllglas, Ruthin)		06.04.13P
	Built by R Hill – project PFA 172-12547 (IE 28.01.18)		

G-BUZB	Aero Designs Pulsar XP	xxxx	14.06.93
	S M Macintyre Yew Tree Farm, Lymm Dam		16.08.17P
	Built by M J Whatley – project PFA 202-12312;		
	tailwheel u/c		

G-BUZG	Zenair CH.601HD Zodiac	xxxx	17.06.93
	G Cox Goodwood		25.02.10P
	Built by N C White – project PFA 162-12457		
	(IE 17.12.18)		

G-BUZH	Star-Lite SL-1	119	17.06.93
	N4HC B A Lyford Watchford Farm, Yarcombe		08.09.00P
	Built by H M Cottle (NF 12.09.17)		

| G-BUZK | Cameron V-77 | 2962 | 17.06.93 |
| | Zebedee Balloon Service Ltd   Szekszárd, Hungary | | 17.09.19E |

G-BUZL	Magni M-16 Tandem Trainer	VPM16UK105	18.06.93
	Cancelled 15.12.11 by CAA		22.04.08
	Kirkbride *Stored 08.13*		

G-BUZM	Avid Speed Wing	xxxx	30.04.93
	D W Bowman (Dalbeattie)		12.03.20P
	Built by O G Jones & R McLuckie		
	– project PFA 189-12179		
G-BUZO	Pietenpol Air Camper	xxxx	28.06.93
	D A Jones (Maidenhead)		
	Built by D A Jones – project PFA 047-12408		
	(NF 07.03.16)		
G-BUZR	Lindstrand LBL 77A	044	29.06.93
	Lindstrand Technologies Ltd Oswestry		17.12.08E
	(NF 21.08.15)		
G-BUZZ	Agusta-Bell 206B-2 JetRanger II	8178	13.04.78
	F-GAMS, HB-XGI, OE-DXF Skypark (UK) Ltd		
	Gloucestershire		10.12.19E

G-BVAA – G-BVZZ

G-BVAB	Zenair CH.601HDS Zodiac	xxxx	26.05.93
	B N Rides Garston Farm, Marshfield		27.06.18P
	Built by A R Bender – project PFA 162-12475		
G-BVAC	Zenair CH.601HD Zodiac	xxxx	01.06.93
	J A Tyndall Oaksey Park		27.03.15P
	Built by A G Cozens – project PFA 162-12504		
	(IE 27.11.15)		
G-BVAF	Piper J-3C-65 Cub	4645	14.06.93
	OO-UBU, N28199, NC28199		
	N M Hitchman tr G-BVAF Group Hinton-in-the-Hedges		25.07.18P
G-BVAG	Lindstrand LBL 90A HAB	022	07.07.93
	Cancelled 23.05.07 as PWFU		10.06.03
	Not Known *Inflated Pidley 05.16*		
G-BVAH	Denney Kitfox Model 3	xxxx	22.10.91
	B J Finch Bidford		19.02.19P
	Built by V A Hutchinson – project PFA 172-12031		
G-BVAI	PZL-110 Koliber 150	03900040	07.07.93
	OY-CYJ A J Verlander Spanhoe		18.08.18E
G-BVAM	Evans VP-1 Series 2	xxxx	07.07.93
	C S Whitwell tr The Breighton VP-1 Group		
	Breighton *'Annie Murphy'*		16.10.16P
	Built by R F Selby – project PFA 062-12132		
	(IE 22.04.17)		
G-BVAW	Staaken Z-1 Flitzer	xxxx	12.07.93
	L R Williams tr Flitzer Sportflugverein Rhigos		22.09.10P
	Built by D J Evans & L R Williams		
	– project PFA 223-12058 (NF 20.03.17)		
G-BVAY	Rutan VariEze	RS8673345	03.09.93
	Cancelled 23.11.17 by CAA		11.11.02
	Sunderland *Built by R N Saunders*		
	For sale as rebuild project 2016		
G-BVBF	Piper PA-28-151 Cherokee Warrior	28-7515206	22.07.93
	N31JM, N32633 Cancelled 18.03.99 by CAA		29.07.93
	Nottingham		
	On display at World Cuisine Buffet, Trinity Square 04.16		
G-BVBJ	Colt Flying Coffee Jar	2427	27.07.93
	The British Balloon Museum & Library Ltd		
	Wellingborough *'Maxwell House'*		06.07.19E
	Built by Thunder & Colt Ltd; active 05.18		
G-BVBK	Colt Flying Coffee Jar	2428	27.07.93
	M E White Abbeyview, Trim, RoI *'Maxwell House'*		28.08.15E
	Built by Thunder & Colt Ltd (iE 21.09.16)		
G-BVBU	Cameron V-77	3076	05.08.93
	(OO-BYS) J Ricards Paulton, Bristol		08.07.19E
G-BVBX[M]	Cameron N-90M HAB	3102	10.08.93
	Cancelled 10.02.97 as temporarily WFU 27.09.95		
	With British Balloon Museum & Library, Newbury		
G-BVCA	Cameron N-105	3129	11.08.93
	Skyview Ballooning Ltd t/a Kent Ballooning		
	Stanford, Ashford		30.04.18E
G-BVCG	Van's RV-6	xxxx	17.08.93
	A W Shellis Sittles Farm, Alrewas		10.02.18P
	Built by E M Farquharson & G J Newby		
	– project PFA 181-11783		
G-BVCL	Rans S-6-116 Coyote II	0493.486	25.08.93
	A M Colman Holmbeck Farm, Burcott		06.09.18P
	Built by W E Willetts – project PFA 204A-12551;		
	tricycle u/c		

G-BVCN	Colt 56A	2445	25.08.93
	G A & I Chadwick & S Richards Caterham		12.07.18E
	Built by Thunder & Colt Ltd		
G-BVCO	Clutton FRED Series II	xxxx	25.08.93
	S Wilson tr BVCO Group Leicester		12.06.18P
	Built by I W Bremner – project PFA 029-10947		
G-BVCP	Piper CP.1 Metisse	xxxx	24.06.93
	B M Diggins RAF Mona		10.11.10P
	Built by C W R Piper – project PFA 253-12512		
	(NF 24.02.16)		
G-BVCS	Aeronca 7AC Champion	7AC-1346	01.09.93
	N69BD, N82702, NC82702 A C Lines Leicester		14.06.18P
G-BVCT	Denney Kitfox Model 4-1200	xxxx	27.08.93
	A F Reid Unicarval House, Comber		28.09.18P
	Built by A F Reid – project PFA 172A-12456		
G-BVCY	Cameron H-24	3136	03.09.93
	A C K Rawson & J J Rudoni t/a Wickers World Hot		
	Air Balloon Company Stafford *'Bryant Group'*		09.01.19E
G-BVDB	Thunder Ax7-77	2364	06.09.93
	G-ORDY M K Bellamy Ironville, Nottingham		18.08.18E
G-BVDC	Van's RV-3	xxxx	12.07.93
	R S Hatwell Tibenham		16.10.18P
	Built by D Calibritto – project PFA 099-12218		
G-BVDF	Cameron Doll-105	3112	07.09.93
	K Gruenauer & A Kaye Irchester, Wellingborough		26.06.17E
G-BVDG	Magni M15 Trainer	VPM15UK103	07.09.93
	5Y-VPM, G-BVDG R F G Moyle		
	Tregolds Farm, St Merryn		
	Built by H P Barlow (NF 06.02.17)		
G-BVDH	Piper PA-28RT-201 Arrow IV	28R-7918030	13.09.93
	N2176L J Goldstein North Weald		26.10.17E
G-BVDI	Van's RV-4	2058	13.09.93
	N55GJ J G Gorman & H Tallini tr BVDI Group		
	Brighton City		28.04.18P
	Built by G P Larson		
G-BVDJ	Campbell Cricket replica	xxxx	13.09.93
	S Jennings RNAS Culdrose *'St Merryns Gyronauts'*		13.05.14P
	Built by S Jennings & C D Julian		
	– project PFA G/03-1189 (NF 20.07.17)		
G-BVDO	Lindstrand LBL 105A	055	16.09.93
	K W Graham Spennymoor *'West Lodge Hotel'*		13.04.14E
	(NF 21.07.15)		
G-BVDP	Sequoia F.8L Falco	xxxx	17.09.93
	N M Turner Biggin Hill		13.12.18P
	Built by T G Painter – project PFA 100-10879		
G-BVDR	Cameron O-77	2452	21.09.93
	C M Duggan North Duffield, Selby		24.08.19E
G-BVDS[M]	Lindstrand LBL69A HAB	102	23.09.93
	Cancelled 03.09.15 by CAA		26.06.01
	With British Balloon Museum & Library, Newbury		
G-BVDT	CFM Streak Shadow SA-I	K 223	23.09.93
	A L Hamer (Kings Norton, Birmingham)		31.05.18P
	Built by H J Bennet – project PFA 206-12462		
G-BVDW	Thunder Ax8-90	2507	30.09.93
	S C Vora Oadby, Leicester *'Cosmic'*		19.10.10E
	(NF 27.05.18)		
G-BVDX	Cameron V-90	3159	30.09.93
	OO-BMY, G-BVDX R K Scott Etwall, Derby *'Merlin'*		25.09.05
	(NF 03.02.15)		
G-BVDY	Cameron C-60	3167	30.09.93
	P Baker Abbeyview, Trim, RoI		07.03.18E
G-BVDZ	Taylorcraft BC-12D	9043	21.01.94
	N96743, NC96743 I Maddock & A Sharp		
	(Great Sankey & Acton Bridge)		
	Noted 07.17 (NF 15.08.16)		
G-BVEA	Mosler Motors N-3 Pup	01GB	07.06.93
	G-MWEA M D Grinstead Boston		
	Built by B D Godden – project PFA 212-11837		
	(SSDR microlight since 11.15) (IE 09.10.19)		
G-BVEH	Jodel D.112	1294	29.10.93
	F-BMOH M L Copland Breighton		19.04.18P
	Built by Société Wassmer Aviation		

G-BVEL Evans VP-1 Series 2 xxxx 06.10.93
M J & S J Quinn Crosland Moor
Built by M J Quinn – project PFA 062-11983 (NF 16.10.14)

G-BVEN Cameron C-80 3164 06.10.93
B J & M A Alford Bristol BS3 28.04.18E

G-BVEP Luscombe 8A 1468 08.10.93
N28707, NC28707 P H C Hall Oaksey Park 21.10.09
(IE 05.02.19)

G-BVER de Havilland DHC-2 Beaver 1 1648 13.08.91
G-BTDM, XV268 Cancelled 20.12.16 as WFU 23.04.95
Cumbernauld *Stored 12.16 as 'XV268'*

G-BVEV Piper PA-34-200 Seneca 34-7250316 08.10.93
N1428T, HB-LLN, D-GHSG, N1428T M Ali Southend 01.06.14E
Stored 02.19 (IE 15.03.17)

G-BVEY Denney Kitfox Model 4-1200 xxxx 14.10.93
J H H Turner Kildalloig, Campbeltown 07.07.18P
Built by J S Penny – project PFA 172A-12527

G-BVEZ Hunting Percival P.84 Jet Provost T.3A PAC/W/9287 13.10.93
XM479 D Marshall tr Newcastle Jet Provost Group
Durham Tees Valley 15.05.18P
As 'XM479' in RAF c/s

G-BVFA Rans S-10 Sakota 1090.116 07.09.93
S M Hall & J C Longmore Headon Farm, Retford 15.01.19P
Built by D Allam & D Parkinson – project PFA 194-12298

G-BVFB Cameron N-31 3175 20.10.93
P Lawman Northampton 05.06.18E

G-BVFF Cameron V-77 3161 26.10.93
G P Allen & R J Kerr Didcot & Abingdon 16.10.09E
(NF 15.02.16)

G-BVFM Rans S-6-116 Coyote II 0793.522 02.11.93
J Fleming (Grantown-on-Spey) 04.04.18P
Built by P G Walton – project PFA 204A-12579;
tricycle u/c

G-BVFO Avid Speed Wing xxxx 09.09.93
T G Solomon Brighton City 30.06.14P
Built by P Chisman – project PFA 189-12053
(NF 16.03.18)

G-BVFR CFM Streak Shadow K 237-SA 03.11.93
S G Smith Swansea 21.08.19P
Built by M G B Stebbing – project PFA 206-12567

G-BVFS Slingsby T.31M Motor Cadet III xxxx 03.11.93
ex RAF? S R Williams (Trimley St Martin, Felixstowe)
Built by M Gaffney & R Jones – project PFA 042-11387
to Motor Tutor standard) (NF 15.09.14)

G-BVFU Cameron Sphere-105 3137 18.11.93
Stichting Phoenix Broek in Waterland, Netherlands
'Greenpeace' 30.09.17E

G-BVFY^M Colt 210A HAB 2493 30.09.93
DQ-BVF, G-BVFY Cancelled 14.03.06 by CAA 11.05.00
With British Balloon Museum & Library, Newbury

G-BVFZ Maule M-5-180C Lunar Rocket 8082C 21.02.94
N5664D R C Robinson Crowfield 09.12.18E

G-BVGA Bell 206B-3 JetRanger III 2922 11.11.93
N54AJ, VH-SBC Bucklefields Business
Developments Ltd (Ogbourne St George) 16.06.18E

G-BVGB Thunder Ax8-105 Series 2 2408 11.11.93
E K Read Timperley, Altrincham 20.03.12E

G-BVGE Westland WS-55 Whirlwind HAR.10 WA100 18.11.93
8732M, XJ729 A D Whitehouse
Higher Purtington Showfield, Chard 20.04.18P
As 'XJ729' in RAF Rescue c/s

G-BVGF Europa Aviation Europa 034 18.11.93
T C Hyde (Street) 01.01.19P
Built by A Graham – project PFA 247-12565; tricycle u/c

G-BVGH^M Hawker Hunter T.7 HABL-003360 26.11.93
XL573 M A Stott St Athan 06.10.15P
Centre fuselage no.HABL 003360; as 'XL573' in RAF
silver c/s; to South Wales Aircraft Museum 12.18
(NF 30.01.19)

G-BVGI Pereira Osprey 2 xxxx 29.11.93
D Westoby Blackpool 25.11.03P
Built by B Weare – project PFA 70-10536 (NF 23.03.18)

G-BVGK Lindstrand LBL Newspaper 059 03.12.93
SE-ZHC, G-BVGK H Holmqvist Lund, Sweden 31.12.10E
(NF 01.07.14)

G-BVGO Denney Kitfox Model 4-1200 xxxx 15.11.93
P Madden Strathaven 05.10.17P
Built by R K Dunford – project PFA 172A-12362
(IE 06.12.17)

G-BVGP Bücker Bü.133C Jungmeister 42 03.12.93
F-AZMN, G-BVGP, F-AZFQ, N15696, HB-MIE, D-EIII,
MB-MIE, Swiss AF U-95
T A Bechtolsheimer Turweston 22.08.18P
Built by Dornier-Werke AG; as 'U-95' in Swiss Air Force c/s

G-BVGT Crofton Auster J1-A xxxx 19.11.93
M Flint Boughton (South), Downham Market 21.05.19P
Built by L A Groves – project PFA 000-220; use of
unknown J1 Autocrat frame ex engine test rig

G-BVGW Luscombe 8A 4823 18.11.93
N2096K, NC2096K H E Simons Fairoaks 23.06.15P
(NF 27.04.17)

G-BVGY Luscombe 8E Silvaire Deluxe 4754 18.11.93
N2027K, NC2027K P Chandler Clench Common 18.04.18P

G-BVGZ Fokker Dr.1 Triplane replica VHB10 20.12.93
R A Fleming Brighton 15.06.18P
Built by V H Bellamy – project PFA 238-12654;
as '152/17' in German Army Air Service c/s

G-BVHC Grob G115D-2 Heron 82005 14.12.93
D-EARG Aeros Global Ltd Gloucestershire 30.05.19E

G-BVHD Grob G115D-2 Heron 82006 14.12.93
D-EARJ J A Woodcock Denham 10.05.18E

G-BVHE Grob G115D-2 Heron 82008 14.12.93
D-EASR, G-BVHE, D-EARQ
Tayside Aviation Ltd Dundee 24.01.19E

G-BVHG Grob G115D-2 Heron 82012 14.12.93
D-EARX KFZ Kogl Alexander eU (Bad Voslau, Austria) 18.05.18E

G-BVHI Rans S-10 Sakota 0990.119 20.12.93
J D Amos (Redlands, Swindon) 15.06.18P
Built by P D Rowley – project PFA 194-12608

G-BVHK Cameron V-77 3209 23.12.93
M J Axtell & C M Duggan Leeds & Selby *'intel inside'* 14.09.17E

G-BVHL Nicollier HN.700 Menestrel II 149 24.12.93
G W Lynch Old Buckenham
Built by C Herbert & I H R Walker – project
PFA 217-12614; stored 01.15 (NF 29.10.14)

G-BVHO Cameron V-90 3158 29.12.93
N W B Bews Boraston, Tenbury Wells 18.07.03
(NF 18.01.16)

G-BVHR Cameron V-90 3174 05.01.94
G P Walton Wicklewood, Wymondham 09.08.10E
(NF 14.09.16)

G-BVHS Murphy Rebel 050 05.01.94
S T Raby Grange Farm, Woodwalton 25.09.18P
Built by J Brown, B Godden & M Hanley
– project PFA 232-12180

G-BVHV Cameron N-105 3215 06.01.94
K F Lowry Tilehurst, Reading *'Rover'* 05.06.19E

G-BVIE Piper PA-18 Super Cub (L-18C-PI) 18-1549 26.01.94
G-CLIK, (G-BLMB), D-EDRB, French Army 18-1549,
51-15549 J C Best tr C'est la Vie Group
Andrewsfield *'C'est La Vie'* 01.09.18P
Fuselage No.18-1521

G-BVIF Montgomerie-Bensen B.8MR xxxx 26.01.94
Cancelled 14.11.14 by CAA 21.08.95
Kirkbride *Built by R M Mann – project*
PFA G/01-1228; stored dismantled 11.14

G-BVIH Piper PA-28-161 Warrior II 28-7916191 26.10.93
G-GFCE, G-BNJP, N2212G
Cancelled 22.11.04 by CAA 23.01.00
Redhill *Open store 12.16*

G-BVIK Maule MXT-7-180 Super Rocket 14056C 31.01.94
D L Crook tr Graveley Flying Group
Graveley Hall Farm, Graveley 17.07.18E

G-BVIL Maule MXT-7-180 Super Rocket 14059C 31.01.94
K & S C Knight t/a K & SC Knight Shobdon 22.08.17E

G-BVIO[M]	Colt Flying Drinks Can SS HAB	2538	04.02.94	
	Cancelled 06.11.01 as WFU *Inflated 04.14*		09.06.00	
	Budweiser Can			
	With British Balloon Museum & Library, Newbury			
G-BVIS	Brügger MB.2 Colibri	xxxx	02.02.94	
	B H Shaw Spanhoe		05.08.15P	
	Built by B H Shaw – project PFA 043-10666			
G-BVIV	Avid Speed Wing	xxxx	25.10.93	
	S Styles Stoney Lane Farm, Tutnall, Broad Green		21.11.18P	
	Built by V & J Hobday – project PFA 189-12034;			
	rebuilt by R C Holmes			
G-BVIW	Piper PA-18-150 Super Cub	18-8277	04.02.94	
	SE-EPD I H Logan Popham		26.06.18E	
G-BVIZ	Europa Aviation Europa	052	24.01.94	
	M Dovey Whitehall Farm, Benington		30.07.18P	
	Built by P G Jeffers & T J Punter			
	– project PFA 247-12601; tricycle u/c			
G-BVJK	Glaser-Dirks DG-800A	8-24A21	30.03.94	
	Birkett Air Services Ltd Tibenham		08.04.18E	
G-BVJT	Reims/Cessna F406 Caravan II	F406-0073	02.02.94	
	M Evans & A Jay t/a Nor Leasing Farnborough		29.03.18E	
G-BVJU	Evans VP-1	xxxx	10.03.94	
	B A Schlussler (Hanthorpe, Bourne)			
	Built by B A Schlussler & R Waring			
	– project PFA 062-10691 (NF 02.09.14)			
G-BVJX	Marquart MA.5 Charger	xxxx	12.01.94	
	I Hoolahan tr Lancashire Barnstormers Group			
	Manchester Barton		13.05.19P	
	Built by M L Martin – project PFA 068-11239			
G-BVKB	Boeing 737-59D	27268	24.03.94	
	SE-DNM Cancelled 19.07.13 by CAA		11.04.13	
	Bruntingthorpe *Fuselage stored 05.18*			
G-BVKF	Europa Aviation Europa	050	11.03.94	
	J R F Bennett (Ardoe, Aberdeen)		18.05.12P	
	Built by T R Sinclair – project PFA 247-12638;			
	tricycle u/c (NF 21.10.16)			
G-BVKK	Slingsby T61F Venture T.2	1984	22.02.94	
	ZA665 Buckminster Gliding Club Ltd Saltby		02.08.16E	
G-BVKM	Rutan VariEze	1933	05.04.94	
	N7137G, N14KM J P G Lindquist			
	Ecuvillens, Switzerland		31.10.18P	
	Built by K H Duncan			
G-BVKU	Slingsby T61F Venture T.2	1877	22.03.94	
	XZ557 I P Wright tr G-BVKU Syndicate			
	Kingston Deverill		17.12.18E	
G-BVLA	Neico Lancair 320	xxxx	29.03.94	
	K W Scrivens Old Buckenham			
	Built by T K Pullen & A R Wellstead			
	– project PFA 191-11751 (NF 13.03.15)			
G-BVLD	Campbell Cricket replica	xxxx	29.03.94	
	S J Smith (Sharnford, Leics)		16.04.15P	
	Built by C Berry – project PFA G/01A-1163;			
	stored at owner's premises 01.19			
G-BVLF	CFM Starstreak Shadow SS-D	K 250-SSD	04.03.94	
	J C Pratelli Field Farm, Oakley		07.12.15P	
	Built by B R Johnson – project PFA 206-12662			
	(IE 21.11.16)			
G-BVLG	Aérospatiale AS.355F1 Ecureuil 2	5011	31.03.94	
	N57745 PLM Dollar Group Ltd			
	Wolverhampton Halfpenny Green		10.03.18E	
	Uses callsign 'Osprey 60'; stored 05.18			
G-BVLN	Aero Designs Pulsar XP	xxxx	06.04.94	
	D A Campbell (Rochdale)			
	Built by D A Campbell – project PFA 202-12530			
	(NF 17.04.18)			
G-BVLP	Piper PA-38-112 Tomahawk II	38-82A0002	08.04.94	
	N91355 Cancelled 18.02.15 by CAA		26.05.10	
	Fir Park Farm, Usselby *Stored 09.17*			
G-BVLR	Van's RV-4	xxxx	13.04.94	
	S D Arnold tr RV4 Group Coventry		29.03.19P	
	Built by S D Arnold, S D Scanlon & M Weaver			
	– project PFA 181-12306			
G-BVLT	Bellanca 7GCBC Citabria 150S	1103-79	06.04.94	
	SE-GHV M J Slade t/a Slade Associates Eyres Field		18.09.18E	

G-BVLU	Druine D.31 Turbulent	PFA 1604	18.04.94	
	C D Bancroft Little Down Farm, Milson		31.10.18P	
	Built by C D Bancroft – project PFA 1604			
G-BVLV	Europa Aviation Europa	039	10.03.94	
	D R Curry tr Euro 39 Group Bidford		15.10.18P	
	Built by J T Naylor – project PFA 247-12585; tailwheel u/c			
G-BVLX	Slingsby T61F Venture T.2	1973	19.04.94	
	ZA654 R M Peach tr Wessex Ventures 2016 Keevil		02.05.09E	
	(NF 05.07.17)			
G-BVMA	Beech 200 Super King Air	BB-797	22.07.93	
	G-VPLC, N84B Dragonfly Aviation Services Ltd			
	Cardiff		26.10.18E	
G-BVMM	Robin HR.200-100 Club	41	18.08.80	
	F-BVMM Gift of Flight Ltd Bournemouth		11.04.19E	
G-BVMN	Ken Brock KB-2	xxxx	29.04.94	
	S A Scally tr G-BVMN Group Kirkbride		12.04.12P	
	Built by S McCullagh – project PFA G/06-1218			
	(NF 10.04.18)			
G-BVMR	Cameron V-90	3269	28.03.94	
	I R Comley Up Hatherley, Cheltenham			
	'Midnight Rainbow'		01.07.15E	
G-BVNG	de Havilland DH.60G III Moth Major	3081	17.05.94	
	EC-AFK, Spanish AF EE1-81, 30-81			
	P & T Groves (Lee-on-the-Solent)			
	True c/n & origins unknown (NF 17.10.14)			
G-BVNI	Taylor JT.2 Titch	xxxx	20.05.94	
	P M Jones Derby		14.08.17P	
	Built by T V Adamson – project PFA 060-11147			
G-BVNS	Piper PA-28-181 Archer II	28-7690358	13.04.94	
	N6163J SAF Prestwick Ltd Glasgow Prestwick		22.02.19E	
G-BVNU	FLS Aerospace Sprint Club	004	25.05.94	
	S R Evans (Welwyn Garden City)		09.12.18E	
G-BVNY	Rans S-7 Courier	0290.072	24.05.94	
	S Hazelden Folly Farm, Fulking		19.09.18P	
	Built by J Whiting – project PFA 218-11951			
G-BVOD	Montgomerie-Parson Two Place Gyroplane	xxxx	08.06.94	
	Cancelled 23.11.00 as PWFU			
	Crosshill, Ayrshire *Built by J M Montgomerie*			
	– project PFA G/08-1238; stored 04.14			
G-BVOH	Campbell Cricket replica	xxxx	14.06.94	
	A Kitson RAF Mona		13.07.17P	
	Built by B F Pearson – project PFA G/03-1220			
G-BVOI	Rans S-6-116 Coyote II	0893.524	14.06.94	
	S J Taft Blackmoor Farm, Aubourn		20.04.11P	
	Built by A P Bacon – project PFA 204A-12712;			
	tailwheel u/c (IE 06.12.17)			
G-BVOP	Cameron N-90	3317	21.06.94	
	R J Mansfield Bowness-on-Windermere			
	'Mr Lazenby'		22.02.09E	
	(IE 25.08.15)			
G-BVOR	CFM Streak Shadow	K 238-SA	31.03.94	
	J M Chandler Field Farm, Oakley		04.01.18P	
	Built by J Lord – project PFA 206-12695			
G-BVOS	Europa Aviation Europa	003	11.04.94	
	D A Young tr Durham Europa Group			
	Morgansfield, Fishburn		14.03.18P	
	Built by D Collinson & D A Young – project			
	PFA 247-12562; 'Swiss' version tailwheel u/c			
G-BVOW	Europa Aviation Europa	084	27.06.94	
	I R Caesar & A T Cross (Tilshead & Andover)		25.06.19P	
	Built by M W Cater – project PFA 247-12679;			
	tailwheel u/c			
G-BVOY	RotorWay Exec 90	5238	17.06.94	
	C O'Neill (Wellingborough)		19.12.18P	
	Built by N J Bethell			
G-BVOZ	Colt 56A	2595	21.06.94	
	G G Scaife Petworth		17.07.19E	
	Built by Thunder & Colt Ltd			
G-BVPA	Thunder Ax8-105 Series 2	2600	24.06.94	
	J Fenton Lambrigg, Kendal		25.05.11E	
	(NF 14.07.16)			
G-BVPM	Evans VP-2	xxxx	06.11.78	
	P Marigold (Locking, Weston-super-Mare)		31.05.94P	
	Built by P Marigold – project PFA 7205 (NF 02.05.18)			

G-BVPP Folland Gnat T.1 FL.536 22.04.94
8620M, XP534   Cancelled 22.05.09 by CAA 14.01.05
Bruntingthorpe
Stored as 'XR993' in RAF Red Arrows c/s 07.15

G-BVPS Jodel D.11 1403 06.07.94
P J Brookman   (Markfield) 25.05.18P
Built by P J Sharp – project PFA 917;
badged 'Jodel D112'

G-BVPV Lindstrand LBL 77B 119 13.07.94
P G Hill   Harrogate   'Reverend Leonard' 07.08.18E

G-BVPW Rans S-6-116 Coyote II 0294.587 12.07.94
T B Woolley   (Narborough, Leicester) 17.03.05P
Built by J G Beesley – project PFA 204-12737;
tricycle u/c (NF 17.03.15)

G-BVPX Bensen B.8 Tyro Gyro Mk.II PCL 125 13.07.94
A W Harvey   (Hawling, Cheltenham) 06.04.10P
Built by P C Lovegrove – project PFA G/11-1237
(NF 03.09.15)

G-BVPY CFM Streak Shadow K 204 14.06.94
A J Grant   Tingwall 15.05.18P
Built by R J Mitchell – project PFA 206-12375

G-BVRA Europa Aviation Europa 008 25.07.94
D F Keedy   Sandtoft   'Hummingbird' 12.03.19P
Built by E J J Pels – project PFA 247-12635; tailwheel u/c

G-BVRH Taylorcraft BL-65 1657 15.07.94
N23929, G-BVRH, N24322, NC24322
M J Kirk   New Barn Farm, Crawley 23.09.06
Stored dismantled 10.16 (NF 24.11.15)

G-BVRL Lindstrand LBL 21A 130 03.08.94
A G A Barclay-Faulkner   Hopton, Stafford 18.08.18E

G-BVRU Lindstrand LBL 105A 131 15.08.94
D K Htempleman-Adams   Corsham   'HTV' 29.10.16E
(NF 20.05.16)

G-BVRV Van's RV-4 793 23.06.94
N144TH   A Troughton   City of Derry 07.12.18P
Built by C T Hahn

G-BVRY Cyclone Ax3K C.3013085 18.08.94
Cancelled 21.11.02 by CAA 02.03.99
Causeway   Built by J Toone – project PFA 245-12471
Stored dismantled 03.16

G-BVRZ Piper PA-18 Super Cub 95 18-3381 22.11.94
SE-ITP, LN-LJG, D-EDCM, West German AF 96+19,
QW+901, QZ+001, AC+507, AS+506, 54-0742
R W Davison   (Wirral) 25.08.19E
Fuselage No.18-3381

G-BVSB Team Mini-Max 91A xxxx 01.07.94
D G Palmer   Easter Nether Cabra Farm, Fetterangus
Built by C Nice – project PFA 186-12463
(SSDR microlight since 07.14) (IE 19.06.18)

G-BVSD Sud Aviation SE.3130 Alouette II 1897 08.09.94
Swiss AF V-54   M J Cuttell
Sandywell Park, Whittington 06.08.18E
As 'V-54' in Swiss AF c/s

G-BVSF Aero Designs Pulsar xxxx 01.07.94
J A & R J Freestone   Deanland 25.05.18P
Built by S N & R J Freestone – project PFA 202-12071;
tricycle u/c

G-BVSG Pilatus B-N BN-2B-20 Islander 2283 03.10.94
VH-ZZX, G-BVSG   Britten-Norman Ltd   Bembridge
(NF 12.12.18)

G-BVSK Pilatus B-N BN-2T Islander 2287 31.01.95
VT-SUN, F-OIAR, G-BVSK   G Cormack   Cumbernauld
(NF 03.03.17)

G-BVSM Rotary Air Force RAF 2000 EW42 24.08.94
A van Rooijen   Enstone 02.10.18P
Built by K Quigley & T M Truesdale (IE 20.06.17)

G-BVSP Hunting Percival P.84 Jet Provost T.3A PAC/W/6327 31.08.94
XM370   Weald Aviation Services Ltd   North Weald 07.10.11P
Stored as 'XM370' less wings 11.18 (NF 08.04.16)

G-BVSS Jodel D.150 Mascaret 118 22.08.94
M S C Ball & M F R B Collett
Garston Farm, Marshfield 13.10.18P
Built by A P Burns – project PFA 151-11878
using SAB plans

G-BVST Jodel D.150 Mascaret 130 11.08.94
A Shipp   Full Sutton 05.06.18P
Built by A Shipp – project PFA 235-12198 using SAB plans

G-BVSX Team Mini-Max 91A xxxx 09.09.94
J A Sephton   Longacre Farm, Sandy
Built by G N Smith – project PFA 186-12463
(SSDR microlight since 12.14) (IE 22.12.15)

G-BVSZ Pitts S-1E xxxx 09.09.94
H J Morton   (Entrammes, France) 15.12.18P
Built by K Garrett & R P Millinship
– project PFA 09-11235

G-BVTA Tri-R KIS xxxx 26.08.94
Cancelled 30.04.15 by CAA 30.01.12
Rowley, Co Durham   Built by P J Webb
– project PFA 239-12450; at Battlezone paintball park,
Mountpleasant Farm, 02.16

G-BVTC BAC 145 Jet Provost T.5A EEP/JP/997 07.09.94
XW333   Global Aviation Ltd   Humberside 08.11.18P
As 'XW333' in RAF c/s

G-BVTL Colt 31A 2572 05.07.94
A Lindsay   Twickenham 15.05.97
Built by Thunder & Colt Ltd (NF 14.03.18)

G-BVTM Reims/Cessna F152 II F15201827 31.08.94
G-WACS, D-EFGZ   The Royal Air Force
Halton Aeroplane Club Ltd   RAF Halton 11.10.18E

G-BVTV RotorWay Exec 90 5243/6599 16.09.94
P M Scheiwiller   Street Farm, Takeley 04.02.17P
Built by J J Bull; discontinued take-off Landmead Farm,
Garford 06.08.16 & extensively damaged;
on rebuild 06.17 (IE 17.01.18)

G-BVTW Aero Designs Pulsar 243 14.09.94
R J Panther   Stoke Golding 07.09.16P
Built by J D Webb – project PFA 202-12172;
tailwheel u/c

G-BVTX de Havilland DHC-1 Chipmunk 22A C1/0705 02.08.94
WP809   N P Woods tr TX Flying Group
Husbands Bosworth 03.02.18P
As 'WP809:78' in Royal Navy silver & red c/s

G-BVUA Cameron O-105 3369 27.09.94
Wickers World Ltd   Great Haywood, Stafford 19.06.18E

G-BVUG Betts TB.1 1045 03.10.94
H F Fekete   Little Gransden 28.11.12P
Built by T A Betts – project PFA 265-12770 from
modified AIA Stampe SV.4C c/n 1045 ex G-BEUS
(NF 22.12.15)

G-BVUH Thunder Ax7-65B 243 03.10.94
JA-A0075   H J M Lacoste   Berdoues, Gers, France 13.10.18E

G-BVUK Cameron V-77 3372 11.10.94
H G Griffiths & W A Steel   Caversham, Reading 10.12.12E
(IE 16.05.16)

G-BVUM Rans S-6-116 Coyote II 0893.528 11.10.94
M A Abbott   Newbigging Farm, Montrose 24.09.18P
Built by J L Donaldson – project PFA 204A-12685

G-BVUN Van's RV-4 xxxx 11.10.94
D J Harvey   Blackpool 25.05.18P
Built by I G Glenn – project PFA 181-12488

G-BVUT Evans VP-1 Series 2 xxxx 24.10.94
M J Barnett   Shobdon   'Pour de Merite' 29.09.99P
Built by P J Weston – project PFA 062-12092;
wears red German A/F c/s; dismantled 09.14
(NF 04.09.14)

G-BVUU Cameron C-80 3383 11.10.94
T M C McCoy   Peasedown St John, Bath   'Ascent' 15.06.05A
(NF 02.11.15)

G-BVUV Europa Aviation Europa 141 23.09.94
R J Mills   Retford Gamston 21.06.18P
Built by R J Mills – project PFA 247-12762; tailwheel u/c

G-BVUZ Cessna 120 11334 20.09.94
Z-YGH, VP-YGH, VP-NAM, VP-YGH
R W Maxted   Sherburn-in-Elmet 06.08.18P

G-BVVB Carlson Sparrow II xxxx 26.09.94
L M McCullen   Oban 01.08.06P
Built by L M McCullen – project PFA 209-11809
(NF 07.06.18)

G-BVVE | Jodel D.112 | 1070 | 28.10.94
F-BKAJ M Balls Hill Farm, Nayland | | 14.07.18P
Built by Société des Etablissements Benjamin Wassmer

G-BVVG | Nanchang CJ-6A (Yak 18) | 2751219 | 10.10.94
(F-....), G-BVVG, Chinese PLAAF
R Davy tr Nanchang CJ6A Group Wycombe Air Park | 19.03.18P
As '68' (Red) in PLAAF c/s

G-BVVH | Europa Aviation Europa | 014 | 31.10.94
M Giudici (Hitchin) | | 14.05.18P
*Built by T G Hoult & M P Whitley – project
PFA 247-12505; tailwheel u/c*

G-BVVI | Hawker Audax I | K5600 | 03.11.94
2015M, K5600 Aero Vintage Ltd (Northiam, Rye)
Built by Avro Aircraft Ltd; on rebuild 2017 (NF 14.11.14)

G-BVVK | de Havilland DHC-6-310 Twin Otter | 666 | 21.12.94
LN-BEZ Loganair Ltd Glasgow *'Spirit of Eilidh'* | | 13.01.20E

G-BVVL | EAA Acrosport II | xxxx | 11.11.94
R C de Almeida Tavares tr G-BVVL Syndicate
(Mafra, Lisbon, Portugal) | | 26.11.18P
*Built by A J Maxwell, D Park & P Price
– project PFA 072A-10887*

G-BVVM | Zenair CH.601HD Zodiac | xxxx | 03.10.94
E Leggoe Monewden | | 30.05.19P
Built by J G Small – project PFA 162-12539; tricycle u/c

G-BVVN | Brügger MB.2 Colibri | xxxx | 12.10.94
N F Andrews RAF Cranwell | | 25.09.18P
Built by N F Andrews – project PFA 043-10979

G-BVVP | Europa Aviation Europa | 088 | 20.09.94
B A Fawkes Hadfold Farm, Adversane | | 21.12.17P
*Built by J S Melville – project PFA 247-12697;
'Swiss' version tailwheel u/c*

G-BVVR | Stits SA-3A Playboy | P-736 | 14.11.94
N4620S J H Prendergast Headcorn | | 07.09.15P
Built by S Goins

G-BVVS | Van's RV-4 | xxxx | 15.11.94
E G & N S C English Melhuish Farm, North Moreton | 05.06.19P
Built by E C English – project PFA 181-12324

G-BVVU | Lindstrand LBL Four | 155 | 18.11.94
HB-QAP, G-BVVU Magical Adventures Ltd
West Bloomfield, MI, USA | | 30.09.09E
(NF 03.06.15)

G-BVVW | IAV Bacau Yakovlev Yak-52 | 844605 | 16.11.94
RA-01361, DOSAAF 15, DOSAAF 95
M Blackman Monewden | | 16.05.18P
Official c/n suspect as plate shows 833519

G-BVVZ | Corby CJ-1 Starlet | xxxx | 09.11.94
P V Flack Lasham | | 25.09.05P
*Built by A E Morris – project PFA 134-12293
(NF 09.02.16)*

G-BVWB | Thunder Ax8-90 Series 2 | 3000 | 02.12.94
M A Stelling, K & K C Tanner South Queensferry,
Sutton & Thame *'Starship'* | | 26.05.18E

G-BVWH[M] | Cameron N-90 Lightbulb SS HAB | 3404 | 08.12.94
Cancelled 17.12.01 as WFU | | 02.09.98
With British Balloon Museum & Library, Newbury

G-BVWI | Cameron Light Bulb-65 | 3405 | 08.12.94
M E White Abbeyview, Trim, RoI *'Philips Energy Saver'* | 02.06.97A
(NF 31.07.15)

G-BVWK[M] | Air & Space 18-A Gyroplane | 18-14 | 19.12.94
SE-HID, N6108S Cancelled 18.10.00 as WFU
With National Museum of Flight Scotland, East Fortune

G-BVWL[M] | Air & Space 18-A Gyroplane | 18-63 | 19.12.94
SE-HIE, N90588, N6152S Cancelled 18.10.00 as TWFU
With The Helicopter Museum, Weston-super-Mare

G-BVWM | Europa Aviation Europa | 070 | 14.12.94
A Head Solent | | 31.07.18P
*Built by A Aubeelack, C Cornish & C J Hadley
– project PFA 247-12620; tailwheel u/c*

G-BVWW | Lindstrand LBL 90A | 169 | 28.12.94
J D A Shields Hastings *'Double Whiskey'* | | 01.07.09E
(IE 05.07.17)

G-BVWZ | Piper PA-32-301 Saratoga | 3206055 | 03.01.95
I-TASP, N9184N Ambar Kelly Ltd Fowlmere | | 21.05.18E

G-BVXA | Cameron N-105 | 3441 | 04.01.95
R E Jones Lytham St Annes *'Ribby Hall Leisure Village'* | 19.03.05
(NF 11.12.15)

G-BVXC | English Electric Canberra B(I).8 | 6649 | 09.01.95
WT333 Cancelled 22.04.00 as PWFU
Bruntingthorpe *Stored in RAE colours as 'WT333' 02.16*

G-BVXD | Cameron O-84 | 3432 | 05.01.95
C J Dunkley Oxford | | 16.06.18E

G-BVXI | Klemm Kl.35D | 1981 | 05.01.95
D-EFEG, SE-BHT, Fv.5052
Cancelled 13.10.00 as PWFU
Boblingen-Sindelfingen, Germany *On rebuild 06.17*

G-BVXK | Aerostar Yakovlev Yak-52 | 9111306 | 12.01.95
RA-44508, DOSAAF 26 A R Dent Tatenhill | | 24.10.18P
As '26' in DOSAAF c/s (IE 01.09.17)

G-BVXM | Aérospatiale AS.350B Ecureuil | 2013 | 10.01.95
I-AUDI, I-CIOC RCR Aviation Ltd (Shipley, Horsham) | 28.02.17E

G-BVXR | de Havilland DH.104 Devon C2 | 04436 | 13.01.95
XA880 Cancelled 09.02.15 as destroyed | | 13.01.95
Elstree Studio *Front fuselage at studio 06.18 as 'XA880'*

G-BVYG | Robin DR.300-180R Remorqueur | 611 | 09.01.95
F-BSQB, F-BSPI PA Technologies Ltd
Husbands Bosworth | | 30.09.13E
On rebuild 01.17 (IE 21.03.17)

G-BVYH[M] | Hawker Hunter GA.11 | HABL-003037 | 31.01.95
N707XE, G-BVYH, XE707
Cancelled 06.06.95 to N707XE *As 'XE707:865'*
With Bentwaters Cold War Museum, Woodbridge

G-BVYK | Team Mini-Max 91A | xxxx | 13.02.95
Cancelled 19.11.14 by CAA | | 21.08.13
Rochester *Built by S B Churchill – project
PFA 186-12598; stored dismantled 11.16*

G-BVYM | Robin DR.300-180R Remorqueur | 656 | 09.12.94
F-BTBL London Gliding Club Proprietary Ltd
Dunstable Downs | | 20.12.18E

G-BVYO | Robin R2160 Alpha Sport | 288 | 11.01.95
Smart People Dont Buy Ltd Wellesbourne Mountford | 24.04.19E

G-BVYP | Piper PA-25-235 Pawnee B | 25-3481 | 13.02.95
N7475D, OY-CLT, N7475Z
Bidford Gliding & Flying Club Ltd Bidford | | 01.11.18E
*Struck parked CAP.10 taxying Bidford 22.07.16
& damaged*

G-BVYX | Avid Speed Wing Mk.4 | xxxx | 16.02.95
C A Simmonds (Hoby, Melton Mowbray) | | 28.04.16P
Built by G J Keen – project PFA 189-12370

G-BVYY | Pietenpol Air Camper | xxxx | 20.02.95
T F Harrison tr Pietenpol Aircamper G-BVYY Group
Little Down Farm, Milson | | 22.06.17P
Built by J R Orchard – project PFA 047-12559

G-BVZJ | Rand Robinson KR-2 | xxxx | 21.02.95
G M Rundle (Popham) | | 29.10.18P
*Built by J P McConnell-Wood – project PFA 129-11049;
rebuilt with fuselage project PFA 129-11174 c.2004-5*

G-BVZN | Cameron C-80 | 3546 | 28.02.95
S J Clarke Watford | | 08.05.11E
(NF 09.07.14)

G-BVZO | Rans S-6-116 Coyote II | 0494.606 | 01.03.95
P J Brion Barton Ashes, Crawley Down | | 31.07.13P
*Built by P Atkinson – project PFA 204A-12710;
tricycle u/c (IE 31.05.17)*

G-BVZR | Zenair CH.601HD Zodiac | xxxx | 02.03.95
R A Perkins Holmbeck Farm, Burcott | | 02.07.18P
Built by J D White – project PFA 162-12417; tricycle u/c

G-BVZT | Lindstrand LBL 90A | 183 | 09.03.95
J Edwards Northampton *'Molly Mae'* | | 29.06.18E

G-BVZX | Cameron H-34 | 3564 | 15.03.95
R H Etherington Rueypeyroux, France | | 08.06.15E

G-BVZY | Mooney M.20R Ovation | 29-0045 | 13.03.95
OE-KGG, OY-ELW, G-BVZY
Hansengroup Ltd Liverpool John Lennon | | 26.05.18E

G-BVZZ | de Havilland DHC-1 Chipmunk 22 | C1/0687 | 05.01.95
WP795 Portsmouth Naval Gliding Centre
RNAS Yeovilton *'Royal Navy'* | | 14.06.04
*Lycoming O-360-A4A; as 'WP795:901'
in RN red & white c/s (NF 19.10.18)*

G-BWAA – G-BWZZ

G-BWAB Jodel D.14 432 25.01.95
R G Fairall Redhill 22.05.18P
Built by W A Braim – project PFA 251-12469
using SAB plans

G-BWAC Waco YKS-7 4693 19.08.92
N50RA, N2896D, NC50 D N Peters Little Gransden 25.01.18E

G-BWAD Rotary Air Force RAF 2000 H2-94-5-147 27.02.95
B J Payne (Aberdeen) 28.02.13P
Built by J R Legge – project PFA G/13-1254
(NF 12.09.18)

G-BWAF[M] Hawker Hunter F 6A S4/U/41H/3393 24.02.95
8831M, XG160 Cancelled 09.12.10 as PWFU
As 'XG160:U' in Black Arrows c/s:
carries 'G-BWAF' on tail bump-stop
With Bournemouth Aviation Museum, Bournemouth

G-BWAH Montgomerie-Bensen B.8MR xxxx 16.03.95
J B Allan (Corringham, Stanford-le-Hope)
'The Flying Scotsman' 21.08.18P
Built by S J O Tinn – project PFA G/01-1208

G-BWAI CFM Streak Shadow SA K.235-SA 21.03.95
S J Smith Chase Farm, Chipping Sodbury 20.08.18P
Built by J M Heath – project BMAA/HB/052
as CFM Shadow CD: completed as Streak
Shadow SA project PFA 206-12556

G-BWAN Cameron N-77 3499 24.03.95
I Chadwick Caterham *'BPG'* 12.06.15E
(IE 05.09.17)

G-BWAO Cameron C-80 3436 24.03.95
R D Allen Alveston, Bristol 15.05.18E

G-BWAP Clutton FRED Series III xxxx 24.03.95
G A Shepherd Seething 24.09.18P
Built by R J Smyth – project PFA 029-10959

G-BWAR Denney Kitfox Model 3 xxxx 16.03.95
M J Downes (Welshpool) 16.07.18P
Built by C E Brookes – project PFA 172-12432

G-BWAT Pietenpol Air Camper xxxx 15.03.95
P W Aitchison (Nakhonsawan, Thailand) 19.05.15P
Built by D R Waters – project PFA 047-11594

G-BWAU Cameron V-90 3569 27.03.95
A M F & K M Hall London N10 24.06.14E
(NF 20.11.16)

G-BWAW Lindstrand LBL 77A 207 28.03.95
D Bareford Cookley, Kidderminster *'ProSport'* 13.07.09E
(NF 05.09.16)

G-BWBI Taylorcraft F-22A 2207 03.04.95
N22UK M W Cave (Holyhead) 26.09.18P

G-BWBO Lindstrand LBL 77A 157 10.04.95
T J Orchard Westcott, Aylesbury 18.08.18E

G-BWBZ ARV ARV K1 Super 2 xxxx 10.03.95
M P Holdstock Holmbeck Farm, Burcott 21.07.15P
Built by J N C Shields – project PFA 152-12802

G-BWCA CFM Streak Shadow K 160 19.04.95
I C Pearson Ranston Farm, Iwerne Courtney 11.07.07P
Built by R Thompson – project PFA 206-11985
(NF 11.11.14)

G-BWCK Everett Gyroplane Series 2 036 26.04.95
N M Gent (Wolverhampton) 14.01.19P
Built by A C S M Hart – project PFA G/03-1260

G-BWCO Dornier Do28D2 4337 19.06.95
EI-CJU, (N5TK), 5N-AOH, D-ILIF
Cancelled 30.01.09 as PWFU 19.05.99
Hibaldstow *Stored 08.13*

G-BWCS BAC 145 Jet Provost T.5 EEP/JP/957 28.04.95
XW293 J H Ashcroft Bournemouth 03.02.09P
As 'XW293:Z' in RAF c/s; derelict
in open store 01.19 (NF 05.01.16)

G-BWCT Tipsy Nipper T.66 Series 1 11 27.04.95
'OO-NIC', PH-MEC, D-EMEC, OO-NIC
R Targonski Wolverhampton Halfpenny Green 08.08.18P
Built by Avions Fairey SA

G-BWCW[M] Barnett J4B-2 PFA G/14-1256 05.05.95
Cancelled 03.03.05 as PWFU
Built by S H Kirkby
With The Helicopter Museum, Weston-super-Mare

G-BWCY Murphy Rebel 058R 15.05.95
A J Glading Enstone 14.08.18P
Built by R Hallam, A Jones & A Koneczek
– project PFA 232-12135

G-BWDH Cameron N-105 3549 22.05.95
M W Shepherd Louth 21.09.18E
(NF 11.12.17)

G-BWDO Sikorsky S-76B 760356 02.06.95
M-ERRY, M-ONTY(1), G-BWDO, VR-CPN, N9HM
Trustair Ltd (Euxton, Chorley)
(IE 02.02.18)

G-BWDP Europa Aviation Europa 062 07.06.95
S Attubato (Snodland) 23.08.07P
Built by I Valentine – project PFA 247-12637;
tailwheel u/c (NF 16.10.14)

G-BWDR[M] Hunting Percival P.84 Jet Provost T.3A PAC/W/660 14.12.05
XM376 Cancelled 08.12.10 as PWFU
As 'G-BWDR'
With Rahmi M. Koc Museum, Istanbul, Turkey

G-BWDS Hunting Percival P.84 Jet Provost T.3A PAC/W/932 06.06.95
XM424, (N77506?), XM424 AT Aviation Sales Ltd,
D C Cooper & J A Gibson Dunkeswell 22.01.19P
Correct c/n believed PAC/W/9231?;
as 'XM424:1 FTS' in RAF c/s

G-BWDX Europa Aviation Europa 056 13.06.95
C J Sweenie (Denmead, Waterlooville) 05.10.19P
Built by J B Crane – project PFA 247-12603; tricycle u/c

G-BWDZ Sky 105-24 002 13.06.95
M T Wiltshire Bristol BS16 *'Sky Balloons'* 09.05.15E
(NF 11.09.17)

G-BWEB BAC 145 Jet Provost T.5A EEP/JP/1044 19.06.95
XW422 Flight Test Support (Istres, France) 27.11.12P
As 'XW422' in RAF c/s (NF 10.05.17)

G-BWEE Cameron V-42 3480 08.03.95
J A Hibberd Krimpen aan den Ijssel, Netherlands 15.05.18E

G-BWEF SNCAN Stampe SV.4C(G) 208 13.05.93
G-BOVL, N20SV, F-BHES, F-BBLC
R T Blain tr Acebell G-BWEF Syndicate Redhill 09.05.19P

G-BWEG Europa Aviation Europa 053 04.04.95
J W Kelly Tatenhill 26.07.18P
Built by R J Marsh & B A Selmes
– project PFA 247-12600; tailwheel u/c

G-BWEM Supermarine 358 Seafire L.III ? 28.06.95
IAC 157, RX168 Aircraft Spares & Materials Ltd Duxford
Built by Westland Aircraft Ltd; noted 07.18
as 'RX168' on restoration (NF 20.10.15)

G-BWEN Macair Merlin GT xxxx 20.06.95
D A Hill (Wigtoft, Boston)
Built by B W Davies – project PFA 208A-12859
(NF 05.04.16)

G-BWEU Reims/Cessna F152 II F15201894 15.06.95
EI-BNC, N9097Y Eastern Air Executive Ltd
Netherthorpe 29.07.16E
Blown over at Retford Gamston during
Storm Doris 23.02.17

G-BWEW Cameron N-105 3637 30.06.95
Unipart Group Ltd t/a Unipart Balloon Club
Wendover *'Unipart'* 16.06.18E

G-BWEY Bensen B.8 xxxx 03.07.95
F G Shepherd (Leadgate, Alston)
Built by F G Shepherd – project PFA G/01-1197
(NF 16.01.15)

G-BWEZ Piper J-3C-85 Cub 6021 03.07.95
N29050, NC29050 J G McTaggart tr Edenfield Aero
Archerfield 03.09.18P
As '436021' in USAAF c/s

G-BWFG Robin HR.200-120B 293 20.07.95
T J Lowe Tatenhill 13.04.18E

G-BWFH Europa Aviation Europa 201 14.07.95
G C Grant Deanland 24.08.18P
Built by R W Baylie & B L Wratten
– project PFA 247-12842; tricycle u/c

G-BWFJ Evans VP-1 PFA 062-10349 01.09.78
G Robson Easterton 27.01.93P
Built by W E Jones – project PFA 062-10349
(NF 21.03.16)

G-BWFK Lindstrand LBL 77A 289 17.07.95
J S Russon & C J Wootton
Cheadle Hulme & Ormskirk *'Mr Orange'* 04.02.18E
Active 09.18 (IE 09.07.18)

G-BWFL Cessna 500 Citation I 500-0264 19.07.95
G-JTNC, G-OEJA, G-BWFL, F-GLJA, N205FM, N5264J
Corbally Group (Aviation) Ltd Tatenhill 13.12.16E
Stored 04.18 (NF 17.08.18)

G-BWFM Yakovlev Yak-50 781208 19.07.95
NX5224R, DDR-WQX, DM-WQX
J Hurrell tr Fox Mike Group Blackpool 26.07.18P

G-BWFN HAPI Cygnet SF-2A xxxx 19.07.95
I P Manley Grange Farm, North Lopham 04.03.15P
Built by T Crawford – project PFA 182-11335;
undercarriage collapsed landing near Blithfield
Reservoir 03.07.14 & damaged (NF 16.01.15)

G-BWFO Colomban MC-15 Cri-Cri xxxx 19.07.95
C S & K D Rhodes Henstridge
Built by O G Jones – project PFA 133-11253 (NF 20.10.14)

G-BWFT Hawker Hunter T.8M 41H-695332 24.07.95
XL602 G I Begg St Athan 23.07.99P
As 'XL602' in RN c/s (NF 18.03.16)

G-BWFX Europa Aviation Europa 038 26.07.95
T P R Pickford (Shaftesbury) 11.03.08P
Built by A D Stewart – project PFA 247-12586;
tailwheel u/c (NF 01.08.18)

G-BWFZ Murphy Rebel 127R 19.07.95
G-SAVS S Irving (Wretton, King's Lynn) 09.08.11P
Built by I E Spencer – project PFA 232-12536
(NF 13.09.16)

G-BWGF BAC 145 Jet Provost T.5A EEP/JP/989 10.08.95
XW325 G-JPVA Ltd Coventry 04.10.18P
As 'XW325:E' in RAF c/s

G-BWGJ Chilton DW.1A xxxx 11.08.95
T J Harrison (Barcombe, Lewes)
Built by T J Harrison – project PFA 225-12615
(IE 05.11.14)

G-BWGL Hawker Hunter T.8C HABL-003086 15.08.95
XF357 Stichting Dutch Hawker Hunter Foundation
Leeuwarden, Friesland, Netherlands 23.05.16P
Officially registered with c/n 41H-695946;
as 'N-321' in R Netherlands AF c/s; active 02.18

G-BWGM Hawker Hunter T.8C HABL-003008 15.08.95
XE665 Cancelled 16.03.11 by CAA 24.06.98
Cotswold *Open store as 'XE665:876:VL*
in grey Royal Navy c/s 06.16

G-BWGN[M] Hawker Hunter T.8C 41H-670689 15.08.95
WT722 Cancelled 16.03.11 by CAA 03.09.97
As 'WT722:878:VL'
With Cornwall Aviation Heritage Centre, Newquay Cornwall

G-BWGO Slingsby T67M-200 Firefly 2048 15.08.95
SE-LBC R Gray Fairoaks 27.12.18E

G-BWGS[M] BAC 145 Jet Provost T.5A EEP/JP/974 XW310 18.08.95
Cancelled 13.07.17 as PWFU
With Bournemouth Aviation Museum, Bournemouth

G-BWGY HOAC DV.20 Katana 20134 22.08.95
Gemstone Aviation Ltd Retford Gamston 15.11.19E

G-BWHD Lindstrand LBL 31A 292 29.08.95
M R Noyce & R P E Phillips Andover 10.09.17E

G-BWHI de Havilland DHC-1 Chipmunk 22 C1/0637 08.09.95
WK624 E H N M Clare Blackpool 19.03.18E
Hulk of WK624 possibly used in rebuild of G-AOSY
c.1998/99; as 'WK624' in RAF c/s

G-BWHK Rans S-6-116 Coyote II 0695.834 15.09.95
S J Wakeling Stoke Golding 01.06.18P
Built by N D White – project PFA 204A-12908; tricycle u/c

G-BWHP CASA 1-131E Jungmann Series 2000 2109 18.08.95
Spanish AF E3B-513 J F Hopkins
Watchford Farm, Yarcombe 27.06.18P
As 'S4+A07' in Luftwaffe c/s

G-BWHR Tipsy Nipper T.66 Series 1 xxxx 19.09.95
(OO-KAM), OO-69 L R Marnef
(Koningshooikt, Belgium)
Built by L R Marnef – project PFA 025-12843:
composite homebuild of original Fairey build
c/ns 29 & 71 (NF 10.07.14)

G-BWHS Rotary Air Force RAF 2000 xxxx 25.09.95
V G Freke (Eynsham) 12.07.12P
Built by V G Freke – project PFA G/13-1253 (IE 17.09.17)

G-BWHU Westland Scout AH.1 F9517 27.09.95
XR595 N J F Boston North Weald 09.07.14P
As 'XR595:M' in AAC c/s; noted 11.18 (NF 17.01.19)

G-BWID Druine D.31 Turbulent 201 16.10.95
F-PHFR T W J Carnall Dunkeswell 20.11.13P
Built by R Druine & H Gindre (IE 26.09.17)

G-BWII Cessna 150G 15065308 22.09.95
N4008J, (G-BSKB), N4008J M W Jones Shobdon 18.04.19E

G-BWIJ Europa Aviation Europa 006 19.10.95
Condor Aviation International Ltd
Birchwood Lodge, North Duffield 17.05.18P
Built by R Lloyd – project PFA 247-12513;
tailwheel u/c (NF 02.09.18)

G-BWIK de Havilland DH.82A Tiger Moth 86417 20.10.95
7015M, NL985 H M M Haines
(Norton Fitzwarren, Taunton)
On rebuild 09.16 (NF 19.11.14)

G-BWIL Rans S-10 Sakota 1089.065 04.10.95
G-WIEN J G Forde Ballyboy, Rol 12.04.07P
Built by J C Longmore – project PFA 194-11770;
fuselage noted 04.14 (NF 17.11.16)

G-BWIP Cameron N-90 3668 20.10.95
O J Evans Peasedown St John, Bath 14.04.18E

G-BWIV Europa Aviation Europa 210 27.10.95
T G Ledbury (Three Mile Cross, Reading) 09.09.99P
Built by J R Lockwood-Goose – project
PFA 247-12871; tailwheel u/c (NF 28.03.18)

G-BWIW Sky 180-24 HAB 008 01.11.95
Cancelled 04.03.15 by CAA 21.04.09
Not Known *Inflated Pidley 05.16*

G-BWIX Sky 120-24 009 31.10.95
J M Percival Bourton-on-the-Wolds, Loughborough
'Mayfly III' 04.02.18E

G-BWIZ QAC Quickie Tri-Q 200 xxxx 21.08.95
M C Davies Sywell 04.08.15P
Built by B Cain – project PFA 094-12330 (IE 02.11.17)

G-BWJG Mooney M.20J Mooney 201 24-3319 07.11.95
N1083P A Mass Elstree 08.07.19E

G-BWJH Europa Aviation Europa 007 10.11.95
I R Willis Perth 03.08.16P
Built by A R D, D, & J Hood – project
PFA 247-12643; tricycle u/c (IE 01.12.17)

G-BWJM Bristol 20 M.1C replica NAW-2 23.11.95
Richard Shuttleworth Trustees Old Warden 09.07.18P
Built by Northern Aeroplane Workshops;
as 'C4918' in RFC 72 Sqdn c/s

G-BWJW Westland Scout AH.1 F9705 29.11.95
XV130 Cancelled 13.11.12 as WFU 25.01.06
Thruxton *Stored as 'XV130' in AAC c/s 12.15*

G-BWKJ Rans S7 Courier xxxx 14.12.95
Cancelled 17.02.10 by CAA 04.11.04
Armagh Field, Woodview, Co Armagh
Built by J P Kovacs – project PFA 218-12918
Stored dismantled 12.13

G-BWKK Auster AOP.9 B5/10/165 30.07.79
XP279 Cancelled 05.08.14 as destroyed 01.08.96
Winchester *Stored as 'XP279' in AAC c/s 10.15*

G-BWKT Laser Lazer Z200 xxxx 19.12.95
T A Cleaver (Morganstown, Cardiff) 26.09.19P
Built by P D Begley – project PFA 123-11421

G-BWKW	Thunder Ax8-90	3770	28.12.95
	Gone With The Wind Ltd Abbots Leigh, Bristol		
	'Road to Mandalay'		03.08.18E
	Built by Cameron Balloons Ltd		
G-BWKZ	Lindstrand LBL 77A	340	21.12.95
	J H Dobson Goring, Reading		04.02.07
	(NF 03.07.18)		
G-BWLD	Cameron O-120	3774	16.01.96
	(I-....) D Pedri Villa Lagarina, Rovereto, Italy		30.07.18E
G-BWLF	Cessna 404 Titan	404-0414	26.10.94
	G-BNXS, HKG-4, (N8799K) Reconnaissance		
	Ventures Ltd t/a RVL Group East Midlands		02.06.18E
G-BWLJ	Taylorcraft DCO-65	04331	16.01.96
	C-GUSA, 42-35870 B J Robe		
	(Loadman Farm, Hexham)		04.10.07P
	On rebuild 11.14 (NF 11.03.13)		
G-BWLL	Murphy Rebel	xxxx	22.01.96
	F W Parker & A F Ratcliffe (Richmond)		22.05.19P
	Built by F W Parker – project PFA 232-12499		
G-BWLW	Avid Speed Wing Mk.4	1477	26.01.96
	G-XXRG, G-BWLW P G Hayward Little Snoring		
	Built by R J Grainger – project PFA 189-12763		
	(NF 19.01.17)		
G-BWLY	RotorWay Exec 90	5142	11.01.93
	I P & P W Bewley Ley Farm, Chirk		07.07.09P
	Built by I P & P W Bewley (IE 01.03.18)		
G-BWMB	Jodel D.119	77	17.02.78
	F-BGMA C Hughes Hinton-in-the-Hedges		24.05.18P
	Built by Société des Etablissements Benjamin Wassmer;		
	believed new build c/n 1492: components of original		
	F-BGMA c/n 77 became F-PHQH & rebuilt as Larrieu JL.2		
G-BWMC	Cessna 182P Skylane II	18263117	30.01.96
	N5462J, G-BWMC, OO-RGM, (OO-RAN), F-BVOU, N7333N		
	N F Abbott t/a aeroplaneviews.co.uk Exeter Int'l		17.06.19E
G-BWMF[M]	Gloster Meteor T.7	G5/356460	15.12.95
	7917M, WA591		
	Cancelled 27.03.18 – to USA		17.10.18
	At World Heritage Air Museum, Detroit; as 'WA591:FMK-Q'		
G-BWMH	Lindstrand LBL 77B	152	07.02.96
	W C Wood Eastbourne		08.08.19E
G-BWMI	Piper PA-28RT-201T Turbo Arrow IV	28R-8031131	31.01.96
	F-GCTG, N82482, N9571N R W Pascoe Fairoaks		28.05.18E
G-BWMJ	Nieuport Scout 17/23 replica	xxxx	08.02.96
	J P Gilbert Stow Maries		18.09.17P
	Built by L J Day & R Gauld-Galliers – project		
	PFA 121-12351; as 'N1977:8' in French AF c/s		
G-BWMK	de Havilland DH.82A Tiger Moth	84483	09.02.96
	T8191 K F Crumplin Henstridge		
	Built by Morris Motors Ltd; as 'T8191'		
	in Royal Navy c/s (NF 04.03.16)		
G-BWMN	Rans S-7 Courier	0193.104	14.02.96
	D C Stokes Lower Withial Farm, East Pennard		09.11.18P
	Built by T M Turnbull – project PFA 218-12446		
G-BWMO	Oldfield Baby Lakes	JAL.3	14.02.96
	G-CIII, N11JL D Maddocks RAF Cosford *'Little Mo'*		05.12.17P
	Built by J A List		
G-BWMS	de Havilland DH.82A Tiger Moth	82712	14.02.96
	OO-EVJ, Belg.AF T-29, R4771		
	Stichting Vroege Vogels Lelystad, Netherlands		
	(NF 02.07.18)		
G-BWMU	Cameron Monster Truck-105	3607	20.02.96
	Magical Adventures Ltd West Bloomfield, MI, USA		
	'Skycrusher'		29.09.09E
	(NF 03.06.15)		
G-BWMX	de Havilland DHC-1 Chipmunk 22	C1/0481	19.02.96
	WG407 K S Kelso tr 407th Flying Group		
	Fen End Farm, Cottenham		01.01.19P
	As 'WG407:67' in RAF white & red c/s		
G-BWMY	Cameron Bradford and Bingley-90	3808	23.02.96
	Magical Adventures Ltd West Bloomfield, MI, USA		
	'Bradford & Bingley Building Society'		29.09.09E
	(NF 03.06.15)		
G-BWNB	Cessna 152 II	15280051	23.08.96
	N757WA South Warwickshire School of Flying Ltd		
	Wellesbourne Mountford		01.07.18E

G-BWNC	Cessna 152 II	15284415	23.08.96
	N6487L South Warwickshire School of Flying Ltd		
	Wellesbourne Mountford		05.12.18E
G-BWND	Cessna 152 II	15285905	23.08.96
	N95493 South Warwickshire School of Flying Ltd		
	Wellesbourne Mountford		23.08.18E
G-BWNI	Piper PA-24 Comanche	24-136	15.02.96
	N5123P B V & J B Haslam Retford Gamston		02.02.18E
G-BWNJ	Hughes 269C (300)	860528	29.02.96
	N42LW, N27RD, N7458F L R Fenwick		
	Long Fosse House, Beelsby		09.08.18E
G-BWNK	de Havilland DHC-1 Chipmunk 22	C1/0317	04.03.96
	WD390 M Nelson tr WD390 Group Compton Abbas		10.08.18E
	As 'WD390:68' in RAF c/s		
G-BWNM	Piper PA-28R-180 Cherokee Arrow	28R-30435	05.03.96
	N934BD M & R C Ramnial Gloucestershire		19.02.18E
G-BWNO	Cameron O-90	3716	05.03.96
	T Knight Ightfield, Whitchurch *'Action Research'*		10.05.19E
G-BWNP	Cameron Club-90	1717	06.03.96
	EI-BVQ H Cusden & J Edwards Northampton		
	'Club Orange'		12.07.12E
	(IE 13.01.16)		
G-BWNS	Cameron O-90	3842	06.03.96
	I C Steward East Runton, Cromer		
	'Hector' & 'Self Assessment Tax'		07.06.12E
	(NF 21.07.15)		
G-BWNT	de Havilland DHC-1 Chipmunk 22	C1/0772	07.03.96
	WP901 S Monk & J Willis Biggin Hill		19.01.18E
	As 'WP901:B' in RAF c/s		
G-BWNU	Piper PA-38-112 Tomahawk	38-78A0334	08.03.96
	N9294T Kemble Aero Club Ltd Cotswold		27.03.18E
G-BWNY	Aeromot AMT-200 Super Ximango	200.055	11.06.96
	M Powell-Brett Husbands Bosworth		18.05.18E
G-BWOF	BAC 145 Jet Provost T.5	EEP/JP/955	18.03.96
	XW291 P H Meeson North Weald		06.05.16P
	Noted 07.18 (IE 05.02.18)		
G-BWOH	Piper PA-28-161 Cadet	2841061	18.03.96
	EC-IBH, G-BWOH, D-ENXG, N9142S		
	Redhill Air Services Ltd Gloucestershire		05.06.18E
	Operated by Clifton Aviation		
G-BWOI	Piper PA-28-161 Cadet	2841307	18.03.96
	N270X, G-BWOI, D-EJTM, N9264N, N9208P		
	Parachuting Aircraft Ltd Old Sarum		05.09.18E
G-BWOK	Lindstrand LBL 105G	370	19.03.96
	C J Sanger-Davies Hawarden CH5		01.11.15E
G-BWOL[M]	Hawker Sea Fury FB.Mk.11	'61631'	18.03.96
	D-CACY, G-9-66, WG599 Cancelled 04.01.01 by CAA		
	With Fantasy of Flight, Polk City, Florida		
G-BWOR	Piper PA-18-135 Super Cub (L-18C)	18-2547	21.03.96
	OO-WIS, OO-HMF, French Army, 52-6229		
	R D & S S Houston Fife		21.08.19E
G-BWOT	Hunting Percival P.84 Jet Provost T.3A	PAC/W/10138	25.03.96
	XN459 Haye House Aviation Ltd North Weald		25.04.19P
	As 'XN459:50' in RAF red c/s		
G-BWOV	Enstrom F-28A	222	26.03.96
	N690BR, G-BWOV, F-BVRG P A Goss Enstone		02.12.17E
G-BWOX	de Havilland DHC-1 Chipmunk 22	C1/0728	27.03.96
	WP844 Cancelled 15.02.10 by CAA		10.07.00
	Adriers, France *Stored as 'WP844' 03.12*		
G-BWOY	Sky 31-24	029	28.03.96
	C Wolstenholme High Littleton, Bristol		31.08.18E
G-BWPC	Cameron V-77	3867	01.04.96
	H Vaughan Pennyland, Milton Keynes *'Olive'*		19.08.10E
	(NF 12.11.15)		
G-BWPE	Murphy Renegade 912	556	02.04.96
	J Hatswell Monaco, Principality of Monaco		25.05.18P
	Built by G Wilson – project PFA 188-12791;		
	carries '83-EB' under starboard wing		
G-BWPH	Piper PA-28-181 Archer II	28-7790311	04.04.96
	N1408H D R Lewis Enstone		24.05.18E
G-BWPJ	Steen Skybolt	xxxx	09.04.96
	A J Hurran Croft Farm, Defford		18.10.17P
	Built by W R Penaluna – project PFA 064-12854		

G-BWPP Sky 105-24 031 09.04.96
R J Mitchener tr Sarnia Balloon Group Andover
'niceday' 14.05.19E

G-BWPS CFM Streak Shadow SA K 275-SA 09.02.96
P J Mogg Henstridge 11.06.17P
Built by P G A Sumner – project PFA 206-12954
(IE 28.07.17)

G-BWRA Sopwith Triplane replica xxxx 19.04.96
G-PENY J G Brander White Waltham 30.03.18P
Built by J S Penny – project PFA 021-10035;
as 'N500' in RAF c/s

G-BWRC Avid Hauler Mk.4 xxxx 22.02.96
R A Stephens (East Winch, King's Lynn) 16.12.16P
Built by B Williams – project PFA 189-12979; damaged
in storms Northrepps 2016 (IE 02.10.18)

G-BWRFM Morane-Saulnier MS.505 Criquet 73/1 12.04.96
D-EFTY (2), F-BAUV, French AF 73
Cancelled 02.06.98 – to D-EGTY (2) *As 'G-BWRF'*
With Sammlung Koch – Historische Flugzeug, Grossenhein,
Germany

G-BWRGM Mraz M.1D Sokol 304 12.04.96
D-EGWP (2), (D-EFTB), HB-TBG, OK-DIX
Cancelled 16.07.98 as WFU *As 'G-BWRG'*
With Sammlung Koch – Historische Flugzeug, Grossenhein,
Germany

G-BWRHM Blériot Type XI replica 001 12.04.96
D-EFTE, N25WM Cancelled 16.07.98 as WFU
As 'G-BWRH' Built by B.Murray
With Sammlung Koch – Historische Flugzeug, Grossenhein,
Germany

G-BWRIM Mignet HM-19C Pou-du-Ciel replica 01 12.04.96
HB-SPG Cancelled 16.07.98 as WFU
As 'G-BWRI' Built by Eigenbau
With Sammlung Koch – Historische Flugzeug, Grossenhein,
Germany

G-BWRO Europa Aviation Europa 196 22.04.96
R A Darley Bagby 06.04.17P
Built by E C Clark – project PFA 247-12849; tricycle u/c

G-BWRR Cessna 182Q Skylane II 18266660 29.03.94
N95861 A & R Reid t/a A & R Reid
Peter Hall Farm, Brinklow 07.10.18E

G-BWRS SNCAN Stampe SV.4C 437 24.04.96
(N.....), F-BCVQ G P J M Valvekens
(Mondorf-les-Bains, Luxembourg)
(NF 10.02.16)

G-BWSB Lindstrand LBL 105A 384 26.04.96
R Calvert-Fisher Radley, Abingdon *'MG'* 26.07.17E

G-BWSD Campbell Cricket 101 03.05.96
R F G Moyle (Carnon Downs, Truro)
Built by R F G Moyle – project PFA G/03-1216
(NF 16.10.14)

G-BWSG BAC 145 Jet Provost T.5 EEP/JP/988 13.05.96
XW324 J Bell East Midlands 31.05.18P
As 'XW324:U' in RAF 6FTS c/s

G-BWSH Hunting Percival P.84 Jet Provost T.3A PAC/W/10159 13.05.96
XN498 Global Aviation Ltd Humberside 08.07.03P
Stored 02.15 (IE 22.01.18)

G-BWSJ Denney Kitfox Model 3 xxxx 15.05.96
A J Calvert (New Mills, High Peak) 18.01.19P
Built by J M Miller – project PFA 172-12204

G-BWSL Sky 77-24 004 16.05.96
E J Briggs Leyland 05.04.18E

G-BWSN Denney Kitfox Model 3 xxxx 16.05.96
R J Mitchell (Scalloway, Shetland) 19.08.16P
Built by W J Forrest – project PFA 172-12141;
converted for float operations 2009

G-BWSTM Sky 200-24 HAB 036 20.05.96
Cancelled 09.06.09 by CAA *Inflated 04.14* 28.04.06
With British Balloon Museum & Library, Newbury

G-BWSU Cameron N-105 3848 20.05.96
A M Marten Norley Wood, Lymington *'Wonderbra'* 04.07.15E
(NF 21.08.18)

G-BWSV IAV Bacau Yakovlev Yak-52 877601 20.05.96
DOSAAF 43 M W Fitch Elstree 17.04.19P
As '43' (Blue) in DOSAAF c/s

G-BWTE Cameron O-140 3885 30.05.96
T G Church Clayton Le Dale, Blackburn 09.10.18E

G-BWTG de Havilland DHC-1 Chipmunk 22 C1/0119 04.06.96
WB671 R G T de Man Midden Zeeland, Netherlands 19.05.17E
As 'WB671:910' & 'Royal Navy' in silver & red c/s

G-BWTJ Cameron V-77 3917 07.06.96
A J Montgomery North Cadbury, Yeovil 27.08.18E

G-BWTK Rotary Air Force RAF 2000 GTX-SE H2-95-6-170 07.06.96
L P Rolfe (West Row, Bury St Edmunds) 26.03.14P
Built by M P Lehermette – project PFA G/13-1264
(NF 23.09.17)

G-BWTO de Havilland DHC-1 Chipmunk 22 C1/0852 05.06.96
WP984 Skycraft Services Ltd Little Gransden 27.05.18E
As 'WP984:H' in RAF c/s

G-BWTW Mooney M.20C Mark 21 20-1188 05.06.96
EI-CHI, N6955V T J Berry Cotswold 12.04.18E

G-BWUH Piper PA-28-181 Archer III 2843048 30.08.96
N9272E, (G-BWUH) Flying at Lee on Solent Ltd
t/a Phoenix Aviation Solent 19.01.18E

G-BWUJ RotorWay Exec 162F 6153 02.07.96
Southern Helicopters Ltd Street Farm, Takeley 20.10.17P
Built by Southern Helicopters Ltd

G-BWUK Sky 160-24 HAB 043 02.07.96
Cancelled 30.01.15 as PWFU 16.03.10
Hungerford *Stored 07.16*

G-BWUN de Havilland DHC-1 Chipmunk 22 C1/0253 05.07.96
WD310 E H W Moore Jersey 23.03.18P
As 'WD310:B' in RAF white & red c/s

G-BWUP Europa Aviation Europa 104 03.07.96
V Goddard Lydeway Field, Etchilhampton 03.04.18P
Built by T J Harrison – project PFA 247-12703;
'Swiss' version tailwheel u/c

G-BWUS Sky 65-24 040 16.07.96
N A P Bates Ross-on-Wye *'Sky Balloons'* 14.08.14E
(NF 26.02.18)

G-BWUT de Havilland DHC-1 Chipmunk 22 C1/0918 04.06.96
WZ879 A J Herbert Audley End 30.06.19E
As 'WZ879:X' in RAF red & white c/s

G-BWUU Cameron N-90 3954 17.07.96
Bailey Balloons Ltd Pill, Bristol *'Discovery Channel'* 05.09.09E
(NF 31.03.15)

G-BWUV de Havilland DHC-1 Chipmunk 22A C1/0655 18.07.96
WK640 A C Darby Hooton Park 24.02.11E
Crashed on take-off 20.02.09 Wombleton; Cockpit
section to Aeroplane Collection for spares 02.17 to 12.18)
(NF 09.03.18) Note: G-CERD flies as 'WK640'

G-BWUW British Aircraft Corporation Jet Provost T.5A
EEP/JP/1045 18.07.96
XW423 Cancelled 29.06.06 as PWFU 14.02.02
Connah Quay
Instructional use at Deeside College as 'XW423'

G-BWVB Pietenpol Air Camper xxxx 24.07.96
A T Marshall & G Oldfield Croft Farm, Croft-on-Tees 05.10.18P
Built by M J Whatley – project PFA 047-11777

G-BWVF Pietenpol Air Camper xxxx 05.08.96
N Clark (Bransgore, Christchurch)
Built by R M Sharphouse – project PFA 047-11936
(NF 03.11.15)

G-BWVIM Stern ST.80 Balade xxxx 07.08.96
I Pearson Newquay Cornwall 11.08.06P
Built by P E Parker – project PFA 166-11190;
on display Cornwall Aviation Heritage Centre 08.18
(NF 27.07.18)

G-BWVR IAV Bacau Yakovlev Yak-52 878202 27.08.96
LY-AKQ, DOSAAF 134 I Parkinson Eshott *'52'* 07.12.06P
Noted 01.17 (IE 27.11.14)

G-BWVS Europa Aviation Europa 085 28.08.96
D R Bishop Popham 26.06.19P
Built by D R Bishop – project PFA 247-12686;
tailwheel u/c

G-BWVT de Havilland DH.82A Tiger Moth 1039 27.08.96
N71350, VH-SNZ, RAAF A17-604, VH-AIN, RAAF A17-604
N L Mackaness Perth 10.08.18P
Built by de Havilland Aircraft Proprietary Ltd, Australia

G-BWVU	Cameron O-90	3204	28.08.96	
	J A Atkinson Dorchester		16.06.17E	
G-BWVY	de Havilland DHC-1 Chipmunk 22	C1/0766	03.09.96	
	WP896 N Gardner RAF Halton		12.09.18P	
	As 'WP896' in RAF silver & yellow bands c/s			
G-BWVZ	de Havilland DHC-1 Chipmunk 22	C1/0614	16.07.96	
	WK590 D Campion Grimbergen, Belgium		07.06.18E	
	As 'WK590:69' in RAF c/s			
G-BWWA	Ultravia Pelican Club GS	xxxx	06.09.96	
	J S Aplin Pillows Barn, Corse		12.09.18P	
	Built by E F Clapham – project PFA 165-12242;			
	tailwheel u/c			
G-BWWB	Europa Aviation Europa	080	09.09.96	
	J Kesselman tr WB Group (Bridgetown, Dulverton)		12.04.14P	
	Built by M G Dolphin – project PFA 247-12670;			
	tailwheel u/c (IE 01.10.18)			
G-BWWE	Lindstrand LBL 90A	410	11.09.96	
	T J Wilkinson Sackville Lodge Farm, Riseley		30.03.16E	
G-BWWF	Cessna 185A Skywagon	185-0240	13.09.96	
	N4893K, G-BWWF, 9J-MCK, 5Y-BBG, ET-ACI, N4040Y			
	T N Bartlett & S M C Harvey Hinton-in-the-Hedges		09.03.18E	
G-BWWK	Hawker Nimrod I	41H-43617	13.09.96	
	S1581 Patina Ltd Duxford		30.05.19P	
	As 'S1581:573' in RN 802 Sqdn c/s			
G-BWWL	Colt Flying Egg	1813	19.09.96	
	JA-A0513 Magical Adventures Ltd			
	West Bloomfield, MI, USA 'Adidas'		02.08.01A	
	Built by Thunder & Colt Ltd (NF 03.06.15)			
G-BWWN	Isaacs Fury II	xxxx	23.09.96	
	J S Marten-Hale Old Warden		26.05.19P	
	Built by D H Pattison – project PFA 011-10957;			
	as 'K8303:D' in RAF yellow c/s			
G-BWWU	Piper PA-22-150 Caribbean	22-5002	09.10.96	
	N7139D K M Bowen Upfield Farm, Whitson		17.05.08	
	Converted to PA-20 Pacer configuration;			
	Hoerner wing-tips (NF 18.07.18)			
G-BWWW	British Aerospace Jetstream 3102	614	08.07.83	
	G-31-614 BAE Systems (Operations) Ltd Warton		26.06.17E	
	(NF 25.08.18)			
G-BWWY	Lindstrand LBL 105A	411	14.10.96	
	MSJ Ballooning Ltd Lewes 'Corks and Cans Norton'		11.05.19E	
G-BWXA	Slingsby T67M-260 Firefly	2236	19.03.96	
	Power Aerobatics Ltd Goodwood		25.02.18E	
G-BWXB	Slingsby T67M-260 Firefly	2237	19.03.96	
	Power Aerobatics Ltd Goodwood		15.09.18E	
G-BWXF	Slingsby T67M-260 Firefly	2241	19.03.96	
	L3 CTS Airline & Academy Training Ltd Bournemouth		01.06.18E	
G-BWXJ	Slingsby T67M-260 Firefly	2245	19.03.96	
	D I Stanbridge (Horsford, Norwich)		24.08.18E	
G-BWXP	Slingsby T67M-260 Firefly	2251	19.03.96	
	T Bock & M Haller Freiburg, Germany		19.05.18E	
G-BWXS	Slingsby T67M-260 Firefly	2253	19.03.96	
	Power Aerobatics Ltd Goodwood		15.02.18E	
G-BWXT	Slingsby T67M-260 Firefly	2254	19.03.96	
	Cranfield University Cranfield		28.09.18E	
G-BWXV	Slingsby T67M-260 Firefly	2256	19.03.96	
	W Hillick Abbeyshrule, RoI		12.02.16E	
G-BWYB	Piper PA-28-160 Cherokee	28-263	16.09.96	
	N6374A, G-BWYB, 6Y-JLO, 6Y-JCH, VP-JCH			
	A J Peters Derby		31.08.17E	
	(IE 23.10.17)			
G-BWYD	Europa Aviation Europa	072	28.08.96	
	S Styles Wellesbourne Mountford		26.08.14P	
	Built by H J Bendiksen – project PFA 247-12621;			
	tailwheel u/c			
G-BWYE	Cessna 310R II	310R-1654	06.09.96	
	F-GBPE, (N26369) Cancelled 07.07.11 by CAA		10.09.09	
	Perth Instructional frame 07.16			
G-BWYK	Yakovlev Yak-50	812004	09.08.96	
	RA-01386, DOSAAF 51 A Marangoni (Rovereto, Italy)		04.06.17P	
	(IE 19.12.17)			

G-BWYN	Cameron O-77	1162	13.11.96	
	G-ODER I R Jones Llansawel, Llandeilo 'DER'		04.08.09E	
	(NF 14.04.16)			
G-BWYO	Sequoia F.8L Falco	xxxx	07.11.96	
	S G Roux Brighton City		09.10.18P	
	Built by S Harper – project PFA 100-10920			
G-BWYP	Sky 56-24 HAB	053	08.11.96	
	Cancelled 09.06.09 by CAA		09.11.01	
	Not Known Inflated Pidley 04.14 'Sky High Leisure'			
G-BWYR	Rans S-6-116 Coyote II	1294-700	08.11.96	
	D A Lord Swanborough Farm, Lewes		01.06.18P	
	Built by S Palmer – project PFA 204A-13058;			
	tailwheel u/c			
G-BWYU	Sky 120-24	052	13.11.96	
	Aerosaurus Balloons Ltd Whimple, Exeter			
	'Bramley Red'		10.05.12E	
	(IE 03.02.17)			
G-BWZA	Europa Aviation Europa	063	01.11.96	
	T G Cowlishaw Rufforth		14.11.18P	
	Built by M C Costin – project PFA 247-12626;			
	tailwheel u/c			
G-BWZG	Robin R2160 Alpha Sport	311	06.11.96	
	F-WZZZ Sherburn Aero Club Ltd Sherburn-in-Elmet		28.02.18E	
G-BWZJ	Cameron A-250	4021	02.12.96	
	Balloon School (International) Ltd t/a Balloon Club			
	of Great Britain Petworth		02.06.15E	
G-BWZP	Cameron Home Special 105SS HAB	4051	06.12.96	
	Cancelled 15.01.04 as PWFU		10.04.02	
	Not Known Inflated Ragley Hall 05.18			
G-BWZR	Bell 412EP	36144	22.08.97	
	ZJ234, G-BWZR, ZJ234, G-BWZR, G-FZLM			
	FB Leasing Ltd Bournemouth		08.07.97A	
	(NF 02.11.18)			
G-BWZS★	Eurocopter AS.350BB	2945	10.12.96	
	ZJ243, G-BWZS, ZJ243, G-BWZS, F-WQDV			
	FB Heliservices Ltd			
	Cancelled 22.08.97 to MOD Restored 28.09.18			
	To C-.... 03.10.18			
G-BWZU	Lindstrand LBL 90B	418	12.12.96	
	Iseo Mongolfiere SAS di Rossi Paolo EC			
	Travagliato, Brescia, Italy		03.07.15E	
	(NF 31.08.16)			
G-BWZY	Hughes 269A (300)	950378	04.12.96	
	G-FSDT, N269CH, N1336D, 64-18066			
	J A Maginn (Annalong, Newry)		12.09.19E	

G-BXAA – G-BXZZ

G-BXAB	Piper PA-28-161 Warrior II	28-8416054	07.10.96	
	G-BTGK, N4344C TG Aviation Ltd Lydd		30.11.18E	
G-BXAC	Rotary Air Force RAF 2000 GTX-SE	H2-96-7-220	21.11.96	
	J A Robinson Trenchard Farm, Eggesford		27.08.18P	
	Built by D C Fairbrass – project PFA G/13-1279			
G-BXAF	Pitts S-1D	xxxx	06.12.96	
	N J Watson MoD Boscombe Down		27.10.18P	
	Built by F Sharples – project PFA 009-12258			
G-BXAJ	Lindstrand LBL 14A	425	23.12.96	
	Oscair Project AB Täby, Sweden			
	(NF 22.09.16)			
G-BXAK	IAV Bacau Yakovlev Yak-52	811508	23.12.96	
	LY-ASC, DOSAAF A M Holman-West			
	Alscot Park, Stratford-upon-Avon		07.04.18P	
G-BXAL	Cameron Bertie Bassett 90SS HAB	4034	13.01.97	
	Cancelled 24.04.09 by CAA		27.01.02	
	Not Known Inflated Ragley Hall 05.18			
G-BXAN	Scheibe SF25C Falke	44299	13.01.97	
	D-KDGQ A J Docherty tr C Falke Syndicate Darlton		12.06.18E	
G-BXAO	Avtech Jabiru SK	0099	14.01.97	
	P J Thompson (Llandaniel, Gaerwen)		23.04.99P	
	Built by I J M Donnelly – project PFA 274-13066			
	(NF 15.09.14)			
G-BXAU	Pitts S-1	GHG9	22.01.97	
	N9GG L Westnage Enstone		30.04.18P	
	Built by G Goodrich			

G-BXAY Bell 206B-3 JetRanger III 3946 24.01.97
N85EA, N521RC, N3210D Crop Spraying Ltd Elstree 18.12.19E
Operated by VVB Helicopters

G-BXBB Piper PA-20-135 Pacer 20-959 24.01.97
EC-AOZ, N1133C Cancelled 22.04.03 by CAA
Farley Farm, Farley Chamberlayne
Stored derelict 12.17 as 'EC-AOZ'

G-BXBE Bell 412EP 36145 22.08.97
ZJ236, G-BXBE, ZJ236, G-BXBE, C-FZLN
FB Leasing Ltd Bournemouth 15.06.97A
(NF 02.11.18)

G-BXBF Bell 412EP 36151 28.01.97
ZJ235, G-BXBF, ZJ235, G-BXBF, C-FZNF
FB Heliservices Ltd Bournemouth 20.05.97A
(NF 02.11.18)

G-BXBH Hunting Percival P.84 Jet Provost T.3A PAC/W/9241 29.01.97
XM365 Cancelled 10.10.02 by CAA 31.08.01
Bruntingthorpe *Displayed as 'XM365' 02.16*

G-BXBK Mudry CAP 10B 17 30.01.97
N170RC, French AF '307-SO' S Skipworth
Ham Hill, Sydmonton, Ecchinswell 20.11.18E

G-BXBL Lindstrand LBL 240A 317 31.01.97
J Fenton Newtown, Hungerford 27.08.16E

G-BXBU Mudry CAP 10B 103 11.02.97
N173RC, French AF J Mann
Watchford Farm, Yarcombe 07.07.18E

G-BXBY Cameron A-105 HAB 4077 13.02.97
Cancelled 14.09.11 as TWFU 09.04.09
Not Known *Inflated Longleat 09.18*

G-BXBZ PZL-104 Wilga 80 CF21930941 13.02.97
EC-GDA, ZK-PZQ J H Sandham
t/a JH Sandham Aviation Carlisle Lake District 22.11.15E

G-BXCA HAPI Cygnet SF-2A xxxx 22.01.97
J D C Henslow Ingrams Green, Midhurst
'Fighting Cygnets' 06.12.18P
Built by G E Collard – project PFA 182-12921

G-BXCC Piper PA-28-201T Turbo Dakota 28-7921068 19.02.97
D-EKBM, N2855A Greer Aviation Ltd
Glasgow Prestwick 10.11.18E

G-BXCD Team Mini-Max 91A xxxx 18.02.97
A Maltby (Appleby-in-Westmorland)
Built by R Davies – project PFA 186-12393
(SSDR microlight since 08.16) (NF 17.08.17)

G-BXCG Jodel 250 replica 60 22.05.97
D-EHGG P G Morris Insch 29.08.17P
Built by J M Scott – project PFA 299-13146 (IE 02.11.17)

G-BXCJ Campbell Cricket replica xxxx 24.02.97
A G Peel Rufforth East 28.04.09P
Built by R A Friend – project PFA G/03-1177;
displayed at Gyrocopter Experience 05.18
(NF 08.01.16)

G-BXCT de Havilland DHC-1 Chipmunk 22 C1/0145 03.03.97
WB697 J W Frecklington & R Merewood
t/a Wickenby Aviation Wickenby 08.05.18E
As 'WB697:95' in RAF c/s

G-BXCU Rans S-6-116 Coyote II 1096.1044 06.03.97
N A Preston Deenethorpe 29.10.18P
Built by M R McNeil – project PFA 204A-13105;
tricycle u/c

G-BXCV de Havilland DHC-1 Chipmunk 22 C1/0807 03.03.97
WP929 Ardmore Aviation Services Ltd Duxford 17.02.19E
As 'WP929:F' in RAF c/s

G-BXCW Denney Kitfox Model 3 xxxx 06.03.97
D R Piercy Eyres Field 29.05.18P
Built by M J Blanchard – project PFA 172-12619

G-BXDA de Havilland DHC-1 Chipmunk 22 C1/0747 07.03.97
WP860 D P Curtis Audley End 21.11.14P
As 'WP860:6' in RAF c/s; on rebuild 2016 (IE 05.03.15)

G-BXDB Cessna U206F U20602233 18.12.96
G-BMNZ, F-BVJT, N1519U D A Howard Colonsay 19.03.18E

G-BXDE Rotary Air Force RAF 2000 GTX-SE H2-96-7-216 14.01.97
V G Freke (Eynsham) 27.06.19P
Built by A McCredie – project PFA G/13-1280

G-BXDG de Havilland DHC-1 Chipmunk 22 C1/0644 07.03.97
WK630 Felthorpe Flying Group Ltd Felthorpe 13.06.18P
As 'WK630' in RAF white & red c/s with
No.8 (AEW) Squadron insignia

G-BXDH de Havilland DHC-1 Chipmunk 22 C1/0270 10.03.97
WD331 Royal Aircraft Establishment Aero Club Ltd
Farnborough 14.01.18E
As 'WD331' in RAF c/s

G-BXDI de Havilland DHC-1 Chipmunk 22 C1/0312 10.03.97
WD373 A M Dinnie tr G-BXDI Wycombe Air Park 15.01.19E
As 'WD373:12' in RAF red & white c/s

G-BXDK★ Bell 412EP 36095 17.03.97
ZJ242, G-BXDK, N2291Q, XA-SYM, N2291Q
FB Heliservices Ltd
Cancelled 01.12.97 to MOD Restored 26.04.18
To MOD as ZJ242 08.03.19

G-BXDL[M] Hunting Percival P.84 Jet Provost T.3A PAC/W/9286 18.03.97
8983M, XM478 Cancelled 14.10.08 – to Italy
As 'G-BXDL'
With Museo Dell'Araba Fenice, Reggio Nell'Emilia, Italy

G-BXDN de Havilland DHC-1 Chipmunk 22 C1/0618 18.03.97
WK609 L A Edwards, G James & W D Lowe
Wycombe Air Park 30.06.18E
As 'WK609:93' in RAF c/s

G-BXDO Rutan Cozy xxxx 21.03.97
G W A Mackenzie tr Cozy Group Perth 27.08.14P
Built by C R Blackburn – project PFA 159-12032;
rebuilt 2008 from remnants of LongEz G-BLZH

G-BXDR Lindstrand LBL 77A 441 25.03.97
A J & A R Brown Litlington, Royston
'Investing in Our Future' 26.08.18E

G-BXDS Bell 206B-3 JetRanger III 2734 01.04.97
G-TAMF, G-BXDS, G-OVBJ, G-BXDS, OY-HDK, N661PS
Aerospeed Ltd Manston Park *'National Grid'* 12.07.18E

G-BXDU Aero Designs Pulsar xxxx 25.03.97
A J Price (Bournemouth) 06.10.18P
Built by M P Board – project PFA 202-11991;
tricycle u/c

G-BXDV Sky 105-24 049 26.03.97
N A Carr Leicester 23.06.18E

G-BXDY Europa Aviation Europa 229 27.03.97
S Attubato & D G Watts
Fowle Hall Farm, Laddingford *'The Rocketeer'* 24.05.19P
Built by D G Watts – project PFA 247-12914:
sequence no. duplicates G-MYZP; tailwheel u/c

G-BXDZ Lindstrand LBL 105A 437 04.04.97
A D & D J Sutcliffe Harrogate *'Akito'* 09.07.18E

G-BXEC de Havilland DHC-1 Chipmunk 22 C1/0647 03.04.97
WK633 M J Miller & A J Robinson (Duxford) 28.06.07
As 'WK633' (NF 30.10.16)

G-BXEE Enstrom 280C Shark 1117 09.04.97
OH-HAN, N336AT Cancelled 31.05.06 as PWFU 10.08.07
Haddington *For sale for static display 01.14*

G-BXEF Europa Aviation Europa 159 07.04.97
C Busuttil-Reynaud (Emsworth)
(NF 16.05.16)

G-BXEJ Magni M16 Tandem Trainer D-9302 08.04.97
D-MIFF N H Collins t/a Aes Radionic Surveillance
Systems Streethay Farm, Streethay 18.08.12P
(NF 11.02.16)

G-BXEN Cameron N-105 10288 11.04.97
E Ghio Dronero, Piedmont, Italy *'Liquigas'* 18.09.18E
Originally c/n 4090: new envelope c/n 10288 fitted 2003

G-BXES Hunting Percival P.66 Pembroke C.1 PAC/W/3032 14.04.97
N4234C, 9042M, XL954 C Keane Dublin Weston, Rol 04.10.17P
As 'XL954' in RAF 60 Sqdn c/s

G-BXET Piper PA-38-112 Tomahawk 38-80A0028 14.04.97
N25089 Cancelled 23.06.11 as PWFU 26.08.11
Dundee *On fire dump 01.18*

G-BXEX Piper PA-28-181 Archer II 28-7790463 16.04.97
N3562Q P Riley tr Nottingham Archer Aviators
Nottingham City 07.09.19E

G-BXEZ Cessna 182P Skylane II 18264344 16.04.97
OH-CHJ, N1479M Forhawk Ltd Bodmin 22.11.17E
Assembled Reims Aviation with c/n 0054

G-BXFB	Pitts S-1C	9543	16.04.97
	N77ZZ J F Dowe Tibenham		
	Built by B J Dziuba (NF 25.07.17)		
G-BXFC	Jodel D.18	179	17.04.97
	M Godbold Little Gransden		24.08.18P
	Built by B S Godbold – project PFA 169-11322		
G-BXFE	Mudry CAP 10B	135	18.04.97
	N175RC, French AF Avions Aerobatic Ltd		
	White Waltham *'The London Aerobatic Company'*		19.10.19E
G-BXFF	Bell 412EP	36156	22.08.97
	ZJ237, G-BXFF, ZJ237, G-BXFF, C-FZVV		
	FB Leasing Ltd Bournemouth		02.08.00A
	(NF 02.11.18)		
G-BXFG	Europa Aviation Europa	018	21.04.97
	A Rawicz-Szczerbo Eaglescott		11.08.18P
	Built by A Rawicz-Szczerbo – project		
	PFA 247-12500; tailwheel u/c		
G-BXFH	Bell 412EP	36125	23.04.97
	ZJ239, G-BXFH, C-FZXD, N6282C		
	FB Leasing Ltd Bournemouth		27.09.97A
	(NF 02.11.18)		
G-BXFK	CFM Streak Shadow	K 206	24.04.97
	P D Curtis (Boston Spa, Wetherby)		21.06.19P
	Built by D Adcock – project PFA 206-12329		
G-BXFN	Colt 77A	4145	25.04.97
	South Downs Ballooning Ltd Grayshott, Hindhead		27.04.09E
	Built by Cameron Balloons Ltd (IE 05.06.17)		
G-BXGA	Eurocopter AS.350B2 Ecureuil	2493	30.04.97
	OO-RCH, OO-XCH, F-WZFX		
	PLM Dollar Group Ltd Dalcross Heliport		27.08.18E
	Callsign 'Osprey 57'		
G-BXGD	Sky 90-24	067	06.05.97
	Servo & Electronic Sales Ltd Lydd, Romney Marsh		05.10.16E
	(NF 24.02.16)		
G-BXGE	Cessna 152 II	15282700	08.05.97
	N89283 Cancelled 23.03.02 as PWFU		16.07.00
	Tatenhill *Fuselage stored 01.17*		
G-BXGG	Europa Aviation Europa	178	29.04.97
	D J Joyce Yeatsall Farm, Abbots Bromley		09.08.17P
	Built by B W Faulkner – project PFA 247-12803;		
	tricycle u/c (IE 23.10.17)		
G-BXGL	de Havilland DHC-1 Chipmunk 22	C1/0924	12.05.97
	WZ884 S Smith tr GL Group Wickenby		10.07.19P
	(IE 30.05.17)		
G-BXGM	de Havilland DHC-1 Chipmunk 22	C1/0806	09.05.97
	WP928 J E Newman tr Chipmunk GBXGM Group		
	Goodwood		11.02.19E
	As 'WP928:D' in AAC c/s		
G-BXGO	de Havilland DHC-1 Chipmunk 22	C1/0097	13.05.97
	WB654 T J Orchard Finmere		30.05.18P
	As 'WB654:U' in AAC c/s		
G-BXGP	de Havilland DHC-1 Chipmunk 22	C1/0927	12.05.97
	WZ882 V Dean (Andover)		11.06.19E
	As 'WZ882:K' in AAC c/s		
G-BXGS	Rotary Air Force RAF 2000	H2-96-7-276	14.05.97
	D W Howell (Stoke-on-Trent)		23.08.12P
	Built by N C White – project PFA G/13-1290		
	(NF 08.01.16)		
G-BXGT	III Sky Arrow 650 T	xxxx	07.05.97
	J S C Goodale Popham		04.09.18P
	Built by Sky Arrow (Kits) UK Ltd		
	– project PFA 298-13085		
G-BXGV	Cessna 172R Skyhawk	17280240	07.01.98
	N9300F A Bristow tr G-BXGV Skyhawk Group		
	White Waltham		04.06.18E
G-BXGX	de Havilland DHC-1 Chipmunk 22	C1/0609	19.05.97
	WK586 The Real Flying Company Ltd Brighton City		19.09.18E
	As 'WK586:V' in AAC c/s		
G-BXGY	Cameron V-65	4125	18.04.97
	R J Plume tr Dante Balloon Group		
	Newtown, Hungerford		23.11.18E
G-BXGZ	Stemme S 10-V	14-023	18.08.97
	D-KSTE, EC-GGD, D-KGDF		
	G S Craven & A J Garner Lasham *'S10'*		19.02.19E

G-BXHA	de Havilland DHC-1 Chipmunk 22	C1/0801	20.05.97
	WP925 H M & S Roberts Old Warden		20.04.18P
	As 'WP925:C' in AAC c/s		
G-BXHC	Bell 412EP	36162	22.05.97
	ZJ238, G-BXHC, C-GAFF		
	FB Leasing Ltd Bournemouth		30.08.97A
	(NF 02.11.18)		
G-BXHF	de Havilland DHC-1 Chipmunk 22	C1/0808	28.05.97
	WP930 R A Wallis tr Hotel Fox Syndicate Redhill		14.04.18P
	As 'WP930:J' in AAC c/s		
G-BXHH	Grumman American AA-5A Cheetah	AA5A-0105	03.06.97
	N9705U P G Hayward Little Snoring		09.07.18E
G-BXHJ	HAPI Cygnet SF-2A	358	29.05.97
	I J Smith Brook Farm, Boylestone		
	Built by I J Smith – project PFA 182-12159 (NF 04.09.14)		
G-BXHL	Sky 77-24	055	29.05.97
	C Timbrell Redditch *'Harlequin'*		20.10.16E
G-BXHM	Lindstrand LBL 25A Cloudhopper HAB	466	30.05.97
	Cancelled 06.11.01 as PWFU		07.05.00
	Not Known *Inflated Pidley 05.16*		
G-BXHO	Lindstrand LBL Telewest Sphere	474	30.05.97
	Magical Adventures Ltd West Bloomfield, MI, USA		
	'Telewest'		30.09.09E
	(NF 03.06.15)		
G-BXHR	Stemme S 10-V	14-030	23.07.97
	D-KSTE J H Rutherford Sleap		20.03.18E
G-BXHT	Bushby-Long Midget Mustang	M-I-1964	03.06.97
	K Manley Palmer's Farm, Lower Dicker		12.07.18P
	Built by P P Chapman – project PFA 168-13077		
G-BXHU	Campbell Cricket Mk.6	xxxx	03.06.97
	B F Pearson Headon Farm, Retford		18.08.06P
	Built by P C Lovegrove – project PFA G/16-1293		
	(NF 12.07.16)		
G-BXHY	Europa Aviation Europa	022	06.06.97
	B Lewis & A L Thorne tr Jupiter Flying Group		
	White Waltham		27.05.18P
	Built by A L Thorne – project PFA 247-12514;		
	tailwheel u/c		
G-BXIA	de Havilland DHC-1 Chipmunk 22	C1/0056	09.06.97
	WB615 S Fisher & C Lightfoot tr WB615 Group		
	Blackpool		26.11.19P
	As 'WB615:E' in AAC c/s		
G-BXIE	Colt 77B	4181	11.06.97
	I R Warrington Hunstanton		23.03.16E
	Built by Cameron Balloons Ltd		
G-BXIF	Piper PA-28-181 Archer II	28-7690404	12.06.97
	PH-SWM, OO-HAY, N6827J Piper Flight Ltd Cardiff		28.09.18E
G-BXIG	Zenair CH.701 STOL	xxxx	16.06.97
	S Ingram (Sutton Coldfield)		16.11.17P
	Built by A J Perry – project PFA 187-12066		
G-BXIH	Sky 200-24	076	16.06.97
	Skyview Ballooning Ltd t/a Kent Ballooning		
	Stanford, Ashford *'adscene'*		09.04.18E
G-BXII	Europa Aviation Europa	175	30.04.97
	D A McFadyean		
	Stoney Lane Farm, Tutnall, Broad Green		11.12.18P
	Built by D A McFadyean – project PFA 247-12812;		
	'Swiss' version tailwheel u/c		
G-BXIJ	Europa Aviation Europa	076	16.06.97
	P N Birch Felthorpe		09.04.16P
	Built by D G & E A Bligh – project PFA 247-12698;		
	tailwheel u/c (IE 04.07.16)		
G-BXIM	de Havilland DHC-1 Chipmunk 22	C1/0548	13.05.97
	WK512 A B Ascroft & P R Joshua RAF Halton		08.10.18P
	As 'WK512:A' in AAC c/s		
G-BXIR★	Bell 412EP	36163	24.06.97
	ZJ240, G-BXIR, C-GAIE FB Heliservices Ltd		
	Cancelled 13.10.97 to MOD Restored 26.04.18		
	To MOD as ZJ240 18.12.18		
G-BXIT	Zebedee V-31	Z1/3999	08.05.97
	P J Bish Newtown, Hungerford		
	Built by Zebedee Balloon Service (IE 06.07.18)		

G-BXIW	Sky 105-24	073	24.06.97
	LY-OEN, PH-EPB, G-BXIW		
	A G A Barclay-Faulkner Hopton, Stafford		23.08.11E
	(IE 05.09.17)		
G-BXIX	Magni M16 Tandem Trainer	xxxx	13.06.97
	P P Willmott North Coates		23.07.17P
	Built by D Beevers – project PFA G/12-1292;		
	frame in container 01.19		
G-BXIY	Blake Bluetit	01	26.06.97
	BAPC.37 M J Aubrey Llanfyrnach		
	Built by W H C Blake; pre-war composite ex Spartans		
	G-AAGN, G-AAJB & unknown Avro 504K; displayed		
	Classic Ultralight Heritage (NF 16.12.14)		
G-BXIZ	Lindstrand LBL 31A	476	03.07.97
	D P Hopkins t/a Lakeside Lodge Golf Centre		
	Pidley, Huntingdon *'Hyundai'*		25.03.17E
G-BXJB	IAV Bacau Yakovlev Yak-52	877403	30.06.97
	LY-ABR, DOSAAF 15		
	D J Dunlop tr Yak Display Group Elmsett *'15'*		02.05.18P
G-BXJD	Piper PA-28-180 Cherokee C	28-4215	27.06.97
	OY-BBZ S Atherton Breighton		25.10.18E
G-BXJH	Cameron N-42	4194	15.07.97
	D M Hoddinott Bristol BS8 *'Unipart'*		05.11.16E
	(IE 02.08.17)		
G-BXJM	Cessna 152 II	15282380	15.07.97
	OO-HOQ, F-GHOQ, N68797 ACS Aviation Ltd		
	Cumbernauld		20.11.18E
G-BXJN	Eurocopter AS.350BB Ecureuil	2999	16.07.97
	ZJ269, G-BXJN FB Heliservices Ltd		19.09.97
	(IE 30.11.17)		
G-BXJO	Cameron O-90	4190	16.07.97
	Dragon Balloon Company Ltd Castleton, Hope Valley		01.09.17E
G-BXJT	Sky 90-24	072	18.07.97
	J G O'Connell (Pattiswick, Braintree)		18.11.07A
	(NF 06.01.15)		
G-BXJY	Van's RV-6	xxxx	23.07.97
	J P Kynaston Holmbeck Farm, Burcott		04.10.18P
	Built by D J Sharland – project PFA 181-12447		
G-BXJZ	Cameron C-60	4168	23.07.97
	N J & S J Bettin Greatham, Liss		23.05.18E
G-BXKL	Bell 206B-3 JetRanger III	3006	08.10.97
	N5735Y Swattons Aviation Ltd Thruxton		10.10.18E
	Operated by Vantage Helicopters		
G-BXKM	Rotary Air Force RAF 2000 GTX-SE	xxxx	05.08.97
	E Mangles Rufforth East		04.05.18P
	Built by J R Huggins – project PFA G/13-1291		
G-BXKU	Colt AS-120 Mk.II HA Airship	4165	15.08.97
	D C Chipping Harleston *'Epul Jovem Lisboa'*		19.04.01A
	Built by Cameron Balloons Ltd (NF 05.09.16)		
G-BXKW	Slingsby T67M-200 Firefly	2061	15.08.97
	VR-HZS, HKG-13, G-7-129 A Huygens & J Jansen		
	Saint Ghislain, Belgium		23.03.18E
	As 'HKG-13' in Royal Hong Kong AAF c/s		
G-BXKX	Auster 5	803	19.08.97
	D-EMXA, HB-EOK, MS938		
	J A Sephton Top Farm, Croydon		20.06.13P
	Built by Taylorcraft Aeroplanes (England) Ltd		
	(IE 31.05.17)		
G-BXLF	Lindstrand LBL 90A	487	03.09.97
	J Edwards & S McMahon Northampton		
	'Variohm Components'		29.06.18E
G-BXLG	Cameron C-80	4250	05.03.98
	S M Anthony Bluntisham, Huntingdon		23.06.18E
G-BXLK	Europa Aviation Europa	074	11.09.97
	R J Sheridan (Twineham, Haywards Heath)		12.10.18P
	Built by R G Fairall – project PFA 247-12613;		
	tailwheel u/c		
G-BXLN	Sportavia-Putzer Fournier RF4D	4022	15.09.97
	F-BORK P W Cooper Seighford		05.07.19E
G-BXLO	BAC P.84 Jet Provost T.4	PAC/W/19986	14.08.97
	9032M, XR673 Century Aviation Ltd Tatenhill		30.11.18P
	As 'XR673' in RAF c/s		
G-BXLP	Sky 90-24	084	18.09.97
	D Bedford & J Edwards Northampton		
	'Heart of Gold'		21.07.14E
	(IE 13.01.16)		
G-BXLS	PZL-110 Koliber 160A	04980078	23.06.98
	SP-WGG, SP-PEB (2), SP-WGG (1), (N150CP)		
	P R Powell Shobdon		16.04.18E
G-BXLT	SOCATA TB-200 Tobago XL	1457	28.04.97
	F-GRBB, EC-FNX, EC-234, F-GLFP		
	C, G & J Fisher & D Fitton Blackpool		23.03.18E
G-BXLW	Enstrom F-28F Falcon	734	11.09.97
	N279SA, G-BXLW, Thai Government KASET 1712		
	Rhoburt Ltd Sleap		14.10.07E
	Stored 04.15 (NF 08.12.14)		
G-BXLY	Piper PA-28-161 Warrior II	28-7715220	19.09.97
	G-WATZ, N7641F North East Flight Academy Ltd		
	Newcastle Int'l		13.05.19E
	Originally built as PA-28-151 Cherokee Warrior		
G-BXMD★	Eurocopter AS.350BB	3026	19.09.97
	ZJ244, G-BXMD FB Heliservices Ltd		
	Cancelled 03.11.97 to MOD Restored 28.09.18		
	To C-.... 03.10.18		
G-BXME★	Eurocopter AS.350BB	3028	19.09.97
	ZJ245, G-BXME FB Leasing Ltd		
	Cancelled 11.11.97 to MOD Restored 02.11.18		
	To C-.... 26.11.18		
G-BXMI★	Eurocopter AS.350BB	3032	25.09.97
	ZJ280, G-BXMI FB Heliservices Ltd		
	Cancelled 13.11.97 to MOD Restored 03.04.18		
	To N62MS 29.05.18		
G-BXMJ★	Eurocopter AS.350BB	3031	25.09.97
	ZJ246, G-BXMJ FB Heliservices Ltd		
	Cancelled 21.11.97 to MOD Restored 26.04.18		
	To MOD as ZJ246 06.09.18		
G-BXMV	Scheibe SF25C Falke	44223	07.08.97
	D-KDFV K E Ballington Kirton in Lindsey		21.03.13E
	(NF 21.11.14)		
G-BXMX	Phoenix Currie Wot	PFA 058-13055	23.09.97
	M W Bodger Yeatsall Farm, Abbots Bromley		09.08.19P
	Built by M J Hayman – project PFA 058-13055		
G-BXMY	Hughes 269C (*300*)	740328	20.10.97
	N9599F K & M Pinfold (Baldwins Gate, Newcastle)		05.11.19E
G-BXNC	Europa Aviation Europa	122	13.10.97
	J K Cantwell (Ashton-under-Lyne)		
	Built by J K Cantwell – project PFA 247-12970		
	(NF 20.04.16)		
G-BXNE★	Eurocopter AS.350BB	3037	15.10.97
	ZJ248, G-BXNE FB Heliservices Ltd		
	Cancelled 04.12.97 to MOD Restored 26.04.18		
	To MOD as ZJ248 06.09.18		
G-BXNN	de Havilland DHC-1 Chipmunk 22	C1/0849	04.08.97
	WP983 E N Skinner Trenchard Farm, Eggesford		
	As 'WP983:B' in AAC c/s (IE 17.12.18)		
G-BXNS	Bell 206B-3 JetRanger III	2385	03.11.97
	N16822 Aerospeed Ltd Manston Park		31.08.17E
G-BXNU	Avtech Jabiru SK	xxxx	31.10.97
	Cancelled 23.01.03 as PWFU		14.07.91
	Southery, Norfolk *Built by J Smith – project*		
	PFA 274-13218; used as engine test-bed 07.14		
G-BXOA	Robinson R22 Beta	1614	10.11.97
	N41132, JA7832 Swift Helicopter Services Ltd		
	Leeds Heliport		22.03.18E
G-BXOC	Evans VP-2	xxxx	29.09.97
	Condor Aviation International Ltd		
	Mount Airey Farm, South Cave		23.04.10P
	Built by H J Cox – project PFA 063-10305 (NF 28.09.15)		
G-BXOF	Diamond DA.20-A1 Katana	10256	04.12.97
	C-FDVP Aircraft Engineers Ltd Glasgow Prestwick		24.11.15E
	Stored 05.18 (IE 6.04.16)		
G-BXOI	Cessna 172R Skyhawk	17280145	17.11.97
	N9990F E J Watts Perranporth		25.02.18E
G-BXOJ	Piper PA-28-161 Warrior III	2842010	15.12.97
	N9265G Tayside Aviation Ltd Dundee		22.02.18E

G-BXOK★	Eurocopter AS.350BB	3049	21.11.97
	ZJ252, G-BXOK FB Heliservices Ltd		
	Cancelled 16.01.98 to MOD Restored 26.04.18		
	To MOD as ZJ252 06.09.18		
G-BXOM	Isaacs Spitfire	xxxx	25.11.97
	S Vince Felthorpe		
	Built by J H Betton – project PFA 027-12768		
	noted 70% complete 02.17 (NF 22.06.16)		
G-BXOT	Cameron C-70	4200	21.10.97
	R J Plume tr Dante Balloon Group		
	Newtown, Hungerford *'British Airways'*	19.09.14E	
	(IE 21.04.17)		
G-BXOU	Robin DR.360 Chevalier	312	06.10.97
	F-BPOU J A Lofthouse		
	(Laborie, Lacapelle-Livron, France)	02.03.18E	
	Built by Centre-Est Aéronautique		
G-BXOX	Grumman American AA-5A Cheetah	AA5A-0694	27.02.98
	F-GBDS R L Carter & P J Large Turweston	15.04.18E	
G-BXOY	QAC Quickie Q.235	xxxx	17.11.97
	C C Clapham Enstone	03.09.04P	
	Built by C C Clapham – project PFA 094A-12183		
	(NF 21.04.16)		
G-BXOZ	Piper PA-28-181 Archer II	28-7790173	14.10.97
	N6927F Oz Air Ltd Elstree	21.07.19E	
G-BXPC	Diamond DA.20-A1 Katana	10258	04.12.97
	C-GKAN Cubair Flight Training Ltd Redhill		
	(NF 24.02.16)		
G-BXPD	Diamond DA.20-A1 Katana	10259	04.12.97
	C-GDMU Cubair Flight Training Ltd Redhill	01.07.16E	
G-BXPI	Van's RV-4	xxxx	02.01.98
	B M Diggins RAF Mona	06.09.18P	
	Built by E M Marsh – project PFA 181-12426		
G-BXPL	Piper PA-28-140 Cherokee	28-24560	10.12.97
	N7224J Cancelled 24.07.12 as destroyed	07.07.11	
	Coventry *Cockpit converted to simulator,*		
	for ATC Coventry 02.17		
G-BXPP	Sky 90-24	092	17.12.97
	S A Nother Poole	08.04.14E	
	(IE 30.04.15)		
G-BXPT	Ultramagic H-77	77/140	22.12.97
	Aerobility Blackwater, Camberley *'AeroBILITY'*	10.01.19E	
G-BXRA	Mudry CAP 10B	3	12.12.97
	French AF 3 Cole Aviation Ltd		
	(Church Hill Farm, Sedlescombe)	15.10.16E	
	(IE 22.12.17)		
G-BXRB	Mudry CAP 10B	100	12.12.97
	French AF 100 T T Duhig Tibenham	07.08.18E	
G-BXRC	Mudry CAP 10B	134	12.12.97
	French AF 134 I F Scott tr Group Alpha Fenland	13.10.18E	
G-BXRF	Scintex CP.1310-C3 Super Emeraude	935	09.01.98
	OO-NSF, F-BMJG D T Gethin Swansea	19.09.18P	
	Built by Société Scintex		
G-BXRL	Westland Scout AH.1	F9639	20.01.98
	XT630 Cancelled 20.03.00 as destroyed	14.06.00	
	Rough Close, Staffs *Wreck stored 03.18 as 'XT630'*		
G-BXRO	Cessna U206G	U20604217	09.02.98
	OH-ULK, N756NE Wild Geese Parachute Ltd		
	McMaster's Farm, Movenis	27.03.18E	
G-BXRP	Schweizer 269C (300)	S 1334	27.01.98
	OH-HSP, N7506U Findelta Pty Ltd	23.02.18E	
	(NF 20.12.17)		
G-BXRS	Westland Scout AH.1	F9741	28.01.98
	XW613 C J Marsden North Weald	24.04.19P	
	As 'XW613' in AAC c/s		
G-BXRT	Robin DR.400-180 Régent	2382	23.02.98
	T P Usborne Goodwood	09.08.18E	
G-BXRV	Van's RV-4	3461	12.01.98
	B J Oke tr Cleeve Flying Group Gloucestershire	01.05.18P	
	Built by B J Oke – project PFA 181-12482		
G-BXRY	Bell 206B JetRanger	208	19.03.98
	N4054G Twylight Management Ltd		
	Palma-Son Bonet, Mallorca, Spain	12.03.19E	

G-BXRZ	Rans S-6-116 Coyote II	0897.1146	03.02.98
	M P Hallam Jackrells Farm, Southwater	28.08.18P	
	Built by C M White – project PFA 204A-13195;		
	tailwheel u/c		
G-BXSC	Cameron C-80	4251	12.12.97
	V A B Rolland Colmenarejo, Madrid, Spain *'Keepsake'*	15.03.18E	
	(IE 18.07.18)		
G-BXSD	Cessna 172R Skyhawk	17280310	12.03.98
	N431ES R Paston Wellesbourne Mountford	13.04.18E	
G-BXSE	Cessna 172R Skyhawk	17280352	19.05.98
	N9321F MK Aero Support Ltd Southend	28.06.19E	
	Operated by Seawing Flying Club		
G-BXSG	Robinson R22 Beta II	2789	03.02.98
	Rivermead Aviation Ltd Gloucestershire	28.07.18E	
	Operated by Rise Helicopters		
G-BXSH	DG Flugzeugbau DG-800B	8-121B50	05.02.98
	D Crimmins Challock *'SH'*	07.12.18E	
G-BXSI	Avtech Jabiru SK	0139	05.02.98
	P F Gandy Deanland	11.07.18P	
	Built by V R Leggott project PFA 274-13204		
G-BXSL	Westland Scout AH.1	F9762	17.02.98
	XW799 Cancelled 07.05.02 by CAA	14.08.01	
	Thruxton *Wreck on fire dump 12.15*		
G-BXSP	Grob G109B	6335	25.03.98
	D-KNEA D Innes tr Deeside Grob Group Aboyne	06.10.18E	
G-BXST	Piper PA-25-235 Pawnee C	25-4952	09.02.98
	PH-BAT, N8532L Staffordshire Gliding Club Ltd		
	Seighford	29.03.18E	
	Fuselage No.25-4971		
G-BXSU	Team Mini-Max 91A	xxxx	20.02.98
	G-MYGL I Pearson Perranporth		
	Built by A R Carr – project PFA 186-12357		
	(SSDR microlight since 06.14) (NF 25.07.17)		
G-BXSV	SNCAN Stampe SV.4C	556	10.10.02
	N21PM, F-BDDB P A Greenhalgh		
	New Barn Farm, Crawley		
	Stored 10.16 – rebuild suspended (NF 13.05.16)		
G-BXSX	Cameron V-77	4329	06.04.98
	D R Medcalf Catshill, Bromsgrove *'All-Tech'*	23.06.14E	
	(IE 04.08.17)		
G-BXSY	Robinson R22 Beta II	2778	27.01.98
	N M G Pearson (Mangotsfield, Bristol)	05.02.09E	
	(IE 11.09.15)		
G-BXTD	Europa Aviation Europa	155	26.02.98
	P G Noonan (Haverfordwest)	29.06.11P	
	Built by P R Anderson – project PFA 247-12772;		
	tailwheel u/c (NF 22.08.14)		
G-BXTF	Cameron N-105	4304	02.04.98
	C J Dunkley Stonefield Park, Chilbolton		
	'Sainsbury's Strawberry'	01.05.15E	
G-BXTG	Cameron N-42	4305	02.04.98
	S M M Carden & P M Watkins Chippenham		
	'Sainsbury's'	25.08.10E	
	(IE 06.06.17)		
G-BXTI	Pitts S-1S	NP1	09.03.98
	ZS-VZX, N96MM A Schmer		
	Oldenburg-Hatten, Germany	06.01.17P	
	Built by N J Pesch (NF 27.01.17)		
G-BXTJ[M]	Cameron N-77 HAB	4332	06.04.98
	Cancelled 07.09.15 as PWFU	27.09.09	
	With British Balloon Museum & Library, Newbury		
G-BXTO	Hindustan HAL-26 Pushpak	PK-128	12.02.98
	9V-BAI, VT-DWM P Q Benn Solent	06.09.16P	
G-BXTS	Diamond DA.20-A1 Katana	10308	10.03.98
	N638DA, C-GKAC Airbourne Aviation Ltd Popham		
	'www.flyMAC.co.uk'	08.06.19E	
G-BXTT	Grumman American AA-5B Tiger	AA5B-0749	27.02.98
	F-GBDH J Ducray Saint Cyr-l'Ecole, France	20.05.18E	
G-BXTW	Piper PA-28-181 Archer III	2843137	26.05.98
	N41279, (G-BXTW), N41279		
	J N Davison t/a Davison Plant Hire Compton Abbas	25.03.19E	
G-BXTY	Piper PA-28-161 Cadet	2841179	11.03.98
	PH-LED Flew LLP Bournemouth	17.08.18E	

G-BXTZ   Piper PA-28-161 Cadet   2841181   11.03.98
              PH-LEE Flew LLP Bournemouth   14.05.18E

G-BXUA   Campbell Cricket Mk.5   PCL 126   12.03.98
              A W Harvey Enstone   12.10.18P
              Built by P C Lovegrove – project PFA G/03-1272;
              carries c/n 'PCL 126' on fin

G-BXUC   Robinson R22 Beta   0908   17.03.98
              OY-HFB Rivermead Aviation Ltd Gloucestershire   08.10.18E
              Operated by Rise Helicopters

G-BXUF   Agusta-Bell 206B-2 JetRanger II   8633   12.05.98
              EC-DUS SJ Contracting Services Ltd
              (Beckley, Oxford)   25.07.17E

G-BXUG   Lindstrand LBL Baby Bel   512   14.05.98
              K Gruenauer Schwäbisch Hall, Germany *'Babybel'* 20.06.16E
              Active 05.18 (IE 07.02.18)

G-BXUH   Lindstrand LBL 31A   513   02.06.98
              R A Lovell Rushden *'Mini Babybel'*   04.07.18E

G-BXUI   DG Flugzeugbau DG-800B   8-105B39   12.05.98
              BGA 4382, D-KKLC J le Coyte Shenington   15.04.18E

G-BXUO   Lindstrand LBL 105A   520   27.03.98
              Lindstrand Technologies Ltd Oswestry *'Oswestry'* 02.08.19E

G-BXUU   Cameron V-65   4362   23.04.98
              M & S Mitchell Hertford   15.05.19E
              Operated by Hertfordshire Balloon Collection

G-BXUW   Colt 90A   4317   23.04.98
               M A Stelling South Queensferry, Edinburgh
              'Zycomm'   02.08.19E
              Built by Cameron Balloons Ltd

G-BXUX   Brandli BX-2 Cherry   161   04.04.98
              M F Fountain Clipgate Farm, Denton   31.08.17P
              Built by M F Fountain – project PFA 179-12571

G-BXVA   SOCATA TB-200 Tobago XL   1325   07.04.98
              F-GJXL, F-WJXL M Goehen
              (Meschers-sur-Gironde, France)   26.06.18E

G-BXVB   Cessna 152 II   15282584   15.04.98
              N69250 PJC (Leasing) Ltd Stapleford   28.08.18E

G-BXVC   Piper PA-28RT-201T Turbo Arrow IV   28R-7931113   20.04.98
              D-ELIV, N2152V Cancelled 22.01.03 as PWFU   28.06.01
              Rochester *Fuselage on fire dump 06.16*

G-BXVG   Sky 77-24   99   28.05.98
              M Wolf Wallingford   24.08.18E

G-BXVK   Robin HR.200-120B   326   01.07.98
              B D & J Cottrell Bourn   15.05.19E

G-BXVO   Van's RV-6A   23021   28.04.98
              R Marsden Hinton-in-the-Hedges   04.12.18P
              Built by P J Hynes – project PFA 181-12575

G-BXVP   Sky 31-24   056   28.04.98
              H G Griffiths & S I Williams Wenvoe, Cardiff
              'Sky Balloons'   13.06.18E

G-BXVR   Sky 90-24   061   20.07.98
              P Hegarty Draperstown, Magherafelt
              'Terrenus handmade tiles'   05.06.18E

G-BXVS   Brügger MB.2 Colibri   xxxx   05.05.98
              G T Snoddon Newtownards   29.10.18P
              Built by G T Snoddon – project PFA 043-11948

G-BXVT   Cameron O-77   1444   30.07.98
              PH-MKB R P Wade Shevington, Wigan
              (NF 28.02.18)

G-BXVU   Piper PA-28-161 Warrior II   28-7816063   05.05.98
              N47372 D C & M Brooks Enstone   19.11.17E

G-BXVV   Cameron V-90   4369   05.05.98
              A E Davies t/a Adeilad Cladding Llandwrda   10.07.15E
              (NF 21.11.16)

G-BXVX   Rutan Cozy Classic   xxxx   06.05.98
              G E Murray (Swansea)   21.10.03P
              Built by G E Murray – project PFA 159-12680
              (NF 23.01.15)

G-BXVY   Cessna 152   15279808   11.05.98
              N757KU Stapleford Flying Club Ltd Stapleford   31.10.18E

G-BXVZ[M]   WSK-PZL Mielec TS-11 Iskra   3H1625   27.03.98
              SP-DOF Cancelled 24.04.09 by CAA
              As '4' of Bialo-Czerwone Iskry (White &
              Red Sparks) aerobatic team
              With RAF Manston History Museum

G-BXWB   Robin HR.100/200B Royal   08   29.04.98
              HB-EMT Yorkshire Land Ltd Leeds Bradford   19.02.18E

G-BXWG   Sky 120-24   114   28.05.98
              M E White Abbeyview, Trim, RoI   13.04.18E

G-BXWH   Denney Kitfox Model 4-1200 Speedster   1760   04.03.98
              M G Porter Croft Farm, Defford *'Bumble 2'*   24.02.18P
              Built by N Hart, S C Hipwell & B Trent
              – project PFA 172A-12343

G-BXWK   Rans S-6-ES Coyote II   0298.1202   19.05.98
              M Taylor Little Gransden   27.09.18P
              Built by J Whiting – project PFA 204-13317;
              tricycle u/c

G-BXWL   Sky 90-24   117   20.07.98
              E J Briggs Leyland *'Espiritu Balloon Flights'* 27.04.14E
              (NF 08.12.17)

G-BXWO   Piper PA-28-181 Archer II   28-8190311   22.05.98
              D-ENHA, N8431C A J Gomes Coventry   24.06.19E

G-BXWP   Piper PA-32-300 Cherokee Six   32-7340088   26.05.98
              N8143D, G-BXWP, OE-DRR, N16452
              D F Scrimshaw Dunkeswell   27.04.18E

G-BXWR   CFM Streak Shadow SA   K 289-SA   22.05.98
              G-MZMI M A Hayward Bodmin   23.10.18P
              Built by M Hayward – project PFA 206-13205

G-BXWT   Van's RV-6   23232   19.07.96
              R C Owen Danehill   06.11.18P
              Built by R C Owen – project PFA 181-12639

G-BXWU   FLS Aerospace Sprint 160   003   05.06.98
              G-70-503 Aeroelvira Ltd Thruxton
              (NF 28.03.18)

G-BXWV   FLS Aerospace Sprint 160   005   05.06.98
              G-70-505 Aeroelvira Ltd Thruxton
              (NF 28.03.18)

G-BXWX   Sky 25-16   082   29.05.98
              C O'N Davis Rockfield, Crosserlough, RoI
              'Sky Balloons'   12.09.18E

G-BXXG   Cameron N-105   3662   19.06.98
              R N Simpkins Mangotsfield, Bristol
              'Wind Beneath My Wings'   21.04.19E

G-BXXH   Hatz CB-1   463   09.06.98
              R F Shingler Breidden   20.07.18P
              Built by R F Shingler – project PFA 143-12445

G-BXXI   Grob G109B   6400   09.06.98
              F-CAQR, F-WAQR P M Yeoman tr Malcolm Martin
              Flying Group Saltby   01.01.19E

G-BXXJ   Colt Flying Yacht   1797   10.06.98
              JA-A0515 Magical Adventures Ltd
              West Bloomfield, MI, USA   29.09.09E
              (NF 03.06.15)

G-BXXK   Reims/Cessna F172N   F17201806   15.06.98
              D-EOPP Flybai SL Palma-Son Bonet, Mallorca, Spain 11.06.19E

G-BXXL   Cameron N-105   4408   16.07.98
              C J Dunkley Stonefield Park, Chilbolton
              'Blue Peter'   14.10.12E
              (NF 02.02.18)

G-BXXO   Lindstrand LBL 90B   534   06.07.98
              G P Walton Wicklewood, Wymondham   28.04.18E

G-BXXP   Sky 77-24   124   20.07.98
              T R Wood London SW18 *'Ottery Antiques'* 16.04.15E
              (IE 05.07.17)

G-BXXR   Lovegrove AV-8 Gyroplane   xxxx   29.06.98
              Cancelled 03.11.09 as PWFU
              Wroughton *Built by P C Lovegrove & officially*
              registered as 'Lovegrove BGL Four-Runner' – project
              PFA G/15-1263
              In Science Museum store 2013

G-BXXT   Beech 76 Duchess   ME-212   17.07.98
              (N212BE), F-GBOZ
              Air Navigation & Trading Company Ltd Blackpool 08.02.18E

G-BXXU	Colt 31A	4427		21.08.98
	Sade Balloons Ltd London NW8			27.04.18E
	Built by Cameron Balloons Ltd			
G-BXXW	Enstrom F-28F Falcon	771		02.07.98
	G-SCOX, N330SA, G-BXXW, JA7823			
	D A Marks (Colmworth, Bedford)			17.04.18E
G-BXYE	Scintex CP.301-C1 Emeraude	559		08.07.98
	F-BTEO, F-PTEO, F-WTEO, F-BJFV			
	D T Gethin Old Park Farm, Margam			
	Built by Société Menavia (NF 02.05.18)			
G-BXYF	Colt AS-105 GD HA Airship	4433		07.08.98
	Alex Air Media Ltd Langford, Bristol, Thailand			07.02.20E
	Built by Cameron Balloons Ltd			
G-BXYI	Cameron H-34	4442		07.08.98
	D J Groombridge Congresbury, Bristol *'Fairy'*			05.04.19E
G-BXYJ	Jodel D.120A Paris-Nice	143		28.07.98
	F-BJNA C Brooke tr G-BXYJ Group Netherthorpe			09.04.18P
	Built by Société Aéronautique Normande			
G-BXYM	Piper PA-28-235 Cherokee	28-10858		18.08.98
	SE-FAM B Guenther Elstree			08.12.18E
	Official type data 'PA-28-235 Cherokee Pathfinder' is incorrect			
G-BXYO	Piper PA-28RT-201 Arrow IV	28R-8018046		18.08.98
	PH-SDD, N8164M D Atherton Liverpool John Lennon			08.09.18E
G-BXYP	Piper PA-28RT-201 Arrow IV	28R-8018050		18.08.98
	PH-SBO, N8168H G I Cooper			
	New Barn Farm, Raydon			12.08.17E
	(IE 15.09.17)			
G-BXYT	Piper PA-28RT-201 Arrow IV	28R-7918198		03.08.98
	PH-SBN, (PH-SBM), OO-HLA, N2878W			
	Wayne Poulter Enterprises Ltd Shobdon			22.09.19E
G-BXYU	Cessna F152 II	F15201804		31.07.98
	OY-CKD, SE-IFY Cancelled 16.10.99 as destroyed			24.08.01
	Dunkeswell *Built by Reims Aviation SA*			
	On fire dump 03.18			
G-BXZB	Nanchang CJ-6A (Yak 18)	2632019		18.09.98
	PLAAF R Davy, D J Gilbody & J L Swallow White Waltham			15.03.16P
	As 'CT-180' in Sri Lankan AF c/s			
G-BXZF	Lindstrand LBL 90A	575		08.01.99
	S McGuigan Draperstown, Magherafelt *'Lindstrand Balloons'*			
	29.05.18E			
G-BXZI	Lindstrand LBL 90A	543		14.08.98
	C M Morley Upchurch, Sittingbourne			31.07.18E
G-BXZN M	Advanced Technologies CH1 ATI	00002		25.08.98
	N8186E Cancelled 28.10.05 by CAA *Unmarked*			
	With The Helicopter Museum, Weston-super-Mare			
G-BXZO	Pietenpol Air Camper	xxxx		10.07.98
	P J Cooke (Palmer's Farm, Lower Dicker)			26.07.18P
	Built by P J Cooke – project PFA 047-12818			
G-BXZU	Micro B.22S Bantam	98-015		21.09.98
	ZK-JJL R W Hollamby & M E Whapham			
	Park Farm, Burwash			04.04.18P
G-BXZV	CFM Streak Shadow	K293-SA		18.09.98
	D J S McClean City of Derry			24.07.18P
	Built by CFM Aircraft Ltd – project PFA 206-13357			
G-BXZY	CFM Shadow Series DD	296-DD		21.09.98
	G L Turner North Craigieford, Ellon			
	(SSDR microlight since 01.18) (IE 27.08.15)			

G-BYAA – G-BYZZ

G-BYAV	Taylor JT.1 Monoplane	xxxx		27.08.98
	R D Boor Fenland			20.04.16P
	Built by C J Pidler – project PFA 055-11010			
G-BYAW	Boeing 757-204	27234		03.04.95
	TUI Airways Ltd t/a TUI Luton			29.11.19E
	Line No: 663			
G-BYAY	Boeing 757-204	28836		13.04.99
	N1786B TUI Airways Ltd t/a TUI Luton			11.10.19E
	Line No: 861			
G-BYAZ	CFM Streak Shadow SA	K 244		01.09.98
	A G Wright (Frimley Green, Camberley)			06.04.18P
	Built by A G Wright – project PFA 206-12656			
G-BYBD	Cessna F172H	F172-0487		06.07.98
	G-OBHX, G-AWMU R Macbeth-Seath Elstree			25.08.19E
	Built by Reims Aviation SA			
G-BYBE M	Jodel D.120A Paris-Nice	269		24.07.98
	OO-FDP Cancelled 04.10.17 by CAA			07.02.18
	Congleton, East Lothian *Stored for rebuild 09.18*			
G-BYBF	Robin R2160 Alpha Sport	329		01.10.98
	D J R Lloyd-Evans Bournemouth			22.08.18E
	Airframe replaced after collision with Kitfox G-LEED 09.02 but c/n retained			
G-BYBH	Piper PA-34-200T Seneca II	34-8070078		09.06.00
	N119SA, (G-BYBH), N4023K, N3567B			
	Aero Club Frosinone ASD Frosinone, Lazio, Italy			23.11.18E
G-BYBI	Bell 206B-3 JetRanger III	3668		19.10.98
	ZS-RGP, N5757M Castle Air Ltd Biggin Hill			03.04.18E
G-BYBK	Murphy Rebel	260R		19.08.98
	N95LD P R Goodwill Dunkeswell			16.03.15P
	Built by L A Dyer			
G-BYBL	Gardan GY-80-160D Horizon	127		25.09.98
	F-BMUY N Heron tr Bluewing Flying Group			
	Compton Abbas			23.02.18R
	Built by Sud Aviation			
G-BYBM	Avtech Jabiru SK	201		18.09.98
	P H Thomas Old Park Farm, Margam			13.06.18P
	Built by M Rudd – project PFA 274-13377			
G-BYBP	Cessna A185F Skywagon	185-03804		15.10.98
	OO-DCD, F-GDCD, F-ODIA, N4593E			
	G M S Scott Deanland			29.04.18E
G-BYBS	Sky 80-16	136		27.10.98
	B K Rippon Upton, Didcot			29.09.15E
G-BYBU	Murphy Renegade Spirit UK	302		12.10.98
	M E Gilman Arclid Green, Sandbach			
	Built by K R Anderson – project PFA 188-13229			
	(SSDR microlight since 01.18) (NF 05.01.18)			
G-BYBV	Mainair Rapier	1183-1198-7-W986		20.10.98
	M W Robson (Market Weighton, York)			01.11.02P
	(NF 03.02.16)			
G-BYBX	Slingsby T.67M-260 Firefly	2261		21.10.98
	Cancelled 29.01.15 as PWFU			
	Cambridge *On rebuild 11.15*			
G-BYBY	Thorp T-18C	492		17.07.98
	N77KK P G Mair Perth			24.07.18P
	Built by K K Knowles			
G-BYBZ	Avtech Jabiru SK	162		07.09.98
	P J Whitehouse Eastfield Farm, Manby			11.04.18P
	Built by A W Harris – project PFA 274-13290			
G-BYCA	Piper PA-28-140 Cherokee D	28-7125223		24.09.98
	PH-VRZ, N11C Go Fly Oxford Ltd			
	Hinton-in-the-Hedges			06.06.18E
G-BYCJ	CFM Shadow Series DD	K 294-DD		14.10.98
	B P Cater Stonefield Park, Chilbolton			25.04.19P
	Built by J W E Pearson – project PFA 161-13258			
G-BYCL	Raj Hamsa X'Air Jabiru(1)	331		15.10.98
	EI-ECV A A Ross (Strathpepper)			31.07.08P
	Built by G A J Salter – project BMAA/HB/088			
G-BYCM	Rans S-6-ES Coyote II	0298.1204		15.09.98
	E W McMullan Dunnyvadden			07.11.00P
	Built by E W McMullan – project PFA 204-13315			
	(NF 16.04.14)			
G-BYCN	Rans S-6-ES Coyote II	0298.1205		15.09.98
	T J Croskery City of Derry			25.06.18P
	Built by J K & R L Dunseath – project PFA 204-13314			
G-BYCS	Jodel DR.1051 Sicile	201		28.10.98
	F-BJUJ G A Stops Manor Farm, Slawston			24.03.18P
	Built by Centre-Est Aéronautique			
G-BYCT	Aero L-29 Delfin	395142		29.10.98
	ES-YLH, Estonian AF, Soviet AF			
	G-BKOU/2 Ltd North Weald			30.11.18P
G-BYCW	Mainair Blade 912	1185-1198-7-W988		05.11.98
	P C Watson St Michaels			06.04.18P
G-BYCX	Westland Wasp HAS.1	F9754		09.11.98
	ZK-HOX, South African Navy 92			
	C J Marsden North Weald			01.10.19P
	Carries 'South African Navy 92'			

G

G-BYCY	III Sky Arrow 650 T		xxxx	10.11.98
	K A Daniels Upfield Farm, Whitson			04.06.18P
	Built by A S Spriglings – project PFA 298-13332			
G-BYCZ	Avtech Jabiru SK		0216	16.10.98
	T Herbert		Leicester	12.09.18P
	Built by C Hewer – project PFA 274-13388			
G-BYDB	Grob G115B		8025	26.03.99
	VH-JVL, D-EFCG A P Shoobert & A R Willis Conington			13.06.19E
G-BYDG	Beech C24R Sierra		MC-627	09.11.98
	OY-AZL R Kolb & H Loeffert Saarbrücken, Germany			24.06.17E
G-BYDJ	Colt 120A		3527	17.11.98
	D K Hempleman-Adams Corsham			07.08.14E
	Built by Cameron Balloons Ltd (NF 26.10.16)			
G-BYDK	SNCAN Stampe SV.4C		55	20.11.98
	F-BCXY, French AF Bianchi Aviation Film Services Ltd			
	Turweston			
	Official p/i quoted as F-BCXV which is c/n 298			
	(NF 22.10.14)			
G-BYDL	Hawker Hurricane IIB		Z5207	17.11.98
	Z5207 K-F Grimminger Thruxton			
	As 'HC-465' in Finnish A/F c/s; on rebuild 2016			
	(NF 04.12.14)			
G-BYDV	Van's RV-6		60158	03.12.98
	R G Andrews Kings Farm, Thurrock			08.06.18P
	Built by G L Carpenter – project PFA 181-13264			
G-BYDX	American General AG-5B Tiger		10051	06.01.99
	N374SA, G-BYDX, F-GKBH, N1191Y			
	Cancelled 29.11.05 as destroyed			05.05.08
	Farley Farm, Farley Chamberlayne *Wreck stored 12.17*			
G-BYDY	Beech 58 Baron		TH-1852	10.11.98
	C-GBWF Pilot Services Flying Group Ltd Thruxton			18.04.18E
G-BYDZ	Cyclone Pegasus Quantum 15-912		7493	22.12.98
	S J Ward Arclid Green, Sandbach			16.11.18P
G-BYEA	Cessna 172P Skyhawk		17275464	07.10.98
	PH-ILL, N63661 M Thambiah Elstree			28.01.19E
	Operated by MAK Aviation			
G-BYEC	DG Flugzeugbau DG-800B		8-102B36	13.11.98
	D-KSDG P D Craven Walney Island '23'			07.05.18E
G-BYEE	Mooney M.20K Mooney 231		25-0282	20.07.88
	N231JZ G Mexias Henstridge			28.11.18E
G-BYEH	Robin DR.250/160 Capitaine		15	06.10.98
	OO-SOL, F-BMZL J D Bally Lane Farm, Painscastle			21.09.17E
	Built by Centre-Est Aéronautique (IE 24.08.18)			
G-BYEJ	Scheibe SF28A Tandem Falke		5713	18.12.98
	OE-9070, (D-KDAM) D Shrimpton			
	Watchford Farm, Yarcombe			02.06.18E
G-BYEK	Stoddard-Hamilton GlaStar		xxxx	14.09.98
	ZK-NEW, G-BYEK T A Reed			
	Watchford Farm, Yarcombe			31.10.18P
	Built by G M New – project PFA 295-13087;			
	tailwheel u/c			
G-BYEL	Van's RV-6		23131	07.01.99
	D Millar Brimpton			10.08.18P
	Built by D T Smith – project PFA 181-12568			
G-BYEM	Cessna R182 Skylane RG II		R18200822	08.01.99
	N494, D-ELVI, N737FT Bickertons Aerodromes Ltd			
	Denham			09.06.18E
G-BYEO	Zenair CH.601HDS Zodiac		6-3822	11.01.99
	J R Clarke Beccles			18.01.18P
	Built by B S Carpenter & M W Elliott			
	– project PFA 162-13345; tailwheel u/c			
G-BYER	Cameron C-80		4513	19.11.98
	J M Langley Ebley, Stroud			08.10.18E
G-BYEW	Cyclone Pegasus Quantum 15-912		7499	15.01.99
	R S Matheson Perth *'Attitude Not Altitude'*			12.10.16P
	(IE 05.06.17)			
G-BYEY	Lindstrand LBL 21 Silver Dream		577	15.01.99
	Oscair Project AB Täby, Sweden			
	(NF 22.09.16)			
G-BYFA	Reims/Cessna F152 II		F15201968	09.11.98
	G-WACA Redhill Air Services Ltd Fairoaks			12.04.18E

G-BYFC	Avtech Jabiru SK		0209	05.02.99
	Cancelled 12.10.15 as PWFU			10.05.09
	Wisbech *Built by A C N Freeman – project*			
	PFA 274-13344; fuselage only for sale 10.15			
G-BYFF	Cyclone Pegasus Quantum 15-912		7500	01.02.99
	T A Willcox Chase Farm, Chipping Sodbury			18.11.18P
G-BYFI	CFM Starstreak Shadow SA-II		SS 014	11.02.99
	J A Cook Parham			13.06.18P
	Built by D G Cook – project PFA 206-13300			
G-BYFJ	Cameron N-105		4545	04.03.99
	R J Mercer Belfast BT5			08.06.15E
G-BYFK	Cameron Printer-105		4522	04.03.99
	T Read & N Smith t/a Mobberley Balloon Collection			
	Knutsford & Goole *'Samsung'*			26.05.03A
	(NF 24.03.14)			
G-BYFL	Diamond HK36TTS Super Dimona		36.623	05.02.99
	J G Kosak tr Seahawk Gliding Club RNAS Culdrose			30.08.18E
G-BYFM	Jodel DR.1050-M1 Excellence replica		870	26.02.99
	A J Roxburgh (Verchocq, Pas de Calais, France)			14.07.19P
	Built by A J Roxburgh & P M Standen			
	– project PFA 304-13237 using SAB plans			
G-BYFR	Piper PA-32R-301 Saratoga II HP		3246133	13.04.99
	N4135P, G-BYFR, N9515N			
	Ebor Air Ltd (Upper Helmsley, York)			22.03.19E
G-BYFT	Pietenpol Air Camper		xxxx	22.12.98
	G Everett Hubbard's Farm, Lenham Heath			05.07.18P
	Built by M W Elliott – project PFA 047-13057			
G-BYFV	Team Mini-Max 91		1024	05.02.99
	W E Gillham Croft Farm, Croft-on-Tees			
	Built by W E Gillham – project PFA 186-13431			
	(SSDR microlight since 06.14) (IE 30.05.18)			
G-BYFX	Colt 77A		4547	04.03.99
	Wye Valley Aviation Ltd Ross-on-Wye			05.05.05A
	Built by Cameron Balloons Ltd (NF 29.08.14)			
G-BYFY	Mudry CAP 10B		263	09.03.99
	F-GKKD R N Crosland Deanland			10.09.18E
G-BYGA	Boeing 747-436		28855	15.12.98
	British Airways PLC London Heathrow			13.12.19E
	Line No: 1190			
G-BYGB	Boeing 747-436		28856	17.01.99
	British Airways PLC London Heathrow			03.07.19E
	Line No: 1194			
G-BYGC	Boeing 747-436		25823	19.01.99
	British Airways PLC London Heathrow			21.06.19E
	Line No: 1195; BOAC – British Overses Airways livery			
G-BYGD	Boeing 747-436		28857	26.01.99
	British Airways PLC London Heathrow			23.10.19E
	Line No: 1196			
G-BYGE	Boeing 747-436		28858	05.02.99
	British Airways PLC London Heathrow			04.02.20E
	Line No: 1198			
G-BYGF	Boeing 747-436		25824	17.02.99
	British Airways PLC London Heathrow			16.02.19E
	Line No: 1200			
G-BYGG	Boeing 747-436		28859	29.04.99
	British Airways PLC London Heathrow			28.03.19E
	Line No: 1212			
G-BYHC	Cameron Z-90		4555	16.03.99
	T J Wilkinson Sackville Lodge Farm, Riseley			
	'Darlows'			30.07.19E
G-BYHE	Robinson R22 Beta		2023	14.01.99
	N82128, LV-VAB Helimech Ltd Brook Farm, Hulcote			13.09.18E
G-BYHG	Dornier 328-100		3098	07.04.99
	D-CDAE, D-CDXZ Loganair Ltd Glasgow			06.04.19E
G-BYHH	Piper PA-28-161 Warrior III		2842050	15.06.99
	N4126Z, G-BYHH, N9527N			
	Stapleford Flying Club Ltd Stapleford			10.06.18E
G-BYHI	Piper PA-28-161 Warrior II		28-8116084	04.01.99
	SE-IDP T W & W S Gilbert Turweston			23.05.18E
	Operated by Turweston Flying Club			
G-BYHJ	Piper PA-28R-201 Arrow III		2844020	25.02.00
	N41675, G-BYHJ, N41675 Flew LLP Bournemouth			04.06.18E
	Official type data 'PA-28R-201 Cherokee Arrow III'			
	is incorrect			

G-BYHK Piper PA-28-181 Archer III 2843240 20.05.99
N4128V, (G-BYHK), N9519N
T-Air Services Ltd Isle of Man 18.04.18E
Official type data 'PA-28-181 Archer II'
is incorrect

G-BYHL de Havilland DHC-1 Chipmunk 22 C1/0361 15.03.99
WG308 I D & M R Higgins Rectory Farm, Averham 29.08.18P
As 'WG308:8' in RAF c/s

G-BYHO Mainair Blade 912 1197-0599-7-W1000 16.03.99
P G Evans (Leigh) 13.06.18P

G-BYHP Robin DR.253B Regent 161 29.03.99
OO-CSK S D Atherton tr HP Flying Group
Low Hill Farm, North Moor, Messingham 08.12.18E
Built by Centre-Est Aéronautique

G-BYHR Cyclone Pegasus Quantum 15-912 7518 06.04.99
I D Chantler (Weston, Hitchin) 14.04.12P
(NF 28.06.18)

G-BYHS Mainair Blade 912 1187-0299-7-W990 11.03.99
S Newton tr Telzor Group
Wolverhampton Halfpenny Green 03.06.19P
Sailwing carried 'G-59-5' in 1996

G-BYHT Robin DR.400-180R Remorqueur 811 09.04.99
HB-EUU R C Wilson tr Deeside Robin Group Aboyne 26.08.18E

G-BYHU Cameron N-105 4567 30.04.99
S Hartnell, D L C Nelmes & R Waycott
t/a Ezmerelda Balloon Syndicate Bath & Bristol 21.06.18E

G-BYHV Raj Hamsa X'Air 582(6) 381 25.03.99
M G Adams Slieve Croob, Castlewellan 30.06.14P
Built by J Bowditch – project BMAA/HB/090
(NF 28.10.15)

G-BYHY Cameron V-77 4493 22.03.99
P Spellward Bristol BS9 'Biggles' 22.07.17E

G-BYIA Avtech Jabiru SK 0237 10.02.99
M D Doyle Ince 19.05.18P
Built by M F Cottam – project PFA 274-13436

G-BYID Rans S-6-ES Coyote II 0498.1218 11.05.99
R M Watson Davidstow Moor 16.10.17P
Built by D J Brotherhood – project PFA 204-13348;
tricycle u/c

G-BYIE Robinson R22 Beta II 2933 22.04.99
K W Horobin Wolverhampton Halfpenny Green 24.01.18E

G-BYIJ CASA 1-131E Jungmann Series 2000 2110 16.07.90
Spanish AF E3B-514 R N Crosland Deanland 15.07.17P
As 'A-23' in Swiss Air Force c/s

G-BYIK Europa Aviation Europa 154 02.02.99
D Allen Full Sutton 15.11.18P
Built by P M Davis – project PFA 247-12771;
tailwheel u/c

G-BYIN Rotary Air Force RAF 2000 GTX-SE H2-98-9-382 19.01.99
C J Watkinson Bridge Cottage, Great Heck 29.11.19P
Built by J R Legge – project PFA G/13-1305

G-BYIO Colt 105A 4601 30.04.99
N Charbonnier Aosta, Aosta Valley, Italy 'Lindt Lindor' 04.12.11E
Built by Cameron Balloons Ltd (NF 20.12.16)

G-BYIP Pitts S-2A 2244 23.02.99
N109WA, TC-ECN D P Heather-Hayes Perth 06.08.18E
Built by Aerotek Inc

G-BYIR Pitts S-1S 1-0063 23.02.99
N103WA, TC-ECP S Kramer (Wennigsen, Germany) 07.12.18E
Built by Aerotek Inc

G-BYIS Cyclone Pegasus Quantum 15-912 7508 25.02.99
D J Ramsden Beverley (Linley Hill) 07.07.18P

G-BYIV Cameron PM-80 4595 14.05.99
A Schneider Sudlohn, North Rhine-Westphalia,
Germany 05.08.17E
Coca Cola bottle special shape

G-BYIW Cameron PM-80 4596 14.05.99
T Gleixner Tagerschen, Switzerland 20.04.19E
Coca Cola bottle special shape

G-BYIX Cameron PM-80 4597 14.05.99
A Schneider Sudlohn, North Rhine-Westphalia,
Germany 08.11.09E
Coca Cola bottle special shape (NF 30.07.13)

G-BYJA Rotary Air Force RAF 2000 GTX-SE H2-97-8-313 06.04.99
C R W Lyne (Fairford) 26.02.13P
Built by B Errington-Weddle – project PFA G/13-1297
(NF 14.11.14)

G-BYJB Mainair Blade 912 1192-0499-7-W995 06.04.99
R G Mason (Aylesbury) 21.04.17P
(NF 18.08.17)

G-BYJD Avtech Jabiru UL 0172 16.04.99
S Bayes & H J Samples Beverley (Linley Hill) 29.08.19P
Built by M W Knights & G Wallis – project
PFA 274-13376: type prefix should be '274A'

G-BYJE Team Mini-Max 91A xxxx 06.04.99
T A Willcox (Yate, Bristol)
Built by A W Austin & M F Cottam – project PFA 186-12327
(SSDR microlight since 06.14) (IE 22.09.16)

G-BYJF Thorp T.211 107 20.05.99
N2545C M J Newton Manchester Barton 14.06.12E
Built by Venture Light Aircraft Resources (NF 12.10.15)

G-BYJH Grob G109B 6512 19.05.99
D-KFRI S T Crisp tr Grob GJH Group Parham Park 26.06.18E

G-BYJI Europa Aviation Europa F0004 19.04.99
G-ODTI M Gibson Pocklington 01.01.19P
Built by Europa Aviation Ltd – project PFA 247-13010;
tailwheel u/c

G-BYJK Cyclone Pegasus Quantum 15-912 7524 07.05.99
S J Wilson (Great Eversden, Cambridge) 02.06.17P
(IE 04.08.17)

G-BYJL Aero Designs Pulsar 3 PQ703521 20.04.99
A Young Sandtoft 12.04.18P
Built by F A H Ashmead – project PFA 202-13311;
tricycle u/c

G-BYJN Lindstrand LBL 105A 605 30.04.99
B Meeson Rhiw, Pwllheli 29.04.00A
(NF 06.04.16)

G-BYJO Rans S-6-ES Coyote II 0498.1217 04.03.99
P D Smalley Spanhoe 25.09.18P
Built by G Ferguson – project PFA 204-13338;
tailwheel u/c

G-BYJP Pitts S-1S 1-0064 16.03.99
N105WA, TC-ECR, Turk.AF?
T Riddle tr Eaglescott Pitts Group Eaglescott 08.04.12E
Built by Aerotek Inc

G-BYJR Lindstrand LBL 77B 608 30.04.99
B M Reed Antigny, Vienne, France 09.07.18E

G-BYJS SOCATA TB-20 Trinidad 1875 15.01.99
F-OIGE A P Bedford Oxford 05.05.18E

G-BYJT Zenair CH.601HDS Zodiac 6-3516 04.05.99
C A Bickley (Wolverhampton) 14.07.18P
Built by J D T Tannock – project PFA 162-13130;
tricycle u/c

G-BYJW Cameron Sphere-105 4585 15.06.99
Balleroy Developpement SAS
Balleroy, Basse-Normandie, France 17.07.17E

G-BYJX Cameron C-70 4580 30.04.99
John Aimo Balloons SAS Mondovi, Italy 21.04.18E

G-BYKA Lindstrand LBL 69A 612 07.05.99
B Meeson Rhiw, Pwllheli 'Vauxhall' 21.06.07A
(NF 02.09.14)

G-BYKB Rockwell Commander 114 14121 18.05.99
SE-GSM, N4801W D L Macdonald Stornoway 30.10.18E

G-BYKC Mainair Blade 912 1196-0599-7-W999 07.05.99
A Williams Perth 27.06.18P

G-BYKD Mainair Blade 912 1198-0599-7-W1001 07.05.99
D C Boyle (Heath Charnock, Chorley) 18.09.10P
(NF 03.08.17)

G-BYKF Enstrom F-28F Falcon 725 19.05.99
JA7684 Cancelled 17.07.18 by CAA 19.03.16
Woodside Farm, Elkington Stored 06.18

G-BYKG Pietenpol Air Camper xxxx 17.03.99
K B Hodge (Mynydd Isa, Mold)
Built by K B Hodge – project PFA 047-12827 (IE 24.01.19)

G-BYKJ Westland Scout AH.1   F9696   06.08.99
XV121   B H Austen t/a Austen Associates
North Weald   04.01.10P
Carries 'XV121'; noted 11.18 (NF 04.12.15)

G-BYKK Robinson R44 Astro   0572   04.03.99
M N Cowley t/a Dragonfly Aviation
Red House Farm, Priors Marston   13.12.18E

G-BYKL Piper PA-28-181 Archer II   28-8090162   15.07.99
HB-PFB, N8129Y   Transport Command Ltd
Brighton City   20.03.18E

G-BYKP Piper PA-28RT-201T Turbo Arrow IV 28R-7931029   22.06.99
HB-PDB, N3010G   J Cameron & R Cromar
Glasgow Prestwick   11.11.18E

G-BYKR   Piper PA-28-161 Warrior II   2816061   22.06.99
HB-PLM   Cancelled 22.08.07 as destroyed   11.08.08
Oxford   *On fire dump 03.15 as 'G-FIRE'*

G-BYKT Cyclone Pegasus Quantum 15-912   7529   28.05.99
K J Bradley & M J Hyde   Deenethorpe   18.12.19P

G-BYKU BFC Challenger II   CH2-09972-1656   25.05.99
L G G Faulkner & P A Tarplee   Otherton   29.09.12P
*Built by K W Seedhouse – project PFA 177A-13252
(BFC kit) (NF 19.09.18)*

G-BYKV[M] Avro 504K replica   0015   27.05.99
Cancelled 16.08.02 – to Australia as A3-17
*Built by Hawker Restorations Ltd   As 'E3747'
With RAAF Museum, Point Cook, VIC*

G-BYKX Cameron N-90   4657   10.08.99
C O'N Davis   Rockfield, Crosserlough, RoI
'Knowledge Pool'   23.09.19E

G-BYLB de Havilland DH.82A Tiger Moth   83286   24.05.99
T5595   H E Snowling (Gillingham, Beccles)   29.07.19P

G-BYLC Cyclone Pegasus Quantum 15-912   7528   25.06.99
G P D Coan   Longacre Farm, Sandy   18.02.18P

G-BYLD Pietenpol Air Camper   xxxx   27.04.99
S Bryan   (Chipping Warden, Banbury)
Built by S Bryan – project PFA 047-13392 (NF 29.09.16)

G-BYLF Zenair CH.601HDS Zodiac   xxxx   03.06.99
S Plater   Water Leisure Park, Skegness   04.09.14P
*Built by M & J S Thomas & G Waters – project
PFA 162-13179; tricycle u/c (NF 11.04.18)*

G-BYLI Nova Vertex 22   14319   09.04.99
M Hay   (Dundee)

G-BYLJ Letov LK-2M Sluka   829909-S22   09.06.99
J G & W H McMinn   Newtownards
*Built by N E Stokes – project PFA 263-13464
(SSDR microlight since 06.14) (NF 08.03.18)*

G-BYLO Tipsy Nipper T.66 Series 1   04   27.04.99
OO-NIA   M J A Trudgill   RAF Henlow   05.09.13P
Built by Avions Fairey SA; noted 07.18 (IE 07.06.18)

G-BYLP Rand Robinson KR-2   xxxx   19.04.99
C S Hales   Shenington   *'Itzy'*   04.08.17P
*Built by C S Hales – project PFA 129-1143;
forced landed on golf course Aioi, Hyogo, Japan
11.07.17 & substantially damaged*

G-BYLS Bede BD-4   xxxx   13.12.90
P J Greenrod   Welshpool   11.04.18P
*Built by G H Bayliss – project PFA 037-11288;
tricycle u/c*

G-BYLT Raj Hamsa X'Air 582(1)   411   08.06.99
T W Phipps   Craysmarsh Farm, Melksham   29.09.05P
*Built by R J Turner – project BMAA/HB/095
(NF 16.10.14)*

G-BYLW Lindstrand LBL 77A   615   11.06.99
Associazione Gran Premio Italiano Mongolfieristico
Todi, Perugia, Umbria, Italy   10.06.00A
(NF 27.08.18)

G-BYLX Lindstrand LBL 105A   614   11.06.99
Italiana Aeronavi   Cervignano, Udine, Italy   29.07.13E
(NF 14.12.17)

G-BYLY Cameron V-77   3375   16.07.97
G-ULIA (2)   R Bayly   Clutton, Bristol   30.07.10E
(IE 07.02.17)

G-BYLZ Rutan Cozy Mk.4   0208   21.05.99
W S Allen   Gloucestershire   26.08.18P
Built by E R Allen – project PFA 159-12464

G-BYMB Diamond DA.20-C1 Katana   C0051   09.07.99
C-GDMB   M Zakaras   (Vilnius, Lithuania)   26.09.19E

G-BYMD Piper PA-38-112 Tomahawk II   38-82A0009   18.06.99
N91342   NWMAS Leasing Ltd   Hawarden   07.06.19E

G-BYMF Cyclone Pegasus Quantum 15-912   7540   09.07.99
G R Stockdale   Rufforth East   12.10.11P
(NF 13.12.16)

G-BYMI Cyclone Pegasus Quantum 15   7533   09.07.99
J Drewe   Sutton Meadows   18.07.18P

G-BYMJ Cessna 152   15285564   16.07.99
N93865   Stapleford Flying Club Ltd   Stapleford   24.10.18E

G-BYMN Rans S-6-ESA Coyote II   0199.1292   16.06.99
R J P Herival   Guernsey   02.03.18P
Built by H Smith – project PFA 204-13477; tricycle u/c

G-BYMP[M] Campbell Cricket Mk.1   0050   16.06.99
Cancelled 20.07.15 by CAA
*Built by J J Fitzgerald – project PFA G/03-1265
With The Helicopter Museum, Weston-super-Mare*

G-BYMR Raj Hamsa X'Air R100(3)   432   18.06.99
W Drury   Slieve Croob, Castlewellan   08.01.12P
*Built by W M McMinn – project BMAA/HB/094
(IE 28.07.17)*

G-BYMT[M] Cyclone Airsports Pegasus Quantum 15-912   7549   16.07.99
Cancelled 10.08.10 as PWFU   30.07.10
With Manchester Museum of Sciences & Industry

G-BYMW Boland 52-12   001   25.06.99
C Jones   Sonning Common, Reading
*Built by C Jones; noted 01.19 in modified form
(IE 04.05.18)*

G-BYNA Cessna F172H   F172-0626   15.01.99
OO-VDW, PH-VDW, (G-AWTH), F-WLIT
D M White   Popham   30.04.19E
Built by Reims Aviation SA

G-BYND Cyclone Pegasus Quantum 15   7546   16.07.99
W J Upton   (Baker Barracks, Thorney Island)   23.11.18P

G-BYNF North American NA-64 Yale I   64-2171   10.01.00
N55904, RCAF 3349   I D Jones   Duxford   18.11.19P
As '3349' in RCAF c/s

G-BYNK Robin HR.200-160   338   28.07.99
K Riley & R J Stainer tr Penguin Flight Group   Bodmin   23.11.18E

G-BYNM Mainair Blade 912   1204-0799-7-W1007 20.07.99
D E Ashton   Ince   14.07.16P

G-BYNN Cameron V-90   4643   16.07.99
J L & T J Hilditch tr Cloud Nine Balloon Group
Southwick, Brighton   14.06.19E

G-BYNP Rans S-6-ES Coyote II   1098.1269   22.07.99
C J Lines   Low Hill Farm, North Moor, Messingham   06.07.18P
Built by R J Lines – project PFA 204-13414

G-BYNR   Avtech Jabiru UL   UL0001   23.07.99
EI-MAT   Cancelled 09.12.11 as destroyed   15.08.11
Yatesbury   *Built by A Parker – project PFA 274-0129
& project SAAC 66; wreck stored 06.14*

G-BYNS Avtech Jabiru SK   0159   23.07.99
D K Lawry   Tibenham   02.01.19P
Built by D K Lawry – project PFA 274-13235

G-BYNU Thunder Ax7-77   3520   29.07.99
B Fisher   Guildford   17.04.18E
Built by Cameron Balloons Ltd

G-BYNW Cameron H-34   4666   27.07.99
S J Roake & M A Stelling
Frimley & South Queensferry   *'energis'*   23.08.18E

G-BYNX Cameron RX-105   4656   26.07.99
Cameron Balloons Ltd   Bristol BS3   01.11.00A
(NF 05.02.18)

G-BYNY Beech 76 Duchess   ME-247   04.08.99
N247ME, OE-FES, N6635H   M D Darragh   Dunkeswell   07.11.18E

G-BYNZ   Westland Scout AH.1   F9736   06.08.99
XW281   Cancelled 05.02.01 as destroyed   23.11.00
Dungannon, RoI
Composite with boom of 'XP883', noted 06.15

G-BYOB Slingsby T67M-260 Firefly   2263   08.06.99
Stapleford Flying Club Ltd   Stapleford   08.10.18E

G-BYOD	Slingsby T67M-200 Firefly	2265	13.06.00	
	D I Stanbridge (Horsford, Norwich)		26.01.18E	
G-BYOG	Cyclone Pegasus Quantum 15-912	7555	15.09.99	
	A C Tyler (Brooks Green, Horsham)		08.11.17P	
G-BYOH	Raj Hamsa X'Air 582(5)	443	23.07.99	
	J Owen Hill Farm, Nayland		07.06.18P	
	Built by G A J Salter – project BMAA/HB/101			
G-BYOI	Sky 80-16	163	05.08.99	
	D J Tofton Warboys, Huntingdon		05.07.19E	
G-BYOJ	Raj Hamsa X'Air 582(11)	458	23.07.99	
	T C Ellison Sackville Lodge Farm, Riseley		29.04.18P	
	Built by R R Hadley – project BMAA/HB/108			
G-BYOO	CFM Streak Shadow SA	K 270	06.08.99	
	J O Gomerson Blackpool		31.10.19P	
	Built by C I Chegwen – project PFA 206-12806			
G-BYOR	Raj Hamsa X'Air 582(7)	478	11.08.99	
	R Dilkes Longacre Farm, Sandy		04.08.18P	
	Built by A R Walker – project BMAA/HB/117			
G-BYOS	Mainair Blade 912	1209-0899-7-W1012	06.08.99	
	K Worthington Eccleston, Chorley		04.09.08P	
	(NF 23.10.14)			
G-BYOT	Rans S-6-ES Coyote II	0498.1221	29.07.99	
	G I Bustin tr G-BYOT Syndicate Saltby		11.12.18P	
	Built by H F Blakeman – project PFA 204-13363;			
	tricycle u/c			
G-BYOV	Cyclone Pegasus Quantum 15-912	7554	17.08.99	
	M Howland Wickenby		27.08.18P	
G-BYOW	Mainair Blade	1207-0899-7-W1010	09.08.99	
	P Gadek & P Szymanski tr G-BYOW Syndicate			
	East Fortune		22.08.18P	
G-BYOYᴹ	Canadair CL-30 Silver Star Mk.3 (*T-33AN*) T33-231		08.02.00	
	N36TH, N333DV, N134AT, N10018, N134AT RCAF 21231			
	Cancelled 08.06.05 by CAA? *As '117415:TR-415'*			
	With The Spitfire & Hurricane Memorial Museum, Ramsgate			
G-BYOZ	Mainair Rapier	1208-0899-7-W1011	12.08.99	
	G P Hodgson (Farnworth, Bolton)			
	(SSDR microlight since 01.18) (IE 09.11.16)			
G-BYPB	Cyclone Pegasus Quantum 15-912	7566	03.09.99	
	Cloudbase Paragliding Ltd Redlands		16.10.18P	
G-BYPF	Thruster T600N	9089-T600N-034	17.08.99	
	T R Villa Priory Farm, Tibenham		26.01.18P	
G-BYPH	Thruster T600N	9089-T600N-036	17.08.99	
	D M Canham Leicester		30.07.14P	
	Official c/n '9099-T600N-036' is incorrect (IE 04.05.18)			
G-BYPJ	Cyclone Pegasus Quantum 15-912	7565	17.09.99	
	R J Coombs Sutton Meadows		21.06.19P	
	Stored 07.18 (NF 25.01.18)			
G-BYPM	Europa Aviation Europa XS	404	16.12.98	
	D G Lewendon Lempitlaw Farm, Kelso		10.09.19P	
	Built by P Mileham – project PFA 247-13418;			
	tricycle u/c			
G-BYPN	SOCATA MS.880B Rallye Club	2043	23.07.99	
	F-BTPN D & S A Bell, R Edwards & G A Rossington			
	Forwood Farm, Treswell		18.07.19E	
G-BYPO	Raj Hamsa X'Air 582(1)	439	25.08.99	
	E Doyle (Gorey, Co Wexford, RoI)		15.09.18P	
	Built by A S Leach & N G Woodhall			
	– project BMAA/HB/111			
G-BYPR	Zenair CH.601HD Zodiac	3223	25.08.99	
	N Surman Enstone		21.11.18P	
	Built by D Clark – project PFA 162-12816; tailwheel u/c			
G-BYPU	Piper PA-32R-301 Saratoga II HP	3246150	02.12.99	
	N4160K, G-BYPU, N9518N R J Golding & R H Kirke			
	tr GOBOB Flying Group Portimão, Portugal		20.03.18E	
G-BYPW	Raj Hamsa X'Air 582(3)	441	01.09.99	
	P J Kimpton Middle Stoke, Isle of Grain		28.04.16P	
	Built by P A Mercer – project BMAA/HB/113			
	(NF 17.07.17)			
G-BYPY	Ryan ST3KR	1001	05.10.99	
	F-AZEV, N18926, NC18926, NX18926			
	T Curtis-Taylor Old Warden		09.04.15P	
	On loan to Richard Shuttleworth Trustees;			
	as '001' in US Army c/s (NF 08.08.17)			

G-BYPZ	Rans S-6-S-116 Super Six	0299.1304	14.07.99	
	R A Blackbourn Perth		30.03.18P	
	Built by P G Hayward – project PFA 204A-13448;			
	tricycle u/c			
G-BYRC	Westland Wessex HC.2	WA539	23.09.99	
	XT671 D Brem-Wilson Biggin Hill			
	Stored externally 12.16 (NF 22.01.15)			
G-BYRE	Rans S-10 Dakota	xxxx	23.07.91	
	Cancelled 08.05.99 by CAA			
	Longside *Built by R J Trickey – project PFA194-11729*			
	Stored incomplete 08.18			
G-BYRG	Rans S-6-ES Coyote II	1298.1289	09.09.99	
	S J Macmillan Easter Poldar Farm, Thornhill		06.10.17P	
	Built by J Whiting – project PFA 204-13518;			
	tricycle u/c			
G-BYRJ	Cyclone Pegasus Quantum 15-912	7548	24.09.99	
	J & R Thompson Dunkeswell			
	(IE 12.01.18)			
G-BYRK	Cameron V-42	4662	14.07.99	
	R Kunert Finchampstead, Wokingham		30.04.18E	
G-BYRO	Mainair Blade	1210-0899-7-W1013	20.08.99	
	T W Thiele Newnham		12.05.18P	
G-BYRR	Mainair Blade 912	1211-0999-7-W1015	17.08.99	
	W J Dowty (Ombersley, Droitwich)		13.08.18P	
	C/n amended to 1222-0999-7-W1015 by Mainair			
G-BYRU	Cyclone Pegasus Quantum 15-912	7574	24.09.99	
	L M Westwood Enstone		02.04.18P	
G-BYRV	Raj Hamsa X'Air 582(2)	387	10.09.99	
	A D Russell Coolboy Little, RoI		25.07.18P	
	Built by A Hipkin – project BMAA/HB/106			
G-BYRY	Slingsby T67M-200 Firefly	2042	28.09.99	
	B-HZQ, VR-HZQ, HKG-11			
	J Clowes Wellesbourne Mountford		24.11.18E	
	As 'HKG-11' in Royal Hong Kong AAF c/s			
G-BYSE	Agusta-Bell 206B-2 JetRanger II	8553	03.11.81	
	G-BFND Startrade Heli GmbH & Co KG			
	Burbach, Germany		23.01.20E	
G-BYSF	Avtech Jabiru UL	195	05.10.99	
	A O Spurway tr Jabber 430 Redlands		02.09.19P	
	Built by M M Smith – project PFA 274A-13356			
G-BYSG	Robin HR.200-120B	339	22.11.99	
	B M Gay (Plaisir, France)		04.07.19E	
	Rebuilt with new fuselage ex G-HRCC?;			
	original stored Croft Farm, Defford 06.17			
G-BYSI	PZL-110 Koliber 160A	04990081	21.01.00	
	SP-WGI D F & J Evans Retford Gamston		14.05.18E	
G-BYSJ	de Havilland DHC-1 Chipmunk 22	C1/0021	12.10.99	
	SE-BON, WB569 Propshop Ltd Duxford		09.05.19E	
	As 'WB569:R' in RAF c/s			
G-BYSK	Cameron A-275 HAB	4699	23.02.00	
	Cancelled 22.10.14 as PWFU		23.05.14	
	Not Known Inflated Donnington Grove Club 01.19			
G-BYSM	Cameron A-210	4698	12.04.00	
	Adventure Balloons Ltd Hartley Wintney, Hook			
	'Heritage Balloons'		12.06.18E	
G-BYSP	Piper PA-28-181 Archer II	28-8590047	12.10.99	
	D-EAUL, N6909D M C Plomer-Roberts			
	Wellesbourne Mountford		03.02.18E	
G-BYSV	Cameron N-120	4704	15.10.99	
	S A Simington Eccles, Norwich *'Cameron Balloons'*		31.07.19E	
G-BYSX	Cyclone Pegasus Quantum 15-912	7586	23.11.99	
	K A Landers Deenethorpe		29.06.18P	
G-BYSY	Raj Hamsa X'Air 582(2)	448	21.10.99	
	A Cochrane (Nuneaton)		16.07.18P	
	Built by J M Davidson – project BMAA/HB/109			
G-BYTA	Kolb Twinstar Mk.3	xxxx	02.09.99	
	Cancelled 21.03.11 by CAA		14.02.08	
	Aughrim, Kilkeel *Built by R E Gray – project*			
	PFA 205-13240; stored dismantled 12.13			
G-BYTB	SOCATA TB-20 Trinidad	2002	18.05.00	
	F-OILE Watchman Aircraft Ltd Jersey		27.10.18E	
G-BYTC	Pegasus Quantum 15-912	7571	25.10.99	
	J C & J E Munro-Hunt (Llandridrod Wells)		24.11.14P	
	Badged 'Q.2 Sport'			

G-BYTI Piper PA-24-250 Comanche   24-3489   09.11.99
D-ELOP, N8297P, N10F G Auchterlonie & M Carruthers
Retford Gamston   04.12.17E

G-BYTJ Cameron C-80   4703   19.11.99
J D Smallridge Cam, Dursley *'Rapido Group'*   12.06.18E

G-BYTK Avtech Jabiru SPL-450   0265   08.11.99
G R Phillips Leicester   06.02.18P
Built by K A Fagan & S R Pike – project PFA 274A-13465

G-BYTL Mainair Blade 912   1224-0999-7-W1017   19.10.99
T J Burrow & D A Meek St Michaels   30.11.17P

G-BYTM Dyn'Aéro MCR-01 Club   83   01.10.99
I Lang (Faak am See, Austria)   27.06.18P
Built by I Lang – project PFA 301-13440

G-BYTN de Havilland DH.82A Tiger Moth   3993   18.11.99
7014M, N6720 R Flanagan Retford Gamston   11.03.15E
As 'N6720:VX' in RAF c/s (NF 09.03.18)

G-BYTR Raj Hamsa X'Air 582(1)   460   05.10.99
L A Dotchin Wing Farm, Longbridge Deverill   23.04.18P
Built by R Dunn & A P Roberts – project BMAA/HB/105

G-BYTS Montgomerie-Bensen B.8MR   MGM-2   22.09.99
C Seaman Melrose Farm, Melbourne   22.04.14P
Built by M G Mee (NF 21.07.15)

G-BYTU Mainair Blade 912   1225-1099-7-W1018   26.11.99
A S R Galley tr GBytes Caernarfon   18.06.18P

G-BYTV Avtech Jabiru UL-450   0264   03.11.99
M W T Wilson Morgansfield, Fishburn   23.04.18P
Built by E Bentley – project PFA 274A-13454

G-BYTW Cameron O-90   4747   11.04.00
Sade Balloons Ltd London NW8   27.04.18E

G-BYTX Whittaker MW6-S Fatboy Flyer   xxxx   02.12.99
J K Ewing Newton Peveril Farm, Sturminster Marshall
Built by J K Ewing – project PFA 164-12819
(SSDR microlight since 07.15) (NF 25.08.17)

G-BYTZ Raj Hamsa X'Air 582(6)   472   26.10.99
J R Kinder Fenland   09.04.18P
Built by K C Millar & A B Wilson – project BMAA/HB/120

G-BYUB Grob G115E Tutor   82087/E   22.07.99
Babcock Aerospace Ltd RAF Woodvale *'UB'*   10.08.19E
Operated by Liverpool University & Manchester
& Salford Universities Air Squadrons

G-BYUC Grob G115E Tutor   82088/E   22.07.99
Babcock Aerospace Ltd RAF Linton-on-Ouse *'UC'*   05.08.19E
Operated by Yorkshire Universities Air Squadron

G-BYUD Grob G115E Tutor   82089/E   22.07.99
Babcock Aerospace Ltd RAF Linton-on-Ouse *'UD'*   04.08.19E
Operated by Yorkshire Universities Air Squadron

G-BYUE Grob G115E Tutor   82090/E   12.08.99
Babcock Aerospace Ltd RAF Wittering *'UE'*   30.08.19E
Operated by Cambridge University, East Midlands
Universities, University of London Air Squadrons
& 115 Squadron

G-BYUF Grob G115E Tutor   82091/E   12.08.99
Babcock Aerospace Ltd RAF Leeming *'UF'*   30.08.19E
Operated by Northumbrian Universities Air Squadron

G-BYUH Grob G115E Tutor   82093/E   22.09.99
Babcock Aerospace Ltd MoD Boscombe Down *'UH'*   27.09.19E
Operated by Southampton University Air Squadron

G-BYUI Grob G115E Tutor   82094/E   24.09.99
Babcock Aerospace Ltd RAF Woodvale *'UI'*   11.11.19E
Operated by Liverpool and Manchester & Salford
Universities Air Squadrons

G-BYUJ Grob G115E Tutor   82095/E   24.09.99
Babcock Aerospace Ltd RAF Leuchars *'UJ'*   27.09.19E
Operated by East of Scotland Universities Air Squadron

G-BYUK Grob G115E Tutor   82096/E   18.10.99
Babcock Aerospace Ltd RAF Cranwell *'UK'*   28.10.19E
Operated by 16 & 57 Squadrons, RAF

G-BYUL Grob G115E Tutor   82097/E   18.10.99
Babcock Aerospace Ltd RAF Woodvale *'UL'*   27.10.19E
Operated by Liverpool and Manchester & Salford
Universities Air Squadrons

G-BYUM Grob G115E Tutor   82098/E   18.10.99
Babcock Aerospace Ltd RAF Wittering *'UM'*   28.10.19E
Operated by Cambridge University, East Midlands
Universities, University of London Air Squadrons
& 115 Squadron

G-BYUN Grob G115E Tutor   82099/E   18.10.99
Babcock Aerospace Ltd RAF Cranwell *'UN'*   26.10.19E
Operated by 16 & 57 Squadrons, RAF

G-BYUO Grob G115E Tutor   82100/E   19.11.99
Babcock Aerospace Ltd RAF Cranwell *'UO'*   28.11.19E
Operated by 16 & 57 Squadrons, RAF

G-BYUR Grob G115E Tutor   82102/E   19.11.99
Babcock Aerospace Ltd RAF Cranwell *'UR'*   28.11.19E
Operated by 16 & 57 Squadrons, RAF

G-BYUS Grob G115E Tutor   82103/E   19.11.99
Babcock Aerospace Ltd RAF Leuchars *'US'*   28.11.19E
Operated by East of Scotland Universities Air Squadron

G-BYUU Grob G115E Tutor   82105/E   07.12.99
Babcock Aerospace Ltd RAF Wittering *'UU'*   14.12.19E
Operated by Cambridge University, East Midlands
Universities, University of London Air Squadrons
& 115 Squadron; force landed near RAF Wittering
02.10.18 & damaged

G-BYUV Grob G115E Tutor   82106/E   07.12.99
Babcock Aerospace Ltd MoD Boscombe Down *'UV'*   14.12.19E
Operated by Southampton University Air Squadron

G-BYUW Grob G115E Tutor   82107/E   07.12.99
Babcock Aerospace Ltd RAF Cranwell *'UW'*   16.12.19E
Operated by 16 & 57 Squadrons, RAF

G-BYUX Grob G115E Tutor   82108/E   18.01.00
Babcock Aerospace Ltd RAF Cranwell *'UX'*   31.01.20E
Operated by 16 & 57 Squadrons, RAF

G-BYUY Grob G115E Tutor   82109/E   18.01.00
Babcock Aerospace Ltd RAF Woodvale *'UY'*   31.01.20E
Operated by Liverpool and Manchester & Salford
Universities Air Squadrons

G-BYUZ Grob G115E Tutor   82110/E   18.01.00
Babcock Aerospace Ltd RAF Cranwell *'UZ'*   31.01.20E
Operated by 16 & 57 Squadrons, RAF

G-BYVA Grob G115E Tutor   82111/E   18.01.00
Babcock Aerospace Ltd MoD Boscombe Down *'VA'*   31.01.20E
Operated by Southampton University Air Squadron

G-BYVB Grob G115E Tutor   82112/E   17.02.00
Babcock Aerospace Ltd St Athan *'VB'*   25.02.20E
Operated by Universities of Wales Air Squadron

G-BYVC Grob G115E Tutor   82113/E   17.02.00
Babcock Aerospace Ltd RAF Wittering *'VC'*   02.03.20E
Operated by Cambridge University, East Midlands
Universities, University of London Air Squadrons
& 115 Squadron

G-BYVD Grob G115E Tutor   82114/E   17.02.00
Babcock Aerospace Ltd MoD Boscombe Down *'VD'*   02.04.19E
Operated by Southampton University Air Squadron

G-BYVE Grob G115E Tutor   82115/E   17.02.00
Babcock Aerospace Ltd RAF Wittering *'VE'*   08.04.19E
Operated by Cambridge University, East Midlands
Universities, University of London Air Squadrons
& 115 Squadron

G-BYVF Grob G115E Tutor   82116/E   22.02.00
Babcock Aerospace Ltd RNAS Yeovilton *'VF'*   28.02.20E
Operated by 727 Naval Air Squadron

G-BYVG Grob G115E Tutor   82117/E   22.03.00
Babcock Aerospace Ltd RAF Wittering *'VG'*   02.04.19E
Operated by Cambridge University, East Midlands
Universities, University of London Air Squadrons
& 115 Squadron

G-BYVH Grob G115E Tutor   82118/E   22.03.00
Babcock Aerospace Ltd RAF Cranwell *'VH'*   05.04.19E
Operated by 16 & 57 Squadrons, RAF

G-BYVI Grob G115E Tutor   82119/E   22.03.00
Babcock Aerospace Ltd RAF Woodvale *'VI'*   04.04.19E
Operated by Liverpool University & Manchester &
Salford Universities Air Squadrons

G-BYVK	Grob G115E Tutor	82121/E	14.04.00
	Babcock Aerospace Ltd RNAS Yeovilton *'VK'*		23.04.19E
	Operated by 727 Naval Air Squadron		
G-BYVL	Grob G115E Tutor	82122/E	14.04.00
	Babcock Aerospace Ltd RAF Cosford *'VL'*		26.04.19E
	Operated by University of Birmingham Air Squadron		
G-BYVM	Grob G115E Tutor	82123/E	14.04.00
	Babcock Aerospace Ltd RAF Cranwell *'VM'*		26.04.19E
	Operated by 16 & 57 Squadrons, RAF		
G-BYVO	Grob G115E Tutor	82125/E	18.05.00
	Babcock Aerospace Ltd St Athan *'VO'*		31.05.19E
	Operated by Universities of Wales Air Squadron		
G-BYVP	Grob G115E Tutor	82126/E	18.05.00
	Babcock Aerospace Ltd RAF Woodvale *'VP'*		31.05.19E
	Operated by Liverpool University & Manchester & Salford Universities Air Squadrons		
G-BYVR	Grob G115E Tutor	82127/E	18.05.00
	Babcock Aerospace Ltd RAF Cranwell *'VR'*		31.05.19E
	Operated by 16 & 57 Squadrons, RAF		
G-BYVU	Grob G115E Tutor	82130/E	20.06.00
	Babcock Aerospace Ltd AAC Middle Wallop *'VU'*		29.06.19E
	Operated by 676 Squadron, AAC		
G-BYVW	Grob G115E Tutor	82132/E	21.07.00
	Babcock Aerospace Ltd St Athan *'VW'*		06.08.19E
	Operated by Universities of Wales Air Squadron		
G-BYVY	Grob G115E Tutor	82134/E	21.07.00
	Babcock Aerospace Ltd AAC Middle Wallop *'VY'*		06.08.19E
	Operated by 676 Squadron, AAC		
G-BYVZ	Grob G115E Tutor	82135/E	21.07.00
	Babcock Aerospace Ltd RAF Cosford *'VZ'*		05.08.19E
	Operated by University of Birmingham Air Squadron		
G-BYWA	Grob G115E Tutor	82136/E	21.08.00
	Babcock Aerospace Ltd RAF Linton-on-Ouse *'WA'*		28.08.19E
	Operated by Yorkshire Universities Air Squadron		
G-BYWB	Grob G115E Tutor	82137/E	21.08.00
	Babcock Aerospace Ltd MoD Boscombe Down *'WB'*		30.08.19E
	Operated by Bristol & Southampton UAS		
G-BYWD	Grob G115E Tutor	82139/E	18.09.00
	Babcock Aerospace Ltd RAF Cosford *'WD'*		28.09.19E
	Operated by University of Birmingham Air Squadron		
G-BYWF	Grob G115E Tutor	82141/E	18.09.00
	Babcock Aerospace Ltd RAF Wittering *'WF'*		27.09.19E
	Operated by Cambridge University, East Midlands Universities, University of London Air Squadrons & 115 Squadron		
G-BYWG	Grob G115E Tutor	82142/E	13.10.00
	Babcock Aerospace Ltd RAF Cosford *'WG'*		29.10.19E
	Operated by University of Birmingham Air Squadron		
G-BYWH	Grob G115E Tutor	82143/E	13.10.00
	Babcock Aerospace Ltd RAF Wittering *'WH'*		09.06.19E
	Operated by Cambridge University, East Midlands Universities, University of London Air Squadrons & 115 Squadron		
G-BYWI	Grob G115E Tutor	82144/E	13.10.00
	Babcock Aerospace Ltd RAF Cranwell *'WI'*		25.10.19E
	Operated by 16 & 57 Squadrons, RAF		
G-BYWK	Grob G115E Tutor	82146/E	17.11.00
	Babcock Aerospace Ltd RAF Leeming *'WK'*		27.07.18E
	Operated by Northumbrian Universities Air Squadron		
G-BYWL	Grob G115E Tutor	82147/E	17.11.00
	Babcock Aerospace Ltd MoD Boscombe Down *'WL'*		26.07.19E
	Operated by Southampton University Air Squadron		
G-BYWM	Grob G115E Tutor	82148/E	17.11.00
	Babcock Aerospace Ltd RNAS Yeovilton *'WM'*		24.10.19E
	Operated by 727 Naval Air Squadron		
G-BYWO	Grob G115E Tutor	82150/E	07.12.00
	Babcock Aerospace Ltd RAF Wittering *'WO'*		13.01.20E
	Operated by Cambridge University, East Midlands Universities, University of London Air Squadrons & 115 Squadron		
G-BYWR	Grob G115E Tutor	82152/E	18.05.00
	Babcock Aerospace Ltd RAF Cranwell *'WR'*		05.02.20E
	Operated by 16 & 57 Squadrons, RAF		
G-BYWS	Grob G115E Tutor	82153/E	07.12.00
	Babcock Aerospace Ltd RAF Wittering *'WS'*		15.01.20E
	Operated by Cambridge University, East Midlands Universities, University of London Air Squadrons & 115 Squadron		
G-BYWU	Grob G115E Tutor	82155/E	19.01.01
	Babcock Aerospace Ltd RAF Cosford *'WU'*		28.01.20E
	Operated by University of Birmingham Air Squadron		
G-BYWV	Grob G115E Tutor	82156/E	19.01.01
	Babcock Aerospace Ltd RAF Linton-on-Ouse *'WV'*		27.01.20E
	Operated by Yorkshire Universities Air Squadron		
G-BYWW	Grob G115E Tutor	82157/E	19.01.01
	Babcock Aerospace Ltd AAC Middle Wallop *'WW'*		28.01.20E
	Operated by 676 Squadron, AAC		
G-BYWX	Grob G115E Tutor	82158/E	14.02.01
	Babcock Aerospace Ltd RAF Wittering *'WX'*		25.02.20E
	Operated by Cambridge University, East Midlands Universities, University of London Air Squadrons & 115 Squadron		
G-BYWY	Grob G115E Tutor	82159/E	14.02.01
	Babcock Aerospace Ltd RAF Cranwell *'WY'*		25.02.20E
	Operated by 16 & 57 Squadrons, RAF		
G-BYWZ	Grob G115E Tutor	82160/E	14.02.01
	Babcock Aerospace Ltd RAF Wittering *'WZ'*		04.03.20E
	Operated by Cambridge University, East Midlands Universities, University of London Air Squadrons & 115 Squadron		
G-BYXA	Grob G115E Tutor	82161/E	14.02.01
	Babcock Aerospace Ltd RAF Cosford *'XA'*		04.03.20E
	Operated by University of Birmingham Air Squadron		
G-BYXC	Grob G115E Tutor	82163/E	19.03.01
	Babcock Aerospace Ltd RAF Wittering *'XC'*		31.03.19E
	Operated by Cambridge University, East Midlands Universities, University of London Air Squadrons & 115 Squadron		
G-BYXD	Grob G115E Tutor	82164/E	19.03.01
	Babcock Aerospace Ltd St Athan *'XD'*		31.03.19E
	Operated by Universities of Wales Air Squadron		
G-BYXE	Grob G115E Tutor	82165/E	19.03.01
	Babcock Aerospace Ltd RAF Wittering *'XE'*		31.03.19E
	Operated by Cambridge University, East Midlands Universities, University of London Air Squadrons & 115 Squadron		
G-BYXF	Grob G115E Tutor	82166/E	12.04.01
	Babcock Aerospace Ltd AAC Middle Wallop *'XF'*		23.04.19E
	Operated by 676 Squadron, AAC		
G-BYXG	Grob G115E Tutor	82167/E	12.04.01
	Babcock Aerospace Ltd MoD Boscombe Down *'XG'*		01.05.19E
	Operated by Bristol & Southampton Universities Air Squadrons		
G-BYXH	Grob G115E Tutor	82168/E	12.04.01
	Babcock Aerospace Ltd RAF Cranwell *'XH'*		23.04.19E
	Operated by 16 & 57 Squadrons, RAF		
G-BYXI	Grob G115E Tutor	82169/E	12.04.01
	Babcock Aerospace Ltd AAC Middle Wallop *'XI'*		29.04.19E
	Operated by 676 Squadron, AAC		
G-BYXJ	Grob G115E Tutor	82170/E	16.05.01
	Babcock Aerospace Ltd RAF Leeming *'XJ'*		28.05.19E
	Operated by Northumbrian Universities Air Squadron		
G-BYXK	Grob G115E Tutor	82171/E	16.05.01
	Babcock Aerospace Ltd RNAS Yeovilton *'XK'*		27.05.19E
	Operated by 727 Naval Air Squadron		
G-BYXL	Grob G115E Tutor	82172/E	16.05.01
	Babcock Aerospace Ltd RAF Leuchars *'XL'*		28.05.19E
	Operated by East of Scotland Universities Air Squadron		
G-BYXM	Grob G115E Tutor	82173/E	16.05.01
	Babcock Aerospace Ltd RAF Wittering *'XM'*		28.05.19E
	Operated by Cambridge University, East Midlands Universities, University of London Air Squadrons & 115 Squadron		
G-BYXO	Grob G115E Tutor	82175/E	08.06.01
	Babcock Aerospace Ltd RAF Leuchars *'XO'*		05.08.19E
	Operated by East of Scotland Universities Air Squadron		

G-BYXP	Grob G115E Tutor	82176/E	08.06.01	
	Babcock Aerospace Ltd RAF Cosford 'XP'		11.06.19E	
	Operated by University of Birmingham Air Squadron			
G-BYXS	Grob G115E Tutor	82178/E	18.07.01	
	Babcock Aerospace Ltd RNAS Yeovilton 'XS'		27.07.19E	
	Operated by 727 Naval Air Squadron			
G-BYXT	Grob G115E Tutor	82179/E	18.07.01	
	Babcock Aerospace Ltd RAF Linton-on-Ouse 'XT'		01.11.19E	
	Operated by Yorkshire Universities Air Squadron			
G-BYXW	Medway EclipseR	166/147	25.10.99	
	G A Hazell Lower Upham Farm, Chiseldon		02.06.11P	
	Officially registered as c/n 166/144 (NF 11.08.14)			
G-BYXX	Grob G115E Tutor	82180/E	18.07.01	
	Babcock Aerospace Ltd RAF Leuchars 'XX'		01.11.18E	
	Operated by East of Scotland Universities Air Squadron			
G-BYXZ	Grob G115E Tutor	82182/E	15.08.01	
	Babcock Aerospace Ltd RAF Wittering 'XZ'		17.08.18E	
	Operated by Cambridge University, East Midlands			
	Universities, University of London Air Squadrons			
	& 115 Squadron			
G-BYYA	Grob G115E Tutor	82183/E	15.08.01	
	Babcock Aerospace Ltd RAF Leeming 'YA'		23.09.19E	
	Operated by Northumbrian Universities Air Squadron			
G-BYYB	Grob G115E Tutor	82184/E	15.08.01	
	Babcock Aerospace Ltd RAF Linton-on-Ouse 'YB'		16.09.18E	
	Operated by Yorkshire Universities Air Squadron			
G-BYYC	HAPI Cygnet SF-2A	285	25.11.99	
	G H Smith Shenstone Hall Farm, Shenstone		29.04.18P	
	Built by C D Hughes & G H Smith			
	– project PFA 182-12311			
G-BYYE	Lindstrand LBL 77A	151	25.11.99	
	Airxcite Ltd t/a Virgin Balloon Flights			
	Stafford Park, Telford		29.10.18E	
G-BYYG	Slingsby T67C Firefly	2101	30.11.99	
	PH-SGI The Pathfinder Flying Club Ltd RAF Wyton		21.03.19E	
G-BYYJ	Lindstrand LBL 25A Cloudhopper	651	10.12.99	
	A Gundrum tr G-BYYJ Go Hopping			
	Herrenberg, Germany 'Lindstrand Balloons'		23.09.18E	
G-BYYL	Avtech Jabiru SPL-450	0281	10.12.99	
	S Langley & D Licheri Willingale		23.08.19P	
	Built by C Jackson – project PFA 274A-13480			
G-BYYM	Raj Hamsa X'Air 582(2)	476	21.10.99	
	J Pozniak (Paignton)		19.11.17P	
	Built by J J Cozens – project BMAA/HB/119			
G-BYYN	Cyclone Pegasus Quantum 15-912	7601	06.01.00	
	R J Bullock (Elmsthorpe, Leicester)		26.03.18P	
G-BYYO	Piper PA-28R-201 Arrow III	2837061	11.02.00	
	(N182ND), N9249C, G-BYYO, N9249C			
	Stapleford Flying Club Ltd Stapleford		12.04.18E	
	Official type data 'PA-28R-201 Cherokee Arrow III'			
	is incorrect			
G-BYYP	Cyclone Pegasus Quantum 15	7603	11.02.00	
	D A Linsey-Bloom New Farm, Felton		16.09.18P	
G-BYYT	Avtech Jabiru UL-450	0259	18.11.99	
	S Turnbull Full Sutton		13.10.15P	
	Built by T D Saveker – project PFA 274A-13452			
	(NF 28.11.16)			
G-BYYX	Team Mini-Max 91	xxxx	06.01.00	
	P J Bishop Rossall Field, Cockerham			
	Built by P L Turner – project PFA 186-13410			
	(SSDR microlight since 05.14) (IE 27.09.16)			
G-BYYY	Cyclone Pegasus Quantum 15-912	7564	08.12.99	
	R D C Hayter Redlands		17.03.16P	
G-BYZA	Aérospatiale AS.355F2 Ecureuil 2	5518	20.12.99	
	JA6764, F-OHNK PLM Dollar Group Ltd			
	Dalcross Heliport		22.04.18E	
	Callsign 'Osprey 67'			
G-BYZB	Mainair Blade	1229-1299-7-W1022	14.01.00	
	A M Thornley (Actthorpe Top, Louth)		04.06.17P	
G-BYZF	Raj Hamsa X'Air 582(1)	461	07.01.00	
	R P Davies (Harrogate)			
	Built by S W Grainger – project BMAA/HB/110			
	(NF 16.04.18)			

G-BYZO	Rans S-6-ES Coyote II	1298.1287	14.01.00	
	J P Snowden (Leeds)		08.01.19P	
	Built by S C Jackson – project PFA 204-13560;			
	tricycle u/c			
G-BYZR	III Sky Arrow 650 TC	C001	24.01.00	
	D-ENGF, I-TREI R Moncrieff & G P Thelwell			
	tr G-BYZR Flying Group Retford Gamston		04.03.19E	
	Built by Iniziative Industriali Italian			
G-BYZS	Avtech Jabiru UL-450	0253	25.01.00	
	(G-OPIP) G J Stafford Ince		16.05.18P	
	Built by N Fielding – project PFA 274A-13489;			
	originally registered as G-OPIP by P Simpson			
G-BYZT	Nova Vertex 26	13345	21.01.00	
	M Hay (Dundee)			
G-BYZU	Cyclone Pegasus Quantum 15	7613	15.02.00	
	L Adams Sutton Meadows		12.05.18P	
G-BYZV	Sky 90-24	174	15.08.00	
	M A Stelling South Queensferry, Edinburgh		01.03.19E	
G-BYZW	Raj Hamsa X'Air 582(11)	499	19.01.00	
	H C Lowther Bedlands Gate, Little Strickland		04.04.18P	
	Built by P A Gilford – project BMAA/HB/129			
G-BYZY	Pietenpol Air Camper	xxxx	02.12.99	
	D B Hanchet White Waltham		30.08.18P	
	Built by D N Hanchet – project PFA 047-12190			

G-BZAA – G-BZZZ

G-BZAE	Cessna 152	15281300	22.03.00	
	N49480 Tatenhill Aviation Ltd Tatenhill		16.08.12E	
	Dumped 08.17 outside maintenance hangar (NF 26.09.17)			
G-BZAH	Cessna 208B Grand Caravan	208B0811	28.02.00	
	N5196U Army Parachute Association			
	MoD Netheravon		13.04.18E	
G-BZAI	Cyclone Pegasus Quantum 15	7614	09.02.00	
	S A Holmes (Chesterfield)		13.06.18P	
G-BZAK	Raj Hamsa X'Air 582(9)	477	20.01.00	
	L M Devine Letterkenny, Rol		20.09.18P	
	Built by B W Austen – project BMAA/HB/114			
G-BZAL	Mainair Blade 912	1205-0799-7-W1008	27.01.00	
	J Potts Rossall Field, Cockerham		13.07.18P	
G-BZAM	Europa Aviation Europa	265	06.12.99	
	N M Graham Charmy Down		11.08.15P	
	Built by D U Corbett – project PFA 247-12969;			
	tailwheel u/c			
G-BZAP	Avtech Jabiru UL-450	0280	13.12.99	
	D R Griffiths & I J Grindley Top Farm, Croydon		30.06.18P	
	Built by S Derwin – project PFA 274A-13479			
G-BZAR	Denney Kitfox Model 4-1200 Speedster	xxxx	17.02.00	
	G-LEZJ N J France Holly Meadow Farm, Bradley			
	'Ol' Red'		01.08.18P	
	Built by L A James – project PFA 172B-12529			
G-BZAS	Isaacs Fury II	xxxx	10.02.00	
	N C Stone Selby House Farm, Stanton			
	'Spirit of Dunsfold'		04.07.04P	
	Built by H A Brunt & H Frick – project PFA 011-10837;			
	rebuilt 2017; as 'K5673' in RAF c/s (NF 06.05.14)			
G-BZBC	Rans S-6-ES Coyote II	0499.1314	02.02.00	
	A J Baldwin (Codnor, Ripley)		17.02.10P	
	Built by A J Baldwin – project PFA 204-13525;			
	tricycle u/c (NF 09.11.16)			
G-BZBE	Cameron A-210	4708	09.05.00	
	Border Ballooning Ltd Plas Madoc, Montgomery		23.06.13E	
	(IE 04.06.17)			
G-BZBF	Cessna 172M Skyhawk	17262258	20.12.99	
	N126SA, G-BZBF, 9H-ACV, N12785			
	Aviolease Ltd Doncaster Sheffield		17.01.20E	
	Operated by Yorkshire Aero Club			
G-BZBH	Thunder Ax7-65 Bolt	173	28.11.78	
	C A Fraser & P J Hebdon Milton, Banbury			
	'Serendipity II'		08.05.17E	
G-BZBJ	Lindstrand LBL 77A	646	29.02.00	
	P T R Ollivere Eastbourne			
	'the cancer research campaign'		27.06.19E	
	Fitted with new, unidentified, envelope			

G-BZBL Lindstrand LBL 120A 676 23.02.00
A G A Barclay-Faulkner Hopton, Stafford 22.06.18E

G-BZBO Stoddard-Hamilton Glasair III 3032 21.02.00
M B Hamlett (Sawston, Cambridge)
Built by M B Hamlett (NF 30.07.14)

G-BZBP Raj Hamsa X'Air 582(5) 470 29.02.00
J L B Roy Andreas 27.08.13P
Built by D F Hughes – project BMAA/HB/131
(NF 12.11.14)

G-BZBS Piper PA-28-161 Warrior III 2842080 10.05.00
N4180H, G-BZBS, N9529N
White Waltham Airfield Ltd White Waltham 16.05.18E

G-BZBT Cameron H-34 4730 18.05.00
P Lesser Partille, Sweden *'Helios'* 01.04.18E

G-BZBW RotorWay Exec 162F 6415 23.02.00
D Parsons tr G-BZBW Group Landmead Farm, Garford 12.11.16P
Built by M Gardiner

G-BZBX Rans S-6-ES Coyote II 0499.1317 26.01.00
P J Taylor Beverley (Linley Hill) 27.08.14P
Built by R Johnstone – project PFA 204-13501;
tricycle u/c (IE 24.08.15)

G-BZBZ Jodel D.9 Bébé 519 29.02.00
OO-48 D C Unwin Saltby 19.09.17P
Built by Etienne de Schrevel, Gent, Belgium 1970-77

G-BZDA Piper PA-28-161 Warrior III 2842087 29.06.00
N41814, G-BZDA, N41814 White Waltham Airfield Ltd
White Waltham 06.07.18E

G-BZDC Mainair Blade 1232-0100-7-W1025 13.03.00
P J Smith & E J Wells Over Farm, Gloucester 01.06.18P

G-BZDD Mainair Blade 912 1238-0200-7-W1031 21.01.00
M H Rollins (Solihull) 29.05.19P

G-BZDE Lindstrand LBL 210A 665 06.03.00
Toucan Travel Ltd Chineham, Basingstoke
'Toucan Travel' 13.09.16E
(IE 04.01.18)

G-BZDF CFM Streak Shadow SA K 241 07.03.00
(EI-...), G-BZDF K Davies & D O'Keefe Swansea 18.10.19P
Built by J W Beckett – project PFA 206-13246

G-BZDH Piper PA-28R-200 Cherokee Arrow II 28R-7235028 08.03.00
5B-CJU, G-BZDH, HB-OHH, N4390T
G-BZDH Ltd Lydd 10.07.19E

G-BZDJ Cameron Z-105 HAB 4832 27.06.00
Cancelled 27.10.17 as PWFU 02.07.16
Not Known *'BWS Security Systems'*
Inflated Longleat 09.18

G-BZDK Raj Hamsa X'Air 582(2) 447 08.02.00
J Bagnall Arclid Green, Sandbach 21.07.17P
Built by R Barnes & B Park – project BMAA/HB/124;
noted 02.18 (IE 08.08.17)

G-BZDM Stoddard-Hamilton GlaStar 5577 13.03.00
F G Miskelly Thruxton 22.09.18P
Built by F G Miskelly – project PFA 295-13283

G-BZDN Cameron N-105 2840 26.04.00
D-OABB, D-Saxonia (2) P A Foot & I R Warrington
Stamford & Hunstanton *'Wir Geben GSA erdgas'* 25.02.14E
(IE 08.01.16)

G-BZDP Scottish Aviation Bulldog Srs 120/121 BH120/244 31.03.00
XX551 D J Rae MoD Boscombe Down 07.08.18E
As 'XX551:E' in RAF c/s

G-BZDR Tri-R KIS 9403 08.03.00
D F Sutherland Inverness 10.05.18P
Built by B S Neilson

G-BZDS Cyclone Pegasus Quantum 15-912 7633 17.04.00
J Ayre Measham Cottage Farm, Measham 25.09.19P

G-BZDV Westland SA.341C Gazelle HT.2 1150 31.03.00
3D-HXL, G-BZDV, XW884 G R Harrison
Sopers Farm, Ashurst 24.07.19P

G-BZEA Cessna A152 Aerobat A1520824 13.03.00
N7606L Blueplane Ltd Blackbushe 10.08.18E

G-BZEB Cessna 152 15282772 31.01.00
N89532 Blueplane Ltd Blackbushe 25.08.18E

G-BZEC Cessna 152 15284475 21.01.00
N4655M Redhill Air Services Ltd Redhill 27.08.19E

G-BZED Cyclone Pegasus Quantum 15-912 7600 17.03.00
D Crozier Greenhills Farm, Wheatley Hill 22.07.18P

G-BZEG Mainair Blade 912 1239-0200-7-W1032 03.03.00
R P Cookson Ince 30.08.18P

G-BZEJ Raj Hamsa X'Air 582(7) 500 31.03.00
C Ricketts tr H-Flight X'Air Flying Group Otherton 23.01.16P
Built by H Hall – project BMAA/HB/134 (IE 04.11.16)

G-BZEL Mainair Blade 1245-0300-7-W1038 27.03.00
M Law (Kelty) 03.04.16P

G-BZEN Avtech Jabiru UL-450 0161 04.04.00
J R Hunt Deenethorpe 19.07.18P
Built by B W Stockil – project PFA 274-13272

G-BZEP Scottish Aviation Bulldog Srs 120/121 BH120/257 04.04.00
XX561 R C Skinner Trenchard Farm, Eggesford 25.05.05
As 'XX561:7' in RAF c/s (IE 14.01.19)

G-BZER Raj Hamsa X'Air 582(2) 526 22.03.00
N P Lloyd & H Lloyd-Hughes (Mold & Wrexham) 17.07.19P
Built by N P Lloyd & H Lloyd-Hughes
– project BMAA/HB/133

G-BZES RotorWay Exec 90 6191 25.04.00
G-LUFF R D Boor Fenland 23.07.18P
Built by D C Luffingham; badly damaged
Fenland 01.07.18

G-BZEU Raj Hamsa X'Air 582(8) 518 20.04.00
D P Molloy Bellarena 20.09.19P
Built by J C Harris – project BMAA/HB/140

G-BZEW Rans S-6-ES Coyote II 0998.1268.0199 05.04.00
N P Gayton (Wellingborough) 16.07.19P
Built by D Kingslake – project PFA 204-13450 –
original kit no.0998.1268 rebuilt & re-dated 1999
after accident (?)); tricycle u/c

G-BZEY Cameron N-90 4829 15.05.00
G L Forde Wendover *'NAPS'* 11.05.17E

G-BZEZ CFM Streak Shadow SA K 332 01.02.00
G J Pearce Henstridge 10.05.18P
Built by M F Cottam – project PFA 206-13503

G-BZFB Robin R2112 Alpha 175 07.04.00
EI-BIU K M Perkins Headcorn 03.07.18E

G-BZFC Cyclone Pegasus Quantum 15 7640 14.04.00
G Addison East Fortune 09.09.18P

G-BZFD Cameron N-90 2725 24.05.00
OO-BFD C, D & E Gingell Nailsea, Bristol
'David Hathaway Transport' 19.04.18E

G-BZFH Cyclone Pegasus Quantum 15-912 7660 15.05.00
J C R Davies Haverfordwest 15.07.18P

G-BZFI Avtech Jabiru UL-450 0271 27.03.00
B S Lapthorn Chatteris 19.07.18P
Built by A I, A S & A W J Findlay
– project PFA 274A-13497

G-BZFK Team Mini-Max 88 xxxx 17.04.00
I Pearson (Falmouth)
Built by C Vandenberghe – project PFA 186-12060
(SSDR microlight since 01.15) (NF 15.08.16)

G-BZFN Scottish Aviation Bulldog Srs 120/121 BH120/325 18.04.00
XX667 Risk Logical Ltd (Derbyhaven, Isle of Man) 13.06.18P
As 'XX667:16' in RAF c/s

G-BZFS Mainair Blade 912 1243-0300-7-W1036 23.03.00
B V Davies & G Roberts tr AwyrenBZFS Caernarfon 16.03.18P

G-BZFT Murphy Rebel 601R 07.04.00
R M Pols Leicester 09.02.18P
Built by N A Evans – project PFA 232-13224

G-BZFV Zenair CH.601UL Zodiac 6-9097 14.04.00
Cancelled 03.02.14 as destroyed 23.07.13
Glebe Farm, Leicestershire
Built by I M Donnelly – project PFA 162A-13547
For sale as rebuild project 02.14

G-BZGA de Havilland DHC-1 Chipmunk 22 C1/0608 31.03.00
WK585 Compton Abbas Airfield Ltd Compton Abbas 10.04.18E
As 'WK585' in RAF c/s

G-BZGB de Havilland DHC-1 Chipmunk 22 C1/0905 31.03.00
WZ872 G Briggs Blackpool 18.08.06
As 'WZ872:E' in RAF c/s (NF 23.02.16)

G-BZGF	Rans S-6-ES Coyote II	0199.1297	25.04.00
	C A Purvis Swansea		31.08.19P
	Built by D F Castle – project PFA 204-13594; originally		
	built as kit no.0899.1334: changed following accident		
	22.07.01; tricycle u/c		
G-BZGJ	Thunder Ax10-180 Series 2	3956	08.05.00
	LN-CBT M Wady t/a Merlin Balloons		
	Hamstreet, Ashford		06.06.17E
	Built by Cameron Balloons Ltd		
G-BZGL	North American OV-10B Bronco	338-11	09.06.00
	GAF 99+26, D-9555, USN 158302 Liberty Aviation Ltd		
	Kortrijk-Wevelgem Int'l, Belgium		
	(NF 12.01.18)		
G-BZGM	Mainair Blade 912	1247-0400-7-W1040	14.04.00
	D Avery Tibenham		16.10.18P
G-BZGO	Robinson R44 Astro	0757	14.04.00
	Flight Academy (Gyrocopters) Ltd Manchester Barton		20.04.18E
G-BZGS	Mainair Blade 912S	1242-0300-7-W1035	10.05.00
	M W Holmes Park Hall Farm, Mapperley		11.07.18P
G-BZGT	Avtech Jabiru SPL-450	291	04.05.00
	C M Bellas (Mansfield)		21.10.19P
	Built by P H Ronfel – project PFA 274A-13539		
G-BZGV	Lindstrand LBL 77A	695	09.05.00
	J H Dryden Fareham 'Skylark'		12.06.18E
G-BZGW	Mainair Blade	1246-0400-7-W1039	05.05.00
	M Liptrot Glassonby		18.09.17P
G-BZGY	Dyn'Aéro CR100C	21	07.06.00
	F-TGCI B Appleby Wolverhampton Halfpenny Green		16.12.18P
G-BZGZ	Cyclone Pegasus Quantum 15-912	7674	07.06.00
	D W Beech Ince		15.03.11P
	(NF 26.06.15)		
G-BZHE	Cessna 152	15281303	20.04.00
	D-EAOC, N49484 Andrewsfield Aviation Ltd		
	Andrewsfield		16.03.18E
G-BZHF	Cessna 152	15283986	20.04.00
	D-EMJA, N4858H MK Aero Support Ltd		
	Andrewsfield		11.08.17E
G-BZHG	Tecnam P92-EM Echo	P92-UK-01	24.05.00
	R W F Boarder Field Farm, Oakley		22.05.18P
	Built by M Rudd – project PFA 318-13606		
G-BZHJ	Raj Hamsa X'Air 582(7)	482	10.05.00
	R W Carbutt North Coates		24.07.18P
	Built by B Baker & A P Harvey – project BMAA/HB/126		
G-BZHL	North American AT-16 Harvard IIB	14A-1158	06.06.00
	FT118, 43-12859 R H Cooper & S Swallow		
	Hibaldstow		
	Built by Noorduyn Aviation, Canada; official c/n '43-12959'		
	is incorrect (USAF p/i); on rebuild 09.13 (NF 08.12.15)		
G-BZHN	Cyclone Pegasus Quantum 15-912	7677	20.06.00
	A M Sirant Monkswell Farm, Horrabridge		17.06.09P
	(IE 07.01.16)		
G-BZHO	Cyclone Pegasus Quantum 15	7658	19.05.00
	C P Dawes tr G-BZHO Group Darley Moor		05.09.18P
G-BZHR	Avtech Jabiru UL-450	0267	16.05.00
	N Morrison Perth		30.11.17P
	Built by G W Rowbotham – project PFA 274A-13493		
G-BZHT	Piper PA-18A-150 Super Cub	18-5886	25.05.00
	ZK-BTF D Bennett tr Super Cub Group		
	Baileys Farm, Long Crendon		27.03.19E
G-BZHU	Wag-Aero CUBy Sport Trainer	AACA/351	25.05.00
	ZK-MPH R T Stimpson tr Teddy Boys Flying Club		
	Gloucestershire		30.07.18P
	Built by D C Hoffman; carries 'MPH' on rudder		
G-BZHV	Piper PA-28-181 Archer III	2843382	17.10.00
	N41848, G-BZHV, N41848 R M & T A Limb		
	White Waltham		23.12.18E
G-BZHX	Thunder Ax11-250 Series 2	4880	21.06.00
	Wizard Balloons Ltd Bury St Edmunds 'Slim Your Bin'		20.08.18E
	Built by Cameron Balloons Ltd		
G-BZHY	Mainair Blade 912	1250-0500-7-W1043	07.06.00
	A Brier Rossall Field, Cockerham		25.08.18P

G-BZIA	Raj Hamsa X'Air 700(1)	475	01.06.00
	J L Pritchett (Churchdown, Gloucester)		24.06.11P
	Built by A U I Hudson – project BMAA/HB/116		
	(IE 05.10.16)		
G-BZIC	Lindstrand LBL Sun	702	08.06.00
	Life Less Ordinary AB Lund, Sweden		15.07.16E
	(NF 21.09.17)		
G-BZID	Montgomerie-Bensen B.8MR	xxxx	31.05.00
	S C Gillies (Crossroads, Keith)		
	Built by A Gault – project PFA G/01-1315, using		
	cannibalised Air Command Elite G-BOGW		
	(NF 11.03.16)		
G-BZIG	Thruster T600N	0040-T600N-042	25.04.00
	K M Jones Leicester		17.09.17P
G-BZIH	Lindstrand LBL 31A	700	07.06.00
	H & L D Vaughan Pennyland, Milton Keynes		
	'Budweiser'		03.07.18E
G-BZII	Extra EA.300/L	119	13.09.00
	BZII Ltd (London N1)		22.11.17E
G-BZIJ	Robin DR.500-200i Président	23	09.03.00
	Rob Airways Ltd Guernsey		19.05.18E
	Officially registered as DR.400-500		
G-BZIL	Colt 120A	4876	07.07.00
	S R Seager t/a Champagne Flights Weedon, Aylesbury		
	'Parrott & Coales'		17.06.19E
	Built by Cameron Balloons Ltd		
G-BZIM	Cyclone Pegasus Quantum 15-912	7678	20.06.00
	M J Stalker Strathaven		16.07.18P
	Shipped to USA for summer 2018, but should return		
G-BZIO	Piper PA-28-161 Warrior III	2842085	29.06.02
	EC-IBJ, G-BZIO, N41796, (VH-PWF), N41796		
	White Waltham Airfield Ltd White Waltham		31.01.18E
G-BZIP	Montgomerie-Bensen B.8MR	xxxx	11.05.00
	V G Freke (Eynsham, Witney)		12.06.07P
	Built by S J Boxall – project PFA G/01A-1319		
	(NF 16.06.16)		
G-BZIS	Raj Hamsa X'Air 582(11)	520	12.06.00
	J Boniface Deanland		01.10.18P
	Built by J Way & R Bonnett – project BMAA/HB/142		
G-BZIT	Beech 95-B55 Baron	TC-564	12.06.00
	HB-GBS, I-ALGE, HB-GBS, N6845Q		
	E P Dablin Turweston		18.10.18E
G-BZIV	Avtech Jabiru UL-450	0341	20.06.00
	A Parr Deanland		17.01.20P
	Built by V R Leggott – project PFA 274A-13587		
G-BZIW	Cyclone Pegasus Quantum 15-912	7681	17.07.00
	J M Hodgson Baxby Manor, Husthwaite		03.08.18P
G-BZIX	Cameron N-90	4867	03.08.00
	P Marmugi & M Stefanini		
	Sesto Fiorentino, Firenze, Italy 'Infostrada'		02.09.17E
G-BZIY	Raj Hamsa X'Air 582(5)	488	19.06.00
	K W Hogg Kirkbride		10.01.09P
	Built by I K Hogg – project BMAA/HB/141 (NF 15.01.15)		
G-BZIZ	Ultramagic H-31	31/02	12.06.00
	C J Davies Castleton, Hope Valley		25.10.17E
G-BZJA	Cameron Fire-90	4757	05.05.00
	Chubb Fire & Security Ltd Ashford TW15 'Chubb'		10.06.19E
	Inflated 05.16 at Pidley		
G-BZJC	Thruster T600N	0070-T600N-044	21.06.00
	P D Snowdon Beverley (Linley Hill)		01.10.18P
	Badged 'Sprint'		
G-BZJD	Thruster T600T 450 Jab	0070-T600T-045	21.06.00
	C C Belcher Old Hay Farm, Paddock Wood		24.01.18P
	Badged 'Sprint'		
G-BZJH	Cameron Z-90	4920	10.07.00
	Egroup SRL San Martino in Rio,		
	Emilia-Romagna, Italy 'Balloon Blunauta'		05.04.18E
G-BZJI	Nova X-Large 37	18946	28.06.00
	M Hay (Dundee)		
	Hang-glider		
G-BZJL	Mainair Blade 912S	1252-0600-7-W1046	04.07.00
	Cancelled 12.05.11 by CAA		
	Warrington *(For sale on ebay 01.14)*		

G-BZJM	Magni M16 Tandem Trainer	xxxx	19.06.00
	J K Padden & A Phillips Melrose Farm, Melbourne		14.12.17P
	Built by J Musil – project PFA G/12-1301		

G-BZJN	Mainair Blade 912	1254-0600-7-W1048	13.07.00
	K Roberts Caernarfon		23.01.19P

G-BZJO	Cyclone Pegasus Quantum 15	7699	06.09.00
	D Minnock Ballyboy, RoI		06.04.18P

G-BZJR	Montgomerie-Bensen B.8MR	xxxx	11.07.00
	G-IPFM, G-BZJR K A O'Neill		
	Holmbeck Farm, Burcott		06.05.15P
	Built by N H Collins – project PFA G/01-1320		

G-BZJV	CASA 1-131E Jungmann Series 1000	1075	31.07.00
	Spanish AF E3B-367 R A Cumming Sleap		10.05.18P
	As 'NM+AA' in Luftwaffe c/s		

G-BZJW	Cessna 150F	15062054	27.06.01
	OO-WIH, OO-SIH, N8754S P Ligertwood		
	Ventfield Farm, Horton-cum-Studley		08.11.18E

G-BZJZ	Cyclone Pegasus Quantum 15	7697	02.08.00
	S Baker (Alcester)		07.10.12P
	(IE 06.11.17)		

G-BZKC	Raj Hamsa X'Air 582(11)	502	12.07.00
	K P Puckey (Abingdon)		26.05.16P
	Built by P J Cheyney & M C Reed		
	– project BMAA/HB/144 (IE 05.10.16)		

G-BZKD	Stolp SA.300 Starduster Too	1	03.07.00
	N70DM C & P Edmunds Enstone		17.12.18P
	Built by R D Merritt		

G-BZKE	Lindstrand LBL 77B	708	17.07.00
	H Cresswell High Wycombe		30.03.11E
	(NF 18.09.15)		

G-BZKF	Rans S-6-ES Coyote II	0499.1315	17.07.00
	S Cartwright & D G Stothard		
	Eddsfield, Octon Lodge Farm, Thwing		04.05.18P
	Built by A W Hodder – project PFA 204-13610;		
	tricycle u/c		

G-BZKL	Piper PA-28R-201 Arrow III	28R-7737152	20.07.00
	D-EFFZ, N40000 M A & M H Cromati Sandown		06.03.18E

G-BZKO	Rans S-6-ES Coyote II	0199.1293	20.07.00
	B, N & P Ringland (Carryduff, Belfast)		30.05.17P
	Built by J A R Hartley – project PFA 204-13564; forced		
	landing near Newtownards 23.03.17 & damaged;		
	tricycle u/c (IE 04.01.18)		

G-BZKU	Cameron Z-105	4931	21.07.00
	N A Fishlock Welland, Malvern *'Cameron Balloons'*		06.07.18E

G-BZKV	Sky 90-24	4857	05.09.00
	D P Busby Broughton, Kettering *'Omega'*		18.05.18E
	Built by Cameron Balloons Ltd		

G-BZKW	Ultramagic M-77	77/179	25.07.00
	(I-....), G-BZKW Slowfly Mongolfiere SNC		
	Mondovi, Italy *'Pendle'*		04.07.18E

G-BZLC	PZL-110 Koliber 160A	04980084	13.09.00
	SP-WGL G F Smith Turweston		27.06.18E

G-BZLE	Rans S-6-ES Coyote II	0499.1311	12.07.00
	G Spittlehouse Finmere		03.04.18P
	Built by W S Long – project PFA 204-13608; tricycle u/c		

G-BZLF	CFM Shadow Series CD	K.236	31.07.00
	D W Stacey Backstable Farm, Haddenham		
	Built by D W Stacey – project BMAA/HB/053		
	(NF 09.07.18)		

G-BZLG	Robin HR.200-120B	353	07.07.00
	Edghill Aviation Services Ltd		
	(Monasterevin, Co Kildare, RoI)		17.05.19E

G-BZLH	Piper PA-28-161 Warrior II	28-8316075	23.08.00
	N43069 A & C A Boyle (Tockwith, York)		31.10.19E

G-BZLK	Cadet III Motor Glider	xxxx	02.08.00
	BGA 2976 G Smith (Fancy Farm, Dunkeswell)		
	'Hathor'		12.10.18P
	Rebuilt by I P Manley – project PFA 042-13629,		
	ex Slingsby T.31B WT873; as 'RF-S' in pseudo RAF c/s		

G-BZLL	Cyclone Pegasus Quantum 15-912	7693	09.08.00
	P F Willey (Aspall, Wigan)		05.04.18P

G-BZLP	Robinson R44 Raven	0814	17.07.00
	Polar Helicopters Ltd Manston		28.02.18E

G-BZLS	Sky 77-24	4858	17.08.00
	D W Young Stenhousemuir, Larbert		14.07.09E
	Built by Cameron Balloons Ltd (NF 16.03.16)		

G-BZLU	Lindstrand LBL 90A	719	09.08.00
	A E Lusty Morton, Bourne *'Tetris 1'*		12.04.09E
	(NF 18.11.15)		

G-BZLV	Avtech Jabiru UL-450	0308	15.08.00
	G Dalton Bodmin		05.10.17P
	Built by G Dalton – project PFA 274A-13537		

G-BZLX	Cyclone Pegasus Quantum 15-912	7714	30.08.00
	M C Wright Willingale		01.10.17P

G-BZLY	Grob G109B	6242	24.08.00
	D-KLMG, G-BZLY, OE-9230		
	D J King & E W Russell tr G-BZLY Group Rattlesden		08.01.18E
	(IE 13.01.18)		

G-BZLZ	Cyclone Pegasus Quantum 15-912	7721	13.09.00
	J Hill Rochester		23.08.19P

G-BZMB	Piper PA-28R-201 Arrow III	28R-7837144	20.04.00
	HB-PBY, N3963M S J White tr Thurrock Arrow Group		
	Kings Farm, Thurrock		01.06.18E
	Official type data 'PA-28R-201 Cherokee Arrow III'		
	is incorrect		

G-BZMC	Avtech Jabiru UL-450	0350	18.08.00
	A & D Coppin Eshott		21.03.19P
	Built by J R Banks – project PFA 274A-13593		

G-BZME	Scottish Aviation Bulldog Srs 120/121	BH120/347	18.08.00
	XX698 H R M Tyrrell tr XX698 Bulldog Group Sleap		08.08.18P
	As 'XX698:9' in RAF c/s		

G-BZMF	Rutan Long-EZ	xxxx	30.08.00
	R Young tr Go-Ez Group Perth		06.08.18P
	Built by A McCaughlin – project PFA 074A-10698		

G-BZMH	Scottish Aviation Bulldog Srs 120/121	BH120/341	21.08.00
	XX692 M E J Hingley Wellesbourne Mountford		19.10.18E
	As 'XX692:A' in RAF c/s		

G-BZMJ	Rans S-6-ES Coyote II	0899.1337ES	31.08.00
	R J G Clark (Pateley Bridge, Harrogate)		09.05.18P
	Built by T I Bull, F J Lloyd and J Seddon		
	– project PFA 204-13631; tricycle u/c		

G-BZML	Scottish Aviation Bulldog Srs 120/121	BH120/342	01.09.00
	XX693 I D Anderson Elmsett		26.07.18E
	Carries '07' in RAF c/s		

G-BZMM	Robin DR.400-180R Remorqueur	918	17.07.00
	OE-KIR, D-EAWR A D Morrison		
	tr Cairngorm Gliding Club Feshiebridge		13.08.18E

G-BZMS	Mainair Blade	1256-0700-7-W1050	02.08.00
	S Elmazouri (Torquay)		07.06.17P

G-BZMW	Cyclone Pegasus Quantum 15-912	7720	26.09.00
	Cancelled 20.06.18 as PWFU		05.07.17
	Eshott *Wreck stored 06.18*		

G-BZMY	Yakovlev Yak C-11	171314	04.10.00
	F-AZSF, Egypt AF A M Holman-West Atherstone		30.04.19P
	Built by Strojírny první petilesky (SPP);		
	as '1' (white) in Soviet AF c/s		

G-BZNA	Lindstrand LBL 90A	732	21.09.00
	A J Kinsella & M A Stelling		
	Farnborough/South Queensferry		
	(NF 05.03.19)		

G-BZNC	Cyclone Pegasus Quantum 15-912	7736	25.10.00
	D E Wall (Alcester)		04.08.17P

G-BZND	Sopwith Pup Replica	xxxx	27.09.00
	Cancelled 26.04.18 by CAA		19.08.11
	Watchford Farm, Yarncombe		
	Built by B F Goddard – project PFA 101-11815		
	Stored 06.12 as 'N5199' in RNAS c/s		

G-BZNF	Colt 120A	4866	13.11.00
	M Torlo Capaccio, Campania, Italy		
	'Grand St Bernard' – 'Le Tunnel'		15.11.17E
	Built by Cameron Balloons Ltd		

G-BZNH	Rans S-6-ES Coyote II	0899.1333	18.10.00
	B A Coombe Deanland		23.08.12P
	Built by V Whiting – project PFA 204-13660;		
	tricycle u/c (IE 21.04.17)		

G-BZNI	Bell 206B-2 JetRanger II	2142	04.10.00
	LN-ORN, G-BZNI, G-ODIG, G-NEEP, N777FW, N3CR		
	Shaw Grove Aviation Ltd (Lilley, Luton)		06.02.19E

G-BZNJ   Rans S-6-ES Coyote II   0700.1382   23.10.00
             R A McKee   Kernan Valley, Tandragee   02.09.16P
             Built by S P Read – project PFA 204-13640;
             tailwheel u/c (IE 02.07.17)

G-BZNK   Morane Saulnier MS.315E D2   354   02.11.00
             F-BCNY, French AF   R H Cooper & S Swallow
             Dunkeswell   01.11.18P
             As '354' in French AF c/s

G-BZNM   Cyclone Pegasus Quantum 15   7754   20.11.00
             M Ward   (Warrington)   29.01.19P

G-BZNN   Beech 76 Duchess   ME-343   25.10.00
             N6133P, F-GHSU, N6722L   Flew LLP Bournemouth   02.05.18E
             Operated by Bournemouth Commercial Flight Training

G-BZNP   Thruster T600N 450   0100-T600N-047   27.10.00
             P D Twissell   Priory Farm, Tibenham   27.06.17P
             Badged 'Sprint'

G-BZNV   Lindstrand LBL 31A   741   12.12.00
             G R Down   Biddenden, Ashford   01.08.19E

G-BZNW   Isaacs Fury II   xxxx   10.11.00
             S M Johnston   RAF Linton-on-Ouse   29.08.18P
             Built by J E D Rogerson – project PFA 011-13402;
             as 'K2048' in RAF c/s

G-BZNY   Europa Aviation Europa XS   401   14.11.00
             W J Harrison   Cambridge   *'November Yankee'*   31.07.18P
             Built by A K Middlemas – project PFA 247-13355;
             tricycle u/c

G-BZOB   Slepcev Storch   xxxx   21.11.00
             P J Clegg   Woolston Moss, Warrington   25.04.18P
             Built by J E Ashby – project PFA 316-13592;
             as '6G+ED' in Luftwaffe c/s

G-BZOE   Cyclone Pegasus Quantum 15   7723   14.09.00
             B Dale   (Sandwich)   18.02.18P

G-BZOF   Montgomerie-Bensen B.8MR   SJML1 & MGM3   07.11.00
             S J M Ledingham   Kirkbride   06.11.18P
             Built by S J M Ledingham & M G Mee

G-BZOI   Nicollier HN.700 Menestrel II   122   27.10.00
             S J McCollum   Newtownards   22.05.18P
             Built by S J McCollum – project PFA 217-12604

G-BZOL   Robin R3000/140   124   20.12.00
             F-GEKZ   M A Stott   Exeter Int'l   13.04.18E

G-BZOM   RotorWay Exec 162F   6243   26.03.19
             G-RALF, G-BZOM, N767SG
             I C Bedford   Marsh Farm, Skegness

G-BZON   Scottish Aviation Bulldog Srs 120/121   BH120/214   19.12.00
             XX528   D J Critchley   Earls Colne   21.12.18P
             As 'XX528:D' in RAF white & red c/s with
             Oxford UAS badge

G-BZOO   Cyclone Pegasus Quantum 15-912   7702   15.08.00
             D W Guest   (Tring)   08.10.18P

G-BZOR   Team Mini-Max 91   2160 P   09.08.00
             T P V Sheppard   Farley Farm, Farley Chamberlayne
             Built by A Watt – project PFA 186-13312
             (SSDR microlight since 10.14) (IE 05.07.17)

G-BZOU   Cyclone Pegasus Quantum 15-912   7768   22.03.01
             M A Bradford   (Little Hallingbury, Bishops Stortford)   27.05.17P

G-BZOW   Whittaker MW7   xxxx   15.12.00
             G W Peacock   (Dunsville, Doncaster)
             Built by G W Peacock – project PFA 171-13118
             (NF 07.02.18)

G-BZOX   Colt 90B   10000   08.02.01
             D J Head   Newbury   27.12.18E
             Built by Cameron Balloons Ltd

G-BZOZ   Van's RV-6   21459   14.09.00
             M & S Sheppard   Cambridge   15.06.18P
             Built by V Edmundson – project PFA 181A-12455

G-BZPA   Mainair Blade 912S   1264-1100-7-W1058   13.12.00
             W McDowell   Slieve Croob, Castlewellan   01.05.10P
             (NF 16.01.17)

G-BZPB[M]   Hawker Hunter GA.Mk.11   41H-670758   15.01.01
             WV256   Cancelled 16.03.11 by CAA   *As 'WV256'*   17.07.03
             With Cornwall Aviation Heritage Centre, Newquay Cornwall

G-BZPC   Hawker Hunter GA.11   HABL-003061   15.01.01
             XF300   Cancelled 16.03.11 by CAA   20.02.04
             Not Known   *As 'WB188' prototype in all-red c/s,*
             sold on ebay 06.17

G-BZPD   Cameron V-65   4700   10.11.00
             P Spellward   Heidelburg, Germany   31.01.15E

G-BZPF   Scheibe SF24B Motorspatz I   4028   19.01.01
             D-KROA, PH-971, OE-9005, (D-KECO)
             D & M Shrimpton   (RAF Keevil)   10.06.19P

G-BZPG   Beech C24R Sierra   MC-556   27.03.01
             N23840   Peter J Ward Nurseryman Ltd
             (Leverington, Wisbech)   12.10.18E

G-BZPH   Van's RV-4   4007   06.09.00
             A G Truman tr G-BZPH RV4 Group
             Slay Barn Farm, Cuddesdon   02.07.18P
             Built by A G Truman – project PFA 181-12867

G-BZPI   SOCATA TB-20 Trinidad   1814   20.12.00
             SX-ATT   P G Leonard   Little Gransden   02.05.19E

G-BZPK   Cameron C-80   4183   23.02.01
             D L Homer   Hook   06.12.07
             (NF 24.06.16)

G-BZPN   Mainair Blade 912S   1268-0101-7-W1062   25.01.01
             J Kilpatrick   (Ruskey Convoy, Lifford, Co Donegal, RoI)
             (NF 17.08.18)

G-BZPP   Westland Wasp HAS.1   F9675   15.01.01
             XT793   Cancelled 07.09.12 as PWFU   24.03.11
             Thruxton   *As 'XT793' in Royal Navy c/s;*
             wreck stored 01.16

G-BZPS   Scottish Aviation Bulldog Srs 120/121   BH120/316   08.01.01
             XX658   M J Miller & A J Robinson   Audley End
             (NF 16.02.16)

G-BZPV   Lindstrand LBL 90B HAB   727   17.01.01
             Cancelled 15.01.13 as PWFU   31.10.11
             Not Known   *Inflated Donnington Grove Club 01.19*

G-BZPW   Cameron V-77   6245   02.02.01
             N4463V   J Vonka   Wargrave, Reading   27.05.19E

G-BZPX   Ultramagic S-105   105/78   12.02.01
             G M Houston t/a Scotair Balloons   Mountaincross, West Linton
             'Re/Max'   12.06.17E

G-BZPY   Ultramagic H-31   31/03   12.02.01
             G M Houston t/a Scotair Balloons
             Mountaincross, West Linton *'Re/Max'*   12.06.17E

G-BZPZ   Mainair Blade   1265-1200-7-W1059   23.01.01
             R A W Young   (Wellington, Telford)   28.02.18P

G-BZRC   de Havilland DH.115 Vampire T.11   15143   26.03.01
             WZ584   Cancelled 22.02.05 by CAA
             Binbrook   *Open store as 'WZ584'*

G-BZRD[M]   de Havilland DH.115 Vampire T.11   15687   27.03.01
             XH313   Cancelled 22.02.05 by CAA   *As 'XH313:E'*
             With Tangmere Military Aviation Museum

G-BZRE[M]   Hunting Percival P 56 Provost T 1   PAC/F/234   15.05.01
             '7688M', WW450, G-BZRE, 7689M
             Cancelled 22.02.05 by CAA   *As 'WW421:P-B'*
             Composite aircraft, fuselage ex WW450 & wings
             ex WW421: carries 'G-BZRE' below tailplane
             With Bournemouth Aviation Museum, Bournemouth

G-BZRF   Percival P.56 Provost T.1   PAC/F/062   15.05.01
             7698M, WV499   P B Childs   Westonzoyland
             As 'WV499'; on rebuild 02.19 (NF 27.06.16)

G-BZRJ   Cyclone Pegasus Quantum 15-912   7783   05.02.01
             D A Hutchinson   (Mexborough)   14.04.18P

G-BZRO   Piper PA-30 Twin Comanche C   30-1923   02.03.01
             SE-IYL, D-GATI, I-KATI, N8767Y
             S M Bogduikiewicz & K V Shail
             tr Gloucester Comanche Group   Gloucestershire   09.04.18E

G-BZRP   Pegasus Quantum 15-912   7758   24.01.01
             M F Sheerman-Chase   Wolverhampton Halfpenny Green   29.06.18P
             QuantumLeap modifications

G-BZRR   Cyclone Pegasus Quantum 15-912   7727   04.10.00
             R Halford & K Robson tr BZRR Syndicate
             (Loughborough/Nottingham)   04.10.17P

G-BZRS   Eurocopter EC135 T2+   0166   22.03.01
             Babcock Mission Critical Services Onshore Ltd
             (Gloucestershire)   15.03.18E

G-BZRV Van's RV-6 60435 12.10.00
N M Hitchman   Hinton-in-the-Hedges 15.07.18P
Built by E & P Hicks & N M Hitchman
– project PFA 181A-13573

G-BZRW Mainair Blade 912S 1266-0101-7-W1060 06.02.01
G J E Alcorn   Newtownards 18.04.13P
(IE 05.07.17)

G-BZRY Rans S-6-ES Coyote II 0600.1375 01.02.01
M J Buchanan   Coldharbour Farm, Willingham 21.12.18P
Built by S Forman – project PFA 204-13666

G-BZRZ Thunder Ax11-250 Series 2 10013 11.10.01
A C K Rawson & J J Rudoni
Priory Farm, Tibenham   *'Kinetic'* 11.10.09E
Built by Cameron Balloons Ltd; stored at
Priory Farm, Tibenham 01.19 (NF 20.03.18)

G-BZSB Pitts S-1S xxxx 02.02.01
A D Ingold   Leicester 02.10.19P
Built by A D Ingold – project PFA 009-13697

G-BZSC Sopwith F.1 Camel replica NAW-3 15.01.01
Richard Shuttleworth Trustees   Old Warden   *'Ikanopit'* 29.08.18P
Built by Northern Aeroplane Workshops & completed
Shuttleworth Collection – project PFA173-14714;
as 'D1851:X' in RFC 70 Sqdn c/s

G-BZSE Hawker Hunter T.8B 41H-670788 06.02.01
9096M, WV322 Canfield Hunter Ltd   North Weald 19.11.11P
Has centre fuselage ex WV318 (c/n 41H-670788), plate
altered to 'HABL/R/41H-670792' (see G-FFOX): c/n
plate indicates built Blackpool but WV318 & WV322 built
Kingston-on-Thames as F.4s; as 'WV322' in Royal Navy
'Admiral's Barge' c/s; on restoration 11.18 (NF 08.12.17)

G-BZSG Cyclone Pegasus Quantum 15-912 7766 22.02.01
A J Harris   Navan, RoI 08.05.17P

G-BZSH Ultramagic H-77 77/191 12.04.01
P M G Vale   Hurcott, Kidderminster 16.09.10E
(IE 28.02.17)

G-BZSI Cyclone Pegasus Quantum 15 7787 12.03.01
T J Drew   (Theale, Wedmore) 27.05.19P

G-BZSM Cyclone Pegasus Quantum 15 7788 23.02.01
G Jenkinson   Deenethorpe 19.11.18P

G-BZSO Ultramagic M-77C 77/190 22.03.02
C C Duppa-Miller   Compton Verney, Warwick 27.09.18E

G-BZSP Stemme S 10-V 10-14 10.05.01
HB-2217, D-KDNE   L Bleaken & A Flewelling
Aston Down   *'626'* 21.10.18E
Official regd as Stemme S 10 but converted to
S 10-V when HB-2217; c/n should be 14-014M

G-BZSS Cyclone Pegasus Quantum 15-912 7770 06.02.01
A P & J M Cadd   (Steeple Aston, Bicester) 19.07.19P

G-BZST Avtech Jabiru UL-450 0400 13.02.01
M D Tulloch   Pittrichie Farm, Whiterashes 28.08.18P
Built by G Hammond – project PFA 274A-13616

G-BZSX Cyclone Pegasus Quantum 15-912 7789 23.02.01
G Reid   Redlands 08.10.18P

G-BZSZ Avtech Jabiru UL-450 220 16.02.01
D W Allen   (Pawlett, Bridgwater) 14.02.19P
Built by F Overall & R Riley – project PFA 274A-13432

G-BZTA Robinson R44 Raven 0968 20.02.01
Jarretts Motors Ltd   Headcorn 25.09.18E

G-BZTC Team Mini-Max 91 2201 P 23.01.01
G G Clayton   Woodlands Barton Farm, Roche
Built by G G Clayton – project PFA 186-13336
(SSDR microlight since 06.14) (IE 28.07.17)

G-BZTD Thruster T600T 450 Jab 0021-T600T-049 22.02.01
A R Hughes   Yatesbury
Badged 'Sprint'; damaged near Newbury 22.09.17;
Permit to Fly suspended 30.09.17

G-BZTH Europa Aviation Europa 010 21.12.00
D J Shipley   Wolverhampton Halfpenny Green 06.07.18P
Built by T J Houlihan – project PFA 247-12494; force
landed near Main Street, Long Compton 04.08.17
& substantially damaged; tailwheel u/c (NF 19.12.17)

G-BZTK Cameron V-90 10083 06.03.01
E Appollodorus   St Leonards-on-Sea 06.07.11E
(NF 10.08.17)

G-BZTM Mainair Blade 1273-0201-7-W1068 12.02.01
I Stanulet   (Sunderland)
(SSDR microlight since 01.19)

G-BZTN Europa Aviation Europa XS 504 16.03.01
P R Norwood   Bournemouth 15.08.19P
Built by J Dewberry, W Pringle & S A Smith
– project PFA 247-1371; tricycle u/c

G-BZTS Cameron Bertie Bassett-90 10050 03.05.01
Trebor Bassett Ltd   Uxbridge   *'Bertie Bassett'* 16.07.10E
Active 05.18 (NF 19.09.16)

G-BZTU Mainair Blade 912 1272-0201-7-W1066 08.02.01
C T Halliday   Ince 17.02.16P

G-BZTV Mainair Blade 912S 1278-0301-7-W1073 02.04.01
R D McManus   (Bignall End, Stoke-on-Trent) 13.10.16P

G-BZTW Huntwing Avon 582(1) 9906092 17.01.01
T S Walker   Arclid Green, Sandbach 25.06.13P
Built by T S Walker- project BMAA/HB/136
(NF 06.10.17)

G-BZTX Mainair Blade 912 1267-0101-7-W1061 09.02.01
K A Ingham   Northrepps 08.04.16P

G-BZTY Avtech Jabiru UL-450 0288 01.03.01
R P Lewis   White House Farm, Southery 24.04.18P
Built by R P Lewis – project PFA 274A-13533

G-BZUB Mainair Blade 1274-0201-7-W1069 27.03.01
J Campbell   (Reigate) 13.08.18P

G-BZUC Cyclone Pegasus Quantum 15-912 7796 10.04.01
J J D Firmino do Carmo   Lagos, Algarve, Portugal 06.05.13P
Operated by Algarve Air Sports (NF 01.07.15)

G-BZUD Lindstrand LBL 105A 780 27.03.01
D Venegoni   Varese, Italy 08.05.18E

G-BZUE Cyclone Pegasus Quantum 15 7800 23.04.01
D T Richardson   (Little Oakley, Corby) 10.08.19P

G-BZUF Mainair Rapier 1277-0301-7-W1072 27.03.01
B Craig   Oban 28.07.16P

G-BZUG TLAC RL7A Sherwood Ranger XP "0020" 23.03.01
J G Boxall   Pittodrie House, Pitcaple 29.09.18P
Built by S P Sharp – project PFA 237-13040;
as 'SR-XP020' in pseudo RAF c/s

G-BZUH Rans S-6-ES Coyote II 0600.1371 26.03.01
R A Darley   Bagby 20.09.16P
Built by G M Prowling – project PFA 204-13716; tricycle u/c

G-BZUI Cyclone Pegasus Quantum 15-912 7798 08.05.01
A P Slade   Field Farm, Oakley 22.08.18P

G-BZUL Avtech Jabiru UL-450 0451 28.03.01
J G Campbell   Low Hill Farm, North Moor, Messingham 16.11.18P
Built by P Hawkins – project PFA 274A-13678

G-BZUP Raj Hamsa X'Air Jabiru(3) 624 24.04.01
M T Sheelan   (Carlingford, Co Louth, RoI) 04.09.17P
Built by I A J Lappin – project BMAA/HB/164

G-BZUU Cameron O-90 10058 14.06.01
D C Ball   Tringford, Tring   *'Elmo II'* 17.08.10E
(NF 30.08.17)

G-BZUV Cameron H-24 2665 27.04.01
LX-JLW   J N Race   Ringmer, Lewes 27.09.09E
(NF 25.02.17)

G-BZUX Cyclone Pegasus Quantum 15 7819 22.05.01
C Gorvett   (Skewen, Neath) 17.04.18P

G-BZUY Van's RV-6 60249 23.05.01
D J Butt   (Northampton) 29.08.19P
Built by K F Crumplin & D M Gale
– project PFA 181A-13471

G-BZUZ Hunt Avon Blade R100(1) xxxx 09.02.01
C F Janes   (Baker Barracks, Thorney Island) 16.08.18P
Built by J A Hunt – project BMAA/HB/162;
Mainair wing c/n W1067 & trike (No.4) ex G-MMGT

G-BZVA Zenair CH.701UL 7-9145 21.03.01
W K MacGillivray   Insch 05.04.19P
Built by M W Taylor – project PFA 187-13635

G-BZVB Reims FR172H Rocket FR17200327 29.08.00
G-BLMX, PH-RPC   Victor Bravo Group Ltd
Brighton City 21.02.18E

G-BZVI	Nova Vertex 24 M Hay (Dundee) *Hang-glider*	13379	24.05.01
G-BZVJ	Cyclone Pegasus Quantum 15 R Blackhall Tain	7821	12.06.01 31.08.18P
G-BZVK	Raj Hamsa X'Air 582(11) R J Hamilton Newcastle, RoI *Built by K P Taylor – project BMAA/HB/152*	592	22.02.01 17.08.18P
G-BZVM	Rans S-6-ES Coyote II M P Booth (Deal) *Built by N N Ducker – project PFA 204-13705*	1000.1394ES	01.03.01 19.06.19P
G-BZVN	Van's RV-6 A G Felce tr Syndicate RV6 G-BZVN Chiltern Park, Wallingford *Built by J A Booth – project PFA 181A-13188*	xxxx	25.04.01 07.02.18P
G-BZVR	Raj Hamsa X'Air 582(4) R F E Berry Davidstow Moor *Built by E Bowen, R P Sims & P Travis – project BMAA/HB/146*	566	13.03.01 13.09.15P
G-BZVT	III Sky Arrow 650 T E M Goldsmith Orchard House, Crockham Hill *(uilt by R N W Wright – project PFA 298-13333*	K116	23.03.01 23.08.19P
G-BZVU	Cameron Z-105 Ballooning Network Ltd Bristol BS3 'The Mall, Cribbs Causeway, Bristol'	10078	09.08.01 31.12.16E
G-BZVV	Cyclone Pegasus Quantum 15-912 J Giladjian & S Smith Henstridge	7793	12.03.01 21.01.19P
G-BZVW	Ilyushin Il-2 Stormovik Sov.AF 1870710 R H Cooper & S Swallow Wickenby *(NF 07.12.15)*	1870710	16.05.01
G-BZVX	Ilyushin Il-2 Stormovik Sov.AF 1878576 R H Cooper & S Swallow Wickenby *Stored externally 11.12 (NF 07.12.15).*	1878576	16.05.01
G-BZWB	Mainair Blade 912 O M Blythin & L G Penson tr Caernarfon Red 1 Caernarfon	1284-0501-7-W1079	26.04.01 10.07.19P
G-BZWC	Raj Hamsa X'Air Falcon 912(1) J Webb Manchester Barton *Built by G A J Salter – project BMAA/HB/157*	587	09.05.01 23.05.18P
G-BZWJ	CFM Streak Shadow SA T A Morgan Stonefield Park, Chilbolton 'Harmony Angel' *Built by T A Morgan – project PFA 206-13553*	K 338	08.05.01 16.05.18P
G-BZWK	Avtech Jabiru SK M Housley (Brothertoft, Boston) *Built by R Thompson – project PFA 274-13292*	0170	08.05.01 26.07.18P
G-BZWM	Cyclone Pegasus XL-Q D T Evans Broadmeadow Farm, Hereford *Built by using Trike SW-TE-0136 ex G-MVKM (NF 28.09.15)*	7792	18.05.01 24.06.04P
G-BZWN	Van's RV-8 A J Symms High Ham, Langport *Built by R D Harper & A J Symms – project PFA 303-13692 (IE 08.12.17)*	81021	14.05.01 23.10.19P
G-BZWR	Mainair Rapier M A Steele (Closeburn, Thornhill) *(IE 06.11.17)*	1275-0301-7-W1070	07.03.01 01.10.16P
G-BZWS	Cyclone Pegasus Quantum 15-912 J D Parker-Cullen tr G-BZWS Syndicate Knapthorpe Lodge, Caunton	7813	26.04.01 25.05.18P
G-BZWT	Tecnam P92-EA Echo R F Cooper Field Farm, Oakley *Built by R F Cooper – project PFA 318-13681; badged 'P92S'*	419	17.05.01 25.03.19P
G-BZWU	Cyclone Pegasus Quantum 15-912 M D Evans Northrepps 'Little Evie'	7831	19.07.01 30.06.18P
G-BZWV	Steen Skybolt D E Blaxland Stow Maries *Built by P D Begley – project PFA 064-10751*	xxxx	30.05.01 22.05.18P
G-BZWX	Whittaker MW5-D Sorcerer J Bate Rossall Field, Cockerham *Built by P G Depper – project PFA 163-13599 (SSDR microlight since 06.14) (NF 01.12.14)*	xxxx	01.06.01
G-BZWZ	Van's RV-6 G J Hardwick tr Bizzy Wizzy Group White Waltham *Built by J Shanley – project PFA 181A-13419*	60237	26.04.01 14.03.18P
G-BZXA	Raj Hamsa X'Air V2 (2) Cancelled 02.09.15 as PWFU Coachford, Aberdeen *Built by D W Mullin – project BMAA/HB/148; open store 08.15*	560	31.05.01 19.10.11
G-BZXB	Van's RV-6 G W Cunningham & R A Pritchard Old Buckenham *Built by D J Akerman & B J King-Smith – project PFA 181A-13625*	xxxx	04.06.01 25.05.18P
G-BZXC	Scottish Aviation Bulldog Srs.120/121 XX612 Cancelled 05.03.08 as PWFU Ayr College *As instructional airframe 09.13 as 'XX612:03-A'*	BH120/260	08.06.01 15.01.09
G-BZXI	Nova Philou 26 M Hay (Dundee)	11207	16.05.01
G-BZXK	Robin HR.200-120B F-GNNV Edghill Aviation Services Ltd (Monasterevin, Co Kildare, RoI)	286	12.06.01 05.04.19E
G-BZXM	Mainair Blade 912 S Dolan St Michaels	1283-0501-7-W1078	20.04.01 01.08.18P
G-BZXN	Avtech Jabiru UL-450 D A Hall & A G Sparshott Solent *Built by A R Silvester – project PFA 274A-13747*	xxxx	07.06.01 10.09.18P
G-BZXO	Cameron Z-105 J Dyer Farnborough GU14 'Innogy'	10125	27.06.01 27.06.18E
G-BZXP	Air Création Buggy 582(1)/Kiss 400 A Fairbrother Sywell *Built by P M Dewhurst – project BMAA/HB/169 (Flylight kit FL001 comprising trike s/n T00100 & wing s/n A00056-0054)*	FL001	14.06.01 24.06.18P
G-BZXR	Cameron N-90 F R Battersby Worsley, Manchester	10124	03.09.01 25.05.18E
G-BZXS	Scottish Aviation Bulldog Srs 120/121 XX631 K J Thompson Sligo, RoI *As 'XX631:W' in RAF c/s (NF 13.02.17)*	BH120/296	21.06.01 07.05.10E
G-BZXT	Mainair Blade 912 J D Sings & S C Stinchcombe (Newton Abbot & South Molton)	1286-0501-7-W1081	25.05.01 29.09.18P
G-BZXV	Cyclone Pegasus Quantum 15-912 P I Oliver Rufforth East	7828	28.06.01 29.08.18P
G-BZXW	Magni M16 Tandem Trainer G-NANA P J Troy-Davies Brook Farm, Pilling *Built by J W P Lewis – project PFA G/12-1249 (NF 28.10.15)*	xxxx	30.04.01
G-BZXX	Cyclone Pegasus Quantum 15-912 D J Johnston & D Ostle (Penrith)	7812	20.04.01 01.06.18P
G-BZXY	Robinson R44 Raven Flight Checks Ltd Earls Colne	1027	12.06.01 10.08.18E
G-BZXZ	Scottish Aviation Bulldog Srs 120/121 XX629 C N Wright Turweston *As 'XX629' in RAF white & red c/s*	BH120/294	01.06.01 22.03.19E
G-BZYA	Rans S-6-ES Coyote II M E Lockett (Nuneaton) *Built by D J Clack – project PFA 204-13529; tricycle u/c*	0499.1313	12.06.01 19.09.19P
G-BZYD	Westland SA.341B Gazelle AH.1 XZ329 C D Meek Deanland *C/n 1652 also quoted; as 'XZ329:J' in AAC c/s*	1648	14.06.01 11.05.19P
G-BZYG	DG Flugzeugbau DG-505MB R C Bromwich Keevil '94' *Built by DG Flugzeugbau GmbH*	5E220B15	25.09.01 12.01.20E
G-BZYI	Nova Phocus 123 M Hay (Dundee) *Hang-glider*	9748	08.06.01
G-BZYK	Avtech Jabiru UL-450 S J Carr (Finchampstead) *Built by A S Forbes – project PFA 274A-13227*	140	21.06.01 07.08.19P
G-BZYN	Cyclone Pegasus Quantum 15-912 J Cannon Longacre Farm, Sandy	7835	15.08.01 04.08.18P
G-BZYR	Cameron N-31 C J Sanger-Davies Hawarden CH5 'Benadryl'	10137	06.08.01 17.07.18E

G-BZYS	Micro B.22S Bantam	94-001	12.07.01
	ZK-JDO D L Howell Middle Stoke, Isle of Grain		12.09.02P
	(NF 02.09.14)		

G-BZYU	Whittaker MW6 Merlin	xxxx	02.07.01
	B J Syson Enstone		
	Built by K J Cole – project PFA 164-13647		
	(SSDR microlight since 08.14) (IE 30.05.17)		

G-BZYX	Raj Hamsa X'Air 700(1A)	653	15.06.01
	A M Sutton Shifnal		29.04.18P
	Built by A G Marsh – project BMAA/HB/173		

| G-BZYY | Cameron N-90 | 10130 | 30.08.01 |
| | M E Mason   Bristol BS6   *'up'* & *'down'* | | 23.05.18E |

G-CAAA – G-CAZZ

G-CAHA	Piper PA-34-200T Seneca II	34-7770010	07.07.98
	N23PL, SE-GPY, (D-IIIC), SE-GPY		
	Tayside Aviation Ltd Dundee		23.10.18E

| G-CALL | Piper PA-23-250 Aztec F | 27-7754061 | 21.12.77 |
| | N62826   J D Moon   Isle of Man | | 05.09.18E |

G-CAMM	Hawker Cygnet replica	xxxx	30.05.91
	(G-ERDB) Richard Shuttleworth Trustees		
	Old Warden *'6'*		09.03.18P
	Built by D M Cashmore – project PFA 077-10245;		
	carries 'G-CAMM' on top of wings		

G-CAMR	BFC Challenger II	xxxx	26.03.99
	P R A Walker (Kingston, Ringwood)		05.04.10P
	Built by P R A Walker – project PFA 177A-12659		
	using BFC kit; Damaged Old Sarum 2009 (NF 24.02.16)		

G-CAPI	Mudry CAP 10B	76	16.03.99
	G-BEXR C A Wills tr PI Group		
	(Orchard House, Littleport)		11.11.19E

G-CAPX	Mudry CAP 10B	280	21.09.98
	H J Pessall Leicester		11.08.18E
	Built by Akrotech Europe		

G-CBAA – G-CBZZ

| G-CBAD | Mainair Blade 912 | 1287-0601-7-W1082 | 08.06.01 |
| | J Stocking   Shifnal | | 29.11.18P |

G-CBAF	Neico Lancair 320	577	11.06.01
	L H V & M v Cleeff Lydd		17.07.05P
	Built by R W Fairless – project PFA 191-13567		
	(NF 20.10.14)		

| G-CBAK | Robinson R44 Clipper | 1089 | 02.08.01 |
| | Phoenix Building Systems Ltd   Beverley (Linley Hill) | | 31.07.19E |

G-CBAL	Piper PA-28-161 Warrior II	28-8116087	25.03.94
	LN-MAD, N83007 L E Harley tr CBAL Flying Group		
	Redhill		24.03.18E

G-CBAN	Scottish Aviation Bulldog Srs 120/121	BH120/326	26.07.01
	XX668 A C S Reynolds RNAS Yeovilton		12.04.17P
	As 'XX668:I' in RAF c/s (IE 16.05.17)		

G-CBAP	Zenair CH.601ULA Zodiac	6-9132	12.07.01
	G D Summers Lamb Holm Farm, Holm		11.04.18P
	Built by L J Lowry – project PFA 162A-13656; tricycle u/c		

G-CBAR	Stoddard-Hamilton GlaStar	54232	18.05.01
	E A Gibson tr Fishburn Flyers Morgansfield, Fishburn		11.05.18P
	Built by C M Barnes – project PFA 295-13133; tricycle u/c		

G-CBAS	Rans S-6-ES Coyote II	1100.1399ES	04.07.01
	S Stockill RAF Halton		06.06.18P
	Built by S R Green – project PFA 204-13688; tailwheel u/c		

| G-CBAT | Cameron Z-90 | 10099 | 01.06.01 |
| | British Telecommunications PLC   Thatcham   *'Ignite'* | | 10.05.18E |

G-CBAU	Rand Robinson KR-2	xxxx	11.07.01
	C B Copsey (Braintree)		
	Built by B Normington – project PFA 129-12789;		
	stored 04.14 (NF 19.02.16)		

| G-CBAW | Cameron A-300 | 10148 | 16.04.02 |
| | Bailey Balloons Ltd   Whimple, Exeter | | 28.06.16E |

G-CBAX	Tecnam P92-EA Echo	TEC/007	26.06.01
	L Collier (Honiton)		02.04.18P
	Built by R P Reeves – project PFA 318-13698		

G-CBAZ	Rans S-6-ES Coyote II	0998.1267	12.07.01
	E S Wills Marldon Lane, Marldon		31.10.18P
	Built by G V Willder – project PFA 204-13596		

| G-CBBB | Cyclone Pegasus Quantum 15-912 | 7827 | 22.06.01 |
| | F A Dimmock   (Long Sutton, Spalding) | | 21.06.18P |

G-CBBC	Scottish Aviation Bulldog Srs 120/121	BH120/201	08.06.01
	XX515 Bulldog Flyers Ltd Blackbushe		19.06.18E
	As 'XX515:4' in RAF c/s		

G-CBBF	Beech 76 Duchess	ME-352	23.07.01
	OY-BED, EI-BHS Flew LLP Bournemouth		12.10.14E
	Stored minus engines outside Airtime Aviation 07.16		
	(IE 23.01.18)		

| G-CBBG | Mainair Blade | 1291-0601-7-W1086 | 23.07.01 |
| | B Donnan   (Rugby) | | 01.09.18P |

G-CBBH	Raj Hamsa X'Air V2(2)	435	19.07.01
	D J Lewis Little Trostrey Farm, Kemeys Commander		05.10.13P
	Built by W G Colyer – project BMAA/HB/143		
	(IE 06.09.17)		

G-CBBK	Robinson R22 Beta II	3233	26.07.01
	EI-CWP, G-CBBK R J Everett (Sproughton, Ipswich)		14.08.09E
	(NF 30.09.14)		

G-CBBL	Scottish Aviation Bulldog Srs 120/121	BH120/243	08.08.01
	XX550 A Cunningham Abbeyshrule, RoI		12.07.18E
	As 'XX550:Z' in RAF c/s		

G-CBBM	ICP MXP-740 Savannah VG Jabiru(1)	01-03-51-062	10.08.01
	J Pavelin Barling		31.07.18P
	Built by S Whittaker & P J Wilson – project BMAA/HB/176		

| G-CBBN | Cyclone Pegasus Quantum 15-912 | 7844 | 09.08.01 |
| | P D Rowe tr G-CBBN Flying Group   (Taunton) | | 01.09.18P |

G-CBBO	Whittaker MW5-D Sorcerer	xxxx	23.07.01
	P J Gripton Baxby Manor, Husthwaite		
	Built by P J Gripton – project PFA 163-13443		
	(SSDR microlight since 06.14) (IE 15.08.16)		

G-CBBP	Cyclone Pegasus Quantum 15-912	7843	31.07.01
	A C Richards Mill Farm, Hughley		06.08.16P
	(NF 06.10.17)		

G-CBBS	Scottish Aviation Bulldog Srs 120/121	BH120/343	08.08.01
	XX694 D R Keene Turweston		27.09.18P
	As 'XX694:E' in RAF c/s		

G-CBBT	Scottish Aviation Bulldog Srs 120/121	BH120/344	08.08.01
	XX695 K A Johnston Perth		26.09.18E
	As 'XX695' in RAF c/s, coded 'C' on one side and		
	'M' on other		

G-CBBW	Scottish Aviation Bulldog Srs 120/121	BH120/277	01.08.01
	XX619 S E Robottom-Scott Coventry		15.09.16P
	As 'XX619:T' in RAF c/s (IE 06.11.17)		

G-CBCB	Scottish Aviation Bulldog Srs 120/121	BH120/223	25.09.01
	XX537 M W Minary Turweston		06.02.19P
	As 'XX537:C' in RAF yellow & black c/s		

| G-CBCD | Cyclone Pegasus Quantum 15 | 7845 | 06.08.01 |
| | I A Lumley   Reagill Grange, Crosby Ravensworth | | 18.09.16P |

| G-CBCF | Cyclone Pegasus Quantum 15-912 | 7846 | 23.08.01 |
| | P A Bromley   Darley Moor | | 23.05.18P |

G-CBCH	Zenair CH.701UL	7-4143	08.08.01
	I J McNally (Ringmer, Lewes)		
	Built by L G Millen – project PFA 187-13568		
	(NF 01.07.14)		

G-CBCI	Raj Hamsa X'Air 582(11)	659	09.08.01
	R McKie (Southampton)		06.08.18P
	Built by P A Gilford – project BMAA/HB/180		

G-CBCL	Stoddard-Hamilton GlaStar	5309	05.09.97
	D W Parfrey Fenland		31.05.18P
	Built by C J Norman – project PFA 295-13089; tricycle u/c		

G-CBCM	Raj Hamsa X'Air 700(1A)	656	23.07.01
	C Childs North Coates		11.01.18P
	Built by A Hipkin – project BMAA/HB/177		

G-CBCP	Van's RV-6A	60444	06.08.01
	A M Smyth tr G-CBCP Group Crowfield		30.05.18P
	Built by A M Smyth – project PFA 181A-13643		

G-CBCR	Scottish Aviation Bulldog Srs 120/121	BH120/351	05.09.01
	XX702 D Clarke & S Lester tr Seven 0 Two		
	Flying Group (Purley & Arundel)		27.06.19P
	As 'XX702' in RAF c/s		

G-CBCY Beech C24R Sierra MC-491 26.09.01
N881RS, PH-HLA J Waldie (Winfarthing, Norfolk) 24.03.11E
Displayed 07.17 Anglia Bed Centre (Route B1077)
in all purple c/s & less marks (NF 22.02.17)

G-CBCZ CFM Streak Shadow SLA K 340-SLA 13.09.01
J O Kane Rayne Hall Farm, Rayne *'Alana Rose'* 19.06.18P
Built by J A Hambleton – project PFA 206-13586

G-CBDC Thruster T600N 450 Jab 0071-T600N-054 12.07.01
T J Gallagher (Dungannon) 25.07.19P
Badged 'Sprint'

G-CBDD Mainair Blade 912 1293-0701-7-W1088 01.08.01
G Hird (Midtown Steading, Glenquiech) 17.08.18P

G-CBDG Zenair CH.601HD Zodiac 6-9032 03.09.01
R E Lasnier Sleap 05.07.18P
Built by R E Lasnier – project PFA 162-13375; tricycle u/c

G-CBDH Flight Design CT2K 03-02-03-13 04.10.01
S J Goate Sywell 03.05.18P
Assembled Pegasus Aviation as c/n 784;
original fuselage kit was s/n 01-07-02-17

G-CBDI Denney Kitfox Model 2 xxxx 04.09.01
J G D Barbour Sheriff Hall Estate, Balgone 13.07.18P
Built by J G D Barbour – project PFA 172-11888

G-CBDJ Flight Design CT2K 01-07-01-17 11.10.01
P J Walker Griffins Farm, Temple Bruer 18.11.18P
Assembled Pegasus Aviation as c/n 7850

G-CBDK Scottish Aviation Bulldog Srs 120/121 BH120/259 26.09.01
XX611 J N Randle Coventry 29.08.18P
As 'XX611:7' in RAF c/s

G-CBDL Mainair Blade 1292-0701-7-W1087 01.08.01
T R Villa Priory Farm, Tibenham 23.09.17P
(IE 15.12.17)

G-CBDM Tecnam P92-EM Echo 568 11.07.01
J J Cozens RNAS Yeovilton 30.03.18P
Built by J J Cozens & C J Willy – project PFA 318-13756

G-CBDN Mainair Blade 1297-0801-7-W1092 20.09.01
T Peckham (Graveney, Faversham) 25.06.18P

G-CBDO Raj Hamsa X'Air 582(1) 583 12.11.01
A Campbell Newtownards 08.08.10P
Built by R T Henry – project BMAA/HB/170;
stored 05.14 at Newtownards

G-CBDP Mainair Blade 912 1295-0801-7-W1090 17.08.01
S T Hayes Headon Farm, Retford 03.12.18P

G-CBDS Scottish Aviation Bulldog Srs.120/121 BH120/356 27.07.01
XX707 Cancelled 13.05.14 by CAA 27.05.11
Caernarfon *Stored 08.15 as 'XX707' in RAF c/s*

G-CBDU Quad City Challenger II 1295.1459 14.09.01
E J Brooks Otherton
Built by B A Hiscox – project PFA 177-13000 (NF 28.06.16)

G-CBDV Raj Hamsa X'Air 582(6) 616 06.08.01
U J Anderson (Dyke, Bourne) 15.07.12P
Built by R J Brown & D J Prothero – project
BMAA/HB/161 (Raj Hamsa X'Air J22) (NF 28.11.14)

G-CBDX Cyclone Pegasus Quantum 15 7857 11.10.01
P Sinkler Rufforth 26.06.12P
(NF 02.08.17)

G-CBDZ Cyclone Pegasus Quantum 15-912 7852 11.09.01
P Smith (Beckingham, Doncaster) 08.08.18P

G-CBEB Air Création Buggy 582(1)/Kiss 400 FL003 03.10.01
M Harris Redlands
Built by P J R Bradshaw & A R R Williams – project
BMAA/HB/184 (Flylight kit FL003 comprising Trike
s/n xxxx & wing s/n A011135?)
(SSDR microlight since 06.14 (IE 31.05.17)

G-CBEE Piper PA-28R-200 Cherokee Arrow II 28R-7635055 05.10.01
N4479X IHC Ltd Biggin Hill 21.01.19E

G-CBEF Scottish Aviation Bulldog Srs 120/121 BH120/286 03.10.01
XX621 A L Butcher & F W Sandwell Little Gransden 08.03.18E
As 'XX621:H' in RAF red & white c/s

G-CBEH Scottish Aviation Bulldog Srs 120/121 BH120/207 28.09.01
XX521 J E Lewis Melhuish Farm, North Moreton 22.05.18E
As 'XX521:H' in RAF c/s

G-CBEI Piper PA-22-108 Colt 22-9136 05.06.02
SE-CZR D Sharp Breighton 02.03.18E

G-CBEJ Colt 120A 10181 11.10.01
Airxcite Ltd t/a Virgin Balloon Flights
Stafford Park, Telford 24.07.17E
Built by Cameron Balloons Ltd (NF 26.07.17)

G-CBEK Scottish Aviation Bulldog Srs 120/121 BH120/349 26.09.01
XX700 M J Searle (Waterlooville) 24.07.18P
As 'XX700:17' in RAF c/s

G-CBEL Hawker Fury FB.11 37539 06.08.01
VH-SFW, N36SF, G-CBEL, (D-FURI), (F-AZXL)
G-CBEL, N36SF, Iraqi AF 315
Anglia Aircraft Restorations Ltd Duxford 06.07.19P
As 'SR661:P' (representing Sea Fury prototype)

G-CBEM Mainair Blade 1294-0801-7-W1089 17.08.01
K W Bodley Otherton 29.09.18P

G-CBEN Cyclone Pegasus Quantum 15-912 7855 08.10.01
A T Cook (Rushton Spencer, Macclesfield) 08.09.17P

G-CBES Europa Aviation Europa 061 27.09.01
D J Shipley Wolverhampton Halfpenny Green 16.02.17P
Built by M R Hexley – project PFA 247-12691;
tailwheel u/c

G-CBEU Cyclone Pegasus Quantum 15-912 7869 16.10.01
Fula Ltd (St Albans) 19.09.17P

G-CBEV Cyclone Pegasus Quantum 15-912 7854 16.10.01
A W G Ambler (Market Rasen) 18.02.19P

G-CBEW Flight Design CT2K 01-08-02-23 19.10.01
A R Hughes tr Cruise Flight Group Yatesbury 09.08.18P
Assembled Pegasus Aviation as c/n 7868

G-CBEX Flight Design CT2K 01-08-01-23 29.10.01
A G Quinn Knapthorpe Lodge, Caunton 14.07.18P
Assembled Pegasus Aviation as c/n 7867

G-CBEY Cameron C-80 10190 31.10.01
M N Hume Twickenham 03.03.18E

G-CBEZ Robin DR.400-180 Régent 2511 26.02.02
K V Field Village Aeronautique des Lacs,
Biscarrosse, France 26.10.18E
Built by Constructions Aeronautiques de Bourgogne

G-CBFA Diamond DA.40 Star 40.063 25.10.01
Lyrastar Ltd Redhill 25.07.19E

G-CBFE Raj Hamsa X'Air 582(1) 636 19.10.01
A R Rainford (Winmarleigh, Preston) 23.10.18P
Built by S Whittle – project BMAA/HB/186

G-CBFJ Robinson R44 Raven 1131 07.11.01
M Klinge Glasgow Prestwick 30.03.18E

G-CBFK Murphy Rebel 264R 13.09.01
P J Gibbs (Zelah, Truro) 30.10.18P
Built by D Webb – project PFA 232-13340

G-CBFN Robin HR.100/200B Royal 112 01.03.02
F-BTBP A F Gillett (Berlbeck, Detmold, Germany) 26.09.19E

G-CBFO Cessna 172S Skyhawk SP 172S8929 22.10.01
N3520A P Warren-Gray Sturgate 25.05.18E

G-CBFP Scottish Aviation Bulldog Srs 120/121 BH120/306 29.10.01
XX636 R Nisbet tr Shacklewell Bulldog Group
Shacklewell Lodge Farm, Empingham 05.02.19E
As 'XX636:Y' in RAF c/s

G-CBFU Scottish Aviation Bulldog Srs 120/121 BH120/293 12.11.01
XX628 J R & S J Huggins Greenwood Farm, Alkham 05.10.18E
As 'XX628:9' in RAF c/s

G-CBFW Montgomerie-Bensen B.8MR xxxx 06.11.01
A J Thomas (Sutton Coldfield) 30.09.17P
Built by B F Pearson – project PFA G/01-1312

G-CBFX Rans S-6-ES Coyote II 1000.1392ES 08.11.01
O C Rash (Wicken, Cambs) 25.10.17P
Built by J Whiting – project PFA 204-13820;
tricycle u/c (IE 06.12.17)

G-CBGB Zenair CH.601UL Zodiac 6-9254 12.11.01
J F Woodham Hollow Hill Farm, Granborough 05.06.18P
Built by R Germany – project PFA 162A-13819;
tricycle u/c

G-CBGC SOCATA TB-10 Tobago 1584 21.09.01
VH-YHB P J Wills Bournemouth 09.04.17E
Test flown 27.09.18 (NF 10.10.17)

G-CBGD Zenair CH.701UL 7-9255 13.11.01
I S Walsh (Hunsdon, Ivybridge) 12.01.16P
Built by I S Walsh – project PFA 187-13785 (IE 21.04.17)

G-CBGE Tecnam P92-EA Echo TEC/003 09.11.01
J P Spiteri Field Farm, Oakley 17.07.18P
Built by T C Robson – project PFA 318-13680

G-CBGG Cyclone Pegasus Quantum 15 7874 27.11.01
T E Davies Headon Farm, Retford 15.04.18P

G-CBGH Teverson Bisport xxxx 07.11.01
M J Larroucau Wellcross Farm, Slinfold 25.05.18P
Built by R C Teverson – project PFA 267-12784

G-CBGJ Aeroprakt A-22 Foxbat UK 004 14.11.01
T G Fitzpatrick & E Smyth Slieve Croob, Castlewellan 01.01.19P
Built by W R Davis-Smith – project PFA 317-13803

G-CBGK Hawker Siddeley Harrier GR.3 41H-712218 13.12.01
9220M, XZ995 Cancelled 14.03.05 as sold to USA
Dolly's Grove, RoI
Forward fuselage no FL/41H-0150252
Stored 11.13 as 'XZ995' in RAF c/s

G-CBGL Max Holste MH.1521M Broussard 19 03.12.01
F-BMJO, F-BNEN, French AF K M Perkins
(Yalding, Maidstone)
As '3303' in Portuguese AF c/s; on rebuild in
Northamptonshire 2017? (NF 18.04.18)

G-CBGO Murphy Maverick 430 122M 24.10.01
K J Miles & R Withall St Michaels 29.10.18P
Built by C R Ellis – project PFA 259-13470

G-CBGP Comco Ikarus C42 FB UK FB 001 22.11.01
G F Welby Bakersfield Farm, Weldon 20.05.18P
Built by A R Lloyd – project PFA 322-13741

G-CBGR Avtech Jabiru UL-450 414 21.11.01
M D Brown Newtownards 15.05.19P
Built by K R Emery – project PFA 274A-13682

G-CBGU Thruster T600N 450 0121-T600N-055 21.11.01
B R Cardosi Wick John O'Groats 25.10.16P
Badged 'Sprint'

G-CBGV Thruster T600N 450 0121-T600N-056 21.11.01
P Ebbatson & M O'Sullivan tr West Wight Aviators
Freshwater Fruit Farm, Freshwater 12.06.18P
Badged 'Sprint'

G-CBGW Thruster T600N 450 0121-T600N-058 21.11.01
A R Pluck Damyns Hall, Upminster 08.05.18P
Badged 'Sprint'

G-CBGX Scottish Aviation Bulldog Srs 120/121 BH120/287 26.11.01
XX622 A D Reohorn tr Bulldog GX Group
Brighton City 09.03.18E
As 'XX622:B' in RAF c/s

G-CBGZ Westland SA.341C Gazelle HT.2 1915 30.10.01
ZB646 D Weatherhead Ltd (Lodge Farm, Cottered) 19.09.18P

G-CBHA SOCATA TB-10 Tobago 1583 06.11.01
VH-YHA Oscar Romeo Aviation Ltd Redhill 08.06.18E

G-CBHC Rotary Air Force RAF 2000 GTX-SE xxxx 22.11.01
R Barton Baker Barracks, Thorney Island 30.09.17P
Built by A J Thomas – project PFA G/13-1326

G-CBHE Slingsby T67M-200 Firefly 2050 28.12.01
ZK-TZX, G-CBHE, SE-LBE J Slagel (Borehamwood) 08.03.08
(NF 04.01.18)

G-CBHG Mainair Blade 1298-1001-7-W1093 12.12.01
A W Leadley Finn Valley, RoI 28.06.18P
Sailwing fitted 04.16 to Gemini/Flash IIA trike
G-MYKH; original trike at Blackmoor Farm, Aubourn?

G-CBHI Europa Aviation Europa XS 373 31.10.01
I Cook tr Alpha Syndicate Stonefield Park, Chilbolton 04.10.18P
Built by B Price – project PFA 247-13245;
tailwheel u/c & motor-glider wing

G-CBHJ Mainair Blade 912S 1305-1201-7-W1100 28.01.02
B C Jones (Hale, Altrincham) 22.07.18P

G-CBHK Cyclone Pegasus Quantum 15 (HKS) 7871 06.12.01
I R Price (Lichfield) 01.07.17P

G-CBHN Cyclone Pegasus Quantum 15-912 7872 06.12.01
S P D Hill Rochester 17.02.19P

G-CBHO Gloster Gladiator II N5719 11.12.01
N5719 Retro Track & Air (UK) Ltd
(Upthorpe Iron Works, Cam, Dursley)
On long term rebuild 05.16 (NF 25.08.15)

G-CBHP Corby CJ-1 Starlet 572 12.12.01
K M Hodson Brook Farm, Pilling 05.10.18P
Built by D H Barker & J D Muldowney
– project PFA 134-12498

G-CBHR Laser Lazer Z200 Q056 31.12.01
VH-IAC S R S Evans tr The G-CBHR Group
Andrewsfield 12.06.18P
Built by H Selvey

G-CBHU Tiger Cub RL5B Sherwood Ranger LWS xxxx 12.12.01
D J Seymour Enstone 08.06.18P
Built by M J Gooch – project PFA 237-12477

G-CBHW Cameron Z-105 10217 16.01.02
Bristol Chamber of Commerce, Industry & Shipping
Abbots Leigh, Bristol 'Ridgemill' 02.04.16E
(NF 04.04.16)

G-CBHX Cameron V-77 3950 19.12.01
A Hook Tibshelf, Alfreton 27.03.18E

G-CBHY Cyclone Pegasus Quantum 15-912 7859 07.01.02
D W Allen (Burntwood) 01.04.18P

G-CBHZ Rotary Air Force RAF 2000 GTX-SE xxxx 02.01.02
M P Donnelly (Thurso)
Built by M P Donnelly – project PFA G/13-1321
(NF 27.08.14)

G-CBIB Flight Design CT2K 01-08-06-23 21.01.02
T R Villa Priory Farm, Tibenham 30.09.17P
Assembled Pegasus Aviation as c/n 7878 (IE 15.12.17)

G-CBIC Raj Hamsa X'Air V2(2) 608 02.01.02
G A J Salter Dunkeswell
Built by J T Blackburn & D R Sutton
– project BMAA/HB/156 (IE 15.02.18)

G-CBID Scottish Aviation Bulldog Srs 120/121 BH120/242 14.12.01
XX549 C R Arkle tr The Red Dog Group
White Waltham 23.07.18E
As 'XX549:6' in RAF c/s

G-CBIE Flight Design CT2K 01-09-01-23 10.01.02
H D Colliver Landmead Farm, Garford 24.11.17P
Assembled Pegasus Aviation as c/n 7879; damaged
when abandoned take-off and overturned at
Peasemore Common 19.08.17 (NF 13.02.19)

G-CBIF Avtech Jabiru UL-450 0507 03.01.02
A G Sindrey Westonzoyland 03.07.18P
Built by J A Iszard – project PFA 274A-13789

G-CBII Raj Hamsa X'Air 582(8) 676 07.01.02
EI-EAX, G-CBII R H Dennis (Clare, Sudbury) 31.05.19P
Built by A Worthington – project BMAA/HB/185

G-CBIJ Comco Ikarus C42 FB UK 0102-6319 ? 03.01.02
J A Smith (Royal Oak, Filey) 17.06.16P
Built by A Jones – project PFA 322-13720; blown over
2016 Eddsfield, Octon Lodge Farm, Thwing &
substantially damaged

G-CBIL Cessna 182K Skylane 18257804 09.10.78
(G-BFZZ), D-ENGO, N2604Q
E Bannister East Midlands 01.11.17E

G-CBIM Lindstrand LBL 90A 817 28.01.02
R K Parsons Yeovil BA20 25.04.18E

G-CBIN Team Mini-Max 91 2073 P 07.01.02
A R Mikolajczyk Headon Farm, Retford
Built by D E Steade – project PFA 186-13111
(SSDR microlight since 09.14) (IE 24.06.16)

G-CBIP Thruster T600N 450 0022-T600N-060 07.01.02
P J Hopkins (Kettering) 05.07.19P
Badged 'Sprint'

G-CBIR Thruster T600N 450 0022-T600N-061 07.01.02
S Langtry Bellarena 10.05.18P
Badged 'Sprint'

G-CBIS Raj Hamsa X'Air 582(2) 708 15.01.02
P T W T Derges (Littleover, Derby) 18.03.17P
Built by P T W T Derges – project BMAA/HB/199
(IE 03.01.18)

G-CBIT Rotary Air Force RAF 2000 GTX-SE H2-01-12-521 27.11.01
M P Lhermette Lamberhurst Farm, Dargate
Built by M P Lhermette – project PFA G/13-1340
(IE 17.09.17)

G-CBIV	Best Off Skyranger 912(1)	SKR02xx092?	25.01.02
	J W & R G Clark　North Weald		15.08.18P
	Built by P M Dewhurst – project BMAA/HB/201		
G-CBIX	Zenair CH.601UL Zodiac	xxxx	24.12.01
	R A Roberts　Whaley Farm, New York		30.11.18P
	Built by M F Cottam – project PFA 162A-13765		
G-CBIY	Evektor EV-97 Eurostar	2002-1138	23.01.02
	W R Grantham & B J Sheppard　(Radstock, Bath)		19.09.19P
	Built by E M Middleton – project PFA 315-13846		
G-CBJD	Stoddard-Hamilton GlaStar	5780	23.01.02
	K F Farey　(Bourne End)		
	Built by K F Farey – project PFA 295-13853		
	(NF 19.01.16)		
G-CBJE	Rotary Air Force RAF 2000 GTX-SE	H2-01-12-516	23.01.02
	V G Freke　Enstone		15.10.18P
	Built by K F Farey – project PFA G/13-1342		
G-CBJG	de Havilland DHC-1 Chipmunk 22	63	08.02.02
	CS-AZT, Portuguese AF 1373		
	C J Rees　Dalkeith Farm, Winwick		24.04.18P
	Built by OGMA; as '1373' in Portuguese AF c/s		
G-CBJH	Aeroprakt A-22 Foxbat	035 & UK0005	30.01.02
	H Smith　Morgansfield, Fishburn		11.05.18P
	Built by H Smith – project PFA 317-13847		
G-CBJL	Air Création Buggy 582(1)/Kiss 400	FL005	08.02.02
	R E Morris　Pembrey		30.07.04P
	Built by R E Morris – project BMAA/HB/205		
	(Flylight kit FL005 comprising Trike s/n T01099 &		
	wing s/n A01158-1164) (NF 16.03.18)		
G-CBJM	Avtech Jabiru SP-470	0500	11.12.01
	J M P Elliott　Newtownards		16.08.19P
	Built by A T Moyce – project PFA 274B-13769		
G-CBJN	Rotary Air Force RAF 2000 GTX-SE	xxxx	30.01.02
	G W Duffill　(Wishanger Farm, Frensham)		
	Built by M P Lhermette – project PFA G/13-1335		
	(IE 22.12.17)		
G-CBJO	Cyclone Pegasus Quantum 15-912	7861	10.12.01
	A E Kemp　(Staplehurst, Tonbridge)		06.05.17P
G-CBJP	Zenair CH.601UL Zodiac	xxxx	31.01.02
	R E Peirse　Armshold Farm, Great Eversden		10.09.18P
	Built by R E Peirse – project PFA 162A-13590; tricycle u/c		
G-CBJR	Evektor EV-97A Eurostar	2002-1139	31.01.02
	C Adams & H F Young tr Madley Flying Group		
	Shobdon		13.04.18P
	Built by B J Crockett – project PFA 315-13845		
G-CBJS	Cameron C-60	10253	17.04.02
	N Ivison　Barton Seagrave, Kettering		20.04.18E
G-CBJT	Mainair Blade	1302-1101-7-W1097	12.12.01
	M A Hartill　(Cannock)		06.06.19P
G-CBJV	RotorWay Exec 162F	6589	13.02.02
	P W Vaughan　(Canewdon, Rochford)		11.07.18P
	Built by Southern Helicopters Ltd		
G-CBJW	Comco Ikarus C42 FB UK	xxxx	13.02.02
	E Foster & J H Peet　St Michaels		08.08.18P
	Built by T J Cale – project PFA 322-13811		
G-CBJX	Raj Hamsa X'Air Falcon Jabiru(1)	622	13.02.02
	R D Bateman　Belle Vue Farm, Yarnscombe		28.11.18P
	Built by M R Coreth – project BMAA/HB/181		
G-CBJY	Avtech Jabiru UL-450	401	14.02.02
	M A Gould　(Forward Green, Stowmarket)		30.09.10P
	Built by D L H Person – project PFA 274A-13613 (NF 27.08.17)		
G-CBJZ	Westland SA.341D Gazelle HT.3	1734	13.02.02
	3D-HGW, XZ932　K G Theurer		
	Stuttgart-Echterdingen, Germany		06.07.18P
G-CBKA	Westland SA.341D Gazelle HT.3	1746	20.02.02
	XZ937　J Windmill　Stapleford		09.01.18P
G-CBKB	Bücker Bü.181C Bestmann	502095	28.01.02
	F-PCRL, F-BCRL, F-BCRU?		
	G D & W R Snadden　(Dumbarton)		
	Officially recorded c/n 121 is Francais Reconstruction		
	rebuild s/n FR-121; reported as composite rebuild		
	of F-BCRL (c/n 112) & F-BCRU (original c/n 121);		
	under restoration 04.16 (NF 18.02.16)		
G-CBKD	Westland SA.341C Gazelle HT.2	1130	20.02.02
	XW868　Flying Scout Ltd　Welshpool		11.01.17P
G-CBKF	Reality Easy Raider J2.2(2)	ER.0003	24.01.02
	D A Karniewicz　Belle Vue Farm, Yarnscombe		
	Built by R J Creasey – project BMAA/HB/202 (IE 19.01.18)		
G-CBKG	Thruster T600N 450	0022-T600N-059	01.03.02
	M C Henry　(Mersham, Ashford)		07.11.16P
	Badged 'Sprint' (IE 15.12.17)		
G-CBKK	Ultramagic S-130	130/32	19.03.02
	Hayrick Ltd　Benenden, Cranbrook　'smile.co.uk'		06.09.17E
	(IE 06.11.17)		
G-CBKL	Raj Hamsa X'Air Jabiru(2)	682	18.02.02
	G Baxter & G Ferries　Insch		03.06.18P
	Built by J Garcia – project BMAA/HB/203		
G-CBKM	Mainair Blade 912	1310-0102-7-W1105	21.01.02
	T E Robinson　Insch		01.04.18P
G-CBKN	Mainair Blade 912	1316-0302-7-W1111	11.03.02
	D S Clews　Headon Farm, Retford		19.04.18P
G-CBKO	Mainair Blade 912	1311-0102-7-W1106	11.02.02
	S J Taft　Blackmoor Farm, Aubourn		13.08.17P
	(IE 06.12.17)		
G-CBKR	Piper PA-28-161 Warrior III	2842143	15.03.02
	N5334N　C B Frost t/a Yeovil Auto Tuning		
	Dunkeswell　'Devon & Somerset Flight Training,*		
	Dunkeswell Aerodrome'		16.04.18E
G-CBKU	Comco Ikarus C42 FB UK	0112 6431	04.03.02
	(EI-...)　C Blackburn　Carnowen, RoI		06.06.18P
	Built by R G Q Clarke & P Walton – project PFA 322-13862		
G-CBKW	Cyclone Pegasus Quantum 15-912	7892	25.03.02
	A Sharma　Rochester		03.12.17P
G-CBKY	Avtech Jabiru SP-470	0499	06.03.02
	I A Lavey　Shobdon		03.07.18P
	Built by P R Sistern – project PFA 274B-13764		
G-CBLA	Aero Designs Pulsar XP	367	15.02.02
	N367JR　T J Searle　Headcorn		22.10.19P
	Built by J L Reeves; tricycle u/c (IE 28.07.17)		
G-CBLB	Tecnam P92-EA Echo	559	13.03.02
	R Lewis-Evans		
	Newton Peveril Farm, Sturminster Marshall		24.09.18P
	Built by M A Lomas – project PFA 318-13770		
G-CBLD	Mainair Blade 912S	1306-1201-7-W1101	21.03.02
	N E King　St Michaels		02.05.18P
G-CBLE	Robin R2120U	364	16.04.02
	Flew LLP　Bournemouth		05.02.17E
	Built by Constructions Aeronautiques de Bourgogne		
	(IE 23.01.18)		
G-CBLF	Raj Hamsa X'Air 582(11)	696	18.03.02
	B J Harper & P J Soukup　Grays Bridge Farm, Winkleigh		30.06.18P
	Built by E G Bishop and E N Dunn		
	– project BMAA/HB/194		
G-CBLK	Hawker Hind	41H-82971	20.03.02
	L7181　Aero Vintage Ltd　Duxford		
	'L7234' on inside cowling; unmarked fuselage		
	on restoration 07.18 (NF 14.11.14)		
G-CBLL	Cyclone Pegasus Quantum 15-912	7891	22.03.02
	P D Alford　Dunkeswell		20.06.18P
G-CBLM	Mainair Blade 912	1308-0102-7-W1103	12.02.02
	A S Saunders　(Crewe)		26.04.18P
G-CBLN	Cameron Z-31	10285	26.04.02
	J R Lawson　Riccall, York		27.05.18E
G-CBLP	Raj Hamsa X'Air Falcon Jabiru(2)	646	26.03.02
	A C Parsons　(Hewish, Weston-super-Mare)		17.05.06P
	Built by M J Kay & S Litchfield – project		
	BMAA/HB/213; noted 06.15 (NF 04.06.18)		
G-CBLS	Fiat CR.42 Falco	920	20.07.05
	Swedish AF 2542　Patina Ltd　Duxford		
	As 'MM6976/16-85'; noted 07.18 (NF 14.10.15)		
G-CBLT	Mainair Blade 912	1315-0202-7-W1110	25.04.02
	E D Locke　Strathaven		28.04.19P
G-CBLW	Raj Hamsa X'Air Falcon 582(3)	641	13.03.02
	R G Halliwell　Ince		29.05.18P
	Built by R R Hadley – project BMAA/HB/209 originally as Raj		
	Hamsa X'Air Falcon V2		
G-CBLY	Grob G109B	6403	12.03.02
	D-KITZ (2), (F-WAQS)　D A Smith tr G-CBLY Syndicate		
	Compton Abbas		14.05.19E

G-CBLZ Rutan Long-EZ 1046 05.06.02
F-PYYV S K Cockburn North Weald 11.05.18P
Built by N W Ruston; noted 07.18

G-CBMB Cyclone AX2000 7894 18.06.02
T H Chadwick Rufforth East 02.09.15P

G-CBMC Cameron Z-105 10274 30.04.02
B R Whatley Nailsea, Bristol *'edwardware homes'* 06.08.19E

G-CBME Reims/Cessna F172M F17201060 28.02.02
TF-FTV, TF-POP, SE-FZP Skytrax Aviation Ltd Sibson 20.07.18E

G-CBMI IAV Bacau Yakovlev Yak-52 855907 24.07.02
LY-AOZ, RA-02050, DOSAAF 107 (blue)
J Slagel (Borehamwood) 26.07.19P

G-CBML de Havilland DHC-6-310 Twin Otter 695 04.06.02
C-FZSG, HB-LSN, C-FZSP, TR-LZO, C-GJZK
Isles of Scilly Skybus Ltd Land's End 04.06.19E

G-CBMM Mainair Blade 912 1312-0202-7-W1107 09.09.02
W L Millar Strathaven 11.07.18P

G-CBMO Piper PA-28-180 Cherokee D 28-4806 16.05.02
ZS-ONK, 9J-RHN, N6391J T Rawlings Strubby 01.07.19E

G-CBMP Cessna R182 Skylane RG II R18201325 09.04.02
ZS-MWT, N38MH, YV-2034P, N2286S
Orman (Carrolls Farm) Ltd Great Massingham 22.10.18E

G-CBMR Medway EclipseR 172/150 27.03.02
D S Blofeld Middle Stoke, Isle of Grain 26.01.18P

G-CBMT Robin DR.400-180 Régent 2538 03.05.02
R J Williamson Crowfield *'Crowfield Flying Club'* 23.01.19E
Built by Constructions Aeronautiques de Bourgogne

G-CBMU Whittaker MW6-S Fatboy Flyer xxxx 30.04.02
J L Jordan (Crossnacreevy, Belfast)
Built by F J Brown – project PFA 164-13339;
stored Crossnacreevy 08.18
(SSDR microlight since 05.17) (IE 13.07.18)

G-CBMV Cyclone Pegasus Quantum 15 7893 03.05.02
A I Howes (Buntingford) 26.06.19P

G-CBMZ Evektor EV-97 Eurostar 2001-1316 12.04.02
J C O'Donnell Church Farm, Shotteswell 14.08.18P
Built by P Grenet & J C O'Donnell
– project PFA 315-13890

G-CBNC Mainair Blade 912 1319-0402-7-W1114 17.04.02
K L Smith Manor Farm, Dalscote 09.07.18P

G-CBNF Rans S-7 Courier 1295 164 12.04.02
I M Ross (Drumoak, Banchory) 16.10.18P
Built by T R Grief – project PFA 218-13762

G-CBNG Robin R2112 Alpha 180 20.05.02
PH-ROL, F-GCAF J P Kistner t/a Grosvenor Aircraft
(Headley, Bordon) 24.10.19E

G-CBNI Lindstrand LBL 90A 857 16.04.02
L Arias & M A Derbyshire Oswestry 01.05.19E

G-CBNJ Raj Hamsa X'Air 582(11) 680 23.04.02
T W Whitty (Dalbeattie) 15.04.19P
Built by J L Francis, M Hunt & M K Slaughter
– project BMAA/HB/187

G-CBNL Dyn'Aéro MCR-01 Club 204 12.04.02
D H Wilson Netherthorpe 15.08.17P
Built by D H Wilson – project PFA 301A-13805
(IE 25.08.17)

G-CBNO CFM Streak Shadow 347 ? 08.03.02
P J Porter Henstridge *'Beano'* 26.02.18P
Built by D J Goldsmith – project PFA 206-13809

G-CBNT Cyclone Pegasus Quantum 15-912 7860 14.05.02
R D Leigh (Middlewich) 16.09.19P

G-CBNV Rans S-6-ES Coyote II 1000.1393 ES 23.04.02
J C Higham tr CBNV Flyers (Willenhall) 26.09.18P
Built by C W J Davis – project PFA 204-13817;
tricycle u/c

G-CBNW Cameron N-105 10283 16.05.02
C & J M Bailey t/a Bailey Balloons
Pill, Bristol *'Bristol & West'* 12.04.18E

G-CBNX Montgomerie-Bensen B.8MR xxxx 26.04.02
J B Allan (Corringham, Stanford-le-Hope) 17.12.18P
Built by C Hewer – project PFA G/01A-1345

G-CBNZ Team HiMax 1700R xxxx 30.04.02
A P S John Croft Farm, Defford *'Chocolat II'*
Built by J J Penny – project PFA 272-13624
(SSDR microlight since 11.14) (IE 25.08.17)

G-CBOC Raj Hamsa X'Air 582(5) 623 01.05.02
A J McAleer Carrickmore 03.04.06P
Built by A J McAleer – project BMAA/HB/166
(NF 11.07.18)

G-CBOE Hawker Hurricane IIB R30040 24.05.02
RCAF 5487 K-F Grimminger
Aalen-Elchingen, Germany 06.08.18P
Built by Canadian Car & Foundry Co;
as 'AG244' in RAF silver c/s

G-CBOF Europa Aviation Europa XS 431 01.05.02
I W Ligertwood Sleap 24.06.15P
Built by I W Ligertwood – project PFA 247-13462

G-CBOG Mainair Blade 912S 1309-0102-7-W1104 26.03.02
S Lillis tr OG Group Ince 29.06.18P

G-CBOM Mainair Blade 912 1314-0202-7-W1109 30.04.02
G Suckling Graveley Hall Farm, Graveley 24.05.18P

G-CBOO Mainair Blade 912S 1317-0302-7-W1112 04.04.02
EI-EMX, G-CBOO H Moore Newtownards 24.11.18P

G-CBOP Avtech Jabiru UL-450 0355 02.05.02
T Briton tr G-CBOP Group
Greenhills Farm, Wheatley Hill 13.05.19P
Built by D W Batchelor – project PFA 274A-13611

G-CBOR Reims/Cessna F172N F17201656 28.05.87
PH-BOR, PH-AXG (1) R P Rochester Full Sutton 03.05.18E

G-CBOS Rans S-6-ES Coyote II 1201.1428 08.05.02
J T Athulathmudali Henstridge 16.04.18P
Built by R Skene – project PFA 204-13859; tricycle u/c

G-CBOV Mainair Blade 912 1327-0502-7-W1122 16.05.02
EI-EAP, G-CBOV M A Pantling
(East Stoke, Stoke-sub-Hambdon) 21.04.18P

G-CBOW Cameron Z-120 10302 07.08.02
Ballooning Network Ltd Bristol BS3 *'Torex'* 10.09.18E

G-CBOY Cyclone Pegasus Quantum 15-912 7898 17.04.02
RM Aviation Ltd Beverley (Linley Hill) 03.06.19P

G-CBOZ IAV Bacau Yakovlev Yak-52 811308 15.11.02
LY-AOC, DOSAAF 30 M J Babbage Headcorn 16.05.16P

G-CBPC Sportavia-Putzer RF5B Sperber 51013 27.06.02
OY-XKC R J Woodhams
(Palomares, Almeria, Spain) 04.06.17E
(IE 25.09.18)

G-CBPD Comco Ikarus C42 FB UK 0112-6444 14.05.02
A Haslam tr Waxwing Group Kirkbride 09.05.18P
Built by M L Robinson – project PFA 322-13863

G-CBPE SOCATA TB-10 Tobago 129 13.06.02
HB-EZR A F Welch Earls Colne 09.03.18E

G-CBPI Piper PA-28R-201 Arrow III 2844073 23.05.02
N53496 M L Roland Southend *'Joy'* 02.11.19E
Official type data 'PA-28R-201 Cherokee Arrow III'
is incorrect

G-CBPM Yakovlev Yak-50 812101 10.07.02
LY-ASG, DOSAAF 58 P W Ansell North Weald 14.03.18P
Carries '50' (black)

G-CBPR Avtech Jabiru UL-450 0270 16.05.02
N R Andrew Rookery Farm, Doynton 12.05.18P
Built by F B Hall & P L Riley – project PFA 274A-13492

G-CBPU Raj Hamsa X'Air R100(3) 442 27.05.02
R Power (Rosecrea, Co Tipperary, RoI) 29.10.09P
Built by M S McCrudden & W P Byrne
– project BMAA/HB/123 (NF 25.01.16)

G-CBPV Zenair CH.601UL Zodiac 682 28.05.02
C J Meadows Westonzoyland 07.04.17P
Built by R D Barnard – project PFA 162A-13689

G-CBPW Lindstrand LBL 105A 863 12.06.02
P Donkin Ulverston *'Samsung'* 14.06.19E

G-CBRB Ultramagic S-105 105/103 19.06.02
P C Bailey Over, Cambridge 22.09.18E

G-CBRC Jodel D.18 xxxx 31.05.02
P J Gripton Wathstones Farm, Newby Wiske
Built by B W Shaw – project PFA 169-11408
(NF 27.11.17)

G-CBRD	Jodel D.18 xxxx		31.05.02
	J D Haslam Oban		27.07.18P
	Built by J D Haslam – project PFA 169-11484		
G-CBRE	Mainair Blade 912 1330-0602-7-W1125		19.06.02
	L M Marsh (Hinckley)		12.09.17P
G-CBRK	Ultramagic M-77 77/212		08.07.02
	R Gower Wellingborough *'Ultra Magic Balloons'*		12.04.19E
G-CBRM	Mainair Blade 1326-0502-7-W1121		19.06.02
	M H Levy (Treuddyn, Mold)		02.06.11P
	(NF 11.07.14)		
G-CBRR	Evektor EV-97A Eurostar xxxx		18.06.02
	T O Powley & M S Turner Seething		14.02.18P
	Built by C M Theakstone – project PFA 315-13919		
G-CBRT	Murphy Elite P670E		19.06.02
	R W Baylie Compton Abbas		
	Built by R W Baylie – project PFA 232-13461;		
	dumped 09.18 (IE 30.03.17)		
G-CBRV	Cameron C-90 10323		31.07.02
	C J Teall Salford, Chipping Norton		21.09.18E
G-CBRW	Aerostar Yakovlev Yak-52 9111415		04.02.03
	RA-44464, DOSAAF 50		
	Max-Alpha Aviation GmbH Bremgarten, Germany		30.07.16P
	As '50' (grey) in DOSAAF c/s		
G-CBRX	Zenair CH.601UL Zodiac 6-0253		21.06.02
	C J Meadows Westonzoyland		08.08.18P
	Built by J B Marshall – project PFA 162A-13833; tricycle u/c		
G-CBSF	Westland SA.341C Gazelle HT.2 1924		06.06.02
	ZB647 Falcon Aviation Ltd		
	Bourne Park, Hurstbourne Tarrant		
	As 'ZB647:CU-59' in RN c/s (NF 25.04.18)		
G-CBSH	Westland SA.341D Gazelle HT.3 1344		28.10.02
	XX406 Cancelled 13.11.17 by CAA		17.04.16
	Rochester *Stored in RAF c/s as 'XX406'*		
G-CBSI	Westland SA.341D Gazelle HT.3 1736		06.06.02
	XZ934 P S Unwin Peytons Cottages, Nutfield		21.06.18P
	As 'XZ934:U' in RAF 32 Sqdn white & grey c/s		
G-CBSK	Westland SA.341D Gazelle HT.3 1914		06.06.02
	ZB627 B W Stuart & P J Whitaker tr Falcon Flying		
	Group Bourne Park, Hurstbourne Tarrant		29.11.18P
	As 'ZB627:A' in RAF c/s; operated by		
	The Gazelle Squadron Display Team		
G-CBSO	Piper PA-28-181 Archer II 28-7690376		18.07.02
	D-EOFL, N9595N Archer One Ltd Lydd		08.12.18E
G-CBSU	Avtech Jabiru UL-450 0510		15.07.02
	K R Crawley Rufforth East		16.05.18P
	Built by P K Sutton – project PFA 274A-13812		
G-CBSZ	Mainair Blade 912S 1334-0602-7-W1129		06.08.02
	P J Nolan Grove Farm, Wolvey		06.05.18P
G-CBTB	III Sky Arrow 650 T K132		25.06.02
	S I Hatherall Welshpool		08.10.18P
	Built by D A & J A S T Hood – project PFA 298-13832		
G-CBTD	Cyclone Pegasus Quantum 15-912 7904		09.07.02
	D Baillie Glassonby		11.11.18P
G-CBTE	Mainair Blade 912S 1328-0602-7-W1123		10.07.02
	K R Hine (Bell Busk, Skipton)		10.08.18P
G-CBTK	Raj Hamsa X'Air 582(5) 589		09.07.02
	N Buckley Arclid Green, Sandbach		02.04.19P
	Built by C D Wood – project BMAA/HB/168		
G-CBTM	Mainair Blade 1322-0502-7-W1117		02.07.02
	K G Osborne (Brixham, Torbay)		30.08.19P
G-CBTN	Piper PA-31 Navajo C 31-7812073		07.08.02
	OO-VLH, N27636		
	Durban Aviation Services Ltd Biggin Hill		16.03.18E
G-CBTO	Rans S-6-ES Coyote II 1201.1427		16.07.02
	A J Gibson Watchford Farm, Yarcombe		30.08.19P
	Built by B J Mould & M Walsh		
	– project PFA 204-13910; tricycle u/c		
G-CBTR	Lindstrand LBL 120A 733		22.07.02
	R H Etherington Rueypeyroux, France		13.08.05A
	(NF 22.06.18)		
G-CBTS	Gloster Gamecock replica GA 97		17.07.02
	Retro Track & Air (UK) Ltd (Cam, Dursley)		
	Built by Retro Track and Air (UK) Ltd (NF 25.08.15)		

G-CBTT	Piper PA-28-181 Archer II 28-7890127		22.07.02
	G-BFMM, N47735 Cedar Aviation Ltd Denham		17.10.18E
G-CBTW	Mainair Blade 912 1329-0602-7-W1124		20.06.02
	J R Davis Over Farm, Gloucester		28.07.18P
G-CBTX	Denney Kitfox Model 2 475		19.07.02
	G I Doake Gilford, Craigavon		
	Built by G I Doake & W M Farrell		
	– project PFA 172-11721 (NF 08.02.16)		
G-CBUB	Bell 412EP 36297		22.07.02
	ZJ707, G-CBUB, (N30338), C-GADQ		
	FB Leasing Ltd Bournemouth		27.04.03A
	(NF 02.11.18)		
G-CBUC	Raj Hamsa X'Air 582(5) 779		22.07.02
	R S Noremberg Great Oakley		30.10.19P
	Built by A P Fenn & D R Lewis – project BMAA/HB/228		
G-CBUD	Cyclone Pegasus Quantum 15-912 7906		30.07.02
	G N S Farrant Manor Farm, Drayton St Leonard		06.05.18P
G-CBUF	Flight Design CTSW 02-04-04-18		26.07.02
	D J Saunders Audley End		21.05.18P
	Assembled Pegasus Aviation as c/n 7901;		
	rebuilt by P&M Aviation 2006 with CTSW		
	wings: now termed as 'CT2K plus Mod 195'		
G-CBUG	Tecnam P92-EM Echo xxxx		20.06.01
	S R A Brierley & K D Mitchell (Hassocks/Itchingfield)		01.10.19P
	Built by R C Mincik – project PFA 318-13662;		
	badged 'P92S'		
G-CBUI	Westland Wasp HAS.1 F9590		05.08.02
	XT420 C J Marsden RNAS Yeovilton		20.06.18P
	As 'XT420:606' in RN c/s		
G-CBUJ	Raj Hamsa X'Air 582(10) 651		01.08.02
	R G Herrod (Glebe Farm, Tolland)		18.01.20P
	Built by J T Laity – project BMAA/HB/212		
G-CBUK	Van's RV-6A 25868		25.07.02
	P G Greenslade Wellcross Farm, Slinfold		16.10.17P
	Built by P G Greenslade – project PFA 181A-13614		
G-CBUN	Barker Charade xxxx		31.07.02
	D R Hall (Matfield, Tonbridge)		10.05.19P
	Built by P E Barker – project PFA 166-13520;		
	based on Stern ST-80		
G-CBUO	Cameron O-90 3353		15.08.02
	CC-PMH P M Smith & W J Treacy		
	Readstown, Trim, RoI		05.08.15E
G-CBUP	Magni M16 Tandem Trainer xxxx		28.08.02
	ZU-AIH J S Firth (Scissett, Huddersfield)		31.03.11P
	Built by R W Husband – project PFA G/12-1346		
	(NF 06.02.18)		
G-CBUS	Cyclone Pegasus Quantum 15 7916		29.08.02
	J Liddiard (Yatesbury)		03.07.18P
G-CBUU	Cyclone Pegasus Quantum 15-912 7917		27.08.02
	N A Hobson (Halesowen)		30.11.18P
G-CBUX	Cyclone AX2000 7918		02.10.02
	A J Sharratt Sackville Lodge Farm, Riseley		08.06.19P
G-CBUY	Rans S-6-ES Coyote II 0302.1436		13.08.02
	S T Cadywould (Upton, Newark)		07.12.18P
	Built by S C Jackson – project PFA 204-13954;		
	tricycle u/c (IE 05.07.17)		
G-CBUZ	Cyclone Pegasus Quantum 15 7907		31.07.02
	D G Seymour Craysmarsh Farm, Melksham		05.08.17P
G-CBVA	Thruster T600N 450 0082-T600N-068		14.08.02
	J H Brady Carrickmore		05.03.18P
	Badged 'Sprint'		
G-CBVB	Robin R2120U 365		26.07.02
	Flew LLP (Bournemouth)		25.09.15E
	Built by Constructions Aeronautiques de Bourgogne (IE 23.01.18)		
G-CBVC	Raj Hamsa X'Air 582(5) 792		15.08.02
	J Rivera (Naas, Co Kildare, RoI)		06.06.18P
	Built by M J Male – project BMAA/HB/230		
G-CBVD	Cameron C-60 10338		31.10.02
	Phoenix Balloons Ltd Bristol BS8 *'Popeye'*		20.03.18E
G-CBVF	Murphy Maverick 430 3		19.08.02
	H A Leek Spanhoe		
	Built by J Hopkinson – project PFA 259-12876		
	(IE 16.12.18)		

G-CBVG Mainair Blade 912S 1338-0802-7-W1133 27.08.02
J C M Collado (Madrid, Spain) 06.05.17P
(NF 21.07.17)

G-CBVH Lindstrand LBL 120A 870 02.09.02
Alba Ballooning Ltd Carrington, Gorebridge *'Line'* 10.12.18E

G-CBVM Evektor EV-97 Eurostar 2003-1163 08.08.02
M Sharpe Brook Breasting Farm, Watnall 04.01.19P
Built by A Costello & J Cunliffe – project PFA 315-13932

G-CBVN Mainair Pegasus Quik 7919 27.08.02
G Ferguson tr RIKI Group Fife 30.07.18P

G-CBVO Raj Hamsa X'Air 582(5) 627 27.08.02
Cancelled 02.02.11 as PWFU 07.06.11
Wing Farm, Longbridge Deverill
Built by W E Richards – project BMAA/HB/227;
parts only 03.14

G-CBVP Bell 412EP 36301 02.09.02
ZJ708, G-CBVP, C-GLYY
FB Leasing Ltd Bournemouth 31.05.03A
(NF 02.11.18)

G-CBVR Best Off Skyranger 912(2) SKR0206209 06.09.02
S H Lunney Ince 12.04.18P
Built by R H J Jenkins – project BMAA/HB/231

G-CBVS Best Off Skyranger Swift 912(1) SKR0207215 19.08.02
S C Cornock Shenstone Hall Farm, Shenstone 13.03.18P
Built by S C Cornock – project BMAA/HB/234

G-CBVU Piper PA-28R-200 Cherokee Arrow B 28R-7135007 12.09.02
ZS-RER, N11C R D Boor Fenland 27.04.19E
Official type data 'PA-28R-200 Cherokee Arrow II'
is incorrect

G-CBVV Cameron N-120 10331 13.09.02
John Aimo Balloons SAS Mondovi, Italy
'Warsteiner' 29.06.18E

G-CBVX Cessna 182P Skylane 18263419 16.12.02
ZS-IYZ, N9653G S J Brenchley Solent 12.09.19E

G-CBVY Comco Ikarus C42 FB UK 0112-6436 04.09.02
C Hubbard tr Grandpa's Flying Group Boston 06.09.18P
Built by R Gossage & M J Hendra
– project PFA 322-13835

G-CBVZ Flight Design CT2K 02-05-06-04 19.09.02
O W Achurch Hill Top, Whilton 12.09.13P
Assembled Pegasus Aviation with c/n '9714'
– should be c/n 7914 (NF 10.02.17)

G-CBWA Flight Design CT2K 02-06-01-04 11.10.02
J Paterson (Azat Le Ris, Haute Vienne, France) 10.07.19P
Assembled Pegasus Aviation as c/n 7921

G-CBWD Piper PA-28-161 Warrior III 2842160 01.10.02
N5357G J Wright Biggin Hill 21.10.18E

G-CBWE Evektor EV-97 Eurostar 2003-1167 16.09.02
C W & J Hood Eshott 22.08.18P
Built by E Clarke – project PFA 315-13958

G-CBWG Evektor EV-97 Eurostar 2003-1162 17.09.02
C Long & M P & T Middleton Haverfordwest 18.08.17P
Built by M Rhodes – project PFA 315-13918

G-CBWI Thruster T600N 450 0102-T600N-071 20.09.02
M Afzal Longacre Farm, Sandy 31.03.15P
Badged 'Sprint' (IE 29.05.15)

G-CBWJ Thruster T600N 450 0092-T600N-069 20.09.02
J K Clayton & K D Smith Northrepps 30.11.17P
Badged 'Sprint'

G-CBWK Ultramagic H-77 77/218 04.11.02
S J Stevens Hanham, Bristol 24.04.18E

G-CBWN Campbell Cricket Mk.6A BGL/100 24.09.02
R S Sanby Bankwood Farm, Oxton 18.10.18P
Built by G J Layzell – project PFA G/16-1328;
badged 'Layzell AV-18A'

G-CBWO RotorWay Exec 162F 6597 24.09.02
N T Oakman (Hampstead, Saffron Walden) 10.10.19P
Built by S P Tetley

G-CBWP Europa Aviation Europa 233 01.10.02
T W Greaves Garton *'Flying Yorkshireman'* 25.06.13P
Built by T W Greaves – project PFA 247-12930;
tailwheel u/c (NF 29.09.14)

G-CBWS Whittaker MW6 Merlin xxxx 07.10.02
K R Emery Otherton
Built by D W McCormack – project PFA 164-12863
(SSDR microlight since 09.17 (IE 02.08.17)

G-CBWW Best Off Skyranger 912(2) UK/210 30.08.02
A Gilruth Perth
Built by R L & S H Tosswill – project BMAA/HB/232
(IE 04.10.18)

G-CBWY Raj Hamsa X'Air 582(6) 775 17.10.02
J C Rose Eastbach Spence, English Bicknor 27.09.15P
Built by T Collins – project BMAA/HB/244 (IE 05.07.17)

G-CBWZ Robinson R22 Beta II 3101 23.10.02
N141DC J Fleming (Grantown-on-Spey) 30.11.14E
(NF 14.09.17)

G-CBXC Comco Ikarus C42 FB UK FB 17 23.10.02
J A Robinson Bleaze Hall, Old Hutton, Kendal 04.06.18P
Built by A R Lloyd – project PFA 322-13955

G-CBXE Reality Easy Raider J2.2(2) ER.0006 22.08.02
A K Day White Ox Mead, Peasedown St John 24.05.18P
Built by A Appleby – project BMAA/HB/198

G-CBXF Reality Easy Raider J2.2(2) ER.0001 19.11.02
M R Grunwell Gerpins Farm, Upminster 16.06.18P
Built by F Colman – project BMAA/HB/196

G-CBXG Thruster T600N 450 0112-T600N-073 29.10.02
J R Hughes tr Newtownards Microlight Group
Newtownards 01.09.18P

G-CBXJ Cessna 172S Skyhawk SP 172S8125 30.10.02
N2391J Steptoe & Son Properties Ltd Caernarfon 20.03.18E
Operated by North Wales Air Academy

G-CBXK Robinson R22 Mariner 2302M 04.11.02
N3052P, LQ-BLD, N80524 Un Pied sur Terre Ltd
t/a Whizzard Helicopters Seigerland, Germany 09.06.19E

G-CBXL Bell 412EP 36306 07.11.02
ZJ705, G-CBXL, C-GBUP
FB Heliservices Ltd Bournemouth

G-CBXM Mainair Blade 1335-0802-7-W1130 19.08.02
K N Dewhurst (Crowborough) 12.08.19P

G-CBXN Robinson R22 Beta II 3385 11.11.02
N M G Pearson Henstridge 15.05.16E

G-CBXR Raj Hamsa X'Air Falcon 582(1) 612 11.11.02
J F Heath (Heathersgill, Carlisle) 19.09.10P
Built by J F Heath – project BMAA/HB/224 (NF 18.10.16)

G-CBXS Best Off Skyranger 912(2) UK/246 13.11.02
K D Adams tr The Ince Skyranger Group Ince 06.06.18P
Built by C J Erith – project BMAA/HB/248
as Skyranger J2.2

G-CBXU Team Mini-Max 91A 952 13.11.02
D Crowhurst Bakersfield Farm, Weldon *'The Mistress'*
Built by T J Shaw – project PFA 186-13037
(SSDR microlight since 06.14) (IE 05.07.17)

G-CBXW Europa Aviation Europa XS 494 18.11.02
R G Fairall Redhill 28.11.18P
Built by R G Fairall – project PFA 247-13674;
tailwheel u/c

G-CBXZ Rans S-6-ESN Coyote II 0302.1438 20.11.02
A Faehndrich (Barton-le-Clay) 12.04.05P
Built by D Tole – project PFA 204-13988 (NF 01.11.17)

G-CBYB RotorWay Exec 162F 6623 20.11.02
T Clark t/a Clark Contracting
Brentford Grange Farm, Coleshill
Built by T Clark (NF 11.01.04)

G-CBYD Rans S-6-ES Coyote II 1201.1429 21.11.02
R Burland Sorbie Farm, Kingsmuir 11.12.18P
Built by R Burland – project PFA 204-13871

G-CBYF Mainair Blade 1349-1202-7-W1144 02.01.03
R Watton (Cheslyn Hay, Walsall) 18.02.19P

G-CBYH Aeroprakt A-22 Foxbat UK0008 02.12.02
G C Moore tr G-CBYH Foxbat Group Otherton 27.04.18P
Built by P C De-Ville & Partners – project
PFA 317-13902; crashed Otherton 05.07.04
& rebuilt 2005 as project PFA 317-14318;
remains of PFA 317-13902 at Ley Farm, Chirk 09.10

G-CBYI Cyclone Pegasus Quantum 15 7931 02.01.03
J M Hardy tr The G-CBYI Group Deenethorpe 03.03.18P

G-CBYM	Mainair Blade	1323-0502-7-W1118	13.09.02	
	D Reid (Hatton, Warrington)		18.04.18P	
G-CBYN	Europa Aviation Europa XS	518	05.12.02	
	G M Tagg Compton Abbas		08.07.13P	
	Built by A B Milne – project PFA 247-13751;			
	tricycle u/c (IE 03.01.18)			
G-CBYO	Cyclone Pegasus Quik	7928	05.12.02	
	C J Roper tr G-CBYO Syndicate East Fortune		14.12.18P	
G-CBYP	Whittaker MW6-S LW Fatboy Flyer	xxxx	06.12.02	
	W G Reynolds Ivy Farm, Overstrand		21.08.18P	
	Built by R J Grainger – project PFA 164-13131			
G-CBYS	Lindstrand LBL 21A	156	17.12.02	
	B M Reed Antigny, Vienne, France		06.07.18E	
G-CBYT	Thruster T600N 450	0102-T600N-072	10.10.02	
	P McAteer Old Park Farm, Margam		29.07.18P	
	Badged 'Sprint'			
G-CBYU	Piper PA-28-161 Warrior III	2842173	12.02.03	
	N53606 Stapleford Flying Club Ltd Stapleford		19.02.19E	
G-CBYV	Cyclone Pegasus Quantum 15-912	7920	19.09.02	
	K M Ward tr G-CBYV Syndicate (Ipswich)		01.07.18P	
G-CBYW	Hatz CB-1	769	16.01.03	
	T A Hinton Rookery Farm, Doynton		26.08.09P	
	Built by T A Hinton – project PFA 143-13710			
	(NF 02.02.15)			
G-CBYZ	Tecnam P92-EA Echo-Super	xxxx	17.12.02	
	B Weaver Middle Pymore Farm, Bridport		12.08.18P	
	Built by M Rudd – project PFA 318A-13984			
G-CBZA	Mainair Blade	1344-1002-7-W1139	28.10.02	
	M Lowe Arclid Green, Sandbach		19.04.18P	
G-CBZD	Mainair Blade	1348-1102-7-W1143	12.12.02	
	G P J Davies (Bryncrug, Tywyn)		08.06.18P	
G-CBZE	Robinson R44 Raven	1276	12.12.02	
	Alps (Scotland) Ltd Perth		12.06.18E	
G-CBZG	Rans S-6-ES Coyote II	1201.1430	09.01.03	
	S G Young Hunsdon		18.07.18P	
	Built by N McKenzie – project PFA 204-13894;			
	tricycle u/c			
G-CBZH	Cyclone Pegasus Quik	7934	30.01.03	
	M P Chew Perranporth		17.09.18P	
G-CBZJ	Lindstrand LBL 25A Cloudhopper	892	09.01.03	
	J L & T J Hilditch t/a Pegasus Ballooning			
	Southwick, Brighton 'Lindstrand'		14.06.19E	
G-CBZK	Robin DR.400-180 Régent	2543	12.02.03	
	A C Fletcher Sherburn-in-Elmet		30.06.18E	
	Built by Constructions Aeronautiques de Bourgogne			
G-CBZM	Avtech Jabiru SPL-450	0514	02.01.03	
	M E Ledward Solent		28.04.18P	
	Built by M E Ledward – project PFA 274A-13827			
G-CBZN	Rans S-6-ES Coyote II	0600.1374-ES	06.01.03	
	K Stevens Shifnal		20.07.18P	
	Built by A James – project PFA 204-13652; tricycle u/c			
G-CBZP	Hawker Fury I	41H-67550	02.04.03	
	SAAF ???, K5674 Historic Aircraft Collection Ltd			
	Duxford		07.05.19P	
	As 'K5674' in RAF c/s			
G-CBZR	Piper PA-28R-201 Arrow III	2837029	13.01.03	
	EC-IJX, N175ND Folada Aero & Technical			
	Services Ltd Blackbushe '07'		17.10.18E	
	Official type data 'PA-28R-201 Cherokee Arrow III'			
	is incorrect			
G-CBZS	Lynden Aurora	xxxx	13.01.03	
	J Lynden Blackpool		22.05.13P	
	Built by J Lynden – project PFA 313-13534 (IE 13.07.17)			
G-CBZT	Cyclone Pegasus Quik	7936	06.01.03	
	H M Roberts Trefgraig, Rhoshirwaun		16.05.19P	
G-CBZW	Zenair CH.701 STOL	79196	13.01.03	
	S Richens Lower Upham Farm, Chiseldon		15.05.18P	
	Built by T M Stiles – project PFA 187-13731			
G-CBZX	Dyn'Aéro MCR-01 ULC	221	15.01.03	
	A C N Freeman & M P Wilson Bournemouth		06.10.18P	
	Built by S L Morris – project PFA 301B-13957			

G-CBZZ	Cameron Z-275	10346	12.02.03	
	A C K Rawson & J J Rudoni t/a Wickers World			
	Hot Air Balloon Company Stafford		19.03.15E	

G-CCAA – G-CCZZ

G-CCAB	Mainair Blade	1345-1002-7-W1140	28.01.03	
	G D Hall March Road, Wimblington		17.06.19P	
G-CCAC	Evektor EV-97 Eurostar	xxxx	26.11.02	
	D C Lugg Polpidnick Farm, St Martin			
	'Slightly Dangerous'		11.05.18P	
	Built by J S Holden & P J Ladd – project PFA 315-13979			
G-CCAD	Cyclone Pegasus Quik	7924	03.12.02	
	M Richardson (Porthcawl)		03.05.18P	
G-CCAE	Avtech Jabiru UL-450	303	17.01.03	
	D Logan Perth		15.10.18P	
	Built by C E Daniels – project PFA 274A-13938			
G-CCAF	Best Off Skyranger 912(1)	SKR0207212	28.11.02	
	G Everett & D N Smith Hubbard's Farm, Lenham Heath		19.06.19P	
	Built by D W Squire – project BMAA/HB/235			
G-CCAG	Mainair Blade 912	1350-1202-7-W1145	22.11.02	
	A Robinson Moss Edge Farm, Cockerham		23.05.18P	
G-CCAK	Zenair CH.601HD Zodiac	6-9055	11.12.02	
	G & JE Trading Ltd (Pawlett, Bridgwater)		07.11.18P	
	Built by A Kinmond – project PFA 162-13469; tricycle u/c			
G-CCAL	Tecnam P92-EA Echo	xxxx	06.12.02	
	G Hawkins Newton Peveril Farm, Sturminster Marshall		24.07.18P	
	Built by D Cassidy – project PFA 318-13842			
G-CCAP	Robinson R22 Beta II	3413	11.02.03	
	D Baker, M Healer & H Price			
	Cherry Orchard Farm, Nailsea		16.07.18E	
G-CCAR	Cameron N-77	2658	05.12.78	
	D P Turner Leigh upon Mendip, Radstock			
	'Mitsubishi Motors'		02.06.05A	
	Originally c/n 464; rebuilt with envelope c/n 670 c.08.80,			
	then c/n 2108 (1989) & c/n 2658 (1992) (NF 08.02.16)			
G-CCAS	Cyclone Pegasus Quik	7935	11.02.03	
	J L Pollard tr Caunton Alpha Syndicate			
	Knapthorpe Lodge, Caunton		03.04.18P	
G-CCAT	Gulfstream American AA-5A Cheetah	AA5A-0893	16.01.92	
	G-OAJH, G-KILT, G-BJFA, N27169			
	Rate 1 Aero Ltd Redhill		30.05.18E	
G-CCAV	Piper PA-28-181 Archer II	28-8090353	31.03.03	
	D-EXRT, N8233A			
	S Turner tr Alpha Victor Group Southend		25.10.19E	
G-CCAW	Mainair Blade 912S	1351-0103-7-W1146	05.02.03	
	I G Molesworth Redlands		20.08.18P	
G-CCAY	Cameron Z-42	10373	27.02.03	
	P Stern Deggendorf, Germany		05.05.18E	
G-CCAZ	Cyclone Pegasus Quik	7927	03.12.02	
	J P Floyd Sywell		07.05.18P	
G-CCBA	Best Off Skyranger R100(1)	SKR0211277	23.01.03	
	E M J Maher tr Fourstrokes Group			
	Barton Ashes, Crawley Down		23.07.18P	
	Built by R M Bremner – project BMAA/HB/256			
G-CCBB	Cameron N-90	10085	11.02.03	
	G-TEEZ (2) L D & S C A Craze			
	Hemel Hempstead 'Fresh Air'		06.11.14P	
	Original G-TEEZ (1) stolen & believed destroyed			
	(NF 20.12.16)			
G-CCBC	Thruster T600N 450	0013-T600N-077	23.01.03	
	M K Boydle Bodmin		18.05.18P	
	Badged 'Sprint'			
G-CCBG	Best Off Skyranger Swift 912(1)	SKR0207214	28.01.03	
	K Wileman (Clophill)		30.06.18P	
	Built by G R Wallis – project BMAA/HB/240			
G-CCBH	Piper PA-28-235 Cherokee	28-10648	29.01.03	
	PH-ABL, F-BNFY, N9054W			
	B C Faulkner Thruxton		03.12.18E	
	Official type data 'PA-28-235 Cherokee Pathfinder'			
	is incorrect			
G-CCBI	Raj Hamsa X'Air 582(11)	600	04.02.03	
	N Byrne Newcastle, RoI		21.08.18P	
	Built by H Adams – project BMAA/HB/192			

G-CCBJ	Best Off Skyranger 912(2)	UK/285	04.02.03
	J d'Rozario Shobdon		07.11.18P
	Built by A T Hayward – project BMAA/HB/262		
G-CCBK	Evektor EV-97 Eurostar	2003-1197	05.02.03
	B S Waycott Eastbach Spence, English Bicknor		19.05.18P
	Built by G R & J A Pritchard – project PFA 315-14025		
G-CCBM	Evektor EV-97 Eurostar	2003-1191	05.02.03
	B Hunter & P W Nestor Manchester Barton		03.06.18P
	Built by W Graves – project PFA 315-14023		
G-CCBN	Replica Plans SE.5A	077246	02.04.03
	PH-WWI, N8010S A Schweisthal (Maidenhead)		10.05.18P
	Built by B Barra; as '80105:19' in US Air Service c/s		
G-CCBR	Jodel D.120 Paris-Nice	59	18.02.03
	OO-JAL, (OO-CMF), F-BHYP		
	A & S Dunne Ballyboy, Rol		14.11.18P
	Built by Société des Etablissements Benjamin Wassmer		
G-CCBT	Cameron Z-90	10340	24.03.03
	I J Sharpe Caterham *'BT'*		10.09.16E
G-CCBU	Raj Hamsa X'Air 582 (9)	756	19.02.03
	Cancelled 08.11.10 by CAA		22.06.07
	Middle Stoke, Isle of Grain *Built by M L Newton*		
	– project BMAA/HB/237; noted 08.11		
G-CCBW	Tiger Cub RL5A Sherwood Ranger LW	xxxx	18.02.03
	A L Virgoe Over Farm, Gloucester		06.04.10P
	Built by P H Wiltshire – project PFA 237-13002		
	(NF 14.05.18)		
G-CCBX	Raj Hamsa X'Air 582(2)	745	28.05.03
	S Hunt (Corby)		09.08.15P
	Built by A D'Amico – project BMAA/HB/286		
	(NF 17.11.17)		
G-CCBY	Avtech Jabiru UL-450	0300	21.02.03
	D M Goodman Baxby Manor, Husthwaite		03.07.07P
	Built by D M Goodman – project PFA 274A-13528		
	(NF 22.09.14)		
G-CCBZ	Aero Designs Pulsar	1936	17.02.03
	N4075X J M Keane Husbands Bosworth		18.01.06P
	Built by R N Wasserman; tricycle u/c;		
	damaged near Deenthorpe 02.07.05 (NF 08.04.16)		
G-CCCA	Supermarine 509 Spitfire Tr.9	CBAF 9590	18.02.03
	G-TRIX, (G-BHGH), IAC 161, G-15-174, PV202		
	Historic Flying Ltd Duxford		07.05.19P
	As 'PV202:5R-H' in RAF c/s		
G-CCCB	Thruster T600N 450	0033-T600N-078	24.02.03
	J Hartland Leicester		12.08.17P
	Badged 'Sprint'		
G-CCCD	Mainair Pegasus Quantum 15	7929	12.06.03
	R N Gamble Plaistows Farm, St Albans		14.09.18P
G-CCCE	Aeroprakt A-22 Foxbat	UK012	16.01.03
	P Sykes Newton Peveril Farm, Sturminster Marshall		04.10.18P
	Built by C V Ellingworth – project PFA 317-14002		
G-CCCF	Thruster T600N 450	0033-T600N-081	24.02.03
	P R Norman Leicester		22.05.18P
	Badged 'Sprint'		
G-CCCG	Mainair Pegasus Quik	7946	16.04.03
	J W Sandars Park Hall Farm, Mapperley		13.06.18P
G-CCCH	Thruster T600N 450	0033-T600N-079	24.02.03
	G Scullion Bellarena		27.06.18P
	Badged 'Sprint'		
G-CCCJ	Nicollier HN.700 Menestrel II	198	26.02.03
	G A Rodmell Beverley (Linley Hill)		14.06.18P
	Built by R Y Kendall – project PFA 217-13707		
G-CCCK	Best Off Skyranger 912(2)	UK/289	26.02.03
	J Donnelly t/a Hilltop Flying Club Carrickmore		04.08.19P
	Built by J S Liming – project BMAA/HB/265		
G-CCCM	Best Off Skyranger 912(2)	SKR0301292	03.03.03
	A Fleming tr Connel Gliding Group Oban		17.06.18P
	Built by J R Moore – project BMAA/HB/263		
G-CCCO	Evektor EV-97A Eurostar	2003-1181	11.03.03
	D R G Whitelaw Oban		17.05.18P
	Built by J E Borril, N D A Graham &		
	D R G Whitelaw – project PFA 315-14006		
G-CCCR	Best Off Skyranger 912(2)	SKR0301290	19.03.03
	D C Nixon (Malvern)		07.03.18P
	Built by T C Viner – project BMAA/HB/266		

G-CCCV	Raj Hamsa X'Air Falcon 133(1)	614	20.03.03
	G J Boyer Westonzoyland		15.09.05P
	Built by G A J Salter – project BMAA/HB/252		
	(NF 03.12.14)		
G-CCCW	Pereira Osprey 2	1505	10.04.03
	D J Southward Kirkbride		04.06.18P
	Built by D J Southward – project PFA 070-13408		
G-CCCY	Best Off Skyranger 912(2)	SKR0211278	25.03.03
	A Watson Haw Farm, Hampstead Norreys		22.11.18P
	Built by D M Cottingham – project BMAA/HB/260		
G-CCDB	Mainair Pegasus Quik	7948	08.04.03
	P K Dale Thornton Watlass, Ripon		24.05.18P
G-CCDC	Rans S-6-ES Coyote II	0302.1439	28.01.03
	J A Matthews Sandown		11.08.18P
	Built by G N Smith – project PFA 204-13992; tricycle u/c		
G-CCDD	Mainair Pegasus Quik	7951	31.03.03
	G Clark Perth		29.08.18P
G-CCDF	Mainair Pegasus Quik	7949	23.04.03
	R P McGann Knapthorpe Lodge, Caunton		27.09.18P
G-CCDG	Best Off Skyranger 912(1)	SKR0302294	01.04.03
	T H Filmer tr Freebird Group	Newtownards	
	10.01.19P		
	Built by W P Byrne – project BMAA/HB/271		
G-CCDH	Best Off Skyranger 912(2)	UK/211	05.02.03
	C F Rogers Little Gransden		12.11.18P
	Built by D M Hepworth – project BMAA/HB/233		
G-CCDJ	Raj Hamsa X'Air Falcon 582(2)	692	18.02.03
	A L Lyons (Tring)		12.08.18P
	Built by J M Spitz – project BMAA/HB/214		
G-CCDK	Mainair Pegasus Quantum 15-912	7947	19.03.03
	D Bishop (Bromyard)		28.04.18P
	Built by Mainair Sports Ltd		
G-CCDL	Raj Hamsa X'Air Falcon 582(2)	819	01.04.03
	J Cropper (Failsworth, Manchester)		10.08.19P
	Built by H Burroughs – project BMAA/HB/274		
G-CCDM	Mainair Blade	1352-0203-7-W1147	21.03.03
	A R Smith (Sawston, Cambridge)		05.12.16P
G-CCDO	Mainair Pegasus Quik	7944	19.03.03
	S T Welsh Ince		12.07.18P
G-CCDP	Raj Hamsa X'Air 582(14)	847	10.04.03
	M V Daly & B Moore Kernan Valley, Tandragee		11.05.18P
	Built by J A McKie – project BMAA/HB/276		
G-CCDS	Nicollier HN.700 Menestrel II	206	13.03.03
	B W Gowland Caernarfon *'Suzy Gee'*		31.10.18P
	Built by B W Gowland – project PFA 217-13915		
G-CCDU	Tecnam P92-EM Echo	TEC/009	23.04.03
	G P & P T Willcox (Lower Wick, Dursley)		07.04.18P
	Built by M J Barrett – project PFA 318-13721		
G-CCDV	Thruster T600N 450	0043-T600N-082	24.04.03
	G C Hobson St Michaels		14.04.18P
	Official c/n '0034-T600N-082' is incorrect –		
	build date 04.03 indicates correct c/n; forced landed		
	after loss of power Myerpole Farm, Preston 01.08.18;		
	badged 'Sprint' (IE 06.07.18)		
G-CCDX	Evektor EV-97 Eurostar	2003-1186	18.02.03
	K Powell tr G-CCDX Syndicate Manchester Barton		14.03.18P
	Built by H F Breakwell & R A Morris		
	– project PFA 315-14013		
G-CCDY	Best Off Skyranger 912(2)	SKR0302310	10.04.03
	I Brumpton Morgansfield, Fishburn		25.10.18P
	Built by A V Dunne & G S Gee-Carter		
	– project BMAA/HB/275		
G-CCDZ	Mainair Pegasus Quantum 15-912	7952	24.04.03
	C Dawes tr G-CCDZ Group Darley Moor		23.05.19P
	Built by Mainair Sports Ltd		
G-CCEA	Mainair Pegasus Quik	7950	08.04.03
	G D Ritchie East Fortune		05.05.18P
G-CCEB	Thruster T600N 450	0053-T600N-085	24.04.03
	C P Whitwell Fenland		28.06.15P
	Official c/n '0035-T600N-085' is incorrect		
	– build date 05.03 indicates correct c/n;		
	badged 'Sprint' (NF 29.02.16)		

G-CCED Zenair CH.601UL Zodiac   6-9332   04.04.03
R P Reynolds   Shenstone Hall Farm, Shenstone   12.05.18P
Built by R P Reynolds – project PFA 162A-13946;
tricycle u/c

G-CCEF Europa Aviation Europa   302   24.04.03
C P Garner   Trenchard Farm, Eggesford   19.07.18P
Built by C P Garner – project PFA 247-13038;
tailwheel u/c

G-CCEH Best Off Skyranger 912(2)   SKR0301291   28.04.03
A Eastham tr ZC Owners   Brook Farm, Pilling   04.11.18P
Built by A Eastham – project BMAA/HB/267

G-CCEJ Evektor EV-97 Eurostar   2003-1187   01.05.03
J R Iveson   Felixkirk   21.07.18P
Built by C R Ashley – project PFA 315-14011

G-CCEK Air Création Buggy 582(1)/Kiss 400   FL018   02.05.03
J L Stone   Old Park Farm, Margam   18.09.18P
Built by G S Sage – project BMAA/HB/272
(Flylight kit FL018 comprising trike s/n T03011
& wing s/n A03008-3006)

G-CCEL Avtech Jabiru UL-450   540   12.02.03
F McMullan   Newtownards   29.06.18P
Built by R Pyper – project PFA 247A-13976

G-CCEM Evektor EV-97A Eurostar   2003-1148   19.02.03
R L Wademan tr Oxenhope Flying Group   Oxenhope   11.09.18P
Built by E Atherden – project PFA 315-13987

G-CCEN Cameron Z-120   10399   09.05.03
T Hook   Alfreton   *'J.C.Balls & Sons'*   01.07.19E

G-CCES Raj Hamsa X'Air 3203(1)   401   08.05.03
G V McCloskey   Letterkenny, RoI   18.12.18P
Built by G V McCloskey – project BMAA/HB/104

G-CCET Nova Vertex 28   14296   25.03.03
M Hay   (Dundee)

G-CCEU Rotary Air Force RAF 2000 GTX-SE   001   24.06.03
N97ZP   N G Dovaston   Morgansfield, Fishburn   28.04.13P
Built by J L Rollins (NF 13.09.16)

G-CCEW Mainair Pegasus Quik   7966   17.06.03
A B Mackinnon   Perth   27.12.18P

G-CCEY Raj Hamsa X'Air 582(11)   833   12.05.03
I B Lavelle   Wickenby   19.08.19P
Built by P J F Spedding – project BMAA/HB/258

G-CCEZ Reality Easy Raider J2.2(2)   ER.0010   07.05.03
P J Clegg   Woolston Moss, Warrington   18.04.18P
Built by S A Chambers – project BMAA/HB/220

G-CCFC Robinson R44 Raven II   10151   16.09.03
Hawker Aviation Ltd   Turweston   29.05.18E

G-CCFD BFC Challenger II   1617   20.05.03
W Oswald   Eshott   11.05.18P
Built by W Oswald – project PFA 177-13180
using BFC kit

G-CCFE Tipsy Nipper T.66 Series 2   37   12.06.03
OO-PLG   N S Dell   (Plymouth)   18.04.14P
Built by Avions Fairey SA (NF 18.04.16)

G-CCFG Dyn'Aéro MCR-01 Club   240   08.04.03
P H Milward   Welshpool   25.08.19P
Built by M P Sargent – project PFA 301A-14047

G-CCFI Piper PA-32-260 Cherokee Six   32-7400002   30.06.03
OO-PCT, N56630   P McManus & N Whelan
Ballyboy, RoI   24.11.17E

G-CCFJ Kolb Twinstar Mk.III Xtra   M3X-02-2-00033 29.05.03
S Buckland   Darley Moor   28.07.18P
Built by M H Moulai – project PFA 205-14014

G-CCFK Europa Aviation Europa XS   502   29.05.03
C R Knapton   Ings Farm, Yedingham   20.04.18P
Built by C R Knapton – project PFA 247-13744

G-CCFL Mainair Pegasus Quik   7960   16.06.03
T E Thomas   Beverley (Linley Hill)   31.10.18P

G-CCFO Pitts S-1S   001   28.05.03
C-FYXO   A D Hoy   Jersey   13.10.18P
Built by R B Innes

G-CCFS Diamond DA.40D Star   D4.034   03.09.03
R H Butterfield   Crosland Moor   17.06.18E

G-CCFT Mainair Pegasus Quantum 15-912   7961   17.06.03
D P Gawlowski   Deenethorpe   29.10.18P
Built by Mainair Sports Ltd (NF 16.01.18)

G-CCFU Diamond DA.40D Star   D4.035   03.09.03
Jetstream Aviation Training & Services SA
Athens Int'l, Greece   27.11.19E

G-CCFV Lindstrand LBL 77A   934   23.06.03
Lindstrand Media Ltd   Hawarden CH5   16.07.18E

G-CCFW WAR Focke-Wulf FW190 replica   xxxx   27.05.03
D B Conway   Lower Upham Farm, Chiseldon   01.06.18P
Built by D B Conway – project PFA 081-12729;
as '+9' (starboard) & '9+' (port) in Luftwaffe c/s

G-CCFX EAA Acrosport II   xxxx   23.06.03
G Cameron   Clipgate Farm, Denton   20.02.18P
Built by C D Ward – project PFA 072A-11221

G-CCFY RotorWay Exec 162F   6719   27.06.03
A & A Thomas   Street Farm, Takeley   19.07.17P
Built by M Hawley; stored in barn 09.18

G-CCFZ Comco Ikarus C42 FB UK   02-0-6496   02.05.03
B W Drake   Over Farm, Gloucester   17.04.18P
Built by B W Drake – project PFA 322-14040

G-CCGA Medway EclipseR   175/153   18.06.03
G Cousins   (Boughton Monchelsea, Maidstone)   14.06.07P
(SSDR microlight since 03.18) (NF 05.09.18)

G-CCGB Team Mini-Max 91A   1054   04.06.03
A D Pentland   Crosland Moor
Built by A D Pentland – project PFA 186-13767
(SSDR microlight since 06.14) (IE 06.10.17)

G-CCGC Mainair Pegasus Quik   7958   27.05.03
D T McAfee & C A McLean   East Fortune   03.06.18P

G-CCGF Robinson R22 Beta II   3454   25.06.03
Glenntrade Ltd   Earls Colne   26.02.18E

G-CCGG Avtech Jabiru J400   068   16.06.03
A Simmers   (Whiterashes)   26.04.16P
Built by K D Pearce – project PFA 325-14055;
on rebuild 10.17

G-CCGH Super Marine Spitfire Mk.26   021   17.06.03
Cokebusters Ltd   Enstone   06.06.13P
Built by K D Pearce – project PFA 324-14054;
as 'AB196' in RAF c/s

G-CCGK Mainair Blade   1355-0603-7-W1150 18.07.03
C M Babiy & M Hurn   (Milton Keynes)   01.08.15P
(IE 04.09.15)

G-CCGM Air Création Buggy 582(2)/Kiss 450   FL021   23.05.03
G-80-1   J Howarth   Millfield Farm, Heckington   09.05.18P
Built by G P Masters – project BMAA/HB/277
(Flylight kit FL021 comprising trike s/n T03026 &
wing s/n A2049-2044); initially flown under BMAA
'B' conditions as 'G-80-1' using trike ex G-SNOG

G-CCGO Gemini F2A/Medway Raven X   176/154   11.04.03
D A Coupland   Blackmoor Farm, Aubourn   23.03.18P

G-CCGS Dornier 328-100   3101   18.03.04
D-CPRX, D-CDXR   Loganair Ltd   Glasgow
'The Spirit of Norwich'   17.03.19E

G-CCGU Van's RV-9A   90412   10.07.03
B J Main & A Strachan   Henstridge   26.03.19P
Built by B J Main – project PFA 320-13798

G-CCGW Europa Aviation Europa   026   08.07.03
D Buckley   Easter Poldar Farm, Thornhill   15.03.13P
Built by G C Smith – project PFA 247-12548;
noted 06.16 (NF 29.07.14)

G-CCGY Cameron Z-105   10422   08.07.03
Atlantic Ballooning BVBA   Destelbergen, Belgium
'Cameron Balloons'   17.01.19E

G-CCHD Diamond DA.40D Star   D4.051   03.09.03
(OE-...), G-CCHD   Cancelled 20.10.15 as destroyed   24.02.16
Brighton City   *Wreck stored 10.16*

G-CCHH Mainair Pegasus Quik   7963   24.06.03
C S Garrett tr Pegasus XL Group   Enstone   27.05.18P
Built by Mainair Sports Ltd

G-CCHI Mainair Pegasus Quik   7971   29.07.03
M R Starling   Ivy Farm, Overstrand   19.06.18P

G-CCHL Piper PA-28-181 Archer III   2843176   04.08.03
OY-JAA, N9501N   Archer Three Ltd   Lydd   25.09.18E

G-CCHM Air Création Buggy 582(1)/Kiss 450   FL022   15.07.03
M J Jessup Barhams Mill Farm, Egerton
Built by W G Colyer – project BMAA/HB/292
(Flylight kit FL022 comprising trike s/n T03057
& wing s/n A03099-3016) (SSDR microlight since 06.16) (IE 20.01.16)

G-CCHN Corby CJ-1 Starlet   640   15.07.03
G Evans (West Huntspill, Highbridge)
Built by D C Mayle – project PFA 134-12848
(NF 30.04.18)

G-CCHO Mainair Pegasus Quik   7968   09.07.03
M Allan East Fortune   09.08.18P

G-CCHP Cameron Z-31   10443   20.08.03
M H Redman Stalbridge, Sturminster Newton   26.09.08E
(NF 05.02.15)

G-CCHR Reality Easy Raider 503(1)   ER.0008   24.06.03
S Wilkes Andrewsfield   26.03.16P
Built by R B Hawkins – project BMAA/HB/223
(IE 04.04.16)

G-CCHS Raj Hamsa X'Air 582(10)   840   04.07.03
N H Gokul Rossall Field, Cockerham   16.08.11P
Built by I Lonsdale – project BMAA/HB/291 (IE 06.11.17)

G-CCHT Cessna 152   15285176   17.07.03
9H-ACW, N6159Q A J Gomes (Croydon)   19.02.12E
(NF 26.02.18)

G-CCHV Mainair Rapier   1353-0403-7-W1148   15.09.03
B J Wesley Sywell   09.05.18P

G-CCHX Scheibe SF25C Rotax-Falke   44694   25.09.03
D-KBCI Lasham Gliding Society Ltd Lasham   13.02.18E

G-CCID Avtech Jabiru J430   067   25.07.03
F Patterson & B J Robe Loadman Farm, Hexham   23.10.18P
Built by J Bailey – project PFA 325-14059

G-CCIF Mainair Blade   1356-0703-7-W1151   28.07.03
P W Dunn & A R Vincent (Stafford & Lichfield)   18.05.19P

G-CCIH Mainair Pegasus Quantum 15   7973   31.07.03
G Cousins Rochester   26.04.19P
Built by Mainair Sports Ltd; sailwing removed
and sold 10.18; trike on conversion to Quik

G-CCII ICP MXP-740 Savannah Jabiru(4)   01-04-51-063   06.06.03
D Chaloner Enstone   04.01.18P
Built by M J Kaye – project BMAA/HB/285

G-CCIJ Piper PA-28R-180 Cherokee Arrow   28R-30873   14.07.03
SE-FDZ S A Hughes Andrewsfield   30.10.18E

G-CCIK Best Off Skyranger 912(2)   SKR0212279   30.07.03
M D Kirby Willingale   17.12.18P
Built by A P Chapman & L E Cowling
– project BMAA/HB/278 (IE 05.06.17)

G-CCIR Van's RV-8   xxxx   07.08.03
P F Whitehead Breighton   10.05.19P
Built by D Marsh – project PFA 303-13732

G-CCISM Scheibe SF28A Tandem Falke   5791   15.10.03
OE-9154, (D-KDFZ) Cornwall Aviation
Heritage Centre Ltd Newquay Cornwall   09.01.15E
On display Cornwall Aviation Heritage Centre 08.18
(NF 05.02.16)

G-CCIU Cameron N-105   10485   18.08.03
P Wiemann Moers, Germany   26.06.17E
(NF 01.02.18)

G-CCIW Raj Hamsa X'Air 582(5)   838   11.08.03
A Evans Shifnal   16.04.18P
Built by G Wilkinson – project BMAA/HB/281

G-CCIY Best Off Skyranger 912(2)   SKR0210244   14.08.03
L F Tanner Sywell   11.05.18P
Built by L F Tanner – project BMAA/HB/250

G-CCIZ PZL-110 Koliber 160A   04010087   21.08.03
SP-WGN J P Nugent Newcastle, RoI   23.09.16E

G-CCJA Best Off Skyranger 912(2)   SKR0307364   06.08.03
G R Barker Hunsdon 'Lady Jean'   24.06.18P
Built by T R Southall – project BMAA/HB/299

G-CCJD Mainair Pegasus Quantum 15   7974   03.09.03
P Clark Yatesbury   03.06.14P
Built by Mainair Sports Ltd; noted 01.18 (NF 10.02.16)

G-CCJH Lindstrand LBL 90A   906   05.08.03
J R Hoare Venton, Plymouth   06.07.18E

G-CCJI Van's RV-6   25701   04.07.03
R N Bennison (Poynton, Stockport) 'jadeair.co.uk'   12.04.19P
Built by E M Marsh – project PFA 181A-13572

G-CCJJ Medway SLA 80 Executive   180803   20.08.03
J K Sargent Middle Stoke, Isle of Grain   26.04.18P
Originally registered as Medway Piranha

G-CCJK Aerostar Yakovlev Yak-52   9612001   03.03.04
RA-02622, LY-AFH
S J Thomas tr G-CCJK Group White Waltham   02.05.18P
As '52 (white)' in Russian AF c/s

G-CCJL Super Marine Spitfire Mk.26   024   22.08.03
P M Whitaker Oxenhope   06.03.17P
Built by M Hanley & P M Whitaker – project
PFA 324-14053; as 'PV303:ON-B' in RAF c/s

G-CCJM Mainair Pegasus Quik   7970   24.07.03
S R Smyth tr The Quik Group
Shempston Farm, Lossiemouth   26.12.18P

G-CCJN Rans S-6-ES Coyote II   0899.1336   28.08.03
W A Ritchie Easterton   15.08.17P
Built by M G A Wood – project PFA 204-13575;
tricycle u/c

G-CCJO ICP MXP-740 Savannah Jabiru(4)   03-05-01-213   28.08.03
I & R Fletcher (Bury)   05.10.18P
Built by I & R Fletcher – project BMAA/HB/295

G-CCJT Best Off Skyranger 912(2)   UK/317   30.07.03
M S R Burak tr Juliet Tango Group
Over Farm, Gloucester   12.12.18P
Built by J W Taylor – project BMAA/HB/300

G-CCJU ICP MXP-740 Savannah Jabiru(4)   03-05-01-214   03.09.03
M G Read tr Savannah Flying Group Nottingham City   12.12.17P
Built by A Colverson & K R Wootton
– project BMAA/HB/294

G-CCJV Aeroprakt A-22 Foxbat   058   03.09.03
J Keats London Colney   28.08.19P
Built by M J Barrett, A Dace, J C Forrester &
S McRoberts – project PFA 317-14082

G-CCJW Best Off Skyranger 912(2)   UK/366   03.09.03
J R Walter Benston Farm, New Cumnock   08.06.18P
Built by J R Walter – project BMAA/HB/303

G-CCJX Europa Aviation Europa XS   509   09.09.03
J S Baranski Wycombe Air Park   13.06.18P
Built by J S Baranski – project PFA 247-13727;
tricycle u/c

G-CCKF Best Off Skyranger Swift 912(1)   UK/314   04.09.03
M Johnson (Cramlington)   13.05.18P
Built by S A Owen – project BMAA/HB/289

G-CCKG Best Off Skyranger 912(2)   SKR0307375   26.08.03
C E Penny Otherton   21.11.16P
Built by J Hannibal – project BMAA/HB/302
(IE 05.06.17)

G-CCKH Diamond DA.40D Star   D4.039   23.10.03
Flying Time Ltd Brighton City   18.06.17E
(IE 18.01.18)

G-CCKJ Raj Hamsa X'Air 133(3)   855   02.10.03
G A Davidson Ashcroft   20.05.18P
Built by S Thompson – project BMAA/HB/306

G-CCKL Evektor EV-97A Eurostar   2003-1218   15.09.03
K Stewart tr G-CCKL Group Bodmin   31.03.18P
Built by A U I Hudson & J S Liming – project PFA 315-14117

G-CCKM Mainair Pegasus Quik   7985   22.09.03
J P Quinlan Park Hall Farm, Mapperley   16.07.18P

G-CCKN Nicollier HN.700 Menestrel II   204   23.09.03
C R Partington Selby House Farm, Stanton   06.11.18P
Built by C R Partington – project PFA 217-13943

G-CCKO Mainair Pegasus Quik   7982   27.08.03
G Bennett & L A Harper Priory Farm, Tibenham   18.06.18P
Fitted with replacement trike c.2012

G-CCKP Robin DR.400-120 Dauphin 2+2   2044   15.09.04
F-GKQD B A Mills t/a Duxford Flying Group
Armshold Farm, Great Eversden
(NF 13.10.15)

G-CCKR Pietenpol Air Camper   xxxx   22.08.03
P G Humphrey RAF Halton   18.04.18P
Built by T J Wilson – project PFA 047-12295

G-CCKT HAPI Cygnet SF-2A   xxxx   15.07.03
P W Abraham   (Bridgend)   13.05.08P
Built by P W Abraham – project PFA 182-13366
(NF 08.10.14)

G-CCKV Isaacs Fury II   xxxx   10.10.03
G Smith   (Fancy Farm, Dunkeswell)   28.09.12P
Built by S T G Ingram – project PFA 011-13695;
as 'K7271' in RAF c/s (NF 26.11.15)
Note: Wings & frame of BAPC148, also as
'K7271', stored Sleap

G-CCKZ Customcraft A25   CC005   10.10.03
P A George   Littlemore, Oxford
(IE 05.06.17)

G-CCLF Best Off Skyranger 912(2)   SKR0309380   16.10.03
C R Stevens & S Uzochukwu
Barhams Mill Farm, Egerton   02.12.18P
Built by G K R Linney – project BMAA/HB/311

G-CCLH Rans S-6-ES Coyote II   0600.1372   24.10.03
K R Browne   (Callington, Plymouth)   15.08.18P
Built by K R Browne – project PFA 204-13658;
tricycle u/c

G-CCLJ Piper PA-28-140 Cherokee Cruiser   28-7525049   01.09.03
OY-TOJ   A M George   North Weald   02.08.08E
(NF 07.08.18)

G-CCLM Mainair Pegasus Quik   7986   07.10.03
T A A Frohawk   Sywell   10.11.17P

G-CCLO Ultramagic H-77   77/244   19.02.04
S J M Hornsby   Christchurch   20.11.18E

G-CCLP ICP MXP-740 Savannah Jabiru(4)   03-09-51-232   31.10.03
C J Powell & A H Watkins   Rhigos   17.09.18P
Built by M J Kaye – project BMAA/HB/314

G-CCLR Schleicher ASH 26E   26209   26.11.03
A Darby & R N John   Dunstable Downs   '26E'   28.12.18E

G-CCLS Comco Ikarus C42 FB UK   0302-6534   19.09.03
B D Wykes   Wickenby   18.06.18P
Built by T Greenhill & J Spinks
– project PFA 322-14050: kit no.unconfirmed

G-CCLTᵀᴹ Powerchute Kestrel   00443   05.11.03
Cancelled 09.12.03 as PWFU
With Newark Air Museum, Winthorpe

G-CCLU Best Off Skyranger 912(2)   SKR0309379   11.11.03
D D Petrov   North Weald   'In my Dreams'   20.10.19P
Built by L Stanton – project BMAA/HB/316

G-CCLW Diamond DA.40D Star   D4.068   19.12.03
J Thorold & R S Watt tr Shacklewell Diamond Group
Shacklewell Lodge Farm, Empingham   20.03.18E

G-CCLX Mainair Pegasus Quik   7996   13.11.03
T D Welburn   Pound Green   07.10.18P

G-CCMC Avtech Jabiru UL-450   493   09.09.03
K J Simpson   Westonzoyland   21.09.18P
Built by J T McCormack – project PFA 274A-13775

G-CCMD Mainair Pegasus Quik   7991   23.10.03
J T McCormack   Broomhill Farm, West Calder   09.08.18P

G-CCMH Miles M.2H Hawk Major   172   20.10.03
EC-ABI, EC-CAS, EC-DDB, EC-W44
M C Ochoa   (Gerona, Spain)
(IE 01.10.15)

G-CCMJ Reality Easy Raider J2.2(1)   ER.0009   13.11.03
G F Clews   (Branston, Burton-on-Trent)   18.04.18P
Built by G F Clews – project BMAA/HB/254;
tailwheel u/c

G-CCMK Raj Hamsa X'Air Falcon Jabiru(3)   827   17.11.03
M J J Clutterbuck
Broomclose Farm, Longbridge Deverill   05.08.18P
Built by M A Beadman – project BMAA/HB/301

G-CCML Mainair Pegasus Quik   7992   14.10.03
G C C Roberts tr G-CCML Syndicate   East Fortune   15.02.19P

G-CCMM Dyn'Aéro MCR-01 ULC   131   08.09.03
J D Harris   Garston Farm, Marshfield   26.07.18P
Built by J P Davis – project PFA 301B-13945

G-CCMN Cameron C-90   10519   27.01.04
C Butler   Birmingham B14   12.04.19E

G-CCMO Evektor EV-97 Eurostar   2003-1239   11.11.03
A P Santus tr IBFC EV97 Group   Manchester Barton   27.05.18P
Built by E M Woods – project PFA 315-14155

G-CCMP Evektor EV-97A Eurostar   2003-1703   23.10.03
M Dunlop   Carrickmore   11.04.19P
Built by W K Wilkie – project PFA 315-14127

G-CCMR Robinson R22 Beta II   3497   09.01.04
N75273   G F Smith   Cranfield   21.02.18E

G-CCMS Mainair Pegasus Quik   7997   01.12.03
A S Facey tr Barton Charlie Charlie Group
Manchester Barton   16.07.18P

G-CCMT Thruster T600N 450   1031-T600N-092 14.11.03
E J Studdert-Kennedy   Redlands   15.07.18P
Badged 'Sprint'

G-CCMU RotorWay Exec 162F   6720   20.11.03
Southern Helicopters Ltd   Street Farm, Takeley   08.05.18P
Built by M Irving; damaged 26.10.17

G-CCMW CFM Shadow Series DD   K 348   02.09.03
K H Creed   Glebe Farm, Hougham   20.07.18P
Built by M Wilkinson – project PFA 161-13869;
based on combination of kits s/n 348 & 349

G-CCMX Best Off Skyranger 912(2)   SKR0210243   25.11.03
S G Weaver   Over Farm, Gloucester   17.05.18P
Built by K J Cole – project BMAA/HB/255

G-CCMZ Best Off Skyranger 912(2)   SKR0304316   23.10.03
D D Appleford   Lower Upham Farm, Chiseldon   19.03.18P
Built by D D Appleford – project BMAA/HB/288

G-CCNA Jodel DR.100A replica   xxxx   21.11.03
R Everitt   Ley Farm, Chirk
Built by R Everitt – project PFA 304-13519;
reported to be rebuild of G-ATHX (NF 29.03.16)

G-CCND Van's RV-9A   90824   10.12.03
D S Murrell   Field Farm, South Walsham   04.09.19P
Built by K S Woodard – project PFA 320-14142

G-CCNE Cyclone Pegasus Quantum 15   7093   11.12.03
T2-2795   G D Barker   (Streetly, Sutton Coldfield)   18.07.18P

G-CCNF Raj Hamsa X'Air Falcon 912(2)   644   09.12.03
B P & L A Perkins   (Market Rasen)   25.06.19P
Built by M F Eddington – project BMAA/HB/211

G-CCNG Flight Design CT2K   03-06-02-27   05.01.04
S Gaiety & P Wayman   Durham Tees Valley   05.09.18P
Assembled Mainair Sports Ltd as c/n 8004

G-CCNH Rans S-6-ES Coyote II   0503.1498   11.09.03
J E Howard   Great Oakley   18.04.18P
Built by N C Harper – project PFA 204-14114

G-CCNJ Best Off Skyranger 912(2)   SKR0310392   17.12.03
J D Buchanan   Coldharbour Farm, Willingham   19.06.18P
Built by J D Buchanan – project BMAA/HB/330

G-CCNL Raj Hamsa X'Air Falcon 133(1)   909   24.12.03
S E Vallance   Longacre Farm, Sandy   30.06.18P
Built by A Davis & S Rance – project BMAA/HB/326

G-CCNM Mainair Pegasus Quik   8002   02.12.03
J Flynn & F J Thorne   Ince   07.11.18P

G-CCNP Flight Design CT2K   03-07-03-34   22.01.04
North East Flying Club Ltd   Shotton Colliery, Peterlee 11.09.19P
Assembled Mainair Sports Ltd; c/n 8005
(kit no.03-06-03-28 (1) is incorrect &
probably became G-CDPZ; operated by
North East Flying Club

G-CCNR Best Off Skyranger 912(2)   SKR0309381   04.12.03
P Horsley   Eshott   04.06.18P
Built by S J Huxtable – project BMAA/HB/315

G-CCNS Best Off Skyranger 912(2)   SKR0401434   24.02.04
F Gallacher, P V Griffiths & D Murdoch   Strathaven   17.07.18P
Built by M Liptrot & G G Rowley
– project BMAA/HB/356

G-CCNT Comco Ikarus C42 FB80   0311-6585   19.12.03
C N Halliday tr November Tango Group   Wickenby   25.01.19P
Assembled Fly Buy Ultralights Ltd

G-CCNW Mainair Pegasus Quantum 15   8010   28.01.04
K J Bradley tr CCNW Group   Deenethorpe   29.01.19P
Built by Mainair Sports Ltd

G-CCNX	Mudry CAP 10B	311	06.01.04
	ARC Input Ltd Monewden		02.04.18F
	Built by Constructions Aeronautiques de Bourgogne		
G-CCNZ	Raj Hamsa X'Air 133(1)	888	05.11.03
	J M Walsh (Chesterfield)		03.12.11P
	Built by K J Foxall – project BMAA/HB/308		
	(NF 02.02.16)		
G-CCOA	Scottish Aviation Bulldog Srs.120/122	BH120/375	04.09.96
	G-111 Ghana, G-BCUU		
	Cancelled 11.06.02 as PWFU		13.03.03
	Sandown, IOW *Displayed 06.18 Wight Aviation*		
	Museum painted as 'G-AXEH'		
G-CCOB	Aero C.104	247	21.01.04
	N2348, LN-BNG, OK-AXV, Czech AF		
	H C Tomkins Spanhoe		05.07.19P
	Built by Aero-Vodochody		
G-CCOC	Mainair Pegasus Quantum 15	7999	16.12.03
	C M Ayres Caernarfon		29.12.15P
	Built by Mainair Sports Ltd		
G-CCOF	Rans S-6-ESA Coyote II	1202.1472	08.01.04
	G J Jones Gransden Lodge		17.07.19P
	Built by A J Wright and M Govan		
	– project PFA 204-14037; tailwheel u/c		
G-CCOG	Mainair Pegasus Quik	8001	16.12.03
	D P Clarke (Nuneaton)		17.02.18P
G-CCOH	Raj Hamsa X'Air Falcon Jabiru(3)	831	13.01.04
	D R Sutton Brook Farm, Pilling		09.05.18P
	Built by A R Emerson – project BMAA/HB/338		
G-CCOK	Mainair Pegasus Quik	8000	05.01.04
	C Curtin Rufforth East		19.08.18P
G-CCOM	Westland Lysander IIIA	Y1363	10.12.03
	N3093K, RCAF V9312 Propshop Ltd Duxford		01.08.19P
	As 'V9312:LX-E' in RAF c/s		
G-CCOP	Ultramagic M-105	105/113	19.01.04
	M E J Whitewood Whelpley Hill, Chesham		08.06.19E
G-CCOR	Sequoia F.8L Falco	xxxx	09.12.03
	D J & K S Thomas White Fen Farm, Benwick		10.07.18P
	Built by D J Thomas – project PFA 100-10588		
G-CCOT	Cameron Z-105	10517	14.01.04
	Airborne Adventures Ltd Rylstone, Skipton *'Invista'*		21.06.18E
G-CCOU	Mainair Pegasus Quik	8012	21.01.04
	D E J McVicker Dunnyvadden		22.04.18P
G-CCOV	Europa Aviation Europa XS	543	19.01.04
	B C Barton Yeatsall Farm, Abbots Bromley		28.10.18P
	Built by G N Drake – project PFA 247-13998; tailwheel u/c		
G-CCOW	Mainair Pegasus Quik	8008	28.01.04
	S Gibson & D Rickard Greenhills Farm, Wheatley Hill		30.06.19P
G-CCOY	North American AT-6D Texan II	88-14555	22.03.04
	Port.AF 1513, SAAF 7426, EX884, 41-33857		
	Classic Flying Machine Collection Ltd		
	(Lleycoussaudie, France)		
	(NF 08.11.17)		
G-CCOZ	Monnett Sonerai II	0197	31.05.78
	W H Cole Spilsted Farm, Sedlescombe		26.03.04P
	Built by P R Cozens – project PFA 015-10107		
	(NF 17.04.18)		
G-CCPC (2)	Mainair Pegasus Quik	7994	26.11.03
	S M Oliver East Fortune		06.04.18P
G-CCPD	Campbell Cricket Mk.4	xxxx	27.01.04
	T H Geake Enstone		11.01.18P
	Built by N C Smith – project PFA G/03-1333		
G-CCPE	Steen Skybolt	xxxx	10.12.03
	C Moore Kirkbride		18.08.18P
	Built by C Moore – project PFA 064-12830		
G-CCPF	Best Off Skyranger 912(2)	SKR0311396	26.01.04
	J R M Macpherson Oban		07.06.18P
	Built by T A Willcox – project BMAA/HB/340		
G-CCPG	Mainair Pegasus Quik	8016	13.05.04
	A W Lowrie Eshott		15.05.18P
G-CCPH	Evektor EV-97 teamEurostar UK	2003-1814	09.01.04
	B J Palfreyman Brook Breasting Farm, Watnall		05.06.18P
	Assembled Cosmik Aviation Ltd		
G-CCPJ	Evektor EV-97 teamEurostar UK	2004-1909	13.02.04
	J S Webb (Camberley)		01.04.18P
	Assembled Cosmik Aviation Ltd		
G-CCPL	Best Off Skyranger 912(2)	SKR0310385	29.01.04
	M Eardley tr The G-CCPL Group		
	Rossall Field, Cockerham		10.08.19P
	Built by B Hartley, P Openshaw, T Seed,		
	J & P Turner – project BMAA/HB/342		
G-CCPM	Mainair Blade 912	1360-1203-7-W1155	12.01.04
	P S Davies Ashcroft		16.07.17P
G-CCPN	Dyn'Aéro MCR-01 Club	271	28.11.03
	J C Thompson Bagby		24.04.18P
	Built by P H Nelson – project PFA 301A-14133		
G-CCPP	Cameron C-70	10515	16.03.04
	R J Mitchener tr Sarnia Balloon Group Andover		12.05.18E
G-CCPS	Comco Ikarus C42 FB100 VLA	xxxx	05.02.04
	H Cullens (Blairdrummond, Stirling)		26.09.18P
	Built by H Cullens – project PFA 322-14138		
G-CCPT	Cameron Z-90	10534	14.04.04
	South Downs Ballooning Ltd Grayshott, Hindhead		
	'Castlepoint, Bournemouth'		31.07.18E
G-CCPV	Avtech Jabiru J400	074	12.02.04
	J R Lawrence Nether Huntlywood Farm, Gordon		17.04.18P
	Built by J R Lawrence – project PFA 325-14058		
G-CCRB	Kolb Twinstar Mk.III	M3X-02-4-00037	09.12.03
	D H Lewis (Nelson, Treharris)		
	Built by R W Burge – project PFA 205-13993)		
	(SSDR microlight since 10.18) (IE 30.08.18)		
G-CCRC	Cessna TU206G	U20607001	24.02.04
	9A-DLC, YU-DLC, N9960R		
	D M Penny McMaster's Farm, Movenis		24.09.11E
	Badged 'Turbo Stationair 6'; dismantled 09.15		
	(NF 02.03.18)		
G-CCRF	Mainair Pegasus Quantum 15	8009	03.03.04
	C J Middleton (Lichfield)		06.07.18P
	Built by Mainair Sports Ltd		
G-CCRG	Ultramagic M-77	77/249	19.04.04
	M Cowling Glencarse, Perth *'Vauxhall'*		06.04.19E
G-CCRI	Raj Hamsa X'Air 582(5)	891	26.02.04
	D K Beaumont Longside		04.04.19P
	Built by R A Wright – project BMAA/HB/354		
G-CCRJ	Europa Aviation Europa	259	27.02.04
	F M Ward Manor House Farm, Dishforth		
	Built by J F Cliff – project PFA 247-12966 (NF 04.06.15)		
G-CCRK	Luscombe 8A	3186	16.02.04
	N71759, NC71759 J R Kimberley		
	Wolves Hall, Tendering		11.06.18P
G-CCRN	Thruster T600N 450	1031-T600N-096	25.02.04
	A W Ambrose & R Locke		
	Knapthorpe Lodge, Caunton		12.11.18P
	Badged 'Sprint'		
G-CCRP	Thruster T600N 450	0043-T600N-099	17.03.04
	G-ULLY, G-CCRP M M Lane		
	South Wraxall, Bradford on Avon		16.12.10P
	In open storage 05.15 (NF 27.09.17)		
G-CCRR	Best Off Skyranger 912(1)	SKR0310393	16.01.04
	M S N Alam Hunsdon		15.07.17P
	Built by J A Hunt – project BMAA/HB/329;		
	CofA suspended 08.07.17		
G-CCRT	Mainair Pegasus Quantum 15	8014	03.02.04
	N Mitchell East Fortune		09.06.18P
	Built by Mainair Sports Ltd		
G-CCRV	Best Off Skyranger Swift 912(1)	SKR0304315	20.02.04
	D Matthews Westonzoyland		10.01.20P
	Built by M R Mosley – project BMAA/HB/283		
G-CCRW	Mainair Pegasus Quik	8003	16.03.04
	M L Cade Rayne Hall Farm, Rayne		30.08.18P
G-CCRX	Avtech Jabiru UL-450	0569	03.03.04
	M Everest Deanland		11.08.17P
	Built by M Everest – project PFA 274A-14032		
G-CCSD	Mainair Pegasus Quik	8023	19.03.04
	D W C Beer (Farringdon, Exeter)		15.04.19P
G-CCSF	Mainair Pegasus Quik	8030	01.04.04
	D G Barnes & A Sorah Caernarfon		01.07.18P

G-CCSG Cameron Z-275   10518   02.04.04
Wickers World Ltd   Priory Farm, Tibenham
'Heart of England Balloons'   25.03.13E
Stored at Priory Farm, Tibenham 01.19 (NF 07.11.17)

G-CCSH Mainair Pegasus Quik   8020   01.03.04
G Carr   Knapthorpe Lodge, Caunton   09.12.18P

G-CCSL Mainair Pegasus Quik   8029   26.04.04
A J Harper   Manor Farm, Croughton   29.04.18P

G-CCSN Cessna U206G   U20604224   26.03.04
F-GECP, D-EKAX, (OY-ASG), N756NM
K Brady   Strathallan   29.05.16E
Operated by Strathallan Parachute Club;
force landing after engine failure at Strathallan
14.05.15 & damaged

G-CCSP Cameron N-77   2882   17.03.04
SE-ZFV   D Berg   Molnlycke, Sweden   *'Reslust'*   03.06.18E

G-CCSR Evektor EV-97A Eurostar   xxxx   18.03.04
D Malbon tr Sierra Romeo Flying Group   Netherthorpe   18.04.18P
Built by M Lang – project PFA 315-14174

G-CCSS Lindstrand LBL 90A   973   11.02.04
British Telecommunications PLC   Thatcham   *'BT'*   10.05.18E

G-CCST Piper PA-32R-301 Saratoga II HP   3246182   14.02.01
N4180T   A R Whibley   Brighton City   15.02.18E
Official type data 'PA-32R-301 Saratoga SP' is incorrect

G-CCSW Nott PA   9   24.03.04
J R P Nott   Santa Barbara, California, USA
(NF 22.05.18)

G-CCSX Best Off Skyranger Swift 912(1)   SKR0401425   24.03.04
T Jackson   Chase Farm, Chipping Sodbury   12.05.19P
Built by T Jackson – project BMAA/HB/366

G-CCSY Mainair Pegasus Quik   8022   27.02.04
G J Gibson   Perth   12.07.16P
(IE 21.04.17)

G-CCTA Zenair CH.601UL Zodiac   6-69207   04.02.04
P Moore   Sackville Lodge Farm, Riseley   25.10.12P
Built by R E Gray & G T Harris
– project PFA 162A-13725 (NF 30.06.16)

G-CCTC Mainair Pegasus Quik   8021   23.02.04
D R Purslow   Pound Green   23.07.18P

G-CCTD Mainair Pegasus Quik   8040   16.03.04
R N S Taylor   Headon Farm, Retford   02.08.13P
(NF 28.06.16)

G-CCTE Dyn'Aéro MCR-01 Club   61   22.03.04
C J McInnes   Rougham   14.02.18P
Built by G J Slater – project PFA 301-13268

G-CCTF Pitts S-2A   2146   26.03.04
N51ST   B Moyaux tr Stampe & Pitts Flying Group
Chastre, Walloon Brabant, Belgium   22.08.18E
Built by Aerotek Inc

G-CCTG Van's RV-3B   xxxx   09.03.04
A Donald   Netherthorpe   19.03.18P
Project no. allocated 06.80 to P Hing (Van's RV-3
G-BHXN c/n EAA 105098) & cancelled 09.91);
built by I G Glenn – project PFA O99-10518

G-CCTH Evektor EV-97 teamEurostar UK   2004-2005   12.03.04
B M Davis   Finmere   14.12.18P
Assembled Cosmik Aviation Ltd

G-CCTI Evektor EV-97 teamEurostar UK   2004-2009   06.04.04
Flylight Airsports Ltd   Sywell   27.04.18P
Assembled Cosmik Aviation Ltd

G-CCTM Mainair Blade   1363-0504-7-W1158   05.04.04
J N Hanson   Yeatsall Farm, Abbots Bromley   04.06.10P
(NF 08.09.17)

G-CCTO Evektor EV-97 Eurostar   "1232"   17.03.04
H Cooke & B Robertson   Eshott   11.07.18P
Built by A J Boulton – project PFA 315-14136

G-CCTP Evektor EV-97 Eurostar   2003-1910   18.02.04
P E Rose   Ashcroft   25.08.12P
Built by G M Yule – project PFA 315-14185
(NF 29.03.18)

G-CCTR Best Off Skyranger 912(2)   SKR0401410   02.03.04
K Mallin   Pound Green   02.08.13P
Built by A H Trapp – project BMAA/HB/350
(NF 18.11.15)

G-CCTS Cameron Z-120   10570   22.06.04
F R Hart   Bishops Sutton, Bristol   *'Snap Surveys'*   22.02.18E

G-CCTT Cessna 172S Skyhawk SP   172S8157   12.02.04
N957SP   Highland Aviation Training Ltd   Inverness   08.10.18E
Operated by Highland Aviation

G-CCTU Mainair Pegasus Quik   8024   21.04.04
N J Lindsay   Strathaven   21.05.18P

G-CCTV Rans S-6-ES Coyote II   0302.1437   19.06.03
B Swindon   London Colney   14.09.18P
Built by R M Broom – project PFA 204-14069; tricycle u/c

G-CCTZ Mainair Pegasus Quik   8031   13.04.04
S Baker   (Alcester)   01.02.10P
(NF 26.02.18)

G-CCUA Mainair Pegasus Quik   8032   27.04.04
J B Crawford   (Somerton)   25.06.18P

G-CCUB Piper J-3C-65 Cub   2362A   02.04.81
N33528, NC33528, NX33528
G Cormack   Easter Poldar Farm, Thornhill
(IE 26.04.17)

G-CCUC Best Off Skyranger J2.2(1)   UK/453   13.04.04
EI-DNW, G-CCUC   R Marrs   Carrickmore   28.08.18P
Built by M Kerrison – project BMAA/HB/373

G-CCUE Ultramagic T-180   180/45   10.05.04
N J Dunnington   Langford, Bristol
'Espiritu Balloon Flights'   27.02.14E
(NF 08.09.17)

G-CCUF Best Off Skyranger 912(2)   SKR0403459   15.04.04
R E Parker   Hunsdon   29.07.18P
Built by C D Hogbourne & D J Parrish
– project BMAA/HB/375

G-CCUH Rotary Air Force RAF 2000 GTX-SE   H2-03-14-575   16.04.04
V G Freke   (Eynsham)   04.06.19P
Built by D R Lazenby – project PFA G/13-1356;
damaged 09.07.18

G-CCUI Dyn'Aéro MCR-01   236   01.04.04
J T Morgan   Sywell   11.01.18P
Built by J T Morgan – project PFA 301-13963

G-CCUK[M] Agusta A109A II   7263   14.09.11
RP-C109, I-SEIE, N109AE   Cancelled 09.09.15 as PWFU   18.03.12
As 'N64EA'
With History of Wheels Museum, Windsor

G-CCUL Europa Aviation Europa XS   336   20.04.04
I P Dole tr Europa 6   Rayne Hall Farm, Rayne   27.03.18P
Built by I Dole – project PFA 247-13119; tailwheel u/c

G-CCUR Mainair Pegasus Quantum 15-912   8034   30.04.04
B J Fallows   Swansea   07.06.19P
Built by Mainair Sports Ltd

G-CCUT Evektor EV-97 Eurostar   xxxx   09.03.04
D A Large tr Doctor & the Medics   Croft Farm, Defford   21.08.19P
Built by C K Jones – project PFA 315-14191

G-CCUY Europa Aviation Europa   315   14.04.04
N Evans   Old Buckenham   15.07.10P
Built by N Evans – project PFA 247-13189 (NF 25.07.18)

G-CCUZ Thruster T600N 450   0044-T600N-102   29.04.04
K Davey & M B Sears   Manor House Farm, Foston
Badged 'Sprint'; crashed into gardens Foston
18.08.18 & extensively damaged (IE 08.08.18)

G-CCVA Evektor EV-97 Eurostar   2003-1914   21.04.04
K J Scott   Middle Stoke, Isle of Grain   01.07.18P
Built by T A Jones – project PFA 315-14226

G-CCVE Raj Hamsa X'Air Falcon Jabiru(3)   885   25.03.04
(F-....), G-CCVE   G J Slater   (Marlborough)
Built by G J Slater – project BMAA/HB/361;
stored unmarked 08.16 (NF 19.03.15)

G-CCVF Lindstrand LBL 105A   953   06.05.04
A W Patterson & S Villiers t/a Alan Patterson Design
Helens Bay, Bangor   29.05.18E

G-CCVH Curtiss H75A-1   12881   25.05.04
NX80FR, G-CCVH, French AF 82   Patina Ltd   Duxford   13.05.19P
Operated by The Fighter Collection;
as '82 X881:8' in Armee de l'Air c/s

G-CCVI Zenair CH.701SP   7-9465   05.05.04
P J Bunce   (Mangotsfield, Bristol)   12.06.18P
Built by C R Hoveman – project PFA 187-14181

G-CCVJ Raj Hamsa X'Air Falcon Jabiru(3)   916   07.05.04
D A Karniewicz   Coombs Farm, Goodleigh   01.10.19P
Built by G A J Salter – project BMAA/HB/381; stalled &
fell vertically near Coombs Farm, Goodleigh 08.04.18

G-CCVK Evektor EV-97 teamEurostar UK   2004-2016   19.05.04
J Holditch   (Faversham)   23.09.17P
Assembled Cosmik Aviation Ltd

G-CCVL Zenair CH.601XL Zodiac   605   22.04.04
G Constantine & A Y Leung
Shenstone Hall Farm, Shenstone   09.11.18P
Built by G Constantine & A Y Leung
– project PFA 162B-14204; tricycle u/c

G-CCVM Van's RV-7   71739   12.03.04
J G Small tr Victor Mike Flying Group   RAF Woodvale   07.03.19P
Built by J G Small – project PFA 323-14213

G-CCVN Avtech Jabiru SP-470   0453   10.05.04
J Hume tr Teesside Aviators Group
Morgansfield, Fishburn   17.07.18P
Built by J C Collingwood – project PFA 274B-13677

G-CCVP Beech 58 Baron   TH-1948   13.05.04
PH-ZEM, N80VS   Richard Nash Cars Ltd
Old Buckenham   30.07.18E

G-CCVR Best Off Skyranger Swift 912(1)   SKR0311407   29.04.04
M J Batchelor   West End, Wickwar   21.02.18P
Built by M J Batchelor – project BMAA/HB/353

G-CCVS Van's RV-6A   xxxx   29.03.04
G-CCVC   L Jensen   (Beverley)   22.12.17P
Built by J Edgeworth – project PFA 181A-13413;
damaged 05.08.17, sold for rebuild (NF 16.02.18)

G-CCVU Robinson R22 Beta II   3600   11.05.04
J H P S Sargent   (Bighton, Alresford)   28.05.18E

G-CCVWᴹ Supermarine 379 Spitfire FR.XIVe   6S/649186   18.05.88
Indian AF '42', MV262   Cancelled 06.01.93 as TWFU
As 'G-CCVV'
With Fantasy of Flight, Polk City, Florida

G-CCVW Nicollier HN.700 Menestrel II   xxxx   13.05.04
B F Enock   Bericote Farm, Blackdown   07.09.18P
Built by B F Enock – project PFA 217-11950

G-CCVX Mainair Tri Flyer 250/Flexiform Striker   AS-001   18.05.04
J A Shufflebotham   Fern Farm, Marton
(SSDR microlight since 05.14) (NF 09.08.17)

G-CCVZ Cameron O-120   10586   27.07.04
T M C McCoy   Peasedown St John, Bath   *'Ascent'*   06.07.19E

G-CCWC Best Off Skyranger 912(2)   UK/422   04.05.04
N C Colgan tr G-CCWC Flying Group   Carrickmore   01.12.18P
Built by C Hewer – project BMAA/HB/367

G-CCWL Mainair Blade   1364-0504-7-W1159   19.05.04
M S Eglin   (Bolton)   23.02.18P

G-CCWM Robin DR.400-180 Régent   2457   03.06.04
F-GTZM   D M Scorer   Shotton Colliery, Peterlee   11.04.18E

G-CCWO Mainair Pegasus Quantum 15-912   8042   16.06.04
R Fitzgerald   Plaistows Farm, St Albans   22.08.18P
Built by Mainair Sports Ltd; QuantumLeap modifications

G-CCWP Evektor EV-97 teamEurostar UK   2004-2010   09.06.04
G Finney tr GF Airsports   Deanland   13.04.18P
Assembled Cosmik Aviation Ltd

G-CCWU Best Off Skyranger 912(1)   SKR0403461   01.06.04
A R Young   (Wheatley, Oxford)   18.06.18P
Built by D M Lane – project BMAA/HB/386

G-CCWV Mainair Pegasus Quik   8043   01.06.04
C Buttery   Greenhills Farm, Wheatley Hill   15.11.18P

G-CCWW Mainair Pegasus Quantum 15-912   8035   04.05.04
T Hudson   (Newark)   05.10.18P
Built by Mainair Sports Ltd

G-CCWZ Raj Hamsa X'Air Falcon Jabiru(3)   925   04.05.04
J P S Ixer tr The Norman Group   (Braintree)   15.02.18P
Built by M A Evans – project BMAA/HB/380

G-CCXA Boeing Stearman A75N1 Kaydet (N2S-4) 75-3616   01.06.04
N75TL, N5148N, USN 37869
Skymax (Aviation) Ltd   Headcorn   14.03.18E
As '669' in USAAC c/s

G-CCXB Boeing Stearman B75N1 Kaydet   75-7854   26.07.05
N1363M, USN 38233   C D Walker   Goodwood   20.05.18E
As '699' in USAAC c/s

G-CCXC Mudry CAP 10B   165   26.05.04
N4247M, Mexican AF EPC-162
J E Keighley   Damyns Hall, Upminster   25.02.19E

G-CCXD Lindstrand LBL 105B   996   14.06.04
M T Stevens tr Silver Ghost Balloon Club   Warwick   25.09.18E

G-CCXF Cameron Z-90   10593   03.08.04
B J Workman   Catcutt, Bridgwater   *'Unison'*   22.04.19E

G-CCXG Replica Plans SE.5A   11785   11.06.04
C Morris   Gresford, Wrexham   10.09.18P
Built by C Morris – project PFA 020-11785;
as 'C5430:V' in RFC c/s

G-CCXH Best Off Skyranger J2.2(1)   SKR 0403 458   04.06.04
M J O'Connor   Damyns Hall, Upminster   16.08.18P
Built by Sky Ranger UK Ltd – project BMAA/HB/377

G-CCXI   Thorp T-211   xxxx   22.09.03
Cancelled 18.02.10 by CAA
Newcastle   Built by J & S G R Gilroy – PFA 305-13504
Instructional frame Newcastle Aviation Academy 02.16

G-CCXK Pitts S-1S   AACA/1061   14.06.04
ZK-ECO   P G Bond   Shipdham   27.03.18P
Built by E C Roberts

G-CCXM Best Off Skyranger Swift 912(1)   SKR0311394   16.06.04
P Batchelor   Hadfold Farm, Adversane   11.06.19P
Built by C J Finnigan – project BMAA/HB/337

G-CCXN Best Off Skyranger 912(2)   SKR0309383   04.06.04
G D P Clouting   (Swaffham)   08.04.18P
Built by C I Chegwen – project BMAA/HB/323

G-CCXO Corby CJ-1 Starlet   693   21.06.04
S C Ord   Sleap   02.07.18P
Built by I W L Aikman – project PFA 134-13267

G-CCXP ICP MXP-740 Savannah Jabiru(4)   03-09-51-231   30.04.04
M D Gregory   Belle Vue Farm, Yarnscombe   16.05.19P
Built by B J Harper – project BMAA/HB/318

G-CCXS Montgomerie-Bensen B.8MR   xxxx   26.05.04
A Morgan   Kirkbride
Built by S A Sharp – project PFA G/01A-1350
(NF 22.02.18)

G-CCXT Mainair Pegasus Quik   8046   18.06.04
C F Yaxley   Northrepps   06.06.18P

G-CCXU Diamond DA.40D Star   D4.037   28.06.04
ZK-SFH   L & R J Hole
(Mingot, Haute Pyrenees, France)   23.10.18E

G-CCXV Thruster T600N 450   0045-T600N-103   18.06.04
R Kelly   Fowlmere   31.05.17P
Badged 'Sprint' (IE 23.10.17)

G-CCXW Thruster T600N 450   0045-T600N-104   15.07.04
D J Atkinson   (Colchester)   15.08.18P

G-CCXX American General AG-5B Tiger   10160   19.04.04
PH-MLG, YL-CAH   P D Lock   Sturgate   17.04.19E

G-CCXZ Mainair Pegasus Quik   8038   24.05.04
M Innes   (Evanton. Dingwall)   11.06.19P

G-CCYB Reality Escapade 912(1)   JA.ESC.0034   24.06.04
B E & S M Renehan   Lasham   28.07.18P
Built by B E Renehan – project BMAA/HB/391

G-CCYC Robinson R44 Raven II   10388   24.06.04
J Butler   (Rosecrea, Co Tipperary, RoI)   29.07.18E

G-CCYE Mainair Pegasus Quik   8050   30.07.04
P M Scrivener   (Beedon, Newbury)   22.07.18P

G-CCYG Robinson R44 Raven II   10424   09.07.04
H & S Wild t/a Mosswood Caravan Park
Hapton Valley Colliery, Burnley   12.12.18E

G-CCYI Cameron O-105   10604   30.07.04
S Bitti   Jesi, Ancona, Italy   05.04.18E

G-CCYJ Mainair Pegasus Quik   8054   02.08.04
G M Cruise-Smith   Rankins Farm, Linton   02.10.18P

G-CCYL Mainair Pegasus Quantum 15   8055   26.07.04
A M Goulden   Harringe Court, Sellindge   25.05.18P
Built by Mainair Sports Ltd

G-CCYM Best Off Skyranger 912(2)   SKR0401412   16.07.04
I Pilton   Brook Farm, Pilling   07.04.18P
Built by D McDonagh – project BMAA/HB/390

G-CCYO   Christen Eagle II   HAYNER 0001   13.09.04
N56RJ   P C Woolley   Cadwell Park, Louth   20.11.07P
Built by R Hayner (NF 26.01.15)

G-CCYP   Colt 56A   302   23.07.04
SE-ZXG   Magical Adventures Ltd
West Bloomfield, MI, USA   27.09.09E
(NF 03.06.15)

G-CCYR   Comco Ikarus C42 FB80   0408-6612   20.09.04
Airbourne Aviation Ltd   Popham   14.05.19P
Assembled Fly Buy Ultralights Ltd

G-CCYS   Reims/Cessna F182Q Skylane II   F18200126   31.08.04
OY-BNG   Just Plane Trading Ltd
Top Farm, Croydon   15.07.18E

G-CCYU   Ultramagic S-90   90/70   17.08.04
J Francis   Dibden Purlieu, Southampton   13.06.18E

G-CCYX   Bell 412   34001   02.08.04
PK-HMI   RCR Aviation Ltd   Redhill
Built by IPTN (NF 16.02.16)

G-CCYY   Piper PA-28-161 Warrior II   2816094   17.06.04
HB-PML   Flightcontrol Ltd   Fairoaks   06.10.18E

G-CCYZ   Dornier EKW C-3605   338   30.09.04
N31624, Swiss AF C-558   CW Tomkins Ltd   Wickenby
*Built by Federal Aircraft Factory; rebuild abandoned
& in open storage 12.16 (NF 29.03.18)*

G-CCZA   SOCATA MS.894A Rallye Minerva 220   12094   14.07.05
D-EBWL, F-BUVI   R N Aylett   Sturgate   29.07.10E
In open store 02.19 (NF 19.01.16)

G-CCZB   Mainair Pegasus Quantum 15   8052   21.07.04
J A Crofts   Penrhiw Farm, Crymych   25.09.19P
Built by Mainair Sports Ltd

G-CCZD   Van's RV-7   xxxx   28.05.04
A P Hatton & E A Stokes   Rectory Farm, Averham   '22'   19.04.19P
Built by R T Clegg – project PFA 323-14087

G-CCZJ   Raj Hamsa X'Air Falcon 582(2)   911   05.08.04
C R Stevens & S Uzochukwu
Barhams Mill Farm, Egerton   17.11.18P
Built by A B Gridley – project BMAA/HB/401

G-CCZK   Zenair CH.601UL Zodiac   6-9551   11.08.04
R J Hopkins & J Lonergan   Popham   18.05.17P
*Built by R J Hopkins – project PFA 162A-14270;
tricycle u/c*

G-CCZL   Comco Ikarus C42 FB80   0410-6620   29.11.04
Shadow Aviation Ltd   Old Sarum   'The African Queen'   27.05.18P
Assembled Fly Buy Ultralights Ltd

G-CCZM   Best Off Skyranger 912S(1)   UK/455   01.07.04
D Woodward tr Skyranger Group G-CCZM
Beverley (Linley Hill)   03.12.18P
Built by D M Hepworth – project BMAA/HB/372

G-CCZN   Rans S-6-ES Coyote II   0404.1561 ES   09.08.04
R D Proctor   RAF Wyton   05.05.18P
Built by M Taylor – project PFA 204-14275; tricycle u/c

G-CCZO   Mainair Pegasus Quik   8066   02.09.04
P G Penhaligan   Middle Stoke, Isle of Grain   25.05.18P

G-CCZS   Raj Hamsa X'Air Falcon 582(2)   943   16.08.04
S Siddiqui   (Mullingar, Co Westmeath, RoI)   05.06.18P
Built by P J Sheehy – project BMAA/HB/403

G-CCZT   Van's RV-9A   90389   10.08.04
B McPheat & J Roberts tr Zulu Tango Flying Group
North Weald   09.05.19P
Built by N A Henderson – project PFA 320-13777

G-CCZV   Piper PA-28-151 Cherokee Warrior   28-7715089   07.07.04
OY-CHR, SE-GNY
London School of Flying Ltd   Elstree   28.02.19E
Operated by Flight Training London Ltd

G-CCZW   Mainair Blade   1368-0904-7-W1163 21.10.04
D Sisson   Headon Farm, Retford   14.02.18P

G-CCZX   Robin DR.400-180 Régent   2127   15.09.04
F-GLKY   Exeter Aviation Ltd   Exeter Int'l   23.05.18E

G-CCZY   Van's RV-9A   xxxx   23.08.04
A Hutchinson   Blackpool   11.06.18P
*Built by P Huws, T E Owen, G Williams &
R Winward – project PFA 320-14154*

G-CCZZ   Evektor EV-97 Eurostar   2003-1233   28.05.04
J P Aitken & B M Starck   Old Warden   05.08.18P
Built by R Bastin & B M Starck – project PFA 315-14158

G-CDAA – G-CDZZ

G-CDAA   Mainair Pegasus Quantum 15-912   8069   27.08.04
G E Parker   Rochester   22.08.18P
Built by Mainair Sports Ltd

G-CDAB   Stoddard-Hamilton Glasair Super IIS RG 2390   07.07.04
D A Payne   City of Derry   04.05.16P
Built by W L Hitchins – project PFA 149-13231

G-CDAC   Evektor EV-97 teamEurostar UK   2004-2116   30.09.04
C R Cousins   Fenland   30.07.18P
Assembled Cosmik Aviation Ltd

G-CDAD   Lindstrand LBL 25A Cloudhopper   1003   21.09.04
G J Madelin   Farnham   29.11.18E

G-CDAE   Van's RV-6A   24379   05.08.04
S L Sapsford tr The Alpha Echo Group   Leicester   09.08.18P
Built by K J Fleming – project PFA 181A-13018

G-CDAI   Robin DR.400/135 cdi Dauphin   2574   13.12.04
D-EEAQ, G-CDAI   P C Mclean   Nottingham City   13.07.18E
*Built by Constructions Aeronautiques de Bourgogne;
type change with new engine*

G-CDAL   Zenair CH.601UL Zodiac   6-9501   07.06.04
J Cook   Westonzoyland   14.10.19P
*Built by D Cassidy – project PFA 162A-14195;
tricycle u/c*

G-CDAO   Mainair Pegasus Quantum 15-912   8061   17.08.04
J C Duncan   Campbeltown   16.02.18P
Built by Mainair Sports Ltd; trailered in to fly

G-CDAP   Evektor EV-97 teamEurostar UK   2004-2114   28.07.04
L N Givens   Ince   22.12.18P
Assembled Cosmik Aviation Ltd

G-CDAR   Mainair Pegasus Quik   8060   17.08.04
J L Merriman tr Caunton Graphites Syndicate
Knapthorpe Lodge, Caunton   27.08.19P

G-CDAT   ICP MXP-740 Savannah Jabiru(4)   03-05-51-211   07.07.04
G M Railson   Eshott   18.09.18P
Built by R Simpson – project BMAA/HB/327

G-CDAX   Mainair Pegasus Quik   8068   08.09.04
L Hurman   Landmead Farm, Garford   '208'   25.04.18P

G-CDAY   Best Off Skyranger 912(2)   SKR0404473   07.07.04
N A Martin tr Redlands Skyranger Group   Redlands   24.07.18P
Built by M E Furniss – project BMAA/HB/394

G-CDAZ   Evektor EV-97 Eurostar   2003-1281   13.08.04
K M Howell   (West Bromwich)   22.05.19P
Built by M C J Ludlow – project PFA 315-14268

G-CDBA   Best Off Skyranger Swift 912(1)   SKR0404484   21.10.04
P J Brennan   Ashcroft
*Built by P J Brennan – project BMAA/HB/406
(IE 01.12.17)*

G-CDBB   Mainair Pegasus Quik   8062   16.08.04
J McLaughlin   (Braco, Dunblane)   12.07.18P

G-CDBD   Avtech Jabiru J400   105   16.08.04
I D Rutherford   Holmbeck Farm, Burcott   13.08.18P
Built by E Bentley & S Derwin – project PFA 325-14077

G-CDBE   Montgomerie-Bensen B.8M   xxxx   07.09.04
P A Harwood   Rufforth East   08.08.07P
*Built by P Harwood – project PFA G/01-1360;
displayed Gyrocopter Experience 05.18 (NF 22.08.14)*

G-CDBG   Robinson R22 Beta II   3682   11.10.04
JW Ramsbottom Contractors Ltd t/a Jepar Rotorcraft
Blackpool   19.11.16E
(NF 01.11.17)

G-CDBJ   Yakovlev Yak-3   0470203   01.11.07
RA-3364K, F-WQVI, RA-44553
C E Bellhouse   Pent Farm, Postling   12.05.09P
*Built by JSC A.S. Yakovlev Design Bureau; officially
registered as c/n 02-03; as '21' (white) in Russian
AF c/s; on rebuild 08.14 (NF 04.12.15)*

G-CDBK   RotorWay Exec 162F   6834   20.09.04
R S Snell   Street Farm, Takeley   13.03.16P
Built by N & M Foreman; noted 06.17 (NF 13.06.16)

G-CDBM Robin DR.400-180 Régent   2573   16.11.04
C M Simmonds   Perranporth   25.02.18E
Built by Constructions Aeronautiques de Bourgogne

G-CDBO Best Off Skyranger 912(2)   SKR0401424   13.08.04
A C Turnbull tr The G-CDBO Flying Group   Perth   10.02.18P
Built by A M Dalgetty – project BMAA/HB/370

G-CDBR Stolp SA.300 Starduster Too   xxxx   15.09.04
R J Warren   White Waltham   29.08.17P
Built by R J Warren – project PFA 35-13036

G-CDBU Comco Ikarus C42 FB100   0411-6632   26.01.05
J K Agarwala & S E Meehan   Ince   07.06.18P

G-CDBV Best Off Skyranger 912S(1)   SKR0406499   23.09.04
C R Burgess & T Smith   Harringe Court, Sellindge   20.05.18P
Built by K Hall – project BMAA/HB/409

G-CDBX Europa Aviation Europa XS   568   16.09.04
R J Bastin tr G-CDBX Group   Kirton in Lindsey   09.04.19P
Built by R Marston – project PFA 247-13971; tricyle u/c

G-CDBY Dyn'Aéro MCR-01 ULC   288   23.08.04
A Thornton   Ince   28.08.18P
Built by R Germany – project PFA 301B-14269

G-CDBZ Thruster T600N 450   0047-T600N-106   24.09.04
J A Lynch tr BZ Flying Group   Sandown   29.09.18P

G-CDCC Evektor EV-97 Eurostar   2003-1282   11.08.04
J R Tomlin   The Firs Farm, Leckhampstead
'The Dream'   16.04.18P
Built by N G & R E Nicholson – project PFA 315A-14262

G-CDCD Van's RV-9A   90547   20.01.04
S D Arnold tr RV9ers   Wellesbourne Mountford   18.12.13P
*Built by S D Arnold & M Weaver – project
PFA 320-13925; forced landed near Wellesbourne
Mountford 06.08.13 & extensively damaged
(NF 27.04.16)*

G-CDCE Mudry CAP 10B   039   03.11.04
F-BNDC, CN-TBW, F-BUDG
The Tiger Club 1990 Ltd   Damyns Hall, Upminster   07.07.18E

G-CDCF Mainair Pegasus Quik   8076   08.11.04
P Thaxter   Northrepps   12.04.18P

G-CDCG Comco Ikarus C42 FB UK   0408-6625   16.08.04
N E Ashton   Ince   14.11.18P
*Built by N E Ashton & R H J Jenkins
– project PFA 322-14281*

G-CDCH Best Off Skyranger Swift 912(1)   SKR0401436   28.09.04
M D Protheroe   Old Park Farm, Margam   08.08.19P
Built by K Laud – project BMAA/HB/384

G-CDCI Mainair Pegasus Quik   8077   14.01.05
R J Allarton   Knapthorpe Lodge, Caunton   25.07.18P

G-CDCM Comco Ikarus C42 FB UK   0408-6624   26.10.04
S T Allen   Lydeway Field, Etchilhampton   10.05.18P
*Built by S T Allen – project PFA 322-14280;
badged 'Icarus C42B'*

G-CDCO Comco Ikarus C42 FB UK   0411-6634   07.10.04
R Urquhart   Morgansfield, Fishburn   07.11.18P
Built by G G Bevis – project PFA 322-14315

G-CDCP Avtech Jabiru J400   xxxx   07.10.04
J Cherry   Eshott   04.05.18P
Built by M W T Wilson – project PFA 325-14094

G-CDCR ICP MXP-740 Savannah Jabiru(4)   04-06-51-291   14.01.05
T Davidson & G McKinstry   Slieve Croob, Castlewellan   14.06.18P
*Built by T Davidson & G McKinstry
– project BMAA/HB/405*

G-CDCS Piper PA-12 Super Cruiser   12-2907   29.09.04
N854CC, CS-ACC   P Westerby-Jones   Breighton   05.11.19P

G-CDCT Evektor EV-97 teamEurostar UK   2004-2117   15.09.04
G R Nicholson   Derryogue, Kilkeel   18.10.18P
Assembled Cosmik Aviation Ltd

G-CDCV Robinson R44 Clipper II   10536   28.10.04
3GRComm Ltd   Gloucestershire   08.03.18E

G-CDCW Reality Escapade 912(1)   JA.ESC.0050   04.10.04
S G Brown   Willingale   24.04.19P
Built by P Nicholls – project BMAA/HB/413; tricycle u/c

G-CDDA SOCATA TB-20 Trinidad   1860   22.10.04
PH-SXE, F-OIGL   Z Clean   (Galstead, Denmark)   07.04.16E
(IE 16.11.17) (Stored 10.18)

G-CDDB Schempp-Hirth Standard Cirrus   577G   13.10.04
BGA 5102/KHJ, F-CEMG   R Robins   Talgarth   *'KM'*   06.11.19E
Built by Burkhart Grob Flugzeugbau

G-CDDF Mainair Pegasus Quantum 15-912   8079   08.11.04
Jarvy Enterprises Ltd   Eshott   02.05.19P

G-CDDG Piper PA-28-161 Warrior II   2816065   04.10.04
HB-PLU   Aviation Advice & Consulting Ltd
Wellesbourne Mountford   12.12.18E
Operated by Tayside Aviation

G-CDDH Raj Hamsa X'Air Falcon Jabiru(3)   944   26.10.04
G Loosley   Sackville Lodge Farm, Riseley   18.12.18P
Built by B Stanbridge – project BMAA/HB/419

G-CDDI Thruster T600N 450   1040-T600N-109   26.10.04
R Nayak   North Coates   22.01.19P
Badged 'Sprint'

G-CDDK Cessna 172M Skyhawk   17265258   01.12.04
TF-SIX, N64478   B K & W G Ranger   Popham   05.05.19E

G-CDDL Cameron Z-350   10632   24.05.05
Adventure Balloons Ltd   Hartley Wintney, Hook
'British School of Ballooning'   25.05.18E

G-CDDN Lindstrand LBL 90A   903   14.01.05
ZS-HAK   D J Groombridge & I J Martin t/a Flying
Enterprises   Congresbury & Wotton-under-Edge
'www.fishtank.cc'   29.07.19E

G-CDDP Laser Lazer Z230   001   16.11.04
N230RT   P R Elvidge tr G-CDDP Flying Group
Breighton   29.03.18P
Built by F L Thomson

G-CDDR Best Off Skyranger 582(1)   SKR0406502   26.10.04
A K Carver & A Greenwell
Brown Shutters Farm, Norton St Philip   31.03.19P
Built by R J Milward – project BMAA/HB/418

G-CDDS Zenair CH.601HD Zodiac   6-9505   08.10.04
D J Hunter   Priory Farm, Tibenham   31.10.19P
Built by S Foreman – project PFA 162-14223; tricycle u/c

G-CDDU Best Off Skyranger 912(2)   SKR0404506   10.11.04
P A Burton & R Newton   Darley Moor   07.06.18P
Built by R C Reynolds – project BMAA/HB/422

G-CDDW Aeroprakt A-22 Foxbat   UK018   08.09.04
A Asslanian   (Cuffley, Potters Bar)   11.04.18P
Built by D A A Wineberg – project PFA 317-14261

G-CDDX Thruster T600N 450   0049-T600N-107   11.11.04
B S P Finch   Orange Grove Barn, Chavenage Green   18.03.18P
Badged 'Sprint'

G-CDDY Van's RV-8   80912   24.11.04
N701CZ   D F Clorley   RAF Mona   31.08.18P
Built by C S Ziekle

G-CDEB Saab 2000   2000-036   30.11.04
HB-IZT, G-CDEB, SE-036, HB-IZT, SE-036
Air Kilroe Ltd t/a Eastern Airways   Humberside   29.11.18E

G-CDEF Piper PA-28-161 Cadet   2841341   12.11.04
D-ESTD, N9184X, N621FT, (OH-PFB)
Falcon Flying Services Ltd   Biggin Hill   26.02.19E

G-CDEH ICP MXP-740 Savannah VG LS(1)   03-03-51-200   18.11.04
D C Crawley   Salterford Farm, Calverton   14.08.18P
*Built by S Whittaker & P J Wilson
– project BMAA/HB/349 (IE 04.10.18)*

G-CDEM Raj Hamsa X'Air 133(1)   939   17.11.04
R J Froud   (Freshwater)   13.07.18P
Built by R J Froud – project BMAA/HB/421

G-CDEN Mainair Pegasus Quantum 15-912   8087   30.11.04
J D J Spragg   Streethay Farm, Streethay   18.05.18P
Built by Mainair Sports Ltd

G-CDEO Piper PA-28-180 Cherokee Archer   28-7405011   17.02.05
HB-OQE, N9568N   Perranporth Flying Club Ltd
Perranporth   12.05.18E

G-CDEP Evektor EV-97 teamEurostar UK   2004-2128   06.12.04
N Morrison & P S Rose tr Echo Papa Group
Wycombe Air Park   30.11.18P
Assembled Cosmik Aviation Ltd

G-CDET Culver LCA Cadet   129   10.11.86
N29261, NC29261   J Gregson   Eshott   21.07.11P
(NF 29.05.15)

G-CDEU	Lindstrand LBL 90B	1015	07.02.05
	N Florence & P J Marshall Udimore, Rye		21.03.18E
G-CDEV	Reality Escapade 912(1)	JA.ESC.0024	26.10.04
	M A Neeves tr Banana Group Leicester		11.04.19P
	Built by M B Devenport – project BMAA/HB/360		
G-CDEW	Mainair Pegasus Quik	8083	13.01.05
	S D Sparrow (Hinckley)		25.07.19P
G-CDEX	Europa Aviation Europa	012	21.10.04
	K Martindale Morgansfield, Fishburn		14.03.18P
	Built by S Collins – project PFA 247-12507; tricycle u/c		
G-CDFD	Scheibe SF25C Rotax-Falke	44705	01.12.04
	D-KEOQ The Royal Air Force Gliding & Soaring		
	Association Keevil		16.02.19E
	Operated by Bannerdown Gliding Club		
G-CDFG	Mainair Pegasus Quik	8082	21.12.04
	D Gabbott Ince		02.04.18P
G-CDFJ	Best Off Skyranger Swift 912(1)	SKR0404490	06.12.04
	K S Reardon Rochester		27.04.19P
	Built by W C Yates – project BMAA/HB/424		
G-CDFK	Avtech Jabiru UL-450	571	02.12.04
	J C Eagle Maypole Farm, Chislet *'Calypso'*		01.11.18P
	Built by H J Bradley – project PFA 274A-14144		
G-CDFL	Zenair CH.601UL Zodiac	6-9536	30.11.04
	F G Green tr Caunton Zodiac Group		
	Knapthorpe Lodge, Caunton		13.03.18P
	Built by V Causey, F G Green & R Welch		
	– project PFA 162A-14309; tricycle u/c		
G-CDFM	Raj Hamsa X'Air 582(5)	920	02.12.04
	W A Keel-Stocker (Norton, Gloucester)		20.04.18P
	Built by J Griffiths – project BMAA/HB/417		
G-CDFN	Thunder Ax7-77	3697	22.02.06
	I-FMCL (2) E Rullo		
	Caulonia Marina, Reggio Calabria, Italy		
	Built by Cameron Balloons Ltd (NF 11.06.14)		
G-CDFO	Mainair Pegasus Quik	8080	17.01.05
	C E Hannigan tr The Foxtrot Oscars Syndicate Balado	28.09.18P
G-CDFR	Cyclone Pegasus Quantum 15	6943	08.03.05
	CS-UGX P D J Davies Redlands		05.05.19P
G-CDFU	Rans S-6-ES Coyote II	0304.1560	03.11.04
	G Mudd Grove Farm, Raveningham		13.03.18P
	Built by P W Taylor – project PFA 204-14232; tricycle u/c		
G-CDFW^M	Lovegrove Sheffey Gyroplane	PCL129	05.09.05
	Cancelled 17.05.10 as WFU *'Sheffy'*		
	Built by P C Lovegrove – project PFA G/19-1366)		
	With Norfolk & Suffolk Aviation Museum, Flixton		
G-CDGA	Taylor JT.1 Monoplane	6020-1	28.12.78
	R M Larimore (Crich, Matlock)		
	Built by D G Anderson – project PFA 055-10382		
	(NF 12.06.18)		
G-CDGB	Rans S-6-116 Coyote II	0696.1006	21.12.04
	S Penoyre (Windlesham)		27.04.16P
	Built by S Penoyre – project PFA 204A-13047		
	(IE 01.12.17)		
G-CDGC	Mainair Pegasus Quik	8090	26.01.05
	A T K Crozier Strathaven		29.05.18P
G-CDGD	Mainair Pegasus Quik	8086	11.11.04
	I D & V A Milne St Michaels		20.02.18P
G-CDGE	AirBorne XT912-B/Streak III-B	XT912-028	22.12.04
	T2-2253 M R Leyshon tr M & G Flight (Brierley Hill)	17.04.18P
	Wing s/n S3B-009		
G-CDGF	Ultramagic S-105	105/127	09.03.05
	D & K Bareford Cookley, Kidderminster		11.07.18E
G-CDGH	Rans S-6-ES Coyote II	1203.1537 ES	22.12.04
	A L Virgoe Over Farm, Gloucester		30.08.18P
	Built by K T Vinning – project PFA 204-14209; tricycle u/c		
G-CDGI	Thruster T600N 450	1041-T600N-108	05.01.05
	P A Pilkington Strubby		18.10.14P
	Badged 'Sprint' (NF 13.01.17)		
G-CDGN	Cameron C-90	10641	24.02.05
	M C Gibbons Severn Beach, Bristol		23.04.19E
G-CDGO	Mainair Pegasus Quik	8084	11.11.04
	J C Townsend Ince		04.07.18P

G-CDGP	Zenair CH.601XL Zodiac	6-9603	06.01.05
	B & P J Chandler Charmy Down		07.12.18P
	Built by T J Bax – project PFA 162B-14313; tailwheel u/c		
G-CDGR	Zenair CH.701UL	7-9597	06.01.05
	I A R Sim Main Hall Farm, Conington		16.11.18P
	Built by M Morris – project PFA 187-14327		
G-CDGS	American General AG-5B Tiger	10097	07.02.05
	PH-BMA, N1195Q M R O'B Thompson Popham	19.06.18E
G-CDGT	Montgomerie-Parsons Two-Place	xxxx	10.01.05
	J B Allan (Corringham, Stanford-le-Hope)		21.08.18P
	Built by A A Craig – project PFA G/08-1361		
G-CDGU	Supermarine 300 Spitfire I	6S-75156	07.01.05
	X4276 Peter Monk Ltd (Pembury, Tunbridge Wells)	
	(NF 18.06.18)		
G-CDGW	Piper PA-28-181 Archer II	28-7990402	13.01.05
	HB-PDZ, N2156Z B F Millet tr Rutland Flying Group	
	Shacklewell Lodge Farm, Empingham		23.02.18E
G-CDGX	Mainair Pegasus Quantum 15-912	8096	28.01.05
	S R Green (Bishops Itchington, Southam)		27.05.18P
	Built by Mainair Sports Ltd		
G-CDGY	Supermarine 349 Spitfire Vc	WWA3832	19.01.05
	ZK-MKV, RAAF A58-149, EF545		
	Aero Vintage Ltd (Northiam, Rye)		
	Built by Westland Aircraft Ltd (NF 06.12.18)		
G-CDHA	Best Off Skyranger 912S(1)	SKR0407508	18.01.05
	A T Cameron (Myroe, Limavady)		30.08.18P
	Built by K J Gay – project BMAA/HB/428		
G-CDHC	Slingsby T67C Firefly	2081	20.01.05
	PH-SGC, (PH-SBC), G-7-138 J Watson &		
	C J Wheeler tr Brimpton Flying Group Brimpton	08.12.18E
G-CDHE	Best Off Skyranger 912(2)	SKR0406500	26.01.05
	T Collins (Chard)		30.04.19P
	Built by S Owen – project BMAA/HB/412		
G-CDHF	Piper PA-30 Twin Comanche B	30-1111	17.02.05
	LX-AML, F-BJCC, N8005Y		
	M Large Le Plessis-Belleville, France		26.11.18E
G-CDHG	Mainair Pegasus Quik	8092	21.02.05
	T W Pelan Balgrummo Steading, Bonnybank		05.07.17P
G-CDHM	Mainair Pegasus Quantum 15	8085	18.01.05
	M R Smith Brimpton		25.05.18P
	Built by Mainair Sports Ltd		
G-CDHO	Raj Hamsa X'Air 582(12)	902	08.02.05
	S Warburton (Stockton, Southam)		10.04.19P
	Built by W E Corps – project BMAA/HB/408		
G-CDHR	Comco Ikarus C42 FB80	0502-6652	21.02.05
	J Bainbridge Membury		14.08.18P
	Assembled Aerosport Ltd		
G-CDHU	Best Off Skyranger Swift 912(1)	SKR0412546	22.02.05
	A R Parker & K Yeo tr G-CDHU Group		
	Old Park Farm, Margam		22.06.18P
	Built by S J Smith – project BMAA/HB/444		
G-CDHX	Aeroprakt A-22 Foxbat	UK019	28.02.05
	N E Stokes Haughton Farm, Ellesmere		09.11.17P
	Built by B N Searle & N E Stokes		
	– project PFA 317-14297		
G-CDHY	Cameron Z-90	10675	06.07.05
	S F Caie Penllergaer, Swansea *'Kerridge'*		24.02.19E
G-CDHZ	Nicollier HN.700 Menestrel II	218	01.03.05
	G E Whittaker (Formby, Liverpool)		
	Built by G E Whittaker – project PFA 217-14163		
	(NF 12.01.16)		
G-CDIA	Thruster T600N 450	0051-T600N-111	08.03.05
	J A Lynch tr IA Flying Group Sandown		11.07.18P
	Badged 'Sprint'		
G-CDIB	Cameron Z-350	10622	11.05.05
	Ballooning Network Ltd Southville, Bristol		30.04.18E
G-CDIF	Mudry CAP 10B	302	21.06.05
	N126SM, F-GYKD J D Gordon Shobdon		26.03.18E
	Built by Constructions Aeronautiques de Bourgogne		
G-CDIG	Evektor EV-97 Eurostar	2004-2208	22.02.05
	P D Brisco & J Young Otherton		17.08.18P
	Built by A Costello & J Cunliffe – project PFA 315-14353	
G-CDIH	Cameron Z-275	10613	06.04.05
	Bailey Balloons Ltd Pill, Bristol *'Bailey Balloons'*	09.12.16E

G-CDIJ	Best Off Skyranger 912(2)	SKR0501553	03.03.05	
	K C Yeates　Leicester		22.07.18P	
	Built by E B Toulson – project BMAA/HB/445			
G-CDIL	Mainair Pegasus Quantum 15-912	8093	21.12.04	
	P J Doherty　Enstone		25.03.19P	
	Built by Mainair Sports Ltd; QuantumLeap modifications			
G-CDIO	Cameron Z-90	10695	28.04.05	
	Slowfly Mongolfiere SNC　Mondovi, Italy		06.08.13E	
	(NF 08.12.17)			
G-CDIR	Mainair Pegasus Quantum 15-912	8108	08.03.05	
	M Crane　Sywell		12.06.18P	
	Built by Mainair Sports Ltd			
G-CDIT	Cameron Z-105	10702	06.04.05	
	Bailey Balloons Ltd　Pill, Bristol　*'The One Show'*		30.08.15E	
	(NF 27.10.16)			
G-CDIU	Best Off Skyranger 912S(1)	SKR0401405	15.03.05	
	D A Manning　(Church Stretton)		08.05.19P	
	Built by R A Budd & C P Dawes – project BMAA/HB/376			
G-CDIX	Comco Ikarus C42 FB100	0504-6669	20.04.05	
	T G Greenhill & J G Spinks　Glebe Farm, Sibson		11.05.18P	
	Assembled Aerosport Ltd			
G-CDIY	Evektor EV-97A Eurostar	2004-2127	30.12.04	
	R E Woolsey　Derryougue, Kilkeel		05.04.18P	
	Built by G R Pritchard – project PFA 315-14345			
G-CDIZ	Reality Escapade 912(3)	JA.ESC.0033	07.01.05	
	E G Bishop & E N Dunn			
	Brookside Farm, Wootton Courtenay		09.06.18P	
	Built by E G Bishop & E N Dunn			
	– project BMAA/HB/393; tricycle u/c			
G-CDJB	Van's RV-4	1270	21.01.05	
	N21RP　J K Cook　Hill Farm, Nayland		18.05.18P	
	Built by R G Pettyjohn & T A Rudisill;			
	carries '1270' in psuedo USAF c/s			
G-CDJD	ICP MXP-740 Savannah Jabiru(4)	03-05-51-209	22.03.05	
	D W Mullin　Otherton		25.05.18P	
	Built by D W Mullin – project BMAA/HB/321			
G-CDJE	Thruster T600N 450	0053-T600N-112	24.03.05	
	R J Stamp　(Market Rasen)		12.06.18P	
	Badged 'Sprint'			
G-CDJF	Flight Design CT2K	03-07-04-35	08.07.05	
	P A James　Redhill		07.07.18P	
	Assembled Mainair Sports Ltd as c/n 8104			
G-CDJG	Zenair CH.601UL Zodiac	6-9661	09.03.05	
	R G Griffin tr G-CDJG Group			
	The Firs Farm, Leckhampstead		12.02.18P	
	Built by J Garcia – project PFA 162A-14374			
G-CDJI	Ultramagic M-120	120/12	17.05.05	
	S J Roake　Frimley, Camberley　*'Zirtek'*		28.03.19E	
G-CDJJ	IAV Bacau Yakovlev Yak-52	899912	26.05.05	
	LY-AQI, HA-HUY, LY-AFR, DOSAAF 99 (yellow)			
	J J Miles　Brighton City		04.11.19P	
G-CDJK	Comco Ikarus C42 FB80	0504-6666	26.04.05	
	R C Best　Wickenby		14.07.19P	
	Assembled Aerosport Ltd			
G-CDJL	Avtech Jabiru J400	152	04.02.05	
	J Gardiner　Aberdeen Int'l		27.06.18P	
	Built by T R Sinclair – project PFA 325-14215			
G-CDJM	Zenair CH.601XL Zodiac	6-9593	30.12.04	
	Cancelled 15.01.13 as PWFU		04.12.12	
	Little Snoring　*Built by T J Adams-Lewis – project*			
	PFA 162B-14303; wreck dumped 03.13			
G-CDJN	Rotary Air Force RAF 2000 GTX-SE	H2-04-15-632	11.03.05	
	D J North　(Penton Grafton, Andover)		23.09.19P	
	Built by D J North – project PFA G/13-1363			
G-CDJP	Best Off Skyranger 912(2)	UK/501	18.01.05	
	I A Cunningham　Easter Poldar Farm, Thornhill		25.09.11P	
	Built by J S Potts – project BMAA/HB/435;			
	tailwheel u/c (NF 15.07.15)			
G-CDJR	Evektor EV-97 teamEurostar UK	2005-2318	24.03.05	
	K C Lye & M D White　Edington Hill, Edington		18.04.18P	
	Assembled Cosmik Aviation Ltd			
G-CDJU	CASA 1-131E Jungmann Series 1000	1078	25.08.05	
	OO-OLE, EC-DKV, Spanish AF E3B-379			
	P Gaskell　Sleap		03.05.18P	
	As 'CX+HI' in German Air Force c/s			
G-CDJV	Beech A36 Bonanza	E-951	27.04.05	
	HB-EJP, D-EICH, N4296S			
	D A Gathercole　White Fen Farm, Benwick		11.06.19E	
G-CDJY	Cameron C-80	10677	16.05.05	
	British Airways PLC　Harmondsworth, West Drayton			
	'British Airways'		03.07.16E	
	(IE 23.01.17)			
G-CDKA	Saab 2000	2000-006	10.03.05	
	SE-006, HB-IZC, SE-006			
	Air Kilroe Ltd t/a Eastern Airways　London City		11.03.19E	
	Built by Saab Scania AB; operated by BA CityFlyer			
G-CDKB	Saab 2000	2000-032	22.04.05	
	SE-032, LY-SBG, HB-IZQ, SE-032			
	Air Kilroe Ltd t/a Eastern Airways　Humberside		21.04.19E	
	Built by Saab AB			
G-CDKE	Rans S-6-ES Coyote II	0603.1506ES	09.05.05	
	J E Holloway　Tinnel Farm, Landulph		11.04.18P	
	Built by J E Holloway – project PFA 204-14119;			
	tricycle u/c			
G-CDKF	Reality Escapade 912(1)	JA.ESC.0035	15.02.05	
	K R Bircher　Over Farm, Gloucester		14.03.18P	
	Built by P J Little – project BMAA/HB/389			
G-CDKH	Best Off Skyranger 912S(1)	UK/545	14.04.05	
	C Lenaghan　(Crossmaglen, Newry)		25.11.18P	
	Built by W P Byrne – project BMAA/HB/448			
G-CDKI	Best Off Skyranger 912S(1)	SKR0209242	15.04.05	
	J M Hucker　Broadmeadow Farm, Hereford		20.04.18P	
	Built by J M Hucker – project BMAA/HB/434			
G-CDKK	Mainair Pegasus Quik	8097	04.03.05	
	P M Knight　Benson's Farm, Laindon		08.09.18P	
G-CDKL	Reality Escapade 912(1)	JA.ESC.0023	21.04.05	
	G Ferguson tr G-CDKL Group			
	Balgrummo Steading, Bonnybank　*'Yellow Peril'*		15.09.18P	
	Built by D Harker – project BMAA/HB/359			
G-CDKM	Mainair Pegasus Quik	8091	28.01.05	
	P Lister　Ince		15.05.18P	
G-CDKN	ICP MXP-740 Savannah Jabiru(4)	04-06-51-293	07.04.05	
	T Wicks　(Rowde, Devizes)		17.08.18P	
	Built by F McGuigan – project BMAA/HB/397			
G-CDKO	ICP MXP-740 Savannah Jabiru(4)	04-01-51-274	25.04.05	
	K Arksey　Bagby		22.08.18P	
	Built by B Hunter & C Jones – project BMAA/HB/402			
G-CDKP	Avtech Jabiru UL-D Calypso	636	18.02.05	
	Rochester Microlights Ltd　Rochester		03.04.18P	
G-CDKR	Diamond DA.42 Twin Star	42.029	28.06.05	
	(D-GAAA)　Cancelled 28.10.10 as destroyed		17.08.10	
	Gamston　*Wreck stored in carpark 12.13*			
G-CDKX	Best Off Skyranger J2.2(1)	SKR0404474	23.05.05	
	E Lewis　Westonzoyland		17.01.19P	
	Built by M S Ashby – project BMAA/HB/395			
G-CDLA	Mainair Pegasus Quik	8102	04.04.05	
	S M Smith　Barhams Mill Farm, Egerton		03.10.19P	
	Built by Mainair Sports Ltd			
G-CDLC	CASA 1-131E Jungmann Series 2000	2095	10.06.05	
	N46923, Spanish AF E3B-494			
	R D Loder　Lower Upham Farm, Chiseldon		24.02.15P	
	Official c/n 2095 is also quoted for Jungmann			
	D-EEGN ex E3B-351; as 'E3B-494:81-47' in			
	Spanish AF c/s (NF 27.03.17)			
G-CDLD	Mainair Pegasus Quik	8106	16.03.05	
	W Williams　Knapthorpe Lodge, Caunton		29.06.18P	
G-CDLG	Best Off Skyranger 912(2)	SKR0403457	19.05.05	
	J Blackburn tr CDLG Skyranger Group　Shifnal		31.08.18P	
	Built by D J Saunders – project BMAA/HB/387			
G-CDLI	AirCo DH.9	1414	31.05.05	
	E8894　Aero Vintage Ltd　Duxford			
	Built by Aircraft Manufacturing Co Ltd 1918;			
	as 'E8894' in RAF c/s; noted 11.18 (IE 13.12.18)			
G-CDLJ	Mainair Pegasus Quik	8111	09.05.05	
	J S James & R S Keyser　(Petersfield & Alton)		30.06.18P	
G-CDLK	Best Off Skyranger 912S(1)	UK/570	11.07.05	
	L E Cowling　Causeway		27.08.18P	
	Built by A P Chapman & L E Cowling			
	– project BMAA/HB/452			

G-CDLL	Dyn'Aéro MCR-01 ULC	308	23.03.05
	R F Connell (Tholthorpe)		03.04.19P
	Built by D Cassidy – project PFA 301B-14348 (IE 23.10.17)		
G-CDLR	ICP MXP-740 Savannah Jabiru(4)	04-06-51-292	09.05.05
	K J Barnard Garton		03.12.18P
	Built by R Locke – project BMAA/HB/399		
G-CDLS	Avtech Jabiru J400	183	09.03.05
	J Hume tr Teesside Aviators Group		
	Morgansfield, Fishburn		11.08.17P
	Built by G M Geary – project PFA 325-14319		
G-CDLW	Zenair CH.601UL Zodiac	6-9342	23.06.05
	W A Stephen Solent		28.02.18P
	Built by W A Stephen – project PFA 162-13944		
G-CDLY	Cirrus SR20	1519	10.06.05
	N54212 Talama		
	Kortrijk-Wevelgem Int'l, Belgium		06.11.18E
G-CDLZ	Mainair Pegasus Quantum 15-912	8113	19.04.05
	S Jeffrey tr Lima Zulu Owner Syndicate		
	Gap-Tallard, France		17.04.16P
	Built by Mainair Sports Ltd		
G-CDMA	Piper PA-28-161 Warrior II	28-7415650	03.05.05
	OY-TFL, SE-GBV Wingtask 1995 Ltd Seething		28.05.18E
	Originally built as PA-28-151 Cherokee Warrior		
G-CDMC	Cameron Z-105	10671	14.03.05
	A-Gas (ORB) Ltd Bristol 'A-Gas'		14.04.18E
	Operated by First Flight		
G-CDMD	Robin DR.500-200i Président	42	14.10.05
	P R Liddle Lydd		14.11.19E
	Built by Constructions Aeronautiques de Bourgogne;		
	officially registered as DR.400-500		
G-CDME	Van's RV-7	xxxx	13.05.05
	W H Greenwood Dunsfold		08.08.19P
	Built by M W Elliott – project PFA 323-14151		
G-CDMF	Van's RV-9A	90758	29.06.05
	J R Bowden Fowle Hall Farm, Laddingford		14.04.18P
	Built by J Shanley – project PFA 320-14157		
G-CDMH	Cessna P210N Pressurized Centurion	P21000131	25.07.05
	LX-ACP, N33CP, C-GRAT, N4901P		
	A M Holman-West Alscot Park, Stratford-upon-Avon		14.08.14E
	(NF 30.11.17)		
G-CDMJ	Mainair Pegasus Quik	8107	17.03.05
	M J R Dean Manchester Barton		13.09.17P
G-CDMK	Montgomerie-Bensen B.8MR	xxxx	08.07.05
	P Rentell (St Clement, Truro)		06.07.12P
	Built by P Rentell – project PFA G/01A-1358		
	(NF 04.07.17)		
G-CDML	P&M Pegasus Quik	8127	15.07.05
	P O'Rourke Broadmeadow Farm, Hereford		09.04.18P
G-CDMN	Van's RV-9	90776	08.06.05
	G J Smith Stoneacre Farm, Farthing Corner		22.05.18P
	Built by G J Smith – project PFA 320-14108		
G-CDMO	Cameron S Can-100	2178	22.07.05
	OE-ZCU, OE-CZU A Schneider Sudlohn,		
	North Rhine-Westphalia, Germany 'Stree Zucker'		28.10.09E
	(NF 08.06.15)		
G-CDMP	Best Off Skyranger 912S(1)	UK/600	08.07.05
	J A Charlton (Kirk Langley, Ashbourne)		24.04.18P
	Built by J A Charlton – project BMAA/HB/457		
G-CDMS	Comco Ikarus C42 FB80	0506-6689	19.07.05
	Airbourne Aviation Ltd Popham		17.03.19P
	Assembled Aerosport Ltd		
G-CDMT	Zenair CH.601XL Zodiac	9667	17.06.05
	H Drever Easter Farm, Fearn		11.12.18P
	Built by D McCormack – project PFA 162B-14359;		
	tricycle u/c		
G-CDMV	Best Off Skyranger Swift 912S(1)	UK/575	28.07.05
	D O'Keeffe & K E Rutter London Colney		13.04.18P
	Built by A J Clarke, D O'Keeffe & K E Rutter		
	– project BMAA/HB/455		
G-CDMX	Piper PA-28-161 Warrior II	28-7916006	04.08.05
	PH-SBY, N39746 C Sher Elstree		28.04.19E
	Operated by Flyers Flying School		
G-CDMY	Piper PA-28-161 Warrior II	28-7916007	25.08.05
	PH-SBZ, N30768 Redhill Air Services Ltd Redhill		29.01.18E
G-CDNA	Grob G109B	6324	28.07.05
	D-KEOJ J W Sage tr Army Gliding Association		
	Trenchard Lines, Upavon		13.08.18E
G-CDND	Gulfstream American GA-7 Cougar	GA7-0057	19.07.05
	(OY-GAV), G-CDND, OY-GAV, (OY-SVO), LN-ALY,		
	OY-GAV, N770GA C J Chaplin Redhill		08.05.18E
G-CDNE	Best Off Skyranger Swift 912S(1)	UK/574	28.07.05
	C A Pollard tr St Michael's Skyranger Syndicate		
	St Michaels		23.11.18P
	Built by A Dunne & G S Gee-Carter – project BMAA/HB/454		
G-CDNF	Aero Designs Pulsar 3	xxxx	28.04.05
	D Ringer (Glasgow G12)		30.06.12P
	Built by D Ringer – project PFA 202-13253 (NF 22.06.15)		
G-CDNG	Evektor EV-97 teamEurostar UK	2005-2319	18.05.05
	D Harington tr G-CDNG New Syndicate Shobdon		08.06.18P
	Assembled Cosmik Aviation Ltd		
G-CDNH	P&M Pegasus Quik	8126	02.08.05
	T P R Wright Measham Cottage Farm, Measham		25.10.18P
	Built by P&M Aviation Ltd		
G-CDNM	Evektor EV-97 teamEurostar UK	2005-2407	05.08.05
	H C Lowther Bedlands Gate, Little Strickland		21.05.17P
	Assembled Cosmik Aviation Ltd (IE 15.12.17)		
G-CDNO	Westland SA.341B Gazelle AH.1	1385	23.09.05
	XX432 J W Blaylock & C M Evans t/a CJ Helicopters		
	Melbourne House, Kirton		17.07.18P
G-CDNP	Evektor EV-97 teamEurostar UK	2005-2320	13.06.05
	B R Pearson tr Eaglescott Eurostar Group Eaglescott		27.06.18P
	Assembled Cosmik Aviation Ltd		
G-CDNS	Westland SA.341B Gazelle AH.1	1614	23.09.05
	XZ321 Falcon Aviation Ltd		
	Bourne Park, Hurstbourne Tarrant		
	Operated by The Gazelle Squadron Display Team;		
	as 'XZ321:D' in Desert c/s (NF 23.10.15)		
G-CDNT	Zenair CH.601XL Zodiac	9668	17.06.05
	W McCormack Broomhill Farm, West Calder		18.12.13P
	Built by W McCormack – project PFA 162B-14360		
	(NF 07.01.17)		
G-CDNW	Comco Ikarus C42 FB UK	0507-6692	06.07.05
	W Gabbott Manchester Barton		12.04.18P
	Built by W Gabbott – project PFA 322-14426		
G-CDNY	Avtech Jabiru SP-470	0491	04.08.05
	G Lucey Popham		03.01.18P
	Built by G Lucey – project PFA 274B-14020		
G-CDOA	Evektor EV-97 teamEurostar UK	2005-2506	12.09.05
	Mainair Microlight School Ltd Manchester Barton		12.05.18P
	Assembled Cosmik Aviation Ltd		
G-CDOB	Cameron C-90	10756	10.08.05
	G T Holmes Benenden, Cranbrook		24.04.18E
G-CDOC	P&M Quik GT450	8123	20.10.05
	R J Carver Sutton Meadows		16.05.18P
G-CDOK	Comco Ikarus C42 FB100	0509-6757	04.10.05
	M Aviation Ltd Old Sarum		20.12.18P
	Assembled Aerosport Ltd		
G-CDOM	Mainair Pegasus Quik	8118	20.05.05
	M C Owen tr G-CDOM Flying Group		
	Manchester Barton		26.10.18P
	Built by Mainair Sports Ltd		
G-CDON	Piper PA-28-161 Warrior II	28-8216185	24.05.05
	N8254D A Logan & J Tansley tr G-CDON Group		
	East Midlands		02.07.18E
G-CDOO	P&M Pegasus Quantum 15-912	8130	02.08.05
	O C Harding Park Hall Farm, Mapperley		05.08.10P
	(NF 25.07.18)		
G-CDOP	P&M Pegasus Quik	xxxx	16.08.05
	G E L Philp tr G-CDOP Syndicate Perth		31.03.18P
	Original wing replaced & c/n 8129 used for G-CIKA		
G-CDOT	Comco Ikarus C42 FB100	0505-6678	24.06.05
	A C Anderson Dunkeswell		01.07.18P
	Assembled Aerosport Ltd		
G-CDOV	Best Off Skyranger 912(2)	SKR0504606	05.09.05
	N Grugan (Simonburn, Hexham)		10.04.18P
	Built by B Richardson – project BMAA/HB/459		
G-CDOY	Robin DR.400-180R Remorqueur	1206	25.10.05
	D-EGRY, SE-GRY Lasham Gliding Society Ltd Lasham		14.01.19E

G-CDOZ Evektor EV-97 Eurostar 2005-2507 02.09.05
I B Marshall & W J Scott tr Wizards of Oz   Perth 03.11.18P
Built by J P McCall – project PFA 315-14437

G-CDPA Alpi Pioneer 300 154 26.08.05
N D White   Podington 22.12.18P
Built by A R Lloyd – project PFA 330-14415

G-CDPB Best Off Skyranger 582(1) UK/423 24.10.05
A W Collett   Rectory Farm, Poundon 05.06.14P
Built by N S Bishop – project BMAA/HB/385
(NF 24.09.18)

G-CDPD Mainair Pegasus Quik 8051 05.08.04
G Tomlinson   (Chester-le-Street) 17.06.19P
Built by Mainair Sports Ltd

G-CDPE Best Off Skyranger 912(2) SKR0309382 13.09.05
I M Hull   Eshott 16.07.18P
Built by P A Mercer – project BMAA/HB/432

G-CDPG Crofton Auster J1-A xxxx 11.08.05
P & T Groves tr G-CDPG Group   (Corhampton) 06.09.18P
Built by P Groves – project PFA 000-325

G-CDPH Tiger Cub Sherwood Ranger ST 012 23.09.05
O C Pope   Henstridge 17.07.17P
Built by K F Crumplin – project PFA 237-12920

G-CDPL Evektor EV-97 teamEurostar UK 2004-2207 13.01.05
C I D H Garrison   Sutton Meadows 22.10.18P
Assembled Cosmik Aviation Ltd

G-CDPN Ultramagic S-105 105/135 03.01.06
D J Macinnes   London W8 24.11.12E
(NF 22.10.15)

G-CDPO Aerochute Dual 240 04.10.05
Cancelled 28.08.08 by CAA
Dungannon   *Stored unflown 12.13*

G-CDPP Comco Ikarus C42 FB100 VLA 0504-6676 22.09.05
H M Owen   Rhyd-y-Maerdy Farm, Foelgastell 22.05.18P
Built by H M Owen – project PFA 322-14423

G-CDPS Raj Hamsa X'Air Falcon 133(3) 919 31.08.05
C G, M G & N Chambers   Sackville Lodge Farm, Riseley 30.10.15P
Built by P R Smith – project BMAA/HB/332
(IE 11.07.17)

G-CDPV Piper PA-34-200T Seneca II 34-8070086 14.10.05
PH-MRM, D-GIGF, N99GN, C-FJRN, N35717
Globebrow Ltd   Shobdon 23.03.18E

G-CDPW P&M Pegasus Quantum 15-912 8138 14.10.05
S B Wilkes tr Hadair Flexwing Flyers
Wolverhampton Halfpenny Green 23.03.19P

G-CDPY Europa Aviation Europa 303 08.03.00
A Burrill   (Calcot, Reading)
Built by A Burrill – project PFA 247-13029;
tailwheel u/c (NF 23.03.16)

G-CDPZ Flight Design CT2K 03-06-03-28 23.06.05
M E Henwick   Popham 18.04.18P
Assembled Mainair Sports Ltd as official c/n 8124
but believed to be c/n 8005

G-CDRC Cessna 182Q Skylane 18267085 02.09.05
N97418   Concorde Investments Ltd   Perth 30.08.18E

G-CDRD AirBorne XT912-B/Streak III-B XT912-096 24.10.05
Fly NI Ltd   Newtownards 27.03.18P
Wing s/n SB3-80

G-CDRF Cameron Z-90 10763 20.01.06
Chalmers Ballong Corps   Göteborg, Sweden 27.04.16E

G-CDRG P&M Pegasus Quik 8137 19.10.05
S P Adams   Yatesbury 11.12.18P

G-CDRH Thruster T600N 0056-T600N-114 30.06.05
G L Pritt tr Carlisle Thruster Group
Carlisle Lake District 20.07.18P
Badged 'Sprint'

G-CDRI Cameron O-105 10794 22.12.05
R J Fuller tr Snapdragon Balloon Group   Godalming
'Snapdragon II' 06.03.18E

G-CDRJ Air Création Tanarg 912S(1)/iXess 15 FLT003 23.11.05
G F Frend   (Kilham, Driffield) 06.09.17P
Built by J H Hayday – project BMAA/HB/464
(Flylight kit FLT003 comprising trike s/n T05071
& wing s/n A05148-5135 (IE 06.10.17)

G-CDRN Cameron Z-225 10750 25.04.06
Adventure Balloons Ltd   Hartley Wintney, Hook 29.05.18E
Union Flag c/s

G-CDRO Comco Ikarus C42 FB80 0507-6750 17.08.05
Airbourne Aviation Ltd   Popham 20.08.19P
Assembled Aerosport Ltd

G-CDRP Comco Ikarus C42 FB80 0509-6762 26.10.05
D S Parker   Carlisle Lake District 26.10.18P
Assembled Aerosport Ltd

G-CDRR P&M Pegasus Quantum 15-912 8134 12.09.05
S D Moran   Longacre Farm, Sandy 19.10.19P

G-CDRS RotorWay Exec 162F 6956 30.08.05
R C Swann   (Blofield, Norwich)   'Husky Dogs' 12.04.18P
Built by R C Swann

G-CDRT P&M Pegasus Quik 8131 22.11.05
R Tetlow   Crosland Moor 09.11.14P

G-CDRU CASA 1-131E Jungmann Series 2000 2321 19.01.90
EC-DRU, Spanish AF E3B-530
P Cunniff   White Waltham   'Yen a Bon' 17.06.18P

G-CDRV Van's RV-9A 90903 29.06.05
R J Woodford   North Weald 19.02.19P
Built by R J Woodford – project PFA 320-14186

G-CDRW P&M Pegasus Quik 8141 21.09.05
C J Meadows   Westonzoyland 10.09.18P

G-CDRY Comco Ikarus C42 FB100 VLA 0509-6763 26.09.05
R J Mitchell   Tingwall 19.07.18P
Built by R J Mitchell – project PFA 322-14448

G-CDRZ Kubicek BB22 395 06.03.06
Club Amatori del Volo In Mongolfiera
Novate Milanese, Italy 04.12.15E
(IE 12.01.16)

G-CDSA P&M Pegasus Quik 8144 09.11.05
F R Simpson   Little Gransden 29.01.18P

G-CDSB Alpi Pioneer 200 91 04.11.05
P M & T A Pugh   Shobdon 17.12.18P
Built by T W Skinner – project PFA 334-14443;
kit no duplicates G-CEMY

G-CDSC Scheibe SF25C Rotax-Falke 44643 02.12.05
D-KIEX   I K G Mitchell tr Devon & Somerset
Motorglider Group   North Hill 11.10.18E

G-CDSD Alpi Pioneer 300 xxxx 03.11.05
R E Rayner   Conington 19.08.19P
Built by F A Cavaciuti – project PFA 330-14439

G-CDSF Diamond DA.40D Star D4.190 24.02.06
OE-VPU   Flying Time Ltd   Brighton City 25.02.18E
Badged 'DA40TDi'

G-CDSH ICP MXP-740 Savannah Jabiru (5) 05-07-51-413 09.11.05
G Miller   (Lesmahagow, Lanark) 23.03.18P
Built by S Whittaker and P J Wilson
– project BMAA/HB/463

G-CDSJ Sud-Aviation SA.316B Alouette III 20 17.11.05
Rom AF12   Cancelled 20.05.09 by CAA
Halton Moor, Leeds
Built by ICA-Brasov as 'IAR.316B'; stored 04.13

G-CDSK Reality Escapade Jabiru(3) UK.ESC.0004 15.11.05
R H Sear   Fir Park Farm, Usselby 31.08.18P
Built by R H Sear – project BMAA/HB/469

G-CDSM P&M Quik GT450 8146 20.10.05
S L Cogger   Willingale 06.05.18P

G-CDSS P&M Pegasus Quik 8142 16.11.05
R N S Taylor   Headon Farm, Retford 06.05.14P
(NF 04.06.18)

G-CDST Ultramagic N-250 250/37 27.05.05
Adventure Balloons Ltd   Hartley Wintney, Hook 12.05.18E

G-CDSW Comco Ikarus C42 FB80 0511-6772 23.11.05
Deanland Flight Training Ltd   Deanland 26.01.19P
Assembled Aerosport Ltd

G-CDSX[M] English Electric Canberra T.4 71367 27.03.06
WJ874   Cancelled 06.11.14 as PWFU   *As 'VN799'*
With Cornwall Aviation Heritage Centre, Newquay Cornwall

G-CDTA Evektor EV-97 teamEurostar UK 2005-2509 19.10.05
R D Stein   Redlands 30.10.18P
Assembled Cosmik Aviation Ltd

G-CDTB	P&M Pegasus Quantum 15-912	8136	06.10.05
	D W Corbett Cottage Farm, Norton Juxta		05.09.17P
	(IE 28.11.17)		
G-CDTH	Schempp-Hirth Nimbus-4DM	65	07.07.06
	M A V Gatehouse Dunkeswell *'NS4'*		18.09.18E
G-CDTI	Messerschmitt Bf 109E-1	4034	12.12.05
	Luftwaffe Rare Aircraft Ltd (Jersey JE4)		
	Built by Focke-Wulf, Bremen 1939?;		
	on rebuild by Retrotec 10.16 (NF 05.12.14)		
G-CDTJ	Reality Escapade Jabiru(5)	UK.ESC.0003	13.12.05
	M E Gilbert Balgrummo Steading, Bonnybank		30.05.16P
	Built by D Little – project BMAA/HB/461; tricycle u/c		
	(IE 01.03.18)		
G-CDTL	Avtech Jabiru J400	222	13.12.05
	M I Sistern Sleap		09.11.18P
	Built by M I Sistern – project PFA 325-14386		
G-CDTO	P&M Quik GT450	8149	11.01.06
	A R Watt Insch		01.04.18P
G-CDTP	Best Off Skyranger 912S(1)	UK/617	21.12.05
	P M Whitaker Oxenhope		29.07.14P
	Built by J R S Heaton – project BMAA/HB/475		
	(NF 27.01.16)		
G-CDTR	P&M Quik GT450	8153	20.12.05
	S M Furner Sutton Meadows		05.05.18P
G-CDTT	ICP MXP-740 Savannah Jabiru(4)	04-01-51-273	29.05.05
	M J Day Oaks Farm, Woodton		07.06.11P
	Built by M P Middleton – project BMAA/HB/383		
	(NF 23.09.16)		
G-CDTU	Evektor EV-97 teamEurostar UK	2005 2522	05.01.06
	I Shaw tr G-CDTU Group Arclid Green, Sandbach		05.01.19P
	Assembled Cosmik Aviation Ltd; carries		
	c/n '2005 2603' on plate inside tailplane		
G-CDTV	Tecnam P2002-EA Sierra	140	19.01.06
	S A Noble Rayne Hall Farm, Rayne		19.07.18P
	Built by M Rudd – project PFA 333-14501		
G-CDTX	Reims/Cessna F152 II	F15201662	22.12.05
	D-EERU, N1659C Blueplane Ltd Blackbushe		23.06.18E
G-CDTY	ICP MXP-740 Savannah Jabiru(5)	05-09-51-414	05.01.06
	D A Cook Beverley (Linley Hill)		20.10.18P
	Built by J N Anyan – project BMAA/HB/467		
G-CDTZ	Aeroprakt A-22 Foxbat	UK024	21.12.05
	L M Astle & P C Piggott tr Colditz Group		
	Husbands Bosworth		02.06.18P
	Built by M E Hughes & P C Piggott		
	– project PFA 317-14433		
G-CDUE	Robinson R44 Raven I	1549	24.01.06
	Southport Golf Complex Ltd Conington		10.06.19E
	Operated by MFH Helicopters		
G-CDUJ	Lindstrand LBL 31A	1080	27.01.06
	R G Griffin Newbury		16.02.18E
G-CDUK	Comco Ikarus C42 FB80	0511-6770	21.11.05
	R A Mitchell tr G-CDUK C42 Group Strathaven		08.04.19P
	Assembled Aerosport Ltd		
G-CDUL	Best Off Skyranger 912(2)	SKR0506615	23.01.06
	M P D Cook & M B Wallbutton Enstone		11.07.18P
	Built by T W Thiele – project BMAA/HB/471		
G-CDUS	Best Off Skyranger 912S(1)	SKR0508643	26.01.06
	G Devlin Baxby Manor, Husthwaite		13.09.18P
	Built by W P Byrne – project BMAA/HB/490		
G-CDUT	Avtech Jabiru J400	207	02.02.06
	A & T W Pullin (Barrow-in-Furness)		19.07.18P
	Built by A & T W Pullin – project PFA 325-14352		
G-CDUU	P&M Quik GT450	8165	16.03.06
	A Rose tr Charlie Delta Group		
	Knapthorpe Lodge, Caunton		24.06.18P
	Damaged on landing at Orston, Notts 24.09.17		
G-CDUV	ICP MXP-740 Savannah Jabiru(5)	05-09-51-415	05.01.06
	D M Blackman Rochester		26.04.18P
	Built by M Leachman – project BMAA/HB/465		
G-CDUW	Aeronca C.3	A517	20.02.06
	(F-AZKE), N64765, NC14631		
	N K Geddes South Barnbeth Farm, Bridge of Weir		
	(NF 04.07.18)		
G-CDUX^M	Piper PA-32-300 Cherokee Six	32-7340074	31.07.02
	EC-DUX, F-BSGY, 5T-TJR, N11C		
	Cancelled 29.01.15 as destroyed		30.05.14
	Long Kesh *Wreck stored with Ulster Aviation Society,*		
	Lisburn 12.17		
G-CDUY	Colt 77A	600	09.02.06
	D-HIPPO, D-WESTFALEN (2)		
	G Birchall Burscough, Ormskirk *'Westfalen'*		02.05.18E
	Built by Thunder & Colt Ltd		
G-CDVA	Best Off Skyranger Swift 912(1)	SKR0211247	21.12.05
	S J Dovey Culbokie		12.10.18P
	Built by R J Hoare – project BMAA/HB/269		
G-CDVD	Evektor EV-97 Eurostar	2005-2510	06.01.06
	S A Wood tr The Northern Flying Group Eshott		11.03.18P
	Built by G R Pritchard – project PFA 315-14485		
G-CDVG	P&M Pegasus Quik	8152	24.01.06
	C M Lewis Graveley Hall Farm, Graveley		29.01.18P
G-CDVH	P&M Pegasus Quantum 15-912	8166	20.02.06
	Durham Microlights Ltd Greenhills Farm, Wheatley Hill		19.07.19P
G-CDVI	Comco Ikarus C42 FB80	0602-6794	13.03.06
	Airbourne Aviation Ltd Popham		12.07.19P
	Assembled Aerosport Ltd		
G-CDVJ	Montgomerie-Bensen B.8MR	xxxx	17.01.06
	J A McGill Damyns Hall, Upminster		
	Built by D J Martin – project PFA G/01A-1355		
	(NF 05.09.18)		
G-CDVK	ICP MXP-740 Savannah Jabiru(5)	05-02-51-372	24.01.06
	M Peters Broomclose Farm, Longbridge Deverill		25.09.18P
	Built by M Peters – project BMAA/HB/449		
G-CDVL	Alpi Pioneer 300	147	27.01.06
	J D Clabon Westonzoyland		05.10.18P
	Built by A N Pascoe & T C Robson		
	– project PFA 330-14379		
G-CDVN	P&M Quik GT450	8176	11.04.06
	P Warrener (Well, Hook)		24.05.18P
	Original wing stored with P&M & replaced by SA.3822		
G-CDVO	P&M Pegasus Quik (modified)	8147	09.12.05
	G Cousins (Boughton Monchelsea, Maidstone)		10.04.17P
	(IE 04.08.17)		
G-CDVR	P&M Quik GT450	8160	27.01.06
	M J King Yatesbury		27.01.18P
	Trike also used with sailwing c/n 8679 as G-CIEG (qv)		
G-CDVS	Europa Aviation Europa XS	364	20.02.06
	J F Lawn Tibenham		14.04.18P
	Built by J F Lawn – project PFA 247-13217;		
	tailwheel u/c		
G-CDVT	Van's RV-6	20206	07.02.06
	N391DS P J Wood Gloucestershire		02.11.18P
	Built by D W Sorrels		
G-CDVU	Evektor EV-97 teamEurostar UK	2005-2525	13.03.06
	M R Smith Otherton		05.04.18P
	Assembled Cosmik Aviation Ltd		
G-CDVV	Scottish Aviation Bulldog Srs 120/121	BH120/291	27.01.06
	9290M, XX626 W H M Mott Sleap		20.06.19P
	As 'XX626:W 02' in RAF c/s		
G-CDVZ	P&M Quik GT450	8151	30.01.06
	S M Green & M D Peacock Compton Abbas		16.05.19P
G-CDWB	Best Off Skyranger 912(2)	SKR0507627	19.01.06
	D R Hammond (Whitchurch)		20.07.19P
	Built by V J Morris – project BMAA/HB/477		
G-CDWD	Cameron Z-105	10827	03.05.06
	P Spellward t/a Bristol University Hot Air Ballooning		
	Society Bristol BS9 *'University of Bristol'*		01.04.18E
G-CDWE	Nord NC.856 Norvigie	01	10.03.06
	F-WFKF, F-BFKF J R Davison Wickenby		07.08.18P
	As 'N856' in French A/F c/s		
G-CDWG	Dyn'Aéro MCR-01 Club	274	10.02.06
	A W Lowrie Morgansfield, Fishburn		19.08.19P
	Built by S E Gribble – project PFA 301A-14132		
G-CDWI	Comco Ikarus C42 FB80	0601-6783	09.01.06
	The Scottish Flying Club Strathaven		16.02.18P
	Assembled Aerosport Ltd		

G-CDWJ Flight Design CTSW 05-11-16 09.03.06
G P Rood Dunkeswell 14.08.18P
Assembled P&M Aviation Ltd as c/n 8157

G-CDWK Robinson R44 Raven II 11116 03.04.06
B Morgan Gloucestershire 05.06.18E

G-CDWM Best Off Skyranger 912S(1) UK/616 15.12.05
D R Devlin & J McCluskey
Kernan Valley, Tandragee *'Wilma'* 13.06.18P
Built by W H McMinn- project BMAA/HB/470

G-CDWO P&M Quik GT450 8175 03.04.06
G W Carwardine (Hadlow Down, Uckfield) 05.07.18P

G-CDWR P&M Quik GT450 8181 10.04.06
I C Macbeth Calton Moor Farm, Ashbourne 12.04.19P

G-CDWT Flight Design CTSW 05-12-10 09.03.06
R Scammell Sywell 02.07.18P
Assembled P&M Aviation Ltd as c/n 8162

G-CDWU Zenair CH.601UL Zodiac xxxx 16.03.06
J Donaldson Eshott 19.12.19P
Built by A D Worrall – project PFA 162A-14332

G-CDWX Lindstrand LBL 77A 1088 13.03.06
LSB Public Relations Ltd Abergavenny
'Stroud and Swindon Building Society' 10.10.15E

G-CDWZ P&M Quik GT450 8154 02.02.06
R Higton Berry Farm, Bovingdon 04.05.19P

G-CDXD Medway SLA 100 Executive 070306 08.03.06
A J Baker & G Withers Middle Stoke, Isle of Grain 15.06.18P

G-CDXF Lindstrand LBL 31A 1076 07.04.06
R K Worsman Monymusk, Inverurie 07.04.18E

G-CDXG P&M Pegasus Quantum 15-912 8180 28.04.06
I C Braybrook Northrepps 04.08.18P

G-CDXI Cessna 182P Skylane 18263554 02.03.06
SE-GXY, OY-ANT, N5820J B G McBeath Lydd 21.11.18E

G-CDXJ Avtech Jabiru J400 206 27.03.06
J C Collingwood (Wittersham, Tenterden) 29.05.18P
Built by J C Collingwood – project PFA 325-14356

G-CDXK Diamond DA.42 Twin Star 42.136 06.06.06
A M Healy Wycombe Air Park 12.05.18E
Operated by Booker Aviation

G-CDXL Flight Design CTSW 06-05-17 04.07.06
A K Paterson Boston 29.07.18P
Assembled P&M Aviation Ltd as c/n 8191

G-CDXN P&M Quik GT450 8171 15.05.06
D J Brookfield (Tickhill, Doncaster) 22.05.18P

G-CDXP Evektor EV-97 Eurostar 2005-2626 06.04.06
B J Crockett Broadmeadow Farm, Hereford 16.05.18P
Built by B J Crockett – project PFA 315-14530

G-CDXR Fokker Dr.1 Triplane replica 0207229 13.04.06
P B Dickinson White Waltham 25.04.18P
*Built by J G Gray – project PFA 238-14043;
as '403/17' in German Army Air Service c/s*

G-CDXS Evektor EV-97 teamEurostar UK 2006-2627 22.02.06
T R James Wycombe Air Park 03.04.18P
Assembled Cosmik Aviation Ltd

G-CDXT Van's RV-9 91139 11.04.06
T M Storey Newells Farm, Lower Beeding 14.08.18P
Built by T M Storey – project PFA 320-14376

G-CDXU Chilton DW.1A xxxx 19.04.06
M Gibbs & J Pollard Old Warden 18.09.17P
Built by R W Burrows – project PFA 225-12038

G-CDXV Campbell Cricket Mk.6A 006/2 19.04.06
33-AJX T L Morley Enstone 18.10.18P
*Built by W G Spencer – project PFA G/16-1339;
badged 'Layzell AV-18A'*

G-CDXW Cameron Orange-120 2947 22.05.06
HB-BXL A Kaye t/a You've Been Tangoed Ballooning
Irchester, Wellingborough 27.08.18E

G-CDXY Skystar Kitfox Model 7 S 70304026 24.02.06
D E Steade (Kempsey, Worcestershire) 09.04.18P
Built by D E Steade – project PFA 172D-14112

G-CDYB Rans S-6-ES Coyote II 0105.1634 28.03.06
P J Hellyer Sunnyside Farm, Whitwell 15.08.19P
Built by D Sykes – project PFA 204-14416; tricycle u/c

G-CDYC Piper PA-28RT-201 Arrow IV 28R-7918164 26.04.06
N2835D Cancelled 28.03.11 by CAA 11.02.11
King Farm, Thurrock *Stored 08.18*

G-CDYD Comco Ikarus C42 FB80 0604-6812 09.06.06
P R Stevens tr C42 Group Baxby Manor, Husthwaite 24.06.17P
Assembled Aerosport Ltd

G-CDYG Cameron Z-105 10870 10.05.06
N-E Kjellen Skovde, Sweden *'Vodaphone'* 05.10.19E

G-CDYL Lindstrand LBL 77A 1098 20.06.06
J S Morge Kingswood, Bristol 22.09.18E

G-CDYM Murphy Maverick 430 259-2981? 20.03.06
C J Gresham (Plymouth) 29.06.18P
Built by G T Leedham – project PFA 259-12981

G-CDYO Comco Ikarus C42 FB80 0604-6810 10.10.06
J Bainbridge & J E Midder Membury 10.02.19P
Assembled Aerosport Ltd

G-CDYP Evektor EV-97 teamEurostar UK 2006-2628 01.06.06
R V Buxton & R Cranborne
Kimberley Hall, Wymondham 25.05.18P
Assembled Cosmik Aviation Ltd

G-CDYR Bell 206L-3 LongRanger III 51237 20.09.07
N341AJ, 5Y-BFL M D Thorpe t/a Yorkshire Helicopters
Leeds Heliport 22.09.18E

G-CDYT Comco Ikarus C42 FB80 0603-6798 04.05.06
P Bayliss Ince 29.10.18P
Assembled Aerosport Ltd

G-CDYU Zenair CH.701UL 7-1410 08.05.06
A Gannon Lawmuir Farm, Sheardale, Coalsnaughton 21.09.17P
Built by M Henderson – project PFA 187-14489

G-CDYX Lindstrand LBL 77B 1094 06.07.06
H M Savage Edinburgh EH3 18.04.16E

G-CDYY Alpi Pioneer 300 128 14.02.06
B Williams Shobdon 06.11.18P
Built by B Williams – project PFA 330-14323

G-CDYZ Van's RV-7 xxxx 01.02.06
Holden Group Ltd Crowfield 16.08.18P
*Built by W D Garlick & G A Martin
– project PFA 323-14276*

G-CDZA Alpi Pioneer 300 124 15.03.06
J F Dowe Monewden 24.08.18P
Built by J Dowe – project PFA 330-14329

G-CDZB Zenair CH.601UL Zodiac 6-9709 10.05.06
L J Dutch Rossall Field, Cockerham 16.07.18P
*Built by L J Dutch – project PFA 162A-14431;
tailwheel u/c*

G-CDZG Comco Ikarus C42 FB80 0604-6808 20.04.06
Mainair Microlight School Ltd Manchester Barton 03.07.18P
Assembled Aerosport Ltd

G-CDZO Lindstrand LBL 60X 1104 07.07.06
R D Parry Sutton, Tenbury Wells *'CfS'* 26.07.19E

G-CDZR Nicollier HN.700 Menestrel II xxxx 17.05.06
C Antrobus & S J Bowles
Spilsted Farm, Sedlescombe 05.06.19P
Built by T M Williams – project PFA 217-13773

G-CDZS Kolb Twinstar Mk.III Xtra M3X-04-1-00053 23.05.06
K V Hill & P J Nolan Grove Farm, Wolvey 28.11.13P
*Built by P W Heywood – project PFA 205-14278
(NF 26.09.17)*

G-CDZU ICP MXP-740 Savannah Jabiru(5) 04-06-51-295 17.05.06
P J Cheyney & A H McBreen
New House Farm, Birds Edge 01.09.18P
Built by P J Cheyney – project BMAA/HB/398

G-CDZW Cameron N-105 2204 23.05.06
SE-ZEK Backetorp Byggconsult AB
Backetorp, Grena, Sweden *'Hard Rock Café'* 08.05.19E

G-CDZY Medway SLA 80 Executive 180406 19.04.06
K J Draper Middle Stoke, Isle of Grain 05.05.18P

G-CDZZ AutoGyro MT-03 xxxx 04.08.06
G-94-1 D J Bell (Newcastle-upon-Tyne) 03.09.19P
Assembled Rotorsport UK as c/n RSUK/MT-03/002

G-CEAA – G-CEZZ

G-CEAH^M	Boeing 737-229	21135	01.08.00

G-CEAHM Boeing 737-229 21135 01.08.00
OO-SDG Cancelled 06.11.13 as PWFU 14.11.09
'Palmair' & *'Spirit Of Peter Bath'* *Front fuselage only*
With Bournemouth Aviation Museum, Bournemouth

G-CEAK Comco Ikarus C42 FB80 0606-6826 20.07.06
M J Rhodes tr Barton Heritage Flying Group
Manchester Barton 21.08.17P
Assembled Aerosport Ltd

G-CEAM Evektor EV-97 teamEurostar UK 2006-2729 13.06.06
Flylight Airsports Ltd Sywell 15.06.18P
Assembled Cosmik Aviation Ltd

G-CEAN Comco Ikarus C42 FB80 0606-6825 20.06.06
M Howland tr G-CEAN Syndicate Wickenby 17.06.19P
Assembled Aerosport Ltd

G-CEAO Jurca MJ.5 Sirocco PFA 2209 23.05.06
P S Watts Cotswold 31.10.18P
Built by P S Watts – project PFA 2209

G-CEAR Alpi Pioneer 300 173 25.05.06
R S Swift Finmere 03.01.19P
Built by A Parker – project PFA 330-14511

G-CEAT Zenair CH.601HDS Zodiac 6-9337 11.05.06
T B Smith Henstridge *'Gimler'* 03.07.18P
Built by T B Smith – project PFA 162-13930; tricycle u/c

G-CEAU Robinson R44 Clipper II 11311 22.06.06
Mullahead Property Company Ltd
Kernan Valley, Tandragee 30.07.18E

G-CEAY Ultramagic H-42 42/13 24.07.06
J D A Shields Hastings 25.06.18E

G-CEBA Zenair CH.601XL Zodiac 6-9605 21.04.06
J E Adams tr Lamb Holm Flyers
Lamb Holm Farm, Holm 17.05.18P
Built by I J M Donnelly – project PFA 162B-14326;
tricycle u/c

G-CEBC ICP MXP-740 Savannah Jabiru(5) 06-03-51-475 25.05.06
H C Lowther Athey's Moor, Longframlington 11.04.17P
Built by E W Chapman – project BMAA/HB/503
(IE 15.12.17)

G-CEBE Schweizer 269C-1 (*300CBi*) 0253 19.06.06
N86G Millburn World Travel Services Ltd
Manchester Barton 17.09.18E

G-CEBF Evektor EV-97A Eurostar 2006-2405 06.06.06
M Lang Forwood Farm, Treswell 19.06.18P
Built by M Lang – project PFA 315A-14525

G-CEBG Kubicek BB26 442 26.06.06
P M Smith Readstown, Trim, RoI *'Beechwood Lodge'* 05.08.15E
(NF 14.08.17)

G-CEBH Air Création Tanarg 912S(2)/BioniX 15 FLTxxx 14.06.06
G McAnelly Eshott 24.08.18P
Built by D A Chamberlain – project BMAA/HB/481
(Flylight kit FLTxxx comprising trike s/n T05098 &
wing s/n A11019-11014

G-CEBI Kolb Twinstar Mk.III Xtra M3X-04-4-00066 06.06.06
R W Livingstone Enniskillen 23.06.15P
Built by R W Livingstone – project PFA 205-14361
(IE 26.08.15)

G-CEBL Kubicek BB20GP 456 23.08.06
Associazione Sportiva Aerostatica Lombarda
Vimerate, Milan, Italy *'X Bianchi Group'* 29.04.11E
(NF 11.12.14)

G-CEBM P&M Quik GT450 8197 23.05.06
R L Davies Shobdon 23.04.18P

G-CEBO Ultramagic M-65C 65/77 26.06.06
D-OWBZ M G Howard
Hewish, Weston-super-Mare *'Warsteiner'* 12.09.18E

G-CEBP Evektor EV-97 teamEurostar UK 2006-2825 03.07.06
M J Morson Blackpool 18.07.18P
Assembled Cosmik Aviation Ltd

G-CEBT P&M Quik GT450 8199 22.06.06
N J Paine Rochester 11.04.18P

G-CEBW North American P-51D-20-NA Mustang 122-38640 05.07.06
44-72181 Iceni International Ltd Mendlesham
(NF 08.06.15)

G-CEBZ Zenair CH.601UL Zodiac 6-1730 12.05.06
W J Miazek Longside 07.04.19P
Built by I M Ross & A Watt – project PFA 162A-13942;
tricycle u/c

G-CECA P&M Quik GT450 8185 16.08.06
A Weatherall St Michaels 02.10.17P
Damaged 03.05.17

G-CECB ELA Aviacion ELA07S 11050710722 14.07.06
Cancelled 12.01.11 as PWFU
Lude Farm, Blair Atholl *Stored 09.14*

G-CECC Comco Ikarus C42 FB80 0607-6832 14.06.06
M J Slack Ludham 16.04.18P
Assembled Aerosport Ltd

G-CECD Cameron C-90 10898 07.08.06
J de Flou & M de Keyzer Knellelare & Maldegem,
Belgium *'Adez'* 21.06.19E

G-CECE Avtech Jabiru UL-D 656 08.06.06
ST Aviation Ltd Oaklands Farm, Horsham 01.08.08P
(NF 16.10.14)

G-CECF Reality Escapade Jabiru(1) UK.ESC.0007 08.06.06
M M Hamer Over Farm, Gloucester *'Charlie Fox'* 09.10.18P
Built by T F Francis – project BMAA/HB/496;
tailwheel u/c

G-CECG Avtech Jabiru UL-D 661 18.07.06
A N C P Lester Wolverhampton Halfpenny Green 08.11.18P

G-CECH Jodel D.150 Mascaret 174 19.07.06
W R Prescott Derryogue, Kilkeel 13.06.18P
Built by D Kennedy – project PFA 235-13889

G-CECI Pilatus PC-6/B2-H4 Turbo-Porter 936 03.03.06
N2TS, N424PS, HB-FMD P Leal Portimão, Portugal 18.03.17E

G-CECJ Aeromot AMT-200S Super Ximango 200.168 14.11.06
PR-AMU M J Philpott tr The G-CECJ Syndicate
Lasham 07.05.19E

G-CECK ICP MXP-740 Savannah Jabiru(5) 06-01-51-453 11.07.06
J F Boyce (Brown Shutters Farm, Norton St Philip) 14.06.18P
Built by K W Eskins – project BMAA/HB/495

G-CECL Comco Ikarus C42 FB80 0607-6834 04.07.06
C Lee Longacre Farm, Sandy 11.10.18P
Assembled Aerosport Ltd

G-CECP Best Off Skyranger 912(2) SKR0508638 13.07.06
B P Lycett tr Woobugly Flying Group Hunsdon 02.04.19P
Built by D C Davies – project BMAA/HB/483

G-CECS Lindstrand LBL 105A 1121 25.07.06
R P Ashford Hindhead *'Harveys Orange'* 09.07.19E

G-CECV Van's RV-7 xxxx 30.05.06
D M Stevens Haverfordwest *'Pops'* 17.11.18P
Built by D M Stevens – project PFA 323-14338

G-CECY Evektor EV-97 Eurostar 2006-2828 21.07.06
M R M Welch Goodwood 07.09.18P
Built by M R M Welch – project PFA 315-14551

G-CECZ Zenair CH.601XL Zodiac 3235 17.07.06
P D Gardner & P Mounce tr Bluebird Aviation
Compton Abbas 09.10.18P
Built by G M Johnson – project PFA 162B-14458;
tailwheel u/c

G-CEDB Reality Escapade Jabiru(5) UK.ESC.0002 12.04.06
G T M Beale (Margate) 29.04.19P
Built by D Bedford – project BMAA/HB/456; tricycle u/c

G-CEDC Comco Ikarus C42 FB100 0607-6831 14.08.06
L M Call Deanland 06.03.18P
Assembled Aerosport Ltd

G-CEDE Flight Design CTSW 06-06-14 16.08.06
M B Hayter Draycott 16.04.18P
Assembled P&M Aviation Ltd as c/n 8212

G-CEDF Cameron N-105 10884 31.07.06
Bailey Balloons Ltd Pill, Bristol *'eDF Energy'* 01.06.18E

G-CEDI Best Off Skyranger 912(2) SKR0603700 10.08.06
R P Hall Deenethorpe 28.07.18P
Built by P B Davey – project BMAA/HB/513

G-CEDJ Aero Designs Pulsar XP 207 21.12.06
N383B P F Lorriman (High Halstow, Rochester) 15.11.08P
Built by W Becker (NF 13.10.14)

G-CEDL	Team Mini-Max 91	447	18.07.06
	A J Weir Charmy Down		
	Built by J W Taylor – project PFA 186-12546		
	(SSDR microlight since 07.15) (IE 28.10.15)		
G-CEDN	P&M Pegasus Quik	8206	15.08.06
	D W Buck t/a Microlight Flight Lessons Netherthorpe		12.06.18P
G-CEDO	Raj Hamsa X'Air Falcon 133(2)	1080	03.08.06
	K J Nicpon tr OCTN Trust (Bishops Waltham)		08.11.13P
	Built by A P Lambert & J Lane – project BMAA/HB/511		
G-CEDT	Air Création Tanarg 912S(2)/iXess 15 FLTxxx		14.07.06
	N S Brayn South Longwood Farm, Owslebury		16.07.18P
	Built by R A Taylor – project BMAA/HB/510 (Flylight		
	kit FLTxxx comprising trike s/n T06033 & wing s/n		
	D04035-06045); wing s/n quoted is 2004 structure		
	& 2006 sail; possible 2006 rebuild of 2004 wing?		
G-CEDV	Evektor EV-97 teamEurostar UK	2006-2826	29.09.06
	J R Brand & J Duczak tr G-CEDV Flying Group		
	Popham		26.07.19P
	Assembled Cosmik Aviation Ltd		
G-CEDX	Evektor EV-97 teamEurostar UK	2006-2827	06.09.06
	R L Owen tr Delta X-Ray Group Gloucestershire		21.09.18P
	Assembled Cosmik Aviation Ltd		
G-CEDZ	Best Off Skyranger 912(2)	UK/685	28.07.06
	I Bell & J E Walendowski Crosland Moor		
	Built by J E Walendowski – project BMAA/HB/505		
	(NF 19.11.14)		
G-CEEC	Raj Hamsa X'Air Hawk	1096	23.08.06
	C C Wallace tr G-CEEC Group Dunkeswell		23.02.18P
	Built by G A J Salter – project PFA 340-14559		
G-CEED	ICP MXP-740 Savannah Jabiru(5)	06-03-51-470	24.08.06
	A C Thompson Ince		14.11.17P
	Built by A U I Hudson – project BMAA/HB/500		
G-CEEG	Alpi Pioneer 300	188SUK	31.08.06
	D McCormack Kirknewton		12.05.12P
	Built by D McCormack – project PFA 330-14556		
	(NF 04.06.18)		
G-CEEI	P&M Quik GT450	8218	16.10.06
	G J Eaton (Stretton, Burton-on-Trent)		05.08.19P
G-CEEJ	Rans S-7S Courier	0105.392	31.08.06
	R Dunn Lower Manor Farm, Chickerell		
	'www.sportair.co.uk'		06.06.18P
	Built by J G J McDill – project PFA 218-14557		
G-CEEK	Cameron Z-105	10909	09.11.06
	J Campbell & T R Wood Loughborough &		
	London SW18 *'Thomson Local'*		08.09.19E
G-CEEL	Ultramagic S-90	90/89	12.09.06
	Anga Company SRO Znojmo, Czech Republic		
	'Impresa S Paolo'		01.08.19E
G-CEEN	Piper PA-28-161 Cadet	2841293	22.09.06
	EC-IHA, N9202N B Coren & T J Harry Brighton City		11.06.18E
G-CEEO	Flight Design CTSW	06-08-12	29.09.06
	M Winship tr CEEO Group		
	Greenhills Farm, Wheatley Hill		10.04.19P
	Assembled P&M Aviation Ltd as c/n 8225		
G-CEEP	Van's RV-9A	90062	07.09.00
	N966AM B M Jones Caernarfon		05.06.18P
	Built by R A Jones		
G-CEER	ELA Aviacion ELA 07R	04040420712	08.09.06
	F G Shepherd (Leadgate, Alston)		
	(NF 16.01.15)		
G-CEEU	Piper PA-28-161 Cadet	2841038	08.02.07
	N224FT, EC-IIF, N9158J		
	White Waltham Airfield Ltd White Waltham		20.09.18E
G-CEEW	Comco Ikarus C42 FB100	0609-6847	18.09.06
	P McCusker & B Metcalfe Kernan Valley, Tandragee		03.05.18P
	Assembled Aerosport Ltd		
G-CEEX	ICP MXP-740 Savannah Jabiru(5)	06-03-51-476	21.08.06
	R G Whyte (Kilsby, Rugby)		11.12.19P
	Built by M Hicks & T Brumpton – project BMAA/HB/508		
G-CEEZ	Piper PA-28-161 Warrior III	2842161	11.12.06
	N53513 Skies Aviation Academy PC (Baja, Hungary)		07.05.18E
G-CEFA	Comco Ikarus C42 FB UK	0609-6851	07.11.06
	EI-EHJ, G-CEFA N Sigsworth tr Ikarus Group		
	Durham Tees Valley		27.06.18P
	Built by J Little – project PFA 322-14570		
G-CEFB	Ultramagic H-31	31/06	30.10.06
	M Ekeroos Göteborg, Sweden		31.12.18E
G-CEFC	Super Marine Spitfire Mk.26	044	21.09.06
	D R Bishop Solent		08.06.17P
	Built by D R Bishop – project PFA 324-14417;		
	as 'RB142:DW-B' in RAF c/s		
G-CEFJ	Sonex Sonex	887	09.10.06
	R W Chatterton North Coates		12.06.18P
	Built by M H Moulai – project PFA 337-14518; tricycle u/c		
G-CEFK	Evektor EV-97 teamEurostar UK	2006-2823	13.11.06
	P Morgan Ince		19.10.18P
	Assembled Cosmik Aviation Ltd		
G-CEFM	Cessna 152	15284357	19.10.06
	N6102L Westair Flying Services Ltd Blackpool		19.03.18E
G-CEFP	Avtech Jabiru J430	xxxx	23.10.06
	R W Brown Stoneacre Farm, Farthing Corner		24.10.18P
	Built by G Hammond – project PFA 336-14452		
G-CEFS	Cameron C-100	11000	02.01.07
	Gone With The Wind Ltd Nisleg, Mongolian People's		
	Republic *'Stairway to Heaven'*		02.09.18E
G-CEFT	Whittaker MW5-D Sorcerer	xxxx	20.10.06
	A M R Bruce (East Halton, Immingham)		
	Built by W Bruce – project PFA 163-14335		
	(SSDR microlight since 08.16) (NF 28.11.14)		
G-CEFV	Cessna 182T Skylane	18281538	02.11.06
	N66167 G H Smith & Son Ltd Sherburn-in-Elmet		01.06.19E
G-CEFY	ICP MXP-740 Savannah Jabiru(5)	04-07-51-316	17.11.06
	B Hartley Brook Farm, Pilling		01.06.18P
	Built by B Hartley – project BMAA/HB/453		
G-CEFZ	Evektor EV-97 teamEurostar UK	2006-2824	09.11.06
	D Young tr The Robo Flying Group Cotswold		11.06.18P
	Assembled Cosmik Aviation Ltd		
G-CEGG	Lindstrand LBL 25A Cloudhopper	1120	20.07.06
	M W A Shemilt Henley-on-Thames		05.12.18E
G-CEGH	Van's RV-9A	91260	05.09.06
	M E Creasey Crowfield		12.11.18P
	Built by M E Creasey – project PFA 320-14468		
G-CEGI	Van's RV-8	81480	10.10.06
	N747RF D R Fraser & R Tye Andrewsfield		07.06.18P
	Built by R Faller; carries '747RF' under tail		
G-CEGJ	P&M Quik GT450	8234	05.01.07
	Flylight Airsports Ltd Sywell		16.01.19P
G-CEGK	ICP MXP-740 Savannah VG Jabiru(1)	06-03-51-474	09.11.06
	A & C Kimpton Eshott		19.04.18P
	Built by S Whittaker & P J Wilson – project BMAA/HB/515		
G-CEGL	Comco Ikarus C42 FB80	0609-6848	21.09.06
	A Brown & S Threadgill tr G-CEGL Flying Group		
	Chatteris		09.06.18P
	Assembled Aerosport Ltd		
G-CEGO	Evektor EV-97A Eurostar	xxxx	25.08.06
	D W Allen, J A Charlton & R F McLachlan		
	Bradley Moor, Ashbourne		16.11.18P
	Built by J A Charlton, N J Keeling & R F McLachlan – project PFA		
	315A-14552		
G-CEGP	Beech 200 Super King Air	BB-726	14.05.01
	G-BXMA, (N58AJ), G-BXMA, N622JA, N522JA, N222JD		
	DO Systems Ltd (Bournemouth)		25.04.18E
G-CEGS	Piper PA-28-161 Warrior II	28-7816418	20.11.06
	N6391C Parachuting Aircraft Ltd Old Sarum		27.01.18E
G-CEGT	P&M Quik GT450	8208	15.08.06
	S J Fisher Eshott		12.09.18P
G-CEGU	Piper PA-28-161 Warrior II	28-7715165	20.11.06
	N575DM, N5990F		
	White Waltham Airfield Ltd White Waltham		02.08.18E
	Originally built as PA-28-151 Cherokee Warrior		
G-CEGV	P&M Quik GT450	8203	18.08.06
	S P A Morris Sutton Meadows		07.09.18P
G-CEGW	P&M Quik GT450	8223	02.11.06
	A Beatty (Blackrod, Bolton)		29.06.18P
G-CEGZ	Comco Ikarus C42 FB80	0609-6852	14.12.06
	F Collister tr C42 Swift Instruction Group Andreas		03.07.18P
	Assembled Aerosport Ltd		

G-CEHC	P&M Quik GT450	8231	04.12.06
	R A McLean tr G-CEHC Syndicate (East Fortune)		19.12.15P
	Trike used by Quik R G-CIZV, wing has		
	departed East Fortune		
G-CEHD	Best Off Skyranger 912(2)	SKR0604716	17.11.06
	R Higton Berry Farm, Bovingdon		27.10.18P
	Built by A A Howland – project BMAA/HB/520		
G-CEHE	Medway SLA 100 Executive	171106	11.02.08
	R P Stonor (London W3)		06.04.18P
G-CEHG	Comco Ikarus C42 FB100	0612-6861	17.11.06
	C J Hayward & C Walters Swansea		02.05.18P
	Assembled Aerosport Ltd		
G-CEHI	P&M Quik GT450	8229	14.12.06
	A Costello Brook Farm, Pilling		23.03.17P
G-CEHL	Evektor EV-97 teamEurostar UK	2007-2928	16.01.07
	A C Richards Mill Farm, Hughley		30.05.18P
	Assembled Cosmik Aviation Ltd; c/n plate on		
	G-ZZAC denotes '2006-2928'		
G-CEHM	AutoGyro MT-03	06 036	18.10.06
	G-94-1 1013 Aviation Ltd Redhill		06.04.18P
	Assembled Rotorsport UK as c/n RSUK/MT-03/004		
G-CEHN	AutoGyro MT-03	06 067	08.12.06
	B N Trowbridge Derby		30.08.18P
	Assembled Rotorsport UK as c/n RSUK/MT-03/008		
G-CEHR	Auster AOP.9	B5/10/149	07.12.06
	XP241 M H Bichan & C R Wheeldon Spanhoe		20.08.18P
	As 'XP241' in AAC c/s		
G-CEHS	Mudry CAP 10B	304	08.03.07
	HS-BCS M D Wynne Headcorn		12.10.18E
	Built by Constructions Aeronautiques de Bourgogne		
G-CEHT	Rand Robinson KR-2	9776	07.12.06
	P P Geoghegan (Hale, Altrincham)		12.10.18P
	Built by P P Geoghegan – project PFA 129-14288		
G-CEHV	Comco Ikarus C42 FB80	0610-6854	14.12.06
	P G Brooks Boston		13.12.18P
	Assembled Aerosport Ltd		
G-CEHW	P&M Quik GT450	8241	08.12.06
	D Smith tr G-CEHW Group Plaistows Farm, St Albans		08.03.18P
G-CEHX	Lindstrand LBL 9A	1147	19.12.06
	P Baker Abbeyview, Trim, RoI		
	(IE 19.02.15)		
G-CEHZ	AirBorne XT912-B/Streak III-B	XT912-144	14.12.06
	J Daly (Kells, Co Meath, RoI)		02.05.13P
	(NF 13.09.17)		
G-CEIA	AutoGyro MT-03	xxxx	12.12.06
	T J Willis (Willington, Tarporley)		11.01.19P
	Assembled Rotorsport UK as c/n RSUK/MT-03/009		
G-CEIB	Yakovlev Yak-18A	1160403	23.05.07
	RA-3336K R A Fleming Breighton		02.01.18P
	As '03' in Soviet AF c/s		
G-CEID	Van's RV-7	72228	29.11.06
	A Moyce Newtownards		02.04.19P
	Built by A Moyce – project PFA 323-14403		
G-CEIE	Flight Design CTSW	06-10-01	14.12.06
	R D Jordan Crosland Moor 'Dolly'		16.04.19P
	Assembled P&M Aviation Ltd as c/n 8243		
G-CEIG	Van's RV-7	72231	05.12.06
	W K Wilkie Newtownards		02.04.19P
	Built by W K Wilkie – project PFA 323-14402		
G-CEII	Medway SLA 80 Executive	010107	27.07.07
	G P Burns Graveley Hall Farm, Graveley		04.09.19P
G-CEIL	Reality Escapade 912(2)	UK.ESC.0008	05.12.06
	T N Crawley Ince 'Fly Girl'		29.10.18P
	Built by D E Bassett – project BMAA/HB/506; tricycle u/c		
G-CEIS	Jodel DR.1050 Ambassadeur	469	09.01.07
	F-BLJL R A Taylor tr Prestwick Tailwheel Group		
	Glasgow Prestwick		19.04.19P
	Built by Société Aéronautique Normande		
G-CEIT	Van's RV-7A	xxxx	21.12.06
	I R Court & W Jones Leicester		10.11.18P
	Built by S S Gould – project PFA 323-13696		

G-CEIV	Air Création Tanarg 912S(2)/iXess 15	xxxx	17.10.06
	W O Fogden Enstone		11.02.17P
	Built by G Brown – project BMAA/HB/516 (Flylight kit		
	FLTxxx comprising Tanarg trike s/n T06079 & 15-metre		
	iXess wing s/n A06121-6106); shares trike with G-WADF		
G-CEIW	Europa Aviation Europa	103	06.11.06
	R Scanlan Trenchard Farm, Eggesford		16.07.18P
	Built by R Scanlan – project PFA 247-12707; tailwheel u/c		
G-CEIX	Alpi Pioneer 300	216	10.04.07
	I M Walton Bidford 'The Hamble Cat'		11.09.18P
	Built by R F Bond – project PFA 330-14656		
G-CEIY	Ultramagic M-120	120/23	20.03.07
	N Banducci Barberino val d'Elsa, Italy		30.03.18E
G-CEIZ	Piper PA-28-161 Warrior II	28-8116076	21.02.07
	D-EIAL, N8291D D Jones tr IZ Aviation Biggin Hill		17.11.18E
G-CEJA	Cameron V-77	2469	17.06.91
	G-BTOF G Gray East Worldham, Alton		02.11.16E
G-CEJC	Cameron N-77	4164	12.01.07
	G-VODA (2) M Cooper Speedwell, Bristol		02.11.18E
	Also see G-VODA (1)		
G-CEJD	Piper PA-28-161 Warrior III	2842244	05.02.07
	D-EGVY, N31044 Western Air (Thruxton) Ltd Thruxton		04.12.18E
G-CEJE	Wittman W.10 Tailwind	02-1216	15.01.07
	R A Povall Turners Arms Farm, Yearby		20.07.18P
	Built by R A Povall – project PFA 031-14003		
G-CEJG	Ultramagic M-56	56/37	02.08.07
	Dragon Balloon Company Ltd		
	Castleton, Hope Valley 'Girlguiding UK'		25.11.18E
G-CEJI	Lindstrand LBL 105A	1144	29.01.07
	Richard Nash Cars Ltd Norwich NR6		02.10.18E
G-CEJJ	P&M Quik GT450	8236	02.01.07
	I D Baxter & G McLaughlin Park Hall Farm, Mapperley		28.12.17P
G-CEJN	Mooney M.20F Executive	670216	12.02.07
	N237MM, F-BOJP, N9639M Social Infrastructure Ltd		
	Wellesbourne Mountford		28.06.19E
G-CEJW	Comco Ikarus C42 FB80	0612-6860	04.01.07
	M I Deeley Otherton		17.01.19P
	Assembled Aerosport Ltd		
G-CEJX	P&M Quik GT450	8249	13.03.07
	A J Huntly & P Stewart Netherton Farm, Bridge of Allan		06.05.18P
G-CEJY	Aerospool Dynamic WT9 UK	DY165/2007	09.03.07
	E Kaplan (Andover)		12.11.19P
	Assembled Yeoman Light Aircraft Co Ltd;		
	official c/n is 'DY165'		
G-CEJZ	Cameron C-90	10970	20.04.07
	M J Woodcock East Grinstead 'AMO Complete'		01.06.19E
G-CEKC	Medway SLA 100 Executive	070207	11.03.08
	M J Woollard Deanland		09.06.18P
G-CEKD	Flight Design CTSW	06-11-05	28.03.07
	M W Fitch Elstree		07.10.19P
	Assembled P&M Aviation Ltd as c/n 8255;		
	operated by Fly by Light)		
G-CEKE	Robin DR.400-180 Régent	943	12.04.07
	HB-EXG M F Cuming Shenington		12.10.18E
G-CEKG	P&M Quik GT450	8261	16.04.07
	C R Whitton East Fortune		15.04.18P
G-CEKI	Cessna 172P Skyhawk	17274356	19.04.07
	N51829 N Houghton Tatenhill		04.08.19E
G-CEKJ	Evektor EV-97A Eurostar	2006-2822	20.11.06
	D K Short & G Thompson (Southam/Redditch)		26.11.18P
	Built by C W J Vershoyle-Greene		
	– project PFA 315A-14584		
G-CEKK	Best Off Skyranger Swift 912S(1)	SKR0610744	15.02.07
	M S Schofield Northfield Farm, Mavis Enderby		28.04.18P
	Built by J A Hunt – project BMAA/HB/522		
G-CEKO	Robin DR.400-100 Cadet	1932	30.03.07
	PH-VSU, OO-KPF, PH-VSU Exavia Ltd Exeter Int'l		25.04.18E
G-CEKS	Cameron Z-105	11003	13.06.07
	Phoenix Balloons Ltd Bristol BS8		
	'Champagne Taittinger, Reims'		29.03.18E
G-CEKT	Flight Design CTSW	07-02-14	05.04.07
	D Colley tr Charlie Tango Group Wycombe Air Park		14.04.19P
	Assembled P&M Aviation Ltd as c/n 8272		

G-CEKV	Europa Aviation Europa	019	19.03.07
	K Atkinson Cark		08.04.18P
	Built by K Atkinson – project PFA 247-12493;		
	tailwheel u/c		

G-CEKW	Avtech Jabiru J430	212	12.01.07
	J G Culley tr J430 Syndicate		
	Hall Farm, Lillingstone Lovell		14.06.18P
	Built by A W Collett, J G & R W Culley & S Wootton		
	– project PFA 336-14340		

G-CELE	Boeing 737-33A	24029	11.07.03
	VH-CZX, G-MONN Dart Group PLC Leeds Bradford		
	'Jet2 Belfast' & 'Friendly Low Fares'		18.08.19E
	Line No: 1601; operated by Jet2.com; red tail		

G-CELI	Boeing 737-330	23526	21.09.04
	D-ABXE, (PR-GLC), D-ABXE Dart Group PLC		
	Cotswold 'Jet2 Manchester'		17.11.18E
	Line No: 1282; red tail; noted 01.19 for part out/scrapping		

G-CELM	Cameron C-80	10931	10.05.07
	L Greaves Doulting, Shepton Mallet		10.06.18E

G-CELR	Boeing 737-330	23523	04.11.03
	TF-ELR, D-ABXB Cancelled 08.09.17 as PWFU		03.11.17
	Prestwick *Cabin trainer use 09.17*		

G-CELS	Boeing 737-377	23660	17.05.02
	VH-CZH Dart Group PLC Norwich Int'l		19.06.17E
	Line No: 1294; used as instructional airframe by		
	KLM Engineering		

G-CELY	Boeing 737-377(QC)	23662	29.04.03
	N662DG, G-CELY, VH-CZJ Dart Group PLC		
	Leeds Bradford 'Jet2 Glasgow' & 'Friendly Low Fares'		13.04.19E
	Line No: 1316; operated by Jet2.com; red tail		

G-CEMA	Alpi Pioneer 200	144	05.03.07
	A Daraskevicius & R W Skelton Carrickmore		26.02.19P
	Built by D M Bracken – project PFA 334-14569		

G-CEMB	P&M Quik GT450	8262	13.04.07
	D W Logue Stonehill Farm, Crawfordjohn		30.04.18P

G-CEMC	Robinson R44 Raven II	11620	26.02.07
	Express Charters Ltd Brighton City		11.07.18E

G-CEME	Evektor EV-97 Eurostar	2007-2927	20.02.07
	J F Cox & F W McCann Strathaven		20.03.18P
	Built by G R Pritchard – project PFA 315-14632		

G-CEMF	Cameron C-80	10892	22.06.07
	Linear Communications Consultants Ltd Chepstow		01.05.18E

G-CEMG	Ultramagic M-105	105/153	16.04.07
	Comunicazione In Volo SRL		
	Carpineti, Emilia-Romagna, Italy 'Ferrara'		18.10.13E
	(NF 13.03.15)		

G-CEMI	Europa Aviation Europa XS	569	02.04.07
	B D A Morris Gloucestershire		26.06.18P
	Built by B D A Morris – project PFA 247-13989		

G-CEMM	P&M Quik GT450	8253	23.04.07
	M A Rhodes Fern Farm, Marton		02.09.18P

G-CEMO	P&M Quik GT450	8265	08.05.07
	T D Stock (London SE8)		03.10.18P

G-CEMR	Mainair Blade 912	1066-0196-7-W868	13.04.07
	I-4651 A Simon tr Easter Airfield Flying Group		
	Easter Farm, Fearn		29.04.19P

G-CEMT	P&M Quik GT450	8251	22.02.07
	M Tautz Glassonby		12.07.18P

G-CEMU	Cameron C-80	11029	13.07.07
	J G O'Connell Pattiswick, Braintree		07.09.18E

G-CEMV	Lindstrand LBL 105A	1164	22.06.07
	R G Turnbull Glasbury, Hereford		11.07.18E

G-CEMX	P&M Pegasus Quik	8281	30.08.07
	S J Meehan Baker Barracks, Thorney Island		28.10.17P
	(IE 03.01.18)		

G-CEMY	Alpi Pioneer 300	91	24.04.07
	J C A Garland & P F Salter Cotswold		01.09.18P
	Built by J C A Garland, C M & P F Salter – project		
	PFA 330-14440; kit no duplicates G-CDSB		

G-CENA	Dyn'Aéro MCR-01 ULC	361	25.05.07
	I N Drury Durham Tees Valley		25.06.18P
	Built by R Germany – project PFA 301B-14640		

G-CENB	Evektor EV-97 teamEurostar UK	2007-2913	16.04.07
	K J Gay Newtownards		10.05.18P
	Assembled Cosmik Aviation Ltd		

G-CEND	Evektor EV-97 teamEurostar UK	2007-2916	10.05.07
	York Aircraft Leasing Ltd Breighton		09.05.19P
	Assembled Cosmik Aviation Ltd;		
	operated by York Flying School		

G-CENE	Flight Design CTSW	07-03-20	01.05.07
	M Donnelly tr The CT Flying Group Manchester Barton		24.02.18P
	Assembled P&M Aviation Ltd as c/n 8273		

G-CENG	Best Off Skyranger 912(2)	SKR0603701	01.05.07
	R A Knight Stonefield Park, Chilbolton		24.07.18P
	Built by R A Knight – project BMAA/HB/518		

G-CENH	Tecnam P2002-EA Sierra	189	03.05.07
	M W Taylor Insch		15.05.19P
	Built by J P Kovacs & M W Taylor – project PFA 333-14564		

G-CENJ	Medway SLA 100 Executive	240407	02.05.07
	'G-68' M Ingleton		
	Barnlands Farm, Isle of Sheppey 'Hot Lips'		01.05.18P
	Badged 'SLA 100 Ex'		

G-CENL	P&M Quik GT450	8267	26.05.07
	S Baker & P von Sydow (Alcester)		07.11.17P

G-CENM	Evektor EV-97 Eurostar	2003-1263	20.03.07
	N D Meer Holly Meadow Farm, Bradley		03.06.18P
	Built by N D Meer – project PFA 315-14247		

G-CENN	Cameron C-60	11013	15.03.07
	C J Y Holvoet Flobecq, Belgium 'Nuclear Power'		01.04.18E

G-CENO	Aerospool Dynamic WT9 UK	DY188/2007	08.05.07
	J H Sands & M D S Williams Bagby		16.01.18P
	Assembled Yeoman Light Aircraft Co Ltd;		
	official c/n recorded as 'DY188'		

G-CENP	Ace Aviation Magic/Laser	MT0115	19.06.07
	G-93-1 A G Curtis (Finedon, Wellingborough)		
	Assembled P&M Aviation Ltd; rebuilt c06.09		
	with new frame s/n MT0115; trike s/n MT0115		
	(rebuilt c06.09) & wing s/n AA00126		
	(SSDR microlight since 05.14) (IE 08.10.18)		

G-CENS	Best Off Skyranger Swift 912S(1)	SKR0701769	09.05.07
	J Spence (Frampton, Dorchester)		27.03.18P
	Built by N D Stannard – project BMAA/HB/536		

G-CENV	P&M Quik GT450	8275	04.06.07
	Mid Anglia Microlights Ltd Beccles		04.03.18P

G-CENW	Evektor EV-97A Eurostar	2007-2914	14.03.07
	A B Cameron & B Waterston tr Southside Flyers		
	Glasgow Prestwick		01.07.18P
	Built by W S Long – project PFA 315-14612		

G-CENX	Lindstrand LBL 360A	1160	04.06.07
	Wickers World Ltd Great Haywood, Stafford		
	'jobs 24', 'homes 24' & 'drive 24'		22.11.18E

G-CENZ	Aeros Discus/Alize	014.07 & 001	19.07.07
	A M Singhvi (New Delhi, India)		
	Comprises Delta Trikes Aviation Alizé trike &		
	Aeros Discus wing		
	(SSDR microlight since 05.14) (NF 03.09.15)		

G-CEOB	Pitts S-1S	DIH-1	30.05.07
	N8036J, C-FQEZ N J Radford Denham		11.02.19P
	Built by D I Heaps		

G-CEOC	Tecnam P2002-EA Sierra	203	31.05.07
	M Nicholas (Mark, Highbridge)		11.07.18P
	Built by M A Lomas – project PFA 333-14604		

G-CEOG	Piper PA-28R-201 Arrow III	2837025	04.06.07
	N173ND A J Gardiner North Weald		21.12.18E
	Official type data 'PA-28R-201 Cherokee Arrow III'		
	is incorrect		

G-CEOH	Raj Hamsa X'Air Falcon ULP(1)	666	13.06.07
	J C Miles Bedlands Gate, Little Strickland		02.11.18P
	Built by J C Miles – project BMAA/HB/525		

G-CEOL	Flylight Dragonfly/Aeros Discus 15T	001	12.06.07
	J M Pearce Strathaven		
	Officially registered as Flylight Lightfly-Discus		
	(SSDR microlight since 05.14) (IE 05.06.17)		

G-CEOM	Avtech Jabiru UL-450	xxxx	12.06.07
	J R Caylow Darley Moor		30.03.18P
	Built by J R Caylow – project PFA 274A-14455		

G-CEON	Raj Hamsa X'Air Hawk	1108	15.06.07
	K S Campbell Carlisle Lake District		24.09.18P
	Built by A Anderson – project PFA 340-14673		
G-CEOO	P&M Quik GT450	8257	30.03.07
	S Moran (Brown Edge, Stoke-on-Trent)		07.08.12P
	(NF 22.03.16)		
G-CEOP	Aeroprakt A-22L Foxbat	xxxx	15.06.07
	G F Elvis Otherton		26.07.18P
	Built by P M Ford – project PFA 317A-14671		
G-CEOS	Cameron C-90	11047	04.09.07
	G G Scaife Petworth *'British School of Ballooning'*		12.07.19E
G-CEOU	Lindstrand LBL 31A	1157	15.06.07
	R D Allen Alveston, Bristol *'Lindstrand Balloons'*		20.08.18E
G-CEOW	Europa Aviation Europa XS	547	04.06.07
	D R Curry tr Europa OW Group Bidford		18.07.18P
	Built by R W Wood – project PFA 247-13877;		
	tailwheel u/c; trailered to fly Shobdon)		
G-CEOX	AutoGyro MT-03	07 039	27.06.07
	A J Saunders Rufforth East		12.02.18P
	Assembled Rotorsport UK as RSUK/MT-03/014		
G-CEOY	Schweizer 269C-1 *(300CBi)*	0234	02.07.07
	SE-JBO, EI-DOJ, G-CEOY, EI-DOJ, N86G		
	S J Beaty Wold Lodge, Finedon		27.11.18E
G-CEOZ	Paramania Action GT26/PAP Chariot Z 1006148		21.06.07
	A M Shepherd (Grendon Underwood, Aylesbury)		
	Built by Reflex Wings Ltd; powered paraglider comprising		
	Paramania Action GT26 wing & Passion'Ailes Chariot Z		
	trike (SSDR microlight since 05.14) (NF 04.09.15)		
G-CEPL	Super Marine Spitfire Mk.26	054	19.06.07
	S R Marsh Rochester		05.06.18P
	Built by S R Marsh – project PFA 324-14507;		
	as 'P9398:KL-B' in RAF c/s		
G-CEPM	Avtech Jabiru J430	286	01.05.07
	T R Sinclair Lamb Holm Farm, Holm		08.06.18P
	Built by T R Sinclair – project PFA 336-14517		
G-CEPP	P&M Quik GT450	8266	10.05.07
	W M Studley Dunkeswell		09.06.18P
G-CEPR	Cameron Z-90	11057	04.09.07
	Sport Promotion Srl La Morra, Piedmont, Italy		
	'Pan di Stelle'		22.12.16E
G-CEPU	Cameron Z-77	11030	31.08.07
	G Forgione Vicoforte, Cuneo, Italy *'Liquigas'*		07.09.18E
G-CEPV	Cameron Z-77	11031	31.08.07
	P Boetti & O Lombardo Mondovì, Italy		03.06.19E
G-CEPW	Alpi Pioneer 300	121	27.06.07
	N K Spedding Hinton-in-the-Hedges		
	Built by N K Spedding – project PFA 330-14293;		
	nearing completion 09.15 (NF 06.11.14)		
G-CEPX	Cessna 152	15285792	13.06.07
	N94808 Devon & Somerset Flight Training Ltd		
	Dunkeswell		15.03.18E
G-CEPY	Comco Ikarus C42 FB80	0707-6900	06.08.07
	L A Hosegood Redlands		09.08.18P
	Assembled Aerosport Ltd		
G-CERB	Best Off Skyranger Swift 912S(1)	UK/772	31.05.07
	J J Littler Baker Barracks, Thorney Island		18.09.18P
	Built by J J Littler – project BMAA/HB/537		
G-CERC (2)	Cameron Z-350	11602	20.12.07
	Ballooning Network Ltd Bristol BS3		
	'Bath Building Society'		09.07.18E
	Original envelope c/n 11028 destroyed 09.11.11		
	& replaced 2012 by c/n 11602		
G-CERD	de Havilland DHC-1 Chipmunk 22	7	25.07.07
	CS-AZM, Port.AF 1317 A C Darby RAF Halton		19.05.17P
	Built by OGMA; as 'WK640/C' in RAF c/s		
G-CERE	Evektor EV-97 teamEurostar UK	2007-2931	04.07.07
	D A Abel Bagby		04.07.18P
	Assembled Cosmik Aviation Ltd		
G-CERF	AutoGyro MT-03	xxxx	24.07.07
	P J Robinson Bleaze Hall, Old Hutton, Kendal		13.06.18P
	Assembled Rotorsport UK as c/n RSUK/MT-03/017		
G-CERH	Cameron C-90	10941	17.07.07
	A Walker Crediton		03.03.18E
G-CERI	Europa Aviation Europa XS	541	20.08.03
	S J M Shepherd RAF Mona		11.01.19P
	Built by S J M Shepherd – project PFA 247-13970		
G-CERK	Van's RV-9A	90571	02.07.07
	P E Brown Swansea		05.12.18P
	Built by P E Brown – project PFA 320-14049		
G-CERN	P&M Quik GT450	8299	26.07.07
	P M Jackson (Upper Beeding, Steyning)		21.10.18P
G-CERP	P&M Quik GT450	8285	12.07.07
	D A Howie tr RP Syndicate East Fortune		12.09.18P
G-CERT	Mooney M.20K Mooney 231	25-1134	05.10.87
	S Lammens (Herent, Belgium)		10.02.19E
G-CERV	P&M Quik GT450	8300	31.07.07
	N F Taylor Easterton		12.08.16P
G-CERW	P&M Pegasus Quik	8294	03.05.07
	D J Cornelius Baker Barracks, Thorney Island		17.05.18P
G-CERX	Raytheon Hawker 850XP	258810	21.08.07
	OE-GJA, N71010 Hangar 8 Management Ltd (Oxford)		06.09.18E
G-CERY	Saab 2000	2000-008	21.09.07
	D-AOLA, SE-008, HB-IZE, (D-ADIB), SE-008		
	Air Kilroe Ltd t/a Eastern Airways Humberside		20.09.19E
	Built by Saab Scania AB		
G-CERZ	Saab 2000	2000-042	24.08.07
	SE-LSA, OH-SAT, SE-LSA, SE-042		
	Air Kilroe Ltd t/a Eastern Airways Humberside		23.08.19E
	Built by Saab AB		
G-CESA	Jodel DR.1050 replica	905	09.07.07
	T J Bates Trench Farm, Penley		23.06.18P
	Built by T J Bates & P D Thomas – project		
	PFA 304-13753 using SAB plans & parts		
	ex CEA DR.1050 OY-GPD c/n 528		
G-CESD	Best Off Skyranger Swift 912S(1)	SKR0701770	15.05.07
	B R Trotman Lower Upham Farm, Chiseldon		27.04.18P
	Built by S E Dancaster – project BMAA/HB/535		
G-CESH	Cameron Z-90	11061	30.07.07
	A P Jay South Cerney, Cirencester		
	'Cabot Circus'		10.07.18E
G-CESI	Aeroprakt A-22L Foxbat	205	25.07.07
	D N L Howell Hoe Farm, Colwall		11.02.18P
	Built by D J Ashley – project PFA 317A-14643		
G-CESJ	Raj Hamsa X'Air Hawk	1124	08.08.07
	J Bolton & R Shewan Pittrichie Farm, Whiterashes		04.08.18P
	Built by R G Cameron & B K Harrison		
	– project PFA 340-14677		
G-CESM	TL 2000UK Sting Carbon	07 ST 234	15.09.08
	R D Myles Perth		30.05.18P
	Built by E Stephenson – project LAA 347-14801		
G-CESPᴹ	Rutan Cozy Mk.4	xxxx	29.06.07
	Cancelled 05.11.10 as PWFU		
	Built by T N Craigie – project PFA 159A-13860		
	Fuselage only		
	With Dumfries & Galloway Aviation Museum, Dumfries		
G-CESR	P&M Quik GT450	8304	20.08.07
	A A Kennedy tr G-CESR Syndicate East Fortune		23.08.19P
G-CESV	Evektor EV-97 teamEurostar UK	2007-3011	17.09.07
	T J Dowling & W D Kyle Newtownards		04.10.18P
	Assembled Cosmik Aviation Ltd		
G-CESW	Flight Design CTSW	07-06-04	20.06.07
	J Whiting Felixkirk		17.07.19P
	Assembled P&M Aviation Ltd as c/n 8296		
G-CESZ	CZAW Sportcruiser	07SC049	08.08.07
	G Clover (Sheffield S5)		19.04.18P
	Built by J A Iszard – project PFA 338-14652		
	(Quick-build kit 3855)		
G-CETB	Robin DR.400-180 Régent	1369	31.07.07
	D-EFQR P P Musto tr QR Flying Group		
	Husbands Bosworth		27.09.18E
G-CETD	Piper PA-28-161 Warrior III	2842152	17.07.07
	N5351Y AJW Construction Ltd Bournemouth		05.09.18E
G-CETE	Piper PA-28-161 Warrior III	2842079	17.07.07
	N120FT Aerodynamics Malaga SL		
	La Axarquia-Leoni Benabu, Vélez-Málaga, Spain		21.05.16E

G-CETF	Flight Design CTSW	07-06-05	24.08.07
	G P Masters Sulby, Sibbertoft		25.05.16P
	Assembled P&M Aviation Ltd as c/n 8318 (IE 01.03.18)		
G-CETK	Cameron Z-145	4770	12.09.07
	OO-BWN R H Etherington Newtown, Hungerford		23.11.18E
G-CETL	P&M Quik GT450	8307	13.08.07
	I A Macadam (Sturminster Newton)		26.09.18P
G-CETM	P&M Quik GT450	8298	31.07.07
	J D Manning tr G-CETM Flying Group East Fortune		30.07.18P
G-CETN	Hummel Aviation Hummel Bird	SK3032.P	31.08.07
	A A Haseldine (Craswall, Hereford)		
	Built by A A Haseldine – project PFA 127-13044		
	(NF 04.02.15)		
G-CETO	Best Off Skyranger Swift 912S(1)	SKR0704783	13.07.07
	S C Stoodley Priory Farm, Tibenham		14.02.18P
	Built by P J Shergold – project BMAA/HB/541		
G-CETP	Van's RV-9A	xxxx	03.09.07
	D Boxall & S Hill Wadswick Manor Farm, Corsham		06.07.18P
	Built by D Boxall & S Hill- project PFA 320-14012		
G-CETR	Comco Ikarus C42 FB80	0706-6898	02.08.07
	Cloudbase Paragliding Ltd Redlands		10.09.18P
	Assembled Aerosport Ltd		
G-CETS	Van's RV-7	70529	23.08.07
	N557WM J Archer tr TS Group Bidford		19.04.19P
	Built by M R Wyatt		
G-CETT	Evektor EV-97 teamEurostar UK	2007-3006	24.07.07
	P Thompson Carrickmore		11.04.18P
	Assembled Cosmik Aviation Ltd		
G-CETU	Best Off Skyranger Swift 912S(1)	SKR0707803	12.09.07
	N McCusker & A Raithby Rufforth East		20.07.18P
	Built by M A Sweet – project BMAA/HB/551		
G-CETV	Best Off Skyranger Swift 912S(1)	SKR0612759	22.06.07
	C J Johnson Willingale		29.08.18P
	Built by K J Gay – project BMAA/HB/532		
G-CETX	Alpi Pioneer 300	195	23.07.07
	J M P Ree Membury		08.05.18P
	Built by M C Ellis – project PFA 330-14573		
G-CETY	Rans S-6-ES Coyote II	xxxx	17.07.07
	R I Jackson Sutton Meadows		04.05.19P
	Built by J North – project PFA 204-14654; tricycle u/c		
G-CETZ	Comco Ikarus C42 FB100	0706-6899	08.11.07
	C P Dawes tr G-CETZ Group Darley Moor		07.11.18P
	Assembled Aerosport Ltd		
G-CEUF	P&M Quik GT450	8325	12.10.07
	G T Snoddon Newtownards		11.10.18P
G-CEUH	P&M Quik GT450	8316	25.10.07
	W Brownlie East Fortune		12.04.18P
G-CEUI	AutoGyro MT-03	xxxx	18.10.07
	Cancelled 23.09.08 as destroyed		25.10.08
	Rufforth East *Assembled Rotorsport (UK) as*		
	RSUK/MT-03/021; used as simulator 05.18		
G-CEUJ	Best Off Skyranger Swift 912S(1)	SKR0707802	14.12.07
	J P Batty & J R C Brightman tr The CEUJ Group		
	Sackville Lodge Farm, Riseley		07.07.18P
	Built by J P Batty & J R C Brightman		
	– project BMAA/HB/548		
G-CEUL	Ultramagic M-105	105/157	04.01.08
	R A Vale Hurcott, Kidderminster		09.06.17E
G-CEUM	Ultramagic M-120	120/30	28.11.07
	Skydive Chatteris Club Ltd Chatteris *'Bridges Van Hire'*		
	17.05.18E		
G-CEUN	Schempp-Hirth Discus CS	075CS	08.10.07
	BGA 4694, RAFGGA 501		
	The Royal Air Force Gliding & Soaring Association		
	RAF Halton *'506'*		16.10.18E
	Built by Orličan Aakciová Společnost;		
	operated by Chilterns Gliding Centre		
G-CEUT	Hoffmann H36 Dimona II	36270	05.10.07
	LY-GDW, F-CGAX Cancelled 13.10.14 as PWFU		14.07.14
	Seighford *For sale for spares use 10.18*		
G-CEUU	Robinson R44 Raven II	11949	12.10.07
	A Stafford-Jones Dunsfold		18.11.17E
G-CEUV	Cameron C-90	11078	18.12.07
	A M Holly Breadstone, Berkeley *'Silverline'*		20.02.18E
	(IE 05.10.18)		
G-CEUW	Zenair CH.601XL Zodiac	6-9856	04.10.07
	P Connolly Goodwood		08.08.18P
	Built by M Taylor – project PFA 162B-14554		
G-CEUZ	P&M Quik GT450	8321	25.10.07
	P M Williamson Northrepps		24.10.18P
G-CEVA	Comco Ikarus C42 FB80	0709-6915	25.10.07
	The Scottish Flying Club Strathaven		06.11.18P
	Assembled Aerosport Ltd		
G-CEVB	P&M Quik GT450	8315	03.10.07
	C Traher Sutton Meadows		09.10.18P
	Carries 'Enola Gay' nose art		
G-CEVC	Van's RV-4	2726	21.09.07
	N2063Z P A Brook Brighton City *'Pops'*		14.01.20P
	Built by K W Pabo		
G-CEVD	Rolladen-Schneider LS3	3024	21.12.07
	BGA 2979/EVD, N63LS, D-7914		
	P G Warner Gransden Lodge *'382'*		16.04.19E
G-CEVE	Centrair 101A Pégase	101A0141	17.09.07
	BGA 2980 T P Newham Lasham *'491'*		03.10.18E
G-CEVH	Cameron V-65	2765	12.10.07
	OO-BGG J A Atkinson Dorchester		10.08.17E
G-CEVJ	Alpi Pioneer 200-M	168	16.10.07
	K Worthington (Eccleston, Chorley)		26.09.18P
	Built by B W Bartlett – project PFA 334-14710		
G-CEVK	Schleicher Ka 6CR	6541	11.10.07
	BGA 2870, AGA 24, BGA 1353		
	K E & O J Wilson Upwood *'451'*		05.07.15E
	(IE 25.04.16)		
G-CEVM	Tecnam P2002-EA Sierra	283	27.07.07
	J A Ellis North Weald		16.06.19P
	Built by R C Mincik – project PFA 333-14709		
G-CEVN	Rolladen-Schneider LS7	7029	25.10.07
	BGA 3438, D-1316 N Gaunt & B C Toon		
	Sutton Bank *'A98'*		07.01.18E
G-CEVO	Grob G109B	6237	14.03.08
	D-KGLM T J Wilkinson Sackville Lodge Farm, Riseley		07.07.14E
	(NF 26.08.15)		
G-CEVP	P&M Quik GT450	8078	30.10.07
	P J Lowe (Stamford)		12.01.19P
	Trike originally registered as c/n 8329;		
	now fitted with 8078 ex G-CDCK		
G-CEVS	Evektor EV-97 teamEurostar UK	2007-3102	16.11.07
	P D Kiddell tr Golf Victor Sierra Flying Group Eshott		14.11.18P
	Assembled Cosmik Aviation Ltd		
G-CEVU	ICP MXP-740 Savannah VG Jabiru(1)	07-05-51-600	02.11.07
	I C May North Weald		31.08.19P
	Built by B L Cook – project BMAA/HB/552		
G-CEVV	Rolladen-Schneider LS3	3035	25.10.07
	BGA 2251 M C Cooper tr LS3 307 Syndicate		
	Challock *'307'*		24.05.18E
G-CEVW	P&M Quik GT450	8314	25.09.07
	J M Mooney Park Hall Farm, Mapperley		12.10.19P
G-CEVX	Aériane Swift Light PAS	111	19.10.07
	P Trueman (Bredbury, Stockport)		
	(IE 25.08.17)		
G-CEVY	AutoGyro MT-03	07 133	20.12.07
	Silver Birch Pet Jets Ltd Chiltern Park, Wallingford		05.12.17P
	Assembled Rotorsport UK as c/n RSUK/MT-03/025		
G-CEVZ	Centrair ASW 20FL	20184	01.10.07
	BGA 2726 B Watkins North Hill *'202'*		28.04.18E
G-CEWC	Schleicher ASK 21	21157	02.11.07
	BGA 2871/EQR London Gliding Club Proprietary Ltd		
	Dunstable Downs *'EQR'*		30.10.18E
G-CEWD	P&M Quik GT450	8330	15.11.07
	S C Key Northrepps		19.09.18P
G-CEWE	Schempp-Hirth Nimbus-2	4	29.10.07
	BGA 1725 T Clark Sandhill Farm, Shrivenham *'TM'*		30.07.18E
G-CEWF	Jacobs V35 Airchair	EJ/194	28.01.08
	ZS-HYU G A & I Chadwick & M G Richards Caterham		
	Built by E J Jacobs (IE 04.09.17)		

G-CEWH	P&M Quik GT450	8324	05.11.07
	A A Shields tr G-CEWH Syndicate East Fortune		08.11.19P
G-CEWI	Schleicher ASW 19B	19086	31.10.07
	BGA 4410, PH-562 S R Edwards		
	Gransden Lodge 'W19'		04.06.18E
G-CEWL	Alpi Pioneer 200	NC165	29.10.07
	R W H Watson New Grimmet Farm, Maybole		09.10.17P
	Built by M A Hogg – project PFA 334-14712		
G-CEWM	de Havilland DHC-6-300 Twin Otter	656	07.04.08
	N70551, PZ-TCE Isles of Scilly Skybus Ltd Land's End		13.04.19E
G-CEWO	Schleicher Ka 6CR	1065	10.08.07
	BGA 2301, D-5144 D P Westcott		
	Burnford Common, Brentor 'DQS'		28.01.18E
	(NF 01.11.17)		
G-CEWP	Grob G102 Astir CS	1258	08.11.07
	BGA 2155/DJQ M J Clee tr G-CEWP Flying Group		
	Usk '214'		27.04.18E
G-CEWR	Aeroprakt A-22L Foxbat	224	22.11.07
	C S Bourne & G P Wiley Otherton		17.03.18P
	Built by C S Bourne & G P Wiley – project PFA 317A-14736		
G-CEWS	Zenair CH.701SP	7-9804	13.11.07
	A I Sutherland Kylarrick House, Edderton		22.05.19P
	Built by I J M Donnelly – project PFA 187A-14692		
G-CEWT	Flight Design CTSW	07-10-10	21.11.07
	K Tuck Langmoor Farm, Horningcroft		16.03.18P
	Assembled P&M Aviation Ltd as c/n 8333		
G-CEWU	Ultramagic H-77	77/316	18.04.08
	P C Waterhouse Flimwell, Wadhurst		
	'Cherished Memories'		10.05.18E
G-CEWW	Grob G102 Astir CS77	1758	25.10.07
	BGA 2442 The South Wales Gliding Club Ltd		
	Usk 'WW'		12.07.18E
G-CEWX	Cameron Z-350	11092	25.03.08
	Celador Radio (South West) Ltd Bristol BS3		
	'Original 106.5 Bristol'		30.03.15E
	(NF 27.10.16)		
G-CEWY	Quicksilver GT500	0420	21.11.07
	N Andrews (Southmoor, Abingdon)		27.08.19P
	Built by W Murphy – project PFA 348-14707		
G-CEWZ	Schempp-Hirth Discus bT	128/490	17.08.07
	BGA 4032 J F Goudie Portmoak '381'		13.01.19E
G-CEXL	Comco Ikarus C42 FB80	0711-6927	23.11.07
	R S O'Carroll tr Syndicate C42-1		
	Kernan Valley, Tandragee		15.01.18P
	Assembled Aerosport Ltd		
G-CEXM	Best Off Skyranger Swift 912S(1)	SKR0708812	01.11.07
	A F Batchelor Rayne Hall Farm, Rayne		07.10.18P
	Built by A F Batchelor – project BMAA/HB/556		
G-CEXN	Cameron A-120	11089	03.01.08
	Dragon Balloon Company Ltd Castleton, Hope Valley		09.05.17E
G-CEXO	Piper PA-28-161 Warrior III	2842041	28.11.07
	N250ND NAL Asset Management Ltd Newcastle Int'l		08.04.19E
G-CEXP	Handley Page HPR.7 Dart Herald 209	195	29.10.87
	I-ZERC, G-BFRJ, 4X-AHO Cancelled 22.03.96 by CAA		07.11.96
	Gatwick Open store 09.18 – to be preserved at St Athan		
G-CEXX	AutoGyro MT-03	07 114	12.11.07
	D Goh Kirkbride		06.04.18P
	Assembled Rotorsport UK as c/n RSUK/MT-03/022		
G-CEYC	DG Flugzeugbau DG-505 Elan Orion	5E194X38	27.11.07
	BGA 4690/JQF, S5-7516		
	Scottish Gliding Union Ltd Portmoak '5GC'		31.03.18E
	Built by Elan Tovarna Sportnega Orodja N.Sol.O		
G-CEYD	Cameron N-31 HAB	3558	22.06.07
	G-LLYD Cancelled 25.09.17 by CAA		17.07.08
	Not Known Inflated Pidley 04.18		
G-CEYE	Piper PA-32R-300 Cherokee Lance	32R-7780533	24.10.02
	SE-KCD, OH-PAS D C M Wilson Goodwood		23.04.18E
G-CEYG	Cessna 152	15280287	14.04.08
	N24495 H E da Costa Alburquerque		
	(Amadora, Portugal)		09.03.19E
G-CEYH	Cessna 152	15282689	29.04.08
	N89253 Cornwall Flying Club Ltd Bodmin		17.05.18E
G-CEYK	Europa Aviation Europa XS	616	10.12.07
	A B Milne Landmead Farm, Garford		05.07.18P
	Built by A B Milne – project PFA 247-14476; tricycle u/c		
G-CEYL	Bombardier BD-700-1A10 Global Express 9196		10.10.08
	VP-CRC, C-FEBQ Voluxis Ltd Biggin Hill		09.10.19E
G-CEYM	Van's RV-6	24878	12.12.07
	R B Skinner Belle Vue Farm, Yarnscombe		24.10.17P
	Built by H Gordon-Roe – project PFA 181A-14595		
G-CEYN	Grob G109B	6256	12.12.07
	D-KGFY V Pringle tr G-CEYN Flying Group Lasham		31.08.18E
G-CEYP	North Wing Design Stratus/ATF	7642	21.12.07
	J S James (Petersfield)		
	(SSDR microlight since 05.14) (NF 20.01.15)		
G-CEYR	AutoGyro MT-03	xxxx	14.02.08
	S R Voller Moorlands Farm, Farway Common		05.04.18P
	Assembled Rotorsport UK as c/n RSUK/MT-03/032		
G-CEYY	Evektor EV-97 teamEurostar UK	2007-3123	07.01.08
	N J James Welshpool		17.01.19P
	Assembled Cosmik Aviation Ltd		
G-CEZA	Comco Ikarus C42 FB80	0711-6923	13.11.07
	D E Bassett & P J Morton St Michaels		26.11.18P
	Assembled Aerosport Ltd		
G-CEZB	ICP MXP-740 Savannah VG Jabiru(1)	07-05-51-599	14.12.07
	W E Dudley Welshpool		08.12.18P
	Built by J N Anyan – project BMAA/HB/549		
G-CEZD	Evektor EV-97 teamEurostar UK	2007-3107	22.12.07
	G P Jones Otherton		08.04.18P
	Assembled Cosmik Aviation Ltd		
G-CEZE	Best Off Skyranger Swift 912S(1)	UK/811	09.11.07
	L Dickinson & T C Viner (Droitwich & Binley)		02.11.18P
	Built by N McAllister – project BMAA/HB/555		
	(IE 20.12.18)		
G-CEZF	Evektor EV-97 teamEurostar UK	2007-3205	18.02.08
	D J Dick Broadmeadow Farm, Hereford		12.03.18P
	Assembled Cosmik Aviation Ltd		
G-CEZH	Aerochute Dual	321	14.01.08
	S T P Askew (Melton Mowbray)		17.12.18P
	Official c/n is for trike unit: wing s/n 1288		
G-CEZI	Piper PA-28-161 Cadet	2841228	04.01.08
	N131ND Redhill Air Services Ltd Redhill		20.04.18E
G-CEZK	Stolp SA.750 Acroduster Too	630	24.01.08
	R I M Hague Full Sutton		29.10.18P
	Built by R I M Hague – project PFA 089-13726		
G-CEZL	Piper PA-28-161 Cadet	2841247	14.01.08
	OO-JAG, N9192Z Chalrey Ltd Elstree		29.03.19E
	Operated by Flyers Flying School		
G-CEZM	Cessna 152	15285179	07.01.08
	N6167Q Modern Air (UK) Ltd Fowlmere		23.03.19E
G-CEZO	Piper PA-28-161 Cadet	2841226	04.01.08
	N145ND Redhill Air Services Ltd Fairoaks		10.02.18E
	Operated by Fairoaks Flight Centre		
G-CEZR	Diamond DA.40D Star	D4.343	02.04.08
	Flying Time Ltd Brighton City		07.06.18E
G-CEZS	Zenair CH.601HDS Zodiac	xxxx	01.02.08
	V D Asque Old Warden		14.03.18P
	Built by R Wyness – project PFA 162-14030; tricycle u/c		
G-CEZT	P&M Quik GT450	8349	22.02.08
	A A Greig East Fortune		12.04.18P
G-CEZU	CFM Streak Shadow SA	K 337-SA	05.02.08
	A W Hodder Belle Vue Farm, Yarnscombe		04.05.18P
	Built by M R Foreman – project PFA 206-13597		
G-CEZW	Jodel D.150 Mascaret	171	05.02.08
	J C Carter (Dry Drayton, Cambridge)		
	Built by J N Kilford – project PFA 235-13866 using		
	hybrid SAB & Frank Roger's plans (NF 03.11.14)		
G-CEZX	P&M Quik GT450	8360	07.03.08
	D C Sollom tr Zulu Xray Group Redlands		04.03.18P
G-CEZZ	Flight Design CTSW	07-08-05	20.09.07
	J A Lynch Sandown		24.11.18P
	Assembled P&M Aviation Ltd as c/n 8326		

G-CFAA – G-CFZZ

G-CFAJ	Glaser-Dirks DG-300 Elan	3E50	07.01.08
	BGA 3103/FAJ J P Borland & R S Rand		
	North Hill 'FAJ'		07.01.20E
	Built by Elan Tovarna Sportnega Orodja N.Sol.O		
G-CFAK	AutoGyro MT-03	xxxx	14.02.08
	R M Savage Croft House, Berrier		23.03.18P
	Assembled Rotorsport UK as c/n RSUK/MT-03/030		
G-CFAM	Schempp-Hirth Nimbus-3/24.5	79	19.10.07
	BGA 3106 K J Hartley tr Nimbus III Syndicate J15		
	Bicester 'J15'		08.09.17E
G-CFAO	Rolladen-Schneider LS4	4465	05.11.07
	BGA 3109/FAQ V R Roberts Snitterfield '631'		20.05.18E
G-CFAP (2)	Ivanov ZJ-Viera	VIERAA14-08M	14.02.08
	P I Passmore (Newark)		
	Built by M Ivanov; official c/n VIERAA5-08M		
	relates to G-CFAP (1)		
	(SSDR microlight since 05.14) (IE 01.06.17)		
G-CFAR	AutoGyro MT-03	xxxx	20.12.07
	P M Twose Eddsfield, Octon Lodge Farm, Thwing		30.07.18P
	Assembled Rotorsport UK as c/n RSUK/MT-03/026		
G-CFAS	Reality Escapade Jabiru(3)	UK.ESC.0005	07.01.08
	C G N Boyd (Malahide, Co. Dublin, RoI)		05.04.14P
	Built by C G N Boyd – project BMAA/HB/473		
	(NF 09.12.15)		
G-CFAT	P&M Quik GT450	8355	28.02.08
	I F Bruce Henstridge		23.04.18P
G-CFAV	Comco Ikarus C42 FB80	0802-6939	20.03.08
	Deanland Flight Training Ltd Deanland		13.07.19P
	Assembled Aerosport Ltd		
G-CFAW	Lindstrand LBL 35A Cloudhopper	899	16.04.08
	HB-QIV A Walker Crediton 'Lindstrand Balloons'		03.03.18E
G-CFAX	Comco Ikarus C42 FB80	0712-6933	05.03.08
	B Cook & R E Parker Hunsdon		17.03.18P
	Assembled Aerosport Ltd		
G-CFAY	Sky 120-24	074	08.01.08
	OE-ZAY G B Lescott Oxford		23.08.15E
G-CFBA	Schleicher ASW 20BL	20665	21.01.08
	BGA 3119/FBA C R Little Halesland '178'		23.06.18E
G-CFBB	Schempp-Hirth Standard Cirrus	327G	25.09.07
	BGA 3120, RAFGGA 312		
	C A J Allen Dunstable Downs '822'		19.03.19E
G-CFBC	Schleicher ASW 15B	15356	10.12.07
	BGA 3121/FBC, OH-439		
	P Pettitt tr G-CFBC Group Rivar Hill 'FBC'		04.11.18E
G-CFBE	Comco Ikarus C42 FB80	0804-6958	27.06.08
	K H Denham Chatteris		31.08.18P
	Assembled Aerosport Ltd		
G-CFBF	Lindstrand 203T HiFlyer	HF010	13.02.08
	S & D Leisure (Europe) Ltd (Manchester M8)		
	'health-on-line'		28.03.17E
	Tethered Gas Balloon; substantially damaged 06.16		
	Bournemouth & stored 02.17		
G-CFBH	Glaser-Dirks DG-100G Elan	E156G123	22.11.07
	BGA 3126/FBH N Riggott Lasham '177'		27.04.18E
	Built by Elan Tovarna Sportnega Orodja N.Sol.O;		
	operated by IBM Gliding Club		
G-CFBJ	AutoGyro MT-03	xxxx	04.03.08
	P S Ball (Mouldsworth, Chester)		21.02.18P
	Assembled Rotorsport UK as c/n RSUK/MT-03/042		
G-CFBL	Best Off Skyranger Swift 912S(1)	SKR0708824	14.02.08
	M A Azeem & D Hennings North Weald		21.03.19P
	Built by S R Isaac – project BMAA/HB/558		
G-CFBM	P&M Pegasus Quantum 15-912	8352	14.02.08
	B J Youngs (Norwich)		05.03.19P
G-CFBN	Glasflügel Mosquito B	167	05.09.07
	BGA 3131, D-6364 J & S R Nash Lasham 'FBN'		11.02.19E
G-CFBT	Schempp-Hirth Ventus bT	35	06.12.07
	BGA 3136/FBT P R Stafford-Allen Tibenham '333'		03.12.18E
G-CFBV	Schleicher ASK 21	21223	08.01.08
	BGA 3138/FBV London Gliding Club Proprietary Ltd		
	Dunstable Downs 'FBV'		08.01.19E

G-CFBW	Glaser-Dirks DG-100G Elan	E174G140	12.12.07
	BGA 3139/FBW M Adams tr G-CFBW Syndicate		
	Lasham '395'		06.07.16E
	Built by Elan Tovarna Sportnega Orodja N.Sol.O		
G-CFBY	Best Off Skyranger Swift 912S(1)	UK/841	26.02.08
	K Washbourne Eshott		25.11.18P
	Built by J A Armin – project BMAA/HB/562		
G-CFCA	Schempp-Hirth Discus b	336	07.02.08
	BGA 4117/HQJ, D-1762 P Lund Shenington '762'		20.04.18E
G-CFCB	Centrair 101 Pégase	10100178	11.09.07
	BGA 3144, F-CGEA T J Berriman & M Phillimore		
	Portmoak 'FCB'		29.04.18E
G-CFCC	Cameron Z-275	11103	27.02.08
	Ballooning Network Ltd Southville, Bristol		
	'Park Furnishers'		23.04.18E
G-CFCD	Best Off Skyranger Swift 912S(1)	UK/801	18.12.07
	D & L Payn Eshott		26.08.18P
	Built by R J Gilbert – project BMAA/HB/554		
G-CFCE	Raj Hamsa X'Air Hawk	1153	20.02.08
	B M Tibenham Longside		14.12.18P
	Built by P C Bishop – project PFA 340-14751;		
	kit no conflicts with EI-EEG		
G-CFCF	Aerochute Dual	327	02.06.08
	C J Kendal & S G Smith (Stockport & Peak Forest, Buxton)		
	Wing c/n 1280 (NF 11.06.18)		
G-CFCG	AutoGyro MT-03	xxxx	10.04.08
	Cancelled 03.09.10 as PWFU		20.04.09
	Rufforth East Assembled Rotorsport (UK) as		
	RSUK/MT-03/035; wreck used as simulator 07.18		
G-CFCI	Reims/Cessna F172N	F17202005	19.04.08
	SE-IFB J Blacklock Derby		11.12.18E
G-CFCJ	Grob G102 Astir CS	1231	13.11.07
	BGA 3151/FCJ, D-4205 A J C Beaumont		
	& P Hardwick Burnford Common, Brentor '571'		26.06.18E
G-CFCK	Best Off Skyranger Swift 912S(1)	SKR0801848	28.02.08
	J Smith Manchester Barton		24.09.18P
	Built by C M Sperring – project BMAA/HB/565		
G-CFCL	AutoGyro MT-03	08 045	12.05.08
	D D Taylor Graveley Hall Farm, Graveley		06.10.18P
	Assembled Rotorsport UK as c/n RSUK/MT-03/043		
G-CFCM	Robinson R44 Raven I	1635	10.04.08
	OO-PMD Newmarket Plant Hire Ltd Cambridge		22.05.19E
G-CFCN	Schempp-Hirth Standard Cirrus	131	22.10.07
	BGA 3155, D-0191 P C Bunniss Nympsfield 'FCN'		29.05.18E
G-CFCP	Rolladen-Schneider LS6-a	6030	08.01.08
	BGA 3156/FCP M A Hall Dunstable Downs '721'		16.01.19E
G-CFCR	Schleicher Ka 6E	4223	07.11.07
	BGA 3158/FCR, OH-375, OH-REC		
	R F Whittaker Lasham '113'		15.05.18E
G-CFCS	Schempp-Hirth Nimbus-2C	233	07.11.07
	BGA 3159/FCS, D-5993		
	P Dolling & J Luck (Codford, Warminster) '2R'		29.04.19E
G-CFCT	Evektor EV-97 teamEurostar UK	2008-3208	25.03.08
	T J A Geering tr Sutton Eurostar Group		
	Sutton Meadows		27.03.18P
	Assembled Cosmik Aviation Ltd		
G-CFCV	Schleicher ASW 20	20076	13.03.08
	BGA 3162/FCV, RAFGSA R24		
	I R Gallacher RAF Cosford 'FCV'		18.07.18E
G-CFCW	AutoGyro MT-03	08 006	06.03.08
	C M Jones Kirkbride		16.06.18P
	Assembled Rotorsport UK as c/n RSUK/MT-03/036		
G-CFCX	Rans S-6-ES Coyote II	0407.1803	05.03.08
	D & S Morrison Nether Huntlywood Farm, Gordon		12.12.17P
	Built by D Morrison – project PFA 204-14699		
G-CFCY	Best Off Skyranger Swift 912S(1)	UK/793	10.03.08
	M E & T E Simpson		
	(Hucclecote, Glos/Rickmansworth. Herts)		18.05.16P
	Built by M E Simpson – project BMAA/HB/545		
G-CFCZ	P&M Quik GT450	8359	09.04.08
	P K Dale Rufforth East		26.02.18P

G-CFDA	Schleicher ASW 15	15050	12.10.07
	BGA 3167/FDA, D-0511		
	N B Coggins Wycombe Air Park '7D'		18.03.14E
	(IE 18.08.15)		

G-CFDE	Schempp-Hirth Ventus bT	53	06.09.07
	BGA 3171 K W Clarke Chipping '510'		05.04.18E

G-CFDF	Ultramagic S-90	90/101	09.06.08
	A A Leggate & H M Savage tr Edinburgh University		
	Hot Air Balloon Club Edinburgh EH3		
	'The University of Edinburgh'		30.05.15E

G-CFDG	Schleicher Ka 6CR	6235	18.03.08
	BGA 3441/FQL, HB-772		
	P R Alderson tr Delta-Golf Group Lasham 'FDG'		11.05.18E

G-CFDI	Van's RV-6	23116	13.03.08
	N76GC M D Challoner Henstridge		08.03.18P
	Built by G M Chancey		

G-CFDJ	Evektor EV-97 teamEurostar UK	2008-3209	22.04.08
	M Jones & J D J Spragg		
	Overgreen Farm, Wishaw, Sutton Coldfield		12.06.18P
	Assembled Cosmik Aviation Ltd		

G-CFDK	Rans S-6-ES Coyote II	0507.1805	25.03.08
	J Fleming (Granton-on-Spey)		20.12.19P
	Built by C Beale – project LAA 204-14767; tricycle u/c		

G-CFDL	P&M QuikR	8370	30.04.08
	N A Higgins (Alrewas, Burton-on-Trent)		16.02.18P

G-CFDM	Schempp-Hirth Discus b	87	01.10.07
	BGA 3185 J L & T G M Whiting Shenington 'H20'		02.06.18E

G-CFDN	Best Off Skyranger Swift 912S(1)	SKRxxxx842	09.04.08
	S B Wilkes tr Hadair Fixed Wing Flyers		
	Wolverhampton Halfpenny Green		06.03.18P
	Built by D A Perkins – project BMAA HB/564		

G-CFDO	Flight Design CTSW	07-12-09	10.04.08
	M Harris Eshott		27.11.18P
	Assembled P&M Aviation Ltd as c/n 8366 (IE 11.06.18)		

G-CFDP	Flight Design CTSW	07-11-06	08.04.08
	N Fielding Ince		16.05.18P
	Assembled P&M Aviation Ltd as c/n 8367		

G-CFDS	TL 2000UK Sting Carbon	07 ST 201	08.04.08
	A G Cummings RAF Woodvale		10.03.18P
	Built by P H Ronfell – project LAA 347-14785;		
	badged 'Sting Sport'		

G-CFDT	Aerola Alatus-M	AS 01-014	28.04.08
	G Rainey & M J Reader-Hoer Westonzoyland		
	(SSDR microlight since 05.14) (IE 30.05.17)		

G-CFDX	SZD-48-1 Jantar-Standard 2	B-1251	03.03.08
	BGA 3188/FDX, (BGA 2916/ESN)		
	A Phillips North Hill 'FDX'		18.04.16E

G-CFDY	P&M Quik GT450	8373	09.04.08
	C N Thornton Shotton Colliery, Peterlee		15.04.14P
	(IE 21.04.17)		

G-CFEA	Cameron C-90	11158	08.05.08
	A M Holly Breadstone, Berkeley 'Barclays'		14.09.18E
	(IE 05.10.18)		

G-CFEB	Cameron C-80	11174	06.05.08
	N Edmunds Thornbury, Bristol		
	'Robert Hitchins Limited'		20.05.19E

G-CFED	Van's RV-9	91171	09.04.08
	E W Taylor White Fen Farm, Benwick		14.03.18P
	Built by P Robinson & E Taylor – project PFA 320-14414		

G-CFEE	Evektor EV-97 Eurostar	2008-3221	21.02.08
	C Prentice tr The G CFEE Group Redhill		04.06.19P
	Built by G R Pritchard – project LAA 315-14778;		
	c/n also quoted as '2008-3210'		

G-CFEF	Grob G102 Astir CS	1164	08.02.08
	BGA 3196/FEF, OY-XGC C J Ballance		
	tr Oxford University Gliding Club Bicester 'FEF'		07.04.18E

G-CFEG	Schempp-Hirth Ventus b/16.6	279	23.11.07
	BGA 3197/FEG D K McCarthy		
	(Ferwig, Cardigan) '120'		29.03.19E

G-CFEH	Centrair 101 Pégase	10100268/2	13.12.07
	BGA 3198/FEH Booker Gliding Club Ltd		
	Wycombe Air Park '318'		12.03.18R
	Originally regd with c/n 101A0268; rebuilt with fuselage		
	c/n 01304: original fuselage rebuilt as BGA 3560		

G-CFEI	Rotary Air Force RAF 2000 GTX-SE	xxxx	10.04.08
	C J Watkinson Bridge Cottage, Great Heck		
	Built by A M Wells – project PFA G/13-1369 (NF 23.06.15)		

G-CFEJ	Schempp-Hirth Discus b	76	17.12.07
	BGA 3199/FEJ W Parker tr Lima Charlie Syndicate		
	Wycombe Air Park 'LC'		12.03.18E

G-CFEK	Cameron Z-105	11176	30.06.08
	RM Penny (Plant Hire & Demolition) Ltd		
	Ston Easton, Radstock 'Penny'		07.08.19E

G-CFEL	Evektor EV-97A Eurostar	2007-2940	14.03.08
	J A Crook (Staverton, Trowbridge)		02.08.18P
	Built by S R Green – project PFA 315-14740		

G-CFEM	P&M Quik GT450	8388	02.06.08
	A M King Fife		01.06.18P

G-CFEN	PZL-Bielsko SZD-50-3 Puchacz	B-1326	17.01.08
	BGA 3203/FEN The Northumbria Gliding Club Ltd		
	Currock Hill 'FEN'		18.04.18E

G-CFEO	Evektor EV-97 Eurostar	xxxx	15.04.08
	J B Binks Beeches Farm, Cliffe		18.11.18P
	Built by J B Binks – project PFA 315-14737		

G-CFER	Schempp-Hirth Discus b	75	25.03.08
	BGA 3206/FER S R Westlake North Hill 'FER'		04.08.18E

G-CFES	Schempp-Hirth Discus b	88	22.11.07
	BGA 3207/FES M J Spittal Crowland 'FES'		24.05.18E

G-CFET	Van's RV-7	70686	17.09.08
	LY-ASJ J Astor Cotswold		19.05.18P
	Built by A Jonusas		

G-CFEV	P&M Pegasus Quik	8375	30.04.08
	W T Davis Ludham		25.06.19P

G-CFEX	P&M Quik GT450 8362		20.05.08
	H Wilson	Shobdon	
	(IE 09.07.18)		

G-CFEY	Aerola Alatus-M	AS 01-017	30.05.08
	M S Hayman (Iver)		
	(SSDR microlight since 05.14) (IE 06.05.15)		

G-CFEZ	CZAW Sportcruiser	3944	14.02.08
	J F Barber & J R Large Stapleford		10.11.18P
	Built by J F Barber & J R Large – project		
	PFA 338-14675; official c/n relates to order no		

G-CFFA	Ultramagic M-90	90/59	15.05.08
	HB-QKA Proximm SpA Milan, Italy 'Re/Max'		25.09.18E

G-CFFB	Grob G102 Astir CS	1123	08.10.07
	BGA 3216, RAFGSA R9, R97, BGA 3216/FFB, D-6977		
	R Millins Dunstable Downs		15.04.18E

G-CFFC	Centrair 101A Pégase	101A0255	21.12.07
	BGA 3217/FFC M P Capps & M J Permain		
	(Ross-on-Wye & Chepstow) 'FFC'		09.03.19E

G-CFFE	Evektor EV-97 teamEurostar UK	2008-3211	13.05.08
	R W Osborne Priory Farm, Tibenham		22.07.18P
	Assembled Cosmik Aviation Ltd		

G-CFFF	Pitts S-1S	xxxx	18.03.08
	P J Roy Graveley Hall Farm, Graveley		
	Built by N N Bentley – project LAA 009-14779		
	(NF 05.02.15)		

G-CFFG	Aerochute Dual	320	08.05.08
	G J Pemberton (Lincoln)		06.12.18P
	Parachute s/n 1384		

G-CFFJ	Flight Design CTSW	07-12-10	15.05.08
	R Germany (Lodge Farm, Norwell, Newark)		18.08.18P
	Assembled P&M Aviation Ltd as c/n 8391		

G-CFFN	P&M Quik GT450	8380	19.06.08
	S D Cox (Hastings)		22.06.18P

G-CFFO	P&M Quik GT450	8361	30.04.08
	D Ben-Lamri & R Wade Arclid Green, Sandbach		29.04.18P

G-CFFS	Centrair 101A Pégase	101A0265	09.11.07
	BGA 3231/FFS R C Verdier Gransden Lodge 'FFS'		06.05.16E

G-CFFT	Schempp-Hirth Discus b	110	28.11.07
	BGA 3232/FFT Goalrace Ltd		
	(Welford, Northampton) 'FFT'		12.05.15E

G-CFFU	Glaser-Dirks DG-100G Elan	E200G166	17.10.07
	BGA 3233 K T Tutthill tr FFU Group Chipping 'FFU'		07.06.18E

G-CFFV	PZL-Bielsko SZD-51-1 Junior	B-1616	12.02.08
	BGA 3234/FFV, F-WGJA		
	Herefordshire Gliding Club Ltd Shobdon *'FFV'*		30.09.18E
G-CFFX	Schempp-Hirth Discus b	109	10.12.07
	BGA 3236/FFX P J Richards		
	(Trelleck, Monmouth) *'627'*		01.05.11E
	(IE 18.09.15)		
G-CFFY	PZL-Bielsko SZD-51-1 Junior	W-938	17.01.08
	BGA 3237/FFY Scottish Gliding Union Ltd		
	Portmoak *'FFY'*		24.08.18E
G-CFGAᴹ	Supermarine 502 Spitfire T.8	xxxx	05.01.09
	RAAF A58-441, JG668		
	Aviation Heritage Foundation Ltd (Haverfordwest SA61)		
	Built as Spitfire LF.Mk.VIIIc; displayed at Welsh		
	Spitfire Museum, Bridge Street (NF 07.03.16)		
G-CFGB	Cessna 680 Citation Sovereign	680-0234	22.09.08
	N5057F Keepflying LLP Leeds Bradford		25.10.18E
G-CFGC	Flylight Dragonlite/Aeros Discus 15T	010.08/DA103	04.06.08
	D P Dixon (Ravenshead, Nottingham)		
	Initial segment of s/n relates to sailwing: s/n DA103		
	relates to Flylight Dragonlite trike but note DA103		
	also quoted for G-CIDB; original Hewing Demoiselle		
	trike replaced by 06.14 & fitted with Aeros Fox 16T		
	sailwing to G-CIGV (c/n 15)		
	(SSDR microlight since 05.14) (IE 02.11.17)		
G-CFGD	P&M Quik GT450	8374	24.04.08
	J Featherstone Brook Breasting Farm, Watnall		17.05.19P
G-CFGE	Stinson 108-1 Voyager	108-1127	13.01.09
	ZS-BHW, NC97127		
	C Tyers t/a Windmill Aviation Spanhoe		
	As '108-1601:H' in USAAF c/s (NF 17.07.18)		
G-CFGF	Schempp-Hirth Nimbus-3T	25/91	05.10.07
	BGA 3244 R E Cross Lasham *'141'*		13.04.18E
G-CFGG	AutoGyro MT-03	xxxx	19.06.08
	I Coates & J Noble tr G-CFGG Flying Group Kirkbride		26.09.18P
	Assembled Rotorsport UK as c/n RSUK/MT-03/049		
G-CFGH	Avtech Jabiru J160	T132	06.05.08
	P J Watson Fenland		16.03.19P
	Built by D F Sargant – project PFA 346-14693		
G-CFGJ	Supermarine 300 Spitfire I	xxxx	11.08.08
	N3200 Imperial War Museum Duxford		21.04.19P
	As 'N3200:QV' in RAF c/s		
G-CFGK	Grob G102 Astir CS	1323	20.12.07
	BGA3248/FGK, RAFGSA R61, RAFGSA 316		
	P Allingham Eyres Field *'FGK'*		03.08.12E
G-CFGM	Comco Ikarus C42 FB80	0804-6969	12.05.08
	G P Burns Little Gransden		25.06.18P
	Assembled Aerosport Ltd		
G-CFGO	Best Off Skyranger Swift 912S(1)	UK/869	04.06.08
	R G Hearsey Commonswood Farm, Northiam		09.04.18P
	Built by S J Smith – project BMAA HB/574		
G-CFGP	Schleicher ASW 19B	19121	03.12.07
	BGA 3252/FGP, C-GJXG A E Prime		
	tr Foxtrot Golf Papa Group Tibenham *'FGP'*		14.04.18E
G-CFGR	Schleicher ASK 13	13655AB	06.02.08
	BGA 3254/FGR Edensoaring Ltd		
	Skelling Farm, Skirwith		15.05.18E
	Built by Jubi GmbH Sportflugzeugbau		
G-CFGT	P&M Quik GT450	8384	23.05.08
	A C McAllister Ince		24.06.18P
G-CFGU	Schempp-Hirth Standard Cirrus	147	26.03.08
	BGA 3257/FGU, D-0193 W R R Carter & P K Zochling		
	Pocklington *'806'*		12.10.19E
G-CFGV	P&M Quik GT450	8387	26.06.08
	R Bennett (Canterbury)		29.06.18P
G-CFGW	Centrair 101A Pégase	101A0275	02.11.07
	BGA 3259/FGW L P Smith Kingston Deverill *'701'*		24.07.18E
G-CFGX	Evektor EV-97 teamEurostar UK	2008-3212	09.07.08
	V R Nolan tr Golf Xray Group Full Sutton		21.07.18P
	Assembled Cosmik Aviation Ltd		
G-CFGY	AutoGyro MT-03	xxxx	10.04.08
	A R Hawes Monewden		07.06.18P
	Assembled Rotorsport UK as c/n RSUK/MT-03/039		

G-CFGZ	Flight Design CTSW	08-05-22	19.06.08
	G R Cassie Perth		01.10.18P
	Assembled P&M Aviation Ltd as c/n 8390		
G-CFHB	Micro B.22J Bantam	08-0321	04.07.08
	ZK-LNZ P Rayson Stoke Golding		15.05.18P
G-CFHC	Micro B.22J Bantam	08-0322	04.07.08
	ZK-VNZ M Russell (Gawcott, Buckingham)		22.09.18P
G-CFHD	Schleicher ASW 20BL	20694	18.12.07
	BGA 3266/FHD, RAFGGA 196		
	P J Joslin Gransden Lodge *'196'*		15.02.19E
G-CFHF	PZL-Bielsko SZD-51-1 Junior	W-952	01.12.07
	BGA 3268/FHF Black Mountains Gliding Club		
	Talgarth *'FHF'*		09.07.19E
G-CFHG	Schempp-Hirth Mini Nimbus C	140	12.10.07
	BGA 3269, (BGA 3213), ZS-GNI		
	S L Reed tr 187 Syndicate Usk *'187'*		06.05.18E
G-CFHI	Van's RV-9	xxxx	09.04.08
	J R Dawe Brighton City		29.04.19P
	Built by M Stewart – project PFA 320-14603		
G-CFHK	Aeroprakt A-22L Foxbat	269	16.07.08
	R Bellew (Starinagh, Collon, Co Meath, RoI)		14.07.18P
	Built by J & R Bellew – project LAA 317A-14834		
G-CFHL	Rolladen-Schneider LS4	4633	28.11.07
	BGA 3273/FHL A Murdoch tr G-CFHL Syndicate		
	Challock *'136'*		05.04.18E
G-CFHM	Schleicher ASK 13	13662AB	16.11.07
	BGA 3274/FHM Lasham Gliding Society Ltd		
	Lasham *'P'*		01.04.18E
	Built by Jubi GmbH Sportflugzeugbau		
G-CFHN	Schleicher K 8B	8797	15.04.08
	BGA 3275/FHN, RAFGGA R85, RAFGSA 385,		
	RAFGSA 360 The Nene Valley Gliding Club Ltd		
	Upwood *'FHN'*		19.04.18E
G-CFHO	Grob G103 Twin II	3566	19.04.07
	BGA 5275/KPI, F-CFHO		
	The Surrey Hills Gliding Club Ltd Kenley *'FHO'*		07.05.18E
G-CFHP	Comco Ikarus C42 FB80	0805-6972	23.07.08
	G J Prisk t/a Cornwall Microlights Perranporth		18.09.18P
	Assembled Aerosport Ltd		
G-CFHR	Schempp-Hirth Discus b	152	07.02.08
	BGA 3278/FHR M Fursedon tr Q5 Syndicate		
	Shenington *'Q5'*		08.12.18E
G-CFHS	Tchemma T01/77	T01/77	24.06.08
	J Dyer Farnborough GU14		
	Built by J A Hibberd (IE 03.01.18)		
G-CFHU	Robinson R22 Beta II	3809	23.06.08
	EI-EMG L Brown & A Cameron t/a Cameron &		
	Brown Partnership (Loanhead, Midlothian)		22.07.17E
G-CFHW	Grob G102 Astir CS	1087	07.12.07
	BGA 3283/FHW, D-6987		
	D Brown & D J Wedlock Long Mynd *'698'*		06.03.18E
G-CFHX	Schroeder Fire Balloons G22/24	928	27.06.08
	LX-BEO T J Ellenrieder Friedrichshafen, Germany		22.04.18E
G-CFHY	Fokker Dr.1 Triplane replica	xxxx	19.06.08
	P G Bond Shipdham		28.01.18P
	Built by P G Bond – project PFA 238-14408;		
	as '556/17' in German Army Air Service c/s		
G-CFHZ	Schleicher Ka 6CR	949	18.03.08
	BGA 3286/FHZ, D-4661		
	P J Howarth Burnford Common, Brentor		26.05.17E
G-CFIA	Best Off Skyranger Swift 912S(1)	SKR0711825	16.05.08
	N Elahi & D Lamb Hunsdon		21.02.19P
	Built by S J Smith – project BMAA/HB/561		
G-CFIC	Jodel DR.1050-M1 Sicile Record	432	18.06.08
	OO-LME, F-BLME		
	J H & P I Kempton Watchford Farm, Yarcombe		24.10.17P
	Built by Centre-Est Aéronautique (IE 02.11.17)		
G-CFID	Air Création Tanarg 912S(1)/iXess 15	FLTxxx	25.06.08
	D Smith St Michaels		
	Built by D Smith – project BMAA HB/507		
	(Flylight kit FLTxxx comprising trike s/n T06045		
	& wing s/n A06070-6047 (NF 18.01.16)		

| G-CFIE | AutoGyro MT-03 | 08 038 | 25.07.08 |

G-CFIE AutoGyro MT-03 08 038 25.07.08
P J Swindells tr The India Echo Flyers
(Bollington, Macclesfield) 17.08.18P
Assembled Rotorsport UK as c/n RSUK/MT-03/048

G-CFIF Christen Eagle II BEERS-0001 06.06.08
N171CB D A Payne tr Eagle Group FGP
City of Derry-Eglinton, RoI 11.01.20P
Built by C Beers

G-CFIG P&M Quik GT450 8382 23.05.08
J Whitfield East Fortune 08.03.18P

G-CFIH Piel CP.1320 xxxx 01.07.08
A R Wade North Weald 11.05.19P
Built by I W L Aikman – project PFA 170-11266

G-CFII de Havilland DH.82A Tiger Moth 85584 20.05.08
N90277, VT-DKN, Indian AF HU726,
South African AF 4613, DE630
Avalon Ventures Ltd Clacton-on-Sea
Built by Morris Motors Ltd; on long restoration 02.19
(IE 11.09.18)

G-CFIJ Christen Eagle II PERNER-0001 29.07.08
N161RJ V Kiminius Conington 07.06.18P
Built by C Perner

G-CFIK Lindstrand LBL 60X 1220 30.06.08
L Sambrook Stonehouse 'Avenue Q' 22.09.18E

G-CFIL P&M Quik GT450 8394 11.07.08
S N Catchpole Pond Farm, Carleton St Peter 09.09.16P

G-CFIM P&M Quik GT450 8395 30.05.08
D M Broom Sutton Meadows 17.06.18P

G-CFIO Cessna 172S Skyhawk SP 172S9079 17.07.08
N5104Y G Price t/a Skytrek Air Services Rochester 19.08.19E

G-CFIP Raj Hamsa X'Air Falcon 700 (1) 918 22.05.08
Cancelled 06.11.12 by CAA
Derryogue, Kilkeel *Built by M Skinner*
– project BMAA/HB/540; wreck stored 2013

G-CFIT Comco Ikarus C42 FB100 0804-6966 16.07.08
D Cioffi tr G-CFIT Group Bradley's Lawn, Heathfield 04.08.19P
Assembled Aerosport Ltd

G-CFIU CZAW Sportcruiser 08SC170 04.07.08
G Everett & D N Smith Hubbard's Farm, Lenham Heath 05.07.18P
Built by G Everett & D Smith – project
LAA 338-14822 (kit '700491-199')

G-CFIW Kubícek BB20XR 615 04.08.08
I S Bridge Minsterley, Shrewsbury 'Kubicek' 19.05.19E

G-CFIZ Best Off Skyranger 912(2) UK/732 20.05.08
J R Hartshorne Wolverhampton Halfpenny Green 15.07.18P
Built by J R Hartshorne – project BMAA/HB/530

G-CFJB AutoGyro MT-03 xxxx 29.09.08
N J Hargreaves (Southport) 11.05.18P
Assembled Rotorsport UK as c/n RSUK/MT-03/052

G-CFJC Sikorsky S-76C 760708 22.09.08
EZ-S706, G-CFJC, N415Y, G-FCJC, N415Y
Bristow Helicopters Ltd Norwich Int'l 01.10.12E
Built by Keystone Helicopter Corpn (IE 06.12.16)

G-CFJF Schempp-Hirth SHK-1 58 18.06.08
BGA 3646/FZC, OH-357, OH-SHA
D W McCormick Milfield 'FZC' 18.03.11E
(NF 16.10.18)

G-CFJG Best Off Skyranger Swift 912S(1) UK/794 07.07.08
E E Colley Deanland 16.03.18P
Built by C M Gray – project BMAA/HB/546

G-CFJH Grob G102 Astir CS77 1763 13.06.08
BGA 3294/FJH, AGA 7 D B Harrison Kenley 'FJH' 22.05.18E

G-CFJI Ultramagic M-105 105/168 16.10.08
Club Aerostatico Wind & Fire
Fragneto Monoforte, Campania, Italy 'Landirenzo' 13.05.18E

G-CFJJ Best Off Skyranger Swift 912S(1) UK/865 11.06.08
J J Ewing Donaghmore 01.06.18P
Built by J J Ewing – project BMAA/HB/571

G-CFJK Centrair 101A Pégase 101070 04.12.07
BGA 3296/FJK, N4429W
G N Figg tr G-CFJK Flying Group (Wells) 'FJK' 27.04.18E

G-CFJL Raj Hamsa X'Air Hawk 1087 25.07.08
I S Doig Newtownards 30.08.19P
Built by G L Craig – project PFA 340-14702

G-CFJM Rolladen-Schneider LS4-a 4665 21.12.07
BGA 3298/FJM, D-1431
I G Sullivan Challock 'Z12' 04.05.18E

G-CFJN Diamond DA.40D Star D4.295 14.10.08
JY-EEE, OE-UHK, OE-VPU Airways Aviation Academy Ltd
Huesca-Pirineos, Spain 15.12.18E

G-CFJO Diamond DA.40D Star D4.296 14.10.08
JY-FFF, OE-UDV, OE-VPU Airways Aviation Academy Ltd
North Weald 12.01.18E

G-CFJR Glaser-Dirks DG-300 Club Elan 3E270C2 17.01.08
BGA 3302/FJR H Inigo-Jones & W Palmer
Lasham '950' 20.01.18E
Built by Elan Tovarna Sportnega Orodja N.Sol.O

G-CFJS Glaser-Dirks DG-300 Club Elan 3E271C3 07.11.07
BGA 3303/FJS K L Goldsmith Rattlesden '257' 22.05.18E
Built by Elan Tovarna Sportnega Orodja N.Sol.O

G-CFJU Raj Hamsa X'Air Hawk 1128 27.06.08
J Beattie Strathaven 16.05.18P
Built by R J Minns – project PFA 340-14731

G-CFJV Schleicher ASW 15 15109 17.07.08
BGA 3306/FJV, D-0710 D J Price Wycombe Air Park 11.05.18E

G-CFJW Schleicher K7 Rhönadler 980 01.02.08
BGA 3307/FJW, OH-241, OH-KKF
G Brind tr K7 Group Rivar Hill 'FJW' 06.05.18E

G-CFJX Glaser-Dirks DG-300 Elan 3E261 10.12.07
BGA 3308/FJX Crown Service Gliding Club
Lasham 'FJX' 06.05.18E
Built by Elan Tovarna Sportnega Orodja N.Sol.O

G-CFJZ Schempp-Hirth SHK-1 14 13.11.07
BGA 3310/FJZ, D-9330
C I Knowles Dunstable Downs 28.09.19E

G-CFKA AutoGyro MT-03 xxxx 18.08.08
M J L Carter Fir Park Farm, Usselby 13.03.18P
Assembled Rotorsport UK as c/n RSUK/MT-03/051

G-CFKB CZAW Sportcruiser 08SC130 02.07.08
J R Couch tr KB Flying Group Fairoaks 22.05.19P
Built by B S Wiliams – project LAA 338-14766

G-CFKD Raj Hamsa X'Air Falcon Jabiru(2) 995 06.06.08
J C Dawson Crosland Moor 22.01.18P
Built by A M Fawthrop – project BMAA/HB/550

G-CFKE Raj Hamsa X'Air Hawk 1120 22.07.08
J F Northey & S P Read Westonzoyland 15.10.18P
Built by S Rance – project PFA 340-14752

G-CFKG Rolladen-Schneider LS4-a 4673 27.11.07
BGA3317/FKG R J Purdie North Hill '125' 15.01.19E

G-CFKH Zenair CH.601XL Zodiac 6-9859 06.08.08
C Long Haverfordwest 26.09.18P
Built by M A Baker – project PFA 162B-14566;
tricycle u/c

G-CFKJ P&M Quik GT450 8405 22.08.08
E Avery & J Witcombe Caernarfon 19.10.18P

G-CFKL Schleicher ASW 20BL 20954 19.12.07
BGA 3321/FKL J Ley Wormingford '159' 29.03.18E

G-CFKM Schempp-Hirth Discus b 212 13.05.08
BGA 3322/FKM Lasham Gliding Society Ltd
Lasham 'SH3' 23.06.18E

G-CFKN Lindstrand GA22 MkII Gas Airship GA014-001 11.08.08
G-72 Lindstrand Technologies Ltd Oswestry
(NF 06.02.18)

G-CFKO P&M Quik GT450 8401 07.07.08
A Maudsley (Chorley) 18.10.18P

G-CFKP Performance Barnstormer/Voyager UK1 26.08.08
G P Foyle (Canisbay, Wick)
(SSDR microlight since 05.14) (NF 03.05.18)

G-CFKR P&M Pegasus Quik 8403 12.08.08
R D Ballard (Bexhill) 10.04.12P
(IE 01.09.17)

G-CFKS Flight Design CTSW 08-05-23 10.09.08
L I Bailey Watling Lodge, Norton 14.03.18P
Assembled P&M Aviation as c/n 8396

G-CFKT Schleicher K 8B 8382 04.03.08
BGA 3328/FKT, D-5366
A R Bushnell tr FKT Group Lyveden 'FKT' 13.06.18E

G-CFKU P&M Quik GT450 8404 18.08.08
P W Frost Boston 13.05.19P

G-CFKW Alpi Pioneer 200-M xxxx 16.07.08
P McCusker & J Metcalfe Kernan Valley, Tandragee 19.02.19P
Built by F A Cavaciuti – project LAA 334-14828

G-CFKX Cameron Z-160 11163 20.10.08
Ballooning In Tuscany SRL Firenze, Italy 11.09.18E

G-CFKY Schleicher Ka 6CR 822 12.02.08
BGA 3329/FKU, D-0025 J A Timmis Camphill *'FKY'* 09.07.15E

G-CFKZ Europa Aviation Europa XS 603 05.06.08
W Aspden & P H Wiltshire Popham 10.06.19P
Built by N P Davis – project PFA 247-14178; tricycle u/c

G-CFLA P&M Quik GT450 8393 04.08.08
P H Woodward Cottage Farm, Norton Juxta 08.08.18P

G-CFLC Glaser-Dirks DG-300 Elan 3E310 12.11.07
BGA 3337/FLC J L Hey Rufforth *'368'* 20.03.18E
Built by Elan Tovarna Sportnega Orodja N.Sol.O

G-CFLD Comco Ikarus C42 FB80 0807-6982 09.09.08
M R Badminton Bagby 05.04.18P
Assembled Aerosport Ltd

G-CFLE Schempp-Hirth Discus b 207 15.10.07
BGA 3339 D A Humphreys Wycombe Air Park *'314'* 21.05.18E

G-CFLF Rolladen-Schneider LS4-a 4694 19.03.08
BGA 3340/FLF D Lamb Saltby *'Z4'* 03.04.18E

G-CFLG CZAW Sportcruiser 4490 16.07.08
G R Greensall Charity Farm, Baxterley 15.12.19P
Built by D A Buttress – project LAA 338-14771

G-CFLH Schleicher K 8B 22 25.01.08
BGA 3342/FLH, OH-361, OH-RTW
The Windrushers Gliding Club Ltd Bicester *'FLH'* 05.05.10E
Built by K K Lehtovaara O/Y (NF 20.09.18)

G-CFLI Europa Aviation Europa 348 24.07.08
A & E Bennett Sleap 14.04.18P
*Built by A Bennett – project PFA 247-13144;
tricycle u/c*

G-CFLK Cameron C-90 11207 18.11.08
J R Rivers-Scott Mareham on the Hill, Horncastle
'Kingspan EnergiPanel' 05.10.19E

G-CFLL Evektor EV-97 Eurostar 2008-3114 15.07.08
I Galea Broadmeadow Farm, Hereford 31.08.19P
*Built by D R Lewis – project LAA 315-14825;
rudder plate shows c/n '2007-3111'
which relates to Eurostar EC-FE4*

G-CFLM P&M Pegasus Quik 8399 29.07.08
S Grimshaw & J Royle tr The Jag Flyers
Manchester Barton 28.10.18P

G-CFLN Best Off Skyranger Swift 912S(1) SKR0806886 25.09.08
D Bletcher Leicester 29.03.18P
Built by D Bletcher – project BMAA/HB/577

G-CFLO AutoGyro MT-03 xxxx 18.08.08
K J Jamieson tr The Flo Rider Group
(Warwick Bridge, Carlisle) 30.09.19P
Assembled Rotorsport UK as c/n RSUK/MT-03/053

G-CFLP Druine D.31 Turbulent xxxx 11.08.08
T K Pullen tr Eaglescott Turbulent Group Eaglescott
*Built by F Blick & T K Pullen – project
PFA 048-13170 (NF 23.02.16)*

G-CFLR P&M Quik GT450 8409 21.10.08
S J Baker Sutton Meadows 15.12.18P

G-CFLS Schleicher Ka 6CR 6180 02.07.08
BGA 3351/FLS, D-4001 UCLU RAF Halton *'FLS'* 18.03.18E

G-CFLU Saab 2000 2000-055 17.12.08
SE-LSG, OH-SAX, SE-LSG, SE-055
Air Kilroe Ltd t/a Eastern Airways Humberside 30.08.19E
Built by Saab AB

G-CFLW Schempp-Hirth Standard Cirrus 75 656 04.10.07
BGA 3355, F-CEMT
S & S M Law Haddenham *'90'* 13.10.18E

G-CFLX Glaser-Dirks DG-300 Club Elan 3E304C19 04.12.07
BGA 3356/FLX S Jarvis tr Felix Flying Group
Upwood *'FLX'* 02.05.18E
Built by Elan Tovarna Sportnega Orodja N.Sol.O

G-CFLZ Scheibe SF27A Zugvogel V 6061 21.07.08
BGA 3358/FLZ, D-5378
B T Green Burnford Common, Brentor *'FLZ'* 13.03.19E

G-CFMA BB Microlight BB03 Trya/BB103 081006005DRDS 08.07.08
P D Curtis (Boston Spa, Wetherby)
(NF 31.05.17)
(SSDR microlight since 05.14)

G-CFMB P&M Quik GT450 8408 05.09.08
Countermine Technologies PLC Wickenby 24.07.10P
(NF 01.09.16)

G-CFMC Van's RV-9A xxxx 25.09.08
M W Bodger & M H Hoffmann tr G-CFMC Flying Group
Yeatsall Farm, Abbots Bromley 11.04.18P
Built by G Griffith – project PFA 320-14575

G-CFMD P&M Quik GT450 8417 06.11.08
M J C & S A C Curtis East Fortune 05.07.18P

G-CFMH Schleicher ASK 13 13673AB 31.10.07
BGA 3366 Lasham Gliding Society Ltd Lasham *'B'* 09.02.19E
Built by Jubi GmbH Sportflugzeugbau

G-CFMI Best Off Skyranger Swift 912(1) SKR0807897 03.10.08
P Shelton Crosland Moor 29.05.18P
Built by P Shelton – project BMAA/HB/580

G-CFMM Cessna 172S Skyhawk SP 172S8242 16.05.08
N216MM, XB-HQZ
Atlantic Flight Training Ltd Cork, Rol 26.01.19E

G-CFMN Schempp-Hirth Ventus cT 123/397 15.02.08
BGA 3371/FMN R E Matthews tr FMN Glider Syndicate
Lasham *'FMN'* 12.12.17E

G-CFMO Schempp-Hirth Discus b 243 28.11.07
BGA 3373/FMQ P D Bagnall Nympsfield *'158'* 06.05.18E

G-CFMP Europa Aviation Europa XS 440 03.10.08
M P Gamble Popham 07.06.18P
*Built by M P Gamble – project PFA 247-13505;
tailwheel u/c*

G-CFMR Ultramagic V-14 14/001 20.11.08
P Baker Abbeyview, Trim, Rol
(NF 09.08.16)

G-CFMS Schleicher ASW 15 15061 15.02.08
BGA 3375/FMS, N111SP D A Logan North Hill *'LU'* 01.10.18E

G-CFMT Schempp-Hirth Standard Cirrus 249 30.01.08
BGA 3376/FMT, N2HM
S J Norman tr G-CFMT Group Parham Park *'FMT'* 18.08.18E

G-CFMU Schempp-Hirth Standard Cirrus 236 31.10.07
BGA 3377, N3LB T J Williamson Upwood *'FMU'* 11.04.19E

G-CFMV Aerola Alatus-M AS 01-019 26.11.08
P J Wood (Malvern)
(SSDR microlight since 05.14) (IE 17.12.15)

G-CFMW Scheibe SF25C Falke 2000 44378 08.12.08
D-KNIB The Windrushers Gliding Club Ltd Bicester 11.06.18E

G-CFMX Piper PA-28-161 Warrior II 28-8316073 03.11.08
N4306Z Stapleford Flying Club Ltd Stapleford 20.11.18E

G-CFMY Rolladen-Schneider LS7 7004 16.01.08
BGA 3381/FMY, D-2516
N J Howes tr G-CFMY Group Camphill *'371'* 22.03.18E

G-CFNA Schleicher K.8B 8499 04.09.07
BGA 3383/FNA Cancelled 18.11.08 as PWFU 28.09.08
Chipping, Lancs Stored damaged 10.15

G-CFNB Cameron TR-70 11140 13.10.08
P Bals Boorgloon, Belgium *'Cameron Balloons Racer'* 04.06.19E

G-CFNC Flylight Dragonfly/Aeros Discus 15T 004 03.09.08
C J Jones (Clydach, Abergavenny)
(SSDR microlight since 05.14) (IE 29.01.19)

G-CFND Schleicher Ka 6E 4069 20.09.07
BGA 3386, PH-366 C Scutt (Haddenham) *'FND'* 27.12.18E

G-CFNE PZL-Bielsko SZD-38A Jantar 1 B-612 14.05.08
BGA 3387/FNE, HB-1215
I Gordon, J Murray & T Robson Rivar Hill *'FNE'* 21.03.18E

G-CFNF Robinson R44 Raven II 12496 05.12.08
Kuki Helicopter Sales Ltd Retford Gamston 20.05.18E
Operated by Helicentre

G-CFNH Schleicher ASW 19B 19174 10.12.07
BGA 3390/FNH, D-7969 Rattlesden Gliding Club Ltd
Rattlesden *'A19'* 26.08.19E

G-CFNI	AirBorne XT912-B/Streak III-B	XT912-0258	11.09.08
	Fly NI Ltd Newtownards		18.01.18P
	Wing s/n S3-526		
G-CFNK	Slingsby T65A Vega	1897	24.04.08
	BGA 3392/FNK, N9023H		
	I P Goldstraw Dunstable Downs *'FNK'*		13.08.18E
G-CFNL	Schempp-Hirth Discus b	253	03.12.07
	BGA 3393/FNL P P Musto & A S Ramsay		
	Husbands Bosworth *'705'*		03.04.18E
G-CFNM	Centrair 101B Pégase	101B0289	25.10.07
	BGA 3394, F-CGSE		
	D T Hartley Husbands Bosworth *'FNM'*		02.05.19E
G-CFNO	Best Off Skyranger Swift 912S(1)	SKR0801844	16.09.08
	P R Hanman Over Farm, Gloucester *'Fly The Flag!'*		27.06.18P
	Built by J W Taylor – project BMAA/HB/566		
G-CFNP	Schleicher Ka 6CR	567	29.07.08
	BGA 3396/FNP, D-4657		
	P Pollard-Wilkins Ringmer *'FNP'*		17.03.19E
G-CFNR	Schempp-Hirth Discus b	255	22.10.07
	BGA 3398 P R Harrison		
	(Cockfield, Bury St Edmunds) *'FNR'*		23.05.19E
G-CFNS	Glaser-Dirks DG-300 Club Elan	3E314C23	14.01.08
	BGA 3399/FNS S Kennedy tr FNS Syndicate		
	Portmoak *'FNS'*		25.09.18E
	Built by Elan Tovarna Sportnega Orodja N.Sol.O		
G-CFNT	Glaser-Dirks DG-600	6-12	21.09.07
	BGA 3400 M R Johnson tr G-CFNT Group		
	Sutton Bank *'FNT'*		24.04.18E
G-CFNU	Rolladen-Schneider LS4-a	4732	23.08.07
	BGA 3401, D-1376 R J Simpson Nympsfield *'190'*		17.05.18E
G-CFNV	CZAW Sportcruiser	700788	10.10.08
	N D McAllister & M Owen Finmere		01.11.18P
	Built by G Smith – project LAA 338-14844		
G-CFNW	Evektor EV-97 teamEurostar UK	2008-3317	05.01.09
	The Scottish Aero Club Ltd Perth		25.01.19P
	Assembled Cosmik Aviation Ltd		
G-CFNX	Air Création Buggy 582/iXess 13	FLTxxx	20.10.08
	A E Barron (Preston, Paignton)		06.07.18P
	Built by Flylight Airsports Ltd – project		
	BMAA HB/569 (Flylight kit FLTxxx comprising		
	original trike s/n T07096 – now T03024		
	(ex G-CCFA) & wing s/n A07162-7196		
G-CFNZ	AirBorne XT912-B/Streak III-B	XT912-290	27.10.08
	N C Grayson Knapthorpe Lodge, Caunton		10.06.18P
	Wing s/n S3-264		
G-CFOB	Schleicher ASW 15B	15340	01.02.08
	BGA 3432/FQB, D-2345 S Whybrow Aboyne *'FOB'*		23.02.19E
G-CFOC	Glaser-Dirks DG-202/17C	2-178CL19	05.03.08
	BGA 3433/FQC, HB-1645		
	R Robinson Lasham *'801'*		17.05.18E
G-CFOF	Scheibe SF27A Zugvogel V	6025	05.02.08
	BGA 3436/FQF, D-0009		
	D Wilde (Assington, Sudbury) *'JJ'*		14.03.19E
G-CFOG	Comco Ikarus C42 FB UK	0511-6773	19.04.06
	P D Coppin Solent		28.11.18P
	Built by P D Coppin – project PFA 322-14482		
G-CFOI	Cessna 172N Skyhawk II	17269315	14.11.08
	N737CN Cessna 172 Ltd (Otley, Ipswich)		
	(NF 02.03.16)		
G-CFOJ	Eurocopter EC155 B1	6852	29.05.09
	Starspeed Ltd Fairoaks		28.05.18E
G-CFOM	Scheibe SF27A Zugvogel V	6098	03.03.08
	BGA 3442/FQM, D-9421		
	P Drake & A Ruddle Kingston Deverill *'FOM'*		05.04.18E
G-CFON	Wittman W.8 Tailwind	xxxx	07.11.07
	A Fergusson tr G-CFON Group Kilkerran		12.12.17P
	Built by C F O'Neill – project PFA 031-11789		
G-CFOO	P&M QuikR	8413	26.11.08
	Terratrip (UK) Ltd t/a Microavionics		
	Park Hall Farm, Mapperley		09.08.18P
G-CFOP	Cameron Shopping Bag-120	3642	18.11.08
	HB-QAO J Ravibalan Mitcham		20.09.13E
G-CFOR	Schleicher K 8B	8537	22.04.08
	BGA 3446/FQR, PH-349		
	Dorset Gliding Club Ltd Eyres Field *'FOR'*		02.11.18E
G-CFOS	Flylight Dragonfly/Aeros Discus 14T	017	18.11.08
	C G Langham Walkeridge Farm, Overton		
	Discus 14T wing s/n 059-06		
	(SSDR microlight since 05.14) (IE 08.07.16)		
G-CFOT	PZL-Bielsko SZD-48-3 Jantar-Standard 3	B-1891	29.02.08
	BGA 3448/FQT, (BGA 3409/FPC)		
	T Greenwood Rivar Hill		09.06.18E
G-CFOU	Schleicher K7 Rhönadler	1139	20.11.07
	BGA 3449/FQU, D-8614, HB-709 B R Pearson		
	tr Eaglescott ASK 7 Group Eaglescott *'FOU'*		07.06.16E
	(NF 22.05.17)		
G-CFOV	CZAW Sportcruiser	700291	18.11.08
	J G Murphy Morgansfield, Fishburn		
	Built by J Holt, R Morey, J G Murphy &		
	S Whitehead – project LAA 338-14832		
	(NF 18.11.15)		
G-CFOW	Best Off Skyranger Swift 912S(1)	UK/896	19.11.08
	D J F Wallace tr Oscar Whiskey Syndicate Perth		07.04.18P
	Built by A Chappell – project BMAA/HB/583		
G-CFOX	Marganski MDM-1 Fox	224	26.09.07
	BGA 4566, SP-P632 M Makari Bicester		14.05.18E
G-CFOY	Schempp-Hirth Discus b	274	21.09.07
	BGA 3453 B K Atkins, R F Dowty & J W Slater		
	Dunstable Downs *'FOY'*		05.12.18E
G-CFOZ	Rolladen-Schneider LS1-f	391	12.02.08
	BGA 3454/FQZ, F-CEKH C Booker (Leeds) *'L51'*		19.05.19E
G-CFPA	CZAW Sportcruiser	700848	20.11.08
	T W Lorimer Strathaven		11.06.18P
	Built by S Lowe & K D Taylor – project LAA 338-14869		
G-CFPB	Schleicher ASW 15B	15243	23.04.08
	BGA 3408/FPB, D-2068		
	I A Burgin tr G-CFPB Syndicate Darlton *'xy'*		03.06.18E
G-CFPD	Rolladen-Schneider LS7	7033	11.03.08
	BGA 3410/FPD, D-5178		
	R A Lovegrove tr LS7 Group Lyveden *'973'*		17.04.18E
G-CFPE	Schempp-Hirth Ventus cT	131/408	28.02.08
	BGA 3411/FPE R Palmer tr G-CFPE Bidford *'238'*		10.12.18E
G-CFPH	Centrair ASW 20F	20132	04.12.07
	BGA 3414/FPH, F-CFFX		
	A L D Munro tr G-CFPH Group Saltby *'GB2'*		09.06.18E
G-CFPI	P&M Quik GT450	8422	01.12.08
	E J Douglas (Gorebridge)		04.12.13P
	Fitted with trike ex G-CDWS c.2014;		
	original trike fitted to G-CIBT (IE 01.08.16)		
G-CFPJ	CZAW Sportcruiser	700541	31.10.08
	S R Winter (Hoddesdon)		03.01.18P
	Built by S R Winter – project LAA 338-14858		
G-CFPL	Schempp-Hirth Ventus c	409	23.08.07
	BGA 3417 R V Barrett Nympsfield *'242'*		10.12.18E
G-CFPM	PZL-Bielsko SZD-51-1 Junior	B-1788	29.10.07
	BGA 3418 Kent Gliding Club Ltd Challock *'FPM'*		11.11.17E
G-CFPN	Schleicher ASW 20	20376	15.02.08
	BGA 3419/FPN, RAFGGA 545, D-8780		
	J C M Docherty Husbands Bosworth *'HD'*		18.03.18E
	(NF 30.11.17)		
G-CFPP	Schempp-Hirth Nimbus-2B	142	21.04.08
	BGA 3420/FPP, D-6779, D-2111		
	R Jones & D W North Walney Island *'N2'*		26.03.18E
G-CFPR	P&M QuikR	8415	06.11.08
	J A Horn Greenhills Farm, Wheatley Hill		21.02.18P
G-CFPS	Sky 25-16	075	01.12.08
	G B Lescott Oxford OX4		12.08.18E
G-CFPT	Schleicher ASW 20	20007	27.03.08
	BGA 3424/FPT, D-7574 L Hornsey tr L Hornsey &		
	L Weeks Syndicate RAF Halton *'574'*		30.06.18E
G-CFPW	Glaser-Dirks DG-600	6-17	27.03.08
	BGA 3427/FPW P B Gray Camphill *'606'*		01.04.18E
G-CFRC	Schempp-Hirth Nimbus-2B	151	06.03.08
	BGA 3457/FRC, D-4980 T J Lean tr Tim & Martin		
	Nimbus 2B Group Dunstable Downs *'998'*		12.09.18E

G

G-CFRE	Schleicher Ka 6E	4349	13.03.08
	BGA 3459/FRE, F-CDTL		
	R A Foreshew Parham Park 'FRE'		15.09.17E

G-CFRF	Lindstrand LBL 31A	1232	19.12.08
	A I Attwood tr RAF Halton Hot Air Balloon Club		
	RAF Halton 'Royal Air Force'		19.06.18E

G-CFRH	Schleicher ASW 20CL	20740	13.03.08
	BGA 3462/FRH, D-9229		
	J N Wilton Husbands Bosworth '634'		21.04.18E

G-CFRI	Ultramagic N-355	355/15	13.03.09
	Skyview Ballooning Ltd t/a Kent Ballooning		
	Stanford, Ashford 'Spitfire'		09.04.19E

G-CFRJ	Schempp-Hirth Standard Cirrus	103	26.11.08
	BGA 3463/FRJ, HB-1041 J H B Jones		
	Kirton in Lindsey 'JJ'		27.04.18E
	Carries 'CJ' under wing		

G-CFRK	Schleicher ASW 15B	15214	29.11.07
	BGA 3464/FRK, D-0941		
	P R Boet Dunstable Downs 'FRK'		01.07.18E

G-CFRM	Best Off Skyranger Swift 912S(1)	SKR0806885	04.12.08
	R K & T A Willcox Chase Farm, Chipping Sodbury		08.04.18P
	Built by R K & T A Willcox – project BMAA/HB/578		

G-CFRN	AutoGyro MTOsport	xxxx	12.03.09
	R Marks North Weald		04.09.19P
	Assembled Rotorsport UK as c/n RSUK/MTOS/003		

G-CFRP	Centrair 101A Pégase	101A0311	08.07.08
	BGA 3458/FRD, EI-162, BGA 3458/FRD		
	L Bourne Parham Park		09.01.19E

G-CFRR	Centrair 101A Pégase	101034	27.11.07
	BGA 3470/FRR, (BGA 3451/FQW), F-CFQA		
	P A Lewis tr G-CFRR Syndicate Walney Island '495'		28.05.18E

G-CFRS	Scheibe Zugvogel IIIB	1097	29.01.08
	BGA 3471/FRS, D-2171, HB-749 P M Jessop		
	tr G-CFRS Flying Group Dunstable Downs 'FRS'		02.12.15E

G-CFRT	Evektor EV-97 teamEurostar UK	2008-3224	03.09.08
	K A O'Neill Holmbeck Farm, Burcott		18.09.19P
	Assembled Cosmik Aviation Ltd		

G-CFRV	Centrair 101A Pégase	101A0325	02.11.07
	BGA 3474/FRV J D Hubberstey		
	Wycombe Air Park 'FRV'		25.02.18E

G-CFRW	Schleicher ASW 20L	20202	11.01.08
	BGA 3475/FRW, D-5981		
	R M Green Aston Down '268'		02.05.18E

G-CFRX	Centrair 101A Pégase	101A0315	10.01.08
	BGA 3476/FRX M A Lithgow & S Woolrich		
	Portmoak 'FRX'		09.04.19E

G-CFRY	Zenair CH.601UL Zodiac	598	05.01.05
	C K Fry (Lytchett Minster, Poole)		
	Built by C K Fry – project PFA 162A-14302 (IE 27.02.17)		

G-CFRZ	Schempp-Hirth Standard Cirrus	348G	16.07.08
	BGA 3478/FRZ, HB-1194, D-2172		
	S G Lapworth Lasham 'FRZ'		26.07.18E
	Built by Burkhart Grob-Flugzeugbau		

G-CFSB	Tecnam P2002-RG Sierra	303	20.01.09
	P G Gale t/a WJ Gale & Son Edington Hill, Edington		19.05.18P
	Built by P G Gale – project LAA 333A-14864		

G-CFSD	Schleicher ASK 13	13367	29.01.08
	BGA 3482/FSD, D-0863 Edensoaring Ltd		
	Skelling Farm, Skirwith 'FSD'		26.03.18E

G-CFSF	P&M QuikR	8421	07.01.09
	C J Gordon (Stonehaven)		27.02.18P
	Replacement wing s/n 8644 fitted 2012		

G-CFSG	Van's RV-9	91646	03.09.09
	LY-AUD T A P Hubbard tr Foley Farm Flying Group		
	Redwood Cottage, Meon		16.10.18P
	Built by S Maciulis		

G-CFSH	Grob G102 Astir CS Jeans	2090	23.01.08
	BGA 3486/FSH, D-7532		
	Buckminster Gliding Club Ltd Saltby 'FSH'		20.04.18E

G-CFSJ	Avtech Jabiru J160	195	22.01.09
	S Langley Willingale		05.06.19P
	Built by M Flint – project LAA 346-14838		

G-CFSL	Kubíček BB26Z	642	03.04.09
	M R Jeynes Redditch 'The Co-operative Funeral Care'		09.07.16E

G-CFSO	Flylight Dragonfly/Aeros Discus 15T	025	28.01.09
	(EI-...), G-CFSO M F J Armstrong Newtownards		
	(SSDR microlight since 05.14) (IE 27.04.16)		

G-CFSR	Glaser-Dirks DG-300 Elan	3E343	18.12.07
	BGA 3494/FSR A P Montague Nympsfield 'FSR'		18.05.18E
	Built by Elan Tovarna Sportnega Orodja N.Sol.O		

G-CFSS	Schleicher Ka 6E	4019	30.07.08
	BGA 3495/FSS, D-5260		
	P R Robey tr FSS Syndicate Lasham 'FSS'		29.03.18E

G-CFST	Schleicher ASH 25E	25073	30.08.07
	BGA 3496, (BGA 3530)		
	K H Lloyd & D Tucker Aston Down 'FST'		25.05.18E

G-CFSW	Best Off Skyranger Swift 912S(1)	SKR0807895	08.01.09
	C T Hanbury-Tenison		
	The Byre, Hardwick, Abergavenny		02.06.18P
	Built by S B Williams – project BMAA/HB/587		

G-CFSX	ICP MXP-740 Savannah VG Jabiru(1)	08-04-51-714	26.01.09
	M E Caton Glebe Farm, Sibson		15.10.18P
	Built by J P Swadling – project BMAA/HB/581		

G-CFTA	Ace Aviation Magic/Laser	MT0111	23.01.09
	G-93-3 P & M Aviation Ltd St Michaels		
	Assembled P&M Aviation Ltd; trike s/n MT0111		
	& wing s/n AA00138		
	(SSDR microlight since 05.14) (IE 08.01.18)		

G-CFTB	Schleicher Ka 6CR	019	31.10.07
	BGA 3504/FTB, D-8900 M W Bennett & B T Green		
	Burnford Common, Brentor		30.05.18E

G-CFTC	PZL-Bielsko SZD-51-1 Junior	B-1860	07.02.08
	BGA 3505/FTC J G Kosak tr Seahawk Gliding Club		
	RNAS Culdrose 'N56'		01.06.18E

G-CFTD	Schleicher ASW 15B	15191	11.01.08
	BGA 3506/FTD, D-0872		
	A A Thorburn Milfield 'FTD'		11.05.18E

G-CFTF^M	Roe Triplane replica	AH2-001	24.02.09
	Cancelled 28.08.16 as PWFU		
	Built by Roe Heritage Group – project LAA 354-14777		
	With Manchester Museum of Sciences & Industry		

G-CFTG	P&M QuikR	8414	05.01.09
	J Waite tr G-CFTG Group Plaistows Farm, St Albans		20.07.19P

G-CFTH	PZL-Bielsko SZD-50-3 Puchacz	B-1881	24.10.07
	BGA 3510/FTH Buckminster Gliding Club Ltd		
	Saltby 'FTH'		08.10.18E

G-CFTI	Evektor EV-97 Eurostar	2008-3414	16.01.09
	R J Dance (Mitcheldean, Gloucester)		07.05.18P
	Built by G R Pritchard – project LAA 315-14878		

G-CFTJ	Evektor EV-97A Eurostar	2005-2625	13.02.06
	C B Flood Ince		28.10.18P
	Built by C B Flood – project PFA 315-14504		

G-CFTK	Grob G102 Astir CS Jeans	2059	05.10.07
	BGA 3512/FTK, OE-5152		
	Ulster Gliding Club Ltd Bellarena 'FTK'		24.07.18E

G-CFTL	Schleicher ASW 20CL	20751	09.10.07
	BGA 3513/FTL, D-3564		
	A E D Hayes Aston Down 'FTL'		05.08.19E

G-CFTM	Cameron C-80	11121	20.01.09
	P A Meecham Chipping Norton		18.04.18E

G-CFTN	Schleicher K 8B	996	11.09.08
	BGA 3515/FTN, D-8539, D-KAEL, D-8539		
	Mendip Gliding Club Ltd Halesland 'FTN'		08.02.18E

G-CFTO	Comco Ikarus C42 FB80	0809-7008	22.10.08
	Fly Hire Ltd Full Sutton		27.05.19P
	Assembled Aerosport Ltd		

G-CFTP	Schleicher ASW 20CL	20733	14.02.08
	BGA 3516/FTP, D-3640		
	D J Pengilley Kingston Deverill '332'		23.06.18E

G-CFTR	Grob G102 Astir CS77	1606	05.12.07
	BGA 3518/FTR, D-4807 The University of Nottingham		
	Students Union Cranwell North 'NU'		14.03.18E

G-CFTS	Glaser-Dirks DG-300 Club Elan	3E349C38	15.01.08
	BGA 3519/FTS P D Souter tr FTS Syndicate		
	Parham Park 'FTS'		20.07.18E
	Built by Elan Tovarna Sportnega Orodja N.Sol.O		

G-CFTT Van's RV-7   72230   12.01.09
J A Paley   Audley End   26.04.19P
Built by D J & R I Blain – project PFA 323-14405

G-CFTU Flylight Dragonfly/Aeros Discus 15T   032   09.02.09
R J Cook   Easter Poldar Farm, Thornhill
(SSDR microlight since 05.14) (IE 06.10.17)

G-CFTV Rolladen-Schneider LS7-WL   7073   06.12.07
BGA 3522/FTV   D Hilton   Wycombe Air Park   *'944'*   01.06.18E

G-CFTW Schempp-Hirth Discus b   292/1   17.09.07
BGA 3523   P A Startup tr 230 Syndicate
North Hill   *'230'*   26.03.19R
(Rebuilt with new fuselage after accident 21.06.91;
original fuselage rebuilt as BGA 3879 now G-CHEE (qv)

G-CFTX Avtech Jabiru J160   T204   02.09.08
J King & J Williamson   North Weald   31.05.19P
Built by R K Creasey – project LAA 346-14829

G-CFTY Rolladen-Schneider LS7-WL   7075   14.01.08
BGA 3525/FTY
A Burgess & J A Thomson   Easterton   *'753'*   08.05.19E

G-CFTZ Evektor EV-97 Eurostar   2007-3202   14.01.09
C A Appleby tr TZ Flyers   (Wistaston, Crewe)   08.06.18P
Built by G G Bevis – project LAA 315-14857

G-CFUA Van's RV-9A   90351   09.02.09
I M Macleod   Stornoway   30.06.18P
Built by M A Onions & P J Roy – project PFA 320-14103

G-CFUB Schleicher Ka 6CR   6007   24.06.08
BGA 3528/FUB, D-8573
C Boyd   Burnford Common, Brentor   *'FUB'*   04.06.18E

G-CFUD Best Off Skyranger Swift 912S(1)   UK/912   02.01.09
D K Maclennan tr G-CFUD Group   Strathaven   02.07.18P
Built by V D Carmichael – project BMAA/HB/584

G-CFUE Alpi Pioneer 300 Hawk   267   16.02.09
A Dayani   Sherburn-in-Elmet   18.10.18P
Built by A Dayani – project LAA 330A-14867

G-CFUF Ultramagic N-300   300/36   19.03.09
Airxcite Ltd t/a Virgin Balloon Flights
Stafford Park, Telford   *'HR Go'*   11.09.18E

G-CFUG Grob G109B   6314   12.01.09
D-KEOP   T World tr Portsmouth Naval Gliding Centre
Parham Park   15.06.18E

G-CFUH Schempp-Hirth Ventus c   438   06.09.07
BGA 3533   C G T Huck & S E Lucas
Aston Down   *'E8'*   15.10.18E

G-CFUI Huntwing Avon 503(4)   9712071   10.03.09
R F G Moyle   (Carnon Downs, Truro)
Built by R Moyle – project BMAA/HB/570 (NF 07.03.16)

G-CFUJ Glaser-Dirks DG-300 Elan   3E353   07.11.07
BGA 3534/FUJ   D Wilson   Portmoak   *'FUJ'*   19.11.19E
Built by Elan Tovarna Sportnega Orodja N.Sol.O

G-CFUL Schempp-Hirth Discus b   293   01.12.07
BGA 3535/FUL   A Hippel tr Discus 803 Syndicate
Dunstable Downs   *'803'*   31.03.18E

G-CFUN Schleicher ASW 20CL   20813   05.11.07
BGA 3537/FUN, D-3432   C A Bailey   North Hill   *'FUN'* 16.05.18E

G-CFUP Schempp-Hirth Discus b   291   13.05.08
BGA 3538/FUP   Lasham Gliding Society Ltd
Lasham   *'SH4'*   27.07.18E

G-CFUR Schempp-Hirth Ventus cT   145/446   05.03.08
BGA 3540/FUR   A P Carpenter   North Hill   *'256'*   02.10.18E

G-CFUS PZL-Bielsko SZD-51-1 Junior   B-1912   02.11.07
BGA 3541/FUS   Scottish Gliding Union Ltd
Portmoak   *'FUS'*   25.11.18E

G-CFUT Glaser-Dirks DG-300 Club Elan   3E350C39   18.06.08
BGA 3542/FUT
P E Newman   Gransden Lodge   *'612'*   13.06.18E
Built by Elan Tovarna Sportnega Orodja N.Sol.O

G-CFUU Glaser-Dirks DG-300 Club Elan   3E360C45   06.09.07
BGA 3543   G Cooksey   Pocklington   *'FUU'*   10.03.19E
Built by Elan Tovarna Sportnega Orodja N.Sol.O

G-CFUV Rolladen-Schneider LS7-WL   7068   09.11.07
BGA 3544/FUV   G J Hoile   Kingston Deverill   *194'*   20.11.18E

G-CFUW AutoGyro MTOsport   xxxx   07.04.09
D A Robertson   Baldardo Farm, Clocksbriggs   19.07.18P
Assembled Rotorsport UK as c/n RSUK/MTOS/005

G-CFUX Cameron C-80   11282   20.03.09
A E Still   North Marston, Buckingham   27.11.17E

G-CFUY PZL-Bielsko SZD-50-3 Puchacz   B-1983   19.02.08
BGA 3546/FUY   The Bath, Wilts & North Dorset
Gliding Club Ltd   Kingston Deverill   *'FUY'*   16.06.18E

G-CFUZ CZAW Sportcruiser   4050   11.12.08
M Gislam   Norwich Int'l   22.08.19P
Built by M W Bush – project PFA 338-14664

G-CFVA P&M Quik GT450   8441   26.06.09
Countermine Technologies PLC   Wickenby
(NF 01.09.16)

G-CFVC Schleicher ASK 13   13682AB   22.12.07
BGA 3550/FVC   Mendip Gliding Club Ltd
Halesland   *'FVC'*   08.03.17E
Built by Jubi GmbH Sportflugzeugbau

G-CFVE Schempp-Hirth Nimbus-2C   202   28.11.07
BGA 3553/FVF, D-2880   L Mitchell   Portmoak   *'FVE'*
24.04.18E

G-CFVF Air Création Buggy 582(1)/Kiss 400   FL012   03.03.09
G R Wilson   Greenhills Farm, Wheatley Hill
Built by J D Pinkney – project BMAA/217
(Flylight kit FL012 initially comprising trike
s/n T02034 & wing s/n A02050-2048; wing changed
to s/n A02050-2046 during build (NF 01.03.18)

G-CFVH Rolladen-Schneider LS7   7067   18.01.08
BGA 3555/FVH, (BGA 3527/FUA)
C C & J C Marshall   Eyres Field   *'246'*   01.05.18E

G-CFVI Evektor EV-97 teamEurostar UK   2009.33.19   04.03.09
Cancelled 18.08.14 as PWFU
Nympsfield   *Built by Cosmik Aviation Ltd; stored 09.14*

G-CFVJ Cvjetkovic CA-65 Skyfly   xxxx   21.01.09
OO-63   N D Hunter
Orange Grove Barn, Chavenage Green   19.08.19P
Built by P Gheysens & D Hunter – project PFA 233-14129

G-CFVK Best Off Skyranger 912(2)   SKR0511662   06.02.09
K Perryman & C S Wilson   Sywell   16.02.19P
Built by B Barrass – project BMAA HB/497

G-CFVL Scheibe Zugvogel IIIB   1082   28.04.08
BGA 3558/FVL, D-5224   M Balogh
tr The G-CFVL Flying Group   Darlton   *'FVL'*   05.08.18E

G-CFVM Centrair 101A Pégase   101A0345   10.12.07
BGA 3559/FVM   S H North   Kingston Deverill   *'369'* 09.04.18E

G-CFVN Centrair 101A Pégase   101A0268/2   06.02.08
BGA 3560/FVN   K Samuels   Kirton in Lindsey   *'FVN'* 22.02.19E
Built by from parts including original fuselage
of BGA 3198

G-CFVP Centrair 101A Pégase   101A0350   27.09.07
BGA 3561   J R Parry tr Foxtrot Victor Papa Group
Long Mynd   *'FVP'*   20.11.18E

G-CFVR Europa Aviation Europa XS   565   12.03.09
R G J Tait tr G-CFVR Group   Easterton   05.09.18P
Built by M T Fuller – project PFA 247-14543

G-CFVT Schempp-Hirth Nimbus-2   18   26.09.08
BGA 3565/FVT, N795
I Dunkley   (Tikao Bay, Akaroa, New Zealand)   *'E60'*
(NF 07.10.15)

G-CFVU Schleicher ASK 13   13062   01.11.07
BGA 3566/FVU, D-1348
Edensoaring Ltd   Skelling Farm, Skirwith   *'FVU'*   22.05.18E

G-CFVV Centrair 101A Pégase   101A0353   29.02.08
BGA 3567/FVV   Cambridge Gliding Club Ltd
Gransden Lodge   *'FVV'*   09.04.18E

G-CFVW Schempp-Hirth Ventus bT   51/252   04.12.07
BGA 3568/FVW, D-KORN   J F de Hollander
Terlet, Gelderland, Netherlands   *'FVW'*   03.06.18E

G-CFVX Cameron C-80   11283   20.03.09
A Hornshaw   Ugborough, Ivybridge   *'bet air'*   10.07.18E

G-CFVY Cameron A-120   4114   21.10.09
HB-QDP   C A Petre   (Bucharest, Romania)   06.07.17E

G-CFVZ Schleicher Ka 6E   4007   12.12.07
BGA 3571/FVZ, D-4104
N R Bowers   Kingston Deverill   *'PS'*   25.06.18E

G

G-CFWA	Schleicher Ka 6CR	6227	10.09.07
	BGA 3572/FWA, D-1062		
	C C Walley Shobdon *'FWA'*		20.03.18E

G-CFWB	Schleicher ASK 13	13224	21.01.08
	BGA 3573/FWB, HB-989		
	Cotswold Gliding Club Aston Down *'FWB'*		16.12.15E

G-CFWC	Grob G103C Twin III Acro	34154	25.01.08
	BGA 3574/FWC The South Wales Gliding Club Ltd		
	Usk *'609'*		17.03.18E

G-CFWD	AutoGyro MTOsport	xxxx	14.04.09
	B G & S D Bray t/a Gower Gyronautics Swansea		09.02.18P
	Assembled Rotorsport UK as c/n RSUK/MTOS/006		

G-CFWE	PZL-Bielsko SZD-50-3 Puchacz	B-1984	25.10.07
	BGA 3576, (BGA 3547/FUZ)		
	Cancelled 10.03.14 as destroyed		27.11.13
	Aboyne *Wreck stored 08.14*		

G-CFWF	Rolladen-Schneider LS7	7097	14.08.08
	BGA 3577/FWF G P Hibberd		
	Husbands Bosworth *'L57'*		29.01.18E

G-CFWH	Scheibe SF27A Zugvogel V	6024	15.09.08
	BGA 3579/FWH, D-4733		
	A S Carter Burnford Common, Brentor *'FWH'*		23.11.18E

G-CFWI	Kubíček BB22Z	686	01.04.09
	V Gounon Limoges, France *'SKY'*		20.04.19E

G-CFWJ	P&M Quik GT450	8447	06.04.09
	T Porter & D Whiteley St Michaels		09.06.18P

G-CFWK	Schempp-Hirth Nimbus-3DT	32	07.01.08
	BGA3581/FWK A J Dibdin tr 29 Syndicate		
	Gransden Lodge *'29'*		24.04.18E

G-CFWL	Schleicher K 8B	106/58	11.02.08
	BGA 3582/FWL, D-7151 D S Downton		
	Burnford Common, Brentor *'FWL'*		26.09.15E
	(NF 03.02.17)		

G-CFWM	Glaser-Dirks DG-300 Club Elan	3E373C50	26.10.07
	BGA 3583 S A Gunn-Russell tr FWM Group		
	Long Mynd *'FWM'*		04.03.18E
	Built by Elan Tovarna Sportnega Orodja N.Sol.O		

G-CFWN	P&M Quik GT450	8438	16.03.09
	G P Fern tr G-CFWN Group Arclid Green, Sandbach		24.05.18P

G-CFWP	Schleicher ASW 19B	19262	03.01.08
	BGA 3585/FWP, D-5980		
	A Zuchora Dunstable Downs *'980'*		23.04.18E

G-CFWR	Best Off Skyranger 912(2)	SKR0409525	02.12.04
	D Squire Moss Edge Farm, Cockerham		12.11.18P
	Built by R W Clarke – project BMAA/HB/426		

G-CFWS	Schleicher ASW 20C	20765	10.12.07
	BGA 3588/FWS, D-6623		
	B N M House (Thornbury, Bristol) *'662'*		01.01.19E

G-CFWT	PZL-Bielsko SZD-50-3 Puchacz	B-1988	03.10.07
	BGA 3589 Coventry Gliding Club Ltd t/a		
	The Gliding Centre Husbands Bosworth *'FWT'*		05.08.18E

G-CFWU	Rolladen-Schneider LS7-WL	7080	21.12.07
	BGA 3590/FWU T W Arscott Lasham *'768'*		12.10.19E

G-CFWV	Van's RV-7	xxxx	30.03.09
	S J Carr & D K Sington Compton Abbas		17.10.18P
	Built by D K Sington – project PFA 323-14428		

G-CFWW	Schleicher ASH 25E	25093	24.03.06
	BGA 3592/FWW N A C Norman Aboyne *'FWW'*		04.04.18E

G-CFWY	Centrair 101A Pégase	101071	17.01.08
	BGA 3594/FWY, F-CFXE G M Dodwell & J Randall		
	Husbands Bosworth *'FWY'*		31.07.18E

G-CFXA	Grob G104 Speed Astir IIB	4083	16.08.07
	BGA 3596, D-2671 S W Swan tr Ringmer Speedy		
	Syndicate Ringmer *'567'*		19.05.18E

G-CFXB	Schleicher K 8B	8193	03.07.08
	BGA 3597/FXB, D-5597 Dartmoor Gliding Society		
	Burnford Common, Brentor *'FXB'*		22.10.19E

G-CFXC	Schleicher Ka 6E	4268	15.04.08
	BGA 3598/FXC, RAFGGA 150, D-0150		
	G E Pook Kingston Deverill *'FXC'*		01.09.18E

G-CFXD	Centrair 101A Pégase	101A0346	02.10.07
	BGA 3599/FXD, (BGA 3563/FVR)		
	R Banks & D G England Husbands Bosworth *'285'*		19.05.16E

G-CFXF	Magni M16C Tandem Trainer	16085104	03.04.09
	P I Jordan (Southsea)		24.10.19P
	Operated by Autogyro Experience		

G-CFXG	Flylight Dragonfly/Aeros Discus 15T	020	08.04.09
	C A Mason Sywell		
	(SSDR microlight since 05.14) (IE 06.12.17)		

G-CFXK	Flylight Dragonfly/Aeros Discus 15T	021	16.04.09
	N R Pettigrew Culbokie		
	(SSDR microlight since 05.14) (IE 03.03.16)		

G-CFXM	Schempp-Hirth Discus bT	16/301	18.08.08
	BGA 3607/FXM, D-KHIA		
	G R E Bottomley Lasham *'173'*		18.08.18E

G-CFXN	CZAW Sportcruiser	700911	11.05.09
	H Bishop (East Grinstead)		29.07.16P
	Built by J D Boyce & R Underwood		
	– project LAA 338-14903 (NF 10.07.17)		

G-CFXO	PZL-Bielsko SZD-50-3 Puchacz	B-2024	03.10.07
	BGA 3658, (BGA 3637/FYT) Derbyshire & Lancashire		
	Gliding Club Ltd Camphill *'FXQ'*		08.03.19E

G-CFXP	Lindstrand LBL 105A	1168	22.04.09
	Shaun Bradley Project Services Ltd		
	Houghton, Stockbridge		04.06.19E

G-CFXR	Lindstrand LBL 105A	1263	21.04.09
	Lindstrand Media Ltd Hawarden CH5 *'Redrow'*		24.07.19E

G-CFXS	Schleicher Ka 6E	4228	03.09.08
	BGA 3612/FXS, D-0073		
	D P Aherne Tibenham *'FXS'*		03.05.19E

G-CFXT	Naval Aircraft Factory N3N-3	–	16.04.09
	N45299, NR45299, USN 4445		
	J A & R H Cooper Wickenby		
	US Navy BuA no quoted as c/n 4445; FAA record		
	registered as 'NR45299 s/n 4445' (NF 08.05.18)		

G-CFXU	Schleicher Ka 6E	4071	04.01.08
	BGA 3614/FXU, OH-343, OH-RSY		
	P Carter tr Xray Uniform Group Bicester *'FXU'*		09.06.18E

G-CFXW	Schleicher K 8B	8651	25.01.08
	BGA 3616/FXW, D-7203, D-KOLA, D-7203		
	The South Wales Gliding Club Ltd Usk *'FXW'*		24.08.18E

G-CFXX	P&M QuikR	8443	03.04.09
	M C Shortman (Pontypool)		07.04.19P

G-CFXY	Schleicher ASW 15B	15348	05.03.08
	BGA 3618/FXY, F-CEJL E L Youle (Scampton) *'EC'*		12.08.18E

G-CFXZ	P&M QuikR	8444	24.03.09
	M Naylor East Fortune		03.06.17P
	(IE 06.11.17)		

G-CFYA	PZL-Bielsko SZD-50-3 Puchacz	B-2022	08.11.07
	BGA 3620/FYA W R Longstaff tr		
	Cairngorm Gliding Club Feshiebridge *'FYA'*		30.09.18E

G-CFYB	Rolladen-Schneider LS7	7102	06.09.07
	BGA3621 V P Haley & A T Macdonald		
	Wormingford *'FYB'*		03.03.18E

G-CFYC	Schempp-Hirth Ventus b	83	08.01.08
	BGA3622/FYC, F-CEDR, F-WEDR		
	J M Brooke Lasham *'V17'*		30.04.18E

G-CFYD	Aeroprakt A-22L Foxbat	xxxx	25.02.09
	A P Fenn Bye Cross Farm, Moccas		20.08.18P
	Built by A P Fenn – project PFA 317A-14750		

G-CFYE	Scheibe Zugvogel IIIB	1079	17.06.08
	BGA 3624/FYE, D-7157		
	The Gliding Heritage Centre Lasham *'FYE'*		25.02.17E
	(IE 21.10.17)		

G-CFYF	Schleicher ASK 21	21470	22.05.08
	BGA 3625/FYF London Gliding Club Proprietary Ltd		
	Dunstable Downs *'FYF'*		18.12.18E

G-CFYG	Glasflügel Club Libelle 205	22	14.08.08
	BGA 3626/FYG, OH-545, D-9476		
	M W Fisher tr FYG Syndicate Talgarth *'FYG'*		11.11.17E

G-CFYH	Rolladen-Schneider LS4-a	4804	21.07.08
	BGA 3627/FYH C A & G W Craig		
	RAF Weston-on-the-Green *'224'*		22.06.18E

G-CFYI	Grob G102 Astir CS	1092	15.04.09
	BGA 4326/HZC, D-6991		
	S R Hill, A H Kay & W E Roper Camphill *'216'*		30.11.18E

G-CFYJ	Schempp-Hirth Standard Cirrus	581G	16.11.07	
	BGA 3628/FYJ, D-8931			
	W Blackburn Pocklington *'WB'*		21.04.18E	
G-CFYK	Rolladen-Schneider LS7-WL	7108	19.11.07	
	BGA 3629/FYK J Bayford Gransden Lodge *'7R'*		05.05.18E	
G-CFYL	PZL-Bielsko SZD-50-3 Puchacz	B-1990	16.11.07	
	BGA 3630/FYL Deeside Gliding Club			
	(Aberdeenshire) Ltd Aboyne *'FYL'*		18.12.17E	
G-CFYM	Schempp-Hirth Discus bT	31/328	05.10.07	
	BGA 3631 T Wright Husbands Bosworth *'FYM'*		15.06.18E	
G-CFYN	Schempp-Hirth Discus b	179	12.11.07	
	BGA 3632/FYN, N75J			
	P R Foulger & N White Wormingford *'J3'*		04.04.18E	
G-CFYO	P&M QuikR	8434	26.05.09	
	M A Sandwith Rufforth		25.05.18P	
G-CFYP	Fresh Breeze Silex M/Flyke/Monster			
	21895 & FK686 & 11045		19.05.09	
	A J R Carver (Duntisborne Leer, Cirencester)			
	(SSDR microlight since 05.14) (NF 09.09.16)			
G-CFYR	LET L-23 Super Blanik	917816	28.03.08	
	BGA 3635/FYR			
	T Newby tr G-CFYR Group Rufforth *'FYR'*		27.07.18E	
G-CFYS	Aerospool Dynamic WT9 UK	DY298/2009	15.04.09	
	E M Middleton Broadmeadow Farm, Hereford		27.06.18P	
	Assembled Yeoman Light Aircraft Co Ltd;			
	official c/n recorded as 'DY298'			
G-CFYU	Glaser-Dirks DG-100G Elan	E111	14.02.08	
	BGA 3638/FYU, OY-XMR, SE-TYO			
	J Hunt RAF Weston-on-the-Green *'DG'*		30.04.19E	
	Built by Elan Tovarna Sportnega Orodja N.Sol.O			
G-CFYV	Schleicher ASK 21	21468	06.11.07	
	BGA 3639/FYV The Bristol Gliding Club			
	Proprietary Ltd Nympsfield *'FYV'*		30.03.18E	
G-CFYW	Rolladen-Schneider LS7-WL	7111	10.12.07	
	BGA 3640/FYW J Douglass Rivar Hill *'B1'*		09.04.18E	
G-CFYX	Schempp-Hirth Discus bT	32	31.03.08	
	BGA 3641 D A Salmon Camphill *'FYX'*		29.04.18E	
	Built by as Discus b as c/n 333; motorised 09.07			
	as Discus bT as c/n 32			
G-CFYY	Schleicher ASK 13	13685AB	12.03.08	
	BGA 3642/FYY Lasham Gliding Society Ltd			
	Lasham *'S'*		27.04.18E	
	Built by Jubi GmbH Sportflugzeugbau			
G-CFYZ	Schleicher ASH 25	25097	04.06.08	
	BGA 3643/FYZ P J Harvey tr 171 Syndicate			
	Bicester *'171'*		17.07.15E	
	(IE 25.04.16)			
G-CFZB	Glasflügel Standard Libelle 201B	112	03.01.08	
	BGA 3645/FZB, OH-388, OH-GLA			
	J C Meyer Nympsfield *'669'*		18.12.18E	
G-CFZD	Avtech Jabiru J430	602	20.04.09	
	C Judd & A Macknish			
	Lark Engine Farm, Prickwillow, Ely		24.05.18P	
	Built by G R Cotterell – project LAA 336-14833			
G-CFZF	PZL-Bielsko SZD-51-1 Junior	B-1861	30.11.07	
	BGA 3649/FZF Devon & Somerset Gliding Club Ltd			
	North Hill *'FZF'*		05.04.18E	
G-CFZH	Schempp-Hirth Ventus cT	455	12.11.07	
	BGA 3651/FZH G D Clack tr FZH Group			
	Lasham *'FZH'*		20.01.19E	
G-CFZI	ICP MXP-740 Savannah Jabiru(5)	07-05-51-601	06.05.09	
	A, J T & O D Lewis Wickenby			
	Built by A, J T & O D Lewis – project BMAA/HB/590			
	(NF 07.07.16)			
G-CFZJ	Supermarine 388 Seafire F.46	xxxx	15.05.09	
	LA546 C T Charleston (Great Horkesley, Colchester)			
	Built by Castle Bromwich 1946; on rebuild 2017			
	(NF 12.01.16)			
G-CFZK	Schempp-Hirth Standard Cirrus	81	09.06.08	
	BGA 3653 R Burgoyne & S E Lucas			
	Aston Down *'FZK'*		24.11.18E	
G-CFZL	Schleicher ASW 20CL	20764	25.09.07	
	BGA 3654, D-5937 A L & R M Housden Aboyne *'Z6'*		22.06.18E	

G-CFZN	Schleicher ASK 13	13045	01.12.07
	BGA 3656/FZN, D-5759		
	Black Mountains Gliding Club Talgarth *'K13'*		30.06.19E
G-CFZO	Schempp-Hirth Nimbus-3DT	31	17.11.07
	BGA 3610/FXQ D Tanner tr 954 Syndicate		
	Lasham *'954'*		15.01.19E
G-CFZP	PZL-Bielsko SZD-51-1 Junior	B-1926	28.01.08
	BGA3657/FZP Midland Gliding Club Ltd		
	Long Mynd *'N16'*		06.02.13E
	Hit power cables on field landing, Barnack,		
	Cambridge 26.08.12 (NF 27.02.18)		
G-CFZR	Schleicher Ka 6CR	6136	24.11.08
	BGA 3659/FZR, D-8459 A L R Roth Tibenham		17.03.18E
G-CFZT	Ace Aviation Magic/Laser	xxxx	06.07.09
	G-93-2 G Cousins Rochester		
	Assembled P&M Aviation Ltd; trike s/n unknown		
	& wing s/n AA00131		
	(SSDR microlight since 05.14) (NF 19.07.18)		
G-CFZW	Glaser-Dirks DG-300 Club Elan	3E378C53	16.01.08
	BGA 3664/FZW D O'Flanagan & G Stilgoe		
	Parham *'FZW'*		14.12.18E
	Built by Elan Tovarna Sportnega Orodja N.Sol.O		
G-CFZX	AutoGyro MTOsport	09 065S	25.08.09
	Gyro-1 Ltd Manchester Barton		25.10.18P
	Assembled Rotorsport UK as c/n RSUK/MTOS/013		
G-CFZZ	LET L-33 Solo	940220	25.03.08
	BGA 3667/FZZ		
	R J Fennell tr The Andreas L33 Group Andreas *'FZZ'*		17.07.18E

G-CGAA – G-CGZZ

G-CGAA	Flylight Dragonfly/Aeros Discus 15T	028	05.06.09
	G Adkins Sackville Lodge Farm, Riseley		
	(SSDR microlight since 05.14) (IE 28.04.16)		
G-CGAB	Sportine Aviacija LAK-12 Lietuva	6170	10.04.08
	BGA 3669/GAB W T Emery Rufforth *'GAB'*		20.06.14E
	(IE 28.07.15)		
G-CGAC	P&M Quik GT450	8455	20.05.09
	G Brockhurst (Horam, Heathfield)		12.11.18P
G-CGAD	Rolladen-Schneider LS3	3032	16.07.08
	BGA 3671/GAD, HB-1363		
	J D Brister Gransden Lodge *'L5'*		29.08.18E
G-CGAF	Schleicher ASK 21	21152	16.01.08
	BGA 3673/GAF, ZD652, BGA 2892/ERN		
	Lasham Gliding Society Ltd Lasham *'778'*		25.05.18E
G-CGAG	Schleicher ASK 21	21143	24.09.07
	BGA 3674, ZD645, BGA 2885/ERF		
	Stratford on Avon Gliding Club Ltd Snitterfield *'GAG'*		27.11.18E
G-CGAH	Schempp-Hirth Standard Cirrus	572	19.12.07
	BGA 3675/GAH, HB-1240		
	J W Williams (Madrid, Spain) *'GAH'*		03.08.17E
G-CGAI	Raj Hamsa X'Air Hawk	1172	02.04.09
	R G Cheshire Shifnal		09.10.18P
	Built by P J Kilshaw – project LAA 340-14813		
G-CGAJ	Alpi Pioneer 400	01	11.06.09
	C Rusalen The Byre, Hardwick, Abergavenny		09.07.18P
G-CGAK	EAA Acrosport II	606	08.06.09
	P D Sibbons Little Gransden		19.09.18P
	Built by P D Sibbons – project PFA 072A-14255		
G-CGAL	P&M QuikR	8452	22.04.09
	R A Keene Over Farm, Gloucester		01.09.18P
G-CGAM	Schleicher ASK 21	21144	08.02.08
	BGA 3679/GAM, ZD646, BGA 2886/ERG		
	T R Dews Kingston Deverill *'GAM'*		20.11.18E
G-CGAN	Glasflügel H301 Libelle	8	01.10.08
	BGA 3680/GAN, D-4111		
	M D Butcher Wormingford *'83'*		18.07.18E
G-CGAO	de Havilland DHC-1 Chipmunk 22	40	27.10.09
	CS-AZY, Port.AF 1350		
	D J Petters tr G-CGAO Group Fenland		20.11.17P
	Built by OGMA; as '1350' in Portuguese AF c/s		
G-CGAP	Schempp-Hirth Ventus bT	14/150	12.08.08
	BGA 3681/GAP, OH-774, N416DP		
	J R Greenwell Milfield *'GAP'*		28.10.17E

G-CGAR	Rolladen-Schneider LS6-c	6205	26.06.08
	BGA 3683/GAR A Warbrick (Premnay, Insch) *'AW'*		07.09.09E
	(IE 28.05.15)		
G-CGAS	Schempp-Hirth Ventus cT	157	03.10.07
	BGA 3684 R A Davenport & A E D Hayes		
	Aston Down *'GAS'*		15.03.19E
G-CGAT	Grob G102 Astir CS	1130	09.05.08
	BGA 3685/GAT, D-4176		
	N J Hooper Snitterfield *'GAT'*		30.07.19E
G-CGAU	Glasflügel Standard Libelle 201B	498	31.03.08
	BGA 3686, F-CELA M J Frawley tr G-CGAU Group		
	Dunstable Downs *'725'*		27.08.17E
	(IE 18.01.18)		
G-CGAV	Scheibe SF27A Zugvogel V	6073	08.02.08
	BGA 3687/GAV, D-5287 J A Milner		
	tr The Golf Alpha Victor Group Darlton *'GAV'*		27.02.19E
G-CGAX	PZL-Bielsko SZD-55-1	551190008	02.06.08
	BGA 3689/GAX D J Brunton tr Golf Alpha Xray Group		
	Portmoak *'302'*		01.09.19E
G-CGAZ	P&M QuikR	8436	05.03.09
	A I Baginski tr G-CGAZ Syndicate East Fortune		06.03.19P
G-CGBB	Schleicher ASK 21	21073	25.02.08
	BGA 3693/GBB, D-3239 University of Edinburgh		
	Sports Union Portmoak *'GBB'*		27.03.18E
G-CGBD	PZL-Bielsko SZD-50-3 Puchacz	B-2028	03.01.08
	BGA 3695/GBD The Northumbria Gliding Club Ltd		
	Currock Hill *'GBD'*		07.06.18E
G-CGBF	Schleicher ASK 21	21142	04.12.07
	BGA 3697/GBF, ZD644, BGA 2883/ERD		
	London Gliding Club Proprietary Ltd		
	Dunstable Downs *'GBF'*		14.12.18E
G-CGBG	Rolladen-Schneider LS6-18W	6214	06.12.07
	BGA 3698/GBG C Villa Gransden Lodge *'521'*		27.04.18E
G-CGBH	Raj Hamsa X'Air Hawk	1126	24.06.09
	EI-DZP S E McEwen Woodlands Barton Farm, Roche		11.09.18P
	Built by M Bowden		
G-CGBJ	Grob G102 Astir CS	1107	06.11.07
	BGA 3700/GBJ, D-4167 Banbury Gliding Club Ltd		
	Hinton-in-the-Hedges *'GBJ'*		05.06.18E
G-CGBL	Rolladen-Schneider LS7-WL	7119	14.01.08
	BGA 3702/GBL P A Roche Rattlesden *'720'*		18.05.18E
G-CGBM	Flight Design CTSW	09-06-06	05.08.09
	P P Duffy Shotton Colliery, Peterlee		21.06.19P
	Assembled P&M Aviation Ltd as c/n 8484;		
	operated by North East Flying Club		
G-CGBN	Schleicher ASK 21	21141	13.12.07
	BGA 3704/GBN, ZD643, BGA 2884/ERE		
	Essex & Suffolk Gliding Club Ltd Wormingford *'GBN'*		20.04.18E
G-CGBO	Rolladen-Schneider LS6	6082	06.02.08
	BGA 3706/GBQ, D-3725		
	E J Foggin tr G-CGBO Syndicate Aston Down *'C30'*		16.02.18E
G-CGBR	Rolladen-Schneider LS6-c	6196	07.12.07
	BGA 3707/GBR, D-3482		
	V L Brown Husbands Bosworth *'167'*		30.10.18E
G-CGBS	Glaser-Dirks DG-300 Club Elan	3E389C58	27.05.08
	BGA 3708/GBS B Fulton & J Thomas		
	Portmoak *'206'*		28.09.19E
	Built by Elan Tovarna Sportnega Orodja N.Sol.O		
G-CGBU	Centrair 101A Pégase	101A0394	01.02.08
	BGA 3710/GBU D J Arblaster Lyveden *'922'*		04.05.18E
G-CGBV	Schleicher ASK 21	21149	10.10.07
	BGA 3711/GBV, ZD649, BGA 2889/ERK		
	Wolds Gliding Club Ltd Pocklington *'GBV'*		05.03.18E
G-CGBY	Rolladen-Schneider LS7-WL	7121	13.03.08
	BGA 3714/GBY B N Searle Saltby *'128'*		10.05.18E
G-CGBZ	Glaser-Dirks DG-500 Elan Trainer	5E34T10	23.11.07
	BGA 3715/GBZ G N Turner Aston Down *'GBZ'*		06.08.19E
	Built by Elan Flight Ltd		
G-CGCA	Schleicher ASW 19B	19281	21.12.07
	BGA 3716/GCA, D-3179 Deeside Gliding Club		
	(Aberdeenshire) Ltd Aboyne *'GCA'*		09.05.18E
G-CGCC	PZL-Bielsko SZD-51-1 Junior	B-1928	02.10.07
	BGA 3718 Coventry Gliding Club Ltd		
	t/a The Gliding Centre Husbands Bosworth *'GCC'*		28.08.18E
G-CGCD	Schempp-Hirth Standard Cirrus	476	17.06.08
	BGA 3719/GCD, PH-507 W G Anderson		
	tr Cirrus Syndicate Feshiebridge *'GCD'*		16.07.18E
G-CGCE	Magni M16C Tandem Trainer	16095384	10.07.09
	A J A Fowler Fowler's Field, Billingshurst		06.09.18P
G-CGCF	Schleicher ASK 23	23010	20.11.07
	BGA 3721/GCF, AGA 9		
	Cotswold Gliding Club Aston Down *'GCF'*		13.03.18E
G-CGCH	CZAW Sportcruiser	07SC023	05.03.09
	J E Preston Beverley (Linley Hill)		06.10.19P
	Built by C Harrison – project PFA 338-14650		
	(Quick-build kit 3833)		
G-CGCI	Sikorsky S-92A	920103	15.07.09
	5N-BMN, G-CGCI, N2077V Bristow Helicopters Ltd		
	Aberdeen Int'l *'35 Years Service – Alistair Hutcheon'*		27.08.10E
	(IE 16.01.18)		
G-CGCK	PZL-Bielsko SZD-50-3 Puchacz	B-2025	05.06.08
	BGA 3725/GCK, G-BTJV		
	Kent Gliding Club Ltd Challock *'GCK'*		07.06.18E
G-CGCL	Grob G102 Astir CS	1194	17.08.07
	BGA 3726, D-7311		
	Southdown Gliding Club Ltd Parham Park *'GCL'*		07.12.18E
G-CGCM	Rolladen-Schneider LS6-c	6216	12.10.07
	BGA 3727 G R Glazebrook Dunstable Downs *'347'*		20.11.17E
G-CGCN	Dyn'Aéro MCR-01 Club	375	08.07.09
	D J Smith Perth		06.07.18P
	Built by D J Smith – project PFA 301A-14742		
G-CGCO	Schempp-Hirth Cirrus VTC	135Y	11.09.08
	BGA 3730/GCQ, D-2945 S V Jones Wormingford		31.03.18E
G-CGCP	Schleicher Ka 6CR	6416	23.01.08
	BGA3729/GCP, D-6369 C G Hayes-Oldroyd		
	tr Burn K6 G-CGCP Group Burn *'GCP'*		26.09.19E
G-CGCR	Schleicher ASW 15B	15447	10.01.08
	BGA 3731/GCR, D-6887		
	R C Page tr ASW15B 748 Group Nympsfield *'748'*		10.04.18E
G-CGCS	Glasflügel Club Libelle 205	159	20.03.09
	BGA 3732/GCS, F-CEQL		
	D G Coats Portmoak *'H12'*		06.06.15E
	(IE 16.06.15)		
G-CGCT	Schempp-Hirth Discus b	360	14.02.08
	BGA 3733/GCT Banbury Gliding Club Ltd		
	Hinton-in-the-Hedges *'TB2'*		25.04.18E
G-CGCU	PZL-Bielsko SZD-50-3 Puchacz	B-2023	23.01.08
	BGA3734/GCU, (BGA3619/FXZ)		
	Darlton Gliding Club Ltd Darlton *'GCU'*		13.08.18E
G-CGCV	Raj Hamsa X'Air Hawk	1219	23.03.09
	K Buckley & B L Prime (Stoke-on-Trent & Ashbourne)		10.06.19P
	Built by P C Bishop – project LAA 340-14881		
G-CGCX	Schleicher ASW 15	15034	18.03.08
	BGA 3736/GCX, D-0420		
	R L Horsnell Snitterfield *'N6'*		09.02.19E
G-CGDA	Rolladen-Schneider LS3-17	3448	15.10.07
	BGA 3739/GDA, RAFGGA 546		
	J S Romanes Milfield *'546'*		25.04.18E
G-CGDB	Schleicher K 8B	8152	11.12.07
	BGA 3740/GDB, HB-738		
	T A Odom Husbands Bosworth *'GDB'*		02.09.18E
G-CGDC	AutoGyro MTOsport	09 091S	16.09.09
	R Derham & T R Kingsley (Bungay & Norwich)		11.04.18P
	Assembled Rotorsport UK as c/n RSUK/MTOS/014		
G-CGDD	Bölkow Phoebus C	836	06.08.08
	BGA 3742/GDD, D-0060		
	G C Kench Crowland *'GDD'*		26.07.11E
	(NF 31.07.14)		
G-CGDE	Schleicher Ka 6CR	6570SI	29.08.07
	BGA 3743, D-5306 P D Rowlands tr K6 Syndicate		
	North Hill *'GDE'*		24.11.16E
G-CGDF	Schleicher Ka 6BR	389	16.09.08
	BGA 3744/GDF, D-8544 H Marshall & D G Pask		
	Sutton Bank *'GDF'*		12.04.18E
G-CGDG	Cameron C-80	11302	22.05.09
	J Braeckman Mariakerke, Belgium		17.07.18E
	Amended to Frog SS		

G

G-CGDH Europa Aviation Europa XS   457   08.07.03
R Cullum tr G-CGDH Group   Wickenby   13.11.18P
Built by G D Harding – project PFA 247-13746;
tricycle u/c

G-CGDI Evektor EV-97A Eurostar   2006-2925   09.06.09
D Street   Netherthorpe   25.11.18P
Built by D Street – project PFA 315A-14606

G-CGDK Schleicher K 8B   8240   23.01.08
BGA 3748/GDK, D-5381, D-KANU, D-5381   Dartmoor
Gliding Society   Burnford Common, Brentor   *'GDK'*   09.09.15E
(NF 22.01.18)

G-CGDL P&M QuikR   8230   05.06.09
S C Reeve   Headon Farm, Retford   08.06.18P
Officially registered as c/n 8470; repaired 2009
with trike c/n 8230 ex G-RITT & new wing

G-CGDM Sonex Sonex   xxxx   26.05.09
P Johnson   Morgansfield, Fishburn   15.09.18P
Built by D Scott – project PFA 337-14761; tricycle u/c

G-CGDN Rolladen-Schneider LS3-17   3291   30.06.09
BGA 3751, D-6932   S J Glassett   Aston Down   19.06.18E

G-CGDO Grob G102 Astir CS   1145   16.11.07
BGA 3753/GDO, D-7229
R Bostock & P Lowe   Seighford   *'GDO'*   10.03.18E

G-CGDR Schempp-Hirth Discus CS   016CS   31.03.08
BGA 3754   D Daniels   Kingston Deverill   *'GDR'*   02.01.19E
Built by Orličan Aakciová Společnost

G-CGDS Schleicher ASW 15B   15205   09.01.08
BGA 3755/GDS, D-0902
B Birk & P A Crouch   Ringmer   *'GDS'*   26.09.17E

G-CGDT Schleicher ASW 24   24120   19.02.08
BGA 3756/GDT   R D McVean tr Tango 54 Syndicate
Chipping   *'T54'*   27.04.18E

G-CGDV Czech Sport Sportcruiser   09SC285   17.08.09
G J Richardson   (Kimbolton, Huntingdon)   07.03.19W

G-CGDW Czech Sport PS-28 Cruiser   C0272   17.08.09
Onega Ltd   North Weald   02.04.15R
Originally built as Sportcruiser c/n 09SC286;
noted 07.18 (NF 05.04.18)

G-CGDX Schempp-Hirth Discus CS   023CS   03.10.07
BGA 3760   D Bieniasz   Kirton in Lindsey   *'GDX'*   10.04.19E
Built by Orličan Aakciová Společnost

G-CGDY Schleicher ASW 15B   15220   13.12.07
BGA 3761/GDY, D-0947
J C Gazzard   Wormingford   *'914'*   09.05.19E

G-CGDZ Schleicher ASW 24   24116   05.12.07
BGA 3762/GDZ   J M Norman tr 24 Group
Pocklington   *'524'*   02.04.18E

G-CGEA Schleicher Ka 6CR   849   24.03.09
BGA 3763/GEA, (BGA 3605), D-5801
J McShane   Portmoak   *'GEA'*   28.11.17E

G-CGEB Grob G102 Astir CS77   1628   09.09.08
BGA 3764/GEB, PH-576
T R Dews   Kingston Deverill   *'GEB'*   08.12.18E

G-CGEC Flight Design CTLS   F.09-02-12   11.05.09
S Munday   Brookfield Farm, Great Stukeley   30.04.18W
Assembled P&M Aviation Ltd

G-CGEE Glasflügel Standard Libelle 201B   94   07.03.08
BGA 3767/GEE, D-0928
D Plumb   Kirton in Lindsey   *'GEE'*   01.04.19E

G-CGEG Schleicher K 8B   689   25.06.08
BGA 3769/GEG, HB-639
Darlton Gliding Club Ltd   Darlton   *'GEG'*   05.09.18E

G-CGEH Schleicher ASW 15B   15276   04.06.08
BGA 3770/GEH, D-2124   D
K Tappenden   Wormingford   *'219'*   10.08.18E

G-CGEJ Alpi Pioneer 200-M   208   17.07.09
D E Foster   (Atherstone)   *'Casper'*   28.02.18P
Built by P S Bewley – project LAA 334-14909

G-CGEK Ace Aviation Magic/Laser   MT0113   21.10.09
G-93-5   T Smith   Harringe Court, Sellindge
Assembled P&M Aviation Ltd; trike s/n
MT0113 & wing s/n AA00140
(SSDR microlight since 05.14) (IE 30.01.18)

G-CGEL PZL-Bielsko SZD-50-3 Puchacz   B-2030   03.01.08
BGA 3772/GEL   The Northumbria Gliding Club Ltd
Currock Hill   *'GEL'*   31.05.18E

G-CGEM Schleicher Ka 6CR   6249   02.04.08
BGA 3773/GEM, D-8486
M A Clark tr GEM Syndicate   (Haddenham)   *'GEM'*   24.04.15E
(IE 29.05.15)

G-CGEO Czech Sport Sportcruiser   09SC303   14.09.09
OK-LUU 26   M G Bird tr The Jester Flying Group
Graveley Hall Farm, Graveley   20.08.18W

G-CGEP Schempp-Hirth Standard Cirrus   205G   14.12.07
BGA 3775/GEP, D-0917   P S Harvey & C J Owen
Burnford Common, Brentor   *'GEP'*   05.08.18E
Built by Burkhart Grob-Flugzeugbau

G-CGER Cameron Z-105   11313   25.08.09
M Casaburo   Ostuni, Puglia, Italy
'CV Fly Communication'   15.09.14E
(NF 06.07.16)

G-CGEU Flylight Dragonfly/Aeros Discus 15T   036   07.08.09
I Hesling-Gibson   (Coombe, Wotton-under-Edge)
Aeros Discus 15T wing c/n 026 09
(SSDR microlight since 05.14) (IE 12.06.18)

G-CGEV Heliopolis Gomhouria Mk.6   067   28.04.10
Egyptian AF 158   A Brier   Breighton   15.02.18P
Built by Kader Industries AOJ; as 'CG+EV' in Luftwaffe c/s

G-CGEW AutoGyro MTOsport   09 048S   02.07.09
J L V Lowry-Corry   Headcorn   26.09.19P
Assembled Rotorsport UK as c/n RSUK/MTOS/008

G-CGEX P&M Quik GT450   8491   16.10.09
M D Howe   Priory Farm, Tibenham   15.10.18P

G-CGEY Julian Dingbat   CJ-003   11.08.09
A H H Mole   (Gravir, Isle of Lewis)
Built by C D Julian (NF 24.01.18)

G-CGEZ Raj Hamsa X'Air Hawk   1217   29.04.09
B J Ellis & M Howes   Rossall Field, Cockerham   19.06.18P
Built by B J Ellis & M Howes – project LAA 340-14887

G-CGFB BB Microlight BB03 Trya/BB103   10030901BF   22.07.09
B J Fallows   Haverfordwest
(SSDR microlight since 05.14) (IE 21.10.15)

G-CGFG Cessna 152   15285724   25.06.09
N94559   Upperstack Ltd t/a LAC Flying School
Manchester Barton   03.02.19E

G-CGFH Cessna T182T Turbo Skylane   T18208667   11.08.09
N1329T, (N148RM), N1329T   H Riffkin   Fife   02.10.18E

G-CGFK Ace Aviation Magic/Laser   MT0114   26.10.09
B B Adams   (Kingston, Lewes)
Assembled P&M Aviation Ltd; trike s/n MT0114
& wing s/n AA00141
(SSDR microlight since 05.14) (NF 07.02.17)

G-CGFN Cameron C-60   11324   04.09.09
G J Madelin   Farnham   10.08.18E

G-CGFO Ultramagic H-42   42/17   22.12.09
D G Such   Farnborough GU14   12.07.18E

G-CGFP Pietenpol Air Camper   0182   21.08.09
M D Waldron   (Cheltenham, Gloucestershire)
Built by D Hetherington – project LAA 047-14906;
noted 09.16 (NF 17.02.15)

G-CGFR Lindstrand LBL HS-120 HA Airship   1269   27.08.09
D Duke   (Weavering, Maidstone)   16.12.10E
(NF 09.06.17)

G-CGFS Nanchang CJ-6A (Yak 18)   4532008   02.09.09
LN-WNC, G-CGFS, Chinese PLAAF 61762
H C Erstad tr Red Star Squadron   (Strommen, Norway)   17.12.19P
As 'CT190' in Sri Lankan AF c/s

G-CGFU Schempp-Hirth Mini Nimbus C   123   20.08.09
BGA 4145/HRQ, (BGA 4122), SE-TVB
S Foster   Long Mynd   *'142'*   16.05.18E

G-CGFY Lindstrand LBL 105A   1179   21.09.09
A C Sutton tr Gone Ballooning   Longwell Green, Bristol   22.04.19E

G-CGFZ Thruster T600N 450   0096-T600N-118   19.08.09
K J Crompton   Newtownards   04.11.18P
Badged 'Sprint'

G-CGGC P&M QuikR 8469 04.08.09
PH-4E6, G-CGGC O G Johns tr Oakley Flyers
Field Farm, Oakley 06.06.19P

G-CGGD Aérospatiale AS.365N2 Dauphin 2 6435 18.01.12
N272DE, N272NE, N365NZ
Multiflight Ltd Leeds Bradford 08.03.18E

G-CGGF Robinson R44 Clipper II 12930 14.10.09
G Stroud (Portsmouth) 19.12.18E

G-CGGG Robinson R44 Astro 0626 24.08.07
G-SJDI K Hayes (Clay Cross) 01.03.18E

G-CGGK Westland Wasp HAS.1 F9604 30.09.09
A2643, A2723, XT434
The Real Aeroplane Company Ltd Breighton
As 'XT434' in RN c/s; noted 07.17 (NF 30.11.16)

G-CGGM Evektor EV-97 teamEurostar UK 3401 29.09.09
A Vincent tr Golf Mike Group Wycombe Air Park 30.07.18P
Assembled Cosmik Aviation Ltd

G-CGGO Robin DR.400-180 Régent 1756 06.10.09
F-GFXG R A Hawkins & G I J Thomson Little Snoring 16.08.18E

G-CGGP AutoGyro MTOsport 09 095S 22.10.09
G P Gibson & J Taylforth Sleap 17.04.19P
Assembled Rotorsport UK as c/n RSUK/MTOS/017

G-CGGS Robinson R44 Raven II 12967 05.02.10
Oakfield Investments Ltd Gloucestershire 11.03.18E

G-CGGT P&M Quik GT450 8466 01.07.09
A H Beveridge tr G-CGGT (Mow Cop, Stoke-on-Trent) 29.07.18P

G-CGGV AutoGyro MTOsport xxxx 02.02.10
S Morris (Whittington, Oswestry) 14.03.18P
Assembled Rotorsport UK as c/n RSUK/MTOS/022

G-CGGW AutoGyro MTOsport 09 117S 24.11.09
P Adams Chiltern Park, Wallingford 19.01.19P
Assembled Rotorsport UK as c/n RSUK/MTOS/021

G-CGGY Ultramagic N-425 425/35 10.05.10
Adventure Balloons Ltd Hartley Wintney, Hook
'www.Essex Balloons.co.uk' 07.03.16E
(IE 04.01.18)

G-CGGZ Ultramagic S-90 90/107 01.11.10
P Lawman Northampton 29.06.18E

G-CGHA P&M QuikR 8499 18.11.09
C A Green Clench Common 17.11.18P

G-CGHB Nanchang CJ-6A (Yak 18) 4532009 03.11.09
PLAAF M J Harvey Redhill 26.09.18P
As '61367:37' in Chinese AF c/s

G-CGHG P&M Quik GT450 8503 17.11.09
J & K D McAlpine Easter Poldar Farm, Thornhill 02.04.18P
Officially registered as c/n 8427; trike c/n 8503 now fitted

G-CGHH P&M QuikR 8496 09.11.09
C Pyle & N Richardson Redlands 24.11.18P

G-CGHJ Staaken Z-21A Flitzer Z238 19.10.09
D J Ashley Dolafallen Farm, Llanwrthwl
Built by D J Ashley – project PFA 223-14682;
(NF 11.10.17)

G-CGHK Alpi Pioneer 300 Hawk 282 19.10.09
D J Ashley Dolafallen Farm, Llanwrthwl 31.07.18P
Built by D J Ashley – project LAA 330A-14914

G-CGHL AutoGyro MTOsport xxxx 24.11.09
C S, C S & E S Mackenzie Perth 29.10.18P
Assembled Rotorsport UK as c/n RSUK/MTOS/019

G-CGHN Aeros Discus/Alize 017.09/003 21.12.09
R Simpson & N Sutton (Gloucester & Ross-on-Wye)
(SSDR microlight since 05.14) (NF 09.02.18)

G-CGHR Ace Aviation Magic/Laser AM147 02.12.09
N P Power (Eastbourne)
Assembled P&M Aviation Ltd; trike s/n AM147 & wing
s/n AL147 (SSDR microlight since 05.14) (IE 15.08.17)

G-CGHT Dyn'Aéro MCR-01 VLA Sportster 81? 30.07.09
G-POOP R P Trives Wickenby 11.04.18P
Built by P Bondar – project PFA 301-13190

G-CGHU Hawker Hunter T.8C HABL-003149 17.02.10
XF994 Hawker Hunter Aviation Ltd RAF Scampton
As 'XF994:873' in RAF c/s; in open
store 10.16 less tail (NF 14.03.18)

G-CGHV Raj Hamsa X'Air Hawk 1088 17.09.09
(F-....), G-CGHV H Adams
Benston Farm, New Cumnock 25.07.18P
Built by A Hipkin – project PFA 340-14721

G-CGHW Czech Sport Sportcruiser 09SC290 10.03.10
Sportcruiser 290 Ltd Wycombe Air Park 21.08.17W

G-CGHZ P&M QuikR 8477 08.09.09
J Rockey (Marldon, Devon) 31.05.18P

G-CGIA Paramania Action/Adventure 4291442 13.11.09
A E C Phillips (Hereford)
Built by Reflex Wings Ltd; Adventure trike unit, but
reported as Nirvana, shared with G-CGIN
(SSDR microlight since 05.14) (IE 07.11.16)

G-CGIB Ace Aviation Magic/Cyclone xxxx 03.12.09
S B Walters (Northampton)
Trike s/n not known & wing s/n AC-144
(SSDR microlight since 05.14) (IE 30.03.16)

G-CGIC AutoGyro MTOsport 10 017S 25.03.10
J Harmon Popham 15.05.18P
Assembled Rotorsport UK as c/n RSUK/MTOS/024

G-CGID Piper PA-31-350 Chieftain 31-7652083 24.11.09
PH-MRE, SE-GNI, N9663N T Michaels Thruxton 14.05.16E
(IE 01.12.17)

G-CGIE Flylight Dragonfly/Aeros Combat 12T 051 04.12.09
N S Brayn Clench Common
Aeros wing s/n 427
(SSDR microlight since 05.14) (IE 19.07.17)

G-CGIF Flylight Dragonfly 045 08.12.09
R D Leigh Darley Moor
(SSDR microlight since 05.14) (IE 10.08.15)

G-CGIG Lindstrand LBL 90A 1280 19.11.09
M R Stokoe Tatsfield, Westerham
'www.flymehome.org.uk' 31.05.18E

G-CGIH Cameron C-90 11359 10.02.10
A & P Gunning-Stevenson Bucknell 06.06.19E

G-CGIK Isaacs Spitfire xxxx 10.12.09
S J Cowley (Hawbridge, Worcester)
Built by C S Robbins – project PFA 27-12065;
as 'EN961:SD-X' in RAF c/s (NF 13.02.18)

G-CGIL CZAW Sportcruiser 700293 09.12.09
T Sheridan tr G-CGIL Group North Weald 12.09.19P
Built by G N Smith – project LAA 338-14856

G-CGIM Ace Aviation Magic/Laser AM145 16.12.09
C Royle Arclid Green, Sandbach
Assembled P&M Aviation Ltd; trike s/n AM145 &
wing s/n AL149 (original s/n AL-146 damaged);
parts used in rebuild of C-CFZT
(SSDR microlight since 05.14) (IE 26.04.15)

G-CGIN Paramania Action GT/Advenure 0307199 13.11.09
A E C Phillips (Hereford)
Built by Reflex Wings Ltd; Nirvana trike shared
with G-CGIA
(SSDR microlight since 05.14) (IE 16.08.17)

G-CGIO Medway Clipper-100 010110 21.12.09
J P Eden tr G-CGIO Syndicate Eshott 30.04.18P
Medway Executive fuselage, three-foot
shorter wing & dropped tips; carried 'G-68'
on tests as Clipper conversion

G-CGIP CZAW Sportcruiser 09SC312 10.12.09
J Greenhalgh Sleap 08.07.18P
Built by R Vincent – project LAA 338-14947

G-CGIR Remos GX 366 16.04.10
L R Marks & J A Pereira Solent 26.07.19W

G-CGIV Kolb Firefly FF09-1-00064 04.01.10
W A Emmerson Causey Park, Morpeth
Built by W A Emmerson
(SSDR microlight since 05.14) (IE 28.03.17)

G-CGIX AutoGyro MTOsport xxxx 23.03.10
J W G Andrews (Welwyn) 13.09.18P
Assembled Rotorsport UK as c/n RSUK/MTOS/026

G-CGIY Piper J-3C-65 Cub 11535 18.01.10
HB-OBP, 43-30244 R C Cummings Retford Gamston 18.04.18E
Fuselage No.11360; as '330244:46-C' in USAAC c/s

G-CGIZ Flight Design CTSW   D.09-12-08   18.03.10
J Hilton   Manchester Barton   29.03.18P
Assembled P&M Aviation Ltd as c/n 8512

G-CGJB Schempp-Hirth Duo Discus XLT   193/569   09.02.09
BGA 5332/KSP G J Basey Pocklington *'GJB'*   20.03.18E

G-CGJC AutoGyro MTOsport   xxxx   20.04.10
J C Collingwood Rochester   31.08.17P
Assembled Rotorsport UK as c/n RSUK/MTOS/029

G-CGJE Supermarine 361 Spitfire LF.IXe   CBAF 9746   26.01.10
RK858 Historic Flying Ltd Duxford
Built by Castle Bromwich 1943; noted 10.18
as 'RK858' on restoration (NF 16.05.18)

G-CGJF Airdrome ¾ Fokker E.III replica   GS-102   19.01.10
E Paterson (Whepstead, Bury St Edmunds)
Built by I Brewster using Grass Strip Aviation kit
s/n GS-102; as 'E37/15' in German Army Air Service
c/s (SSDR microlight since 05.14) (NF 26.04.18)

G-CGJJ P&M QuikR   8507   07.12.09
A J Hubbard tr Juliet Juliet Group (Stoke Albany)   02.07.17P
New wing married to Trike ex G-TEEE

G-CGJL CZAW Sportcruiser   OC4227   27.01.10
S Catalano Wolverhampton Halfpenny Green   24.08.18P
Built by R V Bowles & D Crutchlow
– project PFA 338-14686

G-CGJM Best Off Skyranger Swift 912S(1)   SKRxxxx972 11.11.09
J Pye (Maidstone)   05.07.19P
Built by J P Metcalfe – project BMAA/HB/594; kit no
conflicts with Best Off Skyranger OH-U577 c/n 972

G-CGJN Van's RV-7   73185   01.06.10
LY-AUU E K Coventry
Little Bassetts Farm, Childerditch   24.07.18P

G-CGJP Van's RV-10   40655   04.02.10
A J Macfarlane tr G-CGIP Group (Frimley, Camberley) 12.10.18P
Built by J French & F Morris – project PFA 339-14600

G-CGJS CZAW Sportcruiser   09SC330   29.01.10
J M Tiley Maypole Farm, Chislet   24.04.18P
Built by J M Tiley – project LAA 338-14962

G-CGJT CZAW Sportcruiser   700956   10.11.09
D F Toller Derby   03.07.18P
Built by D F Toller – project LAA 338-14911

G-CGJW Rotary Air Force RAF 2000 GTX-SE H2-05-16-646 28.09.09
J J Woollen (Huby, York)   15.04.13P
Built by J J Woollen – project PFA G/13-1367
(NF 28.03.17)

G-CGJX Westland SA.341B Gazelle AH.1   1165   23.11.10
XW892 The Gazelle Squadron Display Team Ltd
Bourne Park, Hurstbourne Tarrant
As 'XW892' (NF 15.01.15)

G-CGJZ Westland SA.341D Gazelle HT.3   1735   17.02.10
XZ933 The Gazelle Squadron Display Team Ltd
Bourne Park, Hurstbourne Tarrant
Hybrid with boom ex XZ936; stored unmarked
in primer 2016 (NF 15.01.15)

G-CGKD Grob G115E Tutor   82304/E   02.09.09
Babcock Aerospace Ltd RAF Benson *'KD'*   01.09.19E
Operated by Oxford University Air Squadron

G-CGKE Grob G115E Tutor   82305/E   03.09.09
Babcock Aerospace Ltd Glasgow *'KE'*   02.09.19E
Operated by Universities of Glasgow & Strathclyde
Air Squadron

G-CGKG Grob G115E Tutor   82307/E   04.09.09
Babcock Aerospace Ltd RAF Benson *'KG'*   03.09.19E
Operated by Oxford University Air Squadron

G-CGKH Grob G115E Tutor   82308/E   23.09.09
Babcock Aerospace Ltd RAF Benson *'KH'*   19.09.19E
Operated by Oxford University Air Squadron

G-CGKK Grob G115E Tutor   82311/E   14.10.09
Babcock Aerospace Ltd RAF Benson *'KK'*   13.10.19E
Operated by Oxford University Air Squadron

G-CGKL Grob G115E Tutor   82312/E   14.10.09
Babcock Aerospace Ltd RAF Benson *'KL'*   16.10.19E
Operated by Oxford University Air Squadron

G-CGKN Grob G115E Tutor   82314/E   27.10.09
Babcock Aerospace Ltd RAF Benson *'KN'*   09.10.19E
Operated by Oxford University Air Squadron

G-CGKP Grob G115E Tutor   82316/E   11.11.09
Babcock Aerospace Ltd RAF Benson *'KP'*   05.11.19E
Operated by Oxford University Air Squadron

G-CGKR Grob G115E Tutor   82317/E   11.11.09
Babcock Aerospace Ltd RAF Wittering *'KR'*   03.11.19E
Operated by Cambridge University, East Midlands
Universities, University of London Air Squadrons
& 115 Squadron

G-CGKS Grob G115E Tutor   82318/E   12.11.09
Babcock Aerospace Ltd Glasgow *'KS'*   11.11.19E
Operated by Glasgow & Strathclyde Universities
Air Squadrons

G-CGKU Grob G115E Tutor   82320/E   26.11.09
Babcock Aerospace Ltd RAF Leeming   25.11.19E
Operated by Northumbrian Universities Air Squadron

G-CGKW Grob G115E Tutor   82322/E   16.12.09
Babcock Aerospace Ltd RAF Benson *'KW'*   16.12.19E
Operated by Oxford University Air Squadron

G-CGKY Cessna 182T Skylane   18282213   16.04.10
N52830 T A E Dobell Garnons Farm, Wormingford 19.11.18E

G-CGKZ Best Off Skyranger Swift 912S(1) SKR0911986 26.03.10
T Swinson Darley Moor   25.07.18P
Built by A Worthington – project BMAA/HB/596

G-CGLB Airdrome Dream Classic   SB/04   17.02.10
R D Leigh Darley Moor
Built by S J Ball
(SSDR microlight since 05.14) (IE 26.01.18)

G-CGLC Czech Sport Sportcruiser   09SC322   21.06.10
M A Ulrick Sherburn-in-Elmet   17.10.18W

G-CGLE Flylight Dragonfly   053   08.04.10
B Skelding Darley Moor
(SSDR microlight since 05.14) (IE 20.07.17)

G-CGLF Magni M16C Tandem Trainer   16095614   12.04.10
J S Walton (Rednal)   29.07.19P

G-CGLG P&M Quik GT450   8527   19.03.10
P H Evans (Warrington)   25.06.18P

G-CGLI Alpi Pioneer 200-M   271 ?   28.02.10
B A Lyford Watchford Farm, Yarcombe   20.11.18P
Built by B A Lyford – project LAA 334-14919

G-CGLJ TL 2000UK Sting Carbon   9   01.10.09
L A James Wharf Farm, Market Bosworth   11.11.18P
Built by L A James – project LAA 347-14794

G-CGLK Magni M16C Tandem Trainer   16095624   13.04.10
R M Savage Rufforth East   30.03.18P
Operated by Gyrocopter Experience

G-CGLM AutoGyro MTOsport   xxxx   04.02.10
D S T Harris Carlisle Lake District   19.04.18P
Assembled Rotorsport UK as c/n RSUK/MTOS/020

G-CGLN Avtech Jabiru J430   309   08.04.10
A J Thomas Wolverhampton Halfpenny Green 06.08.18P
Built by J R Frohnsdorff & C H K Hood
– project LAA 336-14974

G-CGLO P&M QuikR   8508   28.01.10
R H Lowndes Deenethorpe   26.02.18P

G-CGLP CZAW Sportcruiser   700391   31.03.10
P S Tanner Lydeway Field, Etchilhampton   19.04.18P
Built by P A Cruttenden & P J Reilly
– project LAA 338-14846 (Quick build kit)

G-CGLR Czech Sport Sportcruiser   09SC324   04.06.10
J L R Nichols tr G-CGLR Group
Lower Upham Farm, Chiseldon   08.10.18W

G-CGLT Czech Sport Sportcruiser   09SC329   14.06.10
I Jalowiecki Turweston   24.05.18W

G-CGLY AutoGyro Calidus   10 058   29.06.10
R J Steel Rufforth East   19.04.18P
Assembled Rotorsport UK as c/n RSUK/CALS/012

G-CGLZ TL 2000UK Sting Carbon   08 ST 290   14.01.10
J R Hughes tr Newtownards Microlight Group
(Newtownards)   10.03.18P
Built by D Nieman – project LAA 347-14910

G-CGMA Ace Aviation Magic/Laser   AM144   15.03.10
J N Hanson Rossall Field, Cockerham
Trike s/n AM144 & wing s/n AL144
(SSDR microlight since 05.14) (NF 08.09.17)

G-CGMD	AutoGyro Calidus	xxxx	29.06.10
	W H Morgan RAF Mona		10.09.18P
	Assembled Rotorsport UK as c/n RSUK/CALS/015		
G-CGMG	Van's RV-9	91254	13.04.10
	D J Bone Spite Hall Farm, Pinchinthorpe		17.04.18P
	Built by D J Bone – project PFA 320-14488		
G-CGMH	Jodel D.150A Mascaret	5	24.02.10
	F-BLDC M Hales North Coates		13.08.19P
	Built by Société Aéronautique Normande		
G-CGMI	P&M Quik GT450	8532	02.06.10
	W G Reynolds Ivy Farm, Overstrand		01.06.18P
G-CGML	TL 2000UK Sting Carbon	10	12.10.09
	G T Leedham Grangewood, Netherseal		11.11.18P
	Built by G T Leedham – project LAA 347-14796;		
	badged 'Sting Sport'		
G-CGMM	CZAW Sportcruiser	700891	07.04.10
	M Ferid tr TAF & Co Stoneacre Farm, Farthing Corner		15.11.17P
	Built by M Ferid – project LAA 338-14934		
G-CGMN	Best Off Skyranger Swift 912S(1)	SKR0812927	05.05.10
	M Shea tr G-CGMN Flying Group (Lichfield)		11.01.20P
	Built by T C Butterworth – project BMAA/HB/593		
G-CGMO	Ace Aviation Magic/Laser	AM146	19.04.10
	G J Latham (Sandilands, Lanark)		
	Trike s/n AM146 & wing s/n AL145		
	(SSDR microlight since 05.14) (IE 09.08.18)		
G-CGMP	CZAW Sportcruiser	09SC313	11.02.10
	R Hasler Biggin Hill		16.09.18P
	Built by M Payne – project LAA 338-14948		
G-CGMR	Colt Bibendum-110	4224	20.04.10
	G-GRIP T Read & N Smith		
	t/a Mobberley Balloon Collection Knutsford & Goole		25.01.02A
	(NF 21.03.14)		
G-CGMV	Roko Aero NG4-HD	031/2010	16.06.10
	S Oakley & D Simpson tr Roko NG4		
	Charlton Park, Malmesbury		20.12.17W
G-CGMW	Alpi Pioneer 200-M	291	04.05.10
	M S McCrudden Newtownards		29.11.17P
	Built by M S McCrudden – project LAA 334-14958		
G-CGMZ	P&M QuikR	8513	19.03.10
	T J Heaton Knapthorpe Lodge, Caunton		10.07.19P
G-CGNC	AutoGyro MTOsport	10 074S	24.06.10
	Bath Leasing & Supplies Ltd Avon Farm, Saltford		11.05.18P
	Assembled Rotorsport UK as c/n RSUK/MTOS/035		
G-CGNE	Robinson R44 Raven II	12952	10.05.10
	Heli Air Ltd Wycombe Air Park		24.05.18E
G-CGNG	CZAW Sportcruiser	4021	14.05.10
	H M Wooldridge Eshott		13.12.18P
	Built by T Dounias – project PFA 338-14659		
G-CGNH	Reality Escapade Jabiru(3)	UK.ESC.0001	02.06.10
	J M Ingram Over Farm, Gloucester		01.09.18P
	Built by A H Paul – project BMAA/HB/462; tailwheel u/c		
G-CGNI	Comco Ikarus C42 FB80	1005-7108	13.07.10
	S Conlon Carrickmore		25.07.18P
	Assembled Pioneer Aviation UK Ltd		
G-CGNJ	Cameron Z-105	11261	04.08.10
	A Parsons tr Loughborough Students Union		
	Hot Air Balloon Club Loughborough		
	'Loughborough University'		12.06.19E
G-CGNK	P&M Quik GT450	8536	29.06.10
	Mid Anglia Microlights Ltd Beccles		30.06.19P
G-CGNM	Magni M16C Tandem Trainer	16105824	05.07.10
	Evolo Ltd (Reading)		16.10.17P
G-CGNO	P&M Quik GT450	8522	08.10.10
	J W Thurstan (Cutthorpe, Chesterfield)		04.04.19P
G-CGNS	Sky 65-24	058	05.07.10
	HB-QDB R L Bovell		
	Sunninghill, Johannesburg, South Africa		20.07.18E
G-CGNV	Reality Escapade	JA.ESC.0165	29.06.10
	P M Noonan Headcorn		22.05.18P
	Built by M J Whatley – project LAA 345-14901		
G-CGNW	Scheibe SF25C Falke 2000	44615	02.07.10
	OY-XZY, D-KTIW J W Sage tr Army Gliding		
	Association Trenchard Lines, Upavon		25.11.18E

G-CGNX	AutoGyro MTOsport	xxxx	29.06.10
	L McCallum Kilkerran		14.06.19P
	Assembled Rotorsport UK as c/n RSUK/MTOS/036		
G-CGNZ	Europa Aviation Europa XS	A190	14.07.10
	PH-XXS R Vianello (Guildford)		18.12.17P
	Built by A H Van Den Berg		
G-CGOA	Cessna 550 Citation II	550-0183	13.05.10
	G-JMDW, HB-VGS, (XC-DUF), N98630		
	XJC Ltd Southampton		29.01.19E
G-CGOB	P&M QuikR	8517	19.03.10
	P & M Aviation Ltd Elm Tree Park, Manton		16.07.14P
	Official c/n refers to QuikR Wing; trike to G-CIPA,		
	wing sold as spare (IE 20.01.17)		
G-CGOD	Cameron N-77	2647	05.09.91
	Trinity Balloons CIC Tavistock		30.03.17E
G-CGOG	Evektor EV-97A Eurostar	xxxx	13.04.10
	D C & S G Emmons Whittles, Mapledurham		
	'Slightly Dangerous 2'		28.08.19P
	Built by J S Holden – project LAA 315A-14980		
G-CGOH	Cameron C-80	11447	05.08.10
	Cameron Balloons Ltd Bristol *'King Sturge'*		12.04.12E
	(IE 17.07.15)		
G-CGOI	Stewart S-51D	144	09.08.10
	N51HW K E Armstrong White Fen Farm, Benwick		07.10.15P
	Built by S L Owens; as '413926:E2-S' in USAF		
	c/s 'Lil Darlin'; extensively damaged 02.08.15		
	on take-off at Benwick		
G-CGOJ	Jodel D.11	1841	08.07.10
	J Laszlo Perth		13.11.18P
	Built by J A Macleod – project PFA 052-14400		
G-CGOK	Ace Aviation Magic/Cyclone	AM149	28.05.10
	T H Lee (Sittingbourne)		
	Trike s/n AM149 & Wing s/n AC-146 (IE 04.10.18)		
G-CGOL	Avtech Jabiru J430	715	18.02.10
	J F Woodham Finmere		14.06.18P
	Built by J V Sanders – project LAA 336-14959		
G-CGOM	Flight Design MC	A.10-04-31	07.01.11
	G A Evans & C W Thompson Ince		04.10.18W
	Assembled P&M Aviation Ltd		
G-CGOR	Jodel D.18	337	26.04.10
	R D Cook (Fair Oak, Eastleigh)		
	Built by R D Cook – project PFA 169-12062 (NF 30.04.18)		
G-CGOS	Piper PA-28-161 Warrior III	2842345	21.05.10
	N6105T S H B Smith Perth		05.06.18E
G-CGOT	AutoGyro Calidus	10 056	28.06.10
	P Slater (Kirkby-in-Ashfield, Nottingham)		18.04.18P
	Assembled Rotorsport UK as c/n RSUK/CALS/008		
G-CGOU	Sikorsky S-76C++	760780	15.07.10
	N20868 Bristow Helicopters Ltd Norwich Int'l		27.10.18E
	Built by Keystone Helicopter Corpn		
G-CGOV	Raj Hamsa X'Air Falcon 582(2)	1000	19.07.10
	L Fee Old Park Farm, Margam		02.05.19P
	Built by A Hipkin – project BMAA/HB/599		
G-CGOW	Cameron Z-77	11366	17.08.10
	J F Till Welburn, York		10.07.18E
G-CGOX	Raj Hamsa X'Air Hawk	1227	28.07.10
	W B Russell (Braehead, Forth)		09.06.18P
	Built by B K Harrison – project LAA 340-14993		
G-CGOZ	Cameron GB-1000	11387	14.05.10
	Cameron Balloons Ltd Bristol BS3		02.10.19E
G-CGPA	Ace Aviation Magic/Cyclone	xxxx	23.07.10
	A Williams (Perth)		
	Trike s/n not known & Wing s/n AC-149		
	(SSDR microlight since 05.14) (IE 30.09.15)		
G-CGPB	Magni M24C Orion	24105964	30.07.10
	D Beevers Melrose Farm, Melbourne		08.02.18P
G-CGPC	P&M Pegasus Quik	8544	27.08.10
	E McCallum & D W Watson		
	Athey's Moor, Longframlington		04.03.18P
G-CGPD	Ultramagic S-90	90/110	04.08.10
	S J Farrant Hydestile, Godalming		01.03.18E
G-CGPE	P&M Quik GT450	8542	12.08.10
	E H Gatehouse Pound Green		24.05.18P

G

G-CGPF	Flylight Dragonfly	058	06.08.10
	R G Morris (Ammanford)		
	(SSDR microlight since 05.14) (IE 16.05.16)		
G-CGPG	AutoGyro MTOsport	xxxx	11.05.10
	E Barnes Rochester		03.07.18P
	Assembled Rotorsport UK as c/n RSUK/MTOS/032		
G-CGPH	Ultramagic S-50	50/02	05.08.10
	C D Harding Farnham *'The Packhouse'*		09.09.18E
G-CGPJ	Robin DR.400-140 Earl	957	04.11.10
	F-BVMD W H Cole & P Dass		
	Spilsted Farm, Sedlescombe		14.02.18E
G-CGPK	AutoGyro MT-03	xxxx	17.08.10
	G-RIFS K Blundred tr Ellis Flying Group (Basingstoke)		04.04.18P
	Assembled Rotorsport UK as c/n RSUK/MT-03/020		
G-CGPL	Sonex Sonex	xxxx	25.08.10
	P C Askew Blackpool *'Mya Rose'*		23.10.17P
	Built by P C Askew – project LAA 337-14775		
G-CGPN	SOCATA MS.880B Rallye Club	2429	02.09.10
	F-OCVK, EI-BFR, G-CGPN, (EI-...)		
	J Fingleton Limetree, Portarlington, RoI		12.06.18E
G-CGPO	TL 2000UK Sting Carbon	08 ST 292	02.09.10
	N A Quintin Henstridge		18.08.19P
	Built by G A Squires – project LAA 347-14896		
G-CGPR	Czech Sport PiperSport	P1001043	09.08.10
	J T Langford Audley End		15.05.18W
G-CGPS	Evektor EV-97 Eurostar SL	2010-3725	14.05.10
	P R Jenson & R A Morris Sittles Farm, Alrewas		17.10.18P
	Built by P R Jenson & R A Morris		
	– project LAA 315B-14987		
G-CGPW	Raj Hamsa X'Air Hawk	1214	28.09.10
	G J Langston Otherton		25.07.18P
	Built by K Worthington – project LAA 340-15000		
G-CGPX	Zenair CH.601XL Zodiac	6-9587	27.09.10
	A James Shenstone Hall Farm, Shenstone		27.09.17P
	Built by A James – project PFA 162B-14395; tricycle u/c		
G-CGPY	Boeing Stearman A75L300 Kaydet *(N2S-5)*	75-5303	06.01.11
	N75671, USN 61181, 42-17140		
	M P Dentith Gloucestershire		02.04.18E
	As 'VN2S-5:671' in US Navy c/s		
G-CGPZ	Rans S-4 Coyote	407.329	08.10.10
	G J Jones Gransden Lodge		
	Built by C Saunders – project PFA 193-14625		
	(SSDR microlight since 06.14) (IE 23.10.17)		
G-CGRB	Flight Design CTLS	F.10-07-10	26.08.10
	L K Wright tr The Romeo Bravo Group		
	(Worsley, Manchester)		23.03.18W
	Assembled P&M Aviation Ltd		
G-CGRC	P&M QuikR	8459	15.07.09
	R J Cook Cumbernauld		31.10.18P
G-CGRJ	Carnet Paramotor	001	01.10.10
	M Carnet (Liss)		
	(SSDR microlight since 05.14) (IE 16.12.14)		
G-CGRM	Supermarine 329 Spitfire IIA	CBAF 534	18.10.10
	P8088 M R Oliver (Hale, Altrincham)		
	Carries 'NK-K', 'Bette' & 'The Borough of Lambeth'		
	on cockpit (NF 22.10.16)		
G-CGRN	Pazmany PL-4A	xxxx	21.10.10
	G Hudson (Camberley)		
	Built by G Hudson – project PFA 017-14194		
	(NF 19.09.14)		
G-CGRR	P&M Pegasus Quik	8541	23.07.10
	C R Chapman (Faversham)		20.04.19P
G-CGRS	P&M Pegasus Quik	8529	19.05.10
	J Crosby Perth		23.03.18P
G-CGRV	DG Flugzeugbau DG-1000M	10-156M6	26.09.11
	D-KSJH BR Aviation Ltd Bognor Regis *'RV'*		09.04.18E
G-CGRW	P&M Pegasus Quik	8549	13.10.10
	P M Coppola East Fortune		23.08.18P
G-CGRX	Reims/Cessna F172N	F17201524	29.10.10
	LN-AST J & R Woods Redhill		20.09.19E
G-CGRY	Magni M24C Orion	24106134	03.12.10
	Pollards Wholesale Ltd Rufforth East		06.06.18P
G-CGRZ	Magni M24C Orion	24106004	04.11.10
	C-More Flying School Ltd Carrickmore		24.11.18P
G-CGSA	Flylight Dragonfly	060	15.10.10
	G Sykes (Holmfirth)		
	(SSDR microlight since 05.14) (IE 18.07.16)		
G-CGSC	BFC Challenger II	CH2-0394-UK-1120	12.11.10
	L Gregory (Walsall)		
	Built by L Gregory – project PFA 177-12715		
	(BFC kit) (NF 04.01.19)		
G-CGSD	Magni M16C Tandem Trainer	16106084	08.12.10
	The Gyrocopter Company UK Ltd Rufforth East		06.06.18P
G-CGSG	Cessna 421C Golden Eagle	421C1055	30.03.11
	D-IIAS, HB-LQH, N67979		
	J R Shannon Gloucestershire		23.01.19E
G-CGSH	Evektor EV-97 teamEurostar UK	3604	13.10.10
	D B Medland Bagby		08.08.18P
	Assembled Cosmik Aviation Ltd		
G-CGSI	Zenair CH.601HDS Zodiac	6-8019	08.12.10
	E McHugh (Stokesley, Middlesbrough)		
	Built by E McHugh – project PFA 162-12937		
	(NF 17.10.14)		
G-CGSJ	Bombardier BD-700-1A10 Global Express XRS		
		9377	03.12.10
	(G-HVLD), C-FYNI Abbeville Holdings Ltd Guernsey		04.12.18E
G-CGSO	P&M Quik GT450	8540	23.07.10
	Light Vending Ltd Moss Edge Farm, Cockerham		05.06.18P
G-CGSP	Cessna 152	15282543	13.04.11
	OY-SUK, TF-FTG, N69194		
	H E da Costa Alburquerque (Amadora, Portugal)		13.08.19E
G-CGSW	Flylight MotorFloater	MF01	07.12.10
	R D Leigh Darley Moor		
	(SSDR microlight since 05.14) (IE 30.04.15)		
G-CGSX	Aeroprakt A-22L Foxbat	xxxx	23.12.10
	P J V Dibble Ossemsley, New Milton		28.08.19P
	Built by P J Trimble – project LAA 317A-15001;		
	active from Ossemsley, New Milton, 02.19		
G-CGSZ	Schempp-Hirth Ventus-2cM	245	28.02.11
	D B Smith (Sulby, Isle of Man)		01.04.18E
G-CGTC	Britten-Norman BN-2T-4S Islander	4019	29.11.10
	Police Service of Northern Ireland Belfast Int'l		30.05.18E
	Operated by PSNI Air Support Unit as callsign 'Scout 1'		
G-CGTD	Evektor EV-97 teamEurostar UK	3920	02.02.11
	R J Butler Ashcroft		09.02.18P
	Assembled Cosmik Aviation Ltd		
G-CGTE	Brandli BX-2 Cherry	198	01.12.10
	D Roberts Croft Farm, Defford		19.06.19P
	Built by D Roberts – project PFA 179-13386		
G-CGTF	AutoGyro MT-03	xxxx	24.02.11
	N R Osborne Perth		18.05.18P
	Assembled Rotorsport UK as c/n RSUK/MT-03/054		
G-CGTJ	Eurocopter AS.332L2 Super Puma II	2488	31.01.11
	5N-BNU, G-CGTJ, LN-ONH, F-WQDD		
	Airbus Helicopters Marseille, France		19.01.12E
	(NF 05.05.15)		
G-CGTK	Magni M24C Orion	24116214	11.03.11
	S Brogden Rufforth East		11.04.18P
G-CGTL	Alpi Pioneer 300	311	19.01.11
	M S Ashby Halwell		02.07.18P
	Built by M S Ashby – project LAA 330A-15038		
G-CGTM	Cessna 172S Skyhawk SP	172S9597	04.04.11
	N597FA G Price t/a Skytrek Air Services Rochester		17.04.19E
G-CGTR	Best Off Skyranger Nynja 912S(1)	1009059	16.03.11
	M Jenvey (London N7)		30.07.18P
	Built by T J Newton – project BMAA/HB/608;		
	officially registered as c/n UK\N/BK59		
G-CGTS	Cameron A-140	11498	20.12.10
	A A Brown Worplesdon, Guildford		17.01.18E
G-CGTT	Evektor EV-97 Eurostar SL	3726	31.08.10
	D L Walker Deanland		12.04.18P
	Built by D L Walker – project LAA 315B-14985		
G-CGTU	P&M Quik GT450	8574	06.04.11
	I G R Christie East Fortune		27.07.18P

G

G-CGTV	ICP MXP-740 Savannah VG Jabiru(1)	10-12-51-928	21.03.11
	R Thompson Beverley (Linley Hill)		25.08.19P
	Built by B L Cook & P Etherington		
	– project BMAA/HB/609		

G-CGTW	Flylight MotorFloater	MF002	09.06.11
	S J Varden Rossall Field, Cockerham		
	(IE 26.05.17)		
	(SSDR microlight since 05.14)		

G-CGTX	CASA 1-131E Jungmann Series 2000	2214	25.03.11
	Spanish AF E3B-599		
	G Hunter & T A S Rayner Archerfield		24.07.18P
	As 'E3B-599:791-31' in Spanish Air Force c/s		

G-CGTY	Cameron Z-250	11516	25.05.11
	Airxcite Ltd t/a Virgin Balloon Flights		
	Stafford Park, Telford 'Abercrombie & Kent'		19.05.17E
	(NF 26.07.17)		

G-CGTZ	Escapade Kid	ESC.AW.KID.002	03.11.10
	P D Neilson (Ashbourne, Derby)		
	(SSDR microlight since 05.14) (IE 02.07.17)		

G-CGUD	Lindstrand LBL 77A	1329	14.03.11
	I J Sharpe Caterham		18.04.18E

G-CGUE	Aeroprakt A-22L Foxbat	xxxx	03.02.11
	A T Hayward Mill Farm, Hughley		17.05.18P
	Built by A T Hayward – project LAA 317A-15039		

G-CGUG	P&M QuikR	8557	23.12.10
	J D Lawrance Bourn		05.01.18P

G-CGUI^M	Clutton FRED Series II	xxxx	09.02.11
	I Pearson Newquay Cornwall		11.08.16P
	Built by I Pearson – project PFA 029-10882;		
	on display Cornwall Aviation Heritage Centre 08.18		

G-CGUK	Supermarine 300 Spitfire I	6S-75531	10.02.11
	X4650 Comanche Warbirds Ltd Duxford		15.05.19P
	As 'X4650:KL:A' in RAF c/s		

G-CGUO	de Havilland DH.83C Fox Moth	FM50	11.05.11
	ZK-AQM Airtime Aerobatics Ltd Hill Farm, Durley		
	On rebuild 06.16 (NF 09.02.16)		

G-CGUP	P&M Quik GT450	8565	22.02.11
	D J Allen Redlands		12.05.16P

G-CGUR	P&M QuikR	8572	30.03.11
	M J Williams Deenethorpe		19.04.18P

G-CGUU	Best Off Skyranger Nynja 912S(1)	1009061	14.02.11
	J A Hunt (Clydach, Abergavenny)		11.07.19P
	Built by J A Hunt – project BMAA/HB/605;		
	officially regd as c/n UK\W/BK61		

G-CGUW	Tecnam P2002-EA Sierra	383	15.03.11
	D J Burton Deanland		28.04.18P
	Built by D J Burton – project LAA 333-14952		

G-CGUY	AutoGyro Calidus	xxxx	10.03.11
	R F Harrison Tatenhill		04.05.18P
	Assembled Rotorsport UK as c/n RSUK/CALS/017		

G-CGVA	Aeroprakt A-22L Foxbat	A22L-216	07.01.11
	M E Gilman Arclid Green, Sandbach		11.09.18P
	Built by T R C Griffin – project PFA 317A-14734		

G-CGVC	Piper PA-28-181 Archer III	2843669	30.03.11
	OK-INT, N6003F Western Air (Thruxton) Ltd Thruxton		20.04.18E

G-CGVD	Van's RV-12	120339	30.03.11
	A D Heath Swansea		01.07.19P
	Built by I J M Donnelly – project LAA 363-15005		

G-CGVE	Raj Hamsa X'Air Hawk	1246	23.03.11
	D J Baird Fenland		29.08.18P
	Built by K Worthington – project LAA 340-15069		

G-CGVG	Flight Design CTSW	D.09-12-07	12.01.11
	B Cook Hunsdon		13.08.18P
	Assembled P&M Aviation Ltd as c/n 8575		

G-CGVH	Flylight MotorFloater	MF003	26.04.11
	P F Mayes Shifnal		
	(SSDR microlight since 05.14) (IE 27.04.17)		

G-CGVJ	Europa Aviation Europa XS	xxxx	11.04.11
	D Glowa Sherburn-in-Elmet		04.02.18P
	Built by D Glowa – project PFA 247-13752		

G-CGVK	AutoGyro Calidus	C00148	09.06.11
	B & H Mouldings Ltd Manchester Barton		11.06.18P
	Assembled Rotorsport UK as c/n RSUK/CALS/018		

G-CGVP	Evektor EV-97 Eurostar	2010-3927	14.03.11
	G R Pritchard New House Farm, Hardwicke		14.05.18P
	Built by G R Pritchard – project LAA 315-15047		

G-CGVS	Raj Hamsa X'Air Hawk	1245	18.04.11
	D Matthews (Great Ellingham, Norfolk)		27.06.18P
	Built by J Anderson – project LAA 340-15073		

G-CGVT	Evektor EV-97 teamEurostar UK	2010-3402	16.02.11
	Mainair Microlight School Ltd Manchester Barton		09.03.18P
	Assembled Cosmik Aviation Ltd		

G-CGVV	Cameron Z-90	11386	26.11.10
	John Aimo Balloons SAS Bristol BS3		
	'Cameron Balloons'		07.08.19E

G-CGVX	Europa Aviation Europa	90	09.05.11
	M P Sambrook Wycombe Air Park		20.04.18P
	Built by M P Sambrook – project PFA 247-12719		

G-CGVY	Cameron Z-77	11474	22.06.11
	M P Hill Flax Bourton, Bristol		21.06.18E

G-CGVZ	Zenair CH.601XL Zodiac	6-7358	27.01.11
	K A Dilks Leicester		29.11.18P
	Built by K A Dilks – project LAA 162B-14990; tricycle u/c		

G-CGWA	Comco Ikarus C42 FB80 Bravo	1103-7139	18.05.11
	C Williams (Tonypandy)		13.07.19P
	Assembled Performance Aviation Ltd		

G-CGWC	Ultramagic H-31	31/12	10.03.11
	K Dodman Lowestoft 'Webroot'		07.07.18E

G-CGWD	Robinson R44 Raven I	1695	23.03.07
	J M Potter Sherburn-in-Elmet		12.04.18E
	Operated by Hields Aviation		

G-CGWE	Evektor EV-97A Eurostar	2010-3929	17.01.11
	W S Long Mayfield Farm, Stevenston		09.04.18P
	Built by W S Long – project LAA 315A-15045		

G-CGWF	Van's RV-7	70435	12.05.11
	N3261F M S Hill Crosland Moor		29.11.18P
	Built by J J Bilak		

G-CGWG	Van's RV-7	72168	31.03.11
	G Waters Swansea		25.01.18P
	Built by G Waters – project PFA 323-14486		

G-CGWH	CZAW Sportcruiser	xxxx	11.05.11
	N G & R E Nicholson		
	Moorlands Farm, Farway Common		04.09.18P
	Built by P J F Spedding – project LAA 388-14826		

G-CGWI	Super Marine Spitfire Mk.26	036	13.05.11
	VH-IJH Bertha Property LLP Perth		24.11.16P
	Built by P J Hanbury & P I J Hutchison;		
	as 'BL927:JH-I' in RAF c/s (IE 14.09.17)		

G-CGWK	Comco Ikarus C42 FB80	1103-7133	13.04.11
	B H Goldsmith Clench Common		03.07.19P
	Assembled Performance Aviation Ltd		

G-CGWM	Flylight MotorFloater	MF004	24.03.11
	P A Gardner (Condover, Shrewsbury)		
	(SSDR microlight since 05.14) (IE 26.08.15)		

G-CGWN	Flylight MotorFloater	MF005	24.03.11
	J Williams (Darlton, Newark)		
	(SSDR microlight since 05.14) (IE 14.12.17)		

G-CGWO	Tecnam P2002-JF Sierra	168	26.05.11
	Shropshire Aero Club Ltd Sleap		16.06.18E

G-CGWP	Aeroprakt A-22L Foxbat	xxxx	24.03.11
	P K Goff Old Warden		20.08.19P
	Built by P K Goff – project LAA 317A-15070		

G-CGWR	Nord NC.856A Norvigie	54	02.11.11
	F-BMHS, French Army F-MAOM R Ellingworth Spanhoe		
	As '54:AOM' in French ALAT c/s & insignia (IE 04.04.18)		

G-CGWS	Raj Hamsa X'Air Hawk	1231	13.05.11
	I S McNulty Darley Moor		16.06.16P
	Built by T Collins – project LAA 340-15025		
	(IE 02.08.17)		

G-CGWT	Best Off Skyranger Swift 912(1)	SKR0707805	18.03.11
	D Hamilton Couplaw Farm, Stonehouse		11.05.19P
	Built by P A Allwood – project BMAA/HB/567		

G-CGWU	Ultramagic S-90	90/117	24.06.11
	R P Allan & P Pruchnickyj Watlington & Chinnor		21.06.18E

G-CGWX	Cameron C-90	10856	27.06.11
	J D A Shields Hastings		27.06.18E

G-CGWZ P&M QuikR 8554 04.05.11
P J Lomax & J A Robinson   St Michaels 29.05.18P

G-CGXB Stoddard-Hamilton Glasair Super IIS RG 2228 06.04.11
P J Brion   Thruxton 01.06.18P
Built by P J Brion – project PFA 149-12459

G-CGXE P&M Quik GT450 8584 14.07.11
N G Nikolov   (Widnes) 23.10.19P

G-CGXF North Wing Stratus/Skycycle 48199/10157-11 20.06.11
I D Smith   (Westhill, Aberdeen)
*Trike also used with G-CEZN sailwing & kept
at owner's home
(SSDR microlight since 05.14) (IE 21.04.16)*

G-CGXG Yakovlev Yak-3M 0470107 26.07.11
D-FJAK, N551BH   Chameleon Technologies Ltd
Duxford 15.05.18P
*Built by OKB Yakovlev s.r.o. as Yak-3UA;
as '100' (White) of 402nd IAP [Fighter Air
Regiment], Soviet Air Force)*

G-CGXI Comco Ikarus C42 FB80 Bravo 1106-7157 22.08.11
G V Aggett   Conington 08.09.18P
Assembled Performance Aviation Ltd

G-CGXL Robin DR.400-180 Régent 2119 12.05.11
G-GLKE, F-GLKE   M F Ashton   Sturgate 30.10.18E

G-CGXN American Legend Cub F0181 08.07.11
P L Gaze   (Coldwaltham, Pulborough) 29.08.19P
*Built by D Silsbury – project LAA 373-15028;
supplied Texas Sport Aircraft Co*

G-CGXO Lindstrand LBL 105A 1234 15.07.11
Aerosaurus Balloons Ltd   Whimple, Exeter
'Aerosaurus' 03.03.18E

G-CGXP Grob G109B 6261 26.08.11
D-KAJU   S M Rathband   Enstone 23.10.17E
(IE 07.01.18)

G-CGXR Van's RV-9A xxxx 26.07.11
Solway Flyers 2010 Ltd   Carlisle Lake District 08.02.19P
Built by D J Wilson – project PFA 320-14371

G-CGXT Kovacs Midgie MID-01 15.08.11
J P Kovacs   Insch
*Built by J P Kovacs; tricycle u/c
(SSDR microlight since 05.14) (IE 25.11.16)*

G-CGXV P&M QuikR 8594 06.09.11
Flying Club Ltd   Rankins Farm, Linton 21.09.19P

G-CGXW Grob G109B 6408 06.10.11
D-KISI   I B Kennedy   Usk 01.11.18E

G-CGXX ICP MXP-740 Savannah HKS(1) 03-05-51-210 28.09.11
P Hayward   Broomclose Farm, Longbridge Deverill
Built by P Hayward – project BMAA/HB/305 (IE 05.11.15)

G-CGXY Flylight Dragonfly 062 20.07.11
A I Lea   Benson's Farm, Laindon
*Combat 12T sailwing
(SSDR microlight since 05.14) (IE 15.01.15)*

G-CGXZ AutoGyro MTOsport xxxx 28.10.11
S J Arnett tr G-CGXZ Group   Husbands Bosworth 03.08.18P
Assembled Rotorsport UK as c/n RSUK/MTOS/043

G-CGYA Stoddard-Hamilton Glasair III 1 14.09.11
N541TA   Aerocars Ltd   Manor Farm, East Garston
(NF 04.09.15)

G-CGYB Evektor EV-97 teamEurostar UK 2011-3925 20.06.11
J Waite   Plaistows Farm, St Albans 30.08.18P
Assembled Cosmik Aviation Ltd

G-CGYC Aeropro EuroFOX 912(S) 35411 19.10.11
J C Taylor   Isle of Man 21.11.17P
*Built by D C Fairbrass – project LAA 376-15100;
tricycle u/c*

G-CGYD Fairey Firefly TT.1 F6071 02.09.11
SE-BRG, DT989   Propshop Ltd   Duxford
*Fuselage noted 07.18 as 'SE-BRG' Hangar 2N;
wings noted Building 66 (NF 29.06.15)*

G-CGYF Gloster Gamecock II – 14.09.11
Finnish AF GA-43   Retro Track & Air (UK) Ltd   Cotswold
Fuselage frame stored in hangar roof 06.16 (NF 25.08.15)

G-CGYG Aeropro EuroFOX 912(S) 33911 23.05.11
Highland Gliding Club Ltd   Easterton 30.04.19P
*Built by R Cornwell – project LAA 376-15081;
tricycle u/c; glider-tug*

G-CGYH Magni M24C Orion 24116644 17.10.11
J L Ward   (Sheffield S17) 13.06.18P

G-CGYI Van's RV-12 120281 22.08.11
M J Poole   Sherburn-in-Elmet 05.06.18P
Built by E M Marsh – project LAA 363-14994

G-CGYJ Supermarine 361 Spitfire HF.IX CBAF 10492 01.11.11
SAAF 5xxx, TD314   K M Perkins   Duxford 12.02.20P
As 'TD314:FX-P' in RAF c/s

G-CGYO Van's RV-6A 24704 27.09.11
N57TK   R C Bunce, M Paterson & M Sutherland
RAF Leuchars 25.04.19P
Built by A Kirk

G-CGYP Best Off Skyranger 912(2) SKRxxxx218 28.09.11
C D Cross tr Yankee Papa Group
Osbaston Lodge Farm, Osbaston 23.02.18P
Built by M J Reeve – project BMAA/HB/242

G-CGYT Flylight Dragonfly 070 10.10.11
C R Buckle   Blackmoor Farm, Aubourn
(SSDR microlight since 05.14) (IE 02.10.15)

G-CGYW Sikorsky S-92A 920157 01.03.12
N157Q   Bristow Helicopters Ltd   Aberdeen Int'l
'Paul Richardson' 29.03.18E

G-CGYX AutoGyro Cavalon V00078 26.10.11
K Hall   Sandtoft 01.11.18P
Assembled Rotorsport UK as c/n RSUK/CVLN/001

G-CGYY ICP MXP-740 Savannah VG Jabiru(1) 10-10-51-924 30.03.11
E B Maxwell tr Carlisle Skyrangers
Carlisle Lake District 28.01.18P
Built by C Hewer – project BMAA/HB/603

G-CGYZ P&M Quik GT450 8579 02.12.11
M Florence   Rufforth 08.12.18P

G-CGZE AutoGyro MTOsport 11 099S 02.12.11
T Elliott tr Rufforth No1 Gyro Syndicate   Rufforth East 14.05.18P
Assembled Rotorsport UK as c/n RSUK/MTOS/044

G-CGZF Evektor EV-97 teamEurostar UK 2011-3928 17.01.12
B P Keating   (Sevenoaks) 26.10.18P
Assembled Cosmik Aviation Ltd

G-CGZG AutoGyro MTOsport 11 072S 28.09.11
Highland Aviation Training Ltd   Inverness 11.01.19P
Assembled Rotorsport UK as c/n RSUK/MTOS/041

G-CGZI SOCATA TB-21 Trinidad TC 2209 12.08.11
N121TR, N739TB, (N403MS)   K B Hallam   Fairoaks 02.11.18E

G-CGZJ ITV Dakota XL 2K8 43 10.11.11
C J Lines   (Scunthorpe)
(SSDR microlight since 05.14) (IE 11.01.17)

G-CGZM AutoGyro MTOsport xxxx 24.10.11
J W Cope   Strubby 17.12.19P
Assembled Rotorsport UK as c/n RSUK/MTOS/042

G-CGZN Dudek Synthesis 31/Nirvana Carbon P.06869 15.11.11
P M Jones   Damyns Hall, Upminster
(SSDR microlight since 05.14) (NF 11.06.18)

G-CGZP Curtiss P-40F Kittyhawk 19503 24.11.11
VH-PIV, 41-19841   Patina Ltd   Duxford   'Lee's hope' 13.05.19P
*As 'X-17' in USAAF c/s (as P-40F-20 'Lee's Hope'
flown 1st Lt R J Duffield – 85th FS/79th USAAF FG,
Mediterranean Theatre of Operations)*

G-CGZR Cameron Z-350 11603 27.03.12
Ballooning Network Ltd   Bristol BS3   'Bristol Balloons' 23.09.19E

G-CGZT Aeroprakt A-22L Foxbat A-22L-360 28.07.11
D Jessop   Old Manor Farm, Anwick 20.01.19P
*Built by R Stalker – project LAA 317A-15084;
badged 'Foxbat Sport'*

G-CGZU Supermarine 361 Spitfire IX CBAF 5056 06.03.12
LZ842   M A Bennett   Biggin Hill
*Built by Castle Bromwich as F.Mk.IXc; as 'LZ842:EF-F'
in RAF c/s; on restoration 01.19 (NF 28.01.16)*

G-CGZV Europa Aviation Europa XS 458 06.09.11
I M Moxon   Leicester 27.04.18P
*Built by R W Collings – project PFA 247-13563;
tricycle u/c*

G-CGZW Scheibe SF25C Falke 2000 44374 09.02.12
D-KNAY   J H Jones t/a Airborne Services Int'l
Lleweni Parc 03.04.19E

G-CGZY	Evektor EV-97 teamEurostar UK	2011-3926	01.11.11
	F A Thompson & K J Ward Plaistows Farm, St Albans		31.10.18P
	Assembled Cosmik Aviation Ltd		

G-CGZZ	Kubícek BB22E	855	08.06.11
	A M Holly Breadstone, Berkeley *'Sky Arts HD'*		06.06.19E

G-CHAA – G-CHZZ

G-CHAB	Schleicher Ka 6CR	6596	12.10.07
	BGA 3778, D-1596		
	J March Skelling Farm, Skirwith *'HAB'*		21.06.18E

G-CHAC	PZL-Bielsko SZD-50-3 Puchacz	B-2035	16.04.08
	BGA3779/HAC Peterborough & Spalding		
	Gliding Club Ltd Crowland *'HAC'*		28.06.18E

G-CHAD	Aeroprakt A-22 Foxbat	040 & UK009	30.04.02
	R A Neal tr DJB Foxbat Otherton		31.08.18P
	Built by D Winsper – project PFA 317-13909		

G-CHAE	Glasflügel Club Libelle 205	75	14.04.09
	BGA 3781/HAE, D-8687		
	E A & S R Scothern Burn *'HAE'*		10.06.18E

G-CHAF	PZL-Bielsko SZD-50-3 Puchacz	B-2031	29.11.07
	BGA 3782/HAF J G Kosak tr Seahawk Gliding Club		
	RNAS Culdrose *'N53'*		19.03.18E

G-CHAG	Guimbal Cabri G2	1035	09.07.12
	European Helicopter Importers Ltd Newcastle Int'l		14.08.18E
	Operated by Northumbria Helicopters		

G-CHAH	Europa Aviation Europa XS	252	14.06.04
	T Higgins Welshpool		31.08.18P
	Built by T Higgins – project PFA 247-12949; tailwheel u/c		

G-CHAJ	Cirrus SR22	1057	07.02.12
	D-EYSJ, N579AL R J Garbutt Blackpool		19.06.19E

G-CHAM	Cameron Pot-90	2912	29.09.92
	T G Church t/a Pendle Balloon Company		
	Clayton Le Dale, Blackburn		13.08.16E
	(IE 21.11.17)		

G-CHAN	Robinson R22 Beta II	3794	16.03.05
	J S Everett Sproughton		27.05.15E
	(NF 14.03.18)		

G-CHAO	Rolladen-Schneider LS6-b	6150	30.11.07
	BGA 3791/HAQ, D-8079		
	G A Stewart tr Cloud Nine Syndicate Bidford *'114'*		12.02.18E

G-CHAP	Robinson R44 Astro	0326	09.04.97
	Brierley Lifting Tackle Company Ltd		
	Wolverhampton Halfpenny Green		15.12.18E

G-CHAR	Grob G109B	6435	21.05.86
	The Royal Air Force Gliding & Soaring Association		
	RAF Halton		03.04.18E
	Operated by RAFGSA Chilterns Centre		

G-CHAS	Piper PA-28-181 Archer II	28-8090325	18.03.91
	N82228 A S Montlake tr G-CHAS Flying Group		
	Stapleford		03.07.19E

G-CHAU	Cameron C-80	11614	12.03.12
	G G Cannon & P Haworth Foulridge, Colne		05.03.18E

G-CHAW	Airdrome ¾ Fokker E.III replica	GS-105	21.12.11
	P A Harvie Mount Airey Farm, South Cave		
	Built by S W C Duckworth with Grass Strip Aviation kit		
	s/n GS-105 (Airdrome Kit 283); officially regd as kit s/n		
	'GS-106'; as 'E33/15' in German Army Air Service c/s		
	(SSDR microlight since 05.14 (IE 25.08.17)		

G-CHAX	Schempp-Hirth Standard Cirrus	2	21.11.07
	BGA 3798/HAX, ZS-GHZ, ZS-TIM, ZS-GGR, D-0302		
	R Jarvis & C Keating Rivar Hill *'HAX'*		29.04.18E

G-CHAY	Rolladen-Schneider LS7	7154	28.02.08
	BGA 3799/HAY N J Leaton Gransden Lodge *'779'*		29.05.17E
	(IE 05.07.17)		

G-CHBA	Rolladen-Schneider LS7	7156	29.10.07
	BGA 3801, D-6041		
	I Fisher tr LS7 Crew Currock Hill *'HBA'*		15.12.17E

G-CHBB	Schleicher ASW 24	24132	03.12.07
	BGA 3802/HBB London Gliding Club Proprietary Ltd		
	Dunstable Downs *'HBB'*		25.01.19E

G-CHBC	Rolladen-Schneider LS6-c	6209	20.10.07
	BGA 3803, D-.... A Crowden Talgarth *'HBC'*		03.03.18E

G-CHBD	Glaser-Dirks DG-200	2-12	29.08.07
	BGA 3804, HB-1384		
	W Rossmann tr HBD Syndicate Portmoak *'HBD'*		25.04.18E

G-CHBE	Glaser-Dirks DG-300 Elan	3E237	12.11.07
	BGA 3805/HBE, SE-UFB		
	G R Dixon tr DG356 Group Aston Down *'356'*		06.04.18E
	Built by Elan Tovarna Sportnega Orodja N.Sol.O		

G-CHBF	Schempp-Hirth Nimbus-2C	191	22.05.08
	BGA 3806/HBF, D-3369 J A Clark Talgarth *'HBF'*		16.08.18E

G-CHBG	Schleicher ASW 24	24133	14.02.08
	BGA 3807/HBG Imperial College of Science,		
	Technology & Medicine Lasham *'96'*		01.05.18E

G-CHBH	Grob G103C Twin III	36006	14.02.08
	BGA 3808/HBH Imperial College of Science,		
	Technology & Medicine Lasham *'496'*		28.03.18E

G-CHBK	Grob G103 Twin Astir Trainer	3254-T-31	03.03.08
	BGA 3810/HBK, RAFGGA 550, D-2389		
	S Naylor Burn *'HBK'*		24.04.18E

G-CHBL	Grob G102 Astir CS77	1626	18.03.08
	BGA 3811/HBL, RAFGSA R78, RAFGSA 778		
	Bidford Gliding & Flying Club Ltd Bidford *'HBL'*		27.04.18E

G-CHBM	Grob G102 Astir CS77	1633	02.04.08
	BGA 3812/HBM, RAFGSA R65, RAFGSA R66,		
	RAFGSA 546 M A Rees-Boughton &		
	A C E Walton-Smith Seighford *'755'*		12.12.19E

G-CHBO	Schleicher Ka 6CR	6611	12.03.08
	BGA 3815/HBQ, D-5616		
	C McCallin & M Selby Rivar Hill *'HBO'*		27.04.19E

G-CHBS	PZL-Bielsko SZD-41A Jantar-Standard	B-852/Z	16.06.08
	BGA 3817/HBS, D-4160		
	P J Chaisty & D Hendry Usk *'HBS'*		07.04.18E

G-CHBT	Grob G102 Astir CS Jeans	2235	20.12.07
	BGA 3819/HBT, PH-675		
	Darlton Gliding Club Ltd Darlton *'HBT'*		25.04.19E

G-CHBV	Schempp-Hirth Nimbus-2B	143	22.02.08
	BGA 3821/HBV, D-7850 R Beezer & G J Evison		
	Sutton Bank *'827'*		29.06.18E

G-CHBW	Jurca MJ.10 Spitfire	xxxx	11.01.12
	T A Major Perranporth *'Endeavour'*		
	Built by T A Major – project LAA 130-14886;		
	as 'AD370:PJ-C' in RAF c/s (IE 09.02.18)		

G-CHBX	Lindstrand LBL 77A	1394	16.01.12
	K Hull Hartley Wintney, Hook		25.06.18E
	Operated by Adventure Balloons Ltd; Union Flag c/s		

G-CHBY	Agusta AW139	31310	16.05.12
	OY-HLB Bristow Helicopters Ltd Humberside		27.01.19E

G-CHBZ	TL 2000UK Sting Carbon	xxxx	17.01.12
	C R Ashley Sittles Farm, Alrewas		19.06.18P
	Built by C R Ashley – project LAA 347-14790		

G-CHCF	Eurocopter AS.332L2 Super Puma II	2567	30.11.01
	Lombard North Central PLC Rzeszow, Poland		20.01.17E
	(NF 05.12.17)		

G-CHCG	Eurocopter AS.332L2 Super Puma II	2592	01.07.03
	Airbus Helicopters (Marseille, France)		23.07.17E
	Stored 03.17 (NF 25.02.17)		

G-CHCH	Eurocopter AS.332L2 Super Puma II	2601	16.12.03
	Airbus Helicopters (Marseille, France)		27.01.17E
	Stored 03.17 (NF 25.02.17)		

G-CHCI	Eurocopter AS.332L2 Super Puma II	2395	30.09.05
	LN-OHD, F-WQDN Lombard North Central PLC		
	Rzeszow, Poland		04.10.16E
	(NF 05.12.17)		

G-CHCK	Sikorsky S-92A	920030	28.02.06
	N8001N CHC Scotia Ltd Aberdeen Int'l		28.11.18E

G-CHCL	Eurocopter EC225 LP Super Puma	2674	14.11.07
	F-WWOS Wilmington Trust SP Services (Dublin) Ltd		
	Rzeszow, Poland		14.12.17E
	Stored 11.16		

G-CHCM	Eurocopter EC225 LP Super Puma	2675	21.12.07
	F-WWOV CHC Scotia Ltd Aberdeen Int'l		07.01.19E

G-CHCS	Sikorsky S-92A	920125	01.07.10
	N2133X Macquarie Rotorcraft Leasing Holdings Ltd		
	(London EC2)		22.07.18E
	Stored		

G

G-CHCU	Eurocopter AS.332L2 Super Puma II	2617	23.02.11
	LN-OHL, F-WWOS Airbus Helicopters		
	(Marseille, France)		14.08.17E
	Stored 03.17		
G-CHCY	Eurocopter AS.332L2 Super Puma II	2398	23.05.12
	VP-CHE, G-CHCY, D2-EVP, F-WQEA, LN-OHB, F-WYMD		
	Airbus Helicopters (Marseille, France)		18.06.13E
	Stored 03.17 (NF 25.02.17)		
G-CHDA	Pilatus B4-PC11AF	017	13.02.08
	BGA 3851/HDA, D-0964		
	M J Corcoran tr HDA Syndicate Camphill *'HDA'*		21.06.18E
G-CHDB	PZL-Bielsko SZD-51-1 Junior	B-1997	24.09.07
	BGA 3852 Stratford on Avon Gliding Club Ltd		
	Snitterfield *'HDB'*		20.10.18E
G-CHDC	Schleicher ASK 13	13308	15.04.08
	BGA 3853/HDC, D-0750 Cancelled 06.07.11 by CAA		18.08.09
	Bicester *Stored 02.17*		
G-CHDD	Centrair 101B Pégase	101B0425	30.10.07
	BGA 3854 M Samuels tr 591 Glider Syndicate		
	Gransden Lodge *'591'*		07.04.18E
G-CHDE	Pilatus B4-PC11AF	223	25.01.08
	BGA 3855/HDE, VH-XOZ, VH-WQP		
	I L Pattingale RAF Odiham		16.04.18E
G-CHDH	Lindstrand LBL 77A	1398	17.04.12
	Lindstrand Media Ltd Hawarden CH5		
	'Jones Lang LaSalle'		02.05.15E
	(IE 17.07.15)		
G-CHDJ	Schleicher ASW 20CL	20828	06.02.08
	BGA 3859/HDJ, D-8442 G E G Lambert & L M M		
	Sebreghts (Westmalle, Antwerp, Belgium) *'HDJ'*		21.07.18E
G-CHDK	Magni M16C Tandem Trainer	16126894	21.02.12
	J Gledhill (Abingdon)		26.02.18P
G-CHDL	Schleicher ASW 20	20082	14.02.08
	BGA 3861/HDL, D-1617, OH-495		
	B D Allen & D Reeves Camphill *'137'*		25.02.19E
G-CHDM	P&M QuikR	8602	20.12.11
	A Sheveleu East Fortune		18.01.18P
G-CHDN	Schleicher K 8B	2	14.02.08
	BGA 3863/HDN, D-8017		
	Cotswold Gliding Club Aston Down *'HDN'*		18.11.19E
G-CHDP	PZL-Bielsko SZD-50-3 Puchacz	B-2050	23.01.08
	BGA 3864 D J Marpole tr Heron Gliding Club		
	RNAS Yeovilton *'DP'*		03.11.17E
	(IE 06.11.17)		
G-CHDR	Glaser-Dirks DG-300 Elan	3E95	07.01.08
	BGA 3866/HDR, RAFGSA R30		
	R Robins Pocklington *'HDR'*		21.05.18E
	Built by Elan Tovarna Sportnega Orodja N.Sol.O		
G-CHDU	PZL-Bielsko SZD-51-1 Junior	B-1996	18.10.07
	BGA 3869 Cambridge Gliding Club Ltd		
	Gransden Lodge *'HDU'*		04.03.18E
G-CHDV	Schleicher ASW 19B	19345	19.03.08
	BGA 3870/HDV, D-2876		
	A & M Truelove Lasham *'882'*		20.04.19E
G-CHDX	Rolladen-Schneider LS7-WL	7161	23.01.08
	BGA 3872/HDX R T Halliburton & D Holborn		
	Pocklington *'A2'*		31.03.19E
G-CHDY	Schleicher K 8B	8277	07.02.08
	BGA 3873/HDY, D-4094 V Mallon		
	Kleve-Wisseler Dünen, Germany *'HDY'*		25.06.14E
	(NF 26.04.16)		
G-CHDZ	Cameron O-120	11639	10.05.12
	R J Mansfield Bowness-on-Windermere		20.06.17E
G-CHEB	Europa Aviation Europa	263	16.09.96
	I C Smit & P Whittingham Sittles Farm, Alrewas		27.08.10P
	Built by C H P Bell – project PFA 247-12967		
	(NF 23.07.18)		
G-CHEC	PZL-Bielsko SZD-55-1	551191019	01.11.07
	BGA 3877/HEC D Pye Challock *'308'*		07.04.18E
G-CHED	Aeros Nano Trike/Discus 15T	077	13.04.12
	G W Cameron (Edinburgh EH8)		
	Designated Flylight Dragonfly		
	(SSDR microlight since 05.14) (IE 31.07.15)		

G-CHEE	Schempp-Hirth Discus b	292	26.09.08
	BGA 3879/HEE A Henderson Bicester *'AH'*		03.08.18E
	Composite with fuselage of BGA 3523 (292) – original		
	fuselage rebuilt as G-CFTW with amended c/n 292/1		
G-CHEF	Glaser-Dirks DG-500 Elan Trainer	5E53T20	17.01.08
	BGA 3880/HEF Yorkshire Gliding Club		
	(Proprietary) Ltd Sutton Bank *'HEF'*		09.04.18E
	Built by Elan Flight Ltd		
G-CHEG	Sportine Aviacija LAK-12 Lietuva	6206	07.03.08
	BGA 3881/HEG J M Caldwell, D Cockburn, Z Kmita		
	& R G Parker Kirton in Lindsey *'HEG'*		08.03.18E
G-CHEH	Rolladen-Schneider LS7-WL	7163	17.09.07
	BGA 3882, D-6078 S Brown Gransden Lodge *'795'*		31.03.19E
G-CHEJ	Schleicher ASW 15B	15441	20.11.07
	BGA 3883/HEJ, D-6871		
	A F F Webb Wycombe Air Park *'687'*		03.07.16E
	(IE 21.04.17)		
G-CHEK	PZL-Bielsko SZD-51-1 Junior	B-2009	11.12.07
	BGA 3884/HEK, BGA 3893/HEU, (BGA 3884/HEK)		
	Cambridge Gliding Club Ltd Gransden Lodge *'HEK'*		05.02.18E
G-CHEL	Colt 77B	4823	18.05.00
	Chelsea Financial Services PLC Sutton, Tenbury Wells		
	'CfS – Chelsea Financial Services'		06.08.15E
	Built by Cameron Balloons Ltd (IE 06.06.17)		
G-CHEM	Piper PA-34-200T Seneca II	34-8170032	26.08.87
	N8292Y London Executive Aviation Ltd Stapleford		04.03.09E
	(NF 04.12.15)		
G-CHEN	Schempp-Hirth Discus b	422	22.12.07
	BGA 3887/HEN M P Hardy tr G-CHEN Group		
	Challock *'735'*		15.05.18E
G-CHEO	Schleicher ASW 20	20410	04.12.07
	BGA 3889/HEQ, D-6747		
	S G Lapworth Lasham *'611'*		09.04.19E
G-CHEP	PZL-Bielsko SZD-50-3 Puchacz	B-2057	28.02.08
	BGA 3888/HEP Peterborough & Spalding		
	Gliding Club Ltd Crowland *'HEP'*		12.04.18E
G-CHER	Piper PA-38-112 Tomahawk II	38-82A0004	19.12.00
	G-BVBL, N91339 G E Fox Bagby		21.12.17E
G-CHEW	Rolladen-Schneider LS6-c18	6250B	12.03.08
	BGA 3895/HEW D N Tew Gransden Lodge *'486'*		02.03.18E
	Fitted with new wings & fuselage; original parts		
	of c/n 6250 included in G-CKBC		
G-CHEX	Aero Designs Pulsar	213	14.10.11
	M R Punter Bodmin		17.05.18P
	Built by P Laycock & D R Piercy – project PFA 202-12026		
G-CHFA	Schempp-Hirth Ventus b/16.6	251	23.07.08
	BGA 3899/HFA, RAFGSA R24		
	A K Lincoln Lasham *'65'*		05.05.10E
	(IE 22.02.16)		
G-CHFB	Schleicher Ka 6CR	6344Sl	12.11.07
	BGA 3900/HFB, D-5825 R J Shepherd		
	(Snitterfield, Stratford-upon-Avon) *'HFB'*		31.08.15E
	(NF 12.10.15)		
G-CHFC	P&M Quik GTR	8610	17.04.12
	A Niarchos (Dedham, Colchester)		17.09.19P
G-CHFD	Agusta AW109SP Grand New	22262	30.03.12
	Flight Charter Services Pty Ltd Biggin Hill		10.04.18E
	Operated by EBG (Helicopters) Ltd ex MY 'Ilona IV'		
G-CHFF	Schempp-Hirth Standard Cirrus	539	02.11.07
	BGA 3904/HFF, D-8916		
	R S Morrisroe tr Foxtrot 2 Group Upwood *'HFF'*		02.06.18E
G-CHFG	Van's RV-6	24570	05.03.12
	A H D Stenhouse tr RV Flying Group		
	Kittyhawk Farm, Ripe		07.06.18P
	Built by A H D Stenhouse & J F A Thomas		
	– project PFA 181A-13108		
G-CHFH	PZL-Bielsko SZD-50-3 Puchacz	B-2059	18.12.07
	BGA 3906/HFH Trent Valley Gliding Club Ltd		
	Kirton in Lindsey *'HFH'*		15.05.17E
	(IE 05.06.17)		
G-CHFK	Piper PA-32-260 Cherokee Six	32-7200031	29.03.12
	N5277T Aerobility Blackbushe *'aerobility'*		19.04.18E
G-CHFL	Scheibe SF25C Falke 2000	44512	03.04.12
	D-KCPR Staffordshire Gliding Club Ltd Seighford		11.05.18E

G-CHFM	Cameron Z-120	11625	20.06.12
	David Hathaway Transport Ltd Yate, Bristol		
	'David Hathaway'		23.04.18E
G-CHFO	P&M Quik GTR	8611	02.05.12
	M Bailey Otherton		11.10.18P
G-CHFT	Air Création Tanarg 912S(1)/BioniX 15 FLTxxx		11.04.12
	N C Stubbs (Hilton, Derby)		25.10.18P
	Built by N C Stubbs – project BMAA/HB/624 (Flylight kit		
	FLTxxx comprising trike Txxx & wing s/n A12005-2004)		
G-CHFU	P&M Quik GTR	8612	22.05.12
	P H J Fenn Beccles		25.09.18P
	Badged 'QuikGTR Explorer'		
G-CHFV	Schempp-Hirth Ventus b/16.6	204	05.12.07
	BGA 3918/HFV, D-5235		
	A Cliffe & B Pearson Seighford *'F21'*		28.04.18E
G-CHFW	Schleicher K 8B	8108	12.09.08
	BGA 3919/HFW, HB-705 Oxford Gliding Company Ltd		
	RAF Weston-on-the-Green *'HFW'*		16.10.18E
G-CHFX	Schempp-Hirth Nimbus-4T	12	07.11.07
	BGA 3920/HFX R F Barber Lasham *'Z2'*		05.11.18E
G-CHFZ	Best Off Skyranger Nynja 912S(1)	11080079	30.03.12
	Skyview Systems Ltd Waits Farm, Belchamp Walter		18.06.18P
	Built by D M Robbins – project BMAA/HB/618		
G-CHGA	P&M Quik GTR	8603	02.04.12
	Flying For Freedom Ltd Cotswold		17.05.18P
G-CHGB	Grob G102 Astir CS	1356	13.02.08
	BGA 3924/HGB, D-7386		
	The Windrushers Gliding Club Ltd Bicester *'509'*		28.06.18E
	Rebuilt with wings & components ex RAFGGA 507		
G-CHGE	Evektor EV-97 teamEurostar UK	2012-3935	23.05.12
	J R Mackay (Pinner)		15.05.18P
	Assembled Cosmik Aviation Ltd		
G-CHGF	Schleicher ASW 15B	15264	25.03.08
	BGA 3928/HGF, D-2128		
	P Mylett tr HGF Flying Group Camphill *'HGF'*		24.05.18E
G-CHGG	Schempp-Hirth Standard Cirrus	362	28.01.08
	BGA 3929/HGG, HB-1172		
	P A Nicolai tr HGG Flying Group Nympsfield *'HGG'*		26.05.18E
G-CHGI	Beech A36 Bonanza	E-1784	30.05.12
	(F-), G-CHGI, PH-DRL, OO-CMD, N3803Y		
	Aeronav87 Maintenance Limoges, France		25.06.18E
G-CHGJ	Flylight MotorFloater Fox 16T	MF013	01.05.12
	A M Brooks (Higher Coombe, Buckfastleigh)		
	(SSDR microlight since 05.14) (IE 16.05.16)		
G-CHGK	Schempp-Hirth Discus bT	96	29.10.07
	BGA 3932 P W Berridge		
	Sandhill Farm, Shrivenham *'564'*		20.04.18E
G-CHGM	Groppo Trail	00063/22	27.04.12
	J Walker Strathaven		18.10.18P
	Built by D Cassidy – project LAA 372-15098		
G-CHGN	Ace Aviation Easy Riser/Spirit	ER-52	01.05.12
	Tideswell Trading Ltd Darley Moor		
	Trike c/n ER-52 & Wing s/n AS-110		
	(SSDR microlight since 05.14) (IE 03.12.15)		
G-CHGP	Rolladen-Schneider LS6-c	6270	17.03.08
	BGA 3936/HGP D J Miller Dunstable Downs *'L6'*		07.02.18E
G-CHGR	Sportine Aviacija LAK-12 Lietuva	6186	21.09.07
	BGA 3938 M R Garwood		
	Husbands Bosworth *'HGR'*		24.04.18E
G-CHGS	Schempp-Hirth Discus b	439	08.10.07
	BGA 3939 M J Armes tr G-CHGS Syndicate		
	Lasham *'HGS'*		30.04.18E
G-CHGT	FFA Diamant 16.5	040	15.01.08
	BGA 3940/HGT, HB-929 T E Lynch Burn *'HGT'*		08.12.14E
G-CHGU	Ace Aviation Easy Riser/Touch	ER-51	01.05.12
	T A Dobbins (Birmingham B34)		
	Trike c/n ER-51 & Wing s/n AT-51		
	(SSDR microlight since 05.14) (IE 20.10.17)		
G-CHGV	Glaser-Dirks DG-500/22 Elan	5E70S11	12.11.07
	BGA 3942/HGV A J Hulme tr Hotel Golf Victor		
	Syndicate Gransden Lodge *'HGV'*		16.04.18E
	Built by Elan Tovarna Sportnega Orodja N.Sol.O		

G-CHGW	Centrair ASW 20F	20102	23.08.07
	BGA 3943, F-CFFB P J Coward		
	Husbands Bosworth *'HGW'*		30.05.18E
G-CHGX	Sportine Aviacija LAK-12 Lietuva	6201	07.04.08
	BGA 3944/HGX M Jenks Kingston Deverill *'HGX'*		28.08.13E
	(IE 21.04.17)		
G-CHGY	Schleicher ASW 27-18 (ASG 29)	29073	13.07.12
	(BGA 5714) S C Thompson tr G-CHGY Flying Group		
	Parham Park *'LJW'*		26.07.18E
G-CHGZ	Schempp-Hirth Discus bT	95/434	23.01.08
	BGA 3946/HGZ G C Bell Lasham *'502'*		04.04.18E
G-CHHB	Aeroprakt A-22LS Foxbat	A22LS-244	14.05.12
	A J L Gordon Field Farm, Oakley		19.09.18P
	Built by A Everitt – project LAA 317B-15141		
	Badged 'Foxbat Sport 600'		
G-CHHC	Cameron A-300	11535	27.03.12
	Wickers World Ltd Great Haywood, Stafford		
	'The Trentham Estate'		25.03.18E
G-CHHD	TLAC RL7A Sherwood Ranger XP	042	09.05.12
	R Simpson Eshott		27.10.15P
	Built by M Taylor – project LAA 237A-15054;		
	overturned on take-off Druridge Bay 16.08.15 &		
	substantially damaged (NF 06.05.16)		
G-CHHF	Sikorsky S-92A	920158	27.06.12
	N158G Bristow Helicopters Ltd London Stansted		
	'Christopher Bond'		
	Returned to lessor 02.19 (IE 15.07.16)		
G-CHHH	Rolladen-Schneider LS6-c	6289	18.10.07
	BGA 3954 D H Smith (Stratford-upon-Avon) *'963'*		16.03.19E
G-CHHI	Van's RV-7	72771	25.10.11
	M G Jefferies Little Gransden		02.01.19P
	Built by D Bolton, M G Jefferies & S Morris		
	– project LAA 323-15094		
G-CHHJ	Aeropro EuroFOX 912	37312	25.05.12
	K J Watt Ashcroft		12.12.19P
	Built by K J Watt – project BMAA/HB/625; tricycle u/c		
G-CHHK	Schleicher ASW 19B	19384	29.11.07
	BGA 3956/HHK, ZD661, BGA 2897/ERT		
	R Hubrecht & P Lysak Dunstable Downs *'838'*		12.05.18E
G-CHHL	Cameron C-80	11673	20.06.12
	H G Griffiths & W A Steel Cardiff & Reading		14.06.19E
G-CHHN	Schempp-Hirth Ventus b/16.6	205	03.04.08
	BGA 3959/HHN, RAFGSA R27 N A C Norman		
	tr Ventus 979 Syndicate Feshiebridge *'979'*		02.10.18E
G-CHHO	Schempp-Hirth Discus bT	106	30.10.07
	BGA 3961 S R Domoney tr 97Z Syndicate		
	Parham Park *'97Z'*		18.04.18E
G-CHHP	Schempp-Hirth Discus b	399	03.07.08
	BGA 3960/HHP, SE-UKL		
	F R Knowles Aston Down *'KL'*		17.11.18E
G-CHHR	PZL-Bielsko SZD-55-1	551191020	27.09.07
	BGA 3962 J R Sayce Talgarth *'100'*		28.03.18E
G-CHHS	Schleicher ASW 20	20008	08.02.08
	BGA 3963/HHS, SE-TTU D Britt & P J Rocks		
	Kirton in Lindsey *'HHS'*		21.08.16E
	(IE 11.04.17)		
G-CHHT	Rolladen-Schneider LS6-c	6292	13.11.07
	BGA 3964/HHT D Wilson Gransden Lodge *'855'*		17.03.19E
G-CHHU	Rolladen-Schneider LS6-c	6296	17.08.07
	BGA 3965 A M Sanders tr 445 Syndicate		
	Long Mynd *'445'*		29.05.18E
G-CHHV	Junqua RJ.03 Ibis	xxxx	30.05.12
	J J R Joubert Enstone		
	Built by J J R Joubert – project LAA 178-15150;		
	for sale 03.18 still incomplete		
G-CHHW	Sportine Aviacija LAK-12 Lietuva	6212	08.12.07
	BGA 3967/HHW A J Dibdin Dunstable Downs *'237'*		09.04.18E
G-CHHY	Ace Aviation Magic/Laser	AM158	30.05.12
	S W Walker Broadmeadow Farm, Hereford		
	Assembled P&M Aviation Ltd; trike s/n AM158 & wing		
	s/n AL152 (SSDR microlight since 05.14) (IE 29.06.18)		
G-CHHZ	Schempp-Hirth Cirrus	26	30.04.12
	(BGA 5705), D-0053 B J Dawson & S E Richardson		
	Pocklington *'HZ'*		23.06.18E

G-CHIA North American SNJ-5 Texan　　　　88-17282　　20.07.12
N9012Y, JMSDF 6208, Bu 85061, 42-85501
The Warplane Flying Company Ltd　White Waltham　06.01.16E
As '85061:7F-061' in US Navy c/s (IE 07.08.17)

G-CHID Aeropro EuroFOX 912(1)　　　　35712　　　29.02.12
P David & A P Scott　Shobdon　　　　　　16.02.18P
Built by J W Taylor – project BMAA/HB/621; tricycle u/c

G-CHIE Dudek Nucleon 34/Flymecc Mini Trike　P.07402　06.06.12
J M Keen　(Andover)
(SSDR microlight since 05.14) (IE 26.11.15)

G-CHIG Grob G109B　　　　　　　　　6366　　　17.07.12
D-KINK, (Egyptian AF 675)
Southdown Gliding Club Ltd　Parham Park　　11.10.18E

G-CHIH Aeropro EuroFOX 912(S)　　　36412　　　18.06.12
Banbury Gliding Club Ltd　Hinton-in-the-Hedges　20.09.18P
Built by R Coombs – project LAA 376-15130;
tricycle u/c; glider-tug

G-CHII CASA 1-131E Jungmann Series 1000　1108　11.05.12
Spanish AF E3B-174　R J Allan, N Jones & A J Maxwell
Manchester Barton　　　　　　　　　　16.05.19P

G-CHIJ Comco Ikarus C42 FB80　　　1205-7200　10.07.12
R G Herrod　Dunkeswell　　　　　　　　05.08.19P
Assembled Red-Air UK

G-CHIK Reims/Cessna F152 II　　　F15201628　19.10.81
G-BHAZ, (D-EHLE)　Stapleford Flying Club Ltd
Stapleford　　　　　　　　　　　　　01.11.15E

G-CHIM Ultramagic H-31　　　　　31/13　　　25.05.12
G B Lescott　Oxford OX4　　　　　　　12.08.18E

G-CHIP Piper PA-28-181 Archer II　　28-8290095　22.02.82
N81337　Golden Lion Aviation Ltd　Brighton City　23.04.19E
British Caledonian c/s

G-CHIR Van's RV-7　　　　　　　　71085　　　15.05.12
F Sharples　Sandown　　　　　　　　　30.05.18P
Built by B Fawkes & F Sharples – project LAA 323-13981

G-CHIT AutoGyro MTOsport　　　　M00946　　10.09.12
N G H Staunton　Stanton Farm, Stanton St Bernard　22.01.19P
Assembled Rotorsport UK as c/n RSUK/MTOS/046

G-CHIV P&M QuikR　　　　　　　　8625　　　01.08.12
D A Hopkinson tr G-CHIV Syndicate　East Fortune　05.08.18P

G-CHIW Raj Hamsa X'Air Hawk　　　1104　　　13.07.12
EI-ECO　M D Boley　Batch End Farm, Lympsham　20.09.18P
Built by J McLaughlin; c/n also quoted for
(1) N3178S (Built by J Matthews) &
(2) N977BT (Built by B Treifglaff)

G-CHIX Robin DR.500-200i Président　　36　　　29.11.01
F-GXGD, F-WQPN
P A & R Stephens　Moor Farm, West Heslerton　27.04.18E
Officially registered as DR.400-500

G-CHIY Flylight MotorFloater　　　MF015　　20.08.12
S Polley　(Royston)
(SSDR microlight since 05.14) (IE 12.06.17)

G-CHIZ Flylight Dragonfly　　　　080　　　16.07.12
J Paterson　(Azat Le Ris, Haute Vienne, France)
(SSDR microlight since 05.14) (IE 26.07.16)

G-CHJB Flylight Dragonfly　　　　081　　　20.08.12
Celtic Solutions Ltd　　　　　Sywell
(SSDR microlight since 05.14) (IE 24.09.15)

G-CHJD Schleicher Ka 6E　　　　4141　　　01.03.10
BGA 3974/HJD, D-...., OH-505, SE-TFM
A A G Frier tr The Ruby Syndicate　Shenington　'HJD'　20.08.18E

G-CHJE Schleicher K 8B　　　　8259　　　23.07.08
BGA 3975/HJE, (BGA 3926), RAFGGA 505, RAFGGA 971
Staffordshire Gliding Club Ltd　Seighford　'HJE'　26.07.18E

G-CHJF Rolladen-Schneider LS6-c　　6291　　　17.10.07
BGA 3976　J L Bridge　Gransden Lodge　'245'　01.03.18E

G-CHJG Evektor EV-97 teamEurostar UK　2012-3938　06.08.12
P A Bass　Sherburn-in-Elmet　　　　　01.08.18P
Assembled Cosmik Aviation Ltd

G-CHJJ Medway Clipper-100　　　210712　　29.08.12
J Bulpin　(Clydach, Swansea)　　　　28.01.19P

G-CHJK Cessna T206H Turbo Stationair　T20608910　27.07.12
N5234J　G G Weston　Denham　　　　28.09.18E

G-CHJL Schempp-Hirth Discus bT　　105　　　16.10.07
BGA 3981　M D Forster tr Discus JL Group
Portmoak　'516'　　　　　　　　　　04.12.18E

G-CHJM Cameron C-80　　　　　11684　　27.09.12
C L Smith　Kennington, Oxford　　　　12.04.18E

G-CHJN Schempp-Hirth Standard Cirrus　440G　09.03.09
BGA 3983/HJN, HB-1206
P M Hardingham　Crowland　'HJN'　　19.03.18E

G-CHJO Bushby-Long Midget Mustang　1726　24.07.12
N611DH　R J Hodder　Eastfield Farm, Manby　12.07.17P
Built by D Hoffman

G-CHJP Schleicher Ka 6CR　　　616　　　04.01.08
BGA 3985/HJQ, OH-210, OH-RSB
D M Cornelius　Dunstable Downs　'HJP'　20.05.18E

G-CHJR Glasflügel Standard Libelle 201B　102　14.02.08
BGA 3986/HJR, SE-TIO
R P G Hayhoe　Wormingford　'B9'　01.12.17E
(IE 13.01.18)

G-CHJS Schleicher ASW 27-18E *(ASG 29E)*　29646　29.05.12
(BGA 5713)　J D Spencer　Bicester　'601'　26.04.18E

G-CHJT Centrair ASW 20F　　　20115　　30.04.08
BGA 3988/HJT, F-CFFL
A F Irwin　(Cheltenham)　'292'　　　10.12.18E

G-CHJV Grob G102 Astir CS　　　1007　　06.06.08
BGA 3990/HJV, D-7000
Cotswold Gliding Club　Aston Down　'HJV'　23.09.18E

G-CHJW P&M Quik GTR　　　　8630　　24.09.12
A C Rowlands　Wolverhampton Halfpenny Green　14.09.18P
Badged 'Explorer'

G-CHJX Rolladen-Schneider LS6-c　　6271　　04.09.08
BGA 3991/HJX　M R Haynes & P Robinson
Tibenham　'203'　　　　　　　　　28.04.18E

G-CHJY Schempp-Hirth Standard Cirrus　459　19.02.08
BGA 3992/HJY, HB-1207
D J Jeffries tr Cirrus-459 Group　Usk　'HJY'　28.07.18E

G-CHJZ Luscombe 8E Silvaire Deluxe　4628　28.08.12
N1901K, NC1901K　Narli Aviation Ltd　Savikko, Finland　30.07.16E

G-CHKA Schempp-Hirth Discus CS　120CS　12.10.07
BGA 3994　M P & R W Weaver　Usk　'860'　28.03.18E
Built by Orličan Aakciová Společnost

G-CHKB Grob G102 Astir CS77　　1658　　19.02.08
BGA 3995/HKB, D-7491
C D Woodward　North Hill　'HKB'　　19.08.18E

G-CHKC Schempp-Hirth Standard Cirrus　520G　11.12.07
BGA 3996/HKC, D-3268　J M Hill　Eyres Field　'HKC'　04.09.18E

G-CHKD Schempp-Hirth Standard Cirrus　576G　12.11.07
BGA 3997/HKD, F-CEMF　A Collings
tr Stratocirrus Owners Club　Nympsfield　'E'　26.05.17E

G-CHKF Grob G109B　　　　　6239　　07.09.12
F-CAQN, F-WAQN　A P Moulang tr CHKF Group
Challock　　　　　　　　　　　24.09.18E

G-CHKG Best Off Skyranger Nynja 912S(1)　12050105　11.09.12
D L Turner　Headcorn　　　　　　24.05.18P
Built by S D J Harvey – project BMAA/HB/627

G-CHKH Schleicher ASW 28　　　28068　　19.09.12
(BGA 5720), D-2830　D F McKinney & C Thirkell
Sutton Bank　'DB'　　　　　　　30.11.18E

G-CHKI Sikorsky S-92A　　　　920175　　04.12.12
N975F　Wilmington Trust SP Services (Dublin) Ltd
Rzeszow, Poland　'Vincent Cain'　　05.12.18E
Stored 05.18

G-CHKK Schleicher K 8B　　　　8886　　07.12.07
BGA 4003/HKK, D-0866
L E N Tanner tr Tweetie Bird　Lasham　15.08.18E

G-CHKM Grob G102 Astir CS Jeans　2108　20.06.08
BGA 4005/HKM, D-7636
Essex & Suffolk Gliding Club Ltd　Wormingford　'HKM'　01.08.18E

G-CHKN Air Création Buggy 582(1)/Kiss 400　FL002　18.09.01
P J Higgins　Wingland
Built by I Tomkins – project BMAA/HB/183 (Flylight kit
FL002 comprising Trike s/n xxxx & wing s/n A01134?)
(SSDR microlight since 07.18) (IE 26.08.15)

G-CHKO	Best Off Skyranger Swift 912S(1)	11101041	21.09.12
	B Hetherington & A E Kemp Rankins Farm, Linton		19.04.18P
	Built by S Worthington – project BMAA/HB/629		
G-CHKR	Jastreb Standard Cirrus G/81	276	22.01.08
	BGA 4009/HKR, OH-663 N A White Crowland *'985'*		12.09.18E
G-CHKS	Jastreb Standard Cirrus G/81	361	06.02.08
	BGA 4010/HKS, SE-TZS C E Mustoe		
	tr G-CHKS Flying Group Aston Down *'HKS'*		08.05.19E
	Built by Jastreb Fabrika Aviona I Jedrilica		
G-CHKT	Kubícek BB22E	886	09.05.13
	D L Beckwith Higham Ferrers, Rushden		23.04.19E
G-CHKU	Schempp-Hirth Standard Cirrus	513G	08.05.08
	BGA 4012/HKU, F-CEMA T M O'Sullivan		
	& T J Wheeler Bicester *'C29'*		25.06.18E
G-CHKV	Scheibe Zugvogel IIIA	1034	31.01.08
	BGA 4013/HKV, D-8294 Dartmoor Gliding Society		
	Burnford Common, Brentor *'HKV'*		03.10.18E
G-CHKX	Rolladen-Schneider LS4-b	4933	03.10.07
	BGA 4015 M J Kidd tr G-CHKX Flying Group		
	Kenley *'HKX'*		23.04.18E
G-CHKY	Schempp-Hirth Discus b	461	30.11.07
	BGA 4016/HKY M T Davis Dunstable Downs *'HKY'*		20.05.18E
G-CHKZ	CARMAM JP 15-36AR Aiglon	31	19.09.08
	BGA 4017/HKZ, F-CFGA		
	A J & T A Hollings Rufforth *'HKZ'*		26.06.18R
G-CHLB	Rolladen-Schneider LS4-b	4935	05.03.08
	BGA 4019/HLB E G Leach & K R Rogers		
	Wormingford *'365'*		25.10.18E
G-CHLC	Pilatus B4-PC11AF	177	25.02.08
	BGA 4020/HLC, SE-UFX, OH-455		
	E Lockhart Lasham *'HLC'*		11.05.18E
G-CHLD	AutoGyro MTOsport	xxxx	14.06.12
	D L Sivyer (Newton Valence, Alton)		07.08.18P
	Assembled Rotorsport UK as c/n RSUK/MTOS/045;		
	noted at Carlisle Lake District for training 01.19		
G-CHLE	Cameron A-160	10051	13.04.12
	PH-OOI, OO-BKI Airxcite Ltd t/a Virgin Balloon Flights		
	Stafford Park, Telford		08.04.13E
	(NF 15.09.14)		
G-CHLH	Schleicher K 8B	8637	05.08.08
	BGA 4025/HLH, RAFGGA 569, D-5691		
	Shenington Gliding Club Shenington *'HLH'*		19.11.18E
G-CHLI	Cosmik Aviation Superchaser	SCH002W	27.07.12
	Cosmik Aviation Ltd Deppers Bridge, Southam		
	Assembled Cosmik Aviation Ltd		
	(SSDR microlight since 05.14) (IE 21.01.17)		
G-CHLK	Glasflügel H301 Libelle	85	11.06.08
	BGA 4027/HLK, SE-TFS		
	D T Bray (Wellesbourne, Warwick) *'HLK'*		04.07.18E
G-CHLM	Schleicher ASW 19B	19269	14.02.08
	BGA 4029/HLM, OH-538 J R Paskins Darlton *'819'*		11.03.18E
G-CHLN	Schempp-Hirth Discus CS	143CS	28.01.08
	BGA 4030/HLN T World tr Portsmouth		
	Naval Gliding Centre Solent *'805'*		31.05.18E
	Built by Orličan Aakciová Společnost		
G-CHLP	Schleicher ASK 21	21597	09.11.07
	BGA 4031/HLP		
	Southdown Gliding Club Ltd Parham Park *'HLP'*		26.03.18E
G-CHLS	Schempp-Hirth Discus b	114	07.09.07
	BGA 4034, RAFGSA R11		
	R Roberts Burnford Common, Brentor *'V5'*		12.01.19E
G-CHLV	Schleicher ASW 19B	19325	18.12.07
	BGA 4038/HLW, D-8799		
	P M Shelton Seighford *'HLV'*		09.03.19E
G-CHLY	Schempp-Hirth Discus CS	161CS	17.01.08
	BGA 4040/HLY S J Pearce Snitterfield *'Z45'*		06.07.19E
	Built by Orličan Aakciová Společnost		
G-CHLZ	Best Off Skyranger Swift LS 912(1)	UK/1050	30.05.12
	S K Ridge Crosland Moor		24.03.18P
	Built by S K Ridge – project BMAA/HB/626		
G-CHMA	PZL-Bielsko SZD-51-1 Junior	B-2132	02.10.07
	BGA 4042 The Welland Gliding Club Ltd		
	Lyveden *'HMA'*		03.04.18E
G-CHMB	Glaser-Dirks DG-300 Elan	3E105	15.11.07
	BGA 4043/HMB, D-4676 A D & P Langlands		
	Shenington *'HMB'*		20.03.18E
	Built by Elan Tovarna Sportnega Orodja N.Sol.O		
G-CHMD	DG Flugzeugbau LS8-t	8518	21.09.12
	(BGA 5719), D-KKUG		
	A P Balkwill & G B Monslow Snitterfield *'UG'*		23.11.18E
G-CHME	AMS-Flight DG-303 Elan	3E197	30.05.12
	(BGA5717), HB-1881		
	A G Gibbs Parham Park *'LKA'*		08.06.18E
	Built by AMS-Flight d.o.o.		
G-CHMG	ICA-Brasov IS-28B2	353	04.03.08
	BGA 4044/HMG, HA-5039 R Maksymowicz,		
	A J Palfreyman & A Sutton Snitterfield *'HMG'*		17.04.18E
G-CHMH	Schleicher K 8B	5	02.09.09
	BGA 4045/HMH, D-5735		
	Shenington Gliding Club Shenington *'HMH'*		16.05.15E
G-CHMI	Lindstrand LBL 105A	1431	14.12.12
	J A Lawton Enton, Godalming		09.01.19E
G-CHMK	Rolladen-Schneider LS6-18W	6324	16.10.07
	BGA 4046, D-1245		
	R C Hodge Dunstable Downs *'HMK'*		19.03.18E
G-CHML	Schempp-Hirth Discus CS	114CS	22.08.08
	BGA 4047/HML, OO-ZTU		
	I D Bateman Parham Park *'38'*		01.12.18E
	Built by Orličan Aakciová Společnost (NF 17.01.18)		
G-CHMM	Jastreb Glasflügel 304B	322	03.12.07
	BGA 4048/HMM, SE-UGZ, D-1005		
	A F Greenhalgh Wormingford *'HMM'*		26.05.18R
G-CHMN	Raj Hamsa X'Air Falcon Jabiru(1)	1084	06.11.12
	F C Claydon Great Cornard, Sudbury		11.05.18P
	Built by J Anderson & D Thrower – project BMAA/HB/632		
G-CHMO	Schempp-Hirth Discus CS	099CS	23.10.07
	BGA 4051/HMO, D-7160 S Barter Lasham *'364'*		16.04.18E
	Built by Orličan Aakciová Společnost		
G-CHMR	Embraer EMB-145MP	145405	24.08.12
	OE-IAM, F-GUMA, PT-STC		
	Air Kilroe Ltd t/a Eastern Airways Humberside		02.04.19E
G-CHMS	Glaser-Dirks DG-100	40	16.04.08
	BGA 4053/HMS, D-2579		
	P S Medlock North Hill *'HMS'*		27.09.18E
G-CHMT	Glasflügel Mosquito B	153	29.10.07
	BGA 4054, F-CEDY J Taberham North Hill *'380'*		12.11.18E
G-CHMU	CARMAM JP 15-36AR Aiglon	22	20.11.07
	BGA 4055/HMU, F-CETT C A Chappell		
	tr G-CHMU Group Kingston Deverill *'HMU'*		04.06.18E
G-CHMV	Schleicher ASK 13	13177	18.04.08
	BGA 4056/HMV, D-0268		
	The Windrushers Gliding Club Ltd Bicester *'HMV'*		17.03.18E
G-CHMW	Evektor EV-97 Eurostar SL	2010-3814	22.10.12
	S A Ivell & A Wright Crosland Moor		11.01.19P
	Built by N R Beale – project LAA 315B-15158		
G-CHMX	Rolladen-Schneider LS4-a	4230	15.01.08
	BGA 4058/HMX, OO-ZNN, F-CEIO		
	L Couval Long Mynd *'PZ'*		19.04.18E
G-CHMY	Schempp-Hirth Standard Cirrus	121	20.02.08
	BGA 4059/HMY, HB-1034		
	D Nisbet tr HMY Syndicate Usk *'HMY'*		09.03.18E
G-CHMZ	Fedorov Me7 Mechta	M004	03.09.08
	BGA 4060/HMZ R Andrews Long Mynd		09.04.10R
	(NF 01.11.16)		
G-CHNA	Glaser-Dirks DG-500/20 Elan	5E128W3	30.11.07
	BGA 4061/HNA M S Armstrong tr G-CHNA Group		
	Camphill *'HNA'*		15.04.18E
	Built by Elan Tovarna Sportnega Orodja N.Sol.O		
G-CHNC	Schleicher ASW 19B	19297	09.11.07
	BGA 4063/HNC, OO-ZNN, OH-515		
	T J Highton Tibenham *'HNC'*		06.03.18E
G-CHND	Ultramagic H-65	65/193	20.12.12
	N Dykes Horningsham, Warminster		26.01.18E
G-CHNF	Schempp-Hirth Duo Discus	11	15.10.07
	BGA 4066 Booker Gliding Club Ltd		
	Wycombe Air Park *'315'*		15.03.18E

G-CHNH	Schempp-Hirth Nimbus-2C	187	27.11.07
	BGA 4068/HNH, D-2830		
	A J & M J W Harris Ridgewell *'Z99'*		16.08.19E
G-CHNI	Magni M24C Orion	24127474	18.12.12
	A Smith Oban		29.06.18P
G-CHNK	PZL-Bielsko SZD-51-1 Junior	B-1496	15.10.07
	BGA 4070, SP-3299, (SP-3290)		
	Booker Gliding Club Ltd Wycombe Air Park *'HNK'*		28.02.18E
G-CHNM	Jastreb Standard Cirrus G/81	360	30.11.07
	BGA4072/HNM, SE-TZT		
	C R I Emson & A N Mayer Bicester *'C55'*		29.12.17E
G-CHNO	Cameron C-60	11344	10.12.12
	J F Till Welburn, York *'Carla'*		09.04.18E
G-CHNS	AgustaWestland AW139	31465	16.01.13
	Bristow Helicopters Ltd Norwich Int'l		16.01.19E
G-CHNT	Schleicher ASW 15	15167	09.06.08
	BGA 4078/HNT, F-CEAQ		
	K Tunnicliff Gransden Lodge *'105'*		29.06.16E
	(IE 30.05.17)		
G-CHNU	Schempp-Hirth Nimbus-4DT	3/5	20.09.07
	BGA4079, D-KHIA D E Findon Bidford *'48'*		14.04.18E
G-CHNV	Rolladen-Schneider LS4-b	4960	02.11.07
	BGA 4080/HNV S K Britt & P H Dixon		
	Kirton in Lindsey *'692'*		11.05.18E
G-CHNW	Schempp-Hirth Duo Discus	25	23.10.07
	BGA 4081 G K Drury & J G Garside tr G-CHNW Group		
	Gransden Lodge *'220'*		05.05.18E
G-CHNX[M]	Lockheed L188AF Electra	1068	01.11.94
	(EI-AHO), G-CHNX, N5535		
	Cancelled 12.05.03 as PWFU		31.10.01
	Front fuselage only		
	With Midland Air Museum, Coventry		
G-CHNY	Centrair 101A Pégase	101020	26.09.08
	BGA 4083/HNY, F-CFRP		
	M O Breen Wycombe Air Park *'HNY'*		12.05.10E
	(NF 16.12.16)		
G-CHNZ	Centrair 101A Pégase	101032	26.10.07
	BGA 4084, F-CFRY		
	C R & R H Partington Milfield *'HNZ'*		29.06.18E
G-CHOA	Bell 206B-3 JetRanger III	4582	17.10.12
	EI-MEJ, N909WB, C-GBUB		
	A G B, J P B & N B B Davie-Thornhill		
	t/a Haverholme Farm Partnership Thruxton		04.04.18E
G-CHOD	Schleicher ASW 20	20288	24.06.08
	BGA 4112/HQD, SE-ULA, OH-548		
	S E Archer-Jones & A Duerden Bicester *'A20'*		10.05.17E
	(IE 13.06.17)		
G-CHOE	Robin DR.400-140B Major 80	1046	24.09.12
	F-BXJO D W Midgley & S Nuttall tr YP Flying Group		
	Blackpool		17.05.19E
G-CHOF	CARMAM M-100S Mésange	26	11.09.08
	BGA 4114/HQF, F-CCSO		
	M A Farrelly Long Mynd *'HOF'*		19.11.09R
	(NF 30.09.15)		
G-CHOG	Sportine Aviacija LAK-12 Lietuva	6222	13.03.09
	BGA 4115/HQG J M Pursey North Hill *'HOG'*		15.10.18E
G-CHOI[M]	White Monoplane 1912 Canard Pusher replica	1	30.11.12
	J Aubert Brooklands		
	Built by J Aubert		
	(SSDR microlight since 05.14) (IE 31.05.17)		
G-CHOJ	Cameron A-375	11707	28.02.13
	Ballooning In Tuscany SRL Firenze, Italy		05.02.18E
G-CHOO	Comco Ikarus C42 FB80	1205-7204	11.09.12
	M J Reed Popham		26.08.19P
	Assembled Red-Air UK		
G-CHOP	Westland-Bell 47G-3B-1	WAN-79	19.12.78
	XT221 Leamington Hobby Centre Ltd		
	Wellesbourne Mountford		23.05.18E
G-CHOR	Schempp-Hirth Discus b	531	25.02.08
	BGA 4123/HQR		
	R Connors tr G-CHOR Syndicate Bicester *'T19'*		30.03.18E
G-CHOT	Grob G102 Astir CS77	1678	02.12.11
	BGA 4125/HQT, RAFGGA 561		
	Southdown Gliding Club Ltd Parham Park *'HOT'*		03.12.18E

G-CHOU	Evektor EV-97 teamEurostar UK	4102	04.02.13
	R A Betts Bourn		03.01.19P
	Assembled Cosmik Aviation Ltd		
G-CHOV	PZL-Bielsko SZD-51-1 Junior	B-2139	05.10.07
	BGA 4127 Cancelled 27.11.12 as PWFU		26.04.12
	Husbands Bosworth *Stored 06.14*		
G-CHOX	Europa Aviation Europa XS	566	02.04.03
	Chocks Away Ltd White Waltham		15.10.18P
	Built by P Field – project PFA 247-13974; tricycle u/c		
G-CHOY	Schempp-Hirth Mini Nimbus C	113	18.10.07
	BGA 4130, D-3364 A H Sparrow Lasham *'HOY'*		10.03.18E
G-CHOZ	Rolladen-Schneider LS6-18W	6353	18.01.08
	BGA 4131/HQZ, D-1486		
	J C Trubridge tr U2 Syndicate Parham Park *'U2'*		09.05.18E
G-CHPA	Robinson R22 Beta II	3442	18.04.07
	EI-EHC, N71850 Rivermead Aviation Ltd		
	Gloucestershire		13.09.12E
	(IE 05.12.17)		
G-CHPD	Rolladen-Schneider LS6-c18	6331	29.10.07
	BGA 4088, D-1054		
	R E Robertson Dunstable Downs *'62'*		24.02.19E
G-CHPE	Schleicher ASK 13	13510	23.01.08
	BGA 4089/HPE, D-3992		
	Dumfries & District Gliding Club Falgunzeon *'HPE'*		03.07.18E
G-CHPG	Cirrus SR20	1636	19.12.12
	N470RD AT Aviation Sales Ltd, G Greenfield t/a Guy		
	Greenfield Architects & K M O'Sullivan Branscombe		15.01.19E
G-CHPH	Schempp-Hirth Discus CS	174CS	26.11.07
	BGA 4092/HPH L Finlay (Legbourne, Louth) *'268'*		22.01.19E
	Built by Orličan Aakciová Společnost		
G-CHPI	de Havilland DHC-1 Chipmunk 22	14	16.02.10
	Port AF 1324 J A Da Silva Costa		
	(Albarraque, Sintra, Portugal)		30.11.17E
	Built by OGMA		
G-CHPK	Van's RV-8	82530	26.09.08
	G-JILS J H Penfold tr Vans Papa Kilo Group		
	Brighton City *'Van's Aluminium Mistress'*		07.03.19P
	Built by A C Andover & M R Tingle		
	– project PFA 303-14535		
G-CHPL	Rolladen-Schneider LS4-b	4959	09.11.07
	BGA 4095/HPL, (BGA 4071/HNL)		
	Southdown Gliding Club Ltd Parham Park *'HPL'*		23.02.19E
G-CHPO	Schleicher Ka 6CR	6200	26.11.07
	BGA 4099/HPQ, D-1933		
	A P Frost Wormingford *'HPO'*		15.09.18E
G-CHPS	Best Off Skyranger 582(1)	SKR0811923	21.01.13
	J A Gregorig Longacre Farm, Sandy		30.09.18P
	Built by K Robinson – project BMAA/HB/595		
G-CHPT	Fedorov Me7 Mechta	M006	08.02.08
	BGA 4102/HPT		
	Midland Gliding Club Ltd Long Mynd *'HPT'*		28.08.15R
	(IE 21.04.17)		
G-CHPV	Schleicher ASK 21	21608	27.11.07
	BGA 4104/HPV		
	Scottish Gliding Union Ltd Portmoak *'HPV'*		27.02.18E
G-CHPW	Schleicher ASK 21	21609	02.11.07
	BGA 4105/HPW		
	Scottish Gliding Union Ltd Portmoak *'HPW'*		08.02.18E
G-CHPX	Schempp-Hirth Discus CS	177CS	14.11.07
	BGA 4106/HPX M A Whitehead tr G-CHPX Group		
	Gransden Lodge *'693'*		16.03.18E
	Built by Orličan Aakciová Společnost		
G-CHPY	de Havilland DHC-1 Chipmunk 22	C1/0093	07.03.97
	WB652 Devonair Executive Business Transport Ltd		
	(Swindon)		06.07.08
	(NF 29.10.18)		
G-CHPZ	P&M Quik GT450	8649	12.04.13
	D J Shippen (Wincham, Northwich)		28.07.18P
	Rebuild of G-CEML being original trike c/n 8260 plus new wing		
G-CHRC	Glaser-Dirks DG-500/20 Elan	5E136W5	10.10.07
	BGA 4134 M W Fisher tr DG500-390 Syndicate		
	Parham Park *'390'*		12.07.18E
	Built by Elan Tovarna Sportnega Orodja N.Sol.O		

G-CHRD	Flylight Dragonlite	DF082	03.12.12
	I A Barclay (Great Eccleston, Preston)		
	(SSDR microlight since 05.14) (IE 08.07.16)		
G-CHRE	Nicollier HN.700 Menestrel II	203	30.01.13
	M K A Blyth Little Gransden		19.06.18P
	Built by B S Godbold – project PFA 217-13867		
G-CHRG	PZL-Bielsko SZD-51-1 Junior	B-2013	17.01.08
	BGA 4138/HRG, B-2013		
	PA Technologies Ltd (Claypole, Newark) *'HRG'*		03.06.15E
G-CHRH	Schempp-Hirth Discus-2cT	74	03.07.08
	(BGA 5323), D-KIIH C Hyett Lasham *'KSG'*		21.04.18E
G-CHRJ	Schleicher K 8B	8093	08.08.08
	BGA 4139/HRJ, D-5048		
	G A Smith (Grenofen, Tavistock) *'HRJ'*		19.09.19E
G-CHRM	Comco Ikarus C42 FB80 Bravo	1210-7229	08.01.13
	E Hardiman & J A Horn Greenhills Farm, Wheatley Hill		06.02.20P
	Assembled Red-Air UK		
G-CHRN	Schleicher ASK 18	18026	03.10.07
	BGA 4143, HB-1308 K Richards Talgarth *'HRN'*		07.08.18E
G-CHRS	Schempp-Hirth Discus CS	100CS	25.10.07
	BGA 4147, D-5100 M Menegotto tr G-CHRS Group		
	Calcinate del Pesce, Italy *'B33'*		19.05.18E
	Built by Orličan Aakciová Společnost		
G-CHRT	Evektor EV-97 teamEurostar UK	4103	08.03.13
	A J Ferguson & T W Pawson Rufforth East		17.02.19P
	Assembled Cosmik Aviation Ltd		
G-CHRU	Flylight Dragonlite Fox	DA100	22.03.13
	J R Kendall (Nawton, York)		
	Shares trike unit with G-CITL		
	(SSDR microlight since 05.14) (IE 06.10.16)		
G-CHRV	Van's RV-7	xxxx	11.12.12
	R E Tyers Spanhoe		18.04.18P
	Built by R E Tyers – project LAA 323-15031		
G-CHRW	Schempp-Hirth Duo Discus	43	17.09.07
	BGA4151, (BGA 4160) R A Johnson Shobdon *'802'*		08.02.19E
G-CHRX	Schempp-Hirth Discus a	545	21.01.08
	BGA 4152/HRX A Spirling Portmoak *'P5'*		15.03.19E
G-CHSB	Glaser-Dirks DG-300 Elan	3E461	23.07.08
	BGA 4156/HSB		
	P J Britten Wycombe Air Park *'HSB'*		11.02.18E
	Built by Elan Tovarna Sportnega Orodja N.Sol.O		
G-CHSD	Schempp-Hirth Discus b	258/1	01.11.07
	BGA 4158/HSD, (BGA 4142/HRM) R D Leslie		
	tr G-CHSD Group Dunstable Downs *'D15'*		14.04.19E
G-CHSE	Grob G102 Astir CS77	1635	15.01.08
	BGA 4159/HSE, RAFGSA R68, RAFGSA 548		
	M Nicholls tr Hotel Sierra Echo Group		
	Rattlesden *'HSE'*		31.07.18E
G-CHSG	Scheibe SF27A Zugvogel V	1705/E	03.03.08
	BGA 4161/HSG, D-7827, OE-0827		
	C T Oliver tr HSG Syndicate Challock *'HSG'*		07.08.16E
	Original official c/n 1705/E correct; amended 07.08		
	to c/n 6103 (BGA 3655) but not connected		
G-CHSH	Scheibe Zugvogel IIIB	7/1041	25.06.12
	BGA 4162/HSH, D-6558 S A Lewis tr G-CHSH Group		
	Burnford Common, Brentor *'HSH'*		15.08.19E
G-CHSI	Pulma/Ellipse Fuji 16	11696/30004	12.02.13
	H J Mayer (Northwich)		
	(SSDR microlight since 05.14) (IE 04.08.16)		
G-CHSK	Schleicher ASW 20CL	20827	19.03.08
	BGA 4164/HSK, D-3499 A J Watson tr 751 Syndicate		
	Gransden Lodge *'751'*		25.04.18E
G-CHSM	Schleicher ASK 13	13145	24.09.07
	BGA 4166, D-0168		
	Staffordshire Gliding Club Ltd Seighford *'HSM'*		23.10.17E
	(NF 19.10.17)		
G-CHSN	Schleicher Ka 6CR	6218	20.11.07
	BGA 4167/HSN, OO-ZZF, D-8546		
	Needwood Forest Gliding Club Ltd Snitterfield *'HSN'*		20.08.19E
G-CHSO	Schempp-Hirth Discus b	99	10.12.07
	BGA 4169/HSQ, D-2943		
	W A Baumann Long Mynd *'493'*		27.04.19E
G-CHSP	Ultramagic M-65C	65/196	25.03.13
	S Bareford Cookley, Kidderminster		05.05.18E

G-CHSS	Comco Ikarus C42 FB80 Bravo	1209-7224	14.01.13
	A P Burch (Timperley, Altrincham)		24.10.18P
	Assembled Red-Air UK		
G-CHST	Van's RV-9A	NB8085	25.02.13
	R J Charles Dunkeswell *'9'*		18.06.18P
	Built by E Battle & R J Charles – project PFA 320-14283		
G-CHSU	Eurocopter EC135 T1	0079	04.02.99
	2 Excel Aviation Ltd Sywell		18.05.19E
G-CHSX	Scheibe SF27A Zugvogel V	6031	06.11.07
	BGA 4176/HSX, SE-TDT		
	Essex & Suffolk Gliding Club Ltd Wormingford *'HSX'*		28.04.18E
G-CHSY	Aeroprakt A-22LS Foxbat	A22LS-140	21.02.13
	J D Reed Henstridge		08.08.18P
	Built by A Everitt – project LAA 317B-15186;		
	badged 'Super Sport 600'		
G-CHTA	Grumman American AA-5A Cheetah	AA5A-0631	03.03.86
	G-BFRC D Byrne Elstree		07.05.19E
G-CHTB	Schempp-Hirth Janus	07	20.02.08
	BGA 4180/HTB, D-3114 J B Maddison tr Janus		
	G-CHTB Syndicate Kirton in Lindsey *'HTB'*		08.04.18E
G-CHTC	Schleicher ASW 15B	15188	20.05.08
	BGA 4181/HTC, OE-0930 S Thackray		
	tr G-CHTC Flying Group Aston Down *'HTC'*		11.05.19E
G-CHTD	Grob G102 Astir CS	1012	07.01.08
	BGA 4182/HTD, D-6508 S Waldie Lasham *'HTD'*		17.01.19E
G-CHTE	Grob G102 Astir CS77	1716	20.11.07
	BGA 4183/HTE, RAFGSA R82, RAFGSA 882		
	J P W Towill Challock *'HTE'*		21.04.18E
G-CHTF	Sportine Aviacija LAK-12 Lietuva	6180	19.12.07
	BGA 4184/HTF M Tolson tr TOI Syndicate		
	Husbands Bosworth *'TOI'*		01.05.19E
G-CHTH	Zenair CH.701SP	7-7329 ?	28.02.13
	R E Lasnier (Sleap)		
	Built by R E Lasnier – project LAA 187A-14879		
G-CHTI	Van's RV-12	120282	22.01.13
	M N & N D Stannard RAF Henlow		26.01.19P
	Built by E M Marsh – project LAA 363-15140		
G-CHTJ	Schleicher ASK 13	13125	08.10.08
	BGA 4187/HTJ, D-6048, Belgian Air Cadets PL62		
	Queen's University Gliding Club Bellarena *'HTJ'*		27.10.18E
G-CHTK	Hawker Hurricane X	CCF/41H/8020	12.03.13
	N33TF, G-TWTD, AE977 Warbird Experiences Ltd		
	Biggin Hill		04.04.19P
	Built by Canadian Car & Foundry Co as Hurricane		
	Mk.X; converted to Sea Hurricane Mk.X c.1942 &		
	restored as Hurricane Mk.X c.2000;		
	as 'P2921:GZ-L' in RAF 32 Sqdn c/s		
G-CHTL	Schempp-Hirth Arcus T	35	28.02.13
	R J Large tr 38 Syndicate Husbands Bosworth *'38'*		21.03.18E
G-CHTM	Rolladen-Schneider LS8-18	8036	05.10.07
	BGA 4190 M J Chapman Seighford *'Z8'*		28.04.18E
G-CHTO	Rans S-7S Courier	0711.558	02.01.13
	A G Bell Wickenby		20.11.18P
	Built by J D Llewellyn – project PFA 218-15168		
G-CHTR	Grob G102 Astir CS	1190	25.10.07
	BGA 4194, D-7307 C D Teasdale tr HTR Group		
	(Shipton Bellinger, Tidworth) *'HTR'*		21.03.19E
G-CHTS	Rolladen-Schneider LS8-18	8040	23.10.07
	BGA 4195 P T Cunnison Gransden Lodge *'H8'*		27.05.18E
G-CHTU	Schempp-Hirth Cirrus	88	19.02.08
	BGA 4197/HTU, D-0478		
	G V Higgins tr Open Cirrus Group Burn *'HTU'*		26.05.18E
G-CHTV	Schleicher ASK 21	21624	01.02.08
	BGA 4198/HTV, D-8355 Cambridge Gliding Club Ltd		
	Gransden Lodge *'HTV'*		18.02.18E
G-CHTX	Voltair 86	DRS-01	28.03.13
	Hartlepool College of Further Education (Fishburn)		
	Built by D R Skill		
	(SSDR microlight since 05.14) (NF 03.03.17)		
G-CHTZ	Airbus A330-243	398	31.10.13
	G-WWBM, F-WWKL		
	Thomas Cook Airlines Ltd Manchester		04.06.19E

G

G-CHUA	Schleicher ASW 19B	19091	16.01.08
	BGA 4203/HUA, D-3840		
	G D Vaughan (South Elmshall, Pontefract) *'HUA'*		14.02.18E
G-CHUBM	Colt Cylinder Two N-51	1720	11.04.90
	Cancelled 12.12.01 as WFU		19.12.95
	Fire Extinguisher special shape		
	With British Balloon Museum & Library, Newbury		
G-CHUC	Denney Kitfox Model 2	744	25.02.13
	A Price (Tonbridge)		24.08.18P
	Built by J McIntyre – project LAA 172-15055		
G-CHUD	Schleicher ASK 13	13018	12.10.07
	BGA 4206, D-9203 London Gliding Club		
	Proprietary Ltd Dunstable Downs *'HUD'*		07.05.18E
G-CHUE	Schleicher ASW 27	27022	22.08.08
	BGA 4207/HUE M J Smith Dunstable Downs *'N5'*		20.02.19E
G-CHUF	Schleicher ASK 13	13109	11.12.07
	BGA 4208/HUF, OO-ZWE		
	The Welland Gliding Club Ltd Lyveden *'HUF'*		22.10.18E
G-CHUG	Europa Aviation Europa	260	29.07.96
	C M Washington Sleap		11.05.18P
	Built by C M Washington – project PFA 247-12960;		
	tailwheel u/c		
G-CHUH	Schempp-Hirth Janus	15	18.01.08
	BGA 4210/HUH, D-3116		
	B J Biskup (Bielsko-Biala, Poland) *'D31'*		22.07.17E
G-CHUJ	Centrair ASW 20F	20170	03.10.07
	BGA 4211, F-CFLY S G Lapworth Lasham *'HUJ'*		01.04.19E
G-CHUK	Cameron O-77	2773	06.03.92
	A Hook Tibshelf, Alfreton		27.03.18E
G-CHUN	Grob G102 Astir CS Jeans	2089	03.01.08
	BGA 4215/HUN, D-7531		
	Staffordshire Gliding Club Ltd Seighford *'HUN'*		19.05.18E
G-CHUO	Fedorov Me7 Mechta	M007	10.01.08
	BGA 4217/HUQ		
	J D A Cooper & W H Ollis (Haddenham) *'DP'*		28.04.18R
	Built by Aviastroitel Ltd		
G-CHUP	Aeropro EuroFOX 912(S)	40813	14.03.13
	B Walker & Co (Dursley) Ltd Nympsfield		02.07.18P
	Built by B Walker & I Smith – project LAA 376-15188;		
	tailwheel u/c; glider-tug		
G-CHUR	Schempp-Hirth Cirrus	12	30.11.07
	BGA 4218/HUR, HB-927		
	M Rossiter & J A Stillwagon Talgarth *'HUR'*		23.04.18E
G-CHUS	Scheibe SF27A Zugvogel V	6010	02.04.08
	BGA 4219/HUS, D-1035 P J Duffy		
	tr SF27 HUS Syndicate Shenington *'HUS'*		13.07.13E
	(NF 04.05.17)		
G-CHUT	Centrair ASW 20F	20187	06.09.07
	BGA 4220, F-CEUQ		
	S R Phelps Wycombe Air Park *'HUT'*		14.09.19E
G-CHUU	Schleicher ASK 13	13527AB	12.12.07
	BGA 4221/HUU, D-7506, D-8945		
	Upward Bound Trust Hinton-in-the-Hedges *'HUU'*		20.10.18E
G-CHUX	P&M QuikR	8643	28.01.13
	A J Trye Little Gransden		18.04.18P
	Bounced on touchdown Hawksview,		
	Stretton 01.09.16 & extensively damaged		
G-CHUY	Schempp-Hirth Ventus cT	84	30.08.07
	BGA 4225, D-KILZ		
	P R Gammell (Little Hadham, Ware) *'HUY'*		13.07.18E
G-CHUZ	Schempp-Hirth Discus bT	158	30.11.07
	BGA 4226/HUZ G Starling Nympsfield *'200'*		13.03.18E
G-CHVB	P&M QuikR	8645	29.04.13
	R J Bell tr Victor Bravo Group East Fortune		22.04.18P
G-CHVC	Cameron C-60	11742	17.04.13
	A L L Lenaerts Sinaai, Belgium *'Breitling Academy'*		16.01.20E
G-CHVG	Schleicher ASK 21	21062	10.04.08
	BGA 4233/HVG, D-2606		
	Rattlesden Gliding Club Ltd Rattlesden *'RP1'*		24.05.18E
G-CHVH	Pilatus B4-PC11AF	067	19.06.08
	BGA 4234/HVH, D-2156 London Gliding Club		
	Proprietary Ltd Dunstable Downs *'HVH'*		07.02.19E
G-CHVI	Cameron Z-210	11725	19.03.13
	A-Gas (ORB) Ltd Portishead, Bristol *'A-Gas'*		08.04.17E

G-CHVJ	Supermarine 349 Spitfire Vb	CBAF 1168	24.04.13
	AD189 G N S Farrant (Drayton St Leonard, Wallingford)		
	(NF 23.09.17)		
G-CHVK	Grob G102 Astir CS	1161	10.01.08
	BGA 4236/HVK, D-4182 Yorkshire Gliding Club		
	(Proprietary) Ltd Sutton Bank *'HVK'*		11.10.19E
G-CHVM	Glaser-Dirks DG-300 Elan	3E177	24.04.08
	BGA 4238/HVM, D-4314		
	N R Brown tr Glider Syndicate 393 Portmoak *'393'*		08.08.18E
	Built by Elan Tovarna Sportnega Orodja N.Sol.O		
G-CHVO	Schleicher ASK 13	13251	06.08.08
	BGA 4241/HVQ, D-0605		
	R Brown Shenington *'HVQ'*		15.01.14E
	(IE 21.04.17)		
G-CHVP	Schleicher ASW 20	20374	07.01.08
	BGA 4240/HVP, D-1961, BGA 4076/HNR, EC-DLN		
	G P Northcott Ringmer *'930'*		13.07.18E
G-CHVR	Schempp-Hirth Discus b	560	13.03.08
	BGA 4242/HVR Yorkshire Gliding Club		
	(Proprietary) Ltd Sutton Bank *'HVR'*		31.01.18E
G-CHVS	ICP MXP-740 Savannah XLS Jabiru(1)	10-11-54-0039	12.04.13
	S Whittaker & P J Wilson t/a Sandtoft Ultralights		
	Partnership Sandtoft		13.08.18P
	Built by S Whittaker & P J Wilson		
	– project BMAA/HB/602		
G-CHVV	Rolladen-Schneider LS4-b	41009	06.11.07
	BGA 4246/HVV A J Bardgett Milfield *'HVV'*		09.11.18E
G-CHVW	Schleicher ASK 13	13431	31.01.08
	BGA 4247/HVW, D-2140		
	Rattlesden Gliding Club Ltd Rattlesden *'HVW'*		16.05.15E
	(IE 28.10.15)		
G-CHVX	Centrair ASW 20F	20528	01.12.07
	BGA 4248/HVX, F-CFSJ		
	D Coker Husbands Bosworth *'F20'*		16.05.18E
G-CHVY	Comco Ikarus C42 FB80 Bravo	1304-7246	20.05.13
	H Wilson tr G-CHVY Syndicate Shobdon		29.05.18P
	Assembled Red-Air UK		
G-CHVZ	Schempp-Hirth Standard Cirrus	567G	27.11.07
	BGA 4250/HVZ, HB-1269		
	P H V Alexander tr ABC Soaring Upwood *'HVZ'*		12.05.18E
	Built by Burkhart Grob Flugzeugbau		
G-CHWA	Schempp-Hirth Ventus-2c	8/20	27.05.08
	BGA 4251/HWA C Garton Lasham *'31'*		06.11.18E
G-CHWB	Schempp-Hirth Duo Discus	84	17.07.08
	BGA 4252/HWB		
	Lasham Gliding Society Ltd Lasham *'3'*		26.08.18E
G-CHWC	Glasflügel Standard Libelle 201B	310	12.12.07
	BGA 4253/HWC, HB-1076		
	R P Hardcastle Rufforth *'S4'*		12.04.18E
G-CHWD	Schempp-Hirth Standard Cirrus	97	11.04.11
	BGA 4254/HWD, HB-987		
	M R Hoskins Rivar Hill *'MH'*		21.03.18E
G-CHWE	Lindstrand LBL 77A	1451	02.07.13
	B P Witter Churton, Chester		06.07.18E
G-CHWF	Jastreb Standard Cirrus G/81	281	12.03.08
	BGA 4256/HWF, SE-TZC		
	R J Peake tr Team Cirrus 2ZC Chipping *'2ZC'*		12.09.18E
G-CHWG	Glasflügel Standard Libelle 201B	259	11.05.09
	BGA 4257/HWG, HB-1051		
	M R Fox Seighford *'HWG'*		01.11.17E
G-CHWH	Schempp-Hirth Ventus cT	182	20.08.07
	BGA 4258, RAFGGA 506		
	M J Philpott Lasham *'712'*		01.04.18E
G-CHWI	APEV Demoichelle	GRM-001	15.04.13
	D H Lewis (Nelson, Treharris)		
	Built by G R Moore		
	(SSDR microlight since 05.14) (IE 09.07.18)		
G-CHWJ	Guimbal Cabri G2	1052	22.07.13
	Helitrain Ltd Cotswold		04.07.19E
	Operated by Vantage Aviation		
G-CHWK	Aerochute Hummerchute	436	29.01.13
	W A Kimberlin (Melton Mowbray)		13.04.19P
	Originally registered as Aerochute Dual;		
	type changed to Aeroshute Hummerchute		
	11.14; parachute s/n 12-04-1919		

G-CHWL	Rolladen-Schneider LS8-18	8076	18.01.08
	BGA 4261/HWL D S Lodge Sutton Bank '184'		09.04.18E
G-CHWM	AutoGyro Cavalon	V00094	27.03.13
	Devon Autogyro Ltd		
	Moorlands Farm, Farway Common		04.05.19P
	Assembled Rotorsport UK as c/n RSUK/CVLN/002		
G-CHWN	Comco Ikarus C42 FB100 Bravo	1302-7240	11.03.13
	G Colby Sywell		10.10.19P
	Assembled Red-Air UK		
G-CHWO	P&M Quik GTR	8654	17.04.13
	M J Robbins Rochester		19.04.18P
G-CHWP	Glaser-Dirks DG-100G Elan	E24G13	23.06.08
	BGA 4264/HWP, D-3772		
	M R Baldwin tr HWP Group Chipping 'HWP'		09.04.18E
	Built by Elan Tovarna Sportnega Orodja N.Sol.O		
G-CHWS	Rolladen-Schneider LS8-18	8080	15.11.07
	BGA 4267/HWS		
	G A & H B Chalmers Easterton 'Z5'		07.04.18E
	Trailered in to fly		
G-CHWT	Schleicher K 8B	8780	22.04.09
	BGA 4268/HWT, HB-958		
	Shenington Gliding Club Shenington 'S83'		08.09.12E
	(IE 10.12.14)		
G-CHWW	Grob G103A Twin II Acro	3658-K-27	10.12.07
	BGA 4271/HWW, OE-5285		
	Crown Service Gliding Club Lasham 'HWW'		27.03.19E
G-CHXA	Scheibe Zugvogel IIIB	1107	29.10.08
	BGA 4275/HXA, D-2005		
	C J Tilley tr G-CHXA Group RAF Odiham		07.04.12E
	(IE 20.02.17)		
G-CHXB	Grob G102 Astir CS77	1819	12.09.08
	BGA 4276/HXB, D-6755		
	K Lafferty Gransden Lodge '52' & 'HXB'		04.05.18E
G-CHXD	Schleicher ASW 27	27030	03.12.07
	BGA 4279/HXD		
	M Jerman & J Quartermaine Sutton Bank 'HXD'		18.02.18E
G-CHXE	Schleicher ASW 19B	19053	06.11.07
	BGA 4280/HXE, D-6699		
	M P Featherstone (Arnold, Nottingham) 'Y4'		12.11.19E
G-CHXF	Cameron A-140	11700	27.11.12
	Gone With The Wind Ltd Abbots Leigh, Bristol		26.03.18E
	Operated by The Portuguese Partnership Ltd		
G-CHXG	CZAW Sportcruiser	OC700861	28.03.13
	R J Warne Wycombe Air Park		11.03.19P
	Built by R J Warne – project LAA 338-14884		
G-CHXH	Schempp-Hirth Discus b	573	16.11.07
	BGA 4283/HXH, BGA 4375/JBD, (BGA 4283/HXH)		
	Deeside Gliding Club (Aberdeenshire) Ltd		
	Aboyne 'HXH'		06.01.19E
G-CHXJ	Schleicher ASK 13	13216	23.10.07
	BGA 4284, D-0417		
	Cotswold Gliding Club Aston Down 'HXJ'		28.02.18E
G-CHXK	Scheibe SF25C Falke 2000	44435	29.04.13
	I-APBK, (D-KIAB)		
	Stratford on Avon Gliding Club Ltd Snitterfield		06.04.18E
G-CHXL	Van's RV-6	20960	02.05.14
	N960JT R W Marchant & S C Parsons		
	Little Engeham Farm, Woodchurch		31.05.18P
	Built by J E Teele		
G-CHXM	Grob G102 Astir CS	1272	13.06.08
	BGA 4287/HXM, D-7367 University of Bristol		
	Students Union Nympsfield 'HXM'		27.05.18E
G-CHXN	Kubícek BB20GP	1001	24.07.13
	D R Medcalf Catshill, Bromsgrove		26.06.19E
G-CHXO	Schleicher ASH 25	25187	04.12.07
	BGA 4290/HXQ, OH-874		
	P Morrison tr The Eleven Group North Hill '711'		29.05.18E
G-CHXP	Schleicher ASK 13	13023	28.11.07
	BGA 4289/HXP, D-3656 Dartmoor Gliding Society		
	Burnford Common, Brentor 'HXP'		06.07.18E
G-CHXR	Schempp-Hirth Ventus cT	88	19.10.07
	BGA 4291/HXR, D-KESH		
	P G Kynsey tr 560 Group Lasham '560'		05.11.18E

G-CHXS	Cameron C-90	11754	05.07.13
	B R Whatley Nailsea, Bristol 'dribuild'		23.05.19E
G-CHXT	Rolladen-Schneider LS4-a	4325	03.12.07
	BGA 4293/HXT, ZS-GNV		
	P N Murray Parham Park 'HXT'		04.03.17E
G-CHXU	Schleicher ASW 19B	19359	01.02.08
	BGA 4294/HXU, SE-TXN UCLU RAF Halton 'HXU'		20.04.18E
G-CHXV	Schleicher ASK 13	13080	17.10.07
	BGA 4295, D-5462 Banbury Gliding Club Ltd		
	Hinton-in-the-Hedges 'HXV'		16.04.18E
G-CHXW	Rolladen-Schneider LS8-18	8097	19.12.07
	BGA 4296/HXW W Aspland Wycombe Air Park '325'		31.03.18E
G-CHXZ	Rolladen-Schneider LS4	4249	01.02.08
	BGA 4299/HXZ, SE-TXF N Croxford Snitterfield 'S5'		20.03.18E
G-CHYB	Grob G109B	6372	05.06.13
	D-KERJ C J Tooze & M P Weaver Usk		17.07.19E
G-CHYC	Westlake Altair AX4-31/12	007	22.05.13
	D W Westlake (Quedgeley, Gloucester)		
	(NF 22.08.16)		
G-CHYD	Schleicher ASW 24	24039	20.11.07
	BGA 4303/HYD, OE-5460		
	E B Adlard Long Mynd 'HYD'		25.03.18E
G-CHYE	DG Flugzeugbau DG-505 Elan Orion	5E167X22	12.09.07
	BGA 4304 The Bristol Gliding Club Proprietary Ltd		
	Nympsfield '913'		04.11.18E
	Built by Elan Tovarna Sportnega Orodja N.Sol.O		
G-CHYF	Rolladen-Schneider LS8-18	8106	26.10.07
	BGA 4305 R E Francis Nympsfield '660'		20.02.19E
G-CHYG	Sikorsky S-92A	920196	03.07.13
	N196Q Bristow Helicopters Ltd Aberdeen Int'l		09.07.18E
G-CHYH	Rolladen-Schneider LS3-17	3186	15.05.08
	BGA 4307/HYH, D-6650 B Silke Bellarena 'HYH'		20.12.18E
G-CHYJ	Schleicher ASK 21	21066	05.03.08
	BGA 4308/HYJ, D-2724		
	Highland Gliding Club Ltd Easterton 'HYJ'		02.09.18E
	Original wings stored Rufforth 10.16		
G-CHYK	Centrair ASW 20FL	20176	21.05.08
	BGA 4309/HYK, F-CEUN		
	K H Bates (Stalybridge) 'HYK'		08.06.18E
G-CHYN	CCF T-6 Harvard Mk.4M	CCF4-531	29.05.13
	Portuguese AF 1765, West German AF BF+070,		
	AA+080, 52-8610		
	Victoria Group Holdings Ltd Dunkeswell		24.08.18E
	Built by Canadian Car & Foundry Co;		
	as 'BF+070' in Lufwaffe c/s		
G-CHYO	Ace Aviation Magic/Laser	AM157	18.06.13
	D R Purslow Pound Green		
	Trike s/n AM157 & wing s/n AL153		
	(SSDR microlight since 05.14) (IE 03.01.18)		
G-CHYP	PZL-Bielsko SZD-50-3 Puchacz	B-2082	11.03.08
	BGA 4313/HYP		
	Rattlesden Gliding Club Ltd Rattlesden		17.06.18E
G-CHYR	Schleicher ASW 27	27013	20.11.07
	BGA 4315/HYR, D-8733		
	A J Manwaring Dunstable Downs '432'		12.04.18E
G-CHYS	Schleicher ASK 21	21519	01.05.08
	BGA 4316/HYS, RAFGGA 514 J W Sage		
	tr Army Gliding Association AAC Wattisham 'A14'		13.10.18E
	Operated by Anglia Gliding Club		
G-CHYT	Schleicher ASK 21	21568	29.01.08
	BGA 4317/HYT, AGA 20, (BGA 4317), RAFGGA 515		
	J W Sage tr Army Gliding Association		
	Trenchard Lines, Upavon 'HYT'		05.01.19E
G-CHYU	Schempp-Hirth Discus CS	192CS	01.05.08
	BGA 4318/HYU, AGA??, RAFGGA 561		
	J W Sage tr Army Gliding Association		
	AAC Wattisham 'A6'		13.07.18E
	Operated by Anglia Gliding Club		
G-CHYX	Schleicher K 8B	686	08.02.08
	BGA 4321/HYX, D-5742 Cancelled 05.01.16 by CAA		04.07.15
	Ringmer, Sussex *Stored 08.17*		
G-CHYY	Schempp-Hirth Nimbus-3DT	21	06.11.07
	BGA 4322/HYY, RAFGSA R26, D-KAFA		
	M Ellis tr G-CHYY Syndicate Burn 'A26'		15.05.18E

G-CHYZ Skystar Kitfox Vixen   xxxx   19.06.13
F-PSKJ, F-WSKJ   P B Davey   Headcorn   01.09.19P
Built by C Muller; official c/n 'KCV-024' is incorrect

G-CHZB PZL-Swidnik PW-5 Smyk   17.06.021   09.05.08
BGA 4325/HZB
The Burn Gliding Club Ltd   Burn   *'HZB'*   17.06.18E

G-CHZD Schleicher ASW 15B   15327   04.12.07
BGA 4327/HZD, D-2191
S Barber & C P Ellison   Rivar Hill   *'HZD'*   01.04.18E

G-CHZE Schempp-Hirth Discus CS   121CS   27.07.07
BGA 4328, D-6946
Darlton Gliding Club Ltd   Darlton   *'HZE'*   19.02.18E
Built by Orličan Aakciová Společnost

G-CHZG Rolladen-Schneider LS8-18   8118   15.11.07
BGA 4330/HZG   P F Brice   Wycombe Air Park   *'X8'* 07.04.19E

G-CHZH Schleicher Ka 6CR   6461   06.01.09
BGA 4331/HZH, HB-836
C Hankinson   Chipping   *'HZH'*   27.02.18E

G-CHZI Cessna 172RG Cutlass II   172RG-0549   26.06.13
EC-HVP, D-ECMV(2), (N5514V)
Aeroplano-Planeamento Exploracao e Manutencao
de Aeronaves Lda   Cascais, Portugal   22.01.19E

G-CHZJ Schempp-Hirth Standard Cirrus   23   27.11.07
BGA 4332/HZJ, HB-981
P Mucha   Shenington   *'HZJ'*   21.05.18E

G-CHZK Europa Aviation Europa XS   481   04.07.13
P J Harrod   (Cotton of Balnamoon, Brechin)
Built by P J Harrod – project PFA 247-13657
(NF 20.07.17)

G-CHZL Zenair CH.601XL Zodiac   6-9867   09.07.13
S F Beardsell   Great Oakley   15.03.18P
Built by R J Clarke – project PFA 162B-14580

G-CHZM Rolladen-Schneider LS4-a   4762   15.11.07
BGA 4335/HZM, D-1394
W S H Taylor   Seighford   *'U1'*   21.03.19E

G-CHZO Schleicher ASW 27   27018   23.01.08
BGA 4338/HZQ, D-4499   A A Gilmore
tr Lima Zulu Group   Husbands Bosworth   *'LZ'*   06.06.19E

G-CHZP Cessna 152   15279605   08.07.13
SP-KOE, N757BG
Aeroplano-Planeamento Exploracao e Manutencao
de Aeronaves Lda   Cascais, Portugal   03.10.17E

G-CHZR Schleicher ASK 21   21079   17.12.07
BGA 4339/HZR, D-4491D J Brookman
tr K21 HZR Group   Aston Down   *'HZR'*   19.05.18E

G-CHZS Zenair CH.601HDS Zodiac   xxxx   12.04.13
G Addison   (Wispington, Horncastle)
Built by G Addison – project LAA 162-15011
(NF 19.07.17)

G-CHZT Groppo Trail   00081/40   05.04.13
B J Main & A Strachan   Henstridge   24.04.18P
Built by B J Main – project LAA 372-15184

G-CHZU Schempp-Hirth Standard Cirrus   366   28.11.07
BGA 4342/HZU, HB-1258, N71KW
D I Richmond   AAC Wattisham   *'B11'*   20.12.18E

G-CHZV Schempp-Hirth Standard Cirrus   305   06.06.08
BGA 4343/HZV, VH-GFZ, BGA 4343/HZV, HB-1457,
D-2061   S M Cass   Pocklington   *'P61'*   01.08.18E

G-CHZW P&M Quik GTR   8655   18.07.13
N J Braund   Redlands   25.07.17P
(IE 04.08.17)

G-CHZX Schleicher K 8B   8257   19.04.08
BGA 4345/HZX, D-8476   T G Shepherd
tr K8B Boys Club   Waldershare Park   *'HZX'*   25.05.18E

G-CHZY Rolladen-Schneider LS4   4479   07.11.07
BGA 4346/HZY, D-3458
N P Wedi   Wycombe Air Park   *'EN'*   30.11.17E

G-CHZZ Schleicher ASW 20L   20353   06.11.07
BGA 4347/HZZ, HB-1691, D-1153, N20EE
C M Davey tr LD Syndicate   RAF Wittering   *'LD'* 12.05.19E
C/n plate shows '20353/N20EE' although
BGA records as c/n as '20273'

G-CIAA – G-CIZZ

G-CIAA Mitchinson Safari   SA1-001   03.06.13
S A Labib   Redlands
Built by CM Microlights; noted 11.18
(SSDR microlight since 05.14) (NF 24.04.18)

G-CIAB Avian Riot/Samba   13RT150002   05.06.13
Avian Ltd   Darley Moor
Build appears to be based on BB Trya trike &
Avian Rio T15 wing c/n 13RT150002
(SSDR microlight since 05.14) (NF 07.08.17)

G-CIAC HOAC DV.20 Katana   20156   25.07.13
D-ELWN   LOC Aircraft   Valenciennes-Denain, France 27.12.18E

G-CIAE Cameron TR-70   11781   12.07.13
John Aimo Balloons SAS   Mondovi, Italy
'Cameron Balloons'   11.07.19E

G-CIAF TL 3000 Sirius   xxxx   18.07.13
P H Ronfell   Blackpool   05.05.18P
Built by P H Ronfell – project LAA 386-15211

G-CIAI Schempp-Hirth Arcus T   40   29.07.13
(BGA 5737)   A P Moulang tr G-CIAI Group
Challock   *'A1'*   03.03.18E

G-CIAJ Hawker Hart   –   21.05.15
Swedish AF 726   Westh Flyg AB   Moat Farm, Milden
Built by AB Svenska Järnvägsverkstädernas
Aeroplanavdelning (ASJA) as B4A Hawker Hart;
on rebuild 08.16 (NF 27.10.16)

G-CIAK Groppo Trail   00074/33   20.03.13
I Markham   The Firs Farm, Leckhampstead   17.07.17P
Built by I Markham – project LAA 372-15144

G-CIAM Piper PA-28-181 Archer III   2843361   20.05.13
N4144N   J Mendonca-Caridad   (Lugo, Spain)   11.05.18E

G-CIAN Unicorn Ax6   IC1   25.10.12
G A & I Chadwick   Caterham
(NF 23.05.18)

G-CIAO III Sky Arrow 650 T   xxxx   23.07.97
P L Turner   Enstone   28.06.19P
Built by J Hosier – project PFA 298-13095

G-CIAP Cameron Z-77   11156   22.08.13
A6-SMN   A A Osman   Wembley   12.12.17E

G-CIAR P&M Quik GTR   8648   11.04.13
C R Paterson   Perth   31.05.18P

G-CIAU Canadair CL-600-1A11 Challenger 600S 1067   12.11.13
M-IFES, N240AK, N205EL, N800AB, N50928,
C-GZBE, C-GLXH, (VR-CBP), C-GLXH
Cancelled 24.04.18 as PWFU
Stansted   *Instructional use at Stansted Airport*
college 10.18

G-CIAV Ace Aviation Magic/Cyclone   AM165   23.08.13
A Evans   (Wolverhampton)
Trike s/n AM165 & wing s/n AC-160
(SSDR microlight since 05.14) (IE 27.09.18)

G-CIAW Comco Ikarus C42 FB80   1305-7252   04.07.13
R Hilton   Welshpool   26.06.19P
Assembled Red-Air UK

G-CIAX CZAW Sportcruiser   OC700584-1   12.02.13
A G Higgins   Bitteswell Farm, Bitteswell   14.08.18P
Built by A Palmer & F Sayyah – project LAA 338-15125

G-CIAY Cameron C-70   11786   08.10.13
R P Wade   Shevington, Wigan   09.10.18E

G-CIAZ Aeropro EuroFOX 912(1)   39613   04.03.13
M P Dale   (York)   27.06.19P
Built by M W Houghton – project BMAA/HB/631;
tricycle u/c

G-CIBA Cameron N-145   10268   27.08.13
D-OOTV   Adventure Balloons Ltd
Hartley Wintney, Hook   *'RTL'*   07.03.19E

G-CIBB Cessna F172H   F172-0324   27.08.13
OY-EGZ, N17013   D R Godfrey   Dunkeswell   06.08.18E
Built by Reims Aviation SA;
for sale with AT Aviation 08.18

G-CIBC Aeropro EuroFOX 912(S)   40913   22.10.13
M P Brockington   (Llandeilo)   05.04.18P
Built by M P Brockington – project LAA 376-15197;
tailwheel u/c; glider-tugs from Talgarth

G-CIBF	Aeropro EuroFOX 912(S)	40413	04.09.13
	The Borders (Milfield) Gliding Club Ltd Milfield		13.03.18P
	Built by K L Sangster – project LAA 376-15209;		
	tailwheel u/c; glider-tug		
G-CIBG	Rolladen-Schneider LS4	4454	17.10.13
	(BGA 5755), D-3443		
	G D Ackroyd (Fersfield, Diss) *'1N'*		25.11.17E
	(NF 30.05.18)		
G-CIBH	Van's RV-8A	81216	11.07.13
	N984N W N Blair-Hickman Maypole Farm, Chislet		20.08.19R
	Built by D A Coats; official c/n '69846' is incorrect		
G-CIBI	Lindstrand LBL 90A	1458	29.11.13
	A J & S J M O'Boyle Salford		03.04.18E
G-CIBJ	Colomban MC-30 Luciole	166	09.09.13
	R A Gardiner (Thankerton)		26.11.17P
	Built by R A Gardiner – project LAA 371-15002		
G-CIBL	AutoGyro Cavalon	V00112	01.07.13
	A C R & J Drayton Wolverhampton Halfpenny Green		06.11.18P
	Assembled Rotorsport UK as c/n RSUK/CVLN/005		
G-CIBM	Van's RV-8	83193	13.09.13
	G P Williams & S J Wood Swansea		30.03.19P
	Built by G P Williams & S J Wood – project		
	LAA 303-15083; operates as 'Raven Display		
	Team' – 'No. 4'		
G-CIBN	Cameron Z-90	11782	15.08.13
	B J Newman Rushden		
	'The Northampton Balloon Festival'		04.07.19E
G-CIBO	Cessna 180K Skywagon	18053177	23.07.04
	VH-JNS, N19029 CIBO Ops Ltd Rush Green		09.02.18E
G-CIBP	Cameron Z-77	11776	31.10.13
	A A Osman Wembley		12.12.17E
G-CIBR	P&M Quik GT450	8666	09.10.13
	K D Smith Northrepps		08.10.18P
G-CIBT	P&M QuikR	8667	07.10.13
	M Macrae East Fortune		04.10.18P
	Fitted with trike ex G-CFPI		
G-CIBU	Avtech Jabiru J160	T252	27.09.13
	D J Bly North Weald		19.08.19P
	Built by M Flint – project LAA 346-15009		
G-CIBV	Best Off Skyranger Swift 912S(1)	SKR xx xx 1069	27.09.13
	PPL (UK) Ltd Sherburn-in-Elmet		12.02.18P
	Built by B Robertson – project BMAA/HB/640		
G-CIBW	Westland Scout AH.1	F9632	11.10.13
	XT626 Historic Aircraft Flight Trust RNAS Yeovilton		18.07.19P
	As 'XT626:Q' in AAC c/s		
G-CIBX	Cameron Z-31	11560	04.10.13
	A E Austin Sibbertoft, Market Harborough		23.01.19E
G-CIBZ	Aeropro EuroFOX 912S(1)	427.13	08.10.13
	K N Rigley & D Thorpe Headon Farm, Retford		04.09.18P
	Built by K N Rigley & D Thorpe – project		
	BMAA/HB/642; tricycle u/c		
G-CICA	Europa Aviation Europa XS	475	08.10.13
	R J Grainger Hinton-in-the-Hedges		26.07.18P
	Built by J R Lambert – project PFA 247-13621;		
	tricycle u/c		
G-CICC	Cessna 152	15285282	02.07.13
	F-GPUC, N64903 The Pilot Centre Ltd Denham		06.07.18E
G-CICD	Colt 105A	2621	23.12.13
	D-ODHB T Read & N Smith t/a Mobberley		
	Balloon Collection Knutsford & Goole		
	(NF 23.08.18)		
G-CICF	Comco Ikarus C42 FB80 Bravo	1305-7260	13.08.13
	D Durrans Otherton		21.08.18P
	Assembled Red-Air UK		
G-CICG	Comco Ikarus C42 FB80	1304-7259	10.07.13
	T Osbourne tr G-CICG Group Blackbushe		10.07.19P
	Assembled Red-Air UK		
G-CICH	Sikorsky S-92A	920209	02.12.13
	5N-BTI, G-CICH, N209X		
	Bristow Helicopters Ltd Aberdeen Int'l		01.06.18E
G-CICK	Supermarine 361 Spitfire T.IX	CBAF 8912	04.06.14
	NH341 K M Perkins Headcorn *'Elizabeth'*		13.04.19P
	As 'NH341:DB-E' in 411 Sqdn RCAF c/s		

G-CICM	AutoGyro Calidus	C00291	20.12.13
	F Hammond Exeter Int'l		18.04.18P
	Assembled Rotorsport UK as c/n RSUK/CALS/023		
G-CICN[M]	Agusta-Bell 47G-3B1 Sioux AH.1	1540	12.11.13
	XT131 Historic Aircraft Flight Trust		
	AAC Middle Wallop		28.06.18P
	Built by Westland Helicopters Ltd; as 'XT131' in AAC c/s		
G-CICO	Ultramagic H-42	42/21	06.09.13
	A M Holly Breadstone, Berkeley		14.05.18E
G-CICP[M]	de Havilland DHC-2 Beaver AL.1	1483	12.11.13
	XP820 Historic Aircraft Flight Trust		
	AAC Middle Wallop		28.06.18P
	As 'XP820' in AAC c/s		
G-CICR[M]	Auster AOP.9	B5/10/181	12.11.13
	XR244 Historic Aircraft Flight Trust		
	AAC Middle Wallop		15.08.18P
	Built by Beagle-Auster Aircraft Ltd; as 'XR244' in AAC c/s		
G-CICT	Schempp-Hirth Ventus-2cxT	136	31.10.13
	G-ZENN, BGA 5148/KJY, D-KOZX		
	D Postlethwaite (Grove, Retford) *'110'*		12.04.19E
G-CICU	Raj Hamsa X'Air Hawk	1254	18.10.13
	J R Bell tr X'Air Group Carrickmore		15.11.18P
	Built by M Donnelly & H A Quinn		
	– project LAA 340-15217		
G-CICV	AutoGyro MTOsport	xxxx	16.12.13
	J Owen Fowler's Field, Billingshurst		27.04.18P
	Assembled by Rotorsport UK with c/n RSUK/MTOS/050		
G-CICW	Flylight Dragonlite Fox	DA105	06.05.14
	S F Beardsell Great Oakley		
	(SSDR microlight since 05.14) (IE 24.06.16)		
G-CICY	PZL-Bielsko SZD-50-3 Puchacz	B-1880	19.11.13
	(BGA 5763), SE-UHU		
	Deeside Gliding Club (Aberdeenshire) Ltd Aboyne		18.11.18E
G-CIDB	Flylight Dragon Chaser	DA103	23.09.13
	D M Broom Sutton Meadows		
	(SSDR microlight since 05.14) (IE 06.07.16)		
G-CIDC	Yakovlev Yak-18T	15-35	13.02.14
	HA-YAU, RA-44527 D M Cue White Waltham		15.09.18R
G-CIDD	Bellanca 7ECA Citabria	1002-74	29.11.00
	N86577 B F L & T A Hodges Headcorn		19.10.18E
G-CIDF	AutoGyro MTOsport	xxxx	30.01.14
	K J Whitehead Perth		17.11.18P
	Assembled Rotorsport UK as c/n RSUK/MTOS/051		
G-CIDG	P&M Quik GTR	8665	11.12.13
	G N Kenny (Congleton)		06.04.18P
	Struck ground heavily landing Headcorn 11.11.16		
	& substantially damaged		
G-CIDH	Cameron C-80	11804	23.04.14
	P C Johnson Hucclecote, Gloucester		19.04.18E
G-CIDM	Eurocopter EC225 LP Super Puma	2900	13.12.13
	D2-EZM, G-CIDM, F-WWOC		
	Wilmington Trust SP Services (Dublin) Ltd Fleetlands		
	Stored 11.17 (IE 21.03.17)		
G-CIDO	Glaser-Dirks DG-600/18M	6-54M8	23.01.14
	D-KMCO, F-CGRQ, D-KBDG (2)		
	S S M Turner Sleap *'DO'*		29.11.18E
G-CIDP	Sonex Sonex	1526	08.01.14
	P I Marshall (Monmouth)		
	Built by C C Miller – project LAA 337-15106 (IE 15.01.18)		
G-CIDS	Comco Ikarus C42 FB100 Bravo	1310-7285	13.11.13
	P H J Fenn Beccles		18.11.18P
	Assembled Red-Air UK		
G-CIDT	Schleicher ASH 25E	25035	23.12.13
	G-KIGR, (BGA 5646), D-KIGR		
	G D E Macdonald Lasham		02.06.18E
G-CIDU	Kubicek BB22E	1058	09.05.14
	A M Daniels Honeybourne, Evesham *'GBD'*		05.05.19E
G-CIDW	Evektor EV-97 Eurostar	2013-4109	06.01.14
	D Workman Pound Green		20.07.19P
	Built by D Workman – project LAA 315-15227		
G-CIDX	Sonex Sonex	1493	09.10.13
	J P Dilks New Farm, Felton		17.05.18P
	Built by J P Dilks – project LAA 337-15058; tailwheel u/c		

G-CIDY	P&M Quik GTR	8675	23.01.14
	G P Wade (Watford)		16.02.18P
G-CIDZ	Evektor EV-97 Eurostar SL	2013-4107	12.05.14
	C Bannerman tr Delta Zulu Group (Earley, Reading)		25.05.18P
	Assembled Light Sport Aviation Ltd		
G-CIEA	Rolladen-Schneider LS4-b	4890	13.02.14
	(BGA 5764), D-2358		
	T Zorn (Bissendorf, Germany) '*WH*'		02.04.18E
G-CIEB	AutoGyro MTOsport	xxxx	19.03.14
	K A Hastie Popham		25.03.18P
	Assembled Rotorsport UK as c/n RSUK/MTOS/053		
G-CIEC	Saab 2000	2000-037	11.03.14
	HB-IZU, D-AOLT, HB-IZU, SE-037		
	Air Kilroe Ltd t/a Eastern Airways Humberside		18.08.19E
	Built by Saab AB		
G-CIED	Aeros Fox 16T/RIP1	23-12-13/RIP1	31.01.14
	R J Ripley (Oakley, Bedford)		
	(SSDR microlight since 05.14) (IE 26.05.17)		
G-CIEE	Comco Ikarus C42 FB100	1311-7289	27.11.13
	S B Wilkes t/a Hadair Wolverhampton Halfpenny Green		28.04.18P
	Assembled Red-Air UK		
G-CIEF	Aeropro EuroFOX 912(S)	43214	14.05.14
	J R Paskins tr Darlton Eurofox Group Darlton		17.12.18P
	Built by J R Paskins & Partners – project		
	LAA 376-15218; tricycle u/c; glider-tug		
G-CIEG	P&M QuikR	8679	06.02.14
	N H McCorquodale tr Flying Group G-CIEG		
	East Fortune		18.02.18P
	Uses trike from G-CDVR		
G-CIEH	Aeropro EuroFOX 912(S)	43314	06.02.14
	Lakes Gliding Club Ltd t/a Lakes Gliding Club		
	Walney Island		18.12.18P
	Built by R Jones & Partners – project		
	LAA 376-15247; tricycle u/c; glider-tug		
G-CIEI	Lindstrand LBL HS-110 HA Airship	174	30.01.14
	G-TRIB Lindstrand Asia Ltd Oswestry		12.03.16E
G-CIEJ	AutoGyro MTOsport	xxxx	10.06.14
	K J Robinson tr G-CIEJ Group Lagos, Algarve, Portugal		06.04.18P
	Assembled Rotorsport UK as c/n RSUK/MTOS/054		
G-CIEK	Flylight Dragonlite Fox	DA111	05.02.14
	P A Marks (Moor Farm, Chickerell)		
	(SSDR microlight since 05.14) (IE 22.06.16)		
G-CIEL	Cessna 560XL Citation Excel	560-5247	29.04.05
	N57RL, N7RL, N51038 Enerway Ltd London Stansted		09.05.18E
	Operated by London Executive Aviation		
G-CIEM	P&M QuikR	8678	05.03.14
	S P T Magnus-Hannaford Shobdon		01.04.19P
G-CIEN	Super Marine Spitfire Mk.26	063	18.02.14
	A G Counsell Perth		03.04.18P
	Built by A G Counsell – project PFA 324-14492;		
	as 'PL788' in RAF pale blue c/s		
G-CIEP	Flylight Dragon Chaser	DA107	11.04.14
	R Urquhart Morgansfield, Fishburn		
	(SSDR microlight since 05.14) (IE 27.02.17)		
G-CIER	Cameron Z-160	10807	12.03.14
	OO-BZR J Taylor Huddlesford, Lichfield '*KBC*'		28.08.17E
G-CIET	Lindstrand LBL 31A	1035	02.01.14
	EI-DJZ C A Butter & S I Williams		
	Marsh Benham & Cardiff '*Smart*'		21.06.19E
G-CIEW	AutoGyro Cavalon Pro	V00155	20.03.14
	Rotorsport Sales & Service Ltd		
	Wolverhampton Halfpenny Green		01.06.19E
	Assembled Rotorsport UK as c/n RSUK/CVLN/011		
G-CIEX	Westland SA.341B Gazelle AH.1	1987	13.05.14
	ZB682 S Atherton tr Gazelle Flying Group		
	Crab Tree Farm, Deighton		
	Noted 03.15 as 'ZB662' (NF 18.05.18)		
G-CIEY	Westland SA.341B Gazelle AH.1	1021	04.04.14
	XW851 S Atherton tr Gazelle Flying Group A		
	Crab Tree Farm, Deighton		
	Fitted with boom ex ZA726; noted 03.15 as 'XW851'		
	(NF 18.05.18)		

G-CIEZ	Bücker Bü.181B-1 Bestmann	25082	06.02.14
	D-ECES, Swedish AF 25082		
	A C Whitehead Manchester Barton		
	As '5' in Swedish AF c/s (NF 06.02.14)		
G-CIFA	Aeropro EuroFOX 912(1)	39713	12.02.14
	J R Elcocks Wolverhampton Halfpenny Green		27.04.19P
	Built by L S & S B Williams – project BMAA/HB/649;		
	tricycle u/c		
G-CIFB	Aerochute Dual	1522/342	18.02.14
	J D Abraham (Melton Mowbray)		21.01.18P
	Comprises new parachute s/n 1522 &		
	trike s/n 342 ex G-HUTE		
G-CIFC	SOCATA TB-200 Tobago XL	1634	29.09.14
	9V-BAT, HS-PET, F-GNHH		
	Lincoln Aero Club Ltd Sturgate		26.11.18E
G-CIFD	Titan T-51 Mustang	xxxx	11.03.14
	B J Chester-Master Shobdon		
	'Impatient Virgin' (port) & *'Mimi'* (starboard)		10.08.18P
	Built by B J Chester-Master – project LAA 355-15261;		
	T-51B 'Razorback'; as '2106638:E9-R' in USAAF c/s		
G-CIFE	Beech B200 Super King Air	BB-1829	07.04.14
	G-RAFJ, ZK450, G-RAFJ, N6129N		
	ACH (Witham) Ltd London Stansted		12.03.19E
	Operated by London Executive Aviation		
G-CIFF	P&M Quik GT450	8680	02.04.14
	A W Buchan tr Light Flight Fox Fox Group		
	Knapthorpe Lodge, Caunton		29.05.18P
G-CIFH	Cameron Z-275	11833	24.06.14
	MSJ Ballooning Ltd Lewes		22.06.18E
G-CIFI	Cameron Z-77	11737	20.12.13
	G-UKFT A M Holly Breadstone, Berkeley		23.06.17E
	(IE 07.10.17)		
G-CIFK	Raj Hamsa X'Air Hawk	1251	29.04.14
	E B Toulson Bagby		
	Built by E B Toulson – project LAA 340-15210;		
	noted 02.18 (IE 28.01.18)		
G-CIFL	Van's RV-6	xxxx	30.04.14
	A J Maxwell Manchester Barton		19.08.18P
	Built by A J Maxwell – project PFA 181A-12290		
G-CIFM	Flylight Dragon Chaser	DA109	08.07.14
	J P McCall Sutton Meadows		
	(IE 14.06.18)		
G-CIFN	Comco Ikarus C42 FB80	1405-7307	29.05.14
	K J A Farrance Rougham		06.01.19P
	Assembled Red-Air UK		
G-CIFO	Aeropro EuroFOX 912(S)	40213	27.01.14
	Herefordshire Gliding Club Ltd Shobdon		08.05.18P
	Built by D Johnstone & P L Poole – project		
	LAA 376-15223; tricycle u/c; glider-tug		
G-CIFP	Cameron Frog-90	4101	05.06.14
	PH-ROC Lindstrand Asia Ltd Oswestry		26.03.16E
G-CIFS	Lindstrand LBL 150A	687	05.06.14
	PH-GBT Lindstrand Asia Ltd Oswestry		
	'Fortis Bank'		24.11.17E
G-CIFT	AutoGyro MTOsport	xxxx	09.07.14
	B E, C I & G Reade t/a J Reade & Sons		
	Sgriob-Ruadh Farm, Glengorm		12.06.18P
	Assembled Rotorsport UK as c/n RSUK/MTOS/055		
G-CIFU	Rolladen-Schneider LS4	4619	20.05.14
	(BGA 5797), D-4055		
	N A Taylor Husbands Bosworth '*IZ*'		09.04.18E
G-CIFV	P&M Quik GTR	8689	28.05.14
	R Higton Berry Farm, Bovingdon		18.05.18P
	Trike is rebuild of G-CEVG with new sailwing		
G-CIFY	Piper PA-28-181 Archer III	2843010	27.02.14
	OO-JAI, G-GFPA, N115RT, N9256J		
	D S Gould Turweston		24.04.18E
G-CIFZ	Comco Ikarus C42 FB80	1311-7293	30.01.14
	G W Perry t/a Air Cornwall Bodmin		06.02.18P
	Assembled Red-Air UK		
G-CIGA	Ultramagic H-42	42/05	07.03.14
	I Chadwick Caterham		15.07.19E
G-CIGB	Stinson L-1 Vigilant	40-283	26.05.15
	40-283 G & P M Turner (London SE18)		
	(NF 26.05.15)		

G-CIGC	P&M QuikR	8687	28.05.14
	W G Craig East Fortune		19.05.18P
G-CIGD	Reims/Cessna F172M	F17201352	20.05.14
	G-ENII, PH-WAG, (D-EDQM)		
	D M Collins & D S Sime (Frinton-on-Sea & Harwich)		15.11.18E
G-CIGE	de Havilland DHC-1 Chipmunk 22	C1/0648	16.05.14
	N4358H, WK634 M A V Gatehouse Dunkeswell		07.02.19P
	As 'WK634:902' in RN c/s		
G-CIGF	Slingsby T61F Venture T.2	1983	15.07.14
	SE-UCF, ZA664 M F Cuming Saltby		
	Noted dismantled 03.15 as 'SE-UCF' (NF 15.05.18)		
G-CIGG	P&M Quik GTR	8690	05.06.14
	P C Smith (Great Cambourne, Cambridge)		08.06.19P
	Badged 'QuikGTR Explorer'		
G-CIGH	Max Holste MH.1521M Broussard	284	19.05.14
	F-GGKL, F-WGKL, French AF R A Fleming Brighton		27.04.18P
	Officially regd with c/n 255 – production no.		
	of c/n 284 is 255M; carries production no. plate		
	'255M' in cockpit to indicate 255th military		
	Broussard built; as '255:5-ML' in French AF c/s		
G-CIGI	Lindstrand LBL 77A	1481	22.05.14
	Lindstrand Media Ltd Hawarden CH5 'JLL'		02.07.18E
G-CIGJ	Cameron Z-90	11473	16.06.14
	Viec BVBA Hamme, Belgium		15.06.19E
G-CIGN	Cameron Z-90	11838	05.09.14
	Elgas SRL Lunata, Lucca, Italy 'Elgas'		31.08.18E
G-CIGS	AutoGyro MTOsport	xxxx	30.01.14
	E A Blomfield-Smith Cotswold		08.09.18P
	Assembled Rotorsport UK as c/n RSUK/MTOS/052		
G-CIGT	Best Off Skyranger Swift 912S(1)	SKR xx xx 1078	09.04.14
	N S Wells Hill Farm, Buchlyvie, Stirling		04.08.18P
	Built by J Plenderleith – project BMAA/HB/648		
G-CIGU	Aerochute Dual	14041908	09.06.14
	B Griffiths (Bodelwyddan, Rhyl)		08.11.17P
	Trike c/n 456		
G-CIGV	Hewing Demoiselle 15/Aeros Fox 16T	15	11.06.14
	R B Hewing Benson's Farm, Laindon		
	Demoiselle trike originally fitted to Aeros Discus 15T		
	wing as G-CFGC; extant 07.17 (IE 26.06.15)		
G-CIGW	BRM Bristell NG5 Speed Wing	090	12.06.14
	J R Frohnsdorff Enstone		17.05.19P
	Built by J R Frohnsdorff – project LAA 385-15263		
G-CIGY	Westland-Bell 47G-3B-1	WAN-41	26.10.98
	G-BGXP, XT191 M L Romeling Sherburn-in-Elmet		11.10.18E
G-CIGZ	Sikorsky S-92A	920224	21.08.14
	N224XK Bristow Helicopters Ltd Aberdeen Int'l		18.09.18E
G-CIHA	P&M QuikR	8676	17.02.14
	S D Hitchcock Strathaven		09.03.18P
G-CIHB	Colomban MC-30 Luciole	138	25.06.14
	S Kilpin (Hackleton, Northampton)		13.07.17P
	Built by S Kilpin – project LAA 371-15024 (IE 30.09.17)		
G-CIHC	Cameron Z-105	11800	26.02.14
	Pattersons (Bristol) Ltd Bristol BS3 'Pattersons'		11.05.19E
G-CIHD	British Aerospace Jetstream 4100	41065	04.07.14
	VH-XNE, ZS-NRK, G-4-065 Airtime AB Humberside		
	Stored 01.16 as 'VH-XNE' less engines (IE 12.08.18)		
G-CIHE	British Aerospace Jetstream 4100	41068	04.07.14
	VH-XNF, ZS-NRL, G-4-068 Airtime AB Humberside		
	Stored 01.16 as 'VH-XNF' less engines (IE 11.08.18)		
G-CIHF	Schempp-Hirth Discus-2a	41	14.03.14
	ZK-GIL B J Flewett Lasham '2a'		04.05.18E
G-CIHG	Cameron Z-90	11841	16.07.14
	I Parsons Wraxall, Bristol 'Above+Beyond'		03.07.18E
G-CIHH	AutoGyro MTOsport	xxxx	15.09.14
	A D Gordon Lude Farm, Blair Atholl		29.10.18P
	Assembled Rotorsport UK as c/n RSUK/MTOS/057		
G-CIHI	Cameron V-77	11721	02.04.14
	P Spellward Bristol BS9		19.06.18E
G-CIHL	P&M Quik GTR	8688	08.07.14
	T G Jackson Compton Abbas		01.09.18P
G-CIHM	Schleicher ASW 28-18E	28727	18.06.14
	(BGA 5795), PH-1323, D-KRRB		
	S A Kerby Snitterfield '777'		17.01.19E

G-CIHN	Cameron Z-120	11785	16.07.14
	N J Langley Henbury, Bristol		30.03.18E
G-CIHO	Cameron Z-77	11813	09.04.14
	S D Wrighton Jersey 'C J Hole'		19.05.19E
G-CIHS	Fokker D.VII replica	xxxx	07.08.18
	J A & R H Cooper Wickenby		
	Built by R H Cooper – project LAA 387-15544		
	(NF 07.08.18)		
G-CIHT	Flylight Dragonlite Fox	DA110	10.04.14
	M D Harper (Thornton-Cleveleys)		
	(SSDR microlight since 05.14) (IE 24.06.16)		
G-CIHU	Fokker D.VIII replica	xxxx	07.08.18
	J A & R H Cooper Wickenby		
	Built by R H Cooper – project LAA 082-15546		
	(NF 07.08.18)		
G-CIHV	Best Off Skyranger Nynja 912(1)	UK\N/BK0155	16.05.14
	A Dawson Ince		29.06.19P
	Built by A Dawson – project BMAA/HB/652		
G-CIHW	AutoGyro Cavalon	V00161	09.07.14
	R I Broadhead & A E Polkey		
	Eddsfield, Octon Lodge Farm, Thwing		20.07.18P
	Assembled Rotorsport UK as c/n RSUK/CVLN/010		
G-CIHY	P&M Pegasus Quik	8686	10.04.14
	A P & G M Douglas-Dixon Bagby		16.08.19P
G-CIHZ	P&M Quik GTR	8669	17.04.14
	B Michnay (London W5)		28.09.18P
G-CIIA	P&M QuikR	8692	15.05.14
	K A Ritchie East Fortune		07.08.19P
	Also uses trike from G-CWEB		
G-CIIB	Aerochute Dual	457/14-04-1907	28.07.14
	P Dean (Heacham, King's Lynn)		
	Flies from Northrepps		
	(SSDR microlight since 04.17) (IE 26.04.17)		
G-CIIC	Piper PA-18-150 Super Cub	18-5356	22.05.14
	G-PULL, PH-MRB, Fr Army 18-5356		
	Bianchi Aviation Film Services Ltd Turweston		16.07.18E
G-CIID	BFC Challenger II Long Wing	CH2-0902-2259 UK	29.07.14
	J A Evans (Mickleover, Derby)		
	Built by J A Evans – project PFA 177B-13983		
	using BFC kit; kit no. CH2-0902-O-2259 also		
	quoted for G-CISF (NF 29.06.18)		
G-CIIE	Cameron Z-56	11845	25.09.14
	Pearl Balloon SPRL Court-Saint-Étienne, Belgium		15.09.18E
G-CIIH	P&M Quik GTR	8693	09.07.14
	B Dossett Plaistows Farm, St Albans		09.07.18P
G-CIIK	Yakovlev Yak-55	900909	12.08.14
	UR-SKY, UR-SKYF, DOSAAF 96 (yellow)		
	Yak 55 2014 Ltd Breighton		10.10.18P
G-CIIL	BRM Bristell NG5 Speed Wing	066	11.08.14
	D F P Finan Morgansfield, Fishburn		16.08.18P
	Built by P Johnson – project LAA 385-15275		
G-CIIM	Reims/Cessna F172N	F17201932	26.03.14
	HA-HIE, EC-HIE, D-EHGP		
	Surrey Aviation Ltd Redhill		06.03.18E
G-CIIN	Comco Ikarus C42 FB100	1407-7344	22.08.14
	R S O'Carroll Kernan Valley, Tandragee		10.12.18P
G-CIIO	Curtiss P-40C	16161	05.12.14
	N80FR, Soviet AF, 41-13357 Patina Ltd Duxford		04.06.19P
	Operated by The Fighter Collection;		
	as '39-160:160-10AB' in USAAC TTC c/s		
G-CIIR	Reims/Cessna FRA150L Aerobat	FRA1500187	16.01.15
	D-EAFT, HB-CEW, D-ECWN		
	N Concannon Retford Gamston		22.11.18E
G-CIIT	Best Off Skyranger Swift 912S(1)	SKR xx xx 1072	31.03.14
	P M Dewhurst tr G-CIIT Flying Group Sywell		02.07.19P
	Built by Flylight Airsports Ltd – project		
	BMAA/HB/644;badged 'Swift II'		
G-CIIU	TLAC Sherwood Ranger ST	021	01.09.14
	S K Moeller (Langford, Biggleswade)		
	Built by S K Moeller – project PFA 237B-14590		
	(NF 01.09.14)		
G-CIIV	AMS-Flight Apis M	A031M13	11.06.14
	67BKO J A Harris Henstridge		
	(IE 10.05.18)		

G-CIIW	Piper J-3L-65 Cub	3372	02.09.14
	N24713, NC24713 S D R Dray Old Buckenham		15.03.18E
G-CIIX	Ultramagic M-105	105/203	11.06.14
	E C Meek Sandway, Maidstone		26.08.15E
G-CIIZ	Flylight Dragonlite Fox	DA117	20.10.14
	J Lane Lower Upham Farm, Chiseldon		
	(IE 30.06.17)		
G-CIJA	P&M Quik GT450	8694	01.08.14
	A Fern Darley Moor		08.10.19P
G-CIJB	Cameron Z-90	11806	16.04.14
	J Bennett & Son (Insurance Brokers) Ltd		
	High Wycombe 'J Bennett & Son'		03.05.19E
G-CIJE	Alisport Silent 2 Electro	2062	01.07.14
	73QZ B J Harrison Kingston Deverill		
	(IE 20.12.16)		
G-CIJF	Schempp-Hirth Duo Discus XLT	182	22.09.14
	(BGA 5802), PH-1406		
	Lasham Gliding Society Ltd Lasham '4'		25.04.18E
G-CIJH	Alisport Silent Club	012	18.09.14
	R J Marshall (North Baddesley, Southampton)		
	(IE 24.07.17)		
G-CIJI	Gefa-Flug AS105GD HA Airship	0044	18.09.14
	HJ-305, D-OAAF Alex Air Media Ltd Langford, Bristol		11.02.18E
G-CIJJ	Cameron O-31	11858	18.09.14
	M J Woodcock East Grinstead		01.06.19E
G-CIJK	Zenair CH.750	8790	02.05.14
	N M Goodacre Osgodby Farm, Osgodby		21.07.19P
	Built by N M Goodacre – project LAA 381-15187		
G-CIJL	Cameron Z-105	11861	11.11.14
	Airworks Worldwide Ltd t/a British Balloon Flights		
	Wisborough Green		07.02.19E
G-CIJM	Cameron N-133	10313	17.04.14
	OO-BJR, D-OFON		
	Border Ballooning Ltd Plas Madoc, Montgomery		19.05.18E
G-CIJN	Boeing Stearman E75 Kaydet (N2S-5) 75-5164		23.09.14
	ZK-RDK, N1391V, USN 61042, 42-17001		
	P Fernandes (Langham, Colchester)		30.07.19E
	As '41-64042:317' in USAAF c/s		
G-CIJO	P&M Quik GTR	8702	22.10.14
	B N Montila Longacre Farm, Sandy		19.10.18P
G-CIJR	P&M Pegasus Quantum 15-912	8700	17.10.14
	M Dibben (Shenley Church End, Milton Keynes)		23.10.19P
G-CIJS	Reims/Cessna F152 II	F15201522	02.12.14
	D-EFEK H E da Costa Alburquerque		
	(Amadora, Portugal)		01.09.19E
G-CIJT	Best Off Skyranger Nynja 912S(1) 14010151		07.03.14
	R A & R S Mott tr G-CIJT Group (Hempton, Banbury)		02.05.18P
	Built by C M Theakstone – project BMAA/HB/650		
G-CIJU	Cessna 177RG Cardinal RG	177RG0020	16.10.14
	D-ESLL, N8020G H A Ermert (Langenfeld, Germany)		23.10.18E
G-CIJV	CASA 1-133 Jungmeister	35	27.05.14
	Spanish AF ES.1-16 R A Cumming Sleap		26.10.18P
	As 'LG 01' in Luftwaffe c/s		
G-CIJW	AgustaWestland AW139	31571	11.12.14
	Leonardo SPA (Rome, Italy)		10.12.18E
G-CIJX	AgustaWestland AW139	31579	02.12.14
	Leonardo SPA Rome, Italy		01.12.18E
G-CIJY	Wittman W.10 Tailwind	07-1347	03.10.14
	P Mather Top Farm, Croydon		
	Built by P Mather – project PFA 031-14725;		
	near completion 01.18 (IE 02.11.17)		
G-CIJZ	Zenair CH.750	8462	03.10.14
	M Henderson (Netherley, Stonehaven)		03.01.19P
	Built by A R Oliver – project LAA 381-15118		
G-CIKA	P&M Quik Lite	8698	27.08.14
	C M Wilkinson Boston		
	Incorporates wing frame ex G-CDXM &		
	original wing ex G-CDOP (IE 30.09.17)		
G-CIKB	Schempp-Hirth Duo Discus XLT	262	13.01.15
	(BGA 5838) N Jones & P Morrison North Hill 'DD3'		12.04.18E
G-CIKC	Cameron D-77 HA Airship	11863	08.10.14
	Cameron Balloons Ltd Bristol BS3		
	'D-77 Cameron Balloons'		17.05.18E

G-CIKD	Alisport Silent 2 Targa	2031	08.10.14
	04DY B N Searle (Bingham, Nottingham)		
	(IE 25.04.16)		
G-CIKE	Aeroprakt A-22LS Foxbat	A22LS-212	15.10.14
	C A Pollard (Milanthorpe)		12.06.18P
	Built by A Everitt – project LAA 317B-15298;		
	badged 'Glider Tug Sport 600'		
G-CIKG	AutoGyro Calidus	C00359	09.12.14
	Gyronimo Ltd Chiltern Park, Wallingford		21.10.18P
	Assembled Rotorsport UK as c/n RSUK/CALS/024		
G-CIKH	Aeropro EuroFOX 914	44714	15.01.15
	Deeside Gliding Club (Aberdeenshire) Ltd Aboyne		12.09.18P
	Built by D B Smith – project LAA 376-15292;		
	tricycle u/c; glider-tug		
G-CIKI	P&M Pegasus Quik	8703	27.11.14
	D Brown Manchester Barton		19.01.18P
G-CIKJ	Ace Aviation Easy Riser/Spirit	ER-175	03.11.14
	S A Mercer (Sowerby Bridge)		
	Trike s/n ER-175 & wing s/n not known (IE 06.07.18)		
G-CIKK	Ace Aviation Magic/Laser	AM169	25.11.14
	D R Cooper (Penygroes, Caernarfon)		
	Trike s/n AM169 & wing s/n AL160 (NF 02.08.18)		
G-CIKL	Ultramagic S-70	70/01	29.08.14
	EC-LVK L A Watts Pangbourne, Reading 'Tekno 70'		24.06.19E
G-CIKM	Diamond DA.42 Twin Star	42.367	17.10.14
	SP-NBA, OE-UDS Cloud Global Ltd Perth		04.06.19E
	Operated by ACS Flight Training		
G-CIKN	Lindstrand LBL 150A	1167	10.11.14
	PH-RKF Helena Maria Fragoso Dos Santos SA		
	Lagos, Algarve, Portugal		17.06.18E
G-CIKO	AgustaWestland AW139	41378	26.11.14
	N603SM Bristow Helicopters Ltd Norwich Int'l		22.12.18E
G-CIKR	Best Off Skyranger Nynja 912(1) xxxx0165		26.09.14
	C M Wilkes Stonefield Park, Chilbolton		12.04.18P
	Built by C M Wilkes – project BMAA/HB/659		
G-CIKS	Slingsby T67M Firefly II	2073	13.11.14
	B-HSB, VR-HSB R C P Brookhouse Blackbushe		30.09.18E
	Operated by Blackbushe Aviation		
G-CIKT	Evektor EV-97 teamEurostar UK	2014-1000	14.08.14
	Ampsair Ltd Conington		01.09.19P
	Built by Light Sport Aviation Ltd: rebuilt by Targett		
	Aviation believed using G-IHOT's original fuselage,		
	new wings & components ex G-CFVI		
G-CIKU	Flylight Dragonfly	DA119	30.01.15
	N S Brayn South Longwood Farm, Owslebury		
	(IE 13.07.17)		
G-CIKV	Flylight FoxCub	DA118	18.11.14
	M P Wimsey Strubby		
	Fox 13T wing (IE 21.04.17)		
G-CIKX	Robinson R66 Turbine	0555	04.11.14
	Lset Hire LLP Manchester Barton		26.10.18E
G-CIKZ	Cameron Z-90	11854	19.02.15
	Ufftools-Ufftas BVBA Deinze, Belgium		25.01.20E
G-CILA	Aeropro EuroFOX 912	39814	13.08.14
	M J Turner Fern Farm, Marton		20.02.19P
	Built by R M Cornwell – project BMAA/HB/657;		
	tailwheel u/c		
G-CILB	Alisport Silent 2 Electro	2063	25.11.14
	R Butt & H G Nicklin Lasham		
	(IE 28.11.17)		
G-CILD	Pruett-Curtiss Pusher JP-1	1	23.12.14
	N8234E J A Cooper Wickenby		
	Built by J D Pruett; ¾ scale Curtiss Pusher replica,		
	built in 1960		
G-CILG	Van's RV-7A	73851	19.08.14
	D Perl Elstree		29.10.19P
	Built by D Perl – project LAA 323-15042		
G-CILI	Airdrome ⅞th Nieuport 11 replica GS-301		22.12.14
	R E Peirse Armshold Farm, Great Eversden		
	Built by R E Peirse using Grass Strip Aviation kit		
	s/n GS-301; as 'A126' in RFC c/s (NF 30.07.18)		
G-CILL	BRM Bristell NG5 Speed Wing	067	14.08.14
	C M Knight Maypole Farm, Chislet		09.04.19P
	Built by J Edgeworth – project LAA 385-15219		

G-CILN	AgustaWestland AW139	31586	31.03.15
	Leonardo SPA Rome, Italy		30.03.19E
	Stored 10.18		
G-CILO	Cameron TR-70	10543	04.12.14
	A Collett Rockhampton, Berkeley		
	'Cameron Balloons'		02.02.18E
G-CILP	AgustaWestland AW139	31590	31.03.15
	Leonardo SPA Rome, Italy		30.03.19E
	Stored 10.18		
G-CILR	Guimbal Cabri G2	1090	30.01.15
	European Helicopter Importers Ltd Gloucestershire		28.03.18E
	Operated by PTT Aviation		
G-CILS	DG Flugzeugbau LS10-st	L10-008	21.07.14
	(BGA 5800), D-KJLS W M Coffee Snitterfield *'TT'*		09.03.18E
G-CILT	Comco Ikarus C42 FB100 Bravo	1408-7343	15.10.14
	Boston Wings Ltd Boston		15.10.18P
	Assembled Red-Air UK		
G-CILU	Guimbal Cabri G2	1092	04.03.15
	Helitrain Ltd Cotswold		25.03.19E
	Operated by Cotswold Helicopter Centre		
G-CILV	Flylight Dragon Chaser	DA120	22.01.15
	C J Johnson Benson's Farm, Laindon		
	(IE 31.05.17)		
G-CILW	Ace Aviation Easy Riser/Touch	ER-169	04.11.14
	A Voyce Pound Green		
	Trike s/n ER-169 & wing s/n AT-61 (IE 01.05.18)		
G-CILX	Stolp SA.900 V-Star	JS06	07.10.14
	N6SX S R Green Over Farm, Gloucester		
	Built by J W Shaffstall (NF 20.05.15)		
G-CILY	Comco Ikarus C42 FB80	1410-7351	11.11.14
	G R Shipman Turweston		06.02.19P
	Assembled Red-Air UK		
G-CILZ	Cameron Z-140	11881	20.05.15
	Atlantic Ballooning BVBA Destelbergen, Belgium		12.05.18E
G-CIMB	Cessna 177RG Cardinal RG	177RG0038	06.02.15
	EC-GAX, EC-707, N8038G A R Willis Conington		25.10.17E
G-CIMC	Hoffmann H36 Dimona	36269	05.08.15
	CS-ASJ East Sussex Gliding Club Ltd Ringmer		03.05.18E
G-CIMD	Alpi Pioneer 400	22	11.02.15
	F A Cavaciuti The Byre, Hardwick, Abergavenny		07.07.19P
	Built by F A Cavaciuti – project LAA 364-15302		
G-CIME	Kubicek BB30Z	882	27.08.14
	OK-0882, OE-STD		
	A Pasin Villabassa, Trentino-Alto Adige, Italy		30.07.18E
G-CIMG	Aerochute Dual	459/14041910	05.01.15
	M R Gaylor (Little Dalby, Melton Mowbray)		09.03.18P
G-CIMH	P&M Quik Lite	8706	04.02.15
	G M Douglas tr G-CIMH Syndicate East Fortune		
	(IE 21.04.17)		
G-CIMI	Grob G115A	8048	10.02.15
	EI-DJY, D-EFFX M Kostiuk Humberside		09.04.18E
	Operated by Frank Morgan School of Flying		
G-CIMK	P&M Quik Lite	8710	06.02.15
	N R Beale Deppers Bridge, Southam		
	(NF 06.02.15)		
G-CIML	Aeropro EuroFOX 912(S)	45615	11.02.15
	T E Snoddy tr G-CIML Eurofox Flying Group		
	Newtownards		20.08.19P
	Built by D C Fairbrass – project LAA 376-15309;		
	tailwheel u/c		
G-CIMM	Cessna T182R Turbo Skylane II	18268092	29.07.14
	N9888H, G-PDHJ, (F-BZAR), N9888H		
	A W Oliver Fenn Lane Farm, Upton		20.08.18E
G-CIMN	Zenair CH.750	75-10184	11.02.15
	D A G Johnson Draycott		08.11.18P
	Built by D A G Johnson – project LAA 381-15301		
G-CIMO	Sportavia-Putzer RF5B Sperber	51070	25.11.14
	SX-GEB, D-KMPD S L Reed tr G-CIMO Operating		
	Group (Gwernesney, Monmouthshire)		23.08.18E
	Damaged and for sale for rebuild/spares 06.18		
G-CIMP	Scheibe SF25C Falke 2000	44353	24.02.15
	D-KNAP W B Andrews Tregolds Farm, St Merryn		13.05.18E
G-CIMS	Aeropro EuroFOX 912(1)	45214	23.09.14
	C M Sperring Westonzoyland		06.04.18P
	Built by C M Sperring – project BMAA/HB/658; tricycle u/c		
G-CIMT	AutoGyro Cavalon	V00200	12.05.15
	M L Watson Goodwood		05.08.19P
	Assembled Rotorsport UK as c/n RSUK/CVLN/015		
G-CIMU	AgustaWestland AW139	31583	27.02.15
	VH-ZHH, HL9614, G-CIMU, I-PTFR		
	Bristow Helicopters Ltd Norwich Int'l		
	(IE 27.02.15)		
G-CIMV	Groppo Trail	75/34	15.10.14
	A Batters Baxby Manor, Husthwaite		04.01.19P
	Built by A Batters – project LAA 372-15154		
G-CIMW	Cameron O-31	11897	17.04.15
	B Geeraerts Olen, Antwerp, Belgium		14.04.17E
G-CIMX	Westland Scout AH.1	F9738	30.10.14
	XW283 G P Hinkley North Weald		
	Fuselage no F8/9035; as 'XW283' in AAC c/s;		
	noted 01.18 (NF 01.06.16)		
G-CIMY	Sadler Vampire SV2	SU 021	12.03.15
	LN-YTB, 25-0126 I P Freestone (Northampton)		
	Built by Skywise Ultralight Pty Ltd (NF 05.10.15)		
G-CIMZ	Robinson R44 Raven II	11188	17.11.14
	OY-HPK JMR Aviation LLP Brighton City		31.05.19E
G-CINA	Cessna 152	15285894	14.11.14
	SP-WWH, N95433		
	Swiftair Maintenance Ltd Coventry		12.12.18E
G-CINB	Ace Aviation Magic/Laser	AM167	25.02.15
	J W Galloway (Shrewsbury)		
	Assembled P&M Aviation Ltd; trike s/n AM167		
	(ex G-CIDV) & wing s/n AL159 (NF 12.09.18)		
G-CINC	Magnaghi Sky Arrow 650 TCNS	CNS 033	05.05.15
	Spectrum Aviation Ltd Conington		05.05.19E
G-CIND	Cameron C-70	11847	13.05.15
	Gone With The Wind Ltd Langford, Bristol		12.06.18E
G-CINF	Cessna 182M Skylane	18259573	21.01.15
	D-EBBF, N71314 Aero-Club Braunschweig EV		
	Braunschweig, Germany		12.01.19E
G-CING	TLAC Sherwood Ranger ST	31	21.10.14
	S J Westley Cranfield		
	Built by J North – project PFA 237B-14917 (NF 21.10.14)		
G-CINH	P&M QuikR	8716	26.02.15
	P Martin Newnham		21.05.18P
G-CINI	Rans S-7S Courier	0910547	13.01.15
	D R P Mole (Hinton St George)		
	Built by D R P Mole – project LAA 218-15048		
	(NF 13.01.15)		
G-CINJ	Milholland Legal Eagle	S-25	04.07.14
	N S Jeffrey (Smarden, Ashford)		
	Built by N S Jeffrey (NF 02.07.18)		
G-CINK	Grob G109	6103	20.04.15
	HA-1281, D-KAHL(2), D-KAHI M Tolson		
	tr The Lyvden Motor Gliding Syndicate Lyveden		
	(IE 21.11.15)		
G-CINL	Best Off Skyranger Swift 912S(1)	13111074	03.03.15
	B Richardson Morgansfield, Fishburn		03.06.18P
	Built by CTC Kingshurst Academy, Birmingham		
	– project BMAA/HB/647		
G-CINM	Grob G109B	6245	22.10.14
	D-KGFQ T L Webster tr Grob 109 B Motorglider		
	Syndicate G-CINM Challock		24.05.18E
G-CINN	Cameron Z-31	11179	10.11.14
	S5-OCC		
	Turner Balloons Ltd Chipping Norton *'ALUk Group'*		18.02.19E
G-CINO	Grob G109B	6355	17.11.14
	HB-2103 T R Dews Wing Farm, Longbridge Deverill		05.10.17E
	(IE 02.04.18)		
G-CINU	Eurocopter EC225 LP Super Puma	2832	10.03.15
	PR-OMV, F-WJXX		
	Omni Helicopters International SA (Lisbon, Portugal)		
	(NF 10.03.15)		
G-CINV	Aeroprakt A-22LS Foxbat	A22LS-230	09.03.15
	J P Mimnagh Lleweni Parc		25.06.18P
	Built by J P Mimnagh – project LAA 317B-15316		

G-CIOA	Murphy Rebel	629R	11.03.15
	PH-CRE, (PH-CJB)		
	O P Sparrow Stonefield Park, Chilbolton		31.08.18P
	Built by K Hoyer: initially built R E Crets t/a		
	Lim Air Industry BVBA as project no.NVAV-279		
G-CIOC	Boeing Stearman A75N1 Kaydet (*N2S-4*) 75-4961		10.11.15
	N9548H, USN 55724, (42-16798)		
	Skymax (Aviation) Ltd Damyns Hall, Upminster		07.06.18E
G-CIOD	P&M Quik Lite	8718	13.04.15
	D D'Arcy-Ewing (Millisons Wood, Coventry)		
	(IE 28.02.18)		
G-CIOF	Aeropro EuroFOX 912(iS)	45515	26.06.15
	Yorkshire Gliding Club (Proprietary) Ltd Sutton Bank		03.03.19P
	Built by R A Cole & Partners – project		
	LAA 376-15329; tailwheel u/c; glider-tug		
G-CIOG	Fresh Breeze Bullix Trike/Relax	RLX4153	17.04.15
	D Burton (Topsham, Exeter)		
	Built by Fly Market Flugsport-Zubehor GmbH & Co		
	(IE 05.07.17)		
G-CIOI	Aérospatiale AS.332L Super Puma	2082	30.03.15
	LN-OLB, OY-HMH, LN-OLB, F-WFQA		
	Vector Aerospace International Ltd Solent		16.03.18E
G-CIOJ	Aeropro EuroFOX 912(iS)	444.15	09.07.15
	A C S Paterson Strathaven		
	Built by A C S Paterson – project LAA 376-15325;		
	tailwheel u/c (IE 01.06.18)		
G-CIOK	Best Off Skyranger Swift 912S(1)	SKRxxxx1087	15.04.15
	B Janson & J De Pree Nairns Mains, Haddington		13.07.18P
	Built by J De Pree – project BMAA/HB/664		
G-CIOL	P&M Quik GTR	8719	18.05.15
	D L Clark Great Oakley		03.06.18P
G-CIOM	Magni M24C Orion	24-15-9074	09.06.15
	C R Lear Chiltern Park, Wallingford		30.06.18P
G-CIOO	Van's RV-7	70913	26.06.15
	LN-BAW, (LN-BNW) M Albert-Recht Aboyne		08.08.18P
	Built by A O H Frog		
G-CIOP	Aérospatiale AS.355F Ecureuil 2	5216	19.11.15
	ZS-HMI, V5-HMI, ZS-HMI		
	RCR Aviation Ltd (Shipley, Horsham)		
	Reported as parted out & cabin to a		
	film company 2017? (NF 19.11.15)		
G-CIOR	Nicollier HN.700 Menestrel II	233	15.04.15
	R C & R P C Teverson Waits Farm, Belchamp Walter		25.08.18P
	Built by R C Teverson – project LAA 217-15169		
G-CIOS	McDonnell Douglas MD Explorer	900-00103	14.07.15
	G-SASO, N5646, N1811, N70035, (PH-PXE)		
	Specialist Aviation Services Ltd Newquay Cornwall		26.11.18E
	Operated by Cornwall Air Ambulance as callsign		
	'Helimed 01'		
G-CIOU	Cameron C-70	11896	30.06.15
	R J Mansfield Bowness-on-Windermere		23.08.18E
G-CIOV	Ultramagic H-31	31/14	12.08.15
	J A Lawton Enton, Godalming		19.04.18E
G-CIOW	Westland SA.341C Gazelle HT.2	1436	29.04.15
	ZK-HTF, XX446 S Atherton		
	Bourne Park, Hurstbourne Tarrant		
	Noted 11.15 less rotors (NF 28.04.15)		
G-CIOX	Flylight FoxCub	DA126	31.07.15
	P J Cheyney New House Farm, Birds Edge		
	(IE 18.08.17)		
G-CIOY	Beech G36 Bonanza	E-3888	13.07.15
	EC-LHU, EC-LEG, N836BB Bonanzair Ltd Elstree		09.09.19E
G-CIOZ	Comco Ikarus C42 FB100 Bravo	1503-7383	14.05.15
	C L G Innocent Hadfold Farm, Adversane		06.05.19P
	Assembled Red Aviation		
G-CIPA	P&M Pegasus Quik	8709	12.02.15
	B J Harrison Haverfordwest		24.10.18P
	Trike ex-G-CGOB c/n 8517		
G-CIPB	Messerschmitt Bf 109E-4	3579	16.02.15
	CF-EML, N81562, Luftwaffe		
	Biggin Hill Heritage Hangar Ltd Biggin Hill		20.11.19P
	Built by Arado Flugzeugwerke GmbH;		
	as '3579:14' (white) in Luftwaffe c/s		
G-CIPD	Cameron O-31	11900	11.05.15
	Gone With The Wind Ltd Clifton, Bristol BS8		26.04.18E
G-CIPE	Boeing Stearman A75N1 Kaydet (*N2S-5*) 75-5315		14.05.15
	C-GPTD, N72559, N105H, N5037V, 42-17152		
	Retro Track & Air (UK) Ltd (Cam, Dursley)		
	As '43' in USAAC c/s (NF 14.05.15)		
G-CIPF	Alisport Silent 2 Electro	2072	25.06.15
	Media Techniche Ltd Lasham *'IPF'*		
	(IE 19.07.17)		
G-CIPG	BRM Bristell NG5 Speed Wing	126	19.02.15
	D Peralta tr G-CIPG Syndicate (Cirencester)		20.10.19P
	Built by M D Hamwee & P Marsden		
	– project LAA 385-15315		
G-CIPJ	de Havilland DH.83 Fox Moth	TS2810	29.05.15
	ZK-AGM, ZK-ADJ B K Broady Audley End		30.08.19P
	Originally c/n 4085; crashed 07.06.36 & rebuilt by		
	Air Travel (NZ) Ltd c.1937/38 with new fuselage		
	c/n TS 2810 built DH Technical School, Hatfield		
	– as 'ZK-AGM'		
G-CIPL	Van's RV-9	90892	15.01.15
	M W Meynell Morgansfield, Fishburn		09.05.19P
	Built by M W Meynell & W J Siertsema		
	– project LAA 320-14219		
G-CIPM	P&M QuikR	8715	30.03.15
	M R Niznik East Fortune		28.03.18P
G-CIPO	Comco Ikarus C42 FB80	1503-7368	03.06.15
	J Richards Otherton		03.06.18P
	Assembled Red Aviation		
G-CIPP	AutoGyro Calidus	C00371	10.03.15
	P H Smith t/a Dragon Gyrocopters Llanbedr		28.04.18P
	Assembled Rotorsport UK as c/n RSUK/CALS/025		
G-CIPR	Best Off Skyranger Nynja 912(1)	xxxx	15.04.15
	J M Ross Balgrummo Steading, Bonnybank		16.10.18P
	Built by J M Ross – project BMAA/HB/654		
G-CIPS	Aeropro EuroFOX 912(1)	45315	25.03.15
	P Stretton Harringe Court, Sellindge		28.06.18P
	Built by P Stretton – project BMAA/HB/661; tricycle		
	u/c; struck sheep landing Harringe Court, Sellindge		
	16.09.17 & substantially damaged; Permit		
	suspended 04.11.17		
G-CIPT	BRM Bristell NG5 Speed Wing	134	02.06.15
	A J Radford Darley Moor		25.08.19P
	Built by A J Radford – project LAA 385-15323		
G-CIPU	Cessna F172F	F172-0112	20.05.15
	D-EBVU G Hinz (Wesselburenerkoog, Germany)		26.06.18E
	Built by Reims Aviation SA		
G-CIPW	AgustaWestland AW139	41344	18.08.15
	5H-EXT, N435SH		
	Bristow Helicopters Ltd Norwich Int'l		06.12.18E
G-CIPX	AgustaWestland AW139	41346	18.08.15
	5H-EXU, N438SH		
	Bristow Helicopters Ltd Norwich Int'l		27.10.18E
G-CIPY	Reims/Cessna F152 II	F15201742	05.06.15
	PH-TGB, PH-AYC Swiftair Maintenance Ltd Elstree		07.09.19E
	Operated by Flight Training London Ltd		
G-CIPZ	Pazmany PL-4A	xxxx	29.04.15
	J J Hill Full Sutton		12.02.20P
	Built by P Lloyd – project PFA 017-10357		
G-CIRB	Evektor EV-97 Eurostar SL	2015-4219	29.05.15
	R J Garbutt Manchester Barton		05.07.19P
	Assembled Light Sport Aviation Ltd		
G-CIRC	Such BM60-20	001	25.03.15
	D G Such Barkway, Royston		
	Built by D G Such (NF 24.03.15)		
G-CIRE	Corby CJ-1 Starlet	xxxx	11.06.15
	J Evans Griffins Farm, Temple Bruer		03.10.18P
	Built by J Evans – project LAA 134-14806		
G-CIRF	Advance Alpha 5/Parajet Zenith	3524P53100	21.04.15
	R Frankham (Easton Maudit, Wellingborough)		
	(IE 27.08.15)		
G-CIRH	Magni M16C Tandem Trainer	16159104	16.06.15
	Willy Rose Technology Ltd Chiltern Park, Wallingford		30.06.18P
G-CIRI	Cirrus SR20	1791	15.05.07
	N473SR C D Palfreyman tr Cirrus Flyers Group		
	Turweston		09.05.18E

G-CIRK Alisport Silent 2 Electro   2054   08.05.15
D-MSIB   C H Appleyard   Lasham
(IE 30.05.17)

G-CIRL Ultramagic S-90   90/140   15.07.15
D J Day & M A Scholes   Lindfield, Haywards Heath   11.07.19E

G-CIRM Van's RV-12   120426   25.06.15
P J Hynes   Sleap   10.04.18P
Built by P J Hynes & R Thompson
– project LAA 363-15076

G-CIRN Cameron Z-120   11928   10.09.15
Aeropubblicita Vicenza SRL   Vicenza, Italy
'ADMB HR – partner'   07.09.19E

G-CIRO Cessna F172H   F172-0449   26.02.15
D-EJSU   H G Stroemer   (Moorrege, Germany)   01.10.18E
Built by Reims Aviation SA

G-CIRP Aeropro EuroFOX 912(S)   46015   23.06.15
H R J Spurr   Clench Common   25.03.19P
Built by J M Shaw – project LAA 376-15337;
tailwheel u/c; engine & propeller stolen
Clench Common 07.06.18

G-CIRT AutoGyro MTOsport   M01277   10.07.15
J Gleeson & M Pugh   North Weald   06.09.18P
Assembled Rotorsport UK as c/n RSUK/MTOS/059

G-CIRU Cirrus SR20   2023   06.07.09
M-CIRU, G-CIRU, N164CS
Cirrent BV   Lelystad, Netherlands   06.08.18E

G-CIRV Van's RV-7   74266   13.02.15
R J Fray   Furze Farm, Haddon   07.05.18P
Built by R J Fray – project LAA 323-15281

G-CIRW Reims/Cessna FA150K Aerobat   FA1500053   20.07.15
SP-AKR, D-ECAA
Air Navigation & Trading Company Ltd   Blackpool   28.08.15E
Noted 01.18

G-CIRX Cameron Z-150   11913   28.07.15
Phoenix Balloons Ltd   Bristol BS8   12.07.18E

G-CIRY Evektor EV-97 Eurostar SL   2015-4222   17.07.15
R D Smith tr Hotel Victor Flying Group   Leicester   14.07.18P
Assembled Light Sport Aviation Ltd

G-CIRZ Comco Ikarus C42 FB80   1506-7403   04.08.15
Mainair Microlight School Ltd   Manchester Barton   09.08.18P
Assembled Red Aviation

G-CISA Sprite Stinger   001   22.04.15
Sprite Aviation Services Ltd   Inglenook Farm, Maydensole

G-CISB Sackville AH-56   01   22.04.15
T J Wilkinson   Sackville Lodge Farm, Riseley
Built by T J Wilkinson; active 05.15 (IE 01.07.15)

G-CISC Sackville AH-77   02   22.04.15
T J Wilkinson   Sackville Lodge Farm, Riseley
Built by T J Wilkinson (IE 01.07.15)

G-CISD Sackville AH-31   03   22.04.15
L S Crossland-Clarke   Hull
Built by T J Wilkinson (IE 22.07.18)

G-CISE Aero Designs Pulsar XP   186   20.05.15
S C Goozee
Newton Peveril Farm, Sturminster Marshall   21.07.18P
Built by S C Goozee & A J Nurse – project
PFA 202-12070; tailwheel u/c

G-CISF Quad City Challenger II   CH2-0902-0-2259   26.06.15
S A Beddus   Great Oakley
Built by S A Beddus – project LAA 177-14783;
note G-CIID also quotes kit no.CH2-0902-2259
(NF 26.06.15)

G-CISG Comco Ikarus C42 FB80   1506-7397   23.07.15
C W Good   Cardiff   21.07.18P
Assembled Red Aviation

G-CISH Thatcher CX4   219   29.06.15
P J Watson   Fenland
Built by P J Watson – project LAA 357-14808
(IE 29.06.18)

G-CISI P&M Quik GTR   8727   01.09.15
Kent County Scout Council   (Sandling, Maidstone)   17.08.18P

G-CISJ Ultramagic H-31   31/07   16.07.15
YU-OAL   R P Wade   Shevington, Wigan   31.03.18E

G-CISK Embraer EMB-145LR   145570   21.12.15
XA-ULI, HB-JAU, PT-SBG
Air Kilroe Ltd t/a Eastern Airways   Humberside   07.02.19E

G-CISL Cameron C-70   11880   25.03.15
S Lundin   Vaxjo, Sweden   23.03.18E

G-CISM P&M Quik Lite   8729   13.07.15
P & M Aviation Ltd   Elm Tree Park, Manton
(IE 08.01.18)

G-CISN Flylight FoxCub   DA122   31.07.15
G Nicholas   Sywell
Fox 13TL wing s/n 020-15 (IE 25.08.17)

G-CISO Cessna 150G   15066914   18.05.15
HA-SJT, N3014S   Enterprise Purchasing Ltd   Fairoaks   19.12.17E

G-CISR Flying K Sky Raider 1   SR200   29.06.15
J A Harris   (Bourton, Gillingham)
(IE 29.06.15)

G-CISS Comco Ikarus C42 FB80   1506-7396   17.07.15
R O'Malley-White   Dunkeswell   15.07.18P
Assembled Red Aviation

G-CIST P&M Quik GT450   8723   03.07.15
G J Prisk   Perranporth   02.07.18P

G-CISU CM Microlights Sunbird   SB1-001   26.05.15
C W Mitchinson   (Bradwell, Great Yarmouth)
(IE 26.08.15)

G-CISW La Mouette Samson 12   BA IPSOS.G   20.07.15
N Pain   (Hutton Henry, Hartlepool)
(IE 20.07.15)

G-CISX Cessna 172M Skyhawk   17262309   20.07.15
EI-CGD, OO-BMT, N12846   M A Lorne   Lydd   21.11.19E

G-CISZ Van's RV-7   74228   29.07.15
D C Hanss   (Stony Stratford, Milton Keynes)
Built by D C Hanss – project LAA 323-15328 (IE 16.11.18)

G-CITC Apollo Delta Jet 2/Reflex 13M   UK010515   22.07.15
P Broome   (Much Wenlock)
(IE 22.07.15)

G-CITD Sportavia-Putzer Fournier RF5   5115   24.08.15
D-KCID   J P Harrison tr G-CITD Group
Bentley Farm, Coal Aston   21.03.18E

G-CITE Grob G102 Astir CS Jeans   2016   08.05.15
(BGA 5842), D-4835   The Bath, Wilts & North Dorset
Gliding Club Ltd   Kingston Deverill   *'LPM'*   22.03.18E

G-CITF Evektor EV-97 Eurostar SL   2015-4223   30.07.15
J C Rose   Backstable Farm, Haddenham   27.07.18P
Assembled Light Sport Aviation Ltd

G-CITG Best Off Skyranger Nynja 912S(1)   UK\N/BK187   27.07.15
A C Aiken & J Attard   Sywell   11.10.18P
Built by A C Aiken – project BMAA/HB/670

G-CITH Rans S-6-ES Coyote II   0108.1851   20.05.15
D P Molloy   Newtownards   23.10.19P
Built by J Colton & K Smith – project LAA 204-14849

G-CITK Alisport Silent 2 Targa   2028   27.07.15
01ZA   B T Green   (Nanstallon, Bodmin)
(IE 27.07.15)

G-CITL Ace Aviation Magic/Cyclone   xxxx   21.05.15
S F Beardsell   Great Oakley
Shares DragonLite trike unit with G-CHRU
& wing s/n AC-166 (IE 21.05.15)

G-CITM Magni M16C Tandem Trainer   16159054   16.06.15
R S Payne   Tatenhill   22.07.19P

G-CITN North American P-51D-25-NA Mustang   122-39655   12.08.15
N5449V, 44-73196
P Earthey   (Leycoussaudie, Dordogne, France)

G-CITO P&M Quik   8733   11.09.15
M P Jackson   Manchester Barton   06.09.18P
Sailwing badged 'Quik Lite'

G-CITP Grumman American AA-1B Trainer   AA1B-0466   06.11.15
OO-PTC, G-CITP, OO-PTC, D-EFDM   J-C Vanderstricht
(Namur, La Bruyère, Villers-lez-Heest, Belgium)   13.02.19E

G-CITR Cameron Z-105   10278   22.02.02
A Kaye   Irchester, Wellingborough   *'Citroen'*   09.08.18E

G-CITS Groppo Trail   082/41   28.04.15
D A Buttress   Charity Farm, Baxterley   24.05.18P
Built by D A Butress – project LAA 372-15175

G-CITT Mooney M.20J Mooney 201   24-0598   16.07.15
D-EOSD, N7201K   J M Tiley   Dunkeswell
(NF 16.07.15)

G-CITU Kobra Basik/Ozone Spark   SK30-P-01D-011   14.08.15
T A Dobbins   (Birmingham B34)
(IE 14.08.15)

G-CITV AutoGyro Cavalon   V00217   21.07.15
N R W Whitling   Wolverhampton Halfpenny Green   27.04.18P
Assembled Rotorsport UK as c/n RSUK/CVLN/017

G-CITW Extra EA.400   20   06.08.15
N400LY, D-ELRN   LAC Marine Ltd
Bonn-Hangelar, Nordrhein-Westphalen, Germany   01.06.16E

G-CITX AutoGyro MTOsport   xxxx   10.07.15
D Brooksbank   (Barnsley)   19.07.18P
Assembled by Rotorsport UK as c/n RSUK/MTOS/060

G-CITY Piper PA-31-350 Chieftain   31-7852136   12.09.78
N27741   Blue Sky Investments Ltd   Belfast Int'l   27.06.18E
Official type data 'PA-31-350 Navajo Chieftain'
is incorrect

G-CIUA Ultramagic B-70   70/12   26.08.15
K W Graham   Spennymoor   05.05.18E

G-CIUB Cameron Z-90   10591   21.09.15
G Forster   Bristol BS1   *'HepcoMotion'*   16.01.18E

G-CIUD Stephens Sirocco SW FT   DS005   17.09.15
D H Lewis   (Nelson, Cardiff)
Built by D Stephens – a modified rebuild of G-ROCO;
official type 'Sirocco Swift' is incorrect (IE 14.09.17)

G-CIUE CASA 1-131E Jungmann Series 2000   2043   24.09.15
N131LB, N131LE, N131LB, Spanish AF E3B-447
R A Fleming   Breighton   07.06.19P
As 'A-44' in Swiss AF c/s

G-CIUF Aviad Zigolo MG12   4/2015/27   25.09.15
J D C Henslow & C B Jones   Ingrams Green, Midhurst
Built by D J Pilkington (IE 26.10.18)

G-CIUG Aeropro EuroFOX 3K   47516   21.08.15
J V Clewer & J A Thomas   Harringe Court, Sellindge   20.06.18P
Built by Ascent Industries Ltd; tricycle u/c

G-CIUH Cessna 152   15285745   28.09.15
F-GYVR, HA-ERL, N94622
J M Perfettini   Sherburn-in-Elmet   13.04.18E

G-CIUI Best Off Skyranger 912(2)   UK/376   28.09.15
K Roche tr Wexair Group   Taghmon, RoI   31.07.18P
Built by E Bentley – project BMAA/HB/675

G-CIUK Cameron O-65   11923   23.06.15
Cameron Balloons Ltd   Bristol BS3
'Cameron Superlight'   15.07.18E

G-CIUM Piper PA-12 Super Cruiser   12-1272   20.11.15
D-EFHH, (D-EFLN), OY-AVU, D-ELKE, N2835M, NC2835M
J Havers & S James   North Weald
Noted 07.18 (NF 20.11.15)

G-CIUN Flylight FoxCub   DA130   07.01.16
C I Chegwen   Otherton
(NF 07.01.16)

G-CIUO PPHU-Ekolot KR-010 Elf   01-01-08   13.10.15
P V Griffiths   (Dunblane)
Restyled development of Type JK-01A
(Designer Jerzy Krawczyk) (IE 21.04.17)

G-CIUP Europa Aviation Europa XS   560   07.09.15
F-PMLH, F-WMLH   P Bridges & P C Matthews
Fowle Hall Farm, Laddingford   02.05.18P
Built by M Lacaze (IE 27.08.17)

G-CIUR ProairSport GloW   001   21.10.15
Proairsport Ltd   (Wolverton Mill, Milton Keynes)
(IE 21.10.15)

G-CIUT DAR Solo 120   120-230-003   16.11.15
A Young   (Bircotes, Doncaster)
(NF 18.07.18)

G-CIUU Reims/Cessna F152 II   F15201770   30.11.15
OO-PNP, PH-EVF, OO-PNP, PH-EVF, PH-AYI
DSFT Ltd   Doncaster Sheffield   16.07.19E
Operated by Doncaster Sheffield Flight Training

G-CIUW Noorduyn AT-16-ND Harvard IIB   14-245   02.02.16
SE-BII, Swedish AF 16128, RCAF FE511, (42-708)
J Brown   White Waltham   25.05.18P
Rebuilt Sweden c.2006-2009 as EAA Project No.705;
as 'FE511' in RCAF c/s

G-CIUX Auster AOP.9   AUS.B5.020   09.11.15
'7822M', 7863M, WZ679
R Warner   Westside Farm, Whittlesford   *'ARMY'*
Officially quoted as c/n AUS/180 which relates to
XR243/8057M; as 'WZ679' in AAC c/s (NF 09.11.15)

G-CIUY Bell 206L-3 LongRanger III   51578   25.02.16
D-HALT, C-FNLC   Volantair LLP   (Dungannon)   22.02.18E

G-CIUZ P&M Quik GTR   8726   13.11.15
S Spyrou   (London N12)   09.03.18P

G-CIVA Boeing 747-436   27092   19.03.93
British Airways PLC   London Heathrow   18.03.19E
Line No: 967

G-CIVB Boeing 747-436   25811   15.02.94
(G-BNLY)   British Airways PLC   London Heathrow   14.02.19E
Line No: 1018

G-CIVC Boeing 747-436   25812 5692   26.02.94
(G-BNLZ)   British Airways PLC   London Heathrow
'oneworld'   25.02.19E
Line No: 1022

G-CIVD Boeing 747-436   27349   14.12.94
British Airways PLC   London Heathrow
'oneworld'   03.08.19E
Line No: 1048

G-CIVE Boeing 747-436   27350   20.12.94
British Airways PLC   London Heathrow   22.08.19E
Line No: 1050

G-CIVF Boeing 747-436   25434   29.03.95
(G-BNLY)   British Airways PLC   London Heathrow   20.09.19E
Line No: 1058

G-CIVG Boeing 747-436   25813   20.04.95
N6009F   British Airways PLC   London Heathrow   19.01.19E
Line No: 1059

G-CIVH Boeing 747-436   25809   23.04.96
British Airways PLC   London Heathrow   14.04.19E
Line No: 1078

G-CIVI Boeing 747-436   25814   02.05.96
British Airways PLC   London Heathrow   *'oneworld'*   01.05.19E
Line No: 1079

G-CIVJ Boeing 747-436   25817   11.02.97
British Airways PLC   London Heathrow   10.09.19E
Line No: 1102

G-CIVK Boeing 747-436   25818   28.02.97
British Airways PLC   London Heathrow   *'oneworld'*   30.08.19E
Line No: 1104

G-CIVL Boeing 747-436   27478   28.03.97
British Airways PLC   London Heathrow   *'oneworld'*   08.11.19E
Line No: 1108

G-CIVM Boeing 747-436   28700   05.06.97
British Airways PLC   London Heathrow   *'oneworld'*   04.06.19E
Line No: 1116

G-CIVN Boeing 747-436   28848   29.09.97
British Airways PLC   London Heathrow   28.09.19E
Line No: 1129

G-CIVO Boeing 747-436   28849   05.12.97
N6046P   British Airways PLC   London Heathrow   13.10.19E
Line No: 1135

G-CIVP Boeing 747-436   28850   17.02.98
British Airways PLC   London Heathrow   *'oneworld'*   16.02.19E
Line No: 1144

G-CIVR Boeing 747-436   25820   02.03.98
British Airways PLC   London Heathrow   04.02.19E
Line No: 1146

G-CIVS Boeing 747-436   28851   13.03.98
British Airways PLC   London Heathrow   02.03.19E
Line No: 1148

G-CIVT Boeing 747-436   25821   20.03.98
(G-CIVN)   British Airways PLC   London Heathrow   09.11.19E
Line No: 1149

G-CIVU	Boeing 747-436	25810	24.04.98
	(G-CIVO) British Airways PLC London Heathrow		22.03.19E
	Line No: 1154		
G-CIVV	Boeing 747-436	25819	22.05.98
	N6009F, (G-CIVP) British Airways PLC		
	London Heathrow		10.04.19E
	Line No: 1156		
G-CIVW	Boeing 747-436	25822	15.05.98
	(G-CIVR) British Airways PLC London Heathrow		18.04.19E
	Line No: 1157		
G-CIVX	Boeing 747-436	28852	03.09.98
	British Airways PLC London Heathrow		25.07.19E
	Line No: 1172		
G-CIVY	Boeing 747-436	28853	29.09.98
	British Airways PLC London Heathrow		22.08.19E
	Line No: 1178		
G-CIVZ	Boeing 747-436	28854	31.10.98
	British Airways PLC London Heathrow 'oneworld'		22.09.19E
	Line No: 1183		
G-CIWA	Best Off Skyranger Swift 912(1)	SKR10111018	23.07.15
	S D Lilley Priory Farm, Tibenham		16.04.18P
	Built by S D Lilley – project BMAA/HB/616		
G-CIWB	Van's RV-6	20504	09.09.15
	G D Price Deanland		25.09.19P
	Built by C G Price & M Skalon – project PFA 181A-15259		
G-CIWC	Raj Hamsa X'Air Hawk	1257	14.09.15
	G A J Salter Westonzoyland		07.03.18P
	Built by G A J Salter – project LAA 340-15349		
G-CIWD	TLAC Sherwood Ranger ST	ST52	20.11.15
	A R Pitcher (Udimore, Rye)		12.06.18P
	Built by A R Pitcher – project PFA 237B-15221		
G-CIWE	Kubíček BB22Z	1215	01.03.16
	O J Webb York 'Munchies'		06.06.19E
G-CIWF	Airbus EC225 LP Super Puma	2955	30.11.15
	D-HTIN Babcock Mission Critical Services		
	Offshore Ltd Humberside		13.01.19E
G-CIWG	Aeropro EuroFOX 912(iS)	47015	08.10.15
	A Hegner Aston Down		05.07.18P
	Built by A Hegner – project LAA 376-15351;		
	tailwheel u/c; glider-tug		
G-CIWH	Agusta-Bell 206B-3 JetRanger III	8701	22.12.15
	I-EPIA, F-GEJM P Rosati		
	(Monaco, Principality of Monaco)		27.12.18E
G-CIWI	Evektor EV-97 Eurostar SL	2015-4227	10.09.15
	P A Aston tr Mademoiselle CIWI Group Halwell		09.09.19P
	Assembled Light Sport Aviation Ltd		
G-CIWL	Techpro Merlin 100UL	0012	08.12.15
	OK-UUR 18 Sprite Aviation Services Ltd		
	Inglenook Farm, Maydensole		
	(IE 21.12.17)		
G-CIWN	Such BM42-16	002	16.11.15
	D G Such Barkway, Royston		
	Built by D G Such (NF 16.11.15)		
G-CIWO	Airbus AS.350B3 Ecureuil	8191	03.02.16
	R & J Helicopters LLP Carters Barn, Huggate		02.02.18E
G-CIWP	Comco Ikarus C42 FB100 Bravo	1510-7425	05.02.16
	J I Greenshields tr G-CIWP Syndicate Dunkeswell		24.06.19P
	Assembled Red Aviation		
G-CIWT	Comco Ikarus C42 FB80	1507-7398	11.08.15
	J W Lorains (Wirral)		09.08.18P
	Assembled Red Aviation		
G-CIWU	Hughes 369E (500)	0447E	18.01.16
	OO-SOO, (OO-FOO), D-HGWM		
	Century Aviation (Training) Ltd Retford Gamston		27.04.18E
G-CIWV	Van's RV-7	71877	16.12.15
	J W Baker Seething		25.09.18P
	Built by J W Baker & J W Harris		
	– project PFA 323-14581		
G-CIWW	Sackville BM-56	04	13.10.15
	T J Wilkinson Sackville Lodge Farm, Riseley		
	Built by T J Wilkinson (IE 22.08.17)		
G-CIWX	Sackville 65	05	13.10.15
	T J Wilkinson Sackville Lodge Farm, Riseley		
	Built by T J Wilkinson (IE 09.08.16)		

G-CIWY	Sackville 90	06	13.10.15
	T J Wilkinson Sackville Lodge Farm, Riseley		
	Built by T J Wilkinson (IE 03.11.17)		
G-CIWZ	Sackville BM-34 LW	07	13.10.15
	T J Wilkinson Sackville Lodge Farm, Riseley		
	Built by T J Wilkinson (IE 14.06.17)		
G-CIXA	Dudek Nucleon 31	P.05684	09.10.15
	P Sinkler (Routh, Beverley)		
	(IE 03.11.15)		
G-CIXB	Grob G109B	6380	25.08.10
	D-KNEH S J Williams tr G-CIXB Syndicate		
	Parham Park		13.10.17E
G-CIXD	Cameron A-105	11971	15.04.16
	K R Karlstrom Northwood		11.09.18E
G-CIXE	Moravan Zlin Z-326 Trener Master	928	20.09.17
	F-BPNM J J B Leasor Eaglescott		17.02.18E
G-CIXG	Phantom Phantom X1	KBW-002	12.01.16
	K B Woods Newnham		
	Built by K B Woods (IE 01.06.18)		
G-CIXH	Schempp-Hirth Ventus-2a	20	19.11.15
	(BGA 5902), D-1645 O Walters Bicester 'Y'		14.09.17E
G-CIXI	Polaris FIB	0731239	14.09.15
	J Hennessy tr Pirates Cove Flyers		
	(Thomastown, Co Kilkenny, RoI)		
	(NF 29.10.17)		
G-CIXJ	Curtiss P-36C	12624?	10.02.16
	NX80FR, 38-210 Patina Ltd Duxford		07.07.18P
	As 'PA 50' in USAAC c/s		
G-CIXL	Air Création iFun 13 Pixel 250XC	A15071-15060	13.08.15
	S C Reeve Headon Farm, Retford		
	(IE 23.08.17)		
G-CIXM	Super Marine Spitfire Mk.26	051	06.01.16
	S W Markham Valentine Farm, Odiham		
	Built by S W Markham – project PFA 324-14509;		
	as 'PL793' in RAF c/s (IE 02.07.18)		
G-CIXN	CFM Shadow Series DD	306-D	27.01.16
	I-7929, G-91-01, G-85-25		
	U J Anderson Blackmoor Farm, Aubourn		
	Originally built as CFM Shadow Series E with c/n 346-E		
	(SSDR microlight since 06.16) (NF 01.09.17)		
G-CIXP	Cessna 152	15280872	28.01.16
	SP-KBH, N25944 H E da Costa Alburquerque		
	(Amadora, Portugal)		11.01.19E
G-CIXR	Cameron Z-77	11982	21.03.16
	Airship & Balloon Company Ltd		
	Henbury, Bristol 'Tata Consultancy Services'		13.03.19E
G-CIXS	Zenair CH.701SP	7-10289	28.08.15
	S Foreman Priory Farm, Tibenham 'Sky Jeep'		02.05.18P
	Built by S Foreman – project LAA 187A-15336		
G-CIXT	Flylight FoxCub	DA131	02.03.16
	A G Cummings (Penwortham, Preston)		
	(IE 02.03.16)		
G-CIXU	Cameron Z-77	11450	21.03.16
	Airship & Balloon Company Ltd Henbury, Bristol		
	'Abbott World Marathon Majors'		01.03.18E
G-CIXV	Embraer ERJ 170-100 LR	17000111	18.05.15
	5Y-KYK, PT-SAT Air Kilroe Ltd t/a Eastern Airways		
	Naples, Italy		05.10.19E
	Stored 10.18		
G-CIXW	Embraer ERJ 170-100 LR	17000230	16.05.15
	5Y-KYH, PT-SFG Air Kilroe Ltd t/a Eastern Airways		
	Naples, Italy		19.07.19E
	Stored 11.18		
G-CIXX	AutoGyro Cavalon	V00226	15.02.16
	M J Taylor Perth		12.06.19P
	Assembled Rotorsport UK with c/n RSUK/CVLN/018		
G-CIXY	Comco Ikarus C42 FB80 Bravo	1601-7435	13.04.16
	London Light Flight Ltd Elstree		10.04.19P
	Assembled Red Aviation; operated by Fly by Light		
G-CIXZ	P&M QuikR	8735	02.10.15
	N H N Douglas Beverley (Linley Hill)		15.09.18P

G-CIYB	Jodel DR.1050-M1 Sicile Record	946	04.09.15
	PH-RTS, OO-CAR		
	A G & G I Doake Gilford, Craigavon		29.06.18P
	Built by Centre-Est Aéronautique; official c/n 605		
	relates to OO-CAR (DR.10501-M1) which was		
	rebuilt as c/n 946 PH-RTS (DR.1050-M1);		
	extensive damage 08.06.18		
G-CIYC	Flylight FoxCub	DA132	04.02.16
	S Barbour (Hassocks)		
	(IE 08.11.17)		
G-CIYE	Eurocopter EC225 LP Super Puma	2600	16.02.16
	D-HDON, 7T-WVA, 7T-WPA, 7T-VPE, F-WQDJ		
	Leonardo SpA Stavanger-Sola, Norway		
	Stored 08.16 (NF 16.02.16)		
G-CIYG	Airbike Light Sport	002	10.12.15
	N Allen (Hevingham, Norwich)		
	(NF 10.12.15)		
G-CIYH	Eurocopter EC225 LP Super Puma	2623	16.02.16
	D-HPIT, 7T-WVB, F-WWOQ		
	Leonardo SpA Stavanger-Sola, Norway		
	Stored 08.16 (NF 16.02.16)		
G-CIYK	Greenslade Free Spirit Biplane	FS 001	25.01.16
	N46FS J C Greenslade (Crapstone, Yelverton)		
	Built by J C Greenslade (NF 25.01.16)		
G-CIYL	Aeropro EuroFOX 912iS(1)	49616	17.02.16
	J M & R H Gardner Jersey		31.07.19P
	Built by R M Cornwell & S M Williams – project		
	BMAA/HB/682; tailwheel u/c		
G-CIYN	Best Off Skyranger Nynja 912S(1)	15060188	21.01.16
	R W Sutherland Easter Farm, Fearn		06.11.18P
	Built by R W Sutherland – project BMAA/HB/672		
G-CIYO	Groppo Trail	095/54	14.01.16
	M A McLoughlin (Melton Mowbray)		12.09.19P
	Built by A McIvor – project LAA 372-15237		
G-CIYP	Aeropro EuroFOX 912(1)	48615	21.10.15
	J Andrews Ince		20.03.18P
	Built by J Andrews – project BMAA/HB/677; tricycle u/c		
G-CIYR (2)	Lindstrand 177T	SF001	29.02.16
	Lindstrand Technologies Ltd		
	Uluru, Northern Territories, Australia		
	Operated by SkyShip Uluru; destroyed in storm		
	09.10.18 near Uluru (NF 29.02.16)		
G-CIYT	Rich Flugastol	01	09.03.16
	F B Rich (Picket Piece, Andover)		
	Built by F Rich		
G-CIYV	Van's RV-9A	90790	15.03.16
	M S Ashby Halwell		
	Built by M S Ashby – project PFA 320-14110		
	(NF 15.03.16)		
G-CIYX	Embraer EMB-145LR	145601	18.07.16
	5N-BSO, G-CIYX, HB-JAY, EI-GXB, HB-JAY, PT-SCK		
	Air Kilroe Ltd t/a Eastern Airways Humberside		04.10.17E
	(IE 01.05.18)		
G-CIYY	TLAC Sherwood Ranger XP	XP37	25.02.16
	M R M Welch Goodwood		10.09.18P
	Built by D Hood – project LAA 237A-15388;		
	kit no indicates originally regd as Sherwood		
	Ranger ST with s/n LAA 237B-15388		
G-CIYZ	P&M QuikR	8734	02.10.15
	R A Keene t/a R Keene & Sons Over Farm, Gloucester		01.08.18P
G-CIZA	Spacek SD-1 Minisport	129	01.10.15
	P Smith (Ramsgate)		
	Tricycle u/c (IE 30.05.17)		
G-CIZB	Magni M24C Orion	24169514	22.02.16
	J E Fallis Bellarena		15.03.18P
G-CIZD	P&M Quik GT450	8742	20.01.16
	D Orton Measham Cottage Farm, Measham		14.03.19P
G-CIZE	Cameron O-56	11954	11.03.16
	P Spellward Bristol BS9		20.04.18E
G-CIZF	Ozone Indy/Paramotor Flyer Trike		
		1N09L-1-27B-013/PMF001T	23.03.16
	M R Gaylor (Little Dalby, Melton Mowbray)		
	(IE 23.03.16)		
G-CIZG	Robinson R66 Turbine	0698	11.02.16
	Buildrandom Ltd (Aberton, Pershore)		12.03.18E

G-CIZI	Piper PA-32RT-300 Lance II	32R-7985100	01.12.15
	I-LANC, N2078X Papier Volant SAS		
	(Saint Georges sur la Pree, France)		22.11.18E
G-CIZL	P&M QuikR	8737	01.12.15
	J Macdonald tr East Fortune Flyers East Fortune		20.12.18P
G-CIZM	Cameron Z-210	11936	03.03.16
	The Balloon Company Ltd t/a First Flight		
	Langford, Bristol *'Tribute'*		28.02.18E
G-CIZN	Piper J-5B Cub Cruiser	5-1133	15.04.16
	(D-E...), N40701, NC40701		
	M Howells Woolston Moss, Warrington		
	(NF 15.04.16)		
G-CIZO	Piper PA-28-161 Cadet	2841155	11.01.16
	SE-KII, (F-GHBA)		
	Falcon Flying Services Ltd Exeter Int'l		31.08.18E
	Operated by South West Aviation		
G-CIZP	AutoGyro Cavalon Pro	xxxx	15.02.16
	C Coffield Chiltern Park, Wallingford		18.05.19E
	Assembled Rotorsport UK as c/n RSUK/CAVP/001		
G-CIZR	Van's RV-9	xxxx	26.11.15
	M L Martin (Cuckfield, Haywards Heath)		
	Built by M L Martin – project PFA 320-14506		
	(NF 26.11.15)		
G-CIZS	Tipsy Nipper T.66 Series 2	49	16.02.16
	OO-WOT, PH-MEV, (PH-MES), (PH-SUS), OO-MON,		
	(OY-AEU) N D Dykes Manchester Barton		25.02.20P
	Built by Cobelavia (Compagnie Belge d'Aviation)		
G-CIZT	Ace Aviation Magic/Cyclone	xxxx	01.03.16
	T Robinson Greenhills Farm, Wheatley Hill		
	Trike s/n not known & wing s/n AC-153 (IE 26.04.17)		
G-CIZU	Evektor EV-97 Eurostar SL	2016-4230	23.05.16
	E K McAlinden Derryogue, Kilkeel		15.05.19P
	Assembled Light Sport Aviation Ltd		
G-CIZV	P&M QuikR	8748	29.01.16
	R A McLean tr G-CIZV Syndicate East Fortune		05.02.19P
	Trike from G-CEHC with new wing		
G-CIZW	Alisport Silent 2 Electro	2085	28.07.16
	P C Jarvis & C C Redrup Lasham *'ZW'*		
	(IE 16.07.18)		
G-CIZY	Piper PA-34-200T Seneca II	34-7870044	18.02.16
	SX-BSA, N5151S, C-GQYF		
	BAR Aviation Rentals Ltd Kopaida, Greece		10.09.17E

G-CJAA – G-CJZZ

G-CJAF	Cessna 182T Skylane	18281659	18.01.16
	EC-JSZ, N12615 C S Ringer Sandown		27.02.18E
G-CJAI	P&M Quik GT450	8198	19.10.07
	J C Kitchen Middle Stoke, Isle of Grain		12.06.18P
	Possibly fitted with trike c/n 7979 ex G-CJAY (qv)		
G-CJAJ	P&M Quik GT450	8750	07.03.16
	D Al-Bassam Sutton Meadows		14.04.18P
G-CJAK	Best Off Skyranger Nynja 912S(1)	UK\N\BK192	18.01.16
	A K Birt Sywell		22.10.18P
	Built by A K Birt – project BMAA/HB/674		
G-CJAL	Schleicher Ka 6E	4360	01.05.00
	BGA 4358/JAL, F-CDTX		
	J Stewart tr JAL Syndicate Solent *'JAL'*		09.04.14E
	(IE 05.06.17)		
G-CJAM	Comco Ikarus C42 FB80	1512-7434	04.03.16
	G C Linley Eastbach Spence, English Bicknor		21.02.18P
	Assembled Red Aviation		
G-CJAO	Schempp-Hirth Discus b	190	11.01.00
	BGA 4362/JAQ, D-0960		
	R W Coombs Halesland *'823'*		18.08.17E
	(IE 03.08.18)		
G-CJAP	Comco Ikarus C42 FB80	1003-7095	02.08.10
	B H J Van der Berg Chatteris		01.08.19P
	Assembled Pioneer Aviation UK Ltd		
G-CJAR	Schempp-Hirth Discus bT	83	19.03.08
	BGA 4363/JAR, D-KHEI		
	C J H Donnelly Parham Park *'P3'*		19.08.18E

G-CJAS	Glasflügel Standard Libelle 201B	109	01.12.07
	BGA 4364/JAS, SE-TIS		
	M J Collett Wycombe Air Park *'7Q'*		03.12.16E
	(IE 17.09.18)		
G-CJAT	Schleicher K 8B	8150	10.10.07
	BGA 4365/JAT, D-4390		
	Wolds Gliding Club Ltd Pocklington *'JAT'*		27.05.18E
G-CJAU	White Sports Monoplane	JA002	04.02.16
	J Aubert Brooklands		
	Built by J Aubert (IE 31.05.17)		
G-CJAV	Schleicher ASK 21	21662	10.10.07
	BGA 4367		
	Wolds Gliding Club Ltd Pocklington *'JAV'*		24.05.18E
G-CJAW	Glaser-Dirks DG-200/17	2-180/1759	19.12.07
	BGA 4368/JAW, D-5618 F Friend Llantysilio *'M4'*		01.06.18E
G-CJAX	Schleicher ASK 21	21665	10.10.07
	BGA 4369		
	Wolds Gliding Club Ltd Pocklington *'JAX'*		14.02.18E
G-CJAY	P&M Pegasus Quik	7979	18.08.03
	J C Kitchen (Middle Stoke, Isle of Grain)		02.06.19P
	Built by Mainair as Sports Pegasus Quik; new		
	wing (c/n 8198) fitted 06.06 & re-registered as		
	Quik GT450; reverted to Quik c.2007 & trike		
	possibly donated to G-CJAI (qv)		
G-CJAZ	Grob G102 Astir CS Jeans	2073	11.09.08
	BGA 4371/JAZ, D-7586		
	M R Dews Kingston Deverill *'JAZ'*		08.11.18E
G-CJBA	Alisport Silent 2 Electro	2081	08.03.16
	B A Fairston & A Stotter Husbands Bosworth *'JBA'*		
	(IE 14.03.17)		
G-CJBC	Piper PA-28-180 Cherokee D	28-5470	28.11.80
	OY-BDE J B Cave Wolverhampton Halfpenny Green		15.01.19E
G-CJBD	Spacek SD-1 Minisport	099	18.12.15
	D Cox Redlands *'Little Minx'*		
	Built by D Cox; active 09.18 (IE 18.12.15)		
G-CJBE	Comco Ikarus C42 FB80	1511-7427	04.03.16
	J H Bradbury Arclid Green, Sandbach		21.02.18P
	Assembled Red Aviation		
G-CJBH	Eiriavion PIK-20D-78	20621	14.11.07
	BGA 4379/JBH, OH-529 G A Darby Bicester *'537'*		10.07.18R
G-CJBI	Aeropro EuroFOX 912(iS)	49416	12.05.16
	M B Z de Ferranti Ham Hill, Sydmonton, Ecchinswell		06.09.19P
	Built by S B Williams – project LAA 376-15386;		
	tailwheel u/c		
G-CJBJ	Jastreb Standard Cirrus G/81	280	06.11.08
	BGA 4380/JBJ, SE-TZD		
	S T Dutton (Torpenhow, Wigton) *'G81'*		23.06.18E
	(NF 27.09.17)		
G-CJBK	Schleicher ASW 19B	19204	07.11.07
	BGA 4381/JBK, D-4099, PH-602		
	D Caielli & P Deane Dunstable Downs *'L3'*		11.04.18E
G-CJBL	Flylight FoxTug	DA133	23.08.16
	R W Twamley Coventry		
	Aeros Fox 16T Sailwing c/n 042.16 (IE 20.07.17)		
G-CJBM	Schleicher ASK 21	21089	10.12.07
	BGA 4383/JBM, D-6391		
	The Burn Gliding Club Ltd Burn *'JBM'*		20.04.18E
G-CJBN	Sackville BM-65	BN01	27.01.16
	B J Newman Rushden		
	(IE 21.03.16)		
G-CJBO	Rolladen-Schneider LS8-18	8148	15.08.08
	BGA 4386/JBQ		
	J P Simmonds tr L7 Syndicate (Hereford) *'L7'*		08.04.18E
G-CJBP	Flylight FoxCub	DA134	15.04.16
	R W Skoyles (Halstead)		
	DragonLite trike c/n DA134 & Fox 16T wing c/n 014.16;		
	manufacturer's type unofficially re-named Flylight		
	PeaBee; fitted with new trike c.2017 (IE 11.07.18)		
G-CJBR	Schempp-Hirth Discus b	90	08.02.08
	BGA 4387/JBR, F-CGGD, F-WGGD		
	M R C Corrance tr G-CJBR Group Kenley *'AC'*		19.04.18E
G-CJBT	Schleicher ASW 19B	19075	14.11.07
	BGA 4389/JBT, D-4477		
	Black Mountains Gliding Club Talgarth *'JBT'*		27.09.19E
G-CJBU	BRM Bristell NG5 Speed Wing	187-2015	09.05.16
	OK-QUU 6 H R Pearson Luxters Farm, Hambleden		09.10.18P
	Built by J Cosgrave & H R Pearson – project		
	LAA 385-15376; tailwheel u/c		
G-CJBV	IAV Bacau Yakovlev Yak-52	867203	03.05.16
	F-WRUP, RA-3508K, DOSAAF 144 (yellow)		
	R J Harper Tibenham		20.10.18P
G-CJBW	Schempp-Hirth Discus bT	34	17.10.07
	BGA 4392, D-KBJR		
	N Pringle tr G-CJBW Syndicate Lasham *'710'*		09.02.19E
G-CJBX	Rolladen-Schneider LS4-a	4293	21.03.07
	BGA 4393, D-9111 P W Lee Nympsfield *'JBX'*		07.04.18E
G-CJBZ	Grob G102 Astir CS	1492	16.05.11
	BGA 4395/JBZ, D-4794 The Royal Air Force		
	Gliding & Soaring Association RAF Cosford *'R66'*		13.04.18E
	Operated by Wrekin Gliding Club		
G-CJCD	Schleicher ASW 24	24101	24.09.07
	BGA 4399, D-6091		
	G G Dale & A K Laylee Lasham *'E2'*		27.05.19E
G-CJCE	Ultramagic M-77C	77/397	17.02.17
	Murray Rene Ltd Douglas, Isle of Man		13.04.18E
G-CJCF	Grob G102 Astir CS77	1705	03.01.08
	BGA 4401/JCF, PH-1012, D-7634 The Northumbria		
	Gliding Club Ltd Currock Hill *'JCF'*		02.03.19E
G-CJCG	PZL-Swidnik PW-5 Smyk	17.09.003	03.09.07
	BGA 4402 K Cullen, S Kinnear & M Walsh		
	Gowran Grange, RoI *'JCG'*		27.10.18E
G-CJCH	Sportine Aviacija LAK-19T	017	16.05.14
	(BGA 5791), F-CJCH, LY-JCH		
	S R Brown tr Lak 19T Syndicate Snitterfield *'FA'*		08.02.18E
G-CJCJ	Schempp-Hirth Standard Cirrus	434G	23.10.07
	BGA 4404, SE-TNC		
	R Visse tr G-CJCJ Syndicate		
	Husbands Bosworth *'C7'*		06.05.18E
G-CJCK	Schempp-Hirth Discus bT	92	29.08.07
	BGA 4405, D-KIDE		
	G A Friedrich Gransden Lodge *'JCK'*		22.03.18E
G-CJCL	Evektor EV-97B Eurostar SL	3813	25.04.16
	F Omaraie-Hamdanie Plaistows Farm, St Albans		08.10.18P
	Built by F Omaraie-Hamdanie – project LAA 315B-15305		
G-CJCM	Schleicher ASW 27	27064	08.01.08
	BGA 4407/JCM Zulu Glasstek Ltd		
	Baileys Farm, Long Crendon *'W27'*		19.12.17E
G-CJCN	Schempp-Hirth Standard Cirrus 75	646	08.12.07
	BGA 4408/JCN, D-7247		
	G D E Macdonald Lasham *'JA9'*		30.03.14E
	(NF 23.08.18)		
G-CJCO	Comco Ikarus C42 FB80	1604-7450	14.06.16
	GS Aviation (Europe) Ltd Clench Common		23.06.18P
	Assembled Red Aviation; engine & propeller		
	stolen Clench Common 07.06.18		
G-CJCR	Grob G102 Astir CS	1181	21.05.14
	BGA 4411/JCR, OE-5188		
	B J Harrison Eyres Field *'JCR'*		14.10.18E
G-CJCS	Kubícek BB60Z	1250	12.07.16
	South Downs Ballooning Ltd Grayshott, Hindhead		13.07.19E
G-CJCT	Schempp-Hirth Nimbus-4T	21	22.01.08
	BGA 4413/JCT, D-KKKL		
	E W Richards Keevil *'176'*		29.05.19E
G-CJCU	Schempp-Hirth Standard Cirrus B	688	21.11.07
	BGA 4414/JCU, D-6604		
	P E Pearson tr G-CJCU Group Saltby *'JCU'*		20.04.19E
G-CJCW	Grob G102 Astir CS77	1612	07.04.08
	BGA 4416/JCW, PH-573		
	Essex Gliding Club Ltd Ridgewell *'JCW'*		18.10.18E
G-CJCX	Schempp-Hirth Discus bT	93/432	08.01.08
	BGA 4417/JCX, D-KJOB		
	A D Johnson Wormingford *'JCX'*		10.04.18E
G-CJDA	Comco Ikarus C42 FB80	1605-7452	14.06.16
	Mainair Microlight School Ltd Manchester Barton		09.06.18P
	Assembled Red Aviation		
G-CJDB	Cessna 525 CitationJet	525-0648	08.08.07
	N5152X Breed Aircraft Ltd Jersey		07.08.18E

G

G-CJDC	Schleicher ASW 27	27010	17.10.07
	BGA4422, D-6209		
	T A Sage Dunstable Downs 'A27'		10.12.18E
G-CJDD	Glaser-Dirks DG-202/17C	2-171CL17	20.05.08
	BGA 4423/JDD, PH-717		
	N P Harrison North Hill 'JDD'		18.10.18E
G-CJDE	Rolladen-Schneider LS8-18	8151	29.10.07
	BGA 4424 J W Sage tr Army Gliding Association		
	AAC Wattisham 'A10'		02.06.18E
	Operated by Anglia Gliding Club		
G-CJDG	Rolladen-Schneider LS6-b	6145	05.10.07
	BGA 4426, D-5675 A & R H Moss Nympsfield 'KW'		29.04.18E
G-CJDJ	Rolladen-Schneider LS3	3010	16.10.07
	BGA 4428, D-7729 B J R Moate & S Wilkinson		
	Walney Island '434'		24.02.19E
G-CJDL	Pipistrel Apis/Bee	A067	03.06.16
	M E Hughes (Ewerby, Sleaford)		
	(NF 02.06.16)		
G-CJDM	Schleicher ASW 15B	15280	19.02.08
	BGA 4431/JDM, F-CEGL J D Morris (Sale)		25.05.18E
G-CJDN	Cameron C-90	11335	11.01.10
	N Ivison Barton Seagrave, Kettering		20.04.18E
G-CJDP	Glaser-Dirks DG-200/17	2-134/1732	04.12.07
	BGA 4433/JDP, D-6545 M Downie & R Fielding		
	tr The Owners of JDP Camphill 'JDP'		02.05.18E
G-CJDR	Schleicher ASW 15	15053	20.11.07
	BGA 4435/JDR, D-6910		
	S Mudaliar Rivar Hill 'MI' & 'Rocinante'		23.05.18E
G-CJDS	Schempp-Hirth Standard Cirrus 75	638	13.09.07
	BGA 4436, D-4057, OY-XCZ		
	P Nicholls Wormingford '75'		01.04.18E
G-CJDV	DG Flugzeugbau DG-303 Elan Acro	3E481A24	24.10.07
	BGA 4439 M K Lavender Bicester 'JDV'		14.01.19E
	Built by Elan Tovarna Sportnega Orodja N.Sol.O		
G-CJDW	Magni M16C Tandem Trainer	16169494	18.02.16
	A Brown & W J Whyte Perth		25.05.18P
G-CJDX	Wassmer WA.28 Espadon	101	11.01.08
	BGA 4441/JDX, F-CDZU		
	R Hutchinson Sutton Bank 'JDX'		28.07.18R
G-CJEA	Rolladen-Schneider LS8-18	8159	26.10.07
	BGA 4444, D-2411 M W Durham Bicester 'ER8'		11.05.18E
G-CJEB	Schleicher ASW 24	24172	16.11.07
	BGA 4445/JEB, D-9344 P C Scholz Lasham 'JEB'		23.05.18E
G-CJEC	PZL-Bielsko SZD-50-3 Puchacz	B-2197	16.10.07
	BGA 4446 Cambridge Gliding Club Ltd		
	Gransden Lodge 'JEC'		03.11.18E
G-CJED	Schempp-Hirth Nimbus-3/24.5	37	26.02.08
	BGA 4822/JVT, D-3176		
	J R Edyvean Bicester 'JED'		08.06.18E
G-CJEE	Schleicher ASW 20L	20073	01.11.07
	BGA 4448/JEE, (BGA 4456/JEN), D-7666		
	B Pridgeon Kirton in Lindsey 'JEE'		12.03.18E
G-CJEH	Glasflügel Mosquito B	172	19.12.07
	BGA 4451/JEH, OY-XKE M J Vickery Lasham 'KE'		21.02.18E
G-CJEI	Ultramagic M-77	77/398	10.05.16
	British Telecommunications PLC		
	Thatcham 'BT Sport'		10.05.19E
G-CJEJ	Best Off Skyranger Nynja 912(1)	xxxx	05.05.16
	C Townsley tr G-CJEJ Rossall Skyranger		
	Rossall Field, Cockerham		12.07.19P
	Built by D A Perkins – project BMAA/HB/663		
G-CJEK	Guimbal Cabri G2	1151	13.06.16
	I C Macdonald (Burton in Lonsdale, Carnforth)		27.06.18E
G-CJEL	Schleicher ASW 24	24044	08.02.08
	BGA 4454/JEL, PH-866		
	S M Chapman Waldershare Park 'JEL'		20.04.19E
G-CJEN^M	Ferguson 1911 Monoplane	WM-001/2016	09.05.16
	Cancelled 01.06.16 as PWFU		
	Re-Built by W H McMinn		
	With Ulster Aviation Society, Lisburn		
G-CJEP	Rolladen-Schneider LS4-b	41021	22.11.07
	BGA 4457/JEP		
	N Backes & C F Carter Long Mynd 'JEP'		27.04.18E

G-CJER	Schempp-Hirth Standard Cirrus 75	654	20.11.07
	BGA 4459/JER, D-6475, OO-ZBM		
	C Parvin Lasham 'EM'		05.05.18E
G-CJES	Cameron TR-77	11972	10.06.16
	International Merchandising, Promotion & Services		
	Genval, Belgium		08.06.17E
G-CJEU	Glasflügel Standard Libelle	55	21.11.07
	BGA 4462/JEU, SE-TIC		
	D B Johns Aston Down 'JEU'		06.04.18E
G-CJEW	Schleicher Ka 6CR	6493	14.01.08
	BGA 4464/JEW, D-4116		
	W J Prince Halesland '6CR'		01.06.14E
	(NF 18.11.15)		
G-CJEX	Schempp-Hirth Ventus-2a	64	03.10.07
	BGA 4465 D S Watt Bicester 'DW'		10.04.19E
G-CJEY	Flylight Dragon Combat 12T	DA135	07.07.16
	M Dodd (Bala)		
	(IE 07.08.18)		
G-CJEZ	Glaser-Dirks DG-100	03	16.01.09
	BGA 4467/JEZ, PH-792, D-3721		
	R Kehr Wycombe Air Park '274'		14.04.18E
G-CJFA	Schempp-Hirth Standard Cirrus	225	14.01.08
	BGA 4468/JFA, D-0974 P M Sheahan Lasham 'JFA'		23.04.18E
G-CJFC	Schempp-Hirth Discus CS	054CS	09.05.07
	BGA 4470, RAFGSA R55 C J Tooze Usk '2Z'		10.07.18E
	Built by Orličan Aakciová Společnost		
G-CJFG	Aériane Swift Light PAS	069	02.06.16
	OO-F07 M Jackson (Manton, Marlborough)		
	(IE 28.07.17)		
G-CJFH	Schempp-Hirth Duo Discus	118	27.02.08
	BGA 4475/JFH, RAFGSA R1 The Royal Air Force		
	Gliding & Soaring Association Easterton 'R1'		26.06.18E
	Operated by Fulmar Gliding Club		
G-CJFI	Ace Aviation Magic/Cyclone	xxxx	24.05.16
	W P Byrne (Belfast)		
	Trike s/n not known & wing s/n AC-143 (NF 24.05.16)		
G-CJFJ	Schleicher ASW 20CL	20830	29.01.08
	BGA 4476/JFJ, D-8307, F-CGCS		
	A M McDermott Burn 'JFJ'		01.04.18E
G-CJFP	Dudek Synthesis LT 29	P-07874	02.06.16
	P A Sadowski (Swindon)		
	(IE 30.06.17)		
G-CJFS	Stephens Pulse SSDR	DS006	21.06.16
	D Stephens Barling		
	Built by D Stephens (IE 21.08.16)		
G-CJFT	Schleicher K 8B	8451	15.11.07
	BGA 4485/JFT, D-1883		
	The Surrey Hills Gliding Club Ltd Kenley 'JFT'		29.05.18E
G-CJFU	Schleicher ASW 19B	19038	28.01.08
	BGA 4486/JFU, D-4531 M T Stanley Sutton Bank		12.03.18E
G-CJFW	Ace Aviation Magic/As-Tec 15	xxxx	20.09.16
	S E Dancaster Hawksview, Stretton		
	Trike s/n not knwon & Wing s/n AA15-110 (IE 16.02.18)		
G-CJFX	Rolladen-Schneider LS8-a	8174	16.10.07
	BGA 4489 J E Gatfield Lasham 'L9'		18.03.18E
G-CJFZ	Fedorov Me7 Mechta	M009	26.08.08
	BGA 4491/JFZ R J Colbourne RAF Odiham		21.04.13R
	(IE 25.04.16)		
G-CJGA	Cameron Z-90	12015	05.07.16
	Spoon Service Multimedia SAS Tagliacozzo, Italy		29.07.19E
G-CJGB	Schleicher K 8B	AB.02	28.03.08
	BGA 4493/JGB, D-8868 L R Merritt Saltby		22.05.19E
G-CJGC	Cameron Z-105	12010	17.08.16
	GSM Aeroponorami SRL Palermo, Italy		25.07.18E
G-CJGD	Schleicher K 8B	8214	30.01.08
	BGA 4495/JGD, D-....		
	C A McLay & R E Pettifer Chipping 'JGD'		15.04.18E
G-CJGE	Schleicher ASK 21	21068	06.03.08
	BGA 4496/JGE, RAFGSA R21		
	M R Wall Bidford 'K21'		05.05.18E
G-CJGF	Schempp-Hirth Ventus c	517	24.04.08
	BGA 3785/HAJ R D Slater Usk '391'		30.03.18E

G-CJGG	P&M Quik GT450	8305	30.08.07
	J M Pearce Strathaven		22.10.18P
G-CJGH	Schempp-Hirth Nimbus-2C	188	05.06.08
	BGA 4499/JGH, OO-ZZM, D-2834		
	J Swannack tr G-CJGH Syndicate Darlton 'JGH'		01.06.18E
G-CJGJ	Schleicher ASK 21	21039	10.12.07
	BGA 4500/JGJ, RAFGSA R22		
	Midland Gliding Club Ltd Long Mynd 'JGJ'		05.05.18E
G-CJGK	Eiriavion PIK-20D	20571	22.10.07
	BGA 4501, OO-ZDL, D-6707		
	R Dance tr The Four Aces Camphill 'JGK'		17.05.18E
G-CJGL	Schempp-Hirth Discus CS	148CS	14.01.08
	BGA 4502/JGL, RAFGSA R27 The Royal Air Force		
	Gliding & Soaring Association Easterton '27'		14.11.17E
	Built by Orličan Aakciová Společnost		
G-CJGM	Schempp-Hirth Discus CS	036CS	27.02.08
	BGA 4503/JGM, RAFGSA R53 The Royal Air Force		
	Gliding & Soaring Association RAF Halton 'R53'		01.04.18E
	Built by Orličan Aakciová Společnost;		
	operated by Chilterns Gliding Centre		
G-CJGN	Schempp-Hirth Standard Cirrus	554	29.01.08
	BGA 4504/JGN, D-8674		
	P A Shuttleworth Rufforth '867'		13.08.14E
	(NF 23.11.15)		
G-CJGP	Breezer Breezer M400	UL139	15.06.16
	B S Keene (Milbourne St Andrew, Blandford Forum)		09.01.19P
	Built by Ascent Industries Ltd		
G-CJGR	Schempp-Hirth Discus bT	10/275	03.01.08
	BGA 4507/JGR, D-KGPS, D-5461		
	G W Kamp & S P Wareham Kingston Deverill 'BT'		04.04.18E
G-CJGS	Rolladen-Schneider LS8-18	8180	16.10.07
	BGA 4508 T Stupnik Lesce-Bled, Slovenia 'L2'		20.07.18E
G-CJGT	AMS-Flight Apis M	A001	10.05.16
	S5-NKF? R G Parker & A Spencer Kirton in Lindsey		
	Built by Pipistrel d.o.o Ajdovščina (IE 16.05.17)		
G-CJGU	Schempp-Hirth Mini Nimbus B	69	06.08.08
	BGA 4510/JGU, HB-1427		
	N D Ashton Darlton 'JGU'		16.04.18E
G-CJGV	Flylight FoxCub	DA138	08.09.16
	R A Chapman East Newton Farm, Foulden		
G-CJGW	Schleicher ASK 13	13146	11.01.08
	BGA 4512/JGW, D-0169		
	Darlton Gliding Club Ltd Darlton 'JGW'		12.12.18E
G-CJGX	Schleicher K 8B	753	25.03.08
	BGA 4513/JGX, D-1878		
	D Smith tr Andreas K8 Group Andreas 'JGX'		25.08.13E
	(NF 20.06.16)		
G-CJGY	Schempp-Hirth Standard Cirrus	333	14.04.08
	BGA 4514/JGY, SE-TMU		
	P J Shout Husbands Bosworth 'C3'		15.07.18E
G-CJGZ	Glasflügel Standard Libelle 201B	193	09.01.09
	BGA 4515/JGZ, D-0697		
	D A Joosten Rattlesden 'CD'		25.03.17E
	(NF 26.10.16)		
G-CJHC	Kolb Firefly	DJP-01	01.07.16
	D J Pilkington Brook Farm, Pilling		
	Built by D J Pilkington (IE 02.06.17)		
G-CJHF	Aeropro EuroFOX 912(iS)	50115	12.10.16
	P J Fincham tr BGC Eurofox Group		
	Hinton-in-the-Hedges		29.08.19P
	Built by S F Ducker, P J Fincham & P F Nicholson		
	– project LAA 376-15399; tricycle u/c; glider-tug		
G-CJHG	Grob G102 Astir CS	1084	02.09.08
	BGA 4522/JHG, D-6984 P L E Zelazowski		
	(Tredington, Shipston-on-Stour) '513'		21.03.14E
	(IE 19.04.18)		
G-CJHJ	Glasflügel Standard Libelle 201B	495	18.10.07
	BGA 4524, HB-1187		
	N P Marriott tr G-CJHJ Parham Park 'JHJ'		22.10.18E
G-CJHK	Schleicher K 8B	558	03.10.07
	BGA 4525/JHK, AGA 21, (BGA 4319), RAFGGA 558		
	East Sussex Gliding Club Ltd Ringmer 'JHK'		09.07.18E
G-CJHL	Schleicher Ka 6E	4073	20.02.08
	BGA 4526/JHL, SE-TFB		
	J R Gilbert Wormingford 'JHL'		15.04.18E
G-CJHM	Schempp-Hirth Discus b	373	05.02.08
	BGA 4527/JHM, OO-ZGZ		
	J C Thwaites Sutton Bank 'JHM'		26.04.18E
G-CJHN	Grob G102 Astir CS Jeans	2110	20.05.08
	BGA 4528/JHN, D-7638		
	D N Wills tr Astir Syndicate Aston Down 'JHN'		29.04.18E
G-CJHO	Schleicher ASK 18	18021	23.01.08
	BGA 4530/JHQ, RAFGSA R43, RAFGSA 713,		
	RAFGSA 113 The Royal Air Force Gliding		
	& Soaring Association RAF Cosford 'R43'		16.07.18E
	Operated by Wrekin Gliding Club		
G-CJHP	Flight Design CTSW	07-08-06	02.11.07
	S J Reader Tatenhill		24.05.18P
	Assembled P&M Aviation Ltd as c/n 8327		
G-CJHR	Centrair SNC34C Alliance	34026	25.02.08
	BGA 4531/JHR The Borders (Milfield) Gliding Club Ltd		
	Milfield 'A34'		15.06.18E
G-CJHS	Schleicher ASW 19B	19047	09.07.08
	BGA 4532/JHS, D-6716		
	B Crow tr JHS Syndicate Usk 'JHS'		12.01.18E
G-CJHT	Aeropro EuroFOX 3K	49316	23.09.16
	GS Aviation (Europe) Ltd Clench Common		22.08.19P
	Built by Ascent Industries Ltd; tricycle u/c; engine		
	& propeller stolen from Clench Common 07.06.18		
G-CJHV	Lindstrand LTL Series 1-31	007	12.07.16
	Lindstrand Technologies Ltd Oswestry		23.01.19E
G-CJHW	Glaser-Dirks DG-200	2-19	27.10.08
	BGA 4536/JHW, HB-1400		
	A W Thornhill & S Webster Burn 'JHW'		03.12.18E
G-CJHY	Rolladen-Schneider LS8-18	8181	21.09.07
	BGA 4538, D-9988 S J Eyles Nympsfield 'LT'		22.02.18E
G-CJHZ	Schleicher ASW 20	20313	06.09.07
	BGA 4539, D-6532 T J Stanley Sutton Bank 'G41'		18.10.18E
G-CJIA	Lindstrand LTL Series 2-70	013	12.07.16
	Lindstrand Technologies Ltd Oswestry		
	(NF 12.07.16)		
G-CJIB	Alisport Silent 2 Electro	2086	19.10.16
	S H Gibson tr G-CJIB Gransden Group		
	Gransden Lodge		
	(IE 04.10.18)		
G-CJIC	Van's RV-12	120957	20.07.16
	N W Wilkinson (Harrogate)		
	Built by N W Wilkinson – project LAA 363-15381		
	(NF 27.07.16)		
G-CJID	Alisport Silent 2	2006K	25.07.16
	OO-E91 A K Carver (Bath)		
	(IE 11.08.17)		
G-CJIE	Flylight FoxCub	DA137	07.10.16
	M J Pollard (Liverpool L31)		
	(IE 04.08.17)		
G-CJIG	Lindstrand LTL Series 1-70	010	21.07.16
	A M Holly Breadstone, Berkeley 'Hospital'		06.06.19E
G-CJIH	Lindstrand LTL Series 1-105	016	05.08.16
	Southern Plasticlad Ltd Coalpit Heath, Bristol		
	'southern plasticlad.co.uk'		13.07.18E
G-CJII	TLAC Sherwood Ranger ST	ST57	07.07.16
	M M A Darcy Lower Upham Farm, Chiseldon		15.11.18P
	Built by DH Pattison – project LAA 237B-15320		
G-CJIK	Cameron Z-77	12023	15.09.16
	P Greaves Maidstone		07.09.18E
G-CJIL	Sackville BM-90	BM01	12.08.16
	B Mead Kettering		
	(IE 20.09.19)		
G-CJIM	Taylor JT.1 Monoplane	xxxx	28.12.78
	Cancelled 24.03.99 by CAA		
	Bicester Built by J Crawford – project PFA 1419;		
	on rebuild 03.13		
G-CJIN	Boeing Stearman A75L300 Kaydet (PT-17)	75-4826	31.03.17
	N55180, 42-16663 R D Leigh Enstone		19.10.18E
	As '4826:582' in USN c/s		
G-CJIO	Rans S-6-S-116 Super Six	1112.1966	20.08.16
	D Bedford Shobdon		15.05.19P
	Built by D Bedford – project LAA 204A-15202		

G-CJIP	Aero 31 AM9	001	20.08.16
	C J Sanger-Davies Hawarden CH5		
	Built by C J Sanger-Davies (NF 20.08.16)		
G-CJIR	RotorWay Exec 162F	6169/6724	19.08.16
	G-ESUS Southern Helicopters Ltd		
	Street Farm, Takeley		28.08.09P
	(IE 17.01.17)		
G-CJIT	Comco Ikarus C42 FB100	1608-7466	12.09.16
	R Mitchell tr SARM Group Old Sarum		22.09.19P
G-CJIU	Lindstrand LTL 9T	LTL-9T-001	30.08.16
	Lindstrand Technologies Ltd Oswestry		
	Tethered Gas Balloon (IE 30.08.16)		
G-CJIX	Cameron O-31	12011	27.06.16
	D J Head Newbury		26.06.18E
G-CJJA	Evektor EV-97 Eurostar SL	2016-4235	03.08.16
	S J E Smith tr G-CJJA Group Eshott		13.09.18P
	Assembled Light Sport Aviation Ltd		
G-CJJB	Rolladen-Schneider LS4	4542	09.01.08
	BGA 4541/JJB, D-2397 M Tomlinson Talgarth *'615'*		19.03.18E
G-CJJC	Lindstrand LTL Series 1-105	011	20.08.16
	A M Holly Breadstone, Berkeley		02.11.18E
G-CJJD	Schempp-Hirth Discus bT	5/262	12.03.08
	BGA 4543/JJD, D-KIHS		
	C O'Boyle tr G-CJJD Syndicate Burn *'JJD'*		19.10.18E
G-CJJE	Schempp-Hirth Discus a	379	12.08.08
	BGA 4544/JJE, OE-5530, VH-XQT		
	A Soffici (Varese, Italy) *'TS'*		18.04.17E
G-CJJH	DG Flugzeugbau DG-800S	8-137S30	29.01.08
	BGA 4547/JJH R M Theil Gransden Lodge *'899'*		13.05.19E
	Built by DG Flugzeugbau GmbH		
G-CJJJ	Schempp-Hirth Standard Cirrus	284	21.09.07
	BGA 4548, D-2946		
	J M Roots Husbands Bosworth *'JJJ'*		06.11.16E
	(IE 16.05.17)		
G-CJJK	Rolladen-Schneider LS8-18	8199	26.11.07
	BGA 4549/JJK A D Roch Dunstable Downs *'K8'*		24.02.18E
G-CJJL	Schleicher ASW 19B	19302	03.03.08
	BGA 4550/JJL, D-4227		
	R M Lever tr G-CJJL Group Bicester *'JJL'*		22.03.18E
G-CJJN	Robin HR.100/210 Safari	169	31.08.16
	F-GUAL, F-OCQU J Goldsmith tr The G-CJJN		
	Syndicate Compton Abbas		04.05.19E
G-CJJP	Schempp-Hirth Duo Discus	180	25.09.07
	BGA 4553 A J Swan tr 494 Syndicate		
	Long Mynd *'494'*		19.03.18E
G-CJJS	Piper PA-28-151 Cherokee Warrior	28-7615377	12.09.16
	G-VIVS, LN-NAL		
	Phil Short Electrical Ltd Carlisle Lake District		22.11.18E
G-CJJT	Schleicher ASW 27	27070	06.02.08
	BGA 4557/JJT, D-6209 T World Lasham *'933'*		09.07.18E
G-CJJV	Van's RV-12	120050	30.09.16
	N888HS K Handley (Main Hall Farm, Conington)		31.07.19P
	Built by J W Stevens		
G-CJJW	Lambert Mission M108	008	27.09.16
	D S James (Atherington, Umberleigh)		
	Built by D S James – project LAA 370-15429		
	(IE 16.01.19)		
G-CJJX	Schleicher ASW 15B	15323	31.10.07
	BGA 4561, D-2312 A Snell Darley Moor *'JJX'*		17.05.18E
G-CJJY	Aerochute SSDR	150418	04.10.16
	G R Britton (Melton Mowbray)		
	(IE 22.12.17)		
G-CJJZ	Schempp-Hirth Discus bT	156	27.09.07
	BGA 4563, OO-ZQX S J C Parker Nympsfield *'15'*		11.12.18E
G-CJKA	Schleicher ASK 21	21059	18.01.08
	BGA 4564/JKA, D-8835		
	East Sussex Gliding Club Ltd Ringmer *'JKA'*		03.10.18E
G-CJKB	PZL-Swidnik PW-5 Smyk	17.10.008	25.03.08
	BGA 4565/JKB B Parry (Manningtree) *'JKB'*		21.04.19E
G-CJKE	PZL-Swidnik PW-5 Smyk	17.11.025	30.05.08
	BGA 4568 D Hertzberg Ridgewell *'JKE'*		03.06.19E
G-CJKF	Glaser-Dirks DG-200	2-35	02.04.08
	BGA 4569/JKF, D-6069 D O Sandells Bidford *'JKF'*		23.05.18E

G-CJKG	Schleicher ASK 18	18036	17.10.07
	BGA 4570/JKG, RAFGSA R48, RAFGSA 448		
	The Royal Air Force Gliding & Soaring Association		
	RAF Halton *'R48'*		09.02.11E
	(IE 24.06.15)		
G-CJKH	Ultramagic M-120	120/87	28.03.17
	Cold Climate Expeditions Ltd Corsham		09.04.18E
G-CJKI	Ultramagic S-90	90/158	06.12.16
	M P Rowley Upper Arncott, Bicester		23.11.18E
G-CJKJ	Schleicher ASK 21	21679	17.10.07
	BGA 4572 The Royal Air Force Gliding & Soaring		
	Association RAF Halton *'R21'*		28.02.18E
	Operated by Chilterns Gliding Centre		
G-CJKK	Schleicher ASK 21	21182	01.05.08
	BGA 4573/JKK, AGA 11 J W Sage tr Army Gliding		
	Association AAC Wattisham *'A7'*		11.04.18E
	Operated by Anglia Gliding Club		
G-CJKM	Glaser-Dirks DG-200/17	2-148/1746	08.01.08
	BGA 4575/JKM, D-4155		
	G F Coles & E W Russell Rattlesden *'Z10'*		24.03.18E
G-CJKN	Rolladen-Schneider LS8-18	8214	02.11.07
	BGA 4576/JKN		
	A E Loening tr 790 Syndicate Milfield *'790'*		15.02.18E
G-CJKO	Schleicher ASK 21	21098	18.01.08
	BGA 4578/JKQ, RAFGSA R20 The Royal Air Force		
	Gliding & Soaring Association Keevil *'R20'*		22.02.19E
	Operated by Bannerdown Gliding Club		
G-CJKP	Rolladen-Schneider LS4-b	41000	17.10.07
	BGA 4577, PH-1089 D A Spencer Camphill *'C12'*		22.09.19E
G-CJKS	Schleicher ASW 19B	19362	18.01.08
	BGA 4580/JKS, D-1273		
	R J P Lancaster Dunstable Downs *'S19'*		25.10.18E
G-CJKT	Schleicher ASK 13	13615	04.04.08
	BGA 4581/JKT, RAFGSA R7 The Royal Air Force		
	Gliding & Soaring Association RAF Halton *'R7'*		02.10.18E
G-CJKU	Schleicher ASK 18	18022	19.12.07
	BGA 4582/JKU, RAFGSA R33, RAFGSA 223		
	Derbyshire & Lancashire Gliding Club Ltd		
	Camphill *'JKU'*		06.04.18E
G-CJKV	Grob G103A Twin II Acro	34042-K-273	11.12.07
	BGA 4583/JKV, RAFGSA R52		
	The Welland Gliding Club Ltd Lyveden *'JKV'*		24.05.18E
G-CJKW	Grob G102 Astir CS77	1666	22.12.07
	BGA 4584/JKW, RAFGSA R60, RAFGSA 560		
	The Bath, Wilts & North Dorset Gliding Club Ltd		
	Kingston Deverill *'JKW'*		18.03.18E
G-CJKY	Schempp-Hirth Ventus cT	181	29.10.07
	BGA 4586, RAFGSA R24, RAFGGA 557		
	G V Matthews & M P Osborn Seighford *'243'*		04.02.19E
G-CJKZ	Schleicher ASK 21	21123	17.10.07
	BGA 4587, RAFGSA R25 The Royal Air Force		
	Gliding & Soaring Association RAF Halton *'R25'*		19.03.18E
	Operated by Chilterns Gliding Centre		
G-CJLA	Schempp-Hirth Ventus-2cT	26/94	28.02.08
	BGA 4588/JLA, PH-1129		
	S G Jones (Membury) *'JLA'*		26.09.12E
	Crashed in paddock Wilson Road, Goorambat,		
	Victoria, Australia 01.01.12 & extensively damaged		
	(NF 08.04.16)		
G-CJLC	Schempp-Hirth Discus CS	193CS	05.02.08
	BGA 4590/JLC, RAFGSA R10		
	S M Stannard & M A Stephens Camphill *'R10'*		26.05.19E
	Built by Orličan Aakciová Společnost		
G-CJLD	Lambert Mission M108	007	19.09.16
	P R Mailer Little Gransden		24.05.19P
	Built by P R Mailer – project LAA 370-15408		
G-CJLF	Schleicher ASK 13	13150	10.09.09
	BGA 4593/JLF, AGA 14		
	V Mallon Brüggen, Germany *'JLF'*		12.08.16E
	(NF 12.12.17)		
G-CJLH	Rolladen-Schneider LS4	4256	01.11.07
	BGA 4595/JLH, AGA 1 C A Sorace tr JLH Syndicate		
	Dunstable Downs *'JLH'*		02.07.18E

G-CJLI Piper PA-28-161 Warrior II   28-8216137   15.06.17
SE-LGR, HB-PGW   Smart People Dont Buy Ltd
RAF Waddington   05.06.19E

G-CJLJ Rolladen-Schneider LS4-b   4997   29.01.08
BGA 4596/JLJ, AGA 2   J W Sage tr Army Gliding
Association   Trenchard Lines, Upavon   *'A3'*
Operated by Wyvern Gliding Club   13.04.18E

G-CJLK Rolladen-Schneider LS7   7112   09.01.08
BGA 4597/JLK, AGA 3
D N Munro & J P W Roche-Kelly   Tibenham   *'LS7'*   18.04.18E

G-CJLL Robinson R44 Raven II   11588   29.01.07
R D J Alexander   Manchester Barton   21.03.19E
Operated by Helicentre

G-CJLM Denney Kitfox Model 4   xxxx   11.10.16
C Kinder & T Neale   Stoke Golding   07.08.18P
Built by C Kinder, T Neale & Partners
– project PFA 172-12080

G-CJLN Rolladen-Schneider LS8-18   8169   25.10.07
BGA 4600, RAFGSA R4   The Royal Air Force
Gliding & Soaring Association   RAF Cranwell   *'R4'*
Operated by Cranwell Gliding Club   10.03.18E

G-CJLO Schleicher ASK 13   13608   20.09.07
BGA 4602, RAFGSA R40, RAFGSA R4
Bowland Forest Gliding Club Ltd   Chipping   *'JLO'*   06.01.19E

G-CJLP Schempp-Hirth Discus CS   034CS   01.02.08
BGA 4601/JLP, RAFGSA R39   The Royal Air Force
Gliding & Soaring Association   RAF Cranwell   *'R39'*   14.01.19E
Built by Orličan Aakciová Spoločnost;
operated by Cranwell Gliding Club

G-CJLS Schleicher K 8B   8950   09.01.08
BGA 4604/JLS, RAFGSA R75, RAFGSA 285
E Ustenler   Lasham   *'R75'*   13.11.14E

G-CJLT Cameron O-84   12044   13.04.17
T M Lee   Dursley   05.04.18E

G-CJLU Spacek SD-1 Minisport   240   28.10.16
J Krajca   Berry Farm, Bovingdon
Built by J Krajca; tricycle u/c (IE 03.04.18)

G-CJLV Schleicher Ka 6E   4192   04.08.08
BGA 4607/JLV, OY-XEU, D-4424
J C Cooper   Lyveden   *'JLV'*   28.08.14E
(NF 04.10.17)

G-CJLW Schempp-Hirth Discus CS   033CS   11.02.08
BGA 4608/JLW, RAFGSA R87   The Royal Air Force
Gliding & Soaring Association   RAF Marham   *'87'*   31.10.15E
Built by Orličan Aakciová Spoločnost;
operated by Fenland Gliding Club

G-CJLX Schempp-Hirth Standard Cirrus   279G   01.03.13
BGA 4609/JLX, OO-ZGL, D-1985
J Hunneman   Rivar Hill
(NF 06.07.17)

G-CJLY Schleicher ASW 27   27111   26.11.07
BGA 4610/JLY   L M Astle & P C Piggott
Husbands Bosworth   *'JLY'*   14.03.18E

G-CJLZ Grob G103A Twin II Acro   3633-K-15   02.11.07
BGA 4611/JLZ, D-7912
T K Dunford tr 21 Syndicate   Lasham   *'21'*   12.02.18E

G-CJMA Schleicher ASK 18   18038   20.08.08
BGA 4612/JMA, RAFGSA R36, RAFGSA 236
S D Codd   Kenley   *'R36'*   11.06.19E

G-CJMF BRM Bristell NG5 Speed Wing   214   27.09.16
G E Collard   Popham   18.04.19P
Built by G E Collard – project LAA 385-15413; tricycle u/c

G-CJMG PZL-Bielsko SZD-51-1 Junior   B-2192   08.04.08
BGA 4618/JMG
Kent Gliding Club Ltd   Challock   *'JMG'*   24.08.18E

G-CJMJ Schleicher ASK 13   13616   25.09.08
BGA 4620/JMJ, RAFGSA R46, RAFGSA R16
The Royal Air Force Gliding & Soaring Association
Bicester   *'R46'*   30.05.15E
(IE 24.06.15)

G-CJMK Schleicher ASK 18   18023   09.01.08
BGA 4621/JMK, RAFGSA R49, RAFGSA 318
The Royal Air Force Gliding & Soaring Association
RAF Halton   *'R49'*   28.07.18E
Operated by Chilterns Gliding Centre (IE 25.01.19)

G-CJML Grob G102 Astir CS77   1718   17.09.08
BGA 4622/JML, RAFGSA R63, RAFGSA 883
The Royal Air Force Gliding & Soaring Association
RAF Odiham   *'R63'*   07.04.18E
Operated by Kestrel Gliding Club

G-CJMN Schempp-Hirth Nimbus-2   38   26.09.07
BGA 4624, D-1129, HB-1159
R A Holroyd   Pocklington   *'636'*   29.10.18E

G-CJMO Rolladen-Schneider LS8-18   8225   12.11.07
BGA 4625/JMO   J M Hood   Lasham   *'781'*   02.05.19E

G-CJMP Schleicher ASK 13   13436   18.01.08
BGA 4626/JMP, D-2984
East Sussex Gliding Club Ltd   Ringmer   19.10.18E

G-CJMS Schleicher ASK 21   21212   09.07.08
BGA 4629/JMS, RAFGGA 521   The Royal Air Force
Gliding & Soaring Association   RAF Odiham   *'R23'*   18.11.18E

G-CJMU Rolladen-Schneider LS8-18   8246   15.01.08
BGA 4631/JMU   R Lorenz   Kirton in Lindsey   *'302'*   14.05.18E

G-CJMV Schempp-Hirth Nimbus-2C   179   04.01.08
BGA 4632/JMV, D-6738
G Tucker & K R Walton   Lasham   16.04.18E

G-CJMW Schleicher ASK 13   13688AB   11.10.07
BGA 4633/JMW, RAFGSA R61, RAFGGA 567
The Royal Air Force Gliding & Soaring Association
Keevil   *'R61'*   05.07.15E
Built by Jubi GmbH Sportflugzeugbau

G-CJMX Schleicher ASK 13   13107   05.03.08
BGA 4634/JMX, RAFGSA R86, RAFGSA 386
The Nene Valley Gliding Club Ltd   Upwood   *'JMX'*   14.07.18E

G-CJMY PZL-Bielsko SZD-51-1 Junior   W-959   11.02.08
BGA 4635/JMY, OO-ZRH
Highland Gliding Club Ltd   Easterton   *'JMY'*   17.11.17E

G-CJMZ Schleicher ASK 13   13099   09.01.08
BGA 4636/JMZ, RAFGSA R37, RAFGSA 378
Mendip Gliding Club Ltd   Halesland   *'R37'*   29.10.18E

G-CJNA Grob G102 Astir CS Jeans   2160   11.06.08
BGA 4637/JNA, D-4556
Shenington Gliding Club   Shenington   *'JNA'*   27.07.13E
(NF 20.10.17)

G-CJNB Rolladen-Schneider LS8-18   8227   10.04.08
BGA 4638/JNB   P M Barnes   (Chelmsford)   *'D1'*   13.07.18E

G-CJND Eurocopter MBB-BK117 C-2 *(EC145)*   9471   02.11.16
XA-UQD, D-HADL(3)
The Milestone Aviation Asset Holding Group No 1 Ltd
Bonn-Hangelar, Nordrhein-Westphalen, Germany
Stored 01.18 as 'XA-UQD' (IE 02.11.16)

G-CJNF Schempp-Hirth Discus-2a   12   17.03.08
VH-EAX, G-CJNF, BGA4642/JNF
M Scutter   (London SW5)   *'4Q'*
(NF 20.12.18)

G-CJNG Glasflügel Standard Libelle 201B   006   01.10.07
BGA 4643, SE-TFU
N C Burt & G V Tanner   Rivar Hill   *'JNG'*   14.04.18E

G-CJNH P&M QuikR   8751   27.07.16
N Hammerton   (Oxted)   21.07.17P

G-CJNI AgustaWestland AW139   41374   09.12.16
9Y-EXC, N492SH
Bristow Helicopters Ltd   Norwich Int'l   04.05.18E

G-CJNJ Rolladen-Schneider LS8-18   8226   12.11.07
BGA 4645/JNJ   A B Laws   Crowland   *'198'*   23.05.18E

G-CJNK Rolladen-Schneider LS8-18   8244   24.04.08
BGA 4646/JNK   J W Sage tr Army Gliding
Association   Trenchard Lines, Upavon   *'A8'*   16.12.17E

G-CJNL Jodel DR.1050-M Excellence replica   xxxx   09.11.16
M G Dolphin   RAF Syerston
Built by M G Dolphin – project LAA 304-15103

G-CJNN Schleicher K 8B   8744   23.01.08
BGA 4649/JNN, D-8583
Buckminster Gliding Club Ltd   Saltby   *'JNN'*   23.07.18E

G-CJNO Glaser-Dirks DG-300 Elan   3E341   15.01.08
BGA 4651/JNQ, SE-UHO
D Hammond tr Yankee Kilo Group   Rufforth   *'441'*   09.01.19E
Built by Elan Tovarna Sportnega Orodja N.Sol.O

G-CJNP Rolladen-Schneider LS6-b   6109   31.10.07
BGA 4650, D-5853   L Armbrust, E & P S Fink
(Meschede, Germany)   *'EF'*   29.04.18E

G-CJNR Glasflügel Mosquito B   159   12.11.07
BGA 4652/JNR, D-5908   L S Hitchins & R A Markham
(Bicester & Banbury)   *'JNR'*   07.08.18E

G-CJNU Techpro Merlin 100UL   HV-22   21.12.16
B S Carpenter   Eastfield Farm, Manby
(IE 19.07.17)

G-CJNZ Glaser-Dirks DG-100   70   13.02.08
BGA 4660/JNZ, (D-7324), HB-1324
G Syndercombe   Lasham   *'813'*   30.08.17E

G-CJOA Schempp-Hirth Discus b   265   04.10.07
BGA 4685/JQA, BGA 4535, RAFGGA 547, RAFGGA 500
K A Jarrett   Lasham   *'547'*   17.12.18E

G-CJOB Schleicher K 8B   8880   06.03.08
BGA 4686/JQB, RAFGSA R98, RAFGSA 398
T R Edwards tr JQB Syndicate   Lasham   *'JOB'*   02.04.18E

G-CJOC Schempp-Hirth Discus bT   127/488   16.11.07
BGA 4687/JQC, D-KITT   S G Jones   Lasham   *'82'*   27.04.18E

G-CJOD Rolladen-Schneider LS8-18   8224   20.09.07
BGA 4688   The Royal Air Force Gliding & Soaring
Association   Keevil   *'R3'*   11.01.19E
Operated by Bannerdown Gliding Club

G-CJOE Schempp-Hirth Ventus   25   07.03.08
BGA 4689/JQE, OO-ZRS, D-0483
D I Bolsdon & P T Johnson   Wormingford   *'JOE'*   04.08.18E

G-CJOI Cameron O-31   11638   27.09.16
Cameron Balloons Ltd   Bristol BS3
'Cameron Balloons Superlight'   02.10.19E

G-CJOJ Schleicher K 8B   8795   15.01.08
BGA 4693/JQJ, RAFGSA R47, BGA 1564/CHV
M P Webb   Seighford   *'JOJ'*   02.03.16E
(NF 10.02.17)

G-CJOK HpH Glasflügel 304 MS Shark   064-MS   23.11.16
OK-0064   P S Tickner tr JOK Syndicate
Ringmer   *'JOK'*   04.01.19E

G-CJOL Aeropro EuroFOX 3K   50416   01.02.17
C D Waldron   Redlands   25.02.19P
Built by Ascent Industries Ltd; tricycle u/c

G-CJOM Aeropro EuroFOX 3K   51216   02.02.17
G R Postans   Luke's Field, Marden   23.02.19P
Built by Ascent Industries Ltd; tricycle u/c

G-CJON Grob G102 Astir CS77   1634   18.08.08
BGA 4697/JQN, RAFGSA R67, RAFGSA 547
The Royal Air Force Gliding & Soaring Association
Easterton   *'R67'*   18.08.18E

G-CJOO Schempp-Hirth Duo Discus   227   24.01.08
BGA 4699/JQQ
K G Reid tr 185 Syndicate   Rivar Hill   *'185'*   29.03.18E

G-CJOP Centrair 101A Pégase   101066   31.03.08
BGA 4698, F-CFQY   P A Woodcock   Tibenham   *'eb'*   06.03.18E

G-CJOR Schempp-Hirth Ventus-2cT   49/152   17.09.07
BGA 4700   A M George & N A Maclean
Lasham   *'JOR'*   07.03.18E

G-CJOS Schempp-Hirth Standard Cirrus   251G   20.02.08
BGA 4701/JQS, D-1147
R K Arkley tr G-CJOS Group   Milfield   *'JOS'*   14.07.18E

G-CJOT Comco Ikarus C42 FB80   1606-7459   19.07.16
Cumulus International Services Ltd tr Cherhill Gang
Yatesbury   26.07.19P
Assembled Red Aviation

G-CJOV Schleicher ASW 27   27112   23.09.08
BGA 4704/JQV   J W White   Wycombe Air Park   *'J1M'*   15.11.18E

G-CJOW Schempp-Hirth Cirrus   47   01.02.08
BGA 4705/JQW, D-0186
North Wales Gliding Club Ltd   Llantysilio   *'JOW'*   16.04.18E

G-CJOX Schleicher ASK 21   21702   11.09.07
BGA 4706   Southdown Gliding Club Ltd
Parham Park   *'JOX'*   26.03.19E

G-CJOY Zenair CH.601HDS Zodiac   xxxx   13.06.16
G M Johnson   Mitchells Farm, Wilburton   29.08.19P
Built by G M Johnson – project PFA 162-13273; tricycle u/c

G-CJOZ Schleicher K 8B   8854   01.05.08
BGA 4708/JQZ, RAFGSA R42, RAFGSA 323
Derbyshire & Lancashire Gliding Club Ltd
Camphill   *'JOZ'*   28.03.18E

G-CJPA Schempp-Hirth Duo Discus   201   03.10.07
BGA 4661   Coventry Gliding Club Ltd
t/a The Gliding Centre   Husbands Bosworth   *'HB1'*   31.05.18E

G-CJPB Best Off Skyranger 582(1)   xxxx   09.11.16
T W Thiele   (Radwell, Baldock)
Built by T W Thiele – project BMAA/HB/691 (IE 08.11.16)

G-CJPC Schleicher ASK 13   13256   13.06.08
BGA 4663/JPC, RAFGSA R51
Shalbourne Soaring Society Ltd   Rivar Hill   *'JPC'*   28.11.18E

G-CJPD Cameron O-56   12001   10.08.16
Cameron Balloons Ltd   Bristol BS3   07.08.17E

G-CJPE Best Off Skyranger Nynja 912S(1)   UK\N\BK203   03.05.16
M J Stolworthy & R J Sutherland   Northrepps   27.11.18P
Built by J A Lockert – project BMAA/HB/681

G-CJPG Cameron C-80   10460   25.11.16
P R O Audenaert   Overmere, Belgium   09.11.17E

G-CJPI HpH Glasflügel 304 S Shark   047-MS   28.05.15
J M Whelan tr J Whelan – C Davison Syndicate
Saltby   *'PI'*
(IE 17.09.18)

G-CJPJ Grob G104 Speed Astir IIB   4089   02.05.08
BGA 4669/PJJ, OE-5352   M A Jones   Ridgewell   *'SA'*   26.07.17E

G-CJPK Lorimer & Kelsey Sgian Dubh   PJK001   22.04.16
P J Kelsey tr Sgian Dubh Flying Group   (Edinburgh EH12)
Built by P J Kelsey & H Lorimer (IE 22.04.16)

G-CJPL Rolladen-Schneider LS8-18   8249   12.10.07
BGA 4671, D-2562
I A Reekie   Dunstable Downs   *'RW'*   04.03.18E

G-CJPM Grob G102 Astir CS Jeans   2209   01.04.08
BGA 4672/JPM, D-3825   M A Braddock
tr G-CJPM Syndicate   Camphill   *'JPM'*   17.02.19E

G-CJPN Cessna 152   15280337   18.11.16
EC-GEC, EC-915, N24720
M Pirrie   (Milngavie, Glasgow)
On rebuild Bournemouth 11.18 (NF 17.10.18)

G-CJPO Schleicher ASK 18   18002   05.10.07
BGA 4675, RAFGSA R32, RAFGSA 213, D-3978
The Royal Air Force Gliding & Soaring Association
Keevil   *'R32'*   26.05.19E
Operated by Bannerdown Gliding Club

G-CJPP Schempp-Hirth Discus b   206   23.08.07
BGA 4674, AGA 4
S R Thompson   Sutton Bank   *'388'*   09.11.18E
*Rebuilt with new fuselage in 1990s;
c/n 206 rebuilt as BGA 4270 and now ZK-GXP*

G-CJPR Rolladen-Schneider LS8-18   8245   28.11.07
BGA 4676/JPR   D M Byass & J A McCoshim
Wycombe Air Park   *'161'*   12.04.18E

G-CJPT Schleicher ASW 27   27113   20.02.08
BGA 4678/JPT   R C Willis-Fleming   North Hill   *'JPT'*   16.04.18E

G-CJPV Schleicher ASK 13   13312   09.01.08
BGA 4680/JPV, RAFGSA R88, RAFGSA 186
N Karaolides tr Cyprus Gliding Group   Mammari,
Republic of Cyprus   *'R88'* and *'Crusader Gliding Club'*   14.10.19E

G-CJPW Glaser-Dirks DG-200   2-48   18.08.08
BGA 4681/JPW, D-2201
A Kitchen & R Truchan   Burn   *'JPW'*   09.11.18E

G-CJPX Schleicher ASW 15   15160   21.01.08
BGA 4682/JPX, D-0823
P Johnstone & S J Naisby   Upwood   *'JPX'*   06.10.18E

G-CJPY Schleicher ASK 13   13653AB   22.12.07
BGA 4683/JPY, RAFGSA R59, RAFGGA 509
The Royal Air Force Gliding & Soaring Association
Cranwell North   *'R59'*   27.02.18E
*Built by Jubi GmbH Sportflugzeugbau;
operated by Cranwell Gliding Club*

G-CJPZ Schleicher ASK 18   18027   17.12.07
BGA 4684/JPZ, RAFGSA R56, RAFGGA 563
Cotswold Gliding Club   Aston Down   *'R56'*   16.05.18E
Operated by Cranwell Gliding Club

G-CJRA	Rolladen-Schneider LS8-18	8263	30.10.07
	BGA 4709 J Williams Kirton in Lindsey *'253'*		18.01.19E
G-CJRB	Schleicher ASW 19B	19227	05.02.08
	BGA 4710/JRB, D-2713 J W Baxter Lasham *'S33'*		31.03.18E
G-CJRC	Glaser-Dirks DG-300 Elan	3E20	18.01.08
	BGA 4711/JRC, HB-1718		
	P J Sillett Tibenham *'JRC'*		07.04.18E
	Built by Elan Tovarna Sportnega Orodja N.Sol.O		
G-CJRD	Grob G102 Astir CS	1487	28.08.08
	BGA 4712/JRD, RAFGSA R18, RAFGSA 540, D-4791		
	The Vale of The White Horse Gliding Centre Ltd		
	Sandhill Farm, Shrivenham *'JRD'*		21.04.18E
G-CJRE	Schleicher ASW 15	15048	05.09.07
	BGA 4713, LN-GGL, OH-391, OH-RWA		
	R A Starling Darlton *'RS'*		17.06.18E
G-CJRF	PZL-Bielsko SZD-50-3 Puchacz	B-1395	10.10.07
	BGA 4714, OO-ZTX, D-8213, SP-3285		
	Wolds Gliding Club Ltd Pocklington *'JRF'*		30.06.18E
G-CJRG	Schempp-Hirth Standard Cirrus	146	05.11.07
	BGA 4715/JRG, D-0297		
	N J Laux Gransden Lodge *'JRG'*		18.07.14E
	(IE 19.07.17)		
G-CJRJ	PZL-Bielsko SZD-50-3 Puchacz	503199327	11.02.08
	BGA 4717/JRJ Derbyshire & Lancashire		
	Gliding Club Ltd Camphill *'JRJ'*		17.04.18E
G-CJRK	Cameron Z-31	12062	10.05.17
	BWS Security Systems Ltd t/a BWS Standfast Fire		
	& Security Systems Corston, Bath *'BWS Standfast'*		14.05.19E
G-CJRL	Glaser-Dirks DG-100G Elan	E185G151	29.10.07
	BGA 4719, D-1246 P Lazenby Aston Down *'JRL'*		17.04.18E
	Built by Elan Tovarna Sportnega Orodja N.Sol.O		
G-CJRM	Grob G102 Astir CS	1332	27.10.09
	BGA 4720/JRM, (BGA 4314), AGA 6		
	A R Moore Seighford *'JRM'*		24.02.18E
G-CJRN	Glaser-Dirks DG-202/17C	2-118CL04	28.04.09
	BGA 4721/JRN, D-7267 T G Roberts Lasham *'PT'*		25.05.16E
G-CJRO	Cameron Z-105	12055	10.05.17
	BWS Security Systems Ltd t/a BWS Standfast Fire		
	& Security Systems Corston, Bath *'BWS Standfast'*		16.05.19E
G-CJRR	Schempp-Hirth Discus bT	50	15.10.07
	BGA 4724, PH-1087, D-KBHM		
	N A Hays Gransden Lodge *'LA'*		26.12.15E
G-CJRS	BRM Bristell NG5 Speed Wing	219	05.09.16
	A Watt Insch		18.02.19P
	Built by A Watt – project LAA 385-15406; tailwheel u/c		
G-CJRT	Schempp-Hirth Standard Cirrus	99	29.08.07
	BGA 4726, D-0734 N G Henry Bicester *'JRT'*		15.04.15E
	(IE 28.07.15)		
G-CJRU	Schleicher ASW 24	24168	02.11.07
	BGA 4727/JRU, D-7085		
	C D Bingham Snitterfield *'SK'*		27.01.19E
G-CJRV	Schleicher ASW 19B	19233	26.06.08
	BGA 4728/JRV, D-2644 R E Comer North Hill *'B19'*		25.03.18E
G-CJRX	Schleicher ASK 13	13375	28.04.08
	BGA 4730/JRX, RAFGSA R41, RAFGSA 241		
	The Royal Air Force Gliding & Soaring Association		
	RAF Halton *'R41'*		23.11.17E
	Operated by Chilterns Gliding Centre		
G-CJRZ	Comco Ikarus C42 FB80 Bravo	1611-7481	02.12.16
	D W Cross South Hykeham		29.11.18P
	Assembled Red Aviation		
G-CJSA	Nanchang CJ-6A (Yak 18)	3151215	11.06.10
	N91555, PLAAF M Elmes & J N Ware White Waltham		10.07.18P
G-CJSB	Republic RC-3 Seabee	779	05.10.16
	N11NW, CF-JBN, N6513K, NC6513K		
	J A & R H Cooper Wickenby		27.03.19E
G-CJSC	Schempp-Hirth Nimbus-3DT	10	30.06.10
	BGA 4735/JSC, F-CFUE, F-WFUE, D-KFUE		
	S G Jones Membury		
	(NF 10.11.17)		

G-CJSD	Grob G102 Astir CS	1133	24.01.08
	BGA 4736/JSD, RAFGSA R77, D-4177		
	The Royal Air Force Gliding & Soaring Association		
	RAF Marham *'R77'*		05.08.18E
	Operated by Fenland Gliding Club		
G-CJSE	Schempp-Hirth Discus b	365	14.02.08
	BGA 4737/JSE, PH-918 Imperial College of		
	Science, Technology & Medicine Lasham *'296'*		17.03.18E
G-CJSF	Piper PA-28R-180 Cherokee Arrow	28R-30877	10.10.16
	SX-SIT, G-SBMM, G-BBEL, SE-FDX		
	Y N Dimitrov & V I Genchev (Sofia, Bulgaria)		16.06.18E
G-CJSG	Schleicher Ka 6E	4248	04.10.07
	BGA 4739, D-0090 A J Emck Lasham *'36'*		07.11.18E
G-CJSH	Grob G102 Club Astir IIIb	5504CB	13.05.08
	BGA 4740/JSH, D-6470		
	Lasham Gliding Society Ltd Lasham *'SH9'*		15.08.18E
G-CJSK	Grob G102 Astir CS	1521	22.12.07
	BGA 4742/JSK, D-7455 M Jardine tr Sierra Kilo Group		
	Burnford Common, Brentor *'JSK'*		23.03.18E
G-CJSL	Schempp-Hirth Ventus cT	121	07.11.07
	BGA 4743/JSL, D-KIFL		
	D Latimer Sutton Bank *'782'*		01.05.18E
G-CJSM	Van's RV-8	81984	22.08.16
	S T G Lloyd Swansea		02.02.18P
	Built by S T G Lloyd – project LAA 303-15296;		
	operated by 'Raven Display Team' – 'No. 2'		
G-CJSN	Schleicher K 8B	8916	06.06.08
	BGA 4745/JSN, RAFGSA R45, 245		
	Cotswold Gliding Club Aston Down *'JSN'*		24.04.15E
	Damaged in heavy landing Aston Down		
	23.04.15; stored 01.16 (NF 03.12.15)		
G-CJSP	Piper PA-28-180 Cherokee Archer	28-7505254	12.07.17
	I-CRPI, N3992X J R Wright (Jersey JE2)		
	(NF 12.07.17)		
G-CJSR	Steen Skybolt	SB-1990	30.11.16
	N46294 S L Millar Crowland		
	Built by J C Brown (IE 29.11.16)		
G-CJSS	Schleicher ASW 27	27121	04.02.08
	BGA 4749/JSS G K & S R Drury Challock *'841'*		27.09.18E
G-CJST	Rolladen-Schneider LS1-c	86	07.01.08
	BGA 4750/JST, OO-ZPA, D-0766		
	A M Walker Gransden Lodge *'JST'*		15.02.18E
G-CJSU	Rolladen-Schneider LS8-18	8297	22.01.08
	BGA 4751/JSU, D-0543 J G Bell Lasham *'95'*		02.06.18E
G-CJSV	Schleicher ASK 13	13127	26.09.08
	BGA 4752/JSV, RAFGSA R80, BGA 1509/CFN		
	The Royal Air Force Gliding & Soaring Association		
	RAF Odiham *'R30'*		26.05.18E
G-CJSX	Glaser-Dirks DG-500 Elan Orion	5E200X44	10.06.08
	BGA 4754/JSX Oxford Gliding Company Ltd		
	RAF Weston-on-the-Green *'JSX'*		11.09.18E
	Built by AMS-Flight d.o.o.		
G-CJSY	Sackville BM-34	BN02	30.11.16
	B J Newman Rushden		
	Built by B J Newman (IE 25.04.17)		
G-CJSZ	Schleicher ASK 18	18012	27.02.08
	BGA 4756/JSZ, D-6878 C Weston Challock *'JSZ'*		20.05.18E
G-CJTA	AutoGyro MTOsport	xxxx	23.09.16
	R Brain Rufforth East		12.11.18P
	Assembled Rotorsport UK as c/n RSUK/MTOS/062		
G-CJTB	Schleicher ASW 24	24017	02.10.07
	BGA 4758, D-3465 T Davies Cranwell North *'T9'*		03.12.17E
	(IE 18.12.17)		
G-CJTC	AutoGyro Calidus	C00473	14.11.16
	C J Rose (Lidlington, Bedford)		26.03.18P
	Assembled Rotorsport UK as c/n RSUK/CALS/032		
G-CJTD	Techpro Merlin 100UL	HV-21	02.02.17
	J Murphy Athey's Moor, Longframlington		
	(IE 02.02.17)		
G-CJTE	Aeropro EuroFOX 3K	50917	21.02.17
	C M Theakstone (Rushden)		24.03.19P
	Built by Ascent Industries Ltd; tricycle u/c		

G-CJTG	Hoffmann H36 Dimona II	36244	22.12.16
	LX-CVN, D-KLSW		
	A M Walker tr Dimona Syndicate Rattlesden		13.05.18E
G-CJTH	Schleicher ASW 24	24218	13.02.08
	BGA 4764/JTH, D-7681		
	J E & R J Lodge Dunstable Downs *'L24'*		20.07.16E
G-CJTI	Aerochute Hummerchute	472	13.01.17
	I Davies (Pwllheli)		14.03.18P
G-CJTJ	Schempp-Hirth Mini Nimbus B	73	15.01.08
	BGA 4765/JTJ, D-7620		
	R A Bowker RNAS Yeovilton *'JTJ'*		19.05.17E
G-CJTK	AMS-Flight DG-303 Elan Acro	3E487A28	22.01.08
	BGA 4766/JTK A Drury Sutton Bank *'JTK'*		23.06.18E
G-CJTM	Rolladen-Schneider LS8-18	8268	07.01.08
	BGA 4768/JTM A D Holmes Lasham *'418'*		02.12.18E
G-CJTN	Glaser-Dirks DG-300 Elan	3E19	11.01.08
	BGA 4769/JTN, HB-1717		
	P R Gardner & A D Noble Bicester *'E5'*		21.05.18E
	Built by Elan Tovarna Sportnega Orodja N.Sol.O		
G-CJTO	Glasflügel Mosquito	88	17.01.08
	BGA 4771/JTQ, OO-ZYL I W Myles Burn *'JTO'*		08.01.19E
G-CJTP	Schleicher ASW 20L	20569	12.02.08
	BGA 4770/JTP, D-4688		
	R Abercrombie & C A Sheldon Milfield *'JTP'*		17.05.18E
G-CJTS	Schempp-Hirth Cirrus VTC	108	04.09.08
	BGA 4773/JTS, S5-3059, SL-3059, YU-4200		
	P & S Skinner tr G-CJTS Cirrus Group Kenley *'JTS'*		16.10.11E
	(NF 09.07.18)		
G-CJTT	Aerochute Hummerchute	473	16.01.17
	D Townsend (Mansfield)		18.04.19P
G-CJTU	Schempp-Hirth Duo Discus T	4/234	28.02.08
	BGA 4775/JTU		
	C C Redrup tr G-CJTU Syndicate *'JTU'*		09.04.18E
G-CJTW	Glasflügel Mosquito B	199	28.07.08
	BGA 4777/JTW, F-CELX		
	B L C Gordon Easterton *'M17'*		30.05.17E
G-CJTX	Evektor EV-97 Eurostar SL	2016-4238	13.12.16
	M Moher & P J Newman tr G-TX Group		
	Wycombe Air Park		23.01.19P
	Assembled Light Sport Aviation Ltd		
G-CJTY	Rolladen-Schneider LS8-a	8102	30.11.07
	BGA 4779/JTY, SE-USA H W Ross tr JTY Syndicate		
	Wycombe Air Park *'JTY'*		07.03.18E
G-CJUB	Schempp-Hirth Discus CS	268CS	01.08.08
	BGA 4782/JUB Coventry Gliding Club Ltd		
	t/a The Gliding Centre Husbands Bosworth *'894'*		01.04.18E
G-CJUD	Denney Kitfox Model 3	xxxx	17.01.91
	J E Jeffrey & S Nixon Eshott		09.07.18P
	Built by C W Judge – project PFA 172-11939		
G-CJUF	Schempp-Hirth Ventus-2cT	53/174	04.02.09
	BGA 4786/JUF M H B Pope Bidford *'46'*		27.06.18E
G-CJUJ	Schleicher ASW 27	27127	17.09.08
	BGA 4789/JUJ T K Gooch Aston Down *'Z1'*		10.12.18E
G-CJUK	Grob G102 Astir CS	1430	18.03.08
	BGA 4790/JUK, PH-552		
	S J Calvert & P Freer Wycombe Air Park *'554'*		28.05.13E
	(NF 20.07.16)		
G-CJUN	Schleicher ASW 19B	19096	21.07.08
	BGA 4793/JUN, D-3844		
	M P S Roberts Gransden Lodge *'19'*		09.06.18E
G-CJUO	Cameron Z-42	11609	10.01.17
	Atlantic Ballooning BVBA Destelbergen, Belgium		11.01.18E
G-CJUR	Valentin Mistral C	MC042/81	12.05.08
	BGA 4796/JUR, HB-1596		
	East Sussex Gliding Club Ltd Ringmer *'JUR'*		06.10.18E
G-CJUT	Best Off Skyranger Nynja 912S(1)	xxxx	19.01.17
	A Jackson Darley Moor		
	Built by A Jackson – project BMAA/HB/694		
	(NF 19.01.17)		
G-CJUU	Schempp-Hirth Standard Cirrus	450	01.12.07
	BGA4799/JUU, PH-500 A R Jones Milfield *'JUU'*		11.06.18E
G-CJUV	Schempp-Hirth Discus b	551	22.01.08
	BGA 4800/JUV, D-8257		
	Lasham Gliding Society Ltd Lasham *'SH2'*		09.05.18E
G-CJUX	Aviastroitel AC-4C	051	10.12.08
	BGA 4802/JUX R J Walton (Bingley) *'CD1'*		
	(NF 18.02.16)		
G-CJUY	Sorrell SNS-8 Hypelight	169	05.01.17
	R H Cooper Wickenby		
	(NF 05.01.17)		
G-CJUZ	Schleicher ASW 19B	19146	06.09.07
	BGA 4804, D-7932 J M Hough Chipping *'M80'*		05.04.18E
G-CJVA	Schempp-Hirth Ventus-2cT	66/203	15.10.07
	BGA 4805 M S Armstrong Camphill *'JVA'*		15.01.19E
G-CJVB	Schempp-Hirth Discus bT	111	11.10.07
	BGA 4806, D-KUNK C J Edwards Nympsfield *'DF'*		23.03.18E
G-CJVC	PZL-Bielsko SZD-51-1 Junior	B-1799	29.10.07
	BGA 4807, SP-3434		
	York Gliding Centre (Operations) Ltd Rufforth *'JVC'*		11.05.19E
G-CJVD	Team Mini-Max 1600	514	31.01.17
	EI-CNC D R Thompson Newtownards		
	Built by A M S Allen – project SAAC 042 (NF 31.01.17)		
G-CJVE	Eiriavion PIK-20D-78	20631	18.12.07
	BGA 4809/JVE, OY-XJC		
	S R Wilkinson Pocklington *'JVE'*		05.05.18E
G-CJVF	Schempp-Hirth Discus CS	271CS	27.05.08
	BGA 4810/JVF J Hodgson Dunstable Downs *'JH1'*		24.08.18E
G-CJVG	Schempp-Hirth Discus bT	121	31.03.08
	BGA 4811, D-KSOP		
	M J Beaumont & P M Holland Lasham *'730'*		13.03.18E
G-CJVH	Lindstrand LTL Series 1-105	023	04.01.17
	Lindstrand Technologies Ltd Oswestry *'Lindstrand'*		17.07.19E
G-CJVI	Techpro Merlin 100UL	HV-20	26.05.17
	Sprite Aviation Services Ltd		
	Inglenook Farm, Maydensole		
	(NF 11.07.18)		
G-CJVK	Best Off Skyranger Nynja 912iS(1)	xxxx0169	31.08.16
	R J Speight Freshwater Fruit Farm, Freshwater		
	Built by R J Speight – project BMAA/HB/660		
	(IE 18.01.18)		
G-CJVL	Glaser-Dirks DG-300 Elan	3E158	04.12.07
	BGA 4815/JVL, HB-1833		
	M S Hoy & A T Vidion Tibenham *'JVL'*		09.06.18E
	Built by Elan Tovarna Sportnega Orodja N.Sol.O		
G-CJVM	Schleicher ASW 27B	27138	18.12.07
	BGA 4816/JVM G K Payne Dunstable Downs *'GP'*		26.02.18E
G-CJVN	Lindstrand LTL Racer 65	024	04.01.17
	Slowfly Mongolfiere SNC Mondovi, Italy *'Lindstrand'*		15.07.19E
G-CJVO	Lindstrand LTL Racer 56	027	04.01.17
	Lindstrand Technologies Ltd Oswestry		
	(NF 04.01.17)		
G-CJVP	Glaser-Dirks DG-200	2-1	09.01.08
	BGA 4818/JVP, D-8200		
	M S Howey & S Leadbeater Rufforth *'D8'*		27.04.18E
G-CJVS	Schleicher ASW 28	28003	11.09.07
	BGA 4821/JVS, D-4008		
	A & G S J Bambrook Lasham *'247'*		03.03.18E
G-CJVU	Lanaverre CS11-75L Standard Cirrus	28	07.01.08
	BGA 4823/JVU, F-CFVT P L Turner Bicester *'C74'*		21.03.18E
G-CJVV	Schempp-Hirth Janus C	176	02.05.08
	BGA 4824/JVV, D-4150 J A Melville tr J50 Syndicate		
	Pocklington *'J50'*		24.05.18E
G-CJVW	Schleicher ASW 15	15042	10.09.07
	BGA 4825/JVW, HB-992 P Bolton tr Channel		
	Gliding Club Group Waldershare Park *'15A'*		10.05.18E
G-CJVX	Schempp-Hirth Discus CS	087CS	23.11.07
	BGA 4826/JVX, D-0263		
	M P Kemp tr G-CJVX Syndicate Challock *'988'*		23.08.18E
	Built by Orličan Aakciová Spoločnost		
G-CJVZ	Schleicher ASK 21	21721	06.11.07
	BGA 4828/JVZ Yorkshire Gliding Club (Proprietary) Ltd		
	Sutton Bank *'JVZ'*		18.01.19E

G-CJWA	Schleicher ASW 28	28005	21.08.07
	BGA 4829 R Jones & J R Martindale		
	Walney Island 'C6'		10.12.18E
G-CJWB	Schleicher ASK 13	13671AB	18.01.08
	BGA 4830/JWB, D-1066		
	East Sussex Gliding Club Ltd Ringmer 'JWB'		02.05.18E
	Built by Jubi GmbH Sportflugzeugbau		
G-CJWD	Schleicher ASK 21	21724	08.01.08
	BGA 4832/JWD London Gliding Club Proprietary Ltd		
	Dunstable Downs 'JWD'		12.01.19E
G-CJWE	CCF T-6 Harvard Mk.4	CCF4-97	09.01.17
	N13595, RCAF 20306		
	Cirrus Aircraft UK Ltd Leicester 'Dazzling Debs'		07.06.18P
	Built by Canadian Car & Foundry Co;		
	as '481273:California ANG'		
G-CJWG	Schempp-Hirth Nimbus-3DT	11	15.11.07
	BGA 4835/JWG, D-KMGD		
	P G Kynsey tr 880 Group Lasham '880'		30.11.18E
G-CJWH	Lindstrand LTL Series 1-90	035	16.02.17
	Flintnine Fasteners Ltd Whittle-le-Woods, Chorley		
	'Fixings & Fasteners'		02.05.18E
G-CJWI	CFM Streak Shadow	SA-014	12.01.17
	9J-YCN J A Harris Henstridge		
	Built by Shadow Lite CC (IE 12.01.17)		
G-CJWJ	Schleicher ASK 13	13599	11.01.08
	BGA 4837/JWJ, RAFGSA R38, RAFGSA R3		
	The Royal Air Force Gliding & Soaring Association		
	RAF Cosford 'R38'		02.04.18E
	Operated by Wrekin Gliding Club		
G-CJWK	Schempp-Hirth Discus bT	453/1	14.02.08
	BGA 4838/JWK R Thompson tr 722 Syndicate		
	Nympsfield '722'		26.01.18E
	Composite airframe ex BGA 4687 (fuselage c/n		
	127/488), BGA 3961 (left wing c/n 106/453 &		
	ex New Zealand right wing); officially regd as		
	c/n 122 & carries appropriate plate: note original		
	c/n 122 was BGA 4021 & w/o Parham 07.05.95;		
	originally regd as c/n 106 & changed to c/n 453/1		
	when duplicate c/n 106 noted		
G-CJWL	Hawker Hunter F.58A	HABL-003079	18.01.17
	Swiss AF J-4110, G-9-328, A2567, XF318		
	Hawker Hunter Aviation Ltd RAF Scampton		
	Built by Hawker Aircraft (Blackpool) Ltd as F.Mk.4		
	(NF 18.01.17)		
G-CJWM	Grob G103 Twin II	3536	15.02.08
	BGA 4840/JWM, D-8730		
	The South Wales Gliding Club Ltd Usk 'T12'		29.06.18E
G-CJWO	Supermarine 349 Spitfire LF.Vb	CBAF 1806	26.01.17
	BL688 R M B Parnall		
	(Trelonk Farm, Ruan High Lanes, Truro)		
	Built by Castle Bromwich 1942; on rebuild 11.17		
	(NF 26.01.17)		
G-CJWP	Bölkow Phoebus B1	875	11.09.08
	BGA 4842/JWP, D-0128 A Fidler Crowland 'JWP'		16.05.12E
	(NF 20.07.17)		
G-CJWR	Grob G102 Astir CS	1271	18.12.07
	BGA 4844/JWR, D-7366 A Morrison		
	tr Cairngorm Gliding Club Feshiebridge 'JWR'		14.04.18E
G-CJWT	Glaser-Dirks DG-200	2-42	12.11.07
	BGA4846/JWT, D-6560, D-6660		
	K R Nash Nympsfield 'JWT'		18.04.17E
G-CJWU	Schempp-Hirth Ventus bT	19	31.07.08
	BGA 4847/JWU, ZS-GOW		
	B C P & C Crook Wycombe Air Park 'CB'		02.11.18E
G-CJWW	Super Marine Spitfire Mk.26	026	17.01.17
	M R Overall Whitehall Farm, Wethersfield		10.12.19P
	Built by M R Overall – project LAA 324-14063;		
	as 'MH526:LO-D' in RAF c/s		
G-CJWY	Cameron O-31	12071	20.01.17
	Cameron Balloons Ltd Bristol BS3		
	'Cameron Superlight'		31.05.19E
G-CJXA	Schempp-Hirth Nimbus-3DT	9	02.11.07
	BGA 4853/JXA, D-KKYY, D-4444		
	J B Maddison tr Y44 Syndicate Darlton		21.05.18E

G-CJXB	Centrair 201B Marianne	201015	12.02.08
	BGA 4854/JXB, F-CGMN		
	A C Cherry Ridgewell 'JXB'		13.04.18E
G-CJXC	Wassmer WA.28 Espadon	102	22.12.07
	BGA 4855/JXC, F-CDZV		
	A P Montague Nympsfield 'JXC'		19.11.10R
	(NF 09.02.16)		
G-CJXD	Ultramagic H-77	77/381	28.11.14
	C G Dobson Goring, Reading		13.02.19E
G-CJXE	Lindstrand LTL Series 1-120	030	10.02.17
	N R Beckwith Skewsby, York		19.03.18E
G-CJXF	Best Off Skyranger Swift 912(1)	xxxx	27.01.17
	R J Heath (Burnham-on-Sea)		18.09.18P
	Built by R J Heath -project BMAA/HB/696		
G-CJXG	Eiriavion PIK-20D-78	20660	19.12.07
	BGA4859/JXG, PH-670		
	S Ingason tr W5 Group Lasham 'W5'		02.03.18E
G-CJXI	Cameron A-300	12069	06.04.17
	Bailey Balloons Ltd Pill, Bristol 'Bailey Balloons'		01.04.19E
G-CJXJ	Cameron Z-105	12027	17.04.17
	P Spellward t/a Bristol University Hot Air Ballooning		
	Society Bristol BS9 'University of Bristol'		06.04.18E
G-CJXK	Cameron O-31	12082	06.04.17
	A P Jay South Cerney, Cirencester		22.03.18E
G-CJXL	Schempp-Hirth Discus CS	278CS	01.12.07
	BGA 4863/JXL J Hall Parham Park 'SO1'		31.03.19E
G-CJXM	Schleicher ASK 13	13542	07.02.08
	BGA 4864/JXM, RAFGSA R34, F-CERF		
	The Windrushers Gliding Club Ltd Bicester 'JXM'		05.04.18E
G-CJXN	Centrair 201B Marianne	201A035	13.12.07
	BGA 4865/JXN, F-CBLI		
	G R Davey & C E Metcalfe Kirton in Lindsey 'Z35'		17.07.18E
G-CJXO	Flylight Dragonfly	DA140	25.03.17
	P C Knowles (Andreas)		
	(IE 25.03.17)		
G-CJXP	Glaser-Dirks DG-100	18	13.02.08
	BGA 4866/JXP, PH-520 N L Morris Llantysilio 'JXP'		26.10.17E
G-CJXR	Schempp-Hirth Discus b	540	29.02.08
	BGA 4868/JXR, D-9152		
	Cambridge Gliding Club Ltd Gransden Lodge 'DM'		02.04.18E
G-CJXT	Schleicher ASW 24B	24233	11.10.07
	BGA 4870, D-6706		
	P A Whitehead tr JXT Syndicate Rufforth 'CT'		18.01.18E
G-CJXW	Schempp-Hirth Duo Discus T	7/250	16.11.07
	BGA 4873/JXW, D-KOZX		
	R A Beatty & R R Bryan Gransden Lodge '871'		14.07.18E
G-CJXX	Pilatus B4-PC11AF	013	21.12.07
	BGA 4874/JXX, HB-1112		
	C B Shepperd Upwood 'JXX'		06.06.18E
G-CJXY	Neukom S-4A Elfe	68	17.09.08
	BGA 4875/JXY, HB-1267 J Karran & A Peacock		
	tr Rufforth Elfe S4A Syndicate Rufforth		10.12.17R
G-CJYC	Grob G102 Astir CS	1429	14.08.07
	BGA 4880, RAFGSA R19, RAFGGA 742, D-7425		
	R A Christie Easterton 'JYC'		07.08.18E
G-CJYE	Schleicher ASK 13	13191	23.01.08
	BGA 4882/JYE, D-0347		
	North Wales Gliding Club Ltd Llantysilio 'JYE'		26.11.18E
G-CJYF	Schempp-Hirth Discus CS	281CS	04.12.07
	BGA 4883/JYF C D Sword Milfield 'N55'		30.04.18E
G-CJYI	Piper PA-28-140 Cherokee	28-7225145	15.11.17
	SE-FYL N Butler Bourn		
	Noted as 'SE-FYL' 02.18 (IE 11.12.17)		
G-CJYJ	Cameron O-31	12039	03.04.17
	P Spellward Bristol		20.03.18E
G-CJYK	Boeing Stearman B75N1 Kaydet (N2S-3)	75-2634	10.02.17
	N65633, USN 4304 R Redmond Enstone		18.10.18E
	As '75-4826:27' in US Navy c/s		
G-CJYL	Sportine Aviacija LAK-12 Lietuva	6197	11.06.08
	BGA 4888/JYL, ex ROSTO		
	A Camerotto Udine, Italy		13.08.13E
	(IE 22.10.15)		

G-CJYM	Ultramagic S-90	90/57	25.01.17
	OO-BEZ M A Wrigglesworth Dorking		23.02.18E
G-CJYO	Glaser-Dirks DG-100G Elan	E181G147	06.04.09
	BGA 4892/JYQ, D-1485		
	A M Booth Wormingford '485'		14.06.18E
G-CJYP	Grob G102 Astir CS	5018C	07.02.08
	BGA 4891/JYP, D-8743 G A Fletcher		
	tr Bravo One Two Group Tibenham 'B12'		14.04.18E
G-CJYR	Schempp-Hirth Duo Discus T	16/267	14.03.08
	BGA 4893/JYR, D-KOZX		
	R E Francis tr CJYR Flying Group Nympsfield 'JYR'		02.03.19E
G-CJYS	Schempp-Hirth Mini Nimbus C	106	09.01.08
	BGA 4894/JYS, HB-1437 A Jenkins Shobdon 'JYS'		14.02.18E
G-CJYU	Schempp-Hirth Ventus-2cT	70/216	08.10.07
	BGA4896 P Brown & M T Davis		
	(Havant & Henlow) 'R11'		12.04.18E
	Operated by Chilterns Gliding Centre		
G-CJYV	Schleicher K 8B	133	18.04.11
	BGA 4897/JYV, D-8395		
	Club Agrupacion de Pilotos del Sureste Ontur, Spain		
	(NF 06.05.15)		
G-CJYW	Schleicher K 8B	8432	18.04.11
	BGA 4898/JYW, D-5682		
	Club Agrupacion de Pilotos del Sureste Ontur, Spain		
	(NF 06.05.15)		
G-CJYX	Rolladen-Schneider LS3-17	3289	21.04.08
	BGA 4899/JYX, D-3517		
	V C Diaz & D Meyer-Beeck Ontur, Spain 'JYX'		06.08.14E
	(NF 06.01.16)		
G-CJYY	Super Marine Spitfire Mk.26	056	09.02.17
	D A Whitmore Haverfordwest		
	Built by D A Whitmore – project PFA 324-14683		
	(NF 08.02.17)		
G-CJYZ	Cameron Z-120	12090	09.06.17
	MSJ Ballooning Ltd Lewes		
	'Cotswold Balloon Safaris'		21.05.19E
G-CJZB	Glaser-Dirks DG-500 Elan Orion	5E223X61	07.01.08
	BGA 4903/JZB The Borders (Milfield) Gliding Club Ltd		
	Milfield 'Jezabel'		20.04.18E
	Built by AMS-Flight d.o.o.		
G-CJZD	Aeropro EuroFOX 912(S)	49717	25.07.17
	R Maddocks-Born Rufforth East		13.11.19P
	Built by D G Hall – project LAA 376-15437		
G-CJZE	Schleicher ASK 13	13423	20.11.07
	BGA 4906/JZE, OY-XPJ, D-2125		
	Bowland Forest Gliding Club Ltd Chipping 'JZE'		10.03.18E
G-CJZG	Schempp-Hirth Discus bT	9	07.09.07
	BGA 4908, D-KISM I K G Mitchell North Hill 'JZG'		25.01.16E
G-CJZH	Schleicher ASW 20CL	20754	11.09.07
	BGA 4909, D-5932 A K Bartlett Talgarth 'JZH'		02.02.19E
G-CJZK	Glaser-Dirks DG-500 Elan Orion	5E225X63	18.12.07
	BGA 4911/JZK Devon & Somerset Gliding Club Ltd		
	North Hill 'JZK'		23.03.18E
	Built by AMS-Flight d.o.o.		
G-CJZL	Schempp-Hirth Mini Nimbus B	92	02.11.07
	BGA 4912/JZL, HB-1453		
	J F Wells Wormingford 'JZL'		23.03.18E
G-CJZM	Schempp-Hirth Ventus-2ax	117	07.01.08
	BGA 4913/JZM S Crabb Husbands Bosworth 'C64'		20.07.18E
G-CJZN	Schleicher ASW 28	28038	19.10.07
	BGA 4914 D M Rushton Lyveden 'CD'		09.02.19E
G-CJZO[M]	Royal Aircraft Factory BE.2e replica	753	10.03.17
	ZK-TFZ O Wulff Stow Maries		13.06.18P
	Built by The Vintage Aviator Ltd;		
	as 'A2943' in 7 Sqdn RFC c/s		
G-CJZP	Royal Aircraft Factory BE.2e replica	752	23.02.17
	ZK-KOZ The Vintage Aviator Ltd		
	Hood Aerodrome, Masterton, New Zealand		11.07.18P
	Built by The Vintage Aviator Ltd;		
	as 'A2767' in 37 Sqdn RFC c/s		
G-CJZU	Rogers Sky Prince	00118-1507	08.03.17
	EC-XCP P T Catanach (Puckeridge, Ware)		25.09.19P
	Built by A M Martinez; constructed using plans		
	ex Frank Rogers, Australia		

G-CJZV	Piper PA-28RT-201T Turbo Arrow IV	28R-7931100	25.03.17
	I-GRLC L Tomatis (Cervasca, Italy)		11.01.19E
G-CJZW	Van's RV-12	120958	08.03.17
	M A N Newall Breighton		20.02.20P
	Built by M A N Newall – project LAA 363-15382		
G-CJZY	Grob G102 Standard Astir III	5600S	13.03.08
	BGA 4924/JZY, D-6951		
	Lasham Gliding Society Ltd Lasham 'SH7'		04.09.16E
G-CJZZ	Rolladen-Schneider LS7-WL	7128	08.12.07
	BGA 4925/JZZ, SE-UIU		
	C L Rogers (Wincanton) '7UP'		08.12.17E

G-CKAA – G-CKZZ

G-CKAA	Whittaker MW9 Plank	001	13.03.17
	M W J Whittaker (Clayton, Doncaster)		
	Built by M W J Whittaker; noted 09.18 (IE 24.10.17)		
G-CKAB	Aeropro EuroFOX 912(S)	51617	06.02.17
	R M Cornwell Oaksey Park		14.03.19P
	Built by R M Cornwell & S Williams –		
	project LAA 376-15432; tailwheel u/c;		
	badged 'EUROFOX 120'		
G-CKAC	Glaser-Dirks DG-200	2-159	10.09.08
	BGA 4928/KAC, HB-1611 N Frost Seighford 'KAC'		05.04.19E
G-CKAE	Centrair 101A Pégase	101A0152	25.03.08
	BGA 4930/KAE, F-CGBN		
	J P Gilbert Wormingford 'KAE'		09.06.14E
	(NF 20.12.18)		
G-CKAF	Embraer EMB-145EP	145047	25.05.17
	F-GRGE, PT-SZM British Midland Regional Ltd		
	t/a BMI Regional Aberdeen Int'l		25.03.19E
G-CKAG	Embraer EMB-145EP	145118	03.07.17
	F-GRGG, PT-SCT British Midland Regional Ltd		
	t/a BMI Regional Bristol		22.11.19E
G-CKAI	Griffin RG28	002	13.03.17
	R G Griffin Newbury		
	Built by R G Griffin; noted 01.19 (IE 06.12.17)		
G-CKAM	Glasflügel Club Libelle 205	83	14.09.07
	BGA 4937, D-8928		
	P A Cronk & R C Tallowin Lyveden 'KAM'		29.04.19E
G-CKAN	PZL-Bielsko SZD-50-3 Puchacz	B-2106	26.11.07
	BGA 4938/KAN, PH-1104 The Bath, Wilts & North		
	Dorset Gliding Club Ltd Kingston Deverill 'KAN'		14.05.19E
G-CKAO	Lindstrand LTL Series 1-17	049	20.03.17
	Lindstrand Technologies Ltd Oswestry		
	(NF 20.03.17)		
G-CKAP	Schempp-Hirth Discus CS	290CS	05.10.07
	BGA 4939 R Gollings & H A Johnston		
	Kirton in Lindsey 'KAP'		14.08.19E
G-CKAR	Schempp-Hirth Duo Discus T	35/309	06.03.08
	BGA 4941/KAR, D-KHAF		
	J Giacopazzi tr 977 Syndicate Portmoak '977'		19.04.19E
G-CKAS	Schempp-Hirth Ventus-2cT	93/271	24.01.08
	BGA 4942/KAS, (BGA 4995/KCX), (BGA 4942/KAS)		
	R E Fletcher tr KAS Club Lasham 'KAS'		23.03.19E
G-CKAT	Reims/Cessna F152 II	F15201482	03.02.17
	F-GBFL A S Bamrah Biggin Hill		28.04.17E
	Stored as 'F-GBFL' 09.18 (IE 24.01.18)		
G-CKAU	AMS-Flight DG-303 Elan Acro	3E500A35	22.04.08
	BGA 4944/KAU G Earle Talgarth 'KAU'		27.08.19E
	Built by AMS-Flight d.o.o.		
G-CKAX	Glaser-Dirks DG-500 Elan Orion	5E229X67	29.11.07
	BGA 4947/KAX York Gliding Centre (Operations) Ltd		
	Rufforth 'KAX'		24.02.19E
	Built by AMS-Flight d.o.o.		
G-CKAY	Grob G102 Astir CS	1452	18.01.08
	BGA 4948/KAY, D-7433		
	P Fowler & R G Skerry Strubby 'KAY'		11.05.19E
G-CKAZ	Embraer EMB-505 Phenom 300	50500409	01.06.17
	Golconda Aircraft Leasing LLP East Midlands		01.06.19E
G-CKBA	Centrair 101A Pégase	101A0435	27.02.08
	BGA 4950/KBA, HB-3096 B Tansley		
	tr KBA Pegase 101A Syndicate Challock 'KBA'		21.05.19E

G-CKBB	Sopwith 7F.1 Snipe replica	0112	14.03.17
	ZK-SNI The Vintage Aviator Ltd		
	Hood Aerodrome, Masterton, New Zealand		20.06.18P
	Built by The Vintage Aviator Ltd;		
	as 'F2367:1 2' in 70 Sqdn RFC c/s		
G-CKBC	Rolladen-Schneider LS6-c18	6250-1	22.09.08
	BGA 4952/KBC A W Lyth Ringmer '98'		04.06.19E
	(Rebuilt using major components ex BGA3895 c/n 6250		
G-CKBD	Grob G102 Astir CS	1217	29.10.07
	BGA 4953, D-7290 Peterborough & Spalding		
	Gliding Club Ltd Crowland 'KBD'		18.05.19E
G-CKBE	Van's RV-8	xxxx	17.02.17
	B E Smith (Mannings Heath, Horsham)		
	Built by B E Smith – project PFA 303-13972 (IE 12.02.18)		
G-CKBF	AMS-Flight DG-303 Elan	3E498	21.09.07
	BGA 4955 G A Burtenshaw Parham 'AG1'		14.07.19E
	Built by AMS-Flight d.o.o.		
G-CKBG	Schempp-Hirth Ventus-2cT	83/250	14.02.08
	BGA 4956/KBG R Bollom & D Martin Camphill '71'		23.09.19E
G-CKBH	Rolladen-Schneider LS6	6072	24.10.07
	BGA 4957, D-7798		
	F C Ballard & P Walker Nympsfield 'H1'		05.05.19E
G-CKBJ	Ultramagic H-31	31/17	11.05.17
	R D Parry Sutton, Tenbury Wells 'Chelsea'		22.11.19E
G-CKBL	Grob G102 Astir CS	1464	15.02.08
	BGA 4960/KBL, D-7436		
	Norfolk Gliding Club Ltd Tibenham 'N12'		20.06.16E
G-CKBM	Schleicher ASW 28	28046	02.11.07
	BGA 4961/KBM, D-0001		
	P J Brown Dunstable Downs '73'		01.12.18E
G-CKBN	PZL-Bielsko SZD-55-1	551190004	01.10.07
	BGA 4962, SE-ULV		
	T S Horbury tr G-CKBN Group Kenley 'NH'		21.05.19E
G-CKBP	Smith Smudger 77	001	28.03.17
	VH-UGG C E Smith Plaistow, Billingshurst		
	(IE 04.10.18)		
G-CKBR	Nott AN3	10	29.03.17
	J R P Nott Santa Barbara, California, USA		
	(NF 29.03.17)		
G-CKBT	Schempp-Hirth Standard Cirrus	561G	28.03.08
	BGA 4967/KBT, D-4755		
	P R Johnson Wormingford '633'		18.07.19E
G-CKBU	Schleicher ASW 28	28040	15.10.07
	BGA 4968 G C Metcalfe Lasham '104'		07.01.20E
G-CKBV	Schleicher ASW 28	28045	02.11.07
	BGA 4969/KBV Zulu Glasstek Ltd		
	Baileys Farm, Long Crendon 'H4'		15.10.19E
G-CKBW	Cessna 150M	15076585	04.04.17
	I-AMDG, N3675V G P Boano tr Associazione		
	Sportiva Aeronautica (Novi Ligure, Italy)		20.06.19E
G-CKBX	Schleicher ASW 27	27092	05.03.08
	BGA 4971/KBX, PH-1146		
	M Wright Tibenham 'AV8'		12.03.20E
G-CKBY	Eurocopter AS.365N3 Dauphin 2	6949	11.05.17
	TS-HSI, F-WWOF Babcock Mission		
	Critical Services Offshore Ltd Blackpool		31.05.19E
G-CKCB	Rolladen-Schneider LS4-a	4776	26.09.07
	BGA 4975, PH-887, D-1597 The Bristol Gliding Club		
	Proprietary Ltd Nympsfield 'MY'		04.05.19E
G-CKCC	Cameron Z-105	12088	24.04.17
	The Balloon Company Ltd t/a First Flight		
	Langford, Bristol 'TVE Group'		01.04.19E
G-CKCD	Schempp-Hirth Ventus-2cT	91/267	11.09.08
	BGA4977/KCD		
	R S Jobar & S G Jones Lasham '300'		23.01.19E
G-CKCE	Schempp-Hirth Ventus-2cT	85/256	05.03.08
	BGA 4978/KCE J P Walker tr Ventus 24 Group		
	Husbands Bosworth '24'		14.05.19E
G-CKCF	Scintex CP.301-C1 Emeraude	557	25.03.17
	OY-AIG N C Scanlan Enstone		
	Built by Société Scintex (NF 24.03.17)		
G-CKCH	Schempp-Hirth Ventus-2cT	56/186	12.11.07
	BGA 4981/KCH, PH-1191 J J Pridal Lasham 'EA'		18.03.19E

G-CKCI	Guimbal Cabri G2	1191	13.04.17
	D Robson Jumeirah House, Edenthorpe		09.05.19E
G-CKCJ	Schleicher ASW 28	28051	09.01.08
	BGA 4982/KCJ		
	M McHugo Gowran Grange, RoI 'V8'		15.02.20E
G-CKCK	Enstrom 280FX Shark	2071	05.05.95
	OO-PVL C M Parkinson (Styal, Wilmslow)		31.10.19E
G-CKCL	Cessna 182T Skylane	18281630	26.05.17
	SP-FYI, EC-JQR, N17578		
	PD Stonham Ltd Andrewsfield		04.10.19E
G-CKCM	Glasflügel Standard Libelle	104	09.07.08
	BGA 4985/KCM, HB-968 A Davey North Hill '5'		27.04.19E
G-CKCN	Schleicher ASW 27	27188	23.10.07
	BGA 4986, D-0001		
	W J Head Gransden Lodge '700'		21.03.19E
G-CKCP	Grob G102 Astir CS	1094	15.07.08
	BGA 4987/KCP, OY-XDB		
	Norfolk Gliding Club Ltd Tibenham 'NG1'		14.11.19E
G-CKCR	Sportine Aviacija LAK-17A	132	26.02.08
	BGA 4989/KCR M Kessler Verona, Italy 'FK'		04.02.19E
G-CKCT	Schleicher ASK 21	21751	31.08.07
	BGA4991 Kent Gliding Club Ltd Challock 'KCT'		25.02.19E
G-CKCV	Schempp-Hirth Duo Discus T	54/339	20.09.07
	BGA 4993, D-KOZZ		
	S J Williams tr WE4 Group Parham Park 'WE4'		25.03.20E
G-CKCY	Schleicher ASW 20	20068	12.02.08
	BGA4996/KCY, PH-597, (OY-XTM), PH-597		
	R S Hood Lasham 'KCY'		06.04.19E
G-CKCZ	Schleicher ASK 21	21749	25.01.08
	BGA4997/KCZ Booker Gliding Club Ltd		
	Wycombe Air Park 'KCZ'		21.05.19E
G-CKDA	Schempp-Hirth Ventus-2bx	138	19.10.07
	BGA4998, (BGA5008/KDL), D-4999		
	D J Eade Lasham '406'		17.10.19E
G-CKDD	Aeropro EuroFOX 2K	50817	15.03.17
	W M Holmes (Lancaster)		30.06.19P
	Built by Ascent Industries Ltd – project		
	BMAA/HB/697; tailwheel u/c		
G-CKDE	Grob G109B	6429	08.05.17
	PH-1106, D-KHGJ Navboys Ltd Lasham		11.09.19E
G-CKDF	Schleicher ASK 21	21006	29.01.08
	BGA5003/KDF, D-6539 T World tr Portsmouth		
	Naval Gliding Centre (HMS Sultan, Gosport) 'N7'		19.05.19E
	Stored 05.18		
G-CKDG	BB Microlight BB03 Trya/BB103		07.04.17
		BB03/16/11/UKNANO/16/11/U	
	Z G Nagygyorgy (Salford)		
	(IE 03.04.18)		
G-CKDJ	Sonex Sonex	1602	18.04.17
	S Rance (Poole)		
	Built by S Rance – project LAA 337-15203;		
	cleared to fly 11.12.18 (IE 07.08.18)		
G-CKDK	Rolladen-Schneider LS4-a	4352	21.12.07
	BGA5007/KDK, D-4106		
	M C & P A Ridger Long Mynd 'KDK'		15.07.19E
G-CKDL	Robinson R22 Beta II	3848	27.04.17
	I-HEFD Elicast SRL (Terzigno, Naples, Italy)		
	(NF 27.04.17)		
G-CKDM	Zenair CH.750	75-8699	24.04.17
	M R Cleveley Tibenham		
	Built by M R Cleveley – project LAA 381-15162;		
	cleared to fly 24.07.18 (IE 20.06.18)		
G-CKDN	Schleicher ASW 27B	27208	17.08.07
	BGA5010 J S McCullagh Lasham '150'		13.11.19E
G-CKDO	Schempp-Hirth Ventus-2cT	97	27.09.07
	BGA5012 M W Edwards Kingston Deverill '808'		30.03.20E
G-CKDP	Schleicher ASK 21	21760	17.04.08
	BGA5011/KDP Kent Gliding Club Ltd Challock 'KDP'		22.04.19E
G-CKDR	PZL-Bielsko SZD-48-3 Jantar-Standard 3	B-1642	28.09.09
	BGA5013/KDR, DOSAAF		
	G Hyrkowski Olsztyn, Poland 'GH'		11.11.19E

G-CKDS Schleicher ASW 27   27202   31.10.07
BGA5014   A W Gillett & G D Morris
Nympsfield   *'172'*   31.01.20E

G-CKDT Cameron C-80   10558   09.05.17
W Thijs   Sint-Niklaas, Belgium   25.04.19E

G-CKDU Glaser-Dirks DG-200/17   2-161/1752   08.01.08
BGA5016/KDU, D-6000   J M Knight   Rivar Hill   *'KDU'*   26.02.19E

G-CKDV Schempp-Hirth Ventus b/16.6   224   21.09.07
BGA5017, HB-1770   M A Codd   Talgarth   *'KDV'*   29.04.19E

G-CKDW Schleicher ASW 27   27196   21.11.07
BGA 5018/KDW   C Colton   Gransden Lodge   *'292'*   30.07.19E

G-CKDX Glaser-Dirks DG-200   2-11   26.02.08
BGA5019/KDX, D-7218
A Giles tr Delta X-Ray Group   Aston Down   *'KDX'*   31.08.18E

G-CKDY Glaser-Dirks DG-100   78   02.11.07
BGA5020/KDY, D-2591
D J Crisp tr 503 Syndicate   Dunstable Downs   *'503'*   28.05.19E

G-CKEA Schempp-Hirth Cirrus   11   09.11.07
BGA 5022/KEA, D-8807, HB-911
S G Jessup   Ridgewell   *'KEA'*   10.08.19E

G-CKEB Schempp-Hirth Standard Cirrus   436G   22.02.08
BGA5023/KEB, F-CEFN   R H Buzza   North Hill   *'KEB'*   20.08.19E

G-CKED Schleicher ASW 27   27203   06.11.07
BGA 5025/KED, D-0001
A & R Maskell   Gransden Lodge   *'MB'*   25.04.19E

G-CKEE Grob G102 Astir CS   1135   13.12.07
BGA 5026/KEE, D-4179   Essex & Suffolk
Gliding Club Ltd   Wormingford   *'KEE'*   06.04.19E

G-CKEG Cameron Z-105   12103   25.07.17
The Balloon Company Ltd t/a First Flight
Langford, Bristol   *'Thatchers'*   01.04.19E

G-CKEH Kolb Twinstar Mk.III Xtra   M3X-03-4-00046   08.05.17
R A Budd tr The Darley Tail Draggers   Darley Moor
Built by R A Budd & D Lawrence – project
PFA 205-14273 (NF 08.05.17)

G-CKEI Diamond DA.40NG Star   40.N335   17.07.17
D B Smith   Isle of Man   19.06.19E

G-CKEJ Schleicher ASK 21   21765   16.04.08
BGA 5030/KEJ   London Gliding Club Proprietary Ltd
Dunstable Downs   *'KEJ'*   20.03.19E

G-CKEK Schleicher ASK 21   21767   12.11.07
BGA 5031/KEK   Devon & Somerset Gliding Club Ltd
North Hill   *'KEK'*   15.02.20E

G-CKER Schleicher ASW 19B   19224   06.11.07
BGA 5037/KER, OY-XJI
W A Bowness & E Richards   Strubby   *'KER'*   11.05.19E

G-CKES Schempp-Hirth Cirrus   46   28.11.07
BGA 5038/KES, D-6955, HB-955
N Hawley & D Judd   RAF Cosford   *'KES'*   15.01.19E

G-CKET Rolladen-Schneider LS8-t   8459   30.06.08
BGA 5039
M B Jefferyes & J C Taylor   Dunstable Downs   *'456'*   29.06.19E
Built by Rolladen-Schneider

G-CKEV Schempp-Hirth Duo Discus   368   25.10.07
BGA 5041   The Royal Air Force Gliding
& Soaring Association   Cranwell North   *'R2'*   19.04.19E
Operated by Cranwell Gliding Club

G-CKEY Piper PA-28-161 Warrior II   28-7916061   04.01.07
N510PU, N22166
Warwickshire Aviation Ltd   Wellesbourne Mountford   18.11.19E

G-CKEZ Rolladen-Schneider LS8-t   8464   25.10.07
BGA 5045, D-KSAB   D A Jesty   Nympsfield   *'EZ'*   06.03.19E

G-CKFA Schempp-Hirth Standard Cirrus 75   644   08.02.08
BGA5046/KFA, D-2124, F-CEMQ
University of the West of England,
Bristol Higher Education   Aston Down   *'S75'*   10.04.19E

G-CKFB Schempp-Hirth Discus-2T   30/179   12.12.07
BGA5047/KFB, D-KOZZ
P A G & P L Holland   Kirton in Lindsey   *'PH2'*   15.09.19E

G-CKFD Schleicher ASW 27   27211   30.01.08
BGA5049/KFD   W T Craig   Dunstable Downs   *'906'*   10.02.19E

G-CKFE Eiriavion PIK-20D   20520   11.01.08
BGA 5050/KFE, D-8103, OE-5103
G E Rabe   Eindhoven, Netherlands   *'61'*   03.05.19E

G-CKFF Zenair CH.701SP   7-7208   02.05.17
19-9669   J C Woolard   Oban   23.08.19P
Built by M W Picard (Australia)

G-CKFG Grob G103A Twin II Acro   3771-K-57   06.02.08
BGA 5052/KFG, D-1339
The Surrey Hills Gliding Club Ltd   Kenley   *'KFG'*   07.03.19E

G-CKFH Schempp-Hirth Mini Nimbus HS 7   15   26.11.07
BGA 5053/KFH, D-4819
C J Friar   (Daltongate, Ulverston)   *'T4C'*   29.04.19E

G-CKFI Cameron Drop-95   12089   06.06.17
Belvoir Fruit Farms Ltd   Bottesford, Nottingham
'Belvoir fruit farms'   23.07.19E

G-CKFJ Schleicher ASK 13   13136   29.11.07
BGA 5054/KFJ, PH-383
York Gliding Centre Ltd   Rufforth   *'KFJ'*   13.06.18E

G-CKFK Schempp-Hirth Standard Cirrus 75-VTC   203   29.10.07
BGA 5055, S5-3058, SL-3058, YU-4295
P R Wilkinson   Tibenham   *'2W'*   30.04.19E
Built by Vazduhoplovno Tehnicki Centar

G-CKFL Rolladen-Schneider LS4   4080   17.01.08
BGA 5056/KFL, HB-1619
D O'Brien & D R Taylor   Tibenham   *'EE'*   29.05.19E

G-CKFN DG Flugzeugbau DG-1000S   10-29S28   05.12.07
BGA 5058/KFN   Yorkshire Gliding Club (Proprietary) Ltd
Sutton Bank   *'DS2'* & *'Sharpe's Classique II'*   19.02.19E

G-CKFP Schempp-Hirth Ventus-2cxT   110/304   09.11.07
BGA 5059/KFP, D-KKAH
D A Smith   Aston Down   *'124'*   24.01.20E

G-CKFR Schleicher ASK 13   13433   23.04.08
BGA 5061/KFR, D-3536, RAFGGA 535, D-3535
Club Agrupacion de Pilotos del Sureste
Ontur, Albacete, Spain   *'KFR'*   14.09.15E

G-CKFS Schleicher ASK 14   14022   25.04.17
D-KAQY   J Pool   Pocklington   31.08.19E

G-CKFT Schempp-Hirth Duo Discus T   77/383   12.02.08
BGA 5063/KFT, D-KIIH
L R Merritt tr Duo Discus Syndicate   Saltby   *'UP2'*   28.03.19E

G-CKFV DG Flugzeugbau LS8-t   8476   11.01.08
BGA 5065/KFV, D-KOBP
K I Arkley & G A Rowden   Sutton Bank   *'KFV'*   18.04.19E
Built by Rolladen-Schneider

G-CKFW Mauchline Quaich   PJKHL002   09.01.17
P J Kelsey tr Quaich Flying Group   (Edinburgh EH12)
Built by P J Kelsey & H Lorimer (NF 09.01.17)

G-CKFY Schleicher ASK 21   21776   23.01.06
BGA 5068/KFY
Cambridge Gliding Club Ltd   Gransden Lodge   *'KFY'*   14.01.20E

G-CKFZ Ultramagic M-77   77/404   01.03.17
E C Meek   Sandway, Maidstone   *'Holiday Inn'*   10.04.19E

G-CKGA Schempp-Hirth Ventus-2cxT   115/312   24.04.06
BGA 5070/KGA, D-KIBL
D R Campbell   Wycombe Air Park   *'370'*   17.05.19E

G-CKGC Schempp-Hirth Ventus-2cxT   118/317   07.10.05
BGA 5072/KGC, D-KMAF
J McLaughlin   (Welshpool)   *'64'*   29.10.19E

G-CKGD Schempp-Hirth Ventus-2cxT   119/318   07.10.05
BGA 5073/KGD, D-KEAD   C Morris   Bidford   *'V9'*   30.11.19E

G-CKGF Schempp-Hirth Duo Discus T   84/397   17.10.05
BGA 5075/KGF   P O'Donald tr Duo 233 Group
Gransden Lodge   *'233'*   20.02.20E

G-CKGG Grob G109B   6286   27.04.17
OY-XND   R Banks   Aston Down   10.05.19E

G-CKGH Grob G102 Club Astir II   5057C   06.09.06
BGA 5077/KGH, OO-ZVS
D C & K J Mockford   Lasham   *'KGH'*   26.04.19E

G-CKGI Ultramagic M-77C   77/300   11.05.17
LX-BGK   D J L Gillespie   Horsham   *'Maglite RCM'*   25.06.19E

G-CKGJ Nicollier HN.700 Menestrel II   xxxx   11.05.17
J R, S J & T M Rickett   (Brant Broughton, Lincoln)
Built by S J Rickett – project LAA 217-15369 (NF 11.05.07)

G-CKGK	Schleicher ASK 21	21766	21.12.05
	BGA 5079/KGK The Royal Air Force Gliding		
	& Soaring Association RAF Halton *'R28'*		26.10.19E
	Operated by Chilterns Gliding Centre		
G-CKGL	Schempp-Hirth Ventus-2cT	88/263	13.02.06
	BGA 5080/KGL, EI-152 T R Dews Keevil *'X4'*		05.03.18E
G-CKGM	Centrair 101A Pégase	101055	03.09.08
	BGA 5081/KGM, F-CFQR S France Usk *'760'*		09.04.19E
G-CKGO★	Textron 3000 Texan II	PM-111	01.06.18
	N2826B Affinity Flying Training Services Ltd		
	To MOD ZM324 21.01.19		
G-CKGS	Comco Ikarus C42 FB80	1705-7501	09.06.17
	GS Aviation (Europe) Ltd Clench Common		09.08.19P
G-CKGV	Schleicher ASW 28-18	28512	04.10.05
	BGA 5089/KGV, D-7062		
	A H Reynolds Long Mynd *'KGV'*		06.05.19E
G-CKGX	Schleicher ASK 21	21782	09.05.06
	BGA 5091/KGX Coventry Gliding Club Ltd		
	Husbands Bosworth *'KGX'*		27.04.19E
G-CKGY	Scheibe Bergfalke IV	5839	17.01.06
	BGA 5092/KGY, SE-TLL		
	B R Pearson tr North Devon Gliding Club Eaglescott		02.10.19E
G-CKHB	Rolladen-Schneider LS3	3316	28.03.06
	BGA 5095/KHB, D-2635		
	T J Milner Pocklington *'LS5'*		17.09.19E
G-CKHC	Glaser-Dirks DG-500/20 Elan	5E178W11	12.12.05
	BGA 5096/KHC, D-6401 J Donovan & P Fletcher		
	tr G-CKHC Group Shenington *'KHC'*		08.06.19E
	Built by Elan Tovarna Sportnega Orodja N.Sol.O		
G-CKHD	Schleicher ASW 27B	27222	01.12.05
	BGA 5097/KHD R L Smith Wycombe Air Park *'T4'*		16.11.19E
G-CKHE	Sportine Aviacija LAK-17AT	122	17.01.07
	BGA 5098/KHE, OM-0118		
	V S Bettle Wormingford *'X17'*		17.03.19E
	(Originally built as LAK-17A		
G-CKHH	Schleicher ASK 13	13171	15.03.06
	BGA 5101/KHH, LN-GAX		
	The South Wales Gliding Club Ltd Usk *'KHH'*		17.04.19E
G-CKHI	P&M QuikR	8761	26.05.17
	H A Robson tr G-CKHI Syndicate East Fortune		22.05.19P
G-CKHJ	Ultramagic H-31	31/18	06.07.17
	G A Board West Malling		18.07.19E
G-CKHK	Schempp-Hirth Duo Discus T	100/426	29.06.06
	BGA 5103/KHK		
	I Ashton tr Duo Discus Syndicate Chipping *'KHK'*		13.07.19E
G-CKHM	Centrair 101A Pégase	101A0359	23.11.05
	BGA 5105/KHM, F-CHDE		
	J A Tipler Husbands Bosworth *'KHM'*		31.03.19E
G-CKHN	PZL-Bielsko SZD-51-1 Junior	B-2142	17.03.06
	BGA 5106/KHN, OE-5614, SP-3612		
	The Nene Valley Gliding Club Ltd Upwood *'KHN'*		30.05.19E
G-CKHO	Flight Design CT-Supralight	E14-04-01	02.06.17
	J A Horn Greenhills Farm, Wheatley Hill		20.06.19P
G-CKHR	PZL-Bielsko SZD-51-1 Junior	B-1775	15.11.06
	BGA 5109/KHR, HB-1928		
	Wolds Gliding Club Ltd Pocklington *'KHR'*		28.03.19E
G-CKHS	Rolladen-Schneider LS7-WL	7043	20.12.05
	BGA 5110/KHS, PH-862, D-5157		
	M Lawson & D Wallis Wormingford *'KO'*		23.04.19E
G-CKHU	Kubícek BB17XR	1377	25.07.17
	The International Balloon Flight Company (Australia)		
	Pty Ltd Colhook Common, Petworth		18.06.19E
G-CKHV	Glaser-Dirks DG-100	77	08.02.08
	BGA 5112/KHV, HB-1331 R M Hale tr G-CKHV Trust		
	RAF Weston-on-the-Green *'KHV'*		12.08.19E
G-CKHW	Allstar PZL SZD-50-3 Puchacz	503.A.004.001	14.08.07
	BGA 5113 Derbyshire & Lancashire Gliding Club Ltd		
	Camphill *'KHW'*		29.03.19E
	Built by Allstar PZL Glider SP. z.o.o.		
3-CKHY	P&M HypeR GTR	8743	16.05.17
	G-93-11 E J Douglas East Fortune		16.05.19P

G-CKHZ	Aériane Swift Light PAS	108	08.06.17
	OE-6108 W True (Egerton, Malpas)		
	(IE 08.06.17)		
G-CKIE	Cessna 172S Skyhawk	172S11118	23.06.17
	LN-FTG, N9309N Western Air (Thruxton) Ltd Thruxton		07.06.19E
G-CKIF	Cessna 172S Skyhawk	172S11291	23.06.17
	LN-FTJ, N94900 Western Air (Thruxton) Ltd Thruxton		07.06.19E
G-CKIG	Flylight FoxTug	DA133-2	08.06.17
	D T Mackenzie Croft Farm, Defford		
	(IE 07.06.17)		
G-CKIH	Agusta A109S Grand	22047	28.06.17
	D-HKTG, N109GH, EI-NBG		
	Heli Delta BV (Sint Agatha, Netherlands)		31.01.20E
G-CKIN	Lindstrand LTL Series 1-105	048	24.05.17
	A M Holly Breadstone, Berkeley *'Riney'*		01.07.19E
G-CKIO	Piper PA-28-151 Cherokee Warrior	28-7615340	31.07.17
	SE-GNS W Ali Cranfield		16.01.20E
G-CKIP	Cessna 172N Skyhawk II	17273832	07.06.17
	CS-AYV, N5747J		
	Aero Clube de Leiria Leiria, Portugal		11.11.19E
G-CKIS	Aero Designs Pulsar XP	xxxx	19.05.17
	D R Piercy Eyres Field		
	Built by D R Piercy – project PFA 202-12702		
	(IE 04.10.18)		
G-CKIT	Cameron C-60	12124	17.07.17
	Turner Balloons Ltd Chipping Norton		17.07.19E
G-CKIU	Scheibe SF25C Rotax-Falke	44699	07.07.17
	D-KYNG The Burn Gliding Club Ltd Burn		07.07.19E
G-CKIX	Aeropro EuroFOX 3K	48717	19.09.17
	R G Mulford (Chatham)		14.09.19P
	Built by Ascent Industries Ltd; manufacturer's		
	s/n changed; tricycle u/c; originally allocated		
	as project BMAA/HB/686)		
G-CKIY	Best Off Skyranger Nynja 912S(1)	xxxx	17.07.17
	N Elahi & D Lamb Hunsdon		
	Built by D Lamb – project BMAA/HB/668 (IE 17.07.17)		
G-CKIZ	Eurofly Minifox	MF01	14.06.17
	N R Beale Sutton Meadows		
	Built by N R Beale (IE 14.06.17)		
G-CKJB	Schempp-Hirth Ventus bT	26	09.03.06
	BGA 5118/KJB, D-KBST R Cook & A P Cullen		
	tr KJB Group Husbands Bosworth *'KJB'*		06.12.18E
G-CKJC	Schempp-Hirth Nimbus-3T	6/57	16.01.06
	BGA 5119/KJC, D-KUPA, OY-KHX, D-KHXB		
	A C Wright Sutton Bank *'617'*		25.04.19E
G-CKJE	DG Flugzeugbau LS8-18	8498	06.09.06
	BGA 5121/KJE M D Wells Bidford *'321'*		23.12.19E
G-CKJF	Schempp-Hirth Standard Cirrus	414G	16.01.06
	BGA 5122/KJF, OY-XGW, D-9247		
	R W Skuse Eyres Field *'GW'*		14.04.19E
G-CKJG	Schempp-Hirth Cirrus VTC	153	11.10.05
	BGA 5123/KJG, EC-CKO		
	A R Blanchard & C Nobbs Rattlesden *'901'*		04.05.19E
G-CKJH	AMS-Flight DG-303 Elan	3E506	09.12.05
	BGA 5124/KJH Yorkshire Gliding Club (Proprietary) Ltd		
	Sutton Bank *'KJH'*		10.11.19E
	Built by AMS-Flight d.o.o.		
G-CKJI	Best Off Skyranger Nynja 912S(1)	xxxx	22.06.17
	Flylight Airsports Ltd Sywell		23.07.19P
	Built by Flylight Airsports Ltd – project BMAA/HB/676		
G-CKJJ	Glaser-Dirks DG-500 Elan Orion	5E249X79	29.03.06
	BGA 5125/KJJ, S5-AMS01		
	Ulster Gliding Club Ltd Bellarena *'KJJ'*		30.07.19E
	Built by AMS-Flight d.o.o.		
G-CKJL	Schleicher ASK 13	13468	18.09.06
	BGA 5127/KJL, D-2338		
	Lincolnshire Gliding Club Ltd Strubby *'KJL'*		21.11.19E
G-CKJM	Schempp-Hirth Ventus cT	120/394	10.11.05
	BGA 5128/KJM, D-KAHE, OH-781		
	K R Merritt tr G-CKJM Group Halesland *'7A'*		29.11.19E
G-CKJN	Schleicher ASW 20	20052	22.12.05
	BGA 5129/KJN, D-7964 R Logan Bellarena *'9E'*		01.03.19E

G-CKJO	Lindstrand LTL 9T	LTL-9T-002	23.06.17
	Lindstrand Technologies Ltd Oswestry		
	Tethered Gas Balloon (IE 23.06.17)		
G-CKJP	Schleicher ASK 21	21783	17.01.06
	BGA 5130/KJP, D-0001 The Royal Air Force		
	Gliding & Soaring Association Keevil *'R12'*		25.11.19E
	Operated by Bannerdown Gliding Club		
G-CKJR	Leonardo AW169	69052	12.07.17
	I-EASL Waypoint Asset Co 5A Ltd Redhill		06.11.18E
G-CKJS	Schleicher ASW 28-18E	28713	09.03.06
	BGA 5132/KJS, D-KHJW, BGA 5132, D-KHJW		
	J Eccles Husbands Bosworth *'420'*		05.04.19E
G-CKJT	Ultramagic H-42	42/23	03.07.17
	J Taylor Huddlesford, Lichfield *'Murlac'*		17.06.19E
G-CKJV	Schleicher ASW 28-18E	28725	25.01.06
	BGA 5145/KJV, D-KFAP, D-KOAB		
	A C Price Nympsfield *'AP'*		09.12.19E
G-CKJZ	Schempp-Hirth Discus bT	75	28.11.05
	BGA 5149/KJZ, OE-9367		
	D Lowe Wycombe Air Park *'E17'*		17.12.18E
G-CKKB	Centrair 101A Pégase	101A0209	08.03.06
	BGA 5151/KKB, SE-TZU		
	D M Rushton (Summerbridge, Harrogate) *'KKB'*		27.10.18E
G-CKKC	AMS-Flight DG-303 Elan Acro	3E509A41	08.05.06
	BGA 5152/KKC M P Ellis tr Charlie Kilo Kilo Charlie		
	Syndicate Burn *'KKC'*		28.05.19E
	Built by AMS-Flight d.o.o.		
G-CKKE	Schempp-Hirth Duo Discus T	103/429	30.01.06
	BGA5154/KKE, D-KOZZ P Foster Long Mynd *'57'*		10.04.19E
G-CKKF	Schempp-Hirth Ventus-2cxT	139/364	23.09.05
	BGA 5155/KKF		
	A R Macgregor Kingston Deverill *'306'*		07.12.19E
G-CKKG	TL 3000 Sirius	127 SI 151	31.07.17
	W F Hughes Cambridge		14.03.20E
	Built by W F Hughes – project LAA 386-15474		
G-CKKH	Schleicher ASW 27B	27231	20.10.05
	BGA 5157/KKH, D-0001		
	P L Hurd Dunstable Downs *'218'*		03.02.20E
G-CKKO	Ultramagic H-77	77/409	07.12.17
	I C Steward East Runton, Cromer		28.11.18E
G-CKKP	Schleicher ASK 21	21795	24.04.06
	BGA 5163/KKP		
	Bowland Forest Gliding Club Ltd Chipping *'BF1'*		13.12.19E
G-CKKR	Schleicher ASK 13	13065	05.12.05
	BGA 5164/KKR, PH-391		
	The Windrushers Gliding Club Ltd Bicester *'KKR'*		30.04.19E
G-CKKX	Rolladen-Schneider LS4-a	4827	19.01.06
	BGA 5169/KKX, PH-928, D-3529		
	B W Svenson tr 449 Syndicate Pocklington *'449'*		23.02.20E
G-CKKY	Schempp-Hirth Duo Discus T	124	19.01.06
	BGA 5170/KKY		
	P D Duffin tr G-CKKY Group Wormingford *'440'*		03.05.19E
G-CKLA	Schleicher ASK 13	13363	16.06.06
	BGA 5172/KLA, PH-1084, D-0857		
	Booker Gliding Club Ltd Wycombe Air Park *'KLA'*		05.04.19E
G-CKLC	Glasflügel Hornet	39	16.02.06
	BGA 5174/KLC, SE-TPL		
	W Ellis Wycombe Air Park *'W11'*		02.08.19E
G-CKLD	Schempp-Hirth Discus-2cT	1/2	27.10.05
	BGA 5175/KLD, D-KDCC		
	A Mutch tr 797 Syndicate Portmoak *'797'*		23.11.19E
G-CKLE	AutoGyro MTOsport 2017	M01459	19.09.17
	J R Wilkinson Beverley (Linley Hill)		26.04.19P
	Assembled Rotorsport UK as c/n RSUK/MT02/001		
G-CKLG	Rolladen-Schneider LS4	4264	07.08.06
	BGA 5178, F-CAEQ, D-5530		
	P M Scheiwiller Sandhill Farm, Shrivenham *'KLG'*		22.01.20E
G-CKLI	Piper PA-28R-180 Cherokee Arrow	28R-31079	12.07.17
	OY-BDI J R S Benson Exeter Int'l		25.01.19E
G-CKLK	AutoGyro MTOsport 2017	M01460	19.09.17
	D-MJGA R Peach Sandtoft		26.04.19P
	Assembled Rotorsport UK as c/n RSUK/MT02/002		

G-CKLL	Waco YKS-7	4680	04.07.17
	N19352 K D Pearce Oaklands Farm, Horsham		
	(NF 04.07.17)		
G-CKLN	Rolladen-Schneider LS4-a	4791	12.06.06
	BGA 5183/KLN, D-2823 J W Sage tr Army		
	Gliding Association AAC Wattisham *'A4'*		07.04.19E
	Operated by Anglia Gliding Club		
G-CKLP	Schleicher ASW 28-18E	28737	16.03.06
	BGA 5184/KLP, D-KOAB		
	P E Baker Gransden Lodge *'205'*		11.03.19E
G-CKLS	Rolladen-Schneider LS4	4637	29.06.06
	BGA 5186/KLS, D-6786		
	Wolds Gliding Club Ltd Pocklington *'KLS'*		14.07.19E
G-CKLT	Schempp-Hirth Nimbus-3/24.5	1	22.05.06
	BGA 5187/KLT, D-5052, EC-EBP, D-2111		
	G N Thomas AAC Wattisham *'GT'*		10.07.19E
G-CKLV	Schempp-Hirth Discus-2cT	20/27	08.02.06
	BGA 5188/KLV, D-KKFC		
	S Baker tr KLV Syndicate Lasham *'175'*		12.02.19E
G-CKLW	Schleicher ASK 21	21799	09.12.05
	BGA 5189/KLW Yorkshire Gliding Club		
	(Proprietary) Ltd Sutton Bank *'KLW'*		18.12.18E
G-CKLY	DG Flugzeugbau DG-1000T	10-66T6	03.10.05
	BGA 5191/KLY, D-KAAD R B Petrie & G Simpson		
	tr G-CKLY Flying Group Portmoak *'D6'*		01.06.19E
G-CKMA	DG Flugzeugbau LS8-st	8510	05.12.05
	BGA 5192/KMA		
	W J Morecraft (Wotton-under-Edge) *'KMA'*		18.09.19E
G-CKMB	Sportine Aviacija LAK-19T	018	07.03.07
	BGA 5193/KMB, LY-GJE		
	D J McKenzie Camphill *'KMB'*		10.02.20E
G-CKMD	Schempp-Hirth Standard Cirrus	31	08.11.05
	BGA5195/KMD, SE-TIX, D-0528		
	S A Crabb (Welford, Northampton) *'V12'*		01.06.10E
	(NF 15.03.18)		
G-CKME	DG Flugzeugbau LS8-st	8504	22.12.05
	BGA 5196/KME S M Smith Gransden Lodge *'M8'*		19.03.19E
G-CKMF	Centrair 101A Pégase	101038	08.05.06
	BGA 5197/KMF, F-CFQE		
	D L M Jamin Dunstable Downs *'KMF'*		10.08.19E
G-CKMG	Glaser-Dirks DG-100G Elan	E159G126	27.09.06
	BGA 5198/KMG, HB-1733		
	R A Johnson Long Mynd *'YY'*		30.03.13E
	Built by Elan Tovarna Sportnega Orodja N.Sol.O;		
	crashed Newmarket Heath 23.07.12 after colliding		
	with LS7 G-CGBY & substantially damaged		
	(NF 21.12.16)		
G-CKMH	Kavanagh EX-65	EX65-510	10.06.16
	Border Ballooning Ltd Plas Madoc, Montgomery		31.07.19E
G-CKMI	Schleicher K 8C	81006	06.09.06
	BGA5200/KMI, RAFGGA 562		
	V Mallon Kleve-Wisseler Dünen, Germany		01.06.11E
	(NF 02.11.18)		
G-CKMJ	Schleicher Ka 6CR	6109	15.08.06
	BGA 5201/KMJ, RAFGGA 555. D-8455		
	V Mallon Kleve-Wisseler Dünen, Germany		
	(NF 12.12.17)		
G-CKMK	Sportine Aviacija LAK-17AT	157	29.09.17
	(BGA 5972), D-KYBG, OE-9600, LY-GIS		
	B N Searle Saltby		
	(NF 29.09.17)		
G-CKML	Schempp-Hirth Duo Discus T	52/336	12.04.06
	BGA 5203/KML, PH-1256		
	N Clements tr G-CKML Group Long Mynd *'KA'*		18.03.19E
G-CKMM	Schleicher ASW 28-18E	28742	23.01.06
	BGA 5204/KMM		
	R G Munro Wycombe Air Park *'RM'*		24.04.19E
G-CKMO	Rolladen-Schneider LS7-WL	7007	15.12.05
	BGA 5206/KMO, PH-861, D-1264		
	R D Payne Nympsfield *'G7'*		26.03.20E
G-CKMP	Sportine Aviacija LAK-17A	173	17.01.06
	BGA 5207/KMP, LY-GMZ		
	J L McIver Falgunzeon *'KMP'*		10.11.18E

G-CKMT	Grob G103C Twin III Acro	34157	03.01.06
	BGA 5210/KMT, PH-1151, D-0659 Essex & Suffolk		
	Gliding Club Ltd Wormingford *'KMT'*		12.07.18E
G-CKMV	Rolladen-Schneider LS3-17	3329	08.11.05
	BGA 5212/KMV, D-6931		
	S Procter & M P Woolner North Hill *'KMV'*		26.03.20E
G-CKMW	Schleicher ASK 21	21798	09.12.05
	BGA 5213/KMW The Royal Air Force Gliding		
	& Soaring Association Cranwell North *'R18'*		23.02.19E
	Operated by Cranwell Gliding Club		
G-CKMX	Van's RV-7	74008	18.07.17
	S J Cummins City of Derry		13.11.19P
	Built by S J Cummins – project LAA 323-15138		
G-CKMZ	Schleicher ASW 28-18E	28716	06.01.06
	BGA 5216/KMZ, D-KBJM		
	I Donnelly tr Deeside ASW28 Group Aboyne *'J5'*		21.10.19E
G-CKNB	Schempp-Hirth Standard Cirrus	222	17.03.06
	BGA 5218/KNB, S5-3056, SL-3056, YU-4209		
	S Potter Waldershare Park *'505'*		02.06.19E
G-CKNC	Caproni Vizzola Calif A-21S	240	08.02.06
	BGA 5219/KNC, F-CEUE		
	K Walton tr Calif 240 Syndicate Lasham *'21S'*		24.04.19R
G-CKND	DG Flugzeugbau DG-1000T	10-76T15	12.06.06
	BGA 5220/KND		
	S Heaton tr KND Group Sutton Bank *'KND'*		10.06.19E
G-CKNE	Schempp-Hirth Standard Cirrus 75-VTC	199	27.07.06
	BGA 5221/KNE, S5-3057, SL-3057, YU-4293		
	G D E Macdonald Lasham *'KNE'*		24.06.15R
	Built by Vazduhoplovno Tehnicki Centar (NF 11.01.17)		
G-CKNF	DG Flugzeugbau DG-1000T	10-81T20	12.07.06
	BGA 5222/KNF, D-KTOA		
	R Johnson tr DG 1000 Syndicate Lasham *'KNF'*		15.06.19E
G-CKNG	Schleicher ASW 28-18E	28747	16.08.06
	BGA 5223/KNG, D-KOAB		
	M P Brockington tr NG209 Group Talgarth *'209'*		20.03.20E
G-CKNK	Glaser-Dirks DG-500 Elan Trainer	5E116T48	27.03.06
	BGA 5227/KNK, D-5661		
	Cotswold Gliding Club Aston Down *'KNK'*		04.03.19E
	Built by Elan Flight Ltd		
G-CKNL	Schleicher ASK 21	21811	15.05.06
	BGA 5228/KNL, D-0001		
	Buckminster Gliding Club Ltd Saltby *'KNL'*		02.04.19E
G-CKNM	Schleicher ASK 18	18037	04.07.06
	BGA 5229/KNM, PH-908, D-4539 Derbyshire		
	& Lancashire Gliding Club Ltd Camphill *'K18'*		01.04.19E
G-CKNO	Schempp-Hirth Ventus-2cxT	179/429	04.09.06
	BGA 5231/KNO, D-KOZZ		
	R T Starling Nympsfield *'KNO'*		31.03.19E
G-CKNR	Schempp-Hirth Ventus-2cxT	181/434	27.07.06
	BGA 5233/KNR, D-KIIH		
	R J Nicholls Husbands Bosworth *'KNR'*		11.08.19E
G-CKNS	Rolladen-Schneider LS4-a	4398	05.06.06
	BGA 5234/KNS, SE-UEP, OH-714		
	I R Willows Husbands Bosworth *'341'*		22.05.17E
G-CKNV	Schleicher ASW 28-18E	28749	24.07.06
	BGA 5237/KNV, D-KOAB G G Pursey		
	tr The KNV Group Dunstable Downs *'KNV'*		18.12.19E
G-CKNX	Ozone Buzz Z4 ML/Parajet V1 Macro Trike		
		BZ4ML-0-36C-015/000367	31.08.17
	I T Callaghan (Davidstow, Camelford)		
	(IE 04.10.18)		
G-CKNZ	Boeing 787-9	38895	18.01.18
	Norwegian Air UK Ltd London Gatwick		
	'Sir Freddie Laker'		17.01.20E
	Line No: 647		
G-CKOD	Schempp-Hirth Discus bT	11	01.12.06
	BGA 5245/KOD, HB-2157, D-KECC		
	D Ascroft & M W Talbot Nympsfield *'OD'*		09.01.20E
G-CKOE	Schleicher ASW 27-18 (ASG 29)	29024	20.02.08
	BGA 5246/KOE, D-9729		
	R C Bromwich Keevil *'290'*		13.03.19E
G-CKOF	Boeing 787-9	38786	05.02.18
	N1002R Norwegian Air UK Ltd London Gatwick		
	'Joan Miró'		04.02.20E
	Line No: 662		
G-CKOG	Boeing 787-9	63314	06.02.18
	Norwegian Air UK Ltd London Gatwick		
	'Paco de Lucia'		06.02.19E
	Line No: 664		
G-CKOH	DG Flugzeugbau DG-1000T	10-87T25	20.11.06
	BGA 5249/KOH		
	A D & P Langlands Shenington *'KOH'*		15.05.19E
G-CKOI	Sportine Aviacija LAK-17AT	183	06.12.06
	BGA 5250/KOI, LY-GQF		
	C G Corbett Dunstable Downs *'170'*		10.02.20E
G-CKOK	Schempp-Hirth Discus-2cT	50/67	17.04.07
	BGA 5252/KOK, D-KOZZ		
	P Topping tr G-CKOK Nympsfield *'X9'*		28.11.19E
G-CKOL	Schempp-Hirth Duo Discus xT	164/521	24.04.07
	BGA 5253/KOL, D-KIIH		
	P M Harmer tr Oscar Lima Syndicate North Hill *'OL'*		26.04.19E
G-CKOM	Schleicher ASW 27-18 (ASG 29)	29023	11.01.08
	BGA 5254/KOM, D-9529		
	P G Whipp Dunstable Downs *'LF'*		26.01.20E
G-CKON	Schleicher ASW 27-18E (ASG 29E)	29512	01.05.08
	BGA 5255/KON, D-KBJG		
	J P Gorringe Lasham *'XE'*		08.05.19E
G-CKOO	Schleicher ASW 27-18E (ASG 29E)	29519	01.05.08
	BGA 5256/KOO, D-KAAD		
	A Darlington tr G-CKOO Flying Group Lasham *'7'*		07.05.19E
G-CKOR	Glaser-Dirks DG-300 Elan	3E110	20.12.06
	BGA 5259/KOR, PH-768		
	D Jokinen & W Xu Strubby *'KOR'*		19.04.19E
	Built by Elan Tovarna Sportnega Orodja N.Sol.O		
G-CKOT	Schleicher ASK 21	21818	17.05.07
	BGA 5260/KOT, D-0001		
	Ulster Gliding Club Ltd Bellarena *'KOT'*		23.04.19E
G-CKOU	Sportine Aviacija LAK-19T	027	25.05.07
	BGA 5261/KOU, LY-GNP P Allingham & R M Wootten		
	(Christchurch & Wareham) *'1UP'*		15.05.19E
G-CKOW	Glaser-Dirks DG-505 Elan Orion	5E260X89	16.05.07
	BGA 5263/KOW		
	Southdown Gliding Club Ltd Parham Park *'KOW'*		25.02.20E
	Built by AMS-Flight d.o.o.		
G-CKOX	Glaser-Dirks DG-500 Elan Orion	5E258X87	04.09.07
	BGA 5264/KOX J G Kosak tr Seahawk Gliding Club		
	RNAS Culdrose *'N57'*		01.03.19E
	Built by AMS-Flight d.o.o.		
G-CKOY	Schleicher ASW 27-18E (ASG 29E)	29510	13.05.08
	BGA 5265/KOY, D-KNZG N P Woods		
	tr G-CKOY Group Husbands Bosworth *'S9'*		20.09.19E
G-CKOZ	Schleicher ASW 27-18E (ASG 29E)	29513	09.04.08
	BGA 5266/KOZ, D-KEEJ		
	E W Johnston Dunstable Downs *'G9'*		02.04.20E
G-CKPA	Sportine Aviacija LAK-19T	020	14.02.07
	BGA 5267/KPA, (BGA 5214), LY-GMV		
	M J Hargreaves Wormingford *'L19'*		03.05.19E
G-CKPC	Cameron Z-77	11170	07.09.17
	A A Osman Wembley		03.02.20E
G-CKPE	Schempp-Hirth Duo Discus	56	27.04.07
	BGA 5271/KPE, HB-3088 T World tr Portsmouth		
	Naval Gliding Centre Solent *'KPE'*		28.03.20E
G-CKPF	Champion 7GCBC Citabria	110	26.10.17
	D-EJSW, N1845G C F Dukes Bodmin		
	(IE 05.09.18)		
G-CKPG	Schempp-Hirth Discus-2cT	59	25.07.07
	BGA 5273/KPG, D-KOZZ A J Watson tr KPG		
	Syndicate Gransden Lodge *'KPG'*		18.04.19E
G-CKPJ	Neukom S-4D Elfe	411 AB	26.03.07
	BGA 5276/KPJ, D-4598		
	J Szladowski Camphill *'KPJ'*		
	Built by Jubi GmbH (IE 14.03.17)		
G-CKPK	Schempp-Hirth Ventus-2cxT	197	19.07.07
	BGA 5277/KPK, D-KIHH I C Lees Pocklington *'KPK'*		13.05.19E
G-CKPM	DG Flugzeugbau LS8-t	8517	01.06.07
	BGA 5279/KPM		
	S P Woolcock Gransden Lodge *'8T'*		17.05.19E

G-CKPN	PZL-Bielsko SZD-51-1 Junior	B-1927	01.02.08
	BGA 5280/KPN, HB-3036		
	Rattlesden Gliding Club Ltd Rattlesden *'KPN'*		08.05.18E
G-CKPO	Schempp-Hirth Duo Discus xT	171/532	19.07.07
	BGA 5281/KPO, D-KOZZ, (D-KDWF)		
	J S Forster tr KPO Syndicate Ringmer *'KPO'*		20.02.19E
G-CKPP	Schleicher ASK 21	21824	25.07.07
	BGA 5282/KPP, D-0001 Coventry Gliding Club Ltd		
	t/a The Gliding Centre Husbands Bosworth *'KPP'*		22.09.19E
G-CKPR	Cameron TR-65	12040	15.09.17
	Cameron Balloons Ltd Bristol BS3		19.03.19E
G-CKPS	Aérospatiale AS.350B2 Ecureuil	2109	30.10.17
	F-HBYD, F-ZBFC Helitrain Ltd Cotswold		23.07.19E
G-CKPU	Schleicher ASW 27-18E (*ASG 29E*)	29531	18.03.08
	BGA 5286/KPU		
	C S & M E Newland-Smith Dunstable Downs *'57'*		30.03.20E
G-CKPV	Schempp-Hirth Mini Nimbus B	63	20.06.07
	BGA 5287/KPV, PH-607, (PH-606)		
	N McLaughlin Lasham *'010'*		05.03.19E
G-CKPX	ZS Jezow PW-6U	78.04.03	25.09.07
	BGA 5289		
	North Wales Gliding Club Ltd Llantysilio *'KPX'*		03.03.19E
G-CKPY	Schempp-Hirth Duo Discus xT	174/540	30.11.07
	BGA 5290/KPY		
	C A Marren tr Duo-Discus Syndicate Lasham *'P7'*		28.12.19E
G-CKPZ	Schleicher ASW 20	20360	05.09.07
	BGA 5291/KPZ, D-4090		
	T C J Hogarth Halesland *'T93'*		27.06.19E
G-CKRB	Schleicher ASK 13	13292	13.09.07
	BGA 5293/KRB, D-0220 Derbyshire &		
	Lancashire Gliding Club Ltd Camphill *'KRB'*		17.05.19E
G-CKRC	Schleicher ASW 28-18E	28735	19.10.07
	BGA 5294/KRC, D-KUPC		
	J T Garrett (Upper Rissington, Gloucester)		30.04.19E
G-CKRD	Schleicher ASW 27-18E (*ASG 29E*)	29537	31.03.08
	BGA 5295/KRD R F Thirkell Lasham *'B3'*		09.04.19E
G-CKRE	La Mouette Samson/Atos-VR	15111502	21.09.17
	J S Prosser (Poundbury, Dorchester)		
	Built by J S Prosser (IE 21.09.17)		
G-CKRF	Glaser-Dirks DG-300 Elan	3E392	05.12.07
	BGA 5297/KRF, PH-923 G A King Talgarth *'KRF'*		06.04.20E
	Built by Elan Tovarna Sportnega Orodja N.Sol.O		
G-CKRH	Grob G103 Twin II	3596	22.11.07
	BGA 5299/KRH, F-CFYJ, D-3963		
	Staffordshire Gliding Club Ltd Seighford		28.02.19E
G-CKRI	Schleicher ASK 21	21835	14.05.08
	BGA 5300 Kent Gliding Club Ltd Challock *'KRI'*		21.03.19E
G-CKRJ	Schleicher ASW 27-18E (*ASG 29E*)	29544	30.05.08
	BGA 5301 J J Marshall Dunstable Downs *'KRJ'*		31.03.19E
G-CKRK	Guimbal Cabri G2	1210	09.10.17
	Lyza Aviation Ltd Redhill		09.11.19E
G-CKRL	Europa Aviation Europa XS	340	22.09.17
	D M Cope Leicester		
	Built by D M Cope – project PFA 247-13122 (NF 22.09.17)		
G-CKRO	Schempp-Hirth Duo Discus XLT	185/559	15.08.08
	BGA 5306/KRO B C Morris tr Duo Discus		
	Syndicate KRO Lasham *'KRO'*		18.04.19E
G-CKRR	Schleicher ASW 15B	15393	26.02.08
	BGA 5308/KRR, D-9288		
	D T Edwards Skelling Farm, Skirwith *'KRR'*		09.05.18E
G-CKRU	ZS Jezow PW-6U	78.04.07	21.05.08
	BGA 5311/KRU		
	Essex Gliding Club Ltd Ridgewell *'KRU'*		21.05.19E
G-CKRV	Schleicher ASW 27-18E (*ASG 29E*)	29555	22.08.08
	BGA 5312/KRV Z Marczynski Lasham *'607'*		07.02.20E
G-CKRW	Schleicher ASK 21	21337	22.05.08
	D-4833 The Royal Air Force Gliding		
	& Soaring Association RAF Marham *'R19'*		26.01.19E
	Operated by Fenland Gliding Club		
G-CKRX	ZS Jezow PW-6U	78.04.08	25.06.08
	BGA 5314/KRX		
	Essex Gliding Club Ltd Ridgewell *'KRX'*		17.05.19E

G-CKRZ	Best Off Skyranger Nynja LS 912S(1)	xxxx	13.10.17
	R J Clarke Westonzoyland		19.07.19P
	Built by R J Clarke – project BMAA/HB/693		
G-CKSC	Czech Sport Sportcruiser	09SC327	14.05.10
	S D Tonks tr Czechmate Syndicate Conington		16.10.19W
G-CKSD	Rolladen-Schneider LS8-a	8096	02.05.08
	(BGA 5320), N901T		
	J H Cox & K A Fox Husbands Bosworth *'131'*		29.10.19E
G-CKSE	Cessna 208B Grand Caravan	208B0660	03.11.17
	N208AF, C-GKRM, N73MM, N12249, (N5263U)		
	Wingglider Ltd Portimão, Portugal		11.12.19E
(G-CKSF)	Lange E1 Antares 18T	50T02	
	D-KANH Reserved 2019 (BGA 5322/G-CKSF *'X7'*)		
G-CKSK	Pilatus B4-PC11AF	004	21.07.08
	BGA 5327/KSK, HB-1103		
	K Steinmair (Pettenbach, Austria)		07.09.19E
G-CKSL	Schleicher ASW 15B	15285	04.09.08
	BGA 5328/KSL, D-2987 M P Featherstone		
	tr Sierra Lima Group (Arnold, Nottingham) *'KSL'*		15.11.19E
G-CKSM	Schempp-Hirth Duo Discus XLT	191	16.10.08
	BGA 5329/KSM		
	J M Herman & N J Hoare Wycombe Air Park *'KSM'*		11.10.19E
G-CKSP	Piper PA-28-180 Cherokee	28-7505171	17.11.17
	I-CAVI, N4436X, N9622N G Mannucci		
	tr Italian Wings A.S.D (Casale Monferrato, Italy)		09.07.18E
G-CKSR	Boeing Stearman D75N1 Kaydet (*PT-17*)	75-3855	30.11.17
	N56234, 42-15666, RCAF FJ805, 42-15666		
	C R Maher (Formby, Liverpool)		16.12.19E
	As '28' in USAAC c/s		
(G-CKSS)	Lange E1 Antares 18T	52T03	
	D-KAIJ Reserved 2019 (BGA 5334/G-CKSS *'895'*)		
G-CKST	Boeing Stearman B75N1 Kaydet (*N2S-3*)	75-7556	30.11.17
	N75745, Bu 07952 T W Gilbert Enstone		
	(NF 30.11.17)		
G-CKSU	Boeing Stearman A75 Kaydet (*PT-13B*)	75-871	30.11.17
	N58387, 41-811 T W Gilbert Enstone		
	(NF 29.11.17)		
G-CKSV	Boeing Stearman A75N1 Kaydet (*PT-13B*)	75-123	30.11.17
	N56901, 40-1566 T W Gilbert Enstone		
	(NF 30.11.17)		
G-CKSW	Cameron O-26	12108	10.07.17
	S G Whatley Bristol BS3		03.10.19E
G-CKSX	Schleicher ASW 27-18E (*ASG 29E*)	29562	02.12.09
	(BGA 5639), (BGA 5339/KSX), (BGA 5303), D-KXSX		
	M C Foreman & P J O'Connell Bicester *'F3'*		14.12.19E
G-CKSY	Rolladen-Schneider LS7-WL	7110	02.12.08
	BGA 5340/KSY, PH-902, D-1509 J F G Packer &		
	J P Shackleton tr CKSY Syndicate Portmoak *'SY'*		16.04.19E
G-CKTA	Aerochute Hummerchute	482	04.01.18
	G Stokes (Sutton Coldfield)		
	(IE 13.01.18)		
G-CKTB	Schempp-Hirth Ventus-2cxT	219/557	17.06.09
	(BGA 5343) M H Player Kingston Deverill *'M3'*		25.06.19E
G-CKTC	Schleicher Ka 6CR	6649	14.04.09
	BGA5344/KTC, EI-GLW, EI-128, D-1393		
	B Brannigan Bellarena		14.09.19E
G-CKTD	Colomban MC-30 Luciole	190	03.11.17
	D K Lawry Priory Farm, Tibenham		
	Built by D K Lawry – project LAA 371-15021		
	(NF 26.10.17)		
G-CKTE	Aeropro EuroFOX 3K	53317	01.02.18
	R J Bird (Birdham, Chichester)		15.02.20P
	Built by Ascent Industries Ltd; tricycle u/c		
G-CKTF	Van's RV-6A	24431	28.11.17
	F-PRVM, N542BW D Bennett (Lichfield)		28.10.19P
	Built by B Ward		
G-CKTG	Kubícek BB26E	1426	04.04.18
	Nova Balloon Services Ltd Bristol BS8		
	'Keep Calm And Fly Kubicek Balloons'		06.05.19E
G-CKTJ	Lindstrand LTL Racer 56	063	23.11.17
	A M Holly Breadstone, Berkeley		
	'L'Occitaine en Provence'		05.12.18E

G-CKTK Denney Kitfox Model 4-1200 Classic xxxx 10.11.17
I J M Donnelly Aboyne 02.12.19P
Built by I J M Donnelly – project PFA 172A-14404

G-CKTL Aerochute Hummerchute 484 29.01.18
R D Knight (Westport, Langport) 22.06.19P

G-CKTM Pitts S-1 1 06.11.17
N24JW R Farrer (Kempston, Bedford)
Built by J C Winthrop (NF 06.11.17)

G-CKTN BRM Bristell NG5 Speed Wing xxxx 09.11.17
T H Crow & E O Ridley Greenhills Farm, Wheatley Hill 20.12.19P
Built by T H Crow & E O Ridley – project LAA 385-15505

G-CKTP Ultramagic M-90 90/170 01.12.17
Proximm SpA Milan, Italy 28.05.19E

G-CKTR Tecnam P2006T 007 20.11.17
T7-JAR Romair Aviation Services & Consulting Ltd
Markopoulo-Attika, Greece 02.05.19E

G-CKTS Jodel D.92 Bébé 949 17.11.17
R A Yates Sibsey
Built by R A Yates – project LAA 054-15177 (NF 17.11.17)

G-CKTT P&M Quik GTR 8769 31.10.17
M K Ashmore Northrepps 16.10.19P

G-CKTU Ultramagic M-90 90/169 01.12.17
Proximm SpA Milan, Italy 28.05.19E

G-CKTV Lindstrand LTL Series 1-105 062 22.11.17
A M Holly Breadstone, Berkeley
'L'Occitaine en Provence' & '#RegentStreet' 05.12.18E

G-CKTW Cameron O-31 11991 13.12.17
M & S Mitchell Hertford 13.12.19E

G-CKTX Van's RV-7 xxxx 13.11.17
M M McElrea (Strabane)
Built by M M McElrea – project LAA 323-14871
(NF 13.11.17)

G-CKTY British Aerospace Avro 146-RJ100 E3324 14.12.17
OO-DWD, G-6-234 Qinetiq Ltd MoD Boscombe Down
(NF 22.03.18)

G-CKUB Cessna 560XL Citation XLS+ 560-6169 11.12.17
N898MS, XA-VGR, XA-UTZ, N52645
Catreus AOC Ltd Biggin Hill 16.01.20E

G-CKUE Supermarine 361 Spitfire LF.XVIe CBAF 10917 05.12.17
TB885 G F T van Eerd Biggin Hill
Built by Castle Bromwich as Spitfire LF.XIVe;
as 'TB885:3W-V' in RAF c/s; active 01.19
(NF 05.12.17)

G-CKUG Lindstrand LTL 9T LTL-9T-004 29.05.18
Magic Air Tenerife SL Adeje, Tenerife, Spain
Tethered Gas Balloon (IE 29.05.18)

G-CKUH Czech Sport Sportcruiser OC4092 05.01.18
EI-EHV R Stalker Cumbernauld 11.03.19P
Built by G Doody (as 'EI-AHV') 2009

G-CKUJ ATEC 212 Solo S030306A 05.01.18
Mission Capital Ltd (Manton, Marlborough)
(IE 03.05.18)

G-CKUK Ultramagic Shemilt Eco 50 50/16 23.01.18
Thames Valley Balloons Ltd Henley-on-Thames
(IE 09.07.18)

G-CKUL Ace Aviation Magic/As-Tec 13 xxxx 19.01.18
G L Logan (Great Bourton, Banbury)
Wing s/n AS13-264 (NF 02.07.18)

G-CKUM Swing XWing/Xcitor Paratrike 218/-929-42362 11.01.18
D Burton (Topsham, Exeter)
(IE 11.01.18)

G-CKUN Bareford DB-6R 1 17.01.18
D Bareford Morda, Oswestry
(IE 16.12.18)

G-CKUO Aeroprakt A-22LS Foxbat A22LS-308 18.01.18
P Gosney (Little Aston, Sutton Coldfield) 25.06.19P
Built by P Gosney – project LAA 317B-15487

G-CKUP Cameron Z-77 12158 11.03.18
Airship & Balloon Company Ltd
Henbury, Bristol *'audible'* 06.03.19E

G-CKUR Best Off Skyranger Swift 912(1) xxxx 05.10.17
R F Pearce (Uckfield)
Built by R F Pearce – project BMAA/HB/699
(NF 05.10.17)

G-CKUS Conway Viper DBC-01 16.02.18
D B Conway (Lower Upham Farm, Chiseldon)
Built by D B Conwayl noted 09.18 (NF 15.02.18)

G-CKUT Eurocopter EC155 B1 6655 02.03.18
OY-HJP, F-WWOI Macquarie Rotorcraft
Leasing Holdings Ltd (London EC2) 04.08.18E
Stored 02.19

G-CKUU Piper PA-23-250 Aztec E 27-4700 05.02.18
HA-YCD, OH-PKS, SE-FYI
G Scillieri (Ariccia, Rome, Italy) 11.05.18E

G-CKUV Colomban MC-30 Luciole 79 07.12.17
P J Leggo (Linton, Cambridge)
Built by P J Leggo – project LAA 371-15052 (NF 07.12.17)

G-CKUW Colt 21A 12169 14.03.18
British Broadcasting Corporation Salford *'60'* 20.03.19E

G-CKUX Ace Aviation Magic/Laser AM143 06.02.18
S C Stinchcombe (Knowstone, South Molton)
Trike s/n AM143 & wing s/n AL148 (NF 01.11.18)

G-CKUZ Boeing 737-46J 27213 20.04.18
N120WF, YR-SKI, A6-ESE, N213TH, EC-IZG
West Atlantic UK Ltd Coventry 30.07.19E
Line No: 2585

G-CKVB Eurocopter EC155 B1 6658 02.03.18
OY-HSL Macquarie Rotorcraft Leasing Holdings Ltd
(London EC2) 04.08.18E
Stored 02.19

G-CKVC AutoGyro Cavalon xxxx 16.02.18
H2E Energy Ltd (Christchurch) 25.02.19P
Assembled Rotorsport UK as c/n RSUK/CVLN/025

G-CKVD Rolladen-Schneider LS1-f 326 15.02.18
(BGA 5957), D-9291
G M Spreckley (Poulingny Notre Dame, France) 19.10.18E

G-CKVE Aero 31 AM9 002 13.02.18
A Marshall Great Sutton, Ellesmere Port
Built by A Marshall (NF 12.02.18)

G-CKVF Aeroprakt A-22LS Foxbat A22LS-300 30.01.18
R J Davey Old Manor Farm, Anwick 02.05.19P
Built by R J Davey – project LAA 317B-15464

G-CKVG Comco Ikarus C42 FB80 1803-7522 15.03.18
GS Aviation (Europe) Ltd Clench Common 14.03.19P
Assembled The Light Aircraft Company Ltd

G-CKVH Airbus AS.350B3 Ecureuil 8508 25.04.18
Kelair (IoM) Ltd (Andreas) 24.04.19E

G-CKVI Cameron A-120 12197 07.09.18
G B Davies Thorney, Peterborough 06.09.19E

G-CKVJ Titan T-51 Mustang M07921SOHK0120 21.02.18
Euro Aviation Ltd Rochester
Built by C Firth & D G Smith – project LAA 355-14781;
as '44-63684' in USAF c/s; under construction 10.18
(NF 21.02.18)

G-CKVL★ Textron 3000 Texan II PM-125 29.08.18
N2856B Affinity Flying Training Services Ltd
To MOD ZM327 21.01.19

G-CKVM Aeropro EuroFOX 3K 53618 20.03.18
M Skinner Henstridge 21.03.19P
Built by Ascent Industries Ltd; tricycle u/c

G-CKVN★ Textron 3000 Texan II PM-126 29.08.18
N2857B Affinity Flying Training Services Ltd
To MOD ZM328 21.01.19

G-CKVO★ Textron 3000 Texan II PM-127
21.09.18 N2858B Affinity Flying
Training Services Ltd
To MOD ZM329 21.01.19

G-CKVP AutoGyro Calidus xxxx 16.02.18
P M Bidston Ashcroft 15.04.19P
Assembled Rotorsport UK as RSUK/CALS/035

G-CKVR★ Textron 3000 Texan II PM-128
13.11.18 N2859B Affinity Flying
Training Services Ltd
To MOD ZM330 21.01.19

G-CKVS★ Textron 3000 Texan II PM-129 13.11.18
N2860B Affinity Flying Training Services Ltd
To MOD ZM331 21.01.19

G-CKVT Schempp-Hirth Ventus-3T   024 TS   12.02.19
           D-KKVT   S G Jones   Lasham   20.02.20E
           (IE 12.02.19)

G-CKVU★ Textron 3000 Texan II   PM-130   11.12.18
           N2872B   Affinity Flying Training Services Ltd
           To MOD ZM332 21.01.19

G-CKVV Piper PA-28-181 Cherokee Archer II   28-7890529   09.04.18
           HB-PCZ, N36763   London Transport Flying Club Ltd
           Fairoaks
           (IE 19.10.18)

G-CKVX Breezer Breezer M400   UL142   19.02.18
           M W Houghton   (Bakersfield Farm, Weldon)   22.02.19P
           Built by Ascent Industries Ltd

G-CKVY Aeropro EuroFOX 2K   54118   01.06.18
           P D Sibbons   Duxford   24.06.19P
           Built by Ascent Industries Ltd; tailwheel u/c

G-CKVZ AutoGyro Cavalon Pro   V00339   16.02.18
           AutoGyro GmbH   Hildesheim, Germany   01.05.19E
           Assembled Rotorsport UK as RSUK/CAVP/005

G-CKWA Boeing 787-9   63315   02.03.18
           N1005S   Norwegian Air UK Ltd   London Gatwick
           'Étienne de Montgolfier'   01.03.19E
           Line No: 673

G-CKWB Boeing 787-9   38788   08.03.18
           N1008S   Norwegian Air UK Ltd   London Gatwick
           'Arthur Collins'   07.03.19E
           Line No: 675

G-CKWC Boeing 787-9   38893   20.03.18
           Norwegian Air UK Ltd   London Gatwick
           'Robert Burns'   19.03.19E
           Line No: 680

G-CKWD Boeing 787-9   38789   24.04.18
           Norwegian Air UK Ltd   London Gatwick
           'Ernest Shackleton'   23.04.19E
           Line No: 698

G-CKWE Boeing 787-9   38790   22.05.18
           Norwegian Air UK Ltd   London Gatwick   *'Jane Austen'*   21.05.19E
           Line No: 691

G-CKWF Boeing 787-9   63316   29.06.18
           Norwegian Air UK Ltd   London Gatwick
           'Charles Lindbergh'   28.06.19E
           Line No: 715

G-CKWG Spacek SD-1 Minisport   247   26.02.18
           R Y Kendal   Eshott
           Built by R Y Kendal; noted 01.19 (IE 19.04.18)

G-CKWH Cameron Ronald-105   4047   11.04.18
           F-GPGO   L Bingley & D Bovington
           Whittlesey, Peterborough   *'McDonalds'*   13.07.19E

G-CKWI Tecnam P92-JS   026   16.04.18
           I-TEJG   G P Boano tr Associazione Sportiva Aeronautica
           (Novi Ligure, Italy)
           (NF 16.04.18)

G-CKWJ Lindstrand LBL 77A   623   02.03.18
           SX-MAW   C J Sanger-Davies   Hawarden CH5
           (NF 08.06.18)

G-CKWL Lindstrand LTL 130G   GA-033   30.04.18
           Aeronauts Productions Ltd   London W1
           (IE 19.06.18)

G-CKWM Van's RV-8   QB 1548   13.02.18
           C A G Schofield   Green Meadows, Harpsden
           Built by C A G Schofield – project LAA 303-14430
           (NF 13.02.18)

G-CKWN Boeing 787-9   63317   28.09.18
           Norwegian Air UK Ltd   London Gatwick
           'Oscar Wilde'   27.09.19E
           Line No: 755

G-CKWO Aeropro EuroFOX 912(S)   54018   08.03.18
           G J Slater   Clench Common   17.02.20P
           Built by G J Slater – project LAA 376-15522; tricycle u/c

G-CKWP Boeing 787-9   63318   27.11.18
           Norwegian Air UK Ltd   London Gatwick   *'Mark Twain'*   26.11.19E
           Line No. 772

G-CKWR Magni M16C Tandem Trainer   16181134   02.03.18
           Willy Rose Technology Ltd   Chiltern Park, Wallingford   04.03.19P

G-CKWS Boeing 787-9   63319   27.02.19
           Norwegian Air UK Ltd   London Gatwick
           'Felix Rodriguez de la Fuente'   26.02.20E
           Line No: 837

G-CKWT Boeing 787-9   63320   25.03.19
           Norwegian Air UK Ltd   London Gatwick   *'Harvey Milk'*
           Line No: 0827

G-CKWW Cameron Sport-50   12192   12.02.18
           Cameron Balloons Ltd   Bristol BS3   12.07.19E

G-CKWX Comco Ikarus C42 FB100 Bravo   1804-7536   19.03.18
           The Light Aircraft Company Ltd   Little Snoring   04.07.19P

G-CKWY Cameron Z-90   12189   05.06.18
           Balloon Team Jos Seghers   Breendonk, Belgium   07.06.19E

G-CKWZ Grob G109B   6270   05.01.18
           HB-2088   J I Staton   Enstone   17.08.19E

G-CKXA Cameron Sport-70   12209   12.07.18
           S Church   Almondsbury, Bristol   09.07.19E

G-CKXB★ Grob G109B   6379   12.04.18
           D-KNEI   P R Holloway
           To G-OSTX 05.02.19

G-CKXC Best Off Skyranger Swift 912(1)   xxxx   ··
           M T Dawson   (Penkridge, Stafford)
           Built by M T Dawson – project BMAA/HB/709
           (NF 04.04.18)

G-CKXD SZD-22C Mucha Standard   F-587   05.04.18
           SP-2165   G M Polkinghorne
           tr Eaglescott Mucha Group   Eaglescott
           (NF 05.04.18)

G-CKXE Cameron Sport-90   12205   18.06.18
           K D Peirce   Bodiam, Robertsbridge   13.06.19E

G-CKXF Auster J5G Cirrus Autocar   3062   16.04.18
           (N9741F), AP-AHK, VP-KKO
           R B Webber   Trenchard Farm, Eggesford
           (NF 16.04.18)

G-CKXG Cameron C-70   12213   15.06.18
           J T Wilkinson   Blackland, Calne   07.06.19E

G-CKXH Ultramagic M-65C   65/217   29.05.18
           D Bareford   Morda, Oswestry   28.06.19E

G-CKXI Mooney M.20E Super 21   1053   27.03.18
           EC-JNR, HB-DEU   G C Rogers   North Weald   14.09.19E

G-CKXJ Reims/Cessna F172M   F17201317   08.05.18
           D-EOGA   J A Kroger   (Hamburg, Germany)   10.10.19E

G-CKXK Cameron C-90   12219   01.08.18
           P Michiels   Temse, Belgium   23.07.19E

G-CKXL Sikorsky S-92A   920242   18.05.18
           C-GFCH, N242F   Bristow Helicopters Ltd
           Aberdeen Int'l   *'35 Years Service – Bryan Stott'*   28.06.19E

G-CKXM Aeropro EuroFOX 3K   54418   08.08.18
           J A Walker   Tarn Farm, Cockerham   03.08.19P
           Built by Ascent Indusries Ltd; tricycle u/c

G-CKXN Bombardier CL-600-2D24 CRJ900   15221   09.07.18
           OY-KFD   Triangle Symber Leasing DAC   Exeter Int'l   20.02.19E

G-CKXO★ Robinson R44 Clipper II   10403   22.05.18
           I-LTEC, LX-HCP, N109PG   Ariane SRL
           To I-NWSF 22.06.18

G-CKXP Aerochute Hummerchute   485   01.06.18
           G Stokes   (Sutton Coldfield)   23.06.19P

G-CKXR Lindstrand LTL Series 1-105   083   18.07.18
           B T Harris   Forestside, Rowlands Castle   11.07.19E

G-CKXT Kubícek BB22   246   11.06.18
           HB-QKJ   S Venegoni   Fagnano Olona, Varese, Italy   17.07.19E

G-CKXU Piper PA-28-181 Archer II   28-7990159   06.06.18
           HB-PDH, N2141D
           S P Adshead   (Audley, Stoke-on-Trent)
           (NF 06.06.18)

G-CKXV Piper PA-28-181 Archer III   2843424   06.06.18
           N181HP   S P Adshead   (Audley, Stoke-on-Trent)
           (NF 06.06.18)

G-CKXW Airbus AS.350B3 Ecureuil   8566   25.07.18
           Airbus Helicopters UK Ltd   Oxford   24.07.19E

G-CKXX ★ Piper PA-32R-301 Saratoga IIHP   3213016   24.04.18
N9141Z   Sky Business Ltd
To N9141Z 30.04.18

G-CKXY   Boeing Stearman A75N1 Kaydet (*PT-17*)   75-687   16.07.18
N67238, 41-927   T W Gilbert   Enstone
(*NF 16.07.18*)

G-CKXZ   Team HiMax 1700R   001   26.06.18
S Richens   Lower Upham Farm, Chiseldon
Built by S Richens (IE 23.11.18)

G-CKYA   AutoGyro MTOsport 2017   xxxx   09.07.18
Rotorsport Sales & Service Ltd
Wolverhampton Halfpenny Green   08.08.19P
Assembled Rotorsport UK as c/n RSUK/MTO2/006

G-CKYB   AutoGyro MTOsport 2017   xxxx   09.07.18
Rotorsport Sales & Service Ltd
Wolverhampton Halfpenny Green   19.07.19P
Assembled Rotorsport UK as c/n RSUK/MTO2/007

G-CKYC   Britten-Norman BN-2B-20 Islander   2314   26.06.18
Britten-Norman Aircraft Ltd   Solent
Active 01.19 (NF 26.06.18)

G-CKYD   AutoGyro MTOsport 2017   xxxx   09.07.18
Rotorsport Sales & Service Ltd
Wolverhampton Halfpenny Green   19.07.19P
Assembled Rotorsport UK as c/n RSUK/MTO2/008

G-CKYE   Airbus AS.350B3 Ecureuil   8573   30.08.18
Airbus Helicopters UK Ltd   Oxford   29.08.19E

G-CKYF   Aeropro EuroFOX 912(S)   54918   17.12.18
Wolds Gliding Club Ltd   Pocklington
Built by J R Paskins, A Rands, A Smith, A West &
S Wilkinson – project LAA 376-15545 (NF 17.12.18)

G-CKYG   Aeropro EuroFOX 3K   54518   13.06.18
F S Ogden   (Cuckfield, Haywards Heath)
Built by Ascent Industries Ltd; tricycle u/c (IE 13.06.18)

G-CKYH ★ Airbus EC130 T2   8574   29.08.18
Airbus Helicopters UK Ltd
To G-IPSE 21.12.18

G-CKYI   DAR Solo 120   120-UK-001   04.06.18
P J Kelsey tr Plaistows Farm DAR 120 Group
Plaistows Farm, St Albans
(*NF 01.06.18*)

G-CKYJ   Piper PA-28RT-201 Arrow IV   28R-7918021   02.07.18
SE-LAI, N3022K   G R Bedford & S I H Rizvi
tr Altus Flying Group   Biggin Hill   06.05.19E

G-CKYK   Van's RV-10   41404   03.07.18
R A Arrowsmith   (Bramhall, Stockport)
Built by R A Arrowsmith – project LAA 339-15356
(*NF 03.07.18*)

G-CKYL   Comco Ikarus C42 FB80   1806-7540   20.08.18
L M Cox   (Billingshurst)   15.08.19P
Assembled The Light Aircraft Company Ltd

G-CKYM   Supermarine 361 Spitfire LF.IX   CBAF 10257   07.01.19
Soviet AF, SM639   M A Bennett   (Godalming)
(*NF 07.01.19*)

G-CKYN   Colomban MC-15 Cri-Cri   xxxx   16.07.18
M Hajdukiewicz   (Chalfield Hill, Stroud)
Built by M Hajdukiewicz – project PFA 133-11258
(*NF 16.07.18*)

G-CKYO   Schempp-Hirth Ventus-3T   041 TS   12.03.19
C P A Jeffery   (Debden, Saffron Walden)
(*IE 12.03.19*)

G-CKYP   AgustaWestland AW139   41339   15.10.18
VH-ZFO, N433SH
Bristow Helicopters Ltd   Norwich Int'l   13.12.19E

G-CKYR   AgustaWestland AW139   41322   16.08.18
VT-HLO, RP-C2139, N480SH
Vertical Aviation No1 Ltd   Biggin Hill   17.01.20E

G-CKYS   P&M Quik GT450   8779   20.07.18
P G Eastlake   Hunsdon   23.07.19P

G-CKYT   AutoGyro Cavalon   xxxx   17.07.18
A Sinclair   Inverness   12.08.19P
Assembled Rotorsport UK as c/n RSUK/CVLN/027

G-CKYU   Lindstrand LBL 31A   140   20.07.18
OO-BXX   G B Dey   Frogmore, St Albans   11.10.19E

G-CKYV   AutoGyro Cavalon   RSUK/CVLN/026   30.04.18
G A Speich   Wolverhampton Halfpenny Green   16.05.19P
Assembled Rotorsport UK Ltd as c/n RSUK/CVLN/026

G-CKYW ★ Balony Kubicek BB20XR HAB   1489   23.08.18
Global Ballooning Australia Pty Ltd
To VH-… 11.01.19

G-CKYX   Cameron O-31   12246   05.09.18
W Rousell & J Tyrrell   Wollaston, Wellingborough   02.09.19E

G-CKYZ   Eurofly Minifox   18007   27.08.18
F Kratky   (Chalfont St Giles)
Built by Airplay Aircraft Ltd (IE 27.08.18)

G-CKZA   TAF Sling 4   xxxx   13.04.18
J Smith   (London W1A)
Built by J Smith – project LAA 400-15510 (NF 13.04.18)

G-CKZB   Spacek SD-1 Minisport   274   07.08.18
C J Lines   Low Hill Farm, North Moor, Messingham
Built by C J Lines (NF 05.09.18)

G-CKZD   Aeropro EuroFOX 3K   55318   08.11.18
Breeze Aviation Services Ltd   Sherburn-in-Elmet   24.11.19P
Built by Ascent Industries Ltd

G-CKZE   Medway SLA 80 Executive   180418   30.04.18
The Light Aircraft Company Ltd   Little Snoring   20.04.19P

G-CKZF   P&M Quik GTR   8621   04.06.18
A-012 (Finland)   T Southwell   (Spalding)   20.05.19P

G-CKZG   Parajet Explorer/Apco Cruiser 550   119366BA   09.08.18
G B N Cardozo   (Lawn Farm, Gillingham)
Built by Apco Aviation Ltd (NF 23.08.18)

G-CKZH   Van's RV-12   120921   20.08.18
N11SQ   M N & N D Stannard   RAF Henlow
Built by B McGregor (IE 11.02.19)

G-CKZI   Techpro Merlin 100UL   HV-103   16.04.18
J L Parker   Rochester
(*IE 21.12.18*)

G-CKZJ   Kubíček BB26E   1483   16.10.18
M R Crossley   Old Newton, Stowmarket   04.11.19E

G-CKZK ★ Cessna 172N Skyhawk   17272921   09.05.18
N101VV   Skyhawk Group Ltd
To N101VV 06.06.18

G-CKZL   Piper PA-28RT-201 Arrow IV   28R-7918215   21.09.18
PH-TWP, N2910W, (PH-TWP), N2910W, (PH-NDE),
N2910W   Magna Carta Aviation Ltd   (London E10)   10.04.19E

G-CKZM   Aerochute Hummerchute   489   22.08.18
G J Pemberton   (Lincoln)   06.10.19P

G-CKZN   Bombardier CL-600-2D24 CRJ900LR   15237   30.08.18
OY-KFG   Triangle Symber Leasing DAC
Maastricht Aachen, Netherlands   23.01.19E

G-CKZO   Bombardier CL-600-2D24 CRJ900LR   15242   30.08.18
OY-KFI, C-GIAP   Triangle Symber Leasing DAC
Maastricht Aachen, Netherlands   17.08.19E

G-CKZP   TL 2000UK Sting Carbon S4   18 ST 476   06.08.18
F Pilkington   (Macclesfield)   26.11.19P
Built by F Pilkington – project LAA 347A-15543

G-CKZR   Steen Skybolt   HH-3   19.09.18
N856HH   N Musgrave   RAF Mona
Built by D Hancock (NF 19.09.18)

G-CKZS   Lindstrand 197T   GA-032   04.09.18
Lindstrand Technologies Ltd   Oswestry
Tethered Gas Balloon; noted Cardington 03.19 (NF 04.09.18)

G-CKZT   Piper PA-28-235 Cherokee   28-10431   23.12.09
D-EBWE, N8874W   U Chakravorty   Rochester   21.11.19E

G-CKZU   Air Création Tanarg/Bionix 13   A18029-18039   17.09.18
C R Buckle   Blackmoor Farm, Aubourn
(*IE 17.09.18*)

G-CKZV   Piper PA-28-161 Warrior III   2842068   10.01.19
N268ML, (G-   ), N268ML, N268ND
V2 Aircraft Leasing Ltd   Elstree
(*NF 10.01.19*)

G-CKZW ★ Robinson R44 Cadet   30030   14.09.18
N40411   Alidaunia SRL
To I-LIDH 12.11.18

G-CKZX   Glasair GlaStar Max-4   5374   22.10.18
N98MX   P M Harrison   Strubby
Built by M L Calkin (NF 22.10.18)

G-CKZY	HpH Glasflügel 304 eS Shark	089-MS	26.06.18
	(BGA 5969), OK-0089		
	M M Heslop Parham Park *'ZY'*		08.07.19R
G-CKZZ	Magni M16C Tandem Trainer	16181334	16.04.18
	O L B Brooking North Weald		01.05.19P

G-CLAA – G-CLZZ

G-CLAA	Boeing 747-446F	33749	23.10.15
	VQ-BJB, N402AL, JA402J		
	Cargologicair Ltd London Stansted		01.11.19E
	Line No: 1352		
G-CLAB	Boeing 747-83QF	60119	30.06.16
	N841BA Cargologicair Ltd London Stansted		06.07.19E
	Line No: 1520		
G-CLAC	Piper PA-28-161 Warrior II	28-8116241	18.05.87
	N8396U J M Holley tr G-CLAC Group Blackbushe		09.05.19E
G-CLAD	Cameron V-90	11753	17.06.13
	A E Davies t/a Adeilad Cladding Llanwrda *'Ac-Clad'*		16.07.19E
G-CLAE	Boeing 747-4EVF	35170	12.10.18
	VQ-BUU, N368DF, OE-IBG, B-2439		
	Cargologicair Ltd London Stansted		22.10.19E
	Line No. 1376		
G-CLAI	Comco Ikarus C42 FB100 Bravo	1805-7538	01.08.18
	R S O'Carroll Kernan Valley, Tandragee		15.07.19P
G-CLAJ	Robin DR.400-180R Remorqueur	962	19.07.18
	OO-VZZ, D-EEJA K Verbinnen (Schoten, Belgium)		
	(IE 31.01.19)		
G-CLAK	TLAC Sherwood Scout	TLAC-2-001	20.06.18
	The Light Aircraft Company Ltd Little Snoring		17.07.19P
	Tricycle u/c		
G-CLAL	Comco Ikarus C42 FB100	1608-7468	08.12.16
	C I Law Strubby		11.12.19P
	Assembled Red Aviation		
G-CLAM	DAR Solo 120	120-UK-002	25.07.18
	P J Kelsey tr Ferrari Flying Group (Edinburgh EH12)		
	(NF 24.07.19)		
G-CLAO	Van's RV-7	74405	12.09.18
	M A Carter (Highclere, Newbury)		
	Built by M A Carter – project LAA 323-15307		
	(NF 12.09.18)		
G-CLAP	Cessna 152	15281555	18.06.18
	SP-KFH, N65443 Swiftair Maintenance Ltd Elstree		21.05.19E
	Operated by Flight Training London Ltd		
G-CLAT	P&M QuikR	8777	31.07.18
	L M Caldwell tr G-CLAT Syndicate East Fortune		30.07.19P
G-CLAU	Airbus AS.350B3 Ecureuil	8597	18.10.18
	Airbus Helicopters UK Ltd Oxford		17.10.19E
G-CLAV	Europa Aviation Europa	060	11.10.02
	C Laverty Glenforsa, Isle of Mull		19.06.19P
	Built by C Laverty – project PFA 247-12641; tailwheel u/c		
G-CLAX	Jurca MJ.5 Sirocco	xxxx	22.04.99
	G-AWKB G S Williams St Athan		
	Built by G D Claxton – project PFA 2204 (NF 24.08.15)		
G-CLAY	Bell 206B-3 JetRanger III	4409	16.09.02
	G-DENN, N75486, C-GFNO Tiger Properties (Kent) Ltd		
	Paynetts Farm, Goudhurst		02.08.19E
G-CLAZ	AutoGyro Cavalon	xxxx	04.09.18
	Detoney Ltd (Bromsberrow, Ledbury)		08.10.19P
	Assembled Rotorsport UK Ltd as c/n RSUK/CVLN/029		
G-CLBA	Boeing 747-428F	32870	24.04.17
	OE-IFP, N902AR, F-GIUD		
	Cargologicair Ltd London Stansted		09.04.19E
	Line No: 1344		
G-CLBB★	Team Mini-Max 91	659	21.08.18
	J Owen		
	Cancelled 19.12.18 by CAA		
	Built by J Owen – project PFA 186-12676		
G-CLBC	Aérospatiale SA.342M Gazelle	1615	26.09.18
	French Army 3615:GJH		
	S Atherton Crab Tree Farm, Deighton		
	(NF 26.09.19)		
G-CLBD	Cameron Z-120	12253	02.01.19
	M E Dunstan Bath		13.12.19E

G-CLBE★	Airbus AS.350B3 Ecureuil	8624	22.11.18
	Airbus Helicopters UK Ltd		
	To G-HIDE 20.12.18		
G-CLBG	Van's RV-7	73808	02.07.18
	T Groves (Lee-on-the-Solent)		
	Built by T Groves – project LAA 323-15497 (NF 02.07.18)		
G-CLBH	Lindstrand LTL Boot		21.05.18
	A M Holly Breadstone, Berkeley *'#HunterOriginal'*		04.07.19E
G-CLBI	Extra EA.300/S	008	30.01.19
	D-EXML, N8TH, F-GJRG, D-ETXF, (D-EJKS)		
	Airdisplays.com Ltd Little Gransden		
	(NF 30.01.19)		
G-CLBJ	Cessna 172S Skyhawk SP	172S10705	17.09.18
	PH-DSG, N6239H		
	Atlantic Flight Training Ltd Cork, RoI		15.08.19E
G-CLBK	Ultramagic H-77	77/420	20.11.18
	M A Wrigglesworth Dorking		07.12.19E
G-CLBM	Robinson R44 Cadet	30040	24.10.18
	Startrade Heli GmbH & Co KG Burbach, Germany		29.10.19E
G-CLBN	P&M QuikR	8782	23.11.18
	N J Lister Sutton Meadows		12.11.19P
G-CLBO★	MBB Bolkow Bo.105P	6059	26.10.18
	86+59 German Army AB Airflight Gmbh		
	To RA-…. 13.11.19		
G-CLBP	Lindstrand LTL Series 1-180	094	06.11.18
	Lindstrand Asia Ltd Oswestry		21.01.20E
G-CLBR	Parajet Explorer/Apco Cruiser 500	110078BA	01.11.18
	G B N Cardozo (Lawn Farm, Gillingham)		
	(NF 01.11.18)		
G-CLBS	Flylight FoxTug	DA156	15.01.19
	R Davies, A M Keyte & D C Richardson		
	tr Cambridge Aerotow Club Sutton Meadows		
	(IE 15.06.19)		
G-CLBT	BRM Bristell NG5 Speed Wing	22	02.10.18
	C W Thompson (Lathom, Ormskirk)		
	Built by C W Thompson – project LAA 385-15547		
	(NF 02.10.18)		
G-CLBU★	Piper PA-34-200T Seneca II	34-8170048	07.11.18
	I-NOPA, N8303U S Zanone		
	To N8303U 15.03.19		
G-CLBV	Aériane P Swift	A60C10	13.11.18
	91-RV A Nelson (Great Billing, Northampton)		
	(IE 13.11.18)		
G-CLBW	Airbus AS.350B3 Ecureuil	8635	04.12.18
	Airbus Helicopters UK Ltd Oxford		03.12.19E
G-CLBX	Messerschmitt Bf 109E-4/7	0854	12.11.18
	Luftwaffe C T Charleston (Great Horkesley, Colchester)		
	Built by Erla Maschinenwerk GmbH (NF 12.11.18)		
(G-CLBY)	Robinson R44 Raven II	11711	
	F-GXRP,D-HEXE Reserved for possible use 2019		
G-CLBZ	Reims FR172J Rocket	FR17200490	08.02.18
	I-BZEB, D-EDCC, D-EECC		
	E Marinoni tr Aero Club Bolzano (San Giacomo, Italy)		06.08.19E
G-CLCA	Extra EA.300/LC	LC082	03.01.19
	The Aerobatics Company LLP (Suckley, Worcester)		15.01.20E
G-CLCB	Airbus AS.350B3 Ecureuil	8632	15.01.19
	F-WJXZ Airbus Helicopters UK Ltd Oxford		14.01.20E
G-CLCC	Cameron Sport-90	12234	18.07.18
	Cameron Balloons Ltd Bristol BS3		
	'Cameron Balloons'		06.12.19E
G-CLCD	Advance Iota Mk 4	004	08.08.18
	S Siddiqui (Mullingar, Co Westmeath, RoI)		
	Built by S Siddiqui (NF 08.08.18)		
G-CLCE	Airbus MBB BK117 D-2	20175	13.02.19
	D-HADV Airbus Helicopters UK Ltd Oxford		12.02.20E
G-CLCF	Airbus MBB BK117 D-2	20257	27.03.19
	D-HADL Airbus Helicopters UK Ltd Oxford		
G-CLCH	AutoGyro MTOsport 2017	xxxx	21.08.18
	Rotorsport UK Ltd Wolverhampton Halfpenny Green		03.01.20P
	Assembled Rotorsport UK Ltd as c/n RSUK/MTO2/010		
G-CLCI	AutoGyro MTOsport 2017	xxxx	21.08.18
	Rotorsport UK Ltd Wolverhampton Halfpenny Green		03.10.20P
	Assembled Rotorsport UK Ltd as c/n RSUK/MTO2/009		

G-CLCJ   CCF T-6 Harvard Mk.4M   -   14.02.19
F-AZQK, Italian AF MM53796   T W Gilbert   Enstone
Built by Canadian Car & Foundry Co (NF 14.02.19)

G-CLCL   Van's RV-7   74410   14.09.18
R M Powell   (Pangbourne, Reading)
Built by R M Powell – project LAA 323-15313
(NF 14.09.18)

G-CLCM   Lambert Mission M108   108-010   12.09.18
K L Shern, L D L & V Soutter   (East Grinstead & Bideford)
Built by K L Shern, L D L & V Soutter
– project LAA 370-15559 (NF 12.09.18)

G-CLCN   Sikorsky S-92A   920287   29.03.19
N287Y   Bristow Helicopters Ltd
Aberdeen International

G-CLCO   Groppo Trail Mk.2   134/93   25.06.18
C M Barnes   (Dickleburgh, Diss)
Built by C M Barnes – project LAA 372-15418
(NF 25.06.18)

G-CLCP   Bell 505 Jet Ranger X   65168   14.01.19
C-GLZH   D M Hunter   (Thorner. Leeds)
(IE 14.01.19)

G-CLCR   Cameron Z-90   11454   16.01.19
D-OGER   A2Z Projects BVBA   Lochristi, Belgium
(NF 16.01.19)

G-CLCS   Supermarine 361 Spitfire HF.IX   CBAF IX 3248   20.02.19
RK912   Propshop Ltd   Duxford
(NF 20.02.19)

G-CLCT   Supermarine 379 Spitfire F.XIVe   6S-663419   20.02.19
RN203   Propshop Ltd   Duxford
(NF 20.02.19)

G-CLCU   Robinson R44 Raven II   12470   04.03.19
D-HHRO   D M McGarrity   (Newtownabbey)
(IE 04.03.19)

G-CLCV   AutoGyro Cavalon   xxxx   21.08.18
Rotorsport UK Ltd   Wolverhampton Halfpenny Green   03.01.20P
Assembled Rotorsport UK Ltd as c/n RSUK/CVLN/030

G-CLCW   Zenair CH.701SP   7-9502   18.01.19
C W Wilkins   (Everdon, Daventry)
Built by C W Wilkins – project LAA 187-14397
(NF 18.01.19)

G-CLCX★   Robinson R44 Clipper II   11130   22.02.19
I-AGAC   F Falasca
To N........ 06.03.19

G-CLCX   Robinson R44 Clipper II   11130   22.02.19
I-AGAC   F Falasca   (Rome, Italy)
(NF 22.02.19)

G-CLCZ   Ultramagic M-105   105/226   11.03.19
Skyview Ballooning Ltd t/a Kent Ballooning
Saltwood, Hythe
(NF 11.03.19)

G-CLDA   Lambert Mission M108   108-011   04.03.19
C A & D R Ho   (Napley Heath, Market Drayton)
Built by D R Ho – project LAA 370-15578
(NF 04.03.19)

G-CLDB   Evektor EV-97 Eurostar SL 912(1)   xxxx   15.01.19
R W Thorpe   (Farnham Royal, Slough)
Built by R W Thorpe – project BMAA/HB/713
(NF 15.01.19)

G-CLDC   Evektor EV-97A Eurostar   3201   01.02.19
H M & M A Child   (Leeds)
Built by M A Child – project LAA 315A-14907
(NF 01.02.19)

G-CLDD   Piper PA-32R-300 Cherokee Lance   32R-7780248   10.10.18
D-EEMY, N2489Q   J L Mossman   (London N1)
(NF 10.10.18)

G-CLDE   Avtech Jabiru UL-450   0363   15.02.19
E Bentley   Morgansfield, Fishburn
Built by E Bentley – project PFA 274-13645
(NF 15.02.19)

G-CLDF   AutoGyro MTOsport 2017   xxxx   08.02.19
Rotorsport UK Ltd   Wolverhampton Halfpenny Green
Assembled Rotorsport UK as c/n RSUK/MT02/011
(IE 08.02.19)

G-CLDG   Eurofly Snake/Aeros Fox 13T   18008   05.11.18
J Harbottle   (Amersham)
Assembled Airplay Aircraft Ltd; official
c/n 'DA153' relates to Sailwing) (IE 05.11.18)

G-CLDH   Pietenpol Air Camper   0140   28.02.19
S Eustace & C R Harrison   Monewden
Built by R Arthur – project PFA 047-13437 (NF 28.02.19)

G-CLDI   Just SuperSTOL   JA 471 10 15   13.11.18
Paludis Ltd   (Hathersage)
Built by E Marsh – project LAA 397-15465 (NF 13.11.18)

G-CLDL   Robin DR.400-180R Remorqueur   968   11.01.19
D-EEJB   Lasham Gliding Society Ltd   Lasham
(IE 17.01.19)

G-CLDM   Best Off Skyranger Swift 912(2)   xxxx   08.02.19
Skyranger One Ltd tr Skyranger Swift 2 Group   Balado
Built by J Alexander, K Edwards & C Logan
– project BMAA/HB/715 (NF 08.02.19)

G-CLDN   Best Off Skyranger Swift 912(1)   xxxx   20.11.18
A R Pluck   Damyns Hall, Upminster
Built by A R Pluck – project BMAA/HB/710 (NF 20.11.18)

G-CLDO   BRM Bristell NG5 Speed Wing   321   15.10.18
R Potter   Popham
Built by R Potter – project LAA 385-15555;
cleared to fly 13.02.19 (IE 08.02.19)

G-CLDP   AutoGyro Calidus   xxxx   14.02.19
Rotorsport Sales & Service Ltd
Wolverhampton Halfpenny Green
Assembled Rotorsport UK as c/n RSUK/CALS/039
(IE 14.02.19)

G-CLDR   Raj Hamsa X'Air Hawk   1256   18.03.19
D R Western & J White   (Highbridge & Burnham-on-Sea)
Built D R Western & J White – project LAA 340-15604
(IE 18.03.19)

G-CLDT   Aeropro EuroFOX 3K   56019   11.03.19
L S & S B Williams   (Headcorn, Ashford)
Built Ascent Industries Ltd (IE 11.03.19)

G-CLDU   Robinson R44 Raven II   12426   25.03.19
EI-JOR   AT Aviation Sales Ltd   Dunkeswell
(IE 25.03.19)

G-CLDV   AutoGyro Cavalon   xxxx   08.02.19
Rotorsport UK Ltd   Wolverhampton Halfpenny Green
Assembled Rotorsport UK as c/n RSUK/CVLN/032
(IE 08.02.19)

G-CLDW   AutoGyro Calidus   xxxx   29.01.19
I Ingram   Perth
Assembled Rotorsport UK as c/n RSUK/CALS/038
(IE 29.01.19)

G-CLDX   Boeing Stearman B75N1 Kaydet (N2S-3)   75-6617   25.03.19
N65634, USN 07013   T W Gilbert   Enstone
Officially registered as type 'A75N1' (NF 25.03.19)

G-CLDY   Spacek SD-1 Minisport   287   19.03.19
J R Grundy   (Douglas, Isle of Man)
Built J Krajca (NF 19.03.19)

G-CLDZ   AutoGyro Calidus   xxxx   03.01.19
P A Barnard & J Scrymgeour-Wedderburn
t/a Gyro Partnership   Perth   27.01.20P
Assembled Rotorsport UK as c/n RSUK/CALS/037

G-CLEA   Piper PA-28-161 Warrior II   28-7916081   28.08.80
N30296   Freedom Aviation Ltd   Cotswold   16.02.20E

G-CLEB   Cameron A-315   11940   26.03.19
CC-APJ   Attacama Holdings Pty Ltd
Docklands, Victoria, Australia

G-CLEC   Cameron A-450LW   11941   26.03.19
CC-APL   Attacama Holdings Pty Ltd
Docklands, Victoria, Australia

G-CLED   Cameron A-450LW   11942   26.03.19
CC-APM   Attacama Holdings Pty Ltd
Docklands, Victoria, Australia

G-CLEE   Rans S-6-ES Coyote II   0600.1373 ES   29.06.01
P S Chapman   Ince   24.04.17P
Built by R Holt – project PFA 204-13670; tricycle u/c
(IE 17.09.18)

G-CLEH   Aeroprakt A-32 Vixxen   A32065
28.03.19
C A Pollard   St Michaels
Project LAA 411-15590

G-CLEI	Aeropro EuroFOX 2K	55719	20.02.19
	R M Cornwell Luke's Field, Marden		
	Built by Ascent Industries Ltd (NF 20.02.19)		
G-CLEL	Raj Hamsa X'Air 582(11)	601	08.01.19
	L Edwards (Duloe, Liskeard)		
	Built by E Girling – project BMAA/HB/521 (NF 08.01.19)		
G-CLEM	Bölkow BÖ.208A2 Junior	561	22.09.81
	G-ASWE, D-EFHE		
	D R Smith tr G-CLEM Group RNAS Yeovilton		17.05.11P
	(IE 18.09.18)		
G-CLEO	Zenair CH.601HD Zodiac	6-9075	09.08.99
	K M Bowen Upfield Farm, Whitson		
	Built by K M Bowen – project PFA 162-13500		
	(NF 18.07.18)		
G-CLER	Eurofly Snake/Aeros Fox 13TL	DA162	19.02.19
	J Harbottle (Amersham)		
	(IE 19.02.19)		
G-CLES	Schleicher ASW 27-18E (*ASG 29E*)	29606	18.01.10
	(BGA 5644), (BGA 5622)		
	A P Brown Dunstable Downs *'AB'*		12.12.19E
G-CLEU	Glaser-Dirks DG-200	2-14	17.11.09
	(BGA 5627), HB-1407 D T Freeman Aston Down		31.05.19E
G-CLEV	Comco Ikarus C42 FB80	1811-7551	05.03.19
	A R Hughes tr The Clever Group (Fyfield, Marlborough)		
	Built by The Light Aircraft Company Ltd (NF 05.03.19)		
G-CLEW	P&M QuikR	8781	17.01.19
	A Atkin (Stapleford, Lincoln)		
	(IE 17.01.19)		
G-CLEY	Best Off Skyranger Nynja 912S(1)	xxxx	06.02.19
	Exodus Airsports Ltd tr G-CLEY Group		
	Plaistows Farm, St Albans		
	Built by R Grimwood and J Waite – project		
	BMAA/HB/707 (IE 05.02.19)		
G-CLFB	Rolladen-Schneider LS4-a	4612	25.11.09
	(BGA 5635), PH-987, D-0205 D M Hadlow		
	tr K2 Syndicate Trenchard Lines, Upavon *'K2'*		21.07.19E
G-CLFC	Mainair Blade	1324-0502-7-W1119	11.06.02
	T L Aydon (Buckley)		20.06.18P
	(NF 12.07.18)		
G-CLFH	Schleicher ASW 20C	20786	08.01.10
	(BGA 5641), D-6911		
	P Armstrong & T Fordwich-Gorely Saltby *'LFH'*		31.08.19E
G-CLFM	Stoddard-Hamilton Glasair Sportsman	xxxx	25.01.19
	J Edgeworth Morgansfield, Fishburn		
	Built by J Edgeworthy – project LAA 295A-15433		
	(NF 25.01.19)		
G-CLFO	Eurofly Snake/Grif 3DC	19003	13.03.19
	Airplay Aircraft Ltd Sutton Meadows		
	Built Airplay Aircraft Ltd (IE 13.03.19)		
G-CLFX	Schempp-Hirth Duo Discus XLT	221/604	02.08.10
	(BGA 5654) S Holland & M G Lynes		
	Sandhill Farm, Shrivenham *'XL'*		18.10.19E
G-CLFZ	Schleicher ASW 28-18E	28741	23.08.10
	(BGA 5656), D-KUTW		
	C F Cownden & J P Davies Gransden Lodge *'644'*		10.04.19E
G-CLGC	Schempp-Hirth Duo Discus	173	01.05.08
	BGA 4511/JGV, (D-4020) London Gliding Club		
	Proprietary Ltd Dunstable Downs *'LGC'*		25.01.20E
G-CLGL	Schempp-Hirth Ventus-2c	3	10.12.10
	(BGA 5663), OH-877		
	S C Williams Wycombe Air Park *'HA'*		21.09.19E
G-CLGR	Glasflügel Club Libelle 205	44	04.04.11
	(BGA 5668), D-6433 L Ferguson-Dalling		
	tr LGR Libelle Group Upwood *'LGR'*		15.07.19E
G-CLGT	Rolladen-Schneider LS4	4376	16.03.11
	(BGA 5669), D-9102		
	N M Hill & L Laks RAF Weston-on-the-Green *'WH'*		04.11.19E
G-CLGU	Schleicher ASW 27-18 (*ASG 29*)	29063	12.07.11
	(BGA 5670) T J Scott Lasham *'Z3'*		26.07.19E
G-CLGW	Centrair 101A Pégase	101A0467	20.04.11
	(BGA5672), HB-3245, F-CHFB		
	M White Pocklington *'RN'*		27.04.19E
G-CLGZ	Schempp-Hirth Duo Discus XLT	230	26.07.11
	(BGA 5675) P Dolan & D R Irving Portmoak *'T3'*		09.08.19E

G-CLHF	Scheibe Bergfalke IV	5868	05.08.11
	(BGA 5680), PH-1386, SE-TYS, D-6930		
	Andreas Gliding Club Ltd Andreas *'LHF'*		24.06.19E
G-CLHG	Schempp-Hirth Discus b	227	16.08.11
	(BGA 5681), D-1091		
	S J Edinborough Long Mynd *'WD'*		13.07.18E
	(IE 11.12.18)		
G-CLIC (3)	Cameron A-105	10514	18.04.91
	M Arno Fiumcino, Rome, Italy		08.10.19E
	Original canopy was (i) N-105 c/n 2557; rebuilt		
	(ii) 04.95 as A-105 c/n 3395 & (iii) 04.04 as		
	A-105 c/n 10514		
G-CLIF	Comco Ikarus C42 FB UK	0501 6650	14.03.05
	E R Sims Old Sarum		28.08.19P
	Built by C Sims – project PFA 322-14377		
G-CLIN	Comco Ikarus C42 FB100	0712-6943	19.03.08
	J O'Halloran Ravensdale Park, Dundalk, RoI		16.05.19P
	Assembled Aerosport Ltd		
G-CLJE	Schleicher ASH 25M	25169	17.01.12
	(BGA 5701), D-KKDB, D-2524		
	A Hegner Aston Down *'JE'*		19.08.18E
G-CLJM	Cessna F172G	F172-0249	26.10.16
	I-ALJM G Buso (Segrato, Milan, Italy, Italy)		15.11.19E
	Built by Reims Aviation SA		
G-CLJP	Cessna F172G	F172-0192	05.05.17
	I-ALJP C Marti		
	(Passignano sul Trasimeno, Perugia, Italy)		12.09.19E
	Built by Reims Aviation SA		
G-CLJZ	Schleicher ASH 31 Mi	31071	03.10.12
	J C Thompson Dunstable Downs *'LJZ'*		12.09.19E
G-CLKF	Schempp-Hirth Cirrus VTC	114Y	19.10.12
	(BGA 5722), OO-ZLE, D-0503		
	E C Wright RAF Cranwell *'69'*		05.06.19E
G-CLKG	Schempp-Hirth Janus CM	5	13.11.12
	OO-ZOT, D-KONI, (D-KJMD)		
	A Tebay tr Lakes Janus Group Walney Island *'HI'*		23.09.19E
G-CLKK	Schleicher ASH 31 Mi	31087	12.03.13
	Zulu Glasstek Ltd Baileys Farm, Long Crendon *'Z'*		26.11.19E
G-CLKU	Schleicher Ka 6E	4317	13.02.13
	(BGA 5734), OO-YAR, F-CDRS K Richards Talgarth		20.08.15E
G-CLLB	Schempp-Hirth Discus-2cT	122	10.04.13
	(BGA 5740) R P Das (Bradford)		05.07.19E
G-CLLC	HpH Glasflügel 304 S Shark	029-MS	25.09.13
	(BGA 5741) S E Bort tr F16 Group Challock *'F16'*		
	(IE 19.12.18)		
G-CLLH	HpH Glasflügel 304 S Shark	030-MS	28.10.13
	(BGA 5746) J Haigh Parham Park *'LLH'*		
	(IE 19.12.18)		
G-CLLL	Schleicher ASW 27-18E (*ASG 29E*)	29668	24.02.14
	(BGA 5749) I P Hicks Dunstable Downs *'LLL'*		13.04.19E
G-CLLT	Grob G102 Standard Astir II	5032S	11.10.13
	(BGA 5756), D-6823		
	Staffordshire Gliding Club Ltd Seighford *'LLT'*		29.01.20E
G-CLLX	Schempp-Hirth Duo Discus T	255	16.04.14
	(BGA 5760) J F Paterson Portmoak *'XX'*		25.12.19E
G-CLLY	Rolladen-Schneider LS6-c18	6211	29.11.13
	(BGA 5761), PH-924		
	P W Brown AAC Wattisham *'PB'*		27.05.19E
G-CLMD	Sportine Aviacija LAK-17B FES	225	16.06.14
	(BGA 5766) R C Bromwich Keevil *'B17'*		07.05.19R
G-CLME	Schempp-Hirth Ventus-2cT	51/166	20.12.13
	(BGA 5767), D-KAPV(2), (PH-1492), OO-YEV		
	J H May Sutton Bank *'LME'*		17.04.19E
G-CLMF	Glaser-Dirks DG-200	2-83	28.01.14
	(BGA 5768), D-7419		
	I Godding & R C Tye Rattlesden *'PW'*		01.06.19E
G-CLMO	Schleicher ASW 28-18E	28755	06.03.14
	(BGA 5776) B Bobrovnikov Wycombe Air Park *'FI'*		04.10.19E
G-CLMV	HpH Glasflügel 304 S Shark	005-S	17.04.14
	(BGA 5781), D-KMAY, OK-5511(?)		
	G J Bowser Shenington *'G0'*		
	Official p/i 'OK-5511' is incorrect (IE 19.12.18)		

G-CLMY	Glaser-Dirks DG-300 Elan	3E476	29.05.14
	(BGA 5784), D-2285 W Laing & A D Stevenson		
	tr LMY Glider Syndicate Portmoak 'I3'		02.04.19E
	Built by Elan Line d.o.o		
G-CLNE	Schleicher ASH 31 Mi	31120	12.11.14
	T P Jenkinson Dunstable Downs 'TJ'		06.03.20E
G-CLNG	Schleicher ASW 27-18 (ASG 29)	29090	10.10.14
	(BGA 5792) S C Thompson tr G-CLNG Flying Group		
	Newells Farm, Lower Beeding		19.10.19E
G-CLOC	Schleicher ASK 13	13455	31.10.14
	(BGA 5810), D-2189 J V Edge Challock 'LOC'		23.07.19E
G-CLOE	Sky 90-24	019	11.03.96
	J L M Van Hoesel Den Bosch, Netherlands		29.05.19E
G-CLOG	Schleicher ASW 27-18E (ASG 29Es)	29693	06.01.16
	(BGA 5814), D-KLOG		
	R E D Bailey Sutton Bank 'OG'		27.03.19E
G-CLOL	Schleicher ASK 21	21924	17.02.15
	(BGA 5817) Lasham Gliding Society Ltd		
	Lasham '775'		01.03.20E
G-CLON	HpH Glasflügel 304 S Shark	045-MS	20.03.15
	(BGA 5819) P D Ruskin Gransden Lodge '28'		
	(IE 25.06.18)		
G-CLOO	Grob G103 Twin Astir	3227	08.12.14
	(BGA 5820), OK-1112, D-5968 R G J Tait tr G-CLOO		
	Group Easterton 'Stadt Oldenberg' & '115'		17.06.19E
G-CLOS	Piper PA-34-200T Seneca II	34-7870361	17.06.86
	HB-LKE, N36783 R A Doherty Coventry		24.06.09E
	(NF 13.12.16)		
G-CLOV	Schleicher ASK 21	21929	28.07.15
	(BGA 5826) Scottish Gliding Union Ltd Portmoak		10.08.19E
(G-CLOY)	Glaser-Dirks DG-100G	101G15	
	D-3806 Reserved (BGA 5829/G-CLOY 'LOY')		
G-CLPB	Rolladen-Schneider LS6-18W	6276	05.03.15
	(BGA 5832), SP-3823, D-5906		
	C J Harrison Lasham 'LPB'		11.02.20E
G-CLPE	Schempp-Hirth Discus bT	29/326	16.04.15
	(BGA 5835), D-KIRG		
	R A Braithwaite Lasham 'LPE'		23.03.20E
G-CLPL	Rolladen-Schneider LS7-WL	7135	16.04.15
	(BGA 5841), EI-GLS, EI-177, 3A-MCD		
	W M Davies North Hill 'W7'		28.03.20E
G-CLPU	Schleicher ASW 27-18E (ASG 29E)	29709	06.01.16
	(BGA 5849) A R J Hughes Wycombe Air Park 'ES'		27.01.20E
G-CLPV	Schleicher ASK 21	21932	20.01.16
	(BGA 5850) Portsmouth Naval Gliding Centre		
	(HMS Sultan, Gosport) 'LPV'		30.01.19E
	Stored 05.18		
G-CLPX	Grob G103C Twin III Acro	34128	25.02.16
	(BGA 5852), D-1830		
	The Windrushers Gliding Club Ltd Bicester 'PX'		30.04.19E
G-CLPZ	Jonker JS-MD Single (JS1 Revelation)	1C.MD104	12.01.18
	D-KPAI, (BGA 5854) R E D Bailey t/a Bailey Aviation		
	Sutton Bank 'PZ'		14.01.20E
G-CLRA	Schleicher ASW 27-18E (ASG 29E)	29677	02.10.15
	(BGA 5855), D-KASB		
	C P J Gibson & C A Hunt Lasham 'RA1'		15.12.19E
G-CLRC	Schleicher ASW 27-18E (ASG 29E)	29713	29.03.16
	(BGA 5857) W R Tandy Dunstable Downs 'B8'		25.04.19E
G-CLRD	PZL-Bielsko SZD-51-1 Junior	B-2149	16.11.15
	(BGA 5858), SP-3891, D-2270 Devon & Somerset		
	Gliding Club Ltd North Hill 'LRD'		13.11.19E
G-CLRE	Schleicher Ka 6BR	457	30.09.15
	(BGA 5859), HB-617 B Bay (Augsburg, Germany)		19.04.19E
G-CLRF	Schleicher ASW 27-18E (ASG 29Es)	29715	04.05.16
	(BGA 5860) C G Starkey Lasham '900'		30.01.20E
G-CLRH	HpH Glasflügel 304 S Shark	053-MS	15.02.16
	(BGA 5862) A C Broadbridge tr The Shark Group		
	Bidford 'V'		
	(IE 02.04.18)		
G-CLRJ	Schempp-Hirth Discus bT	28/324	25.11.15
	(BGA 5863), PH-1359, OE-9423, D-KEBG		
	M S Smith Kingston Deverill		14.09.19E

G-CLRK	Sky 77-24	101	03.03.98
	William Clark & Son (Parkgate) Ltd Dumfries		
	'Clark Engineering & Forestry Equipment'		10.09.09E
	(NF 21.07.16)		
G-CLRN	Glaser-Dirks DG-100G Elan	E39G21	09.12.15
	(BGA 5867), D-3741		
	C J Mew tr DG 100G Group North Hill 'LRN'		10.04.19E
	Built by Elan Tovarna Sportnega Orodja N.Sol.O		
G-CLRO	Glaser-Dirks DG-300 Elan	3E175	07.01.16
	(BGA 5868), F-CORB, D-4313		
	P E Kerman Strubby '3W'		31.05.19E
	Built by Elan Tovarna Sportnega Orodja N.Sol.O		
G-CLRP	Schempp-Hirth Janus B	92	08.01.16
	(BGA 5869), D-6890		
	S M Grant & W I H Hall Kirton in Lindsey 'LRP'		21.03.19E
G-CLRS	Schleicher ASW 27-18E (ASG 29E)	29635	13.01.16
	(BGA 5871), D-KKSW		
	F Birlison tr G-CLRS Flying Group Aston Down '565'		10.03.20E
G-CLRT	Schleicher ASK 21	21939	12.09.16
	(BGA 5872)		
	Cotswold Gliding Club Aston Down 'LRT'		31.10.19E
G-CLRY	Rolladen-Schneider LS4	4350	14.03.16
	(BGA 5875), D-4545 S O Boye Nympsfield 'RY'		17.05.17E
G-CLRZ	Rolladen-Schneider LS1-f	345	25.02.16
	(BGA 5876), D-2741		
	C B Hill RAF Weston-on-the-Green 'KC'		24.03.19E
G-CLSG	Rolladen-Schneider LS4-b	4923	26.04.16
	(BGA 5883), PH-1009		
	C Marriott & C Taunton Dunstable Downs		16.01.19E
G-CLSH	Schleicher ASK 21	21940	04.11.16
	(BGA 5884) Lasham Gliding Society Ltd		
	Lasham '776'		16.11.19E
G-CLSJ	HpH Glasflügel 304 S Shark	055-MS	15.02.16
	(BGA 5888) C M Lewis Gransden Lodge 'SJ'		
	(IE 21.03.16)		
G-CLSL	Glaser-Dirks DG-500 Elan Trainer	5E120T51	07.04.16
	(BGA 5887), D-5488 Needwood Forest		
	Gliding Club Ltd Snitterfield 'LSL'		21.04.19E
	Built by Elan Flight Ltd		
G-CLSO	Schempp-Hirth Nimbus-3T	7	20.04.16
	(BGA 5890), D-KHRG, PH-1361, OO-ZKG, D-KHRG,		
	D-3111 R S Rose Currock Hill 'RR'		10.04.19E
G-CLSR	Grob G103 Twin Astir	3048	16.05.16
	(BGA 5892), D-4842		
	The Nene Valley Gliding Club Ltd Upwood 'LSR'		22.06.19E
G-CLSW	Schleicher ASW 20BL	20646	19.07.16
	(BGA 5897), OE-5694, OH-711		
	A Docherty Darlton '20B'		14.06.19E
G-CLSY	Schempp-Hirth SHK-1	3	24.08.16
	(BGA 5899), PH-1170, BGA1592/CJZ, D-9349		
	J R Stiles Ringmer 'LSY'		17.09.18E
	(IE 04.10.18)		
G-CLSZ	DG Flugzeugbau DG-800B	8-85B22	21.09.16
	D-KLPR M Roberts Lasham '44'		03.12.19E
G-CLTA	HpH Glasflügel 304 eS Shark	065-MS	19.12.16
	(BGA 5901), OK-0065 R E Cross Lasham '141'		06.06.19R
G-CLTC	Schempp-Hirth Janus Ce	280	01.11.16
	(BGA 5903), D-5580		
	P J D Smith & C A Willson Rivar Hill 'N'		05.11.19E
G-CLTD	Schleicher K 8B	8975	08.09.16
	(BGA 5904), PH-513 G D Western Rattlesden 'MR'		06.05.19E
G-CLTF	Schempp-Hirth Discus a	041	11.10.16
	(BGA 5906), D-6977, HB-1823		
	L Runhaar Dunstable Downs 'LTF'		15.11.19E
G-CLTG	Glaser-Dirks DG-100	17	26.10.16
	(BGA 5907), D-6032, HB-1276		
	T Pearson Sutton Bank 'LTG'		13.06.19E
G-CLTJ	Sportine Aviacija LAK-17B FES	243	21.03.17
	LY-BCY J T Newbery Wormingford 'JN'		20.05.19R
G-CLTL	Schleicher ASW 19B	19340	16.11.16
	(BGA 5911), D-7719, OH-626		
	J P Salt Kirton in Lindsey 'LTL'		03.05.19E
(G-CLTN)	Schempp-Hirth Ventus-2cxa FES	153	
	Reserved (BGA 55913/G-CLTN 'LTN')		

G-CLTO	Schleicher ASW 27-18E	29733	22.06.17	
	J Pack Lasham *'51'*		25.02.20E	
	Reported as Type ASG-29Es			
G-CLTP	Rolladen-Schneider LS3-17	3238	06.12.16	
	(BGA 5915), HB-1501			
	F C Roles Husbands Bosworth *'LTP'*		17.11.18E	
G-CLTS	Schempp-Hirth Arcus T	73	28.07.17	
	(BGA 5917) M C Boik Bicester *'LTS'*		15.08.19E	
G-CLTW	HpH Glasflügel 304 eS Shark	069-MS	06.02.17	
	(BGA 5921)			
	A Holswilder & S Murdoch Gransden Lodge *'SF'*		22.04.19R	
G-CLTX	Sportine Aviacija LAK-17B FES Mini	004	09.06.17	
	(BGA 5922), LY-BEB D R Bennett Usk *'LTX'*			
	(IE 17.05.18)			
G-CLUD	Grob G102 Club Astir IIIb	5652CB	29.06.17	
	(BGA 5928), D-3923			
	Lasham Gliding Society Ltd Lasham *'SH7'*		24.07.19E	
G-CLUE	Piper PA-34-200T Seneca II	34-7970502	15.09.92	
	N8089Z P Wilkinson Perth		28.02.14E	
	Left gear collapsed landing Durham Tees Valley			
	28.07.13; for spares use 08.17 (NF 21.05.18)			
G-CLUG	Schleicher K 8B	8809	22.01.18	
	(BGA 5931), PH-414			
	The Windrushers Gliding Club Ltd Bicester		14.02.19E	
G-CLUJ	Sportine Aviacija LAK-17B FES Mini	005	09.03.18	
	J I B Bennett & R Emms Upwood *'LUJ'*			
	(IE 07.03.18)			
G-CLUK	Schleicher ASK 23B	23043	25.08.17	
	(BGA 5934), PH-767 London Gliding Club			
	Proprietary Ltd Dunstable Downs *'LUK'*		11.10.19E	
G-CLUP	Schleicher ASH 25	25155	01.09.17	
	(BGA 5938), OE-5525, D-8220			
	G G Dale & A K Laylee Lasham *'G'*		29.04.19E	
G-CLUV	Schleicher ASK 23B	23102	17.10.17	
	(BGA 5941), D-1550			
	Midland Gliding Club Ltd Long Mynd *'LUV'*		05.04.20E	
G-CLUX	Reims/Cessna F172N	F17201996	01.05.80	
	PH-AYG G E Fox Bagby		18.11.19E	
G-CLUZ	Schempp-Hirth Discus-2c FES	24	14.05.18	
	(BGA 5944)			
	A Gillanders tr G-CLUZ Group Portmoak *'XL5'*		01.06.19E	
G-CLVD	Schempp-Hirth Discus-2c FES	26	26.06.18	
	C K Davis, M B Margetson & P R Wilson			
	Gransden Lodge *'Z18'*		04.07.19E	
G-CLVJ	DG Flugzeugbau DG-505 Elan Orion	5E177X29	24.01.18	
	(BGA 5953), D-4182, S5-7515 Coventry Gliding Club			
	Ltd t/a The Gliding Centre Husbands Bosworth *'W4'*		05.04.19E	
G-CLVL	Schempp-Hirth Arcus T	83	03.09.18	
	(BGA 5955) J B Nicholson tr The Assets of			
	G-CLVL Syndicate Lasham		04.02.20E	
G-CLVM	Schleicher ASK 21	21311	20.03.18	
	(BGA 5956), HB-1884			
	York Gliding Centre (Operations) Ltd Rufforth *'LVM'*		04.01.20E	
G-CLVO	Allstar PZL SZD-54-2 Perkoz	542.A.18.022	16.08.18	
	(BGA 5958), SP-4023 Deeside Gliding Club			
	(Aberdeenshire) Ltd Aboyne *'LVO'*		07.08.19E	
	Built by Allstar PZL Glider Sp. z o.o			
G-CLVP	PZL-Bielsko SZD-42-2 Jantar 2B	B-1320	03.05.18	
	(BGA 5959), SP-3254 J Szuster tr J2B Flying Group			
	Dunstable Downs *'LVP'*		02.07.19E	
G-CLVS	HpH Glasflügel 304 eS Shark	091-MS	30.08.18	
	(BGA 5960) G R Hudson Lasham *'LVS'*		06.09.19E	
G-CLVU	Schleicher ASK 21	21461	24.04.18	
	(BGA 5962), D-6153 Stratford on Avon			
	Gliding Club Ltd Snitterfield *'LVU'*		05.05.19E	
G-CLVW	Rolladen-Schneider LS4-a	4178	18.05.18	
	(BGA 5964), OY-MXE, D-3504			
	C Edkins Snitterfield *'ME'*		18.06.19E	
G-CLVZ	Centrair 101A Pégase	101A446	17.06.18	
	(BGA 5967), F-CHLI P Urbanski (London N7)		10.03.19E	
G-CLWA	Schleicher ASK 21B	21959	08.01.19	
	Lasham Gliding Society Ltd Lasham		23.01.20E	

G-CLWC	Allstar PZL SZD-54-2 Perkoz	542.A.18.024	12.03.19	
	SP-4023 Essex & Suffolk Gliding Club Ltd			
	Wormingford			
	(NF 12.03.19)			
G-CLWJ	Schleicher ASW 27-18E	29748	03.10.18	
	(BGA 5975) P Johnson Milfield		15.10.19E	
G-CLWL	Schempp-Hirth Discus bT	74/402	20.02.19	
	D-KRAI, (BGA 5977) N H Wall Nympsfield			
	(IE 20.02.19)			
G-CLWN	Cameron Clown	2857	23.08.07	
	SE-ZGU, G-UBBE Magical Adventures Ltd			
	West Bloomfield, MI, USA		27.09.09E	
	(NF 03.06.15)			
G-CLWR	Rolladen-Schneider LS8-a	8054	30.01.19	
	(BGA 5982), OE-5817, D-3751 M D A Brown Darlton			
	(NF 29.01.19)			
G-CLWZ	Schempp-Hirth Ventus-2c	128	21.02.19	
	D-6164 M J & T J Webb RAF Halton			
	(IE 21.02.19)			

G-CMAA – G-CMZZ

G-CMBC	Cessna 550 Citation Bravo	550-0951	17.12.18	
	G-CGEI, LN-SUV, N51KR, TC-TPE, N5076J			
	Bond Business Services Ltd Gloucestershire		07.11.19E	
G-CMBR	Cessna 172S Skyhawk SP	172S8144	18.04.08	
	N948SP C M B Reid Rochester		21.07.18E	
G-CMCL	Leonardo AW169	69017	12.10.16	
	VH-LSN, I-EASL Bradbury Estates LLP Dunsfold		09.01.19E	
	Built by Finmeccanica SpA			
G-CMDG	P&M QuikR	8713	31.03.15	
	C Fender East Fortune		28.03.19P	
G-CMEW	Aerospool Dynamic WT9 UK	DY457	04.09.12	
	M W Frost Andrewsfield		08.05.19P	
	Assembled Yeoman Light Aircraft Co Ltd			
G-CMKL	Van's RV-12	120800	08.09.15	
	K L Sangster Templehall Farm, Midlem			
	Built by K L Sangster – project LAA 363-15252			
	(IE 07.12.18)			
G-CMNK	de Havilland DHC-1 Chipmunk 22	C1/0173	15.11.16	
	N31352, WB721 Vintage Aircraft Factory Ltd			
	Newquay Cornwall			
	On rebuild 02.18 (IE 15.11.16)			
G-CMON	Van's RV-7	74309	14.03.18	
	F McMullan Newtownards		20.02.20P	
	Built by F McMullan – project LAA 323-15276			
G-CMOR	Best Off Skyranger 912(2)	SKR0412542	25.02.05	
	P J Tranmer Bagby		23.08.18P	
	Built by C Moore – project BMAA/HB/441			
G-CMOS	Cessna T303 Crusader	T30300222	15.12.06	
	D-IPMG, N121JH, N9858C C J Moss Goodwood		06.03.13E	
	In external storage 07.16 (NF 30.10.14)			
G-CMPA	Piper PA-28RT-201 Arrow IV	28R-7918119	06.10.15	
	EC-MBI, G-BREP, EC-HZN, G-BREP, N2230Z			
	J T E Buwalda (Hilversum, Netherlands)		26.09.17E	
G-CMPC	Titan T-51 Mustang	0143	22.02.12	
	J A Carey White Fen Farm, Benwick			
	Built by J A Carey – project LAA 355-14938;			
	as '36922:WD-Y' in USAAF c/s (NF 22.02.12)			
G-CMRA	Eurocopter AS.355N Ecureuil 2	5560	10.11.16	
	N912EM, N12EW, XA-SPB, F-WYMQ			
	Cheshire Helicopters Ltd			
	Blackshaw Heys Farm, Mobberley		22.12.18E	
	Operated by VLL Ltd t/a GB Helicopters			
G-CMSN	Robinson R22 Beta	1669	29.06.04	
	G-MGEE, G-PHEL, G-RUMP, N2405T			
	Kuki Helicopter Sales Ltd Retford Gamston		11.06.16E	
G-CMTO	Cessna 525 Citation M2	525-0848	22.12.14	
	Golconda Aircraft Leasing LLP Biggin Hill		21.12.18E	
	Operated by Catreus			
G-CMWK	Grob G102 Astir CS	1518	08.08.08	
	(BGA 5330), PH-820 J Schaper Darlton *'MWK'*		14.06.18E	

G-CNAA – G-CNZZ

G-CNAB Avtech Jabiru UL-450   0412   27.09.00
M Smith tr G-CNAB Group   Newtownards   30.05.18P
Built by W A Brighouse – project PFA 274-13651;
type prefix should be 'PFA 274A'

G-CNCN Rockwell Commander 112TC-A   13151   01.06.05
HB-NCN, N4620W   112 Group Ltd   Blackpool   08.12.18E

G-CNHB Van's RV-7   73500   13.10.10
T G Lloyd   Shelsley Beauchamp
Built by M E Wood – project LAA 323-15018
(NF 20.02.18)

G-CNWL McDonnell Douglas MD Explorer   900-00124   24.10.14
G-CIGX, N902FN, N9027N
Specialist Aviation Services Ltd   Newquay Cornwall   30.12.18E
Operated by Cornwall Air Ambulance as callsign
'Helimed 01'

G-COAA – G-COZZ

G-COAI Cranfield A 1-400 Eagle   001   01.06.98
G-BCIT   Cranfield University   Cranfield
Built by Cranfield Institute of Technology (NF 26.01.16)

G-COBO Avions Transport ATR 72-212A   852   05.03.09
F-WWEV   Aurigny Air Services Ltd   Guernsey   04.03.19E

G-COBS Diamond DA.42M-NG Twin Star   42.MN020   13.01.12
OE-VPY   Thales UK Ltd   Durham Tees Valley   30.01.19R

G-COCO Reims/Cessna F172M   F17201373   27.10.80
PH-SMO, OO-ADI   R C Larder   Strubby   15.03.18E

G-CODA Hughes 369E (500)   0590E   27.04.16
G-CIYJ, HB-ZKD, N4038S
Studwelders Holdings Ltd   (Mathern, Chepstow)   08.03.18E

G-COGS Bell 407 (Bell 407GXP)   54636   15.09.16
N591KS   HC Services Ltd   Fairoaks   03.10.18E

G-COIN Bell 206B-2 JetRanger II   897   11.03.85
EI-AWA   J P Niehorster
(Stocking Pelham, Buntingford)   02.08.18E

G-COLA Beech F33C Bonanza   CJ-137   31.03.92
G-BUAZ, PH-BNH   Airport Direction Ltd   Tatenhill   25.11.13E
Noted 02.15 less engines (NF 03.06.16)

G-COLF BRM Bristell NG5 Speed Wing   14045-2762   03.03.17
EC-XNS   C Firth
Eddsfield, Octon Lodge Farm, Thwing   24.05.18P
Built by C Firth

G-COLI AutoGyro MT-03   08 034   10.04.08
G D Smith   (Sible Hedingham, Halstead)   29.10.18P
Assembled Rotorsport UK as c/n RSUK/MT-03/037

G-COLS Van's RV-7A   71964   06.10.04
C Terry   Charlton Park, Malmesbury   23.03.19P
Built by C Terry & G Vitta – project PFA 323-14312

G-COLY Aeropro EuroFOX 912(S)   38512   30.10.12
J R Bell   (Lymington)   02.01.20P
Built by C J Norman – project LAA 376-15160; tailwheel u/c

G-COMB Piper PA-30 Twin Comanche B   30-1362   14.09.84
G-AVBL, N8236Y   M Bonsall   Derby   20.03.17E

G-COMP Cameron N-90 HAB   1564   24.09.87
Cancelled 18.12.01 by CAA   20.05.97
Not Known   'Computacenter'   Inflated Pidley 04.18

G-CONA Flight Design CTLS   F.09-02-13   15.07.09
G-CGED   R A Eve   Damyns Hall, Upminster   22.02.18W
Assembled P&M Aviation Ltd; noted 08.18

G-CONB Robin DR.400-180 Régent   2176   14.04.93
G-BUPX   T N Clark   Elstree   26.07.19E

G-CONC Cameron N-90   2139   13.11.89
A A Brown   Worplesdon, Guildford   'Concorde'   17.09.10E
(NF 28.10.15)

G-CONI Lockheed 749A-79 Constellation   2553   12.05.82
N7777G, (N173X), N7777G, TI-1045P,
PH-LDT, PH-TET   Cancelled 13.06.84 as WFU
Wroughton   As 'N7777G' in TWA c/s
In Science Museum store 2013

G-CONL SOCATA TB-10 Tobago   173   22.12.98
F-GCOR   J M Huntington   Full Sutton   19.06.18E

G-CONN Eurocopter EC120B Colibri   1138   12.08.11
EI-EUR, G-BZMK, F-WQOE
M J Connors   (Newborough, Burton-on-Trent)   05.04.14E
(IE 20.07.15)

G-CONR Champion 7GCBC Citabria   280-70   15.05.06
YU-CAB   D T Bishop tr Aerofoyle Group   Bellarena   04.08.19E

G-CONS Groppo Trail   094/53   10.06.15
G Constantine   Shenstone Hall Farm, Shenstone   18.09.18P
Built by G Constantine – project LAA 372-15231

G-CONV General Dynamics Convair CV-440   484   19.07.01
CS-TML, N357SA, N28KE, N28KA, N4402
Cancelled 20.12.06 as PWFU
Carluke   *Displayed Reynard's Garden Centre 07.14*

G-COOT Aerocar Taylor Coot A   EE1A   16.09.81
P M Napp   Selby House Farm, Stanton
Built by D A Hood (NF 21.03.16)

G-COPP Schleicher ASW 27-18E (ASG 29E)   29667   24.01.14
(BGA 5754)   J B Giddins   Bicester   '66'   05.02.19E

G-COPR Robinson R44 Raven II   14172   13.02.18
BML Utility Contractors Ltd   Elstree   27.02.19E

G-COPS Piper J-3C-65 Cub (L-4H-PI)   11911   17.07.79
F-BFYC, French AF, 44-79615
R W Sproat   Lenox Plunton Farm, Borgue   17.08.18P
Official c/n 36-817 is a USAAC contract no;
fuselage No.11739

G-CORA Europa Aviation Europa XS   467   30.05.06
G-ILUM   A P Gardner   Little Gransden
Built by A R Haynes – project PFA 247-13565;
tricycle u/c (NF 30.07.18)

G-CORB SOCATA TB-20 Trinidad   1178   12.04.99
F-GKUX   Corvid Aviation Ltd   Gloucestershire   27.05.18E

G-CORD Nipper T.66 RA.45 Series 3   S129   21.03.88
G-AVTB   P S Gilmour   (St Andrews)   28.06.12P
Built by Slingsby Sailplanes Ltd as G-AVTB (1565)
for Nipper Aircraft Ltd as c/n S105: rebuilt as
G-CORD (1676) with Nipper c/n S129 (NF 19.12.16)

G-CORS Noorduyn AT-16-ND Harvard IIB   14A-1884   11.11.16
KF183   Propshop Ltd   Duxford   17.05.19E
As 'KF183' in RAF c/s

G-CORW Piper PA-28-180 Cherokee C   28-4089   28.02.11
G-AVRY   R P Osborne & C A Wilson
Rayne Hall Farm, Rayne   05.09.18E

G-COSF Piper PA-28-161 Warrior II   28-7716215   05.06.09
N5915V   PA-28 Warrior Ltd   RAF Cosford   23.04.18E

G-COSY Lindstrand LBL 56A   017   18.02.93
M H Read & J E Wetters   Timperley, Altrincham   06.03.18E

G-COTH McDonnell Douglas MD Explorer   900-00085   15.12.10
N3ND, (N999HH), N3ND, N3PD, N7033V
Specialist Aviation Services Ltd   Gloucestershire   24.03.17E
(IE 16.01.18)

G-COTT Cameron Flying Cottage-60   687   13.02.81
'G-HOUS'   Dragon Balloon Company Ltd
Castleton, Hope Valley   'Nottingham Building Society'   07.01.11E
(IE 05.06.17)

G-COUZ Raj Hamsa X'Air 582(2)   444   02.01.09
D J Tully   Letterkenny, RoI   11.08.18P
Built by D J Couzens – project BMAA/HB/153

G-COVA Piper PA-28-161 Warrior III   2842217   18.02.05
G-CDCL, N3072G
Coventry (Civil) Aviation Ltd   Coventry   14.12.18E

G-COVC Piper PA-28-161 Warrior III   2842159   02.10.15
N519MS   Coventry (Civil) Aviation Ltd   Coventry
(IE 05.03.17)

G-COVZ Reims/Cessna F150M   F15001164   06.09.10
G-BCRT   S J Brenchley   Solent   16.04.19E

G-COXI XtremeAir XA42 Sbach 342   124   13.01.15
D-ETXA   ABD Networks LLP   Cotswold   30.03.19E

G-COXS Aeroprakt A-22 Foxbat   UK017   09.03.04
S Cox   (Brentor, Tavistock)   15.07.18P
Built by S Cox – project PFA 317-14168

G-COZI Rutan Cozy   xxxx   19.07.93
R Machin   Isle of Man   13.08.18P
Built by D G Machin – project PFA 159-12162

G-CPAA – G-CPZZ

G-CPAO Eurocopter EC135 P2+　　　　　0843　　　　25.09.09
Police & Crime Commissioner for West Yorkshire
Hawarden　　　　　　　　　　　　　　　　　15.03.18E
*Operated by Cheshire Police Air Support Unit as
callsign 'NPAS 22'*

G-CPAS Eurocopter EC135 P2+　　　　　0920　　　　30.06.10
Police & Crime Commissioner for West Yorkshire
Redhill　　　　　　　　　　　　　　　　　　01.12.18E

G-CPCD Robin DR.221 Dauphin　　　　　81　　　　11.12.90
F-BPCD　D J Taylor　Enstone　　　　　　　03.08.18E
Built by Centre-Est Aéronautique

G-CPDA^M de Havilland DH.106 Comet 4C　6473　　　10.08.00
XS235　Cancelled 27.03.08 as PWFU
As 'XS235'　'Canopus'
*With British Aviation Heritage-Cold War Jets Collection,
Bruntingthorpe*

G-CPDW Mudry CAP 10B　　　　　　　195　　　　23.04.07
N502DW　Hilfa Ltd　Headcorn　　　　　　17.12.18E

G-CPEV Boeing 757-236　　　　　　　29943　　　11.06.99
C-GOEV, C-GPEV, C-GOEV, C-GPEV, C-GOEV,
G-CPEV, N1795B, (G-CPEW)
TUI Airways Ltd t/a TUI　Manchester　　　23.09.19E
Line No: 871

G-CPFC Reims/Cessna F152 II　　　　F15201430　01.12.77
Falcon Flying Services Ltd　Biggin Hill　　18.07.16E

G-CPII Mudry CAP 231　　　　　　　07　　　　16.11.12
D-EIHH, F-GSHH, F-WQOL, CN-ABJ
S Bakhtiari　(Swinton, Manchester)　　　09.10.19E

G-CPLG AutoGyro Cavalon Pro　　　　xxxx　　　18.03.16
Commotion Aviation Ltd　Rochester　　　02.05.19E
Assembled Rotorsport UK as c/n RSUK/CAVP/002

G-CPLH Guimbal Cabri G2　　　　　　1091　　　12.02.15
Helicentre Aviation Ltd　Leicester　　　　30.03.19E

G-CPMK de Havilland DHC-1 Chipmunk 22　C1/0866　28.06.96
WZ847　P A Walley　Elstree　　　　　　　27.04.18P

G-CPMS SOCATA TB-20 Trinidad　　　1607　　　07.04.98
F-GNHA　N G P White　Brighton City　　30.07.18E

G-CPMW Piper PA-32R-301 Saratoga II HP　3213088　24.03.17
D-EAPN, TF-FAX, C-GIXL, N9251R
P M Weaver　(Yoxall, Burton-on-Trent)
(IE 08.05.17)

G-CPOL Aérospatiale AS.355F1 Ecureuil 2　5007　　30.11.95
N5775T, C-GJJB, N5775T
MW Helicopters Ltd　Stapleford　　　　　17.06.10E
(IE 16.06.15)

G-CPPG Alpi Pioneer 400　　　　　　005　　　21.05.13
P B Godfrey　Thruxton　　　　　　　　　06.08.18P
Built by P B Godfrey – project LAA 364-15117

G-CPPM North American AT-6 Texan II　81-4013　02.03.07
RCAF 3019　S D Wilch　Bruntingthorpe
As '3091:91' in RCAF c/s (IE 15.09.17)

G-CPSS Cessna 208B Grand Caravan　208B1059　13.01.11
N208AJ, M-YAKW, G-OAKW, N402AW, N5075K
Army Parachute Association　MoD Netheravon　17.06.18E

G-CPTM Piper PA-28-151 Cherokee Warrior　28-7715012　09.07.91
G-BTOE, N4264F
C & T J Mackay　Liverpool John Lennon　11.04.18E

G-CPXC Mudry CAP 10B　　　　　　301　　　11.12.01
JRW Aerobatics Ltd　Gloucestershire　　14.08.18E
Built by Constructions Aeronautiques de Bourgogne

G-CRAA – G-CRZZ

G-CRAB Best Off Skyranger Swift 912(2)　SKR0210245　01.11.02
S W Plume & J O Williams　Longacre Farm, Sandy　02.03.18P
Built by R A Bell – project BMAA/HB/246

G-CRAR CZAW Sportcruiser　　　　　700524　　04.09.08
J S Kinsey　Baynards Park, Cranleigh　　07.07.18P
Built by R B Armitage – project LAA 338-14841

G-CRBV Kubicek BB26　　　　　　　373　　　22.07.05
OK-0373　South Downs Ballooning Ltd
Grayshott, Hindhead　'Centre MK'　　　03.08.19E

G-CRED Aeropro EuroFOX 3K　　　　54818　　　25.09.18
A M Credland　Sherburn-in-Elmet
Built by Ascent Industries Ltd (IE 25.09.18)

G-CRES Denney Kitfox Model 2　　　xxxx　　　07.06.90
I Foster tr Silver Fox Group
(Rossnowlagh, Co Donegal, RoI)
*Built by R J Cresswell – project PFA 172-11574
(NF 16.10.18)*

G-CREY Progressive SeaRey Amphibian　360　　　02.01.07
K M & M Gallagher & A F Reid　Newtownards　11.05.18P
*Built by P J Gallagher & A F Reid
– project PFA 343-14619*

G-CRGD Piper PA-34-220T Seneca V　3449300　　07.12.17
G-VYND, I-ZYTT, N3010F
Craigard Property Trading Ltd　Southampton　11.11.18E

G-CRIC Colomban MC-15 Cri-Cri　　xxxx　　　22.07.83
R S Stoddart-Stones　(Woldingham, Caterham)　05.05.99P
*Built by A J Maxwell – project PFA 133-10915
(NF 23.08.16)*

G-CRIK Colomban MC-15 Cri-Cri　　576　　　10.11.04
N Huxtable　Wycombe Air Park　　　　　11.01.17P
*Built by C R Harrison & A R Robinson – project
PFA 133-13289; active 09.18 (NF 06.08.18)*

G-CRIL Rockwell Commander 112B　521　　　22.06.79
N1388J　K S Gibson tr Rockwell Aviation Group
Cardiff　　　　　　　　　　　　　　　　08.06.18E

G-CRIS Taylor JT.1 Monoplane　　　xxxx　　　05.06.79
C R Steer　(Bexhill-on-Sea)
Built by C J Bragg – project PFA 055-10318 (NF 01.03.16)

G-CRJW Schleicher ASW 27-18 (ASG 29)　29568　　22.12.08
BGA 5333/KSR
R J Welford　Gransden Lodge　'W8'　　23.03.18E

G-CRLA Cirrus SR20　　　　　　　　1388　　　12.02.09
(D-E...), G-CRLA, N8159Q　Aero Club Heidelberg EV
Mainz-Finthen, Rheinland-Pfalz, Germany　17.01.19E

G-CRNL Fairchild M62A-4 Cornell I　T43-4361　21.10.15
G-CEVL, N9606H, FJ662, 42-15491
CRNL Aviation Ltd　Wickenby
On rebuild 09.18; as 'FJ662:662' in RAF c/s (NF 21.10.15)

G-CRNS Dassault Falcon 7X　　　　161　　　17.10.17
HB-JSA, F-WWZQ
TAG Aviation (UK) Ltd　Farnborough　　10.08.18E

G-CROL Maule MXT-7-180 Super Rocket　14032C　24.11.93
N9232F　J R Pratt　Wolverhampton Halfpenny Green　05.11.18E

G-CROW Robinson R44 Raven　　　　0754　　　19.04.00
Hover Helicopters Ltd　Cardiff City Heliport　19.03.17E

G-CROY Europa Aviation Europa　　101　　　07.02.97
M T Austin　Kirkwall　　　　　　　　　15.05.18P
Built by A T Croy – project PFA 247-12896; tailwheel u/c

G-CRSR Czech Sport Sportcruiser　P1102001　07.10.11
P Simmonds tr G-CRSR Flying Group
White Waltham　　　　　　　　　　　　20.09.18W

G-CRSS Guimbal Cabri G2　　　　　1047　　　25.01.17
D-HTAM　MTC Helicopters Ltd　Blackbushe　15.04.19E
Operated by Phoenix Helicopters

G-CRUE Van's RV-7　　　　　　　　xxxx　　　14.03.19
C Arnold　(Bracknell)
Built C Arnold – project LAA 323-15565 (NF 14.03.19)

G-CRUI CZAW Sportcruiser　　　　　3628　　　01.05.08
J Massey　Baynards Park, Cranleigh　　31.10.18P
Built by J Massey – project PFA 338-14723

G-CRUM Westland Scout AH.1　　　F9712　　　17.03.98
XV137　A P Goddard tr G-CRUM Group　Draycott　18.11.18P
As 'XV137' in AAC c/s

G-CRUZ Cessna T303 Crusader　　　T30300004　07.12.90
N9336T　J R Tubb　Biggin Hill　　　　　19.04.18E

G-CRVC Van's RV-14　　　　　　　　140362　　15.12.17
C C Cooper　(Fintray, Aberdeen)
*Built by C C Cooper – project LAA 393-15452
(NF 15.12.17)*

G-CRWZ CZAW Sportcruiser　　　　　4027　　　23.04.08
A & L Wiffen　(Botley, Southampton)　　05.04.19P
Built by P B Lowry – project PFA 338-14648

G-CRZA CZAW Sportcruiser   xxxx   17.04.08
I M Mackay   Old Warden   02.07.18P
Built by A J Radford – project PFA 338-14657

G-CRZE Ultramagic M-105   105/195   14.02.14
Fresh Air Ltd   London NW2   *'Fresh Air'*   17.07.19E

G-CRZR Czech Sport PS-28 Cruiser   C0448   19.06.15
G-EGHA   S J Newham & S P Rawlinson   Fife   26.10.18R

G-CSAA – G-CSZZ

G-CSAM Van's RV-9A   91130   01.03.07
B G Murray   (Teignmouth)
Built by B G Murray – project PFA 320-14384
(NF 07.08.14)

G-CSAV Thruster T600N 450   0032-T600N-064   14.03.02
S Gennery   North Coates   02.01.20P
Badged 'Sprint'

G-CSAW CZAW Sportcruiser   4006   11.03.08
B C Fitzgerald-O'Connor   (London E16)
Built by B C M Fitzgerald-O'Connor
– project PFA 338-14649 (NF 12.03.15)

G-CSBD Piper PA-28-236 Dakota   28-8211019   18.07.05
G-CSBO, N8471Y   GCSBD Group Ltd   Welshpool   06.09.18E

G-CSBM Reims/Cessna F150M   F15001359   24.05.78
PH-AYC   Blackbushe Flying Club Ltd   Blackbushe   01.11.18E

G-CSCS Reims/Cessna F172N   F17201707   28.11.86
PH-MEM, (PH-WEB), N9899A
J M Grainger & L E Winstanley   North Weald   26.10.18E

G-CSDJ Avtech Jabiru UL-450   0203   23.03.99
M Smith   North Coates   21.06.18P
Built by D W Johnston & C D Slater
– project PFA 274A-13337

G-CSDR Corvus CA-22 Crusader   CA22-010   28.07.08
J B Mills tr Crusader Syndicate   (Warrington)
Data plate shows 'Type 56-01' & 'No.CNE 05-10'
(NF 17.08.15)

G-CSEE Kubicek BB20ED   1405   08.01.18
Fairfax Aviation Ltd   Langford, Bristol
'Kubicek Balloons'   22.01.20E

G-CSGT Piper PA-28-161 Warrior II   2816069   31.01.06
G-BPHB, N9148G   W Ali   Cranfield   19.07.19E

G-CSHB Czech Sport PS-28 Cruiser   C0445   16.06.14
OK-LSA   D Gilham & P Moodie
Rectory Farm, Averham   11.06.19R

G-CSIX Piper PA-32-300 Cherokee Six   32-7840030   15.06.01
ZS-OMX, Z-WJM, VP-WJM, HB-PCX, ZS-KBR, N9857K
A J Hodge   Oxford   24.01.16E

G-CSKW Van's RV-7   71161   03.04.12
G-CDJW   C Stanley tr G-CSKW Group
Church Farm, Shotteswell   05.04.17P
(Built D J Williams – project PFA 323-14045

G-CSMK Evektor EV-97 Eurostar   xxxx   04.12.01
R Frey   Westonzoyland   17.08.18P
Built by N R Beale – project PFA 315-13813

G-CSPR Van's RV-6A   25584   16.05.07
N9004F   P J Pengilly   Membury   *'20'*   18.04.18P
Built by D L Reed

G-CSPT Gippsaero GA8-TC320 Airvan   GA8-TC 320-11-161   14.02.18
VH-AQQ   Downlock Ltd   Biggin Hill
(NF 14.02.18)

G-CSUE ICP MXP-740 Savannah VG Jabiru(5)   06-07-51-505   26.10.06
R K Stephens & J R Stratton   Dunkeswell   17.06.18P
Built by J R Stratton – project BMAA/HB/517

G-CSZM Zenair CH.601XL Zodiac   6-9649   09.12.05
C Budd   (Tairgwaith, Ammanford)
Built by C Budd – project PFA 162B-14367 (NF 11.07.18)

G-CTAA – G-CTZZ

G-CTAB Champion 7GCAA Citabria   114   08.07.15
G-BFHP, HB-UAX   M R Keen & M Walker   Dunkeswell   17.11.18E
For sale with AT Aviation 07.18

G-CTAG Rolladen-Schneider LS8-18   8150   11.09.07
BGA 4450   C D R Tagg   Pocklington   *'C1'*   27.10.18E

G-CTAM Cirrus SR22   2740   15.06.09
N12SJ   D S Olson   Solent   25.05.19E

G-CTAV Evektor EV-97 teamEurostar UK   2004-2129   25.11.04
P Simpson   Bourn   03.12.18P
Assembled Cosmik Aviation Ltd

G-CTCB Diamond DA.42 Twin Star   42.083   29.07.13
G-CDTG   L3 CTS Airline & Academy Training Ltd
Bournemouth   22.05.18E

G-CTCC Diamond DA.42 Twin Star   42.161   07.01.13
G-OCCZ   L3 CTS Airline & Academy Training Ltd
Bournemouth   17.07.18E

G-CTCD Diamond DA.42 Twin Star   42.079   08.02.06
OE-VPI   L3 CTS Airline & Academy Training Ltd
Bournemouth   20.03.18E

G-CTCE Diamond DA.42 Twin Star   42.043   25.08.05
OE-VPI   L3 CTS Airline & Academy Training Ltd
Bournemouth   06.11.18E

G-CTCF Diamond DA.42 Twin Star   42.045   25.08.05
OE-VPY   L3 CTS Airline & Academy Training Ltd
Bournemouth   18.09.18E

G-CTCG Diamond DA.42 Twin Star   42.046   25.08.05
EC-LAM, EC-KSZ, G-CTCG
Dea Aviation Ltd   Retford Gamston   05.06.12E
(NF 02.10.18)

G-CTCH Diamond DA.42 Twin Star   42.238   04.05.07
(ZK-CTP), OE-VPY   L3 CTS Airline & Academy
Training Ltd   Bournemouth   10.12.18E

G-CTCL SOCATA TB-10 Tobago   1107   16.07.90
G-BSIV   J R Wing-Stevenson tr Double S Group
Nottingham City   08.12.18E

G-CTDH Flight Design CT2K   02-08-01-31   01.05.03
A D Thelwall   Felixkirk   25.05.19P
Assembled Mainair Sports Ltd as c/n 7939

G-CTDW Flight Design CTSW   07-05-05   22.06.07
H D Colliver   Landmead Farm, Garford   31.07.18P
Assembled P&M Aviation Ltd as c/n 8295

G-CTED Van's RV-7A   xxxx   24.05.07
J J Nicholson   Liverpool John Lennon   03.12.18P
Built by E W Lyon – project PFA 323-14631

G-CTEE Flight Design CTSW   07-02-13   15.05.14
G-CLEG   P J Clegg   Rossall Field, Cockerham   02.05.18P
Assembled P&M Aviation Ltd as c/n 8269

G-CTEL Cameron N-90   3933   27.08.96
M R Noyce   Newtown, Hungerford   *'Gabletop'*   23.04.14E
(IE 05.07.17)

G-CTFL Robinson R44 Raven   1912   05.03.12
G-CLOT   Heli Air Scotland Ltd   Wycombe Air Park   19.10.18E
Collided with G-HYND Cumbernauld 05.05.18
& substantially damaged; wreck stored 01.19

G-CTFS Westland SA.341C Gazelle HT.2   1081   04.09.15
G-OJCO, G-LEDR, G-CBSB, XW857
RSE 15119 Ltd   (Tickton, Beverley)   04.04.18P

G-CTIO SOCATA TB-20 Trinidad GT   2174   07.11.02
F-OIMH   I R Hunt   Biggin Hill   26.10.18E

G-CTIX Supermarine 509 Spitfire Tr.9   xxxx   09.04.85
N462JC, G-CTIX, Israel DFAF 2067 & 0607,
Italian AF MM4100, PT462   Propshop Ltd   Duxford   20.05.19P
Built by Castle Bromwich 1944 as HF.Mk.IX;
composite including wings ex TE517 (Israeli AF)
pre 1994; as 'PT462:SW-A' in RAF c/s

G-CTKL Noorduyn AT-16-ND Harvard IIB   07-30   22.11.83
(G-BKWZ), Ital AF MM54137, RCAF 3064
M R Simpson   Biggin Hill
C/n also quoted as '76-80';
as 'FE788' in RAF c/s (IE 21.06.16)

G-CTLS Flight Design CTLS   F.08-09-12   19.01.09
D J Haygreen   RAF Mona   16.03.16W
Assembled P&M Aviation Ltd

G-CTNG Cirrus SR20   2012   14.04.09
N570PG   J Crackett   Sleap   04.11.18E

G-CTOY	Denney Kitfox Model 3	1176	14.10.91
	J I V Hill Newtownards		19.08.15P
	Built by C G Brooke & G S Cass – project		
	PFA 172-12150 (NF 21.12.16)		

G-CTSA	Diamond DA.40NG Star	40.N312	03.04.18
	N109QG L3 CTS Airline & Academy Training Ltd		
	Bournemouth		
	(IE 04.10.18)		

G-CTSB	Diamond DA.40NG Star	40.N283	03.04.18
	N265PS L3 CTS Airline & Academy Training Ltd		
	Bournemouth		26.04.19E

G-CTSC	Diamond DA.40NG Star	40.N307	03.04.18
	N391UQ Escola de Aviacao Aerocondor SA		
	Ponte de Sor, Portugal		17.05.19E

G-CTSD	Diamond DA.40NG Star	40.N308	03.04.18
	N468ZF Escola de Aviacao Aerocondor SA		
	Ponte de Sor, Portugal		19.05.19E

G-CTSE	Diamond DA.40NG Star	40.N170	27.06.18
	N637RC Escola de Aviacao Aerocondor SA		Bournemouth
	Operated by L3 CTS Airline & Academy Training		
	(IE 27.06.18)		

G-CTSF	Diamond DA.40NG Star	40.N284	24.05.18
	N605SJ Escola de Aviacao Aerocondor SA		
	Bournemouth		12.01.19E
	Operated by L3 CTS Airline & Academy Training		

G-CTSG	Diamond DA.40NG Star	40.N169	26.06.18
	N846TC Escola de Aviacao Aerocondor SA		
	Bournemouth		
	Operated by L3 CTS Airline & Academy Training		
	(IE 26.06.18)		

G-CTSH	Diamond DA.40NG Star	40.N310	04.05.18
	N874FB Escola de Aviacao Aerocondor SA		
	Bournemouth		
	Operated by L3 CTS Airline & Academy Training		
	(NF 04.05.18)		

G-CTSJ	Diamond DA.40NG Star	40.N181	27.06.18
	N697CT Escola de Aviacao Aerocondor SA		
	Ponte de Sor, Portugal		
	(IE 27.06.18)		

G-CTSK	Diamond DA.40NG Star	40.N224	11.07.18
	N528MH Escola de Aviacao Aerocondor SA		
	Ponte de Sor, Portugal		
	(IE 11.07.18)		

G-CTSL	Flight Design CT-Supralight	E12-09-07	10.03.14
	G D Alcock & J Lander Deanland		17.07.19P
	Assembled P&M Aviation Ltd as c/n 8683		

G-CTSM	Diamond DA.40NG Star	40.N311	21.05.18
	N906KN Escola de Aviacao Aerocondor SA		
	Ponte de Sor, Portugal		22.08.19E

G-CTSN	Diamond DA.40NG Star	40.N180	28.06.18
	N742CC Escola de Aviacao Aerocondor SA		
	Ponte de Sor, Portugal		14.08.19E

G-CTSO	Diamond DA.40NG Star	40.N188	28.06.18
	N539TS Escola de Aviacao Aerocondor SA		
	Ponte de Sor, Portugal		02.08.19E

G-CTSP	Diamond DA.40NG Star	40.N309	21.05.18
	N713HX Escola de Aviacao Aerocondor SA		
	Ponte de Sor, Portugal		02.08.19E

G-CTSR	Diamond DA.40NG Star	40.N304	11.06.18
	N273EV Escola de Aviacao Aerocondor SA		
	Ponte de Sor, Portugal		23.08.19E

G-CTSS	Diamond DA.40NG Star	40.N225	11.07.18
	N386AP Escola de Aviacao Aerocondor SA		
	Bournemouth		04.10.19E
	Operated by L3 CTS Airline & Academy Training		

G-CTST	Diamond DA.40NG Star	40.N302	03.01.19
	N154BY Escola de Aviacao Aerocondor SA		
	Bournemouth		
	Operated by L3 CTS Airline & Academy Training		
	(NF 03.01.19)		

G-CTSU	Diamond DA.42 Twin Star	42.340	15.05.18
	OO-SFA, OE-VPW L3 CTS Airline & Academy		
	Training Ltd Ponte de Sor, Portugal		01.03.19E

G-CTSV	Diamond DA.42 Twin Star	42.214	15.05.18
	OO-SFI L3 CTS Airline & Academy Training Ltd		
	Ponte de Sor, Portugal		09.02.19E

G-CTSX	Diamond DA.40NG Star	40.N303	03.01.19
	N910XD Escola de Aviacao Aerocondor SA		
	Ponte de Sor, Portugal		
	(NF 03.01.19)		

G-CTTS	English Electric Canberra B.2	71399	03.06.16
	G-BVWC, WK163		
	Vulcan to the Sky Trust Doncaster Sheffield		29.06.08P
	Built by Avro Aircraft Ltd; registered as B.6 but c/n		
	relates to nose section originally fitted to XH568;		
	as 'WK163' in RAF 617 Sqdn c/s; stored externally		
	06.18 (NF 02.06.16)		

G-CTUG	Piper PA-25-235 Pawnee C	25-4448	13.09.04
	N4713Y Portsmouth Naval Gliding Centre Keevil		01.07.19E

G-CTUK	Cirrus SR20	2435	09.07.18
	N435AG Cirrus Aircraft UK Ltd Sywell		09.07.19E

G-CTWO	Schempp-Hirth Standard Cirrus	256	11.07.07
	BGA 4836, SE-TMZ R J Griffin Shenington 'C2'		14.04.18E

G-CTZO	SOCATA TB-20 Trinidad GT	2166	07.10.02
	F-OIME R Street tr G-CTZO Group White Waltham		11.12.17E

G-CUAA – G-CUZZ

G-CUBA	Piper PA-32R-301T Turbo Saratoga SP	32R-8029090	17.01.12
	OE-KMS, D-EDET, N82009 M Altass Denham		08.09.18E

G-CUBB	Piper PA-18 Super Cub (*L-18C-PI*)	18-3111	05.12.78
	PH-WAM, Belgian AF OL-L37, 53-4711		
	East Sussex Gliding Club Ltd Ringmer		16.10.14E
	Fuselage No.18-3009; on rebuild Headcorn 06.17		
	(IE 21.12.17)		

G-CUBI	Piper PA-18-125 Super Cub (*L-18C-PI*)	18-3181	26.02.79
	PH-GAV, PH-VCV, R Netherlands AF R-83,		
	Belgian AF L-107, 53-4781 G T Fisher East Winch		04.11.94
	Official c/n '18-559' is incorrect; relates to PH-GAV		
	prior to 1970 rebuild with fuselage no.18-3170		
	ex PH-VCV; dismantled 07.15 (NF 09.12.15)		

G-CUBJ	Piper PA-18-150 Super Cub (*L-18C-PI*)	18-5395	15.12.82
	PH-MBF, PH-NLF, R Netherlands AF R-43, 8A-43,		
	52-2436 Zweefvliegclub Flevo Flevo, Netherlands		01.05.19E
	Original frame no.18-5512 ex PH-MBF rebuilt as		
	PH-BAJ, G-SUPA (qv); registered with c/n 18-5395		
	after 1974 rebuild of PH-NLF (18-2036): acquired		
	data plate from, & took identity of, PH-MBF but		
	retained fuselage no.18-2035; as '18-5395:CDG'		
	in French Army c/s		

G-CUBN	Piper PA-18-150 Super Cub	18-7902	17.11.05
	SE-ECN N J R Minchin Hill Top Farm, Hambleton		09.03.18E

G-CUBS	Piper J-3C-65 Cub	17792	26.10.01
	G-BHPT, F-BSGQ, LX-AIH, N70688, NC70688		
	S M Rolfe (Thurleigh, Bedford)		13.07.05P
	Official p/i 17792 is Fuselage No: c/n possibly		
	18105 (ex NC71076, N71076) (NF 30.04.18)		

G-CUBW	Wag-Aero AcroTrainer	NN13 BOUR	26.11.02
	A G Bourne & B G Plumb Hinton-in-the-Hedges		24.07.18P
	Built by A G Bourne, B G & N D Plumb		
	– project PFA 108-13581		

G-CUBY	Piper J-3C-65 Cub	16317	02.03.95
	N901MV, G-CUBY, G-BTZW, N88689, NC88689		
	J Slade Belvès-Saint Pardoux, France		24.08.18P
	Rebuilt with new fuselage 1996/97		

G-CUCU	Colt 180A	3869	22.04.96
	S R Seager Weedon, Aylesbury		28.05.06
	(NF 09.04.18)		

G-CUGC	Schleicher ASW 19B	19115	22.04.09
	G-CKEX, BGA 5043/KEX, I-IUUH, D-7551		
	P O'Donald tr Cambridge University Gliding Club		
	Gransden Lodge 'CU'		14.03.18E

G-CUMU	Schempp-Hirth Discus b	259	25.09.08
	BGA 3397/FNQ C E Fernando Nympsfield '282'		31.05.13E
	(IE 18.01.16)		

G-CUPP	Pitts S-2A	2166	27.03.07
	N42XX, N86PS		
	Avmarine Ltd Truleigh Manor Farm, Edburton		16.06.18E
	Built by Aerotek Inc		

G-CURV	Avid Speed Wing	1039	28.03.00
	K S Kelso Fen End Farm, Cottenham		
	Built by K S Kelso – project PFA 189-12169;		
	cleared to fly 04.01.19 (IE 07.12.18)		

G-CUTE	Dyn'Aéro MCR-01 Club	132	07.09.99
	J M Keane Deanland		17.05.17P
	Built by E G Shimmin – project PFA 301-13511		

G-CUTH	P&M QuikR	8472	18.08.09
	A, R & S Cuthbertson Old Park Farm, Margam		11.06.18P

G-CVAA – G-CVZZ

G-CVAL	Comco Ikarus C42 FB100	0608-6836	15.08.06
	J C Nudd (Penzance)		29.11.19P
	Assembled Aerosport Ltd		

G-CVBA	Rolladen-Schneider LS6-18W	6360	19.12.13
	(BGA 5758), D-6561		
	J S Moore (Easthope, Much Wenlock) 'BA'		05.03.19E

G-CVBF	Cameron A-210	3588	02.06.95
	Airxcite Ltd t/a Virgin Balloon Flights		
	Stafford Park, Telford		
	(NF 15.09.14)		

G-CVET	Flight Design CTLS	F.11-02-14	07.05.13
	G-CGVR AAA Dev LLP		
	Yeatsall Farm, Abbots Bromley		30.04.18W
	Assembled P&M Aviation Ltd		

G-CVII	Dan Rihn DR.107 One Design	05-510	09.03.06
	N S Bigrigg tr One Design Group RAF Syerston		04.12.18P
	Built by R M Davies – project PFA 264-14478		

G-CVIX	de Havilland DH.110 Sea Vixen FAW.2 10125		26.02.96
	XP924 Naval Aviation Ltd RNAS Yeovilton		27.06.17P
	As 'XP924:134' in 899 RN Sqdn c/s; operated by		
	Fly Navy Heritage Trust; made wheels up landing		
	RNAS Yeovilton 27.05.17 and on rebuild 2019		

G-CVLH	Piper PA-34-200T Seneca II	34-8070332	05.09.02
	F-GCPK, N8252D, N8250H		
	Cancelled 11.01.11 as PWFU		12.09.05
	St Brieuc, France *Derelict 08.15*		

G-CVLN	AutoGyro Cavalon	V00095	22.11.13
	G-CIAT M Spohn (Enfield)		27.04.19P
	Assembled Rotorsport UK as c/n RSUK/CVLN/003		

G-CVMI	Piper PA-18-150 Super Cub	18-5700	23.05.05
	SE-CEE C Watson Rougham		01.03.18E

G-CVST	Jodel D.140E Mousquetaire	456	21.05.03
	N P de G Lambert Popham		04.04.18P
	Built by A Shipp – project PFA 251-13384		

G-CVXN	Reims/Cessna F406 Caravan II	F406-0064	03.12.08
	G-SFPA Directflight Ltd Cranfield		04.04.19E

G-CVZT	Schempp-Hirth Ventus-2cT	39/129	09.11.07
	BGA 4664/JPD A & M W Conboy Lasham 'V2T'		25.02.18E

G-CWAA – G-CWZZ

G-CWAG	Sequoia F.8L Falco	xxxx	11.05.92
	D R Austin High Cross, Ware		19.06.17P
	Built by C C Wagner – project PFA 100-10895		
	(IE 10.07.17)		

G-CWAL	Raj Hamsa X'Air 133(1)	777	27.04.04
	L R Morris Derryogue, Kilkeel		31.10.13P
	Built by C Walsh – project BMAA/HB/339;		
	force landed near Kilkeel 27.08.13 & substantially		
	damaged (NF 13.11.15)		

G-CWAY	Comco Ikarus C42 FB100	0707-6907	06.09.07
	M Conway Carrickmore		08.09.18P
	Assembled Aerosport Ltd		

G-CWBM	Phoenix Currie Wot	xxxx	28.03.94
	G-BTVP J Evans & R Smith tr G-CWBM Group		
	Griffins Farm, Temple Bruer		14.06.18P
	Built by B V Mayo – project PFA 3020		

G-CWCD	Beech B200GT King Air	BY-198	12.05.14
	N198BK Clowes Estates Ltd East Midlands		15.06.18E

G-CWDW	Cessna 182T Skylane	18281946	23.05.17
	G-PCBC, N23121 R A S White Cambridge		06.09.19E

G-CWEB	P&M Quik GT450	8343	20.02.08
	F J Jarvis tr G-CWEB Syndicate East Fortune		05.02.20P
	Uses Trike ex G-CIIA		

G-CWFB	Piper PA-38-112 Tomahawk	38-78A0623	13.01.00
	G-OAAL, N4471E Cancelled 08.12.10 by CAA		08.02.07
	RAF Leuchars *Cockpit with No.2435 ATC Sqn, 08.18*		

G-CWFS	Tecnam P2002-JF Sierra	077	05.09.12
	EC-KMX S Adey Draycott		27.04.18E

G-CWFT	Cessna 172N Skyhawk	17273576	27.07.18
	N6182G Avalon Ventures Ltd		
	(Beaumont, Clacton-on-Sea)		
	(NF 27.07.18)		

G-CWIC	Mainair Pegasus Quik	8067	21.09.04
	Z G Nagygyorgy tr G-CWIC Group Manchester Barton		24.06.18P
	Built by Mainair Sports Ltd		

G-CWLC	Schleicher ASH 25	25105	09.01.08
	BGA3720/GCE C L Withall tr G-CWLC Group		
	Dunstable Downs '8'		24.01.19E

G-CWMC	P&M Quik GT450	8201	26.08.06
	A R Hughes Yatesbury		16.04.17P
	Badged 'Quik Lite' (IE 06.06.17)		

G-CWOW	Kubicek BB45Z	912	08.06.12
	S J Colin t/a Skybus Ballooning Headcorn, Ashford		02.07.19E

G-CWTD	Aeroprakt A-22 Foxbat	UK016	21.10.03
	J R Hughes tr Newtownards Microlight Group		
	Newtownards		08.05.18P
	Built by J V Harris – project PFA 317-14131		

G-CWTT	Cessna 182T Skylane	18283029	23.01.18
	N9020Z C W Ivill Gloucestershire		23.01.19E
	(IE 23.01.18)		

G-CXAA – G-CXZZ

G-CXCX (4)	Cameron N-90	11998	14.03.86
	Cathay Pacific Airways (London) Ltd		
	London W6 'Cathay Pacific'		20.08.19E
	Original envelope c/n 1242: replaced by c/n 3332		
	(xx.xx), c/n 11132 (04.08) & c/n 11998 (01.17)		

G-CXDZ	Cassutt Speed Two	xxxx	27.12.02
	J A H Chadwick Nympsfield		
	Built by J A H Chadwick, S Thompson & R Whinsper		
	– project PFA 34-13816 (NF 27.01.17)		

G-CXIP	Thruster T600N	1031-T600N-095	17.11.03
	R J Howells Old Park Farm, Margam		21.10.18P
	Badged 'Sprint'		

G-CXIV	Thatcher CX4	224	26.03.13
	I B Melville (Thame)		
	Built by I B Melville – project LAA 357-14875		
	(NF 31.03.17)		

G-CXLS	Cessna 560XL Citation XLS	560-5613	13.07.09
	G-PKRG, N613XL, N5265B		
	Gama Aviation (Beauport) Ltd Jersey		21.09.18E

G-CXSM	Cessna 172R Skyhawk	17280320	01.02.07
	G-BXSM, N432ES S Eustathiou (London W5)		15.10.18E

G-CXTE	BRM Bristell NG5 Speed Wing	94	26.08.14
	M Langmead Slay Barn Farm, Cuddesdon		14.10.19P
	Built by M Langmead – project LAA 385-15290;		
	tricycle u/c		

G-CYAA – G-CYZZ

G-CYGI	HAPI Cygnet SF-2A	210	17.12.93
	B Brown (Witney)		
	Built by B Brown – project PFA 182-12084 (NF 24.04.15)		

G-CYLL	Sequoia F.8L Falco	1484	30.10.06
	N J Langrick & A J Newall tr Falco Group Breighton		29.11.19P
	Built by N J Langrick & A J Newall		
	– project PFA 100-14572		

G-CYMA	Gulfstream American GA-7 Cougar	GA7-0083	15.08.83
	G-BKOM, N794GA Cyma Petroleum (UK) Ltd Elstree		09.10.13E
	Noted 10.18 (NF 26.09.16)		

G-CYPC Cessna 208B Grand Caravan   208B2355   05.02.18
N940HL   P M H Bell tr The Cyprus Combined Services
Parachute Club   Kingsfield, Dhekelia, Republic of Cyprus
(IE 05.02.18)

G-CYPM Cirrus SR22   3185   04.11.08
N270CP   M J Matthews   Blackbushe   12.11.19E

G-CYRA Kolb Twinstar Mk.III   xxxx   30.01.03
G-MYRA   S J Fox   Popham   23.08.18P
Built by S J Fox & A P Pickford
– project PFA 205-12434

G-CYRL Cessna 182T Skylane   18282295   05.08.11
N9174B   S R Wilson
Wolverhampton Halfpenny Green   07.12.18E

G-CZAA – G-CZZZ

G-CZAC Zenair CH.601XL Zodiac   6-9443   26.03.04
K W Eskins & J P Pullin   Westonzoyland   25.06.19P
Built by D Pitt – project PFA 162B-14113; tricycle u/c

G-CZAG Sky 90-24   171   05.10.99
D S Tree   Albaretto della Torre, Italy   02.02.18E

G-CZAW CZAW Sportcruiser   06SC009   19.06.06
G N Smith   Inglenook Farm, Maydensole   03.07.14P
Built by G Smith – project PFA 338-14542
(NF 11.01.16)

G-CZBE   CFM Streak Shadow SA-M   K271   17.06.03
G-MZBE   Cancelled 05.12.08 as PWFU   30.11.08
Old Sarum   *Built by N J Bushell*
– project PFA 206-12905; stored 03.16

G-CZCZ Mudry CAP 10B   54   28.07.94
OE-AYY, F-WZCG, HB-SAK, F-BUDT
M Farmer   Garston Farm, Marshfield   16.11.18E

G-CZMI Best Off Skyranger Swift 912(1)   SKR0308377   18.11.03
D G Baker   Solent   07.08.18P
Built by T W Thiele – project BMAA/HB/307

G-CZNE Pilatus B-N BN-2B-20 Islander   2301   27.07.04
G-BWZF   Skyhopper LLP   Gloucestershire   27.08.18E
Carried 'OE-FZO' for 2015 film 'Sceptre'

G-CZOS Cirrus SR20   2038   01.07.10
N510UK   W R M Beesley   Nottingham City   04.10.18E

G-CZSC CZAW Sportcruiser   700153   23.06.08
F J Wadia   Sunnyside Farm, Whitwell   24.07.19P
Built by A K Lynn – project LAA 338-14814

G-DAAA – G-DZZZ

G-DAAN Eurocopter EC135 P2+   1080   04.12.12
Devon Air Ambulance Trading Company Ltd
Exeter Int'l   14.07.18E
Operated by Devon Air Ambulance as callsign
'Helimed 70'

G-DAAY Ultramagic B-70   70/25   25.06.18
A M Holly   Breadstone, Berkeley   08.08.19E
Koala special shape

G-DAAZ Piper PA-28RT-201T Turbo Arrow IV   28R-7931247   17.01.03
N2896B   Fifty Two Management Ltd   (Perth)   28.11.18E

G-DACA^M Percival P.57 Sea Prince T.1   P57/12   06.05.80
WF118
Cancelled 15.12.09 by CAA   *As 'WF118:569'*
With South Wales Aircraft Museum, St Athan

G-DACE Corben Baby Ace D   JC-1   11.12.12
G-BTSB, N3599   G N Holland
White Ox Mead, Peasedown St John   29.08.18P
Carries '3599' on tail

G-DACF Cessna 152 II   15281724   13.06.97
G-BURY, N67285   M L & T M Jones   Derby   12.08.18E
Operated by Derby Aero Club

G-DADA AutoGyro MT-03   xxxx   12.05.08
J C Hilton-Johnson   Enstone   14.06.18P
Assembled Rotorsport UK as c/n RSUK/MT-03/040

G-DADD Reality Escapade 912(2)   AW.ESC.001   08.02.13
P S Balmer   St Michaels   01.11.18P
Built by P S Balmer – project BMAA/HB/613;
kit & frame built by AirWeld

G-DADG Piper PA-18-150 Super Cub   18-5237   13.10.04
N45498, Israel DFAF 069
F J Cox   Gorrell Farm, Woolsery   28.06.18E

G-DADJ Glaser-Dirks DG-200   2-43   29.02.08
BGA 2394/DUQ   M A Hunton   RAF Cranwell   *'58'*   23.01.19E

G-DADZ CZAW Sportcruiser   700523   07.04.08
D Pitt tr Meon Flying Group   West Tisted   17.06.18P
Built by D A Rose – project LAA 338-14792

G-DAGF EAA Acrosport II   xxxx   21.10.10
M G Pahle   (London N8)   17.09.19P
Built by D A G Fraser – project PFA 072A-11129

G-DAGJ Zenair CH.601XL Zodiac   6-9608   28.10.05
D A G Johnson   Popham
Built by D A G Johnson – project PFA 162B-14317;
tricycle u/c (IE 30.09.17)

G-DAGN Comco Ikarus C42 FB80   1509-7419   09.11.15
N J James   Welshpool   03.11.18P
Assembled Red Aviation

G-DAIR Luscombe 8A   1474   03.10.97
G-BURK, N28713, NC28713
D F Soul   Wood Farm, Emberton   19.10.99P
(NF 19.04.18)

G-DAKA Piper PA-28-236 Dakota   28-8111060   22.08.14
F-GJIH, D-ENIH, N8365D   M M Zienkiewicz   (Swindon)   17.05.18E

G-DAKK^M Douglas C-47A-35-DL   9798   26.07.94
(G-OFON), F-GEOM, French Navy 36, OK-WZB,
OK-WDU, 42-23936
R G T de Man   Overloon, Noord Holland, Netherlands   23.05.03
To Oorlogsmuseum, Overloon 2017 (NF 02.09.15)

G-DAKM Diamond DA.40D Star   D4.222   21.09.06
OE-VPT, OE-VPU   K Macdonald   Blackpool   10.11.18E

G-DAKO Piper PA-28-236 Dakota   28-7911187   29.07.99
PH-ARW, (PH-MFB), D-EECG, PH-ARW, OO-HCX,
N29718   M H D Smith   Enstone   31.01.18E

G-DAMB Sequoia F.8L Falco   xxxx   28.08.15
G-OGKB   S O Foxlee   Fife   21.05.18P
Built by G K Brothwood, S Foxlee & A Powell
– project PFA 100-12153

G-DAME Van's RV-7   73181   16.09.09
LY-ATZ   A J Gilbert   (Sleaford)   07.11.19P

G-DAMS Best Off Skyranger Nynja 912S(1)   UK\N/BK0162   27.11.14
Dambusters Ltd   Popham   24.02.18P
Built by P Knight – project BMAA/HB/656

G-DAMY Europa Aviation Europa   105   21.10.94
R J Kelly & U A Schliessler   Wycombe Air Park   09.08.17P
Built by Hart Aviation Ltd – project PFA 247-12781;
tricycle u/c

G-DANA Robin DR.200 replica   871   02.12.02
G-DAST   F A Bakir tr Cheshire Eagles
Yew Tree Farm, Lymm Dam   16.02.18P
Built by F A Bakir & A Macleod – project
PFA 304-13351; composite from parts of
SAN DR.1050 G-AWEN (c/n 67) & CEA DR.1051
G-BLRJ (c/n 502)

G-DANB TLAC Sherwood Ranger ST   56   03.04.14
W A Douthwaite   Rufforth East   06.11.18P
Built by D R Baker – project LAA 237B-15242

G-DAND SOCATA TB-10 Tobago   72   05.12.79
G Ladlow tr Coventry Aviators Flying Group   Coventry   12.11.18E

G-DANP Van's RV-7   73597   29.03.16
D T Pangbourne   Fowle Hall Farm, Laddingford   12.07.19P
Built by D T Pangbourne – project LAA 323-14941

G-DANY Avtech Jabiru UL   0329   28.12.00
D A Crosbie   Crosbie's Field, Little Cornard
Built by D A Crosbie – project PFA 274A-13588
(NF 09.10.15)

G-DASG Schleicher ASW 27-18E (ASG 29E)   29660   22.07.13
(BGA 5751)   E Alston   North Hill   *'G29'*   25.06.18E

G-DASH Rockwell Commander 112A   237   31.03.87
G-BDAJ, N1237J   M J P Lynch   Coventry   14.03.18E

G-DASS Comco Ikarus C42 FB100   0509-6758   30.09.05
E Wright   Wickenby   28.09.19P
Assembled Aerosport Ltd

G-DATR	Agusta-Bell 206B-3 JetRanger III	8588		14.03.14
	G-JLEE, G-JOKE, G-CSKY, G-TALY			
	P J Spinks Gloucestershire			12.09.18E
G-DAVB	Aerosport Scamp	xxxx		29.05.09
	D R Burns Perth			
	Built by D R Burns – project PFA 117-10889 (IE 14.07.16)			
G-DAVD	Reims/Cessna FR172K Hawk XP	FR17200632		23.12.99
	D-EFJT, (PH-ADL), PH-AXO			
	S Copeland, P Ferguson & S Maddock Coventry			16.08.19E
	Blown over in high winds Coventry 03/04.03.19			
	& substantially damaged			
G-DAVE	Jodel D.112	667		16.08.78
	F-BICH I D Worthington Bagby			17.08.17P
	Built by Etablissement Valladeau			
G-DAVM	Mudry CAP 10B	278		26.03.10
	N73AE D Moorman Fowle Hall Farm, Laddingford			30.03.18E
	Built by Akrotech Europe			
G-DAVS	Sportine Aviacija LAK-17AT	158		12.06.06
	BGA 5171/KKZ, LY-GIW			
	D Bellamy tr G-DAVS Syndicate Burn *'17T'*			06.06.18E
G-DAWG	Scottish Aviation Bulldog Srs 120/121	BH120/208		13.03.02
	XX522 High G Bulldog Ltd Blackpool			09.12.18E
	As 'XX522:06' in RAF c/s			
G-DAYI	Europa Aviation Europa	298		19.08.96
	A F Day (Bromley)			
	Built by A F Day – project PFA 247-13027 (NF 29.01.16)			
G-DAYO	Beech A36 Bonanza	E-2651		31.08.16
	D-EAYO Exeter Aviation Ltd Exeter Int'l			23.09.18E
G-DAYP	Beech B300C Super King Air 350C	FM-29		12.07.17
	N6029S, HZ-PM4, N6029S			
	Gama Aviation (Asset 2) Ltd RAF Waddington			25.09.18E
	For RAF as Beechcraft Shadow R1 ZZ505			
G-DAYR	Bombardier CL-600-2B16 Challenger 605	5764		11.10.18
	D-AFAC, OE-ISU, C-FTQZ			
	Gama Aviation (UK) Ltd Farnborough			31.03.19E
G-DAYS	Europa Aviation Europa	177		09.05.95
	R M F Pereira Leicester			11.04.17P
	Built by A, A J & S D Hall – project PFA 247-12810;			
	tailwheel u/c			
G-DAYZ	Pietenpol Air Camper	xxxx		22.06.01
	M B Blackmore & T W J Carnall Dunkeswell			11.09.13P
	Built by J G Cronk – project PFA 047-12342			
	(NF 11.07.18)			
G-DAZO	Diamond DA.20-A1 Katana	10027		15.06.16
	F-GNJJ, N607F Cubair Flight Training Ltd Redhill			18.09.19E
G-DAZY	Piper PA-34-200T Seneca II	34-7770335		04.02.03
	N953A, PH-DLM, OE-DGG, N38727			
	Cancelled 14.12.11 by CAA			02.06.11
	Lydd *Open store 10.15*			
G-DAZZ	Van's RV-8	82147		20.10.04
	D R Holroyd tr Wishangar RV8			
	Wishanger Farm, Frensham			03.10.18P
	Built by D M Hartfree-Bright – project PFA 303-14245			
G-DBCA	Airbus A319-131	2098		23.02.04
	D-AVYV British Airways PLC London Heathrow			21.08.19E
G-DBCB	Airbus A319-131	2188		23.04.04
	D-AVYA British Airways PLC London Heathrow			22.04.19E
G-DBCC	Airbus A319-131	2194		14.05.04
	D-AVYT British Airways PLC London Heathrow			13.05.19E
G-DBCD	Airbus A319-131	2389		09.02.05
	D-AVYJ British Airways PLC London Heathrow			06.01.20E
G-DBCE	Airbus A319-131	2429		31.03.05
	D-AVWG British Airways PLC London Heathrow			30.03.19E
G-DBCF	Airbus A319-131	2466		26.05.05
	D-AVYA British Airways PLC London Heathrow			25.05.19E
G-DBCG	Airbus A319-131	2694		21.02.06
	D-AVXD British Airways PLC London Heathrow			20.02.19E
G-DBCH	Airbus A319-131	2697		23.02.06
	D-AVXE British Airways PLC London Heathrow			22.02.19E
G-DBCJ	Airbus A319-131	2981		09.01.07
	D-AVXG British Airways PLC London Heathrow			12.12.19E
G-DBCK	Airbus A319-131	3049		02.03.07
	D-AVYG British Airways PLC London Heathrow			01.03.19E
G-DBDB	Magni M16 Tandem Trainer	109		19.10.99
	G-IROW, G-DBDB K Kerr Rednal *'Eagle 2'*			10.09.18P
	Built by D R Bolsover – project PFA G/12-1239			
G-DBEE	Avtech Jabiru J430	595		06.07.18
	A G Bridger Shipdham			
	Built by A G Bridger – project LAA 336-14803			
	(NF 06.07.18)			
G-DBEN	Schleicher ASW 15	15105		23.12.15
	(BGA 5870), HB-1008 L C Bennett tr Oscar 8			
	Syndicate Dunstable Downs *'O8'*			05.08.18E
G-DBIN	Medway SLA 80 Executive	070707		22.04.08
	P M Alty Compton Abbas			25.03.19P
G-DBJD	SZD-9bis Bocian 1D	P-391		08.02.08
	BGA 998/BJD C Simpson tr Bertie the Bocian			
	Glider Syndicate Lasham *'Bertie'* & *'BJD'*			25.05.18E
G-DBKL	Supermarine 379 Spitfire F.XIVc	6S-432268		30.03.09
	6640M, (6629M), RM694 P M Andrews (High Wycombe)			
	Built by Chattis Hill 1944; wings to NH904			
	(later G-FIRE, N8118J & now N114BP)			
	c.1966 (NF 20.05.16)			
G-DBND	Schleicher Ka 6CR	1157		18.04.08
	BGA 1094/BND			
	Lincolnshire Gliding Club Ltd Strubby *'BND'*			03.12.16E
G-DBNH	Schleicher Ka 6CR	6115		14.07.08
	BGA 1098/BNH The Bath, Wilts & North Dorset			
	Gliding Club Ltd Kingston Deverill *'BNH'*			15.01.19E
G-DBNK	Eurocopter EC120B Colibri	1673		17.08.15
	G-PERF De Banke Aviation LLP (Solihull)			04.06.19E
G-DBOD	Cessna 172S Skyhawk	172S10961		12.03.10
	N5218X Goodwood Road Racing Company Ltd			
	Goodwood			05.04.18E
G-DBOL	Schleicher Ka 6CR	725		10.06.08
	BGA 1149/BQL, D-7117			
	M T Cook tr G-DBOL Group Long Mynd			11.05.18E
G-DBRT	Slingsby T.51 Dart	1430		24.08.09
	BGA 1180/BRT C W Logue RAF Marham *'BRT'*			23.10.10R
	(NF 30.04.18)			
G-DBRU	Slingsby T.51 Dart	1429		22.07.09
	BGA 1181/BRU P S Whitehead Walney Island			21.08.13E
	(NF 28.06.16)			
G-DBRY	Slingsby T.51 Dart	1434		06.02.08
	BGA 1185/BRY G B Marshall Darlton *'BRY'*			01.04.15R
	(NF 23.08.18)			
G-DBSA	Slingsby T.51 Dart 15	1405		22.10.07
	BGA1187 K P Russell Aston Down *'BSA'*			14.04.17R
G-DBSL	Slingsby T.51 Dart 17	1445		08.09.08
	BGA 1197/BSL			
	J C G Owles tr G-DBSL Group Tibenham *'BSL'*			17.08.18R
G-DBTJ	Schleicher Ka 6CR	6367		18.04.08
	BGA 1219/BTJ I G Robinson			
	Skelling Farm, Skirwith *'BTJ'*			22.11.17E
G-DBUZ	Schleicher Ka 6CR	6418		04.01.08
	BGA 1257/BUZ J J Hartwell Lyveden *'BUZ'*			05.11.09E
	(NF 23.09.15)			
G-DBVB	Schleicher K7 Rhönadler	7230		25.01.08
	BGA 1259/BVB Dartmoor Gliding Society			
	Burnford Common, Brentor *'BVB'*			11.05.14E
	Modified to ASK 13 standard (NF 11.08.15)			
G-DBVH	Slingsby T.51 Dart 17R	1485		29.02.08
	BGA 1265/BVH R D Brister Gransden Lodge *'BVH'*			
	(NF 06.04.17)			
G-DBVR	Schleicher Ka 6CR	6441		01.11.07
	BGA 1273/BVR			
	A L Hoskin Lasham *'BVR'* & *'Woody'*			21.08.17E
G-DBVX	Schleicher Ka 6CR	6439		12.05.08
	BGA 1279/BVX Y Marom Kingston Deverill *'BVX'*			01.12.18E
G-DBVZ	Schleicher Ka 6CR	6446		12.11.07
	BGA 1281/BVZ			
	S J Johnston tr G-DBVZ Group Bellarena *'BVZ'*			12.04.15E
	(NF 25.09.16)			
G-DBWC	Schleicher Ka 6CR	6449		26.03.08
	BGA 1284/BWC T W Humphrey Upwood *'BWC'*			19.05.18E
G-DBWJ	Slingsby T.51 Dart 17R	1495		14.02.08
	BGA 1290/BWJ M F Defendi Wormingford *'317'*			01.08.17R

G-DBWM	Slingsby T.51 Dart 17R	1500	13.02.08
	BGA 1293/BWM P L Poole Shobdon *'182'*		23.03.18R
G-DBWO	Slingsby T.51 Dart 15	1505	21.02.08
	BGA 1296/BWQ C R Stacey Wormingford *'723'*		13.08.14R
	(NF 20.03.17)		
G-DBWP	Slingsby T.51 Dart 17R	1501	07.01.08
	BGA 1295/BWP R Johnson Talgarth *'17R'*		02.06.18R
G-DBWS	Slingsby T.51 Dart 17R	1502	04.12.07
	BGA 1298/BWS R D Broome		
	Hinton-in-the-Hedges *'517'*		01.06.18R
G-DBXG	Slingsby T.51 Dart 17R	1512	31.07.08
	BGA 1312/BXG J M Whelan Saltby *'BXG'*		04.10.18R
G-DBXT	Schleicher Ka 6CR	6492	22.04.09
	BGA 1323/BXT		
	C I Knowles Dunstable Downs *'BXT'*		21.11.15E
G-DBYC	Slingsby T.51 Dart 17R	1526	11.03.08
	BGA 1332/BYC		
	R L Horsnell & N A Jaffray Snitterfield *'BYC'*		23.11.18R
G-DBYG	Slingsby T.51 Dart 17R	1535	12.05.09
	BGA 1336/BYG, RAFGSA, BGA 1336		
	J R G Furnell Portmoak *'BYG'*		23.10.18R
G-DBYL	Schleicher Ka 6CR	6517	20.11.07
	BGA 1340/BYL		
	The Surrey Hills Gliding Club Ltd Kenley *'BYL'*		04.12.18E
G-DBYM	Schleicher Ka 6CR	6518	17.10.07
	BGA 1341, RAFGSA 381, BGA 1341		
	S F Smith Bicester *'558'*		03.08.15E
	(NF 23.02.18)		
G-DBYU	Schleicher Ka 6CR	6525	11.01.08
	BGA 1348/BYU, XW640, BGA 1348		
	K D Walker Seighford *'350'*		01.04.18E
G-DBYX	Schleicher Ka 6E	4055	19.12.07
	BGA 1351/BYX		
	I Bannister (Woolston, Warrington) *'BYX'*		22.10.18E
G-DBZF	Slingsby T.51 Dart 17R	1570	18.03.08
	BGA 1359/BZF S Rhenius Ridgewell *'BZF'*		25.10.18R
G-DBZJ	Slingsby T.51 Dart 17R	1567	12.06.12
	BGA 1362/BZJ L Ingram Enstone *'BZJ'*		14.07.16R
	(NF 08.12.17)		
G-DBZX	Schleicher Ka 6CR	6571	27.06.08
	BGA 1375/BZX B Brockwell Bicester *'BZX'*		05.04.17E
	(IE 31.05.17)		
G-DCAE	Schleicher Ka 6E	4076	09.11.07
	BGA 1381/CAE J R & P R Larner Seighford *'CAE'*		20.04.18E
G-DCAG	Schleicher Ka 6E	4080	28.11.07
	BGA 1383/CAG		
	S A Farmer tr 715 Syndicate Snitterfield *'715'*		04.02.19E
G-DCAM	Eurocopter AS.355NP Ecureuil 2	5750	26.08.10
	LN-OZG, F-WWXD Cameron Charters LLP		
	Blackshaw Heys Farm, Mobberley		07.09.19E
	Operated by VLL Ltd t/a GB Helicopters		
G-DCAO	Schempp-Hirth SHK-1	37	04.07.08
	BGA 1391/CAQ		
	M G Entwisle & M Watt Talgarth *'812'*		27.09.18E
G-DCAS	Schleicher Ka 6E	4029	04.10.07
	BGA 1393, RAFGSA 372		
	R F Tindall Gransden Lodge *'372'*		15.07.13R
	(IE 19.07.17)		
G-DCAZ	Slingsby T.51 Dart 17WR	1611	07.01.08
	BGA 1400/CAZ		
	D A Bullock & M L Chow Bicester *'500'*		11.08.15R
	(IE 05.07.17)		
G-DCBA	Slingsby T.51 Dart 17WR	1612	01.02.08
	BGA 1401/CBA		
	K T Kreis RAF Weston-on-the-Green *'679'*		18.05.18R
G-DCBI	Schweizer 269C-1 (*300CBi*)	0295	10.07.07
	N86G P T Shaw Cranfield		27.11.18E
G-DCBM	Schleicher Ka 6CR	6607	20.11.09
	BGA 1412/CBM R J Shepherd Long Mynd *'CBM'*		20.06.18E
G-DCBP	SZD-24C Foka	W-198	14.07.14
	BGA 1414/CBP, OY-BXR		
	The Gliding Heritage Centre Lasham *'CBP'*		16.02.18E
G-DCBW	Schleicher ASK 13	13034	24.09.07
	BGA 1421 Stratford on Avon Gliding Club Ltd		
	Snitterfield *'CBW'*		03.01.19E
G-DCBY	Schleicher Ka 6CR	960	03.03.08
	BGA 1423/CBY, RAFGSA 175, RAFGSA 322, D-3222		
	R G Appleboom Halesland *'475'*		13.07.18E
G-DCCA	Schleicher Ka 6E	4126	16.05.08
	BGA 1425/CCA R K Forrest Feshiebridge *'CCA'*		31.07.17E
	(IE 04.08.17)		
G-DCCB	Schempp-Hirth SHK-1	52	12.09.07
	BGA 1426		
	R M Johnson tr CCB Syndicate Milfield *'CCB'*		13.10.18E
G-DCCD	Schleicher Ka 6E	4127	30.09.09
	BGA 1428/CCD A G Linfield tr Charlie Charlie Delta		
	Group Shenington *'373'*		02.06.18E
G-DCCE	Schleicher ASK 13	13047	25.02.08
	BGA 1429/CCE Oxford Gliding Company Ltd		
	RAF Weston-on-the-Green *'CCE'*		05.05.18E
G-DCCG	Schleicher Ka 6E	4125	24.06.08
	BGA 1431/CCG R J Playle Shenington *'CCG'*		02.07.17E
	(IE 05.07.17)		
G-DCCL	Schleicher Ka 6E	4129	14.02.08
	BGA 1435/CCL A Sanders Eyres Field *'47'*		20.04.18E
G-DCCM	Schleicher ASK 13	13053	09.05.08
	BGA 1436/CCM		
	The Burn Gliding Club Ltd Burn *'CCM'*		17.06.18E
G-DCCP	Schleicher ASK 13	13052	04.02.08
	BGA 1438/CCP		
	G D Pullen tr Lima 99 Syndicate Lasham *'L99'*		12.04.18E
G-DCCR	Schleicher Ka 6E	4149	16.11.07
	BGA 1440/CCR		
	D Thomas tr G-DCCR Syndicate Bicester *'CCR'*		19.06.18E
G-DCCT	Schleicher ASK 13	13057	24.09.07
	BGA 1442		
	East Sussex Gliding Club Ltd Ringmer *'CCT'*		12.04.18E
G-DCCU	Schleicher Ka 6E	4122	05.10.07
	BGA 1443 J L Hasker Keevil *'CCU'*		13.06.19E
G-DCCV	Schleicher Ka 6E	4160	28.01.08
	BGA 1444/CCV B J Darton Wormingford *'CCV'*		05.06.19E
G-DCCW	Schleicher ASK 13	13051	20.11.07
	BGA 1445/CCW		
	Midland Gliding Club Ltd Long Mynd *'CCW'*		16.05.18E
G-DCCX	Schleicher ASK 13	13054	23.01.08
	BGA 1446/CCX Trent Valley Gliding Club Ltd *'CCX'*		07.10.18E
	Sold to new owners in Netherlands 04.18		
G-DCCY	Schleicher ASK 13	13050	30.11.07
	BGA 1447/CCY		
	Mendip Gliding Club Ltd Halesland *'CCY'*		09.07.18E
G-DCCZ	Schleicher ASK 13	13070	11.09.08
	BGA 1448/CCZ		
	The Windrushers Gliding Club Ltd Bicester *'CCZ'*		23.11.16E
G-DCDA	Schleicher Ka 6E	4136	26.06.08
	BGA 1449/CDA		
	D C Kirby-Smith & R E Musselwhite Kenley *'CDA'*		13.03.18E
G-DCDB	Bell 407	53137	19.10.09
	EI-RHM, G-DCDB, C-FCDB		
	A P Morrin Dublin Weston, RoI		24.03.18E
	Callsign 'Osprey 50'		
G-DCDC	Lange E1 Antares 20E	25	15.11.07
	D-KJWI J D Williams Portmoak *'Z7'*		08.07.18E
G-DCDF	Schleicher Ka 6E	4162	05.02.08
	BGA 1454/CDF		
	K G Reid tr CDF Syndicate Rivar Hill *'683'*		15.08.18E
G-DCDG	FFA Diamant 18	035	02.04.08
	BGA 1455/CDG		
	J Cashin & D McCarty Gowran Grange, RoI *'CDG'*		01.04.18E
G-DCDO	Comco Ikarus C42 FB80	1008-7115	23.09.10
	M Cheetham Dyson's Farm, Cuffley		14.03.19F
	Assembled Pioneer Aviation UK Ltd		
G-DCDW	FFA Diamant 18	033	03.08.07
	BGA 1469 D R Chapman Llantysilio *'CDW'*		30.06.12E
	(NF 06.07.15)		

G-DCDZ	Schleicher Ka 6E	4177		19.04.08
	BGA 1472/CDZ J R J Minnis Wormingford *'CDZ'*			06.11.09E
	(NF 08.06.16)			
G-DCEB	SZD-9bis Bocian 1E	P-433		05.02.08
	BGA 1474/CEB			
	P C Naegeli tr G-DCEB Syndicate Lasham *'007'*			28.11.14E
	Built by ZSLS Jezow Sudecki			
G-DCEC	Schempp-Hirth Cirrus	22		17.03.08
	BGA 1475/CEC C Coville & P J Little North Hill *'18'*			07.11.17E
G-DCEM	Schleicher Ka 6E	4212		23.01.08
	BGA1484/CEM S G Jessup Ridgewell *'CEM'*			10.04.18E
G-DCEO	Schleicher Ka 6E	4230		27.06.08
	BGA 1487/CEQ			
	J C Green & C L Lagden Wormingford *'458'*			18.04.18E
G-DCEW	Schleicher Ka 6E	4209		05.03.08
	BGA 1493/CEW J W Richardson tr JW Richardson			
	& Partners Group Seighford *'CEW'*			16.02.18E
G-DCFA	Schleicher ASK 13	13113		21.02.08
	BGA 1497/CFA			
	Dorset Gliding Club Ltd Eyres Field *'CFA'*			27.09.18E
G-DCFF	Schleicher K 8B	8765		22.08.08
	BGA 1502/CFF Derbyshire & Lancashire			
	Gliding Club Ltd Camphill *'CFF'*			13.05.18E
G-DCFG	Schleicher ASK 13	13115		27.02.08
	BGA 1503/CFG			
	The Nene Valley Gliding Club Ltd Upwood *'CFG'*			24.04.15E
	(NF 18.09.15)			
G-DCFK	Schempp-Hirth Cirrus	38		18.10.07
	BGA 1506 P D Whitters Seighford *'CFK'*			27.03.18E
G-DCFL	Schleicher Ka 6E	4215		09.09.08
	BGA 1507/CFL			
	D M Cornelius Dunstable Downs *'6E'*			22.08.18E
G-DCFS	Glasflügel Standard Libelle 201B	83		15.05.08
	BGA 1513/CFS J E Hoy Tibenham *'CFS'*			13.04.10E
	(NF 19.10.15)			
G-DCFW	Glasflügel Standard Libelle	275		11.06.08
	BGA 1517/CFW R A Robertson Talgarth *'CFW'*			12.03.18E
G-DCFX	Glasflügel Standard Libelle 201B	274		17.09.07
	BGA 1518 A S Burton Lyveden *'CFX'*			27.11.17E
G-DCFY	Glasflügel Standard Libelle	270		08.08.08
	BGA 1519/CFY C W Stevens Pocklington *'862'*			18.10.18E
G-DCGB	Schleicher Ka 6E	4247		16.11.07
	BGA 1522/CGB S C Male & P M Turner Long Mynd			12.07.18E
G-DCGD	Schleicher Ka 6E	4202		19.07.08
	BGA 1524/CGD M P Francis			
	tr Charlie Golf Delta Group Camphill *'CGD'*			02.06.18E
G-DCGE	Schleicher Ka 6E	4246		22.11.07
	BGA 1525/CGE			
	O J Anderson & B Silke Bellarena *'CGE'*			15.04.18E
G-DCGH	Schleicher K 8B	8772		06.02.08
	BGA 1528/CGH			
	T G B Hobbis tr K7 (1971) Syndicate Lasham *'153'*			12.10.18E
G-DCGM	FFA Diamant 18	053		10.09.08
	BGA 1532/CGM			
	J G Batch Hinton-in-the-Hedges *'CGM'*			16.12.10E
	(NF 24.02.17)			
G-DCGO	Schleicher ASK 13	13153		18.12.07
	BGA 1535/CGQ Oxford Gliding Company Ltd			
	RAF Weston-on-the-Green *'CGO'*			07.07.18E
G-DCGT	Schempp-Hirth SHK-1	38		23.01.08
	D-1538, G-DCGT, BGA 1538, D-1966			
	T Callier Lasham			03.06.18E
G-DCGY	Schempp-Hirth Cirrus	51		28.01.08
	BGA 1543/CGY S H Fletcher			
	Burnford Common, Brentor *'CGY'*			28.02.18E
G-DCHB	Schleicher Ka 6E	4235		15.04.08
	BGA 1546/CHB M J Hastings tr 577 Syndicate			
	RAF Weston-on-the-Green *'577'*			30.10.18E
G-DCHC	Bölkow Phoebus C	858		07.03.08
	BGA 1547/CHC			
	H Nolz (Prinzersdorf, Austria) *'CHC'*			11.12.16E
G-DCHG	SZD-30 Pirat	B-294		17.03.15
	BGA1551/CHG, RNGSA 452, BGA1551			
	M I Strange tr Pirat Syndicate Kingston Deverill			
G-DCHJ	Bölkow Phoebus C	879		19.09.08
	BGA 1553/CHJ D C Austin Sutton Bank *'CHJ'*			22.07.12E
	(NF 24.07.15)			
G-DCHL	SZD-30 Pirat	B-295		20.08.08
	BGA 1555/CHL			
	A M Bennett & P M Green Lyveden *'CHL'*			28.11.18E
	Built by ZSLS Bielsko-Biala (NF 25.09.16)			
G-DCHT	Schleicher ASW 15	15013		01.02.08
	BGA 1562/CHT			
	P G Roberts & J M Verrill Aston Down *'846'*			12.06.18E
G-DCHU	Schleicher K 8B	8794		10.07.08
	BGA 1563/CHU M W Norton tr G-DCHU Syndicate			
	Easterton *'CHU'*			12.09.18E
G-DCHW	Schleicher ASK 13	13187		23.12.08
	BGA 1565/CHW			
	Dorset Gliding Club Ltd Eyres Field *'CHW'*			09.06.18E
G-DCHZ	Schleicher Ka 6E	4153		12.05.08
	BGA 1568/CHZ, N6916			
	P K Bunnage & S Sullivan Lasham *'CHZ'*			15.06.18E
	(NF 30.10.17)			
G-DCII	AgustaWestland AW139	31703		06.08.15
	Executive Jet Charter Ltd Bristol			05.08.18E
G-DCJB	Bölkow Phoebus C	919		25.10.07
	BGA 1570 R Idle Burn *'CJB'*			23.05.13E
	(NF 30.06.16)			
G-DCJF	Schleicher K 8B	8803		06.01.12
	BGA 1574/CJF G Smith (Fancy Farm, Dunkeswell)			
	(NF 26.11.15)			
G-DCJJ	Bölkow Phoebus C	913		19.04.10
	BGA 1577/CJJ P N Maddocks (Milnathort, Kinross)			
	Stored in trailer as *'BGA1577'* (NF 29.05.18)			
G-DCJK	Schempp-Hirth SHK-1	35		07.05.08
	BGA 1578/CJK, RAFGSA 25			
	R H Short Lyveden *'CJK'*			12.07.18E
G-DCJM	Schleicher K 8B	8814		10.12.10
	BGA 1580/CJM			
	Midland Gliding Club Ltd Long Mynd *'CJM'*			14.02.18E
G-DCJN	Schempp-Hirth SHK-1	55		15.08.08
	BGA 1581/CJN R J Makin Camphill			10.09.12E
	(NF 20.11.15)			
G-DCJR	Schempp-Hirth Cirrus	87		22.12.07
	BGA 1584/CJR C Thirkell Sutton Bank *'CJR'*			12.05.18E
G-DCJY	Schleicher Ka 6CR	555		04.04.08
	BGA 1591/CJY, RAFGSA 119, BGA 1591			
	J D Peck tr CJY Syndicate Bicester *'CJY'*			16.03.18E
G-DCKD	SZD-30 Pirat	B-327		25.02.08
	BGA 1596/CKD			
	J S Halford tr Pirat Flying Group Eyres Field *'CKD'*			04.01.15E
	Built by ZSLS Bielsko-Biala (IE 07.12.17)			
G-DCKK	Reims/Cessna F172N	F17201589		19.05.80
	PH-GRT, PH-AXA R J Quinton tr KK Group Elstree			03.04.19E
G-DCKL	Schleicher Ka 6E	4336		02.06.08
	BGA 1603/CKL K Marston tr BGA 1603 Owners			
	Syndicate Milfield *'CKL'*			21.09.18E
G-DCKP	Schleicher ASW 15	15058		03.10.08
	BGA 1606/CKP			
	M W Black Easterton *'CKP'* & *'Herr Otto'*			25.08.19E
G-DCKR	Schleicher ASK 13	13247		07.08.08
	BGA 1608/CKR			
	Midland Gliding Club Ltd Long Mynd *'CKR'*			26.02.18E
G-DCKY	Glasflügel Standard Libelle	139		18.06.08
	BGA 1615/CKY B B Hughes (Reigate) *'743'*			11.10.09E
	(NF 29.09.17)			
G-DCKZ	Schempp-Hirth Standard Cirrus	52		04.12.07
	BGA 1616/CKZ, RAFGSA 24, BGA 1616			
	G I Bustin Saltby *'724'*			05.05.17E
G-DCLM	Glasflügel Standard Libelle	178		20.06.08
	BGA 1628/CLM R L Smith North Hill *'CLM'*			23.01.19E
G-DCLO	Schempp-Hirth Cirrus	99		19.06.08
	BGA 1631/CLQ J F Beringer tr Bravo Delta Group			
	AAC Wattisham *'BD'*			31.07.18E

G-DCLP	Glasflügel Standard Libelle 201B		176	01.10.07
	BGA 1630 G K Stanford Seighford *'948'*			11.02.19E
G-DCLT	Schleicher K7 Rhönadler		251	15.02.08
	BGA 1634/CLT, D-5529 Dartmoor Gliding Society			
	Burnford Common, Brentor *'CLT'*			06.05.15E
	Partly modified to ASK 13 standard (NF 22.01.18)			
G-DCLZ	Schleicher Ka 6E		4056	01.02.08
	BGA 1640/CLZ, AGA 2 T D Fielder & R M King			
	tr G-DCLZ Flying Group Kenley *'799'*			02.10.18E
G-DCMI	Mainair Pegasus Quik		7972	07.08.03
	F Omaraie-Hamdanie Plaistows Farm, St Albans			07.10.18P
	Built by Mainair Sports Ltd			
G-DCMK	Schleicher ASK 13		13305	25.01.08
	BGA 1650/CMK			
	Black Mountains Gliding Club Talgarth *'CMK'*			08.08.19E
G-DCMN	Schleicher K 8B		8870	21.04.08
	BGA 1653/CMN The Bristol Gliding Club			
	Proprietary Ltd Nympsfield *'CMN'*			07.07.18E
G-DCMO	Glasflügel Standard Libelle 201B		233	17.01.08
	BGA 1655/CMQ			
	N Jennings & M E Wolff Wycombe Air Park *'CMO'*			21.06.19E
G-DCMR	Glasflügel Standard Libelle 201B		225	18.03.08
	BGA 1656/CMR			
	A Elliott & J M Oatridge Bicester *'LL'*			18.02.18E
G-DCMS	Glasflügel Standard Libelle 201B		234	28.01.08
	BGA 1657/CMS M Worthington tr Libelle 602			
	Syndicate Challock *'602'*			24.08.18E
G-DCMT	Embraer EMB-505 Phenom 300		50500133	03.08.18
	ZS-CSB, PT-TDJ			
	Centreline AV Ltd t/a Centreline Bristol			
G-DCMW	Glasflügel Standard Libelle 201B		242	23.04.08
	BGA 1661/CMW D Williams Lasham *'165'*			14.04.18E
G-DCNC	Schempp-Hirth Standard Cirrus		167	28.11.07
	BGA 1667/CNC M D Cobham Darlton *'273'*			10.02.19E
G-DCNE	Glasflügel Standard Libelle		266	08.07.08
	BGA 1669/CNE S J Cooksey North Hill *'525'*			28.03.20E
G-DCNG	Glasflügel Standard Libelle 201B		265	05.09.07
	BGA 1671 M C J Gardner Dunstable Downs *'622'*			05.12.18E
G-DCNJ	Glasflügel Standard Libelle 201B		272	21.11.07
	BGA 1673/CNJ P I Jameson Crowland *'CNJ'*			11.05.18E
G-DCNM	SZD-9bis Bocian 1E		P-551	13.05.08
	BGA 1676/CNM			
	L I Rigby tr Bocian Syndicate Crowland *'CNM'*			28.01.17E
	Built by ZSLS Jezow Sudecki (IE 21.04.17)			
G-DCNP	Glasflügel Standard Libelle 201B		264	08.09.08
	BGA 1678/CNP			
	I G Carrick & D J Miles Seighford *'CNP'*			21.02.18E
G-DCNS	Slingsby T59A Kestrel		1724	16.06.08
	BGA 1681/CNS J R Greenwell Milfield *'CNS'*			01.08.18R
G-DCNW	Slingsby T59F Kestrel 19		1791	26.10.07
	BGA 1684 S R Watson Seighford *'625'*			04.06.18R
G-DCNX	Slingsby T59F Kestrel 20		1792	28.03.08
	BGA 1685/CNX M Boxall Rufforth *'818'*			30.06.12R
	(Originally built as Kestrel 19 (NF 19.01.16)			
G-DCOC	SZD-30 Pirat		B-472	30.06.15
	BGA1714/CQC			
	The Surrey Hills Gliding Club Ltd Kenley *'CQC'*			19.12.17E
G-DCOE	Van's RV-6		25274	21.02.14
	R E Welch Knapthorpe Lodge, Caunton			28.02.18P
	Built by R E Welch – project PFA 181A-13280			
G-DCOJ	Slingsby T59A Kestrel 17		1727	06.12.07
	BGA 1720/CQJ			
	J Mills (Storrington, Pulborough) *'17K'*			18.04.19R
G-DCOR	Schempp-Hirth Standard Cirrus		220G	04.02.08
	BGA 1727/CQR H R Ford North Hill *'COR'*			18.11.18E
G-DCOY	Schempp-Hirth Standard Cirrus		214	12.09.07
	BGA 1734/CQY			
	R Torr tr RPG Husbands Bosworth *'COY'*			23.05.18E
G-DCPB	Eurocopter MBB-BK117 C-2 *(EC145)*		9265	26.06.09
	D-HMBZ Police & Crime Commissioner			
	for West Yorkshire (Wakefield)			
	Operated by The Chief Constable West Yorkshire			
	Police t/a National Police Air Service (IE 20.04.18)			

G-DCPD	Schleicher ASW 17		17026	21.02.08
	BGA 1691/CPD A J Hewitt Tibenham *'401'*			08.04.18E
G-DCPF	Glasflügel Standard Libelle 201B		267	12.04.13
	EI-GLN, EI-165, BGA 1693/CPF			
	P J A Wickes Sutton Bank			22.10.16E
	(IE 11.08.17)			
G-DCPG	Schleicher K7 Rhonadler		7036	08.04.09
	BGA 1694/CPG, D-4029			
	Cancelled 13.07.16 as PWFU			09.03.15
	Aboyne *Used as simulator 08.16*			
G-DCPJ	Schleicher Ka 6E		4059	24.04.07
	BGA 1696, OO-ZDA			
	A G Linfield tr The K6 Group Shenington *'CPJ'*			15.06.14E
	(IE 11.11.14)			
G-DCPM	Glasflügel Standard Libelle 201B		179	05.02.08
	BGA 1699/CPM A M Carpenter & P E Jessop			
	Trenchard Lines, Upavon *'CPM'*			17.03.18E
G-DCPU	Schempp-Hirth Standard Cirrus		194	15.08.08
	BGA1706/CPU P J Ketelaar Feshiebridge *'761'*			02.11.18E
G-DCRB	Glasflügel Standard Libelle		243	13.02.08
	BGA 1737/CRB A I Mawer Kirton in Lindsey *'241'*			26.12.18E
G-DCRH	Schempp-Hirth Standard Cirrus		233G	07.02.08
	BGA 1743/CRH P E Thelwall Currock Hill *'DV8'*			27.05.17E
G-DCRN	Schempp-Hirth Standard Cirrus		234G	13.03.08
	BGA 1748/CRN D J van der Werf Aston Down *'566'*			23.07.19E
G-DCRO	Glasflügel Standard Libelle 201B		326	24.10.07
	BGA 1750 K G Counsell tr G-DCRO Group			
	Usk *'CRO'*			10.05.18E
G-DCRS	Glasflügel Standard Libelle 201B		325	28.03.08
	BGA 1752/CRS J R Hiley & P S Isaacs			
	Parham Park *'707'*			13.09.18E
G-DCRV	Glasflügel Standard Libelle 201B		329	18.01.08
	BGA 1755/CRV A J Harris Rattlesden *'523'*			04.05.19E
G-DCRW	Glasflügel Standard Libelle 201B		324	10.12.07
	BGA 1756/CRW			
	T Fletcher (North Leigh, Witney) *'TP'*			13.04.19E
G-DCSB	Slingsby T59F Kestrel 19		1798	10.02.09
	BGA 1761/CSB W Fischer Saltby *'CSB'*			06.04.18R
G-DCSD	Slingsby T59D Kestrel 19		1800	14.11.07
	BGA 1763/CSD L P Davidson AAC Wattisham *'L33'*			17.08.18R
G-DCSF	Slingsby T59F Kestrel 19		1802	15.01.08
	BGA 1765/CSF R Birch Aston Down *'34Z'*			05.04.18R
G-DCSI	Robinson R44 Raven II		11746	19.05.11
	G-TGDL Cotswold Ventures Ltd			
	Wellesbourne Mountford			11.08.18E
G-DCSJ	Glasflügel Standard Libelle 201B		372	04.06.08
	BGA 1768/CSJ P J Gill Seighford *'CSJ'*			24.08.18E
G-DCSK	Slingsby T59D Kestrel 20		1806	01.11.07
	BGA 1769/CSK			
	H A Torode tr Kestrel CSK Group Lasham *'CSK'*			31.01.18R
	(Originally built as Kestrel 19			
G-DCSN	Pilatus B4-PC11AF		021	21.02.08
	BGA 1772/CSN J S Firth Burn *'CSN'*			09.12.17E
G-DCSP	Pilatus B4-PC11		027	28.08.08
	BGA 1773/CSP			
	R C Graham tr G-DCSP Group Chipping *'CSP'*			23.03.18E
G-DCSR	Glasflügel Standard Libelle 201B		368	12.11.07
	BGA 1775/CSR J Eagleton tr Glasgow &			
	West of Scotland Gliding Club Portmoak *'CSR'*			09.06.18E
G-DCTB	Schempp-Hirth Standard Cirrus		264G	19.11.07
	BGA 1785/CTB S E McCurdy tr G-DCTB Syndicate			
	RAF Weston-on-the-Green *'579'*			26.05.18E
	Built by Burkhart Grob Flugzeugbau			
G-DCTJ	Slingsby T59D Kestrel 19		1810	20.02.08
	BGA 1792/CTJ R J Aylesbury & J Young			
	Upwood *'CTJ'*			05.07.18R
G-DCTL	Slingsby T59D Kestrel 19		1812	03.04.08
	BGA 1794/CTL E S E Hibbard Wormingford *'CTL'*			28.06.12R
	(NF 18.11.15)			
G-DCTM	Slingsby T59D Kestrel 19		1813	20.11.07
	BGA 1795/CTM C Swain (Bridlington) *'CTM'*			16.02.19R

G

G-DCTO	Slingsby T59D Kestrel 20	1816	09.01.08
	BGA 1798/CTQ K A Moules tr G-DCTO Gliding		
	Syndicate Trenchard Lines, Upavon *'CTO'*		14.03.18R
	(Originally built as Kestrel 19)		
G-DCTP	Slingsby T59D Kestrel 19	1815	06.03.08
	BGA 1797/CTP D C Austin Sutton Bank *'49'*		10.07.18R
G-DCTR	Slingsby T59D Kestrel 19	1817	06.06.08
	BGA 1799/CTR K M Charlton AAC Wattisham *'402'*		30.03.18E
G-DCTT	Schempp-Hirth Standard Cirrus	277G	01.04.08
	BGA 1801/CTT E Sparrow Lasham *'873'*		12.03.18E
G-DCTU	Glasflügel Standard Libelle 201B	371	20.02.08
	BGA 1802/CTU		
	R Cobb & P M Davies Husbands Bosworth *'501'*		05.08.18E
G-DCTV	SZD-30 Pirat	B-528	14.03.08
	BGA 1803/CTV		
	M Cudmore & R Walters Talgarth *'CTV'*		13.10.18E
	Built by ZS Delta-Bielsko		
G-DCTX	SZD-30 Pirat	B-527	19.06.08
	BGA 1805/CTX		
	A M Bennett & P M Green Crowland *'CTX'*		15.11.12E
	Built by ZS Delta-Bielsko (IE 11.01.19)		
G-DCUB	Pilatus B4-PC11	047	07.09.07
	BGA 1809 C Maher & G M Taylor tr G-DCUB Group		
	Seighford *'CUB'*		17.03.18E
G-DCUC	Pilatus B4-PC11	003	03.03.08
	BGA 1810/CUC, HB-1102 G M Cumner Aston Down		18.08.17E
G-DCUD	Yorkshire Sailplanes YS53	02	09.07.08
	BGA 1811/CUD T J Wilkinson		
	Sackville Lodge Farm, Riseley *'CUD'* & *'Flipper'*		28.04.10R
	Built by ex Slingsby T.53B XV951 (c/n 1574)		
	w/o 11.04.72 (IE NF 26.08.15)		
G-DCUJ	Glasflügel Standard Libelle 201B	370	13.11.07
	BGA 1816/CUJ D T Collins & J Poley		
	(Lower Stondon & Melbourn) *'T'*		01.08.18E
G-DCUS	Schempp-Hirth Cirrus VTC	126Y	19.03.08
	BGA 1822/CUS		
	R C Graham (Galgate, Lancaster) *'842'*		25.08.09E
	(NF 21.07.15)		
G-DCUT	Pilatus B4-PC11AF	041	01.06.07
	BGA 1823 A L Walker Lasham *'B4'*		11.05.19E
G-DCVA	LET L-13 Blanik	025418	25.03.08
	BGA 1830/CVA Cancelled 17.06.11 by CAA		28.09.09
	Andreas, IOM *Stored in trailer 08.16*		
G-DCVB	LET L-13 Blanik	025419	22.02.08
	BGA 1831/CVB Cancelled 05.11.12 as PWFU		30.06.11
	Brooklands *Stored 06.14*		
G-DCVE	Schempp-Hirth Cirrus VTC	127Y	13.11.07
	BGA 1834/CVE S Hardy Dunstable Downs *'BZ'*		16.04.17E
G-DCVK	Pilatus B4-PC11AF	048	15.10.07
	BGA1839 J P Marriott Bicester *'92'*		23.04.18E
G-DCVL	Glasflügel Standard Libelle 201B	369	11.04.08
	BGA 1840/CVL J Williams Kirton in Lindsey *'CVL'*		08.01.19E
G-DCVR	SZD-30 Pirat	B-538	20.10.09
	BGA 1845/CVR M T Pitorak Llantysilio		
	Built by ZS Delta-Bielsko; under restoration 10.17		
	(NF 17.08.15)		
G-DCVV	Pilatus B4-PC11AF	028	17.09.07
	BGA 1849		
	J M Sillett tr Syndicate CVV North Hill *'CVV'*		04.06.18E
G-DCVW	Slingsby T59D Kestrel 19	1818	28.05.08
	BGA 1850/CVW		
	J J Green & J A Tonkin Halesland *'423'*		29.03.18R
G-DCVY	Slingsby T59D Kestrel 19	1821	20.02.08
	BGA 1852/CVY N Dickenson Chipping *'355'*		14.10.10R
	(NF 09.08.17)		
G-DCWB	Slingsby T59D Kestrel 19	1833	28.11.07
	BGA 1855/CWB I J Ashdown (Burgess Hill) *'677'*		02.05.19R
G-DCWD	Slingsby T59D Kestrel 19	1835	11.06.08
	BGA1857/CWD G J Palmer Aboyne *'CWD'*		16.01.19R
G-DCWE	Glasflügel Standard Libelle 201B	482	22.11.07
	BGA 1858/DWE L J Maksymowicz Chipping *'468'*		02.10.18E

G-DCWF	Slingsby T59D Kestrel 19	1838	18.10.07
	BGA 1859		
	P F Nicholson Hinton-in-the-Hedges *'CWF'*		02.05.18R
G-DCWG	Glasflügel Standard Libelle 201B	391	28.11.07
	BGA 1860/CWG T D Farquhar Milfield *'322'*		02.09.19E
G-DCWH	Schleicher ASK 13	13424	16.10.07
	BGA 1861 York Gliding Centre (Operations) Ltd		
	Rufforth *'CWH'*		14.06.19E
G-DCWJ	Schleicher K7 Rhonadler	630	30.04.08
	BGA 1862/CWJ, D-6057, D-5723		
	M P Webb Seighford		03.09.15E
G-DCWP	SZD-36A Cobra 15	W-615	15.03.13
	BGA 1867/CWP P Kalcher (Kaindorf, Austria)		02.10.18E
G-DCWR	Schempp-Hirth Cirrus VTC	133Y	14.12.07
	BGA 1869/CWR		
	P J Concannon tr CWR Group (Haddenham) *'917'*		05.04.18E
G-DCWS	Schempp-Hirth Cirrus VTC	129Y	14.07.08
	BGA 1870/CWS K J Ruxton tr Cirrus G-DCWS		
	Syndicate Ridgewell *'CWS'*		06.04.18E
G-DCWT	Glasflügel Standard Libelle 201B	384	20.06.08
	BGA 1871/CWT A A Tills Wormingford *'978'*		05.01.18E
G-DCWX	Glasflügel Standard Libelle	36	11.01.08
	BGA 1875/CWX, RAFGSA 132		
	A Coatsworth Eyres Field *'832'*		20.06.17E
	(IE 21.09.17)		
G-DCWY	Glasflügel Standard Libelle 201B	387	24.09.08
	BGA 1876/CWY S J Taylor Long Mynd *'146'*		28.06.11E
	(NF 18.09.16)		
G-DCXH	SZD-36A Cobra 15	W-619	05.08.13
	BGA 1885/CXH J Dudzik Bicester *'CXH'*		17.11.17E
G-DCXI	Slingsby T61F Venture T.2	1964	18.03.11
	G-BUDB, ZA628 C P Melia & K Stedman		
	tr 611 Vintage Flight (March & Ipswich)		25.03.20P
G-DCXK	Glasflügel Standard Libelle 201B	383	17.03.08
	BGA 1887/CXK J C Richards Portmoak *'L18'*		06.06.18E
G-DCXM	Slingsby T59D Kestrel 19	1820	06.12.07
	BGA 1889/CXM W H Dyozinski Lasham *'532'*		16.01.16R
G-DCXV	Yorkshire Sailplanes YS53	03	27.05.08
	BGA 1897/CXV		
	The Gliding Heritage Centre Lasham *'CXV'*		05.05.18R
G-DCYA	Pilatus B4-PC11	072	08.11.07
	BGA 1902/CYA		
	A C Turner tr B4-072 Group North Hill *'CYA'*		26.05.18E
G-DCYC	Pilatus B4-PC11	029	10.04.18
	BGA1904/CYC, N47247 D P Aherne Tibenham		
	(NF 09.04.18)		
G-DCYD	SZD-30 Pirat	B-559	08.09.08
	BGA 1905/CYD		
	S J Naisby tr G-DCYD Group Upwood *'CYD'*		14.04.18E
	Built by ZS Delta-Bielsko		
G-DCYG	Glasflügel Standard Libelle 201B	441	22.12.07
	BGA 1908/CYG R J Barsby & G Wheldon		
	Husbands Bosworth *'YG'*		25.04.18E
G-DCYM	Schempp-Hirth Standard Cirrus	48	26.09.07
	BGA 1913, D-0578		
	K M Fisher Husbands Bosworth *'CYM'*		24.04.18E
G-DCYO	Schempp-Hirth Standard Cirrus B	364	18.03.08
	BGA 1916/CYQ		
	M J Layton & P Summers North Hill *'477'*		06.03.19E
G-DCYP	Schempp-Hirth Standard Cirrus	369	19.08.09
	BGA 1915/CYP		
	A F Scott Bourg-Saint Bernard, France *'982'*		14.09.15E
	(IE 05.07.17)		
G-DCYT	Schempp-Hirth Standard Cirrus	357G	25.09.07
	BGA 1919 W A L Leader Tibenham *'145'*		29.07.18E
G-DCYZ	Schleicher K 8B	8882	08.04.08
	BGA 1925/CYZ, RAFGSA Oxford Gliding		
	Company Ltd RAF Weston-on-the-Green *'CYZ'*		10.02.18E
G-DCZD	Pilatus B4-PC11AF	081	08.08.07
	BGA 1929 T Dale Rufforth *'CZD'*		28.11.18E
G-DCZE	SZD-30 Pirat	S-01.14	10.12.07
	BGA 1930/CZE L A Bean Tibenham		11.09.11E
	Built by WSK 'Delta' Swidnik (NF 25.08.17)		

G-DCZG   SZD-30 Pirat   S-01.16   02.09.08
BGA 1932/CZG   J T Pajdak   Kenley   *'CZG'*
Built by WSK 'Delta' Swidnik (NF 16.09.15)

G-DCZJ   SZD-30 Pirat   S-01.15   21.01.08
BGA 1934/CZJ
Lincolnshire Gliding Club Ltd   Strubby   *'CZJ'*   06.05.17E
Built by WSK 'Delta' Swidnik

G-DCZN   Schleicher ASW 15B   15329   06.06.08
BGA 1938/CZN   J R Walters   Rivar Hill   *'CZN'*   20.10.18E
(IE 17.08.17)

G-DCZR   Slingsby T59D Kestrel 19   1842   06.11.07
BGA 1941/CZR
G I Corbett   Skelling Farm, Skirwith   *'CZR'*   14.07.19R

G-DCZU   Slingsby T59D Kestrel 19   1849   09.07.08
BGA1944/CZU   R A Morris   Crowland   *'826'*   03.05.19R

G-DDAC   SZD-36A Cobra 15   W-656   04.01.08
BGA 1952/DAC
R J A Colenso   Husbands Bosworth   *'DAC'*   14.09.11E
Built by ZS 'Delta' Wroclaw (NF 28.07.15)

G-DDAJ   Schempp-Hirth Nimbus-2   50   17.08.07
BGA 1958   B R Pearson tr North Devon Gliding Club
Nimbus Group   Eaglescott   *'14'*   22.03.11E
(NF 27.07.15)

G-DDAN   SZD-30 Pirat   S-01.45   29.01.08
BGA 1962/DAN   J M A Shannon   Wormingford   *'DAN'*   08.06.16E
Built by WSK 'Delta' Swidnik (IE 11.07.17)

G-DDAP   SZD-30 Pirat   S-01.47   13.02.08
BGA 1963/DAP   T D Younger tr Delta Alpha Papa
Group   Currock Hill   *'DAP'*   04.08.18E
Built by WSK 'Delta' Swidnik

G-DDAS   Schempp-Hirth Standard Cirrus   378   21.11.07
BGA 1966/DAS, (BGA 1925)
G Goodenough   Sutton Bank   *'DAS'*   24.03.18E

G-DDAY   Piper PA-28R-201T Turbo Cherokee Arrow III
                                                    28R-7703112   24.11.88
G-BPDO, N3496Q
P A Spurrs tr G-DDAY Group   Derby   19.06.19E

G-DDBB   Slingsby T.51 Dart 17R   DG/51/01   14.05.09
BGA 1975/DBB   A L R Roth   Tibenham   *'DBB'*   18.05.18R
Rebuilt by Greenfly Aviation using refurbished parts

G-DDBC   Pilatus B4-PC11   135   12.05.08
BGA 1976/DBC
J H France & G R Harris   Shobdon   *'851'*   28.08.17E
(IE 06.11.17)

G-DDBD   Europa Aviation Europa XS   454   11.02.03
B Davies   Wellcross Farm, Slinfold   29.08.18P
Built by B Davies – project PFA 247-13569; tricycle u/c

G-DDBG   ICA-Brasov IS-29D   31   11.06.08
BGA 1980/DBG
P S Whitehead   Walney Island   *'DBG'*   02.10.11E
(NF 18.06.15)

G-DDBK   Slingsby T59D Kestrel 19   1861   08.10.08
BGA 1983/DBK
G A Adams tr 523 Syndicate   North Hill   23.05.18R

G-DDBN   Slingsby T59D Kestrel 19   1857   11.01.08
BGA 1986/DBN   G K Hutchinson   North Hill   *'575'*   31.07.17R
(IE 13.01.18)

G-DDBP   Glasflügel Club Libelle 205   51   17.10.07
BGA 1987   K Fuks   Wormingford   *'551'*   15.03.18E

G-DDBS   Slingsby T59D Kestrel 19   1864   23.07.08
BGA1990/DBS   K Millar   Rufforth   *'K19'*   03.06.15R
(IE 16.05.17)

G-DDBV   SZD-30 Pirat   S-02.27   19.02.08
BGA 1993/DBV   S J Glassett tr G-DDBV Syndicate
Aston Down   *'DBV'*   26.11.19E
Built by WSK 'Delta' Swidnik

G-DDBX   SZD-9BIS Bocian 1E   P-642   13.02.08
BGA 1995/DBX   Cancelled 01.04.10 as destroyed   15.07.10
Portmoak   *Nose section at Portmoak, marked 'HBS'
at Portmoak 10.15, tail section at Sackville Lodge*

G-DDCA   SZD-36A Cobra 15   W-686   28.11.07
BGA 1998/DCA
R J Aylesbury & J Young   Upwood   *'DCA'*
Built by ZS 'Delta' Wroclaw (NF 16.01.04)

G-DDCC   Glasflügel Standard Libelle 201B   585   15.10.07
BGA 2000/DCC
D S Edwards tr G-DDCC Syndicate   Shobdon   *'324'*   29.05.18E

G-DDCW   Schleicher Ka 6CR   1076   01.10.08
BGA 2018/DCW, D-5228
B W Rendall   Strubby   *'DCW'*
(NF 13.10.15)

G-DDDA   Schempp-Hirth Standard Cirrus   532G   17.09.07
BGA 2022/DDA   M S Davidson tr G-DDDA Group
Kingston Deverill   *'DDA'*   26.05.18E
Built by Burkhart Grob Flugzeugbau

G-DDDB   Schleicher ASK 13   13493   09.06.08
BGA 2023/DDB
Shenington Gliding Club   Shenington   *'DDB'*   13.01.13E
(IE 10.12.14)

G-DDDD   Evektor EV-97 TeamEurostar UK   2007-2907   13.03.07
Cancelled 25.04.12 as PWFU   12.03.12
Middle Stoke, Isle of Grain   *Rear fuselage stored 05.16*

G-DDDE   PZL-Bielsko SZD-38A Jantar 1   B-641   28.02.08
BGA 2026/DDE
P Swallow tr Jantar One Syndicate   Talgarth   *'DDE'*   01.06.18E

G-DDDK   SZD-30 Pirat   S-04-08   17.01.14
BGA 2031/DDK   Buckminster Gliding Club Ltd   Saltby
(IE 10.06.16)

G-DDDL   Schleicher K 8B   218/61   16.04.08
BGA 2032/DDL, D-5156
The Windrushers Gliding Club Ltd   Bicester   *'DDL'*   02.05.15E
(NF 14.03.18)

G-DDDM   Schempp-Hirth Cirrus VTC   164Y   11.01.08
BGA 2033/DDM
H D Maddams   (Saffron Walden)   *'959'*   10.07.19E
Built by Vazduhoplovno Techniki Centar

G-DDDR   Schempp-Hirth Standard Cirrus   531G   16.10.07
BGA 2037   J D Ewence   Nympsfield   *'680'*   23.03.18E
Built by Burkhart Grob Flugzeugbau

G-DDDY   P&M Quik GT450   8308   23.08.07
J W Dodson   Leicester   13.06.13P
(NF 14.11.14)

G-DDEB   Slingsby T59D Kestrel 19   1866   16.04.09
BGA 2047/DEB
J L Smoker   RAF Weston-on-the-Green   *'DEB'*   15.09.11R
(NF 15.05.18)

G-DDEG   ICA-Brasov IS-28B2   48   07.09.07
BGA 2051
P S Whitehead   Skelling Farm, Skirwith   *'DEG'*   26.05.12E
(NF 18.06.15)

G-DDEO   Glasflügel Club Libelle 205   97   18.12.07
BGA 2059/DEQ
J A Linger tr 716 Group   Gransden Lodge   *'716'*   20.02.19E

G-DDEV   Schleicher Ka 6CR   6453   07.01.08
BGA 2064/DEV, RAFGSA 354
P D Valentine tr DEV Group   Upwood   *'DEV'*   02.06.18E

G-DDEW   ICA-Brasov IS-29D   40   30.11.07
BGA 2065/DEW
P S Whitehead   Walney Island   *'DEW'*   28.04.18E

G-DDEX   LET L-13 Blanik   026348   11.09.07
BGA 2066, RAFGSA R4, BGA 2066
Cancelled 25.09.15 as PWFU   11.06.10
Easterton   *Stored 08.18*

G-DDFC   Schempp-Hirth Standard Cirrus   592G   07.03.08
BGA 2071/DFC   C E Hooper   Usk   *'129'*   25.06.19E
Built by Burkhart Grob Flugzeugbau

G-DDFE   Molino PIK-20B   20052   07.07.08
BGA 2073/DFE   M A Roff-Jarrett   Lasham   *'DFE'*   26.10.18E

G-DDFK   Molino PIK-20B   20039   31.10.07
BGA 2078, OH-500
B H & M J Fairclough   North Hill   *'DFK'*   29.04.18R

G-DDFL   PZL-Bielsko SZD-38A Jantar 1   B-682   09.10.07
BGA 2079   S A Lewis tr G-DDFL Group
Burnford Common, Brentor   *'DFL'*   27.07.16E
(IE 21.04.17)

G-DDFR   Grob G102 Astir CS   1038   10.03.08
BGA 2084/DFR
The Windrushers Gliding Club Ltd   Bicester   *'DFR'*   06.07.17E

G-DDFU	PZL-Bielsko SZD-38A Jantar 1	B-685	03.02.14
	BGA 2087/DFU		
	G R Clark tr Jantar 38A Group Solent *'38A'*		24.04.18E
G-DDFW	SZD-30 Pirat	S-05.45	22.02.08
	BGA 2089/DFW Cancelled 30.05.12 as destroyed		31.08.12
	Strubby *Built by WSK 'Delta' Swidnik; stored 06.13*		
G-DDGA	Schleicher K 8B	8587	11.12.07
	BGA 2093/DGA, RAFGSA 334, BGA 1926, RAFGSA 334		
	The Welland Gliding Club Ltd Lyveden *'DGA'*		22.05.18E
G-DDGE	Schempp-Hirth Standard Cirrus 75	606	09.01.08
	BGA 2097/DGE		
	T P Brown (Burnham-on-Crouch) *'DGE'*		09.02.18E
G-DDGG	Schleicher Ka 6E	4061	01.08.08
	BGA 2099/DGG, RAFGSA 263		
	N F Holmes & F D Platt Long Mynd *'DGG'*		25.07.14E
	(NF 29.10.15)		
G-DDGJ	American Champion 8KCAB Super Decathlon		
		1049-2007	17.08.07
	Western Air (Thruxton) Ltd Thruxton		01.11.18E
G-DDGK	Schleicher Ka 6CR	6287	22.11.07
	BGA 2102/DGK, D-3224 J M Davis tr Parham Junior		
	Syndicate Parham Park *'DGK' & 'Betty Blue'*		16.07.19E
G-DDGV	Breguet 905S Fauvette	2	27.04.09
	(F-C...), G-DDGV, BGA2112/DGV, HB-632		
	J N Lee (Lorignac, Charente-Maritime, France)		
	(NF 03.01.16)		
G-DDGX	Schempp-Hirth Standard Cirrus 75	619	24.04.08
	BGA 2114/DGX, AGA 3, BGA 2114		
	C H Grange tr UskGC Group Usk *'610'*		20.04.19E
G-DDGY	Schempp-Hirth Nimbus-2	105	31.10.07
	BGA 2115		
	F J Hill tr Nimbus 195 Group Nympsfield *'195'*		26.04.18E
G-DDHA	Schleicher K 8B	3	30.04.08
	BGA 2117/DHA, D-8848, D-5148		
	Shalbourne Soaring Society Ltd Rivar Hill *'DHA'*		12.05.18E
	Built by FIMA Wolf GmbH & FIMA H Eichelsdörfer		
G-DDHE	Slingsby T.53B Phoenix	1718	13.11.07
	BGA 2132/DHR J Mattocks tr Aviation Preservation		
	Society of Scotland (APSS) Portmoak *'DHE'*		19.05.18R
G-DDHG	Schleicher Ka 6CR	1131	28.04.08
	BGA 2123/DHG, D-5170 M W Roberts Falgunzeon		22.09.15E
G-DDHJ	Glaser-Dirks DG-100	48	13.12.07
	BGA 2125/DHJ G E McLaughlin Bellarena *'DHJ'*		24.07.18E
G-DDHK	Glaser-Dirks DG-100	50	30.08.07
	BGA 2126-DHK		
	R Allcoat & K Dillon Portmoak *'A30'*		07.09.18E
G-DDHL	Glaser-Dirks DG-100	52	25.10.07
	BGA 2127		
	T Bartsch tr DHL Syndicate Challock *'DHL'*		29.05.18E
G-DDHT	Schleicher Ka 6E	4065	11.12.07
	BGA 2134/DHT, D-7202		
	I Deans & N Worrell Lasham *'DHT'*		17.03.18E
G-DDHW	Schempp-Hirth Nimbus-2	106	20.08.08
	BGA 2137/DHW		
	M J Carruthers & D Thompson Portmoak *'951'*		27.05.18E
G-DDHX	Schempp-Hirth Standard Cirrus B	635	27.05.08
	BGA 2138/DHX J Franke Lasham *'7V'*		25.07.18E
	Original destroyed in collision with Rockwell		
	112A G-BIUO 12.05.84: rebuilt as BGA 2138		
	ex Standard Cirrus D-3264 (533G)		
G-DDHZ	SZD-30 Pirat	S-06.41	20.06.08
	BGA 2140/DHZ		
	A M Bennett & P M Green Lyveden *'DHZ'*		18.08.19E
	Built by WSK 'Delta' Swidnik		
G-DDJB	Schleicher K 8B	8879	29.01.08
	BGA 2142/DJB, (RNGSA N11), AGA 17, BGA 2142,		
	RAFGSA 397 T World tr Portsmouth Naval Gliding		
	Centre (Palestine, Andover) *'N11'*		13.07.18E
	Stored in trailer at HMS Sultan, Gosport 05.18		
G-DDJD	Grob G102 Astir CS	1226	16.10.07
	BGA 2144 C W Lewis tr G-DDJD Group		
	Kingston Deverill *'DJD'*		25.11.17E
	(IE 18.01.18)		
G-DDJF	Schempp-Hirth Duo Discus T	121/457	21.04.06
	BGA 5182/KLM R J H Fack Long Mynd *'JF'*		17.07.18E

G-DDJK	Schleicher ASK 18	18030	30.04.08
	BGA 2150/DJK		
	Dorset Gliding Club Ltd Eyres Field *'DJK'*		11.03.18E
G-DDJN	Eiriavion PIK-20B	20140C	20.11.07
	BGA 2153/DJN		
	M Ireland & S Lambourne Kingston Deverill *'407'*		21.03.18R
G-DDJR	Schleicher Ka 6CR	680	27.08.08
	BGA 2156/DJR, D-8423 C H Dennis tr K6CR Syndicate		
	RNAS Culdrose *'DJR'*		29.03.18E
G-DDJX	Grob G102 Astir CS	1259	04.01.08
	BGA 2162/DJX Trent Valley Gliding Club Ltd		
	Kirton in Lindsey *'DJX'*		03.09.18E
G-DDKC	Schleicher K 8B	8261	22.04.08
	BGA 2167/DKC, D-1431 Yorkshire Gliding Club		
	(Proprietary) Ltd Sutton Bank *'DKC'*		21.06.18E
G-DDKD	Glasflügel Hornet	67	03.01.08
	BGA 2168/DKD, (BGA 2165) B J W Thomas		
	tr Hornet Syndicate Eyres Field *'759'*		25.05.18E
G-DDKE	Schleicher ASK 13	13548	25.01.08
	BGA 2169/DKE		
	The South Wales Gliding Club Ltd Usk *'DKE'*		26.09.17E
G-DDKG	Schleicher Ka 6CR	6233	10.03.08
	BGA 2171/DKG, D-4327		
	C B Woolf Wormingford *'DKG'*		25.05.18E
G-DDKL	Schempp-Hirth Nimbus-2	86	01.02.08
	BGA 2175/DKL, D-2111 G J Croll Rattlesden *'444'*		30.05.18E
G-DDKM	Glasflügel Hornet	49	11.04.08
	BGA 2176/DKM, (BGA 2213), BGA 2176, D-7816		
	R S Lee Rattlesden *'DKM'*		22.06.18E
G-DDKR	Grob G102 Astir CS	1327	27.05.08
	BGA 2180/DKR Oxford Gliding Company Ltd		
	RAF Weston-on-the-Green *'DKR'*		30.01.18E
G-DDKS	Grob G102 Astir CS	1330	01.07.08
	BGA 2181/DKS C K Lewis Lasham *'788'*		05.09.18E
G-DDKU	Grob G102 Astir CS	1326	12.09.07
	BGA 2183 P N Stapleton tr Delta Kilo		
	Uniform Syndicate North Hill *'DKU'*		17.03.18E
G-DDKV	Grob G102 Astir CS	1328	12.11.10
	BGA 2184/DKV T J Ireson Sandhill Farm, Shrivenham		
	(NF 16.10.14)		
G-DDKW	Grob G102 Astir CS	1329	08.02.08
	BGA 2185/DKW M A Sandwith Rufforth *'DKW'*		14.06.18E
G-DDKX	Grob G102 Astir CS	1331	23.01.08
	BGA 2186/DKX		
	The South Wales Gliding Club Ltd Usk *'353'*		06.08.18E
G-DDLA	Pilatus B4-PC11	149	17.08.07
	BGA 2189, RAFGSA 354		
	P R Seddon Walney Island *'DLA'*		23.09.18E
G-DDLB	Schleicher ASK 18	18040	28.11.07
	BGA 2190/DLB		
	B A Fairston & A Stotter Husbands Bosworth *'DLB'*		24.04.18E
G-DDLC	Schleicher ASK 13	13549	22.04.08
	BGA 2191/DLC		
	Lasham Gliding Society Ltd Lasham *'C'*		20.03.18E
G-DDLE	Schleicher Ka 6E	4074	01.05.08
	BGA 2193/DLE, AGA 8		
	P J Abbott & J Banks Talgarth *'433'*		30.05.18E
G-DDLG	Schempp-Hirth Standard Cirrus 75	579	13.03.09
	BGA 2195/DLG, AGA 2 S Naylor Burn *'DLG'*		19.05.14E
	(NF 27.04.16)		
G-DDLH	Grob G102 Astir CS77	1646	28.01.08
	BGA 2196/DLH		
	M D & M E Saunders Lasham *'378'*		27.12.18E
G-DDLJ	Eiriavion PIK-20B	20157	09.05.08
	BGA 2197/DLJ R J Pye (Leominster) *'DLJ'*		25.11.18R
G-DDLM	Grob G102 Astir CS	1260	06.08.08
	BGA 2200/DLM, (BGA 2163)		
	J A Laurenson tr Astir Syndicate (Thame) *'DLM'*		24.08.19E
G-DDLP	Schleicher Ka 6CR	6519	18.01.08
	BGA 2202/DLP, RAFGSA 355		
	J R Crosse Crowland *'DLP'*		08.06.18E

G-DDLS Schleicher K 8B 8650 02.09.08
BGA 2205/DLS, D-5718 B R Pearson
tr North Devon Gliding Club Eaglescott *'DLS'*
(NF 30.11.15)

G-DDLY Eiriavion PIK-20D 20509 13.12.07
BGA2211/DLY M Conrad North Weald *'DLY'* 30.09.16E

G-DDMB Schleicher K 8B 8209 27.09.07
BGA 2214, D-4331
Crown Service Gliding Club Lasham *'831'* & *'Kate'* 19.04.18E

G-DDMG Schleicher K 8B 8763 06.11.07
BGA2219/DMG, RAFGSA 382
Dorset Gliding Club Ltd Eyres Field *'DMG'* 14.06.16E
(IE 06.07.16)

G-DDMH Grob G102 Astir CS 1511 08.07.08
BGA 2220/DMH Oxford Gliding Company Ltd
RAF Weston-on-the-Green *'DMH'* 13.04.18E

G-DDMK Schempp-Hirth SHK-1 25 06.06.08
BGA 2222/DMK, D-5401
D Breeze Aston Down *'593'* 27.09.18E

G-DDML Schleicher K7 Rhönadler 929 12.12.07
BGA 2223/DML, D-6194, D-5005
Dumfries & District Gliding Club Falgunzeon *'DML'* 10.05.13E
(NF 27.07.15)

G-DDMM Schempp-Hirth Nimbus-2 125 14.01.08
BGA 2224/DMM T Linee Eyres Field *'76'* 11.05.18E

G-DDMN Glasflügel Mosquito 20 04.03.09
BGA 2225/DMN
G Francis tr DMN Group Portmoak *'DMN'* 11.11.18E

G-DDMO Schleicher Ka 6E 4062 23.01.08
BGA 2227/DMQ, RAFGSA 264
R C Sharman Bicester *'K6'* 04.03.18E

G-DDMP Grob G102 Astir CS 1239 06.06.08
BGA 2226/DMP, ZS-GKF G Nixon tr Kingswood
Syndicate Dunstable Downs *'553'* 02.03.19E

G-DDMR Grob G102 Astir CS 1435 22.12.07
BGA 2228/DMR
Mendip Gliding Club Ltd Halesland *'511'* 26.07.18E

G-DDMS Glasflügel Standard Libelle 201B 385 01.12.07
BGA 2229/DMS, RNGSA 259
K C Springate tr GDDMS Group Burn *'259'* 22.08.18E

G-DDMU Eiriavion PIK-20D 20524 06.08.08
BGA 2231/DMU P Goodchild Sutton Bank *'DMU'* 21.09.18E

G-DDMV North American T-6G-NF Texan 168-313 30.04.90
N3240N, Haitian AF 3209, 49-3209
K M Perkins Headcorn 03.08.18E
As '493209 CA ANG' in USAF c/s

G-DDMX Schleicher ASK 13 13567 25.01.08
BGA 2234/DMX Dartmoor Gliding Society
Burnford Common, Brentor *'DMX'* 30.05.18E

G-DDNC Grob G102 Astir CS 1428 18.10.07
BGA 2239 Norfolk Gliding Club Ltd Tibenham *'588'* 28.09.18E

G-DDND Pilatus B4-PC11AF 136 07.02.08
BGA 2240/DND R J Happs tr DND Group Lasham 10.07.18E

G-DDNE Grob G102 Astir CS77 1631 22.12.07
BGA 2241/DNE M A Wintle tr 621 Astir Syndicate
(Backwell, Bristol) *'DNE'* 29.05.18E

G-DDNG Schempp-Hirth Nimbus-2 126 09.10.07
BGA 2243
P D Wright Trenchard Lines, Upavon *'265'* 02.07.19E

G-DDNK Grob G102 Astir CS 1434 05.10.07
BGA 2246
A Page tr G-DDNK Group Rattlesden *'745'* 05.06.18E

G-DDNU PZL-Bielsko SZD-42-1 Jantar 2 B-783 19.04.08
BGA2255/DNU D Chalmers-Brown & C D Rowland
Wycombe Air Park *'U2'* 24.04.17E

G-DDNV Schleicher ASK 13 13568 24.06.08
BGA 2256/DNV P Bolton tr Channel Gliding Club
Group Waldershare Park *'DNV'* 08.08.18E

G-DDNW Schleicher Ka 6CR 829 21.11.07
BGA 2257/DNW, D-1646
L Wootton tr G-DDNW Group Shenington *'DNW'* 08.08.19E

G-DDNX Schleicher Ka 6CR 6094SI 01.12.07
BGA 2258/DNX, D-5107
Black Mountains Gliding Club Talgarth *'DNX'* 30.01.19E

G-DDNZ Schleicher K 8B 8095 01.09.08
BGA 2260/DNZ, D-1711 L J Gregoire tr Southampton
University Gliding Club Lasham *'DNZ'* & *'Denzel'* 31.07.18E

G-DDOA Schleicher ASK 13 13582 12.11.07
BGA2285/DQA Essex & Suffolk Gliding Club Ltd
Wormingford *'DOA'* 12.03.18E

G-DDOC Schleicher Ka 6CR 6373SI 20.06.08
BGA 2287/DQC, D-5725
W St G V Stoney Lasham *'DOC'* 18.06.17E
Built by Paul Siebert Sport und Segelflugzeugbau

G-DDOE Grob G102 Astir CS77 1636 26.06.08
BGA 2289/DQE D J Marpole tr Heron Gliding Club
RNAS Yeovilton *'480'* 12.09.17E
(IE 06.11.17)

G-DDOF Schleicher Ka 6CR 6417 06.02.08
BGA 2290/DQF, D-5827
A J Watson Portmoak *'DOF'* 04.05.19E

G-DDOG Scottish Aviation Bulldog Srs 120/121 BH120/210 18.06.01
XX524 Deltaero Ltd (Velez-Malaga, Spain) 27.07.13E
As 'XX524:04' in RAF c/s (NF 18.09.16)

G-DDOK Schleicher Ka 6E 4341 13.02.08
BGA 2294/DQK, D-0541
S Y Duxbury & R S Hawley Long Mynd *'542'* 05.07.18E

G-DDOU Eiriavion PIK-20D 20579 21.04.08
BGA 2303/DQU
J M A Shannon Wormingford *'DOU'* 05.02.17E
(IE 11.08.17)

G-DDOX Schleicher K7 Rhönadler 743 04.01.08
BGA 2306/DQX, D-9127
The Nene Valley Gliding Club Ltd Upwood *'DOX'* 31.08.17E
*Modified to ASK 13 standard with fuselage
ex BGA 1833 & wings ex BGA 3331*

G-DDOY Schleicher K 8B 647 22.12.07
BGA 2307/DQY, D-4375
Cancelled 07.03.11 by CAA
Camphill *Stored 08.18*

G-DDPA Schleicher ASK 18 18044 11.01.08
BGA 2261/DPA M J Huddart Saltby *'DPA'* 26.05.18E

G-DDPH Schempp-Hirth Mini Nimbus HS 7 09 25.04.08
BGA 2268/DPH J W Murdoch (Strathaven) *'287'* 15.10.13E
(IE 28.11.17)

G-DDPJ Grob G102 Astir CS77 1641 06.04.16
BGA 2269/DPJ
A M George tr DPJ Syndicate Lasham 15.06.18E

G-DDPK Glasflügel Mosquito 27 25.03.08
BGA 2270/DPK H Nolz Mariazell, Austria *'DPK'* 17.03.18E

G-DDPL Eiriavion PIK-20D 20549 25.02.08
BGA 2271/DPL H A Schuricht tr 437 Syndicate
Dunstable Downs *'437'* 10.05.18E

G-DDPO Grob G102 Astir CS77 1632 09.01.08
BGA 2275/DPQ Yorkshire Gliding Club
(Proprietary) Ltd Sutton Bank *'DPO'* 21.05.18E

G-DDPY Grob G102 Astir CS77 1652 30.10.07
BGA 2283 C A Bailey North Hill *'375'* 06.09.17E

G-DDRA Schleicher Ka 6CR 1118 18.08.08
BGA 2309/DRA, D-9011
D S Edwards tr K6CR Group Shobdon Shobdon *'904'*
(NF 22.09.15)

G-DDRB Glaser-Dirks DG-100 31 01.08.08
BGA2310/DRB, PH-532
J D Peck tr DRB Syndicate (Newport Pagnell) *'86'* 17.11.09E
(NF 06.01.16)

G-DDRD Schleicher Ka 6CR 6377SI 04.10.07
BGA 2312, D-9080 Essex & Suffolk Gliding Club Ltd
Wormingford *'DRD'* 14.06.18E

G-DDRE Schleicher Ka 6CR 6197 28.08.08
BGA 2313/DRE, D-8558
P M Harmer tr DRE Syndicate North Hill *'DRE'* 14.09.18E

G-DDRJ Schleicher ASK 13 13583 22.04.08
BGA 2317/DRJ
Lasham Gliding Society Ltd Lasham *'D'* 23.09.18E

G-DDRL Scheibe SF26A 5040 21.01.09
BGA 2319/DRL, D-7073
T A Lipinski Crowland *'DRL'* 26.02.18E

G-DDRM Schleicher K7 Rhönadler 7017 31.10.07
BGA 2320, D-4666 L G Cross tr K7 DRM
Glider Syndicate Dunstable Downs *'DRM'* 23.03.18E

G-DDRN Glasflügel Mosquito 82 19.03.08
BGA 2321/DRN K J King Ridgewell *'821'* 31.05.18E

G-DDRO Grob G103 Twin Astir 3027 03.04.08
BGA 2323/DRQ A J Gillson tr Twin Astir
258 Syndicate Seighford *'258'* 10.05.18E

G-DDRP Pilatus B4-PC11AF 080 17.03.08
BGA 2322/DRP, RAFGSA, BGA 1927 M Moxon
tr DRP Syndicate RAF Weston-on-the-Green *'DRP'* 22.06.12E
Built by as Type B4-PC11 (IE 15.12.17)

G-DDRT Eiriavion PIK-20D 20587 20.11.07
BGA 2326/DRT S Grant (Maldon) *'688'* 19.04.19E

G-DDRV Schleicher K 8B 8026 26.09.08
BGA 2328/DRV, D-6169
D C Storey tr DRV Syndicate Portmoak *'DRV'* 29.05.18E

G-DDRW Grob G102 Astir CS 1081 01.02.08
BGA 2329/DRW, D-3311 The Royal Air Force Gliding
& Soaring Association RAF Cranwell *'R57'* 18.01.19E
Operated by Cranwell Gliding Club

G-DDRY Schleicher Ka 6BR 370 23.04.08
BGA 2331/DRY M K Bradford Wormingford 10.07.16E

G-DDRZ Schleicher K 8B 668 18.01.08
BGA 2332/DRZ, D-4622, D-KANB, D-4622
East Sussex Gliding Club Ltd Ringmer *'DRZ'* 04.03.15E
(IE 21.11.15)

G-DDSF Schleicher K 8B 8220 10.01.08
BGA 2338/DSF, D-7114 University of Edinburgh
Sports Union Portmoak *'DSF'* & *'Snoopy'* 11.05.15E
(IE 12.10.15)

G-DDSG Schleicher Ka 6CR 6393 13.11.09
BGA 2339/DSG, D-5696
S McGuirk (Papcastle, Cockermouth) 22.05.18E

G-DDSH Grob G102 Astir CS77 1696 21.01.08
BGA 2340/DSH
A Rougvie tr Astir 648 Syndicate Portmoak *'648'* 29.04.18E

G-DDSJ Grob G103 Twin Astir 3050 11.08.08
BGA 2341/DSJ
Herefordshire Gliding Club Ltd Shobdon *'DSJ'* 06.09.18E

G-DDSL Grob G103 Twin Astir 3041 11.09.08
BGA 2343/DSL G Nevisky tr DSL Group
Burnford Common, Brentor *'DSL'* 09.05.18E

G-DDSP Schempp-Hirth Mini Nimbus HS 7 33 25.03.08
BGA 2346/DSP G T H Newbrook tr DDSP Group
(Haddenham) *'270'* 10.05.18E

G-DDST Schleicher ASW 20L 20059 17.09.07
BGA 2350/DST H A Bloxham Nympsfield *'180'* 04.04.19E

G-DDSU Grob G102 Astir CS77 1663 21.09.07
BGA 2351
Bowland Forest Gliding Club Ltd Chipping *'DSU'* 29.01.18E

G-DDSV Pilatus B4-PC11AF 134 21.01.08
BGA 2352/DSV, RAFGSA 718, RAFGSA 518
G M Drinkell Wormingford *'DSV'* 26.03.18E

G-DDSX Schleicher ASW 19B 19188 18.10.07
BGA 2354
J Flory tr G-DDSX Group North Hill *'877'* 22.03.18E

G-DDSY Schleicher Ka 6CR 561 04.01.08
BGA 2355/DSY, D-5702
W S H Taylor Seighford *'DSY'* & *'Daisy'* 30.06.18E

G-DDTA Glaser-Dirks DG-200 2-27 13.12.07
BGA 2357/DTA M Rose Milfield *'699'* 20.11.18E

G-DDTC Schempp-Hirth Janus B 63 22.05.08
BGA 2359/DTC, RAFGSA R9, RAFGSA 16
Darlton Gliding Club Ltd Darlton *'DTC'* 14.09.18E

G-DDTE Schleicher ASW 19B 19185 07.02.08
BGA 2361/DTE G R Purcell Lasham *'DTE'* 28.09.18E

G-DDTG Schempp-Hirth SHK-1 12 06.06.08
BGA 2363/DTG, D-2034
M W Roberts Falgunzeon *'DTG'* 07.10.14E
(NF 03.03.16)

G-DDTK Glasflügel Mosquito B 109 04.12.07
BGA 2366/DTK M G Entwisle Talgarth *'DTK'* 15.07.19E

G-DDTM Glaser-Dirks DG-200 2-34 18.12.07
BGA 2368/DTM M C Bailey Bicester *'DTM'* 14.03.19E

G-DDTN Schleicher K 8B 117/58 07.10.08
BGA 2369/DTN
C G & G N Thomas AAC Wattisham *'DTN'* 14.04.10E
(NF 28.10.15)

G-DDTP Schleicher ASW 20 20078 27.09.07
BGA 2370 S M & T S Hills Lasham *'915'* 10.03.19E

G-DDTS CARMAM M-100S Mésange 31 10.03.08
BGA 2373/DTS, F-CCST J P Dyne (Corby) *'DTS'* 20.06.14R
(NF 21.04.15)

G-DDTU Schempp-Hirth Nimbus-2B 167 14.08.07
BGA 2375 J A Castle Husbands Bosworth *'DTU'* 11.04.18E

G-DDTV Glasflügel Mosquito B 110 04.12.07
BGA 2376/DTV D R Allan Lasham *'704'* 29.03.18E

G-DDTW SZD-30 Pirat S-07.11 25.04.08
BGA 2377/DTW C Kaminski tr NDGC Pirat Syndicate
Burnford Common, Brentor *'DTW'* 17.07.18E
Built by WSK 'Delta' Swidnik

G-DDTX Glasflügel Mosquito B 111 04.01.08
BGA 2378/DTX P T S Nash Crowland *'DTX'* 24.08.18E

G-DDTY Glasflügel Mosquito B 112 06.02.08
BGA 2379/DTY
W H L Bullimore Gransden Lodge *'766'* 24.05.18E

G-DDUB Glasflügel Mosquito B 113 11.03.08
BGA 2382/DUB J E Ritchie tr Mosquito G-DDUB
Syndicate Portmoak *'912'* 07.12.18E

G-DDUE Schleicher ASK 13 13591 01.05.08
BGA 2385/DUE, AGA 15, BGA 2385/DUE
Norfolk Gliding Club Ltd Tibenham *'DUE'* 29.04.18E

G-DDUF Schleicher K 8B 8296A 24.10.07
BGA 2386, D-5294
M Staljan (Jork, Germany) *'DUF'* 19.09.09E
Built by Luftsportverein Medebach (NF 23.02.16)

G-DDUH Scheibe L-Spatz 55 760 29.09.08
BGA 2388/DUH
R J Aylesbury & J Young Upwood *'DUH'* 23.04.18E

G-DDUK Schleicher K 8B 752 29.01.08
BGA 2390/DUK, D-4048 The Bristol Gliding Club
Proprietary Ltd Nympsfield *'DUK'* 09.08.18E

G-DDUL Grob G102 Astir CS77 1720 03.01.08
BGA 2391/DUL M G Dodd & K Nattrass
Skelling Farm, Skirwith *'642'* 28.02.18E

G-DDUR Schleicher Ka 6CR 6273 12.11.07
BGA 2395/DUR, OY-DLX
B N Bromley Strubby *'DUR'* 17.07.17E
(IE 13.01.18)

G-DDUS Schleicher Ka 6E 4263 18.05.09
BGA 2396/DUS, OY-XCB, HB-948
D E Findon Bidford *'638'* 20.06.18E

G-DDUT Schleicher ASW 20 20089 14.04.08
BGA 2397/DUT M E Doig & E T J Murphy
(Kirkcaldy/Edinburgh) *'T34'* 20.11.15E

G-DDUY Glaser-Dirks DG-100 24 02.04.09
BGA 2402/DUY, PH-525
K P & R L McLean Rufforth *'DUY'* 15.09.10E
Noted 10.16 (NF 12.08.14)

G-DDVA Schempp-Hirth Nimbus-2B 172 06.04.18
BGA2404/DVA N & S McLaughlin Lasham *'85'*
(NF 06.04.18)

G-DDVB Schleicher ASK 13 13596 12.11.07
BGA 2405/DVB Essex & Suffolk Gliding Club Ltd
Wormingford *'DVB'* 02.02.19E
Components including c/n plate donated to BGA3493

G-DDVC Schleicher ASK 13 13597 18.08.08
BGA 2406/DVC Staffordshire Gliding Club Ltd
Seighford *'DVC'* 04.11.18E

G-DDVG Schleicher Ka 6CR 003 21.12.07
BGA 2410/DVG, D-1916
S Kahn tr G-DDVG Banana Group Ringmer *'DVG'* 22.03.19E
Built by Herr Holzmann, Diespeck

G-DDVH Schleicher Ka 6E 4117 03.09.08
BGA 2411/DVH, RAFGSA 315
M A K Cropper Burnford Common, Brentor *'DVH'* 01.01.12E
(NF 17.11.15)

G-DDVK SZD-48 Jantar-Standard 2 W-868 25.06.08
BGA 2413/DVK R Goodchild Rattlesden *'732'* 18.01.18E

G-DDVL Schleicher ASW 19B 19222 17.11.07
BGA 2414/DVL J Gavin, P K Newman & G Prophet
Lasham *'X96'* 19.02.18E

G-DDVM Glasflügel Club Libelle 205 52 22.02.08
BGA 2415/DVM, RAFGGA 581
M A Field Wormingford *'DVM'* 27.04.18E

G-DDVN Eiriavion PIK-20D-78 20641 28.01.08
BGA 2416/DVN
P A & T P Bassett Skelling Farm, Skirwith *'DVN'* 02.06.19R

G-DDVP Schleicher ASW 19 19220 17.01.08
BGA 2417/DVP P O R Cumming tr VP Syndicate
Wycombe Air Park *'971'* 12.07.18E

G-DDVS Schempp-Hirth Standard Cirrus xxx 24.10.07
BGA 2420, RAFGSA 824
W T J Wilson Sutton Bank *'VS'* 19.05.19E
Official c/n relates to VH-GGC

G-DDVV Schleicher ASW 20L 20100 12.08.08
BGA 2423 C J Bishop & D M Hurst Lasham *'DV'* 28.09.18E

G-DDVX Schleicher ASK 13 13598 05.08.08
BGA 2425/DVX
Shenington Gliding Club Shenington *'DVX'* 27.04.18E

G-DDVY Schempp-Hirth Cirrus 52 12.02.08
BGA 2426/DVY, OO-ZIR
M G Ashton & G Martin Talgarth *'272'* 27.07.18E

G-DDVZ Glasflügel Mosquito B 133 23.06.08
BGA 2427/DVZ
R M Spreckley Husbands Bosworth *'DVZ'* 24.08.18E

G-DDWB Glasflügel Mosquito B 135 19.03.08
BGA 2429
D T Edwards Skelling Farm, Skirwith *'733'* 23.03.17E

G-DDWC Schleicher Ka 6E 4111 06.11.07
BGA 2430/DWC, AGA 11
C Hitchings Ridgewell *'DWC'* 28.06.18E

G-DDWJ Glaser-Dirks DG-200 2-59 07.03.08
BGA 2436/DWJ
P R Desmond & A P Kamp Chipping *'191'* 06.04.18E

G-DDWL Glasflügel Mosquito B 141 01.11.07
BGA 2438/DWL
H A Stanford Husbands Bosworth *'DWL'* 22.05.18E

G-DDWN Schleicher K7 Rhönadler 7101 12.02.08
BGA 2440/DWN, D-5360
J E & L R Merritt Saltby *'DWN'* 13.05.18E

G-DDWP Glasflügel Mosquito B 136 09.09.09
BGA 2441/DWP I H Murdoch Shenington *'SE'* 01.01.19E

G-DDWR Glasflügel Mosquito B 134 16.10.07
BGA 2443, (BGA 2428) C D Lovell Lasham *'P9'* 04.04.18E

G-DDWS Eiriavion PIK-20D-78 20652 09.04.08
BGA 2444/DWS D G Slocombe Burn *'728'* 28.07.17E

G-DDWT Slingsby T65A Vega 1898 11.10.07
BGA 2445/DWT
A P Grimley (Hale, Altrincham) *'886'* 05.11.09E
(NF 27.11.15)

G-DDWU Grob G102 Astir CS 1201 25.10.07
BGA 2446/DWU, D-7269 H J Smith tr Astir G-DDWU
Syndicate Dunstable Downs *'DWU'* 19.02.19E

G-DDWW Slingsby T65A Vega 1896 28.03.08
BGA 2448/DWW M Finnie & B Grice
(North Walsham & Norwich) *'DWW'* 13.06.12E
(NF 13.09.18)

G-DDWZ Schleicher ASW 19B 19243 15.02.10
BGA 2451/DWZ P Woodcock Burn *'DWZ'* 26.04.18E

G-DDXB Schleicher ASW 20 20142 25.10.07
BGA 2453/DXB
J A Timpany tr 81 Syndicate Nympsfield *'81'* 30.10.18E

G-DDXD Slingsby T65A Vega 1901 26.02.08
BGA 2455/DXD
R M King tr G-DDXD Flying Group Kenley *'132'* 28.06.18E

G-DDXE Slingsby T65A Vega 1902 16.11.07
BGA 2456/DXE H K Rattray Usk *'DXE'* 14.02.18E

G-DDXF Slingsby T65A Vega 1903 26.03.08
BGA2457/DXF B A Walker Gransden Lodge *'DXF'* 07.06.18E

G-DDXG Slingsby T65A Vega 1906 13.03.08
BGA 2458/DXG P J Smith Feshiebridge *'DXG'* 20.09.18E

G-DDXH Schleicher Ka 6E 4198 25.01.08
BGA 2459/DXH, RAFGSA 489, D-4093
D E Findon Bidford *'DXH'* 27.07.17E
(IE 04.08.17)

G-DDXJ Grob G102 Astir CS77 1762 06.12.07
BGA 2460/DXJ
M T Stickland tr DXJ Syndicate Portmoak *'DXJ'* 30.05.18E

G-DDXK Centrair ASW 20F 20108 02.06.08
BGA 2461/DXK A & E Townsend Nympsfield *'160'* 23.07.18E

G-DDXL Schempp-Hirth Standard Cirrus 203G 17.11.07
BGA 2462/DXL, AGA 1 A C Bridges Lasham *'DXL'* 27.05.18E
Built by Burkhart Grob Flugzeugbau

G-DDXN Glaser-Dirks DG-200 2-63 09.01.08
BGA 2464/DXN
J A Johnston Gransden Lodge *'267'* 22.04.17E

G-DDXT Schempp-Hirth Mini Nimbus C 97 10.12.07
BGA 2469/DXT M J Love (Daventry) *'286'* 06.04.18E

G-DDXW Glasflügel Mosquito B 142 06.12.07
BGA 2472/DXW B L C Gordon Easterton *'354'* 19.03.18E

G-DDXX Schleicher ASW 19B 19245 14.12.07
BGA 2473/DXX D Neave Wormingford *'580'* 30.04.19E

G-DDYC Schleicher Ka 6CR 6390 24.01.08
BGA 2478/DYC, D-1545
F J Bradley Skelling Farm, Skirwith *'DYC'* 09.04.18E

G-DDYE Schleicher ASW 20L 20143 05.09.07
BGA 2479 P J L Howell Dunstable Downs *'828'* 12.02.18E

G-DDYF Grob G102 Astir CS77 1805 29.10.07
BGA 2480
York Gliding Centre (Operations) Ltd Rufforth *'DYF'* 16.08.19E

G-DDYH Glaser-Dirks DG-200 2-75 27.05.08
BGA 2482/DYH W A B Roberts Milfield *'DYH'* 24.09.19E

G-DDYJ Schleicher Ka 6CR 6583 19.02.08
BGA 2483/DYJ, D-5838
Upward Bound Trust (Haddenham) *'DYJ'* 25.08.18E

G-DDYL CARMAM JP 15-36AR Aiglon 37 23.04.08
BGA 2485/DYL
J M Caldwell Kirton in Lindsey *'DYL'* 10.09.18E

G-DDYU Schempp-Hirth Nimbus-2C 181 12.12.07
BGA 2491/DYU C B Shepperd Crowland *'DYU'* 17.08.17E

G-DDZA Slingsby T65A Vega 1907 21.09.07
BGA 2496 A W Roberts Dunstable Downs *'DZA'* 22.06.18E

G-DDZB Slingsby T65A Vega 1908 06.03.08
BGA 2497/DZB A L Maitland Portmoak *'639'* 26.09.19E

G-DDZF Schempp-Hirth Standard Cirrus 421G 24.04.08
BGA 2501/DZF, RAFGSA 27
G D E MacDonald Lasham *'152'* 03.05.18E
Built by Burkhart Grob Flugzeugbau (NF 20.08.18)

G-DDZM Slingsby T65A Vega 1909 17.03.08
BGA 2507/DZM A Mattano (Varese, Italy) *'DZM'* 16.06.12E
(NF 15.03.16)

G-DDZN Slingsby T65A Vega 1910 20.02.09
BGA 2508/DZN D A White Aboyne *'990'* 31.05.18E

G-DDZP Slingsby T65A Vega 1911 14.02.0■
BGA 2509/DZP M T Crews Milfield *'DZP'* 11.07.18■

G-DDZR ICA-Brasov IS-28B2 87 05.12.0■
BGA 2511/DZR
Lakes Gliding Club Ltd Walney Island *'DZR'* 10.09.12■
(NF 21.07.17)

G-DDZT Eiriavion PIK-20D-78 20661 31.10.0■
BGA 2513
A C Garside tr Pik20D 106 Group Challock *'106'* 25.05.18■

G-DDZU Grob G102 Astir CS 1076 19.04.0■
BGA 2514/DZU, D-3308
P Clarke Wycombe Air Park *'DZU'* 05.08.17■

G-DDZV	Scheibe SF27A Zugvogel V	6065	17.03.09
	BGA 2515/DZV, D-5839 N Newham Usk '839'		
	(NF 26.02.16)		
G-DDZW	Schleicher Ka 6CR	6628	14.09.09
	BGA 2516/DZW, D-1045		
	S W Naylor Easterton 'DZW'		17.04.15E
	Stored dismantled 10.16 (NF 22.08.18)		
G-DDZY	Schleicher ASW 19B	19275	13.09.07
	BGA 2518 M C Fairman Dunstable Downs '757'		21.01.19E
G-DEAE	Schleicher ASW 20L	20224	01.05.08
	BGA 2524/EAE R Burghall Sutton Bank '107'		06.07.18E
G-DEAF	Grob G102 Astir CS77	1830	25.02.08
	BGA 2525/EAF The Borders (Milfield)		
	Gliding Club Ltd Milfield 'EAF'		29.09.18E
G-DEAG	Slingsby T65A Vega	1913	19.03.08
	BGA 2526/EAG P Hadfield Talgarth 'EAG'		16.04.18E
G-DEAH	Schleicher Ka 6E	4085	05.02.08
	BGA 2527/EAH, D-7542, D-7142		
	R J King Wormingford 'EAH'		16.03.18E
G-DEAJ	Schempp-Hirth Nimbus-2	7	12.11.07
	BGA 2528/EAJ, D-0699 A O'Keefe Rattlesden '2A'		28.03.18E
G-DEAK	Glasflügel Mosquito B	155	14.02.08
	BGA 2529/EAK T A L Barnes Aston Down '594'		26.01.18E
G-DEAM	Schempp-Hirth Nimbus-2B	93	30.10.07
	BGA 2531, D-2787 P I Punt tr Alpha Mike Syndicate		
	Chipping 'EAM'		19.04.18E
G-DEAN	Solar Wings Pegasus XL-Q	SW-WQ-0123	30.11.98
	G-MVJV M G J Bridges (Bridgwater)		13.10.18P
	Trike c/n SW-TE-0117		
G-DEAR	Eiriavion PIK-20D	20550	21.09.07
	BGA 2535, RAFGSA 16 R Penman tr G-DEAR Group		
	RNAS Yeovilton 'EAR'		09.09.18R
G-DEAT	Eiriavion PIK-20D-78	20664	25.07.08
	BGA 2537/EAT D J Knights Kirton in Lindsey '786'		24.03.18R
G-DEAU	Schleicher K7 Rhönadler	7092	15.06.09
	BGA 2538/EAU, PH-304		
	The Welland Gliding Club Ltd Lyveden 'EAU'		06.09.10E
	Modified to ASK 13 standard (IE 13.10.16)		
G-DEAV	Schempp-Hirth Mini Nimbus C	136	25.03.09
	BGA2539/EAV		
	G D H Crawford RAF Weston-on-the-Green '360'		25.11.17E
G-DEAW	Grob G102 Astir CS77	1831	07.11.07
	BGA 2540/EAW J Cooke tr EAW Group		
	Camphill 'EAW' & 'Dark Peak'		26.07.18E
G-DEBT	Alpi Pioneer 300	130	05.10.04
	A J Lloyd & N J T Tonks Shobdon		15.08.18P
	Built by N J T Tonks – project PFA 330-14291		
G-DEBX	Schleicher ASW 20	20058	12.11.07
	BGA 2565/EBX, D-7973 S M Economou & R M Harris		
	Wycombe Air Park '844'		29.07.18E
G-DECC	Schleicher Ka 6CR	60/01	28.02.08
	BGA 2570/ECC, D-5080 P Weaver Burn 'ECC'		17.06.19E
	Built by Paul Siebert Sport		
G-DECF	Schleicher Ka 6CR	856	23.10.07
	BGA 2573, D-5808 Cancelled 20.08.15 by CAA		01.05.12
	Aston Down Stored 12.17		
G-DECJ	Slingsby T65A Vega	1916	04.04.08
	BGA 2576/ECJ		
	J E B Hart & C J Stothard Sutton Bank 'ECJ'		20.01.18E
G-DECL	Slingsby T65A Vega	1918	08.12.07
	BGA 2578/ECL J M Sherman Parham Park 'ECL'		14.07.18E
G-DECM	Slingsby T65A Vega 17L	1919	26.09.08
	BGA 2579/ECM F Wilson Aston Down 'ECM'		01.10.18E
	Originally built as T.65A Vega		
G-DECO	Dyn'Aéro MCR-01 Club	295	15.09.04
	A W Bishop & A P Wheelwright Cambridge		10.05.17P
	Built by A W Bishop & G Castelli		
	– project PFA 301A-14246		
G-DECP	Rolladen-Schneider LS3-17	3426	08.10.07
	BGA 2581 M D Newton tr LS3-17 ECP Syndicate		
	Crowland 'ECP'		22.04.18E

G-DECR	P&M QuikR	8521	07.05.10
	D J Lawrence Stapenhill Farm, Stourbridge		10.05.15P
	Fitted with trike c/n 8263 ex G-DECX (IE 05.06.17)		
G-DECS	Glasflügel Mosquito B	166	05.08.08
	BGA 2584/ECS G Richardson Currock Hill 'ECS'		21.03.18E
G-DECW	Schleicher ASK 21	21008	15.07.08
	BGA 2588/ECW		
	Norfolk Gliding Club Ltd Tibenham 'ECW'		21.01.19E
G-DECZ	Schleicher ASK 21	21009	15.10.07
	BGA 2591		
	Booker Gliding Club Ltd Wycombe Air Park '316'		11.04.18E
G-DEDG	Schleicher Ka 6CR	6512	05.09.08
	BGA 2598/EDG, RAFGGA 541		
	S J Wood Cranwell North 'EDG'		31.08.18E
G-DEDH	Glasflügel Mosquito B	184	09.03.10
	BGA 2599/EDH B L Liddiard Ringmer		
	(IE 22.02.16)		
G-DEDJ	Glasflügel Mosquito B	185	24.01.08
	BGA 2600/EDJ D M Ward Milfield 'EDJ'		25.04.18E
G-DEDK	Schleicher K7 Rhönadler	791	23.01.08
	BGA 2601/EDK, D-1633 D Smith tr Cyprus Gliding		
	Group Mammari, Republic of Cyprus		
	'EDK' & 'North Wales Gliding Club'		28.08.18E
	Partly modified to ASK 13 standard		
G-DEDM	Glaser-Dirks DG-200	2-98	17.09.07
	BGA 2603 D Watson Sutton Bank 'EDM'		11.05.18E
G-DEDN	Glaser-Dirks DG-100G Elan	E12G6	12.03.08
	BGA 2604/EDN		
	S J Gooch tr DG 820 Syndicate Currock Hill '820'		08.08.18E
	Built by Elan Tovarna Sportnega Orodja N.Sol.O		
G-DEDU	Schleicher ASK 13	13613	10.01.08
	BGA 2610/EDU P Bolton tr Channel Gliding Club		
	Group Waldershare Park 'EDU'		05.07.18E
G-DEDX	Slingsby T65D Vega	1928	01.07.08
	BGA 2613/EDX G Kirkham Camphill 'EDX'		
	(NF 12.08.15)		
G-DEDY	Slingsby T65D Vega	1929	29.11.07
	BGA 2614/EDY		
	J Shaw & G Spelman Gransden Lodge 'EDY'		16.08.18E
	(IE 06.06.17)		
G-DEDZ	Slingsby T65C Sport Vega	1931	07.04.08
	BGA2615/EDZ R C R Copley Walney Island 'EDZ'		16.09.10E
	(NF 31.03.17)		
G-DEEA	Slingsby T65C Sport Vega	1932	24.04.08
	BGA 2616/EEA S J Harrison Milfield '337'		04.05.17E
	(IE 16.05.17)		
G-DEEC	Schleicher ASW 20L	20311	19.10.07
	BGA 2618, G-BSTS, BGA 2618		
	D Beams Challock 'EEC'		15.12.14E
	(IE 14.05.15)		
G-DEED	Schleicher K 8B	590	17.03.09
	BGA 2619/EED, RAFGSA R91, NEJSGSA, BGA 2619,		
	D-5703 The Windrushers Gliding Club Ltd		
	Bicester 'EED'		29.07.18E
G-DEEF	Rolladen-Schneider LS3-17	3441	27.09.07
	BGA 2621 R Dann tr Echo Echo Foxtrot Group		
	Rivar Hill 'EEF'		24.01.18E
G-DEEG	Slingsby T65C Sport Vega	1922	21.11.07
	BGA 2622/EEG, EI-129, BGA 2622/EEG, G-7-103		
	G Harris tr Vega Syndicate Rufforth 'EEG'		12.05.18E
G-DEEH	Schleicher ASW 19	19042	30.06.08
	BGA 2623, RAFGGA 166 K Kiely Sutton Bank '166'		04.09.18E
G-DEEJ	Schleicher ASW 20L	20314	11.08.08
	BGA 2624/EEJ T Mills Dunstable Downs 'EEJ'		02.11.18E
G-DEEK	Schempp-Hirth Nimbus-2C	201	06.11.07
	BGA 2625/EEK G D Palmer (Gloucester) '996'		29.07.17E
G-DEEN	Schempp-Hirth Standard Cirrus 75	621	22.02.08
	BGA 2628/EEN, (BGA 2609/EDT), RAFGSA 87		
	T J H Elliott tr G-DEEN Flying Group		
	RAF Weston-on-the-Green 'EEN'		07.05.17E
G-DEEO	Grob G102 Standard Astir II	5015S	11.03.08
	BGA 2630/EEQ, (RNGSA N12)		
	T J Walsh tr G-DEEO Group RAF Cosford 'EEO'		01.07.18E

G-DEEP Wassmer WA.26P Squale   036   15.02.08
    BGA 2629/EEP, F-CDSX S Crossland tr Wassmer
    G-DEEP Group Eaglescott *'EEP'*   14.06.14R
    (NF 07.01.16)

G-DEES Rolladen-Schneider LS3-17   3248   08.10.07
    BGA 2632 J B Illidge Camphill *'50'*   29.10.18E

G-DEEX Rolladen-Schneider LS3-17   3442   22.02.08
    BGA 2637/EEX
    D Edge tr G-DEEX Group Aston Down *'EEX'*   16.05.18E

G-DEEZ Denney Kitfox Model 3   931   15.07.09
    N745B D & J D Cheesman
    Newton Peveril Farm, Sturminster Marshall   12.06.18P
    Built by M Journey

G-DEFA Schleicher ASW 20L   20326   20.05.08
    BGA 2640/EFA R G Cooper tr Eight Eighties Syndicate
    Dunstable Downs *'470'*   04.02.18E

G-DEFB Schempp-Hirth Nimbus-2C   216   30.07.08
    BGA 2641/EFB G D Palmer Aston Down *'EFB'*   18.01.18E

G-DEFE Centrair ASW 20F   20139   01.02.08
    BGA 2644/EFE
    W A Horne & D A Mackenzie Camphill *'586'*   05.04.18E

G-DEFF Schempp-Hirth Nimbus-2C   208   30.11.07
    BGA 2645/EFF
    J W L Clarke & P J D Smith Rivar Hill *'737'*   11.03.18E

G-DEFS Rolladen-Schneider LS3   3022   02.09.09
    BGA 2656/EFS, HB-1356 A Twigg Bicester *'LS3'*   31.12.18E

G-DEFV Schleicher ASW 20   20041   22.01.08
    BGA 2659/EFV, OE-5162
    A R McKillen Bellarena *'EFV'*   11.07.17E

G-DEFW Slingsby T65C Sport Vega   1938   20.02.08
    BGA 2660/EFW H Yildiz Gransden Lodge *'EFW'*   04.06.18E

G-DEFZ Rolladen-Schneider LS3-a   3273   18.03.08
    BGA 2663/EFZ
    D H Gardner tr EFZ Syndicate Aston Down *'EFZ'*   06.05.18E

G-DEGE Rolladen-Schneider LS3-a   3465   29.10.07
    BGA 2668 G Szabo-Toth tr EGE Glider Syndicate
    Nympsfield *'EGE'*   29.01.19E

G-DEGF Slingsby T65C Sport Vega   1936   08.04.09
    BGA 2669/EGF Shalbourne Soaring Society Ltd
    Rivar Hill *'EGF'*   20.07.18E

G-DEGH Slingsby T65C Sport Vega   1943   26.11.07
    BGA 2671/EGH P Thomas Walney Island *'EGH'*   05.05.18E

G-DEGJ Slingsby T65C Sport Vega   1944   04.12.07
    BGA 2672/EGJ M Gilliland tr Sport Vega Syndicate
    Aston Down *'672'*   22.06.18E

G-DEGK Schempp-Hirth Standard Cirrus   542G   31.10.07
    BGA 2673, RAFGSA 569, RAFGSA R2
    D A Parker Burnford Common, Brentor *'569'*   02.05.17E
    Built by Burkhart Grob Flugzeugbau

G-DEGN Grob G103 Twin II   3542   02.09.08
    BGA 2676/EGN
    Staffordshire Gliding Club Ltd Seighford *'EGN'*   21.10.18E

G-DEGP Schleicher ASW 20L   20336   11.05.09
    BGA 2677/EGP
    D Hoolahan & J R Paine (Otford & Mersham) *'0'*   26.10.18E

G-DEGS Schempp-Hirth Nimbus-2CS   192   29.01.08
    BGA 2680/EGS, D-2111 A Klapa Burn *'2CS'*   06.06.18E

G-DEGT Slingsby T65D Vega   1933   08.04.08
    BGA 2681/EGT
    D M Gill tr G-DEGT Group Seighford *'EGT'*   25.07.18E

G-DEGW Schempp-Hirth Mini Nimbus C   078   08.09.08
    BGA 2684/EGW, HB-1447
    A Brook tr IF Barnes & Partners Ridgewell *'EGW'*   29.11.18E
    Originally built as Mini-Nimbus B

G-DEGX Slingsby T65C Sport Vega   1937   14.02.08
    BGA 2685/EGX, RAFGSA R23, BGA 2685/EGX
    C P Raine tr Haddenham Vega Syndicate
    (Haddenham) *'EGX'*   18.06.19E

G-DEGZ Schleicher ASK 21   21030   01.12.07
    BGA 2687/EGZ
    Oxford Gliding Company Ltd
    RAF Weston-on-the-Green *'EGZ'*   02.04.19E

G-DEHC Akaflieg Braunschweig SB-5b Danzig   5017   15.08.11
    BGA 2690, D-9310
    J A Castle Husbands Bosworth *'Edith'*   11.05.18E

G-DEHG Slingsby T65C Sport Vega   1940   27.02.08
    BGA 2694/EHG S R Hopkins Shobdon *'453'*   05.11.18E

G-DEHH Schempp-Hirth Ventus a   07   23.07.08
    BGA 2695/EHH L B Roberts Bicester *'V7'*   11.05.16E
    (NF 30.08.17)

G-DEHK Rolladen-Schneider LS4   4068   27.09.07
    BGA 2697 R P M Symons (Marlborough) *'490'*   27.04.19E

G-DEHM Schleicher Ka 6E   4118   03.03.08
    BGA 2699/EHM, RAFGSA 318
    J B Symons Kingston Deverill *'EHM'*   17.08.18E

G-DEHO Schleicher ASK 21   21035   18.01.08
    BGA 2702/EHQ
    Lasham Gliding Society Ltd Lasham *'431'*   19.03.19E

G-DEHP Schempp-Hirth Nimbus-2C   234   27.11.07
    BGA 2701/EHP D J King Rattlesden *'EHP'*   20.05.18E

G-DEHT Schempp-Hirth Nimbus-2C   235   14.01.08
    BGA 2705/EHT M V Boydon Bicester *'EHT'*   08.04.18E

G-DEHU Glasflügel 304   209   25.10.07
    BGA 2706 F Townsend Bidford *'849'*   18.01.19E

G-DEHY Slingsby T65D Vega   1941   19.05.08
    BGA 2710/EHY
    C J A Rosales (Lisbon, Portugal) *'EHY'*   29.10.18E

G-DEHZ Schleicher ASW 20L   20388   29.10.07
    BGA 2711
    I R Russell tr G-DEHZ Syndicate Challock *'EHZ'*   26.05.18E

G-DEJA ICA-Brasov IS-28B2   88   01.02.08
    BGA 2712/EJA M H Simms Shipdham *'EJA'*   19.04.09E
    (NF 25.02.15)

G-DEJB Slingsby T65C Sport Vega   1945   28.03.08
    BGA 2713/EJB
    D Tait & I G Walker Snitterfield *'EJB'*   25.07.18E

G-DEJC Slingsby T65C Sport Vega   1946   10.01.08
    BGA 2714/EJC I Powis Darlton *'EJC'*   18.07.14E
    (NF 20.06.16)

G-DEJD Slingsby T65D Vega   1930   03.04.09
    BGA 2715/EJD, RAFGGA 510, BGA 2715
    K P & R L McLean Rufforth *'261'*
    (NF 16.03.16)

G-DEJE Slingsby T65C Sport Vega   1947   10.12.07
    BGA 2716/EJE
    Crown Service Gliding Club Lasham *'EJE'*   22.05.18E

G-DEJF Schleicher K 8B   8966   19.09.08
    BGA 2717/EJF, D-2328
    Cotswold Gliding Club Aston Down *'EJF'*   16.11.09E
    Stored 01.16 (NF 03.12.15)

G-DEJH Eichelsdorfer SB-5E   5041A   07.02.08
    BGA 2719/EJH, D-5430, D-0087
    Edensoaring Ltd Skelling Farm, Skirwith *'EJH'*   23.04.18E
    Built by J Altroder (NF 28.11.17)

G-DEJR Schleicher ASW 19B   19334   01.11.07
    BGA 2727/EJR
    M C Woerner tr G-DEJR Group (Swindon) *'193'*   12.12.18E

G-DEJY SZD-9bis Bocian 1D   P-351   04.08.09
    BGA 2734/EJY, D-1587 C Hagerty tr G-DEJY
    Bocian Group Portmoak *'EJY'*   27.11.18E
    Built by ZSLS Jezow Sudecki

G-DEJZ Scheibe SF26A   5020   01.07.08
    BGA 2735/EJZ, D-8473 Cancelled 21.10.15 by CAA   07.08.10
    Wingland, Lincs *Stored 03.16*

G-DEKA Cameron Z-90   10665   16.12.04
    P G Bogliaccino Mondovi, Italy *'Dekalb'*   22.08.18E

G-DEKC Schleicher Ka 6E   4079   14.02.08
    BGA 2738/EKC, OO-ZDV, OE-0813
    M N K Willcox (Sheffield) *'EKC'*   23.06.19E

G-DEKF Grob G102 Club Astir III   5519C   17.04.08
    BGA 2741/EKF The Bristol Gliding Club
    Proprietary Ltd Nympsfield *'EKF'*   12.05.18E

G-DEKG	Schleicher ASK 21	21067	19.11.07
	BGA 2742/EKG, AGA 8, BGA 2742/EKG		
	J W Sage tr Army Gliding Association		
	Trenchard Lines, Upavon '*A15*'		17.02.18E
	Operated by Wyvern Gliding Club		
G-DEKJ	Schempp-Hirth Ventus b	36	22.10.07
	BGA 2744 I J Metcalfe Usk '*EKJ*'		07.05.18E
G-DEKS	Scheibe SF27A Zugvogel V	6096	31.01.08
	BGA 2752/EKS, D-8166 T Emms (Rushden) '*EKS*'		04.05.15E
G-DEKU	Schleicher ASW 20L	20384	06.11.07
	BGA 2754/EKU A J Gillson Sleap '*408*'		09.05.18E
G-DEKV	Rolladen-Schneider LS4	4102	16.11.07
	BGA 2755/EKV S L Helstrip Bicester '*EKV*'		27.07.18E
G-DEKW	Schempp-Hirth Nimbus-2B	111	31.03.08
	BGA 2756, D-7245		
	V Luscombe-Mahoney Dunstable Downs '*430*'		22.03.18E
G-DEKX	Schleicher Ka 6E	4027	28.08.15
	BGA 2757/EKX, D-1221		
	D S Downton Burnford Common, Brentor '*K6e*'		28.02.18E
G-DELA	Schleicher ASW 19B	19346	03.12.07
	BGA 2760/ELA S G Jones (Membury) '*ELA*'		02.02.13E
	Collided with Mainair Blade G-MZBA at Aboyne		
	06.05.12 & substantially damaged (NF 08.04.16)		
G-DELB[M]	Robinson R22 Beta	0799	18.05.88
	N26461 Cancelled 20.04.95 by CAA		
	With South Yorkshire Aircraft Museum, Doncaster		
G-DELD	Slingsby T65C Sport Vega	1950	05.09.07
	BGA 2763		
	The Surrey Hills Gliding Club Ltd Kenley '*ELD*'		08.03.19E
G-DELG	Schempp-Hirth Ventus b/16.6	46	14.11.07
	BGA 2766/ELG A Jelden Shobdon '*ELG*'		23.02.19E
G-DELN	Grob G102 Astir CS Jeans	2024	26.02.08
	BGA 2772/ELN		
	Bowland Forest Gliding Club Ltd Chipping '*ELN*'		23.11.18E
G-DELO	Slingsby T65D Vega	1934	25.03.08
	BGA 2774/ELQ I Sim & I Surley Milfield '*ELO*'		13.11.18E
G-DELR	Schempp-Hirth Ventus b	45	16.10.07
	BGA 2775 I D Smith Nympsfield '*188*'		03.03.18E
G-DELU	Schleicher ASW 20L	20462	08.03.12
	BGA 2778/ELU P G Roberts Aston Down '*ELU*'		20.11.18E
G-DELZ	Schleicher ASW 20L	20310	15.10.07
	BGA 2783, RAFGGA 569		
	D A Fogden Wycombe Air Park '*719*'		10.07.18E
G-DEME	Glaser-Dirks DG-202/17C	2-176CL18	16.01.08
	BGA 2788/EME E D Casagrande Usk '*515*'		21.06.18E
G-DEMF	Rolladen-Schneider LS4	4187	18.01.08
	BGA 2789/EMF R N Johnston & M C Oggelsby		
	Hinton-in-the-Hedges '*452*'		17.04.18E
G-DEMG	Rolladen-Schneider LS4	4242	07.11.07
	BGA 2790/EMG Stratford on Avon Gliding Club Ltd		
	Snitterfield '*EMG*'		26.01.19E
G-DEMH	Reims/Cessna F172M	F17201137	18.11.91
	G-BFLO, PH-DMF, (EI-AYO)		
	M Hammond Airfield Farm, Hardwick		11.04.18E
G-DEMN	Slingsby T65D Vega	1935	13.12.07
	BGA 2796/EMN J C Jenks Llantysilio '*EMN*'		01.10.17E
G-DEMP	Slingsby T65C Sport Vega	1952	15.11.07
	BGA2797/EMP		
	I P Stork (Bridstow, Ross-on-Wye) '*EMP*'		08.03.19E
G-DEMR	Slingsby T65C Sport Vega	1954	05.09.08
	BGA 2799/EMR		
	R Farragher tr Llantysilio Team Llantysilio '*EMR*'		26.10.17E
G-DEMT	Rolladen-Schneider LS4	4243	28.11.07
	BGA 2801/EMT M R Fox Seighford '*MF*'		20.05.18E
G-DEMU	Glaser-Dirks DG-200/17	2-162/1753	11.10.07
	BGA 2802 A Butterfield & N Swinton		
	RAF Weston-on-the-Green '*616*'		08.02.19E
G-DEMZ	Slingsby T65A Vega	1891	07.09.07
	BGA 2807, G-BGCA K Western Rattlesden '*EMZ*'		28.03.18E
G-DENC	Cessna F150G	F150-0107	14.12.95
	G-AVAP		
	T C Aldrich tr G-DENC Cessna Group Popham		15.08.19E
	Built by Reims Aviation SA		
G-DEND	Reims/Cessna F150M	F15001201	06.06.97
	G-WAFC, G-BDFI, (OH-CGD)		
	J P Nugent t/a Wicklow Wings Newcastle, RoI		
	(IE 26.10.15)		
G-DENI	Piper PA-32-300 Cherokee Six	32-7340006	07.12.95
	G-BAIA, N11C A Bendkowski Lydd		07.12.19E
G-DENJ	Schempp-Hirth Ventus b/16.6	62	26.09.08
	BGA 2816/ENJ S Boyden Lasham '*771*'		23.05.11E
	(NF 28.11.16)		
G-DENM	BB Microlight BB03 Trya		
		BB03/16/1/UKNANO/16/1/UK	12.08.16
	D A Morgan (Hatt, Saltash)		
	(NF 06.07.17)		
G-DENO	Glasflügel Standard Libelle 201B	232	14.11.07
	BGA 1662/CMX D M Bland Burn '*226*'		16.08.17E
G-DENS	Binder CP.301S Smaragd	121	20.11.85
	D-ENSA T Wilcock tr Garston Smaragd Group		
	Garston Farm, Marshfield		24.11.17P
	Carries c/n 'AB.429' – denoting Amateur Build		
G-DENU	Glaser-Dirks DG-101G Elan	E108G78	28.03.08
	BGA 2826/ENU		
	R A Johnson tr 435 Syndicate Shobdon '*435*'		25.07.18E
	Built by Elan Tovarna Sportnega Orodja N.Sol.O		
G-DENV	Schleicher ASW 20L	20554	02.11.07
	BGA 2827/ENV R D Hone Wycombe Air Park '*181*'		14.08.18E
G-DENX	SZD-48 Jantar-Standard 2	W-857	03.03.08
	BGA 2829/ENX, (BGA 2746/EKL)		
	J M Hire Currock Hill '*276*'		01.08.18E
G-DENY	Robinson R44 Raven II	14044	18.01.17
	S P Denneny (Horsley Woodhouse, Ilkeston)		01.02.19E
G-DEOA	Rolladen-Schneider LS4	4259	10.01.08
	BGA 2856/EQA M Nowak Lasham		08.06.19E
G-DEOB	SZD-30 Pirat	S-06.48	16.05.08
	BGA 2857/EQB, D-2702		
	R M Golding Parham Park '*EOB*'		19.06.18E
	Built by WSK Swidnik		
G-DEOD	Grob G102 Astir CS77	1614	03.06.08
	BGA 2859/EQD, PH-570 D S Fenton Usk '*EOD*'		17.06.19E
G-DEOE	Schleicher ASK 13	13627AB	01.05.08
	BGA2860/EQE		
	Essex Gliding Club Ltd Ridgewell '*EOE*'		30.08.18E
	Built by Jubi GmbH Sportflugzeugbau		
G-DEOF	Schleicher ASK 13	13626AB	01.05.08
	BGA 2861/EQF		
	A Brook tr K13 – DEOF Syndicate Ridgewell '*EOF*'		15.06.18E
	Built by Jubi GmbH Sportflugzeugbau		
G-DEOJ	Centrair ASW 20FL	20512	15.02.08
	BGA 2864/EQJ C J Bowden Darlton '*968*'		09.06.18E
G-DEOK	Centrair 101A Pégase	101054	07.06.10
	BGA 2865/EOK C M Scott Pocklington '*EOK*'		02.07.19E
G-DEOM	CARMAM M-100S Mésange	81	01.06.09
	BGA 2867/EQM, F-CDKQ		
	S W Hutchinson Skelling Farm, Skirwith '*EOM*'		
	(NF 22.10.16)		
G-DEON	Schempp-Hirth Nimbus-3/25.5	31	08.12.07
	BGA 2868/EQN		
	W H L Bullimore tr 117 Syndicate Lasham '*117*'		18.04.18E
G-DEOT	Grob G103A Twin II Acro	3787-K-65	14.04.08
	BGA 2873/EQT, RAFGGA R58, BGA 2873/EQT		
	R Tyrrell Shenington		09.05.18E
G-DEOU	Pilatus B4-PC11AF	201	26.02.08
	BGA 2874/EQU, PH-535 A N Cole Saltby '*EOU*'		29.07.18E
G-DEOV	Schempp-Hirth Janus C	169	14.12.07
	BGA 2875/EQV, ZD974, BGA 2875/EQV		
	The Burn Gliding Club Ltd Burn '*EOV*'		15.07.18E
G-DEOW	Schempp-Hirth Janus C	171	08.02.08
	BGA 2876/EQW, ZD975, BGA 2876/EQW		
	C C Pike tr 383 Syndicate Rivar Hill '*383*'		24.03.18E
G-DEOX	CARMAM M-200 Foehn	54	08.02.10
	BGA 2877/EOX, F-CDKR		
	B S Goodspeed Isle of Man '*EOX*'		16.04.12R
	(NF 27.04.18)		

G-DEOZ	Schleicher K 8B	8113A	10.06.08
	BGA 2879/EQZ, D-8763		
	Cotswold Gliding Club Aston Down *'EQZ'*		
	Stored 01.16 (NF 03.12.15)		

G-DEPD	Schleicher ASK 21	21119	03.03.08
	BGA 2835/EPD London Gliding Club Proprietary Ltd		
	Dunstable Downs *'EPD'*		21.03.18E

G-DEPF	Centrair ASW 20FL	20515	23.11.07
	BGA 2837/EPF S G Lapworth Lasham *'323'*		20.04.18E
	(NF 09.10.18)		

G-DEPG	CARMAM M-100S Mésange	03	10.03.11
	BGA 2838/EPG, F-CCPB		
	J Kohlmetz (Bruchsal, Germany)		
	(NF 20.12.16)		

G-DEPP	Schleicher ASK 13	13064	22.12.07
	BGA 2845/EPP, PH-368 Mendip Gliding Club Ltd		
	Halesland *'EPP'*		05.09.18E
	Rebuilt from PH-368 (c/n 13064); c/n 1609 relates		
	to spare fuselage		

G-DEPS	Schleicher ASW 20L	20245	01.10.07
	BGA 2848, RAFGSA 87		
	C Beveridge Sandhill Farm, Shrivenham *'765'*		26.05.17E
	(IE 05.06.17)		

G-DEPT	Schleicher K 8B	146/59	21.12.07
	BGA 2849/EPT, RAFGGA 504, D-5004		
	R McEvoy Lasham *'EPT'*		10.06.18E
	Built by Aero-Club Minden		

G-DEPU	Glaser-Dirks DG-101G Elan	E116G85	02.07.07
	BGA 2850, (BGA 2833)		
	J F Rogers Wycombe Air Park *'EPU'*		15.06.18E
	Built by Elan Tozd Plastika		

G-DEPX	Schempp-Hirth Ventus b/16.6	107	22.10.07
	BGA 2853 M E S Thomas Usk *'EPX'*		19.05.18E

G-DERA	Centrair ASW 20FL	20526	14.12.07
	BGA 2880/ERA R J Lockett Wormingford *'283'*		22.06.18E

G-DERH	Schleicher ASK 21	21147	04.01.08
	BGA 2887/ERH, ZD647, BGA 2887/ERH		
	The Burn Gliding Club Ltd Burn *'ERH'*		19.10.18E

G-DERJ	Schleicher ASK 21	21148	09.04.08
	BGA 2888/ERJ, RAFGSA R35, ZD648, BGA 2888		
	The Royal Air Force Gliding & Soaring Association		
	RAF Halton *'R35'*		26.11.18E

G-DERO	Van's RV-10	41967	13.11.18
	D Atkinson Sherburn-in-Elmet		
	Built by D Atkinson – project LAA 339-15583 (NF 13.11.18)		

G-DERR	Schleicher ASW 19B	19382	21.08.08
	BGA 2895/ERR, ZD659, BGA 2895/ERR		
	University of Edinburgh Sports Union		
	Portmoak *'ERR'*		07.05.18E

G-DERS	Schleicher ASW 19B	19383	09.01.08
	BGA 2896/ERS, ZD660, BGA 2896/ERS		
	Booker Gliding Club Ltd Wycombe Air Park *'319'*		29.01.18E

G-DERV	Cameron Truck-56	1719	21.03.88
	J M Percival Bourton-on-the-Wolds, Loughborough		22.02.00A
	(NF 27.05.18)		

G-DERX	Centrair 101A Pégase	101058	16.04.09
	BGA 2901/ERX I P Freestone Husbands Bosworth		04.05.14E
	(NF 17.11.17)		

G-DESB	Schleicher ASK 21	21176	23.10.07
	BGA 2905 C J Rallance tr Oxford University		
	Gliding Club Bicester *'ESB'*		11.07.18E

G-DESC	Rolladen-Schneider LS4	4261	28.03.08
	BGA 2906/ESC		
	J Crawford & J M Staley Bicester *'379'*		01.08.18E

G-DESH	Centrair 101A Pégase	101069	09.11.07
	BGA 2911/ESH		
	J E Moore Wycombe Air Park *'118'*		09.04.18E

G-DESJ	Schleicher K 8B	8730	04.09.07
	BGA 2912, D-5010		
	Bowland Forest Gliding Club Ltd Chipping *'ESJ'*		09.08.18E

G-DESO	Glaser-Dirks DG-300 Elan	3E10	01.02.08
	BGA 2918/ESQ		
	G R P Brown Sandhill Farm, Shrivenham *'231'*		19.04.18E
	Built by Elan Tovarna Sportnega Orodja N.Sol.O		

G-DESU	Schleicher ASK 21	21180	06.11.07
	BGA 2922/ESU, RAFGSA R40, BGA 2922/ESU		
	Banbury Gliding Club Ltd		
	Hinton-in-the-Hedges *'ESU'*		20.11.18E

G-DETA	Schleicher ASK 21	21181	25.03.08
	BGA 2928/ETA		
	P Hawkins Feshiebridge *'ETA'* & *'Daisy'*		11.04.18E

G-DETG	Rolladen-Schneider LS4	4349	12.09.07
	BGA 2934 K J Woods Gransden Lodge *'NW'*		05.06.18E

G-DETJ	Centrair 101A Pégase	101A0110	14.01.08
	BGA 2936/ETJ S C Phillips (Potton, Sandy) *'223'*		21.06.18E

G-DETM	Centrair 101A Pégase	101A0111	08.11.07
	BGA 2939/ETM		
	A Carden & J E Masheder Rufforth *'M7'*		26.02.18E

G-DETV	Rolladen-Schneider LS4	4314	23.06.08
	BGA 2947/ETV, (BGA 2919/ESR)		
	P Fabian Bidford *'ETV'*		10.08.18E

G-DETY	Rolladen-Schneider LS4	4368	23.08.07
	BGA 2950 D T Staff Bicester *'ETY'*		25.10.18E

G-DETZ	Schleicher ASW 20CL	20730	28.01.08
	BGA 2951/ETZ		
	N L Clowes tr The 20 Syndicate Tibenham *'20'*		16.02.18E

G-DEUC	Schleicher ASK 13	13104	28.04.08
	BGA 2954/EUC, AGA 12		
	North Wales Gliding Club Ltd Llantysilio *'EUC'*		06.11.18E

G-DEUD	Schleicher ASW 20C	20734	23.10.07
	BGA 2955 R Tietema Husbands Bosworth *'RT'*		06.04.18E

G-DEUF	PZL-Bielsko SZD-50-3 Puchacz	B-1090	23.01.08
	BGA 2957/EUF		
	Shalbourne Soaring Society Ltd Rivar Hill *'EUF'*		27.01.18E

G-DEUH	Rolladen-Schneider LS4	4382	04.10.07
	BGA 2959 F J Parkinson Nympsfield *'446'*		10.08.18E

G-DEUJ	Schempp-Hirth Ventus b/16.6	162	13.12.07
	BGA 2960/EUJ C Bessent Rivar Hill *'217'*		13.10.18E

G-DEUK	Centrair ASW 20FL	20530	26.09.07
	BGA 2961 P A Clark Lasham *'992'* & *'BGA2691'*		10.03.18E

G-DEUS	Schempp-Hirth Ventus b/16.6	192	04.10.07
	BGA 2968 R J Whitaker Lasham *'443'*		15.01.19E

G-DEUV	PZL-Bielsko SZD-42-2 Jantar 2B	B-934	16.10.08
	BGA 2971/EUV G V McKirdy Bicester *'EUV'*		28.04.12E
	(NF 11.04.18)		

G-DEUY	Schleicher ASW 20BL	20645	16.10.07
	BGA 2974 D G Roberts tr ASW20BL – G-DEUY Group		
	Aston Down *'88'*		06.04.18E

G-DEVF	Schempp-Hirth Nimbus-3T	15/76	19.10.07
	BGA 2981, D-KHIJ A G Leach Bembridge *'EVF'*		26.04.17E

G-DEVH	Schleicher K 10A	10008	06.08.08
	BGA 2983/EVH, HB-791 C W & K T Matten		
	Burnford Common, Brentor *'EVH'*		30.09.17E

G-DEVJ	Schleicher ASK 13	13637AB	24.09.08
	BGA 2984/EVJ		
	Lasham Gliding Society Ltd Lasham *'H'*		03.07.18E
	Built by Jubi GmbH Sportflugzeugbau		

G-DEVK	Grob G102 Astir CS	1397	02.04.08
	BGA 2985/EVK, PH-546 Peterborough & Spalding		
	Gliding Club Ltd Crowland *'EVK'*		19.05.18E

G-DEVL	Eurocopter EC120B Colibri	1273	07.06.02
	D K Richardson Gloucestershire		31.07.19E

G-DEVM	Centrair 101A Pégase	101A0157	29.11.07
	BGA 2987/EVM J G Kosak tr Seahawk Gliding Club		
	RNAS Culdrose *'N51'*		09.03.18E

G-DEVN[M]	de Havilland DH.104 Devon C.2/2	04269	26.10.84
	WB533 Cancelled 16.11.90 by CAA As *'WB533'*		04.02.85
	With Luftfahrt Und Technik Museumpark,		
	Merseburg Sud, Germany		

G-DEVO	Centrair 101A Pégase	101A0149	24.06.08
	BGA 2990/EVQ J A Lyle tr G-DEVO Pegase Glider		
	Parham Park *'SP'*		06.05.18E

G-DEVP	Schleicher ASK 13	13638AB	29.09.08
	BGA 2989/EVP		
	Lasham Gliding Society Ltd Lasham *'K'*		19.11.18E
	Built by Jubi GmbH Sportflugzeugbau		

G-DEVS	Piper PA-28-180 Cherokee B	28-830		05.03.85
	G-BGVJ, D-ENPI, N7066W			
	P Carroll & J M Whiteley tr 180 Group	Popham		23.05.19E
G-DEVV	Schleicher ASK 23	23004		10.12.07
	BGA 2995/EVV			
	Midland Gliding Club Ltd	Long Mynd	*'EVV'*	22.03.18E
G-DEVW	Schleicher ASK 23	23006		08.02.08
	BGA 2996/EVW	London Gliding Club Proprietary Ltd		
	Dunstable Downs	*'EVW'*		05.12.17E
G-DEVX	Schleicher ASK 23	23007		08.02.08
	BGA 2997/EVX	London Gliding Club Proprietary Ltd		
	Dunstable Downs	*'EVX'*		10.04.18E
G-DEWE	Flight Design CTSW	08-06-07		13.01.09
	A R Hughes (Fyfield, Marlborough)			22.01.14P
	Assembled P&M Aviation Ltd as c/n 8435 (NF 12.04.18)			
G-DEWG	Grob G103A Twin II Acro	33885-K-123		20.05.08
	BGA 3006/EWG, ZE501, BGA 3006/EWG			
	Herefordshire Gliding Club Ltd	Shobdon	*'EWG'*	16.01.19E
G-DEWI	AutoGyro MTOsport	09 043S		26.06.09
	D V Nockels (Barton on Sea, New Milton)			08.02.19P
	Assembled Rotorsport UK as c/n RSUK/MTOS/009			
G-DEWP	Grob G103A Twin II Acro	33892-K-130		11.12.07
	BGA 3013/EWP, ZE523, BGA 3013/EWP			
	Bowland Forest Gliding Club Ltd			
	Gransden Lodge	*'EWP'*		29.04.18E
G-DEWR	Grob G103A Twin II Acro	33894-K-132		08.12.07
	BGA 3015/EWR, RAFGSA R70, ZE525,			
	BGA 3015/EWR	The Bristol Gliding Club		
	Proprietary Ltd	Nympsfield	*'P70'*	14.07.18E
G-DEWZ	Grob G103A Twin II Acro	33981-K-214		09.09.08
	BGA 3076/EZE, ZE634, BGA 3076/EZE			
	T R Dews Kingston Deverill	*'EZE'*		10.12.18E
	Originally ZE634 Viking T1 w/o 25.01.90;			
	wreckage rebuilt as BGA 3076			
G-DEXA	Grob G103A Twin II Acro	33908-K-143		23.01.08
	BGA 3024/EXA, ZE534, BGA 3024/EXA			
	Trent Valley Gliding Club Ltd Kirton in Lindsey	*'EXA'*		11.04.18E
G-DEXP	ARV ARV-1 Super 2	003		24.04.85
	R W Clarke Sleap			26.07.18P
	Built by ARV Aviation – project PFA 152-11154			
G-DFAF	Schleicher ASW 20L	20214		22.11.07
	BGA 3101/FAF, RAFGSA 271, RAFGSA R27			
	J J Young tr G-DFAF Group Nympsfield	*'271'*		26.11.18E
G-DFAR	Glasflügel Club Libelle 205	58		28.02.08
	BGA 3110/FAR, HB-1262			
	R G Appleboom Burnford Common, Brentor	*'FAR'*		05.06.18E
G-DFAT	Schleicher ASK 13	13528		09.01.08
	BGA 3112/FAT, PH-456			
	Dorset Gliding Club Ltd Eyres Field *'FAT'*			25.04.18E
G-DFAW	Schempp-Hirth Ventus b/16.6	26		25.02.08
	BGA 3115/FAW, D-6768 J Hanlon Bicester *'833'*			06.08.18E
G-DFBD	Schleicher ASW 15B	15407		12.03.08
	BGA 3122/FBD, OH-445 J J Mion Milfield *'FBD'*			07.06.18E
G-DFBE	Rolladen-Schneider LS6	6028		27.05.08
	BGA 3123/FBE, D-9384			
	J B Van Woerden Easterton *'S6'*			11.03.18E
G-DFBJ	Schleicher K 8B	8221		16.09.08
	BGA 3127/FBJ, D-6340			
	Bidford Gliding & Flying Club Ltd Bidford *'FBJ'*			20.02.14E
	(NF 16.06.15)			
G-DFBM	Schempp-Hirth Nimbus-3/24.5	73		22.09.08
	BGA 3130/FBM D J Blackman (Brighton) *'727'*			15.05.18E
G-DFBO	Schleicher ASW 20BL	20669		10.03.08
	BGA 3133/FBQ A M Cridge Talgarth *'464'*			14.05.18E
G-DFBR	Grob G102 Astir CS77	1701		08.06.09
	BGA 3134/FBR, SE-TSV			
	Essex Gliding Club Ltd Ridgewell *'K3'*			09.05.18E
G-DFBY	Schempp-Hirth Discus b	20		15.07.08
	BGA 3141/FBY D Latimer Sutton Bank *'780'*			14.09.18E
G-DFCD	Centrair 101A Pégase	101A0207		23.06.08
	BGA 3146/FCD G J Bass Challock *'641'*			24.04.13E
	(NF 28.10.15)			
G-DFCK	Schempp-Hirth Ventus b/16.6	241		01.06.10
	BGA 3152/FCK S A Adlard Long Mynd *'671'*			22.05.18E
G-DFCM	Glaser-Dirks DG-300 Elan	3E94		11.03.08
	BGA 3154/FCM			
	A Davis & I D Roberts Snitterfield *'411'*			06.05.19E
	Built by Elan Tovarna Sportnega Orodja N.Sol.O			
G-DFCW	Schleicher ASK 13	13642AB		22.08.08
	BGA 3163/FCW			
	Black Mountains Gliding Club Talgarth *'L'*			29.05.18E
	Built by Jubi GmbH Sportflugzeugbau			
G-DFCY	Schleicher ASW 15	15122		16.04.08
	BGA 3165/FCY, D-0748 M R Shaw Ridgewell *'FCY'*			23.11.12E
	(IE 10.06.16)			
G-DFDF	Grob G102 Astir CS	1321		24.03.09
	BGA 3172/FDF, D-7338			
	W D Harrop Seighford *'FDF'*			16.11.18E
G-DFDO	Evektor EV-97 Eurostar SL	2016-4229		24.03.16
	C W Pittaway tr Dodo Syndicate Old Sarum			24.03.19P
	Assembled Light Sport Aviation Ltd			
G-DFDW	Glaser-Dirks DG-300 Elan	3E143		20.04.09
	BGA 3187			
	C M Hadley Burnford Common, Brentor *'438'*			02.11.12E
	Built by Elan Tovarna Sportnega Orodja N.Sol.O			
	(NF 25.04.18)			
G-DFEB	Grob G102 Club Astir III	5643C		13.05.08
	BGA 3192/FEB			
	Lasham Gliding Society Ltd Lasham *'SH8'*			02.08.18E
G-DFES	Schempp-Hirth Discus-2c FES	31		10.12.18
	(BGA 5984) C J Short Talgarth			
	(NF 10.12.18)			
G-DFEX	Grob G102 Astir CS77	1660		22.08.08
	BGA 3212/FEX, D-7492 L H M Wootton tr			
	Loughborough Students Union Gliding Club			
	Saltby *'LU'*			27.09.18E
G-DFFP	Schleicher ASW 19B	19317		27.06.08
	BGA 3228/FFP, RAFGSA R19 J M Hutchinson			
	tr Foxtrot Papa Group Wycombe Air Park *'93'*			25.05.17E
G-DFGJ	Schleicher Ka 6CR	6634		17.09.08
	BGA 3247/FGJ, D-1041			
	G D S Caldwell (Dalbeattie) *'FGJ'*			05.11.16E
G-DFGT	Glaser-Dirks DG-300 Elan	3E217		27.05.08
	BGA 3256/FGT L Clarke & M J Love			
	Hinton-in-the-Hedges *'FGT'*			10.07.19E
	Built by Elan Tovarna Sportnega Orodja N.Sol.O			
G-DFHS	Schempp-Hirth Ventus cT	82/326		10.09.08
	BGA 3279/FHS			
	R Andrews tr 154 Group Long Mynd *'154'*			10.04.18E
G-DFHY	Scheibe SF27A Zugvogel V	6045		13.03.09
	BGA 3285/FHY, D-1868 J M Pursey North Hill *'H5'*			27.01.17E
G-DFJO	Schempp-Hirth Ventus cT	104		07.04.10
	BGA 3301/EJQ			
	P F Whitehead tr FJO Syndicate Sutton Bank *'FJO'*			15.02.18E
G-DFKA	Schleicher Ka 6CR	6239		20.03.09
	BGA 3311/FKA, D-7037, D-5435			
	P Drake Kingston Deverill *'FKA'*			28.06.18E
G-DFKI	Westland SA.341G Gazelle HT.2	1216		12.02.02
	G-BZOT, XW907 D J Fravigar (Croft)			11.05.18P
G-DFKX	Schleicher Ka 6CR	6433		17.08.09
	BGA 3332/FKX, D-4316 J E Herring Lasham			19.07.18E
G-DFMG	Schempp-Hirth Discus b	242		06.03.08
	BGA 3365/FMG			
	N F von Merveldt (London E2) *'VJ'*			29.01.19E
G-DFOG	Rolladen-Schneider LS7	7050		29.11.07
	BGA 3437/FQG, D-1712			
	R B Porteous Gransden Lodge *'952'*			18.04.18E
G-DFOV	CARMAM JP 15-36AR Aiglon	28		23.03.15
	BGA3450/FQV, F-CETX M Howley Pocklington			14.04.18R
G-DFRA	Rolladen-Schneider LS6-b	6151		05.10.07
	BGA 3455, D-8081			
	M Randle tr 79 Syndicate Aston Down *'79'*			23.03.18E
G-DFSA	Grob G102 Astir CS	1277		28.07.08
	BGA 3479/FSA, D-7371			
	J R Carpenter tr Astir 498 Syndicate Lasham *'498'*			15.09.18E
G-DFTF	Schleicher Ka 6CR	6294		09.12.13
	BGA 3508/FTF, D-6081			
	J Preller tr Daedalus Gransden Lodge *'FTF'*			07.09.18E

G-DFTJ	SZD-48-1 Jantar-Standard 2	W-889	23.11.07
	BGA 3511/FTJ, HB-1472		
	P Nock Kirton in Lindsey *'FTJ'*		07.05.18E
G-DFUF	Scheibe SF27A Zugvogel V	6089	12.08.14
	BGA 3531/FUF, D-6068 R J Savage (Havant)		
	(NF 12.08.14)		
G-DFUN	Van's RV-6	25179	21.08.06
	C Rule tr G-DFUN Flying Group Popham		07.05.18P
	Built by S Hollingsworth & P R Turner		
	– project PFA 181A-13191		
G-DFXE	Rolladen-Schneider LS7	7090	03.08.16
	BGA 3600/FXE		
	Booker Gliding Club Ltd Wycombe Air Park *'35'*		06.06.18E
G-DFXR	Sportine Aviacija LAK-12 Lietuva	6162	30.07.12
	BGA 3611/FXR		
	I P Freestone Husbands Bosworth *'L12'*		25.06.19E
G-DGAJ	Glaser-Dirks DG-300 Club Elan	3E385C56	26.06.15
	BGA3676/GAJ S Lewis (Itxassou, France)		18.05.18E
	Built by Elan Tovarna Sportnega Orodja N.Sol.O		
G-DGAL	Comco Ikarus C42 FB80 Bravo	1209-7223	30.11.12
	S Dixon Athey's Moor, Longframlington		14.01.19P
	Assembled Red-Air UK		
G-DGAV	P&M QuikR	8712	27.02.15
	M D Howe Priory Farm, Tibenham		24.02.18P
G-DGAW	Schleicher Ka 6CR	61/08	21.01.08
	BGA 3688/GAW, D-6320		
	D Searle & H C Yorke Snitterfield *'GAW'*		18.01.19E
G-DGBE	Schleicher Ka 6CR	6133A	17.08.12
	BGA 3696/GBE, D-4085 Cancelled 12.02.18 by CAA		09.04.17
	Eaglescliffe, Co.Durham *Stored at private address 05.18*		
G-DGBT	Chimera Dragon GBT 1170	CA/D 0001	23.08.16
	Chimera Aviation Ltd Tatenhill		
	(IE 17.04.18)		
G-DGDJ	Rolladen-Schneider LS4-a	4832	09.07.08
	BGA 3747/GDJ		
	A Clark tr 450 Syndicate Solent *'450'*		18.04.18E
G-DGDW	Scheibe SF27A Zugvogel V	6116	16.07.13
	BGA 3759/GDW, D-1997		
	G Wardle (Clay Cross, Chesterfield)		23.04.17E
	(IE 05.06.17)		
G-DGEF	Schleicher Ka 6CR	6459	06.02.14
	BGA 3768/GEF, D-1068 R Croker & S Gutman		
	tr Lee K6CR Group Solent *'GEF'*		01.04.18E
G-DGFD	Robinson R44 Clipper II	13027	07.09.10
	G-CGNF Macrae Aviation Ltd Bournemouth		19.11.18E
	Operated by Bliss Aviation Ltd		
G-DGFY	Flylight Dragonfly	064	28.04.11
	M R Sands Shotton Colliery, Peterlee		
	(SSDR microlight since 05.14) (IE 28.11.14)		
G-DGHI	Dyn'Aéro MCR-01 Club	275	11.12.03
	J M Keane Deanland		09.06.16P
	Built by D G Hall – project PFA 301A-14128;		
	damaged landing near Fridd Farm, Bethersden		
	20.09.15		
G-DGIO	Glaser-Dirks DG-100G Elan	E19G7	01.10.07
	BGA 2605 T E Sides tr DG1 Group North Hill *'DG1'*		09.02.19E
	Built by Elan Tovarna Sportnega Orodja N.Sol.O		
G-DGIV	DG Flugzeugbau DG-800B	8-145B69	27.11.98
	P G Noonan & S M Tilling Shenington		23.03.18E
G-DGKB	Centrair ASW 20F	20127	07.06.12
	BGA 2648/EFJ F W Wiltshire Bidford *'GKB'*		10.12.18E
G-DGMT	III Sky Arrow 650 T	K124	26.10.12
	A Powell Biggin Hill		17.11.17P
	Built by A Powell – project PFA 298-14747		
G-DGPS	Diamond DA.42 Twin Star	42.355	27.03.12
	D-GTTI, OE-VPY, OE-VPW		
	AJW Construction Ltd Bournemouth		18.06.19E
	Operated by L3 CTS		
G-DGRE	Guimbal Cabri G2	1137	11.03.16
	Helicentre Aviation Ltd Leicester		16.03.18E
G-DGSC	CZAW Sportcruiser	10SC344	23.03.10
	R J Marsh tr Sierra Charlie Group Dunkeswell		23.09.18P
	Built by D J Gunn – project LAA 338-14979		

G-DGST	Beech 95-B55 Baron	TC-2011	16.12.13
	G-BXDF, SE-IXG, OY-ASB		
	CE Ventures Ltd (Westlea, Swindon)		24.05.19E
G-DGUN	Agusta AW109SP Grand New	22222	29.10.18
	VH-CZT, VH-LSN Castle Air Ltd Trebrown, Liskeard		
G-DHAA	Glasflügel Standard Libelle 201B	356	18.12.07
	BGA 3777/HAA, HB-1090		
	D J Jones & R N Turner Gransden Lodge *'263'*		02.04.18E
G-DHAD	Glasflügel Standard Libelle	3	13.02.08
	BGA 3780/HAD, D-8914 R Hines (Wallingford) *'429'*		21.06.18E
G-DHAH	Aeronca 7BCM Champion	7AC-4185	12.07.05
	G-JTYE, N85445, NC85445		
	E Smith tr Alpha Hotel Group Old Sarum		02.09.18P
	Modified from 7AC standard		
G-DHAL	Schleicher ASK 13	13690AB	19.10.07
	BGA 3787		
	The Windrushers Gliding Club Ltd Bicester *'HAL'*		14.04.18E
	Built by Jubi GmbH Sportflugzeugbau		
G-DHAM	Robinson R44 Raven II	13717	24.07.14
	D B Hamilton (Stonehouse)		10.09.18E
G-DHAP	Schleicher Ka 6E	4335	22.02.08
	BGA 3790/HAP, HB-985		
	M Fursedon & T Turner Shenington *'HAP'*		14.10.17E
G-DHAT	Glaser-Dirks DG-200/17	2-93/1709	05.03.08
	BGA 3794/HAT, D-6843		
	G K Holloway tr G-DHAT Group Aboyne *'HAT'*		22.01.19E
G-DHCA	Grob G103 Twin Astir	3289	09.09.08
	BGA 3826/HCA, D-0094, OO-ZOH, D-3063		
	Midland Gliding Club Ltd Long Mynd *'HCA'*		20.03.18E
G-DHCC	de Havilland DHC-1 Chipmunk 22	C1/0393	28.05.97
	WG321 Liberty Aviation Ltd		
	Kortrijk-Wevelgem Int'l, Belgium		16.05.18E
	As 'WG321:G' in AAC c/s		
G-DHCE	Schleicher ASW 19B	19305	03.10.07
	BGA 3831, D-6527		
	A M Wilmot Kirton in Lindsey *'346'*		15.11.18E
G-DHCF	PZL-Bielsko SZD-50-3 Puchacz	B-2047	17.01.08
	BGA 3832/HCF		
	Shalbourne Soaring Society Ltd Rivar Hill *'HCF'*		07.04.18E
G-DHCJ	Grob G103 Twin II	3709	16.05.08
	BGA 3835/HCJ, RAFGGA 611, D-2611 Peterborough		
	& Spalding Gliding Club Ltd Crowland *'HCJ'*		07.04.19E
G-DHCL	Schempp-Hirth Discus b	136	04.12.07
	BGA 3837/HCL, D-4682		
	A I Lambe (Walford, Ross-on-Wye) *'HCL'*		27.05.18E
G-DHCO	Glasflügel Standard Libelle 201B	197	16.11.07
	BGA 3841/HCQ, HB-999		
	M J Birch Dunstable Downs *'HCQ'*		11.07.18E
G-DHCR	PZL-Bielsko SZD-51-1 Junior	B-2003	18.01.08
	BGA 3842/HCR		
	East Sussex Gliding Club Ltd Ringmer *'394'*		16.01.19E
G-DHCU	Glaser-Dirks DG-300 Club Elan	3E407C66	19.12.07
	BGA 3845/HCU		
	R B Hankey & J B Symonds Kingston Deverill *'78'*		20.03.18E
	Built by Elan Tovarna Sportnega Orodja N.Sol.O		
G-DHCV	Schleicher ASW 19B	19084	04.01.08
	BGA 3846/HCV, D-4486		
	R C May Dunstable Downs *'HCV'*		12.03.18E
G-DHCW	PZL-Bielsko SZD-51-1 Junior	B-2002	21.12.07
	BGA 3847/HCW, (BGA 3844/HCT)		
	Deeside Gliding Club (Aberdeenshire) Ltd		
	Aboyne *'HCW'*		19.02.18E
G-DHCX	Schleicher ASK 21	21541	06.11.07
	BGA 3848/HCX		
	Devon & Somerset Gliding Club Ltd North Hill *'HCX'*		28.04.18E
G-DHCY	Glaser-Dirks DG-300 Club Elan	3E413C67	17.08.18
	BGA3849/HCY R M Wootten Eyres Field		
	Built by Elan Tovarna Sportnega Orodja N.Sol.O		
	(NF 17.08.18)		
G-DHCZ	de Havilland DHC-2 Beaver AL.1	1442	02.03.06
	G-BUCJ, XP772 Propshop Ltd Duxford		26.06.18E
	Red & white c/s		

G-DHDH	Glaser-Dirks DG-200	2-7	26.02.08
	BGA 3858/HDH J R M Crompton & M Johnson		
	tr Delta Hotel Syndicate Milfield '991'		13.05.18E
	Original c/n 2-197; rebuild of BGA2299 with		
	new fuselage 1992 & c/n amended 07.09		

G-DHDV	de Havilland DH.104 Dove 8	04205	26.10.98
	VP981 K M Perkins Headcorn		
	'Royal Air Force Transport Command'		13.01.19E
	Built by as Devon C.2 & modified to C.2/2; as 'VP981'		
	in RAF c/s; operated by Weald Air Services Ltd		

G-DHEB	Schleicher Ka 6CR	6289	17.11.08
	BGA 3876/HEB, HB-773		
	J Burrow North Hill 'HEB'		22.06.17E

G-DHEM	Schempp-Hirth Discus CS	073CS	09.01.08
	BGA 3886/HEM		
	S J Powell tr 473 Syndicate Lasham '473'		15.05.18E
	Built by Orličan Aakciová Společnost		

G-DHER	Schleicher ASW 19B	19240	11.02.08
	BGA 3890/HER, F-CERR		
	R R Bryan Gransden Lodge 'HER'		04.08.18E

G-DHES	Centrair 101A Pégase	101039	29.01.08
	BGA 3891/HES, F-CFQF		
	G H Lawrence & G S Sanderson North Hill 'HES'		20.07.18E

G-DHET	Rolladen-Schneider LS6-c18	6263	22.11.07
	BGA 3892/HET		
	A Lake & M D Langford RAF Halton '335'		24.02.18E

G-DHEV	Schempp-Hirth Cirrus	41	14.08.08
	BGA 3894/HEV, OO-ZXY, (OO-ZOZ), D-0104		
	L K Nazar RAF Weston-on-the-Green 'HEV'		24.05.19E

G-DHGL	Schempp-Hirth Discus b	431	29.10.07
	BGA 3933 E A Martin Camphill 'HGL'		07.12.18E

G-DHGS	Robinson R22 Beta	2592	19.04.96
	EI-MAG, G-DHGS Helimech Ltd Conington		16.10.18E

G-DHGY	SZD-24C Foka	W-180	10.07.12
	BGA 3945/HGY, SP-2385		
	S J Glassett Aston Down 'HGY'		09.05.14E
	(NF 24.06.16)		

G-DHHD	PZL-Bielsko SZD-51-1 Junior	B-2010	24.12.14
	PH-1393, BGA 3950/HHD		
	Scottish Gliding Union Ltd Portmoak 'HHD'		24.04.18E

G-DHHF	North American SNJ-5 Texan	88-17678	21.11.16
	N6972C, USN 90680, 42-85897		
	DH Heritage Flights Ltd Compton Abbas		26.01.19E
	As 'JF:72' in US Marines c/s		

G-DHJH	Airbus A321-211	1238	07.06.00
	D-AVZL Thomas Cook Airlines Ltd Manchester		06.06.19E

G-DHKB	Boeing 757-256(PCF)	29312	27.07.16
	N932DH, TF-FIY, P2-ANB, TF-FIY, EC-HIV		
	DHL Air Ltd East Midlands		26.07.19E
	Line No: 943		

G-DHKC	Boeing 757-256	30052	08.11.16
	N530DH, TF-FIZ, EC-HIX DHL Air Ltd East Midlands		07.11.19E
	Line No: 948		

G-DHKD	Boeing 757-23N(F)	27975	17.01.17
	N975DH, ET-AMU, N519AT		
	DHL Air Ltd East Midlands		16.01.19E
	Line No: 779		

G-DHKE	Boeing 757-23N(PCF)	27976	18.10.16
	N796DH, ET-AMT, N520AT		
	DHL Air Ltd East Midlands		19.10.19E
	Line No: 814		

G-DHKF	Boeing 757-236	29945	20.04.16
	G-TCBB, N945BB, B-2860, N564NA, (G-CPEY)		
	DHL Air Ltd East Midlands		21.10.19E
	Line No: 873		

G-DHKG	Boeing 757-236	29946	13.06.16
	G-TCBC, N946BB, B-2861, N547NA, N1795B		
	DHL Air Ltd East Midlands		03.12.19E
	Line No: 877		

G-DHKH	Boeing 757-28A	26275	13.06.16
	G-FCLI, N651LF, EI-CLV, N151LF		
	DHL Air Ltd East Midlands		19.07.19E
	Line No: 672		

G-DHKK	Boeing 757-28A(F)	32449	10.04.17
	N590CB ET-AMK, C-GMYE, N513AT, N449GE		
	DHL Air Ltd East Midlands		11.04.19E
	Line No: 974		

G-DHKL	Schempp-Hirth Discus bT	120	17.10.07
	BGA 4004 M A Thorne Kingston Deverill '919'		01.02.20E

G-DHKM	Boeing 757-223	29590	21.11.17
	N680AN, N1787B DHL Air Ltd East Midlands		27.11.19E
	Line No: 847		

G-DHKN	Boeing 757-223	31308	13.02.18
	N174AA DHL Air Ltd East Midlands		12.02.19E
	Line No: 998		

G-DHKO	Boeing 757-223	32397	10.04.18
	N179AA DHL Air Ltd East Midlands		16.04.19E
	Line No: 1000		

G-DHKP	Boeing 757-223	32398	02.07.18
	N178AA DHL Air Ltd East Midlands		01.07.19E
	Line No: 1002		

G-DHKR	Boeing 757-223(F)	29426	03.10.18
	N676AN, N1798B DHL Air Ltd East Midlands		02.10.19E
	Line No: 827		

G-DHKS	Boeing 757-223(F)	29427	21.08.18
	N677AN DHL Air Ltd East Midlands		22.08.19E
	Line No: 828		

G-DHKT	Boeing 757-223(F)	29428	14.01.19
	N678AN, N1787B DHL Air Ltd East Midlands		13.01.20E
	Line No: 837		

G-DHKU	Boeing 757-223(F)	29589	16.11.18
	N679AN, N1800B, N1795B DHL Air Ltd East Midlands		
	(IE 16.11.18)		
	Line No: 842		

G-DHKX	Boeing 757-23APF	24971	23.05.16
	D-ALEJ, OO-DLJ, N573CA, G-OBOZ, N5020K		
	DHL Air Ltd East Midlands		19.01.19E
	Line No: 340		

G-DHKZ	Boeing 757-236(PCF)	25620	25.10.18
	VH-TCA, G-CSVS, PP-BIZ, N701AX, OY-GRL, TF-GRL,		
	G-CSVS, G-IEAC DHL Air Ltd East Midlands		25.10.19E
	Line No: 449		

G-DHLE	Boeing 767-3JHF	37805	18.08.09
	DHL Air Ltd East Midlands		17.08.19E
	Line No: 980		

G-DHLF	Boeing 767-3JHF	37806	02.09.09
	DHL Air Ltd East Midlands		01.09.19E
	Line No: 981		

G-DHLG	Boeing 767-3JHF	37807	24.09.09
	DHL Air Ltd East Midlands		23.09.19E
	Line No: 982		

G-DHMM	Piper PA-34-200T Seneca II	34-7770062	19.03.15
	G-BEJV, N7657F		
	Cristal Air Ltd Spilsted Farm, Sedlescombe		13.04.18E

G-DHMP	Schempp-Hirth Discus b	497	01.02.08
	BGA 4050/HMP T Janikowski Aston Down 'HMP'		13.02.18E

G-DHNX	Rolladen-Schneider LS4-b	4937	28.11.07
	BGA 4082/HNX M B Margetson & P R Wilson		
	Gransden Lodge '585'		14.03.18E

G-DHOC	Scheibe Bergfalke II-55	322	17.08.09
	BGA 4111/HQC, D-9004		
	R Karch (Peissenberg, Germany)		12.08.12E
	(NF 20.07.15)		

G-DHOK	Schleicher ASW 20CL	20854	28.11.07
	BGA 4118/HQK, D-3366		
	S D Minson North Hill 'SM'		11.04.19E

G-DHOP	Van's RV-9A	xxxx	11.06.08
	C Partington Isle of Man		14.11.18P
	Built by A S Orme – project PFA 320-14173		

G-DHPA	Issoire E-78 Silène	4	21.08.08
	BGA 4085/HPA, F-CFEA P Woodcock Burn		
	(NF 17.05.16)		

G-DHPM	de Havilland DHC-1 Chipmunk 22	55	28.03.02
	CS-AZS, Portuguese AF 1365 P Meyrick Sleap		15.05.18P
	Built by OGMA; as '1365' in Portuguese AF c/s		

G-DHPR	Schempp-Hirth Discus b	532		23.08.07
	BGA 4100 D P Knibbs tr Knibbs Johnson Syndicate			
	Seighford *'K9'*			06.04.18E
G-DHRR	Schleicher ASK 21	21033		05.12.07
	BGA 4146/HRR, D-7083			
	Lakes Gliding Club Ltd Walney Island *'D70'*			13.03.18E
G-DHSJ	Schempp-Hirth Discus b	546		09.01.08
	BGA 4163/HSJ D Byrne Saltby *'D54'*			30.03.18E
G-DHSR	Sportine Aviacija LAK-12 Lietuva	6178		01.02.08
	BGA 4170/HSR A G A Parker (Bath)			05.09.18E
G-DHSS	de Havilland DH.112 Venom FB.50 (FB.1)	836		26.03.99
	Swiss AF J-1626 Cancelled 05.03.13 as PWFU			22.04.03
	Carrickmore, RoI *Built by F+W Emmen*			
	As 'WR360' in RAF c/s; parts stored 03.16			
G-DHTG	Grob G102 Astir CS	1510		23.01.08
	BGA 4185/HTG, RAFGSA R59, RAFGSA R69,			
	RAFGSA 519 Trent Valley Gliding Club Ltd			
	Kirton in Lindsey *'HTG'*			12.05.18E
G-DHTT	de Havilland DH.112 Venom FB.50 (FB.1)	821		17.10.96
	(G-BMOC), Swiss AF J-1611			
	Cancelled 05.03.13 as PWFU			17.07.99
	Portarlington, RoI *Built by F+W Emmen*			
	As 'WR421' in RAF c/s; stored 08.13			
G-DHUUᴹ	de Havilland DH.112 Venom FB.50 (FB.1)	749		26.02.96
	Swiss AF J-1539, (G-BMOD), J-1539			
	Cancelled 05.03.13 as PWFU As 'WR410'			24.05.02
	With Aviation Museum at Atlantic AirVenture, Shannon			
G-DHVM	de Havilland DH.112 Venom FB.50	752		26.11.03
	G-GONE, Swiss AF J-1542			
	Cancelled 08.02.18 by CAA			29.04.18
	Bruntingthorpe *Built by Federal Aircraft Factory*			
	As 'WR470' in RAF 208 Sqn c/s; stored 09.18			
G-DHYL	Schempp-Hirth Ventus-2a	44		06.11.07
	BGA 4310/HYL M J Cook Lasham *'M2'*			28.03.19E
G-DHYS	Titan T-51 Mustang	0178		20.06.14
	D Houghton Croft Farm, Defford			02.09.17P
	Built by D Houghton – project LAA 355-15190I			
	as '414907:CY-S' in USAAF c/s			
G-DHZF	de Havilland DH.82A Tiger Moth	82309		07.07.99
	G-BSTJ, OO-MEH, OO-GEB, OO-MOR,			
	R Netherlands AF A-13, PH-UFB,			
	R Netherlands AF A-13, N9192 M R Johnson Sywell			15.07.18P
	As 'N9192:RCO-N' in RAF silver with yellow bands c/s			
G-DHZZᴹ	de Havilland DH.115 Vampire T55	990		05.09.91
	Swiss AF U-1230 Cancelled 19.04.07 – to LN-DHZ			
	As 'WZ589' *Built by FFW, Emmen*			
	With Warbirds of Norway, Kjeller			
G-DICA	SIAI Marchetti S.208	4-52		22.12.16
	Italian AF MM61939, I-OTIS			
	P Di Carlo (Motta Montecorvino, Italy)			
G-DICK	Thunder Ax6-56Z	159		06.07.78
	R D Sargeant Altendorf, Switzerland			26.10.12E
	(IE 28.01.15)			
G-DIDG	Van's RV-7	73253		15.02.08
	B R Alexander Stoneacre Farm, Farthing Corner			
	Built by B R Alexander – project LAA 323-14764			
	(NF 22.05.18)			
G-DIDO	Agusta A109E Power	11617		09.04.15
	VT-SWB, N109MJ, N606SR			
	A D Whitehouse Higher Purtington Showfield, Chard			30.04.19E
G-DIDY	Thruster T600T 450	1052-T600T-116		30.01.06
	M M P Evans Dunkeswell			25.10.18P
	Badged 'Sprint'			
G-DIGA	Robinson R66 Turbine	0031		04.09.14
	N4478K Helicopter & Pilot Services Ltd			
	Wycombe Air Park			09.09.19E
G-DIGI	Piper PA-32-300 Cherokee Six	32-7940224		13.10.98
	D-EIES, N2947M			
	P Guest tr Security Unlimited Group Andrewsfield			25.01.20E
G-DIGS	Hughes 369HE *(500)*	890105E		11.12.12
	G-DIZZ, N9029F AT Aviation Sales Ltd Dunkeswell			04.06.19E
G-DIGZ	Hughes 369D *(500)*	1111D		12.10.17
	G-MCDD, N13175, A2-HAO, N5162N, YV-196CP,			
	N395AC Mackinnon Construction Ltd			
	Walpole Barns, Erpingham			06.12.18E

G-DIII	Pitts S-2B	5163		04.03.13
	G-STUB, N260Y			
	J A Coutts Nut Tree Farm, Redenhall			11.05.18E
	Built by Christen Industries Inc			
G-DIKY	Murphy Rebel	530R		13.02.98
	R J Rayson tr Stoke Golding Flyers Stoke Golding			10.05.18P
	Built by R J P Herivel – project PFA 232-13182			
G-DIME	Rockwell Commander 114	14123		09.03.88
	N49829 H B Richardson Badminton			03.12.18E
G-DINA	Gulfstream American AA-5B Tiger	AA5B-1218		27.02.81
	N4555Y Portway Aviation Ltd Shobdon			10.04.18E
G-DINO	Cyclone Pegasus Quantum 15	7225		15.12.98
	G-MGMT			
	R D J Buchanan Coldharbour Farm, Willingham			30.05.18P
G-DINS	Boeing Stearman D75N1 Kaydet *(PT-17)*	75-4041		03.01.18
	G-RJAH, N75957, FJ991 RCAF, 42-15852			
	M V Linney Duxford			14.05.19E
	As '44' in US Army Air Corps c/s			
G-DIPI	Cameron Tub-80	1745		06.05.88
	C G Dobson Goring, Reading *'ohoo dips'*			13.01.13E
	(NF 26.09.17)			
G-DIPM	Piper PA-46-350P Malibu Mirage	4636325		20.02.02
	D-EMPI, G-DIPM, N5350V			
	MAS Mix Ltd (Tortola, British Virgin Islands)			19.04.18E
	Converted c.2011 by JetPROP LLC to Jetprop DLX			
G-DIPZ	Colt 17A Cloudhopper	1245		03.05.88
	OO-BRV, G-DIPZ			
	C G Dobson Goring, Reading *'KP Choc Dips'*			16.04.15E
	(NF 26.09.17)			
G-DIRK	Glaser-Dirks DG-400	4-124		18.09.86
	D-KEKT A N Gibson tr Romeo-Kilo Gliding Group			
	Trenchard Lines, Upavon *'RK'*			23.07.18E
G-DISA	Scottish Aviation Bulldog Srs 120/125	BH120/435		25.08.04
	RJAF 420, RJAF 1142, G-31-44			
	I W Whiting (Coto de Caza, California, USA)			18.07.18E
	Last noted at Broadford 07.17			
G-DISK	Piper PA-24-250 Comanche	24-1197		09.08.89
	G-APZG, EI-AKW, N10F			
	Cancelled 14.06.16 as PWFU			27.10.10
	Not Known *Sold on ebay 06.17*			
G-DISO	Jodel D.150 Mascaret	24		16.12.86
	9Q-CPK, OO-APK, F-BLDT			
	C R Coates & P K Morley Ings Farm, Yedingham			26.06.19P
	Built by Société Aéronautique Normande			
G-DISP	AutoGyro Calidus	xxxx		12.05.16
	P J Troy-Davies Brook Farm, Pilling *'Air Total'*			20.06.19P
	Assembled Rotorsport UK as c/n RSUK/CALS/030			
G-DIWY	Piper PA-32-300 Cherokee Six B	32-40731		26.11.91
	OY-DLW, D-EHMW, N8931N			
	Over the Air Group Ltd (Naburn, York)			26.07.19E
G-DIXY	Piper PA-28-181 Archer III	2843195		10.12.98
	N41284, G-DIXY, N41284			
	Modern Air (UK) Ltd Fowlmere			09.02.18E
G-DIZI	Reality Escapade 912(2)	JA.ESC.0012		01.03.04
	J C Carter (Cambridge)			10.05.18P
	Built by N Baumber – project BMAA/HB/355			
G-DIZO	Jodel D.120 Paris-Nice	326		30.05.91
	G-EMKM, F-BOBG			
	N M Harwood Roughay Farm, Lower Upham			29.11.18P
	Built by Société Wassmer Aviation			
G-DIZY	Piper PA-28R-201T Turbo Arrow III	28R-7703401		13.10.88
	N47570 Dizy Aviation Ltd Gloucestershire			30.11.18E
G-DJAA	Schempp-Hirth Janus B	163		16.01.08
	BGA 4348/JAA, D-3147			
	Bidford Gliding & Flying Club Ltd Bidford *'32'*			26.04.18E
G-DJAB	Glaser-Dirks DG-300 Elan	3E320		16.10.07
	BGA 4349, OY-XTC			
	I G Johnston Sutton Bank *'JAB'*			07.02.19E
	Built by Elan Tovarna Sportnega Orodja N.Sol.O			
G-DJAC	Schempp-Hirth Duo Discus	128		05.11.08
	BGA 4350/JAC D G Roberts tr G-DJAC Group			
	Sisteron, France *'JAC'*			04.03.18E
G-DJAD	Schleicher ASK 21	21659		25.02.08
	BGA 4351/JAD The Borders (Milfield)			
	Gliding Club Ltd Milfield *'JAD'*			23.09.18E

G-DJAH Schempp-Hirth Discus b 572 11.06.08
BGA 4355/JAH S C Moss Nympsfield *'JAH'* 28.07.18E

G-DJAN Schempp-Hirth Discus b 575 01.10.07
BGA 4360 N F Perren Dunstable Downs *'603'* 19.11.18E

G-DJAY Avtech Jabiru UL-450 0402 08.08.00
J R Grigg Old Warden 09.05.19P
Built by D J Pearce – project PFA 274A-13633

G-DJBC Comco Ikarus C42 FB100 0802-6937 05.02.08
Bluecool Water Despensers Ltd
(Kilcurry, Dundalk, RoI) 18.05.18P
Assembled Aerosport Ltd

G-DJBX Aeropro EuroFOX 912(iS) 438 14 24.03.14
D J Barrott Conington 06.05.18P
Built by D J Barrott – project LAA 376-15268; tricycle u/c

G-DJCR Varga 2150A Kachina VAC 155-80 11.04.96
EI-CFK, G-BLWG, OO-HTD, N8360J
M Robertson (Clocksbriggs, Forfar) 30.04.99
(NF 16.03.18)

G-DJEB HpH Glasflügel 304 eS Shark 095-MS 17.12.18
(BGA 5980) P D Candler Dunstable Downs *'Z95'* 31.12.19R

G-DJET Diamond DA.42 Twin Star 42.122 30.03.06
OE-VPW DEA Aviation Ltd Retford Gamston 12.07.19E

G-DJGG Schleicher ASW 15B 15332 05.12.07
BGA 4498/JGG, D-2325
J P N Haxell Halesland *'LE5'* 01.08.18E

G-DJHP Valentin Mistral C MC048/82 21.01.08
BGA 4529/JHP, D-4948 P B Higgs Long Mynd *'JHP'*
(NF 16.01.15)

G-DJJA Piper PA-28-181 Archer II 28-8490014 14.09.87
N4326D Interactive Aviation Ltd Elstree 18.01.19E
Operated by Flyers Flying School

G-DJLL Schleicher ASK 13 13144 29.01.08
BGA 4598/JLL, HB-952
Bidford Gliding & Flying Club Ltd Bidford *'N25'* 05.06.18E

G-DJMC Schleicher ASK 21 21681 23.05.08
BGA 4614/JMC The Royal Air Force
Gliding & Soaring Association RAF Cosford *'R22'* 21.07.18E
Operated by Wrekin Gliding Club

G-DJMD Schempp-Hirth Discus b 241 07.12.07
BGA 4615/JMD, RAFGSA R23 P T Wallace tr G-DJMD
Syndicate RAF Weston-on-the-Green *'P23'* 27.02.19E

G-DJNC ICA-Brasov IS-28B2 33 05.08.08
BGA 2207/DLU, RAFGSA R93, NEJSGSA '3', EI-141,
BGA 2207/DLU J Rigby tr Delta Juliet November Group
(Bury St Edmunds) *'R93'* 15.11.12E
*Official c/n originally 336 & may denote
rebuild of NEJSGSA '1' (NF 30.09.16)*

G-DJNE DG Flugzeugbau DG-808C 8-406B305X67 13.03.13
G-DGRA J N Ellis Sutton Bank *'112'* 14.08.18E
Built by DG Flugzeugbau GmbH

G-DJNH Denney Kitfox Model 3 xxxx 20.09.90
S Borthwick Balado 31.10.17P
*Built by D J N Hall – project PFA 172-11896;
crashed into trees & damaged Eshott 14.04.17*

G-DJSM Eurocopter AS.350B3 Ecureuil 7737 03.02.14
G-CICZ M Z de Ferranti t/a Meoble Estate (Bangor) 27.05.18E

G-DJST Air Création Clipper 912(1)/iXess FL029 12.10.04
K Buckley & B L Prime (Doveridge, Ashbourne) 17.07.19P
*Built by D J Stimpson – project BMAA/HB/416
(Flylight kit FL029 comprising Trike s/n T04070
& wing s/n A04167*

G-DJVY Scintex CP.1315-C3 Super Emeraude 913 01.10.12
F-BJVY A P Goodwin Henstridge 15.08.18P
Built by Société Scintex

G-DJWS Schleicher ASW 15B 15098S 07.04.08
BGA 4845/JWS, D-4656
M Nowak (Hungerford) *'JWS'* 01.07.19E

G-DKBA DKBA AT 0301-0 013.07.93 15.05.07
I Chadwick *'Vodka'* Caterham
*Built by Dolgoprudnenskogo Design Bureau
of Automation (IE 05.09.17)*

G-DKDP Grob G109 6100 09.07.85
(G-BMBD), D-KAMS P Wardell Enstone 19.08.18E

G-DKEM Bell 407 53750 07.06.10
N30562, C-FMRI True Course Helicopter Ltd
(Gibraltar Int'l, Gibraltar) 22.05.16E

G-DKEN Rolladen-Schneider LS4-a 4172 15.11.07
BGA 5034/KEN, OO-ZSM, (OO-ZDG)
B Lytollis & K L Sangster Milfield *'CH'* 18.05.18E

G-DKEY Piper PA-28-161 Cherokee Warrior II 28-7716084 04.01.07
N1120Q PA-28 Warrior Ltd RAF Cosford 29.10.18E

G-DKFU Schempp-Hirth Ventus-2cxT 114/311 19.11.07
G-CKFU, BGA 5064/KFU, D-KOAX
R L Watson Milfield *'X11'* 28.04.16E
(IE 21.04.17)

G-DKGM Cameron O-56 12150 14.03.17
G-CKAD Gone With The Wind Ltd
Pavas Airport, San Jose, Republic of Costa Rica 20.03.18E
Original p/i NTU but will assume G-CKAD in 2019

G-DKNY Robinson R44 Raven II 11651 01.03.07
R R Orr Carnbane Business Park, Dromore 02.02.20E

G-DKTA Piper PA-28-236 Dakota 28-8011089 16.10.09
N6339U, OO-JFD, F-GCMU, OO-HLM, N8152S
G Beattie & C J T Kitchen Wickenby 08.11.18E

G-DLAF BRM Bristell NG5 Speed Wing 074 26.09.13
G Dangerfield & A French
Yeatsall Farm, Abbots Bromley 30.04.19P
*Built by G Dangerfield & A French – project
LAA 385-15226; tricycle u/c*

G-DLAK Cessna 208 Caravan I 20800340 08.01.13
A6-TDA, N985SC Eggesford Ltd Gloucestershire
Fixed-Wing Amphibian (IE 12.03.17)

G-DLAL Beech E90 King Air LW-187 15.10.10
N816RL, N66BP, N816EP, N900MH, N2187L
Penylan Ltd Gloucestershire 17.03.14E
(IE 20.07.15)

G-DLBR Airbus EC175 B 5018 30.06.16
Crystal Sky Ltd (Grand Cayman, Cayman Islands) 05.07.19E

G-DLCB Europa Aviation Europa 046 16.11.95
G F Perry (Brassac, France) 03.11.17P
*Built by D J Lockett – project PFA 247-12652;
tailwheel u/c*

G-DLDL Robinson R22 Beta 1971 02.01.92
Helimech Ltd Brook Farm, Hulcote 06.02.18E
(NF 03.10.17)

G-DLEE SOCATA TB-9 Tampico Club 884 18.02.04
G-BPGX D A Lee Exeter Int'l 08.08.18E

G-DLFN Aero L-29 Delfin 294872 28.05.98
RA-3413K, G-DLFN, ES-YLE, Estonian AF,
Soviet AF AMP Aviation Ltd Leeds East 10.12.18P

G-DLMH Tecnam P2010 061 13.04.18
P J Harle Morganfield, Fishburn
(IE 13.04.18)

G-DLOE Schleicher ASW 27-18E (ASG 29Es) 29694 08.02.16
(BGA 5812), D-KEOE J E Gatfield Lasham *'YO'* 23.02.18E

G-DLOM SOCATA TB-20 Trinidad 1102 13.12.90
N2823Y P A Rieck Cambridge 03.11.18E

G-DLOT HpH Glasflügel 304 S Shark 006-S 09.01.15
(BGA 5824), D-KLZV, OK-6611 J R Matthews
tr Shark G-DLOT Syndicate Parham Park *'LOT'*
(IE 29.09.17)

G-DLOW Grob G103 Twin II 3585 16.02.15
(BGA 5827), F-CFKA The Vale of The White Horse
Gliding Centre Ltd Sandhill Farm, Shrivenham *'T51'* 29.03.18E

G-DLRA Pilatus B-N BN-2T Islander 2140 09.03.84
ZG989, G-DLRA, ZG989, G-DLRA, G-BJYU
Britten-Norman Ltd Solent 27.10.92
(IE 29.11.16)

G-DLRL HpH Glasflügel 304 S Shark 057-MS 13.06.16
(BGA 5865) M P Brooks Lasham *'357'*
(IE 30.10.17)

G-DLTR Piper PA-28-180 Cherokee E 28-5803 15.03.96
G-AYAV, N11C A S Bamrah Biggin Hill 07.06.19E

G-DLTY HpH Glasflügel 304 eS Shark 071-MS 25.04.17
(BGA 5923), OK-0071
J M Gilbey & B D Michael Wycombe Air Park *'LTY'* 14.03.20R

G-DLUT   HpH Glasflügel 304 eS Shark   077-MS   26.09.17
(BGA 5939), OK-9977   A R Fish   Milfield   *'LUT'*
(IE 17.01.18)

G-DLUX   Eurocopter EC120B Colibri   1027   02.03.16
G-IGPW, G-CBRI   EBG (Helicopters) Ltd   Redhill   24.09.18E

G-DMAC   Avtech Jabiru SP-430   0184   15.10.98
C G Pratt   Goodwood   08.11.18P
Built by B McFadden – project PFA 274-13321

G-DMAH   SOCATA TB-20 Trinidad GT   2039   02.04.01
F-OILY   S D Pike   (Harpenden)   15.02.19E

G-DMAZ   Bombardier BD-700-1A10 Global Express XRS   9309   01.10.18
G-IRAP, G-CJME, C-FSRY
TAG Aviation (UK) Ltd   Farnborough   30.09.19E

G-DMBO   Van's RV-7   xxxx   22.11.10
C J Goodwin   White Waltham   29.07.18P
Built by C J Goodwin – project LAA 323-14827

G-DMCAᴹ McDonnell Douglas DC-10-30   48266   12.03.96
N3016Z   Cancelled 03.11.03 as destroyed   11.03.03
Forward 60 feet of fuselage, including flight deck
& 70 seats, retained for use an education classroom
With Runway Visitor Park, Manchester Airport

G-DMCI   Comco Ikarus C42 FB100   0707-6906   16.08.07
C-More Flying School Ltd   Carrickmore   03.05.18P
Assembled Aerosport Ltd

G-DMCP   Tecnam P2008-JC   1110   11.07.18
R J Alderson   Longside   05.08.19E

G-DMCS   Piper PA-28R-200 Cherokee Arrow II   28R-7635284   29.05.84
G-CPAC, PH-SMW, OO-HAU, N75220
W G Ashton tr Arrow Associates   Goodwood   03.05.19E

G-DMCT   Flight Design CT2K   01-04-02-12   10.07.01
A M Sirant   Monkswell Farm, Horrabridge   10.11.08P
Assembled Pegasus Aviation (IE 30.04.15)

G-DMCW   Magni M24C Orion   24116284   30.01.12
G-CGVF   B A Carnegie   Perth   16.08.17P
(IE 17.09.17)

G-DMEE   Cameron Z-105   11729   15.04.13
Airship & Balloon Company Ltd
Henbury, Bristol   *'Despicable Me2'*   31.03.18E

G-DMES   Cameron Minion-105   11739   23.05.13
Airship & Balloon Company Ltd
Henbury, Bristol   *'@SpotStuart'*   09.03.18E

G-DMEZ   Cameron Minion-105   11722   15.04.13
Airship & Balloon Company Ltd
Henbury, Bristol   *'#SpotStuart'*   31.03.18E

G-DMND   Diamond DA.42 Twin Star   42.068   04.11.05
Flying Time Ltd   Brighton City   03.11.18E

G-DMNG   Diamond DA.42M-NG Twin Star   42.MN018   01.12.15
G-PEEK, OE-FGS, OE-VDM
DEA Aviation Ltd   Retford Gamston   29.01.19R

G-DMON   XtremeAir XA42 Sbach 342   116   24.10.12
R M Hockey   White Waltham   20.04.18E

G-DMPI   Agusta A109E Power   11011   17.02.15
G-FVIP, G-HCFC, N551MM, N109TD, 5N-BGX, N108WP,
N27BV, N27BD, N1ZL
D E, M C & M C Pipe t/a DE & MC Pipe Partnership
(Nicholashayne, Wellington)   09.04.18E

G-DMPL   Van's RV-7A   73686   23.10.14
P J & W M Hodgkins   Crowfield   10.03.18P
Built by W M Hodgkins – project LAA 323-14995

G-DMPP   Diamond DA.42M-NG Twin Star   42.M016   23.03.12
OE-FAI, OE-VPI, OE-VDO
DEA Aviation Ltd   Retford Gamston   29.03.19R

G-DMWW   CFM Shadow Series DD   304-DD   12.10.98
M Whittle   Rossall Field, Cockerham   15.05.15P
(NF 23.08.18)

G-DNBH   Raj Hamsa X'Air Hawk   1166   20.10.08
D N B Hearn   Little Atherfield Farm, Atherfield, Ventnor   10.09.18P
Built by D N B Hearn – project LAA 340-14819

G-DNGR   Colt 31A   10162   18.10.01
M J & T J Turner   Wellingborough   12.10.18E
Built by Cameron Balloons Ltd

G-DNKS   Comco Ikarus C42 FB80   0606-6822   15.06.06
D N K & M A Symon   Perth   16.08.18P
Assembled Aerosport Ltd

G-DNOP   Piper PA-46-350P Malibu Mirage   4636303   26.07.00
N4174A   Campbell Aviation Ltd   Denham   03.07.18E

G-DOBS   Van's RV-8   82719   01.10.12
R G Dobney tr BS Flying Group   Gloucestershire   07.11.18P
Built by R G Dobney – project PFA 303-14739

G-DOCB   Boeing 737-436   25304   16.10.91
Cancelled 02.07.15 as PWFU   15.02.15
Cranfield   *Instructional frame 03.16*

G-DODB   Robinson R22 Beta   0911   03.05.96
N8005R   R Breeze tr Durham Flying Syndicate
Humberside   06.12.18E

G-DODD   Reims/Cessna F172P   F17202175   05.10.82
M D Darragh   Dunkeswell   06.09.18E

G-DODG   Evektor EV-97 Eurostar   2004-2102   23.06.04
J Jones   Broadmeadow Farm, Hereford   23.10.18P
Built by R Barton – project PFA 315-14258

G-DOEA   Gulfstream American AA-5A Cheetah   AA5A-0895   30.04.96
G-RJMI, N27170   T M Buick   Kittyhawk Farm, Ripe   03.04.18E

G-DOFY   Bell 206B-3 JetRanger III   3637   26.08.87
N2283F   First Fence Ltd   Costock Heliport   30.03.18E

G-DOGG   Scottish Aviation Bulldog Srs 120/121   BH120/308   03.10.01
XX638   P Sengupta
Bourne Park, Hurstbourne Tarrant   27.04.17P
As 'XX638' in RAF c/s (IE 02.10.17)

G-DOGI   Robinson R22 Beta   2389   08.09.09
G-BVGS, N2363S
Phoenix Helicopter Academy Ltd   Blackbushe   19.06.18E

G-DOGZ   Rogerson Horizon 1   xxxx   10.08.98
M J Nolan   (West Molesey)   08.01.10P
Built by J E D Rogerson – project PFA 241-13129;
badged 'Fisher Super Koala' (NF 20.01.16)

G-DOIG   CZAW Sportcruiser   700561   30.10.08
C J May   (Exmouth)   16.04.19P
Built by J H Doyle – project LAA 338-14859

G-DOIN   Best Off Skyranger 912S(1)   SKR 0403 460   26.04.04
M Geczy   Shifnal   29.05.18P
Built by C D & L J Church – project BMAA/HB/379

G-DOLF   Eurocopter AS.365N3 Dauphin 2   6779   25.10.07
F-WWPP   Executive Jet Charter Ltd   Farnborough   04.03.18E

G-DOLI   Cirrus SR20   2009   07.08.08
Furness Professional Training Ltd   Blackpool   26.08.18E

G-DOLY   Cessna T303 Crusader   T30300107   20.07.94
N303MK, G-BJZK, (N3645C)
KW Aviation Ltd   Biggin Hill   03.07.18E

G-DOMS   Evektor EV-97A Eurostar   2003-1273   24.06.04
C A & R K Stewart   Church Farm, Shotteswell   15.04.18P
Built by D J Cross – project PFA 315-14254

G-DONE   Bell 505 Jet Ranger X   65056   09.02.18
Simpson Heli Charters Ltd   (Drayton, Norwich)
(IE 09.02.18)

G-DONK   Ultramagic M-77   77/414   13.12.17
K R Holzer   Château-d'Oex, Switzerland
'Morris the Donkey'   10.10.19E

G-DONT   Zenair CH.601XL Zodiac   xxxx   24.05.04
J A Kentzer   (Sheffield)   17.05.18P
Built by N C Butcher – project PFA 162B-14172;
tricycle u/c

G-DORN   Dornier EKW C-3605   332   15.05.98
HB-RBJ, Swiss AF C-552   Yak UK Ltd   Little Gransden   28.04.10P
Built by Farner Werke (F+W); as 'C-552' in
Swiss AF c/s; on rebuild 2017 (NF 11.08.17)

G-DORO   Robin DR.401/140B Dauphin 4   2708   26.02.18
R D W Evans   White Waltham
Delivered to Elstree 09.03.18

G-DORS   Eurocopter EC135 T3   0517   14.12.06
Bond Aviation Leasing Ltd   Gloucestershire   17.02.18E

G-DORY   Cameron Z-315   11424   28.06.10
P Baker   Abbeyview, Trim, RoI   *'Hunky Dorys'*   12.04.18E

G-DOSB   Diamond DA.42M Twin Star   42.328   14.07.08
ZA180, G-DOSB   Acrobat Ltd   Bournemouth   22.07.18R
Operated by L3 CTS Airline & Academy Training

G-DOSC Diamond DA.42M Twin Star 42M.001 23.12.08
OE-FOG, OE-VPI Acrobat Ltd Bournemouth 19.06.19R
Operated by L3 CTS Airline & Academy Training

G-DOTS Dornier Do.27A-4 524 28.04.15
F-BSGM, German AF 57+63, GB+375
Liberty Aviation Ltd Kortrijk-Wevelgem Int'l, Belgium
(NF 12.01.18)

G-DOTT CFM Streak Shadow K 341 30.11.04
R J Bell Ladyhill, Antrim 16.11.17P
Built by R J Bell – project PFA 206-13582

G-DOTW ICP MXP-740 Savannah VG Jabiru(1) 08-03-51-694 25.06.08
I W Gardner Headcorn 14.03.18P
Built by I S Wright – project BMAA/HB/575

G-DOTY Van's RV-7 71966 21.10.08
D F Daines Seething 24.06.18P
Built by H Daines – project PFA 323-14387

G-DOUZ Van's RV-12 120910 20.11.17
J & G Aerospace Ltd Fairoaks 03.01.20P
Built by H Lees – project LAA 363-15344

G-DOVE Cessna 182Q Skylane II 18266724 26.06.80
N96446 P Puri Derby 01.06.18E

G-DOVS Robinson R44 Raven II 11858 08.08.07
J Watt Cumbernauld 15.09.18E

G-DOWN Colt 31A 1570 03.08.89
M Williams Wadhurst 08.06.00A
Built by Thunder & Colt Ltd (NF 28.07.16)

G-DOZI Comco Ikarus C42 FB100 0606-6824 22.05.06
D A Izod Gerpins Farm, Upminster 04.10.15P
Assembled Aerosport Ltd

G-DOZZ Best Off Skyranger Swift 912S(1) SKR0803866 16.05.08
J P Doswell Tinnel Farm, Landulph 'Lady Caroline' 30.11.18P
Built by J P Doswell – project BMAA/HB/573

G-DPER Jonker JS-MD Single *(JS-1 Revelation)* 1C.MD120 25.09.17
(BGA 5940) M P Clark Bicester 'ER' 28.09.18E

G-DPRV Van's RV-7A 74569 16.02.17
D H Pattison Lower Upham Farm, Chiseldon
Built by D H Pattison – project LAA 323-15455
(NF 16.02.17)

G-DRAM Reims FR172F Rocket FR17200102 18.09.98
OH-CNS H R Mitchell Oban 'Spirit of Scotland' 30.05.18E
Floatplane

G-DRAT Slingsby T.51 Dart 17R 1517 08.05.08
BGA 1316/BXL W R Longstaff Feshiebridge '121' 09.06.18R

G-DRAW Colt 77A 1830 31.08.90
A G Odell Macclesfield 23.05.18E
Built by Thunder & Colt Ltd

G-DRCC Evektor EV-97 teamEurostar UK 3717 28.08.14
G-SLNM Sanctuary Medical Ltd Bourn 19.05.17P
Assembled Cosmik Aviation Ltd

G-DRCS Schleicher ASH 25E 25060 10.04.08
BGA 4480/JFN, D-KCOH
C R Smithers Gransden Lodge 'M25' 27.05.18E

G-DRDR Cirrus SR22T 1386 19.07.16
N788DR V Kipyatkov (Peyia, Republic of Cyprus) 27.07.19E

G-DREG Cosmik Aviation Superchaser SCH001W 04.06.07
N R Beale Deppers Bridge, Southam
Built by N R Beale
(SSDR microlight since 05.14) (IE 20.01.17)

G-DREI Fokker Dr.1 Triplane replica N-200955 07.03.11
P M Brueggemann Felthorpe 03.09.19P
Built by P M Brueggemann – project LAA 238-14848;
C/n is Ron Sands Plans No; as '425/17' & '1729'
on rudder in German Army Air Service c/s

G-DRGC P&M Quik GT450 8564 03.02.11
D R G Cornwell St Michaels 16.05.18P

G-DRGL Piper PA-18-135 Super Cub 18-3828 20.08.14
G-BLIH, (PH-KNG), R Netherlands AF R-138,
(PH-KNG), (PH-GRC), R Netherlands AF R-138,
54-2428 Goodwood Road Racing Company Ltd
Goodwood 22.01.18E

G-DRGS Cessna 182S Skylane 18280375 17.11.98
N2389X D R G Scott Wycombe Air Park 20.11.18E

G-DRIO Jodel DR.1050-M Excellence 493 21.07.17
G-BXIO, F-BNIO
B N Stevens St Mary's, Isles of Scilly 22.06.18P
Built by Société Aeronautique Normande

G-DRMM Europa Aviation Europa 362 27.07.98
T J Harrison (Gloucester)
Built by M W Mason – project PFA 247-13201;
tricycle u/c (NF 27.06.17)

G-DROL Robinson R44 Raven II 11815 07.06.10
G-OPDG M R Lord (Hill House, Wolverley) 14.09.18E

G-DROP Cessna U206C U2061230 07.08.87
G-UKNO, G-BAMN, 4X-ALL, N71943
K Brady Strathallan 29.05.18E

G-DRPK Reality Escapade JA.ESC.0167 30.06.08
P A Kirkham Popham 06.04.18P
Built by P A Kirkham – project LAA 345-14824
– VLA version; tailwheel u/c

G-DRPO Cameron Z-105 11822 16.04.14
J F A Strickland Harpole, Northampton 'DatumRPO' 29.05.19E

G-DRRT Slingsby T.51 Dart 17R 1516 14.06.11
G-DBXH, BGA 1313/BXH
L W Whittington Burnford Common, Brentor 'D17' 30.05.18R

G-DRSV Robin DR.315X Petit Prince 624 & 01 07.06.90
F-ZWRS R S Voice Rushett Farm, Chessington 03.07.18P
Built by Centre-Est Aéronautique; modified
R S Voice – project PFA 210-11765

G-DRTA Boeing 737-85P 33972 10.03.17
EC-JBJ
Dart Group PLC Leeds Bradford 'Jet2holidays' 16.10.19E
Line No: 1598; operated by Jet2.com

G-DRTB Boeing 737-86N 28610 23.06.17
EI-RUG, VT-SJF, EI-DIS, EC-HHH
Dart Group PLC Leeds Bradford 'Jet2holidays' 22.06.19E
Line No: 449; operated by Jet2.com

G-DRTC Boeing 737-808 34702 29.05.18
EI-RUN, B-5168
Dart Group PLC Leeds Bradford 'Jet2holidays' 27.05.19E
Line No: 1917; operated by Jet2.com

G-DRTD Boeing 737-808 34703 21.05.18
EI-RUO, B-5169, N1795B
Dart Group PLC Leeds Bradford 'Jet2holidays' 17.05.19E
Line No: 1941; operated by Jet2.com

G-DRTE Boeing 737-8K5 28228 16.07.18
EI-RUH, LX-LGT, D-AHFN, N1786B Dart Group PLC
Leeds Bradford 'Jet2 Croatia' & 'Friendly Low Fares' 12.07.19E
Line No: 484; operated by Jet2.com; red tail

G-DRTF Boeing 737-85P 28387 09.07.18
EI-RUI, EC-HJQ Dart Group PLC Leeds Bradford
'Jet2 Madeira', 'Jet2holidays' & 'Friendly Low Fares' 08.07.19E
Line No: 522; operated by Jet2.com; red tail

G-DRTG Boeing 737-8BK 33020 19.12.18
B-5186 Jet2.com Ltd Leeds Bradford 'Jet2 Holidays'
Line No: 2103; operated by Jet.2com

G-DRTH Boeing 737-8BK 33828 21.01.19
B-5187 Jet2.com Ltd Leeds Bradford 'Jet2Holidays'
Line No: 2124; operated by Jet.2com

G-DRTN Boeing 737-86N 28.09.18
VQ-BJX, TC-APJ Dart Group PLC Leeds Bradford
Line No: 1104; operated by Jet2.com; red tail

G-DRTT Boeing 737-8Q8 30722 10.12.18
YL-PSB, OY-PSB, TF-JXE Dart Group PLC
Leeds Bradford 'Jet2Holidays'
Line No: 2261; operated by Jet2.com Ltd (IE 10.12.18)

G-DRTU Boeing 737-86N 34247 21.03.19
LZ-GNA, YL-PSH, OY-PSH, N342AR, JA737H, N1787D
Dart Group PLC Leeds Bradford
Line No: 1830

G-DRTW Boeing 737-86N 28618 21.03.19
LZ-GNB, YL-PSD, OY-PSD, TF-JXH, OK-TVQ, EC-ILX,
OK-TVQ, N1786B
Dart Group PLC Leeds Bradford
Line No: 0514

G-DRYS Cameron N-90 3377 01.12.95
C A Butter Marsh Benham 04.08.16E

G-DRZF	Robin DR.360 Chevalier	451	04.09.91
	F-BRZF P J Kaufeler Earls Colne		13.12.18E
	Built by Centre-Est Aéronautique		
G-DSAA	Leonardo AW169	69027	21.10.16
	SAS (Dorset & Somerset) Ltd Henstridge		20.10.18E
	Operated by Dorset & Somerset Air Ambulance		
	as 'Helimed 10'		
G-DSFT	Piper PA-28R-200 Cherokee Arrow II	28R-7335157	22.11.00
	G-LFSE, G-BAXT, N11C J Jones Headcorn		02.04.18E
G-DSGC	Piper PA-25-260 Pawnee C	25-4890	03.05.95
	OY-BDA		
	Devon & Somerset Gliding Club Ltd North Hill		14.08.18E
G-DSID	Piper PA-34-220T Seneca IV	3447001	21.07.95
	I M Worthington Nottingham City		06.11.18E
G-DSJT	Cessna 182T Skylane	18282385	22.12.15
	N7128T, N40994 D S J Tait Fairoaks		21.12.18E
G-DSKI	Evektor EV-97 Eurostar	2003-1619	25.06.04
	M Nixon tr G-DSKI Group Fenland		25.08.18P
	Built by D R Skill – project PFA 315-14088		
G-DSKY	Diamond DA.42 Twin Star	42.084	01.03.06
	M-STAR, G-CDSZ		
	Aeros Global Ltd Doncaster Sheffield		14.06.19E
	Operated by Aero Flight Training		
G-DSLL	Cyclone Pegasus Quantum 15-912	7836	05.07.01
	D T Evans Broadmeadow Farm, Hereford		25.07.18P
G-DSMA	P&M QuikR	8410	13.02.09
	F Hogarth & D Young Cotswold		11.05.18P
G-DSMR	Gulfstream Gulfstream VI (*Gulfstream 650*) 6329		08.11.18
	N629GA TAG Aviation (UK) Ltd Farnborough		07.11.19E
G-DSOO	Glaser-Dirks DG-500M	5-E61M26	19.04.16
	D-KVRS R Jackson tr Twin Astir Syndicate Rufforth		13.12.17E
G-DSPK	Cameron Z-140	10640	07.01.05
	Bailey Balloons Ltd Pill, Bristol '*D S Smith Packaging*'		11.01.14E
	(NF 27.10.16)		
G-DSPL	Diamond DA.40 Star	40.037	19.11.07
	D-ETFP, G-GBDS, N537DS Dynamic Signal		
	Processing Ltd Bourne Park, Hurstbourne Tarrant		15.08.18E
G-DSPZ	Robinson R44 Raven II	10351	05.05.04
	Focal Point Communications Ltd		
	(Bishop's Sutton, Alresford)		25.06.18E
	Operated by HQ Aviation		
G-DSRV	Van's RV-7	72126?	30.05.14
	S J Boynett & D W Murcott (Coalville & Walsall)		13.09.18P
	Built by S J Boynett & D W Murcott		
	– project PFA 323-14381		
G-DSUE	Aeropro EuroFOX 912(S)	56419	19.09.18
	D M Garrett Little Down Farm, Milson		
	Built by D M Garrett – project LAA 376-15571		
	(NF 19.09.18)		
G-DSVN	Rolladen-Schneider LS8-18	8079	03.01.08
	BGA 4262/HWM A R Paul Dunstable Downs '*D7*'		21.03.18E
G-DTAR	P&M Quik GT450	8416	03.10.08
	The Scottish Aero Club Ltd Perth		04.04.18P
G-DTCP	Piper PA-32R-300 Cherokee Lance	32R-7780255	26.01.93
	G-TEEM, N2604Q R G Cook Cranfield		12.09.18E
G-DTFF	Cessna T182T Turbo Skylane	T18208474	25.10.06
	N2196K		
	Ridgway Aviation Ltd (Dudleston Heath, Ellesmere)		10.11.18E
G-DTFT	Czech Sport PS-28 Cruiser	C0506	29.04.14
	J T Crump (Andover)		07.08.19R
G-DTOF	Schempp-Hirth Discus-2c FES	3	04.03.19
	D-KTOF K Neave & C F M Smith Nympsfield		28.02.20E
G-DTOY	Comco Ikarus C42 FB100	0309-6570	20.10.03
	C W Laskey The Byre, Hardwick, Abergavenny		27.10.18P
	Assembled Fly Buy Ultralights Ltd		
G-DTPC	Van's RV-9A	92234	21.11.18
	P M Clayton & D Turner Netherthorpe		
	Built by D Turner – project LAA 320-15330		
	(IE 11.03.19)		
G-DTSM	Evektor EV-97 teamEurostar UK	2008-3218	01.08.08
	J R Stothart (North Shields)		01.12.18P
	Assembled Cosmik Aviation Ltd		

G-DTUG	Wag-Aero Super Sport	4175	13.05.04
	D A Bullock Bicester		08.05.18P
	Built by D A Bullock – project PFA 108-14026		
G-DUBI	Lindstrand LBL 120A	1123	04.10.06
	M B Vennard Astbury, Congleton '*HSBC*'		06.03.19E
G-DUDE	Van's RV-8	80362	16.07.99
	J J Cooke & R A Seeley Hinton-in-the-Hedges		
	'*Captain Midnight*', '*19*' & '*Vans Air Force*'		01.05.18P
	Built by W M Hodgkins – project PFA 303-13246		
G-DUDI	AutoGyro MTOsport	xxxx	17.05.10
	M B & R J Trickey Longside		29.07.19P
	Assembled Rotorsport UK as c/n RSUK/MTOS/030		
G-DUDZ	Robin DR.400-180 Régent	2367	03.12.97
	G-BXNK W J Lee Edington Hill, Edington		21.02.18E
G-DUFF	Rand Robinson KR-2	xxxx	22.11.10
	J I B Duff (New Deer, Turriff)		
	Built by J I B Duff – project PFA 129-11576 (NF 18.11.14)		
G-DUGE	Comco Ikarus C42 FB UK	0112 6445	30.07.02
	D Stevenson Plaistows Farm, St Albans		22.06.10P
	Built by D Stevenson – project PFA 322-13855		
	(NF 07.06.18)		
G-DUMP	Customcraft A25	CC003	19.05.04
	(PH-xxx), G-DUMP Dept of Doing Ltd Kettering		
	(NF 26.11.18)		
G-DUNK	Reims/Cessna F172M	F17201402	02.05.07
	N90SA, PH-TWS, OY-BUL		
	Devon & Somerset Flight Training Ltd Dunkeswell		05.08.18E
G-DUNS	Lindstrand LBL 90A	1281	19.11.09
	W Rousell & J Tyrrell Wollaston, Wellingborough		05.07.19E
G-DUOT	Schempp-Hirth Duo Discus T	123/466	03.08.05
	BGA 5180 B Kerby tr G-DUOT Soaring Group		
	Snitterfield '*666*'		06.03.18E
G-DURO	Europa Aviation Europa	033	15.11.93
	W R C Williams-Wynne Talybont		10.05.18P
	Built by R Swinden – project PFA 247-12554;		
	tailwheel u/c		
G-DURX	Colt 77A	1522	25.05.89
	P Coman & D J Stagg Priory Farm, Tibenham '*durex*'		18.03.18E
	Built by Thunder & Colt Ltd		
G-DUSKᴹ	de Havilland DH.115 Vampire T.Mk.11	15596	01.02.99
	XE856 Cancelled 19.03.09 as PWFU		
	As 'XE856:V' in 219 Sqdn c/s: carries G-DUSK below		
	tailplane		
	With Bournemouth Aviation Museum, Bournemouth		
G-DUST	Stolp SA.300 Starduster Too	JP-2	28.04.88
	N233JP A R R Holden Compton Abbas		25.04.19P
	Built by J O Perritt		
G-DUVL	Reims/Cessna F172N	F17201723	16.08.78
	G-BFMU		
	I Mackinnon tr G-DUVL Flying Group White Waltham		09.04.18E
G-DVAA	Eurocopter EC135 T2+	0656	14.03.08
	Devon Air Ambulance Trading Company Ltd Eaglescott		03.09.18E
	Operated by Devon Air Ambulance as callsign		
	'*Helimed 04*'		
G-DVBF	Lindstrand LBL 210A	188	06.03.95
	Airxcite Ltd t/a Virgin Balloon Flights		
	Stafford Park, Telford '*Virgin*'		01.06.05E
	(NF 15.09.14)		
G-DVCI	Ultramagic H-31	31/15	09.09.14
	Davinci Associates Ltd Waterlooville		10.07.19E
G-DVIO	Leonardo AW139	31822	06.09.18
	Executive Jet Charter Ltd Farnborough		05.09.19E
G-DVIP	Agusta A109E Power	11217	12.11.13
	VH-VIS Castle Air Ltd Trebrown, Liskeard		15.12.18E
G-DVMI	Van's RV-7	73445	07.04.11
	I Hoolahan tr North West RV Flyers		
	Manchester Barton		27.03.18P
	Built by A Crome & Partners – project LAA 323-14860		
G-DVON	de Havilland DH.104 Dove 8	04201	26.10.84
	(G-BLPD), VP955 C L Thatcher tr 955 Preservation		
	Group (Kimbolton, Huntingdon)		29.05.96
	Originally built as Devon C.2 and modified to		
	C.2/2 status; as 'VP955' in RAF c/s (NF 18.04.16)		

G-DVOR	Diamond DA.62	62.040	02.11.16
	Flight Calibration Services Ltd Goodwood		14.11.18E
	Callsign 'VOR06'		
G-DVOY	CZAW Sportcruiser	10SC343	26.01.17
	G-TDKI J Devoy Tatenhill		19.12.17P
	Built by D R Kendall – project LAA 338-14986;		
	for sale with AT Aviation 10.18		
G-DVTA	Cessna T206H Turbo Stationair	T20608753	15.09.16
	EI-SPB, N2321V D L Parker Old Sarum		08.11.18E
G-DWCB	Chilton DW.1A	xxxx	26.05.15
	C M Barnes Priory Farm, Tibenham		02.05.18P
	Built by C M Barnes – project PFA 225-14454		
G-DWCE	Robinson R44 Raven II	11511	17.11.06
	3GRComm Ltd Gloucestershire		08.12.17E
G-DWIA	Chilton DW.1A	xxxx	25.01.93
	D Elliott (Brooks Green, Horsham)		
	Built by D Elliott – project PFA 225-12256 (NF 01.05.18)		
G-DWIB	Chilton DW.1B	xxxx	22.12.93
	J Jennings (Oak Farm, Bylaugh, Dereham)		
	Built by J Jennings – project PFA 225-12374		
	(NF 17.09.14)		
G-DWJM^M	Cessna 550 Citation II	550-0296	19.05.05
	G-BJIR, N6888C Cancelled 26.02.14 by CAA		18.10.10
	Fuselage only, used as classroom at Milton Hall		
	Primary School, Westcliffe-on-Sea 01.19		
G-DWMS	Avtech Jabiru UL-450	0266	21.06.00
	S McLatchie Fenland		19.06.19P
	Built by D H S Williams – project PFA 274A-13491		
G-DWRU	Chilton DW.1A	xxxx	02.03.17
	K J Steele Old Sarum		
	Built by K J Steele – project PFA 225-13893		
	(NF 02.03.17)		
G-DXLT	Schempp-Hirth Duo Discus XLT	229	27.06.11
	(BGA 5667)		
	M J Hasluck tr G-DXLT Group Parham Park *'X5'*		01.03.18E
G-DXTR	Beech B200 Super King Air	BB-1244	09.11.16
	ZS-DEX, VH-ITA, F-OINC, F-GSFA, G-RIOO, N251DL,		
	N72357 Synergy Aviation Ltd Fairoaks		30.11.18E
G-DYKE	Dyke JD.2 Delta	PFA 1331	06.01.04
	M S Bird Glebe Farm, Stockton		
	Built by M S Bird – project PFA 1331; stored 05.17		
	(NF 10.04.18)		
G-DYLN	Pilatus PC-12/47E	1760	18.12.17
	HB-FQW Oriens Leasing Ltd Biggin Hill		14.12.18E
G-DYNA	Aerospool Dynamic WT9 UK	DY135/2006	09.05.06
	J C Stubbs Manor Farm, Keyston		05.06.19P
	Assembled Yeoman Light Aircraft Co Ltd;		
	official c/n recorded as 'DY135'		
G-DYNM	Aerospool Dynamic WT9 UK	DY161/2007	30.05.07
	D M Pearson tr November Mike Group		
	Chiltern Park, Wallingford		31.08.18P
	Assembled Yeoman Light Aircraft Co Ltd;		
	official c/n recorded as 'DY161'		
G-DYOU	Piper PA-38-112 Tomahawk	38-78A0436	19.10.78
	Cancelled 24.05.95 as PWFU		03.03.94
	Chorley, Oxfordshire *Stored at private address 04.15*		
G-DYUP	Europa Aviation Europa	630	12.03.18
	A Hunter (Lytham St Annes)		
	Built by A Hunter – project LAA 247-15113 (NF 12.03.18)		
G-DZDZ	Rolladen-Schneider LS4	4027	03.03.08
	BGA 3885/HEL, (BGA 3896/HEX), (BGA 3885/HEL),		
	D-6431 I Macarthur Lasham *'DZ'*		24.04.18E
G-DZKY	Diamond DA.40D Star	D4.342	14.03.11
	G-CEZP Go 2 Aviation Ltd Bournemouth		02.05.18E
	Operated by L3 CTS Airline & Academy Training		
G-DZZY	American Champion 8KCAB Super Decathlon		
		1106-2011	23.12.10
	Paul's Planes Ltd Denham		08.05.18E

G-EAAA – G-EZZZ

G-EAGA (2)	Sopwith Dove replica	3004/1	22.11.89
	(G-BLOO) A Wood Old Warden		09.07.18P
	Original Dove G-EAGA c/n 3004/1 to Australia		
	12.1919 as K-157: crashed Essendon, Victoria		
	09.03.30; remains to UK c.1987/88 & rebuilt by		
	Skysport Engineering as G-BLOO then		
	re-registered G-EAGA; on loan to Richard		
	Shuttleworth Trustees		
G-EAVX (2)	Sopwith Pup	xxxx	16.01.78
	B1807 K A M Baker Henstridge		
	Originally built Standard Motor Co Ltd & registered		
	02.11.20 as c/n 'B1807'; rebuilt by K A M Baker		
	– project PFA 101-10523; as 'B1807:A7' in RFC c/s;		
	under restoration 08.18 (NF 15.09.14)		
G-EBJI (2)	Hawker Cygnet replica	xxxx	09.08.77
	C J Essex Old Warden		18.08.18P
	Built by C J Essex – project PFA 077-10240		
G-EBZN (2)	de Havilland DH.60X Moth	608	28.10.88
	VP-NAA, VP-YAA, ZS-AAP, G-UAAP		
	J Hodgkinson (Meopham, Gravesend)		
	(On rebuild from original components (NF 14.12.15)		
G-ECAC	Alpha R2120U	120T-0001	23.01.08
	ZK-SXY Bulldog Aviation Ltd Earls Colne		17.03.18E
	Badged 'Alpha 120T'		
G-ECAD	Reims/Cessna FA152 Aerobat	FA1520369	19.12.08
	G-JEET, G-BHMF Andrewsfield Aviation Ltd		
	& Corvalis Aircraft Leasing Ltd Andrewsfield		26.09.18E
G-ECAE	Royal Aircraft Factory SE.5A	xxxx	23.02.10
	RAAF A2-25, C8996 Westh Flyg AB Elmsett		
	On rebuild by Hawker Restorations 05.17 (NF 20.10.16)		
G-ECAF	Robin HR.200-120B	345	03.08.12
	G-BZET, F-GTZG Bulldog Aviation Ltd Earls Colne		17.08.18E
G-ECAG	Robin HR.200-120B	315	22.09.15
	G-MFLD, G-BXDT Bulldog Aviation Ltd Earls Colne		10.09.18E
G-ECAK	Reims/Cessna F172M	F17201509	03.08.12
	G-BENK Bulldog Aviation Ltd Earls Colne		10.08.18E
G-ECAM	EAA Acrosport II	254	01.08.11
	N456HD, N360RP C England New Barn Farm, Crawley		
	Built by R Price; on rebuild 10.16 (NF 03.07.15)		
G-ECAN	de Havilland DH.84 Dragon	2048	11.01.01
	VH-DHX, VH-AQU, RAAF A34-59		
	C W Norman tr Norman Aeroplane Trust		
	Rendcomb *'Railway Air Services Ltd'*		26.03.18E
	Built by de Havilland Aircraft Proprietary Ltd		
G-ECAP	Robin HR.200-120B	334	26.06.14
	G-NSOF Bulldog Aviation Ltd Earls Colne		16.05.18E
G-ECAR	Robin HR.200-120B	321	23.08.16
	G-MFLB, G-BXOR Bulldog Aviation Ltd Earls Colne		27.09.18E
G-ECAT	Fokker F27 Friendship 500	10672	14.04.00
	G-JEAI, VH-EWZ, PH-EXS		
	Cancelled 12.08.03 by CAA		16.12.02
	Sligo, RoI *Used for rescue training 05.14*		
G-ECBI	Schweizer 269C-1 (*300CBi*)	0282	17.05.07
	N86G Iris Aviation Ltd Southend		07.02.19E
G-ECDB	Schleicher Ka 6E	4137	13.02.08
	BGA 1450/CDB C W R Neve Currock Hill *'CDB'*		17.08.18E
G-ECDS	de Havilland DH.82A Tiger Moth	86347	06.12.07
	N82DS, F-BGFA, NL904		
	N C Wilson Wold Lodge, Finedon		24.06.16P
	(IE 08.11.17)		
G-ECDT	Comper CLA.7 Swift replica	xxxx	04.01.16
	Airtime Aerobatics Ltd Oaksey Park		
	Built by S Jones – project PFA 103-13985 (NF 04.01.16)		
G-ECDX	de Havilland DH.71 Tiger Moth replica	SP7	01.11.94
	Airtime Aerobatics Ltd Hill Farm, Durley		
	Built by R I Souch; noted 06.16 (NF 07.03.16)		
G-ECEA	Schempp-Hirth Cirrus	21	02.04.08
	BGA 1473/CEA, XZ405, BGA 1473, D-8437		
	M Greenwood tr CEA Group Long Mynd *'CEA'*		28.08.18E
G-ECET	Cessna T182T Turbo Skylane	T18208918	16.01.19
	D-ECET, (D-EZAA), N5963A		
	W J Forrest Liverpool John Lennon		06.10.19E

G-ECGC	Reims/Cessna F172N	F17201850	10.10.79
	D H G Penney Kings Farm, Thurrock		27.11.17E
G-ECGO	Bölkow BÖ.208C Junior	599	24.08.89
	D-ECGO P Norman Audley End		20.11.18E
G-ECHB	Dassault Falcon 900DX	623	31.07.12
	D-AMIG, F-WWFA		
	Concierge U Ltd (London W1)		29.03.19E
G-ECJM	Piper PA-28R-201T Turbo Arrow III	28R-7803178	25.09.90
	G-FESL, G-BNRN, N321EC, N3561M		
	Regishire Ltd Bournemouth		04.02.18E
	Official type data 'PA-28R-201T Turbo Cherokee		
	Arrow III' is incorrect		
G-ECKB	Reality Escapade 912(2)	JA.ESC.0003	20.12.07
	C M & C P Bradford Coate, Devizes		31.03.18P
	Built by C M Bradford – project BMAA/HB/533;		
	tailwheel u/c		
G-ECLW	Glasflügel Standard Libelle 201B	174	26.11.07
	BGA 1637/CLW		
	R Harkness & S Leach Kirton in Lindsey *'CLW'*		10.03.19E
G-ECMK	Piper PA-18-150 Super Cub	18-8209022	08.07.08
	N45531, Israel DFAF 111		
	S J Waddy tr Shacklewell Super Cub Group		
	Shacklewell Lodge Farm, Empingham		05.12.18E
	As 'E-44' in USAAF c/s		
G-ECNX	Reims/Cessna F177RG Cardinal RG	F177RG0038	10.03.15
	D-ECNX V Haack (Dulmen, Germany)		25.03.18E
G-ECOA	Bombardier DHC-8-402Q	4180	14.12.07
	C-FMUE Flybe Ltd Exeter Int'l		18.12.19E
G-ECOB	Bombardier DHC-8-402Q	4185	18.01.08
	LN-WDT, G-ECOB, C-FNEN Flybe Ltd Exeter Int'l		11.01.20E
G-ECOC	Bombardier DHC-8-402Q	4197	20.03.08
	C-FOKA Flybe Ltd Exeter Int'l		22.03.19E
G-ECOD	Bombardier DHC-8-402Q	4206	14.07.08
	C-FPEX, (G-ECOD), C-FPEX Flybe Ltd Exeter Int'l		20.07.19E
G-ECOE	Bombardier DHC-8-402Q	4212	30.07.08
	LN-WDV, G-ECOE, C-FQXJ Flybe Ltd Exeter Int'l		06.08.19E
G-ECOF	Bombardier DHC-8-402Q	4216	21.08.08
	LN-WDW, G-ECOF, C-FRJU Flybe Ltd Exeter Int'l		25.08.19E
G-ECOG	Bombardier DHC-8-402Q	4220	17.10.08
	C-FSRQ Flybe Ltd Exeter Int'l		16.10.19E
G-ECOH	Bombardier DHC-8-402Q	4221	24.10.08
	C-FSRW Flybe Ltd Exeter Int'l		23.10.19E
G-ECOI	Bombardier DHC-8-402Q	4224	07.11.08
	C-FTIE Flybe Ltd Exeter Int'l		06.11.19E
G-ECOJ	Bombardier DHC-8-402Q	4229	09.01.09
	C-FTUS Flybe Ltd Exeter Int'l		08.01.20E
G-ECOK	Bombardier DHC-8-402Q	4230	23.01.09
	C-FTUT Flybe Ltd Exeter Int'l		22.01.20E
G-ECOL	Schempp-Hirth Nimbus-2	11	03.12.07
	BGA 1722/CQL L I Rigby & M Upex Crowland *'339'*		25.04.19E
G-ECOM	Bombardier DHC-8-402Q	4233	18.12.08
	C-FUCR Flybe Ltd Exeter Int'l		17.12.19E
G-ECOO	Bombardier DHC-8-402Q	4237	30.01.09
	C-FUOH Flybe Ltd Exeter Int'l		29.01.19E
G-ECOP	Bombardier DHC-8-402Q	4242	02.04.09
	C-FUTG Flybe Ltd Exeter Int'l		01.04.19E
G-ECOR	Bombardier DHC-8-402Q	4248	08.04.09
	C-FVUJ Flybe Ltd Exeter Int'l		07.04.19E
G-ECOT	Bombardier DHC-8-402Q	4251	20.05.09
	C-FVUV Flybe Ltd Exeter Int'l		19.05.19E
G-ECPA	Glasflügel Standard Libelle 201B	328	23.01.08
	BGA 1688/CPA M J Witton Long Mynd *'466'*		10.11.18E
G-ECRM	Slingsby T67M Firefly II	2044	05.12.17
	G-BNSP CRM Aviation Europe Ltd White Waltham		14.03.18E
G-ECTF	Comper CLA.7 Swift replica	xxxx	12.04.07
	P R Cozens Hinton-in-the-Hedges		11.09.18P
	Built by P R Cozens – project PFA 103-13078		
G-ECUB	Piper PA-18-150 Super Cub	18-6279	28.11.03
	G-CBFI, SE-FDY, LN-HHA, SE-CTA, N8675D		
	I Mackinnon tr G-ECUB Flying Group White Waltham		21.09.18E

G-ECVZ	Staaken Z-1S Flitzer	Z061	12.10.12
	J Cresswell Batchley Farm, Hordle		26.09.17P
	Built by V D Long – project LAA 342-14817		
G-ECXL	SZD-30 Pirat	B-548	18.09.09
	BGA 1888/CXL J Hunneman tr Charlie X-Ray		
	Lima Group Rivar Hill *'CXL'*		25.11.15E
	Built by PZL-Bielsko		
G-EDAV	Scottish Aviation Bulldog Srs 120/121	BH120/220	08.08.01
	XX534 Edwalton Aviation Ltd Nottingham City		02.11.17E
	As 'XX534:B 'in RAF c/s		
G-EDBD	SZD-30 Pirat	S-02.02	06.07.11
	BGA 1977/DBD A M Bennett & S P Burgess Lyveden		05.11.18E
	Built by PZL-Bielsko		
G-EDDD	Schempp-Hirth Nimbus-2	84	21.08.08
	BGA 2025/DDD, G-BKPM, BGA 2025/DDD		
	C A Mansfield *'695'* Lasham		28.05.18E
G-EDDS	CZAW Sportcruiser	08SC113	14.02.08
	C P Davis Sittles Farm, Alrewas		14.03.18P
	Built by E H Bishop – project PFA 338-14660		
	(Quick-build kit 4010)		
G-EDDV	PZL-Bielsko SZD-38A Jantar 1	B-664	16.10.08
	BGA 2041/DDV S R Bruce Feshiebridge *'536'*		02.05.11E
	Stored in trailer 10.16 (NF 08.04.16)		
G-EDEE	Comco Ikarus C42 FB100	0511-6769	15.11.05
	C L & D Godfrey Deanland		15.03.18P
	Assembled Aerosport Ltd		
G-EDEL	Piper PA-32-300 Cherokee Six D	32-7140009	16.04.10
	D-EDEL, N8617N J Francis St Mary's, Isles of Scilly		03.04.19E
G-EDEN	SOCATA TB-10 Tobago	66	08.01.80
	N G Pistol tr Group EDEN Elstree		16.05.18E
G-EDFS	Pietenpol Air Camper	xxxx	24.03.98
	J V Comfort (Napton, Southam)		
	Built by D F Slaughter – project PFA 047-13206		
	(NF 08.02.15)		
G-EDGA	Piper PA-28-161 Warrior II	28-8516024	30.08.05
	D-EDGA, N9512N The Royal Air Force Halton		
	Aeroplane Club Ltd RAF Halton		15.11.18E
G-EDGE	Jodel D.150 Mascaret	111	14.09.88
	A D Edge RAF Wyton		26.10.18P
	Built by A D Edge – project PFA 151-11223		
	using SAB plans		
G-EDGI	Piper PA-28-161 Warrior II	28-7916565	19.01.99
	D-EBGI, N2941R H K & T W Gilbert Cotswold		18.02.20E
	Operated by Lyneham Flying Club		
G-EDGK	Cessna TR182 Turbo Skylane RG II	R18200941	14.04.16
	D-EDGK, PH-AYK, N738MB		
	V Holschuh (Michelstadt, Germany)		08.07.18E
G-EDGY	Zivko Edge 540	0018	16.10.07
	N540JN, N540SA P C Massetti & C R A Scrope		
	Whitehall Farm, Benington		15.02.19P
	Built by S K Andeline		
G-EDLY	AirBorne XT912-B/Streak III-B	XT912-073	27.04.05
	M & P L Eardley Rossall Field, Cockerham		26.04.18P
	Wing s/n ST3-058		
G-EDMC	Cyclone Pegasus Quantum 15-912	7513	11.03.99
	R Frost Eshott		18.06.18P
G-EDMK	Boeing Stearman A75N1 Kaydet (N2S-5)	75-5476	29.01.16
	EC-AST, 42-17313 T W Harris Duxford		
	Noted on restoration 07.18 (NF 29.01.16)		
G-EDMV	Eiriavion PIK-20D	20526	12.12.07
	BGA 2232/DMV Cancelled 04.10.11 as PWFU		16.06.10
	Bellarena *Wreck stored 06.15*		
G-EDNA	Piper PA-38-112 Tomahawk	38-78A0364	04.09.84
	OY-BRG Pure Aviation Support Services Ltd		
	Croft Farm, Defford		07.04.14E
	Stored 09.17 for spares use (NF 04.09.17)		
G-EDRE	Lindstrand LBL 90A	1081	17.03.06
	Edren Homes Ltd Melton Mowbray		
	'Edren Homes Limited'		31.08.19E
G-EDRV	Van's RV-6A	xxxx	20.08.99
	P R Sears Shenstone Hall Farm, Shenstone		17.06.18P
	Built by E A Yates – project PFA 181A-13451		
G-EDTO	Reims FR172F Rocket	FR17200090	21.03.01
	D-EDTQ N G Hopkinson Crowland		17.05.18E

G-EDVK	Roger Hardy RH7B Tiger Light	xxxx	10.03.11
	G-MZGT M Peters (Frome)		
	Built by J B McNab – project PFA 230-13013		
	(NF 12.02.15)		
G-EDVL	Piper PA-28R-200 Cherokee Arrow II	28R-7235245	30.06.97
	G-BXIN, D-EDVL, N1243T		
	Redhill Air Services Ltd Redhill		21.08.18E
G-EDYO	Piper PA-32-260 Cherokee Six	32-415	30.03.07
	D-EDYQ, (N3529W), N11C		
	McCarthy Aviation Ltd Morgansfield, Fishburn		06.03.19E
	Also operates from Shotton Colliery, Peterlee		
	when Morgansfield is waterlogged		
G-EDZZ	Comco Ikarus C42 FB100 Bravo	1210-7228	31.01.13
	Microavionics UK Ltd (Horsley, Derby)		15.04.18P
	Assembled Red-Air UK		
G-EEAA	Pietenpol Air Camper	0194	20.09.17
	P G Humphrey RAF Halton		
	Built by P G Humphrey – project LAA 047-15170		
	(NF 20.09.17)		
G-EEAD	Slingsby T65A Vega	1912	02.11.07
	BGA 2523/EAD		
	P Nayeri & A P P Scorer Rufforth *'EAD'*		20.04.18E
G-EEBA	Slingsby T65A Vega	1914	22.04.08
	BGA 2544/EBA		
	J A Cowie & K Robertson Portmoak *'EBA'*		02.08.18E
G-EEBF	Schempp-Hirth Mini Nimbus C	138	23.08.07
	BGA 2549 M Pingel Talgarth *'EBF'*		08.01.19E
G-EEBK	Schempp-Hirth Mini Nimbus C	139	09.10.07
	BGA 2553, AGA 2, BGA 2553		
	R A Foreshew Parham Park *'552'*		30.10.18E
G-EEBL	Schleicher ASK 13	13610	10.04.08
	BGA 2554/EBL		
	Lincolnshire Gliding Club Ltd Strubby *'EBL'*		23.05.19E
G-EEBN	Centrair ASW 20F	20118	09.07.08
	BGA 2556/EBN		
	R Carlisle & S Macarthur Camphill *'37'*		17.06.18E
G-EEBR	Glaser-Dirks DG-200/17	2-89/1706	04.01.08
	BGA 2559/EBR, D-6893 M A Fellis tr EBR Glider		
	Syndicate (Coleshill, Birmingham) *'EBR'*		04.08.19E
G-EEBS	Scheibe Zugvogel IIIA	1054	22.05.08
	BGA 2560/EBS, LX-CAF, D-8363		
	K Kavanagh tr G-EEBS Syndicate Llantysilio		
	'EBS' & *'Schwarzhornfalke'*		10.09.18E
G-EEBZ	Schleicher ASK 13	13614	13.12.07
	BGA 2567/EBZ		
	Bidford Gliding & Flying Club Ltd Bidford *'EBZ'*		17.04.19E
G-EECC	Aerospool Dynamic WT9 UK	DY189/2007	06.11.07
	C V Ellingworth Old Sarum		23.06.18P
	Assembled Yeoman Light Aircraft Co Ltd;		
	official c/n recorded as 'DY189'		
G-EECK	Slingsby T65A Vega	1917	23.10.07
	BGA 2577		
	D A Carus tr Vega G-EECK 2014 Portmoak *'ECK'*		24.10.18E
G-EECO	Lindstrand LBL 25A Cloudhopper	668	01.02.00
	A P Jay South Cerney, Cirencester		27.09.17E
G-EEDE	Centrair ASW 20F	20128	04.01.08
	BGA 2596/EDE G M Cumner Aston Down *'750'*		06.08.18E
G-EEEK	Extra EA.300/200	1034	31.05.06
	D-EXTT A R Willis Conington		26.04.19E
G-EEER	Schempp-Hirth Mini Nimbus C	150	30.08.07
	BGA 2631 D J Uren RNAS Culdrose *'EER'*		23.03.18E
G-EEEZ	American Champion 8KCAB Super Decathlon		
		1034-2007	28.02.07
	P J Webb Andrewsfield		24.06.18E
G-EEFA	Cameron Z-90	11076	18.12.07
	T Coudray Gencay, France		22.07.19E
G-EEFK	Centrair ASW 20FL	20140	07.11.07
	BGA 2649/EFK, F-WFLZ J Gale Snitterfield *'643'*		09.02.18E
G-EEFT	Schempp-Hirth Nimbus-2B	26	31.03.08
	BGA 2657, HB-1160 S A Adlard Long Mynd *'EFT'*		13.01.18E
G-EEGL	Christen Eagle II	AES/01/0353	14.12.90
	5Y-EGL S L Nicholson & M P Swoboda		
	Andrewsfield		30.03.18P
G-EEGU	Piper PA-28-161 Warrior II	28-7916457	07.05.02
	D-EEGU, N2831A		
	Tor Financial Consulting Ltd Norwich Int'l		08.08.18E
G-EEHA	Sonex Sonex	1608	07.02.17
	T J F de Salis (Wycombe Air Park)		
	Built by T J F de Salis – project LAA 337-15220		
	(NF 07.02.17)		
G-EEJE	Piper PA-31 Turbo Navajo B	31-825	18.05.01
	OH-PNG G Turnbull Crosland Moor		14.01.19E
G-EEKA	Glaser-Dirks DG-200/17	2-128/1730	04.10.07
	BGA 2736 D M Betts Tibenham *'EKA'*		10.07.18E
G-EEKI	Sportine Aviacija LAK-17B FES	239	19.04.16
	(BGA 5893) M G Lynes & S Pozerskis		
	Sandhill Farm, Shrivenham *'JL'*		17.05.19R
G-EEKK	Cessna 152	15285621	26.09.13
	EI-CRU, G-BNSW, N94213		
	A D R Northeast Wycombe Air Park		20.03.18E
G-EEKY	Piper PA-28-140 Cherokee B	28-25422	20.06.05
	OY-DFP, LN-BNX, (N8218N)		
	J L Sparks St Athan		14.11.19E
	Operated by Horizon Flight Training		
G-EEKZ	P&M Quik GTR	8684	28.03.14
	A P Douglas-Dixon Bagby		02.04.19P
G-EELS	Cessna 208B Grand Caravan	208B0619	03.03.97
	N5264M Glass Eels Ltd Gloucestershire		09.02.19E
G-EELT	Rolladen-Schneider LS4	4186	15.01.08
	BGA 2777/ELT		
	K J Wood tr ELT Syndicate Lasham *'ELT'*		11.02.19E
G-EELY	Schleicher Ka 6CR	6485/Si	06.12.07
	BGA 2782/ELY, D-5172		
	C Morros tr K6 ELY Syndicate Bellarena *'ELY'*		19.05.19E
	Official c/n '6536' is incorrect; BGA confirm c/n 6485/Si		
G-EENI	Europa Aviation Europa	199	28.07.98
	M P Grimshaw (East Bridgford, Nottingham)		
	Built by M P Grimshaw – project PFA 247-12831		
	(NF 30.10.14)		
G-EENK	Schleicher ASK 21	21106	18.10.07
	BGA 2817		
	Cotswold Gliding Club Aston Down *'ENK'*		18.07.18E
G-EENO	Cessna T210N Turbo Centurion II	21064162	16.03.16
	D-EENO, N5321Y F Renner Landshut, Germany		03.04.18E
G-EENT	Glasflügel 304	210	30.07.08
	BGA 2825/ENT M Hastings & P D Morrison		
	RAF Weston-on-the-Green *'902'*		15.06.18E
G-EENW	Schleicher ASW 20L	20567	26.11.07
	BGA 2828/ENW M Newburn Sutton Bank *'ENW'*		18.05.19E
G-EENZ	Schleicher ASW 19B	19366	26.03.08
	BGA 2831/ENZ C J & G J Walker Lasham *'RNT'*		30.06.18E
G-EEPJ	Pitts S-1S	xxxx	15.12.11
	G-REAP R J Porter Insch *'littleblue.com'*		30.03.18P
	Built by S D Howes – project PFA 009-11557		
G-EERV	Van's RV-6	60215	13.09.01
	G-NESI B F Hill Deenethorpe		01.08.19P
	Built by G Ness, P G Stewart & C B Stirling		
	– project PFA 181A-13381		
G-EERY	Robinson R22 Beta II	4128	27.03.07
	EBG (Helicopters) Ltd Redhill		29.06.18E
G-EESA	Europa Aviation Europa	025	09.04.96
	G-HIIL C Deith Fowle Hall Farm, Laddingford		11.09.18P
	Built by C B Stirling – project PFA 247-12535;		
	tailwheel u/c		
G-EEST	British Aerospace Jetstream Series 3102	781	16.08.00
	SE-LGM, OY-SVY, C-FASJ, G-31-781		
	Cancelled 05.11.07 as PWFU		23.10.03
	Evanton, Highlands		
	Abandoned after film work, in wooded area 08.17		
G-EESY	Rolladen-Schneider LS4	4334	19.10.07
	BGA 2926 S G D Gaze Rivar Hill *'ESY'*		20.03.18E
G-EETG	Cessna 172Q Cutlass II	17275928	30.06.05
	N913AT, N913ER, (N65939)		
	A Kiernan Newcastle, RoI		22.02.18E

G-EETH	Schleicher K 8B	120	18.04.12
	BGA 2935/ETH, D-5755		
	Bowland Forest Gliding Club Ltd Chipping		23.11.18E
	Built by Eichelsdörfer		
G-EEUP	SNCAN Stampe SV.4C	451	01.09.78
	F-BCXQ A M Wajih Redhill		13.12.17E
G-EEVL	Grob G102 Astir CS77	1638	29.04.08
	BGA 2986/EVL, PH-575		
	L F Escartin Santa Cilia, Spain *'SA1'*		09.03.18E
G-EEVY	Cessna 170A	19537	03.10.16
	D-EEVY, D-ELYC, N5503C		
	M Derrett tr Fly By Wire Flying Group Andrewsfield		
	(IE 03.10.16)		
G-EEWA	Beech F33A Bonanza	CE-1226	22.02.19
	D-EEWA, OE-KBE, N23EL		
	P Osborne (Lyneham, Chippenham)		
	(IE 22.02.19)		
G-EEWZ	Mainair Pegasus Quik	8101	16.03.05
	G K Smith Middle Stoke, Isle of Grain		13.09.19P
	Built by Mainair Sports Ltd		
G-EEYE	Mainair Blade 912	1313-0202-7-W1108	13.05.02
	B J Egerton Ince		19.06.13P
	(NF 01.12.16)		
G-EEZR	Robinson R44 Raven II	11391	24.08.06
	Geezer Aviation LLP (Cliddesden, Hants)		10.08.18E
	Lives on private helipad		
G-EEZS	Cessna 182P Skylane	18261338	08.11.99
	D-EEZS, N63054, D-EEZS, (N20981)		
	FHU TARM Marek Tarczykowski (Biale Blota, Poland)		07.06.18E
G-EEZZ	Zenair CH.601XL Zodiac	OC28027	04.08.05
	S Michaelson Kirknewton		12.10.18P
	Built by B Fraser – project PFA 162B-14392		
G-EFAM	Cessna 182S Skylane	18280442	07.06.05
	D-EFAM, N7269H R M Heath tr G-EFAM Flying Group		
	Liverpool John Lennon		26.04.18E
G-EFAO	Scintex CP.301-C Emeraude	540	07.10.14
	D-EFAQ T A S Rayner Archerfield		13.11.18P
	Built by Société Scintex		
G-EFBP	Reims/Cessna FR172K Hawk XP	FR17200664	07.01.04
	D-EFBP, PH-AXF E C Bellamy Sherburn-in-Elmet		29.06.18E
G-EFCG	Aeropro EuroFOX 912(S)	38912	23.10.12
	C A White Little Snoring		29.07.18P
	Built by C A White – project LAA 376-15161;		
	tailwheel u/c		
G-EFCM	Piper PA-28-180 Cherokee D	28-4766	16.11.07
	SE-FCM 2 Excel Aviation Ltd Lasham		09.05.19E
G-EFFH	Cessna T210L Turbo Centurion	21060616	16.04.15
	D-EFFH, N8128L R Paletar (Freinberg, Austria)		24.11.18E
G-EFIZ	Pitts S-2B	5224	01.07.14
	LZ-AIR, N799JB R S Goodwin & G V Paino Bidford		05.04.19E
	Built by Aviat Inc		
G-EFJD	MBB Bölkow BÖ.209 Monsun 160FV	126	22.10.08
	D-EFJD A H & F A Macaskill Over Farm, Gloucester		26.04.18E
G-EFLT	Glasflügel Standard Libelle 201B	41	02.06.08
	BGA 3352/FLT, D-0211		
	P A Tietema Husbands Bosworth *'FLT'*		04.04.18E
G-EFLY	Centrair ASW 20FL	20133	03.09.07
	BGA 2650 S A Whitaker Parham Park *'LY'*		15.11.18E
G-EFNH	Reims/Cessna FR182 Skylane RG II	FR18200058	28.10.14
	D-EFNH C J & V J Crawford		
	Cannes-Mandelieu, France		23.07.17E
G-EFOF	Robinson R22 Beta II	3605	19.05.04
	N73323		
	Helicopter & Pilot Services Ltd White Waltham		15.11.18E
G-EFON	Robinson R22 Beta II	3833	05.09.14
	G-SCHO Burton Aviation Ltd Costock Heliport		18.10.18E
G-EFOX	Aeropro EuroFOX 912(1)	33611	16.12.10
	C J Parsons Dunkeswell		09.04.18P
	Built by R M Cornwell – project BMAA/HB/604;		
	tailwheel u/c		
G-EFRP	Bowers Fly Baby 1A	xxxx	25.09.12
	G-BFRD R A Phillips Kinloss Barracks, Kinloss		20.07.18P
	Built by F R Donaldson & R A Phillips		
	– project PFA 016-10300		

G-EFSD	Aeropro EuroFOX 912(iS)	48015	22.01.16
	S E Dancaster Hawksview, Stretton		26.06.18P
	Built by S E Dancaster – project LAA 376-15359;		
	tricycle u/c		
G-EFSF	Reims/Cessna FR172K Hawk XP	FR17200658	10.01.13
	D-EFSF, PH-PWH, PH-AXT A Vaughan Eshott		
	(IE 22.09.15)		
G-EFSM	Slingsby T67M-260 Firefly	2072	16.07.92
	G-BPLK Anglo Europe Aviation Ltd		
	Retford Gamston		16.03.18E
G-EFTE	Bölkow BÖ.207	218	04.01.90
	D-EFTE R L Earl & B Morris White Waltham		30.05.18E
G-EFTF	Aérospatiale AS.350B Ecureuil	1847	01.04.03
	G-CWIZ, CS-HDF, G-DJEM, G-ZBAC, G-SEBI,		
	G-BMCU T J French t/a T French & Son		
	(Cronberry, Cumnock)		29.07.18E
G-EFUN	e-Go e-Go	SS001	02.07.08
	Giocas Ltd Main Hall Farm, Conington		
	(SSDR microlight since 05.14) (NF 17.10.17)		
G-EFVS	Wassmer WA.52 Europa	22	22.07.09
	D-EFVS W Stotton Felthorpe		24.04.18P
G-EGAG	SOCATA TB-20 Trinidad	1675	29.08.06
	D-EGAG D & E Booth Sherburn-in-Elmet		07.09.18E
G-EGAL	Christen Eagle II	0042-86	11.03.96
	SE-XMU D Williams Hill Farm, Nayland		15.02.19P
	Built by S Wrethagen		
G-EGBJ	Piper PA-28-161 Warrior II	28-8116061	10.08.15
	G-CPFM, G-BNNS, N8283C		
	Aviation Advice & Consulting Ltd Nottingham City		02.02.18E
G-EGBP	American Champion 7ECA Citabria Aurora		10.08.16
		1401-2008	
	SE-LJP, G-IRGJ Freedom Aviation Ltd Cotswold		22.03.19E
G-EGBS	Van's RV-9A	90933	13.04.05
	D M Johnstone tr Shobdon RV9A Group Shobdon		22.08.17P
	Built by D M Johnstone, A & C Price, M Rowland,		
	M Sweeny & J Turner – project PFA 320-14234		
G-EGCA	Rans S-6-ES Coyote II	0611.1945	07.10.14
	P A Linford Crosland Moor		30.03.18P
	Built by P Kobrin – project LAA 204-15193		
	(RAeS/Boeing Build-a-Plane project by Ernesford		
	Grange Community Academy); tricycle u/c		
G-EGEE	Cessna 310Q	310Q0040	14.11.83
	G-AZVY, SE-FKV, N7540Q		
	Cancelled 15.02.11 by CAA		22.03.08
	Hawarden Open store 08.15		
G-EGEG	Cessna 172R Skyhawk	17280894	04.07.00
	N7262H Echo Golf Flying Ltd Elstree		15.12.18E
G-EGEN	Piel CP.301A Emeraude	AB 402	28.01.16
	D-EGEN P Turner tr Croft Aviators Flying Group		
	Croft Farm, Croft-on-Tees		26.06.18P
	Built by H M Eszingen		
G-EGES	Lindstrand LBL Triangle	1446	06.02.13
	Lighter Than Air Ltd Chew Stoke, Bristol		
	'PaddyPower'		22.08.16E
	(NF 20.12.17)		
G-EGGI	Comco Ikarus C42 FB UK	0202-6453	18.04.02
	J S D Llewellyn Wolverhampton Halfpenny Green		11.05.18P
	Built by A G & G J Higgins – project PFA 322-13872		
G-EGGS	Robin DR.400-180 Régent	1443	15.11.79
	P C Naegeli tr G-EGGS Syndicate Lasham		15.07.18E
G-EGGZ	Best Off Skyranger Swift 912S(1)	SKR0704785	26.03.09
	J C Sheardown Sywell		16.04.18P
	Built by J C Sheardown – project BMAA/HB/544		
G-EGIA	Ultramagic M-65	65/177	31.03.10
	A Dizioli Torre di Santa Maria, Lombardy, Italy		06.06.15E
G-EGIB	Piper PA-28-181 Archer II	28-8190017	21.03.17
	D-EGIB, N8257E P A Venton Jersey		22.08.18E
G-EGIL	Christen Eagle II	BOYD-0001	07.11.07
	N21SB Smoke On Go Ltd RAF Cosford		17.10.17P
	Built by S F Boyd		
G-EGJA	SOCATA TB-20 Trinidad	1101	13.12.90
	N2807D Kraydon Services Ltd		
	Nicosia, Republic of Cyprus		28.12.17E

G-EGJJ	P&M Quik GTR	8695	12.08.14
	M D Bowen Jersey		14.08.18P
G-EGKB	British Aerospace BAe 125 Series 800B 258021		29.01.18
	G-IFTF, G-RCEJ, VR-CEJ, G-GEIL, G-5-15		
	Mountfitchet Aircraft Ltd Biggin Hill		27.06.19E
G-EGLA	Cessna 172M Skyhawk	17263391	23.02.17
	G-CGFJ, N5174R Cornwall Flying Club Ltd Bodmin		
	(NF 23.02.17)		
G-EGLE	Christen Eagle II	F0053	30.03.81
	D Thorpe Fowle Hall Farm, Laddingford		14.08.18P
	Built by Airmore Aviation		
G-EGLG	Piper PA-31 Turbo Navajo C	31-7812103	08.09.06
	N45TY, 4X-CCY, N36SG, N27703, G-OATC, G-OJPW,		
	G-BGCC, N27703 Cancelled 20.06.16 as PWFU		15.09.15
	Sywell *Stored for spares use 09.16*		
G-EGLK	Czech Sport PS-28 Cruiser	C0511	22.05.14
	D J & L Medcraft & Yonder Plains Ltd Blackbushe		02.06.18R
G-EGLL	Piper PA-28-161 Warrior II	28-7816257	17.03.06
	G-BLEJ, N2194M Airways Aero Associations Ltd		
	Wycombe Air Park		26.06.18E
	British Airways Flying Club; Union Flag c/s		
G-EGLS	Piper PA-28-181 Archer III	2843348	05.06.00
	N4187C M Wallace Hardwick		05.09.18E
G-EGLT	Cessna 310R II	310R1874	09.09.93
	G-BHTV, N1EU, (N3206M)		
	RVL Aviation Ltd East Midlands		11.05.18E
G-EGPG	Piper PA-18-135 Super Cub	18-3569	03.04.06
	N719CS, G-BWUC, SX-ASM, I-EIYB:EI-181,		
	Italian Army MM54-2369, 54-2369		
	G Cormack Easter Poldar Farm, Thornhill		27.03.18E
G-EGRV	Van's RV-8	81335	15.05.12
	G-PHMG B M Gwynnett Swansea		20.01.20P
	Built by M Gibson & P R Hall – project PFA 303-13639;		
	operated by 'Raven Display Team' – 'No. 3'		
G-EGSJ	Avtech Jabiru J400	389	29.08.07
	G-MGRK C N & K J Stephen Kirknewton		10.05.18P
	Built by H Aines & Partners – project PFA 325-14618		
G-EGSL	Reims/Cessna F152	F15201446	20.08.14
	OE-CMR Andrewsfield Aviation Ltd &		
	Corvalis Aircraft Leasing Ltd Andrewsfield		09.08.19E
G-EGSR	Van's RV-7A	73928	19.08.13
	C A Acland & P S Gilmour Dunkeswell		01.12.18P
	Built by G P Howes, L J Merritt & V Millard		
	– project LAA 323-15093		
G-EGSS	Raytheon Hawker 800XP	258456	11.07.16
	M-MIDO, G-JMAX, N41762, N800EM		
	Interflight (Air Charter) Ltd Biggin Hill		23.10.18E
G-EGTB	Piper PA-28-161 Warrior II	28-7816074	21.01.04
	G-BPWA, N47450 Tayside Aviation Ltd Dundee		19.06.18E
G-EGTF	Evektor EV-97 Eurostar SL	2015-4228	05.01.16
	London Transport Flying Club Ltd Fairoaks		22.12.18P
	Assembled Light Sport Aviation Ltd		
G-EGUR	Jodel D.140B Mousquetaire II	52	09.01.04
	D-EGUR S H Williams Oxenhope		20.10.14E
	Built by Société Aéronautique Normande (IE 02.06.17)		
G-EGVA	Piper PA-28R-200 Cherokee Arrow II 28R-7635229		20.12.12
	D-EGVA, N9255K		
	Social Infrastructure Ltd Wellesbourne Mountford		18.12.18E
G-EGVO	Dassault Falcon 900EX	151	15.12.09
	VP-BSP, F-WWFJ Concierge U Ltd (London W1)		16.12.19E
G-EGWN	American Champion 7ECA Citabria Aurora		
		1399-2007	04.12.07
	Freedom Aviation Ltd Oaksey Park		23.03.19E
G-EHAA	McDonnell Douglas MD Explorer	900-00079	07.05.10
	G-GNAA, PH-RVD, N70279		
	Specialist Aviation Services Ltd Gloucestershire		04.10.18E
G-EHAV	Glasflügel Standard Libelle 201B	40	12.11.07
	BGA 3796/HAV, HB-950 G H W Keates		
	tr G-EHAV Syndicate Challock *'334'*		23.02.19E
G-EHAZ	Piper PA-28-161 Warrior III	2842168	17.07.13
	G-CEEY, N53583 Freedom Aviation Ltd Cotswold		25.07.16E
	Overshot landing Breighton 01.04.16 causing		
	extensive damage		

G-EHBJ	CASA 1-131E Jungmann Series 2000 2150		19.07.90
	Spanish AF E3B-550 E P Howard Hardwick		16.07.18P
G-EHCB	Schempp-Hirth Nimbus-3DT	47	28.02.07
	BGA 3827		
	H A Torode tr G-EHCB Group Lasham *'HCB'*		11.05.18E
G-EHCC	PZL-Bielsko SZD-50-3 Puchacz	B-2048	27.03.08
	BGA 3829/HCC D J Marpole tr Heron Gliding Club		
	RNAS Yeovilton *'CC'*		24.07.18E
G-EHCZ	Schleicher K 8B	8114	20.02.08
	BGA 3850/HCZ, D-4675		
	The Windrushers Gliding Club Ltd Ringmer *'HCZ'*		19.09.09E
	(NF 30.11.16)		
G-EHDS	CASA 1-131E Jungmann Series 2000 2108/512		21.02.05
	G-DUDS, D-EHDS, Spanish AF E3B-512		
	I C Underwood (Thornton-Cleveleys)		
	(NF 20.07.18)		
G-EHEH	Lindstrand LTL Series 1-90	001	26.05.16
	A M Holly Breadstone, Berkeley *'English Heritage'*		31.05.18E
	(IE 05.10.18)		
G-EHEM	McDonnell Douglas MD Explorer	900-00134	23.06.17
	G-LNCT, N40483, (D-H), N40483		
	Specialist Aviation Services Ltd Boreham		25.09.18E
	Operated by Essex & Herts Air Ambulance		
	as callsign 'Helimed 07'		
G-EHGF	Piper PA-28-181 Archer II	28-7790188	23.10.00
	D-EHGF, N9534N G P Robinson Retford Gamston		16.08.18E
G-EHIC	Jodel D.140B Mousquetaire II	53	20.10.04
	D-EHIC G C Roy tr G-EHIC Group White Waltham		26.11.18P
	Built by Société Aéronautique Normande		
G-EHILᴹ	EH Industries EH-101	50003	09.07.87
	ZH647 Cancelled 28.04.99 as PWFU – to MoD		
	as ZH647 09.93 & restored 08.98		09.07.87
	Airframe No.PP3		
	With The Helicopter Museum, Weston-super-Mare		
G-EHLT	de Havilland DH.82A Tiger Moth	84997	23.01.19
	G-BHLT, ZS-DGA, 2272 SAAF, T6697		
	R C P Brookhouse Old Buckenham		
	Built by Morris Motors Ltd (IE 23.01.19)		
G-EHLX	Piper PA-28-181 Archer II	28-8090317	05.11.99
	D-EHLX, N8218S ASG Leasing Ltd Guernsey		20.10.18E
G-EHMF	Isaacs Fury II	xxxx	08.10.03
	G Haye Strathaven		01.05.19P
	Built by M A Farrelly – project PFA 011-14109		
G-EHMJ	Beech S35 Bonanza	D-7879	12.01.99
	D-EHMJ A J Daley Retford Gamston		11.04.18E
G-EHMM	Robin DR.400-180R Remorqueur	867	10.12.84
	D-EHMM London Gliding Club Proprietary Ltd		
	Dunstable Downs		24.07.19E
G-EHMS	McDonnell Douglas MD Explorer	900-00068	12.07.00
	N3212K London's Air Ambulance RAF Northolt		15.12.18E
	Operated by London Air Ambulance as callsign		
	'Helimed 27'		
G-EHRU	Cessna 175 Skylark	55620	18.01.16
	D-EHRU, N7320M Die Netzschmiede GmbH		
	Mönchengladbach, Germany		
	(IE 18.01.16)		
G-EHTT	Schleicher ASW 20CL	20627	22.04.08
	BGA 4196/HTT		
	M Corcoran tr HTT Syndicate Camphill *'HTT'*		10.03.18E
G-EHXP	Rockwell Commander 112A	227	27.01.00
	D-EHXP, N1227J A L Stewart Durham Tees Valley		27.07.18E
G-EHZT	Moravan Zlin Z-526F Trener	1317	22.03.16
	SP-EHA E P Howard Hardwick		25.04.19E
G-EIAP	Jodel DR.1050 Ambassadeur	356	08.05.14
	D-EIAP P M Irvine Mullaghglass		21.05.18P
	Built by Société Aéronautique Normande		
G-EICK	Cessna 172S Skyhawk SP	172S10426	13.07.07
	N12173 Centenary Flying Group Ltd Cork, Rol		17.10.18E
G-EIIR	Cameron N-77 HAB	358	16.11.77
	Cancelled 23.10.01 by CAA		14.05.93
	Not Known *'Silver Jubilee' Inflated Ashton Court 08.18*		

G-EIKY	Europa Aviation Europa	054		27.09.94
	J D Milbank tr Europa G-EIKY Group Longside			11.04.18P
	Built by J D Milbank – project PFA 247-12634;			
	tailwheel u/c			
G-EINI	Europa Aviation Europa XS	452		08.07.11
	G-KDCC K J Burns Husbands Bosworth			05.04.17P
	Built by K A C Dodd – project PFA 247-13562;			
	tricycle u/c			
G-EISG	Raytheon Beech A36 Bonanza	E-3212		02.04.07
	N2533J, (G-EISG), N326R			
	B & R J Howard Sherburn-in-Elmet			05.05.18E
G-EISO^M	SOCATA MS.892A Rallye Commodore 150			
		10563		23.01.01
	D-EISO, F-BNSO Cancelled as PWFU 04.03.17			
	With Sammy Miller Motorcycle Museum, New Milton			
G-EITE	Luscombe 8F Silvaire	3407		27.07.88
	N71980 C P Davey RAF Henlow			24.04.19P
G-EIWT	Reims/Cessna FR182 Skylane RG II	FR18200052		28.01.86
	D-EIWT, OO-BLI Avitrata Sociedad de Tratamentos			
	Fitossanitarios Aeros Lda (Benavente, Portugal)			07.05.19E
G-EIZO	Eurocopter EC120B Colibri	1120		31.12.04
	N20GH, D-HSUN Blok (UK) Ltd (Crewe)			23.04.18E
G-EJAC	Mudry CAP 232	20		09.05.11
	G-OGBR, N232MG G C J Cooper, P Varinot			
	& E Vazeille Meaux-Esbly, France			14.02.18E
	Built by CAP Aviation			
G-EJAE	Glaser-Dirks DG-200	2-62		07.02.08
	BGA 4352/JAE, HB-1443			
	D L P H Waller (Curry Rivel, Langport) *'N8'*			20.07.09E
	(NF 18.04.16)			
G-EJAS	Skystar Kitfox Model 7	S 70307034		16.05.14
	D A Holl (Horsham)			
	(D A Holl – project PFA 172D-14121 (NF 14.06.18)			
G-EJBI	Bölkow BÖ.207	242		09.03.04
	D-EJBI, G-EJBI, D-EJBI A A R Moore Tibenham			21.11.18E
G-EJEL	Cessna 550 Citation II	550-0643		19.12.01
	N747CR, N643MC, PT-ODW, N13091, (N1259S)			
	Futura Finances (Cassis, Bouches-du-Rhône, France)			08.01.19E
G-EJGO	Moravan Zlin Z-226T Trener Spezial	199		07.08.85
	D-EJGO, OK-MHB C M & S K T Neofytou Breighton			09.05.18E
G-EJHH	Schempp-Hirth Standard Cirrus	349G		06.07.11
	BGA 4523/JHH, D-3006			
	L T Merry-Taylor Lasham *'JHH'*			04.12.18E
G-EJIM	Schempp-Hirth Discus-2cT	98		24.11.10
	N A L Stuart (Twickenham) *'T18'*			13.03.19E
G-EJOC	Aérospatiale AS.350B Ecureuil	1465		21.12.94
	G-GEDS, G-HMAN, G-SKIM, G-BIVP			
	CK's Supermarket Ltd Swansea			15.05.18E
G-EJRS	Piper PA-28-161 Cadet	2841115		05.05.04
	D-EJRS, N9175X			
	Carlisle Flight Training Ltd Carlisle Lake District			07.05.18E
G-EJTC	Robinson R44 Clipper II	10623		31.01.05
	N Parkhouse Chelworth House, Chelwood Gate			02.04.18E
G-EJWI	Flight Design CTLS	F.09-07-11		04.01.10
	D D J Rossdale Wickenby			05.04.18W
G-EKEY	Schleicher ASW 20CL	20840		11.01.08
	BGA 5044/KEY, D-3171			
	A P Nisbet Parham Park *'KEY'*			30.05.18E
G-EKIM	Alpi Pioneer 300	175		11.05.06
	R J Raven (Beccles)			14.06.19P
	Built by M Elliott & M Langmead			
	– project PFA 330-14491			
G-EKIR	Piper PA-28-161 Cadet	2841157		17.06.02
	SE-KIR, (SE-KII) Aeros Global Ltd Coventry			30.08.19E
G-EKKL	Piper PA-28-161 Warrior II	28-8416087		24.03.99
	D-EKKL, N43588 Perryair Ltd Brighton City			20.08.18E
G-EKOS	Reims/Cessna FR182 Skylane RG II	FR18200017		15.07.98
	D-EKOS S Charlton Sherburn-in-Elmet			05.03.18E
G-ELAK	Sportine Aviacija LAK-17B FES	249		15.10.18
	LY-GRD G N Fraser & G A Marshall Portmoak			
G-ELAM	Piper PA-30 Twin Comanche B	30-1477		14.10.04
	N26PJ, G-BAWU, (G-BAWV), 9J-RFW, ZS-FAM,			
	N8332Y Hangar 39 Ltd North Weald			02.02.19E
G-ELCH	Commander Aircraft Commander 114B	14566		03.01.19
	D-ELCH L Ormsby (Lindford, Bordon)			04.02.19E
	(IE 03.01.19)			
G-ELDR	Piper PA-32-260 Cherokee Six	32-7400027		21.01.03
	SE-GBK C F Early (Kettering)			17.07.19E
G-ELEC^M	Westland WG.30 Series 200	007		17.06.83
	G-BKNV Cancelled 27.02.98 as WFU			28.06.95
	With The Helicopter Museum, Weston-super-Mare			
G-ELEE	Cameron Z-105	4882		11.07.00
	M A Stelling South Queensferry			26.05.18E
G-ELEN	Robin DR.400-180 Régent	2363		16.09.97
	M Derrett tr Foster ELEN Group Andrewsfield			11.04.18E
G-ELIS	Piper PA-34-200T Seneca II	34-8070265		11.09.03
	G-BOPV, N82323			
	A Gougas (Grand-Lancy, Geneva, Switzerland)			25.09.17E
G-ELKA	Christen Eagle II	0001		18.10.94
	N121DJ, N1DJ, N99DJ J T Matthews Little Snoring			06.04.18P
	Built by R R James c/n JAMES-0001			
G-ELKE	Cirrus SR20	1043		02.12.14
	N147CD S Auer Gloucestershire			07.08.18E
G-ELKI	Diamond DA.40NG Star	40.N175		22.11.17
	HZ-SAE Euro Aircraft Leasing Ltd Dunkeswell			12.12.18E
G-ELKO	Diamond DA.42NG Twin Star	42.N033		08.11.17
	HZ-SA18			
	Euro Aircraft Leasing Ltd Perpignan-Rivesaltes, France			
G-ELLA	Piper PA-32R-301 Saratoga II HP	3246050		13.08.96
	N9279Q, G-ELLA A I Freeman White Waltham			26.09.18E
G-ELLE	Cameron N-90	4498		11.01.99
	D J Stagg Spixworth, Norwich *'L.E. Electrical'*			15.06.07A
	(NF 03.11.15)			
G-ELLI	Bell 206B-3 JetRanger III	4231		24.06.97
	D-HMOF A Chatham (Yardley Gobion, Towcester)			23.04.18E
G-ELMH	North American AT-6D Harvard III	88-16336		22.07.92
	Portuguese AF 1662, EZ341, 42-84555			
	M Hammond Airfield Farm, Hardwick *'Fools Rush-In'*			
	As '42-84555:EP-H' in USAAC c/s (IE 10.08.15)			
G-ELRT	Sopwith Scout	-		19.05.15
	N6161 T A Bechtolsheimer Turweston			24.05.18P
	As 'N6161' in RNAS c/s			
G-ELSB	Robin DR.400-180R Remorqueur	1145		15.09.16
	D-ELSB Cambridge Gliding Club Ltd			
	Gransden Lodge			10.01.19E
G-ELSE	Diamond DA.42 Twin Star	42.114		29.06.06
	OE-VPY R Swann Solent			19.06.18E
G-ELSI	Air Création Tanarg 912S(1)/iXess 15	FLT001		19.01.06
	S J Tennant (Polesworth, Tamworth)			
	Built by D Daniel – project BMAA/HB/466			
	(Flylight kit FLT001 comprising trike s/n			
	T05069 & wing s/n A05146-5134			
	(SSDR microlight since 06.18) (IE 08.07.18)			
G-ELUE	Piper PA-28-161 Warrior II	28-7916484		10.02.10
	D-ELUE, N2856Y Freedom Aviation Ltd Cotswold			05.04.19E
G-ELUN	Robin DR.400-180R Remorqueur	1102		29.05.02
	D-ELUN, I-ALSA P Harper-Little & I A Lane			
	tr Cotswold DR400 Syndicate Cotswold			30.04.18E
	Badged as 'Remo 80'			
G-ELUT	Piper PA-28R-200 Cherokee Arrow II	28R-7435009		21.11.03
	D-ELUT, N56514			
	Green Arrow Europe Ltd Goodwood			05.03.18E
G-ELVN	Van's RV-7A	73573		21.03.13
	M Rothwell (Little Gaddesden, Berkhamsted)			25.05.19P
	Built by G P Elvin – project LAA 323-14930			
G-ELWK	Van's RV-12	120084		07.11.11
	J Devlin (Elwick, Hartlepool)			
	Built by J Devlin – project LAA 363-14924 (NF 29.09.15)			
G-ELXE	Cessna 182T Skylane	18281909		28.07.15
	D-ELXE, N1181Z O Petrov Redhill			14.11.18E
G-ELYS	Reims/Cessna FA150K Aerobat	FA1500078		25.04.13
	G-BIBN, F-BSHN			
	E A Trevor t/a Skyworthy Hire (Ramsgate)			12.06.18E
G-ELZN	Piper PA-28-161 Warrior II	28-8416078		20.07.99
	D-ELZN, N9579N			
	K Jordan tr ZN Flying Group Old Buckenham			01.11.18E

G-ELZY	Piper PA-28-161 Warrior II	28-8616027	13.04.99
	D-ELZY, N9095Z, (N163AV), N9641N		
	Redhill Air Services Ltd Fairoaks		01.09.18E
G-EMAA	Eurocopter EC135 T2	0448	17.01.06
	Babcock Mission Critical Services Onshore Ltd		
	Tatenhill		26.03.18E
	Operated by Midlands Air Ambulance as callsign		
	'Helimed 09'		
G-EMAC	Robinson R22 Beta II	3234	14.10.11
	EI-CWR, G-CBDB P M Phillips (Nuneaton)		19.09.18E
G-EMAT	Diamond DA.62	62.082	28.06.18
	Galaxy Flair Ltd (Tortola, British Virgin Islands)		03.07.19E
G-EMCA	Commander Aircraft Commander 114B	14661	23.07.04
	D-EMCA S Roberts Oaksey Park		10.11.18E
G-EMCM	Eurocopter EC120B Colibri	1160	20.11.00
	Cancelled 06.09.04 as destroyed		28.02.04
	Emmer Compascuum, Netherlands		
	Dismantled with Heli Holland 10.16		
G-EMDM	Diamond DA.40 Star	40.009	07.10.02
	OE-KPO, OE-VPO D J Munson Brighton City		10.02.18E
G-EMEA	Airbus EC175 B (*H175*)	5024	27.07.17
	F-WJXE CHC Scotia Ltd Aberdeen Int'l		27.07.18E
G-EMEB	Airbus EC175 B (*H175*)	5030	14.12.17
	CHC Scotia Ltd Aberdeen Int'l		13.12.18E
G-EMEC	Airbus EC175 B	5031	06.04.18
	CHC Scotia Ltd Aberdeen Int'l		05.04.19E
G-EMED	Airbus EC175 B	5039	31.01.19
	CHC Scotia Ltd Aberdeen Int'l		
	(IE 31.01.19)		
G-EMHE	Agusta A109S Grand	22182	18.09.15
	VH-LBJ, VH-TNX Looporder Ltd		
	t/a East Midlands Helicopters Costock Heliport		14.10.18E
G-EMHK	MBB Bölkow BÖ.209 Monsun 150FV	101	23.02.06
	G-BLRD, D-EBOA, (OE-AHM), D-EBOA		
	C Elder Oaksey Park		22.06.18E
G-EMHN	Agusta A109S Grand	22154	09.03.17
	PP-PRI, VH-OCD		
	Burton Aviation Ltd Costock Heliport		11.04.18E
G-EMID	Eurocopter EC135 P2+	0524	20.12.06
	Police & Crime Commissioner for West Yorkshire		
	Redhill		29.07.18E
G-EMIN	Europa Aviation Europa	083	01.03.94
	S A Lamb Rochester		21.09.17P
	Built by G M Clarke & E W Gladstone – project		
	PFA 247-12673; tailwheel u/c (IE 30.09.17)		
G-EMJA	CASA 1-131E Series 2000 replica	xxxx	02.09.94
	(Spanish AF) D T Kaberry (Manchester)		13.05.19P
	Built by P J Brand – project PFA 242-12340;		
	composite ex spares		
G-EMKT	Cameron Z-105	11862	05.12.14
	Webster Adventures Ltd Kinross 'webster'		22.05.18E
G-EMLE	Evektor EV-97 Eurostar	2004-1279	09.06.04
	A R White Scotland Farm, Hook		02.08.18P
	Built by A R White – project PFA 315-14251		
G-EMLS	Cessna T210L Turbo Centurion	21060094	11.05.07
	D-EMLS, (G-BCJJ), N59107		
	I K F Simcock Denham		12.08.18E
G-EMLY	Cyclone Pegasus Quantum 15-912	7531	30.06.99
	S J Reid (Chidham, Chichester)		15.08.18P
	Rebuilt 2010 with replacement wing, believed c/n 8545		
G-EMMM	Diamond DA.40 Star	40.753	12.04.07
	A J Leigh Retford Gamston		04.06.18E
G-EMMX	P&M Quik GT450	8721	08.06.15
	Airmasters (UK) Ltd Sulby, Sibbertoft		04.06.18P
G-EMMY	Rutan VariEze	xxxx	21.08.78
	M J Tooze Biggin Hill		15.06.18P
	Built by M J Tooze – project PFA 074-10222		
G-EMOL	Schweizer 269C-1 (*300CBi*)	0300	20.07.11
	N17596 Bliss Aviation Ltd Bournemouth		18.09.18E
G-EMPP	Diamond DA.42M Twin Star	42.M011	09.11.15
	G-DSPY, OE-FVA, OE-VDP		
	DEA Aviation Ltd Retford Gamston		25.07.19R

G-EMSA	Czech Sport Sportcruiser	09SC323	11.05.10
	A C & M A Naylor Audley End		02.08.18W
G-EMSI	Europa Aviation Europa	191	24.01.95
	P W L Thomas (Askham Bryan, York)		
	Built by P W L Thomas – project		
	PFA 247-12817; tricycle u/c (NF 29.01.16)		
G-EMSS	Airbus MBB BK117 D-2 (*H145 T2*)	20217	12.09.18
	Babcock Mission Critical Services Onshore Ltd		
	Gloucestershire		11.09.19E
G-EMSY	de Havilland DH.82A Tiger Moth	83666	27.06.91
	G-ASPZ, D-EDUM, T7356		
	M Rogan tr The GEMSY Group Old Sarum		18.05.19P
	Built by Morris Motors Ltd; rebuilt with parts		
	ex OO-MOT		
G-ENAA	Super Marine Spitfire Mk.26B	SA073	13.06.13
	P Fowler tr G-ENAA Syndicate Enstone		20.08.18P
	Built by G-ENAA Syndicate – project LAA 324-15097;		
	as 'EN130:FN-A' in RAF c/s		
G-ENBW	Robin DR.400-180R Remorqueur	1715	15.02.10
	D-ENBW P S Carder & B Elliott Lasham		02.04.18E
G-ENCE	Partenavia P68B	141	01.06.84
	G-OROY, G-BFSU Exeter Flights Ltd Exeter Int'l		24.10.18E
G-ENEA	Cessna 182P Skylane	18260895	13.10.10
	D-ENEA, N9355G Air Ads Ltd Blackpool		15.06.18E
G-ENEE	CFM Streak Shadow	K 280	14.08.00
	A L & S Roberts Old Park Farm, Margam		06.06.18P
	Built by T Green – project PFA 206-13628		
G-ENGO	Steen Skybolt	xxxx	15.11.00
	R G Fulton Brimpton		27.03.18P
	Built by C Docherty & R G Fulton		
	– project PFA 064-13429		
G-ENGR	Head Ax8-105	380	04.08.08
	S Dyer Farnborough GU14 'Sapper'		09.11.19E
G-ENHP	Enstrom 480B	5084	17.08.05
	H J Pelham Cleeves Farm, Chilmark		26.05.18E
G-ENIA	Staaken Z-21 Flitzer	Z200	20.10.08
	A F Wankowski (Combs, Stowmarket)		
	Built by A F Wankowski – project PFA 223-14447;		
	on construction 12.16 (NF 01.10.15)		
G-ENID	Reality Escapade ULP(1)	AW.ESC.002	27.07.11
	Q Irving Broomclose Farm, Longbridge Deverill		07.08.18P
	Built by Q Irving – project BMAA/HB/610;		
	kit & frame built by AirWeld		
G-ENIE	Tipsy Nipper T.66 Series 3	xxxx	17.03.78
	M J Freeman Pound Green		21.08.19P
	Built by A J Waller – project PFA 025-10214		
G-ENIO	Pitts S-2C	6083	22.12.08
	N31PS Advanced Flying (London) Ltd		
	Wycombe Air Park 'Scarlett O'Hara'		30.10.15E
	Built by Aviat Aircraft Inc		
G-ENKY	Best Off Skyranger Swift 912S(2)	xxxx	26.02.19
	P A Jenkins (Blackrod, Bolton)		
	Built by P A Jenkins – project BMAA/HB/716		
	(NF 26.02.19)		
G-ENNA	Piper PA-28-161 Warrior II	28-7916060	01.05.90
	G-ESFT, G-ENNA, N22065		
	Falcon Flying Services Ltd Biggin Hill		11.05.18E
G-ENOA	Cessna F172F	F172-0138	02.09.81
	G-ASZW M K Acors Kings Farm, Thurrock		09.03.18E
	Built by Reims Aviation SA		
G-ENRE	Avtech Jabiru UL-450	0495	28.06.01
	P R Turton Newton Peveril Farm, Sturminster Marshall		02.12.18P
	Built by J C Harris – project PFA 274A-13755		
G-ENRI	Lindstrand LBL 105A	294	04.08.95
	P G Hall Chadurie, France		
	'Henry Numatic Vacuum Cleaners'		05.08.04
	(NF 23.04.15)		
G-ENST	CZAW Sportcruiser	700553	28.01.08
	L M Radcliffe tr Enstone Flyers Enstone		03.07.18P
	Built by D G Price, L M Radcliffe & C Slater		
	– project LAA 338-14769		
G-ENSX	Robinson R44 Clipper II	12281	15.07.16
	G-CLII, OY-HLE		
	M Duggan t/a Ensix (Knockloughrim, Magherafelt)		28.02.20E
	Official type 'R44 Raven II' is incorrect		

G-ENTT	Reims/Cessna F152 II	F15201750	09.11.93
	G-BHHI, (PH-CBA) A R & C Hyett Blackbushe		22.02.18E
G-ENTW	Reims/Cessna F152 II	F15201479	21.01.93
	G-BFLK London School of Flying Ltd Elstree		04.05.13E
	Noted 10.18 (IE 15.08.17)		
G-ENUS	Cameron N-90 HAB	1914	18.01.89
	Cancelled 28.08.02 by CAA		09.06.00
	Not Known Inflated Pidley 05.16		
G-ENVO	MBB Bölkow BÖ.105CBS-4	S.593	29.02.08
	SX-HCK, D-HDQP, Swedish AF 09073, D-HDQP		
	F C Owen Hapton Valley Colliery, Burnley		14.08.19E
G-ENZO	Cameron Z-105	10914	21.09.06
	Garelli VI SpA Mondovi, Italy *'Iveco Garelli V.I'*		29.06.18E
G-EOFW	Cyclone Pegasus Quantum 15-912	7582	15.10.99
	C D Livingstone tr G-EOFW Microlight Group Enstone		18.04.18P
G-EOGE	Gefa-Flug AS105GD HA Airship	0023	14.04.11
	George Brazil 2015 Ltd Langford, Bristol		22.11.17E
G-EOHL	Cessna 182L Skylane	18259279	04.03.99
	D-EOHL, N70505		
	Branton Knight Ltd Retford Gamston		23.07.18E
G-EOID	Aeroprakt A-22L Foxbat	280	03.11.08
	J Pearce (Lymington)		23.08.18P
	Built by M D Northwood – project LAA 317A-14836		
G-EOIN	Zenair CH.701UL	7-9017	19.11.99
	T Barnby tr G-EOIN Flying Group Eshott		05.06.18P
	Built by I M Donnelly – project PFA 187-13490;		
	left runway & struck fence Lamb Holm, Orkney		
	09.05.18; on rebuild Eshott 09.18		
G-EOJB	Robinson R44 Raven II	10480	24.09.09
	G-EDES Difuria Contractors Ltd		
	Paddock Farm, Beckingham		02.03.18E
G-EOLD	Piper PA-28-161 Warrior II	28-8516030	31.03.00
	D-EOLD, N4390F, N9531N		
	Phoenix Aviation Ltd (Bilston)		28.06.19E
G-EOLE	Cameron O-84	12098	19.05.17
	McCornick, Van Haarne & Co Brussels, Belgium		18.05.18E
G-EOMI	Robin HR.200-120B	273	09.09.13
	D-EQMI LAC Aircraft Ltd Lydd		13.04.18E
G-EOPH	Cameron C-90	11280	17.04.09
	A J Cherrett Broadstone		04.07.11E
	(IE 18.11.16)		
G-EORG	Piper PA-38-112 Tomahawk	38-78A0427	18.09.78
	N9734N G W & T W Gilbert Enstone		30.09.12E
	In external storage 09.15 (NF 18.09.14)		
G-EORJ	Europa Aviation Europa	347	23.07.99
	P E George Shenstone Hall Farm, Shenstone		29.11.18P
	Built by P E George – project PFA 247-13139;		
	tailwheel u/c		
G-EPAR	Robinson R22 Beta II	2781	26.02.98
	JW Ramsbottom Contractors Ltd t/a Jepar Rotorcraft		
	Culter Helipad, Peterculter		30.10.18E
G-EPDIᴹ	Cameron N-77 HAB	370	25.01.78
	Cancelled 06.01.15 PWFU *Inflated 05.16 at Pidley*		29.06.91
	With British Balloon Museum & Library, Newbury		
G-EPIC	Avtech Jabiru UL-450	589	04.11.03
	T H Chadwick (Market Weighton, York)		
	Built by T H Chadwick – project PFA 274A-14125		
	(NF 19.04.16)		
G-EPIM	Cessna R172K Hawk XP	R172-2376	02.11.07
	PH-PIM, G-EPIM, PH-PIM, N736AQ		
	A H Creaser (Heckington, Sleaford)		
G-EPOC	Avtech Jabiru UL-450	290	09.06.04
	S Cope (Laceby, Grimsby)		
	Built by S Cope – project PFA 274A-13531		
	(NF 16.02.16)		
G-EPOX	Aero Designs Pulsar XP	xxxx	27.04.94
	Cancelled 06.02.13 by CAA		01.09.11
	Trowbridge *Built by K F Farey & W A Stewart*		
	– project PFA 202-12355; stored 02.16 at private address		
G-EPSN	Ultramagic M-105	105/159	07.01.08
	G Everett Sandway, Maidstone *'Epson'*		30.01.10E
	(IE 06.06.18)		

G-EPTR	Piper PA-28R-200 Cherokee Arrow II	28R-7235090	26.05.98
	D-EPTR, OH-PTR, (SE-KVF), N4558T		
	ACS Aviation Ltd Perth		26.07.18E
G-EPYW	Piper PA-28-181 Archer II	28-7790557	02.06.14
	OH-PYW, N81AB LAC Aircraft Ltd Lydd *'Suomi'*		26.03.18E
	Operated by Lydd Aero Club		
G-ERAS	Cameron O-31	11980	23.05.16
	A A Laing Banchory		26.05.18E
G-ERBA	Leonardo AW189	89011	12.03.19
	I-EASN CHC Scotia Ltd Aberdeen International		12.03.20E
G-ERBE	Cessna P210N Pressurized Centurion	P21000769	11.05.16
	D-ERBE, N6408W J Luschnig (Vienna, Austria)		12.11.18E
G-ERCO	Erco 415D Ercoupe	3210	07.04.93
	N2585H, NC2585H		
	E G Girardey New Barn Farm, Crawley		24.03.15E
	Built by Engineering & Research Corporation;		
	stored 10.16 (NF 03.12.14)		
G-ERDA	Staaken Z-21A Flitzer	065	15.01.03
	J Cresswell Batchley Farm, Hordle		31.08.17P
	Built by J Cresswell – project PFA 223-13947		
G-ERDS	de Havilland DH.82A Tiger Moth	85028	27.07.94
	ZS-BCU, SAAF 2267, T6741 W A Gerdes Enstone		14.08.18E
G-ERDW	Enstrom F-28F Falcon	784	11.11.13
	PH-UGW, D-HEVA, D-HVHM, (JA7858)		
	G Wolfshohl Leer-Papenburg, Germany		23.07.18E
G-ERFC	Royal Aircraft Factory SE.5A replica	MF-01	29.04.14
	F-AZBF R A Palmer Old Warden *'Maybe?'*		
	Initially built W Sneesby & J Tetley as project		
	PFA 197-11500: completed Memorial Flight Association,		
	Dugny, France; as 'C1096:V' in RFC c/s; active 10.18		
G-ERFS	Piper PA-28-161 Warrior II	28-8216051	29.11.02
	D-EPFS, N84570		
	Steptoe & Son Properties Ltd Caernarfon		11.04.18E
G-ERGP	Pilatus PC-12/47E	1564	05.10.18
	LX-ERG, N64NG, HB-FSI		
	Eden Rock Aviation SARL Fairoaks		12.02.19E
G-ERIC	Rockwell Commander 112TC	13010	26.09.78
	SE-GSA D P Williams Earls Colne		20.06.19E
G-ERIE	Raytheon 400A	RK-120	09.09.11
	N702NV, N159AK, N9146Z, TC-MDJ, N3261Y		
	Atlantic Bridge Aviation Ltd Lydd		11.09.19E
	Operated by Lyddair Ltd		
G-ERIK	Cameron N-77 HAB	1753	18.05.88
	Cancelled 10.12.14 as PWFU		27.10.10
	Not Known *Inflated Pidley 05.16*		
G-ERIW	Staaken Z-21 Flitzer	2-060	09.01.04
	R I Wasey Nympsfield		25.06.18P
	Built by R I Wasey – project PFA 223-13834		
G-ERJR	Agusta A109C	7622	10.03.15
	M-DBOY, G-DBOY, N621MM, HB-ZEE, OE-XSG,		
	N67SH, 9M-SJI, Malaysian AF M38-03, 9M-TDJ		
	3GRComm Ltd Wycombe Air Park		16.02.17E
	Stored with Heli Air 11.18		
G-ERKN	Eurocopter AS.350B3 Ecureuil	3587	17.09.13
	G-ORKI, EC-IHX, F-WQRN, F-WQDM		
	Jet Helicopters Ltd Brighton City		06.07.18E
G-ERLI	Cessna 510 Citation Mustang	510-0475	30.12.16
	N40780 Catreus AOC Ltd Dusseldorf, Germany		22.02.18E
G-ERMO	ARV ARV-1 Super 2	018	07.01.87
	G-BMWK M J Slack Ludham		
	(NF 03.12.18)		
G-ERNI	Piper PA-28-181 Archer II	28-8090146	09.10.91
	G-OSSY, N81215		
	J Gardener & N F P Hopwood Headcorn		12.03.18E
G-EROB	Europa Aviation Europa XS	473	15.07.04
	G-RBJW R J Bull Kinloss Barracks, Kinloss		
	Built by R J Bull & J Worthington – project		
	PFA 247-13600 (NF 01.08.17)		
G-EROE	Avro 504K replica	OLA-002	16.02.16
	LV-X430 E A Verdon-Roe t/a British Aviation 100		
	(Holwell, Sherborne) *'AVRO'*		19.12.18P
	Built by Pur Sang Aero Historic		

G-EROL	Westland SA.341G Gazelle 1	WA1108	18.10.02
	G-NONA, G-FDAV, G-RIFA, G-ORGE, G-BBHU		
	MW Helicopters Ltd Stapleford		08.10.10E
	(NF 16.08.17)		
G-EROS	Cameron H-34	2296	06.04.90
	A A Brown t/a Reach for the Sky		
	Perry Hill, Worplesdon, Guildford *'Evening Standard'*		25.11.18E
G-ERRI	Lindstrand LBL 77A	811	20.02.02
	S M Jones Worcester		16.07.18E
G-ERRY	Grumman American AA-5B Tiger	AA5B-0725	20.03.84
	G-BFMJ M Reischl (Hauzenberg, Germany)		12.10.18E
G-ERTE	Best Off Skyranger 912S(1)	UK/566	27.04.05
	A P Trumper Blackmoor Farm, Aubourn		11.05.18P
	Built by A P Trumper – project BMAA/HB/451		
G-ERTI	Staaken Z-21A Flitzer	078	29.09.06
	A M Wyndham Newnham		20.07.18P
	Built by B S Carpenter – project PFA 223-14166		
G-ERYR	P&M Quik GT450	8381	15.05.08
	R D Ellis Chiltern Park, Wallingford		13.04.18P
G-ESCA	Reality Escapade Jabiru(1)	JA.ESC.0002	25.04.03
	G W E & R H May Jackrells Farm, Southwater		17.09.11P
	Built by T F Francis – project BMAA/HB/280		
	(IE 28.07.17)		
G-ESCC	Reality Escapade 912(1)	JA.ESC.0032	07.10.04
	B Bell Jackrells Farm, Southwater		03.11.18P
	Built by G Simons – project BMAA/HB/414		
G-ESCP	Reality Escapade 912(1)	JA.ESC.0004	19.01.04
	A Palmer Wolverhampton Halfpenny Green		10.06.18P
	Built by R G Hughes – project BMAA/HB/313; tricycle u/c		
G-ESET	Eurocopter EC130 B4	4817	30.11.12
	EC-LBX Hogs Head Transportation Ltd		
	(Waterville, Co Kerry, RoI)		18.04.19E
G-ESGA	Reality Escapade	UK.ESC.0010	20.08.07
	I Bamford (Keyworth, Nottingham)		02.11.18P
	Built by T F Francis – project PFA 345-14706		
	– VLA version; tailwheel u/c		
G-ESKA	Reality Escapade 912(2)	JA.ESC.0006	13.05.04
	C G Thompson (West Cranmore, Shepton Mallet)		28.07.19P
	Built by T F Francis – project BMAA/HB/371		
G-ESME	Cessna R182 Skylane RG II	R18201026	10.06.03
	G-BNOX, N756AW G C Cherrington Oaksey Park		22.06.18E
G-ESNA	Embraer EMB-550 Legacy 500	55000069	18.12.17
	PR-LNT Air Charter Scotland Ltd Luton		17.12.18E
G-ESSL	Cessna 182R Skylane II	18267947	07.12.06
	D-EIMP, PH-AXP, N9434H J W F Russell Blackbushe		13.08.19E
	Floatplane		
G-ESTR	Van's RV-6	25909	11.09.00
	J P M & P M White		
	(Belfast & Fethard, Co Tipperary, RoI) *'Jester'*		09.05.19P
	Built by R M Johnson – project PFA 181A-13638		
G-ETAC	Dornier 228-212	8321	07.09.18
	D-CAFE Aurigny Air Services Ltd Guernsey		13.09.19E
	Built by RUAG Aerospace Services GmbH		
G-ETAT	Cessna 172S Skyhawk SP	172S8674	07.07.05
	N742SP I R Malby Brighton City		17.07.19E
G-ETBT	Piper PA-38-112 Tomahawk	38-79A0299	24.07.17
	D-ETBT, N2409D		
	Highland Aviation Training Ltd Inverness		20.03.18E
G-ETBY	Piper PA-32-260 Cherokee Six	32-211	13.07.89
	G-AWCY, N3365W K Richards-Greene &		
	M B Smithson tr G-ETBY Group Enstone		19.10.09E
	Rebuilt with spare Fuselage No.32-858S (NF 20.07.15)		
G-ETDC	Cessna 172P Skyhawk II	17274690	04.05.88
	N53133 The Moray Flying Club (1990)		
	Kinloss Barracks, Kinloss		05.08.18E
G-ETFT	Colt Financial Times SS HAB	1792	11.01.91
	G-BSGZ Cancelled 10.12.02 by CAA		14.10.00
	Not Known *Inflated Pidley 05.16*		
G-ETGO	Groppo Trail Mk.2	xxxx	17.03.17
	S E Gribble & S Taylor (Milton Keynes)		
	Built by S E Gribble – project LAA 372-15462		
	(NF 17.03.17)		
G-ETIM	Eurocopter EC120B Colibri	1387	27.04.05
	VH-NZZ Tenterden (Holdings) Ltd		
	New Lane Farm, North Elmham		14.06.18E
G-ETIN	Robinson R22 Beta	0853	07.09.88
	N9081D HQ Aviation Ltd Denham		25.02.18E
G-ETIV	Robin DR.400-180 Régent	2454	12.07.00
	C A Prior Rochester		28.11.18E
G-ETKT	Robinson R44 Clipper II	13940	09.02.16
	McLaren Construction Ltd Cambridge		20.02.19E
G-ETLX	Piper PA-28R-200 Cherokee Arrow II	28R-7635119	21.11.17
	OK-GKO, D-EFEI, N7828C		
	Blue Skys Aviation Ltd Turweston		31.10.19E
G-ETME	Nord 1002 Pingouin	274	18.04.00
	N108J, F-BFRV, French AF 274		
	S H O'Connell Southend		24.07.19P
	As '14' (yellow) in Luftwaffe c/s		
G-ETNT	Robinson R44 Raven I	1479	27.04.05
	P Irwin t/a Irwin Plant Sales Enniskillen		07.09.17E
	(IE 21.12.17)		
G-ETPA	Pilatus PC-21	310	25.06.18
	HB-HYX QinetiQ Ltd MoD Boscombe Down		
	(IE 25.06.18)		
G-ETPB	Pilatus PC-21	311	18.10.18
	HB-HYY QinetiQ Ltd MoD Boscombe Down		
	(IE 18.10.18)		
G-ETPC	Grob G120TP-A	11125	21.09.17
	D-ETQI Qinetiq Ltd MoD Boscombe Down		23.10.18E
G-ETPD	Grob G120TP-A	11126	21.09.17
	D-ETIQ Qinetiq Ltd MoD Boscombe Down		23.10.18E
G-ETPE	Airbus AS.350B3 Ecureuil	8462	21.11.17
	Qinetiq Ltd MoD Boscombe Down		20.11.19E
G-ETPF	Airbus AS.350B3 Ecureuil	8464	21.11.17
	Qinetiq Ltd MoD Boscombe Down		20.11.18E
	Operated by ETPS		
G-ETPG	Airbus AS.350B3 Ecureuil	8476	12.12.17
	Qinetiq Ltd MoD Boscombe Down		11.12.18E
G-ETPH	Airbus AS.350B3 Ecureuil	8485	13.02.18
	Qinetiq Ltd MoD Boscombe Down		12.02.19E
(G-ETPI)	Agusta A109E Power	11131	
	QQ100, G-CFVB, EI-TWO, D-HARY, B-7770		
	Qinetiq Reserved, due xx.19		
(G-ETPJ)	Agusta A109E Power Elite	11173	
	ZE416, G-ELSH, ZE416, G-ELSH		
	Qinetiq Reserved, due xx.19		
G-ETPK	British Aerospace Avro 146-RJ70	E1254	23.01.19
	QQ102, G-BVRJ, SE-DJP, EI-COQ, 9H-ACM,		
	(9H-ABW), G-BVRJ		
	QinetiQ Ltd MoD Boscombe Down		02.10.17E
	(IE 23.01.19)		
G-ETPL	British Aerospace Avro 146-RJ100	E3368	28.09.18
	QQ101, G-BZAY, G-6-368		
	Qinetiq Ltd MoD Boscombe Down		09.10.19E
G-ETPM	Diamond DA.42M-NG Twin Star	42.255	20.09.18
	QQ103, G-LTPA QinetiQ Ltd MoD Boscombe Down		01.10.19E
G-ETUG	Aeropro EuroFOX 912(S)	37212	09.05.12
	The Northumbria Gliding Club Ltd Currock Hill		15.11.18P
	Built by R M Cornwell – project LAA 376-15147;		
	tailwheel u/c; glider-tug		
G-ETVS	Alpi Pioneer 300 Hawk	272	02.06.09
	V Serazzi (Rogerstone, Newport)		09.07.18P
	Built by T W Skinner – project LAA 330A-14900		
G-ETWO	Guimbal Cabri G2	1063	19.02.14
	F-WWHG European Helicopter Importers Ltd Redhill		04.03.18E
	Operated by EBG Helicopters		
G-EUAB	Europa Aviation Europa XS	544	16.05.07
	A D Stephens Cambridge		22.05.18P
	Built by A D Stephens – project PFA 247-13959;		
	tricycle u/c		
G-EUAN	Avtech Jabiru UL-D	666	30.11.07
	M S Lusted Rochester		23.07.19P
G-EUFO	Rolladen-Schneider LS7-WL	7079	10.01.08
	BGA 3562/FVQ		
	G D Alcock & M J Mingay Parham Park *'FVQ'*		24.04.19E

G-EUJG Avro 594 Avian IIIA R3/CN/185 21.05.07
VH-UJG, G-AUJG D Shew Hill Farm, Durley
On rebuild 06.16 (NF 05.06.18)

G-EUKS Westland Widgeon III WA1780 28.09.10
VH-UKS D Shew Hill Farm, Durley
On rebuild 06.16 (NF 04.06.18)

G-EUNA Airbus A318-112 4007 28.08.09
D-AUAC British Airways PLC London City 27.08.19E

G-EUNB Airbus A318-112 4039 30.09.09
D-AUAF Titan Airways Ltd London Stansted 29.09.19E

G-EUNG Europa Aircraft Europa NG 623 17.08.11
D I Stanbridge (Horsford, Norwich)
*Built by D I Stanbridge – project LAA 247-15067
(NF 07.08.15)*

G-EUNI Beech B200 Super King Air BB-1720 27.11.09
G-TAGH, N208CW, N608TA Universita Telematica
E-Campus (Novedrate, Lombardy, Italy) 08.02.18E

G-EUOA Airbus A319-131 1513 15.06.01
D-AVYE British Airways PLC London Heathrow 14.06.19E

G-EUOB Airbus A319-131 1529 04.07.01
D-AVWH British Airways PLC London Heathrow 03.07.19E

G-EUOC Airbus A319-131 1537 16.07.01
D-AVYP British Airways PLC London Heathrow 15.07.19E

G-EUOD Airbus A319-131 1558 16.08.01
D-AVYJ British Airways PLC London Heathrow 15.08.19E

G-EUOE Airbus A319-131 1574 05.09.01
D-AVWF British Airways PLC London Heathrow 16.09.19E

G-EUOF Airbus A319-131 1590 23.10.01
D-AVYW British Airways PLC London Heathrow 03.10.19E

G-EUOG Airbus A319-131 1594 23.10.01
D-AVWU British Airways PLC London Heathrow 22.10.19E

G-EUOH Airbus A319-131 1604 14.12.01
D-AVYM British Airways PLC London Heathrow 13.12.19E

G-EUOI Airbus A319-131 1606 13.11.01
D-AVYN British Airways PLC London Heathrow 12.11.19E

G-EUPA Airbus A319-131 1082 06.10.99
D-AVYK British Airways PLC London Heathrow 31.05.19E

G-EUPB Airbus A319-131 1115 09.11.99
D-AVYT British Airways PLC London Heathrow 08.11.19E

G-EUPC Airbus A319-131 1118 12.11.99
D-AVYU British Airways PLC London Heathrow 07.09.19E

G-EUPD Airbus A319-131 1142 10.12.99
D-AVWG British Airways PLC London Heathrow 09.12.19E

G-EUPE Airbus A319-131 1193 27.03.00
D-AVYT British Airways PLC London Heathrow 16.01.20E

G-EUPF Airbus A319-131 1197 30.03.00
D-AVWS British Airways PLC London Heathrow 29.03.19E

G-EUPG Airbus A319-131 1222 25.05.00
D-AVYG British Airways PLC London Heathrow 24.05.19E

G-EUPH Airbus A319-131 1225 23.05.00
D-AVYK British Airways PLC London Heathrow 12.04.19E

G-EUPJ Airbus A319-131 1232 30.05.00
D-AVYJ British Airways PLC London Heathrow 29.05.19E
BEA – British European Airways livery

G-EUPK Airbus A319-131 1236 30.05.00
D-AVYO British Airways PLC London Heathrow 29.05.19E

G-EUPL Airbus A319-131 1239 08.06.00
D-AVYP British Airways PLC London Heathrow 16.01.20E

G-EUPM Airbus A319-131 1258 30.06.00
D-AVYR British Airways PLC London Heathrow 29.06.19E

G-EUPN Airbus A319-131 1261 10.07.00
D-AVWA British Airways PLC London Heathrow 30.05.19E

G-EUPO Airbus A319-131 1279 01.08.00
D-AVYU British Airways PLC London Heathrow 31.07.19E

G-EUPP Airbus A319-131 1295 14.08.00
D-AVWU British Airways PLC London Heathrow 30.04.19E

G-EUPR Airbus A319-131 1329 09.10.00
D-AVYH British Airways PLC London Heathrow 08.10.19E

G-EUPS Airbus A319-131 1338 23.10.00
D-AVYM British Airways PLC London Heathrow 22.10.19E

G-EUPT Airbus A319-131 1380 05.12.00
D-AVWH British Airways PLC London Heathrow 04.12.19E

G-EUPU Airbus A319-131 1384 14.12.00
D-AVWP British Airways PLC London Heathrow 13.12.19E

G-EUPW Airbus A319-131 1440 06.03.01
D-AVYP British Airways PLC London Heathrow 05.03.19E

G-EUPX Airbus A319-131 1445 14.12.01
D-AVWB, F-WWDJ, D-AVWB
British Airways PLC London Heathrow 13.12.19E

G-EUPY Airbus A319-131 1466 12.04.01
D-AVYK, (D-AKNK)
British Airways PLC London Heathrow 29.03.19E

G-EUPZ Airbus A319-131 1510 07.06.01
D-AVYY British Airways PLC London Heathrow 30.05.19E

G-EUSO Robin DR.400-140 Earl 904 18.09.03
F-BUSO Weald Air Services Ltd Headcorn 18.12.18E

G-EUUA Airbus A320-232 1661 31.01.02
F-WWIH British Airways PLC London Heathrow 30.01.20E

G-EUUB Airbus A320-232 1689 14.02.02
F-WWBE British Airways PLC London Heathrow 18.01.20E

G-EUUC Airbus A320-232 1696 28.02.02
F-WWIO British Airways PLC London Heathrow 27.02.19E

G-EUUD Airbus A320-232 1760 29.04.02
F-WWBN British Airways PLC London Heathrow 28.04.19E

G-EUUE Airbus A320-232 1782 30.05.02
F-WWDO British Airways PLC London Heathrow 11.04.19E

G-EUUF Airbus A320-232 1814 29.07.02
F-WWIY British Airways PLC London Heathrow 28.07.19E

G-EUUG Airbus A320-232 1829 30.08.02
F-WWIU British Airways PLC London Heathrow 03.05.19E

G-EUUH Airbus A320-232 1665 25.10.02
F-WWIG British Airways PLC London Heathrow 25.07.19E

G-EUUI Airbus A320-232 1871 22.11.02
F-WWBI British Airways PLC London Heathrow 08.11.19E

G-EUUJ Airbus A320-232 1883 25.11.02
F-WWBQ British Airways PLC London Heathrow 01.11.19E

G-EUUK Airbus A320-232 1899 20.12.02
F-WWDO British Airways PLC London Heathrow 19.12.19E

G-EUUL Airbus A320-232 1708 20.12.02
F-WWIV, (EI-CVF)
British Airways PLC London Heathrow 19.12.19E

G-EUUM Airbus A320-232 1907 23.12.02
F-WWDN British Airways PLC London Heathrow 22.12.19E

G-EUUN Airbus A320-232 1910 31.01.03
F-WWDP British Airways PLC London Heathrow 30.01.20E

G-EUUO Airbus A320-232 1958 11.04.03
F-WWIT British Airways PLC London Heathrow 10.04.19E

G-EUUP Airbus A320-232 2038 27.06.03
F-WWDB British Airways PLC London Heathrow 26.06.19E

G-EUUR Airbus A320-232 2040 29.07.03
F-WWID British Airways PLC London Heathrow 02.06.19E

G-EUUS Airbus A320-232 3301 05.12.07
F-WWIF British Airways PLC London Heathrow 05.12.19E

G-EUUT Airbus A320-232 3314 12.12.07
F-WWIT British Airways PLC London Heathrow 11.12.19E

G-EUUU Airbus A320-232 3351 07.03.08
F-WWiD British Airways PLC London Heathrow 06.03.19E

G-EUUV Airbus A320-232 3468 18.04.08
F-WWBO British Airways PLC London Heathrow 10.04.19E

G-EUUW Airbus A320-232 3499 02.06.08
F-WWIN British Airways PLC London Heathrow 11.05.19E

G-EUUX Airbus A320-232 3550 11.07.08
F-WWDM British Airways PLC London Heathrow 24.05.19E

G-EUUY Airbus A320-232 3607 18.09.08
F-WWIC British Airways PLC London Heathrow 17.09.19E

G-EUUZ Airbus A320-232 3649 21.10.08
F-WWDO British Airways PLC London Heathrow 15.07.19E

G-EUXC Airbus A321-231 2305 15.10.04
D-AVZE British Airways PLC London Heathrow 18.09.19E

G-EUXD	Airbus A321-231	2320	28.10.04
	D-AVZO British Airways PLC London Heathrow		23.08.19E
G-EUXE	Airbus A321-231	2323	29.10.04
	D-AVZP British Airways PLC London Heathrow		28.10.19E
G-EUXF	Airbus A321-231	2324	04.11.04
	D-AVZQ British Airways PLC London Heathrow		03.11.19E
G-EUXG	Airbus A321-231	2351	02.12.04
	D-AVZU British Airways PLC London Heathrow		01.12.19E
G-EUXH	Airbus A321-231	2363	17.12.04
	D-AVZW British Airways PLC London Heathrow		04.12.19E
G-EUXI	Airbus A321-231	2536	05.08.05
	D-AVZE British Airways PLC London Heathrow		22.06.19E
G-EUXJ	Airbus A321-231	3081	17.04.07
	D-AVZL British Airways PLC London Heathrow		10.04.19E
G-EUXK	Airbus A321-231	3235	30.08.07
	D-AVZI British Airways PLC London Heathrow		31.08.19E
G-EUXL	Airbus A321-231	3254	21.09.07
	D-AVZV British Airways PLC London Heathrow		23.08.19E
G-EUXM	Airbus A321-231	3290	21.11.07
	D-AVZC, F-WWBD, D-AVZC		
	British Airways PLC London Heathrow		23.11.19E
G-EUYA	Airbus A320-232	3697	24.11.08
	F-WWBM British Airways PLC London Heathrow		23.11.19E
G-EUYB	Airbus A320-232	3703	27.11.08
	F-WWBV British Airways PLC London Heathrow		26.11.19E
G-EUYC	Airbus A320-232	3721	12.12.08
	F-WWBY British Airways PLC London Heathrow		11.12.19E
G-EUYD	Airbus A320-232	3726	16.12.08
	F-WWDH British Airways PLC London Heathrow		15.12.19E
G-EUYE	Airbus A320-232	3912	05.06.09
	F-WWBB British Airways PLC London Heathrow		04.06.19E
G-EUYF	Airbus A320-232	4185	28.01.10
	F-WWIC British Airways PLC London Heathrow		13.12.19E
G-EUYG	Airbus A320-232	4238	18.03.10
	F-WWDH British Airways PLC London Heathrow		17.03.19E
G-EUYH	Airbus A320-232	4265	15.04.10
	F-WWBK British Airways PLC London Heathrow		28.03.18E
G-EUYI	Airbus A320-232	4306	03.06.10
	F-WWIC British Airways PLC London Heathrow		02.06.19E
G-EUYJ	Airbus A320-232	4464	28.10.10
	F-WWBQ British Airways PLC London Heathrow		27.10.19E
G-EUYK	Airbus A320-232	4551	18.01.11
	F-WWBE British Airways PLC London Heathrow		17.01.20E
G-EUYL	Airbus A320-232	4725	01.06.11
	F-WWDY British Airways PLC London Heathrow		31.05.19E
G-EUYM	Airbus A320-232	4791	05.08.11
	F-WWIB British Airways PLC London Heathrow		04.08.19E
G-EUYN	Airbus A320-232	4975	12.01.12
	F-WWDT British Airways PLC London Heathrow		12.12.19E
G-EUYO	Airbus A320-232	5634	13.06.13
	F-WWDG British Airways PLC London Heathrow		12.06.19E
G-EUYP	Airbus A320-232	5784	09.10.13
	F-WWIC British Airways PLC London Heathrow		08.10.19E
G-EUYR	Airbus A320-232	5856	21.11.13
	F-WWBY British Airways PLC London Heathrow		20.11.19E
G-EUYS	Airbus A320-232	5948	30.01.14
	F-WWDY British Airways PLC London Heathrow		27.01.20E
G-EUYT	Airbus A320-232	5985	20.02.14
	D-AUBO British Airways PLC London Heathrow		19.02.19E
G-EUYU	Airbus A320-232	6028	20.03.14
	F-WWDG British Airways PLC London Heathrow		19.03.19E
G-EUYV	Airbus A320-232	6091	16.05.14
	F-WWDR British Airways PLC London Heathrow		15.05.19E
G-EUYW	Airbus A320-232	6129	05.06.14
	F-WWDZ British Airways PLC London Heathrow		04.06.19E
G-EUYX	Airbus A320-232	6155	03.07.14
	F-WWBM British Airways PLC London Heathrow		02.07.19E
G-EUYY	Airbus A320-232	6290	09.10.14
	F-WWBB British Airways PLC London Heathrow		08.10.19E

G-EVAA	AutoGyro Cavalon	V00195	08.05.15
	J W Payne tr Cavalon 014 Syndicate		
	Wolverhampton Halfpenny Green		22.08.19P
	Assembled Rotorsport UK as c/n RSUK/CVLN/014		
G-EVAJ	Best Off Skyranger Swift 912S(1)	SKR0612760	22.02.07
	A B Gridley Sackville Lodge Farm, Riseley		19.11.18P
	Built by A B Gridley – project BMAA/HB/526		
G-EVBF	Cameron Z-350	10687	14.03.05
	Airxcite Ltd t/a Virgin Balloon Flights		
	Stafford Park, Telford *'Virgin'*		23.08.12E
	(NF 15.09.14)		
G-EVEE	Robinson R44 Raven I	1517	26.05.15
	G-REGE EFL Helicopters Ltd Brighton City		03.11.18E
G-EVEN	Cirrus SR22	2234	04.11.16
	G-CGRD, N613SR Glemmestad Invest AS (Poole)		15.05.18E
G-EVET	Cameron C-80	3703	30.10.95
	M D J Walker Roborough, Plymouth		28.07.16E
G-EVEY	Thruster T600N 450	0121-T600N-057	21.11.01
	K J Crompton tr G-EVEY Flying Group Newtownards		16.12.18P
	Badged 'Sprint'		
G-EVIB	Cirrus SR22	2467	11.08.17
	N192SR P Bishop Lydd		19.09.18E
G-EVIE	Piper PA-28-161 Warrior II	28-8316043	31.03.04
	G-ZULU, N4292X Tayside Aviation Ltd Dundee		10.08.18E
G-EVIG	Evektor EV-97 teamEurostar UK	2007-2930	09.03.07
	A S Mitchell Wickenby		12.03.18P
	Assembled Cosmik Aviation Ltd		
G-EVII	Schempp-Hirth Ventus-2cT	10/41	31.10.07
	BGA 4292		
	T Hurn tr Ventus G-EVII Syndicate Lasham *'V11'*		31.10.18E
G-EVLE	Rearwin 8125 Cloudster	803	10.04.03
	G-BVLK, N25403, NC25403 W D Gray Henstridge		07.12.17P
G-EVMK	de Havilland DHC-2 Beaver 1	672	07.12.15
	N613WB, N90409, 53-3718 T W Harris Duxford		
	Noted 10.18 (NF 07.12.15)		
G-EVPI	Evans VP-1 Series 2	xxxx	10.04.03
	C P Martyr Deanland		23.03.18P
	Built by C P Martyr – project PFA 062-13136		
G-EVRO	Evektor EV-97 Eurostar	2003-1222	30.01.04
	J E Rourke Ince		12.04.18P
	Built by D & R I Blain – project PFA 315-14137		
G-EVSL	Evektor EV-97 Eurostar SL	2009-3617	07.07.09
	M Vouros Tibenham		16.10.18P
	Built by N R Beale – project LAA 315B-14891		
G-EVSW	Evektor EV-97 Sportstar	2011 3824	27.03.12
	I Shulver Bagby		09.07.18P
	Built by N Beale & C Theakstone – project		
	LAA 315C-15105; badged 'Sportstar SW'		
G-EVTO	Piper PA-28-161 Warrior II	28-8016271	12.07.05
	N5012V, G-EVTO, D-EVTO, N81615		
	Redhill Air Services Ltd Nottingham City		21.03.18E
	Operated by Fairoaks Flight Centre		
G-EWAD	Robinson R44 Raven II	12296	05.06.08
	MG Helicopters Ltd (Wantage)		10.06.18E
	Operated by Heli Air Ltd		
G-EWAN	Protech PT-2C-160 Prostar	PT1240	23.06.93
	C G Shaw Truleigh Manor Farm, Edburton		31.07.18P
	Built by C G Shaw – project PFA 249-12425		
G-EWBC	Avtech Jabiru SK	0249	03.11.00
	E W B Comber White Fen Farm, Benwick		12.07.18P
	Built by E W B Comber – project PFA 274-13457		
G-EWEN	Aeropro EuroFOX 912(S)	38312	30.11.12
	M H Talbot Easter Farm, Fearn		12.12.18P
	Built by M H Talbot – project LAA 376-15149;		
	tailwheel u/c		
G-EWES	Alpi Pioneer 300	129	24.11.04
	P W Carlton & D F P Finan Morgansfield, Fishburn		07.10.19P
	Built by D A Ions & R Y Kendal – project PFA 330-14322		
G-EWEW	Sportine Aviacija LAK-19T	024	22.05.07
	BGA 5284, (BGA 5241), LY-GNC		
	J B Strzebrakowski Husbands Bosworth *'EW2'*		27.07.18E
G-EWIZ	Pitts S-2S	S18	12.11.82
	VH-EHQ R S Goodwin Gloucestershire		19.05.18E
	Built by H M Shelveyl Union Jack c/s		

G-EWME	Piper PA-28-235 Cherokee Charger	28-7310156	24.09.04
	D-EECN, N55766 Y Remacle (Emines, Belgium)		31.08.19E
	Official type data 'PA-28-235 Cherokee Pathfinder'		
	is incorrect		
G-EXAM	Piper PA-28RT-201T Turbo Arrow IV	28R-8431003	25.05.05
	N45AW, N43230 A Cameron & H S Urquhart		
	Easter Poldar Farm, Thornhill		23.04.19E
G-EXCC	Carbon Cub EX-2	CCK-1865-1012	11.11.15
	M S Colebrook Goodwood		
	Built by M S Colebrook – project LAA 395-15363;		
	cleared to fly 12.02.19 (IE 06.08.18)		
G-EXEC	Piper PA-34-200 Seneca	34-7450072	02.05.78
	(G-EXXC), OY-BGU Sky Air Travel Ltd Stapleford		11.05.18E
G-EXES	Europa Aviation Europa XS	578	25.04.03
	D Barraclough Charlton Mires Farm, South Charlton		31.05.18P
	Built by D Barraclough – project PFA 247-13574;		
	tailwheel u/c		
G-EXEX	Cessna 404 Titan	404-0037	03.05.79
	SE-GZF, (N5418G) Reconnaissance Ventures Ltd		
	t/a RVL Group Inverness 'Coastguard'		28.09.18E
	Red & white c/s: carries 'MCA' logo on tail		
G-EXGC	Extra EA.300/200	027	10.06.08
	D-EXGC P J Bull Andrewsfield		01.07.18E
G-EXHL	Cameron C-70	11408	26.04.10
	R K Gyselynck Marlow		23.11.18E
G-EXII	Extra EA.300	V1	08.10.10
	D-EAEW Z Lidzius (Vilnius, Lithuania)		05.04.19E
G-EXIL	Extra EA.300/S	1036	06.09.10
	D-EXHS G-Force Aerobatics LLP Little Gransden		17.12.18E
G-EXIT	SOCATA MS.893E Rallye 180GT	12979	22.09.78
	F-GARX A Millar tr G-EXIT Group Headcorn		28.10.19E
G-EXLL	Zenair CH.601XL Zodiac	6-9500	04.03.04
	M R Brumby Sturgate		13.06.18P
	Built by R Fox, B Gardner & B McFadden		
	– project PFA 162B-14205; tricycle u/c		
G-EXLT	Extra EA.300/LT	LT004	09.05.11
	J W Marshall Goodwood		01.07.18E
G-EXPO	Piper PA-46R-350T Malibu Matrix	4692138	26.03.18
	D-EEPD, N138CM, N9541N		
	G-EXPO LLP Brighton City 'Lady Irene'		17.05.19E
G-EXTR	Extra EA.260	04	10.08.92
	D-EDID Principia Aerobatics LLP Netherthorpe		14.12.18P
G-EXXL	Zenair CH.601XL Zodiac	6-7369	19.09.11
	J H Ellwood (Caunce Grange Farm, Winmarleigh)		23.08.19P
	Built by M Saywell – project LAA 162B-14868;		
	tricycle u/c		
G-EYAK	Yakovlev Yak-50	801804	19.02.03
	RA-01193, DOSAAF?		
	P N A Whitehead Leicester '50' & 'Temptation'		02.02.16P
	(IE 18.12.17)		
G-EYCO	Robin DR.400-180 Régent	1949	12.03.90
	M J Hanlon Clonbullogue, RoI		20.09.18E
G-EYOR	Van's RV-6	xxxx	15.10.99
	S I Fraser Henstridge		28.02.18P
	Built by S I Fraser – project PFA 181A-13259		
G-EZAA	Airbus A319-111	2677	10.02.06
	D-AVYU easyJet Airline Company Ltd Luton		02.10.19E
G-EZAB	Airbus A319-111	2681	06.02.06
	D-AVYY easyJet Airline Company Ltd Luton		04.10.19E
G-EZAC	Airbus A319-111	2691	16.02.06
	D-AVXB easyJet Airline Company Ltd Luton		04.11.19E
G-EZAF	Airbus A319-111	2715	16.03.06
	D-AVYT easyJet Airline Company Ltd Luton		02.11.19E
G-EZAG	Airbus A319-111	2727	29.03.06
	D-AVXG easyJet Airline Company Ltd Luton		04.01.20E
G-EZAI	Airbus A319-111	2735	06.04.06
	D-AVXM easyJet Airline Company Ltd Luton		29.10.19E
G-EZAJ	Airbus A319-111	2742	13.04.06
	D-AVXP easyJet Airline Company Ltd Luton		11.04.19E
G-EZAK	Airbus A319-111	2744	20.04.06
	D-AVXQ easyJet Airline Company Ltd Luton		02.02.19E

G-EZAL	Airbus A319-111	2754	27.04.06
	D-AVWG easyJet Airline Company Ltd Luton		06.03.19E
G-EZAN	Airbus A319-111	2765	04.05.00
	D-AVWL easyJet Airline Company Ltd Luton		12.12.19E
G-EZAO	Airbus A319-111	2769	09.05.06
	D-AVWO easyJet Airline Company Ltd Luton		02.04.19E
G-EZAP	Airbus A319-111	2777	16.05.06
	D-AVYG easyJet Airline Company Ltd Luton		04.04.19E
G-EZAR	Mainair Pegasus Quik	7942	18.03.03
	D McCormack Broomhill Farm, West Calder		07.12.18P
	Built by Mainair Sports Ltd		
G-EZAS	Airbus A319-111	2779	24.05.06
	D-AVYH easyJet Airline Company Ltd Luton		06.04.19E
G-EZAT	Airbus A319-111	2782	01.06.06
	D-AVYO easyJet Airline Company Ltd Luton		25.05.19E
G-EZAU	Airbus A319-111	2795	09.06.06
	D-AVWQ easyJet Airline Company Ltd Luton		23.03.19E
G-EZAV	Airbus A319-111	2803	22.06.06
	D-AVWV easyJet Airline Company Ltd Luton		28.03.19E
G-EZAW	Airbus A319-111	2812	04.07.06
	D-AVYU easyJet Airline Company Ltd Luton		01.07.19E
G-EZAX	Airbus A319-111	2818	06.07.06
	D-AVXA easyJet Airline Company Ltd Luton		03.07.19E
G-EZBA	Airbus A319-111	2860	18.08.06
	D-AVWB easyJet Airline Company Ltd Luton		26.08.19E
G-EZBB	Airbus A319-111	2854	09.08.06
	D-AVXM easyJet Airline Company Ltd Luton		02.07.19E
G-EZBC	Airbus A319-111	2866	05.09.06
	D-AVWD easyJet Airline Company Ltd Luton		03.09.19E
G-EZBD	Airbus A319-111	2873	13.09.06
	D-AVWK easyJet Airline Company Ltd Luton		11.09.19E
G-EZBE	Airbus A319-111	2884	28.11.06
	D-AVXO easyJet Airline Company Ltd Luton		05.06.19E
G-EZBF	Airbus A319-111	2923	02.11.06
	D-AVYK easyJet Airline Company Ltd Luton		
	'Inverness'		09.07.19E
	Tartan Logojet c/s		
G-EZBH	Airbus A319-111	2959	15.12.06
	D-AVXH easyJet Airline Company Ltd Luton		06.10.19E
G-EZBI	Airbus A319-111	3003	06.02.07
	D-AVYB easyJet Airline Company Ltd Luton		
	'Romeo'		08.10.19E
	William Shakespeare Logojet c/s		
G-EZBK	Airbus A319-111	3041	22.02.07
	D-AVWK easyJet Airline Company Ltd Luton		10.11.19E
G-EZBO	Airbus A319-111	3082	04.04.07
	D-AVYK easyJet Airline Company Ltd Luton		08.02.19E
G-EZBR	Airbus A319-111	3088	26.04.07
	D-AVYY easyJet Airline Company Ltd Luton		01.02.19E
G-EZBU	Airbus A319-111	3118	14.05.07
	D-AVWW easyJet Airline Company Ltd Luton		08.04.19E
G-EZBV	Airbus A319-111	3122	23.05.07
	D-AVWX easyJet Airline Company Ltd Luton		04.04.19E
G-EZBW	Airbus A319-111	3134	05.06.07
	D-AVXE easyJet Airline Company Ltd Luton		04.06.19E
G-EZBX	Airbus A319-111	3137	15.06.07
	D-AVXH easyJet Airline Company Ltd Luton		08.05.19E
G-EZBZ	Airbus A319-111	3184	13.07.07
	D-AVYF easyJet Airline Company Ltd Luton		10.07.19E
G-EZDA	Airbus A319-111	3413	21.02.08
	D-AVYH easyJet Airline Company Ltd Luton		22.01.19E
G-EZDD	Airbus A319-111	3442	17.03.08
	D-AVYL easyJet Airline Company Ltd Luton		
	'Jean Baptiste Fourichon'		26.02.19E
G-EZDF	Airbus A319-111	3432	13.03.08
	D-AVYG easyJet Airline Company Ltd Luton		
	'Spirit of easyJet 2014' & 'James Baron'		09.04.19E
G-EZDG	Rutan VariEze	xxxx	01.11.05
	G-EZOS P J Shute tr Varieze Flying Group		
	Earls Colne		26.06.19P
	Built by O Smith – project PFA 074-10221		

G-EZDH	Airbus A319-111	3466	14.04.08
	D-AVWM easyJet Airline Company Ltd Luton		12.04.19E
G-EZDI	Airbus A319-111	3537	29.05.08
	D-AVWC easyJet Airline Company Ltd Luton		22.05.19E
G-EZDJ	Airbus A319-111	3544	03.06.08
	D-AVWJ easyJet Airline Company Ltd Luton		01.06.19E
G-EZDK	Airbus A319-111	3555	11.06.08
	D-AVWP easyJet Airline Company Ltd Luton		09.06.19E
G-EZDL	Airbus A319-111	3569	23.06.08
	D-AVWT easyJet Airline Company Ltd Luton		08.05.19E
G-EZDM	Airbus A319-111	3571	01.07.08
	D-AVWU, (D-AGWM) easyJet Airline Company Ltd		
	Luton *'Porto'*		29.06.19E
G-EZDN	Airbus A319-111	3608	08.08.08
	D-AVYJ easyJet Airline Company Ltd Luton		06.08.19E
	'Amsterdam' logos		
G-EZDV	Airbus A319-111	3742	15.12.08
	D-AVWY easyJet Airline Company Ltd Luton		14.12.19E
G-EZEB	Airbus A319-111	2120	25.03.04
	D-AVYK easyJet Airline Company Ltd Luton		12.02.19E
G-EZEG	Airbus A319-111	2181	01.04.04
	D-AVWF easyJet Airline Company Ltd Luton		16.02.20E
G-EZEH	Airbus A319-111	2184	16.04.04
	2-GZEH, G-EZEH, HB-JZF, G-EZEH, D-AVWO		
	easyJet Airline Company Ltd Luton		
	(NF 05.05.16)		
G-EZEN	Airbus A319-111	2245	11.06.04
	2-GZEN, G-EZEN, HB-JZI, G-EZEN, D-AVYH		
	easyJet Airline Company Ltd Luton		13.06.19E
G-EZEY	Airbus A319-111	2353	14.01.05
	HB-JZL, G-EZEY, D-AVYM		
	easyJet Airline Company Ltd Luton		04.09.19E
G-EZFT	Airbus A319-111	4132	21.12.09
	D-AVWF easyJet Airline Company Ltd Luton		20.12.19E
G-EZFV	Airbus A319-111	4327	04.06.10
	D-AVXE easyJet Airline Company Ltd Luton		03.06.19E
G-EZFW	Airbus A319-111	4380	23.07.10
	D-AVYQ easyJet Airline Company Ltd Luton		22.07.19E
G-EZFX	Airbus A319-111	4385	30.07.10
	D-AVYS easyJet Airline Company Ltd Luton		29.07.19E
G-EZFY	Airbus A319-111	4418	18.08.10
	D-AVXJ easyJet Airline Company Ltd Luton		17.08.19E
G-EZFZ	Airbus A319-111	4425	25.08.10
	D-AVXL easyJet Airline Company Ltd Luton		24.08.19E
G-EZGA	Airbus A319-111	4427	27.08.10
	D-AVXM easyJet Airline Company Ltd Luton		26.08.19E
G-EZGB	Airbus A319-111	4437	15.09.10
	D-AVXO easyJet Airline Company Ltd Luton		14.09.19E
G-EZGC	Airbus A319-111	4444	24.09.10
	D-AVXP easyJet Airline Company Ltd Luton		23.09.19E
G-EZGE	Airbus A319-111	4624	09.03.11
	D-AVWK easyJet Airline Company Ltd Luton		08.03.19E
G-EZGF	Airbus A319-111	4635	16.03.11
	D-AVWO easyJet Airline Company Ltd Luton		01.12.19E
G-EZGI ★	Airbus A319-111	4693	03.05.11
	HB-JYL, G-EZGI, D-AVYP Easyjet Airline Company Ltd		
	Cancelled 13.01.16 to Switzerland Restored 05.12.18		
	To OE-LKA 30.01.19		
G-EZGR ★	Airbus A319-111	4837	09.09.11
	HB-JYB, G-EZGR, D-AVWD Easyjet Airline Company Ltd		
	Cancelled 26.09.12 to Switzerland Restored 03.04.18		
	To OE-LKB 04.02.19		
G-EZGX	Airbus A320-214	8381	11.07.18
	D-AXAB easyJet Airline Company Ltd Luton		11.07.19E
G-EZGY	Airbus A320-214	8385	31.08.18
	D-AXAX easyJet Airline Company Ltd Luton		30.08.19E
G-EZGZ ★	Airbus A320-214	8390	19.07.18
	D-AVVG Easyjet Airline Company Ltd		
	To HB-JXO 20.03.19		
G-EZIH	Airbus A319-111	2463	09.05.05
	D-AVWV easyJet Airline Company Ltd Luton		06.01.20E
G-EZII	Airbus A319-111	2471	25.05.05
	D-AVYK easyJet Airline Company Ltd Luton		19.04.19E
G-EZIM	Airbus A319-111	2495	17.06.05
	D-AVYO easyJet Airline Company Ltd Luton		16.05.19E
G-EZIO	Airbus A319-111	2512	07.07.05
	D-AVWP easyJet Airline Company Ltd Luton		04.07.19E
	'unicef' logo		
G-EZIV	Airbus A319-111	2565	04.10.05
	D-AVYY easyJet Airline Company Ltd Luton		14.06.19E
G-EZIW	Airbus A319-111	2578	17.10.05
	D-AVXE easyJet Airline Company Ltd		
	Luton *'Linate-Fiumicino'*		07.07.19E
G-EZIX	Airbus A319-111	2605	17.11.05
	D-AVXP easyJet Airline Company Ltd Luton		03.07.19E
G-EZIY	Airbus A319-111	2636	15.12.05
	D-AVWH easyJet Airline Company Ltd Luton		10.10.19E
G-EZIZ	Airbus A319-111	2646	12.01.06
	D-AVWQ easyJet Airline Company Ltd Luton		12.10.19E
G-EZMK	Airbus A319-111	2370	13.01.05
	HB-JZM, G-EZMK, (G-EZXA), D-AVWE		
	easyJet Airline Company Ltd Luton		06.02.20E
G-EZNM	Airbus A319-111	2402	01.03.05
	G-EZNM, D-AVWH easyJet Airline Company Ltd		
	Luton		09.11.19E
G-EZOA	Airbus A320-214	6412	19.12.14
	D-AXAN easyJet Airline Company Ltd Luton		22.08.19E
G-EZOF	Airbus A320-214	6525	17.03.15
	D-AVVC easyJet Airline Company Ltd Luton		22.05.19E
G-EZOI	Airbus A320-214	6562	15.04.15
	D-AVVJ easyJet Airline Company Ltd Luton		14.04.19E
G-EZOK	Airbus A320-214	6568	29.04.15
	F-WWIN easyJet Airline Company Ltd Luton		23.04.19E
G-EZOM	Airbus A320-214	6587	06.05.15
	D-AVVO easyJet Airline Company Ltd Luton		05.05.19E
G-EZOP	Airbus A320-214	6633	02.06.15
	D-AVVU easyJet Airline Company Ltd Luton		01.06.19E
G-EZPB	Airbus A320-214	6977	18.02.16
	D-AUBO easyJet Airline Company Ltd Luton		17.02.20E
G-EZPD	Airbus A320-214	7040	31.03.16
	D-AUBX easyJet Airline Company Ltd Luton		30.03.19E
G-EZPE	Airbus A320-214	7044	16.03.16
	D-AUBY easyJet Airline Company Ltd Luton		15.03.19E
G-EZPG	Airbus A319-111	2385	15.02.05
	D-AVYD easyJet Airline Company Ltd Luton		16.10.19E
G-EZPI	Airbus A320-214	7104	19.05.16
	F-WWIO easyJet Airline Company Ltd Luton		04.06.19E
G-EZRT	Airbus A320-214	8162	18.05.18
	D-AVVZ easyJet Airline Company Ltd Luton		17.05.19E
G-EZRU ★	Airbus A320-214	8165	19.03.18
	F-WWBP easyJet Airline Company Ltd Luton		18.03.19E
	To HB-JXP 25.03.19		
G-EZRV	Airbus A320-214	8263	25.04.18
	easyJet Airline Company Ltd Luton		24.04.19E
G-EZRW ★	Airbus A320-214	8299	29.06.18
	D-AXAE Easyjet Airline Company Ltd		
	To HB-JXM 05.11.18		
G-EZRX	Airbus A320-214	8321	31.05.18
	D-AXAM easyJet Airline Company Ltd Luton		30.05.19E
G-EZRY	Airbus A320-214	8344	21.06.18
	D-AUBJ easyJet Airline Company Ltd Luton		20.06.19E
G-EZRZ	Airbus A320-214	8358	29.06.18
	D-AUBV easyJet Airline Company Ltd Luton		28.06.19E
G-EZTB	Airbus A320-214	3843	09.04.09
	F-WWBO easyJet Airline Company Ltd Luton		08.04.19E
G-EZTC	Airbus A320-214	3871	17.04.09
	F-WWIG easyJet Airline Company Ltd Luton		12.03.19E
G-EZTD	Airbus A320-214	3909	15.05.09
	D-AVVB easyJet Airline Company Ltd Luton		14.05.19E
G-EZTG	Airbus A320-214	3946	17.06.09
	D-AVVJ easyJet Airline Company Ltd		
	Luton *'Alana Kelly'*		16.06.19E

G-EZTH	Airbus A320-214	3953	19.06.09
	D-AVVM easyJet Airline Company Ltd Luton		18.06.19E
G-EZTK	Airbus A320-214	3991	24.07.09
	D-AVVP easyJet Airline Company Ltd Luton		23.07.19E
G-EZTM	Airbus A320-214	4014	20.08.09
	D-AVVD easyJet Airline Company Ltd Luton		19.08.19E
G-EZTR	Airbus A320-214	4179	09.02.10
	D-AVVX easyJet Airline Company Ltd Luton		08.02.20E
G-EZTT	Airbus A320-214	4219	16.03.10
	D-AVVM easyJet Airline Company Ltd Luton		12.02.20E
G-EZTY	Airbus A320-214	4554	06.01.11
	D-AUBS easyJet Airline Company Ltd Luton		05.01.20E
G-EZTZ	Airbus A320-214	4556	12.01.11
	(D-AUBW) easyJet Airline Company Ltd Luton		02.05.19E
G-EZUA	Airbus A320-214	4588	09.02.11
	D-AVVE easyJet Airline Company Ltd Luton		06.02.19E
G-EZUB	Zenair CH.601HD Zodiac	6-2207	13.09.04
	J R Davis Fenland		25.04.19P
	Built by R A C Stephens – project PFA 162-12765;		
	tricycle u/c		
G-EZUF	Airbus A320-214	4676	18.04.11
	D-AXAG easyJet Airline Company Ltd Luton		17.04.19E
G-EZUK	Airbus A320-214	4749	27.06.11
	D-AVVL easyJet Airline Company Ltd Luton		
	'Wayne Fisher'		26.06.19E
G-EZUL	Airbus A320-214	5019	08.02.12
	D-AXAH easyJet Airline Company Ltd Luton		07.02.19E
G-EZUN	Airbus A320-214	5046	22.03.12
	D-AXAN easyJet Airline Company Ltd Luton		21.03.19E
G-EZUO	Airbus A320-214	5052	04.04.12
	D-AUBA easyJet Airline Company Ltd Luton		15.03.19E
G-EZUP	Airbus A320-214	5056	03.04.12
	D-AUBB easyJet Airline Company Ltd Luton		02.04.19E
G-EZUR	Airbus A320-214	5064	12.04.12
	D-AUBD easyJet Airline Company Ltd Luton		31.03.19E
G-EZUS	Airbus A320-214	5104	05.04.12
	D-AUBS easyJet Airline Company Ltd Luton		04.04.19E
G-EZUT	Airbus A320-214	5113	17.04.12
	D-AUBT easyJet Airline Company Ltd Luton		16.04.19E
G-EZUW	Airbus A320-214	5116	13.04.12
	D-AUBY easyJet Airline Company Ltd Luton		12.03.19E
G-EZUZ	Airbus A320-214	5187	19.06.12
	D-AXAV easyJet Airline Company LtdmLuton		18.06.19E
G-EZVS	Colt 77B	063	06.07.04
	SE-ZVS A J Lovell Göteborg, Sweden		12.07.16E
	(NF 14.12.17)		
G-EZWA	Airbus A320-214	5201	26.06.12
	D-AVVQ easyJet Airline Company Ltd Luton		25.06.19E
G-EZWB	Airbus A320-214	5224	07.08.12
	D-AXAZ easyJet Airline Company Ltd Luton		06.08.19E
G-EZWC	Airbus A320-214	5236	31.07.12
	D-AVVX easyJet Airline Company Ltd Luton		28.07.19E
G-EZWD	Airbus A320-214	5249	08.08.12
	D-AXAH easyJet Airline Company Ltd Luton		07.08.19E
G-EZWE	Airbus A320-214	5289	28.09.12
	D-AXAL easyJet Airline Company Ltd Luton		27.09.18E
G-EZWF	Airbus A320-214	5319	07.11.12
	D-AUBE easyJet Airline Company Ltd Luton		06.11.19E
G-EZWG	Airbus A320-214	5318	10.10.12
	F-WWBI easyJet Airline Company Ltd		
	Luton *'Barcelona'*		09.10.19E
G-EZWH	Airbus A320-214	5542	09.04.13
	D-AXAV easyJet Airline Company Ltd Luton		08.04.19E
G-EZWI	Airbus A320-214	5592	15.05.13
	D-AUBH easyJet Airline Company Ltd Luton		14.05.19E
G-EZWJ	Airbus A320-214	5638	04.06.13
	D-AUBS easyJet Airline Company Ltd Luton		03.06.19E
G-EZWL	Airbus A320-214	5702	11.07.13
	D-AVVI easyJet Airline Company Ltd Luton		06.06.19E

G-EZWP	Airbus A320-214	5927	17.01.14
	D-AUBF easyJet Airline Company Ltd Luton		09.04.19E
G-EZWU	Airbus A320-214	6095	08.05.14
	D-AXAP easyJet Airline Company Ltd Luton		07.05.19E
G-EZWV	Airbus A320-214	6177	09.07.14
	D-AVVD easyJet Airline Company Ltd Luton		08.07.19E
G-EZWX	Airbus A320-214	6192	09.07.14
	D-AVVG easyJet Airline Company Ltd Luton		08.07.19E
G-EZWY	Airbus A320-214	6267	05.09.14
	HB-JXH, G-EZWY, D-AVVT		
	easyJet Airline Company Ltd Luton		04.09.19E
G-EZWZ	Airbus A320-214	6353	21.11.14
	F-WWIR easyJet Airline Company Ltd Luton		20.11.19E
G-EZXO	Colt 56A	421	06.07.04
	SE-ZXO K Jakobsson Vastra Frolunda, Sweden		01.02.16E
G-EZZA	Europa Aviation Europa XS	537	10.05.02
	J C R Davey (Harvington, Evesham)		
	Built by J C R Davey – project PFA 247-13841;		
	tailwheel u/c (NF 19.12.14)		
G-EZZE	CZAW Sportcruiser	OC4226	17.08.10
	B W Rooke (Ashen, Sudbury)		11.07.19P
	Built by G Verity – project LAA 338-14687		
G-EZZL	Westland SA.341D Gazelle HT.3	1104	01.06.10
	G-CBKC, XW862 W R Pitcher t/a Regal Group UK		
	Bourne Park, Hurstbourne Tarrant		01.03.18P
G-EZZY	Evektor EV-97A Eurostar	2006-2830	01.08.06
	D P Creedy Hawksview, Stretton		03.05.19P
	Built by G Verity – project PFA 315-14533		

G-FAAA – G-FZZZ

G-FAAG[M]	Armstrong-Whitworth R.33 Airship	R33	14.01.21
	Cancelled 23.11.26 as WFU		
	Section of control gondola		
	With RAF Museum, Hendon		
G-FABA	Piper PA-31-350 Chieftain	31-7652175	17.04.15
	G-OJIL, OY-BTP Atlantic Bridge Aviation Ltd Lydd		12.02.19E
	Operated by Lyddair Ltd		
G-FABO	Bombardier CL-600-2B16 Challenger 604	5487	29.10.13
	I-AFMA, N330FX, C-GLWT		
	Hangar 8 Management Ltd (Oxford)		17.07.18E
G-FABS	Thunder Ax9-120 Series 2	2399	08.06.93
	R C Corrall & A B Court Woodbridge & Oswestry)		19.10.02
	(IE 27.06.18)		
(G-FACD)	Pitts S-1S	9543 G-BXFB	Reserved
	for long term rebuild project		
G-FACE	Cessna 172S Skyhawk SP	172S9194	24.10.02
	N52733 M O Loxton Parsonage Farm, Eastchurch		19.12.18E
G-FADF	Piper PA-18-150 Super Cub	18-7510	05.12.12
	OE-ADF A J Neale Oaksey Park		27.04.18E
G-FAEJ	Cessna 182K Skylane	18257849	02.08.16
	D-EAEJ, (D-EMAF), HB-CSN, N2649Q C Keller,		
	S Koch & B Schmiedel Jesenwang, Germany		22.12.18E
G-FAIR	SOCATA TB-10 Tobago	241	13.10.81
	A J Gomes Redhill		18.05.14E
	Engine caught fire after landing Rayne Hall Farm,		
	Rayne 23.09.13; stored dismantled 01.16 (NF 11.05.18)		
G-FAIT	Eurocopter AS350B3 Ecureuil	3578	06.03.19
	N63FS, N350EW, PR-DMF A S Fitzgibbons (London W8)		
	Kit built by Helicopteros do Brasil SA (NF 06.03.19)		
G-FAJC	Alpi Pioneer 300 Hawk	205	19.04.07
	M Clare Orlingbury Hold Farm, Orlingbury		13.07.18F
	Built by F A Cavaciuti – project PFA 330A-14639		
G-FAJM	Robinson R44 Raven II	12394	08.09.08
	Manor Corporate Ltd Killycurragh Road, Omagh		12.11.19E
G-FALC	Aeromere F.8L Falco Series 3	224	19.02.81
	G-AROT D M Burbridge Enstone *'13'*		06.08.18E
G-FAME	CFM Starstreak Shadow SA-II	K 273-SA	23.05.96
	C Prince (Cannock)		10.09.19F
	Built by T J Palmer – project PFA 206A-12973		
G-FANC	Temco Fairchild 24R-46	R46-347	16.10.81
	N77647, NC77647 Cancelled 30.07.03 by CAA		26.05.0
	Priory Farm, Tibenham *Burnt frame stored 06.17*		

G-FANL	Cessna R172K Hawk XP	R1722873	07.06.79	
	N736XQ J A Rees Haverfordwest		16.08.18E	
	Operated by Haverfordwest Air Charter Services			
G-FARE	Robinson R44 Raven II	10454	16.08.04	
	Toriamos Ltd (Harolds Cross, Dublin, RoI)		22.11.18E	
G-FARL	Pitts S-1E	1	22.10.03	
	N333AB J P Barrenechea Brighton City		30.11.18P	
	Built by S C Burgess; carries 'N333AB' on tail			
G-FARO	Star-Lite SL-1	xxxx	19.06.89	
	S C Goozee Newton Peveril Farm, Sturminster Marshall		26.07.18P	
	Built by M K Faro – project PFA 175-11359			
G-FARR	Jodel D.150 Mascaret	58	21.07.81	
	F-BNIN S J Farr Dairy House Farm, Worleston		19.05.18P	
	Built by Société Aéronautique Normande			
G-FARY	QAC Quickie Tri-Q	xxxx	02.04.02	
	A Bloomfield Sturgate		20.05.16P	
	Built by F Sayyah & J C Simpson			
	– project PFA 094A-10951			
G-FATB	Commander Aircraft Commander 114B 14624		03.07.96	
	N6037Y James D Peace & Co Kirkwall		28.09.11E	
	(NF 21.10.16)			
G-FATE	Sequoia F.8L Falco	757	08.10.08	
	N290 D Mottram tr G-FATE Flying Group			
	Wycombe Air Park		30.07.19P	
G-FAZT	Stoddard-Hamilton Glasair IIS RG	2069	16.10.17	
	PH-DUC C Bruce (West Bridgford, Nottingham)			
G-FBAR	Diamond DA.40 Star	40.248	16.05.17	
	HB-SDU, N248DS Exceedingly Ltd Bournemouth		30.05.18E	
G-FBAT	Aeroprakt A-22 Foxbat	013	16.05.00	
	J Jordan Otherton		13.03.17P	
	Built by G Faulkner – project PFA 317-13591			
G-FBCY	Skystar Kitfox Model 7	xxxx	10.09.14	
	G-FBOY A Bray Coventry		22.05.19P	
	Built by A Bray – project PFA 172D-14696; tricycle u/c			
G-FBEF	Embraer ERJ 190-200 LR	19000104	06.09.07	
	PT-SNY Flybe Ltd Exeter Int'l		09.09.19E	
G-FBEG	Embraer ERJ 190-200 LR	19000120	01.11.07	
	PT-SQO Flybe Ltd Exeter Int'l		04.11.19E	
G-FBEH	Embraer ERJ 190-200 LR	19000128	23.11.07	
	PT-SQX Flybe Ltd Exeter Int'l		26.11.19E	
G-FBEI	Embraer ERJ 190-200 LR	19000143	10.01.08	
	PT-SYV Flybe Ltd Exeter Int'l		14.01.20E	
G-FBEJ	Embraer ERJ 190-200 LR	19000155	06.03.08	
	PT-SAK Flybe Ltd Exeter Int'l		09.03.19E	
	'Welcome to Yorkshire' logo			
G-FBEK	Embraer ERJ 190-200 LR	19000168	25.04.08	
	PT-SDC Flybe Ltd Exeter Int'l		28.04.19E	
G-FBII	Comco Ikarus C42 FB100	0310-6574	18.12.03	
	F Beeson (Haslington, Crewe)		13.05.18P	
	Assembled Fly Buy Ultralights Ltd			
G-FBIX	de Havilland DH.100 Vampire FB.9	22100	24.07.91	
	7705M, WL505 Cancelled 17.05.05 by CAA			
	Mendlesham, Suffolk *Fuselage pod stored 10.15*			
G-FBJA	Embraer ERJ 170-200 STD	17000326	23.11.11	
	PT-TIB Flybe Ltd Exeter Int'l		23.11.19E	
G-FBJB	Embraer ERJ 170-200 STD	17000327	09.12.11	
	PT-TOB Flybe Ltd Exeter Int'l		08.12.19E	
G-FBJC	Embraer ERJ 170-200 STD	17000328	23.11.11	
	PT-TOO Flybe Ltd Exeter Int'l		23.11.19E	
G-FBJD	Embraer ERJ 170-200 STD	17000329	09.12.11	
	PT-TOZ Flybe Ltd Exeter Int'l		08.12.19E	
G-FBJE	Embraer ERJ 170-200 STD	17000336	04.04.12	
	PT-TUS Flybe Ltd Exeter Int'l		03.04.19E	
G-FBJF	Embraer ERJ 170-200 STD	17000341	25.05.12	
	PT-TBM Flybe Ltd Exeter Int'l		24.05.19E	
G-FBJG	Embraer ERJ 170-200 STD	17000344	27.06.12	
	PT-TCY Flybe Ltd Exeter Int'l		26.06.19E	
G-FBJH	Embraer ERJ 170-200 STD	17000351	25.09.12	
	PT-TFA Flybe Ltd Exeter Int'l		24.09.19E	
G-FBJI	Embraer ERJ 170-200 STD	17000355	27.11.12	
	PT-THC Flybe Ltd Exeter Int'l		26.11.19E	

G-FBJJ	Embraer ERJ 170-200 STD	17000358	13.12.13	
	PT-TJN Flybe Ltd Exeter Int'l		12.12.19E	
G-FBJK	Embraer ERJ 170-200 STD	17000359	19.12.13	
	PT-TJQ Flybe Ltd Exeter Int'l		18.12.19E	
G-FBKE	Cessna 510 Citation Mustang	510-0334	01.04.15	
	I-STCA, N40339 Mediocredito Italiano SPA Oxford		16.08.18E	
	(IE 20.08.18) (Stored 11.18)			
G-FBKF	Cessna 510 Citation Mustang	510-0360	21.04.15	
	I-STCC, N40753 Mediocredito Italiano SPA Oxford			
	(IE 20.08.18) (Stored 11.18)			
G-FBKG	Cessna 510 Citation Mustang	510-0361	01.04.15	
	I-STCD, N40770 Mediocredito Italiano SPA Oxford		10.03.19E	
	Stored 11.18			
G-FBKK	Cessna 510 Citation Mustang	510-0182	22.11.16	
	F-GISH, M-USTG Saint Honore Fly SARL Oxford		20.08.18E	
	Stored 10.18 (IE 25.09.18)			
G-FBRN	Piper PA-28-181 Archer II	28-8290166	03.08.98	
	D-EBRN, N82628 G E Fox Nottingham City		15.12.17E	
G-FBSS	Aeroprakt A-22LS Foxbat	A22LS-103	15.03.12	
	S R V McNeill Kernan Valley, Tandragee		11.01.19P	
	Built by A K Lynn – project LAA 317B-15101;			
	badged 'Super Sport 600'			
G-FBTT	Aeroprakt A-22L Foxbat	233	08.01.08	
	J Coyle & J Toner Enniskillen		26.07.18P	
	Built by G C Ellis – project PFA 317A-14743			
G-FBWH	Piper PA-28R-180 Cherokee Arrow	28R-30368	23.08.78	
	SE-FCV K McElhinney Dublin Weston, RoI		04.02.18E	
G-FBXA	Avions Transport ATR 72-212A	1260	18.09.15	
	F-WWEL Flybe Ltd Stockholm-Arlanda, Sweden			
	'Sigsten Viking'		17.09.19E	
	Operated in SAS c/s			
G-FBXB	Avions Transport ATR 72-212A	1277	09.10.15	
	F-WWCF Flybe Ltd Stockholm-Arlanda, Sweden			
	'Eindride Viking'		08.10.19E	
	Operated in SAS c/s			
G-FBXC	Avions Transport ATR 72-212A	1300	23.12.15	
	F-WWEV Flybe Ltd Stockholm-Arlanda, Sweden			
	'Hildur Viking'		22.12.19E	
	Operated in SAS c/s			
G-FBXD	Avions Transport ATR 72-212A	1315	18.03.16	
	F-WWEV Flybe Ltd Stockholm-Arlanda, Sweden			
	'Ansur Viking'		17.03.19E	
	Operated in SAS c/s			
G-FBXE	Avions Transport ATR 72-212A	1322	26.04.16	
	F-WWEE Flybe Ltd Stockholm-Arlanda, Sweden			
	'Torgrim Viking'		25.04.19E	
	Operated in SAS c/s			
G-FCAC	Diamond DA.42 Twin Star	42.062	02.11.05	
	G-ORZA, G-FCAC, OE-VPI			
	AJW Construction Ltd Bournemouth		05.03.18E	
G-FCAV	Schleicher ASK 13	13015	02.09.08	
	BGA 1396/CAV M F Cuming Shenington 'CAV'		25.09.09E	
	(NF 15.05.18)			
G-FCCC	Schleicher ASK 13	13035	05.08.08	
	BGA 1427, RAFGSA R83, BGA 1427			
	Shenington Gliding Club Shenington 'CCC'		29.09.18E	
G-FCKD	Eurocopter EC120B Colibri	1209	11.01.06	
	PH-ECK, ZK-HJD, ZK-HVQ			
	Red Dragon Management LLP White Waltham		12.03.18E	
G-FCOM	Slingsby T59F Kestrel 19	1765	23.01.09	
	BGA 1723			
	A G Truman & P A C Wheatcroft Lasham '234'		09.05.18R	
G-FCSL	Piper PA-31-350 Chieftain	31-7852052	18.04.08	
	PH-PTC, G-CLAN, N27549 Culross Aerospace Ltd			
	Goodwood *www.flight-cal.com*		27.07.18E	
	Official type data 'PA-31-350 Navajo Chieftain'			
	is incorrect; callsign 'VOR01'			
G-FCSP	Robin DR.400-180 Régent	2022	24.10.90	
	N W McConachie Headcorn		25.04.19E	
G-FCTK	de Havilland DH.82C Tiger Moth	883	22.01.15	
	CF-CTK, RCAF 5084			
	A J Palmer Palmer's Farm, Lower Dicker		23.10.19P	
	Built by de Havilland Aircraft of Canada Ltd;			
	as '5084' in RCAF c/s			

G

G-FCUK	Pitts S-1C	02	09.08.02
	OH-XPB H C & M J Luck Shobdon		10.07.19P
	Built by A Ronnberg		
G-FCUM	Robinson R44 Raven II	11723	28.04.07
	Barnes Holdings Ltd & Hummingbird Helicopters Ltd		
	Doncaster Sheffield		27.06.19E
	Operated by Hummingbird Helicopters		
G-FDHB	Bristol Scout C Replica	xxxx	08.08.14
	D S Bremner tr Bristol Scout Group Old Warden		23.05.18P
	Built by D S Bremner, R Bremner & T Willford – project		
	PFA 355-14755; as '1264' of 2 Wing in RNAS c/s		
G-FDHS	Leonardo AW109SP Grand New	22378	26.01.18
	Knaresborough Aviation LLP Leeds East		
G-FDPS	Pitts S-2C	6066	11.02.05
	N130PS Flights & Dreams Ltd Cranfield		23.03.18E
	Built by Aviat Aircraft Inc		
G-FDZE	Boeing 737-8K5	35137	16.01.08
	C-GDZE, G-FDZE, C-GDZE, G-FDZE, C-CGZE,		
	G-FDZE, C-FDZE, G-FDZE, N1786B		
	TUI Airways Ltd t/a TUI Luton		19.02.19E
	Line No: 2482		
G-FDZR	Boeing 737-8K5	35145	26.03.09
	C-FLZR, G-FLZR, C-FLZR, G-FDZR, N1786B		
	TUI Airways Ltd t/a TUI Luton		30.01.19E
	Line No: 2849		
G-FDZS	Boeing 737-8K5	35147	14.04.09
	N1786B TUI Airways Ltd t/a TUI Luton		08.03.19E
	Line No: 2866		
G-FDZT	Boeing 737-8K5	37248	01.02.11
	TUI Airways Ltd t/a TUI Luton		30.01.19E
	Line No: 3532		
G-FDZU	Boeing 737-8K5	37253	01.03.11
	N1796B TUI Airways Ltd t/a TUI Luton		27.02.19E
	Line No: 3562		
G-FDZX	Boeing 737-8K5	37258	23.05.11
	N1786B TUI Airways Ltd t/a TUI Luton		29.09.18E
	Line No: 3655		
G-FDZY	Boeing 737-8K5	37261	22.11.11
	C-GHZY, G-FDZY TUI Airways Ltd t/a TUI Luton		02.05.19E
	Line No: 3844		
G-FDZZ	Boeing 737-8K5	37262	21.12.11
	C-FHZZ, G-FDZZ TUI Airways Ltd t/a TUI Luton		27.04.19E
	Line No: 3876		
G-FEAB	Piper PA-28-181 Archer III	2843567	07.07.04
	N53690 Feabrex Ltd Rochester		21.09.18E
G-FEBB	Grob G104 Speed Astir IIB	4040	03.12.07
	BGA 2545/EBB		
	C P A Jones (Haslington, Crewe) 'EBB'		24.01.19E
G-FEBJ	Schleicher ASW 19B	19282	02.11.07
	BGA 2552/EBJ		
	I R Willows Husbands Bosworth 'H11'		23.07.10E
	(NF 22.02.16)		
G-FECK	Raj Hamsa X'Air Jabiru(3)	1042	19.03.18
	G-CDSN R J Spence Enstone		29.08.19P
	Built by G W Cole – project BMAA/HB/47		
G-FECO	Grob G102 Astir CS77	1837	14.12.07
	BGA 2582/ECQ Stratford on Avon Gliding Club Ltd		
	Snitterfield 'ECO'		17.01.19E
G-FEED	Cameron Z-90	12054	12.12.16
	O Rosellino Mondovi, Italy		06.12.18E
G-FEEF	Robin DR.220 2+2	14	20.03.12
	F-BOCF M Juhrig (Otzberg, Germany) 'Fifi'		30.06.18E
	Built by Centre-Est Aéronautique		
G-FEET	P&M Pegasus Quik	8133	06.10.05
	G Burns Eccles Newton Farm, Coldstream		19.04.19P
G-FEGN	Piper PA-28-236 Dakota	28-8411030	02.11.15
	HB-POJ, N4370G		
	P J Vacher Melhuish Farm, North Moreton		29.04.18E
G-FELD	AutoGyro MTOsport	09 145S	01.02.10
	S P Pearce Carrickmore		22.06.18P
	Assembled Rotorsport UK as c/n RSUK/MTOS/031		
G-FELL	Europa Aviation Europa XS	372	17.03.98
	M C Costin & J A Inglis Husbands Bosworth		29.06.18P
	Built by J A Fell – project PFA 247-13208; tricycle u/c		

G-FELT	Cameron N-77	1174	19.07.85
	R P Allan Aston Rowant, Watlington 'fuzzy felt'		25.06.19E
G-FELX	CZAW Sportcruiser	07SC058	17.09.07
	T F Smith Crowfield		03.08.18P
	Built by T F Smith – project PFA 338-14661		
	(Quick-build kit 3856)		
G-FERN	Mainair Blade 912	1342-1002-7-W1137	18.10.02
	C R Buckle Blackmoor Farm, Aubourn		27.08.17P
	(NF 02.05.17)		
G-FERV	Rolladen-Schneider LS4	4257	12.09.07
	BGA 2899 S Walker Dunstable Downs '54L'		21.03.18E
G-FESB	Pipistrel Apis/Bee	A066	03.06.16
	P C Piggott (Walcote, Lutterworth)		
	(IE 13.12.17)		
G-FESS	Cyclone Pegasus Quantum 15-912	7840	12.02.08
	G-CBBZ P M Fessi (Bretford, Rugby)		26.12.17P
G-FEST	Aérospatiale AS.350B Ecureuil	2079	23.09.16
	HB-ZHC, ZK-HYT, JA9742		
	Wavendon Social Housing Ltd Solent		14.02.19E
	Operated by Phoenix Helicopters		
G-FESX	Schempp-Hirth Discus-2c FES	20	08.01.18
	P K Carpenter & K S Mcphee Challock 'X'		
	(IE 17.01.18)		
G-FEVS	PZL-Bielsko SZD-50-3 Puchacz	B-1091	14.08.08
	BGA 2992/EVS		
	Norfolk Gliding Club Ltd Tibenham 'EVS'		06.07.18E
G-FEWG	Fuji FA.200-160 Aero Subaru	FA200-232	15.10.04
	G-BBNV Cirrus UK Training Ltd Turweston		08.07.15E
G-FEZZ	Agusta-Bell 206B-2 JetRanger II	8317	16.09.98
	SU-YAD, YU-HAT R J Myram White Waltham		19.08.18E
G-FFAB	Cameron N-105	4067	20.02.97
	B J Hammond Boreham, Chelmsford		
	'Hallmark' & 'Forever Friends'		29.06.18E
G-FFAF	Reims/Cessna F150L	F15001033	10.02.06
	I-FFAF R J Fletcher (Penhow, Caldicot)		12.04.18E
G-FFBG	Reims/Cessna F182Q Skylane II	F18200032	14.03.11
	EI-FBG, D-EFBG, (F-GAGU) D P Edwards Sywell		18.05.18E
G-FFEN	Reims/Cessna F150M	F15001204	25.08.78
	PH-VGL J P Nugent t/a Wicklow Wings		
	Newcastle, RoI		10.09.19E
G-FFFA	P&M PulsR	8673	22.01.14
	I A Macadam (Sturminster Newton)		28.08.19P
G-FFFB	P&M Quik GTR	8745	27.05.16
	Flying For Freedom Ltd Cotswold		25.05.18P
G-FFFC	Cessna 510 Citation Mustang	510-0451	31.07.14
	Synergy Aircraft Leasing Ltd Blackbushe		05.08.19E
	Operated by Synergy Aviation Ltd		
G-FFFF	Zenair CH.750	75-10648	16.01.18
	J Bate (Burnley)		
	Built by J Bate – project LAA 381-15485 (NF 16.01.18)		
G-FFFT	Lindstrand LBL 31A	705	30.05.00
	W Rousell & J Tyrrell Wollaston, Wellingborough		
	'FT Financial Times'		23.06.18E
G-FFIT	P&M Pegasus Quik	8238	15.01.07
	M Lewis (Sutton-on-Sea, Mablethorpe)		18.05.19P
G-FFMV	Diamond DA.42M-NG Twin Star	42.MN029	11.12.13
	Cobham Leasing Ltd Bournemouth		13.01.19R
G-FFOX	Hawker Hunter T.7A	41H-670788	10.01.96
	WV318 Swift Composites Ltd		
	Stockholm-Vasteras, Sweden		09.05.16P
	Has centre fuselage, at least, of WV322		
	(c/n 41H-670792): see G-BZSE; as 'WV318'		
	in RAF c/s (NF 20.10.17)		
G-FFRA	Dassault Falcon 20DC	132	28.05.92
	N902FR, (N23FR), (N149FE), N2FE, N560L, N4348F,		
	F-WMKG Cobham Leasing Ltd Bournemouth		20.10.18E
G-FFRV	Van's RV-10	40641	02.08.18
	A Miller tr Fairoaks Flyers Fairoaks		
	Built by C Dupre, D Groves & A Miller		
	– project LAA 339-15082 (NF 02.08.18)		
G-FFTI	SOCATA TB-20 Trinidad	1065	23.02.90
	R Lenk Shipdham		07.12.18E

G-FFTT	Lindstrand LBL Newspaper SS HAB	673	10.07.00	
	Cancelled 04.01.11 as PWFU		11.11.06	
	Not Known *Inflated Pidley 05.16*			
G-FFUN	Solar Wings Pegasus Quantum 15	6655	09.06.99	
	G-MYMD M D & R M Jarvis Longacre Farm, Sandy		10.05.19P	
G-FFWD	Cessna 310R II	310R0579	20.02.90	
	G-TVKE, G-EURO, N87468			
	T S Courtman East Midlands		22.11.18E	
G-FGAZ	Schleicher Ka 6E	4103	21.09.07	
	BGA 2651, RAFGGA 550			
	P W Graves (Wootton-under-Edge) *'EFM'*		06.05.18E	
G-FGID	Vought FG-1D Corsair	3111	01.11.91	
	N8297, N9154Z, USN 88297 Patina Ltd Duxford		07.07.19P	
	Built by Goodyear Aircraft Corporation; operated			
	by The Fighter Collection; as 'KD345:130:A' in			
	RN 1850 Sqdn c/s			
G-FGSI	Montgomerie-Bensen B8MR	xxxx	19.04.07	
	F G Shepherd (Leadgate, Alston)			
	Built by F G Shepherd – project PFA G/01A-1354			
	(NF 16.01.15)			
G-FHAS	Scheibe SF25E Super Falke	4359	14.05.81	
	(D-KOOG) M G Reynolds tr Upwood			
	Motorglider Group Crowland		18.07.08E	
G-FIAT	Piper PA-28-140 Cherokee F	28-7425162	19.07.89	
	G-BBYW, N9622N Demero Ltd & Livingstone Skies Ltd			
	Hinton-in-the-Hedges		26.08.19E	
G-FIBS	Aérospatiale AS.350BA Ecureuil	2074	14.06.94	
	JA9732 Maceplast Romania SA			
	Bucharest Otopeni, Romania		03.08.18E	
G-FIBT	Robinson R44 Raven II	13095	04.02.15	
	D-HVNG A Curnis & G Mazza			
	(Brescia & Sarnico, Lombardy, Italy)		15.12.18E	
G-FICA	Piper PA-28RT-201 Arrow IV	28R-7918165	09.06.17	
	EC-IMT, LX-FLY, N2839K			
	C H Duke (Georgsmarienhuette, Germany)		05.02.19E	
G-FICH	Guimbal Cabri G2	1131	11.02.16	
	Helicentre Aviation Ltd Leicester		23.02.18E	
G-FICS	Flight Design CTSW	07-10-18	17.12.07	
	N Harris Elstree			
	Assembled P&M Aviation Ltd as c/n 8348;			
	also reported as kit no 07-10-17; noted 10.18			
	(IE 08.02.18)			
G-FIDL	Thruster T600T 450 Jab	0032-T600N-062	13.07.12	
	G-CBIO T A Colman			
	Broomclose Farm, Longbridge Deverill		21.03.18P	
	Rebuilt & incorporates parts of G-CBIO			
G-FIDO	Best Off Skyranger Nynja 912(1)	UK\N/BK200	01.12.15	
	P D Hollands Solent			
	Built by P D Hollands – project BMAA/HB/679			
	(NF 01.12.15)			
G-FIFA	Cessna 404 Titan	404-0644	24.05.07	
	G-TVIP, G-KIWI, G-BHNI, LN-LGM, SE-IFV,			
	G-BHNI, (N5302J) RVL Aviation Ltd Lydd		09.01.18E	
G-FIFE	Reims/Cessna FA152 Aerobat	FA1520351	15.02.95	
	G-BFYN The Moray Flying Club (1990)			
	Kinloss Barracks, Kinloss		22.02.18E	
G-FIFI	SOCATA TB-20 Trinidad	688	16.01.87	
	G-BMWS B J Ward tr The Foxtrot India Group			
	(Leamington Spa)		12.01.20E	
	On rebuild 11.18			
G-FIFT	Comco Ikarus C42 FB100	0409-6623	02.08.04	
	A R Jones Carlisle Lake District		19.10.18P	
	Assembled Fly Buy Ultralights Ltd			
G-FIFY	Coloman MC-30 Luciole	95	27.03.12	
	I J M Donnelly (Aboyne)			
	Built by D R Hall – project LAA 371-15007 (NF 22.05.18)			
G-FIGA	Cessna 152 II	15284644	03.06.87	
	N6243M P A Bowen Wellesbourne Mountford		28.09.19E	
G-FIGB	Cessna 152 II	15285925	16.11.87	
	N95561 A J Gomes Biggin Hill		12.02.00	
	(NF 23.09.16)			
G-FIII	Extra EA.300/L	091	06.12.04	
	G-RGEE, D-ESEW			
	M & R M Nagel (Vettweiss, Germany)		14.02.18E	

G-FIJJ	Reims/Cessna F177RG Cardinal RG	F177RG0031	29.04.99	
	G-AZFP Fly 177 SARL (Izeron, France)		27.08.18E	
	Wichita c/n 177RG0194			
G-FILE	Piper PA-34-200T Seneca II	34-8070108	23.07.87	
	N8140Z B Bailey tr G-FILE Group Bristol		21.06.17E	
G-FILL	Piper PA-31 Navajo C	31-7912069	28.06.96	
	OO-EJM, N3521 Cancelled 25.05.11 as PWFU		13.10.11	
	Sywell *Stored for spares use 09.16*			
G-FINA	Reims/Cessna F150L	F15000826	12.10.93	
	G-BIFT, PH-CEW K M Rigby Cumbernauld		21.05.19E	
G-FIND	Reims/Cessna F406 Caravan II	F406-0045	16.08.90	
	OY-PEU, 5Y-LAN, G-FIND, PH-ALV, F-WZDT			
	Reconnaissance Ventures Ltd t/a RVL Group			
	East Midlands		05.06.18E	
G-FINT	Piper L-4B Cub	9444	05.12.08	
	N10491, 43-583, (42-59393) G & H M Picarella			
	Trenchard Farm, Eggesford *'Helen'*		20.12.18E	
	As '3583:44-D' in 30th Infantry Division USAAF c/s			
G-FINZ	III Sky Arrow 650 T	K-133	08.01.03	
	C A Bloom Stornoway		30.06.18P	
	Built by A G Counsell – project PFA 298-13824			
G-FION	Titan T-51 Mustang	160	11.03.16	
	A A Wordsworth Netherthorpe		03.09.19P	
	Built by A A Wordsworth – project LAA 355-15164;			
	as '441968:VF-E' in USAAF c/s			
G-FITY	Europa Aviation Europa XS	550	08.05.09	
	D C A Moore Aboyne		17.09.18P	
	Built by D C A Moore – project PFA 247-14073			
	(IE 20.12.16)			
G-FIXX	Van's RV-7	71760	31.08.06	
	P C Hambilton Blackpool		15.09.17P	
	Built by P C Hambilton – project PFA 323-14225			
G-FIZY	Europa Aviation Europa XS	384	16.12.99	
	G-DDSC C Callicott & W Oswald Eshott		18.07.13P	
	Built by G N Holland – project PFA 247-13291;			
	tricycle u/c (NF 30.10.16)			
G-FIZZ	Piper PA-28-161 Warrior II	28-7816301	01.12.78	
	N2721M M A Artherton tr G-FIZZ Group Shipdham		26.05.18E	
	C/n 28-7816301 built as N2721M: the official			
	p/i N857U relates to Electra G-FIZU			
G-FJCE	Thruster T.600T	9128-T600T-032	25.11.98	
	Cancelled 16.04.10 by CAA		31.07.04	
	Donaghcloney *Stored 12.13*			
G-FJET	Cessna 550 Citation II	550-0419	07.07.97	
	G-DCFR, G-WYLX, VH-JVS, G-JETD, N1217N			
	London Executive Aviation Ltd Southend		17.01.20E	
G-FJMS	Partenavia P68B	113	07.09.92	
	G-SVHA, OY-AJH J B Randle Church Farm, Piltdown		16.09.18E	
G-FJTH	Aeroprakt A-22 Foxbat	043 & UK010	16.07.03	
	A J Tuson Chilbolton		06.05.19P	
	Built by F J T Hancock – project PFA 317-13928			
G-FKNH	Piper PA-15 Vagabond	15-291	19.03.97	
	CF-KNH, N4517H, NC4517H			
	M J Mothershaw RAF Woodvale		19.04.19E	
G-FKOS	Piper PA-28-181 Archer II	28-7790591	27.03.07	
	OE-KOS, OY-BTL Kristelan (UK) Ltd t/a SVM Glasgow			
	Dundee		10.07.19E	
	Operated by Tayside Aviation			
G-FLAG	Colt 77A	2000	20.09.90	
	B A Williams Maidstone *'Thunder & Colt'*		04.06.14E	
	Built by Thunder & Colt Ltd (NF 09.08.17)			
G-FLAP	Cessna A152 Aerobat	A1520856	14.06.02	
	G-BHJB, N4662A Cancelled 20.10.06 by CAA		18.09.08	
	Deanland *Reported stored 06.13*			
G-FLAV	Piper PA-28-161 Warrior II	28-8016283	07.04.94	
	N8171X G E Fox Bagby		02.01.18E	
G-FLAX	Aeropro EuroFOX 914	51317	21.04.17	
	Lleweni Parc Ltd Lleweni Parc		10.09.19P	
	Built by S Sinnot – project LAA 376-15444;			
	tricycle u/c; glider-tug			
G-FLBA	Bombardier DHC-8-402Q	4253	03.07.09	
	C-FVVB Flybe Ltd Exeter Int'l		02.07.19E	
G-FLBB	Bombardier DHC-8-402Q	4255	03.07.09	
	C-FWGE Flybe Ltd Exeter Int'l		02.07.19E	

G-FLBC Bombardier DHC-8-402Q   4257   17.07.09
C-FWGY Flybe Ltd Exeter Int'l   16.07.19E

G-FLBD Bombardier DHC-8-402Q   4259   31.07.09
C-FWZN Flybe Ltd Exeter Int'l 'Spirit of Inverness'   30.07.19E

G-FLBE Bombardier DHC-8-402Q   4261   30.09.09
C-FXAB Flybe Ltd Exeter Int'l 'Spirit of Exeter'   29.09.19E

G-FLBY Comco Ikarus C42 FB100 Bravo   1302-7239   20.03.13
M Fitch t/a Fly by Light Elstree   04.04.19P
Assembled Red-Air UK; operated by Fly by Light

G-FLCA Fleet 80 Canuck   068   18.07.90
CS-ACQ, CF-DQP
S P Evans Calcot Peak Farm, Calcot   04.10.18P

G-FLCN Dassault Falcon 900   078   31.07.13
F-GVMO, LX-GES, N522KM, C-GSSS, N332MC,
N456FJ, F-WWFH XJC Ltd Southampton   03.07.18E

G-FLCT Hallam Fleche   001   21.10.98
R G Hallam (Nether Alderley, Macclesfield)
Built by R G Hallam – project PFA 309-13389
(NF 12.11.14)

G-FLDG Best Off Skyranger 912(2)   UK/390   21.04.04
D James & D W Power Swansea   23.03.13P
Built by A J Gay – project BMAA/HB/328 (IE 14.06.18)

G-FLEA SOCATA TB-10 Tobago   235   31.07.81
PH-TTP, G-FLEA   N J Thomas Bembridge   19.05.18E

G-FLEE Ivanov ZJ-Viera   VIERAA6/08M   26.01.09
P C Piggott Husbands Bosworth
(SSDR microlight since 05.14) (IE 06.10.17)

G-FLEW Lindstrand LBL 90A   586   21.01.99
(A6-), G-FLEW   H C Loveday
South Croydon 'Lindstrand Balloons'   17.10.18E

G-FLGT Lindstrand LBL 105A   888   05.12.02
Life Less Ordinary AB Angelholm, Sweden
'Lindstrand Balloons'   17.07.18E

G-FLIA AutoGyro Calidus   xxxx   21.03.17
P Davies Clench Common   02.04.18P
Assembled Rotorsport UK as c/n RSUK/CALS/033

G-FLIK Pitts S-1S   xxxx   07.01.81
R P Millinship Leicester   18.06.18P
Built by R P Millinship – project PFA 009-10513

G-FLIP Reims/Cessna FA152 Aerobat   FA1520375   29.12.80
G-BOES, G-FLIP   C Bennewith tr South East Area
Flying Section Rochester   14.12.18E

G-FLIS Magni M16C Tandem Trainer   16105974   25.10.10
M L L Temple Eddsfield, Octon Lodge Farm, Thwing   05.10.18P

G-FLIT RotorWay Exec 162F   6324   22.12.98
R S Snell Street Farm, Takeley   20.10.17P
Built by R F Rhodes

G-FLKE Scheibe SF25C Rotax-Falke   44673   05.10.01
The Royal Air Force Gliding & Soaring Association
RAF Wittering   15.07.18E

G-FLKS Scheibe SF25C Rotax-Falke   44662   16.10.00
D-KIEQ London Gliding Club Proprietary Ltd
Dunstable Downs   14.03.18E

G-FLKY Cessna 172S Skyhawk SP   172S8952   15.12.10
N3540U M E Falkingham Full Sutton   22.02.18E

G-FLOE Robinson R66 Turbine   0631   06.11.15
Freechase Ventures Ltd Brighton City   21.11.18E

G-FLOR Europa Aviation Europa   171   11.11.98
A F C V Eldik Pent Farm, Postling   22.09.18P
Built by A F C van Eldik – project PFA 247-12793;
tailwheel u/c

G-FLOW Cessna 172S Skyhawk SP   172S9677   19.08.04
N6127S P H Archard Elstree   03.07.19E

G-FLOX Europa Aviation Europa   129   28.06.95
T W Eaton tr DPT Group Fowle Hall Farm, Laddingford
11.05.18P
Built by P S Buchan, T W Eaton & B Lewer
– project PFA 247-12732; tailwheel u/c

G-FLPI Rockwell Commander 112A   205   16.03.79
SE-FLP, (N1205J) J B Thompson Leicester   16.08.18E

G-FLRT Europa Aviation Europa   xxxx   10.03.04
Cancelled 09.05.06 as destroyed   21.03.06
Langtoft, Yorks *Built by D B Southworth &*
K G Atkinson – project PFA 247-12926; stored 01.18

G-FLSH IAV Bacau Yakovlev Yak-52   877409   09.06.03
RA-44550, LY-AKF, 212(yellow) DOSAAF
Cancelled 26.03.12 by CAA   29.10.10
St Athan *On rebuild as '52 White' in Russia c/s 12.18*

G-FLTC British Aerospace BAe 146 Series 300   E3205   15.12.04
G-JEBH, G-BTVO, G-NJID, B-1777, G-BTVO, G-6-205
E3205 Trading Ltd   17.10.09E
Broken up at Southend 12.18 (NF 04.02.16)

G-FLTY Embraer EMB-110P1 Bandeirante 110215   28.08.92
G-ZUSS, G-REGA, N711NH, PT-GMH
Cancelled 11.04.06 by CAA   05.08.05
Southend *Open store, engineless 01.19*

G-FLUZ Rolladen-Schneider LS8-18   8267   30.04.08
BGA 4718/JRK D M King Shobdon '618'   23.04.18E

G-FLXI Pilatus PC-12/47E   1275   07.08.18
M-TOMS(2), HB-FQF
Flexifly Aircraft Hire Ltd Fairoaks   16.08.19E

G-FLXS Dassault Falcon 2000LX   275   22.08.14
F-WWGR TAG Aviation (UK) Ltd Farnborough   21.08.19E

G-FLYA Mooney M.20J Mooney 201   24-3124   08.06.89
B Willis Full Sutton   29.01.18E

G-FLYB Comco Ikarus C42 FB100   0309-6572   15.09.03
M D Stewart Husbands Bosworth   20.11.12P
Assembled Fly Buy Ultralights Ltd; crashed
Perranporth 07.04.13; stripped fuselage
dumped 07.16 (NF 07.01.18)

G-FLYC Comco Ikarus C42 FB100   0503-6656   07.04.05
Solent Flight Ltd Phoenix Farm, Lower Upham   31.08.18P
Assembled Aerosport Ltd

G-FLYF Mainair Blade 912   1371-0305-7-W1166 30.03.05
D G Adley Westonzoyland   17.03.18P

G-FLYG Slingsby T67C Firefly   2074   23.08.02
PH-SGA, (PH-SBA) G Laden Cranfield   22.01.14E
Stored 02.17 (IE 26.10.15)

G-FLYI Piper PA-34-200 Seneca   34-7250144   01.09.81
G-BHVO, SE-FYY
Falcon Flying Services Ltd Biggin Hill   18.04.18E

G-FLYJ Evektor EV-97 Eurostar SL   2014-4211   21.01.15
The Scottish Aero Club Ltd Perth   15.01.18P
Assembled Light Sport Aviation Ltd

G-FLYK Beech B200 Super King Air   BB-921   27.10.17
D-IKOB, N244JB, N76MP
D T A Rees Haverfordwest   17.03.18E

G-FLYM Comco Ikarus C42 FB100   0707-6903   26.03.08
R S O'Carroll Kernan Valley, Tandragee   16.09.17P
Assembled Aerosport Ltd; crashed Dolly's Brae,
Castlewellan Forest Park, Co Down 29.05.17 &
substantially damaged; Permit suspended 24.06.17

G-FLYO Evektor EV-97 Eurostar SL   2014-4205   07.10.14
N A & P A Allwood North Coates   25.10.19P
Assembled Light Sport Aviation Ltd

G-FLYP Beagle B.206 Series 2   B058   15.10.98
N40CJ, N97JH, G-AVHO, VQ-LAY, G-AVHO
A T J Darrah & R H Ford Seething   06.09.19E

G-FLYT Europa Aviation Europa   057   15.05.95
K F & R Richardson Wellesbourne Mountford   06.05.00P
Built by D W Adams – project PFA 247-12653
(IE 22.09.15)

G-FLYW Beech 200 Super King Air   BB-209   18.12.12
G-LIVY, G-PSTR, F-GPAS, D-IACS, ZP-TTC,
ZP-PTC, EB-001, N5450M, N545GM
D T A & J A Rees Haverfordwest   31.05.18E

G-FLYX Robinson R44 Raven II   11669   11.04.07
HQ Aviation Ltd Denham   19.04.18E
Substantially damaged when it rolled over at
Denham 02.11.18

G-FLYY BAC 167 Strikemaster Mk.80   EEP/JP/163   03.09.01
RSaudi AF 1112, G-27-31 High G Jets Ltd Blackpool   13.07.18E
Plane Set 124

G-FLZA	Staaken Z-21A Flitzer	xxxx	14.04.09
	Cancelled 15.08.13 by CAA		
	Morgansfield, Fishburn *Built by G R Pybus – project*		
	LAA 223-14876) (Advertised for sale 05.13 part build		
G-FLZR	Staaken Z-21 Flitzer	223	21.09.01
	I V Staines Breighton		17.09.18P
	Built by J F Govan & I V Staines		
	– project PFA 223-13219		
G-FMAM	Piper PA-28-161 Warrior II	28-7415056	07.06.90
	G-BBXV, N9603N Air Training Club Aviation Ltd		
	Blackpool		12.03.18E
	Originally built as PA-28-151 Cherokee Warrior		
G-FMBS	Pitts Model 12	12JX	04.01.12
	N12JX W P Wright Cranfield		18.06.18P
	Built by Inverted US		
G-FMGB	Cameron Z-90	11756	06.06.13
	A M Holly Breadstone, Berkeley *'Fortnum & Mason'*		01.07.19E
G-FMGG	Maule M-5-235C Lunar Rocket	7260C	30.04.02
	G-RAGG, N5632M S Bierbaum Bodmin		19.09.18E
	Operated by Bodmin Light Aeroplane Services Ltd		
G-FMLY	Commander Aircraft Commander 114B	14655	13.11.13
	G-VICS, N655V PNG Air Ltd Biggin Hill		11.04.18E
G-FNAV	Piper PA-31-350 Chieftain	31-7752187	17.01.11
	PH-XPI, G-FNAV, PH-XPI, G-BFFR, N27388		
	Airpart Supply Ltd Wycombe Air Park		26.07.18E
	Callsign 'VOR02'		
G-FNEY	Reims/Cessna F177RG Cardinal RG	F177RG0059	24.02.04
	F-BTFQ F Ney East Midlands		10.08.18E
G-FNLD	Cessna 172N Skyhawk II	17270596	03.08.88
	(G-BOUG), N739KD M J Humphrey & R C Laming		
	tr Papa Hotel Flying Group Fenland		13.04.18E
G-FOFO	Robinson R44 Raven II	10320	06.04.04
	A J Pickup Nottingham City		26.05.16E
	(NF 07.07.17)		
G-FOGG	Cameron N-90	1365	21.11.86
	J P E Money-Kyrle Ruardean *'Phileas Fogg'*		25.09.96A
	(NF 13.11.15)		
G-FOGI	Europa Aviation Europa XS	385	29.10.04
	B Fogg Sleap		10.08.18P
	Built by B Fogg – project PFA 247-13313; tailwheel u/c		
G-FOKK	Fokker Dr.1 Triplane replica	240	18.01.06
	P D & S E Ford Derby		03.08.18P
	Built by P D Ford – project PFA 238-14253;		
	as '477/17' in German Army Air Service red c/s		
G-FOKR	Airdrome ¾ Fokker E.III replica	GS-103	10.02.09
	R D Myles Perth		
	Built by D Stephens ex Grass Strip Aviation kit s/n		
	GS-103; as '422/15' in German Army Air Service c/s;		
	dismantled & stored 05.16		
	(SSDR microlight since 05.14) (IE 23.04.15)		
G-FOKS	Aeropro EuroFOX 912(S)	52417	11.07.17
	E R Scougall Ludham		26.02.19P
	Built by E R Scougall – project LAA 376-15473;		
	tailwheel u/c		
G-FOKX	Aeropro EuroFOX 912(S)	39514	01.04.14
	A Spencer tr Trent Valley Eurofox Group		
	Kirton in Lindsey		16.05.18P
	Built by A Spencer & Partners – project		
	LAA 376-15272; tailwheel u/c; glider-tug		
G-FOKZ	Aeropro EuroFOX 912(iS)	43714	16.09.14
	R J Evans (Meldreth, Royston)		16.07.19P
	Built by R J Evans – project LAA 376-15282; tailwheel u/c		
G-FOLI	Robinson R22 Beta II	2813	25.04.98
	Paul D White Ltd Elstree		03.07.19E
	Operated by Flying Pig Helicopters		
G-FOLY	Pitts S-2A	2213	26.07.89
	N31477 C T Charleston Great Horkesley, Colchester		15.04.17E
	Built by Aerotek Inc		
G-FOMO	Bombardier BD-700-1A10 Global 6000	9797	26.03.19
	VP-CAX, C-FUEP London Executive Aviation Ltd		
	London Stansted		
G-FOOT	Robinson R44 Raven	1891	15.08.14
	LN-OSF J Pratt (Sawley, Clitheroe)		14.08.19E
G-FOPP	Neico Lancair 320	672-320-416 FB	14.08.92
	Great Circle Design Ltd Henstridge		24.07.13P
	Built by M A Fopp – project PFA 191-12319 (IE 19.07.17)		
G-FORA	Schempp-Hirth Ventus cT	126	28.11.07
	BGA 4449/JEF, D-KFWH P Clay Sutton Bank '4A'		27.04.18E
G-FORD	SNCAN Stampe SV.4C(G)	129	07.02.78
	F-BBNS P H Meeson Rotary Farm, Hatch		01.05.18P
G-FORZ	Pitts S-1S	xxxx	03.11.98
	N W Parkinson White Waltham		11.08.18P
	Built by N Parkinson – project PFA 009-13393		
G-FOSY	SOCATA MS.880B Rallye Club	1304	07.12.00
	G-AXAK A G Foster Humberside		17.05.04
	(NF 22.05.18)		
G-FOWL	Colt 90A	1198	11.03.88
	M R Stokoe Tatsfield, Westerham *'Chicken'*		27.04.13E
	Built by Thunder & Colt Ltd (IE 24.09.15)		
G-FOXA	Piper PA-28-161 Cadet	2841240	17.11.89
	N9192B The Leicestershire Aero Club Ltd Leicester		14.05.19E
	Official p/i 'N91928' is incorrect		
G-FOXB	Aeroprakt A-22 Foxbat	UK006	15.03.02
	G D McCullough Slieve Croob, Castlewellan		14.09.17P
	Built by M Raflewski – project PFA 317-13878		
G-FOXC	Denney Kitfox Model 3	773	08.01.91
	R M Bremner & T Willford Newton Peveril Farm,		
	Sturminster Marshall *'Foxc Lady'*		15.06.18P
	Built by B W Davis – project PFA 172-11900		
G-FOXD	Denney Kitfox Model 2	xxxx	22.11.89
	C G Langham Walkeridge Farm, Overton		07.10.19P
	Built by D Hanley – project PFA 172-11618		
G-FOXF	Denney Kitfox Model 4	1707	24.03.00
	M S Goodwin Easter Poldar Farm, Thornhill		26.07.18P
	Built by M S Goodwin – project PFA 172A-12399		
G-FOXG	Denney Kitfox Model 2	xxxx	15.08.90
	M V Hearns Balado		13.07.15P
	Built by S M Jackson – project PFA 172-11886		
	(NF 13.10.16)		
G-FOXI	Denney Kitfox Model 2	xxxx	21.09.89
	I M Walton Wellesbourne Mountford		21.08.04P
	Built by I N Jennison – project PFA 172-11508		
	(NF 16.01.15)		
G-FOXL	Zenair CH.601XL Zodiac	6-9823	11.12.06
	R W Taylor (Rayleigh)		
	Built by M J Lloyd – project PFA 162B-14537 (NF 24.07.18)		
G-FOXM	Bell 206B-2 JetRanger II	1514	05.02.93
	G-STAK, G-BNIS, N35HF, N135VG Hessle Dock		
	Company Ltd (Faldingworth, Market Rasen)		11.06.13E
	Stored for spares use 08.17 (NF 16.08.17)		
G-FOXO	Aeropro EuroFOX 912(S)	41313	02.05.13
	S E Coles Turweston		16.11.18P
	Built by S E Coles – project LAA 376-15165;		
	tailwheel u/c		
G-FOXS	Denney Kitfox Model 2	458	15.08.90
	H G Budd tr Darley Taildraggers Darley Moor		
	Built by C C Rea & S P Watkins		
	– project PFA 172-11571 (NF 16.08.17)		
G-FOXT	Aeros Fox 13TL	04216	16.05.17
	R Bower (Port Logan, Stranraer)		
	(IE 16.05.17)		
G-FOXU	Aeropro EuroFOX 912S(1)	47415	17.11.15
	K P I Kent & Simply Signs Ltd Draycott		27.02.19P
	Built by C D Waldron – project BMAA/HB/673;		
	tricycle u/c		
G-FOXW	Aeropro EuroFOX 912(1)	46415	16.06.15
	A P Whitmarsh (Wanshurst Green Farm, Marden)		09.10.19P
	Built by A P Whitmarsh – project BMAA/HB/667;		
	tricycle u/c		
G-FOXX	Denney Kitfox Model 2	xxxx	01.11.89
	H G Budd tr Darley Taildraggers (Flying) Syndicate		
	Darley Moor		08.08.18P
	Built by R O F Harper & P R Skeels – project PFA 172-11509		
G-FOXZ	Denney Kitfox	437.14	04.12.90
	S C Goozee Newton Peveril Farm, Sturminster Marshall		30.03.18P
	Built by M Smalley & J C Whittle – project PFA 172-11834		

G-FOZY Van's RV-7   71605   25.09.09
          G-COPZ   M G Forrest   Stoke Golding   28.08.18P
          Built by R S Horan – project PFA 323-14150

G-FPEH Guimbal Cabri G2   1093   03.03.15
          Paul D White Ltd   Elstree   03.04.19E
          Operated by Flying Pig Helicopters

G-FPIG Piper PA-28-151 Cherokee Warrior   28-7615001   22.03.00
          G-BSSR, N1190X   G F Strain   Dunkeswell   09.03.18E

G-FPLD Beech B200 Super King Air   BB-1433   02.11.01
          N43CE, N43AJ, C-GMEV, C-GMEH, N8043K
          Thales UK Ltd   Durham Tees Valley   19.11.18E

G-FPSA Piper PA-28-161 Warrior II   28-8616038   28.02.03
          G-RSFT, G-WARI, N9276Y
          A S Bamrah t/a Falcon Flying Services   Blackbushe   01.07.18E

G-FRAD Dassault Falcon 20E   304   26.11.86
          9M-BDK, G-FRAD, G-BCYF, F-WRQP
          Cobham Leasing Ltd   Bournemouth   19.07.18E

G-FRAF Dassault Falcon 20E   295   01.09.87
          N911FR, I-EDIM, F-WRQQ
          Cobham Leasing Ltd   Bournemouth   02.07.18E

G-FRAG Piper PA-32-300 Cherokee Six   32-7940284   21.01.80
          N3566L   T A Houghton   Rochester   19.12.18E

G-FRAH Dassault Falcon 20DC   223   31.05.90
          G-60-01, N900FR, (N904FR), N22FE, N4407F, F-WPUX
          Cobham Leasing Ltd   Bournemouth   07.10.18E

G-FRAI Dassault Falcon 20E   270   17.10.90
          N901FR, N37FE, N4435F, F-WPUZ
          Cobham Leasing Ltd   Bournemouth   03.06.18E

G-FRAJ Dassault Falcon 20DC   20   30.04.91
          N903FR, (N25FR), N5FE, (N146FE), N5FE, N367GA,
          N367, N842F, F-WMKJ
          Cobham Leasing Ltd   Bournemouth   12.12.17E
          (IE 16.01.18)

G-FRAK Dassault Falcon 20DC   213   09.10.91
          N905FR, N32FE, N4390F, F-WJMM
          Cobham Leasing Ltd   Bournemouth   13.04.18E

G-FRAL Dassault Falcon 20DC   151   17.03.93
          N904FR, (N24FR), N3FE, (N148FE), N3FE, N810PA,
          N810F, N4360F, F-WMKI
          Cobham Leasing Ltd   Bournemouth   02.09.18E

G-FRAN Piper J-3C-65 Cub *(L-4J-PI)*   12617   14.07.86
          G-BIXY, F-BDTZ, 44-80321
          I P Dole tr Essex L4 Group   Rayne Hall Farm, Rayne   05.06.18P
          Fuselage No.12447; as '480321:44-H' in USAAF c/s

G-FRAO Dassault Falcon 20DC   214   23.10.92
          N906FR, N33FE, N4400F, F-WNGO
          Cobham Leasing Ltd   Bournemouth   28.01.18E

G-FRAP Dassault Falcon 20DC   207   12.07.93
          N908FR, N27FE, N4395F, F-WMKF
          Cobham Leasing Ltd   Bournemouth   19.10.18E
          Being dismantled Bournemouth 02.19

G-FRAR Dassault Falcon 20DC   209   02.12.93
          N909FR, N28FE, N4396F, F-WLCX
          Cobham Leasing Ltd   Bournemouth   15.02.18E

G-FRAS Dassault Falcon 20C   82   31.07.90
          RCAF 117501, 20501, F-WJMM
          Cobham Leasing Ltd   Bournemouth   01.12.18E

G-FRAT Dassault Falcon 20C   87   31.07.90
          CAF 117502, 20502, F-WJMJ
          Cobham Leasing Ltd   Bournemouth   22.02.18E

G-FRAU Dassault Falcon 20C   97   31.07.90
          RCAF 117504, 20504, F-WJMJ
          Cobham Leasing Ltd   Bournemouth   15.12.18E

G-FRAW Dassault Falcon 20C   114   31.07.90
          RCAF 117507, 20507, F-WJMM
          Cobham Leasing Ltd   Bournemouth   09.04.18E

G-FRCE Folland Gnat T.1   FL598   28.11.89
          8604M, XS104   Red Gnat Ltd   North Weald   20.08.08P
          Carries 'XS104' on rear fuselage;
          noted 11.18 (NF 30.07.18)

G-FRCX P&M Quik GTR   8701   12.11.14
          R R Green tr G-FRCX Syndicate   Monewden   02.11.18P

G-FRDM Boeing Stearman B75N1 Kaydet *(N2S-3)* 75-2610   13.12.17
          N63441, Bu 4280   G A Bliss   (Catshill, Bromgrove)   16.12.19E
          As '2610:408' in US Navy c/s

G-FRDY Aerospool Dynamic WT9 UK   DY239/2008   29.04.08
          J A Lockert   Broadmeadow Farm, Hereford   10.10.18P
          Assembled Yeoman Light Aircraft Co Ltd;
          official c/n recorded as 'DY239'

G-FRGT P&M Quik GT450   8341   21.12.07
          N Morgan tr G-FRGT Group   Enstone   21.04.18P

G-FRJBM Aircraft Designs Sheriff SA-1   0001   18.05.81
          Cancelled 06.02.87 by CAA
          Not completed: unfinished airframe without marks
          With East Midlands Aeropark, East Midlands

G-FRNK Best Off Skyranger 912(2)   SKR0409528   26.01.05
          D L Foxley & G Lace   Ince   29.09.19P
          Built by F Tumelty – project BMAA/HB/439

G-FROM Comco Ikarus C42 FB100   0307-6554   15.09.03
          D M Pearson tr G-FROM Group
          Chiltern Park, Wallingford   23.03.18P
          Assembled Fly Buy Ultralights Ltd

G-FRRN Leonardo AW109SP Grand New   22371   31.05.17
          Harrier Enterprises Ltd   (Jersey)   30.05.19E

G-FRSX Supermarine 388 Seafire F.46   –   05.07.10
          LA564   Seafire Displays Ltd   (Old Warden, Biggleswade)
          Unmarked, primered fuselage noted 09.18 (NF 04.06.18)

G-FRYA Robinson R44 Raven II   11605   12.12.14
          G-EJRC   B J Winfield t/a Bryanair   Nottingham City   18.12.18E

G-FRYL Raytheon RB390 Premier 1   RB-97   11.08.04
          N6197F   Hawkair Ltd   Guernsey   12.07.18E

G-FSAR AgustaWestland AW189   89004   04.12.15
          I-RAIX   British International Helicopter Services Ltd
          RAF Mount Pleasant, Falkland Islands   03.12.18E

G-FSBW Aeropro EuroFOX 912S(1)   46915   11.11.15
          N G Heywood   Over Farm, Gloucester   19.10.18P
          Built by L S & S B Williams – project BMAA/HB/678;
          tricycle u/c

G-FSEU Beech 200 Super King Air   BB-331   09.08.06
          N87LP, N111WA, N400WH, N111JW
          Nimbus Air Ltd   Sywell   27.02.19E
          Operated by 2Excel Aviation

G-FSIXM English Electric Lightning F.6   95116   31.12.92
          XP693   Cancelled 13.02.97 – to ZU-BEY   *As 'XP693'*
          With Classic Jets South Africa, Cape Town

G-FSZY SOCATA TB-10 Tobago   1892   23.05.08
          F-GSZY   R Arquier   (Monaco, Principality of Monaco)   17.07.19E

G-FTAX Cessna 421C   421C-0308   23.08.84
          N8363G, G-BFFM, N8363G
          Cancelled 08.07.03 as PWFU
          Stafford   *Fuselage at J Watson & Son scrapyard 09.15*

G-FTFTM Colt Financial Times 90 SS HAB   1163   14.01.84
          Cancelled 13.05.98 as WFU   *Inflated 05.16 at Pidley*   05.06.95
          With British Balloon Museum & Library, Newbury

G-FTIL Robin DR.400-180 Régent   1825   10.03.84
          The Pathfinder Flying Club Ltd   RAF Wyton   21.03.18N

G-FTIN Robin DR.400-100 Cadet   1830   06.05.84
          Cancelled 04.09.13 as PWFU   04.04.1
          Exeter   *Stored Exavia hangar for spares 09.15*

G-FTSE Fairey B-N BN-2A Mk.III-2 Trislander   1053   23.05.0
          G-BEPI   Cancelled 14.08.14 as PWFU   18.12.1
          Guernsey
          Cockpit only used for advertising purposes 10.15

G-FTUS Ultramagic F-12 Paquete   F12/03   17.04.1
          A M Holly   Breadstone, Berkeley   *'Financial Times'*   24.05.16
          (IE 05.10.18)

G-FUEL Robin DR.400-180 Régent   1537   15.05.8
          S L G Darch   East Chinnock, Yeovil   19.08.13

G-FUKM Westland SA.341B Gazelle AH.1   1799   18.08.0
          ZA730   Falcon Aviation Ltd
          Bourne Park, Hurstbourne Tarrant
          Stored as 'ZA730'(NF 24.01.18)

G-FULL Piper PA-28R-200 Cherokee Arrow II   28R-7435248   26.11.8
          G-HWAY, G-JULI, (G-BKDC), OY-POV, CS-AQF,
          N43128   Stapleford Flying Club Ltd   Stapleford   14.11.17

G-FUND Thunder Ax7-65Z 376 03.11.81
G B Davies   Thorney, Peterborough 07.07.18E

G-FUNN Plumb BGP-1A 002 16.10.95
J Riley   Little Staughton 09.08.18P
*Initially built J D Anson & completed J Riley
– project PFA 083-12744*

G-FURI Isaacs Fury II xxxx 07.02.06
S M Johnston   (Brompton on Swale, Richmond)
*Built by S M Johnston – project PFA 011-14467
(NF 01.11.16)*

G-FURZ Best Off Skyranger Nynja 912S(1) 11020064 08.08.11
D J Tomlin   Shobdon 12.01.19P
Built by R S Swift – project BMAA/HB/614

G-FUSE Cameron N-105 10639 30.11.04
S A Lacey   Norwich Common, Wymondham
'L.E. Electrical' 14.08.15E
(IE 20.09.16)

G-FUUN Silence SA.180 Twister 28 01.02.12
A W McKee   Old Warden 11.12.18P
Built by A W McKee – project LAA 329-15078

G-FUZZ Piper PA-18 Super Cub 95 (*L-18C-PI*) 18-1016 11.09.80
(OO-HMY), 51-15319
G W Cline   Church Lane Farm, Elvington 25.05.19P
*Official p/i 'F-MBIT' is incorrect; fuselage
No.18-1086; as '51-15319:A-319' in US Army c/s*

G-FVEE Monnett Sonerai I xxxx 19.12.78
J S Baldwin   (Wigan)
*Built by D R Sparke – project PFA 015-10041
(NF 03.12.14)*

G-FVEL Cameron Z-90 10580 24.08.04
Fort Vale Engineering Ltd
Simonstone, Burnley   'Fort Vale' 25.05.18E

G-FWJR Ultramagic M-56 56/50 11.01.13
Harding & Sons Ltd   Plymouth   'Fairway Furniture' 09.03.19E

G-FWKS Air Création Tanarg 912S(1)/iXess 15 xxxx 20.07.02
G-SYUT   M A Coffin   Middle Stoke, Isle of Grain 02.06.18P
*Built by L Cottle – project BMAA/HB/492 being
Flylight kit comprising trike s/n T05100 & wing
s/n A05188-5195*

G-FWPW Piper PA-28-236 Dakota 2811018 10.10.88
N9145L   F C & P A Winters   Alderney 01.06.18E

G-FXAR Raytheon 400XT RK-252 19.05.17
N490FL, N790TA   Flexjet Ltd   Birmingham 15.10.19E

G-FXBA Aeroprakt A-22LS Foxbat A22LS-318 20.06.18
R G G Pinder   Enstone 23.10.19P
Built by R G G Pinder – project LAA 317B-15534

G-FXBT Aeroprakt A-22 Foxbat 026 & UK 002 07.02.02
R H Jago   Newton Peveril Farm, Sturminster Marshall 06.11.18P
Built by R Jago – project PFA 317-13787

G-FXCR Raytheon 400A RK-423 07.02.17
N429FL, N426FX, N223XP   Flexjet Ltd   Birmingham 26.02.18E
Nextant 400XT conversion

G-FXDM Raytheon 400XT RK-377 03.04.18
N477FL, N477LX, N477CW   Flexjet Ltd   Birmingham
(IE 11.04.18)

G-FXDT Raytheon 400XP RK-397 30.11.18
N473FL, N479LX, N36997   Flexjet Ltd   Birmingham

G-FXER Raytheon 400XT RK-310 ..
N451FL, N451LX, (N468LX), N410CW, N695TA
Flexjet Ltd   Birmingham
Nextant 400XT conversion

G-FXII Supermarine 366 Spitfire F.XII 6S-197707 04.12.89
EN224   Air Leasing Ltd   Sywell
*Composite comprising wings ex EN199 (Mk.IXe),
engine & bearers ex Seafire SX336 (F.XVII)
& new build components; on rebuild & fuselage
in primer 09.18 (NF 25.08.15)*

G-FXIV[M] Supermarine 379 Spitfire FR.XIVc xxxx 11.04.80
Indian AF T44, Indian AF HSxxx, MV370
*Cancelled 05.02.85 as WFU   As 'MV370'
With Luftfahrt Museum, Laatzen-Hannover, Germany*

G-FXKR Raytheon 400XT RK-279 06.03.17
N436FL, N436LX, (N458LX), N773TA
Flexjet Ltd   Birmingham 20.03.18E
Nextant 400XT conversion

G-FXMR Raytheon 400XT RK-327 01.08.18
N454FL, N454LX, (N471LX), N689TA
Flexjet Ltd   Birmingham

G-FXPR Raytheon 400XT RK-468 24.01.18
N467FL, N468LX   Flexjet Ltd   Birmingham

G-FXRS Raytheon 400XT RK-317 03.10.18
N452FL, N452SB, N452LX, (N469LX), N691TA
Flexjet Ltd   Birmingham
Operated by Flairjet Ltd

G-FYAN Williams Westwind MDW-1 06.01.82
M D Williams   Houghton Regis, Dunstable
Built by M D Williams

G-FYAO Williams Westwind MDW-01 06.01.82
M D Williams   Houghton Regis, Dunstable
Built by M D Williams

G-FYAU Williams Westwind Two MDW-02 06.01.82
M D Williams   Houghton Regis, Dunstable
Built by M D Williams

G-FYAV Osprey Mk.4E2 ASC-247 12.01.82
C D Egan & C Stiles   Hounslow & Feltham
Built by Osprey Balloon Group

G-FYBD Osprey Mk.1E ASC-136 20.01.82
M Vincent   St Helier JE2 3ZB
Built by Solent Balloon Group

G-FYBE Osprey Mk.4D ASC-128 20.01.82
M Vincent   St Helier JE2 3ZB
Built by Solent Balloon Group

G-FYBF Osprey Mk.5 ASC-218 20.01.82
M Vincent   St Helier JE2 3ZB
Built by Solent Balloon Group

G-FYBG Osprey Mk.4G2 ASC-204 20.01.82
M Vincent   St Helier JE2 3ZB
Built by Solent Balloon Group

G-FYBH Osprey Mk.4G ASC-214 20.01.82
M Vincent   St Helier JE2 3ZB
Built by Solent Balloon Group

G-FYBI Osprey Mk.4H ASC-234 20.01.82
M Vincent   St Helier JE2 3ZB
Built by Solent Balloon Group

G-FYCL Osprey Mk.4G ASC-213 09.02.82
P J Rogers   Banbury
Built by Solent Balloon Group

G-FYCV Osprey Mk.4D ASK-276 19.02.82
A L Hunter   Luton
Built by Solent Balloon Group

G-FYDF Osprey Mk.4D ASK-278 22.03.82
K A Jones   Thornton Heath
Built by Solent Balloon Group

G-FYDI Williams Westwind Two MDW-005 29.03.82
M D Williams   Houghton Regis, Dunstable
Built by M D Williams

G-FYDN Eaves European 8C DD34/S22 05.04.82
P D Ridout   Eastleigh
Built by D Eaves

G-FYDO Osprey Mk.4D ASK 262 15.04.82
N L Scallan   Hayes
Built by Solent Balloon Group

G-FYDP Williams Westwind Three MDW-006 29.03.82
M D Williams   Houghton Regis, Dunstable
Built by M D Williams

G-FYDS Osprey Mk.4D ASK-261 15.04.82
M E Scallan   Hayes
Built by Solent Balloon Group

G-FYEK Unicorn UE-1C 82024 02.07.82
D & D Eaves   Southampton SO16
Built by Unicorn Group

G-FYEO Scallan Eagle Mk.1A 1 20.07.82
M E Scallan   Hayes
Built by M E Scallan

G-FYEV Osprey Mk.1C ASK-294 10.08.82
M E Scallan   Hayes
Built by Solent Balloon Group

G-FYEZ	Scallan Firefly Mk.1 M E & N L Scallan Hayes *Built by M E Scallan*	MNS 748	22.09.82
G-FYFI	Eaves European E.84PS M A Stelling South Queensferry *Built by D Eaves*	S29	01.12.82
G-FYFJ	Williams Westwind Two M D Williams Houghton Regis, Dunstable *Built by M D Williams*	MDW 010	14.12.82
G-FYFN	Osprey Saturn 2 DC3 J & M Woods Bracknell *Built by Solent Balloon Group*	ATC-250/MJS-11	17.02.82
G-FYFW	Rango NA-55 (*Radio controlled*) A M & N H Ponsford t/a Rango Balloon & Kite Company Leeds '*Vaughan Williams*'	NHP-40	08.10.84
G-FYFY	Rango NA-55RC (*Radio controlled*) A M Ponsford t/a Rango Balloon & Kite Company Leeds '*Fifi*'	AL-43	28.02.85
G-FYGJ	Wells Airspeed-300 N Wells Paddock Wood, Tonbridge *Built by N Wells*	001	08.10.91
G-FYGM	Saffery/Smith Princess A & N Smith Pollington, Goole *Built by C Saffery & N Smith; noted 05.16*	551	24.11.97
G-FZZA	General Avia F22-A W A Stewart Kirkwall	018	13.08.98 17.09.19P
G-FZZI	Cameron H-34 Magical Adventures Ltd West Bloomfield, MI, USA (*NF 03.06.15*)	2105	30.10.89 23.10.09E
G-FZZZ^M	Colt 56A HAB Cancelled 29.04.97 as WFU *With British Balloon Museum & Library, Newbury*	507	23.02.83

G-GAAA – G-GZZZ

G-GAAL	Cessna 560XL Citation XLS+ G-DEIA, N52475 London Executive Aviation Ltd London Stansted	560-6119	21.11.17 15.11.18E
G-GAAZ	Reims/Cessna F172N D-EAAZ M Baumeister tr Haltergemeinschaft G-GAAZ GBR Landshut, Germany (*IE 26.08.16*)	F17201660	17.02.15 05.05.16E
G-GABI	Lindstrand LBL 35A Cloudhopper R D Sargeant Altendorf, Switzerland '*Lindstrand Balloons*' (*IE 28.01.15*)	1233	29.04.09 26.10.12E
G-GABS	Cameron TR-70 N M Gabriel Kimberley, Nottingham (*NF 19.07.16*)	10937	10.03.08 19.04.15E
G-GABY	Bombardier BD-700-1A10 Global Express C-GGOL, C-FXYS Emperor Aviation Ltd (Swatar, Malta)	9364	19.11.10 18.11.19E
G-GACA^M	Percival P.57 Sea Prince T.1 WP308 Cancelled 15.12.09 by CAA *As WP308:572* *With Gatwick Aviation Museum, Charlwood*	P57/58	02.09.80
G-GACB	Robinson R44 Raven II S P Barker (Foxt, Stoke-on-Trent) (*NF 13.01.17*)	10243	09.01.04 27.06.16E
G-GAEA	Aquila AT01 Khair BV Breda Int'l, Netherlands	AT01-214	19.08.10 11.03.18E
G-GAEC	Aquila AT01-100A Khair BV Breda Int'l, Netherlands	AT01-100A-312	24.01.14 02.01.19E
G-GAED	Aquila AT01-100A Khair BV Breda Int'l, Netherlands	AT01-100A-328	30.09.15 30.09.18E
G-GAEE	Tecnam P2010 Khair BV Breda Int'l, Netherlands	037	18.04.16 27.04.18E
G-GAEF	Aquila AT01-100A Khair BV (Roosendaal, Netherlands) (*IE 28.03.18*)	AT01-100A-353	28.03.18
G-GAGE	Cameron Z-105 A J Thompson Patchway, Bristol '*S.M. Gauge Company*'	12038	16.02.17 24.02.19E

G-GAID	Cessna 182T Skylane N386DR, N40996 D R Rayne Wycombe Air Park	18282386	06.01.16 09.02.18E
G-GAII	Hawker Hunter GA.11 XE685 Hawker Hunter Aviation Ltd RAF Scampton *Official c/n '41H-004038' not correct; as 'XE685:861-VL'* *in RN c/s; in external store 10.16* (*NF 08.04.16*)	HABL-003028	07.12.94 15.08.12P
G-GAJB	Gulfstream American AA-5B Tiger G-BHZN, N37519 P W Gillott & S A Niechcial tr G-GAJB Group Biggin Hill	AA5B-1179	06.04.87 15.03.18E
G-GALA	Piper PA-28-180 Cherokee E G-AYAP, N11C J Harrison Hinton-in-the-Hedges	28-5794	31.07.89 07.10.18E
G-GALB	Piper PA-28-161 Warrior II D-EHMP, N9097E, (N157AV), N9635N Gamston Flying School Ltd Retford Gamston	28-8616021	01.09.00 04.01.19E
G-GALI	Agusta AW109SP Grand New G-HLSA, G-HCOM Gall Air LLP Fishpools Farm Barns, Frankton, Warks	22336	18.01.19 06.01.20E
G-GAMA	Beech 58 Baron G-WWIZ, G-GAMA, G-BBSD Gama Aviation (UK) Ltd Fairoaks *Noted dismantled 11.16 as 'G-WWIZ' (NF 06.07.16)*	TH-429	13.10.82 05.07.08E
G-GAME	Cessna T303 Crusader (F-GDFN), N2693C German Automotive Ltd (Derby)	T30300098	25.02.83 17.08.18E
G-GAND	Agusta-Bell 206B-2 JetRanger II G-AWMK, 9Y-TFC, G-AWMK, (VR-BCV), G-AWMK R Henderson Inverness & Nairn Heliport *Airframe exchanged with 5N-AQJ c/n 8051;* *this is now VH-JEF c/n 8051 (1)*	8051 (2)	11.01.00 01.07.18E
G-GAOH	Robin DR.400-120 Dauphin 2+2 Tri-cycle F-GAOH M A Stott Newquay Cornwall	1217	09.05.05 29.04.18E
G-GAOM	Robin DR.400-120 Dauphin 2+2 Tri-cycle F-GAOM P A & P M Chapman Newquay Cornwall	1220	24.06.05 30.10.18E
G-GARE	Cessna 560XL Citation XLS+ Virtus Aviation Ltd Hawarden	560-6232	29.06.17 11.07.18E
G-GARI	Ace Aviation Touch/Buzz G B Shaw (Mynytho, Pwllheli) *Trike s/n not known & wing s/n AS0112* *(SSDR microlight since 05.14) (IE 18.11.15)*	xxxx	11.05.12
G-GASP	Piper PA-28-181 Archer II N4328F M L Robinson tr G-GASP Flying Group Fairoaks	28-7790013	15.10.90 08.04.18E
G-GAST	Van's RV-8 G M R Abrey Illington House, Wretham *Built by G M R Abrey – project PFA 303-14732*	82771	17.09.10 07.05.18P
G-GATH	Airbus A320-232 OE-ICN, TC-OBH, PK-RMJ, VT-WAC, N482TA, F-WWDU British Airways PLC London Gatwick	1482	02.04.15 25.02.19E
G-GATJ	Airbus A320-232 OE-ICO, TC-OBI, N380DF, (PK-RMM), VT-WAD, N483TA, F-WWBD British Airways PLC London Gatwick	1509	19.12.14 01.10.19E
G-GATK	Airbus A320-232 HA-LPD, EI-DGB, F-WQTK, N902VX, F-WWDG British Airways PLC London Gatwick	1902	07.11.14 23.04.19E
G-GATL	Airbus A320-232 HA-LPF, EI-DGC, F-WQTI, N834VX, F-WWBF British Airways PLC London Gatwick	1834	21.11.14 09.05.19E
G-GATM	Airbus A320-232 HA-LPE, EI-DFU, F-WQTJ, N892VX, F-WWBU British Airways PLC London Gatwick	1892	12.01.15 14.03.19E
G-GATN	Airbus A320-232 OE-IDS, PT-MZX, F-WWDI British Airways PLC London Gatwick	1613	24.07.15 01.07.19E
G-GATP	Airbus A320-232 OE-IDU, PR-MAE, F-WWII British Airways PLC London Gatwick	1804	06.08.15 26.07.19E
G-GATR	Airbus A320-232 OE-IDX, PR-MAD, F-WWDD British Airways PLC London Gatwick	1771	04.12.15 07.09.19E
G-GATS	Airbus A320-232 OE-IDW, PR-MAC, F-WWIK British Airways PLC London Gatwick	1672	03.09.15 19.08.19E
G-GATT	Robinson R44 Raven II B W Faulkner Twentyways Farm, Ramsdean	10531	15.11.04 11.03.19E

G-GATU	Airbus A320-232	3089	11.08.16
	OE-IES, TS-INS, EI-EYE, VT-KFT, F-WWBY		
	British Airways PLC London Gatwick		11.07.19E
G-GAVH	P&M Pegasus Quik	8546	06.10.10
	I J Richardson Sittles Farm, Alrewas		09.11.17P
G-GAXC	Robin R2160 Alpha Sport	144	30.07.15
	F-GAXC D D McMaster (Tonbridge)		09.03.18E
	(IE 07.08.18)		
G-GAZA	Aérospatiale SA.341G Gazelle 1	1187	19.06.92
	G-RALE, G-SFTG, N87712 The Auster Aircraft		
	Company Ltd (Chadwell, Melton Mowbray)		25.11.17E
G-GAZN	P&M Quik GT450	8271	24.05.07
	C Hughes Shobdon		17.09.18P
G-GAZO	Ace Aviation Magic/Cyclone	xxxx	13.07.10
	G J Pearce Henstridge		
	Trike s/n not known & wing s/n AC-147		
	(SSDR microlight since 05.14) (IE 17.09.18)		
G-GAZZ	Aérospatiale SA.341G Gazelle 1	1271	14.03.90
	F-GFHD, YV-242CP, HB-XGA, F-WMHC		
	Cheqair Ltd Tharston Industrial Estate, Long Stratton		14.09.09E
	Official p/i, 'F-GFND', is incorrect (NF 10.08.17)		
G-GBAO	Robin R1180TD Aiglon	277	09.09.81
	F-GBAO J Toulorge Wellcross Farm, Slinfold		20.08.15E
	Rebuild of R 1180 prototype F-WVKU c/n 01		
G-GBAS	Diamond DA.62	62.019	27.05.16
	Flight Calibration Services Ltd Goodwood		12.06.18E
	Callsign 'VOR05'		
G-GBBB	Schleicher ASH 25	25074	15.10.07
	BGA 3532, (BGA 3526/FTZ) M J Wells		
	tr ASH 25 bb Glider Syndicate Lasham *'BB'*		30.03.18E
G-GBBT	Ultramagic M-90	90/103	13.08.08
	S J Chatfield Guildford *'BT'*		22.08.19E
G-GBCA	Agusta A109A II	7272	27.01.84
	Cancelled 03.09.85 as PWFU		
	Chippenham *Conv to children's den 06.18*		
G-GBCC	Comco Ikarus C42 FB100 Bravo	1010-7125	05.11.10
	I R Westrope (Wilding's Farm, Steeple Bumpstead)		14.03.18P
	Assembled Performance Aviation Ltd		
G-GBEE	Mainair Pegasus Quik	8039	21.05.04
	G S Bulpitt Clench Common		26.03.18P
	Built by Mainair Sports Ltd		
G-GBET	Comco Ikarus C42 FB UK	xxxx	14.05.12
	G-DBMK, G-MROY P K Meech (Burgess Hill)		09.09.19P
	Built by R Beckham – project PFA 322-13758		
G-GBFI	Kreimendahl K-10 Shoestring	054	18.07.17
	F-PYXC, F-WYXC T Jarvis Hinton-in-the-Hedges		
	Built by A Guignard (NF 18.07.17)		
G-GBFR	Reims/Cessna F177RG Cardinal RG	F177RG0172	07.04.04
	F-GBFR Airspeed Aviation Ltd Derby		
	(IE 06.07.18)		
G-GBGA	Scheibe SF25C Rotax-Falke	44683	28.08.02
	D-KIEJ The Royal Air Force Gliding		
	& Soaring Association RAF Odiham		27.05.18E
G-GBGB	Ultramagic M-105	105/126	30.12.04
	S A Nother Poole		25.03.18E
G-GBGF	Cameron Dragon	3016	23.08.07
	C-GBGF, G-BUVH Magical Adventures Ltd		
	West Bloomfield, MI, USA		27.09.09E
	(NF 03.06.15)		
G-GBHB	SOCATA TB-10 Tobago	6	23.09.16
	F-GBHB, F-WBHB B A Mills Duxford		26.08.18E
G-GBHI	SOCATA TB-10 Tobago	019	12.11.97
	F-GBHI J H Garrett-Cox Dundee		08.12.18E
G-GBIG	AgustaWestland AW139	31475	03.01.19
	I-AWTV, G-DCOI Castle Air Ltd Biggin Hill		02.12.19E
G-GBLP	Reims/Cessna F172M	F17201042	09.11.84
	G-GWEN, G-GBLP, N14496		
	Aviate Scotland Ltd Fife		22.03.18E
G-GBNZ	Aeropro EuroFOX 912(iS)	52917	05.06.17
	C F Pote Wadswick Manor Farm, Corsham		31.05.19P
	Built by C F Pote – project LAA 376-15476; tailwheel u/c		

G-GBOB	Alpi Pioneer 300 Hawk	217	20.08.07
	R E Burgess RAF Mona		22.05.18P
	Built by R E Burgess – project PFA 330A-14681		
G-GBPP	Rolladen-Schneider LS6-c	6230	24.10.07
	BGA 3809		
	G J Lyons & R Sinden Wycombe Air Park *'949'*		26.03.18E
G-GBRB	Piper PA-28-180 Cherokee C	28-2583	02.02.00
	N8381W S D Boulton tr Bravo Romeo Group		
	Netherthorpe		17.05.19E
G-GBRI	Best Off Skyranger Nynja LS 912S(1)	xxxx	27.03.18
	B Greenwood (Deddington, Banbury)		
	Built by B Greenwood – project BMAA/HB/704		
	(NF 27.03.18)		
G-GBRU	Bell 206B-3 JetRanger III	3997	15.02.05
	G-CDGV, N217PM, XC-PFS		
	Ra Fleming Ltd Leeds Bradford		05.05.18E
G-GBRV	Van's RV-9A	90985	02.06.10
	G-THMB J S Chaggar Wellesbourne Mountford		12.04.11P
	Built by C H P Bell – project PFA 320-14266 (NF 24.07.18)		
G-GBSL	Beech 76 Duchess	ME-265	27.03.81
	G-BGVG R D A Berliand & M H Cundey Redhill		11.07.18E
G-GBTL	Cessna 172S Skyhawk SP	172S10322	21.11.06
	N1261M BTL IT Solutions Ltd		
	Wadshock Manor Farm, Corsham		03.10.18E
G-GBTV	Eurocopter AS.355N Ecureuil 2	5360	14.02.18
	N355J, (N95EC), YV-O-KWH-7 Cheshire Helicopters		
	Ltd Blackshaw Heys Farm, Mobberley		20.06.19E
	Operated by VLL Ltd t/a GB Helicopters		
G-GBUE	Robin DR.400-120A Petit Prince	1354	11.05.89
	G-BPXD, F-GBUE J A Kane Bagby		09.10.17E
G-GBUN	Cessna 182T Skylane	18281280	11.12.03
	N2157P G M Bunn Goodwood		04.02.18E
G-GBVX	Robin DR.400-120A Petit Prince	1419	02.03.06
	F-GBVX N Foster RAF Leuchars		18.05.18E
	Operated by The Leuchars Flying Company		
G-GCAC	Europa Aviation Europa XS	559	21.08.02
	W G Miller Oban		29.10.19P
	Built by G J Cattermole – project PFA 247-13940;		
	tricycle u/c		
G-GCAT	Piper PA-28-140 Cherokee B	28-26032	22.10.81
	G-BFRH, OH-PCA		
	P F Jude tr Group CAT Humberside		20.04.19E
G-GCCL	Beech 76 Duchess	ME-322	05.08.87
	(G-BNRF), N6714U Aerolease Ltd Conington		14.10.16E
	(IE 19.07.17)		
G-GCDA	Cirrus SR20	1962	02.07.09
	N173PG S James North Weald		11.07.19E
G-GCDB	Cirrus SR20	1967	02.07.09
	N193PG S James North Weald		11.03.19E
G-GCEA	P&M Pegasus Quik	8209	12.09.06
	K & P Bailey Longside		24.03.19P
G-GCFM	Diamond DA.40D Star	D4.260	30.11.09
	A7-DSM, OE-VPU Centro Formacion Aeronautico		
	Aerofan SA Madrid-Cuatro Vientos, Spain		30.04.19E
G-GCIY	Robin DR.400-140B Major 80	1488	07.07.08
	F-GCIY M S Lonsdale Full Sutton		19.07.18E
	Badged 'Dauphin 4'		
G-GCJA	Rolladen-Schneider LS8-18	8354	14.05.08
	BGA 4871/JXU N T Mallender Lasham *'946'*		24.10.18E
G-GCJL	British Aerospace Jetstream Series 4100	41001	05.02.91
	Cancelled 15.11.02 as PWFU		29.04.95
	Humberside *On fire dump 01.16*		
G-GCKI	Mooney M.20K Mooney 231	25-0401	15.08.80
	N4062H P J Gamble Great Massingham		10.06.19E
G-GCMW	Grob G102 Astir CS	1112	06.11.07
	BGA 5040/KEU, OY-XDE M S F Wood Solent *'KEU'*		26.05.18E
G-GCOY	SOCATA TB-9 Tampico	233	23.12.15
	F-GCOY L J Kelly (London EC1)		19.09.18E
G-GCRT	Robin DR.400-120 Petit Prince	1495	24.04.15
	F-GCRT Aero Club de Valenciennes		
	Valenciennes-Denain, France		16.07.18E
G-GCUF	Robin DR.400-160 Chevalier	1504	19.04.06
	F-GCUF S Clayton & A Davis Henstridge		05.07.18E

G

G-GCVV	Cirrus SR22	4244	23.09.15
	N244CY Daedalus Aviation (Services) Ltd		
	East Midlands		23.09.18E
G-GCWS	Cessna 177 Cardinal	17700504	17.03.15
	SE-CWS, OY-DLB, N3204T B A Mills Bournemouth		21.05.19E
G-GCYC	Reims/Cessna F182Q Skylane II	F18200157	11.02.00
	F-GCYC M Bridgland & P R Ford		
	tr The Cessna 180 Group Brimpton		17.01.19E
G-GDAC	Grumman American AA-5A Cheetah	AA5A-0347	14.07.15
	EC-DAC, (D-EDAA), EC-DAC, N6156A		
	D S Tarmey Retford Gamston		28.01.19E
G-GDAY	Robinson R22 Beta	0676	10.08.87
	Cancelled 28.09.99 by CAA		10.12.99
	Aberglasney, Wales		
	Used as travelling exhibit for Wales Air Ambulance 09.18		
G-GDEF	Robin DR.400-120 Petit Prince	1538	26.07.07
	F-GDEE J M Shackleton Leeds East		10.11.18E
G-GDER	Robin R1180TD Aiglon	280	15.05.97
	F-GDER Berkshire Aviation Services Ltd Fairoaks		06.08.18E
G-GDFB	Boeing 737-33A	25743	04.05.10
	SX-BBU, EC-FMP, EC-970, N3519L		
	Dart Group PLC Leeds Bradford		
	'Jet2holidays' & *'Package holidays you can trust'*		24.03.19E
	Line No: 2206; operated by Jet2.com		
G-GDFC	Boeing 737-8K2	28375	05.01.11
	PH-HZC, C-GHZC, PH-HZC, VT-SPY, PH-HZC, N1786B		
	Jet2.com Ltd Leeds Bradford *'Jet2 Cyprus'*,		
	'22kg allowance' (Stbd) & *'Great package holidays'* (Port)		13.09.19E
	Line No: 85; red tail		
G-GDFD	Boeing 737-8K5	27982	20.04.11
	D-AHFB, N35030, (N53050)		
	Jet2.com Ltd Leeds Bradford *'Jet2holidays'*		13.04.19E
	Line No: 8; blue tail		
G-GDFE	Boeing 737-3Q8	24131	21.07.11
	OO-TNF, N241MT, CS-TGP, OO-LTX, EC-FFC, EC-592,		
	EC-EII, EC-159 Dart Group PLC Leeds Bradford		
	'Jet2 Majorca' & *'Friendly Low Fares'*		30.11.19E
	Line No: 1541; operated by Jet2.com; red tail		
G-GDFF	Boeing 737-85P	28385	22.12.11
	EC-HGP, N1786B		
	Jet2.com Ltd Leeds Bradford *'Jet2holidays'*		08.12.19E
	Line No: 421		
G-GDFG	Boeing 737-36Q	28658	16.03.12
	LN-KKQ, EC-GMY Dart Group PLC Leeds Bradford		
	'Jet2 Budapest' & *'Friendly Low Fares'*		18.08.19E
	Line No: 2865; operated by Jet2.com; red tail		
G-GDFH	Boeing 737-3Y5	25615	27.01.12
	LN-KKC, 9H-ABT Dart Group PLC Lasham		17.12.18E
	Line No: 2478; arrived 07.12.18 for part-out/scrapping		
G-GDFJ	Boeing 737-804	28229	19.03.12
	G-CDZI, SE-DZI		
	Jet2.com Ltd Leeds Bradford *'Jet2holidays'*		26.01.20E
	Line No: 478		
G-GDFK	Boeing 737-36N	28572	16.03.12
	N4620F, ES-ABK, G-STRE, G-XBHX		
	Dart Group PLC Leeds Bradford *'Jet2holidays'*		25.04.19E
	Line No: 3031; operated by Jet2.com		
G-GDFL	Boeing 737-36N	28568	22.06.12
	OO-VEG, EI-TVQ, OO-VEG		
	Dart Group PLC Leeds Bradford *'Jet2holidays'*		30.06.19E
	Line No: 2987; operated by Jet2.com		
G-GDFM	Boeing 737-36N	28586	05.02.13
	OO-VEN, EI-TVN		
	Dart Group PLC Leeds Bradford *'Jet2holidays'*		27.11.19E
	Line No: 3090; operated by Jet2.com		
G-GDFN	Boeing 737-33V	29332	09.04.13
	YL-BBK, HA-LKR, G-EZYH, N1787B		
	Dart Group PLC Leeds Bradford *'Jet2holidays'*		26.01.19E
	Line No: 3072; operated by Jet2.com		
G-GDFO	Boeing 737-3U3	28740	06.02.13
	G-THOP, N335AW, N1790B, N1787B, (PK-GGM), (PK-GGK)		
	Dart Group PLC Leeds Bradford *'Jet2holidays'*		29.09.19E
	Line No: 3003		

G-GDFP	Boeing 737-8Z9	28177	15.03.13
	EI-EZB, OE-LNJ, (OE-LAY), N1786B Dart Group PLC		
	Leeds Bradford *'Jet2 Paris'* & *'Friendly Low Fares'*		29.07.19E
	Line No: 69; operated by Jet2.com; red tail		
G-GDFR	Boeing 737-8Z9	30421	08.03.13
	EI-EZH, OE-LNQ		
	Dart Group PLC Leeds Bradford *'Jet2 Rome'*		10.07.19E
	Line No: 1345; operated by Jet2.com; red tail		
G-GDFS	Boeing 737-86N	32243	09.05.14
	OM-TVA, OK-TVA, N1786B Jet2.com Ltd Leeds		
	Bradford *'Jet2 Tunisia'*		28.04.19E
	Line No: 869; red tail		
G-GDFT	Boeing 737-36Q	29141	16.05.13
	G-TOYM, VT-SJD, N141CY, G-OHAJ Dart Group PLC		
	Leeds Bradford *'Jet2 Murcia'* & *'Friendly Low Fares'*		18.08.19E
	Line No: 3035; operated by Jet2.com; red tail		
G-GDFU	Boeing 737-8K5	30416	17.10.14
	D-AHFX, N1786B		
	Dart Group PLC Leeds Bradford *'Jet2holidays'*		19.02.19E
	Line No: 778; operated by Jet2.com		
G-GDFV	Boeing 737-85F	28821	07.05.13
	F-WTDE, EC-LKO, D-ABBL, F-GRNC, N1786B		
	Jet2.com Ltd Leeds Bradford		
	'Jet2 Fuerteventura' & *'Friendly Low Fares'*		02.06.19E
	Line No: 151; red tail		
G-GDFW	Boeing 737-8K5	27986	14.03.14
	D-AHFM Jet2.com Ltd Leeds Bradford		
	'Jet2holidays' & *'Package holidays you can trust'*		29.01.19E
	Line No: 474; blue tail		
G-GDFX	Boeing 737-8K5	27987	16.05.14
	D-AHFO Jet2.com Ltd Leeds Bradford		
	'Jet2 Vienna' & *'Friendly Low Fares'*		02.12.19E
	Line No: 499; red tail		
G-GDFY	Boeing 737-86Q	30278	17.04.14
	HA-LKE, OK-TVC, N289CD, (OO-CYH)		
	Jet2.com Ltd Leeds Bradford *'Jet2 Kefalonia'*		26.11.19E
	Line No: 963; red tail		
G-GDFZ	Boeing 737-86Q	30276	09.04.14
	EI-FDZ, EC-HZS, N747BX, N1786B		
	Jet2.com Ltd Leeds Bradford *'Jet2holidays'*		18.09.19E
	Line No: 920		
G-GDIA	Reims/Cessna F152	F15201895	13.10.14
	F-GDIA Skytrek Flying School Ltd Rochester		02.11.18E
G-GDKR	Robin DR.400-140B Major 80	1623	12.06.06
	F-GDKR A S Cowan tr Hampshire Flying Group		
	Popham		31.01.18E
G-GDMW	Beech 76 Duchess	ME-316	29.10.04
	D-GDMW, LX-DRS, F-GCGB		
	Flew LLP Bournemouth		18.03.18E
	Operated by Bournemouth Commercial Flight Training		
G-GDOG	Piper PA-28R-200 Cherokee Arrow II	28R-7635227	17.04.89
	G-BDXW, N9235K		
	N J Morton tr Mutley Crew Group Conington		13.03.18E
G-GDRV	Van's RV-6	21367	26.11.01
	C-GDRV M A J de Queiroz tr G-GDRV Group		
	Gloucestershire *'Slavka'*		05.05.18P
	Built by D Piper		
G-GDSG	Agusta A109E Power	11656	16.11.05
	Palmhall Ltd Pendley Farm, Aldbury		19.01.19E
G-GDSO	AutoGyro Cavalon	xxxx	15.11.17
	P Setterfield Beverley (Linley Hill)		29.11.18P
	Assembled Rotorsport UK as c/n RSUK/CVLN/024		
G-GDTU	Mudry CAP 10B	193	27.05.09
	F-GDTU, (N.....), F-GDTK, F-WZCI		
	R W H Cole Headcorn		22.08.18E
G-GECO	Hughes 369HS *(500)*	140557S	27.04.11
	G-TVEE, N45457, ZK-HCM, N22352, C-GCXK, N500AH,		
	N500WH N Duggan Gloucestershire		24.01.18E
G-GEEP	Robin R1180TD Aiglon	266	09.04.80
	M Lawrance tr The Aiglon Flying Group North Weald		11.02.19E
G-GEHL	Cessna 172S Skyhawk SP	172S8324	18.06.03
	N163RA K A & M Whittaker (Abingdon)		23.06.19E
G-GEHP	Piper PA-28RT-201 Arrow IV	28R-8218014	24.04.98
	F-GEHP, N82023		
	Aeros Leasing Ltd Wellesbourne Mountford		26.10.18E

G-GEJS	Extra EA.300/LT	LT032	23.06.15
	G E J Sealey Cambridge		10.07.18E
G-GELI	Colt 31A	10655	30.05.13
	G-CDFI S F Burden Noordwijk, Netherlands		01.09.18E
	Built by Cameron Balloons		
G-GEMM	Cirrus SR20	1138	14.12.05
	N241CD Schmolke Grosskuechensysteme GmbH		
	Mönchengladbach, Germany		02.03.18E
G-GEMS	Thunder Ax8-90 Series 2	2287	06.11.92
	G-BUNP Kraft Bauprojekt GmbH		
	Bonn, Nordrhein-Westphalen, Germany *'Kraft Mobilien'*		16.06.18E
G-GEMX	P&M Quik GT450	8344	31.01.08
	LX-XLL, G-GEMX A R Oliver Dunkeswell		29.01.19P
G-GEOF	Pereira Osprey 2	xxxx	07.09.78
	G Crossley (Hambleton, Poulton-le-Fylde)		
	Built by G Crossley – project PFA 070-10384		
	(NF 22.01.16)		
G-GEOS	Diamond HK36TTC Eco Dimona	36.582	19.10.05
	N842WS, (G-GEOS), N842WS, C-GETC		
	University Court of The University of Edinburgh Fife		10.09.18E
G-GERI	Robinson R44 Raven I	2473	31.05.17
	Robraven Ltd (Dundalk, Co Louth, RoI)		08.06.18E
G-GERS	Robinson R44 Clipper II	12217	17.04.08
	M Virdee (Plaistow, Billingshurst)		21.09.18E
G-GERT	Van's RV-7	70528	22.03.04
	C R A Scrope Whitehall Farm, Benington		28.08.18P
	Built by A Burroughs, M Castle-Smith & B West		
	– project PFA 323-13836		
G-GETU	Leonardo AW169	69053	30.06.17
	Jetheli Ltd Guernsey		29.06.19E
G-GEZZ	Bell 206B-2 JetRanger II	1301	16.02.07
	N68TJ, N59489		
	Rivermead Aviation Ltd Gloucestershire		11.07.18E
	Operated by Rise Helicopters		
G-GFCA	Piper PA-28-161 Cadet	2841100	24.04.89
	N9174X Aviation Advice & Consulting Ltd Perth		12.02.20E
	Operated by Border Air Training		
G-GFCB	Piper PA-28-161 Cadet	2841101	24.04.89
	N9175X Bristol & Wessex Aeroplane Club Ltd Bristol		21.09.18E
G-GFCDᴹ	Piper PA-34-220T Seneca III	34-8133073	31.05.90
	G-KIDS, N83745 Cancelled 15.10.12 as PWFU		20.05.12
	Fuselage only		
	With Aviation Museum at Atlantic AirVenture, Shannon		
G-GFEY	Piper PA-34-200T Seneca II	34-7870343	13.05.98
	D-GFEY, D-IFEY, N36599 M R Badminton Rufforth		01.10.19E
G-GFIA	Cessna 152	15281685	18.09.06
	F-GGLI, N66950 Cancelled 01.12.14 by CAA		11.11.09
	Blackpool *On fire dump 03.16*		
G-GFIB	Reims/Cessna F152 II	F15201556	14.11.06
	G-BPIO, PH-VSO, PH-AXS		
	Westair Flying Services Ltd Manchester Barton		12.03.18E
G-GFID	Cessna 152 II	15282649	28.07.08
	G-BORJ, N89148		
	Pure Aviation Support Services Ltd Coventry		04.12.18E
	Operated by Almat Aviation		
G-GFIG	Cessna 152	15281625	14.07.10
	G-BNOZ, EI-CCP, G-BNOZ, N65570		
	The Pilot Centre Ltd Denham		21.08.18E
G-GFKY	Zenair CH.250 Zenith	34	23.04.93
	C-GFKY R G Kelsall RAF Mona		02.11.18P
	Built by D Koch		
G-GFLY	Reims/Cessna F150L	F15000822	28.08.80
	PH-CES Hangar 1 Ltd Little Snoring		10.10.18E
G-GFNO	Robin ATL	16	23.03.05
	F-GFNO, F-WFNO		
	M J Pink (Melcombe Bingham, Dorchester)		12.05.08E
	(NF 26.04.16)		
G-GFRA	Piper PA-28RT-201T Turbo Arrow IV	28R-8131024	23.02.09
	G-LROY, G-BNTS, N8296R		
	Ravenair Aircraft Ltd Liverpool John Lennon		07.12.17E
G-GFSA	Cessna 172R Skyhawk	17280221	26.10.06
	N410ES Atlantic Flight Training Ltd Cork, RoI		11.09.18E
G-GFTA	Piper PA-28-161 Warrior III	2842047	01.04.99
	N4132L, G-GFTA, N9525N		
	One Zero One Three Ltd Guernsey		08.03.18E
G-GFTB	Piper PA-28-161 Warrior III	2842048	07.05.99
	N4120V, (G-GFTB), N4120V		
	Cancelled 04.09.13 as PWFU		22.05.13
	Ta'qali, Malta *Stored for spares use 01.15*		
G-GFZG	Piper PA-28-140 Cherokee E	28-7225350	15.07.16
	F-GFZG, PH-LAM, N11C B A Mills Duxford		01.07.19E
G-GGCT	Flight Design CT2K	02-08-02-31	18.02.03
	Cancelled 02.01.13 as PWFU		11.06.11
	Yatesbury *Assembled Pegasus Aviation Ltd*		
	as c/n 7938; stored 06.14		
G-GGDV	Schleicher Ka 6E	4099	06.03.08
	BGA 3758/GDV, OO-ZWQ, I-NEST, OE-0807		
	East Sussex Gliding Club Ltd Ringmer *'GDV'*		16.05.16E
	(IE 21.12.17)		
G-GGEM	Piper PA-28-161 Warrior III	2742185	26.03.19
	S5-DRS, N357D, N9511N A Brinkley Meppershall		
G-GGGG	Thunder Ax7-77	162	02.08.78
	T A Gilmour tr Flying G Group		
	Chilbolton, Stockbridge *'Greenham Group'*		17.08.99A
	(NF 02.02.18)		
G-GGHZ	Robin ATL	123	10.02.05
	F-GGHZ M J Pink (Melcombe Bingham, Dorchester)		07.01.15E
	(NF 26.04.16)		
G-GGJK	Robin DR.400-140B Major 80	1805	24.03.05
	F-GGJK D N Smith & S Thompson		
	tr Headcorn Jodelers Headcorn		26.04.19E
G-GGRN	Piper PA-28R-201 Arrow III	28R-7837283	20.05.15
	F-GGRN, N36544 P Sharpe (Maypole Farm, Chislet)		18.07.18E
G-GGRR	Scottish Aviation Bulldog Srs 120/121	BH120/272	11.07.01
	G-CBAM, XX614 D J Sharp Gloucestershire		25.09.19E
	As 'XX614' in RAF white & red c/s		
G-GGRV	Van's RV-8	83418	27.03.14
	C F O'Neill Newtownards		
	Built by C F O'Neill – project LAA 303-15271		
	(NF 05.04.18)		
G-GGTT	Agusta-Bell 47G-4A	2538	21.08.97
	F-GGTT, I-ANDO		
	P R Smith Scarr End Mill, Dewsbury		18.09.18E
G-GGZZ	Aviat A-1B Husky	2078	21.06.17
	OY-NPS, N440PS J A S Everett (Guist, Dereham)		28.09.18E
G-GHEE	Evektor EV-97 Eurostar	xxxx	14.12.01
	P R Howson RAF Henlow		26.06.19P
	Built by C J Ball – project PFA 315-13840		
G-GHER	Eurocopter AS.355N Ecureuil 2	5658	08.12.11
	G-DANZ Gallagher Air LLP Southend		10.02.20E
G-GHKX	Piper PA-28-161 Warrior III	28-8416005	10.06.99
	N380X, G-GHKX, F-GHKX, N4318X		
	Northumbria Aerospace Limited t/a NAL Engineering Ltd		
	Newcastle		31.07.19E
	Operated by ACS Flight Training		
G-GHOP	Cameron Z-77	10897	03.05.12
	D P Hopkins t/a Lakeside Lodge Golf Centre		
	Chiltern Park, Wallingford *'Lakeside Lodge Golf Centre'*		07.07.18E
G-GHOW	Reims/Cessna F182Q Skylane II	F18200151	20.02.01
	OO-MCD, F-BJCE		
	Southern Counties Aviation Ltd Blackbushe		05.10.18E
G-GHRW	Piper PA-28RT-201 Arrow IV	28R-7918140	08.12.83
	G-ONAB, G-BHAK, N29555		
	P Cowley East Midlands		25.05.18E
G-GHZJ	SOCATA TB-9 Tampico	941	04.03.98
	F-GHZJ P K Hayward Turweston		09.09.18E
G-GIAN	Comco Ikarus C42 FB100 Bravo	1812-7555	22.02.19
	I Newman & P Read Brookfield Farm, Usselby		
	Built by The Light Aircraft Company Ltd (IE 22.02.19)		
G-GIAS	Comco Ikarus C42 FB80 Bravo	1410-7350	14.11.14
	R D Wilson tr G-GIAS Group Eshott		29.01.20P
	Assembled Red-Air UK		
G-GIBB	Robinson R44 Raven II	11777	13.06.07
	BEMC Corporate Hire Ltd (Ardee, Co Louth, RoI)		20.07.19E

G

G-GIBI	Agusta A109E Power 11685	30.10.14
	I-RRFF, (I-RRSS) Gazelle Management Services LLP	
	Pentre Celyn Hall, Ruthin	25.11.18E
G-GIBP	Moravan Zlin Z-526 Trener Master 1082	11.06.10
	F-GIBP, F-BRNF	
	D G Cowden Swanborough Farm, Lewes	18.07.18E
G-GIFF	Kubícek BB26XR 978	25.03.13
	A M Holly & The Lord Mayors Appeal	
	Breadstone, Berkeley 'The Lord Mayor's Appeal'	09.07.16E
	(IE 05.10.18)	
G-GIGZ	Van's RV-8 82590	17.12.08
	K A A McDonald & N G Rhind White Waltham	06.03.18P
	Built by C D Mitchell – project PFA 303-14577	
G-GILB	Cessna 510 Citation Mustang 510-0241	10.06.15
	N270MK Catreus AOC Ltd Birmingham	18.06.18E
G-GIPC	Piper PA-32R-301 Saratoga SP 32R-8313005	28.02.11
	F-GIPC, N82778	
	P Sodagar tr GIPC Flying Group Biggin Hill	24.03.18E
G-GIRY	American General AG-5B Tiger 10146	05.02.99
	F-GIRY O Zeloof tr Romeo Yankee Flying Group	
	Elstree	07.05.19E
G-GIWT	Europa Aviation Europa XS 463	29.03.01
	A Twigg Bicester	
	Built by A Twigg – project PFA 247-13623;	
	tailwheel u/c (IE 20.03.17)	
G-GJCD	Robinson R22 Beta 0966	22.02.89
	J C Lane Gloucestershire	25.07.18E
G-GKAT	Enstrom 280C Shark 1200	26.08.97
	F-GKAT, N5694Y	
	D G Allsop & A J Clark (Codnor, Ripley)	09.08.08E
	(NF 05.08.14)	
G-GKFC	Tiger Cub RL5A Sherwood Ranger LW xxxx	24.11.98
	G-MYZI G L Davies Manchester Barton	07.04.15P
	Built by K F Crumplin – project PFA 237-12947	
	(IE 03.01.18)	
G-GKKI	Mudry CAP 231EX 02	23.01.07
	F-GKKI, G-BVXL, F-GKKF (?), F-WGZC	
	D R Farley tr Kilo India Group White Waltham	19.12.18E
	Official p/i 'F-GKKF' is incorrect	
G-GKRC	Cessna 180K Skywagon 18052799	12.01.10
	PH-KRC, SE-KRC, N61790	
	W J Pitts Wold Lodge, Finedon	07.04.18E
G-GKUE	SOCATA TB-9 Tampico 1129	05.02.07
	F-GKUE R S McMaster	
	Sackville Lodge Farm, Riseley	03.01.19E
G-GLAA	Airbus EC135 T2+ 1196	23.09.15
	PLM Dollar Group Ltd t/a PDG Helicopters	
	Dalcross Heliport	04.11.18E
	Callsign 'Osprey 70'	
G-GLAB	Eurocopter EC135 T2+ 0712	25.04.16
	EI-ILS, G-CFFR, D-HTSF PLM Dollar Group Ltd	
	t/a PDG Helicopters Dalcross Heliport	29.10.18E
	Callsign 'Osprey 71'	
G-GLAD	Gloster Gladiator II N5903	05.01.95
	N5903 Patina Ltd Duxford	30.06.18P
	Operated by The Fighter Collection;	
	as 'N5903' in RAF 72 Sqdn c/s	
G-GLAK	Sportine Aviacija LAK-12 Lietuva 647	15.11.07
	BGA3717/GCB C Roney Rattlesden '236'	21.06.18E
G-GLAW	Cameron N-90 1808	10.10.88
	N D Humphries East Leake, Loughborough 'LAW'	17.05.17E
G-GLED	Cessna 150M 15076673	06.01.89
	C-GLED P Constantinou tr G-GLED Group Elstree	25.05.19E
G-GLHI	Best Off Skyranger 912S(1) SKR0403468	30.06.04
	S F Winter Lower Upham Farm, Chiseldon	09.06.18P
	Built by G L Higgins – project BMAA/HB/392	
G-GLID	Schleicher ASW 28-18E 28723	18.04.06
	BGA 5131/KJR, D-KEBB, D-KOAB	
	S Bovin & Compagnie Belge d'Assurances Aviation	
	Zwartberg, Belgium 'E3'	22.04.18E
G-GLII	Great Lakes 2T-1A-2 Sport Trainer 0813	08.08.07
	N3613L T J Richardson Thruxton	01.08.18P

G-GLLY	Bell 505 Jet Ranger X 65106	29.06.18
	Twylight Management Ltd (Douglas, Isle of Man)	
	(IE 29.06.18)	
G-GLOB	Bombardier BD-700-1A10 Global Express XRS 9413	24.02.17
	M-GLOB, C-GGFJ Execujet (UK) Ltd Cambridge	25.02.20E
G-GLOC	Extra EA.300/200 1039	30.03.07
	The Cambridge Aero Club Ltd Cambridge	
	'cambridgeaeroclub.com'	21.04.18E
G-GLSA	Evektor EV-97 Eurostar SL 2014-4216	13.04.15
	I E Sparrowhawk tr LSA1 Group Wycombe Air Park	06.04.18P
	Assembled Light Sport Aviation Ltd	
G-GLST	Great Lakes 2T-1A Sport Trainer xxxx	21.07.03
	T Boehmerle & A Hofmann	
	(Esslingen & Heubach, Germany) 'Poppie II'	02.07.19P
	Built by D A Graham – project PFA 321-13646	
G-GLUC	Van's RV-6 20153	15.10.99
	C-GLUC P J Roper Ludham	19.07.19P
	Built by L De Sadeleer	
G-GLUE	Cameron N-65 390	17.03.81
	G D Hallett & L J M Muir Hertford	17.07.90A
	Stored Hertfordshire Balloon Collection;	
	active 04.18 (NF 25.09.14)	
G-GMAD	Beech B300C Super King Air 350C FM-54	02.10.13
	N51154 Gama Aviation (Asset 2) Ltd	
	RAF Waddington	24.09.18E
	For RAF 2019 as Beechcraft Shadow R1 ZZ506	
G-GMAE	Beech B200 Super King Air BB-1957	21.07.17
	D-IRAR, N957BA, N104AG	
	Gama Aviation (UK) Ltd Farnborough	13.11.18E
G-GMAX	SNCAN Stampe SV.4C 141	19.06.87
	G-BXNW, F-BBPB S T Carrel White Waltham	
	(NF 02.08.18)	
G-GMCM	Eurocopter AS.350B3 Ecureuil 4576	20.04.10
	TJ Morris Ltd Blackpool	02.08.18E
G-GMCT	Beech E33A Bonanza CE-235	25.07.14
	D-EUEE, I-ABCA, HB-EHH	
	MCT Agentur GmbH (Berlin, Germany)	27.11.18E
G-GMGH	Robinson R66 Turbine 0584	28.01.15
	M G Holland Wycombe Air Park	11.02.19E
G-GMIB	Robin DR.500-200i Président 0002	05.09.08
	F-GMIB A L & D A Sadler Insch	12.09.19E
	Officially registered as 'DR.400/500'	
G-GMKE	Robin HR.200-120B 257	07.11.07
	F-GMKE Nogaro Ltd Dublin Weston, RoI	20.07.18E
G-GMOX	Cessna 152 15282152	17.02.16
	C-GMOX, C-GYAD, (N68155) Staverton Flying	
	School @ Skypark Ltd Gloucestershire	19.06.18E
G-GMSI	SOCATA TB-9 Tampico 145	18.09.80
	M L Rhodes Wolverhampton Halfpenny Green	09.08.18E
G-GNJW	Comco Ikarus C42 FB100 VLA xxxx	21.08.01
	N C Pearse (Paignton)	16.08.19P
	Built by I R Westrope – project PFA 322-13717	
G-GNMM	Agusta AW109SP Grand New 22237	05.11.18
	2-GRND, UR-GDF Hadleigh Partners LLP	
	Manton House Farm, Barton Dene	15.11.19E
	Operated by Castle Air Ltd	
G-GNRV	Van's RV-9A 91006	20.06.05
	N K Beavins Rayne Hall Farm, Rayne	13.04.18P
	Built by N K Beavins – project PFA 320-14344	
G-GNSS	Diamond DA.62 62.057	09.05.17
	Flight Calibration Services Ltd Goodwood	24.05.18E
	Callsign 'VOR07'	
G-GNTB	Saab 340A 340A-082	30.09.91
	HB-AHL, SE-E82 Loganair Ltd Glasgow	13.03.19E
	Built by Saab Scania AB	
G-GNTF	Saab 340A 340A-113	27.10.94
	SE-F13, G-GNTF, HB-AHO, SE-F13	
	Loganair Ltd Glasgow	09.08.19E
	Built by Saab Scania AB	
G-GOAC	Piper PA-34-200T Seneca II 34-7770007	09.12.03
	D-GOAC, N5329F	
	Sky Zone Services Aereos Lda Cascais, Portugal	17.01.17E
G-GOAL	Lindstrand LBL 105A 420	18.11.96
	I Chadwick Caterham 'Benfield Group'	05.05.18E

G-GODV	Mudry CAP 232	32	25.09.15
	F-GODV E V Collett tr G-GODV Group		
	White Waltham		05.04.18E
	Built by CAP Aviation		
G-GOER	Bushby-Long Midget Mustang	M-1-1996	02.05.12
	N11LG C Antrobus (Battle)		
	Built by L Graves (NF 27.04.17)		
G-GOES	Robinson R44 Raven II	10942	14.01.08
	EI-KHL Helicentre Aviation Ltd Leicester		02.09.18E
G-GOFF	Extra EA.300/LC	LC008	17.02.12
	George J Goff Ltd Elmham Lodge, North Elmham		10.04.18E
G-GOFR	Ultramagic M-105	105/104	20.02.18
	F-GOFR Associazione Vivere Paestum		
	Paestum, Capaccio, Italy		
	(IE 20.02.18)		
G-GOGB	Lindstrand LBL 90A	1011	20.01.05
	G-CDFX J Dyer Farnborough GU14 *'Team GB'*		07.08.18E
G-GOGW	Cameron N-90	3304	31.08.94
	R Calvert-Fisher Radley, Abingdon *'Great Western'*		29.03.13E
	IE 13.05.14)		
G-GOHI	Cessna 208 Caravan I	20800040	16.07.12
	N208NN, N812FE, (N9401F)		
	Headcorn Parachute Club Ltd Headcorn		26.09.19E
G-GOLA	Zenair CH.701SP	xxxx	16.03.17
	J D Hayward Archerfield		
	Built by J D Hayward & J MacTaggart – project		
	PFA 187-12911; stored part built 2018 (NF 16.03.17)		
G-GOLF	SOCATA TB-10 Tobago	250	21.12.81
	B Lee Boon Hill Farm, Fadmoor		30.06.17E
	(IE 02.08.17)		
G-GOLX	Europa Aviation Europa XS	442	09.02.17
	G-CROB LX Avionics Ltd Turweston		
	Built by R G Hallam – project PFA 247-13510;		
	tricycle u/c (IE 09.02.17)		
G-GOMS	Robinson R66 Turbine	0705	06.04.16
	Bri-Stor Systems Ltd		
	Pasturefields Industrial Estate, Hixon		13.04.19E
G-GOOF	Flylight Dragonfly	043	04.05.10
	M G Preston (Great Sankey, Warrington)		
	(IE 15.06.18)		
	(SSDR microlight since 05.14)		
G-GOPR	Cameron Z-90	11926	28.07.15
	D J Groombridge & I J Martin t/a Flying Enterprises		
	Congresbury & Wotton-under-Edge *'Power Rangers'*		24.07.17E
G-GORA	Robin DR.400-160 Chevalier	2271	20.03.15
	F-GORA Robin Flying Club Ltd Exeter Int'l		31.07.18E
G-GORD	Robin DR.401/140B Dauphin 4	2669	12.03.15
	G-JSMH, F-WZIB		
	J G Bellerby Glebe Farm, Kings Ripton *'82'*		06.08.18E
G-GORE	CFM Streak Shadow	K 138-SA	12.04.90
	P F Stares (Lower Broadheath, Worcester)		31.08.11P
	Built by D N Gore – project PFA 206-11646: sequence		
	no. duplicates TEAM mini-MAX G-MWFD (NF 24.11.16)		
G-GORV	Van's RV-8	82901	20.01.09
	A Zmyslowski tr G-GORV Group RAF Woodvale		23.10.18P
	Built by D Dooley, M Yates & A Zymslowski		
	– project LAA 303-14847		
G-GOSL	Robin DR.400-180 Régent	1974	14.01.02
	G-BSDG R M Gosling		
	Stones Farm, Wickham St Paul		13.03.18E
G-GOTC	Gulfstream American GA-7 Cougar	GA7-0074	25.06.97
	G-BMDY, OO-LCR, OO-HRA		
	G Y Phillips (Llanpumsaint, Carmarthen)		06.06.19E
G-GOTH	Piper PA-28-161 Warrior III	2842208	21.06.04
	N3088U One Zero One Three Ltd Guernsey		28.04.18E
G-GOUP	Robinson R22 Beta	1663	02.01.01
	G-DIRE AKP Aviation Ltd Elstree		29.08.18E
G-GOXC	HpH Glasflügel 304 S Shark	049-MS	29.07.15
	S A W Becker (Itchenor) *'CD'*		
	(IE 19.07.17)		
G-GPAG	Van's RV-6	60206	18.05.01
	J & N Salmon Calcot Peak Farm, Calcot		16.05.19P
	Built by P A Green – project PFA 181A-13306		
G-GPAT	Beech 76 Duchess	ME-398	07.09.10
	N741D, D-GEWU		
	Folada Aero & Technical Services Ltd Thruxton		02.02.18E
G-GPEG	Sky 90-24	4849	31.05.00
	R Cains-Collinson Corby Glen, Grantham		06.03.15E
	Built by Cameron Balloons Ltd (NF 04.10.17)		
G-GPFI	Boeing 737-229	20907	31.07.03
	VH-OZQ, G-GPFI, VH-OZQ, G-GPFI, F-GVAC,		
	OO-SDA, LX-LGN, OO-SDA		02.04.09
	Cancelled 09.06.11 by CAA		
	Bournemouth *Front fuselage as Cabin trainer 03.19*		
G-GPMW	Piper PA-28RT-201T Turbo Arrow IV	28R-8031041	03.07.89
	N3576V Calverton Flying Group Ltd Coventry		15.05.19E
G-GPPN	Cameron TR-70	10940	25.10.06
	Backetorp Byggconsult AB		
	Granna, Jönköping, Sweden *'Cameron Balloons'*		13.02.19E
G-GPSI	Grob G115	8047	29.01.14
	PH-KND, D-EOTA Swiftair Maintenance Ltd		
	Wolverhampton Halfpenny Green		01.02.18E
	Operated by Air MidWest		
G-GPSR	Grob G115	8024	29.01.14
	PH-SPH, G-BOCD, D-EGVV Swiftair Maintenance Ltd		
	Wolverhampton Halfpenny Green		06.12.18E
	Operated by Air MidWest		
G-GPSX	Grob G115A	8040	03.12.13
	OO-OCC, D-ENDS, I-GROD, D-EGVV		
	Swiftair Maintenance Ltd Nottingham City		08.08.18E
	Operated by Sherwood Flying Club		
G-GPWE	Comco Ikarus C42 FB100 Bravo	1606-7458	18.07.16
	P W Ellis (North Luffenham, Oakham)		13.07.18P
	Assembled Red Aviation		
G-GRAY	Cessna 172N Skyhawk II	17272375	03.12.79
	N4859D Cancelled 27.09.00 as PWFU		13.02.95
	Nottingham City *Stored on fire dump 12.15*		
G-GREC	Sequoia F.8L Falco	934	10.10.16
	N155BJ J D Tseliki Kittyhawk Farm, Ripe		27.04.18P
	Built by D W McMurray		
G-GREG	CEA Jodel DR.220 2+2	47	03.10.84
	F-BOKR Cancelled 01.04.97 by CAA		19.02.91
	Crosland Moor *Fuselage stored 09.14*		
G-GREM	MD Helicopters MD.600N	RN053	12.09.18
	HB-ZGU, N70418 Gremlin Air LLP Brighton City		25.04.19E
G-GREY	Piper PA-46-350P Malibu Mirage	4636155	28.11.03
	OY-LAR, N1280K, N4129D		
	S C Askham & S T Day Gloucestershire		19.02.18E
G-GRIN	Van's RV-6	22338	08.01.98
	E Andersen Solent		13.04.18P
	Built by A Phillips – project PFA 181-12409		
G-GRIZ	Piper PA-18-135 Super Cub	18-3123	03.08.10
	G-BSHV, OO-GDG, Belgian Army L-49, 53-4723		
	P N Elkington East Winch		28.06.18E
G-GRLS	Best Off Skyranger Swift 912S(1)	xxxx	02.02.18
	D Young tr GRLS Flying Group Cotswold		21.04.19P
	Built by Benenden School (BMAA New Horizons)		
	– project BMAA/HB/690		
G-GRLW	Avtech Jabiru J400	256	26.06.14
	G-NMBG R L Wood Enstone		23.01.19P
	Built by D K Shead – project PFA 325-14461		
G-GRMN	Aerospool Dynamic WT9 UK	DY159/2007	02.10.06
	I D Worthington Bagby		28.11.17P
	Assembled Yeoman Light Aircraft Co Ltd;		
	official c/n recorded as 'DY159'		
G-GROE	Grob G115A	8054	22.06.04
	I-GROE, (D-EGVV)		
	B Baylis & P B Readings Dunkeswell		11.09.19E
G-GROL	Maule MXT-7-180 Super Rocket	14091C	16.06.98
	D Roosendans Kortrijk-Wevelgem Int'l, Belgium		05.11.18E
G-GRPA	Comco Ikarus C42 FB100	0407-6609	26.08.04
	R L Wood tr G-GRPA Group Enstone		01.09.18P
	Assembled Fly Buy Ultralights Ltd		
G-GRRR	Scottish Aviation Bulldog Srs 120/122	BH120/229	19.10.98
	G-BXGU, Ghana AF G-105		
	Horizons Europe Ltd Compton Abbas		22.03.18E

G-GRVE	Van's RV-6	23037	14.04.07
	A J Ransome tr G-GRVE Group Sherburn-in-Elmet		18.06.18P
	Built by R D Carswell – project PFA 181-12566		
G-GRVY	Van's RV-8	82740	23.03.09
	A Page (Wrington, Bristol)		02.05.19P
	Built by A P Lawton & A Page – project PFA 303-14718		
G-GRWL	Lilliput Type 4	L-04	22.06.06
	A E & D E Thomas Weston, Honiton		
G-GRYN	AutoGyro Calidus	xxxx	30.06.10
	G A Speich Poplar Farm, Prolly Moor, Wentnor		25.04.19P
	Assembled Rotorsport UK as c/n RSUK/CALS/003		
G-GRYZ	Beech F33A Bonanza	CE-1668	04.10.99
	F-GRYZ, D-ESNE, N80011, (OY-GEN), N80011		
	M Kaveh & J Kawadri Fairoaks		13.04.18E
G-GRZZ	Robinson R44 Raven II	12149	06.03.08
	Model Farm Shop Ltd (Bradford)		13.04.19E
G-GSAL	Airdrome ¾ Fokker E.III replica	GS-101	13.05.08
	Grass Strip Aviation Ltd Aston Down		
	Built by Grass Strip Aviation Ltd; as '416/15'		
	in German Army Air Service c/s)		
	(SSDR microlight since 05.14) (IE 29.03.17)		
G-GSCV	Comco Ikarus C42 FB UK	0206 6488	05.09.02
	T J Gayton-Polley Hadfold Farm, Adversane		20.03.18P
	Built by G Sipson – project PFA 322-13939		
G-GSFS	Cessna 152	15284130	18.02.16
	C-GDWJ, N6097H		
	Staverton Flying School @ Skypark Ltd Gloucestershire		
	(NF 18.02.16)		
G-GSGS	HpH Glasflügel 304 eS Shark	059-MS	04.08.16
	(BGA 5919) G E Smith Parham Park 'GS'		04.01.18R
	Damaged by battery fire 10.08.17		
G-GSPY	Robinson R44 Raven II	10772	31.08.05
	HQ Aviation Ltd Denham		08.01.18E
	(IE 16.07.18)		
G-GSST	Grob G102 Astir CS77	1649	08.12.07
	BGA 2291/DQG		
	A G Veitch tr 770 Group Easterton '770'		12.04.18E
G-GSVI	Gulfstream Gulfstream VI (*Gulfstream 650*) 6160		14.03.16
	N660GA Executive Jet Charter Ltd Bristol		13.03.19E
G-GSYL	Piper PA-28RT-201T Turbo Arrow IV	28R-7931104	14.08.12
	G-DAAH, N3026U		
	S J Sylvester Wolverhampton Halfpenny Green		16.12.18E
G-GSYS	Piper PA-34-220T Seneca V	3449363	08.10.07
	N60383 R Schilling Biggin Hill		05.01.19E
G-GTBT	Pilatus B4-PC11AF	040	20.08.14
	G-DCUO, BGA 1821/CUQ		
	T Geissel (Neunkirchen, Germany)		19.06.17E
	(NF 02.10.18)		
G-GTFB	Magni M24C Orion	24148454	09.06.14
	Rotormurf Ltd Caernarfon		12.09.18P
G-GTFC	P&M Pegasus Quik	8184	20.06.06
	A J Fell Bourn 'Quiky McQuik Face'		31.07.18P
G-GTGT	P&M Quik GT450	8145	08.12.05
	T J Lewis Eshott		21.12.18P
G-GTHM	Piper PA-38-112 Tomahawk II	38-81A0171	17.11.86
	C-GTHM, N91338 D R Clyde Swansea		31.05.18E
G-GTJD	P&M Quik GT450	8183	01.06.06
	A J Bacon Northrepps		11.01.18P
G-GTOM	Alpi Pioneer 300	NC245	25.06.08
	S C Oliphant & J Watkins		
	Wadswick Manor Farm, Corsham		06.08.18P
	Built by T F Freake – project LAA 330-14795		
G-GTRE	P&M Quik GTR	8674	20.01.14
	M J Austin (Cheddington)		28.02.18P
G-GTRR	P&M Quik GTR	8618	14.05.12
	M R Wallis Beverley (Linley Hill)		07.05.18P
G-GTRX	P&M Quik GTR	8646	01.03.13
	N Matthews Broadmeadow Farm, Hereford		03.04.18P
G-GTSD	P&M Quik GT450	8766	14.08.17
	P Bayliss Ince		24.08.18P
G-GTSO	P&M Quik GT450	8164	10.03.06
	C Bayliss Ince		18.07.17P

G-GTTP	P&M Quik GT450	8228	27.11.06
	S E Powell Enstone		25.08.17P
	(NF 02.11.17)		
G-GTWO	Schleicher ASW 15	15146	18.12.07
	BGA 3315/FKE, D-0794		
	J M G Carlton & R Jackson Shenington 'G2'		22.05.18E
G-GUAR	Piper PA-28-161 Warrior II	28-7816576	07.09.17
	F-GUAR, PH-ANI, N31685 B A Mills Duxford		13.02.18E
G-GULP	III Sky Arrow 650 T	K 130	04.12.00
	L J Betts Sleap		18.09.18P
	Built by H R Rotherwick – project PFA 298-13664		
G-GULZ	Christen Eagle II	SEGLER 0001	10.02.09
	N83DS T N Jinks Stoke Golding		20.07.18P
	Built by D F Segler		
G-GUMM	Aviat A-1B Husky	2436	16.12.14
	F-GUMM, G-LTMM, N115AA		
	A E Poulsom Manor Farm, Tongham		15.03.18E
G-GUNS	Cameron V-77	2221	09.05.90
	O LeClercq Etigny, France		15.09.16E
	(NF 13.05.18)		
G-GUNZ	Van's RV-8	5-27454	12.08.08
	Cirrus Aircraft UK Ltd Leicester		15.11.18P
	Built by R Ellingworth – project PFA 303-14475		
G-GURU	Piper PA-28-161 Warrior II	28-8316018	12.02.02
	PH-SVJ, N83085 Avro-Marine Ltd		
	Manchester Barton		14.07.18E
G-GUSS	Piper PA-28-151 Cherokee Warrior	28-7415497	16.08.95
	G-BJRY, N43453 K G & P M Martlew		
	tr The Sierra Flying Group Stapleford		14.06.18E
G-GUST	Agusta-Bell 206B-2 JetRanger II	8192	30.08.96
	G-CBHH, F-GALU, G-AYBE		
	Cancelled 29.03.11 as PWFU		27.05.08
	(Leeds) *Stored 05.15, left Coney Park by road 10.15*		
G-GVFR	SOCATA TB-20 Trinidad	1240	09.01.15
	F-GVFR, G-CEPT, G-BTEK A E Allsop Lydd		14.01.19E
G-GVPI	Evans VP-1 Series 2	xxxx	09.08.02
	G Martin Stoke Golding		13.06.08P
	Built by G Martin & P A Schafle – project		
	PFA 062-10668 (NF 24.09.14)		
G-GVSL	Evektor EV-97 Eurostar SL	2014-3720	26.09.14
	G Verity Hawksview, Stretton		06.05.18P
	Built by G Verity – project LAA 315B-15288		
G-GWAC	Eurocopter EC135 T2+	0746	05.06.17
	G-WASN Babcock Mission Critical Services		
	Onshore Ltd Almondsbury		25.03.19E
	Operated by Great Western Air Ambulance Charity		
G-GWFT	Rans S-6-ES Coyote II	1010.1939	29.04.14
	The Georgia Williams Trust		
	Wolverhampton Halfpenny Green		04.10.18P
	Built by M Parry-Sargeant – project LAA 204-15096		
	(Ercall Wood Technology College [RAeS/Boeing		
	Build-a-Plane]); tricycle u/c		
G-GWIZ	Colt Clown	1369	25.04.89
	(G-BPWU) Magical Adventures Ltd		
	West Bloomfield, MI, USA		29.09.09E
	Built by Thunder & Colt Ltd (NF 03.06.15)		
G-GWYN	Reims/Cessna F172M	F17201217	05.03.81
	PH-TWN G Dunne Dublin Weston, RoI		15.06.18E
G-GYAT	Gardan GY-80-180 Horizon	136	13.12.02
	D-EAZZ, HB-DCL, F-BMUU J Luck tr Rochester		
	GYAT Flying Group Stoneacre Farm, Farthing Corner		20.06.18P
	Built by Sud Aviation		
G-GYAV	Cessna 172N Skyhawk II	17271362	26.08.87
	C-GYAV Southport & Merseyside Aero Club (1979) Ltd		
	Liverpool John Lennon		13.04.18E
G-GYRA	AutoGyro Calidus	xxxx	05.07.16
	D B Roberts & W C Walters Nottingham City		11.10.18P
	Assembled Rotorsport UK as c/n RSUK/CALS/027		
G-GYRO	Campbell Cricket replica	01	26.02.82
	J W Pavitt (Huntshaw, Torrington)		19.06.08P
	Built by A L Howell, J W Pavitt & N A Pitcher		
	– project PFA G/03-1046 (NF 12.09.14)		
G-GYTO	Piper PA-28-161 Warrior III	2842082	11.05.00
	N160FT, N9511N		
	White Waltham Airfield Ltd White Waltham		09.05.18E

G-GZDO	Cessna 172N Skyhawk II	17271826	11.10.88
	C-GZDO, (N5299E) Eagle Flying Ltd Elstree		04.11.19E
	Operated by Stars Fly		
G-GZIP	Rolladen-Schneider LS8-18	8309	14.12.07
	BGA 4784/JUD D S S Haughton Long Mynd *'Z19'*		01.04.18E

G-HAAA – G-HZZZ

G-HAAH	Schempp-Hirth Ventus-2cT	52/173	06.12.07
	BGA 4776/JTV		
	J Roland tr V66 Syndicate Wycombe Air Park *'V66'*		11.11.17E
G-HAAR	Aeropro EuroFOX 912(S)	52017	09.05.17
	W Anderson tr Longside Flying Group Longside		20.03.19P
	Built by W Anderson, F Cruikshank & A T Wilson		
	– project LAA 376-15469; tricycle u/c		
G-HAAT	McDonnell Douglas MD Explorer	900-00081	15.08.08
	G-GMPS, N7033K		
	Specialist Aviation Services Ltd Gloucestershire		31.08.18E
G-HABI	Best Off Skyranger Swift 912S(1)	UK/738	26.02.07
	J Habicht Main Hall Farm, Conington		06.07.18P
	Built by J Habicht – project BMAA/HB/524		
G-HABT	Super Marine Spitfire Mk.26	040	29.08.06
	Wright Grumman Aviation Ltd		
	Hohenems-Dornbirn, Austria		31.07.15P
	Built by B Trumble – project PFA 324-14487;		
	as 'BL735:BT-A' in RAF c/s (NF 19.07.17)		
G-HACE	Van's RV-6A	1951	22.05.06
	C-GOLZ S Woolmington Earls Colne		05.04.19P
	Built by J & S Brennan		
G-HACK	Piper PA-18-150 Super Cub	18-7168	20.11.97
	SE-CSA, N10F S J Harris Oaksey Park		22.09.18E
G-HACS	Tecnam P2002-JF Sierra	199	02.03.12
	The Royal Air Force Halton Aeroplane Club Ltd		
	RAF Halton		25.04.18E
G-HADD	P&M QuikR	8510	08.02.10
	T J Barker Manchester Barton		01.04.18P
G-HAEF	Evektor EV-97 teamEurostar UK	2009-3322	08.07.09
	M E Howard tr RAF Microlight Flying Association		
	RAF Halton		15.03.18P
	Assembled Cosmik Aviation Ltd		
G-HAFG	Cessna 340A	340A1806	05.08.04
	JY-AFG, N1230V Pavilion Aviation Ltd Jersey		23.09.18E
G-HAFT	Diamond DA.42 Twin Star	42.057	13.10.05
	Airways Aviation Academy Ltd Oxford		02.12.18E
G-HAGL	Robinson R44 Raven II	12403	03.10.08
	HQ Aviation Ltd Denham		23.06.18E
G-HAGU	Agusta A109C	7665	06.12.18
	EC-GCQ, EC-895, N1ZL Helicom Ltd (Wokingham)		
	(NF 06.12.18)		
G-HAHU	Yakovlev Yak-18T	12-33	27.08.13
	HA-HUE A Leftwich Rochester *'Red Rosie'*		26.01.18R
G-HAIG	Rutan Long-EZ	xxxx	20.05.86
	P R Dalton Tatenhill		18.10.14P
	Built by P N Haig – project PFA 074A-11149 (NF 25.11.15)		
G-HAIR	Robin DR.400-180 Régent	2479	07.12.00
	S P Copson Church Farm, Shotteswell		22.02.18E
G-HAJJ	Glaser-Dirks DG-400	4-225	15.02.88
	J G Kosak & W G Upton RNAS Culdrose		20.06.18E
G-HAKA	Diamond DA.42NG Twin Star	42.N158	16.08.18
	SE-MIS, F-HPVT Directflight Ltd Cranfield		
	(NF 16.08.18)		
G-HALC	Piper PA-28R-200 Cherokee Arrow II	28R-7335042	26.11.90
	N91253, C-FFQO, CF-FQO		
	Halcyon Aviation Ltd Manchester Barton		22.02.18E
G-HALJ	Cessna 140	8336	30.04.96
	N89308, NC89308 A R Willis Conington		16.02.18E
G-HALL	Piper PA-22-160 Tri-Pacer	22-7423	08.11.79
	G-ARAH, N10F F P Hall Clipgate Farm, Denton		17.07.18E
G-HALS	Robinson R44 Raven II	11639	02.07.15
	G-CEKA Paul D White Ltd Denham		29.03.19E
G-HALT	Mainair Pegasus Quik	8063	01.09.04
	J McGrath Bedlands Gate, Little Strickland		30.04.18P
	Built by Mainair Sports Ltd		
G-HAMI	Fuji FA.200-180 Aero Subaru	FA200-188	31.01.92
	G-OISF, G-BAPT		
	K G Cameron tr HAMI Group White Waltham		02.03.18E
G-HAMP	Bellanca 7ACA Champ	30-72	08.08.88
	N9173L R J Grimstead		
	Shipbourne Farm, Wisborough Green		06.09.18P
G-HAMR	Piper PA-28-161 Warrior II	28-8416077	18.07.06
	PH-AMR, N4353B CG Aviation Ltd Perth		30.11.18E
G-HAMS	P&M Pegasus Quik	8224	01.11.06
	D R Morton Knapthorpe Lodge, Caunton		19.10.18P
G-HAMW	Aeropro EuroFOX 3K	52117	07.09.17
	M D Hamwee Popham		24.09.18P
	Built by Ascent Industries Ltd; tricycle u/c		
G-HANC	Robinson R22 Beta	1740	02.03.15
	G-CHIS S Hancock Nottingham City		16.06.18E
G-HANG	Diamond DA.42 Twin Star	42.026	07.06.05
	Airways Aviation Academy Ltd Oxford		14.08.18E
	Operated by CAE Oxford Aviation Academy		
G-HANS	Robin DR.400 2+2	1384	02.03.79
	The Cotswold Aero Club Ltd Gloucestershire		21.12.17E
G-HANY	Agusta-Bell 206B-3 JetRanger III	8598	05.01.01
	G-JEKP, D-HMSF, G-ESAL, G-BHXW		
	Heliflight (UK) Ltd Gloucestershire		03.02.19E
	Operated by HH Helicopters Ltd t/a Cotswold Helicopters		
G-HAPE	Pietenpol Air Camper	158	10.08.09
	J P Chape (Sandown)		
	Built by J P Chape – project PFA 047-13921 (NF 27.10.16)		
G-HAPI	Lindstrand LBL 105A	669	21.03.00
	Adventure Balloons Ltd Hartley Wintney, Hook		
	'Adventure Balloons' & *'Happy Birthday'*		16.04.18E
G-HAPR[M]	Bristol 171 Sycamore HC.14	13387	15.06.78
	8010M, XG547 Cancelled 24.06.08 – to Belgium		
	As 'XG547'		
	With Koninklijk Leger Museum-Musée Royal de l'Armée,		
	Brussels		
G-HAPY	de Havilland DHC-1 Chipmunk 22	C1/0697	03.07.96
	WP803 Astrojet Ltd Wycombe Air Park		30.04.18E
	As 'WP803' in RAF white & red c/s		
G-HARE	Cameron N-77	1467	12.03.87
	C A Buck & D H Sheryn Princes Risborough &		
	London SE16 *'Halls Brewery Company'*		03.12.09E
	(NF 06.07.18)		
G-HARG	Embraer EMB-550 Legacy 500	55000039	23.03.16
	PR-LJD Centreline AV Ltd t/a Centreline Bristol		05.04.18E
G-HARI	Raj Hamsa X'Air V2(2)	455?	11.06.99
	T J Wiltshire tr Xair Group (Holbeach, Spalding)		09.09.18P
	Built by D Mahajan – project BMAA/HB/103;		
	originally notified as Kit 400 (BMAA/HB/099),		
	changed to c/n 455 which conflicts BMAA/HB/112;		
	also quoted as c/n 456 (BMAA/HB/118 G-RAJA)		
	(IE 29.09.18)		
G-HARN	Piper PA-28-181 Archer II	28-8290108	03.02.00
	G-DENK, G-BXRJ, HB-PGO		
	M T Dennis Sherburn-in-Elmet		27.10.18E
G-HARR	Robinson R22 Beta II	3514	14.06.04
	N75301 L G Milne (Stretton under Fosse, Rugby)		13.09.19E
G-HART	Cessna 152 II	15279734	02.02.89
	(G-BPBF), N757GS M Slater tr Taildraggers		
	Flying Group Wellesbourne Mountford		14.11.17E
	Tailwheel conversion		
G-HARY	Alon A-2 Aircoupe	A-188	15.03.93
	G-ATWP M B Willis Bourn		12.05.18E
G-HATB	AutoGyro MTOsport	xxxx	07.10.15
	N J Bent Rochester		24.10.18P
	Assembled Rotorsport UK as c/n RSUK/MTOS/061		
G-HATF	Thorp T-18CW	xxxx	06.12.01
	A T Fraser (Haywards Heath)		05.09.18P
	Built by A T Fraser – project PFA 076-11481 as		
	'Sunderland S-18' re-designed to T-18CW standard		
G-HATH	Techpro Merlin 100UL	HV-19	21.08.18
	N R Hathaway (Bricket Wood, St Albans)		
	(IE 21.08.18)		

G-HATZ	Hatz CB-1	17	11.05.89
	N54623 S P Rollason Stoke Golding		03.08.18P
	Built by R F Dangelo; carries 'N54623'		
	on tail & upper wing		
G-HAUL[M]	Westland WG.30 Series 300	020	03.07.86
	G-17-22 Cancelled 22.04.92 as WFU		27.10.86
	With The Helicopter Museum, Weston-super-Mare		
G-HAUT	Schempp-Hirth Mini Nimbus C	149	08.10.07
	BGA 2597 A D Peacock Rivar Hill *'530'*		13.03.18E
G-HAWK[M]	Hawker Siddeley HS.1182 Hawk 100	41H-4020010	30.06.75
	ZA101 Cancelled 13.05.90 by CAA		
	Displayed at Brooklands Museum, Weybridge		
G-HAYE	Mudry CAP 232	11	11.12.18
	G-SKEW, F-GXRB, F-GKCK, French Army		
	G Haye Glasgow Prestwick		11.01.19E
G-HAYS	Best Off Skyranger Swift 912S(1)	UK/843	19.08.16
	G-CFBS G Hayes Hadfold Farm, Adversane		09.01.19P
	Built by A J Tyler – project BMAA/HB/563		
G-HAYY	Czech Sport Sportcruiser	09SC326	10.05.10
	P H Satchwell tr Sportcrewyy Cotswold		28.09.18W
G-HAZA	Diamond DA.42NG Twin Star	42.N306	18.01.18
	R W F Jackson North Weald		
	(IE 01.02.18)		
G-HAZD	Cameron Z-56	12064	15.06.17
	L S Crossland-Clarke Hull		13.06.18E
G-HBBC	de Havilland DH.104 Dove 8	04211	24.01.96
	G-ALFM, VP961, G-ALFM, VP961 R C Gawn		
	tr Roger Gawn 2007 Family Trust (Melton Constable)		23.03.06
	Originally built as Devon C.2 and modified		
	to C.2/2 status (NF 14.08.15)		
G-HBBH	Comco Ikarus C42 FB100	0608-6835	05.07.06
	G Gates tr Golf Bravo Hotel Group Old Sarum		05.11.18P
	Assembled Aerosport Ltd		
G-HBEE	Lindstrand LTL Series 2-80	047	22.11.16
	R P Waite Newbury, Burton-on-Trent		10.07.18E
G-HBEK	Agusta A109C	7633	31.01.06
	G-DATE, G-RNLD, I-ANAG		
	HPM Investments Ltd (Holton Heath, Poole)		02.09.18E
G-HBJT	Eurocopter EC155 B1	6807	24.06.08
	Starspeed Ltd Fairoaks *'Al Mirqab'*		23.06.18E
G-HBMW	Robinson R22	0170	07.07.94
	G-BOFA, N9068D		
	G Schabana (Ammerbuch-Pfaffingen, Germany)		08.02.16E
	(NF 02.03.16)		
G-HBOS	Scheibe SF25C Rotax-Falke	44574	26.07.01
	D-KTIN Coventry Gliding Club Ltd		
	Husbands Bosworth		18.01.19E
G-HBRB	Comco Ikarus C42 FB100 Bravo	1811-7550	21.12.18
	H K & R M Bilbe (Sloley, Norwich)		
	Assembled The Light Aircraft Company Ltd (IE 21.12.18)		
G-HCAC	Schleicher Ka 6E	4054	01.02.08
	BGA 1380/CAC		
	J P Willsher tr Ka6e 994 Group Crowland *'994'*		08.05.18E
G-HCAT	Sindlinger Hawker Hurricane replica	1058	25.02.13
	N40738 G S Jones Butlers Ghyll Farm, Southwater		
	Built by R I Sturgill (NF 18.07.18)		
G-HCBW	Sequoia F.8L Falco	1254	22.06.15
	R A F Buchanan Lydd		
	Built by R A F Buchannan – project PFA 100-12788;		
	first flight 16.11.18		
G-HCCF	Van's RV-8A	xxxx	06.12.13
	M R Overall Whitehall Farm, Wethersfield		02.07.18P
	Built by S M E Solomon – project PFA 303-13790		
G-HCEN	Guimbal Cabri G2	1079	14.10.14
	Helicentre Aviation Ltd Leicester		08.10.18E
G-HCPD	Cameron C-80	11644	02.04.12
	H Crawley & P Dopson Birmingham B12		29.03.18E
G-HCSA	Cessna 525A CitationJet CJ2	525A0334	20.12.06
	N52699 Bookajet Aircraft Management Ltd		
	Farnborough		02.01.19E
G-HDAE	de Havilland DHC-1 Chipmunk 22	C1/0280	04.06.03
	CS-DAE, Portuguese AF 1304		
	Airborne Classics Ltd Melhuish Farm, North Moreton		17.05.19E
	As 'WP964' in AAC camouflage c/s		

G-HDBV	McDonnell Douglas MD Explorer	900-00080	08.12.17
	G-SASH, PH-SHF, N7008Q		
	Heli Delta BV (Sint Agatha, Netherlands)		20.06.18E
G-HDEW	Piper PA-32R-301 Saratoga SP	3213026	04.12.89
	G-BRGZ, N91787 D P Wood Gloucestershire		13.03.18E
G-HDMD	McDonnell Douglas MD Explorer	900-00089	08.12.17
	G-CEMS, PK-OCR, N70089		
	Heli Delta BV (Sint Agatha, Netherlands)		12.07.18E
G-HDTV	Agusta A109A II	7266	16.09.04
	G-BXWD, N565RJ, I-URIA, D-HEMZ, N109BD		
	Castle Air Ltd Trebrown, Liskeard		25.07.14E
	(IE 15.12.17)		
G-HDUO	Ultramagic M-56	56/46	23.08.18
	F-HDUO S J Colin Hawkhurst, Cranbrook		
G-HEAD	Colt Flying Head	304	18.08.81
	Ikeair Fredericksoord, Netherlands		30.08.16E
G-HEAL	Lindstrand LTL Series 1-31	073	10.04.18
	A M Holly Breadstone, Berkeley		17.05.19E
	(IE 10.04.18)		
G-HEAN	Eurocopter AS.355NP Ecureuil 2	5747	29.08.07
	SE-JJR, (SE-HJR), F-WWPD		
	Brookview Developments Ltd (Dublin 2, RoI)		30.08.08E
G-HEBB	Schleicher ASW 27-18E *(ASG 29E)*	29550	25.06.08
	BGA 5317 A K Stefanczyk tr G-HEBB Group		
	(Kielce, Poland) *'HE'*		25.01.18E
G-HEBO	Pilatus B-N BN-2B-26 Islander	2268	03.10.12
	G-BUBK, JA5319, G-BUBK		
	Islander Aircraft Ltd Cumbernauld		23.02.19E
G-HEBS	Pilatus B-N BN-2B-26 Islander	2267	07.12.07
	G-BUBJ, N450PM, OY-PHV, JA5318, G-BUBJ		
	Hebridean Air Services Ltd Inverness		14.04.19E
G-HEBZ[M]	Fairey B-N BN-2A-26 Islander	823	21.03.07
	G-BELF, D-IBRA, G-BELF		
	Cancelled 08.11.18 as WFU *As 'G-BELF'*		
G-HECB	Fuji FA.200-160 Aero Subaru	FA200-238	16.05.05
	G-BBZO H E W E Bailey (Fontainebleau, France)		01.08.19E
G-HECK	Robinson R44 Raven II	11416	18.06.13
	G-ILLG Helivation Aviation Ltd		
	Bridge Cottage, Great Heck		17.05.18E
G-HECT	Flight Design CTLS	F-09-04-06	29.03.18
	F-HECT R C Kelly Fowlmere		04.07.19W
G-HEDL	Extra EA.300/LC	LC064	25.04.17
	H J R Aylott Full Sutton		16.06.18E
G-HEHE	Eurocopter EC120B Colibri	1480	20.06.07
	EC-KCR He Group Ltd Rochester		05.08.19E
G-HEKL	Percival Mew Gull replica	xxxx	29.04.08
	D Beale Fenland		05.05.18P
	Built by D Beale – project PFA 013-14759		
G-HEKY[M]	McCulloch J.2	039	14.09.07
	G-ORVB, (G-BLGI), (G-BKKL),		
	Bahrain Public Security BPS-3, N4329G		
	Cancelled 30.01.09 as WFU *As 'G-ORVB'*		
	With The Helicopter Museum, Weston-super-Mare		
G-HELA	SOCATA TB-10 Tobago	135	31.12.03
	F-GCOF M A Soakell tr Future Flight Breighton		03.05.18E
	Damaged Bentley Farm, Coal Aston 25.09.16;		
	rebuilt 2017 using wings ex G-MRTN		
G-HELE	Bell 206B-3 JetRanger III	3789	21.02.91
	G-OJFR, N18095		
	B E E Smith Shottesbrooke Park, Shottesbrooke		09.04.18E
G-HELI[M]	Saro Skeeter AOP.12	S2/5110?	15.06.78
	XM556? Cancelled 22.03.95 - to Germany *As 'XM556'*		
	Composite of cabin 7870M ex XM556 & & boom		
	7979M ex XM529 (S2/5105)		
	With Luftwaffen Museum, Gatow, Germany		
G-HELL	Sonex Sonex	1600	18.03.15
	T J Shaw North Coates *'Hellrazer'*		02.11.18P
	Built by T J Shaw & L Wilkinson		
	– project LAA 337-15182		

G-HELN	Piper PA-18 Super Cub 95	18-3365	10.01.86
	G-BKDG, I-EIWB:EI-69 & EI-141, Italian Army MM53-7765,		
	53-7765 J D Morton tr Helen Group White Waltham		06.09.18P
	Originally built as L-21; rebuilt as L-18C		
	(in fuselage swap); Frame No.18-3400		
	As 'MM52-2392:EI-69' in Italian Army c/s		
G-HEMC	Airbus MBB BK117 D-2 (*Eurocopter EC145 T2*)	20012	13.11.14
	Babcock Mission Critical Services Onshore Ltd		
	Cambridge		13.11.18E
	Operated by East Anglian Air Ambulance as callsign		
	'Helimed 88'		
G-HEMN	Eurocopter EC135 T2+	1070	02.08.12
	Babcock Mission Critical Services Onshore Ltd		
	Dafen, Llanelli		06.08.18E
	Operated by Wales Air Ambulance as callsign		
	'Helimed 57'		
G-HEMZ	Agusta A109S Grand	22156	28.01.10
	Sloane Helicopters Ltd Coventry		27.01.19E
	Operated by Children's Air Ambulance as callsign		
	'Helimed 77'		
G-HENT	SOCATA Rallye 110ST Galopin	3210	28.11.01
	OO-MBV G Dolan (Lifford, Co Donegal, RoI)		11.05.18E
G-HENY	Cameron V-77	2486	09.01.91
	Zebedee Balloon Service Ltd Hungerford		23.11.18E
G-HENZ	AutoGyro Cavalon	xxxx	16.08.18
	A Henson Sandtoft		
	Assembled Rotorsport UK Ltd as		
	c/n RSUK/CVLN/028 (IE 16.08.18)		
G-HEOI	Eurocopter EC135 P2+	0825	21.07.09
	Police & Crime Commissioner for West Yorkshire		
	Almondsbury		07.12.19E
	Operated by South West Air Operations Unit		
	as callsign 'Police 09'		
G-HERC	Cessna 172S Skyhawk SP	172S8985	10.12.01
	N5113P The Cambridge Aero Club Ltd Cambridge		03.04.18E
G-HERD	Lindstrand LBL 77B	707	31.07.00
	S W Herd Pantymwyn, Mold		30.03.18E
G-HEVR	Comco Ikarus C42 FB80	1510-7422	04.01.16
	Deanland Flight Training Ltd Deanland		11.10.19P
	Assembled Red Aviation		
G-HEWI	Piper J-3C-65 Cub (*L-4J-PI*)	12566	20.07.84
	G-BLEN, D-EBEN, HB-OFZ, 44-80270		
	R Preston tr Denham Grasshopper Flying Group Denham		
	Fuselage No.12396; active 07.18 (IE 03.01.18)		
G-HEWZ	Hughes 369HS (*500*)	940649S	25.05.16
	G-LEEJ, N9216F A S Mackenzie Denham		03.12.18E
G-HEXE	Colt 17A Cloudhopper	2221	24.02.04
	A Dunnington Clifton, Bristol BS8		19.07.18E
	Built by Thunder & Colt Ltd		
G-HEYY	Cameron Bear-72	1244	21.01.86
	Magical Adventures Ltd		
	West Bloomfield, MI, USA *'George'*		30.11.98A
	(NF 03.06.15)		
G-HFBM	Curtiss Robertson C-2 Robin	352	24.04.90
	LV-FBM, NC9279 D M Forshaw High Cross, Ware		15.01.13P
	(IE 09.03.16)		
G-HFCB	Reims/Cessna F150L	F15000798	10.02.87
	G-AZVR J H Francis Hardwick		07.12.18E
G-HFCL	Reims/Cessna F152 II	F15201663	11.10.88
	G-BGLR Devon & Somerset Flight Training Ltd		
	Dunkeswell		18.04.18E
G-HFCT	Reims/Cessna F152 II	F15201861	27.01.81
	Stapleford Flying Club Ltd Stapleford		11.06.18E
G-HFLA	Schweizer 269C	S.1428	08.12.89
	Cancelled 01.09.05 as destroyed		12.03.05
	Dunkeswell *Stored 02.16*		
G-HFLY	Robinson R44 Raven I	11876	19.10.07
	Helifly (UK) Ltd Brighton City		13.10.18E
G-HFRH	de Havilland DHC-1 Chipmunk 22	C1/0650	13.10.10
	N546PU, WK635 P M Jacobs Hawarden		01.03.18E
	As 'WK635' in Royal Navy c/s		
G-HGPI	SOCATA TB-20 Trinidad	851	04.08.88
	M J Jackson Bournemouth		20.03.18E
G-HGRB	Robinson R44 Raven	0776	21.04.06
	G-BZIN Nick Cook Plant Hire Ltd		
	Cardiff City Heliport		15.03.18E
G-HHAA	Hawker Siddeley Buccaneer S.2B	B3-01-73	06.12.02
	9225M, XX885 Hawker Hunter Aviation Ltd		
	RAF Scampton		
	C/n officially quoted as B3-R-50-67;		
	as 'XX885' in RAF c/s (NF 14.03.18)		
G-HHAC	Hawker Hunter F.58	41H-691770	10.12.02
	G-BWIU, Swiss AF J-4021		
	Hawker Hunter Aviation Ltd RAF Scampton		12.07.09P
	As 'ZZ194' in RAF c/s; noted 10.16 (NF 08.04.16)		
G-HHDR	Cessna 182T Skylane	18282071	23.09.08
	N6332X I D Brierley North Weald		10.10.19E
G-HHEM	Leonardo AW169	69049	18.04.17
	I-RAIM Essex & Herts Air Ambulance Trust		
	North Weald		19.04.19E
	Operated by Essex & Herts Air ambulance		
G-HHII	Hawker Hurricane IIB	CCF/R20023	05.04.07
	G-HRLO, RCAF 5403 Hawker Restorations Ltd		
	Elmsett *'Pegs' (port) & 'Mauritius' (starboard)*		23.07.18P
	Built by Canadian Car & Foundry Co; c/n relates to		
	RCAF 1374 ex AG287 (centre-section used in UK		
	rebuild); as 'BE505:XP-L' in RAF 174 Sqdn c/s		
G-HHPM	Cameron Z-105	11534	02.11.11
	J Armstrong Newquay TR7		
	'Headland Hotel Newquay'		02.03.18E
G-HIAL	Viking Air DHC-6-400 Twin Otter	917	15.05.15
	C-GLVA Loganair Ltd Glasgow		26.05.19E
G-HIBM	Cameron N-145	3197	08.02.94
	Alba Ballooning Ltd Newtown, Hungerford *'Alba'*		14.12.08E
	(NF 25.01.16)		
G-HICU	Schleicher ASW 27-18E (*ASG 29E*)	29629	16.05.11
	(BGA 5679) N Hoare Lasham *'41'*		14.11.18E
G-HIDE	Airbus AS.350B3 Ecureuil	8624	20.12.18
	G-CLBE Loxwood Holdings Ltd Oxford		21.11.19E
G-HIEL	Robinson R22 Beta	1120	28.09.89
	Helimech Ltd Brook Farm, Hulcote		17.12.17E
	(NF 15.01.18)		
G-HIGA	Cessna 172P Skyhawk II	17275004	26.04.18
	G-BRZS, N54585		
	High Alpha Ltd t/a High-G Flight Training Blackpool		11.04.19E
G-HIJK	Cessna 421C Golden Eagle	421C0218	25.02.00
	G-OSAL, G-HIJK, G-OSAL, OY-BEC, SE-GZI, N5471G		
	Acrabot Ltd Bournemouth *'Met Office'*		02.12.18E
	Operated by Met Office as 'Metman 4'		
G-HIJN	Comco Ikarus C42 FB80 Bravo	0403-6597	19.05.04
	G P Burns Middle Stoke, Isle of Grain		10.04.18P
	Assembled Fly Buy Ultralights Ltd		
G-HILI	Van's RV-3B	11445	08.09.09
	A G & E A Hill Notley Green, Sandon		26.08.16P
	Built by A G & E A Hill – project LAA 099-14905		
G-HILO	Rockwell Commander 114	14224	06.02.98
	N4894W M Mills & J Roberts		
	tr Alpha-Golf Flying Group Stapleford		13.07.18E
G-HILS	Cessna F172H	F172-0522	20.12.88
	G-AWCH Blue Thunder Ltd Sandtoft		31.07.19E
	Built by Reims Aviation SA		
G-HILT	SOCATA TB-10 Tobago	298	13.05.82
	(G-BMYB), EI-BOF, G-HILT L Windle Brighton City		30.06.18E
G-HILY	Zenair CH.600 Zodiac	xxxx	01.09.10
	G-BRII K V Hill Bruntingthorpe		13.08.18P
	Built by A C Bowdrey & K V Hill – project		
	PFA 162-11392; badged 'Zodiac 601'		
G-HILZ	Van's RV-8	82453	14.06.06
	A G & E A Hill Notley Green, Sandon		02.05.16P
	Built by A G & E A Hill – project PFA 303-14471		
G-HIMJ	Agusta A109E Power	11163	18.03.03
	Cancelled 14.07.04 as PWFU		15.04.06
	Rugby *Conv into towing caravan c2014*		
G-HIMM	Cameron Z-105	11370	09.03.10
	C M D Haynes Norton St Philip, Bath		
	'Haynes International Motor Museum'		07.03.17E

G-HIND	Maule MT-7-235 Super Rocket	18037C	26.03.98
	M A Ashmole Perth		26.06.18E
	Stored pending repair 12.18 following over-run		
	accident in a loch in early 2018		

G-HINZ	Avtech Jabiru SK	0248	01.02.00
	P J Jackson Manchester Barton		15.06.18P
	Built by B Faupel – project PFA 274-13441		

G-HIOW	Airbus EC135 T3	1190	27.08.15
	Babcock Mission Critical Services Onshore Ltd		
	Thruxton		01.09.18E
	Operated by Hampshire & IOW Air Ambulance		
	as callsign 'Helimed 56'		

G-HIPE	Sorrell SNS-7 Hyperbipe	209	06.04.93
	G-ISMS, G-HIPE, N18RS		
	Aerosprite Informatics Ltd (Hambrook, Bristol)		24.11.16P
	Built by R Stephen (IE 16.03.18)		

G-HIRE	Gulfstream American GA-7 Cougar	GA7-0091	10.12.81
	G-BGSZ, N704G D J Hockings Deanland		06.09.19E

G-HISP	Hispano HA.1112-M1L Buchón	184	12.09.18
	Spanish AF C4K-111 Air Leasing Ltd Sywell		
	Built by Hispano Aviación (NF 12.09.18)		

G-HITI	Airbus AS.350B3 Ecureuil	8239	07.12.16
	I-MGIO, F-WTAG Elstree Ink Ltd Elstree		12.06.19E

G-HITL	Airbus AS.350B3 Ecureuil	8439	24.11.17
	G-CKPH Elstree Ink Ltd Elstree		07.11.19E

G-HITM	Raj Hamsa X'Air Falcon Jabiru(1)	455?	23.02.00
	J Hennegan & I Johnson (Stockport & Middlewich)		19.12.18P
	Built by D J Hickey – project BMAA/HB/112;		
	kit s/n 455 conflicts with BMAA/HB/128 (G-BZGN)		

G-HITT	Hawker Hurricane I	xxxx	19.12.08
	Soviet AF, DR348, P3717 H Taylor Old Warden		11.05.19P
	As 'P3717:SW-P' in 253 Sqdn RAF c/s		

G-HIVE	Reims/Cessna F150M	F15001186	19.04.85
	G-BCXT Peterborough Flying School Ltd Sibson		05.01.19E

G-HIYA	Best Off Skyranger 912(2)	SKR0510648	30.10.06
	C M & R D Parkinson Little Gransden		23.09.18P
	Built by R D Parkinson – project BMAA/HB/493		

G-HIZZ	Robinson R22 Beta II	2677	02.08.04
	G-CNDY, G-BXEW		
	S F Gallimore & T Hehir t/a Flyfare Shobdon		21.12.17E

G-HJSM	Schempp-Hirth Nimbus-4DM	22/32	19.02.01
	G-ROAM G Paul Shenington '60'		08.05.18E

G-HJSS	SNCAN Stampe SV.4C	1101	07.09.92
	G-AZNF, F-BGJM, French Navy 1101, French AF		
	H J Smith Brighton City		14.09.18P
	Built by Atelier industriel de l'Aéronautique		

G-HKAA	Schempp-Hirth Duo Discus T	69/364	20.09.07
	BGA 5033 J Randall Husbands Bosworth '570'		30.11.18E

G-HKCC	Robinson R66 Turbine	0516	17.09.14
	N664VA HQ Aviation Ltd Denham		18.12.18E

G-HKCF	Enstrom 280C-UK Shark	1149	27.11.08
	G-MHCF, G-GSML, G-BNNV, SE-HIY		
	D & H K Collier t/a HKC Helicopter Services		
	(Glazebrook, Warrington)		20.09.11E
	(IE 06.07.17)		

G-HKHK	Robinson R66 Turbine	0888	28.08.18
	HQ Aviation Ltd Denham		

G-HKHM	Hughes 369D (500)	711019D	08.04.99
	B-HHM, VR-HHM, N50605 HQ Aviation Ltd Denham		20.02.19E

G-HKPC	Robinson R66 Turbine	0872	07.09.18
	HQ Aviation Ltd Denham		
	(NF 07.09.18)		

G-HLAM	Kubicek BB-S/Phare	887	18.02.19
	F-HLAM Lighter Than Air Ltd Chew Stoke, Bristol		
	(NF 16.02.19)		

G-HLCF	CFM Starstreak Shadow SA-II	K 256-CD	10.05.96
	F E Tofield (Billinghay, Lincoln)		22.06.07P
	Built by S M E Solomon – project PFA 206-12796		
	(NF 18.01.19)		

G-HLCM	Leonardo AW109SP Grand New	22369	27.02.17
	AWJFP & A W Jenkinson t/a Helicom		
	Carlisle Lake District		28.02.18E

G-HLEE	Best Off Skyranger J2.2(1)	SKR0511655	06.03.07
	P G Hill Palace Land Farm, Shipley		10.04.18P
	Built by L Harland – project BMAA/HB/502		

G-HLIX[M]	Cameron Helix Oilcan 61SS HAB	1192	20.09.85
	Cancelled 29.04.97 as WFU		
	With History of Ballooning, Sint-Niklaas, Belgium		

G-HLMB	Schempp-Hirth Ventus-2b	119	29.04.09
	D-9911, G-HLMB, D-9911		
	U Hoefinghoff Stadtlohn-Vreden, Germany 'B'		16.04.17E
	(IE 22.05.17)		

G-HLOB	Cessna 172S Skyhawk SP	172S10949	25.06.09
	N5152Y Goodwood Road Racing Company Ltd		
	Goodwood		28.07.18E

G-HMCA	Evektor EV-97 teamEurostar UK	2009-3321	09.04.09
	M E Howard tr RAF Microlight Flying Association		
	RAF Halton		16.05.18P
	Assembled Cosmik Aviation Ltd		

G-HMCB	Best Off Skyranger Swift 912S(1)	UK/919	02.01.09
	R W Goddin Whitehall Farm, Benington 'Harry's Bird'		12.02.19P
	Built by R W Goddin – project BMAA/HB/586		

G-HMCD	Comco Ikarus C42 FB80 Bravo	1103-7142	28.06.11
	B Murkin (Chatteris)		27.02.18P
	Assembled Performance Aviation Ltd		

G-HMCE	Comco Ikarus C42 FB80 Bravo	1103-7143	01.09.11
	M E Howard tr RAF Microlight Flying Association		
	RAF Halton		08.09.18P
	Assembled Performance Aviation Ltd		

G-HMCF	Evektor EV-97 Eurostar SL	2014-4204	27.08.14
	M E Howard tr RAF Microlight Flying Association		
	RAF Halton		29.08.18P
	Assembled Light Sport Aviation Ltd		

G-HMCH	Evektor EV-97 Eurostar SL	2016-4239	04.04.17
	M E Howard tr RAF Microlight Flying Association		
	RAF Halton		27.03.18P
	Assembled Light Sport Aviation Ltd		

G-HMDX	McDonnell Douglas MD Explorer	900-00121	20.12.12
	N902RN, N91160		
	Specialist Aviation Services Ltd RAF Wyton		05.08.18E
	Operated by Magpas Helimedix Air Ambulance as		
	callsign 'Helimed 66'		

G-HMEC	Robinson R22 Beta	1767	04.09.17
	G-BWTH, HB-XYD, N4052R		
	Helimech Ltd Nottingham Heliport, Widmerpool		16.06.18E

G-HMED	Piper PA-28-161 Warrior III	2842020	21.07.97
	LX-III Eglinton Flying Club Ltd Enniskillen		20.07.18E

G-HMES	Piper PA-28-161 Warrior II	28-8216070	21.04.89
	OY-CSN, N8471N Cancelled 05.05.04 as TWFU		
	Bagby Open store 05.16		

G-HMHM	AutoGyro MTOsport	xxxx	07.04.09
	R M Kimbell Rothwell Lodge Farm, Kettering		14.04.18P
	Assembled Rotorsport UK as c/n RSUK/MTOS/004		

G-HMJB	Piper PA-34-220T Seneca III	34-8133040	12.07.89
	N8356R W B Bateson Blackpool		10.10.04
	(NF 17.12.14)		

G-HMPS	CZAW Sportcruiser	700876	14.10.09
	A Nicholson (Greenock)		16.07.19P
	Built by P Shedden – project LAA 338-14873		

G-HMPT	Agusta-Bell 206B-2 JetRanger II	8168	07.11.91
	D-HARO M D Thorpe t/a Yorkshire Helicopters		
	Leeds Heliport		16.10.09E
	Stored 09.17 (NF 11.06.15)		

G-HMSJ	Robin DR.400-140B Major 80	2694	31.05.16
	C S & J A Bailey t/a SJ Aircraft Elstree		31.07.19E

G-HNGE	Comco Ikarus C42 FB80	0607-6838	21.08.06
	Compton Abbas Airfield Ltd Compton Abbas		17.08.19P
	Assembled Aerosport Ltd		

G-HNPN	Embraer EMB-505 Phenom 300	50500276	23.09.16
	M-HPIN, PR-PEZ Flairjet Ltd t/a Sirio UK Birmingham		22.09.19E

G-HNTR[M]	Hawker Hunter T.7	HABL-003311	07.08.89
	8834M, XL572 Cancelled 11.10.91 as WFU		
	As 'XL571:V' in 'Blue Diamonds' c/s		
	With Yorkshire Air Museum, Elvington		

G-HOBO	Denney Kitfox Model 4	xxxx	10.09.92	
	M H Wylde (Lewes) *'Navy Baby'*		21.02.18P	
	Built by W M Hodgkins – project PFA 172A-12140			
	(NF 15.06.18)			
G-HOCA	Robinson R44 Raven II	12388	17.07.08	
	JRS Aviation Ltd Wycombe Air Park		18.04.18E	
G-HOCK	Piper PA-28-180 Cherokee D	28-4395	15.05.86	
	G-AVSH, N11C Cancelled 08.09.17 as destroyed		28.10.17	
	Caversham *Dumped at scrapyard 11.17*			
G-HODN	Kavanagh E-120	E120-390	07.07.15	
	VH-AJI A C C Hodgson Stansbatch, Leominster			
	(NF 07.07.15)			
G-HODR	Best Off Skyranger Swift 912S(1)	xxxx	18.07.17	
	A W Hodder (Nottingham NG11)			
	Built by A W Hodder – project BMAA/HB/701			
	(NF 18.07.17)			
G-HOFF	P&M Quik GT450	8383	19.05.08	
	L Mazurek Chatteris		30.05.13P	
	Noted 03.18 (NF 04.08.15)			
G-HOFM	Cameron N-56	1245	21.01.86	
	Magical Adventures Ltd West Bloomfield, MI, USA			
	'Follow the Bear'		29.09.09E	
	(NF 03.06.15)			
G-HOGB	Airbus EC130 T2	7921	15.11.18	
	SP-HIT, F-WTBE, F-WWXA Hogs Head			
	Transportation Ltd (Waterville, Co Kerry, RoI)		30.11.18E	
G-HOGS	Cameron Pig-90	4121	07.04.97	
	Magical Adventures Ltd West Bloomfield, MI, USA		27.09.09E	
	(NF 03.06.15)			
G-HOJO	Schempp-Hirth Discus-2a	2	12.11.07	
	BGA 4533/JHT S G Jones Lasham '6'		12.04.18E	
G-HOLA	Piper PA-28-201T Turbo Dakota	28-7921040	23.06.10	
	G-BNYB, N2856A, N9533N D Ash Denham			
	(IE 15.05.15)			
G-HOLD	Robinson R44 Raven II	10773	04.01.12	
	I-LEAP Mignini & Petrini SpA			
	(Petrignano di Assisi, Italy)		17.01.18E	
G-HOLE	P&M Quik GT450	8193	25.08.10	
	G-CEBD B Birtle St Michaels		11.03.18P	
G-HOLI	Ultramagic M-77	77/294	23.02.07	
	G Everett Sandway, Maidstone *'Holiday Inn'*		26.09.10E	
	(NF 06.03.18)			
G-HOLM	Eurocopter EC135 T2+	0574	20.08.07	
	Capital Air Services Ltd not in its individual			
	capacity but as owner trustee Oxford		31.01.18E	
G-HOME[M]	Colt 77A HAB	032	26.02.79	
	Cancelled 15.01.10 as PWFU		27.05.86	
	With British Balloon Museum & Library, Newbury			
G-HONG	Slingsby T67M-200 Firefly	2060	24.03.94	
	VR-HZR, HKG-12, G-7-128			
	Jewel Aviation & Technology Ltd Fairoaks		14.07.18E	
G-HONI	Robinson R22 Beta	0871	27.01.00	
	G-SEGO, N9081N Paul D White Ltd			
	t/a Elstree Helicopters Elstree		21.05.17E	
G-HONK	Cameron O-105	1813	30.09.88	
	M A Green Rednal, Birmingham *'Dixon'*		26.04.18E	
G-HONO	Just SuperSTOL	JA 448-03-15	17.03.17	
	C A Ho (Napley Heath, Market Drayton)		22.05.19P	
	Built by D Ho – project LAA 397-15378			
G-HONY	Lilliput Type 1 Series A	L-01	31.07.98	
	A E & D E Thomas Weston, Honiton			
G-HOON	Pitts S-1S	001	16.01.15	
	F-AZMV, F-BVKB, F-WVKB			
	R J Allan, N Jones & A J Maxwell Manchester Barton		22.05.19P	
	Built by M Brandt			
G-HOPA	Lindstrand LBL 35A Cloudhopper	972	16.01.04	
	S F Burden Munich, Germany		16.04.18E	
G-HOPE	Beech F33A Bonanza	CE-805	27.02.79	
	N2024Z Hope Aviation Ltd Bournemouth		30.05.18E	
G-HOPR	Lindstrand LBL 25A Cloudhopper	999	21.06.04	
	K C Tanner Thame		21.11.18E	

G-HOPY	Van's RV-6A	xxxx	04.12.95	
	R C Hopkinson tr G-HOPY Group RAF Benson		08.08.19P	
	Built by R C Hopkinson – project PFA 181-12742			
G-HORK	Alpi Pioneer 300 Hawk	227	08.12.07	
	R Y Kendal Ewesley Farm, Ewesley		12.06.18P	
	Built by R Y Kendal – project PFA 330A-14741			
G-HOSS	Beech F33A Bonanza	CE-1151	03.01.06	
	OY-BVT T D Broadhurst tr Beech Baron Aviation			
	Sleap		28.10.18E	
G-HOTA	Evektor EV-97 teamEurostar UK	2008-3318	06.01.09	
	W Chang Plaistows Farm, St Albans		19.08.18P	
	Assembled Cosmik Aviation Ltd			
G-HOTB	Eurocopter EC155 B1	6789	22.04.08	
	G-CEXZ, F-WQDF Multiflight Ltd Leeds Bradford		14.04.19E	
G-HOTC	AutoGyro MTOsport	xxxx	17.09.15	
	G-CINW, D-MMND G Hotchen Shobdon		03.09.18P	
	Assembled Rotorsport UK as c/n RSUK/MTOS/058			
G-HOTM	Cameron C-80	11172	11.06.08	
	M G Howard Hewish, Weston-super-Mare		22.03.18E	
G-HOTR	P&M Quik GTR	8617	03.05.12	
	M E Fowler Bernwood Farm, Botolph Claydon		29.04.18P	
	New Explorer wing fitted to trike ex QuikR G-CFTE			
G-HOTY	Bombardier CL-600-2B16 Challenger 604	5443	04.03.15	
	M-CRCR, JY-IMK, JY-TWO, N605JA, C-GLWT			
	Jet Exchange Ltd (Cambridge)		04.03.18E	
G-HOTZ	Colt 77B	2218	16.06.92	
	C J & S M Davies Castleton, Hope Valley		26.05.18E	
G-HOUR	Max Holste MH.1521C1 Broussard	149	10.05.16	
	F-BXCP, French Army			
	Bremont Watch Company Ltd White Waltham		21.06.18E	
G-HOUS[M]	Colt 31A Air Chair HAB	099	07.10.80	
	Cancelled 14.04.09 as WFU *'Barratts'*		03.05.90	
	With British Balloon Museum & Library, Newbury			
G-HOWD	Magni M24C Orion	24-16-9704	10.06.16	
	J P & M G Howard Exeter Int'l		19.06.18P	
G-HOWI	Reims/Cessna F182Q Skylane II	F18200049	28.04.09	
	N382AS, D-EAAF H Poulson Sherburn-in-Elmet		16.05.18E	
G-HOWL	Rotary Air Force RAF 2000 GTX-SE	H2-95-6-164	02.07.01	
	N4994U C J Watkinson Bridge Cottage, Great Heck		05.10.07P	
	Built by M Urbanczyk (NF 13.07.18)			
G-HOXN	Van's RV-9	xxxx	26.09.06	
	F A L Castleden tr Xray November Flying Club			
	Priory Farm, Tibenham		30.07.18P	
	Built by F A L Castleden – project PFA 320-14229			
G-HPCB	Ultramagic S-90	90/132	21.05.14	
	D R Rawlings Haverhill			
	'hpcb.co.uk – IT Support & Supplies'		16.06.18E	
G-HPDM	Agusta A109E Power	11216	19.05.17	
	G-DPPF Adonby International Ltd Varna, Bulgaria		14.03.16E	
	(IE 07.12.17)			
G-HPIN	Bell 429	57187	30.11.15	
	M-HRPN, C-GZEO Harpin Ltd Bagby		02.12.18E	
	Operated by VLL Ltd t/a GB Helicopters			
G-HPJT	HpH Glasflügel 304 S Shark	014-S	24.04.12	
	(BGA 5779) P D Harvey Lasham *'JT'*			
	(IE 28.11.17)			
G-HPSF	Commander Aircraft Commander 114B	14590	16.11.04	
	N6003F R W Scandrett Guernsey		03.02.18E	
G-HPSL	Commander Aircraft Commander 114B	14682	26.08.04	
	N115KL M B Endean Cotswold		29.06.18E	
G-HPUX	Hawker Hunter T.7	41H-693455	12.03.99	
	8807M, XL587			
	Hawker Hunter Aviation Ltd RAF Scampton			
	Stored 10.16 (NF 14.03.18)			
G-HPWA	Van's RV-8	80836	06.09.10	
	PH-PWA M B Z de Ferranti			
	Ham Hill, Sydmonton, Ecchinswell		26.01.18P	
	Built by A de Brie			
G-HRAF	Schleicher ASK 13	13635AB	12.01.12	
	G-DETS, BGA 2944/ETS			
	Upward Bound Trust (Haddenham) *'AF'*		04.08.18E	
	Built by Jubi GmbH Sportflugzeugbau			

G-HRDB	Agusta A109S Grand	22031	10.02.15
	VH-CTC Freshair UK Ltd Field Farm, Launton		17.03.18E
G-HRDY	Cameron Z-105	11849	30.07.14
	D J Groombridge & I J Martin t/a Flying Enterprises		
	Congresbury & Wotton-under-Edge *'Hardys'*		08.08.19E
G-HRIO	Robin HR.100/210 Safari	149	22.01.87
	F-BTZR Eule Industrial Robotics GmbH & Co KG		
	(Viersen, Germany)		29.09.17E
G-HRLE	Tecnam P2008-JC	1052	27.09.16
	G-OTUK Cancelled 27.07.18 by CAA		06.10.17
	St Athan *Fuselage stored 12.18*		
G-HRLI	Hawker Hurricane I	41H-136172	25.04.02
	V7497 Hawker Restorations Ltd Duxford		09.09.19P
	As 'V7497:SD-X' in RAF c/s		
G-HRND	Cessna 182T Skylane	18281936	31.05.07
	N2252X R H Wicks Denham		06.07.19E
G-HROI	Rockwell Commander 112A	326	19.06.89
	N1326J Intereuropean Aviation Ltd Jersey		14.02.18E
G-HRON	de Havilland DH.114 Heron 2B	14102	04.04.91
	XR442, G-AORH Cancelled 10.04.02 by CAA		
	Albany, Oregon, USA *Stored in RN c/s as 'XR442' 06.18*		
G-HRVD	CCF T-6 Harvard Mk.4	CCF4-548	08.12.92
	G-BSBC Mozambique PLAF 1741, Portuguese AF		
	1741, West German AF BF+055, AA+055, 53-4629		
	P Earthey Bruntingthorpe		
	Built by Canadian Car & Foundry Co; composite		
	– probably from Moz PLAF 1780, Portuguese		
	AF 1780, West German AF AA+614 & 53-4622		
	(NF 11.01.17)		
G-HRVS	Van's RV-8	81842	16.01.09
	D J Harvey (Lytham St Annes)		
	Built by D J Harvey – project PFA 303-14444		
	(NF 18.11.15)		
G-HRYZ	Piper PA-28-180 Cherokee Archer	28-7505090	06.02.06
	G-WACR, G-BCZF, N9517N		
	Gama Engineering Ltd Wellesbourne Mountford		15.06.18E
G-HSDL	Westland SA.341B Gazelle AH.1	1227	10.02.16
	XW909 Howard Stott Demolition Ltd		
	Castle Clough Farm, Hapton		30.10.18P
G-HSEB	Cyclone Pegasus Quantum 15-912	7556	14.07.11
	G-BYNO D Gwyther Clench Common		07.10.18P
G-HSKE	Aviat A-1B Husky	2437	11.06.08
	N65HY R B Armitage & S L Davis		
	Maypole Farm, Chislet		26.09.18E
G-HSKI	Aviat A-1B Husky	2312	20.01.06
	C J R Flint Sleap		27.04.18E
G-HSOO	Hughes 369HE (*500*)	1090208E	03.11.93
	G-BFYJ, F-BRSY		
	Century Aviation Ltd Retford Gamston		26.03.18E
G-HSTH	Lindstrand LBL HS-110 HA Airship	546	20.08.98
	C J Sanger-Davies Hawarden CH5		26.05.06E
	(NF 28.09.15)		
G-HSVI	Reims FR172J Rocket	FR17200487	10.10.16
	HA-SVI, D-EECB S J Sylvester		
	Wolverhampton Halfpenny Green		13.07.18E
G-HSXP	Raytheon Hawker 850XP	258827	26.03.07
	N7077S Paralel Routs Ltd (Tortola, BVI, Russia)		07.04.19E
G-HTEK	Ultramagic M-77	77/375	19.05.14
	Airborne Adventures Ltd Rylstone, Skipton *'Hope'*		30.07.19E
G-HTFU	Gippsaero GA8-TC320 Airvan	GA8-TC 320-11-163	21.06.11
	Skydive London Ltd Redlands		23.02.18E
G-HTML	P&M QuikR	8446	27.03.09
	Skywards Aviation Consultants Ltd Beccles		17.07.18P
G-HTRL	Piper PA-34-220T Seneca III	34-8333061	08.02.00
	G-BXXY, PH-TLN, N4295X Techtest Ltd Shobdon		13.07.18E
G-HTWE	Rans S-6-116 Coyote II	0407.1804	08.01.08
	G R Hill (Bath)		
	Built by H C C Coleridge – project PFA 204-14698		
	(NF 14.07.15)		
G-HUBB	Partenavia P68B	194	27.05.83
	OY-BJH, SE-GXL		
	Ravenair Aircraft Ltd Liverpool John Lennon		10.01.18E
G-HUCH	Cameron Carrots-80	2258	13.03.91
	G-BYPS Magical Adventures Ltd		
	West Bloomfield, MI, USA *'Rabbit'*		27.09.09E
	(NF 03.06.15)		
G-HUDS	P&M Quik GTR	8658	21.08.13
	S J M Morling Dunkeswell		04.08.18P
G-HUET	Avions Transport ATR 42-500	584	24.04.15
	OY-YAS, N584NA, PR-TKH, D-BQQQ, F-WWEP		
	Aurigny Air Services Ltd Guernsey		17.04.19E
G-HUEW	Europa Aviation Europa XS	592	22.07.04
	C R Wright Yeatsall Farm, Abbots Bromley		13.06.18P
	Built by C R Wright – project PFA 247-14156; tricycle u/c		
G-HUEY	Bell UH-1H-BF Iroquois	13560	23.07.85
	Arg.Army AE-413, 73-22077		
	MX Jets Ltd North Weald		11.11.18P
	Carries '560' in 'US Army' camouflage c/s		
G-HUEZ	Hughes 369E (*500*)	0544E	14.03.17
	G-WEBI, N696XX, N90DE, (N833MS), N90DE,		
	N90DK, N7046C		
	Falcon Helicopters Ltd (Shadsworth, Blackburn)		30.03.18E
G-HUFF	Cessna 182P Skylane II	18264076	31.10.78
	PH-CAS, N6059F Highfine Ltd Southend		28.07.19E
	Assembled Reims Aviation with c/n 0033		
G-HUGS	Robinson R22 Beta	1455	27.02.02
	G-BYHD, N900AB Cancelled 21.02.11 as PWFU		21.04.10
	Co Carlow, RoI		
	Instructional frame, Carlow Instructional Of Tech 05.16		
G-HUKA	Hughes 369E (*500*)	0298E	12.02.02
	G-OSOO B P Stein Ockwells Manor, Bray		25.08.18E
G-HUKS	Kubícek BB22XR	1338	13.03.17
	Wharf Farm Ltd Tibshelf, Alfreton		04.04.19E
G-HULK	Best Off Skyranger 912(2)	SKR0207213	16.01.07
	L C Stockman Plaistows Farm, St Albans		10.06.18P
	Built by L C Stockman – project BAA/HB/238		
G-HULL	Reims/Cessna F150M	F15001255	19.01.79
	PH-TGR J P Nugent t/a Wicklow Wings		
	Newcastle, RoI		
	(IE 30.10.15)		
G-HUME	EAA Acrosport II	xxxx	07.09.17
	G Home (Aldfield, Ripon)		
	Built by G Home – project PFA 072-10672 (NF 07.09.17)		
G-HUMH	Van's RV-9A	91111	15.11.05
	D F Daines tr G-HUMH Group Seething		10.09.18P
	Built by H A Daines – project PFA 320-14357		
G-HUMM	Bell 407	54556	24.08.16
	C-FHXS, N827BH, C-FHXS		
	Century Aviation Ltd Retford Gamston		07.09.18E
G-HUNI	Bellanca 7GCBC Citabria	541-73	21.10.96
	OO-IME, D-EIME R G Munro Denham		16.03.18E
G-HUNT^M	Hawker Hunter F.51	41H-680277	05.07.78
	G-9-440, Danish AF E-418, Danish AF 35-418		
	Cancelled 10.12.87 – to N50972 – subsequently N611JR		05.07.78
	As 'WB188'		
	With EAA AirVenture Museum, Oshkosh, Wisconsin		
G-HUPW	Hawker Hurricane I	G592301	21.08.01
	R4118 J Brown Duxford		27.04.18P
	Built by Gloster Aircraft Co Ltd; as 'R4118:UP-W'		
	in RAF camouflage c/s; noted 07.18		
G-HURI	Hawker Hurricane XIIA	72036	09.06.83
	RCAF 5711 Historic Aircraft Collection Ltd Duxford		12.07.19E
	Built by Canadian Car & Foundry Co; composite		
	– probably includes parts of c/n 44019 ex		
	RCAF 5424, RCAF 5625 & RCAF 5547; as		
	'P3700:RF-E' in RAF 303 Sqdn c/s		
G-HUTY	Van's RV-7	72808	26.10.06
	S A Hutt (Angmering, Littlehampton)		
	Built by S A Hutt – project PFA 323-14571 (NF 20.11.14)		
G-HUXY	Cessna 152	15282328	15.06.15
	9H-AFV, TF-MID, N68712 Iris Aviation Ltd Southend		22.10.19E
	Operated by Seawing Flying Club		
G-HVBF	Lindstrand LBL 210A	372	23.05.96
	Airxcite Ltd t/a Virgin Balloon Flights		
	Stafford Park, Telford *'Virgin'*		25.03.07E
	(NF 15.09.14)		

G-HVER	Robinson R44 Raven II	11754	29.05.07	
	Equation Associates Ltd Denham		02.07.18E	
G-HVRZ	Eurocopter EC120B Colibri	1338	17.01.07	
	HB-ZEZ J S Tobias Manchester Barton		10.04.18E	
G-HWAA	Eurocopter EC135 T2	0375	21.02.05	
	Babcock Mission Critical Services Onshore Ltd			
	Tatenhill		25.01.19E	
	Operated by Midlands Air Ambulance as callsign			
	'Helimed 06'			
G-HWKS	Robinson R44 Raven I	1747	06.11.13	
	G-ETFF, G-HSLJ Rapid International (Holdings) Ltd			
	Tandragee, Craigavon		13.09.19E	
G-HWKW	Hughes 369E (500)	0537E	22.10.14	
	D-HWKW, N9237X			
	Flitwick Helicopters Ltd (Flitwick, Bedford)		23.01.19E	
G-HWOW	Robinson R44 Clipper	2219	03.01.19	
	D-HWOW Autorotation Ltd Hill Farm, Sproughton		11.11.19E	
	(IE 03.01.19)			
G-HXJT	HpH Glasflügel 304 S Shark	039-MS	06.11.14	
	(BGA 5825) H Hingley (Blackpool) 'HH'			
	(NF 13.01.18)			
G-HXTD	Robin DR.400-180 Régent	2510	24.10.01	
	S R Evans (Welwyn Garden City)		01.03.18E	
G-HYBD	Gramex Song	09/2013	03.07.13	
	University of Cambridge Sywell			
	(IE 23.08.17)			
G-HYLA	Kubícek BB26E	1305	31.01.17	
	J A Viner North Muskham, Newark		02.02.19E	
G-HYLT	Piper PA-32R-301 Saratoga SP	32R-8213001	23.04.86	
	N84588 T G Gordon Ireland West Airport Knock, Rol		21.08.18E	
G-HYND	Robinson R44 Raven	2433	29.06.16	
	Heli Air Scotland Ltd Cumbernauld		13.07.18E	

G-IAAA – G-IZZZ

G-IACA	Sikorsky S-92A	920050	23.04.07	
	N81254 Bristow Helicopters Ltd			
	Aberdeen Int'l 'Eoin Harcurs'		20.05.18E	
G-IACB	Sikorsky S-92A	920062	14.11.07	
	N4516G Bristow Helicopters Ltd Aberdeen Int'l			
	'35 Years Service – Alan Price'		12.11.18E	
G-IACC	Sikorsky S-92A	920063	15.11.07	
	N45158 Bristow Helicopters Ltd Aberdeen Int'l			
	'Don McGregor'		17.11.18E	
G-IACD	Sikorsky S-92A	920065	20.12.07	
	N4515G Bristow Helicopters Ltd Aberdeen Int'l			
	'35 Years Service – Richard Enoch'		09.01.19E	
G-IACE	Sikorsky S-92A	920066	20.12.07	
	N45148 Bristow Helicopters Ltd Aberdeen Int'l			
	'35 Years Service – Kevin Pickering'		09.01.19E	
G-IACF	Sikorsky S-92A	920068	05.02.08	
	N4509G Bristow Helicopters Ltd Aberdeen Int'l			
	'Ian Pearce'		19.02.18E	
G-IACY	Avions Transport ATR 72-212A	1448	08.09.17	
	F-WWEU			
	Air Kilroe Ltd t/a Eastern Airways Aberdeen Int'l		27.09.19E	
G-IACZ	Avions Transport ATR 72-212A	1482	01.03.18	
	F-WWEH			
	Air Kilroe Ltd t/a Eastern Airways Aberdeen Int'l		28.02.19E	
G-IAGI	SOCATA TB-9 Tampico Club	1396	18.05.17	
	I-IAGI B Pellegry (Villeneuve sur Lot, France, France)		05.02.20E	
G-IAGL	Eurocopter EC120B Colibri	1565	21.10.13	
	G-UYFI, SX-HVR, F-WAIX, F-WAID			
	A Leslie t/a AGL Helicopters Brighton City		05.02.19E	
G-IAGO	Groppo Trail Mk.2	143/102	03.03.17	
	J W Armstrong & J Jones Old Park Farm, Margam		27.09.19P	
	Built by J W Armstrong & J Jones			
	– project LAA 372-15461			
G-IAHS	Evektor EV-97 teamEurostar UK	2013-3601	11.04.13	
	I A Holden Halwell		04.04.18P	
	Assembled Cosmik Aviation Ltd			
G-IAJJ	Robinson R44 Raven II	11953	13.11.07	
	HH-Aviation (Manchester) Ltd Manchester Barton		18.04.19E	

G-IAJS	Comco Ikarus C42 FB UK	0503 6657	27.07.05	
	A J Slater Dairy House Farm, Worleston		02.10.18P	
	Built by A J Slater – project PFA 322-14393			
G-IAMP	Cameron H-34	2541	11.03.91	
	W D Mackinnon Strangford, Downpatrick 'BPG'		26.05.17E	
G-IANB	DG Flugzeugbau DG-800B	8-246B159	12.03.02	
	I S Bullous Sutton Bank		07.05.18E	
G-IANC	SOCATA TB-10 Tobago	150	15.12.04	
	G-BIAK I M Clark tr Rougham Flying Group			
	Rougham		13.03.18E	
G-IANH	SOCATA TB-10 Tobago	1843	13.03.00	
	F-OILI J A Tenison-Collins tr Severn Valley Aero Group			
	Welshpool		02.03.18E	
G-IANI	Europa Aviation Europa XS	505	20.04.01	
	W D Dewey Wishanger Farm, Frensham 'Charlotte'		29.08.18P	
	Built by I F Rickard & I A Watson			
	– project PFA 247-13714; tricycle u/c			
G-IANJ	Reims/Cessna F150K	F15000548	19.05.98	
	G-AXVW D T A & J A Rees Haverfordwest		06.07.18E	
G-IANW	Eurocopter AS.350B3 Ecureuil	3447	18.09.01	
	F-WQPU Milford Aviation Services Ltd Lasham		01.11.18E	
G-IANZ	P&M Quik GT450	8576	14.02.11	
	I W Harriman Rufforth East		27.02.18P	
G-IARC	Stoddard-Hamilton GlaStar	5522	09.11.99	
	A A Craig Glasgow Prestwick		03.07.18P	
	Built by A A Craig – project PFA 295-13261; tricycle u/c			
G-IART	Cessna 182F Skylane	18254663	21.01.15	
	SX-ART, F-BKQX, N3263U			
	Aeroclub of Attica (Athens, Greece)		04.05.18E	
G-IASA	Beech B200 Super King Air	BB-1698	09.01.13	
	F-GUFP, N32287			
	IAS Medical Ltd Durham Tees Valley		13.04.18E	
G-IASB	Beech B200GT King Air	BY-278	08.08.17	
	N278BY IAS Medical Ltd Durham Tees Valley		22.08.18E	
G-IASL	Beech 60 Duke	P-21	18.04.97	
	G-SING, D-IDTA, SE-EXT			
	Cancelled 05.05.10 as WFU		08.03.09	
	Gloucester On fire dump 02.19			
G-IASM	Beech 200 Super King Air	BB-521	26.07.10	
	G-OEAS, N200QN, N355TW, N220GK, LN-AXB,			
	(LN-VIR), SE-IZB, LN-AXB, LN-PAB, OY-CBL,			
	SE-GXM, OY-CBL			
	2 Excel Aviation Ltd Doncaster Sheffield		21.06.19E	
G-IBAZ	Comco Ikarus C42 FB100	0409-6622	30.09.04	
	B R Underwood Coventry		13.10.18P	
	Assembled Fly Buy Ultralights Ltd			
G-IBBS	Europa Aviation Europa	118	08.09.94	
	R H Gibbs Popham		26.05.19P	
	Built by R H Gibbs – project PFA 247-12745;			
	tailwheel u/c			
G-IBCF	Cameron Z-105	11677	24.07.12	
	Avon Autobahn Ltd t/a Cash 4 Cars			
	Brislington, Bristol 'cash4cars.co.uk'		12.05.18E	
G-IBEA	Piper PA-28-181 Archer LX	2881027	29.08.18	
	N7120J J Dobson White Waltham		12.09.19E	
G-IBED	Robinson R22 Alpha	0500	07.09.93	
	G-BMHN Swift Helicopter Services Ltd			
	Leeds Heliport		18.07.19E	
G-IBEE	Pipistrel Apis/Bee	062-AB-F33	09.06.14	
	Fly About Aviation Ltd Damyns Hall, Upminster			
	(IE 04.06.18)			
G-IBEV	Cameron C-90	10375	10.04.03	
	B Drawbridge Cranbrook		10.05.18E	
G-IBFC	BFC Challenger II Long Wing	1774 UK	09.11.98	
	S D Puddle Redlands		14.09.15P	
	Built by K N Dickinson – project PFA 177B-13369			
	(BFC kit); stored in damaged state 02.15			
G-IBFF	Beech A23-24 Musketeer Super	MA-352	30.08.12	
	EI-BFF, G-AXCJ D H G Penney Sandtoft		10.04.16E	
	(NF 23.11.18)			
G-IBFP	Magni M16 Tandem Trainer	106	22.03.05	
	B F Pearson Headon Farm, Retford			
	Built by B F Pearson – project PFA G/12-1240			
	(IE 18.01.18)			

G-IBFW	Piper PA-28R-201 Arrow III	28R-7837235	22.01.79
	N31534 Archer Four Ltd Lydd		19.06.18E
	Official type data 'PA-28R-201 Cherokee Arrow III'		
	is incorrect		
G-IBIG	Bell 206B-3 JetRanger III	2202	20.03.02
	G-BORV, C-GVTY, N16763		
	D W Bevan Manston Park		16.12.18E
G-IBII	Pitts S-2A	2147	17.12.10
	G-XATS, CS-AZE, N338BD		
	First Light Aviation Ltd Gloucestershire		19.06.18E
	Built by Pitts Aerobatics		
G-IBLP	P&M Quik GT450	8523	19.05.10
	C Zizzo Darley Moor		19.05.18P
G-IBMS	Robinson R44 Raven II	11287	20.06.06
	BMS Holdings Ltd Wellesbourne Mountford		05.07.18E
G-IBNH	Westland SA.341C Gazelle HT.2	1033	07.12.11
	G-SWWM, XW853		
	Buckland Newton Hire Ltd Henstridge		07.05.18P
G-IBRO	Cessna F152 II	15201957	11.10.95
	EI-BRO Cancelled 29.06.05 as destroyed		14.03.05
	Old Warden *Built by Reims Aviation SA*		
	Used for fire exercise 04.13		
G-IBSY	Supermarine 349 Spitfire Vc	-	25.01.12
	G-VMIJ, EE602		
	Anglia Aircraft Restorations Ltd Duxford		04.07.19P
	Built by Westland Aircraft Ltd 1942;		
	as 'EE602:DV-V' in RAF c/s		
G-IBUZ	CZAW Sportcruiser	700348	21.10.08
	G L Fearon Forwood Farm, Treswell		03.10.18P
	Built by D W Bessell & R C Wheeler		
	– project LAA 338-14835		
G-ICAS	Pitts S-2B	5344	19.06.97
	N511P J C Smith Full Sutton		19.07.18E
	Built by Aviat Inc		
G-ICBM	Stoddard-Hamilton Glasair III	3337	18.12.00
	D N Brown & G V Waters (Attleborough/Stamford)		04.06.15P
	Built by G V Waters (IE 11.02.16)		
G-ICDM	Avtech Jabiru UL-450	xxxx	26.02.10
	G-CEKM D J R Wenham Damyns Hall, Upminster		08.08.19P
	Built by R H Bain & D R Morton		
	– project PFA 274A-14436		
G-ICDP	Reims/Cessna F150L	F15000906	22.04.14
	EC-CDP P Morton Bembridge		08.06.16E
	(NF 14.11.17)		
G-ICEI	Leonardo AW169	69065	08.01.18
	I-RAIL Iceland International Ltd Dunsfold		08.01.19E
G-ICEL	Robinson R66 Turbine	0892	10.10.18
	HQ Aviation Ltd Denham		
	(NF 10.10.18)		
G-ICES^M	Thunder Ax6-56 SP.1 HAB	283	03.07.80
	Cancelled 14.04.09 as WFU		03.06.94
	Ice Cream Cone		
	With British Balloon Museum & Library, Newbury		
G-ICGA	Piper PA-28-140 Cherokee Fliteliner	28-7225317	29.07.13
	5B-CGA, N709FL M Lalik (Warsaw, Poland)		20.12.17E
G-ICLC	Cessna 150L	15075161	23.04.13
	5B-CLC, PH-HIL, (PH-SKN), N19050		
	Hub2You SA (Waremme, Belgium)		09.10.16E
G-ICMT	Evektor EV-97 Eurostar	2007-2929	04.12.06
	R Haslam (Smalley, Ilkeston)		17.05.18P
	Built by C M Theakstone – project PFA 315-14598		
G-ICMX	Cessna 182P Skylane	18263181	02.08.16
	EC-CMX, N7398N E Bilda Lelystad, Netherlands		24.02.18E
G-ICOM	Reims/Cessna F172M	F17201212	25.04.94
	G-BFXI, PH-ABA, D-EEVC N J Yeoman Bodmin		31.08.18E
G-ICON	Rutan Long-EZ	xxxx	29.11.00
	M A & S J Carradice Retford Gamston		21.06.18P
	Built by S J Carradice – project PFA 074A-11104		
G-ICOR	Lindstrand LTL Series 2-60	068	26.04.18
	Trinity Balloons CIC Tavistock		
	'Faith Hope Love 13.13'		17.05.19E
G-ICRS	Comco Ikarus C42 FB UK	0202-6458	11.03.02
	Ikarus Flying Group Ltd RAF Halton		08.02.18P
	Built by A J Whitlock – project PFA 322-13873		
G-ICRV	Van's RV-7	74239	09.03.17
	I A Coates Retford Gamston		10.06.19P
	Built by I A Coates – project LAA 323-15232		
G-ICSG	Aérospatiale AS.355F1 Ecureuil 2	5104	06.04.93
	G-PAMI, G-BUSA RCR Aviation Ltd (Somerton)		07.08.08E
	For parting out 11.16 (NF 02.11.15)		
G-ICUT	Maule MX-7-180A Super Rocket	21080C	18.11.13
	EI-CUT R A Smith Elmsett		08.05.18E
G-ICWT	Cyclone Pegasus Quantum 15-912	7632	07.04.00
	A R Bill & J E Dawson tr Whisky Tango Group		
	Redlands		02.09.19P
G-IDAY	Skyfox CA-25N Gazelle	CA25N028	29.04.96
	VH-RCR G G Johnstone Sorbie Farm, Kingsmuir		26.11.18E
G-IDEB	Aérospatiale AS.355F1 Ecureuil 2	5192	13.10.09
	G-ORMA, G-SITE, G-BPHC, N365E		
	MW Helicopters Ltd Stapleford		01.06.18E
G-IDHC	Cessna 172N Skyhawk II	17269065	03.05.16
	LN-DAA, SE-GOX, N734RX		
	Aero-Club Maritime Lelystad, Netherlands		14.09.18E
G-IDII	Dan Rihn DR.107 One Design	95-0342	16.06.99
	C Darlow Shacklewell Lodge Farm, Empingham		26.07.18P
	Built by C Darlow – project PFA 264-12953		
G-IDMG	Robinson R44 Raven	2038	30.01.15
	EC-LPO, D-HALC B Davis (Tralee, Rol)		30.04.18E
G-IDOL	Evektor EV-97 Eurostar	2006-2728	04.09.06
	R Powers (Walsall)		03.04.19P
	Built by T D Baker, J J Lynch & C Moore		
	– project PFA 315-14549		
G-IDRS	Van's RV-8	82228	03.10.16
	C-FPVT T I Williams Brighton City		08.01.19P
	Built by P Tuttle		
G-IDSL	Flight Design CT2K	02-06-02-04	28.10.02
	Cancelled 13.10.11 as destroyed		20.05.11
	Yatesbury *Assembled by Pegasus Aviation Ltd*		
	as c/n 7922; stored 06.14		
G-IDTO	Piper PA-28RT-201T Turbo Arrow IV	28R-8331051	01.04.16
	(PH-DTO), G-IDTO, EC-DTQ, N9546N		
	G Cresdee Liverpool John Lennon		14.11.19E
G-IDYL	AutoGyro Cavalon	V00168	30.09.14
	J M & M J Newman Denham		17.10.18P
	Assembled Rotorsport UK as c/n RSUK/CVLN/012		
G-IEEF	Raj Hamsa X'Air Hawk	1171	11.06.12
	EI-EEF P J Sheehy Solent		19.04.18P
G-IEII	Extra EA.230	009	27.03.18
	G-CBUA, N230KR, N286PA		
	D Dobson Little Staughton		15.10.19P
G-IEJH	Jodel D.150 Mascaret	02	28.02.95
	G-BPAM, F-BLDA, F-WLDA		
	A Turner & D Worth Crowfield		02.07.18P
	Built by Société Aéronautique Normande		
G-IENN	Cirrus SR20	1899	31.01.12
	G-TSGE, N621DA		
	Transcirrus BV (Bosschenhoofd, Netherlands)		20.03.18E
G-IFAB	Reims/Cessna F182Q Skylane II	F18200127	06.01.98
	N61AN, G-IFAB, OO-ELM, (OO-HNU)		
	A Bruce & H E Thomas Kirkwall		20.03.19E
G-IFBP	Eurocopter AS.350B2 Ecureuil	9051	27.10.03
	F-GTKR, (F-GYBR)		
	F Bird t/a Frank Bird Aviation Langwathby, Penrith		01.11.19E
G-IFES	Schempp-Hirth Discus-2c FES	33	06.03.19
	(BGA 5973) J M Bevan Husbands Bosworth		
	(IE 25.02.19)		
G-IFFR	Piper PA-32-300 Cherokee Six	32-7340123	01.04.97
	G-BWVO, OO-JPC, N55520		
	J C Gilbert & G D Ritchie tr Brendair RAF Henlow		20.02.19E
G-IFFY	Flylight Dragonfly/Aeros Discus 15T	033	15.09.09
	R D Leigh Darley Moor		
	Discus 15T wing s/n 014-09 & engine s/n 229		
	(SSDR microlight since 05.14) (IE 07.01.18)		
G-IFIF	Cameron TR-60	10811	17.11.05
	M G Howard Hewish, Weston-super-Mare		
	'VgL' & 'if...'		21.08.18E
G-IFIK	Cessna 421C Golden Eagle	421C1115	19.01.15
	D-IFIK, N2652Y M Neumann (Karlsruhe, Germany)		10.09.18E

G-IFIT	Piper PA-31-350 Chieftain	31-8052078	31.12.85
	G-NABI, G-MARG, N3580C		
	Dart Group PLC Cranfield		03.06.18E
	Operated by Jet2.com		
G-IFLE	Evektor EV-97 teamEurostar UK	2004-2113	01.07.04
	M R Smith Otherton		10.07.18P
	Assembled Cosmik Aviation Ltd		
G-IFLI	Gulfstream American AA-5A Cheetah	AA5A-0831	07.07.82
	N26948 J P Nugent Newcastle, RoI		01.01.19E
G-IFLP	Piper PA-34-200T Seneca II	34-8070029	04.01.88
	N81WS, N81149		
	Aviation Advice & Consulting Ltd Oxford		02.03.19E
G-IFOS	Ultramagic M-90	90/135	16.12.14
	I J Sharpe Caterham		26.12.18E
G-IFRH	Agusta A109C	7619	07.01.08
	N637CG, D-HARI, TC-HHI, D-HAAX, JA6608		
	Helicopter & Pilot Services Ltd White Waltham		21.02.18E
G-IFTE	British Aerospace HS125 Series 700B	257037	16.05.96
	G-BVFI, G-5-18 Cancelled 15.05.18 as PWFU		22.07.17
	Biggin Hill *Stored 06.18*		
G-IFWD	Schempp-Hirth Ventus cT	148	08.11.07
	BGA3575/FWD C J Hamilton Portmoak *'888'*		13.04.18E
G-IGBI	Game Composites GB1	001	13.03.15
	Game Composites Ltd Bentonville, Arkansas, USA		
	(IE 21.07.15)		
G-IGET	Best Off Skyranger Nynja 912S(1)	xxxx	03.01.19
	D C Maybury Shobdon		
	Built by D C Maybury – project BMAA/HB/702		
	(NF 03.01.19)		
G-IGGI	Bell 505 Jet Ranger X	65126	22.08.18
	Pristheath Ltd Carleton Park, Carleton		
	(IE 22.08.18)		
G-IGGL	SOCATA TB-10 Tobago	146	26.03.99
	G-BYDC, F-GCOL		
	Cavendish Aviation UK Ltd Earls Colne		05.02.15E
	For probable spares use (NF 08.07.16)		
G-IGHT	Van's RV-8	82525	25.07.08
	E A Yates North Weald		17.05.19P
	Built by E A Yates – project PFA 303-14520		
G-IGIA	Eurocopter AS.350B3 Ecureuil	3243	21.03.07
	I-CFVA Faloria Ltd (Wickford)		27.03.19E
G-IGIE	SIAI Marchetti SF.260	2-42	13.03.02
	D-EHGB Flew LLP Bournemouth		14.06.19E
G-IGIS	Bell 206B-2 JetRanger II	1669	25.06.14
	G-CHGL, EI-WSN, G-CHGL, G-BPNG, G-ORTC,		
	G-BPNG, N20EA, C-GHVB C J Edwards		
	(Home Farm, Hinton Charterhouse)		09.08.18E
G-IGLE	Cameron V-90	2609	11.06.91
	R K Worsman tr The G-IGLE Group		
	Monymusk, Inverurie		07.04.18E
G-IGLI	Schempp-Hirth Duo Discus T	106/435	02.02.10
	(BGA 5643), EI-GLI, EI-159 C Fox Sleap *'563'*		31.01.19E
G-IGLL	AutoGyro MTOsport	11 026S	16.06.11
	I M Donnellan Sleap		05.10.18P
	Assembled Rotorsport UK as c/n RSUK/MTOS/037		
G-IGLY	P&M Quik GT450	8372	09.04.08
	R Davies (Braintree)		07.07.19P
G-IGLZ	American Champion 8KCAB Super Decathlon		
		914-2003	18.02.03
	C A Parsons (Martley, Worcester)		31.07.19E
G-IHAR	Cessna 172P Skyhawk	17274314	02.07.14
	EC-HAR, N172U, N51455 CG Aviation Ltd Perth		19.04.18E
	Stored Bournemouth 12.18 (NF 20.12.18)		
G-IHCI	Europa Aviation Europa	163	20.02.14
	G-VKIT I H Clarke Perth *'Goodtime Girl'*		09.03.18P
	Built by T H Crow – project PFA 247-12783; tricycle u/c		
G-IHHI	Extra EA.300/SC	SC060	21.03.16
	Airdisplays.com Ltd Little Gransden		29.03.18E
G-IHOP	Cameron Z-31	10782	28.11.05
	N W Roberts Cardiff		27.10.18E

G-IHOT	Evektor EV-97 teamEurostar UK	2004-2007	01.04.04
	Exodus Airsports Ltd tr G-IHOT Group		
	Plaistows Farm, St Albans		09.10.19P
	Assembled Cosmik Aviation Ltd;		
	believed rebuilt with new fuselage		
G-IHXD	Reims/Cessna F150M	F15001313	15.04.14
	EC-HXD, TC-DBG, D-EIBT, (D-EIFY)		
	Air Navigation & Trading Company Ltd Blackpool		05.07.18E
G-IIAC	Aeronca 11AC Chief	11AC-169	02.07.91
	(G-BTPY), N86359, NC86359 N Jamieson Sibson		01.09.18P
G-IIAI	Mudry CAP 232	07	22.01.08
	F-GJGM DEP Promotions Ltd Kilrush, RoI		01.12.17E
	(IE 20.12.17)		
G-IIAL	Aerospool Dynamic WT9 UK	DY483	19.02.19
	G-GCJH A Howell (Knockholt, Sevenoaks)		30.06.19P
	Assembled Yeoman Light Aircraft Co Ltd		
G-IIAN	Aero Designs Pulsar	xxxx	10.09.91
	I G Harrison (Pentrich, Ripley)		
	Built by I G Harrison – project PFA 202-12123		
	(NF 22.02.18)		
G-IICC	Van's RV-4	2394-1211	08.08.12
	G-MARX, SE-XUU		
	J C Carter & P R Fabish (Cambridge)		14.06.11P
	Built by T L Berry (NF 13.07.15)		
G-IICT	Schempp-Hirth Ventus-2cT	72/225	12.07.07
	BGA 4921 P McLean RAF Marham *'V2C'*		20.01.18E
G-IICX	Schempp-Hirth Ventus-2cxT	171/415	03.04.06
	BGA 5199/KMH M J M Turnbull Bicester *'CX'*		20.01.15E
	(IE 21.10.17)		
G-IIDC	Bushby-Long Midget Mustang	xxxx	21.11.12
	G-IIMT, G-BDGA D Cooke (Newick, Lewes)		
	Built by M J A Trudgill – project PFA168-1327;		
	as G-BDGA was PFA 1327 (NF 23.08.16)		
G-IIDD	Van's RV-8	82814	01.10.15
	A D Friday Lydd		04.06.19P
	Built by S Birt, D J C Davidson & D de Boer- project LAA		
	303-15248		
G-IIDI	Extra EA.300/L	047	05.10.01
	G-XTRS, D-EXJH Power Aerobatics Ltd Goodwood		22.04.18E
	Operated by Xtreme Team		
G-IIDR	Comco Ikarus C42 FB100 Bravo	1207-7220	06.09.12
	I A Harper & S G Penk		
	Wolverhampton Halfpenny Green		27.12.18P
	Assembled Red-Air UK		
G-IIDW	Flylight Dragon Combat 12T	DA121	29.04.15
	J S Prosser (Poundbury, Dorchester)		
	(IE 05.10.18)		
G-IIDY	Pitts S-2B	5000	11.11.02
	G-BPVP, N5302M		
	R P Millinship tr The S2B Group Leicester		04.10.18E
	Built by Aerotek Inc		
G-IIEX	Extra EA.300/L	04	25.05.05
	JA300L, N123EX, D-ETYM, (D-ETYL)		
	S G Jones Membury		21.08.08E
	(NF 11.11.17)		
G-IIFI	XtremeAir XA41 Sbach 300	02	26.03.17
	D-EYXA Attitude Aerobatics Ltd Audley End		17.07.18W
G-IIFM	Zivko Edge 360	1	10.11.09
	N37TP F L McGee Leicester		24.06.18P
	Built by T A Pound		
G-IIFX	Marganski MDM-1 Fox	223	24.02.11
	(BGA 5666), HB-3298, D-4034		
	G C Westgate t/a GliderFX Parham Park		17.04.17E
	CofA suspended 16.07.16		
G-IIGI	Van's RV-4	381	07.04.04
	N44BZ C J L Wolf (Aberystwyth)		12.09.18P
	Built by C & R F Palmer		
G-IIHL	Extra EA.300/SC	SC082	07.03.19
	Aerobatic Show SP z.o.o (Warsaw, Poland)		
	(NF 07.03.19)		
G-IIHX	Bushby-Long Midget Mustang	266	07.11.13
	N7594U M C Huxtable Wycombe Air Park		02.07.18P
	Built by W Cummins		

G-IIHZ	Mudry CAP 231	08	14.10.13
	G-OZZO, F-GOZO, F-WQOM, CN-ABK		
	R Bates & J Taylor Northrepps		22.06.18E
G-IIID	Dan Rihn DR.107 One Design	94-0168	06.07.00
	D A Kean Wellcross Farm, Slinfold		24.04.19P
	Built by A J & M A N Newall – project PFA 264-12766		
G-IIIE	Pitts S-2B	5017	08.03.04
	N9WQ, N9WR		
	R M C Ribeiro de Aguiar Cascais, Portugal		23.02.17E
	Built by Aerotek Inc		
G-IIIF	XtremeAir XA41 Sbach 300	01	04.04.17
	D-EVXA Airtime Aerobatics Ltd Oaksey Park		16.07.18W
G-IIIG	Boeing Stearman A75N1 Kaydet *(PT-17)* 75-4354		25.03.91
	G-BSDR, N61827, 42-16193		
	S Bolyn & O Josse tr Stearman G-IIIG Group		
	Namur-Suarlee, Belgium		24.07.16E
	In US Army c/s as '309'		
G-IIII	Pitts S-2B	5010	06.01.89
	N5330G A Milhaud (St Cloud, France)		16.11.18E
	Built by Christen Industries Inc		
G-IIIJ	American Champion 8GCBC Scout	522-2010	28.10.14
	N325BC J D May White Waltham		30.11.17E
G-IIIK	Extra EA.300/SC	SC024	20.10.10
	Extra 330SC LLP Wycombe Air Park		23.05.19E
G-IIIL	Pitts S-1T	008	15.02.89
	OH-XPT, G-IIIL, N15JE J O Vize Leicester		05.06.18P
	Built by J L Edwardson		
G-IIIM	Stolp SA.100 Starduster	4258549	21.04.06
	N40D H Mackintosh Spanhoe		
	Built by Starduster Corporation (NF 06.03.18)		
G-IIIN	Pitts S-1C	MC132-H	18.12.14
	N1382 R P Evans Hinton-in-the-Hedges		
	Built by M C Coleman		
G-IIIP	Pitts S-1D	xxxx	22.02.10
	G-BLAG R S Grace Sywell *'Trig Aerobatic Team'*		14.06.19P
	Built by B Bray – project PFA 009-10195		
G-IIIR	Pitts S-1	604	21.01.93
	N27M R Farrer Hulcote Farm, Hulcote		18.06.04P
	Built by Milam (NF 13.11.17)		
G-IIIV	Pitts S-1-11 Super Stinker	0018	04.02.97
	S D Barnard & A N R Houghton Leicester		11.02.16P
	Built by A N R Houghton, G G Ferriman &		
	R P Millinship – project PFA 273-13005;		
	badged 'Pitts S1.11B' (IE 24.07.17)		
G-IIIX	Pitts S-1S	AJT	22.05.89
	G-LBAT, G-UCCI, G-BIYN, N455T		
	D S T Eggleton Waits Farm, Belchamp Walter		16.12.18P
	Built by J Tarascio		
G-IIIY	Boeing Stearman A75N1 Kaydet *(N2S-4)* 75-3491		07.10.15
	N54922, Bu 30054		
	Aero-Super-Batics Ltd Rendcomb		04.10.16E
G-IIJC	Bushby-Long Midget Mustang	XU-5	28.07.08
	G-CEKU, G-GFPF D C Landy (RNAS Culdrose)		10.05.17P
	Built by R W Eaves		
G-IIJI	XtremeAir XA42 Sbach 342	121	13.08.13
	G H Willson Audley End		21.08.18E
G-IILL	Van's RV-7	72029	09.12.13
	N289B C P Wilkinson Finmere *'88'*		28.07.19P
	Built by R L Bonde		
G-IILY	Robinson R44 Raven I	0960	24.07.13
	G-DCSG, G-TRYG Un Pied sur Terre Ltd		
	t/a Whizzard Helicopters Welshpool		17.07.19E
G-IIMI	Extra EA.300/L	141	02.05.01
	D-EXLE A Birch Chesieres, Switzerland		13.08.18E
G-IINI	Van's RV-9A	90360	06.08.04
	N W Thomas Bournemouth		08.10.18P
	Built by S Sampson – project PFA 320-13781		
G-IINK	Cirrus SR22	4187	01.08.17
	OK-STL N P Kingdon Exeter Int'l		09.06.18E
G-IIOO	Schleicher ASW 27-18E *(ASG 29E)*	29573	05.03.09
	BGA 5336/KSU M Clarke Lasham *'MC'*		26.03.18E

G-IIPI	Steen Skybolt	xxxx	13.04.17
	G-BVXE, G-LISA J Buglass Sleap		
	Built by T C Humphreys & T J Reeve –		
	project PFA 064-11123 (NF 12.04.17)		
G-IIPT	Robinson R22 Beta	2506	10.05.01
	G-FUSI, N83306		
	Swift Helicopter Services Ltd Leeds Heliport		04.01.19E
G-IIRG	Stoddard-Hamilton Glasair IIS RG	xxxx	29.06.93
	S R Collier tr AyeAye Group		
	(Littlewindsor, Beaminster)		19.07.19P
	Built by D S Watson – project PFA 149-11937		
G-IIRI	XtremeAir XA41 Sbach 300	GC9	29.06.11
	L Love & One Sky Aviators Ltd Wickenby		13.05.19P
	Built by G C J Cooper – project LAA 379-15090		
G-IIRP	Mudry CAP 232	09	23.02.09
	F-GKMZ R J Pickin Headcorn		30.11.17E
	Built by Mudry Aviation Bernay Air Service		
G-IIRV	Van's RV-7A	73895	19.12.11
	R C W King (Olveston, Bristol)		06.12.18P
	Built by D S Watson – project LAA 323-15074		
G-IIRW	Van's RV-8	80449	11.06.08
	N42KL G G Ferriman Jericho Farm, Lambley		30.09.18P
	Built by J M Sturgis		
G-IISC	Extra EA.300/SC	SC058	02.02.16
	D E H Nichols tr G-IISC Group White Waltham		07.01.19E
G-IITC	Mudry CAP 232	15	23.02.09
	F-GOTC Skyboard Aerobatics Ltd Wombleton		17.08.18E
	Built by CAP Aviation		
G-IIXF	Van's RV-7	705592	14.03.07
	C A & S C Noujaim Rendcomb *'Anna'*		23.04.18P
	Built by C A & S C Noujaim – project PFA 323-13844		
G-IIXI	Extra EA.300/L	134	06.08.03
	YR-EWG B Nielsen Denham		30.01.18E
G-IIXX	Parsons Two-Place Gyroplane	xxxx	13.10.93
	J M Montgomerie Kirkbride		
	Built by J M Montgomerie – project PFA G/08-1225		
	(NF 09.02.16)		
G-IIYI	Boeing Stearman A75N1 Kaydet *(PT-17)* 75-4645		14.08.18
	N49943, 42-16482 V S E Norman Rendcomb		11.09.19E
G-IIYK	Yakovlev Yak-50	842706	15.10.02
	LY-AFZ, DOSAAF 24		
	B R Pearson tr Eaglescott Yak 50 Group Eaglescott		03.01.14P
	(NF 16.08.17)		
G-IIYY	Cessna 421C Golden Eagle	421C0621	10.11.14
	D-IIYY, LX-SKY, D-ISAL, N88636		
	H-J Simon (Rodgau, Germany)		07.09.18E
G-IIZI	Extra EA.300	037	12.12.96
	JY-RNB, D-ETXA M G Jefferies Little Gransden		06.01.19E
G-IJAC	Avid Speed Wing Mk.4	918	31.12.92
	I J A Charlton Chilsfold Farm, Northchapel		
	Built by I J A Charlton – project PFA 189-12095		
	(NF 19.08.14)		
G-IJAG	Cessna 182T Skylane	18281683	07.11.05
	N2284F N J Ratcliffe (Borden, Sittingbourne)		15.11.19E
G-IJBB	Enstrom 480	5010	17.09.99
	G-LIVA, N900SA, G-PBTT, JA6169		
	R P Bateman Hurley Lodge, Westerham		22.11.18E
G-IJMC	Magni M16 Tandem Trainer	xxxx	10.06.98
	G-POSA, G-BVJM		
	R F G Moyle Tregolds Farm, St Merryn		25.11.09P
	Built by D Nash – project PFA G/12-1237 (NF 16.10.14)		
G-IJOE	Piper PA-28RT-201T Turbo Arrow IV	28R-8031178	14.08.90
	N8265X, N9599N		
	J H Bailey tr G-IJOE Group Sturgate		10.10.18E
G-IKAH	Slingsby T.51 Dart 17R	1483	28.04.08
	BGA 1262/BVE		
	K A Hale Sandhill Farm, Shrivenham *'361'*		29.08.14R
	(IE 14.05.15)		
G-IKAP	Cessna T303 Crusader	T30300182	04.03.99
	N63SA, D-IKAP, N9518C		
	Cancelled 07.05.13 by CAA		23.09.05
	Fowlmere *Stored 09.15*		
G-IKBP	Piper PA-28-161 Warrior II	28-8216132	16.07.90
	N81762 NWMAS Leasing Ltd Hawarden		10.10.18E

G-IKEA[M]	Cameron IKEA 120SS HAB	10562	14.06.04
	Cancelled 10.11.14 by CAA		08.05.11
	With British Balloon Museum & Library, Newbury		
G-IKES	Stoddard-Hamilton GlaStar	5763	17.08.05
	N8066A M Stow Byermoor Farm, Burnopfield		
	Built by J K Tofte (NF 26.04.16)		
G-IKEV	Avtech Jabiru UL-450	0547	29.06.04
	P J Findlay & S A Wilson Longside		04.04.18P
	Built by K J Bream – project PFA 274A-14075		
G-IKON	Van's RV-4	4478	22.02.06
	N C Spooner Great Oakley		01.05.18P
	Built by S Sampson – project PFA 181-14474		
G-IKOS	Cessna 550 Citation Bravo	550-0957	27.05.04
	N957PH, N51780 Fteron Ltd Bournemouth		09.06.14E
	Stored 09.18 (IE 27.05.15)		
G-IKRK	Europa Aviation Europa	202	16.04.02
	K R Kesterton Andrewsfield		22.08.19P
	Built by K R Kesterton – project PFA 247-12903;		
	tailwheel u/c		
G-IKRS	Comco Ikarus C42 FB UK	xxxx	01.08.01
	K J Warburton Cottage Farm, Norton Juxta		30.06.18P
	Built by P G Walton – project PFA 322-13719		
G-IKUS	Comco Ikarus C42 FB UK	xxxx	10.10.03
	R Wilkinson Hunsdon		
	Built by C I Law – project PFA 322-14130 (NF 16.08.17)		
G-ILBO	Rolladen-Schneider LS3-a	3458	19.09.07
	BGA 2639 J P Gilbert Wormingford '157'		04.05.18E
G-ILBT	Cessna 182T Skylane	18282016	11.01.13
	N678DA, N1713X		
	G E Gilbert Woods Farm, Whitlock's End		25.04.18E
G-ILDA	Supermarine 361 Spitfire T.IX	CBAF 10164	11.07.02
	G-BXHZ, SAAF xxxx, SM520		
	Boultbee Classic LLP Goodwood		19.07.19P
	Built by Castle Bromwich 1944 as Mk.HF.IXe;		
	fuselage converted by Airframe Assemblies to		
	Tr.9 standard 2009; as 'SM520:KJ-I' in RAF c/s;		
	operated by Boultbee Flight Academy		
G-ILEE	Colt 56A	2624	29.07.94
	B W Smith Billingshurst		07.05.18E
	Built by Thunder & Colt Ltd		
G-ILEW	Schempp-Hirth Arcus M	106	15.12.14
	Lleweni Parc Ltd Lleweni Parc 'LEW'		28.02.18E
G-ILHR	Cirrus SR22	3091	25.05.17
	T7-NTF, TC-NTF, N990CT L H Robinson Leeds East		
	(IE 04.10.17)		
G-ILIB	SZD-36A Cobra 15	W-667	06.01.09
	(BGA 5346), HB-1213		
	D W Poll (Leibnitz, Austria) 'PD'		05.04.18E
	Built by ZS 'Delta' Wroclaw		
G-ILLD	Robinson R44 Raven II	14297	
	25.03.19	SJH-ALL Plant Group Ltd	
	(Alconbury Weston, Huntingdon)		
G-ILLE	Boeing Stearman E75 Kaydet (PT-13D)	75-5028	07.03.90
	N68979, 42-16865, USN 60906		
	A C Anstalt Hohenems-Dornbirn, Austria		28.08.17E
	As '379' in USAAC c/s		
G-ILLY	Piper PA-28-181 Archer II	28-7690193	21.02.80
	SE-GND G M & R A Spiers		
	Green Meadows, Harpsden		19.12.93
	(NF 26.05.17)		
G-ILLZ	Europa Aviation Europa XS	405	29.04.15
	R S Palmer Sandown		31.08.18P
	Built by R S Palmer – project PFA 247-13550;		
	tricycle u/c		
G-ILPD	SIAI Marchetti SF.260C	714	04.01.12
	I-ALPD M Mignini (London SW7)		17.03.18E
G-ILRS	Comco Ikarus C42 FB UK	xxxx	19.06.02
	J J Oliver East Fortune		29.06.18P
	Built by L R Smith – project PFA 322-13927		
G-ILSE	Corby CJ-1 Starlet	xxxx	09.01.84
	S Stride Brine Pits Farm, Droitwich		03.04.18P
	Built by S Stride – project PFA 134-10818		
G-ILUA	Alpha R2160I	160AI-07007	22.05.07
	ZK-SXY A R Haynes Duxford		25.06.19E

G-ILYA	Agusta-Bell 206B-2 JetRanger II	8038	07.11.12
	G-MHMH, G-HOLZ, ZK-IBC, G-HOLZ, G-CDBT,		
	RSAF 1206 Aerospeed Ltd Manston Park		06.02.18E
	(NF 19.09.18)		
G-ILZZ	Piper PA-31 Turbo Navajo B	31-7401211	26.01.16
	N175CT, G-VICT, G-BBZI, N7590L		
	I Kazi & T D Nathan Biggin Hill		01.01.19E
G-IMAB	Europa Aviation Europa XS	331	01.02.00
	N J France Holly Meadow Farm, Bradley		06.09.18P
	Built by A H Brown – project PFA 247-13128;		
	monowheel u/c (NF 09.10.18)		
G-IMBI	QAC Quickie 1	484	07.10.02
	G-BWIT, N4482Z P Churcher Inverness		28.02.06P
	Built by D Fulper (NF 23.11.16)		
G-IMBJ	QAC Quickie	xxxx	14.05.18
	G-WAHL P Churcher (North Kessock, Inverness)		
	Built by A A M Wahlberg – project PFA 094-10619		
	(NF 14.05.18)		
G-IMBO	Robin DR.250/160 Capitaine	73	17.11.15
	D-ENVM, F-BNVM		
	Training & Leisure Consultants Ltd Headcorn		12.08.18E
	Built by Centre-Est Aéronautique		
G-IMCD	Van's RV-7	71015	14.04.04
	I G McDowell Ludham		05.04.18P
	Built by I G McDowell – project PFA 323-13965		
G-IMCH	Lindstrand LTL Series Special-Cube	089	08.03.19
	A M Holly Breadstone, Berkeley		
	(IE 08.03.19)		
G-IMEA	Beech 200 Super King Air	BB-302	01.11.06
	G-OWAX, N86Y, N300BW, N600CP		
	2 Excel Aviation Ltd Doncaster Sheffield		03.02.19E
G-IMEL	Rotary Air Force RAF 2000 GTX-SE	xxxx	30.01.09
	N A Smith Perth		08.07.16P
	Built by P F Murphy – project LAA G/13-1371 (IE 27.07.17)		
G-IMME	Zenair CH.701SP	7-0307	29.08.03
	T R Sinclair Lamb Holm Farm, Holm		06.05.18P
	Built by I J M Donnelly – project PFA 187-14080		
G-IMMI	Escapade Kid	EAL.KID.000	09.08.10
	R K W Moss & C Summerfield Manchester Barton		
	(SSDR microlight since 05.14) (IE 03.11.17)		
G-IMMY	Robinson R44 Clipper I	1890	01.07.08
	Eli Srl (Limbiate, Italy)		02.07.18E
G-IMNY	Reality Escapade 912(2)	JA.ESC.0022	25.05.04
	D S Bremner Little Down Farm, Milson		03.05.18P
	Built by D S Bremner – project BMAA/HB/358		
G-IMOK	HOAC HK 36R Super Dimona	36317	31.07.97
	I-NELI, OE-9352 A L Garfield Dunstable Downs		24.07.14E
	(IE 05.06.17)		
G-IMPS	Best Off Skyranger Nynja 912S(1)	10070047	02.09.10
	B J Killick Plaistows Farm, St Albans		12.04.18P
	Built by S J Brooks & B J Killick – project BMAA/HB/600		
G-IMPX	Rockwell Commander 112B	512	25.10.90
	N1304J G Valluzzi (Olbia, Italy)		30.06.18E
G-IMUP	Air Création Tanarg 912S(1)/iXess 15	FLT005	08.02.06
	C R Buckle Blackmoor Farm, Auburn		06.06.15P
	Built by P D Hill – project BMAA/HB/478		
	(Flylight kit FLT005 comprising trike s/n T05082		
	& wing s/n A05150-5145 (IE 05.07.17)		
G-INAS	Piper PA-28-181 Archer II	28-7790402	06.07.18
	G-BRNV, N2537Q		
	D N F & R Barrington-Bullock Hawarden		18.04.19E
G-INCA	Glaser-Dirks DG-400	4-199	22.01.87
	C Rau Aston Down '320'		04.05.18E
G-INCE	Best Off Skyranger 912(2)	SKR0302293	12.03.03
	A B Shayes Broadmarsh Farm, Great Ellingham		21.07.17P
	Built by N P Sleigh – project BMAA/HB/270		
G-INDC	Cessna T303 Crusader	T30300122	28.06.83
	G-BKFH, N4766C		
	J C M & W J Golden t/a Valco Marketing		
	Middle Chase Farm, Bowerchalke		29.07.19E
G-INDI	Pitts S-2C	6084	19.05.09
	N130PS L Coesens Geraardsbergen, Belgium		20.05.18E
	Built by Aviat Aircraft Inc		

G-INDX	Robinson R44 Clipper II	10491	20.10.04
	Toppesfield Ltd (Claydon, Ipswich)		10.08.19E
G-INES	Zenair CH.650B	65-10720	24.07.17
	N J Brownlow & P W Day Knapthorpe Lodge, Caunton		
	Built by N J Brownlow & P W Day		
	– project LAA 375-15490 (NF 24.07.17)		
G-INGA	Thunder Ax8-84	2149	16.06.92
	M L J Ritchie Addlestone, Weybridge		30.09.04A
	(NF 02.02.16)		
G-INGS	American Champion 8KCAB Super Decathlon		
		1063-2008	07.03.08
	The Leicestershire Aero Club Ltd Leicester		01.07.19E
G-INII	Pitts S-1	515H	23.04.09
	G-BTEF, N88PR C Davidson Sleap		12.07.12P
	Built by D R Brewer (IE 12.05.14)		
G-INJA	Comco Ikarus C42 FB UK	0302 6236	24.04.03
	M O'Donnell (Killeter, Castlederg)		10.05.19P
	Built by J W G Andrews – project PFA 322-14044		
G-INKO	Cessna 172R Skyhawk	17280928	02.05.17
	PH-STP, SE-LPB, N2459S		
	L Salvatore (Castrovillari, Italy)		10.06.17E
	(IE 21.06.17)		
G-INNI	Jodel D.112	540	30.08.94
	F-BHPU K Dermott (Hassocks)		14.08.19P
	Built by Société des Establissements Benjamin Wassmer		
G-INNY	Replica Plans SE.5A	xxxx	18.12.78
	J M Gammidge Sywell		24.10.18P
	Built by R M Ordish – project PFA 020-10439;		
	as 'F5459:Y' in RFC c/s		
G-INSR	Cameron N-90	4320	23.04.98
	P J Waller Wymondham 'Smith & Pinching'		24.09.10E
	(NF 07.01.16)		
G-INTS	Van's RV-4	1780	17.05.06
	H R Carey Shobdon		07.08.18P
	Built by N J F Campbell – project PFA 181-13069		
G-INTV	Aérospatiale AS.355F2 Ecureuil 2	5450	24.08.10
	G-JETU, VR-CET, JA6623		
	Arena Aviation Ltd Redhill		22.05.18E
G-INVN	Hawker Sea Fury T.20	41H-636070	25.07.18
	G-CHFP, N20MD, WG655, D-CACU, G-9-65, WG655		
	S Patrick Duxford		26.02.19P
	As 'WG655:910:GN' in RN c/s		
G-INYS	TLAC Sherwood Scout	SS 003	20.04.18
	S D Pain Rayne Hall Farm, Rayne		05.09.18P
	Built by S D Pain – project LAA 345-15538		
G-IOCJ	Piper PA-28R-200 Cherokee Arrow II	28R-7335148	20.08.18
	G-RONG, N16451 M J Jewers Rougham		21.02.19E
G-IOFR	Lindstrand LBL 105A	1041	01.03.05
	A I Attwood tr RAF Halton Hot Air Balloon Club		
	RAF Halton 'Royal Air Force'		19.06.18E
G-IOIA	III Sky Arrow 650 T	K134	20.03.03
	P G Ward tr G-IOIA Group White Waltham		12.04.18P
	Built by P J Lynch, N J C Ray & P G Ward		
	– project PFA 298-14008		
G-IOOI	Robin DR.400-160 Major	1700	31.05.85
	R P Jones & N B Mason Elstree		12.07.19E
G-IOOK	Agusta A109E Power	11692	05.02.15
	G-VIPE, EI-MSG Hundred Percent Aviation Ltd		
	Radway Grange, Radway		19.03.18E
G-IOOP	Christen Eagle II	RUPPERT 0001	07.03.07
	N414DE A P S Maynard Brighton City		01.11.18P
	Built by E J Ruppert		
G-IOOZ	Agusta A109S Grand	22090	19.03.09
	N109GR Castle Air Ltd Trebrown, Liskeard		21.03.14E
	Stored damaged (NF 19.11.15)		
G-IOPT	Cessna 182P	18261731	09.06.98
	N182EE, D-ECVM, N21585		
	Cancelled 23.09.14 as destroyed		09.08.13
	White Waltham *Stored 07.15*		
G-IORV	Van's RV-10	71481	26.03.07
	J E Howe (Mere, Warminster)		
	Built by A F S Caldecourt – project PFA 339-14610		
	(NF 19.07.17)		

G-IOSI	Jodel DR.1051 Sicile	526	06.10.80
	F-BLRS I Andrews & C Smart tr G-IOSI Group		
	Haverfordwest		16.07.19P
	Built by Centre-Est Aéronautique		
G-IOSL	Van's RV-9	90121	22.01.09
	G-CFIX, N211TX S Leach Bodmin		10.04.19P
G-IOSO	Jodel DR.1050 Ambassadeur	46	13.07.00
	OO-VDV, F-BJUE A E Jackson Podington		15.02.18P
	Built by Centre-Est Aéronautique		
G-IOVE	BRM Bristell NG5 Speed Wing	368	14.03.19
	S D Austen (Torpoint)		
	Built S D Austen – project LAA 385-15556 (NF 14.03.19)		
G-IOWE	Europa Aviation Europa XS	368	30.07.99
	P G & S J Jeffers Wycombe Air Park 'Silver Lady'		04.08.18P
	Built by P A Lowe – project PFA 247-13303; tricycle u/c		
G-IPAT	Avtech Jabiru SP-470	618	14.04.04
	G W A Mackenzie tr Fly Jabiru Scotland Perth		25.10.18P
	Built by M G Thatcher – project PFA 274B-14227		
G-IPAV	Piper PA-32R-301T Saratoga II TC	3257097	27.03.17
	LX-PAV, N9513N Tofana Aviation Ltd (Herne Bay)		20.10.17E
	(IE 13.11.17)		
G-IPAX	Cessna 560XL Citation Excel	560-5228	13.02.04
	EI-PAX Pacific Aviation Ltd Luton		09.10.18E
G-IPEN	Ultramagic M-90	90/134	19.02.15
	G Holtam Heage, Belper		
	'Holtham Kitchens & Bedrooms'		19.12.19E
G-IPEP	Beech 95-B55 Baron	TC-2259	10.12.09
	G-FABM, G-JOND, G-BMVC, N66456		
	M W Fitch Elstree		01.10.19E
G-IPGL	Agusta AW109SP Grand New	22258	15.05.18
	PK-ILS, I-PTFO IPGL Helicopters Ltd Biggin Hill		14.06.19E
	Operated by Castle Air Ltd		
G-IPIG	Cosmos Fly Away 01/Elan 550		
		E1-030202395/A201BL00110L	24.03.15
	87-ER R Frankham (Easton Maudit, Wellingborough)		
	Aka Powrachute Pegasus Cosmos Fly Away 01/		
	Mac Para Elan 550 built by C Andrieux; trike is		
	Robin Rialto replica built onto Pegasus Quasar		
	frame (IE 22.04.16)		
G-IPII	Steen Skybolt	JP1	20.04.17
	ZU-IEO J Buglass Sleap		16.10.18P
	Built by J Prokop (IE 03.12.18)		
G-IPJF	Robinson R44 Raven II	10514	23.09.11
	G-RGNT, G-DMCG		
	Specialist Group International Ltd (Dorking)		22.09.18E
G-IPKA	Alpi Pioneer 300	143	09.02.05
	M E Hughes Griffins Farm, Temple Bruer		26.07.18P
	Built by I P King – project PFA 330-14355		
G-IPLY	Cessna 550 Citation Bravo	550-0927	24.02.14
	G-OPEM, PH-DYE, (PH-CTU), N5061P		
	International Plywood (Aviation) Ltd Gloucestershire		06.06.18E
G-IPOD	Europa Aviation Europa XS	573	18.08.09
	G-CEBV J Wighton Andrewsfield		01.08.18P
	Built by S Vestuti – project PFA 247-14007; tricycle u/c		
G-IPSE	Airbus EC130 T2	8574	21.12.18
	G-CKYH Airbus Helicopters UK Ltd Oxford		28.08.19E
G-IPSI (2)	Grob G109B	6425	29.05.82
	G-BMLO S L Reed tr GIPSI Flying Group Usk		04.06.19E
G-IPSY	Rutan Vari-eze	1512	19.06.78
	(G-IPSI) Cancelled 06.08.09 as PWFU		08.07.09
	Wroughton *Built by R A Fairclough*		
	– project PFA 074-10284		
	In Science Museum store 2013		
G-IPUP	Beagle B.121 Pup Series 2	B121-036	17.07.95
	HB-NAC, G-35-036 T S Walker Cotswold '12'		29.01.18R
G-IRAF	Rotary Air Force RAF 2000 GTX-SE	xxxx	17.06.96
	Condor Aviation International Ltd		
	Birchwood Lodge, North Duffield		03.10.13P
	Built by C D Julian – project PFA G/13-1278;		
	stored 2016 (NF 28.09.15)		
G-IRAK	SOCATA TB-10 Tobago	1315	20.05.13
	F-GNHF, F-OGSE		
	IPGI Ltd Spilsted Farm, Sedlescombe		10.11.18E

Reg	Type	c/n	Date
G-IRAL	Thruster T600N 450	0053-T600N-083	24.04.03
	J Giraldez (Burgh Le Marsh, Skegness)		24.09.19P
	Official c/n '0035-T600N-083' is incorrect		
	– build date (05.03) indicates correct c/n		
G-IRAR	Van's RV-9	xxxx	26.02.07
	J Mapplethorpe Garston Farm, Marshfield		09.05.19P
	Built by J Mapplethorpe – project PFA 320-14106		
G-IRAY	Best Off Skyranger 912S(1)	SKRxxxx1056	05.07.16
	G R Breaden Derryogue, Kilkeel		07.04.18P
	Built by G R Breaden – project BMAA/HB/641		
G-IRED	Comco Ikarus C42 FB100 Bravo	1207-7210	30.08.12
	Deanland Flight Training Ltd Deanland		03.07.19P
	Assembled Red-Air UK		
G-IREN	SOCATA TB-20 Trinidad	2161	05.07.10
	M-ANIN, N882, F-OIMA K F Toumazos tr Chios Aeroclub		
	Chios Island National Airport, Greece		11.09.18E
G-IRIS	Gulfstream American AA-5B Tiger	AA5B-1184	14.12.87
	G-BIXU, N4533N H de Libouton		
	Bergerac-Dordogne Perigord, France		27.10.17E
G-IRJE	Diamond DA.62	62.111	25.01.19
	Gemstone Aviation Ltd Retford Gamston		
	(NF 25.01.19)		
G-IRJXᴹ	BAE Systems Avro 146-RJX100	E3378	24.05.00
	Cancelled 20.02.03 as WFU		
	With Runway Visitor Park, Manchester Airport		
G-IRLE	Schempp-Hirth Ventus cT	172/562	19.02.08
	BGA 3935/HGN D J Scholey Lasham *'D9'*		06.05.18E
G-IRLI	P&M Quik GTR	8622	22.06.12
	77-BMH, G-IRLI R Holness (Porthcawl)		29.06.19P
G-IRLY	Colt 90A	1620	28.12.89
	J A Viner North Muskham, Newark		26.11.18E
G-IRLZ	Lindstrand LBL 60X	1092	05.04.06
	A M Holly Breadstone, Berkeley *'Sloggi'*		27.08.16E
	(IE 07.10.17)		
G-IROB	SOCATA TB-10 Tobago	301	27.02.17
	EI-BOE, F-GDBL R Evans Welshpool		26.07.18E
G-IROJ	Magni M16C Tandem Trainer	16181144	16.01.18
	A G Jones Chiltern Park, Wallingford		
	(NF 16.01.18)		
G-IRON	Europa Aviation Europa XS	583	04.05.04
	J R Gardiner Bodmin		03.09.18P
	Built by T M Clark – project PFA 247-14235		
G-IROS	AutoGyro Calidus	10 052	30.06.10
	M P Kemp & W Perry (Bury St Edmunds)		21.06.18P
	Assembled Rotorsport UK as c/n RSUK/CALS/007		
G-IROX	Magni M24C Orion	24160394	03.04.17
	A J Roxburgh Popham		10.04.18P
G-IROY	Rotorway Exec 152	3525	24.02.98
	Cancelled 06.06.01 by CAA		
	Lochgelly, Fife Stored for sale 03.17		
G-IRPC	Cessna 182Q Skylane II	18266039	15.05.91
	G-BSKM, N559CT, N759JV		
	A T Jeans Chalk Pyt Farm, Broad Chalke		10.04.18E
G-IRPW	Europa Aviation Europa XS	617	04.11.08
	R P Wheelwright Sherburn-in-Elmet		22.08.18P
	Built by R P Wheelwright – project PFA 247-14495		
G-IRTY	Supermarine 361 Spitfire LF.IX	CBAF IX 970	26.09.16
	MJ271, R Netherlands AF 3W-8 & H-8, MJ271		
	Boultbee Flight Academy Ltd Duxford		
	On restoration 10.18 as 'MH424:H-53' (NF 26.09.16)		
G-IRYC	Schweizer 269C-1 *(300CBi)*	0194	08.03.05
	N86G Virage Helicopter Academy LLP Beccles		18.12.18E
G-ISAC	Isaacs Spitfire	027	07.01.15
	A James Haw Farm, Hampstead Norreys		19.03.19P
	Built by A James – project LAA 027-15134;		
	as 'TZ164:OI-A' in RAF c/s		
G-ISAR	Cessna 421C Golden Eagle	421C0848	29.07.11
	G-BHKJ, (N26596) Skycab Ltd Bournemouth		03.11.18E
G-ISAX	Piper PA-28-181 Archer III	2843453	28.06.01
	N5325G J Phelan & W Wallace		
	tr Spectrum Flying Group Belfast Int'l		23.11.18E
G-ISBD	Alpi Pioneer 300 Hawk	310	08.02.11
	B Davies Dunsfold		24.07.19P
	Built by B Davies – project LAA 330A-15043		
G-ISCD	Czech Sport Sportcruiser	10SC297	10.05.10
	P W Shepherd Cotswold		09.06.18W
G-ISDB	Piper PA-28-161 Cherokee Warrior II	28-7716074	19.02.96
	G-BWET, SX-ALX, D-EFFQ, N9612N		
	K Bartholomew (Marsh Gibbon, Bicester)		31.07.18E
G-ISDN	Boeing Stearman A75N1 Kaydet *(N2S-3)*	75-1263	06.02.95
	N4197X, XB-WOV, USN 3486		
	D R L Jones Oaksey Park		13.02.18E
	As '14' in USAAC c/s		
G-ISEH	Cessna 182R Skylane II	18267843	09.11.90
	G-BIWS, N6601N D Jaffa North Weald		03.12.16E
	Damaged beyond repair when blown over during		
	storm at North Weald 28.03.16; noted 07.18		
G-ISEL	Best Off Skyranger 912(2)	UK/368	07.11.03
	P A Robertson Coldharbour Farm, Willingham		04.06.19P
	Built by P A Robertson – project BMAA/HB/312		
G-ISEW	P&M Quik GT450	8170	20.04.06
	R & T Raffle Park Hall Farm, Mapperley		14.08.18P
G-ISFC	Piper PA-31 Turbo Navajo B	31-7300970	23.03.94
	G-BNEF, N7574L Cancelled 25.03.13 as destroyed		25.05.08
	Irthlingborough Fuselage in scrapyard 06.14,		
	wings at Little Staughton		
G-ISHA	Piper PA-28-161 Warrior III	2842211	21.07.04
	N3092D Upperstack Ltd t/a LAC Flying School		
	Manchester Barton		15.01.19E
G-ISII	Pitts S-2S	3000	09.11.18
	VH-VHP(4), ZK-WIZ, N31492 T H Castle Sibbertoft		
	Built by Aerotek Inc (NF 09.11.18)		
G-ISKA	WSK-PZL TS-11 Iskra	1H1018	11.05.00
	Polish AF 1018 Cancelled 24.05.10 as PWFU		
	Bruntingthorpe Noted in Polish AF c/s as '1018' 10.16		
G-ISLC	British Aerospace Jetstream 3202	873	02.03.06
	N873JX, N873AE, G-31-873		
	Oberbank Leasing GmbH Linz, Austria		24.05.15E
	(IE 09.06.15)		
G-ISLF	Avions Transport ATR 42-500	546	19.05.11
	D-BMMM, F-WWLE Elix Assets 12 Ltd Luqa, Malta		26.04.19E
G-ISLGᴹ	Avions Transport ATR 42-320	019	13.02.13
	F-HAAV, F-WKVB, F-WQNE, OY-CIG, YU-ALL, VH-AQD,		
	F-WWEF Cancelled 03.08.16 as PWFU		04.12.16
	Fuselage only		
	With Bournemouth Aviation Museum, Bournemouth		
G-ISLH	Avions Transport ATR 42-320	173	31.07.13
	F-HEKF, F-WEKF, OK-VFI, F-WQNE, D-BHHH, F-WWED		
	Blue Islands Ltd Jersey		19.12.19E
G-ISLK	Avions Transport ATR 72-212A	634	06.10.16
	2-XAJQ, XY-AJQ, I-ADLS, F-WQMB, F-WWLL		
	Blue Islands Ltd Jersey		05.10.19E
G-ISLL	Avions Transport ATR 72-212A	696	20.01.17
	OY-YAT, F-OHFS, F-WWES Blue Islands Ltd Jersey		26.04.19E
G-ISLM	Avions Transport ATR 72-212A	762	12.10.18
	M-ABKN, VT-APB, M-IBAH, VT-KAM, F-WWEZ		
	Blue Islands Ltd Jersey		
	Noted 10.18		
G-ISLN	Avions Transport ATR 72-212A	884	22.02.19
	OY-YCT, 2-XAVT, 4X-AVT, F-WWEN		
	Blue Islands Ltd Jersey		24.01.20E
G-ISLY	Cessna 172S Skyhawk SP	172S8152	08.12.15
	G-IZZS, N952KM		
	R Macfarlane t/a RMACF Aviation Glasgow		17.01.18E
	Operated by Leading Edge Flight Training		
G-ISMA	Van's RV-7	xxxx	07.12.07
	G-STAF D King (Loughton)		19.06.19P
	Initially built A F Stafford & completed S Marriott		
	– project PFA 323-13875		
G-ISMO	Robinson R22 Beta	0870	14.10.88
	OH-HOR, G-ISMO, N8214T (?)		
	Kuki Helicopter Sales Ltd Retford Gamston		31.10.19E
	Official p/i 'N8214T' is incorrect		
G-ISOB	Cameron O-31	12026	26.09.16
	C G Dobson Goring, Reading		21.09.17E
	(IE 17.10.17)		

G-ISPH	Bell 206B-3 JetRanger III	4259	03.03.06
	G-OPJM, D-HABA, C-FOFG		
	Blades Aviation (UK) LLP Costock Heliport		26.04.18E
G-ISRV	Van's RV-7	71680	09.02.17
	I A Sweetland (Gartocharn, Alexandria)		
	Built by I A Sweetland – project LAA 323-15062		
	(NF 08.02.17)		
G-ISSG	de Havilland DHC-6-310 Twin Otter	572	04.04.13
	C-GOYX, TJ-ALL, 5N-AKY, (5B-CJN), 5N-AKY, PH-SAK,		
	C-GSKW Isles of Scilly Skybus Ltd Land's End		03.04.19E
G-ISZA	Pitts S-2A	2137	25.09.09
	G-HISS, G-BLVU, SE-GTX		
	T J B Dugan White Waltham		07.11.18E
	Built by Aerotek Inc		
G-ITAF	SIAI Marchetti SF.260AM	40-013	10.12.08
	Ital.AF MM54532 N A Whatling Spanhoe		17.04.19P
	Italian AF c/s		
G-ITAR	Magni M16C Tandem Trainer	16127284	10.08.12
	J Hawkes tr Hartis Autogyro Syndicate		
	Chiltern Park, Wallingford		21.09.18P
G-ITBT	Alpi Pioneer 300 Hawk	213	19.06.07
	F Paolini Usk		31.07.18P
	Built by F Paolini – project PFA 330A-14641		
G-ITII	Pitts S-2A	2223	05.07.95
	I-VLAT Hurricane Restoration Ltd Audley End		12.07.19E
	Built by Aerotek Inc		
G-ITOI	Cameron N-90	4785	14.01.00
	A E Lusty Bourne 'One to One'		01.12.13E
	(NF 16.08.17)		
G-ITOR	Robinson R44 Raven II	11498	07.03.14
	EI-UNI Tubrid Ltd Denham		25.02.19E
G-ITPH	Robinson R44 Clipper II	11909	17.09.07
	Helicopter Services Europe Ltd (Rome, Italy)		25.08.17E
G-ITST	Europa Aviation Europa	xxxx	16.06.17
	I Tucker (Horsham)		
	Built by R Anrews, B Nortje & I Tucker – project		
	PFA 247-12821 (IE 04.10.18)		
G-ITVM	Lindstrand LBL 105A	1017	08.11.04
	I J Wadey tr Elmer Balloon Team		
	Storrington, Pulborough 'Meridian Tonight'		02.05.19E
G-ITWB	de Havilland DHC-1 Chipmunk 22	48	16.09.04
	CS-AZO, Port AF 1358 I T Whitaker-Bethel Elmsett		15.09.17P
	Built by OGMA		
G-IUII	Aerostar Yakovlev Yak-52	9111604	28.11.06
	RA-1281K, RA-01281, DOSAAF 69 (Grey)		
	Cosmos Technology Ltd Dunkeswell		
	'36' (Red) & '9111604'		01.08.18P
G-IVAL	Mudry CAP 10B	307	08.04.03
	H Thomas Namur-Suarlee, Belgium '307'		15.01.18E
	Built by Constructions Aeronautiques de Bourgogne		
G-IVAR	Yakovlev Yak-50	791504	24.02.89
	D-EIVI, (N5219K), DDR-WQT, DM-WQT		
	A H Soper Jenkin's Farm, Navestock		10.11.17P
G-IVEN	Robinson R44 Raven II	10442	28.07.04
	OKR Group Dublin Weston, RoI		13.09.16E
	(IE 21.04.17)		
G-IVER	Europa Aviation Europa XS	486	14.08.00
	I Phillips Lydd		27.06.18P
	Built by I Phillips – project PFA 247-13632; tricycle u/c		
G-IVES	Europa Aviation Europa	234	18.02.11
	G-JOST I Wyatt Solent		19.09.19P
	Built by J A Austin & A V Orchard		
	– project PFA 247-12915; tricycle u/c		
G-IVET	Europa Aviation Europa	020	23.05.97
	K J Fraser Landmead Farm, Garford		11.01.18P
	Built by K J Fraser – project PFA 247-12511		
G-IVII	Van's RV-7	71635	31.08.04
	M A N Newall Sherburn-in-Elmet		31.07.18P
	Built by M A N Newall – project PFA 323-14222		
G-IVIP	Agusta A109E Power	11208	03.09.13
	G-VIRU, EI-HHH, D-HPWR Castle Air Ltd Lasham		24.10.18E
	Operated by Altas Helicopters		

G-IVOR	Aeronca 11AC Chief	11AC-1035	18.06.82
	EI-BKB, G-IVOR, EI-BKB, N9397E, NC9397E		
	P R White tr South Western Aeronca Group Bodmin		26.07.18P
G-IWFC	Agusta AW109SP Grand New	22331	20.05.15
	HB-ZCR VLL Ltd t/a GB Helicopters		
	Blackshaw Heys Farm, Mobberley		10.03.19E
G-IWIN	Raj Hamsa X'Air Hawk	1097	11.06.07
	C G & M G Chambers (Piddington, Wolverhampton)		22.05.18P
	Built by R Wooldridge – project PFA 340-14679		
G-IWIZ	Flylight Dragonfly/Aeros Discus 15T	008	03.09.08
	I White Northiam, Rye		
	(SSDR microlight since 05.14) (IE 12.05.15)		
G-IWON	Cameron V-90	2504	17.02.92
	G-BTCV D P P Jenkinson Long Marston, Tring		
	'21 Cameron Balloons'		02.11.19E
G-IXII	Christen Eagle II	T0001	09.01.03
	G-BPZI, N48BB		
	I K G Mitchell tr Eagle II Group Halesland		12.04.16P
	Built by R Eicher & J Trent (NF 04.07.17)		
G-IXXI	Schleicher ASW 27-18E (ASG 29E)	29543	15.04.08
	BGA 5318		
	G P Stingemore Husbands Bosworth '10'		07.04.18E
G-IXXY	Ace Aviation Magic/Cyclone	xxxx	13.01.15
	L Hogan Balgrummo Steading, Bonnybank		
	Assembled P&M Aviation Ltd; trike s/n not known		
	& wing c/n AC-166 (IE 16.04.15)		
G-IYRO	Rotary Air Force RAF 2000 GTX-SE	'H2-96-7-216'	20.06.12
	G-BXDD G Golding Enstone		02.08.18P
	Built by R M Savage – project PFA G/13-1284		
G-IZIT	Rans S-6-116 Coyote II	xxxx	07.03.96
	D J Flower Baxby Manor, Husthwaite		05.04.18P
	Built by D A Crompton – project PFA 204A-12965		
	original kit no 0695.841 rebuilt & used in G-MWUN;		
	unknown kit fitted 1999; tricycle u/c		
G-IZOB	Eurocopter EC120B Colibri	1286	08.08.13
	SP-GKK, VH-JAS, VH-AVM		
	Beechview Developments Ltd Newtownards		14.11.18E
G-IZRV	Van's RV-12	120751	02.02.18
	H W Hall & D J Mountain North Weald		
	Built by H W Hall & D J Mountain		
	– project LAA 363-15496 (NF 05.02.18)		
G-IZZI	Cessna T182T Turbo Skylane	T18208100	19.03.02
	N51197 W E Davis Gloucestershire		05.08.18E
G-IZZT	Cirrus SR22T	1714	04.06.18
	N714LD H G Dilloway (Spaxton, Bridgwater)		10.06.19E
G-IZZZ	American Champion 8KCAB Super Decathlon	939-2003	29.01.04
	Leased Flight Ltd Brighton City		08.07.18E

G-JAAA – G-JZZZ

G-JAAB	Avtech Jabiru UL-D	655	28.03.06
	I A Smith (Weldon, Corby)		18.05.18P
G-JABA	Avtech Jabiru SK	xxxx	14.12.99
	Cancelled 13.04.11 as TWFU		21.09.10
	Wisbech		
	Built by A P Gornall – project PFA 274-13297		
	Fuselage only for sale 10.15		
G-JABB	Avtech Jabiru UL-450	0328	27.04.00
	R J Sutherland Ludham		22.05.18P
	Built by D J Royce – project PFA 274A-13555		
G-JABE	Avtech Jabiru UL-D	0657	09.10.06
	G-CDZX Rochester Microlights Ltd		
	Damyns Hall, Upminster		19.09.18P
G-JABI	Avtech Jabiru J400	124	03.10.03
	K & M A Payne Northorpe Fen		25.06.18P
	Built by R A Shaw – project PFA 325-14098		
G-JABJ	Avtech Jabiru J400	J126	17.11.03
	R J Bost tr South Essex Flying Group Stow Maries		10.09.18P
	Built by P G Leonard – project PFA 325-14126		
G-JABO	WAR Focke-Wulf FW190-A3 Replica	xxxx	23.08.01
	Cancelled 19.07.07 by CAA		
	Nutts Corner, Co Antrim Built by S P Taylor		
	– project PFA 081-11786; on rebuild 10.17		

G-JABS	Avtech Jabiru UL-450	464	27.06.02
	P E Todd tr Jabiru Flyer Group		
	Stonefield Park, Chilbolton		08.06.18P
	Built by I R Cook & P E Todd – project PFA 274A-13704		

G-JABU	Avtech Jabiru J430	284	09.01.06
	S D Miller Bourn		13.11.18P
	Built by R J Chapman – project PFA 336-14515		

G-JABY	Avtech Jabiru SPL-450	0413	02.02.01
	D R Watson Leicester		19.07.19P
	Built by J T Grant – project PFA 274A-13672		

G-JABZ	Avtech Jabiru UL-450	0622	03.05.05
	T W Stewart tr G-JABZ Group Eshott		18.04.18P
	Built by A C Barnes – project PFA 274A-14289		

G-JACA	Piper PA-28-161 Warrior II	2842139	28.02.02
	N5328Q The Pilot Centre Ltd Denham		22.05.18E

G-JACB	Piper PA-28-181 Archer III	2843278	23.07.02
	G-PNNI, N41651 P R Coe Jersey		10.11.18E

G-JACH	Piper PA-28-181 Archer III	2843585	19.01.09
	G-IDPH, N3054D		
	Alderney Flying Training Ltd Alderney		16.03.18E

G-JACL	Tecnam P2010	066	13.06.18
	The Channel Islands Aero Club (Jersey) Ltd Jersey		09.08.19E

G-JACM	Tecnam P2008-JC	1111	07.08.18
	I-PDVE, G-JACM, I-PDVE		
	The Channel Islands Aero Club (Jersey) Ltd Jersey		06.09.19E

G-JACN	Tecnam P2008-JC	1112	07.08.18
	I-PDVF		
	The Channel Islands Aero Club (Jersey) Ltd Jersey		13.09.19E

G-JACO	Avtech Jabiru UL	0215	14.04.99
	J R Morrison Enniskillen		10.10.19P
	Built by S Jackson – project PFA 274A-13371		

G-JACS	Piper PA-28-181 Archer III	2843078	15.04.97
	N9287J, (G-JACS) Modern Air (UK) Ltd Fowlmere		18.01.19E

G-JADJ	Piper PA-28-181 Archer III	2843009	27.07.99
	N49TP, N92552		
	P D Wheelen Wolverhampton Halfpenny Green		09.06.18E
	Originally intended as c/n 2890240		

G-JADW	Comco Ikarus C42 FB80	0810-7013	03.12.08
	D M Pearson tr G-JADW Group		
	Chiltern Park, Wallingford		17.01.18P
	Assembled Aerosport Ltd		

G-JAEE	Van's RV-6A	25799	16.09.02
	J A E Edser Wickenby		20.05.18P
	Built by J A E Edser – project PFA 181A-13571		

G-JAES	Bell 206B-2 JetRanger II	1513	13.01.04
	G-STOX, G-BNIR, N59615		
	Associazione Croce Italia Area Flegrea (Quarto, Italy)	02.08.18E

G-JAFS	Piper PA-32R-301 Saratoga II HP	3246235	23.07.15
	OY-OMG, G-VFMC, N31208		
	Countrywide Freight Group Ltd t/a Countrywide Aviation		
	Sandtoft		12.04.18E

G-JAFT	Diamond DA.42 Twin Star	42.288	12.08.11
	JY-YYY (1), OE-UDS, OE-VPI		
	Atlantic Flight Training Ltd Cork, RoI		30.10.19E

G-JAGA	Embraer EMB-505 Phenom 300	50500134	20.02.13
	PR-PAE London Executive Aviation Ltd		
	London Stansted		27.02.18E

G-JAGS	Reims/Cessna FRA150L Aerobat	FRA1500167	24.10.01
	G-BAUY, N10633		
	M A Palmer tr RAF Marham Aero Club RAF Marham	20.04.18E

G-JAIR	Mainair Blade	1249-0500-7-W1042	11.07.00
	G Spittlehouse Finmere *'Joe Loughran'*		22.03.16P

G-JAJA	Robinson R44 Raven II	11691	18.04.07
	J D Richardson Earls Colne		22.12.17E

G-JAJB	Grumman American AA-5A Cheetah	AA5A-0590	30.04.02
	OY-CJE, N26434 D M Hadlow tr D Hadlow &		
	Partners Flying Group Trenchard Lines, Upavon		21.08.18E

G-JAJK	Piper PA-31-350 Chieftain	31-8152014	16.12.99
	G-OLDB, OY-SKY, G-DIXI, N40717		
	Blue Sky Investments Ltd Belfast Int'l		21.07.18E

G-JAJP	Avtech Jabiru UL-450	359	01.12.00
	J Anderson Park Farm, Eaton Bray		01.04.18P
	Built by J W E Pearson – project PFA 274A-13627		

G-JAKF	Robinson R44 Raven II	10866	23.09.05
	J G Froggatt (Stockport)		15.01.18E

G-JAKS	Piper PA-28-160 Cherokee	28-339	02.07.99
	G-ARVS J L & M Harper Stapleford		31.01.18E

G-JAKX	Cameron Z-69	12048	12.04.17
	J A Hibberd Krimpen aan den IJssel, Netherlands	09.04.18E

G-JALS	Cessna 560XL Citation XLS+	560-6024	11.08.17
	M-AKAL, SP-ARK, N50321		
	Air Charter Scotland Ltd Luton		10.08.18E

G-JAME	Zenair CH.601UL Zodiac	6-9586	14.01.05
	G-CDFZ J J Damp Bagby		29.06.18P
	Built by N Barnes, J P Harris, B & K Yoxall		
	– project PFA 162A-14279; tricycle u/c		

G-JAMP	Piper PA-28-151 Cherokee Warrior	28-7515026	03.04.95
	G-BRJU, N44762		
	Lapwing Flying Group Ltd Denham		26.01.18E

G-JAMY	Europa Aviation Europa XS	449	05.01.01
	J P Sharp Garston Farm, Marshfield		20.11.18P
	Built by J P Sharp – project PFA 247-13557		

G-JAMZ	P&M QuikR	8578	30.03.11
	S Cuthbertson Old Park Farm, Margam		30.05.18P

G-JANA	Piper PA-28-181 Archer II	28-7990483	12.02.87
	N2838X S Hoo-Hing Elstree		28.08.19E

G-JANF	BRM Bristell NG5 Speed Wing	137	10.03.16
	B Frederiks tr G-JANF Group Full Sutton		21.08.18P
	Built by B Frederiks – project LAA 385-15333		

G-JANI	Robinson R44 Astro	0110	21.07.95
	N7027W, EI-CUI, G-JANI, D-HIMM (2)		
	JT Helicopters Ltd (Thruxton)		03.03.18E

G-JANN	Piper PA-34-220T Seneca III	3433133	23.06.89
	N9154W D J Whitcombe St Athan		04.02.20E

G-JANS	Reims FR172J Rocket	FR17200414	11.08.78
	PH-GJO, D-EGJO R G & S F Scott Redhill		07.09.19E

G-JANT	Piper PA-28-181 Archer II	28-8390075	23.02.87
	N4297J Janair Aviation Ltd Denham		10.05.18E
	Originally built as c/n 28-8290117 (N81992)		
	for YV-2234P: not delivered &		
	re-manufactured as 28-8390075		

G-JAOC	Best Off Skyranger Swift 912S(1)	SKR0812930	02.03.09
	R L Domiczew Northrepps		01.10.19P
	Built by A C Bell – project BMAA/HB/589		

G-JAPK	Grob G103A Twin II Acro	3691-K-42	21.11.07
	BGA 4990/KCS, D-6940, OH-645		
	W R Longstaff tr Cairngorm Gliding Club		
	Feshiebridge *'PK' & 'Ikarus'*		31.03.18E

G-JARM	Robinson R44 Raven	1620	09.11.09
	EI-LOC J Armstrong Durham Tees Valley		02.11.18E

G-JASE	Piper PA-28-161 Warrior II	28-8216056	13.02.91
	N8461R Mid-Anglia Flight Centre Ltd		
	t/a Mid-Anglia School of Flying Cambridge		12.02.19E

G-JASS	Beech B200 Super King Air	BB-983	23.06.08
	N983AJ, D-ISAZ, N983EB, D-ILTO, N87FE, N6JL,		
	(D-IKFC), N6JE, N6JL		
	Atlantic Bridge Aviation Ltd Lydd		22.06.19E
	Operated by Lyddair Ltd		

G-JAVO	Piper PA-28-161 Warrior II	28-8016130	17.09.97
	G-BSXW, N8119S		
	Victor Oscar Ltd Wellesbourne Mountford		10.09.18E

G-JAWC	Cyclone Pegasus Quantum 15-912	7692	21.07.00
	M J Flower Rochester		26.05.18P

G-JAWZ	Pitts S-1S	449	06.11.95
	A R Harding (Milden, Ipswich)		13.07.17P
	Built by S Howes – project PFA 009-12846		
	(IE 08.02.19)		

G-JAXS	Avtech Jabiru UL-450	0307	10.12.99
	S R Hughes Welshpool		12.02.18P
	Built by C A Palmer – project PFA 274A-13548		

G-JAYI	Auster 5J1 Autocrat	2030	05.02.93
	OY-ALU, D-EGYK, OO-ABF		
	R Greatrex Colthrop Manor Farm, Thatcham		23.02.18P

G-JAYK	Robinson R44 Raven II	10147	05.09.14
	G-MACU, G-SEFI, N75271		
	HQ Aviation Ltd Dunkeswell		06.11.15E
	(IE 06.10.18)		

G-JAYS	Best Off Skyranger 912S(1)	SKR0408509	14.12.04	
	K O'Connor & T L Whitcombe			
	Chiltern Park, Wallingford		30.07.18P	
	Built by J Williams – project BMAA/HB/433			
G-JAYZ	CZAW Sportcruiser	08SC154	16.05.08	
	J Williams Forwood Farm, Treswell		15.06.18P	
	Built by J Williams – project PFA 338-14670			
	(Quick-build kit 4131)			
G-JBAN	P&M Quik GT450	8662	16.09.13	
	A Nourse Ince		20.09.18P	
G-JBAS	Neico Lancair 200	xxxx	21.11.03	
	A Slater Isle of Man		11.05.11P	
	Built by B A Slater – project PFA 191-11465			
	(NF 18.08.16)			
G-JBAV	Evektor EV-97 Eurostar SL	2014-4215	06.03.15	
	R D Masters Old Warden		03.03.19P	
	Assembled Light Sport Aviation Ltd			
G-JBBB	Eurocopter EC120B Colibri	1380	11.10.16	
	M-GOLD, I-ZIAC, F-WQUJ, F-WQDH			
	Bartram Land Ltd Crooked Billet Farm, Little Gransden		20.10.18E	
G-JBBZ	Eurocopter AS.350B3 Ecureuil	3580	13.01.03	
	F-WQDE, F-WQPV			
	D Donnelly (Bellaghy, Magherafelt)		19.03.18E	
G-JBCB	Agusta A109E Power	11168	16.04.14	
	G-PLPL, G-TMWC, VH-BQR, VH-FOX			
	J P Ball t/a SDP Developers Biggin Hill		29.04.19E	
G-JBDB	Agusta-Bell 206B-2 JetRanger II	8238	11.04.96	
	G-OOPS, G-BNRD, Oman AF 602			
	Aerospeed Ltd Manston Park		04.06.14E	
	Stored 09.18 (NF 06.10.15)			
G-JBDH	Robin DR.400-180 Régent	1901	17.03.89	
	W A Clark Netherthorpe		31.08.18E	
G-JBEN	Mainair Blade 912	1337-0802-7-W1132	13.09.02	
	G J Bentley (Cymau, Wrexham)		04.05.07P	
	(NF 05.09.18)			
G-JBIZ	Cessna 550 Citation II	550-0073	07.11.05	
	VP-CTJ, F-GBTL, N4621G			
	Cancelled 12.07.17 as PWFU		08.12.15	
	Ljungbyhed, Sweden			
	Instructional use, Flygteknikcenter 07.17			
G-JBJB	Colt 69A HAB	1274	26.07.88	
	Cancelled 26.03.09 by CAA		19.05.02	
	Not Known *Inflated Pidley 05.16*			
G-JBKA	Robinson R44 Raven	1175	12.03.02	
	J G Harrison Sherburn-in-Elmet		28.09.18E	
G-JBLL	British Aerospace BAe 125 Series 800B	258222	08.11.18	
	G-VIPI, G-5-745			
	Sovereign Business Jets Ltd Biggin Hill		01.11.18E	
G-JBLZ	Cessna 550 Citation Bravo	550-1018	09.11.09	
	OO-IIG, (D-CEFM), SU-HEC, N5259Y			
	Executive Aviation Services Ltd Gloucestershire		19.10.18E	
G-JBOB	Schempp-Hirth Discus-2c FES	25	17.05.18	
	(BGA 5949) O J Bosanko & J M Robson			
	Gransden Lodge *'JO'*			
	(IE 17.05.18)			
G-JBRD	Mooney M.20K Mooney 252 TSE	25-1001	11.02.16	
	PH-VDS, N252JS, N251JS			
	R J Doughton Dunkeswell		17.05.18E	
G-JBRE	AutoGyro MT-03	07 057	23.07.07	
	P A Remfry Draycott		14.09.18P	
	Assembled Rotorsport UK as c/n RSUK/MT-03/016			
G-JBRS	Van's RV-8	81083	06.02.09	
	C Jobling RAF Waddington		31.08.18P	
	Built by C Jobling – project PFA 303-14212			
G-JBSP	Avtech Jabiru SP-470	0289	12.10.99	
	M D Beeby, C K & C R James Ludham		03.08.19P	
	Built by C R James – project PFA 274B-13486			
G-JBTR	Van's RV-8	xxxx	18.09.06	
	H R Mitchell & D Pake tr Double Whisky Flying Group			
	(Tranent)		07.08.18P	
	Built by R A Ellis – project PFA 303-14562;			
	crashed Perth 23.06.18			
G-JBUZ	Robin DR.400-180R Remorqueur	1158	02.06.05	
	OE-DNW D L Saywell Pocklington		27.07.18E	

G-JBVP	Aeropro EuroFOX 3K	52517	07.11.17	
	B J Partridge & J A Valentine Bourn		08.10.18P	
	Built by Ascent Industries Ltd; tricycle u/c			
G-JCIH	Van's RV-7A	72123	25.07.14	
	D F Chamberlain & M A Hughes Haverfordwest		25.08.18P	
	Built by M P Chamberlain & M A Hughes			
	– project PFA 323-14365			
G-JCJC	Colt Flying Jeans	1747	08.06.90	
	SE-ZHS, G-JCJC Magical Adventures Ltd			
	West Bloomfield, MI, USA *'JC Jeans'*		27.09.09E	
	(NF 03.06.15)			
G-JCKT	Stemme S 10-VT	11-004	08.04.98	
	D-KSTE M B Jefferyes & J C Taylor Portmoak		24.09.17E	
G-JCMW	Rand Robinson KR-2	xxxx	03.02.99	
	Cancelled 01.12.16 by CAA			
	Newcastle, ROI *Built by M Wildish*			
	– project PFA 129-11064; stored 08.18			
G-JCOP	Eurocopter AS.350B3 Ecureuil	4345	08.12.07	
	Optimum Ltd Broughton Hall, Eccleshall		03.05.18E	
G-JCUB	Piper PA-18-135 Super Cub (*L-21B-PI*)	18-3630	21.01.82	
	PH-VCH, R Netherlands AF R-103 , 54-2331			
	S Bennett & N Cummins tr The Vintage Aircraft			
	Flying Group Dublin Weston, RoI			
	Fuselage No.18-3630 (IE 23.08.18)			
G-JCWM	Robinson R44 Raven II	11860	17.09.07	
	M L J Goff Elmham Lodge, North Elmham		11.10.18E	
G-JCWS	Reality Escapade 912(2)	JA.ESC.0166	03.08.12	
	D W Allen Hunsdon		25.04.19P	
	Built by W P Seward – project BMAA/HB/606;			
	tailwheel u/c			
G-JDBC	Piper PA-34-200T Seneca II	34-7570150	09.10.02	
	G-BDEF, N33695 Bristol Flying Club Ltd Bristol		26.11.18E	
G-JDEL	Jodel D.150 Mascaret	112	19.09.95	
	G-JDLI K F & R Richardson Wellesbourne Mountford			
	Built by K F Richardson – project PFA 151-11276			
	using SAB plans (IE 22.09.15)			
G-JDOG	Cessna 305C Bird Dog (*O-1E*)	24541	13.02.15	
	N134TT, F-GFVE, F-WFVE, French Army			
	BC Arrow Ltd Hawarden		26.08.17E	
	As '24541:BMG' in French Army c/s			
G-JDPB	Piper PA-28R-201T Turbo Arrow III	28R-7803024	22.09.08	
	G-DNCS, N47841 BC Arrow Ltd Hawarden		30.11.18E	
	Official type data 'PA-28R-201T Turbo Cherokee			
	Arrow III' is incorrect			
G-JDRD	Alpi Pioneer 300 Hawk	292	11.02.10	
	R D W Rippingale tr Anvilles Flying Group			
	Radley Farm, Hungerford		19.09.18P	
	Built by R J Doughton – project LAA 330A-14953			
G-JEAO[M]	British Aerospace BAe 146-100	E-1010	19.09.94	
	G-UKPC, C-GNVX, N802RW, G-5-512, PT-LEP,			
	G-BKXZ, PT-LEP Cancelled 02.11.09 as PWFU		04.06.05	
	Fuselage only: all-white c/s, no titles			
	With de Havilland Aircraft Museum, London Colney			
G-JEBS	Cessna 172S Skyhawk	172S11188	12.09.12	
	N9240B Integrated Hi-Tech Ltd White Waltham		27.09.18E	
G-JECK	Bombardier DHC-8-402Q	4113	27.01.06	
	C-FDRL Flybe Ltd Exeter Int'l		31.01.19E	
G-JECL	Bombardier DHC-8-402Q	4114	27.01.06	
	C-FDRN Flybe Ltd Exeter Int'l *'The George Best'*		05.02.19E	
G-JECM	Bombardier DHC-8-402Q	4118	06.04.06	
	C-FFCE Flybe Ltd Exeter Int'l		10.04.19E	
G-JECN	Bombardier DHC-8-402Q	4120	27.04.06	
	C-FFCL Flybe Ltd Exeter Int'l		02.05.19E	
G-JECO	Bombardier DHC-8-402Q	4126	04.07.06	
	C-FFPT Flybe Ltd Exeter Int'l		11.07.19E	
G-JECP	Bombardier DHC-8-402Q	4136	31.10.06	
	C-FHEL Flybe Ltd Exeter Int'l		04.09.19E	
G-JECR	Bombardier DHC-8-402Q	4139	12.12.06	
	C-FHQM Flybe Ltd Exeter Int'l *'Cancer Reaserch'*		18.11.19E	
G-JECX	Bombardier DHC-8-402Q	4155	13.06.07	
	C-FLKO Flybe Ltd Exeter Int'l		17.06.19E	
G-JECY	Bombardier DHC-8-402Q	4157	22.06.07	
	C-FLKV Flybe Ltd Exeter Int'l *'Spirit Of Liberum'*		27.06.19E	

Reg	Type	C/n	Date
G-JECZ	Bombardier DHC-8-402Q C-FMTY Flybe Ltd Exeter Int'l	4179	20.11.07 25.11.19E
G-JEDH	Robin DR.400-180 Régent J B Hoolahan Challock	2343	03.02.97 22.07.18E
G-JEDM	Bombardier DHC-8-402Q C-FGNP Flybe Ltd Exeter Int'l	4077	18.07.03 22.07.19E
G-JEDP	Bombardier DHC-8-402Q C-FDHO Flybe Ltd Exeter Int'l *'Spirit of Belfast'*	4085	30.01.04 04.03.19E
G-JEDR	Bombardier DHC-8-402Q C-FDHI Flybe Ltd Exeter Int'l *'Spirit of Dublin'*	4087	05.03.04 15.03.19E
G-JEDS	Andreasson BA-4B G-BEBT S B Jedburgh White Waltham *Built by A Horsfall (Hornet Aviation)* *– project PFA 038-10158*	xxxx	17.12.02 11.08.17P
G-JEDT	Bombardier DHC-8-402Q C-FDHP Flybe Ltd Exeter Int'l *'Spirit of Edinburgh'*	4088	19.03.04 23.03.19E
G-JEDU	Bombardier DHC-8-402Q C-GEMU Flybe Ltd Exeter Int'l *'Spirit of The Regions'*	4089	07.04.04 13.04.19E
G-JEDV	Bombardier DHC-8-402Q C-FDHX Flybe Ltd Exeter Int'l	4090	07.05.04 18.05.19E
G-JEDW	Bombardier DHC-8-402Q C-GFBW Flybe Ltd Exeter Int'l	4093	27.07.04 02.08.19E
G-JEEP	Evektor EV-97A Eurostar G-CBNK P A Brigstock tr G-JEEP Group Compton Abbas *Built by M R M Welch – project PFA 315-13888*	2002-1154	08.08.00 25.06.19P
G-JEFA	Robinson R44 Astro Simlot Ltd Denham	0710	07.02.00 22.04.18E
G-JEJE	Rotary Air Force RAF 2000 GTX-SE A F Smallacombe (Exbourne, Oakhampton) *Built by J W Erswell – project PFA G/13-1352;* *stored 05.13 (NF 05.04.16)*	H2-02-13-552	21.01.03 16.10.12P
G-JEJH	Jodel DR.1050 Ambassadeur F-GIGZ, OO-HGZ, F-BKIG R Slater tr Bredon Hill Flying Group Croft Farm, Defford *Built by Centre-Est Aéronautique*	301	29.10.08 23.06.18P
G-JEMI	Lindstrand LBL 90A S W K Smeeton Ely	1189	12.12.07 07.05.18E
G-JEMM	Jodel DR.1050 replica D W Garbe (Bath) *Built by D W Garbe – project LAA 304-13545*	xxxx	31.01.11 27.02.19P
G-JEMP	BRM Bristell NG5 Speed Wing W Precious Fenland *Built by W Precious – project LAA 385-15430* *(IE 13.02.19)*	236	26.10.16
G-JEMS	Ultramagic S-90 D J, J E & L V McDonald Maidstone	90/143	22.02.16 26.02.18E
G-JEMZ	Ultramagic H-31 J A Atkinson Dorchester	31/16	07.10.16 10.10.17E
G-JENA	Mooney M.20J Mooney 201 N1168D M Kolakovic tr Jena Air Force Jena-Schöngleina, Germany	24-1304	05.07.82 11.12.17E
G-JENK	Comco Ikarus C42 FB80 D Bowers & P Neve tr G-JENK Chatteris 2015 Chatteris *Assembled Aerosport Ltd*	0806-6978	01.08.08 20.04.18P
G-JERO	Europa Aviation Europa XS P Jenkinson & N Robshaw Rufforth East *Built by P Jenkinson & N Robshaw – project* *PFA 247-13691; tricycle u/c (NF 21.10.15)*	492	13.06.02 21.05.07P
G-JERR	Aeropro EuroFOX 3K J Robertson Hunsdon *Built by Ascent Industries Ltd; tricycle u/c*	50016	18.10.16 18.10.19P
G-JESS	Piper PA-28R-201T Turbo Arrow III G-REIS, N36689 R E Trawicki Denham *Official type data 'PA-28R-201T Turbo Cherokee* *Arrow III' is incorrect*	28R-7803334	18.09.95 05.12.18E
G-JETC	Cessna 550 Citation II G-JCFR, G-JETC, N68644 Cancelled 07.01.14 by CAA Thorpewood *Fuselage at Jet Art 01.18*	550-0282	28.05.81 01.04.10
G-JETH[M]	Hawker Sea Hawk FGA.6 'XE364', XE489 Cancelled 15.12.09 by CAA *As 'XE489:485' Built by Armstrong-Whitworth Aircraft* *Composite with A2511 ex WM983* *With Gatwick Aviation Museum, Charlwood*	AW-6385	10.08.83
G-JETM[M]	Gloster Meteor T.7 VZ838 Cancelled 15.12.09 by CAA *As 'VZ838' in RN/FRU c/s* *With Gatwick Aviation Museum, Charlwood*	xxxx	10.08.83
G-JETV	HpH Glasflügel 304 S Shark M C Rupasinha tr Sierra Hotel Shark Group Dunstable Downs *'SH'* *(IE 11.04.17)*	051-MS	29.10.15
G-JETX	Bell 206B-3 JetRanger III N3898L G-JETX Aviation LLP (Crockey Hill. Elvington)	3208	09.02.88 16.06.17E
G-JEWL	Van's RV-7 H A & J S Jewell tr G-JEWL Group Seething *Built by J S Jewell & A H S Smith* *– project PFA 323-14523*	72655	03.08.12 19.04.18P
G-JEZZ	Best Off Skyranger 912S(1) C Callicott Eshott *Built by J W Barwick – project BMAA/HB/368*	SKR0403456	06.04.04 29.10.18P
G-JFAN	P&M QuikR P R Brooker & G R Hall Harringe Court, Sellindge	8525	14.05.10 15.03.18P
G-JFDI	Aerospool Dynamic WT9 UK S Turnbull Broadmeadow Farm, Hereford *Assembled Yeoman Light Aircraft Co Ltd;* *official c/n recorded as 'DY192'*	DY192/2009	08.05.07 17.02.18P
G-JFER	Commander Aircraft Commander 114B G-HPSE, N6038V Helitrip Charter LLP Sleap	14638	07.10.08 13.01.18E
G-JFLO	Aerospool Dynamic WT9 UK J Flood Perth *Assembled Yeoman Light Aircraft Co Ltd;* *official c/n recorded as 'DY197'*	DY197/2007	06.11.07 27.06.17P
G-JFLY	Schleicher ASW 24 BGA 3357/FLY, BGA 3430/FPZ, BGA 3357/FLY Cambridge Gliding Club Ltd Gransden Lodge *'FLY'*	24012	18.01.10 10.04.18E
G-JFMK	Zenair CH.701SP J D Pearson Riglaw Farm, Uplawmoor *Built by J D Pearson – project PFA 187-14264*	345	24.09.04 10.08.18P
G-JFRV	Van's RV-7A J H Fisher Haverfordwest *Built by J H Fisher – project PFA 323-13851*	xxxx	08.10.03 26.05.18P
G-JFWI	Reims/Cessna F172N PH-DPA, PH-AXY R P van der Hoorn (Haslingfield)	F17201622	01.09.80 07.12.18E
G-JGAR	Robinson R44 Raven II G-DMRS Garratt Aviation Ltd Gloucestershire	10513	01.06.17 14.08.18E
G-JGBI	Bell 206L-4 LongRanger IV N91285, C-GBUP Dorbcrest Homes Ltd Lake House, Wrightlington	52257	13.08.01 11.12.17E
G-JGCA	Supermarine 361 Spitfire LF.IXe G-CCIX, G-BIXP, Israel DFAF 2046 (?), Czech.AF A-702: IV-2, TE517 P R Monk Biggin Hill *Built as Spitfire LF.IXe; p/i 'Israel DFAF 2046' is* *incorrect; for restoration 01.19 (NF 13.06.16)*	CBAF IX 558	31.03.09
G-JGMN	CASA 1-131E Jungmann Series 2000 Spanish AF E3B-407 P D Scandrett Rendcomb *Officially registered as c/n 2011 which became* *N65522: c/n 2104 plate reported in rear cockpit* *conflicts with G-BTDZ ex E3B-524*	2104?	17.04.91 10.09.16P
G-JGSI	Cyclone Pegasus Quantum 15-912 C P Dawes tr G-JGSI Group Darley Moor	7515	19.04.99 03.09.18P
G-JGXP	Bell 407GX OK-HRN, C-FVUP Helicompany Ltd Leeds East	54727	22.06.18 19.12.18E
G-JHAA	Cameron Z-90 B T Lewis Headington, Oxford *'S.M. Gauge Company'*	11647	15.06.12 24.03.19E
G-JHAC	Reims/Cessna FRA150L Aerobat EI-BRX, G-BACM, EI-BRX, G-BACM A A Whitewick (Milborne Port, Sherborne)	FRA1500160	16.09.02 29.05.19E
G-JHDD	Czech Sport Sportcruiser J W Hagley tr G-JHDD Syndicate Wycombe Air Park	09SC294	21.09.09 21.08.18W

G-JHEW	Robinson R22 Beta	0672	20.07.87
	N23677 Heli Air Ltd Wycombe Air Park		04.01.18E
	(IE 23.01.18)		
G-JHKP	Europa Aviation Europa XS	536	05.11.03
	J E S Turner Lower Upham Farm, Chiseldon		06.02.18P
	Built by J D Heykoop – project PFA 247-13828;		
	tailwheel u/c		
G-JHLE	P&M Quik GTR	8765	27.09.17
	A D Carr Finmere		11.09.18P
G-JHLP	Flylight Dragon Chaser	DA115	21.08.14
	N L Stammers Jersey		
	(IE 21.10.17)		
G-JHMP	SOCATA TB-20 Trinidad	858	13.12.17
	EC-JHM, CN-CDS D M Hook (Northolt)		
	(IE 13.12.17)		
G-JHNY	Cameron A-210	10487	17.03.04
	Bailey Balloons Ltd Pill, Bristol		02.11.18E
G-JHPC	Cessna 182T Skylane	18282125	18.08.08
	N63108 D Wood-Jenkins tr G-JHPC Group		
	(Cheltenham)		24.09.19E
G-JHYS	Europa Aviation Europa	314	06.03.01
	R A Harrowven tr G-JHYS Group Tibenham		25.08.18P
	Built by J D Boyce & G E Walker – project		
	PFA 247-13307; tricycle u/c		
G-JIBO	British Aerospace Jetstream 3102	711	05.05.09
	G-OJSA, OY-SVJ, G-BTYG, N415MX, G-31-711		
	K Beaumont St Athan		29.04.16E
	Stored 10.16 (NF 10.04.17)		
G-JIFI	Schempp-Hirth Duo Discus T	95/420	26.09.05
	BGA 5115/KHY, D-KOZZ		
	E J D Foxon tr 620 Syndicate Lasham '620'		13.02.19E
G-JIII	Stolp SA.300 Starduster Too	2-3-12	27.05.93
	N9043 J G McTaggart t/a VT10 Aero Company		
	Archerfield		15.06.17P
	Built by C S Johnson (IE 30.06.17)		
G-JIIL	Pitts S-2AE	20935	08.10.10
	N83798 A M Southwell Bicester		02.05.18P
	Built by J Eberle		
G-JIMB	Beagle B.121 Pup Series 1	B121-033	07.04.94
	G-AWWF P Fowler Enstone		10.05.12R
	(IE 02.08.17)		
G-JIMC	Van's RV-7	xxxx	02.12.11
	J Chapman (Poling, Arundel)		
	Built by J Chapman – project LAA 323-14996		
	(NF 19.10.15)		
G-JIMH	Reims/Cessna F152 II	F15201839	17.06.05
	G-SHAH, OH-IHA, SE-IHA		
	D J Howell Wolverhampton Halfpenny Green		07.08.18E
G-JIMM	Europa Aviation Europa XS	579	13.07.04
	J Cherry Eshott		
	Built by J Riley – project PFA 247-14071 (NF 03.02.17)		
G-JIMP	Messerschmitt Bf 109G-2	13605	08.08.11
	GAF 13605 M R Oliver (Hale, Altrincham)		
	(NF 24.10.16)		
G-JIMZ	Van's RV-4	2488	28.07.06
	N30GB N A Constantine (Atherton, Manchester)		27.03.19P
	Built by J Banks & J Giatrakis		
G-JINI	Cameron V-77	11025	27.07.07
	I R Warrington Hunstanton		06.09.11E
	(IE 08.01.16)		
G-JINX	Silence SA.180 Twister	26	14.10.11
	P M Wells Baileys Farm, Long Crendon		05.04.18P
	Built by P M Wells – project LAA 329-15102;		
	damaged in forced landing Abingdon 14.05.17		
G-JJAB	Avtech Jabiru J400	184	06.04.05
	K Ingebrigtsen Kjeller, Akershus, Norway		09.06.18P
	Built by K Ingebrigtsen – project PFA 325-14339		
G-JJAN	Piper PA-28-181 Archer II	2890007	28.03.88
	N9105Z Blueplane Ltd Blackbushe		07.06.18E
G-JJEN	Piper PA-28-181 Archer III	2843370	25.08.00
	N4190D K M R Jenkins Jersey		28.10.18E
G-JJFB	Eurocopter EC120B Colibri	1506	16.08.07
	J G Rhoden Walton Wood Farm, Thorpe Audlin		13.11.18E

G-JJGI	SNCAN Stampe SV.4A	199	13.11.18
	ZK-BBV, F-BBVM S L Goldspink Old Warden		
	(IE 13.11.18)		
G-JJSI	British Aerospace BAe 125 Series 800B	258058	16.04.04
	G-OMGG, N125JW, G-5-637, N125JW, VH-NMR,		
	ZK-EUI, (ZK-EUR), G-5-510		
	Cancelled 13.03.19 as PWFU		24.11.13
	Bradford *To be used as restaurant*		
G-JKAT	Robinson R22 Beta	0566	23.11.16
	G-WIZY, G-BMWX J N Kenwright Gloucestershire		07.12.18E
G-JKAY	Robinson R44 Raven II	11093	10.03.06
	Dydb Marketing Ltd (London N1)		28.03.18E
G-JKEE	Diamond DA.42NG Twin Star	42.N179	19.06.15
	Morgan Land Sea & Air LLP Wycombe Air Park		21.06.18E
G-JKEL	Van's RV-7	xxxx	18.04.11
	G-LNNE J D Kelsall Netherthorpe		
	'15' & 'Memories are better than dreams'		17.04.18P
	Built by J D Kelsall – project PFA 323-14170		
G-JKHT	Robinson R22 Beta II	2947	16.06.15
	G-OTUA, G-LHCA, N299FA		
	JK Helicopter Training Ltd Gloucestershire		21.06.18E
G-JKKK	Cessna 172S Skyhawk	172S10663	20.07.10
	JY-KKK, N1743C P Eaton Derby		26.01.18E
G-JKMH	Diamond DA.42 Twin Star	42.168	18.09.06
	Flying Time Ltd Brighton City		27.10.17E
	(IE 18.01.18)		
G-JKMI	Diamond DA.42 Twin Star	42.051	24.06.13
	G-KELV, (G-CTCH), OE-VPI		
	Flying Time Ltd Brighton City		29.06.18E
G-JKMJ	Diamond DA.42 Twin Star	42.141	23.06.06
	Skies Aviation Academy PC		
	(Peraia, Thessaloniki, Greece)		15.09.18E
G-JKPF	Cessna 172S Skyhawk SP	172S8294	10.05.18
	G-CEWK, N397SP Mike Victor Ltd Draycott		12.07.19E
G-JKRV	Schempp-Hirth Arcus T	27	30.09.11
	(BGA 5733) A M Sanders tr Syndicate 291		
	Long Mynd '291'		10.11.18E
G-JLAT	Evektor EV-97 Eurostar	2003-1199	14.05.03
	N E Watts Garton		15.11.18P
	Built by J Latimer – project PFA 315-14068		
G-JLCA	Piper PA-34-200T Seneca II	34-7870428	03.09.97
	G-BOKE, N21030		
	Premier Flight Training Ltd Norwich Int'l		20.02.19E
G-JLHS	Beech A36 Bonanza	E-2571	30.11.90
	N8046U I G Meredith Lydd		12.04.18E
G-JLIA	Cameron O-90	12012	15.08.16
	M Thompson Ripley		29.10.18E
G-JLIN	Piper PA-28-161 Cadet	2841013	24.08.05
	D-ENXI, N9153X J H Sandham		
	t/a JH Sandham Aviation Newcastle Int'l		07.03.19E
	Operated by North East Flight Academy		
G-JLRW	Beech 76 Duchess	ME-165	04.11.87
	N60206 Aviation South West Asset Leasing Ltd		
	Exeter Int'l		27.02.20E
	Operated by Airways Flight Training		
G-JLSP	Extra EA.300/LC	LC038	23.01.15
	J M Lynch & S A Perkes North Weald		14.03.18E
G-JMAA	Boeing 757-3CQ	32241	24.04.01
	Thomas Cook Airlines Ltd Manchester		22.04.19E
	Line No: 960		
G-JMACᴹ	British Aerospace Jetstream Series 410	41004	12.06.92
	G-JAMD, G-JXLI Cancelled 21.05.03 by CAA		06.10.97
	With Wirral Aviation Society, Liverpool-John Lennon		
G-JMAL	Avtech Jabiru UL-D	669	19.08.08
	K Lewis (Effingham, Leatherhead)		04.09.19P
G-JMAN	Mainair Blade 912S	1290-0601-7-W1085	12.07.01
	S T Cain Ince		29.06.18P
G-JMAW	Beech B200GT King Air	BY-326	28.09.18
	N326BY Martin-Baker Aircraft Company Ltd Chalgrove		
	Built by Textron Aviation Inc (IE 28.09.18)		
G-JMBJ	Magni M24C Orion	24159064	09.06.15
	B Lesslie (St Brelade, Jersey)		28.07.18P

G-JMBO	Embraer EMB-505 Phenom 300	50500366	20.05.16
	PR-PHG Catreus AOC Ltd Liverpool John Lennon		19.05.18E
G-JMBS	Agusta A109S Grand	22148	19.12.17
	5H-IVA Avery Charter Services Ltd		
	Fishpools Farm Barns, Frankton, Warks		06.02.19E
G-JMCB	Boeing 737-436(SF)	25859	27.06.17
	N859AU, G-GBTA, G-BVHA		
	West Atlantic UK Ltd East Midlands		02.07.19E
	Line No: 2532		
G-JMCH	Boeing 737-476(SF)	24439	05.09.17
	N475VX, G-RAJG, N24957, OM-SAA, N24957,		
	ZK-JTR, VH-TJN		
	West Atlantic UK Ltd East Midlands		07.09.19E
	Line No: 2265		
G-JMCJ	Boeing 737-436(SF)	25856	27.07.17
	N856NX, G-DOCW		
	West Atlantic UK Ltd East Midlands		03.08.19E
	Line No: 2422		
G-JMCK	Boeing 737-4D7(SF)	28701	24.01.17
	N287AR, HS-TDK		
	West Atlantic UK Ltd East Midlands		29.01.20E
	Line No: 2977		
G-JMCL	Boeing 737-322(SF)	23951	18.12.08
	D-AGEA, N319UA		
	West Atlantic UK Ltd East Midlands		21.04.19E
	Line No: 1532		
G-JMCM	Boeing 737-3Y0(SF)	24679	30.04.12
	EC-KRA, SX-BGK, 9V-TRA		
	West Atlantic UK Ltd East Midlands		25.04.19E
	Line No: 1897		
G-JMCO	Boeing 737-3T0(SF)	23569	12.07.13
	OO-TNA, N13331		
	West Atlantic UK Ltd East Midlands		29.06.19E
	Line No: 1258		
G-JMCP	Boeing 737-3T0(SF)	23578	09.12.13
	OO-TNB, N39340		
	West Atlantic UK Ltd East Midlands		05.12.19E
	Line No: 1358		
G-JMCR	Boeing 737-4Q8(SF)	25372	25.04.14
	N452KA, N431LF, TC-SKD, TC-JDI		
	West Atlantic UK Ltd East Midlands		04.08.19E
	Line No: 2280		
G-JMCS	Boeing 737-4Y0(SF)	24903	15.01.14
	OY-JTK, N451KA, G-JMCS, N451KA, UR-VVN, M-ABCO,		
	UR-VVN, OK-WGF, 9M-MJN		
	West Atlantic UK Ltd East Midlands		14.02.19E
	Line No: 1978		
G-JMCT	Boeing 737-3Y0(SF)	24546	23.12.13
	G-ZAPV, G-IGOC, EI-BZH		
	West Atlantic UK Ltd East Midlands		09.04.19E
	Line No: 1811		
G-JMCU	Boeing 737-301(SF)	23513	24.09.14
	OO-TNC, N559AU, N334US, N323P		
	West Atlantic UK Ltd East Midlands		23.01.20E
	Line No: 1327		
G-JMCV	Boeing 737-4K5(SF)	24128	27.07.15
	S5-ABV, N728CF, EC-JSS, TC-MNI, SP-KEN, D-AHLO		
	West Atlantic UK Ltd East Midlands		13.01.20E
	Line No: 1715		
G-JMCX	Boeing 737-406(SF)	24959	10.10.16
	N116WF, A6-JAK, N959PR, PH-BDY		
	West Atlantic UK Ltd East Midlands		13.10.19E
	Line No: 1949		
G-JMCY	Boeing 737-4Q8(SF)	25114	21.03.16
	2-VBAO, VQ-BAO, N783AS		
	West Atlantic UK Ltd East Midlands		28.03.19E
	Line No: 2666		
G-JMCZ	Boeing 737-4K5(SF)	24126	12.06.15
	S5-ABZ, TC-MCF, N726CF, EC-KRD, N126FH, EC-JSJ,		
	TC-MNF, D-AHLK, SP-KEI, D-AHLK		
	West Atlantic UK Ltd East Midlands		03.06.19E
	Line No: 1697		
G-JMDI	Schweizer 269C *(300)*	S 1398	24.09.91
	G-FLAT Welch Services Group Ltd (Congleton)		23.04.19E

G-JMGP	Aero L-39ZO Albatros	831125	24.03.14
	RA-3537K SARL Jet Concept St Athan		18.04.18P
	On rebuild 12.18; carries '125' (black) on nose		
G-JMKE	Cessna 172S Skyhawk SP	172S9248	17.12.02
	N53012 M C Plomer-Roberts & H White		
	Wellesbourne Mountford		29.09.18E
G-JMNN	CASA 1-131-E3B Jungmann	1040	09.06.14
	Spanish AF E3B-335 B S Charters Sywell		
	Dismantled 08.15 (NF 20.05.18)		
G-JMON	Agusta A109A II	7411	04.08.06
	G-RFDS, N1YU, VP-CLA, VR-CLA, G-BOLA,		
	VR-CMP, G-BOLA Falcon Aviation Ltd		
	Bourne Park, Hurstbourne Tarrant		29.06.09E
	Stored 12.15 (NF 19.12.16)		
G-JMOS	Piper PA-34-220T Seneca V	3449378	01.09.08
	N60936 C J Thomas Bournemouth		10.09.18E
G-JMRT	Comco Ikarus C42 FB80 Bravo	1705-7502	08.08.17
	Kennedy Tuck Air Ltd (Quedgeley, Gloucester)		09.08.18P
G-JMRV	Van's RV-7	xxxx	16.05.07
	J W Marshall (Haslingbourne, Petworth)		
	Built by J W Marshall – project PFA 323-14591		
	(NF 30.09.14)		
G-JNAR	Ace Aviation Magic/As-Tec 13	xxxx	30.09.15
	J D Hoyland (Winchester)		
	Trike s/n no known & wing s/n AS13-262 (IE 11.06.18)		
G-JNAS	Grumman American AA5A Cheetah	AA5A-0604	28.11.00
	SE-GEI, LN-KLE Cancelled 19.10.18 by CAA		09.03.07
	Farley Farm *Wreck stored 06.18*		
G-JNMA	Supermarine 379 Spitfire FR.XIV	6S-381758	30.03.09
	Belgian AF SG-25, RM927 P M Andrews Biggin Hill		
	Carries firewall identity '6S-512313' & '6S-581750'		
	on previous Belgian AF plate; on rebuild 03.16		
	(NF 20.05.16)		
G-JNNB	Colt 90A	2063	20.12.91
	N A P Godfrey West Leith, Tring 'J & B Rare'		25.07.18E
G-JNSC	Schempp-Hirth Janus CT	2	11.12.07
	BGA 4186/HTH, N137DB, D-KHIE D S Bramwell		
	tr Janus Syndicate (Haddenham) 'C4'		02.02.18E
G-JNSH	Robinson R22 Beta II	4591	29.10.14
	N7097C Hawesbates LLP Wellesbourne Mountford		29.09.18E
G-JNUS	Schempp-Hirth Janus C	215	06.09.07
	BGA 4062, D-4149 N A Peatfield Seighford '52'		10.05.18E
G-JOBA	P&M Quik GT450	8174	31.05.06
	S P Durnall Wolverhampton Halfpenny Green		23.07.18P
G-JOBS	Cessna T182T Turbo Skylane	T18208009	27.09.07
	N737RM, G-BZVF, N109LP Tech Travel Ltd		
	Bonn-Hangelar, Nordrhein-Westphalen, Germany		04.04.18E
G-JODB	Jodel D.9 Bébé	959	11.06.14
	M R Routh (Buckerell, Devon)		
	Built by M R Routh – project LAA 054-15253		
	(NF 14.05.18)		
G-JODE	Jodel D.150 Mascaret	191	14.03.13
	B R Vickers (Shenstone, Lichfield)		
	Built by B R Vickers – project PFA 235-14527		
	(NF 30.03.17)		
G-JODL	Jodel DR.1050-M Excellence	99	28.04.86
	F-BJJC D Silsbury Dunkeswell		07.12.17P
	Built by Société Aéronautique Normande; damaged		
	landing Headcorn 24.09.17; on rebuild 02.18		
	(NF 23.01.18)		
G-JOED	Lindstrand LBL 77A	1436	19.12.12
	G R Down Biddenden, Ashford		30.07.19E
G-JOEY[M]	Fairey B-N BN-2A Mk.III-2 Trislander	1016	27.11.81
	G-BDGG, C-GSAA, G-BDGG		
	Cancelled 19.10.16 as PWFU		18.04.16
	Guernsey *Preserved at Oakland Centre 04.18*		
G-JOHA	Cirrus SR20	1968	24.02.10
	N196PG N Harris Elstree		24.03.18E
G-JOID	Cirrus SR20	1910	18.04.12
	N139PG I F Doubtfire Solent		24.05.18E
G-JOJO	Cameron A-210	2674	20.09.91
	A C K Rawson & J J Rudoni t/a Wickers World		
	Hot Air Balloon Company Stafford		11.04.06
	(NF 17.07.18)		

G-JOKR	Extra EA.300/L	1278	28.02.08
	C Jefferies Little Gransden *'Abarth'*		17.04.18E
G-JOLY	Cessna 120	13872	03.09.81
	OO-ACE B V Meade Garston Farm, Marshfield		
	'Noordzee Vliegclub'		08.03.18P
G-JONG	RotorWay Exec 162F	6168	27.04.04
	N630GH S D Barnard Leicester		27.10.16P
	Built by S A Foster		
G-JONL	CZAW Sportcruiser	700320	23.07.09
	J R Linford Carlisle Lake District		19.07.18P
	Built by J R Linford – project LAA 338-14889		
G-JONM	Piper PA-28-181 Archer III	2843614	15.01.08
	OY-PHH, N31011 C C W Hart Wycombe Air Park		02.08.19E
G-JONO M	Colt 77A HAB	1086	22.06.87
	Cancelled 28.05.09 as PWFU		17.09.95
	G-JONO(1) original envelope Built by as c/n 1086(1),		
	re-allocated as c/n 1073 Inflated 04.14		
	G-JONO(2) original envelope Built by as c/n 1086(2))		
	'Sandicliffe Ford' Inflated 04.14		
	With British Balloon Museum & Library, Newbury		
G-JONT	Cirrus SR22	3599	21.01.10
	N14CK J A Green Retford Gamston		23.02.19E
G-JONX	Aeropro EuroFOX 912(1)	18606	03.09.10
	OM-APRO A J South Shipdham		08.05.19P
	Built by J M Walsh – project BMAA/HB/597; tricycle u/c		
G-JONY	Cyclone AX2000 HKS	7503	12.03.99
	S & A Wilson Logistics Ltd (Banff)		18.06.18P
G-JONZ	Cessna 172P Skyhawk II	17276233	28.09.89
	N97835 21st Century Flyers CLG		
	(Tallaght, Dublin, RoI)		17.05.16E
	(IE 31.05.17)		
G-JOOL	Mainair Blade 912	1262-1000-7-W1056	08.12.00
	P C Collins (Usk)		20.07.16P
G-JOON	Cessna 182D Skylane	182-53067	09.06.81
	(N......), G-JOON, OO-ACD, N9967T		
	Cancelled 08.11.11 as WFU		09.06.81
	Pallas West, Toomyvara, RoI *Stored dismantled 05.14*		
G-JOPF	Smyth Model S Sydewinder	xxxx	19.04.01
	Cancelled 06.12.02 as PWFU		
	Gunskirchen, Austria		
	Built by J Furby – project PFA 092-12313		
	Displayed on pole in private garden 08.17		
G-JORD	Robinson R44 Raven II	11725	14.05.07
	G Riddell West Conland Farm, Leslie, Glenrothes		11.12.19E
G-JOSH	Cameron N-105 HAB	1319	13.08.86
	Cancelled 05.11.10 as PWFU		16.08.96
	Not Known *Inflated Pidley 05.16*		
G-JOTC	British Aerospace BAe 146 Series 300QT	E3166	16.05.18
	EC-MHR, OO-TAD, G-TNTM, RP-C480, G-TNTM,		
	G-BSLZ, G-6-166 Jota Aircraft Leasing Ltd Southend		27.10.00
	Noted 02.19		
G-JOTD	British Aerospace BAe 146 Series 300QT	E3168	19.04.18
	EC-MID, OO-TAH, G-TNTL, RP-C479, G-TNTL,		
	G-BSGI, (RP-C479), G-BSGI, G-6-168		
	Jota Aircraft Leasing Ltd Southend		27.10.00
	Noted 02.19		
G-JOTE	British Aerospace BAe 146 Series 300QT	E3182	05.04.18
	EC-MFT, OO-TAE, G-TNTG, G-BSUY		
	Jota Aircraft Leasing Ltd Southend *'Jota Cargo'*		10.03.19E
	Operated by Jota Aviation		
G-JOTF	British Aerospace BAe 146 Series 300QT	E3186	17.08.18
	EC-MEO, OO-TAF, G-TNTK, G-BSXL, G-6-186		
	Jota Aircraft Leasing Ltd Southend		23.10.19E
	Operated by Jota Aviation		
G-JOTR	British Aerospace Avro 146-RJ85	E2294	12.01.16
	G-CHFE, OO-DJT, G-6-294		
	Jota Aircraft Leasing Ltd Southend		03.04.19E
	Operated by Jota Aviation		
G-JOTS	British Aerospace Avro 146-RJ100	E3355	29.03.17
	OO-DWJ, G-6-355 Jota Aviation Ltd Southend		08.03.19E
	Operated by Jota Aviation		
G-JOYT	Piper PA-28-181 Archer II	28-7990132	13.02.90
	G-BOVO, N2239B Alan Cathcart Ltd Enniskillen		08.04.19E

G-JOYZ	Piper PA-28-181 Archer III	2843018	19.01.96
	N9262R, (G-JOYZ)		
	N Reynolds tr Zulu Group Fairoaks		15.02.18E
G-JOZI	Aérospatiale AS.350BA Ecureuil	1456	24.07.13
	9M-RSQ, 9M-HMB, N140EH, N5791R		
	WW Medical Facilities Ltd		
	Hutton Field Farm, Northallerton		28.08.18E
G-JPBA	Van's RV-6	25646	21.07.11
	S B Austin (Nuneaton)		
	Built by S B Austin – project PFA 181A-13517		
	(NF 28.07.15)		
G-JPIT	Pitts S-2S	xxxx	31.10.17
	R S Goodwin (Leigh, Worcester)		
	Built by R S Goodwin – project LAA 009C-15409		
	(NF 31.10.17)		
G-JPJR	Robinson R44 Raven II	11198	04.05.06
	Longstop Investments Ltd Earls Colne		16.06.18E
G-JPMA	Avtech Jabiru UL-450	xxxx	24.05.99
	S Southan (Hilperton. Trowbridge) *'Sheila'*		10.06.19P
	Built by J P Metcalfe – project PFA 274A-13399		
G-JPOT	Piper PA-32R-301 Saratoga SP	32R-8113065	01.08.94
	G-BIYM, N8385X		
	The Big 6 Flyers Ltd White Waltham		24.08.18E
G-JPRO	BAC 145 Jet Provost T.5A	EEP/JP/1055	10.08.95
	XW433 J A Campbell Inverness		03.09.19P
	As 'XW433 'in RAF CFS c/s		
G-JPTV	BAC 145 Jet Provost T.5A	EEP/JP/1002	02.05.96
	XW355 Callegari SRL (Parma, Italy)		23.08.18P
	As 'XW354' in RAF c/s		
G-JPVA	BAC 145 Jet Provost T.5A	EEP/JP/953	22.02.95
	G-BVXT, XW289 Cancelled 04.11.16 as PWFU		06.01.17
	Hawarden *Stored as 'XW289' 02.17*		
G-JPWM	Best Off Skyranger 912(2)	SKR0412541	24.03.05
	M Pittock & R S Waters (Etchingham)		15.05.18P
	Built by M Pittock & R S Waters – project BMAA/HB/442		
G-JRBC	Piper PA-28-140 Cherokee	28-20693	15.10.14
	9J-RBC, N11C, N6602W N Livni North Weald		12.04.18E
	Noted 07.18		
G-JRCR	Bell 206L-1 LongRanger II	45229	17.05.13
	G-EYRE, G-STVI, N60MA, N5019K		
	RSCP Management Ltd Retford Gamston		12.08.19E
G-JREE	Maule MX-7-180 Super Rocket	11096C	13.04.01
	N99MX, N30051		
	C R P Briand Tarbes-Lourdes-Pyrénées, France		16.02.18E
G-JRER	Tecnam P2006T	194	17.03.17
	3GRComm Ltd Gloucestershire		16.04.18E
G-JRLR	Sackville BM-65	JR01	13.10.15
	J S Russon Cheadle Hulme, Cheadle		
	Built by J S Russon (IE 06.07.17)		
G-JRME	Jodel D.140E Mousquetaire	444	13.11.02
	Sapphire Leasing Ltd Blackpool		26.11.18P
	Built by J E & L L Rex – project PFA 251-13155		
	from SAB plans		
G-JROO	Agusta-Bell 206B-2 JetRanger II	8242	22.01.13
	G-VJMJ, G-PEAK, G-BLJE, SE-HBW		
	GH Byproducts (Derby) Ltd		
	Nottingham Heliport, Widmerpool		28.04.18E
G-JRSH	Cirrus SR22T	0725	17.03.14
	N183JS Lismore Instruments Ltd Brighton City		23.03.18E
G-JRVB	Van's RV-8	xxxx	15.03.12
	J W Salter Newtownards		25.06.18P
	Built by M Albury & J W Salter – project PFA 303-13978		
G-JRXI	Bell 505 Jet Ranger X	65058	08.02.18
	Helicompany Ltd Manston Park		27.03.19E
G-JRXV	Bell 505 Jet Ranger X	65151	20.11.18
	C-GFNM R Matthews (West Mersea, Colchester)		02.12.19E
G-JSAK	Robinson R22 Beta II	2959	30.06.99
	Thurston Helicopters Ltd Headcorn		03.07.19E
G-JSAT	Pilatus B-N BN-2T Islander	2277	05.02.98
	G-BVFK Chewton Glen Ltd t/a Chewton Glen Aviation		
	Solent		02.09.18E
G-JSAW	Robinson R66 Turbine	0058	14.06.17
	N404RW GT40 Aviation Ltd (Cheltenham)		29.06.19E

G-JSCA	Piper PA-28RT-201 Arrow IV	28R-8118012	14.12.12	
	G-ISCA, N8288Y, N9608N			
	J C Haddon tr G-JSCA Flying Group Coventry		08.02.18E	
G-JSFC	Tecnam P2008-JC	1039	21.10.14	
	Stapleford Flying Club Ltd Stapleford		26.10.18E	
G-JSIC	Jonker JS-MD Single	1C.MD089	15.02.18	
	(BGA 5952), D-KBHB			
	K Barker & A G W Hall Lasham '240'		11.03.19E	
G-JSKY	Comco Ikarus C42 FB80	1308-7272	07.10.13	
	M S Westman Priory Farm, Tibenham		01.12.18P	
	Assembled Red-Air UK			
G-JSMA	Gloster Meteor T.7	G5/423772	25.05.16	
	WL419 Martin-Baker Aircraft Company Ltd			
	Chalgrove		27.11.18P	
	As 'WL419' in RAF c/s			
G-JSPL	Avtech Jabiru UL-450	0358	27.12.00	
	R S Cochrane (St Ives, Huntingdon)		04.12.18P	
	Built by J A Lord – project PFA 274A-13604			
G-JSPR	Glaser-Dirks DG-400	4-254	07.07.14	
	D-KABK I P Freestone Husbands Bosworth 'SO'		21.07.17E	
	(NF 03.05.18)			
G-JSRK	HpH Glasflügel 304 S Shark	063-MS	24.10.16	
	(BGA 5877)			
	T K Dunford tr Great White Syndicate Lasham 'J2T'			
	(IE 02.04.18)			
G-JSRV	Van's RV-6	60072	23.08.05	
	J Stringer Graveley Hall Farm, Graveley '46'		16.05.19P	
	Built by J Stringer – project PFA 181A-14407			
G-JSSD[M]	Handley Page HP.137 Jetstream 1	227	14.06.79	
	N510F, N510E, N12227, G-AXJZ			
	Cancelled 04.01.96 by CAA		09.10.90	
	Converted to BAe Jetstream Series 3001			
	prototype 1979/80			
	With National Museum of Flight Scotland, East Fortune			
G-JSSE	Dassault Falcon 900	120	05.01.18	
	C-FWKX, F-GXDZ, CS-DLA, F-WQBM, F-GRAX,			
	VP-BNJ, VR-BNJ, F-WWFN XJC Ltd Bournemouth		15.03.19E	
G-JTBP	Piper PA-46-350P Malibu Mirage	4636724	18.05.18	
	N7118N J R Turner Gloucestershire			
	(IE 18.05.18)			
G-JTBX	Bell 206B-3 JetRanger III	3955	10.05.12	
	G-EWAW, G-DORB, SE-HTI, TC-HBN			
	Skywest Aviation Ltd Cork, RoI		13.11.17E	
G-JTPC	Aeromot AMT-200 Super Ximango	200.067	28.05.97	
	G J & J T Potter Rufforth		15.06.18E	
G-JTSA	Robinson R44 Raven II	11659	02.04.07	
	S Novotny Denham		12.01.18E	
G-JUDD	Avtech Jabiru UL-450	0349	09.08.00	
	R J Almey Fenland		05.07.19P	
	Built by C Judd – project PFA 274A-13570			
G-JUDE	Robin DR.400-180 Régent	1869	14.10.88	
	Bravo India Flying Group Ltd RAF Woodvale		15.02.19E	
G-JUDY	Grumman American AA-5A Cheetah	AA5A-0620	31.08.78	
	(G-BFWM), N26480			
	R E Dagless Holly Hill Farm, Guist		13.09.18E	
G-JUFS	SOCATA TB-9 Tampico	928	14.10.15	
	EI-BYG N J Richardson Thruxton		12.10.18E	
G-JUGE	Evektor EV-97 teamEurostar UK	2003-1709	07.10.03	
	I A Baker Sywell		12.10.18P	
	Assembled Cosmik Aviation Ltd			
G-JUGS	AutoGyro MTOsport	09 096S	21.10.09	
	S J M Hornsby Solent		05.11.18P	
	Assembled Rotorsport UK as c/n RSUK/MTOS/018			
G-JUJU	Chilton DW.1A	xxxx	15.12.14	
	D C Reid Felthorpe 'Black Magic'		02.09.18P	
	Built by D C Reid – project PFA 225-12726			
G-JULE	P&M Quik GT450	8219	13.10.06	
	G Almond Ince		30.01.18P	
G-JULL	Stemme S 10-VT	11-039	10.02.00	
	J P C Fuchs Rufforth '199'		21.10.18E	
G-JULU	Cameron V-90	3611	07.07.95	
	J M Searle Thornbury, Bristol		26.04.18E	

G-JULZ	Europa Aviation Europa XS	312	08.10.96	
	J S Firth Burn		23.08.18P	
	Built by M Parkin – project PFA 247-13045;			
	monowheel u/c			
G-JUNG	CASA 1-131E Jungmann Series 1000	1121	23.11.88	
	Spanish AF E3B-143			
	J A Sykes Hawksview, Stretton		30.06.09P	
	Badly damaged Stourton Caundle, Blackmore Vale,			
	5 miles E of Sherborne, Dorset 24.05.09; noted			
	partially rebuilt 04.18 (NF 23.04.15)			
G-JUNO	Fokker D.VII replica	xxxx	15.10.13	
	S J Green (Farnborough GU14)			
	Built by D A Graham – project LAA 387-15228			
	(NF 09.02.17)			
G-JURG	Rockwell Commander 114A	14516	19.09.79	
	N4752W M G Wright Coventry		12.05.18E	
	Originally laid-down as c/n 14449			
G-JUST	Beech F33A Bonanza	CE-1165	11.10.00	
	N334CW N M R Richards Redhill		10.07.18E	
G-JVBF	Lindstrand LBL 210A	265	05.06.95	
	Airxcite Ltd t/a Virgin Balloon Flights			
	Stafford Park, Telford 'Virgin'		19.06.06E	
	(NF 15.09.14)			
G-JVBP	Evektor EV-97 teamEurostar UK	2006-2730	31.05.06	
	J P McCreedy tr Otherton Blue Skies Syndicate			
	Otherton		04.06.18P	
	Assembled Cosmik Aviation Ltd			
G-JVET	Aeropro EuroFOX 912(iS)	448.14	06.08.14	
	J S G Down Darley Moor		22.05.18P	
	Built by J S G & H J Down – project LAA 376-15286;			
	tailwheel u/c			
G-JWBI	Agusta-Bell 206B-2 JetRanger II	8435	03.04.96	
	G-RODS, G-NOEL, G-BCWN The Cloudy Bay			
	Trading Company (Elloughton, Brough)		26.09.08E	
	(NF 04.02.15)			
G-JWDB	Comco Ikarus C42 FB80	0509-6760	24.10.05	
	A R Hughes Yatesbury		28.03.18P	
	Assembled Aerosport Ltd			
G-JWDS	Cessna F150G	F150-0216	15.12.88	
	G-AVNB G Sayer Haverfordwest		13.09.13E	
	Built by Reims Aviation SA (NF 27.01.17)			
G-JWDW	Comco Ikarus C42 FB80	1604-7449	24.05.16	
	D A & J W Wilding Wolverhampton Halfpenny Green		15.05.18P	
	Assembled Red Aviation			
G-JWIV	Jodel DR.1051 Sicile	431	06.09.78	
	F-BLMD C M Fitton Bolt Head, Salcombe		12.01.19P	
	Built by Centre-Est Aéronautique			
G-JWJW	CASA 1-131E Jungmann Series 2000	419	15.05.03	
	PH-MRK, (PH-MRN), D-EDWC, E3B-419			
	J T & J W Whicher Henstridge		02.10.18P	
G-JWMA	Gloster Meteor T.7	G5/356539	04.09.15	
	WA638 Martin-Baker Aircraft Company Ltd			
	Chalgrove		06.12.18P	
	As 'WA638' in RAF c/s			
G-JWNI	Just SuperSTOL	xxxx	14.08.18	
	J D Williams Portmoak			
	Built by J D Williams – project LAA 397-15478			
	(NF 14.08.18)			
G-JWNW	Magni M16C Tandem Trainer	16105644	29.04.10	
	J A Ingram Nottingham City		21.05.18P	
G-JWRN	Robinson R44 Raven II	13857	23.03.17	
	G-JSCH, OE-XYS			
	Heritage Automotive Holdings Ltd Elstree		07.01.19E	
G-JXTC	British Aerospace Jetstream 3108	690	21.06.06	
	PH-KJG, G-LOGT, G-BSFH, PH-KFG, G-31-690			
	Cancelled 07.10.11 as WFU			
	University Of Glamorgan, Cardiff			
	Instructional airframe 04.17			
G-JYRO	AutoGyro MT-03	xxxx	18.10.06	
	A Richards (Barrowford, Nelson)		09.07.18P	
	Assembled Rotorsport UK as RSUK/MT-03/006			
G-JZBA	Boeing 737-800	63157	16.10.17	
	N1795B Jet2.com Ltd Leeds Bradford			
	'Jet2 Turkey' & 'Friendly Low Fares'		15.10.19E	
	Line No: 6624; red tail			

G-JZBB	Boeing 737-800	63158	26.10.17
	Jet2.com Ltd Leeds Bradford		
	'Jet2 Geneva' & *'Friendly Low Fares'*		25.10.19E
	Line No: 6645; red tail		
G-JZBC	Boeing 737-800	63160	24.11.17
	Jet2.com Ltd Leeds Bradford		
	'Jet2holidays' & *'Package holidays you can trust'*		23.11.19E
	Line No: 6668; white fuselage & blue tail		
G-JZBD	Boeing 737-800	63159	17.11.17
	Jet2.com Ltd Leeds Bradford		
	'Jet2holidays' & *'Package holidays you can trust'*		16.11.19E
	Line No: 6680; white fuselage & blue tail		
G-JZBE	Boeing 737-800	63161	04.12.17
	Jet2.com Ltd Leeds Bradford		
	'Jet2holidays' & *'Package holidays you can trust'*		03.12.19E
	Line No: 6703; white fuselage & blue tail		
G-JZBF	Boeing 737-800	63162	20.12.17
	Jet2.Com Ltd Leeds Bradford		
	'Jet2holidays' & *'Package holidays you can trust'*		19.12.19E
	Line No: 6732; white fuselage & blue tail		
G-JZBG	Boeing 737-800	63164	17.01.18
	Jet2.com Ltd Leeds Bradford		
	'Jet2holidays' & *'Package holidays you can trust'*		16.01.20E
	Line No: 6756; white fuselage & blue tail		
G-JZBH	Boeing 737-800	63163	31.01.18
	Dart Group PLC Leeds Bradford		
	'Jet2holidays' & *'Package holidays you can trust'*		30.01.19E
	Line No: 6765; operated by Jet2.com Ltd;		
	white fuselage & blue tail		
G-JZBI	Boeing 737-800	63166	15.02.18
	Jet2.Com Ltd Leeds Bradford *'Friendly Low Fares'*		14.02.19E
	Line No: 6808; red tail		
G-JZBJ	Boeing 737-800	63165	27.02.18
	Jet2.com Ltd Leeds Bradford *'Friendly Low Fares'*		26.02.19E
	Line No: 6823; red tail		
G-JZBK	Boeing 737-800	63167	14.03.18
	Dart Leasing and Finance Ltd Leeds Bradford		
	'Friendly Low Fares'		13.03.19E
	Line No: 6849; operated by Jet2.com Ltd		
G-JZBL	Boeing 737-800	63169	26.03.18
	N1787B Dart Group PLC Leeds Bradford		
	'Friendly Low Fares'		25.03.19E
	Line No: 6869; operated by Jet2.com Ltd; red tail		
G-JZBM	Boeing 737-800	63170	26.04.18
	Dart Group PLC Leeds Bradford		
	'Friendly Low Fares'		25.04.19E
	Line No: 6912; operated by Jet2.com Ltd; red tail		
G-JZBN	Boeing 737-800	63168	30.04.18
	Dart Group PLC Leeds Bradford		
	'Friendly Low Fares'		28.04.19E
	Line No: 6923; operated by Jet2.com Ltd; red tail		
G-JZBO	Boeing 737-800	64439	24.08.18
	Dart Group PLC Leeds Bradford		
	'Jet2holidays' & *'Package holidays you can trust'*		23.08.19E
	Line No: 7117; operated by Jet2.com Ltd;		
	white fuselage & blue tail		
G-JZBP	Boeing 737-800	64440	10.10.18
	Dart Group PLC Leeds Bradford		
	'Jet2holidays' & *'Package holidays you can trust'*		09.10.19E
	Line No.7177; operated by Jet2.com Ltd;		
	white fuselage & blue tail		
G-JZBR	Boeing 737-800	64441	07.11.18
	Jet2.com Ltd Leeds Bradford		
	'Jet2holidays' & *'Package holidays you can trust'*		06.11.19E
	Line No.7247; white fuselage & blue tail		
G-JZBS	Boeing 737-800	64442	21.01.19
	Jet2.com Ltd Leeds Bradford *'Jet2Holidays'*		20.01.20E
	Line No. 7357; operated by Jet2.com Ltd;		
	white fuselage & blue tail		
G-JZHA	Boeing 737-8K5	30417	13.01.15
	D-AHFY, N1787B Dart Group PLC Leeds Bradford		
	'Jet2holidays'		02.02.19E
	Line No: 781; operated by Jet2.com		

G-JZHB	Boeing 737-8K5	28623	17.03.15
	D-AHFS Jet2.com Ltd Leeds Bradford *'Jet2 Malta'*,		
	'22kg bag allowance' (Port) & *'Great flight times'* (Stbd)		15.01.20E
	Line No: 556; red tail		
G-JZHC	Boeing 737-8K5	30593	02.04.15
	D-AHFR, N1787B Jet2.com Ltd Leeds Bradford		
	'Jet2 Crete', *'22kg bag allowance'* (Port) &		
	'Great flight times' (Stbd)		01.03.19E
	Line No: 528; red tail		
G-JZHD	Boeing 737-808	34706	23.04.15
	EI-RUP, B-5171, N1786B		
	Dart Group PLC Leeds Bradford *'Jet2holidays'*		20.04.19E
	Line No: 2014; operated by Jet2.com		
G-JZHE	Boeing 737-8K2	30390	23.03.16
	PH-HZK, N1786B		
	Jet2.com Ltd Leeds Bradford *'Jet2holidays'*		16.03.19E
	Line No: 555		
G-JZHF	Boeing 737-8K2	28378	29.02.16
	PH-HZF, N1786B		
	Jet2.com Ltd Leeds Bradford *'Jet2holidays'*		23.02.19E
	Line No: 291		
G-JZHG	Boeing 737-85P	28388	06.05.16
	EI-RUE, EC-HKQ Dart Group PLC Leeds Bradford		
	'Jet2 Naples', *'Great package holidays'* (Port) &		
	'Great flight times' (Stbd)		04.05.19E
	Line No: 533; operated by Jet2.com; red tail		
G-JZHH	Boeing 737-85P	28536	20.05.16
	EI-RUF, EC-HKR, N1787B Dart Group PLC		
	Leeds Bradford *'Jet2 Costa Bravo'*,		
	'22kg bag allowance' (Port) & *'Great flight times'* (Stbd)		18.05.19E
	Line No: 540; operated by Jet2.com; red tail		
G-JZHJ	Boeing 737-8MG	63144	12.09.16
	N1787B Dart Group PLC Leeds Bradford		
	'Jet2 Ibiza' & *'Friendly Low Fares'*		11.09.19E
	Line No: 6065; operated by Jet2.com; red tail		
G-JZHK	Boeing 737-800	63145	07.10.16
	Jet2.com Ltd Leeds Bradford *'Jet2holidays'*		06.10.19E
	Line No: 6103		
G-JZHL	Boeing 737-800	63568	29.10.16
	Dart Group PLC Leeds Bradford *'Jet2holidays'*		28.10.19E
	Line No: 6138; operated by Jet2.com		
G-JZHM	Boeing 737-800	63570	09.11.16
	Dart Leasing & Finance Ltd Leeds Bradford		
	'Jet2holidays'		08.11.19E
	Line No: 6150; operated by Jet2.com		
G-JZHN	Boeing 737-800	63146	16.11.16
	Dart Group PLC Leeds Bradford *'Jet2holidays'*		10.11.19E
	Line No: 6161; operated by Jet2.com		
G-JZHO	Boeing 737-800	63569	30.11.16
	Dart Group PLC Leeds Bradford		
	'Bob Gruszka' & *'Friendly Low Fares'*		20.11.19E
	Line No: 6183; operated by Jet2.com; red tail		
G-JZHP	Boeing 737-800	63147	16.12.16
	Jet2.com Ltd Leeds Bradford		
	'Jet2 Alicante' & *'Friendly Low Fares'*		15.12.19E
	Line No: 6198; red tail		
G-JZHR	Boeing 737-800	63148	22.12.16
	Dart Group PLC Leeds Bradford		
	'Jet2 Gran Canaria' & *'Friendly Low Fares'*		21.12.19E
	Line No: 6215; operated by Jet2.com; red tail		
G-JZHS	Boeing 737-800	63149	27.01.17
	N1787R Dart Group PLC Leeds Bradford		
	'Jet2 Prague' & *'Friendly Low Fares'*		26.01.19E
	Line No: 6239; operated by Jet2.com; red tail		
G-JZHT	Boeing 737-800	63150	30.01.17
	Dart Leasing & Finance Ltd Leeds Bradford		
	'Jet2holidays'		29.01.19E
	Line No: 6253; operated by Jet2.com		
G-JZHU	Boeing 737-800	63151	13.02.17
	Dart Leasing & Finance Ltd Leeds Bradford		
	'Jet2holidays'		12.02.19E
	Line No: 6267; operated by Jet2.com		
G-JZHV	Boeing 737-800	63152	21.02.1
	Jet2.com Ltd Leeds Bradford		
	'Jet2 Ibiza' & *'Friendly Low Fares'*		20.02.19
	Line No: 6279; red tail		

G-JZHW	Boeing 737-800	63153	17.03.17
	Jet2.com Ltd Leeds Bradford		
	'Jet2 Reus' & 'Friendly Low Fares'		16.03.19E
	Line No: 6311; red tail		
G-JZHX	Boeing 737-800	63154	24.03.17
	Jet2.com Ltd Leeds Bradford		
	'Jet2 Barcelona' & 'Friendly Low Fares'		23.03.19E
	Line No: 6324; red tail		
G-JZHY	Boeing 737-800	63155	18.04.17
	Jet2.com Ltd Leeds Bradford		
	'Jet2 Malta' & 'Friendly Low Fares'		17.04.19E
	Line No: 6358; red tail		
G-JZHZ	Boeing 737-800	63156	28.04.17
	Jet2.com Ltd Leeds Bradford		
	'Jet2 Lanzarote' & 'Friendly Low Fares'		27.04.19E
	Line No: 6378; red tail		

G-KAAA – G-KZZZ

G-KAAT	McDonnell Douglas MD Explorer	900-00056	22.02.00
	G-PASS, N9234P		
	Specialist Aviation Services Ltd Gloucestershire		20.04.18E
G-KAEW[M]	Fairey Gannet AEW.Mk.3	F9459	09.01.04
	XL500, A2701, XL500 M A Stott St Athan		
	Built by Westland Aircraft Ltd; as 'XL500' in RN c/s;		
	to South Wales Aircraft Museum 12.18 (NF 30.01.19)		
G-KAFT	Diamond DA.40D Star	D4.191	13.03.06
	OE-VPU Airways Aviation Academy Ltd		
	Huesca-Pirineos, Spain		09.09.18E
G-KAIR	Piper PA-28-181 Archer II	28-7990176	28.12.78
	N3075D R I Nichols (Crowborough)		26.12.18E
G-KALI	Piper PA-28-140 Cherokee F	28-7325195	01.09.17
	G-BASL, N11C Akki Aviation Services Ltd Turweston		07.12.11E
	(NF 01.09.17)		
G-KALP	Schleicher ASW 24	24213	16.03.16
	(BGA 5889), D-5811		
	H E Gokalp Wycombe Air Park '186'		27.03.19E
G-KALS	Bombardier BD-100-1A10 Challenger 300	20106	12.10.06
	C-FIDX Volar Ltd Biggin Hill		12.10.18E
G-KAMM[M]	Hawker Hurricane IIC	CCF/R32207	23.02.95
	N54FH, BW881		
	Cancelled 23.08.07 – to N54FH		
	At Flying Heritage & Combat Armor Museum, Paine Field;		
	as 'RCAF 5429'		
G-KAMY	North American AT-6D Texan III	88-16849	02.09.11
	LN-AMY, (LN-RCS), (LN-LCN), N10595, 42-85068		
	Orion Enterprises Ltd Old Warden		
	As '285068' in USAAF c/s		
G-KANZ	Westland Wasp HAS.1	F9664	21.12.05
	RNZ Navy NZ3909, XT782 T J Manna North Weald		
	Noted 11.18 as 'NZ3909' (NF 15.06.15)		
G-KAOM	Scheibe SF25C Falke	4417	03.02.98
	D-KAOM D G Coats & J W Murdoch		
	tr Falke G-KAOM Syndicate Portmoak		10.04.18E
G-KAOS	Van's RV-7	xxxx	20.05.03
	J L Miles Redhill		16.05.18P
	Built by D F McGarvey & A E N Nicholas		
	– project PFA 323-13956		
G-KAPW	Percival P.56 Provost T.1	PAC/F/311	22.09.97
	XF603 Richard Shuttleworth Trustees Old Warden		28.05.18P
	As 'XF603' in RAF grey & green camouflage c/s		
G-KARA	Brügger MB.2 Colibri	xxxx	01.06.95
	G-BMUI C L Reddish Netherthorpe		20.12.13P
	Built by Carlton Flying Group – project		
	PFA 043-10980 (NF 23.04.15)		
G-KARE	Pilatus PC-12/47E	1257	07.10.15
	M-HARP, HB-FRY Flexifly Aircraft Hire Ltd Fairoaks		14.10.18E
G-KARK	Dyn'Aéro MCR-01 Club	251	29.12.03
	M J Dawson Deanland		21.08.19P
	Built by R Bailes-Brown – project PFA 301A-14010		
G-KARN	RotorWay Exec 90	5003	08.11.12
	G-VART, G-BSUR U G P Nimz Rochester		07.09.18P
G-KART	Piper PA-28-161 Warrior II	28-8016088	10.07.91
	N8097B Romeo Tango Aviation Ltd Newcastle Int'l		23.03.18E

G-KASW	AutoGyro Calidus	xxxx	29.06.10
	R A Clarkson (Upton, Retford)		08.04.19P
	Assembled Rotorsport UK as c/n RSUK/CALS/006		
G-KASX	Supermarine 384 Seafire F.XVII	FLWA 25488	30.10.03
	G-BRMG, A2055, SX336		
	T J Manna (Old Warden, Biggleswade)		14.05.16P
	Built by Westland Aircraft Ltd; noted 01.17		
	as 'SX336:105:VL'		
G-KATI	Rans S-7 Courier	0795.151	05.03.96
	C E Hunt Old Sarum		12.10.18P
	Built by S M Hall – project PFA 218-12917		
G-KATT	Cessna 152 II	15285661	10.06.93
	G-BMTK, N94387		
	C M de C C Cabral Cascais, Portugal		24.07.18E
G-KAWA	Denney Kitfox Model 2	xxxx	11.03.91
	J K Ewing Newton Peveril Farm, Sturminster Marshall		13.11.18P
	Built by T W C Maton – project PFA 172-11822		
G-KAXF	Hawker Hunter F.6A	S4/U/3361	20.12.95
	8830M, XF515 Stichting Dutch Hawker Hunter		
	Foundation Leeuwarden, Friesland, Netherlands		02.10.16P
	Built by Armstrong-Whitworth Aircraft;		
	as 'N-294' in R Netherlands AF c/s; active 02.18		
G-KAXT	Westland Wasp HAS.1	F9669	05.03.02
	RNZN NZ3905, XT787		
	T E Martin Barton Ashes, Crawley Down		08.08.18P
	As 'XT787' in RN c/s		
G-KAXW	Westland Scout AH.1	F9740	23.01.14
	G-BXRR, XW612		
	Military Vehicle Solutions Ltd (Dunchurch, Rugby)		05.03.19P
	As 'XW612' in AAC c/s		
G-KAYD	Boeing Stearman A75N1 Kaydet (PT-17)	75-4501	30.03.16
	N8256G, N5177Z, 42-16338		
	R H Butterfield Retford Gamston		08.08.18E
	As '31' in USAAC c/s		
G-KAYH	Extra EA.300/L	144	09.04.02
	F M H Versteegh Oosterbeek, Netherlands		03.10.17E
	(IE 23.01.18)		
G-KAYI	Cameron Z-90	10710	30.06.05
	R Bayly Clutton, Bristol 'Snow Business'		09.01.19E
G-KAYS	Hughes 369E (500)	0157E	19.01.17
	G-CIMJ, G-RISK, SE-HNZ, LN-OMV		
	Webb Aviation Ltd (London NW10)		03.08.19E
G-KAYX	Best Off Skyranger Nynja 912(1)	xxxx	05.04.18
	R N J Hughes Hunsdon		
	Built by R N J Hughes – project BMAA/HB/708		
G-KAZB	Sikorsky S-76C++	760614	22.09.06
	N8094S Bristow Helicopters Ltd Norwich Int'l		15.01.18E
G-KBOJ	AutoGyro MTOsport	09 093S	22.10.09
	K M G Barnett Chiltern Park, Wallingford		27.10.18P
	Assembled Rotorsport UK as c/n RSUK/MTOS/016		
G-KBOS	Flight Design CTSW	08-02-15	03.12.18
	G-KBOX G N S Farrant		
	Manor Farm, Drayton St Leonard		04.01.19P
	Assembled P&M Aviation Ltd as c/n 8365		
G-KBWP	Schempp-Hirth Arcus T	18	23.11.11
	(BGA 5698), D-KBWP G & T E Macfadyen		
	tr G-KBWP Gliding Group Nympsfield 'BW'		28.12.18E
G-KCHG	Schempp-Hirth Ventus cT	87	16.03.06
	BGA 5146/KJW, D-KCHG J Burrow North Hill 'JB'		05.02.18E
G-KCIG	Sportavia-Putzer RF5B Sperber	51005	19.06.80
	D-KCIG J R Bisset tr Deeside Fournier Group		
	Easterton		08.08.18P
G-KCIN	Piper PA-28-161 Cadet	2841102	03.11.05
	G-CDOX, HB-PQC, PH-TED, C-FDYA		
	The Pilot Centre Ltd Denham		12.10.18E
G-KCWJ	Schempp-Hirth Duo Discus T	102/428	23.11.10
	(BGA 5662), D-KCWJ		
	C K Davis tr G-KCWJ Group Gransden Lodge '8F'		12.04.19E
G-KDCD	Thruster T600N 450	9098-T600N-025	09.11.05
	G-MZNW M N Watson Felthorpe		23.04.18P
	Badged 'Sprint'		
G-KDEY	Scheibe SF25E Super Falke	4325	06.01.99
	D-KDEY D Tucker tr Falke Syndicate Aston Down		15.11.18E

G-KDIX	Jodel D.9 Bébé	xxxx		23.11.78
	S J Johns Eaglescott			29.08.17P
	Built by K Barlow – project PFA 054-10293			
G-KDOG	Scottish Aviation Bulldog Srs 120/121	BH120/289		18.06.01
	XX624 S R Tilling Bourne Park, Hurstbourne Tarrant			31.03.18E
	As 'XX624:E' in RAF white & red c/s			
G-KEAM	Schleicher ASH 26E	26116		03.03.04
	D-KEAM I W Paterson Portmoak *'AM'*			31.07.18E
G-KEAY	AutoGyro MTOsport	xxxx		24.05.13
	R Keay Liverpool John Lennon			15.08.18P
	Assembled Rotorsport UK as c/n RSUK/MTOS/049			
G-KEDK	Schempp-Hirth Discus bT	81/414		14.01.11
	(BGA 5664), D-KEDK, OO-ZQI			
	S G Vardigans Wycombe Air Park *'Y2'*			14.04.18E
G-KEEF	Commander Aircraft Commander 114B 14610			17.06.04
	N828DL, VT-PVA, (F-GSDV), VT-PVA, N6025M			
	K D Pearse Jersey			19.05.18E
G-KEEN	Stolp SA.300 Starduster Too	800		19.07.78
	PH-HAB, (PH-PET), G-KEEN, N800RE			
	H Sharp tr Sharp Aerobatics Sleap			27.04.04P
	Built by R E Ellenbest; stored 02.18 (IE 15.05.15)			
G-KEES	Piper PA-28-180 Cherokee Archer	28-7505025		29.05.97
	OO-AJV, OO-HAC, N32102		C N Ellerbrook	Brook
	House, Morley St Botolph			07.11.18E
G-KEJY	Evektor EV-97 teamEurostar UK	2004-2017		23.06.04
	M Dagg & T McCaffrey			
	(Stoke-on-Trent & Hednesford)			10.03.19P
	Assembled Cosmik Aviation Ltd			
G-KELI	Robinson R44 Raven II	11040		16.02.06
	Manor Corporate Ltd (Omagh)			29.03.18E
G-KELL	Van's RV-6	xxxx		16.05.95
	(EI-...), G-KELL P R Watkins Crowfield			03.12.19P
	Built by J D Kelsall – project PFA 181-12845			
G-KELP	Aeroprakt A-22LS Foxbat	A22LS-299		29.03.17
	J F Macknay Welshpool			20.12.19P
	Built by J F Macknay – project LAA 317B-15459			
G-KELS	Van's RV-7	xxxx		22.02.02
	G J Collins & F W Hardiman			
	Fowle Hall Farm, Laddingford			21.05.19P
	Built by J D Kelsall – project PFA 323-13801			
G-KELT	Airbus A320-251N	8403		16.01.19
	F-WWBJ, D-AVVL Acropolis Aviation Ltd Farnborough			
	(IE 16.01.19)			
G-KELX	Van's RV-6	21853		01.07.10
	G-HAMY P J McMahon Ludham			16.10.18P
	Built by P W Armstrong – project PFA 181-12305			
G-KELZ	Van's RV-8	xxxx		09.11.06
	G-DJRV M O'Leary Turweston			03.12.18P
	Built by D J Hunt & J D Kelsall – project PFA 303-13665			
G-KEMC	Grob G109	6024		19.10.84
	D-KEMC Norfolk Gliding Club Ltd Tibenham			24.05.18E
G-KEMH	Westland SA.341B Gazelle AH.1	1284		15.01.19
	XX386 MW Helicopters Ltd Stapleford			
	(NF 15.01.19)			
G-KEMI	Piper PA-28-181 Archer III	2843180		28.10.98
	N41493 Modern Air (UK) Ltd Fowlmere			16.02.18E
G-KEMJ	Schempp-Hirth Duo Discus T	23/284		01.03.19
	(BGA 5989), D-KEMJ, (D-7605)			
	H Andersson tr 2UP Group Parham Park			
	(IE 01.03.19)			
G-KENA	Cameron A-300	12156		01.03.18
	Airxcite Ltd Stafford Park, Telford			26.02.19E
G-KENC	Comco Ikarus C42 FB100 Bravo	1607-7455		29.07.16
	K Clark (Chipping Sodbury)			13.09.19P
	Assembled Red Aviation			
G-KENG	AutoGyro MT-03	06 087		22.01.07
	K A Graham Popham			18.04.19P
	Assembled Rotorsport UK as c/n RSUK/MT-03/011			
G-KENK	Cameron TR-70	11873		06.03.15
	K R Karlstrom Northwood			12.04.18E
G-KENL	Sackville BM-65	KL01		24.10.18
	K F Lowry Tilehurst, Reading			
	(NF 24.10.18)			
G-KENM	Luscombe 8E Silvaire Deluxe	2908		09.01.91
	N21NK, N71481, NC71481			
	M G Waters Ranston Farm, Iwerne Courtney			27.06.18P
G-KENR	Kubicek BB20XR	1253		07.06.18
	Airxcite Ltd t/a Virgin Balloon Flights			
	Stafford Park, Telford			19.06.19E
G-KENW	Robin DR.500-200i Président	39		20.02.03
	K J White Homefield Farm, Crowhurst			26.05.18E
	Built by Constructions Aeronautiques de Bourgogne;			
	officially registered as DR.400-500			
G-KENX	Cameron Sport-90	12157		20.03.18
	K R Karlstrom Northwood			
	(NF 20.03.18)			
G-KENZ	Rutan VariEze	xxxx		13.08.04
	G-BNUI K H McConnell Enniskillen			17.05.18P
	Built by T N F Snead – project PFA 074-10960			
G-KEPE	Schempp-Hirth Nimbus-3DT	25		14.10.05
	BGA 5116/KHZ, D-KEPE J McWilliam			
	tr Nimbus Syndicate PE Aston Down *'PE'*			05.05.18E
G-KEPP	Rans S-6-ES Coyote II	0404.1564		19.10.04
	R G Johnston Newtownards			21.05.18P
	Built by S Munday – project PFA 204-14308			
G-KERK	Piper J-3C-65 Cub	12613		08.05.80
	G-OINK, G-BILD, G-KERK, 44-80317			
	Cancelled 11.09.12 by CAA			19.07.99
	(Winchester) *Stored as 'G-OINK' 06.16*			
G-KESS	Glaser-Dirks DG-400	4-257		15.08.05
	F-CGRH M T Collins & T Flude Ringmer			12.06.18E
G-KEST	Steen Skybolt	1		11.06.91
	G-BNKG, G-RATS, G-RHFI, N443AT			
	B Tempest tr G-KEST Syndicate Leicester			01.02.18P
	Built by A Todd			
G-KESY	Slingsby T59D Kestrel 19	1839		01.11.07
	BGA 2902/ERY, EI-125, D-9253			
	C J, K A & P J Teagle Sutton Bank *'983'*			12.10.18R
G-KETH	Agusta-Bell 206B-2 JetRanger II	8418		14.10.03
	OO-HOP, PH-HAP, SX-HAP, (HB-XEX)			
	DAC Leasing Ltd Hall Farm, Mannington			14.02.18E
G-KEVA	Ace Aviation Magic/Cyclone	xxxx		31.07.13
	K A Armstrong Mount Airey Farm, South Cave			
	Trike s/n not known & wing s/n AC-158			
	(SSDR microlight since 05.14) (IE 26.08.16)			
G-KEVB	Piper PA-28-181 Archer III	2843098		29.08.97
	N9289E Victor Bravo Flying Ltd Elstree			04.03.18E
G-KEVG	AutoGyro MT-03	08 001		14.02.08
	C J Morton Turweston			28.02.18P
	Assembled Rotorsport UK as c/n RSUK/MT-03/031			
G-KEVH	Avtech Jabiru UL-450	354		16.06.17
	G-CBPP K L Harris Welshpool			22.11.19P
	Built by C J Cullen & J N Pearson			
	– project PFA 274A-13607			
G-KEVI	Avtech Jabiru J400	197		19.10.04
	P Horth & P G Macintosh tr The Jabo Club Inverness			14.08.18P
	Built by K A Allen – project PFA 325-14321			
G-KEVL	RotorWay Exec 162F	6112		07.12.09
	G-CBIK K D Longhurst Chapter Farm, Higham			22.06.15P
G-KEVS	P&M Quik GT450	8311		17.09.07
	I A Macadam (Hinton St Mary, Sturminster Newton)			26.03.19P
	Trike used with new wing c/n 8598 to become G-KEVZ			
G-KEVZ	P&M QuikR	8598		19.10.11
	K Mallin Pound Green			25.03.18
	Built by with new wing c/n 8598 & trike c/n 8531			
	ex G-KEVS			
G-KEWT	Ultramagic M-90	90/66		27.05.09
	R D Parry Sutton, Tenbury Wells *'Kew Technik'*			08.07.18
G-KEYS	Piper PA-23-250 Aztec F	27-7854052		06.10.78
	N63909 Giles Aviation Ltd Lydd			23.05.18
G-KEYY	Cameron N-77	1748		14.06.89
	G-BORZ L J Whitelock Bristol *'Business Design'*			22.06.09
	Inflated Bath 12.18 (NF 25.11.16)			
G-KFBA	Valentin Taifun 17E	1084		12.08.1
	D-KFBA M T Collins Ringmer			21.07.18

G-KFCA	Comco Ikarus C42 FB80	1309-7282	28.10.13
	D Young Cotswold		15.11.18P
	Assembled Red-Air UK		

G-KFLY	Flight Design CTSW	06-11-04	05.09.07
	G-LFLY J J Brutnell & G W F Morton Cambridge		12.03.18P
	Assembled P&M Aviation Ltd as c/n 8244		

G-KFOG	Van's RV-7	74475	16.10.15
	K Fogarty (Tarnock, Axbridge)		
	Built by K Fogarty – project LAA 323-15361		
	(IE 17.09.17)		

G-KFOX	Denney Kitfox Model 2	xxxx	11.10.88
	R A Hampshire Eaglescott		01.09.18P
	Built by J Hannibal – project PFA 172-11447		

G-KFTI	Pilatus PC-12/47E	1813	21.08.18
	HB-FSX Daki Aviation Ltd (Douglas, IoM)		

G-KFVG	Schempp-Hirth Arcus M	24	17.02.14
	D-KFVG M T Burton Dunstable Downs *'4M'*		11.03.18E

G-KGAO	Scheibe SF25C Falke 2000	44386	30.07.99
	D-KGAO Midland Gliding Club Ltd Long Mynd		17.11.18E

G-KGAW	Scheibe SF25C Falke 2000	44506	21.12.12
	D-KGAW The Windrushers Gliding Club Ltd Bicester		29.08.17E

G-KGKG	Embraer EMB-135BJ Legacy 600	14500986	28.02.19
	9H-OKG, OK-GGG, PT-SKC		
	London Executive Aviation Ltd London Stansted		

G-KGMM	Schempp-Hirth Ventus-2cT	4/11	25.11.14
	(BGA 5816), D-KGMM, SP-0069, BGA 4216/HUP		
	G Smith Parham Park *'MM'*		05.05.18E

G-KHCC	Schempp-Hirth Ventus bT	34	03.04.06
	BGA 5224/KNH, D-KHCC		
	J L G McLane Sutton Bank *'LM'*		15.01.19E

G-KHCG	Aérospatiale AS.355F2 Ecureuil 2	5193	08.06.09
	G-SDAY, G-SYPA, LV-WHC, F-WYMS, G-BPRE, N366E		
	CE Aviation UK Ltd (Lowestoft)		30.03.18E

G-KHEA	Scheibe SF25B Falke	4821	20.06.12
	D-KHEA R J Hale Barton Ashes, Crawley Down		09.03.18E

G-KHOP	Zenair CH.601HDS Zodiac	6-9105	14.09.05
	K Hopkins Sleap		29.03.18P
	Built by K Hopkins – project PFA 162-13561		

G-KHPI	Schleicher ASW 28-18E	28717	04.01.16
	(BGA 5864), D-KHPI		
	J C Ferguson Husbands Bosworth *'Y9'*		25.05.18E

G-KHRE	SOCATA Rallye 150SV Garnement	2931	25.03.82
	F-GAYR S S A Withams tr Kingsmuir Group		
	Sorbie Farm, Kingsmuir		05.06.18E

G-KIAB	Scheibe SF25C Falke 2000	44439	11.11.16
	D-KIAB L Ingram Enstone		12.10.18E

G-KIAN	Piper PA-28R-201 Arrow III	28R-7837022	26.08.15
	SE-LLP, D-EAVD, N47986		
	M Al-Souri White Waltham		01.07.18E

G-KIAU	Scheibe SF25C Falke 2000	44461	28.05.14
	D-KIAU L Ingram Enstone		31.03.18E

G-KICK	Cyclone Pegasus Quantum 15-912	7679	28.06.00
	G v d Gaag (Elm Road, March)		07.10.18P

G-KIDD	Avtech Jabiru J430	272	26.10.06
	G-CEBB R L Kidd (Tewin, Welwyn)		29.09.16P
	Built by K D Pearce – project PFA 336-14541		

G-KIEV	DKBA AT 0300-0	03	11.03.08
	P A Sweatman t/a The Volga Balloon Team		
	Coventry CV5		
	(IE 12.06.15)		

G-KIII	Extra EA.300/L	1246	02.11.06
	Extra 200 Ltd Goodwood		12.06.19E

G-KIKI	Piper PA-28-181 Archer II	28-7990377	11.09.18
	G-BSIZ, N2162Y AJW Construction Ltd Elstree		15.11.19E

G-KIMA	Zenair CH.601XL Zodiac	6-9499	21.03.06
	D Joy	North Weald	11.12.18P
	Built by K Martindale – project PFA 162B-14207;		
	tricycle u/c		

G-KIMB	Robin DR.300-140 Major	470	23.03.90
	F-BPXX, F-WPXX A D Hoy Jersey		07.10.19E

G-KIMH	AutoGyro MTOsport	10 055S	11.05.10
	P B Harrison (Hoylake, Wirral)		12.02.18P
	Assembled Rotorsport UK as c/n RSUK/MTOS/034		

G-KIMI	Piper PA-46-500TP Malibu Meridian	4697314	24.10.14
	F-HPPF, N505HB, N505HP, N168CA, N9538N, N3090K		
	M Konstantinovic & S N Mitchell North Weald		11.09.19E

G-KIMK	Partenavia P68B	27	23.02.01
	G-BCPO P Mason & R Turrell Kings Farm, Thurrock		16.01.19E

G-KIMM	Europa Aviation Europa XS	404	20.07.99
	R A Collins Wadswick Manor Farm, Corsham		03.07.18P
	Built by P A D Clarke – project PFA 247-13404;		
	tailwheel u/c		

G-KIMS	Comco Ikarus C42 FB100	1704-7497	19.06.17
	J W D Blythe Swansea		29.07.18P
	Assembled Red Aviation		

G-KIMY	Robin DR.400-140B Major 80	1401	07.06.00
	PH-SRX J H Wood Perranporth		19.01.18E

G-KIMZ	Piper PA-28-180 Cherokee D	28-4870	15.04.14
	G-AWDP, N11C		
	Ravenair Aircraft Ltd Liverpool John Lennon		02.05.19E

G-KINL	Grumman FM-2 Wildcat	5744	11.05.16
	G-CHPN, N49JC, N70637, N20HA, N68760,		
	BuA 86690 T W Harris Duxford		
	On restoration 07.18 (NF 11.05.16)		

G-KINT	Scheibe SF25C Falke 2000	44412	09.04.15
	D-KINT M R C Bean tr G-KINT Syndicate Tibenham		14.06.18E

G-KIPP	Thruster T.600N 450	1031-T600N-094	19.12.03
	Cancelled 22.12.11 as WFU		19.03.11
	Wing Farm, Longbridge Deverill *Parts only stored 08.13*		

G-KIRB	Europa Aviation Europa XS	474	25.10.06
	G-OIZI P Handford (Wellingborough)		
	Built by K S Duddy – project PFA 247-13615		
	(NF 20.07.15)		

G-KIRC	Pietenpol/Challis Chaffinch	1008	20.03.06
	G-BSVZ, N3265 M J Kirk Barton Ashes, Crawley Down		
	Built by H Challis; noted 06.15 (NF 24.02.16)		

G-KIRT	Stoddard-Hamilton GlaStar	5424	22.01.13
	K Luby Woolston Moss, Warrington		11.05.18P
	Built by K Luby – project LAA 295-15189; tailwheel u/c		

G-KISP	DG Flugzeugbau LS10-st	L10-004	12.03.15
	(BGA 5830), D-KISP		
	D G Pask & J J Shaw Sutton Bank *'SP'*		02.02.19E

G-KISS	Rand Robinson KR-2	xxxx	02.08.83
	B L R J Keeping (St Austell)		
	Built by A C Waller – project PFA 129-10899		
	(NF 30.04.18)		

G-KITE	Piper PA-28-181 Archer II	28-8490053	12.04.88
	N4338X Cancelled 12.12.08 by CAA		01.05.08
	Blackbushe		
	Cockpit used as simulator by Aerobility 06.17		

G-KITH	Alpi Pioneer 300	177	22.09.06
	K G Atkinson Gilrudding Grange, Deighton		09.08.18P
	Built by K G Atkinson – project PFA 330-14510		

G-KITI	Pitts S-2E	002	21.06.90
	N36BM J C W Seward Sleap *'Super Turkey II'*		18.10.18P
	Built by R Jones		

G-KITO	Piper PA-24-260 Comanche B	24-4386	08.09.17
	I-KITO, I-GIOV, N8930P		
	A Costi (Tavarnelle Val Di Pesa, Italy)		02.08.18E

G-KITS	Europa Aviation Europa XS	468	13.06.94
	J R Evernden Wellesbourne Mountford		10.05.18P
	Built by Europa Aviation Ltd – project PFA 247-12844;		
	tricycle u/c		

G-KIZZ	Air Création Buggy 582(1)/Kiss 450	FL028	24.06.04
	D L Price (Lichfield)		22.09.18P
	Built by P David – project BMAA/HB/388 (Flylight		
	kit FL028 comprising trike s/n T04028 & wing s/n		
	A04068-4969)		

G-KJJR	Schempp-Hirth Ventus-2cxT	215	30.01.13
	(BGA 5736), D-KJJR		
	R J L Maisonpierre Gransden Lodge *'JR'*		30.03.18E

G-KJTT	Cessna 182A Skylane	51429	26.08.16
	HB-CRG, N2129G A Savino tr Associazione Sportiva		
	Dilettantistica Alisei (San Giovannni Rotundo, Italy)		25.01.20E

G-KKAM	Schleicher ASW 22BLE	22065	24.06.08
	(BGA 5321), D-KKAM, D-KBJL		
	D P Taylor Sutton Bank *'499'*		15.07.18E

G-KKER	Avtech Jabiru UL-450	0255	01.10.99
	M A Coffin Middle Stoke, Isle of Grain		31.05.17P
	Built by K Kerr – project PFA 274A-13474; noted 08.18		
	(IE 01.05.18)		
G-KKEV	Bombardier DHC-8-402Q	4201	25.04.08
	C-FOUU Flybe Ltd Exeter Int'l *'Kevin Keegan'*		29.04.19E
G-KKKK	Scottish Aviation Bulldog Srs 120/121	BH120/199	02.10.01
	G-CCMI, G-KKKK, XX513		
	M Cowan Hundon, Stradishall		26.09.18P
	As 'XX513:10' in RAF c/s		
G-KKRN	Robinson R22 Beta	1201	22.06.18
	G-WFWS, G-LINS, G-DMCD, G-OOLI, G-DMCD		
	HQ Aviation Ltd Galway, RoI		20.08.19E
G-KKTG	Cessna 182R Skylane	18267964	02.12.16
	ER-COB, N9565H		
	T Knight & S Thomas Bournemouth		09.02.19E
G-KLAW	Christen Eagle II	003-1	24.08.09
	W Hosie tr The Eagle Group RNAS Yeovilton		
	'Raging Bull'		03.10.18P
	Built by R S Goodwin, M Hanley, D Linsowe & B Lovering		
G-KLNE	Hawker 900XP	HA-0186	19.03.12
	N186XP Saxonair Charter Ltd Luton		28.03.18E
G-KLNH	Leonardo AW109SP Grand New	22364	08.09.16
	Saxonair Charter Ltd Norwich Int'l		07.09.18E
G-KLNP	Eurocopter EC120B Colibri	1492	17.09.09
	EI-FGL, PH-ECM, F-WWXM		
	Quinto Crane & Plant Ltd Norwich Int'l		10.03.18E
G-KLNW	Cessna 510 Citation Mustang	510-0157	02.02.09
	Saxonair Charter Ltd Norwich Int'l		31.01.19E
G-KLTB	Lindstrand LTL Series 1-90	009	10.05.16
	A M Holly Breadstone, Berkeley *'keltbray'*		06.06.19E
G-KLUB	Scheibe SF25C Rotax-Falke	44543	25.01.19
	D-KLUB L Ingram Enstone		08.03.19E
	(IE 25.01.19)		
G-KLYE	Best Off Skyranger Swift 912S(1)	SKR0803867	07.05.08
	P A Murdock tr G-KLYE Group		
	(Lurgan, Craigavon, RoI)		30.09.19P
	Built by D M Hepworth & B A Ritchie		
	– project BMAA/HB/572		
G-KMAK	P&M Quik GT450	8202	12.05.15
	44-AKM K I Making Over Farm, Gloucester		22.06.18P
G-KMBB	Scheibe SF25D Falke	46182D	07.08.12
	D-KMBB K P & R L McLean Rufforth		
	Stored 10.16 as 'D-KMBB' (NF 23.07.18)		
G-KMIR	Schleicher ASH 31 Mi	31026	27.11.15
	D-KMIR M Woodcock (Bristol BS8) *'IR'*		04.06.19E
G-KMJK	DG Flugzeugbau DG-808C	8-367B266X30	12.05.16
	EI-GMN, D-KACB		
	N Burke, L Rayment & D W Smith Sutton Bank *'JK'*		10.06.19E
	Built by DG Flugzeugbau GmbH		
G-KMKM	AutoGyro MTOsport	11 069S	28.09.11
	J M Boddy tr Golf Kilo Mike		
	(Upper Cambourne, Cambridge)		30.10.18P
	Assembled Rotorsport UK as c/n RSUK/MTOS/040		
G-KMLA	Cirrus SR20	1763	14.08.17
	N164SR KML Aviation OY (Kuopio, Finland)		19.09.18E
G-KMRV	Van's RV-9A	90755	17.11.04
	G K Mutch Hawarden		16.03.18P
	Built by G K Mutch – project PFA 320-14093		
G-KNAP	Piper PA-28-161 Warrior II	28-8116129	15.02.90
	G-BIUX, N9507N Cancelled 12.01.10 as destroyed		28.04.02
	Randalstown		
	Displayed at Escaramouche paintball park 12.13		
G-KNCG	Piper PA-32-301FT 6X	3232017	05.03.08
	SX-ARP, N3064J, N9519N T Moore t/a		
	Sportsdata Services & Take Flight Aviation Ltd		
	Wellesbourne Mountford		02.06.18E
G-KNEE	Ultramagic M-77C	77/234	20.06.03
	M A Green Birmingham B45		03.09.17E
G-KNEK	Grob G109B	6437	22.05.00
	D-KNEK R A Winley tr Syndicate 109		
	Currock Hill		13.06.18E
G-KNIB	Robinson R22 Beta II	3145	30.10.00
	C G Knibb Sywell		10.10.18E

G-KNOT^M	Hunting Percival P.84 Jet Provost T.3A	PAC/W/13893	09.06.99
	G-BVEG, XN629 Cancelled 21.06.07 as PWFU		
	As 'XN629:49' – fuselage only		
	With Suffolk Aviation Heritage Museum, Kesgrove		
G-KNOW	Piper PA-32-300 Cherokee Six	32-7840111	21.09.88
	N9694C M & W M Wilkins Headcorn *'Jilly King'*		22.11.18E
G-KNYT	Robinson R44 Astro	0723	13.03.00
	Brosters Environmental Ltd Manchester Barton		14.06.18E
G-KOBH	Schempp-Hirth Discus bT	154	23.11.06
	BGA 5257, D-KOBH		
	K Neave & C F M Smith Nympsfield *'920*		02.01.19E
G-KOCO	Cirrus SR22	3447	07.07.09
	N152CK I S L Rutland (London SW6)		14.08.19E
G-KOFM	Glaser-Dirks DG-600/18M	6-66M16	13.07.99
	D-KOFM A Mossman tr G-KOFM Group		
	Feshiebridge		12.01.19E
G-KOKL	Hoffmann H36 Dimona	36276	04.03.98
	D-KOKL G C Alexander tr Dimona Group Rufforth		17.08.18E
G-KOKO	Cirrus SR22T	1680	20.03.18
	N680RF R K Fitzgerald Wycombe Air Park		
	(IE 23.03.18)		
G-KOLB	Kolb Twinstar Mk.IIIA	xxxx	30.06.93
	Condor Aviation International Ltd		
	Birchwood Lodge, North Duffield		29.09.03P
	Built by P A Akines – project PFA 205-12228		
	(NF 28.09.15)		
G-KOLI	PZL-110 Koliber 150	03900038	23.07.90
	N T O'Fee tr KOLI Group RAF Henlow		10.01.19E
G-KONG	Slingsby T67M-200 Firefly	2041	24.03.94
	VR-HZP, HKG-10, G-7-119		
	N A & O O'Sullivan Newcastle, RoI *'293'*		28.07.17E
G-KOOL^M	de Havilland DH.104 Sea Devon C.2/2	04220	12.01.82
	VP967, 'G-DOVE' Cancelled 13.01.12 as WFU		
	As 'VP967' in RAF c/s		
	With Yorkshire Air Museum, Elvington		
G-KORE	Sportavia-Putzer SFS31 Milan	6601	29.11.12
	D-KORE, OE-9083, D-KORO J R Edyvean Bicester		29.04.18E
G-KOTA	Piper PA-28-236 Dakota	28-8011044	23.12.88
	N8130R M D Rush Bagby		26.07.18E
G-KOVU	Reims/Cessna FA150K Aerobat	FA1500081	28.07.16
	G-FMSG, G-POTS, G-AYUY		
	NAL Asset Management Ltd Durham Tees Valley		24.04.19E
G-KOYY	Schempp-Hirth Nimbus-4T	9	28.10.05
	BGA 5205/KMN, D-KOYY D Pitman Bicester *'Y7'*		11.05.18E
G-KRAN	Scheibe SF25C Rotax-Falke	44652	21.11.18
	D-KRAN, D-KIEP Morgan Land Sea & Air LLP		
	(Chalfont St Giles)		
	(NF 21.11.18)		
G-KRBN	Embraer EMB-505 Phenom 300	50500358	30.03.16
	Saxonair Charter Ltd Norwich Int'l		29.03.19E
G-KRBY	Van's RV-8	xxxx	18.07.17
	P Kirby (East Ruston, Norwich)		
	Built by P Kirby – project LAA 303-15238 (NF 18.07.17)		
G-KRES	Stoddard-Hamilton Glasair Super IIS RG	xxxx	12.06.96
	A D Murray Perth		19.12.18P
	Built by G Kresfelder – project PFA 149-12984		
G-KRIB	Robinson R44 Raven II	12640	20.01.09
	Jim Davies Civil Engineering Ltd		
	(Hollybush, Blackwood)		05.04.19E
G-KRII	Rand Robinson KR-2	xxxx	04.08.89
	M R Cleveley Priory Farm, Tibenham		
	Built by M R Cleveley – project PFA 129-10934;		
	on rebuild 02.18 (NF 05.05.16)		
G-KRMA	Cessna 425 Corsair	425-0003	21.12.06
	D-INGA, N98751		
	Speedstar Holdings Ltd Sherburn-in-Elmet		14.04.12E
	(NF 08.12.14)		
G-KRTO	Rand Robinson KR-2	xxxx	01.03.18
	Condor Aviation International Ltd		
	Birchwood Lodge, North Duffield		
	Built by T J Price – project PFA 129-11029 (NF 28.02.18)		

G-KRUZ	CZAW Sportcruiser	4011		22.05.08
	A W Shellis & P Whittingham Sittles Farm, Alrewas			06.09.18P
	Built by A W Shellis & P Whittingham			
	– project LAA 338-14765			
G-KRWR	Glaser-Dirks DG-600/18M	6-95M41		24.04.14
	D-KRWR A D W Hyslop Bicester *'LNA'*			31.03.18E
G-KSFR	Bombardier BD-100-1A10 Challenger 300 20189			30.04.08
	C-FQOI The Lily Partnership LLP London Stansted			29.04.18E
G-KSHI	Beech A36 Bonanza	E-2353		07.11.08
	D-EKDN, N7241Y			
	P A Teichman t/a Hangar 11 Collection Elstree			20.11.18E
G-KSIR	Stoddard-Hamilton Glasair IIS RG	2151		15.04.94
	K M Bowen Cardiff			12.07.18P
	Built by R Cayzer – project PFA 149-12137			
G-KSIX	Schleicher Ka 6E	4165		23.06.08
	BGA 1452/CDD C D Sterritt Lasham			
	Fuselage displayed in The Gliding Heritage Centre 02.15			
	(NF 16.09.15)			
G-KSKS	Cameron N-105	4963		21.03.01
	A Kaye t/a Kiss the Sky Ballooning			
	Irchester, Wellingborough *'Kwik Kaye'*			08.08.19E
G-KSKY	Sky 77-24	170		15.10.99
	M W Durham Brackley *'Sky Balloons'*			16.01.19E
G-KSSA	McDonnell Douglas MD Explorer	900-00123		20.12.12
	N902CS, N90187			
	Specialist Aviation Services Ltd Redhill			13.06.18E
	Operated by Kent, Surrey & Sussex Air Ambulance			
	as callsign 'Helimed 60'			
G-KSSC	Leonardo AW169	69061		22.12.17
	I-EASJ Specialist Aviation Services Ltd Redhill			21.12.18E
	Operated by Kent, Surrey & Sussex Air Ambulance			
	as callsign 'Helimed xx'			
G-KSSH	McDonnell Douglas MD Explorer	900-00062		21.09.07
	G-WMID, N3063T			
	Specialist Aviation Services Ltd RAF Waddington			24.09.18E
	Official type designation superseded			
G-KSST	AgustaWestland AW169	69014		08.02.16
	Specialist Aviation Services Ltd			
	Wheelbarrow Industrial Estate, Marden			08.02.19E
	Built by Finmeccanica SpA; operated by Kent,			
	Surrey & Sussex Air Ambulance as callsign 'Helimed 60'			
G-KSSX	Schleicher ASW 27-18E (ASG 29E) 29593			14.04.15
	(BGA 5840), D-KSSX L M Brady Lasham *'SX'*			14.10.18E
G-KSVB	Piper PA-24-260 Comanche B	24-4657		08.11.91
	G-ENIU, G-AVJU, N9199P, N10F			
	Knockin Flying Club Ltd Sandford Hall, Knockin			29.03.18E
G-KTCH	Magni M16C Tandem Trainer	16181534		02.08.18
	Ketchell Holdings Ltd Popham			
	Active 09.18 (IE 16.11.18)			
G-KTEA	Robin DR.400-140B Major 80	2720		17.09.18
	A B English (Ashtead)			
	(IE 16.01.19)			
G-KTOW	Comco Ikarus C42 FB100 Bravo	1311-7287		27.11.13
	Mayfly G-KTOW Ltd Enstone			04.07.18P
	Assembled Red-Air UK			
G-KTTY	Denney Kitfox Model 3	xxxx		28.11.05
	G-LESJ T Pennington Manchester Barton			12.06.19P
	Built by L A James – project PFA 172-12001			
G-KTWO	Cessna 182T Skylane	18281742		23.11.06
	N282SS S J G Mole Brine Pits Farm, Droitwich			15.01.19E
G-KUBE	Robinson R44 Raven II	10091		27.05.16
	G-VEIT Helicopter Services Ltd White Waltham			02.08.18E
G-KUGG	Schleicher ASW 27-18E (ASG 29E) 29620			09.02.11
	(BGA 5671) J W L Otty Wycombe Air Park *'SG9'*			02.05.18E
G-KUIK	Mainair Pegasus Quik	7990		17.10.03
	P Nugent Grantley Adams Int'l, Barbados			14.06.18P
	Built by Mainair Sports Ltd			
G-KUIP	CZAW Sportcruiser	09SC334		25.01.10
	A J Kuipers Sleap			26.03.18P
	Built by A J Kuipers – project LAA 338-14956			
G-KULA	Best Off Skyranger Swift 912S(1)	UK/353?		26.01.04
	G S Cridland Horse Leys Farm, Burton on the Wolds			05.10.18P
	Built by C R Mason – project BMAA/HB/344;			
	BMAA record as kit no UK/364 but believed UK/353			

G-KUPP	Flight Design CTSW	06-08-21		24.10.06
	P A James tr Cloudbase Group Redhill			
	'Annie's Dream II'			18.03.18P
	Assembled P&M Aviation Ltd as c/n 8227			
G-KURK	Piper J-3C-65 Cub	11527		06.01.09
	G-BJTO, F-BEGK, OO-AAL, 43-30236 M J Kirk			
	(Lodge Farm, Higher Durston) *'Liberty Girl II'*			29.06.17P
	Suffered engine failure landing at Khartoum 20.11.16			
	then force landing en route to Gambelle, Ethiopia			
	22.11.16, damage unknown			
G-KURT	Jurca MJ.8 Fw190	SH 05/MJ8		12.06.13
	S D Howes (Darlington)			
	Built by S D Howes (NF 04.10.17)			
G-KUTI	Flight Design CTSW	08-06-06		03.04.09
	D F & S M Kenny Finmere			02.05.18P
	Assembled P&M Aviation Ltd as c/n 8450			
G-KUTU	QAC Quickie Q.2	xxxx		08.03.82
	R Nash (London W9)			
	Built by Quick Construction Group			
	– project PFA 094A-10758 (NF 24.04.15)			
G-KUUI	Piper J-3C-65 Cub	17521		25.08.05
	N2MD, N70515, NC70515 V S E Norman Rendcomb			
	28.03.19E			
G-KVAN	Flight Design CTSW	07-10-11		09.10.17
	G-IROE K Brown Old Warden			04.09.18P
	Assembled P&M Aviation Ltd as c/n 8334			
G-KVBF	Cameron A-340HL	4313		06.04.98
	Airxcite Ltd t/a Virgin Balloon Flights			
	Stafford Park, Telford *'Virgin'*			08.06.10E
	(NF 15.09.14)			
G-KVIP	Beech 200 Super King Air	BB-487		17.05.02
	G-CBFS, G-PLAT, N8PY, VH-PIL, N198SC, PT-OYR,			
	N40QN, VH-NIC, N40QN, N400N, N243KA			
	Capital Air Ambulance Ltd Exeter Int'l			29.05.19E
G-KWAK	Scheibe SF25C Rotax-Falke	44581		08.01.03
	D-KWAK Mendip Gliding Club Ltd Halesland			27.05.18E
G-KWAX	Cessna 182E Skylane	18253808		18.05.78
	N9902, YV-T-PTS, N2808Y			
	Cancelled 27.04.10 by CAA			16.04.06
	Derby *On rebuild 06.14 using front fuselage of G-ASSF*			
G-KWET	Cessna 150L	15075630		18.03.19
	G-CSFC, (G-BFLX), N11370			
	M Ali Hinton-in-the-Hedges			26.05.19E
G-KWFL	Evektor EV-97 Eurostar SL	2016-4236		26.10.16
	Aqueous 1st Kwikflow Ltd Durham Tees Valley			20.10.17P
	Assembled Light Sport Aviation Ltd (IE 03.11.17)			
G-KWIC	Mainair Pegasus Quik	7962		25.06.03
	M Gibson Perth			23.06.19P
	Built by Mainair Sports Ltd			
G-KWKI	QAC Quickie Q.200	xxxx		22.10.91
	R Greatrex Colthrop Manor Farm, Thatcham			28.10.08P
	Built by D G Greatrex & B M Jackson – project PFA 094-12158 (NF			
	31.10.14)			
G-KWKR	P&M QuikR	8412		07.01.09
	L G White Finmere			09.02.18P
G-KWKX	P&M QuikR	8724		25.06.15
	M G Evans Manor Farm, Croughton			23.06.18P
G-KXMS	Schempp-Hirth Ventus-2cxT	226		04.03.15
	(BGA 5833), D-KXMS A J McNamara Bicester *'TC'*			06.04.18E
G-KXXI	Schleicher ASK 21	21024		06.01.09
	(BGA 5341), SE-TVH			
	Shenington Gliding Club Shenington *'XXI'*			09.06.18E
G-KYLA	Cirrus SR22	3698		05.01.18
	OK-TTP, N440RW J Bannister Cotswold			
	(IE 05.01.18)			
G-KYLE	Thruster T600N 450	0053-T600N-113		03.06.05
	RM Aviation Ltd Beverley (Linley Hill)			23.03.17P
	Badged 'Sprint' (IE 06.06.17)			
G-KYTE	Piper PA-28-161 Warrior II	28-8216043		20.01.06
	G-BRRN, N84533			
	I C Barlow & G Whitlow Wycombe Air Park			19.03.18E
G-KYTT	Piper PA-18-150 Super Cub	18-7909174		19.10.16
	I-SCDT, N9754N F Actis (Turin, Italy)			02.12.18E

G-LAAA – G-LZZZ

G-LAAC Cameron C-90 10778 27.01.06
S Dyer Farnborough GU14 *'Army Air Corps'* 30.06.19E

G-LAAI Druine D.5 Turbi xxxx 20.11.17
D Silsbury (Ivybridge)
Built by D Silsbury – project LAA 276-15365 (IE 20.11.17)

G-LABS Europa Aviation Europa 049 01.03.94
P J Tyler Shifnal 02.09.18P
*Built by C T H Pattinson – project PFA 247-12595;
tailwheel u/c*

G-LACB Piper PA-28-161 Warrior II 28-8216035 12.06.90
N8450A Upperstack Ltd t/a LAC Flying School
Manchester Barton 29.08.18E

G-LACR Denney Kitfox 1117 04.12.90
C M Rose (Scone, Perth)
Built by C M Rose – project PFA 172-11945 (NF 12.02.15)

G-LADD Enstrom 480 5037 20.05.99
O Davies tr Davad Partnership Pembrey 28.04.19E

G-LADI Piper PA-30 Twin Comanche 30-334 08.04.94
G-ASOO Cancelled 21.02.07 as destroyed 22.12.07
Not Known *Converted to touring caravan,
wings to D-GPEZ; noted 06.16*

G-LADS Rockwell Commander 114 14314 06.12.90
N4994W, (N114XT), N4994W
D F Soul Wood Farm, Emberton 20.07.18E

G-LAFT Diamond DA.40D Star D4.193 28.03.06
Airways Aviation Academy Ltd Huesca-Pirineos, Spain 04.10.18E

G-LAGR Cameron N-90 1628 25.01.88
J R Clifton Nelson, New Zealand *'Tennent's Lager'* 11.10.03A
(NF 20.04.16)

G-LAIN Robinson R22 Beta 1992 07.02.92
Startrade Heli GmbH & Co KG
Palma-Son Bonet, Mallorca, Spain 20.06.19E

G-LAIR Stoddard-Hamilton Glasair IIS FT 2106 12.09.91
E O'Broin t/a Huntingdon & S T Raby
(Brampton & Woodwalton) 04.05.18P
*Built by A E O'Broin, S T Raby & D L Swallow
– project PFA 149-11923*

G-LAKE Lake LA-250 Renegade 70 12.07.88
(EI-PJM), G-LAKE, N8415B
Lake Aviation Ltd Biggin Hill 20.11.13E
Built by Aerofab Inc (NF 23.11.15)

G-LAKI Jodel DR.1050 Sicile 534 12.11.79
G-JWBB, G-LAKI, F-BLZD D Evans Headcorn 06.09.17P
Built by Centre-Est Aéronautique (IE 02.01.18)

G-LALA Reims/Cessna FA150K Aerobat 0005 20.07.17
(G-....), HB-TDS, I-FFSJ L J Liveras Elstree 26.09.19E

G-LAMM Europa Aviation Europa 244 20.11.95
S A Lamb (Paddock Wood, Tonbridge)
*Built by S A Lamb – project PFA 247-12941;
tailwheel u/c (NF 14.10.14)*

G-LAMP Cameron Lightbulb-110 4899 21.07.00
D M Hoddinott Bristol BS8 *'L.E.Electrical'* 06.08.18E

G-LAMS Reims/Cessna F152 II F15201431 23.06.88
N54558 APB Leasing Ltd Sleap 09.06.18E

G-LANC[M] Avro 683 Lancaster B.X xxxx 31.01.85
RCAF KB889 Cancelled 02.09.91 by CAA
*As 'KB889:NA-I' in RAF 428 Sqdn c/s
Built by Victory Aircraft, Canada
With Imperial War Museum, Duxford*

G-LANE Reims/Cessna F172N F17201853 27.06.79
M J Hadley North Weald 14.12.18E

G-LAOL Piper PA-28RT-201 Arrow IV 28R-7918211 06.10.99
D-EAOL, N2903Y R J Brink tr Arrow Flying Group
Goodwood *'19'* 28.03.18E

G-LARA Robin DR.400-180 Régent 2050 14.02.91
C A & K D Brackwell Solent 09.05.18E

G-LARD Robinson R66 Turbine 0559 07.11.14
E J R Canvin t/a Perry Farming Company
(Turvey, Bedford) 12.10.18E

G-LARE Piper PA-39 Twin Comanche C/R 39-16 20.02.91
N8861Y Glareways (Neasden) Ltd Biggin Hill 09.04.18E

G-LARK Helton Lark 95 9517 03.12.85
N5017J B S D Chapman tr Lark Group Hawarden 15.10.18P

G-LARR Eurocopter AS.350B3 Ecureuil 4137 15.01.07
F-WWXN TSL Contractors Ltd Balfron 13.04.18E
Operated by Skyhook Helicopters

G-LASN Best Off Skyranger J2.2(1) UK/479 19.07.04
A J Coote (Ryefield, Virginia, RoI) 29.07.16P
*Built by L C F Lasne – project BMAA/HB/396
(IE 06.09.17)*

G-LASR Stoddard-Hamilton Glasair IIS RG 2027 08.01.90
G Lewis Sleap 28.10.17E
Built by G Lewis & P Taylor – project PFA 149-11584

G-LASS Rutan VariEze xxxx 20.09.78
J Mellor Sleap 21.10.18P
*Built by P J Callert, D G Foreman & J F O'Hara
– project PFA 074-10209*

G-LATE Dassault Falcon 2000EX 088 01.12.09
M-ILES, OE-HOT, F-WWGY
Executive Jet Charter Ltd Farnborough 03.12.18E

G-LAUD Cessna 208 Caravan I 20800582 28.04.16
N697ZZ, N5066U
Laudale Estate LLP (Bramham, Wetherby) 05.05.18E

G-LAVA Airbus EC135 P3 2064 12.10.18
Heligroup Operations Ltd Wycombe Air Park 11.10.19E

G-LAVE Cessna 172R Skyhawk 17280663 10.03.99
G-BYEV, N2377J, N41297
Trim Flying Club Ltd Dublin Weston, RoI 22.06.19E

G-LAVN Guimbal Cabri G2 1234 20.09.18
Heligroup Operations Ltd Wycombe Air Park 06.11.19E

G-LAWX Sikorsky S-92A 920007 01.05.09
N908W Starspeed Ltd London Stansted 05.05.18E

G-LAZL Piper PA-28-161 Warrior II 28-8116216 09.06.99
D-EAZL, N9536N
Highland Aviation Training Ltd Inverness 12.08.18E

G-LAZR Cameron O-77 2240 06.03.90
Wickers World Ltd Priory Farm, Tibenham *'Laser'* 14.07.17E
Stored at Priory Farm, Tibenham 01.19

G-LAZZ Stoddard-Hamilton GlaStar 5252 31.10.99
C R & R H Partington Boon Hill Farm, Fadmoor 31.05.18P
*Built by G K Brunwin & A N Evans
– project PFA 295-13059; tricycle u/c*

G-LBAC Evektor EV-97 teamEurostar UK 2013-3934 12.03.12
G Burder & A Cox Plaistows Farm, St Albans 22.02.19P
Assembled Cosmik Aviation Ltd

G-LBDC Bell 206B-3 JetRanger III 3806 17.03.06
N206GF, (G-....), N509KK, JA9448, N206JG, N3186Z
Heli Logistics Ltd Goodwood 04.04.19E

G-LBLI Lindstrand LBL 69A HAB 010 04.11.92
Cancelled 07.10.10 as PWFU 30.06.07
Not Known *Inflated Pidley 05.16*

G-LBMM Piper PA-28-161 Warrior II 28-7816440 28.11.89
N6940C M A Jones Tatenhill 16.09.18E

G-LBRC Piper PA-28RT-201 Arrow IV 28R-7918051 20.07.88
N2245P D J V Morgan
Wolverhampton Halfpenny Green 01.05.18E

G-LBUK Lindstrand LBL 77A 922 15.05.03
D E Hartland Hognaston, Ashbourne
'Lindstrand Balloons' 15.08.18E

G-LBUZ Evektor EV-97A Eurostar 2004-2312 15.07.05
D P Tassart Scotland Farm, Hook 14.08.18P
Built by D P Tassart – project PFA 315-14425

G-LCFC Agusta A109S Grand 22137 20.11.14
HB-ZLI Ceilo Del Rey Co Ltd Biggin Hill 12.09.18E
Operated by King Power International

G-LCGL Comper CLA.7 Swift replica xxxx 01.07.92
R A Fleming Old Warden 26.09.19P
Built by J M Greenland – project PFA 103-11089

G-LCIO[M] Colt 240A HAB 1381 23.01.89
Cancelled 25.05.94 as WFU 07.03.91
*Damaged landing after first overflight Mt Everest by
hot air balloon 21.10.91
With British Balloon Museum & Library, Newbury*

G-LCKY	Flight Design CTSW	07-05-04	09.07.07
	D Subhani tr LCKY Sandown		16.07.19P
	Assembled P&M Aviation Ltd as c/n 8274		
G-LCLE	Colomban MC-30 Luciole	236	20.11.12
	J A Harris (Bourton, Gillingham)		
	Built by J A Harris – project LAA 371-15163		
	(NF 06.09.16)		
G-LCMW	TL 2000UK Sting Carbon	07 ST 243	02.04.08
	B J Tyre Manchester Barton		20.12.17P
	Built by L Chadwick & M J White – project LAA 347-14787		
G-LCPL	Aérospatiale AS.365N2 Dauphin 2	6393	08.04.05
	PT-YIF, ZS-RAZ, F-WYMI		
	Charterstyle Ltd Blackbushe		04.08.18E
G-LCPX	Eurocopter EC155 B1	6748	10.07.17
	G-WINV, G-WJCJ, F-WWOO		
	Charterstyle Ltd (Kingswinford)		18.11.16E
G-LCUB	Piper PA-18 Super Cub 95 (*L-18C-PI*)	18-1631	09.02.07
	G-AYPR, French Army 18-1631, 51-15631		
	The Tiger Club 1990 Ltd Damyns Hall, Upminster		18.05.19E
G-LCYD	Embraer ERJ 170-100 STD	17000294	03.09.09
	PT-TQU BA Cityflyer Ltd London City		02.09.19E
G-LCYE	Embraer ERJ 170-100 STD	17000296	18.09.09
	PT-TQW BA Cityflyer Ltd London City		17.09.19E
G-LCYF	Embraer ERJ 170-100 STD	17000298	29.10.09
	PT-TQR BA Cityflyer Ltd London City		28.10.19E
G-LCYG	Embraer ERJ 170-100 STD	17000300	26.11.09
	PT-TQZ BA Cityflyer Ltd London City		25.11.19E
G-LCYH	Embraer ERJ 170-100 STD	17000302	17.12.09
	PT-XQB BA Cityflyer Ltd London City		16.12.19E
G-LCYI	Embraer ERJ 170-100 STD	17000305	28.01.10
	PT-XQE BA Cityflyer Ltd London City		27.01.19E
G-LCYJ	Embraer ERJ 190-100 SR	19000339	04.03.10
	PT-TXY BA Cityflyer Ltd London City		03.03.19E
G-LCYK	Embraer ERJ 190-100 SR	19000343	08.04.10
	PT-XQK BA Cityflyer Ltd London City		07.04.19E
G-LCYL	Embraer ERJ 190-100 SR	19000346	29.04.10
	PT-XQM BA Cityflyer Ltd London City		28.04.19E
G-LCYM	Embraer ERJ 190-100 SR	19000351	27.05.10
	PT-XQR BA Cityflyer Ltd London City		26.05.19E
G-LCYN	Embraer ERJ 190-100 SR	19000392	08.11.10
	PT-XNY BA Cityflyer Ltd London City		07.11.19E
G-LCYO	Embraer ERJ 190-100 SR	19000430	18.04.11
	PT-TCQ BA Cityflyer Ltd London City		17.04.19E
G-LCYP	Embraer ERJ 190-100 SR	19000443	25.06.11
	PT-TJD BA Cityflyer Ltd London City		24.06.19E
G-LCYR	Embraer ERJ 190-100 SR	19000563	10.08.12
	PT-TDS BA Cityflyer Ltd London City		09.08.19E
G-LCYS	Embraer ERJ 190-100 SR	19000663	29.05.14
	PR-EEX BA Cityflyer Ltd London City		28.02.19E
G-LCYT	Embraer ERJ 190-100 SR	19000670	29.05.14
	PR-EGC BA Cityflyer Ltd London City		28.05.19E
G-LCYU	Embraer ERJ 190-100 SR	19000674	04.09.14
	PR-EHF BA Cityflyer Ltd London City		03.09.19E
G-LCYV	Embraer ERJ 190-100 SR	19000255	17.12.15
	N163HQ, (HB-JQH), PT-STD		
	BA Cityflyer Ltd London City		16.12.19E
G-LCYW	Embraer ERJ 190-100 SR	19000163	20.05.16
	PP-PJJ, HB-JQE, PT-SAS		
	BA Cityflyer Ltd London City		19.05.19E
G-LCYX	Embraer ERJ 190-100 SR	19000178	06.07.16
	PP-PJK, HB-JQF, PT-SDM		
	BA Cityflyer Ltd London City		06.07.19E
G-LCYY	Embraer ERJ 190-100 SR	19000189	22.12.17
	OY-ERA, PP-PJL, HB-JQG, PT-SDX		
	BA Cityflyer Ltd London City		20.01.20E
G-LCYZ	Embraer ERJ 190-100 SR	19000404	03.05.18
	VH-NJA, D-AEMG, PT-TYX		
	BA Cityflyer Ltd London City		16.05.19E
G-LDAH	Best Off Skyranger 912(2)	SKR0209216	08.10.02
	B Plunkett (Carlisle)		21.06.19P
	Built by L Dickinson & A S Haslam		
	– project BMAA/HB/241		

G-LDER	Schleicher ASW 22	22027	01.02.08
	BGA 3261/FGY, D-3527		
	P Shrosbree & D Starer Dunstable Downs '527'		11.05.18E
G-LDSA	TAF Sling 4	095	06.07.16
	L J d'Sa Brighton City		16.02.18P
	Built by L J d'Sa – project LAA 400-15412		
G-LDVO	Europa Aviation Europa XS	371	07.07.08
	D J Park Sleap		11.12.18P
	Built by D J Park – project PFA 247-13254;		
	tricycle u/c		
G-LDWS	Jodel D.150 Mascaret	48	13.02.04
	G-BKSS, F-BMFC		
	A L Hall-Carpenter Priory Farm, Tibenham		02.04.18P
	Built by Société Aéronautique Normande		
G-LDYS	Colt 56A	347	18.05.81
	M J Myddelton Knowle, Bristol 'Gladys'		30.01.13E
	(NF 02.06.14)		
G-LEAC	Cessna 510 Citation Mustang	510-0075	04.06.08
	Leacop SAS (Paris, France)		03.07.19E
G-LEAF	Reims/Cessna F406 Caravan II	F406-0018	07.03.96
	EI-CKY, PH-ALN, OO-TIW, F-WZDX		
	Reconnaissance Ventures Ltd t/a RVL Group		
	East Midlands		14.05.18E
G-LEAH	Alpi Pioneer 300	174	11.01.06
	A Bortolan (Epping)		18.10.18P
	Built by J C Ferguson – project PFA 330-14497;		
	based in Italy		
G-LEAM	Piper PA-28-236 Dakota	28-8011061	01.07.80
	G-BHLS, N35650		
	T F Rowley tr G-LEAM Group Elstree		12.09.19E
G-LEAS	Sky 90-24	158	04.05.99
	C I Humphrey Tilehurst, Reading 'LNG Fuel'		09.07.09E
	(NF 08.05.18)		
G-LEAT	Ultramagic B-70	70/13	07.03.16
	A M Holly Breadstone, Berkeley 'Longleat'		01.03.18E
	Lion's Head special shape		
G-LEAX	Cessna 560XL Citation XLS	560-5712	28.01.10
	N595QS London Executive Aviation Ltd		
	(London Stansted)		25.04.18E
G-LEBE	Europa Aviation Europa	237	17.05.01
	J E Fallis Popham		27.06.19P
	Built by P Atkinson – project PFA 247-12927;		
	tailwheel u/c		
G-LEDE	Zenair CH.601UL Zodiac	xxxx	14.04.09
	R Vicary Wellesbourne Mountford		08.09.18P
	Built by A R Cattell – project PFA 162A-14576		
G-LEED	Denney Kitfox Model 2	450	24.04.91
	O C Rash Chatteris		29.02.20P
	Built by G T Leedham – project PFA 172-11577		
G-LEEE	Avtech Jabiru UL-450	0293	18.01.00
	T Bailey Otherton		22.01.19P
	Built by L E G Fekete – project PFA 274A-13516		
G-LEEH	Ultramagic M-90	90/79	03.08.05
	Sport Promotion Srl La Morra, Piedmont, Italy 'Lee'		24.01.19E
G-LEEK	Reality Escapade	JA.ESC.0168	27.11.08
	G R Jones tr G-LEEK Phoenix Flying Group		
	Haverfordwest		29.08.18P
	Built by P B Bishop, W J Jones & S J Pugh-Jones		
	– project LAA 345-14843 – VLA version		
G-LEEN	Aero Designs Pulsar XP	216	16.07.01
	G-BZMP, G-DESI R B Hemsworth Eaglescott		12.06.07P
	Built by D F Gaughan – project PFA 202-12147		
	(NF 08.10.14)		
G-LEEZ	Bell 206L-1 LongRanger II	45761	22.01.92
	G-BPCT, G-HDBB, N3175G SJ Contracting Services		
	Ltd t/a Heli-Lift Services Oakdene Farm, Standedge		16.01.19E
G-LEFT	Cassutt Racer IIIM	xxxx	05.03.18
	G-CGSU Air Race CC Ltd Shenington		30.09.19P
	Built by D J Howell – project LAA 034-14983		
G-LEGC	Embraer EMB-135BJ Legacy 600	14501025	26.01.11
	EC-LGG, VP-CNJ, PT-SVZ		
	London Executive Aviation Ltd London Stansted		19.05.18E
G-LEGG	Reims/Cessna F182Q Skylane II	F18200145	26.06.96
	G-GOOS W A L Mitchell Insch		16.11.18E

G-LEGO	Cameron O-77	1975	14.04.89
	P M Traviss Low Worsall, Yarm		18.11.18E
G-LEGY	Flight Design CTLS	F.08-09-13	13.01.09
	T R Grief Bagby		30.04.18W
G-LEIC	Cessna FA152 Aerobat	FA1520416	16.09.86
	Cancelled 29.11.11 as PWFU		28.05.11
	Leicester *Built by Reims Aviation SA*		
	Fuselage stored 03.15		
G-LELE	Lindstrand LBL 31A	806	16.08.01
	D S Wilson Cantley, Norwich		31.05.18E
G-LEMI	Van's RV-8	xxxx	09.02.11
	The Lord Rotherwick Cornbury Park, Charlbury		12.02.19P
	Built by H R Rotherwick – project LAA 303-15057		
G-LEMM	Ultramagic Z-90	90/102	20.10.08
	M Marangoni Bagnacavallo, Ravenna, Italy		04.08.18E
G-LEMP	P&M QuikR	8707	16.01.15
	A M & E M Brewis t/a Messrs TH Brewis		
	Lempitlaw Farm, Kelso		25.12.18P
G-LEND	Cameron N-77 HAB	2012	25.05.89
	Cancelled 08.10.01 as PWFU		12.09.96
	Not Known *'Southern Finance Co' Inflated Pidley 04.18*		
G-LENI	Aérospatiale AS.355F1 Ecureuil 2	5311	09.08.95
	G-ZFDB, G-BLEV		
	Grid Defence Systems Ltd Denham		02.06.18E
G-LENN	Cameron V-56	1833	29.09.88
	D J Groombridge Congresbury, Bristol		07.08.18E
G-LENZ	Cirrus SR20	2304	28.10.16
	N121MX Renneta Ltd Cumbernauld		04.01.19E
G-LEOD	Pietenpol Air Camper	0148	23.11.05
	I D McLeod Stoneacre Farm, Farthing Corner		
	'Dame Flora'		17.08.18P
	Built by I D McCleod – project PFA 047-13499		
G-LEOG	Airbus AS.350B3 Ecureuil	8114	01.09.15
	G-CIRG Leo Group Ltd Swales Moor Farm, Halifax		13.10.18E
G-LEOS	Robin DR.400-120 Dauphin 2+2	1884	29.11.88
	Robin Flying Club Ltd Exeter Int'l		31.01.19E
G-LERE	Avions Transport ATR 72-212A	891	15.11.16
	OY-YBO, PP-PTU, F-WWEW		
	Aurigny Air Services Ltd Guernsey		01.11.19E
G-LESZ	Skystar Kitfox Model 5	S 94120076	25.10.02
	G M Park Strathaven		14.12.18P
	Built by L A James – project PFA 172C-12822		
G-LETS	Van's RV-7	72091	20.07.09
	M O'Hearne Sherburn-in-Elmet		
	Built by M O'Hearne – project PFA 323-14588		
	(NF 21.07.17)		
G-LEVI	Aeronca 7AC Champion	7AC-4001	17.04.90
	N85266, NC85266		
	C A Roberts tr G-LEVI Group White Waltham		18.07.17P
	Stored 05.18; carries '85266' on fin		
G-LEXI	Cameron N-77 HAB	438	26.10.78
	Cancelled 30.09.09 as PWFU		09.08.09
	Not Known *Inflated Ashton Court 08.18*		
G-LEXS	Agusta A109E Power	11154	20.02.18
	G-IVJM, G-MOMO Blade 5 Ltd Biggin Hill		16.08.19E
G-LEXX	Van's RV-8	xxxx	11.04.02
	S Emery North Weald		08.01.19P
	Built by A A Wordsworth – project PFA 303-13896		
G-LEXY	Van's RV-8	82725	15.01.08
	R C McCarthy Enstone		27.09.16P
	Built by A A Wordsworth – project PFA 303-14756;		
	Overturned Kingsley, Surrey, 29.06.16		
G-LEYA	Piper PA-32R-301T Saratoga II TC	3257476	29.09.15
	OK-PMP, N60785, N9532N Gamit Ltd North Weald		16.05.19E
G-LEZE	Rutan Long-EZ	xxxx	31.03.82
	Bill Allen's Autos Ltd Gloucestershire		07.06.19P
	Built by Andy Draper – project PFA 074A-10702		
G-LFBD	Cessna 525A CitationJet CJ2	525A0506	18.01.16
	N375DS, (N759R), N375DS, N5145V		
	Centreline AV Ltd t/a Centreline Bristol		25.01.18E
G-LFES	Sportine Aviacija LAK-17B FES	212	12.01.12
	(BGA 5845) C J Tooze Usk *'2ZE'*		21.05.17R
G-LFEZ	Sportine Aviacija LAK-17B FES	218	11.03.13
	(BGA 5744)		
	Baltic Sailplanes Ltd Husbands Bosworth *'L17'*		02.07.18R
G-LFIX	Supermarine 509 Spitfire Tr.9	CBAF.8463	01.02.80
	IAC162, G-15-175, ML407 Air Leasing Ltd Sywell		15.04.19P
	C/n is firewall plate number; as 'ML407:OU-V'		
	(starboard) in RAF 485 (NZ) Sqdn c/s		
G-LFSA	Piper PA-38-112 Tomahawk	38-78A0430	22.10.90
	G-BSFC, N9739N Liverpool Flying School Ltd		
	Liverpool John Lennon *'Liverbird 1'*		08.05.18E
G-LFSB	Piper PA-38-112 Tomahawk	38-78A0072	20.10.94
	G-BLYC, D-ELID, N9715N		
	J D Burford Gloucestershire		22.11.14E
	On overhaul 03.16 (NF 21.06.16)		
G-LFSC	Piper PA-28-140 Cherokee Cruiser	28-7425005	04.09.95
	G-BGTR, OY-BGO, SE-GDS		
	T A Hunt tr G-LFSC Flying Group Old Buckenham		12.12.18E
G-LFSG	Piper PA-28-180 Cherokee E	28-5799	19.06.00
	G-AYAA, N11C North East Aviation Ltd Eshott		26.02.19E
G-LFSH	Piper PA-38-112 Tomahawk	38-78A0352	16.07.01
	G-BOZM, N6247A Liverpool Flying School Ltd		
	Liverpool John Lennon		21.10.18E
G-LFSI	Piper PA-28-140 Cherokee C	28-26850	14.07.89
	G-AYKV, N11C G Corcoran tr G-LFSI Group		
	(Trebujena, Andalucía, Spain)		07.09.18E
G-LFSJ	Piper PA-28-161 Warrior II	28-7916536	04.11.02
	G-BPHE, N2911D Advanced Flight Training Ltd		
	Sherburn-in-Elmet		21.06.19E
G-LFSM	Piper PA-38-112 Tomahawk	38-78A0449	21.09.04
	G-BWNR, N2361E Liverpool Flying School Ltd		
	Liverpool John Lennon		23.06.18E
G-LFSN	Piper PA-38-112 Tomahawk	38-78A0073	04.12.06
	G-BNYV, N9364T Liverpool Flying School Ltd		
	Liverpool John Lennon		17.09.18E
G-LFSR	Piper PA-28RT-201 Arrow IV	28R-7918091	02.06.10
	G-JANO, SE-IZR, N2146X		
	S A Breslaw Elstree *'Liverbird 6'*		17.06.19E
	Operated by Fly Elstree		
G-LFSW	Piper PA-28-161 Warrior II	28-8116041	06.01.17
	G-BSGL, N82690 Liverpool Flying School Ltd		
	Liverpool John Lennon		21.06.18E
G-LFVB	Supermarine 349 Spitfire LF.Vb	CBAF 2403	09.05.94
	8070M, 5377M, EP120 Patina Ltd Duxford		17.06.19P
	As 'EP120:AE-A' in RAF 402 Sqdn c/s;		
	operated by The Fighter Collection		
G-LFVC	Supermarine 349 Spitfire LF.Vc	JG891	28.09.99
	N5TF, N624TB, ZK-MKV, A58-178, JG891		
	Comanche Warbirds Ltd Duxford		09.07.19P
	As 'JG891:T-B' in RAF c/s		
G-LGCA	Robin DR.400-180R Remorqueur	1686	17.02.04
	HB-KAP London Gliding Club Proprietary Ltd		
	Dunstable Downs		13.01.19E
G-LGCB	Robin DR.400-180R Remorqueur	1990	28.04.05
	D-EHRA London Gliding Club Proprietary Ltd		
	Dunstable Downs		11.02.18E
G-LGCC	Robin DR.400-180R Remorqueur	1021	21.08.07
	G-BNXI, SE-FNI London Gliding Club Proprietary Ltd		
	Dunstable Downs		04.12.18E
G-LGEZ	Rutan Long-EZ	xxxx	26.07.06
	P C Elliott Dunsfold		28.06.18P
	Built by P C Elliott – project PFA 074A-11361		
G-LGIS	Dornier 228-202K	8160	04.12.15
	CS-TGG, D-CORA, D-CBDQ		
	Aurigny Air Services Ltd Guernsey		29.04.19E
G-LGNA	Saab 340B	340B-199	11.06.99
	N592MA, SE-F99 Loganair Ltd Glasgow		
	'Spirit of Lewis' & 'Spiorad de Leodhas'		10.02.19E
	Built by Saab Scania AB		
G-LGNB	Saab 340B	340B-216	08.07.99
	N595MA, SE-G16 Loganair Ltd Glasgow		
	'Spirit of Glasgow' & 'Spiorad de Ghlaschu'		24.06.19E
	Built by Saab Scania AB		

G

G-LGNC	Saab 340B	340B-318	09.06.00
	SE-KXC, F-GTSF, EC-GMI, F-GMVZ, SE-KXC, SE-C18		
	Loganair Ltd Glasgow		
	'Spirit of Islay' & *'Spiorad de Ile'*		18.06.19E
	Built by Saab Scania AB		
G-LGND	Saab 340B	340B-169	07.09.01
	G-GNTH, N588MA, SE-F69 Loganair Ltd Glasgow		
	'Spirit of Sandy' & *'Spiorad de Sanddaidh'*		06.03.19E
	Built by Saab Scania AB		
G-LGNE	Saab 340B	340B-172	31.08.01
	G-GNTI, N589MA, SE-F72		
	Loganair Ltd Glasgow *'Spirit of Cumbria'*		04.02.19E
	Built by Saab Scania AB		
G-LGNF	Saab 340B	340B-192	08.08.02
	N192JE, G-GNTJ, N591MA, SE-F92		
	Loganair Ltd Glasgow		
	'Spirit of Young People 2018' & *'Spiorad Oigridh 2018'*		29.07.19E
	Built by Saab Scania AB		
G-LGNG	Saab 340B	340B-327	16.12.02
	SE-C27, VH-CMH, SE-C27 Loganair Ltd Glasgow		
	'Spirit of Harris' & *'Spiorad de Hearach'*		02.12.19E
	Built by Saab Scania AB		
G-LGNH	Saab 340B	340B-333	28.05.04
	SE-C33, VH-XDA, F-GMVX, SE-C33 Loganair Ltd		
	Glasgow *'Spirit of Edinburgh'* & *'Spiorad Dun Eideann'*		29.05.19E
	Built by Saab Scania AB		
G-LGNI	Saab 340B	340B-160	04.05.05
	SE-F60, ER-SGC, HB-AKA, SE-F60		
	Loganair Ltd Glasgow		
	'Spirit of Orkney' & *'Spiorad de Arcaibh'*		03.05.19E
	Built by Saab Scania AB		
G-LGNJ	Saab 340B	340B-173	27.05.05
	SE-F73, F-GPKD, HB-AKD, SE-F73		
	Loganair Ltd Glasgow		
	'Spirit of Benbecula' & *'Spiorad Beinn na Fadhia'*		23.05.19E
	Built by Saab Scania AB		
G-LGNK	Saab 340B	340B-185	07.07.05
	SE-F85, (D-CDAU), F-GPKG, (YR-VGT), F-GPKG,		
	HB-AKG, SE-F85 Loganair Ltd Glasgow		
	'Spirit of Caithness' & *'Spiorad Ghallaibh'*		28.06.19E
	Built by Saab Scania AB		
G-LGNM	Saab 340B	340B-187	18.03.08
	SE-F87, N347BE, SE-F87 Loganair Ltd Glasgow		
	'RMA Shetland Flyer' & *'RMA Itealaiche an Sealtainn'*		24.03.19E
	Built by Saab Scania AB		
G-LGNN	Saab 340B	340B-197	30.04.08
	SE-F97, N350BE, XA-ASM, N350BE, SE-F97		
	Loganair Ltd Glasgow		
	'RMA Orkney Flyer' & *'RMA Itealaiche an Arcaibh'*		22.04.19E
	Built by Saab Scania AB		
G-LGNO	Saab 2000	2000-013	14.03.14
	SE-LOT, YR-SBL, SE-LOT, F-GTSL, EI-CPQ, F-GTSA,		
	D-ADSA, SE-013 Loganair Ltd Glasgow		
	'Spirit of Aberdeen' & *'Spiorad Obar Dheathain'*		10.09.19E
	Built by Saab AB		
G-LGNP	Saab 2000	2000-018	04.06.14
	OY-SFC, YR-SBJ, HB-IZK, SE-018		
	Loganair Ltd Glasgow		14.05.19E
	Built by Saab AB		
G-LGNR	Saab 2000	2000-004	02.05.14
	OY-SFD, YR-SBD, HB-IZA, SE-004		
	Loganair Ltd Glasgow		02.05.19E
	Built by Saab AB		
G-LGNS	Saab 2000	2000-041	27.04.15
	HB-IZX, YR-SBE, HB-IZX, SE-041		
	Loganair Ltd Glasgow		04.06.19E
	Built by SAAB AB		
G-LGNT	Saab 2000	2000-039	19.04.16
	HB-IZW, YR-SBC, HB-IZW, SE-039 Loganair Ltd		
	Glasgow *'Spirit of the Highlands'* &		
	'Spiorad an Gaidhealtachd'		08.03.19E
	Built by Saab AB		
G-LGNU	Saab 340B	340B-223	27.06.17
	SE-KSI, EC-ASO, D-CASB, VH-EKK, SE-KSI, SE-G23		
	Loganair Ltd Glasgow *'Spirit of Dundee'*		02.09.19E

G-LGOC	Aero AT-3 R100	AT3-020	09.03.07
	(F-GURG) Kubi Service – Jakub Kubicki		
	Warsaw-Babice, Poland		21.08.17E
	(NF 18.03.18)		
G-LHAB	TAF Sling 2	225	05.09.17
	A P Beggin (Oxford)		
	Built by A P Beggin – project LAA 399-15401		
G-LHCB	Robinson R22 Beta II	3241	14.06.04
	G-SIVX Helipower Hire Ltd Newtownards		04.08.18E
G-LHCI	Bell 47G-5	2639	10.12.07
	G-SOLH, G-AZMB, CF-NJW		
	W K MacGillivray Glastullich Farm, Tain		29.05.19E
G-LHEL	Aérospatiale AS.355F2 Ecureuil 2	5462	29.03.04
	N42AT, N70PB		
	Beechwave Aviation Ltd (Ballynure, Ballyclare)		15.06.11E
	(NF 24.02.16)		
G-LHER	Czech Sport PiperSport	P1001042	15.07.10
	M P Lhermette Lamberhurst Farm, Dargate		05.07.18W
G-LIBB	Cameron V-77	2463	21.06.91
	R J Mercer Belfast BT5		05.06.18E
G-LIBC★	Piper PA-18-135 Super Cub	18-3451	15.06.18
	G-KAMP, D-EDPM, 96+27, NL+104, AC+502,		
	AS+501, 54-751 G Cormack		
	To G-PAIB 11.09.18		
G-LIBI	Glasflügel Standard Libelle 201B	367	23.08.10
	BGA 1817/CUK		
	O Spreckley Husbands Bosworth *'280'*		28.04.18E
G-LIBS	Hughes 369HS (500)	430469S	20.08.85
	N9147F R J H Strong (Vagg Hill, Yeovil)		17.08.18E
G-LIBY	Glasflügel Standard Libelle 201B	175	29.11.07
	BGA 1629/CLN R P Hardcastle Rufforth *'S2'*		11.05.18E
G-LICK	Cessna 172N Skyhawk II	17270631	19.04.88
	N172AG, G-LICK, G-BNTR, N739LQ		
	Sky Back Ltd Little Staughton		21.11.08E
	Stored dismantled 02.18 (IE 17.04.15)		
G-LIDA	HOAC HK 36R Super Dimona	36355	15.04.92
	Bidford Airfield Ltd Bidford		08.12.18E
G-LIDE	Piper PA-31-350 Chieftain	31-7852156	26.10.78
	(G-VIDE), N27800		
	Blue Sky Investments Ltd Belfast Int'l		03.10.18E
	Official type data 'PA-31-350 Navajo Chieftain'		
	is incorrect		
G-LIKE	Europa Aviation Europa	xxxx	09.03.11
	G-CHAV N G Henry (Oxford)		11.11.04P
	Built by M B Stoner – project PFA 247-12769;		
	rebuild of G-CHAV (kit no.117) (NF 17.04.15)		
G-LIKK	Robinson R66 Turbine	0729	14.12.18
	N54DW G-LIKK Ltd (Cranleigh)		
	(IE 14.12.18)		
G-LIKY	Aviat A-1C-180 Husky	3254	04.04.16
	N254WY L W H Griffith Home Farm, Ebrington		
	'Leslie'		10.05.18E
G-LILY	Bell 206B-3 JetRanger III	4107	14.03.95
	G-NTBI, C-FIJD		
	T Stone-Brown Chestham Park, Henfield		24.07.18E
G-LIMO	Bell 206L-1 LongRanger II	45476	12.06.03
	N5742H, G-LIMO, N5742H		
	Aerospeed Ltd Manston Park		19.07.18E
	Stored 09.18		
G-LIMP	Cameron C-80	10391	04.06.03
	Balloons Over Yorkshire Ltd Harrogate		27.06.18E
G-LINE	Eurocopter AS.355N Ecureuil 2	5566	22.03.94
	Cheshire Helicopters Ltd		
	Blackshaw Heys Farm, Mobberley		06.06.19E
	Operated by VLL Ltd t/a GB Helicopters		
G-LINJ	Robinson R44 Raven II	12168	11.10.18
	YR-JTG, G-ODCR Helicentre Aviation Ltd Leicester		
	(IE 11.10.18)		
G-LINN	Europa Aviation Europa XS	598	20.08.04
	C J Challener (Stockport)		24.04.19P
	Built by T Pond – project PFA 247-14118		
G-LINY	Robinson R44 Raven II	12356	22.09.17
	HB-ZWO, OO-LLL, D-HALB		
	Helicentre Aviation Ltd Leicester		18.12.18E

G

G-LINZ	Robinson R44 Raven II	11911	24.08.15	
	SP-GTE Helicentre Aviation Ltd Leicester		06.12.18E	
G-LIOA[M]	Lockheed 10A Electra	1037	06.05.83	
	N5171N, NC243, NC14959 Cancelled 26.04.02 as WFU			
	As 'NC5171N'			
	With Science Museum, South Kensington			
G-LION	Piper PA-18-135 Super Cub (L-21B-PI)	18-3857	29.08.80	
	PH-KLB, (PH-DKG), R Netherlands AF R-167, 54-2457			
	J G Jones t/a JG Jones Haulage			
	Pennant Uchaf Farm, Llandegla 'Grin'n Bare It'		23.07.18E	
	Fuselage No.18-3841; as 'R-167' in			
	Royal Netherlands Army c/s			
G-LIOT	Cameron O-77	2378	07.08.90	
	N D Eliot West Byfleet		27.05.05A	
	(NF 16.10.14)			
G-LIPS	Cameron Lips-90	4846	15.11.00	
	G-BZBV Reach for the Sky Ltd			
	Worplesdon, Guildford 'Joycam'		12.05.19E	
	Lips special shape			
G-LISS	AutoGyro Calidus	11 044 & C00181	27.09.11	
	Gyronauts Flying Club Ltd North Weald		10.12.19P	
	Assembled Rotorsport UK as c/n RSUK/CALS/019			
G-LITE	Rockwell Commander 112A	291	13.06.80	
	OY-RPP B G Rhodes Sleap		10.10.18E	
G-LITO	Agusta A109S Grand	22015	27.04.16	
	I-AWCC, F-GSNH, VH-FOX			
	Castle Air Ltd Trebrown, Liskeard		02.11.18E	
G-LITS	P&M QuikR	8490	16.10.09	
	A Dixon Bleaze Hall, Old Hutton, Kendal		12.07.18P	
G-LITZ	Pitts S-1E	xxxx	03.03.92	
	H J Morton (Entrammes, France) 'Glitz'		22.06.06P	
	Built by K Eld & J Hughes – project PFA 009-11131			
	(NF 10.07.18)			
G-LIVH	Piper J-3C-65 Cub (L-4H-PI)	11354	31.03.94	
	OO-JAN, OO-AAT, OO-PAX, 43-30238			
	B L Procter Dunkeswell		30.08.18E	
	Fuselage No.11354; as '330238:24-A' in US Army c/s			
G-LIVS	Schleicher ASH 26E	26228	24.02.05	
	P O Sturley Saltby '261'		21.04.18E	
G-LIZI	Piper PA-28-160 Cherokee	28-52	26.01.89	
	G-ARRP, N5050W			
	Peterborough Flying School Ltd Sibson		21.01.19E	
G-LIZY[M]	Westland Lysander III	'504/39'	20.06.86	
	RCAF 1558, V9300 Cancelled 18.04.89 as WFU			
	As 'V9673:MA-J' in RAF 161 Sqdn c/s			
	C/n also quoted as 'Y1351'			
	With Imperial War Museum, Duxford			
G-LJCC	Murphy Rebel	600R	08.07.98	
	P H Hyde (Norwich)			
	Built by J Clarke – project PFA 232-13335 (NF 08.10.14)			
G-LKVA	Tecnam P2010	077	15.03.19	
	K Yurovskiy (Richmond TW10)			
	(IE 15.03.19)			
G-LLBE	Lindstrand LBL 360A	1467	14.03.14	
	Adventure Balloons Ltd Hartley Wintney, Hook			
	'www.adventure balloons co.uk' & 'Rides'		18.04.19E	
G-LLCH	Cessna 172S Skyhawk SP	172S8822	27.06.08	
	G-PLBI, N35368 Bristol Flying Club Ltd Bristol		17.08.18E	
G-LLEW	Aeromot AMT-200S Super Ximango	200.126	15.11.00	
	M P Brockington & K Richards Lleweni Parc		18.04.19E	
G-LLGE	Lindstrand LBL 360A	1401	06.06.13	
	Adventure Balloons Ltd Hartley Wintney, Hook			
	'www.adventure balloons co.uk' & 'Happy Birthday'		09.06.18E	
G-LLIZ	Robinson R44 Raven II	12140	18.02.08	
	D M Hunter (Thorner, Leeds)		17.03.19E	
G-LLLL	Rolladen-Schneider LS8-18	8217	25.09.07	
	BGA 4657 P C Fritche Parham Park 'L4'		08.03.19E	
G-LLLY	Enstrom 480B	5076	25.07.16	
	N480EA, ZS-RCU AR-Pats LLP (Dorking)		08.08.19E	
G-LLMW	Diamond DA.42 Twin Star	42.167	21.09.06	
	OE-VPY M W Lau Wellesbourne Mountford		21.11.19E	
G-LLNT	Schleicher ASW 27-18E	29724	05.12.16	
	(BGA 5898) N D Tillett Dunstable Downs 'NT'		19.01.19E	

G-LLOY	Alpi Pioneer 300 Hawk	199	14.11.06	
	M R Foreman Shifnal		22.05.18P	
	Built by F Cavaciuti & A R Lloyd			
	– project PFA 330A-14568			
G-LMAO	Reims/Cessna F172N	F17201780	27.03.12	
	SE-GYT M G Schlumberger (Paris, France)		27.11.17E	
G-LMBO	Robinson R44 Raven	1743	08.08.07	
	Startrade Heli GmbH & Co KG Burbach, Germany		06.10.18E	
G-LMCB	Raj Hamsa X'Air Hawk	1255	25.05.12	
	B N Thresher (Tatworth, Chard)		25.05.18P	
	Built by B N Thresher – project LAA 340-15126			
G-LMLV	Dyn'Aéro MCR-01 Club	82	25.10.99	
	D Athey & N Fisher tr G-LMLV Flying Group Sturgate		11.08.18P	
	Built by L La Vecchia – project PFA 301A-13524			
G-LNAC	Leonardo AW169	69023	29.09.16	
	I-RAIS Specialist Aviation Services Ltd			
	RAF Waddington		28.09.18E	
	Operated by Lincolnshire & Nottinghamshire			
	Air Ambulance			
G-LNDN	McDonnell Douglas MD Explorer	900-00125	18.08.15	
	A7-NHA, N999GQ, N9043L			
	London's Air Ambulance Ltd RAF Northolt		22.12.18E	
	Operated by London Air Ambulance as callsign			
	'Helimed 27'			
G-LNIG	Flylight Dragonfly/Aeros Discus 15T	038	26.08.09	
	P J Cheyney New House Farm, Birds Edge			
	Wing s/n 021 09			
	(SSDR microlight since 05.14) (IE 21.05.18)			
G-LOAD	Dan Rihn DR.107 One Design	448	07.06.02	
	M J Clark Wellcross Farm, Slinfold		06.10.17P	
	Built by M J Clark – project PFA 264-13776 (IE 06.12.17)			
G-LOAG[M]	Cameron N-77 HAB	359	10.11.77	
	Cancelled 31.03.93 as destroyed		06.04.84	
	Envelope only			
	With British Balloon Museum & Library, Newbury			
G-LOAM	Flylight MotorFloater	MF007	27.07.11	
	A W Nancarrow (Shoreham-by-Sea)			
	(IE 16.07.15)			
	(SSDR microlight since 05.14)			
G-LOAN	Cameron N-77	1434	09.01.87	
	P Lawman Northampton 'Newbury Building Society'		05.06.18E	
G-LOBO	Cameron O-120	3389	03.01.95	
	C A Butter t/a Solo Aerostatics Marsh Benham		27.05.18E	
G-LOCH	Piper J-3C-65 Cub (L-4J-PI)	12687	10.12.84	
	HB-OCH, 44-80391			
	M C & M R Greenland RNAS Yeovilton		19.08.16P	
	Fuselage No.12517			
G-LOFM	Maule MX-7-180A Super Rocket	20027C	19.07.95	
	N31110 B R Alexander Dunkeswell		19.11.19E	
G-LOFT	Cessna 500 Citation I	500-0331	12.01.95	
	LN-NAT, EC-FUM, EC-500, LN-NAT, N40AC, N96RE,			
	N86RE, N331CC, (N5331J)			
	Janez Let D.O.O (Ljubljana, Slovenia)		01.01.19E	
G-LOGN	Piper PA-28-181 Archer III	2843279	09.02.18	
	VH-JYM I P Logan Turweston		07.07.19E	
G-LOIS	Avtech Jabiru UL	144	14.09.00	
	EI-JAK C Conidaris Clench Common		08.03.18P	
	Originally built by as Irish SAAC project SAAC-68;			
	rebuilt by S Walshe – project PFA 274A-0144 (sic)			
G-LOKI	Ultramagic M-77C	77/260	12.04.05	
	Border Ballooning Ltd Plas Madoc, Montgomery		07.07.18E	
G-LOLI	DG Flugzeugbau DG-1000M	10-248M29	31.03.17	
	P Crawley Sutton Bank		18.04.18E	
G-LOLL	Cameron V-77	2964	04.12.92	
	P Spellward Bristol BS9		05.07.18E	
G-LOLZ	Robinson R22 Beta	0655	02.05.17	
	OH-HAF Swift Helicopter Services Ltd Leeds Heliport			
	(NF 28.04.17)			
G-LOMN	Cessna 152	15285217	30.10.14	
	SP-KGV, N6278Q North Weald Flying Group Ltd			
	North Weald		06.11.19E	
G-LONE	Bell 206L-1 LongRanger	45729	05.10.04	
	G-CDAJ, N20AP, N3174W Central Helicopters Ltd			
	Nottingham Heliport, Widmerpool		20.02.18E	

G-LOOC	Cessna 172S Skyhawk SP	172S11006	04.02.10	
	N52742 Goodwood Road Racing Company Ltd			
	Goodwood		24.02.18E	
G-LOON	Cameron C-60	11160	02.07.08	
	T Lex Buch Am Buchrain, Germany		16.07.18E	
G-LOOP	Pitts S-1D	850	11.05.78	
	5Y-AOX N Tomlinson Leicester		20.09.19P	
	Built by D Mallinson as Type S-IC			
G-LORC	Piper PA-28-161 Cadet	2841339	12.01.99	
	D-ESTC, N9184W, (N620FT), (SE-KMP)			
	Advanced Flight Training Ltd Sherburn-in-Elmet		04.06.18E	
G-LORD	Piper PA-34-200T Seneca II	34-7970347	06.05.88	
	N2908W H E Held-Ruf			
	St Gallen-Altenrhein, St Gallen, Switzerland		27.02.15E	
	(NF 11.01.17)			
G-LORN	Mudry CAP 10B	282	04.03.99	
	R G Drury Goodwood		09.08.19E	
G-LORR	Piper PA-28-181 Archer III	2843037	19.04.96	
	N9268X, G-LORR Shropshire Aero Club Ltd Sleap		06.07.18E	
G-LORY	Thunder Ax4-31Z	171	28.11.78	
	M J Woodcock East Grinstead		01.06.19E	
G-LOSM	Gloster Meteor NF.11	S4/U/2342	08.06.84	
	WM167 D G Thomas Bruntingthorpe		17.12.17P	
	Built by Armstrong-Whitworth Aircraft Ltd;			
	as 'WM167' in RAF 151 Sqdn c/s; preserved			
	in taxiable condition by Classic British Jets			
	Collection 01.19 (NF 23.10.18)			
G-LOST	Denney Kitfox Model 3	xxxx	10.08.95	
	J T Lister Sorbie Farm, Kingsmuir		06.08.01P	
	Built by R Baily & H Balfour-Paul – project			
	PFA 172-12055; stored 09.17 (NF 27.04.16)			
G-LOSY	Evektor EV-97 Eurostar	2003-1240	22.12.03	
	M L Willmington Westonzoyland		17.03.18P	
	Built by J A Shufflebotham – project PFA 315-14161			
G-LOTE	Piper PA-28-161 Cadet	2841089	08.07.15	
	SE-KIB AJW Construction Ltd Bournemouth		30.05.18E	
G-LOTI[M]	Blériot Type XI replica	xxxx	21.12.78	
	Cancelled 06.03.09 as PWFU *As '2'*		19.07.82	
	Built by M L Beach – project PFA 088-10410			
	With Brooklands Museum, Weybridge			
G-LOTY	P&M Pegasus Quik	8656	25.07.13	
	L Hewitt (Shaw, Oldham)		23.08.17P	
G-LOUD	Schleicher ASW 27-18E	29730	11.05.17	
	(BGA 5930) T Stuart Nympsfield *'621'*		14.05.18E	
G-LOUS	Evektor EV-97 Eurostar SL	2016-4234	18.07.16	
	S E Bettley & M D Jealous Ashcroft		17.07.18P	
	Assembled Light Sport Aviation Ltd			
G-LOWE	Monnett Sonerai I	367	16.11.78	
	P A Hall White Waltham		20.06.14P	
	Built by J A Lowe – project PFA 015-10344;			
	on rebuild Sywell 09.18 (NF 04.10.16)			
G-LOWS	Sky 77-24	025	19.03.96	
	D J Bellinger & A J Byrne Thatcham *'Dawn Treader'*		05.07.18E	
G-LOWZ	P&M Quik GT450	8599	11.11.11	
	R E J Pattenden Rankins Farm, Linton		13.08.18P	
G-LOYA	Reims FR172J Rocket	FR17200352	04.08.89	
	G-BLVT, PH-EDI, D-EEDI			
	Mid America (UK) Ltd Dornoch		29.08.19E	
G-LOYD	Aérospatiale SA.341G Gazelle 1	1289	19.06.85	
	G-SFTC, N47298			
	S Atherton Crab Tree Farm, Deighton		04.07.08E	
	Rebuilt 1990 using major components of			
	N6957 (c/n 1060) (NF 26.01.16)			
G-LPAD	Lindstrand LBL 105A	632	05.08.99	
	G R Down Biddenden, Ashford			
	'Line Packaging & Design'		28.07.18E	
G-LPIN	P&M QuikR	8424	03.03.09	
	G P D Coan Longacre Farm, Sandy		17.03.18P	
G-LRBW	Lindstrand LBL HS-110 HA Airship	253	02.08.95	
	C J Sanger-Davies Hawarden CH5		30.03.05A	
G-LREE	Grob G109B	6252	07.08.07	
	D-KEKO J T Morgan tr G-LREE Group Denham		06.07.18E	

G-LROK	Robinson R66 Turbine	0581	02.02.15	
	London Rock Supplies Ltd Wycombe Air Park		03.07.19E	
G-LSAA	Boeing 757-236	24122	17.05.05	
	N241CV, TC-FLB, TC-ANM, EC-FFK, EC-744, G-BNSF,			
	(D-AOEB), G-BNSF, EC-ELS, EC-203, G-BNSF			
	Dart Group PLC Leeds Bradford *'Jet2 Tenerife'*,			
	'22kg bag allowance' & *'Allocated seats'* (Port),			
	'Great package holidays' & *'Great flight times'* (Stbd)		07.10.19E	
	Line No: 187; operated by Jet2.com; red tail			
G-LSAB	Boeing 757-27B	24136	17.05.05	
	N136CV, TC-FLC, TC-ANN, PH-AHF, 4X-EBF, G-OAHF,			
	OY-SHF, PH-AHF Dart Group PLC Leeds Bradford			
	'Jet2 Menorca', *'22kg bag allowance'* & *'Allocated seats'*			
	(Port), *'Great package holidays'* & *'Great flight times'*			
	(Stbd)		15.01.20E	
	Line No: 169; operated by Jet2.com; red tail			
G-LSAC	Boeing 757-23A	25488	14.03.06	
	N254DG, G-LSAC, N310FV, C-GTSE, N1792B			
	Dart Group PLC Leeds Bradford			
	'Jet2 Lanzarote' & *'Jet2holidays'*		22.05.19E	
	Line No: 471; operated by Jet2.com			
G-LSAD	Boeing 757-236	24397	16.06.06	
	SX-BLW, G-OOOS, G-BRJD, EC-ESC, EC-349, G-BRJD			
	Dart Group PLC Leeds Bradford *'Jet2holidays'*		01.08.19E	
	Line No: 221; operated by Jet2.com			
G-LSAE	Boeing 757-27B	24135	28.06.06	
	OM-SNA, N335FV, PH-AHE, OY-SHE, PH-AHE, OY-SHE,			
	PH-AHE Dart Group PLC Leeds Bradford			
	'Jet2 Newcastle' & *'Jet2holidays'*		11.09.19E	
	Line No: 165; operated by Jet2.com			
G-LSAG	Boeing 757-21B	24014	23.11.06	
	B-2801, N1792B Dart Group PLC Leeds Bradford			
	'Friendly Low Fares'		22.03.19E	
	Line No: 144; operated by Jet2.com; red tail			
G-LSAH	Boeing 757-21B	24015	23.11.06	
	B-2802, N5573B Dart Group PLC Leeds Bradford			
	'Friendly Low Fares'		19.03.19E	
	Line No: 148; operated by Jet2.com; red tail			
G-LSAI	Boeing 757-21B	24016	23.11.06	
	B-2803, N5573K Dart Group PLC Leeds Bradford			
	'22kg bag allowance' & *'Allocated seats'* (Port),			
	'Great package holidays' & *'Great flight times'* (Stbd)		24.05.19E	
	Line No: 150; operated by Jet2.com			
G-LSAJ	Boeing 757-236	24793	06.05.08	
	G-CDUP, SE-DUP, G-CDUP, SE-DUP, G-OOOT,			
	G-BRJJ, EC-490, G-BRJJ			
	Dart Group PLC Leeds Bradford			
	'Jet2holidays' & *'Package holidays you can trust'*		13.09.19E	
	Line No: 292; operated by Jet2.com			
G-LSAK	Boeing 757-23N	27973	28.01.10	
	N517AT Dart Group PLC Leeds Bradford			
	'Jet2holidays'		24.05.19E	
	Line No: 735; operated by Jet2.com			
G-LSAN	Boeing 757-2K2	26635	30.05.12	
	HC-CIY, N635AV, PR-ONF, N635GS, F-HAXY, F-WAXY,			
	N512TZ, PH-TKC			
	Dart Group PLC Leeds Bradford *'Jet2holidays'*		09.08.19E	
	Line No: 608; operated by Jet2.com			
G-LSCM	Cessna 172S Skyhawk SP	172S8445	07.06.04	
	N612TG, N165ME Pooler-LMT Ltd			
	Lower Grounds Farm, Shirlowe		12.02.18E	
G-LSCP	Rolladen-Schneider LS6-18W	6236	31.01.08	
	BGA 4814/JVK, D-6417			
	L G Blows & M F Collins Parham Park *'CP'*		31.03.18E	
G-LSCW	Gulfstream Gulfstream V-SP (*Gulfstream 550*)	5471	01.10.14	
	N571GA Langley Aviation Ltd Luton		30.09.18E	
G-LSED	Rolladen-Schneider LS6-c	6260	17.10.07	
	BGA 3913, (BGA 3908/HFK)			
	K Atkinson & T Faver Cranwell North *'126'*		14.09.18E	
G-LSFB	Rolladen-Schneider LS7-WL	7009	31.01.08	
	BGA 5042/KEW, F-CGYA, F-WGYA, D-1272			
	Denbigh Gliding LLP Lleweni Parc *'FB'*		12.08.19E	
G-LSFR	Rolladen-Schneider LS4-a	4260	30.10.07	
	BGA 2908 A Mulder Nympsfield *'LS4'*		15.02.19E	

G-LSFT	Piper PA-28-161 Warrior II	28-8516008	10.11.99
	G-BXTX, PH-LEH, N130AV, N43682		
	Falcon Flying Services Ltd Brighton City		01.04.19E
G-LSGB	Rolladen-Schneider LS6-b	6184	04.12.07
	BGA 3361/FMC A Rieder Wormingford '6B'		15.07.18E
G-LSGM	Rolladen-Schneider LS3-17	3346	24.01.06
	BGA 5144/KJU, D-6760, OO-ZLD		
	M R W Crook Tibenham 'GM'		29.05.18E
G-LSHI	Colt 77A	1264	20.07.88
	J H Dobson Goring, Reading		
	'Lambert Smith Hampton'		12.07.95A
	(NF 21.10.15)		
G-LSIF	Rolladen-Schneider LS1-f	383	24.01.08
	BGA 4738/JSF, LN-GGE, SE-TOU		
	R C Godden Wormingford '1F'		04.07.18E
G-LSIV	Rolladen-Schneider LS4	4189	28.09.07
	BGA 2806 G M O'Hagan Nympsfield '264'		15.03.19E
G-LSIX	Rolladen-Schneider LS6-18W	6352	14.03.08
	BGA 4119/HQL, D-0794 D P Masson Lasham 'LS6'		12.05.18E
G-LSJE	Reality Escapade Jabiru(3)	UK.ESC.0006	19.02.08
	L S J Webb RNAS Culdrose		30.05.18P
	Built by L S J Webb – project BMAA/HB/486;		
	tricycle u/c		
G-LSKS	Robinson R66 Turbine	0657	14.02.18
	N657JG Net Blocks Ltd (Nicosia, Republic of Cyprus)		22.04.19E
G-LSKV	Rolladen-Schneider LS8-18	8095	16.11.07
	BGA4288/HXN P A Binnee, C E Garner		
	& J R W Luxton Wycombe Air Park 'KV'		12.04.18E
G-LSKY	P&M Pegasus Quik	8119	12.08.05
	M Gudgeon Hunsdon		28.05.18P
G-LSLS	Rolladen-Schneider LS4	4191	22.10.07
	BGA 2808 A D d'Arcy tr 288 Syndicate		
	Long Mynd '288'		24.03.18E
G-LSPH	Van's RV-8	xxxx	03.09.07
	R S Partridge-Hicks Little Haugh Hall, Norton		27.09.18P
	Built by R S Partridge-Hicks – project PFA 303-13733		
G-LSTA	Stoddard-Hamilton GlaStar	5884	08.05.18
	OE-CCK I V Sharman & R J Sheridan Redhill		
	Built by C Kitzmantel		
G-LSTR	Stoddard-Hamilton GlaStar	xxxx	20.04.98
	D I Waller Eshott		11.05.18P
	Built by R Y Kendal – project PFA 295-13093;		
	tailwheel u/c		
G-LSVI	Rolladen-Schneider LS6-c18	6266	12.10.07
	BGA 3910 R Hanks Long Mynd 'LJ'		25.01.20E
G-LSZA	Diamond DA.42NG Twin Star	42.N013	20.12.17
	HB-LZM, OH-AKW, D-GDAI J Molen Blackbushe		
G-LTFB	Piper PA-28-140 Cherokee	28-23343	28.02.97
	G-AVLU, N11C D Bostock Bournemouth		06.04.19E
	Operated by Fly With Me Aviation		
G-LTFC	Piper PA-28-140 Cherokee B	28-26259	08.06.94
	G-AXTI, N11C N M G Pearson Henstridge		04.02.08E
	Noted 09.18 (NF 18.03.15)		
G-LTNG[M]	English Electric Lightning T.5	B1/95011	08.11.89
	8503M, XS451 Cancelled 13.02.97 – to ZU-BEX		
	As 'XS451'		
	With Classic Jets South Africa, Cape Town		
G-LTSB	Cameron LTSB-90	4483	15.01.99
	ABC Flights Ltd Clapton in Gordano, Bristol		
	'Lloyds TSB'		01.06.05A
	(NF 16.08.17)		
G-LTWA	Robinson R44 Clipper	0816	18.03.09
	PH-WRF L T W Alderman (Sandon, Buntingford)		22.03.18E
G-LTZY	Eurocopter EC120B Colibri	1073	22.03.18
	G-OTFL, G-IBRI, LX-HCR J Henshall Redhill		13.12.19E
G-LUBB	Cessna 525 CitationJet	525-0271	12.12.11
	G-OSOH, HB-VNK, N860DB, N860DD		
	Surrey Heli Charters LLP Bristol		28.02.19E
G-LUBY	Avtech Jabiru J430	399	19.12.06
	S King North Weald		03.07.19P
	Built by K Luby – project PFA 336-14605		
G-LUCK	Reims/Cessna F150M	F15001238	13.12.79
	PH-LEO, D-EHRA A W C Knight Sywell		27.07.19E

G-LUCL	Colomban MC-30 Luciole	Plans No: 80	10.05.10
	A McQueen East Fortune		09.05.19P
	Built by R C Teverson – project LAA 371-14988		
G-LUDM	Van's RV-8	82531	22.02.06
	A G Ransom Northrope Fen		08.04.18P
	Built by D F Sargant – project PFA 303-14521		
G-LUED	Aero Designs Pulsar	xxxx	09.03.92
	J C Anderson		26.05.18P
	Built by J C Anderson – project PFA 202-12122;		
	damaged beyond repair when it over-ran on landing		
	at Sturgate and flipped upside down 31.08.18		
G-LUEK	Cessna 182T Skylane	18281740	23.11.09
	N2467A S R Greenall Jersey		21.02.18E
G-LUEY	Rans S-7S Courier	0108.494	18.03.10
	S Garfield Stoke Golding		08.11.18P
	Built by S Garfield – project LAA 218-14772		
G-LUGS	Agusta A109S Grand	22125	22.01.18
	G-FRZN Volare Aviation Ltd Oxford		24.06.18E
G-LUKA	Beech G58 Baron	TH-2257	10.01.13
	SP-MAP, N6257R Bentley O-S Ltd Isle of Man		15.07.18E
G-LUKE	Rutan Long-EZ	xxxx	04.07.84
	R A Pearson Coventry		14.10.16P
	Built by S G Busby – project PFA 074A-10978		
	(IE 13.01.18)		
G-LULA	Cameron C-90	10833	08.06.06
	S D Davis Netherbury, Bridport		19.09.18E
G-LULU	Grob G109	6137	06.09.82
	B M E Loth Namur-Suarlee, Belgium		17.12.18E
G-LULV	Diamond DA.42 Twin Star	42.313	29.01.08
	B A & M L M Langevad (London W4)		25.06.19E
G-LUND	Cessna 340 II	340-0305	27.03.03
	G-LAST, G-UNDY, G-BBNR, N69452		
	Cancelled 12.04.11 by CAA		
	North Weald Open store 06.17		
G-LUNE	Mainair Pegasus Quik	8017	18.02.04
	D Muir St Michaels		07.08.18P
	Built by Mainair Sports Ltd		
G-LUNG	AutoGyro MT-03	xxxx	24.09.07
	P Krysiak Manchester Barton		22.05.19P
	Assembled Rotorsport UK as c/n RSUK/MT-03/018		
G-LUNY	Pitts S-1S	xxxx	09.01.08
	R P Millinship tr G-LUNY Group Leicester		
	Built by C Tector – project PFA 009-14757;		
	fuselage less marks noted 03.15 (NF 29.06.15)		
G-LUON	Schleicher ASW 27-18E (ASG 29E)	29596	19.10.09
	BGA 5348/KTG P C Naegeli Lasham '520'		22.12.18E
G-LUSC	Luscombe 8E Silvaire Deluxe	3975	01.11.84
	D-EFYR, LN-PAT, (NC1248K)		
	M Fowler Sulby, Sibbertoft		04.12.18P
G-LUSI	Luscombe 8F Silvaire	6770	03.10.89
	N838B P H Isherwood Henstridge		06.07.18P
	Built by Temco Engineering		
G-LUSK	Luscombe 8F Silvaire	3795	19.06.09
	G-BRGG, N1068K, NC1068K		
	M A Lamprell & P J Laycock Kittyhawk Farm, Ripe		22.11.18P
G-LUST	Luscombe 8E Silvaire Deluxe	6492	09.11.89
	N2065B, NC2065B		
	M R Griffiths & C J Watson (Stourbridge)		06.05.14P
	On rebuild Stonefield Park, Chilbolton 08.16		
G-LUUP	Pilatus B4-PC11AF	022	28.02.13
	G-ECSW, BGA1780/CSW		
	B L Cooper Lasham 'UUP'		16.04.18E
G-LUXE	British Aerospace BAe 146 Series 301	E3001	09.04.87
	G-5-300, G-SSSH, (G-BIAD)		
	United Kingdom Research & Innovation		
	Glasgow Prestwick		05.05.19E
	Operated by Directflight Ltd,		
	for FAAM (Atmospheric Research)		
G-LVCY	Colomban MC-30 Luciole	xxxx	25.06.12
	C Wright (Bristol BS9)		
	Built by C Wright – project LAA 371-15091		
	(IE 18.02.19)		

G-LVDC | Bell 206L-3 LongRanger III | 51300 | 05.01.11
G-OFST, 5B-CJW, G-BXIB, EC-EQQ
WAG Aviation Ltd   Goodwood | | 16.02.19E
Operated by Elite Helicopters

G-LVIE | Robinson R44 Clipper II | 11159 | 10.05.18
EC-LFJ, G-GEST   Luviair Ltd   Isle of Man
(NF 10.05.18)

G-LVME | Reims/Cessna F152 II | F15201560 | 23.07.14
G-BGHI   Superior Air SA   (Megara, Greece) | | 09.12.16E
(NF 06.04.17)

G-LVPL | AirBorne XT912-B/Streak III-B | XT912-035 | 21.12.04
C D Connor   Pound Green | | 19.05.18P
*Original wing s/n S3-0016; replacement S3-286
fitted 2009; kit no.XT912-033 also quoted*

G-LVRS | Piper PA-28-181 Archer II | 28-7890059 | 08.07.14
G-ZMAM, G-BNPN, N47379   L J Liveras   Elstree | | 17.03.19E
Operated by Flight Training London Ltd

G-LWLW | Diamond DA.40D Star | D4.052 | 26.03.12
G-CCLV   M P Wilkinson   Breighton | | 17.10.18E

G-LWNG | Aero Designs Pulsar | xxxx | 14.10.02
G-OMKF   A B Wood   Wellesbourne Mountford | | 27.04.18P
Built by M K Faro – project PFA 202-11866; tricycle u/c

G-LXAA | Aerospool Dynamic WT9 LSA Club | 18003 | 30.04.18
LX Aviation Ltd   Turweston
(NF 30.04.18)

G-LXUS | Alpi Pioneer 300 | xxxx | 18.07.05
A & J Oswald   Eshott | | 08.01.19P
Built by W C Walters – project PFA 330-14390

G-LXVI | Schempp-Hirth Arcus T | 62 | 29.01.16
A Aveling tr Sixty-Six Group   Lasham   '66' | | 05.03.18E

G-LXWD | Cessna 560XL Citation XLS | 560-5760 | 13.01.16
OE-GHA, YU-SPA, N50756
Catreus AOC Ltd   Biggin Hill | | 26.05.18E

G-LYDA | Hoffmann H36 Dimona | 3515 | 05.04.94
OE-9213   J W Hagley tr G-LYDA Flying Group
Wycombe Air Park | | 25.10.18E

G-LYDF | Piper PA-31-350 Chieftain | 31-7952031 | 23.01.06
N12CD, N27784   Atlantic Bridge Aviation Ltd   Lydd | | 03.08.19E
*Official data 'PA-31-350 Navajo Chieftain' is incorrect;
operated by Lyddair Ltd*

G-LYFA | IAV Bacau Yakovlev Yak-52 | 822608 | 31.03.03
LY-AFA, DOSAAF 110
M I Boyd tr Fox Alpha Group   Manchester Barton | | 16.06.17P

G-LYNC | Robinson R22 Beta II | 3069 | 05.05.00
Hummingbird Helicopters Ltd   Doncaster Sheffield | | 19.06.19E

G-LYND | Piper PA-25-235 Pawnee D | 25-6309 | 08.09.93
SE-IXU, G-BSFZ, N6672Z
York Gliding Centre (Operations) Ltd   Rufforth | | 28.06.19E
*Rebuild of G-ASFZ (25-2246) with new fuselage
c/n 25-6309*

G-LYNI | Evektor EV-97 Eurostar | 2004-2311 | 14.09.05
M D Marshall & G Watts   (Hull) | | 05.07.19P
Built by G Evans – project PFA 315-14409

G-LYNK | CFM Shadow Series DD | 303-DD | 12.10.98
D Royle   (Waverbridge, Wigton) | | 01.06.19P

G-LYNX[M] | Westland WG.13 Lynx 800 | WA/102 | 06.11.78
ZA500, G-LYNX, ZB500   Cancelled 27.02.98 as WFU
As 'ZB500'
With The Helicopter Museum, Weston-super-Mare

G-LYPG | Avtech Jabiru UL-450 | 0251 | 06.07.99
A J Geary   Baxby Manor, Husthwaite | | 26.07.18P
Built by P G Gale – project PFA 274A-13466

G-LYPH | DG Flugzeugbau LS8-t | 8499 | 27.02.12
(BGA 5708), SE-UOH, D-KDAH
S & S Barter   Lasham   'L1' | | 23.03.18E

G-LYTE | Thunder Ax7-77 | 1113 | 29.09.87
R G Turnbull   Manchester   'Crispen' | | 19.05.91A
(NF 11.07.16)

G-LYZA | Guimbal Cabri G2 | 1200 | 19.06.17
G-IZOO   Lyza Aviation Ltd   Redhill | | 31.05.18E

G-LZED | AutoGyro MTOsport | xxxx | 11.11.10
L Zivanovic   (Birmingham B14) | | 23.11.11P
*Assembled Rotorsport UK as c/n RSUK/MTOS/033;
struck wall on take-off Shell Island, Llanbedr 27.06.11
& substantially damaged (NF 27.10.14)*

G-LZII | Laser Lazer Z200 | xxxx | 24.04.08
K G Begley   Fenland | | 23.05.18P
Built by K G Begley – project PFA 123-14410

G-MAAA – G-MZZZ

G-MAAC[M] | Advanced Airship Corp ANR-1 | 01 | 16.01.89
Cancelled 15.11.00 by CAA
*Gondola only – identity unconfirmed
With Aviodrome Museum, Lelystad, Netherlands*

G-MAAM | CFM Shadow Series C | K011 | 23.09.11
G-MTCA   R Sinclair-Brown   (Cleethorpes) | | 08.07.17P
*Forced landed near Boston 22.10.16 & substantially
damaged; sold for spares 10.16*

G-MAAN | Europa Aviation Europa XS | 567 | 07.01.03
P S Maan   (Desborough, Kettering)
*Built by P S Maan – project PFA 247-14009;
tricycle u/c (NF 16.02.16)*

G-MAAS | Piper PA-28-181 Archer II | 28-8390030 | 02.06.14
HB-PHO   Skies Aviation Academy PC
(Thessaloniki, Greece) | | 19.04.17E

G-MABE | Reims/Cessna F150L | F15001119 | 20.06.97
G-BLJP, N962L   Aviolease Ltd   Doncaster Sheffield | | 06.12.18E
Operated by Yorkshire Aero Club

G-MABL | P&M Quik GTR | 8635 | 11.12.12
M Tomlinson   Pound Green | | 10.04.19P

G-MACA | Robinson R22 Beta II | 3836 | 03.05.05
JW Ramsbottom Contractors Ltd t/a Jepar Rotorcraft
Blackpool | | 05.07.18E

G-MACH | SIAI Marchetti SF.260 | 114 | 29.10.80
F-BUVY, OO-AHR, OO-HAZ, (OO-RAB)
Cheyne Motors Ltd   Thruxton | | 20.11.18E

G-MACI | Van's RV-7 | 73171 | 21.02.13
S J E Smith   Eshott | | 21.12.18P
Built by N J F Campbell – project LAA 323-14782

G-MACR | Cirrus SR22T | 1704 | 04.05.18
N115JT   J D M Tickell   Aberdeen Int'l
(IE 04.05.18)

G-MADA | Boeing 737-548 | 24919 | 10.11.15
UR-GBF, UR-AAM, UP-B3708, YL-BBG, EI-CDB, EI-BXF
Opel Investments Ltd   Lasham
Line No: 1970; Stored 01.19 (IE 16.01.17)

G-MADC | Eurofly Snake/Grif 3DC | 18002 | 21.03.18
C Traher   (Bury St Edmunds)
Assembled Airplay Aircraft Ltd (IE 21.03.18)

G-MADV | P&M Quik GT450 | 8476 | 11.09.09
G T Lewis   (Bath) | | 15.02.19P

G-MADZ | Bell 505 Jet Ranger X | 65179 | 24.01.19
Overby Ltd   (Ascot)
(IE 23.01.19)

G-MAFA | Reims/Cessna F406 Caravan II | F406-0036 | 02.06.98
G-DFLT, F-WZDZ
Directflight Ltd   (Cranfield)   'QinetiQ' | | 01.07.19E
Operated by DEFRA as callsign 'DCT04'

G-MAFB | Reims/Cessna F406 Caravan II | F406-0080 | 27.05.98
F-WWSR   Directflight Ltd   (Cranfield) | | 28.09.19E
Operated by DEFRA as callsign 'DCT05'

G-MAFI | Dornier 228-202K | 8115 | 16.02.87
D-CAAE   RUAG Aerospace Services GmbH
Wessling, Germany | | 27.01.17E

G-MAFT | Diamond DA.40D Star | D4.243 | 28.02.07
OE-VPU, (D-EXON)   Airways Aviation Academy Ltd
Huesca-Pirineos, Spain | | 11.04.18E

G-MAGC | Cameron Grand Illusion | 4000 | 19.01.95
Magical Adventures Ltd   West Bloomfield, MI, USA | | 27.09.09E
(NF 03.06.15)

G-MAGG | Pitts S-1SE | xxxx | 17.03.83
R G Gee   Sherburn-in-Elmet | | 14.02.18P
Built by G C Masterton – project PFA 009-10873

G-MAGK	Schleicher ASW 20L		20387	13.11.07
	BGA 2740/EKE A G K Mackenzie Burn '20L'			13.05.18E
G-MAGN	Magni M24C Orion		24127494	21.12.12
	Net2Net IPs Ltd Rufforth East			11.04.18P
G-MAGZ	Robin DR.500-200i Président		35	29.07.05
	F-GXGC T J Thomas Sywell			16.05.18E
	Built by Constructions Aeronautiques de Bourgogne;			
	officially registered as DR.400-500			
G-MAHY	Cessna 182T Skylane		18282124	13.06.17
	G-SKEN, N63106			
	Keyboard Print Solutions Ltd Rochester			03.09.18E
G-MAIE	Piper PA-32R-301T Saratoga II TC		3257046	01.12.00
	N47BK, N41283 Rainbow Self Storage Ltd Solent			06.12.18E
G-MAIN	Mainair Blade 912		1202-0699-7-W1005	16.06.99
	J G Parkin Bicester			13.09.18P
G-MAIR	Piper PA-34-200T Seneca II		34-7970140	15.02.89
	N3029R Ravenair Aircraft Ltd (Liverpool)			01.05.13E
	Parted out Liverpool John Lennon 04.18, remains			
	departed by road 01.19 (IE 23.09.16)			
G-MAJA	British Aerospace Jetstream 4102		41032	22.04.94
	G-4-032 Air Kilroe Ltd t/a Eastern Airways			
	Humberside			29.06.19E
	Built by Jetstream Aircraft Ltd			
G-MAJB	British Aerospace Jetstream 4102		41018	01.06.94
	G-BVKT, (N140MA), G-4-018			
	Air Kilroe Ltd t/a Eastern Airways Humberside			08.06.19E
	Built by Jetstream Aircraft Ltd			
G-MAJC	British Aerospace Jetstream 4102		41005	12.09.94
	G-LOGJ			
	Air Kilroe Ltd t/a Eastern Airways Humberside			20.12.18E
G-MAJD	British Aerospace Jetstream 4102		41006	27.03.95
	G-WAWR			
	Air Kilroe Ltd t/a Eastern Airways Humberside			02.03.19E
G-MAJE	British Aerospace Jetstream 4102		41007	12.09.94
	G-LOGK			
	Air Kilroe Ltd t/a Eastern Airways Humberside			24.02.17E
	Stored less engines 07.17			
G-MAJF	British Aerospace Jetstream 4102		41008	06.02.95
	G-WAWL			
	Air Kilroe Ltd t/a Eastern Airways Humberside			07.07.15E
	(IE 22.09.16)			
G-MAJG	British Aerospace Jetstream 4102		41009	16.08.94
	G-LOGL			
	Air Kilroe Ltd t/a Eastern Airways Humberside			20.09.19E
	Built by Jetstream Aircraft Ltd			
G-MAJH	British Aerospace Jetstream 4102		41010	04.04.95
	G-WAYR			
	Air Kilroe Ltd t/a Eastern Airways Humberside			13.04.17E
	Built by Jetstream Aircraft Ltd; stored less engines 07.17			
G-MAJI	British Aerospace Jetstream 4102		41011	20.03.95
	G-WAND			
	Air Kilroe Ltd t/a Eastern Airways Humberside			27.04.16E
	Built by Jetstream Aircraft Ltd; stored less engines 07.17			
	(IE 22.09.16)			
G-MAJJ	British Aerospace Jetstream 4102		41024	27.02.95
	G-WAFT, G-4-024			
	Air Kilroe Ltd t/a Eastern Airways Humberside			21.01.19E
	Built by Jetstream Aircraft Ltd			
G-MAJK	British Aerospace Jetstream 4102		41070	27.07.95
	SX-SEB, G-MAJK, G-4-070			
	Air Kilroe Ltd t/a Eastern Airways Humberside			28.08.19E
	Built by Jetstream Aircraft Ltd			
G-MAJL	British Aerospace Jetstream 4102		41087	01.04.96
	G-4-087 Eastern Airways (UK) Ltd Humberside			16.05.19E
	Built by Jetstream Aircraft Ltd			
G-MAJR	de Havilland DHC-1 Chipmunk 22		C1/0699	25.09.96
	WP805 C Adams Solent			13.08.19P
	As 'WP805' in RAF red c/s			
G-MAJT	British Aerospace Jetstream 4102		41040	21.09.05
	SX-SEC, G-MAJT, N551VL, G-4-040			
	Air Kilroe Ltd t/a Eastern Airways Humberside			08.02.19E
	Built by Jetstream Aircraft Ltd			

G-MAJU	British Aerospace Jetstream 4102		41071	10.04.06
	N558HK, G-4-071			
	Air Kilroe Ltd t/a Eastern Airways Humberside			26.06.19E
	Built by Jetstream Aircraft Ltd			
G-MAJW	British Aerospace Jetstream 4102		41015	08.06.06
	N303UE, G-4-015			
	Eastern Airways (UK) Ltd Humberside			17.06.18E
	Built by Jetstream Aircraft Ltd			
G-MAJY	British Aerospace Jetstream 4102		41099	08.06.06
	N331UE, G-4-099			
	Eastern Airways International Ltd Humberside			15.10.19E
	Built by Jetstream Aircraft Ltd			
G-MAJZ	British Aerospace Jetstream 4102		41100	08.06.06
	N332UE, G-4-100			
	Eastern Airways (Europe) Ltd Humberside			14.01.19E
	Built by Jetstream Aircraft Ltd			
G-MAKE	AutoGyro Calidus		10 082	29.06.10
	P M Ford Willingale			25.05.18P
	Assembled Rotorsport UK as c/n RSUK/CALS/016			
G-MAKK	Aeroprakt A-22L Foxbat		307	18.08.10
	M A McKillop (Bathampton, Bath)			
	Built by M A McKillop – project LAA 317A-14929			
	(NF 01.09.14)			
G-MAKN	Pilatus PC-12/47E		1744	15.12.17
	HB-FQG Ravenair Aircraft Ltd Leeds East			14.12.18E
	Operated by for Makins Enterprises, owners of			
	Leeds East			
G-MAKS	Cirrus SR22		0367	20.05.08
	N800C J P Briggs North Coates			11.04.18E
G-MALC	Grumman American AA-5 Traveler		AA5-0664	19.11.79
	G-BCPM, N6170A M A Ray (Banwell)			15.05.17E
G-MALE	Kubicek BB-S/Skyballs		1195	09.05.16
	OK-1195 A M Holly Breadstone, Berkeley			
	'#Skyballs'			17.09.18E
G-MALS	Mooney M.20K Mooney 231		25-0573	16.08.84
	N1061T P Mouterde Bourg-en-Bress, Ain, France			28.05.18E
G-MALT	Colt Flying Hop		1447	14.04.89
	P J Stapley Hertford 'White Label 1%'			11.09.97A
	Stored Hertfordshire Balloon Collection (NF 22.10.15)			
G-MAMM	Comco Ikarus C42 FB80		1505-7395	03.06.15
	Mid Anglia Microlights Ltd Beccles			03.06.18P
	Assembled Red Aviation			
G-MAMZ	Comco Ikarus C42 FB80		1806-7543	10.08.18
	Mid Anglia Microlights Ltd Beccles			02.08.19P
	Assembled The Light Aircraft Company Ltd			
G-MANX	Clutton FRED Series II		xxxx	31.05.78
	S Styles (Lydiate Ash, Bromsgrove)			
	Built by P Williamson – project PFA 029-10327			
	(NF 27.03.15)			
G-MANZ	Robinson R44 Raven II		12319	02.06.08
	S M Hill (Nether Winchendon, Aylesbury)			03.05.18E
G-MAOL	Agusta AW109SP Grand New		22271	14.06.12
	Sloane Helicopters Ltd Sywell			13.06.19E
	Operated by VLL Ltd t/a GB Helicopters			
G-MAPR	Beech A36 Bonanza		E-2713	17.09.92
	N55916 G B Gufler (Malmo, Sweden)			20.06.18E
G-MAPY	Piper PA-31-350 Chieftain		31-7552075	18.05.17
	9H-FMH, PH-OTH, G-BXUV, PH-OTH, G-BXUV,			
	OH-OTH, N59979			
	Blue Sky Investments Ltd Belfast Int'l			28.09.17E
	(IE 23.01.18)			
G-MARE	Schweizer 269C (300)		S 1320	12.08.88
	Earl of Caledon Caledon Castle, Caledon			01.11.16E
G-MARL	AutoGyro Calidus		xxxx	13.12.16
	M R Love Farley Farm, Farley Chamberlayne			15.12.18P
	Assembled Rotorsport UK as c/n RSUK/CALS/031			
G-MARO	Best Off Skyranger J2.2(2)		SKR0305318	22.12.04
	S Gavin tr G-MARO Flying Group Strathaven			
	Built by E Daleki – project BMAA/HB/348 (IE 01.05.18)			
G-MARZ	Thruster T600N 450		1031-T600N-093	27.01.04
	A S R Czajka Longacre Farm, Sandy			21.07.18P
G-MASC	Jodel D.150 Mascaret		37	01.02.91
	F-BLDZ K F & R Richardson Wellesbourne Mountford			31.08.17P
	Built by Société Aéronautique Normande			

G-MASF	Piper PA-28-181 Archer II	28-7790191	24.06.97
	OY-EPT, LN-NAP Mid-Anglia Flight Centre Ltd		
	t/a Mid-Anglia School of Flying Cambridge		05.10.18E
G-MASH	Westland-Bell 47G-4A	WA725	03.11.89
	G-AXKU, G-17-10 A J E Smith Breighton		05.12.18E
	Wears US Army c/s		
G-MASS	Cessna 152 II	15281605	06.03.95
	G-BSHN, N65541 MK Aero Support Ltd Southend		12.05.19E
	Operated by Seawing Flying Club		
G-MATB	Robin DR.400-160 Chevalier	735	28.02.14
	G-BAFP J C Bacon		
	The Byre, Hardwick, Abergavenny		23.11.18E
G-MATO	Dassault Falcon 7X	277	12.12.16
	F-WWUP SDI Aviation Ltd Luton		12.12.18E
	Operated by Air Charter Scotland		
G-MATS	Colt GA-42 Gas Airship	738	11.06.87
	JA1009, G-MATS P A Lindstrand		
	Queens Park, Oswestry 'Castlemaine XXXX'		23.05.90A
	(NF 10.10.14)		
G-MATT	Robin R2160 Alpha Sport	97	07.05.85
	G-BKRC, F-BZAC, F-WZAC		
	R Ivison tr Swift Flying Group Dunkeswell		05.08.17E
G-MATW	Cessna 182P Skylane	18261335	13.01.15
	D-EJPZ, OY-POE, G-BAFJ, N20977 |		
	Subados SL (Barcelona, Spain)		30.07.18E
G-MATZ	Piper PA-28-140 Cherokee Cruiser	28-7325200	11.12.90
	G-BASI, N11C		
	R B Walker t/a Midland Air Training School Coventry		11.10.18E
G-MAUS	Europa Aviation Europa	030	28.06.05
	A P Ringrose Dunsfold		01.12.18P
	Built by A P Ringrose – project PFA 247-12651;		
	tailwheel u/c		
G-MAUX	Raj Hamsa X'Air Hawk	1252	01.02.13
	M A Urch (Ashby Magna, Lutterworth)		
	Built by M A Urch – project LAA 340-15185 (NF 11.05.17)		
G-MAVK	Pitts S-1S	4010	12.10.16
	TF-WTF, N107JK M O'Leary Turweston		13.06.18P
	Built by J M Killough		
G-MAXA	Piper PA-32-301FT 6X	3232021	06.02.14
	N116KY, N562RR, N30614		
	L Bennett & Son Ltd Elstree		19.02.19E
G-MAXD	Robinson R44 Raven I	1907	20.08.15
	OO-TOM RSM Aviation Ltd		
	Walton Wood Farm, Thorpe Audlin		12.08.18E
G-MAXG	Pitts S-1S	xxxx	27.04.01
	S J Hampton tr The Assets of The G-MAXG Group		
	(Hampton TW12) '*Little Stinger*'		10.03.17P
	Built by T P Jenkinson – project PFA 009-13233;		
	extensively damaged landing Breighton 17.04.16		
G-MAXI	Piper PA-34-200T Seneca II	34-7670150	11.02.81
	N8658C The Draycott Seneca Syndicate Ltd		
	Gloucestershire		27.05.18E
G-MAXS	Mainair Pegasus Quik	8105	16.03.05
	W J Walker Rossall Field, Cockerham		11.03.18P
	Built by Mainair Sports Ltd		
G-MAXT	Piper PA-28RT-201T Turbo Arrow IV	28R-8031102	15.04.16
	I-FRIZ, D-EDIS, N8211C M Toninelli (Cremona, Italy)		28.07.18E
G-MAXV	Van's RV-4	4137	20.01.00
	CRM Aviation Europe Ltd White Waltham		14.03.19P
	Built by T P Jenkinson – project PFA 181-13266;		
	operated by 'Raven Display Team' – 'No. 1'		
G-MAZA	AutoGyro MT-03	xxxx	20.02.08
	N Crownshaw & M Manson Crosland Moor		06.10.17P
	Assembled Rotorsport UK as c/n RSUK/MT-03/029		
G-MAZS	Bombardier BD-700-1A10 Global 6000 9549		20.03.18
	9M-SMB, M-BMAL, C-GUEU		
	Gama Aviation (UK) Ltd Farnborough		21.10.19E
G-MBAA	Hiway Skytrike II/Excalibur	01	23.04.81
	M J Aubrey Llanfyrnach		
	Displayed Classic Ultralight Heritage		
	(SSDR microlight since 05.14) (NF 02.11.17)		

G-MBAB	Hovey Whing-Ding II	MA-59	26.05.81
	M J Aubrey Llanfyrnach		
	Built by R F Morton – project PFA 116-10706;		
	displayed Classic Ultralight Heritage		
	(SSDR microlight since 05.14) (NF 02.11.17)		
G-MBAL	Hiway Demon	HD51	29.06.81
	D M Pecheur (Downham Market)		
	(SSDR microlight since 05.15) (IE 11.05.15)		
G-MBBB^M	Skycraft Scout II	0388W	03.08.81
	Cancelled 04.08.17 as PWFU		
G-MBBJ (2)	Hiway Skytrike/Demon 175	80-00029	15.02.82
	M J Aubrey Llanfyrnach		
	Displayed Classic Ultralight Heritage		
	(SSDR microlight since 05.14) (IE 30.06.17)		
G-MBBZ^M	Volmer VJ-24W	7	23.09.81
	Cancelled 29.11.95 as WFU		
	With Newark Air Museum, Winthorpe		
G-MBCJ	Mainair Tri-Flyer/Solar Wings Typhoon S JRN-1		30.09.81
	R A Smith (Harworth, Doncaster)		
	Sailwing c/n T881-225 but may have replacement		
	c/n T382-390L		
	(SSDR microlight since 05.14) (NF 23.09.17)		
G-MBCL	Hiway Skytrike 160/Solar Wings Typhoon T118107		30.09.81
	P J Callis Halwell		
	(SSDR microlight since 05.14) (NF 30.01.15)		
G-MBCX	Hornet 250/Airwave Nimrod 165	0090 LJH	12.10.81
	M Maylor (Manby, Louth)		
	Built by Airwave Gliders Ltd		
	(SSDR microlight since 05.14) (NF 31.07.17)		
G-MBDL^M	Aero & Engineering Services Lone Ranger 109		21.10.81
	Cancelled 13.06.90 by CAA *No marks carried*		
	With North East Land Sea and Air Museum, Usworth		
G-MBDM	Southdown Sigma	SST/001	26.10.81
	A R Prentice (Dartford)		
	(SSDR microlight since 05.14) (IE 18.05.15)		
G-MBEP^M	American Aerolights Eagle 215B		09.11.81
	M J Aubrey (Stanner, Kington)		08.04.96P
	Stored Caernarfon 08.15		
G-MBET	Micro Engineering Mistral Trainer	MEA 103	10.11.81
	Cancelled 16.04.18 as PWFU		27.09.98
	Old Sarum *Stored in trailer 05.18*		
G-MBFO	Eipper Quicksilver MX	MLD-01	17.11.81
	R A Szczepanik (Southall)		
	(SSDR microlight since 07.14) (NF 06.12.16)		
G-MBFZ	Eurowing Goldwing	MSS01	25.11.81
	D G Palmer Easter Nether Cabra Farm, Fetterangus		
	(SSDR microlight since 06.14) (NF 08.12.14)		
G-MBGF	Twamley Trike/Birdman Cherokee	RWT-01	26.11.81
	T B Woolley (Narborough, Leicester)		
	Built by Birdman Enterprises Ltd		
	(SSDR microlight since 05.14) (NF 30.11.17)		
G-MBGP	Hiway Sky-Trike/Solar Wings Typhoon T48114L		01.12.81
	Cancelled 23.04.01 by CAA		
	(Bath) *For sale from Bath area 12.15*		
-MBHE	American Aerolights Eagle 430B	4210	18.12.81
	R J Osborne (Cove, Tiverton)		
	(SSDR microlight since 05.14) (NF 13.10.17)		
G-MBHK	Mainair Tri-Flyer 330/Flexiform Solo Striker		
		EB-1 & 036-241181	30.12.81
	A L Virgoe Over Farm, Gloucester		
	Original Tri-Flyer 250 Trike c/n 036 replaced		
	by Tri-Flyer 330 c/n 060-382 in 1982		
	(SSDR microlight since 05.14) (NF 23.09.15)		
G-MBIO	American Aerolights Eagle 215B	E4007-Z	12.01.82
	D J Lewis (Elmstone Hardwicke, Cheltenham)		
	(SSDR microlight since 05.14) (IE 26.08.15)		
G-MBIT	Hiway Skytrike/Demon	2501	18.01.82
	K S Hodgson (Skutterskelfe, Yarm)		
	(SSDR microlight since 07.14) (NF 18.06.18)		
G-MBIV^M	Hiway Skytrike/Flexiform Sealande	EJPTQ-01	18.01.82
	Cancelled 07.07.92 by CAA		
	Originally regd as Flexform Trike 440		
	With Ulster Aviation Society, Lisburn		

G-MBIZ Mainair Tri-Flyer 250/Hiway Vulcan   039-251181   20.01.82
E F Clapham, W B S Dobie, S P Slade
& D M A Templeman   (Bristol BS)
(SSDR microlight since 05.14) (IE 09.02.16)

G-MBJD American Aerolights Eagle 215B   4169   21.01.82
R W F Boarder   (Aston Rowant, Watlington)
(SSDR microlight since 05.14) (NF 08.11.17)

G-MBJK American Aerolights Eagle   2742   16.01.82
B W Olley   (Coolboy Little, Co Donegal, RoI)
(SSDR microlight since 05.14) (NF 27.10.17)

G-MBJV^M Rotec Rally 2B   CJGW-01   01.02.82
Cancelled 13.06.90 by CAA
Built by for C J G Welch
With Ulster Aviation Society, Lisburn

G-MBJX^M Hiway Skytrike 1/Hiway Super Scorpion   MM-01   02.02.82
Cancelled 13.06.90 by CAA   *Stored*
With National Museum of Flight Scotland, East Fortune

G-MBKY American Aerolights Eagle 215B   BF-01   12.02.82
M J Aubrey   Llanfyrnach
Official c/n ZFE-15288 is corruption of engine model
displayed Classic Ultralight Heritage
(SSDR microlight since 05.14) (IE 26.08.15)

G-MBKZ Hiway Skytrike/Super Scorpion   xxxx   12.02.82
L Magill   (Newtownabbey)
Official c/n 'EC25P8-04' is the engine model
(SSDR microlight since 05.14) (NF 08.12.17)

G-MBLU Ultrasports Tri-Pacer/Southdown Lightning L195
                                                        L195-191   26.02.82
C R Franklin   (Landkey, Barnstaple)
(SSDR microlight since 05.14) (NF 16.02.15)

G-MBMF Rotec Rally 2B   JGW-01   03.03.82
Cancelled 13.06.90 by CAA
Waringstown   *Stored dismantled 12.13*

G-MBMG Rotec Rally 2B   RJP-01   03.03.82
J R Pyper   (Waringstown, Craigavon)
(SSDR microlight since 05.14) (NF 16.08.17)

G-MBMT Mainair Tri-Flyer/Southdown Lightning 195   TRY-01   08.03.82
Cancelled 10.02.14 as PWFU
Tillicoultry   *Wing c/n L195-195?*
On display at garden centre 05.15

G-MBMZ Ultrasports Tripacer/Flexiform Sealander US/46 & FF/419   12.03.82
Cancelled 23.06.97 by CAA
Banstead   *Advertised for sale 12.13*

G-MBOF Pakes Jackdaw   LGP-01   26.03.82
M J Aubrey   (Ryde, Isle of Wight)
Built by L G Pakes
(SSDR microlight since 08.14) (NF 26.08.14)

G-MBOH Micro Engineering Mistral   008   29.03.82
T J Gayton-Polley   Hadfold Farm, Adversane
Wing covers are ex G-MBSL & engine ex G-MMIB
(IF 11.09.17)

G-MBPB (2) Pterodactyl Ptraveller   PEB-01   07.04.82
T D Dawson   Plaistows Farm, St Albans
Built by P E Bailey
(SSDR microlight since 05.14) (IE 30.06.17)

G-MBPM^M Eurowing Goldwing   EW-21   14.04.82
Cancelled 30.08.00 as WFU   *Stored*   21.08.98
With National Museum of Flight Scotland, East Fortune

G-MBPX Eurowing Goldwing SP   EW-42   21.04.82
V H Hallam   (Torquay)
(SSDR microlight since 06.14) (IE 06.12.17)

G-MBRB Electraflyer Eagle Mk.I   E2229   09.12.81
R C Bott   (Abergynolwyn, Tywyn)
(SSDR microlight since 05.14) (NF 19.09.17)

G-MBRD American Aerolights Eagle 215B   E2635   20.04.82
R J Osborne   (Cove, Tiverton)
(SSDR microlight since 05.14) (NF 13.10.17)

G-MBSJ American Aerolights Eagle 215B   5001   14.06.82
T J Gayton-Polley   Hadfold Farm, Adversane
(SSDR microlight since 05.14) (IE 05.06.17)

G-MBSX Ultraflight Mirage II   240   14.06.82
A D Russell   (Ballyroney, Banbridge)
(SSDR microlight since 08.14) (NF 13.07.17)

G-MBTF Mainair Gemini/Southdown Sprint   168-30683   26.04.82
Cancelled 17.11.08 by CAA   26.03.00
Toomebridge, Co Antrim   *Stored dismantled 12.13*

G-MBTH^M Whittaker MW4   001   06.04.82
(G-MBPB (1))   Cancelled 11.01.14 as PWFU   *Stored*   25.06.12
With Aerospace Bristol

G-MBTJ Ultrasports Tri-Pacer/Solar Wings Typhoon
                                                        CSRS-01   02.04.82
H A Comber   (Canford Heath, Poole)
Wing s/n may be T1081-286L
(SSDR microlight since 05.14) (IE 26.08.15)

G-MBUD^M Wheeler (Skycraft) Scout Mk.III/R/3   0432/R/3   12.05.82
Cancelled 06.09.94 by CAA   *Modified to Super Scout*
Note G-MBOU holds same c/n
With Norfolk & Suffolk Aviation Museum, Flixton

G-MBUE^M MBA Tiger Cub 440   MBA-001   29.04.82
Cancelled 06.09.94 by CAA
Originally registered as Micro-Bipe c/n 001
With Newark Air Museum, Winthorpe

G-MBUR Rotec Rally 2B   DJSM-01   12.05.82
Cancelled 16.11.83 as PWFU
RAF Stafford   *For sale from RAF Museum store 05.16*

G-MBUU Mainair TriFlyer/Southdown Puma   0532181   07.05.82
Cancelled 02.09.88 as PWFU
Llanfairfechan, Conwy   *Advertised for sale 10.15*

G-MBUZ Skycraft Scout II   0366   04.05.82
Cancelled 15.10.13 by CAA
Wingland, Lincs   *Stored 03.16*

G-MBVE^M Hiway Skytrike 160   TJD-01   06.05.82
Cancelled 13.06.90 by CAA
With Newark Air Museum, Winthorpe

G-MBWL Huntair Pathfinder Mk.I   MLP-01   20.05.82
A D Russell   (Ballyroney, Banbridge)
(SSDR microlight since 05.16) (IE 27.06.16)

G-MBXL Eipper Quicksilver MXII   3624   26.05.82
Cancelled 13.06.90 by CAA
Darley Moor   *Stored in stables 08.15*

G-MBYK Huntair Pathfinder 1   012   04.06.82
Cancelled 30.05.01 by CAA   17.06.97
Drumavish, Co Donegal   *Stored 05.16*

G-MBYM Eipper Quicksilver MX   JW-01   04.06.82
Cancelled 01.08.14 as PWFU   21.09.96
Priory Farm, Tibenham   *Stored 01.15*

G-MBZO Mainair Tri-Flyer 330/Flexiform Medium Striker
                                                        GRH-01   15.06.82
A N Burrows   Jurby
(SSDR microlight since 05.14) (NF 25.07.17)

G-MBZV American Aerolights Eagle 215B   4227-Z   16.06.82
M J Aubrey   Llanfyrnach
Displayed Classic Ultralight Heritage
(SSDR microlight since 05.14) (IE 30.06.17)

G-MCAB Gardan GY-201 Minicab   xxxx   19.05.08
P G Hooper   (Winchester)
Built by P G Hooper – project PFA 056-11161
(NF 16.06.15)

G-MCAN Agusta A109S Grand   22021   10.11.09
EI-JFC, N84RE
Cannon Air LLP   (Westbury-on-Trym, Bristol)   10.11.18E

G-MCAP Cameron C-80   10186   30.07.02
L D Pickup   Bristol BS1   'Mencap'   09.09.18E

G-MCAZ Robinson R44 Raven II   13785   11.02.15
M C Allen   Denham   15.03.19E
Operated by HQ Aviation

G-MCCF Thruster T600N   0100-T600N-048   25.04.01
C C F Fuller   Craysmarsh Farm, Melksham   28.03.18P
Badged 'Sprint'

G-MCCY IAV Bacau Yakovlev Yak 52   9011112   11.11.04
LY-AQF, UR-BBP, Ukraine AF 129, DOSAAF 129
Cancelled 04.02.15 by CAA   20.11.08
Newcastle, RoI   *Open store 06.17*

G-MCDB Supermarine 361 Spitfire LF.IX   CBAF IX 401   27.02.08
MA764   M Collenette   (Sway, Lymington)
C/n quoted is fuselage no: firewall plate shows
'CBAF 5423' (NF 15.02.19)

G-MCEL	Cyclone Pegasus Quantum 15-912	7858	10.10.01
	F Hodgson Sywell		22.10.18P
G-MCFK	P&M Quik GT450	8696	08.10.14
	F A A Kay London Colney		10.10.18P
G-MCGB	Sikorsky S-92A	920167	21.02.13
	N167G Bristow Helicopters Ltd Sumburgh		25.02.18E
	Operated by Marine & Coastguard Agency		
G-MCGC	Sikorsky S-92A	920169	11.04.13
	N169F Bristow Helicopters Ltd Sumburgh		
	'Oscar Charlie'		16.04.18E
	Operated by Marine & Coastguard Agency		
G-MCGD	Sikorsky S-92A	920171	05.06.13
	N971E Bristow Helicopters Ltd Stornoway		24.06.18E
	Operated by Marine & Coastguard Agency		
G-MCGE	Sikorsky S-92A	920214	15.10.14
	N214HM Bristow Helicopters Ltd Aberdeen Int'l		05.11.18E
	Operated by Marine & Coastguard Agency		
G-MCGF	Sikorsky S-92A	920222	16.10.14
	N222XC Bristow Helicopters Ltd Aberdeen Int'l		26.10.18E
	Operated by Marine & Coastguard Agency		
G-MCGG	Sikorsky S-92A	920225	28.10.14
	N225WK Bristow Helicopters Ltd Stornoway		26.11.18E
	Operated by Marine & Coastguard Agency		
G-MCGH	Sikorsky S-92A	920234	19.12.14
	N234TR Bristow Helicopters Ltd Aberdeen Int'l		15.02.18E
	Operated by Marine & Coastguard Agency		
G-MCGI	Sikorsky S-92A	920235	19.12.14
	N235U Bristow Helicopters Ltd Aberdeen Int'l		16.02.18E
	Operated by Marine & Coastguard Agency		
G-MCGJ	Sikorsky S-92A	920248	20.04.15
	N248N Bristow Helicopters Ltd Aberdeen Int'l		14.05.18E
	Operated by Marine & Coastguard Agency		
G-MCGK	Sikorsky S-92A	920251	05.05.15
	N251Z Bristow Helicopters Ltd Stornoway		28.05.18E
	Operated by Marine & Coastguard Agency		
G-MCGL	Sikorsky S-92A	920254	13.11.15
	N254J Bristow Helicopters Ltd Stornoway		08.12.18E
	Operated by Marine & Coastguard Agency		
G-MCGM	AgustaWestland AW189	89001	21.11.14
	I-EASN Bristow Helicopters Ltd Solent		16.01.19E
	Operated by Marine & Coastguard Agency		
G-MCGN	AgustaWestland AW189	92001	23.12.14
	G-CJNV, G-MCGN Bristow Helicopters Ltd Solent		31.03.18E
	Operated by Marine & Coastguard Agency as callsign 'Rescue 152'		
G-MCGO	AgustaWestland AW189	92002	10.03.15
	Bristow Helicopters Ltd Aberdeen Int'l		04.01.19E
	Operated by Marine & Coastguard Agency		
G-MCGP	AgustaWestland AW189	92003	10.03.15
	Bristow Helicopters Ltd Solent		02.06.18E
	Operated by Marine & Coastguard Agency		
G-MCGR	AgustaWestland AW189	92004	10.03.15
	Bristow Helicopters Ltd Glasgow Prestwick		17.11.18E
	Operated by Marine & Coastguard Agency		
G-MCGS	AgustaWestland AW189	92005	10.03.15
	Bristow Helicopters Ltd Solent		07.09.18E
	Operated by Marine & Coastguard Agency		
G-MCGT	AgustaWestland AW189	92006	10.03.15
	Bristow Helicopters Ltd Glasgow Prestwick		08.02.18E
	Operated by Marine & Coastguard Agency		
G-MCGU	Leonardo AW189	92007	28.03.17
	Bristow Helicopters Ltd Aberdeen Int'l		20.12.18E
G-MCGV	Leonardo AW189	92008	28.03.17
	Bristow Helicopters Ltd Lydd		20.12.18E
G-MCGW	Leonardo AW189	92009	05.01.18
	Bristow Helicopters Ltd St Athan		16.05.19E
G-MCGX	Leonardo AW189	92010	05.01.18
	Bristow Helicopters Ltd St Athan		02.08.19E
G-MCGY	Sikorsky S-92A	920257	15.09.15
	N257Z Bristow Helicopters Ltd Aberdeen Int'l		05.10.18E
	Operated by Marine & Coastguard Agency		
G-MCGZ	Sikorsky S-92A	920262	08.10.15
	N262U Bristow Helicopters Ltd Aberdeen Int'l		12.11.18E
	Operated by Marine & Coastguard Agency		

G-MCJL	Cyclone Pegasus Quantum 15-912	7497	16.03.99
	RM Aviation Ltd Beverley (Linley Hill)		19.05.18P
G-MCLK	Van's RV-10	41131	20.03.13
	M W Clarke (Winkhill, Leek)		11.01.19P
	Built by M W Clarke – project LAA 339-15041		
G-MCLN	Cirrus SR20	1642	11.06.15
	F-GTHM, N50011 Laminar Flight Ltd Turweston		05.03.18E
G-MCLY	Cessna 172P Skyhawk	17275597	14.06.07
	N61GA, SE-IXY, N64643		
	McAully Flying Group Ltd Little Snoring		25.01.18E
G-MCOW	Lindstrand LBL 77A	1142	13.12.06
	S & S Villiers Ballyclare		29.05.18E
G-MCOX	Fuji FA.200-180AO Aero Subaru	FA200-296	29.12.81
	(G-BIMS) A M Cox Fairoaks		03.12.17E
G-MCPR	Piper PA-32-301T Turbo Saratoga	32-8024040	27.05.11
	G-MOLL, N82535		
	M C Plomer-Roberts Wellesbourne Mountford		09.06.18E
G-MCRO	Dyn'Aéro MCR-01 VLA Sportster	387	02.09.08
	J M Keane Deanland		28.08.13P
	Built by M K Faro – project LAA 301-14802		
	(NF 20.02.18)		
G-MCSA	Sikorsky S-92A	920273	03.06.16
	N273H Babcock Mission Critical Services		
	Offshore Ltd Aberdeen Int'l		08.06.18E
G-MCSB	Sikorsky S-92A	920281	03.06.16
	N281LM Babcock Mission Critical Services		
	Offshore Ltd Aberdeen Int'l		15.06.18E
G-MCSC	AgustaWestland AW139	41379	17.08.16
	YR-VGA, I-VEGC, N621SM Babcock Mission		
	Critical Services Offshore Ltd Aberdeen Int'l		13.10.18E
G-MCSD	AgustaWestland AW139	41375	17.08.16
	YR-VGB, I-VEGB, N622SM Babcock Mission		
	Critical Services Offshore Ltd Aberdeen Int'l		02.10.18E
G-MCSE	Airbus EC175 B	5022	10.02.17
	F-WWOV Babcock Mission Critical Services		
	Offshore Ltd Aberdeen Int'l		10.02.18E
G-MCSF	Airbus EC175 B	5023	08.03.17
	F-WWPE Babcock Mission Critical Services		
	Offshore Ltd Aberdeen Int'l		07.03.18E
G-MCSG	Airbus EC175 B	5021	23.06.17
	Babcock Mission Critical Services Offshore Ltd		
	Aberdeen Int'l		22.06.18E
G-MCSH	Airbus EC175 B	5034	22.11.18
	F-WWOF Babcock Mission Critical Services		
	Offshore Ltd Aberdeen Int'l		22.11.19E
G-MCSI	Sikorsky S-92A	920304	05.03.19
	N304BT Babcock Mission Critical Services		
	Offshore Ltd Aberdeen Int'l		
	Noted 02.19		
G-MCSJ	Sikorsky S-92A	920297	13.07.18
	N297W Babcock Mission Critical Services		
	Offshore Ltd Aberdeen Int'l		
G-MCSK	Sikorsky S-92A	920233	13.03.19
	VH-NYZ, N233Q		
	Babcock Mission Critical Services Offshore Ltd		
	Aberdeen International		
G-MCSL	Sikorsky S-92A	920265	13.03.19
	VH-NWD, N265R		
	Babcock Mission Critical Services Offshore Ltd		
	Aberdeen International		
G-MCTO	Flylight Dragon Chaser	DA108	15.05.14
	B J Syson Enstone		
	(IE 30.05.17)		
G-MCUB	Reality Escapade	UK.ESC.0009	27.04.07
	M A Appleby Full Sutton		06.11.15P
	Built by A D Janaway – project		
	PFA 345-14680 – VLA version		
G-MCVE	Comco Ikarus C42 FB80	1507-7405	04.09.15
	A & J McVey Ince		27.08.17P
	Assembled Red Aviation		
G-MCVY	Flight Design CT2K	02-01-06-04	04.12.13
	G-CBNA A & J McVey Ince		14.05.18P
	Assembled Pegasus Aviation as c/n 7887		

G-MCXV	Colomban MC-15 Cri-Cri	371	01.03.00
	F-PYVA P C Appleton Newquay Cornwall		25.10.08P
	Built by J P Lorre; stored 05.17 (NF 08.09.15)		
G-MDAC	Piper PA-28-181 Archer II	28-8290154	06.11.87
	N8242T S A Nicklen Henstridge		10.08.18E
G-MDAY	Cessna 170B	26350	02.05.03
	N2807C M Day Thruxton		06.08.18E
	Carries 'N2807C' on tail		
G-MDBC	Cyclone Pegasus Quantum 15-912	7814	04.05.01
	J D Ryan (Liverpool L15)		31.08.18P
G-MDBD	Airbus A330-243	266	24.06.99
	F-WWKG Thomas Cook Airlines Ltd Manchester		24.06.19E
G-MDDE	Hughes 369E (500)	0563E	16.11.17
	C-GZUN, N7033V		
	Draper Gain Aviation Ltd Brighton City		
	(NF 16.11.17)		
G-MDJE	Cessna 208 Caravan I	20800336	13.06.07
	N208FM, XA-TSV, N5263S		
	Holcombe Ltd Gloucestershire		28.11.18E
	Amphibian		
G-MDKD	Robinson R22 Beta	1247	18.04.90
	M A & M L Mulcahy Swansea		09.06.18E
G-MDME	Diamond DA.62	62.077	21.11.17
	Flight Calibration Services Ltd Denham		11.12.18E
	Callsign 'VOR08'		
G-MDMX	Hughes 369E	0396E	25.05.18
	N369NM, 5Y-TLS, N51LK, G-CHRI, EC-LEH, EC-KRR,		
	PT-HSC, PP-EPC, N1607G		
	MH Pilot Services Ltd (London SW1)		12.06.19E
G-MDPI	Agusta A109A II	7393	11.08.04
	G-PERI, G-EXEK, G-SLNE, G-EEVS, G-OTSL		
	Castle Air Ltd Pond House, Nicholashayne		27.11.18E
G-MECK	TL 2000UK Sting Carbon S4	15 ST 439	09.09.15
	M J Seemann Leicester		03.05.19P
	Built by M J Seemann – project LAA 347A-15350		
G-MEDF	Airbus A321-231	1690	28.02.02
	D-AVZX British Airways PLC London Heathrow		27.02.19E
G-MEDG	Airbus A321-231	1711	05.04.02
	D-AVZK British Airways PLC London Heathrow		04.04.19E
G-MEDJ	Airbus A321-231	2190	08.04.04
	D-AVZD British Airways PLC London Heathrow		07.04.19E
G-MEDK	Airbus A320-232	2441	27.05.05
	F-WWBQ British Airways PLC London Heathrow		26.05.19E
G-MEDL	Airbus A321-231	2653	19.01.06
	D-AVZC British Airways PLC London Heathrow		07.01.20E
G-MEDM	Airbus A321-231	2799	26.06.06
	D-AVZP British Airways PLC London Heathrow		14.07.19E
G-MEDN	Airbus A321-231	3512	09.05.08
	D-AVZK British Airways PLC London Heathrow		08.05.19E
G-MEDU	Airbus A321-231	3926	16.07.09
	D-AZAB British Airways PLC London Heathrow		10.06.19E
G-MEDZ	Beech B200 Super King Air	BB-1478	20.06.18
	EC-JGB, D-IHAN, N8150N		
	Zeusch Aviation BV Lelystad, Netherlands		20.08.19E
G-MEEE	Schleicher ASW 20L	20312	11.09.07
	BGA 2620 T E Macfadyen Nympsfield *'EEE'*		13.04.18E
G-MEGG	Europa Aviation Europa XS	358	14.06.00
	R L Hitchcock Bentley Farm, Coal Aston		11.04.18P
	Built by M E Mavers – project PFA 247-13202;		
	tailwheel u/c		
G-MEGN	Beech B200 Super King Air	BB-1518	30.11.06
	N65LA, SU-ZBA, N3218V		
	Dragonfly Aviation Services Ltd Cardiff		02.01.19E
G-MEGS	Cessna 172S Skyhawk	172S10723	09.06.08
	N6245C The Cambridge Aero Club Ltd Cambridge		07.09.18E
G-MEGZ	Comco Ikarus C42 FB100 Bravo	1311-7286	03.12.13
	J M Mooney Park Hall Farm, Mapperley		02.04.18P
	Assembled Red-Air UK		
G-MEIS	CASA 1-133 Jungmeister	117	09.06.14
	Spanish AF ES.1-36 B S Charters (Rayleigh)		
	(NF 20.05.18)		
G-MELL	CZAW Sportcruiser	700547	01.12.08
	G A & J A Mellins Elstree *'Lady Jane'*		25.06.19P
	Built by G A & J A Mellins – project		
	LAA 338-14866 (Quick build kit)		
G-MELS	Piper PA-28-181 Archer III	2843633	17.07.07
	D-EASX, N3139C P J Sowood Denham		08.07.18E
G-MELT	Cessna F172H	F172-0580	23.09.83
	G-AWTI Falcon Aviation Ltd		
	Bourne Park, Hurstbourne Tarrant		15.07.14E
	Built by Reims Aviation SA; noted 11.15 (NF 23.10.15)		
G-MEME	Piper PA-28R-201 Arrow III	2837051	17.08.90
	N9219N Henry J Clare Ltd Bodmin		20.05.18E
	Official type data 'PA-28R-201 Cherokee Arrow III'		
	is incorrect		
G-MEMS	Diamond DA.42 Twin Star	42.069	26.02.19
	HB-LTY, N42TY, HB-LTY		
	AKM Aviation Ltd (London N17)		
	(NF 26.02.19)		
G-MENU	Robinson R44 Raven II	12664	27.01.09
	HQ Aviation Ltd Denham		23.05.18E
G-MEOW	CFM Streak Shadow	K 172	23.04.93
	G J Moor Henstridge		26.09.18P
	Built by S D Hicks – project PFA 206-12025		
G-MERC	Colt 56A	842	11.06.86
	A F & C D Selby Priory Farm, Tibenham		
	'Mercedes-Benz'		09.08.09E
	Stored at Priory Farm, Tibenham 01.19 (NF 21.10.15)		
G-MERE	Lindstrand LBL 77A	092	07.04.94
	R D Baker Goodnestone, Canterbury		
	'Cancer Research Campaign'		
	(NF 04.11.14)		
G-MERF	Grob G115A	8091	24.07.95
	EI-CAB G Wylie White Waltham		04.09.18E
G-MERL	Piper PA-28RT-201 Arrow IV	28R-7918036	27.06.86
	N2116N D Brennan & J Gubbay Fairoaks		09.08.18E
G-MESH	CZAW Sportcruiser	700463	21.07.08
	M E S Heaton Oxenhope		05.10.18P
	Built by M E S Heaton – project LAA 338-14823		
G-METH	Cameron C-90	10841	21.04.06
	A & D Methley Marshfield, Chippenham		03.07.15E
G-MEUP	Cameron A-120	2117	05.10.89
	J M Woodhouse Lancaster		02.08.14E
G-MFAC	Cessna F172H	F172-0387	23.08.01
	G-AVBZ G Y Phillips (Llanpumsaint, Carmarthen)		22.11.18E
	Built by Reims Aviation SA		
G-MFEF	Reims FR172J Rocket	FR17200426	19.10.00
	D-EGJQ B A & C L Duguid Perth		02.04.19E
G-MFHI	Europa Aviation Europa	202	14.11.97
	P Rees tr Hi Fliers Rochester		30.03.18P
	Built by M F Howe – project PFA 247-12841; tricycle u/c		
G-MFLA	Robin HR.200-120B	282	26.08.09
	G-HHUK, SE-KYN R J Williamson Crowfield		20.12.18E
	Operated by Crowfield Flying Club		
G-MFLC	Robin HR.200-120B Club	317	25.11.09
	G-BXGW Cancelled 16.09.14 as PWFU		01.12.14
	Leeds Bradford *Used as instructional airframe at*		
	'The Aviation Academy' 10.15, painted as 'G-OTAA'		
G-MFLE	Robin HR.200-120B Club	335	09.11.11
	G-BYLH R J Williamson Crowfield		14.11.18E
	Operated by Crowfield Flying Club		
G-MFLI	Cameron V-90	2650	14.08.91
	J M Percival Bourton-on-the-Wolds, Loughborough		
	'Mayfly'		14.08.17E
G-MFLJ	P&M Quik GT450	8303	29.08.07
	J A Davies Plaistows Farm, St Albans		28.08.19P
G-MFLM	Reims/Cessna F152 II	F15201451	07.01.10
	G-BFFC NAL Asset Management Ltd Newcastle Int'l		16.01.19E
G-MFLT	Eurocopter AS.365N3 Dauphin 2	6806	08.11.16
	YR-PRC Ven Air ULC Bragganstown, Co Louth, Rol		11.08.18E
G-MFLY	Mainair Rapier	1359-1103-7-W1154	30.03.04
	J J Tierney (Limavady)		05.10.08P
	(NF 14.08.15)		

G-MFMF	Bell 206B-3 JetRanger III	3569	04.06.84	

G-MFMF Bell 206B-3 JetRanger III   3569   04.06.84
G-BJNJ   Polo Aviation Ltd
Urchinwood Manor, Congresbury   05.08.18E

G-MFMM Scheibe SF25C Falke   4412   20.04.82
(G-MBMM), D-KAEU
J E Selman   (Ardagh, Co Limerick, RoI)   16.07.08E
(NF 16.08.17)

G-MFOX Aeropro EuroFOX 912(1)   38612   20.09.12
D W & M L Squire   Perranporth   30.05.18P
Built by R M Cornwell – project BMAA/HB/630;
tricycle u/c

G-MFUX Eurofly Minifox   19004   13.03.19
Airplay Aircraft Ltd   Sutton Meadows
Built Airplay Aircraft Ltd (IE 13.03.19)

G-MGBG Cessna 310Q   310Q0110   29.08.17
N727MB, G-AYND, N7610Q
Cotswold Aero Maintenance Ltd   Bournemouth   12.05.08
Stored externally 01.19 (IE 29.08.17)

G-MGCK Whittaker MW6-S FT   xxxx   30.03.93
H A Kruczek   (Wolverhampton)   24.06.18P
Built by M W J Whittaker – project PFA 164-11262

G-MGDL Cyclone Pegasus Quantum 15   7400   17.02.98
M J Buchanan   Coldharbour Farm, Willingham   09.07.18P

G-MGEC Rans S-6-ESD-XL Coyote II   1096.1047   13.10.97
S P Tkaczyk & D Williams   Old Park Farm, Margam   08.07.15P
Built by E Carter – project PFA 204-13209;
tricycle u/c (IE 26.08.15)

G-MGEF Cyclone Pegasus Quantum 15-912   7261   18.09.96
M A Steadman   Longacre Farm, Sandy   06.07.18P

G-MGFC Aeropro EuroFOX 912(1)   36312   29.05.12
M G F Cawson   Arclid Green, Sandbach   18.10.18P
Built by M G F Cawson – project BMAA/HB/622;
tailwheel u/c

G-MGFK Cyclone Pegasus Quantum 15-912   7396   02.02.98
R J Whitmarsh   Perranporth   09.03.19P

G-MGGG Cyclone Pegasus Quantum 15-912   7377   03.11.97
R A Beauchamp   (Birmingham B44)   27.07.09P
(NF 02.03.15)

G-MGGT CFM Streak Shadow SA   K 252   03.06.94
G von Wilcken   Middle Stoke, Isle of Grain
Built by J W V Edmonds – project PFA 206-12723
(SSDR microlight since 05.18) (IE 06.11.17)

G-MGGV Cyclone Pegasus Quantum 15-912   7484   12.10.98
I S Duffy   Otherton   06.05.18P

G-MGIC Ace Aviation Magic/Cyclone   AM156   25.03.11
P J Hopkins   Deenethorpe
Trike s/n AM156 & wing s/n AC-152
(SSDR microlight since 05.14) (IE 05.02.18)

G-MGNI Magni M16C Tandem Trainer   16170804   21.09.17
Gyromania Ltd   Popham   01.10.19P

G-MGOD Medway Raven X   MRB110/106   06.07.93
N R Andrew, D J Millward & A Wherrett
Rookery Farm, Doynton   01.05.00P
(IE 27.04.17)

G-MGOO Murphy Renegade Spirit UK   xxxx   14.11.89
J A Aley   (London N9)   10.08.12P
Built by A R Max – project PFA 188-11580 (NF 13.03.18)

G-MGPA Comco Ikarus C42 FB100   0412-6635   25.01.05
S Ashley   (Brixham)   02.04.18P
Assembled Fly Buy Ultralights Ltd;
engine stolen at Halwell 06.17

G-MGPD Cyclone Pegasus XL-R   6905   09.01.95
T A Dockrell   Westonzoyland   20.09.18P

G-MGPH CFM Streak Shadow SA-M   286   27.11.97
G-RSPH   V C Readhead   (Saxmundham)
Built by CFM Aircraft Ltd – project PFA 206-13166
(SSDR microlight since 08.16) (NF 26.01.18)

G-MGPS Leonardo AW169   69077   05.12.18
I-RAIT   Specialist Aviation Services Ltd   RAF Wyton   10.12.19E
Operated by MAGPAS Helimedix Air Ambulance

G-MGPX Kolb Twinstar Mk.III Xtra   xxxx   28.01.08
C F Janes   Baker Barracks, Thorney Island   26.09.19P
Built by S P Garton – project PFA 205-14701

G-MGRH Quad City Challenger II   CH2-1189-0482   20.02.90
Cancelled 18.10.16 as PWFU   24.07.06
Popham   *Open store 04.16, gone by 10.16*

G-MGTG Cyclone Pegasus Quantum 15-912   7369   19.12.97
G-MZIO   F B Oram   (Vancals, France)   14.11.18P

G-MGTV Thruster T600N 450   0052-T600N-070   14.03.02
R Bingham   Kernan Valley, Tandragee   18.10.18P
Badged 'Sprint'

G-MGTW CFM Shadow Series DD   287-DD   23.01.98
G T Webster   Easter Poldar Farm, Thornhill   26.02.17P
Permit suspended 29.10.16

G-MGUN Cyclone AX2000   7284   18.12.96
M A Boffin   Bruntingthorpe   30.09.13P
(NF 07.01.16)

G-MGUY CFM Shadow Series CD   078   23.11.87
F J Luckhurst & R G M Proost   Old Sarum   16.08.91P
(NF 16.09.14)

G-MGWH Thruster T300   9013-T300-507   08.12.92
S A Wilson tr Bluestreak Thruster Group
(Dromara, Dromore)   03.11.18P
Built by Tempest Aviation Ltd

G-MGWI Robinson R44 Astro   0663   04.05.00
G-BZEF   Ed Murray & Sons Ltd   (Hartlepool)   11.04.18E

G-MHCE Enstrom F-28A   150   22.08.96
G-BBHD   M P Larsen   (Sevbolle, Denmark)   03.05.18E

G-MHCM Enstrom 280FX Shark   2052   05.04.06
G-IBWF, G-ZZWW, G-BSIE, HA-MIN, G-BSIE
Dave Tinsley Ltd   Welshpool   17.08.18E

G-MHGS Stoddard-Hamilton GlaStar   5720   30.07.03
H D Jones   Blackpool   30.03.18P
Built by M Henderson – project PFA 295-13473;
tricycle u/c

G-MHMR Mainair Pegasus Quantum 15-912   7969   19.12.05
D-MHMR   S B Wilkes t/a Hadair
Wolverhampton Halfpenny Green   15.11.18P
Built by Mainair Sports Ltd

G-MHPS Stoddard-Hamilton Glasair Sportsman   7253   02.12.14
Hardmead Ltd   (Hardmead, Newport Pagnell)
Built by P Shedden – project LAA 295A-15281
(NF 21.12.18)

G-MHRV Van's RV-6A   xxxx   28.07.04
M R Harris   (Luton LU2)
Built by M R Harris – project PFA 181A-13422
(NF 04.02.16)

G-MIAN Best Off Skyranger Nynja 912S(1)   xxxx1029   02.06.16
I P Stubbins   Sandtoft   04.01.19P
Built by I P Stubbins – project BMAA/HB/637

G-MICH Robinson R22 Beta   0647   03.09.87
G-BNKY   Tiger Helicopters Ltd   Shobdon   10.10.05
(NF 18.12.18)

G-MICI Cessna 182S Skylane   18280546   14.06.01
G-WARF, N7089F
C G Tandy tr Magic Carpet Flying Company   Denham   15.10.18E

G-MICK Reims/Cessna F172N   F17201592   09.01.80
PH-JRA, PH-AXB   D H G Penney   Fenland   18.03.18E

G-MICX Air Création Tanarg 912S(1)/BioniX 13   xxxx   24.07.15
M J Moulton   Measham Cottage Farm, Measham   14.03.19P
Built by M J Moulton – project BMAA/HB/671;
trike s/n T15062 & sailwing s/n A15070-15064

G-MICY Everett Gyroplane Series 1   018   26.02.90
(G-BOVF)   G M V Richardson   (Foxhole, St Austell)   02.05.92P
(NF 05.09.16)

G-MIDD Piper PA-28-140 Cherokee Cruiser   28-7325444   20.01.97
G-BBDD, N11C
R B Walker t/a Midland Air Training School   Coventry   24.05.18E

G-MIDG Bushby-Long Midget Mustang   385   14.03.90
N11DE, N567, N2TH   C E Bellhouse   Headcorn   27.04.18P
Built by T Holt

G-MIDO Airbus A320-232   1987   29.04.03
F-WWIR   British Airways PLC   London Heathrow   28.04.19E

G-MIDS Airbus A320-232   1424   21.03.01
F-WWBO   British Airways PLC   London Heathrow   20.03.19E

G-MIDT Airbus A320-232   1418   14.03.01
F-WWBI   British Airways PLC   London Heathrow   26.06.19E

G-MIDX	Airbus A320-232	1177	21.03.00
	F-WWDP British Airways PLC London Heathrow		20.03.19E
G-MIDY	Airbus A320-232	1014	28.06.99
	F-WWDQ British Airways PLC London Heathrow		27.06.19E
G-MIFF	Robin DR.400-180 Régent	2076	31.05.91
	J C Harvey tr Westfield Flying Group		
	Spilsted Farm, Sedlescombe		17.01.18E
G-MIGG	PZL-Mielec Lim-5	1C1211	17.01.03
	G-BWUF, Polish AF 1211 D Miles North Weald		
	As '1211' in North Vietnam AF c/s; noted 11.18		
	(NF 12.10.15)		
G-MIII	Extra EA.300/L	013	05.09.95
	D-EXFI Angels High Ltd Enstone		10.10.18E
G-MIKE	Gyroflight Brookland Hornet	MG-1	15.05.78
	M H J Goldring Tregolds Farm, St Merryn		25.09.92P
	(NF 06.02.15)		
G-MIKI	Rans S-6-ESA Coyote II	0996.1040	28.02.97
	S P Slade Chase Farm, Chipping Sodbury		18.06.18P
	Built by N R Beale – project PFA 204-13094; tricycle u/c		
G-MILA	Cessna F172N Skyhawk II	F17201686	09.06.98
	D-EGHC, PH-AYJ Cancelled 15.08.14 as destroyed		03.07.14
	Kings Farm, Thurrock *Built by Reims Aviation SA*		
	Stored 06.17		
G-MILD	Scheibe SF25C Falke	44190	20.12.05
	D-KDET C A & L J Bailey Westacott Farm, Coldridge		06.09.18E
G-MILE	Cameron N-90	2411	26.09.90
	Miles Air Ltd Bristol BS3		
	'Miles Architectural Ironmongery Ltd'		19.07.18E
	Originally registered as N-77; new envelope		
	c/n 10548 fitted 2004		
G-MILF	Harmon Rocket II	xxxx	09.12.10
	E Stinton (Linthwaite, Huddersfield)		
	Built by E Stinton – project LAA 314-14933		
	(NF 20.10.14)		
G-MILR	Aeroprakt A-22LS Foxbat	A22LS-266	06.01.17
	G Millar T/A Myrtlegrove Aviation Services		
	Donnydeade, Dungannon		13.06.18P
	Built by G Millar – project LAA 317B-15402;		
	badged 'Super Sport 600'		
G-MIMU	CFM Shadow Series CD	K245	04.06.15
	G-MYXY N M Barriskell Kernan Valley, Tandragee		26.05.16P
	Built by N H Townsend – project BMAA/HB/059		
	(IE 03.08.16)		
G-MIND	Cessna 404 Titan	404-0004	27.04.93
	G-SKKC, G-OHUB, SE-GMX, (N3932C)		
	Reconnaissance Ventures Ltd t/a RVL Group		
	East Midlands *'Geomatics Group'*		17.02.18E
G-MINN	Lindstrand LBL 90A	883	30.10.02
	D & S M Johnson Bromley		10.05.18E
G-MINS	Nicollier HN.700 Menestrel II	xxxx	23.10.92
	R Fenion Bedlands Gate, Little Strickland		31.03.16P
	Built by R Fenion – project PFA 217-12354) (IE 27.04.17)		
G-MINT	Pitts S-1S	xxxx	07.02.83
	T R G Barnby Headcorn		07.04.18P
	Built by T G Sanderson – project PFA 009-10292		
G-MIOO M	Miles M.100 Student	1008	26.10.84
	G-APLK, XS941, G-35-4 Cancelled 31.03.09 as PWFU		06.05.86
	On loan from Aces High Ltd		
	With Museum of Berkshire Aviation, Woodley		
G-MIRA	Avtech Jabiru SP-430	0222	29.09.05
	G-LUMA C P L Helsen Balen-Keiheuvel, Belgium		28.11.14P
	Built by B Luyckx – project PFA 274-13458		
G-MIRN	Remos GX	271	31.10.08
	M Kurkic Elstree		12.07.18W
	Noted 10.18		
G-MIRV	Van's RV-8	81995	04.10.17
	S P Ayres & E R J Hicks (Chippenham & Bristol BS16)		
	Built by S P Ayres – project LAA 303-15153 (NF 04.10.17)		
G-MISG	Boeing 737-3L9	27833	31.03.16
	N4973S, G-OGBD, OY-MAR, D-ADBJ, OY-MAR		
	GMISG Ltd St Athan		13.06.19E
	Line No: 2688; stored 12.18		
G-MISH	Cessna 182R Skylane II	18267888	16.06.95
	G-RFAB, G-BIXT, N6397H		
	A C Hill & A A D Mckerrell Great Oakley		24.02.20E

G-MISJ	CZAW Sportcruiser	4434	20.01.09
	B P Clarke Andrewsfield		22.01.20P
	Built by M T Dawson – project LAA 338-14862		
G-MISK	Robinson R44 Astro	0520	01.04.11
	G-BYCE H W Euridge (Redlynch, Salisbury)		18.05.18E
G-MISS	Taylor JT.2 Titch	PFA 3234	18.12.78
	D Beale (Sutton, Ely)		02.08.10P
	Built by A Brenen – project PFA 3234 (NF 06.11.15)		
G-MITE	Raj Hamsa X'Air Falcon Jabiru(4)	830	03.03.04
	W Parker Benston Farm, New Cumnock		06.08.19P
	Built by T Jestico – project BMAA/HB/296		
G-MITY	Mole Mite	xxxx	24.01.13
	R H Mole Leicester		
	Built by R H Mole – project LAA 360-14839		
	(SSDR microlight since 11.16)		
G-MJAD	Eipper Quicksilver MX	3034	17.06.82
	J McCullough Newtownards		
	(SSDR microlight since 06.14) (IE 22.09.15)		
G-MJAE	American Aerolights Eagle	1021	12.07.82
	T B Woolley (Narborough, Leicester)		
	C/n unconfirmed		
	(SSDR microlight since 05.14) (NF 30.11.17)		
G-MJAJ	Eurowing Goldwing	EW-36	18.06.82
	M J Aubrey Llanfyrnach		
	Displayed Classic Ultralight Heritage		
	(SSDR microlight since 06.14) (NF 29.05.18)		
G-MJAL	Ron Wheeler Scout Mk.III/3R	0433 R/3	18.06.82
	Cancelled 22.08.00 by CAA		
	Not Known *Displayed at Popham 05.14*		
G-MJAM	Eipper Quicksilver MX	JCL-01	18.06.82
	P R Szczepanik (Southall)		
	(SSDR microlight since 07.14) (NF 06.12.16)		
G-MJAN	Hiway Skytrike I/Flexiform Hilander	RPFD-01	21.06.82
	G M Sutcliffe (Macclesfield)		
	(NF 30.07.18)		
G-MJAZ	Aerodyne Vector 627SR Ultravector	1251	23.06.82
	PH-1J1, G-MJAZ Cancelled 12.04.10 as PWFU		
	Swansea *Stored 02.15*		
G-MJBK	Swallow AeroPlane Swallow B	582007-2	18.11.83
	M A Newbould (Markington, Harrogate)		
	(SSDR microlight since 06.14) (NF 28.06.18)		
G-MJBL	American Aerolights Eagle 215B	2892	25.06.82
	B W Olley (Soham, Ely)		
	(SSDR microlight since 05.14) (NF 27.10.17)		
G-MJBZ	Huntair Pathfinder Mk.I	PK-17	02.07.82
	Cancelled 07.04.10 as PWFU		28.12.93
	Eastbach, English Bicknor *Stored 04.16*		
G-MJCF M	Maxair Hummer	SMC-01	05.07.82
	Cancelled 24.01.95 by CAA		
	With Newark Air Museum, Winthorpe		
G-MJCU	Tarjani/Solar Wings Typhoon	SCG-01	07.07.82
	J K Ewing (Corfe Mullen, Wimborne)		
	(SSDR microlight since 05.14) (IE 25.08.17)		
G-MJDE	Huntair Pathfinder Mk.I	020	09.07.82
	P Rayson Stoke Golding		
	(SSDR microlight since 08.14) (NF 12.06.18)		
G-MJDJ	Hiway Skytrike/Demon	VW17D	09.07.82
	A J Cowan (Yarm)		
	(SSDR microlight since 05.14) (IE 01.09.17)		
G-MJDP	Eurowing Goldwing	GW-001	12.07.82
	A D Russell (Ballyroney, Banbridge)		
	(SSDR microlight since 05.16) (IE 28.06.16)		
G-MJDW M	Eipper Quicksilver MXII	RI-01	15.07.82
	Cancelled 13.02.08 as PWFU		05.05.07
	C/n noted as 3506		
	With Newark Air Museum, Winthorpe		
G-MJEO	American Aerolights Eagle 215B	4562	26.07.82
	A M Shaw (Alsager, Stoke-on-Trent)		
	(SSDR microlight since 05.14) (NF 10.07.17)		
G-MJER	Ultrasports Tri-Pacer/Flexiform Solo Striker		
		DSD-01	23.07.82
	D S Simpson Graveley Hall Farm, Graveley		
	(SSDR microlight since 05.14) (NF 25.07.17)		

G-MJEX Eipper Quicksilver MXII 13894 27.07.82
Cancelled 14.11.91 by CAA
Holywood, Co Down *Stored 12.13*

G-MJFK Mainair Tri Flyer/Flexiform Dual Sealander JH-01 28.07.82
Cancelled 10.05.00 by CAA
Rufforth East *Stored suspended from roof, 10.12*

G-MJFM Huntair Pathfinder Mk.I ML-01 02.09.82
M J Aubrey Llanfyrnach
Displayed Classic Ultralight Heritage
(SSDR microlight since 06.14) (NF 29.05.18)

G-MJFX Skyhook TR1/Sabre TR1/38 02.08.82
M R Dean (Mytholmroyd, Hebden Bridge)
(SSDR microlight since 08.16) (NF 29.06.18)

G-MJFZ Mainair Tri-Flyer/Hiway Demon JAL-01 29.07.82
A W Lowrie (West Rainton, Houghton Le Spring)
(SSDR microlight since 05.14) (NF 26.02.15)

G-MJGI Eipper Quicksilver MXII (JMH)14888 & (JRW)1021 03.08.82
Cancelled 03.02.92 by CAA
Skipton *Built by J M Hayes & J R Wilman*
Stored for sale 09.12

G-MJHV Hiway Skytrike 250 II/Demon 175 AG 17 13.08.82
A G Griffiths (Hyde Heath, Amersham)
(SSDR microlight since 05.14) (NF 24.07.17)

G-MJIA Ultrasports Tri-Pacer/Flexiform Solo Striker SE-007 13.08.82
Cancelled 05.11.13 as destroyed 20.09.96
Wolverhampton
On rebuild 05.14 at Tettenhall Transport Heritage Centre

G-MJJA Huntair Pathfinder Mk.I 031 23.08.82
R D Bateman & J M Watkins (Barnstaple & Chichester)
(SSDR microlight since 06.14) (NF 06.02.18)

G-MJJB Eipper Quicksilver MX 3526 23.08.82
Cancelled 14.03.01 by CAA
(Fleet) *For sale from Fleet area 01.17*

G-MJJK Eipper Quicksilver MXII Sprint 3397 25.08.82
J McCullough (Newtownards) 21.08.06P
Built by Lincs Airsports UK for B Harrison
(s/n BH.02) (IE 22.09.15)

G-MJKL Ultrasports Puma/Southdown Lightning DS AT.1 06.09.82
Cancelled 13.06.90 by CAA
Loughbrickland *Stored 12.13*

G-MJKPᴹ Hiway Skystrike-Super Scorpion PEB-01 07.09.82
Cancelled 09.12.94 as WFU
Built by for P E Blyth
With South Yorkshire Aircraft Museum, Doncaster

G-MJKX Ultralight Flight Phantom PH 82005 14.09.82
L R Graham Rayne Hall Farm, Rayne
(SSDR microlight since 06.14) (IE 30.06.17)

G-MJLK Squires Dragonfly 250-II D.105 10.09.82
Cancelled 18.04.90 as PWFU 10.09.82
Breighton *Built by G A Squires Stored 12.16*

G-MJMD Hiway Skytrike II/Demon 175 OE 17D 27.09.82
T A N Brierley tr Hiway Demon Group
Baxby Manor, Husthwaite
(SSDR microlight since 05.14) (NF 04.12.14)

G-MJOC Huntair Pathfinder 048 25.10.82
A J Glynn Gerpins Farm, Upminster
(SSDR microlight since 06.14) (IE 27.04.17)

G-MJOE Eurowing Goldwing EW-55 29.10.82
R J Osborne (Cove, Tiverton)
(SSDR microlight since 08.16) (NF 25.07.18)

G-MJOX Mainair Tri-Flyer 330/Solar Wings Typhoon LJ-01 & 076-20582 13.01.83
Cancelled 13.06.90 by CAA
Enniskellen *Stored 12.13*

G-MJPA Rotec Rally 2B AT-01 05.01.83
Cancelled 30.03.10 as PWFU
Armagh Field, Woodview *Built by A Troughton*
Stored 02.14

G-MJPBᴹ Manuel Ladybird WLM-14 09.11.82
Cancelled 13.06.90 by CAA
Built by W L Manuel On loan from Estate of W.L.Manuel
With Brooklands Museum, Weybridge

G-MJPE Mainair Tri-Flyer 330/Hiway Demon 175 OG17D 10.11.82
T G Elmhirst (Worsbrough, Barnsley)
(SSDR microlight since 05.14) (NF 06.11.17)

G-MJPOᴹ Eurowing Goldwing 018 16.12.82
Cancelled 09.04.02 as PWFU *Stored*
With South Yorkshire Aircraft Museum, Doncaster

G-MJPV Eipper Quicksilver MX JBW-01 30.11.82
F W Ellis Water Leisure Park, Skegness
(SSDR microlight since 05.14) (NF 07.09.17)

G-MJRAᴹ Mainair Tri-Flyer 250/Hiway Demon PRJM-01 21.12.82
Cancelled 24.01.95 by CAA 28.06.91
Built by for J Martin & P Richardson
With Yorkshire Air Museum, Elvington

G-MJRL Eurowing Goldwing EW-79 30.12.82
Cancelled 03.07.14 by CAA 15.06.00
(Heanor) *Sold on ebay 04.15*

G-MJRU MBA Tiger Cub 440 SO.86 06.01.83
Cancelled 29.06.11 as PWFU
Messingham *Stored 07.17*

G-MJSD Rotec Rally 2B AT-02 19.01.83
Cancelled 13.06.90 by CAA
Armagh Field, Woodview *Stored dismantled 02.14*

G-MJSE Skyrider Phantom SF101 24.01.83
R P Tribe Damyns Hall, Upminster
(SSDR microlight since 12.14) (IE 25.04.16)

G-MJSF Skyrider Phantom SF105 24.01.83
(SE-...), G-MJSF R P Stonor Middle Stoke, Isle of Grain
Original airframe cancelled 01.11.83 when sold to
Sweden; c/n SF105 is a new frame
(SSDR microlight since 07.14) (IE 22.04.17)

G-MJSL Dragon Light Dragon 200 0018 24.02.83
M J Aubrey Llanfyrnach 22.09.99P
Displayed Classic Ultralight Heritage (NF 04.11.15)

G-MJSM Weedhopper JC-24 JRB-01 01.02.83
Cancelled 13.03.90 by CAA
Caernarfon *Stored 08.15*

G-MJSO Hiway Skytrike III/Demon 175 SA17D 01.02.83
D C Read (Bromsberrow Heath, Ledbury)
(SSDR microlight since 05.14) (NF 30.08.17)

G-MJSP MBA Romain Super Tiger Cub Special 440 S0.54 07.02.83
A R Sunley (Chelmsford)
(SSDR microlight since 08.14) (NF 29.05.18)

G-MJST Pterodactyl Ptraveller GCS-01 02.12.81
T D Dawson Plaistows Farm, St Albans
Built by Micro Engineering (Aviation) Ltd
(SSDR microlight since 12.11) (NF 14.09.17)

G-MJSUᴹ MBA Tiger Cub 440 SO.75/1 02.02.83
Cancelled 23.06.93 by CAA 31.01.86
Suspended from rafters
With Norfolk & Suffolk Aviation Museum, Flixton

G-MJSVᴹ MBA Tiger Cub SO.2/87 02.02.83
Cancelled 09.11.89 by CAA
Built by Flylite East Anglia
With Morayvia Sci-Tech Experience Project, Kinloss

G-MJSY Eurowing Goldwing EW-63 08.02.83
A J Rex (Minera, Wrexham)
(SSDR microlight since 06.14) (NF 03.05.18)

G-MJSZ Harker DH Wasp HA5 10.02.83
J J Hill (Easby, Great Ayton, Middlesbrough)
Built by D Harker
(SSDR microlight since 06.14) (NF 24.05.18)

G-MJTM Southdown Pipistrelle P2B SAL/P2B/002 21.02.83
A M Sirant Monkswell Farm, Horrabridge
(SSDR microlight since 08.16) (NF 23.05.18)

G-MJTX Skyrider Phantom 110 01.03.83
P D Coppin Solent
(SSDR microlight since 08.14) (NF 21.08.14)

G-MJTY Huntair Pathfinder Mk.I CHS-01 02.03.83
A S Macdonald Cranfield
(SSDR microlight since 07.14) (NF 27.06.18)

G-MJTZ Skyrider Phantom MBS-01 29.04.83
B J Towers Croft Farm, Defford
(SSDR microlight since 06.14) (IE 11.07.17)

G-MJUF MBA Super Tiger Cub 440 MCT-01 08.03.83
D G Palmer Easter Nether Cabra Farm, Fetterangus
Built by for M P Chetwynd-Talbot
(SSDR microlight since 05.14) (IE 19.07.18)

G-MJUW   MBA Tiger Cub 440   SO.69   29.03.83
            D G Palmer   Easter Nether Cabra Farm, Fetterangus
            (SSDR microlight since 06.14) (IE 19.07.18)

G-MJUX   Ultralight Flight Phantom   PH00094   29.02.84
            T J Searle   (Nettlestead, Maidstone)
            *Built by Ultralight Flight Inc; fitted with wings
            ex G-MTTN 08.07*
            (SSDR microlight since 05.14) (NF 18.11.15)

G-MJVF   CFM Shadow Series CD   002   12.04.83
            J A Cook   Parham
            (SSDR microlight since 03.17) (IE 29.07.17)

G-MJVI[M]   Lee Rooster 1 Series 4   4   08.04.83
            Cancelled 13.06.90 by CAA
            Suspended from rafters
            With Norfolk & Suffolk Aviation Museum, Flixton

G-MJVN   Ultrasports Puma 440/Flexiform Striker   82-00030-PR1   18.04.83
            R McGookin   (Carlung Farm, West Kilbride)   05.10.93P
            *Original trike & engine fitted to G-MJRP;
            stored 06.15 (NF 21.10.14)*

G-MJVP   Eipper Quicksilver MXII   1149   19.04.83
            G J Ward   (Moreton, Dorchester)   10.07.96P
            Original c/n 1124 became G-MTDO? (NF 25.06.18)

G-MJVU   Eipper Quicksilver MXII   1118   03.04.83
            F J Griffith   (Denbigh)   26.08.18P

G-MJVY   Dragon Light Dragon 150   D150/013   04.05.83
            J C Craddock   Freshwater Fruit Farm, Freshwater   19.08.18P
            *Includes components of G-MMAE
            – discernible on rudder*

G-MJWB   Eurowing Goldwing   EW-59   24.05.83
            D G Palmer   Easter Nether Cabra Farm, Fetterangus
            (SSDR microlight since 06.14) (IE 19.07.18)

G-MJWF   MBA Tiger Cub 440   BRH-001   04.05.83
            R A & T Maycock   (Chryston, Glasgow)
            (SSDR microlight since 08.16) (NF 09.04.15)

(G-MJWH)[M] Chargus Vortex 120   xxxx   R
            *Regn reserved 1983 for Chargus T.250 & engine:
            fitted to 1974 Vortex hang glider: abandoned &
            only wing on display*
            With Midland Air Museum, Coventry

G-MJWJ   MBA Tiger Cub 440   013/191   09.05.83
            Cancelled 28.02.05 by CAA   18.03.96
            Colne   *For sale in poor condition 02.15*

G-MJWS[M]   Eurowing Goldwing   EW-22   16.05.83
            Cancelled 23.06.97 by CAA
            Built by for J W Salter
            With Ulster Aviation Society, Lisburn

G-MJXE[M]   Mainair Tri-Flyer 330/Hiway Demon 175
                                        102-131082 & HS-001   17.05.83
            Cancelled 19.10.00 as TWFU   21.03.95
            *Unmarked: on loan from The Aeroplane Collection
            to Manchester Museum of Sciences & Industry*

G-MJXL   MBA Super Tiger Cub   SO.29   23.05.83
            Cancelled 13.06.90 by CAA
            Shrewsbury   *Displayed at Listers Furniture shop 02.17*

G-MJYF   Mainair Gemini/Flash   305-585-3 & W45   18.04.85
            Cancelled 31.01.03 by CAA   02.05.93
            Battlehill   *Stored 12.13*

G-MJYV   Mainair Rapier/Flexiform Solo Striker   175-19783   23.11.83
            L H Phillips   (Tanworth-in-Arden, Solihull)
            (SSDR microlight since 05.14) (NF 22.05.15)

G-MJYW   Lancashire 330/Wasp Gryphon III   2-330PM-PGK-6-83-K   28.06.83
            P D Lawrence   (Munlochy)
            Trike also used with G-MMPL
            (SSDR microlight since 05.14) (IE 05.09.17)

G-MJYX   Mainair Tri-Flyer/Hiway Demon   108-251182   09.06.83
            K G Grayson & R D Leigh   Darley Moor
            (SSDR microlight since 05.14) (IE 26.01.18)

G-MJZK (2) Southdown Puma Sprint   SN1111/0081   03.03.86
            R J Osborne   (Cove, Tiverton)
            (NF 30.10.14)

G-MJZP   MBA Tiger Cub 440   HCB-01   21.06.83
            Cancelled 12.06.97 as PWFU   31.01.86
            (Liverpool)   *Frame advertised for sale 02.19*

G-MJZS   MMT Scorpion   1   27.06.83
            Cancelled 02.11.88 as PWFU
            Evesham   *Advertised for sale 10.16*

G-MJZX   Hummer TX   TX/16   21.06.83
            M J Aubrey   Llanfyrnach
            Displayed Classic Ultralight Heritage
            (SSDR microlight since 05.14) (IE 26.08.15)

G-MKAK   Colt 77A   2039   15.08.91
            P M Davies & M A Webb   Oswestry   26.09.18E

G-MKAS   Piper PA-28-140 Cherokee Cruiser   28-7425338   30.04.98
            G-BKVR, OY-BGV
            G R Manley tr 3G's Flying Group   Redhill   06.05.18E

G-MKER   P&M QuikR   8581   18.05.11
            M C Kerr   Field Farm, Oakley   23.08.18P
            *Comprises QuikR wing ex G-MKRR (c/n 8561)
            & trike ex G-CCGI (c/n 7967)*

G-MKEV   Evektor EV-97 Eurostar   2007-3126   14.04.09
            K Laud   Streethay Farm, Streethay   06.07.18P
            Built by K Laud – project LAA 315-14830

G-MKHB   Aeropro EuroFOX 912(iS)   48916   05.10.16
            Ascent Industries Ltd   Oaksey Park   21.08.18P
            *Built by M K H Bell – project LAA 376-15391;
            tailwheel u/c*

G-MKVB   Supermarine 349 Spitfire LF.Vb   CBAF 2461   02.05.89
            5718M, BM597
            Historic Aircraft Collection Ltd   Duxford   26.04.19P
            As 'BM597:JH-C' in RAF c/s

G-MKVI[M]   de Havilland DH.100 Vampire FB6   676   02.06.92
            Swiss AF J-1167   Cancelled 02.01.09 by CAA
            As 'WL 505'   Built by FFW, Essen
            With Rahmi M. Koc Museum, Istanbul, Turkey

G-MKXI   Supermarine 365 Spitfire PR.XI   6S-504719   13.11.89
            N965RF, G-MKXI, R Netherlands AF, PL965
            P A Teichman t/a Hangar 11 Collection   North Weald   19.04.19P
            As 'PL965:R' in RAF reconnaissance c/s

G-MKZG   Super Marine Spitfire Mk.26   60   05.02.15
            D G Richardson   Audley End
            *Built by D G Richardson – project PFA 324-14587;
            on construction 10.15 (NF 05.02.16)*

G-MLAL   Avtech Jabiru J400   225   23.10.06
            K Lafferty   Fenland   17.09.19P
            Built by M A Scudder – project PFA 325-14399

G-MLAP   Leonardo AW169   69020   16.02.17
            I-PTFI   Starspeed Ltd   Biggin Hill   16.02.18E

G-MLAW   P&M Quik GT450   8310   12.09.07
            J R Payne   East Winch   17.09.18P

G-MLHI   Maule MX-7-180 Star Rocket   11073C   20.04.04
            G-BTMJ   R C Dawe & A F Millar tr Maulehigh Group
            White Waltham   28.09.19E

G-MLJL   Airbus A330-243   254   15.06.99
            F-WWKT   Thomas Cook Airlines Ltd   Manchester   14.06.19E

G-MLKE   P&M QuikR   8442   31.03.09
            G Oliver   Grove Farm, Wolvey   07.04.18P

G-MLLI   Piper PA-32RT-300 Lance II   32R-7885098   17.12.12
            G-JUPP, G-BNJF, N31539   T Steward   Southend   26.10.19E
            *Official type data 'PA-32R-300 Cherokee Lance II'
            is incorrect*

G-MLSY   BRM Bristell NG5 Speed Wing   382   28.01.19
            T E Mills   (Whitstable)
            *Built by T E Mills – project LAA 385-15584
            (NF 28.01.19)*

G-MLTA   Ultramagic M-77   77/377   04.07.14
            R Parr   Chatteris   *'visit Malta'*   05.03.19E

G-MLWI   Thunder Ax7-77   1000   03.09.86
            C A Butter   Marsh Benham   16.06.16E

G-MLXP   Europa Aviation Europa   251   14.06.11
            M Davies   Sandtoft   11.05.18P
            *Built by M Davies, M McCallum & I Seager
            – project PFA 247-12974; tailwheel u/c*

G-MLZZ   Best Off Skyranger Swift 912S(1)   SKR0708823   06.11.07
            I D Grossart   Strathaven   22.06.16P
            *Built by D M Robbins – project BMAA/HB/557
            (IE 05.01.18)*

G-MMAE Dragon Light Aircraft Dragon Series 200 005 07.09.82
Cancelled 27.10.07 by CAA 01.05.07
Freshwater, IOW   *Stored Freshwater area 06.18*

G-MMAG MBA Tiger Cub 440 SO.47 22.06.83
M J Aubrey   (Llanfyrnach, Cemais)
Stored Llanfyrnach Classic Ultralight Heritage 2018
(SSDR microlight since 06.14) (NF 30.05.18)

G-MMAM MBA Tiger Cub 440 SO.197 19.07.94
I Pearson   Perranporth
(SSDR microlight since 06.14) (NF 11.06.18)

G-MMAR Mainair Gemini/Southdown Puma Sprint MS
195-11083-2 23.09.83
B A Fawkes   (Storrington, Pulborough) 04.06.18P

G-MMAY Airwave Magic Nimrod/Patterson WW2 Trike WW-2 23.08.83
Cancelled 12.06.90 as WFU
Killinchy   *Stored 12.13*

G-MMBE MBA Tiger Cub 440 SO.74 30.06.83
A Gannon   Lawmuir Farm, Sheardale, Coalsnaughton
(SSDR microlight since 08.16) (NF 16.02.16)

G-MMBN Eurowing Goldwing EW-89 28.06.83
Cancelled 20.04.10 by CAA
Enstone   *Stored 08.17*

G-MMBU Eipper Quicksilver MXII CAL-222 08.07.83
D A Norwood   (Gwespyr, Holywell) 17.06.14P
(NF 01.10.15)

G-MMBV Huntair Pathfinder Mk.I 044 08.07.83
Cancelled 14.12.10 as PWFU 09.05.07
(Birmingham)   *For sale 10.16*

G-MMCB Huntair Pathfinder Mk.II 136 13.07.83
Cancelled 23.11.88 as WFU
Wroughton   *In Science Museum store 2013*

G-MMCI Southdown Puma Sprint X P421 28.09.83
Cancelled 17.11.11 by CAA 08.07.06
Finedon, Northants   *Also c/n DMP-01*
Advertised for sale 05.13

G-MMCO Hornet Invader/Southdown Sprint RPO.15 27.07.83
Cancelled 23.06.97 by CAA
Swadlincote   *For sale from Swadlincote area 06.18*

G-MMCV Hiway Skytrike II/Solar Wings Typhoon T583783 27.07.83
G Addison   (Bannockburn, Stirling)
(SSDR microlight since 05.14) (NF 06.11.17)

G-MMDF Southdown Wildcat MkII/Lightning Phase II 007 24.08.83
Cancelled 29.07.11 as PWFU 04.11.03
Not Known   *Displayed at Popham 05.14*

G-MMDJ Mainair Tri-Flyer 250/Solar Wings Typhoon 070-24582 09.09.83
A M Webb   (Great Fransham, Dereham)
Solar Wings Typhoon wing s/n T1082-633; trike
c/n 070-24582 originally ex G-MJVK (Mainair
Tri-Flyer 250/Silhouette) 06.83
(SSDR microlight since 10.18) (IE 03.10.18)

G-MMDKᴹ Mainair Merlin/Striker 18116883 07.09.83
Cancelled 02.12.10 as PWFU 30.05.99
With South Yorkshire Aircraft Museum, Doncaster

G-MMDO Hornet Dual Invader/Southdown Sprint RP014 02.11.83
M Roberts   Trefgraig, Rhoshirwaun
Built by Templeward Ltd & Southdown Sailwings Ltd
(IE 11.07.18)

G-MMEK Medway Hybred 44XL 129836 16.09.83
M G J Bridges tr West Country Wings
(Chagford, Newton Abbot)
Solar Wings Typhoon XLII wing c/n either
T883-884XL or '887XL
(SSDR microlight since 08.14) (IE 29.04.16)

G-MMFSᴹ Micro Biplane Aviation:Tiger Club 440 SO.64 14.05.99
Cancelled 11.03.10 by CAA 27.07.01
'Black' (port side) & 'Adder' (starboard side)
With Tettenhall Transport Heritage Centre, Wolverhampton

G-MMFV Mainair Tri-Flyer 440/Flexiform Dual Striker 212271083 08.12.83
R A Walton   (Kingsteignton, Newton Abbot) 26.04.97P
(NF 09.09.14)

G-MMGF MBA Tiger Cub 440 SO.124 18.11.83
I J Webb   (Basingstoke)
(SSDR microlight since 06.14) (IE 31.07.17)

G-MMGL MBA Tiger Cub 440 SO.148 23.11.83
H E Dunning   Baxby Manor, Husthwaite
(Originally built Micro Biplane Aviation as
kit no SO.148: completed H E Dunning
– project BMAA/HB/050
(SSDR microlight since 07.14) (IE 24.06.16)

G-MMGS Solar Wings Panther XL-S T1283939XL 28.12.83
G C Read   (Shortstown, Bedford) 21.04.08P
(NF 10.12.14)

G-MMGT Huntwing Pegasus Classic JAH-7 28.11.83
H Cook   (Newport)
Built by J A Hunt; trike c/n SW-TB-1228 ex G-MTOH
(SSDR microlight since 06.14) (NF 06.06.18)

G-MMGV Whittaker MW5 Sorcerer Series A 001 02.12.83
G N Haffey & M W J Whittaker   Popham
Built by Microknight Aviation Ltd
(SSDR microlight since 07.14) (IE 08.06.16)

G-MMHN MBA Tiger Cub 440 SO.136 19.12.83
M J Aubrey   Llanfyrnach
Displayed Classic Ultralight Heritage)
(SSDR microlight since 06.14) (NF 30.05.18)

G-MMHS SMD Gazelle/Flexiform Dual Striker 104-11283 21.12.83
C J Meadows   (Shepton Mallet)
(IE 22.02.18)

G-MMHZ Solar Wings Panther XL-S T1283948XL 03.01.84
Cancelled 19.12.00 by CAA 28.07.00
Bedford   *For sale on eBay 05.15*

G-MMIE MBA Tiger Cub 440 G7-7 03.01.84
B W Olliver   (Wellington, Telford)
Built by Midland Ultralights Ltd
(SSDR microlight since 08.16) (NF 29.06.18)

G-MMIH MBA Tiger Cub 440 SO.130 25.04.84
T Barnby   (Deerness, Orkney)
Damaged 05.06.16
(SSDR microlight since 08.15) (IE 22.06.17)

G-MMIJ Ultrasports Tripacer/Airwave Nimrod 165 ZX-00165 01.11.83
Cancelled 28.04.00 by CAA 09.12.96
Not Known   *For sale from Lampeter area 06.18*

G-MMJD Southdown Puma Sprint SP/1001 28.06.83
M P Robertshaw   (Keighley) 20.07.08P
(NF 19.11.14)

G-MMJS MBA Tiger Cub 440 WAM.1 08.01.87
Cancelled 07.09.94 by CAA 08.01.87
Not Known   *Sold 04.16 in Co Louth area*

G-MMJV MBA Tiger Cub 440 SO.195 25.03.84
D G Palmer   Easter Nether Cabra Farm, Fetterangus
Built by K Bannister – project PFA 140-10902
(SSDR microlight since 06.14) (NF 08.12.14)

G-MMKA Solar Wings Panther Dual XL T284986XL 08.03.84
R S Wood   (Wallacestone, Falkirk)
(NF 25.06.18)

G-MMKM Mainair Tri-Flyer/Flexiform Dual Striker 221-01-84-0002 12.03.84
S W Hutchinson   Trenholme Farm, Ingleby Arncliffe 11.06.99P
Original trike was Mainair 440 Tri-Flyer (c/n 210-1083);
exchanged for 440 Gemini rebuild, exported to US
& re-imported; noted 01.14 (NF 19.05.15)

G-MMKP MBA Tiger Cub 440 SO.203 13.03.84
J W Beaty   (Lowick, Kettering)
(SSDR microlight since 08.16) (NF 02.08.18)

G-MMKR Mainair Tri-Flyer 440/Southdown Lightning DS
209-171083 14.03.84
C R Madden   (Bromham, Bedford) 29.05.10P
Originally registered 11.10.83 as G-MNDK; restored
14.02.84 as G-MMKR originally as c/n CM-01
(Cyril Moore); built by using trike unit ex G-MNDK;
wing s/n L195/341 (IE 08.09.17)

G-MMKT MBA Tiger Cub 440 SO.85 07.11.83
A R Sunley   (Chelmsford)
Built by K N Townshend
(SSDR microlight since 08.14) (NF 29.05.18)

G-MMKX Skyrider Phantom 330 PH107R 18.03.85
G J Lampitt   Pound Green
(SSDR microlight since 06.14) (NF 22.05.18)

G-MMLE Eurowing Goldwing SP   EW-81   21.03.84
M J Aubrey   Llanfyrnach
Displayed Classic Ultralight Heritage)
(SSDR microlight since 06.14) (NF 29.05.18)

G-MMLF MBA Tiger Cub 440   SO.115   23.03.84
Cancelled 10.05.01 by CAA   31.12.91
Bridgemere
On display at 'Jurassic Golf' in garden centre 07.15

G-MMLI[M] Mainair Tri-Flyer 250/Solar Wings Typhoon S
BAPC.244   RPAT-01 & T484-423L 26.03.84
Cancelled 07.09.94 by CAA   *Stored*
Originally registered as Hiway Skytrike Mk.II 250)
With National Museum of Flight Scotland, East Fortune

G-MMLK MBA Tiger Cub 440   SO.112   26.03.84
M J Aubrey   (Stanner, Kington)
Built by A C Barr
(SSDR microlight since 11.16) (NF 08.11.16)

G-MMLM[M] MBA Tiger Cub 440   SO.172   26.03.84
Cancelled 22.05.00 as TWFU   *'Red Baron'*
Built by L L Campbell
Unmarked – overall red with German crosses
With Montrose Air Station Heritage Centre

G-MMMG Eipper Quicksilver MXL   1383   05.06.84
L Swift   Water Leisure Park, Skegness
(SSDR microlight since 06.14) (IE 30.07.17)

G-MMMH Hadland Willow/Flexiform Striker   MJH 383   09.12.83
M J Hadland   (Ashton-in-Makerfield, Wigan)   11.05.11P
Built by M J Hadland (NF 23.05.18)

G-MMMI Ultrasports Tripacer/Southdown Lightning Phase II
SW-01   30.03.84
Cancelled 07.11.00 by CAA   08.07.96
Wisbech   *For sale from Wisbech area 06.18*

G-MMML Dragon Light Dragon 150   002   28.06.83
(OY-...), G-MMML   M J Aubrey   Llanfyrnach   06.08.00P
Displayed Classic Ultralight Heritage (NF 04.11.15)

G-MMMN Solar Wings Panther XL-S   PXL843150   04.04.84
C Downton   (Haytor, Newton Abbot)   16.07.04
Probably c/n T484-1059XL (NF 04.02.16)

G-MMNA Eipper Quicksilver MXII   1046   30.03.84
G A Marples   (Melton Mowbray)   02.01.05P
C/n conflicts with Quicksilver G-MMIL (IE 03.02.17)

G-MMNB Eipper Quicksilver MX   4286   30.03.84
J M Lindop   (Stratford-upon-Avon)
(SSDR microlight since 05.14) (NF 15.08.17)

G-MMNC Eipper Quicksilver MX   4276   30.03.84
W S C Toulmin   (Great Gidding, Huntingdon)
(SSDR microlight since 05.14) (NF 17.10.17)

G-MMNH Dragon Light Dragon 150   D150/42   27.07.83
T J Barlow   (Dromara, Dromore)
(NF 16.04.18)

G-MMOB Mainair Gemini/Southdown Sprint 244-584-2(K) & EM-01   11.05.84
D Woolcock   St Michaels   30.10.17P
C/n 'K' denotes kit built

G-MMOK Solar Wings Panther XL-S   T5841066XL   09.05.84
A J & R F Foster t/a RF & AJ Foster
Red Barn Farm, Badingham   03.11.18P
Wing c/n PXL844-157

G-MMPH Southdown Puma Sprint   P545   20.06.84
J Siddle   (Alsager, Stoke-on-Trent)   27.04.05P
(NF 09.04.18)

G-MMPL Lancashire 440/Flexiform Dual Striker   PDL-02   05.12.83
P D Lawrence   Culbokie
Trike c/n 2/330PM/PGK/683/K ex G-MJYW,
possibly used with exchangeable wings
(SSDR microlight since 11.14) (IE 08.09.17)

G-MMPR Dragon Light Aircraft Dragon 150   0011   18.04.83
Cancelled 08.10.93 by CAA   28.02.87
Carnoven, Co Donegal   *Stored 03.16*

G-MMPZ Teman Mono-Fly   JWH-01   02.07.84
H Smith   Morgansfield, Fishburn   *'Miss Monofly'*
Built by J W Highton
(SSDR microlight since 05.14) (IE 17.02.15)

G-MMRH Hiway Skytrike/Demon   JSM-01   20.06.84
A M Sirant   Monkswell Farm, Horrabridge
(SSDR microlight since 05.14) (IE 17.02.15)

G-MMRL Solar Wings Pegasus XL-R   T6841102XL   17.07.84
R J Hood   London Colney
Trike c/n SW-TB-1233 ex G-MTOM c.2001
(SSDR microlight since 06.14) (IE 16.06.15)

G-MMRN Southdown Puma Sprint   P544   16.07.84
D C Read   (Bromsberrow Heath, Ledbury)   18.04.01P
(NF 12.06.18)

G-MMRP Mainair Gemini/Southdown Sprint   P561   07.02.85
J C S Jones   (Greenlands, Rhedyn Coch)   07.08.11P
(NF 23.03.18)

G-MMSP Mainair Gemini Flash   265-984-2   17.08.84
J Whiteford   (Stewarton, Kilmarnock)   24.04.01P
Original wing s/n W03 fitted to G-MNGF 1998;
current wing s/n not known (NF 16.09.14)

G-MMSS Southdown Puma/Lightning   SRS HJ2426   11.09.98
G A Hazell   Lower Upham Farm, Chiseldon
(SSDR microlight since 05.14) (IE 20.07.15)

G-MMSZ Medway Half Pint/Aerial Arts 130SX   2/21385   27.03.85
A M Sutton   Shifnal
(SSDR microlight since 05.14) (IE 26.08.15)

G-MMTD Mainair Tri-Flyer 330/Hiway Demon 175 EIA-01   16.08.84
W E Teare   (Ramsey, Isle of Man)
Original trike s/n ??? sold to Denmark
(SSDR microlight since 05.14) (NF 16.10.17)

G-MMTJ Southdown Puma Sprint   SN1221/0006   17.01.85
Cancelled 17.04.09 by CAA   16.04.00
Limetree, ROI   *Stored 04.18*

G-MMTL Mainair Gemini/Southdown Sprint 268-1084-2-P576   03.10.84
K Birkett   (Swanick, Southampton)   03.08.05P
(NF 05.04.18)

G-MMTY Fisher FP.202U   2140   28.09.84
M A Welch   (Swindon)
(SSDR microlight since 06.14) (NF 16.10.17)

G-MMUL Ward Elf E47   E47   16.10.84
Cancelled 12.04.89 by CAA
Breighton   *Built by M Ward; noted 12.16*

G-MMUO Mainair Gemini Flash   272-1084-2   29.10.84
D M Pecheur   (Downham Market)
(SSDR microlight since 05.16) (IE 17.05.16)

G-MMUV Southdown Puma Sprint   SN1121/0010   07.11.84
D C Read   (Bromsberrow Heath, Ledbury)
(NF 12.06.18)

G-MMUX Mainair Gemini/Southdown Sprint 285-185-3-P587   28.12.84
D R Gregson   (Lyne, Chertsey)   26.12.12P
Trike c/n confirmed as 284-185-3 (NF 20.07.17)

G-MMVI Southdown Puma Sprint   SN1121/0012   28.11.84
G R Williams   (Oakdale, Blackwood)   02.11.97P
(NF 19.01.16)

G-MMVS Skyhook TR1 Pixie/Zeus   TR1/52   28.02.85
B W Olley   (Soham, Ely)
(SSDR microlight since 05.14) (NF 27.10.17)

G-MMVU Mainair Gemini Flash II   278-1284-2-W16   28.12.84
Cancelled 30.10.91 by CAA   13.01.86
Shrewsbury   *Advertised for sale in Shrewsbury area 10.15*

G-MMWA Mainair Gemini Flash II   271-1184-1-W07   22.11.84
Cancelled 15.11.10 by CAA   22.06.07
Deenethorpe   *Trike c/n stamped as 'KR271-1184-2'*
Stored 06.13

G-MMWG Mainair Tri-Flyer/Flexiform Solo Striker
FF-LAI-83-JDR-11 17.12.84
R D Leigh tr G-MMWG Group   Darley Moor
Built by P G Greenslade; replaced with trike
ex G-MJGN; wing s/n duplicates G-MMFC
(SSDR microlight since 05.14) (IE 26.01.18)

G-MMWL[M] Eurowing Goldwing   SWA-09 & EW-91   09.04.85
Cancelled 19.04.10 as PWFU   20.11.06
With Norfolk & Suffolk Aviation Museum, Flixton

G-MMWN Mainair Tri-Flyer/Flexiform Striker   1283.NH   21.11.84
Cancelled 04.02.05 as TWFU   30.03.97
(Portsmouth)   *Advertised for sale 01.14*

G-MMWS Ultrasports Tri-Pacer/Flexiform Solo Striker 983SH   21.11.84
P H Risdale   Tower Farm, Wollaston
(Originally fitted with Mainair trike))
(SSDR microlight since 05.14) (IE 26.08.15)

G-MMWX Southdown Puma Sprint SN1121/0047 10.04.85
G A Webb (London SW11) 31.10.07P
(NF 07.08.15)

G-MMXL Mainair Gemini Flash 292-385-3-W36 17.01.85
Cancelled 08.10.14 as PWFU 16.05.97
Rossall Field, Cockerham *Stored 04.15*

G-MMXO Southdown Puma Sprint SN1121/0018 23.01.85
I White Commonswood Farm, Northiam 14.11.15P

G-MMXU Mainair Gemini Flash 254-784-2-W21 29.01.85
T J Franklin Graveley Hall Farm, Graveley 04.09.17P

G-MMXV Mainair Gemini Flash 298-385-3-W37 29.01.85
M A Boffin Bruntingthorpe 30.06.11P
(NF 25.07.14)

G-MMYL Aerial Arts 130SX/Cyclone 70 CH01 08.03.85
Cancelled 10.12.13 by CAA 06.05.07
(Shoreham) *Sold on ebay 05.15*

G-MMZA Mainair Gemini Flash 266-984-3-W60 04.03.85
G T Johnston (Tullygally, Craigavon) 30.06.00P
(NF 02.05.18)

G-MMZC Mainair Gemini Flash 301-485-3 & W40 04.03.85
Cancelled 31.07.96 as PWFU
Tullygally, Craigavon *Stored 12.13*

G-MMZD Mainair Gemini Flash 309-585-3-W49 04.03.85
S McDonnell (Ballina, Co Mayo, RoI) 24.07.11P
(NF 03.08.16)

G-MMZS Eipper Quicksilver MXII 4343 18.03.85
Cancelled 16.02.93 as WFU 18.03.85
Bangor, Co Down *Stored 12.13*

G-MMZW Southdown Puma Sprint SN1121/0043 28.03.85
M G Ashbee (Frittenden, Cranbrook) 30.09.00
(NF 07.01.17)

G-MNAE Mainair Gemini Flash 343-885-3-W77 18.04.85
G C Luddington (Bolnhurst, Bedford) 26.07.14P
(IE 22.09.15)

G-MNAZ Solar Wings Pegasus XL-R SW-WA-1017 06.08.85
R W Houldsworth Northrepps 13.10.13P
Trike c/n SW-TB-1016 (NF 20.10.16)

G-MNBA Solar Wings Pegasus XL-R SW-WA-1018 06.09.85
V C Chambers (Newcastle ST5) 29.03.09P
Trike c/n SW-TB-1024 (NF 11.08.14)

G-MNBB Solar Wings Pegasus XL-R SW-WA-1019 20.09.85
A A Sawera (Nuneaton) 27.01.12P
Trike c/n SW-TB-1020 (NF 20.06.16)

G-MNBC Solar Wings Pegasus XL-R SW-WA-1020 11.10.85
R T Parry (Cross Hands, Llanelli) 09.09.04P
Trike c/n SW-TB-1026 (NF 15.12.15)

G-MNBGᴹ Mainair/Gemini Flash 345-585-3-W66 09.05.85
Cancelled 01.11.11 by CAA 05.01.11
Kircaldy *For sale 09.17, from Kilcaldy area*
With Grampian Transport Museum, Aberdeen

G-MNBI Solar Wings Pegasus XL-R T8841161XL 03.05.85
G-MMVF M O'Connell Rathcash East, Gowran, RoI 21.06.09P
Built as Panther XL-S with trike c/n
PXL884-17 & wing s/n T884-1161XL both
ex G-MMVF; fitted with trike s/n SW-TB-1174
ex EI-BUU (G-MTHK) as Pegasus XL-R
(NF 29.07.15)

G-MNBJ Skyhook Pixie HLC-01 07.05.85
Cancelled 10.05.12 by CAA
(Scotland) *For sale 02.16*

G-MNBM Southdown Puma Sprint SN1231/0058 25.06.85
Cancelled 27.05.14 by CAA 07.10.01
Wingland, Lincs *Stored 03.16*

G-MNBP Mainair Gemini Flash 338-885-3-W75 15.05.85
B J James (Raunds, Wellingborough) 21.07.11P
(NF 25.02.16)

G-MNBS Mainair Gemini Flash 308-585-3-W48 15.05.85
P A Comins (Nottingham NG3) 20.06.94P
(NF 18.11.15)

G-MNBV Mainair Gemini Flash 333-685-3-W70 15.05.85
Cancelled 25.11.10 by CAA 21.08.04
Newtownards *Stored 05.18*

G-MNCA Hunt Avon Sky-Trike/Hiway Demon 175 DA-01 28.05.85
A M Sirant Monkswell Farm, Horrabridge
Built by Hiway Hang Gliders Ltd & originally
registered as Adams Trike
(SSDR microlight since 05.14) (NF 04.01.18)

G-MNCF Mainair Gemini Flash 321-685-3-W61 03.06.85
C F Janes Solent 04.07.10P
(IE 21.04.17)

G-MNCG Mainair Gemini Flash 320-685-3-W59 03.06.85
T Lynch (Rossendale) 02.05.16P

G-MNCM CFM Shadow Series C 006 31.05.85
A Gibson Strathaven
(Originally built as Shadow Series B
(SSDR microlight since 06.16) (IE 09.06.17)

G-MNCP Southdown Puma Sprint SN1231/0071 24.06.85
D A Payne (Stratford-upon-Avon) 16.11.18P

G-MNCS Ultralight Flight Phantom PH00098 02.01.86
J A Harris (Bourton, Gillingham)
(SSDR microlight since 06.14) (NF 10.05.18)

G-MNCU Medway Hybred 44XL 26485/10 13.06.85
J E Evans (Shavington, Crewe) 24.06.05P
Solar Wings Typhoon wing (NF 31.07.15)

G-MNCVᴹ Medway Hybred 44XL 26485/11 13.06.85
M J Turland Newquay Cornwall 14.05.08P
Pegasus XL-R Sailwing c/n SW-WA-1030; on display
Cornwall Aviation Heritage Centre 08.18 (NF 11.05.15)

G-MNDD Mainair Scorcher 358-885-1-W85 12.06.85
S F Winter Lower Upham Farm, Chiseldon
(SSDR microlight since 09.14) (NF 16.05.16)

G-MNDE Medway Half Pint/Aerial Arts 130SX 386/85 19.06.85
C R Madden tr Delta Echo Half Pint Group
(Bromham, Bedford)
Wing ex G-MNBZ
(SSDR microlight since 05.14) (NF 10.07.18)

G-MNDF Mainair Gemini Flash 327-785-3-W67 25.06.85
Cancelled 25.06.10 by CAA 21.06.09
North Cornelly, Bridgend, Wales *On rebuild 07.16*

G-MNDU Midland Ultralights Sirocco 377GB MU-011 22.07.85
M A Collins Eaglescott
(SSDR microlight since 06.14) (NF 13.07.18)

G-MNDY Southdown Puma Sprint P536 02.05.84
A M Coupland Blackmoor Farm, Aubourn 19.06.03P
Trike rebuilt 1999 (IE 27.07.16)

G-MNEG Mainair Gemini Flash 360-885-3-W92 08.07.85
A Sexton (Nurney, Co Kildare, RoI) 18.10.99P
(NF 03.06.16)

G-MNER CFM Shadow Series CD 008 15.07.85
P A Taylor Ince 26.06.14P
(IE 07.01.16)

G-MNEW Mainair Tri-Flyer/Southdown Lightning MAR-01 08.07.85
Cancelled 24.01.95 by CAA 31.12.85
Chepstow *For sale ebay from Chepstow area 09.18*

G-MNEY Mainair Gemini Flash 365-1085-3-W94 23.07.85
D A Spiers East Fortune 17.09.04P
Noted 03.18 (NF 06.05.14)

G-MNFB Southdown Puma Sprint SN1231/0077 22.07.85
Cancelled 26.02.14 as PWFU 16.08.05
Westonzoyland *Stored 07.16*

G-MNFG Southdown Sprint 115 SN1231/0078 31.07.85
M Ingleton Parsonage Farm, Eastchurch
(SSDR microlight since 05.14) (IE 24.05.17)

G-MNFL AMF Microflight Chevvron 2-32A 002 19.08.85
J Pool Low Hill Farm, North Moor, Messingham 31.10.11P
(NF 10.01.18)

G-MNFM Mainair Gemini Flash 366-1085-3-W98 10.10.85
P M Fidell Wombleton 01.09.05P
(NF 13.05.16)

G-MNFN Mainair Gemini Flash 367-1085-3-W99 06.11.85
J R Martin (Exelby, Bedale) 13.08.04P
(NF 04.08.18)

G-MNGK Mainair Gemini Flash 374-1085-3-W112 05.09.85
A R Hawes (Needham Market) 29.04.17P
(IE 12.06.18)

G-MNGO Hiway Skytrike/Solar Wings Storm   21U8   05.09.85
Cancelled 20.03.85 by CAA
Wollaston   *For sale from Wollaston area 10.18*

G-MNHH Solar Wings Pegasus XL-S   SW-WA-1051   22.01.86
F J Williams   (Shefford, Bedford)   24.06.01P
Trike is an Ultrasports unit c/n PXL847-170 (NF 31.01.14)

G-MNHI Solar Wings Pegasus XL-R   SW-WA-1052   08.01.86
B R Claughton   (Whitstable)   07.08.07P
Trike c/n SW-TB-1042 (NF 11.10.16)

G-MNHJ Solar Wings Pegasus XL-R   SW-WA-1053   11.03.86
S J Woodd   (Northleach, Cheltenham)   26.06.93P
Trike c/n SW-TB-1056 (NF 30.04.18)

G-MNHK Solar Wings Pegasus XL-R   SW-WA-1054   09.07.86
C R Baker   (Stanford in the Vale, Faringdon)   25.08.19
Trike c/n SW-TE-000

G-MNHL Solar Wings Pegasus XL-R   SW-WA-1055   09.07.86
The Microlight School (Lichfield) Ltd   Fisherwick   04.05.14P
Trike c/n SW-TB-1077: fitted with wing ex G-MTRN
(whole frame or skin only?); converted to Pegasus
XL-R/Se configuration (NF 03.09.16)

G-MNHR Solar Wings Pegasus XL-R   SW-WA-1060   07.08.86
B D Jackson   (Wincanton)   13.11.08P
Trike c/n SW-TB-1081 (NF 20.11.14)

G-MNIA Mainair Gemini Flash   370-1185-3-W105   10.10.85
W R Furness   Mitchells Farm, Wilburton
(NF 12.04.17)

G-MNIC MBA Tiger Club 440   SO.170   26.03.84
Cancelled 13.06.90 by CAA
New Farm, Piddington   *Stored for rebuild 08.18*

G-MNIF Mainair Gemini Flash   403-286-4-W147   07.01.86
W Montgomery   (Arva, Co Cavan, RoI)   04.04.08P
(NF 26.11.18)

G-MNIG Mainair Gemini Flash   391-1285-3-W139   09.01.86
M Grimes   (North Walsham)   07.04.16P
(NF 17.07.15)

G-MNII Mainair Gemini Flash   390-1285-3-W128   06.11.85
R F Finnis   (Peasmarsh, Guildford)   06.09.91P
(NF 10.04.18)

G-MNIK Solar Wings Pegasus Photon   SW-WP-0002   29.10.85
M Belemet   (Kingston upon Thames)
Trike c/n SW-TP-0002
(SSDR microlight since 05.14) (IE 14.01.15)

G-MNIX Mainair Gemini Flash   395-1285-3-W136   29.11.85
Cancelled 17.03.05 as PWFU   11.07.98
Sutton Meadows   *Stored 07.15*

G-MNJD Mainair Tri-Flyer 440/Sprint   JBD-01/243-10484-2   02.04.84
S D Smith   Darley Moor   07.05.05P
(NF 05.06.15)

G-MNJF Dragon Light Aircraft Dragon Series 150 0068   02.01.86
(OY)9-17   Cancelled 24.03.10 by CAA   06.09.06
South Wraxall   *Stored 05.15*

G-MNJJ Solar Wings Pegasus Flash   SW-WF-0006   22.10.85
P A Shelley   (Washbrook, Ipswich)   26.11.96P
Trike c/n SW-TB-1029 & Mainair wing s/n W96
(NF 26.02.16)

G-MNJR Solar Wings Pegasus Flash   SW-WF-0013   30.12.85
M G Ashbee   (Cranbrook)   04.07.14P
Trike c/n SW-TB-1041 & Mainair Sailwing
c/n W133 (NF 07.01.17)

G-MNJS Southdown Puma Sprint   SN1231/0085   18.09.85
E A Frost   (Steeple Bumstead, Haverhill)   24.02.06P
(NF 14.03.18)

G-MNJX Medway Hybred 44XL   15885/14   09.12.85
H A Stewart   (Hartlip, Sittingbourne)   23.07.98P
(NF 29.01.16)

G-MNKB Solar Wings Pegasus Photon   SW-WP-0005   14.01.86
I E Wallace   (Amble, Northumberland)
Trike c/n SW-TP-0005
(SSDR microlight since 05.14) (NF 01.03.16)

G-MNKC Solar Wings Pegasus Photon   SW-WP-0006   14.01.86
K B Woods   Newnham
Trike c/n SW-TP-0006
(SSDR microlight since 05.14) (NF 18.10.17)

G-MNKD Solar Wings Pegasus Photon   SW-WP-0007   14.01.86
A M Sirant   Monkswell Farm, Horrabridge
Trike c/n SW-TP-0007 believed exported; current
trike possibly c/n SW-TP-0016
(SSDR microlight since 05.14) (NF 04.01.18)

G-MNKE Solar Wings Pegasus Photon   SW-WP-0008   14.01.86
H C Lowther   Bedlands Gate, Little Strickland
Trike c/n SW-TP-0008
(SSDR microlight since 05.14) (IE 07.08.15)

G-MNKJ Solar Wings Pegasus Photon   SW-WP-0013   28.01.86
Cancelled 04.07.96 by CAA   02.01.90
Ashley Farm, Binfield   *Stored 06.17*

G-MNKK Solar Wings Pegasus Photon   SW-WP-0014   28.01.86
M E Gilbert   Balgrummo Steading, Bonnybank
Trike c/n SW-TP-0014
(SSDR microlight since 05.14) (NF 22.10.15)

G-MNKM MBA Tiger Cub 440   SO.213   30.12.85
A R Sunley   (Chelmsford)
Built by L J Forinton
(SSDR microlight since 08.14) (NF 29.05.18)

G-MNKN Skycraft Scout III   410   06.01.86
M J Aubrey   Llanfyrnach
Displayed Classic Ultralight Heritage
(SSDR microlight since 05.14) (NF 02.09.15)

G-MNKP Solar Wings Pegasus Flash   SW-WF-0014   09.01.86
I N Miller   Plaistows Farm, St Albans   14.05.15P
Trike c/n SW-TB-1043 & Mainair Sailwing c/n W131

G-MNKW Solar Wings Pegasus Flash   SW-WF-0018   28.01.86
G J Eaton   (Stretton, Burton-on-Trent)   08.05.18P
Trike c/n SW-TB-1049 & Mainair wing c/n W140

G-MNLT Southdown Raven X   SN2232/0115   06.02.86
J L Stachini   (Borehamwood)   12.08.01P
(NF 16.12.14)

G-MNMC Mainair Gemini/Southdown Puma Sprint MS
222-284-2-P524   20.03.84
J C Peat   (Hinton St George, Tavistock)   18.06.07P
(NF 18.01.16)

G-MNMG Mainair Gemini Flash II   419-386-4-W177   11.02.86
N A M Beyer-Kay   (Southport)   20.08.94P
(NF 29.09.14)

G-MNMK Solar Wings Pegasus XL-R   SW-WA-1038   19.08.85
A F Smallacombe   (Woodhall Barn, Exbourne)   22.06.15P
Trike c/n SW-TB-1021 (NF 11.10.17)

G-MNMM Aerotech MW-5(K) Sorcerer   5K-0001-01   11.02.86
S F N Warnell   Plaistows Farm, St Albans
Originally registered as c/n SR101-R4008-01
(SSDR microlight since 08.16) (NF 04.12.14)

G-MNMO Mainair Gemini Flash II   398-186-4-W141   27.02.86
Cancelled 10.03.00 by CAA   28.05.99
Tavistock   *For sale 06.13*

G-MNMU Southdown Puma Raven   SN2232/0127   17.02.86
M J Curley   London Colney   26.03.06P
(NF 25.09.14)

G-MNMV Mainair Gemini Flash   375-1085-3-W113   03.03.86
N Riding   (Thornton-Cleveleys)   29.07.14P
Stored 04.15 (IE 07.06.18)

G-MNMW Whittaker MW6-1-1 Merlin   xxxx   16.04.86
E F Clapham tr G-MNMW Flying Group (Oldbury, Bristol)
31.07.18P
Built by E F Clapham – project PFA 164-11144

G-MNMY Cyclone 70/Aerial Arts 110SX   CH-02   06.03.86
N R Beale   Deppers Bridge, Southam
(SSDR microlight since 05.14) (IE 20.01.17)

G-MNNA Southdown Raven X   SN2232/0129   04.03.86
D & G D Palfrey   (Morebath, Tiverton)
(NF 15.09.14)

G-MNNF Mainair Gemini Flash II   402-286-4-W148   28.02.86
W J Gunn   (Kilsby, Rugby)   08.04.97P
(NF 06.04.16)

G-MNNG Squires Lightfly/Pegasus Photon   SW-WP-0019   25.02.86
K B Woods   Newnham
Trike possibly Mainair Tri-Flyer c/n 032-221181 ex G-MJKY?
(SSDR microlight since 05.14) (NF 18.10.17)

G-MNNJ Mainair Gemini Flash II 405-286-4-W150 28.02.86
L J Nelson Newtownards 06.05.05P
C/n plate shows 'G-MNNZ' incorrectly (NF 10.10.16)

G-MNNL Mainair Gemini Flash II 429-486-4-W186 28.02.86
C L Rumney (Allonby, Maryport) 21.11.05P
(NF 15.09.15)

G-MNNM Mainair Scorcher Solo 424-486-1-W182 20.03.86
(G-MNPE) S R Leeper Grove Farm, Needham
(SSDR microlight since 06.14) (NF 18.08.14)

G-MNNO Southdown Raven X SN2232/0133 26.03.86
M J Robbins (Dallington, Heathfield) 16.12.01P
(NF 16.09.14)

G-MNNS Eurowing Goldwing EW-74 08.04.86
N K Geddes Kilkerran
*Originally built Eurowing Ltd c.1983
– rebuilt as project BMAA/HB/287 c.2003
(SSDR microlight since 07.14) (IE 10.02.17)*

G-MNPC Mainair Gemini Flash II 423-586-4-W181 17.03.86
Cancelled 25.06.14 by CAA 19.06.14
Newtownards *Stored 07.14*

G-MNPG Mainair Gemini Flash II 437-686-4-W204 20.03.86
P Kirton Easter Poldar Farm, Thornhill 04.09.06P
(NF 22.08.14)

G-MNPY Mainair Scorcher Solo 452-886-1-W229 25.03.86
R J Turner (Sutton Bridge, Spalding)
(SSDR microlight since 05.14) (IE 22.09.17)

G-MNPZ Mainair Scorcher Solo 449-886-1-W226 25.03.86
S Stevens (Cornhill-on-Tweed)
*Three-blade propeller test aircraft
(SSDR microlight since 06.14) (NF 22.05.18)*

G-MNRD Ultraflight Lazair IIIE 81 17.06.83
F P Welsh tr Sywell Lazair Group Sywell
(SSDR microlight since 05.14) (IE 13.12.16)

G-MNRE Mainair Scorcher Solo 453-886-1-W230 25.03.86
J E Orbell (Spean Bridge)
(SSDR microlight since 05.14) (IE 14.06.18)

G-MNRT[M] Midland Ultralights Sirocco 377GB MU-016 01.04.86
Cancelled 13.08.14 by CAA
With Newark Air Museum, Winthorpe

G-MNRX Mainair Gemini Flash II 434-686-4-W220 08.04.86
R Downham St Michaels 17.04.16P

G-MNRZ Mainair Scorcher Solo 426-586-1-W184 31.03.86
R D Leigh Darley Moor
(SSDR microlight since 06.14) (IE 23.11.15)

G-MNSJ Mainair Gemini Flash II 443-886-4-W223 11.04.86
P Cooney (Ballyconnell, RoI) 14.05.06P
(NF 12.05.14)

G-MNSL Southdown Raven X SN2232/0145 17.04.86
P B Robinson (Sutton, Ely) 11.08.00P
(NF 07.03.16)

G-MNSX Southdown Raven X SN2232/0148 30.04.86
Cancelled 26.05.09 by CAA 18.07.03
(Kings Lynn) *For sale 03.16*

G-MNSY Southdown Raven X SN2232/0149 30.04.86
L A Hosegood (Swindon) 08.03.03P
(IE 06.09.17)

G-MNTD Aerial Arts Chaser/110SX 110SX/255 24.04.86
B Richardson (Sunderland)
*C/n duplicates G-MTSF
(SSDR microlight since 05.14) (NF 22.11.17)*

G-MNTK CFM Shadow Series CD 024 08.05.86
K Davies (Warrington) 17.08.14P
(NF 17.09.17)

G-MNTP CFM Shadow Series C K 022 19.05.86
C Lockwood (Llandudno) 15.05.14P
(NF 02.08.17)

G-MNTV Mainair Gemini Flash II 455-886-4-W241 09.07.86
A M Sirant Monkswell Farm, Horrabridge 17.10.04P
(NF 20.05.18)

G-MNUF Mainair Gemini Flash II 472-786-4-W252 13.06.86
K Jones Guy Lane Farm, Waverton 08.09.10P
(NF 10.12.15)

G-MNUI Mainair Tri-Flyer/Skyhook Cutlass MH-01 21.05.86
M Holling (Pollington, Goole)
(NF 07.07.14)

G-MNUW Southdown Raven X SN2232/0163 17.06.86
B A McDonald (Burwell, Cambridge) 19.12.96P
(NF 25.04.18)

G-MNUY Mainair Gemini Flash 422-586-4-W180 23.06.86
Cancelled 14.12.04 by CAA
Ballgowan *Stored 12.13*

G-MNVE Solar Wings Pegasus XL-R SW-WA-1079 19.06.86
M P Aris (Dry Drayton, Cambridge) 11.08.00P
Trike c/n SW-TB-1075 (NF 28.10.15)

G-MNVG Solar Wings Pegasus Flash II SW-WF-0109 11.06.86
D J Ward (Norwich NR7) 10.07.10P
*Trike c/n SW-TB-1069 & Mainair wing c/n W194
(NF 23.04.18)*

G-MNVI CFM Shadow Series CD 026 17.06.86
D R C Pugh (Caersws, Powys) 24.09.16P

G-MNVJ CFM Shadow Series CD 028 17.06.86
R Delaney RAF Honington 02.02.19P

G-MNVK CFM Shadow Series CD 029 17.06.86
A K Atwell Little Trostrey Farm, Kemeys Commander 18.04.18P

G-MNVN Southdown Puma Raven SN2132/0165 27.06.86
Cancelled 16.12.10 by CAA 11.04.08
Russia *Active in Russia 08.15 as G-MNVN*

G-MNVO Hovey Whing-Ding II CW-01 14.08.86
C Wilson (Basildon)
(SSDR microlight since 05.14) (NF 25.07.17)

G-MNVT Mainair Gemini Flash II 477-786-4-W258 27.06.86
S P Barker (Foxt, Stoke-on-Trent)
(NF 13.01.17)

G-MNVW Mainair Gemini Flash II 466-986-4-W246 26.06.86
J C Munro-Hunt (Llandrindod Wells) 29.09.09P
(NF 17.01.13)

G-MNVZ Solar Wings Pegasus Photon SW-WP-0021 27.06.86
J J Russ (Washington, Sunderland)
*Trike c/n SW-TP-0021
(SSDR microlight since 05.14) (NF 05.09.17)*

G-MNWB Thruster TST 086-118-UK-001 25.06.86
B Donnelly Carrickmore 03.01.95P
(IE 28.11.15)

G-MNWG Southdown Raven X SN2232/0170 04.08.86
G P Lane (Pucklechurch, Bristol) 09.05.05P
(NF 17.11.15)

G-MNWI Mainair Gemini Flash II 478-986-4-W264 09.07.86
P Dickinson (Upton, Wirral) 09.10.13P
(NF 27.06.17)

G-MNWK CFM Shadow Series C 030 09.07.86
Cancelled 10.05.05 by CAA 19.08.98
Dartford, Kent *For sale by Dartford Motors 05.18*

G-MNWL Arbiter Services Trike/Aerial Arts 130SX 130SX/333 23.07.86
E H Snook (Newport Pagnell)
(SSDR microlight since 05.14) (NF 07.08.17)

G-MNWW Solar Wings Pegasus XL-R SW-WA-1085 08.10.86
K P Taylor tr G-MNWW Group (Willoughby, Rugby) 06.07.17P
Trike c/n SW-TE-0008; converted to XL Tug configuration

G-MNWX Solar Wings Pegasus XL-R SW-WA-1086 04.08.86
Cancelled 10.11.00 by CAA 05.05.96
Otherton *Trike c/n SW-TB-1093 Stored 02.16*

G-MNWY CFM Shadow Series C K 031 28.07.86
R R L & S R Potts Selby House Farm, Stanton 19.08.03P
*Built by CFM Aircraft Ltd – project PFA 161-11130
(NF 18.03.16)*

G-MNXE Southdown Raven X SN2232/0202 07.08.86
A E Silvey White Cross Farm, Wilburton 06.11.09P
(NF 11.08.15)

G-MNXJ[M] Medway Half Pint 14/7886 03.09.86
Cancelled 17.01.95 by CAA
With Travis AFB Museum, Sacramento, California

G-MNXX CFM Shadow Series CD K027 13.08.86
R Sinclair-Brown North Coates 14.04.18P

G-MNYD Aerial Arts Chaser/110SX 110SX/320 19.08.86
B Richardson Wingland
(SSDR microlight since 05.14) (NF 22.11.17)

G

G-MNYF	Aerial Arts Chaser/110SX	110SX/322	19.08.86
	R W Twamley	(Coventry)	
	(SSDR microlight since 05.14) (IE 26.07.16)		
G-MNYK★	Mainair Gemini Flash II	494-1086-4-W296	11.09.86
	A Ryan Cancelled 06.04.10 as WFU Restored 04.09.18		
	To EI-.... 25.02.19		
G-MNYP	Southdown Raven X	SN2232/0207	03.09.86
	A G Davies (Bristol BS4)		14.05.01P
	(NF 13.04.16)		
G-MNYS	Southdown Raven X	SN2232/0208	08.09.86
	Cancelled 19.04.05 by CAA		09.01.99
	Sittingbourne For sale 04.14		
G-MNYU	Solar Wings Pegasus XL-R	SW-WA-1092	16.09.86
	G L Turner North Craigieford, Ellon		
	Trike c/n SW-TB-1100		
	(SSDR microlight since 08.14) (NF 11.10.17)		
G-MNZD	Mainair Gemini Flash II	493-1086-4-W295	08.09.86
	N D Carter (Horton, Slough)		04.04.96P
	(NF 14.11.14)		
G-MNZJ	CFM Shadow Series CD	033	19.09.86
	W Hepburn (Law, Carluke)		13.06.10P
	(NF 11.06.18)		
G-MNZK	Solar Wings Pegasus XL-R/Se	SW-WA-1096	24.09.86
	P J Appleby (Foxfield, Carrick-on-Shannon, RoI)		29.03.04P
	(NF 07.03.16)		
G-MNZP	CFM Shadow Series BD	K039	19.09.86
	G C White (Park Gate, Southampton)		
	Built by CFM Aircraft Ltd – project PFA 161-11206		
	(SSDR microlight since 10.18) (NF 02.10.18)		
G-MNZU	Eurowing Goldwing	EW-88	24.09.86
	P D Coppin & P R Millen Solent		
	Built by H B Baker		
	(SSDR microlight since 08.14) (IE 20.06.16)		
G-MNZW	Southdown Raven X	SN2232/0220	17.10.86
	T A Willcox Nichols Farm, Doynton		07.07.02P
	(NF 04.05.18)		
G-MNZZ	CFM Shadow Series CD	036	19.09.86
	Shadow Aviation Ltd Old Sarum		31.08.05P
	(NF 09.03.18)		
G-MOAC	Beech F33A Bonanza	CE-1349	25.05.89
	N1563N R L Camrass Alderney		25.05.18E
G-MOAL	Agusta AW109SP Grand New	22348	02.12.15
	SDI Aviation Ltd		
	Fishpools Farm Barns, Frankton, Warks		01.12.19E
	Operated by Sloane Helicopters Ltd		
G-MOAN	Aeromot AMT-200S Super Ximango	200.133	29.03.04
	PT-PRU T Boin Hausen-Am Albis, Switzerland		10.05.16E
G-MOCL	Bombardier CL-600-2B16 Challenger 604 5620		08.03.17
	M-YBST, VP-BST. OE-IVE, C-FFGE, C-GLWV		
	London Executive Aviation Ltd Athens Int'l, Greece		16.03.18E
G-MODE	Eurocopter EC120B Colibri	1295	19.08.02
	F-WQPU P G Barker Hunterswood Farm, Dunsfold		05.06.18E
G-MOFB	Cameron O-120	4275	13.01.98
	D M Moffat Thornbury, Bristol		20.12.18E
G-MOGS	CZAW Sportcruiser	07SC097	24.02.10
	J M Oliver Wolverhampton Halfpenny Green		26.02.18P
	Built by J M Oliver – project PFA 338-14728		
	(Quick-build kit 3945)		
G-MOJI	Lindstrand LTL Sphere	069	16.04.18
	Lindstrand Technologies Ltd Oswestry		
	(NF 16.04.18)		
G-MOKE	Cameron V-77	3686	04.10.95
	G Moyano tr G-MOKE ASBL Winseler, Luxembourg		12.04.18E
G-MOLA	Evektor EV-97 teamEurostar UK	2012-3937	28.06.12
	A Szczepanek Guy Lane Farm, Waverton		27.05.18P
	Assembled Cosmik Aviation Ltd		
G-MOMA	Thruster T600N 450	0036-T600N-088	22.08.03
	G-CCIB J H Keep tr Compton Abbas Microlight Group		
	Compton Abbas		18.04.19P
	Badged 'Sprint'		
G-MONI	Monnett Moni	xxxx	12.01.84
	T McKinley Bembridge		19.05.19P
	Built by ARV Aviation Ltd – project PFA 142-10925		
G-MOOD	Comco Ikarus C42 FB100 Bravo	1509-7418	15.08.17
	G-HARL R Moody Eshott		26.11.18P
G-MOOR	SOCATA TB-10 Tobago	82	23.07.91
	G-MILK P D Kirkham Retford Gamston		22.03.18E
G-MOOS	Percival P.56 Provost T.1	PAC/F/335	05.04.91
	G-BGKA, 8041M, XF690		
	R M Scarre tr Yeo Pro Group Dunkeswell		14.09.19P
	As 'XF690' in RAF c/s		
G-MOOV	CZAW Sportcruiser	08SC153	27.05.08
	S P Clifton tr G-MOOV Syndicate Bidford		09.04.18P
	Built by S P Clifton – project PFA 338-14666		
	(Quick-build kit no.4188)		
G-MOPS	Best Off Skyranger Swift 912S(1)	SKR0706800	04.10.07
	M Gates (London Colney)		07.03.19P
	Built by P Stretton – project BMAA/HB/547		
G-MORG	Kubicek BB-S/Ship	1027	29.11.13
	OK-2027 A M Holly Breadstone, Berkeley		26.03.15E
	(IE 05.10.18)		
G-MOSA	Morane Saulnier MS.317	351	14.12.09
	N351MS, F-BCNU, French AF		
	A C Whitehead Manchester Barton		26.08.18P
	As '351:HY22' in French Navy c/s		
G-MOSH	Piper PA-28R-201 Arrow III	2837043	24.07.15
	OY-NFF, N812ND S J Griggs (Bingley)		04.12.19E
	Official type data 'PA-28R-200 Cherokee Arrow II'		
	is incorrect		
G-MOSI^M	de Havilland DH.98 Mosquito TT.35	xxxx	10.11.81
	N98DH, N9797, G-ASKA, RS709		
	Cancelled 21.01.87 by CAA as 'NS519'		17.12.84
	With National Museum of USAF, Dayton, Ohio		
G-MOSJ	Beech C90GTI King Air	LJ-1984	31.01.11
	9H-MOS, G-MOSJ, N6014V		
	Newcastle Aviation Ltd t/a Naljets Newcastle Int'l		02.02.19E
G-MOSY	Cameron O-84	2315	17.04.96
	EI-CAO P L Mossman Llanishen, Chepstow		
	'Budget Travel'		27.04.18E
G-MOTA	Bell 206B-3 JetRanger III	4494	20.10.98
	N81521 J W Sandle Runcton Holme, King's Lynn		13.11.18E
G-MOTH	de Havilland DH.82A Tiger Moth	85340	31.01.78
	7035M, DE306 P T Szluha Audley End		22.05.19E
	Built by Morris Motors Ltd; as 'K-2567' in RAF (silver) c/s		
G-MOTI	Robin DR.500-200i Président	0006	23.11.98
	The Lord Saville of Newdigate		
	tr The Tango-India Flying Group Biggin Hill		01.04.18E
	Officially registered as DR.400-500		
G-MOTO	Piper PA-24 Comanche	24-3239	24.03.87
	G-EDHE, N51867, G-ASFH, EI-AMM, N7998P		
	B Spiralke (Leipzig, Germany)		14.05.18E
G-MOTW	Meyers OTW-145	45	10.11.11
	N34301, NC34301 J K Padden Duxford		
	On rebuild 12.17; Permit application 20.08.18		
G-MOUL	Maule M-6-235C Super Rocket	7518C	01.05.90
	H G Meyer (Nottuln, Germany)		07.04.18E
G-MOUR	Folland Gnat T.1	FL596	16.05.90
	8624M, XS102 Heritage Aircraft Ltd North Weald		16.03.19P
	As 'XR992' in RAF Yellowjacks c/s		
G-MOUT	Cessna 182T Skylane	18281315	23.03.04
	N2104H G Mountain New York Farm, North Rigton		09.07.18E
G-MOUZ	Cameron O-26	12144	21.09.17
	M E Banks & T J Orchard Bristol & Aylesbury		21.08.19E
G-MOVI	Piper PA-32R-301 Saratoga SP	32R-8313029	06.02.89
	G-MARI, N8248H J E Bray White Waltham		08.11.18E
G-MOWG	Aeroprakt A-22L Foxbat	xxxx	21.06.06
	J Smith East Winch		06.07.18P
	Built by J Smith – project PFA 317A-14545		
G-MOYR	Aeropro EuroFOX 912(S)	39013	11.04.13
	The Northumbria Gliding Club Ltd Currock Hill		11.12.18P
	Built by R A Cole – project LAA 376-15172;		
	tailwheel u/c; glider-tug		
G-MOZE	P&M Quik GTR	8663	13.09.13
	M R Mosley Headon Farm, Retford		20.04.18P
G-MOZI	Glasflügel Mosquito	34	21.08.07
	BGA 3587, N77RL J Christensen & P Smith		
	RAF Weston-on-the-Green '277'		02.03.18E

G-MOZZ	Mudry CAP 10B	256	30.10.90
	N Skipworth & P M Wells		
	Shrove Furlong Farm, Kingsey		24.09.18E
G-MPAA	Piper PA-28-181 Archer III	2843539	17.06.05
	N567SC Shropshire Aero Club Ltd Sleap		17.09.18E
G-MPAC	Ultravia Pelican PL	001	06.04.00
	J J Bodnarec Oxenhope		31.08.18P
	Built by M J Craven – project PFA 165-12944		
G-MPAT	Evektor EV-97 teamEurostar UK	2010-3919	12.01.11
	P J Dale Woodview House Farm, Chesham		03.06.18P
	Assembled Cosmik Aviation Ltd		
G-MPFC	Grumman American AA-5B Tiger	AA5B-0845	24.09.13
	G-ZARI, G-BHVY, N28835 MPFC Ltd Biggin Hill		31.03.18E
G-MPHY	Comco Ikarus C42 FB80 Bravo	1102-7136	23.03.11
	P Murphy Ince		25.07.17P
	Assembled Performance Aviation Ltd		
G-MPLA	Cessna 182T Skylane	18281686	15.03.12
	VH-RBR, N15206 Ainslie Aviation Ltd Bournemouth		05.12.19E
G-MPLB	Cessna 182T Skylane	18281646	15.03.12
	VH-CLL Colne Valley Electrical Ltd Earls Colne		03.05.19E
G-MPLC	Cessna 182T Skylane	18281855	05.04.12
	VH-EUX, N12368		
	Oxford Aviation Academy (Oxford) Ltd Oxford		09.06.18E
G-MPLD	Cessna 182T Skylane	18281788	05.04.12
	VH-EWV, N2437J Cropspray Ltd Bristol		17.09.18E
G-MPLE	Cessna 182T Skylane	18282039	17.06.13
	VH-NEG, N1749C		
	Oxford Aviation Academy (Oxford) Ltd Oxford		15.08.18E
G-MPLF	Cessna 182T Skylane	18282102	17.06.13
	VH-CBF, N6194N		
	Oxford Aviation Academy (Oxford) Ltd Oxford		15.08.18E
G-MPRL	Cessna 210M Centurion	21061892	05.08.02
	EC-GKD, N732YY		
	Mike Stapleton & Company Ltd Southend		05.11.18E
G-MPSA	Eurocopter MBB-BK117 C-2 (EC145)	9065	28.11.05
	Police & Crime Commissioner for West Yorkshire		
	Lippitts Hill		10.04.18E
	Operated by Metropolitan Police Air Support Unit		
	as callsign 'NPAS 61'		
G-MPSB	Eurocopter MBB-BK117 C-2 (EC145)	9068	28.11.05
	Police & Crime Commissioner for West Yorkshire		
	Lippitts Hill		26.11.18E
	Operated by Metropolitan Police Air Support Unit		
	as callsign 'NAPS 62'		
G-MPSC	Eurocopter MBB-BK117 C-2 (EC145)	9075	19.12.05
	Police & Crime Commissioner for West Yorkshire		
	Lippitts Hill		23.01.18E
	Operated by Metropolitan Police Air Support Unit		
	as callsign 'NAPS 63'		
G-MPWI	Robin HR.100/210 Safari	163	03.03.80
	F-GBTY, F-ODFA, F-BUPD D A Gathercole Fenland		31.01.19E
G-MRAG	Cessna 182T Skylane	18282414	23.08.17
	N122CS A S Gardner		
	Stoney Lane Farm, Tutnall, Broad Green		19.09.18E
G-MRAJ	Hughes 369E (500)	0010E	19.03.98
	N51946 A Jardine Dundee		11.09.14E
	(NF 21.01.16)		
G-MRAM	Mignet HM-1000 Balerit	134	15.11.99
	R A Marven Coleman Green, St Albans		24.05.18P
G-MRDS	CZAW Sportcruiser	08SC120	22.04.08
	P Wood Swanborough Farm, Lewes		21.04.18P
	Built by D I Scott – project PFA 338-14665		
	(Quick-build kit 4012)		
G-MRED	Elmwood CA-05 Christavia Mk.1	581	02.08.96
	C R Nash tr Mister Ed Group		
	Barton Ashes, Crawley Down		12.11.18P
	Built by E Hewett – project PFA 185-12935		
G-MRGT	Best Off Skyranger Swift 912S(1)	SKR xx xx 1068	07.01.14
	G I Taylor Plaistows Farm, St Albans		15.09.18P
	Built by G I Taylor – project BMAA/HB/638		
G-MRJC	AutoGyro Cavalon	V00127	28.08.13
	T Woodcock (Forder, Saltash)		07.06.19P
	Assembled Rotorsport UK as c/n RSUK/CVLN/008		

G-MRJJ	Mainair Pegasus Quik	7940	16.04.03
	J H Sparks Dunkeswell		10.09.18P
	Built by Mainair Sports Ltd		
G-MRJP	Silence SA.180 Twister	23	18.11.10
	J P Marriott Bicester		05.02.19P
	Built by M D Carruthers – project LAA 329-14972		
G-MRKS	Robinson R44 Raven	0771	20.05.03
	G-RAYC TJD Trade Ltd (Colmworth, Bedford)		10.12.18E
G-MRKT	Lindstrand LBL 90A	037	07.06.93
	R M Stanley Tewin, Welwyn 'Marketplace'		12.06.19E
G-MRLI	Sikorsky S-92A	920056	07.06.17
	G-CKGZ LN-OQF, N4502R Bristow		
	Helicopters Ltd Aberdeen Int'l		
	'Bruce H. Stover Board of Directors 2009-2018'		05.12.18E
G-MRLN	Sky 240-24	161	04.08.99
	M Wady Hamstreet, Ashford 'Icom'		28.04.09E
	(NF 25.03.15)		
G-MRLS	AutoGyro Calidus	C00210	01.05.12
	C N Fleming Fenland		03.05.18P
	Assembled Rotorsport UK as c/n RSUK/CALS/020		
G-MRLX	Gulfstream Gulfstream V-SP (Gulfstream 550)	5396	23.08.13
	N550DV, N596GA		
	Saxonair Charter Ltd London Stansted		22.08.18E
G-MRLZ	Robinson R44 Raven II	10396	09.10.17
	OK-OOK, HB-ZFW, N73858		
	Catedra Service XXI SL (Murcia, Spain)		
	(NF 06.10.17)		
G-MRME	Gefa-Flug AS105GD HA Airship	G0031 H0064	31.10.12
	Airship Over Atlanta Ltd Roswell, Georgia, USA		27.01.17E
G-MROC	Cyclone Pegasus Quantum 15-912	7498	22.01.99
	P J Hill Rufforth		14.06.18P
G-MROD	Van's RV-7A	xxxx	29.11.06
	K R Emery Sittles Farm, Alrewas		21.07.19P
	Built by M Rhodes – project PFA 323-14432		
G-MROS	Pipistrel Alpha BCAR-S 164	AT1640003	09.11.18
	MKR Aviation Ltd (Egloskerry, Launceston)		
	Pipistrel Alpha Trainer (NF 09.11.18)		
G-MRPH	Murphy Rebel	248R	07.01.10
	B S & P Metson (Lakenheath, Brandon)		30.01.19P
	Built by P Metson – project PFA 232-12480		
G-MRPT	Cessna 172S Skyhawk SP	172S8611	08.01.13
	G-UFCC, N2466X Sands Wealth Management Ltd		
	& TWC Facilities Ltd Bagby		15.12.18E
G-MRRI	Sikorsky S-76C++	760699	19.09.18
	G-URSA, G-URSS, N2592J		
	VLL Ltd t/a GB Helicopters (Ashley, Altrincham)		07.05.19E
G-MRSN	Robinson R22 Beta	1654	21.01.91
	M D Thorpe t/a Yorkshire Helicopters (Rawdon, Leeds)		02.05.14E
	(NF 23.06.16)		
G-MRSS	Comco Ikarus C42 FB80 Bravo	1110-7175	24.04.12
	North East Aviation Ltd Eshott		17.12.18P
G-MRST	Piper PA-28RT-201 Arrow IV	28R-7918068	27.11.86
	9H-AAU, 5B-CEC, N3019U		
	D C L Pluche (Jouy-en-Josas, France)		14.06.19E
G-MRSW	Lindstrand LBL 90A	1430	25.04.13
	G-CHWU D S Wilson Cantley, Norwich		23.08.18E
G-MRTN	SOCATA TB-10 Tobago	62	09.07.98
	G-BHET G C Jarvis (Henstridge, Templecombe)		21.12.16E
	Forced landing near Henstridge 27.08.16 &		
	substantially damaged; wings to Breighton		
	12.16 for rebuild of G-HELA		
G-MRTY	Cameron N-77	1008	24.04.84
	N T M, P M G & R A Vale		
	Kidderminster 'The Martin Group'		27.10.10E
	(IE 28.02.17)		
G-MRVK	Czech Sport PiperSport	P1001041	09.08.10
	M Farrugia Maypole Farm, Chislet		01.11.19W
G-MRVL	Van's RV-7	72086	28.10.05
	T W Wielkopolski Dunkeswell		15.08.17P
	Built by L W Taylor – project PFA 323-14349		
G-MRVN	PZL-Bielsko SZD-50-3 Puchacz	B-1618	03.12.12
	(BGA 5725), OH-751 The Bath, Wilts & North Dorset		
	Gliding Club Ltd Kingston Deverill 'VN'		10.04.18E

G-MRVP　Van's RV-6　　　　　　　　　24985　　　　02.09.14
　　　　　M R Parker　Gloucestershire　　　　　　　　24.04.19P
　　　　　Built by J W Addison, M R & R H Parker
　　　　　– project PFA 181A-13403

G-MSAL　Morane Saulnier MS.733 Alcyon　　143　　　16.06.93
　　　　　F-BLXV, French Army
　　　　　M Isbister tr Alcyon Flying Group　North Weald　　11.05.18P
　　　　　As '143' in Aéronavale c/s

G-MSAV　ICP MXP-740 Savannah VG Camit(1)　xxxx　　06.12.18
　　　　　J G Miller　Stonehill Farm, Crawfordjohn
　　　　　Built by J G Miller – project BMAA/HB/689 (NF 06.12.18)

G-MSCL　AutoGyro Cavalon　　　　　　xxxx　　　15.03.16
　　　　　Power Management Engineering Ltd　Popham　　23.04.18P
　　　　　Assembled Rotorsport UK as c/n RSUK/CVLN/019
　　　　　(IE 21.05.18)

G-MSES　Cessna 150L　　　　　　　15072747　　09.11.95
　　　　　EI-CMV, G-MSES, N1447Q　Go Fly Oxford Aircraft
　　　　　Rentals Ltd　Hinton-in-the-Hedges　　　　16.06.18E

G-MSFC　Piper PA-38-112 Tomahawk II　38-81A0067　11.05.90
　　　　　N25735　Cancelled 08.02.18 by CAA　　　22.11.17
　　　　　Leicester　*Stored 02.19*

G-MSFT　Piper PA-28-161 Warrior II　28-8416093　02.04.97
　　　　　G-MUMS, N118AV
　　　　　Western Air (Thruxton) Ltd　Thruxton　　23.05.18E

G-MSGI　Magni M24C Orion　　　　24-16-0384　　03.04.17
　　　　　M S Gregory　Popham　　　　　　　　10.04.18P
　　　　　Rolled over Oakley, 06.08.17

G-MSIX　DG Flugzeugbau DG-800B　　8-156B80　　21.04.99
　　　　　P Richer tr G-MSIX Group　Dunstable Downs　'M6'　05.04.18E
　　　　　Built by DG Flugzeugbau GmbH;
　　　　　new fuselage c/n 274 fitted ca 8.02

G-MSKY　Comco Ikarus C42 FB UK　　007　　　　03.10.01
　　　　　K R Still tr G-MSKY Group　Saltby　　　　02.04.18P
　　　　　Built by C K Jones – project PFA 322-13722

G-MSOF　Cessna 172N Skyhawk II　　17267803　　08.02.17
　　　　　PH-JNP, N75554　Excelis Ltd　(Witney)　　26.10.18E

G-MSON　Cameron Z-90　　　　　11036　　　　22.06.07
　　　　　Regional Property Services Ltd
　　　　　Maidstone　*'Clive Emson'*　　　　　　10.05.18E

G-MSPT　Eurocopter EC135 T2　　　0361　　　　17.03.05
　　　　　S J Golding　Brighton City　　　　　　19.07.18E

G-MSPY　Cyclone Pegasus Quantum 15-912　7625　　17.03.00
　　　　　B E Wagenhauser　Westonzoyland　　　　08.10.18P

G-MSTC　Gulfstream AA-5A Cheetah　　AA5A-0833　30.01.95
　　　　　G-BIJT, N26950　Cancelled 31.08.10 as destroyed　27.04.08
　　　　　Andreas, IoM　*Wreck dumped 01.14*

G-MSTG　North American P-51D-25-NT Mustang　124-48271　02.09.97
　　　　　RNZAF NZ242, 45-11518
　　　　　M Hammond　(AAIB Farnborough)　*'Janie'*　19.08.17P
　　　　　As '414419:LH-F' in USAAF 350th Fighter Sqdn/
　　　　　353rd Fighter Group c/s; crashed Denton Road,
　　　　　Topcroft, Bungay 02.10.16 & substantially damaged;
　　　　　to AAIB 01.17

G-MSVI　Agusta A109S Grand　　　22028　　　05.03.13
　　　　　G-ETOU　JPM Ltd　Biggin Hill
　　　　　(IE 13.12.16)

G-MTAB　Mainair Gemini Flash II　492-1086-4-W290　08.10.86
　　　　　M J Thompson　(Winstanley, Wigan)　　06.02.18P

G-MTAC　Mainair Gemini Flash II　486-1086-4-W278　15.10.86
　　　　　(YR-...), G-MTAC　B T Bradshaw　(Liverpool)　15.09.18P

G-MTAF　Mainair Gemini Flash II　499-1186-4-W301　05.10.86
　　　　　P J Byrne　Redlands　　　　　　　　18.04.19P

G-MTAG　Mainair Gemini Flash II　487-1086-4-W281　15.10.86
　　　　　Cancelled 17.12.14 as PWFU　　　　　28.05.04
　　　　　North Coates　*Stored for sale 06.18*

G-MTAH　Mainair Gemini Flash IIA　488-1086-4-W282　16.10.86
　　　　　A J Rowe　Gilrudding Grange, Deighton
　　　　　(SSDR microlight since 07.14) (IE 14.06.17)

G-MTAL　Solar Wings Pegasus Photon　SW-WP-0023　15.10.86
　　　　　I T Callaghan　Davidstow Moor
　　　　　Trike c/n SW-TP-0023
　　　　　(SSDR microlight since 05.14) (IE 03.10.17)

G-MTAS　Whittaker MW5 Sorcerer　　xxxx　　　14.10.86
　　　　　C D Wills　Stonefield Park, Chilbolton
　　　　　Built by E A Henman – project PFA 163-11166
　　　　　(SSDR microlight since 06.14) (IE 06.12.17)

G-MTAV　Solar Wings Pegasus XL-R　SW-WA-1110　21.10.86
　　　　　S Fairweather　(Carlton, Nottingham)　　05.07.18P
　　　　　Trike c/n SW-TB-1115 (IE 21.11.16)

G-MTAW　Solar Wings Pegasus XL-R　SW-WA-1111　21.10.86
　　　　　M G Ralph　Good's Farm, Stour Row　　27.07.13P
　　　　　Trike c/n SW-TB-1116 (NF 30.06.17)

G-MTAY　Solar Wings Pegasus XL-R　SW-WA-1113　27.10.86
　　　　　S A McLatchie　Enstone　　　　　　16.11.05P
　　　　　Trike c/n SW-TB-1118 (NF 13.04.16)

G-MTAZ　Solar Wings Pegasus XL-R　SW-WA-1114　28.10.86
　　　　　M O'Connell　Rathcash East, Gowran, RoI　25.03.01P
　　　　　Trike c/n SW-TB-1119 (NF 29.07.15)

G-MTBB　Southdown Raven X　　　SN2232/0226　16.10.86
　　　　　A Miller　(Worplesdon, Guildford)　　15.10.02P
　　　　　(NF 30.05.18)

G-MTBD　Mainair Gemini Flash II　498-1186-4-W229　16.10.86
　　　　　J G Jones　Caernarfon　　　　　　28.09.15P
　　　　　(NF 12.05.17)

G-MTBE　CFM Shadow Series CD　　K 035　　　16.10.86
　　　　　P J Mogg　Henstridge　　　　　　24.08.08P
　　　　　(NF 12.04.16)

G-MTBH　Mainair Gemini Flash II　524-187-5-W327　28.10.86
　　　　　M Sheehy　(Celbridge, Co Kildare, RoI)　19.10.08P
　　　　　(NF 10.10.18)

G-MTBL　Solar Wings Pegasus XL-R　SW-WA-1117　06.11.86
　　　　　R N Whiting　(Sawston, Cambridge)　　16.07.04P
　　　　　Trike c/n SW-TB-1121 (NF 17.11.15)

G-MTBN　Southdown Raven X　　　SN2232/0227　28.10.86
　　　　　A J & S E Crosby-Jones　(Rickney, Hailsham)　04.12.18P

G-MTBO　Southdown Raven X　　　SN2232/0233　28.10.86
　　　　　J Liversuch　Rookery Farm, Doynton　　08.09.18P

G-MTBP　Aerotech MW-5B Sorcerer　SR102-R440B-02　28.10.86
　　　　　A D Russell　New Farm, Piddington
　　　　　(SSDR microlight since 05.16) (IE 28.06.16)

G-MTBR　Aerotech MW-5B Sorcerer　SR102-R440B-03　20.01.87
　　　　　R Poulter　Wing Farm, Longbridge Deverill
　　　　　(SSDR microlight since 07.14) (NF 11.07.16)

G-MTBS　Aerotech MW-5B Sorcerer　SR102-R440B-04　27.10.86
　　　　　D J Pike　(Balcombe, Haywards Heath)
　　　　　(SSDR microlight since 07.14) (NF 06.02.15)

G-MTBU　Solar Wings Pegasus XL-R　SW-WA-1118　13.11.86
　　　　　R P R Staveley　(Riddings, Alfreton)　　29.03.06P
　　　　　Trike c/n SW-TB-1122 (NF 16.04.18)

G-MTCM　Southdown Raven X　　　SN2232/0239　11.12.86
　　　　　J C Rose　Backstable Farm, Haddenham　02.07.97P
　　　　　(NF 28.03.18)

G-MTCN　Solar Wings Pegasus XL-R　SW-WA-1126　16.12.86
　　　　　Cancelled 30.03.10 by CAA　　　　　21.07.06
　　　　　Redlands　*Trike c/n SW-TB-1128　Stored 06.16*

G-MTCP　Aerial Arts Chaser/110SX　110SX/476　16.12.86
　　　　　B Richardson　(Sunderland)
　　　　　(SSDR microlight since 05.14) (NF 22.11.17)

G-MTCU　Mainair Gemini Flash IIA　451-1286-4-W228　05.01.87
　　　　　T J Philip　Ashcroft　　　　　　　28.05.10P
　　　　　(NF 02.11.17)

G-MTCZ　Ultrasports TriPacer 250/Solar Wing Storm　20-00138　22.01.87
　　　　　Cancelled 03.08.94 as WFU
　　　　　Strabane, Co Tyrone　*C/n also quoted as 20-00138*
　　　　　Stored 12.13

G-MTDD　Aerial Arts Chaser/110SX　110SX/137　26.01.87
　　　　　B Richardson　(Sunderland)
　　　　　(NF 22.11.17)
　　　　　(SSDR microlight since 05.14)

G-MTDE　Aerial Arts Chaser/110SX　110SX/438　05.01.87
　　　　　P J Higgins　Wingland　　　　　　06.07.08P
　　　　　(SSDR microlight since 05.14) (NF 18.05.15)

G-MTDF　Mainair Gemini Flash II　515-287-5-W319　05.01.87
　　　　　P G Barnes　(Little Oakley, Harwich)　01.05.03P
　　　　　(NF 03.09.16)

G-MTDK Aerotech MW-5B Sorcerer SR102-R440B-06 22.01.87
C C Wright (Johnshaven, Montrose)
(SSDR microlight since 10.14) (NF 27.07.18)

G-MTDR Mainair Gemini Flash 516-287-5-W276 26.01.87
D J Morriss (Whitchurch) 23.05.13P
(NF 22.08.14)

G-MTDU CFM Shadow Series CD K 037 26.01.87
P S Sweet Old Park Farm, Margam
(SSDR microlight since 01.19)

G-MTDW Mainair Gemini Flash II 517-387-5-W212 02.02.87
S R Leeper (Carleton Rode, Norwich) 01.06.11P
(NF 11.09.14)

G-MTDY Mainair Gemini Flash II 513-187-5-W317 11.02.87
S Penoyre Shobdon
(SSDR microlight since 09.15) (IE 06.11.17)

G-MTEK Mainair Gemini Flash II 523-387-5-W279 03.03.87
M O'Hearne Rufforth 17.06.03P
(NF 13.11.14)

G-MTER Solar Wings Pegasus XL-R SW-WA-1144 19.02.87
S J Nix (Boston) 08.09.11P
Trike c/n SW-TB-1146; stored 11.17 (NF 29.01.18)

G-MTES Solar Wings Pegasus XL-R SW-WA-1145 19.02.87
N P Read Davidstow Moor 29.08.04P
Trike c/n SW-TB-1147 (NF 17.12.14)

G-MTEU Solar Wings Pegasus XL-R/Se SW-WA-1147 19.02.87
T E Thomas Beverley (Linley Hill) 07.10.10P
Trike c/n SW-TB-1149; noted 04.17 (NF 10.10.14)

G-MTEY Mainair Gemini Flash II 518-387-5-W217 20.02.87
E Jackson (Lowestoft) 28.10.15P
(NF 12.05.15)

G-MTFC Medway Hybred 44XLR 22087/24 23.03.87
J K Masters (Hartlip, Sittingbourne) 25.07.97P
(NF 15.04.16)

G-MTFG AMF Microflight Chevvron 2-32C 004 09.03.87
J Pool (Barton-upon-Humber) 20.03.12P
(NF 12.04.18)

G-MTFK[M] Moult Trike/Flexiform Striker DIM-01 23.03.87
Cancelled 13.06.90 by CAA
Built by for D I Moult Officially registered
with c/n SO.175 Suspended from rafters
With Norfolk & Suffolk Aviation Museum, Flixton

G-MTFN Whittaker MW5 Sorcerer PFA 163-11207 13.03.87
S M King (Foulridge, Colne)
Built by D C Britton & K Southam – project
PFA 163-11207; type may be Model MW5B
(SSDR microlight since 07.14) (NF 20.06.18)

G-MTFU CFM Shadow Series CD K 034 18.03.87
EI-DDN, G-MTFU J E Course (Bosham, Chichester) 28.06.18P

G-MTGB Thruster TST Mk1 837-TST-011 10.04.87
M J Aubrey Llanfyrnach 11.09.00P
Displayed Classic Ultralight Heritage (NF 04.11.15)

G-MTGD Thruster TST Mk1 837-TST-013 10.04.87
B A Janaway Dunkeswell 30.08.18P
(NF 23.09.15)

G-MTGL Solar Wings Pegasus XL-R SW-WA-1167 01.04.87
P J & R Openshaw (Birchwood, Warrington) 09.06.06P
Trike c/n SW-TB-1167 (NF 23.07.18)

G-MTGO Mainair Gemini Flash IIA 550-587-5-W336 10.04.87
J Ouru (Leteensuo, Kant-Hame, Finland) 16.08.06P
(NF 13.12.16)

G-MTGR Thruster TST Mk1 847-TST-017 10.04.87
W H J Knowles Stoodleigh Barton Farm, Stoodleigh 16.11.18P

G-MTGS Thruster TST Mk1 847-TST-018 10.04.87
R J Nelson (Kibworth, Leicester) 12.08.18P

G-MTGU Thruster TST Mk.1 847-TST-020 10.04.87
Cancelled 18.08.09 by CAA 27.01.06
Foston, Lincs Stored 10.16

G-MTGV CFM Shadow Series CD 052 08.04.87
D J Flanagan (Hadfield, Glossop) 22.09.19P

G-MTGW CFM Shadow Series CD 054 08.04.87
(I-....), G-MGTW N Hart (Sudbury)
(IE 17.10.18)
(SSDR microlight since 12.14)

G-MTHH Solar Wings Pegasus XL-R SW-WA-1172 13.04.87
J Palmer (Beaford, Winkleigh) 28.12.98P
Trike c/n SW-TB-1171 (NF 18.04.18)

G-MTHN Solar Wings Pegasus XL-R SW-WA-1178 13.04.87
M T Seal (Cilcennin, Lampeter) 28.03.08P
Trike c/n SW-TB-1177 (NF 10.11.14)

G-MTHS CFM Shadow Srs.CD 059 22.04.87
Cancelled 11.06.99 by CAA
Dromore, Omagh Stored 12.13

G-MTHT CFM Shadow Series CD 058 22.04.87
A P Jones Enstone 25.05.18P

G-MTHV CFM Shadow Series CD K 049 07.05.87
S J Ellis Old Park Farm, Margam 22.07.17P

G-MTHW Mainair Gemini Flash II 540-587-5-W325 14.05.87
Cancelled 06.12.10 by CAA 10.06.08
Deenethorpe Stored 06.13

G-MTIE Solar Wings Pegasus XL-R SW-WA-1183 18.05.87
P Wibberley Brook Breasting Farm, Watnall 27.03.12P
Trike c/n SW-TE-0019 (IE 06.11.17)

G-MTIJ Solar Wings Pegasus XL-R/Se SW-WA-1188 18.05.87
M J F Gilbody (Urmston, Manchester) 01.04.98P
Trike c/n SW-TB-1185 (NF 20.03.18)

G-MTIL Mainair Gemini Flash IIA 549-687-5-W338 21.05.87
D J Robinson (Keadby, Scunthorpe) 23.06.19P

G-MTIM Mainair Gemini Flash IIA 553-687-5-W341 21.05.87
W M Swan East Fortune 29.08.18P

G-MTIP Solar Wings Pegasus XL-R SW-WA-1191 26.05.87
Cancelled 31.03.08 by CAA 19.12.01
Redlands, Swindon Trike SW-TB-1188 Noted 03.12

G-MTIR Solar Wings Pegasus XL-R/Se SW-WA-1192 26.05.87
P Jolley Brook Breasting Farm, Watnall 02.09.15P
Trike c/n SW-TB-1189 (IE 05.04.16)

G-MTIW Solar Wings Pegasus XL-R SW-WA-1196 26.05.87
S G Hutchinson (Sheffield) 26.10.08P
Trike c/n SW-TB-1193 (NF 20.01.17)

G-MTIZ Solar Wings Pegasus XL-R SW-WA-1199 26.05.87
S L Blount Sutton Meadows 29.09.17P
Trike c/n SW-TB-1196 (IE 06.11.17)

G-MTJC Mainair Gemini Flash IIA 555-687-5-W344 01.06.87
T A Dockrell Westonzoyland 16.08.12P
Rebuilt with c/n 788-0590-7-W581 (ex-G-MWHY)
(NF 10.02.15)

G-MTJE Mainair Gemini Flash IIA 556-687-5-W345 24.06.87
C I Hemingway Rossall Field, Cockerham 11.04.18P

G-MTJH Solar Wings Pegasus Flash W342-687-3 17.06.87
C G Ludgate (Whitwell, Norwich) 28.03.04P
Trike c/n SW-TB-1050 ex G-MMUF (NF 29.03.18)

G-MTJL Mainair Gemini Flash IIA 548-687-5-W337 17.06.87
R Thompson (Cranswick, Driffield) 25.07.12P
(NF 04.07.18)

G-MTJN Midland Ultralights Sirocco 377GB MU.020 23.06.87
A R Hawes (Needham Market)
(NF 26.02.18)

G-MTJT Mainair Gemini Flash IIA 558-787-5-W347 16.07.87
P J Barratt Headon Farm, Retford 22.07.18P

G-MTJV Mainair Gemini Flash IIA 562-787-5-W351 16.07.87
D A Ballard (Senven-Lehart, France) 29.10.17P

G-MTKA Thruster TST Mk1 867-TST-021 21.07.87
M J Coles & S R Williams Manchester Barton 04.04.18P

G-MTKD Thruster TST Mk.1 867-TST-024 21.07.87
Cancelled 28.05.14 by CAA 27.01.06
Limetree, RoI For sale 09.17

G-MTKE Thruster TST Mk.1 867-TST-025 21.07.87
Cancelled 20.02.09 as PWFU 27.08.03
Ballyboy, Co Meath Stored 03.16

G-MTKI Solar Wings Pegasus XL-R SW-WA-1203 13.07.87
M Wady (Hamstreet, Ashford) 09.11.12P
Trike c/n SW-TB-1201
(SSDR microlight since 10.16) (IE 05.09.17)

G-MTKR	CFM Shadow Series CD	067	20.07.87	
	9H-ABL, G-MTKR			
	T J Wiltshire tr Shadow Group Wingland		10.06.15P	
	(IE 01.07.15)			
	(SSDR microlight since 05.15)			
G-MTKW	Mainair Gemini Flash IIA	569-887-5-W358	13.07.87	
	J H McIvor (Newtownabbey)			
	(SSDR microlight since 08.14) (IE 26.08.15)			
G-MTKX	Mainair Gemini Flash IIA	568-887-5-W357	13.07.87	
	S P Disney (Hoby, Melton Mowbray)		27.08.00P	
	(NF 07.03.16)			
G-MTLB	Mainair Gemini Flash IIA	573-887-5-W362	31.07.87	
	C R Partington (Perth)		11.01.17P	
	(NF 29.06.17)			
G-MTLC	Mainair Gemini Flash IIA	574-887-5-W363	31.07.87	
	R J Alston (Alby, Norwich)		13.07.02P	
	(NF 18.05.18)			
G-MTLG	Solar Wings Pegasus XL-R	SW-WA-1211	31.07.87	
	D Young Cotswold		05.12.13P	
	Trike c/n SW-TB-1207 (NF 15.05.17)			
G-MTLL	Mainair Gemini Flash IIA	578-987-5-W367	14.08.87	
	M S Lawrence Shifnal		22.04.07P	
	Stored 04.16 (NF 20.10.17)			
G-MTLM	Thruster TST Mk1	887-TST-027	05.08.87	
	R J Nelson (Kibworth, Leicester)		24.06.05P	
	(NF 16.06.18)			
G-MTLN	Thruster TST Mk1	887-TST-028	05.08.87	
	P W Taylor (Thorndon, Eye)		17.09.07P	
	(NF 30.10.16)			
G-MTLT	Solar Wings Pegasus XL-R	SW-WA-1216	12.08.87	
	K M Mayling Plaistows Farm, St Albans		10.10.03P	
	Trike c/n SW-TB-1212 (NF 08.04.16)			
G-MTLV	Solar Wings Pegasus XL-R	SW-WA-1218	12.08.87	
	W D Foster Beccles		11.05.15P	
	Trike c/n SW-TB-1214; stored 01.18 (NF 13.09.19)			
G-MTLW	Solar Wings Pegasus XL-R	SW-WA-1219	12.08.87	
	Cancelled 13.06.01 by CAA		30.08.98	
	Sutton Meadows *Trike c/n SW-TB-1215 Stored 07.15*			
G-MTLX	Medway Hybred 44XLR	20687/26	14.08.87	
	D A Coupland Blackmoor Farm, Aubourn			
	(SSDR microlight since 04.18) (NF 27.07.16)			
G-MTLY	Solar Wings Pegasus XL-R	SW-WA-1220	12.08.87	
	G J Prisk Perranporth		28.05.17P	
	Trike c/n SW-TE-0026 (NF 15.01.18)			
G-MTMA	Mainair Gemini Flash IIA	579-987-5-W368	14.08.87	
	S Cunningham Derryrogue, Kilkeel		14.06.18P	
G-MTMC	Mainair Gemini Flash IIA	581-987-5-W370	14.08.87	
	M A Thomas (Irlam, Manchester)		18.04.19P	
G-MTMF	Solar Wings Pegasus XL-R	SW-WA-1222	18.08.87	
	H T M Smith (Mallaig)		23.05.09P	
	Trike c/n SW-TB-1217 (NF 21.10.15)			
G-MTMG	Solar Wings Pegasus XL-R	SW-WA-1223	18.08.87	
	C W & P E F Suckling (Rushden)		08.11.04P	
	Trike c/n SW-TB-1218 (NF 11.11.14)			
G-MTML	Mainair Gemini Flash IIA	582-1087-5-W371	27.08.87	
	J F Ashton Rufforth		30.07.00P	
	(NF 09.03.18)			
G-MTMR	Hornet Dual Trainer/Southdown Raven			
		HRWA0065/SN2000/0297	28.08.87	
	D J Smith (Calverton, Nottingham)		08.12.07P	
	(NF 09.10.14)			
G-MTMT	Mainair Gemini Flash IIA	583-1087-5-W372	03.09.87	
	Cancelled 09.05.14 by CAA		06.09.04	
	Rossall Field, Cockerham *Stored 04.15*			
G-MTMW	Mainair Gemini Flash IIA	587-1087-5-W376	09.09.87	
	D J Boulton (Stoke-on-Trent)		10.09.17P	
	(IE 06.10.17)			
G-MTMX	CFM Shadow Series CD	070	04.09.87	
	D R White Plaistows Farm, St Albans		09.08.18P	
G-MTNC	Mainair Gemini Flash IIA	588-1087-5-W377	15.09.87	
	K R Emery Otherton			
	(IE 22.09.15)			
	(SSDR microlight since 05.15)			
G-MTNE	Medway Hybred 44XLR	7987/32	12.10.87	
	A G Rodenburg (Hillforts Nursery, Tillicoultry, Alloa)		23.09.08P	
	Fitted with new trike as original to G-MVDC 1988			
	(NF 26.01.15)			
G-MTNF	Medway Hybred 44XLR	1987/31	12.10.87	
	P A Bedford Croft Farm, Defford		04.09.14P	
	(NF 19.09.17)			
G-MTNI	Mainair Gemini Flash IIA	595-1187-5-W384	18.09.87	
	D R McDougall Eshott		09.09.17P	
G-MTNK	Weedhopper JC-24B	1936	28.09.87	
	S D Hutchinson (Walton-le-Dale, Preston)			
	(NF 14.07.17)			
	(SSDR microlight since 05.14)			
G-MTNR	Thruster TST Mk1	897-TST-032	01.10.87	
	A M Sirant Monkswell Farm, Horrabridge		23.09.07P	
	(NF 20.05.18)			
G-MTNT	Thruster TST Mk.1	897-TST-034	01.10.87	
	Cancelled 09.04.13 by CAA		01.06.07	
	Insch *Stored 2014*			
G-MTNU	Thruster TST Mk1	897-TST-035	01.10.87	
	T H Brearley Dunkeswell		26.09.18P	
G-MTNV	Thruster TST Mk1	897-TST-036	01.10.87	
	J B Russell (Magheramorne, Larne)			
	Stored dismantled 12.13 (NF 20.03.18)			
G-MTOA	Solar Wings Pegasus XL-R	SW-WA-1226	15.09.87	
	R A Bird (Bugbrooke, Northampton)		08.08.01P	
	Trike c/n SW-TB-1221 (NF 27.04.18)			
G-MTOG	Solar Wings Pegasus XL-R	SW-WA-1232	15.09.87	
	Cancelled 29.06.10 by CAA		05.05.06	
	Newport, Gwent *Trike c/n SW-TB-1227*			
	Advertised for sale 07.13			
G-MTOH	Solar Wings Pegasus XL-R	SW-WA-1233	15.09.87	
	H Cook (Newport)		02.03.02P	
	Trike c/n SW-TB-1228 (NF 07.06.18)			
G-MTOJ	Solar Wings Pegasus XL-R/Se	SW-WA-1235	15.09.87	
	(EI-xxx), G-MTOJ J Hennessy Newtownards *'Spirit of Argo'*		25.10.18P	
	Trike c/n SW-TB-1230			
G-MTON	Solar Wings Pegasus XL-R	SW-WA-1239	02.10.87	
	D J Willett Ivy Farm, Egerton Green		18.04.18P	
	Trike c/n SW-TB-1234			
G-MTOY	Solar Wings Pegasus XL-R	SW-WA-1249	19.10.87	
	T J Wiltshire tr XL2 Group Wingland		15.08.07P	
	Trike c/n SW-TB-1244 (IE 13.02.18)			
G-MTPB	Mainair Gemini Flash IIA	599-1187-5-W387	15.10.87	
	G von Wilcken Middle Stoke, Isle of Grain			
	(SSDR microlight since 06.17) (IE 06.11.17)			
G-MTPF	Solar Wings Pegasus XL-R	SW-WA-1261	21.10.87	
	A S Mitchel & P M Watts tr G-MTPF Group Halwell		18.11.05P	
	Trike c/n SW-TB-1259 (NF 04.06.15)			
G-MTPH	Solar Wings Pegasus XL-R	SW-WA-1263	30.10.87	
	D Bannister (Nelson)		07.01.10P	
	Trike c/n SW-TB-1261 (NF 17.10.18)			
G-MTPK	Solar Wings Pegasus XL-R	SW-WA-1266	30.10.87	
	Cancelled 26.04.12 by CAA		21.10.01	
	Deenethorpe *Trike c/n SW-TB-1264*			
	Trike only stored 06.13			
-MTPL	Solar Wings Pegasus XL-R	SW-WA-1267	30.10.87	
	C J Jones (Clydach, Abergavenny)		06.04.19P	
	Trike c/n SW-TB-1265			
G-MTPM	Solar Wings Pegasus XL-R	SW-WA-1268	30.10.87	
	D K Seal (Lichfield)		04.08.04P	
	Trike c/n SW-TB-1266 (NF 30.05.18)			
G-MTPU	Thruster TST Mk1	8107-TST-039	23.10.87	
	N Hay London Colney			
	(SSDR microlight since 11.14) (IE 20.03.18)			
G-MTPW	Thruster TST Mk1	8107-TST-041	23.10.87	
	D W Tewson (Loders, Bridport)		06.04.18P	
G-MTPX	Thruster TST Mk1	8107-TST-042	23.10.87	
	T Snook (Newport Pagnell)		02.05.93P	
	(NF 06.02.18)			

G-MTPY	Thruster TST Mk.1	8107-TST-043	23.10.87
	Cancelled 05.08.13 as destroyed		08.08.13
	Wing Farm, Longbridge Deverill		
	Wreck used for spares 06.14		
G-MTRC	Midland Ultralights Sirocco 377GB	MU-021	02.11.87
	D Thorpe (Grantham)		
	(NF 12.06.18)		
	(SSDR microlight since 07.14)		
G-MTRM	Solar Wings Pegasus XL-R	SW-WA-1276	10.11.87
	C H Edwards (Ystradgynlais, Swansea)		27.04.10P
	Trike c/n SW-TE-0030 (NF 07.05.15)		
G-MTRS	Solar Wings Pegasus XL-R	SW-WA-1273	02.12.87
	W R Edwards Caernarfon		15.08.14P
	Trike c/n SW-TB-1274 (NF 06.07.18)		
G-MTRX	Whittaker MW5 Sorcerer	xxxx	11.11.87
	W Turner Otherton		
	Built by W Turner – project PFA 163-11202		
	(SSDR microlight since 06.14) (IE 22.09.15)		
G-MTRZ	Mainair Gemini Flash IIA	611-1287-5-W400	17.11.87
	D S Lally (Anderton, Chorley)		28.03.08P
	(NF 30.06.15)		
G-MTSC	Mainair Gemini Flash IIA	618-188-5-W407	17.11.87
	J Kilpatrick Finn Valley, RoI		
	(SSDR microlight since 04.17) (IE 06.07.18)		
G-MTSH	Thruster TST Mk1	8117-TST-044	03.12.87
	R R Orr Keenaghan-The Moy, Dungannon		13.04.07P
	Stored 12.13 (NF 14.10.14)		
G-MTSJ	Thruster TST Mk1	8117-TST-046	03.12.87
	J D Buchanan Enstone		
	(SSDR microlight since 09.15) (IE 18.09.15)		
G-MTSM	Thruster TST Mk1	8117-TST-049	03.12.87
	M A Horton (Winchcombe, Cheltenham)		25.10.18P
	Modified to T300 standard		
G-MTSS	Solar Wings Pegasus XL-R	SW-WA-1284	14.12.87
	V Marchant (Grantham)		
	Trike c/n SW-TE-0031		
	(SSDR microlight since 08.14) (NF 24.09.18)		
G-MTSZ	Solar Wings Pegasus XL-R/Se	SW-WA-1290	14.01.88
	D L Pickover (Nelson)		02.07.16P
	Trike c/n SW-TB-1284		
G-MTTA	Solar Wings Pegasus XL-R	SW-WA-1291	14.01.88
	D Hall Greenhills Farm, Wheatley Hill		04.09.00P
	Trike c/n SW-TE-0035 (NF 17.03.16)		
G-MTTE	Solar Wings Pegasus XL-Q	SW-WQ-0012	15.01.88
	C F Barnard Rufforth East		20.05.15P
	Trike c/n SW-TB-1287		
G-MTTF	Whittaker MW6 Merlin	xxxx	14.12.87
	P Cotton (Badgeworth, Cheltenham)		29.03.95P
	Built by V E Booth – project PFA 164-11273		
	(NF 20.04.16)		
G-MTTI	Mainair Gemini Flash IIA	620-188-5-W409	14.12.87
	F J Smith tr G-MTTI Flying Group St Michaels		19.10.18P
G-MTTN	Ultralight Flight Phantom	PH00100	22.01.88
	F P Welsh (Troutbeck, Windermere)		
	Built by Ultralight Flight Inc; wing fitted to		
	G-MJUX 08.07 (qv)		
	(SSDR microlight since 06.14) (IE 30.04.18)		
G-MTTP	Mainair Gemini Flash IIA	612-188-5-W401	18.01.88
	A Ormson St Michaels		11.07.18P
G-MTTU	Solar Wings Pegasus XL-R	SW-WA-1294	25.02.88
	A Friend Westonzoyland		10.02.07P
	Trike c/n SW-TB-1332 (NF 15.05.14)		
G-MTTZ	Solar Wings Pegasus XL-Q	SW-WQ-0015	21.01.88
	M O Bloy White House Farm, Southery		09.08.18P
	Trike c/n SW-TE-0039		
G-MTUA	Solar Wings Pegasus XL-R/Se	SW-WA-1295	15.01.88
	J & S Bunyan Headon Farm, Retford		15.02.12P
	Trike c/n SW-TB-1294 (NF 26.07.16)		
G-MTUC	Thruster TST Mk1	8018-TST-051	15.01.88
	N S Chittenden Woodlands Barton Farm, Roche		29.07.17P
	(IE 25.08.17)		
G-MTUN	Solar Wings Pegasus XL-Q	SW-WQ-0016	20.01.88
	M J O'Connor (Little Budworth, Tarporley)		26.04.05P
	Trike c/n SW-TB-1301; fitted with wing ex G-MVUK?		
	(NF 22.09.14)		

G-MTUR	Solar Wings Pegasus XL-Q	SW-WQ-0019	20.01.88
	G Ball (Tewkesbury)		26.09.07P
	Trike c/n SW-TB-1304 (NF 19.02.15)		
G-MTUS	Solar Wings Pegasus XL-Q	SW-WQ-0020	20.01.88
	P W Davidson	(Windygates, Leven)	
	(SSDR microlight since 04.15) (IE 26.08.15)		
G-MTUT	Solar Wings Pegasus XL-Q	SW-WQ-0021	21.01.88
	R E Bull Hadfold Farm, Adversane		
	Trike c/n SW-TE-0040		
	(SSDR microlight since 10.14) (IE 29.06.18)		
G-MTUV	Mainair Gemini Flash IIA	624-288-5-W413	28.01.88
	J Norton Boston		14.05.16P
	(NF 30.11.18)		
G-MTUY	Solar Wings Pegasus XL-Q	SW-WQ-0022	28.01.88
	H C Lowther Bedlands Gate, Little Strickland		31.08.08P
	Trike c/n SW-TE-0041 (IE 20.01.17)		
G-MTVC	Solar Wings Pegasus XL-R	SW-WA-1303	28.01.88
	A Duffy (Mountnugent, Co Cavan, RoI)		
	(SSDR microlight since 04.17) (NF 26.04.17)		
G-MTVH	Mainair Gemini Flash IIA	626-288-6-W415	17.02.88
	P H Statham Darley Moor		27.06.11P
	(NF 02.09.14)		
G-MTVP	Thruster TST Mk1	8028-TST-056	10.02.88
	J M Evans Landmead Farm, Garford		18.06.11P
	C/n plate shows '8208-TST-056' incorrectly		
	(NF 18.12.18)		
G-MTVT	Thruster TST Mk1	8028-TST-059	10.02.88
	W H J Knowles Stoodleigh Barton Farm, Stoodleigh		02.06.12P
	(NF 08.12.15)		
G-MTVX	Solar Wings Pegasus XL-Q	SW-WQ-0025	03.03.88
	D A Foster (Asfordby, Melton Mowbray)		26.05.12P
	Trike c/n SW-TE-0042 (NF 25.08.17)		
G-MTWK	CFM Shadow Series CD	073	25.02.88
	M J Cooper (Langrick, Boston)		30.04.13P
	(IE 24.02.15)		
G-MTWR	Mainair Gemini Flash IIA	632-388-6-W421	03.03.88
	J B Hodson Arclid Green, Sandbach		21.10.12P
	(NF 15.01.16)		
G-MTWS	Mainair Gemini Flash IIA	633-488-6-W422	03.03.88
	A Robins (Halkyn, Holywell)		20.02.16P
G-MTWX	Mainair Gemini Flash IIA	634-488-6-W423	11.03.88
	K Walsh (Blackburn)		16.06.18P
G-MTWY	Thruster TST Mk.1	8038-TST-062	15.03.88
	Cancelled 23.12.14 by CAA		25.02.06
	(East Riding) *For sale ebay 09.16*		
G-MTWZ	Thruster TST Mk1	8038-TST-063	15.03.88
	M J Aubrey Llanfyrnach		11.02.16P
	Displayed Classic Ultralight Heritage (IE 30.06.17)		
G-MTXA	Thruster TST Mk1	8038-TST-064	15.03.88
	M A Franklin (Coveney, Ely)		24.03.17P
	(IE 02.06.17)		
G-MTXD	Thruster TST Mk1	8038-TST-067	15.03.88
	D Newton Hunsdon		
	Modified to T300 standard		
	(SSDR microlight since 06.14) (IE 07.08.17)		
G-MTXJ	Solar Wings Pegasus XL-Q	SW-WQ-0032	11.03.88
	E W Laidlaw (Broom Loan, Kelso)		18.03.08P
	Trike c/n SW-TB-1330 (NF 07.04.14)		
G-MTXK	Solar Wings Pegasus XL-Q	SW-WQ-0033	11.03.88
	D R G Whitelaw Oban		23.11.16P
	Trike c/n SW-TB-1331		
G-MTXM	Mainair Gemini Flash IIA	636-488-6-W425	10.05.88
	H J Vinning (Freuchie, Cupar)		01.04.12P
	(NF 11.09.15)		
G-MTXO	Whittaker MW6 Merlin	xxxx	11.03.88
	R E Arnold & C A Harper Otherton		
	Built by N A Bailes – project PFA 164-11326		
	(IE 06.07.18)		
G-MTXR	CFM Shadow Series CD	K 038	23.03.88
	G E Arnott Old Sarum		25.10.18P
G-MTXZ	Mainair Gemini Flash IIA	641-588-6-W430	10.05.88
	J S Hawkins (Ashreigney, Chumleigh)		26.07.10P
	(NF 02.11.17)		

G-MTYA	Solar Wings Pegasus XL-Q	SW-WQ-0037	29.03.88
	Cancelled 20.02.12 as PWFU		13.11.09
	Deenethorpe *Trike c/n SW-TE-0047* *Stored 06.13*		
G-MTYC	Solar Wings Pegasus XL-Q	SW-WQ-0039	30.03.88
	C I D H Garrison Sutton Meadows		06.10.13P
	Trike c/n SW-TE-0049 (IE 06.09.17)		
G-MTYI	Solar Wings Pegasus XL-Q	SW-WQ-0045	30.03.88
	T J Wiltshire tr Q Group Wingland		20.04.18P
	Trike c/n SW-TE-0055		
G-MTYL	Solar Wings Pegasus XL-Q	6412	30.03.88
	S Cooper (Market Harborough)		20.10.02P
	Trike c/n SW-TE-0058; original wing c/n SW-WQ-0048		
	now replaced by c/n 6412 (NF 18.11.16)		
G-MTYR	Solar Wings Pegasus XL-Q	SW-WQ-0053	30.03.88
	D T Evans Broadmeadow Farm, Hereford		30.04.99P
	Trike c/n SW-TE-0063 (NF 28.09.15)		
G-MTYS	Solar Wings Pegasus XL-Q	SW-WQ-0054	30.03.88
	R G Wall Pen-y-Parc Farm, Caerleon		04.10.05P
	Trike c/n SW-TE-0064 (NF 27.03.18)		
G-MTYV	Raven Aircraft Raven X	SN2232/0341	08.04.88
	(N.....), G-MTYV S R Jones (Tonyrefail, Porth)		05.07.07P
	(NF 08.12.14)		
G-MTYW	Raven Aircraft Raven X	SN2232/0344	08.04.88
	R Solomons Middle Stoke, Isle of Grain		28.07.07P
	(NF 10.09.14)		
G-MTYY	Solar Wings Pegasus XL-R	SW-WA-1326	06.05.88
	L A Hosegood (Swindon)		24.01.05P
	(IE 06.09.17)		
G-MTZA	Thruster TST Mk1	8048-TST-068	13.04.88
	J F Gallagher (Newtownstewart, Omagh)		13.05.06P
	(NF 06.08.18)		
G-MTZB	Thruster TST Mk1	8048-TST-069	13.04.88
	J E Davies Penrhiw Farm, Crymych		02.06.07P
	(NF 31.10.14)		
G-MTZC	Thruster TST Mk1	8048-TST-070	13.04.88
	D J L Scott Kernan Valley, Tandragee		07.03.18P
	(NF 25.06.18)		
G-MTZF	Thruster TST Mk1	8048-TST-073	13.04.88
	J D Buchanan Coldharbour Farm, Willingham		
	(SSDR microlight since 08.14) (IE 17.11.15)		
G-MTZG	Mainair Gemini Flash IIA	642-588-6-W431	10.05.88
	A P Fenn Shobdon		14.03.09P
	(NF 15.10.15)		
G-MTZL	Mainair Gemini Flash IIA	645-588-6-W435	10.05.88
	N S Brayn (Morestead, Winchester)		13.04.06P
	(NF 19.09.14)		
G-MTZM	Mainair Gemini Flash IIA	646-588-6-W436	03.05.88
	G Burns Eccles Newton Farm, Coldstream		
	(SSDR microlight since 04.15) (IE 22.02.16)		
G-MTZS	Solar Wings Pegasus XL-Q	SW-WQ-0061	06.05.88
	T M Evans & T A Spencer (Braunston/Weedon)		22.09.15P
	Trike c/n SW-TB-1339		
G-MTZV	Mainair Gemini Flash IIA	650-688-6-W440	06.05.88
	P Robinson Darley Moor		18.01.17P
	(NF 12.01.17)		
G-MTZW	Mainair Gemini Flash IIA	651-688-6-W441	25.05.88
	M Devlin Carrickmore		02.07.18P
	(NF 01.11.17)		
G-MTZX	Mainair Gemini Flash IIA	652-688-6-W442	23.06.88
	R G Cuckow Over Farm, Gloucester		17.10.18P
G-MTZY	Mainair Gemini Flash IIA	653-688-6-W443	24.05.88
	M D Leslie (Seaton Burn, Tyne & Wear)		25.06.16P
	(NF 17.07.17)		
G-MTZZ	Mainair Gemini Flash IIA	654-688-6-W444	14.06.88
	G J Cadden (Smithborough, Co Monaghan, RoI)		18.06.14P
	(NF 19.11.15)		
G-MUCK	Lindstrand LBL 77A	982	25.01.05
	C J Wootton Ormskirk *'Poppies'*		22.04.19E
G-MUDD	Hughes 369E (500)	0325E	24.11.10
	HB-ZUN, F-GYCC, D-HASP, I-BNAR		
	Derwen Plant Company Ltd (Skewen, Neath)		10.05.18E
G-MUDX	AutoGyro Cavalon	xxxx	28.07.17
	G-CJVT P R Biggs (Caxton, Cambridge)		06.06.19P
	Assembled Rotorsport UK as c/n RSUK/CVLN/022		

G-MUDY	Piper PA-18-150 Super Cub	18-5352	13.10.09
	G-OTUG, (G-BKNM), PH-MBA, French Army 18-5352,		
	N10F C J de Sousa e Morgado Goodwood		17.08.18E
G-MUIR	Cameron V-65	2037	23.06.89
	Border Ballooning Ltd Plas Madoc, Montgomery		31.05.18E
G-MUJD	Van's RV-12	xxxx	15.08.13
	M F El-Deen Henstridge		13.11.18P
	Built by M F El-Deen – project LAA 363-15145;		
	FF 27.08.15		
G-MUKY	Van's RV-8	83102	12.10.11
	I E K Mackay Sleap		09.11.18P
	Built by I E K Mackay – project LAA 303-14998		
G-MUMM	Colt 180A	1636	12.04.05
	SE-ZES D K Hempleman-Adams Corsham		23.09.13E
	(NF 26.10.16)		
G-MUMY	Van's RV-4	xxxx	11.01.05
	S D Howes Durham Tees Valley		08.10.18P
	Built by S D Howes – project PFA 181-13401		
G-MUNI	Mooney M.20J Mooney 201	24-3118	12.05.89
	P R Williams Oxford		05.02.18E
G-MUPP	Lindstrand LBL 90A	1417	07.08.12
	J A Viner North Muskham, Newark		27.12.18E
G-MURG	Van's RV-6	21676	22.06.05
	Cadmium Lake Ltd North Weald		09.04.18P
	Built by E C Murgatroyd – project PFA 181-12470		
G-MURYM	Robinson R44 Astro	0201	19.07.95
	Cancelled 09.10.03 - to USA *As 'G-MURY'*		17.05.04
	With National Air & Space Museum, Chantilly, Virginia		
G-MUSH	Robinson R44 Raven II	10278	18.02.04
	Topgrade Property Management Ltd Swansea		04.09.19E
G-MUSM	Colt 77A	1073	04.04.18
	The British Balloon Museum & Library Ltd		
	Wellingborough		11.04.19E
	Built by Thunder & Colt Ltd		
G-MUSO	Rutan Long-EZ	xxxx	11.06.83
	D J Gay Seething		08.08.18P
	Built by G B Castle – project PFA 074A-10590		
G-MUTS	Jurca MJ.100 Spitfire	xxxx	21.05.13
	G-CDPM S M Johnston & J E D Rogerson Morgansfield,		
	Fishburn *'Cherub'*		
	Built by J E D Rogerson – project PFA 130-12007;		
	as 'X4683:EB-N' in RAF c/s (IE 18.12.17)		
G-MUTT	CZAW Sportcruiser	4005	14.09.07
	A M Griffin Welshpool		15.01.19P
	Built by A McIvor – project PFA 338-14667		
G-MUTZ	Avtech Jabiru J430	265	29.12.0?
	N C Dean Sibson		09.07.18P
	Built by N C Dean – project PFA 336-14171		
G-MUZY	Titan T-51 Mustang	0122	18.07.0?
	A D Bales Tibenham *'Big Beautiful Doll'*		27.04.18?
	Built by D Stephens – project LAA 355-14831;		
	as '472218:WZ-I' in USAF c/s		
G-MUZZ	Agusta AW109SP Grand New	22325	19.12.1?
	Hagondale Ltd (Great Sampford)		18.12.18?
G-MVAC	CFM Shadow Series CD	K 077	12.05.8?
	R G Place Old Sarum		03.12.17?
G-MVAH	Thruster TST Mk1	8058-TST-075	18.05.8?
	M W H Henton Trenchard Farm, Eggesford		22.07.18?
G-MVAI	Thruster TST Mk1	8058-TST-076	18.05.8?
	P J Houtman London Colney		02.04.12?
	(NF 10.08.17)		
G-MVAJ	Thruster TST Mk1	8058-TST-077	18.05.8?
	D Watson Rossall Field, Cockerham		13.06.18?
G-MVAM	CFM Shadow Series CD	082	18.05.8?
	C P Barber Brook Farm, Pilling		22.09.17?
G-MVAN	CFM Shadow Series CD	K 048	18.05.8?
	R W Frost (Mallow, Co Cork, RoI)		17.10.08?
	Built by CFM Metal-Fax – project PFA 161-11219		
	(NF 08.08.18)		
G-MVAR	Solar Wings Pegasus XL-R	SW-WA-1331	24.05.8?
	A J Thomas (Thrapston, Kettering)		13.07.13
	Trike c/n SW-TB-1343 (NF 11.10.16)		

G-MVAX Solar Wings Pegasus XL-Q SW-WQ-0065 24.05.88
J H Cuthbertson (Glasgow G40) 03.03.13P
Trike c/n SW-TB-1349 (NF 10.09.15)

G-MVAY Solar Wings Pegasus XL-Q SW-WQ-0066 24.05.88
V O Morris (Four Roads, Kidwelly) 16.04.97P
Trike c/n SW-TB-1350 (NF 09.02.16)

G-MVBC Mainair Tri-Flyer/Aerial Arts 130SX 130SX/616 24.05.88
D Beer (Lee, Ilfracombe)
Believed fitted with Mainair Tri-Flyer 250 trike ex G-MJIX
(SSDR microlight since 05.14) (IE 23.10.17)

G-MVBJ Solar Wings Pegasus XL-R SW-WA-1338 07.06.88
M Sims Haverfordwest 04.08.08P
Trike c/n SW-TE-0033 (NF 07.04.16)

G-MVBK Mainair Gemini Flash IIA 666-788-6-W456 07.06.88
B R McLoughlin Ince 11.04.14P
(NF 29.06.15)

G-MVBN Mainair Gemini Flash IIA 668-788-6-W458 08.06.88
S R Potts Selby House Farm, Stanton 21.11.12P
(NF 26.03.18)

G-MVBO Mainair Gemini Flash IIA 671-788-6-W461 08.06.88
M Bailey Otherton 14.10.18P

G-MVBT Thruster TST Mk.1 8068-TST-083 14.06.88
Cancelled 10.11.15 by PWFU 19.12.07
Ley Farm, Chirk Wreck stored 09.17

G-MVBZ Solar Wings Pegasus XL-R SW-WA-1345 17.06.88
J Greatwood (Alrewas, Burton-on-Trent) 17.09.05P
Trike c/n SW-TB-1358 (NF 12.02.19)

G-MVCA Solar Wings Pegasus XL-R SW-WA-1346 17.06.88
R Walker (Magdalen, King's Lynn) 26.03.11P
Trike c/n SW-TB-1359 (NF 17.12.14)

G-MVCC CFM Shadow Series CD K 045 17.06.88
G Anderson tr Walpole Shadow Group
Rayne Hall Farm, Rayne 11.09.15P
(NF 01.09.17)

G-MVCF Mainair Gemini Flash IIA 673-788-6-W463 14.07.88
R C Hinds (Newnham GL14) 07.07.17P

G-MVCL Solar Wings Pegasus XL-Q SW-WQ-0075 27.06.88
T E Robinson Abbeyleix, RoI 31.05.14P
Trike c/n SW-TE-0069 (NF 24.08.15)

G-MVCP Solar Wings Pegasus XL-Q SW-WQ-0079 27.06.88
Cancelled 07.12.10 as WFU
Deenethorpe *Trike c/n SW-TE-0073*
Wings only stored 06.13

G-MVCR Solar Wings Pegasus XL-Q SW-WQ-0080 27.06.88
P Hoeft (Stickney, Boston) 06.06.17P
Trike c/n SW-TE-0069

G-MVCT Solar Wings Pegasus XL-Q SW-WQ-0082 27.06.88
G J Lampitt (Wonbourne, Wolverhampton) 15.06.06P
Trike c/n SW-TE-0076 (NF 21.05.18)

G-MVCV Solar Wings Pegasus XL-Q SW-WQ-0084 27.06.88
G Stewart Redlands
Original trike c/n SW-TE-0078 damaged, repaired
& fitted with wing c/n SW-WQ-0105 to became
G-MVHP; trike c/n SW-TE-108
(SSDR microlight since 06.14) (IE 26.07.16)

G-MVCW CFM Shadow Series BD 084 28.06.88
D A Coupland RAF Barkston Heath 16.06.18P

G-MVCZ Mainair Gemini Flash IIA 675-788-6-W465 26.08.88
S G Roberts St Michaels 11.10.18P

G-MVDA Mainair Gemini Flash IIA 676-788-6-W466 13.07.88
C Tweedley (Millom) 08.05.06P
(NF 08.09.17)

G-MVDE Thruster TST Mk1 8078-TST-087 12.07.88
M N Watson Felthorpe 08.04.19P

G-MVDF Thruster TST Mk1 8078-TST-088 12.07.88
A R Sunley & J Walsh tr G-MVDF Syndicate
Rayne Hall Farm, Rayne 01.11.18P
Operated by Saxon Microlights

G-MVDG Thruster TST Mk1 8078-TST-089 12.07.88
Cancelled 03.09.12 as PWFU 26.07.00
Wing Farm, Longbridge Deverill *Spares use 06.14*

G-MVDH Thruster TST Mk1 8078-TST-090 12.07.88
R J Whettem (Haywards Heath)
(SSDR microlight since 08.15) (IE 27.08.15)

G-MVDJ Medway Hybred 44XLR MR010/38 20.07.88
W D Hutchings (Bingham, Nottingham) 09.02.09P
(NF 03.12.14)

G-MVDL Aerial Arts Chaser S CH701 11.08.88
N P Lloyd (Cefn-y-Bed, Wrexham) '112'
(SSDR microlight since 06.14) (IE 24.06.16)

G-MVDP Aerial Arts Chaser S 447 CH706 11.08.88
G J Slater Clench Common
(SSDR microlight since 05.14) (NF 13.11.14)

G-MVDV Solar Wings Pegasus XL-R SW-WA-1349 13.07.88
Cancelled 19.07.16 as PWFU 29.11.15
Otherton *Trike c/n SW-TB-1362 For sale 06.17*

G-MVEF Solar Wings Pegasus XL-R SW-WA-1358 19.07.88
EI-ELV, G-MVEF D M Pecheur (Downham Market)
Trike c/n SW-TE-0079
(SSDR microlight since 06.15) (IE 11.06.15)

G-MVEG Solar Wings Pegasus XL-R SW-WA-1359 19.07.88
A M Shaw (Alsager, Stoke-on-Trent) 17.01.11P
Trike c/n SW-TE-0080 (NF 10.07.17)

G-MVEH Mainair Gemini Flash IIA 677-788-6-W468 26.08.88
D Evans Rossall Field, Cockerham 01.04.18P

G-MVEI CFM Shadow Series CD 085 26.07.88
R L Morgan Oban 24.05.18P

G-MVEL Mainair Gemini Flash IIA 680-888-6-W471 27.07.88
M R Starling (Swafield, North Walsham) 25.07.03P
(NF 03.09.14)

G-MVEN CFM Shadow Series CD K 047 26.07.88
M R Garwood Sywell
Originally registered as CFM Shadow Series BD,
then Series SS
(SSDR microlight since 07.17) (IE 30.10.17)

G-MVEO Mainair Gemini Flash IIA 682-888-6-W472 28.07.88
Cancelled 09.02.09 by CAA 08.05.09
Coatbridge, Lancs *Sold on eBay 06.14*

G-MVER Mainair Gemini Flash IIA 684-888-6-W474 28.07.88
J R Davis Over Farm, Gloucester 18.12.07P
(NF 15.03.18)

G-MVES Mainair Gemini Flash IIA 685-888-6-W475 05.08.88
A Robins (Holywell) 21.07.18P
(NF 13.08.18)

G-MVET Mainair Gemini Flash IIA 686-888-6-W476 19.08.88
J R Kendall (Nawton, York) 23.05.18P

G-MVEV Mainair Gemini Flash IIA 687-888-6-W477 05.08.88
K Davies (Golborne, Warrington) 08.07.01P
(NF 12.09.16)

G-MVFB Solar Wings Pegasus XL-Q SW-WQ-0092 09.08.88
M O Bloy White House Farm, Southery 22.10.13P
Trike c/n SW-TE-0086 (IE 31.05.17)

G-MVFD Solar Wings Pegasus XL-Q SW-WQ-0094 09.08.88
C D Humphries (Coventry) 15.06.18P
Trike c/n SW-TE-0088

G-MVFE Solar Wings Pegasus XL-Q SW-WQ-0095 09.08.88
S J Weeks Cotswold 30.04.00P
Trike c/n SW-TE-0089 (NF 18.05.18)

G-MVFF Solar Wings Pegasus XL-Q SW-WQ-0096 09.08.88
A Makepeace (Burpham, Guildford) 23.11.18P
Trike c/n SW-TE-0090

G-MVFH CFM Shadow Series CD 086 09.08.88
K Garnett Monewden 07.10.19P
On rebuild 02.19

G-MVFJ Thruster TST Mk1 8088-TST-092 11.08.88
B E Renehan Popham 22.05.19P

G-MVFL Thruster TST Mk1 8088-TST-094 11.08.88
E J Wallington Inglenook Farm, Maydensole 08.06.17P

G-MVFM Thruster TST Mk1 8088-TST-095 11.08.88
G J Boyer Westonzoyland 01.09.05P
(NF 09.02.16)

G-MVFO Thruster TST Mk1 8088-TST-097 11.08.88
A Whittaker Chatteris 21.07.18P

G-MVGA Aerial Arts Chaser S 508 CH707 11.08.88
T A Willcox tr Golf Alpha Group
Chase Farm, Chipping Sodbury
(SSDR microlight since 05.14) (NF 18.06.18)

G-MVGB Medway Hybred 44XLR   MR011/39   01.09.88
Cancelled 19.05.09 as PWFU   28.08.02
Rochester   *Stored 10.16*

G-MVGC AMF Microflight Chevvron 2-32C   010   02.09.88
W Fletcher   (Raglan, Usk)   11.09.08P
(NF 19.12.14)

G-MVGD AMF Microflight Chevvron 2-32C   011   05.09.88
D H Lewis   (Nelson, Treharris)
(SSDR microlight since 07.18) (IE 17.07.18)

G-MVGE   AMF Chevvron 2-32C   012   26.09.88
Cancelled 19.03.08 as destroyed
Low Hill Farm, Messingham   *Stored for spares use 08.12*

G-MVGF Aerial Arts Chaser S   CH720   02.09.88
P J Higgins   Fenland   *'The Dingbat'*
(SSDR microlight since 05.14) (IE 27.08.15)

G-MVGG Aerial Arts Chaser S 508   CH721   02.09.88
J A Horn   Greenhills Farm, Wheatley Hill
(SSDR microlight since 07.14) (IE 20.09.16)

G-MVGI Aerial Arts Chaser S   CH723   01.09.88
(EI-xxx)   J R Kendall   Rufforth East
(SSDR microlight since 05.14) (IE 20.07.18)

G-MVGK Aerial Arts Chaser S   CH726   02.09.88
D J Smith   (Calverton, Nottingham)
(SSDR microlight since 05.14) (IE 04.08.18)

G-MVGO Solar Wings Pegasus XL-R   SW-WA-1378   23.08.88
J B Peacock   (Surlingham, Norwich)   10.10.17P
Trike c/n SW-TB-1382

G-MVGP Solar Wings Pegasus XL-R   SW-WA-1379   23.08.88
(EC-...), G-MVGP
J W Norman   (Goring Heath, Reading)   18.05.17P
Trike c/n SW-TB-1383

G-MVGY Medway Hybred 44XLR   MR015/41   31.08.88
M Vines   Beverley (Linley Hill)   16.06.08P

G-MVGZ Ultraflight Lazair IIIE   A338   21.10.88
C-....   D M Broom   (Sutton, Ely)
(SSDR microlight since 06.14) (NF 20.06.18)

G-MVHB Powerchute Raider   80105   26.08.88
G A Marples   (Melton Mowbray)
(SSDR microlight since 12.14) (IE 21.10.16)

G-MVHE Mainair Gemini Flash IIA   692-988-6-W482   04.10.88
T J McMenamin   (Convoy, Lifford, Rol)   23.10.14P
(NF 23.06.14)

G-MVHH Mainair Gemini Flash IIA   607-1187-5-W485   24.10.88
D Rowland   (Gamrie, Banff)   14.02.18P
Original trike c/n 695-988-6 replaced by
c/n 607-1187-5 ex G-MTSA c.1995

G-MVHI Thruster TST Mk1   8098-TST-100   26.09.88
G L Roberts   (Cester Bridge, Macclesfield)   10.03.06
Stored in damaged condition 07.18 (NF 22.06.15)

G-MVHJ Thruster TST Mk1   8098-TST-101   26.09.88
T Welch   Longacre Farm, Sandy   27.05.17P
(IE 05.06.17)

G-MVHK Thruster TST Mk1   8098-TST-102   27.09.88
D J Gordon   Woodlands Barton Farm, Roche   14.08.07P
(IE 25.08.17)

G-MVHP Solar Wings Pegasus XL-Q   SW-WQ-0105   23.09.88
J B Gasson   (Peterborough)   29.10.11P
Damaged trike c/n SW-TE-0078 ex G-MVCV
repaired & fitted to wing (NF 24.09.14)

G-MVHR Solar Wings Pegasus XL-Q   SW-WQ-0106   23.09.88
J M Hucker   Broadmeadow Farm, Hereford   26.05.04P
Trike c/n SW-TE-0099 (NF 09.07.18)

G-MVIB Mainair Gemini Flash IIA   700-1088-4-W490   14.10.88
A, L & S Rosser t/a LSA Systems
Arclid Green, Sandbach   05.05.11P
(NF 12.04.16)

G-MVIE Aerial Arts Chaser S   CH732   14.10.88
C J Meadows   Westonzoyland
(SSDR microlight since 05.14) (NF 01.08.17)

G-MVIF   Medway Raven X   MR020/43   04.10.88
Cancelled 11.07.18 as PWFU   13.08.15
Rochester   *Trike stored 09.18*

G-MVIG CFM Shadow Series BD   K 044   05.10.88
M Roberts   (Sarn, Pwllheli)   08.04.13P
(IE 20.06.17)

G-MVIH Mainair Gemini Flash IIA   697-1088-6-W487   14.10.88
T M Gilsenan   (Eaton Bray)   21.06.18P

G-MVIL Noble Hardman Snowbird Mk.IV   SB-014   06.02.89
S J Reid   (Chidham, Chichester)   15.01.13P
Stored 04.14 (IE 04.06.15)

G-MVIN Noble Hardman Snowbird Mk.IV   SB-016   06.02.89
C P Dawes   Darley Moor
(SSDR microlight since 02.17) (IE 03.03.17)

G-MVIP AMF Microflight Chevvron 2-32C   008   11.05.88
J Pool   Mount Airey Farm, South Cave   19.06.07P
Noted 01.17 (NF 21.10.16)

G-MVIR Thruster TST Mk1   8108-TST-104   21.10.88
T Dziadkiewicz   Wickenby   07.06.17P
C/n plate shows '8116-TST-104' incorrectly

G-MVIV Thruster TST Mk1   8108-TST-108   21.10.88
G Rainey   Westonzoyland   24.06.01P
(NF 29.01.16)

G-MVIX Mainair Gemini Flash IIA   702-1088-6-W492   14.10.88
C J Barnes   (Bolton le Sands, Carnforth)   29.04.15P
(NF 13.09.18)

G-MVJF Aerial Arts Chaser S   CH743   21.11.88
V S Rudham   Dunkeswell
(SSDR microlight since 08.16) (NF 10.07.18)

G-MVJG Aerial Arts Chaser S   CH749   22.11.88
T H Scott   Rayne Hall Farm, Rayne
(SSDR microlight since 05.14) (NF 13.12.17)

G-MVJI   Aerial Arts Chaser S   CH752   17.11.88
Cancelled 24.01.10 by CAA   01.11.03
Causey Park, Morpeth   *Stored 03.13*

G-MVJJ Aerial Arts Chaser S 447   CH753   14.11.88
C W Potts   Selby House Farm, Stanton
(SSDR microlight since 06.14) (NF 20.07.18)

G-MVJK Aerial Arts Chaser S   CH754   14.11.88
M P Lomax   Rossall Field, Cockerham
(SSDR microlight since 05.14) (NF 05.01.15)

G-MVJM^M Microflight Aircraft Spectrum   007   05.07.00
Cancelled 22.08.12 by CAA
With Tettenhall Transport Heritage Centre, Wolverhampton

G-MVJN Solar Wings Pegasus XL-Q   SW-WQ-0116   26.10.88
L P Geer   (Marston St Lawrence, Banbury)   13.05.18P
Trike c/n SW-TE-0110

G-MVJP Solar Wings Pegasus XL-Q   SW-WQ-0118   26.10.88
S H Bakowski   Rochester   29.09.15P
Trike c/n SW-TE-0112 (IE 06.09.17)

G-MVJU Solar Wings Pegasus XL-Q   SW-WQ-0122   26.10.88
J C Sutton   Headon Farm, Retford   18.04.18P
Trike c/n SW-TE-0116

G-MVKH Solar Wings Pegasus XL-R   SW-WA-1394   14.11.88
D J Higham   Darley Moor   12.10.17P
Trike c/n SW-TB-1391

G-MVKK Solar Wings Pegasus XL-R   SW-WA-1397   14.11.88
G P Burns   Graveley Hall Farm, Graveley   09.12.12P
Trike c/n SW-TE-0131 (NF 12.11.14)

G-MVKL Solar Wings Pegasus XL-R   SW-WA-1398   14.11.88
B J Morton   (Hartley, Longfield)
Original Trike s/n SW-TE-0132 replaced with s/n
SW-TB-1391; badged 'XL-Q' possibly indicating
a replacement pod c.2015/16?
(SSDR microlight since 06.18) (IE 14.07.17)

G-MVKN Solar Wings Pegasus XL-Q   SW-WQ-0126   14.11.88
D Seiler   Rufforth
Trike c/n SW-TE-0120
(SSDR microlight since 12.16) (NF 07.12.16)

G-MVKO Solar Wings Pegasus XL-Q   SW-WQ-0127   14.11.88
A R Hughes   Yatesbury   31.05.13P
(NF 16.04.18)

G-MVKP Solar Wings Pegasus XL-Q   SW-WQ-0128   14.11.88
K R Emery   Sittles Farm, Alrewas
Trike c/n SW-TE-0122
(SSDR microlight since 03.15) (IE 16.05.16)

G-MVKU Solar Wings Pegasus XL-Q SW-WQ-0132 14.11.88
I K Priestley   Sackville Lodge Farm, Riseley 01.06.10P
Trike c/n SW-TE-0126 (NF 02.11.15)

G-MVLA Aerial Arts Chaser S CH762 12.12.88
K R Emery   Bradley Moor, Ashbourne
(SSDR microlight since 05.14) (IE 21.11.16)

G-MVLB Aerial Arts Chaser S CH763 05.12.88
R P Wilkinson   Charmy Down
(SSDR microlight since 05.14) (IE 18.09.16)

G-MVLC Aerial Arts Chaser S 447 CH764 22.11.88
B R Barnes   (Dundry, Bristol)
(SSDR microlight since 05.14) (NF 25.07.17)

G-MVLD Aerial Arts Chaser S CH765 22.11.88
J D Doran   (Ballymore, Mullingar, Rol)
(SSDR microlight since 05.14) (NF 20.06.18)

G-MVLE Aerial Arts Chaser S CH766 05.12.88
J M Hucker   Broadmeadow Farm, Hereford
(SSDR microlight since 05.14) (NF 13.09.16)

G-MVLF Aerial Arts Chaser S 508 CH767 11.01.89
A Matheu   (Bajos, Barcelona, Spain)
(SSDR microlight since 02.15) (IE 28.03.17)

G-MVLG Aerial Arts Chaser S CH768 14.11.88
Cancelled 22.04.10 by CAA 26.11.04
East Fortune   Stored 06.18

G-MVLJ CFM Shadow Series CD 092 11.11.88
D R C Pugh   (Trefeglwys, Caersws) 24.07.18P

G-MVLL Mainair Gemini Flash IIA 708-1188-6-W498 23.11.88
A A Sawera   (Nuneaton)
Fitted with wing ex G-MTSA c/n W396
(SSDR microlight since 09.16) (IE 23.09.16)

G-MVLS Aerial Arts Chaser S 447 CH773 21.02.89
P K Dale   Thornton Watlass, Ripon
(SSDR microlight since 05.14) (NF 17.08.15)

G-MVLT Aerial Arts Chaser S CH774 05.12.88
P H Newson   Sutton Meadows
(SSDR microlight since 06.14) (IE 05.10.16)

G-MVLX Solar Wings Pegasus XL-Q SW-WQ-0114 30.11.88
D J Harber   Manor Farm, Drayton St Leonard
Trike c/n SW-TE-0133
(SSDR microlight since 06.16) (NF 29.06.18)

G-MVLY Solar Wings Pegasus XL-Q SW-WQ-0142 05.12.88
I B Osborn   (Minster, Ramsgate)
Trike c/n SW-TE-0137
(SSDR microlight since 07.15) (IE 16.11.15)

G-MVMA Solar Wings Pegasus XL-Q SW-WQ-0144 05.12.88
M Peters   Broomclose Farm, Longbridge Deverill 30.03.10P
Trike c/n SW-TE-0139 (NF 30.10.17)

G-MVMC Solar Wings Pegasus XL-Q SW-WQ-0146 05.12.88
R A Cuttell   Park Hall Farm, Mapperley
Trike c/n SW-TE-0141
(SSDR microlight since 03.18) (IE 29.03.18)

G-MVMI Thruster TST Mk1 8128-TST-114 12.12.88
I J Webb   (Basingstoke) 11.08.14P
(IE 09.08.18)

G-MVML Aerial Arts Chaser S CH781 28.12.88
G C Luddington   (Bolnhurst, Bedford)
(SSDR microlight since 05.14) (IE 22.09.15)

G-MVMR Mainair Gemini Flash IIA 717-1288-6-W509 09.01.89
P W Ramage   (Rufford, Ormskirk) 20.09.96P
(NF 24.02.16)

G-MVMT Mainair Gemini Flash IIA 718-189-6-W510 22.12.88
R F Sanders   Otherton 25.09.98P
(NF 07.01.16)

G-MVMW Mainair Gemini Flash IIA 710-1188-6-W500 11.11.88
G Jones   (Llanfairfechan) 09.06.17P

G-MVMX Mainair Gemini Flash IIA 721-189-6-W513 23.12.88
E A Dygutowicz   Newtownards 18.09.18P
Trike stamped 'W512' incorrectly (IE 04.10.18)

G-MVNA Powerchute Raider 81230 12.07.89
J McGoldrick   (Dromara, Dromore)
(SSDR microlight since 05.14) (NF 20.11.14)

G-MVNC Powerchute Raider 81232 12.07.89
S T P Askew   (Melton Mowbray)
(SSDR microlight since 05.14) (IE 27.04.17)

G-MVNE Powerchute Raider 90219 12.07.89
A E Askew   (Melton Mowbray)
(SSDR microlight since 12.14) (IE 28.07.17)

G-MVNK Powerchute Raider 90623 12.07.89
A E Askew   (Melton Mowbray)
(SSDR microlight since 05.14) (IE 27.08.15)

G-MVNM Mainair Gemini Flash IIA 725-189-6-W517 06.01.89
C D Phillips   (Chichester) 31.08.08P
(NF 03.02.15)

G-MVNP Whittaker MW5-K Sorcerer 5K-0005-02 13.07.89
A M Edwards   (Winnersh, Wokingham)
Built by Aerotech International Ltd
(SSDR microlight since 08.16) (NF 22.01.15)

G-MVNR Whittaker MW5-K Sorcerer 5K-0006-02 04.05.89
E I Rowlands-Jones   Ley Farm, Chirk
Built by Aerotech International Ltd; frame noted 09.17
(SSDR microlight since 06.14) (NF 11.05.18)

G-MVNS Whittaker MW5-K Sorcerer 5K-0007-02 19.07.89
A M Sirant   Monkswell Farm, Horrabridge
Built by Aerotech International Ltd
(SSDR microlight since 06.14) (NF 07.01.16)

G-MVNTᴹ Aerotech MW-5(K) Sorcerer 5K-0008-02 28.03.90
Cancelled 27.05.11 as PWFU 05.05.07
With South Yorkshire Aircraft Museum, Doncaster

G-MVNW Mainair Gemini Flash IIA 726-189-6-W518 25.01.89
D J Furey   (Coventry) 30.07.15P
(IE 06.10.15)

G-MVNX Mainair Gemini Flash IIA 727-289-6-W519 10.01.89
G Copperthwaite   Redlands 23.10.15P
(IE 02.12.15)

G-MVNY Mainair Gemini Flash IIA 724-189-6-W516 11.01.89
M K Buckland   (Daventry) 12.06.18P

G-MVNZ Mainair Gemini Flash IIA 728-289-6-W520 11.01.89
D A Ballard   Brook Breasting Farm, Watnall 10.01.19P

G-MVOA Aerial Arts Chaser S 447 CH780 16.01.89
W A Emmerson   Causey Park, Morpeth
(IE 22.08.18)

G-MVOD Aerial Arts Chaser/110SX 110SX/653 16.01.89
N R Beale   Deppers Bridge, Southam
(SSDR microlight since 05.14) (IE 20.10.15)

G-MVOJ Noble Hardman Snowbird Mk.IV SB-019 26.07.89
C D Beetham   Lleweni Parc 27.09.18P

G-MVOL Noble Hardman Snowbird Mk.IV SB-021 29.08.89
Cancelled 11.10.11 by CAA 26.01.02
Not Known   *Sold on ebay 05.15*

G-MVON Mainair Gemini Flash IIA 731-289-6-W523 30.01.89
D S Lally   Eccleston, Chorley 21.04.10P
(NF 30.06.15)

G-MVOO AMF Microflight Chevvron 2-32C 014 10.01.89
M K Field   Sleap 10.05.07P
(NF 13.07.18)

G-MVOP Aerial Arts Chaser S CH787 21.02.89
D Thorpe   (Grantham)
(SSDR microlight since 05.14) (IE 26.10.15)

G-MVOR Mainair Gemini Flash IIA 732-289-6-W524 06.02.89
(EC-...), G-MVOR   P T & R M Jenkins   (Newton Abbot) 05.10.03P
(NF 28.01.16)

G-MVOT Thruster TST Mk1 8029-TST-116 17.02.89
Doyt Ltd   (Armoy, Ballymoney) 02.10.16P
(IE 14.10.16)

G-MVOV Thruster TST Mk1 8029-TST-118 17.02.89
I Garforth   (Bristol BS3) 09.09.10P
(NF 02.11.17)

G-MVOY Thruster TST Mk.1 8029-TST-121 17.02.89
Cancelled 22.05.09 by CAA 22.06.07
Redlands   *Noted 10.13*

G-MVPA Mainair Gemini Flash IIA 735-289-7-W527 29.03.89
D Hume   (Shildon)
(SSDR microlight since 07.17) (IE 31.10.17)

G-MVPB Mainair Gemini Flash IIA 736-389-7-W528 29.03.89
J M Breaks   (Marchwood, Southampton) 09.08.17P

G-MVPC Mainair Gemini Flash IIA   737-389-7-W529   07.02.89
W O Flannery   (Scariff, Co Clare, RoI)   09.05.10P
C/n plate inscribed '740-389-7-W532'
which is identity of G-MVPI (NF 23.08.17)

G-MVPD Mainair Gemini Flash IIA   738-389-7-W530   07.02.89
P Thelwell   Rossall Field, Cockerham   16.02.07P
(NF 27.05.14)

G-MVPF Medway Hybred 44XLR   MR036/52   27.02.89
G H Crick   Over Farm, Gloucester   16.06.17P
(NF 13.07.17)

G-MVPK CFM Shadow Series CD   K 091   15.02.89
P Sarfas   Benson's Farm, Laindon   20.09.18P

G-MVPM Whittaker MW6 Merlin   xxxx   21.02.89
K W Curry   (Nantmel, Llandrindod Wells)   30.04.03P
Built by S J Field – project PFA 164-11272;
reported as Type MW6-T (NF 27.03.15)

G-MVPR Solar Wings Pegasus XL-Q   SW-WQ-0163   14.03.89
M G J Bridges   (Bridgwater)   11.04.19P
Trike c/n SW-TE-0149

G-MVPS Solar Wings Pegasus XL-Q   SW-WQ-0140   14.03.89
G W F J Dear   Old Sarum   09.05.19P
Trike c/n SW-TE-0143

G-MVPW Solar Wings Pegasus XL-R   SW-WA-1411   28.03.89
C A Mitchell   Strathaven   07.09.18P

G-MVPX Solar Wings Pegasus XL-Q   SW-WQ-0158   28.03.89
J R Appleton   Clench Common   31.07.17P
Trike c/n SW-TE-0144

G-MVPY Solar Wings Pegasus XL-Q   SW-WQ-0188   28.03.89
P Lombardi   (Birdbrook, Halstead)   18.10.19P
Trike c/n SW-TE-0178

G-MVRD Mainair Gemini Flash IIA   749-489-7-W541   09.05.89
J D Pearce   (Gwernagle, Carmarthen)   13.06.12P
(NF 10.02.15)

G-MVRG Aerial Arts Chaser S   CH798   14.04.89
T M Stiles   Herrings Farm, Dallington
(IE 26.08.15)
(SSDR microlight since 05.14)

G-MVRH Solar Wings Pegasus XL-Q   SW-WQ-0177   10.04.89
K Farr   (Swinford, Lutterworth)   13.08.17P
Trike c/n SW-TE-0160

G-MVRI Solar Wings Pegasus XL-Q   SW-WQ-0159   10.04.89
R J Pattinson   Clench Common
Trike c/n SW-TE-0145 (IE 06.09.17)

G-MVRM Mainair Gemini Flash IIA   752-489-7-W545   12.04.89
M Davidson   East Fortune   25.09.18P

G-MVRO CFM Shadow Series CD   K 105   03.04.89
M G Read   Nottingham City   28.10.19P

G-MVRP CFM Shadow Series CD   097   07.04.89
Cancelled 01.07.13 by CAA   21.05.13
Old Park Farm, Margham   *Stored 2014*

G-MVRR CFM Shadow Series CD   098   07.04.89
S P Christian   Glebe Farm, Hougham   27.09.16P
(IE 21.04.17)

G-MVRT CFM Shadow Series CD   104   07.04.89
J Campbell & G M Cruise-Smith   Rankins Farm, Linton
Originally built as Series SS; airworthy & for sale 11.18
(SSDR microlight since 05.15)

G-MVRW Solar Wings Pegasus XL-Q   SW-WQ-0178   12.04.89
C A Hamps   Sutton Meadows   20.04.18P
Trike c/n SW-TE-0161; rebuilt 1999 with new wing

G-MVRZ Medway Hybred 44XL   MR043/57   09.05.89
P J Higgins   Wingland
(SSDR microlight since 09.15) (IE 16.09.15)

G-MVSE Solar Wings Pegasus XL-Q   SW-WQ-0196   18.04.89
T Wilbor   Bagby   29.09.19P
Trike c/n SW-TE-0187

G-MVSG Aerial Arts Chaser S   CH804   24.04.89
M Roberts   Moss Edge Farm, Cockerham
(SSDR microlight since 05.14) (NF 02.08.17)

G-MVSI Medway Hybred 44XL   MR040/58   18.04.89
R J Hood   London Colney
(IE 03.06.16)

G-MVSJ Aviasud Mistral 532GB   072   18.04.89
D Price & N Primrose   (Preston)   24.08.19P
Built by Aviasud Engineering – project BMAA/HB/013

G-MVSL Aerial Arts Chaser S   CH807   15.05.89
D M Pearson   Chiltern Park, Wallingford
(SSDR microlight since 11.15) (IE 20.06.17)

G-MVSO Mainair Gemini Flash IIA   755-589-7-W548   27.04.89
M Larrad   (Huntingdon)   14.08.16P
(IE 06.11.17)

G-MVSP Mainair Gemini Flash IIA   756-589-7-W549   27.04.89
D R Buchanan   (Washington, Pulborough)   04.04.04P
(NF 07.06.18)

G-MVSY Solar Wings Pegasus XL-Q   SW-WQ-0200   11.05.89
Cancelled 24.04.09 by CAA   12.09.04
Westonzoyland   *Trike c/n SW-TE-0191   Stored 07.16*

G-MVSZ Solar Wings Pegasus XL-Q   SW-WQ-0201   11.05.89
Cancelled 09.05.11 as PWFU   12.10.11
Wing Farm, Longbridge Deverill   *Trike c/n SW-TE-0192*
Wreck stored 06.14

G-MVTD Whittaker MW6 Merlin   xxxx   11.05.89
G R Reynolds   Otherton   12.10.15P
Built by J S Yates – project PFA 164-11367 (IE 03.11.16)

G-MVTF Aerial Arts Chaser S   CH808   30.05.89
D A Morgan   Tinnel Farm, Landulph
(SSDR microlight since 05.14) (IE 21.09.16)

G-MVTJ Solar Wings Pegasus XL-Q   SW-WQ-0207   25.05.89
M P & R A Wells   (Earls Croome, Worcester)   26.01.09P
Trike c/n SW-TE-0197 (NF 29.06.15)

G-MVTL Aerial Arts Chaser S   CH809   13.06.89
N D Meer   (Tamworth)
(SSDR microlight since 05.14) (IE 16.09.15)

G-MVTM Aerial Arts Chaser S 447   CH810   13.06.89
G L Davies   (Den Helder, Netherlands)
(SSDR microlight since 08.14) (NF 17.07.18)

G-MVUA Mainair Gemini Flash IIA   760-689-7-W553   14.06.89
K D Sinclair-Russell   (Witchford, Ely)   26.05.18P

G-MVUB Thruster T300   089-T300-373   13.06.89
A K Grayson   (Haydock, St Helens)   26.06.03P
(NF 28.07.14)

G-MVUF Solar Wings Pegasus XL-Q   SW-WQ-0213   13.06.89
G P Blakemore   (Eastbourne)   01.09.15P
Trike c/n SW-TE-0203 (IE 24.10.17)

G-MVUG Solar Wings Pegasus XL-Q   SW-WQ-0214   13.06.89
R A Allen   (Midgham, Reading)   01.07.17P
Trike c/n SW-TE-0204

G-MVUI Solar Wings Pegasus XL-Q   SW-WQ-0216   13.06.89
K Casserley & P E Hadley   Streethay Farm, Streethay   25.02.19P
Trike c/n SW-TE-0206: wing c/n marked as
'SW-TE-0216' incorrectly

G-MVUJ Solar Wings Pegasus XL-Q   SW-WQ-0217   13.06.89
N Huxtable   (Loosely Row, Princes Risborough)   29.08.18P
Trike c/n SW-TE-0207

G-MVUK Solar Wings Pegasus XL-Q   SW-WQ-0218   13.06.89
Cancelled 30.07.10 by CAA   27.10.05
Redlands   *Trike c/n SW-TE-0208   Noted 07.16*

G-MVUO AMF Microflight Chevvron 2-32C   015   14.06.89
W D M Turtle   (Broughshane, Ballymena)   04.06.07P
Stored dismantled 12.13 (NF 18.08.16)

G-MVUP Aviasud Mistral   1087.048   10.08.89
83-CQ   D J Brightman
Low Hill Farm, North Moor, Messingham   04.04.18P
Built by Aviasud Engineering – project BMAA/HB/003

G-MVUS Aerial Arts Chaser S   CH813   03.07.89
H Poyzer   (North Walbottle, Tyne & Wear)
(SSDR microlight since 05.14) (NF 27.07.17)

G-MVUU Hornet R-ZA   HRWB0061/ZA110   13.07.89
K W Warn   Rossall Field, Cockerham   01.11.18P

G-MVVI Medway Hybred 44XLR   MR050/64   12.07.89
C J Turner   (Siteia, Crete, Greece)   05.04.14P
(NF 26.08.15)

G-MVVK Solar Wings Pegasus XL-R   SW-WA-1423   11.07.89
A J Weir   Clench Common   05.05.09P
Trike c/n SW-TB-1414 (IE 12.07.16)

G-MVVO Solar Wings Pegasus XL-Q SW-WQ-0227 11.07.89
A L Scarlett Clench Common 29.07.04P
Trike c/n SW-TE-0215 (NF 08.05.18)

G-MVVT CFM Shadow Series CD K 101 26.07.89
P L Naylor Durham Tees Valley
Built by CFM Metal-Fax – project PFA 161-11569;
originally built as Series SS; noted 01.18
(SSDR microlight since 03.15) (IE 08.08.17)

G-MVVV AMF Microflight Chevvron 2-32C 016 11.05.89
PH-1W9, G-MVVV J S Firth (Scissett, Huddersfield) 16.02.11P
(NF 06.02.18)

G-MVVZ Powerchute Raider 90628 25.07.89
G A Marples (Melton Mowbray)
(SSDR microlight since 05.14) (IE 26.10.15)

G-MVWJ Powerchute Raider 90738 25.07.89
N J Doubek (Corringham, Stanford-le-Hope)
Sailwing No.880288
(SSDR microlight since 05.14) (NF 04.04.18)

G-MVWN Thruster T300 089-T300-374 26.07.89
R D Leigh Darley Moor 22.03.17P

G-MVWS Thruster T300 089-T300-378 26.07.89
R J Humphries (Christchurch) 19.07.17P

G-MVWW Aviasud Mistral 0389.081 25.07.89
S G A Milburn & S Wood Rossall Field, Cockerham 12.06.18P
Built by Aviasud Engineering – project BMAA/HB/005

G-MVXA Whittaker MW6 Merlin xxxx 17.08.89
J C Gates (Weeley, Clacton)
Built by I Brewster – project PFA 164-11337
(SSDR microlight since 07.15) (IE 25.08.17)

G-MVXN Aviasud Mistral 532GB 065 18.08.89
P W Cade (New York, Lincoln) 16.09.16P
Built by Aviasud Engineering – project BMAA/HB/002

G-MVXP Aerial Arts Chaser S CH822 17.08.89
B Mills Barhams Mill Farm, Egerton
(SSDR microlight since 05.14) (NF 05.09.18)

G-MVXR Mainair Gemini Flash IIA 764-889-7-W557 22.08.89
D M Bayne East Fortune 05.10.18P

G-MVXV Aviasud Mistral 532GB 092 22.08.89
D L Chalk & G S Jefferies Clench Common 14.06.15P
Built by Aviasud Engineering – project BMAA/HB/004
(IE 05.04.16)

G-MVXX AMF Microflight Chevvron 2-32 018 27.07.89
T R James (Northend, Southam)
(SSDR microlight since 06.14) (IE 01.06.17)

G-MVYC Solar Wings Pegasus XL-Q SW-WQ-0239 08.09.89
P E L Street Blackmoor Farm, Aubourn
Trike c/n SW-TE-0224
(SSDR microlight since 10.15) (IE 27.04.17)

G-MVYD Solar Wings Pegasus XL-Q SW-WQ-0240 08.09.89
J S Hawkins (Ashreigney, Chumleigh) 28.09.13P
Trike c/n SW-TE-0225

G-MVYE Thruster TST Mk1 8089-TST-123 13.09.89
M J Aubrey Llanfyrnach
Displayed Classic Ultralight Heritage (NF 04.11.15)

G-MVYI Hornet R-ZA HRWB0074/ZA122 22.09.89
K W Warn (Rossall Field, Cockerham) 21.09.95P
(NF 17.03.16)

G-MVYU Noble Hardman Snowbird Mk.IV SB-023 07.11.89
R P Tribe Damyns Hall, Upminster
(SSDR microlight since 02.17) (IE 01.11.17)

G-MVYV Noble Hardman Snowbird Mk.IV SB-024 21.08.90
D W Hayden Swansea 23.11.18P

G-MVYW Noble Hardman Snowbird Mk.IV SB-025 22.10.90
T J Harrison (Gloucester) 25.07.06P
(NF 27.06.17)

G-MVYX Noble Hardman Snowbird Mk.IV SB-026 25.11.91
R McBlain Kilkerran 20.11.17P

G-MVYY Aerial Arts Chaser S 508 CH824 26.09.89
G H Crick Over Farm, Gloucester
(SSDR microlight since 06.14) (NF 23.05.18)

G-MVYZ CFM Shadow Series BD 121 25.09.89
D H Lewis (Treharris, Cardiff)
(SSDR microlight since 09.17) (IE 20.09.17)

G-MVZA Thruster T300 089-T300-379 26.09.89
A I Milne Chatteris 15.04.18P

G-MVZC Thruster T300 089-T300-381 26.09.89
S M Dougan Popham 29.07.18P

G-MVZD Thruster T300 089-T300-382 26.09.89
J M Chapman Tatenhill 23.02.18P

G-MVZE Thruster T300 089-T300-383 26.09.89
T L Davis Popham 09.07.02P
(SSDR microlight since 02.17) (NF 23.02.17)

G-MVZI Thruster T300 089-T300-387 26.09.89
G R Moore Black Springs Farm, Castle Bytham 03.08.19P

G-MVZL Solar Wings Pegasus XL-Q SW-WQ-0242 04.10.89
P R Dobson (Brentwood) 16.06.05P
Trike c/n SW-TE-0227 (NF 11.05.18)

G-MVZM Aerial Arts Chaser S 447 CH825 02.11.89
P Leigh (Edenbridge)
(SSDR microlight since 06.14) (IE 16.05.16)

G-MVZO Medway Hybred 44XLR MR072/78 25.10.89
S J Taft Blackmoor Farm, Aubourn 15.04.12P
(NF 04.04.16)

G-MVZP Murphy Renegade Spirit UK xxxx 17.10.89
H M Doyle tr The North American Syndicate
Park Farm, Eaton Bray 31.07.15P
Built by G S Hollingsworth – project PFA 188-11630

G-MVZR Aviasud Mistral 90 09.10.89
Cancelled 14.03.05 as PWFU 07.06.01
Crosland Moor *Built by Aviasud Engineering –*
project BMAA/HB/011; stored 09.12

G-MVZS Mainair Gemini Flash IIA 771-1089-7-W564 17.10.89
N McMaster (Gorstage, Northwich) 06.09.16P
(NF 03.07.18)

G-MVZT Solar Wings Pegasus XL-Q SW-WQ-0243 06.10.89
C J Meadows (Shepton Mallet) 25.08.02P
Trike c/n SW-TE-0228 (IE 22.02.18)

G-MVZU Solar Wings Pegasus XL-Q SW-WQ-0244 06.10.89
R D Proctor RAF Wyton 13.04.07P
Trike c/n SW-TE-0229 (NF 06.10.14)

G-MVZV Solar Wings Pegasus XL-Q SW-WQ-0245 06.10.89
K Mudra (Warrington) 03.06.18P
(IE 17.09.18)

G-MVZX Murphy Renegade Spirit UK xxxx 18.10.89
G Holmes Newton-on-Rawcliffe 23.07.18P
Built by G Holmes – project PFA 188-11590

G-MVZZ AMF Microflight Chevvron 2-32 019 27.07.89
W A L Mitchell Brownhill of Ardo Farm, Methlick
(SSDR microlight since 06.14) (IE 05.10.16)

G-MWAB Mainair Gemini Flash IIA 772-1089-7-W565 24.10.89
J E Buckley (Sandbach) 29.07.17P

G-MWAC Solar Wings Pegasus XL-Q SW-WQ-0260 25.10.89
D Jones & H Lloyd-Hughes (Mold) 23.07.19P
Trike c/n SW-TE-0236

G-MWAE CFM Shadow Series CD 130 24.10.89
R J Collins (Bideford) 26.08.19P

G-MWAJ Murphy Renegade Spirit UK xxxx 01.11.89
EI-EYN, G-MWAJ L D Blair (Artigarvan, Strabane)
Built by J Hall – project PFA 188-11438 (IE 30.09.17)

G-MWAL Solar Wings Pegasus XL-Q SW-WQ-0263 02.11.89
Cancelled 08.11.10 as PWFU 11.08.06
Sutton Meadows *Trike c/n SW-TE-0240 Stored 07.15*

G-MWAN Thruster T300 089-T300-389 14.11.89
M Jady (Spencers Wood, Reading) 07.09.08
(NF 07.06.18)

G-MWAT Solar Wings Pegasus XL-Q SW-WQ-0265 13.11.89
C A Reid Redlands 18.02.19P
Trike c/n SW-TE-0241

G-MWBJ Medway Puma Sprint MS003/1 21.11.89
C C Strong (Witheridge, Tiverton) 14.07.00P
(NF 09.04.19)

G-MWBO Rans S4 Coyote 89-097 29.11.89
Cancelled 08.12.09 by CAA 28.11.07
Falmouth *Built by L R H d'Ath*
– project PFA 193-11583; stored 06.16

G-MWBP Hornet R-ZA HRWB0083/ZA144 29.11.89
P Wilcox tr Foston Hornet Group
Manor House Farm, Foston
(SSDR microlight since 08.16) *(IE 12.08.16)*

G-MWBS Hornet R-ZA HRWB0085/ZA146 29.11.89
P D Jaques Sandtoft *'Freedom Hornet'* 03.10.08P
(NF 19.12.14)

G-MWBT Hornet R-ZA HRWB0086/ZA147 29.11.89
W Finley & K W Warn (Peterlee & Newton Abbot) 27.08.92P
(NF 05.10.16)

G-MWBY Hornet R-ZA HRWB0091/ZA152 29.11.89
IP Rights Ltd (London SW6) 25.11.09P
(NF 08.04.16)

G-MWCC Solar Wings Pegasus XL-R/Se SW-WA-1447 01.12.89
I K Priestley Sackville Lodge Farm, Riseley 26.03.05P
Trike c/n SW-TB-1387 ex G-MVKD (NF 03.08.18)

G-MWCE Mainair Gemini Flash IIA 775-1289-7-W568 19.12.89
B A Tooze Little Trostrey Farm, Kemeys Commander
(SSDR microlight since 07.16) *(IE 03.08.16)*

G-MWCF Solar Wings Pegasus XL-Q SW-WQ-0276 13.12.89
S P Tkaczyk Old Park Farm, Margam 30.09.12P
Trike c/n SW-TE-0252 (IE 06.10.17)

G-MWCG Microflight Spectrum 011 15.12.89
R J Hood London Colney
(SSDR microlight since 10.14) *(IE 23.05.18)*

G-MWCH Rans S-6-ESD Coyote II 0989.067 15.12.89
D C & P R Smith Rufforth East 17.08.18P
Built by J Whiting – project PFA 204-11632
– sequence no. duplicates Kitfox G-BSFY

G-MWCK Powerchute Kestrel 91247 03.01.90
A E Askew (Melton Mowbray)
Wing s/n 120503
(SSDR microlight since 05.14) *(IE 28.07.17)*

G-MWCL Powerchute Kestrel 91248 03.01.90
R W Twamley (Coventry) 07.10.16P

G-MWCM Powerchute Kestrel 91249 03.01.90
A E Askew (Melton Mowbray) 17.06.96P
(NF 20.11.14)

G-MWCN Powerchute Kestrel 91250 03.01.90
A E Askew (Melton Mowbray) 16.08.04P
(IE 26.08.15)

G-MWCO Powerchute Kestrel 91251 03.01.90
J R E Gladstone Enstone 31.05.11P
Trike noted 03.15 (NF 30.06.16)

G-MWCP Powerchute Kestrel 91252 03.01.90
A E Askew (Tamworth)
(SSDR microlight since 05.14) *(IE 26.08.15)*

G-MWCS Powerchute Kestrel 91253 03.01.90
S T P Askew (Melton Mowbray) 08.11.15P
(IE 27.04.17)

G-MWCY Medway Hybred 44XLR MR077/81 15.01.90
J K Masters (Hartlip, Sittingbourne) 10.09.04P
(NF 15.04.14)

G-MWCZ Medway Hybred 44XLR MR078/82 10.01.90
D Botha Sandown
(SSDR microlight since 02.17) *(IE 22.04.16)*

G-MWDB CFM Shadow Series CD 100 03.07.89
T D Dawson Plaistows Farm, St Albans 17.06.18P

G-MWDI Hornet RS-ZA HRWB0098/ZA158 10.01.90
K W Warn (Rossall Field, Cockerham) 29.06.05P
(NF 18.05.16)

G-MWDK Solar Wings Pegasus XL-Q SW-WQ-0281 17.01.90
J E Merriman & D R Western Westonzoyland
(Trike c/n SW-TE-0259)
(SSDR microlight since 06.16) *(IE 26.08.15)*

G-MWDN CFM Shadow Series CD K 102 17.01.90
J P Bath (Sturminster Newton) 05.10.18P

G-MWDP Thruster TST Mk.1 8129-TST-124 30.01.90
Cancelled 23.02.08 by CAA
Clougmills *Stored 12.13*

G-MWDS Thruster T300 089-T300-395 30.01.90
A W Nancarrow Folly Farm, Fulking
(SSDR microlight since 12.14) *(IE 16.07.15)*

G-MWDZ Eipper Quicksilver MXL II 022 29.01.90
R G Cook Sackville Lodge Farm, Riseley 06.08.16P
Built by Eipper Aircraft Inc – originally
registered as project PFA 214-11869

G-MWEG Solar Wings Pegasus XL-Q SW-WQ-0284 30.01.90
S P Michlig (Kenilworth) 05.06.09P
Trike c/n SW-TE-0262 (NF 25.03.15)

G-MWEH Solar Wings Pegasus XL-Q SW-WQ-0286 07.02.90
K A Davidson RAF Waddington 14.08.07P
Trike c/n SW-TE-0264 (IE 27.04.17)

G-MWEK Whittaker MW5 Sorcerer xxxx 20.02.90
D W & M L Squire (Hewas Water, St Austell)
Built by J T Francis – project PFA 163-11284
(SSDR microlight since 06.14) *(IE 26.07.16)*

G-MWEL Mainair Gemini Flash IIA 780-0290-7-W573 13.02.90
D R Spencer (Castle Camps, Cambridge) 04.08.12P
(NF 30.11.15)

G-MWEN CFM Shadow Series CD K 113 20.02.90
C Dawn (Ludford, Market Rasen) 08.08.01P
(NF 13.03.18)

G-MWEO Whittaker MW5 Sorcerer xxxx 21.02.90
P M Quinn Bellarena
Built by C D Wills – project PFA 163-11263
(SSDR microlight since 06.14) *(IE 28.07.17)*

G-MWEP Rans S-4 Coyote 89.096 21.02.90
E J Wallington Harringe Court, Sellindge
Built by K E Wedl – project PFA 193-11616
(SSDR microlight since 06.14) *(IE 18.05.18)*

G-MWER Solar Wings Pegasus XL-Q SW-WQ-0287 01.03.90
The Microlight School (Lichfield) Ltd Fisherwick 28.05.13P
Trike c/n SW-TE-0265 (IE 03.10.17)

G-MWES Rans S-4 Coyote 89.099 01.02.90
A R Dobrowolski Perth
Built by I Fleming & R W Sage – project PFA 193-11737;
on rebuild 09.18
(SSDR microlight since 06.14) *(NF 31.01.17)*

G-MWEZ CFM Shadow Series CD 136 22.02.90
T D Dawson Plaistows Farm, St Albans 29.05.14P
(NF 14.08.17)

G-MWFA Solar Wings Pegasus XL-R SW-WA-1454 27.02.90
D G Shaw (Llanrhaedr, Denbigh) 21.05.17P

G-MWFD Team Mini-Max 88 293 01.03.90
A T Carter Crosland Moor 20.08.14P
Built by J Riley – project PFA 186-11646; sequence
no. duplicates Shadow G-GORE
(SSDR microlight since 08.14) *(IE 23.08.17)*

G-MWFF Rans S-5 Coyote 89.106 10.01.90
P J Greenrod Welshpool
Built by M W Holmes – project PFA 193-11639;
converted to Rans S-5 c.2001; stored 07.16
(SSDR microlight since 08.14) *(NF 27.06.18)*

G-MWFH Powerchute Kestrel 00359 20.03.90
Cancelled 26.02.96 by CAA 10.02.96
Welshpool *Stored 08.15*

G-MWFL Powerchute Kestrel 00363 20.03.90
G A Marples (Melton Mowbray)
(SSDR microlight since 09.14) *(IE 21.10.16)*

G-MWFS Solar Wings Pegasus XL-Q SW-WQ-0289 14.03.90
D R Williams (Two Gates, Tamworth) 22.04.16P

G-MWFT MBA Tiger Cub 440 WFT-02 24.11.83
J R Ravenhill Orange Grove Barn, Chavenage Green
Built by Micro Biplane Aviation for W F Tremayne
(SSDR microlight since 06.14) *(NF 09.10.15)*

G-MWFU Quad City Challenger II xxxx 16.03.90
C J Whittaker (Staunton, Glos) 02.06.11P
Built by K N Dickinson – project PFA 177-11654
(NF 27.05.15)

G-MWFV Quad City Challenger II xxxx 16.03.90
M Liptrot Glassonby 26.05.05P
Built by E G Astin – project PFA 177-11655 (IE 03.11.15)

G-MWFW Rans S-4 Coyote 89.107 16.03.90
C Dewhurst (Sidcup)
Built by G R Hillary – project PFA 193-11662
(SSDR microlight since 06.14) *(NF 05.08.14)*

G-MWFX Quad City Challenger II xxxx 20.03.90
I M Walton Wellesbourne Mountford 28.09.12P
Built by I M Walton – project PFA 177-11706
(NF 16.01.15)

G-MWFY Quad City Challenger II xxxx 20.03.90
C C B Soden Westonzoyland 16.12.14P
Built by P J Ladd – project PFA 177-11668)
(IE 20.09.16)

G-MWGI Whittaker MW5-K Sorcerer 5K-0012-02 28.03.90
J A Aley Blockmoor Farm, Soham, Ely
Built by Aerotech International Ltd;
original wings fitted to G-MTBT by 07.96
(SSDR microlight since 10.14) (IE 10.06.16)

G-MWGJ Whittaker MW5-K Sorcerer 5K-0014-02 06.09.90
I Pearson Newquay Cornwall
Built by Aerotech International Ltd
(SSDR microlight since 06.14) (IE 15.12.17)

G-MWGK Whittaker MW5-K Sorcerer 5K-0015-02 19.09.90
(G-MWLV) R J Cook Easter Poldar Farm, Thornhill
Built by Aerotech International Ltd
(SSDR microlight since 08.16) (IE 06.10.17)

G-MWGL Solar Wings Pegasus XL-Q SW-WQ-0293 28.03.90
F McGlynn (Rostrevor, Newry) 12.06.15P
(IE 26.08.15)

G-MWGM Solar Wings Pegasus XL-Q SW-WQ-0294 28.03.90
I Davis (Wing, Leighton Buzzard) 02.02.08P
(Trike c/n SW-TE-0271 (NF 10.01.18)

G-MWGN Rans S-4 Coyote 89.113 26.03.90
V H Hallam (Torquay)
Built by B H Ashman – project PFA 193-11709
(SSDR microlight since 06.14) (IE 27.11.15)

G-MWGR Solar Wings Pegasus XL-Q SW-WQ-0296 06.04.90
M Jady Redlands 22.05.15P
Trike c/n SW-TE-0272 (NF 22.08.16)

G-MWGT Powerchute Kestrel 00367 26.04.90
Cancelled 01.04.03 by CAA 20.06.93
Carrickfergus *Stored 12.13*

G-MWHF Solar Wings Pegasus XL-Q SW-WQ-0305 24.04.90
N J Troke (Burbage, Hinckley) 18.07.17P
Trike c/n SW-TE-0275

G-MWHG Solar Wings Pegasus XL-Q SW-WQ-0306 24.04.90
M D Morris (Cumwhinton, Carlisle) 04.02.03P
Trike c/n SW-TE-0276 (IE 24.07.17)

G-MWHH Team Mini-Max 88 326 23.04.90
R J Hood London Colney
Built by B F Crick – project PFA 186-11814
(SSDR microlight since 06.14) (IE 16.10.16)

G-MWHL Solar Wings Pegasus XL-Q SW-WQ-0308 01.05.90
G J Eaton (Stretton, Burton-on-Trent) 03.09.18P
Trike c/n SW-TE-0278

G-MWHM Whittaker MW6-S Fatboy Flyer xxxx 18.05.90
K R Emery Sittles Farm, Alrewas
Built by D W Squire – project PFA 164-11463
(SSDR microlight since 08.17) (IE 31.07.17)

G-MWHP Rans S-6-ESD Coyote II 1089.093 08.05.90
P G Angus Higher Barn Farm, Hoghton 21.02.18P
Built by J F Bickerstaffe – project PFA 204-11768;
tricycle u/c

G-MWHR Mainair Gemini Flash IIA 787-0590-7-W580 16.05.90
J E S Harter (Lostock Hall, Preston) 20.11.18P

G-MWHS AMF Chevvron 2-32C 021 18.05.90
Cancelled 22.11.00 by CAA 26.02.98
Robin Hood, Doncaster Sheffield *Stored 08.16*

G-MWHX Solar Wings Pegasus XL-Q SW-WQ-0318 15.05.90
N P Kelly Navan, Rol 17.07.18P
Trike c/n SW-TE-0280

G-MWIA Mainair Gemini Flash IIA 789-0690-7-W582 21.05.90
A Evans Shifnal 16.04.18P

G-MWIB Aviasud Mistral 094 16.05.90
P Brady Newtownards *'Weston Belle'* 27.07.18P
Built by Aviasud Engineering – project BMAA/HB/010

G-MWIC Whittaker MW5-C Sorcerer xxxx 20.02.90
P J Cheyney New House Farm, Birds Edge
Built by I P Croft – project PFA 163-11224
(SSDR microlight since 05.17) (NF 17.05.17)

G-MWIF Rans S-6-ESD Coyote II 1089.095 30.05.90
K Kelly Finn Valley, Rol 08.08.17P
Built by M G K Prout – project PFA 204-11749;
tricycle u/c (IE 03.10.17)

G-MWIM Solar Wings Pegasus Quasar TC SW-WQQ-0326 11.06.90
M C Keeley (Toddington, Cheltenham) 18.05.12P
Trike c/n SW-TQ-0008 (NF 08.06.16)

G-MWIP Whittaker MW6 Merlin xxxx 07.06.90
D Beer & B J Merret Belle Vue Farm, Yarnscombe
Built by D Beer & B J Merrett – project PFA 164-11360
(SSDR microlight since 10.15) (IE 30.09.17)

G-MWIS Solar Wings Pegasus XL-Q SW-WQ-0331 08.06.90
P G Strangward (Sutton Coldfield)
Trike c/n SW-TE-0284
(SSDR microlight since 04.17) (IE 26.08.15)

G-MWIU Solar Wings Pegasus Quasar TC SW-WQQ-0333 08.06.90
W Hepburn (Law, Carluke) 08.05.13P
Trike c/n SW-TQ-0010 (NF 26.07.16)

G-MWIX Solar Wings Pegasus Quasar TC SW-WQQ-0335 18.06.90
G Hawes Deenethorpe 31.05.18P
Trike c/n SW-TQ-0012

G-MWIZ CFM Shadow Series CD 096 22.11.88
T A England RAF Henlow 09.08.19P

G-MWJF CFM Shadow Series CD K 123 26.06.90
T de B Gardner Walkeridge Farm, Overton 30.07.17P

G-MWJH Solar Wings Pegasus Quasar SW-WQQ-0340 29.06.90
L A Hosegood Redlands 04.05.17P
Trike c/n SW-TQ-0017 (IE 06.09.17)

G-MWJI Solar Wings Pegasus Quasar SW-WQQ-0341 29.06.90
M G J Bridges Westonzoyland 16.11.14P
Trike c/n SW-TQ-0018 (IE 05.12.17)

G-MWJJ Solar Wings Pegasus Quasar SW-WQQ-0342 29.06.90
P Darcy Newtownards 14.03.18P
Trike c/n SW-TQ-0019

G-MWJN Solar Wings Pegasus XL-Q SW-WQ-0344 29.06.90
J C Corrall Chatteris 15.06.18P
Trike c/n SW-TE-0288

G-MWJR Medway Hybred 44XLR MR098/92 28.06.90
Otherton Airfield Ltd Otherton 06.10.12P
(NF 20.09.18)

G-MWJT Solar Wings Pegasus Quasar TC SW-WQQ-0350 16.07.90
F McGlynn (Rostrevor, Newry) 06.05.18P
Trike c/n SW-TQ-0022

G-MWJW Whittaker MW-5 Sorcerer JDW-02 11.05.90
Cancelled 17.05.07 by CAA 20.07.06
Shennington, Oxon *Built by J D Webb*
– project PFA 163-11186; stored 06.17

G-MWKE Hornet RS-ZA HWRB0108/ZA167 30.07.90
D R Stapleton (Thornton-Cleveleys) 11.09.11P
Trike c/n overstamped on HRWB-0107 (NF 10.08.17)

G-MWKX Microflight Spectrum 016 03.08.90
C R Ions (Callerton, Tyne & Wear)
(IE 30.05.17)
(SSDR microlight since 04.15)

G-MWLD CFM Shadow Series CD 106 09.05.89
J A Weston (Sandwick, Shetland) 18.12.15P
(NF 19.09.18)

G-MWLE Solar Wings Pegasus XL-R SW-WA-1474 09.08.90
D Stevenson Plaistows Farm, St Albans 30.07.06P
Trike c/n SW-TB-1425 (NF 06.06.18)

G-MWLG Solar Wings Pegasus XL-R SW-WA-1476 09.08.90
C Cohen (Birmingham B35) 18.04.18P
Trike c/n SW-TB-1427

G-MWLL Solar Wings Pegasus XL-Q SW-WQ-0338 16.08.90
A J Bacon (Catfield, Norfolk) 15.10.14P
Trike c/n SW-TE-0287, sailwing from G-MTYN
(IE 04.02.16)

G-MWLN Whittaker MW6-S Fatboy Flyer xxxx 16.08.90
S J Field (Edgarley, Glastonbury) *'Red Lips'* 05.06.92P
Built by S J Field – project PFA 164-11844 (NF 09.12.15)

G-MWLP Mainair Gemini Flash 801-0990-5-W594 24.08.90
K M Husecken East Fortune 28.03.18P

G-MWLS	Medway Hybred 44XLR	MR081/95	29.08.90
	M A Oliver Glassonby		28.12.06P
	(NF 15.04.15)		
G-MWLU	Solar Wings Pegasus XL-R/Se	SW-WA-1478	06.09.90
	T P G Ward (Meathop, Grange-over-Sands)		14.10.91P
	Trike c/n SW-TE-0294 (NF 14.03.18)		
G-MWLW	Team Mini-Max	xxxx	14.09.90
	R J Ripley Sackville Lodge Farm, Riseley		15.06.09P
	Built by W T Kirk – project PFA 186-11717		
	(SSDR microlight since 07.14) (NF 23.11.15)		
G-MWLX	Mainair Gemini Flash IIA	805-0990-7-W598	05.10.90
	D J May (Crosthwaite, Kendal)		20.05.19P
G-MWLZ	Rans S-4 Coyote	90.116	08.10.90
	A Russell tr Hedge Hopper Flying Group		
	(Ballyroney, Banbridge)		
	Built by T E G Buckett – project PFA 193-11887		
	(SSDR microlight since 06.14) (IE 27.08.17)		
G-MWMB	Powerchute Kestrel	00399	07.11.90
	S T P Askew (Melton Mowbray)		21.04.11P
	(IE 27.10.15)		
G-MWMC	Powerchute Kestrel	00400	07.11.90
	S T P Askew (Melton Mowbray)		03.10.05P
	(IE 27.04.17)		
G-MWMD	Powerchute Kestrel	00401	07.11.90
	S T P Askew (Melton Mowbray)		20.11.91P
	(IE 31.05.17)		
G-MWMH	Powerchute Kestrel	00405	07.11.90
	E W Potts Penrhiw Farm, Crymych		12.06.04P
	(NF 30.10.14)		
G-MWMI	Solar Wings Pegasus Quasar TC	SW-WQQ-0383	21.09.90
	R A Khosravi (Norwich)		01.04.18P
	Trike c/n SW-TQ-0043		
G-MWML	Solar Wings Pegasus Quasar	SW-WQQ-0386	21.09.90
	F A Collar Chatteris		15.06.18P
	Trike c/n SW-TQ-0046		
G-MWMM	Mainair Gemini Flash IIA	800-0890-7-W593	24.08.90
	J Dodd (Ash Magna, Whitchurch)		16.06.18P
G-MWMN	Solar Wings Pegasus XL-Q	SW-WQ-0387	02.10.90
	P A Arnold & N A Rathbone		
	(Coventry & Brinklow, Rugby)		14.05.08P
	Trike c/n SW-TE-0297 (IE 26.08.15)		
G-MWMO	Solar Wings Pegasus XL-Q	SW-WQ-0388	02.10.90
	D S F McNair Oban		07.07.18P
	Trike c/n SW-TE-0298		
G-MWMV	Solar Wings Pegasus XL-R	SW-WA-1484	05.10.90
	M Nutting (Birstall, Leicester)		08.04.09P
	Trike c/n SW-TE-0307 (NF 06.05.14)		
G-MWMW	Murphy Renegade Spirit UK	xxxx	21.08.89
	D M Casey (Shepton Mallet) *'Spirit of Cornwall'*		20.07.18P
	Built by M W Hanley – project PFA 188-11544		
G-MWMX	Mainair Gemini Flash IIA	810-1090-7-W603	17.10.90
	P G Hughes (Scotstown, Co Monaghan, Rol)		18.06.14P
	(NF 09.08.17)		
G-MWMY	Mainair Gemini Flash IIA	809-1090-7-W602	17.10.90
	G R Walker (Tywyn)		19.04.14P
	(NF 12.02.18)		
G-MWNB	Solar Wings Pegasus XL-Q	SW-WQ-0395	08.10.90
	G W F J Dear (Bournemouth)		27.10.18P
	Trike c/n SW-TE-0303		
G-MWND	Tiger Cub RL5A Sherwood Ranger LW xxxx		09.10.90
	A F Walters Longacre Farm, Sandy		13.06.03P
	Built by R Light – project PFA 237-12229;		
	active 03.19 (NF 20.01.09)		
G-MWNE	Mainair Gemini Flash IIA	803-1090-7-W596	17.10.90
	S W Crossman (Brookhouse, Lancaster)		16.09.18P
	(IE 18.09.18)		
G-MWNF	Murphy Renegade Spirit UK	xxxx	15.10.90
	R Haslam Brook Breasting Farm, Watnall		26.09.18P
	Built by D J White – project PFA 188-11853		
	(IE 05.07.17)		
G-MWNK	Solar Wings Pegasus Quasar TC	SW-WQQ-0403	01.11.90
	N Brigginshaw RAF Wyton		13.08.15P
	Trike c/n SW-TQA-0054 (IE 27.04.17)		

G-MWNL	Solar Wings Pegasus Quasar	SW-WQQ-0404	01.11.90
	N H S Insall Compton Abbas		28.11.15P
	Trike c/n SW-TQA-0055 (NF 13.09.17)		
G-MWNO	AMF Microflight Chevvron 2-32C	025	12.11.90
	J R Milnes Low Hill Farm, North Moor, Messingham		13.08.15P
	Noted 02.17		
G-MWNP	AMF Microflight Chevvron 2-32C	026	31.10.90
	M K Field Sleap		01.06.11P
	(NF 13.07.18)		
G-MWNR	Murphy Renegade Spirit UK	xxxx	12.11.90
	J J Lancaster Park Farm, Eaton Bray		09.04.18P
	Built by J J Lancaster – project PFA 188-11926		
G-MWNU	Mainair Gemini Flash IIA	813-1190-5-W606	06.11.90
	C C Muir Rookery Farm, Doynton		19.06.18P
G-MWNY	Powerchute Kestrel	00409	12.11.90
	Cancelled 18.06.01 by CAA		18.06.97
	Ballgawley *Stored 12.13*		
G-MWOC	Powerchute Kestrel	00413	12.11.90
	A Evans (Manorbier, Tenby)		
	(SSDR microlight since 09.15) (IE 26.08.15)		
G-MWOD	Powerchute Kestrel	00414	12.11.90
	T Morgan (Churchill, Kidderminster)		04.10.00P
	(NF 10.07.18)		
G-MWOI	Solar Wings Pegasus XL-R	SW-WA-1486	29.11.90
	B T Geoghegan (Burton-on-Trent)		16.06.18P
	Trike c/n SW-TB-1430		
G-MWON	CFM Shadow Series CD	K 128	18.12.90
	D A Crosbie Crosbie's Field, Little Cornard		
	Built by as Series SS		
	(SSDR microlight since 04.17) (NF 27.01.15)		
G-MWOO	Murphy Renegade Spirit UK	318	14.09.90
	R C Wood (Thetford)		15.09.12P
	Built by A Hipkin – project PFA 188-11811) (IE 06.10.17)		
G-MWOV	Whittaker MW6 Merlin	xxxx	09.01.91
	T J Gayton-Polley (Hadfold Farm, Adversane)		05.08.13P
	Built by C R Melhuish – project PFA 164-11301)		
	(IE 18.10.18)		
G-MWPB	Mainair Gemini Flash IIA	823-0191-7-W617	03.01.91
	J Fenton & S G Roberts St Michaels		06.03.18P
G-MWPD	Mainair Gemini Flash	824-0191-5-W618	09.01.91
	A Vaughan (Slayley, Hexham)		
	(SSDR microlight since 10.15) (NF 30.10.15)		
G-MWPH	Microflight Spectrum	020	09.01.91
	C G Chambers New Farm, Piddington		03.04.15P
	Stored 09.18 (NF 09.02.16)		
G-MWPK	Solar Wings Pegasus XL-Q	SW-WQ-0419	17.01.91
	Cancelled 29.10.10 as PWFU		12.07.08
	Strathaven *Trike c/n SW-TE-0313 Stored 05.13*		
G-MWPN	CFM Shadow Series CD	K 147	22.01.91
	W R H Thomas (Llethtryd, Swansea)		11.06.99P
	(NF 09.02.16)		
G-MWPP	CFM Streak Shadow	K 166-SA	14.02.91
	G-BTEM R B J Gordon (Farnham)		13.06.17P
	Built by C A Mortlock – project PFA 206-11992		
	(NF 05.10.18)		
G-MWPR	Whittaker MW6 Merlin	xxxx	15.10.90
	S F N Warnell (Staines)		
	Built by P J S Ritchie – project PFA 164-11260 (NF 05.12.14)		
G-MWPU	Solar Wings Pegasus Quasar TC	SW-WQQ-0426	20.02.91
	P R Murdock Newtownards		06.07.06P
	Trike c/n SW-TQC-0062 (NF 19.01.17)		
G-MWPW	AMF Microflight Chevvron 2-32C	027	26.11.90
	P G Morris (Stonehaven)		10.03.15P
	(NF 28.11.16)		
G-MWPZ	Murphy Renegade Spirit UK	xxxx	18.03.91
	J L Sparks St Athan		24.02.99P
	Built by J Ievers – project PFA 188-11631 (NF 23.11.18)		
G-MWRC	Mainair Gemini Flash IIA	820-0191-7-W614	05.02.91
	C J Eddies (Perton, Wolverhampton)		09.06.13P
	(IE 24.05.18)		
G-MWRE	Mainair Gemini Flash IIA	822-0191-7-W616	05.02.91
	Kendal College (Kendal)		05.08.12P
	(NF 06.04.16)		

G-MWRF Mainair Gemini Flash IIA 829-0191-7-W623 04.02.91
N Hay Hallyards Farm, Bucknall
(*SSDR microlight since 07.14*) (*IE 20.03.18*)

G-MWRH Mainair Gemini Flash IIA 831-0191-7-W625 05.02.91
K J Hughes (Wigan) 30.08.17P

G-MWRJ Mainair Gemini Flash IIA 832-0291-7-W626 28.02.91
P Mansfield (Rushden) 01.10.18P

G-MWRL CFM Shadow Series CD K 152 13.02.91
A M Morris (Wigan) 18.11.17P
(*IE 18.01.18*)

G-MWRN Solar Wings Pegasus XL-R SW-WA-1489 05.03.91
D T Mackenzie tr Malvern Aertow Club
Croft Farm, Defford 06.09.18P
Trike c/n SW-TE-0316

G-MWRS Ultravia Super Pelican E001-201 09.05.84
T B Woolley (Narborough, Leicester)
(*SSDR microlight since 05.14*) (*NF 30.11.17*)

G-MWRT Solar Wings Pegasus XL-R SW-WA-1492 15.03.91
G L Gunnell (Edgmond, Newport, Telford) 10.09.03P
Trike c/n SW-TB-1431 (*NF 10.03.16*)

G-MWRX Solar Wings Pegasus XL-Q SW-WQ-0432 25.03.91
Cancelled 24.03.09 by CAA 17.09.04
(Market Drayton) *Trike c/n SW-TE-0321 For sale 01.13*

G-MWRY CFM Shadow Series CD K 162 26.03.91
A T Armstrong Tinnel Farm, Landulph 12.09.13P
Lost power on take-off Tinnel Farm, Landulph 08.12.12
& extensively damaged; wreck noted 08.14 (NF 04.08.15)

G-MWSA Team Mini-Max 88 xxxx 08.04.91
A R Stratton (Aldershot)
Built by A N Baumber – project PFA 186-11855
(*SSDR microlight since 06.14*) (*NF 13.06.16*)

G-MWSC Rans S-6-ESD Coyote II 0191.152 13.05.91
E J D Heathfield tr G-MWSC Group
(Lowdham, Nottingham) 14.08.19P
Built by B E Francis – project PFA 204-12019;
tricycle u/c

G-MWSD Solar Wings Pegasus XL-Q SW-WQ-0430 06.03.91
A M Harley Coldharbour Farm, Willingham 19.09.17P
Trike c/n SW-TE-0319

G-MWSF Solar Wings Pegasus XL-R SW-WA-1497 10.04.91
J J Freeman (Gorleston) 22.08.15P
Trike c/n SW-TE-0324 (NF 07.03.17)

G-MWSI Solar Wings Pegasus Quasar TC SW-WQQ-0436 30.04.91
S Chambers (Easenhall, Rugby) 19.03.19P
Trike c/n SW-TQC-0065

G-MWSJ Solar Wings Pegasus XL-Q SW-WQ-0437 12.04.91
R J Collison Little Snoring 17.05.18P
Trike c/n SW-TE-0326

G-MWSK Solar Wings Pegasus XL-Q SW-WQ-0438 12.04.91
J Doogan (Galashields) 26.05.02P
Trike c/n SW-TE-0327 (NF 05.04.18)

G-MWSL Mainair Gemini Flash IIA 835-0491-7-W629 16.04.91
Cancelled 08.08.17 as PWFU 11.06.98
Holmfirth *For sale from Holmfirth area 06.18*

G-MWSM Mainair Gemini Flash IIA 836-0491-7-W630 16.04.91
R M Wall (Ripponden, Sowerby Bridge) 07.10.16P

G-MWSO Solar Wings Pegasus XL-R SW-WA-1503 25.04.91
M A Clayton (New Romney) 28.03.10P
Trike c/n SW-TE-0329 (NF 21.04.16)

G-MWSS Medway Hybred 44XLR MR117/97 07.05.91
Cancelled 07.10.11 as PWFU 28.05.10
Old Sarum *Stored 05.15*

G-MWST Medway Hybred 44XLR MR118/98 08.05.91
A Ferguson (Inverness IV2) 03.08.05P
(*NF 16.02.16*)

G-MWSU Medway Hybred 44XLR MR119/99 01.05.91
T de Landro Middle Stoke, Isle of Grain 04.05.13P
(*NF 15.10.15*)

G-MWSX Whittaker MW5 Sorcerer xxxx 03.05.91
A T Armstrong Tinnel Farm, Landulph
Built by A T Armstrong – project PFA 163-11549
(*SSDR microlight since 07.14*) (*NF 31.08.16*)

G-MWSY Whittaker MW5 Sorcerer xxxx 03.05.91
J E Holloway Tinnel Farm, Landulph
Built by J E Holloway – project PFA 163-11218
(*SSDR microlight since 06.14*) (*NF 17.05.18*)

G-MWSZ CFM Shadow Series CD K 158 04.04.91
(G-MWRY) M W W Clotworthy
Wadswick Manor Farm, Corsham 11.10.15P
(*IE 24.02.16*)

G-MWTC Solar Wings Pegasus XL-Q SW-WQ-0446 08.05.91
M M Chittenden Rochester 04.08.12P
Trike c/n SW-TE-0334 (NF 22.10.15)

G-MWTE Microflight Spectrum 023 13.05.91
Cancelled 18.10.10 by CAA 20.06.04
Yatesbury *Noted 06.14*

G-MWTI Solar Wings Pegasus XL-Q SW-WQ-0274 23.05.91
J G Hilliard (Corby)
Trike c/n SW-TE-0251
(*SSDR microlight since 01.16*) (*IE 09.12.15*)

G-MWTJ CFM Shadow Series CD K 167 16.05.91
J S Harris tr Shadow Tango Juliet Group
Brook Farm, Pilling
Originally built as Series SS
(*SSDR microlight since 08.15*) (*IE 24.10.17*)

G-MWTL Solar Wings Pegasus XL-R SW-WA-1508 28.05.91
B Lindsay (Chipping Sodbury, Bristol) 13.07.07P
Trike c/n SW-TE-0336 (NF 06.08.18)

G-MWTN CFM Shadow Series CD K 153 23.05.91
M J Broom Buttermilk Hall Farm, Blisworth
Originally built as Series SS
(*SSDR microlight since 06.14*) (*IE 06.07.16*)

G-MWTO Mainair Gemini Flash IIA 840-0591-7-W634 28.05.91
M B Ryder-Jarvis Rossall Field, Cockerham 28.10.16P
(*NF 03.08.17*)

G-MWTP CFM Shadow Series CD K 107 23.05.91
P J F Spedding Hamilton Farm, Bilsington 15.06.13P
Landed in crops Grange Farm, Market Rasen
12.07.13 & substantially damaged (NF 23.01.19)

G-MWTT Rans S-6-ESD Coyote II 0391.175 30.04.91
L E Duffin (Alford, Aberdeen) 'Warrior 2' 28.11.07P
Built by I K Radcliffe – project PFA 204-12016;
tricycle u/c (NF 16.09.14)

G-MWTZ Mainair Gemini Flash IIA 844-0691-7-W638 12.06.91
C W R Felce Sackville Lodge Farm, Riseley 06.08.10P
(*NF 26.01.16*)

G-MWUA CFM Shadow Series CD K 161 10.06.91
P A James (Chatham) 21.06.05P
(*NF 21.03.18*)

G-MWUD Solar Wings Pegasus XL Tug SW-WA-1512 12.06.91
A J Weir (Melksham) 02.10.16P
Trike c/n SW-TE-0340

G-MWUI AMF Microflight Chevvron 2-32C 029 02.07.91
S Wilson tr Group G-MWUI Beverley (Linley Hill)
'Miss Behavin' 27.05.18P

G-MWUK Rans S-6-ESD Coyote II 0491.187 01.07.91
G K Hoult Gloucestershire 16.05.18P
Built by G K Hoult – project PFA 204-12090;
tricycle u/c

G-MWUL Rans S-6-ESD Coyote II 0391.172 10.06.91
D M Bayne East Fortune 15.05.18P
Built by K J Lywood – project PFA 204-12054;
tricycle u/c

G-MWUN Rans S-6-ESD Coyote II 0391.173 10.06.91
J Parke Carrickmore 15.05.09P
Built by S Eland – project PFA 204-12075;
rebuilt c.1994 with kit no.0695.841 (ex G-IZIT);
tricycle u/c (NF 16.10.15)

G-MWUR Solar Wings Pegasus XL-R SW-WA-1518 21.06.91
S McMeekin tr Scottish Hang Gliding Club Balado 19.08.18P
Converted to Tug configuration; trike c/n SW-TE-0342

G-MWUU Solar Wings Pegasus XL-R SW-WA-1521 28.06.91
B R Underwood (Hampton Magna, Warwick) 04.02.18P
Trike c/n SW-TE-0346

G-MWUV Solar Wings Pegasus XL-R SW-WA-1522 28.06.91
T J Wiltshire tr XL Group (Holbeach, Spalding)
Trike c/n SW-TE-0347
(SSDR microlight since 05.14) (IE 02.07.18)

G-MWUX Solar Wings Pegasus XL-Q SW-WQ-0454 28.06.91
B D Attwell (Caerphilly) 27.05.13P
Originally supplied as wing only – trike origin unknown

G-MWVA Solar Wings Pegasus XL-Q SW-WQ-0457 28.06.91
W Frosina (Aberdeen AB24) 30.07.15P
Trike c/n SW-TE-0351 (NF 26.09.15)

G-MWVE Solar Wings Pegasus XL-R SW-WA-1524 18.07.91
W A Keel-Stocker (Norton, Gloucester) 30.06.12P
Trike c/n SW-TB-1441 (IE 20.07.18)

G-MWVF Solar Wings Pegasus XL-R/Se SW-WA-1525 18.07.91
J B Wright (Elford, Tamworth) 22.07.18P
Trike c/n SW-TB-1442

G-MWVG CFM Shadow Series CD 151 05.08.91
Shadow Aviation Ltd Old Sarum 16.10.18P

G-MWVH CFM Shadow Series CD 181 05.08.91
M McKenzie (Pitcaple, Inverurie) 25.08.07P
On rebuild but abandoned? (NF 17.04.15)

G-MWVL Rans S-6-ESD Coyote II 0892.341 13.08.91
J C Gates Hill Farm, Nayland 09.08.18P
Built by J D Hall – project PFA 204-12118;
tricycle u/c; damaged & repaired with new frame;
original s/n 0491.186 to G-MZAH

G-MWVM Solar Wings Pegasus Quasar IITC SW-WX-0020 02.09.91
G-65-8 A A Edmonds Shifnal 02.06.08P
Trike c/n SW-TQ-0031 – c/n duplicates G-MWLI
(NF 29.01.15)

G-MWVO Mainair Gemini Flash IIA 852-0891-7-W646 27.08.91
W W Hammond (Atherton, Manchester) 16.05.15P
(NF 07.07.17)

G-MWVP Murphy Renegade Spirit UK xxxx 22.08.91
P D Mickleburgh (Oakham) 06.03.18P
Built by I E Spencer – project PFA 188-11735

G-MWVR Mainair Gemini Flash IIA 855-0991-7-W650 30.08.91
Cancelled 20.10.11 by CAA 21.05.11
Eshott *Stored 05.15*

G-MWVT Mainair Gemini Flash IIA 860-1091-7-W655 02.09.91
P J Newman (Beeston, Nottingham) 01.04.16P
(IE 06.10.17)

G-MWVZ Mainair Gemini Flash IIA 863-1091-7-W658 04.09.91
R W Twamley (Coventry) 18.06.13P
(IE 26.07.16)

G-MWWB Mainair Gemini Flash IIA 864-1091-7-W659 18.09.91
W P Seward Ley Farm, Chirk
Noted 09.17
(SSDR microlight since 10.14) (IE 06.07.16)

G-MWWC Mainair Gemini Flash IIA 868-1191-7-W663 23.09.91
A & D Margereson (Wingerworth, Chesterfield) 16.04.16P

G-MWWD Murphy Renegade Spirit UK 344? 23.09.91
R M Hughes (Rhewl, Ruthin) 19.11.18P
Built by A M Smyth & J M Walter
– project PFA 188-11719

G-MWWH Solar Wings Pegasus XL-Q SW-WQ-0469 03.10.91
A J Alexander Brook Breasting Farm, Watnall 21.03.12P
Trike c/n SW-TE-0356 (NF 23.04.15)

G-MWWI Mainair Gemini Flash IIA 870-1291-7-W665 11.10.91
M A S Nesbitt Strathaven
(SSDR microlight since 10.14) (NF 15.08.16)

G-MWWL Rans S-6-ESD Coyote II xxxx 17.10.91
(G-BTXD) Cancelled 26.03.07 as PWFU 12.06.05
Lower Mountpleasant Farm, Chatteris
Built by J E Carr – project PFA 204-11849; stored 06.13

G-MWWN Mainair Gemini Flash IIA 872-1291-7-W667 22.10.91
M M Pope (Little Ellingham, Norfolk) 22.07.17P

G-MWWP Rans S-4 Coyote 90.115 21.10.91
Cancelled 04.06.10 by CAA 01.08.00
Keddington, Lincs *Built by R H Braithwaite – project*
PFA 193-12073; stored Brocklebank reclamation yard 06.14

G-MWWS Thruster T300 089-T300-370 04.11.91
EI-BYW J H Milne
Great Friars' Thornes Farm, Swaffham
Built by Tempest Aviation Ltd (NF 07.11.16)
(SSDR microlight since 11.16)

G-MWWV Solar Wings Pegasus XL-Q SW-WQ-0470 30.10.91
R W Livingstone (Lisnaskea, Enniskillen) 07.08.08P
Trike c/n SW-TE-0357 (IE 26.08.15)

G-MWWZ Cyclone Chaser S 447 CH829 29.10.91
P K Dale (Thornton Watlass, Ripon)
(SSDR microlight since 05.14) (IE 21.04.17)

G-MWXA Mainair Gemini Flash IIA 873-0192-7-W668 30.10.91
Cancelled 24.05.12 as destroyed 29.11.09
Strathaven *Pod only stored 05.13*

G-MWXC Mainair Gemini Flash IIA 874-0192-7-W669 06.11.91
Cancelled 27.10.11 as PWFU
Strathaven *Pod only stored 05.13*

G-MWXF Mainair Mercury 867-1191-5-W662 12.11.91
C Dunford (Calder Grove, Wakefield) 25.07.19P

G-MWXG Solar Wings Pegasus Quasar IITC SW-WQT-0471 07.11.91
Cancelled 17.01.12 by CAA 16.09.08
Bagby *Trike c/n SW-TQC-0074*
Stored 06.14, reported gone by 05.15

G-MWXH Solar Wings Pegasus Quasar IITC SW-WQT-0472 07.11.91
R G Wall Pen-y-Parc Farm, Caerleon 26.07.18P
Trike c/n SW-TQC-0075

G-MWXJ Mainair Mercury 861-1091-5-W656 15.11.91
P J Taylor Beverley (Linley Hill) 31.03.06P
(NF 20.11.14)

G-MWXK Mainair Mercury 862-1191-5-W657 15.11.91
M P Wilkinson (Sandtoft) 18.07.96P
(NF 10.09.14)

G-MWXP Solar Wings Pegasus XL-Q SW-WQ-0475 26.11.91
A P Attfield (Wick, Bristol) 18.08.99P
Trike c/n SW-TE-0359 (NF 22.06.18)

G-MWXU Mainair Gemini Flash IIA 882-0192-7-W677 09.12.91
Cancelled 17.01.11 as PWFU 23.01.03
Strathaven *Pod only stored 08.13*

G-MWXV Mainair Gemini Flash IIA 879-1291-7-W674 09.12.91
T A Daniel Pembrey 17.04.18P

G-MWXX Cyclone Chaser S 447 CH831 09.12.91
(G-MWEB), (G-MWCD)
P I Frost Chiltern Park, Wallingford
(SSDR microlight since 05.14) (NF 25.07.17)

G-MWXY Cyclone Chaser S 447 CH832 19.12.91
(G-MWEC) D Reckett (Kingsbridge)
(SSDR microlight since 05.14) (IE 20.09.18)

G-MWXZ Cyclone Chaser S 508 CH836 31.12.91
D L Hadley (Petham, Canterbury)
(SSDR microlight since 05.14) (IE 06.08.15)

G-MWYA Mainair Gemini Flash IIA 886-0292-7-W681 03.01.92
R F Hunt St Michaels 11.02.18P

G-MWYC Solar Wings Pegasus XL-Q SW-WQ-0486 15.01.92
D W Curtis Shifnal
Trike c/n SW-TE-0365
(SSDR microlight since 10.14) (IE 06.10.17)

G-MWYD CFM Shadow Series C K 179 08.01.92
W J I Robb Causeway 21.07.18P

G-MWYE Rans S-6-ESD Coyote II 0591.189 10.01.92
G A M Moffat (Mobberley, Knutsford) 28.04.17P
Built by G A Squires – project PFA 204-12223;
tricycle u/c

G-MWYG Mainair Gemini Flash IIA 884-0292-7-W679 15.01.92
J H McIvor Newtownards
(SSDR microlight since 06.18) (IE 14.07.17)

G-MWYI Solar Wings Pegasus Quasar IITC SW-WQT-0488 30.01.92
T J Lundie Longacre Farm, Sandy 08.04.18P
Trike c/n SW-TQC-0083

G-MWYJ Solar Wings Pegasus Quasar IITC SW-WQT-0489 24.01.92
A S Wason Lower Upham Farm, Chiseldon 24.10.18P
Trike c/n SW-TQC-0084

G-MWYL Mainair Gemini Flash IIA 877-0192-7-W672 17.01.92
A J Hinks (Aberdeen) 01.05.19P

G-MWYM Cyclone Chaser S 1000   CH838   21.01.92
C J Meadows   (Shepton Mallet)
Reported as rebuild of G-MVJI – perhaps trike only?
(SSDR microlight since 06.14) (IE 04.08.17)

G-MWYP CGS Hawk II Arrow   H-T-468-R447   24.01.92
N216HK   Cancelled 09.02.93 as sold in France
Causeway   *Stored still as N216HK 02.16*

G-MWYR CGS AG-Hawk   H-T-469-R447-AG   24.01.92
N217HK   Cancelled 09.02.93 as sold in France
Causeway   *Stored still as N217HK 02.16*

G-MWYS CGS ArrowFlight Hawk I Arrow   H-T-470   17.02.93
D W Hermiston-Hooper t/a Civilair   (Ryde, Isle of Wight)
Built by Arrowflight Ltd – project BMAA/HB/020;
categorised as Seaplane from 10.14; project
believed to have been abandoned

G-MWYT Mainair Gemini Flash IIA   881-0392-7-W676   03.02.92
A J Geary & P K Morley   Ings Farm, Yedingham   28.08.15P
(IE 06.10.17)

G-MWYU Solar Wings Pegasus XL-Q   SW-WQ-0491   30.01.92
J S Hawkins   (Ashreigny, Chulmleigh)
Original trike c/n SW-TE-0364 donated to G-MTFB;
replacement trike c/n SW-TE-0093 ex G-MVGU
(SSDR microlight since 06.15) (IE 18.06.15)

G-MWYV Mainair Gemini Flash IIA   896-0392-7-W691   03.02.92
R Bricknell   Bankwood Farm, Oxton   20.09.17P

G-MWYY Solar Wings Pegasus XL-Q   SW-WQ-0492   17.02.92
R D Allard   (Weldon, Corby)   13.07.12P
Trike c/n SW-TE-0365 (NF 17.11.15)

G-MWZA Mainair Mercury   888-0292-5-W683   07.02.92
M Willan   (Tyldesley, Manchester)   21.04.16P

G-MWZB AMF Microflight Chevvron 2-32C   033   10.02.92
E Ratcliffe   Acaster Malbis   27.10.12P
(NF 03.08.18)

G-MWZF Solar Wings Pegasus Quasar IITC   SW-WQT-0496   17.02.92
I A Macadam   (Hinton St Mary, Sturminster Newton)   26.07.18P
Trike c/n SW-TQD-0108 duplicates G-MYEK

G-MWZL Mainair Gemini Flash IIA   900-0492-7-W695   17.02.92
D Renton   East Fortune   05.07.04P
(NF 29.03.18)

G-MWZO Solar Wings Pegasus Quasar IITC   SW-WQT-0498   26.02.92
A Robinson   (Marston Montgomery, Ashbourne)   27.03.06P
Trike c/n SW-TQC-0089 (NF 30.05.18)

G-MWZP Solar Wings Pegasus Quasar IITC   SW-WQT-0499   26.02.92
C Garton   Enstone   *'Grace'*   19.02.17P
Trike c/n SW-TQC-0090 (IE 28.03.17)

G-MWZR Solar Wings Pegasus Quasar IITC   SW-WQT-0500   26.02.92
N Dyczko   (Sheffield S2)   11.06.08P
Trike c/n SW-TQC-0091 (NF 11.07.18)

G-MWZS Solar Wings Pegasus Quasar IITC   SW-WQT-0501   26.02.92
EI-CIP, G-MWZS
A M Charlton   Greenhills Farm, Wheatley Hill   31.10.17P
Trike c/n SW-TQC-0092

G-MWZU Solar Wings Pegasus XL-R   SW-WA-1536   26.02.92
K J Slater   (Stretton, Burton-on-Trent)   08.06.12P
Trike c/n SW-TE-0371 (NF 07.01.15)

G-MWZY Solar Wings Pegasus XL-R   SW-WA-1540   26.02.92
Darley Moor Airsports Club Ltd   Darley Moor   04.11.13P
Trike c/n SW-TE-0375 (NF 15.09.16)

G-MWZZ Solar Wings Pegasus XL-R   SW-WA-1541   26.02.92
The Microlight School (Lichfield) Ltd   Fisherwick   08.03.13P
Trike c/n SW-TE-0376 (NF 03.09.16)

G-MXII Pitts Model 12   xxxx   12.10.12
P T Borchert   Old Sarum   24.08.19P
Built by P T Borchert – project LAA 349-15116

G-MXMX Piper PA-46R-350T Malibu Matrix   4692088   17.12.08
N61002   Feabrex Ltd   Lydd   28.02.18E

G-MXPH BAC 167 Strikemaster Mk.84   EEP/JP/1931   04.05.07
G-SARK, N2146S, Singapore AF 311, G-27-140
Voodooair Ltd   RAF Leeming   30.08.18P
Plane Set 148; as '311' in Singapore Air
Defence Command c/s (NF 30.10.18)

G-MXPI Robinson R44 Raven II   12827   05.08.14
OK-SIM, G-CGAE   MG Group Ltd   Blackbushe   22.06.18E
Operated by Phoenix Helicopters

G-MXVI Supermarine 361 Spitfire LF.XVIe   CBAF IX 4394   17.02.89
6850M, TE184, TE184   S R Stead   Biggin Hill   21.03.19P
As 'TE184:9N-B' in RAF c/s

G-MYAB Solar Wings Pegasus XL-R/Se   SW-WA-1542   26.02.92
A N F Stewart   Red House Farm, Preston Capes   04.08.14P
Trike c/n SW-TE-0377 (IE 30.04.15)

G-MYAC Solar Wings Pegasus XL-Q   SW-WQ-0502   26.02.92
M E Gilman   (North Rode, Congleton)   10.11.14P
Trike c/n SW-TE-0378 (NF 16.02.16)

G-MYAF Solar Wings Pegasus XL-Q   SW-WQ-0505   26.02.92
J H S Booth   (Abernethy, Perth)
Trike c/n SW-TE-0381
(SSDR microlight since 07.17) (NF 08.01.18)

G-MYAH Whittaker MW5 Sorcerer   xxxx   02.03.92
A R Hawes   (Needham Market)
Built by T Knight – project PFA 163-11233
(SSDR microlight since 06.14) (IE 04.08.18)

G-MYAN Whittaker MW5-K Sorcerer   5K-0017-02   24.03.92
(G-MWNI)   A F Reid   Unicarval House, Comber
Built by Aerotech International Ltd; Full Lotus floats
(SSDR microlight since 08.16) (NF 05.09.17)

G-MYAO Mainair Gemini Flash IIA   894-0392-7-W689   11.03.92
K R Emery   Sittles Farm, Alrewas
(SSDR microlight since 02.16) (IE 09.09.16)

G-MYAR Thruster T300   9022-T300-502   12.03.92
G Hawkins   Newton Peveril Farm, Sturminster Marshall   02.09.07
Built by Tempest Aviation Ltd (NF 17.01.19)

G-MYAS Mainair Gemini Flash IIA   895-0392-7-W690   11.03.92
J R Davis   Over Farm, Gloucester   15.06.10P
(NF 14.03.18)

G-MYAT Team Mini-Max 88   xxxx   06.03.92
C J Gillam   (Whitwell, York)
Built by D M Couling – project PFA 186-12017
(SSDR microlight since 06.14) (NF 30.10.18)

G-MYAY Microlight Spectrum   027   13.03.92
Cancelled 27.10.10 as PWFU   21.12.00
Eshott   *Derelict 07.17*

G-MYAZ Murphy Renegade Spirit UK   xxxx   16.03.92
R Smith   Kilkerran   10.10.03P
Built by R Smith – project PFA 188-12027;
noted dismantled 05.14 (NF 13.05.18)

G-MYBA Rans S-6-ESD Coyote II   1291.247   12.03.92
A M Hughes   Popham   20.01.19P
Built by S M Vickers – project PFA 204-12210;
frame carries '1291.247.0800' – re-dated
after rebuild?; tailwheel u/c

G-MYBB UK Drifter   MD.001   09.04.92
M Ingleton   Harringe Court, Sellindge
Imported Medway Microlights as Maxair Drifter &
rebuilt by M Ingleton as UK Drifter s/n BMAA/HB/014
(SSDR microlight since 05.15) (IE 24.05.17)

G-MYBC CFM Shadow Series CD   K.196   18.03.92
P C H Clarke   (Bretton, Peterborough)
Built by T S Moore – project PFA 206-12221;
type series denotes Streak Shadow & project
BMAA/HB/047 (IE 30.04.15)

G-MYBF Solar Wings Pegasus XL-Q   SW-WQ-0513   26.03.92
S J Hillyard   Monewden   18.11.17P
Trike c/n SW-TE-0384; noted 01.18

G-MYBJ Mainair Gemini Flash IIA   908-0592-7-W706   02.04.92
I P Maltas   (Hull)   01.08.16P
(SSDR microlight since 03.18) (NF 13.05.18)

G-MYBM Team Mini-Max 91   xxxx   03.04.92
B Hunter   Manchester Barton
Built by M K Dring – project PFA 186-12212
(SSDR microlight since 08.16) (IE 15.12.17)

G-MYBT Solar Wings Pegasus Quasar IITC   SW-WQT-0519   16.04.92
G A Rainbow-Ockwell   Redlands   07.08.17P
Trike c/n SW-TQC-0097

G-MYBU Cyclone Chaser S 447   CH837   28.04.92
G-69-15, G-MYBU   P B J Eveleigh   Great Oakley   21.01.00P
(IE 10.05.16)
(SSDR microlight since 05.14)

G-MYBW Solar Wings Pegasus XL-Q   SW-WQ-0523   05.05.92
J S Chapman   (Flaxby, Knaresborough)   12.10.10P
Trike c/n SW-TE-0394 (NF 05.08.18)

G-MYCA Whittaker MW6-T Merlin   xxxx   14.05.92
C M Byford   (Long Marston)   23.06.06P
Built by E Barfoot & N B Morley
– project PFA 164-11821 (NF 04.10.17)

G-MYCB Cyclone Chaser S 447   CH839   18.05.92
S D Voysey   (Axminster)
(SSDR microlight since 06.14) (IE 17.08.15)

G-MYCE Solar Wings Pegasus Quasar IITC   SW-WQT-0527   14.05.92
S W Barker   (Scalby, Scarborough)   01.09.18P
Trike c/n SW-TQC-0098

G-MYCJ Mainair Mercury   906-0592-5-W704   19.05.92
D W B Aitken   East Fortune   04.01.18P

G-MYCK Mainair Gemini Flash IIA   909-0592-7-W707   19.05.92
A W Gunn   (Driby Manor, Alford)
(SSDR microlight since 11.17) (IE 07.11.17)

G-MYCL Mainair Mercury   910-0592-5-W708   19.05.92
P B Cole   (Wrenbury, Nantwich)   13.09.05P
(NF 17.03.16)

G-MYCM CFM Shadow Series CD   196   20.05.92
A K Robinson   Low Hill Farm, North Moor, Messingham   09.05.18P

G-MYCN   Mainair Mercury   901-0492-5-W696   22.05.92
Cancelled 20.01.16 by CAA   14.09.08
Newtownards   *Stored 10.17*

G-MYCO Murphy Renegade Spirit UK   xxxx   28.05.92
T P Williams   (Penmaenmawr)   16.12.08P
Built by C Slater – project PFA 188-12020
(NF 20.07.15)

G-MYCP Whittaker MW6 Merlin   xxxx   02.06.92
K R Emery   Sittles Farm, Alrewas
Built by R M Clarke – project PFA 164-11505)
(SSDR microlight since 05.17) (IE 09.09.16

G-MYCS Mainair Gemini Flash IIA   911-0592-7-W710   12.06.92
M J Rankin   Dunkeswell   09.09.17P

G-MYCT Team Mini-Max 91   xxxx   30.03.92
R J Turner   Chatteris   04.07.13P
Built by M A Curant – project PFA 186-12163
(SSDR microlight since 02.17) (IE 23.10.17)

G-MYCX Powerchute Kestrel   00421   15.06.92
S J Pugh-Jones   (Meinciau, Kidwelly)
Sailwing s/n 160207
(SSDR microlight since 05.14) (NF 13.09.17)

G-MYDA Powerchute Kestrel   00424   15.06.92
A E Askew   (Melton Mowbray)   02.08.07P
(IE 13.12.16)

G-MYDC Mainair Mercury   916-0792-5-W715   23.06.92
D Moore   St Michaels   24.02.18P

G-MYDE CFM Shadow Series CD   K 187   24.06.92
D N L Howell   Hoe Farm, Colwall   06.04.13P
(NF 16.02.16)

G-MYDF Team Mini-Max 91   xxxx   24.06.92
J L Barker   Priory Farm, Tibenham
Built by L G Horne – project PFA 186-12129
(SSDR microlight since 08.14) (NF 12.07.18)

G-MYDJ Solar Wings Pegasus XL-R   SW-WA-1558   01.07.92
D C Richardson & R C Wood tr Cambridgeshire
Aerotow Club   Sutton Meadows   01.06.18P
Converted to Tug configuration; trike c/n SW-TE-0403

G-MYDK Rans S-6-ESD Coyote II   0392.276   21.04.92
J W Caush & K Southam   Eshott   10.08.18P
Built by D N Kershaw – project PFA 204-12239;
tricycle u/c

G-MYDM Whittaker MW6-S Fatboy Flyer   xxxx   26.06.92
Cancelled 07.01.13 by CAA   05.11.10
Rathcash East, Co Kilkenny   *Built by S J Field &*
R Hemsworth – project PFA 164-12105; stored 06.17

G-MYDN Quad City Challenger II   xxxx   30.06.92
J E Barlow   Slieve Croob, Castlewellan   28.09.08P
Built by T C Hooks – project PFA 177-12245
(IE 21.04.17)

G-MYDT Thruster T300   9072-T300-506   21.07.92
A J L Eves   Wing Farm, Longbridge Deverill   09.09.19P
Built by Tempest Aviation Ltd

G-MYDU Thruster T300   9072-T300-504   21.07.92
S Collins   (Killineer, Drogheda, RoI)   16.11.07P
Built by Tempest Aviation Ltd (NF 20.10.14)

G-MYDV Mainair Gemini Flash IIA (modified)
          917-0892-7-W716   29.07.92
S J Mazilis   St Michaels   11.07.18P

G-MYDX Rans S-6-ESD Coyote II   0392.279   27.07.92
A Tucker   (Taunton)   06.06.16P
Built by R J Goodburn – project PFA 204-12238;
tricycle u/c

G-MYDZ Mignet HM-1000 Balerit   66   03.08.92
D S Simpson   Graveley Hall Farm, Graveley   20.09.13P
(IE 22.09.15)

G-MYEA Solar Wings Pegasus XL-Q   SW-WQ-0537   28.07.92
A M Taylor   Wolverhampton Halfpenny Green   13.08.18P
Trike c/n SW-TE-0404

G-MYEI Cyclone Chaser S 447   CH841   18.08.92
D J Hyatt   (Nevill Park, Tunbridge Wells)
(SSDR microlight since 05.14) (NF 19.07.18)

G-MYEJ Cyclone Chaser S 447   CH842   18.08.92
A W Lowrie   Baxby Manor, Husthwaite
(SSDR microlight since 05.14) (IE 21.10.17)

G-MYEK Solar Wings Pegasus Quasar IITC   SW-WQT-0540   07.08.92
The Microlight School (Lichfield) Ltd   Fisherwick   06.06.19P
Trike c/n SW-TQD-0108 duplicates G-MWZF

G-MYEM Solar Wings Pegasus Quasar IITC   SW-WQT-0542   07.08.92
D J Moore   (Oakington, Cambridge)   03.04.13P
Trike c/n SW-TQD-0101 (NF 03.08.17)

G-MYEN Solar Wings Pegasus Quasar IITC   SW-WQT-0543   07.08.92
T J Feeney   Wolverhampton Halfpenny Green   27.12.17P
Trike c/n SW-TQD-0105

G-MYEP CFM Shadow Series CD   K 205   13.08.92
A Halsall   Ince   21.06.19P

G-MYER Cyclone AX2000   CA 001   19.08.92
G-69-27, G-MYER, G-69-5, 59-GF
T F Horrocks   Wick John O'Groats   22.11.15P
(IE 20.12.16)

G-MYFA Powerchute Kestrel   00429   28.08.92
M Phillips   (Redditch)
(SSDR microlight since 05.14) (NF 12.07.16)

G-MYFL Solar Wings Pegasus Quasar IITC   SW-WQT-0541/A   11.09.92
C C Wright   Wolverhampton Halfpenny Green   14.03.18P
Trike c/n SW-TQD-0103: replacement wing s/n
SW-WQT-0541/A fitted after original SW-WQT-0554
stolen 01.93

G-MYFO Cyclone Chaser S   CH843   22.09.92
M H Broadbent   Westfield Farm, Hailsham
(SSDR microlight since 07.14) (IE 21.10.16)

G-MYFP Mainair Gemini Flash IIA   920-0992-7-W719   02.10.92
A O'Connor   Rossall Field, Cockerham   29.04.18P

G-MYFR Mainair Gemini Flash IIA   921-0992-7-W720   30.09.92
Cancelled 12.08.14 by CAA   09.11.14
Pinczow-Ladowsko, Poland   *Stored 11.14*

G-MYFT Mainair Scorcher   922-0992-3-W234   30.09.92
E Kirkby   (Barford, Warwick)
(SSDR microlight since 04.16) (IE 27.04.17)

G-MYFV Cyclone AX3/503   C 2083050   06.10.92
I J Webb   (Basingstoke)   15.11.12P
(NF 16.10.18)

G-MYFX Solar Wings Pegasus XL-Q   SW-WQ-0378   25.06.93
Cancelled 21.11.11 by CAA   24.08.04
Horsham   *Trike c/n SW-TE-0295*
For sale from Horsham area 03.18

G-MYGD Cyclone AX3/503   C 2083049   21.10.92
G M R Keenan   Easterton   18.01.17P
Noted parked outside at Stonefield Park,
Chilbolton 07.04.18 (IE 02.01.18)

G-MYGF Team Mini-Max 91   xxxx   22.10.92
W P Seward   Ley Farm, Chirk
Built by R D Barnard – project PFA 186-12175
(SSDR microlight since 06.14) (IE 23.09.17)

G-MYGK Cyclone Chaser S 508   CH846   03.11.92
P C Collins   (Llanbadoc, Usk)
(SSDR microlight since 08.16) (NF 14.06.18)

G-MYGM	Quad City Challenger II	CH2-0391-UK-0662	06.11.92

G-MYGM Quad City Challenger II   CH2-0391-UK-0662   06.11.92
S J Luck   Sandhill Farm, Shrivenham
Built by R Holt – project PFA 177-12261
(SSDR microlight since 04.16) (IE 31.05.17)

G-MYGO CFM Shadow Series CD   K 114   28.07.92
D B Bullard   (Abbeyleix, Co Laois, RoI)   06.05.16P

G-MYGP Rans S-6-ESD Coyote II   0992.349   30.10.18
The Spirit of Goole
Low Hill Farm, North Moor, Messingham   07.06.19P
Built by J S Melville – project PFA 204-12368;
tailwheel u/c

G-MYGR Rans S-6-ESD Coyote II   0992.348   16.11.92
F C J Denton   Felthorpe   09.07.18P
Built by D K Haughton – project PFA 204-12378

G-MYGT Solar Wings Pegasus XL-R   SW-WA-1569   13.11.92
G A McCann tr Condors Aerotow Syndicate
Dunkeswell   15.08.18P
Trike c/n SW-TE-0413; converted to Tug configuration

G-MYGU Solar Wings Pegasus XL-R   SW-WA-1570   13.11.92
J A Sims   Stoodleigh Barton Farm, Stoodleigh   02.07.11P
Trike c/n SW-TE-0414 (NF 26.08.14)

G-MYGV Solar Wings Pegasus XL-R   SW-WA-1571   13.11.92
G M Birkett & J A Crofts   Penrhiw Farm, Crymych   09.04.07P
Trike c/n SW-TE-0415; converted to XL Tug
configuration (NF 16.12.14)

G-MYGZ Mainair Gemini Flash IIA   928-1192-7-W726   18.11.92
I N Blanchard   Priory Farm, Tibenham   01.05.18P

G-MYHG Cyclone AX3/503   C 2103070   27.11.92
N P Thomson   (Falkirk)   02.12.05P
(NF 19.12.14)

G-MYHI Rans S-6-ESD Coyote II   0692.312   08.12.92
I J Steele   (Marchington, Uttoxeter)   03.09.13P
Built by L N Anderson – project PFA 204-12279;
tailwheel u/c (NF 20.07.15)

G-MYHJ Cyclone AX3/503   C 2103073   11.12.92
D H Edwards   (Tynreithyn, Tregaron)   18.12.18P
Reported as keel tube c/n C 3093157 – see G-MYME

G-MYHK Rans S-6-ESD Coyote II   0692.311   03.12.92
R A Durance   (Ashby de la Launde, Lincoln)   04.07.18P
Built by J M Longley – project PFA 204-12349;
tricycle u/c (NF 08.07.18)

G-MYHL Mainair Gemini Flash IIA   932-0193-7-W730   21.12.92
M F Harper   (Lytham St Annes)   02.05.19P

G-MYHM Cyclone AX3/503   C 2103068   18.12.92
T H Knapton   Greenhills Farm, Wheatley Hill   09.08.19P
Also c/n CA.007

G-MYHN Mainair Gemini Flash IIA   933-0193-7-W731   29.12.92
A Atkin   (Stapleford, Lincoln)   08.08.19P

G-MYHP Rans S-6-ESD Coyote II   0892.343   08.01.93
D M Smith   Chase Farm, Little Burstead   26.03.15P
Built by D A Crompton – project PFA 204-12406;
tricycle u/c (NF 24.04.15)

G-MYHR Cyclone AX3/503   C 2103071   15.01.93
G-68-8, G-MYHR   C W Williams   Ley Farm, Chirk   27.06.05P
Damaged by hangar roof collapse 01.14 (NF 07.04.16)

G-MYHS Powerchute Kestrel   00433   26.01.93
Cancelled 07.02.11 by CAA   06.04.01
Ballygawley   *Frame no 00433, parachute no 931013*
Stored 12.13

G-MYIA Quad City Challenger II   xxxx   21.01.93
I Pearson   Bodmin
Built by I J Arkieson – project PFA 177-12400
(SSDR microlight since 06.14) (IE 15.12.17)

G-MYIF CFM Shadow Series CD   217   02.02.93
P J Edwards   Westonzoyland   30.06.18P

G-MYIH Mainair Gemini Flash IIA   0937-0293-7-W734   09.03.93
T L T Sheldrick   (Hoddesdon)   05.08.17P

G-MYII Team Mini-Max 91   xxxx   10.11.92
G H Crick   Broomclose Farm, Longbridge Deverill
Built by G W Peacock – project PFA 186-12119
(SSDR microlight since 08.16) (NF 31.07.17)

G-MYIK Kolb Twinstar Mk.III   K0003-0192   13.01.93
M Khalid   Redlands
Built by R P Smith – project PFA 205-12220;
kit imported by Mainair
(SSDR microlight since 02.17) (NF 01.08.17)

G-MYIL Cyclone Chaser S 508   CH849   03.03.93
R A Rawes   Over Farm, Gloucester
(SSDR microlight since 06.14) (IE 04.08.17)

G-MYIM Solar Wings Pegasus Quasar IITC   SW-WQT-0579   22.02.93
(EI-...), G-MYIM
D Forde   (Claregalway, Co Galway, RoI)   24.04.16P
Trike c/n SW-TQD-0122 (IE 06.07.16)

G-MYIN Solar Wings Pegasus Quasar IITC   SW-WQT-0580   22.02.93
W P Hughes   RAF Henlow   15.03.19P
Trike c/n SW-TQD-0123

G-MYIP CFM Shadow Series CD   K 198   16.03.93
D R G Whitelaw   Oban   20.09.18P

G-MYIR Rans S-6-ESD Coyote II   0892.344   17.03.93
M L Foden   (Midgham, Reading)   08.09.15P
Built by J Simpson – project PFA 204-12458;
tricycle u/c (NF 06.11.17)

G-MYIS Rans S-6-ESD Coyote II   0892.346   31.12.92
I S Everett & M Stott   Sackville Lodge Farm, Riseley   28.07.17P
Built by A J Wyatt – project PFA 204-12382;
tricycle u/c (IE 27.08.17)

G-MYIT Cyclone Chaser S 508   CH850   19.03.93
S D J Harvey   (Wormelon, Hereford)   28.03.99P
(SSDR microlight since 05.14) (NF 12.10.17)

G-MYIU Cyclone AX3/503   C 3013084   22.03.93
Ulster Seaplane Association Ltd   Causeway   27.04.18P

G-MYIV Mainair Gemini Flash IIA   938-0393-7-W735   30.03.93
P Norton & T Williams   Finmere   20.06.18P

G-MYIY Mainair Gemini Flash IIA   942-0493-7-W737   01.04.93
D Jackson   Arclid Green, Sandbach   21.07.16P
(IE 05.06.17)

G-MYIZ Team Mini-Max 91   xxxx   31.03.93
J C Longmore   Headon Farm, Retford
Built by J C Longmore – project PFA 186-12347
(SSDR microlight since 06.14) (IE 05.03.15)

G-MYJC Mainair Gemini Flash IIA   944-0593-7-W739   07.04.93
M N Irven   (Wittersham, Tenterden)
(SSDR microlight since 06.14) (IE 07.06.18)

G-MYJD Rans S-6-ESD Coyote II   0792.324   23.04.93
A M Charlton   Greenhills Farm, Wheatley Hill   03.09.19P
Built by D J Dimmer and B Robins
– project PFA 204-12360; tailwheel u/c

G-MYJF Thruster T300   9013-T300-509   14.04.93
P F McConville   Keenaghan-The Moy, Dungannon   04.01.18P
Built by Tempest Aviation Ltd

G-MYJG Thruster T300   9043-T300-510   14.04.93
J W Rice   Redlands   24.08.18P
Built by Tempest Aviation Ltd

G-MYJJ Solar Wings Pegasus Quasar IITC   SW-WQT-0591   27.04.93
S J Reader   Tatenhill   24.07.18P
Trike c/n SW-TQD-0131

G-MYJK Solar Wings Pegasus Quasar IITC   SW-WQT-0592   27.04.93
The Microlight School (Lichfield) Ltd   Fisherwick   03.03.13P
Trike c/n SW-TQD-0132 – built with
Cyclone c/n 6752 (NF 03.09.16)

G-MYJM Mainair Gemini Flash IIA   945-0593-7-W740   29.04.93
J G Treanor   Slieve Croob, Castlewellan   01.05.18P

G-MYJT Solar Wings Pegasus Quasar IITC   6582   19.05.93
S Ferguson   (Southport)   23.06.19P

G-MYJU Solar Wings Pegasus Quasar IITC   6573   19.05.93
C Lamb   Commonswood Farm, Northiam   04.09.17P
QuasarShift modifications

G-MYJXM Whittaker MW 8   xxxx   24.05.93
Cancelled 31.07.01 by CAA
Built by M W J Whittaker – project PFA 243-12345
With South Yorkshire Aircraft Museum, Doncaster

G-MYJZ Whittaker MW5-D Sorcerer   xxxx   22.04.93
P A Aston   Halwell
Built by J G Beesley – project PFA 163-12385
(SSDR microlight since 07.14) (IE 27.04.17)

G-MYKB Kolb Twinstar Mk.III   K0007-0193   31.03.93
T Antell   (Watergore, South Petherton)   12.09.17P
Built by J D Holt – project PFA 205-12398;
kit imported Mainair with c/n K0007-0193

G-MYKD Cyclone Chaser S 508   CH857   26.05.93
S D Pain   Rayne Hall Farm, Rayne
(SSDR microlight since 05.14) (IE 06.10.17)

G-MYKE CFM Shadow Series BD   K 031   14.01.88
M Hughes t/a MKH Engineering
(Greenlands, Rhedyn Coch)   26.10.96P
(NF 18.03.16)

G-MYKF Cyclone AX3/503   C 3013083   08.06.93
M A Collins   Eaglescott   24.07.07P
(IE 09.09.14)

G-MYKG Mainair Gemini Flash IIA   950-0693-7-W745   21.06.93
B D Walker   (St Martin's, Oswestry)   02.11.07P
(NF 06.11.18)

G-MYKH Mainair Gemini Flash IIA   951-0693-7-W746   21.06.93
A W Leadley   Finn Valley, RoI   25.06.16P
Sailwing ex G-CBHG fitted 04.16 (IE 21.04.17)

G-MYKJ Team Mini-Max   xxxx   10.06.93
J P Pullin   Westonzoyland
Built by M Hill – project PFA 186-12215
(SSDR microlight since 06.14) (NF 01.05.18)

G-MYKO Whittaker MW6-S Fatboy Flyer   xxxx   25.06.93
J A Weston   (Hoswick, Sandwick)   23.09.10P
Built by J Glover & M Phillips – project
PFA 164-11919; stored 05.16 (NF 15.05.14)

G-MYKR Solar Wings Pegasus Quasar IITC   6635   07.07.93
C Stallard   Chase Farm, Little Burstead   03.10.17P

G-MYKS Solar Wings Pegasus Quasar IITC   6780   07.07.93
D J Oskis   Middle Stoke, Isle of Grain   16.09.16P
Fitted with new trike c/n 6780 (IE 22.04.17)

G-MYKV Mainair Gemini Flash IIA   954-0793-7-W749   13.07.93
P J Gulliver   Shifnal   29.09.18P

G-MYKW Mainair Mercury   960-0893-7-W755   09.07.93
Cancelled 24.02.11 by CAA   09.11.08
Eshott   *Stored 07.15*

G-MYKX Mainair Mercury   961-0893-7-W756   03.09.93
K Medd   Kenyon Hall Farm, Kenyon   10.07.18P

G-MYKY Mainair Mercury   962-0893-7-W757   06.08.93
P M Kelsey   Turners Arms Farm, Yearby   14.08.18P

G-MYKZ Team Mini-Max 91   xxxx   26.07.93
G-BVAV   J Batchelor   Gerpins Farm, Upminster
Built by P A Ellis – project PFA 186-11841
(SSDR microlight since 02.15) (IE 06.10.16)

G-MYLC Solar Wings Pegasus Quantum 15   6634   09.08.93
M D Morris   Kirkbride   24.03.18P

G-MYLD Rans S-6-ESD Coyote II   0892.350   01.03.93
A W Nancarrow   (Shoreham-by-Sea)   16.10.16P
Built by L R H d'Eath – project PFA 204-12394;
tailwheel u/c; crashed into trees near Cobham
26.08.16 & substantially damaged

G-MYLE Solar Wings Pegasus Quantum 15   6609   09.08.93
R S Mott tr Quantum Quartet   Enstone   20.01.11P
Badged 'Lite' (NF 27.08.15)

G-MYLF Rans S-6-ESD Coyote II   0493.483   04.08.93
A J Spencer   Eagle Moor, Grantham   *'Low Flyer'*   22.09.17P
Built by G R and J A Pritchard – project
PFA 204-12544; tricycle u/c

G-MYLG Mainair Gemini Flash IIA   959-0893-7-W754   06.08.93
P J Mezzo   (Sunderland)
(SSDR microlight since 11.17) (IE 05.10.18)

G-MYLH Solar Wings Pegasus Quantum 15   6632   11.08.93
D Parsons   Harringe Court, Sellindge   02.08.15P
(NF 26.11.15)

G-MYLI Solar Wings Pegasus Quantum 15   6645   11.08.93
A M Keyte   (Stony Stratford, Milton Keynes)   21.04.18P

G-MYLM Solar Wings Pegasus Quantum 15   6651   31.08.93
(EC-...), G-MYLM
R G Hearsey   Commonswood Farm, Northiam   15.11.18P

G-MYLN Kolb Twinstar Mk.III   K0010-0193   03.09.93
J F Joyes   Chiltern Park, Wallingford   04.06.19P
Built by G E Collard – project PFA 205-12430;
kit c/n K0010-0193 imported by Mainair

G-MYLO Rans S-6-ESD Coyote II   0692.313   09.09.93
J G Burns & W Lucy   Morgansfield, Fishburn   20.08.19P
Built by J G Dance and P E Lewis – project
PFA 204-12334: frame may be kit no. 0692.315;
tricycle u/c

G-MYLR Mainair Gemini Flash IIA   964-0993-7-W759   17.09.93
A L Lyall   East Fortune   04.03.18P

G-MYLS Mainair Mercury   966-0993-7-W761   05.10.93
W K C Davies   Old Park Farm, Margam   27.03.12P
(NF 05.03.15)

G-MYLT Mainair Blade 912   967-1093-7-W762   23.09.93
T D Hall   Finmere   28.11.17P

G-MYLV CFM Shadow Series CD   220   24.09.93
Aviation for Paraplegics & Tetraplegics Trust
Old Sarum   22.04.18P

G-MYLW Rans S-6-ESD Coyote II   1292.401   04.08.93
A D Dias   Otherton   19.07.19P
Built by J R Worswick – project PFA 204-12560;
tricycle u/c

G-MYLX Medway Raven X   MRB113/109   06.10.93
K Hayley   (Langton Green, Tunbridge Wells)   25.07.13P
Wing s/n also quoted for G-MYVV qv (NF 11.08.15)

G-MYLZ Pegasus Quantum 15   6672   06.10.93
Cancelled 24.05.12 by CAA   28.02.10
Callander, Stirling   *Stored private address 05.17*

G-MYMB Solar Wings Pegasus Quantum 15   6674   06.10.93
D B Jones   (Bletchley, MIlton Keynes)   09.03.18P

G-MYMC Solar Wings Pegasus Quantum 15   6675   06.10.93
I A Macadam   (Hinton St Mary, Sturminster Newton)   11.06.11P
(IE 10.04.18)

G-MYMH Rans S-6-ESD Coyote II   0793.520   20.10.93
R W Keene   Over Farm, Gloucester   23.09.18P
Built by D J Thompsett – project PFA 204-12576;
tricycle u/c

G-MYMI Kolb Twinstar Mk.III   K0016-0693   21.10.93
F J Brown   Sackville Lodge Farm, Riseley   21.11.18P
Built by R T P Harris – project PFA 205-12537;
kit c/n K0016-0693 imported by Mainair

G-MYMJ Medway Raven X   MRB004/110   28.10.93
N Brigginshaw   RAF Wyton   31.07.17P

G-MYMK Mainair Gemini Flash IIA   968-1193-7-W763   29.10.93
C L M Haywood   (Hemel Hempstead)   18.11.17P

G-MYMM Air Création Ultraflight Fun 18S GTBIS   93/001   30.09.93
N P Power   Sywell   11.06.18P

G-MYMN Whittaker MW6 Merlin   xxxx   29.10.93
R E Arnold   Otherton
Built by K J Cole – project PFA 164-12124) (IE 06.07.18)
(SSDR microlight since 07.14)

G-MYMS Rans S-6-ESD Coyote II   0893.526   17.11.93
C G Chambers   (Piddington, Northampton)   15.03.08P
Built by G C Moore – project PFA 204-12581;
tricycle u/c (NF 08.04.17)

G-MYMW Cyclone AX3/503   C 3093156   23.11.93
D I Lee   (Brackley)   17.07.18P

G-MYMZ Cyclone AX3/503   C 3093154   07.12.93
The Microlight School (Lichfield) Ltd   Fisherwick   05.04.17P

G-MYNB Solar Wings Pegasus Quantum 15   6719   14.12.93
N Robinson   (Titchmarsh, Kettering)   05.03.19P

G-MYNE Rans S-6-ESD Coyote II   1292.408   25.06.93
J L Smoker   Enstone   04.01.11P
Built by G Ferguson – project PFA 204-12497;
tailwheel u/c (NF 15.05.18)

G-MYNF Mainair Mercury   974-1293-7-W770   17.01.94
S Carter   (Burnley)   23.03.18P

G-MYNI Team Mini-Max 91   xxxx   22.02.93
I Pearson   Newquay Cornwall
Built by R Barton – project PFA 186-12314)
(SSDR microlight since 06.14) (IE 15.12.17)

G-MYNJ	Mainair Mercury	972-1293-7-W768	14.01.94
	Cancelled 17.05.10 by CAA		10.08.04
	Deenethorpe *Stored 06.13*		
G-MYNK	Solar Wings Pegasus Quantum 15	6614	17.11.93
	M T Cain Beverley (Linley Hill)		22.09.17P
G-MYNL	Solar Wings Pegasus Quantum 15	6648	17.11.93
	I J Rawlinson (Stoke-on-Trent)		22.04.18P
G-MYNN	Solar Wings Pegasus Quantum 15	6679	17.11.93
	V Loy Strubby		20.09.18P
G-MYNP	Solar Wings Pegasus Quantum 15	6688	17.11.93
	K A Davidson Knapthorpe Lodge, Caunton		07.08.16P
	(IE 27.04.17)		
G-MYNR	Solar Wings Pegasus Quantum 15	6692	17.11.93
	D A Eastough (Barrow-on-Trent)		13.10.13P
	Badged 'Super Sport'; noted 04.17 (NF 12.09.18)		
G-MYNS	Solar Wings Pegasus Quantum 15	6694	17.11.93
	W R Furness Mitchells Farm, Wilburton		17.05.18P
G-MYNT	Solar Wings Pegasus Quantum 15	6693	17.11.93
	N Ionita Clench Common		08.05.13P
	(NF 02.03.15)		
G-MYNV	Solar Wings Pegasus Quantum 15	6725	10.01.94
	J Goldsmith-Ryan Eaglescott		31.05.09P
	(NF 18.06.15)		
G-MYNX	CFM Streak Shadow SA	K 193-SA-M	15.06.92
	S P Fletcher Redlands		03.09.13P
	Built by P A White – project PFA 206-12268		
	(NF 24.09.15)		
G-MYNY	Kolb Twinstar Mk.III	K0014-0693	22.11.93
	A Vaughan Athey's Moor, Longframlington		
	Built by W R C Williams-Wynne – project PFA 205-12478;		
	kit imported Mainair with c/n K0014-0693		
	(SSDR microlight since 06.16) (IE 22.09.15)		
G-MYNZ	Solar Wings Pegasus Quantum 15	6709	18.01.94
	P W Rogers (Shawforth, Rochdale)		21.06.11P
	(NF 05.09.14)		
G-MYOA	Rans S-6-ESD Coyote II	0793.523	23.11.93
	P-M Cavallucci Shobdon		27.03.19P
	Built by H Lang – project PFA 204-12578;		
	tricycle u/c		
G-MYOG	Kolb Twinstar Mk.III	K0011-0193	19.01.94
	T A Womersley (West Cowick, Goole)		09.06.16P
	Built by A P de Legh – project PFA 205-12449;		
	kit imported by Mainair with c/n K0011-0193		
	(IE 27.04.17)		
G-MYOH	CFM Shadow Series CD	K 201	27.01.94
	S E Lyden (Terrington St Clement)		04.09.10P
	(NF 11.09.17)		
G-MYOL	Air Création Ultraflight Fun 18S GTBIS	94/001	07.02.94
	G A McCann tr Condors Aerotow Syndicate		
	Dunkeswell		04.11.19P
G-MYON	CFM Shadow Series CD	240	12.01.94
	D J Shaw Eshott		03.05.18P
G-MYOS	CFM Shadow Series CD	246	18.02.94
	C A & E J Bowles Craysmarsh Farm, Melksham		01.10.17P
	(IE 02.10.17)		
G-MYOU	Solar Wings Pegasus Quantum 15	6726	01.03.94
	D J Tasker Camp Farm, Bulkington, Bedworth		24.03.18P
G-MYOX	Mainair Mercury	984-0294-7-W780	23.02.94
	K Driver Headon Farm, Retford		06.02.18P
G-MYOY	Cyclone AX3/503	C.3123191	23.02.94
	Cancelled 15.11.10 as PWFU		16.07.08
	Roddige *Wing stored 06.14*		
G-MYPA	Rans S-6-ESD Coyote II	0893.527	24.02.94
	A R Hawes (Needham Market, Ipswich)		12.06.15P
	Built by E J Garner – project PFA 204-12678;		
	tailwheel u/c (IE 26.08.15)		
G-MYPE	Mainair Gemini Flash IIA	985-0394-7-W781	11.03.94
	A Matthews (Tanyfron, Wrexham)		08.02.18P
G-MYPH	Solar Wings Pegasus Quantum 15	6764	11.03.94
	I E Chapman (Haworth, Keighley)		02.10.18P
G-MYPI	Solar Wings Pegasus Quantum 15	6767	11.03.94
	P L Jarvis & D S Ross Longacre Farm, Sandy		21.08.18P
G-MYPJ	Rans S-6-ESD Coyote II	1293.569	18.03.94
	K A Eden Brook Farm, Pilling		09.09.05P
	Built by A W Fish – project PFA 204-12692;		
	tricycle u/c (NF 08.10.14)		
G-MYPL	CFM Shadow Series CD	K.213	14.02.94
	G I Madden Longacre Farm, Sandy		03.08.18P
	Built by CFM Metal-Fax – completed G I Madden		
	as project BMAA/HB/080		
G-MYPM	Cyclone AX3/503	C 3123188	23.03.94
	A A Ahmed Causeway		07.05.18P
G-MYPN	Solar Wings Pegasus Quantum 15	6727	12.04.94
	C M Boswell Wickenby		12.05.18P
G-MYPR	Cyclone AX3/503	C 3123190	13.04.94
	W J I Robb (Nutts Corner, Crumlin)		18.08.19P
G-MYPS	Whittaker MW6 Merlin	xxxx	19.04.94
	I S Bishop Brook Farm, Pilling		10.04.06P
	Built by I S Bishop – project PFA 164-11585		
	(NF 30.04.18)		
G-MYPT	CFM Shadow Series CD	K 212	22.04.94
	R Gray (Kettering)		07.09.11P
	(NF 13.10.14)		
G-MYPV	Mainair Mercury	986-0394-7-W782	18.03.94
	R Whitworth (Kenilworth)		05.01.17P
	(NF 23.08.17)		
G-MYPZ	BFC Challenger II	xxxx	02.03.94
	J I Gledhill & J Harvard (Bradwell-on-Sea)		29.03.17P
	Built by E G Astin – project PFA 177A-12689		
	using BFC kit; kit no CH2-0194-UK-1046 quoted		
	but not confirmed		
G-MYRD	Mainair Blade	989-0594-7-W785	20.05.94
	Savemylight Ltd (Oakengates, Telford)		20.10.18P
G-MYRE	Cyclone Chaser S	CH863	10.05.94
	S W Barker (Scalby, Scarborough)		
	(IE 30.06.17)		
	(SSDR microlight since 05.14)		
G-MYRF	Solar Wings Pegasus Quantum 15	6795	13.05.94
	K N Mosby (Elsenham, Bishop's Stortford)		23.05.19P
G-MYRG	Team Mini-Max 88	xxxx	17.05.94
	A R Hawes (Needham Market, Ipswich)		
	Built by D G Burrows – project PFA 186-11891		
	(SSDR microlight since 01.15) (NF 09.07.18)		
G-MYRH	BFC Challenger II	xxxx	10.03.94
	B Dillon-White Brook Farm, Pilling		07.09.16P
	Built by R T Hall – project PFA 177A-12690		
	using BFC kit		
G-MYRJ	BFC Challenger II	xxxx	28.03.94
	86-GU, G-MYRJ R A Allen Saint Secondin, France		21.10.08P
	Built by H F Breakwell & P Woodcock – project		
	PFA 177A-12658 using BFC kit; carries '86-GU'		
	only (NF 21.09.15)		
G-MYRK	Murphy Renegade Spirit UK	215	03.10.89
	B J Palfreyman Brook Breasting Farm, Watnall		11.04.18P
	Built by J Brown – project PFA 186-11891		
G-MYRL	Team Mini-Max 91	xxxx	17.05.94
	J N Hanson Brook Farm, Pilling		
	Built by W W Vinton – project PFA 186-11967		
	(SSDR microlight since 09.14) (NF 08.09.17)		
G-MYRN	Solar Wings Pegasus Quantum 15	6801	26.05.94
	I L Waghorn Perth		30.04.13P
	(NF 17.05.16)		
G-MYRP	Letov LK-2M Sluka	829409x09?	06.06.94
	R M C Hunter (Blue Tile Farm, Hindolveston)		
	Built by R L Jones – project PFA 263-12725		
	(SSDR microlight since 08.16) (NF 17.06.16)		
G-MYRS	Solar Wings Pegasus Quantum 15	6803	13.06.94
	N H Kirk (Thorpe Satchville, Melton Mowbray)		12.09.18P
G-MYRT	Solar Wings Pegasus Quantum 15	6732	07.02.94
	G P Preston (Douglas, Isle of Man)		07.04.18P
G-MYRW	Mainair Mercury	999-0694-7-W795	17.06.94
	G C Hobson St Michaels		17.07.18P
	Operated by Northern Microlight School		
G-MYRY	Solar Wings Pegasus Quantum 15	6813	15.06.94
	S D P Bridge & D N Brocklesby		
	(Herne Bay & Chatteris)		13.07.19P
	Badged 'Lite'		

G-MYRZ Solar Wings Pegasus Quantum 15   6812   15.06.94
R E Forbes   Oban   09.06.18P

G-MYSA Cyclone Chaser S 508   CH864   15.06.94
P W Dunn & A R Vincent   (Stafford & Lichfield)
(SSDR microlight since 06.15) (NF 18.06.15)

G-MYSB Solar Wings Pegasus Quantum 15   6809   22.06.94
H G Reid   (Ryton)   10.08.19P

G-MYSC Solar Wings Pegasus Quantum 15   6811   22.06.94
K R White   (Maiden Newton, Dorchester)   19.09.10P
(NF 23.07.14)

G-MYSD BFC Challenger II   CH2-0193-1043   23.06.94
C W Udale   (Manton, Oakham)   21.06.11P
Built by C E Bell – project PFA 177A-12688
using BFC kit (IE 10.07.14)

G-MYSJ Mainair Gemini Flash IIA   1001-0894-7-W797   02.08.94
A Warnock   Newtownards   14.08.17P

G-MYSK Team Mini-Max 91   xxxx   25.07.94
T D Wolstenholme   Brook Farm, Pilling
Built by K Worthington – project PFA 186-12203;
operated by Brook Farm Microlight Centre
(SSDR microlight since 08.14) (IE 05.07.17)

G-MYSL Aviasud Mistral   066   27.02.92
83-DE   R D Ainley   North Coates   12.05.18P
Built by Aviasud Engineering – project BMAA/HB/007

G-MYSO Cyclone AX3/503   C 4043215   01.08.94
J P Gilroy   North Weald   24.03.17P
Blown over 23.02.17 & substantially damaged;
noted 07.18

G-MYSR Solar Wings Pegasus Quantum 15   6837   03.08.94
M P Bawden   Perranporth   12.07.18P
(NF 15.12.17)

G-MYSU Rans S-6-ESD Coyote II   0394.600   05.08.94
W Matthews   Shobdon   20.09.18P
Built by I Whyte – project PFA 204-12753

G-MYSV Aerial Arts Chaser S   CH812   24.08.94
G S Highley   Sackville Lodge Farm, Riseley
(SSDR microlight since 05.14) (IE 14.09.16)

G-MYSW Solar Wings Pegasus Quantum 15   6834   13.07.94
M Richardson   (Porthcawl)   14.05.15P
(IE 19.07.17)

G-MYSY Solar Wings Pegasus Quantum 15   6864   15.08.94
B D S Vere   Belle Vue Farm, Yarnscombe   26.09.16P

G-MYSZ Mainair Mercury   1006-0894-7-W802   02.09.94
W Fletcher   Broadmeadow Farm, Hereford   18.04.13P
(NF 24.08.15)

G-MYTB Mainair Mercury   1004-0894-7-W800   19.08.94
P J Higgins   Wingland
(SSDR microlight since 11.17) (IE 26.08.15)

G-MYTD Mainair Blade   1002-0894-7-W798   18.08.94
D B Meades & B E Warburton   St Michaels   14.08.17P

G-MYTE Rans S-6-ESD Coyote II   0394.598   22.07.94
M F Hadley   Boston   26.07.11P
Built by A J Bourner – project PFA 204-12718;
tailwheel u/c (NF 08.02.17)

G-MYTH CFM Shadow Series CD   089   07.11.88
W J I Robb   Causeway
(SSDR microlight since 08.16) (IE 06.04.17)

G-MYTI Cyclone Pegasus Quantum 15   6874   06.10.94
K M Gaffney   (Sutton Coldfield)   21.05.18P

G-MYTJ Cyclone Pegasus Quantum 15   6877   29.09.94
L Blight   (Amington, Tamworth)   07.10.18P

G-MYTK Mainair Mercury   1009-1094-7-W805   29.09.94
D A Holroyd   (Perth, Western Australia, Australia)   19.04.14P
(NF 20.08.16)

G-MYTL Mainair Blade   1010-1094-7-W807   04.10.94
S Gibson   Greenhills Farm, Wheatley Hill   03.06.17P
(IE 23.08.17)

G-MYTN Cyclone Pegasus Quantum 15   6878   30.09.94
M Humphries   (Standon, Ware)   27.07.18P

G-MYTO Quad City Challenger II   xxxx   22.07.94
A Studley   Middle Pymore Farm, Bridport   16.04.01P
Built by D M Cottingham & K B Tolley
– project PFA 177-12583 (NF 23.04.14)

G-MYTP Arrowflight Hawk II (UK)   H-CGS-489-P   06.10.94
N215   R J Turner   Otherton   12.07.05P
Built by M Whittaker – project PFA 266-12801
(NF 13.01.16)

G-MYTT Quad City Challenger II   CH2-0394-UK-111   11.10.94
P W Brush   Eaglescott   24.08.18P
Built by P L Fisk – project PFA 177-12761

G-MYTU Mainair Blade   1011-1094-7-W808   21.10.94
A P Pearce   Wingland   20.07.19P

G-MYTY CFM Streak Shadow M   K 242   11.07.94
R J Creasey tr Adventurer's SSDR Group
Plaistows Farm, St Albans
Built by N R Beale – project PFA 206-12607;
active 09.18 (SSDR microlight since 07.14)

G-MYUA Air Création Ultraflight Fun 18S GTBIS   94/002   08.11.94
A Shaw   (Woldingham, Caterham)   03.05.19P

G-MYUC Mainair Blade   1015-1294-7-W813   16.11.94
C J Ashton   (Penwortham, Preston)   05.02.19P

G-MYUD Mainair Mercury   1016-1294-7-W814   24.11.94
P W Margetson   (Gordrergraig, Swansea)   30.07.17P

G-MYUF Murphy Renegade Spirit UK   xxxx   16.11.94
S R Greasley & B W Webb   Old Warden   17.05.18P
Built by C J Dale – project PFA 188-12795

G-MYUH Solar Wings Pegasus XL-Q   6810   28.11.94
K S Daniels   London Colney   26.08.16P
Trike ex-G-MVKR c/n SW-TE-0123

G-MYUI Cyclone AX3/503   C 102822   13.12.94
G J Hanlon   (Swindon)   18.06.19P
Fitted with new monopole c/n C 102822

G-MYUJ Murphy Maverick 430   xxxx   30.12.94
G-ONFL, G-MYUJ   P J Porter   Henstridge   16.05.14P
Built by K Godfrey & G Lockwood
– project PFA 259-12750 (IE 23.10.17)

G-MYUL Quad City Challenger II   xxxx   10.01.95
B M R & N van Cleve   (Littlehampton)   12.09.18P
Built by A G Easson – project PFA 177-12687

G-MYUN Mainair Blade   1019-0195-7-W817   05.12.94
G A Barratt   St Michaels   24.07.18P

G-MYUO Cyclone Pegasus Quantum 15   6911   23.01.95
R J Hughes   Knettishall   14.04.18P

G-MYUP Letov LK-2M Sluka   829409X24   20.12.94
F Overall   Whitehall Farm, Wethersfield
Built by F Overall – project PFA 263-12785)
(SSDR microlight since 06.14) (IE 18.08.17)

G-MYUR Huntwing Avon Skytrike   xxxx   24.01.95
Cancelled 29.11.11 as PWFU   30.03.05
Graveley Hall Farm, Graveley   *Built by S D Pain*
– project BMAA/HB/034; being restored 09.12

G-MYUV Cyclone Pegasus Quantum 15   6918   06.02.95
I Tulkan   (Kirkby-in-Ashfield)   03.05.19P

G-MYUW Mainair Mercury   1024-0295-7-W822   07.02.95
G C Hobson   St Michaels   23.02.18P

G-MYVA Kolb Twinstar Mk.III   K0018-1193 ?   13.02.95
E Bayliss   Ince   14.01.14P
Built by S P Read – project PFA 205-12756;
kit no not confirmed

G-MYVB Mainair Blade   1021-0195-7-W819   15.12.94
S Gaskell   (Aspull, Wigan)   29.05.18P

G-MYVC Cyclone Pegasus Quantum 15   6904   13.02.95
M A Cox   (Sutton Coldfield)   13.06.19P

G-MYVG Letov LK-2M Sluka   829409X26   15.02.95
A Evans   (Wolverhampton)   08.07.14P
Built by L W M Summers – project PFA 263-12786
(SSDR microlight since 06.14) (IE 28.03.17)

G-MYVH Mainair Blade   1028-0295-7-W826   21.02.95
R H de C Ribeiro   Baxby Manor, Husthwaite   06.07.18P

G-MYVI Air Création Ultraflight Fun 18S GTBIS   94/004   17.02.95
D Rowland   (Gamrie)   16.10.18P
Believed roaded to Boyndie for flying

G-MYVJ Cyclone Pegasus Quantum 15   6974   24.02.95
A I & P W Davidson   (Windygates, Leven)
(SSDR microlight since 04.16) (IE 26.08.15)

G-MYVK	Cyclone Pegasus Quantum 15	6970	27.02.95
	T P C Hague (Winchester)		21.07.15P
	(NF 18.08.17)		
G-MYVL	Mainair Mercury	1030-0395-7-W828	01.03.95
	P J Judge Davidstow Moor		05.08.07P
	(NF 12.11.14)		
G-MYVM	Cyclone Pegasus Quantum 15	6893	09.03.95
	G-69-17, G-MYVM G J Gibson (Coupar Angus)		26.03.14P
	On rebuild 06.15 (IE 07.08.15)		
G-MYVN	Cyclone AX3/503	C 4043212	16.03.95
	F Watt Strathdon		05.10.03P
	(NF 17.07.15)		
G-MYVO	Mainair Blade	1010-1104 7 W811	08.11.94
	S S Raines tr Victor Oscar Group Shobdon		30.07.18P
G-MYVP	Rans S-6-ESD Coyote II	0294.593	27.03.95
	M Jady Redlands		11.04.18P
	Built by J S Liming – project PFA 204-12828;		
	tricycle u/c		
G-MYVR	Cyclone Pegasus Quantum 15	6980	21.03.95
	J M Webster & M Winwood Park Hall Farm, Mapperley		11.08.16P
G-MYVV	Medway Hybred 44XLR	MR127/109	03.04.95
	S Perity (Leverington, Wisbech)		04.06.04P
	Wing s/n also quoted for G-MYLX qv (NF 21.05.18)		
G-MYVZ	Mainair Blade	1034-0495-7-W832	31.03.95
	W C Hyner (Ffostrasol, Llandysul)		26.09.16P
G-MYWC	Huntwing Avon/Skytrike 503	9409038	03.04.95
	D Dales (Marton-in-Cleveland, Middlesbrough)		06.06.16P
	Built by F J C Binks – project BMAA/HB/043		
G-MYWE	Thruster T600N	9035-T600-512	18.04.95
	(G-MYOK) J K Avis Priory Farm, Tibenham		18.03.16P
	Noted dismantled 09.18)		
G-MYWF	Newman Shadow	K.227	18.04.95
	J Preller Gransden Lodge		
	Built by CFM Metal-Fax as CFM Shadow Srs SS;		
	completed M A Newman – project BMAA/HB/068		
	(SSDR microlight since 05.15) (IE 05.10.16)		
G-MYWG	Cyclone Pegasus Quantum 15	6998	20.04.95
	S L Greene Plaistows Farm, St Albans		14.08.18P
G-MYWI	Cyclone Pegasus Quantum 15	7006	01.05.95
	M S Ahmadu (Corby)		13.07.18P
	(NF 07.08.18)		
G-MYWJ	Cyclone Pegasus Quantum 15	6919	24.01.95
	I Clarkson & L M Sams (Evesham & Warwick)		01.04.18P
G-MYWK	Cyclone Pegasus Quantum 15	7011	01.05.95
	J R Bluett (Filton, Bristol)		07.08.16P
	(IE 20.09.16)		
G-MYWL	Cyclone Pegasus Quantum 15	6995	02.05.95
	R P McGuffie Shobdon		09.05.17P
G-MYWM	CFM Shadow Series CD	K.248	09.05.95
	N McKinley Plaistows Farm, St Albans		12.08.18P
	Built by R E Peirse – project BMAA/HB/056		
G-MYWO	Cyclone Pegasus Quantum 15	6932	09.05.95
	K Grimley (Hednesford)		10.07.19P
G-MYWR	Cyclone Pegasus Quantum 15	7002	10.05.95
	The Microlight School (Lichfield) Ltd Fisherwick		25.06.19P
	Carries 'E032RH' (=US Ultralight registration)		
G-MYWS	Cyclone Chaser S 447	CH866	17.05.95
	M H Broadbent Westfield Farm, Hailsham		
	Conceived as Aerial Arts Chaser with c/n CH866		
	but built as Cyclone c/n 6946		
	(SSDR microlight since 05.14) (IE 24.07.17)		
G-MYWU	Cyclone Pegasus Quantum 15	7024	25.05.95
	P L Owen Haverfordwest		25.06.18P
G-MYWV	Rans S-4C Coyote	93.212	30.05.95
	G J Simoni (Carterton)		
	Built by A H Trapp – project PFA 193-12826		
	(SSDR microlight since 06.14) (NF 27.03.18)		
G-MYWW	Cyclone Pegasus Quantum 15	7021	30.05.95
	B Mandley (Minehead)		01.03.18P
G-MYWY	Cyclone Pegasus Quantum 15	6982	20.03.95
	P Byrne Longacre Farm, Sandy		05.08.18P

G-MYXA	Team Mini-Max 91	xxxx	13.06.95
	D C Marsh Rookery Farm, Doynton		
	Built by D S Worman – project PFA 186-12266;		
	tailwheel u/c		
	(SSDR microlight since 02.15) (IE 02.10.17)		
G-MYXB	Rans S-6-ESD Coyote II	1293.567	20.06.95
	M Gaffney (Obidos, Portugal)		07.06.19P
	Built by A Aldridge – project PFA 204-12787;		
	tricycle u/c		
G-MYXC	BFC Challenger II	CH2-0294-UK-1099	16.05.95
	N O'Brien (Kilkenny, RoI)		17.05.19P
	Built by K N Dickinson		
G-MYXD	Solar Wings Pegasus Quasar IITC	7029	21.06.95
	A Knight (Nuneaton)		24.03.19P
G-MYXE	Cyclone Pegasus Quantum 15	7061	23.06.95
	J F Bolton (Shrewsbury)		07.09.19P
G-MYXG	Rans S-6-ESD Coyote II	0394.599	29.06.95
	G H Lee Higher Barn Farm, Hoghton		22.01.09P
	Built by G H Lee – project PFA 204-12879;		
	tricycle u/c (NF 20.01.16)		
G-MYXH	Cyclone AX3/503	7028	03.07.95
	T de B Gardner (Kingsclere, Newbury)		06.05.18P
G-MYXI	Cook Aries Mk.1	xxxx	04.07.95
	H Cook (Newport NP20)		
	Built by H Cook – project BMAA/HB/048		
	(SSDR microlight since 08.16) (NF 25.07.18)		
G-MYXJ	Mainair Blade	1048-0795-7-W846	17.07.95
	S N Robson Eshott		14.11.08P
	(NF 20.10.15)		
G-MYXL	Mignet HM-1000 Balerit	112	11.07.95
	R W Hollamby (Bardown, Wadhurst)		22.04.18P
G-MYXM	Mainair Blade	1047-0795-7-W845	19.07.95
	C Johnson Broadmeadow Farm, Hereford		03.12.17P
G-MYXN	Mainair Blade	1046-0795-7-W844	27.07.95
	J C Birkbeck Thornton Watlass, Ripon		27.09.18P
G-MYXO	Letov LK-2M Sluka	8295s001	27.07.95
	A Furness & J R Surbey Mitchells Farm, Wilburton		
	Built by K C Rutland – project PFA 263-12873)		
	(SSDR microlight since 06.14) (IE 14.11.17		
G-MYXT	Cyclone Pegasus Quantum 15	7073	04.08.95
	L A Washer (Haywards Heath)		30.04.14P
	(NF 24.01.17)		
G-MYXU	Thruster T300	9024-T300-513	16.08.95
	D W Wilson (Collone, Armagh)		09.11.11P
	Built by Tempest Aviation Ltd (NF 12.01.15)		
G-MYXV	Quad City Challenger II	xxxx	19.07.95
	T S Savage Deanland		26.07.17P
	Built by A Hipkin – project PFA 177-12864		
G-MYXW	Cyclone Pegasus Quantum 15	7090	24.08.95
	J Uttley (Baker Barracks, Thorney Island)		15.05.18P
G-MYXX	Cyclone Pegasus Quantum 15	7081	25.08.95
	K A Davidson Knapthorpe Lodge, Caunton		24.03.19P
G-MYXZ	Cyclone Pegasus Quantum 15	7023	21.06.95
	Light Vending Ltd Moss Edge Farm, Cockerham		04.08.19P
G-MYYA	Mainair Blade	1052-0995-7-W850	01.09.95
	S J Ward Arclid Green, Sandbach		23.07.17P
G-MYYB	Cyclone Pegasus Quantum 15	7079	04.09.95
	A L Johnson & D S Ross Longacre Farm, Sandy		06.02.18P
G-MYYC	Cyclone Pegasus Quantum 15	7094	12.09.95
	T R E Goldfield (Walsall)		20.04.18P
G-MYYF	Quad City Challenger II	xxxx	27.09.95
	L E J Wojciechowski (West Bridgford, Nottingham)		14.10.17P
	Built by G Ferries – project PFA 177-12811		
G-MYYH	Mainair Blade	1056-1095-7-W854	03.10.95
	D J Dodd (Norton Bridge, Stone)		07.02.16P
G-MYYI	Cyclone Pegasus Quantum 15	7101	28.09.95
	C M Day (Baker Barracks, Thorney Island)		17.09.17P
G-MYYJ	Huntwing Avon/Skytrike 503	9409032	29.09.95
	R M Jarvis (Cranfield, Ohio, USA)		
	Built by M J Slatter – project BMAA/HB/033		
	(NF 04.02.15)		

G-MYYK	Cyclone Pegasus Quantum 15	7100		02.10.95
	N Ionita Clench Common			09.03.16P
	(IE 05.04.16)			
G-MYYL	Cyclone AX3/503	7110		04.10.95
	D Roach Rossall Field, Cockerham			03.04.18P
G-MYYR	Team Mini-Max 91	xxxx		31.10.95
	S I Hatherall Welshpool			01.04.15P
	Built by D Palmer – project PFA 186-12724			
	(SSDR microlight since 03.15) (IE 27.04.17)			
G-MYYS	Team Mini-Max	xxxx		07.11.95
	D Brunton Eshott			
	Built by J R Hopkinson – project PFA 186-11989			
	(SSDR microlight since 06.14) (NF 09.10.18)			
G-MYYV	Rans S-6-ESD-XL Coyote II	0896.1026		17.11.95
	R C Parsons Northrepps			10.05.19P
	Built by J Whiting – project PFA 204-12943;			
	originally kit no.0795.851; tricycle u/c			
G-MYYW	Mainair Blade	1051-0895-7-W849		08.08.95
	M D Kirby Chase Farm, Little Burstead			31.07.15P
G-MYYY	Mainair Blade	1031-0495-7-W829		15.03.95
	E D Locke Strathaven			12.03.18P
	(SSDR microlight since 03.18) (IE 26.08.15)			
G-MYYZ	Medway Raven X	MRB135/116		10.01.96
	J W Leaper (Defford, Worcester)			27.06.04P
	(NF 24.09.14)			
G-MYZB	Cyclone Pegasus Quantum 15	7124		22.11.95
	I K Priestley Sackville Lodge Farm, Riseley			01.06.14P
	(NF 03.08.18)			
G-MYZC	Cyclone AX3/503	7125		05.12.95
	P F J Rogers (Littlehampton)			13.08.19P
G-MYZF	Cyclone AX3/503	7133		11.12.95
	Microflight (Ireland) Ltd Causeway			27.04.18P
	Crashed on take-off at Causeway 19.01.19			
G-MYZG	Cyclone AX3/503	7137		11.01.96
	I J Webb (Basingstoke)			05.06.18P
G-MYZH	Chargus Titan 38	JPA-1		16.01.96
	T J Gayton-Polley (Billingshurst)			
	(NF 30.03.15)			
G-MYZJ	Cyclone Pegasus Quantum 15	7150		24.01.96
	K Foyen Athey's Moor, Longframlington			18.10.19P
G-MYZL	Cyclone Pegasus Quantum 15	7158		05.02.96
	R F Greaves (Okehampton)			09.10.17P
G-MYZN	Whittaker MW6-S-LW Fatboy Flyer	xxxx		31.01.96
	Cancelled 23.06.07 as PWFU			28.06.07
	Wingland, Lincs *Built by M K Shaw*			
	– project PFA 164-12431; stored 03.16			
G-MYZP	CFM Shadow Series DD	249		07.02.96
	I G Poutney Wickenby			24.04.19P
	Built by D G Cook – project PFA 161-12914;			
	sequence no.duplicates G-RXDY			
G-MYZR	Rans S-6-ESD-XL Coyote II	1295.902		09.02.96
	N R Beale Deppers Bridge, Southam			
	Built by V R Leggott – project PFA 204-12958; tricycle u/c			
	(SSDR microlight since 08.15) (IE 20.10.15)			
G-MYZV	Rans S-6-ESD-XL Coyote II	0795.849		26.02.96
	I M Charlwood (Bordon)			30.05.17P
	Built by H Lammers – project PFA 204-12946;			
	tricycle u/c			
G-MYZY	Cyclone Pegasus Quantum 15	7156		08.02.96
	C Chapman (Faversham)			07.07.18P
G-MZAB	Mainair Blade	1043-0695-7-W841		26.05.95
	D Brennan (South Yearle, Northumberland)			23.08.16P
G-MZAC	BFC Challenger II	xxxx		21.07.95
	T R Gregory Wing Farm, Longbridge Deverill			17.06.14P
	Built by M N Calhaem – project PFA 177A-12716			
	using BFC kit (IE 05.10.16)			
G-MZAE	Mainair Blade	1063-1295-7-W863		04.12.95
	A P Finn (Brighton)			13.09.17P
	(IE 24.10.13)			
	(SSDR microlight since 06.18)			
G-MZAF	Mainair Blade	1045-0795-7-W843		01.12.95
	P F Mayes Pound Green			15.05.18P
G-MZAG	Mainair Blade	1042-0695-7-W840		26.05.95
	M J P Sanderson St Michaels			11.05.18P
G-MZAK	Mainair Mercury	1070-0296-7-W872		15.01.96
	ZU-DVL, G-MZAK I Rawson St Michaels			
	(SSDR microlight since 06.18) (IE 22.07.15)			
G-MZAM	Mainair Blade	1044-0695-7-W842		31.05.95
	R J Coppin Broadmeadow Farm, Hereford			28.09.19P
G-MZAN	Cyclone Pegasus Quantum 15	7188		07.03.96
	P M Leahy (Lytchett Minster, Poole)			20.08.18P
G-MZAP	Mainair Blade 912	1036-0495-7-W834		31.03.95
	K D Adams Ince			12.08.18P
G-MZAR	Mainair Blade	1072-0296-7-W874		13.02.96
	D Reston Ince			30.04.18P
G-MZAS	Mainair Blade	1049-0895-7-W847		15.08.95
	T Carter Pound Green			18.10.04P
	(NF 15.04.16)			
G-MZAT	Mainair Blade	1060-1195-7-W860		29.11.95
	S Elmazouri (Torquay)			17.03.17P
G-MZAU	Mainair Blade	1064-0196-7-W864		29.11.95
	A F Glover (Woolston, Warrington)			07.09.17P
	Stolen 1999: rebuilt by P&M Aviation Ltd with			
	new trike ex spares & wing located 2004;			
	original c/n retained			
G-MZAW	Cyclone Pegasus Quantum 15	7160		14.02.96
	O O'Donnell (Bridge of Don, Aberdeen)			05.02.16P
	Stored 08.16			
G-MZAY	Mainair Blade	1077-0396-7-W880		15.03.96
	Cancelled 28.02.11 as destroyed			01.06.10
	Wing Farm, Longbridge Deverill *Wings stored 08.13*			
G-MZAZ	Mainair Blade	1040-0595-7-W838		26.05.95
	A W Gunn (Driby, Alford)			18.02.18P
	(IE 23.04.18)			
G-MZBC	Cyclone Pegasus Quantum 15	7077		15.08.95
	B M Quinn (Barlow, Sheffield)			23.11.18P
G-MZBD	Rans S-6-ESD-XL Coyote II	0795.850		15.03.96
	W E Tinsley Henstridge			25.08.17P
	Built by H W Foster – project PFA 204-12957;			
	tricycle u/c			
G-MZBF	Letov LK-2M Sluka	xxxx		18.03.96
	V Simpson Kernan Valley, Tandragee			
	Built by C R Stockdale – project PFA 263-12881			
	(SSDR microlight since 06.14) (IE 31.05.17)			
G-MZBG	Whittaker MW6-S Fatboy Flyer	xxxx		20.03.96
	M W Kilvert & E I Rowlands-Jones			
	(Newtown, Shrewsbury)			01.06.01P
	Built by A W Hodder – project PFA 164-12891			
	(NF 21.04.16)			
G-MZBH	Rans S-6-ESD Coyote II	0392.277		21.03.96
	G L Campbell Low Hill Farm, North Moor, Messingham			27.06.18P
	Built by D Sutherland – project PFA 204-12244;			
	tricycle u/c			
G-MZBI	Pegasus Quantum 15	7189		21.03.96
	Cancelled 26.04.09 as destroyed			08.08.08
	Park Hall Farm, Mapperley *Remains stored 04.13*			
G-MZBK	Letov LK-2M Sluka	8295s002		26.03.96
	R M C Hunter Redlands			
	Built by R Painter – project PFA 263-12872			
	(SSDR microlight since 08.16) (NF 17.06.16)			
G-MZBL	Mainair Blade	1080-0496-7-W883		01.04.96
	C J Rubery Westonzoyland			13.06.18P
G-MZBN	CFM Shadow Series CD	K.069		22.04.96
	G-MTWP W J Buskell (Beetley, Dereham)			
	'Cloud Base'			10.08.18P
	(Originally built CFM Metal-Fax: rebuilt by J A James			
	– project BMAA/HB/073 being rebuild of c/n K.069			
	G-MTWP; roaded to Northrepps for flying			
G-MZBS	CFM Shadow Series D	K 274		14.05.96
	T P Ryan Plaistows Farm, St Albans			21.05.19P
	Built by P A White – project PFA 161-13008			
G-MZBT	Cyclone Pegasus Quantum 15-912	7224		22.05.96
	M L Saunders Middle Stoke, Isle of Grain			31.05.19P
G-MZBU	Rans S-6-ESD-XL Coyote II	0296.938		30.05.96
	R S Marriott Low Hill Farm, North Moor, Messingham			05.06.18P
	Built by J B Marshall – project PFA 204-12992			

G-MZBW Quad City Challenger II xxxx 19.02.96
R M C Hunter (Coulsdon) 16.08.10P
Built by C Bird – project PFA 177-12971 (NF 17.06.16)

G-MZBX Whittaker MW6-S-LW Fatboy Flyer xxxx 16.05.96
Cancelled 10.05.10 by CAA 22.06.05
*Not Known Built by S Rose & P Tearall – project
PFA 164-12563; sold on ebay 11.17, part restored*

G-MZBY Cyclone Pegasus Quantum 15 7227 30.05.96
P L Wilkinson Swansea 17.12.18P

G-MZBZ Quad City Challenger II CH2-0695-UK-1360 11.03.96
T R Gregory (Midsomer Norton, Radstock) 02.04.04P
*Built by J Flisher – project PFA 177-12928
(NF 12.01.15)*

G-MZCB Cyclone Chaser S 508 7220 04.06.96
P W Dunn & A R Vincent Sittles Farm, Alrewas
(SSDR microlight since 04.15) (NF 18.06.15)

G-MZCC Mainair Blade 912 1086-0696-7-W889 07.06.96
K S Rissmann Fenland 13.05.17P
(IE 31.05.17)

G-MZCE Mainair Blade 1088-0696-7-W891 17.06.96
I C Hindle Rossall Field, Cockerham 13.03.12P
(NF 26.07.17)

G-MZCF Mainair Blade 1089-0696-7-W892 30.08.96
C Hannaby Ley Farm, Chirk 19.02.08P
(NF 16.09.14)

G-MZCI Cyclone Pegasus Quantum 15 7231 10.06.96
J Riley Little Staughton 30.05.13P
(IE 17.10.18)

G-MZCJ Cyclone Pegasus Quantum 15 7233 14.06.96
T N Jerry Northrepps 12.05.18P

G-MZCK AMF Microflight Chevvron 2-32C 038 11.07.96
S Mebarki (Cardiff) 29.06.19P

G-MZCM Cyclone Pegasus Quantum 15 7219 03.05.96
J M Reed & J L Smith (Stoke-on-Trent & Stafford) 20.04.19P
Badged 'Lite'

G-MZCN Mainair Blade 1079-0396-7-W882 27.06.96
G M Gomez (Valdemoro, Madrid, Spain) 26.03.16P
(NF 13.07.17)

G-MZCS Team Mini-Max 91 xxxx 20.12.95
J A Aley (London N9)
*Built by C S Cox – project PFA 186-12646
(SSDR microlight since 08.16) (NF 18.08.17)*

G-MZCT CFM Shadow Series CD 277 11.07.96
W G Gill Plaistows Farm, St Albans 22.02.13P
(NF 28.07.15)

G-MZCU Mainair Blade 1082-0496-7-W885 01.05.96
C E Pearce Pond Farm, Carleton St Peter 26.10.17P

G-MZCV Cyclone Pegasus Quantum 15 7235 11.07.96
D R Langton Kenyon Hall Farm, Kenyon 16.08.19P

G-MZCX Huntwing Avon/Skytrike 503 9510055 17.07.96
A I Sutherland Kylarrick House, Edderton 21.02.19P
Built by R Harrison – project BMAA/HB/072

G-MZCY Cyclone Pegasus Quantum 15 7236 19.07.96
G Murphy Newtownards 17.09.18P
(NF 30.11.17)

G-MZDA Rans S-6-ESD-XL Coyote II 0396.951 29.07.96
R Plummer Baxby Manor, Husthwaite 13.08.14P
*Built by J Dent & W C Lombard – project
PFA 204-13019; tricycle u/c (IE 21.04.17)*

G-MZDB Cyclone Pegasus Quantum 15-912 7237 31.07.96
S Martin Eshott 03.06.19P

G-MZDC Cyclone Pegasus Quantum 15 7246 02.08.96
C Garton Enstone 30.05.18P

G-MZDD Cyclone Pegasus Quantum 15 7114 11.07.96
G-69-23 A J Todd Sackville Lodge Farm, Riseley 06.05.16P

G-MZDE Cyclone Pegasus Quantum 15 7238 12.07.96
R G Hedley Kenyon Hall Farm, Kenyon 21.03.18P

G-MZDF Mainair Blade 1093-0896-7-W896 15.08.96
M Liptrot Glassonby 31.05.12P
(IE 03.11.15)

G-MZDG Rans S-6-ESD-XL Coyote II 0696.1002 07.08.96
P Coates Athey's Moor, Longframlington 18.12.15P
*Built by R Rhodes – project PFA 204-13030;
tricycle u/c (IE 30.01.17)*

G-MZDH Cyclone Pegasus Quantum 15-912 7248 12.08.96
A T Willis tr G-MZDH Flying Group
Wolverhampton Halfpenny Green 10.08.16P
*Wing structure failed, spiralled to ground Holy Cross
Green, Clent 15.08.16 & substantially damaged*

G-MZDI Whittaker MW6-S Fatboy Flyer xxxx 15.08.96
G-BUNN C M Byford (Long Marston) 19.02.02P
*Built by M Grunwell – project PFA 164-11929
(NF 04.10.16)*

G-MZDJ Medway Raven X MRB138/119 19.08.96
R Bryan & S Digby Rookery Farm, Doynton 11.08.04P
(NF 04.04.14)

G-MZDK Mainair Blade 1084-0596-7-W887 09.05.96
J Bunyan Headon Farm, Headon 07.10.18P
Trike c/n reported as 1084-0696-7

G-MZDM Rans S-6-ESD-XL Coyote II 0396.954 02.09.96
M E Nicholas (Acton Trussell, Stafford) 20.09.18P
*Built by M E Nicholas – project PFA 204-13022;
tricycle u/c*

G-MZDN Cyclone Pegasus Quantum 15 7255 05.09.96
N Cross Sutton Meadows 10.11.18P

G-MZDS Cyclone AX3/503 7253 16.09.96
M J Cooper (Langrick, Boston) 16.09.16P

G-MZDT Mainair Blade 1096-0996-7-W899 19.09.96
R L Beese Arclid Green, Sandbach 05.08.18P

G-MZDU Cyclone Pegasus Quantum 15-912 7260 19.09.96
J J D Firmino do Carmo Lagos, Algarve, Portugal 09.11.18P
Operated by Algarve Air Sports

G-MZDV Cyclone Pegasus Quantum 15 7199 09.04.96
Griffin Toomes Consulting Engineers Ltd (Hull) 29.05.18P

G-MZDX Letov LK-2M Sluka 8295s004 30.09.96
J L Barker (Attleborough)
*Built by T J T Dorricott – project PFA 263-12882
(SSDR microlight since 01.16) (NF 19.01.16)*

G-MZDY Cyclone Pegasus Quantum 15 7263 02.10.96
D T Moeller (Deddington) 05.07.18P

G-MZDZ Huntwing Avon/Skytrike 9501042 23.10.96
E W Laidlaw (Broom Loan, Kelso)
*Built by E W Laidlaw – project BMAA/HB/045
(NF 31.05.18)*

G-MZEA BFC Challenger II xxxx 22.04.96
G S Cridland Horse Leys Farm, Burton on the Wolds 29.08.10P
*Built by G S Cridland – project PFA 177A-12728
using BFC kit (IE 02.08.17)*

G-MZEB Mainair Blade 1074-0396-7-W876 22.07.96
R A Campbell (Crowton, Northwich) 21.06.18P

G-MZEC Cyclone Pegasus Quantum 15 7278 24.10.96
A B Godber Holly Meadow Farm, Bradley 16.06.18P
Badged 'Super Sport'

G-MZEE Cyclone Pegasus Quantum 15 7245 09.08.96
A R Greenly (Navenby, Lincoln) 29.03.19P

G-MZEG Mainair Blade 1095-0896-7-W898 08.08.96
G Cole Deenethorpe 17.04.18P

G-MZEH Cyclone Pegasus Quantum 15 7259 19.09.96
P S Hall Old Warden 21.10.18P

G-MZEK Mainair Mercury 1098-1096-7-W901 14.10.96
G Crane Arclid Green, Sandbach 14.09.18P

G-MZEL Cyclone AX3/503 7250 30.10.96
S Millen Causeway 11.08.19P

G-MZEM Cyclone Pegasus Quantum 15-912 7277 08.11.96
L H Black Newtownards 12.08.18P

G-MZEN Rans S-6-ESD Coyote II 1294.705 09.07.96
R Mills (Thorne, Doncaster) 26.05.18P
*Built by P Bottomley – project PFA 204-12823;
tricycle u/c*

G-MZEP Mainair Rapier 1103-1296-7-W906 13.12.96
A G Bird (Stourport-on-Severn) 11.03.13P
For sale 11.18 from Welwyn Garden City (IE 06.10.15)

G-MZES Letov LK-2M Sluka 8296K010 05.12.96
A P Love (Rugby) 13.03.15
Built by C Parkinson – project PFA 263-13064
(SSDR microlight since 06.14) (NF 26.03.18)

G-MZEU Rans S-6-ESD-XL Coyote II 0296.939 23.12.96
P Wilcox (Lincoln) 19.07.18P
Built by J E Holloway – project PFA 204-13023; tricycle u/c

G-MZEV Mainair Rapier 1101-1296-7-W904 07.01.97
W T Gardner Newtownards 02.05.15P

G-MZEW Mainair Blade 1105-0197-7-W908 13.01.97
T D Holder (Scrooby Top, Doncaster) 02.06.18P

G-MZEX Cyclone Pegasus Quantum 15 7292 19.11.96
D A Eastough Park Hall Farm, Mapperley 26.12.17P

G-MZEZ Cyclone Pegasus Quantum 15-912 7285 08.11.96
M J Hunt Middle Stoke, Isle of Grain 05.03.18P

G-MZFA Cyclone AX2000 7301 17.12.96
G S Highley Sackville Lodge Farm, Riseley 30.10.18P

G-MZFB Mainair Blade 1108-0197-7-W911 07.01.97
A J Plant Eccleston, Chorley 01.10.17P

G-MZFC Letov LK-2M Sluka 8296K009 07.01.97
D W Bayliss (Whitwell, Ventnor) 31.10.07P
Built by G Johnson – project PFA 263-13063
(SSDR microlight since 06.14) (NF 08.01.19)

G-MZFD Mainair Rapier 1109-0197-7-W912 24.01.97
A Hayward (Carlton, Nottingham) 25.04.18P

G-MZFE Huntwing Avon 503 9507049 16.01.97
G J Latham Strathaven
Built by G J Latham – project BMAA/HB/061
(SSDR microlight since 07.14) (IE 19.08.17)

G-MZFF Huntwing Avon 503(3) 9604058 22.01.97
B J Adamson Ince 16.01.03P
Built by B J Adamson – project BMAA/HB/074
(NF 05.08.14)

G-MZFH AMF Microflight Chevvron 2-32C 039 27.03.97
M C Holmes tr Eagle Flying Group Causeway 27.04.18P

G-MZFI Lorimer Iolaire BMAA/HB/035 30.01.97
Cancelled 25.03.09 as PWFU
Not Known *Stored in Ireland 03.17*

G-MZFL Rans S-6-ESD-XL Coyote II 0696.999 12.02.97
J J Lynch (Harrogate) 15.08.08P
Built by G A Clayton – project PFA 204-13041;
tricycle u/c (NF 07.11.17)

G-MZFM Cyclone Pegasus Quantum 15 7310 21.02.97
N Musgrave RAF Mona 24.09.18P

G-MZFO Thruster T600N 9037-T600N-001 04.03.97
S J P Stevenson Yatesbury 31.03.15P
Badged as 'T600'; noted 01.18 (IE 04.09.15)

G-MZFR Thruster T.600N 9047-T600N-003 04.03.97
Cancelled 19.10.10 by CAA 30.04.10
Hunsdon *Fuselage stored on farm 04.14*

G-MZFS Mainair Blade 1110-0297-7-W913 08.01.97
P L E Zelazowski (Tredington, Shipston-on-Stour) 04.10.14P
(NF 21.09.18)

G-MZFT Cyclone Pegasus Quantum 15-912 7264 02.10.96
G R Smith Headcorn 24.08.18P

G-MZFU Thruster T600N 450 Jab 9047-T600N-004 04.03.97
W C Walters Nottingham City 19.05.19P

G-MZFX Cyclone AX2000 7322 14.03.97
T J Wiltshire tr AX Group Wingland 24.07.17P

G-MZFY Rans S-6-ESD-XL Coyote II 0696.1003 17.03.97
L G Tserkezos Popham 23.03.18P
Built by L G Tserkezos – project PFA 204-13043;
tricycle u/c

G-MZFZ Mainair Blade 1119-0497-7-W922 02.04.97
D J Bateman (Shotley, Ipswich) 21.04.11P
(NF 09.09.16)

G-MZGA Cyclone AX2000 7303 17.12.96
R D Leigh Darley Moor 24.04.17P

G-MZGC Cyclone AX2000 7304 20.12.96
T J McMenamin Drumavish, Rol 12.05.16P

G-MZGD Rans S-5 Coyote 89.095 01.04.97
P J Greenrod Welshpool
Built by A G Headford – project PFA 193-13096;
abandoned take-off Welshpool 13.03.16 &
undercarriage collapsed; stored 07.16
(SSDR microlight since 08.14) (IE 26.08.15)

G-MZGF Letov LK-2M Sluka 8296K008 08.04.97
T W Thiele Newnham
Built by R J Cook – project PFA 263-13073; noted 01.17
(SSDR microlight since 06.14) (IE 19.01.16)

G-MZGG Cyclone Pegasus Quantum 15 7327 10.04.97
J M Chapman Monewden 08.06.18P
Uses trike ex G-MYRM (IE 06.07.18)

G-MZGH Huntwing Avon 462(3) 9406021 20.10.96
J H Cole Otherton
Built by G C Horner – project BMAA/HB/070
(SSDR microlight since 11.16) (NF 22.12.14)

G-MZGI Mainair Blade 912 1117-0397-7-W920 11.04.97
H M Roberts Trefgraig, Rhoshirwaun 03.09.18P

G-MZGL Mainair Rapier 1104-0197-7-W907 18.12.96
A Robins Welshpool 03.07.19P

G-MZGM Cyclone AX2000 7334 01.05.97
A F Smallacombe Davidstow Moor 12.11.15P
(NF 11.10.17)

G-MZGN Cyclone Pegasus Quantum 15 7332 02.05.97
J B Peacock (Surlingham, Norwich) 08.08.19P

G-MZGO Cyclone Pegasus Quantum 15 7320 20.03.97
S F G Allen (Farthinghoe, Brackley)
(SSDR microlight since 05.16) (IE 28.07.17)

G-MZGP Cyclone AX2000 7333 07.05.97
D G Palmer tr Buchan Light Aeroplane Club
Easter Nether Cabra Farm, Fetterangus 14.06.07P

G-MZGU Arrowflight Hawk II (UK) xxxx 08.05.97
M C Holmes Causeway 03.05.02P
Built by Arrowflight Aviation Ltd – project
PFA 266-13075 (NF 29.10.14)

G-MZGW Mainair Blade 1112-0297-7-W915 19.02.97
R C Ford Priory Farm, Tibenham
(SSDR microlight since 10.15) (NF 28.06.17)

G-MZGY Thruster T600N 450 9057-T600N-006 28.04.97
K J Brooker Jackrells Farm, Southwater 13.08.18P

G-MZHA Thruster T600T 9057-T600T-008 28.04.97
P Stark (Cumnock) 06.09.17P
Stored at Meikle Garclauch Farm (IE 06.12.17)

G-MZHB Mainair Blade 1114-0297-7-W917 19.02.97
P Sidebottom (Leek) 06.05.18P
(IE 22.05.18)

G-MZHD Thruster T600T 9067-T600T-010 13.05.97
R P Scothern (Derby) 31.08.18P
(NF 09.09.18)

G-MZHF Thruster T600N 9067-T600N-012 13.05.97
C Carmichael Beverley (Linley Hill) 05.03.18P
Badged 'Sprint'

G-MZHG Whittaker MW6-T Merlin xxxx 16.06.97
J L Jordan (Crossnacreevy, Belfast)
Built by M G Speers – project PFA 164-11420;
stored 08.18
(SSDR microlight since 10.18) (IE 17.07.18)

G-MZHI Cyclone Pegasus Quantum 15 7337 27.05.97
M A Gardiner (Hayle, Truro) 16.04.18P

G-MZHJ Mainair Rapier 1123-0697-7-W926 17.06.97
G Standish St Michaels 25.08.17P
(IE 15.12.17)

G-MZHMᴹTeam HiMax 1700R xxxx 08.01.97
M H McKeown Long Kesh, Lisburn
Built by M H McKeown – project PFA 272-12912;
displayed Ulster Aviation Society Heritage Collection
(SSDR microlight since 06.14) (NF 08.06.15)

G-MZHN Cyclone Pegasus Quantum 15 7351 27.06.97
F W Frerichs Sackville Lodge Farm, Riseley 10.07.18P

G-MZHO Quad City Challenger II xxxx 15.07.97
J Pavelin Barling Magna 22.08.17P
Built by J Pavelin – project PFA 177-12936 (IE 23.10.17)

G-MZHP	Cyclone Pegasus Quantum 15	7353	15.07.97
	W J Flood Rochester		17.03.18P
G-MZHR	Cyclone AX2000	7307	07.03.97
	J P Jones (Rhuallt, St Asaph)		31.08.12
	(SSDR microlight since 06.18) (NF 13.12.16)		
G-MZHS	Thruster T600T	9077-T600T-013	04.07.97
	D Greenly tr G-MZHS Group Popham		13.03.18P
G-MZHV	Thruster T600N	9077-T600T-018	04.07.97
	H G Denton Longacre Farm, Sandy		31.08.18P
	Originally built as T600T		
G-MZHW	Thruster T600N	9077-T600N-017	04.07.97
	A J Glynn Gerpins Farm, Upminster		29.07.18P
G-MZHY	Thruster T600N	9077-T600N-015	04.07.97
	B W Webster Ince		
	Rebuilt 2009 after incident using parts from G-BYOS		
	(SSDR microlight since 07.15) (IE 26.08.15)		
G-MZIB	Cyclone Pegasus Quantum 15	7354	15.07.97
	S Murphy (Kilmessan, RoI)		12.07.12P
	(IE 20.06.16)		
G-MZID	Whittaker MW6 Merlin	xxxx	15.07.97
	C P F Sheppard Darley Moor		24.08.06P
	Built by M G A Wood – project PFA 164-11383;		
	stored 10.16 (NF 28.05.14)		
G-MZIE	Cyclone Pegasus Quantum 15	7359	06.08.97
	Flylight Airsports Ltd Sywell		09.06.13P
	Noted 07.15 as stripped frame (NF 07.03.16)		
G-MZIH	Mainair Blade 912	1128-0797-7-W931	16.07.97
	N J Waller Headon Farm, Retford		17.09.18P
G-MZIJ	Cyclone Pegasus Quantum 15	7362	14.08.97
	D L Wright Sywell		05.11.18P
G-MZIK	Cyclone Pegasus Quantum 15	7368	08.09.97
	J H Cole Otherton		04.12.17P
	(NF 05.10.18)		
G-MZIL	Mainair Rapier	1132-0897-7-W935	01.09.97
	B L Cook Sandtoft		26.08.18P
	(NF 25.09.17)		
G-MZIM	Mainair Rapier	1124-0697-7-W927	09.06.97
	M J McKegney Newtownards		03.10.18P
G-MZIS	Mainair Blade	1115-0397-7-W918	17.02.97
	M K Richings (Scarborough)		03.07.09P
	(NF 17.02.15)		
G-MZIT	Mainair Blade 912	1129-0897-7-W932	16.07.97
	M A Robinson Newtownards		22.07.18P
G-MZIU	Cyclone Pegasus Quantum 15	7371	15.10.97
	E A McCabe Easter Poldar Farm, Thornhill		27.09.19P
G-MZIV	Cyclone AX2000	7372	21.10.97
	A M Clements tr G-MZIV Syndicate (Nottingham NG8)		14.11.18P
G-MZIW	Mainair Blade	1127-0797-7-W930	16.07.97
	J C Boyd Perranporth		27.09.18P
G-MZIZ	Murphy Renegade Spirit UK	257	21.10.92
	G-MWGP C B Hopkins Hunsdon		19.12.17P
	Built by B Bayley – project PFA 188-11701		
G-MZJA	Mainair Blade	1135-0997-7-W938	30.09.97
	D M Whelan Otherton		06.08.18P
	(IE 06.10.17)		
G-MZJE	Mainair Rapier	1136-1097-7-W939	17.10.97
	N E Smith North Coates		25.05.17P
	(IE 18.07.16)		
G-MZJF	Cyclone AX2000	7378	02.12.97
	D J Lewis (Hardwicke, Cheltenham)		26.04.18P
G-MZJG	Cyclone Pegasus Quantum 15	7335	02.05.97
	S A Holmes (Chesterfield)		24.03.19P
G-MZJH	Cyclone Pegasus Quantum 15	7350	25.06.97
	P Copping Darley Moor		07.02.16P
	Crashed near Slipton, Northants 10.09.15 &		
	extensively damaged		
G-MZJI	Rans S-6-ESD-XL Coyote II	1096.1046XL	03.11.97
	J P Hunsdale (Easingwold, York)		20.04.18P
	Built by J Whiting – project PFA 204-13221; tricycle u/c		
G-MZJJ	Murphy Maverick	xxxx	05.11.97
	M F Farrer Monewden		15.05.17P
	Built by M F Cottam – project PFA 259-13016;		
	forced landed Shop Farm, Clopton 22.05.16 &		
	substantially damaged: on repair 01.18		
G-MZJK	Mainair Blade	1100-1196-7-W903	19.11.96
	P G Angus Higher Barn Farm, Hoghton		01.07.15P
G-MZJL	Cyclone AX2000	7363	11.08.97
	M H Owen Westonzoyland		23.05.18P
G-MZJM	Rans S-6-ESD-XL Coyote II	1096.1049	19.11.97
	B Lorraine Bodmin		06.11.18P
	Built by R J Hopkins – project PFA 204-13215		
G-MZJO	Cyclone Pegasus Quantum 15	7338	17.06.97
	D J Cook Eaglescott		03.06.18P
G-MZJP	Whittaker MW6-S Fatboy Flyer	xxxx	21.10.97
	D J Burton & R C Funnell (Brighton)		
	Built by D J Burton & C A J Funnell		
	– project PFA 164-13049 (NF 12.11.14)		
G-MZJT	Cyclone Pegasus Quantum 15-912	7399	23.12.97
	N Hammerton (Oxted)		08.06.19P
G-MZJV	Mainair Blade 912	1141-0198-7-W944	07.01.98
	M A Roberts (West Malling)		13.06.04P
	(NF 09.09.14)		
G-MZJW	Cyclone Pegasus Quantum 15-912	7390	27.01.98
	G A & G E Blackstone		
	Brown Shutters Farm, Norton St Philip		24.04.18P
G-MZJX	Mainair Blade	1139-0198-7-W942	09.01.98
	H Mercer Rossall Field, Cockerham		02.04.17P
G-MZJY	Cyclone Pegasus Quantum 15-912	7394	23.12.97
	(EI-...), G-MZJY R G Wyatt Northrepps		12.03.19P
G-MZJZ	Mainair Blade 912	1121-0597-7-W924	23.06.97
	S F Sharp tr Lima Zulu Owner Syndicate		
	(North Berwick)		22.02.18P
G-MZKA	Cyclone Pegasus Quantum 15-912	7380	01.12.97
	S P Tkaczyk Old Park Farm, Margam		15.08.17P
	(IE 06.10.17)		
G-MZKC	Cyclone AX2000	7398	22.01.98
	D J Pike Bradley's Lawn, Heathfield		28.10.14P
	(NF 22.10.16)		
G-MZKD	Cyclone Pegasus Quantum 15-912	7404	19.03.98
	T M Frost Charmy Down		17.09.18P
	(IE 02.11.17)		
G-MZKE	Rans S-6-ESD-XL Coyote II	0797.1142	19.01.98
	P A Flaherty Beccles		28.04.18P
	Built by I Findlay – project PFA 204-13248; tricycle u/c		
G-MZKF	Cyclone Pegasus Quantum 15-912	7407	21.01.98
	A H, D P & V J Tidmas Willingale		06.12.18P
G-MZKG	Mainair Blade	1145-0198-7-W948	23.01.98
	N S Rigby Ince		21.10.11P
	(NF 14.08.15)		
G-MZKH	CFM Shadow Series DD	292-DD	23.01.98
	S P H Calvert Kittyhawk Farm, Ripe		05.10.18P
G-MZKI	Mainair Rapier	1147-0298-7-W950	12.02.98
	D L Aspinall Oban		07.06.16P
G-MZKJ	Mainair Blade	1039-0595-7-W837	19.05.95
	K M Jones tr The G-MZKJ Group Leicester		01.05.05P
	(IE 29.10.16)		
G-MZKL	Cyclone Pegasus Quantum 15	7360	18.08.97
	R Viner tr Kilo Lima Group Park Hall Farm, Mapperley		08.05.19P
G-MZKN	Mainair Rapier	1138-1297-7-W941	12.12.97
	O P Farrell (Ballymakenny, Drogheda, RoI)		11.05.18P
G-MZKS	Thruster T600N	9038-T600N-022	27.01.98
	J R Gardiner Bodmin		11.09.19P
G-MZKU	Thruster T600T	9038-T600T-024	27.01.98
	A S Day Tibenham		07.10.18P
G-MZKW	Quad City Challenger II	xxxx	22.03.94
	R A Allen (Midgham, Reading)		16.10.17P
	Built by K W Warn – project PFA 177-12518		
G-MZKY	Cyclone Pegasus Quantum 15 (HKS)	7403	16.01.98
	P S Constable Deenethorpe		28.09.17P

G

G-MZKZ	Mainair Blade	1137-0298-7-W940	18.02.98
	R P Wolstenholme Arclid Green, Sandbach		07.08.04P
	(NF 17.02.16)		
G-MZLA	Cyclone Pegasus Quantum 15	7415	27.02.98
	A C Hodges Brook Breasting Farm, Watnall		31.08.18P
G-MZLD	Cyclone Pegasus Quantum 15-912	7416	24.03.98
	L Sokoli Eshott		20.12.18P
G-MZLE	Murphy Maverick 430	xxxx	27.02.98
	G-BXSZ M W Hands Saltby		22.01.19P
	Built by A A Plumridge – project PFA 259-12955		
G-MZLF	Cyclone Pegasus Quantum 15	7417	30.03.98
	S Seymour (Corby)		19.06.10P
	(NF 25.08.17)		
G-MZLG	Rans S-6-ESD-XL Coyote II	0897.1143	03.03.98
	A M Beale Lofts Farm, Broad Street Green		18.11.09P
	Built by R H J Jenkins – project PFA 204-13192;		
	tricycle u/c (IE 17.03.16)		
G-MZLI	Mignet HM-1000 Balerit	133	05.03.98
	A G Barr Otherton		31.05.13P
	(NF 17.08.15)		
G-MZLJ	Cyclone Pegasus Quantum 15	7421	20.03.98
	R M Williams Arclid Green, Sandbach		18.05.18P
G-MZLK	Ultrasports Tri-Pacer/Solar Wings Typhoon		
		T7851471M	09.03.98
	Cancelled 20.02.12 as PWFU		16.11.08
	Eshott *Trike ex G-MJEC & wing is Typhoon S4+,*		
	s/n T785-1471M – ex-hang-glider; stored 09.14		
G-MZLL	Rans S-6-ESD-XL Coyote II	0696.998	23.09.97
	D W Adams (Partridge Green, Horsham)		30.05.18P
	Built by G W Champion & J A Willats		
	– project PFA 204-13067		
G-MZLM	Cyclone AX2000	7425	22.04.98
	P E Hadley Glebe Farm, Sibson		13.06.18P
	Modified to tug version		
G-MZLN	Cyclone Pegasus Quantum 15	7431	14.04.98
	P A Greening Longacre Farm, Sandy		16.10.18P
G-MZLP	CFM Shadow D Series SS	K 299-D	01.04.98
	D J Gordon Woodlands Barton Farm, Roche		
	(SSDR microlight since 08.16) (IE 25.08.17)		
G-MZLT	Cyclone Pegasus Quantum 15-912	7438	24.04.98
	B Jackson Darley Moor		23.05.18P
G-MZLU	Cyclone AX2000	7439	28.07.98
	E Pashley (Spencers Wood, Reading)		02.05.09P
	(NF 18.03.15)		
G-MZLV	Cyclone Pegasus Quantum 15	7437	29.04.98
	R R Till (Standon under Bardon, Markfield)		13.06.19P
G-MZLW	Cyclone Pegasus Quantum 15	7440	28.04.98
	R W R Crevel tr G-MZLW Syndicate Sywell		14.10.18P
G-MZLX	Micro B.22S Bantam	97-013	09.12.97
	(EI-...), G-MZLX, ZK-JIV V J Vaughan Abbeyleix, RoI		23.09.13P
	Noted 05.16 (NF 22.09.15)		
G-MZLY	Letov LK-2M Sluka	xxxx	20.04.98
	W McCarthy (Kirk, Wick)		
	Built by B G M Chapman – project PFA 263-13065		
	(SSDR microlight since 06.14) (NF 14.09.16)		
G-MZLZ	Mainair Blade 912	1154-0498-7-W957	21.04.98
	D Round Otherton		22.04.18P
G-MZMA	Solar Wings Pegasus Quasar IITC	6611	01.09.93
	V Donskovas Redlands		07.08.17P
	Noted dismantled 02.18 (IE 01.11.17)		
G-MZMC	Cyclone Pegasus Quantum 15-912	7206	10.05.96
	J J Baker (Kettering)		29.07.17P
G-MZME	Medway EclipseR	151/130E	08.04.98
	G-582 T A Dobbins (Birmingham B34)		21.06.19P
	Originally Medway Hybred 44XLRE		
	(c/n MR151/129 later MR151/130)		
G-MZMF	Cyclone Pegasus Quantum 15 (HKS)	7387	30.04.98
	A J Tranter Maryculter		03.12.18P
G-MZMG	Cyclone Pegasus Quantum 15	7446	27.05.98
	C J Meadows Westonzoyland		17.12.17P
	Badged 'Super Sport' (IE 04.04.18)		
G-MZMH	Cyclone Pegasus Quantum 15-912	7402	27.01.98
	A K Hole Caernarfon		08.02.19P
G-MZMJ	Mainair Blade 912	1155-0598-7-W958	08.05.98
	D Wilson Bankwood Farm, Oxton		27.09.18P
G-MZMK	AMF Microflight Chevvron 2-32C	040	19.05.98
	P M Waller (Weston-Super-Mare)		10.08.18P
G-MZML	Mainair Blade 912	1158-0698-7-W961	19.05.98
	C J Meadows Westonzoyland		12.04.16P
G-MZMN	Cyclone Pegasus Quantum 15-912	7445	21.05.98
	V Donskovas tr G-MZMN Group Redlands		27.04.18P
G-MZMO	Team Mini-Max 91	914	20.05.98
	North East Flight Training Ltd		
	Easter Nether Cabra Farm, Fetterangus		
	Built by I M Ross – project PFA 186-12951)		
	(SSDR microlight since 08.14) (IE 19.07.18)		
G-MZMT	Cyclone Pegasus Quantum 15	7449	18.06.98
	T Hemsley (Langport)		25.04.19P
G-MZMU	Rans S-6-ESD-XL Coyote II	0897.1145	05.06.98
	K G Diamond tr WEZ Group Redhill		06.08.17P
	Built by S Cox – project PFA 204-13242;		
	rebuilt with kit no.0298.1203 c.2003		
G-MZMV	Mainair Blade	1152-0498-7-W955	30.03.98
	S P Allen & C J Tomlin (Kettering)		11.07.18P
G-MZMW	Mignet HM-1000 Balerit	125	02.10.96
	M E Whapham Park Farm, Burwash		23.05.18P
G-MZMY	Mainair Blade	1153-0498-7-W956	16.03.98
	N Janes Arclid Green, Sandbach		21.05.19P
G-MZMZ	Mainair Blade	1081-0496-7-W884	22.04.96
	D T Page (Kettering)		10.09.19P
G-MZNA	Quad City Challenger II	CH2-0894-UK-1193	19.03.98
	EI-CLE S Hennessy (Ballisodare, Co Sligo, RoI)		14.04.08P
	Built by M Tormey (IE 23.10.17)		
G-MZNB	Cyclone Pegasus Quantum 15-912	7456	17.07.98
	S J Metters Caernarfon		11.07.18P
	Badged 'Super Sport'		
G-MZNC	Mainair Blade 912	1161-0698-7-W964	22.06.98
	A J Harrison Headon Farm, Retford		17.06.18P
G-MZND	Mainair Rapier	1170-0898-7-W973	24.06.98
	D W Stamp Pound Green		23.10.11P
	(NF 01.10.14)		
G-MZNG	Cyclone Pegasus Quantum 15-912	7457	11.08.98
	The Scottish Flying Club Strathaven		10.06.18P
G-MZNH	CFM Shadow Series DD	297-DD	30.06.98
	P A James Redhill		08.09.13P
	(NF 22.09.16)		
G-MZNJ	Mainair Blade	1168-0798-7-W971	06.07.98
	R A Hardy Headon Farm, Retford		15.04.18P
G-MZNO	Mainair Blade 912	1167-0798-7-W970	09.06.98
	E McCallum Athey's Moor, Longframlington		29.09.19P
	Trike is ex G-ENVY		
G-MZNR	Cyclone Pegasus Quantum 15	7465	17.08.98
	N J Clemens (Paignton)		17.09.17P
G-MZNS	Cyclone Pegasus Quantum 15-912	7473	31.07.98
	S Uzochukwu Barhams Mill Farm, Egerton		09.12.18P
	Badged 'Super Sport'		
G-MZNT	Cyclone Pegasus Quantum 15-912	7470	25.09.98
	N W Barnett (Coventry CV4)		19.04.18P
	Badged 'Super Sport'		
G-MZNV	Rans S-6-ESD-XL Coyote II	1294.704	07.08.98
	A P Thomas Brimpton		24.04.18P
	Built by D E Rubery – project PFA 204-12884;		
	tricycle u/c		
G-MZNY	Thruster T600N 450	9098-T600N-027	10.08.98
	Cheshire Flying School Ltd Ashcroft		31.08.17P
G-MZOC	Mainair Blade 912	1172-0898-7-W975	10.08.98
	A S Davies (Liverpool L4)		03.06.17P
G-MZOD	Cyclone Pegasus Quantum 15-912	7435	28.04.98
	G P Burns Sackville Lodge Farm, Riseley		12.04.18P
G-MZOE	Cyclone AX2000	7472	17.09.98
	B E Wagenhauser Westonzoyland		02.07.18P
G-MZOG	Cyclone Pegasus Quantum 15	7471	12.10.98
	D Smith Eshott		27.08.18P

G-MZOH	Whittaker MW5-D Sorcerer	xxxx	14.08.98
	I Pearson Newquay Cornwall		
	Built by D M Precious – project PFA 163-13060)		
	(SSDR microlight since 06.14) (IE 15.12.17)		
G-MZOI	Letov LK-2M Sluka	8296s012	17.08.98
	J G Burns Morgansfield, Fishburn		
	Built by K P Taylor – project PFA 263-13238)		
	(SSDR microlight since 06.14) (IE 18.08.15)		
G-MZOK	Whittaker MW6 Merlin	xxxx	24.08.97
	R E Arnold tr G-MZOK Syndicate Otherton		28.04.16P
	Built by R K Willcox – project PFA 164-11568		
	(IE 24.01.18)		
G-MZOP	Mainair Blade 912	1178-0998-7-W981	11.09.98
	K M Thorogood Caernarfon		07.08.11P
	(NF 16.09.15)		
G-MZOS	Cyclone Pegasus Quantum 15-912	7458	06.10.98
	T G Ryan Sandtoft		24.05.18P
G-MZOV	Cyclone Pegasus Quantum 15	7512	09.03.99
	B E Wagenhauser Westonzoyland		31.08.18P
	Badged 'Quantum Super Sport' (NF 15.10.18)		
G-MZOW	Cyclone Pegasus Quantum 15-912	7502	09.03.99
	G P Burns Middle Stoke, Isle of Grain		31.05.18P
G-MZOX	Letov LK-2M Sluka	8289 SO-21	15.02.99
	N R Beale Gilderage Farm, Stelling Minnis '301'		
	Built by C M James – project PFA 263-13415		
	(SSDR microlight since 07.14) (IE 22.11.17)		
G-MZOY	Team Mini-Max 91	186	29.03.99
	P R & S E Whitehouse Otherton		
	Built by E F Smith – project PFA 186-12526)		
	(SSDR microlight since 05.15) (IE 05.06.17)		
G-MZOZ	Rans S-6-ESA Coyote II	1096.1052	20.05.98
	G L Daniels (Beddau, Pontypridd)		13.12.18P
	Built by D C & S G Emmons – project PFA 204-13168;		
	tricycle u/c		
G-MZPH	Mainair Blade	1177-0998-7-W980	26.08.98
	A M Donkin Moss Edge Farm, Cockerham		07.07.18P
G-MZPJ	Team Mini-Max 91	xxxx	23.11.92
	J Aubert Fairoaks		
	Built by P R Jenson – project PFA 186-12277)		
	(SSDR microlight since 06.14) (IE 31.05.17)		
G-MZRC	Cyclone Pegasus Quantum 15	7482	25.11.98
	M Hopkins Rufforth East		23.02.03P
	(NF 12.04.16)		
G-MZRM	Cyclone Pegasus Quantum 15-912	7455	10.07.98
	R Milwain (Alloa)		19.05.18P
G-MZRS	CFM Shadow Series CD	141	04.04.90
	C J Tomlin (Desborough, Kettering)		17.08.18P
G-MZSP	Spacek SD-1 Minisport	111	11.09.14
	A M Hughes Popham		
	Tricycle u/c (IE 09.06.17)		
G-MZTG	Titan T-51 Mustang	0190	20.11.14
	A R Evans (Wilmslow)		
	Built by A R Evans – project LAA 355-15255		
	(NF 21.11.14)		
G-MZUB	Rans S-6-ESD-XL Coyote II	0897.1144	30.04.98
	R E Main (Warrington)		03.10.14P
	Built by B O Dowsett – project PFA 204-13244;		
	tricycle u/c		
G-MZZT	Kolb Twinstar Mk.III	K0006-0992	01.05.98
	F Omaraie-Hamdanie Plaistows Farm, St Albans		
	Built by P I Morgans – project PFA 205-12596;		
	imported by Mainair as kit s/n K0006-0992		
	(SSDR microlight since 11.15) (IE 22.07.18)		
G-MZZY	Mainair Blade 912	1050-0895-7-W848	13.11.95
	A Mucznik Bankwood Farm, Oxton		04.09.14P
	(NF 03.12.15)		

G-NAAA – G-NZZZ

G-NAAT	Folland Gnat T.1	FL.507	27.11.89
	XM697 Cancelled 10.04.95 as PWFU		
	Carluke Stored private address 05.16 as 'XM697'		
G-NACA	Norman NAC-2 Freelance 180	2001	23.11.87
	P J L Caruth & A R Norman Henstridge		14.01.18P

G-NACI	Norman NAC-1 Freelance 180	NAC 001	20.06.84
	G-AXFB M D Gorlov Elstree		26.06.19P
G-NADN	Piper PA-23-250 Aztec F	27-7754103	17.06.16
	G-XSFT, G-CPPC, G-BGBH, N63773		
	N M T Sparks St Athan		16.06.09E
G-NADO	Titan Tornado SS	SOHK 0521	21.04.08
	C Firth (Scarborough)		
	Built by C Firth & D G Smith –		
	project LAA 356-14780 (NF 29.06.18)		
G-NADS	Team Mini-Max 91	xxxx	08.02.99
	N P St J Ramsay (North Petherwin, Launceston)		
	Built by G Evans & P M Spencer –		
	project PFA 186-12995		
	(SSDR microlight since 01.15) (IE 29.05.18)		
G-NAGG	AutoGyro MT-03	xxxx	18.05.07
	C A Clements Thruxton		01.08.18P
	Assembled Rotorsport UK as c/n RSUK/MT-03/012		
G-NALD	Aeroprakt A-32 Vixxen	A32062	29.01.19
	D J Medcraft (Hartley Wintney, Hook)		
	Built by D J Medcraft – project LAA 411-15587		
	(IE 29.01.19)		
G-NANI	Robinson R44 Clipper II	11537	09.01.07
	Mega Parquet SL Palma-Son Bonet, Mallorca, Spain		04.02.18E
G-NANO	Avid Speed Wing	911	23.01.08
	A M Wyndham (London SE11)		02.01.19P
	Built by T M C Handley – project PFA 189-12094		
G-NAPO	Cyclone Pegasus Quantum 15-912	7799	06.04.01
	K S Henderson & J K Kerr East Fortune		21.07.18P
G-NAPP	Van's RV-7	xxxx	03.09.03
	R C Meek North Weald		10.07.19P
	Built by R J Napp – project PFA 323-14115		
G-NARG	Air Création Tanarg 912S(1)/iXess 15	FLxxx	24.06.05
	K Kirby Osbaston Lodge Farm, Osbaston		24.03.18P
	Built by Flylight Airsports Ltd – project		
	BMAA/HB/450 (Flylight kit FLxxx comprising		
	trike s/n T05020 & wing s/n A05040-5041		
G-NATI	Corby CJ-1 Starlet	602	12.07.13
	S P Evans Coventry		
	Built by S P Evans – project PFA 134-12631		
	(NF 15.08.17)		
G-NATT	Rockwell Commander 114A	14538	14.01.80
	N5921N Northgleam Ltd Liverpool John Lennon		26.09.18E
	(IE 28.07.17)		
G-NATY	Folland Gnat T.1	FL.548	19.06.90
	8642M, XR537 Cancelled 04.04.18 by CAA		13.07.16
	North Weald Stored 05.18 in Red Arrows c/s as 'XR537'		
G-NBCA	Pilatus PC-12/47E	1717	26.06.17
	HB-FSG Narm Aviation Ltd Leeds Bradford		21.06.18E
G-NBDD	Robin DR.400-180 Régent	1103	26.09.88
	F-BXVN B & S E Chambers tr Delta Delta Group		
	Rothwell Lodge Farm, Kettering		11.04.18E
G-NBOX	Comco Ikarus C42 FB100 Bravo	1405-7329	07.07.14
	Natterbox Ltd (Oxted)		01.07.18P
	Assembled Red-Air UK		
G-NBPL	Aérospatiale AS.355F2 Ecureuil 2	5483	07.09.18
	HB-ZKB, I-SFLY, OM-WIQ, OK-WIQ, SE-JET, F-WYMA		
	Nigel Brunt Properties Ltd Elstree		10.10.19E
G-NCFC	Piper PA-38-112 Tomahawk II	38-81A0107	14.01.99
	N737V, G-BNOA, N23272 (?)		
	A M Heynen Brighton City		03.02.14E
	Official p/i 'N23272' is incorrect (NF 16.12.15)		
G-NCUB	Piper J-3C-65 Cub (L-4H-PI)	11599	06.07.84
	G-BGXV, F-BFQT, OO-GAB, 43-30308		
	R J Willies Old Warden		12.06.18P
G-NDAD	Medway Clipper-100	80910	22.11.11
	R D Pyne Middle Stoke, Isle of Grain		28.03.18P
	Originally registered as Clipper-100		
G-NDIA	Robinson R22 Beta II	3453	02.02.16
	G-CCGE Altitude Consultants Ltd &		
	EBG (Helicopters) Ltd Redhill		14.12.18E
G-NDJS	Jonker JS-MD Single (JS1 Revelation)	1C.MD102	28.11.17
	(BGA 5945), D-KBAD A J Davis Nympsfield '80'		29.11.18E
G-NDOT	Thruster T600N 450	0052-T600N-066	18.06.02
	P C Bailey Hill Farm, Over		29.05.17P

G

G-NDPA	Comco Ikarus C42 FB UK	0302 6235	01.12.05
	G-OOMW C Hubbard tr Grandpa's Flying Group		
	Boston		16.05.18P
	Built by R O'Malley-White – project PFA 322-14056		
G-NEAL	Piper PA-32-260 Cherokee Six	32-1048	07.11.83
	G-BFPY, N5588J S G Watson (Darlington)		24.09.19E
G-NEAT	Europa Aviation Europa	065	28.06.94
	P F D Foden Dunkeswell		26.04.18P
	Built by M Burton – project PFA 247-12642; tricycle u/c		
G-NEDS	Best Off Skyranger Nynja 912S(1)	12 11 0117	10.01.13
	J Hunter (Kettering)		14.05.19P
	Built by H Van Allen – project BMAA/HB/634		
G-NEEE	Reims/Cessna F172M	F17201350	26.04.17
	G-BCZM Genius Aviation Ltd (Miskin, Pontyclun)		27.06.19E
G-NEEL	RotorWay Exec 90	5002	07.08.90
	I C Bedford (Skegness)		
	Built by P N Haigh (NF 21.11.14)		
G-NEII	Montgomerie-Bensen B.8MR	xxxx	14.11.16
	G-BVJF Dept of Doing Ltd Deenethorpe		
	Built by R S Frankham – project PFA G/01-1082;		
	'Little Nellie' style c/s (NF 14.11.16)		
G-NEIL	Thunder Ax3 Maxi Sky Chariot	379	02.12.81
	R M Powell Upper Timsbury, Romsey *'Neil'*		
	(NF 24.08.16)		
G-NELI	Piper PA-28R-180 Cherokee Arrow	28R-31011	09.02.01
	OH-PWW, D-EMWE, N7693J		
	MK Aero Support Ltd Andrewsfield		22.06.18E
G-NELS	Robinson R44 Raven I	1512	28.05.15
	D-HALI Heliwarns Aviation Ltd Leeds Heliport		21.10.17E
G-NEMO	Raj Hamsa X'Air Jabiru(4)	602	11.03.04
	G F Allen Great Oakley		21.08.18P
	Built by D G Smith – project BMAA/HB/158		
G-NEON	Piper PA-32-300 Cherokee Six B	32-40683	07.04.00
	D-EMKW, N4246R T F Rowley Popham		06.08.19E
G-NEOP	Airbus A321-261NX	8469	27.03.19
	D-AVZB British Airways PLC London Heathrow		
G-NEOR	Airbus A321-251NX	8526	22.11.18
	D-AVZQ British Airways PLC London Heathrow		21.11.19E
G-NEOS	Airbus A321-251NX	8637	29.01.19
	D-AYAD British Airways PLC London Heathrow		28.01.20E
G-NEOT	Airbus A321-251NX	8718	01.03.19
	D-AYAP British Airways PLC London Heathrow		
(G-NEOU)	Airbus A321-251NX	8804	
	British Airways PLC Reserved, due xx.19		
(G-NEOV)	Airbus A321-251NX	8930	
	British Airways PLC Reserved, due xx.19		
(G-NEOW)	Airbus A321-251NX		
	British Airways PLC Reserved, due xx.19		
(G-NEOX)	Airbus A321-251NX		
	British Airways PLC Reserved, due xx.19		
G-NESA	Europa Aviation Europa XS	450	17.04.01
	A M Kay Cambridge		24.11.18P
	Built by K G & V E Summerhill		
	– project PFA 247-13544; tri-gear u/c		
G-NESE	Tecnam P2002-JF Sierra	039	09.06.06
	N & S Easton Perth		19.07.18E
G-NESH	Robinson R44 Clipper II	11609	08.02.07
	Helicentre Aviation Ltd Leicester *'National Grid'*		13.03.19E
G-NEST	Christen Eagle II	SHAY 0001	14.09.06
	N23MS P J Nonat Le Plessis-Belleville, France		26.11.18P
	Built by M Shay		
G-NESW	Piper PA-34-220T Seneca III	34-8233072	13.12.02
	D-GAMO, N8064M G C U Guida Jersey		07.12.18E
G-NESY	Piper PA-18 Super Cub 95	18-7482	18.08.00
	N124SA, SE-CUG		
	V Featherstone Northside, Thorney		06.05.15E
	(IE 01.08.16)		
G-NETR	Aérospatiale AS.355F1 Ecureuil 2	5164	04.04.00
	G-JARV, G-OGHL, N5796S		
	PLM Dollar Group Ltd Dalcross Heliport		27.05.18E
	Operated by for British Transport Police (Network Rail),		
	callsign 'Osprey 62')		
G-NETY	Piper PA-18-150 Super Cub	1809108	08.09.95
	N4159K S de Sutter Ostend, Belgium		08.07.18E
G-NEUS	Brügger MB.2 Colibri	xxxx	02.11.78
	T R Fray (Plungar, Nottingham)		
	Built G E Smeaton – project PFA 043-10392		
	(NF 08.03.19)		
G-NEVE	Comco Ikarus C42 FB100	1608-7465	26.08.16
	M Neve (Llangennech, Llanelli)		22.09.18P
	Assembled Red Aviation		
G-NEWA	Rans S-6-ES Coyote II	0611.1944	02.06.15
	J Cook Low Hill Farm, North Moor, Messingham		03.09.19P
	Built by S Blakemore – project LAA 204-15224		
	(North East Wolverhampton Academy		
	'build-a-plane'); tricycle u/c		
G-NEWT	Beech 35 Bonanza	D-1168	28.02.90
	G-APVW, EI-BIL, G-APVW, N9866F, 4X-ACI,		
	Israel DFAF 0604, ZS-BTE J S Allison Bicester		25.07.18E
G-NEWZ	Bell 206B-3 JetRanger III	4475	28.01.98
	C-GBVZ H P L Frost (Warfield, Bracknell)		08.02.18E
G-NFLA	British Aerospace Jetstream 3102	637	15.02.06
	G-BRGN, G-BLHC, G-31-637		
	Cranfield University Cranfield		21.08.18E
	Operated by National Flying Laboratory Centre		
G-NFLC	Handley Page HP137 Jetstream 1	222	12.12.95
	G-AXUI, G-8-9 Cancelled 03.08.04 as PWFU		03.06.09
	Perth *Instructional frame 07.16*		
G-NFLY	Tecnam P2002-EA Sierra	228	28.03.07
	C N Hodgson Hinton-in-the-Hedges		10.09.18P
	Built by C N Hodgson – project PFA 333-14613		
G-NFNF	Robin DR.400-180 Régent	2047	15.11.02
	VP-BNU, VR-BNU, G-BTDU		
	J Archer, M Child & W Cobb Old Warden		17.01.18E
G-NFON	Van's RV-8	82750	02.07.09
	N F O'Neill Newtownards		14.07.18P
	Built by N F O'Neill – project LAA 303-14921		
G-NFOX	Aeropro EuroFOX 912(S)	48115	26.10.15
	A E Mayhew Rochester		25.05.18P
	Built by A E Mayhew – project LAA 376-15358;		
	tailwheel u/c		
G-NFVB	Cameron Z-105	12107	02.08.17
	Ballooning Network Ltd Bristol BS3 *'novia'*		16.06.19E
G-NGAA	BRM Bristell NG5 Speed Wing	xxxx	23.01.18
	A J Palmer & F Sayyah Chilsfold Farm, Northchapel		04.10.19P
	Built by A J Palmer & F Sayyah – project LAA 385-15524		
	First flight 08.09.18		
G-NGCC	BRM Bristell NG5 Speed Wing	313-2017	05.02.18
	G C Coull Perth		26.11.19P
	Built by G C Coull – project LAA 385-15516		
G-NGII	BRM Bristell NG5 Speed Wing	235	27.02.17
	A J Palmer & F Sayyah Chilsfold Farm, Northchapel		22.04.19P
	Built by A J Palmer & F Sayyah – project LAA 385-15431		
G-NHAA	Aérospatiale AS.365N2 Dauphin 2	6431	21.01.10
	G-MLTY, N365EL, JA6673 The Great North		
	Air Ambulance Service Durham Tees Valley		
	'The Guardian of the North'		06.06.18E
	Operated by Great North Air Ambulance as		
	callsign 'Helimed 63'		
G-NHAB	Aérospatiale AS.365N2 Dauphin 2	6407	11.06.10
	G-DAUF, N31EH, XA-SWT, N488FA, JA6676		
	The Great North Air Ambulance Service		
	Langwathby, Penrith *'The Pride of Cumbria'*		22.03.19E
	Operated by Great North Air Ambulance as		
	callsign 'Helimed 58'		
G-NHAC	Eurocopter AS.365N2 Dauphin 2	6497	27.04.11
	VP-BEO, N28LA, TC-HDO, F-WWOF, F-WQDC		
	The Great North Air Ambulance Service		
	Langwathby, Penrith		21.09.18E
	Operated by Great North Air Ambulance		
G-NHAD	Airbus AS.365N3 Dauphin 2	6979	05.03.19
	G-SSKP, HS-LCF, G-CIUC The Great North		
	Air Ambulance Service Durham Tees Valley		
G-NHEM	Eurocopter EC135 T2	0175	31.10.16
	G-KRNW Babcock Mission Critical Services		
	Onshore Ltd Long Kesh, Lisburn		11.07.18E
	Operated by Northern Ireland Air Ambulance		

G-NHRH	Piper PA-28-140 Cherokee	28-22807	19.05.82	
	OY-BIC, SE-EZP C J Milsom Compton Abbas		07.04.17E	
	Heavy landing Compton Abbas 30.05.16 &			
	nose u/c collapsed; in open store 08.16			
G-NHRJ	Europa Aviation Europa XS	333	30.09.99	
	R J Dawson Retford Gamston *'Snow Goose'*		12.06.19P	
	Built by R J Dawson & D A Lowe – project			
	PFA 247-13112; tricycle u/c			
G-NIAA	Beech B200 Super King Air	BB-897	14.03.14	
	D-IEFB, N200TM, N1837S			
	Blue Sky Investments Ltd Belfast Int'l		12.06.18E	
G-NIAB	Beech B200C Super King Air	BL-16	20.12.16	
	OO-LAC, F-GLTX, (OO-SKN), F-GLTX, N57LM,			
	LN-TWI, N62GA, F-GFAA, N200RG, N621AW			
	Blue Sky Investments Ltd Belfast Int'l		15.09.18E	
G-NIAC	TL 2000UK Sting Carbon S4	xxxx	03.04.18	
	J Middleton Newtownards			
	Built by A Coulter & M Fulton – project			
	LAA 347A-15425; initial build at Long Kesh;			
	to Newtownards 04.18 (IE 08.04.18)			
G-NICC	Evektor EV-97 teamEurostar UK	2004-1913	01.03.04	
	C Wileman (Bideford)		14.12.18P	
	Assembled Cosmik Aviation Ltd			
G-NICI	Robinson R44 Raven II	10854	31.08.05	
	David Fishwick Vehicles Sales Ltd			
	Bentley Farm, Coal Aston		02.11.18E	
G-NICS	Best Off Skyranger Swift 912S(1)	UK/868	11.06.08	
	I A Forrest & C K Richardson East Fortune		24.06.18P	
	Built by N G Heywood – project BMAA/HB/576			
G-NICX	Europa Aviation Europa XS	525	08.07.16	
	N Kenney Damyns Hall, Upminster			
	Built by N Kenney – project LAA 247-15362;			
	cleared to fly 10.18 (IE 07.08.18)			
G-NIDG	Evektor EV-97 Eurostar	1999-0609	29.02.00	
	Skydrive Ltd Deppers Bridge, Southam		01.08.18P	
	Built by N R Beale – project PFA 315-13580;			
	also known as Evektor 99 Eurostar			
G-NIEN	Van's RV-9A	91112	19.04.06	
	K N P Higgs Westonzoyland		17.10.18P	
	Built by G R Pybus – project PFA 320-14419			
G-NIFE	SNCAN Stampe SV.4A	156	27.05.05	
	F-BBBL, French AF CEV, F-BFCE, French AF CEV			
	Training & Leisure Consultants Ltd Headcorn		18.08.11C	
	As '156' in French AF c/s (NF 05.02.18)			
G-NIGC	Avtech Jabiru UL-450	0454	03.05.01	
	C K Fry (Lytchett Minster, Poole)		06.04.18P	
	Built by N Creeney – project PFA 274A-13703			
G-NIGE	Luscombe 8E Silvaire Deluxe	3525	06.06.90	
	G-BSHG, N72098, NC72098			
	Gardan Party Ltd Popham		01.07.18P	
	Noted 09.18			
G-NIGL	Europa Aviation Europa	147	06.07.95	
	N M Graham Sywell			
	Built by N M Graham – project PFA 247-12775;			
	tailwheel u/c; noted as 'Callisto' fuselage 09.16			
	(NF 30.10.14)			
G-NIHM	Eurocopter EC135 T2+	0147	27.02.17	
	G-SASA Babcock Mission Critical Services			
	Onshore Ltd Long Kesh, Lisburn		21.10.18E	
	Operated by Northern Ireland Air Ambulance			
G-NIKE	Piper PA-28-181 Archer II	28-8390086	04.07.89	
	N4315N MET Aviation Ltd Seething		29.06.19E	
	Official type data 'PA-28-181 Cherokee Archer II'			
	is incorrect			
G-NIKK	Diamond DA.20-C1 Katana	C0109	05.12.05	
	N909CT, C-FDVP Cubair Flight Training Ltd Redhill		19.08.19E	
G-NIKO	Airbus A321-211	1250	21.06.00	
	D-AVZA Thomas Cook Airlines Ltd Manchester		20.06.19E	
G-NIKS	Aeropro EuroFOX 912(1)	38412	08.11.12	
	Gosk Ltd (Aston, Stone)		14.03.18P	
	Built by N G Heywood – project BMAA/HB/633;			
	tricycle u/c			
G-NILT	Evektor EV-97 Eurostar SL	2014-4202	16.07.14	
	G I Nelson (London N3)		10.08.19P	
	Assembled Light Sport Aviation Ltd			

G-NIMA	Kubícek BB30Z	458	16.10.06	
	C Williamson Goudhurst, Cranbrook		22.06.18E	
G-NIMB	Schempp-Hirth Nimbus-2C	180	03.10.07	
	BGA2495			
	W P Stephen & W J Winthrop Saltby '943'		14.10.18E	
G-NIME	Cessna T206H Turbo Stationair	T20608188	06.06.11	
	N191ME Whitby Seafoods Ltd			
	Newgate Foot Farm, Saltergate		23.06.18E	
G-NINA	Piper PA-28-161 Cherokee Warrior II	28-7716162	29.07.88	
	G-BEUC, N3507Q			
	Global Aviation SA Athens, Greece		19.02.18E	
G-NINC	Piper PA-28-180 Cherokee G	28-7205016	02.02.00	
	SE-KVH, N2166T NWMAS Leasing Ltd Hawarden		08.05.18E	
G-NIND	Piper PA-28-180 Cherokee Challenger	28-7305420	06.06.07	
	SE-GAT Aquarelle Investments Ltd Jersey		23.11.18E	
	Official type data 'PA-28-180 Cherokee' is incorrect			
G-NINJ	Best Off Skyranger Nynja 912S(1)	xxxx070	24.06.14	
	C P Dawes tr G-NINJ Group Darley Moor		14.08.18P	
	Built by N L Stammers – project BMAA/HB/653			
G-NIOG	Robinson R44 Clipper II	10471	01.09.04	
	Helicopter Sharing Ltd Denham		08.02.18E	
G-NIOS	Piper PA-32R-301 Saratoga SP	32R-8513004	28.09.90	
	N4381Z, N105DX, N4381Z			
	B Reddan t/a Plant Aviation Stapleford		12.04.19E	
G-NIPA	Nipper T.66 RA.45 Series 3	S120	07.06.96	
	G-AWDD R J O Walker Grange Farm, North Lopham		13.04.04P	
	Built by Slingsby Aircraft Co Ltd as c/n 1627			
	for Nipper Aircraft Ltd; stored 02.17 (NF 10.02.14)			
G-NIPL	Eurocopter AS.350B3 Ecureuil	7604	20.03.13	
	Pacific Helicopters Ltd Denham		20.03.18E	
G-NIPP	Nipper T.66 RA.45 Series 3	S103	17.01.00	
	G-AVKJ North East Flight Training Ltd Longside		14.12.18P	
	Originally built Avions Fairey SA as c/n T66/32;			
	rebuilt by Slingsby Aircraft Co Ltd as c/n 1587			
	for Nipper Aircraft Ltd			
G-NIPR	Nipper T.66 RA.45 Series 3	S108	15.07.05	
	G-AVXC P A Gibbs Inverness		21.12.18P	
	Built by Slingsby Aircraft Co Ltd as c/n 1605			
	for Nipper Aircraft Ltd			
G-NIPS	Tipsy Nipper T.66 Series 2	36	02.09.10	
	VH-CGB, ZK-CAP, VH-CGB, (OY-AER)			
	B W Faulkner Twentyways Farm, Ramsdean		20.11.15P	
	Damaged in force landing near West Tisted 14.07.15			
G-NISA	Robinson R44 Clipper II	12881	31.08.10	
	G-HTMT Antinori Agricola SRL Firenze, Italy		27.07.18E	
G-NISH	Van's RV-8	80426	22.12.09	
	N H F Hampton & S R Whitling Headcorn		18.10.18P	
	Built by N H F Hampton & S R Whitling			
	– project PFA 303-13187			
G-NIUS	Reims/Cessna F172N	F17201651	14.03.78	
	EI-BSC, G-NIUS M A Lee (Nunthorpe, Middlesborough)			
	Damaged 29.01.16 in storms Durham Tees Valley;			
	wreck removed from Morgansfield 01.18 for conversion			
	into a flight simulator			
G-NIVA	Eurocopter EC155 B1	6642	02.09.05	
	N84AZ Lanthwaite Aviation Ltd Cambridge		01.09.18E	
G-NIXX	Best Off Skyranger 912S(1)	UK/681	04.04.13	
	G-CDYJ R Wilkinson Hunsdon		11.04.19P	
	Built by D S Taylor – project BMAA/HB/498			
G-NJBA	RotorWay Exec 162F	6927	10.03.05	
	A J Thomas Street Farm, Takeley		30.11.17P	
	Stored 09.18 (NF 22.03.18)			
G-NJCZ	Czech Sport PiperSport	P1001087	04.10.17	
	HB-WYO Aerocruz Ltd North Weald		13.12.19W	
G-NJET	Schempp-Hirth Ventus cT	161/521	15.01.08	
	BGA 4461/JET, RAFGSA R38			
	P S Carder Solent 'JET'		20.02.18E	
G-NJNH	Robinson R66 Turbine	0228	13.06.17	
	N66JN Hawesbates LLP			
	Briarhill Farm, Steeple Claydon		01.07.19E	
G-NJOY	Piper PA-28-181 Archer II	28-8290049	23.02.16	
	OK-JOY, D-ENPF, N8454E M J Groves Turweston		29.03.18E	

G-NJPG Best Off Skyranger Nynja 912S(1) UK\N/BK0124 21.05.13
P Gibbs Plaistows Farm, St Albans 22.10.18P
Built by P Gibbs – project BMAA/HB/636

G-NJPW P&M Quik GT450 8150 02.02.06
I W Barlow tr Golf Papa Whiskey Group
Park Hall Farm, Mapperley 30.03.18P

G-NJSH Robinson R22 Beta 0780 19.04.88
Hawesbates LLP Wellesbourne Mountford 15.03.18E

G-NJSP Avtech Jabiru J430 259 06.04.06
N J S Pitman Napps Field, Billericay 02.10.18P
Built by N J S Pitman – project PFA 336-14514

G-NJTC Aeroprakt A-22L Foxbat xxxx 06.09.06
P A Henretty & J R Russell (Northampton & Daventry) 29.06.18P
*Built by T F Casey & B Jackson
– project PFA 317A-14565*

G-NKEL Robinson R44 Raven II 10488 04.04.16
I-HPGF G Martinelli (Milan, Italy) 17.01.19E

G-NLCH Lindstrand LBL 35A Cloudhopper 1325 08.09.10
S A Lacey Wymondham *'Norwich Lighting Centre'* 20.09.15E
(IE 20.09.16)

G-NLDR Aérospatiale AS.355F2 Ecureuil 2 5282 15.10.13
G-PDGS, VP-BJC, VR-BJC, SX-HBX, F-WZKG
PLM Dollar Group Ltd t/a PDG Helicopters
Dalcross Heliport 15.01.19E
*'NetworkRail Long Distance and Regional' as
callsign 'Osprey 65'*

G-NLEE Cessna 182Q Skylane II 18265934 01.12.93
G-TLTD, N759EL R J Houghton Popham 12.06.19E

G-NLMB Zenair CH.601UL Zodiac 6-9814 22.11.10
N Lamb Ings Farm, Yedingham 12.07.18P
Built by N Lamb – project PFA 162A-14531

G-NLSE Aérospatiale AS.355F2 Ecureuil 2 5364 22.08.13
G-ULES, G-OBHL, G-HARO, G-DAFT, G-BNNN
PLM Dollar Group Ltd Cumbernauld *'Network Rail'* 04.02.19E
Callsign 'Osprey 66'

G-NLYB Cameron N-105 10012 19.04.01
P H E Van Overwalle (Eeke, Belgium) 06.06.17E
Pink Elephant Head special shape

G-NMCL Aeropro EuroFOX 912(S) 35812 07.03.12
N R McLeod (Auchenblae, Laurencekirk) 19.06.18P
*Built by N R McLeod – project LAA 376-15108;
tailwheel u/c*

G-NMMB Van's RV-10 xxxx 14.03.17
M S Bamber & N R Maclennan (St Helens)
*Built by M S Bamber & N R MacLennan
– project LAA 339-15435*

G-NMOS Cameron C-80 4966 05.01.01
M C East & C J Thomas Farnham *'RiverSoft'* 19.01.19E

G-NMRV Van's RV-6 22870 29.09.08
N32/HV R L N & S C Lucey Perth 12.04.18P
Built by N Moon

G-NMUS Steen Skybolt BZ-2015 03.11.17
N996BZ N Musgrave RAF Mona
Built by Cuban Eight LLC (IE 03.04.18)

G-NNAC Piper PA-18-135 Super Cub (L-21B-PI) 18-3820 19.05.81
PH-PSW, R Netherlands AF R-130, 54-2420
PAW Flying Services Ltd Green Farm, Beckwithshaw 02.06.18E
Fuselage No.18-3820

G-NNON Mainair Blade 1318-0302-7-W1113 24.04.02
D R Kennedy Strathaven 07.02.18P

G-NOAH Airbus A319-115CJ 3826 25.03.09
D-AVYJ Acropolis Aviation Ltd Farnborough 14.03.18E

G-NOCK Reims/Cessna FR182 Skylane RG II FR18200036 18.01.94
G-BGTK, (D-EHZB) C H M Brown Sleap 31.08.19E

G-NODE Gulfstream American AA-5B Tiger AA5B-1283 22.05.81
N4533L Ultranomad Sro (Zabehlice, Czech Republic) 03.04.18E

G-NOIL Fairey B-N BN-2A-26 Islander 334 21.12.12
G-BJWO, 4X-AYR, SX-BBX, 4X-AYR, G-BAXC
Aerospace Resources Ltd Redhill 16.01.16E
Operated by Oil Spill Response (IE 09.08.17)

G-NOMZ Kubicek BB-S/Gnome 772 29.07.10
OK-2772 A M Holly Breadstone, Berkeley 21.08.17E
(IE 07.10.17)

G-NONE Dyn'Aéro MCR-01 ULC 272 02.07.04
M A Collins Eaglescott 17.08.17P
Built by J Flisher – project PFA 301B-14238

G-NONI Grumman American AA-5 Traveler AA5-0383 01.08.88
G-BBDA, (EI-AYL), G-BBDA A Vaicvenas (Ilford) 04.07.17E
(NF 19.02.18)

G-NORA Comco Ikarus C42 FB UK 0504-6676 13.07.05
N A Rathbone Stoke Golding 11.09.18P
Built by N A Rathbone – project PFA 322-14420

G-NORB Air et Aventure Saturne S110K SC981494 28.11.05
R N Pearce (Halesowen)
Initially regd with c/n SC981482 (IE 08.01.18)

G-NORD SNCAC NC.854 7 20.10.78
F-BFIS A D Pearce
Eastbach Spence, English Bicknor 06.10.17P
*As '7' in Armee de l'Air c/s; on rebuild 05.16
(NF 03.05.18)*

G-NORG (2) Gefa-Flug AS105GD HA Airship 0006 23.02.17
I-NORG & I-COOK, G-BZUR, D-OATV
Fairfax Aviation Ltd Langford, Bristol *'tinder'* 29.06.18E
*Gondola c/n 0006 ex G-BZUR & envelope
c/n '0021' is incorrect; G-NORG uses envelopes
ex I-NORG & I-COOK)*

G-NORK Bell 206B-3 JetRanger III 3615 25.05.11
N8040T, 5N-RAA, N2271V R S Forsyth
(Orchardleigh House, Orchardleigh, Frome) 08.12.18E
Operated by Vantage Helicopters

G-NOSE Cessna 402B 402B0823 23.04.96
N98AR, G-MPCU, SE-IRL, OO-TAT, (OO-SEL), N3946C
Reconnaissance Ventures Ltd t/a RVL Group
East Midlands 05.02.18E

G-NOTE Piper PA-28-181 Archer III 2843082 19.09.97
D-ESPI, N9282N J Beach Elstree 21.11.18E

G-NOTS Best Off Skyranger 912S(1) SKR0401433 24.06.05
S F N Warnell Plaistows Farm, St Albans 06.05.18P
Built by P M Dewhurst – project BMAA/HB/352

G-NOTT Nott ULD2 06 11.06.86
J R P Nott Santa Barbara, California, USA
(NF 22.05.18)

G-NOTY Westland Scout AH.1 F9630 05.11.97
XT624 Cancelled 15.11.18 by CAA 28.01.10
North Weald Stored 09.18

G-NOWW Mainair Blade 912S 1227-1299-7-W1020 10.12.99
R S Sanby Bankwood Farm, Oxton 25.09.17P

G-NOXY Robinson R44 Raven I 1421 26.02.09
G-VALV TA Knox Shopfitters Ltd Manchester Barton 20.11.18E

G-NPKJ Van's RV-6 xxxx 12.02.98
M R Turner (London EC1) 01.05.19P
Built by K Jones – project PFA 181-13138

G-NPPL Comco Ikarus C42 FB100 0306-6543 02.09.03
G-90-1 D C Jarman tr Papa Lima Group Old Sarum 25.03.18P
*Assembled Fly Buy Ultralights Ltd;
officially registered as 0307-6543*

G-NPTA Boeing 737-86N(F) 32740 17.04.18
N346PH, OK-TVH, C-FGVK, OK-TVH, C-FGVK,
OK-TVH, C-FGVK, OK-TVH, C-FGVK, OK-TVK,
N977RY, EC-ISL
West Atlantic UK Ltd East Midlands 09.05.19E
Line No: 1444

G-NPTB Boeing 737-83N(F) 32609 24.08.18
B-5121, N316TZ West Atlantic UK Ltd Coventry 28.08.19E
Line No: 1059

G-NPTC Boeing 737-83N(F) 32612 02.11.18
N474SR, B-5125, N326TZ
West Atlantic UK Ltd East Midlands 06.11.19E
Line No: 1184

G-NPTD Boeing 737-83N(F) 32615 18.01.19
N835DM, B-5127, N329TZ
West Atlantic UK Ltd East Midlands
Line No: 1207

G-NPTV Eurocopter AS.355NP Ecureuil 2 5761 14.01.15
OM-GGA, F-GKCZ Arena Aviation Ltd Redhill 15.06.18E

G-NPTX	Boeing 737-4C9F	25429	26.06.18
	N470AX, SP-ENF, SE-RID, YR-BAD, EI-DGN, LX-LGF		
	West Atlantic UK Ltd East Midlands		03.07.19E
	Line No: 7000		
G-NPTY	Boeing 737-436F	25267	29.11.17
	N267AT, G-DOCA West Atlantic UK Ltd Coventry		30.11.19E
	Line No: 2131		
G-NPTZ	Boeing 737-436F	25842	09.04.18
	N842AT, G-DOCL West Atlantic UK Ltd Coventry		19.04.19E
	Line No: 2228		
G-NREG	Bombardier CL-600-1A11 Challenger 600S 1045		08.03.12
	N247CK, C-GBKB, N900FC, N55PG, C-GLXB		
	Cancelled 15.02.16 by CAA		
	White Waltham *Used for filming work 07.17 as 'N247CK'*		
G-NRFK	Van's RV-8	xxxx	23.04.13
	C N Harper & P G Peal Felthorpe		17.08.19P
	Built by C N Harper & P G Peal – project PFA 303-14135		
G-NRIA	Beech 23 Musketeer	M-337	10.09.09
	I-MIFA, N2373J Cancelled 05.07.17 by CAA		
	Northampton		
	Instruction use Northampton University 10.18		
G-NRMA	Dan Rihn DR.107 One Design	1449	15.03.12
	A W Brown Sleap		24.04.18P
	Built by A W Brown – project PFA 264-14000		
G-NROY	Piper PA-32RT-300 Lance II	32R-7985070	26.11.93
	G-LYNN, G-BGNY, N3024L		
	B Nedjati-Gilani White Waltham		02.07.18E
G-NRRA	SIAI Marchetti SF.260W Warrior	116	29.11.00
	F-GOBF, Burkina Faso AF BF8431 (c/s XTMCI), OO-SMB		
	G Boot Lydd		19.06.18P
	As 'BF8431:31' in Burkina Faso Air Force c/s		
G-NSBB	Comco Ikarus C42 FB100 VLA	0310-6581	15.01.04
	M Pratt tr Bravo Bravo Flying Group Chatteris		21.07.18P
	Built by B Bayes & N E Sams – project PFA 322-14162		
G-NSEW	Robinson R44 Astro	0615	06.07.99
	Styl SC Zielona Góra-Przylep, Poland		22.05.18E
G-NSEY	Embraer ERJ 190-200 STD	19000671	24.06.14
	PR-EGE Aurigny Air Services Ltd Guernsey		23.06.19E
G-NSFS	Supermarine 361 Spitfire IX	-	22.01.19
	PL258 Norwegian Spitfire Foundation (Maura, Norway)		
	(NF 22.01.19)		
G-NSKB	Aeroprakt A-22L Foxbat	A22-347	05.07.10
	N F Smith Elmsett *'Kitty Belle'*		19.10.18P
	Built by N F Smith – project LAA 317A-14982		
G-NSKY	Alpi Pioneer 400	xxxx	23.05.16
	A P Sellars North Coates		27.10.18P
	Built by D Almey & A P Sellars – project LAA 364-15236		
G-NSSA	TLAC RL5A Sherwood Ranger XP	xxxx	01.07.14
	A R Stanley (Halesworth)		
	Built by A R Stanley – project LAA 237A-15273		
	(NF 25.11.16)		
G-NSTG	Cessna F150F	F150-0058	16.08.89
	G-ATNI Westair Flying Services Ltd Blackpool		21.06.18E
	Built by Reims Aviation SA; Wichita c/n 15063499;		
	tailwheel u/c		
G-NSYS	Eurocopter EC135 T1	0115	19.05.15
	M-GLBL, G-CEYF, P4-XTX, P4-LGB, G-HARP, VP-CAF,		
	D-HECG Nova Aerospace Ltd Cotswold		22.06.18E
G-NTPS	BRM Bristell NG5 Speed Wing	082	10.02.14
	N D H Stokes Garston Farm, Marshfield		05.10.19P
	Built by N D H Stokes – project LAA 385-15243;		
	tailwheel u/c		
G-NTVE	Beagle A.61 Terrier 3	B.626	11.10.12
	LN-TVE, SE-ELR, (SE-ELJ), G-ASIE, G-35-11, VX924		
	D Capon Fenland		08.08.18P
	As 'VX924' in AAC c/s		
G-NTWK	Aérospatiale AS.355F2 Ecureuil 2	5347	16.05.06
	G-FTWO, G-OJOR, G-FTWO, G-BMUS		
	PLM Dollar Group Ltd		
	Wolverhampton Halfpenny Green		17.04.18E
	Operated by for British Transport Police		
	(Network Rail), callsign 'Osprey 63'		
G-NUFC	Best Off Skyranger Swift 912S(1)	UK/768	22.02.07
	C R Rosby Eshott		12.07.18P
	Built by C R Rosby – project BMAA/HB/529		
G-NUGC	Grob G103A Twin II Acro	34040-K-271	17.01.08
	BGA 4729/JRW, RAFGGA R15, RAFGGA 556		
	The University of Nottingham Students Union		
	Cranwell North *'NU2'*		30.04.18E
G-NUKA	Piper PA-28-181 Archer II	28-8290134	09.01.04
	OY-CJI, N8209A N Ibrahim North Weald		14.05.19E
G-NULA	Flight Design CT2K	02-05-05-04	17.10.02
	R E Antell Damyns Hall, Upminster		30.04.19P
	Assembled Pegasus Aviation with c/n 7913		
G-NUNI	Lindstrand LBL 77A	1181	15.01.08
	The University of Nottingham Nottingham NG7		
	'The University of Nottingham'		22.07.19E
G-NUTA	Christen Eagle II	0471	15.08.06
	D-ECCA A R Whincup Leicester		17.08.18P
	Built by D Sondermann		
G-NUTS	Cameron Mr Peanut 35SS HAB	711	18.02.81
	Cancelled 16.04.09 by CAA		07.04.86
	Not Known *Inflated Ashton Court 08.18*		
G-NUTT	Mainair Pegasus Quik	8114	29.04.05
	P Underwood tr NUTT Syndicate Fife		04.11.18P
	Built by Mainair Sports Ltd		
G-NVBF	Lindstrand LBL 210A	249	19.05.95
	Airxcite Ltd t/a Virgin Balloon Flights		
	Stafford Park, Telford *'Virgin'*		
	(NF 15.09.14)		
G-NVWV	Agusta A109E Power	11725	20.03.19
	G-SRGE, I-SIRI Novawave Ltd (Borehamwood)		01.05.19E
G-NWAA	Eurocopter EC135 T2	0427	10.10.05
	Babcock Mission Critical Services Onshore Ltd		
	Blackpool *'Katie'*		30.11.18E
	Operated by North West Air Ambulance as		
	callsign 'Helimed 08'		
G-NWAE	Eurocopter EC135 T2	0312	07.10.13
	G-DAAT Babcock Mission Critical Services		
	Onshore Ltd Manchester Barton		12.07.18E
	Operated by North West Air Ambulance as		
	callsign 'Helimed 75'		
G-NWEM	Eurocopter EC135 T2	0270	29.06.10
	G-SSXX, G-SSSX Babcock Mission Critical		
	Services Onshore Ltd Manchester Barton		27.04.18E
	Operated by North West Air Ambulance as		
	callsign 'Helimed 72'		
G-NWFA	Cessna 150M	15076736	29.05.08
	G-CFBD, N45103		
	North Weald Flying Group Ltd North Weald		01.05.19E
G-NWFC	Cessna 172P Skyhawk	17276305	04.07.07
	N98523 North Weald Flying Group Ltd North Weald		27.02.19E
G-NWFG	Cessna 172P Skyhawk	17274192	31.07.07
	N6396K North Weald Flying Group Ltd North Weald		11.10.19E
G-NWFS	Cessna 172P Skyhawk	17275815	26.09.11
	G-TYMS, N65674		
	North Weald Flying Group Ltd North Weald		05.07.19E
G-NWFT	Reims/Cessna F172N	F17201677	08.11.13
	G-BURD, PH-AXI		
	North Weald Flight Training Ltd North Weald		19.04.19E
G-NWOI	Eurocopter EC135 P2+	0887	29.03.10
	Police & Crime Commissioner for West Yorkshire		
	St Athan *'Heddlu'*		10.11.19
	Operated by South Wales Police as callsign 'NPAS 47'		
G-NWPR	Cameron N-77	1181	15.08.85
	D B Court Ormskirk		17.05.18E
	Rebuilt with new envelope c/n 1667		
G-NWPS	Eurocopter EC135 T1	0063	15.10.98
	RCR Aviation Ltd Brook Farm, Hulcote		18.12.17E
	For sale 11.18 (NF 24.05.18)		
G-NXOE	Cessna 172S Skyhawk	172S11002	12.03.10
	N52697 Goodwood Road Racing Company Ltd		
	Goodwood		14.03.19E
G-NYCO	Beech B200GT King Air	BY-238	21.02.19
	N238KA Dry Lease Aero Ltd Gloucestershire		
	(IE 21.02.19)		
G-NYKS	Cessna 182T Skylane	18281607	09.08.12
	HB-CZC, N1159Q M Lapidus Denham		29.07.18E

G-NYMB	Schempp-Hirth Nimbus-3DT	63	09.11.07
	BGA 4008/HKQ I D Smith tr Nimbus Syndicate		
	Nympsfield '970'		15.02.19E
G-NYMF	Piper PA-25-235 Pawnee D	25-7556112	08.02.02
	OO-PAL, N267JW, N9799P		
	The Bristol Gliding Club Proprietary Ltd Nympsfield		14.02.18E
G-NYNA	Van's RV-9A	91700	15.07.08
	B Greathead & S Hiscox Seething		08.01.19P
	Built by B Greathead & S Hiscox – project LAA 320-14773		
G-NYNE	Schleicher ASW 27-18E (ASG 29E)	29569	05.03.09
	(BGA 5652), (BGA 5335)		
	R C W Ellis Husbands Bosworth '9'		09.05.18E
G-NYNJ	Best Off Skyranger Nynja 912S(1)	xxxx0144	16.10.13
	N J Sutherland tr G-NYNJ Group Perth		10.07.18P
	Built by N J Sutherland – project BMAA/HB/643		
G-NZGL	Cameron O-105	1361	03.09.86
	N T M, P M G & R A Vale Hurcott, Kidderminster		27.10.10E
	(IE 13.12.13)		
G-NZIC	LeVier Cosmic Wind	102	15.11.18
	N21C J C Tempest Ranksborough Farm, Langham		
	(NF 15.11.18)		
G-NZSS	Boeing Stearman E75 Kaydet (N2S-5)	75-8611	31.01.89
	N4325, USN 43517, (42-109578)		
	R W Davies Little Engeham Farm, Woodchurch		06.03.18E
	As '43517:227' in USAAC c/s		

G-OAAA – G-OZZZ

G-OAAA	Piper PA-28-161 Warrior II	2816107	08.09.93
	N9142N Redhill Air Services Ltd		
	Wolverhampton Halfpenny Green		26.09.18E
G-OAAC^M	Airtour AH-77B	AH-010	15.01.03
	Cancelled as PWFU 16.01.06		
	With British Balloon Museum & Library, Newbury		
G-OAAM	Cameron C-90	11745	12.04.13
	A M Holly Breadstone, Berkeley		
	'Aberdeen Asset management'		31.05.18E
G-OABB	Jodel D.150 Mascaret	01	21.01.97
	F-BJST, F-WJST K Manley Westfield Farm, Hailsham		26.06.18P
	Built by Société Aéronautique Normande		
G-OABC	Colt 69A	1159	17.11.87
	P A C Stuart-Kregor Sanham Green, Hungerford		26.06.00A
	(NF 17.03.16)		
G-OABO	Enstrom F-28A	097	10.07.98
	G-BAIB C R Taylor (Wacton, Norwich)		23.07.09E
	(NF 23.10.15)		
G-OABR	American General AG-5B Tiger	10124	15.04.98
	C-GZLA, N256ER	A Corcoran & F Hopper	
	(Sligo, Co Sligo, RoI)		05.12.18E
G-OACE	Valentin Taifun 17E	1017	22.01.87
	D-KCBA I F Wells Spanhoe		01.10.16E
G-OACI	SOCATA MS.893E Rallye 180GT	13086	05.05.98
	G-DOOR, EI-BHD, F-GBCF J M & S Bain Perth		01.10.18E
G-OADY	Beech 76 Duchess	ME-56	27.10.86
	N5022M Skies Airline Training AB Nykoping, Sweden		23.05.18E
G-OAER	Lindstrand LBL 105A	359	04.03.96
	M P Rowley Upper Arncott, Bicester 'Bubbles'		05.06.18E
G-OAFA	Reims/Cessna F172M	F17201093	18.02.14
	G-BFZV, SE-FZR The Royal Artillery Aero Club Ltd		
	t/a The Army Flying Association AAC Middle Wallop		17.01.19E
G-OAGA	Eurocopter EC225 LP Super Puma	2878	22.08.13
	Element Capital Corp Fleetlands		22.08.16E
	Stored 04.17 (NF 09.09.16)		
G-OAGE	Airbus EC225 LP Super Puma	2949	05.12.14
	Wilmington Trust SP Services (Dublin) Ltd		
	Rzeszow, Poland		09.12.17E
	Stored 11.16		
G-OAGI	FLS Aerospace Sprint 160	001	30.11.06
	G-FLSI A L Breckell Compton Abbas		17.12.18P
G-OAHC	Beech F33C Bonanza	CJ-133	02.09.91
	G-BTTF, PH-BND Cirrus Aviation Ltd Clacton-on-Sea		
	26.06.18E		

G-OAJL	Comco Ikarus C42 FB100	0403-6589	18.05.04
	G D McCullough Slieve Croob, Castlewellan		30.08.18P
	Assembled Fly Buy Ultralights Ltd		
G-OAJS	Piper PA-39 Twin Comanche C/R	39-15	09.03.94
	G-BCIO, N49JA, N57RG, G-BCIO, N8860Y		
	M C Bellamy Sherburn-in-Elmet		15.08.18E
G-OALC	Aérospatiale AS.355F2 Ecureuil 2	5327	04.02.19
	G-VONG, G-OILX, ZH141, G-OILX, ZH141, G-OILX,		
	G-RMGN, G-BMCY Alcaline UK Ltd (Lympne, Hythe)		16.07.19E
G-OALD	SOCATA TB-20 Trinidad	490	17.03.88
	N54TB, F-GBLL		
	D A Grief tr Gold Aviation Biggin Hill		17.03.18E
G-OALE	Kubícek BB22XR	1146	05.05.15
	Belvoir Brewery Ltd Old Dalby, Melton Mowbray		
	'Belvoir Brewery'		10.05.19E
G-OALH	Tecnam P92-EA Echo	TEC/006	12.06.01
	A Pritchard RAF Mona		10.08.18P
	Built by L Hill – project PFA 318-13675		
G-OALI	Aérospatiale AS.355F1 Ecureuil 2	5115	14.01.15
	G-WDKR, ZJ635, G-NEXT, G-WDKR, G-NEXT, I-NEXT,		
	G-NEXT, G-OMAV Atlas Helicopters Ltd Lasham		23.03.18E
G-OALP	Alpi Pioneer 300 Hawk	382	16.06.17
	Cavendish Aviation UK Ltd Earls Colne		11.07.19P
	Built by Alpi Aviation SRL – project LAA 330A-15471		
G-OAMF	Cyclone Pegasus Quantum 15-912	7764	20.12.00
	J C Birkbeck Thornton Watlass, Ripon		07.06.19P
G-OAML	Cameron AML-105	3881	04.12.96
	Stratton Motor Company (Norfolk) Ltd		
	Long Stratton, Norwich 'Aston Martin'		08.08.19E
G-OANI	Piper PA-28-161 Warrior II	28-8416091	08.01.91
	N43570 A S Bamrah t/a Falcon Flying Services		
	Biggin Hill		08.09.97
	(NF 29.01.18)		
G-OANN (2)	Zenair CH.601HD Zodiac	6-8020	02.02.96
	B Donald & R Torrie Insch		06.12.19P
	Built by P Noden – project PFA 162-12932;		
	rebuilt with unknown kit; original frame;		
	displayed Deesside Activity Centre (IE 05.09.18)		
G-OAPR	Brantly B.2B	446	21.04.89
	(G-BPST), N2280U E D A Rees t/a Helicopter		
	International Magazine Weston-super-Mare		01.10.15E
G-OARA	Piper PA-28R-201 Arrow III	2837002	28.10.98
	N802ND, N9622N		
	Dorian & Brunning Holdings LLP Brighton City		30.06.16E
	Official type data 'PA-28R-201 Cherokee Arrow III'		
	is incorrect (IE 22.12.17)		
G-OARC	Piper PA-28RT-201 Arrow IV	28R-7918009	17.08.99
	EC-HXO, G-OARC, EC-JAE, EC-HXO, G-OARC,		
	G-BMVE, N3071K Norton Systems LLP Enstone		09.02.18E
G-OARS	Cessna 172S Skyhawk SP	172S11048	13.07.10
	N90042 De Hertog Juweeldesign GCV		
	(Lier, Belgium)		16.08.18E
G-OART	Piper PA-23-250 Aztec D	27-4293	26.11.93
	G-AXKD, N6936Y		
	Prescribing Services Ltd Great Massingham		17.12.18E
G-OARU	Piper PA-28R-201 Arrow III	2837026	24.05.02
	N174ND Hardman Aviation Ltd Blackbushe		17.08.18E
	Official type data 'PA-28R-201 Cherokee Arrow III'		
	is incorrect		
G-OASA	Flight Design CTSW	09-07-10	15.03.13
	G-CGHE O W & S M Achurch Hill Top, Whilton		28.07.18P
	Assembled P&M Aviation as c/n 8497		
G-OASH	Robinson R22 Beta	0761	13.06.06
	N2627Z J C Lane Wolverhampton Halfpenny Green		20.07.18E
G-OASI	Lindstrand LTL Series 1-90	086	26.06.18
	A M Holly Breadstone, Berkeley		
	'Aberdeen Standard Investments'		16.07.19E
G-OASK	Aeropro EuroFOX 912(S)	52817	07.09.17
	Aero Space Scientific Educational Trust Fife		03.12.19P
	Built by D Barr, A P Benbow, J Hoy, G Ross,		
	A Stewart & N Watt – project LAA 376-15416;		
	tricycle u/c		
G-OASM	HpH Glasflügel 304 eS Shark	087-MS	30.05.18
	(BGA 5966) A S Miller Keevil '4SM'		15.06.19E

G-OASP	Aérospatiale AS.355F2 Ecureuil 2	5479		03.08.95
	F-GJAJ, F-WYMH			
	Helicopter & Pilot Services Ltd White Waltham			26.01.18E
G-OASW	Schleicher ASW 27B	27227		10.03.06
	BGA 5160/KKL			
	M P W Mee Wycombe Air Park *'MM'*			23.05.18E
G-OATE	Mainair Pegasus Quantum 15-912	8064		27.08.04
	A Roberts Sywell			21.05.18P
G-OATI★	Hawker 900XP	HA-0041		07.06.18
	G-ODUR, N34441 Sable Air APS			
	To OK-HWL 11.03.19			
G-OATS	Piper PA-38-112 Tomahawk	38-78A0007		14.03.78
	N9659N Cancelled 16.01.06 as destroyed			15.10.06
	Tollerton *Dumped 02.14*			
G-OATV	Cameron V-77	2149		14.02.90
	A W & E P Braund-Smith Denby Dale, Huddersfield			15.05.18E
G-OATY	Pipistrel Alpha BCAR-S 164	AT1640002		09.11.18
	MGAP London LLP Shipmeadow			17.12.19P
G-OATZ	Van's RV-12	120526		06.05.11
	J W Armstrong Old Park Farm, Margam			06.12.18P
	(J W Armstrong & J Jones – project LAA 363-15079			
G-OAUD	Robinson R44 Raven	1467		29.01.14
	G-CDHV, N393N, G-CDHV Pinpoint3D Ltd Fairoaks			26.07.18E
G-OAUR	Dornier 228-212	8305		11.12.15
	Aurigny Air Services Ltd Guernsey			22.12.19E
	Built by RUAG Aerospace Services GmbH			
G-OAVA	Robinson R22 Beta II	3303		08.03.02
	Phoenix Helicopter Academy Ltd Blackbushe			23.11.19E
G-OAWM	Cirrus SR20 GTS	1972		16.12.15
	G-GCDD, M-YGTS, N496PG			
	AWM General Aviation Ltd North Weald			25.07.19E
G-OAWS	Colt 77A	4340		23.04.98
	P Lawman Northampton			23.06.18E
	Built by Cameron Balloons Ltd			
G-OBAB	Lindstrand LBL 35A Cloudhopper	1276		18.09.09
	M A Green Rednal, Birmingham			08.06.19E
G-OBAD	Evektor EV-97 Eurostar SL	2014-4210		14.01.15
	M J Robbins Rochester			12.02.18P
	Assembled Light Sport Aviation Ltd			
G-OBAK	Piper PA-28R-201T Turbo Cherokee Arrow III			
		28R-7703054		27.08.02
	D-EKOR, N1146Q			
	J Laffan tr G-OBAK Group Fairoaks			26.07.18E
G-OBAL	Mooney M.20J Mooney 201	24-1601		27.11.86
	N56569 R Knights tr G-OBAL Group Elstree			14.04.18E
	(IE 10.08.18)			
G-OBAN	Jodel D.140B Mousquetaire II	80		20.02.92
	G-ATSU, F-BKSA L P Keegan Perth			16.04.18E
	Built by Société Aéronautique Normande			
G-OBAP	Zenair CH.701SP	7-8267		11.04.11
	J L Adams Swansea			
	Built by J M Gale & A D Janaway			
	– project LAA 187A-15075 (NF 27.09.17)			
G-OBAX	Thruster T600N 450 Jab	0051-T600N-053		12.07.01
	J D Alexander t/a Hilton Estates Balado			01.12.18P
	Badged 'Sprint'			
G-OBAY^M	Bell 206B JetRanger	276		27.07.98
	G-BVWR, C-GNXQ, N4714R			
	Cancelled 12.09.03 as PWFU			06.03.03
	Less tail boom unmarked in 'Stromberg' c/s			
	With Miami Auto Museum, Florida			
G-OBAZ	Best Off Skyranger 912(2)	SKR0309391		17.11.03
	B J Marsh Plaistows Farm, St Albans			21.04.18P
	Built by B J Marsh – project BMAA/HB/322			
G-OBBO	Cessna 182S Skylane	18280534		08.06.99
	N7274Z A E Kedros Oxford			19.08.18E
G-OBDA	Diamond DA.20-A1 Katana	10260		02.07.98
	C-FDVT Oscar Papa Ltd			
	Wolverhampton Halfpenny Green			25.05.18E
G-OBDN	Piper PA-28-161 Warrior III	2842177		10.07.03
	N53586 R M Bennett Redhill			21.10.18E

G-OBEE	Boeing Stearman A75N1 Kaydet (*N2S-3*)	75-1174		21.02.05
	N5580S, N6734S, USN 3397			
	R H Mackay Easterton			16.06.19E
	As '3397:174' in US Navy c/s			
G-OBEI	SOCATA TB-200 Tobago GT	2096		26.06.02
	F-OIUX K Stoter Groningen, Netherlands			14.09.18E
G-OBEN	Cessna 152 II	15281856		16.08.93
	G-NALI, G-BHVM, N67477			
	Globibussola Lda Cascais, Portugal			09.02.18E
G-OBET	Sky 77-24	178		22.02.00
	S M M Carden & P M Watkins Chippenham			
	'Victor Chandler'			25.09.18E
G-OBFE	Sky 120-24	167		28.04.03
	D-OBFE J Sonnabend Huenfelden, Germany			
	'Hees Burowelt'			26.08.16E
	(NF 28.11.16)			
G-OBFS	Piper PA-28-161 Warrior III	2842039		04.12.98
	N41274 Flevo Aviation BV Lelystad, Netherlands			23.05.19E
G-OBHE	Robinson R44 Astro	0381		27.07.17
	G-PRET The BHE Hub Ltd Elstree			24.09.19E
	Operated by Flying Pig Helicopters			
G-OBIL	Robinson R22 Beta	0792		10.05.88
	Helicopter & Pilot Services Ltd White Waltham			21.08.19E
G-OBIO	Robinson R22 Beta	1402		29.06.98
	N7724M Go Exclusive Ltd Manchester Barton			06.04.19E
G-OBJB	Lindstrand LBL 90A	640		12.11.99
	B J Bower Perugia, Umbria, Italy			
	'Bubbles Celebration Balloon'			29.03.12E
	(NF 30.04.15)			
G-OBJM	Taylor JT.1 Monoplane	xxxx		02.05.08
	R K Thomas Whaley Farm, New York			28.06.18P
	Built by B J Main – project PFA 055-14623			
G-OBJP	Cyclone Pegasus Quantum 15-912	7847		29.08.01
	G I Somers Sutton Meadows			28.08.18P
G-OBJT	Europa Aviation Europa	055		16.11.00
	G-MUZO A Burrill Brimpton *'41'*			21.04.18P
	Built by J T Grant & B J Tarmar – project			
	PFA 247-12623; tricycle u/c			
G-OBLC	Beech 76 Duchess	ME-249		03.06.87
	N6635R Air Navigation & Trading Company Ltd			
	Blackpool			06.07.13E
	(NF 17.01.17)			
G-OBLN^M	de Havilland DH.115 Vampire T.11			14.09.95
	XE956 J M Vivash St Athan			
	Official c/n DHP 48700 is nacelle number; as 'XE956';			
	to South Wales Aircraft Museum 12.18 (NF 26.11.18)			
G-OBMI	Mainair Blade	1289-0601-7-W1084		19.06.01
	R G Jeffery (Crosby, Liverpool))			01.11.18P
G-OBMS	Reims/Cessna F172N	F17201584		16.04.84
	OO-BWA, (OO-HWA), D-EBYX			
	T J Arnold tr Mike Sierra Group Sherburn-in-Elmet			16.08.18E
G-OBNA	Piper PA-34-220T Seneca V	3449002		25.05.00
	N9281D, (N338DB) O R & P M Saiman Elstree			09.08.19E
G-OBNC	Britten-Norman BN-2B-20 Islander	3000		09.02.05
	Britten-Norman Aircraft Ltd Solent			
	Stored 2017 (NF 18.12.15)			
G-OBNF	Cessna 310K	310K-0109		20.07.94
	F-BNFI, N7009L Cancelled 07.01.91 as PWFU			20.05.03
	Melbourne, East Yorkshire			
	Stored 12.14 in private garden as children's play thing			
G-OBNW	Piper PA-31-350 Navajo Chieftain	31-7305118		04.04.03
	OY-EBE, EI-BYE, G-BFDA, SE-GDR, N9684N			
	Cancelled 15.08.08 as PWFU			05.05.07
	Exeter Int'l *Fuselage stored 01.15*			
G-OBOF	Remos GX	361		27.04.10
	D Hawkins (Highmoor, Henley-on-Thames)			26.08.18W
G-OBPL	Embraer EMB-110P2 Bandeirante	110-199		27.11.98
	(G-OEAB), PH-FVB, G-OEAB, G-BKWB, G-CHEV, (PT-GLR)			
	Cancelled 22.07.04 as PWFU			12.12.01
	Abridge, Stapleford *Fuselage only at Mayhem*			
	Paintball Site 01.12; as 'G-OBWB' on starboard side			
G-OBPP	Schleicher ASW 27-18E (*ASG 29E*)	29563		23.10.08
	BGA 5326/KSJ R A F King Bicester *'MP'*			09.03.19E

G-OBRO	Alpi Pioneer 200-M xxxx	04.05.11
	A Brown (Lincoln)	23.07.15P
	Built by A Brown – project LAA 334-15059	
G-OBRY	Cameron N-180 3010	01.03.93
	A C K Rawson & J J Rudoni t/a Wickers World	
	Hot Air Balloon Company Stafford *'Bryant Homes'*	04.03.15E
G-OBSM	Robinson R44 Raven 1030	15.12.05
	G-CDSE, N43861, C-FAEP	
	Whitearrow Associates Ltd (Hitchin)	04.06.19E
G-OBSR	Partenavia P68 Observer 236/01/OBS	20.03.12
	I-OBSR Ravenair Aircraft Ltd Liverpool John Lennon	25.05.18E
G-OBTS	Cameron C-80 3589	18.04.95
	Skydive Chatteris Club Ltd Chatteris *'Hi-Q'*	09.02.18E
G-OBUC	Piper PA-34-220T Seneca III 34-8233174	13.05.16
	I-ACTD, N8242A	
	Tamara Trading SL (Palma de Mallorca, Spain)	26.09.18E
G-OBUDM	Colt 69A HAB 698	26.06.85
	Cancelled 29.04.97 as WFU	01.02.90
	With British Balloon Museum & Library, Newbury	
G-OBUP	DG Flugzeugbau DG-808C 8-381B280X42	31.10.07
	C J Lowrie Parham Park *'CL'*	27.11.18E
	Built by DG Flugzeugbau GmbH	
G-OBUU	Comper CLA.7 Swift replica xxxx	25.01.07
	R H Hunt & J A Pothecary (Salisbury SP2 & SP4)	
	Built by R H Hunt & J A Pothecary	
	– project PFA 103-12165 (NF 14.10.14)	
G-OBUY	Colt 69A 2031	07.08.91
	T G Read Mobberley, Knutsford *'Virgin Megastore'*	31.08.19E
G-OBUZ	Van's RV-6 20410	28.08.08
	N868CM A F Hall Elmsett	27.09.18P
	Built by H M Sutter	
G-OBYG	Boeing 767-304ER 29137	13.01.99
	D-ATYG, G-OBYG, (D-AGYG), G-OBYG	
	TUI Airways Ltd t/a TUI Luton	27.10.19E
	Line No: 733	
G-OBYH	Boeing 767-304ER 28883	04.02.99
	SE-DZO, D-AGYH, G-OBYH	
	TUI Airways Ltd t/a TUI Luton	10.09.19E
	Line No: 737	
G-OBYT	Agusta-Bell 206A JetRanger 8237	30.01.95
	G-BNRC, Oman AF 601 J S Everett Sproughton	12.07.03
	Stored 10.17 (NF 11.04.18)	
G-OBZR	Breezer Breezer B600 LSA 019LSA	06.07.11
	P Coomber Spanhoe	06.04.18W
G-OCAC	Robin R2112 Alpha 371	16.02.12
	G-EWHT The Cotswold Aero Club Ltd	
	Gloucestershire	27.06.18E
	Built by Constructions Aeronautiques de Bourgogne;	
	fitted with wings ex G-BGBA in 2012	
G-OCAD	Sequoia F.8L Falco xxxx	08.06.92
	D R Vale Derby	20.04.19P
	Built by C W Garrard – project PFA 100-12114	
G-OCAF	Robinson R44 Cadet 30041	12.11.18
	Agriline Aviation LLP Wellesbourne Mountford	
	Operated by Heli Air Ltd (IE 12.11.18)	
G-OCAK	Bombardier BD-700-1A10 Global Express XRS 9339	15.12.17
	VQ-BNP, C-GFRX, N112ZZ, C-FVGP	
	Gama Aviation (UK) Ltd Farnborough	18.12.18E
G-OCAM	Gulfstream American AA-5A Cheetah AA5A-0741	24.03.94
	G-BLHO, OO-RTJ, OO-HRN	
	G Fenton & J Khambatta Cranfield	12.05.18E
G-OCBI	Schweizer 269C-1 (300CBi) 0139	14.08.02
	N86G Alpha Properties (London) Ltd Biggin Hill	21.03.18E
G-OCCF	Diamond DA.40D Star D4.229	02.10.06
	OE-VPU Flying Time Ltd Brighton City	05.03.18E
G-OCCG	Diamond DA.40D Star D4.230	09.10.06
	OE-VPU Flying Time Ltd Brighton City	06.04.18E
G-OCCH	Diamond DA.40D Star D4.233	09.10.06
	Innovative Aviation (Leeds) Ltd Leeds Bradford	11.02.18E
G-OCCN	Diamond DA.40D Star D4.241	23.11.06
	OE-VPU, (G-OCCT) Flying Time Ltd Brighton City	13.04.18E
G-OCCU	Diamond DA.40D Star D4.252	18.12.06
	Chalrey Ltd Elstree	05.03.19E
	Operated by Flyers Flying School	
G-OCCX	Diamond DA.42 Twin Star 42.155	03.08.06
	OE-VPW Aeros Global Ltd Coventry	13.06.19E
G-OCDC	Best Off Skyranger Nynja 912S(1) 10090056	16.03.11
	C D Church Newton Peveril Farm, Sturminster Marshall	07.10.18P
	Built by C D Church – project BMAA/HB/612	
G-OCDO	Guimbal Cabri G2 1133	16.02.16
	Vantage Aviation Ltd Old Sarum	17.02.18E
G-OCDP	Flight Design CTSW 06-08-22	23.10.06
	M A Beadman Bourn	18.02.18P
	Assembled P&M Aviation Ltd as c/n 8226	
G-OCDW	Avtech Jabiru UL-450 587	31.03.04
	S S Aujla & D Goodman Knapthorpe Lodge, Caunton	28.06.18P
	Built by C D Wood – project PFA 274A-14122	
G-OCFC	CAB Robin R2160 Alpha Sport 374	21.06.02
	Cancelled 09.11.16 as PWFU	23.07.15
	Clench Warton, Norfolk *Noted in storage yard 06.18*	
G-OCFD	Bell 206B-3 JetRanger III 3165	10.06.04
	G-WGAL, G-OICS, N678TM, N678TW	
	Rushmere Helicopters LLP Turweston	22.05.19E
G-OCFM	Piper PA-34-200 Seneca 34-7350021	20.04.04
	G-ELBC, G-BANS, N15110	
	Stapleford Flying Club Ltd Stapleford	27.12.14E
	(NF 02.07.15)	
G-OCFT	Bombardier CL-600-2B16 Challenger 601-3A 5067	09.05.12
	VP-CFT, HB-IUF, N220TW, 9A-CRT, 9A-CRO,	
	N603CC, C-GLXF Air Link One Ltd Oxford	19.06.17E
G-OCGC	Robin DR.400-180R Remorqueur 1372	18.11.09
	HB-EYO Cambridge Gliding Club Ltd	
	Gransden Lodge	14.12.18E
G-OCGD	Cameron O-26 12130	21.09.17
	C G Dobson Goring, Reading	18.09.18E
G-OCHM	Robinson R44 Raven 1055	04.05.01
	C M Beighton Bruntingthorpe	15.09.19E
G-OCJZ	Cessna 525A CitationJet CJ2 525A0051	04.07.08
	N415SL, N6JR, N6M	
	Centreline AV Ltd t/a Centreline Bristol	30.06.18E
G-OCLC	Aviat A-1B Husky 2380	08.06.07
	N440HY E Marinoni (Merano, Italy)	30.09.18E
G-OCMM	Agusta A109A II 7347	20.03.01
	G-BXCB, F-GJSH, G-ISEB, G-IADT, G-HBCA	
	Castle Air Ltd Trebrown, Liskeard	06.09.13E
G-OCMS	Evektor EV-97 teamEurostar UK 2010-3718	14.04.10
	C M Saysell Plaistows Farm, St Albans	14.05.18P
	Assembled Cosmik Aviation Ltd	
G-OCMT	Evektor EV-97 teamEurostar UK 2003-1701	14.07.03
	P Crowhurst Manor Farm, Keyston	21.04.19P
	Assembled Cosmik Aviation Ltd	
G-OCOK	American Champion 8KCAB Super Decathlon	16.06.08
	825-99	
	N669MM L Levinson Elstree	31.07.19E
G-OCON	Robinson R44 Raven 1608	12.05.06
	P Kelly Dublin Weston, RoI	08.06.18E
G-OCOV	Robinson R22 Beta II 3217	23.05.01
	Central Helicopters Ltd	
	Nottingham Heliport, Widmerpool	27.08.19E
G-OCPC	Reims/Cessna FA152 Aerobat FA1520343	20.01.78
	Devon & Somerset Flight Training Ltd Dunkeswell	19.10.16E
G-OCRI	Colomban MC-15 Cri-Cri 524	24.06.92
	K A Beetson & L A Fowler Sywell	
	Built by M J J Dunning – project PFA 133-12288	
	(NF 15.06.18)	
G-OCRL	Europa Aviation Europa 188	12.10.11
	G-OBEV R J Lewis Garston Farm, Marshfield	
	Built by R J Lewis – project PFA 247-12813; initially	
	registered to M B Hill 02.98 as 'G-OBEV' (NF 05.11.15)	
G-OCRM	Slingsby T67M Firefly II 2112	23.05.14
	G-BUUB CRM Aviation Europe Ltd White Waltham	25.07.18E
G-OCRZ	CZAW Sportcruiser 4017	03.03.08
	P Marsden The Firs Farm, Leckhampstead	25.01.19P
	Built by P Marsden – project PFA 338-14668	

G-OCTI	Piper PA-32-260 Cherokee Six	32-288	26.07.88
	G-BGZX, 9XR-MP, 5Y-ADH, N3427W		
	M B Dyos Bembridge		03.03.18E
G-OCTO	Van's RV-8	80303	20.12.17
	D-EBRV A P S Maynard & A Stokes Brighton City		26.06.19P
	Built by S Servatius; official c/n quoted as '470'		
G-OCTS	Cameron Z-90	11108	08.08.11
	A Collett Rockhampton, Berkeley		
	'CTS' & 'Collett Isuzu'		17.08.19E
G-OCTU	Piper PA-28-161 Cadet	2841280	16.11.89
	EC-IHB, G-OCTU, N91997		
	Glenn Aviation Ltd RAF Brize Norton		28.05.18E
	Operated by Brize Norton Flying Club		
G-OCUB	Piper J-3C-90 Cub (L-4J-PI)	xxxx	21.04.81
	OO-JOZ, PH-NKC, PH-UCH (1), 45-4508		
	C Marshall & V Peirce tr Zebedee Flying Group		
	Goodwood 'Florence'		01.03.18P
	Fuselage No.13078; official c/n relates to PH-UCE		
	(fuselage no.13045 ex 45-4475) & rebuilt as		
	PH-UCH (2): original PH-UCH rebuilt as		
	PH-NKC (c/n 13215)		
G-OCXI	Van's RV-8	xxxx	24.03.17
	P S Gilmour (St Andrews)		
	Built by P S Gilmour – project LAA 303-14688		
	(NF 23.03.17)		
G-OCZA	CZAW Sportcruiser	700347	11.07.08
	S M Dawson Eshott		10.05.18P
	Built by S M Dawson – project LAA 338-14820		
G-ODAC	Reims/Cessna F152 II	F15201824	19.12.96
	G-BITG M L & T M Jones Derby		06.08.18E
	Rebuilt 06.96 with cockpit & front fuselage ex G-BITG		
G-ODAF	Lindstrand LBL 105A	1042	10.03.05
	T J Horne North Crawley, Newport Pagnell		
	'Brian Currie' & 'DAF'		01.03.18E
G-ODAK	Piper PA-28-236 Dakota	28-7911162	29.02.00
	D-EXMA, OH-SMO, N386WT, N22328		
	Flydak LLP Wycombe Air Park		15.02.18E
	Operated by British Airways Flying Club; Union Flag c/s		
G-ODAY	Cameron N-56	551	16.07.79
	The British Balloon Museum & Library Ltd		
	(Wellingborough)		12.05.14E
	(NF 07.03.16)		
G-ODAZ	Robinson R44 Raven II	12167	11.03.08
	S L Walton Redhill		26.04.18E
G-ODBN	Lindstrand LBL Flowers	389	22.05.96
	Magical Adventures Ltd West Bloomfield, MI, USA		
	'Sainsbury's Quality and Freshness'		30.09.09E
	(NF 03.06.15)		
G-ODCH	Schleicher ASW 20L	20067	13.03.08
	BGA 4860/JXH, D-7657		
	P J Stratten Bicester 'W20'		12.01.19E
G-ODDF	Issoire PIK-30	728	01.02.13
	EC-GXN, F-CFPK G F Bailey, J D Sorrell		
	& D M Thomas Usk 'P30'		02.03.18R
G-ODDS	Pitts S-2A	2225	31.08.05
	N31486 M J Collett White Waltham		12.02.19E
	Built by Aerotek Inc		
G-ODDZ	Schempp-Hirth Duo Discus T	49/330	22.05.08
	BGA 4931/KAF P A King Shobdon 'DD2'		21.03.18E
G-ODEE	Van's RV-6	24734	14.04.00
	PH-RVM, G-ODEE		
	J Redfearn Morgansfield, Fishburn		27.04.18P
	Built by D Powell – project PFA 181A-13173		
G-ODGC	Aeropro EuroFOX 912(iS)	44214	03.07.14
	Dorset Gliding Club Ltd Eyres Field		13.12.17P
	Built by J Halford, J Marshall & D R Piercy – project		
	LAA 376-15274; damaged landing 28.05.17 Eyres Field;		
	tailwheel u/c; glider-tug (IE 03.01.18)		
G-ODGS	Avtech Jabiru UL-450	0247	02.08.99
	W K Evans Old Park Farm, Margam		19.10.17P
	Built by D G Salt – project PFA 274A-13472		
G-ODHB	Robinson R44 Raven II	10985	05.12.05
	A J Mossop Gloucestershire		26.01.18E
	Operated by Rise Helicopters		

G-ODHC	de Havilland DHC-1B-2-S5 Chipmunk	160-198	30.06.15
	N198RJ, CF-CNZ, CAF 12022, RCAF 18022		
	P M Wells (Long Crendon, Aylesbury)		
	Stored for rebuild 07.15 (NF 30.06.15)		
G-ODIN	Mudry CAP 10B	192	16.12.93
	F-GDTH N P Shields tr CAP Ten Group Goodwood		13.04.18E
G-ODIP	Aviat A-1C-180 Husky	3247	26.10.15
	N47HU A J Whyte Hawarden		20.04.18E
	Amphibian		
G-ODIZ	AutoGyro Cavalon	V00116	17.07.13
	P Williams Moorlands Farm, Farway Common		16.09.15P
	Assembled Rotorsport UK as c/n RSUK/CVLN/006		
	(NF 10.11.17)		
G-ODJD	Raj Hamsa X'Air 582(7)	559	25.04.01
	N M Toulson East Kirkby		05.05.18P
	Built by D J Davis – project BMAA/HB/151		
G-ODJF	Lindstrand LBL 90B	1075	11.04.06
	Helena Maria Fragoso Dos Santos SA		
	Lagos, Algarve, Portugal		14.03.18E
G-ODJG	Europa Aviation Europa	167	03.05.96
	C S Andersson & K R Challis		
	Fowle Hall Farm, Laddingford		12.05.18P
	Built by D J Goldsmith – project PFA 247-12889;		
	tricycle u/c		
G-ODJH	Mooney M.20C Mark 21	690083	19.01.93
	G-BMLH, N9293V A P Howells Henstridge		13.09.08E
	(NF 13.03.15)		
G-ODOC	Robinson R44 Astro	0372	27.08.97
	E Theben (Borken, Germany)		25.11.18E
G-ODOG	Piper PA-28R-200 Cherokee Arrow II	28R-7235197	02.08.96
	EI-BPB, G-BAAR, N11C		
	M Brancart Kortrijk-Wevelgem Int'l, Belgium		09.07.18E
G-ODRT	Cameron Z-105	11740	03.04.13
	N W N Townshend Broadway		15.02.18E
G-ODSA	Bell 429	57139	02.10.13
	C-GVGQ Starspeed Ltd Fairoaks		07.10.18E
G-ODTW	Europa Aviation Europa	215	07.09.95
	D T Walters (Meopham, Gravesend)		
	Built by D T Walters – project PFA 247-12890;		
	tailwheel u/c (NF 02.03.18)		
G-ODUB	Embraer EMB.110P1 Bandeirante	110-217	07.02.00
	PH-FVC, G-BNIX, N8536J		
	Cancelled 19.10.02 by CAA		06.02.01
	Cotswold On fire dump 04.14		
G-ODUD	Piper PA-28-181 Archer II	28-7790107	15.03.04
	G-IBBO, D-EPCA, N5389F		
	S Barlow, R N Ingle & R J Murray Retford Gamston		09.03.18E
G-ODUO	Schempp-Hirth Duo Discus	29	26.11.07
	BGA 4113/HQE		
	A J Eddie tr 3D Syndicate Aboyne '3D'		21.03.18E
G-ODVB	CFM Shadow Series DD	300-DD	03.11.98
	G-MGDB, L J E Moss (Shenley, Radlett)		02.03.11P
	(NF 16.06.18)		
G-ODWS	Silence SA.180 Twister	xxxx	11.12.13
	T R Dews Wing Farm, Longbridge Deverill		
	Built by T R Dews – project LAA 329-15146 (NF 02.02.18)		
G-OEAC	Mooney M.20J Mooney 201	24-1636	16.06.88
	N57656 S Lovatt Nottingham City		09.01.19E
G-OEAT	Robinson R22 Beta	0650	08.01.98
	G-RACH Leamington Hobby Centre Ltd		
	Gloucestershire		03.03.18E
G-OECM	Commander Aircraft Commander 114B	14627	04.03.04
	N6107Y R G Macdowall Carlisle Lake District		11.12.18E
G-OECO	Flylight Dragonfly/Aeros Discus 15T	018	04.02.09
	M W & P A Aston Halwell		
	(IE 27.04.17)		
	(SSDR microlight since 05.14)		
G-OEDB	Piper PA-38-112 Tomahawk	38-79A0167	09.05.89
	G-BGGJ, N9694N BS Offshore Ltd Hawarden		25.03.18E
	Damaged on landing at Tatenhill 28.06.18		
G-OEDP	Cameron N-77	2189	28.12.89
	M J Betts Costessey, Norwich 'Smith & Pinching'		12.06.01A
	(NF 20.10.14)		

G-OEFT	Piper PA-38-112 Tomahawk	38-80A0092	22.05.17
	PH-NRA, (PH-ARN), (PH-GEC), OO-HKH, N9684N		
	M A Lee Durham Tees Valley		17.12.18E
G-OEGG	Cameron Egg-65	2140	04.12.89
	T Read & N Smith t/a Mobberley Balloon Collection		
	Knutsford & Goole 'Cadbury's creme egg'		06.05.12E
	(NF 26.09.16)		
G-OEGL	Christen Eagle II	001	12.01.98
	N46JH C Butler & G G Ferriman		
	Jericho Farm, Lambley		24.06.18P
	Built by J W Hayward		
G-OEGO	e-Go e-Go	SS002	12.01.15
	W M Burnett t/a Cambridge Business Travel		
	Main Hall Farm, Conington		
	(IE 09.06.16)		
G-OEKS	Comco Ikarus C42 FB80	0807-6981	17.09.08
	J D Smith Baxby Manor, Husthwaite		29.10.18P
	Assembled Aerosport Ltd		
G-OELZ	Wassmer WA.52 Europa	66	10.08.05
	F-BTLO J A Simms Breighton		10.02.12P
	Noted 12.16 (NF 08.01.15)		
G-OEMZ	Pietenpol Air Camper	xxxx	25.09.14
	G-IMBY C Brockis (Poundon, Bicester)		
	Built by C Brockis – project PFA 047-12402 (NF 25.09.14)		
G-OENB	AgustaWestland AW189	49008	17.04.14
	I-RAIP Bristow Helicopters Ltd Aberdeen Int'l		16.04.18E
G-OENC	AgustaWestland AW189	89002	03.08.17
	I-RAIW Bristow Helicopters Ltd Aberdeen Int'l		02.08.18E
G-OERR	Lindstrand LBL 60A	469	30.06.97
	P C Gooch Alresford		08.03.18E
G-OERS	Cessna 172N Skyhawk II	17268856	24.05.94
	G-SSRS, N734HA		
	N J Smith & A Stevens Brighton City		04.06.18E
G-OESC	Aquila AT01	AT01-199	17.03.14
	G-OZIO Osterreichischer Sportflieger Club		
	Salzburg, Austria		19.11.18E
G-OESP	Robinson R44 Clipper II	12729	13.01.16
	G-CGND MJL Plant Hire (Cornwall) Ltd		
	(Water-Ma-Trout, Helston)		03.08.18E
G-OESY	Reality Easy Raider J2.2(1)	ER.0005	16.11.01
	J Gray (Bookham, Leatherhead)		02.11.18P
	Built by T F Francis – project BMAA/HB/193		
G-OETI	Bell 206B-3 JetRanger III	2533	23.07.02
	G-RMIE, G-BPIE, N327WM		
	J H & S Garrioch t/a Jaspa Manston Park		18.12.17E
G-OETV	Piper PA-31-350 Chieftain	31-7852073	16.06.04
	N27597 Atlantic Bridge Aviation Ltd Lydd		28.06.19E
	Official type 'PA-31-350 Navajo Chieftain' is incorrect		
G-OEVA	Piper PA-32-260 Cherokee Six	32-219	13.03.03
	G-FLJA, G-AVTJ, N3373W		
	Enterprise Purchasing Ltd (Leighton Buzzard)		06.07.17E
	Rebuilt using spare Fuselage No.32-860S		
G-OEWA	de Havilland DH.104 Dove 8	04528	10.06.98
	G-DDCD, G-ARUM Cancelled 24.05.05 by CAA		
	Calcutt, Swindon		
	Stored Kingshill Recycling Centre 01.15 as 'G-DDCD'		
G-OEWD	Raytheon RB390 Premier 1	RB-126	03.06.05
	N3726G Avidus Jet Management Ltd Farnborough		09.06.18E
G-OEZI	Reality Easy Raider J2.2(2)	ER.0007	31.05.02
	S E J M McDonald Darley Moor		04.07.18P
	Built by M A Claydon – project BMAA/HB/216;		
	replacement fuselage no.ER.0011 fitted c.2004		
G-OEZY	Europa Aviation Europa	042	08.08.95
	A W Wakefield Conington		20.11.13P
	Built by A W Wakefield – project PFA 247-12590;		
	tailwheel u/c (IE 31.05.17)		
G-OFAA	Cameron Z-105	10886	09.08.06
	R A Schwab Misterton, Crewkerne		
	'Royal Navy' & 'Fly Navy'		12.06.19E
G-OFAL	Ozone Roadster/Bailey Quattro		
		RDL-J31E-028 & 0990108	18.09.08
	Malcolm Roberts Heating, Plumbing & Electrical Ltd		
	(Sarn, Pwllheli)		
	(NF 13.07.16)		

G-OFAS	Robinson R22 Beta	0559	17.06.86
	Advance Helicopters Ltd Brighton City		15.09.18E
G-OFBT	Cameron O-84	12137	06.12.17
	A A & W S Calvert Dromore		27.11.18E
G-OFBU	Comco Ikarus C42 FB UK	0301-6328	28.08.01
	K R Meredith tr Old Sarum C42 Group Old Sarum		04.05.18P
	Built by Fly Buy Ultralights Ltd		
	– project PFA 322-13653		
G-OFCM	Reims/Cessna F172L	F17200839	21.10.81
	G-AZUN, (OO-FCB) Sirius Aviation Ltd Jersey		12.07.18E
G-OFDR	Piper PA-28-161 Cadet	2841286	11.09.15
	EC-LCY, D-EFXZ, N92032		
	Electric Scribe 2000 Ltd (Aberdeen)		01.12.18E
	Stored less propeller Elstree 10.18		
G-OFDT	P&M Pegasus Quik	8320	09.11.07
	R M Tomlins (Dover)		07.04.18P
G-OFER	Piper PA-18-150 Super Cub	18-7709058	29.12.89
	N83509 White Waltham Airfield Ltd White Waltham		13.05.18E
G-OFES	Alisport Silent 2 Electro	2076	30.11.15
	N D A Graham Oban 'FES'		
	(IE 28.11.17)		
G-OFFA	Pietenpol Air Camper	xxxx	03.11.94
	C Brockis & P A Hall Turweston 'Sweet FA'		21.04.16P
	Built by Offa Group – project PFA 047-13181;		
	badly damaged landing at Turweston 19.04.16;		
	on rebuild 01.17 (IE 04.11.16)		
G-OFFO	Extra EA.300/L	1226	10.03.06
	2 Excel Aviation Ltd Sywell		23.03.19E
	Operated by 'The Blades' as callsign 'Blade 3'		
G-OFFS	Piper PA-38-112 Tomahawk	38-78A0524	24.02.15
	G-BMSF, N4277E NWMAS Leasing Ltd Welshpool		08.06.18E
	Operated by Welshpool Flying School		
G-OFGC	Aeroprakt A-22L Foxbat	A22L-348	25.01.11
	J M Fearn Ormonde Fields, Codnor		12.04.18P
	Built by J M Fearn – project LAA 317A-14992		
G-OFIT	SOCATA TB-10 Tobago	938	11.09.89
	G-BRIU G M Richards tr GFI Aviation Group		
	White Waltham		24.08.18E
G-OFIX	Grob G109B	6394	05.01.09
	F-CJLS, HB-2111		
	T R Dews Wing Farm, Longbridge Deverill		16.03.17E
	Operated by 'AeroSparx Team' (IE 02.04.18)		
G-OFIZ[M]	Cameron Can 80 SS HAB	2106	30.10.89
	Cancelled 10.02.97 as temporarily WFU		02.12.91
	With British Balloon Museum & Library, Newbury		
G-OFJC	Eiriavion PIK-20E	20291	19.03.93
	SE-UPG, (D-KMTR), SE-UPG, G-OFJC, OH-641		
	G F Bailey, J D Sorrell & D M Thomas Usk 'P20'		13.11.18R
G-OFLG	SOCATA TB-10 Tobago	11	11.12.91
	G-JMWT, F-GBHF Cancelled 15.11.05 as PWFU		29.05.06
	Derby Wreck dumped 01.15		
G-OFLY	Cessna 210M Centurion II	21061600	13.10.79
	(D-EBYM), N732LQ A P Mothew Southend		18.12.15E
	Stored 02.19 (IE 06.02.19)		
G-OFNC	Kubicek BB17XR	994	07.06.13
	M R Jeynes Redditch 'The co-operative funeralcare'		05.08.16E
	(IE 16.03.17)		
G-OFOM	British Aerospace BAe 146 Series 100	E1144	16.03.00
	N3206T, PK-DTA, G-BSLP, (PK-DTA), G-6-144,		
	G-11-144, (G-BRLM)		
	Formula One Management Ltd Biggin Hill		06.10.18E
G-OFRB	Everett Gyroplane Series 2	006	07.08.85
	(G-BLSR) T N Holcroft-Smith (High Wycombe)		18.02.08P
	(NF 19.06.15)		
G-OFRY	Cessna 152 II	15281420	08.02.93
	G-BPHS, N49971		
	Devon & Somerset Flight Training Ltd Dunkeswell		12.07.18E
G-OFSP	Czech Sport Sportcruiser	09SC302	04.01.10
	L Dempsey Abbeyshrule, RoI		15.05.18W
G-OFTI	Piper PA-28-140 Cherokee Cruiser	28-7325201	11.06.96
	G-BRKU, N15926		
	I Mir Wolverhampton Halfpenny Green		09.05.18E
G-OFZY	Eurocopter AS.355N Ecureuil 2	5744	08.10.18
	G-ORDH, F-WWXS Atlas Helicopters Ltd Lasham		08.10.19E

G-OGAN	Europa Aviation Europa	100	28.07.94
	R K W Moss Manchester Barton		31.10.18P
	Built by R S Cullum & Partners		
	– project PFA 247-12734; tricycle u/c		
G-OGAR	PZL-Bielsko SZD-45A Ogar	B-601	29.01.90
	SP-0004 J F C Sergeant (Arianfryn, Barmouth)		25.07.18E
G-OGEM	Piper PA-28-181 Archer II	28-8190226	10.03.88
	N83816 GEM Integrated Solutions Ltd Coventry		30.03.18E
G-OGEO	Aérospatiale SA.341G Gazelle 1	1417	28.01.02
	G-BXJK, F-GEHC, N341AT, N49536		
	G Steel (Cauldhame Farm, Falkirk)		13.03.16E
	(IE 16.08.17)		
G-OGES	Enstrom 280FX Shark	2078	15.11.02
	LN-OWW, G-OGES, G-CBYL, HB-XAJ		
	AWB SAS (Fayence, France)		10.03.18E
G-OGEZ	Robinson R44 Raven II	14254	14.09.18
	G K Jewson (Maeshafn, Mold)		
	(NF 14.09.18)		
G-OGGB	Grob G102 Astir CS	1072	02.04.08
	BGA 4096/HPM, D-3304		
	M P Webb Seighford 'HPM'		16.01.19E
G-OGGI	Aviat A-1C-180 Husky	3211	23.07.14
	N41HU E D Fern Bodmin		17.08.18E
G-OGGM	Cirrus SR22	1382	21.12.11
	N434A Datascope Systems Ltd Hawarden		23.05.19E
G-OGGY	Aviat A-1B Husky Pup	NF0005	27.02.04
	N144HP J H Garrett-Cox Dundee		19.10.18E
G-OGILᴹ	Short SD.3-30 Var.100	SH.3068	23.01.89
	G-BITV, G-14-3068 Cancelled 12.11.92 as WFU		21.04.93
	Damaged Newcastle 01.07.92		
	With North East Land Sea and Air Museum, Usworth		
G-OGIN	Kubicek BB40Z	920	08.01.19
	PH-EJJ A B Court Morda, Oswestry		
	(NF 08.01.19)		
G-OGJC	Robinson R44 Raven II	11653	03.06.09
	EI-JWP, N3017B Telecom Advertising & Promotions Ltd		
	Liverpool John Lennon		
	Operated by Helicentre (IE 17.10.16)		
G-OGJM	Cameron C-80	4869	21.11.00
	A M Holly Breadstone, Berkeley		18.12.18E
G-OGJP	Hughes 369E (500)	0512E	23.01.01
	N685F, N5223X M J Church Gloucestershire		13.07.18E
G-OGJS	Rutan Cozy	xxxx	27.01.89
	G J Stamper (Worsley, Manchester)		14.09.98P
	Built by G J Stamper – project PFA 159-11169		
	(NF 28.06.18)		
G-OGLE	Airbus AS.350B3 Ecureuil	7827	01.04.14
	G-CIEU Freshair UK Ltd Field Farm, Launton		07.10.18E
G-OGLY	Cameron Z-105	11188	21.07.08
	H M Ogston London SW7 'The Deemster'		23.05.18E
G-OGOD	P&M Quik GT450	8537	21.07.10
	L McIlwaine Wickenby		11.04.18P
G-OGOL	Tecnam P2006T	262	07.01.19
	Cucumber Cow Ltd Shipmeadow		
	(NF 07.01.19)		
G-OGOS	Everett Gyroplane	004	30.07.84
	7Q-YES, G-OGOS		
	N A Seymour (Hill Farm, Sproughton)		12.09.90P
	(NF 27.08.14)		
G-OGPN	Cassutt Special	xxxx	01.05.01
	(F-....), G-OGPN, G-OMFI, G-BKCH		
	S Alexander (Bromsgrove)		28.08.02P
	Built by S C Thompson – project PFA 126-10778		
	(NF 18.05.18)		
G-OGRL	Van's RV-7	71874	08.06.17
	N92LT M A Wyer Denham		31.08.19P
	Built by K A Howell		
G-OGSA	Avtech Jabiru SPL-450	299	10.02.00
	R Ryan tr G-OGSA Group Wick John O'Groats		24.01.18P
	Built by G J Slater – project PFA 274A-13540		
G-OGSE	Gulfstream Gulfstream V-SP (Gulfstream 550)	5453	21.03.14
	N353GA TAG Aviation (UK) Ltd Farnborough		20.03.19E

G-OGTR	P&M Quik GTR	8613	01.05.12
	K J Bowles Longacre Farm, Sandy		25.06.18P
G-OGUN	Eurocopter AS.350B2 Ecureuil	3187	17.07.14
	G-SMDJ Go Exclusive Ltd Liverpool John Lennon		30.07.18E
	Operated by Kingmoor Aviation Ltd (IE 17.12.18)		
G-OGZZ	Van's RV-8	xxxx	19.12.18
	E D Fern Bodmin		
	Built by E D Fern – project LAA 303-15536		
	(NF 19.12.18)		
G-OHAC	Reims/Cessna F182Q Skylane II	F18200048	11.07.01
	D-ENCM Maguirelzatt LLP Enstone		17.08.18E
G-OHAL	Pietenpol Air Camper	xxxx	25.11.96
	A Ryan-Fecitt Old Sarum		04.06.18P
	Built by H C Danby – project PFA 047-12840		
G-OHAM	Robinson R44 Raven II	10743	24.07.09
	G-GBEN, G-CDJZ		
	Hamsters Wheel Productions Ltd Gloucestershire		23.06.18E
G-OHAS	Robinson R66 Turbine	0349	23.06.14
	N66CN Heli Air Scotland Ltd Cumbernauld		26.03.19E
G-OHAV	Hybrid Air Vehicle HAV-3	HAV-3/001	21.07.08
	Hybrid Air Vehicles Ltd Cardington		
	(NF 20.01.16)		
G-OHCP	Aérospatiale AS.355F1 Ecureuil 2	5249	14.03.94
	G-BTVS, G-STVE, G-TOFF, G-BKJX		
	Staske Construction Ltd (Bletchley, Milton Keynes)		19.08.17E
	Crashed 29.03.17 in Rhinog mountains between		
	Trawsfynydd & Harlech		
G-OHDK	HpH Glasflügel 304 S Shark	036-MS	24.06.14
	(BGA 5806) D G Clews tr The Shark Syndicate		
	Parham Park 'DK'		
	(IE 13.07.17)		
G-OHEA	Hawker Siddeley HS 125 Series 3B/RA	25144	25.11.86
	G-AVRG, G-5-12 Cancelled 23.06.94 as WFU		07.08.92
	Cranfield Fuselage dumped 03.13 as 'G-DHEA'		
G-OHGA	Hughes OH-6A Cayuse	301381	05.01.09
	N387RF, 69-16011 MSS Holdings (UK) Ltd		
	Wesham House Farm, Wesham		18.05.18P
	As '69-16011' in US Army c/s		
G-OHGC	Scheibe SF25C Rotax-Falke	44695	26.07.04
	D-KBLC D J Marpole tr Heron Gliding Club		
	RNAS Yeovilton		01.04.18E
G-OHIO	Dyn'Aéro MCR-01	AGA4-181-20-MA0173	19.01.07
	N3085Q J M Keane Deanland		
	Built by P Ghiles (NF 20.02.18)		
G-OHJE	Alpi Pioneer 300 Hawk	262	25.11.08
	M C Birchall tr Abergavenny Flying Group		
	The Byre, Hardwick, Abergavenny		20.11.18P
	Built by H J Edwards – project LAA 330A-14853		
G-OHJV	Robinson R44 Raven I	1722	16.08.07
	N457R I Taylor Hallgarth, Great Broughton		10.12.19E
G-OHKS	Cyclone Pegasus Quantum 15 (HKS)	7505	24.03.99
	L J Nelson Newtownards		20.08.18P
	(NF 27.09.17)		
G-OHLI	Robinson R44 Clipper II	10832	08.08.05
	K C McCarthy & D R Smith t/a NCS Partnership		
	Wycombe Air Park		31.08.18E
	Officially registered as 'Raven II'		
G-OHLV	Sackville BM-65	HLV01	23.11.17
	H & L D Vaughan Milton Keynes		
G-OHMS	Aérospatiale AS.355F1 Ecureuil 2	5194	15.06.90
	N367E HFS (Aviation) Ltd Stapleford		03.12.18E
G-OHOV	RotorWay Exec 162F	6885	14.09.04
	M G Bird Street Farm, Takeley		18.12.17P
	Built by M G Bird; noted 02.18		
G-OHPC	Cessna 208 Caravan I	20800224	04.04.08
	N288SR, N788SR, (N9820F) S Ulrich Headcorn		05.02.18E
	Operated by Headcorn Parachute Club		
G-OHUR	Ingleton Hurricane 315	250218	19.02.18
	M Ingleton (Eastchurch, Sheerness)		
	(IE 19.02.18)		
G-OHWK	Bell 206L-1 LongRanger II	45193	04.08.16
	G-PWIT, D-HHSW, G-DWMI, N18092		
	Eze Air Ltd Sleap		26.01.20E

G-OHWV	Raj Hamsa X'Air 582(6) 474	18.11.99
	M Duffy (Monivea, Co Galway)	29.06.19P
	Built by H W Vasey – project BMAA/HB/121	
	(NF 22.09.17)	
G-OHYE	Thruster T600N 450 0042-T600N-098	09.03.04
	G-CCRO T Kossakowski Chiltern Park, Wallingford	11.07.18P
	Badged 'Sprint'	
G-OHZO	Aviat A-1A Husky 1425	06.10.17
	N119WP Neil's Seaplanes Ltd Cumbernauld	
	Stored 05.18 (NF 06.10.17)	
G-OIBO	Piper PA-28-180 Cherokee C 28-3794	21.01.87
	G-AVAZ, N11C M Kraemer & J G C Schneider	
	(St Wendel, Germany & Basel, Switzerland)	23.05.17E
G-OICU	Learjet Learjet 45 45-167	19.07.18
	G-GMAA, N5012V	
	Capital Air Ambulance Ltd Birmingham	05.05.19E
G-OIFM	Cameron Dude-90 2841	18.06.92
	Magical Adventures Ltd West Bloomfield, MI, USA	
	'Dude'	29.05.99A
	(NF 03.06.15)	
G-OIHC	Piper PA-32R-301 Saratoga II HP 3246163	06.12.06
	G-PUSK, N237TB N J Lipczynski Biggin Hill	15.10.18E
	Official type data 'PA-32R-301 Saratoga SP' is incorrect	
G-OIIO	Robinson R22 Beta 2444	27.03.02
	G-ULAB, N8311Z Un Pied sur Terre Ltd	
	t/a Whizzard Helicopters Welshpool	10.04.18E
G-OIIY	Ultramagic S-70 70/10	03.08.15
	M Cowling (Glencarse, Perth)	16.04.19E
G-OIMC	Cessna 152 II 15285506	15.05.87
	N93521 East Midlands Flying School Ltd	
	East Midlands	01.12.18E
G-OIMF	Dassault Falcon 7X 125	27.01.17
	OE-IMF, D-AFSX, OE-ILM, F-WWHL	
	TAG Aviation (UK) Ltd Farnborough	30.10.18E
G-OINN	Ultramagic H-31 31/10	15.03.10
	G Everett Sandway, Maidstone 'Holiday Inn'	19.06.18E
G-OINT	Kubicek BB20XR 993	06.06.13
	M A Green Rednal, Birmingham	25.04.19E
G-OIOB	Mudry CAP 10B 194	30.01.08
	N501DW Rolls-Royce PLC Derby	12.07.18E
G-OIOIM	EH Industries EH-101 Heliliner 50008	23.11.88
	Cancelled 01.04.96 – to MOD	05.05.94
	Airframe No.PP8 To RAF as 'ZJ116'	
	With RAF Museum, Hendon	
G-OIOZ	Thunder Ax9-120 Series 2 4434	17.11.98
	D Venegoni Fagnano Olona, Varese, Italy 'Spire FM'	23.11.18E
G-OITV	Enstrom 280C Shark 1038	09.04.96
	G-HRVY, G-DUGY, G-BEEL C W Brierley-Jones	
	Westbrook House, Higher Whitley	25.04.08E
	(NF 20.10.14)	
G-OIVN	Liberty XL-2 0008	17.05.07
	N511XL I Shaw Newton-on-Rawcliffe	17.07.18P
G-OJAB	Avtech Jabiru SK 0088	19.09.96
	J D Winder White House Farm, Southery	11.08.18P
	Built by K D Pearce – project PFA 274-13031	
G-OJAC	Mooney M.20J Mooney 201 24-1490	20.08.90
	N5767E Hornet Engineering Ltd Biggin Hill	05.03.18E
G-OJAG	Cessna 172S Skyhawk SP 172S9794	04.04.05
	N66124 Valhalla Aviation LLP Wycombe Air Park	16.02.18E
G-OJAN	Robinson R22 Beta 2012	22.05.01
	G-SANS, G-BUHX J C Lane Gloucestershire	17.08.18E
G-OJAS	Auster J1U Workmaster 3501	21.03.00
	F-BJAS, F-WJAS, (F-OBHT)	
	D S Hunt (Balcombe, Crawley)	
	Displayed Wings Museum World War Two Remembrance	
	(NF 12.01.16)	
G-OJAV	Fairey Britten-Norman BN-2A MkIII-2 Trislander 1024	06.06.90
	(4X-CCI), G-BDOS	
	Cancelled 11.01.10 as sold in Philippines	29.01.07
	Manila, Philippines *Stored 02.13*	
G-OJBB	Enstrom 280FX Shark 2084	14.06.99
	M Jones Hawarden	08.11.18E

G-OJBM	Cameron N-90 2899	28.09.92
	S J Bettin Greatham, Liss 'JBM'	31.08.19E
G-OJBS	Cameron N-105 4733	08.03.00
	J Bennett & Son (Insurance Brokers) Ltd	
	High Wycombe 'J.Bennett & Son'	19.09.18E
G-OJBW	Lindstrand LBL J & B Bottle 436	26.08.97
	G Gray East Worldham, Alton 'J&B'	31.03.17E
	(NF 06.09.16)	
G-OJCL	Robinson R22 Beta 1950	18.11.16
	G-HRHE, G-BTWP	
	J C Lane t/a JCL Aviation Gloucestershire	19.05.17E
G-OJCS	BRM Bristell NG5 Speed Wing 255	02.03.17
	A Rowsome tr Bristell Flyer Grp (Dublin)	25.06.19P
	Built by J C Simpson – project LAA 385-15458	
G-OJCW	Piper PA-32RT-300 Lance II 32R-7985062	09.01.80
	N3016K P G Dobson Wishanger Farm, Frensham	20.12.18E
G-OJDA	EAA Acrosport II xxxx	01.04.98
	D B Almey Fenland	15.10.19P
	Built by D B Almey – project PFA 072-11067	
	– project type should be 072A	
G-OJDC	Thunder Ax7-77 875	09.01.89
	A Heginbottom Cheadle Hulme, Cheadle	30.05.11E
	(NF 07.06.18)	
G-OJEH	Piper PA-28-181 Archer II 28-8690051	17.12.02
	D-EDPA, N9125Y P C Lilley Solent	23.03.18E
G-OJEN	Cameron V-77 3302	26.05.94
	S D Wrighton St Brelade JE3 8GU	19.05.18E
G-OJER	Cessna 560XL Citation XLS+ 560-6148	18.12.13
	N5031E Gama Aviation (Beauport) Ltd Jersey	17.12.18E
G-OJGC	Van's RV-4 xxxx	26.04.10
	J G Claridge Thruxton	
	Built by J G Claridge – project LAA 181-14971	
	(NF 01.05.18)	
G-OJGT	Maule M-5-235C Lunar Rocket 7285C	30.06.98
	LN-AEL, (LN-BEK), N5635V S R Clark tr Newnham	
	Joint Flying Syndicate (Leamington Spa)	02.11.17E
G-OJHC	Cessna 182P Skylane 18264535	21.08.07
	N86AD N Foster Carlisle Lake District	16.08.15E
	Extensively damaged in heavy landing at Carlisle	
	early 05.15, stored 09.15	
G-OJHL	Europa Aviation Europa 311	12.05.97
	M D Burns & G Rainey Cumbernauld 'Lady Lace'	06.03.18P
	Built by J H Lace – project PFA 247-13039; tailwheel u/c	
G-OJIM	Piper PA-28R-201T Turbo Cherokee Arrow III	
	28R-7703200	04.08.86
	N38299 Black Star Aviation Ltd Biggin Hill	27.02.18E
G-OJJV	P&M Pegasus Quik 8276	07.06.07
	J J Valentine Ince	05.06.18P
G-OJKM	Rans S-7 Courier 1095.158	05.03.01
	A J Owen RAF Mona	30.05.18P
	Built by M Jackson – project PFA 218-12982	
G-OJLD	Van's RV-7 73622	24.11.09
	J L Dixon Sherburn-in-Elmet	18.07.18P
	Built by J L Dixon – project LAA 323-14946	
G-OJLH	Team Mini-Max 91 xxxx	12.12.01
	G-MYAW P D Parry (Clawddnewydd, Ruthin)	
	Built by J L Hamer – project PFA 186-12164	
	(SSDR microlight since 06.14) (IE 30.09.17)	
G-OJMP	Cessna 208B Grand Caravan 208B0917	19.01.18
	N106AN Parachuting Aircraft Ltd Old Sarum	
	(IE 19.01.18)	
G-OJMS	Cameron Z-90 10860	28.09.06
	Joinerysoft Ltd Chipping Norton 'Joinerysoft'	06.09.19E
G-OJNE	Schempp-Hirth Nimbus-3T 22/88	27.11.07
	BGA 4344/HZW, D-KILO	
	M R Garwood Husbands Bosworth 'HZW'	22.06.18E
G-OJON	Taylor JT.2 Titch xxxx	06.10.78
	Freelance Aviation Ltd Coventry	04.09.12P
	Built by J H Fell – project PFA 3208;	
	on rebuild 05.15 (NF 08.12.14)	
G-OJPS	Bell 206B-2 JetRanger II 1484	30.10.06
	G-UEST, G-ROYB, G-BLWU, ZS-PAW	
	C & L Fairburn Property Developments Ltd (Louth)	27.11.18E

G-OJRM	Cessna T182T Turbo Skylane	T18208007	19.07.01
	N72778 M D Harvey tr Romeo Mike Group		
	Earls Colne		08.09.19E
G-OJSD	Aeropro EuroFOX 912(S)	50516	23.11.16
	J D Sinclair-Day Eshott		05.09.19P
	Built by J D Sinclair-Day – project LAA 376-15428;		
	tailwheel u/c		
G-OJSH	Thruster T600N 450	0061-T600N-052	29.05.01
	P J Reed tr G-OJSH Group Enstone		03.03.18P
G-OJVA	Van's RV-6	xxxx	06.09.96
	J A Village Moor Green Farm, Barlow		20.06.18P
	Built by J A Village – project PFA 181-12292		
G-OJVL	Van's RV-6	22176	28.10.02
	S E Tomlinson Bournemouth		05.02.18P
	Built by S E Tomlinson – project PFA 181-12441		
G-OJWS	Piper PA-28-161 Warrior II	28-7816415	13.07.88
	N6377C P J Ward Denham		01.11.17E
G-OKAG	Piper PA-28R-180 Cherokee Arrow	28R-30075	15.04.88
	N3764T Cancelled 05.12.13 by CAA		09.06.13
	Kings Farm, Thurrock *Fuselage stored 05.17*		
G-OKAY	Pitts S-1E	12358	27.05.80
	N35WH S R S Evans Andrewsfield		16.08.18P
	Built by W D Henline		
G-OKCP	Lindstrand LBL Battery	621	09.05.05
	OO-BXY, G-MAXX		
	Lindstrand Asia Ltd Oswestry *'Panasonic'*		24.08.19E
	Battery special shape		
G-OKED	Cessna 150L	15074250	29.01.93
	N19223 M J Fogarty Clipgate Farm, Denton		17.12.18E
G-OKEN	Piper PA-28R-201T Turbo Cherokee Arrow III		
		28R-7703390	20.10.87
	N47518 J D Hood & L James (Lichfield/Mickleover)		27.10.19E
G-OKER	Van's RV-7	71793	11.05.04
	R M Johnson Templehall Farm, Midlem *'Miss Joker'*		18.05.18P
	Built by R M Johnson – project PFA 323-14233		
G-OKEV	Europa Aviation Europa	328	11.06.97
	K A Kedward Wolverhampton Halfpenny Green		
	'Freedom'		02.10.18P
	Built by K A Pilcher – project PFA 247-13091; tricycle u/c		
G-OKEW	Ultramagic M-65C	65/184	13.04.11
	Hampshire Balloons Ltd Bramley, Tadley *'Kewtech'*		06.08.18E
G-OKID	Escapade Kid	ESC.K001	25.11.08
	V H Hallam Dunkeswell		
	Built by T F Francis – US supplied kit		
	(SSDR microlight since 05.14) (IE 06.12.17)		
G-OKIM	Best Off Skyranger 912(2)	SKR0310395	23.12.03
	K P Taylor Sywell		17.06.18P
	Built by K P Taylor – project BMAA/HB/333		
G-OKIS	Tri-R KIS	xxxx	15.06.92
	T E Reeder (Catterick)		16.10.18P
	Built by B W Davies – project PFA 239-12248		
G-OKLY	Reims/Cessna F150K	F15000577	28.04.15
	G-ECBH, D-ECBH		
	J L Sparks St Athan *'Oakley'*		27.09.19E
G-OKMA	Tri-R KIS	xxxx	22.11.95
	K Miller Lelystad, Netherlands		02.10.19P
	Built by K Miller – project PFA 239-12808; tricycle u/c		
G-OKPS	Best Off Skyranger Nynja 912S(1)	xxxx	11.12.18
	K P Taylor tr G-OKPS Group (Willoughby, Rugby)		
	Built by P Osborne, K P Taylor & S Walters		
	– project BMAA/HB/712 (NF 11.12.18)		
G-OKPW	Tri-R KIS	xxxx	17.08.93
	P J Reilly (Southwater, Horsham)		20.11.07P
	Built by K P Wordsworth – project PFA 239-12359;		
	tricycle u/c (NF 15.03.16)		
G-OKTA	Comco Ikarus C42 FB80	1305-7250	24.05.13
	Avion Training & Consultancy Ltd Solent		29.05.18P
	Assembled Red-Air UK		
G-OKTI	Aquila AT01	AT01-172	12.10.07
	P H Ferdinand North Weald		02.12.18E
G-OKUB	TLAC Sherwood Kub	TLAC-3-001	27.02.15
	The Light Aircraft Company Ltd Little Snoring		
	Noted 09.16 with large tundra tyres (NF 27.02.15)		

G-OKYA	Cameron V-77	3331	04.03.87
	R J Pearce Doagh, Ballyclare		29.05.19E
	Replacement envelope c/n 3331 fitted;		
	original c/n 1259		
G-OKYM	Piper PA-28-140 Cherokee	28-23303	10.05.88
	G-AVLS, N11C R B Petrie Caernarfon		09.06.10E
	(NF 17.05.16)		
G-OLAA	Alpi Pioneer 300 Hawk	219	04.10.07
	G G Hammond Crowfield		27.05.17P
	Built by G G Hammond – project PFA 330A-14719;		
	noted 01.18		
G-OLAD	Extra EA.300/L	1270	04.12.15
	G-JJIL A Hanson t/a Hanson Aviation Blackpool		03.01.19E
G-OLAU	Robinson R22 Beta	1119	05.09.89
	Un Pied sur Terre Ltd t/a Whizzard Helicopters		
	Welshpool		25.06.18E
G-OLAW	Lindstrand LBL 25A Cloudhopper	170	09.12.94
	George Law Plant Ltd Kidderminster		
	'Law Plant & Tools'		09.04.11E
	(NF 17.08.16)		
G-OLCP	Eurocopter AS.355N Ecureuil 2	5580	18.02.02
	G-CLIP Cheshire Helicopters Ltd		
	Blackshaw Heys Farm, Mobberley		11.04.19E
	Operated by VLL Ltd t/a GB Helicopters		
G-OLCY	Lindstrand LTL Series 1-105	052	24.05.17
	A M Holly Breadstone, Berkeley *'London City Airport'*		31.05.18E
	(IE 05.10.18)		
G-OLDG	Cessna T182T Turbo Skylane	T18208127	17.10.02
	G-CBTJ, N5170R		
	H W Palmer Palma-Son Bonet, Mallorca, Spain		15.04.18E
G-OLDM	Cyclone Pegasus Quantum 15-912	7589	10.12.99
	J W Holme (Bishops Stortford)		12.04.18P
G-OLDO	Eurocopter EC120B Colibri	1489	29.11.07
	G-HIGI Gold Group International Ltd		
	Tupwood Lane, Caterham		17.09.18E
G-OLDP	Mainair Pegasus Quik	7957	28.05.03
	G J Gibson Perth		27.06.16P
	Built by Mainair Sports Ltd		
G-OLEA	Piper PA-28-151 Cherokee Warrior	28-7415457	24.03.17
	N2929W London School of Flying Ltd Elstree		21.06.19E
	Operated by Flight Training London Ltd		
G-OLEC	Alisport Silent 2 Electro	2069	17.03.15
	N Parry Lotmead Farm, Wanborough *'LEC'*		
	(IE 04.03.17)		
G-OLEE	Reims/Cessna F152 II	F15201797	11.09.80
	Redhill Air Services Ltd Fairoaks		01.02.18E
	Operated by Fairoaks Flight Centre		
G-OLEG	Yakovlev Yak-3UA	0470202	26.11.15
	D-FLAK, (G-LLBW), D-FLAK, RA-44552		
	W H Greenwood Goodwood		21.04.18P
	As 'OO' (White) in Russian AF c/s		
G-OLEM	Jodel D.18	xxxx	11.02.02
	G-BSBP G E Roe		
	Brown Shutters Farm, Norton St Philip		12.12.18P
	Built by R T Pratt – project PFA 169-11613		
G-OLEW	Van's RV-7A	71629	29.04.09
	C-FSIS A Burani North Weald		27.06.19P
	Built by S J Hurlbut		
G-OLEZ	Piper J-3C-65 Cub	18432	08.08.01
	G-BSAX, N98260, NC98260		
	L Powell (Adisham, Canterbury)		
	(NF 30.10.14)		
G-OLFB	Cyclone Pegasus Quantum 15-912	7767	02.03.01
	M S McGimpsey Newtownards		14.03.18P
G-OLFE	Dassault Falcon 20-E5	302	31.05.17
	F-GOPM, F-WQBM, N84V, OE-GDP, D-COMM,		
	F-WRQP		
	Green Go Aircraft KFT (Budapest, Hungary)		24.02.18E
G-OLFT	Rockwell Commander 114	14274	28.03.85
	G-WJMN, N4954W		
	D A Tubby Liverpool John Lennon		08.06.18E
G-OLFZ	P&M Quik GT450	8354	15.02.08
	A J Boyd Newtownards		01.05.18P

G-OLGA	CFM Starstreak Shadow SA-II	K 288	15.10.97
	(EI-xxx) G L Turner Limetree, Portarlington, RoI		02.09.18P
	Built by N F Smith – project PFA 206-13164		
G-OLHR	Cassutt Racer IIIM	xxxx	14.08.12
	G-BNJZ P A Hall & A R Lewis White Waltham		14.08.13P
	Built by Miller Aerial Spraying		
	– project PFA 034-11228 (NF 26.07.16)		
G-OLIC	Tecnam P2008-JC	1059	27.05.16
	Stapleford Flying Club Ltd Stapleford		05.06.18E
G-OLIV	Beech B200 Super King Air	BB-1835	12.11.14
	G-RAFN, ZK454, G-RAFN, N60275		
	Dragonfly Aviation Services Ltd Cardiff		06.08.18E
G-OLNT	Aérospatiale SA.365N1 Dauphin 2	6309	24.08.06
	N111EP, G-POAV, G-BOPI		
	LNT Aviation Ltd Leeds East		25.09.18E
G-OLPE	Aérospatiale AS.350BA Ecureuil	1272	09.09.16
	I-CRMC, F-GCJZ G Martinelli (Milan, Italy)		29.10.18E
G-OLPH	Piper PA-28-140 Cherokee Cruiser	28-7725094	30.01.19
	(G-EECI), EI-CMB, G-BELR, N9541N		
	J L Sparks St Athan		
	(NF 30.01.19)		
G-OLPM	P&M QuikR	8627	17.08.12
	M D Freeman Beccles		03.11.18P
G-OLSF	Piper PA-28-161 Cadet	2841284	23.11.89
	G-OTYJ, G-OLSF, N92008 Flew LLP Bournemouth		25.03.18E
	Operated by Bournemouth Flying Club		
G-OLUD	Extra EA.300/200	1044	09.06.16
	OK-VAV A P Walsh Ludham		19.04.18E
G-OMAA	Eurocopter EC135 T2+	1144	19.12.13
	Babcock Mission Critical Services Onshore Ltd		
	RAF Cosford		07.01.19E
	Operated by Midlands Air Ambulance as		
	callsign 'Helimed 03'		
G-OMAF	Dornier 228-202K	8112	16.02.87
	D-CAAD RUAG Aerospace Services GmbH		
	Oberpfaffenhofen, Germany		29.06.19E
G-OMAG	Cessna 182B Skylane	52214	13.05.05
	F-BJEC, N7214E J W N Sharpe Dunkeswell		21.06.19E
G-OMAL	Thruster T600N 450	0061-T600N-050	16.05.01
	M I Garner (Bottesford, Nottingham)		23.06.16P
	Badged 'Sprint'; operated by Fly 365; extant 11.17		
G-OMAO	SOCATA TB-20 Trinidad	378	14.01.09
	N37EL, G-GDGR		
	R Deery tr Alpha Oscar Group Brighton City		04.06.18E
G-OMAS	Cessna A150M Aerobat	A1500719	03.03.08
	G-BTFS, N20331, HP-902, (N7332A)		
	M A Segar Kirknewton		13.12.17E
G-OMAT	Piper PA-28-140 Cherokee D	28-7125139	27.08.87
	G-JIMY, G-AYUG, N11C		
	R B Walker t/a Midland Air Training School Coventry		23.11.19E
G-OMCB	TL 2000UK Sting Carbon S4	xxxx	29.05.15
	M C Bayley Wolverhampton Halfpenny Green		12.02.18P
	Built by M C Bayley – project LAA 347A-15342		
G-OMCC	Aérospatiale AS.350B Ecureuil	1836	26.03.02
	G-JTCM, G-HLEN, G-LOLY, JA9897, N5805T,		
	HP-1084P, HP-1084, N5805T		
	Airbourne Solutions Ltd Five Acres Farm, Gamlingay		29.05.17E
	(IE 05.07.17)		
G-OMCH	Piper PA-28-161 Warrior III	2842291	25.07.12
	OK-AGT, N460ND, N9517N Chalrey Ltd Elstree		16.10.19E
	Operated by Flyers Flying School		
G-OMDD	Thunder Ax8-90 Series 2	4345	02.04.98
	M D Dickinson Budleigh Salterton		08.10.16E
	Built by Cameron Balloons Ltd (IE 21.04.17)		
G-OMDG	Hoffman H36 Dimona	3510	19.11.98
	OE-9215 Cancelled 07.04.10 by CAA		09.01.05
	Sligo, RoI *Stored dismantled 05.14*		
G-OMDH	Hughes 369E (500)	0293E	14.11.88
	Stiltgate Ltd Longacre, Chalfont St Giles		21.12.17E
G-OMDR	Agusta-Bell 206B-3 JetRanger III	8610	08.12.97
	G-HRAY, G-VANG, G-BIZA Castle Air Ltd Biggin Hill		13.02.15E
	(IE 07.12.17)		

G-OMEM	Eurocopter EC120B Colibri	1006	28.04.11
	G-BXYD Go Exclusive Ltd Liverpool John Lennon		05.01.19E
	Operated by Helicentre		
G-OMEN	Cameron Z-90	10614	25.06.04
	M G Howard Hewish, Weston-super-Mare		
	'Manchester Evening News'		22.08.18E
G-OMER	Avtech Jabiru UL-450	0508	04.07.11
	G-GPAS B P Bradley Top Farm, Croydon		23.03.19P
	Built by G D Allen – project PFA 274A-13823		
G-OMEX	Zenair CH.701UL	xxxx	11.12.01
	J W Johns (South Molton, Exeter)		07.05.15P
	Built by S J Perry – project PFA 187-13556 (IE 17.10.18)		
G-OMEZ	Zenair CH.601HDS Zodiac	6-9104	16.07.01
	A D Sutton North Weald		17.07.19P
	Built by C J Gow – project PFA 162-13552		
G-OMGR	Cameron Z-105	11095	14.04.08
	J F A Strickland Harpole, Northampton *'Omega'*		29.05.19E
G-OMHC	Piper PA-28RT-201 Arrow IV	28R-7918105	10.02.81
	N3072Y J W Tonge Beverley (Linley Hill)		22.11.18E
G-OMHD	English Electric Canberra PR.Mk.9	SH.1724	15.08.06
	XH134 Kemble Airfield Estates Ltd Cotswold		13.08.15P
	Built by Short Brothers & Harland Ltd; as 'XH134'		
	in RAF silver c/s; donated to Indian Air Force		
	Historic Flight 07.18 (NF 27.09.16)		
G-OMHI	Mills MH-1	MH001	08.10.97
	J P Mills (Stockport)		
	Built by J P Mills (NF 06.04.16)		
G-OMHP	Avtech Jabiru UL	0351	23.05.00
	J Livingstone Sorbie Farm, Kingsmuir		18.08.15P
	Built by M H Player – project PFA 274A-13584 (NF 19.01.17)		
G-OMIA	SOCATA MS.893A Rallye Commodore 180	12074	21.07.98
	D-ENME, F-BUGE, (D-ENMH)		
	S R Winter Wellesbourne Mountford		15.11.19E
G-OMIK	Europa Aviation Europa	270	12.01.98
	M J Clews tr Mikite Flying Group White Waltham		19.06.18P
	Built by M J Clews – project PFA 247-12991;		
	tailwheel u/c		
G-OMIW	P&M Pegasus Quik	8232	24.01.07
	A J Ladell Pond Farm, Carleton St Peter		14.05.18P
G-OMJA	Piper PA-28-181 Archer II	28-7690328	26.10.07
	A6-DXB, N75319 P R Monk Biggin Hill		03.04.18E
G-OMJT	Rutan Long-EZ	xxxx	14.10.92
	D A Daniel Shobdon		11.12.18P
	Built by M J Timmons – project PFA 074A-10703		
G-OMMG	Robinson R22 Beta	1041	25.02.94
	G-BPYX Sky Touch GmbH & Co KG		
	(Burbach, Germany)		11.01.16E
G-OMMM	Colt 90A	2328	20.01.93
	Davinci Associates Ltd Waterlooville		22.09.19E
G-OMNI	Piper PA-28R-200 Cherokee Arrow II	28R-7335130	03.01.84
	G-BAWA, N11C Cotswold Aviation Services Ltd		
	Gloucestershire		13.08.18E
G-OMPH	Van's RV-7	71648	24.09.14
	LY-BAW, LY-AXY, N751CW R J Luke Solent		13.11.18P
	Built by V Macilius		
G-OMPW	Mainair Pegasus Quik	8088	12.01.05
	M P Wimsey Strubby		29.01.19P
	Built by Mainair Sports Ltd		
G-OMRB	Cameron V-77	2184	29.08.90
	I J Jevons Westerleigh, Bristol		03.08.15E
	(NF 30.11.16)		
G-OMRC	Van's RV-10	41040	26.11.12
	A W Collett Rectory Farm, Poundon		06.03.18P
	Built by A W Collett – project LAA 339-15032		
G-OMRP	Flight Design CTSW	08-02-16	03.10.08
	M E Parker Sackville Lodge Farm, Riseley		19.07.18P
	Assembled P&M Aviation Ltd as c/n 8397		
G-OMSA	Flight Design CTSW	09-10-07	21.11.09
	Microlight Sport Aviation Ltd Damyns Hall, Upminster		22.05.19P
	Assembled P&M Aviation Ltd as c/n 8501		
G-OMSL	Pilatus PC-12/47E	1842	20.12.18
	HB-FRA Pink Time Ltd Carrickmore		
	(IE 20.12.18)		

G-OMST	Piper PA-28-161 Warrior III	2842121		01.08.01
	G-BZUA, N53363 Mid-Sussex Timber Co Ltd Redhill			27.04.18E
G-OMUM	Rockwell Commander 114	14067		24.01.97
	PH-JJJ, (PH-MMM), N4737W M J P Lynch Coventry			03.08.18E
G-OMYT	Airbus A330-243	301		14.05.03
	G-MOJO, F-WWYE			
	Thomas Cook Airlines Ltd (Copenhagen, Denmark)			07.11.19E
	Operated by Thomas Cook Scandinavia			
G-ONAA	North American OV-10B Bronco	338-3		30.11.11
	German AF 99+18, D-9547, USN 158294			
	Liberty Aviation Ltd Kortrijk-Wevelgem Int'l, Belgium			22.04.19P
	As '99+18' in German AF c/s			
G-ONAF	Naval Aircraft Factory N3N-3	4406		31.01.89
	N45192, USN 4406 J P Birnie Sandown			11.01.18E
	As '4406:12' in US Navy c/s			
G-ONAT	Grob G102 Astir CS77	1804		23.10.07
	BGA 5296/KRE, HB-1459			
	N A Toogood RAF Weston-on-the-Green			
	(NF 14.10.14)			
G-ONAV	Piper PA-31 Navajo C	31-7812004		29.01.93
	G-IGAR, D-IGAR, N27378			
	Panther Aviation Ltd North Weald			24.08.19E
G-ONCB	Lindstrand LBL 31A	393		04.06.96
	B J Alford Bristol BS3 *'Flying Circus'*			21.11.18E
	Operated by Hertfordshire Balloon Collection			
G-ONCE	Flight Design CTSW	08-02-01		02.12.18
	OO-F86 M A Wood Enstone			
	(NF 02.12.18)			
G-ONCS	Tipsy Nipper T.66 Series 3B	PFA 1390		18.12.06
	G-AZBA C Swann & M G Walker Netherthorpe			28.03.19P
	Built by E Shouler – project PFA 1390			
G-ONES	Slingsby T67M-200 Firefly	2046		12.11.01
	SE-LBB, LN-TFB, G-7-122			
	A N Booth & R M Davies Leicester			09.04.17E
	Operated by Leicester Aero Club (NF 23.08.18)			
G-ONET	Piper PA-28-180 Cherokee E	28-5802		03.06.98
	G-AYAU, N11C N Z Ali & T Mahmood Stapleford			24.02.14E
	In external storage 04.16 (NF 12.05.15)			
G-ONEZ	Glaser-Dirks DG-200/17	2-143/1738		17.01.08
	BGA 4878/JYB, D-1086			
	R Nuza tr One Zulu Group Rufforth *'1Z'*			09.05.18E
G-ONGC	Robin DR.400-180R Remorqueur	1385		11.11.98
	EI-CKA, SE-GHM Norfolk Gliding Club Ltd Tibenham			24.05.18E
G-ONHH	Forney F-1A Aircoupe	5725		13.12.89
	G-ARHA, N3030G			
	R D I Tarry Pytchley Grange, Pytchley *'Easy Rider'*			22.09.18E
	Built by Air Products Inc			
G-ONHL	Allstar PZL SZD-54-2 Perkoz	542.A.17.021W		01.03.18
	(BGA 5947), SP-3989 Devon & Somerset			
	Gliding Club Ltd North Hill *'NH2'*			24.04.19E
	Built by Wytwórnia Konstrukcji Kompozytowych			
	Andrzej Papiorek SP z.o.o.			
G-ONIC	Evektor EV-97 Sportstar Max	2011-1503		13.04.12
	D M Jack Longside			19.07.18W
G-ONIG	Murphy Elite	E745		29.04.03
	N S Smith Longside			01.02.18P
	Built by N Smith – project PFA 232-14042			
G-ONKA	Aeronca K	K283		21.10.91
	N19780, NC19780			
	N J R Minchin Hill Top Farm, Hambledon *'Aggnes'*			29.11.18P
G-ONNE	Westland SA.341D Gazelle HT.3	1089		20.06.11
	G-DMSS, XW858			
	A M Parkes (Steeple Bumpstead, Haverhill)			20.06.18P
	As 'XW858:C' in RAF red & white c/s			
G-ONSW	Best Off Skyranger Swift 912S(1)	UK/1075		15.01.14
	N S Wells (Buchlyvie, Stirling)			
	Built by N S Wells – project BMAA/HB/646			
	(NF 28.02.18)			
G-ONTV	Agusta-Bell 206B-3 JetRanger III	8733		01.04.98
	G-GOUL, G-ONTV, D-HUNT, TC-HKJ, (D-HSAV),			
	I-GPFP, I-PIEF Adventure 001 Ltd Newcastle Int'l			24.03.18E
	Operated by Northumbria Helicopters			
G-ONUN	Van's RV-6A	24660		20.02.96
	D Atkinson Sherburn-in-Elmet			28.02.18P
	Built by R E Nunn – project PFA 181-12976			
G-ONVG	Guimbal Cabri G2	1141		19.04.16
	F-WZEA Vantage Aviation Ltd Thruxton			20.04.18E
G-ONYX	Bell 206B-3 JetRanger III	4160		22.01.98
	G-BXPN, N18EA, D-HOBA, (D-HOBE)			
	CBM Aviation Ltd (Brittas Bay, Co Wicklow, RoI)			24.11.16E
G-OOBA	Boeing 757-28A	32446		09.02.01
	C-GUBA, G-OOBA, C-GUBA, G-OOBA, N446GE,			
	(N558NA) TUI Airways Ltd t/a TUI Manchester			30.03.19E
	Line No: 950			
G-OOBB	Boeing 757-28A	32447		09.02.01
	C-GTBB, G-OOBB, N447GE, (N559NA)			
	TUI Airways Ltd t/a TUI Manchester			05.01.20E
	Line No: 951			
G-OOBC	Boeing 757-28A	33098		28.03.03
	TUI Airways Ltd t/a TUI Manchester			19.07.19E
	Line No: 1026			
G-OOBD	Boeing 757-28A	33099		31.03.03
	TUI Airways Ltd t/a TUI Manchester			08.07.19E
	Line No: 1028			
G-OOBE	Boeing 757-28A	33100		19.05.03
	TUI Airways Ltd t/a TUI Manchester			18.05.19E
	Line No: 1029			
G-OOBF	Boeing 757-28A	33101		19.04.04
	TUI Airways Ltd t/a TUI Manchester			10.04.19E
	Line No: 1041			
G-OOBG	Boeing 757-236	29942		11.03.04
	C-FUBG, G-OOBG, C-FUBG, G-OOBG, C-FUBG,			
	G-OOBG, C-FUBG, G-OOBG, C-FUBG, G-OOBG,			
	G-FUBG, G-OOBG, N544NA, N1795B, (G-CPEV)			
	TUI Airways Ltd t/a TUI Manchester			25.03.19E
	Line No: 867			
G-OOBN	Boeing 757-2G5	29379		19.05.10
	HB-IHR TUI Airways Ltd t/a TUI Manchester			02.08.19E
	Line No: 919			
G-OOBP	Boeing 757-2G5	30394		02.06.10
	HB-IHS, (D-ABPB), HB-IHS			
	TUI Airways Ltd t/a TUI Manchester			03.08.19E
	Line No: 922			
G-OOCP	SOCATA TB-10 Tobago	1588		04.03.14
	PH-DFJ, G-BZRL, VH-YHF R M Briggs Wickenby			09.05.18E
G-OODD	Robinson R44 Raven II	13877		19.10.15
	S K Miles (Girona, Spain)			20.11.18E
G-OODE	SNCAN Stampe SV.4C	500		09.05.77
	G-AZNN, F-BDGI, French AF			
	M S Johnson tr G-OODE Flying Group Headcorn			19.03.18P
G-OODI	Pitts S-1D	KH1		23.12.80
	G-BBBU C Hutson & R S Wood Tatenhill			
	'Little Bumble'			05.06.18P
	Built by A Etheridge & Lincs Aerial Spraying (K Harness)			
G-OODW	Piper PA-28-181 Archer II	28-8490031		14.07.87
	N4332C Redhill Air Services Ltd Fairoaks			29.01.18E
G-OODX	Robinson R22 Beta	0720		18.01.18
	G-BXXN, N720HH HQ Aviation Ltd Denham			08.01.19E
G-OOEG	Bombardier BD-100-1A10 Challenger 350	20733		20.04.18
	C-GOXW Catreus AOC Ltd Blackpool			
	(IE 25.04.18)			
G-OOEY	Kubíček BB22Z	767		24.05.10
	A M Holly Breadstone, Berkeley			
	'exclusive Ballooning'			01.07.19E
G-OOFE	Thruster T600N 450	0036-T600N-087		08.07.03
	D Dance (Gedling, Nottingham)			10.02.18P
	Badged 'Sprint'			
G-OOFT	Piper PA-28-161 Warrior III	2842083		25.05.00
	N170FT Aerodynamics Malaga SL			
	La Axarquia-Leoni Benabu, Vélez-Málaga, Spain			08.10.16E
G-OOGO	Grumman American GA-7 Cougar	GA7-0049		12.11.97
	N762GA CCB Servicos Aereos Lda			
	Santarém, Ribatejo, Portugal			17.12.17E
G-OOGS	Gulfstream American GA-7 Cougar	GA7-0105		19.06.98
	G-BGJW, N737G P Wilkinson Blackpool			27.03.08E
	Noted in fire dump area 03.16 (NF 11.12.13)			
G-OOGY	P&M QuikR	8458		01.06.09
	Cambridge Road Professional Services Ltd			
	Churchlands Farm, Rickney			12.04.18P

G-OOIO	Eurocopter AS.350B3 Ecureuil	3463		17.10.01
	Hovering Ltd Elstree			31.08.18E
G-OOJP	Commander Aircraft Commander 114B	14567		24.12.99
	N92JT, D-EYCA G Drui tr Haltergemeinschaft			
	(Mondercange, Luxembourg)			01.11.18E
G-OOLE	Cessna 172M Skyhawk II	17266712		25.08.89
	G-BOSI, N80714 J Edmondson Sherburn-in-Elmet			16.07.18E
G-OOMA	Piper PA-28-161 Warrior II	28-8116030		28.06.89
	G-BRBB, N8260W			
	Aviation Advice & Consulting Ltd Gloucestershire			30.11.18E
G-OOMC	Raytheon RB360 Premier 1	RB-146		27.08.13
	M-YAIR, N1CR, N6146J			
	Cancelled 19.08.15 as destroyed			11.09.15
	Blackpool *Stored hangar 5, 10.16*			
G-OOMF	Piper PA-18-150 Super Cub	18-8560		13.04.06
	N45554, IAF/DF 020 C G Bell Shenington			12.05.18E
G-OONA	Robinson R44 Clipper II	10907		18.10.05
	Malaika Developments LLP White Waltham			07.11.17E
G-OONE	Mooney M.20J Mooney 201	24-3039		31.07.87
	C Hollis, M Kalyuzhny & D Newton Denham			12.10.19E
G-OONY	Piper PA-28-161 Warrior II	28-8316015		26.07.89
	N83071 J R Golding Compton Abbas			11.05.19E
G-OONZ	P&M Pegasus Quik	8539		30.07.10
	D Garnett tr G-OONZ Group Manchester Barton			13.10.17P
G-OOON	Piper PA-34-220T Seneca III	34-8533024		08.01.03
	N822CB, ZS-LWI, N2431Q, N9513N			
	R Paris Alderney			13.06.18E
G-OOPY	Czech Sport PS-28 Cruiser	C0519		20.04.15
	V Barnes North Weald			28.04.17R
	(IE 01.05.18) (Noted 07.18)			
G-OORV	Van's RV-6	24319		21.12.06
	N120XK C Sharples Brighton City			19.02.18P
	Built by C & D Henwood			
G-OOSE	Rutan VariEze	xxxx		07.12.78
	B O Smith & J A Towers Turners Arms Farm, Yearby			
	Built by J A Towers – project PFA 074-10326			
	(NF 29.04.16)			
G-OOSH	Zenair CH.601UL Zodiac	6-9396		18.11.05
	J P Batty & J R C Brightman			
	Sackville Lodge Farm, Riseley			26.10.18P
	Built by D J Paget – project PFA 162A-14022			
G-OOSY	de Havilland DH.82A Tiger Moth	85831		06.09.94
	F-BGFI, French AF, DE971			
	S Philpott & C Stopher Bicester			19.04.18E
	Composite rebuild; as 'DE971' in RAF c/s			
G-OOTC	Piper PA-28R-201T Turbo Cherokee Arrow III			18.01.94
		28R-7703086		
	G-CLIV, N3011Q R E Grimster & D R L Hughes			
	tr G-OOTC Group Sleap			28.09.18E
G-OOTT	Eurocopter AS.350B3 Ecureuil	3953		20.07.05
	R J Green Rodge Hill Farm, Hillside, Martley			16.03.18E
G-OOUK	Cirrus SR22	1463		09.08.10
	N900UK P R D Smith Biggin Hill			15.04.18E
G-OOWS	Eurocopter AS.350B3 Ecureuil	4386		18.03.08
	Millburn World Travel Services Ltd Wycombe Air Park			25.04.18E
G-OOXP	Aero Designs Pulsar XP	xxxx		25.10.90
	P C Avery Fenland			16.11.11P
	Built by G W Associates Ltd – project			
	PFA 202-11915 (NF 05.11.15)			
G-OPAG	Piper PA-34-200 Seneca	34-7250348		16.10.90
	N506DM, G-BNGB, F-BTQT, F-BTMT			
	A H Lavender Biggin Hill			12.11.17E
G-OPAM	Reims/Cessna F152 II	F15201536		05.09.86
	G-BFZS PJC (Leasing) Ltd Stapleford			25.06.18E
G-OPAR	Van's RV-6	21877		16.09.13
	G-CGNR L V Adams (Hertford)			11.07.19P
	Built by N Rawlinson – project PFA 181A-12444			
G-OPAT	Beech 76 Duchess	ME-304		06.12.82
	G-BHAO Golf Alpha Tango Ltd Fairoaks			14.02.18E
G-OPAW	Cameron Z-105	12182		06.07.18
	Lighter Than Air Ltd Chew Stoke, Bristol			04.07.19E
G-OPAZ	Pazmany PL-2	xxxx		20.03.98
	A D Wood Sturgate *'The Little Yellow Peril'*			06.11.18P
	Built by K Morris – project PFA 069-10673			
G-OPBW	Cameron Z-150	11891		21.05.15
	Polar Bear Windows Ltd Willsbridge, Bristol			
	'Polar Bear Windows'			12.05.18E
G-OPCG	Cessna 182T Skylane	18280948		18.02.02
	N2451Y S K Pomfret Andrewsfield			13.03.18E
G-OPEJ	Team Mini-Max 91A	JDT64		05.01.07
	A W McBlain Kilkerran			
	Built by P E Jackson – project PFA 186-14388			
	(SSDR microlight since 06.14) (IE 30.06.17)			
G-OPEP	Piper PA-28RT-201T Turbo Arrow IV	28R-7931070		03.12.97
	OY-PEP, N2217Q S Denham Turweston			08.05.18E
G-OPER	Lindstrand LTL Series 1-70	002		22.09.15
	Lindstrand Technologies Ltd Oswestry *'Lindstrand'*			05.07.19E
G-OPET	Piper PA-28-181 Archer II	28-7690067		03.01.02
	OH-PET, OY-BLC			
	Cambrian Flying Group Ltd Cardiff			29.06.18E
G-OPFA	Alpi Pioneer 300	127		23.11.04
	R & S Eddison Gloucestershire			08.06.18P
	Built by S Eddison & R Minett – project			
	PFA 330-14298; c/n 127 also quoted for G-YVES			
G-OPFR	Diamond DA.42 Twin Star	42.077		05.12.05
	N700PR, G-OPFR, OE-VPI P F Rothwell Coventry			15.11.18E
G-OPFWᴹ	Hawker Siddeley HS.748 Series 2A/266	1714		01.07.98
	G-BMFT, VP-BFT, VR-BFT, G-BMFT, 5W-FAO, G11-10			
	Cancelled 15.06.09 as PWFU			16.02.07
	Cockpit only – no marks			
G-OPHT	Schleicher ASH 26E	26105		06.02.97
	J S Wand Bidford *'T1'*			19.04.18E
G-OPIBᴹ	English Electric Lightning F.6	95238		31.12.92
	XR773 Cancelled 13.02.97 – to ZU-BEW *As 'XR773'*			
	With Classic Jets South Africa, Cape Town			
G-OPIC	Reims/Cessna FRA150L Aerobat	FRA1500234		20.06.95
	G-BGNZ, PH-GAB, D-EIQE A V Harmer Hardwick			11.04.18E
G-OPIK	Eiriavion PIK-20E	20233		27.01.82
	PH-651 D R Piercy tr G-OPIK Syndicate			
	Eyres Field			29.07.17E
G-OPIT	CFM Streak Shadow	K126-SA		22.11.89
	I J Guy Welshpool			16.10.14P
	Built by L W Opit – project PFA 161A-11624			
G-OPJC	Cessna 152 II	15282280		07.06.88
	N68354 Cancelled 25.04.08 as PWFU			17.10.07
	Hampenden *Used as simulator by 745 ATC Sqn, 08.18*			
G-OPJD	Piper PA-28RT-201T Turbo Arrow IV	28R-8231028		02.10.89
	N8097V J M McMillan Alderney			14.06.18E
G-OPJK	Europa Aviation Europa	017		29.04.93
	F D Hollinshead Sleap *'The First Of The Many'*			10.07.17P
	Built by P J Kember – project PFA 247-12487;			
	tailwheel u/c			
G-OPJS	Pietenpol Air Camper	xxxx		10.11.00
	P J Shenton (Croughton, Brackley)			
	Built by J W & P J Shenton – project PFA 047-12834			
	(NF 27.08.14)			
G-OPKF	Cameron Bowler-90	2314		12.06.90
	D K Fish Sydney, NSW, Australia			
	'Pannell Kerr Forster'			02.08.03A
	(NF 25.03.15)			
G-OPLC	de Havilland DH.104 Dove 8	04212		10.01.91
	G-BLRB, VP962 Columba Aviation Ltd Biggin Hill			19.09.15E
	Originally built as Devon C.2 and modified to C.2/2			
	status; operated by Mayfair Dove; active 08.16			
G-OPME	Piper PA-23-250 Aztec D	27-4099		31.03.94
	G-ODIR, G-AZGB, N878SH, N9...N			
	R G Pardo (Cadiz, Spain)			05.02.18E
G-OPMJ	Reims/Cessna F172M	F17201110		02.07.15
	G-BIIB, PH-GRE A J Chadwick			
	t/a Jefferson Air Photography Hawarden			27.06.18E
G-OPMT	Lindstrand LBL 105A	052		30.09.93
	K R Karlstrom Northwood *'Pace'*			26.11.18E

G-OPNI	Bell 206B Jetranger II	83	24.04.96
	G-BXAA, F-GKYR, HB-XOR, G-BHMV, VH-SJJ, VH-FVR		
	Cancelled 20.01.00 as PWFU		30.05.99
	Newton Abbot *At UCZ paintball park 12.12*		

G-OPOT	Agusta A109S Grand	22027	07.09.17
	G-EMHD, G-STGR, ZS-BAX		
	Sundorne Products (Llanidloes) Ltd Welshpool		24.09.19E
	Operated by Castle Air Ltd		

G-OPPO	Groppo Trail	00066/25	02.03.12
	A C Hampson Priory Farm, Tibenham		24.08.18P
	Built by A C Hampson – project LAA 372-15123		

G-OPRC	Europa Aviation Europa XS	378	22.06.01
	M J Ashby-Arnold & D Lee Rufforth		09.04.18P
	Built by I Chaplin – project PFA 247-13281; tricycle u/c		

G-OPSF	Piper PA-38-112 Tomahawk	38-79A0998	13.10.82
	EI-BLT, G-BGZI, N9664N		
	P I Higham High Cross, Ware		11.04.19E

G-OPSG	Aeropro EuroFOX 912(S)	38012	09.05.12
	P S Gregory Wolverhampton Halfpenny Green		26.06.18P
	Built by P S Gregory – project LAA 376-15148; tailwheel u/c		

G-OPSL	Piper PA-32R-301 Saratoga SP	32R-8013085	04.01.99
	G-IMPW, N8186A P R Tomkins (Robertsbridge)		04.05.19E

G-OPSS	Cirrus SR20-G2	1458	28.10.04
	N410CD Clifton Aviation Ltd Gloucestershire		28.07.18E

G-OPST	Cessna 182R Skylane II	18267932	16.06.88
	OO-HFF, N9317H S Kidney Cambridge		04.07.19E

G-OPTI	Piper PA-28-161 Cherokee Warrior II	28-7716210	29.09.06
	N5888V Rio Leon Services Ltd Conington		28.08.18E

G-OPTZ	Pitts S-2A	2048	13.09.17
	G-SKNT, G-PEAL, N81LF, N48KA		
	J L Dixon Sherburn-in-Elmet		26.08.17E
	(NF 13.09.17)		

G-OPUB	Slingsby T67M-160 Firefly	2002	18.10.96
	G-DLTA, G-SFTX A L Barker Full Sutton		22.03.18E

G-OPUG	Czech Sport PS-28 Cruiser	C0604	22.03.18
	OM-CAC Pentaction Ltd (Battle)		
	(NF 22.03.18)		

G-OPUK	Piper PA-28-161 Warrior III	2842288	29.08.02
	N30904 D J King Brighton City		15.12.18E

G-OPUP	Beagle B.121 Pup Series 2	B121-062	31.10.84
	G-AXEU, (5N-AJC) F A Zubiel White Waltham		18.06.18R

G-OPUS	Avtech Jabiru SK	0194	16.07.98
	Cancelled 30.10.15 as PWFU		07.08.14
	Sandown, IOW *Built by S Percy – project PFA 274-13343; cockpit preserved 'Amazon World Zoo Park' 06.18*		

G-OPVM	Van's RV-9A	91106	08.08.05
	R M Cochran Henstridge		17.10.18P
	Built by P Mather – project PFA 320-14351		

G-OPWR	Cameron Z-90	11925	28.07.15
	D J Groombridge & I J Martin t/a Flying Enterprises		
	Congresbury & Wotton-under-Edge *'Power Rangers'*		24.07.17E

G-OPWS	Mooney M.20K Mooney 231	25-0663	12.04.91
	N1162W S Crowley Oxford		23.05.19E

G-OPYE	Cessna 172S Skyhawk SP	172S8059	19.02.99
	N653SP Quarry Garage (Rotherham) Ltd Netherthorpe		02.03.18E

G-OPYO	Alpi Pioneer 300 Hawk	xxxx	08.09.09
	T J Franklin & D S Simpson		
	Graveley Hall Farm, Graveley *'86'*		26.11.18P
	Built by D S Simpson – project PFA 330A-14597		

G-ORAC	Cameron Van-110	4577	22.06.99
	T G Church Clayton Le Dale, Blackburn *'RAC'*		09.10.18E

G-ORAE	Van's RV-7	71173	20.03.03
	R W Eaton tr G-ORAE Group Netherthorpe		22.09.18P
	Built by R W Eaton – project PFA 323-14016		

G-ORAF	CFM Streak Shadow	K 134-SA	18.05.90
	G A Carter (Harwich)		01.11.00P
	Built by G A Taylor – project PFA 161A-11627; sequence no.conflicts with MW6 G-MYCU		
	(NF 29.10.15)		

G-ORAL^M	Hawker Siddeley HS.748 Series 2A/334	1756	13.08.99
	G-BPDA, G-GLAS, 9Y-TFS, G-11-8		12.11.07
	Cancelled 15.06.09 as PWFU		
	At Avro Heritage Museum, Woodford; front fuselage only		

G-ORAM	Thruster T600N 450	0071-T600N-117	13.06.07
	D W Wilson (Collone, Armagh)		29.06.17P
	Badged 'Sprint' (IE 05.07.17)		

G-ORAR	Piper PA-28-181 Archer III	2890224	06.06.95
	N9255G P N & S M Thornton Goodwood		26.08.18E

G-ORAS	Clutton FRED Series II	xxxx	14.06.01
	A I Sutherland Fearn		07.12.16P
	Built by A I Sutherland – project PFA 029-11002		

G-ORAU	Evektor EV-97A Eurostar	2007-2917	04.06.07
	W R C Williams-Wynne Talybont		19.04.18P
	Built by W R C Williams-Wynne – project PFA 315A-14655		

G-ORAW	Cessna 525 Citation M2	525-0892	24.04.17
	OY-RAW, N4085S Catreus AOC Ltd Biggin Hill		20.11.18E

G-ORAY	Reims/Cessna F182Q Skylane II	F18200132	26.03.80
	G-BHDN M Parrinder Humberside		06.02.19E

G-ORBK	Robinson R44 Raven II	10213	28.11.03
	G-CCNO T2 Technology Ltd		
	Wellesbourne Mountford		10.04.18E

G-ORBS	Mainair Blade	1336-0802-7-W1131	19.08.02
	J W Dodson Leicester		03.06.10P
	(NF 19.11.14)		

G-ORCA	Van's RV-4	4093	25.11.04
	I A Harding North Weald *'44'*		22.05.19P
	Built by M R H Wishart – project PFA 181-12924		

G-ORCC	AutoGyro Calidus	C00245	14.11.12
	D G & S J E Wigley Tatenhill		22.11.19P
	Assembled Rotorsport UK as c/n RSUK/CALS/022		

G-ORCD	Agusta A109S Grand	22009	29.03.19
	G-GBMM, G-GRND		
	Orchard Holdings Ltd (Feering, Colchester)		

G-ORCV	Cameron Z-120	12201	05.06.18
	A Collett Rockhampton, Berkeley		22.05.19E

G-ORCW	Schempp-Hirth Ventus-2cxT	134/346	21.11.05
	BGA 5108/KHQ J C A Garland & M S Hawkins		
	Kingston Deverill *'A39'*		17.08.18E

G-ORDA	Reims/Cessna F172N	F17201879	18.06.15
	EC-ICE, N47PT, F-WBQT, F-GBQT		
	D G Martinez (Valencia, Spain)		07.04.18E

G-ORDM	Cessna 182T Skylane	18281206	08.10.12
	G-KEMY, N53397		
	The Cambridge Aero Club Ltd Cambridge		10.12.18E

G-ORDS	Thruster T600N 450	0042-T600N-100	14.01.04
	G J Pill Ginge Farm, Wantage		04.07.18P
	Badged 'Sprint'		

G-ORED	Pilatus B-N BN-2T Islander	2142	10.01.85
	G-BJYW Britten-Norman Ltd Solent		18.07.17E

G-OREZ	Cessna 525 Citation M2	525-0928	30.09.16
	N4078L Helitrip Charter LLP Hawarden		10.10.18E
	Operated by Catreus AOC		

G-ORFC	Jurca MJ5 Sirocco	xxxx	16.05.85
	Cancelled 20.06.06 by CAA		03.07.04
	St Omer-Wizemas, France *Built by P Phillips – project PFA 2210; stored 04.17*		

G-ORHE	Cessna 500 Citation 1	500-0220	25.03.96
	(N619EA), G-OBEL, G-BOGA, N932HA, N93WD, N5220J		
	Cancelled 19.08.11 by CAA		24.07.08
	Shannon *Displayed at Airventure 10.18*		

G-ORIB	Aeropro EuroFOX 912(iS)	422.14	03.10.14
	J McAlpine (Longworth, Abingdon)		08.07.19P
	Built by J McAlpine – project LAA 376-15294; tailwheel u/c		

G-ORIG	Glaser-Dirks DG-800A	8-39A29	05.04.94
	BGA 4972, G-ORIG		
	M Bond & R Kalin Rufforth *'345'*		24.04.19E

G-ORIX	ARV ARV K1 Super 2	034	16.09.93
	G-BUXH, (G-BNVK) T M Lyons (Newcastle)		09.04.07P
	Built by P M Harrison – project PFA 152-12424 (NF 11.09.14)		

G-ORJW Laverda F.8L Falco Series 4 403 02.12.85
(PH-...), G-ORJW, D-ELDV (?), D-ELDY
Viking BV Hilversum, Netherlands 02.10.17E
Official p/i 'D-ELDV' is incorrect

G-ORKY Eurocopter AS.350B2 Ecureuil 2153 03.01.08
N66NN, JA9791
PLM Dollar Group Ltd Dalcross Heliport 27.02.18E
Callsign 'Osprey 53'

G-ORLA P&M Pegasus Quik 8268 21.05.07
J Summers Redlands 20.06.18P

G-ORLY Gulfstream American AA-5B Tiger AA5B-1029 18.02.19
G-DONI, G-BLLT, OO-RTG. (OO-HRS)
Boker Layla Aviation Ltd Elstree 18.04.19E

G-ORMB Robinson R22 Beta 1607 14.12.90
Heli Air Scotland Ltd Cumbernauld 08.08.18E

G-ORMW Comco Ikarus C42 FB100 0501-6653 11.04.05
A J Dixon Swansea 25.04.19P
Assembled Aerosport Ltd

G-ORNH Lindstrand LTL Series 2-50 077 12.12.18
A M Holly Breadstone, Berkeley
(IE 19.12.18)

G-OROD Piper PA-18-150 Super Cub 18-7856 27.06.89
SE-CRD B W Faulkner
Twentyways Farm, Ramsdean 13.03.16E

G-OROS Comco Ikarus C42 FB80 0509-6759 07.10.05
R I Simpson Clipgate Farm, Denton 29.10.18P
Assembled Aerosport Ltd

G-ORPC Europa Aviation Europa XS 443 05.02.04
P W Churms (Farnborough GU14)
Built by P W Churms – project PFA 247-13521
(NF 09.09.16)

G-ORPR Cameron O-77 2341 26.06.90
S R Vining Puxey, Sturminster Newton 03.03.18E

G-ORRG Robin DR.400-180 Régent 1216 06.02.08
OO-VPI P G Folland tr Radley Robin Group
Radley Farm, Hungerford 16.03.18E

G-ORSE Comco Ikarus C42 FB100 Bravo 1504-7386 07.05.15
GA3-1 D S Murrell Field Farm, South Walsham 26.04.18P
Assembled Red Aviation

G-ORST Airbus EC135 T3 1269 03.01.18
G-DEWF Babcock Mission Critical Services
Onshore Ltd Gloucestershire 27.11.18E

G-ORTH Beech E90 King Air LW-136 12.11.03
G-DEXY, N750DC, N30CW, N84GA, N328TB, TR-LTT
Gorthair Ltd Newcastle Int'l 02.04.19E
Operated by NALJets

G-ORUG Thruster T600N 450 0033-T600N-080 02.09.03
R D McKellar (Barton-upon-Humber) 11.12.16P
Badged 'Sprint' on wingtips

G-ORUN Reality Escapade JA.ESC.00061 16.10.17
M J Clark Sedgwick Park, Horsham
Built by M J Clark – project LAA 345-15129

G-ORVE Van's RV-6 21710 16.07.07
N2084J F M Sperryn & R J F Swain Sleap 03.01.19P
Built by M R Spiller

G-ORVG Van's RV-6 xxxx 02.01.01
J T M Ball Biggin Hill 24.09.18P
Built by R J Fry – project PFA 181A-13509

G-ORVI Van's RV-6 20036 16.06.08
N1021 B O Harvey (Ventor, IoW) 10.09.19P
Built by L B Porter

G-ORVR Partenavia P68B 115 02.10.95
G-BFBD Ravenair Aircraft Ltd Liverpool John Lennon 30.01.18E

G-ORVS Van's RV-9 xxxx 10.09.07
C J Marsh Stockbridge Manor, Whitwell 29.05.18P
Built by C J Marsh – project PFA 320-13999

G-ORVX Van's RV-10 40765 25.08.15
G-OHIY C D Meek Deanland 30.11.18P
Built by M A Hutton & C D Meek
– project PFA 339-14730

G-ORVZ Van's RV-7 74343 15.10.14
C Taylor (Sapcote, Leicester)
Built by C Taylor – project LAA 323-15283 (NF 15.10.14)

G-ORYG AutoGyro Cavalon xxxx 17.02.17
M P L Dowie (Kingsbridge) 02.03.19P
Assembled Rotorsport UK as c/n RSUK/CVLN/023

G-OSAR Bell 206L-1 LongRanger II 45704 30.11.16
OY-HPJ, N600WH, N410PC, N600JS, N2153H
Vantage Aviation Ltd Thruxton 03.07.18E

G-OSAT Cameron Z-105 10564 18.06.04
A V & M R Noyce Hatherden, Andover 'Fastrat' 19.04.19E

G-OSAZ Robinson R22 Beta 1005 15.02.11
G-DERB, G-BPYH W Oswald (Wien, Austria) 18.03.18E

G-OSCC Piper PA-32-300 Cherokee Six 32-7540020 27.11.84
G-BGFD, D-EOSH, N32186
BG & G Airlines Ltd Jersey 25.03.19E

G-OSCO Team Mini-Max 91 5126 24.12.96
S H Slade (Goudhurst, Cranbrook)
Built by PJ Schofield – project PFA 186-12878
(SSDR microlight since 02.15) (NF 18.01.16)

G-OSDF Schempp-Hirth Ventus a 17 20.05.08
BGA 3878/HED, D-2524 S D Foster Keevil '840' 05.05.19E

G-OSEA Pilatus B-N BN-2B-26 Islander 2175 27.08.85
G-BKOL WT Johnson & Sons (Huddersfield) Ltd
Crosland Moor 15.03.18E

G-OSEM Robinson R44 Clipper II 13665 13.03.14
D A George t/a Sloane Charter Sywell 06.04.18E

G-OSEP Mainair Blade 912 1340-0902-7-W1135 29.10.02
J D Smith Baxby Manor, Husthwaite 29.10.18P

G-OSFB Diamond HK36TTC Super Dimona 36.807 13.05.09
SE-UPO Oxfordshire Sportflying Ltd Enstone 08.06.18E

G-OSFL Beech B200 Super King Air BB-1607 22.03.19
EC-MME, N699AL, F-GRLF, ZS-DJA, N724TA
RVL Aviation Ltd East Midlands

G-OSFS Reims/Cessna F177RG Cardinal RG F177RG0082 26.01.04
F-BUMP D G Wright Derby 26.03.18E

G-OSGU Aeropro EuroFOX 912(S) 42814 14.05.14
Scottish Gliding Union Ltd Portmoak 28.02.19P
Built by A P Benbow & Partners – project
LAA 376-15214; tailwheel u/c; glider-tug

G-OSHK Schempp-Hirth SHK-1 V1 28.03.08
BGA 1467/CDU, D-8441
P B Hibbard AAC Wattisham 'PH' 12.05.18E

G-OSHL Robinson R22 Beta 1000 19.04.89
Sloane Helicopters Ltd Sywell 05.04.18E

G-OSIC Pitts S-1C 1921-77 07.10.02
G-BUAW, N29DH P J Hebdon Shenington 14.09.18P
Built by R Hendry

G-OSII Cessna 172N Skyhawk II 17267768 17.10.95
G-BIVY, N73973 W Stitt tr G-OSII Group Hardwick 12.10.18E

G-OSIS Pitts S-1S xxxx 19.09.94
D S T Eggleton Waits Farm, Belcham Walter 24.07.19P
Built by M C Boddington, C Butler & P J Burgess
– project PFA 009-12043

G-OSIT Pitts S-1T 1023 07.12.01
N96JD C J J Robertson Perth 28.04.18E
Built by Pitts Aerobatics

G-OSJC Piper PA-32R-301 Saratoga II HP 3246193 13.11.18
G-GOBD, G-OARW, EC-IJT, N5339Z
S-J Clegg (Lancaster) 22.02.19E
Official type data 'PA-32R-301 Saratoga SP'
is incorrect

G-OSKR Best Off Skyranger 912(2) SKR0201162 14.01.03
J E O Larsson Chiltern Park, Wallingford 27.06.18P
Built by Sky Ranger UK Ltd – project BMAA/HB/249

G-OSKY Cessna 172M Skyhawk II 17267389 27.02.79
A6-KCB, N73343
Skyhawk Leasing Ltd Wellesbourne Mountford 11.07.18E

G-OSLD Europa Aviation Europa XS 485 23.08.00
C Davies & S Percy Nottingham City 10.03.18P
Built by S C Percy – project PFA 247-13641; tricycle u/c

G-OSLO Schweizer 269C (300) S 1360 15.03.89
N7507L AH Helicopter Services Ltd
Little Park Farm, Somerton 08.06.18E

G-OSMD	Bell 206B-2 JetRanger II	2034	12.02.99
	G-LTEK, G-BMIB, ZS-HGH TR Aviation Services Ltd		
	Oaklands Park, Englefield Green		17.05.18E
G-OSND	Reims/Cessna FRA150M Aerobat	FRA1500272	16.10.84
	G-BDOU S A Goldsmith tr Group G-OSND		
	RAF Henlow		09.11.18E
G-OSNI	Piper PA-23-250 Aztec C	27-3852	02.07.98
	G-AWER, N6556Y Cancelled 08.03.06 as PWFU		22.05.04
	Belfast Int'l *Used by Airport Fire department 12.13*		
G-OSNX	Grob G109B	6413	19.06.17
	OH-740 R J Barsby Husbands Bosworth		
	Operated by 'AeroSparx Team' – 'Blacks' (IE 20.06.17)		
G-OSOD	P&M Quik GTR	8623	28.05.12
	R Gellert Fenland		08.07.18P
G-OSON	P&M QuikR	8601	07.12.11
	R Parr Little Gransden		14.01.18P
G-OSOR	DG Flugzeugbau DG-1000M	10-249M30	30.06.17
	Lleweni Parc Ltd Lleweni Parc 'SOR'		29.06.18E
G-OSPD	Evektor EV-97 teamEurostar UK	2003-1708	03.09.03
	R A Stewart-Jones (Whittington, Lichfield) 'Bunny'		06.02.19P
	Assembled Cosmik Aviation Ltd		
G-OSPH	Comco Ikarus C42 FB100 Bravo	1205-7202	14.08.12
	Progress Flying Club Membury Ltd Membury		
	'Membury Flying Club'		28.10.19P
	Assembled Red-Air UK		
G-OSPP	Robinson R44 Clipper	0632	27.05.16
	D-HXXY, OE-XXY, 5B-CJO		
	Foton Ltd (Haughton, Tarporley)		28.07.18E
G-OSPS	Piper PA-18 Super Cub 95 (*L-18C-PI*)	18-1555	09.07.92
	OO-SPS, G-AWRH, OO-HMI, French Army 51-15555		
	R C Lough Andrewsfield		18.05.18E
	Fuselage No.18-1527; as '51-15555' in USAAF c/s		
G-OSPX	Grob G109B	6414	09.03.15
	EI-HCS, G-BMHR G C Westgate t/a Aerosparx		
	(Cootham, Pulborough)		23.07.16E
	Operated by 'AeroSparx Team' – 'Blacks' (IE 20.02.18)		
G-OSPY	Cirrus SR20 GTS	1546	09.09.05
	N81706 C Deretz Elstree		16.04.19E
G-OSRA	Boeing 727-2S2F(RE)	22938	19.06.13
	N217FE T2 Aviation Ltd Doncaster Sheffield		10.09.19E
	Line No: 1832; Oil Spill Response		
G-OSRB	Boeing 727-2S2F(RE)	22929	05.08.14
	N480EC, N207FE		
	T2 Aviation Ltd Doncaster Sheffield		01.05.19E
	Line No: 1823; Oil Spill Response		
G-OSRL	Learjet Learjet 45	45-391	13.02.09
	N40086 S R Lloyd Biggin Hill		12.02.18E
	Operated by Zentin Aviation		
G-OSRS	Cameron A-375	11730	10.05.13
	Wickers World Ltd Great Haywood, Stafford		
	'Stan Robinson'		12.05.18E
G-OSSA	Cessna TU206B	U2060824	17.11.03
	4X-CHT, C-GDTO, N139LA, N139LF, (N3824G)		
	Skydive St Andrews Ltd Fife		19.09.18E
G-OSST	Colt 77A	737	28.10.85
	A A Brown Worplesdon, Guildford 'Concorde'		10.10.96A
	(NF 06.08.15)		
G-OSTC	Gulfstream American AA-5A Cheetah	AA5A-0848	22.04.91
	N26967 C J Aucken (Twickenham)		21.02.19E
G-OSTL	Comco Ikarus C42 FB100	0503-6661	30.03.05
	G P Curtis Mullaghglass		16.06.18P
	Assembled Aerosport Ltd		
G-OSTX	Grob G109B	6379	05.02.19
	G-CKXB, D-KNEI		
	Aerosparx Ltd (Husbands Bosworth)		08.05.19E
G-OSTY	Cessna F150G	F150-0129	21.03.97
	G-AVCU A P Daines Beccles		
	Built by Reims Aviation SA (NF 01.10.18)		
G-OSUS	Mooney M.20K Mooney 231	25-0429	07.11.94
	OY-SUS, (N3597H) Le Toy Van Ltd (East Molesey)		23.04.19E
G-OSUT	Scheibe SF25C Rotax-Falke	44588	24.04.06
	D-KTIK Yorkshire Gliding Club (Proprietary) Ltd		
	Sutton Bank		16.06.18E

G-OSVN	AutoGyro Cavalon	V00117	18.07.13
	Engetel Ltd Rochester		11.07.19P
	Assembled Rotorsport UK as c/n RSUK/CVLN/007		
G-OSZA	Pitts S-2A	2134	22.07.05
	N60CP, N80058		
	R Alberti tr Septieme Ciel Chavenay, France		30.08.19E
	Built by Aerotek Inc		
G-OSZB	Pitts S-2B	5200	10.02.04
	G-OGEE, OH-SKY K A Fitton & A M Gent Chalgrove		02.08.18E
	Built by Christen Industries Inc		
G-OSZS	Pitts S-2S	3018	23.02.10
	SP-FYB B Dierickx tr G-OSZS Group		
	(Chastre, Belgium)		11.04.19E
	Built by Aviat Aircraft Inc		
G-OTAL	ARV ARV-1 Super 2	024	10.09.87
	G-BNGZ J M Cullen Eaglescott		28.06.18P
G-OTAM	Cessna 172M Skyhawk II	17264098	13.02.89
	N29060 G V White Felthorpe		12.10.18E
G-OTAN	Piper PA-18-135 Super Cub (*L-21B-PI*)	18-3845	28.10.96
	OO-TAN, (OO-DPD), R Netherlands AF R-155, 54-2445		
	A & J D Owen Hawarden		04.09.18E
	Fuselage No.18-3850; as '54-2445:A-445'		
	in US Army c/s		
G-OTAW	BRM Bristell NG5 Speed Wing	414	13.03.19
	A & L Wiffen (St Peter Port, Guernsey)		
	Built T Wiffen – project LAA 385-15603 (NF 13.03.19)		
G-OTAY	Tecnam P2006T	049	10.11.14
	G-ZOOG Nyuki Ltd Brighton City		19.01.18E
G-OTCH	CFM Streak Shadow	K 207	28.10.93
	(CS-xxx) A G & R M M Moura		
	(Gafanha da Nazare & Porto, Portugal)		06.07.12P
	Built by H E Gotch – project PFA 206-12401		
	(IE 20.10.16)		
G-OTCT	Cameron Z-105	12070	02.05.17
	Lighter Than Air Ltd Chew Stoke, Bristol		
	'Teenage Cancer Trust'		14.05.18E
G-OTCV	Best Off Skyranger Swift 912S(1)	SKR0407511	13.12.04
	G Roberts Arclid Green, Sandbach 'Terry Viner'		03.10.19P
	Built by T C Viner – project BMAA/HB/436		
G-OTCZ	Schempp-Hirth Ventus-2cxT	137/352	07.12.05
	BGA 5147/KJX, D-KAAQ A J Rees Nympsfield 'CZ'		19.12.18E
G-OTEA	Kubícek BB17XR	1174	09.07.15
	A M Holly Breadstone, Berkeley 'Fortnum & Mason'		12.09.19E
G-OTEC	Tecnam P2002 Sierra DeLuxe	431	11.01.10
	D P Sudworth Maypole Farm, Chislet		07.08.19P
	Built by C W Thirtle – project LAA 333-14950		
G-OTED[M]	Robinson R-22 HP	0209	17.01.96
	G-BMYR, ZS-HLG Cancelled 26.03.02 as PWFU		17.02.02
	With The Helicopter Museum, Weston-super-Mare		
G-OTEL	Thunder Ax8-90	1790	13.06.90
	J W Adkins Market Harborough		
	'I.C.P Cleaning Services'		18.05.18E
G-OTFT	Piper PA-38-112 Tomahawk	38-78A0311	14.03.97
	G-BNKW, N9274T P Tribble RAF Henlow		17.07.19E
G-OTGA	Piper PA-28R-201 Arrow III	28R-7837281	21.02.01
	ZS-KFI TG Aviation Ltd Lydd		08.01.19E
	Official type data 'PA-28R-201 Cherokee Arrow III'		
	is incorrect		
G-OTHE	Enstrom 280C-UK Shark	1226	22.09.87
	G-OPJT, G-BKCO		
	K P Groves Red House Farm, Preston Capes		17.09.19E
G-OTHL[M]	Robinson R22 Beta	0738	28.11.94
	G-DSGN Cancelled 08.02.00 as WFU *As 'G-RAFM'*		27.04.03
	With RAF Museum, Hendon		
G-OTIB	Robin DR.400-180R Remorqueur	1545	26.04.00
	D-EGIA The Windrushers Gliding Club Ltd Bicester		20.04.18E
G-OTIG	Gulfstream American AA-5B Tiger	AA5B-0996	28.07.00
	G-PENN, (I-TIGR), N3756L L Burke Newcastle, RoI		19.04.19E
G-OTIM	Bensen B.8MV	xxxx	05.06.90
	T J Deane (Felingwm, Carmarthen)		
	Built by T J Deane – project PFA G/01-1084		
	(NF 21.03.18)		

G-OTIV	Aerospool Dynamic WT9 UK	DY194/2007	06.11.07	
	P O'Donohue & D P Pactor Ince		07.01.18P	
	Assembled Yeoman Light Aircraft Co Ltd;			
	official c/n recorded as 'DY194'			
G-OTJH	Cyclone Pegasus Quantum 15-912	7791	20.03.01	
	L R Gartside (Balsall Common, Coventry)		21.04.13P	
	(NF 29.11.16)			
G-OTJS	Robinson R44 Raven II	12305	09.07.08	
	Kuki Helicopter Sales Ltd Retford Gamston		01.08.17E	
	Blown inverted Retford Gamston 17.11.16 &			
	substantially damaged: wreck noted 12.16			
G-OTJT	HpH Glasflügel 304 S Shark	027-S	10.07.13	
	(BGA 5753) N J L Busvine Parham Park *'J3T'*			
	(IE 15.05.17)			
G-OTLC	Grumman American AA-5 Traveler	AA5-0480	20.12.10	
	G-BBUF S R Cameron & L P Keegan Oban		17.05.18E	
G-OTME	Nord 1002 Pingouin II	197	23.09.14	
	N108E, F-BAUL, French AF F-TEUC			
	S H O'Connell Southend			
	Under rebuild 02.19 (NF 06.07.18)			
G-OTNA	Robinson R44 Raven II	11092	07.02.06	
	Abel Homes Ltd			
	The Old Rectory, Little Cressingham, Watton		23.02.18E	
G-OTNM	Tecnam P2008-JC	1074	27.04.17	
	C S Nahhas (Oxford)		13.05.19E	
G-OTOE	Aeronca 7AC Champion	7AC-4621	02.04.90	
	G-BRWW, N1070E, NC1070E			
	D Cheney Mullaghglass		28.08.18P	
G-OTOO	Stolp SA.300 Starduster Too	xxxx	26.08.98	
	I M Castle Spanhoe			
	Built by I M Castle – project PFA 035-13352			
	(NF 23.02.18)			
G-OTOP	P&M QuikR	8471	07.08.09	
	M I White Longacre Farm, Sandy		10.08.18P	
G-OTOW	Cessna 175B Skylark		22.09.82	
	G-AROC, G-OTOW, G-AROC, N8297T			
	C J P Wilkes (Collingham, Newark)			
	(NF 26.06.18)			
G-OTRT	Robinson R44 Raven II	12341	08.04.15	
	4O-FLY, YU-HFG, G-CFEC			
	Ian Hutchinson Enterprises Ltd (Guiseley, Leeds)		30.05.19E	
G-OTRV	Van's RV-6	60179	27.05.98	
	E Andersen Solent		01.05.19P	
	Built by W R C Williams-Wynne – project PFA 181-13302			
G-OTRY	Schleicher ASW 24	24023	18.01.08	
	BGA 3372/FMP			
	A H Beckingham Dunstable Downs *'328'*		02.11.18E	
G-OTSP	Aérospatiale AS.355F1 Ecureuil 2	5177	31.03.98	
	G-XPOL, G-BPRF, N363E			
	MW Helicopters Ltd Stapleford		06.05.12E	
	(IE 16.06.15)			
G-OTTI	Cameron Otti-34	3983	23.03.95	
	P Spellward Whiteley, Fareham *'Otti'*		24.04.19E	
	Replacement envelope c/n 3983 c.04.97:			
	original c/n 3490			
G-OTTS	Comco Ikarus C42 FB100 Bravo	1407-7346	11.08.14	
	B C Gotts Felthorpe		18.08.18P	
	Assembled Red-Air UK			
G-OTTY	AutoGyro Calidus	xxxx	28.06.10	
	GS Aviation (Europe) Ltd Clench Common		14.02.18P	
	Assembled Rotorsport UK as c/n RSUK/CALS/011			
G-OTUI	SOCATA TB-20 Trinidad	1096	07.03.03	
	G-KKDL, G-BSHU H Graff Elstree		17.05.19E	
G-OTUM	Best Off Skyranger Nynja LS 912S(1)	xxxx	14.11.16	
	D W Wallington Nottingham City			
	Built by D W Wallington – project BMAA/HB/692			
	(NF 14.11.16)			
G-OTUN	Evektor EV-97 Eurostar	xxxx	15.05.02	
	K R Annett & L R Morris Derryogue, Kilkeel		30.09.18P	
	Built by E O Otun – project PFA 315-13865			
G-OTVR	Piper PA-34-220T Seneca V	3449279	25.07.05	
	N53497 Brinor International Shipping & Forwarding Ltd			
	Elmsett		06.11.19E	

G-OTWS	Schempp-Hirth Duo Discus XLT	258	11.07.14
	(BGA 5783)		
	T W Slater School Road, Hinderclay *'T2'*		12.08.18E
G-OTYE	Evektor EV-97 Eurostar	xxxx	15.04.02
	A B Godber *'Ali Minimum'* (Ashbourne)		05.06.18P
	Built by A B Godber & J Tye – project PFA 315-13858		
G-OTYP	Piper PA-28-180 Cherokee Challenger	28-7305166	13.01.04
	F-BTYP, N11C T C Lewis Cambridge		12.02.19E
	Official type data 'PA-28-180 Cherokee' is incorrect		
G-OTZZ	AutoGyro Cavalon	xxxx	18.03.16
	B C Gotts Felthorpe		17.05.19P
	Assembled Rotorsport UK as c/n RSUK/CVLN/021		
G-OUAV	TLAC Sherwood Scout	SS 04	09.08.17
	University of Southampton (Southampton SO16)		
	Built by University of Southampton – project		
	LAA 345-15480		
G-OUCP	Piper PA-31 Navajo C	31-7912117	05.08.15
	G-GURN, G-BHGA, N3539M		
	2 Excel Aviation Ltd Sywell		13.04.19E
G-OUDA	Aeroprakt A-22L Foxbat	A22-333	26.07.10
	A R Cattell Brimpton		28.09.17P
	Built by A R Cattell – project LAA 317A-14967		
G-OUEG	Bombardier BD-700-1A10 Global 6000	9828	02.01.19
	C-FYEM Catreus AOC Ltd Biggin Hill		
G-OUGH	IAV Bacau Yakovlev Yak-52	877404	23.06.10
	G-LAOK, LY-AOK, DOSAAF 16 (yellow)		
	Optimum Promotions Ltd Swansea		17.05.19P
G-OUHI	Europa Aviation Europa XS	488	07.06.01
	N M Graham (Chandlers Ford, Eastleigh)		
	Built by D R Philpott – project PFA 247-13684;		
	tricycle u/c (NF 13.06.16)		
G-OUIK	Mainair Pegasus Quik	7983	22.08.03
	M D Evans (Horsford, Norwich)		02.09.18P
	Built by Mainair Sports Ltd		
G-OURO	Europa Aviation Europa	016	13.12.93
	I M Mackay Holmbeck Farm, Burcott		08.09.16P
	Built by D Dufton – project PFA 247-12522; tricycle u/c		
G-OURT	Lindstrand LTL Racer 56	019	17.11.16
	A B Court Morda, Oswestry		09.04.18E
G-OUVI	Cameron O-105	1766	04.05.89
	P Spellward t/a Bristol University Hot Air		
	Ballooning Society Bristol BS9 *'Uvistat II'*		23.04.14E
G-OVAL	Comco Ikarus C42 FB100	0407-6608	18.08.04
	N G Tomes Dunkeswell		14.10.18P
	Assembled Fly Buy Ultralights Ltd		
G-OVBF	Cameron A-250	3494	01.03.95
	Airxcite Ltd t/a Virgin Balloon Flights		
	Stafford Park, Telford *'Virgin'*		18.03.07E
	(NF 15.09.14)		
G-OVEG	Diamond DA.20-C1 Katana	C0121	18.08.17
	N961CT International Flight Referral BVBA		
	(Zwijnaarde, Belgium)		10.10.18E
G-OVFM	Cessna 120	14720	29.04.88
	N2119V, NC2119V		
	P A Harvie Mount Airey Farm, South Cave		24.04.19P
G-OVFR	Reims/Cessna F172N	F17201892	23.05.79
	Marine & Aviation Ltd Solent		05.07.18E
G-OVII	Van's RV-7	71361	30.09.04
	T J Richardson Thruxton		08.05.18P
	Built by T J Richardson – project PFA 323-14100		
G-OVIN	Rockwell Commander 112TC	13090	19.11.04
	OY-DVN, D-EIXN, N4585W L C Branfield (Usk)		03.10.18E
G-OVIV	Breezer Breezer B600 LSA	016LSA	01.06.11
	P & V Lynch Park Farm, Eaton Bray		06.04.18W
G-OVLA	Comco Ikarus C42 FB UK	0303-6550	04.02.03
	Propeller Owners Ltd Popham		20.09.17P
	Built by B Bayes & N Sams – project PFA 322-14028		
G-OVMC	Reims/Cessna F152 II	F15201667	29.05.79
	Swiftair Maintenance Ltd Doncaster Sheffield		08.10.19E
	Operated by Yorkshire Aero Club		
G-OVNEᴹ	Cessna 401A	401A-0036	11.03.88
	N401XX, (N171SF), N71SF, N6236Q		
	Cancelled 08.02.94 by CAA		08.10.92
	With City of Norwich Aviation Museum		

G-OVNR Robinson R22 Beta 1634 24.12.90
HQ Aviation Ltd Denham 12.05.17E

G-OVOL Best Off Skyranger 912S(1) SP012 02.06.05
K B Woods Newnham 24.04.19P
Built by Skyranger UK Ltd – project BMAA/HB/447;
badged 'V Max 912S'

G-OVON Piper PA-18 Super Cub 95 18-1596 01.06.05
OY-ELG, D-ECXO, French Army 51-15596
V F A Stanley Home Farm, Ebrington 30.08.19E

G-OVPM Europa Aviation Europa NG 625 21.01.16
P Munford (Radwinter, Saffron Walden) 12.10.18P
Built by P Munford – project LAA 247-15051

G-OWAG Cameron TR-70 11908 21.05.15
M G Howard Hewish, Weston-super-Mare 20.05.16E

G-OWAI Schleicher ASK 21 21675 16.06.08
BGA 4487/JFV Scottish Gliding Union
– Walking On Air Portmoak 'WA1' 02.03.18E

G-OWAL Piper PA-34-220T Seneca III 3448030 07.07.98
D-GAPN, N9163K R G & W Allison tr G-OWAL Group
Retford Gamston 20.12.18E

G-OWAN Cessna 210D Centurion 21058321 11.06.01
N672P, HB-CII, D-EDEG, OE-DEG, N3821Y
Cancelled 20.05.16 as PWFU 18.08.16
Ingleton, Yorks *Displayed at repair yard 11.17*

G-OWAP Piper PA-28-161 Warrior II 28-7816314 13.06.05
G-BXNH, N2828M Tayside Aviation Ltd Dundee 12.01.19E

G-OWAR Piper PA-28-161 Warrior II 28-8616054 18.02.88
TF-OBO, N9521N
Bickertons Aerodromes Ltd Denham 21.02.18E
Operated by The Pilot Centre

G-OWAZ Pitts S-1C 43JM 22.11.94
G-BRPI, N199M P E S Latham Sleap 'Tiny Dancer' 02.06.18P
Built by J Magueri

G-OWBA Alpi Pioneer 300 Hawk 317 10.10.12
A H Lloyd Oxenhope 26.06.19P
Built by L J Tonkinson – project LAA 330-15155

G-OWEN K & S Jungster 1 xxxx 13.11.78
R C Owen (Danehill, Haywards Heath)
Built by R C Owen – project PFA 044-10124
(NF 08.10.14)

G-OWGC Slingsby T61F Venture T.2 1875 14.08.91
XZ555 Wolds Gliding Club Ltd Pocklington 12.01.19E

G-OWLL Ultramagic M-105 105/214 30.11.16
J A Lawton Enton, Godalming 08.01.19E

G-OWLS Magni M24C Orion 24181724 03.12.18
K D Woods Popham
(NF 03.12.18)

G-OWLY Cameron C-70 12092 05.06.17
M E Banks Bristol BS6 04.06.19E

G-OWMC Thruster T600N 450 0122-T600N-076 05.03.03
A R Hughes t/a Wilts Microlight Centre Yatesbury 14.04.15P

G-OWOW Cessna 152 II 15283199 10.05.95
G-BMSZ, N47254
M D Perry Wellesbourne Mountford 25.05.18E

G-OWPS Comco Ikarus C42 FB100 Bravo 1405-7322 22.05.14
B C & P A Webb t/a Webb Plant Sales
Westonzoyland 14.05.18P
Assembled Red-Air UK

G-OWRT Cessna 182G Skylane 18255077 24.08.00
G-ASUL, N3677U
D G Wright tr Tripacer Group Derby 02.06.18E

G-OWST Cessna 172S Skyhawk SP 172S8163 17.06.05
G-WABH, N961SP
Westair Flying Services Ltd Blackpool 10.10.18E

G-OWTF Pitts S-2B 5189 02.07.14
OO-SMD, G-BRVT D P Curtis Kilkerran 09.06.17E
Built by Christen Industries Inc (IE 30.10.17)

G-OWTN Embraer EMB-145EP 145010 08.08.13
F-GRGB, PT-SYG
BAE Systems (Corporate Air Travel) Ltd Warton 06.04.19E

G-OWWW Europa Aviation Europa XS 051 09.06.94
R F W Holder High Cross, Ware 30.05.18P
Built by N F Harrison, R F W Holder & W R C
Williams-Wynne – project PFA 247-12683; tricycle u/c

G-OXBA Cameron Z-160 11129 16.06.08
J E Rose Abingdon 'oxford balloon' 02.03.18E

G-OXBC Cameron A-140 4981 02.02.01
J E Rose Abingdon 22.03.11E
(NF 06.04.16)

G-OXBY Cameron N-90 1993 09.06.94
PH-DUM C A Oxby Newbury
To British Balloon Museum & Library 2015
(NF 20.10.14)

G-OXFA Piper PA-34-220T Seneca V 3449479 12.05.14
N34059, N9512N
Oxford Aviation Academy (Oxford) Ltd Oxford 25.05.18E

G-OXFB Piper PA-34-220T Seneca V 3449480 13.05.14
N34646, N9516N
Oxford Aviation Academy (Oxford) Ltd Oxford 15.06.18E

G-OXFC Piper PA-34-220T Seneca V 3449481 13.05.14
N34734, N9520N
Oxford Aviation Academy (Oxford) Ltd Oxford 20.06.18E

G-OXFD Piper PA-34-220T Seneca V 3449482 13.05.14
N34437, N9523N
Oxford Aviation Academy (Oxford) Ltd Oxford 10.07.18E

G-OXFE Piper PA-34-220T Seneca V 3449484 13.05.14
N34574, N9513N
Oxford Aviation Academy (Oxford) Ltd Oxford 22.06.18E

G-OXFF Piper PA-34-220T Seneca V 3449485 13.05.14
N34668, N9516N
Oxford Aviation Academy (Oxford) Ltd Oxford 27.06.18E

G-OXFG Piper PA-34-220T Seneca V 3449486 13.05.14
N34752, N9518N
Oxford Aviation Academy (Oxford) Ltd Oxford 04.07.18E

G-OXII Van's RV-12 xxxx 17.02.10
J A King (Llanrhaedr ym Mochnant, Oswestry)
Built by J A King – project LAA 363-14968
(NF 04.04.18)

G-OXIV Van's RV-14 140273 09.02.16
M A N Newall Sherburn-in-Elmet
Built by M A N Newall – project LAA 393-15383
(NF 09.02.16)

G-OXOM Piper PA-28-161 Cadet 2841285 09.12.03
G-BRSG, N92011 AJW Construction Ltd Elstree 07.05.19E
Operated by Flight Training London Ltd

G-OXPS American Aircraft Falcon XPS xxxx 19.11.09
G-BUXP J C Greenslade (Crapstone, Yelverton)
Built by J C Greenslade – project PFA 250-12439
(NF 24.09.15)

G-OXVI Supermarine 361 Spitfire LF.XVIe CBAF 4262 22.08.89
7246M, TD248 Spitfire Ltd Humberside 22.05.19P
As 'TD248:CR-S' in RAF 74 Sqdn c/s

G-OYAK Yakovlev Yak C-11 1701139 25.02.88
Egypt AF 705, OK-KIH A H Soper Little Gransden 13.10.15P
Built by Strojírny první petilesky (SPP); c/n also quoted
as 690120; damaged in wheels-up landing 21.06.18;
as '9' (white) in Russian AF c/s (IE 11.01.18)

G-OYES Mainair Blade 912 1186-1198-7-W989 12.11.98
C R Chapman East Fortune 13.04.18P

G-OYGC Aeropro EuroFOX 912(iS) 49216 08.07.16
York Gliding Centre (Operations) Ltd Rufforth 26.02.19P
Built by R Eckford, R Horney, T Mortimer &
A Wrigley – project LAA 376-15374;
tailwheel u/c; glider-tug

G-OYIO Robin DR.400-120 Dauphin 2+2 2038 16.02.07
OO-YIO Exeter Aviation Ltd Exeter Int'l 21.05.18E
Officially registered as DR.400-120 Petit Prince

G-OYTE Rans S-6-ES Coyote II 0404.1563 21.07.04
K C Noakes (Aylesbury) 09.10.18P
Built by I M Vass – project PFA 204-14263; tricycle u/c

G-OZAM Piper PA-28-161 Warrior II 28-7816036 10.07.15
G-LACA, N44883
G Hussain Wolverhampton Halfpenny Green 11.01.19E

G-OZBN Airbus A321-231 1153 02.04.07
G-MIDK, D-AVZF ALS Irish Aircraft Leasing
MSN 1153 Ltd Ostrava, Czech Republic 26.10.17E
(IE 20.11.17)

G-OZEE	Avid Speed Wing Mk.4	xxxx	18.04.94
	G D Bailey (Little Hucklow, Buxton)		12.06.19P
	Built by S C Goozee – project PFA 189-12308		
G-OZIE	Avtech Jabiru J400	181	30.06.05
	S A Bowkett Sleap		15.06.18P
	Built by S A Bowkett – project PFA 325-14284		
G-OZIP	Christen Eagle II	249	23.08.16
	ZU-ZIP		
	J D N Cooke Shenstone Hall Farm, Shenstone		27.04.18P
	Built by A Van Rensberg		
G-OZOI	Cessna R182 Skylane RG II	R18201950	31.05.85
	G-ROBK F L G & J R G Fleming t/a Ranston Farms		
	Ranston Farm, Iwerne Courtney		22.08.18E
G-OZON	Piper PA-32R-301T Saratoga II TC	3257393	10.06.15
	SX-ACZ, OY-PHI, N9522N, N3113J		
	D J Pilkington Blackpool		24.04.18E
G-OZOZ	Schempp-Hirth Nimbus-3DT	6	27.11.07
	BGA 4458/JEQ, OO-ZOZ, HB-1921, D-7695		
	T Barnes tr G-OZOZ Flying Group Bicester *'OZ'*		21.04.18E
	Originally built as Nimbus-3D c/n 1; converted to		
	Nimbus-3DT with sustainer engine (c/n 6)		
G-OZSB	Gefa-Flug AS105GD HA Airship	0002	02.07.14
	D-OZSB Cheers Airships Ltd Langford, Bristol		09.07.18E
	Envelope c/n 0038		
G-OZZE	Lambert Mission M108	004	20.10.11
	Lambert Aircraft Engineering BVBA Eshott		
	Built by J Oswald – project LAA 370-15089;		
	tailwheel u/c (NF 25.05.17)		
G-OZZI	Avtech Jabiru SK	0157	15.08.97
	A H Godfrey Batch End Farm, Lympsham		09.07.18P
	Built by A H Godfrey & E J Stradling		
	– project PFA 274-13176		
G-OZZT	Cirrus SR22T	0073	04.12.14
	M-YZZT, N100EU C C Aitkenhead Blackpool		21.12.18E

G-PAAA – G-PZZZ

G-PACE	Robin R1180T Aiglon	218	16.10.78
	C A C Bontet La Rochelle-Île de Ré, France		08.09.18E
G-PACO	Sikorsky S-76C++	760782	07.10.10
	N782V Cardinal Helicopter Services (IoM) Ltd		
	Billown, Ballasalla, Isle of Man		11.10.18E
	Built by Keystone Helicopter Corpn		
G-PACT	Piper PA-28-181 Archer III	2843546	25.03.03
	N5368F A Parsons Headcorn		27.06.18E
G-PADE	Reality Escapade 912(2)	JA.ESC.0027	02.06.04
	F Overall Whitehall Farm, Wethersfield		20.06.18P
	Built by C L G Innocent – project BMAA/HB/369; tailwheel u/c		
G-PAFF	AutoGyro MTOsport	11 042S	06.07.11
	S R Paffett Graveley Hall Farm, Graveley *'Big Nellie'*		13.09.18P
	Assembled Rotorsport UK as c/n RSUK/MTOS/039		
G-PAIB	Piper PA-18-135 Super Cub	18-3451	11.09.18
	G-LIBC, G-KAMP, D-EDPM, West German AF 96+27,		
	NL+104, AC+502, AS+501, 54-751		
	G Cormack Easter Poldar Farm, Thornhill		12.05.15E
	(IE 11.09.18)		
G-PAIG	Grob G109B	6257	05.01.12
	D-KHMA M E Baker tr G-PAIG RAF Cranwell		03.04.18E
G-PAIZ	Piper PA-12 Super Cruiser	12-2018	11.04.94
	N3215M, NC3215M B R Pearson Eaglescott		16.08.07
	Carries 'NC3215M' on tail (NF 30.10.18)		
G-PALI	Czech Sport PiperSport	P1001040	01.07.10
	MPG Aviation Ltd Rochester		22.05.19W
G-PALT	AutoGyro MTOsport	xxxx	26.05.17
	D A Jordan Northrepps		22.06.18P
	Assembled Rotorsport UK as c/n RSUK/MTOS/063		
G-PAMY	Robinson R44 Clipper II	11641	06.03.07
	Batchelor Aviation Ltd Rochester		06.01.19E
G-PAPE	Diamond DA.42 Twin Star	42.221	14.03.12
	I-VFLY DEA Aviation Ltd Retford Gamston		09.05.19E
G-PAPI	Comco Ikarus C42 FB80	1406-7323	30.07.14
	Avion Training & Consultancy Ltd Solent		27.07.18P
	Assembled Red-Air UK		

G-PAPJ	Van's RV-8	83386	19.06.18
	P G Jenkins (Watford)		
	Built by P G Jenkins – project LAA 303-15240		
	(NF 19.06.18)		
G-PARG	Pitts S-1S	19528-1	30.06.03
	N18FW R J Dolby Gloucestershire		05.04.17P
	Built by F G Weaver; bounced on landing		
	Gloucestershire 31.07.16 & substantially damaged		
G-PARI	Cessna 172RG Cutlass II	172RG0010	19.11.79
	N4685R Mannion Automation Ltd Abbeyshrule, RoI		24.08.18E
G-PARR[M]	Colt Bottle 90 SS HAB	1953	15.03.91
	Cancelled 10.02.97 as temporarily WFU		29.09.94
	Old Parr Whisk Bottle		
	With British Balloon Museum & Library, Newbury		
G-PASA (1)[M]	MBB BÖ.105D	S.41	03.04.89
	G-BGWP, F-ODMZ, HB-XFO, N153BB, D-HDAS		
	Cancelled 20.04.93 as PWFU		17.01.94
	Original pod only – rebuilt by as G-PASA (2)		
	With The Helicopter Museum, Weston-super-Mare		
G-PASB[M]	MBB BÖ.105D	S.135	02.03.89
	VH-LSA, G-BDMC, D-HDEC Cancelled 09.08.94 as WFU		
	Original pod from 1994 rebuild		
	With The Helicopter Museum, Weston-super-Mare		
G-PASH	Aérospatiale AS.355F1 Ecureuil 2	5040	17.05.96
	F-GHLI, LX-HUG, F-GHLI, N356E		
	MW Helicopters Ltd Stapleford		22.05.18E
G-PASL	Aérospatiale AS.355F2 Ecureuil 2	5108	18.02.14
	F-GHMC, (F-GHCH), N57902		
	C Giblain Bourne Park, Hurstbourne Tarrant		
	(NF 06.03.17)		
G-PASN	Enstrom F-28F Falcon	427	19.04.05
	G-BSHZ, N51702 N Pasha (Harrow)		22.09.11E
	(NF 26.01.15)		
G-PATF	Europa Aviation Europa	107	05.01.99
	Condor Aviation International Ltd		
	Birchwood Lodge, North Duffield		
	Built by E P Farrell – project PFA 247-12757;		
	tailwheel u/c & motor-glider wing; stored 11.16		
	(NF 12.06.14)		
G-PATG	Cameron O-90	3856	13.03.96
	S Neighbour & N Symonds Cheltenham & Bristol		22.08.14E
	(NF 16.12.15)		
G-PATJ	Comco Ikarus C42 FB80 Bravo	1509-7421	11.12.15
	P J Oakey Chatteris		10.12.18P
	Assembled Red Aviation		
G-PATN	SOCATA TB-10 Tobago	307	25.03.97
	G-LUAR D R Godfrey (Sonning Common, Reading)		05.12.19E
G-PATO	Zenair CH.601UL Zodiac	6-9628	02.03.05
	R J Duckett Eshott		26.08.18P
	Built by D L Walker – project PFA 162A-14328; tricycle u/c		
G-PATP	Lindstrand LBL 77A	471	08.07.97
	P Pruchnickyj Chinnor		01.07.16E
	(IE 07.08.17)		
G-PATS	Europa Aviation Europa	216	19.07.95
	D J G Kesterton tr G-PATS Flying Group		
	(Bow Brickhill, Milton Keynes)		
	Built by D J G Kesterton – project PFA 247-12888;		
	tailwheel u/c & motor-glider wing (NF 30.05.18)		
G-PATX	Lindstrand LBL 90A	778	19.06.01
	M R Noyce & R P E Phillips Andover		12.09.19E
G-PATZ	Europa Aviation Europa	069	02.06.98
	C W & S R Potts Selby House Farm, Stanton		18.08.10P
	Built by H P H Griffin – project PFA 247-12625;		
	tailwheel u/c (NF 05.04.17)		
G-PAWS	Gulfstream American AA-5A Cheetah	AA5A-0806	08.02.82
	N2623Q D Anders t/a Close Encounters Bagby		01.11.16E
G-PAWW	Ultramagic M-90	90/187	30.10.18
	S J Thomas Wick, Bristol		
	(IE 30.10.18)		
G-PAWZ	Best Off Skyranger Swift 912S(1)	UK/758	23.07.07
	L Moore tr G-PAWZ Syndicate		
	Red House Farm, Preston Capes		19.05.17P
	Built by S D McMurran – project BMAA/HB/528) (IE 25.08.17)		

G-PAXX	Piper PA-20-135 Pacer	20-1107	20.05.83
	N135XX, G-PAXX, (G-ARCE), F-BLLA, CN-TDJ, F-DADR		
	C W Monsell Brimpton		11.10.18E
G-PAYD	Robin DR.400-180 Régent	847	14.01.03
	D-EAYD P Bigland Gloucestershire		31.05.19E
G-PAZY	Pazmany PL-4A	xxxx	20.11.89
	G-BLAJ M Richardson (Durrington, Salisbury)		03.10.95P
	Built by J D Le Pine – project PFA 017-10378 (NF 23.06.16)		
G-PBAL	AutoGyro MTOsport	xxxx	24.11.17
	P S Ball (Mouldsworth, Chester)		12.12.18P
	Assembled Rotorsport UK as c/n RSUK/MTOS/064		
G-PBAT	Czech Sport Sportcruiser	09SC296	22.03.10
	P M W Bath Nottingham City		06.09.18W
G-PBEC	Van's RV-7	72125	21.08.07
	P G Reid Shenstone Hall Farm, Shenstone		20.12.18P
	Built by P G Reid – project PFA 323-14382		
G-PBEE	Robinson R44 Clipper	0829	11.09.00
	B K Pitfield tr Echo Echo Syndicate Guernsey		14.09.18E
G-PBEL	CFM Shadow Series DD	305-DD	27.10.98
	S Fairweather (Carlton, Nottingham)		25.06.18P
G-PBIG	Airbus EC130 T2	8298	04.01.18
	G-CJYT Bapchild Motoring World (Kent) Ltd		
	(Canterbury)		25.09.19E
G-PBII	Dan Rihn DR.107 One Design	14-575	12.06.18
	P D Baisden Southend		
	Built by P D Baisden – project LAA 264-15312		
	(IE 01.10.18)		
G-PBIX	Supermarine 361 Spitfire LF.XVIe	CBAF.IX 4640	15.10.08
	N382RW, G-XVIA, 8075M, 7245M, RW382		
	Downlock Ltd Biggin Hill		01.10.19P
	As 'RW382:3W-P' in RAF c/s		
G-PBWS	Schleicher ASH 31 Mi	31096	28.08.13
	P B Walker Aston Down '4J'		23.01.19E
G-PBYA	Consolidated PBY-5A Catalina	CV283	19.11.04
	C-FNJF, CF-NJF, F-ZBBD, CF-NJF, F-ZBAY, CF-NJF, RCAF 11005		
	Catalina Aircraft Ltd Duxford 'Miss Pick Up'		27.04.19E
	Built by Canadian Vickers Ltd as Canso A for RCAF; as '433915' in USAAF c/s		
G-PBYY	Enstrom 280FX Shark	2077	15.08.97
	G-BXKV, D-HHML S A Craske Eaglescott		08.07.16E
G-PCAT	SOCATA TB-10 Tobago	60	17.07.03
	G-BHER, 4X-AKK, G-BHER		
	D R A Bott tr G-PCAT Group Curry Rivel, Langport		05.01.18E
G-PCCC	Alpi Pioneer 300	112	31.03.04
	R Pidcock White Fen Farm, Benwick		03.08.18P
	Built by F A Civaciuti – project PFA 330-14220		
G-PCCM	Alpi Pioneer 200-M	260	14.04.14
	M G Freeman Sibson		25.08.19P
	Built by M G Freeman – project LAA 334-15250		
G-PCDP	Moravan Zlin Z-526F Trener	1163	24.10.94
	SP-CDP D J Lee Deanland 'Ticker'		21.03.18E
G-PCGC	Allstar PZL SZD-54-2 Perkoz	542.A.17.018W	07.09.17
	(BGA 5932), SP-3970 Cambridge Gliding Club Ltd		
	Gransden Lodge 'PZ'		30.08.19E
G-PCIZ	Pilatus PC-12/47E	1639	15.08.18
	M-YAKW, HB-FSF Limbourne Ltd Gloucestershire		15.08.19E
G-PCJS	Diamond DA.42NG Twin Star	42.N027	23.02.18
	UR-GRG, UR-GRGR, OE-FYF, OE-VDO		
	P J Cooper & G E J Sealey Cambridge		
	(IE 23.02.18)		
G-PCMC	P&M QuikR	8514	30.09.10
	G Charman Longacre Farm, Sandy		16.09.18P
G-PCOP	Beech B200 Super King Air	BB-1860	07.10.05
	N6200G Albert Bartlett & Sons (Airdrie) Ltd Glasgow		20.09.18E
G-PCPC	AutoGyro Calidus	C00372	11.03.15
	P E Churchill North Weald		24.03.19P
	Assembled Rotorsport UK as RSUK/CALS/026		
G-PCTW	Pilatus PC-12/47E	1674	19.12.16
	HB-FQO Yellow Skies LLP Oxford		15.12.18E

G-PCUB	Piper PA-18-135 Super Cub (L-21B)	18-3874	16.02.81
	(PH-KER), R.Netherlands AF R-184/54-2474		
	Cancelled 10.03.99 by CAA		28.03.98
	Lower Barn Farm, Paddock Wood		
	Displayed at airfield entrance 03.19		
G-PDGF	Eurocopter AS.350B2 Ecureuil	9024	25.05.07
	G-FROH PLM Dollar Group Ltd Dalcross Heliport		21.01.19E
	Callsign 'Osprey 55'		
G-PDGG	Aeromere F.8L Falco Series 3	208	06.01.98
	OO-TOS, I-BLIZ T W Gilbert Enstone		09.06.19E
G-PDGI	Aérospatiale AS.350B2 Ecureuil	1991	29.07.11
	EI-FAC, G-BVJE, SE-HRS		
	PLM Dollar Group Ltd Dalcross Heliport		02.06.18E
	Callsign 'Osprey 54'		
G-PDGN	Aérospatiale SA.365N Dauphin 2	6074	05.04.01
	PH-SSU, 5N-ATX, PH-SSU, (G-BLDR), G-TRAF, G-BLDR		
	PLM Dollar Group Ltd Dalcross Heliport		07.07.18E
	Callsign 'Osprey 68'		
G-PDGO	Aérospatiale AS.365N2 Dauphin 2	6405	21.11.16
	LN-OLE, VT-CKR, F-WQDK, F-WQDK, F-WQDG, JA6671		
	PLM Dollar Group Ltd t/a PDG Helicopters		
	Dalcross Heliport		28.03.18E
	Callsign 'Osprey 69'		
G-PDGP	Aérospatiale AS.355F2 Ecureuil 2	5135	04.05.18
	G-ZITZ, N596SJ, 9M-BDA, F-GIFR, F-WIFR, F-WZKZ		
	PLM Dollar Group Ltd Dalcross Heliport		
	Callsign 'Osprey 60'(IE 04.05.18)		
G-PDGR	Aérospatiale AS.350B2 Ecureuil	2559	26.01.07
	G-RICC, G-BTXA		
	PLM Dollar Group Ltd Dalcross Heliport		21.03.18E
	Callsign 'Osprey 75'		
G-PDGT	Aérospatiale AS.355F2 Ecureuil 2	5374	27.11.07
	N325SC, G-BOOV PLM Dollar Group Ltd		
	t/a PDG Helicopters Wolverhampton Halfpenny Green		24.11.18E
	Callsign 'Osprey 64'		
G-PDGV	Vulcanair P68C-TC	485-52TC	16.02.18
	OY-GIS PLM Dollar Group Ltd		
	Wolverhampton Halfpenny Green		
	Callsign 'Osprey 75 or 76'(IE 16.02.18)		
G-PDGX	Vulcanair P68C-TC		12.03.18
	OY-GNS PLM Dollar Group Ltd		
	Wolverhampton Halfpenny Green		20.03.19E
G-PDOC	Piper PA-44-180 Seminole	44-7995090	17.12.85
	G-PVAF, N2242A T White t/a Medicair Newcastle Int'l		22.06.18E
G-PDOG	Cessna 305C Bird Dog (O-1E)	24550	25.09.98
	F-GKGP, French Army		
	A J Williams & J C Wright Old Warden		01.06.19E
	As '24550:GP' in USAF c/s		
G-PDRO	Schleicher ASH 31 Mi	31121	21.11.14
	P Crawley Sutton Bank		09.12.15E
G-PDSI	Cessna 172N Skyhawk II	17270420	04.01.88
	N739BU G Gates & A Harding tr DA Flying Group		
	Blackbushe		11.10.18E
G-PEAR	P&M Pegasus Quik	8309	20.09.07
	N D Major Cottage Farm, Norton Juxta		02.07.18P
G-PECK	Piper PA-32-300 Cherokee Six D	32-7140008	22.04.03
	G-ETAV, G-MCAR, G-LADA, G-AYWK, N8616N		
	K H McCune (Truro)		10.07.19E
G-PECX	Aeropro EuroFOX 912S(2)	48816	29.06.16
	SAE Systems Ltd Ludham		13.12.18P
	Built by S Peck – project BMAA/HB/687; tailwheel u/c		
G-PEGA	Cyclone Pegasus Quantum 15-912	7700	14.08.00
	M Konisti Hunsdon		13.05.12P
	(NF 29.01.16)		
G-PEGE	Best Off Skyranger 912(2)	UK/640	31.01.06
	A N Hughes Westonzoyland		26.11.18P
	Built by A N Hughes – project BMAA/HB/479; c/n either SKR0508640 or SKR0511640		
G-PEGI	Piper PA-34-200T Seneca II	34-7970339	27.11.89
	N2907A ACS Aviation Ltd Oxford		16.03.18E
G-PEGY	Europa Aviation Europa	096	16.05.00
	A Carter Spilsted Farm, Sedlescombe		29.06.19P
	Built by M T Dawson – project PFA 247-12713; tricycle u/c		

G-PEJM	Piper PA-28-181 Archer III	2843355		28.06.00
	N41860 S J Clark Dunkeswell			01.08.18E
G-PEKT	SOCATA TB-20 Trinidad	532		28.07.89
	N24AS D J Drumm & D F Wallace			
	tr The WERY Flying Group Sherburn-in-Elmet			09.02.18E
G-PERC	Cameron N-90	10127		29.08.01
	I R Warrington Hunstanton *'Stanton Marris'*			05.06.19E
G-PERD	AgustaWestland AW139	41270		02.03.12
	LN-OEA, G-PERD, N395SH Babcock Mission			
	Critical Services Offshore Ltd Aberdeen Int'l			31.03.18E
	Built by AgustaWestland Philadelphia Corp, USA			
G-PERE	Robinson R22 Beta II	3382		24.02.03
	N70881 Phoenix Helicopter Academy Ltd			
	Doncaster Sheffield			21.10.19E
	Operated by Hummingbird Helicopters			
G-PERG	Embraer EMB-505 Phenom 300	50500266		02.11.17
	G-POWO, N566EE			
	Air Charter Scotland Ltd London Stansted			24.05.18E
G-PERH	Guimbal Cabri G2	1164		08.09.16
	M Munson Wycombe Air Park			19.09.18E
	Operated by Helicopter Services			
G-PERR[M]	Cameron Bottle 60 SS HAB	699		28.01.81
	Cancelled 24.01.92 as WFU			03.06.84
	With British Balloon Museum & Library, Newbury			
G-PERU	Guimbal Cabri G2	1140		18.04.16
	F-WWHG Heligroup Operations Ltd			
	Wycombe Air Park			07.07.19E
	Operated by Phoenix Helicopters			
G-PEST	Hawker Tempest II	"1181"		09.10.89
	Indian AF HA604, MW401 Anglia Aircraft			
	Restorations Ltd (Great Canfield, Dunmow)			
	Built by Bristol Aeroplane Co Ltd;			
	on rebuild 01.17 (NF 12.06.14)			
G-PETH	Piper PA-24-260 Comanche C	24-4979		15.10.04
	N9469P J V Hutchinson & W T G Ponnet			
	(Frangy & Franclens, France)			24.08.18E
G-PETO	Hughes 369HM *(500)*	520214M		16.02.12
	G-HAUS, G-KBOT, G-RAMM, EI-AVN, N9037F			
	P E Tornberg Sywell			05.06.18E
G-PETR	Piper PA-28-140 Cherokee Cruiser	28-7425320		23.09.85
	G-BCJL, N9591N P Stamp Isle of Man			05.06.18E
G-PFAA	EAA Biplane Model P2	PEB/03		19.09.78
	T A Fulcher Rayne Hall Farm, Rayne			09.04.09P
	Built by P E Barker – project PFA 1338 (NF 27.05.15)			
G-PFAE	Taylor JT1	xxxx		19.09.78
	Cancelled 02.09.91 by CAA			
	(Thatcham) *Built by G Johnson – project PFA 1426;*			
	for sale for completion 08.16			
G-PFAF	Clutton FRED Series II	xxxx		30.10.78
	M S Perkins Stoke Golding			13.11.08P
	Built by K Fern & M S Perkins – project			
	PFA 029-10310 (NF 11.11.14)			
G-PFAG	Evans VP1	xxxx		13.11.78
	Cancelled 15.02.10 by CAA			30.06.89
	(Attleborough) *Built by N S Giles-Townsend*			
	– project PFA 7022; for sale 10.16			
G-PFAH	Evans VP-1	PFA 7004		23.11.78
	J A Scott Chestnut Farm, Tipps End			06.07.18P
	Built by J A Scott – project PFA 7004			
G-PFAL	Clutton FRED Series 2	xxxx		07.12.78
	Cancelled 12.10.10 by CAA			
	Derrytrasna Glen Bannfoot			
	Built by H Pugh – project PFA 029-10243; stored 12.13			
G-PFAP	Phoenix Currie Wot	xxxx		12.12.78
	J H Seed Black Springs Farm, Castle Bytham			22.06.09P
	Built by P G Abbey – project PFA 058-10315			
	as SE.5A replica; as 'C1904:Z' in RFC c/s (IE 24.09.15)			
G-PFAR	Isaacs Fury II	xxxx		18.12.78
	D J Phillips & C C Silk Bericote Farm, Blackdown			09.06.07P
	Built by C J Repik – project PFA 011-10220;			
	as 'K2059' in RAF 25 Sqdn c/s (NF 19.06.14)			
G-PFAT	Monnett Sonerai II	xxxx		26.10.78
	H B Carter (St Clement, Jersey)			24.10.92P
	Built by H B Carter – project PFA 015-10312 (NF 04.05.18)			

G-PFAW	Evans VP-1	xxxx		18.12.78
	R F Shingler Forest Farm, Westbury, Shrewsbury			28.06.07P
	Built by R F Shingler – project PFA 062-10183			
	(IE 27.04.17)			
G-PFAY	EAA Biplane	1525		18.12.78
	Cancelled 26.08.10 by CAA			
	Dunkeswell *Built by A K Lang & A L Young*			
	– project PFA 1525; stored, part built 11.13			
G-PFCL	Cessna 172S Skyhawk SP	172S9330		19.03.03
	N53287 C H S Carpenter Fairoaks			07.07.18E
G-PFKD	Yakovlev Yak-12M	210999		24.03.03
	HA-HUB, LY-AQG, LY-FKD, G-PFKD, SP-FKD,			
	SP-AAD, Polish AF 999 R D Bade White Waltham			17.04.18P
	Built by Wytwórnia Sprzetu Komunikacyjneg (WSK)			
G-PFSL	Reims/Cessna F152 II	F15201746		30.08.00
	PH-TWF, D-ENAX P A Simon Headcorn			03.05.18E
G-PGAC	Dyn'Aéro MCR-01 Club	48		27.01.99
	G A Coatesworth Cambridge			25.05.18P
	Built by G A Coatesworth – project PFA 301-13186			
G-PGFG	Tecnam P92-EM Echo	xxxx		30.10.01
	T Farncombe (Marlborough) *'Charlie's Angel'*			11.07.19P
	Built by P G Fitzgerald – project PFA 318-13772			
G-PGGY	Robinson R44 Clipper II	11115		03.04.06
	EBG (Helicopters) Ltd Redhill			06.01.18E
G-PGHM	Air Création Buggy 582(2)/Kiss 450	FL026		04.02.04
	R J Turner (Sutton Bridge, Spalding)			17.11.15P
	Built by P G H Milbank – project BMAA/HB/341			
	(Flylight kit FL026 comprising trike s/n T03111			
	& wing s/n A04004-xxxx (IE 01.06.17)			
G-PGSA	Thruster T600N	0080-T600N-046		11.08.00
	M Atkinson (Blackpool)			17.11.19P
G-PGSI	Robin R2160 Alpha Sport	309		09.03.00
	F-GSAF M A Spencer North Weald			17.09.18E
G-PHAA	Reims/Cessna F150M	F15001159		19.06.97
	G-BCPE W B Bateson Blackpool			25.11.13E
	(NF 05.09.17)			
G-PHAB	Cirrus SR22	2710		04.06.10
	G-MACL, N926SR G3 Aviation Ltd Fairoaks			04.04.18E
G-PHAT	Cirrus SR20	1999		14.09.09
	N714TS T W Wielkopolski Dunkeswell			14.06.18E
G-PHIZ	Piper PA-30 Twin Comanche C	30-1871		12.02.19
	D-GPEZ, N8798Y, N9703N			
	G M & T J Laundy Conington			
	(IE 12.02.19)			
G-PHNX	Schempp-Hirth Duo Discus xT	157		14.03.07
	BGA 5248/KOG			
	J L Birch tr 72 Syndicate Gransden Lodge *'72'*			07.04.18E
G-PHOR	Reims/Cessna FRA150L Aerobat	FRA1500157		19.10.06
	G-BACC M Bonsall Netherthorpe			29.01.18E
G-PHOT	Colt Film Cassette SS HAB	4507		03.02.99
	Cancelled 16.12.02 as PWFU			23.03.02
	Not Known *Built by Cameron Balloons*			
	Inflated Pidley 05.16			
G-PHOX	Aeroprakt A-22L Foxbat	A22L-198		08.05.07
	J D Webb The Old Mushroom Farm, Haywood, Callow			09.06.18P
	Built by J D Webb – project PFA 317A-14635;			
	N188DA also reported with kit no A22L-198			
G-PHRG	Hybrid Air Vehicles Airlander 10	001		21.10.15
	US Army 09-009 Cancelled 01.10.18 as PWFU			
	Cardington *Stored 10.18*			
G-PHSE	Kubicek BB26Z	937		09.08.12
	The Packhouse Ltd Farnham *'Packhouse'*			28.04.19E
G-PHSI	Colt 90A	2181		12.05.92
	P H Strickland Bedford *'Daks – Simpsons'*			21.07.01A
	(NF 25.01.16)			
G-PHTG	SOCATA TB-10 Tobago	1008		15.11.89
	A J Baggarley Brighton City			25.10.18E
G-PHUN	Reims/Cessna FRA150L Aerobat	FRA1500177		27.06.06
	G-BAIN M Bonsall Netherthorpe			12.03.18E
	Operated by Phoenix Flying Club			
G-PHVM	Van's RV-8	xxxx		16.10.07
	G P Howes & A Leviston Elmsett			09.05.18P
	Built by G Howes & V Millard – project PFA 303-14609			

G-PHYL	Denney Kitfox Model 4	1127	14.09.98
	R S Horan (Melrose)		15.09.19P
	Built by J Dunn – project PFA 172A-12189		
G-PHYS	Avtech Jabiru SP-470	544	19.02.03
	G E D Evans Sandtoft		24.08.19P
	Built by P C Knight – project PFA 274B-13926		
G-PHYZ	Avtech Jabiru J430	xxxx	09.06.08
	P C Knight Wolverhampton Halfpenny Green		28.11.18P
	Built by P C Knight – project PFA 336-14617		
G-PIAF	Thunder Ax7-65	1885	19.11.90
	L Battersby Leckhampstead, Newbury		
	'No Regrets'		07.07.18E
G-PICO	Cameron O-31	11885	06.07.15
	J F Trehern (Devon)		18.07.17E
G-PICU	Leonardo AW169	69055	30.08.17
	I-EASI Specialist Aviation Services Ltd Oxford		31.08.18E
	Operated by for The Children's Air Ambulance		
G-PICX	P&M QuikR	8411	05.01.09
	C Phillips Sywell		18.09.19P
G-PIEL	Piel CP.301A Emeraude	218	17.11.88
	G-BARY, F-BIJR E B Atalay Sackville Lodge Farm, Riseley		
	18.01.18P		
	Built by Société Menavia		
G-PIES	Thunder Ax7-77Z	263	13.02.80
	M K Bellamy Ironville, Nottingham 'Pork Farms'		28.08.18E
G-PIET	Pietenpol Air Camper	xxxx	01.04.93
	P Batchelor & J Granell (Chertsey)		06.10.16P
	Built by N D Marshall – project PFA 047-12267		
	(NF 29.05.18)		
G-PIFZ	Agusta AW109SP Grand New	22355	15.04.16
	Alba Aviation Limited Partnership Norwich Int'l		14.04.18E
	Built by Finmeccanica SpA		
G-PIGI	Evektor EV-97 teamEurostar UK	2005-2315	23.02.05
	P A Aston tr Pigs Might Fly Group Exeter Int'l		02.12.18P
	Assembled Cosmik Aviation Ltd		
G-PIGS	SOCATA Rallye 150ST	2696	13.06.88
	G-BDWB D Hodgson tr Boon Hill Flying Group		
	Wombleton		05.07.18E
G-PIGY	Short SC.7 Skyvan 3 Variant 101	SH.1943	21.12.95
	LX-JUL, 5T-MAM, (G-14-111)		
	Liberty Aviation Ltd Kortrijk-Wevelgem Int'l, Belgium		21.08.19E
	Carries 'Austrian Air Force 5S-TC'		
G-PIGZ	Cameron Z-315	11938	09.03.16
	Wickers World Ltd Great Haywood, Stafford		08.03.18E
G-PIII	Pitts S-1D	xxxx	11.01.02
	G-BETI, G-PIII, G-BETI M O'Leary		
	(Woolstone, Milton Keynes) 'Trig Aerobatic Team'		14.06.19P
	Built by B Bray – project PFA 009-10156		
G-PIIT	Pitts S-2AE	1984	14.02.07
	N3QQ J Law Leicester		25.05.18P
	Built by R S McGlashon		
G-PIKD	Eiriavion PIK-20D-78	20638	21.05.07
	BGA 2412 A J Hulme Gransden Lodge '869'		27.07.18E
G-PIKK	Piper PA-28-140 Cherokee	28-22932	19.08.88
	G-AVLA, N11C, (N9509W) V Vieira Elstree		17.12.16E
	Stored 10.18		
G-PILE	RotorWay Exec 90	5143	27.07.93
	J B Russell (Magheramorne, Larne)		05.11.98P
	Built by J B Russell; on rebuild 01.17 (NF 19.10.15)		
G-PILL	Avid Flyer Mk.4	xxxx	12.08.97
	D R Meston Old Sarum		13.07.16P
	Built by D R Meston – project PFA 189-12333		
	(IE 05.09.16)		
G-PILY	Pilatus B4-PC11	138	12.11.07
	BGA 2296/DQM, RAFGSA 506		
	J Hunt Pocklington 'DOM'		22.07.18E
G-PILZ	AutoGyro MT-03	07 040	21.06.07
	D J Gavan Deenethorpe		21.10.19P
	Assembled Rotorsport UK as c/n RSUK/MT-03/013;		
	operated by The Gyrocopter Flying Club		
G-PIMM	Ultramagic M-77	77/263	01.03.05
	G Everett Sandway, Maidstone 'Anyone for Pimm's?'		21.08.17E
G-PIMP	Robinson R44 Raven II	12123	05.02.08
	A Ferrari (Lugano, Switzerland)		12.04.18E

G-PING	Gulfstream American AA-5A Cheetah	AA5A-0878	06.12.95
	G-OCWC, G-WULL, N27153		
	Boker Layla Aviation Ltd Elstree		28.04.19E
G-PINO	AutoGyro MTOsport	xxxx	10.06.11
	N Crighton Rochester		24.06.18P
	Assembled Rotorsport UK as c/n RSUK/MTOS/038		
G-PINT	Cameron Barrel-60	794	04.01.82
	D K Fish Sydney, NSW, Australia 'Charles Wells'		31.10.11E
	(NF 04.06.18)		
G-PINX	Lindstrand LBL Pink Panther	032	23.04.93
	Magical Adventures Ltd West Bloomfield, MI, USA		
	'The Son of the Pink Panther'		30.09.09E
	(NF 03.06.15)		
G-PION	Alpi Pioneer 300	123	07.06.05
	A A Mortimer Perth		28.08.18P
	Built by F A Cavaciuti – project PFA 330-14294;		
	kit no also quoted for G-XCIT		
G-PIPB	Aérospatiale AS.355F1 Ecureuil 2	5261	09.10.14
	G-NBEL, G-SKYW, G-TALI		
	Heli Air Ltd Cotswold		31.05.18E
G-PIPI	Mainair Pegasus Quik	8109	09.04.08
	R E Forbes (Forfar)		31.07.17P
	Built by Mainair Sports Ltd; Permit suspended 04.02.17		
G-PIPR	Piper PA-18 Super Cub 95	18-826	11.10.96
	G-BCDC, 4X-ANQ, Israel DFAF, 4X-ADE		
	R & T Kellett Newtownards		30.11.18E
	Fuselage No.18-832		
G-PIPS	Van's RV-4	xxxx	03.08.90
	P N Davis Otherton		06.09.18P
	Built by C J Marsh – project PFA 181-11883		
G-PIPY	Cameron Pipe-105 SS HAB	3815	30.01.96
	Cancelled 24.11.15 as PWFU		30.08.12
	Not Known Inflated Pidley 05.16		
G-PIPZ	BRM Bristell NG5 Speed Wing	xxx	08.05.14
	D T White Lydd		30.10.18P
	Built by D T White – project LAA 385-15279		
G-PITS	Pitts S-2AE	xxxx	04.07.85
	P N A & S N Whitehead Leicester		05.08.04P
	Built by B Bray – project PFA 009A-11001 (NF 12.11.14)		
G-PITZ	Pitts S-2A	100ER	02.10.87
	N183ER M J Wood Woolston Moss, Warrington		
	'Wildcats'		12.03.18P
	Built by Razorback Air Services		
G-PIVI	Pipistrel Virus 912S(1) SW127	792 SWN100	08.07.16
	H Sanganee tr Pipistrel Virus UK Group		
	Top Farm, Croydon		14.04.18P
	Built by D Mahajan – project BMAA/HB/684		
G-PIXE	Colt 31A	4883	11.07.00
	A D McCutcheon Rylstone, Skipton		14.08.18E
	Built by Cameron Balloons Ltd		
G-PIXI	Cyclone Pegasus Quantum 15-912	7557	27.08.99
	M R H Lewis Arclid Green, Sandbach		20.05.19P
G-PIXL	Robinson R44 Clipper II	11221	28.06.06
	Flying TV Ltd Denham		21.04.18E
G-PIXX	Robinson R44 Raven II	10263	16.04.04
	Flying TV Ltd Denham 'HTV/HD'		02.11.18E
G-PIXY	Super Marine Spitfire Mk.26	062	13.02.06
	R Collenette Henstridge		
	Built by R Collenette – project PFA 324-14477;		
	as 'RK855:F-TC' in RAF c/s (IE 07.08.18)		
G-PJCC	Piper PA-28-161 Warrior II	2816043	30.03.04
	OY-ODN, SE-IUI PJC (Leasing) Ltd Stapleford		10.04.18E
G-PJMT	Neico Lancair 320	xxxx	08.05.98
	K A & P P Gilroy Dunkeswell		08.05.18P
	Built by M T & P J Holland – project PFA 191-12348;		
	tricycle u/c		
G-PJPJ	Boeing 737-5H6	27355	08.05.09
	G-GFFJ, VT-JAZ, 9M-MFH		
	Cancelled 15.10.15 as PWFU		06.05.12
	Lasham Displayed in sunken pool for film work		
	in US Airways colours 10.15		
G-PJSY	Van's RV-6	xxxx	19.07.04
	P J York Leicester		12.07.18P
	Built by P J York – project PFA 181-13107		

G-PJTM	Reims/Cessna FR172K Hawk XP	FR17200611	13.10.98	
	EI-CHJ, G-BFIF			
	J R & R Emery Clutton Hill Farm, High Littleton			11.10.18E
G-PKHA	Pilatus PC-12/47E	1776	09.03.18	
	HB-FRM Pilatus Beheer BV (Schiedam, Netherlands)			08.03.19E
G-PKPK	Schweizer 269C (*300*)	S 1454	03.08.93	
	EI-CAR, N69A C H Dobson & M R Golden			
	Thorpe Farm, South Elkington			21.05.18E
G-PLAD	Kolb Twinstar Mk.III Xtra	xxxx	25.01.05	
	A R Smith (Sawston, Cambridge)			16.03.18P
	Built by P J Ladd – project PFA 205-14350			
G-PLAH	British Aerospace Jetstream Series 3102640		01.11.99	
	G-LOVA, G-OAKA, G-BUFM, G-LAKH, G-BUFM,			
	N410MX, G-31-640 Cancelled 22.01.08 by CAA			26.07.02
	Old Sarum *Cockpit stored 07.17*			
G-PLAJ	British Aerospace Jetstream Series 3102 738		30.03.00	
	N2274C, G-CJPH, N331QB, G-31-738			
	Cancelled 16.06.16 as PWFU			30.11.10
	Wolverhampton Halfpenny Green *Stored 01.18*			
G-PLAN	Reims/Cessna F150L	F15001066	11.08.78	
	PH-SPR S J Brenchley Solent			03.02.18E
	(NF 02.05.18)			
G-PLAR	Van's RV-9A	xxxx	22.12.09	
	M P Board North Weald			22.09.19P
	Built by M P Board & P Riglar – project PFA 320-14459			
G-PLAY	Robin R2112 Alpha	170	01.08.79	
	F-ODIT S J Wilson Gloucestershire			15.08.18E
G-PLAZ	Rockwell Commander 112A	345	15.04.04	
	G-RDCI, G-BFWG, ZS-JRX, N1345J			
	I Hunt St Athan			07.08.19E
G-PLEE	Cessna 182Q Skylane II	18266570	04.12.87	
	N95538 Skydive Academy Ltd t/a Peterlee			
	Parachute Centre Shotton Colliery, Peterlee			23.07.18E
G-PLIP	Diamond DA.40D Star	40.DS004	03.02.11	
	OE-DXH AJW Construction Ltd Bournemouth			22.11.19E
	Built by Shandong Bin AO Aircraft Industries Co Ltd			
G-PLJR	Pietenpol Air Camper	0142	16.01.15	
	P E Taylor Turweston			
	Built by P E Taylor – project PFA 047-13426			
	(NF 16.01.15)			
G-PLOP	Magni M24C Orion	24116204	07.02.11	
	R F Tuthill Turweston			27.06.19P
G-PLOW	Hughes 269B (*300*)	670317	13.09.83	
	G-AVUM C Walton Ltd Bruntingthorpe			
	(NF 16.09.15)			
G-PLPC	Schweizer 269C (*300*)	S 1558	14.04.97	
	G-JMAT A R Baker (Wistow, Selby)			31.10.17E
G-PLPM	Europa Aviation Europa XS	383	17.05.00	
	P L P Mansfield Popham			
	Built by P L P Mansfield – project PFA 247-13287;			
	tailwheel u/c; on rebuild 05.16 (NF 12.10.15)			
G-PLSR	P&M PulsR	8607	30.11.11	
	59 DHJ, G-PLSR			
	P & M Aviation Ltd Elm Tree Park, Manton			03.12.15P
	(IE 08.01.18)			
G-PLUG^M	Colt 105A HAB	1958	17.04.91	
	Cancelled 23.07.96 by CAA			14.08.95
	With British Balloon Museum & Library, Newbury			
G-PMAM	Cameron V-65	1155	29.05.85	
	P A Meecham Milton-under-Wychwood,			
	Chipping Norton *'Tempus Fugit'*			18.04.18E
G-PMGG	Agusta-Bell 206A JetRanger	8185	08.09.10	
	G-EEGO, G-PELS, G-DNCN, 9H-AAJ,			
	Libyan Arab Rep AF 8185, 5A-BAM			
	P M Gallagher & S Perry			
	Woodland Grange, Everingham			08.03.18E
G-PMIZ	Pitts Model 12	45	09.12.15	
	G-DEWD, G-CGRP I S Smith Oaksey Park			13.06.18P
	Built by J Miller & R F Warner – project LAA 349-15010			
G-PMNF	Supermarine 361 Spitfire HF.IX	CBAF 10372	29.04.96	
	SAAF??, TA805 P R Monk Biggin Hill *'Spirit of Kent'*			18.03.19P
	As 'TA805:FX-M' in RAF 234 Sqdn c/s			
G-PMSL	Ultramagic M-120	120/53	28.01.13	
	High Road Ventures Ltd t/a High Road Balloons			
	Stretton on Fosse, Moreton-in-Marsh			20.11.18E
G-PNAD	Lindstrand LBL Box	1308	04.01.19	
	G-PLLT Gone With The Wind Ltd Bristol BS8			10.10.19E
G-PNEU	Colt Bibendum-110	4223	05.01.98	
	P A Rowley Caversfield, Bicester *'Michelin'*			26.06.02A
	Built by Cameron Balloons Ltd; active 05.18			
	(NF 18.11.15)			
G-PNGB	Partenavia P68B	37	06.11.15	
	VH-DBF, VH-PNC, P2-DNC P Morton Bembridge			18.05.18E
G-PNGC	Schleicher ASK 21	21770	24.01.06	
	BGA 5078 T World tr Portsmouth Naval Gliding Centre			
	Trenchard Lines, Upavon *'N3'*			17.03.18E
G-PNIX	Reims/Cessna FRA150L Aerobat	FRA1500205	02.11.04	
	G-BBEO			
	D C Bonsall t/a Dukeries Aviation Netherthorpe			16.02.18E
	Operated by Phoenix Flying Club			
G-PODD	Robinson R66 Turbine	0727	10.08.16	
	Jamiroquai Ltd Wycombe Air Park			06.08.19E
G-POET	Robinson R44 Raven II	10219	03.03.10	
	VH-VTO GP Owen Ltd Caernarfon			19.05.18E
G-POGO	Flight Design CT2K	01-06-02-12	30.07.01	
	P J Reilly (Southwater, Horsham)			28.06.19P
	Assembled Pegasus Aviation			
G-POLA	Eurocopter EC135 P2+	0877	11.02.10	
	Police & Crime Commissioner for West Yorkshire			
	Birmingham			13.07.18E
	Operated by West Midlands Police Air Operations Unit			
	as callsign 'NPAS 51'			
G-POLB	Eurocopter EC135 T2+	0283	04.06.15	
	G-SURY Police & Crime Commissioner for West			
	Yorkshire (Wakefield)			
	Operated by The Chief Constable West Yorkshire Police			
	t/a National Police Air Service; active 09.18 (IE 20.04.18)			
G-POLC	Eurocopter EC135 T2+	0209	01.04.16	
	G-CPSH, D-HECJ Police & Crime Commissioner for			
	West Yorkshire Manchester Barton			20.06.18E
	Operated by The Chief Constable West Yorkshire Police			
	t/a National Police Air Service			
G-POLD	Eurocopter EC135 T2+	0300	07.06.16	
	G-NMID Police & Crime Commissioner for West			
	Yorkshire (Wakefield)			29.03.18E
	Operated by The Chief Constable West Yorkshire Police			
	t/a National Police Air Service			
G-POLF	Eurocopter EC135 T2+	0267	14.11.16	
	G-ESEX Police & Crime Commissioner for West			
	Yorkshire (Wakefield)			18.06.18E
	Operated by The Chief Constable West Yorkshire Police			
	t/a National Police Air Service			
G-POLG	Eurocopter EC135 T2+	0228	12.07.17	
	G-LASU, D-HTSH Police & Crime Commissioner			
	for West Yorkshire (Wakefield)			19.11.18E
	Operated by The Chief Constable West Yorkshire Police			
	t/a National Police Air Service			
G-POLH	Eurocopter EC135 T2+	0204	12.12.17	
	G-WCAO Police & Crime Commissioner for			
	West Yorkshire Bournemouth			13.06.18E
	Operated by Dorset Police as callsign 'NPAS10'			
G-POLJ	Eurocopter EC135 T2+	0333	07.11.18	
	G-NEAU, D-HECB Police & Crime Commissioner			
	for West Yorkshire (Wakefield)			15.03.19E
G-POLL	Best Off Skyranger 912(1)	SKR0305313	26.02.04	
	S Spence (Aldreth, Ely)			15.06.19P
	Built by D L Pollitt – project BMAA/HB/290			
G-POLR	P&M QuikR	8746	20.01.16	
	D Sykes Rufforth East			23.02.19P
G-POLS	Airbus EC135 T3	1220	05.05.16	
	D-HECR Babcock Mission Critical Services			
	Onshore Ltd Glasgow City Heliport			05.05.18E
	Operated by Police Scotland Air Support Unit			
(G-POLV)	Vulcanair P68R			
	Police Aviation Services Reserved, due xx.19			
(G-POLW)	Vulcanair P68R			
	Police Aviation Services Reserved, due xx.19			

(G-POLX)	Vulcanair P68R		
	Police Aviation Services Reserved, due xx.19		
G-POLY	Cameron N-77	428	13.07.78
	S Church & S Jenkins Bristol BS32 & BS8		
	'Polywallets'		20.04.18E
(G-POLZ)	Vulcanair P68R		
	Police Aviation Services Reserved, due xx.19		
G-POMP	Cameron Bearskin-100	12086	31.05.17
	Lighter Than Air Ltd Chew Stoke, Bristol		14.06.19E
	Bearskin special shape		
G-POND	Oldfield Baby Lakes	01	02.10.90
	N87ED J Maehringer (Oftersheim, Germany)		27.06.18P
	Built by G E Davis		
G-POOH	Piper J-3C-65 Cub	6932	17.10.79
	F-BEGY, NC38324 P L Beckwith		
	Upper Harford Farm, Bourton-on-the-Water		15.08.17E
	Fuselage No.7015		
G-POOL	ARV ARV-1 Super 2	025	28.08.87
	G-BNHA E Stinton Crosland Moor		10.05.19P
G-POPA	Beech A36 Bonanza	E-2177	20.05.92
	N7007F, N7204R S F Payne Earls Colne		08.06.18E
G-POPE	Eiriavion PIK-20E	20257	05.03.80
	E P Lambert tr G-POPE Syndicate Aston Down		08.04.18E
G-POPG	Aeropro EuroFOX 2K	51717	25.07.17
	C M Hoyle (Romsey)		29.07.19P
	Built by Ascent Industries Ltd; tailwheel u/c		
G-POPI	Socata TB10 Tobago	315	20.04.90
	G-BKEN, (G-BKEL) Cancelled 30.10.16 as destroyed		04.05.15
	Guernsey *On fire dump 10.16*		
G-POPW	Cessna 182S Skylane	18280204	10.07.98
	N9451F M S Archer Conington		25.10.18E
G-POPY	Best Off Skyranger Swift 912S(1)	UK/737	06.03.07
	J Young Wolverhampton Halfpenny Green		19.04.19P
	Built by C D & L J Church – project BMAA/HB/519		
G-POPZ	Druine D.31A Turbulent	xxxx	10.08.17
	S A Blanchard Beverley (Linley Hill)		
	Built by S A Blanchard – project LAA 048-15494		
	(NF 10.08.17)		
G-PORG	Sportine Aviacija LAK-17AT	167	14.07.17
	(BGA 5917), D-KYLJ, LY-YLJ		
	R M Garden Aboyne *'RG'*		29.12.18E
G-PORK	Grumman American AA-5B Tiger	AA5B-0625	28.02.84
	EI-BMT, G-BFHS S D Pryke (Great Witchingham)		22.07.19E
G-POSH	Colt 56A	822	10.06.86
	G-BMPT B K Rippon Didcot		09.04.16E
G-POTA	Extra EA.300/LT	LT030	06.02.18
	OO-MSL, G-CIRJ L Franceschetti & M Frizza		
	(Provaliglio D'Iseo & Brescia, Italy)		
	(IE 06.02.18)		
G-POTR	Agusta A109E Power	11043	04.03.15
	G-OFTC, N195NJ, N109GR, TC-HCU		
	Castle Air Ltd Trebrown, Liskeard		11.05.18E
G-POUX	Pou Du Ciel – Bifly	JBMD-01	29.06.07
	59ABT G D Priest Spilsted Farm, Sedlescombe		
	Built by J Bierinx & M Dugourd		
	(SSDR microlight since 05.14) (NF 27.06.18)		
G-POWD	Boeing 767-36N	30847	17.12.09
	N308TL, JA767D, N847SF, (JA01LQ)		
	Titan Airways Ltd London Stansted		21.10.19E
	Line No: 902		
G-POWH	Boeing 757-256	29308	18.06.12
	TC-OGT, EC-HIR, N1795B		
	Titan Airways Ltd Leeds Bradford		11.05.19E
	Line No: 935; operated by Jet2.com		
G-POWK	Airbus A320-233	4701	15.01.15
	9V-SLN, D-AUBE Hagondale Ltd London Stansted		11.01.20E
	Operated by Titan Airways Ltd		
G-POWL	Cessna 182R Skylane II	18267813	11.11.82
	N9070G, D-EOMF, N6265N		
	Oxford Aeroplane Company Ltd Oxford		09.04.18E
G-POWM	Airbus A320-232	2564	19.03.15
	4R-ABJ, VT-DKY, F-WWDC		
	Titan Airways Ltd London Stansted		16.03.19E

G-POWN	Airbus A321-211	3830	30.03.16
	OE-LET, D-AVZG Hagondale Ltd London Stansted		15.02.19E
	Operated by Jet2.com; jet2.com logo		
G-POWP	Boeing 737-436(SF)	25844	23.02.17
	N844AU, G-DOCY, OO-LTQ, G-BVBY		
	Titan Airways Ltd London Stansted		21.02.19E
	Line No: 2514		
G-POWS	Boeing 737-436	25853	29.01.18
	N853AT, G-DOCT		
	Titan Airways Ltd (London Stansted)		
	Line No: 2409 (IE 15.08.18)		
G-POWU	Airbus A321-211	3708	26.04.18
	OE-LCA, D-ABCA, D-AVZO		
	Hagondale Ltd London Stansted		19.11.19E
	Operated by Jet2.com		
G-POWV	Airbus A321-211	3749	02.05.18
	OE-LCB, D-ABCB, D-AVZC		
	Hagondale Ltd London Stansted		16.02.19E
	Operated by Jet2.com		
G-POZA	Reality Escapade ULP(2)	JA.ESC.0014	05.02.04
	M R Jones Broomclose Farm, Longbridge Deverill		04.02.18P
	Built by M R Jones – project BMAA/HB/347		
G-PPBZ	AutoGyro Calidus	C00260	12.01.18
	LY-BAR Dept of Doing Ltd Deenethorpe		
	Assembled Rotorsport UK as c/n RSUK/CALS/036		
	(IE 12.01.18)		
G-PPFS	Reims/Cessna FRA150L Aerobat	FRA1500126	11.10.12
	G-AZJY M Bonsall Netherthorpe		20.04.18E
G-PPIO	Cameron C-90	11096	20.02.09
	A G Martin Blagdon, Bristol		12.10.18E
G-PPLG	AutoGyro MT-03	06 086	09.01.07
	A King tr Gyro Syndicate PPLG Perth		04.09.18P
	Assembled Rotorsport UK as c/n RSUK/MT-03/010		
G-PPLL	Van's RV-7A	71747	28.06.04
	D Bull Redhill		11.05.18P
	Built by P G Leonard – project PFA 323-14240		
G-PPLS	Reims/Cessna F152	F15201828	24.08.15
	F-GDIL Devon & Somerset Flight Training Ltd		
	Dunkeswell		13.07.18E
G-PPOD	Europa Aviation Europa XS	xxxx	26.03.08
	S Easom Nottingham City		10.04.18P
	Built by S Easom – project PFA 247-13745; tricycle u/c		
G-PPPP	Denney Kitfox Model 3	771	09.01.91
	C J Thompson (Handley Park, Towcester)		02.08.18P
	Built by P Eastwood – project PFA 172-11830		
G-PRAG	Brügger MB.2 Colibri	xxxx	29.11.78
	D Frankland tr Colibri Flying Group RAF Mona		26.02.04P
	Built by P Russell – project PFA 043-10362 (NF 06.02.18)		
G-PRAH	Flight Design CT2K	01-06-01-12	31.07.01
	P A Banks Finmere		20.05.18P
	Assembled Pegasus Aviation		
G-PRAY	Lindstrand LTL Series 2-60	032	16.05.17
	Trinity Balloons CIC Tavistock		08.06.19E
G-PRBB	HpH Glasflügel 304 eS Shark	061-MS	27.10.16
	(BGA 5920)		
	P J Belcher & R I Brickwood Gransden Lodge *'B2'*		04.01.18R
G-PRDH	Aérospatiale AS.355F2 Ecureuil 2	5367	30.04.08
	G-DOOZ, G-BNSX K & M Pinfold t/a Claremont		
	Air Services (Baldwins Gate, Newcastle)		18.04.18E
G-PREY	Pereira Osprey 2	xxxx	28.09.99
	G-BEPB Condor Aviation International Ltd		
	Birchwood Lodge, North Duffield		
	Built by A J C & J J Zwetsloot – project PFA 070-10193; stored 11.16 (NF 28.09.15)		
G-PRII	Hawker Hunter PR.11	41H-670690	14.07.99
	N723WT, A2616, WT723		
	Horizon Aircraft Engineering Ltd St Athan		09.06.16P
	As 'WT723:LM-692' in RN 764 Sqdn c/s; stored 11.16 (NF 21.09.16)		
G-PRIM	Piper PA-38-112 Tomahawk	38-78A0669	28.01.87
	N2398A Braddock Ltd Stonefield Park, Chilbolton		25.12.01
	Dismantled in external store 04.16 (NF 02.09.15)		
G-PRIT	Cameron N-90 HAB	1375	06.11.86
	G-HTVI, G-PRIT Cancelled.07.04.05 as PWFU		15.03.04
	Not Known *Inflated Pidley 05.16*		

G-PRIV	Supermarine 353 Spitfire PR.IV	6S-171374	14.04.10
	BP926 P R Arnold Sandown		
	Noted 07.17 (NF 14.05.18)		
G-PRKZ	Allstar PZL SZD-54-2 Perkoz	542.A.16.014	12.07.16
	(BGA 5896), SP-3886		
	Buckminster Gliding Club Ltd Saltby *'S8Y'*		10.07.18E
G-PRLY	Avtech Jabiru SK	0219	11.03.02
	G-BYKY J McVey Ince		31.05.11P
	Built by N J Bond – project PFA 274-13385		
	(NF 21.07.17)		
G-PROM	Aerospatiale AS.350B Ecureuil	1486	11.10.96
	G-MAGY, G-BIYC Cancelled 21.02.11 by CAA		23.10.05
	Dungannon *Stored 12.13*		
G-PROO	Hawker 4000 Horizon	RC-34	17.11.10
	M-PAUL, N3194F		
	Sun-Air of Scandinavia AS Billund, Denmark		17.11.19E
G-PROS	Van's RV-7A	xxxx	27.04.06
	A J & S A Sutcliffe Westonzoyland		12.03.18P
	Built by S A Jarret – project PFA 323-14146		
G-PROV	BAC P.84 Jet Provost T.52A	PAC/W/23905	13.12.83
	Singapore AF 352, South Arabian AF 104, G-27-7, XS228		
	Hollytree Management Ltd t/a The Provost Group		
	Nottingham City		13.12.18P
	As '104' in South Arabian AF c/s		
G-PROW	Evektor EV-97 Eurostar	2002-1180	30.10.02
	Fly Hire Ltd tr Quantum Syndicate Full Sutton		12.01.19P
	Built by G M Prowling – project PFA 315-13968		
G-PRPA	Bombardier DHC-8-402Q	4187	27.05.15
	N187WQ, C-FNQG Flybe Ltd Exeter Int'l		28.05.19E
G-PRPB	Bombardier DHC-8-402Q	4333	07.07.15
	N333NG, C-GGFI Flybe Ltd Exeter Int'l		23.07.19E
G-PRPC	Bombardier DHC-8-402Q	4338	25.08.15
	N338NG, C-GGQY Flybe Ltd Exeter Int'l		21.09.19E
G-PRPD	Bombardier DHC-8-402Q	4332	13.11.15
	N332NG, C-GFKK Flybe Ltd Exeter Int'l		23.12.19E
G-PRPE	Bombardier DHC-8-402Q	4209	28.04.16
	N209WQ, C-FPQA Flybe Ltd Exeter Int'l		27.05.19E
G-PRPF	Bombardier DHC-8-402Q	4195	01.12.16
	N195WQ, C-FOJM Flybe Ltd Exeter Int'l		22.02.19E
G-PRPG	Bombardier DHC-8-402Q	4191	04.11.16
	N191WQ, C-FNQQ Flybe Ltd Exeter Int'l		19.12.19E
G-PRPH	Bombardier DHC-8-402Q	4323	04.10.16
	N323NG, C-GEVP Flybe Ltd Exeter Int'l		30.11.19E
G-PRPI	Bombardier DHC-8-402Q	4204	02.09.16
	G-CJFN, N204WQ, C-FPEF Flybe Ltd Exeter Int'l		15.09.19E
G-PRPJ	Bombardier DHC-8-402Q	4202	01.08.16
	N202WQ, C-FOUY Flybe Ltd Exeter Int'l		01.01.20E
G-PRPK	Bombardier DHC-8-402Q	4203	06.02.17
	N203WQ, C-FPDY Flybe Ltd Exeter Int'l		05.04.19E
G-PRPL	Bombardier DHC-8-402Q	4380	07.04.15
	N380NG, C-GKNB Flybe Ltd Exeter Int'l		06.04.19E
G-PRPM	Bombardier DHC-8-402Q	4188	10.04.17
	N188WQ, C-FNQH Flybe Ltd Exeter Int'l		26.06.19E
G-PRPN	Bombardier DHC-8-402Q	4213	07.03.17
	N213WQ, C-FQXO Flybe Ltd Exeter Int'l		07.05.19E
G-PRPO	Bombardier DHC-8-402Q	4214	12.05.17
	N214WQ, C-FQXP Flybe Ltd Exeter Int'l		16.07.19E
G-PRXI	Supermarine 365 Spitfire PR.XI	6S/583723	06.06.83
	PL983, G-15-109, N74138, PL983		
	Propshop Ltd Duxford		11.06.01P
	As 'PL983' on PR blue overall c/s;		
	active 05.18 (NF 27.01.16)		
G-PRZI	Cameron A-375	11798	07.04.14
	Bailey Balloons Ltd Pill, Bristol *'red letter days'*		01.04.19E
G-PSAX	Lindstrand LBL 77B	960	08.10.03
	M V Farrant & I Risbridger Chichester & Guildford		07.05.18E
G-PSFG	Robin R2160i	337	05.12.07
	G-COVD, G-BYOF Mardenair Ltd Goodwood		11.04.18E
G-PSGC	Piper PA-25-260 Pawnee C	25-5324	29.04.04
	G-BDDT, CS-AIX, N8820L		
	Peterborough & Spalding Gliding Club Ltd Crowland		08.06.18E

G-PSHK	Schempp-Hirth SHK-1	40	18.03.08
	BGA 1392/CAR P Gentil Aston Down *'422'*		26.06.17E
G-PSHU	Eurocopter EC135 T2+	0597	23.05.17
	G-WONN Babcock Mission Critical Services		
	Onshore Ltd Gloucestershire *'Poileas Alba'*		11.03.19E
G-PSIR	Jurca MJ.77 Gnatsum	04	28.08.09
	F-PANG P W Carlton & D F P Finan		
	Morgansfield, Fishburn		
	Built by ASS Legend'Air; as '474008:VF-R'		
	in USAAF c/s; cleared to fly 08.02.19 (NF 05.01.17)		
G-PSJS	Robinson R22 Beta II	4053	27.02.17
	G-PBRL G E J Sealey (Waterbeach)		25.04.18E
G-PSKY	Best Off Skyranger 912S(1)	SKR0409524	03.02.05
	P W Curnock & J W Wilcox		
	(Bristol BS37 & Wotton-under-Edge)		31.07.18P
	Built by S Ivell – project BMAA/HB/430		
G-PSMS	Aeropro EuroFOX 912(S)	41813	14.02.13
	I Archer Perth		04.09.19P
	Built by P V Stevens – project BMAA/HB/635; tricycle u/c		
G-PSNI	Eurocopter EC135 T2	0337	26.07.04
	Police Service of Northern Ireland Belfast Int'l		20.04.18E
	Operated by PSNI Air Support Unit as callsign		
	'Police 441'		
G-PSNO	Eurocopter MBB-BK117 C-2 (*EC145*)	9296	10.11.09
	D-HADC Police Service of Northern Ireland		
	Belfast Int'l		09.06.18E
	Operated by PSNI Air Support Unit as callsign		
	'Police 442'		
G-PSNR	Eurocopter MBB-BK117 C-2 (*EC145*)	9488	03.01.13
	G-LFRS Police Service of Northern Ireland		
	Belfast Int'l		17.07.18E
	Operated by PSNI Air Support Unit as callsign		
	'Police 443'		
G-PSON	Colt Cylinder One	1780	14.03.95
	PH-SON Flintnine Fasteners Ltd		
	Whittle-le-Woods, Chorley *'Panasonic LR20'*		22.11.18E
	Built by Thunder & Colt Ltd; cylinder special shape		
	(IE 16.12.18)		
G-PSRT	Piper PA-28-151 Cherokee Warrior	28-7615225	18.03.99
	G-BSGN, N9657K R W Nash Enstone		20.11.18E
G-PSUE	CFM Shadow Series CD	K 139	01.04.99
	G-MYAA D A Crosbie (Little Cornard, Sudbury)		19.05.03P
	(NF 09.10.15)		
G-PSUK	Thruster T600N 450	0044-T600N-101	26.05.04
	K Edwards Balado		29.08.18P
	Badged 'Sprint'		
G-PTAG	Europa Aviation Europa	337	14.12.98
	R C Harrison Wickenby		11.04.18P
	Built by R C Harrison – project PFA 247-13121;		
	tricycle u/c		
G-PTAR	Best Off Skyranger 912S(1)	UK/687	06.07.06
	P Vergette Lindens Farm, Riby		10.12.18P
	Built by A C Aiken – project BMAA/HB/509		
G-PTBA	Boeing Stearman A75 Kaydet (*PT-13B*)	75-0045	13.05.16
	N731, USAAC 37-0089		
	Mach Eight 3 Ltd Gloucestershire		25.08.18E
	As '3789:466' in USAAC c/s		
G-PTCC	Piper PA-28RT-201 Arrow IV	28R-7918145	14.02.12
	EI-SKU, G-BXYS, PH-SBS, N29561		
	B O'Donnchu Cork, RoI		15.12.17E
G-PTDP	Bücker Bü.133C Jungmeister	1018	31.08.05
	G-AEZX, N5A, PP-TDP		
	M S Pettit & T J Reeve (Oaklands Farm, Stonesfield)		
	(NF 20.07.18)		
G-PTEA	Piper PA-46-350P Malibu Mirage	4636327	11.12.09
	OY-TPJ, PH-RHB, N350PM, N5349V		
	K Buchberger Guernsey		26.03.18E
G-PTEK	Van's RV-9A	90562	11.11.15
	P K Eckersley Blackpool		09.08.19P
	Built by P K Eckersley – project PFA 320-13934		
G-PTFE	BRM Bristell NG5 Speed Wing	079	11.04.14
	P R Thody Croft Farm, Defford		16.09.19P
	Built by P R Thody – project LAA 385-15245;		
	tricycle u/c		

G-PTIX	Supermarine 361 Spitfire IX	CBAF IX.2922	29.01.18
	G-BYDE, Soviet AF, PT879		
	P A Teichman t/a Hangar 11 Collection North Weald		
	On restoration 11.18 as 'PT879' (NF 29.01.18)		
G-PTOO	Bell 206L-4 LongRanger IV	52132	24.02.10
	N340AJ, N98867, 5Y-BKR, C-FVSU, (N98867)		
	Helicompany Ltd Perth		06.09.19E
G-PTRE	SOCATA TB-20 Trinidad	762	14.06.88
	G-BNKU W M Chesson Rochester		02.07.18E
G-PTTA	Reims/Cessna F152 II	F15201904	22.12.16
	G-BJVT North Weald Flight Training Ltd North Weald		09.01.19E
G-PTTB	Reims/Cessna F152 II	F15201908	18.01.17
	G-WACT, G-BKFT		
	Ulster Flying Club (1961) Ltd Newtownards		20.02.19E
G-PTTE	Cessna 152	15282516	12.06.18
	G-BXTB, OH-CMS, N69151		
	NAL Asset Management Ltd Dunkeswell		20.01.20E
G-PTTS	Pitts S-2A	2179	09.05.03
	N555JR, N32TP, N31450 B & J Voce Leicester		10.04.18E
	Built by Aerotek Inc		
G-PTXC	SOCATA TBM-700C2	321	08.11.18
	D-FLEX, F-HBCF, N700ZB		
	Coelus Flight Services Ltd Biggin Hill		11.09.19E
G-PUBS[M]	Colt Beer Glass 56 SS HAB	037	07.06.79
	Cancelled 01.12.95 by CAA		30.11.90
	With British Balloon Museum & Library, Newbury		
G-PUDL	Piper PA-18-150 Super Cub	18-7292	24.02.98
	SE-CSE C M Edwards Rochester		03.03.17E
	(IE 30.06.17)		
G-PUDS	Europa Aviation Europa	253	09.10.97
	C R A Spirit Goodwood		29.08.18P
	Built by I Milner – project PFA 247-12999; tricycle u/c		
G-PUFF	Thunder Ax7-77 Bolt	165	17.11.78
	C A Gould tr The Intervarsity Balloon Club		
	Ipswich 'Puffin II'		26.07.14E
	(NF 11.01.17)		
G-PUGS	Cessna 182H Skylane	18256480	15.05.00
	SE-ESM, N8380S		
	D Waterhouse Manchester Barton		20.04.18E
G-PUGZ	P&M Quik GT450	8639	11.03.13
	A E Hill Longacre Farm, Sandy		28.02.18P
G-PUKA	Avtech Jabiru J400	0130	11.09.03
	D P Harris New Farm, Felton		09.03.17P
	Built by D P Harris – project PFA 325-14120		
G-PULA	Dassault Falcon 2000LX	269	17.09.15
	F-HLXS, F-WWGZ		
	Centreline AV Ltd t/a Centreline Guernsey		05.05.18E
G-PULR	Pitts S-2AE	K0054	18.01.10
	Ayre to Air (Nevenby, Lincoln)		
	Built by A Ayre – project LAA 009A-14904		
	(NF 20.05.15)		
G-PUMB	Aérospatiale AS.332L Super Puma	2075	31.01.83
	VH-LYS, C-GJEB, G-PUMB		
	CHC Scotia Ltd Rzeszow, Poland		15.05.11E
	(IE 02.05.18)		
G-PUMM	Eurocopter AS.332L2 Super Puma II	2477	29.07.98
	LN-OHM, PR-HPG, G-PUMM, F-WWOO		
	Element Capital Corp Aberdeen Int'l		17.06.17E
G-PUMN	Eurocopter AS.332L2 Super Puma II	2484	16.07.99
	LN-OHF CHC Scotia Ltd Rzeszow, Poland		26.07.17E
G-PUMO	Eurocopter AS.332L2 Super Puma II	2467	30.09.98
	Element Capital Corp Aberdeen Int'l		24.10.16E
	Stored 03.15 less rotors (NF 09.09.16)		
G-PUMS	Eurocopter AS.332L2 Super Puma II	2504	18.08.00
	Element Capital Corp		
	Boundary Bay, British Columbia, Canada		28.01.15E
	(NF 09.09.16)		
G-PUNK	Thunder Ax8-105	1719	28.03.90
	S C Kinsey Ebberley, Torrington		15.05.99
	(NF 07.07.16)		
G-PUNT	Robinson R44 Raven II	12979	19.03.10
	R D Cameron Crendle Court, Purse Caundle		17.06.19E
G-PUPP	Beagle B.121 Pup Series 2	B121-174	23.11.93
	G-BASD, (SE-FOG), G-BASD M G Evans Swansea		04.01.18E
G-PUPY	Europa Aviation Europa XS	499	10.09.02
	D A Cameron Oban		24.07.18P
	Built by D A Cameron, C Flett & P G Johnson		
	– project PFA 247-13694; tri-Gear		
G-PURE	Cameron Can-70	1913	18.01.89
	T Read & N Smith t/a Mobberley Balloon Collection		
	Knutsford & Goole 'Draught Guinness'		10.12.93A
	(NF 21.03.14)		
G-PURL	Piper PA-32R-301 Saratoga II HP	3213078	30.11.05
	N620PL, N92434 A P H & E Hay North Weald		08.03.19E
G-PURP	Lindstrand LBL 90A	1387	07.11.11
	C & P Mackley Bradley Stoke, Bristol		03.05.18E
G-PURR	Grumman American AA-5A Cheetah	AA5A-0794	22.02.82
	G-BJDN, N26893		
	P Constantinou tr G-PURR Owners Group Elstree		22.08.19E
G-PURS	RotorWay Exec	3827	19.01.90
	(EI-...), G-PURS D & J Parke Street Farm, Takeley		02.11.16P
	Built by J E Houseman; stored 09.17 (IE 24.04.17)		
G-PUSA	Gefa-Flug AS105GD HA Airship	0052	17.07.09
	Skyking Aviation Ltd Bristol BS1 'Greenpeace'		13.10.17E
	Gondola officially registered as c/n 26		
	ex HB-QIP: airship is c/n 52		
G-PUSH	Rutan Long-EZ	xxxx	11.07.83
	J P Watts (Grimston, King's Lynn)		
	Built by E G Peterson – project PFA 074A-10740		
	(NF 18.05.18)		
G-PUSI	Cessna T303 Crusader	T30300273	26.07.88
	N3479V S Devin & C Smith Kilrush, RoI		30.05.18E
G-PUSS	Cameron N-77	1577	06.10.87
	B D Close Templecombe		26.10.14E
G-PUTT	Cameron Golfball-76	2060	08.08.95
	LX-KIK D P Hopkins t/a Lakeside Lodge Golf Centre		
	Pidley, Huntingdon 'Lakeside Lodge'		
	(NF 06.10.15)		
G-PVBF	Lindstrand LBL 260S	504	07.04.98
	Airxcite Ltd t/a Virgin Balloon Flights Stafford Park,		
	Telford 'Virgin'		15.02.07E
	(NF 15.09.14)		
G-PVCV	Robin DR.400-140 Earl	919	19.10.06
	F-BVCV Bustard Flying Club Ltd		
	MoD Boscombe Down		12.12.18E
G-PVET	de Havilland DHC-1 Chipmunk 22	C1/0017	23.05.97
	WB565 Connect Properties Ltd Rendcomb		16.03.18P
	As 'WB565:X' in AAC c/s		
G-PVIP	Cessna 421C Golden Eagle	421C0118	30.06.04
	G-RLMC, PH-SBI, D-IMAZ, I-CCNN, N3849C		
	Passion 4 Autos Ltd (Harrow)		22.01.07E
	Parts noted 05.16 Foxbury Road, Ringwood		
	(NF 02.02.15)		
G-PVSS	P&M Quik GT450	8302	08.08.07
	A J Callaghan Northrepps		21.08.19P
G-PWAL	Aeropro EuroFOX 912(1)	44314	18.07.14
	P Walton Finmere		14.06.18P
	Built by P Walton – project BMAA/HB/655; tricycle u/c		
G-PWBE	de Havilland DH.82A Tiger Moth	LES1	23.07.99
	VH-KRW K M Perkins Headcorn		26.05.18E
	Built by Lawrence Engineering & Sales Proprietary		
	Ltd, Camden, NSW, Australia ex RAAF spares;		
	operated by Aero Legends		
G-PWEF	Magni M24C Orion	24181754	04.12.18
	P W D Walshe (Ryde)		17.12.19P
G-PWUL	Van's RV-6	22954	03.07.02
	A Fergusson tr The G-PWUL Group Kilkerran		09.07.19P
	Built by P C Woolley – project PFA 181-12773		
G-PXMI	Agusta A109C	7654	06.08.18
	G-BWNZ Brentwood Aviation Services Ltd (Clitheroe)		17.12.18E
G-PYAK	Yakovlev Yak-18T	12-35	20.10.15
	HA-YAB, RA-44777 P S Beardsell Fairoaks		04.01.18R
G-PYNE	Thruster T600N 450	0072-T600N-067	27.08.02
	R Derham Shipmeadow		14.05.17P
	Badged 'Sprint' (IE 06.10.17)		
G-PYPE	Van's RV-7	72229	12.09.06
	L & R Pyper Newtownards		16.04.19P
	Built by R Pyper – project PFA 323-14398		

G-PYRO Cameron N-65   567   08.01.80
A C Booth   Bristol BS4   'Pyromania'   16.07.18E

G-PZAS Schleicher ASW 27-18 (ASG 29)   29044   10.03.09
(BGA 5342)
A P C Sampson   Dunstable Downs   'A5'   24.11.18E

G-PZPZ P&M Pegasus Quantum 15-912   7370   07.11.12
J Urrutia   Little Trostrey Farm, Kemeys Commander   06.06.17P
Quoted s/n 8636 relates to Wing: Trike s/n 7370
is ex G-MZSC; original wing of G-MZSC
stolen in France in 2012; new wing ordered
ex P&M & previous trike re-used

G-RAAA – G-RZZZ

G-RAAF Supermarine 359 Spitfire VIII   6S-196056   22.04.09
RAAF A58-328, JF872
Composite Mast Engineering & Technology Ltd   (Bacup)
Built by Chattis Hill 1943 (NF 18.02.19)

G-RAAM Piper PA-28-161 Warrior II   28-8016276   13.08.13
G-BRSE, N8163R   A S Bamrah   Blackbushe   07.09.19E

G-RAAY Taylor JT.1 Monoplane   xxxx   13.03.13
G-BEHM   R Bowden   (Exeter)
Built by H McGovern – project PFA 1420 (NF 18.07.17)

G-RABS Alpi Pioneer 300   196.S.UK   31.08.06
J Mullen   Strathaven   13.03.18P
Built by J Mullen – project PFA 330-14563

G-RACK Comco Ikarus C42 FB80   0804-6954   02.12.13
G-CFIY   G P Burns   Middle Stoke, Isle of Grain   04.11.19P
Assembled Aerosport Ltd

G-RACO Piper PA-28R-200 Cherokee Arrow II   28R-7535300   12.09.91
N1498X   J R Wright   Jersey   10.05.18E
Rebuilt 2018 with wings from EC-FKR

G-RACR Ultramagic M-65C   65/143   08.04.05
R A Vale   Kidderminster   31.03.17E

G-RACY Cessna 182S Skylane   18280588   19.10.99
N7273Y   C M Bishop & N K Wright   Cambridge   30.01.19E

G-RADA Soko P-2 Kraguj   024   25.09.96
Yugoslav AF 30140
Airfield Aviation Ltd   Morgansfield, Fishburn   05.09.05P
Stored 01.18 as '30140' (IE 29.08.17)

G-RADI Piper PA-28-181 Archer II   28-8690002   06.05.98
N2582X, N9608N   The Sherwood Flying Club Ltd
Nottingham City   29.08.19E

G-RADR Douglas AD-4NA Skyraider   7722   30.10.03
G-RAID, F-AZED, Gabon AF TR-KMM, French AF 42,
Bu.126922   Orion Enterprises Ltd   North Weald   19.06.17P
SFERMA c/n 42; as '126922:H-503' in
US Navy c/s; noted 11.18

G-RAEF Schempp-Hirth SHK-1   39   20.06.08
BGA 1544/CGZ
R A Earnshaw-Fretwell   Keevil   'CGZ'   31.07.17E

G-RAEM Rutan Long-EZ   xxxx   15.03.82
W M Burnett t/a Cambridge Business Travel   Tatenhill   06.11.19P
Built by G F H Singleton – project PFA 074A-10638;
for sale 11.18

G-RAES Boeing 777-236ER   27491   10.06.97
(G-ZZZN)   British Airways PLC   London Heathrow   09.06.19E
Line No: 76

G-RAFA Grob G115A   8081   02.03.89
D-EGVV   K J Peacock & S F Turner   Earls Colne   16.02.18E

G-RAFB Grob G115A   8079   02.03.89
D-EGVV   The Royal Air Force College Flying Club Ltd
RAF Barkston Heath   05.09.18E

G-RAFC Robin R2112 Alpha   192   19.05.80
J E Churchill tr RAF Charlie Group   Conington   30.07.16E

G-RAFE Thunder Ax7-77 Bolt   176   18.12.78
L P Hooper tr Giraffe Balloon Syndicate
Oswestry   'Giraffe'   16.07.12E
(IE 06.06.17)

G-RAFG Slingsby T67C Firefly   2076   02.11.89
R C P Brookhouse   RAF Benson   02.06.18E
Operated by Aeros Stratford upon Avon

G-RAFH Thruster T600N 450   0032-T600N-063   10.04.02
J W Sandars tr G-RAFH Group
Park Hall Farm, Mapperley   29.11.17P
Badged 'Sprint'

G-RAFIᴹ Hunting-Percival P.84 Jet Provost T.4   PAC/W/17641   18.12.92
8458M, XP672   Cancelled 22.11.10 as PWFU   11.03.00
St Athan
With South Wales Aircraft Museum as 'XP672:03' in RAF c/s

G-RAFK Beech B200 Super King Air   BB-1830   12.12.03
ZK451, G-RAFK, N50130
RVL Aviation Ltd   East Midlands   11.12.07E
(IE 14.09.18)

G-RAFL Beech B200 Super King Air   19.03.04
ZK452, G-RAFL, N5032K
RVL Aviation Ltd   East Midlands   05.12.19E

G-RAFR Best Off Skyranger 912S(1)   SKR0404487   08.10.04
M Ellis   Low Hill Farm, North Moor, Messingham   10.09.18P
Built by P Waters – project BMAA/HB/410

G-RAFS Thruster T600N 450   0041-T600N-097   05.04.04
M C Law & D J Redding tr Hoveton Flying Group
Felthorpe   24.10.18P
Badged 'Sprint'

G-RAFT Rutan Long-EZ   xxxx   09.08.82
H M & S Roberts   Turweston   'A Craft of Graft'   15.10.16P
Built by D G Foreman – project PFA 074A-10734;
noted 15.02.19 with no marks

G-RAFV Avid Speed Wing   xxxx   28.07.04
G-MOTT   M K Slaughter tr Fox Victor Group
The Firs Farm, Leckhampstead   30.04.18P
Built by M D Ott – project PFA 189-11738

G-RAFW Mooney M.20E Super 21   805   14.11.84
G-ATHW, N5881Q
Vinola (Knitwear) Manufacturing Co Ltd   Leicester   09.05.18E

G-RAFY Best Off Skyranger Swift 912S(1)   UK/757   07.03.07
A P Portsmouth   Eshott   26.04.18P
Built by J Kumela & P Waters – project BMAA/HB/523

G-RAFZ Rotary Air Force RAF 2000 GTX-SE   h2-97-8-316   07.05.02
V G Freke   (Eynsham)
Built by J W Pavitt – project PFA G/13-1295 (NF 25.08.15)

G-RAGE Wilson Cassutt IIIM   xxxx   17.10.06
G-BEUN   R S Grace   Bentwaters   07.07.97P
Built by M S Crossley – project PFA 034-10241
(NF 14.03.18)

G-RAGS Pietenpol Air Camper   xxxx   08.06.94
S H Leonard   Shobdon   11.07.18P
Built by R F Billington – project PFA 047-11551

G-RAGT Piper PA-32-301FT 6X   3232038   03.06.05
N3116F   Oxhill Aviation Ltd   Wellesbourne Mountford   24.07.18E

G-RAHA Schempp-Hirth Standard Cirrus   111   10.03.17
(BGA 5924), D-0318   G C Stallard   Lasham   'M11'   03.04.18E

G-RAIR Schleicher ASH 25   25095   31.10.07
BGA 3623   D B Walker tr ASH 25 G-RAIR Grp
(Aylesford)   '942'   31.05.18E

G-RAJA Raj Hamsa X'Air 582(2)   456   13.09.99
C Roadnight   Ince   23.09.18P
Built by S R Roberts – project BMAA/HB/118

G-RALF RotorWay Exec 162F   6243   24.11.11
G-BZOM, N767SG
I C Bedford   Marsh Farm, Skegness   30.08.13P
Built by G & S Waugh (IE 21.11.14)

G-RAMI Bell 206B-3 JetRanger III   2955   18.10.90
N1080N   M D Thorpe t/a Yorkshire Helicopters
Leeds Heliport   05.09.16E
Stored 09.17

G-RAML Piper PA-34-220T Seneca III   34-8233045   16.05.17
G-BWDT, PH-TWI, G-BKHS, N8472H
P d'Costa   Redhill   15.02.20E

G-RAMP Piper J-3C-65 Cub   6658   05.07.90
N35941, NC35941
J A Gibson   Watchford Farm, Yarcombe   24.04.18P

G-RAMS Piper PA-32R-301 Saratoga SP   32R-8013134   17.10.80
N8271Z   Mike Sierra LLP   Retford Gamston   15.03.18E

G-RANE	Bombardier CL-600-2B16 Challenger 605	5904	28.02.19	
	OE-IXI, G-LCDH, C-GOVJ			
	Saxonair Charter Ltd Norwich Int'l		19.12.19E	
	(IE 08.02.19)			
G-RANN	Beech B300 Super King Air 350	FL-899	09.04.14	
	N5099D Flycorp Aviation LLP Bournemouth		10.04.18E	
G-RANZ	Rans S-10 Sakota	xxxx	02.11.89	
	Cancelled 22.09.05 by CAA		27.06.03	
	Maillen, Namur, Belgium *Built by B A Phillips*			
	– project PFA 194-11536; stored 05.18			
G-RAPH	Cameron O-77	1673	21.03.88	
	P A Sweatman Coventry *'Walsall Litho'*		13.07.12E	
	(IE 12.06.15)			
G-RAPL	Schempp-Hirth Duo Discus XLT	270	28.09.15	
	(BGA 5837) C R Lewis tr G-RAPL Duo XLT Syndicate			
	Lasham *'D66'*		21.11.18E	
G-RARA	AutoGyro MTOsport	xxxx	26.03.13	
	Gyro School Pro Ltd Rochester		04.04.18P	
	Assembled Rotorsport UK as c/n RSUK/MTOS/048			
G-RARB	Cessna 172N Skyhawk II	17272334	04.06.96	
	G-BOII, N4702D			
	H C R Page Damyns Hall, Upminster		14.10.18E	
G-RASA	Diamond DA.42 Twin Star	42.144	30.06.06	
	OE-VPY Southern Sailplanes Ltd Membury		11.10.19E	
G-RASC	Evans VP-2	V2-1178	14.12.78	
	R F Powell (Maenan, Llanrwst)		14.12.06P	
	Built by R A Codling – project PFA 063-10422			
	(NF 21.09.15)			
G-RASH	Grob G109B	6217	24.06.04	
	OH-686 D G Coats & D F Tait tr G-RASH Syndicate			
	Portmoak		09.03.18E	
G-RATC	Van's RV-4	4411	30.05.06	
	P Johnson & A F Ratcliffe Morgansfield, Fishburn			
	Built by A F Ratcliffe – project PFA 181-13996			
	(NF 23.08.18)			
G-RATD	Van's RV-8	xxxx	07.08.09	
	J R Pike Kittyhawk Farm, Ripe		12.11.18P	
	Built by J R Pike – project PFA 303-13839			
G-RATE	Gulfstream American AA-5A Cheetah	AA5A-0781	11.06.84	
	G-BIFF, (G-BIBR), N26879			
	A M Chester tr GRATE Flying Group Cranfield		13.03.18E	
	Operated by Billins Air Services			
G-RATH	RotorWay Exec 162F	6886	12.10.04	
	W H Cole Street Farm, Takeley		04.01.13P	
	Built by M S Cole; on rebuild by Southern Helicopters			
	2018; new tailboom 06.18 (NF 17.04.18)			
G-RATI	Reims/Cessna F172M	F17201311	22.12.05	
	G-PATI, G-WACZ, G-BCUK N F Collins Enstone		19.02.18E	
G-RATT	Aeropro EuroFOX 912(S)	41413	08.07.13	
	Rattlesden Gliding Club Ltd Rattlesden		09.04.19P	
	Built by D King – project LAA 376-15199;			
	tricycle u/c; glider-tug			
G-RATV	Piper PA-28RT-201T Turbo Arrow IV	28R-8431005	20.06.05	
	G-WILS, PH-DPD, N4330W			
	Tango Victor Ltd Fairoaks		08.05.18E	
G-RATZ	Europa Aviation Europa	237	16.06.95	
	W Goldsmith Morgansfield, Fishburn		23.08.18P	
	Built by R Muller – project PFA 247-12582; tailwheel u/c			
G-RAVE	Mainair Mercury 582/Southdown Raven X			
		SN2232/0219	22.12.98	
	G-MNZV M J Robbins (Dallington, Heathfield)		20.03.04P	
	Sailwing is ex G-MNCV (SN2000/0219) (NF 16.09.14)			
G-RAVN	Robinson R44 Raven	1022	23.03.01	
	Transair (UK) Ltd Brighton City		07.09.19E	
G-RAWS	RotorWay Exec 162F	6492/6978	14.11.00	
	R P Robinson & D D Saint Street Farm, Takeley			
	Built by B W Grindle			
G-RAYB	P&M Quik GT450	8237	19.02.07	
	R Blatchford Perranporth		13.03.18P	
G-RAYE[M]	Piper PA-32-260 Cherokee Six	32-460	30.05.96	
	G-ATTY, N11C Cancelled 17.06.03 & 02.06.08 as PWFU		27.09.08	
	Fuselage only			
	With South Yorkshire Aircraft Museum, Doncaster			

G-RAYH	Zenair CH.701UL	7 9117	07.07.03	
	R Horner Staindrop		17.06.19P	
	Built by R Horner – project PFA 187-13583			
G-RAYM	SOCATA TB-20 Trinidad GT	2097	04.07.14	
	PH-KMF, N75MF, PH-KMF, F-OJBM			
	West Wales Airport Ltd Gloucestershire		06.06.18E	
G-RAYO	Lindstrand LBL 90A	949	13.10.03	
	R Owen Standish, Wigan *'Cash Convertor'*		27.04.18E	
G-RAYS	Zenair CH.250 Zenith	xxxx	26.10.78	
	D-EEVT Cancelled 30.09.13 as destroyed		10.01.14	
	Shennington, Oxon *Built by R E Delves originally*			
	project PFA 024-10460, completed M J Malbon			
	as project PFA 113-10460; wreck for sale 05.14			
G-RAYY	Cirrus SR22	2921	18.04.08	
	N924SR Alquiler de Veleros SL			
	Madrid-Cuatro Vientos, Spain		15.06.18E	
G-RAYZ	Tecnam P2002-EA Sierra	190	05.02.07	
	R Wells Morgansfield, Fishburn		04.05.18P	
	Built by R Wells – project PFA 333-14567			
G-RAZI	SIAI Marchetti SF.260	102	10.07.18	
	D-ESIC, (D-EGCL), I-SIAW			
	P A Freeland (Horton, Northampton)			
	(IE 10.07.18)			
G-RAZY	Piper PA-28-181 Archer II	28-8090102	11.02.04	
	G-REXS, N8093Y T H Pemberton Hawarden		19.06.18E	
G-RAZZ	Maule MX-7-180 Super Rocket	11050C	10.11.04	
	N266MM, D-EOLW, N6118L			
	R Giles Bury Farm, High Easter		26.05.18E	
G-RBBB	Europa Aviation Europa	073	06.05.94	
	T J Hartwell Sackville Lodge Farm, Riseley		12.08.05P	
	Built by W M Goodburn & I H Macleod – project			
	PFA 247-12664; tailwheel u/c (NF 10.10.14)			
G-RBCA	Agusta A109A II	7412	22.02.11	
	G-TBGL, G-VJCB, G-BOUA			
	R Bauer Trebrown, Liskeard		28.06.17E	
	Stored Trebrown, Liskeard 10.18			
G-RBCT	Schempp-Hirth Ventus-2cT	3/10	27.07.07	
	BGA 4505, N200EE, D-KHIA			
	J D Huband & M J Weston Aston Down *'RB'*		17.11.18E	
G-RBHF	Leonardo AW139	31750	07.05.18	
	I-EASZ Starspeed Ltd Fairoaks		06.05.19E	
G-RBIL	Westland SA.341D Gazelle HT.3	1199	13.12.13	
	G-CGJY, XW902			
	R B Illingworth Bourne Park, Hurstbourne Tarrant		28.08.18P	
G-RBLU	Piper PA-28RT-201 Arrow IV	28R-8018021	02.02.17	
	I-ACLU, N35720			
	C & M Busoni (Montecatini Terme, Italy)			
	(IE 22.03.17)			
G-RBMV	Cameron O-31	4658	27.07.99	
	P D Griffiths Totton, Southampton		21.08.18E	
G-RBOS	Colt AS-105 HA Airship	390	09.02.82	
	Cancelled 03.04.97 by CAA		06.03.87	
	Wroughton *In Science Museum store 2013*			
G-RBOW	Thunder Ax7-65	1439	24.04.89	
	R S McDonald Burcott, Leighton Buzzard		30.08.18E	
G-RBRI	Robinson R44 Raven II	11963	15.12.14	
	G-RWGS Helicentre Aviation Ltd Leicester		29.11.18E	
G-RBSN	Comco Ikarus C42 FB80	0407-6610	23.08.04	
	M & P B Robinson Sutton Meadows		16.01.18P	
	Assembled Fly Buy Ultralights Ltd			
G-RBWW	BRM Bristell NG5 Speed Wing	xxxx	27.11.17	
	R J Baker & W Woods Wellesbourne Mountford		27.09.19P	
	Built by R J Baker & W Woods – project LAA 385-15456			
G-RCAV	Bombardier CL-600-2B16 Challenger 604	5526	19.12.12	
	I-WISH, N604CB, C-GLYH			
	Gama Aviation (UK) Ltd Farnborough		20.11.18E	
G-RCED	Rockwell Commander 114	14241	19.06.92	
	VR-CED, N4917W			
	D & D J Pitman Newquay Cornwall		24.07.18E	
G-RCFC	Hawker 900XP	HA-0164	18.04.18	
	N100ZT, N835ZP, N964XP			
	Saxonair Charter Ltd Norwich Int'l			

G

G-RCHE Cessna 182T Skylane 18282059 12.01.15
G-PTRI, N61910
R S Bentley   Main Hall Farm, Conington 26.10.18E

G-RCHL P&M Quik GT450 8592 16.08.11
R M Broughton   Rossall Field, Cockerham 21.05.18P

G-RCHY Evektor EV-97 Eurostar 2003-1906 30.03.04
N McKenzie   (Cumwhinton, Carlisle) 18.12.18P
Built by N McKenzie – project PFA 315-14187

G-RCIE Piper J-3C-65 Cub 7278 20.09.17
G-CCOX, EI-CCH, N38801. NC38801
R P Marks   Dunkeswell

G-RCKT Harmon Rocket II HARMON 109 10.10.03
K E Armstrong   White Fen Farm, Benwick 25.06.18P
Built by K E Armstrong – project PFA 314-13536;
modified Van's RV-4

G-RCMC Murphy Renegade 912 485 01.02.93
R S Mott tr The Renegades   (Hempton, Banbury) 13.03.18P
Built by B D Godden – project PFA 188-12483

G-RCMF Cameron V-77 1618 23.11.87
J M Percival   Burton-on-the-Wolds, Loughborough
'Mouldform' 02.10.09E
(NF 29.11.16)

G-RCMP Piper PA-28RT-201T Turbo Arrow IV 28R-8231043 16.06.15
EC-LFY, D-EHZW, N81852
Southeast Air Ltd   Blackbushe 15.03.18E

G-RCNB Eurocopter EC120B Colibri 1333 20.03.03
F-WQPX   D Kelly   (Frosses, Co Donegal, RoI) 13.04.19E

G-RCOH Cameron Cube-105 11681 04.09.12
A M Holly   Breadstone, Berkeley   'Ricoh' 31.05.18E

G-RCRC P&M Pegasus Quik 8252 09.03.07
R M Brown   Battleby Farm, Luncarty 16.03.18P

G-RCSR de Havilland DH.88 Comet replica KF1995 02.11.11
K Fern   Derby
Replica of G-ACSR c/n 1995; fuselage stored 12.17
(NF 09.10.15)

G-RCST Avtech Jabiru J430 273 18.04.06
P M Jones   Napps Field, Billericay 06.06.19P
Built by G R Cotterell – project PFA 336-14513

G-RCUB Piper PA-18 Super Cub 95 (L-18C) 18-1980 13.12.12
G-BPJH, I-EICA/E.I.59, Italian Military MM52-2380,
52-2380   D Bennett tr Super Cub Group
Baileys Farm, Long Crendon 26.11.14P
On rebuild 11.13 using major parts of G-BPJH
(NF 06.08.18)

G-RCUS Schempp-Hirth Arcus T 28 16.12.11
(BGA 5739)   D Briggs & M J Weston
tr Arcus G-RCUS Syndicate   Aston Down   'CUS' 26.03.18E

G-RDAD Reality Escapade ULP(1) AW.ESC.003 13.05.11
F Overall   Whitehall Farm, Wethersfield
Built by R W Burge – project BMAA/HB/615;
kit & frame built AirWeld (NF 09.06.17)

G-RDAS Reims/Cessna F172M F17200999 19.02.14
PH-DAS, 5B-CBW, (D-EGBX)
J Martin   Lognes-Emerainville, France 23.04.18E

G-RDAY Van's RV-9 91624 25.07.11
R M Day   (Up Hatherley, Cheltenham)
Built by R M Day – project PFA 320-14733
(NF 11.08.15)

G-RDCO Avtech Jabiru J430 xxxx 15.04.03
A H & F A Macaskill   Gloucestershire 07.10.16P
Built by J M Record – project PFA 325-14052
(IE 01.12.16)

G-RDDM Cessna 182T Skylane 18282387 04.02.16
N387D   Optum Global Ltd   Retford Gamston 01.01.19E

G-RDEN Cameron Z-105 11879 09.03.15
Hillmount Bangor Ltd   Bangor 29.05.18E

G-RDFX Aero AT-3 AT3-009 08.07.10
M W Richardson   Enstone 23.03.18P
Built by B Wilson – project PFA 327-14295

G-RDHS Europa Aviation Europa XS 549 31.05.02
R D H Spencer   Rayne Hall Farm, Rayne 28.06.17P
Built by R D H Spencer – project PFA 247-13887;
tricycle u/c

G-RDNS Rans S-6-S-116 Super Six 0404 1566-S 02.11.04
S R Green   Chase Farm, Chipping Sodbury 30.05.19P
Built by G J McDill – project PFA 204-14307;
tailwheel u/c

G-RDNY AutoGyro Cavalon V00165 20.05.13
C Rodney   Holmbeck Farm, Burcott 29.03.19P
Assembled Rotorsport UK as c/n RSUK/CVLN/004;
original frame c/n V00107 was damaged 03.14 &
rebuilt with c/n V00165

G-RDPH P&M QuikR 8463 18.08.09
R S Partridge-Hicks   Little Haugh Hall, Norton 10.09.17P

G-RDRL Reaction Pegasus PH200PJ 00001 05.05.16
N246PJ   Genesis Aerotech Ltd   Newtownards
Originally built by Pegasus Helicopters Inc;
stored 06.17 (NF 23.06.17)

G-READ Colt 77A 1158 16.11.87
EI-BYI, G-READ   C A Gould tr The Intervarsity
Balloon Club   Ipswich   'Sunday Express' 07.07.18E
Carries 'EI-BYI' on canopy

G-REAF Avtech Jabiru J400 288 05.01.10
R E Rayner   Glebe Farm, Kings Ripton 07.12.18P
Built by R E Afia – project PFA 325-14502

G-REAR (2) Lindstrand LBL 69X 977 12.02.04
A M Holly   Breadstone, Berkeley   'Sloggi' 19.09.13E
New envelope fitted c.2006 c/n unknown (IE 07.10.17)

G-REAS Van's RV-6A xxxx 16.08.94
T J Smith   Sleap 17.08.18P
Built by D W Reast – project PFA 181-12188

G-REBB Murphy Rebel 376R 23.08.05
N13BN   M Stow   Byermoor Farm, Burnopfield 17.09.18P
Built by W W Newkirk

G-RECL Cameron Z-105 12239 07.09.18
A J Thompson   Bristol BS10   'Ben's Tiles' 06.09.19E

G-RECW Piper PA-28-181 Archer II 28-8090257 13.09.16
G-BOBZ, N81671   R E C Washington   Blackbushe
'Julie – The Spirit of BCAL' 12.02.18E
British Caledonian c/s

G-REDC Cyclone Pegasus Quantum 15-912 7572 30.09.99
S Houghton   Northrepps 16.08.18P

G-REDF Eurocopter AS.365N3 Dauphin 2 6884 22.10.09
D-HAVU, G-REDF   Babcock Mission Critical
Services Offshore Ltd   Blackpool 23.02.18E

G-REDJ Eurocopter AS.332L2 Super Puma II 2608 19.05.04
F-WWOJ   Babcock Mission Critical Services
Leasing Ltd   Humberside 20.05.18E
Stored 09.16

G-REDN Eurocopter AS.332L2 Super Puma II 2616 20.08.04
F-WQDH   Babcock Mission Critical Services
Leasing Ltd   Humberside 18.08.18E
Stored 09.16

G-REDO Eurocopter AS.332L2 Super Puma II 2622 12.09.05
F-WWOH   Babcock Mission Critical Services
Leasing Ltd   Humberside 15.09.18E
Stored 09.16

G-REDP Eurocopter AS.332L2 Super Puma II 2634 17.11.05
F-WWOB   Babcock Mission Critical Services
Leasing Ltd   Humberside 12.12.18E
Stored 09.16

G-REDR Eurocopter EC225 LP Super Puma 2699 27.06.08
Babcock Mission Critical Services Leasing Ltd
Humberside 26.06.18E
Stored 09.16

G-REDT Eurocopter EC225 LP Super Puma 2701 04.09.08
Babcock Mission Critical Services Leasing Ltd
Humberside 02.09.18E
Stored 09.16

G-REDU Eurocopter EC225LP Super Puma 2690 23.05.08
Cancelled 26.02.09 as PWFU 22.05.09
Cranfield   Wreck used for training by AAIB 05.17

G-REDX Experimental Aviation Berkut 002 27.01.95
G V Waters   Tibenham 14.06.18P
Built by G V Waters – project PFA 252-12481

G-REDZ Thruster T600T 450 0037-T600N-091 05.08.03
N S Dell   (Plymouth) 24.05.17P

G-REEC	Sequoia F.8L Falco	654	02.07.96
	LN-LCA　K J E Augustinus　(Boechout, Belgium)		28.08.14P
	Built by B Eriksen; incurred extensive damage		
	near Lewes 24.08.14 (NF 07.01.15)		
G-REED	Mainair Blade 912S	1282-0501-7-W1077	11.06.01
	D J Kaye　Darley Moor		21.04.18P
G-REEF	Mainair Blade	1285-0501-7-W1080	15.06.01
	B Skidmore　Rossall Field, Cockerham		02.07.18P
G-REEM	Aérospatiale AS.355F1 Ecureuil 2	5175	09.03.98
	G-EMAN, G-WEKR, G-CHLA, N818RL, C-FLXH,		
	N818RL, N818R, N5798U　Heliking Ltd　Lasham		27.06.18E
G-REER	Centrair 101A Pégase	101033	15.10.07
	BGA3593, F-CFRZ		
	R L Howorth & G C Stinchcombe　Talgarth　*'FWX'*		28.02.19E
G-REES	Jodel D.140C Mousquetaire III	156	23.04.80
	F-BMFR　C C Rea tr G-REES Flying Group		
	Sheepcote Farm, Severn Stoke		07.12.18P
	Built by Société Aéronautique Normande		
G-REEV	Robinson R44 Clipper II	12448	03.11.15
	D-HIAG　SNG Aviation Ltd		
	Palma-Son Bonet, Mallorca, Spain		09.04.19E
G-REGC	Zenair CH.601XLSA Zodiac	6-7087	03.09.08
	G P Couttie　Perth		03.05.18P
	Built by G P Couttie – project LAA 162B-14784		
G-REGJ	Robinson R44 Raven II	10235	20.06.17
	G-OPTF　HQ Aviation Ltd　Denham		31.05.19E
G-REGZ	Aeroprakt A-22L Foxbat	A22L-188	01.10.13
	L Campbell　Perth		14.08.18P
	Built by M D Northwood – project LAA 317B-15230		
G-REJP	Europa Aviation Europa XS	582 T	31.08.06
	A Milner　Cambridge		11.05.18P
	Built by A Milner – project PFA 247-14086		
G-REKO	Solar Wings Pegasus Quasar IITC	SW-WQT-0467	14.11.01
	G-MWWA　M Carter　(Kilcock, Co Kildare, RoI)		04.07.15P
	Trike c/n SW-TQC-0073 (IE 03.08.16)		
G-RELL	Druine D.62B Condor	RAE/619	14.08.07
	G-OPJH, G-AVDW		
	M J Golder　Barton Ashes, Crawley Down		01.12.15P
	Built by Rollason Aircraft and Engines Ltd (NF 13.07.17)		
G-REMH	Bell 206B-3 JetRanger III	4626	16.09.08
	N65560, C-FMQK, (N65560)		
	Flightpath Ltd　Costock Heliport		08.11.18E
G-RENE	Murphy Renegade 912	xxxx	06.11.91
	Cancelled 04.10.06 sold in Thailand		03.05.06
	Old Sarum　*'Spirit of Adventure'*		
	Built by D Evans – project PFA 188-12030		
	Stored dismantled 08.15		
G-RENI	Kubícek BB30Z	936	17.07.12
	A M Holly　Breadstone, Berkeley　*'Renishaw'*		30.05.19E
G-RENTᴹ	Robinson R22 Beta	0758	17.03.88
	N2635M　Cancelled 11.12.03 as WFU		12.06.94
	Damaged Newtownards 30.09.92		
	With Ulster Aviation Society, Lisburn		
G-RESG	Dyn'Aéro MCR-01 Club	237	10.04.03
	R E S Greenwood　Wickhambrook		07.07.18P
	Built by R E S Greenwood – project PFA 301A-13994		
G-REST	Beech P35 Bonanza	D-7171	14.12.82
	G-ASFJ　C R E S Taylor　Lydd		27.11.18E
G-RESU	Airbus MBB BK117 D-2 (Eurocopter EC145 T2)		
		20052	23.10.15
	Babcock Mission Critical Services Onshore Ltd		
	Norwich Int'l		26.10.18E
	Operated by East Anglian Air Ambulance as		
	callsign 'Helimed 85'		
G-RETA	CASA 1-131E Jungmann Series 2000　2197		24.03.80
	Spanish AF E3B-305		
	A N R Houghton　Ranksborough Farm, Langham		10.04.12P
	As '4477:GD+EG' in Luftwaffe WWII silver c/s		
	(IE 20.02.17)		
G-REVE	Van's RV-6	xxxx	29.08.07
	S D Foster　Keevil		13.09.19P
	Built by R C Dyer, B P Smallcorn & J D Winder		
	– project PFA 181A-12945		

G-REVO	Best Off Skyranger 912(2)	UK/408	02.02.04
	H Murray & D A Wilson　Slieve Croob, Castlewellan		11.07.18P
	Built by R T Henry – project BMAA/HB/346		
G-REXA	Beech B200GT King Air	BY-339	05.12.18
	RVL Aviation Ltd　Jersey		12.12.19E
	Operated by for Isle-Fly Ltd		
G-REYE	Robinson R44 Raven	2390	05.03.15
	Redeye.com Ltd　Retford Gamston		23.04.18E
G-REYS	Bombardier CL-600-2B16 Challenger 604　5467		17.09.01
	N467RD, C-GLWX		
	Logically Applied Solutions Ltd　Farnborough		16.09.18E
G-RFAD	Sportavia-Putzer Fournier RF4D	4064	27.05.15
	N1700G, N389GS, N1700, D-KEDE		
	M P Dentith　Gloucestershire		
	(NF 27.05.15)		
G-RFCA	Tecnam P2008-JC	1061	22.04.16
	The Waddington Flying Club　RAF Scampton		
	'Royal Air Force flying clubs'		02.05.18E
G-RFCB	Tecnam P2008-JC	1076	22.05.17
	The Waddington Flying Club　RAF Waddington		02.07.18E
G-RFGB	Fournier RF6B-100 replica	xxxx	01.02.19
	R J Grimstead　Shipbourne Farm, Wisborough Green		
	Built by R J Grimstead – project LAA 410-15594		
	(NF 02.01.19)		
G-RFIO	Aeromot AMT-200 Super Ximango	200.048	06.03.95
	M D Evens　Kirkbride		14.08.18E
G-RFLO	Ultramagic M-105	105/213	20.11.15
	D J Groombridge & I J Martin t/a Flying Enterprises		
	Congresbury & Wotton-under-Edge　*'Raffaello'*		02.08.19E
G-RFLY	Extra EA.300/L	1284	22.07.08
	H B Sauer　Aschaffenburg, Germany		11.08.12E
	(IE 08.09.15)		
G-RFOX	Denney Kitfox Model 3	918	05.09.05
	D A Jackson　Sittles Farm, Alrewas		19.10.18P
	Built by L G G Faulkner & R Nicklin – project PFA 172-12029		
G-RFSB	Sportavia-Putzer RF5B Sperber	51045	02.12.88
	N55HC, D-KEAO		
	C P Prideaux tr G-RFSB Group　Saltby		15.08.19E
G-RGTS	Schempp-Hirth Discus b	140	29.11.07
	BGA 4301/HYB, D-4684		
	G R & L R Green　Wormingford　*'T5'*		31.03.18E
G-RGUS	Fairchild 24R-46A Argus III (*UC-61K-FA*)　1145		16.09.86
	(PH-...), G-RGUS, ZS-UJX (?), ZS-BAY, KK527, 44-83184		
	R Ellingworth　Sibson		15.05.19P
	Official p/i 'ZS-UJX' is incorrect; as 'KK527' in RAF c/s		
G-RGWY	Bell 206B-3 JetRanger III	3035	28.04.14
	G-OAGL, G-CORN, G-BHTR, N18098		
	Ridgway Aviation Ltd　(St Martins, Oswestry)		30.04.18E
G-RGZT	Cirrus SR20	1915	30.04.08
	(T7-xxx), G-RGZT, N195PG　M Presenti　Foligno, Italy		
	04.06.18E		
G-RHAM	Best Off Skyranger 582(1)	SKR0509647	09.01.06
	P Gibson & L Smart　Baxby Manor, Husthwaite		02.10.18P
	Built by G Eden – project BMAA/HB/482		
G-RHCB	Schweizer 269C-1 (*300CB*)	0036	20.03.98
	N201WL　P R Butler　(Vale Park, Evesham)		09.09.14E
	(NF 17.04.18)		
G-RHHT	Piper PA-32RT-300 Lance II	32R-7885190	03.07.78
	N36476　Cancelled 13.03.12 by CAA		02.06.11
	Tatenhill　*Spares use 03.13*		
G-RHML	Robinson R22 Beta	1735	10.12.14
	OH-HPV　C Lescure　(Compiegne, France)		22.03.18E
G-RHMS	Embraer EMB-135BJ Legacy	14501072	06.11.08
	PT-SEV　TAG Aviation (UK) Ltd　Farnborough		05.11.19E
G-RHOD	Just SuperSTOL	xxxx	31.03.17
	C S & K D Rhodes　Henstridge		
	Built by C S & K D Rhodes – project LAA 397-15470		
	(NF 31.03.17)		
G-RHOS	ICP MXP-740 Savannah VG Jabiru(1)　08-08-51-744		15.07.09
	J C Munro-Hunt　(Llanbister Road, Llandrindod Wells)		
	Built by J C Munro-Hunt – project BMAA/HB/591		
	(NF 29.11.16)		

G-RHYM Piper PA-31 Turbo Navajo B   31-815   24.04.02
G-BJLO, F-BTQG, (F-BTDV), N7428L
2 Excel Aviation Ltd   Sywell   30.01.19E

G-RHYS RotorWay Exec 90   5140   08.11.93
A K Voase   (Hornsea)   21.07.04P
Built by B Williams (NF 31.05.18)

G-RIAM SOCATA TB-10 Tobago   85   31.01.07
F-GFLA, F-ZVLA
R E Pozerskis tr TB10 Group   Bruntingthorpe   06.06.13E
(IE 30.10.17)

G-RIBA P&M Quik GT450   8217   21.11.06
R J Murphy   East Fortune   06.04.18P

G-RICO American General AG-5B Tiger   10162   14.05.99
N130U   P F Robertshaw tr Delta Lima Flying Group
Durham Tees Valley   14.12.18E

G-RICS Europa Aviation Europa   125   19.03.96
R G Allen t/a The Flying Property Doctor   29.08.18P
Built by R G Allen – project PFA 247-12747

G-RIDA Eurocopter AS.355NP Ecureuil 2   5754   07.12.07
F-WQDE
National Grid Electricity Transmission PLC   Oxford   23.10.18E

G-RIDB Bell 429   57105   14.06.13
OK-BHX, C-GTNQ(2), C-GAJN
National Grid Electricity Transmission PLC   Turweston   05.06.18E

G-RIDE Stephens Akro   111   10.08.78
N81AC, N55NM   R E Mitchell   Sleap   13.08.92P
Built by N Mardis (NF 13.10.17)

G-RIDG Van's RV-7   72233   04.01.06
M Holliday tr G RIDG Flying Group   North Weald   09.08.18P
Built by B A Ridgway – project PFA 323-14449

G-RIEF DG Flugzeugbau DG-1000T   10-85T23   19.07.06
BGA 5239-KNC   M C Costin tr EF Gliding Group
Husbands Bosworth   *'EF'*   30.05.18E

G-RIET Hoffmann H36 Dimona   36224   06.08.02
I-RIET   S Macfarlane tr Dimona Syndicate Group
Balado   08.06.18E

G-RIEV Rolladen-Schneider LS8-18   8039   04.01.08
BGA 4192/HTP, D-3175   R D Grieve   Tibenham   *'L58'*   30.01.19E

G-RIFD HpH Glasflügel 304 eS Shark   067-MS   21.12.16
(BGA 5925), OK-0067   D Griffiths   Lasham   *'DG5'*   13.03.18R

G-RIFN Mudry CAP 10B   276   06.06.96
R A J Spurrell & D E Starkey   White Waltham   06.10.19E

G-RIFO Schempp-Hirth Standard Cirrus 75-VTC 294   10.12.09
G-CKGT, BGA 5087/KGT, HA-4283
A Mura   Mugello, Italy   *'DM'*   24.09.17R
Built by Jastreb Fabrika Aviona I Jedrilica

G-RIFY Christen Eagle II   GN-1   10.09.08
N961GN   C I D H Garrison tr The G-RIFY Flying Group
Fenland   13.12.18P
Built by G Nelson

G-RIGB Thunder Ax7-77   1201   16.03.88
N J Bettin   Greatham, Liss   13.07.09E
(NF 11.03.16)

G-RIGH Piper PA-32R-301 Saratoga II HP   3246123   23.12.98
N41272, G-RIGH, N41272   A Brinkley   Fowlmere   10.09.18E
*Official type data 'PA-32R-301 Saratoga SP' is incorrect;
forced landed Faversham Road, Seasalter, Whitstable
28.08.17 & substantially damaged*

G-RIGS Piper Aerostar 601P   61P-0621-7963281   18.05.79
N8220J   G G Caravatti & P G Penati
Milano-Bresso, Italy   *'Marilyn'*   09.08.18E
Official type data 'PA-60-601P Aerostar' is incorrect

G-RIHN Dan Rihn DR.107 One Design   xxxx   18.05.04
P J Burgess   Wickenby   *'www.hatchedbrands.com'*   16.11.18P
Built by J P Brown – project PFA 264-14201

G-RIII Van's RV-3B   11374   19.12.08
J F Dowe   Tibenham
Built by R S Grace – project PFA 099-14341
(NF 22.04.16)

G-RIIV Van's RV-4   1340   20.02.08
N24EL   M R Overall   Whitehall Farm, Wethersfield   11.04.18P
Built by E C Lorr

G-RIKI Mainair Blade 912   1280-0401-7-W1075 29.08.01
C M Mackinnon   Strathaven   22.02.18P

G-RIKS Europa Aviation Europa XS   393   18.10.01
H Foster   Bournemouth   03.05.19P
Built by R Morris – project PFA 247-13329; tricycle u/c

G-RIKY Mainair Pegasus Quik   8007   17.12.03
S Clarke   (Burbage, Hinckley)   03.06.18P
Built by Mainair Sports Ltd

G-RILA Flight Design CTSW   06-08-11   29.09.06
(D-xxxx)   P A Mahony   (Plymouth)   17.09.18P
Assembled P&M Aviation Ltd as c/n 8182

G-RILY Monnett Sonerai IIL   xxxx   20.12.72
A Sharp   (Acton Bridge, Northwich)
Built by K D Riley – project PFA 015-10353
(NF 02.09.15)

G-RIMB Lindstrand LBL 105A   827   15.03.02
D Grimshaw   Leyland   *'Parkinsons of Leyland'*   27.04.18E

G-RIME Lindstrand LBL 25A Cloudhopper   954   09.12.03
N Ivison   Barton Seagrave, Kettering   *'Poppies'*   12.07.18E

G-RIMM Westland Wasp HAS.1   F9605   11.03.99
RNZN NZ3907, XT435   J M Heath   (Wadhurst)   13.12.18P
As 'XT435:430' in RN c/s

G-RINN Mainair Blade   1261-1000-7-W1055 02.01.01
P Hind   Headon Farm, Retford   30.04.18P

G-RINO   Thunder Ax7-77 HAB   975   24.06.87
Cancelled 11.07.18 as PWFU   05.03.94
Not Known   *Inflated Pidley 04.18*

G-RINS Rans S-6-ESA Coyote II   0498.1220   15.03.99
P A Harvie   Mount Airey Farm, South Cave   19.09.18P
Built by D G Watts – project PFA 204-13361

G-RINT CFM Streak Shadow   K 199-SA   07.12.93
D & J S Grint   Deanland   15.09.18P
Built by D Grint – project PFA 206-12251

G-RINZ Van's RV-7   70950   08.01.09
R C May   Finmere   29.05.18P
Built by P Chaplin – project PFA 323-13982

G-RIOT Silence SA.180 Twister   xxxx   11.10.07
G-SWIP, G-RIOT   Zulu Glasstek Ltd
Baileys Farm, Long Crendon   *'SWIP Twister Duo'*   02.07.18P
Built by P M Wells – project PFA 329-14700

G-RIPA Vulcanair P68 Observer 2   423-23/OB2   29.05.09
I-SORV   APEM Aviation Ltd   Liverpool John Lennon   29.06.18E

G-RIPH Supermarine 384 Seafire F.XVII   xxxx   24.09.09
G-CDTM, A2054, A646, SX300
Seafire Displays Ltd   (Old Warden, Biggleswade)
Unpainted wings noted 10.18 (NF 13.12.16)

G-RISA Piper PA-28-180 Cherokee C   28-3128   22.08.11
G-ATZK, N9090J, (D-EFUN), N9090J
D B Riseborough   Morgansfield, Fishburn   28.12.17E

G-RISH RotorWay Exec 162F   6926   15.03.05
M H Hoffmann   (Newborough)   23.07.18P
Built by C S Rische

G-RISY Van's RV-7   xxxx   10.02.05
D I Scott   Swanborough Farm, Lewes   15.04.19P
Built by A J A Weal – project PFA 323-14320

G-RITS Pitts S-1C   JH111   05.07.17
N82J   J H D Newman   (Benenden, Cranbrook)
Built by J C Holcomb (NF 05.07.17)

G-RITT P&M Pegasus Quik   8230   08.12.06
T H Parr   (Priest Hutton, Carnforth)   08.06.18P
*Original wing mated with Quik 912 trike
(c/n 8488) & engine ex Eurostar G-CDVP*

G-RITZ Cessna 182S Skylane   18280029   12.02.98
G-JBRN, N432V, G-RITZ, N9872F
C M Brittlebank   Solent   01.11.19E

G-RIVA SOCATA TBM-850 *(TBM-700N)*   615   07.12.12
D-FTBM (3), N850CV   MSV GmbH & Co KG
Mainz-Finthen, Rheinland-Pfalz, Germany   06.08.18E

G-RIVE Jodel D.153   153   14.07.04
M J Applewhite   Sturgate   27.02.18P
*Built by P Fines – project PFA 235-12856
using SAB plans*

G-RIVR Thruster T600N 450   9029-T600N-031   03.12.99
S W Turley   Wickenby   13.08.18P

G-RIVT	Van's RV-6	xxxx	31.07.95
	R Howard Grove Moor Farm, Treswell		06.04.18P
	Built by N Reddish – project PFA 181-12743		

G-RIXA	Piper J-3C Cub	18711	19.01.07
	7Q-YDF, 5Y-KEV, VP-KEV, VP-NAE, ZS-AZT		
	J J Rix (Waterbeach, Cambridge)		
	(NF 09.11.18)		

G-RIXS	Europa Aviation Europa XS	533	02.07.02
	T J Houlihan Croft Farm, Defford		12.07.18P
	Built by R Iddon – project PFA 247-13822; tricycle u/c		

G-RIXY	Cameron Z-77	10788	23.01.06
	Rix Petroleum (Hull) Ltd Hull *'Rix'*		21.04.18E

G-RIZE	Cameron O-90	3163	13.12.93
	S F Burden Noordwijk, Netherlands		25.04.09E
	(IE 06.11.17)		

G-RIZI	Cameron N-90	3080	12.05.93
	(F-GXIL), G-RIZI Asociata Sportiva Nyaradballoon		
	Sky Team Mures, Romania		13.12.19E

G-RIZK	Schleicher ASW 27-18E (*ASG 29E*)	29665	25.02.14
	(BGA 5775) P Lund Bicester *'GR8'*		07.03.19E

G-RIZZ	Piper PA-28-161 Warrior II	28-7816494	11.02.99
	D-EMFW, N9563N W Ali Cranfield		21.06.19E

G-RJAM	Sequoia F.8L Falco	xxxx	26.07.00
	D G Drew Jericho Farm, Lambley		11.01.18P
	Built by R J Marks – project PFA 100-11665		

G-RJIT	Groppo Trail Mk.2	123/82	15.11.16
	I M Belmore & R A Brown tr Dragon Trail Group		
	Truleigh Manor Farm, Edburton		16.11.19P
	Built by A T Banks & Partners – project LAA 372-15355		

G-RJPI★	Piaggio P180 Avanti	1033	09.04.18
	I-WJET, (D-IPCI), T7-PAI, I-DPCS Jetcom SRL		
	Cancelled 03.08.18 by CAA		

G-RJRC	Commander Aircraft Commander 114B	14615	22.12.16
	OO-MOM, N6031Y R M Jowitt Brighton City		17.07.18E

G-RJRJ	Evektor EV-97A Eurostar	2008-3121	29.01.08
	D P Myatt Wycombe Air Park		02.11.18P
	Built by D P Myatt & J Patterson		
	– project LAA 315A-14763		

G-RJVH	Guimbal Cabri G2	1157	12.08.16
	RJV Holdings Ltd Elstree		17.08.19E
	Operated by Flying Pig Helicopters		

G-RJWW	Maule M-5-235C Lunar Rocket	7250C	06.10.87
	G-BRWG, N5632H D E Priest North Weald		15.06.19E

G-RJWX	Europa Aviation Europa XS	359	11.09.00
	D S P Disney Westonzoyland		20.02.18P
	Built by J R Jones – project PFA 247-13197; tailwheel u/c		

G-RJXA	Embraer EMB-145EP	145136	18.06.99
	PT-SDN Loganair Ltd Glasgow		17.06.19E

G-RJXB	Embraer EMB-145EP	145142	23.06.99
	PT-SDS Loganair Ltd Glasgow		27.06.19E

G-RJXC	Embraer EMB-145EP	145153	15.07.99
	PT-SEE Loganair Ltd Glasgow		14.07.19E

G-RJXD	Embraer EMB-145EP	145207	04.02.00
	PT-SGX Loganair Ltd Glasgow		03.02.20E

G-RJXE	Embraer EMB-145EP	145245	10.04.00
	PT-SIJ Loganair Ltd Glasgow		09.04.19E

G-RJXG	Embraer EMB-145EP	145390	20.02.01
	PT-SQO British Midland Regional Ltd t/a BMI Regional		
	Alverca, Portugal		19.02.20E

G-RJXH	Embraer EMB-145EP	145442	01.06.01
	PT-SUN Loganair Ltd Glasgow		01.05.19E

G-RJXI	Embraer EMB-145EP	145454	22.06.01
	PT-SUZ Loganair Ltd Glasgow		21.06.19E

G-RJXK	Embraer EMB-135ER	145494	14.09.01
	PT-SXN Loganair Ltd Glasgow		13.09.19E

G-RJXL	Embraer EMB-135ER	145376	20.12.04
	PT-SQA, (EI-LCY), PT-SQA, (CN-RLF), PT-SQA		
	Loganair Ltd Glasgow		19.12.19E

G-RJXM	Embraer EMB-145MP	145216	23.12.05
	PH-RXA, PT-SHC Loganair Ltd Glasgow		22.12.19E

G-RKAF	Diamond DA.40D Star	D4.186	13.07.17
	JY-AAA Airways Aviation Academy Ltd		
	Huesca-Pirineos, Spain		07.08.18E

G-RKAG	Diamond DA.40D Star	D4.255	31.08.17
	JY-BBB Airways Aviation Academy Ltd Oxford		12.09.18E

G-RKAH	Diamond DA.40D Star	D4.258	13.07.17
	JY-CCC Airways Aviation Academy Ltd		
	Huesca-Pirineos, Spain		07.08.18E

G-RKAI	Diamond DA.40D Star	D4.257	01.09.17
	JY-DDD Airways Aviation Academy Ltd Oxford		19.09.18E

G-RKBD	Diamond DA.42 Twin Star	42.183	16.10.17
	JY-YYY (2), HA-DAM, OE-VPI		
	Airways Aviation Academy Ltd Oxford		03.12.18E

G-RKEL	Agusta-Bell 206B-3 JetRanger III	8617	02.08.01
	HB-XPR, F-GCVE		
	Nunkeeling Ltd (Elloughton, Brough)		12.06.09E
	(NF 08.06.16)		

G-RKET	Taylor JT-2 Titch	xxxx	25.08.99
	G-BIBK Cancelled 20.04.09 by CAA		
	(Seaford) *Built by P A Dunley – project PFA 3223*		
	For sale 06.17 part built		

G-RKID	Van's RV-6A	22586	11.07.17
	N219EJ I Shaw Manchester Barton		22.05.19P
	Built by E M Johnson		

G-RKKT	Reims FR172G Rocket	FR17200225	15.01.09
	G-AYJW K L Irvine Insch		02.07.19E

G-RKUS	Schempp-Hirth Arcus T	52	20.01.15
	(BGA 5861)		
	F B Jeynes tr Arcus Syndicate Bidford *'61'*		06.12.18E

G-RLDS	Cameron A-315	11799	07.04.14
	Bailey Balloons Ltd Pill, Bristol *'red letter days'*		03.04.19E

G-RLDX	Cameron A-375	11860	10.03.15
	Wickers World Ltd Great Haywood, Stafford		
	'red letter days'		18.03.19E

G-RLDZ	Cameron A-315	11914	05.08.15
	Bailey Balloons Ltd Pill, Bristol *'red letter days'*		01.04.19E

G-RLMW	Tecnam P2002-EA Sierra	162	01.06.06
	S P Hoskins Maypole Farm, Chislet		08.03.18P
	Built by J S Melville & R O'Malley-White		
	– project PFA 333-14536		

G-RLON	Fairey B-N BN-2A Mk.III-2 Trislander	1008	26.04.02
	G-ITEX, G-OCTA, VR-CAA, (G-OLPL), VR-CAA,		
	DQ-FCF, G-BCXW		
	Aurigny Air Services Ltd (Southampton)		16.12.17E
	Displayed Solent Sky Museum 2018		

G-RLWG	Ryan ST3KR	1716	20.10.08
	N58612, 41-15687 R A Fleming Brighton		01.02.18P

G-RMAA	Airbus MBB BK117 D-2 (*Eurocopter EC145 T2*)		
		20166	20.09.17
	Babcock Mission Critical Services Onshore Ltd		
	RAF Cosford		19.09.19E
	Operated by Midlands Air Ambulance Charity as		
	callsign 'Helimed 03'		

G-RMAC	Europa Aviation Europa	109	03.07.97
	P J Lawless Orange Grove Barn, Chavenage Green		30.08.18P
	Built by P J Lawless – project PFA 247-12717;		
	tailwheel u/c		

G-RMAN	Aero Designs Pulsar	475	06.06.97
	J M Angiolini Cumbernauld		05.11.18P
	Built by M B Redman – project PFA 202-13071		

G-RMAR	Robinson R66 Turbine	0154	19.11.15
	G-NSEV, N66EV		
	Marfleet Civil Engineering Ltd Earls Colne		15.02.19E

G-RMAV	Comco Ikarus C42 FB80	1502-7358	13.04.15
	RM Aviation Ltd Beverley (Linley Hill)		02.05.18P
	Assembled Red Aviation		

G-RMAX	Cameron C-80	4705	10.06.08
	J Kenny Athlone, Rol *'Re/Max'*		04.09.18E

G-RMCS	Cessna 182R Skylane	18268278	31.08.10
	OH-CKI, N4855E		
	R M C Sears Wateringhill Farm, Manea		13.03.18E

Reg	Type	C/n	Dates
G-RMHE	Aerospool Dynamic WT9 UK	DY155/2006	02.10.06
	D R Lewis The Old Mushroom Farm, Haywood, Callow		04.07.19P
	Assembled Yeoman Light Aircraft Co Ltd;		
	official c/n recorded as 'DY155'		
G-RMIT	Van's RV-4	3103	04.09.96
	J P Kloos Truleigh Manor Farm, Edburton		13.06.18P
	Built by J P Kloos – project PFA 181-12207		
G-RMMT	Europa Aviation Europa XS	A260	28.01.05
	N929N N Schmitt Nottingham City 'Grommit'		20.04.18P
	Built by N Schmitt; tricycle u/c		
G-RMPI	Whittaker MW5-D Sorcerer	xxxx	11.06.10
	R W Twamley (Coventry)		
	Built by N R Beale & D Charlesworth		
	– project PFA 163-12909		
	(SSDR microlight since 06.14) (NF 13.09.16)		
G-RMPS	Van's RV-12	120033	17.08.09
	K D Boardman tr RV-12 Group Perth		28.06.19P
	Built by K D Boardman – project LAA 363-14923		
G-RMPY	Evektor EV-97 Eurostar SL	2003-1214	04.02.04
	N R Beale Deppers Bridge, Southam		15.08.18P
	Built by N R Beale – project PFA 315-14139		
G-RMRV	Van's RV-7A	72186	25.05.07
	R Morris Whitehall Farm, Benington		14.05.18P
	Built by R Morris – project PFA 323-14434		
G-RMUG	Cameron Mug-90	3450	03.05.95
	The British Balloon Museum & Library Ltd		
	Wellingborough 'Nescafé'		05.06.15E
G-RMYD	Robinson R44 Raven II	14252	20.09.18
	Kaizen Motorsport & Aviation Ltd (Leeds, Maidstone)		
	(NF 14.09.18)		
G-RNAC	IAV Bacau Yakovlev Yak-52	888912	25.07.03
	RA-44463, DOSAAF 99 Chewton Glen Ltd		
	t/a Chewton Glen Aviation Solent '123'		31.01.18P
G-RNBW	Bell 206B-2 JetRanger II	2270	09.01.98
	F-GQFH, F-WQFH, HB-XUF, F-GFBP, N900JJ, N16UC		
	Rainbow Helicopters Ltd		
	(Rodden Barn Lodge, Portesham)		11.04.17E
	Being parted out 01.19		
G-RNCH	Piper PA-28-181 Archer II	28-8190141	19.04.06
	HB-PHR, D-EIFP, N83235		
	Airborne Adventures Ltd (Ramsey, Isle of Man)		09.06.17E
	Crashed Causeway, Ireland 18.08.16 & extensively		
	damaged; noted for spares use 03.17 (IE 06.04.18)		
G-RNDD	Robin DR.500-200i Président	37	02.05.03
	Witham (Specialist Vehicles) Ltd		
	Ponton Heath Farm, Great Ponton		21.08.19E
	Built by Constructions Aeronautiques de Bourgogne;		
	officially registered as DR.400-500		
G-RNER	Cessna 510 Citation Mustang	510-0409	26.06.12
	S J Davies Retford Gamston		05.07.18E
G-RNFR	Bombardier CL-600-2B16 Challenger 604	5983	20.04.16
	N605ZK, C-FAQD		
	TAG Aviation (UK) Ltd Farnborough		26.04.18E
G-RNGD	Murphy Renegade Spirit UK	xxxx	29.09.16
	G-MWPS A G Chalk tr Spirit Flying Group		
	Roughay Farm, Lower Upham		16.11.18P
	Built by A R Broughton-Tompkins		
	– project PFA 188-11931 (NF 29.09.16)		
G-RNHF	Hawker Sea Fury T.20	ES3615	01.06.07
	N281L, N8476W, G-BCOW, D-CACO, G-9-64, VX281		
	Naval Aviation Ltd North Weald		20.08.19P
	As 'VX281:120:VL' in RN 799 Sqdn c/s		
G-RNIE	Cameron Ball-70	2333	03.08.90
	N J Bland Didcot		18.10.10E
	(IE 27.10.14)		
G-RNJP	Bombardier CL-600-2B16 Challenger 604	5980	20.04.16
	N605BD, C-FJRG, C-FAPO		
	TAG Aviation (UK) Ltd Farnborough		26.04.18E
G-RNRM	Cessna A185F Skywagon	185-02541	20.01.87
	N1826R Skydive St Andrews Ltd Fife		
	'Thunderchild'		09.08.18E
G-ROAD	Robinson R44 Raven II	11589	29.01.07
	Aztec Aviators Ltd (Shillington, Hitchin)		02.03.18E
G-ROAT	Robinson R44 Raven II	13694	15.05.14
	R D Jordan Cranfield		14.06.18E
G-ROBA	Grob G115D-2 Heron	82011	29.03.16
	G-BVHF, D-EARV		
	Social Infrastructure Ltd Wellesbourne Mountford		20.02.18E
G-ROBD	Europa Aviation Europa	078	23.02.94
	Condor Aviation International Ltd		
	Birchwood Lodge, North Duffield		
	Built by R D Davies – project PFA 247-12671;		
	tailwheel u/c (NF 28.09.15)		
G-ROBG	P&M Quik GT450	8516	21.04.10
	Exodus Airsports Ltd Plaistows Farm, St Albans		24.04.19P
G-ROBJ	Robin DR.500-200i Président	45	02.09.08
	D R L Jones Oaksey Park		10.11.18E
	Officially regd as DR.400-500		
G-ROBN	Robin R1180T Aiglon	220	16.08.78
	N D Anderson Bournemouth		10.09.18E
G-ROBT	Hawker Hurricane I	xxxx	19.09.94
	P2902 Anglia Aircraft Restorations Ltd Duxford		06.07.19P
	Built by Gloster Aircraft Co Ltd;		
	as 'P2902:DX-R' in RAF c/s		
G-ROBZ	Grob G109B	6442	19.06.07
	I-BREM P M Scheiwiller tr Bravo Zulu Group		
	Sandhill Farm, Shrivenham		28.09.18E
G-ROCH	Cessna T303 Crusader	T30300129	29.03.90
	N4962C R S Bentley Cambridge		18.06.18E
G-ROCK	Thunder Ax7-77	781	25.02.86
	M A Green Rednal, Birmingham		13.07.09E
	(NF 18.04.16)		
G-ROCR	Schweizer 269C (300)	S 1336	14.06.90
	N219MS A Harvey & M Wilkinson Dunkeswell		07.12.19E
G-ROCT	Robinson R44 Raven II	11854	10.08.07
	A von Liechtenstein Trento, Italy		29.09.18E
G-RODC	Steen Skybolt	4568	20.02.02
	N10624 D G Girling Liverpool John Lennon		05.01.19P
	Built by R H Williams		
G-RODD	Cessna 310R II	310R0544	02.10.89
	G-TEDD, G-MADI, N87396, G-MADI, N87396		
	Alpha Properties (London) Ltd Biggin Hill		09.03.18E
G-RODG	Avtech Jabiru UL	0208	14.04.99
	N R Smith tr G-RODG Group Perranporth		27.03.18P
	Built by I J M Donnelly – project PFA 274A-13379		
G-RODI	Isaacs Fury	CM.1	22.12.78
	M J Bond RAF Waddington		11.05.18P
	Built by D C J Summerfield – project PFA 011-10130;		
	as 'K3731' in RAF 43 Sqdn c/s		
G-RODJ	Comco Ikarus C42 FB80	0709-6912	02.10.07
	Mediaviate Ltd (Scalford, Melton Mowbray)		11.02.19P
	Assembled Aerosport		
G-RODO	Europa Aviation Europa XS	435	07.03.11
	G-ROWI R M Carson (Cheltenham)		
	Built by R M Carson – project PFA 247-13482		
	(NF 09.02.15)		
G-RODZ	Van's RV-3A	10622	04.07.07
	N68AR C C Cooper Pittrichie Farm, Whiterashes		27.09.19P
	Built by T F Hinckley		
G-ROEIᴹ	Avro Roe 1 replica	xxxx	06.02.08
	Brooklands Museum Trust Ltd Brooklands		
	Built by Brooklands Museum		
	– project PFA 344-14629 (NF 15.01.17)		
G-ROEN	Cameron C-70	11122	25.05.12
	R M W Romans Hasselt-Kiewit, Belgium		04.06.18E
G-ROFS	Groppo Trail	00072/31	06.02.12
	J S Evans (Chesham)		21.03.19P
	Built by R F Bond – project LAA 372-15133		
G-ROGY	Cameron C-60	3055	11.05.93
	S A Laing Woodlands of Durris, Banchory		26.05.18E
G-ROKO	Roko Aero NG4-HD	020/2009	19.05.10
	C D Sidoli (Sandyhill, Ellesmere)		14.12.17W
G-ROKS	Robinson R44 Raven II	10325	08.08.13
	G-WEGO Swift Helicopter Services Ltd		
	Leeds Heliport		10.05.16E
	(NF 26.07.18)		
G-ROKT	Reims FR172E Rocket	FR17200046	01.05.00
	N261SA, D-ECLY		
	P Donohoe (Castleknock, Dublin, RoI)		09.04.19E

G-ROKY Groppo Trail 00064/23 30.01.12
J Webb   Lower Upham Farm, Chiseldon 30.05.18P
Built by N I Hart – project LAA 372-15131

G-ROLF Piper PA-32R-301 Saratoga SP 32R-8113018 07.01.81
N83052 P F Larkins High Cross, Ware 07.12.18E

G-ROLL Pitts S-2A 2175 20.02.80
N31444 P H Meeson (London SW1) 09.08.19E
Built by Aerotek Inc

G-ROLY Reims/Cessna F172N F17201945 01.12.04
G-BHIH M Bonsall Netherthorpe 19.10.18E

G-ROME III Sky Arrow 650 TC C011 26.05.99
Sky Arrow (Kits) UK Ltd Old Sarum 28.06.11E
Noted 04.16 (NF 12.07.16)

G-ROMP Extra EA.230H 001 13.01.05
S5-MBP, OO-JVD, D-EIWH
D G Cowden & S C Hipwell tr The G-ROMP Group
Swanborough Farm, Lewes 25.05.19P
Built by W Hawickhorst

G-ROMS Lindstrand LBL 105G HAB 401 13.09.96
Cancelled 28.01.10 as PWFU 13.09.00
Queensferry, West Lothian *Preserved 10.14*

G-ROMT Robinson R44 Clipper II 10788 01.06.17
G-RALA Dydb Marketing Ltd (London N1) 17.07.17E

G-ROMW Cyclone AX2000 7486 04.02.99
K V Falvey Sackville Lodge Farm, Riseley 12.08.18P

G-RONA Europa Aviation Europa 043 17.01.95
C M Noakes Shenstone Hall Farm, Shenstone
'Mr Jake' 15.08.18P
Built by C M Noakes – project PFA 247-12588;
tailwheel u/c

G-RONI Cameron V-77 2349 27.07.90
R E Simpson Ballinger, Great Missenden 24.10.17E

G-RONK Aeropro EuroFOX 3K 53718 11.04.18
P Knowles (Pevensey Bay) 08.05.19P
Built by Ascent Industries Ltd; tricycle u/c

G-RONS Robin DR.400-180 Régent 2088 17.07.91
C A Gough tr G-RONS Group (Seavington, Ilminster) 10.07.19E

G-RONW Clutton FRED Series II xxxx 18.12.78
W J Pope & S Procter tr RONW Syndicate North Hill 08.07.19P
Built by P Gronow – project PFA 029-10121

G-RONZ Comco Ikarus C42 FB80 1210-7227 14.01.13
R F Dean Shifnal 20.04.18P
Assembled Red-Air UK

G-ROOG Extra EA.300/LT LT027 08.04.14
M J Coward Brighton City 21.06.18E

G-ROOK Reims/Cessna F172P F17202081 12.01.81
PH-TGY, G-ROOK Rolim Ltd Aberdeen Int'l 14.12.18E
Operated by Bon Accord Flying Group

G-ROON Sikorsky S-76C 760781 06.03.17
N120TN, PR-YMH, N781L
Rooney Air Ltd Brighton City 06.03.18E
Built by Keystone Helicopter Corpn

G-ROOO Avtech Jabiru J430 787 04.09.12
G-HJZN H S A Brewis (Hawstead, Bury St Edmunds) 20.07.18P
Built by H D Jones – project LAA 336-15049

G-ROOV Europa Aviation Europa XS 354 16.07.98
P W Hawkins Biggin Hill 03.08.17P
Built by D Richardson – project PFA 247-13214;
tricycle u/c; roaded in to Biggin Hill to fly

G-ROPO Groppo Trail 00084/43 03.12.12
J M Chapman (Ellastone, Ashbourne) 08.08.18P
Built by J C & R D P Cadle – project LAA 372-15181

G-ROPP Groppo Trail 00083/42 14.12.12
D Dobson & S J Perkins Little Staughton 06.02.20P
Built by G Jeans & P T Price – project LAA 372-15178

G-RORA Embraer EMB-550 Legacy 500 55000057 04.01.18
PR-LNP Centreline AV Ltd t/a Centreline Bristol 08.01.19E

G-RORB Super Marine Spitfire Mk.26 050 15.01.10
Bertha Property LLP Perth
'Miss Helen' (port) & 'Miss Debbie' (starboard)
Built by G Robinson – project PFA 324-14745;
as 'P9637:GR-B' in RAF sand c/s (IE 13.09.17)

G-RORI Folland Gnat T.1 FL549 18.10.93
8621M, XR538 Heritage Aircraft Ltd North Weald 20.06.19P
As 'XR538:01' in RAF c/s

G-RORO Cessna 337B Super Skymaster 33700554 08.01.80
G-AVIX, N5454S Cancelled 09.12.02 as PWFU 15.07.00
Castlerock *Stored 12.13*

G-RORY Focke-Wulf Piaggio FWP.149D 014 02.08.88
G-TOWN, D-EFFY, West German AF 90+06, BB+394
M Edwards Enstone 07.01.08
Piaggio c/n 338; noted 08.17 (NF 16.03.15)

G-ROSI Thunder Ax7-77 1284 29.06.88
J E Rose Abingdon 21.09.96A
(NF 26.01.15)

G-ROSK Ultramagic M-90 90/160 17.05.17
N Roskell Skipton 25.05.18E

G-ROSS Practavia Pilot Sprite 132 28.02.80
A N Barley Sandcroft Farm, Messingham
Built by A N Barley & A D Janaway – project
PFA 005-10404 (NF 23.11.17)

G-ROTI Luscombe 8A 2117 18.04.89
N45590, NC45590 R Ludgate & L Prebble
Old Hay Farm, Paddock Wood 14.06.17P
Carries 'N45590' on tail (NF 08.08.17)

G-ROTR Brantley B2B 403 09.12.91
N2192U Cancelled 17.04.09 by CAA 17.11.02
Eaglescott *Stored 04.16*

G-ROTS CFM Streak Shadow K 120-SA 21.12.89
J Edwards Popham 21.07.18P
Built by H R Cayzer – project PFA 161A-11603

G-ROUS Piper PA-34-200T Seneca II 34-7870187 26.04.78
(LN-...), G-ROUS, (G-BFTB), N9412C
R Pedersen (Kraakstad, Norway) 08.06.17E

G-ROVA Aviat A-1B Husky Pup NF0008 09.05.16
N48HU, N142HP
Aviat Aircraft (UK) Ltd Lower Grounds Farm, Shirlowe
29.05.18E

G-ROVE Piper PA-18-135 Super Cub (L-21B-PI) 18-3846 06.05.82
PH-VLO, (PH-DKF), R Netherlands AF R-156, 54-2446
S J Gaveston Headcorn 21.08.18E
Fuselage No.18-3853; as 'R-156' in
R Netherlands AF c/s & '54-2446'

G-ROVY Robinson R22 Beta II 2957 09.07.99
M H Hoffmann & R F McLachlan
Bradley Moor, Ashbourne 10.11.18E

G-ROWA Aquila AT01 AT01-174 31.10.07
R Simpson (Upton Bishop, Ross-on-Wye) 28.12.18E

G-ROWL Grumman American AA-5B Tiger AA5B-0595 26.10.77
(N28410) Box MR Ltd Manchester Barton 27.04.18E

G-ROWS Piper PA-28-151 Cherokee Warrior 28-7715296 15.09.78
N8949F S Tahsin t/a Air Academy Elstree 25.05.19E

G-ROXI Cameron C-90 11106 07.07.08
D Marshall Thornton-Cleveleys 04.04.18E

G-ROYC Avtech Jabiru UL-450 489 24.04.03
P S Reed tr G-ROYC Flying Group Old Warden 11.05.18P
Built by R Clark – project PFA 274A-13990

G-ROYM Robinson R44 Raven II 12295 02.06.08
HQ Aviation Ltd Denham 28.11.18E

G-ROYP Robinson R22 Beta 2071 17.11.17
F-GMCE, N23263 R M Price Shobdon 21.05.19E

G-ROZE Magni M24C Orion 24126884 22.02.12
R I Simpson Maypole Farm, Chislet 22.05.18P

G-ROZY[M] Cameron R-36 Gas.HAB 1141 20.05.85
Cancelled 01.12.09 by CAA 18.09.86
With Anderson-Abruzzo Int'l Balloon Museum,
Albuquerque, New Mexico

G-ROZZ Comco Ikarus C42 FB80 0407-6607 19.08.04
A J Blackwell Enstone 23.08.18P
Assembled Fly Buy Ultralights Ltd

G-RPAF Europa Aviation Europa XS 605 26.01.05
R P Frost tr G-RPAF Group Kirkbride 'Mrs J Hart' 09.08.18P
Built by R P Frost – project PFA 247-14202; tricycle u/c

G-RPAX	CASA 1-133 Jungmeister	101	06.08.12
	Spanish AF ES.1-31 A J E Smith Breighton		
	As '35-23' in Spanish Air Force c/s;		
	on rebuild 12.16 (NF 14.06.16)		
G-RPCC	Europa Aviation Europa XS	614M	10.01.07
	R P Churchill-Coleman (Curdridge, Southampton)		
	Built by R P Churchill-Colman		
	– project PFA 247-14615 (NF 09.10.14)		
G-RPEZ	Rutan Long-EZ	xxxx	03.04.84
	M P Dunlop (Tutshill, Chepstow)		
	Built by B A Fairston & D Richardson		
	– project PFA 074A-10746 (NF 03.10.14)		
G-RPPO	Groppo Trail	0047	02.12.10
	D R Baker Dunkeswell *'Spriteaviation.co.uk'*		14.03.19P
	Built by G N Smith – project LAA 372-15014		
G-RPRP	P&M QuikR	8778	27.07.18
	R M Brown Battleby Farm, Luncarty		
	(IE 27.07.18)		
G-RPRV	Van's RV-9A	90565	17.10.03
	T A Willcox Chase Farm, Chipping Sodbury		16.06.17P
	Built by G R Pybus – project PFA 320-13936;		
	overturned Nympsfield 23.08.16		
G-RRAK	Enstrom 480B	5055	31.07.08
	G-RIBZ P J Began (Charlton Musgrove, Wincanton)		30.09.19E
G-RRAT	CZAW Sportcruiser	700294	22.09.08
	G Sipson Camp Farm, Bulkington, Bedworth		19.10.18P
	Built by G Sipson – project LAA 338-14821 (Kit 4413)		
G-RRCU	Robin DR.221B Dauphin	129	09.12.99
	F-BRCU Merlin Flying Club Ltd Tatenhill		17.07.18E
	Built by Centre-Est Aéronautique		
G-RRED	Piper PA-28-181 Archer III	2843673	04.09.08
	N6048L J P Reddington Denham		19.04.18E
	Official type data 'PA-28-181 Cherokee Archer III'		
	is incorrect		
G-RRFF	Supermarine 329 Spitfire IIB	6S-109137	04.09.09
	P8208 Retro Track & Air (UK) Ltd		
	(Upthorpe Iron Works, Cam, Dursley)		
	(NF 20.07.17)		
G-RRGN	Supermarine 390 Spitfire PR.XIX	6S-594677	23.12.96
	G-MXIX, PS853 Rolls-Royce PLC East Midlands		11.05.16P
	As 'PS853:C' in RAF 2nd TAF/PRU c/s;		
	on rebuild 2018 (IE 20.12.17)		
G-RROB	Robinson R44 Raven II	10011	06.12.02
	R S Rai Stapleford		20.04.18E
G-RROD	Piper PA-30 Twin Comanche B	30-1221	20.06.00
	G-SHAW, LN-BWS, N10F		
	Cancelled 11.04.11 as sold in USA		25.08.09
	Farley Farm, Farley Chamberlayne		
	Stored unmarked 12.17		
G-RRRV	Van's RV-6	20843	02.04.13
	C St J Hall Bidford *'Roar Power II'*		17.09.19P
	Initially built by E Kosik (Sonora, California, USA) &		
	completed C Hall – project LAA 181A-15192;		
	tailwheel u/c		
G-RRRZ	Van's RV-8	82003	22.12.11
	J Bate Blackpool *'74'*		27.03.18P
	Built by D J C Davidson – project LAA 303-15107		
G-RRSR	Piper J-3C-65 Cub	12905	07.09.05
	N1315V, 44-80609 R W Roberts		
	Church Farm, Shotteswell *'Special Delivery'*		29.04.16E
	As '480173:57-H' in USAAC c/s (IE 04.08.17)		
G-RRVX	Van's RV-10	40368	05.12.06
	T Booth Nottingham City		13.03.18P
	Built by R E Garforth – project PFA 339-14601		
G-RSAF	BAC 167 Strikemaster Mk.80A	EEP/JP/3687	08.04.05
	R Saudi AF 1120, G-27-231		
	NWMAS Leasing Ltd Hawarden		17.07.19P
	Plane Set 152; as '417' in Oman AF c/s;		
	wings used in rebuild from SOAF Mk.82A 403		
G-RSAM	P&M Quik GTR	8638	21.12.12
	J W Foster Deenethorpe		06.05.18P
G-RSCU	Agusta A109E Power	11777	02.12.09
	Sloane Helicopters Ltd Coventry		02.12.18E
	Operated by Warwickshire & Northamptonshire		
	Air Ambulance as callsign 'Helimed 53'		

G-RSHI	Piper PA-34-220T Seneca V	3449077	04.02.08
	D-GMGM, N9265Q		
	A G Hill t/a RS Hill & Sons Bournemouth		05.03.18E
G-RSKR	Piper PA-28-161 Warrior II	28-7916181	27.04.95
	G-BOJY, N3030G		
	Aviation Advice & Consulting Ltd Dundee		27.07.18E
	Operated by Tayside Aviation		
G-RSKY	Best Off Skyranger 912(2)	SKR0403452	12.10.04
	P Lister Ince		28.05.19P
	Built by C G Benham – project BMAA/HB/382		
G-RSMC	Medway SLA 100 Executive	131106	24.08.07
	W S C Toulmin Conington		13.06.13P
	(NF 27.10.16)		
G-RSMT	AutoGyro MT-03	xxxx	01.05.07
	Cancelled 17.11.11 as destroyed		29.07.11
	RAF Keevil *Assembled Rotorsport (UK) as*		
	RSUK/MT-03/015; fuselage pod to Bannerdown		
	GC as simulator 12.11		
G-RSSF	Denney Kitfox Model 2	xxxx	09.10.92
	C Bingham East Lound, Haxey		20.11.18P
	Built by R W Somerville – project PFA 172-12125		
G-RSWO	Cessna 172R Skyhawk	17280206	25.02.98
	N9401F G Fischer (Hohenroda, Germany)		17.04.17E
G-RSXP	Cessna 560XL Citation XLS+	560-6198	10.11.15
	N52457 Catreus AOC Ltd Biggin Hill		12.11.18E
G-RTEN	Pipistrel Alpha BCAR-S 164	AT1640001	20.09.18
	67 CA, F-JBWO Microlight Sport Aviation Ltd		
	Damyns Hall, Upminster		
	(IE 20.09.18)		
G-RTFM	Avtech Jabiru J400	268	28.02.08
	A H Hamilton (Cairndow)		15.08.19P
	Built by I A Macphee – project PFA 325-14463		
G-RTHS	Rans S-6-ES Coyote II	1107.1841	17.01.08
	R G Hughes Little Down Farm, Milson		07.12.15P
	Built by T Harrison-Smith – project PFA 204-14753		
	(IE 05.10.16)		
G-RTIN	AutoGyro MT-03	08 039	21.07.08
	C J Morton (Richmond TW10)		02.05.17P
	Assembled Rotorsport UK as c/n RSUK/MT-03/047;		
	rolled over taxying Turweston 13.02.17		
G-RTMS	Rans S-6-ES Coyote II	1202.1470	19.08.04
	C J Arthur tr G-RTMS Flying Group Eshott		11.07.17P
	Built by C J Arthur – project PFA 204-14149; tricycle u/c		
G-RTMY	Comco Ikarus C42 FB100	0502-6655	11.04.05
	R F Learney tr Mike Yankee Group Redhill		10.04.18P
	Assembled Aerosport Ltd		
G-RTRV	Van's RV-9A	91974	12.12.11
	R Taylor Dunkeswell		09.04.18P
	Built by R Taylor – project LAA 320-15033		
G-RUBB	Grumman American AA-5B Tiger	AA5B-0928	20.09.83
	(G-BKVI), OO-NAS, (OO-HRC) D E Gee Blackbushe		22.11.18E
G-RUBY	Piper PA-28RT-201T Turbo Arrow IV	28R-8331037	05.01.90
	G-BROU R Harman tr Arrow Aircraft Group Tatenhill		27.09.11E
	(NF 02.08.17)		
G-RUCK	Bell 206B-3 JetRanger III	4054	05.10.10
	OH-HKH, N206HM, JA9817, C-GLZK		
	J A Ruck Elms Green, Leominster		16.06.18E
G-RUDD	Cameron V-65 HAB	844	19.05.82
	Cancelled 25.11.08 as PWFU		20.05.00
	Not Known *Inflated Pidley 04.14*		
G-RUES	Robin HR.100/210 Safari	185	31.07.00
	F-BVCH R H R Rue Turweston		14.06.18E
G-RUFF	Mainair Blade 912	1203-0799-7-W1006	18.06.99
	P Mulvey Ince		20.04.16P
G-RUFS	Avtech Jabiru UL	200	19.11.99
	M Bastin Lower Upham Farm, Chiseldon		19.08.18P
	Built by J W Holland – project PFA 274A-13359		
G-RUGS	Campbell Cricket Mk.4	140	11.02.99
	J L G McLane (Gilling East, York)		
	Built by J L G Mclane – project PFA G/03-1307		
	(NF 19.01.16)		
G-RUIA	Reims/Cessna F172N	F17201856	04.10.79
	PH-AXA D R Clyde Swansea		01.03.18E
	Operated by Cambrian Flying Club		

G-RUKA Boeing 737-8AS 44687 20.12.18
EI-FEF Ryanair UK Ltd London Stansted 25.09.19E
Line No: 5099

G-RULE Robinson R44 Raven II 11039 03.02.06
P W Brown t/a Huckair Cotswold 30.06.18E

G-RUMI Noble Hardman Snowbird Mk.IV SB-018 09.09.02
G-MVOI G Crossley Rossall Field, Cockerham
(NF 22.01.16)

G-RUMM Grumman F8F-2P Bearcat 1088 20.03.98
NX700HL, NX700H, N1YY, N4995V, USN 121714
Patina Ltd Duxford 25.06.19P
As '121714:201 B' in USN c/s

G-RUMN American AA-1A Trainer AA1A-0086 30.05.80
N87599, D-EAFB, (N9386L)
A M Leahy Goodwood '222' 17.06.18E

G-RUMW Grumman FM-2 Wildcat 5765 15.04.98
N4845V, USN 86711 Patina Ltd Duxford 30.05.19P
As 'JV579:F' in RN c/s

G-RUNS P&M Quik GT450 8624 01.08.12
S Nicol Easterton 09.07.18P

G-RUNT Cassutt Racer IIIM 161149 12.04.83
D P Lightfoot Headcorn 'Nemesis' & '1' 18.05.18P
Built by N A Brendish – project PFA 034-10860

G-RUPS Cameron TR-70 11305 28.04.11
R M Stanley Tewin, Welwyn 19.04.18E

G-RUSL Van's RV-6A 25829 22.10.01
G R Russell Middle Pymore Farm, Bridport
Built by G Russell – project PFA 181-13522
(NF 15.03.16)

G-RUVE Van's RV-8 82747 06.01.09
J P Brady & D J Taylor RAF Benson
Built by J P Brady & D J Taylor
– project PFA 303-14716 (NF 11.12.15)

G-RUVI Zenair CH.601UL Zodiac 6-9330 08.11.02
P G Depper Pound Green 'Indulgence' 26.09.17P
Built by P G Depper – project PFA 162A-13933;
tricycle u/c (IE 23.10.17)

G-RUVY Van's RV-9A 90425 04.01.02
R D Taylor Henstridge 25.03.19P
Built by R D Taylor – project PFA 320-13807

G-RVAA Van's RV-7 xxxx 28.10.15
A J Almosawi (Bierton, Aylesbury)
Built by A J Almosawi – project LAA 323-15338
(NF 28.10.15)

G-RVAB Van's RV-7 71091 20.09.04
A T Banks & I M Belmore Wellcross Farm, Slinfold 12.05.18P
Built by I M Belmore – project PFA 323-14005

G-RVAC Van's RV-7 71481 07.09.05
A F S & B L Caldecourt Popham 29.04.19P
Built by A F S Caldecourt – project PFA 323-14445

G-RVAH Van's RV-7 73681 20.04.12
C Morris tr Regent Group Bidford 24.01.19P
Built by H W Hall – project LAA 323-14963

G-RVAL Van's RV-8 81099 23.07.01
P D Scandrett Rendcomb 08.11.18P
Built by R N York – project PFA 303-13532

G-RVAN Van's RV-6 xxxx 25.04.97
C Richards North Weald 07.05.19P
Built by D Broom – project PFA 181-12657

G-RVAR Van's RV-8 83122 07.09.17
B A Ridgway Rhigos
Built by B A Ridgway – project LAA 303-15139;
cleared to fly 12.18 (IE 07.05.18)

G-RVAT Van's RV-8 82982 07.12.09
T R Grief Morgansfield, Fishburn 22.01.18P
Built by J D Llewellyn – project LAA 303-14928

G-RVAW Van's RV-6 xxxx 24.11.97
M E & R E Lee Rectory Farm, Averham 24.04.19P
Built by A A Wordsworth – project PFA 181-13234

G-RVBA Van's RV-8A 80697 26.10.99
D P Richard (London SW16)
Built by S Hawksworth – project PFA 303-13309
(NF 06.01.15)

G-RVBC Van's RV-6A xxxx 16.02.00
T G Gibbs (Faulkland, Radstock) 21.09.18P
Built by T G Gibbs – project PFA 181-12618

G-RVBF Cameron A-340HL 10493 23.02.04
Airxcite Ltd t/a Virgin Balloon Flights
Stafford Park, Telford 'Virgin' 28.02.11E
(NF 15.09.14)

G-RVBI Van's RV-8 xxxx 15.10.10
K R H Wingate Bolt Head, Salcombe 29.08.18P
Built by K Wingate & M A N Newall
– project LAA 303-15013

G-RVBP Van's RV-7 xxxx 04.09.18
B J A Polwin (Scopwick, Lincoln)
Built by B J A Polwin – project LAA 323-15569
(NF 04.09.18)

G-RVBZ Van's RV-7 LAA 323-14583 26.03.19
R A Broad (Taunton)

G-RVCE Van's RV-6A xxxx 28.06.01
C & M D Barnard Glebe Farm, Ladbroke 24.06.19P
Built by M D Barnard & C Voelger
– project PFA 181-13372

G-RVCH Van's RV-8A xxxx 09.11.07
JB Aviation Ltd (Harrogate) '50' 07.08.19P
Built by C R Harrison – project PFA 303-14116

G-RVCL Van's RV-6 xxxx 18.02.99
N Halsall Sherburn-in-Elmet 19.04.19P
Built by C Lamb – project PFA 181A-13439

G-RVDB Van's RV-7 72214 22.03.17
D Broom Whitehall Farm, Benington 01.08.19P
Built by D Broom – project LAA 323-14526

G-RVDC Van's RV-8 83479 29.05.15
D P Catt (South Newington, Banbury)
Built by D P Catt – project LAA 303-15321
(NF 28.05.15)

G-RVDD Van's RV-14 140275 25.07.18
D M Dash (Roydon, Harlow)
Built by D M Dash – project LAA 393-15384
(NF 25.07.18)

G-RVDG Van's RV-9 91025 06.01.05
D M Gill Bicester 25.04.18P
Built by D M Gill – project PFA 320-14310

G-RVDH Van's RV-8 80563 26.08.11
G-ONER, N563JH D J Harrison (Winster, Matlock) 07.07.16P
Built by J A Hawkins

G-RVDJ Van's RV-6 24515 08.02.99
C S & P S Foster Morgansfield, Fishburn 08.09.19P
Built by J D Hewitt – project PFA 181-12938

G-RVDP Van's RV-4 4313 10.05.00
O Florin (Neuilly-sur-Seine, France) 27.04.18P
Built by D H Pattison – project PFA 181-13416

G-RVDR Van's RV-6A xxxx 15.05.00
P R Redfern Breighton 10.08.18P
Built by D E Reast – project PFA 181A-13098

G-RVDX Van's RV-4 926 31.10.08
G-FTUO, C-FTUQ P Musso Karlsruhe, Germany 07.09.18P
Built by T Martin

G-RVEA BRM Bristell NG5 Speed Wing 85 07.07.14
R V Emerson White Waltham 09.04.19P
Built by R V Emerson – project LAA 385-15257

G-RVEE Van's RV-6A xxxx 16.02.93
J C A Wheeler Perth 19.07.18P
Built by J C A Wheeler – project PFA 181-12262

G-RVEI Van's RV-8 xxxx 27.01.10
M R Turner Retford Gamston 06.11.19P
Built by D Stephens – project LAA 303-14961

G-RVEM Van's RV-7A xxxx 18.02.11
G-CBJU D A Cowan Oban 11.05.18P
Built by T W Waltham – project PFA 323-13868

G-RVER Van's RV-4 497 18.08.11
N4306U M D Falconer tr G-RVER Flying Group
Shempston Farm, Lossiemouth 19.01.19P
Built by J R Blunt

G-RVET Van's RV-6 23820 09.03.98
D R Coleman Rochester 20.09.18P
Built by D R Coleman – project PFA 181-12852

G-RVGA	Van's RV-6A	xxxx	11.05.98	
	R Emery North Weald		29.04.19P	
	Built by D P Dawson – project PFA 181-13079			
G-RVGO	Van's RV-10	xxxx	16.02.11	
	Tapeformers Ltd Leicester		06.11.18P	
	Built by D C Arnold & D Stephens			
	– project LAA 339-15063			
G-RVHD	Van's RV-7	74332	19.01.16	
	N Lamb North Weald		13.06.19P	
	Built by H W Hall & D J Mountain			
	– project LAA 323-15306			
G-RVIA	Van's RV-6A	xxxx	13.08.97	
	K R W Scull & J Watkins			
	The Byre, Hardwick, Abergavenny		16.07.18P	
	Built by A J Rose – project PFA 181-12289			
G-RVIB	Van's RV-6	xxxx	22.06.99	
	R D Myles Perth		25.05.18P	
	Built by I M Belmore – project PFA 181A-13220			
G-RVIC	Van's RV-6A	xxxx	11.06.04	
	I T Corse Perth		29.04.19P	
	Built by I T Corse & C Whatley			
	– project PFA 181A-13319			
G-RVII	Van's RV-7	25799	13.09.01	
	P H C Hall Oaksey Park		26.07.18P	
	Built by P H Hall – project PFA 323-13576			
G-RVIL	Van's RV-4	xxxx	02.11.17	
	S C Hipwell Swanborough Farm, Lewes		26.11.19P	
	Built by N Hart, S C Hipwell & B Trent			
	– project LAA 181-15020			
G-RVIN	Van's RV-6	25207	28.11.97	
	M Lawton Sittles Farm, Alrewas		28.05.18P	
	Built by N Reddish – project PFA 181-13236			
G-RVIO	Van's RV-10	40500	14.07.06	
	R C Hopkinson tr G-RVIO Group Bicester		05.03.18P	
	Built by R C Hopkinson – project PFA 339-14548			
G-RVIS	Van's RV-8	81798	17.06.03	
	M W Edwards Keevil		22.03.19P	
	Built by I V Sharman – project PFA 303-14031			
G-RVIT	Van's RV-6	xxxx	01.05.95	
	P J Shotbolt Netherthorpe		16.07.18P	
	Built by P J Shotbolt – project PFA 181-12422			
G-RVIV	Van's RV-4	3264	31.12.97	
	S B Robson Watchford Farm, Yarcombe		07.06.18P	
	Built by G S Scott – project PFA 181-12366			
G-RVIW	Van's RV-9	xxxx	09.09.10	
	C R James Ludham		14.06.19P	
	Built by G S Scott – project PFA 320-13924			
G-RVIX	Van's RV-9A	90243	11.09.01	
	J R Holt & C S Simmons			
	Valley Farm, Dunston Heath		11.05.18P	
	Built by R E Garforth – project PFA 320-13779			
G-RVIZ	Van's RV-12	120429	14.01.11	
	P I Harrison & J F Leather tr Chelwood Flying Group			
	Gloucestershire		19.12.17P	
	Built by J E Singleton – project LAA 363-15034			
G-RVJG	Van's RV-7	71729	06.11.14	
	J W Ellis Wolverhampton Halfpenny Green			
	Built by J C Bacon – project PFA 323-14237			
	(NF 04.01.17)			
G-RVJM	Van's RV-6	3791	04.12.02	
	M D Challoner (Stalbridge, Sturminster Newton)			
	Built by M D Challoner – project PFA 181A-13861			
	(NF 21.01.16)			
G-RVJO	Van's RV-9A	90096	05.01.07	
	P D Chandler Brighton City		06.03.18P	
	Built by J E Singleton – project PFA 320-13778			
G-RVJP	Van's RV-9A	91103	28.10.05	
	J M Palmer White Fen Farm, Benwick		09.04.19P	
	Built by R M Palmer – project PFA 320-14364			
G-RVJW	Van's RV-4	3117	26.08.05	
	J M Williams Sleap		21.06.18P	
	Built by J M Williams – project PFA 181-12987			
G-RVLC	Van's RV-9A	xxxx	27.04.07	
	M C Wilksch Turweston		11.07.19P	
	Built by L J Clark – project PFA 320-13780			

G-RVLW	Reims/Cessna F406 Caravan II	F406-0052	14.07.16	
	N6590Y RVL Aviation Ltd East Midlands		30.10.18E	
G-RVLX	Reims/Cessna F406 Caravan II	F406-0054	14.07.16	
	N6591R RVL Aviation Ltd East Midlands		24.10.18E	
G-RVLY	Reims/Cessna F406 Caravan II	F406-0034	14.07.16	
	N861FT, OO-LMO, (D-ILIM), OY-PAB, PH-PHO,			
	AP-BFB, N443AB, G-BPSX, F-WZDX			
	RVL Aviation Ltd East Midlands		30.10.18E	
G-RVLZ	Cessna 310R II	310R1837	17.03.16	
	EC-KSU, N53CK, OE-FCK, (N2739D)			
	RVL Aviation Ltd East Midlands		21.11.18E	
G-RVMB	Van's RV-9A	xxxx	16.06.06	
	M James Enstone		07.11.18P	
	Built by M James & R W Littledale			
	– project PFA 320-14324			
G-RVMJ	Van's RV-4	xxxx	16.02.99	
	Cancelled 21.05.09 by CAA			
	Aghalee, Craigavon *Built by M J de Ruiter*			
	– project PFA 181-13433; stored part built 12.13			
G-RVMM	Van's RV-7	xxxx	18.02.19	
	M Malone (Sheriffs Lench, Evesham)			
	Built by M Malone – project LAA 323-15022 (NF 18.02.19)			
G-RVMT	Van's RV-6	21293	30.01.01	
	P I Lewis Sleap		25.04.19P	
	Built by M R Tingle – project PFA 181A-13644			
G-RVMZ	Van's RV-8	xxxx	12.11.99	
	A E Kay Parsons Farm, Waterperry Common		04.01.19P	
	Built by M W Zipfell – project PFA 303-13395			
G-RVNA	Piper PA-38-112 Tomahawk	38-79A0450	03.02.11	
	G-DFLY, N9655N			
	Ravenair Aircraft Ltd Liverpool John Lennon		24.01.18E	
G-RVNC	Piper PA-38-112 Tomahawk	38-79A0838	19.09.11	
	G-BTJK, N2427N			
	Ravenair Aircraft Ltd Liverpool John Lennon		10.01.19E	
G-RVND	Piper PA-38-112 Tomahawk	38-79A0545	01.11.11	
	G-BTAS, F-GTAS, G-BTAS, N2492G			
	N Parker t/a NPA Aviation Liverpool John Lennon		10.08.17E	
G-RVNE	Partenavia P68B	101	30.11.11	
	G-SAMJ, D-GERA, CS-AYB, D-GERA			
	Ravenair Aircraft Ltd Liverpool John Lennon		31.01.18E	
G-RVNG	Partenavia P68B	103	28.01.13	
	G-BMOI, I-EEVA			
	Ravenair Aircraft Ltd Liverpool John Lennon		07.11.18E	
G-RVNH	Van's RV-9A	90570	20.07.06	
	N R Haines Manor Farm, Lea		29.07.18P	
	Built by N R Haines – project PFA 320-13952			
G-RVNI	Van's RV-6A	25472	01.07.10	
	FI-ECF R F McKeown tr G-RVNI Group			
	Newtownards		18.05.18P	
	Built by J Bailey			
G-RVNJ	Partenavia P68B	52	19.03.13	
	D-GILA Ravenair Aircraft Ltd Liverpool John Lennon		09.08.17E	
G-RVNK	Partenavia P68B	191	28.06.13	
	G-BHBZ Ravenair Aircraft Ltd			
	Liverpool John Lennon		12.04.18E	
G-RVNM	Partenavia P68B	24	28.11.13	
	G-BFBU, SE-FTM			
	Ravenair Aircraft Ltd Liverpool John Lennon		08.08.18E	
G-RVNO	Piper PA-34-200T Seneca II	34-7570303	21.03.14	
	G-VVBK, G-BSBS, G-BDRI, SE-GLG			
	Ravenair Aircraft Ltd Liverpool John Lennon		03.07.18E	
G-RVNP	Partenavia P68B	67	13.04.12	
	EC-IMD, I-TIZY			
	Ravenair Aircraft Ltd Liverpool John Lennon		12.02.18E	
G-RVNS	Van's RV-4	3340	12.10.07	
	G-CBGN C A Hawkins (Finchampstead)		20.07.19P	
	Built by G A Nash – project PFA 181-12443			
G-RVOM	Van's RV-8	82943	07.10.13	
	O D Mihalop Perranporth		01.07.16P	
	Built by O D Mihalop – project LAA 303-14894			
	(IE 02.10.17)			
G-RVPH	Van's RV-8	xxxx	25.05.04	
	J C P Herbert Audley End		23.01.19P	
	Built by J C P Herbert – project PFA 303-13906			

G-RVPL	Van's RV-8	81718	06.08.04
	B J Summers Old Buckenham		13.04.19P
	Built by A P Lawton – project PFA 303-13885		
G-RVPM	Van's RV-4	3181	20.02.06
	G-RVDS D P Lightfoot Headcorn		18.05.18P
	Built by D F Sargant – project PFA 181-12270		
G-RVPW	Van's RV-6A	xxxx	09.06.03
	C G Deeley Sittles Farm, Alrewas		08.09.18P
	Built by P Waldron – project PFA 181A-13481		
G-RVRA	Piper PA-28-140 Cherokee Cruiser	28-7625038	14.01.97
	G-OWVA, N4459X E W Roberts Caernarfon		16.05.19E
G-RVRB	Piper PA-34-200T Seneca II	34-7970440	24.02.97
	G-BTAJ, N22MJ, N45113		
	Ravenair Aircraft Ltd Liverpool John Lennon		16.02.18E
G-RVRE	Partenavia P68B	57	08.12.03
	D-GIFR, (N4412H), D-GIFR, LN-LMS		
	Ravenair Aircraft Ltd Liverpool John Lennon		14.01.19E
G-RVRH	Van's RV-3B	xxxx	17.02.03
	R Hodgson (Bramley, Guildford)		
	Built by R Hodgson – project PFA 099-10821		
	(NF 30.09.14)		
G-RVRJ	Piper PA-E23-250 Aztec E	27-7305004	12.10.04
	G-BBGB, N40206		
	Ravenair Aircraft Ltd Liverpool John Lennon		26.11.18E
G-RVRK	Piper PA-38-112 Tomahawk	38-79A1068	09.08.05
	G-BGZW, N9674N		
	Ravenair Aircraft Ltd Liverpool John Lennon		07.09.18E
G-RVRL	Piper PA-38-112 Tomahawk	38-78A0711	09.08.05
	G-BGBY, N9689N		
	Aviation South West Ltd Exeter Int'l		19.06.18E
G-RVRM	Piper PA-38-112 Tomahawk	38-78A0575	20.10.05
	G-BGEK, N9662N		
	Ravenair Aircraft Ltd Liverpool John Lennon		10.08.18E
G-RVRN	Piper PA-28-161 Warrior II	28-7916325	12.12.05
	G-BPID, N2137V		
	Ravenair Aircraft Ltd Liverpool John Lennon		25.04.18E
G-RVRO	Piper PA-38-112 Tomahawk II	38-82A0017	14.06.06
	G-BOUD, N91365		
	Ravenair Aircraft Ltd Liverpool John Lennon		14.09.18E
G-RVRP	Van's RV-7	xxxx	16.07.03
	R C Parris Holmbeck Farm, Burcott		15.05.18P
	Built by R C Parris – project PFA 323-14085		
G-RVRR	Piper PA-38-112 Tomahawk	38-79A0199	20.08.07
	G-BRHT, N2474C Cancelled 13.12.18 as PWFU		08.03.17
	Compton Abbas *Wreck dumped 08.18*		
G-RVRS	Robinson R22 Beta	1478	31.01.01
	G-XTEC, G-BYCK, N101EJ		
	Cancelled 14.09.04 by CAA		11.11.01
	Upper Heyford		
	Exhibited at shows on car roof rack, noted 10.16		
G-RVRT	Piper PA-28-140 Cherokee C	28-26933	13.09.06
	G-AYKX, N11C		
	Full Sutton Flying Centre Ltd Full Sutton		20.12.18E
G-RVRU	Piper PA-38-112 Tomahawk	38-80A0081	18.11.08
	G-NCFE, G-BKMK, OO-GME, (OO-HKD), N9676N		
	Ravenair Aircraft Ltd Liverpool John Lennon		04.01.18E
G-RVRV	Van's RV-4	4114	29.09.98
	P Jenkins (Nairn)		
	Built by P Jenkins – project PFA 181-13024		
	(NF 27.08.14)		
G-RVRW	Piper PA-23-250 Aztec E	27-7305045	17.12.04
	G-BAVZ, N40241		
	Ravenair Aircraft Ltd Liverpool John Lennon		15.10.13E
	(NF 23.09.16)		
G-RVRX	Partenavia P68B	62	27.04.10
	G-PART, F-GMPT, G-PART, OY-CEY, D-GATE,		
	PH-EEO, (N718R)		
	Ravenair Aircraft Ltd Liverpool John Lennon		21.01.19E
G-RVRY	Piper PA-38-112 Tomahawk	38-78A0155	12.07.10
	G-BTND, N9671T		
	Ravenair Aircraft Ltd Liverpool John Lennon		22.08.18E
G-RVRZ	Piper PA-23-250 Aztec E	27-7305142	09.11.10
	G-NRSC, N250MC, (N244AR), N250MC, EI-BXP,		
	G-BSFL, PH-NOA, 9M-AUS, PH-NOA, N40378		
	Ravenair Aircraft Ltd Liverpool John Lennon		15.01.19E

G-RVSA	Van's RV-6A	22357	19.05.99
	J Stevenson Longside		30.05.19P
	Built by W H Knott – project PFA 181A-12574		
G-RVSB	Van's RV-6	21099	05.01.17
	N606JP, N606DP S Beard (Walkeringham, Doncaster)		
	Built by D R Pierson (NF 05.01.17)		
G-RVSD	Van's RV-9A	xxxx	23.05.06
	S W Damarell (Peatmor, Swindon)		
	Built by S W Damarell – project PFA 320-14092		
	(NF 11.08.14)		
G-RVSE	Van's RV-6	23771	14.01.19
	G-USRV, N200HC S Eustace Monewden		01.11.18P
	Built by F M Carter		
G-RVSG	Van's RV-9A	xxxx	10.11.04
	S Gerrish Popham 'Special Lady'		19.04.19P
	Built by S Gerrish – project PFA 320-14265		
G-RVSH	Van's RV-6A	24220	20.09.02
	S F A Madi White Waltham		02.07.18P
	Built by S J D Hall – project PFA 181A-13026		
G-RVSK	Van's RV-9A	91268	20.03.14
	D A Kenworthy Morgansfield, Fishburn		
	Built by D A Kenworthy – project PFA 320-14505		
	(NF 31.05.18)		
G-RVSR	Van's RV-8	82451	04.06.07
	R K & S W Elders Sturgate		06.12.17P
	Built by R K & S W Elders – project PFA 303-14470		
G-RVST	Van's RV-6	22293	12.06.12
	G-BXYX, N2399C A F Vizoso RAF Halton		02.01.18P
	Built by M T Hathaway		
G-RVSX	Van's RV-6	244902	18.09.97
	M J Benham Headcorn		08.06.19P
	Built by R L West – project PFA 181-13090		
G-RVTA	Van's RV-7	74413	09.02.17
	A G Andrew (Llanfynydd, Wrexham)		
	Built by A G Andrew – project LAA 323-15308		
	(NF 08.02.17)		
G-RVTB	Van's RV-7	73550	12.11.15
	G-CIWM T M Bootyman Netherthorpe		14.02.19P
	Built by T Bootyman, W Duncan & V Millard		
	– project LAA 323-14932		
G-RVTE	Van's RV-6	xxxx	23.01.08
	T Feeny & E McShane Bellarena		
	Built by T Feeny & E McShane – project PFA 181A-13523		
G-RVTN	Van's RV-10	40609	15.05.07
	C I Law Strubby		13.12.18P
	Built by C I Law – project PFA 339-14602		
G-RVTT	Van's RV-7	70477	09.11.07
	R L Mitcham White Waltham		04.05.18P
	Built by A Phillips – project PFA 323-13852		
G-RVTW	Van's RV-12	xxxx	10.05.12
	A P Watkins Shenstone Hall Farm, Shenstone		08.05.18P
	Built by N A Jack & A P Watkins		
	– project LAA 363-14960		
G-RVTX	Van's RV-8	82517	31.10.16
	N315TX M N Stannard RAF Waddington		09.03.18P
	Built by D R Love		
G-RVUK	Van's RV-7	72441	08.06.06
	P D G Grist Sibson		12.03.18P
	Built by R J Fray – project PFA 323-14441		
G-RVVI	Van's RV-6	22383	26.01.93
	P R Thorne Cheddington		14.05.19P
	Built by J E Alsford & J N Parr – project PFA 181-12418		
G-RVWJ	Van's RV-9A	xxxx	06.09.12
	N J Williams-Jones Blackpool		
	Built by N J Williams-Jones – project LAA 320-15128;		
	on construction 12.17 (NF 19.07.16)		
G-RVXP	Van's RV-3B	11378	12.03.12
	N283RV A N Buchan Yeatsall Farm, Abbots Bromley		
	Built by P S Clohan (IE 01.06.17)		
G-RWAY	RotorWay Exec 162F	6414	18.11.04
	G-URCH C R Johnson		
	Top o' th' Close Farm, Upper Cumberworth		02.08.17P
	Built by S Andrews		

G-RWCA	Piper PA-18-150 Super Cub	18-8309010	20.07.15
	CS-DIO, N45474, Israel DFAF 126		
	R J Williamson Crowfield		07.09.18E
	Operated by Crowfield Flying Club;		
	crashed Beccles 07.04.18, rebuilt East Winch		
G-RWEW	Robinson R44 Clipper II	11148	05.04.06
	CJ Aviation Ltd (Newry)		28.05.19E
G-RWIA	Robinson R22 Beta	0753	26.11.07
	G-BOEZ S A Wolski		
	Walton Wood Farm, Thorpe Audlin		14.10.12E
	On rebuild 08.18 (NF 18.12.15)		
G-RWIN	Rearwin 175 Skyranger	1522	12.09.90
	N32391, NC32391		
	N D Battye & A B Bourne Old Warden		18.07.05P
	(NF 17.10.14)		
G-RWOD	Dan Rihn DR.107 One Design	05-506	05.02.13
	R S Wood Nottingham City		
	Built by R S Wood – project PFA 264-14472;		
	cleared to fly 12.18 (NF 31.08.18)		
G-RWSS	Denney Kitfox Model 2	xxxx	16.04.91
	J I V Hill (Moneyrea, Newtownards)		14.06.93P
	Built by R W Somerville – project PFA 172-12008;		
	stored dismantled 12.13 (NF 30.10.14)		
G-RWWW[M]	Westland WS-55 Whirlwind HCC.12 WA/418		21.06.90
	8727M, XR486 Cancelled 10.07.00 as WFU		25.08.96
	As 'XR486' in Queens Flight c/s		
	With The Helicopter Museum, Weston-super-Mare		
G-RXTV	Agusta A109E Power	11158	25.07.17
	G-GCMM, EI-DJO, D-HIRL, N32GH, D-HOME		
	Arena Aviation Ltd Redhill		26.10.18E
G-RXUK	Lindstrand LBL 105A	232	29.03.95
	E C & R K Scott Etwall, Derby 'X'		21.04.18E
G-RYAL	Avtech Jabiru UL	0212	06.07.99
	G R Oscroft (Old Whittington, Chesterfield)		31.05.16P
	Built by A C Ryall – project PFA 274A-13365;		
	hit street light 31.10.15 on approach to Sandtoft		
	& destroyed		
G-RYDR	AutoGyro MT-03	xxxx	04.03.08
	U Junger & H W Parsons (Hay-on-Wye, Hereford)		24.04.18P
	Assembled Rotorsport UK as c/n RSUK/MT-03/033		
G-RYFF	Agusta A109S Grand	22058	05.03.18
	G-DEUP, G-FUFU		
	Bandersnatch Ltd Partnership Inc Biggin Hill		19.11.19E
	Operated by Castle Air Ltd		
G-RYNS	Piper PA-32-301FT 6X	3232071	14.09.07
	N30970 D A Earle Dunkeswell		10.03.18E
G-RYPE	DG Flugzeugbau DG-1000T	10-113T35	20.03.08
	BGA 5315, (BGA 5292)		
	R Abbott tr DG1000T Partners Lasham 'E6'		08.12.17E
G-RYPH	Mainair Blade 912	1248-0500-7-W1041	08.06.00
	A R Young (Wheatley, Oxon)		21.11.18P
G-RYSE	Cessna TR182 Turbo Skylane RG II	R18200990	13.08.15
	N51VM, G-BZVO, D-EPOL, N739CX		
	Renger Racing GmbH & Co KG (Rothenburg, Germany)		24.07.19E
G-RYZZ	Robinson R44 Raven II	11418	15.11.06
	N31448 Rivermead Aviation Ltd Gloucestershire		16.02.18E
	Operated by Rise Helicopters		
G-RZEE	Schleicher ASW 19B	19126	07.04.08
	BGA 2282/DPX		
	R Christopherson Aston Down '999'		01.09.18E
G-RZLY	Flight Design CTSW	06-11-15	13.06.08
	N102RK J D Macnamara (Sandford, Crediton)		
	(NF 18.08.15)		
	Damaged landing 10.03.07 Double Eagle II Airport, Albuquerque,		
	New Mexico & probably not imported		

G-SAAA – G-SZZZ

G-SAAA	Flight Design CTSW	05-12-09	17.02.06
	Comunica Industries International Ltd Old Sarum		23.03.18P
	Assembled P&M Aviation Ltd as c/n 8161		
G-SAAR	AgustaWestland AW189	89003	20.11.15
	I-RAIQ British International Helicopter Services Ltd		
	RAF Mount Pleasant, Falkland Islands		20.11.18E

G-SABA	Piper PA-28R-201T Turbo Cherokee Arrow III		
		28R-7703268	22.08.79
	G-BFEN, N38745 C A Burton Sherburn-in-Elmet		30.07.18E
G-SACD	Cessna F172H	F172-0385	13.06.83
	G-AVCD Cancelled 29.11.10 as PWFU		27.07.00
	Brighton City *Built by Reims Cessna SA*		
	Instructional airframe at Northbrook College 09.16		
G-SACF	Cessna 152 II	15283175	21.03.85
	G-BHSZ, N47125 Cancelled 11.08.97 by CAA		08.06.98
	Derby *Derelict in open store 10.13*		
G-SACH	Stoddard-Hamilton GlaStar	5325	27.09.99
	R S Holt Croft Farm, Defford		20.12.18P
	Built by R S Holt – project PFA 295-13088; tailwheel u/c		
G-SACI	Piper PA-28-161 Warrior II	28-8216123	26.07.89
	N81535 PJC (Leasing) Ltd Stapleford		17.04.18E
G-SACL	Tecnam P2006T	152	19.07.16
	UR-LJA ?? Surrey Aero Club Ltd Thruxton		05.09.18E
G-SACM	TL 2000UK Sting Carbon	07-ST-247	30.04.08
	M Clare Orlingbury Hold Farm, Orlingbury		10.08.18P
	Built by M Clare – project LAA 347-14798;		
	badged 'Sting Sport'		
G-SACN	Scheibe SF25C Turbo-Falke	44731	25.09.14
	The Royal Air Force Gliding & Soaring Association		
	Cranwell North		23.09.18E
G-SACO	Piper PA-28-161 Warrior II	28-8416085	01.06.09
	N4358Z Stapleford Flying Club Ltd Stapleford		30.08.18E
G-SACP	Aero AT-3 R100	AT3-062	22.06.15
	SP-GEB Sherburn Aero Club Ltd Sherburn-in-Elmet		27.04.18E
G-SACR	Piper PA-28-161 Cadet	2841046	06.02.89
	N91618 Sherburn Aero Club Ltd Sherburn-in-Elmet		14.05.18E
G-SACS	Piper PA-28-161 Cadet	2841047	06.02.89
	N91619 Sherburn Aero Club Ltd Sherburn-in-Elmet		04.05.18E
G-SACT	Piper PA-28-161 Cadet	2841048	06.02.89
	N9162D Sherburn Aero Club Ltd Sherburn-in-Elmet		
	'Sherburn Aero Club'		09.04.19E
G-SACU	Piper PA-28-161 Cadet	2841049	06.02.89
	N9162X Cancelled 07.06.01 as PWFU		19.02.98
	Sowersby Bridge		
	Used as simulator 10.16, Ryburn High School		
G-SACW	Aero AT-3 R100	AT3-058	12.04.13
	OO-CFA, SP-GEW		
	Sherburn Aero Club Ltd Sherburn-in-Elmet		21.06.18E
G-SACX	Aero AT-3 R100	AT3-028	07.11.07
	Sherburn Aero Club Ltd Sherburn-in-Elmet		07.01.19E
G-SAEA	Supermarine 361 Spitfire LF.XVIe	CBAF IX 4693	03.02.15
	SL611 M Harris (Kidsgrove, Stoke-on-Trent)		
	(NF 07.01.19)		
G-SAFA	Agusta A109S Grand	22050	06.06.18
	G-PBWR, G-VERU, N35AG Myheli Ltd Oxford		03.08.19E
G-SAFE	Cameron N-77	511	14.02.79
	P J Waller Wymondham		21.04.91A
	(NF 19.12.14)		
G-SAFI	Piel CP.1320	xxxx	23.07.01
	C S Carleton-Smith (Lee Common, Great Missenden)		
	Built by C S Carleton-Smith – project		
	PFA 183-12103 (NF 02.05.18)		
G-SAGA	Grob G109B	6364	28.06.90
	OE-9254 M C Downey (Beedon, Newbury)		23.04.19E
G-SAGE	Luscombe 8A	2581	15.08.90
	G-AKTL, N71154, NC71154		
	C D Howell Bolt Head, Salcombe		28.04.18P
G-SAHI	Trago Mills SAH-1	001	21.10.80
	M J A Trudgill tr Hotel India Group RAF Henlow		14.08.19E
	Built by Trago Mills Ltd & designated Type SAH-1		
	(Designer S A Holloway)		
G-SAIG	Robinson R44 Raven II	11364	04.08.06
	Thurston Helicopters Ltd Headcorn		07.11.18E
G-SAJA	Schempp-Hirth Discus-2c	22/56	22.01.07
	BGA 5243/KOB J G Arnold Keevil 'JA'		26.05.19E
G-SAJB	Embraer EMB-135ER	145473	19.10.18
	G-RJXJ, PT-SVS Loganair Ltd Glasgow		22.07.19E
G-SAJC	Embraer EMB-145EP	145280	17.12.18
	G-RJXF, PT-SJW Loganair Ltd Glasgow		28.06.19E

G-SAJG	Embraer EMB-145EP	145126	08.03.19
	G-EMBI, PT-SDD Loganair Ltd Glasgow		22.04.19E
G-SAJH	Embraer EMB-145EP	145134	08.03.19
	G-EMBJ, PT-SDL Loganair Ltd Glasgow		26.05.19E
G-SAJI	Embraer EMB-145EP	145201	08.03.19
	G-EMBN, PT-SGQ Loganair Ltd Glasgow		12.01.20E
G-SAJM	Diamond DA.42 Twin Star	42.185	27.06.18
	G-CJFO, 5B-CLA		
	Skyborne Aviation Ltd Gloucestershire		04.05.19E
G-SAJR	Embraer EMB-135ER	145431	12.03.19
	G-RJXP, G-CDFS, EI-ORK, PT-SUC, (CN-RLG), PT-SUC		
	Loganair Ltd Glasgow		13.01.20E
G-SALD	Bombardier BD-700-1A10 Global 6000 9781		19.09.17
	C-FRYZ Esselco Aviation LLP Farnborough		
	(IE 03.01.18)		
G-SALE	Cameron Z-90	10944	15.12.06
	R D Baker Goodnestone, Canterbury *'Fell Reynolds'*		21.10.19E
G-SAMC	Comco Ikarus C42 FB80 Bravo	1207-7213	20.07.12
	C A & C D Spence (Swallowfield, Reading)		03.10.19P
	Assembled Red-Air UK		
G-SAMG	Grob G109B	6278	16.05.84
	The Royal Air Force Gliding & Soaring Association		
	RAF Odiham		16.01.17E
G-SAMY	Europa Aviation Europa XS	221	17.08.95
	P Vallis Tatenhill		14.09.18P
	Built by K R Tallent & P Vallis – project PFA 247-12901;		
	tricycle u/c		
G-SAMZ	Cessna 150D	15060536	19.04.84
	G-ASSO, N4536U A J Taylor Little Gransden		16.06.17E
G-SANT	Schempp-Hirth Discus bT	12/287	03.11.15
	G-JPIP, (BGA5347), HB-2159, D-KIDE		
	S Cervantes Portmoak *'SC'*		11.02.19E
G-SAOC	Schempp-Hirth Discus-2cT	54/72	29.06.07
	BGA 5288 The Royal Air Force Gliding		
	& Soaring Association RAF Halton *'R6'*		11.04.18E
	Operated by Chilterns Gliding Centre		
G-SAPA	Robinson R66 Turbine	0877	16.07.18
	S Chenevix-Trench & P Wills Denham		24.07.19E
G-SAPI	Piper PA-28-181 Archer II	28-7690191	10.05.16
	EC-CXA, N9531N		
	Biggleswade Flying Group Ltd Fenland		14.06.18E
G-SAPM	SOCATA TB-20 Trinidad	1009	08.12.04
	G-EWFN, G-BRTY G-SAPM Ltd Gloucestershire		18.05.18E
G-SARA	Piper PA-28-181 Archer II	28-7990039	06.04.81
	N21270 C P W Villa Brighton City		18.05.18E
G-SARJ	P&M Quik GT450	8460	04.06.09
	A R Jones Carlisle Lake District		14.06.18P
G-SARM	Comco Ikarus C42 FB80	0504-6674	13.05.05
	L Bligh tr G-SARM Group Redlands		29.06.18P
	Assembled Aerosport Ltd		
G-SARO[M]	Saro Skeeter AOP.12	S2/5097	17.07.78
	XL812 Cancelled 14.04.10 as WFU		
	As 'XL812' in AAC c/s		
	With Museum of Army Flying, AAC Middle Wallop		
G-SARP	Cessna R182 Skylane RG II	R18201652	31.03.15
	CS-ARP, N6226S		
	Aerobatica LDA (Rana, Lisbon, Portugal)		04.08.18E
G-SARV	Van's RV-4	3634	02.10.00
	J J Doswell tr The Hinton Flying Group		
	Hinton-in-the-Hedges		01.06.18P
	Built by S N Aston – project PFA 181-12606		
G-SASC	Beech B200C Super King Air	BL-150	30.12.05
	N6178D Gama Aviation (UK) Ltd Glasgow		12.01.19E
	Built by Raytheon Aircraft Company;		
	operated by Scottish Air Ambulance		
G-SASD	Beech B200C Super King Air	BL-151	04.01.06
	N6178F Gama Aviation (UK) Ltd Aberdeen Int'l		29.01.19E
	Built by Raytheon Aircraft Company;		
	operated by Scottish Air Ambulance		
G-SASF	Scheibe SF25C Turbo-Falke	44730	27.02.14
	The Royal Air Force Gliding & Soaring Association		
	RAF Halton		10.04.18E

G-SASG	Schleicher ASW 27-18E (*ASG 29E*)	29530	16.11.07
	BGA 5316 C Jackson & P T Reading Lasham *'29E'*		17.12.17E
G-SASI	CZAW Sportcruiser	xxxx	09.07.07
	K W Allan Balgrummo Steading, Bonnybank		04.01.18P
	Built by F Sayyah & J C Simpson		
	– project PFA 338-14651		
G-SASM	Westland Scout AH.1	F9713	16.02.10
	XV138 C J Marsden North Weald		
	As 'XV138' in AAC c/s; noted 11.18 (NF 24.10.18)		
G-SASN	Airbus MBB BK117 D-2 (*Eurocopter EC145 T2*)		
		20025	12.03.15
	D-HCBW Babcock Mission Critical Services		
	Onshore Ltd Glasgow City Heliport		12.03.18E
	Operated by Police Scotland Air Support Unit'		
G-SASR	McDonnell Douglas MD Explorer	900-00074	24.08.15
	G-LNAA, G-76-074, G-LNAA, N7030B		
	Specialist Aviation Services Ltd Henstridge		04.07.18E
	Operated by Dorset & Somerset Air Ambulance		
	as callsign 'Helimed 10'		
G-SASS	Airbus MBB BK117 D-2 (*Eurocopter EC145 T2*)		
		20022	13.01.15
	D-HCBT Babcock Mission Critical Services		
	Onshore Ltd Glasgow City Heliport		12.01.19E
	Operated by Scottish Air Ambulance as		
	callsign 'Helimed 05'		
G-SASX	Leonardo AW169	69064	03.04.18
	I-EASL Specialist Aviation Services Ltd Land's End		03.04.19E
	Operated by Island Helicopters		
G-SASY	Eurocopter EC130 B4	4760	23.06.09
	R J H Smith Denham		22.05.18E
G-SATI	Cameron Sphere-105	1901	16.12.88
	M A Stelling South Queensferry		22.06.19E
G-SATL	Cameron Sphere-105	2696	05.12.91
	M A Stelling South Queensferry		22.06.19E
G-SATM	Diamond DA.42M Twin Star	42.M005	24.04.18
	OE-FYE, (YVO151), OE-UDN, OE-VPY		
	Skyborne Aviation Ltd Gloucestershire		27.02.19E
G-SATN	Piper PA-25-260 Pawnee C	25-5179	10.08.05
	N8722L The Royal Air Force Gliding		
	& Soaring Association RAF Halton		16.03.18E
G-SAUF	Colt 90A	1497	25.05.89
	K H Medau Bad Sackingen, Germany		21.06.04A
	New envelope c/n 2492 c.1990/1991 (NF 18.12.17)		
G-SAUK	Rans S-6-ES Coyote II	0904.1611	05.01.05
	J M A Juanos Bagby		26.04.18P
	Built by E Robshaw & D A Smith		
	– project PFA 204-14346; tricycle u/c		
G-SAUL	Robin HR.200-160	106	18.09.17
	SE-KNA, OY-AJP J C Wignall Elmsett		26.09.19E
G-SAUO	Cessna A185F Skywagon	18502324	01.02.10
	CS-AUO, N53028 T G Lloyd Shelsley Beauchamp		28.05.18E
G-SAVA	ICP MXP-740 Savannah XLS D(1)	xxxx	25.01.16
	E N L Troffigue (West Parley, Ferndown)		
	Built by E Troffigue – project BMA/HB/666		
	(NF 25.01.16)		
G-SAVY	ICP MXP-740 Savannah VG Jabiru(1) 06-03-51-469		02.01.09
	S P Yardley Otherton		01.07.18P
	Built by C S Hollingworth & S P Yardley		
	– project BMAA/HB/499		
G-SAWG	Scheibe SF25C Turbo-Falke	44732	24.03.15
	The Royal Air Force Gliding & Soaring Association		
	RAF Cosford		16.03.18E
G-SAWI	Piper PA-32RT-300T Turbo Lance II 32R-7887069		23.06.99
	OY-CJJ, N36719 R R Tyler Blackbushe		31.07.19E
	Official type data 'PA-32RT-300T Turbo Cherokee		
	Lance II' is incorrect		
G-SAXL	Schempp-Hirth Duo Discus XLT	243	07.02.13
	(BGA 5735) The Royal Air Force Gliding		
	& Soaring Association Keevil *'16'*		17.04.19E
G-SAXT	Schempp-Hirth Duo Discus xT	158/513	15.03.07
	BGA 5274, (BGA 5242), D-KIIH		
	The Royal Air Force Gliding & Soaring Association		
	RAF Halton *'26'*		14.04.18E
	Operated by Chilterns Gliding Centre		

G-SAYE Dornier 228-200 8046 29.05.15
D-IFLM, TF-CSF, TF-VMF, TF-CST, TF-ABD, TF-ELF,
LN-NVC, D-IDBN Aurigny Air Services Ltd Guernsey 30.11.19E

G-SAYS Rotary Air Force RAF 2000 GTX-SE H2-00-11-466 04.09.00
G D Prebble Enstone 16.10.18P
Built by K Aziz – project PFA G/13-1322

G-SAYX Cessna 152 15284658 24.11.14
CS-AYX, N6296M
Aero Club de Portugal Cascais, Portugal 10.12.18E

G-SAZM Piper J-3C-65 Cub 18584 04.05.12
N717PC, G-SAZM, ZS-AZM
I E M J Van Vuuren Felixkirk 08.06.18E

G-SAZY Avtech Jabiru J400 xxxx 16.04.03
S M Pink Biggin Hill 09.07.18P
Built by N J Bond – project PFA 325-14057

G-SAZZ Piel CP.328 Super Emeraude xxxx 04.07.01
D J Long Nympsfield 20.08.18P
Built by D J Long – project PFA 216-11940

G-SBAG Phoenix Currie Wot xxxx 07.09.12
G-BFAH R W Clarke (Heald Green, Cheadle)
Built by N Hamilton-Wright – project PFA 058-11376
(NF 28.06.16)

G-SBDB Remos GX 353 07.12.09
D J Brook tr G-SBDB Group Deanland 20.09.18W

G-SBII Steen Skybolt xxxx 24.03.14
K G, P D & P J Begley Fenland 22.11.18P
Built by P & P K Begley – project LAA 064-15196

G-SBIZ Cameron Z-90 10348 12.12.02
Snow Business International Ltd Ebley, Stroud
'Snow Business' 29.06.18E

G-SBKR SOCATA TB-10 Tobago 1077 10.03.04
D-EAGG Profit Invest Sp Zoo (Wroclaw, Poland) 09.11.18E

G-SBLT Steen Skybolt MH-01 14.04.92
S D Arnold tr Skybolt Group (Coventry)
Built by M A McCallum & N Workman (NF 06.02.18)

G-SBOL Steen Skybolt 555 06.12.07
M J Tetlow RAF Halton 27.06.18P
Built by K R H Wingate – project PFA 064-14453

G-SBOY Piper PA-28-181 Archer III 2843157 11.06.18
G-LACD, G-BYBG, N47BK
Phoenix Flight Training Ltd Cumbernauld 19.12.19E

G-SBRK Aero AT-3 R100 AT3-021 14.03.07
(F-GURH) Sywell Aerodrome Ltd Sywell 25.04.18E

G-SBSB Diamond DA.40NG Star 40.N319 20.12.16
Diamond Aviation Training Ltd Redhill 09.01.19E
Also operates from Brighton City

G-SBUS NAMC B-N BN-2A-26 Islander 3013 31.10.86
G-BMMH, RP-C578
Isles of Scilly Skybus Ltd Land's End 17.04.19E
Built by Philippine Aerospace Development Corporation
(PADC)

G-SCAA Eurocopter EC135 T2+ 0151 21.09.15
G-SASB Babcock Mission Critical Services
Onshore Ltd Perth 05.10.18E
Operated by Scottish Charity Air Ambulance
as callsign 'Helimed 76'

G-SCAN Wallis WA-116/100/R 001 05.07.82
Cancelled 03.08.16 as PWFU 04.08.10
Old Warden Stored 10.16

G-SCAP Leonardo AW109SP Grand New 22396 20.03.19
I-EASO Apollo Air Services Ltd Carlisle Lake District 19.03.20E

G-SCCA Cessna 510 Citation Mustang 510-0106 30.12.14
OE-FMY, N4076J, (OE-FWW) Airplay Ltd Jersey 15.09.18E

G-SCCZ CZAW Sportcruiser 700492 29.10.08
J W Ellis & M P Hill Wolverhampton Halfpenny Green 22.03.18P
Built by J W Ellis – project LAA 338-14845

G-SCFC Ultramagic S-90 90/148 25.04.16
J S Russon Cheadle Hulme, Cheadle 23.05.19E

G-SCHI Eurocopter AS.350B2 Ecureuil 3337 05.02.01
F-WQOQ Patriot Aviation Ltd Birmingham 05.06.19E

G-SCHZ Eurocopter AS.355N Ecureuil 2 5663 26.04.12
ZS-HND, G-SCHZ, G-STON, VP-BCE
Patriot Aviation Ltd Birmingham 03.11.18E
Operated by British International Helicopter Services Ltd

G-SCII Agusta A109C 7628 18.08.06
G-JONA, VP-CWA, JA6610 Plattreid Ltd Biggin Hill 29.04.18E

G-SCIP SOCATA TB-20 Trinidad GT 2014 19.09.00
F-OILO The Studio People Ltd Welshpool 26.04.18E

G-SCIR Piper PA-31 Navajo C 31-7712038 02.03.17
N522AW, N522FW, N522W, N63718
2 Excel Aviation Ltd Sywell 12.06.19E

G-SCLX FLS Aerospace Sprint 160 002 14.07.94
G-PLYM J K Edgley tr Aero Sprint Group Thruxton 07.11.14R
(NF 21.12.15)

G-SCMG Comco Ikarus C42 FB80 Bravo 1402-7304 18.02.14
C J Bishop & B N Thresher Dunkeswell 19.02.20P
Assembled Red-Air UK

G-SCMR Piper PA-31 Navajo C 31-7812114 07.02.17
N27773 2 Excel Aviation Ltd Sywell 29.05.19E

G-SCNN Schempp-Hirth Standard Cirrus 173 22.12.07
BGA 1677/CNN
G C Short (Leefdaal, Belgium) 'CNN' 16.06.19E

G-SCOL Gippsland GA-8 Airvan GA8-05-088 28.03.06
VH-FNG Parachuting Aircraft Ltd Old Sarum 17.03.18E

G-SCOR Eurocopter EC155 B1 6968 03.12.14
3A-MDR, M-NACO, F-WWOX
Starspeed Ltd Fairoaks 02.12.18E

G-SCPD Reality Escapade 912(1) JA.ESC.0015 30.01.04
C W Potts Eshott 14.08.17P
Built by R Gibson – project BMAA/HB/319; tricycle u/c

G-SCPI CZAW Sportcruiser 700460 09.12.08
P F J Burton & I M Speight Henstridge 22.02.18P
Built by P R W Goslin & I M Speight
– project LAA 338-14855

G-SCPJ Hawker 900XP HA-0140 14.11.17
M-CKAY, G-KTIA, LX-KAT, N6340T
Saxonair Charter Ltd Norwich Int'l 14.12.18E

G-SCPL Piper PA-28-140 Cherokee Cruiser 28-7725160 04.05.89
G-BPVL, N1785H Aeros Leasing Ltd Gloucestershire 23.12.16E
(IE 29.08.17)

G-SCRZ CZAW Sportcruiser 3854 29.08.07
R Vora Stow Maries 03.06.18P
Built by P M Grant – project PFA 338-14684

G-SCSC CZAW Sportcruiser 700826 03.10.08
G Chalmers Monewden 18.11.19P
Built by A Daltry-Cooke – project LAA 338-14852

G-SCTA Westland Scout AH.1 F9701 18.12.95
XV126 G R Harrison North Weald 12.10.18P

G-SCTR Piper PA-31 Navajo C 31-7912112 16.03.17
N331DB 2 Excel Aviation Ltd Sywell 15.06.19E

G-SCUB Piper PA-18-135 Super Cub (L-21B-PI) 18-3847 13.12.78
PH-GAX, R Netherlands AF R-157, 54-2447
J D Needham Fenland 31.05.10E
Fuselage No.18-3849; as '54-2447'
in US Army c/s (NF 12.07.16)

G-SCUL Rutan Cozy 0639 28.05.98
K R W Scull (Trostrey, Usk)
Built by K R W Scull – project PFA 159-13212
(NF 11.12.14)

G-SCZR CZAW Sportcruiser 4167 07.05.08
G Farrar Netherthorpe 14.09.18P
Built by D L Walker – project PFA 338-14647

G-SDAT Flight Design CTSW 07-03-21 23.07.07
S P Pearson Fenland 03.04.18P
Assembled P&M Aviation Ltd as c/n 8312

G-SDCI Bell 206B-2 JetRanger II 925 24.02.00
G-GHCL, G-SHVV, N72GM, N83106
Heliwork (Services) Ltd Thruxton 24.07.12E
(NF 01.11.17)

G-SDEV de Havilland DH.104 Dove 6 04472 29.03.90
XK895
Cancelled 04.01.19 as PWFU 17.09.01
Built as de Havilland DH.104 Sea Devon C.20;
displayed at South Wales Aircraft Museum, St Athan;
as 'XK895:CU-19' in RN 771 Sqdn c/s

G

G-SDFM	Evektor EV-97 Eurostar	xxxx	23.08.02	
	S Moore tr G-SDFM Eurostar Group			
	Priory Farm, Tibenham		21.06.18P	
	Built by A K Paterson – project PFA 315-13884			
G-SDII	Eurocopter AS.350B2 Ecureuil	2825	17.11.17	
	HB-ZKY, G-PROB, G-PROD			
	Airbourne Solutions Ltd Five Acres Farm, Gamlingay		31.10.18E	
G-SDNI	Supermarine 361 Spitfire LF.IXe	CBAF IX 1892	02.04.09	
	Burmese AF UB441, Israel DFAF 2020, Czech.AF A-719,			
	ML119 P M Andrews (High Wycombe)			
	(NF 20.05.16)			
G-SDOA	Aeropro EuroFOX 912(S)	55218	31.07.18	
	S P S Dornan Latch Farm, Kirknewton		26.02.20P	
	Built by S P S Dornan – project LAA 376-15554;			
	tricycle u/c			
G-SDOB	Tecnam P2002-EA Sierra	163	26.04.06	
	A B Dean Strathaven		30.04.18P	
	Built by G E Collard & S P S Dornan			
	– project PFA 333-14529			
G-SDOI	Aeroprakt A-22 Foxbat	UK014	26.06.03	
	S A Owen Latch Farm, Kirknewton		29.03.18P	
	Built by S P S Dornan – project PFA 317-14064			
G-SDOZ	Tecnam P92-EA Echo-Super	825	09.09.04	
	D M Stewart tr Cumbernauld Flyers G-SDOZ			
	Cumbernauld		08.05.18P	
	Built by S P S Dornan – project PFA 318A-14287			
G-SDRV	Van's RV-8	83544	31.08.16	
	S M Dawson Eshott			
	Built by S M Dawson – project LAA 303-15375			
	(NF 31.08.16)			
G-SDRY	Cessna 525C CitationJet CJ4	525C0134	19.09.13	
	N94FP, N5067U			
	Dowdeswell Aviation LLP Gloucestershire		18.09.18E	
G-SDTL	Guimbal Cabri G2	1110	08.09.15	
	W R Pitcher t/a Regal Group UK			
	Bourne Park, Hurstbourne Tarrant		31.08.18E	
G-SDTO	Stolp SA.300 Starduster Too	xxxx	11.07.18	
	M J Golder Barton Ashes, Crawley Down			
	Built by M J Golder – project LAA 035-12384			
	(NF 11.07.18)			
G-SDWV	Robinson R66 Turbine	0864	10.05.18	
	Dreamwalker Ltd (Denham)		23.05.19E	
	Based on M/Y 'Ocean Dreamwalker III'			
G-SEAF	Hawker Sea Fury FB.11	41H/63631x	07.09.17	
	VH-SFY, G-BWOL, D-CACY, G-9-66, WG599			
	Patina Ltd Chino, CA, USA			
	Hawker c/n believed to be 41H/63631x; on rebuild 09.17			
	(NF 07.09.17)			
	Note D-CACY regd 07.09.62 as c/n ES3617 by Deutscher			
	Luftfahrt- Beratungsdienst (German Registration authority)			
	(ES = Ernst Seibert)			
G-SEAI	Cessna U206G	U20604059	20.03.92	
	N756FQ K A O'Connor Dublin Weston, RoI			
	'National Flight Centre'		12.06.08	
	Fixed-Wing Amphibian; stored 05.14 (NF 14.03.17)			
G-SEAL	Robinson R44 Raven II	12508	23.07.13	
	G-KLNJ, OO-PVZ A Soria Turin-Aeritalia, Italy		06.02.18E	
G-SEAT	Colt 42A	817	28.05.86	
	T G Read Mobberley, Knutsford *'Fly Virgin'*		26.03.17E	
G-SEBN	Best Off Skyranger 912S(1)	SKR0311406	08.06.09	
	C M James Maypole Farm, Chislet		22.08.18P	
	Built by C M James – project BMAA/HB/363			
G-SEBS	Ultramagic M-77	77/416	10.07.18	
	C Collins Clifton, Preston			
	(IE 10.07.18)			
G-SEDC	Fairchild 24W-46	W46342	28.01.19	
	N77642 G E J Spooner (Kelvedon, Colchester)			
	(IE 28.01.19)			
G-SEDO	Cameron N-105	10388	28.03.03	
	I M Ashpole Ross-on-Wye *'Agfa'*		02.08.18E	
G-SEED	Piper J-3C-90 Cub (L-4H-PI)	12499	28.01.80	
	EI-BAP, F-BFBZ, 44-80203, 43-29807			
	J H Seed Black Springs Farm, Castle Bytham		10.09.18P	
	Fuselage No.10932: probably rebuilt 1945			

G-SEEE	P&M Quik GT450	8235	22.01.07	
	I M Spence Rufforth East		18.02.18P	
G-SEEK	Cessna T210N Turbo Centurion II	21064579	14.10.83	
	N9721Y (?) A Hopper Little Shelford		11.06.19E	
	Official p/i 'N9271Y' is incorrect			
G-SEFA	Piper PA-38-112 Tomahawk	38-78A0597	19.01.17	
	EC-DFU, N9671N Ace Line Ltd Mutxamel, Spain		14.07.17E	
G-SEHK	Cessna 182T Skylane	18282132	18.05.11	
	N232TD, N63276 GolfHK Ltd Biggin Hill		03.02.18E	
G-SEJW	Piper PA-28-161 Warrior II	28-7816469	19.04.78	
	N9557N Tor Financial Consulting Ltd Norwich Int'l		03.07.18E	
G-SELA	Cessna 152	15282590	12.06.09	
	G-FLOP, N69265 Cloud Global Ltd Perth		08.01.18E	
	Operated by ACS Flight Training			
G-SELB	Piper PA-28-161 Warrior II	28-7816599	12.06.09	
	G-LFSK, SE-IAD			
	POM Flight Training Ltd Humberside		10.05.18E	
G-SELC	Diamond DA.42NG Twin Star	42.032	30.06.05	
	Stapleford Flying Club Ltd Stapleford		30.08.18E	
G-SELF	Europa Aviation Europa	279	10.08.01	
	N D Crisp, E J Hatcher & A H Lams Rochester		07.10.17P	
	Built by N D Crisp, E J Hatcher & A H Lams			
	– project PFA 247-12996; tailwheel u/c (IE 13.12.17)			
G-SELL	Robin DR.400-180 Régent	1153	07.03.85	
	D-EEMT CR Beard Farmers Ltd			
	Grange Farm, Grassthorpe		20.04.18E	
G-SELY	Agusta-Bell 206B-3 JetRanger III	8740	26.07.96	
	M D Tracey (Home Farm, Evenlode)		15.03.18E	
G-SEMI	Piper PA-44-180 Seminole	44-7995052	23.02.99	
	G-DENW, N21439 J Benfell & M Djukic North Weald		23.03.08E	
	Stored externally 07.18 (NF 27.11.14)			
G-SEMR	Cessna T206H Turbo Stationair	T20608669	06.02.07	
	N11347 Semer LLP Elmsett		16.03.18E	
G-SENA	Rutan Long-EZ	1325	11.11.96	
	F-PZSQ, F-WZSQ			
	G Bennett (Caister-on-Sea, Great Yarmouth)			
	Built by R Bazin (NF 16.02.16)			
G-SEND	Colt 90A	2100	02.12.91	
	Air du Vent Paris 19, France *'Motorola'*		14.07.12E	
	(NF 30.03.15)			
G-SENE	Piper PA-34-200T Seneca II	34-8170069	20.11.03	
	N797WA, N8314P Orion Coil Coating Ltd Elstree		12.09.19E	
G-SENS	Eurocopter EC135 T2+	0833	10.09.09	
	T Duggan & D Saville t/a Saville Air Services Oxford		15.09.18E	
G-SENX	Piper PA-34-200T Seneca II	34-7870356	15.05.95	
	G-DARE, G-WOTS, G-SEVL, N36742			
	First Air Ltd Haverfordwest		24.05.12E	
	Stored 06.16 (NF 24.01.18)			
G-SEPT	Cameron N-105	1880	22.11.88	
	A G Merry Temple Valley, Winchester *'septodont'*		01.07.18E	
G-SERE	Diamond DA.42 Twin Star	42.314	19.12.07	
	SERE Ltd Belfast Int'l		06.01.19E	
G-SERL	SOCATA TB-10 Tobago	109	28.05.92	
	G-LANA, EI-BIH G C Jarvis Henstridge		05.10.18E	
G-SERV	Cameron N-105	10382	16.04.03	
	Servo & Electronic Sales Ltd Lydd, Romney Marsh			
	'Servo connectors'		15.06.18E	
G-SETH	de Havilland DHC-1 Chipmunk 22	30	26.07.07	
	CS-DAI, Portuguese AF 1340			
	Cancelled 24.01.08 as PWFU			
	MoD St Athan *Built by OGMA; on rebuild 09.14*			
G-SETI	Sky 80-16	4853	25.09.00	
	R P Allan Aston Rowant, Watlington		08.07.16E	
	Built by Cameron Balloons Ltd			
G-SEUK	Cameron TV-80	3810	12.04.96	
	T Read & N Smith t/a Mobberley Balloon Collection			
	Knutsford & Goole		24.03.00A	
	(NF 21.03.14)			
G-SEVA	Replica Plans SE.5A	xxxx	19.06.85	
	D P Curtis tr G-SEVA Trust Kilkerran		19.06.15P	
	Built by I D Gregory – project PFA 020-10955;			
	as 'F-141:G' in RFC 141 Sqdn c/s (NF 14.08.17)			

G-SEVE	Cessna 172N Skyhawk II	17269970	10.01.90	
	N738GR Imagineer London Ltd Beccles		23.04.18E	
G-SEVN	Van's RV-7	70413	13.09.01	
	N Reddish Netherthorpe '777'		04.09.18P	
	Built by N Reddish – project PFA 323-13795			
G-SEXE	Scheibe SF25C Falke 2000	44396	31.07.03	
	N716SF, (D-KNII)			
	B J Griffiths tr SF25C G-SEXE Syndicate Saltby		28.07.18E	
G-SEXX	Piper PA-28-161 Warrior II	28-7816196	12.05.01	
	SE-GVD Weald Air Services Ltd Headcorn		16.01.19E	
G-SEXY[M]	American AA-1 Yankee	AA1-0442	30.06.81	
	G-AYLM Cancelled 15.11.00 by CAA		17.03.95	
	Registered incorrectly as c/n AA1-0042			
	With Wirral Aviation Society, Liverpool-John Lennon			
G-SEZA	Schleicher ASW 20C	20824	16.01.18	
	(BGA 5950), D-3493 A H Brown Portmoak 'ZA'			
G-SFAR	Comco Ikarus C42 FB100	0704-6883	27.03.07	
	R Moore Newtownards		15.06.18P	
	Assembled Aerosport Ltd			
G-SFCM	P&M PulsR	8762	20.12.17	
	J D Harrison Rougham		11.12.19P	
G-SFLA	Comco Ikarus C42 FB80	0701-6867	15.06.07	
	Solent Flight Ltd Phoenix Farm, Lower Upham		06.07.16P	
	Assembled Aerosport Ltd; bounced landing			
	Phoenix Farm, Lower Upham 13.05.16 & extensively			
	damaged; Permit suspended 21.05.16			
G-SFLB	Comco Ikarus C42 FB80	0709-6914	13.11.07	
	Solent Flight Ltd Phoenix Farm, Lower Upham		30.05.18P	
	Assembled Aerosport Ltd			
G-SFLY	Diamond DA.40 Star	40.362	31.03.04	
	L & N P L Turner Sleap		23.06.18E	
G-SFOX	RotorWay Exec 90	5059	11.10.93	
	G-BUAH J G H Vissers (America, Netherlands)		07.04.10	
	Built I L Griffith (NF 13.03.19)			
G-SFSL	Cameron Z-105	10308	31.07.02	
	A J Gregory Calcot, Cheltenham 'Somerfield'		10.06.18E	
G-SFTA[M]	Westland SA.341G Gazelle 1	1039	10.09.82	
	HB-XIL, G-BAGJ, (XW858) Cancelled 21.05.86 as WFU		24.02.86	
	As 'XZ345:T' in.AAC c/s			
	Crashed near Alston, Cumbria 07.03.84			
	With North East Land Sea and Air Museum, Usworth			
G-SFTZ	Slingsby T67M-160 Firefly	2000	07.02.83	
	A B Slinger tr Slingsby T67M Group			
	Sherburn-in-Elmet		07.12.18E	
G-SGEN	Comco Ikarus C42 FB80	0407-6611	27.08.04	
	G A Arturi Old Sarum		10.01.19P	
	Assembled Fly Buy Ultralights Ltd			
G-SGFE	Liberty XL-2	0050	20.11.15	
	G-OLAR, M-OLAR, N564XL I Fidler Retford Gamston		29.03.19E	
G-SGNT	Townsend Skylark	xxxx	31.07.15	
	N H Townsend Old Sarum			
	Built by N H Townsend – project LAA 351-14944			
	(IE 15.11.17)			
G-SGRP	Agusta AW109SP Grand New	22236	22.09.11	
	Apollo Air Services Ltd Carlisle Lake District		21.09.18E	
	Operates as callsign 'Solway 01'			
G-SGSE	Piper PA-28-181 Archer II	28-7890332	02.12.96	
	G-BOJX, N3774M U Patel Manchester Barton		17.02.18E	
G-SGSG	Bombardier BD-700-1A11 Global 5000 9780		28.06.17	
	C-FRZM TAG Aviation (UK) Ltd Farnborough		27.06.18E	
G-SGTS	Viking Air DHC-6-400 Twin Otter	918	21.05.15	
	C-FVIK Loganair Ltd Glasgow		26.05.19E	
G-SHAA	Enstrom 280C-UK Shark	1011	08.07.88	
	N280Q D McCann (Clonaslee, Co Laois, RoI)		30.09.18E	
G-SHAF	Robinson R44 Raven II	10892	20.10.05	
	H S Thirsk t/a HS Thirsk & Son Glebe Farm, Bielby		12.04.18E	
G-SHAK	Cameron Cabin	2820	23.08.07	
	SE-ZHO, G-ODIS Magical Adventures Ltd			
	West Bloomfield, MI, USA		27.09.09E	
	(NF 03.06.15)			
G-SHAR	Cessna 182T Skylane	18281636	11.11.05	
	N1968L G N Clarkson Oxford		08.02.18E	

G-SHAY	Piper PA-28R-201T Turbo Cherokee Arrow III			
		28R-7703365	17.09.01	
	G-JEFS, G-BFDG, N47381			
	K Drage tr Alpha Yankee Flying Group Earls Colne		23.02.18E	
G-SHAZ	Guimbal Cabri G2	1238	03.12.18	
	Solent Helicopters Ltd t/a Elite Helicopters Goodwood		08.01.20E	
	(NF 03.12.18)			
G-SHBA	Reims/Cessna F152	F15201570	10.12.12	
	OO-SHB Paul's Planes Ltd Denham		12.11.18E	
G-SHCK	Comco Ikarus C42 FB80	1510-7426	11.12.15	
	F S Group Ltd Gloucestershire		17.01.19P	
	Assembled Red Aviation; operated by The Flying Shack			
G-SHED	Piper PA-28-181 Archer II	28-7890068	12.06.89	
	G-BRAU, N47411			
	D R Allard tr G-SHED Flying Group Gloucestershire		18.05.18E	
G-SHEE	P&M Quik GT450	8284	31.07.07	
	C J Millership (Scot Hay, Newcastle)		29.08.18P	
G-SHEZ	Mainair Pegasus Quik	7993	28.10.03	
	R & S Wells Baker Barracks, Thorney Island		16.11.18P	
	Built by Mainair Sports Ltd			
G-SHHH	Glaser-Dirks DG-101G Elan	E71G46	13.03.08	
	BGA 2749/EKP J C Brattle Nympsfield 'EKP'		12.04.18E	
	Built by Elan Tovarna Sportnega Orodja N.Sol.O			
G-SHIM	CFM Streak Shadow	K 228-SA	19.05.93	
	P D Babin Old Sarum		25.10.13P	
	Built by E G Shimmin – project PFA 206-12501			
	(NF 23.07.18)			
G-SHIV	Gulfstream GA-7 Cougar	GA7-0092	22.11.84	
	N713G Cancelled 16.09.04 by CAA		18.01.98	
	Cranfield Open store 12.15, for sale on eBay			
G-SHKI	Comco Ikarus C42 FB80	1311-7292	03.01.14	
	Poet Pilot (UK) Ltd (Coleford)		15.01.18P	
	Assembled Red-Air UK			
G-SHKK[M]	Hughes 269A	111-0029	17.05.89	
	N8716F Cancelled 12.08.94 by CAA			
	(No marks carried)			
	With Ashburton Aviation Museum, New Zealand			
G-SHLE	Agusta A109E Power	11100	01.08.18	
	I-AWCT, OO-DIX, G-CHVA, OE-XSA			
	Sloane Helicopters Ltd Sywell		23.04.19E	
G-SHLS	Agusta A109E Power	11789	28.09.18	
	N103H Sloane Helicopters Ltd Sywell			
	(IE 28.09.18)			
G-SHMI	Evektor EV-97 teamEurostar UK	2007-3013	03.10.07	
	M Perry tr Mike India Flying Group Gloucestershire		02.10.18P	
	Assembled Cosmik Aviation Ltd;			
	operated by Skytime Flight Training			
G-SHMN	Alpi Pioneer 300 Hawk	297	13.10.16	
	G-GKEV E G Shimmin Shobdon		15.06.18P	
	Built by K D Taylor – project LAA 330A-14965			
G-SHOG	Colomban MC-15 Cri-Cri	001	03.10.96	
	G-PFAB, F-PYPU C S & K D Rhodes Henstridge		16.07.14P	
	Built by G Nappez (IE 08.05.17)			
G-SHOW	Morane Saulnier MS.733 Alcyon French AF 125		01.10.80	
	F-BMQJ, French AF 125			
	P Cartwright & F A Forster (Ashford)			
	(NF 09.02.16)			
G-SHPP	Hughes 269A	36-0481	24.07.89	
	N80559, 64-18169 Cancelled 09.12.08 as destroyed		23.04.08	
	Dromore, Co Down Wreck stored 11.17			
G-SHRD	Eurocopter AS.350B2 Ecureuil	4712	22.07.14	
	G-LHTB, F-HFLO, F-WQYF			
	Jet Helicopters Ltd Brighton City		17.08.18E	
G-SHRK	Enstrom 280C-UK Shark	1173	06.01.97	
	N373SA, G-SHRK, G-BGMX, EI-CCS, G-SHXX,			
	G-BGMX, EI-BHR, G-BGMX, (F-GBOS)			
	Shark Helicopters Ltd Brighton City		22.12.18E	
G-SHRT	Robinson R44 Raven II	10473	14.09.04	
	PH-WKW, G-SHRT			
	Hingley Aviation Ltd Wellesbourne Mountford		04.04.18E	
G-SHSH	Europa Aviation Europa	113	07.04.98	
	S G Hayman & J Price Rochester		20.08.18P	
	Built by D G Hillam – project PFA 247-12722;			
	tailwheel u/c			

G-SHSP | Cessna 172S Skyhawk SP | 172S8079 (?) | 25.03.99
N9552Q   Shropshire Aero Club Ltd   Sleap | 20.08.19E
Official c/n '172S8059' is incorrect

G-SHUC | Rans S-6-ESD Coyote II | 0892.338 | 27.08.10
G-MYKN   E W Calvin   (Macosquin, Coleraine) | 19.04.19P
Built by S E Hartles – project PFA 204-12361;
tricycle u/c (IE 12.08.18)

G-SHUF | Mainair Blade | 1241-0200-7-W1034 | 10.03.00
G Holdcroft   (Haslington, Crewe) | 26.10.18P

G-SHUG | Piper PA-28R-201T Turbo Cherokee Arrow III
| | 28R-7703048 | 17.05.88
N1026Q   G-SHUG Ltd   Elstree | 09.06.18E

G-SHUI | Cessna 680A Citation Latitude | 680A0102 | 27.09.17
N52144   Air Charter Scotland Ltd   London Stansted | 15.10.18E

G-SHUU | Enstrom 280C-UK-2 Shark | 1221 | 16.10.89
G-OMCP, G-KENY, G-BJFG, N8617N
Tinles DOO   Burbach, Germany | 10.10.19E
(IE 13.06.18)

G-SHUV | Aerosport Woody Pusher | xxxx | 20.09.02
J R Wraight   (Chatham)
Built by J R Wraight – project PFA 007A-13960
(NF 14.10.16)

G-SHWK | Cessna 172S Skyhawk SP | 172S9642 | 02.06.04
N21733   The Cambridge Aero Club Ltd   Cambridge | 19.06.18E

G-SHWN | North American P-51D Mustang | 122-40417 | 02.03.15
N167F, CF-PCZ, RCAF 9279, 44-73877
Sharkmouth Ltd   Duxford | 23.04.19P
As 'KH774:GA-S' in RAF c/s

G-SIBK | Raytheon Beech A36 Bonanza | E-3034 | 13.09.11
N36SU, OY-TFE, N1096Y
W Robson   Retford Gamston | 01.09.19E

G-SICA | Britten-Norman BN-2B-20 Islander | 2304 | 19.07.06
G-SLAP   Shetland Leasing & Property Development Ltd
Tingwall   '*www.Shetland.gov.uk*' | 17.12.19E

G-SICB | Pilatus B-N BN-2B-20 Islander | 2260 | 12.06.06
G-NESU, G-BTVN   Shetland Islands Council
Tingwall   '*www.Shetland.gov.uk*' | 02.04.19E

G-SIGN | Piper PA-39 Twin Comanche C/R | 39-8 | 09.02.78
OY-TOO, N8853Y   D Buttle   Blackbushe | 01.12.17E

G-SIIE | Pitts S-2B | 5057 | 06.02.04
G-SKYD, N5331N
S M Brownlow tr Wild Thing   Tibenham | 31.05.18E
Built by Christen Industries Inc

G-SIII | Extra EA.300 | 058 | 10.01.95
D-ETYE   S C Cattlin tr Owners of G-SIII
White Waltham   '*Fun Flight*' & '*61*' | 06.01.19E

G-SIIO | Schempp-Hirth Ventus-3T | 003 TS | 12.02.19
D-KIIJ, (D-KENY)   S G Jones   Lasham | 20.02.20E

G-SIJJ | North American P-51D-20-NA Mustang | 122-31894 | 20.03.02
F-AZMU, N5306M, HK-2812P, HK-2812X, N5411V,
44-72035   P A Teichman t/a Hangar 11 Collection
North Weald   '*Tall In The Saddle*' | 18.06.19P
As 'A3-3' in USAAF 99th Fighter Sqdn/
332nd Fighter Group c/s

G-SIJW | Scottish Aviation Bulldog Srs 120/121 | BH120/295 | 31.03.00
XX630   M Miles   Audley End | 23.03.19E
As 'XX630:5' in RAF c/s

G-SILS | Pietenpol Air Camper | xxxx | 29.06.98
D Silsbury   Dunkeswell
Built by D Silsbury – project PFA 047-13331 as
single-seat version designated 'Pietenpol Skyscout'
(NF 09.02.16)

G-SILY | Mainair Pegasus Quantum 15 | 8074 | 17.12.04
S D Sparrow   (Hinckley) | 23.05.18P

G-SIMM | Comco Ikarus C42 FB100 VLA | 0411 6630 | 06.09.04
D Simmons   Peacocks Farm, Farley Green | 31.08.18P
Built by D Simmons – project PFA 322-14286

G-SIMY | Piper PA-32-300 Cherokee Six | 32-7640082 | 22.03.04
G-OCPF, G-BOCH, N9292K   I Simpson   Kirkbride | 02.03.18E

G-SINK | Schleicher ASH 25 | 25139 | 17.09.07
BGA 5009, F-CHAY   A F W Watson tr G-SINK Group
Cranwell North   '*RC*' | 18.03.19E

G-SINN | Evektor EV-97 Eurostar SL | 2014-4203 | 11.08.14
J C Miller   (Shanklin, Isle of Wight) | 04.08.18P
Assembled Light Sport Aviation Ltd

G-SION | Piper PA-38-112 Tomahawk II | 38-81A0146 | 30.01.91
N23661   Cancelled 09.09.02 by CAA | 28.12.00
Enstone   *Open store 08.17*

G-SIPA | SIPA 903 | 63 | 31.05.83
G-BGBM, F-BGBM
G S Dilland & A C Leak   (Southampton SO40)
(NF 15.01.15)

G-SIPP | Lindstrand LBL 35A Cloudhopper | 891 | 29.09.09
HB-QIT   A R Rich   (Hadfield, Glossop) | 19.04.18E

G-SIRD | Robinson R44 Raven II | 11745 | 21.05.07
Peglington Productions Ltd   Wycombe Air Park | 18.04.18E

G-SIRE | Best Off Skyranger Swift 912S(1) | SKR0608740 | 26.03.07
P W F Coleman   Hadfold Farm, Adversane | 15.04.18P
Built by P Rigby – project BMAA/HB/531

G-SIRO | Dassault Falcon 900EX | 172 | 16.05.07
F-WWFL   Condor Aviation LLP   Leeds Bradford | 23.05.19E

G-SIRS | Cessna 560XL Citation Excel | 560-5185 | 01.08.01
N51042   London Executive Aviation Ltd
Farnborough | 01.08.18E

G-SISI | Schempp-Hirth Duo Discus | 193 | 17.08.07
BGA 5002, PH-1141
R Puritz tr Glider Sierra India   Dunstable Downs   '*SI*' | 16.03.18E

G-SISU | P&M Quik GT450 | 8215 | 29.08.06
Executive & Business Aviation Support Ltd
North Coates | 18.07.15P
Stored 01.19

G-SISX | Pitts S-1S | xxxx | 22.01.19
A J & C A J Millson   Andrewsfield
Built by A J & C A J Millson – project LAA 009-14997
(NF 22.01.19)

G-SITA | Cyclone Pegasus Quantum 15-912 | 7797 | 18.06.01
P N Thompson   Shifnal | 04.08.17P

G-SIVJ | Westland SA.341C Gazelle HT.2 | 2012 | 26.06.02
G-CBSG, ZB649
Skytrace (UK) Ltd   Wolverhampton Halfpenny Green | 06.02.18P

G-SIXC | Douglas DC-6B | 45550 | 20.03.87
N93459, N90645, B-1006, XW-PFZ, B-1006
Cancelled 02.08.11 as WFU | 04.04.05
Coventry
Open store 11.17 – was used as Diner, now closed

G-SIXD | Piper PA-32-300 Cherokee Six D | 32-7140007 | 25.03.98
HB-OMH, N8615N
I Gordon & M B Payne   Kings Farm, Thurrock | 27.04.18E

G-SIXT | Piper PA-28-161 Warrior II | 2816056 | 22.02.08
G-BSSX, N9141H
Airways Aero Associations Ltd   Wycombe Air Park | 05.01.18E
Operated by British Airways Flying Club;
BOAC c/s (port side) & BEA c/s (starboard side)

G-SIXX | Colt 77A | 1327 | 21.10.88
S Drawbridge   Mildenhall, Bury St Edmunds
'*6X – the 100% Organic Manure*' | 21.02.15E
(IE 28.06.17)

G-SIXY | Van's RV-6 | 25485 | 09.03.99
C J Hall & C R P Hamlett
(Saint-Laurent-le-Minier, France & Cambridge)
Built by C J Hall & C R P Hamlett
– project PFA 181-13368 (NF 11.06.18)

G-SIZZ | Avtech Jabiru J400 | 270 | 13.02.06
K J Betteley   Sandown | 17.05.18P
Built by K J Betterley – project PFA 325-14483

G-SJBI | Pitts S-2C | 6082 | 11.06.08
N10UK   S L Walton   White Waltham | 19.03.18E
Built by Aviat Aircraft Inc

G-SJEF | AutoGyro Cavalon | V00214 | 09.07.15
J Smith   Wolverhampton Halfpenny Green | 30.07.19P
Assembled Rotorsport UK as c/n RSUK/CVLN/016

G-SJEN[M] | Comco Ikarus C42 FB80 | 0405-6602 | 01.07.04
Cancelled 10.08.10 as PWFU – crashed 17.07.07 | 09.04.10
near Strathaven
Built by M C Henry
With National Museum of Flight Scotland, East Fortune

G-SJES Evektor EV-97 teamEurostar UK 2007-2918 15.06.07
North East Aviation Ltd Eshott 05.07.18P
Assembled Cosmik Aviation Ltd

G-SJKR Lindstrand LBL 90A 756 26.01.01
P Richardson Raglan, Usk 23.02.18E

G-SJPI Aerospool Dynamic WT9 UK DY281/2008 29.04.08
S R Wilkinson (Bourne, Peterborough) 18.10.18P
Assembled Yeoman Light Aircraft Co Ltd; originally
registered as c/n 'DY257'; official c/n recorded
as 'DY281'

G-SKAN Reims/Cessna F172M F17201120 08.07.85
G-BFKT, F-BVBJ
M Richardson & J Williams MoD Boscombe Down 20.02.18E

G-SKAZ Aero AT-3 R100 AT3-055 27.09.10
SP-GES J K Kazula tr G-SKAZ Flying Group Sywell 11.09.18E

G-SKBD Raytheon 400A RK-376 07.11.14
N426FL, N476LX, N476CW
Sky Border Logistics Ltd Cardiff 17.11.18E
Operated by Dragonfly Aviation Services

G-SKBH Agusta AW109SP Grand New 22216 14.04.16
N109LW, I-PTFG
Sky Border Logistics Ltd Carlisle Lake District 20.04.18E

G-SKBL Agusta A109S Grand 22011 20.06.14
G-PDAY, G-CDWY
Sky Border Logistics Ltd Carlisle Lake District 25.07.18E

G-SKCI Rutan VariEze 1864 30.03.01
C Boyd Cranfield
Built by S K Cockburn – project PFA 074-12081
(NF 22.12.14)

G-SKFY Robinson R44 Clipper II 13497 26.05.15
G-GRGE, OE-XYK
Skyfly Air Ltd Mount Offham, Offham, West Malling 23.05.18E

G-SKIE Steen Skybolt AACA/357 29.08.97
ZK-DEN M J Coles tr G-SKIE Group
(Weston, Cheshire) 15.11.18P
Built by D Axe; badly damaged when it landed in
a tree at the Lancashire Aero Club's strip at
Kenyon Hall Farm, Culcheth on 24.06.18

G-SKKY Cessna 172S Skyhawk 172S9850 30.06.05
N14897 J Herbert & G P Turner White Waltham 18.08.18E

G-SKLR Eurocopter EC120B Colibri 1049 17.12.18
G-VIPR, F-GRAE EFL Helicopters Ltd Brighton City 06.01.20E

G-SKNG Westland Sea King HAR.3 WA863 21.03.19
XZ597 Lift West (Helicopters) Ltd (Crewkerne)
(NF 20.03.19)

G-SKOT Cameron V-42 4813 27.06.00
S A Laing Woodlands of Durris, Banchory 01.04.17E
(IF 06.09.17)

G-SKPG Best Off Skyranger 912(2) SKR0404483 11.11.04
G C Hobson tr NMSSR Group St Michaels 18.05.19P
Built by P Gibbs – project BMAA/HB/400

G-SKPH Yakovlev Yak-50 853010 15.03.05
G-BWWH, LY-ABL, LY-XNI, DOSAAF
I C Austin & R S Partridge-Hicks (Little Gransden) 08.06.17P

G-SKPP Eurocopter EC120B Colibri 1463 18.01.10
G-MKII, F-HAAL, F-WQDD
Bliss Aviation Ltd Bournemouth 14.06.18E

G-SKRA Best Off Skyranger 912(2) SKR0504599 21.11.05
K G Winter Northrepps 10.07.19P
Built by P A Banks – project BMAA/HB/458

G-SKRG Best Off Skyranger 912(2) SKR0307352 02.09.03
M J Kingsley & D J Liddle
Wolverhampton Halfpenny Green 24.11.19P
Built by R W Goddin – project BMAA/HB/298

G-SKSW Best Off Skyranger Swift 912S(1) SKR0707804 03.10.07
J & J A Pegram North Weald 04.03.18P
Built by M D & S M North – project BMAA/HB/553

G-SKTN Avro 696 Shackleton MR.2 - 04.02.13
WR963 Shackleton Aviation Group CIC
(Redgrave, Diss)
In RN c/s as 'WR963:B' (NF 08.08.18)

G-SKUA Stoddard-Hamilton GlaStar 5523 30.08.07
G-LEZZ F P Smiddy Tibenham 01.06.18P
Built by L A James – project PFA 295-13241;
tricycle u/c

G-SKYC Slingsby T67M Firefly 2009 13.06.97
G-BLDP K Taylor Full Sutton 24.11.18E

G-SKYF SOCATA TB-10 Tobago 1589 01.05.01
VH-YHG W L McNeil Enstone 22.05.18E

G-SKYL Cessna 182S Skylane 18280176 19.06.98
N4104D G A Gee Sherburn-in-Elmet 05.01.19E

G-SKYN Aérospatiale AS.355F1 Ecureuil 2 5185 21.11.03
G-OGRK, G-BWZC, (G-MOBZ), N107KF, N5799R
RCR Aviation Ltd Redhill 23.04.17E
Stored 06.18 (NF 09.08 18)

G-SKYO Slingsby T67M-200 Firefly 2264 20.09.00
Vg Flight Ltd Wombleton 01.09.18E

G-SKYT III Sky Arrow 650 TC C004 06.09.96
W M Bell & S J Brooks Croft Farm, Defford 04.04.18E

G-SKYV Piper PA-28RT-201T Turbo Arrow IV 28R-8031132 20.09.04
G-BNZG, N82376
Airborne Adventures Ltd Crosland Moor 31.05.19E

G-SLAC Cameron N-77 2295 07.06.90
A Barnes Salford 'Scottish Life' 09.10.18E

G-SLAR Agusta A109C 7649 18.11.11
G-OWRD, G-USTC, JA6695, (G-LAXO)
MW Helicopters Ltd Stapleford 21.01.18E

G-SLCC Evektor EV-97 Eurostar SL 2014-4214 18.02.15
E S A McMahon Horsley Brook Farm, Lichfield 17.02.18P
Built by Light Sport Aviation Ltd

G-SLCE Cameron C-80 4022 24.02.97
A M Holly Breadstone, Berkeley 'db database' 14.04.11E
(IE 07.10.15)

G-SLCT Diamond DA.42NG Twin Star 42.031 30.06.05
Stapleford Flying Club Ltd Stapleford 19.02.18E

G-SLEA Mudry CAP 10B 124 19.12.80
R Harris, M J M Jenkins & N R Thorburn RAF Wittering 28.08.17E

G-SLIP Reality Easy Raider J2.2(3) ER.0004 21.05.02
D R Squires (Wokingham)
Built by J S Harris – project BMAA/HB/215
(NF 08.03.18)

G-SLIV TAF Sling 4 096 10.01.18
D J Pilkington (Goosnargh, Preston)
Built by D J Pilkington – project LAA 400-15445
(NF 01.08.18)

G-SLMG Diamond HK36TTC Super Dimona 36.727 05.08.04
N267JP A R Morley & P R Thody
tr G-SLMG Syndicate Aston Down 15.09.18E

G-SLNG TAF Sling 4 119 02.08.17
R J H Davis & R S D Wheeler (London W9 & SW6)
Built by R J H Davis & R S D Wheeler
– project LAA 400-15477 (NF 02.08.17)

G-SLNT Flight Design CTSW 06-10-02 28.02.07
K Kirby Sywell 23.03.18P
Assembled P&M Aviation Ltd as c/n 8254

G-SLNW Robinson R22 Beta II 3524 07.04.06
G-LNIC Sky Helicopters Ltd Manor Farm, Binham 17.02.18E

G-SLYR Folland Gnat F.1 H/GN/130 03.02.15
N296PS, Indian AF E296
Heritage Aircraft Ltd North Weald
Assembled Hindustan Aeronautics Ltd;
as 'E-296' in Indian AF c/s; noted 11.18

G-SMAJ DG Flugzeugbau DG-808C 8-378B277X39 13.10.14
G-TRTM S Marriott Milfield 30.03.18E
Built by DG Flugzeugbau GmbH

G-SMAR Schempp-Hirth Arcus M 66 28.10.13
S H C Marriott tr Alpha Syndicate
Lleweni Parc 'AR' 12.03.18E

G-SMBM Cyclone Pegasus Quantum 15-912 7602 24.01.00
B Cook Hunsdon 30.08.19P
Badged 'Super Sport'

G-SMDH Europa Aviation Europa XS 403 08.10.98
S W Pitt Fairoaks 09.08.18P
Built by S W Pitt – project PFA 247-13367; tricycle u/c

G-SMIG Cameron O-65 922 06.06.83
R D Parry Sutton, Tenbury Wells 'San Miguel' 27.10.10E
(IE 05.06.17)

G-SMIL	Lindstrand LBL 105A	1425	10.09.12
	A L Wade Shevington, Wigan		11.11.18E
G-SMKR	Aeropro EuroFOX 912(S)	53217	06.02.18
	S M Kenyon-Roberts Pittrichie Farm, Whiterashes		
	Built by S M Kenyon-Roberts – project		
	LAA 376-15504 (NF 06.02.18)		
G-SMLA	British Aerospace BAe 146 Series 200	E2047	06.08.14
	N880PA, G-OZRH, EI-DDF, G-OZRH, N188US, N364PS		
	Jota Aviation Ltd Southend		28.08.19E
	Operated by Jota Aviation		
G-SMLE	Robinson R44 Raven II	13995	15.07.16
	English Braids Ltd Gloucestershire		24.09.18E
G-SMLI	Groppo Trail	'39322'	30.10.12
	A M Wilson Maun, Botswana		03.01.19P
	Built by A M Wilson – project LAA 372-15120;		
	operated by Royal Veterinary College		
G-SMLZ	Groppo Trail Mk.2	112/71	07.04.17
	A M Wilson Wisbridge Farm, Reed		14.02.19P
	Built by M Dixon & A M Wilson – project LAA 372-15327		
G-SMMA	Reims/Cessna F406 Caravan II	F406-0094	24.04.08
	Scottish Ministers per Director General Environment		
	Inverness		07.05.19E
	Operated by Scottish Fisheries as callsign		
	'Watchdog 64'		
G-SMMB	Reims/Cessna F406 Caravan II	F406-0095	06.01.09
	Scottish Ministers per Director General Environment		
	Inverness		19.01.19E
G-SMMF	Lindstrand LBL 77A	1277	27.02.15
	S5-OCC M & S Mitchell *'Lumpi'* Hertford		15.05.19E
	P/i 'S5-OCC' also quoted for G-CINN Cameron		
	Z-31 c/n 11179; operated by Hertfordshire		
	Balloon Collection		
G-SMON	Cessna A152 Aerobat	A1520805	19.07.17
	G-BNJE, G-OWFS, G-DESY, G-BNJE, N7386L		
	North Weald Flying Group Ltd North Weald		21.09.19E
G-SMRS	Cessna 172F Skyhawk	17252558	17.03.06
	N8656U M R Sarling North Weald		26.07.19E
G-SMSM	Dassault Falcon 2000LX	325	09.12.16
	F-WWML		
	London Executive Aviation Ltd London Stansted		08.12.18E
G-SMSP	Super Marine Spitfire Mk.26B	074	01.03.16
	S J D Hall (Pirbright, Woking)		
	Built by S J D Hall – project LAA 324-15019;		
	as 'JG241:ZX-J' in RAF c/s (NF 01.03.16)		
G-SMTH	Piper PA-28-140 Cherokee C	28-26916	28.09.90
	G-AYJS, N11C Cancelled 02.08.17 as PWFU		02.05.17
	Bournemouth *Stored dismantled 07.17*		
G-SMYK	PZL-Swidnik PW-5 Smyk	17.06.020	28.04.08
	BGA 4311/HYM		
	P Webber tr PW-5 Syndicate Lasham *'PW5'*		19.12.17E
G-SNAL	Cessna 182T Skylane	18282123	12.09.08
	N6310X N S Lyndhurst Goodwood		27.02.18E
G-SNAP	Cameron V-77 HAB	1217	29.11.85
	Cancelled 16.03.11 as PWFU		19.09.04
	Ramsbottom, Bury *Inflated Pidley 04.14*		
G-SNCA	Piper PA-34-200T Seneca II	34-7970355	01.11.13
	5B-CKW, D-GHBW, I-MEPI, N2184K		
	Social Infrastructure Ltd Wellesbourne Mountford		17.07.18E
G-SNEV	CFM Streak Shadow SA	K 283	17.09.96
	A Child (Telford)		03.07.18P
	Built by N G Smart – project PFA 206-13042		
G-SNGZ	TAF Sling 2	222	01.04.16
	T D R Hardy Sywell		01.11.19P
	Built by T D R Hardy – project LAA 399-15395		
G-SNJS	Cessna 560XL Citation XLS+	560-6252	06.09.18
	Gama Aviation (UK) Ltd Jersey		
G-SNOG	Air Création Buggy 582(1)/Kiss 400	FL011	02.05.02
	G-80-1 P S Wesley Sywell		05.08.16P
	Built by B H Ashman – project BMAA/HB/219		
	(Flylight kit FL011 comprising Trike s/n T02033		
	& wing s/n A02048-2045); trike unit used to		
	test-fly Kiss 450 wing in early 2003 under		
	BMAA's 'B' conditions as 'G-80-1'		

G-SNOP	Europa Aviation Europa	040	03.01.07
	G-DESL, G-WWWG , 'G-DSEL', G-WWWG		
	A Graham Eshott		12.04.19P
	Built by W R C Williams-Wynne		
	– project PFA 247-12597; tricycle u/c		
G-SNOW (2)	Cameron V-77	2050	21.06.79
	I Welsford Bristol BS14		20.06.15E
	Registered as c/n 541; in 1989 acquired new		
	envelope c/n 2050 (IE 10.06.16)		
G-SNOZ	Europa Aviation Europa	032	07.10.04
	G-DONZ P O Bayliss Swansea		28.01.20P
	Built by P O Bayliss & D J Smith		
	– project PFA 247-12545		
G-SNSA	AgustaWestland AW139	31308	10.09.10
	I-RAIQ CHC Scotia Ltd Norwich Int'l		12.09.18E
G-SNSE	AgustaWestland AW139	31561	28.11.14
	CHC Scotia Ltd Norwich Int'l		28.08.18E
G-SNSH	AgustaWestland AW139	31474	13.12.16
	VP-CHF, G-LLOV CHC Scotia Ltd Norwich Int'l		18.01.19E
G-SNSI	AgustaWestland AW139	31479	13.12.16
	VP-CHJ, G-FTOM CHC Scotia Ltd Humberside		18.01.19E
G-SNSJ	Agusta AW139	41268	11.01.17
	N41268, RP-C2013, VT-HLF, N388SH		
	CHC Scotia Ltd Humberside		08.05.18E
G-SNSK	AgustaWestland AW139	41354	01.12.16
	RP-C3139, HS-UOE, N152MM		
	CHC Scotia Ltd Norwich Int'l		20.04.18E
G-SNUG	Best Off Skyranger Nynja 912S(1)	UK\N/BK0175	13.02.15
	J D Fielding & J C Mundy Priory Farm, Tibenham		12.09.18P
	Built by J C Mundy – project BMAA/HB/662		
G-SNUZ	Piper PA-28-161 Warrior II	28-8416021	19.12.01
	G-PSFT, G-BPDS, N4328P		
	Freedom Aviation Ltd Cotswold		29.05.19E
G-SNXA	Sonex Sonex	1383	14.03.17
	S J Moody (Leamington Spa)		
	Built by S J Moody – project LAA 337-14984		
	(NF 14.03.17)		
G-SOAF	BAC 167 Strikemaster Mk.82A	xxxx	21.02.05
	Oman AF 425, G-27-405		
	Strikemaster Flying Club Hawarden		22.05.18P
	Plane Set 376; as '425' in Oman c/s		
G-SOBI	Piper PA-28-181 Archer II	28-7690212	03.05.00
	D-EAQL R A Heap tr G-SOBI Flying Group		
	Sherburn-in-Elmet		01.09.18E
G-SOCK	Mainair Pegasus Quik	8041	25.05.04
	K R McCartney Baxby Manor, Husthwaite		05.05.18P
	Built by Mainair Sports Ltd		
G-SOCT	Yakovlev Yak-50	842804	17.03.04
	LY-XCD, DOSAAF 32 M J Gadsby Oaksey Park		30.11.17P
	As 'RB-A' in pseudo-RAF scheme		
G-SOKO	Soko P-2 Kraguj	033	06.01.94
	G-BRXK, Yug.AF 30149 P C Avery Fenland		20.10.11P
	As '30149:149' in Yugoslav AF c/s (NF 21.10.16)		
G-SOLA	Star-Lite SL-1	xxxx	09.06.88
	G P Thomas Caernarfon *'A Star Is Born'*		03.03.17P
	Built by A Clarke & P Clifton – project PFA 175-11311		
G-SONA	SOCATA TB-10 Tobago	151	24.10.80
	G-BIBI J Freeman Headcorn		13.10.18E
G-SONE	Cessna 525A CitationJet CJ2	525A0031	07.01.10
	M-XONE, VP-BFC, N312CJ, N5204D		
	Centreline AV Ltd t/a Centreline Bristol		03.01.19E
G-SONX	Sonex Sonex	1177	13.11.08
	A J L Eves (West Stour, Gillingham)		12.02.19P
	Built by M Chambers – project LAA 337-14776;		
	tailwheel u/c		
G-SOOC	Hughes 369HS (500)	1110354S	06.10.93
	G-BRRX, N9083F R J H Strong (Vagg Hill, Yeovil)		23.02.06
	(NF 15.02.18)		
G-SOOM	Glaser-Dirks DG-500M	5-E42M20	14.05.92
	BGA4907, G-SOOM J A Van Gorp & A M Wensing		
	(Hegelo & Enschede, Netherlands)		18.04.18E
G-SOOS	Colt 21A Cloudhopper	1263	07.06.88
	P J Stapley Colney Heath, St Albans		25.03.95A
	(NF 22.10.15)		

G-SOOT	Piper PA-28-180 Cherokee C	28-4033	19.08.88
	G-AVNM, N11C R J Hunter Little Snoring		10.05.18E
G-SOOZ	Rans S-6-ESN Coyote II	0899.1335	27.04.01
	R E Cotterrell Fenland		22.05.18P
	Built by A Batters – project PFA 204-13543; tricycle u/c		
G-SOPC	Sopwith F.1 Camel replica	xxxx	16.01.15
	P Hoeft & C I Law Wickenby		
	Built by P Hoeft & C I Law – project LAA 173-15050		
	(NF 16.01.15)		
G-SORA	Glaser-Dirks DG-500/22 Elan	5E35S7	23.02.07
	BGA 5269/KPC, PH-1082, D-5219		
	M D Newton tr DG Syndicate Crowland 'KPC'		08.06.18E
	Built by Elan Tovarna Sportnega Orodja N.Sol.O		
G-SOUT	Van's RV-8	80661	14.11.14
	G-CDPJ J M Southern Elstree		20.04.18P
	Built by P Johnson – project PFA 303-13295;		
	operated by 'Raven Display Team' – 'No. 6'		
G-SOVB	Learjet Learjet 45	45-138	12.09.06
	N138AX, G-OLDJ, N5018G		
	Zenith Aviation Ltd Biggin Hill		11.09.18E
G-SPAM	Avid Aerobat	xxxx	09.05.91
	M Durcan Navan, RoI		14.04.14P
	Built by C M Hicks – project PFA 189-12074		
	(NF 05.08.18)		
G-SPAR	Cameron N-77 HAB	1248	04.03.86
	Re-registered 31.05.90 as G-BSJA		
	Not Known *Inflated Pidley, still wearing G-SPAR 05.16*		
G-SPAT	Aero AT-3 R100	AT3-008	20.10.04
	SP-EAR, (SP-ERM) S2T Aero Ltd North Weald		08.11.19E
G-SPCI	Cessna 182P Skylane	18261643	30.09.16
	G-GUMS, G-CBMN, ZS-KJS, N21458		
	K Brady Strathallan		04.12.18E
G-SPCY	Embraer EMB-135BJ Legacy 650	14501162	02.01.18
	OE-IOL, G-OTCL, PT-TCW		
	London Executive Aviation Ltd London Stansted		27.01.19E
G-SPCZ	CZAW Sportcruiser	700282	22.09.08
	R J Robinson Shobdon		17.07.18P
	Built by R J Robinson – project LAA 338-14842		
G-SPDY	Raj Hamsa X'Air Hawk	1122	27.04.07
	K J Underwood Deanland		06.11.18P
	Built by G H Gilmour-White – project PFA 340-14678		
G-SPED	Alpi Pioneer 300	244	16.07.08
	C F Garrod Solent 'Phoenix'		01.06.19P
	Built by M Taylor – project LAA 330-14797		
G-SPEL	Sky 220-24	045	26.07.96
	T G Church Irchester, Wellingborough		
	'Pendle Balloon Flights'		22.06.18E
G-SPEY	Agusta-Bell 206B-3 JetRanger III	8608	01.04.81
	G-BIGO Castle Air Ltd Trebrown, Liskeard		11.04.18E
G-SPFX	Rutan Cozy	0546	30.04.97
	B D Tutty (Gillingham, Kent)		
	Built by B D Tutty – project PFA 159-13113 (NF 04.08.14)		
G-SPHU	Eurocopter EC135 T2+	0245	12.11.02
	D-HKBA Babcock Mission Critical Services		
	Onshore Ltd Inverness		07.01.19E
G-SPID	Ultramagic S-90	90/125	28.06.13
	A Fawcett Adlington, Chorley		04.08.17E
G-SPIN	Pitts S-2A	2110	13.03.80
	N5CQ P Avery Shrove Furlong Farm, Kingsey		05.07.19E
	Built by Aerotek Inc		
G-SPIP	SNCAN Stampe SV.4C	303	27.07.12
	G-BTIO, N73NS, F-BCLC A G & P M Solleveld		
	(Easter Kepdowrie, Buchlyvie, Stirling)		12.12.14E
	(NF 18.04.16)		
G-SPIT	Supermarine 379 Spitfire FR.XIVe	6S-649205	02.03.79
	(G-BGHB), IAF T-20, MV293		
	Anglia Aircraft Restorations Ltd Duxford		01.11.19P
	As 'MV268:JE-J' in RAF c/s		
G-SPJE	Robinson R44 Raven II	12026	04.12.07
	Abel Alarm Company Ltd (Leicester)		22.01.19E
G-SPMM	Best Off Skyranger Swift 912S(1)	SKR0703773	01.06.07
	A W Paterson Strathaven		21.04.18P
	Built by M J Milne & S M Pink – project BMAA/HB/539		

G-SPOG	Jodel DR.1050 Ambassadeur	155	25.09.95
	G-AXVS, F-BJNL		
	A R Neal tr G-SPOG Group Old Warden		30.07.18P
	Built by Société Aéronautique Normande		
G-SPRC	Van's RV-8	83043	29.11.17
	A P & C Durston & J C Gowdy (Pulborough)		
	Built by J C Gowdy – project LAA 303-14969		
	(NF 29.11.17)		
G-SPRE	Cessna 550 Citation Bravo	550-0872	20.01.14
	5N-IZZ, OE-GKK, N5093L XJC Ltd Southampton		06.04.18E
G-SPRI	Agusta A109E Power	11721	09.11.18
	G-EMHC Looporder Ltd t/a East Midlands Helicopters		
	Costock Heliport		06.02.19E
G-SPRK	Van's RV-4	845	02.02.15
	N845GW Jack Aviation Ltd		
	Frieslands Farm, Washington 'Fireflies Team'		16.08.18P
	Built by G E Winfield		
G-SPRX	Van's RV-4	1622	05.02.15
	N621RT Jack Aviation Ltd		
	Frieslands Farm, Washington 'Fireflies Team'		09.08.18P
	Built by T Crowell		
G-SPTR	Robinson R44 Raven II	12799	18.06.09
	Heli Air Ltd Wellesbourne Mountford		08.10.18E
G-SPTT	Diamond DA.40D Star	D4.249	17.06.13
	G-OCCS, OE-VPU Acrobat Ltd Bournemouth		28.01.19E
	Operated by L3 CTS Academy		
G-SPTX	Dassault Falcon 7X	282	24.10.18
	F-WWHD Concierge U Ltd (London W1)		
G-SPUR	Cessna 550 Citation II	550-0714	27.10.98
	N593EM, N12035		
	London Executive Aviation Ltd London Stansted		15.11.18E
G-SPUT	Aerostar Yakovlev Yak-52	9111608	18.06.12
	G-BXAV, RA-01325, DOSAAF 73		
	D J Hopkinson Henstridge		12.05.17P
	(NF 11.10.17)		
G-SPVI	SOCATA TB-20 Trinidad GT	2168	08.02.16
	D-EDMH S W Parker tr Teegee Group		
	Nottingham City		21.03.18E
G-SPVK	Eurocopter AS.350B3 Ecureuil	4301	24.09.07
	G-CERU, F-WWXL Squirrel Hire LLP (London W1)		03.02.19E
	Operated by Kingmoor Aviation Ltd		
G-SPWP	Cirrus SR22 GTS	1413	01.12.16
	N753TW S Pope Liverpool John Lennon		04.01.19E
G-SPXX	Supermarine 356 Spitfire F.22	CBAF108	18.05.12
	PK519 P R Arnold (Newport Pagnell)		
	Built by Castle Bromwich 1945 (NF 18.03.16)		
G-SRAH	Schempp-Hirth Mini Nimbus C	96	25.03.08
	BGA 2466/DXQ		
	P Hawkins tr Sarah Group Feshiebridge '147'		21.03.18E
G-SRBM	Beech B300 Super King Air 350	FL-1072	27.09.16
	N1072B Skyhopper LLP Gloucestershire		17.10.18E
	Built by Textron		
G-SRCB	Van's RV-12	xxxx	12.11.18
	C Burgess (Guildford)		
	Built by C Burgess – project LAA 363-15191 (NF 12.11.18)		
G-SRGE★	Agusta A109E Power	11725	21.12.18
	I-SIRI Novawave Ltd		
	To G-NVWV 20.03.19		
G-SRII	Reality Easy Raider 503(1)	010	02.03.01
	K Myles Baxby Manor, Husthwaite		07.10.18P
	Built by T F Francis – project BMAA/HB/163;		
	originally registered as Flying K Sky Raider II 503		
G-SRNE	Eurocopter MBB-BK117 C-2 (EC145)	9283	08.09.14
	M-SRNE, D-HADM Starspeed Ltd Cotswold		10.04.18E
G-SROE	Westland Scout AH.1	F9508	26.10.95
	XP907 Saunders-Roe Helicopter Ltd		
	(Clopton, Woodbridge)		20.03.06P
	As 'XP907' in AAC c/s (NF 09.03.15)		
G-SRRA	Tecnam P2002-EA Sierra	137?	23.02.09
	J Dunn Brimpton		27.06.18P
	Built by J Dunn – project PFA 333-14493		

G-SRWN	Piper PA-28-161 Warrior II	28-8116284	30.07.02
	G-MAND, G-BRKT, N8082Z		
	A J Bell Hinton-in-the-Hedges		29.08.19E
	Operated by Go Fly London		
G-SRYY	Europa Aviation Europa XS	430	19.09.02
	I O'Brien Cork, RoI		16.05.18P
	Built by S R Young – project PFA 247-13806; tricycle u/c		
G-SRZZ	Cirrus SR22	3696	17.06.10
	N411UK A Bodaghi Elstree		18.07.18E
G-SSCL	Hughes 369E (500)	0491E	25.04.98
	N684F		
	Stevens Construction Ltd (Yalding, Maidstone)		25.06.18E
G-SSDI	Spacek SD-1 Minisport	179	05.02.15
	B A Fairston & P C Piggott Husbands Bosworth		
	Built by B A Fairston & P C Piggott; tricycle u/c		
	(IE 06.10.17)		
G-SSDR	Attard Scooter	JA001	14.04.09
	J Attard (Goffs Oak, Waltham Cross)		
	Built by J Attard (NF 23.11.15)		
G-SSEX	Rotorway Exec 162F	6809	21.03.06
	Cancelled 21.01.11 by CAA		
	Killyleagh, Downpatrick *Built by J Donnon; stored 12.13*		
G-SSIX	Rans S-6-116 Coyote II	0899.1335	05.09.94
	R I Kelly Wellesbourne Mountford		14.07.05P
	Built by J V Squires – project PFA 204A-12749; frame		
	rebuilt; carries c/n '0899.1335.800ES' (NF 12.01.16)		
G-SSKY	Pilatus B-N BN-2B-26 Islander	2247	11.05.92
	G-BSWT Isles of Scilly Skybus Ltd Land's End		31.03.19E
G-SSRD	Kubíček BB17XR	934	11.06.12
	A M Holly Breadstone, Berkeley 'Gossard'		19.07.18E
G-SSTI	Cameron N-105	3238	30.03.94
	A A Brown Worplesdon, Guildford		
	'British Airways' & 'Concorde'		25.11.18E
G-SSTL	Just SuperSTOL	JA429	21.12.16
	Avalanche Aviation Ltd Sleap		21.12.18P
	Built by G Lewis & R F Pooler – project LAA 397-15377		
G-SSVB	Supermarine 349 Spitfire LF.Vb	CBAF 2384	09.10.13
	G-CGBI, BM539 I D Ward (Aldershot)		
	(NF 21.07.17)		
G-SSWE	Short SD.3-60 Variant 100	SH.3705	06.11.96
	SE-IXE, G-BNBA Cancelled 06.06.07 as PWFU		22.08.05
	Kingsland Primary School, Bucknall		
	In use as classroom complete with wings 06.17		
G-SSWM	Short SD.3-60 Variant 100	SH.3648	28.09.01
	SE-KCI, G-OAAS, OY-MMB, G-BLIL G-14-3648		
	Cancelled 06.06.07 as PWFU		14.10.06
	Liverpool John Lennon		
	Nose with Speke Aerodrome Heritage Group 04.14		
G-SSWO	Short SD.3-60 Variant 100	SH.3609	08.10.01
	SE-KLO, N343MV, (G-BKMY), G-14-3609		
	Cancelled 06.06.07 as PWFU		04.12.04
	St Johns The Baptist School, Colwick		
	Used as classroom complete with wings 06.17		
G-SSWP[M]	Short SD.3-30 Variant 100	SH.3030	21.06.00
	CS-DBY, G-BGNB Cancelled 08.10.04 as PWFU)		
	Forward fuselage only in Aurigny Air Services Ltd c/s		
	With RAF Manston History Museum		
G-SSWV	Sportavia-Putzer RF5B Sperber	51032	31.05.90
	N55WV, D-KEAI		
	A R Kendall tr Fournier Flying Group Pocklington		21.04.16P
	Dismantled 08.16 (NF 17.01.18)		
G-SSXL	Just SuperSTOL XL	JA459	16.02.16
	P T Price (Ashton-in-Makerfield, Wigan)		
	Built by P T Price – project LAA 397-15385; engine		
	failure 10.06.18, crashed Chat Moss, Manchester		
	& substantially damaged (IE 03.07.17)		
G-STAV	Cameron O-84	2913	29.09.92
	A Pollock Swindon		20.05.18E
G-STAY	Reims/Cessna FR172K Hawk XP	FR17200620	15.12.00
	D-EOVX, OE-DVX J M Wilkins Haverfordwest		27.01.12E
	(IE 19.06.15)		
G-STBA	Boeing 777-336ER	40542	09.07.10
	British Airways PLC London Heathrow		08.07.19E
	Line No: 879		
G-STBB	Boeing 777-36NER	38286	31.08.10
	British Airways PLC London Heathrow		30.08.19E
	Line No: 887		
G-STBC	Boeing 777-36NER	38287	04.11.10
	British Airways PLC London Heathrow		03.11.19E
	Line No: 901		
G-STBD	Boeing 777-36NER	38695	15.10.11
	British Airways PLC London Heathrow		14.10.19E
	Line No: 968		
G-STBE	Boeing 777-36NER	38696	09.12.11
	British Airways PLC London Heathrow		08.12.19E
	Line No: 980		
G-STBF	Boeing 777-336ER	40543	21.02.12
	British Airways PLC London Heathrow		10.12.19E
	Line No: 995		
G-STBG	Boeing 777-336ER	38430	13.09.13
	British Airways PLC London Heathrow		12.09.19E
	Line No: 1135		
G-STBH	Boeing 777-336ER	38431	19.10.13
	British Airways PLC London Heathrow		18.10.19E
	Line No: 1143		
G-STBI	Boeing 777-336ER	43702	28.01.14
	British Airways PLC London Heathrow		27.01.20E
	Line No: 1171		
G-STBJ	Boeing 777-336ER	43703	06.03.14
	British Airways PLC London Heathrow		05.03.19E
	Line No: 1182		
G-STBK	Boeing 777-336ER	42121	28.05.14
	British Airways PLC London Heathrow		27.04.19E
	Line No: 1204		
G-STBL	Boeing 777-336ER	42124	28.07.14
	British Airways PLC London Heathrow		13.06.19E
	Line No: 1221		
G-STBT	Cameron N-42	3256	11.09.13
	PH-OPP, G-BVLC D Sjokvist Örebro, Sweden		18.07.15E
	(NF 23.08.17)		
G-STBY	Flylight MotorFloater	MF012	02.05.12
	B C C Middleton (Normandy, Guildford)		
	(SSDR microlight since 05.14) (NF 19.10.18)		
G-STDO	BRM Bristell NG5 Speed Wing	125	24.03.15
	J A Strong & S M Wade North Weald		28.06.19P
	Built by J A Strong & S M Wade		
	– project LAA 385-15314; tailwheel u/c		
G-STEA	Piper PA-28R-200 Cherokee Arrow II	28R-7235096	18.06.02
	HB-OIH, N4569T D W Breden Durham Tees Valley		19.07.18E
G-STEE	Evektor EV-97 Eurostar	2010-3602	03.03.11
	S G Beeson Otherton		28.06.18P
	Built by S A Ivell – project PFA 315-15037		
	– should be LAA 315-15037		
G-STEL	BRM Bristell NG5 Speed Wing	074	10.10.13
	J M Naylor & L C Rowson Old Warden		02.04.19P
	Built by A J Palmer & F Sayyah		
	– project LAA 385-15235; tricycle u/c		
G-STEM	Stemme S 10-V	14-027	02.07.97
	D-KSTE A M Booth tr G-STEM Group Tibenham		24.05.18E
G-STEN	Stemme S 10	10-32	09.01.92
	D-KGCH R E Cross tr G-STEN Syndicate		
	Lasham '4'		15.08.18E
G-STEU	Rolladen-Schneider LS6-18W	6362	24.01.08
	BGA4153/HRY F K Russell Dunstable Downs 'L8'		16.04.18E
G-STFO	TL 2000UK Sting Carbon S4	15 ST442	08.03.16
	I H Foster Shobdon		21.08.18P
	Built by I H Foster – project LAA 347A-15380		
G-STHA	Piper PA-31-350 Chieftain	31-8052077	29.05.07
	G-GLUG, N2287J, G-BLOE, G-NITE, N3559A		
	Atlantic Bridge Aviation Ltd Lydd		15.01.14E
	Official type data 'PA-31-350 Navajo Chieftain'		
	is incorrect; noted less engines 08.16 (IE 06.07.16)		
G-STIN	TL 2000UK Sting Carbon	008	08.10.09
	N A Smith Sleap		06.06.18P
	Built by N A Smith – project LAA 347-14898		
G-STIX	Van's RV-7	xxxx	07.01.11
	R D S Jackson Perranporth		08.10.18P
	Built by R D S Jackson – project PFA 323-14638		

G-STMP	SNCAN Stampe SV4A	241	11.03.83
	F-BCKB Cancelled 24.09.18 by CAA		
	Not Known *For sale as rebuild project 06.18*		
G-STMT	Dassault Falcon 7X	148	21.03.12
	TAG Aviation (UK) Ltd Farnborough		20.03.19E
G-STNG	TL 2000UK Sting Carbon	07ST214	02.04.08
	D L Hill tr Geesting 3 Syndicate RAF Syerston		26.02.18P
	Built by J V Bradbury, D L Hill &, A G Rackstraw		
	– project LAA 347-14789		
G-STNK	Pitts S-1-11 Super Stinker	4088	12.12.16
	T H Castle (Sibbertoft, Market Harborough)		
	Built by T H Castle – project LAA 273-15438		
	(NF 12.12.16)		
G-STNS	Agusta A109A II	7324	26.04.06
	N716HA, N4RP, N109WS, D-HOOC, N1YB, N109KA		
	Eurotech SRL (Caiolo, Italy)		01.12.17E
	(NF 15.10.18)		
G-STOD	ICP MXP-740 Savannah VG Jabiru(1)	08-09-51-757	26.07.10
	M P Avison & L J Boardman Oxenhope		21.05.18P
	Built by S B Todd – project BMAA/HB/598		
G-STOK	Colt 77B	4791	04.05.00
	M H Read & J E Wetters Timperley, Altrincham		12.06.10E
	Built by Cameron Balloons Ltd (NF 09.09.15)		
G-STOO	Stolp SA.300 Starduster Too	2206	30.01.03
	A K Robinson RNAS Yeovilton		13.07.18P
	Built by K F Crumplin – project PFA 035-13870		
G-STOP	Robinson R44 Raven II	10852	05.09.05
	HLQ Services Ltd (Dublin 16, RoI)		24.07.17E
G-STOW	Cameron Wine Box-90	4420	02.10.98
	D J Groombridge & I J Martin t/a Flying Enterprises		
	Congresbury & Wotton-under-Edge		
	'Stowells of Chelsea'		08.09.19E
G-STPK	Lambert Mission M108	108003	30.04.12
	S T P Kember Fowle Hall Farm, Laddingford		11.05.18P
	Built by S T P Kember – project LAA 370-15092; tricycle u/c		
G-STRG	Cyclone AX2000	7837	24.07.01
	D R Thompson Newtownards		21.06.18P
	(IE 25.06.18)		
G-STRK	CFM Streak Shadow SA	xxxx	04.04.90
	E J Hadley (Aros, Isle of Mull)		14.05.16P
	Built by M E Dodd – project PFA 161-11762		
	– type series is '161A' (IE 05.07.17)		
G-STRV	Van's RV-14	140413	12.02.19
	S D Hicks (Whixall, Whitchurch)		
	Built by S D Hicks – project LAA 393-15500		
	(NF 12.02.19)		
G-STSN	Stinson 108-3 Voyager	108-4352	11.06.09
	G-BHMR, F-BABO, F-DABO, NC6352M		
	M S Colebrook Goodwood *'Miss Grace'*		16.06.19E
G-STUA	Pitts S-2A	2164	06.03.91
	N13GT P J G Margetson-Rushmore		
	tr G-STUA Group Stapleford		22.10.17E
	Built by Aerotek Inc		
G-STUE	Europa Aviation Europa	165	20.11.06
	F Xuereb Maypole Farm, Chislet		12.08.19P
	Built by F Xuereb – project PFA 247-12869		
G-STUI	Pitts S-2AE	K0051	25.06.09
	C-GMWT S L Goldspink & J M-M Munn		
	Old Warden		22.10.19P
	Built by G Deines		
G-STUN	TL 2000UK Sting Carbon	08-ST-299	19.03.10
	G-KEVT D Russell North Weald		08.02.19P
	Built by K D Taylor – project LAA 347-14897		
G-STUU	BRM Bristell NG5 Speed Wing	310	05.02.18
	S M Spencer North Weald		31.07.19P
	Built by S M Spencer – project LAA 385-15512		
G-STUY	Robinson R44 Raven II	10508	08.10.04
	Central Helicopters Ltd		
	Nottingham Heliport, Widmerpool		22.06.18E
G-STUZ	Lambert Mission M108	108005	30.03.15
	C J Finnigan (Banbury) *'Miss Suki'*		18.07.19P
	Built by S A Blanchard – project LAA 370-15326;		
	tricycle u/c		

G-STVL	Lindstrand LBL 77A	624	02.01.18
	SX-MAG S J Donkin Walton-le-Dale, Preston		
	(NF 02.01.18)		
G-STVT	CZAW Sportcruiser	xxxx	14.03.08
	S Taylor Netherthorpe		01.02.18P
	Built by S Taylor – project PFA 338-14676		
G-STVZ	Bell 206B-3 JetRanger III	4466	07.12.15
	G-XBCI, N206EE, RP-C1778, N80706, C-GAJH		
	Mediatech Consulting Ltd (London SE1)		05.12.18E
G-STWB	Hawker 750	HB-17	01.11.18
	HZ-KSRD, N3217D Avery Charter Services Ltd Oxford		
	(IE 01.11.18)		
G-STWO	ARV ARV-1 Super 2	xxxx	24.04.85
	R E Griffiths Middle Stoke, Isle of Grain		08.05.14P
	Built by ARV Aviation Ltd – project PFA 152-11048		
	(NF 04.05.18)		
G-STYL	Pitts S-1S	GJSN-1P	26.01.88
	N665JG Cancelled 17.11.11 as PWFU		05.07.11
	Holbeach *Built by G Harben & G Smith*		
	For sale as rebuild project 10.16		
G-STZZ	TL 2000UK Sting Carbon	10 ST342	25.08.10
	W R Field tr Dorset Aviation Group Bournemouth		09.10.18P
	Built by W R Field – project LAA 347-15003		
G-SUAU	Cameron C-90	11656	23.03.12
	A Heginbottom Cheadle Hulme, Cheadle		17.06.18E
G-SUCK	Cameron Z-105	10280	16.05.02
	R P Wade Shevington, Wigan *'Hall's Soothers'*		13.05.12E
	(NF 28.02.18)		
G-SUCT	Robinson R22 Beta II	4078	29.09.06
	P Irwin t/a Irwin Plant Sales Enniskillen		10.04.18E
G-SUEC★	Piper PA-32-301XTC 6XT	3255029	10.01.07
	M-OPED, G-SUEC, D-EGTC, N30908 G G L James		
	Cancelled 15.02.08 to IOM Restored 11.07.18		
	To 2-.... 17.12.18		
G-SUED	Thunder Ax8-90	1546	22.10.02
	G-PINE S A Kidd & E C Lubbock Billericay		22.03.18E
G-SUEI	Diamond DA.42 Twin Star	42.415	23.06.09
	OE-VDN S D Bell t/a Sue Air North Weald		27.06.18E
G-SUEJ	Embraer EMB-550 Legacy 500	55000042	16.12.16
	PR-LJW Saxonair Charter Ltd London Stansted		15.12.18E
G-SUEL	P&M Quik GT450	8301	23.07.07
	D A Ellis Over Farm, Gloucester		19.05.18P
G-SUEM	Diamond DA.42 Twin Star	42.332	01.02.18
	PH-CCD, OE-VPY S D Bell t/a Sue Air North Weald		27.07.19E
	Operated by Aeros		
G-SUEO	Diamond DA.40NG Star	D4.354	22.10.13
	(CN-CEI), OE-VPU		
	S D Bell t/a Sue Air Gloucestershire		06.11.18E
	Operated by L3 CTS		
G-SUER	Bell 206B JetRanger	480	26.08.11
	G-CBYX, HB-ZBX, N203WB, C-GRGP, N2502M		
	Aerospeed Ltd Manston Park		28.07.09E
	Stored 09.18 (NF 28.07.15)		
G-SUET	Bell 206B-2 JetRanger II	314	30.03.11
	G-BLZN, ZS-HMV, C-GWDH, N1408W		
	Aerospeed Ltd Manston Park		04.04.18E
	'DHL' c/s; stored 09.18		
G-SUEY	Bell 206L-1 LongRanger	45612	05.03.04
	C-GCET, N300CS, N3901Q		
	Aerospeed Ltd Manston Park		26.06.18E
	Stored 09.18		
G-SUEZ	Agusta-Bell 206B-2 JetRanger II	8319	16.09.98
	SU-YAE, YU-HAZ Aerospeed Ltd Manston Park		17.06.13E
	Stored 09.18 (NF 09.03.16)		
G-SUFK	Eurocopter EC135 P2+	0730	31.10.08
	Police & Crime Commissioner for West Yorkshire		
	AAC Wattisham		15.06.18E
	Operated by Suffolk Police Air Operations Unit		
	as callsign 'NPAS 14'		
G-SUGR	Embraer EMB-135BJ Legacy 650	14501199	14.04.14
	PR-LBQ Air Charter Scotland Ltd London Stansted		13.04.18E
G-SUKI	Piper PA-38-112 Tomahawk	38-79A0260	22.05.91
	G-RVNB, G-SUKI, G-BPNV, N2313D		
	Merseyflight Ltd Liverpool John Lennon		09.03.18E

G-SUKK	Sukhoi Su-29	75-03	23.01.18
	HA-YAR, RA-01609, RA-7503		
	M Benshemesh (London NW11)		19.06.18R

G-SULU	Best Off Skyranger 912(2)	SKR0212286	04.04.14
	G-SOPH S Marathe Sackville Lodge Farm, Riseley		06.04.18P
	Built by N A Read – project BMAA/HB/259		

G-SUMM	Best Off Skyranger Nynja 912S(1)	xxxx	16.02.18
	A Summers (Rushden, Buntingford)		
	Built by A Summers – project BMAA/HB/700		
	(IE 20.09.18)		

G-SUMO	Best Off Skyranger Nynja LS 912S(1)	xxxx	19.03.19
	J A Hunt (Clydach, Abergavenny)		
	Built J A Hunt – project BMAA/HB/714 (NF 19.03.19)		

| G-SUMX | Robinson R22 Beta II | 3274 | 01.11.01 |
| | Bickerstaffe Aviation Ltd   Higher Barn Farm, Hoghton | | 13.12.18E |

G-SUNN	Robinson R44 Clipper	1367	16.07.04
	N7531L Phoenix Helicopter Academy Ltd		
	Blackbushe		17.07.19E
	Operated by Phoenix Helicopters		

G-SUPA	Piper PA-18-150 Super Cub	18-5395	13.12.78
	PH-BAJ, PH-MBF, French Army 18-5395, N10F		
	S E Leach Perth		04.05.18E
	Fuselage No.18-5512		

G-SUSE	Europa Aviation Europa XS	554	25.06.02
	P R Tunney (Wilmslow)		
	Built by P R Tunney – project PFA 247-13905		
	(NF 09.02.16)		

G-SUSI	Cameron V-77	1133	22.07.85
	J H Dryden Fareham		09.08.04A
	(IE 05.06.17)		

| G-SUTD | Avtech Jabiru UL-D | 662 | 14.08.06 |
| | R F G Bermudez & W J Lister   Perth | | 14.08.19P |

| G-SUTE | Van's RV-8A | 83219 | 30.10.17 |
| | OE-AJL   A H Brown & G N Fraser   Perth | | 04.12.18P |

| G-SUUK | Sukhoi Su-29 | 001-01 | 10.01.18 |
| | HA-YAO, RA-44479   D J Barke   Southend | | 21.03.19R |

G-SUZN	Piper PA-28-161 Warrior II	28-8016187	16.01.91
	N3573C, N9540N A J Gomes Biggin Hill		27.07.16E
	(NF 23.02.18)		

G-SVAS	Piper PA-18-150 Super Cub	18-7605	22.10.09
	G-BGWH, ST-ABR, G-ARSR, N10F		
	Richard Shuttleworth Trustees Old Warden		12.03.18E

G-SVDG	Avtech Jabiru SK	0238	05.12.05
	R Tellegen Compton Abbas		17.07.14P
	Built by R Tellegen – project PFA 274-13442;		
	noted 09.18 (NF 23.10.15)		

G-SVEA	Piper PA-28-161 Warrior II	28-7916082	16.12.98
	N30299 I J Hiatt tr G-SVEA Group Little Staughton		08.09.16E
	Extensively damaged on A40 after t/o from Abergavenny,		
	25.06.16; parts only noted at Little Staughton 05.18		

G-SVEN	Centrair 101A Pégase	101A0262	15.01.08
	BGA 4329/HZF, PH-796		
	A J Cronshaw tr G7 Group Gransden Lodge 'G7'		10.05.18E

G-SVET	Yakovlev Yak-50	822210	16.09.03
	RA-44459, LY-AGG, DOSAAF 107		
	S Crossland tr The Assets of The Svetlana Group		
	Eaglescott *'Svetlana'*		27.05.12P
	(NF 18.08.17)		

G-SVGL	SNCAN Stampe SV.4A	516	01.10.15
	F-BDJJ, F-BDGV G W Lynch Old Buckenham		
	(IE 01.10.15)		

G-SVIP	Cessna 421B Golden Eagle	421B0820	12.03.97
	G-BNYJ, N4686Q, D-IMVB, N1590G		
	R P Bateman Biggin Hill		11.06.18E

G-SVIV	SNCAN Stampe SV.4C(G)	475	07.08.90
	N65214, F-BDBL		
	J E Keighley Damyns Hall, Upminster		18.06.19E

G-SVNH	ICP MXP-740 Savannah VG Jabiru(1)	08-04-51-712	18.01.13
	G-CFKV K Harmston Headon Farm, Retford		02.04.18P
	Built by K N Rigley & D Thorpe – project BMAA/HB/579		

| G-SVNX | Dassault Falcon 7X | 123 | 17.02.12 |
| | F-WWHF   Executive Jet Charter Ltd   Farnborough | | 16.02.19E |

G-SVPN	Piper PA-32R-301T Saratoga II TC	3257310	24.08.05
	N48HB, N164AM, N9529N		
	Stratton Motor Company (Norfolk) Ltd Tibenham		29.05.18E

G-SVRN	Embraer EMB-500 Phenom 100	50000112	23.12.16
	M-YTOY, PT-TIQ TD Aviation (IoM) Ltd Biggin Hill		
	Operated by Sovereign Business Jets (IE 11.04.17)		

G-SWAB	TLAC RL5A Sherwood Ranger XP	047	24.02.14
	D S Brown Jersey		09.07.18P
	Built by D S Brown – project LAA 237A-15152		

G-SWAI	Swift Aircraft SW01A	SW01A-0001	20.10.17
	Swift Aircraft Ltd (Coltishall)		
	(NF 20.10.17)		

G-SWAK	Oldfield Baby Lakes	88	02.11.07
	N4287X B Bryan (Lower Sticker, St Austell)		
	Built by R W Hunt (NF 16.08.16)		

| G-SWAT | Robinson R44 Raven II | 10041 | 24.02.03 |
| | N75097   Unique Helicopters (NI) Ltd   Enniskillen | | 14.11.15E |

G-SWAY	Piper PA-18 Super Cub 95	18-6039	03.06.08
	OY-EFY, D-EJEQ, SE-CLH, N7879D		
	R L Brinklow & S J Gaveston Damyns Hall, Upminster		20.05.19E

G-SWCT	Flight Design CTSW	07-11-05	31.01.08
	J A Shufflebotham Fern Farm, Marton		09.03.18P
	Assembled P&M Aviation Ltd as c/n 8364		

| G-SWEE | Beech 95-B55 Baron | TC-1406 | 16.04.03 |
| | G-AZDK   T Slotover   North Weald | | 08.04.19E |

G-SWEL	Hughes 369HS (500)	610328S	18.07.96
	G-RBUT, C-FTXZ, CF-TXZ M A Crook & A E Wright		
	Westbrook House, Higher Whitley		09.05.18E

G-SWIF^M	Vickers Supermarine 552 Swift F.7	VA.9597	01.06.90
	XF114 Cancelled 19.07.04 as WFU		
	With Solent Sky, Southampton		

| G-SWIG | Robinson R44 Raven I | 1700 | 06.04.10 |
| | EI-EXM, N30607   S Goddard   Hawarden | | 31.07.18E |

| G-SWLL | Aero AT-3 R100 | AT3-012 | 24.10.05 |
| | SP-KAC   Sywell Aerodrome Ltd   Sywell   '46' | | 23.11.17E |

| G-SWNG | Eurocopter EC120B Colibri | 1532 | 11.01.16 |
| | EC-KQA, F-WQAA   J G Jones   Caernarfon | | 06.04.18E |

| G-SWNS | Robinson R44 Raven II | 11695 | 27.08.14 |
| | G-PROJ   Swan Staff Recruitment Ltd   Redhill | | 23.02.18E |

G-SWON	Pitts S-1S	093	14.07.05
	N522H S L Goldspink Old Warden		08.03.19P
	Built by J Heverling		

G-SWOT	Phoenix Currie Super Wot	xxxx	10.09.80
	P N Davis Otherton		05.06.18P
	Built by G Chittenden – project PFA 3011;		
	modified as SE.5a replica; as 'C3011:S' in RAF c/s		

G-SWRD	Boeing 737-3L9	27834	23.01.18
	OY-JTE, G-OGBE, OY-MAS		
	21T Ltd Doncaster Sheffield		17.12.19E
	Line No: 2692; operated by 2 Excel Aviation Ltd		

G-SWRE	Tecnam P2002-EA Sierra	139	12.08.14
	W Swire (Newbattle, Dalkeith)		
	Built by W Swire – project PFA 333-14494 (NF 12.08.14)		

G-SWSW	Schempp-Hirth Ventus bT	61	17.08.07
	BGA 4562, PH-981, D-KMIH		
	R Kalin Rufforth 'SW'		30.07.18E

G-SWYF	Best Off Skyranger Swift 912(1)	xxxx	03.04.17
	K J Bradley & C Moore Deenethorpe		25.09.18P
	Built by K J Bradley – project BMAA/HB/698		

G-SWYM	CZAW Sportcruiser	700912	10.03.09
	R W Beal (Baxterley, Atherstone)		10.08.18P
	Built by R W Beal – project LAA 338-14893		

G-SXIX	Rans S-19 Venterra	1910	07.01.09
	R J Almey Fenland		
	Built by J L Almey – project LAA 361-14851		
	(NF 25.02.16)		

| G-SXSX | Robinson R66 Turbine | 0922 | 28.03.19 |
| | M Struth   (West Mersea, Colchester) | | |

G-SYDH	Bell 206B-3 JetRanger III	2398	20.12.17
	G-BXNT, N94CA, N123AL		
	SJH North West Ltd (Bury)		10.12.18E

| G-SYEL | Aero AT-3 R100 | AT3-019 | 21.08.06 |
| | Sywell Aerodrome Ltd   Sywell | | 19.09.18E |

G-SYES	Robinson R66 Turbine	0556	04.11.14	
	Lset Hire LLP Manchester Barton		25.10.18E	
G-SYFW	WAR Focke-Wulf FW190 replica	269	28.02.83	
	A Collins (Rugby)		13.09.16P	
	Built by M R Parr – project PFA 081-10584;			
	as '2+1' in Luftwaffe c/s (NF 18.02.16)			
G-SYLJ	Embraer EMB-135BJ Legacy	14500937	12.12.05	
	(PT-SCI), G-SYLJ, PT-SCI			
	Blue Wings Ltd (Ebene, Mauritius)		10.03.18E	
G-SYLL	Piper PA-31-350 Chieftain	31-7952102	21.02.19	
	G-BVYF, G-SAVE, N3518T			
	Sywell Aerodrome Ltd Sywell		01.02.19E	
G-SYLM	Reims/Cessna F177RG Cardinal RG	F177RG0043	13.03.19	
	G-AZTW Sylmar Aviation & Services Ltd			
	(Bucklebury, Reading)			
	(NF 13.03.19)			
G-SYLV	Cessna 208B Grand Caravan	208B0936	08.12.11	
	D-FAAH, (D-FAMC), UR-CEGC, D-FAAH, EC-IEV, N40753			
	WAS Aircraft Leasing Ltd Swansea		12.11.18E	
	Operated by Skydive			
G-SYWL	Aero AT-3 R100	AT3-011	24.10.05	
	SP-KOT Sywell Aerodrome Ltd Sywell '50'		23.11.18E	
G-SZDA	Allstar PZL SZD-59 Acro	590.A.14.015	27.02.14	
	(BGA 5769) P C Sharphouse Portmoak 'DA'		19.04.19E	
	Built by Allstar PZL Glider SP. z o.o.			

G-TAAA – G-TZZZ

G-TAAB	Cirrus SR22	1769	10.07.06	
	N944CD Alpha Bravo Aviation Ltd Oxford		17.09.18E	
G-TAAC	Cirrus SR20	1694	14.09.06	
	N997SR Pegasus Grab Hire Ltd			
	Wolverhampton Halfpenny Green		15.12.18E	
G-TAAS	Agusta AW109SP Grand New	22305	04.07.13	
	Sloane Helicopters Ltd East Midlands		04.07.18E	
	Operated by Derbyshire, Leicestershire & Rutland			
	Air Ambulance as callsign 'Helimed 54'			
G-TAAT	Piper PA-32-301FT 6X	3232027	07.11.16	
	OK-SIV, N3095G, OK-SIV, N3095G			
	A D Trotter Elstree		15.12.18E	
G-TACK	Grob G109B	6279	30.05.84	
	A P Mayne tr G-TACK Group Exeter Int'l		15.06.18E	
G-TACN	Diamond DA.62	62.044	05.10.18	
	OE-FHM Flight Calibration Services Ltd			
	Brighton City		24.09.19E	
G-TADS	Mead BM-77	DS01	18.04.16	
	D J Stagg Spixworth, Norwich			
	Built by D J Stagg (IE 04.01.17)			
G-TAFF	CASA 1-131E Jungmann Series 1000	1129	07.09.84	
	G-BFNE, Spanish AF E3B-148			
	R A Fleming Breighton		25.05.18P	
G-TAJF	Lindstrand LBL 77A	905	28.04.03	
	T A J Fowles Chester		04.08.17E	
G-TAKE	Aérospatiale AS.355F1 Ecureuil 2	5088	18.08.05	
	G-OITN, N400HH, N5788B			
	Arena Aviation Ltd Redhill 'BBC News'		20.02.18E	
G-TALA	Cessna 152 II	15285134	06.03.07	
	G-BNPZ, N6109Q Tatenhill Aviation Ltd Tatenhill		23.03.18E	
	'Donald Duck' logo			
G-TALB	Cessna 152 II	15283767	06.03.07	
	G-BORO, N5130B Tatenhill Aviation Ltd Tatenhill		01.03.18E	
	'Tigger' logo			
G-TALC	Cessna 152 II	15284941	24.04.07	
	G-BPBG, N5418P Tatenhill Aviation Ltd Tatenhill		21.07.18E	
	'Piglet' logo			
G-TALD	Reims/Cessna F152 II	F15201718	05.04.07	
	G-BHRM, F-GCHR Tatenhill Aviation Ltd Tatenhill		18.04.18E	
	'Eeyore' logo			
G-TALE	Piper PA-28-181 Archer II	28-8290048	30.10.07	
	G-BJOA, N8453H Tatenhill Aviation Ltd Tatenhill		07.05.18E	
	'Winnie the Pooh' logo			
G-TALF	Piper PA-24-250 Comanche	24-1094	27.11.07	
	G-APUZ, N6000P Tatenhill Aviation Ltd Tatenhill		18.10.18E	

G-TALG	Piper PA-28-151 Cherokee Warrior	28-7715219	14.02.08	
	G-BELP, N9543N Tatenhill Aviation Ltd Tatenhill		16.09.18E	
	'Roo' logo			
G-TALH	Piper PA-28-181 Archer II	28-7790208	21.10.08	
	G-CIFR, PH-MIT, OO-HBB, N7654F			
	Tatenhill Aviation Ltd Tatenhill		08.05.18E	
	'Owl' logo			
G-TALJ	Grumman American AA-5 Traveler	AA5-0479	25.09.12	
	G-BBUE S E Philpott tr The Lima Juliet Group Sleap		29.10.18E	
	'Simba' logo			
G-TALN	RotorWay A600 Talon	8022	19.08.08	
	Southern Helicopters Ltd Street Farm, Takeley		20.07.18P	
	Built by Southern Helicopters Ltd			
G-TALO	Reims/Cessna FA152 Aerobat	FA1520355	11.02.14	
	G-BFZU Tatenhill Aviation Ltd Tatenhill		11.07.18E	
	'Dumbo' logo			
G-TALP	Cessna 172N Skyhawk II	17271900	17.10.18	
	G-BOUF, N5605E Tatenhill Aviation Ltd Tatenhill		16.07.19E	
G-TAMA	Schweizer 269D (*Schweizer 333*)	0051A	10.03.05	
	N86G Cancelled 16.06.08 as PWFU		12.06.08	
	Kelham Hall, Kelham, Nottinghamshire			
	Stored as 'K-HALL' 01.15			
G-TAMD	Schweizer 269D (*Schweizer 333*)	0056A	01.12.05	
	Cancelled 16.04.13 as PWFU		13.06.09	
	Emmer Compascuum, Netherlands			
	Stored dismantled with Heli Holland 10.16			
G-TAMI	Diamond DA.40D Star	D4.210	10.11.17	
	D-EEWU AJW Construction Ltd Bournemouth		06.09.18E	
	Operated by L3 CTS Academy			
G-TAMR	Cessna 172S Skyhawk SP	172S8480	07.06.00	
	N2458J Caledonian Air Surveys Ltd Inverness		17.07.18E	
G-TAMS	Beech A23-24 Musketeer Super	MA-190	30.06.00	
	OY-DKF C P Allen Tatenhill		23.03.18E	
G-TANA	Air Création Tanarg 912S(2)/iXess 15	FLTxxx	17.01.06	
	B S Smy Red Barn Farm, Badingham		25.09.18P	
	Built by A P Marks – project BMAA/HB/485			
	(Flylight kit FLTxxx comprising trike s/n			
	T05099 & wing s/n A05187-5194)			
G-TANG	Air Création Tanarg 912S(2)/iXess 15	FLTxxx	18.09.09	
	N L Stammers Jersey		25.10.18P	
	Built by N L Stammers – project BMAA/HB/568			
	(Flylight kit FLTxxx comprising trike s/n T07094			
	& wing s/n A07161-7176) (IE 16.12.18)			
G-TANJ	Raj Hamsa X'Air 582(5)	629	21.06.01	
	K P Smith Willingale		12.11.15P	
	Built by R Thorman – project BMAA/HB/171			
	(IE 04.08.17)			
G-TANKᴹ	Cameron N-90 HAB	3625	20.06.95	
	Cancelled 23.05.16 as PWFU 'DFDS HOYER'		28.05.14	
	With Ulster Aviation Society, Lisburn			
G-TANO	Rolladen-Schneider LS3-a	3380	04.02.14	
	OY-XJP T Cavattoni			
	(Castlenuovo del Garda, Verona, Italy)		28.12.17E	
G-TANY	EAA Acrosport II	xxxx	19.02.04	
	P J Tanulak Sleap		19.07.18P	
	Built by P J Tanulak – project PFA 072A-13821			
G-TAPS	Piper PA-28RT-201T Turbo Arrow IV	28R-8131080	02.06.04	
	HB-PLV, N83423			
	T R Edwards & R L Nunn Kings Farm, Thurrock		04.05.18E	
G-TARN	Pietenpol Air Camper	xxxx	03.08.98	
	P J Heilbron Farnborough		27.06.18P	
	Built by P J Heilbron – project PFA 047-13349			
G-TARR	P&M Pegasus Quik	8264	27.04.07	
	A Edwards Yatesbury		28.05.18P	
G-TART	Piper PA-28-236 Dakota	28-7911261	18.12.90	
	N2945C N K G Prescot Goodwood		25.06.18E	
G-TATR	Travel Air Type R Mystery Ship replica	xxxx	12.03.09	
	R A Seeley Turweston '29'		04.05.18P	
	Built by Aero Antiques – project LAA 362-14892			
G-TATS	Aérospatiale AS.350BA Ecureuil	1905	14.05.01	
	F-GHSN, N37AW Helitrain Ltd Cotswold		07.06.18E	

G-TATT | Gardan GY-20 Minicab | xxxx | 30.11.78
P W Tattersall tr Tatt's Group
(Newton in Bowland, Clitheroe)
Built by L Tattershall – project PFA 056-10347
(NF 12.06.18)

G-TAWA | Boeing 737-8K5 | 37264 | 30.01.12
C-FVWA, G-TAWA   TUI Airways Ltd t/a TUI   Luton | 30.04.19E
Line No: 3907

G-TAWB | Boeing 737-8K5 | 37242 | 06.02.12
C-GWVB, G-TAWB   TUI Airways Ltd t/a TUI   Luton | 29.04.19E
Line No: 3917

G-TAWC | Boeing 737-8K5 | 39922 | 13.02.12
C-FAWC, G-TAWC, C-FAWC, G-TAWC
TUI Airways Ltd t/a TUI   Luton | 07.05.19E
Line No: 3925

G-TAWD | Boeing 737-8K5 | 37265 | 23.02.12
C-GFWD, G-TAWD   TUI Airways Ltd t/a TUI   Luton | 14.05.19E
Line No: 3939

G-TAWF | Boeing 737-8K5 | 37244 | 08.03.12
TUI Airways Ltd t/a TUI   Luton | 07.03.19E
Line No: 3955

G-TAWG | Boeing 737-8K5 | 37266 | 19.03.12
C-GZUG, G-TAWG   TUI Airways Ltd t/a TUI   Luton | 29.04.19E
Line No: 3967

G-TAWI | Boeing 737-8K5 | 37267 | 19.04.12
C-GEWI, G-TAWI   TUI Airways Ltd t/a TUI   Luton | 30.10.19E
Line No: 4006

G-TAWJ | Boeing 737-8K5 | 38108 | 08.05.12
C-GVOJ, G-TAWJ   TUI Airways Ltd t/a TUI   Luton | 01.11.19E
Line No: 4024

G-TAWL | Boeing 737-8K5 | 37243 | 09.01.13
C-GSWL, G-TAWL   TUI Airways Ltd t/a TUI   Luton | 05.04.19E
Line No: 4299

G-TAWM | Boeing 737-8K5 | 37249 | 27.02.13
C-GQWM, G-TAWM, C-GQWM G-TAWM, N5515R
TUI Airways Ltd t/a TUI   Luton | 26.03.19E
Line No: 4360

G-TAWN | Boeing 737-8K5 | 37251 | 11.03.13
C-GMWN, G-TAWN, C-GMWN, G-TAWN, N5573K
TUI Airways Ltd t/a TUI   Luton | 07.05.19E
Line No: 4369

G-TAWO | Boeing 737-8K5 | 37255 | 25.03.13
C-GEWO, G-TAWO, C-GEWO, G-TAWO
TUI Airways Ltd t/a TUI   Luton | 21.05.19E
Line No: 4384

G-TAWU | Boeing 737-8K5 | 37263 | 22.04.14
N5515R, N1787B   TUI Airways Ltd t/a TUI   Luton | 03.10.19E
Line No: 4875

G-TAWV | Boeing 737-8K5 | 41662 | 30.03.17
D-ATUP   TUI Airways Ltd t/a TUI   Luton | 03.09.19E
Line No: 5340

G-TAWW | Boeing 737-8K5 | 41663 | 10.04.17
D-ATUQ   TUI Airways Ltd t/a TUI   Luton | 19.07.19E
Line No: 5369

G-TAWX | Boeing 737-8K5 | 44272 | 07.12.18
SE-RFY   TUI Airways Ltd t/a TUI   Luton | 16.03.19E
Line No: 4827

G-TAWY ★ | Boeing 737-8K5 | 37246 | 04.03.19
SE-RFX   TUI Airways Ltd
To SE-RFX 19.03.19
Line No: 3994

G-TAXI | Piper PA-23-250 Aztec E | 27-7305085 | 06.04.78
N40270   S Waite   Sherburn-in-Elmet | 17.07.09E
(NF 26.05.17)

G-TAYC | Gulfstream Gulfstream IV-X *(Gulfstream 450)*   4060 | 18.01.07
N460GA   Executive Jet Charter Ltd   Farnborough | 17.01.19E

G-TAYI | Grob G115 | 8008 | 12.09.90
G-DODO, D-ENFT   K P Widdowson   Sandtoft | 25.04.18E
D-ENFT reserved between 19.09.95 & 04.97 but
never canx by CAA

G-TAYL | Pitts S-1S | 20940 | 08.01.13
N42221   R S Taylor   (Ardargie, Forgandenny) | 26.06.15P
(NF 18.10.16)

G-TAZZ | Dan Rihn DR.107 One Design | 02-0488 | 20.02.06
N J Riddin   Netherthorpe
Built by C J Gow – project PFA 264-14038;
FF 22.12.18 (IE 22.01.19)

G-TBAG | Murphy Renegade 912 | xxxx | 11.12.90
M R Tetley   Newton-on-Rawcliffe | 16.11.18P
Built by M Tetley – project PFA 188-11912

G-TBET | Ultramagic M-77 | 77/386 | 26.06.15
H Crawley & P Dopson   Birmingham B12   *'Tibet'* | 20.06.18E

G-TBFT | Textron 3000 Texan II | PM-110 | 07.06.18
N2842B   Affinity Flying Training Services Ltd
RAF Valley
For RAF as 'ZM323' in 2018 (IE 07.06.18)

G-TBHH | Aérospatiale AS.355F2 Ecureuil 2 | 5346 | 01.12.06
G-HOOT, G-SCOW, ZS-HSW, G-POON, G-MCAL
Alpha Properties (London) Ltd   Biggin Hill | 23.02.08E

G-TBIO | SOCATA TB-10 Tobago | 340 | 10.02.83
F-BNGZ   RPR Associates Ltd   (Swansea) | 10.05.18E

G-TBJP | Mainair Pegasus Quik | 8071 | 29.09.04
D J Bromley   Deenethorpe | 01.08.18P
Built by Mainair Sports Ltd

G-TBLB | P&M Quik GT450 | 8188 | 01.06.06
L Chesworth   Arclid Green, Sandbach |
Landed heavily Longford, Market Drayton 09.04.18
with damage to pod & wing (IE 07.06.18)

G-TBLC | Rans S-6-ES Coyote II | xxxx | 21.07.15
Royal Aeronautical Society   Gloucestershire
Built by P Buckley – project LAA 204-15110;
on construction 12.17; RAeS/Boeing 'Build a Plane'
project for The Bridge Learning Campus (NF 21.07.15)

G-TBLY | Eurocopter EC120B Colibri | 1192 | 12.03.01
F-WQOV   AD Bly Aircraft Leasing Ltd   Elstree | 19.03.19E

G-TBMR | P&M Quik GT450 | 8407 | 19.09.08
R W Street tr G-TBMR Syndicate   East Fortune | 01.09.18P

G-TBOK | SOCATA TB-10 Tobago | 1111 | 26.06.02
SX-ABF, F-GKUA   TB10 Ltd   Dunkeswell | 05.04.18E

G-TBSV | SOCATA TB-20 Trinidad GT | 2169 | 10.10.06
N403MS, F-HKJT, F-WWRB
Condron Concrete Ltd   Abbeyshrule, Rol | 11.09.18E

G-TBTN | SOCATA TB-10 Tobago | 322 | 07.08.03
G-BKIA   Y A Soojeri   Glasgow Prestwick | 22.09.11E
(NF 19.02.18)

G-TBUC | Airbus EC155 B1 | 7020 | 27.07.16
Noirmont (EC155) Ltd   Portledge Estate, Bideford | 11.10.19E

G-TBXX | SOCATA TB-20 Trinidad | 276 | 16.03.82
Aeroplane Ltd   Headcorn | 11.05.18E

G-TBYD | Raj Hamsa X'Air Falcon D(1) | 1249 | 25.11.13
T Collins   (High Kelling, Holt) | 12.08.19P
Built by T Ansari & P D Sibbons – project BMAA/HB/617

G-TBZO | SOCATA TB-20 Trinidad | 444 | 08.08.84
J L Auberget & J P Bechu
Nevers-Fourchambault, France | 09.05.18E

G-TCAA | Leonardo AW169 | 69038 | 30.08.17
I-EASJ   Specialist Aviation Services Ltd
Retford Gamston | 01.08.18E
Operated by Children's Air Ambulance

G-TCAN | Colt 69A | 1996 | 19.07.91
H C J Williams   Langford, Bristol
'Thunder & Colt Balloons' | 28.08.18E

G-TCCF | Airbus A330-243 | 248 | 23.10.18
C-GJDA, A6-EKQ, F-WWKL
Thomas Cook Airlines Ltd   Manchester | 13.11.19E

G-TCCG | Airbus A330-243 | 251 | 01.11.18
C-GUFR, A6-EKR, F-WWKO
Thomas Cook Airlines Ltd   Manchester | 13.11.19E

G-TCCI | Airbus A330-243 | 728 | 29.10.18
C-GUBL, B-6121, F-WWKQ
Thomas Cook Airlines Ltd   Manchester | 15.11.19E

G-TCDA | Airbus A321-211 | 2060 | 23.05.09
TC-JMG, N118CH, G-JOEE, D-AVZH
Thomas Cook Airlines Ltd   Manchester | 22.05.19E

G-TCDB | Airbus A321-211 | 5603 | 03.02.14
D-AIAB, D-AVZM   Thomas Cook Airlines Ltd
Manchester   *'Voyager Android'* | 29.05.19E

G-TCDC	Airbus A321-211	5872	22.11.13
	D-AVZT Thomas Cook Airlines Ltd Manchester		21.11.19E
G-TCDD	Airbus A321-211	6038	26.03.14
	D-AVZO Thomas Cook Airlines Ltd Manchester		09.10.19E
G-TCDE	Airbus A321-211	6056	10.04.14
	D-AVZS Thomas Cook Airlines Ltd Manchester		09.04.19E
G-TCDF	Airbus A321-211	6114	09.05.14
	D-AVXD Thomas Cook Airlines Ltd Manchester		30.11.19E
G-TCDG	Airbus A321-211	6122	13.05.14
	D-AVXG Thomas Cook Airlines Ltd Manchester		12.05.19E
G-TCDH	Airbus A321-211	6515	13.03.15
	D-AVZZ Thomas Cook Airlines Ltd Manchester		12.03.19E
G-TCDP	Airbus A321-211	6376	15.11.18
	D-AIAE, D-AVXS		
	Thomas Cook Airlines Ltd Manchester		30.11.19E
G-TCDR	Airbus A321-211	6615	06.12.18
	D-AIAH, D-AVXP		
	Thomas Cook Airlines Ltd Manchester		21.05.19E
G-TCDV	Airbus A321-211	1972	07.04.15
	OY-VKT, G-SMTJ, D-AVXG		
	Thomas Cook Airlines Ltd London Gatwick		20.04.19E
G-TCDW	Airbus A321-211	1921	08.12.14
	OY-VKB, D-AVZQ Thomas Cook Airlines Ltd		
			28.02.19E
G-TCDX	Airbus A321-211	1887	18.12.14
	OY-VKE, G-CTLA, D-AVZC		
	Thomas Cook Airlines Ltd Manchester		21.04.19E
G-TCDY	Airbus A321-211	1881	22.03.19
	C-GTXY, G-TCDY, OY-VKA, D-AVZO		
	Thomas Cook Airlines Ltd Manchester		
	(NF 17.11.17)		
G-TCDZ	Airbus A321-211	1006	23.05.14
	F-HBAF, EC-IXY, G-OOAI, (G-UNIG), D-AVZJ		
	Thomas Cook Airlines Ltd Manchester		07.12.19E
G-TCEE	Hughes 369HS *(500)*	610326S	06.09.00
	G-AZVM, N9091F		
	A M E Castro Phoenix Farm, Lower Upham		09.10.18E
G-TCHI	Supermarine 509 Spitfire Tr.9	6S-200618	19.11.08
	BS410 M B Phillips Biggin Hill		
	As 'BS410:PK-A' in RAF c/s; on restoration 01.19		
	(NF 30.11.15)		
G-TCHO	Supermarine 361 Spitfire IX	xxxx	12.12.08
	EN179 M B Phillips (Newton St Cyres, Exeter)		
	Recovered remains noted 08.13 (NF 30.11.15)		
G-TCHZ	Supermarine 329 Spitfire IIA	xxxx	05.04.12
	P7819 M B Phillips (Newton St Cyres, Exeter)		
	(NF 30.11.15)		
G-TCNM	Tecnam P92-EA Echo	609	12.08.02
	M Kolev Manchester Barton		13.07.18P
	Built by J Quaife – project PFA 318-13922		
G-TCNY	Mainair Pegasus Quik	8037	13.05.04
	A J Sawdon tr G-TCNY Group Solent		30.07.18P
	Built by Mainair Sports Ltd		
G-TCSX	Boeing 757-2K2	26330	11.08.14
	YA-AQT, EI-EXX, OH-AFI, PH-TKD, XA-TMU, PH-TKD,		
	C-GTSR, PH-TKD		
	TAG Aviation (UK) Ltd Farnborough		21.09.19E
	Line No: 717; operated by TCS Expeditions		
G-TCTC	Piper PA-28RT-201T Turbo Arrow IV	2831001	01.12.89
	N9130B P Salemis Kortrijk-Wevelgem Int'l, Belgium		
	25.06.18E		
	Originally built as N9524N (c/n 28R-8631006)		
G-TCUB	Piper J-3C-65 Cub	13970	31.07.87
	N9039Q, N67666, NC67666, USN 29684, 45-55204		
	C Kirk Northfield Farm, Mavis Enderby		30.08.18E
	Officially registered with Fuselage No.13805		
G-TCVA	Airbus A321-231	5582	05.04.18
	G-ZBAD, D-AVZH		
	Thomas Cook Airlines Ltd Manchester		25.03.19E
G-TCVB	Airbus A321-231	5606	26.04.18
	G-ZBAE, D-AVZO		
	Thomas Cook Airlines Ltd Manchester		22.04.19E
G-TCVC	Airbus A321-231	6059	09.03.18
	G-ZBAM, D-AVZT		
	Thomas Cook Airlines Ltd Manchester		05.02.19E
G-TCVD	Airbus A321-231	6126	01.03.18
	G-ZBAO, D-AVXH		
	Thomas Cook Airlines Ltd Manchester		26.02.19E
G-TCXB	Airbus A330-243	948	17.06.15
	G-CINS, N948AC, F-WWKN		
	Thomas Cook Airlines Ltd Manchester		11.06.19E
G-TCXC	Airbus A330-243	967	29.04.16
	G-CIUJ, N967CG, F-WWYI		
	Thomas Cook Airlines Ltd Manchester		26.04.19E
G-TDFS	IMCO Callair A-9A	1200	08.10.86
	G-AVZA, PH-ABI, SE-EUA, N26D		
	Cancelled 20.11.07 by CAA		05.07.07
	Tattershall Thorpe		
	Nose stored at Thorpe Camp visitor's centre 06.16		
G-TDJN	North American AT-6D Texan III	121-42228	12.06.12
	N7231C, 44-81506, RCAF 44-81506, 44-81506		
	D J Nock Wolverhampton Halfpenny Green		25.10.16E
	As '313048' in USAAF c/s		
G-TDJP	Van's RV-8	83119	25.03.13
	D J Pearson Wolverhampton Halfpenny Green		01.02.18P
	Built by D J Pearson & T J T Simmonds		
	– project LAA 303-15056		
G-TDOG	Scottish Aviation Bulldog Srs 120/121	BH120/230	17.09.01
	XX538 G S Taylor Shobdon		17.12.17E
	As 'XX538:O' in RAF white & red c/s		
G-TDSA	Reims/Cessna F406 Caravan II	F406-0096	04.12.08
	M Evans & W Johnston t/a Nor Leasing Farnborough		25.01.19E
G-TDVB	Dyn'Aéro MCR-01 ULC	242	23.01.03
	D V Brunt Plaistows Farm, St Albans		24.10.18P
	Built by D Brunt – project PFA 301B-14015		
G-TDYN	Aerospool Dynamic WT9 UK	DY147/2006	02.10.06
	N C Herrington & N Lilley Old Sarum		27.10.18P
	Assembled Yeoman Light Aircraft Co Ltd;		
	official c/n recorded as 'DY147'		
G-TEBZ	Piper PA-28R-201 Arrow III	28R-7737050	07.01.00
	N105CC Smart People Dont Buy Ltd		
	Wellesbourne Mountford		31.10.18E
G-TECA	Tecnam P2002-JF Sierra	218	03.12.12
	Aeros Global Ltd Wellesbourne Mountford		13.12.18E
G-TECB	Tecnam P2006T	122	04.12.13
	Aeros Holdings Ltd Coventry		09.08.18E
G-TECC	Aeronca 7AC Champion	7AC-5269	26.06.91
	N1704E, NC1704E N J Orchard-Armitage		
	Maypole Farm, Chislet *'Champ Chump'*		19.07.18P
G-TECH	Rockwell Commander 114	14074	08.08.85
	G-BEDH, N4744W A S Turner Newquay Cornwall		16.12.17E
G-TECI	Tecnam P2002-JF Sierra	127	21.06.10
	G-TECI Flying Club Ltd Brimpton		23.03.18E
G-TECM	Tecnam P92-EM Echo	002	01.12.00
	N Stamford Sywell		18.07.19P
	Built by D A Lawrence – project PFA 318-13667		
G-TECO	Tecnam P92-EA Echo	608	16.02.05
	A N Buchan Calton Moor Farm, Ashbourne		20.09.18P
	Built by A N Buchan – project PFA 318-13830		
G-TECS	Tecnam P2002-EA Sierra	xxxx	16.06.04
	D A Lawrence Membury		18.06.18P
	Built by D A Lawrence – project PFA 333-14325;		
	originally registered as PFA 318A-14250		
G-TECT	Tecnam P2006T	077	13.05.11
	Cabledraw Ltd Lydd		19.03.18E
G-TEDB	Reims/Cessna F150L	F15000772	20.01.05
	G-AZLZ R Nightingale Bristol		20.12.18E
G-TEDI	Best Off Skyranger J2.2(1)	SKR0207217	01.05.03
	P W Reid Eshott		20.05.18P
	Built by E Robshaw & D A Smith		
	– project BMAA/HB/243		
G-TEDW	Air Création Buggy 582(2)/Kiss 450	FL024	21.01.04
	G Frost Arclid Green, Sandbach		15.10.16P
	Built by D J Wood – project BMAA/HB/343		
	(Flylight kit FL024 comprising trike s/n T03103 &		
	wing s/n A03184-3179); badged 'GTE' (IE 03.01.17)		

G-TEDY	Evans VP-1	xxxx	04.10.90
	G-BHGN N K Marston (Harrow) *'The Plank'*		01.07.97P
	Built by A Cameron – project PFA 062-10383		
	(NF 21.08.14)		
G-TEFC	Piper PA-28-140 Cherokee F	28-7325088	18.06.80
	OY-PRC, N15530 S S Bamrah Biggin Hill		06.10.17E
	(IE 13.02.18)		
G-TEGS	Bell 206B-3 JetRanger III	4622	17.04.07
	C-FLZN HC Services Ltd Fairoaks		30.01.18E
G-TEHL	CFM Streak Shadow SA-M	xxxx	20.11.98
	G-MYJE D W Allen Hunsdon		
	Built by A K Paterson – project PFA 206-13412		
	(SSDR microlight since 08.16) (IE 06.10.17)		
G-TELY	Agusta A109A II	7326	10.03.89
	N1HQ, N200SH Castle Air Ltd Trebrown, Liskeard		07.09.17E
G-TEMB	Tecnam P2002-EA Sierra	204	29.11.06
	M B Hill Draycott		15.09.17P
	Built by M B Hill – project PFA 333-14593 (IE 08.12.17)		
G-TEMP	Piper PA-28-180 Cherokee E	28-5806	15.05.89
	G-AYBK, N11C		
	F R Busch & M Khoshkou Andrewsfield		17.11.17E
G-TEMT	Hawker Tempest II	420	09.10.89
	Indian AF HA586, MW763 Anglia Aircraft		
	Restorations Ltd (Great Canfield, Dunmow)		
	As 'MW763:HF' (NF 12.04.16)		
G-TENG	Extra EA.300/L	172	08.12.03
	D C Mowat Perth		21.02.18E
G-TENN	Van's RV-10	xxxx	26.10.16
	R E Frew tr RV10 Group Swansea		13.02.20P
	Built by J Adams & Partners – project LAA 339-15222		
G-TENT	Auster J1N Alpha	2058	01.02.90
	G-AKJU, TW513		
	R Callaway-Lewis Greenlease Farm, Selsey *'123'*		15.12.14P
	(NF 18.10.16)		
G-TERN	Europa Aviation Europa	106	18.07.97
	J Smith (North Thoresby, Grimsby)		14.06.18P
	Built by J E G Lundesjo – project PFA 247-12780;		
	tailwheel u/c; roaded to North Coates to fly		
G-TERO	Van's RV-7	73964	10.02.14
	A Phillips Boarhunt Farm, Fareham		28.07.18P
	Built by A Phillips – project LAA 323-15124		
G-TERR	Cyclone Pegasus Quik	7925	06.01.03
	M Faulkner Fenland		26.05.18P
	Built by Cyclone Airsports Ltd		
G-TERY	Piper PA-28-181 Archer II	28-7990078	13.01.89
	G-BOXZ, N22402 J R Bratherton Sandown		08.06.18E
G-TESI	Tecnam P2002-EA Sierra	138	23.11.05
	C C Burgess White Waltham		11.06.18P
	Built by P J Mitchell – project PFA 333-14481		
G-TESR	Tecnam P2002 RG Sierra	302	04.01.08
	J M P Ree tr TecnamRG Group Brimpton		24.04.19P
	Built by P J Mitchell -project PFA 333A-14758		
G-TEST	Piper PA-34-200 Seneca	34-7450116	28.07.89
	OO-RPW, G-BLCD, PH-PLZ, N41409		
	Stapleford Flying Club Ltd Stapleford		23.12.11E
	(IE 02.07.15)		
G-TEWS	Piper PA-28-140 Cherokee B	28-25128	23.05.88
	G-KEAN, G-AWTM, N11C		
	D Barron tr G-TEWS Group Beverley (Linley Hill)		03.02.18E
G-TEXN	North American T-6G-NT Texan	168-176	22.06.05
	G-BHTH, N2807G, 49-3072		
	Boultbee Classic LLP Goodwood		23.06.19E
	As 'KF402:HT-Y' in RAF c/s		
G-TEZZ	CZAW Sportcruiser	700539	11.11.08
	K McKay & B M Tune Beverley (Linley Hill)		11.09.19P
	Built by T D Baker – project LAA 338-14863		
G-TFAM	Piper PA-46R-350T Malibu Matrix	4692068	23.06.15
	G-UDMS, N6077F		
	Take Flight Aviation Ltd Wellesbourne Mountford		10.11.18E
G-TFCC	Cub Crafters Carbon Cub SS CC11-160	CC11-00116	20.08.13
	N396SR Patina Ltd Duxford		18.12.18W
	Operated by The Fighter Collection		
G-TFIX	Mainair Pegasus Quantum 15-912	8048	21.07.04
	T G Jones Caernarfon		08.07.18P
G-TFLX	P&M Quik GT450	8379	16.04.08
	L Bligh Redlands		05.05.19P
G-TFLY	Air Création Buggy 582(1)/Kiss 450	FL030	28.06.05
	A J Ladell (Thetford)		05.05.14P
	Built by A J Ladell – project BMAA/HB/438		
	(Flylight kit FL030 [as FL027 duplicated]		
	comprising trike s/n T040843 & wing s/n D065015)		
G-TFOG	Best Off Skyranger 912(2)	SKR0511661	02.03.06
	T J Fogg Rossall Field, Cockerham		21.08.18P
	Built by T J Fogg – project BMAA/HB/494		
G-TFRBᴹ	Air Command 532 Elite Sport	0628	26.04.90
	Cancelled 07.06.01 by CAA		06.08.98
	Built by F R Blennerhasset – project PFA G/04-1167		
	With Yorkshire Air Museum, Elvington		
G-TFSI	North American TF-51D Mustang	124-44703	17.06.14
	N251RJ, 44-84847 Anglia Aircraft Restorations Ltd		
	Duxford *'Contrary Mary'*		09.07.19P
	As '44-14251/WZ-I' in USAAF c/s		
G-TFUN	Valentin Taifun 17E	1011	28.12.83
	D-KIHP G F Wynn tr North West Taifun Group		
	Blackpool		23.01.08E
	(NF 20.10.14)		
G-TFYN	Piper PA-32RT-300 Lance II	32R-7885128	28.04.00
	N5HG, D-ELAE, N31740		
	Cancelled 28.03.14 by CAA		05.07.03
	Meppershall *Wreck stored 05.18*		
G-TGER	Gulfstream American AA-5B Tiger	AA5B-0952	20.02.86
	G-BFZP L Walkden Dunkeswell *'8'*		19.08.19E
	Noted 06.18		
G-TGGR	Eurocopter EC120B Colibri	1224	22.07.04
	SE-JMF Messiah Corporation Ltd Stapleford		12.06.17E
G-TGJH	Evans VP-1 Series 2	xxxx	18.01.13
	Condor Aviation International Ltd		
	Birchwood Lodge, North Duffield		17.04.17P
	Built by A Graham & J C H Hart – project		
	PFA 062-11933; damaged 28.07.16,		
	Ewesley Farm, Northumbria (NF 18.12.17)		
G-TGLG	AutoGyro Calidus	C00419	20.11.15
	T R Galloway Shobdon		02.12.17P
	Assembled Rotorsport UK as c/n RSUK/CALS/028		
G-TGPG	Boeing 737-3Y0(SF)	24464	07.02.17
	OY-JTB, RP-C4010, EI-BZE		
	21T Ltd Doncaster Sheffield		20.12.18E
	Line No: 1753; operated by 2 Excel Aviation Ltd		
G-TGRA	Agusta A109A	7201	15.02.01
	D-HEED, N3983N, HB-XNF, I-PATZ		
	Tiger Helicopters Ltd Shobdon		14.05.11E
	Stored 09.14 less rotor (NF 18.05.16)		
G-TGRC	Robinson R22 Beta	1775	13.02.17
	G-RSWW, N40815 Tiger Aviation Ltd Shobdon		14.11.18E
G-TGRD	Robinson R22 Beta II	2712	16.06.04
	G-OPTS Tiger Aviation Ltd Shobdon		24.08.11E
	(NF 12.08.18)		
G-TGRE	Robinson R22 Alpha	0471	11.09.03
	G-SOLD, N8559X Tiger Aviation Ltd Shobdon		21.02.13E
	(NF 27.06.18)		
G-TGRS	Robinson R22 Beta	1069	05.11.97
	G-DELL, N80466 Tiger Aviation Ltd Shobdon		28.04.18E
G-TGRZ	Bell 206B-2 JetRanger II	2288	15.06.00
	G-BXZX, N27EA, N286CA, N93AT, N16873		
	Tiger Aviation Ltd Shobdon		10.10.18E
G-TGTT	Robinson R44 Raven II	10023	08.01.08
	G-STUS, N369SB, G-STUS		
	Smart People UK Ltd Cabourne		13.07.18E
G-TGUL	Earthstar Thundergull J	003	10.04.18
	P J Reilly (Southwater, Horsham)		
	Built by R Kingston (NF 10.04.18)		
G-TGVP	Supermarine 377 Seafire F.XV	FLWA 25243	01.12.14
	N462XV, N9413Z, 'UB415', UB414 Burm.AF UB414,		
	G-15-225, SR462		
	T A V Percy (Old Warden, Biggleswade)		
	Built by Westland Aircraft Ltd;		
	on rebuild 07.17 (NF 01.12.14)		

G-THAT	Raj Hamsa X'Air Falcon 912(1)	613	27.05.02
	M C Sawyer Hunsdon		20.08.19P
	Built by M G Thatcher – project BMAA/HB/221		
G-THEO	Team Mini-Max 91	2071 P	09.02.99
	D R Western Westonzoyland		
	Built by T Willford – project PFA 186-13099;		
	raised rear fuselage		
	(SSDR microlight since 06.14) (IE 04.08.17)		
G-THFC	Embraer EMB-135BJ Legacy	14500954	02.02.10
	G-RRAZ, G-RUBN, PT-SFC		
	Raz Air Ltd London Stansted		12.12.18E
G-THIN	Reims FR172E Rocket	FR17200016	04.12.02
	G-BXYY, OY-AHO, F-WLIP		
	T B Sumner Leeds Bradford		18.07.19E
G-THOM	Thunder Ax6-56	366	14.07.81
	T H Wilson Wendling, Dereham		14.08.07A
	(NF 02.01.15)		
G-THOT	Avtech Jabiru SK	xxxx	16.09.97
	S G Holton Elmsett		07.11.17P
	Built by N V Cook – project PFA 274-13159		
G-THRE	Cessna 182S Skylane	18280454	06.05.99
	N2391A J P Monjalet Sainte Bazeille, France		13.11.14E
G-THSL	Piper PA-28R-201 Arrow III	28R-7837278	11.09.78
	N36396 D M Markscheffel Southend		05.03.19E
	Official type data 'PA-28R-201 Cherokee Arrow III'		
	is incorrect		
G-THUN	Republic P-47D-40-RA Thunderbolt	39955731	18.06.99
	N147PF, G-THUN, N47DD, Peruvian AF 119 (was 5xx),		
	45-49192		
	Fighter Aviation Engineering Ltd Duxford *'Nellie'*		07.07.07P
	As '549192/F4-J' in USAAF c/s (NF 27.04.18)		
G-THYB	Cessna 172S Skyhawk SP	172S10569	06.10.16
	N495ER Atlantic Flight Training Ltd (Cork, RoI)		07.11.18E
G-TIAC	TLAC Sherwood Ranger XP	XP61	04.11.11
	The Light Aircraft Company Ltd Little Snoring		03.04.17P
	Built by The Light Aircraft Company Ltd – project		
	LAA 237A-14949; initially built as kit no XP36;		
	rebuilt 2017 as XP61 after M3 damage 05.16		
G-TIBF	Kubicek BB34Z	566	08.05.15
	HS-EWF G B Lescott Oxford OX4 *'Mastercard'*		01.06.19E
G-TIBS	SOCATA TB-20 Trinidad	866	31.01.17
	N34FA, G-BPFG C C Jewell Lydd		23.02.18E
	Operated by Lydd Aero Club (Group Two)		
G-TICH	Taylor JT.2 Titch	xxxx	12.02.01
	J W Graham-White Top Farm, Croydon *'Titch Bitch'*		18.07.17P
	Built by R Davitt, A J House & C J Wheeler – project PFA		
	060-3213: original allocation project PFA 3213		
G-TICO	Cameron O-77	11902	06.07.15
	J F Trehern (Devon)		12.07.18E
G-TIDS	Jodel D.150 Mascaret	44	15.04.86
	OO-GAN M R Parker Sywell		05.06.18P
	Built by Société Aéronautique Normande		
G-TIDY	Best Off Skyranger Nynja 912S(1)	xxxx090	20.03.12
	J M Stables Baxby Manor, Husthwaite		26.06.18P
	Built by P Rigby – project BMAA/HB/623		
G-TIFG	Comco Ikarus C42 FB80	1009-7119	22.09.10
	D Birchall tr The Ikarus Flying Group		
	Manchester Barton		27.09.18P
	Assembled Pioneer Aviation UK Ltd		
G-TIGA	de Havilland DH.82A Tiger Moth	83547	05.06.85
	G-AOEG, T7120 D E Leatherland Langar		10.08.16P
	Built by Morris Motors Ltd		
G-TIGC	Aérospatiale AS.332L Super Puma	2024	14.04.82
	G-BJYH, F-WTNJ		
	Airbus Helicopters Marseille, France		27.08.15E
	Noted 03.15		
G-TIGE[M]	Aérospatiale AS.332L Super Puma	2028	15.04.82
	G-BJYJ, F-WTNM Cancelled 08.12.15 as PWFU		06.06.15
	With The Helicopter Museum, Weston-super-Mare		
G-TIGS	Aérospatiale AS.332L Super Puma	2086	06.05.83
	Airbus Helicopters Marseille, France		27.06.15E
	Noted 03.15		
G-TIGV	Aérospatiale AS.332L Super Puma	2099	12.01.84
	LN-ONC, G-TIGV, LN-ONC, G-TIGV, LN-OPF, G-TIGV		
	Airbus Helicopters Leasing Services Ltd Fleetlands		25.06.14E
	Stored 11.18 (IE 09.07.18)		
G-TIII	Pitts S-2A	2196	27.02.89
	G-BGSE, N947		
	D D & D S Welch (Catbrook, Chepstow)		15.07.19E
	Built by Aerotek Inc		
G-TIJL	Airbus AS.355NP Ecureuil 2	5801	25.02.19
	G-PERX, F-WWPO Wycombe Helicopter Services LLP		
	Wycombe Air Park		01.05.19E
G-TILE	Robinson R22 Beta	1100	04.08.89
	Heli Air Ltd Wellesbourne Mountford		21.11.18E
G-TIMC	Robinson R44 Raven II	11102	30.03.06
	G-CDUR T Clark Aviation LLP		
	Brentford Grange Farm, Coleshill		29.03.18E
G-TIMG	Beagle Terrier 3	xxxx	07.03.01
	T J Goodwin (Manningtree)		
	Built by T J Goodwin – project PFA 000-318;		
	comprises unknown Auster AOP,6 fuselage		
	frame & wing of VF505) (NF 02.03.18)		
G-TIMI	BRM Bristell NG5 Speed Wing	095	05.09.14
	A I D Rich Elstree		01.06.19P
	Built by T Harrison – project LAA 385-15295		
G-TIMK	Piper PA-28-181 Archer II	28-8090214	25.08.81
	OO-TRT, PH-EAS, OO-HLN, N8142H		
	Minimal Risk Consultancy Ltd Shobdon		06.02.18E
G-TIMP	Aeronca 7BCM Champion	7AC-3392	14.08.92
	N84681, NC84681 R B Valler Goodwood		07.06.18P
G-TIMS	Falconar F-12A Cruiser	xxxx	01.10.91
	T Sheridan (London E4)		
	Built by T Sheridan – project PFA 022-12134		
	(NF 06.01.15)		
G-TIMX	Head Ax8-88B	384	23.04.09
	J Edwards & S McMahon Northampton		29.06.18E
G-TIMY	Gardan GY-80-160 Horizon	36	17.01.00
	I-TIKI A R Whyte Wellesbourne Mountford		22.08.17R
G-TINA	Socata TB10 Tobago	67	30.10.79
	Cancelled 29.10.14 as PWFU		30.03.11
	Milton Keynes College *Instructional use 10.16*		
G-TINK	Robinson R22 Beta	0937	22.05.01
	G-NICH Helimech Ltd Brook Farm, Hulcote		23.10.18E
G-TINS	Cameron N-90	1626	27.01.88
	J R Clifton Upper Moutere, Nelson, New Zealand		
	'Carling Black Label'		11.10.03A
	(NF 20.04.16)		
G-TINT	Evektor EV-97A Eurostar	2005-3019	08.08.05
	I A Cunningham Perth		13.08.19P
	Built by I A Cunningham – project PFA 315-14394		
G-TINY	Moravan Zlin Z-526F Trener	1257	20.04.94
	OK-CMD, G-TINY, YR-ZAD D Evans North Weald		01.04.09E
	Noted 07.18 (NF 20.11.15)		
G-TIPJ	Cameron Z-77	11456	30.03.11
	A W Macdonald tr Servowarm Balloon Syndicate		
	Leigh-on-Sea *'Tiptree'*		31.03.18E
G-TIPP	Aeroprakt A-22LS Foxbat	A22LS-242	20.05.15
	E Fogarty Rochester		21.08.18P
	Built by E Fogarty – project LAA 317B-15334		
G-TIPR	Eurocopter AS.350B2 Ecureuil	4474	09.10.15
	SE-HJL, G-PATM, SE-HJL		
	Thames Materials Holdings Ltd Denham		03.06.18E
G-TIPS	Tipsy Nipper T.66 Series 3	T66/50	27.03.95
	OO-VAL, 9Q-CYJ, 9O-CYJ, (OO-CYJ), (OO-CCD)		
	F V Neefs (London W14)		10.08.06P
	Built by Avions Fairey SA: rebuilt by R F L Cuypers		
	– project PFA 025-12696 (IE 28.11.14)		
G-TIPY	Czech Sport PS-28 Cruiser	C0516	25.06.14
	I C Tandy Cotswold		19.07.18R
G-TIVV	Evektor EV-97 Eurostar	2005-2313	04.08.05
	A W K Van der Schatte (Fearnan, Aberfeldy)		24.05.19P
	Built by S Hoyle – project PFA 315-14435		

G-TJAL	Avtech Jabiru UL	0210	21.02.03
	M R Williamson Sutton Meadows		
	Built by T J Adams-Lewis – project PFA 274A-13360		
	(IE 14.08.18)		
G-TJAV	Mainair Pegasus Quik	8070	23.09.04
	Access Anywhere Ltd Perth		19.06.18P
	Built by Mainair Sports Ltd		
G-TJAY	Piper PA-22-135 Tri-Pacer	22-730	11.05.93
	N730TJ, N2353A		
	D Pegley (Wisborough Green, Billingshurst)		31.01.18E
G-TJCL	P&M QuikR	8756	29.03.17
	B R Dale (Sarre, Birchington)		26.03.18P
G-TJDM	Van's RV-6A	25433	21.09.07
	J D Michie White Waltham		11.05.18P
	Built by J D Michie – project PFA 181A-13370		
G-TKAY	Europa Aviation Europa	179	02.06.99
	A M Kay Cambridge		14.08.07P
	Built by A M Kay – project PFA 247-12804;		
	tailwheel u/c (IE 08.12.17)		
G-TKEV	P&M QuikR	8498	10.11.09
	S J Thompson Solent		13.08.18P
G-TKHE	Piper PA-28RT-201T Turbo Arrow IV	28R-7931116	06.11.18
	G-EPTL, I-EPTL, N2215V		
	C H Smith (Chelmsford)		02.08.19E
G-TKIS	Tri-R KIS	029	23.12.93
	J L Bone Biggin Hill		28.04.06P
	Built by J L Bone – project PFA 239-12358;		
	tailwheel u/c (NF 20.10.14)		
G-TKNO	Ultramagic S-50	50/06	01.08.11
	P Dickinson St Martins, Oswestry		13.09.18E
G-TLAC	TLAC Sherwood Ranger ST	"303"	16.03.09
	The Light Aircraft Company Ltd Little Snoring		06.09.18P
	Built by The Light Aircraft Company Ltd		
	– project PFA 237B-13895		
G-TLCL	Raytheon Hawker 800XP	258783	23.07.18
	N783TX, CS-DRQ, N37146 Voluxis Ltd Biggin Hill		
G-TLDL	Medway SLA 100 Executive	290906	29.03.07
	J M Clifford (Moreton, Dorchester)		27.10.17P
G-TLETᴹ	Piper PA-28-161 Cadet	2841259	25.08.04
	G-GFCF, G-RHBH, N9193Z		
	Cancelled 10.06.13 as destroyed		18.10.12
	Fuselage only		
	With Bournemouth Aviation Museum, Bournemouth		
G-TLMA	Lindstrand LTL Series 1-105	017	05.12.16
	A M Holly Breadstone, Berkeley		
	'Lord Mayor's Appeal Charity'		05.06.19E
G-TLST	TL 2000UK Sting Carbon	ST0293	02.06.09
	W H J Knowles Stoodleigh Barton Farm, Stoodleigh		30.08.18P
	Built by B McFadden – project LAA 347-14895		
G-TLTL	Schempp-Hirth Discus CS	257CS	11.01.08
	BGA 4679/JPU E K Armitage Camphill *'TL2'*		21.03.18E
G-TMAX	Evektor EV-97 Sportstar Max	2010 1305	22.10.10
	P A Baxter & P Earley tr G-TMAX Group		
	Wycombe Air Park		28.09.18W
G-TMCB	Best Off Skyranger 912(2)	SKR0309378	23.10.03
	J R Davis Hawling Manor Farm, Hawling		26.06.17P
	Built by A H McBreen – project BMAA/HB/310		
G-TMCC	Cameron N-90	4327	30.03.98
	M S Jennings Malmesbury		
	'The Mall – Cribb's Causeway'		16.07.09E
	(IE 04.08.17)		
G-TMHK	Piper PA-38-112 Tomahawk	38-78A0025	05.11.13
	G-GALL, G-BTEV, N9315T		
	Smart People Dont Buy Ltd Wellesbourne Mountford		01.06.12E
	(NF 12.10.17)		
G-TMPV	Hawker Tempest V	41H-511591	13.03.14
	4887M, JN768 Anglia Aircraft Restorations Ltd Sywell		
	(NF 20.10.17)		
G-TNGO	Van's RV-6	21897	27.03.08
	N97HS J D M Willis Holmbeck Farm, Burcott *'23'*		16.03.18P
	Built by H R Schweitzer		
G-TNIK	Dassault Falcon 2000	25	18.04.16
	T7-NIK, M-NIKO, N25FJ, N122SC, (N406ST), N122SC,		
	N96FG, N2042, F-WWML		
	Blu Halkin Ltd Cuneo-Levaldigi, Turin, Italy		17.04.18E
G-TNJB	P&M QuikR	8553	23.11.10
	J H Bradbury Arclid Green, Sandbach		22.11.18P
G-TNRG	Air Création Tanarg 912S(2)/iXess 15	FLT002	02.11.05
	I M Lane (Westcott)		11.11.19P
	Built by C M Saysell – project BMAA/HB/468		
	(Flylight kit FLT002 comprising trike s/n T05070		
	& wing s/n A05147-5129)		
G-TNTN	Thunder Ax6-56	1991	25.04.91
	A A Leggate & H M Savage Edinburgh EH3		12.07.18E
G-TOBA	SOCATA TB-10 Tobago	625	04.04.91
	N600N I Blamire Solent		15.10.19E
G-TOBI	Reims/Cessna F172K	F17200792	05.01.84
	G-AYVB M J Clarke tr The TOBI Group Leicester		30.07.18E
G-TOES	Piper PA-28-161 Warrior II	28-7816512	21.03.17
	LN-BDA, N9664C Freedom Aviation Ltd Cotswold		27.01.20E
G-TOFT	Colt 90A	1693	08.03.90
	C S Perceval Chipperfield, Kings Langley		
	'Norwest Holst'		24.10.17E
G-TOGO	Van's RV-6A	60296	06.04.99
	J C Simpson Brighton City *'Gernot'*		07.11.18P
	Built by G Schwetz – project PFA 181A-13447		
G-TOLL	Piper PA-28R-201 Arrow III	28R-7837025	12.10.00
	N52HV, D-ECIW, N9007K Arrow Aircraft Ltd		
	Wolverhampton Halfpenny Green		09.03.18E
	Official type data 'PA-28R-201 Cherokee Arrow III'		
	is incorrect		
G-TOLS	Robinson R44 Raven	1194	28.09.11
	G-CBOT K N Tolley Kyrebatch Farm, Thornbury		03.12.18E
G-TOLY	Robinson R22 Beta II	2809	08.02.01
	G-NSHR Helicopter & Pilot Services Ltd		
	Wycombe Air Park		21.03.18E
G-TOMC	North American AT-6D Texan III	88-14602	22.04.02
	French AF 114700, 42-44514		
	A A Marshall tr Texan Restoration		
	Bruntingthorpe *'Texan Tomcat'*		
	(NF 21.05.18)		
G-TOMJ	Flight Design CT2K	03-04-01-14	28.07.03
	Avair Ltd Sackville Lodge Farm, Riseley		18.06.18P
	Assembled Mainair Sports Ltd as c/n 7975		
G-TOMX	Dyn'Aéro MCR-01	345	06.01.09
	P T Knight Sittles Farm, Alrewas		17.07.18P
	Built by P T Knight – project PFA 301-14624		
G-TONE	Pazmany PL-4	xxxx	24.06.87
	P I Morgans Haverfordwest		
	Built by J A Walmsley & A D Worrall – project		
	PFA 017-10695; noted dismantled 05.12 (NF 21.12.15)		
G-TONN	Mainair Pegasus Quik	7954	28.05.03
	T D Evans Wolverhampton Halfpenny Green		07.10.18P
	Built by Mainair Sports Ltd		
G-TOOB	Schempp-Hirth Discus-2b	72	30.04.08
	BGA 4820/JVR M F Evans Lasham *'540'*		08.02.18E
G-TOOL	Thunder Ax8-105	1670	29.03.90
	D V Howard Bath *'Toolmaster'*		21.09.09E
	Inflated Bath 12.18 (NF 20.12.16)		
G-TOOO	Guimbal Cabri G2	1175	25.11.16
	Helicentre Aviation Ltd Leicester		04.12.18E
G-TOPB	Cameron Z-140	11718	20.12.12
	Anana Ltd Bristol BS16 *'anana'*		08.05.19E
G-TOPC	Aérospatiale AS.355F1 Ecureuil 2	5313	29.07.97
	I-LGOG, 3A-MCS, D-HOSY, OE-BXV, D-HOSY		
	Kinetic Avionics Ltd Wycombe Air Park		06.11.18E
G-TOPK	Europa Aviation Europa XS	1000	16.03.04
	P J Kember Fowle Hall Farm, Laddingford		27.04.18P
	Built by P J Kember – project PFA 247-14193;		
	tricycle u/c		
G-TOPM	Agusta-Bell 206B-2 JetRanger II	8732	06.07.15
	G-CCBL, OO-VCI, PH-VCP, OO-VCI, (OO-XCI)		
	A Scott t/a A & W Demolition (Bracknell)		
	(Ashley Farm, Warfield, Bracknell)		02.09.17E
	(IE 14.02.18)		

G-TOPO Piper PA-23-250 Turbo Aztec E   27-4587   23.01.07
G-BGWW, OO-ABH, N13971   Ravenair Aircraft Ltd
(Liverpool) *'www.osni.gov.uk'*   01.01.15E
Parted out at Liverpool John Lennon 01.19
(NF 13.09.17)

G-TOPP Van's RV-10   41575   17.09.14
S E Coles & D Topp   (Milton Keynes & Buckingham)
Built by S E Coles & D Topp – project
LAA 339-15289 (NF 17.09.14)

G-TORC Piper PA-28R-200 Cherokee Arrow II   28R-7535036   18.07.03
OE-DIU, N32236   Pure Aviation Support Services Ltd
Croft Farm, Defford   29.03.18E

G-TORI Zenair CH.701SP   7-9496   10.09.08
G-CCSK   R W H Watson
New Grimmet Farm, Maybole   20.11.17P
Built by S J Thomas – project PFA 187-14188;
lost control landing Old Sarum 26.05.17
(NF 11.04.18)

G-TORK Cameron Z-105   10968   05.01.07
M E Dunstan   Bath   *'rotork'*   15.01.19E

G-TORN Flight Design CTSW   06-05-04   01.02.07
N C Harper   Grove Farm, Needham   24.04.18P
Assembled P&M Aviation Ltd as c/n 8189 (2);
original c/n 8189 allocated to kit no.06-06-14

G-TORO Best Off Skyranger Nynja 912S(1)   13090146   18.10.13
C Fenwick & L J E Moss   (Shenley, Radlett)   18.07.18P
Built by B J Nortje – project BMAA/HB/645

G-TOSH Robinson R22 Beta   0933   14.03.97
N2629S, LV-RBD, N8012T   Choicecircle Ltd   (Rugby)   14.11.18E

G-TOTN Cessna 210M Centurion II   21061674   15.07.04
G-BVZM, OO-CNJ, N732PV
Quay Financial Strategies Ltd   Isle of Man   21.06.18E

G-TOTO Reims/Cessna F177RG Cardinal RG   F177RG0049   29.08.89
G-OADE, G-AZKH   Airspeed Aviation Ltd   Derby   15.08.17E
Made wheels up landing Denham 14.12.16; noted 07.17

G-TOUR Robin R2112 Alpha   187   09.10.79
R M Wade   Bournemouth   24.05.18E

G-TOWS Piper PA-25-260 Pawnee C   25-4853   17.07.91
PH-VBT, D-EAVI, N4370Y, N9722N
Lasham Gliding Society Ltd   Lasham   12.03.18E

G-TOYZ Bell 206B-3 JetRanger III   3949   21.11.96
G-RGER, N75EA, JA9452, N32018
G-TOYZ Ltd   (Hailsham)   10.01.18E

G-TPAL P&M Quik GT450   8363   28.03.08
P Robertson   East Fortune   21.04.18P

G-TPPW Van's RV-7   xxxx   10.05.13
R S Grace   Sywell   31.05.19P
Built by P Wright – project LAA 323-14966

G-TPSL Cessna 182S Skylane   18280398   11.12.98
N23700   A N Purslow   Popham   31.05.19E

G-TPSY American Champion 8KCAB Super Decathlon
                                                803-97   01.07.11
G-CEOE, N748PH   M C R Sims t/a MCRS Aviation
Goodwood   03.07.18E

G-TPTP Robinson R44 Raven I   2065   13.05.11
A N Purslow   Thruxton   02.07.18E

G-TPTR[M] Agusta-Bell 206B JetRanger II   8587   25.08.81
G-LOCK (2), N2951N, N2951W
Cancelled 09.10.89 as Destroyed   31.12.89
With The Helicopter Museum, Weston-super-Mare

G-TPWL P&M Quik GT450   8187   16.05.06
S Speake tr G-TPWL Group   Arclid Green, Sandbach   07.08.18P

G-TPWX Heliopolis Gomhouria Mk.6   183   10.08.11
D-EECW, SU-345, Egypt AF 345
Cirrus Aircraft UK Ltd   Leicester   13.05.19P
As 'TP+WX' in Luftwaffe c/s

G-TRAC Robinson R44 Astro   0598   10.05.99
C J Sharples   Thruxton   01.03.18E

G-TRAM Cyclone Pegasus Quantum 15-912   7552   29.07.99
I W Barlow tr G-TRAM Group
Park Hall Farm, Mapperley   05.05.19P
Badged 'Super Sport'

G-TRAT Pilatus PC-12/47   710   18.04.06
HB-FQX   Flew LLP   Bournemouth   02.04.18E

G-TRAX Cessna F172M Skyhawk II   F17201081   22.11.06
D-EIQU   Cancelled 22.01.15 as destroyed   26.07.14
Derby   *Built by Reims Aviation SA; wreck dumped 01.15*

G-TRBN HpH Glasflügel 304 S Shark   038-MS   22.07.14
(BGA 5808)   A Cluskey   Saltby   *'J5T'*
(IE 17.09.17)

G-TRBO Schleicher ASW 28-18E   28743   18.07.06
BGA 5238/KNW   M P & R W Weaver   Usk   *'28T'*   28.04.18E

G-TRCY Robinson R44 Astro   0668   22.10.99
Marman Aviation Ltd   (Nicosia, Republic of Cyprus)   21.11.18E

G-TRDS Guimbal Cabri G2   1049   21.05.13
F-WWHX   W R Harford   Elstree   09.06.19E

G-TREB Cessna 182T Skylane   18282376   17.11.15
N7156J, N4228A
Camel Aviation Ltd   Wycombe Air Park   16.01.18E

G-TREC Cessna 421C Golden Eagle   421C0838   02.07.96
G-TLOL, (N2659K)   Sovereign Business
Integration PLC   Wycombe Air Park   01.06.18E

G-TREE Bell 206B-3 JetRanger III   2826   15.06.87
N2779U   Heliflight (UK) Ltd   Gloucestershire   10.06.19E
Operated by HH Helicopters Ltd t/a Cotswold Helicopters

G-TREK Jodel D.18   182   01.05.92
R H Mole   Derby   15.10.18P
Built by R H Mole – project PFA 169-11265

G-TREX Alpi Pioneer 300   133   06.01.05
S R Winter   Willingale   05.07.19P
Built by R K King – project PFA 330-14305

G-TRIG Cameron Z-90   10446   28.07.03
J R Wilson tr Hedge Hoppers Balloon Group
Oxford OX2   *'intel inside'* & *'centrino'*   24.08.18E

G-TRIM Monnett Moni   00258T   16.02.84
E A Brotherton-Ratcliffe   Acaster Malbis
Built by Monnett Aircraft – project PFA 142-11012;
stored incomplete 2017 (NF 29.10.15)

G-TRIN SOCATA TB-20 Trinidad   1131   25.06.90
M J Porter tr G-TRIN Group   Strubby   15.02.18E

G-TRJB Beech A36 Bonanza   E-2719   24.02.11
D-EPLL, (D-EZGO), PH-RUB, D-EGBS
G A J Bowles   Carlisle Lake District   31.03.18E

G-TRLL Groppo Trail   00079/38   09.05.13
P M Grant   Wickenby   12.12.17P
Built by P M Grant – project LAA 372-15166

G-TRNG Agusta A109E Power Elite   11156   08.03.11
G-NWOY, G-JMXA
G Walters (Leasing) Ltd   Gloucestershire   01.06.18E

G-TRON Robinson R66 Turbine   0731   22.07.16
PFR Aviation Ltd   Wycombe Air Park   31.05.19E

G-TROW Comco Ikarus C42 FB80 Bravo   1811-7553   19.02.19
Blue Socks Aviation Ltd   (Malvern)
Built by The Light Aircraft Company Ltd (IE 19.02.19)

G-TROY North American T-28A Trojan   51-7692   21.04.99
F-AZFV, French AF 142, 51-7692
Air Leasing Ltd   Duxford   27.09.19P
As '517692:LT-692' in USAF c/s

G-TRTL Best Off Skyranger Nynja LS 912S(1) xxxx   10.02.17
J T & J W Whicher   Henstridge   04.02.19P
Built by J T & J W Whicher – project BMAA/HB/695

G-TRUE Hughes 369E (500)   0490E   12.09.94
N6TK, ZK-HFP   N E Bailey   Oaksey Park   30.10.17E

G-TRUK Stoddard-Hamilton Glasair RG   xxxx   23.07.84
S Moore   Fairoaks   27.06.18P
Built by M P Jackson – project PFA 149-11015

G-TRUU Piper PA-34-220T Seneca III   3433020   21.05.14
G-BOJK, G-BRUF, N9113D
Omega Sky Taxi Ltd   Blackbushe   16.02.19E

G-TRUX Colt 77A   1860   13.11.90
J R Lawson   (Riccall, York)   27.05.18E

G-TRVR Van's RV-7   73478   03.07.13
Perlucid LLP   Blackpool   12.09.19P
Built by J Edser & T Roche – project LAA 323-14882

G-TSAC Tecnam P2002-EA Sierra   227   19.12.07
A G Cozens   Solent   19.06.18P
Built by A G Cozens – project PFA 333-14611

G-TSAS	Piper PA-28-181 Archer II	28-8190055	18.01.19
	G-MALA, G-BIIU, N82748		
	M E McElhinney (Talygarn, Pontyclun)		
	(IE 18.01.19)		
G-TSBY	Robinson R44 Clipper II	14238	20.08.18
	A Woodward Aviation Ltd White Waltham		
	(IE 20.08.18)		
G-TSDA	Aquila AT01-100A	AT01-100A-329	09.12.15
	Tayside Aviation Ltd Dundee		17.01.19E
G-TSDB	Aquila AT01-100A	AT01-100A-330	09.12.15
	Tayside Aviation Ltd Dundee		17.01.19E
G-TSDC	Aquila AT01-100A	AT01-100A-332	24.02.16
	Tayside Aviation Ltd Dundee		20.03.18E
G-TSDE	Aquila AT01-100A	AT01-100A-333	24.02.16
	Tayside Aviation Ltd Dundee		07.08.18E
G-TSDS	Piper PA-32R-301 Saratoga SP	32R-8013132	03.10.05
	N145AV, EC-HHM, G-TRIP, G-HOSK, PH-WET,		
	OO-HKN, N8261X I R Jones Hawarden		15.12.18E
G-TSFC	Tecnam P2008-JC	1047	07.04.15
	Stapleford Flying Club Ltd Stapleford		12.04.18E
G-TSGA	Piper PA-28R-201 Arrow III	28R-7737082	03.07.07
	G-ONSF, G-EMAK, D-EMAK, N38180		
	J N Bailey & I R Lockhart Conington		23.03.18E
G-TSGJ	Piper PA-28-181 Archer II	28-8090109	12.09.88
	N8097W J O Elliott & G White		
	tr Golf Juliet Flying Group Durham Tees Valley		30.11.18E
G-TSHO	Comco Ikarus C42 FB80 Bravo	1103-7141	13.04.11
	A P Shoobert Little Gransden		12.04.18P
	Assembled Performance Aviation Ltd		
G-TSIM	Titan T-51 Mustang	149	31.03.10
	B J Chester-Master Shobdon *'The Millie G'*		19.04.18P
	Built by B J Chester-Master – project LAA 355-14964;		
	as 'CY:G' in USAAF c/s		
G-TSIX	North American AT-6C-1-NT Harvard IIA 88-9725		19.03.79
	Portuguese AF 1535, South African AF 7183, EX289,		
	41-33262 Bulldog Aviation Ltd Earls Colne		26.07.18P
	As '111836:JZ-6' in USN c/s		
G-TSKD	Raj Hamsa X'Air Falcon Jabiru(2)	633	08.05.01
	K B Dupuy & T Sexton Barling		21.04.18P
	Built by K B Dupuy & T Sexton – project BMAA/HB/165		
G-TSKS	Evektor EV-97 teamEurostar UK	2009-3320	28.08.09
	North East Aviation Ltd Eshott		20.10.17P
	Assembled Cosmik Aviation Ltd		
G-TSLC	Schweizer 269C-1 *(300CBi)*	0246	22.06.06
	(G-CDYV (1)), N86G CJ Cox Ltd Henstridge		10.02.18E
G-TSOB	Rans S-6-ES Coyote II	1202.1471	28.06.04
	T McKinley & N K Watts tr G-TSOB Syndicate		
	Bembridge *'The Spirit of Brooklands'*		04.06.19P
	Built by S C Luck – project PFA 204-14066;		
	tricycle u/c		
G-TSOG	TLAC Sherwood Ranger XP	051	25.02.15
	The Spirit of Goole Low Hill Farm, North Moor,		
	Messingham *'The Spirit of Goole'*		09.03.18P
	Built by J Milnes – project LAA 237A-15239		
G-TSOL	EAA Acrosport	xxxx	18.07.00
	G-BPKI D F Cumberlidge & H Stuart		
	Morgansfield, Fishburn		07.07.18P
	Built by J Sykes – project PFA 072-11391		
G-TSUE	Europa Aviation Europa	048	15.08.05
	H J C Maclean White Waltham		06.10.17P
	Built by A L Thorne – project PFA 247-12612		
G-TSWI	Lindstrand LBL 90A	1149	05.02.07
	R J Gahan Ramsbottom, Bury		
	'Dylan Harvey Property Development'		06.06.18E
G-TSWZ	Cameron Z-77	11652	27.04.12
	Group First Global Ltd Burnley *'group first'*		23.05.18E
G-TTAT	ICP MXP-740 Savannah VG Jabiru(1)	08-09-51-752	16.07.09
	D J Broughall & D Varley North Weald		07.12.18P
	Built by A N Green – project BMAA/HB/592		
G-TTDD	Zenair CH701 STOL	xxxx	01.09.97
	Cancelled 25.01.16 as PWFU		26.06.15
	Lawmuir Farm, Clackmannanshire *Built by D B Dainton*		
	& B E Trinder – project PFA 187-13106; spares use 03.16		

G-TTEC	Piper PA-32-301FT 6X	3232066	28.04.17
	OK-ORL, N10562, OK-ORL, N9521N		
	Taytech Environmental Ltd (Seamill, West Kilbride)		03.08.18E
G-TTEN	Tecnam P2010	008	30.03.15
	R C Mincik Goodwood		23.05.18E
G-TTFG	Colt 77B	1993	05.02.08
	G-BUZF M J & T J Turner (Wellingborough)		
	'Patricia'		02.05.18E
G-TTGV	Bell 206L-4 LongRanger IV	52381	03.02.15
	G-JACI, N195AW, C-FUZW, C-GADQ		
	Langley Aviation Ltd (Retford)		18.06.18E
G-TTKP	Enstrom 280FX Shark	2076	01.08.18
	G-HDIX, N506DH, D-HDIX		
	K & M A Payne (Maxey, Peterborough)		22.05.19E
G-TTNA	Airbus A320-251N	8108	10.04.18
	F-WWIV British Airways PLC London Heathrow		09.04.19E
G-TTNB	Airbus A320-251N	8139	25.04.18
	F-WWDV British Airways PLC London Heathrow		24.04.19E
G-TTNC	Airbus A320-251N	8173	07.06.18
	F-WWBY British Airways PLC London Heathrow		06.06.19E
G-TTND	Airbus A320-251N	8308	26.07.18
	F-WWDV British Airways PLC London Heathrow		25.07.19E
G-TTNE	Airbus A320-251N	8365	21.09.18
	F-WWIG British Airways PLC London Heathrow		20.09.19E
G-TTNF	Airbus A320-251N	8408	27.10.18
	F-WWBD British Airways PLC London Heathrow		26.10.19E
G-TTNG	Airbus A320-251N	8431	29.11.18
	F-WWDR British Airways PLC London Heathrow		28.11.19E
G-TTNH	Airbus A320-251N	8489	17.01.19
	D-AXAY British Airways PLC London Heathrow		16.01.20E
G-TTNI	Airbus A320-251N	8767	20.02.19
	F-WWDM British Airways PLC London Heathrow		19.02.20E
G-TTNJ	Airbus A320-251N	8772	28.02.19
	F-WWBH British Airways PLC London Heathrow		27.02.20E
(G-TTNK)	Airbus A320-251N		
	British Airways PLC Reserved, due xx.19		
(G-TTNL)	Airbus A320-251N		
	British Airways PLC Reserved, due xx.19		
(G-TTNM)	Airbus A320-251N		
	British Airways PLC Reserved, due xx.19		
G-TTOB	Airbus A320-232	1687	11.02.02
	F-WWIM British Airways PLC London Heathrow		25.03.19E
G-TTOE	Airbus A320-232	1754	11.04.02
	F-WWDH British Airways PLC London Heathrow		23.03.19E
G-TTOM	Zenair CH.601HD Zodiac	8346	13.09.13
	D H Pattison Lower Upham Farm, Chiseldon		16.08.19P
	Built by T M Bootyman – project LAA 162-15088;		
	tricycle u/c		
G-TTOY	CFM Streak Shadow SA	K 233	15.04.96
	J Softley Brimpton		17.07.13P
	Built by D A Payne – project PFA 206-12805		
	(IE 06.09.17)		
G-TTRL	Van's RV-9A	90945	11.12.07
	J E Gattrell Sittles Farm, Alrewas		22.06.18P
	Built by J E Gattrell – project PFA 320-14248		
G-TTUG	Aeropro EuroFOX 912(iS)	41514	16.08.13
	G-WTUG Buckminster Gliding Club Ltd Saltby		02.07.19P
	Built by R M Cornwell – project LAA 376-15213;		
	tricycle u/c; glider-tug		
G-TUBB	Avtech Jabiru UL-450	0256	01.10.99
	A H Bower Orange Grove Barn, Chavenage Green		17.02.18P
	Built by A H Bower & A Silvester – project PFA 274A-13484		
G-TUCK	Van's RV-8	81534	25.09.03
	N G R Moffat Dundee		12.08.19P
	Built by M A Tuck – project PFA 303-13706		
G-TUGG	Piper PA-18-150 Super Cub	18-8274	10.01.83
	PH-MAH, N5451Y Ulster Gliding Club Ltd Bellarena		05.09.18E
	Fuselage No.18-8497		
G-TUGI	CZAW Sportcruiser	4020	28.03.08
	T J Wilson Hamilton Farm, Bilsington		01.06.19P
	Built by T J Wilson – project LAA 338-14786		

G-TUGY	Robin DR.400-180 Régent	2052	27.04.98
	D-EPAR G S S Rizk tr TUGY Group Saltby		03.06.18E
G-TUGZ	Robin DR.400-180R Remorqueur	1030	04.02.11
	OE-DCC, D-EGPS		
	M J Aldridge School Road, Hinderclay		04.02.18E
G-TUIA	Boeing 787-8	34422	29.05.13
	TUI Airways Ltd t/a TUI Luton 'Living The Dream'		02.12.19E
	Line No: 92		
G-TUIB	Boeing 787-8	34423	30.05.13
	TUI Airways Ltd t/a TUI Luton 'Alfie'		29.05.19E
	Line No: 94		
G-TUIC	Boeing 787-8	34424	13.06.13
	TUI Airways Ltd t/a TUI Luton 'Dream Maker'		12.06.19E
	Line No: 102		
G-TUID	Boeing 787-8	36424	16.08.13
	TUI Airways Ltd t/a TUI Luton 'Angel of the Sky'		15.08.19E
	Line No: 106		
G-TUIE	Boeing 787-8	37227	30.06.14
	TUI Airways Ltd t/a TUI Luton 'Miles of Smiles'		29.06.19E
	Line No: 191		
G-TUIF	Boeing 787-8	36428	15.07.14
	TUI Airways Ltd t/a TUI Luton 'Neil'		14.07.19E
	Line No: 198		
G-TUIH	Boeing 787-8	37229	07.05.15
	TUI Airways Ltd t/a TUI Luton 'Mr Patmore'		06.05.19E
	Line No: 291		
G-TUII	Boeing 787-8	37230	28.05.15
	TUI Airways Ltd t/a TUI Luton 'Mrs Patmore'		27.05.19E
	Line No: 300		
G-TUIJ	Boeing 787-9	44578	27.06.16
	TUI Airways Ltd t/a TUI Luton 'Pixie Dust'		26.06.19E
	Line No: 439		
G-TUIK	Boeing 787-9	44579	18.05.17
	TUI Airways Ltd t/a TUI Luton		17.05.19E
	Line No: 564		
G-TUIL	Boeing 787-9	64053	15.03.18
	N1009N TUI Airways Ltd t/a TUI Luton		14.03.19E
	Line No: 676		
G-TUIM	Boeing 787-9	62742	17.05.18
	N1005S TUI Airways Ltd t/a TUI Luton		16.05.19E
	Line No: 703		
(G-TUIN)	Boeing 787-9		
	TUI Airways Reserved, due xx.19		
(G-TUIO)	Boeing 787-9		
	TUI Airways Reserved, due xx.19		
G-TUKU	Stemme S 10-VT	11-126	06.11.15
	D-KUKU Stemme AG (Strausberg, Germany)		16.07.19E
G-TULA	Diamond DA.40D Star	40.DS002	31.10.17
	D-EEKU, TC-MAG, OE-DXG		
	AJW Construction Ltd Bournemouth		08.10.18E
	Operated by L3 CTS Aviation		
G-TULI	Embraer EMB-550 Legacy 500	55000031	13.09.18
	N351PF, D-BEER, N729MM, PR-LIJ		
	Centreline AV Ltd t/a Centreline Bristol		
	(IE 12.09.18)		
G-TULP	Lindstrand LBL Tulips SS HAB	662	16.10.00
	(PH-AJT), (PH-ORA), (PH-TLP)		
	Cancelled as sold in USA 21.09.11		17.06.11
	Not Known Active Phillipines 02.13		
G-TUMA	Boeing 737-8	44593	16.11.18
	N1786B TUI Airways Ltd t/a TUI Luton		15.11.19E
	Line No.7211		
G-TUMB	Boeing 737-8	44595	06.12.18
	TUI Airways Ltd t/a TUI Luton		05.12.19E
	Line No: 7278		
G-TUMC	Boeing 737-8	44597	31.01.19
	N1786B TUI Airways Ltd t/a TUI Luton		
	Line No: 7353		
G-TUMD	Boeing 737-8	44648	12.02.19
	TUI Airways Ltd t/a TUI Luton		11.02.20E
	Line No: 7366		
G-TUMF	Boeing 737-8	44599	23.02.19
	TUI Airways Ltd t/a TUI Luton		22.02.20E
	Line No: 7395		

G-TUMG	Boeing 737-8	44600	04.03.19
	TUI Airways Ltd t/a TUI Luton		
	Line No: 7400		
(G-TUMH)	Boeing 737-8 (Max 8)	44602	
	TUI Airways Reserved, due xx.19		
(G-TUMJ)	Boeing 737-8 (Max 8)		
	TUI Airways Reserved, due xx.19		
(G-TUMK)	Boeing 737-8 (Max 8)		
	TUI Airways Reserved, due xx.19		
(G-TUML)	Boeing 737-8 (Max 8)		
	TUI Airways Reserved, due xx.19		
G-TUNE	Robinson R22 Beta	0818	12.01.99
	N60661, G-OJVI, (G-OJVJ) Heli Air Ltd Thruxton		01.04.18E
G-TUNL	Robinson R44 Raven II	11628	21.03.19
	G-TCAL Barhale PLC (Walsall)		30.03.19E
G-TURF	Reims/Cessna F406 Caravan II	F406-0020	17.10.96
	PH-FWF, (EI-CND), PH-FWF, F-WZDS		
	Reconnaissance Ventures Ltd t/a RVL Group		
	East Midlands 'Coastguard'		26.10.18E
G-TURKᴹ	Cameron Sultan 80SS HAB	1711	12.04.88
	Cancelled 28.08.02 by CAA		18.06.00
	With Musée des Ballons, Chateau de Balleroy, France		
G-TUTU	Cameron O-105	10659	17.01.05
	A C K Rawson & J J Rudoni Stafford		12.01.19E
G-TVAL	Airbus EC135 T3	1189	05.08.15
	D-HCBA Babcock Mission Critical Services		
	Onshore Ltd RAF Benson		05.08.18E
	Operated by Thames Valley & Chiltern Air Ambulance		
	as callsign 'Helimed 24'		
G-TVBF	Lindstrand LBL 310A	439	02.04.97
	Airxcite Ltd t/a Virgin Balloon Flights		
	Stafford Park, Telford 'Virgin'		25.03.07E
	(NF 15.09.14)		
G-TVCO	Gippsland GA-8 Airvan	GA8-06-101	01.11.06
	P Ligertwood Ventfield Farm, Horton-cum-Studley		08.11.18E
G-TVGC	Schempp-Hirth Janus	33	09.03.17
	(BGA 5926), F-CEPF Trent Valley Gliding Club Ltd		
	Kirton in Lindsey 'TV'		16.11.18E
G-TVHB	Eurocopter EC135 P2+	0874	04.02.10
	Police & Crime Commissioner for West Yorkshire		
	RAF Benson		13.09.18E
	Operated by Chiltern Air Support Unit as		
	callsign 'NPAS 16'		
G-TVHD	Aérospatiale AS.355F2 Ecureuil 2	5449	07.02.08
	ZK-ILN, JA6638 Arena Aviation Ltd Redhill		03.03.18E
G-TVIIᴹ	Hawker Hunter T.7	41H-693834	08.12.97
	XX467, R Jordanian AF 836, RSAF 70-617, G-9-214,		
	XL605 Cancelled 28.07.14 by CAA As 'XX467:86'		
	With Newark Air Museum, Winthorpe		
G-TVIJ	CCF T-6 Harvard Mk.4	CCF4-442	10.12.93
	G-BSBE, Mozambique PLAF 1730, Portuguese AF 1730,		
	West German AF AA+652, 52-8521		
	R W Davies Headcorn		23.07.07P
	Built by Canadian Car & Foundry Co;		
	as '28521:TA-521' in USAF yellow c/s (IE 02.08.18)		
G-TVSI	Campbell Cricket replica	CA-340	08.04.82
	G-AYHH G Smith Spilsted Farm, Sedlescombe		16.04.98P
	(NF 28.07.18)		
G-TWAL	Rutan Long-EZ	xxxx	30.01.17
	G-BNCZ T Walsh (Tuam, Co Galway, RoI)		
	Built by R Baibridge & P Ellway		
	– project PFA 074A-10723		
G-TWAZ	Rolladen-Schneider LS7-WL	7074	25.04.08
	BGA 4452/JEJ, OE-5477		
	S Derwin tr Walking On Air WA2 Portmoak 'WA2'		01.05.18E
G-TWEL	Piper PA-28-181 Archer II	28-8090290	12.06.80
	N81963 IAE Ltd Cranfield		12.08.18E
G-TWIS	Silence SA.180 Twister	xxxx	15.01.10
	C S & K D Rhodes Henstridge		29.06.18P
	Built by C S & K D Rhodes – project LAA 329-14954		
G-TWIY	Hawker 750	HB-14	08.04.15
	G-NLPA, N555RU, (M-OANH), N555RU, N3194Q		
	Saxonair Charter Ltd Norwich Int'l		08.03.18E

G-TWIZ	Rockwell Commander 114	14375	09.05.90
	SE-GSP, N5808N B C & P M Cox Lydd		05.10.17E
G-TWLV	Van's RV-12	xxxx	11.08.09
	J N Parr tr G-TWLV Group Turweston		18.02.19P
	Built by J N Parr – project LAA 363-14931		
G-TWNN	Beech 76 Duchess	ME-329	25.03.08
	N127MR, N127MB, N67161		
	M Magrabi Bournemouth		02.06.17E
	(NF 13.11.17)		
G-TWOC	Schempp-Hirth Ventus-2cxT	141/369	06.03.06
	BGA 5165/KKS G C Lewis Camphill *'2C'*		18.04.19E
G-TWOO	Extra EA.300/200	05	22.04.10
	G-MRKI, N694M		
	Skyboard Aerobatics Ltd Wombleton		26.01.18E
G-TWOP	Cessna 525A CitationJet CJ2	525A0397	05.09.12
	G-ODAG, N5148B		
	Centreline AV Ltd t/a Centreline Bristol		28.04.18E
G-TWRL	Pitts S-1S	xxxx	30.06.09
	C Dennis Bodmin *'Tarquin'*		17.01.19P
	Built by B C Dennis – project PFA 009-14196		
G-TWSR	Silence SA.180 Twister	xxxx	24.03.05
	J A Hallam Gloucestershire		05.03.17P
	Built by J A Hallam – project PFA 329-14385		
G-TWSS	Silence SA.180 Twister	xxxx	09.09.08
	T R Dews Wing Farm, Longbridge Deverill		13.03.18P
	Built by A P Hatton – project PFA 329-14608		
G-TWST	Silence SA.180 Twister	xxxx	07.09.04
	G-ZWIP, G-TWST		
	Zulu Glasstek Ltd Baileys Farm, Long Crendon		14.04.18P
	Built by P M Wells – project PFA 329-14211		
G-TWTD[M]	CCF Hawker Sea Hurricane X	CCF/41H/8020	06.05.94
	(Russia), AE977 Cancelled 25.09.01 to NX33TF		
	As 'AE977:LE-D'		
	With Planes of Fame Air Museum, Chino, California		
G-TWTR	Robinson R44 Raven II	13003	19.03.10
	Volitant Aviation Ltd Gloucestershire		12.04.19E
	Operated by Heliair Ltd		
G-TWTW	Denney Kitfox Model 2	xxxx	24.03.04
	R M Bremner Little Down Farm, Milson		16.11.17P
	Built by T Willford – project PFA 172-11730		
G-TXAN	North American AT-6D-NT Texan III	88-14722	16.02.09
	G-JUDI, Portuguese AF 1502, SAAF 7439, EX915,		
	41-33888		
	K-F Grimminger Rottweil-Zepfenhahn, Germany		06.08.18P
	Respray into RAF scheme at Dunkeswell 03.18		
G-TXAS	Cessna A150L Aerobat	A1500381	22.01.14
	G-HFCA, N6081J T H Scott Rayne Hall Farm, Rayne		15.10.19E
	Texas Taildragger conversion		
G-TXTV	Agusta A109E Power	11769	23.09.16
	N53BK, PR-FZZ Arena Aviation Ltd Redhill		05.10.18E
G-TYAK	IAV Bacau Yakovlev Yak-52	899907	23.12.02
	RA-01038, LY-AIE, DOSAAF 94 (yellow)		
	S J Ducker Breighton *'Betsy'*		29.04.16P
	(IE 29.08.17)		
G-TYER	Robin DR.500-200i Président	21	25.04.00
	F-GTZB C A White (Steeple Bumpstead, Haverhill)		01.11.19E
	Officially registered as DR.400/500		
G-TYGA	Gulfstream American AA-5B Tiger	AA5B-1161	22.02.82
	G-BHNZ, (D-EGDS), N4547L		
	A C Dent tr Three Musketeers Flying Group Oxford		22.02.18E
G-TYGR	Best Off Skyranger Swift 912S(1)	SKR0406498	08.11.04
	B W G Stanbridge East Kirkby		18.11.18P
	Built by M J Poole – project BMAA/HB/420		
G-TYKE	Avtech Jabiru UL-450	0465	08.06.01
	B Mcguire Strathaven		07.04.18P
	Built by A Parker – project PFA 274A-13739		
G-TYNE	SOCATA TB-20 Trinidad	1523	06.11.97
	F-GRBM, F-WWRW, CS-AZH, F-OHDE		
	N V Price Kirknewton		05.12.18E
G-TYPH	British Aerospace BAe 146 Series 200	E2200	23.02.11
	G-BTVT, D-ACFA, G-BTVT, (I-FLRZ), G-BTVT, G-6-200		
	BAE Systems (Corporate Air Travel) Ltd Warton		01.05.19E
G-TYRE	Reims/Cessna F172M	F17201222	10.02.79
	OY-BIA J S C English East Midlands		07.02.18E

G-TYRO	AutoGyro MTOsport	xxxx	18.11.16
	G-CINT C Bennett (Tibshelf, Alfreton)		22.12.18P
	Assembled Rotorsport UK as c/n RSUK/MTOS/056		
G-TZED	SOCATA TB-200 Tobago XL	1813	15.06.15
	TF-MAX, F-GRBY Zytech Ltd Earls Colne		27.11.18E
G-TZII	Thorp T.211B	xxxx	02.06.99
	M J Newton Cranfield		29.08.08P
	Built by AD Aerospace Ltd – project PFA 305-13285		
	(NF 10.08.15)		

G-UAAA – G-UZZZ

G-UACA	Best Off Skyranger Swift 912(1)	UK/384	25.06.04
	R G Hicks The Byre, Hardwick, Abergavenny		01.06.18P
	Built by R Openshaw – project BMAA/HB/324		
G-UAKE	North American P-51D-5-NA Mustang	109-27587	17.02.04
	44-13954 P S Warner (Dumbleton, Evesham)		
	(NF 22.08.14)		
G-UANO	de Havilland DHC-1 Chipmunk 22	57	18.10.06
	G-BYYW, CS-DAQ, Port.AF 1367 R J Stirk Breighton		26.04.19P
	Built by OGMA; as '1367' in Portuguese AF c/s		
G-UANT	Piper PA-28-140 Cherokee F	28-7325568	12.04.02
	OO-MYR, N56084		
	Air Navigation & Trading Company Ltd Blackpool		10.02.18E
G-UAPA	Robin DR.400-140B Major 80	2213	11.01.95
	F-GMXC Sor Air Sociedade de Aeronautica, SA		
	Pontesor-Tramaga, Portugal		26.04.18E
G-UAPO	Ruschmeyer R90-230RG	019	02.03.95
	D-EECT P Randall Retford Gamston		29.10.18E
G-UART	Moravan Zlin Z-242L	0652	16.05.12
	G-EKMN, SE-KMN		
	Oxford Aviation Academy (Oxford) Ltd Oxford		14.07.18E
G-UAVA	Piper PA-30 Twin Comanche B	30-1413	16.06.03
	D-GLDU, HB-LDU, N8279Y		
	M D Northwood Coventry		08.03.18E
G-UBOO	Schleicher ASW 27-18E	29716	07.11.18
	(BGA 5985), D-KASB S G Hunt Pocklington		03.05.19E
G-UCAM	Piper PA-31-350 Chieftain	31-7405402	04.06.10
	G-NERC, G-BBXX, N66869		
	Blue Sky Investments Ltd Isle of Man		10.07.18E
G-UCAN	Tecnam P2002-JF Sierra	229	05.03.14
	I-RAIJ Aerobility Blackbushe		16.04.18E
G-UCCC	Cameron Sign-90	3918	05.07.96
	Unipart Group of Companies Ltd Wendover		28.10.10E
	(NF 06.08.18)		
G-UCLU	Schleicher ASK 21	21010	11.07.08
	BGA 2612/EDW UCLU RAF Halton *'EDW'*		01.06.18E
G-UDET	Airdrome ¾ Fokker E.III replica	GS-104	18.02.10
	M J Clark Sedgwick Park, Horsham		
	Built by M J Clark from Grass Strip Aviation Ltd		
	kit s/n GS-104/Airdrome Kit 358; as '105/15' in		
	German Army Air Service c/s		
	(SSDR microlight since 05.14) (IE 06.12.17)		
G-UDGE	Thruster T600N	9099-T600N-037	17.09.99
	G-BYPI S M Eyers tr G-UDGE Syndicate Shobdon		06.09.19P
G-UDIX	Schempp-Hirth Duo Discus xT	159	11.08.06
	(BGA 5777), D-KDIX R Banks Aston Down *'DI'*		06.03.18E
G-UDOG	Scottish Aviation Bulldog Srs 120/121	BH120/204	24.01.02
	XX518 M Van den Broeck (Waasmunster, Belgium)		08.06.18E
	As 'XX518:S' in RAF white & red c/s: carries 'G-UDOG'		
G-UFAW	Raj Hamsa X'Air 582(15)	582	24.07.01
	P Batchelor Hadfold Farm, Adversane		
	Built by J H Goddard – project BMAA/HB/167		
	(IE 19.04.18)		
G-UFCB	Cessna 172S Skyhawk SP	172S8318	25.01.00
	N455SP The Cambridge Aero Club Ltd Cambridge		22.04.18E
G-UFCE	Cessna 172S Skyhawk SP	172S9305	20.02.03
	N5318Y Ulster Flying Club (1961) Ltd		
	Newtownards		04.08.18E
G-UFCG	Cessna 172S Skyhawk SP	172S9450	28.07.03
	N2154T Ulster Flying Club (1961) Ltd		
	Newtownards		18.09.18E

G-UFCI	Cessna 172S Skyhawk SP	172S10508	12.02.08
	N21946 Ulster Flying Club (1961) Ltd		
	Newtownards		25.07.18E
G-UFCN	Cessna 152	15283847	06.03.14
	N5362B Ulster Flying Club (1961) Ltd		
	Newtownards		23.03.18E
G-UFLY	Cessna F150H	F150-0264	29.09.89
	G-AVVY Westair Flying Services Ltd Isle of Man		18.05.19E
	Built by Reims Aviation SA;		
	operated by IOM Flight Training		
G-UFOE	Grob G115	8033	28.11.11
	OY-CRF, (D-E...), OY-CRF, (LN-AES), OY-CRF		
	Swiftair Maintenance Ltd Leicester		30.04.18E
G-UFOX	Aeropro EuroFOX 912(1)	37612	15.08.12
	T Jestico tr G-UFOX Group Popham		15.05.18P
	Built by D Dollery, G Haffey, T Jestico & I Norfield		
	– project BMAA/HB/628; tailwheel u/c		
G-UHIH	Bell UH-1H Iroquois	13208	14.12.05
	NX41574, 72-21509 MSS Holdings (UK) Ltd		
	Wesham House Farm, Wesham *'Miss Jo'*		21.05.18P
	As '72-21509:129' in US Army c/s		
G-UHOP	Ultramagic H-31	31/09	30.03.09
	A R Brown Litlington, Royston		17.03.18E
G-UIII	Extra EA.300/200	1042	14.12.16
	YR-ITA, OO-TIT, D-EXSS M Thomas RAF Cranwell		08.11.18E
G-UIKR	P&M QuikR	8493	20.10.09
	A M Sirant Plaistows Farm, St Albans		07.04.12P
	Noted 03.14 (IE 07.01.16)		
G-UILD	Grob G109B	6419	28.01.86
	K Butterfield Cark		08.07.18E
G-UILE	Neico Lancair 320	746	17.01.94
	R J Martin (Pressignac, France)		16.10.18P
	Built by R J Martin – project PFA 191-12538		
G-UILT	Cessna T303 Crusader	T30300280	03.07.00
	G-EDRY, N4817V D L Tucker Denham		25.10.18E
G-UIMB	Guimbal Cabri G2	1028	30.09.11
	F-WWHY Helitrain Ltd Cotswold		22.10.18E
	Operated by Cotswold Helicopter Centre		
G-UINN	Stolp SA.300 Starduster Too	HB1980-1	16.03.98
	EI-CDQ, C-GTLJ A Dunne Ballyboy, Rol		06.11.18P
	Built by H Baaken		
G-UINS	Ultramagic B-70	70/06	27.03.14
	A M Holly Breadstone, Berkeley		16.07.18E
	Penguin special shape		
G-UINZ	Ultramagic B-70	70/09	04.06.15
	A M Holly Breadstone, Berkeley		16.07.18E
	Penguin special shape		
G-UIRI	Aeropro EuroFOX 912(S)	40313	22.07.13
	P Crawley (Shipley)		18.12.15P
	Built by P Crawley – project LAA 376-15195;		
	tailwheel u/c; aborted take-off Ontur, Spain 05.04.15,		
	hit tree, & substantially damaged		
G-UIRO	AutoGyro MT-03	08 008	17.03.16
	G-CFAG S D Kellner Ashcroft		13.12.18P
	Assembled Rotorsport UK as c/n RSUK/MT-03/034		
G-UISE	Van's RV-8	83484	25.03.15
	J A Green (Aspley Guise, Milton Keynes)		
	Built by J A Green – project LAA 303-15324		
	(NF 25.03.15)		
G-UJAB	Avtech Jabiru UL	193	27.01.99
	C A Thomas Top Farm, Croydon		20.08.18P
	Built by C A Thomas – project PFA 274A-13373		
G-UJET	Learjet Learjet 45	45-055	08.05.17
	G-PFCT, G-GOMO, G-OLDF, G-JRJR, N45LR, N63MJ		
	Patriot Aviation Ltd Birmingham		09.03.19E
	Operated by Capital Air Ambulance Ltd		
G-UJGK	Avtech Jabiru UL-450	0329	17.04.00
	J G Kosak & W G Upton RNAS Culdrose		01.09.18P
	Built by J G Kosak & W G Upton – project PFA 274A-13558		
G-UKAL	Reims/Cessna F406 Caravan II	F406-0098	13.09.12
	(F-....), G-UKAL		
	I Groves & P Jackson t/a Aero Lease UK Cranfield		24.11.18E

G-UKAW	Agusta A109E Power	11003	21.12.07
	I-VRGT, N1NQ		
	AgustaWestland Ltd Cascina Costa, Italy		31.01.18E
G-UKCS	Piper PA-31 Turbo Navajo B	31-7400984	03.02.16
	N45NH, SE-GBS, OH-MRS, SE-GBS		
	2 Excel Aviation Ltd Sywell		26.05.19E
G-UKOZ	Avtech Jabiru SK	0190	16.06.99
	D J Burnett White House Farm, Southery		26.06.18P
	Built by D J Burnett – project PFA 274-13310		
G-UKPA	Cessna 208B Grand Caravan	208B1201	03.01.19
	N722JR, HP-1611PS, HP-1611, N5091J		
	UK Parachute Services Ltd Beccles		
	(NF 03.01.19)		
G-UKPB	Cessna 208B Grand Caravan	208B0629	25.01.18
	N850SD UK Parachute Services Ltd Beccles		
	(IE 25.01.18)		
G-UKPS	Cessna 208 Caravan I	20800423	29.04.08
	UK Parachute Services Ltd Beccles		06.05.18E
	Carries 'UK Parachute Services Limited' on tail		
G-UKRO	Evektor SportStar RTC	2019-2117	05.02.19
	Co & Builder Ltd (London E17)		
	(IE 05.02.19)		
G-UKRV	Van's RV-7A	xxxx	10.08.16
	Netwasp.net Ltd (Stevenage)		
	Built by J Hunt – project LAA 323-15304 (NF 10.08.16)		
G-UKTV	Aérospatiale AS.355F2 Ecureuil 2	5169	05.08.16
	G-JESE, G-EMHH, G-BYKH, SX-HNP, VR-CCM, N57967		
	Arena Aviation Ltd Redhill *'Sky News'*		18.12.18E
G-UKUK	Head Ax8-105	248	01.09.97
	N8303U P A George Littlemore, Oxford		18.07.18E
G-ULAG	Piper PA-34-220T Seneca V	3449240	20.09.18
	N145DR N Holden Cotswold		
	(IE 20.09.18)		
G-ULAS	de Havilland DHC-1 Chipmunk 22	C1/0554	14.06.96
	WK517 M B Phillips Goodwood		13.12.17E
	Operated by Boultbee Flight Academy;		
	as 'WK517' in RAF c/s		
G-ULCC	Schleicher ASH 30 Mi	30011	21.04.16
	Viscount Cobham tr G-ULCC Flying Group		
	Lasham *'CC'*		28.04.18E
G-ULDA★	Cessna 560XL Citation XLS	560-5731	09.01.19
	I-CMAB, N51995 Unicredit Leasing SPA		
	To N560RD 10.01.19		
G-ULFM	Gulfstream Gulfstream IV-X	4359	03.05.17
	N459GA Pendley Aviation LLP Luton		03.05.18E
G-ULHI	Scottish Aviation Bulldog Srs 100/101	BH100/148	30.09.03
	G-OPOD, SE-LLK, Swedish AF 61038, G-AZMS		
	Kryten Systems Ltd Cotswold		21.06.18E
G-ULIA	Cameron V-77	2860	20.05.92
	A Lutz & D W Westlake Newnham & Quedgley		21.07.19E
G-ULPSM	Everett Gyroplane Series 1	007	13.07.93
	G-BMNY I Pearson Newquay Cornwall		10.07.01P
	On display Cornwall Aviation Heritage Centre 08.18		
	(NF 27.07.18)		
G-ULRJ★	Hawker 900XP	HA-0056	18.05.18
	I-BBGR, N3386A, (D-BGRL), N3386A		
	Unicredit Leasing SPA		
	To N3386A 18.05.18		
G-ULRK	Sequoia F.8L Falco	xxxx	13.09.17
	U K S S N Lawson (Jacobstowe, Okehampton)		
	Built by U K S S N Lawson – project PFA 100-15448		
	(NF 13.09.17)		
G-ULSY	Comco Ikarus C42 FB80	0405-6603	26.07.04
	M L Cade Rayne Hall Farm, Rayne		16.10.18P
	Assembled Fly Buy Ultralights Ltd		
G-ULTA	Ultramagic M-65C	65/172	06.07.09
	G A Board West Malling		19.09.17E
G-ULTR	Cameron A-105	4100	24.02.97
	P Glydon Knowle, Bristol *'ultrait://'*		21.07.18E
	Active 09.19		
G-ULUL	AutoGyro Calidus	11 030	28.02.13
	G-HTBT R S Payne Rufforth East *'Air Total'*		11.04.18P
	Assembled Rotorsport UK as c/n RSUK/CALS/009		

G-ULZE	Robinson R22 Beta	2048	15.09.16
	G-BUBW HQ Aviation Ltd Denham		27.10.18E
G-UMBL	Guimbal Cabri G2	1068	02.05.14
	European Helicopter Importers Ltd Goodwood		02.06.18E
	Operated by Elite Helicopters		
G-UMBOᴹ	Colt Jumbo SS HAB	747	02.04.86
	Cancelled 26.02.03 as PWFU		
	Replacement envelope c/n 1645 fitted in 1990		
	With History of Ballooning, Sint-Niklaas, Belgium		
G-UMBY	Hughes 369E (500)	0346E	10.10.12
	D-HHHM, N252JP HQ Aviation Ltd Denham		22.03.18E
G-UMMI	Piper PA-31 Navajo C	31-7912060	11.08.92
	G-BGSO, N3519F 2 Excel Aviation Ltd Sywell		18.08.19E
G-UMMS	Evektor EV-97 teamEurostar UK	2005-2316	22.04.10
	G-ODRY G W Carwardine Rochester		17.06.18P
	Assembled Cosmik Aviation Ltd		
G-UMMY	Best Off Skyranger J2.2(1)	SKR0409521	25.07.05
	K T G Room (Storwood, York)		12.11.18P
	Built by A R Williams – project BMAA/HB/437		
G-UMPY	Europa Aviation Europa	176	08.02.11
	GDBMK Ltd Park Farm, Eaton Bray		07.03.18P
	Built by G D Bird – project PFA 247-12800		
G-UNAC	Piper PA-32R-301T Saratoga II TC	3257422	28.09.17
	OK-VSK, N31381, OK-VSK, N31381		
	A C Campbell Fowlmere		16.08.19E
G-UNDD	Piper PA-23-250 Aztec E	27-4832	22.03.00
	G-BATX, N14271 D P & G J Deadman Goodwood		29.06.18E
G-UNER	Lindstrand LBL 90A	895	16.04.03
	Blind Veterans UK London W1		01.07.09E
	(NF 10.03.15)		
G-UNES	Van's RV-6	xxxx	22.04.10
	C A Greatrex Shobdon		17.05.18P
	Built by R C Dyer – project PFA 181A-13222		
G-UNGE	Lindstrand LBL 90A	122	06.12.96
	G-BVPJ M T Stevens tr Silver Ghost Balloon Club		
	Warwick		13.07.10E
	(NF 16.12.16)		
G-UNGO	Pietenpol Air Camper	159	16.09.02
	A R Wyatt (Shalfleet, Newport, Isle of Wight)		03.01.19P
	Built by P Thody & A R Wyatt – project PFA 047-13951		
G-UNIN	Schempp-Hirth Ventus b	135	08.11.07
	BGA 4378/JBG, OE-5315		
	R Hill tr U9 Syndicate Feshiebridge *'U9'*		27.04.18E
G-UNIVᴹ	Montgomerie-Parsons Two-Place Gyroplane		
		PFA G/08-1276	03.08.99
	G-BWTP Cancelled 16.01.14 as PWFU		18.01.05
	Built by J M Montgomerie		
	With National Museum of Flight Scotland, East Fortune		
G-UNIX	Magni M16 Tandem Trainer	SA-M16-04	10.03.06
	ZU-AHX A P Wilkinson (Wyton, Hull)		19.10.18P
	Built by A P Wilkinson – project PFA G/12-1349		
G-UNKY	Ultramagic S-50	50/08	17.04.12
	A M Holly Breadstone, Berkeley		21.09.17E
	(IE 07.10.17)		
G-UNNA	Avtech Jabiru UL-450WW	xxxx	13.04.07
	J F Heath Carlisle Lake District		28.05.18P
	Built by N D A Graham – project PFA 274A-14442		
G-UNRL	Lindstrand LBL RR21	260	25.05.95
	Lindstrand Media Ltd Hawarden CH5		23.06.13E
	(IE 20.10.16)		
G-UNZZ	Bell 206L LongRanger	45030	08.06.18
	G-DSTN, G-CYRS, OH-HOH, C-GIIP		
	K Hayes (Clay Cross, Chesterfield)		17.04.19E
	(IE 08.06.18)		
G-UPFS	Waco UPF-7	5660	27.08.04
	N32029 N R Finlayson & D N Peters Little Gransden		11.06.18E
G-UPHI	Best Off Skyranger Swift 912S(1)	SKR0507629	02.10.06
	M B Harper & C E Walsh Newtownards		24.02.18P
	Built by P M Dewhurst – project BMAA/HB/480		
G-UPID	Bowers Fly Baby 1A	xxxx	12.10.10
	R D Taylor Henstridge *'G'*		25.03.19P
	Built by R D Taylor – project PFA 016-13347		

G-UPIZ	BRM Bristell NG5 Speed Wing	218	26.08.16
	C P & K J Faint (Ashington, Pulborough)		
	Built by K J Faint – project LAA 385-15414		
	(NF 05.09.18)		
G-UPOI	Cameron TR-84	11296	07.07.09
	Cameron Balloons Ltd Bristol BS3		14.09.18E
G-UPPYᴹ	Cameron DP-80 Airship	2274	09.03.90
	Cancelled 01.12.09 by CAA		27.08.94
	With Anderson-Abruzzo Int'l Balloon Museum,		
	Albuquerque, New Mexico		
G-UPRT	Slingsby T67M-260 Firefly	2255	08.04.15
	G-BWXU L3 CTS Airline & Academy Training Ltd		
	Bournemouth		21.01.18E
G-UPTA	Best Off Skyranger 912S(1)	UK/645	15.02.06
	S J Joseph Graveley Hall Farm, Graveley		01.04.18P
	Built by P E Tait – project BMAA/HB/488; carries		
	'SKR0508629' which conflicts with G-UPHI		
G-UPUP	Cameron V-77	1828	21.07.89
	S F Burden Noordwijk, Netherlands		09.08.09E
	(IE 06.11.17)		
G-UPUZ	Lindstrand LBL 120A	969	26.01.04
	C J Sanger-Davies Oswestry		12.01.19E
G-URMS	Europa Aviation Europa	232	18.05.15
	G-DEBR C Parkinson (Newbury)		20.09.18P
	Built by A J Calvert & C T Smallwood		
	– project PFA 247-12922; tricycle u/c		
G-UROP	Beech 95-B55 Baron	TC-2452	17.09.90
	N64311 Just Plane Trading Ltd Conington		11.12.18E
G-URRR	Air Command 582 Sport	0630	13.06.90
	L Armes (Basildon)		
	Built by L Armes – project PFA G/4-1200 (NF 19.09.14)		
G-USAA	Cessna F150G	F150-0188	13.08.08
	G-OIDW, N70163, D-EGTI		
	Aeros Global Ltd Coventry *'Lil' Baby Doll'*		06.02.19E
G-USAR	Cessna 441 Conquest	441-0355	03.07.08
	D-ILYS, N355VB, AP-BCW, N1213Y		
	I Annenskiy Leeds East		25.02.18E
G-USCO	Hughes 269C (300)	1140377	01.02.16
	G-CECO, D-HAEK, JA7574		
	G R Colquhoun (Lullington, Frome)		13.08.18E
G-USHA	Learjet Learjet 45	45-535	28.09.16
	N40085 EssexJets Ltd Biggin Hill		06.10.18E
	Completed as Model 75; operated by Zenith Aviation		
G-USHI	Piper PA-28-140 Cherokee Cruiser	28-7625188	04.06.18
	G-BZWG, N9656K M Rajain Bournemouth		16.01.19E
G-USIL	Thunder Ax7-77	1587	22.08.89
	Window on the World Ltd London SE1		22.04.11E
	(IE 20.02.18)		
G-USKY	Aviat A-1B Husky	2261	08.04.04
	R F Pooler Lower Grounds Farm, Shirlowe		26.04.19E
G-USTH	Agusta A109A II	7304	12.09.05
	N109UK, F-GKGV, (F-GUHS), F-GKGV, N109PS, N109FM		
	Stratton Motor Company (Norfolk) Ltd		
	Tharston Industrial Estate, Long Stratton		20.05.10E
	(NF 22.06.15)		
G-USTS	Agusta A109A II	7275	24.11.03
	G-MKSF, N18SF, F-GDPR		
	MB Air Ltd t/a Eagle Helicopters & Tedham Ltd		
	Newcastle City Heliport		14.09.18E
G-USTVᴹ	Messerschmitt Bf.109G-2/Trop	10639	26.10.90
	8478M, RN228, Luftwaffe Cancelled 24.09.98 as PWFU		30.05.98
	As '10639:6' in Luftwaffe III/JG77 c/s		
	Built by ERLA-Maschinenwerk GmbH		
	With Royal Air Force Cosford Museum		
G-USTY	Clutton FRED Series III	xxxx	11.10.78
	I Pearson (Falmouth)		23.09.13P
	Built by S Styles – project PFA 029-10390;		
	carries 'E 039' on tail; stored 07.16 (IE 27.07.18)		
G-USUKᴹ	Colt 2500A HAB	1100	01.06.87
	Cancelled 21.08.90 as WFU *'Virgin Atlantic Flyer'*		19.08.87
	On loan from Virgin Atlantic Airways Ltd		
	Gondola displayed – remainder stored		
	With Imperial War Museum, Duxford		
G-UTRA	Ultramagic M-77C	77/339	15.06.11
	Ultrait Ltd West Malling *'ultrait://'*		28.07.18E

G-UTSI	Rand Robinson KR-2	xxxx	02.10.89
	K B Gutridge Fowle Hall Farm, Laddingford		11.11.15P
	Built by K B Gutridge – project PFA 129-10966		
G-UUPP	Cameron C-70	11814	05.12.14
	Cameron Balloons Ltd Bristol BS3		08.08.18E
G-UURO	Evektor EV-97 Eurostar	2005-2527	04.01.06
	T B McAlinden tr Romeo Oscar Syndicate Shobdon		10.05.19P
	Built by E M Middleton – project PFA 315-14480		
G-UUUU	Comco Ikarus C42 FB100 Bravo	1408-7336	06.11.14
	R Engelhard Popham		26.03.19P
	Assembled Red-Air UK		
G-UVBF	Lindstrand LBL 400A	1051	19.08.05
	Airxcite Ltd t/a Virgin Balloon Flights		
	Stafford Park, Telford *'Virgin'*		06.03.14E
	(NF 15.09.14)		
G-UWAS	Scottish Aviation Bulldog Srs 120/121	BH120/235	13.09.17
	G-CBAB, XX543 Mid America (UK) Ltd Duxford		26.07.17E
	As 'XX625:45' in RAF c/sl stored at Aircraft		
	Restoration Company 12.18		
G-UWEB	Cameron Z-120	11927	05.08.15
	GWE Business West Ltd Abbots Leigh, Bristol		
	'UWE Bristol'		11.07.19E
G-UYAK	Yakovlev Yak-18T	22202023842	20.10.15
	HA-JAB, FLA-02160, CCCP-44420		
	C A Brightwell Rochester		
	Noted 08.16 as 'HA-JAB' for overhaul (NF 20.10.15)		
G-UZHA	Airbus A320-251N	7649	13.06.17
	F-WWIG easyJet Airline Company Ltd Luton		12.06.19E
	'NEO' logo		
G-UZHB	Airbus A320-251N	7705	07.07.17
	F-WWTN easyJet Airline Company Ltd Luton		06.07.19E
	'NEO' logo		
G-UZHC	Airbus A320-251N	7802	21.11.17
	D-AVVJ easyJet Airline Company Ltd Luton		20.11.19E
	'NEO' logo		
G-UZHD	Airbus A320-251N	7841	09.11.17
	F-WWIJ easyJet Airline Company Ltd Luton		08.11.19E
	'NEO' logo		
G-UZHE	Airbus A320-251N	8110	23.03.18
	D-AUBW easyJet Airline Company Ltd Luton		22.03.19E
	'NEO' logo		
G-UZHF	Airbus A320-251N	8193	17.04.18
	D-AXAN easyJet Airline Company Ltd Luton		16.04.19E
	'NEO' logo		
G-UZHG	Airbus A320-251N	8243	26.06.18
	D-AXAZ easyJet Airline Company Ltd Luton		25.06.19E
G-UZHH	Airbus A320-251N	8268	28.06.18
	D-AVVQ easyJet Airline Company Ltd Luton		27.06.19E
G-UZHI	Airbus A320-251N	8304	12.07.18
	D-AXAF easyJet Airline Company Ltd Luton		
	'Winston Chau'		11.07.19E
G-UZHJ	Airbus A320-251N	8338	10.08.18
	D-AUBH easyJet Airline Company Ltd Luton		09.09.19E
G-UZHK	Airbus A320-251N	8356	09.08.18
	D-AUBU easyJet Airline Company Ltd Luton		08.09.19E
G-UZHL	Airbus A320-251N	8375	23.08.18
	D-AUBM easyJet Airline Company Ltd Luton		22.08.19E
G-UZHM	Airbus A320-251N	8405	25.09.18
	F-WWBV easyJet Airline Company Ltd Luton		24.09.19E
	'Charlie Taylor'		
G-UZHN	Airbus A320-251N	8409	19.10.18
	D-AVVW easyJet Airline Company Ltd Luton		18.10.19E
G-UZHO	Airbus A320-251N	8411	04.10.18
	F-WWDN easyJet Airline Company Ltd Luton		03.10.19E
G-UZHP	Airbus A320-251N	8433	29.11.18
	D-AUBG easyJet Airline Company Ltd Luton		28.11.19E
G-UZHR	Airbus A320-251N	8505	16.11.18
	F-WWBH easyJet Airline Company Ltd Luton		15.11.19E
G-UZHS	Airbus A320-251N	8506	26.10.18
	D-AUBV easyJet Airline Company Ltd Luton		25.10.19E
G-UZHT	Airbus A320-251N	8662	14.12.18
	F-WWIX easyJet Airline Company Ltd Luton		13.12.19E

G-UZHU	Airbus A320-251N	8681	28.12.18
	D-AUAX easyJet Airline Company Ltd Luton		27.12.19E
(G-UZHV)	Airbus A320-251N	8722	
	Easyjet Reserved, due xx.19		
G-UZHW	Airbus A320-251N	8759	19.02.19
	F-WWII easyJet Airline Company Ltd Luton		18.02.20E
(G-UZHX)	Airbus A320-251N	8890	
	Easyjet Reserved, due xx.19		
(G-UZHY)	Airbus A320-251N	8920	
	Easyjet Reserved, due xx.19		
(G-UZHZ)	Airbus A320-251N		
	Easyjet Reserved, due xx.19		
G-UZLE	Colt 77A	2021	01.08.91
	G B Davies Thorney, Peterborough *'John Courage'*		07.07.18E
G-UZMA	Airbus A321-251NX	8314	13.07.18
	D-AVZU easyJet Airline Company Ltd Luton		12.07.19E
	'NEO' logo		
G-UZMB	Airbus A321-251NX	8369	23.08.18
	D-AZAD easyJet Airline Company Ltd Luton		22.08.19E
G-UZMC	Airbus A321-251NX	8386	10.10.18
	D-AYAR easyJet Airline Company Ltd Luton		09.10.19E
G-UZMD	Airbus A321-251NX	8421	20.03.19
	D-AZAO easyJet Airline Company Ltd Luton		19.03.20E
G-UZME	Airbus A321-251NX	8454	18.01.19
	D-AZAW easyJet Airline Company Ltd Luton		17.01.20E
(G-UZMF)	Airbus A321-251NX	8508	
	Easyjet Reserved, due xx.19		
(G-UZMG)	Airbus A321-251NX		
	Easyjet Reserved, due xx.19		
(G-UZMH)	Airbus A321-251NX		
	Easyjet Reserved, due xx.19		
G-UZUP	Evektor EV-97A Eurostar	2005-2629	21.06.06
	R B Shaw tr G-UZUP Flying Group		
	Netherthorpe *'Serenity'*		15.04.19P
	Built by S A Woodhams – project PFA 315A-14528		
G-UZZI	Lancair LC41-550FG Corvalis TT	41017	01.07.16
	N79HR The Lord Rotherwick		
	Cornbury Park, Charlbury		29.09.17E
G-UZZY	Enstrom 480	5013	29.10.04
	LZ-VIG, G-UZZY, G-BWMD, (F-GOTA), G-BWMD, N480E		
	N Shakespeare Oaksey Park		01.01.10E
	(NF 08.12.16)		

G-VAAA – G-VZZZ

G-VAAC	Piper PA-28-181 Archer III	2843398	11.09.07
	G-CCDN, HB-PQA, N4176W		
	J N D de Jager Lelystad, Netherlands		07.07.18E
G-VAAV	P&M QuikR	8595	21.09.11
	M Kent (Dinnington, Sheffield)		11.10.18P
G-VAGA	Piper PA-15 Vagabond	15-248	14.11.80
	G-CCEE, G-VAGA, N4458H, NC4458H		
	N S Lomax Woodlands Barton Farm, Roche		08.05.18P
G-VAHH	Boeing 787-9	37967	30.12.14
	Virgin Atlantic Airways Ltd London Heathrow		
	'Dream Girl'		29.12.19E
	Line No: 246		
G-VALG	Evektor EV-97 Eurostar SL	2016-4240	24.05.17
	J A Ganderton Finmere		25.05.18P
	Built by Light Sport Aviation Ltd		
G-VALS	Pietenpol Air Camper	xxxx	30.07.97
	R A Phillips tr G-VALS Flying Group Easterton		08.06.18P
	Built by J R D Bygraves – project PFA 047-13157		
G-VALY	SOCATA TB-21 Trinidad	2081	30.03.04
	N246SS, (N717TB)		
	Richard Thwaites Aviation Ltd Gloucestershire		12.07.18E
G-VALZ	Cameron N-120	4998	09.01.01
	J D & K Griffiths Bingham, Nottingham		22.05.18E
	Operated by Ladybird Balloons		
G-VANA	Gippsland GA-8 Airvan	GA8-04-046	20.12.05
	VH-KLN P Marsden East Leys Farm, Grindale		26.01.18E

Reg	Type		C/n	Date

G-VANC   Gippsland GA-8 Airvan   GA8-06-097   25.09.06
TF-VAN, G-VANC
Irish Skydiving Club Ltd   Kilkenny, RoI   20.04.18E

G-VAND   Gippsland GA-8 Airvan   GA8-07-114   19.09.07
Irish Skydiving Club Ltd   Kilkenny, RoI   19.09.17E

G-VANN   Van's RV-7A   71204   05.07.04
D N & J A Carnegie tr G-VANN Flying Group   Kirkbride   26.05.18P
Built by D N & J A Carnegie – project PFA 323-14034

G-VANS   Van's RV-4   355   07.09.92
N16TS   R J Marshall   Watchford Farm, Yarcombe
'Betsy'   14.12.18P
Built by T Saylor

G-VANU   Piper PA-28RT-201T Turbo Arrow IV   28R-8131039   06.07.18
D-EMTK, SE-KGU, N8305D
G Chandrasekaran   Biggin Hill
(IE 06.07.18)

G-VANX   Gippsland GA-8 Airvan   GA8-07-115   31.03.08
VH-AUM   Airkix Aircraft Ltd   Tilstock   10.01.19E

G-VANZ   Van's RV-6A   22382   15.07.93
M Wright   Tilstock
Built by S J Baxter – project PFA 181-12531
(NF 26.10.15)

G-VARG   Varga 2150A Kachina   VAC 157-80   14.05.84
OO-RTY, N80716   R A Denton   RAF Waddington   26.10.18E

G-VARK   Van's RV-7   72469   09.04.14
C-FJRE   W J Miazek   Insch   01.09.19P

G-VAST   Boeing 747-41R   28757   17.06.97
Virgin Atlantic Airways Ltd   London Gatwick
'Ladybird'   16.06.19E
Line No: 1117

G-VBAA   Cameron A-400   11607   15.02.12
Airxcite Ltd t/a Virgin Balloon Flights
Stafford Park, Telford   *'Virgin'*   14.02.16E
(IE 19.10.18)

G-VBAB   Cameron A-400   11608   15.02.12
Airxcite Ltd t/a Virgin Balloon Flights
Stafford Park, Telford   *'Virgin'*   18.09.19E

G-VBAD   Cameron A-300   11623   17.04.12
Airxcite Ltd t/a Virgin Balloon Flights
Stafford Park, Telford   *'Virgin'*   05.10.19E

G-VBAE   Cameron A-400   11624   03.05.12
Airxcite Ltd t/a Virgin Balloon Flights
Stafford Park, Telford   *'Virgin'*   26.07.19E

G-VBAF   Cameron A-300   11705   26.02.13
Airxcite Ltd t/a Virgin Balloon Flights
Stafford Park, Telford   *'Virgin'*   22.08.19E

G-VBAG   Cameron A-400   11706   28.02.13
Airxcite Ltd t/a Virgin Balloon Flights
Stafford Park, Telford   *'Virgin'*   12.08.19E

G-VBAH   Cameron A-400   11778   26.09.13
Airxcite Ltd t/a Virgin Balloon Flights
Stafford Park, Telford   *'Virgin'*   22.09.18E
(IE 19.10.18)

G-VBAI   Cameron A-400   11868   06.03.15
Airxcite Ltd t/a Virgin Balloon Flights
Stafford Park, Telford   *'Virgin'*   18.09.19E

G-VBAJ   Cameron A-400   11869   06.03.15
Airxcite Ltd t/a Virgin Balloon Flights
Stafford Park, Telford   *'Virgin'*   02.07.19E

G-VBAK   Cameron A-400   11870   04.03.15
Airxcite Ltd t/a Virgin Balloon Flights
Stafford Park, Telford   *'Virgin'*   26.07.19E

G-VBAL   Cameron A-400   11871   19.03.15
Airxcite Ltd t/a Virgin Balloon Flights
Stafford Park, Telford   *'Virgin'*   25.06.19E

G-VBAM   Cameron A-400   11872   19.03.15
Airxcite Ltd t/a Virgin Balloon Flights
Stafford Park, Telford   *'Virgin'*   14.06.19E

G-VBAN   Cameron A-400   11959   17.03.16
Airxcite Ltd t/a Virgin Balloon Flights
Stafford Park, Telford   *'Virgin'*   24.10.19E

G-VBAO   Cameron A-400   11961   09.05.16
Airxcite Ltd t/a Virgin Balloon Flights
Stafford Park, Telford   *'Virgin'*   02.11.19E

G-VBAP   Cameron A-400   11962   31.05.16
Airxcite Ltd t/a Virgin Balloon Flights
Stafford Park, Telford   *'Virgin'*   02.09.19E

G-VBAR   Cameron A-400   12041   16.03.17
Airxcite Ltd t/a Virgin Balloon Flights
Stafford Park, Telford   *'Virgin'*   10.10.19E

G-VBAS   Cameron A-400   12042   16.03.17
Airxcite Ltd t/a Virgin Balloon Flights
Stafford Park, Telford   *'Virgin'*   23.05.19E

G-VBAT   Cameron A-400   12152   28.02.18
Airxcite Ltd t/a Virgin Balloon Flights
Stafford Park, Telford   *'Virgin'*   19.10.19E

G-VBAU   Cameron A-400   12153   28.02.18
Airxcite Ltd t/a Virgin Balloon Flights
Stafford Park, Telford   *'Virgin'*   25.02.19E

G-VBAV   Cameron A-400   12154   01.05.18
Airxcite Ltd   Stafford Park, Telford   *'Virgin'*   25.04.19E

G-VBAW   Cameron A-400   12155   01.05.18
Airxcite Ltd   Stafford Park, Telford   *'Virgin'*   26.04.19E

G-VBCA   Cirrus SR22   2656   11.10.07
N967SR   C A S Atha   Bagby   30.03.18E

G-VBEL   Boeing 787-9   37980   13.03.18
Virgin Atlantic Airways Ltd   London Heathrow
'Show Girl'   12.03.19E
Line No: 665

G-VBFA   Ultramagic N-250   250/44   06.04.06
Airxcite Ltd t/a Virgin Balloon Flights
Stafford Park, Telford   *'Virgin'*   29.09.15E
(NF 19.10.18)

G-VBFB   Ultramagic N-355   355/09   05.05.06
Airxcite Ltd t/a Virgin Balloon Flights
Stafford Park, Telford   *'Virgin'*   02.04.11E
(NF 19.10.18)

G-VBFC   Ultramagic N-250   250/45   05.05.06
Airxcite Ltd t/a Virgin Balloon Flights
Stafford Park, Telford   *'Virgin'*   13.03.15E
(NF 19.10.18)

G-VBFD   Ultramagic N-250   250/46   20.06.06
Airxcite Ltd t/a Virgin Balloon Flights
Stafford Park, Telford   *'Virgin'*   15.11.16E
(IE 19.10.18)

G-VBFE   Ultramagic N-355   355/10   07.07.06
Airxcite Ltd t/a Virgin Balloon Flights
Stafford Park, Telford   *'Virgin'*   08.07.12E
(NF 19.10.18)

G-VBFF   Lindstrand LBL 360A   1116   08.08.06
Airxcite Ltd t/a Virgin Balloon Flights
Stafford Park, Telford   *'Virgin'*   07.04.15E
(IE 19.10.18)

G-VBFG   Cameron Z-350   10984   08.03.07
Airxcite Ltd t/a Virgin Balloon Flights
Stafford Park, Telford   *'Virgin'*   23.08.15E
(IE 19.10.18)

G-VBFH   Cameron Z-350   10985   08.03.07
Airxcite Ltd t/a Virgin Balloon Flights
Stafford Park, Telford   *'Virgin'*   09.10.13E
(NF 19.10.18)

G-VBFI   Cameron Z-350   10986   08.03.07
Airxcite Ltd t/a Virgin Balloon Flights
Stafford Park, Telford   *'Virgin'*   20.09.17E
(IE 19.10.18)

G-VBFJ   Cameron Z-350   11006   08.03.07
Airxcite Ltd t/a Virgin Balloon Flights
Stafford Park, Telford   *'Virgin'*   22.10.12E
(NF 19.10.18)

G-VBFK   Cameron Z-350   11007   08.03.07
Airxcite Ltd t/a Virgin Balloon Flights
Stafford Park, Telford   *'Virgin'*   03.09.16E
(IE 19.10.18)

G-VBFL   Cameron Z-400   11347   10.12.09
Airxcite Ltd t/a Virgin Balloon Flights
Stafford Park, Telford   *'Virgin'*   07.07.18E
(NF 19.10.18)

G-VBFM	Cameron Z-375	11133	18.04.08
	Airxcite Ltd t/a Virgin Balloon Flights		
	Stafford Park, Telford 'Virgin'		22.03.16E
	(NF 19.10.18)		
G-VBFN	Cameron Z-375	11134	25.04.08
	Airxcite Ltd t/a Virgin Balloon Flights		
	Stafford Park, Telford 'Virgin'		13.04.15E
	(NF 19.10.18)		
G-VBFO	Cameron Z-375	11135	06.05.08
	Airxcite Ltd t/a Virgin Balloon Flights		
	Stafford Park, Telford 'Virgin'		29.04.18E
	(NF 19.10.18)		
G-VBFP	Ultramagic N-425	425/26	28.07.08
	Airxcite Ltd t/a Virgin Balloon Flights		
	Stafford Park, Telford 'Virgin'		11.08.15E
	(NF 19.10.18)		
G-VBFR	Cameron Z-375	11217	27.02.09
	Airxcite Ltd t/a Virgin Balloon Flights		
	Stafford Park, Telford 'Virgin'		15.02.17E
	(NF 19.10.18)		
G-VBFS	Cameron Z-375	11216	27.02.09
	Airxcite Ltd t/a Virgin Balloon Flights		
	Stafford Park, Telford 'Virgin'		18.02.16E
	(NF 19.10.18)		
G-VBFT	Cameron Z-275	11215	27.02.09
	Airxcite Ltd t/a Virgin Balloon Flights		
	Stafford Park, Telford 'Virgin'		23.05.19E
G-VBFU	Cameron A-400	11492	24.08.11
	Airxcite Ltd t/a Virgin Balloon Flights		
	Stafford Park, Telford 'Virgin'		24.10.18E
G-VBFV	Cameron Z-400	11348	09.12.09
	Airxcite Ltd t/a Virgin Balloon Flights		
	Stafford Park, Telford 'Virgin'		23.09.16E
	(NF 19.10.18)		
G-VBFW	Cameron Z-77	11354	10.12.09
	Airxcite Ltd t/a Virgin Balloon Flights		
	Stafford Park, Telford 'Virgin'		04.04.19E
G-VBFX	Cameron Z-400	11349	10.12.09
	Airxcite Ltd t/a Virgin Balloon Flights		
	Stafford Park, Telford 'Virgin'		04.03.19E
G-VBFY	Cameron Z-400	11371	15.12.09
	Airxcite Ltd t/a Virgin Balloon Flights		
	Stafford Park, Telford 'Virgin'		24.08.19E
G-VBFZ	Cameron A-300	11493	04.05.11
	Airxcite Ltd t/a Virgin Balloon Flights		
	Stafford Park, Telford 'Virgin'		22.09.19E
G-VBIG	Boeing 747-4Q8	26255	10.06.96
	Virgin Atlantic Airways Ltd London Gatwick		
	'Tinker Belle'		09.06.19E
	Line No: 1081		
G-VBOW	Boeing 787-9	37978	29.03.17
	Virgin Atlantic Airways Ltd London Heathrow		
	'Pearly Queen'		28.03.19E
	Line No: 534		
G-VBPM	Cirrus SR22	3173	19.05.09
	N286MD S A Perkes North Weald		12.06.19E
G-VBZZ	Boeing 787-9	37976	29.03.16
	Virgin Atlantic Airways Ltd London Heathrow		
	'Queen Bee'		28.03.19E
	Line No: 401		
G-VCIO	EAA Acrosport II	xxxx	09.10.97
	J W Graham-White (St Albans) 'Smart as Ten'		05.05.19P
	Built by R F Bond, V Millard & F Sharples		
	– project PFA 072A-12388		
G-VCJH	Robinson R22 Beta	1569	26.10.90
	Nedroc Ltd (Derby)		07.02.18E
G-VCML	Beech 58 Baron	TH-1346	31.10.97
	N2289R St Angelo Aviation Ltd Lydd		03.07.18E
G-VCRU	Boeing 787-9	37972	14.09.15
	Virgin Atlantic Airways Ltd London Heathrow		
	'Olivia-Rae'		13.09.19E
	Line No: 338		
G-VCRZ	Schleicher ASH 31 Mi	31178	08.06.18
	C A & S C Noujaim Aston Down 'RP'		31.01.20E

G-VCUB	Piper PA-18-150 Super Cub	18-7609021	16.03.17
	PH-ZVB, I-BAEB, N9773P		
	N J Morgan Retford Gamston		13.03.18E
G-VCXT	Schempp-Hirth Ventus-2cxT	144/xxx	04.11.05
	BGA 5158/KKJ, D-KOZZ R F Aldous		
	Kirchheim-Hahnweide, Germany 'RA'		10.08.18E
G-VDIA	Boeing 787-9	37975	24.03.16
	Virgin Atlantic Airways Ltd London Heathrow		
	'Lucy In The Sky'		23.03.19E
	Line No: 377		
G-VDIR	Cessna 310R II	310R0211	31.01.91
	N5091J Cancelled 03.03.06 as destroyed		21.06.07
	North Weald Derelict in open store 06.17		
G-VDOG	Cessna 305C Bird Dog (L-19E)	24582	18.08.06
	F-BIFB, French Army J A Watt Dundee		02.08.18E
	As '24582' in US Army c/s		
G-VEGA	Slingsby T65A Vega	1889	20.10.78
	BGA 2729/EJT, G-VEGA, (G-BFZN)		
	W A M Sanderson Wormingford 'AS'		23.07.18E
G-VELA	SIAI Marchetti S.205-22/R	4-149	30.10.89
	N949W N D Dixon tr G-VELA Group Hardwick		21.02.18E
	Officially registered as S 205-22R; now modified		
	to S.208A standard		
G-VENC	Schempp-Hirth Ventus-2c	9/21	17.09.07
	BGA 4249 A James (Monmouth) '584'		21.04.19E
G-VENI	de Havilland DH.112 Venom FB.50 (FB.1)	733	08.06.84
	J-1523 Cancelled 05.03.13 as PWFU		25.07.01
	Portarlington, RoI Built by F+W;		
	stored dismantled 08.13 as 'VV612' in RAF c/s		
G-VENM	de Havilland DH.112 Venom FB.50	824	16.06.99
	G-BLIE, Swiss AF J-1614		
	Cancelled as sold in USA 13.08.18		30.07.16
	Bruntingthorpe Built by Federal Aircraft Factory		
	Stored dismantled 10.18 as 'WK436' in RAF c/s		
G-VERA	Gardan GY-201 Minicab	xxxx	07.06.94
	D K Shipton (Peterborough)		
	Built by D K Shipton – project PFA 056-12236		
	(NF 30.04.18)		
G-VETC	Lambert Mission M108	006	24.06.16
	C J Cheetham (Nether Stowey, Bridgwater)		05.09.18P
	Built by C J Cheetham – project LAA 370-15407		
G-VETS	Enstrom 280C-UK Shark	1015	11.09.95
	G-FSDC, G-BKTG, OY-HBP		
	B G Rhodes (Henbury, Macclesfield)		28.07.02
	(NF 26.06.15)		
G-VETT	Guimbal Cabri G2	1066	04.04.14
	Farm Veterinary Aviation Ltd Nottingham City		12.04.18E
	Operated by Arcus Helicopters		
G-VEYE	Robinson R22	0140	08.02.00
	G-BPTP, N9056H K A Jones Tatenhill		08.05.15E
G-VEZE	Rutan VariEze	xxxx	02.09.77
	J M Keane Deanland		19.07.19P
	Built by S D Brown, S Evans, P Henderson		
	& M Roper – project PFA 074-10285		
G-VFAN	Boeing 787-9	37977	10.06.16
	Virgin Atlantic Airways Ltd London Heathrow		
	'Pin Up Girl'		09.06.19E
	Line No: 431		
G-VFAS	Piper PA-28R-200 Cherokee Arrow II	28R-7435104	15.01.08
	G-MEAH, G-BSNM, N46PR, N54439		
	P Wood Audley End		21.11.18E
G-VFDS	Van's RV-8	xxxx	14.09.12
	S B Shirley Swansea		18.04.19P
	Built by S Brown & S T G Lloyd – project PFA 303-14637;		
	operated by 'Raven Display Team' – 'No. 5'		
G-VFIT	Airbus A340-642	753	24.05.06
	F-WWCG Virgin Atlantic Airways Ltd		
	London Heathrow 'Dancing Queen'		23.05.19E
G-VGAG	Cirrus SR20 GTS	1572	25.10.05
	N54149 C M O'Connell Southend		11.08.19E
G-VGAL	Boeing 747-443	32337	26.04.01
	(EI-CVH) Virgin Atlantic Airways Ltd		
	London Gatwick 'Jersey Girl'		25.04.19E
	Line No: 1272		

G-VGBR	Airbus A330-343	1329	24.08.12
	F-WWTP Virgin Atlantic Airways Ltd		
	London Heathrow *'Golden Girl'*		23.08.19E
G-VGEM	Airbus A330-343	1215	30.10.12
	B-18392, (G-VGEM), F-WWKK Virgin Atlantic		
	Airways Ltd London Gatwick *'Diamond Girl'*		30.10.19E
G-VGFS	Cameron Z-90	12094	02.08.17
	Western Commodities Ltd Willand, Cullompton		
	'goodfullstop.com'		31.07.18E
G-VGMC	Eurocopter AS.355N Ecureuil 2	5693	02.03.04
	G-HEMH, F-WQPV Cheshire Helicopters Ltd		
	Blackshaw Heys Farm, Mobberley		10.05.19E
	Operated by VLL Ltd t/a GB Helicopters		
G-VGVG	ICP MXP-740 Savannah VG Jabiru(1)	**-07-51-588	22.06.07
	M A Jones RAF Scampton		21.07.18P
	Built by M F Cottam – project BMAA/HB/542		
G-VIBA^M	Cameron DP-80	1729	28.05.91
	Cancelled 01.12.09 by CAA		03.02.99
	With Anderson-Abruzzo Int'l Balloon Museum,		
	Albuquerque, New Mexico		
G-VICC	Piper PA-28-161 Warrior II	28-7916317	03.03.92
	G-JFHL, N2249U Freedom Aviation Ltd Cotswold		28.04.19E
G-VICI	de Havilland DH.112 Venom FB.50 (FB.1)	783	06.02.95
	HB-RVB, G-BMOB, Swiss AF J-1573		
	Cancelled 05.03.13 as PWFU		24.11.99
	Portarlington, RoI *Built by F+W*		
	Stored dismantled 08.13 as 'J-1573' in Swiss A/F c/s		
G-VIEW	Wallis WA-116/L	002	05.07.82
	Cancelled 03.08.16 as PWFU		
	Old Warden *Stored 10.16*		
G-VIIA	Boeing 777-236ER	27483	03.07.97
	N5022E, (G-ZZZF) British Airways PLC		
	London Heathrow		02.07.19E
	Line No: 41		
G-VIIB	Boeing 777-236ER	27484	23.05.97
	N5023Q, (G-ZZZG) British Airways PLC		
	London Heathrow		30.01.20E
	Line No: 49		
G-VIIC	Boeing 777-236ER	27485	06.02.97
	N5016R, (G-ZZZH) British Airways PLC		
	London Heathrow		18.05.19E
	Line No: 53		
G-VIID	Boeing 777-236ER	27486	18.02.97
	(G-ZZZI) British Airways PLC London Heathrow		15.09.19E
	Line No: 56		
G-VIIE	Boeing 777-236ER	27487	27.02.97
	(G-ZZZJ) British Airways PLC London Heathrow		23.09.19E
	Line No: 58		
G-VIIF	Boeing 777-236ER	27488	19.03.97
	(G-ZZZK) British Airways PLC London Heathrow		28.10.19E
	Line No: 61		
G-VIIG	Boeing 777-236ER	27489	09.04.97
	(G-ZZZL) British Airways PLC London Heathrow		30.03.19E
	Line No: 65		
G-VIIH	Boeing 777-236ER	27490	07.05.97
	(G-ZZZM) British Airways PLC London Heathrow		06.05.19E
	Line No: 70		
G-VIIJ	Boeing 777-236ER	27492	29.12.97
	(G-ZZZP) British Airways PLC London Heathrow		21.08.19E
	Line No: 111		
G-VIIK	Boeing 777-236ER	28840	03.02.98
	British Airways PLC London Heathrow		02.02.19E
	Line No: 117		
G-VIIL	Boeing 777-236ER	27493	13.03.98
	British Airways PLC London Heathrow		12.03.19E
	Line No: 127		
G-VIIM	Boeing 777-236ER	28841	26.03.98
	British Airways PLC London Heathrow		13.09.19E
	Line No: 130		
G-VIIN	Boeing 777-236ER	29319	21.08.98
	British Airways PLC London Heathrow		20.08.19E
	Line No: 157		
G-VIIO	Boeing 777-236ER	29320	26.01.99
	British Airways PLC London Gatwick		25.10.19E
	Line No: 182		

G-VIIP	Boeing 777-236ER	29321	09.02.99
	British Airways PLC London Gatwick		20.12.19E
	Line No: 193		
G-VIIR	Boeing 777-236ER	29322	18.03.99
	British Airways PLC London Gatwick		17.03.19E
	Line No: 203		
G-VIIS	Boeing 777-236ER	29323	01.04.99
	British Airways PLC London Heathrow		31.03.19E
	Line No: 206		
G-VIIT	Boeing 777-236ER	29962	26.05.99
	British Airways PLC London Gatwick		25.05.19E
	Line No: 217		
G-VIIU	Boeing 777-236ER	29963	28.05.99
	British Airways PLC London Gatwick		27.05.19E
	Line No: 221		
G-VIIV	Boeing 777-236ER	29964	29.06.99
	British Airways PLC London Gatwick		28.06.19E
	Line No: 228		
G-VIIW	Boeing 777-236ER	29965	30.07.99
	British Airways PLC London Gatwick		11.07.19E
	Line No: 233		
G-VIIX	Boeing 777-236ER	29966	11.08.99
	British Airways PLC London Gatwick		10.08.19E
	Line No: 236		
G-VIIY	Boeing 777-236ER	29967	22.10.99
	British Airways PLC London Heathrow		21.09.19E
	Line No: 251		
G-VIIZ	CZAW Sportcruiser	07SC048	04.09.07
	Skyview Systems Ltd Waits Farm, Belchamp Walter		01.06.19P
	Built by N I G Hart – project PFA 338-14672		
	(Quick-build kit 4131)		
G-VIKE	Bellanca 17-30A Super Viking 300A	79-30911	08.07.80
	N302CB R Waas (Kelmis, Belgium)		13.10.18E
G-VILL	Laser Lazer Z200	10	10.06.96
	G-BOYZ S A Youngman		
	(Boughton Monchelsea, Maidstone)		11.03.14P
	Built by M G Jefferies (NF 25.07.17)		
G-VINA	Aeroprakt A-22L Foxbat	A22L-334	14.08.13
	J M Davidson Oxleaze Grange, Hawling		29.11.18P
	Built by J M Davidson – project LAA 317A-14977		
G-VINB	AgustaWestland AW139	31398	31.10.12
	Wilmington trust SP Services (Dublin) Ltd (Dublin)		31.10.19E
	Operated as callsign 'Bond 10'		
G-VIND	Sikorsky S-92A	920006	23.06.14
	N192PH Babcock Mission Critical Services		
	Offshore Ltd Aberdeen Int'l		29.06.18E
G-VINE	Airbus A330-343	1231	08.07.11
	N771RD, G-VINE, F-WWYA Virgin Atlantic		
	Airways Ltd London Heathrow *'Champagne Belle'*		20.09.19E
G-VINF	Sikorsky S-92A	920008	09.12.14
	N292PH, G-VINF, N292PH Babcock Mission Critical		
	Services Offshore Ltd Aberdeen Int'l		23.09.18E
G-VING	Sikorsky S-92A	920207	25.11.13
	N207RJ Babcock Mission Critical Services		
	Offshore Ltd Aberdeen Int'l		07.12.18E
G-VINI	Sikorsky S-92A	920220	26.03.14
	LN-OEE, N220Q Babcock Mission Critical		
	Services Offshore Ltd Aberdeen Int'l		26.03.18E
G-VINK	Sikorsky S-92A	920223	15.04.14
	N223P Babcock Mission Critical Services		
	Offshore Ltd Aberdeen Int'l		28.04.18E
G-VINL	Sikorsky S-92A	920226	09.05.14
	N226Z Babcock Mission Critical Services		
	Offshore Ltd Aberdeen Int'l		25.05.18E
G-VINM	Airbus EC225 LP Super Puma	2942	12.02.15
	Babcock Mission Critical Services Offshore Ltd		
	Humberside		12.02.18E
	Stored 09.16		
G-VINP	Sikorsky S-92A	920182	03.06.15
	LN-OED, N982P Babcock Mission Critical Services		
	Offshore Ltd Aberdeen Int'l		25.02.18E
G-VINT	Sikorsky S-92A	920258	23.06.16
	N258A Babcock Mission Critical Services		
	Offshore Ltd Aberdeen Int'l		26.07.18E

G-VIOF	Gulfstream VI (G650)	6355	29.03.19
	N655GD Executive Jet Charter Ltd Farnborough		
G-VIPA	Cessna 182S Skylane	18280720	13.09.00
	N148ME Rollright Aviation Ltd Oxford		16.12.17E
G-VIPG	AgustaWestland AW139	31497	19.02.19
	TC-HEE, I-EASJ Castle Air Ltd Trebrown, Liskeard		
G-VIPH	Agusta A109C	7643	21.09.01
	EI-CUV, G-BVNH, G-LAXO Cheqair Ltd		
	Tharston Industrial Estate, Long Stratton		18.01.19E
	Operated by Long Stratton Motor Company		
G-VIPP	Piper PA-31-350 Chieftain	31-7952244	06.08.93
	G-OGRV, G-BMPX, N3543D		
	Cancelled 04.05.17 as PWFU		09.10.17
	Bournemouth *Open store 03.19*		
G-VIPU	Piper PA-31-350 Chieftain	31-8152115	08.11.07
	G-MOHS, G-BWOC, N40898, (CP-1665)		
	Atlantic Bridge Aviation Ltd Lydd		21.11.16E
	Official type data 'PA-31-350 Navajo Chieftain'		
	is incorrect (IE 22.06.18)		
G-VIPW	Piper PA-31-350 Chieftain	31-7952129	28.07.08
	G-NEWR, N35251		
	Capital Air Ambulance Ltd Exeter Int'l		16.11.19E
	Official type data 'PA-31-350 Navajo Chieftain'		
	is incorrect		
G-VIPY	Piper PA-31-350 Chieftain	31-7852143	10.10.97
	EI-JTC, G-POLO, (EI-...), G-POLO, N27750		
	Capital Air Ambulance Ltd Exeter Int'l		12.10.19E
	Official type data 'PA-31-350 Navajo Chieftain'		
	is incorrect		
G-VITE	Robin R1180T Aiglon	219	16.10.78
	N C Lamb & D T Scrutton tr The G-VITE Flying Group		
	Stapleford		23.07.18E
G-VITL	Lindstrand LBL 105A	720	24.08.00
	M J Axtell Methley, Leeds *'vital resources'*		16.07.19E
G-VIVA	Thunder Ax7-65 Bolt	190	28.11.78
	R J Mitchener Andover		18.03.99A
	(IE 16.04.14)		
G-VIVE	Leonardo AW109SP Grand New	22393	03.01.19
	I-EASO Oxford Helicopter Services LLP Dunsfold		02.01.20E
G-VIVI	Taylor JT.2 Titch	xxxx	04.11.96
	C S Hales & P J Hebdon Shenington		21.02.06P
	Built by D G Tucker – project PFA 060-12405		
	(NF 08.05.17)		
G-VIVM	Hunting Percival P.84 Jet Provost T.5	PAC/W/23907	25.03.96
	G-BVWF, XS230 K Lyndon-Dykes tr Victor Mike Group		
	North Weald *'International Test Pilots School'*		08.10.19P
G-VIVO	Nicollier HN.700 Menestrel II	208	05.07.05
	D G Tucker Northrepps		03.06.18P
	Built by D G Tucker – project PFA 217-14039		
G-VIXN^M	de Havilland DH.110 Sea Vixen FAW.2 (TT)	10145	05.08.85
	8828M, XS587 Cancelled 15.12.09 by CAA		
	As ' XS587' in RN c/s		
	With Gatwick Aviation Museum, Charlwood		
G-VIXX	Alpi Pioneer 300	155	20.07.07
	G-CESE, G-CERJ N Harrison Westonzoyland		29.04.18P
	Built by K P O'Sullivan – project PFA 330-14465		
G-VIZZ	Sportavia RS.180 Sportsman	6018	25.10.79
	D-EFBK N Heald & J D Howard		
	tr The Exeter Fournier Group Exeter Int'l		31.05.18E
G-VJET^M	Avro 698 Vulcan B.2	Set 44	07.07.87
	XL426 Vulcan Restoration Trust Southend		
	Carries 'XL426'; noted 02.19 (NF 22.09.15)		
G-VJIM	Colt Jumbo-2	1298	07.08.89
	(G-BPJI) Magical Adventures Ltd		
	West Bloomfield, MI, USA *'Jumbo Jim'*		14.10.02A
	Built by Thunder & Colt Ltd (NF 03.06.15)		
G-VKRP	Piper PA-32R-301T Saratoga II TC	3257071	23.11.18
	OY-GKM R G Poxon (Anmering, Littlehampton)		
	(IE 23.11.18)		
G-VKSS	Airbus A330-343	1201	28.02.11
	F-WWYU Virgin Atlantic Airways Ltd		
	London Gatwick *'Mademoiselle Rouge'*		19.01.20E
G-VKUP	Cameron Z-90	10803	10.05.06
	T P E Y Eyckerman Hamme, Belgium		
	'VK Vodka Kick'		22.07.18E

G-VLCN	Avro 698 Vulcan B.2	Set 12	06.02.95
	XH558 Cancelled 19.08.17 as PWFU		
	Doncaster Sheffield *Preserved 09.17 as 'XH558'*		
G-VLIP	Boeing 747-443	32338	15.05.01
	(EI-CVI) Virgin Atlantic Airways Ltd		
	London Gatwick *'Hot Lips'*		14.05.19E
	Line No: 1274		
G-VLNM	Airbus A330-223	322	26.03.18
	D-ABXB, HB-1QQ, D-AIMD, F-WIHM, OO-SFT, F-WYYT		
	Virgin Atlantic Airways Ltd London Gatwick		
	'Strawberry Fields'		07.06.19E
G-VLTT	Diamond DA.42 Twin Star	42.AC116	10.09.12
	SP-DLP, N516TS R H Butterfield Retford Gamston		09.10.18E
G-VLUV	Airbus A330-343	1206	30.11.12
	B-18391, (G-VLUV), F-WWYH Virgin Atlantic		
	Airways Ltd London Heathrow *'Lady Love'*		29.11.19E
(G-VLUX)	Airbus A350-1041	274	
	Virgin Atlantic Reserved due, xx.19		
G-VMAP	Boeing 787-9	38047	20.05.16
	Virgin Atlantic Airways Ltd London Heathrow		
	'West End Girl'		19.05.19E
	Line No: 421		
G-VMCG	Piper PA-38-112 Tomahawk	38-79A0950	12.09.03
	G-BSVX, N2336P Pure Aviation Support Services Ltd		
	Liverpool John Lennon		18.07.18E
G-VMIK	Airbus A330-223	432	08.12.17
	D-ALPB, F-WWYG Virgin Atlantic Airways Ltd		
	London Gatwick *'Honkytonk woman'*		05.02.19E
G-VMJM	SOCATA TB-10 Tobago	1361	21.04.92
	G-BTOK D J Bryan Wolverhampton Halfpenny Green		17.02.18E
G-VMNK	Airbus A330-223	403	02.02.18
	D-ALPA, F-WWKO Virgin Atlantic Airways Ltd		
	London Heathrow *'Daydream Believer'*		31.03.19E
G-VMOZ	Van's RV-8	83134	05.12.16
	G-CIKP V Millard AAC Wattisham		21.02.18P
	Built by C A Acland & P S Gilmour		
	– project LAA 303-15029		
G-VMVM	Cameron Z-77	11393	29.03.10
	Airxcite Ltd t/a Virgin Balloon Flights		
	Stafford Park, Telford *'Virgin money'*		14.12.19E
G-VNAM	Cessna 305A Bird Dog	21666	01.08.17
	N5074G, Japanese GSDF 11017, 51-4781		
	L J Gregoire & O-1 Aviation Ltd Membury		
	(NF 01.03.18)		
G-VNAP	Airbus A340-642	622	24.02.05
	F-WWCE Virgin Atlantic Airways Ltd		
	London Gatwick *'Sleeping Beauty'*		31.01.20E
	'a big virgin atlantic thank you' fuselage logo		
G-VNEW	Boeing 787-9	40956	09.10.14
	Virgin Atlantic Airways Ltd London Heathrow		
	'Birthday Girl'		08.10.18E
	Line No: 218		
G-VNON	Reality Escapade Jabiru(5)	JA.ESC.0008	04.10.05
	P A Vernon Craysmarsh Farm, Melksham		06.04.18P
	Built by P A Vernon – project BMAA/HB/325; tricycle u/c		
G-VNTS	Schempp-Hirth Ventus bT	46	14.08.07
	BGA 4400, D-KFMS		
	A G Reid tr 911 Syndicate Bicester *'911'*		21.04.18E
G-VNYC	Airbus A330-343	1315	28.06.12
	F-WWKE Virgin Atlantic Airways Ltd		
	London Heathrow *'Uptown Girl'*		27.06.19E
G-VNYL	Boeing 787-9	37981	24.04.18
	N8289V Virgin Atlantic Airways Ltd		
	London Heathrow *'Penny Lane'*		23.04.19E
	Line No: 681		
G-VOAR	Piper PA-28-181 Archer III	2843011	03.11.95
	N9256Q Carlisle Flight Training Ltd		
	Carlisle Lake District		13.07.18E
G-VOCA	Extra EA.230	009	26.03.19
	G-IEII, G-CBUA, N230KR, N286PA		
	Aerial Vocations Ltd Inverness		
G-VOCE	Robinson R22 Beta	1249	30.07.07
	G-BSCL J J Voce (Doncaster)		11.08.02
	Displayed South Yorkshire Aircraft Museum		
	(NF 27.05.15)		

G-VODA	Cameron N-77	2208	08.02.90
	H Cusden Northampton		29.06.18E
	Original envelope rebuilt 01.07 & regd G-CEJC		
	(4164); crown ring used in c/n 4164 & became		
	G-VODA (2) c/n 2208		
G-VOID	Piper PA-28RT-201 Arrow IV	28R-8118049	17.08.87
	ZS-KTM, (G-GCAA), ZS-KTM, N83232		
	Doublecube Aviation LLP Thruxton		13.03.18E
G-VOIP	Westland SA.341D Gazelle HT.3	1792	15.11.05
	G-HOBZ, G-CBSJ, ZA802		
	E K Coventry Little Bassetts Farm, Childerditch		10.02.18P
G-VOLO	Alpi Pioneer 300	145	21.06.05
	J Buglass Sleap		23.02.17P
	Built by J Buglass & J W Clarke – project PFA 330-14389		
G-VONK	Aérospatiale AS.355F1 Ecureuil 2	5325	15.01.07
	G-BLRI, ZJ139, G-NUTZ, G-BLRI		
	Airbourne Solutions Ltd Five Acres Farm, Gamlingay		18.04.10E
	For potential rebuild 10.16 (NF 21.10.15)		
G-VONS	Piper PA-32R-301T Saratoga II TC	3257155	28.07.03
	N602MA Vox Filemaker Solutions SRL		
	(Timisoara, Romania)		03.02.18E
G-VONY	Cessna T182T Turbo Skylane	T18208662	29.08.17
	PH-MIK, SP-THC, N13256		
	W S Stanley (Ebrington, Chipping Campden)		01.11.18E
G-VOOH	Boeing 787-9	37968	04.02.15
	Virgin Atlantic Airways Ltd London Heathrow		
	'Miss Chief'		03.02.19E
	Line No: 256		
G-VOOM	Pitts S-1S	xxxx	08.04.03
	P G Roberts tr VOOM Syndicate White Waltham		01.09.18P
	Built by P G Roberts – project PFA 009-12989		
G-VORN	Evektor EV-97 Eurostar	2004-2126	02.05.07
	G-ODAV J Parker Fenland		02.11.18P
	Built by B R Davies – project PFA 315-14299		
G-VOUS	Cessna 172S Skyhawk SP	172S11266	23.12.13
	N266CS Flyglass Ltd Wycombe Air Park		21.03.18E
G-VOWS	Boeing 787-9	37974	23.12.15
	Virgin Atlantic Airways Ltd London Heathrow		
	'Maid Marion'		22.12.19E
	Line No: 373		
G-VPAT	Evans VP-1 Series 2	xxxx	11.02.04
	A P Twort (Isle of Lewis)		
	Built by A P Twort – project PFA 062-13907		
	(NF 18.09.16)		
G-VPCB	Evans VP-1 Series 2	xxxx	28.02.03
	C A Bloom Deanland		
	Built by C Bloom – project PFA 062-13901 (NF 08.07.16)		
(G-VPOP)	Airbus A350-1041	298	
	Virgin Atlantic Reserved due, xx.19		
G-VPPL	SOCATA TB-20 Trinidad	283	12.12.08
	G-BPAS, A2-ADR, F-GDBO		
	J M Thorpe Gloucestershire		01.04.18E
(G-VPRD)	Airbus A350-1041	310	
	Virgin Atlantic Reserved due, xx.19		
G-VPSJ	Europa Aviation Europa	023	29.07.93
	J D Bean Enstone		23.03.18E
	Built by J D Bean – project PFA 247-12520; tailwheel u/c		
G-VRAY	Airbus A330-343	1296	30.03.12
	F-WWKF Virgin Atlantic Airways Ltd		
	London Heathrow *'Miss Sunshine'*		29.03.19E
G-VRED	Airbus A340-642	768	19.10.06
	F-WWCH Virgin Atlantic Airways Ltd		
	London Heathrow *'Scarlet Lady'*		18.10.19E
G-VROE	Avro 652A Anson T.21	3634	03.03.98
	G-BFIR, 7881M, WD413 G G L James Sleap		31.05.18P
	As 'WD413' in RAF silver with yellow training bands c/s		
G-VROM	Boeing 747-443	32339	29.05.01
	CP-2603, G-VROM, (EI-CVJ) Virgin Atlantic		
	Airways Ltd London Gatwick *'Barbarella'*		24.05.19E
	Line No: 1275		
G-VROS	Boeing 747-443	30885	22.03.01
	(EI-CVG) Virgin Atlantic Airways Ltd		
	London Gatwick *'English Rose'*		21.03.19E
	Line No: 1268		
G-VROY	Boeing 747-443	32340	18.06.01
	(EI-CVK) Virgin Atlantic Airways Ltd		
	London Gatwick *'Pretty Woman'*		16.06.10E
	Line No: 1277		
G-VRRV	Van's RV-12	120900	25.05.17
	R W Shone Rochester		15.05.19P
	Built by J F Edmunds – project LAA 363-15322		
G-VRVB	Van's RV-8	8-2327	20.10.09
	G-CETI R J Verrall Luxters Farm, Hambleden		02.03.18P
	Built by E M Marsh – project PFA 303-14466		
G-VRVI	Cameron O-90	2522	27.02.91
	Air Events BVBA Beselare, Belgium		
	'VRV Air Conditioning'		30.04.16E
	(IE 10.05.17)		
G-VSGE	Cameron O-105	2382	14.08.02
	I-VSGE, G-BSSD D Chiriac Bucharest, Romania		17.09.19E
G-VSGG	Schempp-Hirth Ventus-2b	33	23.02.15
	SE-UTN, BGA 4353/JAF, (BGA 4306)		
	S G Gaunt Lasham *'SG'*		16.06.19E
G-VSIX	Schempp-Hirth Ventus-2cT	102/293	13.11.07
	BGA 5006/KDJ		
	M Nash-Wortham tr V6 Group Lasham *'V6'*		21.02.19E
G-VSKP	Leonardo AW169	69018	08.07.16
	I-EASI Foxborough Ltd (AAIB Farnborough)		10.07.18E
	Built by Finmeccanica SpA; crashed on take off		
	Leicester 27.10.18 & destroyed: wreck to		
	Farnborough 11.18		
G-VSOZ	Yakovlev Yak-18T	10-34	06.01.14
	HA-YAN, RA-44465(2), LY-AOL, RA-44483(2)		
	J Dodd & N R Parsons		
	Lausanne-Blecherette, Switzerland		02.08.18R
G-VSPY	Boeing 787-9	37973	16.12.15
	Virgin Atlantic Airways Ltd London Heathrow		
	'Miss Moneypenny'		14.12.19E
	Line No: 370		
G-VSTR	Stolp SA.900 V-Star	WTW1	30.06.11
	N998WW R L Hanreck Old Warden		04.03.15P
	Built by W Williams (IE 23.06.16)		
G-VSXY	Airbus A330-343	1195	24.02.11
	F-WWKY Virgin Atlantic Airways Ltd		
	London Heathrow *'Beauty Queen'*		23.02.19E
G-VTAL	Beech V35 Bonanza	D-7978	27.02.03
	HB-EJB, D-EFTH M A Rooney Sturgate		25.06.19E
G-VTCT	Schempp-Hirth Ventus-2cT	90/266	09.01.08
	BGA 4976/KCC		
	J B Hoolahan tr V26 Syndicate Challock *'V26'*		12.04.18E
G-VTEW	Schempp-Hirth Ventus-2a	112	01.12.14
	(BGA 5811), D-5816 O M McCormack Lasham *'77'*		19.03.18E
G-VTGE	Bell 206L LongRanger	45091	30.09.10
	G-ELIT, SE-HTK, N2652 Vantage Helicopters Ltd		
	Orchardleigh House, Buckland Dinham		18.12.18E
G-VTII	de Havilland DH.115 Vampire T.11	15127	09.01.80
	WZ507 M B Hooton Coventry		25.02.19P
	As 'WZ507:74' in RAF c/s		
G-VTOL[M]	Hawker Siddeley Harrier T.52	B3/41H/735795	27.07.70
	ZA250, G-VTOL, (XW273) Cancelled 13.03.90 by CAA		02.11.86
	With Brooklands Museum, Weybridge		
G-VTUS	Schempp-Hirth Ventus-2cT	64/199	19.10.07
	BGA 4886		
	P G Myers tr Ventus 02 Syndicate Feshiebridge *'2'*		07.04.18E
G-VUEM	Cessna 501 Citation I	501-0178	24.04.06
	G-FLVU, N83ND, N4246A, LV-PML, N67749		
	Cancelled 14.07.11 as destroyed		16.07.11
	Cranfield Wreck used for training by AAIB 05.17		
G-VUFO	Airbus A330-343	1352	15.11.12
	F-WWCR Virgin Atlantic Airways Ltd		
	London Heathrow *'Lady Stardust'*		14.11.19E
G-VULC[M]	Avro 698 Vulcan B.2A	xxxx	27.02.84
	(N655AV), XM655 Cancelled 25.03.02 as PWFU		
	Built by Hawker Siddeley Aviation Ltd		
	With XM655 Maintenance & Preservation Society,		
	Wellesbourne Mountford		

G-VVBA	Aérospatiale AS.355F2 Ecureuil 2	5463	06.01.11
	G-DBOK, N620LH, D-HKEV, N158BC, XU-018, N158BC		
	Hudson Aviation Ltd Elstree		24.05.19E
	Operated by VVB Aviation Services Ltd		
G-VVBF	Colt 315A	4058	03.03.97
	Airxcite Ltd t/a Virgin Balloon Flights		
	Stafford Park, Telford *'Virgin'*		17.08.05E
	Built by Cameron Balloons Ltd (NF 19.10.18)		
G-VVBH	Guimbal Cabri G2	1136	29.03.16
	S D Evans Bolt Head, Salcombe		14.04.18E
G-VVBO	Bell 206L-3 LongRanger III	51284	19.04.10
	EI-BYR, (EI-LMG), EI-BYR, D-HBAD, C-GADP		
	Nugent Aviation Ltd (Pomeroy, Dungannon)		
	(IE 12.06.18)		
G-VVBR	Robinson R22 Beta	1596	28.07.14
	G-SIMS, N7800R, LV-RBZ A & M Helicopters Ltd		
	Wolverhampton Halfpenny Green		09.08.18E
G-VVBZ	Guimbal Cabri G2	1097	27.04.15
	Hudson Aviation Ltd Elstree		16.05.19E
	Operated by VVB Aviation Services Ltd		
G-VVME	Maule M-5-235C Lunar Rocket	7276C	27.08.18
	G-CCBF, G-NHVH, N5643N		
	I M Jong, D Van Zonneveld & M Vogler		
	(Hessen, Germany, Heede & Ijmuiden, Netherlands)		27.03.05
	(NF 24.08.18)		
G-VVRV	Van's RV-9A	90549	30.07.18
	G-ENTS I G Harban (Leamington Spa)		
	Built by L G Johnson – project LAA 320-13917 (NF 30.07.18)		
G-VVTV	Diamond DA.42 Twin Star	42.170	18.09.06
	OE-VPY A D R Northeast Wycombe Air Park		14.06.18E
	Operated by Booker Aviation		
G-VVVV	Best Off Skyranger 912(2)	SKR0407510	15.12.04
	J Thomas (Great Cambourne, Cambridge)		20.03.18P
	Built by J B Hobbs & J Thomas – project BMAA/HB/427		
G-VVWW	Enstrom 280C Shark	2056	22.10.03
	N7802J, JA7822 P J Odendaal Southend		25.10.19E
G-VWAG	Airbus A330-343	1341	15.10.12
	F-WWCG Virgin Atlantic Airways Ltd		
	London Heathrow *'Miss England'*		14.10.19E
G-VWEB	Airbus A340-642	787	20.12.06
	F-WWCZ Virgin Atlantic Airways Ltd		
	London Heathrow *'Surfer Girl'*		19.12.19E
G-VWET	Lake LA-4-200 Buccaneer	1106	10.11.15
	D-EARS, G-VWET, D-EARS, N8543J		
	Belgian Seaplane Aeroclub (Brussels, Belgium)		07.06.18E
G-VWHO	Boeing 787-9	37971	30.06.15
	Virgin Atlantic Airways Ltd London Heathrow		
	'Mystery Girl'		29.06.19E
	Line No: 313		
G-VWIN	Airbus A340-642	736	28.02.06
	(N), G-VWIN, F-WWCL Virgin Atlantic Airways Ltd		
	London Heathrow *'Lady Luck'*		27.02.19E
G-VWND	Airbus A330-223	476	11.12.17
	D-ALPF, F-WWKT Virgin Atlantic Airways Ltd		
	London Gatwick *'Scarlett O'Hara'*		26.04.19E
G-VWOO	Boeing 787-9	37979	19.01.18
	Virgin Atlantic Airways Ltd London Heathrow		
	'Leading Lady'		18.01.20E
	Line No: 645		
G-VXLG	Boeing 747-41R	29406	30.09.98
	Virgin Atlantic Airways Ltd London Gatwick		
	'Ruby Tuesday'		22.09.19E
	Line No: 1177		
G-VXXN	Aeroprakt A-32 Vixxen	A32056	05.12.18
	A Everitt Ley Farm, Chirk		
	Built by A Everitt – project LAA 411-15580		
G-VYAK	Yakovlev Yak-18T	01-32	13.05.11
	HA-HUA, N7818T A I Mcrobbie Rochester		08.12.12R
	In open storage 06.16 (IE 02.06.15)		
G-VYGJ	Airbus A330-243MRTT Voyager	1439	15.08.14
	EC-333, F-WWKF Airtanker Ltd RAF Brize Norton		17.08.19E
G-VYGK	Airbus A330-243MRTT Voyager	1498	06.02.15
	EC-330, F-WWTR Airtanker Ltd Manchester		10.02.19E
	'Sunny Heart'; operated by Thomas Cook Airlines Ltd		

G-VYGL	Airbus A330-243MRTT Voyager	1555	23.06.15
	ZZ341, G-VYGL, EC-336, F-WWYI		
	Airtanker Ltd RAF Brize Norton		08.03.19E
	All white c/s		
G-VYGM	Airbus A330-243MRTT Voyager	1601	26.02.16
	EC-332, F-WWCC Airtanker Ltd RAF Brize Norton		28.02.19E
G-VYOU	Airbus A340-642	765	23.08.06
	F-WWCK Virgin Atlantic Airways Ltd		
	London Heathrow		
	'Emmeline Heaney born August 2006'		22.08.19E
G-VYUM	Boeing 787-9	37970	14.05.15
	Virgin Atlantic Airways Ltd London Heathrow		
	'Ruby Murray'		13.05.19E
	Line No: 296		
G-VZED	Magni M16C Tandem Trainer	16181314	13.04.18
	A C S M Hart (Wargrave, Reading)		01.05.19P
G-VZIG	Boeing 787-9	37969	09.03.15
	Virgin Atlantic Airways Ltd London Heathrow		
	'Dream Jeannie'		08.03.19E
	Line No: 267		
G-VZIM	Alpha R2160	160A-07012	07.03.11
	ZK-CTT I M Hollingsworth Gloucestershire		15.02.18E
G-VZON	Avions Transport ATR 72-212A	853	27.03.09
	F-WWEW Aurigny Air Services Ltd Guernsey		25.03.19E
G-VZSF	Hawker Sea Fury T.20	ES.8503	03.10.17
	VZ345, D-CATA, D-FATA, G-9-30, VZ345		
	Patina Ltd Duxford		
	Allocated c/n ES.8503 by Deutscher Luftfahrt-		
	Beratungsdienst (German Registration authority)		
	(ES = Ernst Seibert); operated by The Fighter		
	Collection (NF 03.10.17)		

G-WAAA – G-WZZZ

G-WAAN	MBB Bolkow Bo.105DB	S.20	14.11.03
	G-AZOR, EC-DOE, G-AZOR, D-HDAC		
	Cancelled 07.09.12 as PWFU		26.07.11
	Iver Heath *Pod used at Pinewood Studios 06.15*		
G-WACB	Reims/Cessna F152 II	F15201972	11.09.86
	Airways Aero Associations Ltd Wycombe Air Park		21.12.18E
G-WACE	Reims/Cessna F152 II	F15201978	16.09.86
	Airways Aero Associations Ltd Wycombe Air Park		12.04.18E
G-WACF	Cessna 152 II	15284852	20.01.87
	N628GH, (LV-PMB), N628GH		
	Airways Aero Associations Ltd Wycombe Air Park		07.09.18E
G-WACH	Reims/Cessna FA152 Aerobat	FA1520425	18.06.87
	Airways Aero Associations Ltd Wycombe Air Park		06.12.18E
G-WACI	Beech 76 Duchess	ME-289	26.07.88
	N6703Y Cancelled 05.09.17 as PWFU		22.11.12
	Dublin-Weston *Fuselage derelict 06.17*		
G-WACJ	Beech 76 Duchess	ME-278	03.01.89
	N6700Y Cancelled 15.02.18 as PWFU		22.07.11
	Dublin-Weston *Fuselage derelict 06.17*		
G-WACU	Reims/Cessna FA152 Aerobat	FA1520380	10.07.86
	G-BJZU Airways Aero Associations Ltd		
	Wycombe Air Park		05.10.18E
G-WACW	Cessna 172P Skyhawk II	17274057	16.05.88
	N5307K Civil Service Flying Club (Biggin Hill) Ltd		
	Rochester		07.09.18E
G-WACY	Reims/Cessna F172P	F17202217	03.10.86
	F-GDOZ Paul's Planes Ltd Denham		22.03.19E
G-WADD	Airbus EC120B Colibri	1695	11.07.16
	GGR Group Ltd (Broadway, Chadderton)		03.11.19E
G-WADF	Air Création Tanarg 912S(2)/BioniX 13	xxxx	25.02.16
	W O Fogden Enstone		26.05.18P
	Built by W O Fogden – project BMAA/HB/683;		
	Tanarg Trike s/n T06079 & 13-metre BioniX wing		
	s/n A16002-16002; shares trike with G-CEIV		
G-WADS	Robinson R22 Beta	1224	25.04.96
	G-NICO Un Pied sur Terre Ltd		
	t/a Whizzard Helicopters Welshpool		21.04.17E
	(NF 17.08.17)		

G-WADZ	Lindstrand LBL 90A	1354	11.10.12
	G-CGVN A K C, J E H, M H & Y K Wadsworth		
	Nailsea, Bristol		02.10.18E
G-WAFI	Van's RV-12	121019	14.12.18
	M N Fotherby & B M Lloyd (New Malden)		
	Built by M N Fotherby & B M Lloyd		
	– project LAA 363-15450 (NF 14.12.18)		
G-WAGA	Wag-Aero Wagabond	xxxx	17.08.09
	G-BNJA A I Sutherland Fearn *'Bea'*		12.12.17P
	Built by R A Yates – project PFA 137-10886		
G-WAGG	Robinson R22 Beta II	2960	07.07.99
	Aztec Aviators Ltd Cranfield		25.04.18E
G-WAGN	Stinson 108-3 Voyager	108-4216	22.06.05
	N6216M, NC6216M S E H Ellcome Cumbernauld		23.04.18E
	Built by Consolidated Vultee Aircraft		
G-WAHT	Albatros D.Va-1 replica	0147	29.08.18
	ZK-ALB O Wulff Old Warden		
	Built by The Vintage Aviator Ltd; as 'D2263'		
	(NF 29.08.18)		
G-WAIR	Piper PA-32-301 Saratoga	32-8506010	14.01.91
	N2607X, N9577N P J Hopkins tr Finningley Aviation		
	Ninescores Farm, Finningley		03.03.18E
G-WAIT	Cameron V-77	2390	20.11.90
	C P Brown Littleport, Ely		24.07.99A
	(NF 28.02.18)		
G-WAKE	Mainair Blade 912	1244-0300-7-W1037	06.03.00
	G J Molloy (Wallasey)		01.01.15P
	New wing fitted 11.09 (IE 05.10.16)		
G-WAKY	Cyclone AX2000	7890	05.04.02
	E E & R J Hunt (Halford, Shipston-on-Stour)		14.06.18P
G-WALI	Robinson R44 Raven II	10849	30.08.05
	G Reidy Ballyboughal, RoI *'Lithofin'*		02.09.19E
G-WALY	Maule MX-7-180 Star Rocket	11028C	23.01.03
	N5668H J R Colthurst Radley Farm, Hungerford		25.10.18E
G-WALZ	Best Off Skyranger Nynja 912S(1)	11080078	22.11.11
	R J Thomas The Byre, Hardwick, Abergavenny		11.06.18P
	Built by R J Thomas – project BMAA/HB/619		
G-WAMS	Piper PA-28R-201 Arrow III	2844050	29.04.04
	N491A, N5328Q		
	Stapleford Flying Club Ltd Stapleford		29.04.18E
	Official type data 'PA-28R-201 Cherokee Arrow III'		
	is incorrect		
G-WANA	P&M Quik	8681	28.02.14
	A Lord Sywell		12.05.19P
	Wanafly Airsports		
G-WAPA	Robinson R44 Raven II	13228	05.01.12
	Aerocorp Ltd (Birkenhead)		31.01.18E
G-WARA	Piper PA-28-161 Warrior III	2842021	03.09.97
	EC-HXU, G-WARA, N9289N, (G-WARA), N9289N		
	Global Aviation SA (Athens, Greece)		21.08.17E
	(NF 08.07.18)		
G-WARB	Piper PA-28-161 Warrior III	2842034	04.09.98
	N41286, (G-WARB), N41286		
	OSF Ltd Wolverhampton Halfpenny Green		07.09.18E
G-WARD	Taylor JT.1 Monoplane	xxxx	01.12.80
	R P J Hunter (Chertsey)		22.02.00P
	Built by G Ward – project PFA 1407 (NF 11.06.18)		
G-WARE	Piper PA-28-161 Warrior II	28-8416080	21.07.89
	N4357L, (N4354Z) I D Wakeling Henstridge		05.12.16E
	(IE 30.09.17)		
G-WARH	Piper PA-28-161 Warrior III	2842063	04.02.00
	N4177Y, G-WARH		
	Focus Aviation BV Lelystad, Netherlands		29.04.19E
G-WARO	Piper PA-28-161 Warrior III	2842015	24.10.97
	EC-HVT, G-WARO, N92946, (G-WARO), N92946		
	TGD Leasing Ltd Coventry		05.06.19E
G-WARP	Cessna 182F Skylane	18254633	06.06.95
	G-ASHB, N3233U R D Fowden Haverfordwest		06.11.18E
G-WARR	Piper PA-28-161 Warrior II	28-7916321	15.09.88
	N3074U R D Carnegie		
	(Fercé-sur-Sarthe, France, France)		28.08.19E
G-WARS	Piper PA-28-161 Warrior III	2842022	07.11.97
	N9281X, (G-WARS), N9281X		
	London School of Flying Ltd Elstree		05.01.20E
	Operated by Flight Training London Ltd		
G-WARU	Piper PA-28-161 Warrior III	2842023	06.11.97
	EC-HVU, G-WARU, N92880		
	Smart People Dont Buy Ltd Coventry		14.01.19E
	Operated by Aeros		
G-WARV	Piper PA-28-161 Warrior III	2842036	08.10.98
	N41247, (G-WARV), N41247		
	Bickertons Aerodromes Ltd Denham		19.02.18E
G-WARW	Piper PA-28-161 Warrior III	2842037	17.11.98
	N41254, (G-WARW), N41254		
	P Lodge & J G McVey Liverpool John Lennon		28.06.18E
G-WARX	Piper PA-28-161 Warrior III	2842038	15.12.98
	N4126D, (G-WARX), N4126D		
	White Waltham Airfield Ltd White Waltham		21.12.18E
G-WARY	Piper PA-28-161 Warrior III	2842024	13.11.97
	N9287X, (G-WARY), N9287X		
	Target Aviation Ltd Brighton City		10.02.18E
G-WASC	Eurocopter EC135 T2+	1074	01.10.12
	Babcock Mission Critical Services Onshore Ltd		
	Welshpool		03.10.18E
	Operated by Wales Air Ambulance as callsign		
	'Helimed 59'		
G-WASS	Eurocopter EC135 T2+	0745	25.03.09
	Babcock Mission Critical Services Onshore Ltd		
	Caernarfon		01.06.18E
	Operated by Wales Air Ambulance as callsign		
	'Helimed 61'		
G-WATR	Christen A-1 Husky	1040	02.04.03
	N2941W Clipper Aviation Ltd Rochester		05.10.18E
	Amphibian		
G-WAVA	Robin HR.200-120B	352	10.07.00
	Carlisle Flight Training Ltd Carlisle Lake District		10.02.18E
G-WAVE (2)	Grob G109B	6381	01.08.85
	C G Wray Park Farm, Eaton Bray		18.04.18E
G-WAVV	Robin HR.200-120B Club	291	06.03.06
	G-GORF, F-GORF		
	Carlisle Flight Training Ltd Carlisle Lake District		20.03.18E
G-WAVY	Grob G109B	6374	05.05.05
	F-CAQP, F-WAQP G M Brightman & T Donovan		
	tr G-WAVY Group Shenington		24.08.18E
G-WAWW	P&M Quik GT450	8547	09.11.10
	O P Gall (Lerwick)		28.05.18P
	Trailered to fly from Tingwall		
G-WAYS	Lindstrand LBL 105A	1307	04.05.10
	D B Green Neston *'Palletways'*		08.01.19E
G-WAZP	Best Off Skyranger 912(2)	SKR0212288	10.06.04
	(G-KNSR) M Gilson & P C Terry North Weald		28.05.19P
	Built by K H A Negal – project BMAA/HB/273		
G-WBATᵀᴹ	Julian Wombat Gyrocopter	CJ-001	31.05.90
	G-BSID Cancelled by CAA 12.07.99		04.03.97
	Built by C.D.Julian		
	With The Helicopter Museum, Weston-super-Mare		
G-WBEV	Cameron N-77	4376	15.12.04
	G-PVCU M J & T J Turner Wellingborough		
	'Beverley'		19.08.09E
	(NF 16.05.13)		
G-WBLY	Mainair Pegasus Quik	8057	30.07.04
	A J Lindsay Newtownards		13.08.18P
	Built by Mainair Sports Ltd		
G-WBRD	Avro Curtiss 1911 Replica	RHC1	13.04.15
	Cooper Aerial Surveys Engineering Ltd &		
	The Lakes Flying Company Ltd Wickenby		
	Built by R H Cooper; carries 'Lakes Flying Company';		
	noted 02.16 (NF 10.04.15)		
G-WBTS	Falconar F-11W-200	xxxx	22.10.90
	G-BDPL M K Field Sleap		11.01.18P
	Built by A J Watson – project PFA 032-10070		
G-WCAT	Colt Flying Mitt	1744	30.05.90
	I Chadwick Caterham *'Washcat'*		02.08.13E
	(IE 05.09.17)		

G-WCCP Beech B200 Super King Air BB-1295 16.10.06
N295CP, N95MW, N3079S GCP Aviation Ltd Sywell 10.03.19E
Operated by 2 Excel Aviation

G-WCEI SOCATA MS.894E Rallye 220GT 12141 28.05.85
G-BAOC Cancelled 11.12.14 as PWFU 14.11.08
Rixton, Warrington
Displayed at Ramswood Garden Centre 10.16

G-WCKM Best Off Skyranger Swift 912(1) UK/1020 01.03.11
D R Hardy Westonzoyland 08.10.18P
Built by J Depree & B Janson – project BMAA/HB/611

G-WCME Grumman FM-2 Wildcat 3226 27.09.13
N585FM, N681S, N68JS, N47S, N1970M, USN 55585
Wildcat WP Ltd (Charlbury, Chipping Norton)
Built by General Motors Corp (NF 06.12.16)

G-WCMI Grumman FM-2 Wildcat 5808 27.09.13
N750FM, N12731, USN 86750
Wildcat WP Ltd (Charlbury, Chipping Norton)
(NF 06.12.16)

G-WCMO Grumman FM-2 Wildcat 3045 23.09.13
USN 55404 Wildcat WP Ltd
(Charlbury, Chipping Norton)
(NF 06.12.16)

G-WCUB Piper PA-18-150 Super Cub 18-8278 11.05.01
HB-OLR, N5514Y
P A Walley Swinmore Farm, Ledbury 15.09.17E

G-WDCL Agusta A109E Power 11710 18.06.14
G-WELY Wickford Development Company Ltd
Runwell, Wickford 08.08.19E
Operated by Solent Helicopters Ltd t/a Elite Helicopters

G-WDEB Thunder Ax7-77 1606 26.09.89
A Heginbottom Cheadle Hulme, Cheadle 09.09.12E
(IE 21.04.17)

G-WDGC Rolladen-Schneider LS8-18 8395 08.02.08
G-CEWJ, BGA 4904/JZC
W D G Chappel Trenchard Lines, Upavon *'M9'* 14.07.18E

G-WEAT Robinson R44 Raven II 12722 13.03.09
R F Brook (Hornchurch) 08.04.18E

G-WEBY Ace Aviation Magic/Cyclone xxxx 17.05.10
B W Webster (Ewloe)
Trike s/n not known & Wing s/n AC-152
(SSDR microlight since 05.14) (IE 26.08.15)

G-WECG Eurocopter AS.355NP Ecureuil 2 5798 09.03.16
G-MXCO, XB-OFG WEC Group Ltd Blackpool 25.10.18E

G-WEEK Best Off Skyranger 912(2) UK/628 19.01.06
R E Williams Old Park Farm, Margam 28.09.19P
Built by R J Brown & D J Prothero
– project BMAA/HB/476

G-WEFR Alpi Pioneer 200-M 218 23.06.09
S G Llewelyn St Athan 12.02.15P
Built by S Llewelyn – project LAA 334-14912)
(IE 25.04.15)

G-WEFX British Aerospace Avro 146-RJ100 E3379 04.12.18
G-ILLR, HB-IYU, G-CGAC, G6-379
Airbus Exo Alpha SAS Cranfield 14.12.18E
For conversion to 'E-Fan X' hybrid test bed 2020

G-WEND Piper PA-28RT-201 Arrow IV 28R-8118026 08.11.82
PH-SYL, N8296L Tayside Aviation Ltd Dundee 01.06.18E

G-WENN Hoffmann H36 Dimona 3672 27.05.15
OE-9238, (D-KPEL), OE-9238
N Clarke & L Ingram Enstone 17.04.18E

G-WENU Airbus MBB BK117 D-2 (*Eurocopter EC145 T2*)
20112 28.10.16
D-HBTA Babcock Mission Critical Services
Onshore Ltd Glasgow City Heliport 01.11.18E
Operated by Wales Air Ambulance as 'Helimed 57'

G-WERY SOCATA TB-20 Trinidad 305 02.04.82
R-Aviation SARL Aerodrome Roenne St Leger, France 30.09.18E

G-WESS Lindstrand LTL Series 1-90 051 16.03.18
A Moore Wickwar, Wotton-under-Edge
'Wes The Wolf' 09.05.19E

G-WESX CFM Streak Shadow K 116-SA 02.02.90
M Catania Lleweni Parc 06.03.16P
Built by N Ramsey – project PFA 161A-11561
(IE 21.04.17)

G-WETI Cameron N-31 449 27.11.78
C A Butter & J J T Cooke Marsh Benham &
Urgup Nevsehir, Turkey *'Wet Ones'* 18.08.14E

G-WEWI Cessna 172 Skyhawk 46555 27.02.12
G-BSEP, N6455E T J Wassell Sleap 07.04.18E

G-WEZZ Taylor JT.1 Monoplane PFA 1459 07.06.13
G-BDRF W A Tierney (Letchworth Garden City)
Built by R A Codling – project PFA 1459 (NF 14.07.17)

G-WFFW Piper PA-28-161 Warrior II 28-8116161 26.10.93
N8342A D Jelly & S Letheren Oaksey Park 12.02.10E
(NF 27.08.15)

G-WFLY Mainair Pegasus Quik 8073 08.10.04
S Turton (Fremington, Barnstaple) 18.11.18P
Built by Mainair Sports Ltd

G-WFWA Piper PA-28-161 Cherokee Warrior II 28-8416119 04.04.17
PH-SFT, G-BPMR, N4373S, N9620N
Wings For Warriors Aberdeen Int'l 14.08.18E

G-WGCS Piper PA-18 Super Cub 95 (*L-18C-PI*) 18-1528 21.12.84
(G-BLSV), French Army F-MBCH, 51-15528
S C Thompson Newells Farm, Lower Beeding 28.11.18P
Fuselage No.18-1500

G-WGHB Canadair CL-30(T-33AN) Silver Star Mk.3 640 09.05.74
CF-EHB, CAF133640, RCAF21640
Cancelled 24.02.12 as PWFU
Mendlesham, Suffolk *Stored dismantled 10.15*

G-WGSI Air Création Tanarg 912S(3)/iXess 13 FLTxxx 16.12.08
M Nazm Gerpins Farm, Upminster 08.09.18P
Built by J A Ganderton – project BMAA/HB/585
(Flylight kit FLTxxx comprising trike s/n T08072 &
wing s/n xxxx-xxx); fitted with unknown replacement
trike c.2016

G-WHAT Colt 77A 1911 15.03.91
M A Scholes London SE25 04.12.13E
(IE 04.08.17)

G-WHEE Cyclone Pegasus Quantum 15-912 7510 26.03.99
A Snell tr G-WHEE Group Darley Moor 16.06.19P

G-WHEN Tecnam P92-EM Echo xxxx 07.02.01
F G Walker Lleweni Parc 02.10.18P
Built by C D Marsh – project PFA 318-13679

G-WHIL Kubícek BB-S/Cup 977 09.05.13
OK-0977 A M Holly Breadstone, Berkeley
'williamhill.com' 23.11.17E
Challenge Cup (IE 05.10.18)

G-WHIM Colt 77A 1476 10.04.89
D L Morgan Ilford 28.07.04A
(NF 06.08.18)

G-WHOG CFM Streak Shadow K 253-SA 21.09.94
B R Cannell Old Sarum *'Wart Hog'* 01.08.18P
Built by B R Cannell – project PFA 206-12776

G-WHOO RotorWay Exec 162F 6495 05.06.01
J White (Glenrothes) 19.10.17P
Built by C A Saull

G-WHPG Comco Ikarus C42 FB80 1607-7463 23.08.16
T Penn & C P Roche Wolverhampton Halfpenny Green 12.07.18P
Assembled Red Aviation

G-WHRL Schweizer 269C (*300*) S 1453 19.04.90
EC-GGX, CS-HDG, G-WHRL, N41S
A Harvey (Lustleigh, Newton Abbot) 11.09.17E

G-WHST Eurocopter AS.350B2 Ecureuil 2915 09.08.96
G-BWYA Toppesfield Ltd Elmsett 04.05.19E

G-WHYS ICP MXP-740 Savannah VG Jabiru(1) 04-06-51-290 15.06.10
R W Swift Swansea 21.04.18P
Built by D J Whysall – project BMAA/HB/404;
badged Savannah VG Sport

G-WIBB Jodel D.18 18 18.06.96
C J Bragg Hill Farm, Nayland 21.07.16P
Built by J Wibberley – project PFA 169-11640

G-WIBS CASA 1-131E Jungmann Series 2000 2005 25.03.99
Spanish AF E3B-401 C Willoughby
(Southam, Coventry)
(NF 09.05.16)

G-WICH Clutton FRED Series II xxxx 03.01.79
D R G Griffith (Daganwy, Conwy)
Built by L A Tomlinson – project PFA 029-10331
(NF 20.07.15)

G-WIDZ	Staaken Z-21 Flitzer	089	26.08.05
	T G Lloyd Shelsley Beauchamp		
	Built by T F Crossman – project PFA 223-14314		
	(NF 04.09.18)		
G-WIFE	Cessna R182 Skylane RG II	R18200244	11.12.01
	G-BGVT, N3162C		
	A L Brown tr Wife 182 Group Kirknewton		07.03.18E
G-WIFI	Cameron Z-90	10624	09.09.04
	A R Rich Hadfield, Glossop *'intel inside – centrino'*		16.04.19E
G-WIGI	Aeroprakt A-22LS Foxbat	A22LS-306	16.11.18
	K Wigginton Kirknewton		20.03.20P
	Built by K Wigginton – project LAA 317B-15574		
G-WIGS	Aerospool Dynamic WT9 UK	DY200/2007	15.12.14
	G-DYMC A Wiggins Bagby		09.01.20P
	Assembled Yeoman Light Aircraft Co Ltd		
G-WIGY	Pitts S-1S	7-0115	31.05.07
	G-ITTI, N91VA R E Welch Rectory Farm, Averham		10.05.18P
	Built by S Eisenberger		
G-WIII	Schempp-Hirth Ventus bT	49/247	08.07.08
	BGA 4862/JXK, D-KLOE I G Carrick Seighford *'W3'*		22.03.18E
G-WIIZ	Agusta-Bell 206B-2 JetRanger II	8111	28.10.03
	G-DBHH, G-AWVO, VH-BHI, PK-HCA, G-AWVO,		
	9Y-TDN, PK-HBG, G-AWVO		
	Bradawl Ltd Dublin Weston, RoI		10.11.17E
G-WIKD	Van's RV-8	83419	11.07.17
	E P Morrow Newtownards		31.10.19P
	Built by E P Morrow – project LAA 303-15394		
G-WIKI	Europa Aviation Europa XS	581	18.11.10
	S P Kirton & A H Smith Rufforth East		18.04.18P
	Built by K J Bull & J Greenhalgh		
	– project PFA 247-14095; tricycle u/c		
G-WILB	Ultramagic M-105	105/161	11.04.08
	A S Davidson tr Nottingham & Derby Hot Air		
	Balloon Club Ashby de la Zouch *'William Bailey'*		17.06.18E
G-WILD	Pitts S-1T	1017	06.12.85
	ZS-LMM, N947 S L Goldspink Old Warden		16.02.14E
	Built by Pitts Aerobatics (NF 06.11.15)		
G-WILG	PZL-104 Wilga 35	62153	15.04.97
	G-AZYJ M H Bletsoe-Brown Sywell		
	'The Startled Fart!'		29.07.12E
	(NF 28.03.18)		
G-WILI	Piper PA-32R-301 Saratoga SP	3213004	21.11.88
	OO-RAG, G-WILI, N9128N, N9582N		
	D A Abel (Stockton-on-Tees)		18.12.18E
G-WILN	Tecnam P2006T	178	25.07.16
	W Flight Hire Ltd Finmere		11.09.18E
G-WILT	Comco Ikarus C42 FB80	0506-6687	14.07.05
	V J P R Denecker (Frilford Heath, Abingdon)		22.09.17P
	Assembled Aerosport; operated by		
	Clearprop Microlight School (IE 20.10.17)		
G-WIMP	Colt 56A	755	13.02.86
	D M Wade Shevington, Wigan		15.08.16E
	(IE 05.06.17)		
G-WINH	Evektor EV-97 teamEurostar UK	2008-3216	09.07.08
	J A Warters Carlisle Lake District		26.08.18P
	Assembled Cosmik Aviation Ltd		
G-WINI	Scottish Aviation Bulldog Srs 120/121	BH120/238	23.09.03
	G-CBCO, XX546 A Bole Isle of Man		18.06.19P
	As 'XX546:03' in RAF c/s		
G-WINK	Grumman American AA-5B Tiger	AA5B-0327	14.12.90
	N74658 B St J Cooke tr WINK Group Elstree		12.05.18E
G-WINO	Aeropro EuroFOX 912S(1)	46515	22.09.15
	M A J Spiers Ashcroft		
	Built by P Knowles – project BMAA/HB/669;		
	tricycle u/c; active 09.18 (IE 11.08.18)		
G-WINR	Robinson R22 Beta	1709	04.03.10
	EI-CFE, G-BTHG, EI-CFE, G-BTHG		
	Heli Air Ltd Wellesbourne Mountford		03.07.18E
G-WINS	Piper PA-32-300 Cherokee Six	32-7640065	24.04.91
	N8476C Cheyenne Ltd Jersey		29.11.18E
G-WINX	Tecnam P2010	048	17.03.17
	CR Flight Hire Ltd Turweston		29.03.18E

G-WINZ	Lindstrand LTL Penguin	050	06.09.17
	A M Holly Breadstone, Berkeley		27.11.18E
	Penguin special shape		
G-WIRG	Embraer EMB-135BJ Legacy 650	14501184	07.10.13
	PR-LBY Air Charter Scotland Ltd Luton		06.10.18E
G-WIRL	Robinson R22 Beta	0671	27.07.87
	Rivermead Aviation Ltd Gloucestershire		05.08.16E
	Operated by Rise Helicopters		
G-WISS[M]	British Aerospace ATP	2020	12.06.89
	SE-LHX, LX-WAN, SE-LHX, LX-WAN, SE-LHX,		
	N851AW, G-11-20 Cancelled 03.01.90 – to N851AW		
	At Manx Aviation and Military Museum, Ronaldsway		
G-WISZ	Steen Skybolt	xxxx	08.07.08
	G S Reid (Great Ellingham, Attleborough)		
	Built by G S Reid – project PFA 064-13961		
	(NF 14.07.15)		
G-WIXI	Mudry CAP 10B	279	27.01.98
	A R Harris Sleap		17.06.18E
	Built by Akrotech Europe		
G-WIZA	Robinson R22 Beta	0861	16.11.94
	G-PERL, N90815 Cancelled 13.12.11 as PWFU		07.02.10
	Gloucestershire *Stored 11.13*		
G-WIZG	Agusta A109E Power	11123	12.01.17
	M-EMLI(2), M-ONEY, G-TYCN, G-VMCP		
	Tycoon Aviation Ltd		
	Bowyers Court, Wisborough Green		12.01.20E
	Operated by Solent Helicopters Ltd t/a Elite Helicopters		
G-WIZI	Enstrom 280FX Shark	2040	08.07.02
	Chil.Army H-177		
	Cloud Telematics LLP Nottingham City		14.05.18E
G-WIZR	Robinson R22 Beta II	2799	09.03.98
	Helimech Ltd Conington		12.08.19E
	Operated by MFH Helicopters		
G-WIZS	Mainair Pegasus Quik	8019	17.03.04
	L Hogan Balgrummo Steading, Bonnybank		19.06.19P
	Built by Mainair Sports Ltd		
G-WIZZ	Agusta-Bell 206B-2 JetRanger II	8540	07.12.77
	Rivermead Aviation Ltd Gloucestershire		19.06.19E
	Operated by Rise Helicopters		
G-WJAC	Cameron TR-70	10694	29.04.05
	J A & S J Bellaby Nottingham NG8		13.06.18E
G-WJCM	CASA 1-131E Jungmann Series 2000	2053	20.08.10
	G-BSFB, Spanish AF E3B-449		
	G W Lynch Old Buckenham		11.06.18P
G-WJET	HpH Glasflügel 304 S Shark	028-S	08.08.13
	(BGA 5748) P Thomson Feshiebridge *'ET'*		
	(IE 17.09.17)		
G-WJSG	P&M Quik GT450	8760	19.12.17
	W J Hardy Yatesbury		29.01.20P
	Noted 01.18 (IE 19.12.17)		
G-WKNS	Europa Aviation Europa XS	353	16.03.11
	A L Wickens (Bracknell)		
	Built by A L Wickens – project PFA 247-13200		
	(NF 26.02.15)		
G-WKTG	Diamond DA.42M-NG Twin Star	42.MN001	09.03.18
	PH-VIG, OE-VMN, OE-VDP		
	DEA Aviation Ltd Retford Gamston		25.08.19R
G-WKTH	Diamond DA.62	62.029	19.06.18
	OE-FFT DEA Aviation Ltd Retford Gamston		12.11.19E
G-WLAC	Piper PA-18-150 Super Cub	18-8899	02.06.98
	G-HAHA, G-BSWE, N9194P		
	White Waltham Airfield Ltd White Waltham		17.12.14E
G-WLDN	Robinson R44 Raven I	1507	16.09.05
	M R J Pearson Eddsfield, Octon Lodge Farm, Thwing		25.11.17E
G-WLGC	Piper PA-28-181 Archer III	2843484	16.04.07
	G-FLUX, N5339U E F Mangion Sandtoft		11.01.19E
G-WLKI	Lindstrand LBL 150A	1140	27.03.07
	C Wilkinson Aldbrough St John, Richmond		
	'adVentures Aloft'		07.04.14E
	(NF 22.01.18)		
G-WLKR	Embraer EMB-550 Legacy 500	55000091	20.12.18
	PR-LFD Air Charter Scotland Ltd London Stansted		19.12.19E

G-WLKS	Schleicher ASW 20L	20386	12.03.12
	G-IUMB, BGA 2691/EHD		
	S E Wilks Husbands Bosworth *'891'*		19.03.18E
G-WLLS	Rolladen-Schneider LS8-18	8038	06.11.07
	BGA 4189/HTL, D-3156		
	A & L M P Wells Bidford *'LS'*		22.12.18E
G-WLMS	Mainair Blade 912	1223-0999-7-W1016	23.09.99
	N J Cowdery (Sharnbrook, Bedford)		09.08.19P
G-WLRS	Supermarine 236 Walrus Mk.I	S2-5591	22.05.18
	G-RNLI, W2718 T W Harris Duxford		
	Noted 07.18 unmarked (NF 21.05.18)		
G-WLSN	Best Off Skyranger 912S(1)	UK/639	24.11.05
	A R Wilson Butterfield Farm, Swanwick		08.08.18P
	Built by A, A R & A R Wilson – project BMAA/HB/474		
G-WLTS	Bell 429	57191	06.10.14
	C-GZLQ Wiltshire Air Ambulance Charitable Trust		
	Outmarsh Farm, Semington		26.10.19E
	Operated by Wiltshire Air Ambulance as callsign		
	'Helimed 22'		
G-WLVE	Cameron Buddy-90	10913	17.10.06
	(EC-...), G-WLVE A E Austin & C J Freeman		
	Market Harborough & Wellingborough		22.12.18E
G-WMBL	P&M QuikR	8755	12.10.16
	WM Buchanan Ltd Oban		28.09.18P
G-WMRN	SOCATA TBM-900	1159	07.12.16
	Cheshire Flying Services Ltd t/a Ravenair		
	Liverpool John Lennon		05.01.19E
G-WMTM	Gulfstream American AA-5B Tiger	AA5B-1035	08.01.91
	N4517V R K Hyatt Newquay		06.08.19E
G-WMWM	Robinson R44 Raven	0767	27.04.00
	Cancelled 16.11.10 as destroyed		03.08.08
	Booker *Wreck stored 05.18*		
G-WNCH	Beech B200 Super King Air	BB-1259	15.10.08
	G-OMGI, N800MG, D-IDSM, N734P		
	Synergy Aircraft Leasing Ltd Fairoaks		19.07.18E
G-WNSC	Eurocopter AS.332L2 Super Puma II	2393	15.01.13
	VP-CHC, G-WNSC, VP-CHC, LN-OHC		
	Airbus Helicopters Aberdeen Int'l		30.01.14E
	(NF 25.02.17)		
G-WNSD	Sikorsky S-92A	920231	09.07.14
	N231Y Waypoint Asset Co 3 Ltd Aberdeen Int'l		10.08.18E
G-WNSE	Sikorsky S-92A	920190	17.05.13
	N190V CHC Scotia Ltd Aberdeen Int'l		29.05.18E
G-WNSF	Sikorsky S-92A	920046	14.12.12
	PH-EUI, G-WNSF, OY-HKA, N8052Z		
	CHC Scotia Ltd Aberdeen Int'l		07.07.18E
G-WNSG	Sikorsky S-92A	920058	14.12.12
	OY-HKB, N4502X CHC Scotia Ltd Aberdeen Int'l		12.11.18E
G-WNSI	Sikorsky S-92A	920024	07.09.12
	9M-AIH, C-GOHA, N8015U		
	CHC Scotia Ltd Aberdeen Int'l *'Big Irene'*		18.02.18E
G-WNSL	Sikorsky S-92A	920241	09.10.14
	N241Q CHC Scotia Ltd Aberdeen Int'l		26.10.18E
G-WNSM	Sikorsky S-92A	920237	23.12.14
	N237MW CHC Scotia Ltd Aberdeen Int'l		22.02.18E
G-WNSN	Eurocopter EC225 LP Super Puma	2688	10.12.13
	VH-WEQ, LN-OHU, (G-ECLP), 5N-BKH, F-WWOG		
	Lombard North Central PLC Rzeszow, Poland		19.05.16E
	Stored 12.18 (IE 14.06.16)		
G-WNSP	Eurocopter EC225 LP Super Puma	2707	30.08.13
	9M-AIT, LN-OHX		
	Lombard North Central PLC Fleetlands		05.12.16E
	Stored 04.17 (IE 24.03.17)		
G-WNST	Sikorsky S-92A	920216	17.06.16
	C-FBXY, (PR-BGU), N216Y		
	CHC Scotia Ltd Aberdeen Int'l *'Linda'*		01.06.18E
G-WNSU	Sikorsky S-92A	920229	17.06.16
	C-FEAE, N229V CHC Scotia Ltd Aberdeen Int'l		01.06.18E
G-WNSV	Sikorsky S-92A	920057	26.09.16
	LN-OQN, VH-LYJ, 9M-AIG, C-GOHC, N4502S		
	CHC Scotia Ltd Aberdeen Int'l *'Suzy Q'*		09.08.18E
G-WNSW	Sikorsky S-92A	920283	02.02.17
	N283QT CHC Scotia Ltd Aberdeen Int'l		
	'Captain Steve O'Collard'		28.02.18E
G-WNTR	Piper PA-28-161 Warrior II	28-7816281	13.01.06
	G-BFNJ, N9520N		
	D M Jarman tr Fleetlands Flying Group Solent		20.04.18E
	Operated by Fleetlands Flying Group;		
	carries 'NJ' on nose		
G-WOBR	Airbus MBB BK117 D-2 *(Eurocopter EC145 T2)*		
		20116	05.12.16
	D-HCBY Babcock Mission Critical Services		
	Onshore Ltd Welshpool		05.12.18E
	Operated by Wales Air Ambulance		
G-WOFM	Agusta A109E Power	11678	29.08.06
	G-NWRR Quinnasette Ltd (Douglas, Isle of Man)		07.08.18E
G-WOLF	Piper PA-28-140 Cherokee Cruiser	28-7425439	20.03.80
	OY-TOD K C Fitch tr G-WOLF Group Elstree		27.07.19E
G-WONE	Schempp-Hirth Ventus-2cT	55/179	11.09.07
	BGA 4795 J P Wright Lasham *'W1'*		28.04.18E
G-WOOD	Beech 95-B55A Baron	TC-1283	17.09.79
	SE-GRC, G-AYID, SE-EXK M S Choksey Tatenhill		15.06.18E
G-WOOF	Enstrom 480	5027	03.03.98
	Curvature Ltd & N Ltd Brookside Farm, Allostock		17.09.17E
G-WOOL	Colt 77A	2044	23.02.93
	D P MacGregor Storrington		05.04.19E
G-WOOO	CZAW Sportcruiser	700513	18.03.09
	J J Nicholson Liverpool John Lennon		19.04.18P
	Built by A Palmer & F Sayyah – project LAA 338-14840		
G-WORM	Thruster T600N 450	9109-T600N-039	05.10.99
	C H A Bott & C R A Scrope tr WORM Group		
	Whitehall Farm, Benington		05.03.18P
	Official type data 'T600N' upgraded to		
	'Thruster T.600N 450'; 'Sprint' fuselage fairing		
G-WOTW	Ultramagic M-77	77/334	12.04.10
	Window on the World Ltd London SW4 *'Window on the World'*		
			23.03.19E
G-WOWI	Van's RV-7	xxxx	02.07.10
	P J Wood Compton Abbas		04.06.19P
	Built by P J Wood – project PFA 323-14585		
G-WOWS	Cirrus SR22T	1712	22.05.18
	N318DG A M & R W Glaves Retford Gamston		
G-WPDA	Eurocopter EC135 P1	0109	12.01.12
	D-HIPT South Western Helicopters Ltd		
	t/a WPD Helicopter Unit Bristol		01.01.19E
	Operated by Western Power Distribution		
G-WPDB	Eurocopter EC135 P1	0112	08.12.11
	D-HAIT South Western Helicopters Ltd		
	t/a WPD Helicopter Unit Bristol		18.02.18E
	Operated by Western Power Distribution		
G-WPDC	Eurocopter EC135 P1	0090	27.06.12
	D-HKUG South Western Helicopters Ltd		
	t/a WPD Helicopter Unit Bristol		28.07.18E
	Operated by Western Power Distribution		
G-WPDD	Eurocopter EC135 P1	0071	05.09.12
	D-HSOS South Western Helicopters Ltd		
	t/a WPD Helicopter Unit Bristol		06.02.18E
	Operated by Western Power Distribution		
G-WPDE	Airbus EC135 P2+	1145	21.04.15
	South Western Helicopters Ltd		
	t/a WPD Helicopter Unit Bristol		21.04.19E
G-WPKR	Enstrom 280FX Shark	2012	12.04.17
	G-WPIE, G-RCAR, G-BXRD, PH-JVM, N213M		
	N Ker (Blaengwynlais, Caerphilly)		27.04.18E
G-WPNS	Britten-Norman BN-2T-4S Defender 4000 4011		29.02.16
	G-GMPB, G-BWPU, (9M-TPD), G-BWPU		
	Britten-Norman Ltd Solent		07.10.19E
G-WREN	Pitts S-2A	2229	08.01.81
	N947 W Ali Cranfield		23.07.11E
	Built by Aerotek Inc (NF 15.01.18)		
G-WRFM	Enstrom 280C-UK Shark	1202	21.04.89
	G-CTSI, G-BKIO, (G-BKHN), SE-HLB		
	A J Clark (Codnor, Derbyshire)		01.09.17E

G-WRIT Colt 77A 1328 15.09.88
G Pusey Balsall Common, Coventry
'Edge, Leyden & Ellis Solicitors' 22.07.11E
(NF 17.01.19)

G-WROL Airbus MBB BK117 D-2 (Eurocopter EC145 T2)
20115 13.02.17
G-OLWG, D-HCBS Babcock Mission Critical
Services Onshore Ltd Caernarfon 05.12.18E
Operated by Wales Air Ambulance

G-WSEX Westland Wessex HU.5 WA483 19.03.18
A2678, A2767, XT761 A D Whitehouse
Higher Purtington Showfield, Chard
(NF 19.03.18)

G-WSKY Enstrom 280C-UK-2 Shark 1037 25.07.83
G-BEEK B J Rutterford RAF Lakenheath 09.03.18E

G-WSMW Robinson R44 Raven 2068 18.05.10
G-SGPL M Wass (Durham) 11.05.18E

G-WSSX Comco Ikarus C42 FB100 0608-6837 31.10.06
J M Crane Compton Abbas 01.11.18P
Assembled Aerosport Ltd

G-WSTY Lindstrand LBL 77A 1461 07.01.14
C & C Westwood Clayton West, Huddersfield 06.05.18E

G-WTAV Robinson R44 Raven II 11449 29.09.06
T Levitan (Harlow) 11.11.14E
(NF 14.07.17)

G-WTFH Van's RV-6 25157 17.03.16
N M R Richards North Weald
Built by A Pelly, N M Richards & P Roy
– project PFA 181-13174 (NF 17.03.16)

G-WTSN Van's RV-8 xxxx 03.10.13
S R Watson Tatenhill 10.06.18P
Built by S R Watson – project LAA 303-14943

G-WTWO Aquila AT01 AT01-176 09.01.08
J P Wright Lasham 18.04.18E

G-WUFF Europa Aviation Europa 235 19.01.99
W H Bliss Loadman Farm, Hexham 'Kathy' 18.01.18P
Built by M A Barker – project PFA 247-12942;
tailwheel u/c

G-WUKA★ Airbus A320-232 8097 01.03.18
D-AVVL Wizz Air UK Ltd Luton 28.02.19E
To HA-LSB 14.03.19

G-WUKB Airbus A320-232 8151 08.03.18
D-AVVW Wizz Air UK Ltd Luton 07.03.19E

G-WUKC Airbus A321-231 8169 28.03.18
D-AZAR Wizz Air UK Ltd Luton 27.03.19E

G-WUKD Airbus A320-232 8311 07.06.18
D-AXAG Wizz Air UK Ltd Luton 06.06.19E

G-WUKE Airbus A320-232 8327 01.06.18
D-AXAP Wizz Air UK Ltd Luton 31.05.19E

G-WUKF Airbus A320-232 8210 26.03.18
D-AUBI Wizz Air UK Ltd Luton 25.03.19E

G-WUKG Airbus A321-231 8236 13.04.18
D-AVXT Wizz Air UK Ltd Luton 12.04.19E

G-WUKH Airbus A321-231 8600 13.11.18
D-AVXW Wizz Air UK Ltd Luton 12.11.19E

G-WUKI Airbus A321-231 8625 21.12.18
D-AVYJ Wizz Air UK Ltd Luton 20.12.19E

G-WUKL Airbus A321-231 8791 25.03.19
D-AVZJ Wizz Air UK Ltd Luton 24.03.20E

G-WULF WAR Focke-Wulf FW190 replica 204 24.02.78
B Hunter (Whaley Bridge) 18.07.17P
Built by SBV Aeroservices Ltd – project PFA 081-10328;
as '1' in Luftwaffe c/s (NF 12.05.17)

G-WVBF Lindstrand LBL 210A 312 06.12.95
Airxcite Ltd t/a Virgin Balloon Flights
(Stafford Park, Telford) 'Virgin'
(NF 15.09.14)

G-WVEN Extra EA.300/200 1046 14.10.14
R J Hunter Conington 19.12.18E

G-WVIP Beech 200 Super King Air BB-625 18.08.01
N869AM, N8SZ, N8SP, N18BH, N302EC, N6682U
Capital Air Ambulance Ltd Exeter Int'l 19.08.19E

G-WWAL Piper PA-28R-180 Cherokee Arrow 28R-30461 23.10.98
G-AZSH, N4612J
White Waltham Airfield Ltd White Waltham 11.05.18E

G-WWAY Piper PA-28-181 Archer II 28-8690031 30.03.04
D-ELCX, N165AV, N9643N
R A Witchell Andrewsfield 30.03.18E

G-WWLF Extra EA.300/L 020 20.09.11
N663JC, (N44DK), N663JC, D-ETZA
P Sapignoli Fano, Pesaro e Urbino, Italy 08.05.18E

(G-WWVV) Lange E1 Antares 18T 56T04
D-KAIB Reserved 2019 (BGA 5337/G-WWVV)

G-WWZZ CZAW Sportcruiser 700875 07.01.09
L Hogan Balgrummo Steading, Bonnybank 17.07.18P
Built by D M Hepworth & L Hogan
– project LAA 338-14877

G-WXYZ Zenair CH.750 75-10577 25.07.17
P M Porter Sleap
Built by P M Porter – project LAA 381-15436
(NF 24.07.17)

G-WYAT CFM Streak Shadow SA K 279 09.06.97
J L Wolstenholme Brook Farm, Pilling 22.12.16P
Built by M G Whyatt – project PFA 206-12993
(IE 05.07.17)

G-WYDE Schleicher ASW 22BL 22053 04.03.08
BGA 3388/FNF D M Byass tr 461 Syndicate
Wycombe Air Park '461' 08.07.18E

G-WYKD Air Création Tanarg 912S(2)/iXess 15 FLTxxx 04.01.08
M R Thorley (Sutton Coldfield) 30.08.18P
Built by D C Dewey – project BMAA/HB/559
(Flylight kit FLTxxx comprising trike s/n T07095
& wing s/n A07060-7185)

G-WYLD Cessna T210N Turbo Centurion II 21064341 03.10.17
G-EEWS, D-EBWS, N6339Y R M de Roeck Dundee 09.08.18E

G-WYMM Piper PA-15 Vagabond 15-227 14.06.16
G-AWOF, F-BETF
N G Busschau (Dittisham, Dartmouth) 27.03.13P

G-WYND Wittman W.8 Tailwind xxxx 02.08.99
R S Marriott (Whitton, Scunthorpe)
Built by R S Marriott – project PFA 031-12407;
on build 07.13 (NF 13.11.15)

G-WYNN Rand Robinson KR2 xxxx 28.08.85
Cancelled 14.07.04 by CAA
Congo Rapids Adventure Golf, Easton, Norfolk
Built by W Thomas – project PFA 129-11141
Displayed unmarked in zebra colours 10.16
Note: A second unregistered Rand Robinson KR2
is displayed at 'Congo Rapids Adventure Golf',
Ufford, Woodbridge, Suffolk

G-WYNT Cameron N-56 1038 03.04.84
P Richardson Raglan, Usk
'Gwyntoedd Dros Cymru' & 'Wings Over Wales' 07.06.18E

G-WYSZ Robin DR.400-100 Cadet 1829 02.10.08
G-FTIM Exavia Ltd Exeter Int'l 05.06.13E
Stored 09.15 (NF 19.09.16)

G-WYVN DG Flugzeugbau DG-1000T 10-63T5 10.02.06
BGA5179/KLH J W Sage tr Army Gliding Association
Trenchard Lines, Upavon '12' 22.06.18E
Operated by Wyvern Gliding Club

G-WZAP Embraer EMB-505 Phenom 300 50500438 29.12.17
Hagondale Ltd London Stansted 28.12.19E
Operated by Tiitan Airways

G-WZOL Tiger Cub RL5B Sherwood Ranger LWS "495" 20.01.99
G-MZOL D Lentell Sackville Lodge Farm, Riseley 10.11.10P
Built by G W F Webb – project PFA 237-12887 (NF 09.05.18)

G-WZOY Rans S-6-ESA Coyote II 0707.1821 29.11.07
M J Laundy Westonzoyland 27.04.18P
Built by S P Read – project PFA 204-14735

G-WZRD Eurocopter EC120B Colibri 1455 03.11.06
Conductia Enterprises Ltd
Athens Heliport, Afidnai, Greece 21.02.18E

G-XAAA – G-XZZZ

G-XAIM	Ultramagic H-31	31/11	01.06.10
	G Everett Sandway, Maidstone		03.06.11E
	(NF 06.03.18)		
G-XALT	Piper PA-38-112 Tomahawk	38-79A0801	09.10.06
	PH-ALT, OO-TLT, N9651N D R Clyde Swansea		01.03.18E
G-XALZ	Rans S-6-S-116 Super Six	0205.1638	01.07.09
	D G I Wheldon Morgansfield, Fishburn		16.10.18P
	Built by A F Stafford – project PFA 204A-14378		
G-XARA	Czech Sport PS-28 Cruiser	C0500	17.01.14
	C W D Ross (Liphook)		12.03.19R
G-XARV	ARV ARV-1 Super 2	010	08.11.95
	G-OPIG, G-BMSJ C M Rose Perth		06.06.18P
G-XASH	Schleicher ASH 31 Mi	31051	13.02.12
	R C Wilson Aboyne *'A31'*		17.04.18E
G-XAVB	Cessna 510 Citation Mustang	510-0283	04.02.10
	Gama Aviation (Beauport) Ltd Jersey		03.02.19E
G-XAVI	Piper PA-28-161 Warrior II	28-7916258	12.06.06
	G-SACZ, N2098N Freedom Aviation Ltd Cotswold		27.08.19E
G-XAVV	Schempp-Hirth Ventus-2cxa	125	10.05.12
	(BGA 5715), D-4609		
	S E Buckley & R G Corbin Aston Down *'VV'*		06.04.18E
G-XBAL	Best Off Skyranger Nynja 912S(1)	UK\N/BK092 ?	25.01.12
	N D Ewer & W G Gill Plaistows Farm, St Albans		21.11.18P
	Built by W G Gill – project BMAA/HB/620		
G-XBGA	Glaser-Dirks DG-500/22 Elan	5E71S12	13.02.08
	BGA 3955/HHJ N Kelly Bicester *'X97'*		12.06.18E
	Built by Elan Tovarna Sportnega Orodja N.Sol.O		
G-XBJT	Evektor EV-97 Eurostar	2002-1174	06.12.10
	G-WHOA, G-DATH C J & J A Aldous Popham		09.04.19P
	Built by D N E D'Ath – project PFA 315-13967		
G-XBLD	MBB Bölkow BÖ.105DB	S.381	14.06.12
	EI-BLD, D-HDLQ PLM Dollar Group Ltd		
	Wolverhampton Halfpenny Green		19.11.13E
	Stored 05.18 (NF 11.05.16)		
G-XBOX	Bell 206B-3 JetRanger III	3370	31.01.05
	G-OOHO, G-OCHC, G-KLEE, G-SIZL, G-BOSW, N2063T		
	Castle Air Ltd Trebrown, Liskeard		22.08.18E
G-XCCC	Extra EA.300/L	142	20.08.01
	P T Fellows (London SE9)		13.07.18E
G-XCID	SAAB 91D Safir	91-441	08.09.15
	OY-DBT (2), (OY-IRN), SE-IOC, OH-SFK,		
	Finnish AF SF-32 J T Hunter Oaksey Park		23.02.19E
G-XCIT	Alpi Pioneer 300	123	16.09.04
	A Thomas Shobdon		08.08.17P
	Built by A Thomas – project PFA 330-14296;		
	kit no conflicts with G-PION		
G-XCRI	Colomban MC-15 Cri-Cri	NVAV-130	07.12.17
	PH-CRI P A Harvie Mount Airey Farm, South Cave		
	Built by J R Van Haarlem (IE 17.01.19)		
G-XCRJ	Van's RV-9A	91502	08.01.10
	H Comber & R Jones tr Romeo Juliet Group		
	Bournemouth		10.04.18P
	Built by R Jones – project PFA 320-14333		
G-XCSP	Raytheon Hawker 800XP	258786	08.06.18
	N878TX, CS-DRR, N36986 XJC Ltd (Southampton)		
	Noted 06.18 at Robin Hood Doncaster Sheffield		
	(IE 29.06.18)		
G-XCUB	Piper PA-18-150 Super Cub	18-8109036	01.05.81
	N9348T White Waltham Airfield Ltd White Waltham		11.05.18E
G-XDEA	Diamond DA.42 Twin Star	42.AC012	04.09.12
	N785CM Tesla Aviation Ltd Coventry		28.09.19E
G-XDUO	Schempp-Hirth Duo Discus xT	162/519	08.03.07
	BGA 5247/KOF		
	P Jackson tr G-XDUO Group Bidford *'DUO'*		19.11.18E
G-XDWE	P&M Quik GT450	8242	15.02.07
	G J Prisk Perranporth		12.04.19P
G-XELL	Schleicher ASW 27-18E (ASG 29E)	29532	12.03.08
	BGA 5307 S R Ell Pocklington *'E11'*		12.04.18E
G-XENA	Piper PA-28-161 Cherokee Warrior II	28-7716158	29.06.98
	N3486Q P Brewer Goodwood		05.08.18E

G-XERK	Van's RV-7	xxxx	23.03.16
	C A Morris (Stratton Strawless, Norwich)		
	Built by C A Morris – project PFA 323-14147		
	(NF 22.03.16)		
G-XERO	CZAW Sportcruiser	08SC138	15.05.08
	M R Mosley Headon Farm, Retford		24.06.18P
	Built by M R Mosley – project PFA 338-14658		
	(Quick-build kit 4041)		
G-XFLY	Lambert Mission M212-100	xxxx	03.02.00
	Lambert Aircraft Engineering BVBA		
	Kortrijk-Wevelgem Int'l, Belgium		30.11.18P
	Built by Lambert Aircraft Engineering BVBA		
	– project PFA 306-13380		
G-XFOX	Aeropro EuroFOX 912(S)	41913	04.04.13
	G J Baxter & R F Lyon tr Fox Five Group		
	Swanborough Farm, Lewes		30.09.18P
	Built by G J Baxter & Partners		
	– project LAA 376-15200; tailwheel u/c		
G-XFTF	BRM Bristell NG5 Speed Wing	113	15.04.15
	R O'Donnell Eaglescott		30.10.19P
	Built by R O'Donnell – project LAA 385-15331;		
	tricycle u/c		
G-XFYF	Guimbal Cabri G2	1225	22.03.18
	R O'Donnell Eaglescott		
	(NF 22.03.18)		
G-XHOT	Cameron Z-105	10999	05.01.07
	S F Burden Noordwijk, Netherlands		25.04.16E
G-XIFR	Lambert Mission M108	108002	15.12.14
	Lambert Aircraft Engineering BVBA		
	Kortrijk-Wevelgem Int'l, Belgium		17.07.18P
	Built by Lambert Aircraft Engineering BVBA		
	– project LAA 370-14986		
G-XIII	Van's RV-7	xxxx	20.02.04
	D N Carnegie tr Icarus Flying Group RAF Henlow		12.04.19P
	Built by G Wright – project PFA 323-14165		
G-XILM	TL 3000 Sirius	17 SI 156	30.11.17
	Orbis Management Ltd Rufforth East		24.09.19P
	Built by L McWilliams – project LAA 386-15484		
G-XINE	Piper PA-28-161 Cherokee Warrior II	28-7716112	14.10.03
	G-BPAC, N2567Q		
	P Tee Standalone Farm, Meppershall		18.06.18E
G-XION	Dassault Falcon 7X	409	21.03.17
	F-WWQI Execujet (UK) Ltd Cambridge		20.03.19E
G-XIOO	Raj Hamsa X'Air 133(1)	681	27.01.03
	G M R Keenan (Lhambryde, Elgin)		22.06.15P
	Built by R Paton & A Start – project BMAA/HB/247		
	(NF 17.09.15)		
G-XIVA	Van's RV-14A	140372	13.03.18
	R Jones Bournemouth		
	Built by R Jones – project LAA 393-15468 (NF 13.03.18)		
G-XIXI	Evektor EV-97 teamEurostar UK	2007-2938	12.07.07
	J A C Cockfield RNAS Culdrose		14.05.18P
	Assembled Cosmik Aviation Ltd		
G-XIXT	Sportine Aviacija LAK-19T	035	12.02.18
	(BGA 5946), LY-BDU		
	W M Kay & P R Thomas Dunstable Downs *'19t'*		25.04.20E
G-XIXX	Glaser-Dirks DG-300 Elan	3E9	01.09.08
	BGA 3124/FBF, BGA 2952/EUA		
	S D Black Milfield *'19X'*		07.01.19E
	Built by Elan Tovarna Sportnega Orodja N.Sol.O		
G-XJCI	Cessna 550 Citation Bravo	550-0874	24.01.18
	N237MB, D-CHMC, LX-EJH, D-CHAN, N5194B		
	XJC Ltd Southampton		
	(IE 24.01.18)		
G-XJCJ	Cessna 550 Citation Bravo	550-1129	23.11.16
	M-BRVO, N60LW, N52059 XJC Ltd Southampton		21.12.18E
G-XJET	Learjet Learjet 45	45-311	04.07.12
	G-IZAP, G-OLDK, N40078 Patriot Aviation Ltd Exeter Int'l		
	01.10.19E		
G-XJON	Schempp-Hirth Ventus-2b	114	17.09.07
	BGA 4895, (BGA 4885) J C Bastin Lasham *'E4'*		28.04.18E
G-XKKA	Diamond HK36TTC Super Dimona	36.677	16.02.07
	S5-KKA S M Godleman tr G-XKKA Group Challock		17.03.18E

G-XKRV	Best Off Skyranger Nynja LS 912S(1)		
		UK\N/BK0152-VLA	17.04.14
	A V Francis Little Gransden		
	Built by A V Francis – project BMAA/HB/651		
	(NF 27.04.18)		
G-XLAM	Best Off Skyranger 912S(1)	SKR0504609	19.12.05
	D A Archer tr XLAM Skyranger Syndicate Sywell		25.09.18P
	Built by D M Broom – project BMAA/HB/460		
G-XLEA	Airbus A380-841	095	03.07.13
	F-WWSK British Airways PLC London Heathrow		01.07.18E
G-XLEB	Airbus A380-841	121	19.09.13
	F-WWAY British Airways PLC London Heathrow		18.09.18E
G-XLEC	Airbus A380-841	124	17.10.13
	F-WWSC British Airways PLC London Heathrow		16.10.18E
G-XLED	Airbus A380-841	144	16.01.14
	F-WWAK British Airways PLC London Heathrow		15.01.19E
G-XLEE	Airbus A380-841	148	06.03.14
	F-WWAS British Airways PLC London Heathrow		05.03.18E
G-XLEF	Airbus A380-841	151	14.05.14
	F-WWSI British Airways PLC London Heathrow		05.04.18E
G-XLEG	Airbus A380-841	161	11.09.14
	F-WWSK British Airways PLC London Heathrow		10.09.18E
G-XLEH	Airbus A380-841	163	16.10.14
	F-WWSM British Airways PLC London Heathrow		15.10.18E
G-XLEI	Airbus A380-841	173	13.02.15
	F-WWSB British Airways PLC London Heathrow		12.02.18E
G-XLEJ	Airbus A380-841	192	10.11.15
	F-WWAE British Airways PLC London Heathrow		09.11.18E
G-XLEK	Airbus A380-841	194	03.02.16
	F-WWSG British Airways PLC London Heathrow		02.02.19E
G-XLEL	Airbus A380-841	215	22.06.16
	F-WWAL British Airways PLC London Heathrow		21.06.18E
G-XLII	Schleicher ASW 27-18E (ASG 29E)	29554	10.07.08
	(BGA 5325) P M Wells Baileys Farm, Long Crendon		02.03.11E
	(NF 26.04.17)		
G-XLLL	Aérospatiale AS.355F1 Ecureuil 2	5033	14.02.06
	G-PASF, G-SCHU, N915EG, N5777H		
	MW Helicopters Ltd Stapleford		10.06.18E
G-XLNT	Zenair CH.601XL Zodiac	6-9468	27.01.04
	I A R Sim tr Zenair G-XLNT Group		
	Main Hall Farm, Conington		02.10.18P
	Built by P H & S J Ronfell – project PFA 162B-14182;		
	tricycle u/c		
G-XLTG	Cessna 182S Skylane	18280234	17.07.98
	N9571L S N Chater tr The G-XLTG Flying Group		
	Sherburn-in-Elmet		10.01.19E
G-XLXL	Robin DR.400-160 Chevalier	813	03.01.92
	G-BAUD L R Marchant Rochester		13.09.18E
G-XMGO	Aeromot AMT-200S Super Ximango	200.127	18.04.01
	C & R P Beck Rufforth		07.07.19E
G-XONE	Bombardier CL-600-2B16 Challenger 604	5426	10.06.08
	N51VR, JY-ONE, N604JA, C-GLYC		
	Gama Aviation (UK) Ltd Farnborough		10.06.18E
G-XPBI	Letov LK-2M Sluka	KA14	04.12.98
	R M C Hunter Redlands		
	Built by P Bishop – project PFA 263-13341		
	(SSDR microlight since 08.16) (NF 17.06.16)		
G-XPDA	Cameron Z-120	11038	06.08.07
	M Cowling Perth 'Expedia'		30.12.17E
	(NF 18.12.17)		
G-XPII	Cessna R172K Hawk XP	R1723071	06.11.06
	G-DIVA, N758FX		
	London Denham Aviation Ltd Denham		29.10.18E
	Badly damaged Nottingham City, 04.11.17		
G-XPTV	Embraer EMB-135BJ Legacy 600	14501051	23.10.17
	A6-FLL, PT-SEG Arena Aviation Ltd Biggin Hill		
	(IE 01.11.17)		
G-XPWW	Cameron TR-77	11063	08.04.08
	Chalmers Ballong Corps Göteborg, Sweden		
	'Blaklader Workwear'		30.07.17E

G-XPXP	Aero Designs Pulsar XP	218	30.03.92
	B J Edwards Belle Vue Farm, Yarnscombe		24.07.18P
	Built by B J Edwards – project PFA 202-11958;		
	tailwheel u/c		
G-XRAF	Raj Hamsa X'Air 582(5)	513	07.04.00
	EI-EZZ, G-XRAF		
	S A Taylor Ranston Farm, Iwerne Courtney		31.08.17P
	Built by M E Howard & S Stockill		
	– project BMAA/HB/132 (NF 07.09.18)		
G-XRAY	Rand Robinson KR-2	xxxx	30.04.87
	R S Smith (Pitcaple, Inverurie)		
	Built by R S Smith – project PFA 129-11227		
	(NF 04.05.18)		
G-XRED	Pitts S-1C	338H	28.11.05
	G-SWUN, G-BSXH, N14RM J E Rands Wickenby		27.09.18P
	Built by R Merrick		
G-XRLD	Cameron A-250	4820	25.04.00
	Aeolus Aviation GmbH Hamburg, Germany		02.09.16E
G-XRVB	Van's RV-8	82057	22.09.08
	R E Kelly Henstridge		21.08.18P
	Built by P G Winters – project PFA 303-14190		
G-XRVX	Van's RV-10	xxxx	24.11.06
	N K Lamping Sleap		09.12.18P
	Built by N K Lamping – project PFA 339-14592		
G-XRXR	Raj Hamsa X'Air 582(5)	431	13.09.99
	J E Merriman (Etsome Hill, Somerton)		05.07.18P
	Built by I S Walsh – project BMAA/HB/102		
G-XSAM	Van's RV-9A	xxxx	18.09.02
	Parachuting Aircraft Ltd Old Sarum		04.01.19P
	Built by D G Lucas – project PFA 320-13797		
G-XSDJ	Europa Aviation Europa XS	402	03.02.99
	D N Joyce Gloucestershire		20.08.16P
	Built by D N Joyce – project PFA 247-13378;		
	tailwheel u/c (IE 07.12.18)		
G-XSEA	Van's RV-8	82120	15.08.05
	H M Darlington Bury Farm, High Easter		16.11.17P
	Built by N I Hart – project PFA 303-14228		
G-XSEL	Silence SA.180 Twister	1-3	03.10.07
	Skyview Systems Ltd Waits Farm, Belchamp Walter		02.10.15P
	Built by N I G Hart – project PFA 329-14594		
	(IE 05.06.17)		
G-XSMC	Raytheon Hawker 800XP	258779	08.06.18
	N779TX, CS-DRP, N37179		
	XJC Ltd Liverpool John Lennon		15.08.19E
G-XSRF	Europa Aviation Europa NG	626	29.09.11
	R L W Frank Fairoaks		26.11.19P
	Built by R L W Frank – project LAA 247-15008		
G-XSTV	Cessna 560XL Citation XLS	560-5788	02.09.14
	D-CLIC, D-CWWW, N5259Y		
	Arena Aviation Ltd Biggin Hill		22.06.18E
G-XTAZ	Van's RV-7	73435	26.04.17
	N9823W D Robbins tr G-XTAZ Group Goodwood		28.06.19P
	Built by B Delamater		
G-XTEE	AirBorne XT912-B/Streak III-B	XT912-026	25.08.04
	T2-2252 G J Webster tr Shropshire Bush Pilots		
	Shifnal		15.04.18P
	Wing s/n S3B-051		
G-XTNI	AirBorne XT912-B/Streak III-B	XT912-067	10.05.05
	A J Parry (Loughrea, Co Galway, RoI)		09.05.10P
	Wing s/n ST3-043 (NF 11.01.16)		
G-XTRA	Extra EA.230	12A	21.01.87
	SE-XVB, G-XTRA, D-EDLF C Butler Netherthorpe		17.06.18P
G-XTUN	Westland-Bell 47G-3B-1	WA382	11.05.99
	G-BGZK, XT223		
	P A Rogers Pen y Bryn Farm, Betws yn Rhos		13.06.18E
	As 'XT223' in AAC c/s		
G-XVAT	Schleicher ASW 27	27221	14.11.18
	(BGA 5983), LN-GCD B Pridgeon Kirton in Lindsey		
	(NF 14.11.18)		
G-XVAX	Tecnam P2006T	076	04.04.11
	M A Baldwin Old Quarry Farm, Canterbury		26.07.19E
G-XVII	Schleicher ASW 17	17012	21.05.13
	G-DCTE, BGA 1788/CTE		
	C A & S C Noujaim Nympsfield '40'		31.05.18E

G-XVIP	Beech 200 Super King Air	BB-588	12.04.16
	G-OCEG, N578BM, N132GA, XA-RQQ, N200RJ,		
	N200AJ, N200RJ, N200LJ		
	Patriot Aviation Ltd Exeter Int'l		09.06.19E
G-XVOM	Van's RV-6	24067	06.04.01
	A Baker-Munton Enstone		11.09.18P
	Built by A Baker-Munton – project PFA 181A-12894		
(G-XWBA)	Airbus A350-1041	342	
	British Airways PLC Reserved, due xx.19		
(G-XWBB)	Airbus A350-1041		
	British Airways PLC Reserved, due xx.19		
(G-XWBC)	Airbus A350-1041		
	British Airways PLC Reserved, due xx.19		
G-XWEB	Best Off Skyranger 912(2)	SKR0411539	13.04.05
	M Chambers & A P Dalgetty Crosland Moor		06.04.18P
	Built by T J Hector & K B Woods		
	– project BMAA/HB/443		
G-XWON	Rolladen-Schneider LS8-18	8305	07.01.08
	BGA 4783/JUC P Mather & T W Williams		
	tr G-XWON Syndicate Challock 'X'		19.04.18E
G-XXBH	Agusta-Bell 206B-3 JetRanger III	8596	07.05.08
	G-BYBA, G-BHXV, G-OWJM, G-BHXV		
	Temchu Ltd (Cookhill, Alcester)		14.12.18E
G-XXEB	Sikorsky S-76C++	760753	28.09.09
	N753V M Stevens, Keeper of The Privy Purse		
	RAF Odiham		27.09.19E
	Built by Keystone Helicopter Corporation;		
	operated by The Queen's Helicopter Flight		
G-XXEC	Agusta A109S Grand	22104	16.05.14
	N473SH, PR-YAA		
	M Stevens, Keeper of The Privy Purse RAF Odiham		01.06.19E
	Operated by The Queen's Helicopter Flight		
G-XXHP	Extra EA.300/L	203	28.01.16
	G-BZFR R A C Tyrer Wycombe Air Park		09.10.18E
G-XXIV	Agusta-Bell 206B-3 JetRanger III	8717	27.04.89
	Adventure 001 Ltd (Beaconsfield)		27.08.18E
G-XXIX	Schleicher ASW 27-18E (*ASG 29E*)	29514	28.04.08
	BGA 5319, D-KPRA		
	A H & P R Pentecost Lasham '630'		07.05.18E
G-XXRS	Bombardier BD-700-1A10 Global Express	9169	24.01.06
	C-FCSR TAG Aviation (UK) Ltd Farnborough		14.06.19E
G-XXRR	Van's RV-9	90645	09.01.09
	N2667T D R Gilbert & D Slabbert Brighton City		12.11.18P
	Built by B Wilson		
G-XXSF	Bell 505 Jet Ranger X	65198	04.03.19
	C-FZGX Seafresh Group (Holdings) Ltd (Redditch)		
	(IE 04.03.19)		
G-XXTB	SOCATA TB-20 Trinidad	1821	20.04.11
	G-KPTT, F-GRBI N Schaefer		
	Mainz-Finthen, Rheinland-Pfalz, Germany		26.09.18E
G-XXTR	Extra EA.300/L	126	13.08.02
	G-ECCC, D-EDGE P J Randell tr		
	The Shoreham Extra Group Brighton City		08.03.18E
G-XXVB	Schempp-Hirth Ventus b	32	28.11.07
	BGA 2743/EKH R Johnson Parham Park '714'		16.04.18E
G-XYJY	Best Off Skyranger Swift 912(1)	UK/370	20.10.03
	A V Francis Little Gransden		21.06.18P
	Built by A V Francis – project BMAA/HB/309		
G-XYZT	Aeromot AMT-200S Super Ximango	200.176	19.06.08
	(PR-LFC) Betav BV (Leiden, Netherlands)		17.01.18E
G-XZXZ	Robinson R44 Raven II	12567	28.01.09
	Ashley Martin Ltd City of Derry		06.01.17E

G-YAAA – G-YZZZ

G-YAAC	Airbus MBB BK117 D-2 (*Eurocopter EC145 T2*)		
		20084	26.05.16
	D-HADO Yorkshire Air Ambulance Ltd		
	Nostell Priory, Wakefield		01.05.18E
	Operated by Yorkshire Air Ambulance as callsign		
	'Helimed 98'		

G-YAAK	Yakovlev Yak-50	812003	23.03.05
	G-BWJT, RA-01385, DOSAAF 50		
	D J Hopkinson Henstridge		10.01.19P
	As '20' in Soviet AF c/s		
G-YACC	Yakovlev Yak-18T	14-35	30.08.18
	HA-YAC, RA-44532		
	M J Babbage (Rushlake Green, Heathfield)		
G-YADA	Comco Ikarus C42 FB100	0707-6901	29.06.07
	A Rowell tr Ikarus Flying Syndicate		
	Carlisle Lake District		19.09.18P
	Assembled Aerosport Ltd		
G-YAKC	IAV Bacau Yakovlev Yak-52	867212	25.06.02
	LY-AKC, DOSAAF 153 (yellow)?		
	Airborne Services Ltd Henstridge		26.02.18P
	As Soviet AF '86'		
G-YAKE	IAV Bacau Yakovlev Yak-52	877610	04.05.12
	G-BVVA, LY-ANN, DOSAAF 52		
	D J Hopkinson Henstridge		19.07.19P
	As '10' (red) in Soviet AF c/s		
G-YAKF	Aerostar Yakovlev Yak-52	9111205	25.10.07
	ZU-IAK, RA-02090, DOSAAF 10		
	P H Collin Shipdham		09.06.19P
G-YAKG	Yakovlev Yak-18T	22202034023	22.08.12
	HA-YAP, RA-44545, LY-AIH, ES-FYE		
	M P Blokland Oaksey Park		24.06.19R
G-YAKH	IAV Bacau Yakovlev Yak-52	899915	24.12.02
	RA-01948, LY-AFV, DOSAAF 102 (yellow)		
	Plus 7 Minus 5 Ltd White Waltham		27.04.18P
	As '33' (white) in Soviet AF c/s		
G-YAKI	IAV Bacau Yakovlev Yak-52	866904	20.09.94
	LY-ANM, DOSAAF 100 Yak One Ltd Popham		31.03.18P
	As '100' (blue): carries Soviet red star on tail		
G-YAKJ	Yakovlev Yak-18T	01-33	04.06.13
	HA-YAJ, LY-APP N Collett tr Teshka Aviation		
	Syndicate White Waltham		23.02.18R
G-YAKM	Yakovlev Yak-50	842710	06.02.04
	RA-44461, Ukraine AF 28 (blue)		
	Airborne Services Ltd Henstridge		09.11.18P
	As '61' (red) in Soviet AF c/s		
G-YAKN	IAV Bacau Yakovlev Yak-52	855905	06.02.04
	RA-44466, DOSAAF 105 (blue)		
	Airborne Services Ltd Henstridge		31.05.18P
	As '66' (red) in Soviet AF c/s		
G-YAKU	Yakovlev Yak-50	822305	06.11.03
	RA-44549, G-BXNO, LY-ASD, DOSAAF 82		
	D J Hopkinson Henstridge		07.09.18P
	As '49' (red) in Soviet AF c/s		
G-YAKX	Aerostar Yakovlev Yak-52	9111307	13.03.96
	RA-44473, G-YAKX, RA-9111307, DOSAAF 27		
	The X-Fliers Ltd Popham		22.03.19P
	As '27' (red) in Soviet AF camouflage & yellow c/s		
G-YAKY	IAV Bacau Yakovlev Yak-52	844109	26.02.96
	LY-AKX, DOSAAF 24 (red)		
	W T Marriott (East Barkwith, Market Rasen)		07.03.02P
	(NF 04.02.16)		
G-YAKZ	Yakovlev Yak-50	853206	07.11.03
	RA-44533 Airborne Services Ltd Henstridge		10.01.19P
	As '33' in Soviet AF c/s		
G-YANK	Piper PA-28-181 Archer II	28-8090163	19.03.93
	N81314 M R Shelton tr G-YANK Flying Group		
	Tatenhill		05.07.18E
G-YARD	Robinson R44 Raven II	13481	15.12.17
	SP-AMZ Caffco Ltd Elstree		27.05.18E
G-YARR	Mainair Rapier	1255-0700-7-W1049	14.08.00
	D Yarr St Michaels		10.10.11P
	(NF 18.10.16)		
G-YARV	ARV ARV-1 Super 2	K004	15.10.01
	G-BMDO A M Oliver Lydeway Field, Etchilhampton		14.01.19P
	Built by Hornet Aviation Ltd – project PFA 152-11127		
G-YAWW	Piper PA-28RT-201T Turbo Arrow IV	28R-8031024	15.11.90
	N2929Y Barton Aviation Ltd Liverpool John Lennon		10.07.18E
G-YBAA	Reims FR172J Rocket	FR17200579	15.11.84
	5Y-BAA A Evans tr G-YBAA Flying Group Bourn		08.05.16E

G-YCMI	Sonex Sonex	1555	01.12.14
	T R D H Mobbs Seething *'You Cawn't Miss It'*		
	Built by T R D H Mobbs – project LAA 337-15157		
	(IE 01.03.18)		
G-YCUB	Piper PA-18-150 Super Cub	1809077	23.08.96
	N4993X, N4157T F W Rogers Bealbury, St Mellion		13.11.17E
	(IE 08.12.17)		
G-YDEA	Diamond DA.42 Twin Star	42.151	12.12.12
	SP-SII, D-GSSS DEA Aviation Ltd Retford Gamston		16.07.19E
G-YEDC	Cessna 525B CitationJet CJ3	525B0162	31.01.13
	M-YEDC, N503LC		
	Air Charter Scotland Ltd Biggin Hill		06.02.18E
G-YEHA	Schleicher ASW 27	27136	09.04.08
	BGA 4819/JVQ B L Cooper Lasham *'68'*		05.07.18E
G-YELL	Murphy Rebel	229R	01.05.95
	I N Scott (Bristol)		
	Built by A D Keen – project PFA 232-12381		
	(NF 23.10.14)		
G-YELO	AutoGyro MT-03	08 044	22.08.08
	Cancelled 14.02.13 by CAA		10.09.11
	Sywell *Assembled Rotorsport (UK) as*		
	c/n RSUK/MT-03/050; stored 09.18		
G-YELP	TLAC Sherwood Ranger ST	044	10.02.12
	C Blount Bourne Park, Hurstbourne Tarrant		07.11.18P
	Built by C Blount – project LAA 237B-15135		
G-YEOM	Piper PA-31-350 Chieftain	31-8352022	03.01.89
	N41108 Strata Aviation Services Ltd Elstree		05.11.19E
G-YETI	Europa Aviation Europa	121	01.12.15
	G-CILF C G Sutton Wellesbourne Mountford		06.08.18P
	Built by G Cole & C G Sutton		
	– project PFA 247-12746; tailwheel u/c		
G-YEWS	RotorWay Exec	3850	22.06.89
	P Mason & R Turrell (Wickford)		17.06.93P
	Built by D G Pollard – c/n DGP-1 (NF 01.04.14)		
G-YFOX	Dassault Falcon 2000EX	067	25.08.15
	OH-FOX, F-WWGA		
	London Executive Aviation Ltd London Stansted		18.10.18E
G-YIPI	Reims/Cessna FR172K Hawk XP	FR17200616	09.01.03
	OY-IPI, D-EIPI		
	J Francis & M T Hodgson St Mary's, Isles of Scilly		26.04.18E
G-YIRO	Campbell Cricket Mk.4	066	23.06.10
	G-KGED R Boese Melrose Farm, Melbourne		20.06.14P
	Built by K G Edwards – project PFA G/03-1337		
	(NF 29.04.16)		
G-YJET	Montgomerie-Bensen B.8MR	xxxx	25.09.96
	G-BMUH P D Davis-Ratcliffe Manchester Barton		07.05.07P
	Built by J M Montgomerie – project PFA G/01-1072		
	(NF 30.09.14)		
G-YKSO	Yakovlev Yak-50	791506	08.04.02
	LY-APT A M Holman-West		
	Alscot Park, Stratford-upon-Avon		14.09.18P
	As '23' in Soviet AF c/s		
G-YKSS	Yakovlev Yak-55	901103	01.07.03
	RA-44525, DOSAAF 96 (blue)		
	T Ollivier (Ranchicourt, France)		22.08.18W
G-YMFC	Waco YMF	F5033	06.04.04
	N90B S J Brenchley Stoke Golding		22.11.18E
	Built by Classic Aircraft Corporation 1990		
G-YMMA	Boeing 777-236ER	30302	07.01.00
	N5017Q British Airways PLC London Heathrow		06.01.20E
	Line No: 242		
G-YMMB	Boeing 777-236ER	30303	18.01.00
	British Airways PLC London Heathrow		17.01.20E
	Line No: 265		
G-YMMC	Boeing 777-236ER	30304	04.02.00
	British Airways PLC London Heathrow		01.11.19E
	Line No: 268		
G-YMMD	Boeing 777-236ER	30305	19.02.00
	British Airways PLC London Heathrow		17.02.19E
	Line No: 269		
G-YMME	Boeing 777-236ER	30306	16.04.00
	British Airways PLC London Heathrow		14.04.19E
	Line No: 275		

G-YMMF	Boeing 777-236ER	30307	17.05.00
	British Airways PLC London Heathrow		16.05.19E
	Line No: 281		
G-YMMG	Boeing 777-236ER	30308	28.09.00
	British Airways PLC London Heathrow		28.07.19E
	Line No: 301		
G-YMMH	Boeing 777-236ER	30309	14.10.00
	British Airways PLC London Heathrow		13.10.19E
	Line No: 303		
G-YMMI	Boeing 777-236ER	30310	02.11.00
	British Airways PLC London Heathrow		01.11.19E
	Line No: 308		
G-YMMJ	Boeing 777-236ER	30311	08.12.00
	British Airways PLC London Heathrow		07.12.19E
	Line No: 311		
G-YMMK	Boeing 777-236ER	30312	08.12.00
	British Airways PLC London Heathrow		02.10.19E
	Line No: 312		
G-YMML	Boeing 777-236ER	30313	10.04.01
	British Airways PLC London Heathrow		13.04.19E
	Line No: 334		
G-YMMN	Boeing 777-236ER	30316	15.06.01
	British Airways PLC London Heathrow		14.06.19E
	Line No: 346		
G-YMMO	Boeing 777-236ER	30317	17.09.01
	British Airways PLC London Heathrow		23.09.19E
	Line No: 361		
G-YMMP	Boeing 777-236ER	30315	30.10.01
	British Airways PLC London Heathrow		29.10.19E
	Line No: 369		
G-YMMR	Boeing 777-236ER	36516	23.03.09
	N5014K British Airways PLC London Heathrow		22.03.19E
	Line No: 771		
G-YMMS	Boeing 777-236ER	36517	29.05.09
	British Airways PLC London Heathrow		18.04.19E
	Line No: 784		
G-YMMT	Boeing 777-236ER	36518	25.06.09
	British Airways PLC London Heathrow		28.05.19E
	Line No: 791		
G-YMMU	Boeing 777-236ER	36519	31.07.09
	British Airways PLC London Heathrow		30.07.19E
	Line No: 796		
G-YNOT	Druine D.62B Condor	RAE/649	10.11.83
	G-AYFH T Littlefair (Pennington, Lymington)		04.09.03P
	Built by Rollason Aircraft and Engines Ltd (NF 04.04.18)		
G-YNYS	Cessna 172S Skyhawk SP	172S8725	23.11.05
	N835SP T V Hughes RAF Mona		16.09.18E
G-YOAA	Airbus MBB BK117 D-2 *(Eurocopter EC145 T2)*		
		20086	22.06.16
	D-HADQ Yorkshire Air Ambulance Ltd		
	RAF Topcliffe		04.07.18E
	Operated by Yorkshire Air Ambulance		
G-YOBI	Schleicher ASH 25	25088	04.04.08
	BGA 3606/FXL		
	J Kangurs Husbands Bosworth *'108'*		18.04.18E
G-YODA	Schempp-Hirth Ventus-2cT	82/249	06.11.07
	BGA 4943/KAT		
	J W M Gijrath (Sint-Truiden, Belgium) *'520'*		13.04.19E
G-YOGI	Robin DR.400-140B Major 80	1090	01.10.86
	G-BDME M M Pepper tr G-YOGI Flying Group		
	Spanhoe		12.12.18E
G-YOHO	Glasflugel H201B Standard Libelle	597	27.11.07
	BGA 3750/GDM, D-6666		
	Cancelled 03.06.09 as PWFU		23.01.08
	Rufforth *Stored 04.18*		
G-YOLK	P&M Quik GT450	8398	14.07.08
	G J Wright (Dunnington, York)		18.09.18P
G-YOLO	Aeroprakt A-22L Foxbat	A22L-435	20.09.13
	J W Mann Enstone		29.03.18P
	Built by J W Mann – project LAA 317C-15206;		
	badged 'Foxbat Super Sport'		
G-YORK	Reims/Cessna F172M	F17201354	14.12.78
	PH-LUY, F-WLIT		
	H A E Waetjen tr EIMH-Flying Group Ballyboy, Rol		01.05.18E

G-YOTS	IAV Bacau Yakovlev Yak-52	9010308	04.05.03
	LY-AOW, Ukraine AF 105, DOSAAF 05 (yellow)		
	J Windover tr G-YOTS Group　North Weald		11.07.19P
G-YOYO	Pitts S-1E	xxxx	22.05.96
	G-OTSW, G-BLHE　P M Jarvis　Andrewsfield		24.08.18P
	Built by W R Penaluna – project PFA 009-10885		
G-YPDN	AutoGyro MT-03	08 036	18.06.08
	T M Jones　Rufforth East		23.08.18P
	Assembled Rotorsport UK as c/n RSUK/MT-03/045		
G-YPSY	Andreasson BA-4B	xxxx	07.06.78
	T P Nettleton　Full Sutton　'65'		06.04.19P
	Built by H P Burrill – project PFA 038-10352		
G-YRAF	Rotary Air Force RAF 2000 GTX-SE	H2-96-7-269	01.06.01
	J R Cooper　Rhigos		22.05.08P
	Built by J R Cooper & C V King		
	– project PFA G/13-1289 (NF 21.11.14)		
G-YRAX	Magni M24C Orion	24116194	19.01.11
	R D Armishaw　Northrepps		25.04.19P
G-YRIL	Luscombe 8E Silvaire Deluxe	5945	03.02.92
	N1318B, NC1318B　I de Groot　Insch		22.09.12P
	Carries '1318B' on tail; stored 07.18 (IE 07.08.15)		
G-YROA	AutoGyro MTOsport	10 033S	12.04.10
	S Smith　Tibenham		05.05.18P
	Assembled Rotorsport UK as c/n RSUK/MTOS/025		
G-YROC	AutoGyro MT-03	xxxx	14.05.08
	C V Catherall　Chiltern Park, Wallingford		19.07.18P
	Assembled Rotorsport UK as c/n RSUK/MT-03/044		
G-YROF	Magni M22 Voyager	22-13-8184	01.09.17
	Clocktower Fund Management Ltd　(Cobham)		
	(NF 01.09.17)		
G-YROG	Magni M24C Orion	24159384	30.11.15
	A D & A J Mann　Fairoaks		27.01.18P
G-YROH	AutoGyro MTOsport	xxxx	24.07.09
	M Winship　Carlisle Lake District		19.04.18P
	Assembled Rotorsport UK as c/n RSUK/MTOS/012		
G-YROI	Air Command 532 Elite	0002	03.09.87
	N532CG　W B Lumb　(Manchester M40)		
	Built by Air Command Manufacturing Inc (NF 11.06.18)		
G-YROK	Magni M16C Tandem Trainer	16126904	08.02.12
	K J Yeadon　Rufforth East		28.03.19P
G-YROL	AutoGyro Cavalon	V00151	21.03.14
	C G Gilbert　(Bath)		
	Assembled Rotorsport UK as c/n RSUK/CVLN/009		
	(IE 20.07.18)		
G-YROM	AutoGyro MT-03	xxxx	21.09.07
	A Wallace　Slieve Croob, Castlewellan		19.04.16P
	Assembled Rotorsport UK as c/n RSUK/MT-03/019		
G-YRON	Magni M16C Tandem Trainer	16116624	18.10.11
	H E Simons　Fairoaks		01.11.18P
G-YROO	Rotary Air Force RAF 2000 GTX-SE	H2-01-12-520	27.11.01
	L Goodison　Melrose Farm, Melbourne		16.07.18P
	Built by C S Oakes & K D Rhodes		
	– project PFA G/13-1341		
G-YROP	Magni M16C Tandem Trainer	16095344	17.07.09
	Clocktower Fund Management Ltd　(Cobham)		06.08.19P
G-YROR	Magni M24C Orion	24106034	25.10.10
	R M Stanley　(Tewin, Welwyn)		15.05.18P
G-YROT	AutoGyro MTOsport 2017	xxxx	18.04.18
	R Wright　Oxenhope		
	Assembled Rotorsport UK as c/n RSUK/MTO2/004		
	(IE 18.04.18)		
G-YROU	Magni M24C Orion	24171064	04.01.18
	Fairoaks Gyros Ltd　Fairoaks		21.01.19P
G-YROV	AutoGyro MT-03	xxxx	20.08.15
	G-UMAS　PKPS Aviation Ltd　Blackpool		11.10.18P
	Assembled Rotorsport UK as c/n RSUK/MT-03/024;		
	P/I 'G-UMAS' on manufacturer's plate		
G-YROX	AutoGyro MT-03	xxxx	21.08.06
	G-94-2　C A M Holmes-Surplus & N F Surplus		
	t/a Surplus Art　Sandy Bay, Larne		10.01.18P
	Assembled Rotorsport UK as c/n RSUK/MT-03/005		
G-YROY	Montgomerie-Bensen B.8MR	xxxx	12.09.89
	S S Wilson　Carlisle Lake District		19.10.17P
	Built by R D Armishaw – project PFA G/01A-1145		

G-YROZ	AutoGyro Calidus	10 029	28.06.10
	A M Mackey　Wolverhampton Halfpenny Green		24.05.18P
	Assembled Rotorsport UK as c/n RSUK/CALS/005		
G-YRRO	AutoGyro Calidus	xxxx	24.11.09
	C M Leivers　Shacklewell Lodge, Empingham		11.06.18P
	Assembled Rotorsport UK as c/n RSUK/CALS/002		
G-YRTE	Agusta A109S Grand	22133	30.06.14
	N359SH　Galegrove 2 LBG　East Midlands		27.06.18E
G-YRUS	Jodel D.140E Mousquetaire	483	08.09.03
	G-YRNS　W E Massam　(Bristol BS1)		
	Built by W E Massam – project PFA 251-14090		
	(NF 28.01.16)		
G-YSIR	Van's RV-8	83616	07.06.17
	The Lord Rotherwick　Cornbury Park, Charlbury		
	Built by H R Rotherwick – project LAA 303-15446		
	(NF 05.06.17)		
G-YSMO	Mainair Pegasus Quik	8049	12.07.04
	T M Shaw　Eshott		18.04.19P
	Built by Mainair Sports Ltd		
G-YTLY	Rans S-6-ES Coyote II	1108-1910	20.05.11
	D M Geddes　Longside		24.07.18P
	Built by C Uttley – project LAA 204-14925;		
	tricycle u/c; sponsored RAeS/Boeing		
	'Build-a-Plane' project for Yateley School		
G-YUGE	Schempp-Hirth Ventus cT	130/407	11.06.10
	G-CFNN, BGA 3395/FNN		
	E P Lambert　Aston Down　'109'		28.09.18E
G-YULL	Piper PA-28-180 Cherokee E	28-5603	30.03.79
	G-BEAJ, 9H-AAC, N2390R		
	P Beange tr Beange Flying Group　Compton Abbas		12.11.19E
G-YUMM	Cameron N-90	2723	12.12.91
	H Stringer　Ebberston, Scarborough　'Boulevard'		28.04.19E
G-YUPI	Cameron N-90	1602	12.01.88
	McCormick, Van Haarne & Co　Brussels, Belgium		
	'Cameron Balloons'		22.11.98A
	(NF 31.03.16)		
G-YURO[M]	Europa Aviation Europa	001	06.04.92
	Cancelled as PWFU 22.04.98		09.06.95
	Built by Europa Aviation – project PFA 220-11981		
	With Yorkshire Air Museum, Elvington		
G-YVES	Alpi Pioneer 300	127	07.12.04
	A P Anderson　(Curdridge, Southampton)		02.11.18P
	Built by M C Birchall – project PFA 330-14290;		
	c/n 127 also quoted for G-OPFA		
G-YVIP	Beech B200 Super King Air	BB-1306	23.01.19
	N501HC, N1553E		
	Capital Air Ambulance Ltd　Exeter Int'l		
G-YXLX	Valentin Mistral C	MC020/79	10.05.12
	BGA 4376/JBE, OY-XLX, PH-667		
	R R Penman　RNAS Yeovilton		22.06.14E
G-YYAK	IAV Bacau Yakovlev Yak-52	878101	18.04.02
	LY-AOM, DOSAAF 118		
	Repxper SARL　Feurs-Chambeon, France		10.08.18P
G-YYRO	Magni M16C Tandem Trainer	16105654	23.04.10
	A Yin-Tuen Leung　Shenstone Hall Farm, Shenstone		30.05.19P
G-YYYY	Max Holste MH.1521C1 Broussard	208M	10.03.00
	F-GDPZ, French AF　P F N Burrow tr Eggesford		
	Heritage Flight　Trenchard Farm, Eggesford		11.07.18P
	As '208:IR' in French A/F c/s		
G-YZYZ	Mainair Blade 912	1357-0803-7-W1152	14.08.03
	A M Beale　Lofts Farm, Broad Street Green		23.08.18P

G-ZAAA – G-ZZZZ

G-ZAAP	CZAW Sportcruiser	4244	31.01.08
	H C R Page　Barling		12.09.18P
	Built by L A Seers – project PFA 338-14663;		
	badged 'PiperSport'; rudder plate no. '3833'		
	also reported for G-CGCH		
G-ZAAZ	Van's RV-8	80637	02.07.02
	P A Soper　Rands Farm, Layham		19.07.18P
	Built by P A Soper – project PFA 303-13279		
G-ZABC	Sky 90-24	062	10.04.97
	P Donnelly　Maghera		29.05.18E

G-ZACE	Cessna 172S Skyhawk SP	172S8808	03.09.02	
	F-HAMC, N3527P Sywell Aerodrome Ltd Sywell		09.09.18E	
G-ZACH	Robin DR.400-100 Cadet	1831	20.10.92	
	G-FTIO A P Wellings Popham		02.11.18E	
G-ZACK	Cirrus SR20	1503	27.09.17	
	TC-CHK Modern Air (UK) Ltd Fowlmere			
	(NF 27.09.17)			
G-ZADA	Best Off Skyranger 912S(1)	UK/547	11.10.06	
	C P Lincoln Middle Stoke, Isle of Grain		17.05.18P	
	Built by D F Hughes – project BMAA/HB/446;			
	ran off end of runway into river landing Ince 18.06.17			
G-ZAIR	Zenair CH.601HD Zodiac	xxxx	21.02.92	
	A D Brown North Coates		01.05.18P	
	Built by B E Shaw – project PFA 162-12194; tricycle u/c			
G-ZANY	Diamond DA.40D Star	D4.040	23.10.03	
	Altair Aviation Ltd Stapleford		13.05.18E	
G-ZAPX	Boeing 757-256	29309	17.05.06	
	EC-HIS Titan Airways Ltd London Stansted		05.05.19E	
	Line No: 936			
G-ZAPY	Robinson R22 Beta	0788	06.07.98	
	G-INGB HQ Aviation Ltd Denham		18.05.18E	
G-ZARV	ARV ARV-1 Super 2	xxxx	26.02.97	
	P R Snowden Higham, Gazeley		01.08.18P	
	Built by P R Snowden – project PFA 152-13035			
G-ZASH	Comco Ikarus C42 FB80	1304-7257	12.07.13	
	J W D Blythe Swansea		29.07.18P	
	Assembled Red-Air UK			
G-ZAST	Christen A-1 Husky	1155	03.02.16	
	I-ASKY, N948 E Marinoni (Merano, Italy)		18.03.18E	
G-ZATG	Diamond DA.42M Twin Star	42.319	19.08.16	
	G-DOSA, ZA179, G-DOSA Directflight Ltd Cranfield		11.09.18R	
G-ZAVI	Comco Ikarus C42 FB100	0601-6777	25.01.06	
	M de Cleen & M J Hawkins Old Sarum		09.12.18P	
	Assembled Aerosport Ltd			
G-ZAZA	Piper PA-18 Super Cub 95 (*L-18C-PI*)	18-2041	01.05.84	
	D-ENAS, R Netherlands AF R-66, 52-2441			
	G J Harry The Viscount Goschen			
	(Wisborough Green, Billingshurst)		19.06.18P	
G-ZAZU	Diamond DA.42 Twin Star	42.187	13.09.13	
	G-GFDA, G-CEFX, OE-VPY Cloud Global Ltd Perth		24.11.18E	
G-ZAZZ	Lindstrand LBL 120A	1200	21.01.09	
	Idea Balloon SAS Di Stefano Travaglia & Co			
	Tavarnelle Val di Pesa, Firenze, Italy			
	'Lindstrand Balloon School'		05.05.18E	
G-ZBAG	Airbus A321-231	2793	26.04.13	
	5B-DCP, JY-AYH, D-AVZN Wilmington Trust			
	SP Services (Dublin) Ltd Shannon, RoI		14.07.18E	
G-ZBAP	Airbus A320-214	1605	14.02.14	
	M-RAFF, TG-SGN, G-OOPT, C-GTDH, G-OOAT, F-WWBV			
	First Star Speir Aviation 1 Ltd St Athan		06.03.18E	
	Scrapped 07.18			
G-ZBED	Robinson R22 Beta	1684	18.11.99	
	N63993, F-GHHM			
	M J Wearing (Black Bourton, Bampton)		25.06.18E	
G-ZBEN	IAV Bacau Yakovlev Yak-52	822708	08.11.16	
	SP-YOC, RA-3466K, 9A-BUG, LY-NXE, 125 DOSAAF			
	B A Nicholson Inverness		17.09.18P	
G-ZBJA	Boeing 787-8	38609	29.06.13	
	British Airways PLC London Heathrow		28.06.19E	
	Line No: 108			
G-ZBJB	Boeing 787-8	38610	25.06.13	
	British Airways PLC London Heathrow		24.06.19E	
	Line No: 111			
G-ZBJC	Boeing 787-8	38611	01.09.13	
	British Airways PLC London Heathrow		31.08.19E	
	Line No: 114			
G-ZBJD	Boeing 787-8	38619	28.09.13	
	British Airways PLC London Heathrow		26.09.19E	
	Line No: 121			
G-ZBJE	Boeing 787-8	38612	15.05.14	
	British Airways PLC London Heathrow		14.05.19E	
	Line No: 173			

G-ZBJF	Boeing 787-8	38613	25.05.14	
	British Airways PLC London Heathrow		24.05.19E	
	Line No: 177			
G-ZBJG	Boeing 787-8	38614	08.07.14	
	British Airways PLC London Heathrow		07.07.19E	
	Line No: 187			
G-ZBJH	Boeing 787-8	38615	15.08.14	
	British Airways PLC London Heathrow		14.08.19E	
	Line No: 197			
G-ZBJI	Boeing 787-8	60626	26.09.17	
	British Airways PLC London Heathrow		25.09.19E	
	Line No: 609			
G-ZBJJ	Boeing 787-8	60629	14.06.18	
	British Airways PLC London Heathrow		13.06.19E	
	Line No: 708			
G-ZBJK	Boeing 787-8	60630	13.09.18	
	N1014X British Airways PLC London Heathrow		12.09.19E	
	Line No: 733			
G-ZBJM	Boeing 787-8	60631	15.11.18	
	British Airways PLC London Heathrow		14.11.19E	
	Line No.769			
G-ZBKA	Boeing 787-9	38616	28.09.15	
	British Airways PLC London Heathrow		27.09.19E	
	Line No: 346			
G-ZBKB	Boeing 787-9	38617	20.10.15	
	British Airways PLC London Heathrow		19.10.19E	
	Line No: 357			
G-ZBKC	Boeing 787-9	38621	23.10.15	
	British Airways PLC London Heathrow		22.10.19E	
	Line No: 360			
G-ZBKD	Boeing 787-9	38618	24.11.15	
	British Airways PLC London Heathrow		22.11.19E	
	Line No: 361			
G-ZBKE	Boeing 787-9	38620	27.11.15	
	British Airways PLC London Heathrow		26.11.19E	
	Line No: 374			
G-ZBKF	Boeing 787-9	38622	29.01.16	
	British Airways PLC London Heathrow		10.01.20E	
	Line No: 392			
G-ZBKG	Boeing 787-9	38623	29.08.16	
	N896BA, N1006F British Airways PLC			
	London Heathrow		28.08.19E	
	Line No: 396			
G-ZBKH	Boeing 787-9	38624	29.06.16	
	N1792B, N943BA British Airways PLC			
	London Heathrow		28.06.19E	
	Line No: 404			
G-ZBKI	Boeing 787-9	38625	21.03.16	
	British Airways PLC London Heathrow		20.03.19E	
	Line No: 406			
G-ZBKJ	Boeing 787-9	38626	28.04.16	
	British Airways PLC London Heathrow		27.04.19E	
	Line No: 424			
G-ZBKK	Boeing 787-9	38627	22.06.16	
	British Airways PLC London Heathrow		21.06.19E	
	Line No: 442			
G-ZBKL	Boeing 787-9	38628	20.07.16	
	British Airways PLC London Heathrow		19.07.19E	
	Line No: 451			
G-ZBKM	Boeing 787-9	38629	29.07.16	
	British Airways PLC London Heathrow		28.07.19E	
	Line No: 461			
G-ZBKN	Boeing 787-9	38630	07.09.16	
	British Airways PLC London Heathrow		06.09.19E	
	Line No: 475			
G-ZBKO	Boeing 787-9	38631	26.09.16	
	British Airways PLC London Heathrow		25.09.19E	
	Line No: 481			
G-ZBKP	Boeing 787-9	38632	06.12.16	
	British Airways PLC London Heathrow		05.12.19E	
	Line No: 493			
G-ZBKR	Boeing 787-9	60627	27.03.18	
	British Airways PLC London Heathrow		26.03.19E	
	Line No: 682			

Reg	Type	Serial	Date

G-ZBKS Boeing 787-9   60628   31.05.18
British Airways PLC   London Heathrow   30.05.19E
Line No: 700

G-ZBLT Cessna 182S Skylane   18280910   06.07.01
N72764, G-ZBLT, N72764
G Doyle tr Cessna 182S Group   Abbeyshrule, RoI   05.12.18E

G-ZBOP SZD-36A Cobra 15   W-618   16.07.08
BGA 1886/CXJ   S R Bruce   Feshiebridge   *'791'*   19.11.09E
Built by Zs Delta-bielsko Wroclaw; stored 10.16
(NF 06.04.16)

G-ZDEA Diamond DA.42 Twin Star   42.080   17.08.12
SP-KRL, OE-VPI   DEA Aviation Ltd   Retford Gamston   11.09.19E

G-ZEBY Piper PA-28-140 Cherokee F   28-7325240   07.04.00
G-BFBF, EI-BMG, G-BFBF, PH-SRF
N Wright   Wolverhampton Halfpenny Green   26.10.17E

G-ZECH CZAW Sportcruiser   08SC108   11.01.08
A J Dace tr Sportcruiser UK015 Syndicate
Wolverhampton Halfpenny Green   02.06.18P
Built by P J Reilly – project PFA 338-14685
(Quick-build kit 4007)

G-ZEIN Slingsby T67M-260 Firefly   2234   19.07.95
R C P Brookhouse   Headcorn   14.07.18E

G-ZENA Zenair CH.701UL   7-4323   16.10.00
E Bentley   Morgansfield, Fishburn   19.12.19P
Built by A N Aston & E Bentley – project PFA 187-13637

G-ZENJ Learjet Learjet 75   45-565   13.04.18
Jet Aircraft Ltd   Biggin Hill   02.07.19E
Operated by Zenith Aviation Ltd

G-ZENR Zenair CH.601HD Zodiac   xxxx   09.04.08
G-BRJB   N G Bumford   Shobdon   08.07.19P
Project allocated originally to D Collinson as G-BRJB;
completed D J Hunter – project PFA 162-11573;
tricycle u/c

G-ZENY Zenair CH.601HD Zodiac   6-9167   07.07.08
B K & T R Pugh   Old Sarum   30.05.18P
Built by T R Pugh – project PFA 162-13668;
tricycle u/c

G-ZEPI Colt GA-42 Gas Airship   878   09.04.92
G-ISPY, (G-BPRB)
P A Lindstrand   Queens Park, Oswestry   12.05.93A
(NF 10.10.14)

G-ZERO Grumman American AA-5B Tiger   AA5B-0051   03.09.80
OO-PEC   N R Evans & D K Rose   Turweston   23.05.19E

G-ZEVS Cessna F172H   F17200736   20.02.19
D-ECJT   D M White   Popham
(IE 20.02.19)

G-ZEXL Extra EA.300/L   1225   10.03.06
2 Excel Aviation Ltd   Sywell   15.03.19E
Operated by 'The Blades' as callsign 'Blade 1'

G-ZEZE Cessna 182S Skylane   18280741   28.02.18
G-LVES, G-ELIE, N23754   S Bonham   Leicester   12.11.19E

G-ZFOO Flying Legend Tucano replica   xxxx   15.10.15
A J Palmer & F Sayyah   Chilsfold Farm, Northchapel
Built by A J Palmer & F Sayyah – project
LAA 394-15360; under construction 09.16
(NF 15.10.15)

G-ZFOX Denney Kitfox Model 2   xxxx   29.04.09
S M Hall   Headon Farm, Retford   09.01.19P
Built by S M Hall – project PFA 172-11552

G-ZGAB BRM Bristell NG5 Speed Wing   188   29.03.16
G A Beale   Old Warden   30.07.19P
Built by G A Beale – project LAA 385-15392

G-ZGTK Schleicher ASH 26E   26076   05.02.13
G-BWBY   P M Wells   Baileys Farm, Long Crendon   31.01.12E
(NF 26.04.17)

G-ZGZG Cessna 182T Skylane   18282036   20.12.07
N12722   J Noble   Brighton City   12.01.19E

G-ZHKF Reality Escapade 912(2)   JA.ESC.0045   26.11.04
C D & C M Wills   Stonefield Park, Chilbolton   14.12.18P
Built by C D Wills – project BMAA/HB/415

G-ZHWH RotorWay Exec 162F   6596   19.11.01
B Alexander   Dunkeswell   28.10.19P
Built by B Alexander

G-ZIGI Robin DR.400-180 Régent   2107   19.11.91
Aeroclub du Bassin d'Arcachon
Villemarie, Arcachon, France   16.07.18E

G-ZIGY Europa Aviation Europa XS   497   25.02.05
K D Weston   (Gosport)
Built by K D Weston – project PFA 247-13693
(NF 14.10.14)

G-ZIII Pitts S-2B   5151   03.05.05
G-CDBH, SE-LVI, F-GMOV, OO-MOV, N10ZX,
(N71ZX), N10ZX
W A Cruickshank   Old Buckenham   *'Wildcats'*   11.05.18E
Built by Christen Industries Inc

G-ZINC Cessna 182S Skylane   18280757   26.10.09
G-VALI, N238ME   M Mears   Blackpool   02.08.18E

G-ZINT Cameron Z-77   10488   17.09.03
G Bogliaccino   Mondovi, Italy   22.08.18E

G-ZION Cessna 177B Cardinal   17701690   23.05.13
HB-CWC, (N34192)   J Tully   North Weald   08.11.19E

G-ZIPA Rockwell Commander 114A   14505   03.09.98
G-BHRA, N5891N   R Robson   Longside   28.06.18E
Originally laid down as c/n 14436

G-ZIPE Agusta A109E Power Elite   11798   07.09.11
Noble Foods Ltd   (Tring)   07.09.18E

G-ZIPI Robin DR.400-180 Régent   1557   22.02.82
A J Cooper   Lydd   18.10.19E

G-ZIPY Wittman W.8 Tailwind   xxxx   29.05.91
K J Nurcombe   Spanhoe   08.09.14P
Built by M J Butler – project PFA 031-11339)
(IE 02.11.17)

G-ZIRA Staaken Z-1RA Stummelflitzer   094   26.06.08
P J Dale   Woodview House Farm, Chesham   04.05.18P
Built by D H Pattison – project PFA 342-14596

G-ZIZY TL 2000UK Sting Carbon S4   13 ST 403   20.06.13
C E & R P Reeves   Dunkeswell   08.07.18P
Built by R P Reeves – project LAA 347A-15201

G-ZLLE Aérospatiale SA.341G Gazelle 1   1012   04.10.01
N504KH, JA9098   MW Helicopters Ltd   Stapleford   06.11.07E
(IE 16.06.15)

G-ZLOJ Beech A36 Bonanza   E-1677   11.09.98
ZS-LOJ, N6748J   C J Parker   Fairoaks   14.05.18E

G-ZNTH Learjet Learjet 45   45-540   30.09.16
N10872   Zenith Aircraft Ltd   Biggin Hill   06.10.18E
Completed as Model 75

G-ZNTJ Learjet Learjet 45   45-562   21.03.18
N5013Y   Zenith Aircraft Ltd   Biggin Hill   23.04.19E

G-ZODY Zenair CH.601UL Zodiac   6-9531   26.05.04
B H Stephens tr Sarum 2000 Group   Old Sarum   20.02.18E
Built by B H Stephens, J Corben, D A Dance,
D J Evans & D O Russell – project PFA 162A-14239;
tricycle u/c

G-ZOFG Piper PA-28-181 Cherokee Archer II   28-7790373   05.12.18
EC-JQH, SE-GPO   K Davidson & S T Hanssen
tr The Zero Oktas Flying Group   Cumbernauld   08.06.19E

G-ZOIZ Ultramagic M-105   105/185   19.04.12
British Telecommunications PLC   Thatcham   *'BT'*   06.03.18E

G-ZOMB Comco Ikarus C42 FB100 Bravo   1706-7506   07.08.17
Apocalypse Aviation Ltd   (Shillingford, Wallingford)   09.09.18P

G-ZOOB Tecnam P2008-JC   1046   14.05.15
Century Aviation Ltd   Retford Gamston   16.07.18E

G-ZOOL Reims/Cessna FA152 Aerobat   FA1520357   11.11.94
G-BGXZ   A S C Rathmell-Davey   Turweston   22.04.18E

G-ZORO Europa Aviation Europa   074   20.06.95
N T Read   (Gillingham ME8)
Built by N T Read – project PFA 247-12672;
tailwheel u/c (NF 10.09.14)

G-ZOSA American Champion 7GCAA Citabria   509-2006   30.11.06
R McQueen   Quilkieston Farm, Stair   10.08.18E

G-ZPPY Piper PA-18 Super Cub 150 (*L-18C*)   18-2065   22.04.14
G-NICK, PH-CWA, R Netherlands AF R-79, 8A-79,
52-2465   R Sims   White Waltham   04.05.19P

G-ZSDB Piper PA-28-236 Dakota   28-8211004   05.08.10
G-BPCX, N8441S
Dakota Air Services LLP   White Waltham   18.11.18E

G-ZSIX	Schleicher ASW 27-18E (*ASG 29E*) (BGA 5345) F J Davies & K W Payne Husbands Bosworth *'Z6'*	29581	13.03.09 06.12.18E
G-ZSKD	Cameron Z-90 M J Gunston Blackwater, Camberley	10749	16.02.06 14.08.18E
G-ZSKY	Best Off Skyranger 912S(1) J E Lipinski Rayne Hall Farm, Rayne *Built by N R Henry & J J C Scott – project BMAA/HB/543*	SKR0703771	20.06.07 12.04.18P
G-ZTED	Europa Aviation Europa J J Kennedy Perth *Built by E W Gladstone & J J Kennedy – project PFA 247-12492; tailwheel u/c*	015	30.04.96 06.07.18P
G-ZTOO	Staaken Z-2 Flitzer E B Toulson Rufforth East *Built by E B Toulson – project LAA 359-15393 (NF 04.05.16)*	91	04.05.16
G-ZTUG	Aeropro EuroFOX 914 G-CICX P J Tiller Fenland *Built by R M Cornwell & L J Kaye – project LAA 376-15215; tailwheel u/c; glider-tug*	42314	18.02.14 08.11.18P
G-ZTWO	Staaken Z-2 Flitzer S J Randle (Blackfordby, Swadlincote) *Built by S J Randle – project LAA 359-14899 (NF 21.07.16)*	001	28.05.09
G-ZUFL	Lindstrand LBL 90A G-CHLL R P Wade tr Zuffle Dog Balloon Team Mondovi, Italy	941	16.09.13 24.11.18E
G-ZUMI	Van's RV-8 D R Cairns Denham *Built by P M Wells – project PFA 303-13527*	81091	06.03.02 01.11.18P
G-ZUMP^M	Cameron N-77 HAB Cancelled 08.04.98 as WFU *Rebuilt by 1985 with new canopy c/n 1107 With British Balloon Museum & Library, Newbury*	377	18.01.78 03.05.91
G-ZVIP	Beech 200 Super King Air G-SAXN, G-OMNH, N108BM, RP-C1979, TR-LWC Capital Air Ambulance Ltd Exeter Int'l	BB-108	07.04.10 20.08.19E
G-ZVKO	Zivko Edge 360 N360CH J & S P Wood Breighton *Built by C Huey*	1	14.02.06 18.08.19P
G-ZXCL	Extra EA.300/L 2 Excel Aviation Ltd Sywell *Operated by 'The Blades' as callsign 'Blade 5'*	1223	27.02.06 15.03.19E
G-ZXEL	Extra EA.300/L 2 Excel Aviation Ltd Sywell *Operated by 'The Blades' as callsign 'Blade 2'*	1224	27.02.06 15.03.19E
G-ZXLL	Extra EA.300/L 2 Excel Aviation Ltd Sywell *Operated by 'The Blades' as callsign 'Blade 4'*	1319	03.05.11 05.05.19E
G-ZZAC	Evektor EV-97 Eurostar N R Beale Turweston *Built by S A Ivell – project PFA 315-14642 – c/n details also shown on G-CEHL*	2006-2928	10.05.07 19.08.18P
G-ZZAJ	Schleicher ASH 26E A T Johnstone Wycombe Air Park *'AJ'*	26232	15.07.05 25.01.19E
G-ZZDD	Schweizer 269C (*300C*) G-OCJK, N69A D D Saint Norton Malreward	S 1294	29.03.11 17.07.19E
G-ZZDG	Cirrus SR20 N985SR N Deeks & B Lane Elstree	1733	19.12.06 16.01.19E
G-ZZEL	Westland SA.341B Gazelle AH.1 G-BZYJ, XW885 The Gazelle Squadron Display Team Ltd Bourne Park, Hurstbourne Tarrant	1152	25.11.02 02.03.18P
G-ZZIJ	Piper PA-28-180 Cherokee C G-AVGK, N9516J E Hutchinson tr G-ZZIJ Group Andrewsfield	28-3639	18.09.09 29.06.18E
G-ZZLE	Westland SA.341C Gazelle HT.2 G-CBSE, XX436 A Moorhouse, S Qardan & P J Whitaker Bourne Park, Hurstbourne Tarrant *Operated by The Gazelle Squadron Display Team; as 'XX436:39 CU' in Royal Navy c/s*	1402	29.04.05 13.08.18P

G-ZZMM	Enstrom 480B G-TOIL Fly 7 Helicopters LLP Gloucestershire	5082	13.07.09 18.01.18E
G-ZZOE	Eurocopter EC120B Colibri F-WQOX J F H James The Mill House, Aynho	1196	21.03.01 06.07.18E
G-ZZOT	Piper PA-34-220T Seneca V N199PS Cheshire Aircraft Leasing Ltd Hawarden	3449108	17.10.17
G-ZZOW	Medway EclipseR M Belemet (Kingston-upon-Thames) *(NF 09.03.16)*	178/156	31.08.06 24.04.14P
G-ZZSA	Eurocopter EC225 LP Super Puma F-WWOJ Bristow Helicopters Ltd Aberdeen Int'l *Stored 02.18*	2603	21.07.05 27.07.19E
G-ZZSB	Eurocopter EC225 LP Super Puma F-WWOG Bristow Helicopters Ltd Aberdeen Int'l *'Martin Bull'* *Stored 02.18*	2615	11.08.05 18.10.18E
G-ZZSC	Eurocopter EC225 LP Super Puma F-WWOG Bristow Helicopters Ltd Aberdeen Int'l *Stored 02.18*	2654	13.09.06 14.10.18E
G-ZZSD	Eurocopter EC225 LP Super Puma F-WWOQ Bristow Helicopters Ltd Aberdeen Int'l *Stored 02.18*	2658	05.12.06 17.12.17E
G-ZZSE	Eurocopter EC225 LP Super Puma F-WWOT Bristow Helicopters Ltd Aberdeen Int'l *Stored 02.18*	2660	14.02.07 25.02.19E
G-ZZSF	Eurocopter EC225 LP Super Puma F-WWOR Bristow Helicopters Ltd Aberdeen Int'l *Stored 02.18*	2662	05.04.07 15.04.18E
G-ZZSG	Eurocopter EC225 LP Super Puma Bristow Helicopters Ltd Aberdeen Int'l *Stored 02.18*	2714	17.12.08 20.12.16E
G-ZZSI	Eurocopter EC225 LP Super Puma G-CGES Bristow Helicopters Ltd Aberdeen Int'l *Stored 11.17*	2736	30.10.09 15.11.18E
G-ZZSK	Eurocopter EC225 LP Super Puma Bristow Helicopters Ltd Rzeszow, Poland *Stored 02.18*	2849	17.10.12 08.11.18E
G-ZZSL	Airbus EC225 LP Super Puma Bristow Helicopters Ltd Aberdeen Int'l *Stored 11.17*	2928	21.01.15 05.03.18E
G-ZZSM	Airbus EC225 LP Super Puma Bristow Helicopters Ltd Aberdeen Int'l *Stored 11.17*	2937	21.01.15 06.04.18E
G-ZZSN	Airbus EC225 LP Super Puma Bristow Helicopters Ltd Aberdeen Int'l *Stored 11.17*	2989	17.12.15 16.12.18E
G-ZZTT	Schweizer 269C (*300C*) C-FFZZ, N86G Heli Andaluz SL (Malaga, Spain)	S 1884	20.06.08 16.03.18E
G-ZZXX	P&M Quik GT450 B B Seabridge (Haslington, Crewe)	8177	19.04.06 23.03.18P
G-ZZZA	Boeing 777-236 N77779 British Airways PLC London Heathrow *Line No: 6*	27105	20.05.96 19.05.19E
G-ZZZB	Boeing 777-236 N77771 British Airways PLC London Heathrow *Line No: 10*	27106	28.03.97 03.12.19E
G-ZZZC	Boeing 777-236 N5014K British Airways PLC London Heathrow *Line No: 15*	27107	11.11.95 10.11.19E
G-ZZZS	Eurocopter EC120B Colibri OO-WER, F-WQDI Rosegate Helicopter Services Ltd (Fairoaks)	1321	26.11.07 20.12.18E

AIRCRAFT TYPE INDEX (UK)

This Index covers only entries in that are currently on the CAA Permanent Register. We are very grateful to Dave Reid for producing the Index from the Database at short notice.

A

A V ROE and CO LTD including BAe and HAWKER SIDDELEY AVIATION design and production

504K, 504L and replicas
G-ADEV EASD EBHB EROE

581, 594 and 616 AVIAN
G-EUJG

621 TUTOR
G-AHSA

652A ANSON and AVRO NINETEEN
G-AHKX VROE

683 LANCASTER
G-ASXX

696 SHACKLETON
G-SKTN

698 VULCAN
G-VJET

AVRO ROE 1 replica
G-ROEI

CURTISS 1911 replica
G-WBRD

TRIPLANE replica
G-ARSG

AB SPORTINE AVIACIJA – see LAK

ABBOTT-BAYNES

SCUD III
G-ALJR

ACE AVIATION

AS-TEC
G-CJFW CKUL JNAR

EASY RISER SPIRIT
G-CHGN CIKJ

EASY RISER TOUCH
G-CHGU CILW

MAGIC CYCLONE
G-CGIB CGOK CGPA CIAV CITL CIZT CJFI GAZO IXXY KEVA MGIC WEBY

MAGIC LASER
G-CENP CFTA CFZT CGEK CGFK CGHR CGIM CGMA CGMO CHHY CHYO CIKK CINB CKUX

TOUCH/BUZZ
G-GARI

ACRO

ADVANCED
G-BPAA

ACROSTAR – see YAKOVLEV

AD AEROSPACE LTD – see THORP AERO INC

ADVANCE

IOTA
G-CLCD

ADVANCE THUN AG

ADVANCE ALPHA
G-CIRF

AERIAL ARTS (LTD)

CHASER with 110SX and 130SX wings
G-MNTD MNYD MNYF MTCP MTDD MTDE MVOD

CHASER S
G-MVDL MVDP MVGA MVGF MVGG MVGI MVGK MVIE MVJF MVJG MVJJ MVJK MVLA MVLB MVLC MVLD MVLE MVLF MVLS MVLT MVML MVOA MVOP MVRG MVSG MVSL MVTF MVTL MVTM MVUS MVXP MVYY MVZM MWWZ MWXX MWXY MWXZ MWYM MYBU MYCB MYEI MYEJ MYFO MYGK MYIL MYIT MYKD MYRE MYSA MYSV MYWS MZCB

AÉRIANE SA

P SWIFT
G-CLBV

SWIFT LIGHT PAS
G-CEVX CJFG CKHZ

AERO

31
G-CJIP CKVE

AEROCAR

TAYLOR COOT A
G-COOT

AEROCHUTE INDUSTRIES PTY LTD

DUAL
G-CEZH CFCF CFFG CHWK CIFB CIGU CIIB CIMG CJTI CJTT CKTA CKTL CKXP CKZM

SSDR
G-CJJY

AERO DESIGNS

PULSAR 3
G-BYJL CDNF

PULSAR X
G-BSFA BTDR BTRF BTWY BUDI BUSR BUYB BVSF BVTW BXDU CCBZ CHEX IIAN LUED LWNG RMAN

PULSAR XP
G-BUOW BUZB BVLN CBLA CEDJ CISE CKIS LEEN OOXP XPXP

AERO SP ZOO

AT-3 variants
G-LGOC RDFX SACP SACW SACX SBRK SKAZ SPAT SWLL SYEL SYWL

AEROFAB INC – see LAKE AIRCRAFT CORPORATION

AEROLA LTD

ALATUS-M
G-CFDT CFEY CFMV

AEROMOT INDUSTRIA MECANICO METALURGICA LTDA

AMT-200 SUPER XIMANGO
G-BWNY CECJ JTPC LLEW MOAN RFIO XMGO XYZT

AÉRONAUTIQUE HAVRAISE – see GARDAN

AERONCA – AERONAUTICAL CORPORATION OF AMERICA

AERONCA C.2
G-ABHE

AERONCA C.3
G-ADRR ADYS AEFT AESB CDUW

AERONCA – AERONAUTICAL CORPORATION OF GB LTD

AERONCA 100
G-AETG AEVS AEXD

AERONCA AIRCRAFT CORPORATION – also see BELLANCA and CHAMPION

AERONCA K
G-ONKA

O-58B (L-3) GRASSHOPPER
G-BRHP BRPR

65C(TAC) SUPER CHIEF
G-BTRG

7AC CHAMPION
G-AJON AKTR AOEH ATHK AVDT AWVN BPFM BPGK BRAR BRCV BRER BRWA BRXG BTGM BTNO BUYE BVCS LEVI OTOE TECC

7ACA CHAMP
G-HAMP

7BCM CHAMPION (L-16)
G-AKTO BFAF DHAH TIMP

7DC CHAMPION
G-BRFI

11AC CHIEF
G-AKTK AKUO AKVN BJEV BPRX BRCW BRFJ BRWR BRXF BRXL BSTC BTFL BTSR BUAB BUTF IIAC IVOR

11CC SUPER CHIEF
G-BJNY BTRI

15AC SEDAN
G-AREX

AEROPLANES DAR LTD

SOLO 120
G-CIUT CKYI CLAM

AEROPRAKT

A-22 FOXBAT
G-CBGJ CBJH CBYH CCCE CCJV CDDW CDHX CDTZ CEOP CESI CEWR CFHK CFYD CGSX CGUE CGVA CGWP CGZT CHAD CHHB CHSY CIKE CINV CKUO CKVF COXS CWTD EOID FBAT FBSS FBTT FJTH FOXB FXBA FXBT KELP MAKK MILR MOWG NJTC NSKB OFGC OUDA PHOX REGZ SDOI TIPP VINA WIGI YOLO

A-32 VIXXEN
G-CLEH NALD VXXN

AEROPRO

EUROFOX
G-CGYC CGYG CHHJ CHID CHIH CHUP CIAZ CIBC CIBF CIBZ CIEF CIEH CIFA CIFO CIKH CILA CIML CIMS CIOF CIOJ CIPS CIRP CIUG CIWG CIYL CIYP CJBI CJHF CJHT CJOL CJOM CJTE CJZD CKAB CKDD CKIX CKTE CKVM CKVY CKWO CKXM CKYF CKYG CKZD CLDT CLEI COLY CRED DJBX DSUE EFCG EFOX EFSD ETUG EWEN

FLAX FOKS FOKX FOKZ FOXO FOXU FOXW
FSBW GBNZ HAAR HAMW JBVP JERR
JONX JVET MFOX MGFC MKHB MOYR
NFOX NIKS NMCL OASK ODGC OJSD
OPSG ORIB OSGU OYGC PECX POPG
PSMS PWAL RATT RONK SDOA SMKR
TTUG UFOX UIRI WINO XFOX ZTUG

AEROS COMPANY

DISCUS c/w Delta Trikes Aviation ALIZE trike
G-CENZ CGHN

FOX
G-CIED CIGV FOXT

AÉROSPATIALE – see also EUROCOPTER (EC prefix), MESSERSCHMITT-BÖLKOW-BLOHM (BK and BÖ prefixes) and SUD-AVIATION (SA and SE prefixes)

AS 332L SUPER PUMA including EC 225LP variant
G-BLXS BLZJ BMCX BRXU CGTJ CHCF
CHCG CHCH CHCI CHCL CHCM CHCU
CHCY CIDM CINU CIOI CIWF CIYE CIYH
OAGA OAGE PUMB PUMM PUMN PUMO
PUMS REDJ REDN REDO REDP REDR
REDT TIGC TIGS TIGV VINM WNSC WNSN
WNSP ZZSA ZZSB ZZSC ZZSD ZZSE ZZSF
ZZSG ZZSI ZZSK ZZSL ZZSM ZZSN

AS 350B ECUREUIL variants
G-BRVO BVXM BXGA BXJN CIWO CKPS
CKVH CKXW CKYE CLAU CLBW CLCB
DJSM EFTF EJOC ERKN ETPE ETPF ETPG
ETPH FAIT FEST FIBS GMCM HIDE HITI
HITL IANW IFBP IGIA JBBZ JCOP JOZI
LARR LEOG NIPL OGLE OGUN OLPE OMCC
OOIO OOTT OOWS ORKY PDGF PDGI
PDGR SCHI SDII SHRD SPVK TATS TIPR
WHST

AS 355 ECUREUIL 2 variants
G-BOSN BPRI BPRJ BPRL BSTE BVLG
BYZA CIOP CMRA CPOL DCAM GBTV
GHER HEAN ICSG IDEB INTV KHCG LENI
LHEL LINE NBPL NETR NLDR NLSE NPTV
NTWK OALC OALI OASP OFZY OHCP
OHMS OLCP OTSP PASH PASL PDGP
PDGT PIPB PRDH REEM RIDA SCHZ SKYN
TAKE TBHH TIJL TOPC TVHD UKTV VGMC
VONK VVBA WECG XLLL

AS 365 (and SA 365) DAUPHIN variants
G-BTNC CGGD CKBY DOLF LCPL MFLT
NHAA NHAB NHAC NHAD OLNT PDGN
PDGO REDF

AÉROSPATIALE-ALENIA including ATR

ATR 42
G-HUET ISLF ISLH

ATR 72
G-COBO FBXA FBXB FBXC FBXD FBXE
IACY IACZ ISLK ISLL ISLM ISLN LERE VZON

AEROSPOOL SPOL S.R.O.

WT9 UK DYNAMIC
G-CEJY CENO CFYS CMEW DYNA DYNM
EECC FRDY GRMN IIAL JFDI JFLO LXAA
OTIV RMHE SJPI TDYN WIGS

AEROSPORT

SCAMP
G-BKPB BOOW DAVB

WOODY PUSHER including WOODS production
G-AWWP AYVP SHUV

AEROSPORT LTD/FLYBUY ULTRALIGHTS LTD – see COMCO IKARUS

AEROSTYLE – see BREEZER

AEROTECH INTERNATIONAL LTD – see WHITTAKER

AEROTEK INC – see PITTS

AERO VODOCHODY NÁRODNÍ PODNIK

C-104
G-CCOB

L-29 DELFIN
G-BYCT DLFN

L-39 ALBATROS
G-JMGP

Lim-5
G-MIGG

AESL – see VICTA

AGUSTA SpA – see LEONARDO

AGUSTA BELL HELICOPTERS – see BELL HELICOPTER TEXTRON

AIA D'ALGER – see STAMPE ET VERTONGEN

AIA DE MAISON-BLANCHE – see SNCAN

AIRBIKE

LIGHT SPORT
G-CIYG

AIRBORNE WINDSPORTS PTY LTD

XT912/STREAK
G-CDGE CDRD CEHZ CFNI CFNZ EDLY
LVPL XTEE XTNI

AIRBUS SAS including AIRBUS INDUSTRIE

A318 variants
G-EUNA EUNB

A319 variants
G-DBCA DBCB DBCC DBCD DBCE DBCF
DBCG DBCH DBCJ DBCK EUOA EUOB
EUOC EUOD EUOE EUOF EUOG EUOH
EUOI EUPA EUPB EUPC EUPD EUPE EUPF
EUPG EUPH EUPJ EUPK EUPL EUPM EUPN
EUPO EUPP EUPR EUPS EUPT EUPU
EUPW EUPX EUPY EUPZ EZAA EZAB EZAC
EZAF EZAG EZAI EZAJ EZAK EZAL EZAN
EZAO EZAP EZAS EZAT EZAU EZAV EZAW
EZAX EZBA EZBB EZBC EZBD EZBE EZBF
EZBH EZBI EZBK EZBO EZBR EZBU EZBV
EZBW EZBX EZBZ EZDA EZDD EZDF EZDH
EZDI EZDJ EZDK EZDL EZDM EZDN EZDV
EZEB EZEE EZEN EZEY EZFT EZFV
EZFW EZFX EZFY EZFZ EZGA EZGB EZGC
EZGE EZGF EZIH EZII EZIM EZIO EZIV EZIW
EZIX EZIY EZIZ EZMK EZNM EZPG NOAH

A320 variants
G-EUUA EUUB EUUC EUUD EUUE EUUF
EUUG EUUH EUUI EUUJ EUUK EUUL EUUM
EUUN EUUO EUUP EUUR EUUS EUUT
EUUU EUUV EUUW EUUX EUUY EUUZ
EUYA EUYB EUYC EUYD EUYE EUYF EUYG
EUYH EUYI EUYJ EUYK EUYL EUYM EUYN
EUYO EUYP EUYR EUYS EUYT EUYU EUYV
EUYW EUYX EUYY EZGX EZGY EZOA EZOF
EZOI EZOK EZOM EZOP EZPB EZPD EZPE
EZPI EZRT EZRV EZRX EZRY EZRZ EZTB
EZTC EZTD EZTG EZTH EZTK EZTM EZTR
EZTT EZTY EZTZ EZUA EZUF EZUK EZUL
EZUN EZUO EZUP EZUR EZUS EZUT EZUW
EZUZ EZWA EZWB EZWC EZWD EZWE
EZWF EZWG EZWH EZWI EZWJ EZWL
EZWP EZWU EZWV EZWX EZWY EZWZ
GATH GATJ GATK GATL GATM GATN GATP
GATR GATS GATU KELT MEDK MIDO MIDS

MIDT MIDX MIDY POWK POWM TTNA TTNB
TTNC TTND TTNE TTNF TTNG TTNH TTNI
TTNJ TTOB TTOE UZHA UZHB UZHC UZHD
UZHE UZHF UZHG UZHH UZHI UZHJ UZHK
UZHL UZHM UZHN UZHO UZHP UZHR
UZHS UZHT UZHU UZHW WUKB WUKD
WUKE WUKF ZBAP

A321 variants
G-DHJH EUXC EUXD EUXE EUXF EUXG
EUXH EUXI EUXJ EUXK EUXL EUXM MEDF
MEDG MEDJ MEDL MEDM MEDN MEDU
NEOP NEOR NEOS NEOT NIKO OZBN
POWN POWU POWV TCDA TCDB TCDC
TCDD TCDE TCDF TCDG TCDH TCDP TCDR
TCDV TCDW TCDX TCDY TCDZ TCVA TCVB
TCVC TCVD UZMA UZMB UZMC UZMD
UZME WUKC WUKG WUKH WUKI WUKL
ZBAG

A330 variants
G-CHTZ MDBD MLJL OMYT TCCF TCCG
TCCI TCXB TCXC VGBR VGEM VINE VKSS
VLNM VLUV VMIK VMNK VNYC VRAY VSXY
VUFO VWAG VWND VYGJ VYGK VYGL
VYGM

A340 variants
G-VFIT VNAP VRED VWEB VWIN VYOU

A380 variants
G-XLEA XLEB XLEC XLED XLEE XLEF XLEG
XLEH XLEI XLEJ XLEK XLEL

AIR COMMAND MANUFACTURING INC

503 (COMMANDER)
G-BOIK BRSP

532 ELITE
G-BRLB YROI

582 SPORT
G-BTCB URRR

AIR CRÉATION

503 FUN 18 GT
G-MYMM MYOL MYUA MYVI

582, IXESS
G-CFNX

582, KISS
G-BZXP CBEB CBJL CCEK CCGM CCHM
CFVF CHKN KIZZ PGHM SNOG TEDW TFLY

IFUN
G-CIXL

IXESS (TANARG) 912
G-CDRJ CEDT CEIV CFID DJST ELSI FWKS
IMUP NARG TANA TANG TNRG WGSI WYKD

TANARG BIONIX
G-CEBH CHFT CKZU MICX WADF

AIR ET ADVENTURE

SATURNE S11OK
G-NORB

AIR NAVIGATION AND ENGINEERING CO

ANEC II
G-EBJO

AIRBUS HELICOPTERS – see AÉROSPATIALE (AS prefix), EUROCOPTER (EC prefix), MESSERSCHMITT-BÖLKOW-BLOHM (BK and BÖ prefixes) and SUD-AVIATION (SA and SE prefixes)

AIRCRAFT MANUFACTURING CO (AIRCO) – also see DE HAVILLAND AIRCRAFT LTD

DH.2 replica
G-BFVH

DH.9
G-CDLI

AIRDROME AEROPLANES

DREAM CLASSIC
G-CGLB

AIRTOUR BALLOON CO LTD

31 series
G-BKVY BLVA

56 series
G-BLVB BSGH

AKAFLIEG BRAUNSCHWEIG

EICHELSDORFER SB-5
G-DEHC DEJH

AKROTECH EUROPE – see MUDRY

ALBATROS

D.VA replica
G-WAHT

ALEXANDER SCHLEICHER – see SCHLEICHER

ALISPORT

SILENT
G-CIJE CIJH CIKD CILB CIPF CIRK CITK
CIZW CJBA CJIB CJID OFES OLEC

ALLPORT

HOT AIR FREE
G-BJIA BJSS

ALLSTAR PZL GLIDER – see SZD-SZYBOWCOWY ZAKLAD DOSWIADCZALNY

ALON INC – see FORNEY

ALPHA AVIATION MANUFACTURING LTD – see ROBIN

ALPI AVIATION SRL

PIONEER 200
G-CDSB CEMA CEVJ CEWL CFKW CGEJ
CGLI CGMW OBRO PCCM WEFR

PIONEER 300 (HAWK)
G-CDPA CDSD CDVL CDYY CDZA CEAR
CEEG CEIX CEMY CEPW CETX CFUE CGHK
CGTL DEBT EKIM ETVS EWES FAJC GBOB
GTOM HORK IPKA ISBD ITBT JDRD KITH
LEAH LLOY LXUS OALP OHJE OLAA OPFA
OPYO OWBA PCCC PION RABS SHMN
SPED TREX VIXX VOLO XCIT YVES

PIONEER 400
G-CGAJ CIMD CPPG NSKY

AMERICAN AEROLIGHTS INC

EAGLE
G-MBEP MBHE MBIO MBJD MBJK MBKY
MBRD MBSJ MBZV MJAE MJBL MJEO

AMERICAN AIRCRAFT

FALCON
G-BUYF OXPS

AMERICAN AVIATION CORPORATION – see GRUMMAN AMERICAN AVIATION CORPORATION

AMERICAN CHAMPION – see AERONCA, BELLANCA and CHAMPION

AMERICAN GENERAL AVIATION – see GRUMMAN AMERICAN AVIATION CORPORATION

AMERICAN LEGEND

CUB
G-CGXN

AMERICAN MOTH CORPORATION – see DE HAVILLAND AIRCRAFT LTD

AMF MICROFLIGHT LTD including AMF AVIATION ENTERPRISES LTD and also see ULTRAFLIGHT LTD

CHEVVRON (Konig SD570)
G-MNFL MTFG MVGC MVGD MVIP MVOO
MVUO MVVV MVXX MVZZ MWNO MWNP
MWPW MWUI MWZB MZCK MZFH MZMK

AMS-FLIGHT DOO – also see GLASER-DIRKS FLUGZEUGBAU GmbH

APIS
G-CIIV CJGT

ANDREASSON including CROSBY

BA.4B
G-AWPZ AYFV BEBS BFXF JEDS YPSY

APCO

CRUISER
G-CKZG CLBR

APOLLO AIRCRAFT UK

DELTA JET
G-CITC

AQUILA TECHNISCHE ENTWICKLUNGEN GmbH

AT01
G-GAEA GAEC GAED GAEF OESC OKTI
ROWA TSDA TSDB TSDC TSDE WTWO

ARBITER SERVICES

TRIKE
G-MNWL

ARROW AIRCRAFT (LEEDS) LTD

ACTIVE
G-ABVE

ARV AVIATION LTD

ARV-1 variants
G-BMOK BMWF BNGV BNGW BNGY BNHB
BOGK BSRK BWBZ DEXP ERMO ORIX OTAL
POOL STWO XARV YARV ZARV

ATEC

212 Solo
G-CKUJ

ATTARD

SCOOTER
G-SSDR

AUBERT

WHITE MONOPLANE 1912 CANARD PUSHER
G-CHOI

AUSTER AIRCRAFT LTD – also see TAYLORCRAFT AEROPLANES (ENGLAND) LTD, BEAGLE-AUSTER AIRCRAFT LTD and BEAGLE AIRCRAFT LTD

AUSTER 5
G-AGLK AIKE AJGJ AJXC AKPI AKSY AKSZ
AKWS AKXP ALBJ ALBK ALFA ALXZ AMVD
ANHR ANHX ANIE ANIJ ANRP AOCR AOCU
AOVW APAF APAH APBE APBW APTU BDFX
BICD BXKX

AUSTER 6A, AOP.6 and TUGMASTER variants
G-APRO ARHM ARIH ARRX ARXU ASTI
BKXP BNGE

AUSTER AOP.9, AOP.11 and BEAGLE E.3 variants
G-ASCC AVXY AXRR AXWA AZBU BDFH
BGKT BGTC BJXR BKVK BURR CEHR CICR
CIUX

J1 AUTOCRAT and variants

G-AGTO AGTT AVG AGXV AHAM AHAO
AHAP AHAU AHSP AIBM AIBX AIBY AIGD
AIPV AIRC AIZU AJEE AJEM AJIH AJIT AJIU
AJIX AJRB AJUE AMKU AMTM AXUJ BRKC
BVGT CDPG JAYI

J1B AIGLET

G-ARBM

J1N ALPHA

G-AGXN AGXU AGYD AGYH AGYT AHAL
AHCL AHHH AHHT AHSS AIBH AIBR AIBW
AIFZ AIGF AIGT AJAE AJAJ AJAS AJDY
AJEH AJEI AJIS AJIW AJUL AJYB APIK
APJZ APTR ARRL ARUY BLPG TENT

J1U WORKMASTER

G-APMH APSR OJAS

J2 ARROW

G-AJAM AWLX BEAH

J4 ARCHER

G-AIJM AIJS AIJT AIPR

J5B, J5G, J5P, and J5V AUTOCAR variants

G-AOHZ APUW ARKG ARNB ARUG CKXF

J5F, J5K and J5L AIGLET TRAINER variants

G-AMMS AMRF AMTA AMUI AMYD AMZI
AMZT AOFS APVG BGKZ

J5Q and J5R ALPINE variants

G-ANXC AOGV AOZL APCB

AUTOGYRO GmbH

CAVALON
G-CGYX CHWM CIBL CIEW CIHW CIMT
CITV CIXX CIZP CKVC CKVZ CKYT CKYV
CLAZ CLCV CLDV CPLG CVLN EVAA GDSO
HENZ IDYL MRJC MSCL MUDX ODIZ ORYG
OSVN OTZZ RDNY SJEF YROL

UK CALIDUS
G-CGLY CGMD CGOT CGUY CGVK CICM
CIKG CIPP CJTC CKVP CLDP CLDW CLDZ
DISP FLIA GRYN GYRA IROS KASW LISS
MAKE MARL MRLS ORCC OTTY PCPC
PPBZ TGLG ULUL YROZ YRRO

UK MT-03
G-CDZZ CEHM CEHN CEIA CEOX CERF
CEVY CEXX CEYR CFAK CFAR CFBJ CFCL
CFCW CFGG CFGY CFIE CFJB CFKA CFLO
CGPK CGTF COLI DADA JBRE JYRO KENG
KEVG LUNG MAZA NAGG PILZ PPLG RTIN
RYDR UIRO YPDN YROC YROM YROV
YROX

UK MTO SPORT
G-CFRN CFUW CFWD CFZX CGDC CGEW
CGGP CGGV CGGW CGHL CGIC CGIX
CGJC CGLM CGNC CGNX CGPG CGXZ
CGZE CGZG CGZM CHIT CHLD CICV CIDF
CIEB CIEJ CIFT CIGS CIHH CIRT CITX CJTA
CKLE CKLK CKYA CKYB CKYD CLCH CLCI
CLDF DEWI DUDI FELD HATB HMHM HOTC
IGLL JUGS KBOJ KEAY KIMH KMKM LZED
PAFF PALT PBAL PINO RARA TYRO YROA
YROH YROT

AUTOMOBILOVE ZAVODY MRAZ – see MRAZ

AVENGER

T.200-2112
G-BHMJ BHMK BIGR BIPW BIRL

AVIAD

ZIGOLO MG12
G-CIUF

AVIAMILANO SRL including AEROMERE, LAVERDA and SEQUOIA production

F.8L FALCO
G-BVDP BWYO CCOR CWAG CYLL DAMB
FALC FATE GREC HCBW OCAD ORJW
PDGG REEC RJAM ULRK

AVIAN
RIOT
   G-CIAB

AVIASTROITEL LTD – see also FEDEROV
AC-4C
   G-CJUX

AVIASUD ENGINEERING SA
MISTRAL
   G-MVSJ MVUP MVWW MVXN MVXV MWIB
   MYSL

AVIAT AIRCRAFT INC – see CHRISTEN INDUSTRIES and PITTS

AVIATION COMPOSITES CO LTD – see EUROPA AVIATION

AVID AIRCRAFT INC
AVID FLYER (Rotax 582) including Aerobat, Hauler and Speedwing variants
   G-BTGL BTRC BUJJ BUJV BULC BULY
   BUON BUZM BVFO BVIV BVYX BWLW
   BWRC CURV IJAC NANO OZEE PILL RAFV
   SPAM

AVIONS FAIREY SA – see TIPSY AIRCRAFT CO LTD

AVIONS FOURNIER – see FOURNIER

AVIONS MARCEL DASSAULT and AVIONS MARCEL DASSAULT-BREGUET AVIATION – see DASSAULT AVIATION

AVIONS MAX HOLSTE – see HOLSTE

AVIONS MUDRY ET CIE – see MUDRY

AVIONS PIERRE ROBIN – see ROBIN

AVTECH PTY LTD – see JABIRU

B

BAC (1935) LTD including KRONFELD LTD
DRONE
   G-ADPJ AEDB

BAE SYSTEMS (OPERATIONS) LTD
including BRITISH AEROSPACE plc, BRITISH AEROSPACE (REGIONAL AIRCRAFT) Ltd, HANDLEY-PAGE and SCOTTISH AVIATION production
BAe 146 including Avro variants
   G-CKTY ETPK ETPL FLTC JOTC JOTD JOTE
   JOTF JOTR JOTS LUXE OFOM SMLA TYPH
   WEFX
JETSTREAM Series 31 and Series 32
   G-BWWW ISLC JIBO NFLA
JETSTREAM Series 41 variants
   G-CIHD CIHE MAJA MAJB MAJC MAJD
   MAJE MAJF MAJG MAJH MAJI MAJJ MAJK
   MAJL MAJT MAJU MAJW MAJY MAJZ

BAILEY AVIATION
QUATTRO 175 (PARAMANIA ACTION)
   G-CGIA CGIN

BALONY-KUBÍCEK Spol SrO – see KUBÍCEK

BAREFORD
DB-6R
   G-CKUN

BARKER
CHARADE
   G-CBUN

BARON
TIGER T.200
   G-BIMK

BB MICROLIGHT
BB03 TRYA
   G-CFMA CGFB CKDG DENM

BEAGLE AIRCRAFT LTD
A.109 AIREDALE
   G-ARNP ARRO ARXB ARXD ARZS ASAI
   ASBH ASRK ATCC AVKP
B.121 PUP
   G-AVDF AVLM AVLN AVZP AWEA AWKO
   AWVC AWWE AWYJ AWYO AXDV AXEV
   AXHO AXIA AXIE AXJH AXJI AXJJ AXJO
   AXMW AXMX AXNN AXNP AXNR AXNS
   AXOJ AXOZ AXPA AXPC AXPN AXSC AXUA
   AZCK AZCL AZCN AZCP AZCT AZCU AZCV
   AZCZ AZDG AZEV AZEW AZEY AZFA AZGF
   BAKW BASP BDCO IPUP JIMB OPUP PUPP
B.206
   G-FLYP

BEAGLE-AUSTER AIRCRAFT LTD
A.61 TERRIER
   G-ARLR ARNO ARUI ASAJ ASAX ASCH
   ASDK ASMZ ASOI ASOM ASYG ASZE ASZX
   ATBU ATDN ATHU AVYK AYDX NTVE TIMG
D.4
   G-ARLG
D.5 HUSKY
   G-ASNC ATCD ATMH AVOD AVSR AWSW
D.6
   G-ARCS ARDJ

BEAGLE-MILES AIRCRAFT LTD – see WALLIS AUTOGYROS LTD

BEAGLE-WALLIS LTD – see WALLIS AUTOGYROS LTD

BEDE
BD-4
   G-BOPD BYLS
BD-5
   G-BJPI

BEECH AIRCRAFT CORPORATION
including RAYTHEON AIRCRAFT COMPANY production, and also see HAWKER BEECHCRAFT
17 TRAVELER
   G-BRVE
18/3NM, 3TM and C-45
   G-BKGL BKGM BKRN
19A MUSKETEER SPORT III
   G-AWFZ AWTS AWTV
A23-24 MUSKETEER SUPER III
   G-IBFF TAMS
C23 SUNDOWNER 180
   G-AYYU BARH BASN BBTY
C24R MUSKETEER SUPER R
   G-BYDG BZPG CBCY
E33, E33A and E33C BONANZA
   G-GMCT
F33, F33A and F33C BONANZA
   G-BGSW BTZA COLA EEWA GRYZ HOPE
   HOSS JUST MOAC OAHC
35, G35, H35, N35, P35 S35 and V35B BONANZA
   G-APTY ARKJ ASJL ATSR BONZ EHMJ
   NEWT REST VTAL

36 BONANZA variants
   G-CIOY
A36 BONANZA
   G-BSEY CDJV CHGI DAYO EISG JLHS KSHI
   MAPR POPA SIBK TRJB ZLOJ
55 BARON variants
   G-AWAJ
58 BARON variants
   G-BNUN BTFT BYDY CCVP GAMA LUKA
   VCML
76 DUCHESS
   G-BGVH BIMZ BNUO BNYO BOFC BXXT
   BYNY BZNN CBBF GBSL GCCL GDMW
   GPAT JLRW OADY OBLC OPAT TWNN
90 KING AIR variants
   G-DLAL MOSJ ORTH
95 TRAVELAIR variants
   G-ASYJ
95-A55A and 95-B55A BARON
   G-ASOH BFLZ BLJM BZIT DGST IPEP
   SWEE UROP WOOD
200 and 300 KING AIR variants
   G-BGRE BVMA CEGP CIFE CWCD DAYP
   DXTR EUNI FLYK FLYW FPLD FSEU GMAD
   GMAE IASA IASB IASM IMEA JASS JMAW
   KVIP MEDZ MEGN NIAA NIAB NYCO OLIV
   OSFL PCOP RAFK RAFL RANN REXA SASC
   SASD SRBM WCCP WNCH WVIP XVIP YVIP
   ZVIP
400A
   G-ERIE FXAR FXCR FXDM FXDT FXER FXKR
   FXMR FXPR FXRS SKBD

BELL
FD 31T
   G-BITY

BELL HELICOPTER TEXTRON INC
including AGUSTA BELL HELICOPTER CO, BELL HELICOPTER, TEXTRON CANADA, IPTN (412) and WESTLAND HELICOPTERS LTD production
47D and 47G (WESTLAND)
   G-ARXH AXKO AXKX BAXS BBRI BFEF BFYI
   BHBE BHNV CHOP CICN CIGY GGTT LHCI
   MASH XTUN
47J RANGER
   G-BFPP
206A and 206B JETRANGER variants
   G-BBOR BEWY BKEW BLGV BNYD BOLO
   BTHY BUZZ BVGA BXAY BXDS BXKL BXNS
   BXRY BXUF BYBI BYSE BZNI CHOA CIWH
   CLAY COIN DATR DOFY ELLI FEZZ FOXM
   GAND GBRU GEZZ HANY HELE HMPT IBIG
   IGIS ILYA ISPH JAES JBDB JETX JROO
   JTBX JWBI KETH LBDC LILY MFMF MOTA
   NEWZ NORK OBYT OCFD OETI OJPS
   OMDR ONTV ONYX OSMD PMGG RAMI
   REMH RGWY RKEL RNBW RUCK SDCI
   SELY SPEY STVZ SUER SUET SUEZ SYDH
   TEGS TGRZ TOPM TOYZ TREE WIIZ WIZZ
   XBOX XXBH XXIV
206L LONGRANGER
   G-CDYR CIUY JGBI JRCR LEEZ LIMO LONE
   LVDC OHWK OSAR PTOO SUEY TTGV
   UNZZ VTGE VVBO
212
   G-BIGB
407
   G-COGS DCDB DKEM HUMM JGXP
412
   G-BWZR BXBE BXBF BXFF BXFH BXHC
   CBUB CBVP CBXL CCYX
429
   G-HPIN ODSA RIDB WLTS

505 JET RANGER X
G-CLCP DONE GLLY IGGI JRXI JRXV MADZ
XXSF

UH-1H IROQUOIS
G-HUEY UHIH

BELLANCA AIRCRAFT CORPORATION
**– including AERONCA, CHAMPION and
AMERICAN CHAMPION production**

7ECA CITABRIA
G-BLHS BOID BOTO BPMM BSLW CIDD

7ECA CITABRIA AURORA
G-EGBP EGWN

7GCAA CITABRIA
G-CTAB ZOSA

7GCBC CITABRIA
G-BBEN BBXY BGGA BGGB BGGC BKBP
BVLT CKPF CONR HUNI

7KCAB CITABRIA
G-AYXU BOLG

8GCBC SCOUT
G-BGGD IIIJ

8KCAB DECATHLON
G-BTXX

8KCAB SUPER DECATHLON
G-DDGJ DZZY EEEZ IGLZ INGS IZZZ OCOK
TPSY

17-30A SUPER VIKING
G-VIKE

BENSEN AIRCRAFT CORPORATION
**including CAMPBELL-BENSEN and
MONTGOMERIE-BENSEN production; see
CAMPBELL for Cricket**

B.8 GYROPLANE variants
G-ATLP AWDW AXBG BCGB BIGX BIHX
BIVK BJAO BKBS BLLA BLLB BMZW BNBU
BOUV BOWZ BOZW BPTV BREA BREU
BRFW BSZM BTBL BTIG BTJS BTTD BUPF
BVPX BWAH BWEY BYTS BZID BZIP BZJR
BZOF CBFW CBNX CCXS CDBE CDMK
CDVJ FGSI NEII OTIM YJET YROY

BENSEN-PARSONS – see PARSONS

BEST OFF
SKY RANGER (SWIFT) variants
G-CBIV CBVR CBVS CBWW CBXS CCAF
CCBA CCBG CCBJ CCCK CCCM CCCR
CCCY CCDG CCDH CCDY CCEH CCIK
CCIY CCJA CCJT CCJW CCKF CCKG CCLF
CCLU CCMX CCMZ CCNJ CCNR CCNS
CCPF CCPL CCRR CCRV CCSX CCTR
CCUC CCUF CCVR CCWC CCWU CCXH
CCXM CCXN CCYM CCZM CDAY CDBA
CDBO CDBV CDCH CDDR CDDU CDFJ
CDHA CDHE CDHU CDIJ CDIU CDJP CDKH
CDKI CDKX CDLG CDLK CDMP CDMV
CDNE CDOV CDPB CDPE CDTP CDUL
CDUS CDVA CDWB CDWM CECP CEDI
CEDZ CEHD CEKK CENG CENS CERB
CESD CETO CETU CETV CEUJ CEXM CEZE
CFBL CFBY CFCD CFCK CFCY CFDN
CFGO CFIA CFIZ CFJG CFJJ CFLN CFMI
CFNO CFOW CFRM CFSW CFUD CFVK
CFWR CGJM CGKZ CGMN CGTR CGUU
CGWT CGYP CHFZ CHKG CHKO CHLZ
CHPS CIBV CIGT CIHV CIIT CIJT CIKR CINL
CIOK CIPR CITG CIUI CIWA CIYN CJAK
CJEJ CJPB CJPE CJUT CJVK CJXF CKIY
CKJI CKRZ CKUR CKXC CLDM CLDN CLEY
CMOR CRAB CZMI DAMS DOIN DOZZ
EGGZ ENKY ERTE EVAJ FIDO FLDG FRNK
FURZ GBRI GLHI GRLS HABI HAYS HIYA
HLEE HMCB HODR HULK IGET IMPS INCE
IRAY ISEL JAOC JAYS JEZZ JPWM KAYX
KLYE KULA LASN LDAH MARO MIAN MLZZ
MOPS MRGT NEDS NICS NINJ NIXX NJPG
NOTS NUFC NYNJ OBAZ OCDC OKIM

OKPS ONSW OSKR OTCV OTUM OVOL
PAWZ PEGE POLL POPY PSKY PTAR RAFR
RAFY REVO RHAM RSKY SEBN SIRE SKPG
SKRA SKRG SKSW SNUG SPMM SULU
SUMM SUMO SWYF TEDI TFOG TIDY
TMCB TORO TRTL TYGR UACA UMMY
UPHI UPTA VVVV WALZ WAZP WCKM
WEEK WLSN XBAL XKRV XLAM XWEB XYJY
ZADA ZSKY

BETTS
TB.1
G-BVUG

BIERINX and DUGOURD
POU du CIEL BI-FLY
G-POUX

BLACKBURN AEROPLANE AND
MOTOR CO LTD
B.2
G-AEBJ

MONOPLANE
G-AANI

BLAKE
BLUETIT
G-BXIY

BLERIOT CIE
XI
G-AANG BPVE

BOEING AIRCRAFT CO including BOEING
COMPANY
727-200 series
G-OSRA OSRB

737-300 series
G-CELE CELI CELS CELY GDFB GDFE
GDFG GDFH GDFK GDFL GDFM GDFN
GDFO GDFT JMCL JMCM JMCO JMCP
JMCT JMCU MISG SWRD TGPG

737-400 series
G-CKUZ JMCB JMCH JMCJ JMCK JMCR
JMCS JMCV JMCX JMCY JMCZ NPTX
NPTY NPTZ POWP POWS

737-500 series
G-MADA

737-800 series
G-DRTA DRTB DRTC DRTD DRTE DRTF
DRTG DRTH DRTN DRTT DRTU DRTW FDZE
FDZR FDZS FDZT FDZU FDZX FDZY FDZZ
GDFC GDFD GDFF GDFJ GDFP GDFR
GDFS GDFU GDFV GDFW GDFX GDFY
GDFZ JZBA JZBB JZBC JZBD JZBE JZBF
JZBG JZBH JZBI JZBJ JZBK JZBL JZBM
JZBN JZBO JZBP JZBR JZBS JZHA JZHB
JZHC JZHD JZHE JZHF JZHG JZHH JZHJ
JZHK JZHL JZHM JZHN JZHO JZHP JZHR
JZHS JZHT JZHU JZHV JZHW JZHX JZHY
JZHZ NPTA NPTB NPTC NPTD RUKA TAWA
TAWB TAWC TAWD TAWF TAWG TAWI TAWJ
TAWL TAWM TAWN TAWO TAWU TAWV
TAWW TAWX

737-8 series
G-TUMA TUMB TUMC TUMD TUMF TUMG

747-400 series
G-BNLN BNLP BNLY BYGA BYGB BYGC
BYGD BYGE BYGF BYGG CIVA CIVB CIVC
CIVD CIVE CIVF CIVG CIVH CIVI CIVJ CIVK
CIVL CIVM CIVN CIVO CIVP CIVR CIVS CIVT
CIVU CIVV CIVW CIVX CIVY CIVZ CLAA
CLAE CLBA VAST VBIG VGAL VLIP VROM
VROS VROY VXLG

747-800 series
G-CLAB

757-200 series
G-BIKT BIKX BMRA BMRB BMRD BMRF
BMRI BMRJ BYAW BYAY CPEV DHKB DHKC
DHKD DHKE DHKF DHKG DHKH DHKK
DHKM DHKN DHKO DHKP DHKR DHKS
DHKT DHKU DHKX DHKZ LSAA LSAB LSAC
LSAD LSAE LSAG LSAH LSAI LSAJ LSAK
LSAN OOBA OOBB OOBC OOBD OOBE
OOBF OOBG OOBN OOBP POWH TCSX
ZAPX

757-300 series
G-JMAA

767-300 series
G-DHLE DHLF DHLG OBYG OBYH POWD

777-200 series
G-RAES VIIA VIIB VIIC VIID VIIE VIIF VIIG
VIIH VIIJ VIIK VIIL VIIM VIIN VIIO VIIP VIIR
VIIS VIIT VIIU VIIV VIIW VIIX VIIY YMMA
YMMB YMMC YMMD YMME YMMF YMMG
YMMH YMMI YMMJ YMMK YMML YMMN
YMMO YMMP YMMR YMMS YMMT YMMU
ZZZA ZZZB ZZZC

777-300 series
G-STBA STBB STBC STBD STBE STBF
STBG STBH STBI STBJ STBK STBL

787-8 series
G-TUIA TUIB TUIC TUID TUIE TUIF TUIH
TUII ZBJA ZBJB ZBJC ZBJD ZBJE ZBJF
ZBJG ZBJH ZBJI ZBJJ ZBJK ZBJM

787-9 series
G-CKNZ CKOF CKOG CKWA CKWB CKWC
CKWD CKWE CKWF CKWN CKWP CKWS
CKWT TUIJ TUIK TUIL TUIM VAHH VBEL
VBOW VBZZ VCRU VDIA VFAN VMAP VNEW
VNYL VOOH VOWS VSPY VWHO VWOO
VYUM VZIG ZBKA ZBKB ZBKC ZBKD ZBKE
ZBKF ZBKG ZBKH ZBKI ZBKJ ZBKK ZBKL
ZBKM ZBKN ZBKO ZBKP ZBKR ZBKS

BOEING AIRPLANE CO
KAYDET including N2S, PT-13 & PT-17 variants
G-AROY AWLO AZLE BAVO BIXN BNIW
BRUJ BSDS BSWC BTFG CCXA CCXB
CGPY CIJN CIOC CIPE CJIN CJYK CKSR
CKST CKSU CKSV CKXY CLDX DINS EDMK
FRDM IIIG IIIY IIYI ILLE ISDN KAYD NZSS
OBEE PTBA

B-17G FORTRESS
G-BEDF

BOLAND
52-12
G-BYMW

BÖLKOW APPARATEBAU GmbH
**including MALMO, MBB and WAGGON-U
MASCHINENBAU AG production**

BÖ 207
G-EFTE EJBI

BÖ 208 JUNIOR
G-ASFR ASZD ATDO ATSI ATTR ATUI ATVX
ATXZ AVKR AVLO BIJD BJEX BOKW BSME
CLEM ECGO

BÖ 209 MONSUN
G-AYPE AZBB AZDD AZOA AZOB AZRA
AZTA AZVA AZVB EFJD EMHK

PHOEBUS variants
G-CGDD CJWP DCHC DCHJ DCJB DCJJ

BOMBARDIER INC – also see DE
HAVILLAND CANADA and LEARJET
CL-600 CHALLENGER series
G-CKXN CKZN CKZO DAYR FABO HOTY
MOCL OCFT RANE RCAV REYS RNFR RNJP
XONE

BD-100 CHALLENGER 300/350
G-KALS KSFR OOEG

BD-700 GLOBAL Series
G-CEYL CGSJ DMAZ FOMO GABY GLOB
MAZS OCAK OUEG SALD SGSG XXRS

BONSALL
DB-1 MUSTANG
G-BDWM

BOWERS
FLY BABY
G-BNPV BUYU EFRP UPID

BRANDLI
BX-2 CHERRY
G-BXUX CGTE

BRANTLY HELICOPTER CORPORATION
B.2
G-ASXD AVIP AWDU OAPR

BREGUET (SOCIÉTÉ ANONYME DES ATELIERS D'AVIATION LOUIS BREGUET)
905A FAUVETTE
G-DDGV

BREEZER AIRCRAFT GmbH and Co KG
AEROSTYLE BREEZER
G-CJGP CKVX OBZR OVIV

BRISTOL AEROPLANE CO LTD
20 M.1C replica
G-BWJM

BOXKITE
G-ASPP

F.2B FIGHTER
G-AEPH

SCOUT replica
G-FDHB

149 BOLINGBROKE (BLENHEIM)
G-BPIV

BRITISH AIRCRAFT CORPORATION (BAC) – also see HUNTING PERCIVAL AIRCRAFT LTD
BAC.145 JET PROVOST variants
G-BVTC BWCS BWEB BWGF BWOF BWSG
JPRO JPTV

BAC.167 STRIKEMASTER variants
G-FLYY MXPH RSAF SOAF

BRITISH AIRCRAFT MANUFACTURING COMPANY LTD
SWALLOW 2
G-ADMF ADPS AFCL AFGD AFGE

BRITISH KLEMM AEROPLANE CO
L.25 SWALLOW
G-ACXE

BRITTEN-NORMAN LTD including BRITTEN-NORMAN (BEMBRIDGE) LTD, FAIREY BRITTEN-NORMAN LTD, IRMA and PILATUS (BN-2) production
BN-2A III TRISLANDER
G-BEVT RLON

BN-2A, BN-2B, BN-2T ISLANDER and DEFENDER
G-AWNT AXUB BCEN BEXJ BIIO BJEC
BJED BJEF BJEJ BJOH BJYT BKOK BLDV
BLNI BPCA BSAH BSWR BUBG BUBN
BUBP BVSG BVSK CGTC CKYC CZNE
DLRA HEBO HEBS JSAT NOIL OBNC ORED
OSEA SBUS SICA SICB SSKY WPNS

BRM AERO
BRISTELL NG5
G-CIGW CIIL CILL CIPG CIPT CJBU CJMF
CJRS CKTN CLBT CLDO COLF CXTE DLAF
IOVE JANF JEMP MLSY NGAA NGCC NGII
NTPS OJCS OTAW PIPZ PTFE RBWW RVEA
STDO STEL STUU TIMI UPIZ XFTF ZGAB

BROCHET (CONSTRUCTIONS AÉRONAUTIQUES MAURICE BROCHET)
MB.50 PIPISTRELLE
G-AVKB BADV

BROCK – see KEN BROCK

BROOKMOOR BEDE AIRCRAFT – see BEDE

BRÜGGER
MB.2 COLIBRI
G-BKCI BKRH BNDP BNDT BPBP BRWV
BUDW BUTY BVIS BVVN BXVS KARA NEUS
PRAG

BÜCKER including CASA and DORNIER-WERKE AG production
BÜ.131 JUNGMANN (CASA 1-131)
G-BECT BECW BEDA BHPL BHSL BIRI
BJAL BPDM BPTS BPVW BSAJ BSLH BTDT
BTDZ BUCC BUCK BUVN BWHP BYIJ BZJV
CDJU CDLC CDRU CGTX CHII CIUE EHBJ
EHDS EMJA JGMN JMNN JUNG JWJW
RETA TAFF WIBS WJCM

BÜ.133 JUNGMEISTER including CASA variants
G-AXMT BUKK BUTX BVGP CIJV MEIS
PTDP RPAX

BÜ.181 BESTMANN
G-CBKB CIEZ

BURKHART GROB FLUGZEUGBAU – see SCHEMPP-HIRTH FLUGZEUGBAU GmbH

BURKHART GROB LUFT-UND RAUMFAHRT GMBH & CO KG – see GROB-WERKE GMB & CO KG

BUSHBY-LONG
MIDGET MUSTANG
G-AWIR BXHT CHJO GOER IIDC IIHX IIJC
MIDG

C

C D JULIAN – see JULIAN

CAMERON BALLOONS LTD – also see COLT BALLOONS LTD, SKY BALLOONS LTD and THUNDER BALLOONS LTD
20 series
G-BIBS BJUV BOYO BRCJ

24 series
G-BSCK BVCY BZUV

26 series
G-CKSW MOUZ OCGD

31 series
G-BEJK BEUY BGHS BKIX BKIZ BPUB
BRMT BVFB BZYR CBLN CCHP CIBX CIJJ
CIMW CINN CIPD CJIX CJOI CJRK CJWY
CJXK CJYJ CKTW CKYX ERAS IHOP ISOB
PICO RBMV WETI

34 series
G-BRKL BVZX BXYI BYNW BZBT EROS
FZZI IAMP

42 series
G-BCDL BCEU BMWU BUPP BWEE BXJH
BXTG BYRK CCAY CJUO SKOT STBT

56 series
G-BDSF BDUI BDUZ BECK BEEH BEND
BERT BFKL BHGF BICU BLUJ BNZN BOWM
CIIE CIZE CJPD DKGM HAZD HOFM LENN
ODAY WYNT

60 series
G-BTZU BVDY BXJZ CBJS CBVD CENN
CGFN CHNO CHVC CKIT IFIF LOON ROGY

65 series
G-AZIP BDSK BEIF BHNC BHOT BIBO BIGL
BISH BIYI BKWR BMCD BMJN BMKY BNAN
BNAW BOAL BOOB BOWV BPGD BROE
BROG BTUH BXGY BXUU BZPD CEVH CIUK
CKPR GLUE MUIR PMAM PYRO SMIG

69 series
G-JAKX

70 series
G-BXOT BYJX CCPP CFNB CIAE CIAY CILO
CIND CIOU CISL CKXG EXHL GABS GPPN
KENK OWAG OWLY ROEN RUPS UUPP
WJAC

77 series
G-BCNP BDBI BEEI BFYK BGAZ BHDV
BHHN BHII BIET BLLD BLPP BMAD BMKJ
BMKP BMLJ BMOH BMTX BNCB BNEO
BNGJ BNIN BNIU BNKT BNNE BNPE BOAU
BOBR BOEK BOJB BOOZ BORB BORN
BOTW BOWB BOXG BPHH BPLV BPPP
BPSR BPTD BPYT BRBO BRKW BRMU
BRMV BRNW BRRF BRRR BRSD BRUV
BRZA BSBR BSDX BSEH BSEV BSHO BSIC
BSIJ BSUV BSWV BSXM BTOI BTOP BTPT
BTZV BUAM BUGP BUGS BUHM BUNG
BUTJ BUWU BUZK BVBU BVDR BVFF
BVHK BVUK BWAN BWPC BWTJ BWYN
BXSX BXVT BYHY BYLY BZPW CBHX CCAR
CCSP CEJA CEJC CEPU CEPV CGOD
CGOW CGVY CHUK CIAP CIBP CIFI CIHI
CIHO CIKC CIXR CIXU CJES CJIK CKPC
CKUP FELT GHOP GUNS HARE HENY JINI
KEYY LAZR LEGO LIBB LIOT LOAN LOLL
MOKE MRTY NWPR OATV OEDP OJEN
OKYA OMRB ORPR POLY PUSS RAPH
RCMF RIXY RONI SAFE SLAC SNOW SUSI
TICO TIPJ TSWZ ULIA UPUP VBFW VMVM
VODA WAIT WBEV XPWW ZINT

80 series
G-BUYC BVEN BVUU BVZN BWAO BXLG
BXSC BYER BYIV BYIW BYIX BYTJ BZPK
CBEY CDJY CELM CEMF CEMU CFEB
CFTM CFUX CFVX CGDG CGOH CHAU
CHHL CHJM CIDH CJPG CKDT EVET HCPD
HOTM LIMP MCAP NMOS OBTS OGJM
RMAX SLCE

84 series
G-AZNT AZRN BAGY BALD BNFP BOYM
BREX BRGD BVXD CJLT EOLE MOSY OFBT
STAV UPOI

90 series
G-BPSO BROY BTFU BTHF BTXF BUGY
BUIZ BUVW BVDX BVHO BVHR BVMR
BVOP BWAU BWIP BWNO BWNS BWUU
BWVU BXJO BXVV BYHC BYKX BYNN
BYTW BZEY BZFD BZIX BZJH BZTK BZUU
BZXR BZYY CBAT CBRV CBUO CCBB
CCBT CCMN CCPT CCXF CDGN CDHY
CDIO CDOB CDRF CECD CEJZ CEOS CEPR
CERH CESH CEUV CFEA CFLK CGIH CGVV
CGWX CHXS CIBN CIGJ CIGN CIHG CIJB
CIKZ CIUB CJDN CJGA CKWY CKXK CLAD
CLCR CONC CTEL CXCX DEKA DRYS EEFA
ELLE EOPH FEED FMGB FOGG FVEL GLAW
GOGW GOPR IBEV IGLE INSR ITOI IWON
JHAA JLIA JULU KAYI LAAC LAGR LTSB
LULA METH MFLI MILE MSON OAAM OCTS
OJBM OJMS OMEN OPWR OXBY PATG
PERC PPIO RIZE RIZI ROXI SALE SBIZ
SUAU TINS TMCC TRIG VGFS VKUP VRVI
WIFI YUMM YUPI ZSKD

100 series
G-CEFS

105 series
G-BOTD BOTK BRLL BTKW BTRL BUAV
BUHU BUWF BVCA BVHV BVUA BVXA
BWDH BWEW BWSU BXEN BXTF BXXG
BXXL BYFJ BYHU BYNX BZDN BZKU BZVU
BZXO CBHW CBMC CBNW CCGY CCIU
CCOT CCYI CDIT CDMC CDRI CDWD CDYG
CDZW CEDF CEEK CEKS CFEK CGER
CGNJ CIXD CJRO CJXJ CKCC CKEG CLIC
ELEE ENZO FFAB FUSE GAGE HIMM HONK
KSKS NFVB NLYB NZGL OAML OFAA OGLY
OJBS OPAW OSAT OTCT OUVI RECL SEDO
SEPT SERV SFSL SSTI SUCK TORK TUTU
ULTR VSGE XHOT

120 series
G-BOZY BRXA BTOU BWLD BYSV CBOW
CBVV CCEN CCTS CCVZ CEXN CFVY CHDZ
CHFM CIHN CIRN CJYZ CKVI CLBD LOBO
MEUP MOFB ORCV UWEB VALZ XPDA

133 series
G-CIJM

140 series
G-BWTE CGTS CHXF CILZ DSPK OXBC
TOPB

145 series
G-CETK CIBA HIBM

150 series
G-CIRX OPBW

160 series
G-CHLE OXBA

180 series
G-OBRY

210 series
G-BYSM BZBE CHVI CIZM CVBF JHNY
JOJO

225 series
G-CDRN

250 series
G-BWZJ CGTY OVBF XRLD

275 series
G-CBZZ CCSG CDIH CFCC CIFH VBFT

300 series
G-CBAW CHHC CJXI KENA VBAD VBAF
VBFZ

315 series
G-CLEB DORY PIGZ RLDS RLDZ

340 series
G-KVBF HVBF

350 series
G-CDDL CDIB CERC CEWX CGZR EVBF
VBFG VBFH VBFI VBFJ VBFK

375 series
G-CHOJ OSRS PRZI RLDX VBFM VBFN
VBFO VBFR VBFS

400 series
G-VBAA VBAB VBAE VBAG VBAH VBAI
VBAJ VBAK VBAL VBAM VBAN VBAO VBAP
VBAR VBAS VBAT VBAU VBAV VBAW VBFL
VBFU VBFV VBFX VBFY

450 series
G-CLEC CLED

GB-1000
G-CGOZ

SS Ball
G-RNIE

SS Barrel
G-PINT

SS Bear
G-HEYY

SS Bearskin
G-POMP

SS Bertie Bassett
G-BZTS

SS Bowler
G-OPKF

SS Bradford and Bingley
G-BWMY

SS Buddy
G-WLVE

SS Bus
G-BUSS

SS Cabin
G-SHAK

SS Can
G-PURE

SS Carrots
G-HUCH

SS Chateau
G-BTCZ

SS Clown
G-CLWN

SS Club
G-BWNP

SS Cube
G-RCOH

SS Doll
G-BVDF

SS Drag
G-GBGF

SS Drop
G-CKFI

SS Dude
G-OIFM

SS Egg
G-OEGG

SS Elephant
G-BPRC

SS Fire
G-BZJA

SS Flying Cottage
G-COTT

SS Frog
G-CIFP

SS Furness House
G-BSIO

SS Golfball
G-PUTT

SS Grand Illusion
G-MAGC

SS Light Bulb
G-BVWI

SS Lightbulb
G-LAMP

SS Lips
G-LIPS

SS Minion
G-DMES DMEZ

SS Monster Truck
G-BWMU

SS Nescafe Mug
G-RMUG

SS Orange
G-CDXW

SS OTTI
G-OTTI

SS Pig
G-HOGS

SS Pot
G-CHAM

SS Printer
G-BYFK

SS Ronald
G-CKWH

SS Rupert Bear
G-BTML

SS S Can
G-CDMO

SS Shoe
G-BUDN

SS Shopping Bag
G-CFOP

SS Sign
G-UCCC

SS Sphere
G-BVFU BYJW SATI SATL

SS Sport
G-CKWW CKXA CKXE CLCC KENX

SS Truck
G-DERV

SS Tub
G-DIPI

SS TV
G-SEUK

SS Van
G-ORAC

SS Watch
G-BMJJ

SS Wine Box
G-STOW

CAMPBELL AIRCRAFT LTD including
BENSEN and **EVERETT GYROPLANES LTD**
production
CRICKET
G-AXPZ AXRC AXVM AYCC AYPZ AYRC
BHBA BORG BRLF BSRL BTMP BUIG BVDJ
BVLD BVOH BWSD BXCJ BXHU BXUA
CBWN CCPD CDXV GYRO RUGS TVSI YIRO

CAMPBELL-BENSEN – see BENSEN

CANADAIR – see BOMBARDIER INC

CANADIAN-VICKERS LTD
PBY-5A CATALINA
G-PBYA

**CAPRONI VIZZOLA ZOSTRUZIONII
AERONAUTICHE SpA**
CALIF A-21
G-CKNG

CARLSON
SPARROW
G-BSUX BVVB

CARMAM (SOCIÉTÉ CARMAM)
JP-15/36A AIGLON
G-CHKZ CHMU DDYL DFOV

M100S MESANGE
G-CHOF DDTS DEOM DEPG

M200 FOEHN
G-DEOX

CARNET
PARAMOTOR
G-CGRJ

CASA – see BÜCKER

CASSUTT including MUSSO SPECIAL,
SPEED TWO and WILSON variants
RACER
G-BFMF BOMB BOXW BPVO CXDZ LEFT
OGPN OLHR RAGE RUNT

CEA – see JODEL

CENTRAIR (SOCIÉTÉ NOUVELLE CENTRAIR) see also SCHLEICHER

101 PÉGASE variants
G-CEVE CFCB CFEH CFFC CFFS CFGW
CFJK CFNM CFRP CFRR CFRV CFRX CFVM
CFVN CFVP CFVV CFWY CFXD CGBU
CHDD CHNY CHNZ CJOP CKAE CKBA
CKGM CKHM CKKB CKMF CLGW CLVZ
DEOK DERX DESH DETJ DETM DEVM DEVO
DFCD DHES REER SVEN

201 MARIANNE
G-CJXB CJXN

SNC-34 ALLIANCE
G-CJHR

CESSNA AIRCRAFT COMPANY including REIMS AVIATION SA production (F.prefix)

120
G-AJJS AJJT AKTS AKVM BHLW BJML
BPZB BRJC BRPE BRPF BRPG BRPH
BRUN BRXH BTBW BTEW BUHZ BUJM
BUKO BVUZ JOLY OVFM

140 variants
G-AKUR ALTO BOCI BPUU BTBV BUHO
HALJ

150 and A150 variants
G-ARFI ARFO ASMS ASMW ASUE ASYP
ASZB ASZU ATEF ATHV ATHZ ATMC ATMM
ATNE ATNL ATRK ATRM ATUF ATYM ATZZ
AVEM AVEN AVEO AVER AVHM AVIB AVIT
AVMD AVMF AVNC AVUG AVUH AVZU
AWAX AWBX AWCP AWES AWFF AWGK
AWMT AWOT AWPJ AWPU AWTX AWUJ
AWUL AWUN AWUT AWUU AXGG AXPF
AXSW AXUF AYCF AYGC AYOZ AYRV AZLY
AZOZ AZUZ AZZR BABC BABD BACN
BACO BAEP BAEV BAEZ BAHI BAIK BAMC
BAPI BAPJ BAXU BAXV BAYP BAYP BAZS
BBBC BBDT BBJX BBKA BBKB BBKY BBNJ
BBTB BBXB BCBX BCDY BCFR BCKU
BCKV BCUH BCUJ BCUY BCVG BCVH
BDAI BDBU BDEX BDOD BDRD BDTX
BDUM BDUO BEIG BEKN BELT BEMY BEOE
BEOK BEOY BFGG BFGZ BFIE BFIY BFOG
BFRR BFVU BGBI BHIY BHRH BIFY BIOC
BJOV BJTB BLVS BMBB BMEX BMLX BOBV
BOFW BOIV BORY BOTP BOUJ BPAB
BPAW BPEM BPGZ BPJW BPOS BPWG
BPWM BPWN BRBH BRLR BRNC BRTJ
BSEJ BSJZ BSKA BSSB BSYV BSZV BTES
BTHE BTYC BUCA BUCT BURH BUTT BWII
BZJW CIIR CIRW CISO CKBW COVZ CSBM
DENC DEND ELYS FFAF FFEN FINA GFLY
GLED HFCB HIVE HULL IANJ ICDP ICLC
IHXD JAGS JHAC JWDS KOVU KWET LALA
LUCK MABE MSES NSTG NWFA OKED
OKLY OMAS OPIC OSND OSTY PHAA
PHOR PHUN PLAN PNIX PPFS SAMZ TEDB
TXAS UFLY USAA

152 and A152 variants
G-BFEK BFFE BFFW BFGL BFHU BFLU
BFMK BFOE BFOF BFRV BGAA BGAB
BGAE BGFX BGGO BGGP BGIB BGLG
BGNT BHAA BHAD BHAI BHAV BHCP
BHDM BHDS BHED BHEN BHFC BHFI
BHHG BHIN BHMG BHUI BHWA BHWB
BHZH BICG BIDH BIJV BIJW BILR BILS
BIMT BIOK BITF BITH BIZG BJVJ BJYD
BKAZ BKFC BKGW BLAC BLJO BLZH BLZP
BMCN BMCV BMGG BMJB BMJD BMMM
BMTA BMTB BMTJ BMUO BMVB BMXA
BMXB BMXC BMYG BNAJ BNFR BNHJ
BNHK BNID BNIV BNJB BNJC BNJH BNKC
BNKI BNKP BNKR BNKS BNKV BNMD
BNME BNMF BNPY BNRL BNSM BNSN
BNSU BNUL BNUT BNYL BOAI BODO BOFL
BOHI BOHJ BOIO BOIR BOKY BOLV BOLW
BONW BOSO BOTG BOYB BOYL BOZR
BPBJ BPBK BPEO BPFZ BPME BRBP

BRCD BRND BRNE BRNK BRNN BRPV
BRTD BRTP BRUM BSCP BSCZ BSDO
BSDP BSFP BSFR BSTO BSTP BSWH BSZO
BSZW BTAL BTCE BTDW BTFC BTGR
BTGW BTGX BTVW BTVX BTYT BUEF BUEG
BVTM BWEU BWNB BWNC BWND BXJM
BXVB BXVY BYFA BYMJ BZAE BZEA BZEB
BZEC BZHE BZHF CCHT CDTX CEFM CEPX
CEYG CEYH CEZM CGFG CGSP CHIK
CHZP CICC CIJS CINA CIPY CIUH CIUU
CIXP CJPN CKAT CLAP CPFC DACF ECAD
EEKK EGSL ENTT ENTW FIFE FIGA FIGB
FLIP GDIA GFIB GFID GFIG GMOX GSFS
HART HFCL HFCT HUXY JIMH KATT LAMS
LOMN LVME MASS MFLM OBEN OCPC
ODAC OFRY OIMC OLEE OPAM OVMC
OWOW PFSL PPLS PTTA PTTB PTTE SAYX
SELA SHBA SMON TALA TALB TALC TALD
TALO UFCN WACB WACE WACF WACH
WACU ZOOL

C.165 AIRMASTER
G-BTDE

170
G-APVS AWOU BCLS EEVY MDAY

172 SKYHAWK and CUTLASS variants
G-ARID ARMO ARMR AROA ARWR ARYK
ARYS ASFA ASMJ ASNW ASOK ASSS ASUP
ASVM ATFY ATKT ATLM ATSL ATWJ AVHH
AVIC AVIS AVJF AVKG AVPI AVTP AVVC
AVZV AWLF AWUZ AWVA AXBJ AXDI AXSI
AXVB AYCT AYRG AYRT AYUV AZJV AZKW
AZKZ AZLV AZTS AZUM AZXD AZZV BAEO
BAEW BAEY BAIW BANX BAVB BAXY BBDH
BBJY BBJZ BBKI BBKZ BBNZ BBOA BBTG
BBTH BCRB BCUF BCVJ BCYR BDNU
BDZD BEHV BEMB BEUX BEWR BEZK
BEZO BEZV BFGD BFKB BFMX BFOV BFPH
BFRS BFTH BGHJ BGIU BGIY BGLO BGMP
BGND BGRO BGSV BGVS BHCC BHCM
BHDX BHDZ BHPZ BHSB BHUG BHVR
BHYP BHYR BIGJ BIHI BIOB BIZF BJDE
BJDW BJGY BJVM BJWI BJWW BJXZ BKCE
BKEV BKII BKIJ BKLO BLHJ BLVW BMCI
BMHS BMIG BNKD BNKE BNRR BNST
BNTP BNYM BOEN BOHH BOIL BOIX BOIY
BOJS BOLI BOLY BOMS BONR BONS
BOOL BORW BOUE BPML BPRM BPTL
BPVA BPWS BRAK BRBI BRBJ BRCM BREZ
BSNG BSOG BSOO BSPE BSTM BTMA
BTMR BUJN BXGV BXOI BXSD BXSE BXXK
BYBD BYEA BYNA BZBF CBFO CBME
CBOR CBXJ CCTT CDDK CEKI CFCI CFIO
CFMM CFOI CGRX CGTM CIBB CIGD CIIM
CIPU CIRO CISX CKIE CKIF CKIP CKXJ
CLBJ CLJM CLJP CLUX CMBR COCO
CSCS CWFT CXSM DBOD DCKK DEMH
DODD DUNK DUVL ECAK ECGC EETG
EGEG EGLA EICK ENOA ETAT ETDC FACE
FLKY FLOW FNLD GAAZ GBLP GBTL GEHL
GFSA GWYN GYAV GZDO HERC HIGA HILS
HLOB ICOM IDHC IHAR INKO ISLY JEBS
JFWI JKKK JKPF JMKE JONZ LANE LAVE
LICK LLCH LMAO LOOC LSCM MCLY
MEGS MELT MFAC MICK MRPT MSOF
NEEE NIUS NWFC NWFG NWFS NWFT
NXOE OAFA OARS OBMS OERS OFCM
OJAG OOLE OPMJ OPYE ORDA OSII OSKY
OTAM OVFR OWST PDSI PFCL RARB RATI
RDAS ROLY ROOK RSWO RUIA SEVE SHSP
SHWK SKAN SKKY SMRS TALP TAMR
THYB TOBI TYRE UFCB UFCE UFCG UFCI
VOUS WACW WACY WEWI YNYS YORK
ZACE ZEVS

172RG CUTLASS
G-BHYC BILU CHZI PARI

R172K HAWK XP
G-BHYD BPCI BPWR BTMK EPIM FANL XPII

REIMS FR172 ROCKET variants
G-AWCN AWDR AWWU AYGX BARC BBKG
BCTK BFSS BLPF BZVB CLBZ DRAM EDTO

HSVI JANS LOYA MFEF RKKT ROKT THIN
YBAA

REIMS FR172K HAWK XP
G-BFIG BFIU DAVD EFBP EFSF PJTM STAY
YIPI

175 SKYLARK
G-ARCV ARMN ARRI ARWS EHRU OTOW

177(RG) CARDINAL
G-AYPG AYPH AYSX AYSY AZTF AZVP
BAGN BAIS BAJA BAJB BAJE BBJV BEBN
BFIV BFMH BFPZ BRDO BRPS BTSZ BUJE
CIJU CIMB ECNX FIJJ FNEY GBFR GCWS
OSFS SYLM TOTO ZION

180 including 180K SKYWAGON
G-ASIT AXZO BNCS CIBO GKRC

182 SKYLANE variants
G-ARAW ATCX ATLA ATPT AVCV AVDA
AXZU AYOW AYWD AZNO BAFL BAHX
BBYH BCWB BDIG BEKO BFSA BFZD BGAJ
BHDP BHIB BHVP BHYA BJVH BKKN BKKO
BKKP BMMK BNMO BNRY BOPH BOTH
BOWO BPUM BRRK BSDW BSRR BUVO
BWMC BWRR BXEZ BYEM CBIL CBMP
CBVX CCYS CDRC CDXI CEFV CGFH CGKY
CIMM CINF CJAF CKCL CWDW CWTT
CYRL DOVE DRGS DSJT DTFF ECET EDGK
EEZS EFAM EFNH EIWT EKOS ELXE ENEA
EOHL ESME ESSL FAEJ FFBG GAID GBUN
GCYC GHOW HHDR HOWI HRND HUFF
IART ICMX IFAB IJAG ILBT IRPC ISEH IZZI
JHPC JOBS KJTT KKTG KTWO LEGG LUEK
MAHY MATW MICI MISH MOUT MPLA
MPLB MPLC MPLD MPLE MPLF MRAG
NLEE NOCK NYKS OBBO OHAC OJHC
OJRM OLDG OMAG OPCG OPST ORAY
ORDM OWRT OZOI PLEE POPW POWL
PUGS RACY RCHE RDDM RITZ RMCS
RYSE SARP SEHK SHAR SKYL SNAL SPCI
THRE TPSL TREB VIPA VONY WARP WIFE
XLTG ZBLT ZEZE ZGZG ZINC

185 SKYWAGON variants
G-AYNN BDKC BKPC BLOS BWWF BYBP
RNRM SAUO

190
G-BTBJ

195A
G-BSPK

205(A)
G-ASNK

206 variants
G-ATCE ATLT AZRZ BFCT BMOF BPGE
BXDB BXRO CCRC CCSN CHJK DROP
DVTA NIME OSSA SEAI SEMR

208 CARAVAN and 208B GRAND CARAVAN
G-BZAH CKSE CPSS CYPC DLAK EELS
GOHI LAUD MDJE OHPC OJMP SYLV UKPA
UKPB UKPS

210 CENTURION variants
G-BEYV BNZM BSGT CDMH EENO EFFH
EMLS ERBE MPRL OFLY SEEK TOTN WYLD

T303 CRUSADER
G-CMOS CRUZ DOLY GAME INDC PUSI
ROCH UILT

305 BIRD DOG (L-19)
G-JDOG PDOG VDOG VNAM

310 variants
G-AZUY BALN BJMR BODY EGLT FFWD
MGBG RODD RVLZ

REIMS F337 SUPER SKYMASTER variants
G-BFGH BFJR

340
G-HAFG

402
G-NOSE

404 TITAN
G-BWLF EXEX FIFA MIND

REIMS F406 CARAVAN II
G-BVJT CVXN FIND LEAF MAFA MAFB
RVLW RVLX RVLY SMMA SMMB TDSA
TURF UKAL

421 GOLDEN EAGLE variants
G-BBUJ CGSG HIJK IFIK IIYY ISAR PVIP
SVIP TREC

425 CORSAIR
G-KRMA

441 CONQUEST
G-USAR

500 CITATION
G-BWFL LOFT

510 CITATION MUSTANG
G-ERLI FBKE FBKF FBKG FBKK FFFC GILB
KLNW LEAC RNER SCCA XAVB

525 CITATIONJET variants
G-CJDB CMTO HCSA LFBD LUBB OCJZ
ORAW OREZ SDRY SONE TWOP YEDC

550 CITATION BRAVO
G-CMBC IKOS IPLY JBLZ SPRE XJCI XJCJ

550 CITATION II
G-CGOA EJEL FJET SPUR

560 XL CITATION EXCEL
G-CIEL IPAX SIRS

560 XL CITATION XLS
G-CKUB CXLS GAAL GARE JALS LEAX
LXWD OJER RSXP SNJS XSTV

680 CITATION SOVEREIGN
G-CFGB

680A CITATION LATITUDE
G-SHUI

CFM METAL-FAX including CFM AIRCRAFT LTD

SHADOW Series B and BD (Rotax 447)
G-MNZP MVCW MVIG MVYZ MYKE

SHADOW Series C and CD (Rotax 503)
G-BZLF MAAM MGUY MIMU MJVF MNCM
MNER MNTK MNTP MNVI MNVJ MNVK
MNWY MNXX MNZJ MNZZ MTBE MTDU
MTFU MTGV MTGW MTHT MTHV MTKR
MTMX MTWK MTXR MVAC MVAM MVAN
MVCC MVEI MVEN MVFH MVLJ MVPK
MVRO MVRR MVRT MVVT MWAE MWDB
MWDN MWEN MWEZ MWIZ MWJF MWLD
MWON MWPN MWRL MWRY MWSZ MWTJ
MWTN MWTP MWUA MWVG MWVH MWYD
MYBC MYCM MYDE MYEP MYGO MYIF
MYIP MYLV MYOH MYON MYOS MYPL
MYPT MYTH MYWF MYWM MZBN MZCT
MZRS PSUE

SHADOW D Series SS (Rotax 912)
G-MZLP

SHADOW Series DD (Rotax 582)
G-BXZY BYCJ CCMW CIXN DMWW LYNK
MGTW MYZP MZBS MZKH MZNH ODVB
PBEL

STREAK SHADOW and STARSTREAK SHADOW
G-BONP BRSO BRWP BSMN BSOR BSPL
BSRX BTDD BTEL BTGT BTKP BTZZ BUGM
BUIL BULJ BUOB BUTB BUVX BUWR BUXC
BVDT BVFR BVLF BVOR BVPY BWAI BWCA
BWPS BXFK BXWR BXZV BYAZ BYFI BYOO
BZDF BZEZ BZWJ CBCZ CBNO CEZU CJWI
DOTT ENEE FAME GORE HLCF MEOW
MGGT MGPH MWPP MYNX MYTY OLGA
OPIT ORAF OTCH RINT ROTS SHIM SNEV
STRK TEHL TTOY WESX WHOG WYAT

CGS including ARROWFLIGHT AVIATION LTD

HAWK
G-MWYS MYTP MZGU

CHAMPION AIRCRAFT CORPORATION
– also see AERONCA and BELLANCA

7FC TRI-TRAVELER
G-APYT ARAP ARAS

CHARGUS GLIDING CO LTD – also see HIWAY

TITAN 38
G-MYZH

CHILTON AIRCRAFT

DW.1 and 2 variants
G-AESZ AFGH AFGI AFSV BWGJ CDXU
DWCB DWIA DWIB DWRU JUJU

CHIMERA

DRAGON
G-DGBT

CHOWN including SOLENT BALLOON GROUP

OSPREY MLB variants
G-BJID BJND BJNH BJPL BJRA BJRG BJTN
BJTY BJUE BJUU FYAV FYBD FYBE FYBF
FYBG FYBH FYBI FYCL FYCV FYDF FYDO
FYDS FYEV FYFN

CHRIS TENA

MINI COUPE
G-BPDJ

CHRISLEA AIRCRAFT CO LTD

CH.3 SUPER ACE
G-AKUW

CH.3 Series 4 SKYJEEP
G-AKVR

LC.1 AIRGUARD
G-AFIN

CHRISTEN INDUSTRIES INC including AVIAT AIRCRAFT INC and homebuilt, also see PITTS

A-1 HUSKY variants
G-BUVR GGZZ GUMM HSKE HSKI LIKY
OCLC ODIP OGGI OGGY OHZO ROVA
USKY WATR ZAST

EAGLE
G-CCYO CFIF CFIJ EEGL EGAL ECIL EGLE
ELKA GULZ IOOP IXII KLAW NEST NUTA
OEGL OZIP RIFY

CIRRUS DESIGN CORPORATION

SR20
G-CDLY CHPG CIRI CIRU CRLA CTNG
CTUK CZOS DOLI ELKE GCDA GCDB
GEMM IENN JOHA JOID KMLA LENZ MCLN
OAWM OPSS OSPY PHAT RGZT TAAC
VGAG ZACK ZZDG

SR22
G-CHAJ CTAM CYPM DRDR EVEN EVIB
GCVV IINK ILHR IZZT JONT JRSH KOCO
KOKO KYLA MACR MAKS OGGM OOUK
OZZT PHAB RAYY SPWP SRZZ TAAB VBCA
VBPM WOWS

CIVILIAN AIRCRAFT CO

CAC.1 COUPE
G-ABNT

CLUTTON

FRED
G-BBBW BDBF BGFF BISG BITK BKAF
BKDP BKVF BKZT BLNO BMAX BMMF
BMSL BOLS BVCO BWAP CGUI MANX
ORAS PFAF RONW USTY WICH

CM MICROLIGHTS

SUNBIRD
G-CISU

COATES

SWALESONG
G-AYDV

COBELAVIA SA – see TIPSY AIRCRAFT CO LTD

COLOMBAN – also see ZENAIR

MC-12 and MC-15 CRI-CRI variants
G-BOUT BWFO CKYN CRIC CRIK MCXV
OCRI SHOG XCRI

MC-30 LUCIOLE
G-CIBJ CIHB CKTD CKUV FIFY LCLE LUCL
LVCY

COLT BALLOONS LTD including THUNDER and COLT LTD and CAMERON BALLOONS LTD production – also see CAMERON

17A Cloudhopper
G-BJWV BKIU BKXM DIPZ HEXE

21 series
G-BLXG BOLN BOLR BSAK BSIG BTXM
CKUW SOOS

25 series
G-BSOF BUPH

31 series
G-BROJ BSMM BVTL BXXU DNGR DOWN
GELI PIXE

42 series
G-BJZR SEAT

56 series
G-BICM BISX BIXW BJYF BLLW BLOT BTZY
BVCN BVOZ CCYP EZXO ILEE LDYS MERC
POSH WIMP

65D
G-BLCH

69 series
G-BNRW BSHC BTMO OABC OBUY TCAN

77 series
G-BLUE BOHD BORE BPEZ BRVF BSCI
BSUB BSUK BTZS BUJH BUVB BUVT BUYO
BXFN BXIE BYFX CDUY CHEL DRAW DURX
EZVS FLAG HOTZ LSHI MKAK MUSM
OAWS OSST READ SIXX STOK TRUX TTFG
UZLE WHAT WHIM WOOL WRIT

90 series
G-BIFP BRRU BTPV BXUW BZOX FOWL
IRLY JNNB OMMM PHSI SAUF SEND TOFT

105 series
G-BSCC BSNU BTHX BURL BUSV BYIO
CICD CIHC CIJL CITR CJGC DMEE DRPO
EMKT HHPM HRDY IBCF ODRT OMGR
RDEN

120 series
G-BYDJ BZIL BZNF CBEJ

160 series
G-CFKX CIER

180 series
G-CUCU MUMM

210 series
G-BULN

315 series
G-VVBF

AS-105 (Rotax 462)
G-BXYF

AS-120 (Rotax 582)
G-BXKU

GA-42
G-MATS ZEPI

SS Beer Glass
G-BNHL

SS Bibendum
G-CGMR PNEU

SS Clown
G-GWIZ

SS Cylinder One
G-PSON

SS Flying Coffee Jar
G-BVBJ BVBK

SS Flying Egg
G-BWWL

SS Flying Head
G-HEAD

SS Flying Hop
G-MALT

SS Flying Jeans
G-JCJC

SS Flying Mitt
G-WCAT

SS Flying Yacht
G-BXXJ

SS Jumbo
G-VJIM

SS Satzenbrau Bottle
G-BIRE

SS Saucepan
G-BHRK

COMCO IKARUS GmbH including AEROSPORT LTD (formerly FLYBUY ULTRALIGHTS LTD) production

IKARUS C42 variants
G-CBGP CBIJ CBJW CBKU CBPD CBVY
CBXC CCFZ CCLS CCNT CCPS CCYR
CCZL CDBU CDCG CDCM CDCO CDHR
CDIX CDJK CDMS CDNW CDOK CDOT
CDPP CDRO CDRP CDRY CDSW CDUK
CDVI CDWI CDYD CDYO CDYT CDZG CEAK
CEAN CECC CECL CEDC CEEW CEFA
CEGL CEGZ CEHG CEHV CEJW CEPY
CETR CETZ CEVA CEXL CEZA CFAV CFAX
CFBE CFGM CFHP CFIT CFLD CFOG CFTO
CGNI CGWA CGWK CGXI CHIJ CHOO
CHRM CHSS CHVY CHWN CIAW CICF
CICG CIDS CIEE CIFN CIFZ CIIN CILT CILY
CIOZ CIPO CIRZ CISG CISS CIWP CIWT
CIXY CJAM CJAP CJBE CJCO CJDA CJIT
CJOT CJRZ CKGS CKVG CKWX CKYL CLAI
CLAL CLEV CLIF CLIN CVAL CWAY DAGN
DASS DCDO DGAL DJBC DMCI DNKS DOZI
DTOY DUGE EDEE EDZZ EGGI FBII FIFT
FLBY FLYB FLYC FLYM FROM GBCC GBET
GIAN GIAS GNJW GPWE GRPA GSCV
HBBH HBRB HEVR HIJN HMCD HMCE
HNGE IAJS IBAZ ICRS IIDR IKRS IKUS ILRS
INJA IRED JADW JENK JMRT JSKY JWDB
JWDW KENC KFCA KIMS KTOW MAMM
MAMZ MCVE MEGZ MGPA MOOD MPHY
MRSS MSKY NBOX NDPA NEVE NORA
NPPL NSBB OAJL OEKS OFBU OKTA
ORMW OROS ORSE OSPH OSTL OTTS
OVAL OVLA OWPS PAPI PATJ RACK RBSN
RMAV RODJ RONZ ROZZ RTMY SAMC
SARM SCMG SFAR SFLA SFLB SGEN SHCK
SHKI SIMM TIFG TROW TSHO ULSY UUUU
WHPG WILT WSSX YADA ZASH ZAVI ZOMB

COMMANDER AIRCRAFT COMPANY – see ROCKWELL INTERNATIONAL CORPORATION

COMPER AIRCRAFT CO

CLA.7 SWIFT
G-ABUS ACTF ECDT ECTF LCGL OBUU

CONSOLIDATED – see CANADIAN-VICKERS LTD

CONSOLIDATED AERONAUTIC INC – see LAKE AIRCRAFT CORPORATION

CONSTRUCTIONS AERONAUTIQUE DE BEARN – see GARDAN

CONSTRUCTIONS AÉRONAUTIQUES DE BOURGOGNE – see MUDRY and ROBIN

CONSTRUCTIONS AÉRONAUTIQUES MAURICE BROCHET – see BROCHET

CONSTRUZIONI AERONAUTICHE TECNAM SRL – see TECNAM

CONWAY

VIPER
G-CKUS

COOK

ARIES P
G-MYXI

COOPAVIA – see PIEL AVIATION

CORBEN

BABY ACE
G-DACE

CORBETT FARMS – see MICROFLIGHT AIRCRAFT LTD

CORBY

CJ-1 STARLET
G-BVVZ CBHP CCHN CCXO CIRE ILSE NATI

CORVUS AIRCRAFT KFT

CA22 CRUSADER
G-CSDR

COSMIK AVIATION LTD – also see EVEKTOR

SUPERCHASER
G-CHLI DREG

COSMOS

FLY AWAY
G-IPIG

COSTRUZIONI AERONAUTICHE GIOVANNI AGUSTA SpA – see LEONARDO

CRANFIELD INSTITUTE OF TECHNOLOGY

A.1-400 EAGLE
G-COAI

CREMER

HOT AIR FREE BALLOON
G-BJLX BJLY BJRP BJRR BJRV

CROSBY – see ANDREASSON

CROSSLEY

RACER
G-BKRU

CUB CRAFTERS

CARBON CUB
G-TFCC

EX-2
G-EXCC

CULVER

LCA CADET
G-CDET

CUPRO SAPHIRE LTD – see SAFFERY MODEL BALLOONS

CURRIE

WOT variants
G-APNT ARZW ASBA AVEY AYMP AYNA
BANV BDFB BFWD BGES BKCN BLPB
BXMX CWBM PFAP SBAG SWOT

CURTISS ROBERTSON

ROBIN C.2
G-BTYY HFBM

CURTISS-WRIGHT AIRCRAFT CORPORATION

TRAVEL AIR 12Q TRAVELAIR
G-AAOK

CURTISS-WRIGHT CORPORATION

H-75A
G-CCVH

P-36C HAWK
G-CIXJ

P-40C WARHAWK
G-CIIO

P-40F KITTYHAWK
G-CGZP

CUSTOMCRAFT BALLOON SERVICES

A25
G-CCKZ DUMP

CVJETKOVIC AIRCRAFT

CA-65 SKYFLY
G-CFVJ

CYCLONE AIRSPORTS LTD – also see PEGASUS AVIATION and SOLAR WINGS (AVIATION)

AX3
G-MYFV MYGD MYHG MYHJ MYHM MYHR
MYIU MYKF MYMW MYMZ MYPM MYPR
MYSO MYUI MYVN MYXH MYYL MYZC
MYZF MYZG MZDS MZEL

AX2000
G-CBMB CBUX JONY MGUN MYER MZFA
MZFX MZGA MZGC MZGM MZGP MZHR
MZIV MZJF MZJL MZKC MZLM MZLU
MZOE ROMW STRG WAKY

TRIKE
G-MNMY

CZECH AIRCRAFT WORKS (CZAW) – also see CZECH SPORT AIRCRAFT below

SPORTCRUISER (Home built)
G-CESZ CFEZ CFIU CFKB CFLG CFNV
CFOV CFPA CFPJ CFUZ CFXN CGCH CGIL
CGIP CGJL CGJS CGJT CGLP CGMM
CGMP CGNG CGWH CHXG CIAX CRAR
CRUI CRWZ CRZA CSAW CZAW CZSC
DADZ DGSC DOIG DVOY EDDS ENST EZZE
FELX HMPS IBUZ JAYZ JONL KRUZ KUIP
MELL MESH MISJ MOGS MOOV MRDS
MUTT OCRZ OCZA RRAT SASI SCCZ SCPI
SCRZ SCSC SCZR SPCZ STVT SWYM TEZZ
TUGI VIIZ WOOO WWZZ XERO ZAAP ZECH

CZECH SPORT AIRCRAFT

PIPERSPORT
G-CGPR LHER MRVK NJCZ PALI

PS-28 CRUISER
G-CGDW CRZR CSHB DTFT EGLK OOPY
OPUG TIPY XARA

SPORTCRUISER (Factory built)
G-CGDV CGEO CGHW CGLC CGLR CGLT
CKSC CKUH CRSR EMSA HAYY ISCD JHDD
OFSP PBAT

D

DAN RIHN – see RIHN

DART AIRCRAFT LTD

KITTEN
G-AEXT

DASSAULT AVIATION including AVIONS MARCEL DASSAULT and AVIONS MARCEL DASSAULT-BREGUET AVIATION production

FALCON 20
G-FFRA FRAD FRAF FRAH FRAI FRAJ FRAK FRAL FRAO FRAP FRAR FRAS FRAT FRAU FRAW OLFE

FALCON 2000 variants
G-FLXS LATE PULA SMSM TNIK YFOX

FALCON 7X
G-CRNS MATO OIMF SPTX STMT SVNX XION

FALCON 900 variants
G-ECHB EGVO FLCN JSSE SIRO

DAVIS

DA-2A
G-BPFL

DE HAVILLAND AIRCRAFT LTD including AMERICAN MOTH CORPORATION, DE HAVILLAND AIRCRAFT PTY LTD, F + W, MORANE-SAULNIER, MORRIS MOTORS and OGMA production – also see AIRCO and HAWKER SIDDELEY AVIATION

DH.51
G-EBIR

DH.53 HUMMING BIRD
G-EBHX EBQP

DH.60G and DH.60M MOTH variants
G-AADR AAEG AAHI AAHY AAJT AALY AANL AANO AAWO AAXG AAYT AAZG ABAG ABDA ABDX ABEV ABJJ ABSD ABYA ABZB ACGZ ACNS ACXB ADHD ATBL BVNG EBLV EBWD EBZN

DH.71 TIGER MOTH
G-ECDX

DH.80A PUSS MOTH
G-AATC AAZP ABLS AEOA

DH.82 QUEEN BEE
G-BLUZ

DH.82 TIGER MOTH variants
G-ACDA ACDC ACDI ACDJ ACMD ADGT ADGV ADIA ADJJ ADNZ ADPC ADWJ AFGZ AFWI AGEG AGHY AGNJ AGPK AGYU AGZZ AHAN AHIZ AHLT AHMN AHOO AHPZ AHUF AHUV AHVU AHVV AIDS AIRK AIXJ AJHS AJTW AJVE AKUE AKXS ALBD ALIW ALJL ALNA ALND ALUC ALWS ALWW AMBB AMCK AMCM AMHF AMIV AMNN AMTF AMTK AMTV AMVS ANBZ ANCS ANDE ANDM ANDP ANEH ANEL ANEM ANEN ANEW ANEZ ANFC ANFI ANFL ANFM ANFP ANFV ANHI ANHK ANJA ANJD ANJI ANJK ANKK ANKT ANKV ANKZ ANLD ANLS ANMO ANMY ANNG ANNI ANNK ANOD ANOH ANOM ANON ANOO ANPE ANPK ANRF ANRM ANRN ANSM ANTE ANZU ANZZ AOAA AOBH AOBJ AOBX AODR AODT AOEI AOES AOET AOGI AOGR AOHY AOIM AOIS AOJJ AOJK AOXN AOZH APAL APAM APAO APAP APBI APCC APFU APLU APMX APVT ARAZ AREH ARTL ASKP ASPV AVPJ AXAN AXBW AXBZ AXXV AYDI AZDY AZGZ AZZZ BAFG BBRB BEWN BFHH BHUM BJAP BMPY BPAJ BPHR BTOG BWIK BWMK BWMS BWVT BYLB BYTN CFII DHZF ECDS EHLT EMSY ERDS FCTK MOTH OOSY PWBE TIGA

DH.83 FOX MOTH variants
G-ABWD ACCB ACEJ AOJH CGUO CIPJ

DH.84 DRAGON
G-ACET ECAN

DH.85 LEOPARD MOTH
G-ACGS ACLL ACMA ACMN ACOJ ACOL ACUS AIYS

DH.87B HORNET MOTH
G-ADKC ADKK ADKL ADKM ADLY ADMT ADND ADNE ADUR AELO AESE AHBL AHBM

DH.88 COMET
G-ACSP ACSS RCSR

DH.89 DRAGON RAPIDE variants
G-AGJG AGSH AGTM AHAG AIDL AIYR AKDW AKIF AKRP

DH.90 DRAGONFLY
G-AEDU

DH.94 MOTH MINOR
G-AFNI AFOB AFOJ AFPN

DH.104 DOVE and (SEA) DEVON including Riley conversions
G-ARBE ARJB DHDV DVON HBBC OPLC

DH.110 SEA VIXEN
G-CVIX

DH.114 HERON and SEA HERON
G-AORG

DH.115 VAMPIRE and SEA VAMPIRE
G-OBLN VTII

DE HAVILLAND CANADA including DE HAVILLAND INC, BOMBARDIER INC and OGMA production

DHC-1 CHIPMUNK
G-AKDN ALWB AMUF ANWB AOFE AOJR AORW AOSK AOSY AOTD AOTF AOTR AOTY AOUO AOUP AOZP APLO APPA APPM APYG ARMC ARMF ARMG ARWB ATHD ATVF BAPB BARS BAVH BBMN BBMO BBMR BBMT BBMV BBMW BBMZ BBNA BBND BBSS BCAH BCCX BCEY BCGC BCHL BCIH BCKN BCOI BCOO BCOU BCOY BCPU BCRX BCSA BCSL BCXN BCYM BCZH BFAW BFAX BFDC BNZC BPAL BTWF BVTX BVZZ BWHI BWMX BWNK BWNT BWTG BWTO BWUN BWUT BWUV BWWY BWVZ BXCT BXCV BXDA BXDG BXDH BXDI BXDN BXEC BXGL BXGM BXGO BXGP BXGX BXHA BXHF BXIA BXIM BXNN BYHL BYSJ BZGA BZGB CBJG CERD CGAO CHPI CHPY CIGE CMNK CPMK DHCC DHPM HAPY HDAE HFRH ITWB MAJR ODHC PVET UANO ULAS

DHC-2 BEAVER
G-CICP DHCZ EVMK

DHC-6 TWIN OTTER – including VIKING AIR production
G-BIHO BVVK CBML CEWM HIAL ISSG SGTS

DHC-8 DASH EIGHT variants
G-ECOA ECOB ECOC ECOD ECOE ECOF ECOG ECOH ECOI ECOJ ECOK ECOM ECOO ECOP ECOR ECOT FLBA FLBB FLBC FLBD FLBE JECK JECL JECM JECN JECO JECP JECR JECX JECY JECZ JEDM JEDP JEDR JEDT JEDU JEDV JEDW KKEV PRPA PRPB PRPC PRPD PRPE PRPF PRPG PRPH PRPI PRPJ PRPK PRPL PRPM PRPN PRPO

DENNEY AEROCRAFT COMPANY including SKYSTAR

KITFOX
G-BONY BPII BPKK BRCT BSAZ BSCG BSCM BSDD BSFX BSGG BSIF BSRT BSSF BSUZ BSVK BTBG BTDC BTDN BTIF BTKD BTNR BTOL BTSV BTTY BTVC BTWB BUDR BUIP BUKF BUKP BULZ BUOL BUPW

BUWS BUYK BUZA BVAH BVCT BVEY BVGO BWAR BWSJ BWSN BXCW BXWH BZAR CBDI CBTX CDXY CHUC CJLM CJUD CKTK CRES CTOY DEEZ DJNH EJAS FBCY FOXC FOXD FOXF FOXG FOXI FOXS FOXX FOXZ HOBO KAWA KFOX KTTY LACR LEED LESZ LOST PHYL PPPP RFOX RSSF RWSS TWTW ZFOX

KITFOX VIXEN
G-CHYZ

DEPERDUSSIN CIE

MONOPLANE
G-AANH

DESOUTTER AIRCRAFT COMPANY

DESOUTTER 1
G-AAPZ

DG FLUGZEUGBAU GmbH – also see GLASER-DIRKS FLUGZEUGBAU GmbH and ROLLADEN-SCHNEIDER

DG-1000 variants
G-CGRV CKFN CKLY CKND CKNF CKOH LOLI OSOR RIEF RYPE WYVN

DIAMOND AIRCRAFT INDUSTRIES GmbH – also see HOFFMANN

DA.20 KATANA
G-BXOF BXPC BXPD BXTS BYMB DAZO NIKK OBDA OVEG

DA.40 STAR and variants
G-CBFA CCFS CCFU CCKH CCLW CCXU CDSF CEZR CFJN CFJO CKEI CTSA CTSB CTSC CTSD CTSE CTSF CTSG CTSH CTSJ CTSK CTSM CTSN CTSO CTSP CTSR CTSS CTST CTSX DAKM DSPL DZKY ELKI EMDM EMMM FBAR GCFM KAFT LAFT LWLW MAFT OCCF OCCG OCCH OCCN OCCU PLIP RKAF RKAG RKAH RKAI SBSB SFLY SPTT SUEO TAMI TULA ZANY

DA.42 TWIN STAR variants
G-CDXK CIKM COBS CTCB CTCC CTCD CTCE CTCF CTCG CTCH CTSU CTSV DGPS DJET DMND DMNG DMPP DOSB DOSC DSKY ELKO ELSE EMPP ETPM FCAC FFMV HAFT HAKA HANG HAZA JAFT JKEE JKMH JKMI JKMJ LLMW LSZA LULV MEMS OCCX OPFR PAPE PCJS RASA RKBD SAJM SATM SELC SERE SLCT SUEI SUEM VLTT VVTV WKTG XDEA YDEA ZATG ZAZU ZDEA

DA.62 variants
G-DVOR EMAT GBAS GNSS IRJE MDME TACN WKTH

DOLGOPRUDNENSKOGO DESIGN BUREAU OF AUTOMATION

DKBA AT 0300-0
G-KIEV

DKBA AT 0301-0
G-DKBA

DORNIER – including AG für DORNIER-FLUGZEUGE, DORNIER GmbH, DORNIER WERKE AG, DORNIER LUFTFAHRT GmbH, and see BUCKER

DO.27
G-DOTS

228
G-ETAC LGIS MAFI OAUR OMAF SAYE

328
G-BYHG CCGS

DOUGLAS AIRCRAFT COMPANY INC including DOUGLAS AIRCRAFT CORPORATION

AD-4 SKYRAIDER
G-RADR

C-47 DAKOTA and C-53 SKYTROOPER
G-AMPY AMRA ANAF DAKK

DC-6
G-APSA

DRAGON LIGHT AIRCRAFT CO LTD
DRAGON 150 and 200
G-MJSL MJVY MMML MMNH

DRUINE including ROLLASON AIRCRAFT and ENGINES LTD (D.31 & D.62 production)
D.31 TURBULENT
G-AJCP APIZ APNZ APTZ APUY APVN
APVZ ARBZ AREZ ARGZ ARIM ARLZ ARMZ
ARNZ ARRU ARRZ ASFX ASHT ASMM ASSY
ATBS AWBM AWDO AWMR BFXG BGBF
BKUI BKXR BLTC BUKH BVLU BWID CFLP
POPZ

D.53 TURBI, D.54 TURBI
G-AOTK APBO APFA LAAI

D.62 CONDOR
G-ARHZ ARVZ ASEU ASRC ATAU ATAV
ATOH ATUG ATVW AVAW AVEX AVMB AVOH
AVXW AWEI AWFN AWFO AWFP AWSN
AWSP AWSS AWST AXGS AXGV AXGZ
AYFC AYFD AYFE AYFF AYZS BADM BUOF
RELL YNOT

DUDEK PARAGLIDERS SJ
NUCLEON
G-CHIE CIXA

SYNTHESIS
G-CJFP

DYKE
DELTA
G-DYKE

DYN'AÉRO (SOCIÉTÉ DYN'AÉRO)
CR100
G-BZGY

MCR-01 variants (Rotax 912)
G-BYTM CBNL CBZX CCFG CCMM CCPN
CCTE CCUI CDBY CDLL CDWG CENA
CGCN CGHT CUTE DECO DGHI KARK LMLV
MCRO NONE OHIO PGAC RESG TDVB
TOMX

E

EAA
ACROSPORT
G-BJHK BKCV BLCI BPGH BTAK BTWI
BVVL CCFX CGAK DAGF ECAM HUME
OJDA TANY TSOL VCIO

BIPLANE
G-AVZW BBMH BPUA PFAA

EARTHSTAR
THUNDERGULL
G-TGUL

EAVES
DODO
G-BJIC

EUROPEAN variants
G-FYDN FYFI

EBERHARDT STEEL COMPANY
SE.5E
G-BLXT

E-GO AEROPLANES LTD
E-GO
G-EFUN OEGO

EIPPER AIRCRAFT INC
QUICKSILVER MX
G-MBFO MJAD MJAM MJJK MJPV MJVP
MJVU MMBU MMMG MMNA MMNB MMNC
MWDZ

EIRIAVION O/Y including MOLINO
PIK-20 series
G-BHIJ BHNP CJBH CJGK CJVE CJXG
CKFE DDFE DDFK DDJN DDLJ DDLY DDMU
DDOU DDPL DDRT DDVN DDWS DDZT
DEAR DEAT OFJC OPIK PIKD POPE

EKOLOT
KR-010 ELF
G-CIUO

EKW
C-3605
G-CCYZ DORN

ELA AVIACIÓN S.L
ELA 07
G-CEER

ELAN FLIGHT and ELAN TOVARNA SPORTNEGA ORODJA N.SOL.O – see GLASER-DIRKS FLUGZEUGBAU GmbH

ELECTRA FLYING CORPORATION
EAGLE
G-MBRB

ELMWOOD
CA-05 CHRISTAVIA
G-MRED

EMBRAER
EMB-135BJ LEGACY
G-KGKG LEGC RHMS SPCY SUGR SYLJ
THFC WIRG XPTV

EMB-135ER
G-RJXK RJXL SAJB SAJR

EMB-145 variants
G-CHMR CISK CIYX CKAF CKAG OWTN
RJXA RJXB RJXC RJXD RJXE RJXG RJXH
RJXI RJXM SAJC SAJG SAJH SAJI

EMB-500 PHENOM 100
G-SVRN

EMB-505 PHENOM 300
G-CKAZ DCMT HNPN JAGA JMBO KRBN
PERG WZAP

EMB-550 LEGACY 500
G-ESNA HARG RORA SUEJ TULI WLKR

ERJ-170-100 (Embraer 170)
G-CIXV CIXW LCYD LCYE LCYF LCYG
LCYH LCYI

ERJ-170-200 (Embraer 175)
G-FBJA FBJB FBJC FBJD FBJE FBJF FBJG
FBJH FBJI FBJJ FBJK

ERJ-190-100 (Embraer 190)
G-LCYJ LCYK LCYL LCYM LCYN LCYO
LCYP LCYR LCYS LCYT LCYU LCYV LCYW
LCYX LCYY LCYZ

ERJ-190-200 (Embraer 195)
G-FBEF FBEG FBEH FBEI FBEJ FBEK NSEY

ENGINEERING AND RESEARCH CORPORATION – see FORNEY

ENGLISH ELECTRIC CO LTD including AVRO & SHORT BROS & HARLAND production
CANBERRA
G-CTTS OMHD

WREN
G-EBNV

ENSTROM HELICOPTER CORPORATION
F-28
G-BDKD BONG BURI BVOW BXLW BXXW
ERDW MHCE OABO PASN

280 SHARK
G-BEYA BPXE BRZF BSDZ BSLV CKCK
GKAT HKCF MHCM OGES OITV OJBB OTHE
PBYY SHAA SHRK SHUU TTKP VETS
VVWW WIZI WPKR WRFM WSKY

480
G-ENHP IJBB LADD LLLY RRAK UZZY
WOOF ZZMM

EUROCOPTER and EUROCOPTER DEUTSCHLAND GmbH – also see AÉROSPATIALE (AS prefix), MESSERSCHMITT-BÖLKOW-BLOHM (BK and BÖ prefixes) and SUD-AVIATION (SA and SE prefixes)
EC 120 variants
G-CONN DBNK DEVL DLUX EIZO ETIM
FCKD HEHE HVRZ IAGL IZOB JBBB JJFB
KLNP LTZY MODE OLDO OMEM RCNB
SKLR SKPP SWNG TBLY TGGR WADD
WZRD ZZOE ZZZS

EC 130
G-ESET HOGB IPSE PBIG SASY

EC 135 variants
G-BZRS CHSU CPAO CPAS DAAN DORS
DVAA EMAA EMID GLAA GLAB GWAC
HEMN HEOI HIOW HOLM HWAA LAVA
MSPT NHEM NIHM NSYS NWAA NWAE
NWEM NWOI NWPS OMAA ORST POLA
POLB POLC POLD POLF POLG POLH POLJ
POLS PSHU PSNI SCAA SENS SPHU SUFK
TVAL TVHB WASC WASS WPDA WPDB
WPDC WPDD WPDE

EC 155
G-CFOJ CKUT CKVB HBJT HOTB LCPX
NIVA SCOR TBUC

EC 175
G-DLBR EMEA EMEB EMEC EMED MCSE
MCSF MCSG MCSH

EUROFLY
MINIFOX
G-CKIZ CKYZ MFUX

SNAKE
G-CLDG CLER CLFO MADC

EUROPA AVIATION including AVIATION COMPOSITES CO LTD
EUROPA variants
G-BVGF BVIZ BVKF BVLV BVOS BVOW
BVRA BVUV BVVH BVVP BVWM BWDP
BWDX BWEG BWFH BWFX BWIJ BWIV
BWJH BWRO BWUP BWVS BWWB BWYD
BWZA BXDY BXEF BXFG BXGG BXHY BXII
BXIJ BXLK BXNC BXTD BYIK BYJI BYPM
BZAM BZNY BZTH BZTN CBES CBHI CBOF
CBWP CBXW CBYN CCEF CCFK CCGW
CCJX CCOV CCRJ CCUL CCUY CDBX
CDEX CDPY CDVS CEIW CEKV CEMI CEOW
CERI CEYK CFKZ CFLI CFMP CFVR CGDH
CGNZ CGVJ CGVX CGZV CHAH CHEB
CHOX CHUG CHZK CICA CIUP CKRL CLAV
CORA CROY DAMY DAYI DAYS DDBD DLCB
DRMM DURO DYUP EENI EESA EIKY EINI
EMIN EMSI EORJ EROB EUAB EUNG EXES
EZZA FELL FITY FIZY FLOR FLOX FLYT
FOGI GCAC GIWT GOLX HUEW IANI IBBS
IHCI IKRK ILLZ IMAB IOWE IPOD IRON
IRPW ITST IVER IVES IVET JAMY JERO
JHKP JHYS JIMM JULZ KIMM KIRB KITS
LABS LAMM LDVO LEBE LIKE LINN MAAN
MAUS MEGG MFHI MIXF NEAT NESA NHRJ
NICX NIGL OBJT OCRL ODJG ODTW OEZY
OGAN OJHL OKEV OMIK OPJK OPRC
ORPC OSLD OUHI OURO OVPM OWWW

PATF PATS PATZ PEGY PLPM PPOD PTAG
PUDS PUPY RATZ RBBB RDHS REJP RICS
RIKS RIXS RJWX RMAC RMMT ROBD
RODO RONA ROOV RPAF RPCC SAMY
SELF SHSH SMDH SNOP SNOZ SRYY STUE
SUSE TERN TKAY TOPK TSUE UMPY URMS
VPSJ WIKI WKNS WUFF XSDJ XSRF YETI
ZIGY ZORO ZTED

EUROWING LTD
GOLDWING
   G-MBFZ MBPX MJAJ MJDP MJOE MJSY
   MJWB MMLE MNNS MNZU

EVANS
VP-1
   G-AYUJ BAAD BAPP BDAR BDTB BDTL
   BDUL BEIS BEKM BFAS BFHX BGLF BHMT
   BHYV BIDD BIFO BKFI BLWT BMJM BVAM
   BVEL BVJU BVUT BWFJ EVPI GVPI PFAH
   PFAW TEDY TGJH VPAT VPCB

VP-2
   G-BFYL BGPM BJZB BMSC BTSC BUKZ
   BVPM BXOC RASC

EVEKTOR including COSMIK AVIATION LTD production
EV-97 SPORTSTAR
   G-EVSW ONIC TMAX UKRO

EV-97(A) (TEAM) EUROSTAR (Rotax 912-UL)
   G-CBIY CBJR CBMZ CBRR CBVM CBWE
   CBWG CCAC CCBK CCBM CCCO CCDX
   CCEJ CCEM CCKL CCMO CCMP CCPH
   CCPJ CCSR CCTH CCTI CCTO CCTP CCUT
   CCVA CCVK CCWP CCZZ CDAC CDAP
   CDAZ CDCC CDCT CDEP CDIG CDIY CDJR
   CDNG CDNM CDNP CDOA CDOZ CDPL
   CDTA CDTU CDVD CDVU CDXP CDXS
   CDYP CEAM CEBF CEBP CECY CEDV
   CEDX CEFK CEFZ CEGO CEHL CEKJ CEME
   CENB CEND CENM CENW CERE CESV
   CETT CEVS CEYY CEZD CEZF CFCT CFDJ
   CFEE CFEL CFEO CFFE CFGX CFLL CFNW
   CFRT CFTI CFTJ CFTZ CGDI CGGM CGOG
   CGPS CGSH CGTD CGTT CGVP CGVT
   CGWE CGYB CGZF CGZY CHGE CHJG
   CHMW CHOU CHRT CIDW CIDZ CIKT CIRB
   CIRY CITF CIWI CIZU CJCL CJJA CJTX
   CLDB CLDC CSMK CTAV DFDO DODG
   DOMS DRCC DSKI DTSM EGTF EMLE EVIG
   EVRO EVSL EZZY FLYJ FLYO GHEE GLSA
   GVSL HAEF HMCA HMCF HMCH HOTA
   IAHS ICMT IDOL IFLE IHOT JBAV JEEP JLAT
   JUGE JVBP KEJY KWFL LBAC LBUZ LOSY
   LOUS LYNI MKEV MOLA MPAT NICC NIDG
   NILT OBAD OCMS OCMT ORAU OSPD
   OTUN OTYE PIGI PROW RCHY RJRJ RMPY
   SDFM SHMI SINN SJES SLCC STEE TINT
   TIVV TSKS UMMS UURO UZUP VALG VORN
   WINH XBJT XIXI ZZAC

EVERETT GYROPLANES LTD including R J EVERETT ENGINEERING and see CAMPBELL for Cricket
GYROPLANE variants
   G-BIPI BMZN BMZS BTMV BUAI BULT
   BWCK MICY OFRB OGOS ULPS

EXPERIMENTAL AVIATION
BERKUT
   G-REDX

EXTRA FLUGZEUGBAU GmbH
EA.230/260
   G-EXTR ROMP VOCA XTRA

EA.300
   G-BZII CLBI CLCA EEEK EXGC EXII EXIL
   EXLT FIII GEJS GLOC GOFF HEDL IHHI IIDI
   IIEX IIHL IIIK IIMI IISC IIXI IIZI JLSP JOKR
   KAYH KIII MIII OFFO OLAD OLUD POTA

RFLY ROOG SIII TENG TWOO UIII WVEN
WWLF XCCC XXHP XXTR ZEXL ZXCL ZXEL
ZXLL

EA.400
   G-CITW

F

F + W – see DE HAVILLAND AIRCRAFT LTD

FABRIKA VAZDUHOPLOVA SOKA
SOKO P-2 KRAGUJ
   G-BSXD RADA SOKO

FAIRCHILD ENGINE and AIRPLANE CORPORATION
24R ARGUS
   G-AJPI BCBH BCBL RGUS
24W ARGUS
   G-SEDC
M-62 CORNELL
   G-CRNL

FAIREY AVIATION CO LTD – also see WESTLAND AIRCRAFT LTD
FIREFLY
   G-CGYD
GANNET
   G-KAEW

FAIREY BRITTEN-NORMAN LTD – see BRITTEN-NORMAN

FAIRTRAVEL LTD
LINNET 2
   G-ASMT ASZR

FALCONAR – also see JODEL
F-11
   G-AWHY WBTS
F-12
   G-BGHT TIMS
F-9
   G-AYEG

FEDOROV – see also AVIASTROITEL
Me-7 MECHTA
   G-CHMZ CHPT CHUO CJFZ

FFA FLUGZEUGWERKE AG
DIAMANT
   G-CHGT DCDG DCDW DCGM

FIAT AERONAUTICA D'ITALIA
FIAT CR.42
   G-CBLS

FISHER FLYING PRODUCTS INC
SUPER KOALA variants
   G-MMTY

FLAGLOR
SKY SCOOTER
   G-BDWE

FLEET AIRCRAFT OF CANADA LTD
80 CANUCK
   G-FLCA

FLIGHT DESIGN GmbH
CT-SUPRALIGHT
   G-CKHO CTSL

CT2K (Rotax 912-ULS)
   G-CBDH CBDJ CBEW CBEX CBIB CBIE
   CBVZ CBWA CCNG CCNP CDJF CDPZ

CTDH DMCT MCVY NULA POGO PRAH
TOMJ

CTLS
   G-CGEC CGRB CONA CTLS CVET EJWI
   HECT LEGY

CTSW
   G-CBUF CDWJ CDWT CDXL CEDE CEEO
   CEIE CEKD CEKT CENE CESW CETF CEWT
   CEZZ CFDO CFDP CFFJ CFGZ CFKS CGBM
   CGIZ CGVG CJHP CTDW CTEE DEWE FICS
   KBOS KFLY KUPP KUTI KVAN LCKY OASA
   OCDP OMRP OMSA ONCE RILA RZLY SAAA
   SDAT SLNT SWCT TORN

MC
   G-CGOM

FLS AEROSPACE (LOVAUX) LTD – also see OPTICA INDUSTRIES LTD
SPRINT
   G-BVNU BXWU BXWV OAGI SAHI SCLX

FLY MARKET FLUGSPORT-ZUBEHOR GMBH AND CO
RELAX
   G-CIOG

FLYING K ENTERPRISES INC
SKY RAIDER 1
   G-CISR

FLYING LEGEND
TUCANO REPLICA
   G-ZFOO

FLYLIGHT AIRSPORTS LTD
DRAGON CHASER
   G-CIDB CIEP CIFM CILV JHLP MCTO
DRAGON COMBAT
   G-CJEY IIDW
DRAGONFLY
   G-CEOL CFNC CFOS CFSO CFTU CFXG
   CFXK CGAA CGEU CGIE CGIF CGLE CGPF
   CGSA CGXY CGYT CHED CHIZ CHJB CIKU
   CJXO DGFY GOOF IFFY IWIZ LNIG OECO
DRAGONLITE
   G-CFGC CHRD CHRU CICW CIEK CIHT CIIZ
FOXCUB
   G-CIKV CIOX CISN CIUN CIXT CIYC CJBP
   CJGV CJIE
FOXTUG
   G-CJBL CKIG CLBS
MOTORFLOATER
   G-CGSW CGTW CGVH CGWM CGWN
   CHGJ CHIY LOAM STBY

FOCKE-WULF FLUGZEUGBAU GMBH – see PIAGGIO AERO INDUSTRIES SpA

FOKKER BV including FOKKER VFW NV, ROYAL NETHERLANDS AIRCRAFT FACTORY production and replicas
D.VII replica
   G-CIHS JUNO
D.VIII replica
   G-CIHU
Dr.1 replica
   G-BVGZ CDXR CFHY DREI FOKK
E.III replica
   G-AVJO CGJF CHAW FOKR GSAL UDET
S.11 INSTRUCTOR
   G-BEPV BIYU

FOLLAND AIRCRAFT LTD
GNAT
   G-FRCE MOUR RORI SLYR

FORNEY

ALON A-2
G-AVIL HARY

ERCOUPE 415
G-ERCO

FORNEY F-1A
G-ARHB ARHC ONHH

FOSTER WIKNER AIRCRAFT CO LTD

GM.1 WICKO
G-AFJB

FOURNIER (AVIONS FOURNIER)
including ALPAVIA and SPORTAVIA-PÜTZER

RF3
G-ATBP AYJD BCWK BFZA BIIA BIPN BLXH
BNHT

RF4D
G-AVHY AVKD AVNY AVNZ AVWY AWEK
AWEL AWGN AWLZ BHJN BIIF BXLN RFAD

RF5 and RF5B SPERBER
G-AYME AZJC AZPF AZRK AZRM BACE
BEVO BJXK BPWK CBPC CIMO CITD KCIG
RFSB SSWV

RF6B
G-BKIF BOLC RFGB

**FRESH BREEZE MÜLLER & WERNER
GBR**

FLYKE TRIKE/SILEX L
G-CFYP

FUJI HEAVY INDUSTRIES LTD

FA.200
G-BBGI BBRC BBZN BCKS BCKT BDFR
FEWG HAMI HECB MCOX

G

G PARNALL and COMPANY – see
PARNALL

GAME COMPOSITES

GB1
G-IGBI

GARDAN including AÉRONAUTIQUE
Havraise, CONSTRUCTIONS AERONAUTIQUE
DE BEARN, NOUVELLE SOC COMETAL and
SRCM production

GY-20 and GY-201 MINICAB
G-ATPV AVRW AWEP AWUB AZJE BANC
BBFL BCER BCNC BCPD BDGB BEBR
BGKO BGMJ BGMR BRGW MCAB TATT
VERA

HORIZON
G-ATGY AVRS AWAC AZYA BYBL GYAT
TIMY

GEFA-FLUG GmbH

AS 105 GD
G-CIJI EOGE MRME NORG OZSB PUSA

GEMS – see MORANE-SAULNIER

GENERAL AVIA

F22
G-FZZA

GIPPSLAND AERONAUTICS PTY LTD
including GIPPSAERO PTY LTD

GA-8 AIRVAN
G-CSPT HTFU SCOL TVCO VANA VANC
VAND VANX

GLASER-DIRKS FLUGZEUGBAU GmbH
including DG FLUGZEUGBAU GmbH, AMS-
FLIGHT DOO, ELAN FLIGHT, ELAN TOVARNA
SPORTNEGA ORODJA N.SOL.O production –
also see DG FLUGZEUGBAU

DG-100 and DG-101
G-CFBH CFBW CFFU CFYU CHMS CHWP
CJEZ CJNZ CJRL CJXP CJYO CKDY CKHV
CKMG CLRN CLTG DDHJ DDHK DDHL
DDRB DDUY DEDN DENU DEPU DGIO
SHHH

DG-200 and DG-202
G-CFOC CHBD CJAW CJDD CJDP CJHW
CJKF CJKM CJPW CJRN CJVP CJWT CKAC
CKDU CKDX CLEU CLMF DADJ DDTA
DDTM DDWJ DDXN DDYH DEDM DEME
DEMU DHAT DHDH EEBR EEKA EJAE ONEZ

DG-300 and DG-303 ELAN
G-CFAJ CFJR CFJS CFJX CFLC CFLX CFNS
CFSR CFTS CFUJ CFUT CFUU CFWM
CFZW CGBS CHBE CHDR CHMB CHME
CHSB CHVM CJDV CJNO CJRC CJTK CJTN
CJVL CKAU CKBF CKJH CKKC CKOR CKRF
CLMY CLRO DESO DFCM DFDW DFGT
DGAJ DHCU DHCY DJAB XIXX

DG-400
G-BNXL BRTW BSOM DIRK HAJJ INCA
JSPR KESS

DG-500 ELAN series
G-BZYG CEYC CGBZ CHEF CHGV CHNA
CHRC CHYE CJSX CJZB CJZK CKAX CKHC
CKJJ CKNK CKOW CKOX CLSL CLVJ DSOO
SOOM SORA XBGA

DG-600
G-CFNT CFPW CIDO KOFM KRWR

DG-800 variants
G-BVJK BXSH BXUI BYEC CJJH CLSZ DGIV
DJNE IANB KMJK MSIX OBUP ORIG SMAJ

GLASFLÜGEL ING EUGEN HANLE

H201 STANDARD LIBELLE
G-AXZH CFZB CGAU CGEE CHJR CHWC
CHWG CJAS CJEU CJGZ CJHJ CJNG
CKCM DCFS DCFW DCFX DCFY DCKY
DCLM DCLP DCMO DCMR DCMS DCMW
DCNE DCNG DCNJ DCNP DCPF DCPM
DCRB DCRO DCRS DCRV DCRW DCSJ
DCSR DCTU DCUJ DCVL DCWE DCWG
DCWT DCWX DCWY DCXK DCYG DDCC
DDMS DENO DHAA DHAD DHCO ECLW
ECPA EFLT EHAV LIBI LIBY

H205 CLUB LIBELLE
G-CFYG CGCS CHAE CKAM CLGR DDBP
DDEO DDVM DFAR

H206 HORNET
G-CKLC DDKD DDKM

H301 LIBELLE
G-CGAN CHLK

H303 MOSQUITO
G-CFBN CHMT CJEH CJNR CJTO CJTW
DDMN DDPK DDRN DDTK DDTV DDTX
DDTY DDUB DDVZ DDWB DDWL DDWP
DDWR DDXW DEAK DECS DEDH DEDJ
MOZI

304
G-CHMM CJOK CJPI CKZY CLLC CLLH
CLMV CLON CLRH CLSJ CLTA CLTW CLVS
DEHU DJEB DLOT DLRL DLTY DLUT EENT
GOXC GSGS HPJT HXJT JETV JSRK OASM
OHDK OTJT PRBB RIFD TRBN WJET

GLOBE AIRCRAFT CORPORATION

GC-1B SWIFT
G-AHUN BFNM

GLOSTER AIRCRAFT CO LTD

GAMECOCK
G-CGYF

GAMECOCK replica
G-CBTS

GLADIATOR
G-AMRK CBHO GLAD

METEOR variants
G-JSMA JWMA LOSM

GRAMEX SRO

SONG
G-HYBD

GRANGER

ARCHAEOPTERYX
G-ABXL

GREAT LAKES AIRCRAFT INC

2T-1A SPORT TRAINER
G-BIIZ BUPV GLII GLST

GREEN

S-25
G-BSON

GREENSLADE

FREE SPIRIT BIPLANE
G-CIYK

GRIFFIN

RG28
G-CKAI

GROB-WERKE GMB & CO KG including
GROB FLUGZEUGBAU GmbH & CO KG and
BURKHART GROB LUFT-UND RAUMFAHRT
GMBH & CO KG

G102 ASTIR
G-CEWP CEWW CFCJ CFEF CFFB CFGK
CFHW CFJH CFSH CFTK CFTR CFYI CGAT
CGBJ CGCL CGDO CGEB CHBL CHBM
CHBT CHGB CHJV CHKB CHKM CHOT
CHSE CHTD CHTE CHTR CHUN CHVK
CHXB CHXM CITE CJAZ CJBZ CJCF CJCR
CJCW CJHG CJHN CJKW CJML CJNA
CJON CJPM CJRD CJRM CJSD CJSH CJSK
CJUK CJWR CJYC CJYP CJZY CKAY CKBD
CKBL CKCP CKEE CKGH CLLT CLUD
CMWK DDFR DDJD DDJX DDKR DDKS
DDKU DDKV DDKW DDKX DDLH DDLM
DDMH DDMP DDMR DDNC DDNE DDNK
DDOE DDPJ DDPO DDPY DDRW DDSH
DDSU DDUL DDWU DDXJ DDYF DDZU
DEAF DEAW DEEO DEKF DELN DEOD DEVK
DFBR DFDF DFEB DFEX DFSA DHTG EEVL
FECO GCMW GSST OGGB ONAT

G103 TWIN ACRO and TWIN ASTIR variants
G-CFHO CFWC CHBH CHBK CHWW CJKV
CJLZ CJWM CKFG CKMT CKRH CLOO
CLPX CLSR DDRO DDSJ DDSL DEGN DEOT
DEWG DEWP DEWR DEWZ DEXA DHCA
DHCJ DLOW JAPK NUGC

G104 SPEED ASTIR
G-CFXA CJPJ FEBB

G109
G-BIXZ BJVK BLMG BLUV BMCG BMFY
BMGR BMLK BMLL BMMP BXSP BXXI
BYJH BZLY CBLY CDNA CEVO CEYN CFUG
CGXP CGXW CHAR CHIG CHKF CHYB
CINK CINM CINO CIXB CKDE CKGG CKWZ
DKDP IPSI KEMC KNEK LREE LULU OFIX
OSNX OSPX OSTX PAIG RASH ROBZ SAGA
SAMG TACK UILD WAVE WAVY

G115 variants
G-BOPU BPKF BVHC BVHD BVHE BVHG
BYDB BYUB BYUC BYUD BYUE BYUF
BYUH BYUI BYUJ BYUK BYUL BYUM BYUN
BYUO BYUR BYUS BYUU BYUV BYUW
BYUX BYUY BYUZ BYVA BYVB BYVC BYVD
BYVE BYVF BYVG BYVH BYVI BYVK BYVL
BYVM BYVO BYVP BYVR BYVU BYVW

BYVY BYVZ BYWA BYWB BYWD BYWF
BYWG BYWH BYWI BYWK BYWL BYWM
BYWO BYWR BYWS BYWU BYWV BYWW
BYWX BYWY BYWZ BYXA BYXC BYXD
BYXE BYXF BYXG BYXH BYXI BYXJ BYXK
BYXL BYXM BYXO BYXP BYXS BYXT BYXX
BYXZ BYYA BYYB CGKD CGKE CGKG
CGKH CGKK CGKL CGKN CGKP CGKR
CGKS CGKU CGKW CIMI GPSI GPSR GPSX
GROE MERF RAFA RAFB ROBA TAYI UFOE

G120 variants
G-ETPC ETPD

GROPPO
TRAIL
G-CHGM CHZT CIAK CIMV CITS CIYO
CLCO CONS ETGO IAGO OPPO RJIT ROFS
ROKY ROPO ROPP RPPO SMLI SMLZ TRLL

GRUMMAN AIRCRAFT ENGINEERING
FM-2 WILDCAT
G-KINL RUMW WCME WCMI WCMO

F-8F BEARCAT
G-RUMM

GRUMMAN AMERICAN AVIATION
CORPORATION (3) including AMERICAN
AVIATION CORPORATION (1), AMERICAN
GENERAL AVIATION (2) and GULFSTREAM
AMERICAN CORPORATION (4) production
AMERICAN AA-1 YANKEE (1)
G-AYHA AYLP AZKS BFOJ

AMERICAN AA-1A TRAINER (1)
G-RUMN

GRUMMAN AA-1B TRAINER (3)
G-BDNW BDNX BERY CITP

GRUMMAN AA-1C LYNX (3)
G-BEXN BTLP

AMERICAN AA-5 TRAVELLER (1)
G-AZMJ AZVG BAFA BAJN BAJO

GRUMMAN AA-5 TRAVELLER (3)
G-BAOU BASH BAVR BBBI BBCZ BBDL
BBDM BBLS BBRZ BBSA BCCK BCEE
BCEP BCLI BCPN BDFY BEZC BEZF BEZG
BEZH BEZI BIAY BMYI BSTR MALC NONI
OTLC TALJ

GULFSTREAM AA-5A CHEETAH (4)
G-BGCM BGFG BHZO CCAT DOEA IFLI
OCAM OSTC PAWS PING RATE

GRUMMAN AA-5A CHEETAH (3)
G-BDLO BFIN BFLX BFZO BNVB BXHH
BXOX CHTA GDAC JAJB JUDY PURR

GRUMMAN AA-5B TIGER (3)
G-BCRR BFTF BFTG BFVS BFXW BFXX
BHLX BHZK BIPA BKPS BXTT ERRY MPFC
PORK ROWL RUBB WINK ZERO

GULFSTREAM AA-5B TIGER (4)
G-BGPH BGVY BIBT BIPV BJAJ BOZO
BOZZ BPIZ BTII DINA GAJB IRIS NODE
ORLY OTIG TGER TYGA WMTM

AMERICAN GENERAL AG-5B TIGER (2)
G-BTUZ CCXX CDGS GIRY OABR RICO

GRUMMAN GA-7 COUGAR (3)
G-BOXR OOGO

GULFSTREAM GA-7 COUGAR (4)
G-BGNV BGON BGSY BLHR BOOE CDND
CYMA GOTC HIRE OOGS

GUIMBAL
CABRI G2
G-CHAG CHWJ CILR CILU CJEK CKCI
CKRK CPLH CRSS DGRE ETWO FICH FPEH
HCEN LAVN LYZA OCDO ONVG PERH PERU
RJVH SDTL SHAZ TOOO TRDS UIMB UMBL
VETT VVBH VVBZ XFYF

GULFSTREAM AEROSPACE
CORPORATION
GULFSTREAM GIV-X (G450)
G-TAYC ULFM

GULFSTREAM GV-SP (G550)
G-LSCW MRLX OGSE

GULFSTREAM GVI (G650)
G-DSMR GSVI VIOF

GULFSTREAM AMERICAN
CORPORATION – see GRUMMAN
AMERICAN AVIATION CORPORATION

GYROFLIGHT
BROOKLAND HORNET
G-BRPP MIKE

H

HADLAND
WILLOW
G-MMMH

HALLAM
FLECHE
G-FLCT

HANDLEY PAGE
O/400 replica
G-BKMG

HAPI
CYGNET SF-2A
G-BRZD BWFN BXCA BXHJ BYYC CCKT
CYGI

HARKER
DH WASP
G-MJSZ

HARMON
ROCKET
G-MILF RCKT

HASELDINE
HUMMELBIRD
G-CETN

HATZ
CB-1
G-BRSY BXXH CBYW HATZ

HAWKER AIRCRAFT LTD including AVRO
and CCF production
AUDAX
G-BVVI

CYGNET
G-CAMM EBJI

DEMON
G-BTVE

FURY
G-CBZP

HART
G-CIAJ

HIND
G-AENP CBLK

HUNTER
G-BVGH BWFT BWGL BZSE CGHU CJWL
FFOX GAII HHAC HPUX KAXF PRII

HURRICANE
G-BYDL CBOE CHTK HHII HITT HRLI HUPW
HURI ROBT

IRAQI FURY
G-CBEL

NIMROD
G-BURZ BWWK

SEA FURY
G-BUCM INVN RNHF SEAF VZSF

SEA HURRICANE
G-BKTH

TEMPEST
G-PEST TEMT TMPV

TOMTIT
G-AFTA

HAWKER BEECHCRAFT
CORPORATION – also see BEECH
AIRCRAFT CORPORATION and RAYTHEON
AIRCRAFT COMPANY
HAWKER 4000 HORIZON
G-PROO

HAWKER SIDDELEY AVIATION including
BRITISH AEROSPACE PLC, CORPORATE JETS
LTD and RAYTHEON-HAWKER production –
also see DE HAVILLAND AIRCRAFT LTD
BUCCANEER
G-HHAA

*DH 125, HS 125, BAe and HAWKER 750/800/900
variants*
G-CERX EGKB EGSS HSXP JBLL KLNE
RCFC SCPJ STWB TLCL TWIY XCSP XSMC

HEAD BALLOONS INC
Ax8-88
G-TIMX

Ax8-105
G-ENGR UKUK

HEATH
PARASOL
G-AFZE

HEINTZ – see ZENAIR

HELICOPTERES GUIMBAL SA – see
GUIMBAL

HELIO
SUPER COURIER
G-BAGT

HELIOPOLIS including KADER INDUSTRIES
AOJ
GOMHOURIA MK6
G-CGEV TPWX

HELTON AIRCRAFT CORPORATION
LARK 95
G-LARK

HILLER HELICOPTERS INC
UH-12 (360)
G-ASAZ

HINDUSTAN AERONAUTICS LTD
PUSHPAK
G-AVPO BXTO

HIWAY HANG GLIDERS LTD – also see
CHARGUS
*SKYTRIKE/Demon, Excalibur, Flexiform, Gold
Marque, Hiway, Solar Wings, Super Scorpion &
Vulcan wings*
G-MBAA MBAL MBBJ MBCL MBIT MBKZ
MJAN MJDJ MJHV MJMD MJSO MMRH

HOFFMANN (HOAC FLUGZEUGWERKE)
including DIAMOND AIRCRAFT INDUSTRIES GmbH production

DV.20 KATANA
G-BWGY CIAC

H 36 DIMONA
G-BKPA CIMC CJTG KOKL LYDA RIET WENN

HK 36 SUPER DIMONA variants
G-BYFL GEOS IMOK LIDA OSFB SLMG XKKA

HOLD CONTROL PLC – see SOLAR WINGS LTD

HOLSTE (AVIONS MAX HOLSTE)
MH.1521 BROUSSARD variants
G-CBGL CIGH HOUR YYYY

HORNET MICROLIGHTS LTD
HORNET 250 with Airwave Nimrod wing
G-MBCX

HORNET DUAL TRAINER with Southdown Raven wing
G-MTMR

HORNET DUAL TRAINER with Southdown Sprint wing
G-MMDO

HORNET R variants (Combi)
G-MVUU MVYI MWBP MWBS MWBT MWBY MWDI MWKE

HOVEY
WD-II/III WHING DING
G-MBAB MNVO

HOWARD
SPECIAL T-MINUS
G-BRXS

HUGHES (HUGHES TOOL CO and HUGHES HELICOPTERS INC) including SCHWEIZER AIRCRAFT CORPORATION (269 from 1986) and McDONNELL DOUGLAS (369 from 1983) production

269 (Series 300)
G-BAXE BOXT BRTT BSVR BWNJ BWZY BXMY BXRP CEBE CEOY DCBI ECBI EMOL IRYC JMDI MARE OCBI OSLO PKPK PLOW PLPC RHCB ROCR TSLC USCO WHRL ZZDD ZZTT

369 (Series 500 and OH-6A Cayuse)
G-AYIA BIOA BPLZ BPYL BRTL CIWU CODA DIGS DIGZ GECO HEWZ HKHM HSOO HUEZ HUKA HWKW KAYS LIBS MDDE MDMX MRAJ MUDD OGJP OHGA OMDH PETO SOOC SSCL SWEL TCEE TRUE UMBY

HUMMER
TX
G-MJZX

HUNT
AVON Trike variants with HIWAY & HUNT wings
G-BZTW BZUZ CFUI MMGT MNCA MYWC MYYJ MZCX MZDZ MZFE MZFF MZGH

HUNTAIR LTD
PATHFINDER
G-MBWL MJDE MJFM MJJA MJOC MJTY

HUNTING PERCIVAL AIRCRAFT LTD – also see BRITISH AIRCRAFT CORPORATION (BAC) and PERCIVAL

P.66 PEMBROKE
G-BNPH BXES

P.84 JET PROVOST variants
G-AOBU BKOU BVEZ BVSP BWDS BWOT BWSH BXLO PROV VIVM

HYBRID AIR VEHICLES
HAV-3
G-OHAV

I

IAV-BACHAU – see YAKOVLEV

ICA (INTREPRINDEREA DE CONSTRUCTII AERONAUTICE-BRASOV)
IS-28B2
G-CHMG DDEG DDZR DEJA DJNC

IS-28M
G-BMMV

IS-29D
G-DDBG DDEW

ICP SRL
MXP-740 SAVANNAH variants
G-CBBM CCII CCJO CCJU CCLP CCXP CDAT CDCR CDEH CDJD CDKN CDKO CDLR CDSH CDTT CDTY CDUV CDVK CDZU CEBC CECK CEED CEEX CEFY CEGK CEVU CEZB CFSX CFZI CGTV CGXX CGYY CHVS CSUE DOTW MSAV RHOS SAVA SAVY STOD SVNH TTAT VGVG WHYS

III (INIZIATIVE INDUSTRIALI ITALIANE) SpA
SKY ARROW (Rotax 912)
G-BXGT BYCY BYZR BZVT CBTB CIAO CINC DGMT FINZ GULP IOIA ROME SKYT

ILYUSHIN
Il-2
G-BZVW BZVX

INDUSTRIE AERONAUTICHE E MECCANICHE RINALDO PIAGGIO SpA – see PIAGGIO AERO INDUSTRIES SpA

INGLETON
HURRICANE
G-OHUR

INTERPLANE AIRCRAFT INC
ZJ-VIERA
G-CFAP FLEE

IRMA – see BRITTEN-NORMAN LTD

ISAACS
FURY
G-ASCM AYJY BBVO BCMT BEER BIYK BKFK BKZM BMEU BWWN BZAS BZNW CCKV EHMF FURI PFAR RODI

SPITFIRE
G-BBJI BXOM CGIK ISAC

ISSOIRE AVIATION (SOCIÉTÉ ISSOIRE AVIATION)
E7B SILENE
G-DHPA

ITV PARAPENTES
DAKOTA
G-CGZJ

J

JABIRU AIRCRAFT COMPANY PTY LTD
including AVTECH PTY LTD

JABIRU SK, SPL and UL variants (Jabiru 2200A)
G-BXAO BXSI BYBM BYBZ BYCZ BYIA BYJD BYNS BYSF BYTK BYTV BYYL BYYT BYZS BZAP BZEN BZFI BZGT BZHR BZIV BZLV BZMC BZST BZSZ BZTY BZUL BZWK BZXN BZYK CBGR CBIF CBJM CBJY CBKY CBOP CBPR CBSU CBZM CCAE CCBY CCEL CCMC CCRX CCVN CDFK CDKP CDNY CECE CECG CEOM CLDE CNAB CSDJ DANY DJAY DMAC DWMS ENRE EPIC EPOC EUAN EWBC HINZ ICDM IKEV IPAT JAAB JABB JABE JABS JABY JABZ JACO JAJP JAXS JBSP JMAL JPMA JSPL JUDD KEVH KKER LEEE LOIS LYPG MIRA NIGC OCDW ODGS OGSA OJAB OMER OMHP OZZI PHYS PRLY RODG ROYC RUFS RYAL SUTD SVDG THOT TJAL TUBB TYKE UJAB UJGK UKOZ UNNA

JABIRU J160
G-CFGH CFSJ CFTX CIBU

JABIRU J400 and J430 variants (Jabiru 3300A)
G-CCGG CCID CCPV CDBD CDCP CDJL CDLS CDTL CDUT CDXJ CEFP CEKW CEPM CFZD CGLN CGOL DBEE EGSJ GRLW JABI JABJ JABU JJAB KEVI KIDD LUBY MLAL MUTZ NJSP OZIE PHYZ PUKA RCST RDCO REAF ROOO RTFM SAZY SIZZ

JACKAROO AIRCRAFT LTD
JACKAROO
G-ANZT AOEX AOIR

JACOBS
V35 AIRCHAIR
G-CEWF

JASTREB FABRIKA AVIONAI JEDRILICA – see SCHEMPP-HIRTH FLUGZEUGBAU GmbH

JODEL including CEA, SAN and WASSMER production – also see FALCONAR and ROBIN

D.9 and D.92 variants
G-AVPD AWFT AXKJ AXYU AZBL BAGF BDEI BDNT BGFJ BZBZ CKTS JODB KDIX

D.11, D.112, D.117 and D.119 variants
G-ARDO ARNY ASIS ASJZ ATIN ATIZ ATJN ATWB AVPM AWFW AWMD AWVZ AWWI AXAT AXCG AXCY AXFN AXHV AXWT AXXW AXZT AYBP AYBR AYCP AYEB AYGA AYHX AYKJ AYKK AYKT AYMU AYWH AYXP AZHC AZII AZKP AZVL BAAW BAKR BAPR BARF BAUH BAZM BBPS BCGW BCLU BDBV BDDG BDIH BDJD BEZZ BFEH BFGK BFNG BFXR BGEF BGWO BHCE BHEL BHKT BHNX BIAH BIDX BIEO BIOU BIPT BITO BIVB BIVC BIWN BIYW BIZY BJOT BKAO BKIR BMIP BOOH BPFD BRCA BRVZ BVEH BVPS BVVE BWMB CGOJ DAVE INNI

D.18
G-BODT BTRZ BUAG BUPR BXFC CBRC CBRD CGOR OLEM TREK WIBB

D.120 PARIS-NICE
G-ASPF ASXU ATLV AVLY AXNJ AYGG AYRS AZEF AZGA AZLF BACJ BANU BCGM BDDF BDEH BFOP BHGJ BHNK BHPS BHXD BHXS BHZV BICR BIEN BJFM BJOE BJYK BKAE BKCW BKCZ BKGB BKJS BKPX BMDS BMID BMYU BOWP CCBR DIZO

D.140 MOUSQUETAIRE
G-ARDZ AROW ARRY ATKX BJOB BSPC BWAB CVST EGUR EHIC JRME OBAN REES YRUS

D.150 MASCARET variants
G-ASKL ASRT AVEF AZBI BACL BFEB BHEG
BHVF BIDG BLAT BLXO BMEH BVSS BVST
CECH CEZW CGMH CJZU DISO EDGE
FARR IEJH JDEL JODE LDWS MASC OABB
TIDS

DR.100A replica
G-CCNA

DR.200, DR.220 and DR.221 variants
G-AVOM AYDZ BANA BFHR BLCT BLLH
BMKF BUTH CPCD DANA FEEF RRCU

DR.250 and DR.253 variants
G-AWYL AXWV AYUB BJBO BOSM BSZF
BUVM BXCG BYEH BYHP IMBO

DR.300, DR.315, DR.340 and DR.360 variants
G-AXDK AYCO AZIJ AZJN BGVB BICP
BLAM BLGH BLHH BOEH BOZV BVYG
BVYM BXOU DRSV DRZF KIMB

DR.1050 and DR.1051 variants
G-ARFT ARRD ARRE ARXT ASXS ATAG
ATEV ATFD ATIC ATJA ATLB ATWA AVGJ
AVGZ AVHL AVJK AVOA AWUE AWVE
AWWN AWWO AXLS AXSM AXUK AYEH
AYEJ AYEW AYGD AYJA AYKD AYLC AYLF
AYLL AYUT AYYO AYYT AYZK AZOU AZWF
BAEE BDMW BEAB BEYZ BFBA BGBE BGRI
BHHE BHOL BHSY BHTC BHUE BIOI BKDX
BLKM BXYJ BYCS BYFM CEIS CESA CFIC
CIYB CJNL DRIO EIAP IOSI IOSO JEJH
JEMM JODL JWIV LAKI RIVE SPOG

JONKER
JS-1
G-CLPZ DPER JSIC NDJS

JULIAN (C D JULIAN)
DINGBAT GYROPLANE
G-CGEY

JUNQUA
RJ.03 IBIS
G-CHHV

JURCA
MJ.2 TEMPETE
G-ASUS AYTV

MJ.5 SIROCCO
G-CEAO CLAX

MJ.8 FW190
G-KURT

MJ.10 SPITFIRE
G-CHBW

MJ.77 GNATSUM
G-PSIR

MJ.100 SPITFIRE
G-MUTS

JUST AIRCRAFT
SUPERSTOL
G-CLDI HONO JWNI RHOD SSTL SSXL

K

K & S
JUNGSTER
G-OWEN

SA.102.5 CAVALIER
G-AZHH BCMJ BDLY

KADER INDUSTRIES AOJ – see HELIOPOLIS

KAVANAGH BALLOONS PTY LTD
E-120
G-HODN

EX-65
G-CKMH

KEN BROCK
KB-2 (Rotax 582)
G-BVMN

KENSINGER
KF
G-ASSV

KIRK
SKYRIDER
G-BJTF

KLEMM – see BRITISH AIRCRAFT MANUFACTURING COMPANY LTD

KOLB including THE NEW KOLB AIRCRAFT COMPANY
FIREFLY
G-CGIV CJHC

TWINSTAR (Rotax 582)
G-CCFJ CCRB CDZS CEBI CKEH CYRA
KOLB MGPX MYIK MYKB MYLN MYMI
MYNY MYOG MYVA MZZT PLAD

KOVACS
MIDGIE
G-CGXT

KREIMENDAHL
K-10 SHOESTRING
G-GBFI

KRONFELD LTD – see BAC

KUBÍCEK (BALONY-KUBICEK Spol SrO)
BB17
G-CKHU OFNC OTEA SSRD

BB20
G-CEBL CFIW CHXN CSEE KENR OINT

BB22
G-CDRZ CFWI CGZZ CHKT CIDU CIWE
CKXT HUKS OALE OOEY

BB26
G-CEBG CFSL CKTG CKZJ CRBV GIFF
HYLA PHSE

BB30
G-CIME NIMA RENI

BB34
G-TIBF

BB40
G-OGIN

BB45
G-CWOW

BB60
G-CJCS

SS Cup
G-WHIL

SS Gnome
G-NOMZ

SS Phare
G-HLAM

SS Ship
G-MORG

SS Skyballs
G-MALE

L

LA MOUETTE
SAMSON
G-CISW CKRE

LAK including AB SPORTINE AVIACIJA
LAK-12 LIETUVA
G-CGAB CHEG CHGR CHGX CHHW CHOG
CHTF CJYL DFXR DHSR GLAK

LAK-17 series
G-CKCR CKHE CKMK CKMP CKOI CLMD
CLTJ CLTX CLUJ DAVS EEKI ELAK LFES
LFEZ PORG

LAK-19T
G-CJCH CKMB CKOU CKPA EWEW XIXT

LAKE AIRCRAFT CORPORATION including AEROFAB INC and CONSOLIDATED AERONAUTIC INC
LA-4
G-BASO BOLL VWET

LA-250 RENEGADE
G-LAKE

LAMBERT AIRCRAFT ENGINEERING BVBA
MISSION M108
G-CJJW CJLD CLCM CLDA OZZE STPK
STUZ VETC XIFR

MISSION M212-100
G-XFLY

LANAVERRE INDUSTRIE – see SCHEMPP-HIRTH FLUGZEUGBAU GmbH

LANCAIR
LANCAIR 200, 235, 320
G-BSRI BUNO BVLA CBAF FOPP JBAS
PJMT UILE

LC41
G-UZZI

LANCASHIRE
MICRO-TRIKE with Flexiiform & Wasp wings
G-MJYW MMPL

LANGE FLUGZEUGBAU GmbH
E1 ANTARES
G-DCDC

LASER
LAZER Z200, Z230
G-BWKT CBHR CDDP LZII VILL

LEARJET INC including BOMBARDIER AEROSPACE production
LEARJET 45
G-OICU OSRL SOVB UJET XJET

LEARJET 75
G-USHA ZENJ ZNTH ZNTJ

LEDERLIN
38OL LADYBUG
G-AYMR

LEIGHTFLUGZEUGBAU KLEMM GMBH – see also BRITISH AIRCRAFT MANUFACTURING COMPANY
L.25-1A
G-AAUP

LEONARDO
A109 variants
G-CHFD CKIH DGUN DIDO DMPI DVIP
EMHE EMHN ERJR FDHS FRRN GALI GDSG
GIBI GNMM HAGU HBEK HDTV HEMZ
HLCM HPDM HRDB IFRH IOOK IOOZ IPGL
IVIP IWFC JBCB JMBS JMON KLNH LCFC
LEXS LITO LUGS MAOL MCAN MDPI MOAL
MSVV MUZZ NVWV OCMM OPOT ORCD
PIFZ POTR PXMI RBCA RSCU RXTV RYFF
SAFA SCAP SCII SGRP SHLE SHLS SKBH

SKBL SLAR SPRI STNS TAAS TELY TGRA
TRNG TXTV UKAW USTH USTS VIPH VIVE
WDCL WIZG WOFM XXEC YRTE ZIPE

AW139
G-CHBY CHNS CIJW CIJX CIKO CILN CILP
CIMU CIPW CIPX CJNI CKYP CKYR DCII
DVIO GBIG MCSC MCSD PERD RBHF SNSA
SNSE SNSH SNSI SNSJ SNSK VINB VIPG

AW169
G-CKJR CMCL DSAA GETU HHEM ICEI
KSSC KSST LNAC MGPS MLAP PICU SASX
TCAA VSKP

AW189
G-ERBA FSAR MCGM MCGN MCGO MCGP
MCGR MCGS MCGT MCGU MCGV MCGW
MCGX OENB OENC SAAR

LEOPOLDOFF (SOCIÉTÉ DES AVIONS LEOPOLDOFF)

L-7
G-AYKS

LET NÓRODNÍ PODNIK KUNOVICE –
also see YAKOVLEV

L-23 SUPER BLANIK
G-CFYR

L-33 SOLO
G-CFZZ

LETOV LTD

LK-2M SLUKA
G-BYLJ MYRP MYUP MYVG MYXO MZBF
MZBK MZDX MZES MZFC MZGF MZLY
MZOI MZOX XPBI

LEVASSEUR (SOCIÉTÉ LEVASSEUR) –
see MORANE-SAULNIER

LIBERTY AEROSPACE INC

XL-2
G-OIVN SGFE

LILLIPUT BALLOONS UK

TYPE 1
G-HONY

TYPE 4
G-GRWL

LINDSTRAND (HOT AIR) BALLOONS
LTD – also see **LINDSTRAND TECHNOLOGIES LTD**

GA 22
G-CFKN

HS 110
G-CIEI HSTH LRBW

HS 120
G-CGFR

LBL 9A
G-CEHX

LBL 14A
G-BXAJ

LBL 21 series
G-BVRL BYEY CBYS UNRL

LBL 25 CLOUDHOPPER
G-BYYJ CBZJ CDAD CEGG EECO HOPR
OLAW RIME

LBL 31A
G-BWHD BXIZ BXUH BZIH BZNV CDUJ
CDXF CEOU CFRF CIET CKYU FFFT LELE
ONCB

LBL 35A CLOUDHOPPER
G-CFAW GABI HOPA NLCH OBAB SIPP

LBL 56 series
G-COSY

LBL 60 series
G-CDZO CFIK IRLZ OERR

LBL 69 series
G-BYKA REAR

LBL 77 series
G-BUBS BUWI BUZR BVPV BWAW BWBO
BWFK BWKZ BWMH BXDR BYJR BYLW
BYYE BZBJ BZGV BZKE CCFV CDWX CDYL
CDYX CGUD CHBX CHDH CHWE CIGI
CKWJ ERRI HERD JOED LBUK MCOW
MERE MUCK NUNI PATP PSAX SMMF STVL
TAJF WSTY

LBL 90 series
G-BVWW BVZT BWWE BWZU BXLF BXXO
BXZF BXZI BZLU BZNA CBIM CBNI CCJH
CCSS CDDN CDEU CGIG CIBI DUNS EDRE
FLEW GOGB JEMI MINN MRKT MRSW
MUPP OBJB ODJF PATX PURP RAYO SJKR
TSWI UNER UNGE WADZ ZUFL

LBL 105 series
G-BVDO BVRU BWOK BWSB BWWY BXDZ
BXUO BYJN BYLX BZUD CBPW CCVF
CCXD CECS CEJI CEMV CFXP CFXR CGFY
CGXO CHMI ENRI FLGT GOAL HAPI IOFR
ITVM LPAD OAER ODAF OPMT RIMB RXUK
SMIL VITL WAYS

LBL 120 series
G-BZBL CBTR CBVH DUBI UPUZ ZAZZ

LBL 150A
G-CIFS CIKN WLKI

LBL 210A
G-BZDE DVBF HVBF JVBF NVBF WVBF

LBL 240A
G-BXBL

LBL 260 series
G-PVBF

LBL 310A
G-TVBF

LBL 360A
G-CENX LLBE LLGE VBFF

LBL 400 series
G-UVBF

SS Baby Bel
G-BXUG

SS Battery
G-OKCP

SS Box
G-PNAD

SS Cube
G-IMCH

SS Flowers
G-ODBN

SS Four
G-BVVU

SS J & B Bottle
G-OJBW

SS Newspaper
G-BVGK

SS Pink Panther
G-PINX

SS Sun
G-BZIC

SS Telewest Sphere
G-BXHO

SS Triangle
G-EGES

LINDSTRAND TECHNOLOGIES LTD –
also see LINDSTRAND (HOT AIR) BALLOONS LTD

LTL 130G
G-CKWL

LTL 177T
G-CIYR

LTL 197T
G-CKZS

LTL 203T
G-CFBF

LTL 1-17
G-CKAO

LTL 1-105
G-CJIH CJJC CJVH CKIN CKTV CKXR OLCY
TLMA

LTL 1-120
G-CJXE

LTL 1-180
G-CLBP

LTL SERIES 1-31
G-CJHV HEAL

LTL SERIES 1-70
G-CJIG OPER

LTL SERIES 1-90
G-CJWH EHEH KLTB OASI WESS

LTL SERIES 2-50
G-ORNH

LTL SERIES 2-60
G-ICOR PRAY

LTL SERIES 2-70
G-CJIA

LTL SERIES 2-80
G-HBEE

LTL SERIES 9T
G-CJIU CKJO CKUG

LTL SERIES R-56
G-CJVO CKTJ OURT

LTL SERIES R-65
G-CJVN

LTL SS Boot
G-CLBH

LTL SS Cube
G-IMCH

LTL SS Penguin
G-WINZ

LTL SS Sphere
G-MOJI

LORIMER & KELSEY

SGIAN DUBH
G-CJPK

LUSCOMBE AIRPLANE CORPORATION

8 variants
G-AFUP AFYD AFZK AGMI AHEC AICX
AJAP AJJU AJKB AKTI AKTT AKUF AKUH
AKUJ AKUK AKUL AKUM AKUP AKVP BNIO
BNIP BPOU BPPO BPVZ BPZC BPZE BRDJ
BRGF BRHX BRHY BRJA BRJK BROO
BRPZ BRRB BRSW BRUG BSHH BSNE
BSNT BSOE BSOX BSSA BSTX BSUD BSYF
BSYH BTCH BTCJ BTDF BTIJ BTJA BTJB
BTJC BUAO BUKU BULO BVEP BVGW
BVGY CCRK CHJZ DAIR EITE KENM LUSC
LUSI LUSK LUST NIGE ROTI SAGE YRIL

LUTON – see PHOENIX

LYNDEN

AURORA
G-CBZS

M

MACAIR

MERLIN
G-BWEN

MAGNI GYRO

M14 SCOUT
G-BUEN

M15 TRAINER
G-BVDG

M16 TANDEM TRAINER
G-BUPM BXEJ BXIX BZJM BZXW CBUP
CFXF CGCE CGLF CGLK CGNM CGSD
CHDK CIRH CITM CJDW CKWR CKZZ
DBDB FLIS IBFP IJMC IROJ ITAR JWNW
KTCH MGNI UNIX VZED YROK YRON YROP
YYRO

M22 VOYAGER
G-YROF

M24
G-CGPB CGRY CGRZ CGTK CGYH CHNI
CIOM CIZB DMCW GTFB HOWD IROX JMBJ
MAGN MSGI OWLS PLOP PWEF ROZE
YRAX YROG YROR YROU

MAINAIR SPORTS LTD see also PEGASUS/FLASH and SOUTHDOWN INTERNATIONAL

(DUAL) TRI-FLYER trike with Flexiform, Hiway Solar Wings & Southdown wings
G-CCVX MBCJ MBHK MBIZ MBZO MJFZ
MJPE MJYX MMDJ MMFV MMKM MMKR
MMTD MMWG MNJD MNUI MVBC

BLADE
G-BYCW BYHO BYHS BYJB BYKC BYKD
BYNM BYOS BYOW BYRO BYRR BYTL
BYTU BYZB BZAL BZDC BZDD BZEG BZEL
BZFS BZGM BZGS BZGW BZHY BZJN
BZMS BZPA BZPN BZPZ BZRW BZTM
BZTU BZTV BZTX BZUB BZWB BZXM BZXT
CBAD CBBG CBDD CBDL CBDN CBDP
CBEM CBHG CBHJ CBJT CBKM CBKN
CBKO CBLD CBLM CBLT CBMM CBNC
CBOG CBOM CBOO CBOV CBRE CBRM
CBSZ CBTE CBTM CBTW CBVG CBXM
CBYF CBYM CBZA CBZD CCAB CCAG
CCAW CCGK CCIF CCPM CCTM CCWL
CCZW CEMR CLFC EEYE FERN FLYF JAIR
JBEN JMAN JOOL MAIN MYLT MYRD MYTD
MYTL MYTU MYUC MYUN MYVB MYVH
MYVO MYVZ MYXJ MYXM MYXN MYYA
MYYH MYYW MYYY MZAB MZAE MZAF
MZAG MZAM MZAP MZAR MZAS MZAT
MZAU MZAZ MZBL MZCC MZCE MZCF
MZCN MZCU MZDF MZDK MZDT MZEB
MZEG MZEW MZFB MZFS MZFZ MZGI
MZGW MZHB MZIH MZIS MZIT MZIW MZJA
MZJK MZJV MZJX MZJZ MZKG MZKJ
MZKZ MZLZ MZMJ MZML MZMV MZMY
MZMZ MZNJ MZNO MZOC MZOP
MZPH MZZY NNON NOWW OBMI ORBS
OSEP OYES REED REEF RIKI RINN RUFF
RYPH SHUF WAKE WLMS YZYZ

GEMINI FLASH variants
G-MMSP MMUO MMXU MMXV MMZA
MMZD MNAE MNBP MNBS MNCF MNCG
MNEG MNEY MNFM MNFN MNGK MNIA
MNIF MNIG MNII MNMG MNMV MNNF
MNNJ MNNL MNPG MNRX MNSJ MNTV
MNUF MNVT MNVW MNWI MNZD MTAB
MTAC MTAF MTAH MTBD MTBH MTCU
MTDF MTDR MTDW MTDY MTEK MTEY
MTGO MTIL MTIM MTJC MTJE MTJL MTJT
MTJV MTKW MTKX MTLB MTLC MTLL
MTMA MTMC MTML MTMW MTNC MTNI
MTPB MTRZ MTSC MTTI MTTP MTUV
MTVH MTWR MTWS MTWX MTXM MTXZ
MTZG MTZL MTZM MTZV MTZW MTZX
MTZY MTZZ MVBK MVBN MVBO MVCF
MVCZ MVDA MVEH MVEL MVER MVES
MVET MVEV MVHE MVHH MVIB MVIH MVIX
MVLL MVMR MVMT MVMW MVMX MVNM
MVNW MVNX MVNY MVNZ MVON MVOR
MVPA MVPB MVPC MVPD MVRD MVRM
MVSO MVSP MVUA MVXR MVZS MWAB
MWCE MWEL MWHR MWIA MWLP MWLX

MWMM MWMX MWMY MWNE MWNU
MWPB MWPD MWRC MWRE MWRF MWRH
MWRJ MWSM MWTO MWTZ MWVO MWVT
MWWZ MWWB MWWC MWWI MWWN
MWXV MWYA MWYG MWYL MWYT MWYV
MWZL MYAO MYAS MYBJ MYCK MYCS
MYDV MYFP MYGZ MYHL MYHN MYIH
MYIV MYIY MYJC MYJM MYKG MYKH
MYKV MYLG MYLR MYMK MYPE MYSJ

GEMINI wih Flexiform and Southdown wings
G-MMAR MMOB MMRP MMTL MMUX
MNMC

MERCURY
G-MWXF MWXJ MWXK MWZA MYCJ MYCL
MYDC MYKX MYKY MYLS MYNF MYOX
MYPV MYRW MYSZ MYTB MYTK MYUD
MYUW MYVL MZAK MZEK RAVE

RAPIER
G-BYBV BYOZ BZUF BZWR CCHV MFLY
MJYV MZEP MZEV MZFD MZGL MZHJ MZIL
MZIM MZJE MZKI MZKN MZND YARR

SCORCHER SOLO
G-MNDD MNNM MNPY MNPZ MNRE MNRZ
MYFT

MANNING-FLANDERS

MF.1 replica
G-BAAF

MARGANSKI & MYSLOWSKI ZAKLADY LOTNICZE Sp.z.o.o.

MDM-1 FOX
G-CFOX IIFX

MARQUART

MA.5 CHARGER
G-BHBT BVJX

MARTIN HEARN LTD – see SLINGSBY SAILPLANES LTD

MAUCHLINE

QUAICH
G-CKFW

MAULE AIRCRAFT CORPORATION

M-5-180C LUNAR ROCKET
G-BVFZ

M-5-235C LUNAR ROCKET
G-BHJK BIES FMGG OJGT RJWW VVME

M-6-235 SUPER ROCKET
G-BKGC MOUL

MT-7-235 SUPER ROCKET
G-HIND

MX-7-180 SUPER ROCKET variants
G-BSKG ICUT JREE LOFM MLHI RAZZ
WALY

MXT-7-180 SUPER, ROCKET
G-BUEP BVIK BVIL CROL GROL

MAXAIR

DRIFTER
G-MYBB

McDONNELL DOUGLAS HELICOPTERS – see HUGHES

MD HELICOPTERS INC

MD.600N NOTAR
G-GREM

MD.900 EXPLORER
G-CIOS CNWL COTH EHAA EHEM EHMS
HAAT HDBV HDMD HMDX KAAT KSSA
KSSH LNDN SASR

MEAD

BM-77
G-TADS

MEDWAY MICROLIGHTS LTD – also see RAVEN and SOUTHDOWN

AV8R
G-CCGO

CLIPPER
G-CHJJ

ECLIPSER
G-BYXW CBMR CCGA MZME ZZOW

HALF PINT with Aerial Arts 130SX wing
G-MMSZ MNDE

HYBRED 44XL
G-MMEK MNCU MNCV MNJX MVSI

HYBRED 44XLR
G-MTFC MTLX MTNE MTNF MVCD MVDJ
MVGY MVPF MVRZ MVVI MVZO MWCY
MWCZ MWJR MWLS MWST MWSU MYVV

SLA 80 Executive
G-CCJJ CDZY CEII CKZE DBIN

SLA 100 Executive
G-CDXD CEHE CEKC CENJ CGIO NDAD
RSMC TLDL

MEMORIAL FLIGHT

SE.5A REPLICA
G-ERFC

MENAVIA – see PIEL AVIATION

MESSERSCHMITT AG including HISPANO HA.1112 versions

Bf.109
G-AWHC AWHH AWHK AWHM AWHR CDTI
CIPB CLBX HISP JIMP

MESSERSCHMITT-BÖLKOW-BLOHM GmbH – also see AÉROSPATIALE (AS prefix), EUROCOPTER (EC prefix) and SUD-AVIATION (SA and SE prefixes)

BÖ.105 variants
G-BFYA BTKL ENVO XBLD

BK117 C-2 (EC 145)
G-CJND DCPB MPSA MPSB MPSC PSNO
PSNR SRNE

BK-117D-2 (EC145)
G-CLCE CLCF EMSS HEMC RESU RMAA
SASN SASS WENU WOBR WROL YAAC
YOAA

MEYERS AIRCRAFT COMPANY

OTW
G-MOTW

MICRO AVIATION

B-22 BANTAM
G-BXZU BZYS CFHB CFHC MZLX

MICRO BIPLANE AVIATION

TIGER CUB 440
G-MJSP MJUF MJUW MJWF MMAG MMAM
MMBE MMGF MMGL MMHN MMIE MMIH
MMJV MMKP MMKT MMLK MNKM MWFT

MICRO ENGINEERING (AVIATON) LTD (MEA)

MISTRAL
G-MBOH

MICROFLIGHT AIRCRAFT LTD including CORBETT FARMS production

SPECTRUM (Rotax 503)
G-MWCG MWKX MWPH

MIDLAND ULTRALIGHTS LTD
SIROCCO
G-MNDU MTJN MTRC

MIGNET (SOCIÉTÉ D'EXPLOITATION DES AERONEFS HENRI MIGNET)
HM.14 POU-DU-CIEL
G-AEBB

HM.293
G-AXPG

HM-1000 BALERIT
G-MRAM MYDZ MYXL MZLI MZMW

MILES AIRCRAFT LTD including PHILLIPS AND POWIS AIRCRAFT LTD
M.2 HAWK
G-CCMH

M.2L HAWK SPEED SIX
G-ADGP

M.2W HAWK TRAINER
G-ADWT

M.3 FALCON
G-AEEG

M.5 SPARROWHAWK
G-ADNL

M.11A WHITNEY STRAIGHT
G-AERV AEUJ

M.14A HAWK TRAINER 3
G-AHUJ AIUA AJRS AKAT AKPF

M.17 MONARCH
G-AFJU AFRZ

M.28 MERCURY
G-AHAA

M.38 MESSENGER variants
G-AGOY AIEK AJOE AJWB AKBO AKDF
AKIN AKVZ ALAH ALAR

M.65 GEMINI variants
G-AKDK AKEN AKHP AKHU AKKB AKKH

MILHOLLAND
LEGAL EAGLE
G-CINJ

MILLS
MH-1
G-OMHI

MINICAB – see GARDAN

MITCHELL-PROCTER
G-ATXN BBRN

MITCHINSON
SAFARI
G-CIAA

MOLE
MITE
G-MITY

MOLINO – see EIRIAVION O/Y

MONNETT – also see SONEX
MONI
G-BMVU MONI TRIM

SONERAI
G-BGEH BJBM BJLC BKNO BLAI BOBY
BSGJ CCOZ FVEE LOWE PFAT RILY

MONOCOUPE CORPORATION
90A
G-AFEL

MONTGOMERIE-BENSEN – see BENSEN

MONTGOMERIE-PARSONS – see PARSONS

MOONEY AIRCRAFT CORPORATION
M.20 variants
G-ASUB ATOU AWLP BDTV BHJI BIWR
BJHB BKMA BKMB BPCR BSXI BVZY
BWJG BWTW BYEE CEJN CERT CITT CKXI
FLYA GCKI JBRD JENA MALS MUNI OBAL
ODJH OEAC OJAC OONE OPWS OSUS
RAFW

MOORE
DEMOICHELLE
G-CHWI

MORANE-SAULNIER including GEMS, SOCIÉTÉ LEVASSEUR, MORANE, SEEMS, and SOCATA production and see DE HAVILLAND
TYPE N
G-AWBU

MS.315
G-BZNK

MS.317
G-MOSA

MS.500 CRIQUET
G-BPHZ

MS.733 ALCYON
G-MSAL SHOW

MS.800 series RALLYE variants
G-ASAU AVIN AXGE AXOH AXOT AZGL
AZKE AZMZ AZVI AZYD BAAI BAOJ BCOR
BCVC BECB BERA BEVB BEVC BGMT
BGSA BIAC BIIK BJDF BKBF BKGA BKOA
BLGS BTOW BTUG BUKR BYPN CCZA
CGPN EXIT FOSY HENT KHRE OACI OMIA
PIGS

MORAVAN NÁRODNÍ PODNIK – see ZLIN

MORETON
ORIENTAL
G-BINY

MORRIS
SCRUGGS BL2 series
G-BILE BILG BINL BINM BINX BIPH BISL
BISM BISS BIST

SCRUGGS RS5000
G-BIWB BIWC

MORRIS MOTORS – see DE HAVILLAND AIRCRAFT LTD

MOSS BROS AIRCRAFT LTD
MOSS MA.1
G-AFHA

MOSS MA.2
G-AFJV

MRAZ
M.1 SOKOL
G-AIXN

MUDRY (AVIONS MUDRY ET CIE) including AKROTECH EUROPE and CONSTRUCTIONS AÉRONAUTIQUES DE BOURGOGNE
CAP 10
G-BECZ BKCX BLVK BRDD BXBK BXBU
BXFE BXRA BXRB BXRC BYFY CAPI CAPX
CCNX CCXC CDCE CDIF CEHS CPDW
CPXC CZCZ DAVM GDTU IVAL LORN MOZZ
ODIN OIOB RIFN SLEA WIXI

CAP 231 and CAP 232
G-CPII EJAC GKKI GODV HAYE IIAI IIHZ IIRP
IITC

MURPHY
QUICKSILVER GT500
G-CEWY

MURPHY AIRCRAFT MANUFACTURING LTD
ELITE
G-CBRT ONIG

MAVERICK
G-CBGO CBVF CDYM MYUJ MZJJ MZLE

REBEL
G-BUTK BVHS BWCY BWFZ BWLL BYBK
BZFT CBFK CIOA DIKY LJCC MRPH REBB
YELL

RENEGADE 912
G-BTKB BWPE RCMC TBAG

RENEGADE SPIRIT UK
G-BYBU MGOO MVZP MVZX MWAJ MWMW
MWNF MWNR MWOO MWPZ MWVP
MWWD MYAZ MYCO MYRK MYUF MZIZ
RNGD

N

NANCHANG AIRCRAFT MANUFACTURING COMPANY – see YAKOVLEV

NAVAL AIRCRAFT FACTORY
N3N-3
G-CFXT ONAF

NEICO – see LANCAIR

NEUKOM
ELFE S4
G-CJXY CKPJ

NICOLLIER
HN.700 MENESTREL
G-BVHL BZOI CCCJ CCDS CCKN CCVW
CDHZ CDZR CHRE CIOR CKGJ MINS VIVO

NIEUPORT
11
G-CILI

SCOUT 17/23
G-BWMJ

NIPPER AIRCRAFT LTD – see TIPSY AIRCRAFT CO LTD

NIRVANA
CARBON TRIKE (DUDEK SYNTHESIS Wing)
G-CGZN

NOBLE HARDMAN AVIATION LTD including THE SNOWBIRD AEROPLANE CO LTD
SNOWBIRD
G-MVIL MVIN MVOJ MVYU MVYV MVYW
MVYX RUMI

NOORDUYN AVIATION LTD – see NORTH AMERICAN AVIATION INC

NORMAN AEROPLANE CO LTD
NAC-2 FREELANCE
G-NACA NACI

NORTH AMERICAN AVIATION INC including CAC, CCF, NOORDUYN AVIATION LTD and see NORTH AMERICAN ROCKWELL production
(A) T-6 TEXAN, AT-16 HARVARD variants
G-AZBN AZSC BBHK BDAM BGHU BGOR
BGPB BICE BJST BKRA BRBC BRVG BSBG

G

BTXI BZHL CCOY CHIA CHYN CIUW CJWE
CLCJ CORS CPPM CTKL DDMV DHHF
ELMH HRVD KAMY TDJN TEXN TOMC TSIX
TVIJ TXAN

NA-64 YALE
G-BYNF

OV-10B BRONCO
G-BZGL ONAA

P-51 MUSTANG
G-ARKD BIXL CEBW CITN MSTG SHWN
SIJJ TFSI UAKE

T-28/A TROJAN
G-TROY

NORTH AMERICAN ROCKWELL INC –
see NORTH AMERICAN AVIATION INC

NORTH WING DESIGN
STRATUS-ATF
G-CEYP

STRATUS-SKYCYCLE
G-CGXF

NOSTALGAIR
N.3 PUP
G-BVEA

NOTT
AN3
G-CKBR

PA
G-CCSW

ULD
G-NOTT

NOUVELLE SOC COMETAL – see
GARDAN

NOVA VERTRIEBSGESELLSCHAFT
GmbH
PHILOU
G-BZXI

PHOCUS
G-BZYI

VERTEX
G-BYLI BYZT BZVI CCET

X LARGE 37
G-BZJI

O

OGMA – see DE HAVILLAND AIRCRAFT LTD
and DE HAVILLAND CANADA

OLDFIELD
BABY LAKES
G-BGEI BKCJ BKHD BMIY BWMO POND
SWAK

OMEGA AEROSTATICS LTD
84
G-AXJB

OPTICA INDUSTRIES LTD including FLS
production
OA.7 OPTICA
G-BMPL BOPO BOPR

ORLICAN
L-40 META-SOKOL
G-APUE APVU

OZONE POWER LTD
SPARK
G-CITU

OZONE/ADVENTURE SA
BUZZ/PARAJET MACRO
G-CKNX

INDY/PARAMOTOR FLYER
G-CIZF

ROADSTER-ADVENTURE/BAILEY QUATTRO
G-OFAL

P

P&M LTD – see PEGASUS AVIATION

PAKES
JACKDAW
G-MBOF

PARNALL (G PARNALL and COMPANY)
PARNALL ELF
G-AAIN

PARSONS including BENSEN-PARSONS and
MONTGOMERIE-PARSONS
TWO PLACE GYROPLANE
G-BPIF BTFE BUWH CDGT IIXX

PARTENAVIA COSTRUZIONI
AERONAUTICHE SpA including
VULCANAIR SpA
P.64B OSCAR
G-BMDP

P.68
G-OBSR

P.68B and C
G-BCDK BHJS ENCE FJMS HUBB KIMK
ORVR PDGV PDGX PNGB RIPA RVNE RVNG
RVNJ RVNK RVNM RVNP RVRE RVRX

PASSION'ALLES
*CHARIOT Z Trike - PARAMANIA ACTION GT26
sailwing*
G-CEOZ

PAYNE
FREE BALLOON
G-AZRI

PAZMANY
PL-2
G-OPAZ

PL-4
G-TONE

PL-4A
G-BMMI BRFX CGRN CIPZ PAZY

PEARSON
SERIES 2
G-BIXX

PEGASUS AVIATION including CYCLONE
AIRSPORTS LTD, MAINAIR SPORTS LTD and
P&M Ltd production
HYPER
G-CKHY

PULSR
G-FFFA PLSR SFCM

QUANTUM series
G-BYDZ BYEW BYFF BYHR BYIS BYJK
BYKT BYLC BYMF BYMI BYND BYOG BYOV
BYPB BYPJ BYRJ BYRU BYSX BYTC BYYN
BYYP BYYY BYZU BZAI BZDS BZED BZFC
BZFH BZGZ BZHN BZHO BZIM BZIW BZJO
BZJZ BZLL BZLX BZLZ BZNC BZNM BZOE
BZOO BZOU BZRJ BZRP BZRR BZSG BZSI
BZSM BZSS BZSX BZUC BZUE BZUI BZUX
BZVJ BZVV BZWS BZWU BZXV BZXX BZYN
CBBB CBBN CBBP CBCD CBCF CBDX

CBDZ CBEN CBEU CBEV CBGG CBHK
CBHN CBHY CBJO CBKW CBLL CBMV
CBNT CBOY CBTD CBUD CBUS CBUU
CBUZ CBYI CBYV CCCD CCDK CCDZ
CCFT CCIH CCJD CCNE CCNW CCOC
CCRF CCRT CCUR CCWO CCWW CCYL
CCZB CDAA CDAO CDDF CDEN CDFR
CDGX CDHM CDIL CDIR CDLZ CDOO
CDPW CDRR CDTB CDVH CDXG CFBM
CIJR DINO DSLL EDMC EMLY EOFW FESS
FFUN HSEB ICWT JAWC JGSI KICK MCAL
MCJL MDBC MGDL MGEF MGFK MGGG
MGGV MGTG MHMR MROC MSPY MYLC
MYLE MYLH MYLI MYLM MYMB MYMC
MYNB MYNK MYNL MYNN MYNP MYNR
MYNS MYNT MYNV MYNZ MYOU MYPH
MYPI MYPN MYRF MYRN MYRS MYRT
MYRY MYRZ MYSB MYSC MYSR MYSW
MYSY MYTI MYTJ MYTN MYUO MYUV
MYVC MYVJ MYVK MYVM MYVR MYWG
MYWI MYWJ MYWK MYWL MYWO MYWR
MYWU MYWW MYWY MYXE MYXT MYXW
MYXX MYXZ MYYB MYYC MYYI MYYK
MYZB MYZJ MYZL MYZY MZAN MZAW
MZBC MZBT MZBY MZCI MZCJ MZCM
MZCV MZCY MZDB MZDC MZDD MZDE
MZDH MZDN MZDU MZDV MZDY MZEC
MZEE MZEH MZEM MZEX MZEZ MZFM
MZFT MZGG MZGN MZGO MZHI MZHN
MZHP MZIB MZIE MZIJ MZIK MZIU MZJG
MZJH MZJO MZJT MZJW MZJY MZKA
MZKD MZKF MZKL MZKY MZLA MZLD
MZLF MZLJ MZLN MZLT MZLV MZLW
MZMC MZMF MZMG MZMH MZMN MZMT
MZNB MZNG MZNR MZNS MZNT MZOD
MZOG MZOS MZOV MZOW MZRC MZRM
NAPO OAMF OATE OBJP OHKS OLDM
OLFB OTJH PEGA PIXI PZPZ REDC SILY
SITA SMBM TFIX TRAM WHEE

QUIK variants
G-CBVN CBYO CBZH CBZT CCAD CCAS
CCAZ CCCG CCDB CCDD CCDF CCDO
CCEA CCEW CCFL CCGC CCHH CCHI
CCHO CCJM CCKM CCKO CCLM CCLX
CCMD CCML CCMS CCNM CCOG CCOK
CCOU CCOW CCPC CCPG CCRW CCSD
CCSF CCSH CCSL CCSY CCTC CCTD
CCTU CCTZ CCUA CCWV CCXT CCXZ
CCYE CCYJ CCZO CDAR CDAX CDBB
CDCF CDCI CDEW CDFG CDFO CDGC
CDGD CDGO CDHG CDKK CDKM CDLA
CDLD CDLJ CDMJ CDML CDNH CDOC
CDOM CDOP CDPD CDRG CDRT CDRW
CDSA CDSM CDSS CDTO CDTR CDUU
CDVG CDVN CDVO CDVR CDVZ CDWO
CDWR CDWZ CDXN CEBM CEBT CECA
CEDN CEEI CEGJ CEGT CEGV CEGW CEHC
CEHI CEHW CEJJ CEJX CEKG CEMB
CEMM CEMO CEMT CEMX CENL CENV
CEOO CEPP CERN CERV CERW CERW
CESR CETL CETM CEUF CEUH CEUZ CEVB
CEVP CEVW CEWD CEWH CEZT CEZX
CFAT CFCZ CFDL CFDY CFEM CFEV CFEX
CFFN CFFO CFGD CFGT CFGV CFIG CFIL
CFIM CFKJ CFKO CFKR CFKU CFLA CFLM
CFLR CFMB CFMD CFOO CFPI CFPR CFSF
CFTG CFVA CFWJ CFWN CFXX CFXZ CFYO
CGAC CGAL CGAZ CGDL CGEX CGGC
CGGT CGHA CGHG CGHH CGHZ CGJJ
CGLG CGLO CGMI CGMZ CGNK CGNO
CGOB CGPC CGPE CGRC CGRR CGRS
CGRW CGSO CGTU CGUG CGUP CGUR
CGWZ CGXE CGXV CGYZ CHDM CHFC
CHFO CHFU CHGA CHIV CHJW CHPZ
CHUX CHVB CHWO CHZW CIAR CIBR CIBT
CIDG CIDY CIEG CIEM CIFF CIFV CIGC
CIGG CIHA CIHL CIHY CIHZ CIIA CIIH CIJA
CIJO CIKA CIKI CIMH CIMK CINH CIOD
CIOL CIPA CIPM CISI CISM CIST CITO CIUZ
CIXZ CIYZ CIZD CIZL CIZV CJAI CJAJ CJAY
CJGG CJNH CKHI CKTT CKYS CKZF CLAT
CLBN CLEW CMDG CUTH CWEB CWIC
CWMC DCMI DDDY DECR DGAV DRGC

DSMA DTAR EEKZ EEWZ EGJJ EMMX ERYR
EZAR FEET FFFB FFIT FRCX FRGT GAVH
GAZN GBEE GCEA GEMX GTFC GTGT
GTJD GTRE GTRR GTRX GTSD GTSO GTTP
HADD HALT HAMS HOFF HOLE HOTR
HTML HUDS IANZ IBLP IGLY IRLI ISEW
JAMZ JBAN JFAN JHLE JOBA JULE KEVS
KEVZ KMAK KUIK KWIC KWKR KWKX LEMP
LITS LOTY LOWZ LPIN LSKY LUNE MABL
MADV MAXS MCFK MFLJ MKER MLAW
MLKE MOZE MRJJ NJPW NUTT OFDT
OGOD OGTR OJJV OLDP OLFZ OLPM
OMIW OMPW OOGY OONZ ORLA OSOD
OSON OTOP OUIK PCMC PEAR PICX PIPI
POLR PUGZ PVSS RAYB RCHL RCRC
RDPH RIBA RIKY RITT ROBG RPRP RSAM
RUNS SARJ SEEE SHEE SHEZ SISU SOCK
SUEL TARR TBJP TBLB TBMR TCNY TERR
TFLX TJAV TJCL TKEV TNJB TONN TPAL
TPWL UIKR VAAV WANA WAWW WBLY
WFLY WIZS WJSG WMBL XDWE YOLK
YSMO ZZXX

PERCIVAL AIRCRAFT CO LTD including
HUNTING PERCIVAL AIRCRAFT LTD
production

Type E MEW GULL
G-AEXF HEKL

Type K VEGA GULL
G-AEZJ

Type Q SIX
G-AFFD

PROCTOR variants
G-AHTE AKEX AKIU ALJF ANVY ANXR

P.40 PRENTICE
G-AOKL AOLU APJB APPL

P.56 PROVOST
G-AWPH AWRY BKFW BLIW BZRF KAPW
MOOS

P.57 SEA PRINCE
G-BRFC

PEREIRA
OSPREY
G-BVGI CCCW GEOF PREY

PERFORMANCE DEIGNS INC
BARNSTORMER/VOYAGER
G-CFKP

PHILLIPS AND POWIS AIRCRAFT LTD –
see MILES AIRCRAFT LTD

PHOENIX
*LUTON LA-4, LA-4A MINOR including Ord-Hume
O-H7, Parker CA-4 plus Phoenix Duet versions
and replicas*
G-AFIR AMAW ARIF ARXP ASAA ASEA
ASEB ASML ATCJ ATCN ATKH AVUO AWMN
AXGR AXKH AYDY AYSK AYTT AZHU BANF
BBCY BBEA BDJG BIJS BRWU

PIAGGIO AERO INDUSTRIES SpA
including FOCKE-WULF FLUGZEUGBAU
GMBH production

P.149
G-RORY

PIEL AVIATION including COOPAVIA,
ROUSSEAU, SOCIÉTÉ MENAVIA and SOCIÉTÉ
SCINTEX production

CP.301 EMERAUDE
G-ARDD ARRS ASCZ ASVG AXXC AYCE
AYTR AZGY AZYS BBKL BDCI BDKH BHRR
BIDO BIJU BIVF BKFR BKNZ BKUR BLRL
BSVE BXYE CKCF DENS EFAO EGEN PIEL

CP.328 SUPER EMERAUDE
G-SAZZ

CP.1310-C3 SUPER EMERAUDE
G-ASMV ASNI BCHP BGVE BJCF BJVS BLXI
BXRF

CP.1315-C3 SUPER EMERAUDE
G-BHEK DJVY

CP.1320
G-CFIH SAFI

CP.1330 SUPER EMERAUDE
G-BANW

PIETENPOL
AIRCAMPER
G-ADRA BMDE BMLT BNMH BRXY BUCO
BUXK BUZO BVYY BWAT BWVB BWVF
BXZO BYFT BYKG BYLD BYZY CCKR CGFP
CLDH DAYZ EDFS EEAA HAPE KIRC LEOD
OEMZ OFFA OHAL OPJS PIET PLJR RAGS
SILS TARN UNGO VALS

PILATUS AIRCRAFT LTD – see
BRITTEN-NORMAN for BN-2 production

P.3
G-BTLL

PC-6 TURBO PORTER
G-CECI

PC-12 variants
G-DYLN ERGP FLXI KARE KFTI MAKN
NBCA OMSL PCIZ PCTW PKHA TRAT

PC-21
G-ETPA ETPB

PILATUS FLUGZEUGWERKE AG
B4-PC11 variants
G-CHDA CHDE CHLC CHVH CJXX CKSK
DCSN DCSP DCUB DCUC DCUT DCVK
DCVV DCYA DCYC DCZD DDBC DDLA
DDND DDRP DDSV DEOU GTBT LUUP PILY

PIPER
CP.1 METISSE
G-BVCP

PIPER AIRCRAFT CORPORATION
including TAYLOR AIRCRAFT CO LTD, and THE
NEW PIPER AIRCRAFT INC production

J-2 CUB
G-AEXZ AFFH

J-3 CUB variants
G-AFDO AGAT AGIV AHIP AIIH AISS AISX
AJAD AJES AKIB AKTH AKUN ALMA ASPS
ATKI ATZM AXGP AXHP AXHR AYEN BAET
BBHJ BBLH BBUU BCNX BCOB BCOM
BCPH BCPJ BCUB BCXJ BDCD BDEY
BDHK BDJP BDMS BDOL BECN BEDJ BEUI
BFBY BFDL BFHI BFZB BGPD BGSJ BGTI
BGXA BHPK BHVV BHXY BHZU BIJE BILI
BJAF BJAY BJSZ BKHG BMKC BOTU BOXJ
BPCF BPUR BPVH BPYN BREB BROR
BSBT BSFD BSNF BSTI BSVH BSYO BTET
BTSP BTUM BTZX BVAF BWEZ CCUB CGIY
CIIW COPS CUBS CUBY FRAN HEWI KURK
KUUI LIVH LOCH NCUB OCUB OLEZ POOH
RAMP RCIE RIXA RRSR SAZM SEED TCUB

J-4 CUB COUPÉ variants
G-AFGM AFWH AFZA BRBV BUWL

J-5 CUB CRUISER
G-BPKT BRIL BRLI BSDK BSXT BTKA CIZN

L-4B CUB
G-FINT

PA-12 SUPER CRUISER
G-AMPG ARTH AWPW AXUC BCAZ BOWN
BSYG CDCS CIUM PAIZ

PA-15 VAGABOND
G-ALGA ASHU BDVB BOVB BRJL BRPY
BRSX BSFW BTFJ BTOT FKNH VAGA
WYMM

PA-16 CLIPPER
G-BAMR BIAP BSWF

PA-17 VAGABOND
G-AKTP ALEH ALIJ AWKD AWOH BCVB
BDVA BDVC BIHT BLMP BSMV BSWG BTBY
BTCI BUXX

PA-18 SUPER CUB variants
G-AMEN APZJ ARAM ARAN ARCT AREO
ARGV ARVO ATRG AVOO AWMF AXLZ
AYPM AYPO AYPS AZRL BAFT BAFV BAKV
BBOL BBYB BCFO BCMD BEOI BEUA
BEUU BFFP BGPN BGYN BHGC BHOM
BIDJ BIDK BIID BIJB BIMM BITA BIYJ BIYR
BIYY BIZV BJBK BJCI BJEI BJFE BJIV BJTP
BJWX BJWZ BKET BKJB BKRF BKTA BKVM
BLHM BLLO BLMI BLMR BLMT BLPE BLRC
BMAY BMEA BMKB BNXM BOOC BPJG
BPUL BROZ BTBU BTDY BTUR BVIE BVIW
BVRZ BWOR BZHT CIIC CUBB CUBI CUBJ
CUBN CVMI DADG DRGL ECMK ECUB
EGPG FADF FUZZ GRIZ HACK HELN JCUB
KYTT LCUB LION MUDY NESY NETY NNAC
OFER OOMF OROD OSPS OTAN OVON
PAIB PIPR PUDL RCUB ROVE RWCA SCUB
SUPA SVAS SWAY TUGG VCUB WCUB
WGCS WLAC XCUB YCUB ZAZA ZPPY

PA-20 PACER
G-ATBX BFMR BSED BUDE PAXX

PA-22-108 COLT
G-ARGO ARKK ARKM ARKP ARKS ARNE
ARNG ARNJ ARNK ARNL ARON CBEI

PA-22-135 TRI-PACER
G-BMCS BUVA TJAY

PA-22-150 CARIBBEAN
G-APXT ARDS AREL ARFB ARHR ARIK ARIL
ATXA AVDV BWWU

PA-22-150 TRI-PACER
G-APXU ARAX ARCF AWLI AZRS BRNX

PA-22-160 TRI-PACER
G-APUR APXR APZL ARBS ARET ARFD
BTKV HALL

PA-23-160 APACHE
G-APFV ARCW ARJS ARJT ARJU ASMY

PA-(E)23-250 AZTEC
G-ASEP AXZP AZYU BADJ BAPL BAVL
BBDO BBHF BBIF BBRA BCBG BCCE BJNZ
BJXX BKJW BMFD BSVP CALL CKUU KEYS
NADN OART OPME RVRJ RVRW RVRZ TAXI
TOPO UNDD

PA-24 & 24-180 COMANCHE
G-AXMA AZKR BRDW BWNI MOTO

PA-24-250 COMANCHE
G-APXJ ARDB ARLK ARXG ARYV ASEO
BAHJ BYTI TALF

PA-24-260 COMANCHE
G-ATJL ATNV AVCM AVGA AXTO AZWY
BRXW KITO KSVB PETH

PA-25-235 PAWNEE
G-ASIY AVPY AVXA AXED AZPA BAUC
BCBJ BDPJ BEII BETM BFEV BFPR BFPS
BFSC BFSD BHUU BLDG BPWL BSTH
BUXY BVYP BXST CTUG LYND NYMF

PA-25-260 PAWNEE
G-BDDS BFRY DSGC PSGC SATN TOWS

*PA-28-140 CHEROKEE, CRUISER and
FLITELINER*
G-ASSW ASVZ ATEZ ATJG ATOI ATOJ ATOK
ATON ATOO ATOP ATOR ATTI ATTK ATTV
ATUB ATVK ATVO AVFR AVFX AVFZ AVGC
AVGE AVLB AVLC AVLE AVLF AVLG AVLI
AVLJ AVLT AVSI AVUS AVUT AVWA AVWD
AVWI AVWL AVWM AWBG AWBS AWEV
AWEX AXAB AXIO AXIR AXJV AXJX AXSZ
AXTA AXTC AXTJ AXTL AYIG AYJP AYJR
AYKW AYMK AYNF AYNJ AYPV AYRM AZEG
AZFC AZRH AZWB BAFU BAFW BAGX
BAHF BAKH BAWK BAXZ BBBY BBDC BBIL

BBIX BBYP BCGI BCGJ BCGN BCJM BCJN
BCJP BDGY BDSH BDWY BEAC BEYT
BFXK BGAX BIYX BOFY BRBW BRPK BRPL
BSLU BSTZ BTGO BTON BULR BYCA CCLJ
CJYI EEKY FIAT GCAT GFZG ICGA JRBC
KALI LFSC LFSI LTFB LTFC MATZ MIDD
MKAS NHRH OFTI OKYM OLPH OMAT
PETR PIKK RVRA RVRT SCPL TEFC TEWS
UANT USHI WOLF ZEBY

PA-28-150 CHEROKEE
G-BIFB

PA-28-151 CHEROKEE WARRIOR
G-BBXW BCIR BCRL BCTF BDGM BDPA
BEBZ BEFA BHFK BIEY BNMB BNNT BOHR
BOTF BPPK BRBD BRTX BTNT BTUW CCZV
CJJS CKIO CPTM FPIG GUSS JAMP OLEA
PSRT ROWS TALG

PA-28-160 CHEROKEE
G-ARVT ARVU ARVV ATDA ATIS BSER BSLM
BWYB JAKS LIZI

PA-28-161 (CHEROKEE) WARRIOR II
G-BFBR BFDK BFMG BFNI BFNK BFSZ
BFWB BGKS BGOG BGPJ BGPL BGYH
BHJO BHOR BHRC BHVB BICW BIIT BJBW
BJCA BJSV BLVL BMFP BMKR BMUZ BNCR
BNEL BNJT BNNO BNNY BNNZ BNOF
BNOH BNOJ BNOM BNON BNOP BNRG
BNSY BNSZ BNTD BNXE BNXU BNZB
BNZZ BOAH BODB BODD BODE BODR
BOER BOFZ BOHA BOHG BOIG BOJW
BOJZ BOKB BOKX BOMY BOPC BORK
BORL BOTI BOTN BOVK BOXA BOXC BOYH
BOYI BOZI BPAF BPBM BPCK BPDT BPFH
BPIU BPKM BPMF BPOM BPRY BPWE
BRBA BRBE BRDF BRDG BRDM BRFM
BRUB BSAW BSBA BSCV BSCY BSHP
BSJX BSLK BSLT BSOK BSOZ BSSC BSVG
BSVM BSXA BSXB BSXC BSYY BSYZ BSZT
BTAW BTBC BTDV BTFO BTGY BTIV BTKT
BTNH BTNV BTRK BTRS BTRY BTSJ BUFH
BUFY BUIF BUIJ BUIK BUJO BUJP BXAB
BXLY BXVU BYHI BZLH CBAL CCYY CDDG
CDMA CDMX CDMY CDON CEGS CEGU
CEIZ CFMX CJLI CKEY CLAC CLEA COSF
CSGT DKEY EDGA EDGI EEGU EGBJ EGLL
EGTB EKKL ELUE ELZN ELZY ENNA EOLD
ERFS EVIE EVTO FIZZ FLAV FMAM FPSA
GALB GHKX GUAR GURU HAMR IKBP ISDB
JASE JAVO KART KYTE LACB LAZL LBMM
LFSJ LFSW LSFT MSFT NINA OAAA OANI
OJWS OOMA OONY OPTI OWAP OWAR
OZAM PJCC RAAM RIZZ RSKR RVRN SACI
SACO SEJW SELB SEXX SIXT SNUZ SRWN
SUZN SVEA TOES VICC WARE WARR
WFFW WFWA WNTR XAVI XENA XINE

PA-28-161 (CHEROKEE) WARRIOR III
G-BXOJ BYHH BZBS BZDA BZIO CBKR
CBWD CBYU CEEZ CEJD CETD CETE
CEXO CGOS CKZV COVA COVC EHAZ
GFTA GGEM GOTH GYTO HMED ISHA JACA
OBDN OBFS OMCH OMST OOFT OPUK
WARA WARB WARH WARO WARS WARU
WARV WARW WARX WARY

PA-28-161 CADET
G-BPJS BRJV BTIM BWOH BWOI BXTY
BXTZ CDEF CEEN CEEU CEZI CEZL CEZO
CIZO EJRS EKIR FOXA GFCA GFCB JLIN
KCIN LORC LOTE OCTU OFDR OLSF OXOM
SACR SACS SACT

PA-28-180 CHEROKEE, CHALLENGER and ARCHER
G-ARYR ASEJ ASFL ASHX ASII ASIJ ASIL
ASKT ASRW ASUD ASWX ATAS ATEM ATHR
ATNB ATOT ATTX ATUL ATYS AVBG AVBH
AVBR AVBS AVBT AVNN AVNO AVNS AVNU
AVNW AVOZ AVPV AVRK AVRU AVRZ AVSA
AVSB AVSC AVSD AVSE AVSF AVSP AVYL
AVYM AWIT AWSL AWTL AWXR AWXS
AXSG AXZD AYAB AYAR AYAT AYAW AYEE
AYEF AYPJ AYUH AZLN AZYF BABG BAJR
BASJ BATV BBBN BBHY BBKX BBPP BCCF

BEYL BKCC BOHM BRBG BRGI BSEF
BSGD BUTZ BUUX BUYY BXJD CBMO
CDEO CJBC CJSP CKSP CORW DEVS DLTR
EFCM GALA GBRB HRYZ KEES KIMZ LFSG
NINC NIND OIBO ONET OTYP RISA SOOT
TEMP YULL ZZIJ

PA-28-181 (CHEROKEE) ARCHER II
G-BDSB BEIP BEMW BEXW BFDI BFSY
BFVG BGBG BGVZ BGWM BHNO BHWZ
BHZE BIUY BJAG BLFI BMIW BMPC BMSD
BNGT BNPO BNRP BNVE BNYP BOEE
BOJM BOMP BOMU BOOF BOPA BOSE
BPAY BPFI BPGU BPOT BPTE BPXA BRBX
BRME BRUD BRXD BSCS BSEU BSIM
BSKW BSNX BSVB BSZJ BTAM BTGZ BTKX
BTYI BUMP BVNS BWPH BXEX BXIF BXOZ
BXWO BYKL BYSP CBSO CBTT CCAV
CDGW CHAS CHIP CKVV CKXU DJJA EGIB
EHGF EHLX EPYW ERNI FBRN FKOS GASP
HARN ILLY INAS JANA JANT JJAN JOYT
KAIR KIKI LVRS MAAS MASF MDAC NIKE
NJOY NUKA ODUD OGEM OJEH OMJA
OODW OPET RADI RAZY RECW RNCH SAPI
SARA SGSE SHED SOBI TALE TALH TERY
TIMK TSAS TSGJ TWEL WWAY YANK ZOFG

PA-28-181 (CHEROKEE) ARCHER III
G-BWUH BXTW BYHK BZHV CCHL CGVC
CIAM CIFY CKXV DIXY EGLS FEAB ISAX
JACB JACH JACS JADJ JJEN JONM JOYZ
KEMI KEVB LOGN LORR MELS MPAA NOTE
ORAR PACT PEJM RRED SBOY VAAC VOAR
WLGC

PA-28-181 (CHEROKEE) ARCHER LX
G-IBEA

PA-28-201T TURBO DAKOTA
G-BOKA BXCC HOLA

PA-28-235 CHEROKEE and PATHFINDER)
G-ASLV AWSM BXYM CCBH CKZT EWME

PA-28-236 DAKOTA
G-BGXS BHTA BRKH CSBD DAKA DAKO
DKTA FEGN FWPW KOTA LEAM ODAK TART
ZSDB

PA-28R-180 CHEROKEE ARROW
G-AVWO AVWR AVWT AVWU AVWV AVXF
AVYS AVYT AWAZ AWBB AWBC AWFB
AWFC AWFD AWFJ AZWS BAPW BWNM
CCIJ CJSF CKLI FBWH NELI WWAL

PA-28R-200 CHEROKEE ARROW
G-AXCA AXWZ AYAC AYII AYPU AYRI AZAJ
AZDE AZFI AZFM BCPG BFZH BTLG CBVU

PA-28R-200 CHEROKEE ARROW II
G-AZNL AZOG AZSF BAHS BAIH BAMY
BAWG BNDE BBEB BBFD BBZH BBZV
BCGS BCJO BHEV BHGY BHWY BIKE BIZO
BKXF BMGB BMKK BMOE BTRT BZDH
CBEE DMCS DSFT EDVL EGVA ELUT EPTR
ETLX FULL GDOG HALC IOCJ ODOG OMNI
RACO STEA TORC VFAS

PA-28R-201 (CHEROKEE) ARROW III
G-BEWX BGKU BGKV BIDI BMLS BMPR
BNEE BNSG BOBA BYHJ BYYO BZKL
BZMB CBPI CBZR CEOG GGRN IBFW KIAN
MEME MOSH OARA OARU OTGA TEBZ
THSL TOLL TSGA WAMS

PA-28R-201T TURBO (CHEROKEE) ARROW III
G-BEOH BFDO BFTC BGOL BMIV BNNX
BNVT BOIC BOYV BSPN DDAY DIZY ECJM
JDPB JESS OBAK OJIM OKEN OOTC SABA
SHAY SHUG

PA-28RT-201 ARROW IV
G-BGVN BOET BOJI BONC BPZM BVDH
BXYO BXYP BXYT CKYJ CKZL CMPA FICA
GEHP GHRW JSCA LAOL LBRC LFSR MERL
MRST OARC OMHC PTCC RBLU VOID
WEND

PA-28RT-201T TURBO ARROW IV
G-BHFJ BMHT BOGM BOOG BOWY BPBO
BPXJ BRLG BWMI BYKP CJZV DAAZ EXAM

GFRA GPMW GSYL IDTO IJOE MAXT OPEP
OPJD RATV RCMP RUBY SKYV TAPS TCTC
TKHE VANU YAWW

PA-30 TWIN COMANCHE – also see PA-39
G-ASRO ASSP ATEW ATSZ ATXD AVJJ
AYSB AZAB BAAJ BLOR BZRO CDHF
COMB ELAM PHIZ UAVA

PA-31 TURBO NAVAJO
G-BEZL BFIB BPYR CBTN EEJE ILZZ ONAV
OUCP RHYM SCIR SCMR SCTR UKCS
UMMI

PA-31-350 (NAVAJO) CHIEFTAIN
G-BBNT CGID CITY FABA FCSL FNAV IFIT
JAJK LIDE LYDF MAPY OETV STHA SYLL
UCAM VIPU VIPW VIPY YEOM

PA-32-260 CHEROKEE SIX
G-ATJV ATRW ATRX BBFV BHGO BRGT
CCFI CHFK EDYO ELDR ETBY NEAL OCTI
OEVA

PA-32-300 CHEROKEE SIX
G-AVFU AVUZ AZDJ BAGG BEZP BGUB
BXWP CSIX DENI DIGI DIWY EDEL FRAG
IFFR KNOW NEON OSCC PECK SIMY SIXD
WINS

PA-32-301 SARATOGA
G-BVWZ WAIR

PA-32-301FT 6x
G-KNCG MAXA RAGT RYNS TAAT TTEC

PA-32-301T TURBO SARATOGA
G-MCPR

PA-32R-300 (CHEROKEE) LANCE
G-BEHH BHBG CEYE CLDD DTCP

PA-32R-301 SARATOGA variants
G-BJCW BKMT BMJA BPVI BYFR BYPU
CCST CPMW ELLA GIPC HDEW HYLT JAFS
JPOT MOVI NIOS OIHC OPSL OSJC PURL
RAMS RIGH ROLF TSDS WILI

PA-32R-301T TURBO SARATOGA variants
G-BOGO BPVN CUBA IPAV LEYA MAIE
OZON SVPN UNAC VKRP VONS

PA-32RT-300 LANCE II
G-BFUB BOTV BRHA CIZI MLLI NROY
OJCW

PA-32RT-300T TURBO LANCE II
G-SAWI

PA-34-200 SENECA
G-AZOL BABK BACB BAIG BBLU BBNI
BBXK BRHO BVEV EXEC FLYI OCFM OPAG
TEST

PA-34-200T SENECA II
G-BCVY BDUN BEHU BEVG BHFH BLWD
BMUT BNRX BOFE BOIZ BOUK BOUM
BPXX BSDN BSHA BSII BSPG BYBH CAHA
CDPV CHEM CIZY CLOS CLUE DHMM ELIS
FILE GFEY GOAC IFLP JDBC JLCA LORD
MAIR MAXI PEGI ROUS RVNO RVRB SENE
SENX SNCA

PA-34-220T SENECA III
G-BMJO BOCU HMJB HTRL JANN NESW
OBUC OOON OWAL RAML TRUU

PA-34-220T SENECA IV
G-DSID

PA-34-220T SENECA V
G-CRGD GSYS JMOS OBNA OTVR OXFA
OXFB OXFC OXFD OXFE OXFF OXFG RSHI
ULAG ZZOT

PA-38-112 TOMAHAWK
G-BGBK BGBW BGGE BGGI BGGM BGIG
BGKY BGLA BGRM BGRR BGRX BHCZ
BJUR BJUS BLWP BMVL BNKH BNNU
BNPM BNSL BNUY BNXV BODS BOLD
BOLE BOMO BOMZ BPES BPHI BPPE BPPF
BRHR BRLO BRLP BSFE BSOU BTFP BTIL
BTJL BWNU BYMD CHER EDNA EORG
ETBT GTHM LFSA LFSB LFSH LFSM LFSN
NCFC OEDB OEFT OFFS OPSF OTFT PRIM

RVNA RVNC RVND RVRK RVRL RVRM
RVRO RVRU RVRY SEFA SUKI TMHK VMCG
XALT

PA-39 TWIN COMANCHE C/R – *also see PA-30*
G-ASMA LARE OAJS SIGN

PA-44-180 SEMINOLE
G-BGCO BGTF BHFE BRUX PDOC SEMI

PA-46-350P MALIBU MIRAGE
G-DIPM DNOP GREY JTBP PTEA

PA-46-350T MALIBU MATRIX
G-EXPO MXMX TFAM

PA-46-500TP MALIBU MERIDIAN
G-KIMI

**PA-60-601P AEROSTAR 601 (TED SMITH
production)**
G-RIGS

PIPISTREL d.o.o.
ALPHA
G-MROS OATY RTEN

APIS/BEE
G-CJDL FESB IBEE

VIRUS
G-PIVI

PITTS AVIATION ENTERPRISES INC
including AEROTEK INC, AVIAT INC and
CHRISTEN INDUSTRIES INC

S-1 variants
G-AXNZ AZCE BBOH BIRD BKDR BKKZ
BKPZ BKVP BLAG BMTU BOXH BOXV
BOZS BPDV BPRD BPZY BRAA BRBN
BRCE BRJN BRRP BRVL BRZL BRZX BSRH
BTOO BVSZ BXAF BXAU BXFB BXTI BYIR
BYJP BZSB CCFO CCXK CEOB CFFF CKTM
EEPJ FARL FCUK FLIK FORZ HOON IIIL IIIN
IIIR IIIX INII JAWZ LITZ LOOP LUNY MAGG
MAVK MAXG MINT OKAY OODI OSIC OSIS
OSIT OWAZ PARG PIII RITS SISX SWON
TAYL TWRL VOOM WIGY WILD XRED YOYO

S-2 variants
G-BADW BADZ BOEM BTTR BTUK BYIP
CCTF CUPP DIII EFIZ ENIO EWIZ FDPS
FOLY IBII ICAS IIDY IIIE IIII INDI ISII ISZA ITII
JIIL JPIT KITI ODDS OPTZ OSZA OSZB
OSZS OWTF PIIT PITS PITZ PTTS PULR
ROLL SIIE SJBI SPIN STUA STUI TIII WREN
ZIII

S-1-11 SUPER STINKER
G-IIIV STNK

S-12
G-FMBS MXII PMIZ

PLUMB
BGP.1 BIPLANE
G-BGPI FUNN

POLARIS
FIB (Flying Inflatable Boat)
G-CIXI

POLIKARPOV
Po-2 (CSS-13)
G-BSSY

PORTERFIELD AIRPLANE CO
CP-50
G-AFZL

POWERCHUTE SYSTEMS
INTERNATIONAL LTD
KESTREL
G-MWCK MWCL MWCM MWCN MWCO
MWCP MWCS MWFL MWMB MWMC
MWMD MWMH MWOC MWOD MYCX MYDA
MYFA

RAIDER
G-MVHB MVNA MVNC MVNE MVNK MVVZ
MVWJ

PPHU EKOLOT – see EKOLOT

PRACTAVIA
PILOT SPRITE
G-BCVF BCWH ROSS

PRICE
AX7-77
G-BMDJ

PROAIRSPORT LTD
GLOW
G-CIUR

PROGRESSIVE AERODYNE INC
SEAREY AMPHIBIAN
G-CREY

PROTECH
PT-2C
G-EWAN

PRUETT
PUSHER
G-CILD

PTERODACTYL LTD
PFLEDGLING, PTRAVELER
G-MBPB MJST

PULMA
ELLIPSE
G-CHSI

PZL-BIELSKO – see SZD-SZYBOWCOWY
ZAKLAD DOSWIADCZALNY

PZL-SWIDNIK
PW-5 SMYK
G-CHZB CJCG CJKB CJKE SMYK

PZL WARSZAWA-OKECIE SA
PZL-104 WILGA variants
G-BUNC BXBZ WILG

PZL-110 KOLIBER variants
G-BUDO BVAI BXLS BYSI BZLC CCIZ KOLI

Q

QAC
QUICKIE
G-BKSE BPMW BSPA BSSK BXOY IMBI
IMBJ KUTU KWKI

TRI-Q
G-BMFN BWIZ FARY

QUAD CITY including BFC kits
CHALLENGER
G-BYKU CAMR CBDU CCFD CGSC CIID
CISF IBFC MWFU MWFV MWFX MWFY
MYDN MYGM MYIA MYPZ MYRH MYRJ
MYSD MYTO MYTT MYUL MYXC MYXV
MYYF MZAC MZBW MZBZ MZEA MZHO
MZKW MZNA

R

R AND W MCCANDLESS
M.4 GYROPLANE
G-ARTZ AXVN

RAJ HAMSA
X'AIR (FALCON and HAWK) variants
G-BYCL BYHV BYLT BYMR BYOH BYOJ
BYOR BYPO BYPW BYRV BYSY BYTR
BYTZ BYYM BYZF BYZW BZAK BZBP BZDK
BZEJ BZER BZEU BZHJ BZIA BZIS BZIY
BZKC BZUP BZVK BZVR BZWC BZYX
CBBH CBCI CBCM CBDO CBDV CBFE
CBIC CBII CBIS CBJX CBKL CBLF CBLP
CBLW CBNJ CBOC CBPU CBTK CBUC
CBUJ CBVC CBWY CBXR CCBI CCBX
CCCV CCDJ CCDL CCDP CCES CCEY
CCHS CCIW CCKJ CCMK CCNF CCNL
CCNZ CCOH CCRI CCVE CCVJ CCWZ
CCZJ CCZS CDDH CDEM CDFM CDHO
CDPS CEDO CEEC CEOH CEON CESJ
CFCE CFJL CFJU CFKD CFKE CGAI CGBH
CGCV CGEZ CGHV CGOV CGOX CGPW
CGVE CGVS CGWS CHIW CHMN CICU
CIFK CIWC CLDR CLEL COUZ CWAL DNBH
FECK HARI HITM IEEF IWIN LMCB MAUX
MITE NEMO ODJD OHWV RAJA SPDY TANJ
TBYD THAT TSKD UFAW XIOO XRAF XRXR

RAND-ROBINSON
KR-2
G-BLDN BNML BRJX BRJY BSTL BTGD
BUDS BUWT BVZJ BYLP CBAU CEHT DUFF
KISS KRII KRTO UTSI XRAY

RANGO BALLOON AND KITE COMPANY
NA variants
G-BJAS BJRH FYFW FYFY

RANS
S-4 COYOTE
G-CGPZ MWEP MWES MWFW MWGN
MWLZ MYWV

S-5 COYOTE
G-MWFF MZGD

S-6 variants
G-BSSI BSTT BSUA BTNW BTXD BUEW
BUTM BUWK BVCL BVFM BVOI BVPW
BVUM BVZO BWHK BWYR BXCU BXRZ
BXWK BYCM BYCN BYIO BYJO BYMN
BYNP BYOT BYPZ BYRG BYZO BZBC BZBX
BZEW BZGF BZKF BZKO BZLE BZMJ BZNH
BZNJ BZRY BZUH BZVM BZYA CBAS CBAZ
CBFX CBNV CBOS CBTO CBUY CBXZ
CBYD CBZG CBZN CCDC CCJN CCLH
CCNH CCOF CCTV CCZN CDFU CDGB
CDGH CDKE CDYB CETY CFCX CFDK CITH
CJIO CLEE EGCA GWFT HTWE IZIT KEPP
MGEC MIKI MWCH MWHP MWIF MWSC
MWTT MWUK MWUL MWUN MWVL MWYE
MYBA MYDK MYDX MYGP MYGR MYHI
MYHK MYHP MYIR MYIS MYJD MYLD
MYLF MYLO MYLW MYMH MYMS MYNE
MYOA MYPA MYPJ MYSU MYTE MYVP
MYXB MYXG MYYV MYZR MYZV MZBD
MZBH MZBU MZDA MZDG MZDM MZEN
MZEU MZFL MZFY MZJI MZJM MZKE
MZLG MZLL MZMU MZNV MZOZ MZUB
NEWA OYTE RDNS RINS RTHS RTMS SAUK
SHUC SOOZ SSIX TBLC TSOB WZOY XALZ
YTLY

S-7 COURIER
G-BVNY BWMN CBNF CEEJ CHTO CINI
KATI LUEY OJKM

S-9 CHAOS
G-BSEE

S-10 SAKOTA
G-BRPT BRZW BSBV BSGS BSMT BSWB
BTJX BTWZ BUKB BVFA BVHI BWIL

S-19
G-SXIX

RAVEN – see MEDWAY MICROLIGHTS LTD

RAYTHEON AIRCRAFT COMPANY – also
see BEECH AIRCRAFT CORPORATION and
HAWKER BEECHCRAFT

RB390 PREMIER
G-FRYL OEWD

REALITY AIRCRAFT LTD

EASY RAIDER
G-CBKF CBXE CBXF CCEZ CCHR CCMJ
OESY OEZI SLIP SRII

ESCAPADE
G-CCYB CDCW CDEV CDIZ CDKF CDKL
CDSK CDTJ CECF CEDB CEIL CFAS CGNH
CGNV CGTZ DADD DIZI DRPK ECKB ENID
ESCA ESCC ESCP ESGA ESKA IMMI IMNY
JCWS LEEK LSJE MCUB OKID ORUN PADE
POZA RDAD SCPD VNON ZHKF

REARWIN AIRCRAFT and ENGINES INC

175 SKYRANGER
G-BTGI RWIN

8125 CLOUDSTER
G-EVLE

8500 SPORTSTER
G-AEOF

REID and SIGRIST

RS.4 DESFORD
G-AGOS

REIMS AVIATION SA – see CESSNA AIRCRAFT COMPANY

REMOS

GX
G-CGIR MIRN OBOF SBDB

REPLICA PLANS – also see ROYAL AIRCRAFT FACTORY

SE.5a
G-BDWJ BIHF BKER BMDB BUOD BUWE
CCBN CCXG INNY SEVA

REPUBLIC AVIATION CORPORATION

P-47 THUNDERBOLT
G-THUN

RC-3 SEABEE
G-CJSB

RICH

FLUGASTOL
G-CIYT

RIDOUT

ARENA
G-BIRP BJNA

EUROPEAN
G-BJDK BJFC BJMZ

JARRE
G-BJMX

STEVENDON SKYREACHER
G-BIWA

WARREN
G-BIWF

ZELENSKI
G-BIWG

RIGG

SKYLINER II
G-BIAR

RIHN

DR.107 ONE DESIGN
G-CVII IDII IIID LOAD NRMA PBII RIHN
RWOD TAZZ

ROBIN (AVIONS PIERRE ROBIN)
including **ALPHA AVIATION MANUFACTURING LTD (R2160)** and **CONSTRUCTIONS AÉRONAUTIQUES DE BOURGOGNE** – also see **JODEL**

ATL variants
G-GFNO GGHZ

DR.400 variants
G-BAEB BAEM BAEN BAFX BAGC BAGR
BAGS BAHL BAJZ BAKM BALF BALG BALH
BALJ BAMU BAMV BANB BAPX BAZC
BBAX BBAY BBCH BBCS BBDP BBJU
BBMB BCXE BDUY BEUP BFJZ BGWC
BHAJ BHJU BHLE BHLH BHOA BIHD BJUD
BKDH BKDJ BKVL BNFV BOGI BPHG BRBK
BRBL BRBM BRNT BRNU BSDH BSFF
BSLA BSSP BSVS BSYU BTRU BUGJ BUYS
BXRT BYHT BZMM CBEZ CBMT CBZK
CCKP CCWM CCZX CDAI CDBM CDOY
CEKE CEKO CETB CGGO CGPJ CGXL
CHOE CLAJ CLDL CONB DORO DUDZ
EGGS EHMM ELEN ELSB ELUN ENBW ETIV
EUSO EYCO FCSP FTIL FUEL GAOH GAOM
GBUE GBVX GCIY GCRT GCUF GDEF
GDKR GGJK GORA GORD GOSL HAIR
HANS HMSJ HXTD IOOI JBDH JBUZ JEDH
JUDE KIMY KTEA LARA LEOS LGCA LGCB
LGCC MATB MIFF NBDD NFNF OCGC
ONGC ORRG OTIB OYIO PAYD PVCV RONS
SELL TUGY TUGZ UAPA WYSZ XLXL YOGI
ZACH ZIGI ZIPI

DR.500-200i PRÉSIDENT
G-BZIJ CDMD CHIX GMIB KENW MAGZ
MOTI RNDD ROBJ TYER

HR.100-200B ROYAL
G-AZHB AZHK BXWB CBFN

HR.100-210 SAFARI II
G-BAPY BAYR BBAW BBCN BBIO CJJN
HRIO MPWI RUES

HR.100-285 TIARA
G-BEUD

HR.200 variants
G-BCCY BETD BFBE BGXR BLTM BNIK
BVMM BWFG BXVK BYNK BYSG BZLG
BZXK ECAF ECAG ECAP ECAR EOMI GMKE
MFLA MFLE SAUL WAVA WAVV

R.1180T(D) AIGLON
G-BGHM BIRT GBAO GDER GEEP PACE
ROBN VITE

R.2100 SUPER CLUB
G-BKXA

R.2112 ALPHA
G-BIVA BZFB CBNG OCAC PLAY RAFC
TOUR

R.2120
G-CBLE CBVB ECAC

R.2160 (ALPHA SPORT)
G-BLWY BVYO BWZG BYBF GAXC ILUA
MATT PGSI PSFG VZIM

R.3000 variants
G-BOLU BZOL

ROBINSON AIRCRAFT CO

REDWING
G-ABNX

ROBINSON HELICOPTER CO INC

R22 variants
G-BLDK BMIZ BOCN BODZ BOYC BOYX
BPNI BPTZ BROX BRVI BSCE BSGF BTBA
BTNA BXOA BXSG BXSY BXUC BYHE BYIE
CBBK CBWZ CBXK CBXN CCAP CCGF
CCMR CCVU CDBG CFHU CHAN CHPA
CKDL CMSN DHGS DLDL DODB DOGI
EERY EFOF EFON EMAC EPAR ETIN FOLI
GJCD GOUP HANC HARR HBMW HIEL HIZZ
HMEC HONI IBED IIPT ISMO JHEW JKAT
JKHT JNSH JSAK KKRN KNIB LAIN LHCB

LOLZ LYNC MACA MDKD MICH MRSN NDIA
NJSH OASH OAVA OBIL OBIO OCOV OEAT
OFAS OIIO OJAN OJCL OLAU OMMG OODX
ORMB OSAZ OSHL OVNR PERE PSJS
RHML ROVY ROYP RWIA SLNW SUCT
SUMX TGRC TGRD TGRE TGRS TILE TINK
TOLY TOSH TUNE ULZE VCJH VEYE VOCE
VVBR WADS WAGG WINR WIRL WIZR ZAPY
ZBED

R44 variants
G-BYKK BZGO BZLP BZTA BZXY CBAK
CBFJ CBZE CCFC CCYC CCYG CDCV
CDUE CDWK CEAU CEMC CEUU CFCM
CFNF CGGF CGGG CGGS CGNE CGWD
CHAP CIMZ CJLL CLBM CLCU CLDU COPR
CROW CTFL DCSI DENY DGFD DHAM
DKNY DOVS DROL DSPZ DWCE EEZR EJTC
ENSX EOJB ETKT ETNT EVEE EWAD FAJM
FARE FCUM FIBT FLYX FOFO FOOT FRYA
GACB GATT GERI GERS GIBB GOES GRZZ
GSPY HAGL HALS HECK HFLY HGRB
HOCA HOLD HVER HWKS HWOW HYND
IAJJ IBMS IDMG IILY ILLD IMMY INDX IPJF
ITOR ITPH IVEN JAJA JAKF JANI JARM
JAYK JBKA JCWM JEFA JGAR JKAY JORD
JPJR JTSA JWRN KELI KNYT KRIB KUBE
LINJ LINY LINZ LLIZ LMBO LTWA LVIE
MANZ MAXD MCAZ MENU MGWI MISK
MRKS MRLZ MUSH MXPI NANI NELS NESH
NICI NIOG NISA NKEL NOXY NSEW OAUD
OBHE OBSM OCAF OCHM OCON ODAZ
ODHB ODOC OESP OGEZ OGJC OHAM
OHJV OHLI OODD OONA ORBK OSEM
OSPP OTJS OTNA OTRT PAMY PBEE PGGY
PIMP PIXL PIXX POET PUNT RAVN RBRI
REEV REGJ REYE RMYD ROAD ROAT ROCT
ROKS ROMT ROYM RROB RULE RWEW
RYZZ SAIG SEAL SHAF SHRT SIRD SKFY
SMLE SPJE SPTR STOP STUY SUNN SWAT
SWIG SWNS TGTT TIMC TOLS TPTP TRAC
TRCY TSBY TUNL TWTR WALI WAPA WEAT
WLDN WSMW WTAV XZXZ YARD

R66 variants
G-CIKX CIZG DIGA FLOE GMGH GOMS
HKCC HKHK HKPC ICEL JSAW LARD LIKK
LROK LSKS NJNH OHAS PODD RMAR
SAPA SDWV SXSX SYES TRON

ROCKWELL INTERNATIONAL CORPORATION including **COMMANDER AIRCRAFT COMPANY (COMMANDER 114B)** production

COMMANDER 112 variants
G-BDAK BDIE BDKW BDLT BEBU BEDG
BENJ BEPY BFPO BFZM BHRO BMWR
BPTG CNCN CRIL DASH EHXP ERIC FLPI
HROI IMPX LITE OVIN PLAZ

COMMANDER 114 and 114A variants
G-BERI BFXS BHSE BKAY BMJL BOLT
BUSW BYKB DIME HILO JURG LADS NATT
OLFT OMUM RCED TECH TWIZ ZIPA

COMMANDER 114B
G-ELCH EMCA FATB FMLY HPSF HPSL
JFER KEEF OECM OOJP RJRC

ROGER HARDY

RH7B TIGER LIGHT
G-EDVK

ROGERSON

HORIZON 1
G-DOGZ

ROKO AERO

NG4
G-CGMV ROKO

ROLLADEN-SCHNEIDER FLUGZEUGBAU GmbH including DG FLUGZEUGBAU GmbH

LS1 variants
G-CFOZ CJST CKVD CLRZ LSIF

LS3 variants
G-CEVD CEVV CGAD CGDA CGDN CHYH
CJDJ CJYX CKHB CKMV CLTP DECP DEEF
DEES DEEX DEFS DEFZ DEGE ILBO LSGM
TANO

LS4 variants
G-CFAO CFHL CFJM CFKG CFLF CFNU
CFYH CHKX CHLB CHMX CHNV CHPL
CHVV CHXT CHXZ CHZM CHZY CIBG CIEA
CIFU CJBX CJEP CJJB CJKP CJLH CJLJ
CKCB CKDK CKFL CKKX CKLG CKLN CKLS
CKNS CLFB CLGT CLRY CLSG CLVW DEHK
DEKV DEMF DEMG DEMT DEOA DESC
DETG DETV DETY DEUH DGDJ DHNX DKEN
DZDZ EELT EESY FERV LSFR LSIV LSLS

LS6 variants
G-CFCP CGAR CGBG CGBO CGBR CGCM
CHAO CHBC CHEW CHGP CHHH CHHT
CHHU CHJF CHJX CHMK CHOZ CHPD
CJDG CJNP CKBC CKBH CLLY CLPB CVBA
DFBE DFRA DHET GBPP LSCP LSED LSGB
LSIX LSVI STEU

LS7 variants
G-CEVN CFMY CFPD CFTV CFTY CFUV
CFVH CFWF CFWU CFYB CFYK CFYW
CGBL CGBY CHAY CHBA CHDX CHEH
CJLK CJZZ CKHS CKMO CKSY CLPL DFOG
DFXE EUFO LSFB TWAZ

LS8 variants
G-CHMD CHTM CHTS CHWL CHWS CHXW
CHYF CHZG CJBO CJDE CJEA CJFX CJGS
CJHY CJJK CJKN CJLN CJMO CJMU CJNB
CJNJ CJNK CJOD CJPL CJPR CJRA CJSU
CJTM CJTY CKET CKEZ CKFV CKJE CKMA
CKME CKPM CKSD CLWR CTAG DSVN
FLUZ GCJA GZIP LLLL LSKV LYPH RIEV
WDGC WLLS XWON

LS10 variants
G-CILS KISP

ROLLASON AIRCRAFT and ENGINES LTD – see also DRUINE for D.31 and D.62 production

BETA
G-AWHX BADC BETE BUPC

ROTARY AIR FORCE INC

RAF 2000 variants (Subaru EJ22)
G-BUYL BVSM BWAD BWHS BWTK BXAC
BXDE BXGS BXKM BYIN BYJA CBHC CBHZ
CBIT CBJE CBJN CCEU CCUH CDJN CFEI
CGJW HOWL IMEL IRAF IYRO JEJE RAFZ
SAYS YRAF YROO

ROTEC ENGINEERING INC

RALLY 2B
G-MBMG

ROTORWAY

(SCORPION) EXECUTIVE
G-BNZL BNZO BSRP BURP BUSN BVOY
BVTV BWLY BWUJ BZBW BZES BZOM
CBJV CBWO CBYB CCFY CCMU CDBK
CDRS CJIR FLIT JONG KARN KEVL NEEL
NJBA OHOV PILE PURS RATH RAWS RHYS
RISH RWAY SFOX WHOO YEWS ZHWH

A600 TALON
G-TALN

ROUSSEAU – see PIEL AVIATION

ROYAL AIRCRAFT FACTORY – also see REPLICA PLANS and SLINGSBY

BE.2C
G-AWYI

BE.2E
G-CJZO CJZP

SE.5 & SE.5A
G-EBIA ECAE

RUSCHMEYER LUFTFAHRTTECHNIK GmbH

RUSHMEYER R90
G-UAPO

RUTAN

COZY
G-BXDO BXVX BYLZ COZI OGJS SCUL
SPFX

LONG-EZ
G-BKXO BLLZ BLMN BLTS BMHA BMIM
BMUG BOOX BRFB BSIH BUPA BZMF CBLZ
HAIG ICON LEZE LGEZ LUKE MUSO OMJT
PUSH RAEM RAFT RPEZ SENA TWAL

VARIEZE
G-BEZE BEZY BIMX BKST BKXJ BVKM
EMMY EZDG KENZ LASS OOSE SKCI VEZE

RYAN AERONAUTICAL CORPORATION

ST3KR, PT-22
G-AGYY BTBH BYPY RLWG

S

SAAB-SCANIA AB including SVENSKA AEROPLAN AB (SAAB)

91 SAFIR
G-ANOK BCFW XCID

SF.340 variants
G-GNTB GNTF LGNA LGNB LGNC LGND
LGNE LGNF LGNG LGNH LGNI LGNJ LGNK
LGNM LGNN LGNU

2000
G-CDEB CDKA CDKB CERY CERZ CFLU
CIEC LGNO LGNP LGNR LGNS LGNT

SACKVILLE

65
G-CIWX

90
G-CIWY

AH-31
G-CISD

AH-56
G-CISB

AH-77
G-CISC

BM-34
G-CIWZ CJSY

BM-56
G-CIWW KENL

BM-65
G-CJBN JRLR OHLV

BM-90
G-CJIL

SADLER

VAMPIRE
G-CIMY

SAFFERY MODEL BALLOONS including CUPRO SAPHIRE LTD

S.200
G-BIHU

S.200 RIGG SKYLINER
G-BHLJ

S.330
G-BERN BFBM

SMITH PRINCESS
G-FYGM

SAN – see JODEL and SNCAM

SAUNDERS-ROE LTD

SKEETER
G-BLIX

SCALLAN

EAGLE
G-FYEO

FIREFLY
G-FYEZ

SCHEIBE-FLUGZEUGBAU GmbH – also see SLINGSBY SAILPLANES LTD

BERGFALKE
G-CKGY CLHF DHOC

L-SPATZ
G-DDUH

SF24 MOTORSPATZ
G-BZPF

SF25 FALKE variants including SLINGSBY T.61 derivatives
G-AXEO AXJR AYBG AYUM AYUN AYUP
AYUR AYZU AYZW AZHD AZIL AZMC AZMD
AZPC AZYY BADH BAIZ BAMB BDZA BEGG
BFPA BFUD BHSD BKVG BLCU BLTR BLZA
BMBZ BODU BPIR BRWT BSEL BSUO
BTWC BTWD BTWE BUDA BUDC BUDT
BUED BUEK BUFG BUFR BUGL BUGT
BUGV BUGW BUGZ BUHA BUHR BUIH
BUJA BUJB BUJI BUJX BUNB BVKK BVKU
BVLX BXAN BXMV CCHX CDFD CDSC
CFMW CGNW CGZW CHFL CHXK CIGF
CIMP CKIU DCXI FHAS FLKE FLKS GBGA
HBOS KAOM KDEY KGAO KGAW KHEA
KIAB KIAU KINT KLUB KMBB KRAN KWAK
MFMM MILD OHGC OSUT OWGC SACN
SASF SAWG SEXE

SF26A STANDARD
G-DDRL

SF27A ZUGVOGEL V
G-CFLZ CFOF CFOM CFWH CGAV CHSG
CHSX CHUS DDZV DEKS DFHY DFUF
DGDW

SF28A TANDEM FALKE
G-BARZ BYEJ CCIS

ZUGVOGEL II
G-CFRS CFVL CFYE CHKV CHSH CHXA
EEBS

SCHEMPP-HIRTH FLUGZEUGBAU GmbH including SCHEMPP-HIRTH KG and SCHEMPP-HIRTH GMBH, BURKHART GROB FLUGZEUGBAU, JASTREB FABRIKA AVIONAI JEDRILICA, LANAVERRE INDUSTRIE, VAZDUHOPLOVNO TEHNICKI CENTAR [VTC]

ARCUS variants
G-CHTL CIAI CLTS CLVL ILEW JKRV KBWP
KFVG LXVI RCUS RKUS SMAR

CIRRUS and CIRRUS VTC
G-CGCO CHHZ CHTU CHUR CJOW CJTS
CKEA CKES CKJG CLKF DCEC DCFK DCGY
DCJR DCLO DCUS DCVE DCWR DCWS
DDDM DDVY DHEV ECEA

DISCUS 2
G-CHRH CIHF CJNF CKFB CKLD CKLV
CKOK CKPG CLLB CLUZ CLVD DFES DTOF
EJIM FESX HOJO IFES JBOB SAJA SAOC
TOOB

DISCUS A, B and CS variants
G-CEUN CEWZ CFCA CFDM CFEJ CFER
CFES CFFT CFFX CFHR CFKM CFLE CFMO
CFNL CFNR CFOY CFTW CFUL CFUP
CFXM CFYM CFYN CFYX CGCT CGDR
CGDX CHEE CHEN CHGK CHGS CHGZ
CHHO CHHP CHJL CHKA CHKY CHLN
CHLS CHLY CHML CHMO CHOR CHPH
CHPX CHRS CHRX CHSD CHSO CHUZ
CHVR CHXH CHYU CHZE CJAO CJAR
CJBR CJBW CJCK CJCX CJFC CJGL CJGM
CJGR CJHM CJJD CJJE CJJZ CJLC CJLP
CJLW CJOA CJOC CJPP CJRR CJSE CJUB
CJUV CJVB CJVF CJVG CJVX CJWK CJXL
CJXR CJYF CJZG CKAP CKJZ CKOD CLHG
CLPE CLRJ CLTF CLWL CUMU DFBY DFMG
DHCL DHEM DHGL DHKL DHMP DHPR
DHSJ DJAH DJAN DJMD KEDK KOBH RGTS
SANT TLTL

DUO DISCUS
G-CGJB CHNF CHNW CHRW CHWB CIJF
CIKB CJFH CJJP CJOO CJPA CJTU CJXW
CJYR CKAR CKCV CKEV CKFT CKGF CKHK
CKKE CKKY CKML CKOL CKPE CKPO
CKPY CKRO CKSM CLFX CLGC CLGZ CLLX
DDJF DJAC DUOT DXLT HKAA IGLI JIFI
KCWJ KEMJ ODDZ ODUO OTWS PHNX
RAPL SAXL SAXT SISI UDIX XDUO

JANUS
G-BMBJ CHTB CHUH CJVV CLKG CLRP
CLTC DDTC DEOV DEOW DJAA JNSC JNUS
TVGC

MINI NIMBUS
G-CFHG CGFU CHOY CJGU CJTJ CJYS
CJZL CKFH CKPV DDPH DDSP DDXT DEAV
DEGW EEBF EEBK EEER HAUT SRAH

NIMBUS 2
G-CEWE CFCS CFPP CFRC CFVE CFVT
CHBF CHBV CHNH CJGH CJMN CJMV
DDAJ DDGY DDHW DDKL DDMM DDNG
DDTU DDVA DDYU DEAJ DEAM DEEK DEFB
DEFF DEGS DEHP DEHT DEKW ECOL
EDDD EEFT NIMB

NIMBUS 3
G-CFAM CFGF CJED CKJC CKLT CLSO
DEON DEVF DFBM OJNE

NIMBUS 3D
G-CFWK CFZO CHYY CJSC CJWG CJXA
EHCB KEPE NYMB OZOZ

NIMBUS 4
G-CHFX CJCT KOYY

NIMBUS 4D
G-CDTH CHNU HJSM

SHK-1
G-CFJF CFJZ CLSY DCAO DCCB DCGT
DCJK DCJN DDMK DDTG OSHK PSHK
RAEF

STANDARD CIRRUS
G-CDDB CFBB CFCN CFGU CFLW CFMT
CFMU CFRJ CFRZ CFYJ CFZK CGAH
CGCD CGEP CHAX CHFF CHGG CHJN
CHJY CHKC CHKD CHKR CHKS CHKU
CHMY CHNM CHVZ CHWD CHWF CHZJ
CHZU CHZV CJBJ CJCJ CJCN CJCU CJDS
CJER CJFA CJGN CJGY CJJJ CJLX CJOE
CJOS CJRG CJRT CJUU CJVU CKBT CKEB
CKFA CKFK CKJF CKMD CKNB CKNE
CTWO DCKZ DCNC DCOR DCOY DCPU
DCRH DCRN DCTB DCTT DCYM DCYO
DCYP DCYT DDAS DDDA DDDR DDFC
DDGE DDGX DDHX DDLG DDVS DDXL
DDZF DEEN DEGK EJHH RAHA RIFO SCNN

VENTUS 2
G-CGSZ CHWA CICT CIXH CJEX CJLA
CJOR CJUF CJVA CJYU CJZM CKAS CKBG
CKCD CKCE CKCH CKDA CKDO CKFP
CKGA CKGC CKGD CKGL CKKF CKNO
CKNR CKPK CKTB CLGL CLME CLWZ
CVZT DHYL DKFU EVII HAAH HLMB IICT

IICX KGMM KJJR KXMS ORCW OTCZ RBCT
TWOC VCXT VENC VSGG VSIX VTCT VTEW
VTUS WONE XAVV XJON YODA

VENTUS 3
G-CKVT CKYO SIIO

VENTUS A, B and C variants
G-CFBT CFDE CFEG CFMN CFPE CFPL
CFUH CFUR CFVW CFYC CFZH CGAP
CGAS CHFA CHFV CHHN CHUY CHWH
CHXR CJGF CJKY CJSL CJWU CKDV CKJB
CKJM DEHH DEKJ DELG DELR DENJ DEPX
DEUJ DEUS DFAW DFCK DFHS DFJO FORA
IFWD IRLE KCHG KHCC NJET OSDF SWSW
UNIN VNTS WIII XXVB YUGE

**SCHLEICHER (ALEXANDER
SCHLEICHER SEGELFLUGZEUGBAU
GmbH and Co) – including SA
CENTRAIR, PAUL SIEBERT SPORT und
SEGELFLUGZEUGBAU and JUBI GMBH
SPORTFLUGZEUGBAU production)**

Ka 6, BR, CR RHÖNSEGLER
G-CEVK CEWO CFDG CFHZ CFKY CFLS
CFNP CFTB CFUB CFWA CFZR CGCP
CGDE CGDF CGEA CGEM CHAB CHBO
CHFB CHJP CHPO CHSN CHZH CJEW
CKMJ CKTC CLRE DBND DBNH DBOL
DBTJ DBUZ DBVR DBVX DBVZ DBWC DBXT
DBYL DBYM DBYU DBZX DCBM DCBY
DCJY DDCW DDEV DDGK DDHG DDJR
DDKG DDLP DDNW DDNX DDOC DDOF
DDRA DDRD DDRE DDRY DDSG DDSY
DDUR DDVG DDYC DDYJ DDZW DECC
DEDG DFGJ DFKA DFKX DFTF DGAW DGEF
DHEB EELY

Ka 6E
G-AWTP CFCR CFND CFRE CFSS CFVZ
CFXC CFXS CFXU CHJD CJAL CJHL CJLV
CJSG CLKU DBYX DCAE DCAG DCAS
DCCA DCCD DCCG DCCL DCCR DCCU
DCCV DCDA DCDF DCDZ DCEM DCEO
DCEW DCFL DCGB DCGD DCGE DCHB
DCHZ DCKL DCLZ DCPJ DDGG DDHT
DDLE DDMO DDOK DDUS DDVH DDWC
DDXH DEAH DEHM DEKC DEKX DHAP
ECDB FGAZ GGDV HCAC KSIX

K 7 RHÖNADLER
G-CFJW CFOU DBVB DCLT DCWJ DDML
DDOX DDRM DDWN DEAU DEDK

K 8
G-CFHN CFKT CFLH CFOR CFTN CFWL
CFXB CFXW CGDB CGDK CGEG CHDN
CHDY CHFW CHJE CHKK CHLH CHMH
CHRJ CHWT CHZX CJAT CJFT CJGB CJGD
CJGX CJHK CJLS CJNN CJOB CJOJ CJOZ
CJSN CJYV CJYW CKMI CLTD CLUG DCFF
DCGH DCHU DCJF DCJM DCMN DCYZ
DDDL DDGA DDHA DDJB DDKC DDLS
DDMB DDMG DDNZ DDRV DDRZ DDSF
DDTN DDUF DDUK DEED DEJF DEOZ DEPT
DESJ DFBJ EETH EHCZ

Ka 10
G-DEVH

ASH 25 variants
G-CFST CFWW CFYZ CHXO CIDT CLJE
CLUP CWLC DRCS GBBB RAIR SINK YOBI

ASH 26E
G-CCLR KEAM LIVS OPHT ZGTK ZZAJ

ASH 30
G-ULCC

ASH 31
G-CLJZ CLKK CLNE KMIR PBWS PDRO
VCRZ XASH

ASK 13
G-CFGR CFHM CFMH CFSD CFVC CFVU
CFWB CFYY CFZN CHMV CHPE CHSM
CHTJ CHUD CHUF CHUU CHVO CHVW
CHXJ CHXP CHXV CJGW CJKT CJLF CJLO
CJMJ CJMP CJMW CJMX CJMZ CJPC

CJPV CJPY CJRX CJSV CJWB CJWJ CJXM
CJYE CJZE CKFJ CKFR CKHH CKJL CKKR
CKLA CKRB CLOC DCBW DCCE DCCM
DCCP DCCT DCCW DCCX DCCY DCCZ
DCFA DCFG DCGO DCHW DCKR DCMK
DCWH DDDB DDKE DDLC DDMX DDNV
DDOA DDRJ DDUE DDVB DDVC DDVX
DEDU DEOE DEOF DEPP DEUC DEVJ DEVP
DFAT DFCW DHAL DJLL EEBL EEBZ FCAV
FCCC HRAF

ASK 14
G-BSIY CKFS

ASK 16
G-BCHT BCTI

ASK 18
G-CHRN CJHO CJKG CJKU CJMA CJMK
CJPO CJPZ CJSZ CKNM DDJK DDLB DDPA

ASK 21
G-CEWC CFBV CFYF CFYV CGAF CGAG
CGAM CGBB CGBF CGBN CGBV CHLP
CHPV CHPW CHTV CHVG CHYJ CHYS
CHYT CHZR CJAV CJAX CJBM CJGE CJGJ
CJKA CJKJ CJKK CJKO CJKZ CJMS CJOX
CJVZ CJWD CKCT CKCZ CKDF CKEJ
CKEK CKFY CKGK CKGX CKJP CKKP
CKLW CKMW CKNL CKOT CKPP CKRI
CKRW CLOL CLOV CLPV CLRT CLSH CLVM
CLVU CLWA DECW DECZ DEGZ DEHO
DEKG DEPD DERH DERJ DESB DESU DETA
DHCX DHRR DJAD DJMC EENK KXXI OWAI
PNGC UCLU

ASK 23
G-CGCF CLUK CLUV DEVV DEVW DEVX

ASW 15
G-CFBC CFDA CFJV CFMS CFOB CFPB
CFRK CFTD CFXY CGCR CGCX CGDS
CGDY CGEH CHEJ CHGF CHNT CHTC
CHZD CJDM CJDR CJJX CJPX CJRE CJVW
CKRR CKSL DBEN DCHT DCKP DCZN
DFBD DFCY DJGG DJWS GTWO

ASW 17 variants
G-DCPD XVII

ASW 19
G-CEWI CFGP CFNH CFWP CGCA CHDV
CHHK CHLM CHLV CHNC CHUA CHXE
CHXU CJBK CJBT CJFU CJHS CJJL CJKS
CJRB CJRV CJUN CJUZ CKER CLTL CUGC
DDSX DDTE DDVL DDVP DDWZ DDXX DDZY
DEEH DEJR DELA DERR DERS DFFP DHCE
DHCV DHER EENZ FEBJ RZEE

ASW 20
G-BUCG CEVZ CFBA CFCV CFHD CFKL
CFPH CFPN CFPT CFRH CFRW CFTL CFTP
CFUN CFWS CFZL CHDJ CHDL CHEO
CHGW CHHS CHJT CHOD CHSK CHUJ
CHUT CHVP CHVX CHYK CHZZ CJEE CJFJ
CJHZ CJTP CJZH CKCY CKJN CKPZ CLFH
CLSW CDST DDTP DDUT DDVW DDXB
DDXK DDYE DEAE DEBX DEEC DEEJ DEFA
DEFE DEFV DEGP DEHZ DEKU DELU DELZ
DENV DEOJ DEPF DEPS DERA DETZ DEUD
DEUK DEUY DFAF DFBO DGKB DHOK
EEBN EEDE EEFK EENW EFLY EHTT EKEY
MAGK MEEE ODCH SEZA WLKS

ASW 22
G-KKAM LDER WYDE

ASW 24
G-CGDT CGDZ CHBB CHBG CHYD CJCD
CJEB CJEL CJRU CJTB CJTH CJXT JFLY
KALP OTRY

ASW 27
G-CHUE CHXD CHYR CHZO CJCM CJDC
CJJT CJLY CJOV CJPT CJSS CJUJ CJVM
CKBX CKCN CKDN CKDS CKDW CKED
CKFD CKHD CKKH OASW XVAT YEHA

ASW 27-18E (ASG-29)
G-CHGY CHJS CKOE CKOM CKON CKOO
CKOY CKOZ CKPU CKRD CKRJ CKRV

CKSX CLES CLGU CLLL CLNG CLOG CLPU
CLRA CLRC CLRF CLRS CLTO CLWJ COPP
CRJW DASG DLOE HEBB HICU IIOO IXXI
KSSX KUGG LLNT LOUD LUON NYNE
OBPP PZAS RIZK SASG UBOO XELL XLII
XXIX ZSIX

ASW 28
G-CHKH CIHM CJVS CJWA CJZN CKBM
CKBU CKBV CKCJ CKGV CKJS CKJV CKLP
CKMM CKMZ CKNG CKNV CKRC CLFZ
CLMO GLID KHPI TRBO

SCHROEDER FIRE BALLOONS GmbH
MODEL G
G-CFHX

SCHWEIZER AIRCRAFT CORPORATION
– see HUGHES

SCINTEX – see PIEL AVIATION

SCOTTISH AVIATION
BULLDOG variants
G-ASAL AZHX BCUO BCUS BCUV BDOG
BHXA BHXB BHZR BHZT BPCL BULL BZDP
BZEP BZFN BZME BZMH BZML BZON
BZPS BZXS BZXZ CBAN CBBC CBBL CBBS
CBBT CBBW CBCB CBCR CBDK CBEF
CBEH CBEK CBFP CBFU CBGX CBID CDVV
DAWG DDOG DISA DOGG EDAV GGRR
GRRR KDOG KKKK SIJW TDOG UDOG ULHI
UWAS WINI

SEEMS – see MORANE-SAULNIER

SHIELD
XYLA
G-AWPN

SHORT BROTHERS LTD
SC.7 SKYVAN
G-BEOL PIGY

SIAI-MARCHETTI SpA
F.260
G-ILPD

S.205
G-AVEH AYXS BFAP VELA

S.208
G-DICA

SF.260
G-BAGB IGIE ITAF MACH NRRA RAZI

SIKORSKY AIRCRAFT – see also WESTLAND
S-61 variants
G-ATBJ ATFM BFRI

S-76 variants
G-BOYF BWDO CFJC CGOU KAZB MRRI
PACO ROON XXEB

S-92
G-CGCI CGYW CHCK CHCS CHHF CHKI
CHYG CICH CIGZ CKXL CLCN IACA IACB
IACC IACD IACE IACF LAWX MCGB MCGC
MCGD MCGE MCGF MCGG MCGH MCGI
MCGJ MCGK MCGL MCGY MCGZ MCSA
MCSB MCSI MCSJ MCSK MCSL MRLI VIND
VINF VING VINI VINK VINL VINP VINT WNSD
WNSE WNSF WNSG WNSI WNSL WNSM
WNST WNSU WNSV WNSW

SILENCE AIRCRAFT
TWISTER
G-FUUN JINX MRJP ODWS RIOT TWIS
TWSR TWSS TWST XSEL

SINDLINGER
HAWKER HURRICANE REPLICA
G-HCAT

SIPA (SOCIÉTÉ INDUSTRIELLE POUR L'AÉRONAUTIQUE)
903 & S91
G-AMSG ASXC ATXO AWLG BBDV BDAO
BDKM BGME BHMA SIPA

SIREN
PIK-30
G-BMMJ ODDF

SKANDINAVISK AERO INDUSTRI
KRAMME KZ.VIII
G-AYKZ

SKY BALLOONS LTD including CAMERON BALLOONS production
25 series
G-BXWX CFPS

31 series
G-BWOY BXVP

65 series
G-BWUS CGNS

77 series
G-BWSL BXHL BXVG BXXP BZLS CLRK
KSKY LOWS OBET

80 series
G-BYBS BYOI SETI

90 series
G-BXGD BXJT BXLP BXPP BXVR BXWL
BYZV BZKV CLOE CZAG GPEG LEAS ZABC

105 series
G-BWDZ BWPP BXDV BXIW

120 series
G-BWIX BWYU BXWG CFAY OBFE

200 series
G-BXIH

220 series
G-SPEL

240 series
G-MRLN

SKYCRAFT (UK) LTD
SCOUT series
G-MNKN

SKYFOX
CA-25N GAZELLE
G-IDAY

SKYHOOK SAILWINGS LTD
TR1 Trike
G-MJFX MMVS

SKYRIDER AVIATION
AIRSPORTS PHANTOM
G-MJSE MJSF MJTX MJTZ MMKX

SKYSTAR – see DENNEY AEROCRAFT COMPANY

SLEPCEV
STORCH
G-BZOB

SLINGSBY ENGINEERING LTD – see SLINGSBY SAILPLANES LTD

SLINGSBY SAILPLANES LTD including MARTIN HEARN LTD, VICKERS SLINGSBY, YORKSHIRE SAILPLANES and SLINGSBY ENGINEERING LTD – also see FOURNIER, ROYAL AIRCRAFT FACTORY, SCHEIBE, SOPWITH and TIPSY AIRCRAFT CO LTD
REPLICA SE.5A
G-AVOU

T.30 KIRKBY PREFECT
G-ALLF

T.31 MOTOR CADET derivatives
G-AYAN BCYH BDSM BMDD BNPF BOOD
BRVJ BVFS BZLK

T.51 DART
G-DBRT DBRU DBRY DBSA DBSL DBVH
DBWJ DBWM DBWO DBWP DBWS DBXG
DBYC DBYG DBZF DBZJ DCAZ DCBA
DDBB DRAT DRRT IKAH

T.53
G-DCUD DCXV DDHE

T.59 KESTREL
G-BDZG DCNS DCNW DCNX DCOJ DCSB
DCSD DCSF DCSK DCTJ DCTL DCTM
DCTO DCTP DCTR DCVW DCVY DCWB
DCWD DCWF DCXM DCZR DCZU DDBK
DDBN DDBS DDEB FCOM KESY

T.65 (SPORT) VEGA variants
G-BFYW BGBV BGCB BGCU BILH CFNK
DDWT DDWW DDXD DDXE DDXF DDXG
DDZA DDZB DDZM DDZN DDZP DEAG
DECJ DECL DECM DEDX DEDY DEDZ DEEA
DEEG DEFW DEGF DEGH DEGJ DEGT
DEGX DEHG DEHY DEJB DEJC DEJD DEJE
DELD DELO DEMN DEMP DEMR DEMZ
EEAD EEBA EECK VEGA

T.67A and T.67M FIREFLY
G-BJIG BJNG BJXA BJXB BJZN BKAM
BKTZ BLLP BLLR BLLS BLRF BLTW BLUX
BLVI BNSR BOCL BOCM BONT BONU
BUUA BUUC BUUE BUUF BUUI BUUJ
BUUK BUUL BWGO BWXA BWXB BWXF
BWXJ BWXP BWXS BWXT BWXV BXKW
BYOB BYOD BYRY BYYG CBHE CDHC
CIKS ECRM EFSM FLYG HONG KONG
OCRM ONES OPUB RAFG SFTZ SKYC
SKYO UPRT ZEIN

SMD
GAZELLE with FlexiformSealander sailwing
G-MMHS

SMITH
DSA-1 MINIPLANE
G-BTGJ

SMUDGER
G-CKBP

SMYTH
MODEL S SIDEWINDER
G-BRVH

SNCAN – also see STAMPE ET VERTONGEN
1002 PINGOUIN
G-ASTG ATBG ETME OTME

3202
G-BIZK BIZM BPMU

3400
G-BOSJ

NC854
G-BCGH BIUP BJEL NORD

NC856 NORVEGIE
G-CDWE CGWR

NC858
G-BDJR BDXX BPZD

SNOWBIRD AEROPLANE CO LTD – see NOBLE HARDMAN AVIATION LTD

SOCATA – also see MORANE-SAULNIER
ST.10 DIPLOMATE
G-AZIB

TB-9 TAMPICO
G-BHOZ BIBA BIXA BIXB BIZE BIZR BKIT
BKUE BKVC BRIV BTZP DLEE GCOY GHZJ
GKUE GMSI IAGI JUFS

TB-10 TOBAGO
G-BGXC BGXD BGXT BHDE BHJF BITE
BKBV BKBW BKIS BNDR BNRA BOIT BTIE
CBGC CBHA CBPE CONL CTCL DAND
EDEN FAIR FLEA FSZY GBHB GBHI GOLF
HELA HILT IANC IANH IGGL IRAK IROB
MOOR MRTN OFIT OOCP PATN PCAT PHTG
RIAM SBKR SERL SKYF SONA TBIO TBOK
TBTN TOBA VMJM

TB-20 TRINIDAD
G-BLXA BLYD BMIX BPTI BSCN BYJS BYTB
BZPI CDDA CORB CPMS CTIO CTZO DLOM
DMAH EGAG EGJA FFTI FIFI GVFR HGPI
IREN JHMP OALD OMAO OTUI PEKT PTRE
RAYM SAPM SCBI SCIP SPVI TBSV TBXX
TBZO TIBS TRIN TYNE VPPL WERY XXTB

TB-21 TRINIDAD GT TURBO
G-CGZI VALY

TB-200 TOBAGO GT
G-OBEI

TB-200 TOBAGO XL
G-BXLT BXVA CIFC TZED

TBM-700
G-PTXC RIVA WMRN

SOLAR WINGS LTD and SOLAR WINGS AVIATION LTD including HOLD CONTROL PLC – also see CYCLONE AIRSPORTS LTD and PEGASUS AVIATION
PANTHER XL
G-MMKA

PANTHER XL-S
G-MMGS MMMN MMOK MNHH

PEGASUS FLASH
G-MNJJ MNJR MNKP MNKW MNVG MTJH

PEGASUS PHOTON
G-MNIK MNKB MNKC MNKD MNKE MNKK
MNVZ MTAL

PEGASUS QUASAR
G-MWIM MWIU MWIX MWJH MWJI MWJJ
MWJT MWMI MWML MWNK MWNL MWPU
MWSI MWVM MWXH MWYI MWYJ MWZF
MWZO MWZP MWZR MWZS MYBT MYCE
MYEK MYEM MYEN MYFL MYIM MYIN
MYJJ MYJK MYJT MYJU MYKR MYKS
MYXD MZMA REKO

PEGASUS XL-Q
G-BZWM DEAN MTTE MTTZ MTUN MTUR
MTUS MTUT MTUY MTVX MTXJ MTXK
MTYC MTYI MTYL MTYR MTYS MTZS MVAX
MVAY MVCL MVCR MVCT MVCV MVEF
MVFB MVFD MVFE MVFF MVHP MVHR
MVJN MVJP MVJU MVKN MVKO MVKP
MVKU MVLX MVLY MVMA MVMC MVPR
MVPS MVPX MVPY MVRH MVRI MVRW
MVSE MVTJ MVUF MVUG MVUI MVUJ
MVVO MVYC MVYD MVZL MVZT MVZU
MVZV MWAC MWAT MWCF MWDK MWEG
MWEH MWER MWFS MWGL MWGM MWGR
MWHF MWHG MWHL MWHX MWIS MWJN
MWLL MWMN MWMO MWNB MWSD
MWSJ MWSK MWTC MWTI MWUX MWVA
MWWH MWWV MWXP MWYC MWYU
MWYY MYAC MYAF MYBF MYBW MYEA
MYUH

PEGASUS XL-R variants
G-MGPD MMRL MNAZ MNBA MNBB MNBC
MNBI MNHI MNHJ MNHK MNHL MNHR
MNMK MNVE MNWW MNYU MNZK MTAV
MTAW MTAY MTAZ MTBL MTBU MTER
MTES MTEU MTGL MTHH MTHN MTIE MTIJ
MTIR MTIW MTIZ MTKI MTLG MTLT MTLV
MTLY MTMF MTMG MTOA MTOH MTOJ
MTON MTOY MTPF MTPH MTPL MTPM
MTRM MTRS MTSS MTSZ MTTA MTTU
MTUA MTVC MTYY MVAR MVBJ MVBZ
MVCA MVEG MVGO MVGP MVKH MVKK
MVKL MVPW MVVK MWCC MWFA MWLE
MWLG MWLU MWMV MWOI MWRN MWRT

MWSF MWSO MWTL MWUD MWUR MWUU
MWUV MWVE MWVF MWZU MWZY MWZZ
MYAB MYDJ MYGT MYGU MYGV

SOLENT BALLOON GROUP – see CHOWN

SOMERS-KENDAL
SK.1
G-AOBG

SONEX AIRCRAFT – also see MONNETT
SONEX
G-CEFJ CGDM CGPL CIDP CIDX CKDJ
EEHA HELL SNXA SONX YCMI

SOPWITH AVIATION CO LTD
CAMEL including replicas
G-BPOB BZSC SOPC

DOVE replica
G-EAGA

PUP including replicas
G-ABOX EAVX EBKY

SCOUT
G-ELRT

SNIPE replica
G-CKBB

TRIPLANE replica
G-BOCK BWRA

SORRELL AVIATION
SNS-7 HYPERBIPE
G-HIPE

SNS-8 HYPERLIGHT
G-CJUY

SOUTHDOWN AEROSTRUCTURE LTD
PIPISTRELLE
G-MJTM

SOUTHDOWN INTERNATIONAL LTD/ SOUTHDOWN SAILWINGS LTD including MEDWAY MICROLIGHTS LTD and RAVEN AIRCRAFT INTERNATIONAL production – also see MAINAIR SPORTS LTD
PUMA RAVEN
G-MNMU

PUMA SPRINT
G-MJZK MMJD MMPH MMRN MMUV MMVI
MMWX MMXO MMZW MNCP MNDY MNFG
MNJS MWBJ

RAVEN variants
G-MGOD MNLT MNNA MNNO MNSL MNSY
MNUW MNWG MNXE MNYP MNZW MTBB
MTBN MTBO MTCM MTYV MTYW MYLX
MYMJ MYYZ MZDJ

TRI-PACER
G-MMSS

TRIKE with SIGMA wing
G-MBDM

SOUTHERN AIRCRAFT LTD
MARTLET
G-AAYX

SPACEK
SD-1 MINISPORT
G-CIZA CJBD CJLU CKWG CKZB CLDY
MZSP SSDI

SPARTAN AIRCRAFT LTD
ARROW
G-ABWP

SPORTAVIA-PÜTZER GmbH – see also FOURNIER
RS.180 SPORTSMAN
G-VIZZ

SFS31 MILAN
G-AYRL KORE

SPP – see also YAKOVLEV
MORAVA L-200A
G-ASFD

SUPER AERO 145
G-ATBH

SPRITE AVIATION SERVICES LTD
STINGER
G-CISA

SQUIRES
SOLAR WING
G-MNNG

SRCM – see GARDAN

STAAKEN
Z-1 FLITZER, Z-21(A) FLITZER
G-BVAW CGHJ ECVZ ENIA ERDA ERIW ERTI
FLZR WIDZ ZIRA ZTWO

Z-2 FLITZER
G-ZTOO

STAMPE ET RENAULT – see STAMPE ET VERTONGEN

STAMPE ET VERTONGEN including SNCAN, AIA D'ALGER(1) and SOCIÉTÉ STAMPE ET RENAULT(2) (SV-4) production
SV-4A (DH Gipsy Major 10)
G-AZNK

SV-4A (Renault 4P)
G-BHYI BKBK JJGI NIFE SVGL

SV-4B (DH Gipsy Major 10)
G-AIYG AWIW AYIJ AZSA

SV-4C (DH Gipsy Major 10)
G-AXRP BPLM BRXP OODE

SV-4C (Renault 4P)
G-AMPI ATIR AWXZ AXNW AYCG AYDR
AYGE AYZI AZGC AZGE BAKN BHFG BKRK
BWRS BXSV BYDK EEUP GMAX HJSS SPIP

SV-4C(G) (DH Gipsy Major 10)
G-ASHS AWEF AYCK AYJB AYWT AZCB
BWEF FORD SVIV

SV-4E (Lycoming O-360)
G-BNYZ

STAR-LITE
SL-1
G-BUZH FARO SOLA

STARCK
AS.80
G-BJAE

STEEN AERO LAB INC
SKYBOLT
G-BGRT BIMN BUXI BWPJ BZWV CCPE
CJSR CKZR ENGO IIPI IPII KEST NMUS
RODC SBII SBLT SBOL SKIE WISZ

STEMME GmbH and Co KG
S 10 variants
G-BXGZ BXHR BZSP JCKT JULL STEM
STEN TUKU

STEPHENS
AKRO
G-RIDE

PULSE SSDR
G-CJFS

SIROCCO
G-CIUD

STERN

ST.80 BALADE
G-BWVI

STEWART

S-51 MUSTANG replica
G-CGOI

STINSON AIRCRAFT CORPORATION

108 VOYAGER (Consolidated Vultee Aircraft production)
G-BPTA BRZK CFGE STSN WAGN

HW-75
G-AFYO BMSA

L-1 VIGILANT
G-CIGB

V-77 RELIANT
G-BUCH

STITS

SA.3A PLAYBOY
G-BGLZ BVVR

STODDARD-HAMILTON

GLASAIR
G-BKHW BMIO BODI BOVU BSAI BUBT
BUHS BZBO CDAB CGXB CGYA CLFM
FAZT ICBM IIRG KRES KSIR LAIR LASR
MHPS TRUK

GLASTAR
G-BYEK BZDM CBAR CBCL CBJD CKZX
IARC IKES KIRT LAZZ LSTA LSTR MHGS
SACH SKUA

STOLP AIRCRAFT CORPORATION

SA.100 STARDUSTER
G-IIIM

SA.300 STARDUSTER TOO
G-BOBT BRVB BSZB BTGS BUPB BZKD
CDBR DUST JIII KEEN OTOO SDTO STOO
UINN

SA.500 STARLET
G-AZTV

SA.750 ACRODUSTER TOO
G-BLES CEZK

SA.900 V-STAR
G-BLAF CILX VSTR

STOREY

TSR.3
G-AWIV

STROJNIK

S-2A
G-BMPS

SUCH

SUCH BM42-16
G-CIWN

SUCH BM60-20
G-CIRC

SUD-AVIATION GARDAN

HORIZON
G-ATGY AVRS AWAC AZYA BYBL GYAT
TIMY

SUD-AVIATION – also see AÉROSPATIALE (AS prefix), EUROCOPTER (EC prefix) and MESSERSCHMITT-BÖLKOW-BLOHM (BK and BÖ prefixes)

SE.313 ALOUETTE II variants
G-BVSD

SA.341 and SA.342 GAZELLE (including ICA-Brasov and Westland production)
G-BZDV BZYD CBGZ CBJZ CBKA CBKD
CBSF CBSI CBSK CDNO CDNS CGJX CGJZ
CIEX CIEY CIOW CLBC CTFS DFKI EROL
EZZL FUKM GAZA GAZZ HSDL IBNH KEMH
LOYD OGEO ONNE RBIL SIVJ VOIP ZLLE
ZZEL ZZLE

SUKHOI

SU-29
G-SUKK SUUK

SUPER MARINE AIRCRAFT (PTY)

SPITFIRE Mk.26
G-CCGH CCJL CEFC CEPL CGWI CIEN
CIXM CJWW CJYY ENAA HABT MKZG PIXY
RORB SMSP

SUPERMARINE LTD including WESTLAND AIRCRAFT LTD production

236 WALRUS
G-WLRS

SEAFIRE variants
G-BUAR BWEM CFZJ FRSX KASX RIPH

SPITFIRE variants
G-AIDN AIST ALGT ASJV AVAV AWII BMSB
BRRA BRSF BUOS CCCA CDGU CDGY
CFGA CFGJ CGJE CGRM CGUK CGYJ
CGZU CHVJ CICK CJWO CKUE CKYM
CLCS CLCT CTIX DBKL FXII IBSY ILDA IRTY
JGCA JNMA LFIX LFVB LFVC MCDB MKVB
MKXI MXVI NSFS OXVI PBIX PMNF PRIV
PRXI PTIX RAAF RRFF RRGN SAEA SDNI
SPIT SPXX SSVB TCHI TCHO TCHZ TGVP

SVENSKA AEROPLAN AB (SAAB) – see SAAB-SCANIA AB

SWALLOW AEROPLANE CO

SWALLOW B
G-MJBK

SWIFT AIRCRAFT

SW01A
G-SWAI

SWING

XWING
G-CKUM

SZD-SZYBOWCOWY ZAKLAD DOSWIADCZALNY including ALLSTAR PZL GLIDER and PZL-BIELSKO

SZD-9bis BOCIAN
G-DBJD DCEB DCNM DEJY

SZD-22 MUCHA
G-CKXD

SZD-24 FOKA
G-DCBP DHGY

SZD-30 PIRAT
G-DCHG DCHL DCKD DCOC DCTV DCTX
DCVR DCYD DCZE DCZG DCZJ DDAN
DDAP DDBV DDDK DDHZ DDTW DEOB
ECXL EDBD

SZD-36A COBRA
G-DCWP DCXH DDAC DDCA ILIB ZBOP

SZD-38A JANTAR-1
G-CFNE DDDE DDFL DDFU EDDV

SZD-41A JANTAR STANDARD 1
G-CHBS

SZD-42-1 JANTAR 2
G-CLVP DDNU DEUV

SZD-45A OGAR
G-BKTM BMFI OGAR

SZD-48 JANTAR STANDARD 2 & 3
G-CFDX CFOT CKDR DDVK DENX DFTJ

SZD-50-3 PUCHACZ
G-CFEN CFTH CFUY CFWT CFXO CFYA
CFYL CGBD CGCK CGCU CGEL CHAC
CHAF CHDP CHEP CHFH CHYP CICY CJEC
CJRF CJRJ CKAN CKHW DEUF DHCF
EHCC FEVS MRVN

SZD-51-1 JUNIOR
G-CFFV CFFY CFHF CFPM CFTC CFUS
CFZF CFZP CGCC CHDB CHDU CHEK
CHMA CHNK CHRG CJMG CJMY CJVC
CKHN CKHR CKPN CLRD DHCR DHCW
DHHD

SZD-54 PERKOZ
G-CLVO CLWC ONHL PCGC PRKZ

SZD-55-1 PROMYK
G-CGAX CHEC CHHR CKBN

SZD-59 ACRO
G-SZDA

T

TARJANI

TRIKE with SOLAR WINGS TYPHOON wing
G-MJCU

TAYLOR

JT.1 MONOPLANE (Volkswagen 1600)
G-AWGZ AXYK AYSH AYUS BBBB BDAD
BDAG BDNC BDNG BEUM BEVS BFOU
BGCY BGHY BILZ BKHY BLDB BMAO
BMET BRUO BUXL BYAV CDGA CRIS OBJM
RAAY WARD WEZZ

JT.2 TITCH
G-AYZH BABE BARN BDRG BFID BGMS
BIAX BKWD BVNI MISS OJON TICH VIVI

TAYLOR AIRCRAFT CO LTD – see PIPER AIRCRAFT CORPORATION

TAYLORCRAFT AEROPLANES (ENGLAND) LTD – also see AUSTER AIRCRAFT

AUSTER 3
G-AHLK AREI BUDL

AUSTER 4
G-AJXV AJXY ANHS

PLUS D
G-AHCR AHGW AHGZ AHSD AHUG

TAYLORCRAFT AIRCRAFT CORPORATION

BC-12D
G-AHNR AKVO BIGK BOLB BPHO BPHP
BPPZ BREY BRIH BRPX BRXE BSDA BVDZ

BC-65
G-BSCW

BL-65
G-BVRH

DCO-65
G-BWLJ

DF-65
G-BRIY

F-19
G-BRIJ

F-22 varants
G-BWBI

TCHEMMA

T01/77
G-CFHS

TEAM

HI-MAX
G-CBNZ CKXZ MZHM

MINI-MAX
G-BVSB BVSX BXCD BXSU BYFV BYJE
BYYX BZFK BZOR BZTC CBIN CBXU CCGB
CEDL CJVD MWFD MWHH MWLW MWSA
MYAT MYBM MYCT MYDF MYGF MYII MYIZ
MYKJ MYKZ MYNI MYRG MYRL MYSK
MYXA MYYR MYYS MZCS MZMO MZOY
MZPJ NADS OJLH OPEJ OSCO THEO

TECHPRO AVIATION

MERLIN 100UL
G-CIWL CJNU CJTD CJVI CKZI HATH

TECNAM (CONSTRUZIONI AERONAUTICHE TECNAM SRL)

P92 ECHO variants
G-BZHG BZWT CBAX CBDM CBGE CBLB
CBUG CBYZ CCAL CCDU CKWI OALH
PGFG SDOZ TCNM TECM TECO WHEN

P2002 SIERRA variants
G-CDTV CENH CEOC CEVM CFSB CGUW
CGWO CWFS HACS NESE NFLY OTEC
RAYZ RLMW SDOB SRRA SWRE TECA TECI
TECS TEMB TESI TESR TSAC UCAN

P2006T
G-CKTR JRER OGOL OTAY SACL TECB
TECT WILN XVAX

P2008-JC
G-DMCP JACM JACN JSFC OLIC OTNM
RFCA RFCB TSFC ZOOB

P2010
G-DLMH GAEE JACL LKVA TTEN WINX

TEMAN

MONO-FLY
G-MMPZ

TEVERSON

BISPORT
G-CBGH

TEXTRON

3000 TEXAN II
G-TBFT

THATCHER

CX4 series
G-CISH CXIV

THE AIRPLANE FACTORY

SLING 2
G-LHAB SNGZ

SLING 4
G-CKZA LDSA SLIV SLNG

THE LIGHT AIRCRAFT COMPANY (TLAC)

SHERWOOD KUB
G-OKUB

SHERWOOD RANGER variants
G-BZUG CBHU CCBW CDPH CHHD CIIU
CING CIWD CIYY CJII DANB GKFC MWND
NSSA SWAB TIAC TLAC TSOG WZOL YELP

SHERWOOD SCOUT variants
G-CLAK INYS OUAV

THERMAL AIRCRAFT

104
G-BRAP

THORP AERO INC including AD AEROSPACE LTD and VENTURE LIGHT AIRCRAFT RESOURCES production

T.18
G-BLIT BSVN BYBY HATF

T.211
G-BTHP BYJF TZII

THRUSTER AIR SERVICES LTD including THRUSTER AIRCRAFT (UK) LTD

T.300 variants
G-MGWH MVUB MVWN MVWS MVZA
MVZC MVZD MVZE MVZI MWAN MWDS
MWWS MYAR MYDT MYDU MYJF MYJG
MYXU

T.600 (Jabiru 2200A)
G-BYPF BYPH BZIG BZJC BZJD BZNP
BZTD CBDC CBGU CBGV CBGW CBIP
CBIR CBKG CBVA CBWI CBWJ CBXG CBYT
CCBC CCCB CCCF CCCH CCDV CCEB
CCMT CCRN CCRP CCUZ CCXV CCXW
CDBZ CDDI CDDX CDGI CDIA CDJE CDRH
CGFZ CSAV CXIP DIDY EVEY FIDL IRAL
KDCD KYLE MARZ MCCF MGTV MOMA
MYWE MZFO MZFU MZGY MZHA MZHD
MZHF MZHS MZHV MZHW MZHY MZKS
MZKU MZNY NDOT OBAX OHYE OJSH
OMAL OOFE ORAM ORDS ORUG OWMC
PGSA PSUK PYNE RAFH RAFS REDZ RIVR
UDGE WORM

TST Mk.1 (Rotax 503)
G-MNWB MTGB MTGD MTGR MTGS MTKA
MTLM MTLN MTNR MTNU MTNV MTPU
MTPW MTPX MTSH MTSJ MTSM MTUC
MTVP MTVT MTWZ MTXA MTXD MTZA
MTZB MTZC MTZF MVAH MVAI MVAJ MVDE
MVDF MVDH MVFJ MVFL MVFM MVFO
MVHI MVHJ MVHK MVIR MVIV MVMI MVOT
MVOV MVYE

THUNDER BALLOONS LTD including CAMERON BALLOONS LTD and THUNDER and COLT LTD production

Ax3 SKY CHARIOT
G-BKBD BKFG NEIL

Ax4 series
G-LORY

Ax5 series
G-BDAY

Ax6 series
G-BFIT BHTG BJVU DICK THOM TNTN

Ax7 series
G-BFIX BHEU BHHH BHIS BJSW BLCY
BLTN BMCC BMKV BMMW BMUU BNGO
BNMX BNXZ BNZK BPHU BPYK BRLS BSAV
BSCO BSEA BSOJ BTHK BTRR BTSX BTTW
BTVA BTXK BUDK BUIN BUKI BULB BUPU
BVDB BVUH BYNU BZBH CDFN FUND
GGGG LYTE MLWI OJDC PIAF PIES PUFF
RAFE RBOW RIGB ROCK ROSI USIL VIVA
WDEB

Ax8 series
G-BJMW BSTK BTJD BTPX BUBY BUEI
BVDW BVGB BVPA BVWB BWKW GEMS
INGA OMDD OTEL PUNK SUED TOOL

Ax9 series
G-BTJO BTOZ FABS OIOZ

Ax10 series
G-BZGJ

Ax11 series
G-BZHX BZRZ

TIPSY AIRCRAFT CO LTD including AVIONS FAIREY SA, COBELAVIA SA and SLINGSBY (for NIPPER AIRCRAFT LTD) production

BELFAIR
G-APIE

JUNIOR
G-AMVP

NIPPER variants
G-APYB ARBG ARDY ARFV ARXN ASZV
ATUH AVKI AVKK AVTC AVXD AWDA AWJE
AWLR AWLS AXLI AXLJ AXZM BALS BLMW
BRIK BRPM BWCT BWHR BYLO CCFE CIZS
CORD ENIE NIPA NIPP NIPR NIPS ONCS
TIPS

TRAINER I
G-AFSC AFWT AISA AISC

TITAN AIRCRAFT

T-51 MUSTANG
G-CIFD CKVJ CMPC DHYS FION MUZY
MZTG TSIM

TORNADO SS
G-NADO

TL ULTRALIGHT COMPANY

TL 2000 STING
G-CESM CFDS CGLJ CGLZ CGML CGPO
CHBZ CKZP LCMW MECK NIAC OMCB
SACM STFO STIN STNG STUN STZZ TLST
ZIZY

TL 3000 SIRIUS
G-CIAF CKKG XILM

TONY LE VIER ASSOCIATES INC

COSMIC WIND
G-ARUL BAER NZIC

TOWNSEND

SKYLARK
G-SGNT

TRAVEL AIR

R TYPE REPLICA
G-TATR

TRI-R TECHNOLOGIES

KIS
G-BZDR OKIS OKMA OKPW TKIS

TWAMLEY

TRIKE
G-MBGF

U

ULTRAFLIGHT LTD including AMF Microflight Ltd production

LAZAIR
G-MNRD MVGZ

ULTRALIGHT FLIGHT INC

MIRAGE
G-MBSX

PHANTOM
G-MJKX MJUX MNCS MTTN

ULTRAMAGIC SA

50 series
G-CKUK

65 series
G-CHND

70 series
G-CIUA DAAY LEAT UINS UINZ

77 series
G-BXPT BZKW BZSH BZSO CBRK CBWK
CCLO CCRG CEWU CJCE CJEI CJXD CKFZ
CKGI CKKO CLBK DONK HOLI HTEK KNEE
LOKI MLTA PIMM SEBS TBET UTRA WOTW

90 series
G-CCYU CEEL CFDF CFFA CGGZ CGPD CGWU CIRL CJKI CJYM CKTP CKTU GBBT HPCB IFOS IPEN JEMS KEWT LEEH LEMM PAWW ROSK SCFC SPID

105 series
G-BZPX CBRB CCOP CDGF CDPN CEMG CEUL CFJI CIIX CLCZ CRZE EPSN GBGB GOFR OWLL RFLO WILB ZOIZ

130 series
G-CBKK

300 series
G-CFUF

F-12
G-FTUS

H-31
G-BZIZ BZPY CEFB CGWC CHIM CIOV CISJ CKBJ CKHJ DVCI JEMZ OINN UHOP XAIM

H-42
G-CEAY CGFO CICO CIGA CKJT

M-56
G-CEJG FWJR HDUO

M-65C
G-CEBO CHSP CKXH EGIA OKEW RACR ULTA

M-120
G-CDJI CEIY CEUM CJKH PMSL

N-250
G-CDST VBFA VBFC VBFD

N-355
G-CFRI VBFB VBFE

N-425
G-CGGY VBFP

S-50 series
G-CGPH TKNO UNKY

S-70 series
G-CIKL OIIY

T-180
G-CCUE

V-14
G-CFMR

ULTRASPORTS

TRI-PACER TRIKE with Excalibur, Flexiform, Hiway, Solar Wings, Southdown & Wasp wings
G-MJVN

TRIKE with Excalibur, Flexiform, Hiway, Solar Wings, Southdown & Wasp wings
G-MBLU MBTJ MJER MMWS

ULTRAVIA

PELICAN variants
G-BWWA MPAC MWRS

UNICORN

AX variants
G-CIAN

UNICORN GROUP

UE variants
G-BINR BINS BINT BIWJ BJGM BJLF BJLG FYEK

V

VALENTIN FLUGZEUGBAU GMBH

MISTRAL C
G-CJUR DJHP YXLX

TAIFUN 17E
G-BMSE KFBA OACE TFUN

VAN DEN BEMDEN

OMEGA III
G-BDTU

VAN'S AIRCRAFT INC

RV-3 variants
G-BVDC CCTG HILI RIII RODZ RVRH RVXP

RV-4
G-BOHW BROP BULG BVDI BVLR BVRV BVUN BVVS BXPI BXRV BZPH CDJB CEVC IICC IIGI IKON INTS JIMZ MAXV MUMY OJGC ORCA PIPS RATC RIIV RMIT RVDP RVDX RVER RVIL RVIV RVJW RVNS RVPM RVRV SARV SPRK SPRX VANS

RV-6 variants
G-BUEC BUTD BVCG BXJY BXVO BXWT BYDV BYEL BZOZ BZRV BZUY BZVN BZWZ BZXB CBCP CBUK CCJI CCVS CDAE CDVT CEYM CFDI CGYO CHFG CHXL CIFL CIWB CKTF CSPR DCOE DFUN EDRV EERV ESTR EYOR GDRV GLUC GPAG GRIN GRVE HACE HOPY JAEE JPBA JSRV KELL KELX MHRV MRVP MURG NMRV NPKJ OBUZ ODEE OJVA OJVL ONUN OORV OPAR ORVE ORVG ORVI OTRV PJSY PWUL REAS REVE RIVT RKID RRRV RUSL RVAN RVAW RVBC RVCE RVCL RVDJ RVDR RVEE RVET RVGA RVIA RVIB RVIC RVIN RVIT RVJM RVMT RVNI RVPW RVSA RVSB RVSE RVSH RVST RVSX RVTE RVVI SIXY TJDM TNGO TOGO UNES VANZ WTFH XVOM

RV-7 variants
G-CCVM CCZD CDME CDYZ CECV CEID CEIG CEIT CETS CFET CFTT CFWV CGJN CGWF CGWG CHHI CHIR CHRV CILG CIOO CIRV CISZ CIWV CKMX CKTX CLAO CLBG CLCL CMON CNHB COLS CRUE CSKW CTED DAME DANP DIDG DMBO DMPL DOTY DPRV DSRV DVMI EGSR ELVN FIXX FOZY GERT HUTY ICRV IILL IIRV IIXF IMCD ISMA ISRV IVII JCIH JEWL JFRV JIMC JKEL JMRV KAOS KELS KFOG LETS MACI MROD MRVL NAPP OGRL OJLD OKER OLEW OMPH ORAE ORVZ OVII PBEC PPLL PROS PYPE RIDG RINZ RISY RMRV RVAA RVAB RVAC RVAH RVBP RVBZ RVDB RVEM RVHD RVII RVJG RVMM RVRP RVTA RVTB RVTT RVUK SEVN STIX TERO TPPW TRVR UKRV VANN VARK WOWI XERK XIII XTAZ

RV-8 variants
G-BZWN CCIR CDDY CEGI CHPK CIBH CIBM CJSM CKBE CKWM DAZZ DOBS DUDE EGRV GAST GGRV GIGZ GORV GRVY GUNZ HCCF HILZ HPWA HRVS IDRS IGHT IIDD IIRW JBRS JBTR JRVB KELZ KRBY LEMI LEXX LEXY LSPH LUDM MIRV MUKY NFON NISH NRFK OCTO OCXI OGZZ PAPJ PHVM RATD RRRZ RUVE RVAL RVAR RVAT RVBA RVBI RVCH RVDC RVDH RVEI RVIS RVMZ RVOM RVPH RVPL RVSR RVTX SDRV SOUT SPRC SUTE TDJP TUCK UISE VFDS VMOZ VRVB WIKD WTSN XRVB XSEA YSIR ZAAZ ZUMI

RV-9 variants
G-CCGU CCND CCZT CCZY CDCD CDMF CDMN CDRV CDXT CEEP CEGH CERK CETP CFED CFHI CFMC CFSG CFUA CGMG CGXR CHST CIPL CIYV CIZR CSAM DHOP DTPC EGBS GBRV GNRV HOXN HUMH IINI IOSL IRAR KMRV NIEN NYNA OPVM ORVS PLAR PTEK RDAY RPRV RTRV RUVY RVDG RVIW RVIX RVJO RVJP RVLC RVMB RVNH RVSD RVSG RVSK RVWJ TTRL VVRV XCRJ XSAM XXRV

RV-10
G-CGJP CKYK DERO FFRV IORV MCLK NMMB OMRC ORVX RRVX RVGO RVIO RVTN TENN TOPP XRVX

RV-12
G-CGVD CGYI CHTI CIRM CJIC CJJV CJZW CKZH CMKL DOUZ ELWK IZRV MUJD OATZ OXII RMPS RVIZ RVTW SRCB TWLV VRRV WAFI

RV-14
G-CRVC OXIV RVDD STRV XIVA

VARGA

2150A KACHINA
G-BLHW BPVK DJCR VARG

VAZDUHOPLOVNO TEHNICKI CENTAR [VTC] – see SCHEMPP-HIRTH FLUGZEUGBAU GmbH

VENTURE LIGHT AIRCRAFT RESOURCES – see THORP AERO INC

VICKERS SLINGSBY – see SLINGSBY SAILPLANES LTD

VICTA including AESL production

AIRTOURER
G-ATCL ATEX ATHT ATJC AWVG AXIX AYLA AYWM AZBE AZHI AZHT AZOE AZOF AZTM

VIKING

DRAGONFLY
G-BKPD BRKY

VIKING AIR – see DE HAVILLAND CANADA

VINTEN-WALLIS LTD – see WALLIS AUTOGYROS LTD

VOLJET

SX255
G-RDRL

VOLMER

VJ.22 SPORTSMAN
G-BAHP

VOLTAIR

86
G-CHTX

VOUGHT

F4U CORSAIR
G-FGID

VPM SNC and SRL – see MAGNI GYRO

VULCANAIR SpA – see PARTENAVIA COSTRUZIONI AERONAUTICHE

W

WACO

UPF-7
G-UPFS

YKS-7
G-BWAC CKLL

YMF
G-YMFC

WAG-AERO INC

ACRO TRAINER
G-CUBW

CUBY SPORT TRAINER
G-BTWL BZHU

SUPER SPORT
G-DTUG

WAG-A-BOND
G-WAGA

WALLINGFORD MODEL BALLOONS

WMB.2 WINDTRACKER
G-BIAI BIBX BILB

WALLIS AUTOGYROS LTD including BEAGLE-MILES AIRCRAFT LTD, BEAGLE-WALLIS LTD and VINTEN-WALLIS LTD production

WA.116
G-ATTB

W.A.R.

FOCKE-WULF FW190 replicas
G-BSLX CCFW SYFW WULF

WASSMER (SOCIÉTÉ DES ETABLISSMENTS BENJAMIN WASSMER) – also see JODEL

WA26P SQUALE
G-DEEP

WA28F ESPADON
G-CJDX CJXC

WA.41 SUPER BALADOU
G-ATZS AVEU

WA.51 PACIFIC
G-AZYZ

WA.52 EUROPA
G-BTLB EFVS OELZ

WA.81 PIRANHA
G-BKOT

WEEDHOPPER OF UTAH INC

JC-24
G-MTNK

WELLS

AIRSPEED 300
G-FYGJ

WESTERN

20
G-AYMV

O-31
G-AZPX

O-65
G-BBUT

WESTLAKE

ALTAIR
G-CHYC

WESTLAND AIRCRAFT LTD – also see see FAIREY and SUPERMARINE

LYSANDER
G-AZWT CCOM

WIDGEON
G-EUKS

WESTLAND HELICOPTERS LTD – also see BELL, SIKORSKY and SUD AVIATION

SCOUT
G-BWHU BXRS BYKJ CIBW CIMX CRUM
KAXW SASM SCTA SROE

SEA KING
G-SKNG

WASP
G-BYCX CBUI CGGK KANZ KAXT RIMM

WESTLAND WESSEX
G-BYRC WSEX

WESTLAND WS-55 WHIRLWIND HAR.10
G-BVGE

WHITE

SPORTS MONOPLANE
G-CJAU

WHITTAKER including AEROTECH INTERNATIONAL LTD

MW5 SORCERER series (Rotax 447)
G-BZWX CBBO CEFT MMGV MNMM MTAS
MTBP MTBR MTBS MTDK MTFN MTRX
MVNP MVNR MVNS MWEK MWEO MWGI
MWGJ MWGK MWIC MWSX MWSY MYAH
MYAN MYJZ MZOH RMPI

MW6 MERLIN, MW6-S FATBOY FLYER and MW6-T
G-BUOA BYTX BZYU CBMU CBWS CBYP
MGCK MNMW MTTF MTXO MVPM MVTD
MVXA MWHM MWIP MWLN MWOV MWPR
MYCA MYCP MYKO MYMN MYPS MZBG
MZDI MZHG MZID MZJP MZOK

MW7 (Rotax 532)
G-BOKH BPUP BTFV BTUS BZOW

MW9
G-CKAA

WILD

BVS SPECIAL
G-BJUB

WILLIAMS

All variants
G-FYAN FYAO FYAU FYDI FYDP FYFJ

WITTMAN

W.8 and W.10 TAILWIND (Continental O-200-A)
G-BCBR BDAP BDBD BJWT BMHL BNOB
BOHV BOIB BPYJ CEJE CFON CIJY WYND
ZIPY

WOLF

W-II BOREDOM FIGHTER
G-BMZX BNAI

WOODS

PHANTOM
G-CIXG

X

XTREME AIR

SBACH series
G-COXI DMON IIJI IIRI

XA-41
G-IIFI IIIF

Y

YAKOVLEV including ACROSTAR, IAV-BACHAU, LET, NANCHANG AIRCRAFT MANUFACTURING COMPANY (NAMC CJ-6A) and SPP production

Yak-1
G-BTZD

Yak-11 (C-11)
G-BTUB BZMY OYAK

Yak-12 variants
G-PFKD

Yak-18 variants
G-BMJY BVVG BXZB CEIB CGFS CGHB
CIDC CJSA HAHU PYAK UYAK VSOZ VYAK
YACC YAKG YAKJ

Yak-3
G-CDBJ CGXG OLEG

Yak-50
G-BTZB BWFM BWYK CBPM EYAK IIYK
IVAR SKPH SOCT SVET YAAK YAKM YAKU
YAKZ YKSO

Yak-52
G-BVVW BVXK BWSV BWVR BXAK BXJB
CBMI CBOZ CBRW CCJK CDJJ CJBV IUII
LYFA OUGH RNAC SPUT TYAK YAKC YAKE
YAKF YAKH YAKI YAKN YAKX YAKY YOTS
YYAK ZBEN

Yak-55
G-CIIK YKSS

YORKSHIRE SAILPLANES – see SLINGSBY SAILPLANES LTD

Z

ZAKLAD SZYBOWCOWY JEZOW

PW-6U
G-CKPX CKRU CKRX

ZEBEDEE BALLOON SERVICE

V-31
G-BXIT

ZENAIR – also see COLOMBAN

CH.250 ZENITH variants
G-BTXZ GFKY

CH.601 ZODIAC variants (Rotax 912)
G-BUTG BUZG BVAB BVAC BVVM BVZR
BYEO BYJT BYLF BYPR CBAP CBDG CBGB
CBIX CBJP CBPV CBRX CCAK CCED CCTA
CCVL CCZK CDAL CDDS CDFL CDGP
CDJG CDLW CDMT CDNT CDWU CDZB
CEAT CEBA CEBZ CECZ CEUW CEZS CFKH
CFRY CGPX CGSI CGVZ CHZL CHZS CJOY
CLEO CSZM CZAC DAGJ DONT EEZZ EXLL
EXXL EZUB FOXL HILY JAME KHOP KIMA
LEDE NLMB OANN OMEZ OOSH PATO
REGC RUVI TTOM XLNT ZAIR ZENR ZENY
ZODY

CH.650 variants
G-INES

CH.701 variants (Rotax 912)
G-BXIG BZVA CBCH CBGD CBZW CCVI
CDGR CDYU CEWS CHTH CIXS CKFF
CLCW EOIN GOLA IMME JFMK OBAP
OMEX RAYH TORI ZENA

CH.750 variants
G-CIJK CIJZ CIMN CKDM FFFF WXYZ

ZIVKO AERONAUTICS INC

EDGE 360
G-IIFM ZVKO

EDGE 540
G-EDGY

ZLIN

ZLIN Z-226T TRENER SPEZIAL
G-EJGO

ZLIN Z-242L
G-UART

ZLIN Z-326 TRENER MASTER
G-BEWO BKOB CIXE

ZLIN Z-526 TRENER MASTER variants
G-AWJX AWSH BLMA BPNO EHZT GIBP
PCDP TINY

SECTION 2 – BRITISH GLIDING ASSOCIATION REGISTERS

The BGA glider register follows a similar format to the main aircraft registers in this book.

Column 1 shows the three-letter Trigraph issued by the BGA.

Column 2 shows the BGA number – the Certificate of Airworthiness (CofA) number issued by the British Gliding Association.

Column 3 shows the markings actually carried on the glider, which is usually either the trigraph or a BGA-allocated competition number. Occasionally ex-military or civil markings are carried – an index to these marks is in Part 2 below; a dash indicates that no code is worn.

The official BGA list is extended by including non-current gliders and those with recently lapsed CofAs for which no cancellation details are known but which may survive. We include the complete expiry dates for CofA and the complete date for the first issue where known. Where a BGA CofA number has been reserved for future use, the reservation date is shown suffixed by the letter 'R'. Most entries with a CofA expiry before the year 2014 have been deleted if there is no recent news on their fate or continued existence. Similar entries, where a reason for the non-renewal of CofA is known, such as accident details or sale abroad, have been retained but will be removed in the next edition. Owners' details are no longer officially available due to data protection rules, so information in the 'Owner(Operator)' and '(Unconfirmed) Base' columns is largely based on feedback received from readers, as well as information given on gliding club websites and in the BGA magazine *Sailplane & Gliding*.

The majority of active gliders are now G- registered under European Aviation Safety Agency (EASA) rules, the only exceptions being a number of vintage and one-off designs which are exempted under 'Annex II' and which will remain unregistered and under BGA control. BGA numbers are still allocated to newly-registered gliders, but EASA CofAs are issued, normally on the recommendation of BGA-authorized inspectors. The list below only covers aircraft not detailed in Section 1.

The BGA register has been updated by Richard Cawsey, with thanks to the staff at the British Gliding Association in Leicester for their help. Information is current to January 2019.

Information on gliders coming under the auspices of the Irish Gliding & Soaring Association can be found under Section 4 on page 547. Those operating on foreign registers are listed in Section 8, starting on page 570. The Index for this section starts on page 504.

Trigraph	BGA	Code	Type	Constructor's No	Date	Previous Identity	Owner(Operator)	(Unconfirmed) Base	CofA Expy
–	162	–	Manuel Willow Wren	–		09.34	Gliding Heritage Centre	Lasham	
		Built W L Manuel 1932					*On loan from Brooklands Museum*		
AAA	231	–	Abbott-Baynes Scud II	215B	G-ALOT	22.08.35	Gliding Heritage Centre	Lasham	29.03.14
			Completed by Slingsby		BGA 231					
AAF	236	12	Slingsby T.6 Kirby Kite	27A	G-ALUD	14.11.35	P & D Underwood	Wycombe Air Park	10.09.19
					BGA 236, BGA 222					
AAX	251	–	Slingsby T.6 Kirby Kite	227A	RAFGSA 240	30.03.36	J R Furnell	Portmoak	31.07.16
					BGA 251					
ABG	260	–	Schweyer Rhönsperber	35/22		04.05.36	F K Russell (Rhönsperber Syndicate)	Dunstable	04.06.19
–	266	–	Slingsby T.1 Falcon I Waterglider	237A		29.05.36	Windermere Jetty	Windermere	
							Stored 2.14		
ABZ	277	–	Grunau Baby II	–	RAFGSA 270	25.08.36	J R Furnell	Portmoak	19.06.18
			Built F Coleman		BGA 277, G-ALKU, BGA 277					
ACF	283	G-ALJR	Abbott-Baynes Scud III	2	G-ALJR	18.12.36	Gliding Heritage Centre	Lasham	29.06.14
					BGA 283		*Registered as G-ALJR*		
ACH	285	E	Slingsby T.6 Kirby Kite	247A	G-ALNH	30.12.36	Museum of Army Flying	AAC Middle Wallop	05.99
					BGA 285		*As 'G 285' in 1 GTS RAF c/s*		
ADJ	310	–	Slingsby T.6 Kirby Kite	258B	RAFGSA 182	09.02.37	The Shuttleworth Collection	Shuttleworth (Old Warden)	19.03.19
					VD218, BGA 310					
			Rebuilt 1982 with fuselage from BGA 327 c/n 285A; original fuselage under restoration by D Underwood, Eaton Bray in 2018							
AEM	337	–	Schleicher Rhönbussard	620	RAFGSA 265	25.04.38	T J Wills & partners	Bidford	09.02.17
					BGA 337, G-ALME, BGA 337, TK710, BGA 337					
AHC	400	F	Slingsby T.6 Kirby Kite	336A	VD165	06.05.39	D Bramwell	Thame	10.09.19
			Uses wings from Special T.6 c/n 355A		BGA 400		*In 1 GTS RAF c/s*		
AHU	416	–	Scott Viking I	114	G-ALRD	19.06.39	Gliding Heritage Centre	Lasham	20.05.18
					BGA 416					
AJW	442	AJW	Slingsby T.8 Tutor	MHL/RC8	G-ALMX	08.46	M Hodgson	Dunstable	14.08.98
			Built by Martin Hearn Ltd		BGA 442		*Stored 8.12*		
–	448	'D-11-875'	Jacobs Schweyer Weihe	000348	G-ALJW	06.47	Gliding Heritage Centre	Lasham	18.04.79
					BGA 448, LO+WQ		*On display 8.17*		
AKD	449	LF+VO	DFS Olympia-Meise	227	LF+VO	07.47	R Hardcastle	Rufforth	07.09.18
AKW	466	–	Slingsby T.8 Tutor	MHL/RT7		11.46	Hooton Park Trust	Hooton Park	06.07.96
AKZ	469	–	Slingsby T.8 Tutor	MHL/RT10	G-ALKP	11.47	D Burke	(Stamford)	19.08.93
					BGA 469		*New owner 9.14; crashed on landing, Wormingford 4.7.93*		
–	470	–	Short Nimbus	S.1312		.47	Ulster Folk & Transport Museum	Holywood, Belfast	08.75
							Stored in poor condition 2.18		
–	473	–	Slingsby T.8 Tutor	MHL/RT12	G-ALPU	10.47	J Howard	Hooton Park	10.12.67
					BGA 473		*Under restoration 3.17*		
ALR	485	–	Slingsby T.8 Tutor	513	G-ALPE	11.46	R van Aalst	Asperden, Germany	08.04.12
					BGA 485					

ALW	490	G-ALRK	Hütter H.17 *Built D Campbell*	–	G-ALRK BGA 490	13.08.48	N I Newton	Wycombe Air Park 21.08.19
–	491		Hawkridge Dagling	08471		02.47	N H Ponsford *Stored 2015*	Selby
–	493	–	Hawkridge Nacelle Dagling	10471		07.47	P J Underwood *Also allotted BAPC 81; stored 2018*	Eaton Bray
AMK	503	AMK	EoN Olympia 2	EoN/O/003	G-ALJP BGA 503	19.05.47	R Maxfield *Under restoration 2014*	Liversedge 28.05.95
AML	504		EoN Olympia 2	EoN/O/004	G-ALTV BGA 504	19.05.47	A Emmerson *Stored 2018*	(Ipswich) 16.08.87
AMM	505	AMM	EoN Olympia 2	EoN/O/006	G-ALJV BGA 505	29.05.47	J R Furnell	Portmoak 26.07.09
AMR	509	AMR	EoN Olympia 2	EoN/O/011	G-ALLA BGA 509	19.05.47	K J Nurcombe *To USA as N110LY 9.18*	Husbands Bosworth 09.07.14
AMV	513	–	EoN Olympia 2	EoN/O/014	G-ALNB BGA 513	03.06.47	K G Reid & W Cook *Under restoration 2019*	(Rivar Hill) 22.08.90
AMW	514	AMW	EoN Olympia 2	EoN/O/015	G-ALKM BGA 514	03.06.47	J Stiles & T Henderson *Under restoration 2017*	Ringmer 16.04.03
AND	521	–	Slingsby T.26 Kite 2	MHL/RK5		.	C P Raine *Stored*	Chalfont St.Giles 20.06.80
ANW	538	ANW	EoN Olympia 2	EoN/O/040	G-ALNE BGA 538	18.07.47	Midland Air Museum *Stored 8.16*	Baginton 09.03.04
ANZ	541	–	EoN Olympia 2	EoN/O/043		27.07.57	R Davies *Under restoration 2019*	RAF Halton 19.05.92
APC	544	APC	EoN Olympia 2	EoN/O/046	G-ALMJ BGA 544	11.09.47	R D Bryce-Smith	Gransden Lodge 25.08.19
APZ	565	–	Slingsby T.25 Gull IV	505	G-ALPB BGA 565	.	A Fidler *Rebuilt with Kite 2 fuselage no. MHL/210*	Crowland 01.10.18
AQE	570	–	Slingsby T.21B	538	AGA 20 BGA 570, G-ALNJ, BGA 570	.	Derby & Lancs Gliding Club	Camphill 13.02.19
AQN	578	AQN	Grunau Baby IIB *Built by Hawkridge*	G.3348	G-ALSO BGA 578	27.07.48	G D Pullen *'Baby G'*	Lasham 30.04.15
AQQ	580	AQQ	EoN Primary	EoN/P/003	G-ALPS BGA 580	.	The Shuttleworth Collection Shuttleworth (Old Warden) 30.03.19	
–	588		EoN Primary	EoN/P/011		.	N H Ponsford *Stored 2015*	Selby
–	589	G-ALMN	EoN Primary	EoN/P/012	G-ALMN BGA 589	19.05.48	Museum of Berkshire Aviation *On display 3.18*	Woodley 20.04.51
ARK	599	ARK / G-ALLF	Slingsby T.30A Prefect	548	PH-1 BGA 599, G-ALLF, BGA 599	.	Gliding Heritage Centre *Registered as G-ALLF*	Lasham 30.06.15
ARM	601	ARM	Slingsby T.21B	543	G-ALKX BGA 601	25.08.48	D Firth & M Wills *Rebuilt 1974 with wings and tail from BGA 900; under restoration in 2018*	Doncaster 29.10.13
ASB	614	ASB	Slingsby T.21B	549	RNGSA, BGA 614, G-ALLT, BGA 614	06.09.48	R A Robertson & partners	Talgarth 17.08.19
ASC	615		Grunau Baby IIB *Built by Hawkridge*	G-4848	RAFGSA 152 BGA 615, G-ALMM, BGA 615	21.02.49	M Diller *Under restoration 2014*	Burgheim, Germany 13.08.94
ASN	625	ASN	Slingsby T.30B Prefect	567	G-ALPC BGA 625	28.01.49	G Martin	Talgarth 03.08.18
–	628	G-ALRU	EoN Baby	EoN/B/004	(BGA 645), G-ALRU, BGA 628	31.03.49	Gliding Heritage Centre *Fuselage on display 8.17*	Lasham 24.05.72
AST	629	G-ALRH	EoN Baby	EoN/B/005	G-ALRH BGA 629	31.03.49	B Stephenson & partners *Under restoration 2014*	Saltby 01.09.96
ATH	643	–	Slingsby T.15 Gull III	364A	TJ711	07.11.49	Gliding Heritage Centre *On display 8.17, on loan from Brooklands Museum*	Lasham 20.06.04
ATL	646	–	Slingsby T.21B	536	G-ALKS	25.06.50	E Munk & partners Lemelerveld, Netherlands 12.07.96 *Under restoration; reserved as PH-200 1.11*	
ATR	651	–	Slingsby T.13 Petrel	361A	EI-101, IGA 101, IAC 101, BGA 651, G-ALPP	06.07.50	G P Saw	Wycombe Air Park 25.06.19
ATV	655	CK-8592	Zlin 24 Krajanek	101	G-ALMP OK-8592	04.04.50	Gliding Heritage Centre	Lasham 10.06.16
–	660		EoN Olympia 2	EoN/O/094		20.01.51	P Storey *New owner 1.18*	(Darlton) 16.10.77
AUD	663	663	Slingsby T.26 Kite 2B	727		01.52	F G Bradney	Lasham 28.01.20
AUF	665	–	Slingsby T.21B	653		14.04.51	R Harvey *Under restoration 2.19*	Bellarena 29.04.86
AUG	666	–	Slingsby T.21B	643		15.06.51	Cambridge Gliding Club	Gransden Lodge 01.06.19
AUP	673	N21	Slingsby T.21B	636	RNGSA LS3 BGA 673	26.07.51	T21 Group	Lasham 13.07.19
AVA	684	–	Abbott-Baynes Scud III	3		10.01.53	J Steegh	Venlo, Netherlands 20.04.13
AVB	685	AVB	Slingsby T.34A Sky	644	G-644	10.02.53	R Moyse	Lasham 22.04.19
AVC	686	AVC	Slingsby T.34A Sky	670		02.03.53	M S Armstrong *'Kinder Scout II'*	Camphill 23.06.19
AVD	687	AVD	EoN Olympia 2	EoN/O/092		11.03.53	Not known	Portmoak 12.03.19
AVF	689	AVF	Slingsby T.26 Kite 2A	728	RAFGSA 294 BGA 689	08.04.53	C P Raine *'Percy'*	Thame 31.08.11

BGA

AVL	694	–	Slingsby T.34A Sky	671	G-671	15.05.53	M P Wakem	Long Mynd 02.07.19
AVQ	698	G46	Slingsby T.34A Sky	645	G-645	09.09.53	L M Middleton *'Gertie'*	Easterton 19.08.19
AVT	701	AVT	Slingsby T.30B Prefect	857		14.02.54	K Schickling	Aschaffenburg, Germany 25.04.19
AWS	724	AWS	Slingsby T.41 Skylark 2S	997		31.07.56	D M Cornelius	Dunstable 11.06.18
AWT	725		Slingsby T.37 Skylark	879		23.06.55	P F Woodcock *Under restoration 2019*	(South Yorkshire) 25.06.89
AWU	726	AWU	EoN Olympia 2	EoN/O/082		20.05.55	M J Riley	Sackville Lodge, Riseley 03.07.12
AWX	729	–	Slingsby T.41 Skylark 2	946	AGA, BGA 729	27.01.56	A G Leach	Bembridge 19.07.09
AWZ	731	AWZ	Slingsby T.7 Cadet	SSK/FF169	RA847	08.01.57	R Moyse	Lasham 23.02.19
AXB	733	AXB	Slingsby T.41 Skylark 2	926		24.02.56	Skysport Engineering *Stored 2014*	Hatch 30.06.02
AXD	735	AXD	Slingsby T.43 Skylark 3	1014		.	A P Stacey *Badly damaged Aston Down 11.7.03; stored 1.12*	RAF Keevil 05.06.04
AXE	736	AXE	Slingsby T.43 Skylark 3	1029		27.03.56	B Pearson *Stored 5.17*	Eaglescott 21.08.01
AXJ	740	AXJ	Slingsby T.42A Eagle 2	994		.56	A Kendall	Pocklington 29.06.19
AXL	742	AXL	Slingsby T.43 Skylark 3	1030	RNGSA LM72 BGA 742	07.06.56	R Birch *Stored 6.18*	Aston Down 10.07.12
AXP	745	AXP	Slingsby T.41 Skylark 2	949		05.04.56	I McHardy	Drumshade 02.06.09
AXR	747	AXR	Slingsby T.41 Skylark 2	945		01.03.57	R Kilham *Stored 2012*	(Husbands Bosworth) 31.03.00
AXV	751	–	Slingsby T.26 Kite 2B	?		16.04.56	R A Wilgoss	Wycombe Air Park 08.09.17
AYD	759	AYD	Slingsby T.41 Skylark 2	1048		21.07.56	F G Bradney	Lasham 09.05.19
AYF	761	AYF	Slingsby T.43 Skylark 3B	1058		08.09.56	J Hall *Damaged on launch, Long Mynd 19.8.15*	Long Mynd 03.03.16
AYH	763	AYH	Slingsby T.43 Skylark 3B	1066		11.10.56	Not known *Noted 2014*	Falgunzeon 22.06.10
AYY	778	33	Slingsby T.41 Skylark 2C	1073		01.02.57	E Lambert & partners *'Merlin'*	Aston Down 19.06.18
AZA	780	AZA	Slingsby T.42B Eagle 3	1085	RNGSA 2-08 BGA 780	18.04.57	D A Bullock	Bicester 23.07.01
AZC	782	782	Slingsby T.21B	1096		27.05.57	L Starkl	Langenlebarn, Austria 20.10.18
AZF	785	'WE996'	Slingsby T.30B Prefect	1100		29.06.57	A Ferra	Bechyne, Czech Republic 19.07.19
–	791	VM684	Slingsby T.8 Tutor	–	VM684	20.01.57	Not known *New owner 2015*	Knutsford 27.02.71
AZP	793	AZP	Slingsby T.41 Skylark 2	999		13.01.57	R Milligan *Noted 2.14*	Falgunzeon 13.08.97
AZQ	794	VM687	Slingsby T.8 Tutor	–	VM687	.57	D J Gibbs	Saltby 07.07.10
AZR	795	AZR	EoN Olympia 2	EoN/O/101		03.06.58	G Kench	Crowland 27.05.17
AZX	801	AZX	Slingsby T.41 Skylark 2	995	BGA 1909 AGA 4, BGA 801	09.04.57	B J Griffin	Saltby 02.06.18
BAA	804	'XE761'	Slingsby T.8 Tutor	SSK/FF931	VW537	10.05.57	A P Stacey *Under restoration 2016 ;Note also Cadet TX.1 'BGA 804 ' at Midland Air Museum, Coventry*	RAF Keevil 09.03.97
BAC	806	BAC	Slingsby T.43 Skylark 3B	1101	RNGSA CU19 BGA 806	17.07.57	W den Baars *Stored 7.15*	Midden-Zeeland, Netherlands 24.04.04
BAL	813	BAL	Slingsby T.43 Skylark 3B	1111		12.11.57	A Wales	Falgunzeon 02.09.18
BAN	815	BAN	Slingsby T.30B Prefect	1120		03.01.58	Gliding Heritage Centre	Lasham 28.04.19
BAW	823	BAW	Slingsby T.43 Skylark 3B	1126		14.02.58	N Read *New owner 8.18*	Long Mynd 15.10.10
BAY	825	BAY	Slingsby T.42B Eagle 3	1116		28.03.58	D Williams *Under restoration 2018*	Halton 15.08.00
BAZ	826	BAZ	Slingsby T.41 Skylark 2	1112		26.03.58	D Neilson & A Wales	Falgunzeon 30.03.19
BBA	827	BBA	Slingsby T.41 Skylark 2	1128		28.03.58	McLean Aviation *Stored 4.18*	Rufforth 15.06.12
BBB	828	BBB	Slingsby T.42B Eagle 3	1118		11.04.58	J Burrow & partners	North Hill 03.07.19
BBG	833	BBG	Slingsby T.8 Tutor	–	VW535	03.09.57	P Pearson	Husbands Bosworth 18.05.19
BBQ	841	BBQ	Slingsby T.42B Eagle 3	1115		14.05.58	Portmoak Vintage Collection	Portmoak 03.07.16
BBT	844	BBT	Slingsby T.43 Skylark 3B	1134	RAFGSA 73 RAFGSA 234, BGA 844	06.06.58	J P Gilbert	Wormingford 12.08.18
BBU	845	BBU	Slingsby T.41 Skylark 2B	1135		13.06.58	D A Bullock	Bicester 13.04.18
–	852	TS291	Slingsby T.8 Tutor	SSK/FF250	TS291	02.07.58	National Museum of Flight	East Fortune 27.12.66
BCH	858	BCH	Slingsby T.8 Tutor	SSK/FF489	VM547	30.09.58	SegelflygMuseet	Alleberg, Sweden 24.01.05
BCP	864	BCP	Slingsby T.43 Skylark 3B	1140		01.11.58	M Smith	Milfield 01.09.14
BCS	867	549	Slingsby T.43 Skylark 3B	1144		05.12.58	A P Benbow & J R Furnell *Stored 2018*	Milnathort 16.04.05
BCV	870	155	Slingsby T.43 Skylark 3B	1195		06.04.59	Gliding Heritage Centre	Lasham 13.05.16
BDF	880	45	Slingsby T.42B Eagle 3	1213		28.09.59	G MacDonald	Lasham 22.06.19
BDM	886	BDM	Slingsby T.21B	1216		04.11.59	M Wright & W Day	Tibenham 07.04.19
BDR	890	BDR	Slingsby T.45 Swallow	1243		11.06.60	M King *'Sarah'*	Portmoak 18.05.13
BDW	895		Slingsby T.8 Tutor	–	VM637	30.04.59	Newark Air Museum	Winthorpe 12.06.93
Stored 6.10								
BDX	896	BDX	Slingsby T.41 Skylark 2	CH.095/1		10.06.59	H D Maddams *Built C Hurst*	Ridgewell 28.04.11

BEA	899	BEA	Slingsby T.41 Skylark 2	1194		01.07.59	P Q Benn	Portmoak 19.06.13
–	902	–	Slingsby T.12 Gull	?		15.05.59	National Museum of Scotland *On display 3.18*	Edinburgh 14.05.60
BEF	904	–	Slingsby T.8 Tutor	SSK/FF934	VW52?	29.10.59	South Yorkshire Aircraft Museum	Doncaster 02.05.96
BEL	909	BEL	EoN Olympia 2B	EoN/O/126		21.12.59	J G Gilbert *Stored 2009*	(Wormingford) 11.05.05
BEM	910	BEM	Slingsby T.45 Swallow	1221	RNGSA VL25 BGA 910	05.02.60	G Winch	Wormingford 25.09.19
BET	916	830	Slingsby T.43 Skylark 3B	1227		09.03.60	A C Robertson & partners *Stored 10.16*	Feshiebridge 31.05.98
BEX	920	91	Slingsby T.43 Skylark 3F	1229		08.04.60	A J Pettitt	Rivar Hill 07.05.19
BEY	921	BEY	Slingsby T.45 Swallow	1230		14.04.60	G P Hayes	Kenley 06.08.19
BEZ	922	BEZ	Slingsby T.43 Skylark 3F	1232		29.04.60	Not known	Rufforth 21.09.18
BFC	925	BFC	Slingsby T.43 Skylark 3F	1239	AGA , BGA 925	20.05.60	C Faichney	Portmoak 06.06.16
BFE	927	BFE	Slingsby T.43 Skylark 3F	1244		24.06.60	I Dunkley	Akaroa, New Zealand 13.03.09
BFY	945	BFY	Slingsby T.21B	1251	RAFGSA 515 RAFGGA 515, RAFSA 286, BGA 945	20.09.60	M Wood	Sutton Bank 10.07.19
BGB	948	–	Slingsby T.21B	1274	RAFGSA 282 BGA 948	16.11.60	F Brune *New owner 2.10*	Eudenbach, Germany 25.08.05
BGD	950	BGD	Slingsby T.43 Skylark 3F	1276		26.11.60	A P Stacey *Stored 8.17*	Keevil 21.05.05
BGL	957	BGL	Slingsby T.43 Skylark 3F	1296		01.03.61	B Smee	Falgunzeon 20.11.18
BGR	962	BGR	EoN Olympia 2B	EoN/O/124		04.06.60	Gliding Heritage Centre	Lasham 12.04.19
BGX	968	BGX	EoN Olympia 2B	EoN/O/123	(BGA 892)	08.08.60	B Silke	Bellarena 22.07.18
BHC	973	BHC	EoN Olympia 2B	EoN/O/138		09.01.61	A Brind	Rivar Hill 07.05.11
BHQ	985	BHQ	Slingsby T.43 Skylark 3F	1304		15.04.61	Not known	Chipping 09.06.19
BHT	988	BHT	Slingsby T.43 Skylark 3F	1306		19.04.61	S Parramore	Brentor 20.07.16
BHV	990	BHV	Slingsby T.45 Swallow	1308		04.61	K Briggs	Strubby 21.03.18
BJB	996	BJB	Slingsby T.43 Skylark 3F	SSK/JPS/1		19.04.61	M Roberts *Built Jones, Pentelow & Saint*	Portmoak 26.05.19
BJC	997	BJC	EoN Olympia 2B	EoN/O/135		15.04.61	A Hoskins	Parham 16.04.19
BJF	1000	BJF	Slingsby T.21B	1309		16.06.61	Not known	Portmoak 02.08.11
BJJ	1003	–	Slingsby T.45 Swallow	1310		23.06.61	P Hardman *New owner 10.13*	Dunstable 30.08.82
BJK	1004	BJK	Slingsby T.43 Skylark 3F	1311		14.07.61	Gliding Heritage Centre	Lasham 09.08.17
BJP	1008	BJP	Slingsby T.45 Swallow	1316		04.09.61	P Hardman *New owner 8.12*	Dunstable 05.06.07
BJQ	1009	49A	Slingsby T.49A Capstan	1314		23.02.62	D Bullock	Bicester 21.06.19
–	1013	113	Slingsby T.43 Skylark 3G	1320		12.61	J McIver *Under restoration 2014*	Falgunzeon 06.07.77
BJV	1014	–	Slingsby T.21B	556	SE-SHK	15.01.62	National Museum of Flight *Stored*	East Fortune 30.04.81
BKA	1019	BKA	Slingsby T.50 Skylark 4	1326	EI-117 BGA 1019	28.05.62	Mendip Gliding Club	Halesland 29.06.19
BKC	1021	BKC	Jacobs Schweyer Weihe *Built AB Flygindustri*	231	SE-SNE Fv.8312	15.04.61	B Briggs	RAF Cranwell 01.10.12
BKE	1023	BKE	Slingsby T.43 Skylark 3F	1715/CR/1		13.07.61	Dumfries & District Gliding Club *Built C Ross*	Falgunzeon 21.10.18
BKJ	1027	BKJ/270	Schleicher Ka 6CR	565	9G-AAR	28.07.61	D J Moore *Stored 2017*	(Bristol) 24.03.06
BKK	1028	BKK	EoN Olympia 2B	EoN/O/139		07.07.61	B Kozuh	Rana, Czech Republic 13.09.19
BKL	1029	127	EoN Olympia 2B	EoN/O/134		18.06.61	M Wells & partners *'Brimstone'*	Lasham 17.08.19
BKP	1032	BKP	Slingsby T.45 Swallow	1203		08.10.61	S Grant *Under restoration 2017*	Not known 09.05.02
BKS	1035	BKS	EoN Olympia 2B	EoN/O/144		11.11.61	N W Woodward	Wycombe Air Park 29.04.19
BKU	1037	BKU	EoN Olympia 2B	EoN/O/153		01.62	D N MacKay	Aboyne 09.12.18
BLA	1043	BLA	Slingsby T.50 Skylark 4	1331		05.05.62	I E Russell	Milfield 08.06.14
BLE	1047	BLE	Slingsby T.50 Skylark 4	1335	RNGSA 1-228 BGA 1047	28.06.62	A Wilson *Under restoration 2019*	Sutton Bank 25.08.12
BLH	1050	BLH	Slingsby T.50 Skylark 4	1338	RAFGSA 305 BGA 1050	10.07.62	D Wakefield	Rufforth 11.06.17
BLJ	1051	BLJ	EoN Olympia 419X	EoN/4/009		10.01.62	I D Walton & Syndicate *'Big Bird'*	Long Mynd 03.08.16
BLK	1052	67	EoN Olympia 419X	EoN/4/007	G-APSX	13.03.62	G T Bowes *'Wild Goose'*	Seighford 29.04.19
BLN	1055	BLN	EoN Olympia 2B	EoN/O/152		07.03.62	J Stiles	Ringmer 19.05.17
BLP	1056	BLP	EoN Olympia 2B	EoN/O/149		07.03.62	R E Wooller & partners	Chipping 30.05.19
BLS	1059	BLS	EoN Olympia 2B	EoN/O/151		14.07.62	R Andrews *EoN rebuild of BGA 897 [EoN/O/128]*	Long Mynd 21.06.19
BLU	1061	BLU	Slingsby T.45 Swallow	1340		27.07.62	J M Brookes	Strubby 01.03.18
BLW	1063	303	Slingsby T.50 Skylark 4	1342		30.08.62	E D Weekes	Feshiebridge 24.06.19
BLZ	1066	BLZ	Slingsby T.50 Skylark 4	1346		26.11.62	M Hollowell	Lasham 10.05.19
BME	1071	–	Slingsby T.8 Tutor	–	VW531	28.04.62	Not known *Stored 2015*	Brentor 20.06.94

BMU	1085	'XN149'	Slingsby T.21B	1355	9G-ABD, BGA 1085	09.11.62	Boscombe Down Aviation Collection *On display 11.16*	Old Sarum 27.09.97
BMW	1087	BMW	Slingsby T.50 Skylark 4	1357		01.01.63	N Dickenson	Chipping 28.08.19
BMX	1088	739	Slingsby T.50 Skylark 4	1358	RAFGSA 16 RAFGSA 308, BGA 1088	04.01.63	Not known *Under restoration 2015*	RAF Odiham 16.04.11
BMY	1089	163	Slingsby T.50 Skylark 4	1361		26.01.63	M D Etherington & P Woodcock *Under restoration 10.15*	(S Yorks) 07.04.98
BNA	1091	–	Shenstone Harbinger Mk.2	1		12.12.62	S Edyvean	Bicester 26.11.19
BNC	1093	–	Jacobs Schweyer Weihe *Built AB Kockums Flygindustri*	1	SE-SHU	11.03.63	M Wills	Lasham 21.06.18
BNE	1095	BNE	Slingsby T.50 Skylark 4	1375		07.04.63	D Kershaw	Lasham 06.06.19
BNK	1100	BNK	Slingsby T.50 Skylark 4	1362		02.02.63	D Weekes & partners	RAF Weston-on-the-Green 18.05.19
BNM	1102	BNM	Slingsby T.50 Skylark 4	1367		28.02.63	I McIver	Falgunzeon 06.06.19
BNN	1103	BNN	Slingsby T.50 Skylark 4	1366		22.02.63	Not known	Shenington 29.05.19
BNP	1104	BNP / 653	Slingsby T.50 Skylark 4	1368	G-DBNP BGA 1104	08.03.63	Shenington Gliding Club	Shenington 23.04.17
BNQ	1105	BNQ	Slingsby T.50 Skylark 4	1369		30.03.63	D H Smith *Stored 2014*	Shenington 29.04.00
BNR	1106	BNR	Slingsby T.49B Capstan	1370		01.08.63	A Walford	Gransden Lodge 02.04.19
BNS	1107	XS652	Slingsby T.45 Swallow	1373	XS652 BGA 1107	20.03.63	P N Ling *Stored 2018*	Chipping 08.03.13
BPA	1115		Slingsby T.50 Skylark 4	1383		21.05.63	I Pattingale *Overshot field landing, Halesland 9.6.05; under restoration 2014*	Odiham 03.01.06
BPC	1117	BPC	Slingsby T.50 Skylark 4	1389		19.07.63	J L Grayer & partner	Ringmer 03.07.19
BPD	1118	N55	Slingsby T.49B Capstan	1390	RNGSA, BGA 1118	22.07.63	W den Baars *Noted 7.15*	Midden-Zeeland, Netherlands 12.11.11
BPG	1121	741	Slingsby T.50 Skylark 4	1393		18.07.63	P Orchard	Long Mynd 30.11.18
BPK	1124	BPK	Slingsby T.50 Skylark 4	1381		22.06.63	Y Marom	Crowland 21.07.15
BPL	1125	'VV401'	EoN Olympia 2B	EoN/O/136	G-APXC	15.06.63	T Henderson *As '99' In ETPS c/s*	Ringmer 16.12.18
BPS	1131	BPS	Slingsby T.49B Capstan	1399		13.09.63	Deeside Capstan Group	Aboyne 28.05.19
BPT	1132		Slingsby T.49B Capstan	1400		21.10.63	Not known *Stored 8.14*	Bicester 11.02.95
BPU	1133	BPU	Slingsby T.49B Capstan	1402		15.11.63	R Lloyd	Challock 27.07.19
BPV	1134	BPV	Slingsby T.49B Capstan	1404	RNGSA BGA 1134	20.12.63	G L Barrett	Weston-on-the-Green 25.06.19
BPW	1135		Slingsby T.49B Capstan	1408		17.01.64	W den Baars *Stored 2012*	Midden-Zeeland, Netherlands 26.01.06
BPX	1136	859	Slingsby T.45 Swallow	1397	XS859 BGA 1136	01.01.64	M Powell *Stored 8.18*	Felthorpe 14.01.08
BQE	1143	RA905	Slingsby T.7 Cadet	–	RAFGSA 273 RA905	11.08.63	Trenchard Museum *On display 12.13*	RAF Halton 14.03.00
BQF	1144	1	Slingsby T.21B	1168	XN189	14.10.63	C Mioni *For restoration 2017*	Chambley, France 13.04.02
–	1147	–	DFS Kranich II	821	RAFGSA 215 VD224	10.11.63	H Kersten & partners *Under restoration 2011*	Hahnweide, Germany 25.06.67
BQP	1152	BQP	Slingsby T.30B Prefect	646	RAFGSA 159	14.02.64	R J Brimfield	Dunstable 24.07.19
BQQ	1153	–	EoN Olympia 2B	EoN/O/121	RAFGSA 244	08.02.64	I D Smith *'Dopey'* *Rebuilt 1993 using wings from BGA 678*	Nympsfield 23.08.08
BQT	1156	BQT	EoN 460 Srs.1 (463)	EoN/S/007	BGA 2666 AGA 6, BGA 1156	26.01.64	Museum of Science & Industry	Manchester 18.04.97
BRA	1163	BRA	Slingsby T.49B Capstan	1417		24.04.64	P Hardman	Dunstable 04.06.14
BRC	1165	BRC	Slingsby T.45 Swallow 1	1407		01.05.64	RAF Scampton Heritage Centre	RAF Scampton 11.05.15
BRF	1168	904	Slingsby T.50 Skylark 4	1419		15.05.64	P Hardman	Dunstable 02.08.19
BRG	1169	BRG	Slingsby T.45 Swallow	1410		23.05.64	Not known	Not known 16.05.15
BRK	1172	G-APWL	EoN 460 Srs.1A	EoN/S/001	G-APWL BGA 1172, G-APWL, RAFGSA 268, G-APWL	26.04.64	AFE Pilot Shop *On display 11.18*	Kidlington 26.04.00
BRL	1173	BRL	EoN Olympia 2B	EoN/O/132		12.05.64	R J Lockett	Wormingford 12.09.14
BRQ	1177	BRQ	EoN 460 Srs.1C	EoN/S/003	G-ARFU	10.06.64	J Steel & partners *Stored 2.14*	Falgunzeon 04.08.96
BRW	1183	BRW	Slingsby T.49B Capstan	1413		25.06.64	D A Sinclair	Lasham 24.04.19
BRZ	1186	BRZ	Slingsby T.51 Dart 15	1435		16.07.64	D Bullock *Stored 9.14*	Bicester 21.03.94
BSC	1189	BSC	Slingsby T.50 Skylark 4	1422		25.08.64	A P Stacey *'Moonraker'*	Keevil 22.04.09
BSE	1191	BSE	Slingsby T.49B Capstan	1414		11.09.64	C Raine	Haddenham 03.07.19
BSH	1194	BSH	Slingsby T.50 Skylark 4	1444		03.11.64	C Ashman	Rattlesden 04.95.19
BSK	1196	BSK	Slingsby T.49B Capstan	1418	RNGSA LS32 BGA 1196	21.10.64	Not known	Portmoak 06.09.17
BSM	1198	597	Slingsby T.51 Dart 15	1439		30.10.64	Gliding Heritage Centre	Lasham 29.05.06
BSQ	1201	463	EoN 460 Srs.1 (463)	EoN/S/014		01.05.64	J S Halford	Eyres Field 03.10.19
BSR	1202	BSR	Slingsby T.50 Skylark 4	1443		17.12.64	Not known	Portmoak 17.08.17
BSV	1206	BSV	Slingsby T.51 Dart 15	1454		29.07.65	McLean Aviation *Stored 7.14*	Rufforth 11.02.97

BSW	1207	BSW	Slingsby T.51 Dart 15	1459		19.02.65	B L Owen	Tibenham 25.09.08
							Stored 2018	
BSZ	1210	BSZ	Slingsby T.50 Skylark 4	1460		26.04.65	I Sullivan	Challock 11.01.20
BTA	1211	'XS651'	Slingsby T.45 Swallow	1473	RNGSA LS33, BGA 1211	24.06.65	621 VGS Historic Flight	Little Rissington 28.07.17
BTE	1215	BTE	Slingsby T.21B	557	OH-KSA SE-SHL	22.01.65	M Nussbaumer *'Buttercup'*	Spitzberg, Austria 21.12.19
BTH	1218	BTH	Slingsby T.21B	JHB/2		12.03.65	A G Linfield	Shenington 02.07.18
			Built from parts by J Hulme; restored 1995 with wings from BGA 3238					
BTK	1220	BTK	Slingsby T.50 Skylark 4	1364	SE-SZW	06.03.65	S Foster	Long Mynd 08.05.19
BTN	1223	BTN	EoN 460 Srs.1 (463)	EoN/S/022	AGA 15 BGA 1223	21.03.65	P Thomas	Dunstable 07.10.19
BTQ	1225	BTQ	EoN 460 Srs.1 (463)	EoN/S/029		04.04.65	R Hobson	Darlton 24.02.19
BTU	1229	BTU	EoN 460 Srs.1 (463)	EoN/S/026		24.04.65	S Gibson	Gransden Lodge 25.03.93
							Stored 8.18	
BTV	1230	BTV	Jacobs Schweyer Weihe	000358	RAFGGA	07.05.65	I Dunkley	Omaka, New Zealand 11.08.07
							Under restoration 4.11; reserved as ZK-GAR; not taken up	
BUC	1237	A23	Slingsby T.49B Capstan	1472		27.06.65	Not known	Seighford 17.08.19
BUE	1239	BUE	Slingsby T.50 Skylark 4	1468	RNGSA 103 BGA 1239	07.65	G J Jones	Seighford 03.05.19
BUR	1249	BUR	Slingsby T.49B Capstan	1482		18.11.65	R J Playle	Shenington 20.06.19
BUT	1251	BUT	Slingsby T.43 Skylark 3F	VRT.1		03.07.65	I Bannister tr Sky Syndicate	Chipping 24.05.19
			Built V & R Tull					
BUU	1252	BUU	EoN Baby	EoN/B/048	RAFGSA 255	09.04.65	R H Short *'Top Banana'*	Lyveden 04.08.19
BUV	1253		EoN 460 Srs.1 (463)	EoN/S/030		10.07.65	Not known	Not known 22.05.19
BUW	1254	WB945	Slingsby T.21B	612	RAFGSA 242 WB945	12.08.65	Not known	RAF Halton 09.08.06
							Stored 10.16	
–	1255	–	Slingsby T.31B	684	RAFGSA WT874	21.07.65	D Bullock	Bicester 22.07.71
							Under restoration 2014; wings from BGA 1070	
BVF	1263	BVF	Slingsby T.45 Swallow	1481		12.11.65	J S Morgan	Not known 19.09.19
BVJ	1266	BVJ	Slingsby T.51 Dart 17R	1486		01.01.66	A P Stacey	RAF Keevil 14.06.07
							Hit hedge on landing, Chedworth, Glos. 5.5.07; stored 1.12	
BVM	1269	150	Slingsby T.51 Dart 17R	1492		24.01.66	N H Ponsford	Selby 25.07.90
							Stored 2015	
BVS	1274	BVS	SZD-9bis Bocian 1D	F-831		16.10.65	T Wrobel	(Stamford) 28.07.01
							Stored 2018	
BVT	1275		EoN 460 Srs.1 (463)	EoN/S/045		22.09.65	B L Cooper	RAF Odiham 28.08.92
							Stored 6.14	
BVW	1278	403	EoN Olympia 403	EoN/4/001	RAFGSA 306 G-APEW	20.08.65	F G Bradney	Lasham 25.08.19
BWB	1283	B96	EoN 460 Srs.1 (463)	EoN/S/036		28.11.65	R Sage	Priory Farm, Tibenham 17.12.03
							Stored 10.16	
BWE	1286	BWE	EoN 460 Srs.1 (463)	EoN/S/035		30.12.65	J M Turner	Challock 23.05.19
BWG	1288	465	EoN 465 Srs.2	EoN/S/038		07.12.65	Museum of Berkshire Aviation	Woodley 27.04.97
							On display 3.18	
BWU	1300	BWU	EoN 460 Srs.1 (463)	EoN/S/034		21.01.66	S H Gibson	Skelling Farm, Skirwith 16.04.20
BWX	1303	BWX	EoN Olympia 2B	101		02.02.66	R Birch	Aston Down 23.04.16
			Built from parts				*Damaged in heavy landing, Aston Down 27.6.15; on rebuild 2019*	
BXK	1315		Slingsby T.21B	1510		20.06.66	Not known	Rufforth 18.07.80
							Damaged Falgunzeon 18.5.80: current status unknown	
BXP	1319	BXP	Slingsby T.45 Swallow 2	1522		19.07.66	R J Poole	Chipping 14.07.19
BYA	1330	BYA	Slingsby T.51 Dart 17R	1518		23.07.66	A P Stacey	RAF Keevil 18.05.05
							Damaged Easterton 15.8.04; fuselage stored 1.12	
BYB	1331	'XS651'	Slingsby T.45 Swallow	1525		29.07.66	D Clarke	Parham 21.08.19
BYE	1334	BYE	EoN 460 Srs.1 (463)	EoN/S/044		22.09.66	B Liddiard	Ringmer 17.05.19
BYJ	1338	BYJ	Slingsby T.45 Swallow	1568		24.02.67	J R Furnell	Milnathort 11.03.15
							Stored 2018	
BYK	1339	BYK	Slingsby T.45 Swallow	1566	OO-YWL BGA 1339	12.01.67	G Western	Rattlesden 14.05.19
–	1346	–	Slingsby T.31B	?	RAFGSA 297	08.06.66	D & S Firth	Doncaster 24.01.79
							For restoration 2018	
BYY	1352	BYY	Slingsby T.21B	628	RAFGSA 338 WB967	12.11.66	T Akerman	Poitiers, France 28.06.02
							Stored 2017	
BZA	1354	BZA	Slingsby T.21B	1162	RAFGSA 318 XN183	28.11.66	M Diehl & partners	Nastätten, Germany 07.05.19
BZG	1360	BZG	Slingsby T.49B Capstan	1581	RNGSA BGA 1360	28.04.67	J D Huband & partners	Aston Down 19.06.19
BZL	1364	BZL	Slingsby T.45 Swallow	1596		12.07.67	Cairngorm Swallow Syndicate	Feshiebridge 05.06.13
BZM	1365	BZM	Slingsby T.45 Swallow	1597		12.07.67	Gliding Heritage Centre	Lasham 02.08.19
BZP	1367	F4	SZD-24-4A Foka 4	W-301		24.01.67	M Owen	(Southport) 03.06.04
							Stored 2014	
BZR	1369	BZR	EoN 460 Srs.1 (463)	EoN/S/049		15.02.67	M Armstrong	Camphill 14.02.19
BZV	1373	BZV	EoN 460 Srs.1 (463)	EoN/S/046		15.02.67	Gliding Heritage Centre	Lasham 28.08.19

BGA

BZY	1376	BZY	Slingsby T.31B	SSK/FF1817	BGA 1175	16.03.67	D Bramwell (*The Blue Brick Syndicate*)	Thame	29.07.1
							Rebuild of BGA 1175		
CAB	1379	CAB	EoN 460 Srs.1 (463)	EoN/S/033	RAFGSA 344	22.03.67	R Hobson	(Darlton)	21.10.98
							New owner 5.17		
CAF	1382	CAF	EoN Olympia 2B	EoN/O/131	RAFGSA 254	05.04.67	M Auberger	Germany	17.07.05
							Under restoration 2009		
CAT	1394	CAT	EoN 460 Srs.1 (463)	EoN/S/051		13.05.67	P S Whitehead	Skelling Farm, Skirwith	08.10.18
CAX	1398	CAX	Slingsby T.45 Swallow	1598		24.07.67	A J Pettitt	Rivar Hill	28.07.19
CBK	1410	–	Grunau Baby III	?	RAFGSA 378	05.09.67	P Bedford	Dromod, Co Leitrim	02.04.83
			Built Sfg. Schaffin		D-4676		*Preserved at Cavan & Leitrim Railway 6.18*		
CBU	1419	905	Schempp-Hirth SHK-1	53		17.10.67	M J Dodd	(Shobdon)	26.12.99
							Stored 2010		
–	1424	–	Slingsby T.8 Tutor	SSK/FF27	RAFGSA 214	11.10.67	P Bedford	Dromod, Co Leitrim	04.04.78
					RA877		*Preserved at Cavan & Leitrim Railway 6.18*		
CCS	1441	CCS	Slingsby T.41 Skylark 2	1008	PH-230	08.03.68	Lincolnshire Gliding Club	Strubby	18.06.13
–	1461	–	EoN Primary	?		30.05.68	Norfolk & Suffolk Aviation Museum	Flixton	29.05.69
CDR	1464	CDR	Scheibe Bergfalke III	5625		12.08.68	B Pearson	Eaglescott	02.04.04
							Fuselage stored 5.17		
CDX	1470	CDX	SZD-30 Pirat	W-392		04.06.68	Newark Air Museum	Darlton	06.01.07
CEH	1480	CEH	Wassmer WA-22 Super Javelot	68	F-OTAN-C6	12.07.68	N A Mills	Wycombe Air Park	11.07.15
					F-CCLU				
CEK	1482	–	Slingsby T.21B (T)	1151	RAFGSA 369	19.07.68	D Woolerton	North Coates	07.05.05
					XN147		*Stored 3.17*		
CGU	1539	CGU	EoN Olympia 2B	EoN/O/115	RAFGSA 157	10.04.69	R Shackleton	Chipping	30.05.19
					RAFGSA 228				
CGV	1540	CGV	PIK-16C Vasama	48		11.04.69	D J Osborne & partners	Currock Hill	16.07.18
CHE	1549	CHE	Slingsby T.41 Skylark 2	DSS002		09.06.69	M D Etherington & P Woodcock	(S Yorks)	30.05.05
							Stored 2015		
CHK	1554	CHK	EoN Olympia 2B	EoN/O/130	RAFGSA 134	03.06.69	L R Saker & P Hooke	Halesland	04.04.18
					RAFGSA 253				
CHQ	1559		Slingsby T.31B	1186	RAFGSA 316	21.06.69	N H Ponsford	Wigan	01.07.82
					XN247		*Stored 2006*		
CJC	1571	–	Ginn-Lesniak Kestrel	1		10.10.69	J Sharp	Wattisham	25.03.02
							Stored 6.13		
CJL	1579	222	Schempp-Hirth SHK-1	42	OO-ZLG	14.02.70	M F Brook	(W Yorks.)	29.06.06
							Stored 2017		
–	1588		Slingsby T.21B	1167	XN188	21.03.70	V Meers	(Wolverhampton)	03.02.78
							Stored 2008		
–	1599	–	Slingsby T.8 Tutor	JHB5 / SSK/FF918	VW506	05.70	M H Simms	Shipdham	17.05.79
							Under restoration 5.09		
CKJ	1601		Slingsby T.30B Prefect	740	PH-197	27.04.71	Not known	Crosshill	14.04.90
							Stored 2008		
CLC	1619	CLC	Slingsby T.21B	1200	RNGSA 2-07	18.11.70	K G Reid & W Cook	Rivar Hill	09.07.19
–	1625	–	EoN Primary	EoN/P/035	WP267	08.02.71	T Akerman	Poitiers, France	07.02.72
							Under restoration 2018		
CLK	1626	CLK	Schleicher K 7 (Mod.)	607	D-5714	01.02.71	Dartmoor Gliding Society	Brentor	20.08.08
							Stored 7.13		
CYL	1639	CYL	Schempp-Hirth Gö 3 Minimoa	378	PH-390	20.03.72	F K Russell *'Terry McGee'*	Dunstable	13.06.19
					D-5076, RAFGGA				
CNV	1683	229	Slingsby T59F Kestrel 19	1790		22.06.72	R Birch	(Aston Down)	25.03.07
							Groundlooped on field landing near Kintbury 30.5.06;		
							awaiting repair 2010		
CPE	1692		EoN Olympia 2B	EoN/O/120	RAFGSA 133	22.03.72	M Breen	Hazlemere	09.08.95
					RAFGSA 233		*Stored 10.09*		
CPK	1697	VV400	EoN Olympia 2	EoN/O/027	VV400	18.04.72	R Birch	Aston Down	08.05.19
					BGA 558		*In ETPS c/s, coded '97'*		
CPL	1698	CPL	Slingsby T.8 Tutor	SSK/FF477	RAFGSA 183	26.04.72	B Cooper *'Mistress Tutor'*	Lasham	11.04.18
CPQ	1702	695	Torva Sprite TA Srs.2	003		14.07.74	McLean Aviation	Rufforth	11.06.84
							Stored 4.18		
CPZ	1711	'D-12-354'	Aachen FVA.10B Rheinland	?	RAFGGA 521	12.04.72	Deutsches Segelflugmuseum		
					S-58		*On display 2018*	Wasserkuppe, Germany	24.08.96
CQF	1717		SZD-36A Cobra 15	W-565		18.03.72	Not known	Hinton-in-the-Hedges	03.07.87
							Stored 9.16		
CQG	1718	CQG	EoN Olympia 2B	EoN/O/044	RAFGSA 126	24.04.72	R D Bryce-Smith	Gransden Lodge	06.09.14
					RAFGSA 26, RAFGSA 206, (BGA 542)				
CQW	1732		SZD-36A Cobra 15	W-572		08.06.72	P Zelazowski	Shenington	03.11.07
							Stored 3.15		
CQX	1733	789	SZD-30 Pirat	B-483		09.06.72	2247 Sqn ATC	Hawarden	06.07.01
							Noted 4.16		
CRF	1741	351	Birmingham Guild BG-135	001		28.02.72	C D Stevens	Lee-on-Solent	02.05.15
CRK	1745	–	Slingsby T.8 Tutor	930	XE760	25.07.72	R Birch	(Aston Down)	28.08.82
					VM539		*Stored 2018*		
CRM	1747	–	Grunau Baby III	1	RAFGSA 361	27.07.72	Not known *'Grumpy'*	(Long Mynd)	26.11.96
					D-8061		*New owners 2015*		
CRX	1757	CRX	Slingsby T.41 Skylark 2B	1146	RNGSA WAB42	07.10.72	K Oman	Slovenia	23.07.19

–	1759	–	Slingsby T.8 Tutor		–	RAFGSA 178	15.10.72	The Helicopter Museum	Weston-super-Mare 15.07.77
								Fuselage on display 6.18	
CSL	1770		Slingsby T.8 Tutor	928	XE758		15.10.72	W den Baars Midden-Zeeland, Netherlands 19.09.00	
					VF181			*Stored 9.15*	
CSU	1778	–	Manuel Hawk	1			24.11.72	Gliding Heritage Centre	Lasham 23.05.82
CSV	1779	CSV	SZD-30 Pirat	B-515			03.12.72	Not known	Darlton 20.03.06
								Stored 8.14	
CTZ	1807	CTZ	Schleicher K 8B	8035/B5	D-KOCU		03.04.73	Not known	Portmoak 12.09.07
					D-5203			*Stored 8.15*	
CVC	1832	CVC	SZD-30 Pirat	B-535			04.03.73	T J Wilkinson	Sackville Lodge, Riseley 20.07.08
								Stored 9.17	
CVJ	1838	CVJ	Breguet 905S Fauvette	37	F-CCJH		29.06.73	McLean Aviation	Rufforth 22.05.02
								Stored 4.18	
–	1872	D-5627	Schleicher Rhönlerche II	390	D-5627		22.04.73	Sailplane Preservation Group Brighton Shoreham 18.11.76	
								Stored 5.11	
CWV	1873	Z	Schleicher Rhönlerche II	123	D-8226		22.04.73	J S Morgan	Pershore 26.05.94
								Stored 2014	
CYJ	1910	–	Grunau Baby IIB	031000	D-6021		11.08.73	Gliding Heritage Centre	Lasham 13.01.90
			Built Petera 1943					*Fuselage on display 8.17*	
CYK	1911	248	Pilatus B4-PC11	078			28.08.73	I Trotter	Portmoak 31.03.07
								Stored 2016	
CYN	1914	N4	Slingsby T59D Kestrel 19	JP/054			02.10.74	S J Cooke & partners	Gransden Lodge 16.12.19
			Built D Jones & T Pentelow						
CYV	1921	CYV	Birmingham Guild BG-135	5			21.09.73	E J Gunner	Kingston Deverill 19.05.14
CYX	1923		EoN Olympia 419	EoN/4/006	RAFGSA 86		18.11.73	M L Boxall	Sutton Bank 07.08.93
					RAFGSA 249			*Stored 3.14*	
CZK	1935		Grunau Baby III	?	RAFGSA 366		05.04.74	W den Baars Midden-Zeeland, Netherlands 28.10.95	
					D-8510, WBLV S-161			*Stored 8.09; reserved as PH-221 5.12*	
CZM	1937	CZM	München Mü 13D III	10/52	D-1488		08.12.73	R Kracht	Germany 22.08.17
DAR	1965	DAR	Slingsby T.21B	SSK/FF1280	RAFGSA 404		01.06.74	P T Nash	Upwood 07.08.19
DBA	1974	207	EoN Olympia 2B	EoN/O/156	RNGSA 208		25.05.74	W R Williams	RAF Halton 20.06.04
								Noted 11.14	
DBU	1992	–	Schempp-Hirth Gö 4 Goevier II	557	D-5233		13.07.74	R Arnold	Abbots Bromley 19.07.87
								Stored 2017	
DCB	1999	–	Fauvel AV.36CR	133	RAFGSA		04.10.74	The Shuttleworth Collection	
					F-CBSH			Shuttleworth (Old Warden) 19.03.19	
DCE	2002	DCE	Slingsby T.41 Skylark 2B	1003	RAFGGA 540		25.10.74	J Salvin	Darlton 23.05.16
					PH-225				
DCN	2010		Slingsby T.21B	1250	RAFGSA 501		31.12.74	M R Dawson	(Vinax, France) 16.07.95
					RAFGSA 287, BGA 943			*Stored 2017*	
DCZ	2021	DCZ	King-Elliott-Street Osprey 2	1470			10.75	G R Thurston	(Halesworth) 06.11.07
			Built using Dart fuselage (c/n 1457) from unregistered Chard Osprey; Dart c/n 1470 was BGA 1245						
DDC	2024	DDC	Slingsby T.21B	1157	RAFGSA 313		01.03.75	J S Shaw	Orbigny, France 29.03.09
					XN153			*Stored 8.17*	
DDQ	2036	–	Slingsby T.21B	630	RAFGSA 247		23.06.76	South Yorkshire Aircraft Museum	Doncaster 08.10.80
					WB969			*Damaged 24.8.80; frame on display 4.18*	
DFP	2082	DFP	Aeromere M.100S	029	I-LSUO		23.11.75	D Ottevanger	Nistelrode, Netherlands 23.02.03
								To PH-1605 7.18	
DFY	2091	DFY	Schempp-Hirth Standard Cirrus	396	AGA .		05.11.75	Science Museum	South Kensington 03.03.92
								On display 3.17	
DHY	2139	DHY	Schleicher K 7	1137	RAFGSA 266		14.04.76	G Whittaker	Chipping 21.01.07
					D-5162			*Stored 6.17*	
DJF	2146	500	Halford JSH Scorpion	001			14.03.77	Gliding Heritage Centre	Lasham 12.80
DJG	2147	K2	Schleicher Ka 2B	231	D-6179		22.06.76	Not known	North Hill 10.06.01
								Noted 4.15	
DJP	2154	DJP	Schleicher K 8B	8588	RAFGSA 335		20.07.76	Sackville Vintage Gliding Club	
								Stored 9.15	Sackville Lodge, Riseley 17.06.03
DLX	2210	539	Slingsby T.45 Swallow	1494	RAFGGA 539		03.02.77	RAF Museum Laarbruch	Weeze, Germany 29.05.99
DLZ	2212	DLZ	Swales SD3-15T	03			16.12.76	R Harris	Rivar Hill 28.09.19
DNB	2238	S1+1-11	Grunau Baby IIB	2	RAFGSA 380		19.04.11	D Bramwell & partners	Thame 07.09.18
			Built Flg.u.Arbeitsg.Hall		D-5766, D-8039				
DPG	2267	DPG	München Mü 13D III	005	D-1327		13.06.77	Gliding Heritage Centre	Lasham 24.09.14
DPT	2278	DPT	Scheibe L-Spatz 55	01	RAFGSA		24.08.77	McLean Aviation	Rufforth 12.07.98
								Stored 4.18	
DPZ	2284	HB-561	Slingsby T.34A Sky	822	HB-561		08.08.77	M Borrowdale & partners	Lasham 03.07.00
								Under restoration 2015	
DQD	2288	DQD	Slingsby T.8 Tutor	–			25.08.77	M Smith	Brentor 20.04.12
			Assembled F Breeze from parts						
DQV	2304	DQV	Slingsby T.45 Swallow	1514	RAFGGA 527		03.07.78	Not known	Strubby 19.03.83
								Fuselage stored 8.14	
DSA	2333	DSA	Slingsby T.30B Prefect	575	WE985		10.02.78	J M Turner	Challock 09.03.19
DSM	2344	–	Fauvel AV.22S	3	F-CCGM		25.05.80	I Dunkley	Akaroa, New Zealand 05.01.11
DSN	2345	893	Grob G102 Astir CS77	1698			23.03.78	J J M Riach	Feshiebridge 27.06.04
								Damaged 22.5.04; stored 10.16	

BGA

DTR	2372	DTR	EoN Olympia 401	EoN/4/005	NEJSGSA 7	30.05.78	S Hoy		Wattisham 24.05.19
					RAFGSA 401, RAFGSA 252, G-APSI				
DTZ	2380	S30	Slingsby T.30B Prefect	573	WE983	20.06.78	D J Gibbs		Saltby 16.07.12
							Stored 2017		
DUC	2383	–	CARMAM M-100S Mésange	012	F-CCSA	06.06.78	North East Aircraft Museum		Usworth 06.05.88
							Stored 5.16		
DUD	2384	–	Grunau Baby III	?	(BGA 2074)	06.06.78	Norfolk & Suffolk Aviation Museum		Flixton 29.03.92
					RAFGSA 374, D-9142				
DWF	2433	DWF	Grunau Baby IIB	–	AGA 16	19.04.80	S Slater		Bicester 09.01.02
					RAFGSA 220, RNGSA 1-13, VW743			*Under restoration 2015*	
DXU	2470	56	Slingsby T59J Kestrel 22	1867	G-BDWZ	11.04.79	I Kennedy		Usk 14.12.19
DXY	2474	HB-474	Müller Moswey III	–	HB-474	20.04.79	B Pearson		Eaglescott 22.06.12
							Noted 2019		
DZC	2498	DZC	Scheibe L-Spatz 55	642	RAFGGA 502	04.05.79	Kringloopwinkel De Wissel	Assen, Netherlands 23.10.98	
					D-5629		*On display 2.17*		
DZS	2512	DZS	SZD-8bis-0 Jaskolka	183	HB-583	30.05.79	R A Wilgoss		Wycombe Air Park 02.07.16
DZX	2517	–	Slingsby T.30B Prefect	577	WE987	08.06.79	South Yorkshire Aircraft Museum		Doncaster 17.07.89
							On display 4.18		
EAP	2533	R31	Schleicher ASK 13	13609	RAFGSA R31	19.07.79	Not known		Bicester 27.01.05
					BGA 2533		*Stored 9.14*		
EBC	2546	EBC	Slingsby T.30B Prefect	1060	RAFGSA 33	01.08.79	K R Reeves *'Jonathan Livingstone Prefect'*		
					BGA 1618, BGA 808				RAF Cranwell 04.06.17
EBE	2548	EBE	Issoire E78 Silene	07	G-EEBE	20.11.79	K S Wells & partners		Lyveden 21.09.14
					BGA 2548				
EBP	2557	EBP	Allgaier Geier I	3/4	D-9025	04.09.79	E Seibold & partners	Kempten, Germany 21.07.01	
					D-4093, D-1434		*Noted 5.15*		
ECR	2583	WE990	Slingsby T.30B Prefect	580	WE990	07.11.79	D Ladley		Tibenham 21.07.14
EDD	2595	W17	Schleicher ASW 17	17043	D-6865	23.04.80	M D Etherington		(Saltby) 14.12.05
							Under restoration 2015		
EDL	2602	–	Focke-Wulf Weihe 50	4	D-0893	26.01.80	A Middleton		Saltby 14.10.96
					HB-555		*Under restoration 2014*		
EGQ	2678	EGQ	Schleicher K 7 (Mod.)	7200	D-4114	25.07.80	McLean Aviation		Rufforth 22.06.96
							Fuselage for restoration 2014		
EHB	2689	EHB	Schleicher Ka 3	3	RAFGGA 559	23.10.80	Gliding Heritage Centre		Lasham 03.05.17
EHE	2692	WE992	Slingsby T.30B Prefect	582	WE992	29.09.80	A P Stacey		Little Rissington 13.07.16
EHX	2709	EHX	Grunau Baby IIB	134	D-1128	21.12.80	W R Williams		RAF Odiham 21.06.19
EJJ	2720	'WJ306'	Slingsby T.21B	618	RAFGSA 120	01.03.81	A C Jarvis		Parham 19.04.19
					BGA 662, WB957		*See BGA 3240 for original WJ306*		
EKT	2753	EKT	Wassmer WA-30 Bijave	241	G-DEKT	11.05.81	Not known		Dunstable 30.09.14
					BGA 2753, F-CDML				
ELC	2762	ELC	Slingsby T.45 Swallow	1474	AGA	25.05.81	Not known		Wingland 21.01.11
					RAFGSA 346		*Stored 4.16*		
ELH	2767	ELH	Slingsby T.21B	?	RAFGSA 314	16.09.81	L Tibaldi		Brescia, Italy 10.07.91
					RAF		*Possibly ex WB966 [627]; under restoration 2012*		
ELL	2770	ELL	Vogt Lo 100 Zwergreiher	25	HB-591	27.07.81	LO100 Syndicate		RAF Halton 14.05.16
ELS	2776	ELS	EoN 460 Srs.1 (463)	EoN/S/020	RAFGGA 530	07.02.82	D G Shepherd		Easterton 10.07.14
ELV	2779	ELV	Scheibe Zugvogel IIIB	1088	F-CCPX	05.09.81	D Chidley		Lasham 20.07.19
EMW	2804	17	Grunau Baby III	?	D-1373	05.07.89	M T Sands	Santo Tome del Puerto, Spain 11.07.19	
ENY	2830		Schleicher ASK 13	13606	RAFGSA R17	22.07.82	Aquila Gliding Club	Hinton-in-the-Hedges 02.06.04	
							Fuselage stored 2015		
EPR	2847	EPR	Hütter H.17	–	(Kenya),	30.09.82	D Shrimpton		Parham 18.06.10
					PH-269				
EPZ	2855	D-4012	Scheibe Bergfalke II/55	370	D-4012	15.01.83	A P Stacey & R Fretwell		RAF Keevil 11.08.96
							Stored 4.11		
EQM	2866		Rocheteau-Scheibe CRA-60 Fauconnet	03K	F-CDNR	18.01.86	Not known	Ley Farm, Chirk 30.06.01	
							Stored 9.17		
EQP	2869	–	Glaser-Dirks DG-202/17	2-187/1761		10.03.83	Cotswold Gliding Club		Aston Down 22.10.92
							Cockpit in use as simulator 2017; remainder dumped		
EQY	2878	–	BAC.VII rep	01		08.09.91	D Rogers		(Middlesex) 21.05.96P
				Rebuild of BAC Drone with wings of G-AEJR & new fuselage) (Being refurbished as powered aircraft						
ERB	2881	ERB	Slingsby T.50 Skylark 4 Special	001		25.04.83	S Trengove		Shenington 22.05.16
				Fuselage built by C Almack; wings from Skylark 3B parts at Doncaster Sailplanes						
ERW	2900	ERW	Slingsby T.21B	1130	RAFGSA 237	24.05.83	N J Jardine		Llantisilio 11.06.05
					BGA 842				
ERZ	2903	ERZ	Oberlerchner Mg 19a Steinadler	015	OE-0324	01.06.83	Gliding Heritage Centre		Lasham 09.11.19
ESK	2913	ESK	Schleicher Ka 2B	697	RAFGGA 594	23.07.83	W R Williams		RAF Halton 20.05.00
					D-5947		*Stored 10.16*		
EUN	2964	–	Slingsby T.21B	588	RAFGSA R92	20.04.84	N I Newton		Wycombe Air Park 26.06.19
					RAFGSA 212, WB925				
EVN	2988	EVN	Monnett Monerai	312	BGA 3190	07.11.87	Ulster Aviation Society	Long Kesh 11.88	
					(BGA 2988)		*New owner 3.17*		
FAK	3104	FAK	Avialsa A.60 Fauconnet	104K	F-CDFG	12.05.85	Not known		(Huntingdon) 09.05.01
							For sale 6.17		
FCC	3145	XN243	Slingsby T.31B	1182	XN243	06.05.85	G Smith		Lasham 25.11.12
FCF	3148	993	Slingsby T.21B	MHL.017	WB990	12.05.85	G D Pullen		Lasham 22.07.19

BGA

FCT	3160	WB944	Slingsby T.21B	611	WB944	16.12.86	D A Bullock	Bicester 05.05.15
FCZ	3166	–	Slingsby T.1 Falcon I replica *Built Southdown Aero Services*	–		09.07.85	Gliding Heritage Centre	Lasham 20.05.19
FDC	3169	FDC	Pottier JP 15-34 Kit Club	TAH.50/60		10.03.87	G Winch	Wormingford 24.08.18
FDQ	3181	FDQ	Slingsby T.31B	710	WT915	19.09.85	J F Forster *'Chris Wills'*	Brüggen, Germany 19.04.10
FDY	3189	FDY	Slingsby T.21B	MHL.005	WB978	26.01.86	R Lloyd *'Florence'*	Challock 14.06.19
FED	3194	WT914	Slingsby T.31B	709	WT914	08.02.86	East Midlands Aeropark	East Midlands 07.02.87
FEE	3195	–	Slingsby T.21B	MHL.016	WB989	20.01.86	K Schickling	Aschaffenburg, Germany 25.04.19
FEZ	3214	–	EoN Primary	EoN/P/037	RAFGSA R13 RAFGSA 113, WP269	19.09.86	A P Stacey *Stored 10.16*	Little Rissington 03.06.01
FFQ	3229	FFQ	Slingsby T.31B	913	XE800	18.08.86	W J Stoney	Lasham 09.07.19
FFW	3235	FFW	Slingsby T.21B	1155	XN151	03.10.87	R Schmid *Stored 2013*	Aalen-Elchingen, Germany 02.07.11
FFZ	3238	WB981	Slingsby T.21B	MHL.008	WB981	21.08.86	Not known	Eaglescott 18.06.13
FGA	3239	WT913	Slingsby T.31B	708	WT913	26.10.86	South Yorkshire Aircraft Museum *Fuselage on display 8.17*	Doncaster 21.07.96
FGB	3240	WJ306	Slingsby T.21B	654	WJ306	23.08.86	Oxford Gliding Club RAF Weston-on-the-Green 21.08.19 *'Daisy' – BGA 2720 also carries 'WJ306'*	
FGC	3241		Slingsby T.31B	713	WT918	24.08.86	K Litek	Ahlhorn, Germany 12.09.19
FGE	3243	–	Slingsby T.21B	619	WB958	26.09.87	M Simms *For restoration 1.19*	Bellarena 21.04.93
FGG	3245	WG498	Slingsby T.21B	665	WG498	29.09.86	R Birch & partners	Aston Down 06.05.19
FGM	3250	FGM	Slingsby T.21B	1160	XN156	19.07.87	R B Petrie	Portmoak 15.03.18
FGS	3255	XN157	Slingsby T.21B	1161	XN157	11.10.86	D W Cole	Long Mynd 18.11.18
FHC	3265	–	Slingsby T.21B	MHL.013	WB986	07.06.87	S Hazelton & partners *New owners 2018*	(Kent) 16.03.97
FHK	3272	WT900	Slingsby T.31B	695	WT900	22.04.87	A Hepburn & partners	Saltby 04.05.19
FHQ	3277	–	Hols der Teufel reproduction *Built M L Beach*	001		21.03.90	Deutsches Segelflugmuseum *On display 2018* Wasserkuppe, Germany N/E	
FJA	3287	FJA	Slingsby T.21B	1152	XN148	08.07.87	M Steiner Lachen-Speyerdorf, Germany 19.04.19	
FJB	3288	FJB	Slingsby T.21B	MHL.002	WB975	08.07.87	E Moskovits *As 'WB975' 'Big Daddy'*	Atkar, Hungary 18.03.18
FJD	3290	T21	Slingsby T.21B	MHL.007	WB980	29.08.87	The Gliding Centre	Husbands Bosworth 02.05.19
FJF	3292	FJF	Slingsby T.21B	586	WB923	07.09.87	R L Horsnell	Snitterfield 26.05.19
FKP	3324	WB971	Slingsby T.21B	632	WB971	28.02.88	M Powell	Felthorpe 19.03.13
FLB	3336	XA295/D	Slingsby T.31B	837	XA295	23.08.88	B Pearson *Stored 5.16*	Eaglescott 06.12.13
FLN	3348	FLN	Schleicher K 8B *Built KK Lehtovaara O/Y*	07	OH-316 OH-RTP	07.05.88	Not known *Stored 4.16*	Wingland 04.05.02
FMA	3359	–	Slingsby T.38 Grasshopper	793	WZ797	08.08.88	Not known *Stored 9.10*	Shipdham 07.08.89
FMR	3374	FMR	Neukom Standard Elfe S-2	05	HB-801	08.11.88	M A Braddock & partners	Camphill 10.04.09
FNC	3385	WB934	Slingsby T.21B	601	WB934	05.11.88	R Fehlhaber Koblenz-Winningen, Germany 11.05.19	
FNX	3404		Wassmer WA 30 Bijave	84	F-CCTJ	02.01.89	Not known *Stored 4.16*	Wingland 17.01.05
FPS	3423	–	Slingsby T.21B	MHL.001		03.02.89	D Semmler Brandenburg-Mühlenfeld, Germany 09.06.17 G-DFPS, BGA 3423, OH-914X, LN-GAO, BGA 3423, WB974	
FQE	3435	FQE	Schleicher K 8B	3	D-6329	03.04.89	Not known *New owner 1.16*	Portishead 09.04.01
FRG	3461	FRG	Siebert Sie 3	3009	D-0739	07.04.89	A Cridge	Talgarth 13.05.13
FRQ	3469	XT653	Slingsby T.45 Swallow	1420	XT653	27.04.89	D Shrimpton	RAF Keevil 07.06.14
FSB	3480	–	Slingsby T.38 Grasshopper	1269	XP492	R	Not known *Stored 2005; new owner 1.16*	Eyres Field
FSC	3481	WZ755	Slingsby T.38 Grasshopper	751	WZ755	27.04.90	Tettenhall Transport Heritage Centre *On display 7.16* Wolverhampton 30.04.93	
FSJ	3487	WT908	Slingsby T.31B	703	WT908	22.05.89	R J Brimfield	Dunstable 02.08.19
FSK	3488	WZ795	Slingsby T.38 Grasshopper	791	WZ795	26.06.89	E Janssen	Lemelerveld, Netherlands 28.05.19
FSV	3498	WZ819	Slingsby T.38 Grasshopper	800	WZ819	26.06.89	P D Mann *Stored 1.12*	RAF Halton 06.06.04
FTM	3514	–	Schleicher K 8B	513	D-5708	30.08.89	Not known *Stored 6.16*	Ringmer 09.04.06
FUW	3545	XE807	Slingsby T.31B	920	XE807	20.11.89	G Tischler	Germany 10.07.10
FVA	3548	N15	Schleicher K 8B	1051	D-5117	13.04.90	Portsmouth Naval Gliding Club Lee-on-Solent 18.10.06 *To Germany as D-9761 .18*	
FZT	3661	FZT	Hütter H 17 *Built by John Lee*	7		R	W Stoney	Lasham
FZU	3662		Slingsby T.38 Grasshopper	761	WZ765	08.08.91	Luftwaffenmuseum Berlin-Gatow, Germany 26.12.96 *On display 2006*	
GCG	3722	S81	Schleicher K 8B	8186	D-5227	05.02.91	Shenington Gliding Club *Stored 7.17*	Shenington 24.10.04
GDC	3741	GDC	Slingsby T.38 Grasshopper	SSK/FF1795		11.05.91	F K Russell & partners *Stored 8.12*	Dunstable 02.05.97
GDL	3749		Akaflieg Braunschweig SB-5B	5049	D-0307	24.04.91	D Reynolds *New owner 4.13*	Hartlepool 12.06.94

GEN	3774	GEN	Slingsby T.21B	1154	RAFGGA 550 XN150	16.05.92	Not known _Blown over, Papenburg 30.6.07; stored 2017_	Borkenberge, Germany 11.06.08
GEQ	3776	2001	SZD-12A Mucha 100A	462	SP-2001	06.06.91	R A Earnshaw-Fretwell	Trenchard Lines, Upavon 11.07.10
HAK	3786	XA302	Slingsby T.31B	844	XA302	17.08.91	RAF Museum _On display 6.18_	Hendon 24.05.96
HAR	3792	HAR	Schleicher K 8B	8151	D-8453	04.09.91	Gliding Heritage Centre	Lasham 04.07.97
HAW	3797	–	SZD-12 Mucha 100	367	SP-1817	11.03.92	Lietuvos Aviacijos Muziejus _On display 2015_	Kaunas, Lithuania 10.03.93
HBX	3823	HBX	Slingsby T.45 Swallow	1386	8801M XS650	16.05.93	J P Ben David _'Sir Iain'_	Lasham 21.08.19
HBZ	3825	HBZ	Slingsby T.15 Gull III replica	–		28.06.92	B Stephenson	Saltby 03.08.11
HCG	3833	HCG	Maupin Woodstock One _Built R Harvey_	–		07.10.92	Norfolk & Suffolk Aviation Museum	Flixton 23.03.11
HCK	3836	WB962	Slingsby T.21B	623	RAFGGA WB962	02.01.92	V Mallon	Kleve-Wisseler Dünen, Germany 11.06.11
HDQ	3865	–	Schempp-Hirth Cirrus VTC	132Y	OY-XBJ	11.04.92	R C Graham _Stored 6.17_	Chipping 10.04.93
HFC	3901	WB924	Slingsby T.21B	587	WB924	25.07.92	P Hardman	Bicester 24.09.17
HFE	3903	XN187	Slingsby T.21B	1166	XN187	23.06.92	A Hill & partners	RAF Halton 13.09.19
HFG	3905	HFG / XN186	Slingsby T.21B	1165	XN186	28.06.92	T Horsley & partners	Wattisham 01.06.19
HFS	3915	–	Vogt Lo 100 Zwergreiher	02	D-6040	23.08.92	Gliding Heritage Centre _Fuselage as simulator_	Lasham 22.08.93
HFZ	3922	–	Abbott-Baynes Scud replica _Built by M L Beach, 1995_	001		R	Gliding Heritage Centre _On display 8.17, on loan from Brooklands Museum_	Lasham
HHG	3953	WT910	Slingsby T.31B	705	WT910	09.01.93	N J Jardine	Llantisilio 05.08.06
HJJ	3979	–	Slingsby T.38 Grasshopper	797	WZ816	R	Malta Aviation Museum	Ta' Qali, Malta
HJM	3982	HJM	Hütter H.28 III replica _Built E R Duffin_	ED.02		25.05.93	B Pearson _Stored 4.13_	Eaglescott 12.06.99
HKF	3999	HKF	CARMAM JP 15-36AR Aiglon	23	F-CETU	31.07.93	K & C Vincent _Stored 2.17_	Shenington 26.07.00
HKJ	4002	–	Penrose Pegasus 2 _Built J M Lee_	001		14.07.93	Norfolk & Suffolk Aviation Museum	Flixton 15.09.98
HLR	4033	XE786	Slingsby T.31B	899	XE786	18.12.93	D Thomson _Under restoration 2012_	Arbroath 15.04.04
HLU	4036	HLU	Scheibe SF 27A	6101	SE-TGP D-1225	22.02.94	N Jaffray _Stored 2015_	(Snitterfield) 08.05.08
HND	4064	HND	Scheibe Zugvogel IIIA	1044	HB-735 D-9119	23.05.94	M Y Kiteley _Stored 8.14_	Sackville Lodge, Riseley 13.07.08
HNS	4077	XN185	Slingsby T.21B	1164	8942M XN185	21.06.94	RAF Scampton Heritage Centre _Preserved 4.16_	RAF Scampton 12.04.04
HPJ	4093	HPJ	Edgley EA9 Optimist	EA9/001		22.11.94	J K Edgley	Tibenham 25.08.09
HPP	4098	–	Slingsby T.38 Grasshopper	863	XA230	05.02.95	E Fowkes _Noted 2.14_	Henlow 14.04.11
HQB	4110	WB935	Slingsby T.21B	602	WB935	01.10.94	M Konermann	Hahnweide, Germany 28.07.19
HRD	4135	HRD	Slingsby T.21B	634	WB973	18.03.95	C Langenau	Aukrug, Germany 12.05.18
HRT	4148	HRT	Schleicher K 8B	8390/A	RAFGGA 599 D-5599	09.03.96	S Franklin & D Richards _Under restoration 2016_	RNAS Yeovilton 20.06.04
HVC	4229	HVC	Slingsby T.38 Grasshopper	765	WZ769	04.05.01	Not known	Switzerland 02.04.12
HXL	4286	CK-0927	Letov LF-107 Lunak	39	OK-0927 OK-0827	01.11.96	G P Saw _'Czech Mate'_	Wycombe Air Park 25.04.19
HZN	4336	D-6173	Schleicher Ka 2B Rhönschwalbe	195	D-6173	28.03.97	M Wilton-Jones	Ringmer 23.08.19
JAM	4359		Schleicher ASW 15B	15353	D-2360	29.05.97	Not known _Dumped 9.16_	Hinton-in-the-Hedges 23.07.06
JAP	4361	–	Slingsby T.38 Grasshopper	779	WZ783	R	R H Targett _Believed to be ex WZ818 [799]_	Nympsfield
JAU	4366	WB922	Slingsby T.21B	585	WB922	27.05.97	A Clarke	Sandhill Farm, Shrivenham 03.05.19
JBA	4372	XP463	Slingsby T.38 Grasshopper _Assembled from components; p/i is starboard wing only_	1262	XP463	08.06.98	G Pullen	Lasham 09.09.15
JDB	4421	WZ828	Slingsby T.38 Grasshopper	809	WZ828	06.11.97	A Clarke	Little Rissington 06.05.13
JDW	4440	JDW	PZL-Swidnik PW-5 Smyk	17.009.018		23.12.97	Burn Gliding Club _Stored for spares 3.14_	Burn 14.12.00
JJN	4552	XP490	Slingsby T.38 Grasshopper	1267	XP490	22.07.98	611 VGS _Regd as '2067', from Frame no. SSK/FF2067; stored 4.12_	RAF Watton 21.07.99
JJS	4556	XA240	Slingsby T.38 Grasshopper	873	XA240	08.12.08	A P Benbow & J R Furnell _Stored 10.13_	Portmoak 07.12.09
JPK	4670	–	Slingsby T.34A Sky	672	RAFGSA 876 XA876, G-672	04.05.99	J Tournier	Wycombe Air Park 02.06.07
JQY	4707	R92	Slingsby T.21B	666	RAFGSA R92 NEJSGSA 4, WG499	20.06.99	Cyprus Gliding Group _Sold to museum 2014_	North Nicosia, Cyprus 15.03.14
JSP	4746	JSP	Slingsby T.31B	1189	BGA 2724 XN250	04.07.04	R Wulfers _Restored using wings of XE798_	Deelen, Netherlands 03.07.17
JSQ	4747	F1	Rolladen-Schneider LS8-b	8301	D-KKAF	05.00	I Mountain	RAF Cranwell 10.05.19
JTA	4757	–	Colditz Cock replica _Built by Southdown Aero Services & John Lee_	SA3		24.01.00	Norfolk & Suffolk Aviation Museum	Flixton 20.02.00

BGA

JWE	4833	JWE	Slingsby T.21B	1159	XN155	01.07.00	M Selss	Bad Tolz, Germany 28.04.19
JXD	4856	WB961	Slingsby T.21B	622	WB961	20.01.01	F Brune	Eudenbach, Germany 30.11.17
JXE	4857	JXE	SZD-22C Mucha Standard	F-717	SP-2330	12.08.01	Not known	Eaglescott 11.06.05
							Stored 7.16	
JYA	4877	WB988	Slingsby T.21B	MHL.015	WB988	31.03.01	C Bravo	Santo Tome del Puerto, Spain 04.03.19
JYG	4884	CK-0833	Letov LF-107 Lunak	49	OK-0833	21.09.02	M Launer	Rossfeld, Germany 04.11.18
KBP	4963	XA310	Slingsby T.31B	852	XA310	20.04.02	A P Stacey	Sandhill Farm, Shrivenham 02.05.19
KBW	4970	OM-0973	Letov LF-107 Lunak	22	OM-0973	09.06.02	P Walsh	Saltby 26.08.18
					OK-0973, OK-0813			
KDT	5015	OK-0975	Letov LF-107 Lunak	12	OK-0975	29.09.02	D Poll	Switzerland 17.09.19
					OK-0875			
KFW	5066	D-6932	Grunau Baby IIB	5	(BGA 2532)	09.09.07	Gliding Heritage Centre	Lasham 19.04.13
					D-6932, D-1932			
KGE	5074	WZ789	Slingsby T.38 Grasshopper	785	WZ789	11.09.03R	W den Baars	Midden-Zeeland, Netherlands
							Stored 4.16	
KLE	5176	KLE	SZD-22B Mucha Standard	524	OO-ZIS	30.08.07	B Stephenson	Saltby 11.05.19
KMR	5208	QK-0838	Letov LF-107 Lunak	54		13.04.06	W Seitz	Pohlheim, Germany 13.06.19
					G-CKMR, OK-0838			
KPR	5283	XE802	Slingsby T.31B	915	XE802	15.09.09	M Smith	Brentor 19.07.16
KSF	5322	X7	Lange E1 Antares 18T	50T02	D-KANH	30.06.08R	N G G Hackett	Husbands Bosworth
							Reserved as G-CKSF	
KSS	5334	895	Lange E1 Antares 18T	52T03	D-KAIJ	27.08.08R	J Inglis	Husbands Bosworth
							Reserved as G-CKSS	
KSV	5337	W	Lange E1 Antares 18T	56T04	D-KAIB	03.11.08R	W Inglis	Bidford
							Reserved as G-WWVV	
LEV	5628	XA290	Slingsby T.31B	832	XA290	11.12.09	J R Furnell 'Silver Hornet'	Portmoak 19.11.19
LFC	5636	XE799/R	Slingsby T.31B	912	8943M	17.11.09R	R O Johnson (T31 Club)	Lasham
					XE799		*Stored 2018*	
LFE	5638		Slingsby T.31B	696	WT901	27.11.09R	R Strasser	
LLG	5745		Slingsby T.38 Grasshopper	1041	XK822	26.04.13R		
LNV	5804	XA289	Slingsby T.31B	831	XA289	.14R	R Schmitt	Germany
LNW	5805		Slingsby T.31B	FF1373		.14R	*Probably c/n 677 ex WT867*	
LNZ	5807		Slingsby T.38 Grasshopper	760	WZ764	.14R		
LOY	5829		Glaser-Dirks DG-100G	101G15	D-3806	.15R	*Reserved as G-CLOY*	
LPD	5834	LPD	Slingsby T.31B	853	OO-ZMQ	08.04.15	A Ferra	Bechyne, Czech Republic 19.04.19
					XA311			
LPS	5847	WZ798	Slingsby T.38 Grasshopper	794	WZ798	.15R	Not known	Eaglescott
							Stored 3.16	
LSU	5895	FA2	Schempp-Hirth Ventus-2cxa FES	152	D-KLSU	.16R		
LTN	5913	MH	Schempp-Hirth Ventus-2cxa FES	153	D-KLTN	.16R	*Reserved as G-CLTN*	
LVX	5965		Slingsby T.38 Grasshopper	'2470'		4.5.18R		
LWC	5970		Allstar SZD-54-2 Perkoz	542.A.18.025	(BGA 5963)	14.6.18R	*Reserved as G-CLWC*	
	5973		Schempp-Hirth Discus-2c FES	33		4.7.18R		
LWK	5976		Rolladen-Schneider LS8-t	8416	D-KKSX	17.9.18R		
					D-4674			
LWP	5981		Sportine Aviacija LAK-17B FES	252		7.11.18R	*Reserved as G-CLWP*	
LWW	5987		Schempp-Hirth Ventus-2a	7	D-9031,	26.11.18R		
					F-CGLS, D-8559			

MISCELLANEOUS GLIDERS

The following gliders, preserved or under restoration, still carry RAFGSA or RAFGGA markings, or their original identities have been lost:

No.	Type	Constructor's No	Previous Identity	Owner (Operator)	Base
RAFGSA 37	EoN Primary	EoN/P/034	RAFGSA 337	K Kiely	(Helperby)
			WP266	*Stored 2005*	
RAFGSA 103	EoN Olympia 1	EoN/O/017	BGA 529	Museum of Berkshire Aviation	Woodley
				Damaged 31.7.57; on display 2010	
RAFGSA 258	Slingsby T.8 Tutor	510	BGA 427	R Birch	(Cirencester)
			G-ALTY, BGA 427	*Stored 2017*	
RAFGSA 324	Grunau Baby III	2	D-5081	H Robbins	Los Gatos, California
				Under restoration 2005	
RAFGSA R99	Slingsby T.45 Swallow	1387	NEJSGSA 3	Not known	Kingsfield, Cyprus
			XS651	*Stored 10.09*	
RAFGGA 591	Schleicher Rhönlerche II	209	D-0359, F-	Museum of Flight	East Fortune
				On display 9.17	
–	EoN Primary	'EON/PE/FF068'		Ulster Gliding Club	Bellarena
				For restoration 2018	
'D-3-340'	Grunau Baby II	?		Kent Battle of Britain Museum	Hawkinge
				On display 6.16	

BGA COMPETITION NUMBER INDEX

BGA Competition Numbers are issued to pilots and not to individual gliders, and hence may change when the glider changes hands. Gliders may sometimes be found wearing lapsed numbers or other markings, therefore this listing is a composite one based on BGA information and reported sightings. Identities marked with an asterisk indicate where gliders have been observed with the numbers shown although not listed in the current BGA record. The missing numbers are not allocated.

No.	Regn	No.	Regn	No.	Regn	No.	Regn
0	G-DEGP	85	G-DDVA	190	G-CFNU	302	G-CJMU
00	G-TANO*	86	G-DDRB	191	G-DDWJ	306	G-CKKF
1	1144*, D-0606	87	G-CJLW	193	G-DEJR	307	G-CEVV
2	869*, G-VTUS	88	G-DEUY	194	G-CFUV	308	G-CHEC
3	G-CHWB	90	G-CFLW	195	G-DDGY	311	G-DBZF
4	G-CIJF, G-STEN*	91	920	196	G-CFHD	314	G-CFLE
5	G-CKCM	92	G-DCVK	198	G-CJNJ	315	G-CHNF
6	G-HOJO	93	G-DFFP	199	G-JULL	316	G-DECZ
7	G-CKOO	94	G-BZYG	200	G-CHUZ	317	G-DBWJ
007	G-DCEB	95	G-CJSU	202	G-CEVZ	318	G-CFEH
8	G-CWLC	96	G-CHBG	203	G-CHJX	319	G-DERS
9	G-NYNE	97	1697	205	G-CKLP	320	G-INCA
10	G-IXXI	98	G-CKBC	206	G-CGBS	321	G-CKJE
010	G-CKPV	99	1125	207	1974*	322	G-DCWG
12	236, G-WYVN	100	G-CHHR	209	G-CKNG	323	G-DEPF
13	D-KOOL	104	G-CKBU	210	D-5410, D-KKVT	324	G-DDCC
14	G-DDAJ	105	G-CHNT	214	G-CEWP	325	G-CHXW
15	G-CJJZ	106	G-DDZT	216	G-CFYI	326	G-CFYM
16	G-SAXL	107	G-DEAE	217	G-DEUJ	328	G-OTRY
17	2804	108	G-YOBI	218	G-CKKH	332	G-CFTP
18	G-DCEC	109	G-YUGE	219	G-CGEH	333	G-CFBT
19	G-CJUN	110	G-SIIO	220	G-CHNW	335	G-DHET
20	G-DETZ	112	G-DJNE	222	1579*	337	G-DEEA
21	G-CJLZ	113	1013*, G-CFCR	223	G-DETJ	339	G-ECOL
23	G-BYEC	114	G-CHAO	224	G-CFYH	341	G-CKNS
24	G-CKCE	115	G-CLOO	226	G-DENO	344	G-BUCG
26	G-SAXT	117	G-DEON	229	1683	345	G-ORIG
27	G-CJGL	118	G-DESH	230	G-CFTW	346	G-DHCE
28	G-CLON	120	G-CFEG	231	G-DESO	347	G-CGCM
29	G-CFWK	121	G-DRAT	233	G-CKGF	350	G-DBYU
31	G-CHWA	123	G-AXZH	234	G-FCOM	351	1741
32	G-DJAA	124	G-CKFP	236	G-GLAK	353	G-DDKX
33	778	125	G-CFKG	237	G-CHHW	354	G-DDXW
35	G-DFXE	126	G-LSED	238	G-CFPE	355	G-DCVY*
36	G-CJSG	127	1029	240	G-JSIC	356	G-CHBE
37	G-EEBN	128	G-CGBY	242	G-CFPL	357	G-DLRL
38	G-CHML, G-CHTL	129	G-DDFC	243	G-CJKY	360	G-DEAV
40	G-XVII	132	G-DDXD	245	G-CHJF	361	G-IKAH*
41	G-HICU	136	G-CFHL	246	G-CFVH	364	G-CHMO
42	G-XLII*, ZS-GAK	137	G-CHDL	247	1504*, G-CJVS	365	G-CHLB
44	G-CLSZ	141	G-CFGF, G-CLTA	248	1911*	368	G-CFLC
45	880	142	G-CGFU	250	G-CICT	369	G-CFVM
46	G-CJUF	146	G-DCWY*	253	G-CJRA	370	G-CKGA
47	G-DCCL	147	G-SRAH	256	G-CFUR	371	G-CFMY
48	G-CHNU	150	1269*, G-CKDN	257	G-CFJS	372	G-DCAS
49	G-DCTP	152	G-DDZF	258	G-DDRO	373	G-DCCD
50	G-DEES	153	G-DCGH	259	G-DDMS	375	G-DDPY
51	G-CLTO	154	G-DFHS	261	G-DEJD*, G-LIVS	378	G-DDLH
52	G-CHXB*, G-JNUS	155	870	263	G-DHAA	379	G-DESC
56	2470	157	G-ILBO	264	G-LSIV	380	G-CHMT
57	G-CKPU	158	G-CFMO	265	G-DDNG	381	G-CEWZ
58	G-DADJ	159	G-CFKL	267	G-DDXN	382	G-CEVD
60	G-HJSM	160	G-DDXK	268	G-CFRW, G-CHPH*	383	G-DEOW
61	G-CKFE, G-RKUS	161	G-CJPR	270	1027*, G-DDSP	388	G-CJPP
62	G-CHPD	163	1089*, 1299*	271	G-DFAF	390	G-CHRC
63	G-CJWX	165	G-DCMW	272	G-DDVY	391	G-CJGF
64	G-CKGC	166	G-DEEH	273	G-DCNC	393	G-CHVM
65	G-CHFA	167	G-CGBR	274	G-CJEZ	394	G-DHCR
66	G-COPP, G-LXVI	170	G-CKOI	276	G-DENX	395	G-CFBW*
67	1052	171	G-CFYZ	277	G-MOZI	400	G-BLRM
68	G-YEHA	172	G-CKDS	279	G-DEOA	401	G-DCPD
69	G-CLKF	173	G-CFXM*	280	G-LIBI	402	G-DCTR
71	G-CKBG	175	G-CKLV	282	G-CUMU	403	1278
72	G-PHNX	176	G-CJCT	283	G-DERA	406	G-CKDA
73	G-CKBM	177	G-CFBH	285	G-CFXD	407	G-DDJN
75	G-CJDS	178	G-CFBA	286	G-DDXT	408	G-DEKU
76	G-DDMM	180	G-DDST, G-DERX*	287	G-DDPH	409	G-CKBK
77	G-VTEW	181	G-DENV	288	G-LSLS	411	G-DFCM
78	G-DHCU	184	G-CHWL, G-DCMV*	290	G-CKOE	418	G-CJTM
79	G-DFRA	185	G-CJOO	291	G-JKRV	420	G-CKJS
80	G-NDJS	186	G-KALP	292	G-CHJT, G-CKDW	422	G-PSHK
81	G-DDXB	187	G-CFHG	296	G-CJSE	423	G-DCVW
83	G-CGAN	188	G-DELR	300	G-CKCD	429	G-DHAD

No.	Identity	No.	Identity	No.	Identity	No.	Identity
430	G-DEKW	563	G-IGLI	711	G-CHXO*	842	G-DCUS
431	G-DEHO	564	G-CHGK	712	G-CHWH	844	G-DEBX
432	G-CHYR	565	G-CLRS	714	G-XXVB	846	G-DCHT
433	G-DDLE	566	G-DCRN	715	G-DCAG	849	G-DEHU
434	G-CJDJ	567	G-CFXA	716	G-DDEO	850	G-DDYF
435	G-DENU	569	G-DEGK	719	G-DELZ	851	G-DDBC
437	G-DDPL	570	G-HKAA	720	G-CGBL	855	G-CHHT
438	G-DFDW	571	G-CFCJ	721	G-CFCP	859	1136*
440	G-CKKY	574	G-CFPT	722	G-CJWK	860	G-CHKA
441	G-CJNO	575	G-DDBN	723	G-DBWO	862	G-DCFY
443	G-DEUS	576	G-DDZJ	724	G-DCKZ	867	G-CJGN
444	G-DDKL	577	G-DCHB	725	G-CGAU	869	G-PIKD
445	G-CHHU	579	G-DCTB	727	G-DFBM	871	G-CJXW
446	G-DEUH	580	G-DDXX	728	G-DDWS	873	G-DCTT
449	G-CKKX	584	G-VENC	730	G-CJVG	877	G-DDSX
450	G-DGDJ	585	G-DHNX	732	G-DDVK	880	G-CJWG
451	G-CEVK	586	G-DEFE	733	G-DDWB	882	G-CHDV
452	G-DEMF	588	G-DDNC	735	G-CHEN	886	G-DDWT*
453	G-DEHG*	591	G-CHDD	737	G-DEFF	888	G-IFWD
456	G-CKET	592	G-BDZG	739	1088	891	G-WLKS
458	G-DCEO	593	G-DDMK	741	1121	893	2345*
461	G-WYDE	594	G-DEAK*	743	G-DCKY*	894	G-CJUB
463	1201	597	1198*	745	G-DDNK	895	D-KAIJ
464	G-DFBO	601	G-CHJS	747	G-DHEV	899	G-CJJH
465	1288*	602	G-DCMS	748	G-CGCR	900	G-CLRF
466	G-ECPA	603	G-DJAN	750	G-EEDE	901	G-CKJG
468	G-DCWE	606	G-CFPW	751	G-CHSK	902	G-EENT
469	G-CHMZ*	607	G-CKRV	753	G-CFTY	904	1168
470	G-DEFA*	609	G-CFWC	755	G-CHBM	905	1419*
473	G-DHEM	610	G-DDGX	757	G-DDZY	906	G-CKFD
474	G-DCJF*	611	G-CHEO*	759	G-DDKD*	909	G-DDZG
475	G-DCBY	612	G-CFUT	760	G-CKGM	911	G-VNTS
477	G-DCYO	615	G-CJJB	761	G-DCPU	912	G-DDUB
480	G-DDOE*	616	G-DEMU	762	G-CFCA	913	G-CHYE
486	G-CHEW	617	G-CKJC	765	G-DEPS	914	G-CGDY
490	G-DEHK	618	G-FLUZ	766	G-DDTY	915	G-DDTP
491	G-CEVE	620	G-JIFI	768	G-CFWU	917	G-DCWR
493	G-CHSO	621	G-LOUD	770	G-GSST	919	G-DHKL
494	G-CJJP	622	G-DCNG	771	G-DENJ	920	G-KOBH
495	G-CFRR	625	G-DCNW	775	G-CLOL	921	D-KTOF
496	G-CHBH	626	G-BZSP*	776	G-CLSH	922	G-CGBU
498	G-DFSA	627	G-CFFX	777	G-CIHM	927	G-CJFU
499	G-KKAM	630	G-XXIX	778	G-CGAF	930	G-CHVP
500	2146*, G-DCAZ	631	G-CFAO	779	G-CHAY	933	G-CJJT
501	G-DCTU	633	G-CKBT	780	G-DFBY	942	G-RAIR
502	G-CHGZ	634	G-CFRH	781	G-CJMO	943	G-NIMB
503	G-CKDY	636	G-CJMN	782	782*, G-CJSL	944	G-CFTV
505	G-CKNB	638	G-DDUS	783	G-CHGX	946	G-GCJA
506	G-CEUN	639	G-DDZB	785	G-CFOY	948	G-DCLP
509	G-CHGB	641	G-DFCD	786	G-DEAT	949	G-GBPP
510	G-CFDE	642	G-DDUL	788	G-DDKS	950	G-CFJR
511	G-DDMR	643	G-EEFK	789	1733*	951	G-DDHW
513	G-CJHG	644	G-CLFZ	790	G-CJKN	952	G-DFOG
514	G-BHIJ	648	G-DDSH	791	G-ZBOP	954	G-CFZO
515	G-DEME	653	1104*	795	G-CHEH	959	G-DDDM
516	G-CHJL	660	G-CHYF	797	G-CKLD	963	G-CHHH
517	G-DBWS	662	G-CFWS	799	G-DCLZ	968	G-DEOJ
520	G-LUON, G-YODA*	663	663	801	G-CFOC	970	G-NYMB
521	G-CGBG	664	G-CHRL	802	G-CHRW	971	G-DDVP
523	G-DDBK*	666	G-DUOT	803	G-CFUL	973	G-CFPD
524	G-CGDZ	669	G-CFZB	805	G-CHLN	977	G-CKAR
525	G-DCNE	671	G-DFCK	806	G-CFGU	978	G-DCWT
527	G-LDER	672	G-DEGJ	808	G-CKDO	979	G-CHHN
528	G-DCRV	674	G-CFNT	812	G-DCAO	980	G-CFWP
530	G-HAUT	677	G-DCWB	813	G-CJNZ	982	G-DCYP
532	G-DCXM	679	G-DCBA	818	G-DCNX	983	G-KESY
533	G-DDMP	680	G-DDDR	819	G-CHLM	985	G-CHKR
536	G-EDDV*	683	G-DCDF	820	G-DEDN	988	G-CJVX
537	G-CJBH	687	G-CHEJ	821	G-DDRN	990	G-DDZN
539	2210*	688	G-DDRT	822	G-CFBB	991	G-DHDH*
540	G-TOOB	692	G-CHNV	823	G-CJAO	992	G-DEUK
541	G-BGCU*	693	G-CHPX	826	G-DCZU	993	3148
542	G-DDOK	695	1702*, G-EDDD	827	G-CHBV	994	G-HCAC
546	G-CGDA	698	G-CFHW	828	G-DDYE	996	G-DEEK
547	G-CJOA	699	G-DDTA	830	916*	998	G-CFRC
549	867*	700	G-CKCN	831	G-DDMB	999	G-RZEE
551	G-DDBP	701	G-CFGW	832	G-DCWX	2001	3776*
552	G-EEBK	704	G-DDTV	833	G-DFAW		
554	G-CJUK	705	G-CHNL	838	G-CHHK		
558	G-DBYM	707	G-DCRS	839	G-DDZV*		
560	G-CHXR	710	G-CJBW	841	G-CJSS		

BGA ALPHA/NUMERIC COMPETITION NUMBER INDEX

No.	Identity	No.	Identity	No.	Identity	No.	Identity
1F	G-LSIF	AP	G-CKJV	DG5	G-RIFD	H5	G-DFHY*
1UP	G-CKOU	AR	G-SMAR	DI	G-UDIX	H8	G-CHTS
1Z	G-ONEZ	AS	G-VEGA	DK	G-OHDK	H11	G-FEBJ
2A	G-CIHF*, G-DEAJ	AV8	G-CKBX	DM	G-CJXR, G-RIFO*	H12	G-CGCS
2C	G-TWOC	AW	G-CGAR	DP	G-CHDP, G-CHUO	H17	2847*
2CS	G-DEGS	AZ	G-FGAZ*	DS2	G-CKFN	H20	G-CFDM
2R	G-CFCS			DUO	G-XDUO	HA	G-CLGL
2UP	G-CJUM	B	G-CFMH	DV	G-DDVV	HB1	G-CJPA
2W	G-CKFK	B1	G-CFYW	DV8	G-DCRH	HD	G-CFPN
2Z	G-CJFC	B2	G-PRBB	DW	G-CJEX	HE	G-HEBB
2ZC	G-CHWF	B3	G-DCUT	DZ	G-DZDZ	HH	G-HXJT
2ZE	G-LFES	B4	G-DCUT			HI	G-CLKG
3D	G-ODUO	B5	ZS-GCE	E	285*, G-CHKD	HZ	G-CHHZ
3W	G-CLRO	B8	ZS-GEH	E1	ZS-GEH		
4A	G-FORA	B9	G-CHJR	E2	G-CJCD	I3	G-CLMY
4J	G-PBWS	B11	G-CHZU	E3	G-GLID	IPF	G-CIPF*
4M	G-KFVG	B12	G-CJYP	E4	G-XJON	IR	G-KMIR
4SM	G-OASM	B17	G-CLMD	E5	G-CJTN	IT	G-CKSD
5GC	G-CEYC	B19	G-CJRV	E6	G-RYPE	IZ	G-CIFU
6B	G-LSGB	B33	G-CHRS	E8	G-CFUH		
6CR	G-CJEW	B96	1283*	E11	G-XELL	J1M	G-CJOV
6E	G-DCFL	BA	G-CVBA	E17	G-CKJZ	J2T	G-JSRK
7A	G-CKJM	BB	G-GBBB	E60	G-CFVT*	J3	G-CFYN
7D	G-CFDA*	BD	G-DCLO	EA	G-CKCH	J3T	G-OTJT
7Q	G-CJAS	BF1	G-CKKP	EB	G-CJOP	J5	G-CKMZ
7R	G-CFYK	BJ	G-BMBJ	EC	G-CFXY	J5T	G-TRBN
7UP	G-CJZZ	BS	G-CJZL	EE	G-CKFL	J15	G-CFAM
7V	G-DDHX	BT	G-CJGR	EF	G-CJNP*, G-RIEF	J34	G-EHAV
8F	G-KCWJ	BW	G-KBWP	EM	G-CJER	J50	G-CJVV
8Q	ZS-GEE	BZ	G-DCVE	EN	G-CHZY	JA	G-SAJA
8T	G-CKPM			ER	G-DPER	JB	G-KCHG
9A	1317*	C	G-DDLC	ES	G-CLPU	JA9	G-CJCN
9E	G-CKJN	C1	G-CTAG	ET	G-WJET	JBA	G-CJBA*
15A	G-CJVW	C2	G-CTWO	EW	G-CJMV	JE	G-CLJE
17K	G-DCOJ	C3	G-DCGY	EW2	G-EWEW	JED	G-CJED*
17R	G-DBWP	C4	G-JNSC	EZ	G-CKEZ	JF	G-DDJF
17T	G-DAVS	C6	G-CJWA			JH1	G-CJVF
19T	G-XIXT	C7	G-CJCJ	F	400*	JJ	G-CFOF, G-CFRJ
19X	G-XIXX	C12	G-CJKP	F1	4747	JK	G-KMJK
20B	G-CLSW	C29	G-CHKU*	F2	D-KEWV	JL	G-EEKI
20L	G-MAGK	C30	G-CGBO	F3	G-CKSX	JN	G-CLTJ
21S	G-CKNC	C55	G-CHNM	F4	1367*	JO	G-JBOB
26E	G-CCLR	C64	G-CJZM	F16	G-CLLC	JOK	G-CJOK*
28T	G-TRBO	C74	G-CJVU	F20	G-CHVX	JR	G-KJJR
29E	G-SASG	CB	G-CJWU	F21	G-CHFV	JT	G-HPJT
34Z	G-DCSF	CC	G-EHCC, G-ULCC	FA	G-CJCH		
38A	G-DDFU	CD	G-CJGZ, G-CJZN,	FA2	D-KLSU	K	G-DEVP
49A	1009		G-GOXC	FB	G-LSFB	K2	2147*, G-CLFB
97Z	G-CHHO	CD1	G-CJUX	FES	G-OFES	K3	G-DFBR
		CL	G-OBUP	FI	G-CLMO	K6	G-DDMO
A1	G-CIAI	CO2	G-CIDO	FK	G-CKCR	K6e	G-DEKX
A2	G-CHDX	CP	G-LSCP	FZ	G-CKKE	K8	G-CJJK
A3	G-CJLJ	CT	G-CJXT			K9	G-DHPR
A4	G-CKLN	CU	G-CUGC	G	G-CLUP	K13	G-CFZN
A5	G-PZAS	CUS	G-RCUS	G0	G-CLMV	K18	G-CKNM
A6	G-CHYU	CX	G-IICX	G1	G-CJJF	K19	G-DDBS
A7	G-CJKK	CYL	1639	G2	G-GTWO	K21	G-CJGE
A8	G-CJNK	CZ	G-OTCZ	G7	G-CKMO, G-SVEN*	KA	G-CKML
A10	G-CJDE			G9	G-CKOZ	KC	G-CLRZ
A14	G-CHYS	D	G-DDRJ	G29	G-DASG	KE	G-CJEH*
A15	G-DEKG	D1	G-CJNB	G41	G-CJHZ	KL	G-CHHP
A19	G-CFNH	D6	G-CKLY	G46	698	KM	G-CDDB
A20	G-CHOD	D7	G-DSVN	G81	G-CJBJ*	KO	G-CKHS
A23	1237	D8	G-CJVP	GB2	G-CFPH	KV	G-LSKV
A26	G-CHYY	D9	G-IRLE	GH	G-CKDR	KW	G-CJDG
A27	G-CJDC	D15	G-CHSD	GJB	G-CGJB*		
A30	G-DDHK	D17	G-DRRT	GKB	G-DGKB	L	G-DFCW
A31	G-XASH	D31	G-CHUH	GM	G-LSGM	L1	G-LYPH
A34	G-CJHR	D54	G-DHSJ	GP	G-CJVM	L2	G-CJGS
A39	G-ORCW	D66	G-RAPL	GR	G-CKMA	L3	G-CJBK
A98	G-CEVN	D70	G-DHRR	GR8	G-RIZK	L4	G-LLLL
AB	G-CLES	DA	G-SZDA	GS	G-GSGS	L5	G-CGAD
AC	G-CJBR	DB	G-CHKH	GT	G-CKLT	L6	G-CHGP
AF	G-HRAF	DD2	G-ODDZ	GW	G-CKJF	L7	G-CJBO
AG1	G-CKBF*	DD3	G-CIKB			L8	G-STEU
AH	G-CHEE	DF	G-CJVB	H	G-DEVJ	L9	G-CJFX
AJ	G-ZZAJ*	DG	G-CFYU	H1	G-CKBH	L11	G-BNXL
AM	G-KEAM	DG1	G-DGIO	H4	G-CKBV	L12	G-DFXR

No.	Identity	No.	Identity	No.	Identity	No.	Identity
L17	G-LFEZ	NH	G-CKBN	R63	G-CJML	T34	G-DDUT
L18	G-DCXK	NH2	G-ONHL	R66	G-CJBZ	T51	G-DLOW
L19	G-CKPA	NS4	G-CDTH	R67	G-CJON	T54	G-CGDT
L24	G-CJTH	NT	G-LLNT	R75	G-CJLS	T65	G-BGBV
L33	G-DCSD	NU	G-CFTR	R77	G-CJSD	T93	G-CKPZ
L51	G-CFOZ	NU2	G-NUGC	R88	G-CJPV	TB2	G-CGCT
L57	G-CFWF	NW	G-DETG	R92	4707*	TC	G-KXMS
L58	G-RIEV			R93	G-DJNC	TJ	G-CLNE
L99	G-DCCP	O8	G-DBEN	RA	G-VCXT	TL	ZS-GBM
LA	G-CJRR	OD	G-CKOD	RA1	G-CLRA	TL2	G-TLTL
LC	G-CFEJ	OG	G-CLOG	RB	G-RBCT	TM	G-CEWE
LD	G-CHZZ	OL	G-CKOL	RC	G-SINK	TO1	G-CHTF
LE5	G-DJGG	OM	G-BSOM	RG	G-PORG	TP	G-DCRW
LEC	G-OLEC	OZ	G-OZOZ	RK	G-DIRK	TS	G-CJJE*
LEW	G-ILEW			RM	G-CKMM	TT	G-CILS
LF	G-CKOM	P	G-CFHM	RN	G-CLGW	TV	G-TVGC
LGC	G-CLGC*	P2	D-KDPF	RNT	G-EENZ*		
LJ	G-LSVI	P3	G-CJAR	RP	G-VCRZ	U1	G-CHZM
LL	G-DCMR	P5	G-CHRX	RP1	G-CHVG	U2	G-CHOZ, G-DDNU*
LM	G-KHCC	P7	G-CKPY	RR	G-CLSO	U9	G-UNIN
LNA	G-KRWR	P9	G-DDWR	RS	G-CJRE	UG	G-CHMD, G-CLUG
LS	G-WLLS	P20	G-OFJC	RT	G-DEUD	UP2	G-CKFT
LS3	G-DEFS	P23	G-DJMD	RV	G-CGRV	UUP	G-LUUP
LS4	G-LSFR	P30	G-ODDF	RW	G-CJPL		
LS5	G-CKHB	P61	G-CHZV	RY	G-CLRY	V	G-CLRH
LS6	G-LSIX	P70	G-DEWR			V2	D-KJMH
LS7	G-CJLK	PB	G-CLLY	S	G-CFYY	V2C	G-IICT
LS8	G-CHVL	PD	G-ILIB*	S2	G-LIBY	V2T	G-CVZT
LT	G-CJHY	PE	G-KEPE	S4	G-CHWC	V5	G-CHLS
LU	G-CFMS, G-DFEX	PG	G-DEPE	S4L	G-FERV	V6	G-VSIX
LX	G-YXLX*	PH	G-OSHK	S5	G-CHXZ	V7	G-DEHH
LY	G-EFLY	PH2	G-CKFB	S6	G-DFBE	V8	G-CKCJ
LZ	G-CHZO	PI	G-CJPI	S8	G-XWON	V9	G-CKGD
		PK	G-JAPK	S8Y	G-PRKZ	V11	G-EVII
M1	G-CJDR	PS	G-CFVZ	S9	G-CKOY	V12	G-CKMD
M2	G-DHYL	PT	G-CJRN	S10	G-BXGZ*	V17	G-CFYC
M3	G-CKTB	PW	G-CLMF	S19	G-CJKS	V26	G-VTCT
M4	G-CJAW	PW5	G-SMYK	S30	2380*	V66	G-HAAH
M6	G-MSIX	PX	G-CLPX	S33	G-CJRB	VJ	G-DFMG
M7	G-DETM	PZ	G-CHMX, G-CLPZ,	S75	G-CKFA*	VN	G-MRVN
M8	G-CKME		G-PCGC	S81	3722*	VS	G-DDVS
M9	G-WDGC			SA	G-CJPJ	VV	G-XAVV
M11	G-RAHA	Q5	G-CFHR	SA1	G-EEVL*		
M17	G-CJTW	QV	G-DFOV*	SC	G-SANT	W	D-KAIB
M25	G-DRCS			SE	G-DDWP	W1	G-WONE
M80	G-CJUZ	R1	G-CJFH	SG	G-VSGG	W3	G-WIII
MB	G-CKED	R2	G-CKEV	SG9	G-KUGG	W4	G-CLVJ
MC	G-IIOO	R3	G-CJOD	SH	G-BXSH*, G-JETV	W5	G-CJXG
MD	G-CJEA	R4	G-CJLN	SH2	G-CJUV	W7	G-CLPL
ME	G-CLVW	R6	G-SAOC	SH3	G-CFKM	W8	G-CRJW
MF	G-DEMT	R7	G-CJKT	SH4	G-CFUP	W11	G-CKLC
MH	D-KLTN, G-CHWD	R10	G-CJLC	SH7	G-CJZY, G-CLUD	W17	2595*
MM	G-KGMM, G-OASW	R11	G-CJYU	SH8	G-DFEB	W19	G-CEWI
MP	G-OBPP	R12	G-CKJP	SH9	G-CJSH	W20	G-ODCH
MR	G-CLTD	R18	G-CKMW	SI	G-SISI	W27	G-CJCM
MWK	G-CMWK	R19	G-CKRW	SJ	G-CLSJ	WA1	G-OWAI
MY	G-CKCB	R20	G-CJKO	SK	G-CJRU	WA2	G-TWAZ
		R21	G-CJKJ	SM	G-DHOK	WB	G-CFYJ
N	G-CLTC	R22	G-DJMC	SO	G-JSPR	WD	G-CLHG
N1	ZS-GEG	R23	G-CJMS	SO1	G-CJXL	WE4	G-CKCV
N2	G-CFPP	R25	G-CJKZ	SOR	G-OSOR	WH	G-CIEA, G-CLGT
N3	G-PNGC	R28	G-CKGK	SP	G-DEVO, G-KISP	WW	G-CEWW
N4	1914	R30	G-CJSV	SW	G-SWSW	WZ	ZS-GCD
N5	G-CHUE	R31	2533*	SX	G-KSSX		
N6	G-CGCX	R32	G-CJPO	SY	G-CKSY	X	G-FESX
N7	G-CKDF	R35	G-DERJ			X4	G-CKGL
N8	G-EJAE*	R36	G-CJMA	T	G-DCUJ	X5	G-DXLT
N11	G-DDJB	R37	G-CJMZ	T1	G-OPHT	X7	D-KANH
N12	G-CKBL	R38	G-CJWJ	T2	G-OTWS	X8	G-CHZG
N15	3548*	R39	G-CJLP	T3	G-CKGB*, G-CLGZ	X9	G-CKOK
N21	673	R41	G-CJRX	T4	G-CKHD	X11	G-DKFU
N25	G-DJLL	R43	G-CJHO	T4C	G-CKFH	X17	G-CKHE
N28	G-CFSD	R46	G-CJMJ*	T5	G-RGTS	X96	G-DDVL
N51	G-DEVM	R48	G-CJKG*	T9	G-CJTB	X97	G-XBGA
N52	G-DCHG*	R49	G-CJMK	T12	G-CJWM	XE	G-CKON
N53	G-CHAF	R53	G-CJGM	T15	G-DCPF	XJS	G-BXJS
N55	1118*, G-CJYF	R56	G-CJPZ	T18	G-EJIM	XL	G-CLFX
N56	G-CFTC	R57	G-DDRW	T19	G-CHOR	XL5	G-CLUZ
N57	G-CKOX	R59	G-CJPY	T21	3290	XS	ZS-GBL
NG1	G-CKCP	R61	G-CJMW	T27	G-CJRH	XXI	G-KXXI

No.	Identity	No.	Identity	No.	Identity	No.	Identity
XY	G-CFPB	YO	G-DLOE	Z7	G-DCDC	Z95	G-DJEB
XZ	ZS-GEF	YY	G-CKMG	Z8	G-CHTM	Z99	G-CHNH
				Z9	ZS-GBK	ZA	G-SEZA
Y	G-CIXH	Z	1873*, G-CLKK	Z10	G-CJKM	ZB	ZS-GBR
Y2	G-KEDK	Z1	G-CJUJ	Z12	G-CFJM	ZP	ZS-GCG
Y4	G-CHXE	Z2	G-CHFX	Z18	G-CLVD	ZW	G-CIZW
Y7	G-KOYY	Z3	G-CLGU	Z19	G-GZIP*	ZY	G-CKZY
Y9	G-KHPI	Z4	G-CFLF	Z25	G-DDVZ*	ZZ	ZS-GCJ
Y44	G-CJXA	Z5	G-CHWS	Z35	G-CJXN		
YG	G-DCYG*	Z6	G-CFZL*, G-ZSIX	Z45	G-CHLY		

CIVIL REGISTRATION and MILITARY SERIAL DECODE INDEX

Several former British military gliders carry their former service serials for authenticity. A few imported vintage specimens also carry their previous UK and overseas civil registrations. Whilst details of marks carried are included in Part 1, Column 3 this specific decode Index is including for ease of reference. Identities shown with an asterisk are not original.

Regn or Serial	BGA No.	Regn or Serial	BGA No.	Regn or Serial	BGA No.	Regn or Serial	BGA No.
UK		WB971	3324	XA290	5628	**GERMANY**	
G-ALJR	283	WB975	3288	XA295	3336	D-11-875	448*
G-ALMN	589	WB981	3238	XA302	3786	D-12-354	1711*
G-ALRH	629	WB988	4877	XA310	4963	D-4012	2855
G-ALRK	490	WE990	2583	XA311	5834	D-5627	1872
G-ALRU	628	WE992	2692	XE761	804*	D-6173	4336
G-APWL	1172	WE996	785*	XE786	4033	D-6932	5066
		WG498	3245	XE799	5636	LF+VO	449
RAF		WJ306	2720*, 3240	XE802	5283	S1+1-11	2238*
RA905	1143	WP266	BAPC 423*	XE807	3545		
TS291	852	WT900	3272	XN149	1085*	**SWITZERLAND**	
VM684	791	WT908	3487	XN157	3255	HB-474	2474
VM687	794	WT910	3953	XN185	4077	HB-561	2284
VV400	1697	WT913	3239	XN186	3905		
VV401	1125*	WT914	3194	XN187	3903	**CZECH REPUBLIC**	
WB922	4366	WZ755	3481	XN243	3145	CK-0833	4884
WB924	3901	WZ789	5074	XP463	4372	QK-0838	5208
WB934	3385	WZ795	3488	XP490	4552	CK-0927	4286
WB935	4110	WZ798	5847	XS651	1211*, 1331*	OK-0975	5015
WB944	3160	WZ819	3498	XS652	1107	CK-8592	655
WB945	1254	WZ828	4421	XT653	3469		
WB961	4856	XA240	4556			**SLOVAKIA**	
WB962	3836	XA289	5804			OM-0973	4970

AIRCRAFT TYPE INDEX (BGA)

Note: This Index covers gliders listed in this volume with the exception of those on the British Civil Register.

LAK including **AB SPORTINE AVIAICIJA**

LAK-17
BGA 5981 EI-GLH

LANGE AVIATION CO (LANGE FLUGZEUGBAU GmbH)

E1 ANTARES
BGA 5322 BGA 5334 BGA 5337 D-KAIB
D-KAIJ D-KANH D-KZEN D-0606

LET NARODNI PODNIK KUNOVICE

L-13 BLANIK
EI-120

LETOV LTD (VOKENSKÁ TOVÁRNA NA LETADIA LETOV)

LF-107 LUNAK
BGA 4286 BGA 4884 BGA 4970 BGA 5015
BGA 5208

MANUEL

WILLOW WREN
BGA 162

HAWK
BGA 1778

MAUPIN

WOODSTOCK
BGA 3833

MONNETT

MONERAI
BGA 2988

MÜLLER (MOSWEY SEGELFLUGZEUG-WERKE)

MOSWEY III
BGA 2474

MÜNCHEN (SCHWARZWALD-FLUGZEUGBAU WILHELM JEHLE)

MU 13D
BGA 1937 BGA 2267

NEUKOM

STANDARD ELFE S-2
BGA 3374

JOSEF OBERLERCHNER HOLZINDUSTRIE

Mg19a STEINADLER
BGA 2903

PENROSE

PEGASUS
BGA 4002

PIK

PIK-16C VASAMA
BGA 1540

PILATUS AIRCRAFT LTD

B4-PC11
BGA 1911

PZL-BIELSKO – see SZD

PZL-SWIDNIK

PW-5 SMYK
BGA 4440

ROLLADEN-SCHNEIDER FLUGZEUGBAU GmbH

LS4
D-9691

LS8
BGA 4747 BGA 5976

SCHEIBE-FLUGZEUGBAU GmbH including **AVIALSA/ROCHETEAU** production

SF-25 FALKE (inc SLINGSBY T.61)
D-KIAH

BERGFALKE
BGA 1464 BGA 2855 D-3229

L-SPATZ and A60 FAUCONNET
BGA 2278 BGA 2498 BGA 2866 BGA 3104
EI-130

ZUGVOGEL III
BGA 2779 BGA 4064 EI-GLO

SF27A ZUGVOGEL V
BGA 4036 EI-144

SCHEMPP-HIRTH FLUGZEUBAU GmbH including **GROB** production

CIRRUS
BGA 3865

DISCUS B
BGA 5977 EI-GLT

DISCUS-2
BGA 5973 D-KTOF

DUO DISCUS
BGA 5989 D-KDLQ

GÖ 3 MINIMOA
BGA 1639

GÖ 4 GOEVIER
BGA 1992

MINI NIMBUS
D-4818

SHK
BGA 1419 BGA 1579

STANDARD CIRRUS
BGA 2091

VENTUS
BGA 5895 BGA5913 BGA5987 BGA5990
D-KDPF D-KEWV D-KIIJ D-KJMH D-KKVT
D-KLSU D-KLTN

ALEXANDER SCHLEICHER GmbH and CO – *see* **ALEXANDER SCHLEICHER SEGELFLUGZEUGBAU GmbH and CO**

SCHWEYER

RHÖNSPERBER
BGA 260

SCOTT

VIKING
BGA 416

SHENSTONE

HARBINGER
BGA 1091

PAUL SIEBERT SPORT UND SEGELFLUGZEUGBAU

SIE 3
BGA 3461

SLINGSBY SAILPLANES LTD

T.1 FALCON I
BGA 266 BGA 3166

T.6 KIRBY KITE
BGA 236 BGA 251 BGA 285 BGA 310
BGA 400

T.7 CADET
BGA 731 BGA 1143

T.8 TUTOR
BGA 442 BGA 466 BGA 469 BGA 473
BGA 485 BGA 791 BGA 794 BGA 804
BGA 833 BGA 852 BGA 858 BGA 895
BGA 904 BGA 1071 BGA 1424 BGA 1599
BGA 1698 BGA 1745 BGA 1759 BGA 1770
BGA 2288

T.12 GULL
BGA 902

T.13 PETREL
BGA 651

T.15 GULL III
BGA 643 BGA 3825

T.21
BGA 570 BGA 601 BGA 614 BGA 646
BGA 665 BGA 666 BGA 673 BGA 782
BGA 886 BGA 945 BGA 948 BGA 1000
BGA 1014 BGA 1085 BGA 1144 BGA 1215
BGA 1218 BGA 1254 BGA 1315 BGA 1352
BGA 1354 BGA 1482 BGA 1588 BGA 1619
BGA 1965 BGA 2010 BGA 2024 BGA 2036
BGA 2720 BGA 2767 BGA 2964 BGA 3148
BGA 3160 BGA 3189 BGA 3195 BGA 3235
BGA 3238 BGA 3240 BGA 3243 BGA 3245
BGA 3250 BGA 3255 BGA 3265 BGA 3287
BGA 3288 BGA 3290 BGA 3292 BGA 3324
BGA 3385 BGA 3423 BGA 3774 BGA 3836
BGA 3901 BGA 3903 BGA 3905 BGA 4077
BGA 4110 BGA 4135 BGA 4366 BGA 4707
BGA 4833 BGA 4856 BGA 4877 EI-157

T.25 GULL IV
BGA 565

T.26 KITE 2
BGA 521 BGA 663 BGA 689 BGA 751 EI-102

T.30 PREFECT
BGA 599 BGA 625 BGA 701 BGA 785
BGA 815 BGA 1152 BGA 1601 BGA 2333
BGA 2380 BGA 2517 BGA 2546 BGA 2583
BGA 2692

T.31B
BGA 1255 BGA 1346 BGA 1376 BGA 1559
BGA 3145 BGA 3181 BGA 3194 BGA 3229
BGA 3239 BGA 3241 BGA 3272 BGA 3336
BGA 3487 BGA 3545 BGA 3786 BGA 3953
BGA 4033 BGA 4746 BGA 4963 BGA 5283
BGA 5628 BGA 5636 BGA 5638 BGA 5804
BGA 5805 BGA 5834 EI-139

T.31 MOTOR CADET
EI-CJJ EI-CJT

T.34 SKY
BGA 685 BGA 686 BGA 694 BGA 698
BGA 2284 BGA 4670

T.37 SKYLARK 1
BGA 725

T.38 GRASSHOPPER
BGA 3359 BGA 3480 BGA 3481 BGA 3488
BGA 3498 BGA 3662 BGA 3741 BGA 3979
BGA 4098 BGA 4229 BGA 4361 BGA 4372
BGA 4421 BGA 4552 BGA 4556 BGA 5074
BGA 5745 BGA 5807 BGA 5847 BGA 5965
EI-135

T.41 SKYLARK 2
BGA 724 BGA 729 BGA 733 BGA 745
BGA 747 BGA 759 BGA 778 BGA 793
BGA 801 BGA 826 BGA 827 BGA 845
BGA 896 BGA 899 BGA 1441 BGA 1549
BGA 1757 BGA 2002

T.42 EAGLE
BGA 740 BGA 780 BGA 825 BGA 828
BGA 841 BGA 880

T.43 SKYLARK 3
BGA 735 BGA 736 BGA 742 BGA 761
BGA 763 BGA 806 BGA 813 BGA 823
BGA 844 BGA 864 BGA 867 BGA 870
BGA 916 BGA 920 BGA 922 BGA 925
BGA 927 BGA 950 BGA 957 BGA 985
BGA 988 BGA 996 BGA 1004 BGA 1013
BGA 1023 BGA 1251

T.45 SWALLOW
BGA 890 BGA 910 BGA 921 BGA 990
BGA 1003 BGA 1008 BGA 1032 BGA 1061
BGA 1107 BGA 1136 BGA 1165 BGA 1169
BGA 1211 BGA 1263 BGA 1319 BGA 1331
BGA 1338 BGA 1339 BGA 1364 BGA 1365
BGA 1398 BGA 2210 BGA 2304 BGA 2762
BGA 3469 BGA 3823

T.49 CAPSTAN
BGA 1009 BGA 1106 BGA 1118 BGA 1131
BGA 1132 BGA 1133 BGA 1134 BGA 1135

BGA 1163 BGA 1183 BGA 1191 BGA 1196
BGA 1203 BGA 1237 BGA 1249 BGA 1360

T.50 SKYLARK 4
BGA 1019 BGA 1043 BGA 1047 BGA 1050
BGA 1063 BGA 1066 BGA 1087 BGA 1088
BGA 1089 BGA 1095 BGA 1100 BGA 1102
BGA 1103 BGA 1104 BGA 1105 BGA 1115
BGA 1117 BGA 1121 BGA 1124 BGA 1168
BGA 1189 BGA 1194 BGA 1202 BGA 1210
BGA 1220 BGA 1239 BGA 2881

T.51 DART
BGA 1186 BGA 1198 BGA 1206 BGA 1207
BGA 1266 BGA 1269 BGA 1330

T.59 KESTREL
BGA 1683 BGA 1914 BGA 2470

SOCIÉTÉ CARMAM

JP 15-34 KIT-CLUB
BGA 3169

JP-15 36 AIGLON
BGA 3999

M-100S MESANGE
BGA 2383

SOCIÉTÉ DES ETABLISSMENTS BENJAMIN WASSMER

WA22 SUPER JAVELOT
BGA 1480

WA30 BIJAVE
BGA 2753 BGA 3404

SOCIÉTÉ NOUVELLE CENTRAIR

101A PEGASE
EI-GLC

SPALINGER

S.21H
HB-357

SPORTINE AVIACIJA – see LAK

STEMME GmbH AND Co KG

S.6
D-KRUK

SWALES – see BIRMINGHAM GUILD

SZD

SZD-8 JASKOLKA
BGA 2512

SZD-9bis BOCIAN
BGA 1274

SZD-12A MUCHA
BGA 3776 BGA 3797 EI-100 EI-140

SZD-22 MUCHA STANDARD
BGA 4857 BGA 5176

SZD-24 FOKA
BGA 1367

SZD-30 PIRAT
BGA 1470 BGA 1733 BGA 1779 BGA 1832

SZD-36A COBRA 15
BGA 1717 BGA 1732

Torva SAILPLANES

SPRITE
BGA 1702

Vogt

LO-100 ZWERGREIHER
BGA 2770 BGA 3915

SOCIÉTÉ Wassmer – see SOCIÉTÉ DES ETABLISSMENTS BENJAMIN WASSMER

Zlin (ZLINSKA LETECKNA AKCIOVA)

24 KRAJANEK
BGA 655

SECTION 3 – AVIATION HERITAGE UK REGISTER

The British Aviation Preservation Council (BAPC) was formed in 1967 and is the national body for the preservation of aviation related items. It has been renamed the Aviation Heritage UK Register, but will continue to use BAPC as a prefix for its registered items. It is a voluntary staffed body that undertakes a representation, co-ordination and enabling role. AHUK membership includes national, local authority, independent and service museums, private collections, voluntary groups and other organisations involved in the advancement of aviation preservation in the UK. A number of overseas aircraft preservation organisations have affiliated membership.

The Register of Anonymous Airframes started in the 1980s as a way of flagging up aircraft which had not been formally identified, for example there was no known civilian registration, military serial or construction number. These examples include 'pioneer' aircraft built and flown before registration systems were devised, unfinished projects, deliberate omissions, hang gliders and similar devices. Additionally, the register allows other airframes and similar items that would not normally need a formal identity such as man-powered aircraft, full scale models for use as 'gate guardians' and non flying replicas intended only for display purposes. Most exhibits held in Museums are usually on display. Further identity details for most of the viewable Museum and Collection entries can be found in SECTION 9 on page 599. This year we are very grateful to Lloyd Robinson (*Lloyd.robinson@aviation-data-research.com*) who has assumed the role of Registrar and has provided substantial updates for 2018 and 2019 editions of *Air-Britain News*.

The items listed by the Irish Aviation Historical Council Register can be found on page 517.

Reg No	Type		C/n	Regn Date
	Previous Identity Location Remarks			
BAPC.001	Roe Triplane replica		HAC.1	
	G-ARSG The Shuttleworth Collection Old Warden *'12'*			
	Now airworthy as G-ARSG			
BAPC.002	Bristol Boxkite replica		BM.7279	
	G-ASPP The Shuttleworth Collection Old Warden *'12A'*			
	Now airworthy as G-ASPP			
BAPC.003	Bleriot Type XI		14	
	G-AANG The Shuttleworth Collection Old Warden			
	Now airworthy as G-AANG			
BAPC.004	Deperdussin Monoplane		43	
	G-AANH The Shuttleworth Collection Old Warden			
	Now airworthy as G-AANH			
BAPC.005	Blackburn Type D Monoplane		9	
	G-AANI The Shuttleworth Collection Old Warden			
	Now airworthy as G-AANI			
BAPC.006	Roe Triplane IV replica			
	'14' & 'Bullseye Aeroplane'			
	On loan from The Aeroplane Collection			
	to Manchester Museum of Sciences & Industry			
BAPC.007	Southampton University Man-Powered Aircraft			
	Solent Sky Museum Southampton			
BAPC.008	Dixon Ornithopter replica			
	The Shuttleworth Collection Old Warden			
	No marks carried			
BAPC.009	Humber / Bleriot Type XI Monoplane replica			
	Midland Air Museum Coventry			
	No marks carried			
BAPC.010	Hafner R.II Revoplane			
	The Helicopter Museum Weston-Super-Mare			
BAPC.011	English Electric Wren Composite		3	
	G-EBNV The Shuttleworth Collection Old Warden *'4'*			
	Now airworthy as G-EBNV			
BAPC.012	Mignet HM.14 Pou-du-Ciel			
	'G-ADYO' / 'BHP.1'			
	On loan from The Aeroplane Collection			
	to Manchester Museum of Sciences & Industry			
BAPC.013	Mignet HM.14 Pou-du-Ciel			
	Brimpex Metal Treatments Sheffield			
BAPC.014	Addyman Standard Training Glider			
	Nigel Ponsford Collection Yorkshire			
BAPC.015	Addyman Standard Training Glider		YA.2	
	Nigel Ponsford Collection Yorkshire			
	Rebuilt by Yorkshire Aeroplanes			
BAPC.016	Addyman Ultralight Aircraft			
	Nigel Ponsford Collection Yorkshire			
BAPC.017	Woodhams Sprite			
	Suffolk Aviation Heritage Museum Ipswich			
	Built by Bill Woodhams 1966: uncompleted ultralight In store			
BAPC.018	Killick Man-Powered Helicopter			
	Nigel Ponsford Collection Yorkshire			

Reg No	Type		C/n	Regn Date
	Previous Identity Location Remarks			
BAPC.019	Bristol F.2b Fighter replica			
	Musee Royale de l'Armée Brussels *'66'*			
	Rebuilt by to static condition by Skysport			
	Engineering 06.89 with parts from J8264			
BAPC.020	Lee-Richards Annular Biplane replica			
	Newark Air Museum Winthorpe			
	Built for 'Those Magnificent Men in Their Flying			
	Machines' film			
BAPC.021	de Havilland DH.82A Tiger Moth / Jackeroo			
	M J Brett Not known			
	Used in the rebuild of G-APAL			
BAPC.022	Mignet HM.14 Pou-du-Ciel		WM.1	
	The Aviodrome Lelystad *'G-AEOF'*			
BAPC.023	Royal Aircraft Factory SE.5a ½ Scale Model			
	Allocated in error to the Newark Air Museum			
BAPC.024	Currie Wot ⅔ Scale Model			
	Allocated in error to the Newark Air Museum			
BAPC.025	Nyborg TGN.III Glider			
	P Williams (Warwick)			
	Burnt at Shenington, Oxfordshire, unknown date			
BAPC.026	Auster AOP.9			
	Fuselage frame only, believed scrapped at Swansea			
BAPC.027	Mignet HM.14 Pou-du-Ciel replica			
	May not have been completed – was under construction in			
	Coventry area in 1988			
BAPC.028	Wright Flyer replica		FVAC.2	
	Yorkshire Air Museum Elvington			
BAPC.029	Mignet HM.14 Pou-du-Ciel replica			
	The Brooklands Museum Weybridge *'G-ADRY'*			
	Built by P.D.Roberts, Swansea 1960-78			
BAPC.030	DFS Grunau Baby			
	Destroyed in a fire at Swansea during 1969			
BAPC.031	Slingsby T.7 Cadet			
	Reportedly scrapped at Swansea			
BAPC.032	Crossley Tom Thumb			
	Midland Air Museum Coventry			
	Not completed Banbury 1937 In store			
BAPC.033	DFS-108-49 Grunau Baby IIB		122	
	(BGA 2400), VN148, LN+ST, D-IX-47, SV-5			
	Danish Vintage Glider Association Viborg			
	(To Denmark for rebuild 2003)			
BAPC.034	DFS-108-49 Grunau Baby IIB		030892	
	(BGA 2362), RAFGSA 281, RAFGGA GK-4, LZ+AR			
	D Elsdon Hazlemere, Buckingham *'DTF'*			
	Now known to be BGA 2362			
BAPC.035	EoN AP.7 Primary		EoN/P/063	
	BGA.2493 M & S Malcolm Pocklington *'DYW'*			
	Now known to be BGA 2493			

BAPC.036   Fieseler Fi.103 (FZG-76 / V-1) replica
           Kent Battle of Britain Museum   Hawkinge
           Built for 'Operation Crossbow' film

BAPC.037   Blake Bluetit   01
           G-BXIY   M J Aubrey   Old Warden
           Under restoration to fly as G-BXIY

BAPC.038   Bristol Scout D replica
           Aerospace Bristol   Bristol   *'A1742'*

BAPC.039   Addyman Zephyr
           Nigel Ponsford Collection   Yorkshire

BAPC.040   Bristol Boxkite replica   BM.7281
           Bristol Museum and Art Gallery   Clifton, Bristol
           *Built for 'Those Magnificent Men in
           Their Flying Machines' film*

BAPC.041   Royal Aircraft Factory BE.2c FSM   *'9970'*
           Yorkshire Air Museum   Elvington   *'6232' & '10000'*
           Built by RAF Halton apprentices

BAPC.042   Avro 504K replica   *'9828' or '9848'*
           Yorkshire Air Museum   Elvington   *'H1968'*
           Built by RAF Halton apprentices

BAPC.043   Mignet HM.14 Pou-du-Ciel   AWK.1
           Newark Air Museum   Winthorpe

BAPC.044   Miles M.14A Magister Composite
           Museum of Berkshire Aviation   Woodley   *'L6906'*

BAPC.045   Pilcher Hawk replica
           Stanford Hall   Lutterworth
           Built by Armstrong-Whitworth Aviation apprentices 1957/58

BAPC.046   Mignet HM.14 Pou-du-Ciel
           J A Holmes
           *Last noted at Tump Farm, Coleford, Gloucestershire in 1970;
           probably scrapped*

BAPC.047   Watkins CHW Monoplane
           National Waterfront Museum   Swansea

BAPC.048   Pilcher Hawk replica
           Riverside Museum   Glasgow
           Built by No.2175 Sqdn ATC, Glasgow 1966   In store

BAPC.049   Pilcher Hawk
           National Museum of Scotland   Edinburgh
           *1896 original   Rebuilt by after fatal crash at
           Stanford Hall, Leicester 30.09.1899*

BAPC.050   Roe Triplane Type I
           The Science Museum   South Kensington
           1909 original

BAPC.051   Vickers FB.27A Vimy
           The Science Museum   South Kensington
           Rebuild of 1919 original

BAPC.052   Lilienthal Type XI Glider
           The Science Museum   Wroughton
           In store

BAPC.053   Wright Flyer replica
           The Science Museum   South Kensington
           Built by Hatfield

BAPC.054   JAP / Harding Monoplane
           The Science Museum   South Kensington
           Built by J.A.Prestwich & Co 1910   Modified Blériot XI

BAPC.055   Levavasseur Antionette
           The Science Museum   South Kensington
           Built by 1909

BAPC.056   Fokker E.III
           The Science Museum   South Kensington
           *As '210:16'   Captured Somme, France 04.16
           Skeletal airframe*

BAPC.057   Pilcher Hawk replica
           No marks carried
           Imperial War Museum   Duxford
           On loan from E Littledike

BAPC.058   Yokosuka MXY-7 Ohka II
           Fleet Air Arm Museum   RNAS Yeovilton   *'15-1585'*
           On loan from Science Museum

BAPC.059   Sopwith F.1 Camel replica
           'D3419', 'F1921'   Air Station Heritage Centre   Montrose
           As 'B5577:II-W'

BAPC.060   Murray M.1 Helicopter
           The Helicopter Museum   Weston-Super-Mare

BAPC.061   Stewart Man-Powered Ornithopter   2
           South Yorkshire Aviation Museum / Aeroventure   Doncaster
           'Bellbird II'

BAPC.062   Cody V Biplane
           The Science Museum   South Kensington   *As '304'*
           Built 1912

BAPC.063   Hawker Hurricane I FSM
           'L1592', 'JX-G' No. 1 Sqn / 'KW-Z'
           Kent Battle of Britain Museum   Hawkinge
           *As 'P3208:SD-T' in RAF 501 Sqdn c/s
           Built for 'Battle of Britain' film*

BAPC.064   Hawker Hurricane I FSM
           'SD-N' No. 501 Sqn
           Kent Battle of Britain Museum   Hawkinge
           *As 'P3059:SD-N' in RAF 501 Sqdn c/s
           Built for 'Battle of Britain' film*

BAPC.065   Supermarine Spitfire FSM
           'QV-K' No. 19 Sqn   Kent Battle of Britain Museum
           Hawkinge   *As 'N3289:DW-K' in RAF 610 Sqdn c/s
           Built for 'Battle of Britain' film*

BAPC.066   Messerschmitt Bf.109G FSM
           1480   Kent Battle of Britain Museum   Hawkinge   *As '480/6'*
           Built for 'Battle of Britain' film

BAPC.067   Messerschmitt Bf.109G FSM
           Kent Battle of Britain Museum   Hawkinge
           *As '14' in JG-52 colours
           Built for 'Battle of Britain' film*

BAPC.068   Hawker Hurricane I FSM
           'H3426', 'P3975'   Pinewood Studios   (With Graham Adlum)
           *As 'P2725:TM-B'
           May be displayed as Gate Guard at RAF Museum*

BAPC.069   Supermarine Spitfire FSM
           'BO-D' / 'MH314'   Kent Battle of Britain Museum
           Hawkinge   *As 'N3313:KL-B' in RAF 54 Sqdn c/s
           Built for 'Battle of Britain' film*

BAPC.070   Auster AOP.5   *TAY/33153*
           'TJ472', 'G-ALES', 'G-ILES'
           Royal Canadian Artillery Museum   Camp Shilo   *'TJ398'*

BAPC.071   Supermarine Spitfire replica
           'P9390', 'P9390' / 'P8140:ZP-K'
           Norfolk and Suffolk Aviation Museum   Flixton
           *As 'N3317:BO-U' in camouflage c/s
           Built by for 'Battle of Britain' film*

BAPC.072   Hawker Hurricane I FSM
           'V7767', 'V7467'   Jet Age Museum   Gloucestershire
           As 'V6799:SD-X' in RAF 501 Sqdn c/s

BAPC.073   Hawker Hurricane I FSM
           'P2916'   Omaka Aviation Heritage Centre
           Blenheim, NZ   *'P3854'*

BAPC.074   Messerschmitt Bf.109G FSM
           Kent Battle of Britain Museum   Hawkinge   *As '6357:6'*
           Built for 'Battle of Britain' film

BAPC.075   Mignet HM.14 Pou-du-Ciel
           Nigel Ponsford Collection   Yorkshire   *'G-AEFG'*

BAPC.076   Mignet HM.14 Pou-du-Ciel replica   YA.1
           Yorkshire Air Museum   Elvington   *'G-AFFI'*

BAPC.077   Mignet HM.14 Pou-du-Ciel replica
           *'G-ADRG'   For sale 10.16 by USP Vehicles Ltd/
           Cameron Thompson from Chipping Camden;
           was with Stondon Transport Museum Bedfordshire*

BAPC.078   Hawker Hind   41H-81902
           RAfghan AF, G-AENP   The Shuttleworth Collection
           Old Warden   *'K5414'*

BAPC.079   Fiat G.46-4B   32
           'FHE', MM52799   Classic Aero Services   Shipdham
           'MM53211:ZI-4'

BAPC.080   Airspeed AS.58 Horsa II Composite
           Museum of Army Flying   AAC Middle Wallop   *'KJ351'*
           Composite ex LH208, TL659 & 8569M

BAPC.081   Hawkridge Nacelle Dagling   10471
           BGA.493   P Underwood   Eaton Bray   *In store*

BAPC.082   Hawker Hind
           Royal Air Force Museum   Hendon

BAPC.083   Kawasaki Ki.100 III   *'16336' / '24'*
           8476M   Royal Air Force Museum   RAF Cosford   *As '16336'*

BAPC.084 Mitsubishi Ki.46 Dinah III
8484M Japanese Army Air Force c/s
Royal Air Force Museum RAF Cosford *'5439'*

BAPC.085 Weir W-2 Helicopter
National Museum of Flight Scotland East Fortune *'W-2'*

BAPC.086 de Havilland DH.82A Tiger Moth FSM
Status unknown

BAPC.087 Bristol 30 / 46 Babe replica 1
Aerospace Bristol Filton *'G-EASQ'*
Built by W.Sneesby

BAPC.088 Fokker Dr.1 Triplane ⅝ Scale Model
Fleet Air Arm Museum RNAS Yeovilton *'102/17'*
Modified Lawrence Parasol airframe

BAPC.089 Cayley Glider replica
Yorkshire Air Museum Elvington

BAPC.090 Colditz Cock replica
Imperial War Museum (Duxford)
Built by for 'The Colditz Story' BBC film
Also allocated BGA 4757 'JTA'

BAPC.091 Fieseler Fi.103R-4 Reichenburg IV 6/2080
Lashenden Air Warfare Museum Headcorn

BAPC.092 Fieseler Fi.103 (FZG-76 / V-1)
Not known

BAPC.093 Fieseler Fi.103 (FZG-76 / V-1)
Imperial War Museum Duxford
On loan from RAF Museum

BAPC.094 Fieseler Fi.103 (FZG-76 / V-1)
8483M Royal Air Force Museum RAF Cosford

BAPC.095 Gizmer Autogyro
F Fewsdale Darlington

BAPC.096 Brown Helicopter
North-East Land, Sea and Air Museum Usworth

BAPC.097 Luton LA-4 Minor
North-East Land, Sea and Air Museum Usworth *As 'G-AFUG'*

BAPC.098 Yokosuka MXY-7 Ohka II
8485M Museum of Science and Industry Manchester
As '997'

BAPC.099 Yokosuka MXY-7 Ohka II
8486M Royal Air Force Museum RAF Cosford
As '10461' in Japanese Army Air Force c/s

BAPC.100 Clarke Chanute Glider
The Gliding Heritage Centre Lasham
Built by TWK Clarke & Co, based on configuration evolved
by Octave Chanute

BAPC.101 Mignet HM.14 Pou-du-Ciel
Newark Air Museum Winthorpe
Built by W R Earle, Sleaford but not completed;
fuselage only

BAPC.102 Mignet HM.14 Pou-du-Ciel
Never completed – parts incorporated into BAPC.075

BAPC.103 Hulton Biplane Hang Glider
Personal Plane Services Limited Wycombe Air Park
Built by E A S Hulton, London 1969

BAPC.104 Bleriot Type XI No. 225
G-AVXV Musee Aeronautique Presqu'ile Cote d'Amour
La Baule, Loire-Atlantique, France *F-AZIN*

BAPC.105 Bleriot Type XI Composite 54
N605WB? The Aviodrome Lelystad
Built by L.D.Goldsmith 1976 at RAF Colerne: composite
from original components including c/n 54; also reported at
San Diego Air & Space Museum, USA

BAPC.106 Bleriot Type XI
9209M Royal Air Force Museum Hendon *'No.164'*
Built by 1910

BAPC.107 Bleriot Type XXVII 433
9202M Royal Air Force Museum Hendon *As 'No.433'*
Built 1911

BAPC.108 Fairey Swordfish IV
Royal Air Force Museum RAF Stafford *Stored*
Incorrectly allocated BAPC.108 when known to have been
serialled HS503

BAPC.109 Slingsby Cadet TX.1
8599M, BGA 679
Built by Ottley Motors Now known to have been BGA 679

BAPC.110 Fokker D.VIIF FSM
Planes of Fame Air Museum Chino *As '5128/18'*

BAPC.111 Sopwith Triplane FSM
Fleet Air Arm Museum RNAS Yeovilton
'Black Maria' As 'N5492:B' in R Navy Air Service c/s

BAPC.112 de Havilland DH.2 FSM
Stored in poor condition by a collector near Rugby *'5964'*

BAPC.113 Royal Aircraft Factory SE.5a FSM
The Tiger Boys Guelph, Ontario, Canada *'B4863'*

BAPC.114 Vickers Type 84 Viking IV replica
'R4' Argentine Navy Brooklands Museum
Weybridge *'G-EBED'*
Built for 'The Land Time Forgot' film

BAPC.115 Mignet HM.14 Pou-du-Ciel replica
Norfolk and Suffolk Aviation Museum Flixton
On loan from I Hancock

BAPC.116 Santos Dumont Dempiselle No.20 replica
Ex Flambards Theme Park Not known

BAPC.117 Royal Aircraft Factory BE.2c FSM
P Smith Hawkinge
Built by Ackland & Shaw in 1976 for BBC TV 'Wings';
reportedly broken up at the RAF Manston History
Museum in Kent

BAPC.118 Albatros D.Va FSM
'C19/18' *Reportedly scrapped in 1993Scrapped in 1993 -*
Confirmation required

BAPC.119 Bensen B.7 Gyroglider
North-East Land, Sea and Air Museum Usworth

BAPC.120 Mignet HM.14 Pou-du-Ciel TLC.1
South Yorkshire Aviation Museum / Aeroventure
Doncaster *'G-AEJZ'*

BAPC.121 Mignet HM.14 Pou-du-Ciel replica
Museum and Art Gallery Doncaster *'G-AEKR'*

BAPC.122 Avro 504K FSM
Personal Plane Services *'1881'*
Built by Personal Plane Services in 1976 for BBC TV 'Wings'

BAPC.123 Vickers FB.5 Gunbus replica 1186 / 2
ZS-UHN A Topen Cranfield *'P641'*
Built by IES Projects Ltd in 1975 for 'Shout at the Devil' film
Small components only

BAPC.124 Lilienthal Type XI Glider replica
The Science Museum South Kensington
Display replica of BAPC.52 qv

BAPC.125 Clay Cherub BRC/3
Midland Air Museum Coventry *Scrapped*

BAPC.126 Rollason / Druine D.31 Turbulent
Midland Air Museum Coventry
Static airframe – yellow c/s, no marks carried

BAPC.127 Halton Aero Club Jupiter Man-Powered Aircraft
Foulkes-Halbard Collection Filching Manor, Wannock

BAPC.128 Watkinson CG-4 Cyclogyroplane Mk. IV
The Helicopter Museum Weston-Super-Mare

BAPC.129 Blackburn 1911 Monoplane FSM
Not known Sold 1993 *'Mercury'*
Built for 'Flambards' TV Series

BAPC.130 Blackburn 1911 Monoplane FSM
Yorkshire Air Museum Elvington *'Mercury'*
Built for the 'Flambards' TV Series

BAPC.131 Pilcher Hawk replica
United States *May be at the Church Street Station*
Complex, Orlando, Florida
Built by C Paton 1972 for film work

BAPC.132 Bleriot Type XI Composite PFA 088-10864/EMK.010
G-BLXI (1) Musée de l'Automobiliste
Mougins, Cannes, France
May be BAPC189 qv

BAPC.133 Fokker Dr.1 Triplane FSM
Kent Battle of Britain Museum Hawkinge *As '425/17'*

BAPC.134 Aerotek / Pitts S-2A Special replica
'G-CARS', 'G-RKSF' Rahmi M Koc Muzesi
Istanbul *'G-AXNZ'*

BAPC.135 Bristol 20 M.1C FSM
Formerly with Leisure Sport *'C4912'*

BAPC.136 Deperdussin 1913 Monoplane FSM
Planes of Fame Air Museum Chino, California *As '19'*

BAPC.137 Sopwith Baby FSM
Hooton Park Trust Ellesmere Port *'8151'*
Built by FEM Displays Ltd 1978; under restoration

BAPC.138 Hansa-Brandenburg W.29 FSM
Formerly with Leisure Sport *'2292' Sold before 10.87*

BAPC.139 Fokker Dr.1 Triplane FSM
Church Street Collection Orlando, Florida, *As '102/17'*

BAPC.140 Curtiss R3C2 (42A) FSM
Planes of Fame Air Museum Chino, California *As '3'*

BAPC.141 Macchi M.39 FSM
Planes of Fame Air Museum Chino, California *As '5'*

BAPC.142 Royal Aircraft Factory SE.5a FSM
Not known (Switzerland) *'F5459' Sold 01.05.93*

BAPC.143 Paxton Man-Powered Aircraft
R A Paxton Gloucestershire

BAPC.144 Weybridge / Group Mercury Man-Powered Aircraft
(RAF Cranwell) *'Mercury' Previously 'Dumbo', since rebuilt*

BAPC.145 Oliver Man-Powered Aircraft
Not known (Warton) *Possibly scrapped*

BAPC.146 Hertfordshire Pedal Aeronauts Toucan Man-Powered Aircraft
Not known *Centre section/power train only*

BAPC.147 Bensen B.7 Gyroglider   LHS-1
Norfolk and Suffolk Aviation Museum Flixton *As 'LHS-1'*

BAPC.148 Hawker Fury FSM
Wartime Aircraft Recovery Group Aviation Museum
Sleap *As 'K7271' in RAF 1 Sqdn c/s*

BAPC.149 Short S.27 replica
Fleet Air Arm Museum RNAS Yeovilton

BAPC.150 SEPECAT Jaguar GR.1 FSM
'XX718', 'XX732' RAF Exhibition Production & Transportation
Team Oman *'XX725:GU' in RAF 54 Sqdn c/s*

BAPC.151 SEPECAT Jaguar GR.1A FSM
'XZ363' RAF Exhibition Production & Transportation Team
RAF Cranwell *'XX824'*

BAPC.152 British Aerospace Hawk T.1A FSM
'XX226', 'XX262', 'XX162', 'XX227'
RAF Exhibition Production & Transportation Team RAF Cranwell
'XX225' in RAF Red Arrows c/s

BAPC.153 Westland WG-33 Mock-Up
The Helicopter Museum Weston-Super-Mare
Engineering mock-up

BAPC.154 Druine / Rollason D.31 Turbulent   PFA 1654
Lincolnshire Aviation Heritage Centre East Kirkby
Fuselage stored 2015

BAPC.155 Panavia Tornado GR.1 FSM
'ZA368', 'ZA446', 'ZA600', 'ZA322' RAF Exhibition & Production
and Transportation Team, RAF Cranwell *As 'ZA556:Z'*

BAPC.156 Supermarine S.6B FSM
Planes of Fame Air Museum Chino *As 'S1595'*

BAPC.157 WACO CG-4A Hadrian Composite
'237123' Yorkshire Air Museum Elvington *As '319764'*
Fuselage frame section only & tail pieces ex 456476

BAPC.158 Fieseler Fi.103 (FZG-76 / V-1)
Defence Explosive Ordnance Disposal School Chattenden

BAPC.159 Yokosuka MXY-7 Ohka II
Imperial War Museum Duxford

BAPC.160 Chargus 18/50 Hang Glider
National Museum of Flight Scotland East Fortune *Stored*

BAPC.161 Stewart Man-Powered Ornithopter
Not known (Louth) *'Coppelia'*
Built by A Stewart Stored 08.98

BAPC.162 Goodhart Newbury Manflier Man-Powered Aircraft
The Science Museum Wroughton *In store*

BAPC.163 AFEE 10/42 Rotabuggy Reconstruction
Museum of Army Flying AAC Middle Wallop *As 'B/415'*
On loan from Wessex Aviation Society

BAPC.164 Wight Quadruplane Type I FSM
'N248' Solent Sky Museum Southampton *As 'N548'*

BAPC.165 Bristol F.2b Fighter
Royal Air Force Museum Hendon
As 'E2466' in RAF 22 Sqdn c/s

BAPC.166 Bristol F.2b Fighter Reconstruction   '67626'
G-AANM Canadian Aviation and Space Museum
Rockcliffe Airport, Ontario *'D7889'*

BAPC.167 Royal Aircraft Factory SE.5a FSM
Not known (USA)
Built by TDL Replicas Exported 12.97

BAPC.168 de Havilland DH.60G Gipsy Moth replica
Kent Battle of Britain Museum Hawkinge
As 'G-AAAH' 'Jason'

BAPC.169 SEPECAT Jaguar GR.1 FSM
RAF (No.1 School of Technical Training) RAF Cosford *'XX110'*
Engine systems static demonstration airframe

BAPC.170 Pilcher Hawk replica
Status unknown (Glasgow)
Built by A Gourlay for BBC TV Series 'Kings Royal' in 1982

BAPC.171 British Aerospace Hawk T.1A FSM
'XX263', 'XX297', 'XX262' RAF Exhibition & Production
and Transportation Team RAF Cranwell *'XX308'*

BAPC.172 Chargus Midas Super E Hang Glider
The Science Museum Wroughton *In store*

BAPC.173 Birdman Sports Promotions Grasshopper Hang Glider
The Science Museum Wroughton *In store*

BAPC.174 Bensen B.7 Gyroglider
The Science Museum Wroughton *In store*

BAPC.175 Volmer VJ-23 Swingwing Powered Hang Glider
Museum of Science and Industry Manchester

BAPC.176 Royal Aircraft Factory SE.5a Scale Model
Bygone Times Eccleston *'A4850'*

BAPC.177 Avro 504K replica
'G1381' Brooklands Museum Weybridge
As 'G-AACA' in Brooklands School of Flying c/s

BAPC.178 Avro 504K FSM
Not known *'E373' German c/s*

BAPC.179 Sopwith Pup FSM
'A3717' Great War Aerodrome Stow Maries
As 'A653' Taxiable On loan from M Boddington
Built by C Boddington for TV series 'Wings' 1977

BAPC.180 McMurdy Silver Dart Reconstruction
The Reynolds-Alberta Museum Wetaskiwin, Alberta, Canada

BAPC.181 Royal Aircraft Factory BE.2b replica
Royal Air Force Museum Hendon *As '687'*
Restoration from original components

BAPC.182 Wood Man-Powered Rotary Ornithopter
Museum of Science and Industry Manchester *In store*

BAPC.183 Zurowski ZP-1 Helicopter
Newark Air Museum Winthorpe
Polish AF c/s

BAPC.184 Supermarine Spitfire IX FSM
'EN398:JE-J / WO-A' Boultbee Flight Academy Goodwood
'MK392':JE-J'
Built by Specialised Mouldings Ltd 1985

BAPC.185 WACO CG-4A Hadrian Composite
The Museum of Army Flying AAC Middle Wallop *As '243809'*

BAPC.186 de Havilland DH.82B Queen Bee
'K3584' The de Havilland Aircraft Heritage Centre
London Colney *As 'LF786:R2-K'*

BAPC.187 Roe Type I Biplane replica
Brooklands Museum Weybridge
Built by M.L.Beach

BAPC.188 McBroom Cobra 88 Hang Glider
Science Museum Wroughton

BAPC.189 Bleriot Type XI replica
Sold at Christies 31.10.86, probably to France
– see also BAPC.132 Some original parts ex Goldsmith Trust

BAPC.190   Supermarine Spitfire IX FSM
           Macclesfield Historic Aviation Society
           Manchester Barton   *'EN398'/'K5054'*

BAPC.191   British Aerospace Harrier GR.5 Replica
           'ZD472:01'   RAF Exhibition Production & Transportation Team
           RAF Cranwell   *'ZH139:01'*

BAPC.192   Weedhopper JC-24
           M J Aubrey   Kington

BAPC.193   Hovey Whing-Ding
           M J Aubrey   Kington

BAPC.194   Santos Dumont Type 20 Demoiselle replica   PPS/DEM/1
           24 bis   Tettenhall Transport Heritage Collection
           Wolverhampton   *As '20'*
           *Built by Personal Plane Services for 'Those Magnificent
           Men in Their Flying Machines' film*

BAPC.195   Birdman Sports Promotions Moonraker 77 Hang Glider
           National Museum of Flight Scotland   East Fortune
           Built c.1977   Stored

BAPC.196   Southdown Sailwings Cirris III Hang Glider / Sigma 2m
           National Museum of Flight Scotland   East Fortune
           Built c.1980   Stored

BAPC.197   Scotkites Electra Cirrus III Hang Glider
           National Museum of Flight Scotland   East Fortune
           Built 1977   Stored

BAPC.198   Fieseler Fi.103 (FZG-76 / V-1)   477663
           Imperial War Museum   Duxford

BAPC.199   Fieseler Fi.103 (FZG-76 / V-1)
           The Science Museum   South Kensington   *As '442795'*

BAPC.200   Bensen B.7 Gyroglider
           Not known   Leeds   *Composite of three airframes*

BAPC.201   Mignet HM.14 Pou-du-Ciel
           The Aeroplane Collection   Ellesmere Port – Hooton Park
           Built by I Jones in 1936   Fuselage only
           On loan from J Howard

BAPC.202   Supermarine Spitfire IX FSM
           Status unknown   (Llanbedr)   *'MW467:R-O'*

BAPC.203   Chrislea LC.1 Airguard replica
           The Aeroplane Collection   Warmingham   *'G-AFIN'*
           Broken up c.95

BAPC.204   McBroom Hang Glider
           The Aeroplane Collection   Ellesmere Port – Hooton Park

BAPC.205   Hawker Hurricane IIc FSM
           'BE421:XP-G', 'Z3427:XP-G'   Royal Air Force Museum
           Hendon   *As 'P2725'*

BAPC.206   Supermarine Spitfire IX FSM
           'MH486:FT-E'   Royal Air Force Museum   Hendon
           As 'TB288:FF-A' in RAF 132 Sqdn c/s

BAPC.207   Austin Whippet FSM
           South Yorkshire Aviation Museum / Aeroventure
           Doncaster   *As 'K.158'*
           Built by Ken Fern/Vintage & Rotary Wing Collection c.1993
           On loan from D Charles

BAPC.208   Royal Aircraft Factory SE.5a replica
           'D2700'   Prince's Mead Shopping Centre
           Farnborough   *As 'D276:A'*
           Built by AJD Engineering

BAPC.209   Supermarine Spitfire V FSM
           'MJ791:DU-V'   Feggans Brown   Niagara South, Ontario
           'MH415:FU-N'   Built for 'Piece of Cake' TV series

BAPC.210   Avro 504J replica
           Solent Sky Museum   Southampton   *As 'C4451'*
           Built by AJD Engineering

BAPC.211   Mignet HM.14 Pou-du-Ciel replica
           North-East Land, Sea and Air Museum   Usworth   *As 'G-ADVU'*
           Built by Ken Fern and Vintage & Rotary Wing Collection 1993

BAPC.212   Bensen B.6 Gyrocopter
           The Helicopter Museum   Weston-super-Mare

BAPC.213   Vertigo Man-Powered Helicopter
           The Helicopter Museum   Weston-Super-Mare

BAPC.214   Supermarine Spitfire FSM
           Tangmere Military Aviation Museum   Tangmere   *As 'K5054'*

BAPC.215   Airwave Hang Glider
           Solent Sky Museum   Southampton

BAPC.216   de Havilland DH.88 Comet replica
           The Trout Lake Air Force   Kings Langley, Hertfordshire
           As 'G-ACSS'   Built in Australia for film 'The Great Air Race'

BAPC.217   Supermarine Spitfire I FSM
           'R6595' / 'N9926'   GateGuards UK Limited   *'DW-O'*
           Not known

BAPC.218   Hawker Hurricane IIc FSM
           'P3386:FT-I', 'BN230:FT-A'   Bentley Priory Museum
           Bentley Priory   *As 'P2921:FT-A'*

BAPC.219   Hawker Hurricane IIc FSM
           'L1710:AL-D'   RAF Northolt   Middlesex
           As 'L1684' in RAF Northolt Station Flight c/s

BAPC.220   Supermarine Spitfire IX FSM
           'N3194:GR-Z'   Feggans Brown   Perth
           As 'BR954:JP-A' in RAF c/s

BAPC.221   Supermarine Spitfire IX FSM
           'MH777:RF-N'   RAF Northolt   Middlesex
           As 'MH314:SZ-G' in RAF 316 Sqdn c/s

BAPC.222   Supermarine Spitfire IX FSM
           'BR600:SH-V'   The Battle of Britain Bunker and Visitor Centre
           Uxbridge   *'BS239:5R-E'*

BAPC.223   Hawker Hurricane IIc FSM
           'V7467:LE-D'   Paul Lomax / Lytham Spitfire Display Team
           Blackpool   *As 'V7752:JZ-L'*
           Under refurbishment at Blackpool, Lancashire

BAPC.224   Supermarine Spitfire IX FSM
           'BR600:JP-A'   National Air Force Museum of Canada
           Rockcliffe, Ontario   *As 'ML380:LV-C'   Built by TDL Replicas*

BAPC.225   Supermarine Spitfire IX FSM
           RAF Selection Centre   RAF Cranwell   *'P8448:UM-D'*

BAPC.226   Supermarine Spitfire PR.XI FSM
           'EN343'   Gate Guard   RAF Benson   *As 'PL904'*

BAPC.227   Supermarine Spitfire I FSM
           'L1070:XT-A'   Edinburgh Airport   Edinburgh   *'Blue Peter'*
           As 'L1067: XT-D.' in RAF 603 Sqdn c/s

BAPC.228   Olympus Hang Glider
           North-East Land, Sea and Air Museum   Usworth

BAPC.229   Supermarine Spitfire IX FSM
           'L1096:PR-O'   Gate Guard   RAF Digby   *'MJ832:DN-Y'*

BAPC.230   Supermarine Spitfire IX FSM
           'AA908:UM-W'   Eden Camp – Modern History Theme Museum
           Malton   *As 'RK838:GE' in RAF c/s*
           Built by TDL Replicas 1993

BAPC.231   Mignet HM.14 Pou-du-Ciel replica
           Solway Aviation Museum   Crosby-on-Eden   *As 'G-ADRX'*
           Believed originally built at Ulverston in 1936

BAPC.232   Airspeed AS.51/58 Horsa I/II Composite
           de Havilland Aircraft Museum   London Colney
           Composite airframe from unidentified components

BAPC.233   Broburn Wonderlust
           Museum of Berkshire Aviation   Woodley
           Built 1946

BAPC.234   Vickers FB.5 Gunbus replica
           '2882'   Spitfire Spares Limited   Taunton   *'A1452'*

BAPC.235   Fieseler Fi.103 (FZG-76 / V-1) FSM
           Eden Camp – Modern History Theme Museum   Malton

BAPC.236   Hawker Hurricane IIc FSM
           Eden Camp – Modern History Theme Museum   Malton
           Mounted on a Queen Mary trailer as 'P2793:SD-M'
           in RAF 501 Sqdn c/s
           Built by TDL Replicas 1993

BAPC.237   Fieseler Fi.103 (FZG-76 / V-1) FSM
           Militaire Luchtvaart Museum   Soesterburg

BAPC.238   Waxflatter Ornithopter
           Personal Plane Services Limited   Wycombe Air Park   *'8'*

BAPC.239   Fokker D.VIII ⅝ Scale Model
           '157/18'   Norfolk and Suffolk Aviation Museum   Flixton
           As '694'

BAPC.240   Messerschmitt Bf.109G-6 FSM
           Yorkshire Air Museum   Elvington   *As '15919:1'*
           Built by D.Thorton 1994

BAPC

BAPC.241   Hawker Hurricane I FSM
           Tangmere Military Aviation Museum   Tangmere
           As 'L1679:JX-G' in RAF 1 Sqdn camouflage c/s
           Built by Aerofab 1994

BAPC.242   Supermarine Spitfire FSM
           The Beale Park Wildlife Park and Gardens   Lower Basildon
           As 'BL924:AZ-G' in RAF 234 Sqdn c/s   'Valdermar Atterdag'
           Built by TDL Replicas 1994

BAPC.243   Mignet HM.14 Pou-du-Ciel replica   WF.1
           'LA-FLEA', 'A-FLEA'   Lakeland Motor Museum
           Backbarrow   *'G-ADYV'*

BAPC.244   Mainair / Solar Wings Tri-Flyer 250 / Typhoon S
           G-MMLI   National Museum of Flight Scotland   East Fortune

BAPC.245   Electric Flyer Floater Hang Glider
           National Museum of Flight Scotland   East Fortune
           Built 1979   Wing only   Stored

BAPC.246   HiWay Chordwise Cloudbase Hang Glider
           National Museum of Flight Scotland   East Fortune
           Built 1978   Stored

BAPC.247   Albatros Sail Gliders ASG.21 Hang Glider
           National Museum of Flight Scotland   East Fortune
           Built 1977   Stored

BAPC.248   McBroom Hang Glider
           Museum of Berkshire Aviation   Woodley
           Built 1974

BAPC.249   Hawker Fury I replica
           Brooklands Museum   Weybridge
           As 'K5673' in RAF 1 Sqdn 'A' Flight c/s
           Built by Brooklands c.1990s

BAPC.250   Royal Aircraft Factory SE.5a replica
           Brooklands Museum   Weybridge
           As 'F5475:A'   '1st Battalion Honourable Artillery Company'
           Built by Brooklands c.1990s

BAPC.251   Hi-Way Spectrum
           Ian Fyffe   Lytham St Annes
           Built by 1980   Stored

BAPC.252   Flexi-Form Skysails Hang Glider
           Museum of Science and Industry   Manchester   *In store*
           Built by 1982

BAPC.253   Mignet HM.14 Pou-du-Ciel replica
           Solent Sky Museum   Southampton   *As 'G-ADZW'*
           Built by 1990s   On loan from H.Shore

BAPC.254   Supermarine Spitfire FSM
           Yorkshire Air Museum   Elvington
           As 'R6690:PR-A' in RAF 609 Sqdn c/s

BAPC.255   North American P-51D Mustang FSM
           Imperial War Museum / American War Museum
           Duxford   *As '463209:WZ-S' in 78th FG c/s*
           Built by Rialto, California, USA 1990

BAPC.256   Santos Dumont Type 20 Demoiselle replica
           Brooklands Museum   Weybridge
           Built by J Aubert 1996-97

BAPC.257   de Havilland DH.88 Comet ⅞ Scale Model
           Not known   Sywell   *'G-ACSS'*

BAPC.258   Adams / RFD-GQ Balloon (5000 cu.feet)
           British Balloon Museum and Library   Newbury
           Built by RFD-GQ Parachutes

BAPC.259   Gloster Gamecock replica
           Jet Age Museum   Gloucestershire   *As 'J7904'*

BAPC.260   Mignet HM.280 replica
           Not known   Wickenby   *'F-4L'*

BAPC.261   General Aircraft GAL.48 Hotspur Composite
           Museum of Army Flying   AAC Middle Wallop   *As 'HH268'*
           Composite from anonymous cockpit of Mk.1
           & rear of Mk.II HH379

BAPC.262   Eurowing Catto CP-16 Microlight
           SE-SHK   National Museum of Flight Scotland   East Fortune
           Stored

BAPC.263   Chargus Cyclone Hang Glider
           Ulster Aviation Collection   Long Kesh
           Built 1979

BAPC.264   Bensen B.8M Gyrocopter
           The Helicopter Museum   Weston-Super-Mare
           Built 1984

BAPC.265   Hawker Hurricane I FSM
           Yorkshire Air Museum   Elvington
           As 'P3873:YO-H' in RCAF 1 Sqdn c/s

BAPC.266   Rogallo Hang Glider
           Ulster Aviation Collection   Long Kesh

BAPC.267   Hawker Hurricane I FSM
           'R4115:LE-X', 'P2954:WX-E'   Imperial War Museum   Duxford
           As 'V7467:LE-D' in RAF c/s

BAPC.268   Supermarine Spitfire IX FSM
           'MH978', 'N3317', 'PL279'   Spitfire Corner
           Newquay Cornwall   *As 'PL279:ZF-Z' in RAF 485 Sqn c/s*
           Built by for 'Dark Blue World' 2001 Czech film

BAPC.269   Supermarine Spitfire V FSM
           The Wings of Liberty Memorial Park   RAF Lakenheath
           'BM361:XR-C' of RAF 71 Sqn c/s

BAPC.270   de Havilland DH.60G Gipsy Moth FSM
           Dumfries and Galloway Aviation Museum
           Tinwald Downs   *As 'G-AAAH'   'Jason'*

BAPC.271   Messerschmitt Me.163B Komet FSM
           The Shuttleworth Collection   Old Warden   *'191454'*
           No wings or rear fuselage/tail: renovated rocket-motor
           fitted to cockpit mock-up

BAPC.272   Hawker Hurricane I FSM
           Kent Battle of Britain Museum   Hawkinge
           As 'N2532:GZ-H' and 'P2921:GZ-L' in RAF 32 Sqdn c/s

BAPC.273   Hawker Hurricane I FSM
           Kent Battle of Britain Museum   Hawkinge
           As 'P3059:SD-N'

BAPC.274   Boulton-Paul P.6 replica
           'K-124', 'G-EAPD'   Norfolk and Suffolk Aviation Museum
           Flixton   *As 'X25'   Carries 'Boulton & Paul Ltd, Sales Dept' titles*
           On loan from Boulton Paul Aircraft Heritage Project

BAPC.275   Bensen B.8M Gyrocopter
           Museum and Art Gallery   Doncaster
           Built by S J R Wood, Warmsworth

BAPC.276   Hartman Ornithopter
           The Science Museum   Wroughton
           In store

BAPC.277   Mignet HM.14 Pou-du-Ciel replica
           The Gliding Heritage Centre   Lasham
           'L'Autre Aviation' on tail

BAPC.278   Hawker Hurricane I FSM
           Kent Battle of Britain Museum   Hawkinge
           As 'P3679:GZ-K' in RAF 32 Sqdn c/s

BAPC.279   Airspeed AS.51 Horsa I replica
           The Assault Glider Trust   RAF Cosford   *'LH291'*

BAPC.280   de Havilland DH.89A Dragon Rapide replica
           'G-AEAJ', 'G-ANZP'   The Marriott Hotel   Liverpool Airport
           As 'G-AJCL' in Railway Air Services c/s

BAPC.281   Boulton-Paul Defiant I FSM
           Kent Battle of Britain Museum   Hawkinge
           As 'L7005:PS-B' in RAF 264 Sqdn c/s
           On permanent loan from Boulton-Paul Association

BAPC.282   Manx / Peel Engineering Eiderduck
           Hanging from ceiling in Terminal   Isle of Man Airport

BAPC.283   Supermarine Spitfire FSM
           A Saunders   Jurby
           Built by Feggans Brown for 'Piece of Cake' TV series
           Stored 09.10

BAPC.284   Gloster E28/39 FSM
           Sir Frank Whittle Commemorative Trust   Lutterworth
           Built by Sir Frank Whittle Commemorative Trust;
           displayed on a roundabout in the town

BAPC.285   Gloster E28/39 FSM
           Sir Frank Whittle Commemorative Trust
           Ively Roundabout, Farnborough
           Built by Sir Frank Whittle Commemorative Trust

BAPC.286   Mignet HM.14 Pou-du-Ciel replica
           Caernarfon Airworld Museum   Caernarfon   *As 'G-EGCK'*

BAPC.287   Blackburn F.2 Lincock FSM
           Streetlife Museum of Transport   Hull   *As 'G-EBVO'*
           Built by BAE, Brough c 2002

BAPC

BAPC.288 Hawker Hurricane I FSM
Robin Hood's Wheelgate Park   Farnsfield
As 'V7467:LE-D' in RAF 242 Sqdn c/s

BAPC.289 Bensen B.8B Gyro-Boat
The Helicopter Museum   Weston-Super-Mare

BAPC.290 Fieseler Fi.103 (FZG-76 / V-1) FSM
The Dover Museum   Dover

BAPC.291 Hawker Hurricane I FSM
National Memorial To The Few   Capel Le Ferne
As 'P2970:US-X' in RAF 56 Sqdn c/s   'Little Willie'
Built by GB Replicas

BAPC.292 Eurofighter Typhoon FSM
Not known

BAPC.293 Supermarine Spitfire IX FSM
Not known
Built by Concepts & Innovations

BAPC.294 Fairchild F-24W Argus II replica
Thorpe Camp Visitor Centre   Tattershall Thorpe   *As 'EV771'*

BAPC.295 Leonardo da Vinci Glider replica
Skysport Engineering   Sandy
Built Skysport Engineering 2003 for Channel 4
TV documentary 'Leonardo's Dream Machines'

BAPC.296 Army Balloon Factory Nulli Secundus 1 Gondola replica
Not known   *'Nulli Secundus 1'*

BAPC.297 Supermarine Spitfire replica
Kent Battle of Britain Museum   Hawkinge
As Spitfire Prototype 'K5054'
Built for 'Battle of Britain' film

BAPC.298 Supermarine Spitfire IX FSM
Gate Guard   RAF Cosford   *'MK356'*

BAPC.299 Supermarine Spitfire FSM
'P3338'   National Memorial To The Few   Capel Le Ferne
As 'R6775:YT-J' in RAF 72 Sqdn c/s
Built by GB Replicas

BAPC.300 Piffard Hummingbird replica
Shoreham Airport Historical Association   Brighton City

BAPC.301 Supermarine Spitfire Vb FSM
As 'BM481:YO-T' (401 Sqn) & 'PK651:B-RAO' (608 Sqn)
Displayed in A1045 roundabout at Thornaby-on-Tees
Built by GB Replicas 2007

BAPC.302 Mignet HM.14 Pou-du-Ciel
Gliding Heritage Centre   Lasham

BAPC.303 Goldfinch Amphibian 161
Norfolk and Suffolk Aviation Museum   Flixton

BAPC.304 Supermarine Spitfire Vb FSM
Mark Oliver   Knutsford   *'W3850:PR-A'in RAF 609 Sqn c/s*
Built by Royal British Legion, Ripon Branch in 2008

BAPC.305 Mersnier Pedal-Powered Airship replica
British Balloon Museum and Library   Newbury   *Gondola only*

BAPC.306 Lovegrove Discord Autogyro
Norfolk and Suffolk Aviation Museum   Flixton   *'PCL-129'*
'The Discord'

BAPC.307 Bleriot Type XI replica
South Yorkshire Aviation Museum / Aeroventure   Doncaster
Built by Ken Fern 2008

BAPC.308 Supermarine Spitfire I FSM
R Whitton   Currie, Elgin   *'L1019:LO-S'*

BAPC.309 Fairey Gannet Cockpit Procedures Trainer
The Aeroplane Collection   Ellesmere Port – Hooton Park

BAPC.310 Miles Wings Gulp 100A Hang Glider   29.02.16
The Aeroplane Collection   Ellesmere Port – Hooton Park

BAPC.311 Ferranti Phoenix UAV ⅜ Scale Prototype   07.03.16
National Museum of Scotland   Edinburgh

BAPC.312 Airwave Magic Kiss Hang Glider   07.03.16
National Museum of Flight Scotland   East Fortune

BAPC.313 Firebird Sierra Hang Glider   07.03.16
National Museum of Flight Scotland   East Fortune

BAPC.314 Gold Marque Gyr Hang Glider   07.03.16
National Museum of Flight Scotland   East Fortune

BAPC.315 Bensen B-8 Gyroglider   07.03.16
National Museum of Flight Scotland   East Fortune
In store

BAPC.316 Pilcher Bat Mk. 2 replica   07.03.16
Riverside Museum   Glasgow
Built by Spirit Aerosystems, Prestwick 2007

BAPC.317 WACO CG-4A Hadrian Cockpit   07.03.16
National Museum of Flight Scotland   East Fortune
'The Bunhouse'

BAPC.318 Supermarine Spitfire FSM   07.03.16
Hamish Macleod   Moffatt   *'PT462:SW-A'*

BAPC.319 Supermarine Spitfire FSM   07.03.16
No. 1333 Squadron, Air Training Corps   Grangemouth
'X4859:PQ-N'

BAPC.320 Supermarine Spitfire Vb FSM   07.03.16
Air Station Heritage Centre   Montrose
As 'EP121:LO-D'.in RAF 602 (City of Glasgow) Sqdn c/s
'Red Lichtie'   Built by GB Replicas

BAPC.321 Royal Aircraft Factory BE.2c replica   07.03.16
Air Station Heritage Centre   Montrose   Angus
As '471' in RFC 2 Sqdn c/s

BAPC.322 Handley Page Halifax III Cockpit replica   07.03.16
Dumfries and Galloway Aviation Museum   Tinwald Downs

BAPC.323 Supermarine Spitfire Vb FSM   07.03.16
Fairhaven Lake   Lytham St Annes   *'W3644:QV-J'*
Built by GB Replicas; moved autumn 2018

BAPC.324 Supermarine Spitfire IXc FSM   07.03.16
'RB159'   Lytham Spitfire Display Team   Blackpool
As 'BS435: FY-F' in 611 Sqn c/s   Used as travelling exhibit
Built by TDL Replicas

BAPC.325 Supermarine Spitfire FSM   07.03.16
'TM-L'   Lytham Spitfire Display Team   Blackpool
As 'PL256:TM-L' in 504 Sqn c/s   Used as travelling exhibit
Built by TDL Replicas

BAPC.326 Supermarine Spitfire II FSM   07.03.16
'N3290:AI-H'   Lytham Spitfire Display Team   Blackpool
As 'X4253:FY-N'   Used as travelling exhibit

BAPC.327 Fieseler Fi.103 (FZG-76 / V-1) FSM   10.03.16
Ian Starmes   Cheshire

BAPC.328 Avro F Type Cabin replica   11.03.16
Avro Heritage Museum   Woodford, Cheshire   *As '10'*
On loan from Museum of Science & Industry, Manchester

BAPC.329 Mignet HM.14 Pou-du-Ciel   14.03.16
T Smith   Exhibited in roof at Breighton   *'F50'*

BAPC.330 Ward Gnome   14.03.16
Newark Air Museum   Winthorpe

BAPC.331 Gloster E28/39 FSM   14.03.16
Jet Age Museum   Gloucestershire   *As 'W4041/G'*

BAPC.332 Royal Aircraft Factory BE.2b replica   14.03.16
Boscombe Down Aviation Collection   Old Sarum
As '2783'

BAPC.333 Supermarine Spitfire II FSM   14.03.16
Royal Air Force Museum   RAF Cosford
As 'RG904:BT-K' in RAF c/s   'Haldane Place'

BAPC.334 Hawker Hurricane FSM   17.03.16
On pole in Alexandra Park   Windsor   *'R4229:GN-J'*

BAPC.335 Supermarine Spitfire IIa FSM   17.03.16
Gate Guard   RAF High Wycombe   *'Observer Corps'*
As 'P7666:EB-Z' in RAF 41 Sqn c/s
Built by Gateguards (UK) Ltd

BAPC.336[1] Pilcher Bat Mk. 2 replica   17.03.16
Allocation Cancelled – Duplicate of BAPC.316

BAPC.336[2] Northrop F-5E Tiger II FSM   31.03.16
Gate Guard   RAF Alconbury   *'01532'*

BAPC.337 Pilcher Bat Mk. 3 replica   17.03.16
The Shuttleworth Collection   Old Warden
Built by E Littledike 2009

BAPC.338 Halton Aero Club Mayfly replica   20.03.16
Trenchard Museum   RAF Halton

BAPC.339 Husband Modac 500 Hornet Gyroplane   21.03.16
The Helicopter Museum   Weston-Super-Mare

BAPC.340 Dickson Primary Glider   22.03.16
Nigel Ponsford Collection   Yorkshire

BAPC.341 Lockheed-Martin F-35B Lightning II FSM   25.03.16
Royal Air Force Museum   Hendon
Built by Gateguards (UK) Ltd

BAPC.342	Lockheed-Martin F-35B Lightning II Ground Training Aid Fleet Air Arm RNAS Culdrose *'GTA-01'*	25.03.16
BAPC.343	Lockheed-Martin F-35B Lightning II Ground Training Aid Fleet Air Arm RNAS Culdrose *'GTA-02'*	25.03.16
BAPC.344	Fieseler Fi.103 (FZG-76 / V-1) FSM Cornwall Aviation Heritage Centre Newquay Cornwall *Built by Gateguards (UK) Ltd*	25.03.16
BAPC.345	Fieseler Fi.103 (FZG-76 / V-1) FSM Cornwall At War Museum Davidstow Moor *Built by Gateguards (UK) Ltd*	25.03.16
BAPC.346	Hawker Hurricane FSM Gate Guard North Weald *As 'V7313:US-F' in RAF 56 Sqdn c/s*	29.03.16
BAPC.347	Colditz Cock replica Gliding Heritage Centre Lasham *On loan from South East Aircraft Services*	29.03.16
BAPC.348	Sopwith 7F.1 Snipe replica Not known *'E6655:B'*	31.03.16
BAPC.349	de Havilland DH.103 Hornet F.1 Cockpit Composite The DH Hornet Project Chelmsford	11.04.16
BAPC.350	TEAM Minimax Hi-MAX PFA 272-13162 LAA Build-A-Plane Project Not known *Mobile Exhibit*	11.04.16
BAPC.351	Airspeed AS.58 Horsa II replica Cobbaton Combat Collection Chittlehampton *'5' Built by for film ' A Bridge Too Far'*	11.04.16
BAPC.352	Armstrong-Whitworth / Hawker Sea Hawk Cockpit Fort Perch Museum New Brighton	11.04.16
BAPC.353	Sopwith 5F1 Dolphin Composite Not known *'C3988'*	11.04.16
BAPC.354	Sopwith Tabloid Floatplane replica Brooklands Museum Brooklands *As '3'*	11.04.16
BAPC.355	Slingsby T.7 Cadet Tettenhall Transport Heritage Collection Wolverhampton *As 'PD685'*	11.04.16
BAPC.356	GEC Avionics Phoenix UAV Composite Boscombe Down Aviation Collection Old Sarum	26.04.16
BAPC.357	BAC Lightning F.6 FSM BAE Systems Factory Samlesbury *'XS921:BA'*	26.04.16
BAPC.358	Boulton-Paul Overstrand Cockpit replica Norfolk and Suffolk Aviation Museum Flixton *'K4556:F-101'*	26.04.16
BAPC.359	Cody Army Aeroplane No. 1A replica Farnborough Air Sciences Trust Farnborough	26.04.16
BAPC.360	Eurofighter Typhoon FGR.4 FSM RAF Exhibition Unit RAF Cranwell *'IR106'*	26.04.16
BAPC.361	Boeing-Vertol CH-47 Chinook HC.2 FSM RAF Exhibition Unit RAF Cranwell *'IR808'*	26.04.16
BAPC.362	Hawker Fury replica Cambridge Bomber and Fighter Society Little Gransden *As 'K1926'*	26.04.16
BAPC.363	Hawker Typhoon Cockpit Jet Age Museum Brockworth *Under restoration*	26.04.16
BAPC.364	Kiceniuk Icarus II Biplane Hang Glider Norfolk and Suffolk Aviation Museum Flixton	26.04.16
BAPC.365	Northrop MQM-36 Shelduck SD-1 UAV XR898? Boscombe Down Aviation Collection Old Sarum *As 'XT005'*	26.04.16
BAPC.366	Percival E.2H Mew Gull replica Not known *As 'G-AEXF' Built by Hawker Restorations 2005-2008*	26.04.16
BAPC.367	Percival E.2H Mew Gull replica Thorpe Camp Visitor Centre Tattershall Thorpe *As 'G-AEXF' Built by J Lord & Partners*	26.04.16
BAPC.368	Supermarine 361 Spitfire LF.XVIe Replica Norfolk and Suffolk Aviation Museum Flixton *As 'TD248:8Q-T' in RAF 695 Sqdn c/s*	26.04.16
BAPC.369	Supermarine Spitfire FSM *'P7895:RN-N'* Ulster Aviation Collection Long Kesh *As 'R7823:TM-F'*	26.04.16
BAPC.370	WACO CG-4A Hadrian replica Royal Air Force Museum RAF Cosford *On loan from Assault Glider Trust as '241079'*	26.04.16
BAPC.371	Westland Lysander FSM *'V9875:MA-J'* Tangmere Military Aviation Museum Tangmere *'V9875:MA-E'* *Built by Gateguards (UK) Ltd*	26.04.16
BAPC.372	Wasp Falcon 4 Hang Glider Norfolk and Suffolk Aviation Museum Flixton *No marks carried*	26.04.16
BAPC.373	Westland Whirlwind Mk. 1 replica Whirlwind Fighter Project Not known *Under construction*	26.04.16
BAPC.374	Antonov C.14 Hang Glider Norfolk and Suffolk Aviation Museum Flixton	26.04.16
BAPC.375	Boeing-Stearman PT-27 Kaydet Composite N62842, 42-15662 Norfolk and Suffolk Aviation Museum Flixton *'FJ801'*	26.04.16
BAPC.376	Messerschmitt Bf.109E-4 FSM Iconic WW2 Aircraft Belper *'6' Yellow* *Built by Gateguards (UK) Ltd*	26.04.16
BAPC.377	Supermarine Spitfire IX FSM Iconic WW2 Aircraft (Northern Forties Re-enactment Group) Belper *'EN398'*	26.04.16
BAPC.378	Hawker Hurricane IIc FSM Gate Guard RAF High Wycombe *As 'V7467:LE-D' in RAF 242 Sqdn c/s* *Built by Gateguards (UK) Ltd*	30.04.16
BAPC.379	Supermarine Spitfire FSM Not known Not known *Was with Dumfries and Galloway Aviation Museum;* *wings incorporated into Spitfire at Australian Museum* *of Army Flying, Oakey, Queensland*	30.04.16
BAPC.380	Blackburn Triplane replica Brough Heritage Group Fort Paull Museum *Built by Brough Heritage Group 2008*	30.04.16
BAPC.381	Westland Wallace replica Not known (Leicester East)	30.04.16
BAPC.382	British Aerospace 125 Forward Fuselage Deeside College, Kelsterton Road Connah's Quay	14.05.16
BAPC.383	Airspeed AS.58 Horsa Cockpit replica Jet Age Museum Gloucestershire	17.05.16
BAPC.384	Flight Refuelling Limited Falconet UAV Mark Oliver Knutsford	18.05.16
BAPC.385	Sopwith F.1 Camel replica Mark Oliver Knutsford *'D6447'*	18.05.16
BAPC.386	Bristol F.2b Fighter Bristol Aero Collection Filton *As 'A7288'*	27.05.16
BAPC.387	Bristol F.2b Fighter replica Aerospace Bristol Filton *'A7228:7'*	27.05.16
BAPC.388	Short Stirling B.III Composite The Stirling Project Alconbury	27.05.16
BAPC.389	Heinkel He.111 Recreation Lincolnshire Aviation Heritage Centre East Kirkby	27.05.16
BAPC.390	Felixstowe F.5 Cockpit Norfolk and Suffolk Aviation Museum Flixton	27.05.16
BAPC.391	Cody Type V Bi-Plane replica Farnborough Air Sciences Trust Farnborough	31.05.16
BAPC.392	Avro International RJX-100 Bristol Aero Collection Filton	31.05.16
BAPC.393	Supermarine Spitfire FSM Lodge Hill Garage Abingdon *'N3310:AI-A'*	31.05.16
BAPC.394	Supermarine Spitfire I FSM *'X4178:EB-K'* Imperial War Museum Duxford *As 'X4474:QV-I' in RAF 19 Sqdn c/s*	31.05.16
BAPC.395	Pilatus P2-05 replica Personal Plane Services Limited Wycombe Air Park	31.05.16
BAPC.396	Airspeed AS.51 Horsa II Cockpit Imperial War Museum Duxford	31.05.16
BAPC.397	General Aircraft GAL.48 Hotspur II Cockpit Dumfries and Galloway Aviation Museum Tinwald Downs	31.05.16
BAPC.398	Bristol 156 Beaufighter VI Cockpit Midland Air Museum Coventry	31.05.16

BAPC.399[1] Lockheed-Martin Desert Hawk III UAV								31.05.16
ZK150 *Allocation Cancelled – Is UK Military Serial*

BAPC.399[2] Hawker Hurricane IIc FSM									23.06.16
Eden Camp – Modern History Theme Museum
Malton *Pole mounted as 'P2793:SD-M' in
RAF 501 Sqdn c/s*

BAPC.400 Royal Aircraft Factory FE.2b replica								31.05.16
Royal Air Force Museum Hendon *As 'A6526'*
Incorporating original nacelle & engine

BAPC.401 Mignet HM.14 Pou-du-Ciel									31.05.16
Catford Independent Air Force London

BAPC.402 Hawker Hurricane I Composite								31.05.16
Cambridge Bomber and Fighter Society
Little Gransden *As 'L1639'*

BAPC.403 Fieseler Fi.103 (FZG-76 / V-1) FSM								24.06.16
Ulster Aviation Collection Long Kesh
Built by J Herron 2010

BAPC.404 Civilian Aircraft Company Coupe 6							23.07.16
Shipping and Airlines Limited Biggin Hill *Incomplete*

BAPC.405 Manuel Crested Wren									03.08.16
Gliding Heritage Centre Lasham
As 'BGA 178' – not the original BGA 178
Donated by B Reed

BAPC.406 Electro Flight Lightning P 1E FSM								27.08.16
Roger Targett / Electroflight Stroud

BAPC.407 de Havilland DH.2 ⅞ Scale Model								27.08.16
Great War Aerodrome Stow Maries

BAPC.408 BAe Systems Phoenix UAV Composite							27.08.16
Larkhill Wiltshire *'NF314'*

BAPC.409 de Havilland DH.82A Tiger Moth Composite							27.08.16
Thorpe Camp Visitor Centre Tattershall Thorpe
As 'G-ANNN'

BAPC.410 Supermarine Spitfire II FSM								27.08.16
War and Peace Ash *As 'P7370:ZP-A'*
Used as a Travelling exhibit

BAPC.411 Hawker Hurricane FSM									27.08.16
'P3144' War and Peace Ash *As 'V6555:DT-A'*
'Burma' *Used as a Travelling exhibit*

BAPC.412 Gotha G.V Cockpit replica									27.08.16
Great War Aerodrome Stow Maries6

BAPC.413 Sopwith 1½ Strutter Cockpit replica							27.08.16
Great War Aerodrome Stow Maries *As 'A8274'*

BAPC.414 Sopwith F.1 Camel replica									27.08.16
Great War Aerodrome Stow Maries 'South African'
Dismantled

BAPC.415 ML Aviation Sprite UAV									27.08.16
Museum of Berkshire Aviation Woodley

BAPC.416 ML Aviation Sprite UAV									27.08.16
Museum of Army Flying AAC Middle Wallop

BAPC.417 Airspeed AS.** Horsa replica								27.08.16
Museum of Army Flying AAC Middle Wallop

BAPC.418 Airspeed AS.** Horsa Cockpit Replica							27.08.16
Museum of Army Flying AAC Middle Wallop

BAPC.419 Fieseler Fi.103 (FZG-76 / V-1) FSM								27.08.16
North-East Land, Sea and Air Museum Usworth

BAPC.420 Vickers FB.27A Vimy Cockpit replica							22.11.16
Brooklands Museum Weybridge

BAPC.421 Vickers Wellington Forward Fuselage replica						22.11.16
Brooklands Museum Weybridge

BAPC.422 Avro 683 Lancaster Composite Cockpit							29.11.16
Avro Heritage Trust Woodford
'Hi Ho! Hi Ho! It's Off to Work We Go' (port) &
'Maggie's Murderous Mission' (starboard)
Built by J.Hall

BAPC.423 EoN AP.5 Primary									12.12.16
Aircraft Restoration Group Masham
'WP266' *In store*

BAPC.424 Manchester University / BAe JAVA UAV							05.01.17
Museum of Science and Industry Manchester

BAPC.425 Avro 683 Lancaster Cockpit replica								12.02.17
The Pitstone Museum Pitstone
Built by N Groom

BAPC.426 Supermarine Spitfire IX FSM								16.02.17
Simply Spitfires Lowestoft *'MK805:SH-B'*

BAPC.427 Skyhook Safari Powered Hang Glider							16.02.17
The Science Museum Wroughton *In store*

BAPC.428 Cody Man-Lifting Kite replica								17.02.17
Museum of Science and Industry Manchester

BAPC.429 Bleriot XI Cockpit									17.02.17
The Science Museum South Kensington

BAPC.430 Army Balloon Factory Airship Beta II Gondola						17.02.17
The Science Museum South Kensington *'HMA No.17'*

BAPC.431 Supermarine Spitfire FSM									17.02.17
St George's Chapel of Remembrance Biggin Hill
As 'K9998:QJ-K'

BAPC.432 Breen Hang Glider									18.02.17
Tettenhall Transport Heritage Collection
Wolverhampton

BAPC.433 Westland Whirlwind Mk. 1 Cockpit replica							19.02.17
City of Norwich Aviation Museum Horsham St Faith

BAPC.434 de Havilland DH.98 Mosquito Composite / Replica						19.02.17
Lincolnshire Aviation Heritage Centre
East Kirkby *As 'HJ711:VI-C'*

BAPC.435 WACO CG-4A Hadrian Cockpit								19.02.17
Museum of Military Life Carlisle

BAPC.436 Bristol 152 Beaufort Composite								19.02.17
9131M Royal Air Force Museum Hendon
As 'DD931'

BAPC.437 Lilienthal Kleiner Doppeldecker replica							19.02.17
The Shuttleworth Collection Old Warden
No marks carried

BAPC.438 Lilienthal Normal Apparatus replica							19.02.17
The Shuttleworth Collection Old Warden
No marks carried

BAPC.439 Lilienthal Type XI Glider replica								19.02.17
The Shuttleworth Collection Old Warden
Built by E Littledyke & S Nitsch 2007

BAPC.440 Lovegrove Rota-Glida GyroGlider							19.02.17
The Gyrocopter Experience Rufforth *'PCL 132'*

BAPC.441 Pilcher Triplane replica									19.02.17
The Shuttleworth Collection Old Warden

BAPC.442 Sopwith Baby Composite									19.02.17
Fleet Air Arm Museum RNAS Yeovilton *As 'N2078'*

BAPC.443 WACO CG-4A Hadrian Cockpit replica							19.02.17
South Yorkshire Aviation Museum / Aeroventure
Doncaster

BAPC.444 Westland WG-25 / WR-05 Mote Remotely Piloted					19.02.17
Helicopter
The Helicopter Museum Weston-Super-Mare

BAPC.445 Westland WG-25 / WR-07 Wideye Remotely
Piloted Helicopter										19.02.17
The Helicopter Museum Weston-Super-Mare

BAPC.446 Westland WG-25 / WR-06 Wisp Remotely
Piloted Helicopter										19.02.17
The Helicopter Museum Weston-Super-Mare

BAPC.447 Yamaha Motors Remotely Piloted Helicopter						19.02.17
The Helicopter Museum Weston-Super-Mare

BAPC.448 Bleriot XI replica									21.02.17
Caernarfon Airworld Museum Caernarfon

BAPC.449 Handley Page HP.61 Halifax B.III
Composite/Reconstruction									22.02.17
HR792, JP158, LW687, TG536 Yorkshire Air Museum
Elvington *As 'LV907:NP-F'* & *'NP763:H7-N'*

BAPC.450 Hawker Siddeley Harrier Composite							26.02.17
XV798, XW264
The Helicopter Museum Weston-Super-Mare
Composite

BAPC.451 Westland WG-25 Sharpeye MockUp Remotely
Piloted Helicopter										26.02.17
The Helicopter Museum Weston-Super-Mare

BAPC.452 Sopwith 1½ Strutter replica								26.02.17
'B9708' Not known Bletchingley Road, Merstham
'N5177' *In store*

BAPC.453	Lockheed-Martin F-35B Lightning II Ground Training Aid Fleet Air Arm RNAS Culdrose 'GTA-03'	03.04.17
BAPC.454	Lockheed-Martin F-35B Lightning II Ground Training Aid Fleet Air Arm RNAS Culdrose 'GTA-04'	03.04.17
BAPC.455	Lockheed-Martin F-35B Lightning II FSM BAE Systems Factory Samlesbury *On gate*	03.04.17
BAPC.456	Supermarine Spitfire FSM Not known	07.04.17
BAPC.457	Supermarine Spitfire VIII FSM RAAF Museum Point Cook, Victoria 'A58-492'	07.04.17
BAPC.458	North American P-51D Mustang FSM Not known Business Park, Auckland, New Zealand	07.04.17
BAPC.459	Levasseur PL.8 Biplane ⅞ Scale FSM Peninsular Hotel, 19 Avenue Kleber Paris 'L'oiseau Blanc'	07.04.17
BAPC.460	Supermarine Spitfire V FSM L Wilton Kent *Coded 'RS-T'* *Built Gateguards (UK) Ltd*	07.04.17
BAPC.461	Supermarine Spitfire Cockpit FSM Not known	07.04.17
BAPC.462	Supermarine Spitfire Cockpit FSM *Reduced to parts for re-use at Gate Guards UK at Newquay*	07.04.17
BAPC.463	Bristol 156 Beaufighter IIF Cockpit Not known	07.04.17
BAPC.464	North American P-51D Mustang FSM Tuskegee Airmen National Historic Site, Moton Field Tuskegee, Alabama '10' 'Duchess Arlene'	07.04.17
BAPC.465	Fieseler Fi.103 (FZG-76 / V-1) FSM RAF Manston Museum Manston	21.05.17
BAPC.466	Huntair Pathfinder 2 RAF Manston Museum Manston	21.05.17
BAPC.467	Nieuport 17 replica RAF Manston Museum Manston 'A213'	21.05.17
BAPC.468	Sopwith 1½ Strutter replica RAF Manston Museum Manston 'B619'	21.05.17
BAPC.469	Nieuport 17 replica RAF Manston Museum Manston	21.05.17
BAPC.470	de Havilland DH.60G Gipsy Moth FSM St Stephen's Shopping Mall Hull As 'G-AAAH' 'Jason' *Built by HM Prison Hull*	07.06.17
BAPC.471	Avro 683 Lancaster Cockpit replica Avro Heritage Museum Woodford As 'R5868:PO-S' On loan from M Willoughby *Used as a travelling exhibit*	16.07.17
BAPC.472	Morane-Saulnier Type N replica North-East Land, Sea and Air Museum Usworth As '5191'	17.07.17
BAPC.473	Messerschmitt Bf.109x FSM War and Peace Ash *Used as a travelling exhibit*	07.08.17
BAPC.474	Philips British Matchless Flying Machine The Shuttleworth Collection Old Warden	10.08.17
BAPC.475	Hawker Hurricane I FSM The Battle of Britain Bunker and Visitor Centre Uxbridge As 'P3901:RF-E' in RAF 303 Sqdn c/s	19.08.17
BAPC.476	Supermarine Spitfire Cockpit replica Biggin Hill Heritage Limited Biggin Hill As 'TB885'	09.09.17
BAPC.477	Hawker Hurricane FSM St George's Chapel of Remembrance Biggin Hill As 'P2921:GZ-L'	09.09.17
BAPC.478	Supermarine Spitfire Cockpit replica RAF Elsham Wolds Memorial Garden and Memorial Room Elsham Wolds	18.09.17
BAPC.479	Bleriot XI replica Telford Thomson Ipswich *Under construction*	08.10.17
BAPC.480	Ferranti / Slingby T.68 Phoenix UAV National Museum of Flight Scotland East Fortune *Built by Slingsby Engineering, Kirkbymoorside*	18.10.17
BAPC.481	Mignet HM.14 Pou-du-Ciel Aircraft Restoration Group Masham 'G-ADRZ' *In store*	21.10.17
BAPC.482	Avro Lancaster Cockpit replica Malcolm Goosey Staffordshire	28.10.17
BAPC.483	Supermarine Spitfire II Cockpit replica Malcolm Goosey Staffordshire	28.10.17
BAPC.484	British Aerospace Harrier Composite South Yorkshire Aviation Museum Doncaster 'XV281'	26.11.17
BAPC.485	Government Aircraft Factory Jindivik Mk.103A (Composite) A92-664? Boscombe Down Aviation Collection Old Sarum As 'A92-466' *Composite includes parts from A92-244, A92-442, A92-466 & A92-490*	04.02.18
BAPC.486	Curtiss P-40N Warhawk FSM Not known *Destroyed during the making of the film 'Red Tails'*	20.02.18
BAPC.487	Curtiss P-40N Warhawk FSM GateGuards UK Limited Newquay Cornwall	20.02.18
BAPC.488	Curtiss P-40N Warhawk FSM GateGuards UK Limited Newquay Cornwall	20.02.18
BAPC.489	North American P-51D Mustang FSM GateGuards UK Limited Newquay Cornwall	20.02.18
BAPC.490	North American P-51D Mustang FSM GateGuards UK Limited Newquay Cornwall	20.02.18
BAPC.491	North American P-51D Mustang FSM GateGuards UK Limited Newquay Cornwall	20.02.18
BAPC.492	Supermarine Spitfire FSM Not known *Burned in the Netherlands during filming of 'Dunkirk'*	20.02.18
BAPC.493	Supermarine Spitfire FSM Planes of Fame Air Museum Chino, California	20.02.18
BAPC.494	Supermarine Spitfire Cockpit replica Not known	09.03.18
BAPC.495	Supermarine Spitfire Vb FSM Spitfire Heritage Trust *On display in Makoanyane Square, Kingsway, Maseru* As 'L2016:RN-E' of 72 Sqn c/s	09.03.18
BAPC.496	Bristol F.2b Fighter reconstruction Aerospace Bristol Bristol *Under restoration in USA 2018*	23.03.18
BAPC.497	Comper / Cranwell Light Aeroplane Club CLA.4 As '4' Alberta Aviation Museum Edmonton, Alberta	23.03.18
BAPC.498	Avro 616 Avian IVA replica Guy Menzies Memorial Hari Hari, Westland District, West Coast Region, New Zealand As 'G-ABCF'	23.03.18
BAPC.499	Hawker Hurricane FSM The Battle of Britain Bunker and Visitor Centre Uxbridge 'P3873:YO-H' on starboard side	23.03.18
BAPC.500	Supermarine Spitfire FSM The Battle of Britain Bunker and Visitor Centre Uxbridge 'L1035:SH-D'	23.03.18
BAPC.501	Northrop Shelduck D.1 Composite Muckleburgh Collection Weybourne As 'XT581'	23.03.18
BAPC.502	Short 184 replica Estonian Maritime Museum Tallinn As 'N9190' *Under construction*	23.03.18
BAPC.503	Airspeed AS.5* Horsa fuselage Dumfries and Galloway Aviation Museum Tinwald Downs	22.04.18
BAPC.504	de Havilland DH.9 Royal Saudi Air Force Museum Riyadh	22.04.18
BAPC.505	Westland Wapiti replica Royal Saudi Air Force Museum Riyadh	22.04.18
BAPC.506	Vickers Type 60 Viking IV ⅞ Scale Model Alberta Aviation Museum Edmonton As 'G-CAEB'	22.04.18
BAPC.507	Bristol 86A Tourer replica Museum of Western Australia Perth As 'G-AUDK'	22.04.18
BAPC.508	Sopwith F.1 Camel replica Museum of Western Australia Perth As 'M6394'	22.04.18
BAPC.509	Hinkler Ibis replica Hinkler Hall of Aviation Bundaberg, Queensland	22.04.18
BAPC.510	Sopwith Triplane replica CP101 Aerospace Museum Calgary 'N500'	22.04.18

BAPC.511	de Havilland DH.83 Fox Moth replica M Dowell Hokitika Airport, NZ As 'ZK-ADI' Built by M Dowell	23.03.18
BAPC.512	North American P-51D Mustang cockpit replica Gary Dean Wiltshire '44-14134' 'One More Time' Data Plate '44-11175' Used as a travelling exhibit Built by G Dean	19.07.18
BAPC.513	Supermarine Spitfire FSM Essex Memorial Spitfire Monument Ontario As 'ML135:YO-D' of No. 401 Sqn	23.07.18
BAPC.514	Miles M.25 Martinet Cockpit Composite Tettenhall Transport Heritage Centre Tettenhall 'RG907' Under construction	01.10.18
BAPC.515	TASUMA Observer Concept UAV Newark Air Museum Winthorpe Built by TASUMA (UK) Ltd	25.10.18
BAPC.516	TASUMA Navigator CSV 30 UAV Newark Air Museum Winthorpe Built by TASUMA (UK) Ltd	25.10.18
BAPC.517	TASUMA Navigator CSV 30 UAV Newark Air Museum Winthorpe Built by TASUMA (UK) Ltd	25.10.18
BAPC.518	English Electric Canberra PR.9 Cockpit Newark Air Museum Winthorpe 'Test Specimen Rig. No. 1' Built by English Electric Ltd	25.10.18
BAPC.519	Supermarine Spitfire IX FSM South African Air Force Museum Port Elizabeth Built R Tribelhorn; As 'JK769:AGM'	29.10.18
BAPC.520	Aerospatiale / BAC Concorde Scale Model Flugausstellung Hermeskeil Rhienland-Palatinate As 'F-WTSA'	29.10.18
BAPC.521	Hawker Hurricane I FSM Composite North-East Land, Sea and Air Museum Usworth Under construction	02.01.19
BAPC.522	Supermarine Spitfire FSM Andy Harper Blackpool Built by A Harper	02.01.19
BAPC.523	Supermarine Spitfire Cockpit replica Lytham Spitfire Display Team Blackpool Displayed in Hangar 42	02.01.19
BAPC.524	Morane-Saulnier MS.406 Cockpit replica Lytham Spitfire Display Team Blackpool Displayed in Hangar 42	02.01.19
BAPC.525	Messerschmitt Bf.109 Cockpit replica Lytham Spitfire Display Team Blackpool Displayed in Hangar 42	02.01.19
BAPC.526	Hawker Typhoon replica La Memorial de la Paix Caen As 'JP656:BR-SW'	08.01.19
BAPC.527	Supermarine Spitfire Vc FSM Classic Flyers Museum, Mount Manganui Tauranga As 'JK715:SN-A' of No. 485 Sqn	08.01.19

BAPC.528	Fairey Swordfish replica Classic Flyers Museum, Mount Manganui Tauranga Built by Museum of Transport & Technology, Auckland As 'DK791'	08.01.19
BAPC.529	BAe Systems Tempest Concept Model Not known Used as a travelling exhibit by BAe Systems	08.01.19
BAPC.530	Supermarine Spitfire IX ⅔ Scale Model Greenwood Military Aviation Museum Nova Scotia Built by S Derrick; as 'BS306:AE-A' of 402 (City of Winnipeg) Sqn	15.01.19
BAPC.531	QinetiQ Zephyr 6 6-1 Farnborough Air Sciences Trust Farnborough Built QinetiQ	15.01.19
BAPC.532	QinetiQ Zephyr 6 6-2 Winchester Science Centre Winchester Built QinetiQ	15.01.19
BAPC.533	Bensen B.8 Gyrocopter South Yorkshire Aircraft Museum / Aeroventure Doncaster	16.01.19
BAPC.534	Hawker Typhoon IB Cockpit South Yorkshire Aircraft Museum / Aeroventure Doncaster	16.01.19
BAPC.535	Hawker Typhoon IB Cockpit South Yorkshire Aircraft Museum / Aeroventure Doncaster	16.01.19
BAPC.536	Hawker Tempest II Cockpit South Yorkshire Aircraft Museum / Aeroventure Doncaster	16.01.19
BAPC.537	Ford Flivver replica South Yorkshire Aircraft Museum / Aeroventure Doncaster Buillt by K Fern	16.01.19
BAPC.538	Supermarine Spitfire FSM Czech Spitfire Club Czech Republic As 'ML296:DU-N' of No. 312 Sqn	17.01.19

In addition a number of Full Scale Models and display reproductions have been noted at various locations. Many are not associated with any particular BAPC numbers and some are not accessible. They are listed alphabetically.

Bristol M.1 scale replica/simulator	Stow Maries Great War Aerodrome Stow Maries
Port Victoria P.V.8 Eastchurch Kitten replica	Yorkshire Air Museum Elvington Built W Sneesby 'N540'
Supermarine Spitfire IX fsm	Kent Battle of Britain Museum Hawkinge 'MK356:2I-V' in RCAF 443 Sqdn c/s
Supermarine Spitfire IX fsm	Wartime Aircraft Recovery Group Aviation Museum AMSS Valley Farm Industrial Estate, Pyle 'EN398:JE-J'
Supermarine Spitfire fsm	Boultbee Academy Goodwood 'MK392:JE-J'

IRISH AVIATION HISTORICAL COUNCIL REGISTER

The IAHC Register came into existence with similar objectives as above. Updates are very welcome.

Register No	Type C/n Previous Identity Location Remarks
IAHC.1	Mignet HM.14 Pou du Ciel reproduction South East Aviation Enthusiasts Group Dromod, County Leitrim 'St Patrick' Stored
IAHC.2	Aldritt Monoplane Foulkes-Halbard Collection Filching Manor, Wannock
IAHC.3	Mignet HM.14 Pou du Ciel M Donohoe Delgany Built by R Robinson, Carbury in 1937 but unflown
IAHC.4	Hawker Hector IAAC.... D McCarthy Not known Fuselage frame; believed on rebuild Florida, USA
IAHC.5	Morane-Saulnier MS.230 1045 ? Fuselage frame; believed scrapped

Register No	Type C/n Previous Identity Location Remarks
IAHC.6	Ferguson Monoplane replica Ulster Folk & Transport Museum Holywood, Belfast Built by Capt J Kelly Rogers in 1974
IAHC.7	Sligo Concept G O'Hara Sligo Stored incomplete 08.91
IAHC.8	O'Hara Autogyro G O'Hara Sligo Stored incomplete 08.91
IAHC.9	Ferguson Monoplane replica Ulster Folk & Transport Museum Holywood, Belfast Built by L Hannah in 1980 Dismantled

SECTION 4 – REPUBLIC OF IRELAND

Information is updated to 15th March 2019.

Aircraft listed as registered on the official Irish Aviation Authority's Register website are marked in **bold**, even if there have not been any recent positive sightings. Those that are extant but no longer current are displayed in roman (non-bold) text, and those which both joined and departed the register in the period since the publication of the 2018 edition of this volume are indicated with a star (⋆).

Other information has come from Ian Burnett's monthly Overseas Register section published in *Air-Britain News* and other important data has been supplied by David Buck, Peter Budden, Richard Cawsey, Colman Corcoran, Phil Dunnington, Ken Parfitt, Dave Partington, Trevor Read and the indispensable *Irish Air Letter*. Finally, please note Aer Lingus aircraft carry names in English on the port side and Gaelic on the starboard side.

Details of the Irish Gliding and Soaring Register can be found on page 547, and the type index cross-reference on page 548.

Regn	Type	C/n	Regn date
	Previous identity Owner/Cancellation details Prob Base		
EI-ABI	de Havilland DH.84 Dragon 2	6105	12.08.85
	EI-AFK, G-AECZ, AV982, G-AECZ		
	Aer Lingus Charitable Foundation Dublin *'Iolar'*		
EI-AED	Cessna 120	11783	11.03.08
	N77342, NC77342 E McNeill & P O'Reilly Limetree		
EI-AEE	Auster V J/1 Autocrat	1873	22.12.09
	G-AGVN, EI-CKC, G-AGVN		
	O & N A O'Sullivan Newcastle *'Aimee'*		
EI-AEF	Cessna 120	12692	16.03.11
	N4221N, NC4221N J Halligan Kilrush		
EI-AEH	Luscombe 8F Silvaire	1821	07.01.14
	G-BSHI, N39060, NC39060		
	D Kelly Craughwell		
EI-AEI	Aeronca 65-TAC Defender	C1661TA	01.05.13
	G-BTUV, N36816, NC36816		
	F J McMorrow & Partners Ballyboy		
	As 'C1661:T/A' in USAF c/s		
EI-AEL	Piper PA-16 Clipper	16-186	07.03.14
	G-BSVI, N5379H G Dolan (Lifford, Co Donegal)		
	'Tranquility Mk11'		
EI-AEM	Cessna 140	13744	28.10.14
	G-BYCD, N4273N, NC4273N		
	Cessna 140 Flying Group Ballyboy		
EI-AET	Piper J-3C-65 Cub	16108	22.02.17
	C-FLEI S T Scully (Trim, Co Meath)		
EI-AFE	Piper J-3C-90 Cub	16687	11.03.49
	OO-COR, D-ELAB, N9954F, EI-AFE, NC79076		
	4 of Cubs Flying Group Clonbullogue		
EI-AFZ	de Havilland DHC-1 Chipmunk 22	C1/0659	25.01.17
	G-BXDP, WK642 Gipsy Captains Group Kilrush		
	As 'WK642:94' in RAF c/s		
EI-AGD	Taylorcraft Plus D	108	26.05.53
	G-AFUB, HL534, G-AFUB		
	G Lynch (Ballyjamesduff, Co Cavan)		
	Fuselage stored 04.16		
EI-AGJ	Auster V J/1 Autocrat	2208	03.11.53
	G-AIPZ W G Rafter Rafter's Field, Ellistown		
EI-AHI	de Havilland DH.82A Tiger Moth	85347	17.09.93
	G-APRA, DE313 High Fidelity Flyers Ballyboy		
EI-AII	Cessna 150F	15064509	27.09.12
	N3109X L Bagnell Coonagh		
EI-AKM	Piper J-3C-65 Cub	15810	17.11.58
	N88194 J A Kent Kilmoon		
EI-ALH	Taylorcraft Plus D	106	05.05.60
	G-AHLJ, HH987, G-AFTZ		
	Cancelled 26.10.11 as decision of authority		
	Ballyjamesduff, Co Cavan *Fuselage stored 04.16*		
EI-ALP	Avro 643 Cadet	848	12.09.60
	G-ADIE J C O'Loughlin Rafter's Field, Ellistown		
	Stored		
EI-AMF	Taylorcraft Plus D	157	26.04.62
	G-ARRK, G-AHUM, LB286		
	Cancelled 03.04.70 as de-registered Carr Farm, Thorney		
	On restoration 02.15		

Regn	Type	C/n	Regn date
	Previous identity Owner/Cancellation details Prob Base		
EI-AMI	Piper PA-22-108 Colt	22-8835	02.07.15
	G-ARSU Cancelled 15.02.16 as WFU Carlow		
	Carlow Institute of Technology 05.16		
EI-AMK	Auster V J/1 Autocrat	1838	19.09.62
	G-AGTV D Doyle & Partners Gorey		
EI-AMY	Auster J/1N Alpha	2634	09.04.63
	G-AJUW Cancelled 18.10.12 as decision of authority		
	Maynooth, Co Meath		
	Stored wreck 03.16		
EI-ANA	Taylorcraft Plus D	206	29.08.63
	G-AHCG, LB347		
	Cancelled xx.xx.xx as xxx		
	Ballyjamesduff, Co Cavan *Fuselage stored 04.16*		
EI-ANT	Champion 7ECA Citabria	7ECA-38	13.01.65
	T Croke & Partners Gorey		
EI-ANY	Piper PA-18 Super Cub 95	18-7152	18.11.64
	G-AREU, N3096Z The Bogavia Group Kilrush		
EI-AOB	Piper PA-28-140 Cherokee	28-20667	28.04.65
	Knock Flying Group Waterford		
EI-APF	Cessna F150G	F150-0112	06.03.66
	Cancelled 16.01.06 as de-registered Perth		
	Built by Reims Aviation SA; stored fuselage 03.18		
EI-ARN	Cessna 182H Skylane	18256196	xx.xx.67
	N2096X Cancelled 22.09.80 as WFU		
	Abbeyshrule		
	Stored wreck 04.14		
EI-ARW	Jodel DR.1050	118	14.08.67
	F-BJJH J Davy Abbeyshrule		
EI-ATJ	Beagle B.121 Pup Series 1	B121-029	10.02.69
	G-35-029 C Barrett & N James Waterford		
EI-ATK	Piper PA-28-140 Cherokee	28-24120	18.10.68
	G-AVUP Cancelled 22.02.11 as WFU		
	Edgeworthstown		
	Midland Karting & Paintball 04.16		
EI-ATP^M	Phoenix Luton LA-4A Minor	PAL 1124	29.08.69
	G-ASCY Cancelled 07.73 – to N924GB		11.08.70
	Suspended from roof as 'EI-ATP' & N924GB		
	Built by Cornelius Bros		
	At Miami International Airport, Florida		
EI-AUE	Morane MS.880B Rallye Club	1359	xx.04.70
	G-AXHU		
	Cancelled 20.11.07 as de-registered		
	Carlow		
	Carlow Institute of Technology 05.16		
EI-AUH	Cessna F172H Skyhawk	F172-0727	xx.08.70
	Cancelled 28.08.86 as DBR		
	Dublin Weston		
	Built by Reims Aviation SA; fire training area 09.14		
EI-AUM	Auster V J/1 Autocrat	2612	11.09.70
	G-AJRN T G Rafter Rafter's Field, Ellistown		
EI-AUO	Reims/Cessna FA150K Aerobat	FA1500074	02.03.71
	B Shane & Partners Spanish Point		

EI-AUS	Auster J/5F Aiglet Trainer	2779	17.11.70

EI-AUS · Auster J/5F Aiglet Trainer · 2779 · 17.11.70
Cancelled 18.10.12 as decision of authority
Warrenstown
On restoration 03.16

EI-AUT · Forney F-1A Aircoupe · 5731 · 21.12.70
G-ARXS, D-EBSA, N3037G
Cancelled 27.05.11 as WFU   Tullylish, Co Down
Stored wreck 03.16

EI-AVC · Cessna F337F Super Skymaster · 01355/0038 · 26.08.71
N4757   Cancelled 26.06.03 as de-registered
Enniskillen
Built by Reims Aviation SA; dismantled 03.16

EI-AVM · Reims/Cessna F150L · F15000745 · 03.03.72
J Nugent   Newcastle
Stored dismantled 04.18

EI-AWP · de Havilland DH.82A Tiger Moth · 85931 · 04.07.72
F-BGCL, French AF, DF195   A P Bruton   Abbeyshrule
Registered with c/n 19577

EI-AWR · Malmö MFI-9 Junior · 010 · 12.06.73
LN-HAG, (SE-EBW)   L P Murray   (Ashbourne, Co Meath)
Stored dismantled 04.16

EI-AWU · Morane MS.880B Rallye Club · 880 · 12.01.74
G-AVIM   Cancelled 27.06.08 as de-registered
Milford, Co Donegal
Fuselage in Strains Scrapyard 03.16

EI-AYB · Gardan GY-80-180 Horizon · 156 · 05.10.73
F-BNQP   J B Smith   Abbeyshrule

EI-AYI · Morane MS.880B Rallye Club · 189 · 21.11.73
F-OBXE   J McNamara   Cloncarneel

EI-AYK · Reims/Cessna F172M Skyhawk II · F17201092 · 25.03.74
Cancelled 15.06.11 as WFU   Trevet
Stored 05.14

EI-AYN · Britten-Norman BN-2A-8 Islander · 704 · 26.03.74
G-BBFJ   Galway Aviation Services Ltd   Connemar
Built by IRMA; operated by Aer Arann Islands

EI-AYR · Schleicher ASK 16 · 16022 · 05.04.74
(EI-119)   B O'Broin   Ballyboy

EI-AYT · SOCATA MS.894A Rallye Minerva 220 · 11065 · 06.08.74
G-AXIU   K A O'Connor   Abbeyshrule
Stored wreck

EI-AYY · Evans VP-1 · MD01 · 18.08.75
Ballyboughal VP-1 Flying Group   Ballyboughal
Built by M Donoghue as SAAC project 003

EI-BAJ · SNCAN Stampe SV-4C · 171 · 17.10.74
F-BBPN   W Rafter & Partners   Abbeyshrule

EI-BAT · Reims/Cessna F150M · F15001196 · 02.05.75
J Nugent   Henlow
Operated by Henlow Flying Club

EI-BAV · Piper PA-22-108 Colt · 22-8347 · 30.04.75
G-ARKO   E Finnamore   Limetree

EI-BBE · Champion 7FC Tri-Traveller · 7FC-393 · 07.09.75
G-APZW   P Ryan   (Oranmore, Co Galway)
Tail-wheel conversion to 7EC Traveller status

EI-BBV · Piper J-3C-65 Cub (L-4J-Pl) · 13058 · 14.06.76
D-ELWY, F-BEGB, 44-80762
A N Johnston   Ballyboy
Frame No.12888; as '480762' in USAAF c/s

EI-BCE · Britten Norman BN-2A-26 Islander · 519 · 14.09.76
G-BDUV   Galway Aviation Services Ltd   Connemara
Operated by Aer Arann Islands

EI-BCF · Bensen B-8M Gyrocopter · 47941 · 24.08.76
N....   P Flanagan   Kilrush
Stored

EI-BCJ · Aeromere F.8L Falco 3 · 204 · 19.01.77
G-ATAK, D-ENYB   M P McLoughlin   Kilrush

EI-BCK · Reims/Cessna F172N Skyhawk II · F17201543 · 22.11.76
National Flight Centre Ltd   Dublin Weston

EI-BCM · Piper J-3C-65 Cub (L-4H-Pl) · 11983 · 26.11.76
F-BNAV, N9857F, 44-79687 ?
M Bergin & Partners   Ballyboughal

EI-BCN · Piper J-3C-65 Cub (L-4H-Pl) · 12335 · 26.11.76
F-BFQE, OO-PIE, 44-80039   H Diver   Kilrush

EI-BCP · Druine D.62B Condor · RAE 618 · 27.01.77
G-AVCZ   T Delaney   Monaquill
Built by Rollason Aircraft & Engines

EI-BCU · SOCATA MS.880B Rallye 100ST · 2595 · 10.02.77
F-BXTH   Cancelled 28.01.09 as destroyed
Dublin Weston
Fire training area 09.14

EI-BDL · Evans VP-2 · V2-2101 · 07.09.77
P Buggle   Kilrush
Built by J Duggan as PFA 7213 & then SAAC project 004

EI-BDM^M · Piper PA-23-250 Aztec D · 27-4166 · 10.10.77
G-AXIV, N6826Y
Cancelled 02.02.12 as removed from service   Dromod
Dromod Railway Station Museum 05.17

EI-BDR · Piper PA-28-180 Cherokee C · 28-3980 · 08.12.77
G-BAAO, LN-AEL, SE-FAG   Cherokee Group   Cork

EI-BDX · Druine D.62B Condor · RAE 608 · 24.06.16
G-ASRB   The Brian Douglas Trust-BDX Group
Taghmon
Built by Rollason Aircraft & Engines

EI-BEN · Piper J-3C-65 Cub (L-4J-Pl) · 12546 · 28.04.78
G-BCUC, F-BFMN, 44-80250
Ballyboughal L4 Flying Group   Ballyboughal
Frame No.12376

EI-BGG · SOCATA MS.892E Rallye 150GT · 12824 · 30.01.79
F-GAFS   Cancelled 31.01.06 as WFU   Co Kilkenny
Paintball site 10.13

EI-BGJ · Reims/Cessna F152 · F15201359 · 14.05.79
Cancelled 21.02.12 as removed from service   Carlow
Carlow Institute of Technology 05.16

EI-BHB · SOCATA MS.887 Rallye 125 · 2162 · 07.06.79
F-BUCH   Cancelled 29.11.99 as WFU   Abbeyshrule
Stored wreck 11.13

EI-BHM · Cessna 337E Super Skymaster · 33701217 · 01.11.79
Cancelled 19.10.12 as WFU   Ashbourne
Puddenhill Activity Center 11.13

EI-BHV · Champion 7EC Traveller · 7EC-739 · 30.10.79
G-AVDU, N9837Y   P O'Donnell & Partners   Ballyboe

EI-BHW · Cessna F150F · F150-0013 · 22.11.79
G-ATMK   Cancelled 19.10.12 as decision of authority
Mullaghbane, Co Armagh
Built by Reims Aviation SA; stored 04.16

EI-BIB · Reims/Cessna F152 II · F15201724 · 30.11.79
Sligo Aeronautical Club Ltd   Sligo

EI-BIC · Reims/Cessna F172N Skyhawk II · F17201965 · 15.02.80
(OO-HNZ)   Cancelled 18.11.02 as WFU Abbeyshrule
Stored wreck 04.14

EI-BID · Piper PA-18 Super Cub 95 (L-18C-Pl) · 18-1524 · 30.11.79
D-EAES, French Army 18-1524, 51-15524
A Connaire & Partners   Craughwell

EI-BIK · Piper PA-18-150 Super Cub · 18-7909088 · 01.02.80
N82276   Dublin Gliding Club Ltd   Gowran Grange
Modified to 180hp engine

EI-BIO · Piper J-3C-65 Cub (L-4J-Pl) · 12657 · 27.05.80
F-BGXP, OO-GAE, 44-80361
H Duggan & Partners   Limetree
As '480361:H-47' in USAAF c/s

EI-BIR · Reims/Cessna F172M Skyhawk II · F17201225 · 24.03.80
F-BVXI   Figile Flying Group   Clonbullogue

EI-BIV · Bellanca 8KCAB Super Decathlon · 464-79 · 03.06.80
N5032Q   Atlantic Flight Training Ltd   Cork

EI-BJB · Aeronca 7DC Champion · 7AC-925 · 16.04.80
G-BKKM, EI-BJB, N82296, NC82296
W Kennedy   Moyne
Stored incomplete

EI-BJC · Aeronca 7AC Champion · 7AC-4927 · 02.04.80
N1366E, NC1366E, SE-FBW, OY-DKN
E Griffin   Blackwater

EI-BJK · SOCATA Rallye 110ST · 3226 · 08.07.80
F-GBKY   M Keenen   Kilrush

EI-BJM · Cessna A152 Aerobat · A1520936 · 18.09.80
N761CC   National Flight Centre Ltd   Dublin Weston

EI-BJO · Cessna R172K Hawk XP II · R1723340 · 06.08.80
N758TD   The XP Group   Galway

EI-BKC   Aeronca 15AC Sedan   15AC-467   05.11.80
              N1394H   G F Hendrick   Birr

EI-BKE   Morane MS.885 Rallye   278   09.02.81
              F-BKUN, F-WKUN   Cancelled 16.09.86 as WFU
              Edgeworthstown
              Midland Karting & Paintball 04.16

EI-BKK   Taylor JT.1 Monoplane   PFA 1421   02.02.81
              G-AYYC   D Doyle   Limetree
              Built by S B Sharp

EI-BKN   SOCATA MS.880B Rallye 110ST   3035   18.02.81
              Cancelled 05.11.10 as WFU   Clonbullogue
              Wreck in container 05.17

EI-BMI   SOCATA TB-9 Tampico   203   12.05.82
              F-GCOV   A Breslin   Kilrush

EI-BMN   Reims/Cessna F152 II   F15201912   10.03.82
              National Flight Centre Ltd   Dublin Weston

EI-BMU   Monnett Sonerai IIL   01224   19.05.82
              N O'Donnell   Sligo
              Built by D Connaire & P Ford as SAAC project 014

EI-BNK   Cessna U206F Stationair   U20601706   23.12.82
              G-HILL, PH-AND, D-EEXY, N9506G
              Cancelled 31.10.12 as WFU   Clonbullogue
              Stored 05.18

EI-BNL   Rand Robinson KR-2   xxxx   13.01.83
              K Hayes   (Bearna, Co Galway)
              Built as SAAC project 012 – for sale

EI-BNU   Morane MS.880B Rallye Club   1204   07.04.83
              F-BPQV   J Cooke   Dublin Weston

EI-BOV   Rand Robinson KR-2   xxxx   07.05.84
              G O'Hara & Partners   (Strandhill, Co Sligo)
              *Built by G Callan & G O'Hara as SAAC project 011;
              damaged Carnmore 03.91 & dismantled 03.16*

EI-BPL   Reims/Cessna F172K   F17200758   28.03.85
              G-AYSG   Phoenix Flying Ltd   Shannon

EI-BPP   Eipper Quicksilver MX   3207   12.03.85
              J A Smith   Abbeyshrule
              Stored

EI-BRU   Evans VP-1   V-12-84-CQ   05.11.85
              C O'Shea   (Bray, Co Wicklow)
              *Built by C Quinn as SAAC project 018;
              stored dismantled 04.16*

EI-BSB   Wassmer Jodel D.112   1067   23.06.87
              G-AWIG, F-BKAA   T Darmody   Newcastle
              Rebuilt by W Kennedy as SAAC project 025

EI-BSF   Hawker Siddeley HS.748 Series 1   1544   xx.xx.86
              EC-DTP, G-BEKD, LV-HHF, LV-PUM
              Cancelled 26.07.94 as WFU   Dublin Weston
              Stored fuselage 05.17

EI-BSG   Bensen B-8M Gyrocopter   HB   30.01.86
              J Todd   (Ashbourne, Co Meath)
              Stored

EI-BSK   SOCATA TB-9 Tampico   618   09.04.86
              J Byrne   Dublin Weston

EI-BSL   Piper PA-34-220T Seneca III   34-8233041   27.06.86
              N8468X   P Sreenan   Dublin Weston

EI-BSN   Cameron O-65 HAB   1278   14.04.86
              L Durcan   (Dunshaughlin, Co Meath)   *'Erin-Go-Bragh'*

EI-BSO   Piper PA-28-140 Cherokee B   28-25449   16.04.86
              C-GOBL, N8241N   S Brazil   Newcastle

EI-BSW   Solar Wings Pegasus XL-R   SW-WA-1122   22.06.87
              E Fitzgerald   (Butlerstown, Co Waterford)
              Trike c/n SW-TB-1124

EI-BSX   Piper J-3C-65 Cub   13255   22.08.17
              G-ICUB, F-BEGT, NC79805, 45-4515, 42-36788
              J O'Dwyer   (Naas, Co Kildare)

EI-BUA   Cessna 172M Skyhawk II   17265451   08.08.86
              N5458H   Cancelled 27.01.14 as removed from service
              Dublin Weston
              Fire training area 09.14

EI-BUC   Jodel D.9 Bébé   xxxx   20.01.87
              G-BASY   B Lyons & Partners   Moyne
              Built by R L Sambell as project PFA 929

EI-BUF   Cessna 210N Centurion II   21063070   18.12.86
              G-MCDS, G-BHNB, N6496N   210 Group   Abbeyshrule

EI-BUG   SOCATA ST-10 Diplomate   125   04.02.87
              G-STIO, OH-SAB   J Cooke   Abbeyshrule
              Stored

EI-BUL   Whittaker MW.5 Sorcerer   1   04.03.87
              J Culleton   (Mountmellick, Co Laois)
              Built by Aerotech & J Greene

EI-BUN   Beech 76 Duchess   ME-371   26.06.87
              (EI-BUO), N37001
              National Flight Centre Ltd   Dublin Weston

EI-BUO^M   Aero Composites Sea Hawker   080   25.08.87
              Cancelled xx.09.91 as DBR
              With Ulster Aviation Society, Long Kesh

EI-BUO^M   Aero Composites Sea Hawker   080   25.08.87
              Cancelled xx.09.91 as DBR   Long Kesh
              Preserved Ulster Aviation Museum 04.16

EI-BUT   GEMS MS.893A Rallye Commodore 180 10559   30.07.87
              SE-IMV, F-BNBU   T Keating   Dublin Weston

EI-BVJ   AMF Microflight Chevvron 2-32   009   16.02.88
              A Dunne   Kilrus

EI-BVK   Piper PA-38-112 Tomahawk   38-79A0966   02.03.88
              OO-FLG, OO-HLG, N9705N   B Lowe   Newcastle

EI-BVT   Evans VP-2   V2-2129   29.04.88
              G-BEIE   P Morrison   (Cobh, Co Cork)   *'Birdy'*
              *Built by F G Morris as PFA 7221 & then J J O'Sullivan
              as SAAC project 020*

EI-BVY   Heintz Zenith CH.200AA-RW   2-582   07.06.88
              J Matthews & Partners   Abbeyshrule
              Built by J Matthews & M Skellly as SAAC project 026

EI-BXO   Fouga CM.170 Magister   257   21.11.88
              FM-28   Cancelled 27.01.10 as de-registered
              Baldonnel
              Stored dismantled 06.17

EI-BYA   Thruster TST Mk.1   8504   01.02.89
              G-MNDA   Cancelled 25.01.12 as decision of authority
              Ballyheelan, Co Cavan
              Stored wreck 04.16

EI-BYL   Heintz Zenith CH.250   2866   14.06.89
              (EI-BYD)   I Calton   Newcastle
              Built by A Corcoran as SAAC project 030

EI-BYX   Champion 7GCAA Citabria   7GCAA-40   04.04.90
              N546DS   P J Gallagher   Coonagh

EI-BYY   Piper J-3C-85 Cub   12494   12.04.90
              EC-AQZ, HB-OSG, 44-80198
              The Cub Club   Dublin Weston
              *Frame No.12322; regd with c/n 22288 & officially
              ex G-AKTJ, N3595K, NC3595K; under restoration 04.16*

EI-CAA   Reims/Cessna FR172J Rocket   FR17200486   17.08.89
              G-BHTW, 5Y-ATO   Cancelled 27.11.98 as WFU
              Abbeyshrule
              Stored wreck 04.14

EI-CAC   Grob G-115A   8092   22.10.89
              C Phillips   Dublin Weston

EI-CAD   Grob G-115A   8104   22.08.03
              G-WIZB, EI-CAD   C Phillips   Kilrush

EI-CAE   Grob G-115A   8105   05.04.90
              R M Davies   Cork

EI-CAN   Aerotech MW.5(K) Sorcerer   5K-0011-02   15.06.90
              (G-MWGH)   V Vaughan   Abbeyleix

EI-CAP   Cessna R182 Skylane RGII   R18200056   27.04.90
              G-BMUF, N7342W   EICAP Ltd   Helsinki-Malmi

EI-CAU   AMF Microflight Chevvron 2-32C   022   14.11.90
              J Tarrant   Rathcoole

EI-CAX   Cessna P210N Pressurized Centurion II P21000215 09.07.90
              (EI-CAS), G-OPMB, N4553K
              K A O'Connor   Dublin Weston
              Stored

EI-CBK   Aérospatiale-Alenia ATR 42-300   199   25.07.90
              F-WWEM   Elix Assets 7 Ltd   Maastricht
              Broken up)

EI-CCF   Aeronca 11AC Chief   11AC-S-40   10.01.91
              N3826E, NC3826E   G McGuinness   (Trim)

EI-CCK	Cessna 152 II	15279610	09.10.90

N757BM   Cancelled 05.11.12 as de-registered
Dublin Weston
Fire training area 09.14

EI-CCM	Cessna 152 II	15282320	09.10.90

N68679   J Dunphy   Kilrush

EI-CDP	Cessna 182L	18258955	20.05.91

G-FALL, OY-AHS, N4230S
Irish Parachute Club Ltd   Clonbullogue

EI-CDV	Cessna 150G	15066677	14.08.98

N2777S   K A O'Connor   Dublin Weston
Fire training area 09.14

EI-CEG	SOCATA MS.893E Rallye 180GT	13083	31.10.91

SE-GTS   M Jarrett   Manor Farm, Glatton

EI-CES	Taylorcraft BC-65	2231	25.03.92

G-BTEG, N27590, NC27590
G Higgins & Partners   Kilcoleman, Enniskeane
Stored 05.17

EI-CFF	Piper PA-12 Super Cruiser	12-3928	23.05.91

N78544, NC78544   J O'Dwyer & Partners   Kilrush

EI-CFG	Rousseau Piel CP.301B Emeraude	112	01.06.91

G-ARIW, F-BIRQ   F Doyle   (Barntown, Co Wexford)
Stored

EI-CFH	Piper PA-12 Super Cruiser	12-3110	01.06.91

(EI-CCE), N4214M, NC4214M   G Treacy   Moyne

EI-CFO	Piper J-3C-65 Cub (*L-4H-PI*)	11947	13.05.92

OO-RAZ, OO-RAF, 44-79651   B Reilly   Abbeyshrule
As '479651' in USAAF c/s

EI-CFV	Morane MS.880B Rallye Club	1850	13.05.92

G-OLFS, G-AYYZ   Cancelled 15.11.00 as WFU
Edgeworthstown
Midland Karting & Paintball 04.16

EI-CFY	Cessna 172N Skyhawk II	17268902	18.06.92

N734JZ   National Flight Centre Ltd   Dublin Weston

EI-CGF	Phoenix Luton LA-5 Major	PAL-1124	31.07.92

G-BENH   P Jones   (Tuam, Co Galway)
*Built by C D McCartney as project PFA 1208
then F Doyle as SAAC project 019*

EI-CGG	Erco 415C Ercoupe	3147	10.09.92

N2522H, NC2522H
Cancelled 06.11.12 as de-registered   Dublin Weston
Fire training area 09.14

EI-CGH	Cessna 210N Centurion II	21063524	16.11.92

N6374A   J Greif-Wuestenbecker   (Cavan, Co Cavan)

EI-CGP	Piper PA-28-140 Cherokee C	28-26928	25.11.92

G-MLUA, G-AYJT, N11C
S Collins & Partners   Waterford

EI-CGU	Robinson R-22HP	0148	10.12.92

G-BSNH, N9065D
Cancelled 16.04.97 as WFU   Bolton Street, Dublin
Dublin Institute of Technology 04.14

EI-CHN	Morane MS.880B Rallye Club	901	22.02.93

G-AVIO   Cancelled xx.xx.xx as xxx   Edgeworthstown
Midland Karting & Paintball 04.16

EI-CHR	CFM Shadow Series BD	063	20.05.93

G-MTKT   B Kelly   Limetree

EI-CIAM	Morane MS.880B Rallye Club	1218	26.04.93

G-MONA G-AWJK
Cancelled 03.02.11 as de-registered
Shannon   *With Aviation Museum at Atlantic AirVenture, Shannon*

EI-CIF	Piper PA-28-180 Cherokee C	28-2853	12.06.93

G-AVVV, N8880J   AA Flying Group   Eglinton
Rebuilt 1967 with spare frame c/n 28-3808S

EI-CIG	Piper PA-18-150 Super Cub	18-7203	12.06.93

G-BGWF, ST-AFJ, ST-ABN
National Flight Centre Ltd   Dublin Weston
Frame No.18-7360

EI-CIM	Avid Flyer Model IV	1125D	17.08.93

P Swan   Dublin Weston
Built by P Swan as SAAC project 041

EI-CIN	Cessna 150K	15071728	06.09.93

G-OCIN, EI-CIN, G-BSXG, N6228G
K A O'Connor   Dublin Weston
Stored dismantled

EI-CIV	Piper PA-28-140 Cherokee Cruiser	28-7725232	20.11.93

G-BEXY N9639N
Cancelled 06.11.12 as decision of authority   Waterford
Stored dismantled 09.14

EI-CJD	Boeing 737-204	22966	18.02.94

G-BKHE   Cancelled 29.10.04 as de-registered   Dublin
Dublin Airport Fire Trainer 05.17

EI-CJJ	Slingsby T.31 Motor Cadet III	907	19.01.06

XE794   J J Sullivan   Blackpool
*Built by J J Sullivan as SAAC project 40?;
stored dismantled*

EI-CJS	Jodel Wassmer D.120A Paris-Nice	339	28.02.94

F-BOYF   A Flood   Birr

EI-CJT	Slingsby T.31 Motor Cadet III	830	25.02.94

G-BPCW, XA288   J Tarrant   Rathcoole
Built by P C Williams as c/n PCW-001; stored

EI-CJX	Boeing 757-2Y0	26160	20.11.15

N135CA, G-FCLJ, N160GE, EI-CJX, N3519M, N1786B
ASL Airlines (Ireland) Ltd   Dublin
Operated by Aer Lingus

EI-CJY	Boeing 757-2Y0	26161	09.08.16

N153CA, G-FCLK, N161GE, EI-CJY, N3521N
AS Air Lease III (Ireland) Ltd   Cotswold
Stored

EI-CKH	Piper PA-18 Super Cub 95	18-7248	03.06.94

G-APZK, N10F   G Brady   Kilrush

EI-CKI	Thruster TST Mk.1	8078-TST-091	03.06.94

G-MVDI   S Woodgates   Limetree

EI-CKJ	Cameron N-77 HAB	3305	06.07.94

F Meldon   (Naas, Co Kildare)   *'Goodfellas'*

EI-CKZ	Jodel D.18	229	05.04.95

J O'Brien   (Glen of Imaal, Co Wicklow)
Still under construction?

EI-CLQ	Reims/Cessna F172N Skyhawk II	F17201653	26.05.95

G-BFLV   E Finnamore   Abbeyshrule

EI-CML	Cessna 150M	15076786	05.01.96

G-BNSS, N45207   L Kapser   Prague-Letnany

EI-CMN	Piper PA-12 Super Cruiser	12-1617	26.01.96

N2363M, NC2363M   A McNamee & Partners   Birr

EI-CMR	Rutan LongEz	1716	02.05.96

F O'Caoimh & Partners   Waterford
Built by F O'Caoimh as SAAC project 028

EI-CMT	Piper PA-34-200T Seneca II	34-7870088	23.04.96

G-BNER, N2590M   Atlantic Flight Training Ltd   Cork

EI-CMU	Mainair Mercury	1071-0296-7 & W873	03.05.96

B O'Neill   Limetree

EI-CMW	Rotorway Executive	3550	13.05.96

B McNamee   (Dunboyne, Co Meath)

EI-CNGM	Air & Space 18-A Gyroplane	18-75	10.09.96

G-BALB, N6170S   P Joyce   Long Kesh
Preserved Ulster Aviation Museum 04.16

EI-CNU	Pegasus Quantum 15	7326	10.04.97

M Ffrench   Limetree

EI-COP	Reims/Cessna F150L	F15001058	26.06.97

G-BCBY, PH-TGI, (G-BCBY)
Cancelled 08.02.06 as WFU   Keady, Co Armagh
Stored wreck 11.13

EI-COT	Reims/Cessna F172N Skyhawk II	F17201884	24.11.97

D-EIEF   Tojo Air Leasing Ltd   Abbeyshrule

EI-COY	Piper J-3C-65 Cub Special (Floatplane)	22519	05.11.97

N3319N, NC3319N   W Flood   Abbeyshrule

EI-COZM	Piper PA-28-140 Cherokee C	28-26796	05.11.97

G-AYMZ N11C
Cancelled 16.05.13 as WFU
With Aviation Museum at Atlantic AirVenture, Shannon

EI-CPE	Airbus A321-211	0926	11.12.98

D-AVZQ   Aer Lingus Ltd   Dublin   *'St Enda/Eanne'*

EI-CPG	Airbus A321-211	1023	28.05.99

D-AVZE   Aer Lingus Ltd   Dublin   *'St Aidan/Aodhan'*

EI-CPH	Airbus A321-211	1094	22.11.99

D-AVZB   Aer Lingus Ltd   Dublin   *'St Dervilla/Dearbhla'*

EI-CPI	Rutan LongEz	17	18.12.97
	D J Ryan (Waterford) *'Lady Elizabeth'*		
	Written off at Knockahavaun, Co Waterford 27.03.17		
EI-CPN	Auster J/4	2073	01.04.98
	G-AIJR Cancelled 06.11.12 as decision of authority		
	Ballyheelan, Co Cavan		
	Stored 04.16		
EI-CPP	Piper J-3C-65 Cub (L-4H-PI)	12052	23.03.98
	G-BIGH, F-BFQV, OO-GAS, OO-GAZ, 44-79756		
	W Kennedy Taghmon		
EI-CPX	III Sky Arrow 650T	K.122	24.06.98
	M McCarthy (Watergrasshill, Co Cork)		
	Built by M McCarthy as SAAC project 67		
EI-CRB	Lindstrand LBL 90A HAB	550	23.09.98
	J Concannon & Partners (Tuam, Co Galway)		
EI-CRG	Robin DR.400/180 Régent	2021	11.12.98
	D-EHEC D Lodge & Partners Waterford		
EI-CRR	Aeronca 11AC Chief	11AC-1605	13.04.99
	OO-ESM, (OO-DEL), OO-ESM L Maddock (Carlow)		
EI-CRX	SOCATA TB-9 Tampico	1170	21.05.99
	F-GKUL J W Leonard Dublin Weston		
EI-CSG	Boeing 737-8AS	29922	31.05.00
	N1786B Sapphire Leasing I (AOE 5) Ltd Ulan Bator		
	'Ogedei Khaan'		
	Operated by MIAT Mongolian Airlines		
EI-CSI	Boeing 737-8AS	29924	30.06.16
	VP-BPG, EI-CSI Sapphire Leasing I (AOE 4) Ltd		
	Rome-Fiumicino *'citta di Bologna'*		
	Operated by Blue Panorama Airlines		
EI-CTI	Reims/Cessna FRA150L	FRA1500261	29.04.99
	G-BCRN Cancelled 06.11.12 as de-registered		
	Abbeyshrule		
	Stored wreck 11.13		
EI-CTL	Aerotech MW-5B Sorcerer	SR102-R440B-07	21.05.99
	G-MTFH M Wade	Kilrush	
EI-CUB	Piper J-3C-65 Cub	16010	17.07.91
	G-BPPV, N88392 Cancelled xx.xx.xx as xxx Ballyboy		
	On restoration 05.17		
EI-CUJ	Cessna 172N Skyhawk II	17271985	19.11.99
	G-BJGO, N6038E The Hotel Bravo Flying Club Ltd		
	Cork		
EI-CUP	Cessna 335	335-0018	05.05.00
	N2706X Cancelled 07.09.12 as removed from service		
	Carlow		
	Carlow Institute of Technology 5.16		
EI-CUS	Agusta-Bell 206B-3 JetRanger III	8721	24.08.00
	G-BZKA, (EI-...), G-OONS, G-LIND, G-OONS		
	H Hassard (Slane, Co Meath)		
EI-CUW	Pilatus Britten-Norman BN-2B-20 Islander	2293	08.11.00
	G-BWYW Galway Aviation Services Ltd Connemara		
	Operated by Aer Arann Islands		
EI-CVA	Airbus A320-214	1242	22.06.00
	F-WWIT Aer Lingus Ltd Dublin *'St Schira/Scire'*		
EI-CVB	Airbus A320-214	1394	08.02.01
	F-WWIV Aer Lingus Ltd Dublin *'St Mobhi/Mobhi'*		
EI-CVC	Airbus A320-214	1443	06.04.01
	F-WWBS Aer Lingus Ltd Dublin		
	'St Kealin/Caoilphion'		
EI-CVL	Erco 415CD Ercoupe	4754	15.03.01
	G-ASNF, PH-NCF, NC94647 V O'Rourke Abbeyshrule		
EI-CVW	Bensen B-8M Gyrocopter	FK-199801	26.05.05
	F Kavanagh Kilrush		
	Built by F Kavanagh		
EI-CXC	Raj Hamsa X'Air 502T	333	06.09.02
	(44 SU) R Dunleavy Letterkenny		
EI-CXN	Boeing 737-329	23772	01.05.02
	OO-SDW, N506GX, OO-SDW		
	Transalpine Leasing Ltd Moscow-Domodedovo		
	Stored		
EI-CXR	Boeing 737-329	24355	31.05.02
	OO-SYA, (OO-SQA)		
	Transalpine Leasing Ltd Moscow-Vnukovo		
	Stored		
EI-CXV	Boeing 737-8CX	32364	03.07.02
	MASL Ireland Ltd Ulan Bator *'Khubelai Khaan'*		
	Operated by MIAT Mongolian Airlines in Borussia		
	Dortmund c/s		
EI-CXY	Evektor EV-97 Eurostar	2000-0701	31.10.02
	OK-FUR S Pallister Kilrush		
EI-CXZ	Boeing 767-216ER	24973	25.07.02
	N502GX, VH-RMM, N483GX, CC-CEF		
	Transalpine Leasing Ltd Moscow-Vnukovo		
	Stored		
EI-CZA	ATEC Zephyr 2000	Z580602A	17.07.03
	D Cassidy Limetree		
	Built by M Higgins		
EI-CZC	CFM Streak Shadow	K269SA11	16.07.02
	G-BWHJ R Camp (Mallow, Co Cork)		
EI-CZD	Boeing 767-216ER	23623	02.09.02
	N762TA, CC-CJU, N4529T		
	Cancelled 08.04.16 as WFU Enniscrone, Co Sligo		
	Quirky Glamping Village 05.16		
EI-CZP	Schweizer 269C-1 (*300CBi*)	0149	02.05.03
	NG Kam Tim Dublin Weston		
	Operated by European Helicopter Academy		
EI-DAA	Airbus A330-202	397	17.04.01
	F-WWKK Aer Lingus Ltd Dublin *'St Keeva/Caoimhe'*		
EI-DAC	Boeing 737-8AS	29938	02.12.02
	Ryanair DAC (Dublin)		
EI-DAD	Boeing 737-8AS	33544	03.12.02
	Ryanair DAC (Dublin)		
EI-DAE	Boeing 737-8AS	33545	09.12.02
	Ryanair DAC (Dublin)		
EI-DAF	Boeing 737-8AS	29939	09.01.03
	Ryanair DAC (Dublin)		
EI-DAG	Boeing 737-8AS	29940	17.01.03
	Ryanair DAC (Dublin)		
EI-DAH	Boeing 737-8AS	33546	22.01.03
	Ryanair DAC (Dublin)		
EI-DAI	Boeing 737-8AS	33547	03.02.03
	Ryanair DAC (Dublin)		
EI-DAJ	Boeing 737-8AS	33548	04.02.03
	Ryanair DAC (Dublin)		
EI-DAK	Boeing 737-8AS	33717	17.04.03
	Ryanair DAC (Dublin)		
EI-DAL	Boeing 737-8AS	33718	22.04.03
	Ryanair DAC (Dublin)		
EI-DAM	Boeing 737-8AS	33719	23.04.03
	Ryanair DAC (Dublin)		
EI-DAN	Boeing 737-8AS	33549	02.09.03
	Ryanair DAC (Dublin)		
EI-DAO	Boeing 737-8AS	33550	05.09.03
	N1800B Ryanair DAC (Dublin)		
EI-DAP	Boeing 737-8AS	33551	18.09.03
	N6066U Ryanair DAC (Dublin)		
EI-DAR	Boeing 737-8AS	33552	11.09.03
	(EI-DAQ) Ryanair DAC (Dublin)		
EI-DAS	Boeing 737-8AS	33553	12.09.03
	(EI-DAR) Ryanair DAC (Dublin)		
EI-DBI	Raj Hamsa X'Air Mk.2 Falcon	671	16.04.03
	D Cornally Kilrush		
EI-DBJ	Huntwing Pegasus XL Classic	xxxx	19.05.03
	G-MZCZ P A McMahon Clonbullogue		
	Built by C Kiernan as project BMAA/HB/039		
EI-DBK	Boeing 777-243ER	32783	10.10.03
	Celestial Aviation Trading 7 Ltd Rome-Fiumicino		
	'Ostuni'		
	Operated by Alitalia		
EI-DBL	Boeing 777-243ER	32781	14.11.03
	Celestial Aviation Trading 6 Ltd Rome-Fiumicino		
	'Sestriere'		
	Operated by Alitalia		

EI-DBM	Boeing 777-243ER 32782 12.12.03 Celestial Aviation Trading 5 Ltd Rome-Fiumicino 'Argentario' Operated by Alitalia		
EI-DBO	Air Création 582(1)/Kiss 400 T03025 13.05.03 E Spain (Monasterevin, Co Kildare) Wing s/n A03034-3033		
EI-DBV	Raj Hamsa X'Air 602T 516 13.08.03 44-AEE S Scanlon (Tralee, Co Kerry)		
EI-DCA	Raj Hamsa X'Air 742 18.07.03 C Kiernan Ferskill		
EI-DCF	Boeing 737-8AS 33804 01.07.04 Ryanair DAC (Dublin)		
EI-DCG	Boeing 737-8AS 33805 02.07.04 Ryanair DAC (Dublin)		
EI-DCH	Boeing 737-8AS 33566 03.08.04 Ryanair DAC (Dublin)		
EI-DCI	Boeing 737-8AS 33567 03.08.04 Ryanair DAC (Dublin)		
EI-DCJ	Boeing 737-8AS 33564 01.09.04 Ryanair DAC (Dublin)		
EI-DCK	Boeing 737-8AS 33565 01.09.04 Ryanair DAC (Dublin)		
EI-DCL	Boeing 737-8AS 33806 01.10.04 N1786B Ryanair DAC (Dublin)		
EI-DCM	Boeing 737-8AS 33807 01.10.04 Ryanair DAC (Dublin)		
EI-DCN	Boeing 737-8AS 33808 01.11.04 N60436 Ryanair DAC (Dublin)		
EI-DCO	Boeing 737-8AS 33809 01.11.04 Ryanair DAC (Dublin)		
EI-DCP	Boeing 737-8AS 33810 01.11.04 Ryanair DAC (Dublin)		
EI-DCR	Boeing 737-8AS 33811 02.12.04 Ryanair DAC (Dublin)		
EI-DCW	Boeing 737-8AS 33568 13.01.05 Ryanair DAC (Dublin)		
EI-DCX	Boeing 737-8AS 33569 21.01.05 Ryanair DAC (Dublin)		
EI-DCY	Boeing 737-8AS 33570 25.01.05 Ryanair DAC (Dublin)		
EI-DCZ	Boeing 737-8AS 33815 26.01.05 Ryanair DAC (Dublin)		
EI-DDC	Reims/Cessna F172M Skyhawk II F17201082 15.10.03 G-BCEC Trim Flying Club Ltd Dublin Weston		
EI-DDD	Aeronca 7AC Champion 7AC-2895 27.04.04 G-BTRH, N84204, NC84204 J Sullivan & Partners Coonagh		
EI-DDH	Boeing 777-243ER 32784 15.05.04 Celestial Aviation Trading 15 Ltd Rome-Fiumicino 'Tropea' Operated by Alitalia in SkyTeam c/s		
EI-DDJ	Raj Hamsa X'Air 582 863 24.09.03 I Talt Limetree		
EI-DDP	Southdown Puma Sprint 1121/0031 27.05.04 G-MMYJ M Mannion Kilrush		
EI-DDR	Bensen B-8V Gyrocopter SAAC 037 24.06.13 P MacCabe (Oughterard, Co Kildare) Parts only, stored 03.16		
EI-DDU	Airbus A330-203 463 31.08.17 TC-JNF, A7-AFN, EI-DDU, I-VLEG, F-WWKN Celestial Aviation Trading 45 Ltd Lourdes Stored		
EI-DDX	Cessna 172S Skyhawk SP 172S8313 19.02.04 G-UFCA, N2461P Atlantic Flight Training Ltd Cork		
EI-DEA	Airbus A320-214 2191 30.04.04 F-WWBX Aer Lingus Ltd Dublin 'St Fidelma/Fiedeilme'		
EI-DEB	Airbus A320-214 2206 19.05.04 F-WWBP Aer Lingus Ltd Dublin 'St Nathy/Nathy'		
EI-DEC	Airbus A320-214 2217 04.06.04 F-WWBH Aer Lingus Ltd Dublin 'St Fergal/Fearghal'		
EI-DEE	Airbus A320-214 2250 27.08.04 F-WWBE Aer Lingus Ltd Dublin 'St Ultan/Ultan'		
EI-DEF	Airbus A320-214 2256 02.09.04 F-WWBK Aer Lingus Ltd Dublin 'St Declan/Deaglan'		
EI-DEG	Airbus A320-214 2272 10.09.04 F-WWIB Aer Lingus Ltd Dublin 'St Fachtna/Fachtna'		
EI-DEH	Airbus A320-214 2294 20.10.04 F-WWBX Aer Lingus Ltd Dublin 'St Malachy/Maolmhaoghog'		
EI-DEI	Airbus A320-214 2374 14.02.05 F-WWDU Aer Lingus Ltd Dublin 'St Cornelius' Irish Rugby Team c/s		
EI-DEJ	Airbus A320-214 2364 03.02.05 F-WWDI Aer Lingus Ltd Dublin 'St Kilian/Cillian'		
EI-DEK	Airbus A320-214 2399 24.03.05 F-WWIZ Aer Lingus Ltd Dublin 'St Eunan/Eunan'		
EI-DEL	Airbus A320-214 2409 13.04.05 F-WWDE Aer Lingus Ltd Dublin 'St Canice/Cainneach'		
EI-DEM	Airbus A320-214 2411 07.04.05 F-WWDG Aer Lingus Ltd Dublin 'St Ibar/Ibhar'		
EI-DEN	Airbus A320-214 2432 13.05.05 F-WWBK Aer Lingus Ltd Dublin 'St Kieran/Ciaran'		
EI-DEO	Airbus A320-214 2486 06.07.05 F-WWIV Aer Lingus Ltd Dublin 'St Sebastian' Irish Rugby Team c/s		
EI-DEP	Airbus A320-214 2542 07.10.05 F-WWIU Aer Lingus Ltd Dublin 'St Eugene/Eoghan'		
EI-DER	Airbus A320-214 2583 03.11.05 F-WWDE Aer Lingus Ltd Dublin 'St Mel/Mel'		
EI-DES	Airbus A320-214 2635 22.12.05 F-WWDZ Aer Lingus Ltd Dublin 'St Pappin/Paipan'		
EI-DFA	Airbus A319-112 1305 30.03.04 D-ANDI F-WQQG, OO-SSJ, D-AVWX Cancelled 25.09.15 as removed from service Westfield Shopping Centre, Shepherds Bush Forward fuselage 10.14		
EI-DFM	Evektor EV-97 Eurostar 2003-1706 08.03.04 J Gibbons (Navan, Co Meath)		
EI-DFO	Airbus A320-211 0371 20.04.04 A6-ABX, C-FTDD, SU-LBA, TC-OND, N531LF, C-FLSJ, F-WWIQ Triton Aviation Ireland Ltd Malta Training frame with Lufthansa Technik		
EI-DFS	Boeing 767-33AER 25346 31.05.04 ET-AKW, V8-RBE Transalpine Leasing Ltd Hong Kong Stored		
EI-DFX	Air Création 582(1)/Kiss 400 xxxx 13.05.04 E Hynes Limetree Wing s/n A04007-4007		
EI-DFY	Raj Hamsa X'Air R100(2) 430 13.05.04 G-BYLN P McGirr & Partners (Ballybofey, Co Donegal) Built by R Gillespie & P McGirr as project BMAA/HB/096		
EI-DGA	Urban Air UFM-11UK Lambada 16/11 16.04.04 P Dunkan & Partners Birr		
EI-DGG	Raj Hamsa X'Air 133 899 09.06.04 P A Weldon Newcastle		
EI-DGH	Raj Hamsa X'Air 582(11) 861 09.06.04 W, C & D Baker Lough Sheelin		
EI-DGJ	Raj Hamsa X'Air 582(11) 707 09.06.04 G-CCEV N Brereton Ferskill Built by R Morelli as project BMAA/HB/210		
EI-DGK	Raj Hamsa X'Air 133 856 09.06.04 B Chambers Abbeyshrule		
EI-DGP	Urban Air UFM-11UK Lambada 15/11 24.11.04 OK-IUA 68 R Linehan Abbeyshrule		
EI-DGT	Urban Air UFM-11UK Lambada 14/11 12.08.04 OK-FUA 09 M P Walsh & Partners (Headford, Co Galway)		

EI-DGU	Airbus A300B4-622RF	557	11.02.16
	N109CL, TF-ELK, EI-DGU, F-WQTL, SU-GAR, F-WWAQ		
	ASL Airlines (Ireland) Ltd Dublin		
	Operated by DHL		
EI-DGV	ATEC Zephyr 2000	Z590702A	08.09.05
	K Higgins (Roscommon, Co Roscommon)		
EI-DGW	Cameron Z-90 HAB	10607	15.09.04
	J Leahy (Navan, Co Meath) *'Meath Heritage'*		
EI-DGX	Cessna 152	15281296	19.10.04
	G-BPJL, N49473 National Flight Centre Ltd		
	Dublin Weston		
EI-DGY	Urban Air UFM-11UK Lambada	10/11	15.10.04
	OK-EUU 55 D McMorrow Abbeyshrule		
EI-DHA	Boeing 737-8AS	33571	01.02.05
	Ryanair DAC (Dublin)		
EI-DHB	Boeing 737-8AS	33572	23.02.05
	Ryanair DAC (Dublin)		
EI-DHC	Boeing 737-8AS	33573	17.02.05
	Ryanair DAC (Dublin)		
EI-DHD	Boeing 737-8AS	33816	25.02.05
	N1786B Ryanair DAC (Dublin)		
EI-DHE	Boeing 737-8AS	33574	02.03.05
	N1786B Ryanair DAC (Dublin)		
EI-DHF	Boeing 737-8AS	33575	03.03.05
	N1782B Ryanair DAC (Dublin)		
EI-DHG	Boeing 737-8AS	33576	18.03.05
	N1787B Ryanair DAC (Dublin)		
EI-DHH	Boeing 737-8AS	33817	29.03.05
	Ryanair DAC (Dublin)		
EI-DHN	Boeing 737-8AS	33577	01.09.05
	Ryanair DAC (Dublin)		
EI-DHO	Boeing 737-8AS	33578	14.10.05
	N1786B Ryanair DAC (Dublin)		
EI-DHP	Boeing 737-8AS	33579	21.10.05
	Ryanair DAC (Dublin)		
EI-DHR	Boeing 737-8AS	33822	24.10.05
	Ryanair DAC (Dublin)		
EI-DHS	Boeing 737-8AS	33580	07.11.05
	N1786B Ryanair DAC (Dublin)		
EI-DHT	Boeing 737-8AS	33581	14.11.05
	N1786B Ryanair DAC (Dublin)		
EI-DHV	Boeing 737-8AS	33582	14.11.05
	N1786B Ryanair DAC (Dublin)		
EI-DHW	Boeing 737-8AS	33823	23.11.05
	N1786B Ryanair DAC (Dublin)		
EI-DHX	Boeing 737-8AS	33585	05.12.05
	N60436 Ryanair DAC (Dublin)		
EI-DHY	Boeing 737-8AS	33824	06.12.05
	N1781B Ryanair DAC (Dublin)		
EI-DHZ	Boeing 737-8AS	33583	19.12.05
	N1786B Ryanair DAC (Dublin)		
EI-DIA	Solar Wings Pegasus XL-Q	SW-WQ-0503	15.09.04
	G-MYAD P Byrne Limetree		
	Trike c/n SW-TE-0379		
EI-DIF	Piper PA-31-350 Navajo Chieftain	31-7752105	04.02.05
	G-OAMT, G-BXKS, N350RC, EC-EBN, N27230		
	Flightwise Aviation Ltd & Partners Eglinton		
	Stored, unmarked 03.16		
EI-DIP	Airbus A330-202	339	10.03.08
	A6-EYW, EI-DIP, I-VLEF, C-GGWD, F-WWYZ		
	AS Air Lease 43 (Ireland) Ltd Rome-Fiumicino		
	'Gian Lorenzo Bernini'		
	Operated by Alitalia		
EI-DIR	Airbus A330-202	272	22.05.08
	A6-EYV, EI-DIR, I-VLEE, F-WQQL, C-GGWC, F-WWKE		
	SASOF III (A18) Aviation Ireland DAC Rome-Fiumicino		
	Operated by Alitalia in SkyTeam c/s		
EI-DIY	Van's RV-4	3254	16.03.05
	J A Kent Trevet		
	Built by J A Kent		

EI-DJF	Luscombe 8F Silvaire	6179	11.01.19
	G-BWOB, N1552B, NC1552B		
	S Forde (Liscaninane, Co Galway)		
EI-DJM	Piper PA-28-161 Warrior II	28-8316106	21.02.05
	HB-POV, N4314K Waterford Aero Club Ltd Waterford		
EI-DKC	Solar Wings Pegasus Quasar	SW-WQQ-0351	22.04.05
	G-MWJU Cancelled 15.01.14 as de-registered		
	Lough Sheelin		
	Stored 04.16		
EI-DKE	Air Création 582(1)/Kiss 400	xxxx	12.05.05
	J Bennett Kilrush		
	Wing s/n A04172-4187		
EI-DKJ	Thruster T600N 450 Sprint	0047-T600N-105	11.05.05
	G-CDBN C Brogan Kilrush		
EI-DKK	Raj Hamsa X'Air Jabiru 3(5)	857	11.05.05
	M E Tolan (Crossmolina, Co Mayo)		
	Built by M Tolan		
EI-DKT	Raj Hamsa X'Air 582(11)	798	22.06.05
	S Kiernan & S Newlands Ballyboy		
EI-DKU	Air Création 582(1)/Kiss 400	xxxx	22.06.05
	P Kirwan Limetree		
	Wing s/n A05036-5040		
EI-DKW	Evektor EV-97 Eurostar	2005-2513	28.06.05
	Ormand Flying Club Ltd Birr		
EI-DKY	Raj Hamsa X'Air 582	720	27.07.05
	G-CBTY M Clarke Ferskill		
	Built by K Quigley as project BMAA/HB/222		
EI-DKZ	Reality Escapade 912(1)	JAESC0040	29.07.05
	G-CDFH J Deegen Limetree		
	Built by J Deegan as project BMAA/HB/423		
EI-DLB	Boeing 737-8AS	33584	19.12.05
	N5573L Ryanair DAC (Dublin)		
EI-DLC	Boeing 737-8AS	33586	13.01.06
	N1786B Ryanair DAC (Dublin)		
EI-DLD	Boeing 737-8AS	33825	13.01.06
	Ryanair DAC (Dublin)		
EI-DLE	Boeing 737-8AS	33587	09.02.06
	Ryanair DAC (Dublin)		
EI-DLF	Boeing 737-8AS	33588	13.02.06
	Ryanair DAC (Dublin)		
EI-DLG	Boeing 737-8AS	33589	14.02.06
	N1786B Ryanair DAC (Dublin)		
EI-DLH	Boeing 737-8AS	33590	06.03.06
	Ryanair DAC (Dublin)		
EI-DLI	Boeing 737-8AS	33591	22.03.06
	N1786B Ryanair DAC (Dublin)		
EI-DLJ	Boeing 737-8AS	34177	28.03.06
	Ryanair DAC (Dublin)		
EI-DLK	Boeing 737-8AS	33592	29.03.06
	N1786B Ryanair DAC (Dublin)		
EI-DLN	Boeing 737-8AS	33595	24.04.06
	Ryanair DAC (Dublin)		
EI-DLO	Boeing 737-8AS	34178	25.04.06
	Ryanair DAC (Dublin)		
EI-DLR	Boeing 737-8AS	33596	25.09.06
	Ryanair DAC (Dublin)		
EI-DLV	Boeing 737-8AS	33598	28.09.06
	Ryanair DAC (Dublin)		
EI-DLW	Boeing 737-8AS	33599	17.10.06
	Ryanair DAC (Dublin)		
EI-DLX	Boeing 737-8AS	33600	18.10.06
	Ryanair DAC (Dublin)		
EI-DLY	Boeing 737-8AS	33601	26.10.06
	Ryanair DAC (Dublin)		
EI-DMA	SOCATA MS.892A Rallye Commodore 150	12376	22.12.05
	G-BVAN, F-BVAN J Lynn & Partners (Newcastle)		
EI-DMB	Best Off Skyranger 912S(1)	SKR0503588	19.08.05
	E Spain Limetree		
	Built by N Furlong & E Spain		
EI-DMG	Cessna 441 Conquest	441-0165	04.07.01
	N140MP, N27214 Dawn Meats Group Ltd Waterford		

EI-DMU	Whittaker MW6S	xxxx	13.12.05
	M Heaton Abbeyleix		
	Built by G Maher as project PFA 164-12235		
EI-DMZ★	Boeing 737-8FH	29671	16.03.18
	D-ASXU, TC-SNI, EI-DMZ, EC-JGE		
	Airspeed Ireland Leasing 16 Ltd		
	To HL8302 04.05.18		
EI-DNM	Boeing 737-4S3	24166	01.03.06
	EC-JHX, VT-SIY, N768BC, VT-SII, VT-JAJ, N691MA,		
	G-BPKD Transalpine Leasing Ltd Amsterdam		
	Operated by Corendon Dutch Airlines		
EI-DNR	Raj Hamsa X'Air 582(5)	791	27.02.06
	G-CCAX N Furlong & Partners Limetree		
	Built by N Farrell as project BMAA/HB/251		
EI-DNV	Urban Air UFM-11UK Lambada	12/11	27.02.06
	OK-EUU 56 F Maughan Abbeyshrule		
EI-DOB	Zenair CH.701	7-9272	13.02.07
	D O'Brien Mullagh		
EI-DOW	Mainair Blade 912	1361-0104-7-W1156	01.06.06
	G-CCPB D G Fortune Newcastle		
EI-DOY	PZL-110 Koliber 150A	04940072	05.04.11
	N150AZ T J Britton (Kilkenny)		
EI-DPB	Boeing 737-8AS	33603	20.11.06
	N1787B Ryanair DAC (Dublin)		
EI-DPC	Boeing 737-8AS	33604	06.12.06
	N1786B Ryanair DAC (Dublin)		
EI-DPD	Boeing 737-8AS	33623	06.12.06
	N1786B Ryanair DAC (Dublin)		
EI-DPF	Boeing 737-8AS	33606	23.01.07
	Ryanair DAC (Dublin)		
EI-DPG	Boeing 737-8AS	33607	26.01.07
	Ryanair DAC (Dublin)		
EI-DPH	Boeing 737-8AS	33624	01.02.07
	Ryanair DAC (Dublin)		
EI-DPI	Boeing 737-8AS	33608	07.02.07
	Ryanair DAC (Dublin)		
EI-DPJ	Boeing 737-8AS	33609	13.02.07
	N1781B, N1786B Ryanair DAC (Dublin)		
EI-DPK	Boeing 737-8AS	33610	16.02.07
	Ryanair DAC (Dublin)		
EI-DPL	Boeing 737-8AS	33611	23.02.07
	Ryanair DAC (Dublin)		
EI-DPM	Boeing 737-8AS	33640	05.03.07
	N1786B Ryanair DAC (Dublin)		
EI-DPN	Boeing 737-8AS	35549	07.03.07
	N1787B Ryanair DAC (Dublin)		
EI-DPO	Boeing 737-8AS	33612	14.03.07
	N1786B Ryanair DAC (Dublin)		
EI-DPP	Boeing 737-8AS	33613	20.03.07
	Ryanair DAC (Dublin)		
EI-DPR	Boeing 737-8AS	33614	28.03.07
	N1786B Ryanair DAC (Dublin)		
EI-DPT	Boeing 737-8AS	35550	04.04.07
	N1787B Ryanair DAC (Dublin)		
EI-DPV	Boeing 737-8AS	35551	13.04.07
	N1779B Ryanair DAC (Dublin)		
EI-DPW	Boeing 737-8AS	35552	15.05.07
	Ryanair DAC (Dublin)		
EI-DPX	Boeing 737-8AS	35553	30.05.07
	Ryanair DAC (Dublin)		
EI-DPY	Boeing 737-8AS	33615	11.09.07
	N1781B Ryanair DAC (Dublin)		
EI-DPZ	Boeing 737-8AS	33616	12.09.07
	Ryanair DAC (Dublin)		
EI-DRH	Mainair Blade	1320-0402-7-W1115	08.06.06
	G-CBOL J McErlain Limetree		
EI-DRL	Raj Hamsa X'Air Jabiru	1005	23.06.06
	N Brunton (Oldcastle, Co Meath)		
EI-DRM	Urban Air UFM-10 Samba	3/10	07.07.06
	OK-FUU 31 K Haslett Kilrush		

EI-DRT	Air Création Tanarg/iXess 15 912S(2)	xxxx	01.08.06
	P McMahon Limetree		
	Wing s/n A06082-6078		
EI-DRU	Tecnam P.92/EM Echo	543	29.12.06
	I-6351 P Gallogly Abbeyshrule		
EI-DRW	Evektor EV-97 Eurostar	2006-2709	31.07.06
	Eurostar Flying Club Ltd Coonagh		
EI-DRX	Raj Hamsa X'Air 582(5)	1048	21.08.06
	M Sheelan & Partners Ferskill		
EI-DSA	Airbus A320-216	2869	14.09.06
	F-WWBE Aircraft Purchase Company No 1 Ltd		
	Rome-Fiumicino		
	Operated by Alitalia in Muoviamo chi muove l'Italia c/s		
EI-DSG	Airbus A320-216	3115	26.04.07
	F-WWIZ Aircraft Purchase Company No 4 Ltd		
	Rome-Fiumicino *'Elio Vittorini'*		
	Operated by Alitalia		
EI-DSL	Airbus A320-216	3343	18.12.07
	F-WWBO Aircraft Purchase Company No 5 Ltd		
	Rome-Fiumicino *'Ignazio Silone'*		
	Operated by Alitalia		
EI-DSU	Airbus A320-216	3563	25.07.08
	F-WWBI AS Air Lease VII (Ireland) Ltd Rome-Fiumicino		
	'Beppe Fenoglio'		
	(Operated by Alitalia)		
EI-DSV	Airbus A320-216	3598	07.11.08
	F-WWDJ Sunflower Aircraft Leasing Ltd Rome-Fiumicino		
	'Primo Levi'		
	Operated by Alitalia		
EI-DSW	Airbus A320-216	3609	07.11.08
	F-WWIE Sunflower Aircraft Leasing Ltd Rome-Fiumicino		
	(Operated by Alitalia in Jeep Renegade c/s)		
EI-DSX	Airbus A320-216	3643	07.11.08
	F-WWBT Sunflower Aircraft Leasing Ltd		
	Rome-Fiumicino *'Trilussa'*		
	Operated by Alitalia		
EI-DSY	Airbus A320-216	3666	02.01.09
	F-WWDY AS Air Lease XII (Ireland) Ltd		
	Rome-Fiumicino *'Aldo Palazzeschi'*		
	Operated by Alitalia		
EI-DSZ	Airbus A320-216	3695	02.01.09
	F-WWBI AS Air Lease VII (Ireland) Ltd Rome-Fiumicino		
	Operated by Alitalia		
EI-DTA	Airbus A320-216	3732	02.01.09
	F-WWDM AS Air Lease XXV (Ireland) Ltd		
	Rome-Fiumicino *'Ada Negri'*		
	Operated by Alitalia		
EI-DTB	Airbus A320-216	3815	13.03.09
	F-WWIF AS Air Lease XII (Ireland) Ltd		
	Rome-Fiumicino *'Giacomo Leopardi'*		
	Operated by Alitalia		
EI-DTD	Airbus A320-216	3846	02.04.09
	F-WWBY AWAS Ireland Leasing Five Ltd		
	Rome-Fiumicino *'Alessandro Manzoni'*		
	Operated by Alitalia		
EI-DTE	Airbus A320-216	3885	19.05.09
	F-WWIY Orix Aircraft Management Ltd		
	Rome-Fiumicino *'Francesco Petrarca'*		
	Operated by Alitalia		
EI-DTF	Airbus A320-216	3906	22.05.09
	F-WWIM AWAS Ireland Leasing Five Ltd		
	Rome-Fiumicino *'Giovanni Boccaccio'*		
	Operated by Alitalia		
EI-DTG	Airbus A320-216	3921	01.07.09
	F-WWBK ICIL Munster Company Ltd		
	Rome-Fiumicino *'Ludovico Ariosto'*		
	Operated by Alitalia		
EI-DTH	Airbus A320-216	3956	23.09.09
	F-WWBZ ICIL Munster Company Ltd		
	Rome-Fiumicino *'Torquato Tasso'*		
	Operated by Alitalia		
EI-DTI	Airbus A320-216	3976	23.09.09
	F-WWIV ICIL Munster Company Ltd		
	Rome-Fiumicino *'Niccolo Machiavelli'*		
	Operated by Alitalia		

EI-DTJ	Airbus A320-216	3978	23.09.09
	F-WWIX ICIL Munster Company Ltd		
	Rome-Fiumicino 'Giovanni Pascoli'		
	Operated by Alitalia		
EI-DTK	Airbus A320-216	4075	24.03.10
	F-WWBN EAF Leasing 2 Ltd		
	Rome-Fiumicino 'Giovanni Verga'		
	Operated by Alitalia		
EI-DTL	Airbus A320-216	4108	23.04.10
	F-WWDS EAF Leasing 3 Ltd		
	Rome-Fiumicino 'Gabriele D'Annunzio'		
	Operated by Alitalia		
EI-DTM	Airbus A320-216	4119	29.04.10
	F-WWIE Aercap Ireland Asset Investments 2 Ltd		
	Rome-Fiumicino 'Giuseppe Ungaretti'		
	Operated by Alitalia		
EI-DTN	Airbus A320-216	4143	25.03.10
	F-WWBB Aercap Ireland Asset Investments 2 Ltd		
	Rome-Fiumicino 'Ugo Foscolo'		
	Operated by Alitalia		
EI-DTO	Airbus A320-216	4152	25.03.10
	F-WWBJ Aercap Ireland Asset Investments 2 Ltd		
	Rome-Fiumicino 'Citta di L'Aquila'		
	Operated by Alitalia		
EI-DTS	Piper PA-18-95 Super Cub	18-5822	04.10.06
	OO-VIK, N7484D M D Murphy Ballyboy		
EI-DTT	ELA Aviacion ELA 07 R100	04061050722	06.10.06
	N Steele Navan		
EI-DUH	Scintex CP.1310-C3 Super Emeraude	921	12.12.06
	F-BJMR W Kennedy Moyne		
EI-DUJ	Evektor EV-97 Eurostar	2006-2814	09.03.07
	E Fitzpatrick (Portlaoise, Co Laois)		
EI-DUL	Alpi Aviation Pioneer 300	181-UK	21.05.07
	Alpi Pioneer Group Birr		
	Built by J Hackett		
EI-DUO	Airbus A330-202	841	25.05.07
	F-WWYT Aer Lingus Ltd Dublin 'St Columba/Colum'		
EI-DUV	Beech 95-B55 Baron	TC-1618	13.03.07
	N3045W J Given Abbeyshrule		
EI-DUZ	Airbus A330-302	847	26.06.07
	F-WWKM Aer Lingus Ltd Dublin 'St Aoife/Aoife'		
EI-DVE	Airbus A320-214	3129	18.05.07
	F-WWBJ Aer Lingus Ltd Dublin 'St Aideen/Etaoin'		
EI-DVG	Airbus A320-214	3318	28.11.07
	F-WWIV Aer Lingus Ltd Dublin 'St Flannan/Flannan'		
EI-DVH	Airbus A320-214	3345	14.12.07
	F-WWBP Aer Lingus Ltd Dublin 'St Ciara/Ciara'		
EI-DVI	Airbus A320-214	3501	03.06.08
	F-WWBQ Aer Lingus Ltd Dublin 'St Emer/Eimear'		
EI-DVJ	Airbus A320-214	3857	03.04.09
	F-WWDL Aer Lingus Ltd Dublin		
	'St Macartan/Macárthain'		
EI-DVK	Airbus A320-214	4572	21.01.11
	D-AUBY Aer Lingus Ltd Dublin 'St Brigid/Brighid'		
EI-DVL	Airbus A320-214	4678	27.04.11
	F-WWDR Aer Lingus Ltd Dublin 'St Moling/Moling'		
EI-DVM	Airbus A320-214	4634	24.03.11
	F-WWDV Aer Lingus Ltd Dublin 'St Colman/Colman'		
	1970s retro c/s		
EI-DVN	Airbus A320-214	4715	24.05.11
	D-AUBH Aer Lingus Ltd Dublin 'St Caimin/Caimin'		
EI-DVO	Barnett J4B2	227	09.03.07
	C-FRKB T A Brennan (Castleconnell, Co Limerick)		
EI-DVZ	Robinson R44 Raven II	11629	07.03.07
	M O'Donovan Enniskillen		
EI-DWA	Boeing 737-8AS	33617	12.09.07
	Ryanair DAC (Dublin)		
EI-DWB	Boeing 737-8AS	36075	18.09.07
	Ryanair DAC (Dublin)		
EI-DWC	Boeing 737-8AS	36076	20.09.07
	Ryanair DAC (Dublin)		
EI-DWD	Boeing 737-8AS	33642	25.09.07
	N1787B Ryanair DAC (Dublin)		
EI-DWE	Boeing 737-8AS	36074	27.09.07
	Ryanair DAC (Dublin)		
EI-DWF	Boeing 737-8AS	33619	03.10.07
	Ryanair DAC (Dublin)		
EI-DWG	Boeing 737-8AS	33620	03.10.07
	Ryanair DAC (Dublin)		
EI-DWH	Boeing 737-8AS	33637	19.10.07
	N1787B Ryanair DAC (Dublin)		
EI-DWI	Boeing 737-8AS	33643	19.10.07
	Ryanair DAC (Dublin)		
EI-DWJ	Boeing 737-8AS	36077	22.10.07
	Ryanair DAC (Dublin)		
EI-DWK	Boeing 737-8AS	36078	27.10.07
	N1786B Ryanair DAC (Dublin)		
EI-DWL	Boeing 737-8AS	33618	26.10.07
	N1787B Ryanair DAC (Dublin)		
EI-DWM	Boeing 737-8AS	36080	07.11.07
	Ryanair DAC (Dublin)		
EI-DWO	Boeing 737-8AS	36079	19.11.07
	Ryanair DAC (Dublin)		
EI-DWP	Boeing 737-8AS	36082	21.11.07
	Ryanair DAC (Dublin)		
EI-DWR	Boeing 737-8AS	36081	29.11.07
	N1786B Ryanair DAC (Dublin)		
EI-DWS	Boeing 737-8AS	33625	07.01.08
	N1786B Ryanair DAC (Dublin)		
EI-DWT	Boeing 737-8AS	33626	18.01.08
		Ryanair DAC	(Dublin)
EI-DWV	Boeing 737-8AS	33627	22.01.08
	Ryanair DAC (Dublin)		
EI-DWW	Boeing 737-8AS	33629	05.02.08
	N1781B Ryanair DAC (Dublin)		
EI-DWX	Boeing 737-8AS	33630	05.02.08
	Ryanair DAC (Dublin)		
EI-DWY	Boeing 737-8AS	33638	14.02.08
	N1781B Ryanair DAC (Dublin)		
EI-DWZ	Boeing 737-8AS	33628	14.02.08
	N1796B Ryanair DAC (Dublin)		
EI-DXA	Comco Ikarus C42	0604-6809	26.01.07
	S Ryan (Kilcock, Co Kildare)		
EI-DXL	CFM Shadow Series CD	K.232	15.10.07
	PH-2S5 F Lynch Fermoy		
EI-DXM	Raj Hansa X'Air 582(4)	402	11.05.07
	G-BYTT B Nugent Limetree		
	Built by R P Reeves as project BMAA/HB/100		
EI-DXN	Zenair CH.601HD	6-9095	30.05.07
	N Gallagher Newcastle		
EI-DXP	Cyclone AX3/503	7252	29.06.07
	G-MZDO J Hennessy (Thomastown, Co Kilkenny)		
EI-DXS	CFM Shadow Series C	K.023	04.10.07
	G-MYNA R W Frost Ahane		
EI-DXT	Urban Air UFM-10 Samba	10/10	14.12.07
	OK-GUA 19 N Irwin Rathcoole		
EI-DXV	Thruster T600T	9067-T600T-009	06.10.08
	G-MZHC P Higgins Enfield		
EI-DXX	Raj Hamsa X'Air 582(6)	685	20.12.07
	G-CBFT E D Hanly & S MacSweeney Birr		
	Built by T Collins as project BMAA/HB/190		
EI-DXZ	Urban Air UFM-10 Samba	20/10	14.12.07
	OK-GUA 27 D O'Leary Kilrush		
EI-DYA	Boeing 737-8AS	33631	04.03.08
	N1786B Ryanair DAC (Dublin)		
EI-DYB	Boeing 737-8AS	33633	10.03.08
	Ryanair DAC (Dublin)		
EI-DYC	Boeing 737-8AS	36567	10.03.08
	N1787B Ryanair DAC (Dublin)		
EI-DYD	Boeing 737-8AS	33632	10.03.08
	N1786B Ryanair DAC (Dublin)		

EI-DYE	Boeing 737-8AS Ryanair DAC (Dublin)	36568	14.03.08
EI-DYF	Boeing 737-8AS N1786B Ryanair DAC (Dublin)	36569	14.03.08
EI-DYL	Boeing 737-8AS N1786B Ryanair DAC (Dublin)	36574	11.06.08
EI-DYM	Boeing 737-8AS N1787B Ryanair DAC (Dublin)	36575	11.06.08
EI-DYN	Boeing 737-8AS N1796B Ryanair DAC (Dublin)	36576	12.06.08
EI-DYO	Boeing 737-8AS Ryanair DAC (Dublin)	33636	12.09.08
EI-DYP	Boeing 737-8AS N1786B Ryanair DAC (Dublin)	37515	18.09.08
EI-DYR	Boeing 737-8AS Ryanair DAC (Dublin)	37513	05.12.08
EI-DYV	Boeing 737-8AS Ryanair DAC (Dublin)	37512	15.12.08
EI-DYW	Boeing 737-8AS N1786B Ryanair DAC (Dublin)	33635	05.01.09
EI-DYX	Boeing 737-8AS Ryanair DAC (Dublin)	37517	05.01.09
EI-DYY	Boeing 737-8AS N1787B Ryanair DAC (Dublin)	37521	14.01.09
EI-DYZ	Boeing 737-8AS Ryanair DAC (Dublin)	37518	14.01.09
EI-DZA	Colt 21A Cloudhopper HAB G-MLGL P Baker (Trim, Co Meath) 'Sean's Bar'	527	11.12.07
EI-DZB	Colt 14A Cloudhopper HAB G-BVKX P Baker (Trim, Co Meath)	2580	11.12.07
EI-DZE	Urban Air UFM-10 Samba OK-GUA 24 J P Gilroy (Drumlish, Co Longford)	14/10	18.12.07
EI-DZF	Pipistrel Sinus 912 Light Sport Aviation Ltd Birr	254	26.02.08
EI-DZK	Robinson R22 Beta II G-FEBY Skywest Aviation Ltd Dublin Weston	3179	12.02.08
EI-DZL	Urban Air Samba XXL M Tormey Abbeyshrule	SAXL64	15.02.08
EI-DZM	Robinson R44 Raven II A & G Thomond Builders Ltd Kilkenny	12207	29.04.08
EI-DZN	Bell 222 CS-HDX, N307CK, N8114X, N11SP, N222LB, (N222LG), (N222LB) A Dalton & B McCarty Dublin Weston Operated by Skywest Aviation	47071	24.09.08
EI-DZO	Dominator Gyroplane Ultrawhite P O'Reilly Limetree Built by P O'Reilly	SAAC 112	08.04.08
EI-DZS	BRM Land Africa M Whyte (Williamstown, Co Galway)	0100/912/K4/08	28.04.08
EI-EAJ	Rotary Air Force RAF 2000GTX-SE G-BYDW J P Henry Gowran Grange Built by M T Byrne as project PFA G13-1302	095264	12.05.09
EI-EAK	Airborne Windsports Edge XT N30192 M O'Brien (Whitegate, Co Clare)	E-619	28.07.08
EI-EAM	Cessna 172R G-TAIT G-DREY, N23726 Atlantic Flight Training Ltd Cork	17280781	05.02.08
EI-EAV	Airbus A330-302 F-WWKF Aer Lingus Ltd Dublin 'St Ronan/Ronan'	985	27.02.09
EI-EAY	Raj Hamsa X'Air 582(5) G-CBHV West-Tech Aviation Ltd (Kilkelly, Co Mayo) Built by J D Buchanan as project MAA/HB/139	525	12.12.01
EI-EAZ	Cessna 172R N74LU Atlantic Flight Training Ltd Cork	17281146	09.08.07
EI-EBA	Boeing 737-8AS Ryanair DAC (Dublin)	37516	20.01.09
EI-EBC	Boeing 737-8AS N1795B Ryanair DAC (Dublin)	37520	02.02.09
EI-EBD	Boeing 737-8AS N1796B Ryanair DAC (Dublin)	37522	02.02.09
EI-EBE	Boeing 737-8AS N1796B Ryanair DAC (Dublin)	37523	11.02.09
EI-EBF	Boeing 737-8AS N60697, N1796B Ryanair DAC (Dublin)	37524	17.02.09
EI-EBG	Boeing 737-8AS Ryanair DAC (Dublin)	37525	11.02.09
EI-EBH	Boeing 737-8AS Ryanair DAC (Dublin)	37526	11.02.09
EI-EBI	Boeing 737-8AS Ryanair DAC (Dublin)	37527	11.02.09
EI-EBK	Boeing 737-8AS Ryanair DAC (Dublin)	37528	17.02.09
EI-EBL	Boeing 737-8AS N1796B Ryanair DAC (Dublin)	37529	02.03.09
EI-EBM	Boeing 737-8AS N1787B Ryanair DAC (Dublin)	37002	02.03.09
EI-EBN	Boeing 737-8AS N1787B Ryanair DAC (Dublin)	37003	17.03.09
EI-EBO	Boeing 737-8AS N1796B Ryanair DAC (Dublin)	37004	17.03.09
EI-EBP	Boeing 737-8AS Ryanair DAC (Dublin)	37531	20.03.09
EI-EBR	Boeing 737-8AS N1779B Ryanair DAC (Dublin)	37530	30.03.09
EI-EBS	Boeing 737-8AS N1786B Ryanair DAC (Dublin)	35001	15.04.09
EI-EBV	Boeing 737-8AS Ryanair DAC (Dublin)	35009	15.04.09
EI-EBW	Boeing 737-8AS Ryanair DAC (Dublin)	35010	15.04.09
EI-EBX	Boeing 737-8AS Ryanair DAC (Dublin)	35007	24.04.09
EI-EBY	Boeing 737-8AS Ryanair DAC (Dublin)	35006	27.04.09
EI-EBZ	Boeing 737-8AS Ryanair DAC (Dublin)	35008	27.04.09
EI-ECC	Cameron Z-90 HAB J Daly (Halfway House, Co Waterford) 'Discover Waterford'	11213	19.09.08
EI-ECD★	Boeing 737-8FH D-ASXQ, TC-SNH, EI-ECD, EC-JHV, (N3775) Airspeed Ireland Leasing 16 Ltd To HL8303 11.04.18	30826	27.02.18
EI-ECG	BRM Land Africa J McGuiness Taghmon	0114/912/K4/08	23.10.08
EI-ECK	Raj Hamsa X'Air Hawk N Geh (Gort, Co Galway)	1158	28.10.08
EI-ECL	Boeing 737-86N LN-NOP, EI-ECL, EC-JDU Rise Aviation 1 Ltd Moscow-Vnukovo Operated by Alrosa Avia	32655	13.05.15
EI-ECM	Boeing 737-86N LN-NOQ, EI-ECM, EC-KKU, D-ALIG, EC-JFB Celestial Aviation Trading 26 Ltd Moscow-Vnukovo Operated by Alrosa Avia	32658	28.04.15
EI-ECP	Raj Hamsa X'Air Hawk 44-ALU S P McGirr (Lifford, Co Donegal)	934	23.10.08
EI-ECZ	Raj Hamsa X'Air Hawk M Tolan Letterkenny	1163	26.11.08
EI-EDB	Cessna 152 G-BTIK, N46068 National Flight Centre Ltd Dublin Weston	15282993	17.04.09
EI-EDC	Reims/Cessna FA152 G-BILJ National Flight Centre Ltd Dublin Weston	FA1520376	28.01.09
EI-EDI	Comco Ikarus C42 FB I-7501 M Owens Ferskill	0009-6272	26.11.08
EI-EDJ	CZAW Sportcruiser Croftal Ltd Coonagh	700796	21.12.09
EI-EDP	Airbus A320-214 (D6-CAU), F-WWIR Aer Lingus Ltd Dublin 'St Albert/Ailbhe'	3781	11.02.09

EI-EDR	Piper PA-28R-200 Cherokee Arrow II	28R-7435265	19.11.87
	G-BCGD, N9628N Dublin Flyers Ltd Dublin Weston		
EI-EDS	Airbus A320-214	3755	11.02.09
	(D6-CAT), F-WWBU Aer Lingus Ltd Dublin		
	'St Malachy/Maolmhaodhog'		
EI-EDY	Airbus A330-302	1025	12.06.09
	F-WWYU Aer Lingus Ltd Dublin *'St Munchin/Maincin'*		
EI-EEH	BRM Land Africa	0115/912ULS/K4/08-LA	13.05.09
	R Duffy Shercock		
EI-EEO	Van's RV-7	71700	10.02.11
	A Butler Leicester		
EI-EES	ELA Aviacion ELA 07R	06040480712	11.05.09
	G-CEHO D Doyle & Partners	Kilrush	
EI-EEU	Pereira GP-2 Osprey II	304	14.06.11
	P Forde & Partners Abbeyshrule		
EI-EFC	Boeing 737-8AS	35015	13.05.09
	N1787B Ryanair DAC (Dublin)		
EI-EFD	Boeing 737-8AS	35011	20.05.09
	N1787B Ryanair DAC (Dublin)		
EI-EFE	Boeing 737-8AS	37533	14.05.09
	Ryanair DAC (Dublin)		
EI-EFF	Boeing 737-8AS	35016	26.05.09
	N1786B Ryanair DAC (Dublin)		
EI-EFG	Boeing 737-8AS	35014	26.05.09
	N1786B Ryanair DAC (Dublin)		
EI-EFH	Boeing 737-8AS	35012	02.06.09
	N1787B Ryanair DAC (Dublin)		
EI-EFI	Boeing 737-8AS	35013	04.06.09
	N1786B Ryanair DAC (Dublin)		
EI-EFJ	Boeing 737-8AS	37536	15.06.09
	N1786B Ryanair DAC (Dublin)		
EI-EFK	Boeing 737-8AS	37537	24.06.09
	N1786B Ryanair DAC (Dublin)		
EI-EFN	Boeing 737-8AS	37538	06.07.09
	N1787B Ryanair DAC (Dublin)		
EI-EFO	Boeing 737-8AS	37539	
	24.07.09	Ryanair DAC (Dublin)	
EI-EFX	Boeing 737-8AS	35019	04.11.09
	N1787B Ryanair DAC (Dublin)		
EI-EFY	Boeing 737-8AS	35020	05.11.09
	N1786B Ryanair DAC (Dublin)		
EI-EFZ	Boeing 737-8AS	38489	09.11.09
	N1787B Ryanair DAC (Dublin)		
EI-EGA	Boeing 737-8AS	38490	13.11.09
	N1787B Ryanair DAC (Dublin)		
EI-EGB	Boeing 737-8AS	38491	17.11.09
	N1787B Ryanair DAC (Dublin)		
EI-EGC	Boeing 737-8AS	38492	17.11.09
	N1786B Ryanair DAC (Dublin)		
EI-EGD	Boeing 737-8AS	34981	30.09.10
	(EI-END) Ryanair DAC (Dublin)		
EI-EGO	Gulfstream Aerospace Gulfstream G550	5406	14.02.19
	M-UGIC, N346GA VipJet Ltd Shannon		
EI-EHF	Aeroprakt A22 Foxbat	56	20.09.17
	I-9266 K Glynn (Loughrea, Co Galway)		
EI-EHG	Robinson R22 Beta	3509	16.04.04
	N75302 G Jordan (Kilglass, Co Roscommon)		
EI-EHH	Aérospatiale-Alenia ATR 42-300	196	22.12.09
	G-SSEA, OY-CIT, C-FZVZ, C-GITI, F-WWEK		
	Elix Assets 7 Ltd Monchengladbach		
	Stored		
EI-EHK	Magni M-22 Voyager	22-07-4384	20.07.09
	M Concannon Craughwell		
EI-EHL	Air Création Tanarg/iXess 15 912S(2)	xxxx	30.06.06
	G-CEBY S Woods	Birr	
	Built by P S Bewley as project BMAA/HB/504		
	(Flylight kit xxxx wing s/n xxxx)		
EI-EHM	Rand KR-2	1554	25.07.11
	C-GQKW A Lagun Kilrush		

EI-EHY	Urban Air Samba XXL	SAXL36	10.02.10
	OK-NUA 22 C N Murphy & R White Abbeyshrule		
EI-EIA	Airbus A320-216	4195	09.07.10
	F-WWIL Mainstream Aircraft Leasing Ltd		
	Rome-Fiumicino *'Elsa Morante'*		
	Operated by Alitalia		
EI-EIB	Airbus A320-216	4249	08.07.10
	F-WWDX Mainstream Aircraft Leasing Ltd		
	Rome-Fiumicino *'Citta di Fiumicino'*		
	Operated by Alitalia		
EI-EIC	Airbus A320-216	4520	10.12.10
	D-AXAI AS Air Lease XXXIX (Ireland) Ltd		
	Rome-Fiumicino *'Leonardo Sciascia'*		
	Operated by Alitalia		
EI-EID	Airbus A320-216	4523	08.12.10
	D-AUBU AS Air Lease 46 (Ireland) Ltd		
	Rome-Fiumicino *'Umberto Saba'*		
	Operated by Alitalia		
EI-EIE	Airbus A320-216	4536	20.12.10
	D-AXAL AS Air Lease 46 (Ireland) Ltd		
	Rome-Fiumicino *'Carlo Goldoni'*		
	Operated by Alitalia		
EI-EJG	Airbus A330-202	1123	06.07.10
	F-WWKY Cayenne Aviation MSN 1123 Ltd		
	Rome-Fiumicino *'Raffaello Sanzio'*		
	Operated by Alitalia		
EI-EJH	Airbus A330-202	1135	23.07.10
	F-WWYU Cayenne Aviation MSN 1135 Ltd		
	Rome-Fiumicino *'Sandro Botticelli'*		
	Operated by Alitalia		
EI-EJI	Airbus A330-202	1218	15.04.11
	F-WWYT ALC Blarney Aircraft Ltd		
	Rome-Fiumicino *'Canaletto'*		
	Operated by Alitalia		
EI-EJJ	Airbus A330-202	1225	19.05.11
	F-WWKV ALC Shamrock Ireland Ltd Rome-Fiumicino		
	'Michelangelo Merisi Da Caravaggio'		
	Operated by Alitalia		
EI-EJK	Airbus A330-202	1252	15.09.11
	F-WWKP ALC Blarney Aircraft Ltd		
	Rome-Fiumicino *'Giotto'*		
	Operated by Alitalia		
EI-EJL	Airbus A330-202	1283	30.01.12
	F-WWKA ALC Blarney Aircraft Ltd		
	Rome-Fiumicino *'Piero Della Francesca'*		
	Operated by Alitalia		
EI-EJM	Airbus A330-202	1308	14.05.12
	F-WWKH MDAC 10 Ltd Rome-Fiumicino		
	'Giovanni Battista Tiepolo'		
	Operated by Alitalia		
EI-EJN	Airbus A330-202	1313	28.06.12
	F-WWYM Aircraft Purchase Company Ltd		
	Rome-Fiumicino *'Il Tintoretto'*		
	Operated by Alitalia		
EI-EJO	Airbus A330-202	1327	12.07.12
	F-WWTN MDAC 10 Ltd Rome-Fiumicino *'Tiziano'*		
	Operated by Alitalia		
EI-EJP	Airbus A330-202	1354	22.10.12
	F-WWCT CVI Aergo Acquisitions 1 Ltd		
	Rome-Fiumicino *'Michelangelo Buonarroti'*		
	Operated by Alitalia		
EI-EKA	Boeing 737-8AS	35022	01.01.10
	N1786B Ryanair DAC (Dublin)		
EI-EKB	Boeing 737-8AS	38494	11.01.10
	N1786B Ryanair DAC (Dublin)		
EI-EKC	Boeing 737-8AS	38495	13.01.10
	N1786B Ryanair DAC (Dublin)		
EI-EKD	Boeing 737-8AS	35024	19.01.10
	N1786B Ryanair DAC (Dublin)		
EI-EKE	Boeing 737-8AS	35023	19.01.10
	N1787B Ryanair DAC (Dublin)		
EI-EKF	Boeing 737-8AS	35025	21.01.10
	N1786B Ryanair DAC (Dublin)		
EI-EKG	Boeing 737-8AS	35021	25.01.10
	Ryanair DAC (Dublin)		

EI-EKH	Boeing 737-8AS N1787B Ryanair DAC (Dublin)	38493	25.01.10
EI-EKI	Boeing 737-8AS N1786B Ryanair DAC (Dublin)	38496	02.02.10
EI-EKJ	Boeing 737-8AS N1796B Ryanair DAC (Dublin)	38497	10.02.10
EI-EKK	Boeing 737-8AS N1787B Ryanair DAC (Dublin)	38500	10.02.10
EI-EKL	Boeing 737-8AS N1796B Ryanair DAC (Dublin)	38498	11.02.10
EI-EKM	Boeing 737-8AS N1786B Ryanair DAC (Dublin)	38499	15.02.10
EI-EKN	Boeing 737-8AS N1787B Ryanair DAC (Dublin)	35026	18.02.10
EI-EKO	Boeing 737-8AS N1795B Ryanair DAC (Dublin)	35027	02.03.10
EI-EKP	Boeing 737-8AS N1786B Ryanair DAC (Dublin)	35028	02.03.10
EI-EKR	Boeing 737-8AS N1786B Ryanair DAC (Dublin)	38503	08.03.10
EI-EKS	Boeing 737-8AS N1786N Ryanair DAC (Dublin)	38504	08.03.10
EI-EKT	Boeing 737-8AS N1786B Ryanair DAC (Dublin)	38505	08.03.10
EI-EKV	Boeing 737-8AS Ryanair DAC (Dublin)	38507	15.03.10
EI-EKW	Boeing 737-8AS N1786B Ryanair DAC (Dublin)	38506	23.03.10
EI-EKX	Boeing 737-8AS N1786N Ryanair DAC (Dublin)	35030	23.03.10
EI-EKY	Boeing 737-8AS Ryanair DAC (Dublin)	35031	07.04.10
EI-EKZ	Boeing 737-8AS Ryanair DAC (Dublin)	38058	07.04.10
EI-ELA	Airbus A330-302 F-WWYH Aer Lingus Ltd Dublin 'St Patrick/Padraig'	1106	07.04.10
EI-ELB	Raj Hamsa X'Air 582(1) G-BZVH G McLaughlin (Buncrana, Co Donegal) Built by B & D Bergin as project BMAA/HB/160	561	27.11.09
EI-ELC	Comco Ikarus C42B D-MSAZ A Kilpatrick & M Mullin (Lifford, Co Donegal)	9908-6204	27.05.10
EI-ELL	Medway Eclipse R P McMahon Ballyboy	157/136	01.11.11
EI-ELM	Piper PA-18 Super Cub 95 (L-18C-PI) G-AYPT, (D-EALX), French Army 18-1533, 51-15533 S Coughlan Craughwell Frame No.18-1508	18-1533	14.05.10
EI-EMA	Boeing 737-8AS Ryanair DAC (Dublin)	35032	12.04.10
EI-EMB	Boeing 737-8AS N1796B Ryanair DAC (Dublin)	38511	20.04.10
EI-EMC	Boeing 737-8AS Ryanair DAC (Dublin)	38510	20.04.10
EI-EMD	Boeing 737-8AS N1786B Ryanair DAC (Dublin)	38509	26.04.10
EI-EME	Boeing 737-8AS Ryanair DAC (Dublin)	35029	26.04.10
EI-EMF	Boeing 737-8AS N1786B Ryanair DAC (Dublin)	34978	26.04.10
EI-EMH	Boeing 737-8AS Ryanair DAC (Dublin)	34974	29.04.10
EI-EMI	Boeing 737-8AS Ryanair DAC (Dublin)	34979	04.05.10
EI-EMJ	Boeing 737-8AS N1786B Ryanair DAC (Dublin)	34975	10.05.10
EI-EMK	Boeing 737-8AS N1786B Ryanair DAC (Dublin)	38512	11.05.10
EI-EML	Boeing 737-8AS N1786B Ryanair DAC (Dublin)	38513	20.05.10

EI-EMM	Boeing 737-8AS N1786B Ryanair DAC (Dublin)	38514	20.05.10
EI-EMN	Boeing 737-8AS Ryanair DAC (Dublin)	38515	24.05.10
EI-EMO	Boeing 737-8AS Ryanair DAC (Dublin)	40283	21.06.10
EI-EMP	Boeing 737-8AS N1787B Ryanair DAC (Dublin)	40285	25.06.10
EI-EMR	Boeing 737-8AS Ryanair DAC (Dublin)	40284	28.06.10
EI-EMT	Piper PA-16 Clipper G-BBUG, F-BFMC G Dolan (Lifford, Co Donegal)	16-29	13.04.10
EI-EMU	Reims/Cessna F152 II G-BJNF National Flight Centre Ltd Dublin Weston	F15201882	14.05.10
EI-EMV	CZAW Sportcruiser PH-IRL L Doherty & Partners Waterford	07SC053	28.04.10
EI-ENA	Boeing 737-8AS N1796B Ryanair DAC (Dublin)	34983	28.09.10
EI-ENB	Boeing 737-8AS N1796B Ryanair DAC (Dublin)	40289	28.09.10
EI-ENC	Boeing 737-8AS Ryanair DAC (Dublin)	34980	30.09.10
EI-ENE	Boeing 737-8AS Ryanair DAC (Dublin)	34976	08.10.10
EI-ENF	Boeing 737-8AS Ryanair DAC (Dublin)	35034	26.10.10
EI-ENG	Boeing 737-8AS N1787B Ryanair DAC (Dublin)	34977	27.10.10
EI-ENH	Boeing 737-8AS N1796B Ryanair DAC (Dublin)	35033	26.10.10
EI-ENI	Boeing 737-8AS N1796B Ryanair DAC (Dublin)	40300	12.01.11
EI-ENJ	Boeing 737-8AS N1796B Ryanair DAC (Dublin)	40301	14.01.11
EI-ENK	Boeing 737-8AS Ryanair DAC (Dublin)	40303	20.01.11
EI-ENL	Boeing 737-8AS N1786B Ryanair DAC (Dublin)	35037	21.01.11
EI-ENM	Boeing 737-8AS N1786B Ryanair DAC (Dublin)	35038	20.01.11
EI-ENN	Boeing 737-8AS Ryanair DAC (Dublin)	35036	25.01.11
EI-ENO	Boeing 737-8AS Ryanair DAC (Dublin)	40302	25.01.11
EI-ENP	Boeing 737-8AS Ryanair DAC (Dublin)	40304	25.01.11
EI-ENR	Boeing 737-8AS N1786B Ryanair DAC (Dublin)	35041	01.02.11
EI-ENS	Boeing 737-8AS Ryanair DAC (Dublin)	40307	04.02.11
EI-ENT	Boeing 737-8AS N1786B Ryanair DAC (Dublin)	35040	08.02.11
EI-ENV	Boeing 737-8AS N1786B Ryanair DAC (Dublin)	35039	09.02.11
EI-ENW	Boeing 737-8AS N1786B Ryanair DAC (Dublin)	40306	15.02.11
EI-ENX	Boeing 737-8AS Ryanair DAC (Dublin)	40305	16.02.11
EI-ENY	Boeing 737-8AS Ryanair DAC (Dublin)	35042	17.02.11
EI-EOA	Raj Hamsa X'Air Jabiru(1) G-CBDW B Lynch Junior Fermoy Built by P R Reynolds as project BMAA/HB/150	575	26.05.10
EI-EOB	Cameron Z-69 HAB J Leahy (Navan, Co Meath)	11432	20.07.10
EI-EOC	Van's RV-6 G-TEXS V P & N O'Brien Abbeyshrule	23830	30.06.10
EI-EOF	Avtech Jabiru SP-430 G-BZDZ, ZU-BVB J Bermingham Abbeyshrule	232	16.12.10

EI-EOH	BRM Land Africa 0162/912ULS/10-LA	26.07.10	
	M McCarrick (Ballina, Co Mayo)		
	Written off near Ballina, Co Mayo 04.05.18		
EI-EOI	Take Off Merlin 1100 119405	29.09.10	
	N Fitzmaurice Limetree		
EI-EOO	Comco Ikarus C42 FB UK xxxx	13.09.10	
	G-CCCT B M Gurnett & Partners (Ardfert, Co Kerry)		
	Built by G A Pentelow as project PFA 322-13975		
EI-EOU	Evektor Eurostar SL 2009 3615	14.02.11	
	S Kearney (Portlaoise, Co Laois)		
EI-EOW	Flight Design CTSW 07-07-17	15.12.10	
	G-CETH J Moriarty Kilrush		
	Assembled P&M Aviation Ltd with c/n 8317		
EI-EPA	Boeing 737-8AS 34987	23.03.11	
	Ryanair DAC (Dublin)		
EI-EPB	Boeing 737-8AS 34986	23.03.11	
	N1787B Ryanair DAC (Dublin)		
EI-EPC	Boeing 737-8AS 40312	23.03.11	
	Ryanair DAC (Dublin)		
EI-EPD	Boeing 737-8AS 40310	23.03.11	
	Ryanair DAC (Dublin)		
EI-EPE	Boeing 737-8AS 34984	24.03.11	
	Bluesky 4 Leasing Company Ltd Montpellier		
	Stored – due to become D-ASXX with SunExpress		
EI-EPF	Boeing 737-8AS 40309	21.03.11	
	Ryanair DAC (Dublin)		
EI-EPG	Boeing 737-8AS 34985	29.03.11	
	N1786B Bluesky 4 Leasing Company Ltd Montpellier		
	Stored – due to become D-ASXY with SunExpress		
EI-EPH	Boeing 737-8AS 40311	29.03.11	
	Ryanair DAC (Dublin)		
EI-EPI	Medway Hybred 44XLR MR058/66	13.06.11	
	G-MVVR H J Long Taghmon		
EI-EPJ	Mainair Gemini Flash IIA 551-687-5-W339	02.06.11	
	G-MTJA L Flannery (Scariff, Co Clare)		
EI-EPK	Pegasus Quantum 15 7430	17.05.11	
	G-MGMC H J Long Taghmon		
EI-EPP	Piper PA-22-160 Tri-Pacer 22-7421	26.05.11	
	G-ARAI, N10F P McCabe Kilrush		
	Fitted with wings ex G-ARSX c.2005/6		
EI-EPW	ICP MXP-740 Savannah Jabiru(5) 04-11-51-344	01.06.11	
	G-CENU L Reilly Ferskill		
	Built by N Farrell as project BMAA/HB/534		
EI-EPY	Urban Air UFM-11UK Lambada 5/11	27.06.11	
	OK-DUU 15 P Kearney (Bagenalstown, Co Carlow)		
EI-EPZ	Jodel DR1050 M1 Sicile Record 02	10.02.11	
	OO-IPZ, F-BIPZ, F-WIPZ A Dunne & Partners Ballyboy		
EI-ERE	Cyclone Pegasus Quantum 15-912 7909	16.06.11	
	G-CBTZ M Carter (Kilcock, Co Kildare)		
EI-ERH	Airbus A320-232 2157	06.12.12	
	G-TTOJ, F-WWDE CRA Aircraft Ireland No.1 Ltd		
	Monterrey		
	Operated by Viva Aerobus		
EI-ERI	Air Création 582(1)/Kiss 400 T02051	28.02.11	
	G-CBSX E Thompson Kilrush		
	Built by N Hartley as project BMAA/HB/225		
	(Flylight kit FL014 Wing s/n A02085-2079)		
EI-ERJ	Southdown Raven X 2232/0157	08.02.11	
	G-MNTY M Hanley Limetree		
	Stored wreck 04.18		
EI-ERL	Best Off Skyranger 912(2) 0130103	10.02.11	
	I-7048 B Chambers Carnowen		
EI-ERM	Comco Ikarus C42B 0802-6941	08.04.11	
	YR-5155 C42 Club Ferskill		
EI-ERO	Solar Wings Pegasus XL-R SW-WA-1124	12.04.11	
	G-MTCH M Doyle Limetree		
	Trike c/n SW-TB-1126		
EI-ERZ	Flight Design CT2K 03-02-04-07	27.04.11	
	G-KKCW M Bowden Letterkenny		
	Assembled Mainair Sports Ltd with c/n 7964		
EI-ESB	Urban Air Samba XXL SAXL53	01.07.11	
	OK-MUA 78 G Creegan Abbeyshrule		

EI-ESC	BRM Land Africa 0190/912ULS/11-LA	21.07.11	
	D Killian Clane		
EI-ESD	Mainair Blade 1008-0994-7-W804	27.06.11	
	G-MYTG O Farrell (Drogheda, Co Louth)		
EI-ESE	Zenair CH.601XL 6-9666	28.07.11	
	PH-3W6 C O'Connell Ballyboy		
EI-ESF	Piper PA-22-160 Tri-Pacer 22-6685	04.11.11	
	G-BUXV, N9769D G Dolan (Lifford, Co Donegal)		
	Super Pacer tail-wheel conversion		
EI-ESN	Boeing 737-8AS 34991	26.09.11	
	N742BA Ryanair DAC (Dublin)		
EI-ESP	Boeing 737-8AS 34990	27.09.11	
	N751BA Ryanair DAC (Dublin)		
EI-ESR	Boeing 737-8AS 34995	15.12.11	
	N759BA Ryanair DAC (Dublin)		
EI-ESS	Boeing 737-8AS 35043	14.12.11	
	N760BA Ryanair DAC (Dublin)		
EI-EST	Boeing 737-8AS 34994	19.12.11	
	N761BA Ryanair DAC (Dublin)		
EI-ESV	Boeing 737-8AS 34993	19.12.11	
	N762BA Ryanair DAC (Dublin)		
EI-ESW	Boeing 737-8AS 34997	02.12.11	
	N1795B Ryanair DAC (Dublin)		
EI-ESX	Boeing 737-8AS 34998	01.12.11	
	Ryanair DAC (Dublin)		
EI-ESY	Boeing 737-8AS 34999	24.11.11	
	Ryanair DAC (Dublin)		
EI-ESZ	Boeing 737-8AS 34996	24.11.11	
	Ryanair DAC (Dublin)		
EI-ETB	Comco Ikarus C42B 0405-6598	29.08.11	
	D-MTAT, OE-7100 P Connolly Shercock		
EI-ETD	Raj Hamsa X'Air Hawk 949	07.08.12	
	44-AFX T McDevitt Finn Valley		
EI-ETE	Morane MS.880B Rallye Club 1733	10.01.12	
	G-BXZT, OO-EDG, D-EBDG, F-BSVL		
	Wicklow Wings Ltd Dromod		
	Stored 06.18		
EI-ETF	Urban Air Samba XXL 28/XXL	29.02.12	
	OK-KUA 26 V J Vaughan Abbeyleix		
EI-ETV	Raj Hamsa X'Air Hawk 1247	08.03.12	
	P Higgins & Partners Limetree		
EI-EUA	Airbus A320-232 2210	15.05.12	
	EC-IYG, F-WWBG GASL Leasing Ireland No.1 Ltd		
	Monterrey		
	Operated by Viva Aerobus		
EI-EVA	Boeing 737-8AS 40288	05.01.12	
	Ryanair DAC (Dublin)		
EI-EVB	Boeing 737-8AS 34982	24.01.12	
	Ryanair DAC (Dublin)		
EI-EVC	Boeing 737-8AS 40286	24.01.12	
	Ryanair DAC (Dublin)		
EI-EVE	Boeing 737-8AS 35035	06.02.12	
	Ryanair DAC (Dublin)		
EI-EVF	Boeing 737-8AS 40291	08.02.12	
	Ryanair DAC (Dublin)		
EI-EVG	Boeing 737-8AS 40292	10.02.12	
	Ryanair DAC (Dublin)		
EI-EVH	Boeing 737-8AS 40290	20.02.12	
	Ryanair DAC (Dublin)		
EI-EVI	Boeing 737-8AS 38502	27.02.12	
	Ryanair DAC (Dublin)		
EI-EVJ	Boeing 737-8AS 38501	05.03.12	
	Ryanair DAC (Dublin)		
EI-EVK	Boeing 737-8AS 40298	07.03.12	
	Ryanair DAC (Dublin)		
EI-EVL	Boeing 737-8AS 40299	20.03.12	
	Ryanair DAC (Dublin)		
EI-EVM	Boeing 737-8AS 40296	27.03.12	
	Ryanair DAC (Dublin)		

EI-EVN	Boeing 737-8AS Ryanair DAC (Dublin)	40294	02.04.12
EI-EVO	Boeing 737-8AS N1786B Ryanair DAC (Dublin)	40297	20.04.12
EI-EVP	Boeing 737-8AS N1787B Ryanair DAC (Dublin)	40293	25.04.12
EI-EVR	Boeing 737-8AS Ryanair DAC (Dublin)	40295	14.09.12
EI-EVS	Boeing 737-8AS Ryanair DAC (Dublin)	40313	12.09.12
EI-EVT	Boeing 737-8AS Ryanair DAC (Dublin)	40315	12.09.12
EI-EVV	Boeing 737-8AS Ryanair DAC (Dublin)	40314	21.09.12
EI-EVW	Boeing 737-8AS Ryanair DAC (Dublin)	40318	14.12.12
EI-EVX	Boeing 737-8AS Ryanair DAC (Dublin)	40317	12.12.12
EI-EVY	Boeing 737-8AS N1796B Ryanair DAC (Dublin)	40319	14.12.12
EI-EVZ	Boeing 737-8AS Ryanair DAC (Dublin)	40316	03.12.12
EI-EWB	Comco Ikarus C42B SX-UBP E Maguire & P O'Reilly Cavan	0301-6523	15.06.12
EI-EWC	Beech 76 Duchess G-BZPJ, N6630Z National Flight Centre Ltd Dublin Weston	ME-227	10.07.13
EI-EWG	Airbus A330-223 5N-JID, EI-EWG, VT-VJN, F-WWKE Nightjar Ltd Dublin *Stored*	927	28.09.17
EI-EWH	Airbus A330-223 5N-JIC, EI-EWH, VT-VJL, F-WWYO Skua Ltd Lourdes *Stored*	891	26.09.17
EI-EWI	Boeing 717-2BL N906ME Ruby Leasing (Ireland) Ltd Barcelona-El Prat *Operated by Volotea Airlines*	55170	11.05.12
EI-EWJ	Boeing 717-2BL N907ME Ruby Leasing (Ireland) Ltd Barcelona-El Prat *Operated by Volotea Airlines*	55171	23.05.12
EI-EWR	Airbus A330-202 9M-XAD, EI-EWR, PK-YVI, EI-EWR, F-WWKV Aer Lingus Ltd Dublin *'St Thomas/Tomas'*	330	29.01.15
EI-EWV	Comco Ikarus C42 FB 100 VLA G-CBRF D Parke (Letterkenny, Co Donegal) *Built by T W Gale as project PFA 322-13900 – for sale*	0202-6454	09.05.12
EI-EWX	Aeropro Eurofox 912 3K I-6929 E J Symes Newcastle	13002	20.09.12
EI-EWY	Van's RV-6A SE-XVM D McKendrick Eshott	60380-1065	08.05.12
EI-EWZ	Brugger Colibri MB-2 Colibri Group Taghmon	232	08.05.12
EI-EXA	Boeing 717-2BL N908ME Ruby Leasing (Ireland) Ltd Barcelona-El Prat *Operated by Volotea Airlines*	55172	06.07.12
EI-EXB	Boeing 717-2BL N909ME Ruby Leasing (Ireland) Ltd Barcelona-El Prat *Operated by Volotea Airlines*	55173	18.06.12
EI-EXD	Boeing 737-8AS Ryanair DAC (Dublin)	40320	03.12.12
EI-EXE	Boeing 737-8AS Ryanair DAC (Dublin)	40321	28.11.12
EI-EXF	Boeing 737-8AS Ryanair DAC (Dublin)	40322	28.11.12
EI-EXI	Boeing 717-2BL N910ME Ruby Leasing (Ireland) Ltd Barcelona-El Prat *Operated by Volotea Airlines*	55174	21.06.12
EI-EXJ	Boeing 717-2BL N913ME Ruby Leasing (Ireland) Ltd Barcelona-El Prat *Operated by Volotea Airlines*	55176	13.07.12

EI-EXR	Airbus A300B4-622RF B-MBJ, TC-OAY, PK-KDP, B-18577, N8888B, PK-GAT, F-WWAF ASL Airlines (Ireland) Ltd Dublin *Operated by DHL*	677	16.07.12
EI-EXY	Urban Air Samba XXL OK-NUA 22 M Tormey Abbeyshrule	86/XXL	26.07.12
EI-EYI	Piper PA-28-181 Archer II D-EFLD, N2125A C Rooney Trevet	28-7990106	06.09.12
EI-EYJ	Reims/Cessna F172N Skyhawk II D-EOWY Trim Flying Club Ltd Dublin Weston	F17201696	31.08.12
EI-EYL	Airbus A319-111 N940FR, D-AVWW Celestial Aviation Trading 37 Ltd St Petersburg-Pulkovo *'Izhevsk'* *Operated by Rossiya Airlines*	2465	11.12.12
EI-EYM	Airbus A319-111 N942FR, D-AVYT Celestial Aviation Trading 37 Ltd St Petersburg-Pulkovo *Stored, due to become JY- with Royal Jordanian*	2497	18.10.12
EI-EYT	Comco Ikarus C42B SX-UBO Croom C42 Club Limetree	0805-6964	09.10.12
EI-EYW	Thruster T600N Sprint G-INGE M O'Carroll & B Corrigan Limetree	9039-T600N-033	13.11.12
EI-EZC	Airbus A319-112 B-6232, D-AVXN Celestial Aviation Trading 5 Ltd Moscow-Domodedovo *Stored, due to become EC- with Volotea Airlines*	2879	28.02.13
EI-EZD	Airbus A319-112 B-6233, D-AVWZ Celestial Aviation Trading 5 Ltd Woensdrecht *Stored – due to become JY-AYY with Royal Jordanian*	2913	21.03.13
EI-EZU	Reims/Cessna FR172K Hawk XP D-EBXR, HB-CXO The Hawk Group Rathcoole	FR17200597	22.05.13
EI-EZX	Piper PA-22-108 Colt G-ARJF A Fenton Newtownards	22-8199	07.02.13
EI-EZY	Dominator Gyroplane Ultrawhite J Dowling Limetree *Built by A Mahon*	I132	31.01.13
EI-FAB	Eurocopter EC.120B Colibri F-HIAN VP-BRD, F-WQDK Billy Jet Ltd (Rathangan, Co Kildare) *Operated by Kildare Helicopters*	1155	10.07.07
EI-FAD	Van's RV-7A J Lynch & Partners Birr	71464	18.12.13
EI-FAM	Rans S-6-ES Coyote II G-CBOK N Blair (Ballinascarthy, Co Cork) *Built by C J Arthur as project PFA 204-13864*	1201.1426	23.01.14
EI-FAS	Aérospatiale-Alenia ATR 72-212A F-WWET Stobart Air ULC Dublin *'St Connell/Conall'* *Aer Lingus Regional c/s*	1083	03.05.13
EI-FAT	Aérospatiale-Alenia ATR 72-212A F-WWEJ Stobart Air ULC Dublin *'St Fursey/Fursa'* *Aer Lingus Regional c/s*	1097	25.07.13
EI-FAU	Aérospatiale-Alenia ATR 72-212A F-WWEK Stobart Air ULC Dublin *'St Darragh/Daire'* *Aer Lingus Regional c/s*	1098	26.07.13
EI-FAV	Aérospatiale-Alenia ATR 72-212A F-WWER Stobart Air ULC Dublin *'St Eithne/Ethna'* *Aer Lingus Regional c/s*	1105	12.09.13
EI-FAW	Aérospatiale-Alenia ATR 72-212A F-WWEK Stobart Air ULC Dublin *'St Cronan/Cronan'* *Aer Lingus Regional c/s*	1122	26.11.13
EI-FAX	Aérospatiale-Alenia ATR 72-212A F-WWEP Stobart Air ULC Dublin *'St Finnian/Finnian'* *Aer Lingus Regional c/s*	1129	30.12.13
EI-FAZ	Urban Air UFM-10 Samba OK-GUA 16 J Halpin Abbeyshrule	9/10	08.08.14
EI-FBC	Cessna 172N Skyhawk II D-EAAY, N4927G National Flight Centre Ltd Dublin Weston	17273474	27.03.13
EI-FBJ	Boeing 717-2BL N409BC, XA-CLF, N914ME Ruby Leasing (Ireland) Ltd Barcelona-El Prat *Operated by Volotea Airlines*	55177	09.05.13

EI-FBL	Boeing 717-2BL	55183	15.05.13
	N921ME Ruby Leasing (Ireland) Ltd Barcelona-El Prat		
	Operated by Volotea Airlines		
EI-FBM	Boeing 717-2BL	55192	04.07.13
	N926ME Ruby Leasing (Ireland) Ltd Barcelona-El Prat		
	Operated by Volotea Airlines		
EI-FBU	Airbus A330-322	120	07.05.13
	D-AERK, F-WWKN IFTI Aviation Ireland Ltd		
	Moscow-Vnukovo		
	Operated by I-Fly		
EI-FBW	BRM Land Africa	0165/912ULS/10-LA	31.03.14
	CS-USC J O'Connor Gorey		
EI-FBX	BRM Citius	0112/KIT/08-CT	05.07.13
	I-9631 P Higgins Enfield		
EI-FBY	BRM Citius	0118/KIT/08-CT	05.07.13
	I-9772 S Smith (Phibsboro, Dublin)		
EI-FBZ	Thruster T600N 450 Sprint	0122-T600N-074	22.05.13
	G-PVST V Vaughan Abbeyleix		
EI-FCA	Urban Air UFM-11UK Lambada	13/11	16.05.13
	OK-FUA 05, OK-EUU 02 S Walshe Waterford		
EI-FCB	Boeing 717-2BL	55191	13.06.13
	N925ME Ruby Leasing (Ireland) Ltd Barcelona-El Prat		
	Operated by Volotea Airlines		
EI-FCH	Boeing 737-83N	32576	29.08.13
	M-ABFV, TC-SKR, PR-GIC, PH-HST, PR-GIC, N302TZ		
	Celestial Aviation Trading 41 Ltd Moscow-Vnukovo		
	Operated by Alrosa Avia		
EI-FCI	Zenair CH.601HD	4074	18.06.13
	J Kenny Ballyboy		
EI-FCT	Embraer ERJ-190-100STD	19000593	27.03.17
	VT-LBR, EI-FCT, (ES-AEE), PT-THV		
	Celestial Aviation Trading 14 Ltd Clermont Ferrand		
	Stored		
EI-FCU	Boeing 717-2BL	55190	19.07.13
	N799BC, XA-CLD, N924ME		
	Ruby Leasing (Ireland) Ltd Barcelona-El Prat		
	Operated by Volotea Airlines		
EI-FCY	Aérospatiale-Alenia ATR 72-212A	1139	04.04.14
	F-WWED Stobart Air ULC Dublin		
	'St Oliver Plunkett/Oilibhear Pluinceid'		
	Aer Lingus Regional c/s		
EI-FCZ	Aérospatiale-Alenia ATR 72-212A	1159	03.07.14
	F-WWEX Stobart Air ULC Dublin *'St Senan/Seanan'*		
	Aer Lingus Regional c/s		
EI-FDC	PZL-110 Koliber 150	03930051	04.07.14
	D-EIVF A D Brennan Kilrush		
EI-FDD	Cameron Z-105 HAB	11777	23.08.13
	The Travel Department Ltd (Harmony Court, Dublin)		
	'Travel Department'		
EI-FDF	Urban Air Samba XXL	SAXL73	03.10.13
	OK-NUA 19 K Dardis Abbeyshrule		
EI-FDJ	Embraer ERJ-190-100STD	19000608	27.03.17
	VT-LVR, EI-FDJ, (ES-AEF), PT-TJO		
	Celestial Aviation Trading 14 Ltd Clermont Ferrand		
	Stored – due for delivery to CP- Amaszonas		
EI-FDO	Avtech Jabiru UL-D	668	03.02.14
	G-CFIS O Matthews Newcastle		
EI-FDR	BFC Challenger II	CH2-1194-1254	16.07.14
	G-MYXK P Collins Abbeyleix		
	Built by E G Astin as project PFA 177A-12877		
EI-FDS	Boeing 737-86N	28595	14.03.14
	OK-TVD, CN-RNO, N1784B, N1795B		
	ECAF I 28595 DAC Olbia		
	Operated by Air Italy		
EI-FDY	Comco Ikarus C42	0101-6298	11.04.14
	PH-3L3 N Dockery Enfield		
EI-FED★	Boeing 737-8KN	40236	17.01.18
	A6-FDF, PH-HSR, A6-FDF, EI-FED, A6-FDF, N1786B		
	AWAS 40236 Ireland Ltd		
	To VT-JTN 07.02.18		
EI-FEG	Boeing 737-8AS	44688	13.10.14
	Ryanair DAC (Dublin)		
EI-FEH	Boeing 737-8AS	44689	15.10.14
	Ryanair DAC (Dublin)		
EI-FEI	Boeing 737-8AS	44690	06.11.14
	Ryanair DAC (Dublin)		
EI-FEJ	Pipistrel Virus 912	513 SW 912UL	07.03.14
	R Armstrong Donaghmore		
EI-FEO	ELA Aviacion ELA 07S	03061030722	16.09.14
	G-CENR H Graham (Lisbellaw, Co Fermanagh)		
EI-FEP	Aviatika MAI-890	040	16.04.14
	78-MK H A Humphreys (Brittas, Co Limerick)		
EI-FET	Raj Hamsa X'Air 502T	523	28.05.14
	A J Cunningham Limetree		
EI-FEU	Aviatika MAI-890	069	10.04.15
	P O'Donnell Kilrush		
EI-FEV	Raj Hamsa X'Air 582(5)	790	27.05.14
	G-CBXA M Garvey (Kells, Co Meath)		
	Built by N Stevenson-Guy as project BMAA/HB/245		
EI-FEW	Van's RV-7	73242	30.05.14
	P Hayes Birr		
	Built by P Hayes		
EI-FFM	Boeing 737-73S	29082	13.06.14
	D-AHIA, D-ASKH, N1787B Airopco II ME Ltd Olbia		
	Operated by Air Italy		
EI-FFN	Raj Hamsa X'Air 582(6)	400	03.07.14
	G-BZGX P J Gleeson Abbeyleix		
	Built by A Crowe as project BMAA/HB/099		
EI-FFV	Grumman-American AA-5 Traveler	AA5-0645	13.11.14
	D-EFDL K A J O'Doherty Kilrush		
EI-FFW	Boeing 737-85F	30477	22.07.14
	N477MQ, PR-GIO, N477GX, PP-VSB, N1782B, N1786B		
	Aergen Aircraft Fourteen Ltd Olbia		
	Operated by Air Italy		
EI-FFZ	Magni M-16 Tandem Trainer	16-11-6314	03.10.14
	S Brennan Kilrush		
EI-FGB	BRM Land Africa	0226/K2/13-LA	23.02.15
	PJ Piling Contracts Ltd Ballyboy		
EI-FGF	Comco Ikarus C42	9907-6192	29.10.14
	PH-3F6 Tibohine Flying Club Tibohine		
EI-FGG	Comco Ikarus C42	9908-6202	22.10.14
	D-MTWS M Murphy Cloongawnagh		
EI-FGH	Boeing 717-2BL	55169	13.11.14
	EC-LQS, N796BC, XA-CLC, N905ME		
	Ruby Leasing (Ireland) Ltd Barcelona-El Prat		
	Operated by Volotea Airlines		
EI-FGI	Boeing 717-2BL	55167	04.12.14
	EC-LQI, N408BC, XA-CLG, N903ME		
	Ruby Leasing (Ireland) Ltd Barcelona-El Prat		
	Operated by Volotea Airlines		
EI-FGN	Boeing 767-3BGER	30564	28.11.14
	ET-ALL OO-IHV, HB-IHV WWTAI Airopco II DAC		
	Ulan Bator *'Munkh Khaan'*		
	Operated by MIAT Mongolian Airlines		
EI-FGU	Best Off Skyranger 912S(1)	SKR0407507	06.02.15
	G-CDIP A Ryan (Enniscorthy, Co Wexford)		
	Built by M S McCrudden as project BMAA/HB/429		
EI-FGW	Piper PA-22-108 Colt	22-8327	13.07.15
	G-ARKN, N10F W H Worrell (Termonfeckin, Co Louth)		
EI-FGX	Boeing 737-3Q8SF	28054	16.03.15
	N54AU, G-TOYI, YJ-AV18		
	Aircraft 23810 QC Holdings Ltd Rome-Ciampino		
	Operated by Mistral Air in Poste Italiane colours		
EI-FHA	Boeing 737-8JP	39012	27.02.15
	LN-DYY Norwegian Air International Ltd (Dublin)		
	'Vilhelm Bjerknes'		
EI-FHD	Boeing 737-8JP	39011	17.02.15
	LN-DYX Norwegian Air International Ltd (Dublin)		
EI-FHE	Boeing 737-8Q8	35280	19.02.15
	LN-NOD Norwegian Air International Ltd (Dublin)		
	'Sonje Henie'		
EI-FHH	Boeing 737-8FZ	31713	25.02.15
	LN-NOV Norwegian Air International Ltd (Dublin)		
	'Evert Taube'		

EI-FHJ	Boeing 737-8JP	42069	20.08.15
	(LN-NHH) Norwegian Air International Ltd (Dublin)		
EI-FHK	Boeing 737-8JP	41140	01.09.15
	(LN-NHI) Norwegian Air International Ltd (Dublin)		
EI-FHL	Boeing 737-8JP	42078	16.09.15
	(LN-NHJ) Norwegian Air International Ltd (Dublin)		
EI-FHM	Boeing 737-8JP	42070	21.09.15
	(LN-NHK) Norwegian Air International Ltd (Dublin)		
EI-FHN	Boeing 737-8JP	39046	20.01.16
	LN-DYK, N1784B, N1786B Norwegian Air		
	International Ltd (Dublin) 'Carl Larsson'		
EI-FHP	Boeing 737-8JP	40865	25.11.15
	LN-DYH Norwegian Air International Ltd		
	(Dublin) 'Soren Kiekegaard'		
EI-FHR	Boeing 737-8JP	39045	18.11.15
	LN-DYJ Norwegian Air International Ltd		
	(Dublin) 'Georg Brandes'		
EI-FHS	Boeing 737-8JP	39021	06.10.15
	LN-NGJ Norwegian Air International Ltd		
	(Dublin) 'John Bauer'		
EI-FHT	Boeing 707-0JP	40867	11.11.15
	LN-DYL Norwegian Air International Ltd		
	(Dublin) 'Amalie Skram'		
EI-FHU	Boeing 737-8JP	39019	09.12.15
	LN-NGH Norwegian Air International Ltd		
	(Dublin) 'Anders Zorn'		
EI-FHV	Boeing 737-8JP	40870	14.10.15
	LN-DYR Norwegian Air International Ltd		
	(Dublin) 'Peter C Asbjornsen/Jorgen Moe'		
EI-FHW	Boeing 737-8JP	39007	21.10.15
	LN-DYS, N1787B Norwegian Air International Ltd		
	(Dublin) 'Niels Henrik Abel'		
EI-FHX	Boeing 737-8JP	40866	09.12.15
	LN-DYI, N1787B Norwegian Air International Ltd		
	(Dublin) 'Aasmund Olavson Vinje'		
EI-FHY	Boeing 737-8JP	39020	05.11.15
	LN-NGI Norwegian Air International Ltd		
	(Dublin) 'Wenche Foss'		
EI-FHZ	Boeing 737-8JP	39005	15.03.16
	LN-DYM, N1786B Norwegian Air International Ltd		
	(Dublin) 'Andre Bjerke'		
EI-FIA	Boeing 737-8AS	44691	19.01.15
	N1796B Ryanair DAC (Dublin)		
EI-FIB	Boeing 737-8AS	44692	30.01.15
	Ryanair DAC (Dublin)		
EI-FIC	Boeing 737-8AS	44693	23.02.15
	Ryanair DAC (Dublin)		
EI-FID	Boeing 737-8AS	44694	27.02.15
	Ryanair DAC (Dublin)		
EI-FIE	Boeing 737-8AS	44695	12.03.15
	Ryanair DAC (Dublin)		
EI-FIF	Boeing 737-8AS	44696	27.03.15
	Ryanair DAC (Dublin)		
EI-FIG	Boeing 737-8AS	44698	03.04.15
	Ryanair DAC (Dublin)		
EI-FIH	Boeing 737-8AS	44697	21.04.15
	N1796B Ryanair DAC (Dublin)		
EI-FII	Cessna 172RG Cutlass II	172RG0550	28.11.08
	G-BHVC, N9048K, G-BHVC, N372SA, G-BHVC, N5515V		
	National Flight Centre Ltd Dublin Weston		
EI-FIJ	Boeing 737-8AS	44699	01.05.15
	Ryanair DAC (Dublin)		
EI-FIK	Boeing 737-8AS	44700	11.05.15
	Ryanair DAC (Dublin)		
EI-FIL	Boeing 737-8AS	44702	02.06.15
	Ryanair DAC (Dublin)		
EI-FIM	Boeing 737-8AS	61576	04.06.15
	Ryanair DAC (Dublin)		
EI-FIN	Boeing 737-8AS	44701	12.06.15
	N1796B Ryanair DAC (Dublin)		
EI-FIO	Boeing 737-8AS	61579	12.06.15
	Ryanair DAC (Dublin)		

EI-FIP	Boeing 737-8AS	61577	30.06.15
	N6055X Ryanair DAC (Dublin)		
EI-FIR	Boeing 737-8AS	61578	02.07.15
	Ryanair DAC (Dublin)		
EI-FIS	Boeing 737-8AS	44704	03.09.15
	Ryanair DAC (Dublin)		
EI-FIT	Boeing 737-8AS	44703	09.09.15
	Ryanair DAC (Dublin)		
EI-FIV	Boeing 737-8AS	44705	29.10.15
	Ryanair DAC (Dublin)		
EI-FIW	Boeing 737-8AS	44706	27.10.15
	Ryanair DAC (Dublin)		
EI-FIY	Boeing 737-8AS	44707	27.10.15
	Ryanair DAC (Dublin)		
EI-FIZ	Boeing 737-8AS	44709	10.11.15
	Ryanair DAC (Dublin)		
EI-FJA	Boeing 737-8JP	39419	27.01.16
	LN-NOY Norwegian Air International Ltd (Dublin)		
	'Knud Rasmussen'		
EI-FJB	Boeing 737-8JP	42081	21.12.15
	Norwegian Air International Ltd (Dublin)		
	'N F S Grundtvig'		
EI-FJD	Boeing 737-8JP	41143	20.01.16
	N1787B Norwegian Air International Ltd (Dublin)		
	'Miguel de Cervantes'		
EI-FJE	Boeing 737-8JP	39420	10.02.16
	LN-NOZ Norwegian Air International Ltd (Dublin)		
	'Gidsken Jakobsen'		
EI-FJH	Boeing 737-8JP	42071	16.02.16
	N1786B Norwegian Air International Ltd (Dublin)		
EI-FJJ	Boeing 737-8JP	41148	08.03.16
	Norwegian Air International Ltd (Dublin)		
EI-FJK	Boeing 737-8JP	42072	24.03.16
	Norwegian Air International Ltd (Dublin)		
EI-FJL	Boeing 737-8JP	42073	31.03.16
	Norwegian Air International Ltd (Dublin)		
EI-FJM	Boeing 737-8JP	42074	04.04.16
	Norwegian Air International Ltd (Dublin)		
EI-FJN	Boeing 737-8JP	41152	12.05.16
	Norwegian Air International Ltd (Dublin)		
EI-FJO	Boeing 737-8JP	42076	19.05.16
	Norwegian Air International Ltd (Dublin)		
EI-FJP	Boeing 737-8JP	42077	06.06.16
	Norwegian Air International Ltd (Dublin)		
EI-FJS	Boeing 737-8JP	41153	29.06.16
	Norwegian Air International Ltd (Dublin) 'Karin Larsson'		
EI-FJT	Boeing 737-8JP	42079	11.08.16
	Norwegian Air International Ltd (Dublin)		
	'Fredrika Bremer'		
EI-FJU	Boeing 737-8JP	42273	25.08.16
	Norwegian Air International Ltd (Dublin)		
EI-FJV	Boeing 737-8JP	42080	14.09.16
	Norwegian Air International Ltd (Dublin)		
	'Gustav Vigeland'		
EI-FJW	Boeing 737-800	42286	26.09.16
	Norwegian Air International Ltd (Dublin) 'Roald Dahl'		
EI-FJX	Boeing 737-800	42271	17.10.16
	Norwegian Air International Ltd (Dublin)		
	'Gloria Fuertes'		
EI-FJY	Boeing 737-800	42272	01.11.16
	Norwegian Air International Ltd (Dublin)		
	'Clara Campoamor'		
EI-FJZ	Boeing 737-800	42082	20.12.16
	Norwegian Air International Ltd (Dublin)		
	'Christopher Polhem'		
EI-FLA	Dominator Gyroplane Ultrawhite	PF2012	14.05.13
	P Flanagan Spanish Point		
EI-FLH	BRM Land Africa	012/05/KF2	01.05.15
	I-8730 G lumiento, T Holmes & S O'Reilly Limetree		
EI-FLI	Urban Air Samba XXL	SAXL72	14.07.15
	OK-NUA 18 M Tormey Abbeyshrule		

EI-FLK	BRM Land Africa CS-UOM Lough Sheelin Aero (Lough Sheen, Co Cavan)	0018/05	18.08.15
EI-FLL	Comco Ikarus C42 PH-3F8 A Clarke (Ballina, Co Mayo)	9907-6200	15.07.15
EI-FLM	Boeing 737-85F N571MQ, PR-GIP, N571GX, PP-VSA, N1795B MASL Ireland Ltd Olbia *Operated by Air Italy*	30571	30.06.15
EI-FLO	Denney Kitfox 4 G-CIKY, I-5863 M Nee (Clifden, Co Galway) *Built by SAL SNC di de Angelis*	1702	21.03.16
EI-FLS	Comco Ikarus C42 PH-4K1 J & O Houlihan Kilrush	1110-7172	08.07.15
EI-FLU	Piper PA-22-108 Colt G-ARND M Bergin Ballyboughal	22-8484	13.04.16
EI-FLW	Comco Ikarus C42 PH-3H6 D Browne Shercock	9912-6234	30.07.15
EI-FLX	Raj Hamsa X'Air 582(5) G-CDWL P M Noons, I Bennett & P J Keating (Rathangan, Co Kildare) *Built by C Lenaghan as project BMAA/HB/484*	xxxx	08.10.15
EI-FMA	Aeropro Eurofox 912 3K I-6570 P Reilly (Virginia, Co Cavan)	11301	07.10.15
EI-FMF	Bellanca 7GCAA Citabria G-BUGE, N4165Y Citabria Flying Group Birr	339-77	10.03.16
EI-FMG	Solar Wings Pegasus XL-R G-MNUX T Noonan (Dromcollogher, Co Limerick) *Trike c/n SW-TB-1072*	SW-WA-1076	23.11.15
EI-FMJ	Aérospatiale-Alenia ATR 72-212A F-WWEZ Stobart Air ULC Dublin *Operated by Flybe*	1295	27.11.15
EI-FMK	Aérospatiale-Alenia ATR 72-212A F-WWEC Stobart Air ULC Dublin *Operated by Flybe*	1297	18.12.15
EI-FMO	BRM Land Africa I-8035 J Minogue Limetree	06-00014	23.11.15
EI-FMP	AgustaWestland AW169 I-RAIR, I-EASI LCI Helicopters Eleven Ltd Fonte di Papa, Rome *'Pegaso 21'* *Operated by Elitaliana*	69010	23.06.17
EI-FNA	Aérospatiale-Alenia ATR 72-212A F-WWEH Stobart Air ULC Dublin *'St Abban/Aban'* *Aer Lingus Regional c/s*	1325	29.04.16
EI-FNC	BRM Citius I-9885 R F Gibney Limetree	0119/KIT/08-CT	19.04.16
EI-FNE	Javron PA-18 P J McKenna (Oranmore, Co Galway)	JA1009065	16.09.16
EI-FNG	Airbus A330-302 F-WWYM Aer Lingus Ltd Dublin *'St Colmcille/Colmcille'*	1742	31.08.16
EI-FNH	Airbus A330-302 F-WWKH Aer Lingus Ltd Dublin *'St Laurence O'Toole/Lorcan O Tuathail'*	1744	28.09.16
EI-FNI	Boeing 777-2Q8ER VN-A141 AerCap Ireland Ltd Rome-Fiumicino *'Lampedusa'* *Operated by Alitalia)*	28688	19.04.16
EI-FNJ	Airbus A320-214 EC-KFI, F-WWIP Aer Lingus Ltd Dublin *'St Dympna/Dymphna'*	3174	10.06.16
EI-FNO	Aeropro Eurofox 912 3K PH-3S1 A Donnelly Carrickmore	12902	19.04.16
EI-FNS	Comco Ikarus C42 PH-3F3 M J Brady Tibohine	9904-6147	06.04.16
EI-FNT	AgustaWestland AW169 I-EASJ Como Aviation Ltd Fonte di Papa, Rome *'Pegaso 12'* *Operated by Elitaliana*	69013	05.08.16
EI-FNU	Boeing 737-86N HL8214, D-ABBQ, EC-HHG, N1786B ECAF I 28608 DAC Olbia *Operated by Air Italy*	28608	29.04.16
EI-FNW	Boeing 737-86N LN-NOM, SE-RHA, TC-APF, N1787B Genesis Ireland Aviation Trading 3 Ltd Olbia *Operated by Air Italy*	28642	07.06.16
EI-FNX	Airbus A330-243 A6-EKS, F-WWKH DAE Leasing 16 Ltd Moscow-Vnukovo *Operated by I-Fly*	283	04.05.16
EI-FOA	Boeing 737-8AS Ryanair DAC (Dublin)	44708	18.11.15
EI-FOB	Boeing 737-8AS Ryanair DAC (Dublin)	44710	24.11.15
EI-FOC	Boeing 737-8AS N1786B Ryanair DAC (Dublin)	44714	25.01.16
EI-FOD	Boeing 737-8AS N1795B Ryanair DAC (Dublin)	44715	22.01.16
EI-FOE	Boeing 737-8AS Ryanair DAC (Dublin)	44713	27.01.16
EI-FOF	Boeing 737-8AS Ryanair DAC (Dublin)	44716	27.01.16
EI-FOG	Boeing 737-8AS N1786B Ryanair DAC (Dublin)	44711	03.02.16
EI-FOH	Boeing 737-8AS Ryanair DAC (Dublin)	44717	28.01.16
EI-FOI	Boeing 737-8AS Ryanair DAC (Dublin)	44712	29.01.16
EI-FOJ	Boeing 737-8AS Ryanair DAC (Dublin)	44722	09.02.16
EI-FOK	Boeing 737-8AS N1795B Ryanair DAC (Dublin)	44719	18.02.16
EI-FOL	Boeing 737-8AS Ryanair DAC (Dublin)	61580	19.02.16
EI-FOM	Boeing 737-8AS Ryanair DAC (Dublin)	44720	22.02.16
EI-FON	Boeing 737-8AS N1786B Ryanair DAC (Dublin)	44721	24.02.16
EI-FOO	Boeing 737-8AS Ryanair DAC (Dublin)	44724	26.02.16
EI-FOP	Boeing 737-8AS Ryanair DAC (Dublin)	44723	25.02.16
EI-FOR	Boeing 737-8AS Ryanair DAC (Dublin)	44718	29.02.16
EI-FOS	Boeing 737-8AS Ryanair DAC (Dublin)	44727	03.03.16
EI-FOT	Boeing 737-8AS N1786B Ryanair DAC (Dublin)	44730	11.03.16
EI-FOV	Boeing 737-8AS N1795B Ryanair DAC (Dublin)	44725	21.03.16
EI-FOW	Boeing 737-8AS N1786B Ryanair DAC (Dublin)	44729	22.03.16
EI-FOY	Boeing 737-8AS Ryanair DAC (Dublin)	44728	24.03.16
EI-FOZ	Boeing 737-8AS Ryanair DAC (Dublin)	44731	29.03.16
EI-FPA	Bombardier CL-600-2D24 CRJ-900LR C-GWFX CityJet DAC Stockholm-Arlanda *'Onam Viking'* *Operated by SAS Scandinavian Airlines*	15398	16.03.16
EI-FPB	Bombardier CL-600-2D24 CRJ-900LR C-GWFL CityJet DAC Stockholm-Arlanda *'Alof Viking'* *Operated by SAS Scandinavian Airlines*	15399	23.03.16
EI-FPC	Bombardier CL-600-2D24 CRJ-900LR C-GWFQ CityJet DAC Stockholm-Arlanda *'Bivor Viking'* *Operated by SAS Scandinavian Airlines*	15400	30.03.16
EI-FPD	Bombardier CL-600-2D24 CRJ-900LR C-GZSJ CityJet DAC Stockholm-Arlanda *'Asker Viking'* *Operated by SAS Scandinavian Airlines*	15401	07.04.16

EI-FPE	Bombardier CL-600-2D24 CRJ-900LR 15402 C-GZYJ CityJet DAC Stockholm-Arlanda *'Aldis Viking'* *Operated by SAS Scandinavian Airlines*		21.04.16
EI-FPF	Bombardier CL-600-2D24 CRJ-900LR 15403 C-GZVR CityJet DAC Stockholm-Arlanda *'Arna Viking'* *Operated by SAS Scandinavian Airlines*		27.04.16
EI-FPG	Bombardier CL-600-2D24 CRJ-900LR 15406 C-GZWO CityJet DAC Stockholm-Arlanda *'Budle Viking'* *Operated by SAS Scandinavian Airlines*		17.05.16
EI-FPH	Bombardier CL-600-2D24 CRJ-900LR 15409 C-GZUY CityJet DAC Stockholm-Arlanda *'Bikke Viking'* *Operated by SAS Scandinavian Airlines*		16.06.16
EI-FPI	Bombardier CL-600-2D24 CRJ-900LR 15425 C-GZSJ CityJet DAC Stockholm-Arlanda *'Inga Viking'* *Operated by SAS Scandinavian Airlines*		03.02.17
EI-FPJ	Bombardier CL-600-2D24 CRJ-900LR 15426 C-GWFL NAC Aviation 29 DAC Stockholm-Arlanda *'Jare Viking'* *Operated by SAS Scandinavian Airlines*		09.02.17
EI-FPK	Bombardier CL-600-2D24 CRJ-900LR 15428 C-GWFX NAC Aviation 29 DAC Stockholm-Arlanda *'Klur Viking'* *(Operated by SAS Scandinavian Airlines*		09.03.17
EI-FPM	Bombardier CL-600-2D24 CRJ-900LR 15429 C-GZQA NAC Aviation 29 DAC Stockholm-Arlanda *'Lyr Viking'* *Operated by SAS Scandinavian Airlines*		16.03.17
EI-FPN	Bombardier CL-600-2D24 CRJ-900LR 15433 C-GIAV CityJet DAC Stockholm-Arlanda *'Menja Viking'* *(Operated by SAS Scandinavian Airlines*		30.06.17
EI-FPO	Bombardier CL-600-2D24 CRJ-900LR 15434 C-GIBN NAC Aviation 29 DAC Stockholm-Arlanda *'Naref Viking'* *Operated by SAS Scandinavian Airlines*		14.06.17
EI-FPP	Bombardier CL-600-2D24 CRJ-900LR 15435 C-GIBT CityJet DAC Stockholm-Arlanda *'Olver Viking'* *(Operated by SAS Scandinavian Airlines*		14.09.17
EI-FPR	Bombardier CL-600-2D24 CRJ-900LR 15436 C-GICP CityJet DAC Stockholm-Arlanda *'Ragnvi Viking'* *Operated by SAS Scandinavian Airlines*		28.09.17
EI-FPS	Bombardier CL-600-2D24 CRJ-900LR 15437 C-GZWV CityJet DAC Stockholm-Arlanda *'Sifka Viking'* *Operated by SAS Scandinavian Airlines*		13.10.17
EI-FPT	Bombardier CL-600-2D24 CRJ-900LR 15438 C-GZWO CityJet DAC Stockholm-Arlanda *'Skogul Viking'* *Operated by SAS Scandinavian Airlines*		09.11.17
EI-FPU	Bombardier CL-600-2D24 CRJ-900LR 15439 C-GZVU CityJet DAC Stockholm-Arlanda *'Svior Viking'* *Operated by SAS Scandinavian Airlines*		07.12.17
EI-FPV	Bombardier CL-600-2D24 CRJ-900LR 15440 C-GZVR CityJet DAC Stockholm-Arlanda *'Trud Viking'* *Operated by SAS Scandinavian Airlines*		15.12.17
EI-FPW	Bombardier CL-600-2D24 CRJ-900LR 15443 C-GIAU CityJet DAC Stockholm-Arlanda *'Una Viking'* *Operated by SAS Scandinavian Airlines*		08.02.18
EI-FPX	Bombardier CL-600-2D24 CRJ-900LR 15444 C-GIAV CityJet DAC Stockholm-Arlanda *'Vale Viking'* *Operated by SAS Scandinavian Airlines*		06.03.18
EI-FRB	Boeing 737-8AS Ryanair DAC (Dublin)	44726	30.03.16
EI-FRC	Boeing 737-8AS Ryanair DAC (Dublin)	62690	31.03.16
EI-FRD	Boeing 737-8AS Ryanair DAC (Dublin)	44738	06.04.16
EI-FRE	Boeing 737-8AS Ryanair DAC (Dublin)	62691	11.04.16
EI-FRF	Boeing 737-8AS Ryanair DAC (Dublin)	44732	14.04.16
EI-FRG	Boeing 737-8AS Ryanair DAC (Dublin)	44737	19.04.16
EI-FRH	Boeing 737-8AS N1786B Ryanair DAC (Dublin)	44736	21.04.16
EI-FRI	Boeing 737-8AS N1781B Ryanair DAC (Dublin)	44733	22.04.16
EI-FRJ	Boeing 737-8AS Ryanair DAC (Dublin)	44734	26.04.16
EI-FRK	Boeing 737-8AS Ryanair DAC (Dublin)	44735	27.04.16
EI-FRL	Boeing 737-8AS Ryanair DAC (Dublin)	44741	05.05.16
EI-FRM	Boeing 737-8AS Ryanair DAC (Dublin)	44743	11.05.16
EI-FRN	Boeing 737-8AS N1787B Ryanair DAC (Dublin)	44744	18.05.16
EI-FRO	Boeing 737-8AS Ryanair DAC (Dublin)	44742	23.05.16
EI-FRP	Boeing 737-8AS Ryanair DAC (Dublin)	62692	23.05.16
EI-FRR	Boeing 737-8AS Ryanair DAC (Dublin)	44739	24.05.16
EI-FRS	Boeing 737-8AS Ryanair DAC (Dublin)	44745	27.05.16
EI-FRT	Boeing 737-8AS Ryanair DAC (Dublin)	44740	26.05.16
EI-FRV	Boeing 737-8AS Ryanair DAC (Dublin)	44747	06.09.16
EI-FRW	Boeing 737-8AS Ryanair DAC (Dublin)	44748	15.09.16
EI-FRX	Boeing 737-800 N1786B Ryanair DAC (Dublin)	44746	21.09.16
EI-FRY	Boeing 737-800 N1786B Ryanair DAC (Dublin)	44750	23.09.16
EI-FRZ	Boeing 737-800 Ryanair DAC (Dublin)	44749	28.09.16
EI-FSA	TL Ultralight TL-3000 Sirius M J Kirrane (Claregalway, Co Galway)	16 SI 140	07.07.16
EI-FSE	Airbus A330-243 A6-EKT, F-WWKR DAE Leasing 16 Ltd Moscow-Vnukovo *Operated by I-Fly*	293	07.06.16
EI-FSF	Airbus A330-243 A6-EKU, F-WWYF DAE Leasing 16 Ltd Moscow-Vnukovo *Operated by I-Fly*	295	11.07.16
EI-FSJ	Boeing 737-86N N546CC, B-2673, N1786B WWTAI Airopco II DAC Rome-Fiumicino *'citta di Bergamo'* *Operated by Blue Panorama Airlines)*	29888	06.07.16
EI-FSK	Aérospatiale-Alenia ATR 72-212A (600) 1326 F-WWEI Stobart Air ULC Dublin		14.06.16
EI-FSL	Aérospatiale-Alenia ATR 72-212A (600) 1339 F-WWEH Stobart Air ULC Dublin		26.08.16
EI-FSN	Aérospatiale-Alenia ATR 72-212A (600) 1069 XY-AMG, F-WTBA, F-WTDW, 8Q-VAS, F-WWEF Celestial Aviation Trading 4 Ltd Hyderabad *Stored*		07.09.18
EI-FSO	Aérospatiale-Alenia ATR 72-212A (600) 1109 XY-AMH, F-WTBB, F-WTDX, 8Q-VAT, F-WWEV Celestial Aviation Trading 53 Ltd Hyderabad *Stored*		07.09.18
EI-FSR	ELA Aviacion ELA 07S ZK-CEJ, G-CEJH J Heffernan (Ennis, Co Clare)	09061140724	24.11.16

EI-FSS	Boeing 777-2Q8ER	32701	08.08.16
	VN-A142 MASL Ireland Ltd Lourdes		
	Stored		
EI-FST	Comco Ikarus C42	1605-7454	27.06.16
	Ikarus Aviation Ireland Ltd (Castlerea, Co Roscommon)		
EI-FSW	Rans S-6ESD Coyote II	0696.1001	18.01.17
	G-MZEO A J Cunningham (Enfield, Co Meath)		
	Built by J A A Dungey as project PFA 204-13046		
EI-FSX	Pegasus Quantum 15	8065	19.10.16
	G-CDCY G Hanna (Dunleer, Co Louth)		
EI-FSZ	Pipistrel Virus 912	132 VN 912	08.08.16
	I-9020 J Tierney (Bundoran, Co Donegal)		
EI-FTA	Boeing 737-800	44751	03.10.16
	Ryanair DAC (Dublin)		
EI-FTB	Boeing 737-800	44752	11.10.16
	Ryanair DAC (Dublin)		
EI-FTC	Boeing 737-800	44753	01.11.16
	Ryanair DAC (Dublin)		
EI-FTD	Boeing 737-800	44754	12.10.16
	Ryanair DAC (Dublin)		
EI-FTE	Boeing 737-800	44755	13.10.16
	N1786B Ryanair DAC (Dublin)		
EI-FTF	Boeing 737-800	44756	28.10.16
	N1795B Ryanair DAC (Dublin)		
EI-FTG	Boeing 737-800	44757	02.11.16
	N1795B Ryanair DAC (Dublin)		
EI-FTH	Boeing 737-800	44758	17.11.16
	Ryanair DAC (Dublin)		
EI-FTI	Boeing 737-800	44759	01.12.16
	N1786B Ryanair DAC (Dublin)		
EI-FTJ	Boeing 737-800	44760	28.11.16
	Ryanair DAC (Dublin)		
EI-FTK	Boeing 737-800	44761	17.01.17
	N1786B Ryanair DAC (Dublin)		
EI-FTL	Boeing 737-800	44762	18.01.17
	Ryanair DAC (Dublin)		
EI-FTM	Boeing 737-800	44763	23.01.17
	Ryanair DAC (Dublin)		
EI-FTN	Boeing 737-800	44764	25.01.17
	Ryanair DAC (Dublin)		
EI-FTO	Boeing 737-800	44765	27.01.17
	Ryanair DAC (Dublin)		
EI-FTP	Boeing 737-800	44766	30.01.17
	Ryanair DAC (Dublin)		
EI-FTR	Boeing 737-800	44767	31.01.17
	Ryanair DAC (Dublin)		
EI-FTS	Boeing 737-800	44768	06.02.17
	Ryanair DAC (Dublin)		
EI-FTT	Boeing 737-800	44769	20.02.17
	N1786B Ryanair DAC (Dublin)		
EI-FTV	Boeing 737-800	44770	16.02.17
	Ryanair DAC (Dublin)		
EI-FTW	Boeing 737-800	44771	20.02.17
	Ryanair DAC (Dublin)		
EI-FTX	Rans S-6-ES Coyote II	1003.1524	24.04.14
	G-CCTX N Blair (Ballinascarthy, Co Cork)		
	Built by L M Leachman as project PFA 204-14143		
EI-FTY	Boeing 737-800	44772	22.02.17
	Ryanair DAC (Dublin)		
EI-FTZ	Boeing 737-800	44773	24.02.17
	Ryanair DAC (Dublin)		
EI-FVA	Boeing 737-4Q8	24706	23.08.16
	G-CIPH, N916SK, SP-LLI, F-GRNH, EC-FXP, EC-644,		
	9M-MJD Aerotron Ireland Ltd Rome-Fiumicino		
	Operated by Blue Panorama Airlines		
EI-FVF	Raj Hamsa X'Air 582(1)	675	14.02.17
	G-CCWF D Greziner & A D Cummins		
	(Castlerea, Co Roscommon)		
	Built by G A J Salter as project BMAA/HB/331		

EI-FVG	Airbus A319-111	1362	14.03.17
	EC-HKO, D-AVWJ ECAF I AOE 2 DAC Milan-Malpensa		
	Operated by Ernest		
EI-FVH	Boeing 737-800	42083	19.01.17
	Norwegian Air International Ltd (Dublin) 'Jean Sibelius'		
EI-FVI	Boeing 737-800	42274	27.01.17
	Norwegian Air International Ltd (Dublin) 'Gustaf Dalen'		
EI-FVJ	Boeing 737-800	42275	02.02.17
	Norwegian Air International Ltd (Dublin) 'Amy Johnson'		
EI-FVK	Boeing 737-800	42276	13.02.17
	Norwegian Air International Ltd (Dublin) 'Dirch Passer'		
EI-FVL	Boeing 737-800	42084	27.02.17
	Norwegian Air International Ltd (Dublin)		
	'Rosalia de Castro'		
EI-FVM	Boeing 737-800	42277	21.03.17
	N1786B Norwegian Air International Ltd (Dublin)		
	'Anne-Cath. Vestly'		
EI-FVN	Boeing 737-800	42085	30.03.17
	Norwegian Air International Ltd (Dublin)		
	'Camilla Collett'		
EI-FVO★	Boeing 737-800	42278	08.05.18
	LV-HQH, EI-FVO Norwegian Air International Ltd		
	To LV-HQH 05.10.18		
EI-FVR	Boeing 737-800	42279	03.05.17
	Norwegian Air International Ltd (Dublin) 'Karin Boye'		
EI-FVU	Boeing 737-800	42088	07.06.17
	Norwegian Air International Ltd (Dublin)		
EI-FVV	Boeing 737-800	42281	08.06.17
	Norwegian Air International Ltd (Dublin)		
EI-FVW	Boeing 737-800	42282	27.06.17
	Norwegian Air International Ltd (Dublin)		
	"Richard Moller Nielsen"		
EI-FVX	Boeing 737-800	42090	05.09.17
	N1786B Norwegian Air International Ltd (Dublin)		
	'Freddie Mercury'		
EI-FVY	Boeing 737-800	42092	22.11.17
	N1795B Norwegian Air International Ltd (Dublin)		
	'Aleksis Kivi'		
EI-FVZ	Boeing 737-800	42093	09.01.18
	Norwegian Air International Ltd (Dublin) 'Jan Baalsrud'		
EI-FWA	Sukhoi Superjet 100-95B	95102	02.06.16
	I-PDVZ, 97013 CityJet DAC Shannon		
	Stored		
EI-FWB	Sukhoi Superjet 100-95B	95108	01.07.16
	I-PDVW, 97016 CityJet DAC Dublin		
	Stored		
EI-FWC	Sukhoi Superjet 100-95B	95111	26.10.16
	I-PDVX, 97011 CityJet DAC Venice		
	Stored		
EI-FWD	Sukhoi Superjet 100-95B	95105	24.03.17
	I-PDVX, 97008 CityJet DAC Shannon		
	Stored		
EI-FWE	Sukhoi Superjet 100-95B	95117	05.05.17
	I-PDVX, 97004 CityJet DAC Shannon		
	Stored		
EI-FWF	Sukhoi Superjet 100-95B	95118	01.06.17
	I-PDVX, 97010 CityJet DAC Shannon		
	Stored		
EI-FWG★	Sukhoi Superjet 100-95B	95120	27.06.18
	I-PDVX, 97011 CityJet DAC		
	To 9H-SJI 06.12.18		
EI-FXA	Aérospatiale-Alenia ATR 42-300F	282	22.04.05
	N282AT, F-WWLI ASL Airlines (Ireland) Ltd Dublin		
	Operated by FedEx		
EI-FXB	Aérospatiale-Alenia ATR 42-300F	243	12.05.05
	(N924FX), N246AE, N243AT, F-WWEQ		
	ASL Airlines (Ireland) Ltd Dublin		
	Operated by FedEx		
EI-FXC	Aérospatiale-Alenia ATR 42-300F	310	25.08.05
	(N925FX), N310DK, F-WWEC		
	ASL Airlines (Ireland) Ltd Dublin		
	Operated by FedEx		

EI-FXD	Aérospatiale-Alenia ATR 42-300F (N927FX), N271AT, N273AT, F-WWEQ ASL Airlines (Ireland) Ltd Dublin *Operated by FedEx*	273	29.06.05
EI-FXE	Aérospatiale-Alenia ATR 42-300F (N926FX), N327AT, F-WWLM ASL Airlines (Ireland) Ltd Dublin *(Operated by FedEx)*	327	21.10.05
EI-FXG	Aérospatiale-Alenia ATR 72-202F (N814FX), D-ANFA, F-WWEQ ASL Airlines (Ireland) Ltd Dublin *Operated by FedEx*	224	09.08.05
EI-FXH	Aérospatiale-Alenia ATR 72-202F N815FX, D-ANFB, F-WWEX ASL Airlines (Ireland) Ltd Dublin *Operated by FedEx*	229	02.02.06
EI-FXI	Aérospatiale-Alenia ATR 72-202F N818FX, D-ANFE, F-WWLS ASL Airlines (Ireland) Ltd Dublin *Operated by FedEx*	294	18.10.06
EI-FXJ	Aérospatiale-Alenia ATR 72-202F N813FX, D-ANFF, F-WWLT ASL Airlines (Ireland) Ltd Dublin *Operated by FedEx*	292	17.05.07
EI-FXK	Aérospatiale-Alenia ATR 72-202F N817FX, D-ANFD, F-WWEE ASL Airlines (Ireland) Ltd Dublin *Operated by FedEx*	256	10.08.07
EI-FXL	Robinson R44 Raven G-CJJM Skywest Aviation Ltd Newcastle	2447	19.12.16
EI-FXV	Best Off Skyranger Nynja 912S(1) K Kiernan Limetree	16090219	24.03.17
EI-FXW	Best Off Skyranger Swift 912(2) P Marnane Limetree	16091107	25.05.17
EI-FXZ	Roko Aero NG4UL OK-AUA 01 Fly Hubair Ltd Kilrush	KP0028008K/2015	16.01.17
EI-FYA	Boeing 737-8 MAX N60697, N1786B Norwegian Air International Ltd (Dublin) *'Sir Freddie Laker'*	42830	29.06.17
EI-FYB	Boeing 737-8 MAX N6063S Norwegian Air International Ltd (Dublin) *'Tom Crean'*	42826	29.06.17
EI-FYC	Boeing 737-8 MAX N60697 Norwegian Air International Ltd (Dublin) *'Jonathan Swift'*	42825	17.07.17
EI-FYD	Boeing 737-8 MAX N1799B Norwegian Air International Ltd (Dublin) *'Benjamin Franklin'*	42828	17.07.17
EI-FYE	Boeing 737-8 MAX Norwegian Air International Ltd (Dublin) *'Sojourner Truth'*	42827	31.07.17
EI-FYF	Boeing 737-8 MAX N1786B Norwegian Air International Ltd (Dublin) *'Clara Barton'*	42829	10.08.17
EI-FYG	Boeing 737-8 MAX N6069R Norwegian Air International Ltd (Dublin) *'Maria Zambrano'*	42831	16.05.18
EI-FYH	Boeing 737-8 MAX N1786B Norwegian Air International Ltd (Dublin) *'Tycho Brahe'*	64992	26.06.18
EI-FYI	Boeing 737-8 MAX N1786B Norwegian Air International Ltd (Dublin) *'Arthur Collins'*	42834	24.09.18
EI-FZA	Boeing 737-800 N1796B Ryanair DAC (Dublin)	44774	27.02.17
EI-FZB	Boeing 737-800 N1786B Ryanair DAC (Dublin)	44775	09.03.17
EI-FZC	Boeing 737-800 Ryanair DAC (Dublin)	44776	14.03.17
EI-FZD	Boeing 737-800 N1798B Ryanair DAC (Dublin)	44777	28.03.17
EI-FZE	Boeing 737-800 N1796B Ryanair DAC (Dublin)	44778	16.03.17
EI-FZF	Boeing 737-800 N1786B Ryanair DAC (Dublin)	44779	20.03.17
EI-FZG	Boeing 737-800 N1780B Ryanair DAC (Dublin)	44780	24.03.17
EI-FZH	Boeing 737-800 N1782B Ryanair DAC (Dublin)	44781	30.03.17
EI-FZI	Boeing 737-800 N1786B Ryanair DAC (Dublin)	44782	18.04.17
EI-FZJ	Boeing 737-800 Ryanair DAC (Dublin)	44788	12.04.17
EI-FZK	Boeing 737-800 N1786B Ryanair DAC (Dublin)	44783	19.04.17
EI-FZL	Boeing 737-800 Ryanair DAC (Dublin)	44784	20.04.17
EI-FZM	Boeing 737-800 Ryanair DAC (Dublin)	44785	21.04.17
EI-FZN	Boeing 737-800 Ryanair DAC (Dublin)	44786	25.04.17
EI-FZO	Boeing 737-800 N1786B Ryanair DAC (Dublin)	44787	27.04.17
EI-FZP	Boeing 737-800 Ryanair DAC (Dublin)	44790	05.05.17
EI-FZR	Boeing 737-800 Ryanair DAC (Dublin)	44792	10.05.17
EI-FZS	Boeing 737-800 Ryanair DAC (Dublin)	44789	15.05.17
EI-FZT	Boeing 737-800 N1786B Ryanair DAC (Dublin)	44793	16.05.17
EI-FZV	Boeing 737-800 N1795B Ryanair DAC (Dublin)	44794	18.05.17
EI-FZW	Boeing 737-800 Ryanair DAC (Dublin)	44795	19.05.17
EI-GAH	Comco Ikarus C42B PH-3Y2 Tibohine Flying Club Ltd Tibohine	0511-6767	24.01.17
EI-GAJ	Airbus A330-302 F-WWCQ Aer Lingus Ltd Dublin *'St Carthage/Mochuta'*	1791	23.05.17
EI-GAL	Airbus A320-214 VQ-BAZ, F-WWBC Aer Lingus Ltd Dublin *'St Maeve/Maedbh'*	3789	05.05.17
EI-GAM	Airbus A320-214 VQ-BBB, F-WWIT Aer Lingus Ltd Dublin *'St Brona'*	3823	14.06.17
EI-GAW	Boeing 737-8Z0 B-2509, N1787B WWTAI Airopco BPA Ireland Ltd Rome-Fiumicino *'citta di Pisa'* *Operated by Blue Panorama Airlines*	30072	04.07.17
EI-GAX	Boeing 737-8Z0 B-2511, N1786B WWTAI Airopco BPA Ireland Ltd Rome-Fiumicino *'citta di Genova'* *Operated by Blue Panorama Airlines*	30073	06.06.17
EI-GAZ	Embraer ERJ-190-200LR TC-YAR, (VQ-BUS), G-FBEE, PT-SNN Celestial Aviation Trading 5 Ltd Clermont Ferrand *Stored*	19000093	11.05.17
EI-GBB	Boeing 737-86N LN-NOF Norwegian Air International Ltd (Dublin) *'Edvard Munch'*	36809	01.02.17
EI-GBF	Boeing 737-8JP LN-NGK Norwegian Air International Ltd (Dublin) *'Johan Falkberget'*	39022	25.04.17
EI-GBG	Boeing 737-8JP LN-NGL Norwegian Air International Ltd (Dublin) *'Johan Frederik "Frits" Thaulow'*	39023	26.04.17
EI-GBI	Boeing 737-8JP LN-NIF Norwegian Air International Ltd (Dublin) *'Minna Canth'*	39434	08.03.17
EI-GCA	Embraer ERJ-190-200LR TC-YAO, (VQ-BUQ), G-FBEC, PT-SJI Celestial Aviation Trading 69 Ltd Clermont Ferrand *Stored*	19000069	12.05.17

EI-GCC	Airbus A320-233 PR-MBL, HC-CDZ, F-WWIC MASL Ireland (35) Ltd Milan-Malpensa *Operated by Ernest*	2044	29.05.17
EI-GCF	Airbus A330-302 F-WWCN Aer Lingus Ltd Dublin *'St Aengus/Oengus'*	1817	20.11.17
EI-GCG	BRM Citius D Bolger (Rathvilly, Co Carlow)	0227/K4/13-CT	25.02.19
EI-GCJ	CZAW Sportcruiser G-SCVF S Meagher & Partners Kilrush	09SC321	21.07.17
EI-GCP	Best Off Skyranger 912(2) 30-NA J Marbach (Arklow, Co Wicklow)	A203MN0011L	06.11.17
EI-GCT	ATEC Zephyr 2000 PH-3L5 C S Kilpatrick & S R McGirr (Convoy, Co Donegal)	Z410601A	07.12.17
EI-GCU	Airbus A330-223 VN-A383, D-ANJB, VT-VJP, F-WWYX DAE Leasing 31 Ltd Moscow-Vnukovo *Operated by I-Fly*	946	13.11.17
EI-GCV	Boeing 737-7CT C-FBWS, N1786B Wilmington Trust SP Services Ltd Moscow-Vnukovo *Operated by Alrosa Avia*	37088	18.01.18
EI-GCZ	Airbus A330-223 D-ALPH, F-WWYD SASOF III (A3) Aviation Ireland Ltd Moscow-Vnukovo *Operated by I-Fly*	739	27.03.18
EI-GDC	Boeing 737-800 N1780B Ryanair DAC (Dublin)	44800	07.09.17
EI-GDD	Boeing 737-800 N1787B Ryanair DAC (Dublin)	44802	29.09.17
EI-GDE	Boeing 737-800 Ryanair DAC (Dublin)	44803	06.10.17
EI-GDF	Boeing 737-800 Ryanair DAC (Dublin)	44801	10.10.17
EI-GDG	Boeing 737-800 N1786B Ryanair DAC (Dublin)	44804	13.10.17
EI-GDH	Boeing 737-800 Ryanair DAC (Dublin)	44805	23.10.17
EI-GDI	Boeing 737-800 N1795B Ryanair DAC (Dublin)	44809	01.11.17
EI-GDJ	Piper J-4E Cub Coupe G-BSDJ, N35975, NC35975 Ballyboughal J4 Flying Group Ballyboughal	4-1456	13.08.13
EI-GDK	Boeing 737-800 Ryanair DAC (Dublin)	44806	02.11.17
EI-GDM	Boeing 737-800 Ryanair DAC (Dublin)	44810	06.11.17
EI-GDN	Boeing 737-800 Ryanair DAC (Dublin)	44807	10.11.17
EI-GDO	Boeing 737-800 N6069R Ryanair DAC (Dublin)	44808	29.11.17
EI-GDP	Boeing 737-800 Ryanair DAC (Dublin)	44813	16.01.18
EI-GDR	Boeing 737-800 N1796B Ryanair DAC (Dublin)	44812	23.01.18
EI-GDS	Boeing 737-800 Ryanair DAC (Dublin)	44811	23.01.18
EI-GDT	Boeing 737-800 N1786B Ryanair DAC (Dublin)	44815	29.01.18
EI-GDV	Boeing 737-800 Ryanair DAC (Dublin)	44816	30.01.18
EI-GDW	Boeing 737-800 Ryanair DAC (Dublin)	44814	31.01.18
EI-GDX	Boeing 737-800 Ryanair DAC (Dublin)	44817	31.01.18
EI-GDY	Boeing 737-800 N6055X, N1786B Ryanair DAC (Dublin)	44818	27.02.18
EI-GDZ	Boeing 737-800 N1786B Ryanair DAC (Dublin)	44820	16.02.18

EI-GEA	Bombardier CL-600-2D24 CRJ-900LR OY-KFE, C-GIBH CityJet DAC Brussels *Operated by Brussels Airlines*	15224	06.04.18
EI-GEB	Bombardier CL-600-2D24 CRJ-900LR OY-KFF, C-GZQO CityJet DAC Brussels *Operated by Brussels Airlines*	15231	09.07.18
EI-GEC	Bombardier CL-600-2D24 CRJ-900LR OY-KFL CityJet DAC Stockholm-Arlanda *'Regin Viking'* *Operated by SAS Scandinavian Airlines*	15246	29.08.18
EI-GED	Bombardier CL-600-2D24 CRJ-900LR OY-KFH, C-GZQU CityJet DAC Stockholm-Arlanda *'Ella Viking'* *Operated by SAS Scandinavian Airlines*	15240	30.08.18
EI-GEF	Bombardier CL-600-2D24 CRJ-900LR OY-KFK, C-GBSZ, C-GIAW CityJet DAC Stockholm-Arlanda *'Hardeknud Viking'* *Operated by SAS Scandinavian Airlines*	15244	30.08.18
EI-GEG★	Embraer ERJ-190-200LR PK-KDA, G-FBEA, PT-SGD Aldus Portfolio B Ltd To 4L-MGT 28.09.18	19000029	08.06.18
EI-GEN	Best Off Skyranger 912(2) Skybound Air Sports Ltd (Navan, Co Meath)	17041117	22.08.18
EI-GEO	ICP Savannah S I-C513 K P Walsh Limetree	15-08-54-0413	07.12.17
EI-GEP	Boeing 767-323ER N359AA Spectre Overseas Aircraft Ltd Rome-Fiumicino *Operated by Blue Panorama Airlines*	24040	04.05.18
EI-GER	Maule MX-7-180A Star Rocket P J L Ryan Ballyboughal	20006C	07.01.94
EI-GES	Boeing 777-31HER A6-EBA AerCap Ireland Ltd Moscow-Vnukovo *'Tomsk'* *Operated by Rossiya Airlines*	32706	11.04.18
EI-GET	Boeing 777-31HER A6-EBL, N5017V AerCap Ireland Ltd Moscow-Vnukovo *'Magadan'* *Operated by Rossiya Airlines*	32709	12.03.18
EI-GEU	Boeing 777-31HER A6-EBP, N5017V Altair Aviation No.3 Ltd Moscow-Vnukovo *'Ulyanovsk'* *Operated by Rossiya Airlines*	32710	13.06.18
EI-GEV	Aérospatiale-Alenia ATR 42-600 OY-YCC, F-WWLR Stobart Air ULC Dublin *'St Ita'* *Aer Lingus Regional c/s*	1213	09.02.18
EI-GEW	Airbus A330-203 PT-MVG, F-WWKQ Aircraft Engine Lease Finance Ltd Moscow-Vnukovo *Operated by I-Fly*	472	09.02.18
EI-GEX★	Airbus A330-203 PT-MVL, F-WWKB Aircraft Engine Lease Finance Ltd To TC-AGL 12.12.18	700	21.02.18
EI-GEY	Airbus A330-202 A7-ACH, (CS-TMT), F-WWYK Aer Lingus Ltd Dublin *'St Benan/Beineon'*	441	06.04.18
EI-GEZ★	Boeing 737-73V HL8207, G-EZJR ECAF I 32413 DAC To UR-SQD 26.10.18	32413	26.02.18
EI-GFA	Boeing 777-31HER A6-EBS AerCap Ireland Ltd Moscow-Vnukovo *'Anadyr'* *Operated by Rossiya Airlines*	32715	25.09.18
EI-GFB	Boeing 777-31HER A6-EBT AerCap Ireland Ltd Moscow-Vnukovo *'Velikiy Novgorod'* *Operated by Rossiya Airlines*	32730	03.10.18
EI-GFN	Airbus A319-112 VP-BDY, G-EZID, D-AVWT SASOF III (C) Aviation Ireland DAC Moscow-Vnukovo *Operated by I-Fly*	2442	01.05.18
EI-GFO	Airbus A319-112 VP-BDZ, G-EZIE, D-AVWQ SASOF III (C) Aviation Ireland DAC Moscow-Vnukovo *Operated by I-Fly*	2446	08.06.18

EI-GFP	Boeing 737-89L	29878	17.05.18
	B-2643, N1786B WWTAI Airopco BPA Ireland Ltd		
	Rome-Fiumicino *'Citta di Torino'*		
	Operated by Blue Panorama Airlines		

EI-GFR	Boeing 737-7CT	37421	22.03.18
	C-GWSY, N1786B		
	Wilmington Trust SP Services Ltd Moscow-Vnukovo		
	Operated by Alrosa Avia		

EI-GFS★	AgustaWestland AW139	31758	09.03.18
	I-EASM LCI Helicopters Sixteen Ltd		
	To B-706H 25.09.18		

EI-GFT★	Boeing 747-4HAFER	35236	16.03.18
	(N594CC), OO-THD		
	Constitution Aircraft Leasing (Ireland) 5 Ltd		
	To OO-THD 03.05.18		

EI-GFV	Wassmer Jodel D.112	1175	30.05.18
	G-AZFF, F-BLFI J B Bolger & T Delaney		
	(Dungarvan, Co Waterford)		

EI-GFW★	Airbus A320-214	1615	25.05.18
	N218FR, N261AV, F-WWDR		
	SASOF II (C) Aviation Ireland Ltd		
	To SX-EMY 15.06.18		

EI-GFX	Airbus A330-202	571	04.05.18
	A7-ACE, F-WWKF		
	Wilmington Trust SP Services Ltd Olbia		
	Operated by Air Italy		

EI-GFY	Boeing 737-8 MAX	64605	10.05.18
	N1786B Pembroke Aircraft Leasing 8 Ltd Olbia		
	Operated by Air Italy		

EI-GGA	Embraer ERJ-190-200LR	19000184	15.02.19
	G-FBEL, PT-SDS Stobart Air ULC Dublin		
	(Operated by Flybe		

EI-GGB	Embraer ERJ-190-200LR	19000204	21.12.18
	G-FBEM, PT-SGN Stobart Air ULC Dublin		
	Operated by Flybe		

EI-GGC	Embraer ERJ-190-200LR	19000213	19.06.18
	G-FBEN, PT-SGW Stobart Air ULC Dublin		
	Operated by Flybe		

EI-GGD★	Airbus A320-232	2724	20.06.18
	9V-TAE, F-WWBG GPFC Ireland Ltd		
	To SX-ODS 28.06.18		

EI-GGE	BRM Citius Sport	0004/07	02.05.18
	I-9262 Laois Flying Club Ltd Limetree		

EI-GGF★	Boeing 737-8F2	34409	17.05.18
	TC-JGK, N1786B		
	SMBC Aviation Capital Ireland Leasing 3 Ltd		
	To 9H-TJA 14.06.18		

EI-GGH	AgustaWestland AW169	69060	28.06.18
	I-EASJ LCI Helicopters Eighteen Ltd		
	Fonte di Papa, Rome *'Pegaso 21'*		
	Operated by Elitaliana		

EI-GGK	Boeing 737-8 MAX	64606	11.07.18
	N1781B Pembroke Aircraft Leasing 8 Ltd Olbia		
	Operated by Air Italy)		

EI-GGL	Boeing 737-8 MAX	64607	20.11.18
	N1786B Pembroke Aircraft Leasing 8 Ltd Olbia		
	Operated by Air Italy		

EI-GGN	Airbus A330-202	489	27.09.18
	A7-ACB, F-WWYN		
	Wilmington Trust SP Services Ltd Olbia		
	Operated by Air Italy		

EI-GGO	Airbus A330-202	511	03.09.18
	A7-ACC, F-WWKR		
	Wilmington Trust SP Services Ltd Olbia		
	Operated by Air Italy		

EI-GGP	Airbus A330-202	521	01.06.18
	A7-ACD, F-WWKU		
	Wilmington Trust SP Services Ltd Olbia		
	Operated by Air Italy		

EI-GGR	Airbus A330-202	638	30.10.18
	A7-ACF, F-WWYQ		
	Wilmington Trust SP Services Ltd Olbia		
	Operated by Air Italy		

EI-GGS	AgustaWestland AW139	31461	05.06.18
	9M-WAP, I-RAIP LCI Helicopters (Labuan) Ltd		
	Fonte di Papa, Rome		
	Operated by Elitaliana		

EI-GGU★	Airbus A320-214	2388	23.07.18
	EC-JFF, F-WWIH		
	Genesis Ireland Aviation Trading 4 Ltd		
	To VT-IHT 14.08.18		

EI-GGW★	Boeing 737-86N	36548	27.07.18
	B-5510, N1795B Oriental Leasing 17 Company Ltd		
	To OY-PSJ 14.09.18		

EI-GGX	Zenair CH.601UL	00006	23.10.18
	HA-YBC, OM-M117 N Farrell		
	(Brianstown, Co Longford)		

EI-GHA	Boeing 737-490SF	28895	10.10.18
	N708AS, N1786B Aircraft 23810 QC Holdings Ltd		
	Rome-Ciampino		
	Operated by Mistral Air in Poste Italiane c/s		

EI-GHB	Boeing 737-490SF	28896	06.09.18
	N709AS, N1787B Aircraft 23810 QC Holdings Ltd		
	Rome-Ciampino		
	Operated by Mistral Air in Poste Italiane c/s		

EI-GHE	Airbus A320-232	1957	09.10.18
	A7-ADE, F-WWIG AS Air Lease XXXIV (Ireland) Ltd		
	Larnaca		
	Stored – due to become VT-IKC with IndiGo		

EI-GHF	Airbus A320-232	2138	02.11.18
	A7-ADH, F-WWBI AS Air Lease XXXIV (Ireland) Ltd		
	Larnaca		
	Stored – due to become VT-IKE with IndiGo		

EI-GHG★	Airbus A320-232	2288	07.01.19
	A7-ADJ, F-WWBS Wilmington Trust SP Services Ltd		
	To OE-LOJ 04.02.19		

EI-GHH	Europa Aviation Europa	066	09.11.18
	G-BVJN Lee Aero Club (Co Cork)		
	Built by N Adam as project PFA 247-12666		

EI-GHI	Piper PA-22-150 Tri-Pacer	22-5181	17.10.18
	G-APZX, N7420D H Taggart (Enfield, Co Meath)		
	Tail-wheel conversion		

EI-GHJ	Embraer ERJ-190-100IGW	19000202	01.02.19
	N202NC, VH-ZPI, PT-SGK Stobart Air ULC London City		
	Operated by BA CityFlyer		

EI-GHK	Embraer ERJ-190-100IGW	19000218	15.11.18
	N821NC, VH-ZPK, PT-SHB Stobart Air ULC London City		
	Operated by BA CityFlyer		

EI-GHU	AgustaWestland AW119Ke	14780	15.01.19
	I-HVDP, N193NT, N302YS		
	Perspect Aviation DAC (Carrigtwohill, Co Cork)		

EI-GHW	Bell 505 JetRanger X	65155	06.02.19
	C-GFNR Yoyo Capital ULC (Dublin)		

EI-GHX★	Airbus A319-132	2568	06.12.18
	9V-SBE, D-AVXA WWTAI Airopco II DAC		
	To VN-A581 31.01.19		

EI-GHY★	Airbus A320-232	2934	06.12.18
	TC-JPD, F-WWIC WWTAI Airopco II DAC		
	To VN-A586 23.01.19		

EI-GHZ	Cessna 208B Grand Caravan EX	208B5405	21.11.18
	OE-EGA, N208GC Grob Power Service Ltd (Dublin)		

EI-GIA★	Boeing 737-8K5	35134	22.11.18
	G-FDZA, C-FPZA, G-FDZA, C-FPZA, G-FDZA, C-FPZA,		
	G-FDZA, C-FPZA, G-FDZA, N1786B		
	Tempelhof Aircraft Leasing Ltd		
	To HL8321 21.12.18		

EI-GIB	Airbus A320-271N	8371	07.12.18
	(B-LCQ), D-AUBF Star Rising Aviation 10 Ltd Francazal		
	Stored		

EI-GII	Airbus A320-271N	8430	21.12.18
	(B-LCR), D-AUBW Star Rising Aviation 10 Ltd		
	Francazal		
	Stored		

EI-GIJ	Van's RV-9	2002495	22.01.19
	D-EYYE D Horan (Tralee, Co Kerry)		

EI-GIM Boeing 737-86Q   30289   xx.xx.19
VP-CNG, LN-NOO, N289CG, OY-SEJ   –
Rome-Fiumicino
Operated by Blue Panorama Airlines

EI-GIN Airbus A321-231   2730   21.12.18
OO-SBA, (G-POWT), G-ZBAF, 5B-DCO, JY-AYG, D-AVZB
Fortress Aircraft 32A-2730 Ltd   Montpellier
Stored

EI-GIO Magni M-16 Tandem Trainer   VPM16-UK-111 22.01.19
G-ODPJ, G-BVWX   P M Flanagan   (Kilrush, Co Clare)
Built by M L Smith as project PFA G/12-1251

EI-GIS Tecnam P.2002-JF Sierra   191   13.02.19
G-UFCL   Waterford Aero Club Ltd   Waterford
Badly damaged at Waterford Airport 11.03.19

EI-GIW Aérospatiale-Alenia ATR 72-212A   1064   22.02.19
VT-JCY, F-WWEZ   Celestial Aviation Trading 27 Ltd
Sonderborg
Stored

EI-GIX Aérospatiale-Alenia ATR 72-212A   1075   22.02.19
VT-JCZ, F-WWEL   Celestial Aviation Trading 71 Ltd
Sonderborg
Stored

EI-GIY★ Boeing 737-8K5   34690   06.02.19
G-FDZJ, C-FRZJ, G-FDZJ, C-FRZJ, G-FDZJ, C-FRZJ,
G-FDZJ, C-FRZJ, G-FDZJ, C-FRZJ, G-FDZJ, D-ATUI,
N1786A Tempelhof Aircraft Leasing Ltd
To HL8322 15.02.19

EI-GJA Boeing 737-800   44819   20.02.18
Ryanair DAC   (Dublin)

EI-GJB Boeing 737-800   44822   23.02.18
Ryanair DAC   (Dublin)

EI-GJC Boeing 737-800   44824   26.02.18
Ryanair DAC   (Dublin)

EI-GJD Boeing 737-800   44821   28.02.18
N1799B Ryanair DAC   (Dublin)

EI-GJE Boeing 737-800   44823   02.03.18
Ryanair DAC   (Dublin)

EI-GJF Boeing 737-800   44828   01.03.18
Ryanair DAC   (Dublin)

EI-GJG Boeing 737-800   44829   16.03.18
Ryanair DAC   (Dublin)

EI-GJH Boeing 737-800   44830   20.03.18
Ryanair DAC   (Dublin)

EI-GJI Boeing 737-800   44826   23.03.18
N1786B Ryanair DAC   (Dublin)

EI-GJJ Boeing 737-800   44831   29.03.18
N1786B Ryanair DAC   (Dublin)

EI-GJK Boeing 737-800   44825   23.03.18
Ryanair DAC   (Dublin)

EI-GJL Eurocopter AS.365N Dauphin 2   6785   27.05.08
G-CEUK, F-WWOZ   Anglo Beef Processors Ireland
(Ardee, Co Louth)

EI-GJM Boeing 737-800   44827   29.03.18
Ryanair DAC   (Dublin)

EI-GJN Boeing 737-800   44838   11.04.18
Ryanair DAC   (Dublin)

EI-GJO Boeing 737-800   44833   19.04.18
N1799B Ryanair DAC   (Dublin)

EI-GJP Boeing 737-800   44834   23.04.18
N1786B Ryanair DAC   (Dublin)

EI-GJR★ Boeing 737-800   44835   27.04.18
N1786B Ryanair DAC
To SP-RSS 18.12.18

EI-GJS Boeing 737-800   44836   26.04.18
Ryanair DAC   (Dublin)

EI-GJT Boeing 737-800   44837   01.05.18
N1786B Ryanair DAC   (Dublin)

EI-GJV★ Boeing 737-800   44832   09.05.18
N1795B Ryanair DAC
To SP-RSB 22.11.18

EI-GJW★ Boeing 737-800   44843   11.05.18
Ryanair DAC
To SP-RSC 22.11.18

EI-GJX★ Boeing 737-800   44845   18.05.18
Ryanair DAC
To SP-RSD 22.11.18

EI-GJY★ Boeing 737-800   44839   23.05.18
Ryanair DAC
To SP-RSE 22.11.18

EI-GJZ★ Boeing 737-800   44840   24.05.18
Ryanair DAC
To SP-RSF 03.12.18

EI-GKM Airbus A320-232   3010   28.02.19
TC-JPG, F-WWBJ
WWTAI Airopco II DAC   Chicago Rockford
Stored

EI-GKX Boeing 737-8K5   39093   22.02.19
OO-JAD, C-FNAD, OO-JAD
Fitzroya Issuance DAC   Shannon
Stored

EI-GLA Schleicher ASK 21   21002   28.03.07
EI-150, D-6957   Dublin Gliding Club Ltd
Gowran Grange   *'ICS'*
Substantially damaged at Kilrush 10.08.18

EI-GLB Schleicher ASK 21   21060   28.03.07
EI-164, D-4089   Dublin Gliding Club Ltd
Gowran Grange

EI-GLC Centrair 101A Pégase   101-102   28.03.07
EI-163, PH-738   Dublin Gliding Club Ltd
Gowran Grange   *'ZC'*

EI-GLD Schleicher ASK 13   13131   28.03.07
EI-112   Dublin Gliding Club Ltd   Gowran Grange

EI-GLF Schleicher K 8B   8468   28.03.07
EI-108   Dublin Gliding Club Ltd   Gowran Grange   *'08'*

EI-GLG Schleicher Ka 6CR   662   25.09.09
EI-127, PH-259   C Sinclair & Partners
Gowran Grange   *'Albatross'*

EI-GLH Sportine Aviacija LAK-17A   136   28.03.07
EI-169, HA-4511   K Commins & S Kinnear
Gowran Grange   *'T8'*

EI-GLL Glaser-Dirks DG-200   2-22   28.03.07
EI-147, D-6780   P Denman & Partners
Gowran Grange   *'DS'*

EI-GLM Schleicher Ka 6CR   6565   28.03.07
EI-111, IGA 9   P Denman & Partners
Gowran Grange   *'11'*

EI-GLO Scheibe Zugvogel IIIB   1085   28.03.07
EI-146, D-4096   J Walsh & Partners
Gowran Grange   *'TK'*

EI-GLP EoN AP.5 Olympia 2B   EoN/O/155   28.03.07
EI-115, BGA 1097   J Cashin   Kilkenny

EI-GLT Schempp-Hirth Discus b   219   04.05.07
EI-149, BGA 3320/FKK   T Deane   Gowran Grange   *'49'*

EI-GLU Schleicher Ka 6CR   808   28.03.07
EI-161, BGA 3536/FUM, D-6289   K Cullen & Partners
Gowran Grange

EI-GLV Schleicher ASW 19B   19316   28.03.07
EI-153, BGA 4274/HWZ, HB-1524
C Sinclair & Partners   Gowran Grange   *'53'*

EI-GLZ Schleicher ASK 21   21332   17.12.18
D-4780   Dublin Gliding Club Ltd   Gowran Grange

EI-GMB Schleicher ASW 17   17031   28.03.07
EI-132, D-2365   ASW-17 Group   Gowran Grange   *'TK'*
Substantially damaged at Kilrush 10.08.18

EI-GMC Schleicher ASK 18   18007   20.09.07
EI-136, BGA 2945-ETT, D-6868
The Eighteen Group   Gowran Grange

EI-GMD Bölkow Phoebus C   908   28.03.07
EI-158, BGA 4202-HTZ, OO-ZDJ, BGA 1573
F McDonnell & Partners   Gowran Grange

EI-GMF Schleicher ASK 13   13189   28.03.07
EI-113   Dublin Gliding Club Ltd   Gowran Grange

| EI-GMG | Glasflugel Standard Libelle 201B | 180 | 11.02.19 |
| | G-DCLV, BGA 1636   T McHugh   (Blackrock, Co Dublin) | | |

EI-GMH	Wag-Aero CUBy Sport Trainer	xxxx	17.12.14
	G-BVMH J Matthews (Trim)		
	Built by D M Jagger as project PFA 108-12647;		
	as '624:D-39' in US Army c/s		

EI-GMI	PZL-Swidnik PW-5 Smyk	17.03.013	26.02.19
	HA-3791, SP-3791, OO-YPW, HB-3020		
	P Walsh & Partners (Waterford)		

EI-GMO	Schleicher Ka 6E	4307	14.09.17
	G-CJHD, BGA 4519-JHD, OY-XGS, D-0272		
	C Sinclair & Partners Gowran Grange		

| EI-GPS | Grob G-120TP-A | 11103 | 28.08.18 |
| | D-ETPQ   Grob Power Service Ltd   (Dublin) | | |

EI-GPT	Robinson R22 Beta II	3317	08.11.04
	N70637 Treaty Plant & Tool (Hire & Sales) Ltd		
	(Childers Road, Limerick)		

| EI-GRA | Urban Air UFM-13 Lambada | 86/13 | 12.12.18 |
| | 33-64, OK-LUA 66   J Selman   (Ardagh, Co Limerick) | | |

EI-GSA★	Boeing 737-800	44841	24.05.18
	Ryanair DAC		
	To SP-RSG 26.11.18		

EI-GSB★	Boeing 737-800	44842	01.06.18
	N1786B Ryanair DAC		
	To SP-RSH 03.12.18		

EI-GSC★	Boeing 737-800	44844	30.05.18
	Ryanair DAC		
	To SP-RSI 03.12.18		

EI-GSD★	Boeing 737-800	44847	31.08.18
	N1786B Ryanair DAC		
	To SP-RSK 29.11.18		

EI-GSE	Reims/Cessna F172M Skyhawk II	F17201105	12.04.02
	D-EDXO Cancelled 27.01.14 as removed from service		
	Dublin Weston		
	Fire training area 09.14		

EI-GSF★	Boeing 737-800	44850	13.09.18
	N1786B Ryanair DAC		
	To SP-RSL 01.12.18		

| EI-GSG | Boeing 737-800 | 44849 | 21.09.18 |
| | N1786B   Ryanair DAC   (Dublin) | | |

| EI-GSH | Boeing 737-800 | 44846 | 29.09.18 |
| | N1786B   Ryanair DAC   (Dublin) | | |

| EI-GSI | Boeing 737-800 | 44848 | 27.09.18 |
| | N1786B   Ryanair DAC   (Dublin) | | |

| EI-GSJ | Boeing 737-800 | 44854 | 27.09.18 |
| | N1786B   Ryanair DAC   (Dublin) | | |

| EI-GSK | Boeing 737-800 | 44855 | 28.09.18 |
| | Ryanair DAC   (Dublin) | | |

| EI-GSM | Cessna 182S Skylane | 18280188 | 17.06.98 |
| | N9541Q   Westpoint Flying Group Ltd   Dublin Weston | | |

| EI-GVM | Robinson R22 Beta | 2711 | 03.09.10 |
| | G-ERBL   J Porter   (Ramelton, Co Donegal) | | |

| EI-GWY | Cessna 172R Skyhawk | 17280162 | 31.12.97 |
| | N9497F   Atlantic Flight Training Ltd   Cork | | |

| EI-GXG | Boeing 737-800 | 44853 | 29.09.18 |
| | Ryanair DAC   (Dublin) | | |

| EI-GXH | Boeing 737-800 | 44852 | 29.09.18 |
| | Ryanair DAC   (Dublin) | | |

| EI-GXI | Boeing 737-800 | 44851 | 22.10.18 |
| | Ryanair DAC   (Dublin) | | |

| EI-GXJ | Boeing 737-800 | 44859 | 07.11.18 |
| | Ryanair DAC   (Dublin) | | |

| EI-GXK | Boeing 737-800 | 44860 | 13.11.18 |
| | N1786B   Ryanair DAC   (Dublin) | | |

| EI-GXL | Boeing 737-800 | 44857 | 15.11.18 |
| | N1786B   Ryanair DAC   (Dublin) | | |

| EI-GXM | Boeing 737-800 | 44858 | 29.11.18 |
| | N1786B   Ryanair DAC   (Dublin) | | |

| EI-GXN | Boeing 737-800 | 44856 | 13.12.18 |
| | N60436   Ryanair DAC   (Dublin) | | |

EI-HAA	Boeing 737-4Y0(SF)	25177	26.05.17
	N760SL, A6-ESF, EI-EMY, SX-BGQ, F-GLXJ, G-OBMM		
	ASL Aircraft Investment (No.2) Ltd Budapest		
	Operated by ASL Airlines Hungary		

| EI-HAT | Boeing 737-8 200 MAX | 65076 | xx.xx.19 |
| | N6065Y, N1786B   Ryanair DAC   (Dublin) | | |

| EI-HAV | Boeing 737-8 200 MAX | 65077 | xx.xx.19 |
| | Ryanair DAC   (Dublin) | | |

| EI-HAW | Boeing 737-8 200 MAX | 65078 | xx.xx.19 |
| | Ryanair DAC   (Dublin) | | |

EI-HBA	Bombardier CL-600-2E25 CRJ-1000	19020	02.11.18
	EC-LOX, C-GZQV Hibernian Airlines Ltd		
	Madrid-Barajas		

EI-HEA	Airbus A330-322(F)	116	05.12.17
	D-AAEA, G-CIOH, 9M-MKI, F-WWKT		
	ASL Airlines (Ireland) Ltd Hong Kong		
	Operated by DHL		

EI-HEB	Airbus A330-322(F)	127	01.03.18
	D-AAEB, CS-TRI, D-AERQ, F-WWKO		
	ASL Airlines (Ireland) Ltd Hong Kong		
	Operated by DHL		

EI-HED	Airbus A330-243F	1414	17.12.18
	D-ALMB, A6-DCC, F-WWTL		
	ASL Airlines (Ireland) Ltd Hong Kong		
	Operated by DHL		

EI-HFA	de Havilland DHC-1 Chipmunk 22	C1/0464	02.06.15
	168 Irish Historic Flight Foundation Co Ltd Ballyboy		
	As '168' in Irish Air Corps c/s		

EI-HFB	de Havilland DHC-1 Chipmunk 22	C1/0247	08.05.15
	G-ARGG, WD305 Irish Historic Flight Foundation Co Ltd		
	Ballyboy		
	As '169' in Irish Air Corps c/s		

EI-HFC	de Havilland DHC-1 Chipmunk 22	C1/0742	08.05.15
	G-BDRJ, WP857 Irish Historic Flight Foundation Co Ltd		
	Trim		
	As '170' in Irish Air Corps c/s		

EI-HFD	Boeing Stearman E75 (N2S-5) Kaydet	75-5736A	27.05.16
	G-THEA, (EI-RYR), G-THEA, N1733B, USN38122		
	Irish Historic Flight Foundation Co Ltd Trim		
	'Spirit of Tipperary'		

EI-HUM	Van's RV-7	70588-1	08.02.07
	G Humphreys Brittas		
	Built by G Humphreys		

| EI-IAL | AgustaWestland AW109SP | 22343 | 28.08.15 |
| | I-EASU   Ion Aviation Ltd   (Simmonscourt Road, Dublin) | | |

EI-ICA	Sikorsky S-92A	920045	17.06.13
	G-SARB, N80562 CHC Ireland DAC Shannon		
	Operated by Irish Coast Guard – Rescue 115		

EI-ICD	Sikorsky S-92A	920052	08.07.13
	G-SARC, N45168 CHC Ireland DAC Dublin		
	Operated by Irish Coast Guard – Rescue 116		

EI-ICG	Sikorsky S-92A	920150	24.01.12
	N150AL CHC Ireland DAC Sligo		
	Operated by Irish Coast Guard – Rescue 118		

| EI-ICP | ICP Savannah S | 18-07-54-0626 | 11.09.18 |
| | Funfly Aerospots Ltd   Limetree | | |

EI-ICR	Sikorsky S-92A	920051	17.06.13
	G-CGOC, N45165 CHC Ireland DAC (Sligo)		
	Written off in sea off Co Mayo 14.03.17		

EI-ICS	Sikorsky S-92A	920259	17.10.17
	G-CKII, VH-NBP, N259CV CHC Ireland DAC Waterford		
	Operated by Irish Coast Guard – Rescue 117		

EI-ICU	Sikorsky S-92A	920034	23.07.13
	G-CGMU, N8010S CHC Ireland DAC Shannon		
	Operated by Irish Coast Guard – Rescue 115		

EI-IKB	Airbus A320-214	1226	03.11.10
	I-BIKB, F-WWIG Aircraft Purchase Company No 12 Ltd		
	Rome-Fiumicino *'Wolfgang Amadeus Mozart'*		
	Operated by Alitalia		

EI-IKF	Airbus A320-214	1473	26.07.11
	I-BIKF, F-WWDP Aircraft Purchase Company No 12 Ltd		
	Rome-Fiumicino *'Mole Antonelliana'*		
	Operated by Alitalia		

EI-IKG   Airbus A320-214   1480   27.07.11
I-BIKG, F-WWDT   Aircraft Purchase Company No 12 Ltd
Rome-Fiumicino   *'Scirocco'*
Operated by Alitalia

EI-IKL   Airbus A320-214   1489   16.11.10
I-BIKL, F-WWDN   Aircraft Purchase Company No 12 Ltd
Rome-Fiumicino   *'Libeccio'*
Operated by Alitalia

EI-IKU   Airbus A320-214   1217   02.11.10
I-BIKU, F-WWBD   Aircraft Purchase Company No 12 Ltd
Rome-Fiumicino   *'Fryderyk Chopin'*
Operated by Alitalia

EI-IMB   Airbus A319-112   2033   22.11.10
I-BIMB, D-AVYP   Aircraft Purchase Company No 12 Ltd
Rome-Fiumicino   *'Isola del Giglio'*
Operated by Alitalia

EI-IMC   Airbus A319-112   2057   15.11.10
I-BIMC, D-AVYC   Aircraft Purchase Company No 12 Ltd
Rome-Fiumicino   *'Isola di Lipari'*
Operated by Alitalia

EI-IMD   Airbus A319-112   2074   12.11.10
I-BIMD, D-AVYM   Aircraft Purchase Company No 12 Ltd
Rome-Fiumicino   *'Isola di Capri'*
Operated by Alitalia

EI-IME   Airbus A319-112   1740   09.11.10
I-BIME, D-AVWW   Aircraft Purchase Company No 12 Ltd
Rome-Fiumicino   *'Isola di Panarea'*
Operated by Alitalia

EI-IMF   Airbus A319-112   2083   08.11.10
I-BIMF, D-AVYZ   Aircraft Purchase Company No 12 Ltd
Rome-Fiumicino   *'Isola Tremiti'*
Operated by Alitalia

EI-IMG   Airbus A319-112   2086   19.11.10
I-BIMG, D-AVWD   Aircraft Purchase Company No 12 Ltd
Rome-Fiumicino   *'Isola di Pantelleria'*
Operated by Alitalia

EI-IMH   Airbus A319-112   2101   30.11.10
I-BIMH, D-AVYY   Aircraft Purchase Company No 12 Ltd
Rome-Fiumicino   *'Isola di Ventotene'*
Operated by Alitalia

EI-IMI   Airbus A319-112   1745   25.11.10
I-BIMI, D-AVWZ   Aircraft Purchase Company No 12 Ltd
Rome-Fiumicino   *'Isola di Ponza'*
Operated by Alitalia in Friuli-Venezia-Giulia c/s

EI-IMJ   Airbus A319-112   1779   29.11.10
I-BIMJ, D-AVYG   Aircraft Purchase Company No 12 Ltd
Rome-Fiumicino   *'Isola di Caprera'*
Operated by Alitalia

EI-IML   Airbus A319-112   2127   01.12.10
I-BIML, D-AVWN   Aircraft Purchase Company No 12 Ltd
Rome-Fiumicino   *'Isola La Maddalena'*
Operated by Alitalia)

EI-IMM   Airbus A319-111   4759   29.06.11
D-AVYE   AS Air Lease XXXIX (Ireland) Ltd
Rome-Fiumicino   *'Vittorio Alfieri'*
Operated by Alitalia

EI-IMN   Airbus A319-111   4764   05.08.11
D-AVYG   AS Air Lease XXXIX (Ireland) Ltd
Rome-Fiumicino   *'Carlo Collodi'*
Operated by Alitalia

EI-IMO   Airbus A319-112   1770   26.11.10
I-BIMO, D-AVWC   Aircraft Purchase Company No 12 Ltd
Rome-Fiumicino   *'Isola d'Ischia'*
Operated by Alitalia

EI-IMP   Airbus A319-111   4859   04.11.11
D-AVWR   GY Aviation Lease 103 Co Ltd
Rome-Fiumicino   *'Italo Svevo'*
Operated by Alitalia

EI-IMR   Airbus A319-111   4875   04.11.11
D-AVYB   GY Aviation Lease 103 Co Ltd
Rome-Fiumicino   *'Italo Calvino'*
Operated by Alitalia

EI-IMS   Airbus A319-111   4910   07.11.11
D-AVYC   AS Air Lease XXXIX (Ireland) Ltd
Rome-Fiumicino   *'Giuseppe Parrini'*
Operated by Alitalia

EI-IMT   Airbus A319-111   5018   14.06.12
D-AVYI   Orix Aircraft Management Ltd
Rome-Fiumicino   *'Silvio Pellico'*
Operated by Alitalia

EI-IMU   Airbus A319-111   5130   22.05.12
D-AVYA   GY Aviation Lease 103 Co Ltd
Rome-Fiumicino   *'Pietro Verri'*
Operated by Alitalia

EI-IMV   Airbus A319-111   5294   15.01.13
D-AVWB   AS Air Lease 46 (Ireland) Ltd
Rome-Fiumicino   *'Filippo Tommaso Marinetti'*
Operated by Alitalia

EI-IMW   Airbus A319-111   5383   04.12.12
D-AVWJ   AS Air Lease VII (Ireland) Ltd   Rome-Fiumicino
Operated by Alitalia

EI-IMX   Airbus A319-111   5424   17.01.13
D-AVWM   AS Air Lease VII (Ireland) Ltd   Rome-Fiumicino
Operated by Alitalia

EI-ING   Reims/Cessna F172P Skyhawk II   F17202084   19.08.05
G-BING   21st Century Flyers Ltd   Dublin Weston

EI-IRI   Boeing 737-86J   36881   02.05.18
D-AIRI, N279EA, D-ABKT
Wings Aviation 36881 Ltd   Erfurt
Stored

EI-ISA   Boeing 777-243ER   32855   10.01.13
I-DISA   Aircraft Purchase Company No 12 Ltd
Rome-Fiumicino   *'Taormina'*
Operated by Alitalia

EI-ISB   Boeing 777-243ER   32859   23.03.12
I-DISB   Aircraft Purchase Company No 12 Ltd
Rome-Fiumicino   *'Porto Rotondo'*
Operated by Alitalia

EI-ISD   Boeing 777-243ER   32860   14.07.11
I-DISD   Aircraft Purchase Company No 12 Ltd
Rome-Fiumicino   *'Cortina d'Ampezzo'*
Operated by Alitalia

EI-ISE   Boeing 777-243ER   32856   19.12.12
I-DISE   Aircraft Purchase Company No 12 Ltd
Rome-Fiumicino   *'Portofino/Pier Paolo Racchetti'*
Operated by Alitalia

EI-ISO   Boeing 777-243ER   32857   28.12.12
I-DISO   Aircraft Purchase Company No 12 Ltd
Rome-Fiumicino   *'Positano'*
Operated by Alitalia

EI-ITA   Airbus A321-251N   8312   21.12.18
OY-PAE, D-AVZS   ACG Aircraft Leasing Ireland Ltd
Newquay Cornwall
Stored

EI-ITN   Bombardier BD-700-1A10 Global Express   9159   09.09.16
OE-ITN, (D-AZNF), OH-TNR, D-ATNR, C-FCOI
Airlink Airways Ltd   Shannon/Riga

EI-IXH   Airbus A321-112   0940   09.02.10
I-BIXH, D-AVZS   Aircraft Purchase Company No 11 Ltd
Rome-Fiumicino   *'Piazza della Signoria Gubbio'*
Operated by Alitalia

EI-IXJ   Airbus A321-112   0959   08.02.10
I-BIXJ, D-AVZP   Aircraft Purchase Company No 11 Ltd
Rome-Fiumicino   *'Piazza del Municipio Noto'*
Operated by Alitalia

EI-IXV   Airbus A321-112   0819   11.01.10
I-BIXV, D-AVZU   Aircraft Purchase Company No 11 Ltd
Rome-Fiumicino   *'Piazza del Rinascimento Urbino'*
Operated by Alitalia

EI-IXZ   Airbus A321-112   0848   10.02.10
I-BIXZ, D-AVZC   Aircraft Purchase Company No 11 Ltd
Rome-Fiumicino   *'Piazza del Duomo Orvieto'*
Operated by Alitalia

EI-JIM   Urban Air Samba XLA   43   21.12.06
J Smith   Navan

EI-JOR   Robinson R44 Raven II   12426   24.09.08
Bluebrook Investments Ltd   Dunkeswell
For sale

EI-JPK   Tecnam P.2002-JF Sierra   079   08.04.08
Limerick Flying Club (Coonagh) Ltd   Coonagh

EI-JSK	Gulfstream Aerospace Gulfstream G650 6070	01.05.14	
	N670GA Westair Aviation Ltd Shannon		
EI-JWMᴹ	Robinson R22 Beta 1386	21.11.92	
	G-BSLB Cancelled 28.05.07 as destroyed		
	With South Yorkshire Aircraft Museum, Doncaster		
EI-KDH	Piper PA-28-181 Archer III 2843422	01.06.05	
	N301PA, N41870 K O'Driscoll & Partners		
	Dublin Weston		
EI-KEL	Eurocopter EC135T2+ 0848	09.12.10	
	G-CGHP Bond Air Services (Ireland) Ltd Cork		
EI-KEV	Raj Hamsa X'Air 133(1) 567	21.05.04	
	G-BZLD P Kearney Birr		
	Built by C Blackburn		
EI-KMA	Bombardier CL-600-2B16 Challenger 5585	07.06.16	
	SX-KMA, D-AAOK, N585BD, C-GLXO		
	Gain Jet Ireland Ltd Shannon		
EI-LAD	Robinson R44 Raven II 10779	16.09.08	
	G-CDMI Helicopter Support Ireland Ltd		
	(Naas, Co Kildare)		
EI-LAX	Airbus A330-202 269	29.04.99	
	F-WWKV Aer Lingus Ltd Dublin *'St Mella/Mella'*		
EI-LBR	Boeing 757-2Q8 28167	04.12.13	
	OH-LBR ASL Airlines (Ireland) Ltd Dublin		
	'St Otteran/Odhran'		
	Operated by Aer Lingus		
EI-LBS	Boeing 757-2Q8 27623	21.02.14	
	OH-LBS ASL Airlines (Ireland) Ltd Dublin		
	'St Columbanus/Columban'		
	Operated by Aer Lingus		
EI-LBT	Boeing 757-2Q8 28170	14.03.14	
	OH-LBT ASL Airlines (Ireland) Ltd Dublin		
	'St Brendan/Breandan'		
	Operated by Aer Lingus		
EI-LCM	Socata TBM700N (TBM850) 436	13.06.08	
	N850JS GEO Power Dublin Weston		
EI-LEO	Cessna 750 Citation X 750-0232	12.11.14	
	OE-HAC, N232CX Gain Jet Ireland Ltd Shannon		
EI-LFC	Tecnam P.2002-JF Sierra 063	10.07.07	
	Limerick Flying Club (Coonagh) Ltd Coonagh		
EI-LIA	Airbus A321-251N 8260	21.12.18	
	OY-PAC, D-AVYL ACG Aircraft Leasing Ireland Ltd		
	Newquay Cornwall		
	Stored		
EI-LID	AgustaWestland AW169 69015	21.12.16	
	G-CJHA, I-RAIM Vertical Aviation No 1 Ltd Foggia		
	Operated by Alidaunia		
EI-LIM	AgustaWestland AW139 31541	10.04.14	
	I-EASY Westair Aviation Ltd Shannon		
EI-LIX	Airbus A320-214 8604	30.11.18	
	(B-), F-WWBP Sky High 104 Leasing Company Ltd		
	Milan-Malpensa		
	Operated by Ernest		
EI-LOW	Eurocopter AS.355N Ecureuil 2 5685	18.02.11	
	LN-OGP, 5Y-EXD, F-WQDI, F-WQDB		
	Executive Helicopter Maintenance Ltd		
	(Loughrea, Co Galway)		
EI-LSA	Cubcrafters CC11-160 CC11-00096	08.08.12	
	N298A Directsky Aviation Ltd Abbeyshrule		
EI-LSN	Gulfstream Aerospace Gulfstream G650 6092	13.12.16	
	SX-GSB, N692GA Gain Jet Ireland Ltd Shannon		
EI-LSY	Gulfstream Aerospace Gulfstream G550 5350	30.11.16	
	SX-GJJ, N750GA Gain Jet Ireland Ltd Shannon		
EI-MCF	Cessna 172R Skyhawk 17280799	13.03.09	
	N2469D National Flight Centre Ltd Dublin Weston		
EI-MCG	Cessna 172R Skyhawk 17281539	18.11.08	
	N6311Y Galway Flying Club Ltd Galway		
EI-MIK	Eurocopter EC.120B Colibri 1104	22.06.01	
	G-BZIU Executive Helicopter Maintenance Ltd		
	(Loughrea, Co Galway)		
EI-MIR	Roko Aero NG 4HD 017/2009	24.09.09	
	A Fegan Newcastle		

EI-MNG	Boeing 737-8 MAX 43795	30.01.19	
	N1786B Avolon Aerospace (Ireland) AOE 171 Ltd		
	Ulan Bator *'Tolui Khaan'*		
	Operated by MIAT Mongolian Airlines		
EI-MPC	AgustaWestland AW109SP 22391	11.01.19	
	Quarry & Mining Equipment Ltd (Dundalk, Co Louth)		
EI-MPW	Robinson R44 Raven 1554	14.02.06	
	Connacht Helicopters Ltd (Ballina, Co Mayo)		
EI-MRB	Denney Kitfox Model 2 449	03.09.14	
	G-BSHK D Doyle Limetree		
	Built by A C Cree as project PFA 172-11752		
EI-MTZ	Urban Air Samba XXL SAXL68	16.06.08	
	M Motz Abbeyshrule		
EI-NEO	Boeing 787-9 38785	11.12.17	
	ILFC Ireland Ltd Milan-Malpensa *'Spirit of Italy'*		
	Operated by Neos		
EI-NEU	Boeing 787-9 38794	30.10.18	
	Cesium Funding Ltd Milan-Malpensa		
	Operated by Neos		
EI-NEW	Boeing 787-9 38791	27.06.18	
	ILFC Ireland Ltd Milan-Malpensa *'Erminio Ferri'*		
	Operated by Neos		
EI-NFW	Cessna 172S Skyhawk SP 172S9861	28.02.06	
	G-CDOU, N1538W Galway Flying Club Ltd Galway		
EI-NJA	Robinson R44 Raven II 11945	21.12.07	
	N155N Nojo Aviation Ltd Newcastle		
EI-NVL	JORA Jora C129	25.07.03	
	A McAllister & Partners Ballyboy		
EI-ODD	Bell 206B-3 JetRanger III 3627	25.11.05	
	G-CDES, N22751 Dwyer Nolan Developments Ltd		
	Newcastle		
EI-OFM	Reims/Cessna F172N Skyhawk II F17201988	06.05.05	
	G-EOFM, D-EDFM		
	21st Century Flyers Company Ltd Dublin Weston		
EI-OOR	Cessna 172S Skyhawk SP 172S10374	23.12.08	
	N11688 M Casey Cork		
EI-OZL	Airbus A300B4-622RF 717	01.09.15	
	HL7299, UK-31004, HL7299, F-WWAY		
	ASL Airlines (Ireland) Ltd Dublin		
	Operated by DHL		
EI-OZM	Airbus A300B4-622RF 722	28.08.15	
	HL7244, UK-31005, HL7244, F-WWAH		
	ASL Airlines (Ireland) Ltd Dublin		
	Operated by DHL		
EI-PCI	Bell 206B-3 JetRanger III 4072	22.06.18	
	N208M, JA9850, C-GAJN Marketside Ltd		
	(Ashbourne, Co Meath)		
EI-PGA	Dudek Hadron XX P-127451	19.08.16	
	F Taylor (Ballymote, Co Sligo)		
EI-PGB	Dudek Hadron 28 P-109225	22.02.17	
	C Fowler (Enfield, Co Meath)		
EI-PGD	Paramania Revolution 2 0307646	01.02.18	
	D Keoghegan (Enfield, Co Meath)		
EI-PGH	Dudek Synthesis LT P-07518	14.09.16	
	R Leslie (Kinsale, Co Cork)		
EI-PGI	Dudek Hadron 28 P-114571	20.03.17	
	J McGovern (Leopardstown, Dublin)		
EI-PGJ	Swing Sting 2 ST2 11-5268066	30.08.16	
	A Auffret (Timoleague, Co Cork)		
EI-PGK	Ozone Spyder 26 SD26-R-26B-047	12.08.16	
	O Creagh (St Lukes, Cork)		
EI-PGL	Dudek Synthesis 34 P-08129	04.10.16	
	K Sullivan (Leixlip, Co Kildare)		
EI-PGM	Dudek Nucleon XX P-145084	13.04.17	
	L Graham (Athgarvan, Co Kildare)		
EI-PGN	ITV Boxer 2K11488	13.06.17	
	N Burke (Vicarstown, Co Cork)		
EI-PGO	Fly Market Relax 25 RLX 4273	14.06.17	
	M N Bendon (Glandore, Co Cork)		
EI-PGP	Paramania Fusion 26 0908032	21.12.17	
	E DeKhors (Sallins, Co Kildare)		

EI-PGS	Dudek Universal 25.5 M Markowicz (Waterfall, Cork)	P-139853	21.08.18
EI-PGT	ITV Boxer M Hastings (Youghal, Co Cork)	2K11977	18.09.18
EI-PMI	Agusta-Bell 206B-3 JetRanger III EI-BLG, G-BIGS Eirland Ltd (Castleknock, Dublin)	8614	19.09.96
EI-POK	Robinson R44 Raven D-HALS Skywest Aviation Ltd Newcastle	2374	08.12.16
EI-POP	Cameron Z-90 HAB The Travel Department Ltd (Harmony Court, Dublin) 'Travel Department'	10753	23.09.05
EI-PRO	Eurocopter AS.365N Dauphin 2 I-PCFL, PT-YRM, F-WYMN Executive Helicopter Maintenance Ltd (Loughrea, Co Galway)	6443	14.12.16
EI-PWC	Magni M-24 Orion R Macnioclais Dublin Weston	24-16-9754	05.07.16
EI-RCA	Roko Aero NG 4UL OK-TUR 22, EI-RCA, OK-PUR 04 A Breslin Kilrush	019/2009	08.03.16
EI-RDA	Embraer ERJ-170-200LR PT-TPD Blackbird Capital I Leasing Ltd Rome-Fiumicino 'Parco Nazionale del Gran Paradiso' Operated by Alitalia Cityliner	17000330	27.10.11
EI-RDB	Embraer ERJ-170-200LR PT-TPR Aircraft Purchase Company Ltd Rome-Fiumicino 'Parco Nazionale dello Stelvio' Operated by Alitalia Cityliner	17000331	10.11.11
EI-RDC	Embraer ERJ-170-200LR PT-TSA Aircraft Purchase Company Ltd Rome-Fiumicino 'Parco Nazionale delle Cinque Terre' Operated by Alitalia Cityliner	17000333	01.03.12
EI-RDD	Embraer ERJ-170-200LR PT-TSP NAC Aviation 19 Ltd Rome-Fiumicino 'Parco Nazionale d'Abruzzo' Operated by Alitalia Cityliner	17000334	26.03.12
EI-RDE	Embraer ERJ-170-200LR PT-TUH NAC Aviation 19 Ltd Rome-Fiumicino 'Parco Nazionale dell'Etna' Operated by Alitalia Cityliner	17000335	16.04.12
EI-RDF	Embraer ERJ-170-200LR PT-TUW Minerva Airlease One Ltd Rome-Fiumicino 'Parco Nazionale Dolomiti Friulane' Operated by Alitalia Cityliner	17000337	22.06.12
EI-RDG	Embraer ERJ-170-200LR PT-TVD Minerva Airlease Two Ltd Rome-Fiumicino 'Parco Nazionale dell'Asinara' Operated by Alitalia Cityliner	17000338	26.06.12
EI-RDH	Embraer ERJ-170-200LR PT-TZV Minerva Airlease Three Ltd Rome-Fiumicino 'Parco Delta del Po' Operated by Alitalia Cityliner	17000339	26.06.12
EI-RDI	Embraer ERJ-170-200LR PT-TAY NAC Aviation 19 Ltd Rome-Fiumicino Operated by Alitalia Cityliner) 'Parco Storico Monte Sole'	17000340	26.06.12
EI-RDJ	Embraer ERJ-170-200LR PT-TBT CIT Aerospace International Rome-Fiumicino 'Parco Nazionale del Circeo' Operated by Alitalia Cityliner	17000342	26.07.12
EI-RDK	Embraer ERJ-170-200LR PT-TBY CIT Aerospace International Rome-Fiumicino 'Parco Nazionale del Gargano' Operated by Alitalia Cityliner	17000343	26.07.12
EI-RDL	Embraer ERJ-170-200LR PT-TDO CIT Aerospace International Rome-Fiumicino 'Parco Nazionale Val Grande' Operated by Alitalia Cityliner	17000345	23.08.12
EI-RDM	Embraer ERJ-170-200LR PT-TDW CIT Aerospace International Rome-Fiumicino 'Parco Nazionale della Majella' Operated by Alitalia Cityliner	17000346	30.08.12
EI-RDN	Embraer ERJ-170-200LR PT-TGA Tiradentes Portfolio D Ltd Rome-Fiumicino 'Parco Nazionale dell'Alta Murgia' Operated by Alitalia Cityliner	17000347	22.03.13

EI-RDO	Embraer ERJ-170-200LR PT-THB Tiradentes Portfolio D Ltd Rome-Fiumicino 'Parco Regionale della Maremma' Operated by Alitalia Cityliner	17000348	22.03.13
EI-REJ	Aérospatiale-Alenia ATR 72-201F ES-KRA, OH-KRA, F-WWEJ ASL Airlines (Ireland) Ltd Sonderborg Stored	126	18.05.06
EI-REL	Aérospatiale-Alenia ATR 72-212A F-WWEI Stobart Air ULC Dublin Flybe c/s	748	25.05.07
EI-REM	Aérospatiale-Alenia ATR 72-212A F-WWEW Stobart Air ULC Dublin Flybe c/s	760	25.10.07
EI-RJD	British Aerospace Avro 146-RJ85 G-CEFL, N516XJ, G-6-334 CityJet DAC Dublin 'Valentia Island' Operated by Aer Lingus	E2334	10.08.07
EI-RJF	British Aerospace Avro 146-RJ85 G-CEFN, N518XJ, G-6-337 CityJet DAC Dublin 'Great Blasket island'	E2337	24.08.07
EI-RJI	British Aerospace Avro 146-RJ85 (G-CDZP), N521XJ, G-6-346 CityJet DAC Dublin 'Skellig Michael'	E2346	02.05.07
EI-RJN	British Aerospace Avro 146-RJ85 N526XJ, G-6-351 CityJet DAC Dublin 'Lake Isle of Inisfree' Operated by Aer Lingus	E2351	11.01.07
EI-RJO	British Aerospace Avro 146-RJ85 N527XJ, G-6-352 CityJet DAC Dublin 'Inis Mor'	E2352	11.01.07
EI-RJR	British Aerospace Avro 146-RJ85 N530XJ, G-6-364 CityJet DAC Dublin 'Tory Island'	E2364	27.11.06
EI-RJT	British Aerospace Avro 146-RJ85 N532XJ, G-6-366 CityJet DAC Dublin 'Inishbofin'	E2366	16.04.07
EI-RJU	British Aerospace Avro 146-RJ85 N533XJ, G-6-367 CityJet DAC Dublin 'Cape Clear'	E2367	24.05.07
EI-RJW	British Aerospace Avro 146-RJ85 N535XJ, G-6-371 CityJet DAC Dublin 'Garinish Island'	E2371	13.07.07
EI-RJX	British Aerospace Avro 146-RJ85 N536XJ, G-6-372 CityJet DAC Dublin 'Scattery Island' Leinster Rugby c/s	E2372	20.09.07
EI-RJY	British Aerospace Avro 146-RJ85 N502XJ, G-6-307 CityJet DAC Dublin 'Inishcealtra'	E2307	14.11.08
EI-RJZ	British Aerospace Avro 146-RJ85 N512XJ, G-6-326 CityJet DAC Dublin 'Inis Meain'	E2326	15.05.08
EI-RNA	Embraer ERJ-190-100STD PT-TOQ Aircraft Purchase Company Ltd Rome-Fiumicino 'Parco Nazionale del Vesuvio' Operated by Alitalia Cityliner	19000470	23.09.11
EI-RNB	Embraer ERJ-190-100STD PT-TPC Aircraft Purchase Company Ltd Rome-Fiumicino 'Parco Nazionale del Pollino' Operated by Alitalia Cityliner)	19000479	05.10.11
EI-RNC	Embraer ERJ-190-100STD PT-TRL NAC Aviation 19 Ltd Rome-Fiumicino 'Parco Nazionale Arcipelago Toscano' Operated by Alitalia Cityliner	19000503	15.12.11
EI-RND	Embraer ERJ-190-100STD PT-TPC NAC Aviation 19 Ltd Rome-Fiumicino 'Parco Nazionale Dolomiti Bellunesi' Operated by Alitalia Cityliner in SkyTeam c/s	19000512	12.03.12
EI-RNE	Embraer ERJ-190-100STD PT-TUH NAC Aviation 19 Ltd Rome-Fiumicino 'Parco Nazionale Della Sila' Operated by Alitalia Cityliner	19000520	23.04.12
EI-ROK	Roko Aero NG 4UL OK-NUR 40 K Harley Newcastle	004/2008	24.09.09
EI-RUJ	Boeing 737-81Q N982CQ, VT-SIJ, N8253J, N1786B Vardy Ltd Cotswold Broken up	29049	06.06.13

EI-RUK	Boeing 737-86N	28621	31.10.13

VT-SPE, EI-DIT, EC-HMJ
Magnetic Parts Trading Ltd   Teruel
Stored – for sale

EI-SAC	Cessna 172P Skyhawk	17276263	22.09.00

N98149   Sligo Aeronautical Club Ltd   Sligo

EI-SEA	Progressive Aerodyne SeaRey Amphibian	1DK359C	19.04.06

J Brennan   Sligo
Built by J Brennan

EI-SEV	Boeing 737-73S	29078	05.06.15

N278KA, HK-4627, OY-MLW, PR-SAE, EI-CRP, N1014S,
N60436, N1787B   Ryanair DAC   Dublin

EI-SIA	Airbus A320-251N	7897	30.11.17

D-AVVQ   Scandinavian Airlines Ireland Ltd   Dublin
'Iilv Viking'

EI-SIB	Airbus A320-251N	7951	12.12.17

D-AUBU   Scandinavian Airlines Ireland Ltd   Dublin
'Ellisiv Viking'

EI-SIC	Airbus A320-251N	7979	21.12.17

D-AUBJ   Scandinavian Airlines Ireland Ltd   Dublin
'Sigurd Viking'

EI-SID	Airbus A320-251N	8031	17.01.18

D-AXAQ   Scandinavian Airlines Ireland Ltd   Dublin
'Dotter Viking'

EI-SIE	Airbus A320-251N	8058	01.02.18

D-AVVG   Scandinavian Airlines Ireland Ltd   Dublin
'Gorm Viking'

EI-SIF	Airbus A320-251N	8109	12.04.18

D-AUBG   Scandinavian Airlines Ireland Ltd   Dublin
'Turgesius Viking'

EI-SIG	Airbus A320-251N	8333	26.07.18

D-AUBC   Scandinavian Airlines Ireland Ltd   Dublin
'Amlaib Viking'

EI-SIH	Airbus A320-251N	8551	27.11.18

D-AVVT   Scandinavian Airlines Ireland Ltd   Dublin
'Imar Viking'

EI-SII	Airbus A320-251N	8566	10.12.18

D-AUAD   Scandinavian Airlines Ireland Ltd   Dublin

EI-SKP	Reims/Cessna F172P Skyhawk II	F17202101	05.10.18

G-PTCA, EI-SKP, PH-VSZ, D-EOFR
National Flight Centre Ltd   Dublin Weston

EI-SKS	Robin R.2160	307	13.07.04

OO-OBC   Shemburn Ltd   Warrenstown

EI-SKV	Robin R.2160D	171	28.03.03

PH-BLO   Shemburn Ltd   (Glenmore, Co Kilkenny)
Stored fuselage

EI-SKW	Piper PA-28-161 Warrior II	28-8216115	18.02.04

D-EIBV, N9630N   Shemburn Ltd   Popham
Dismantled 05.17

EI-SLF	Aérospatiale-Alenia ATR 72-201F	210	26.11.02

OY-RUA, B-22703, F-WWEH
ASL Airlines (Ireland) Ltd   Dublin

EI-SLJ	Aérospatiale-Alenia ATR 72-201F	324	14.08.09

LY-PTK, HL5233, ES-KRF, OH-KRF, F-WWEU
ASL Airlines (Ireland) Ltd   Sonderborg
Stored

EI-SLM	Aérospatiale-Alenia ATR 72-212	413	04.02.10

N643AS F-WWLC
Cancelled 12.03.12 as removed from service
Bolton Street, Dublin
Dublin Institute of Technology 11.13

EI-SLP	Aérospatiale-Alenia ATR 72-212	461	07.10.15

EC-LKK, F-GVZF, F-OGXF, F-WWLP
ASL Airlines (Ireland) Ltd   Dublin

EI-SLS	Aérospatiale-Alenia ATR 72-201F	198	02.09.16

HB-AFS, P2-PXZ, HB-AFS, F-WKVJ, EC-IKK, F-WQND,
F-WQOG, (SX-BSX), F-WQJU, EC-GQU, F-WQGC,
B-22702, F-WWEL
ASL Airlines (Ireland) Ltd   Dublin

EI-SLT	Aérospatiale-Alenia ATR 72-201F	389	19.01.16

HB-AFN, B-22716, F-WWEH
ASL Airlines (Ireland) Ltd   Dublin

EI-SLU	Aérospatiale-Alenia ATR 72-202F	364	20.06.17

HB-AFM, B-22712, F-WWEA
ASL Airlines (Ireland) Ltd   Dublin

EI-SLV	Aérospatiale-Alenia ATR 72-202F	154	13.07.17

HB-AFJ, OY-RTE, F-WQNF, EC-ESS, EC-383, F-WWEK
ASL Airlines (Ireland) Ltd   Dublin

EI-SLW	Aérospatiale-Alenia ATR 72-202F	232	04.08.17

HB-AFK, F-GKOB   ASL Airlines (Ireland) Ltd   Dublin

EI-SLX	Aérospatiale-Alenia ATR 72-202F	222	28.07.17

HB-AFL, F-GKPF   ASL Airlines (Ireland) Ltd   Dublin

EI-SLY	Aérospatiale-Alenia ATR 72-202F	341	12.09.17

HB-AFV, (VT-), HB-AFV, F-WKVJ, VN-B204, F-OKVM
ASL Airlines (Ireland) Ltd   Dublin

EI-SLZ	Aérospatiale-Alenia ATR 72-202F	419	16.10.17

HB-AFW, VN-B206, (SX-), F-WWLW
ACL Airlines (Ireland) Ltd   Dublin

EI-SMK	Zenair CH.701	7-3551	15.10.03

S King   Limetree
Built by S King as project PFA 187-13149

EI-SOA	Aérospatiale-Alenia ATR 72-202F	265	14.11.17

HB-AFX, SP-LFB, F-WWEJ
ASL Airlines (Ireland) Ltd   Dublin

EI-SOO	Aérospatiale-Alenia ATR 72-212A	577	02.11.16

HB-ACE, 4X-AVZ, F-WWEN
ASL Airlines (Ireland) Ltd   Dublin

EI-SOP	Aérospatiale-Alenia ATR 72-212A	583	12.10.15

4X-AVW, F-WWER   ASL Airlines (Ireland) Ltd   Dublin

EI-STA	Boeing 737-31S	29057	23.03.10

G-THOG, D-ADBM   ASL Airlines (Ireland) Ltd   Dublin

EI-STJ	Boeing 737-490(SF)	28885	11.10.17

N788AS   ASL Airlines (Ireland) Ltd   Dublin

EI-STK	Boeing 737-448(SF)	25052	17.08.17

OY-JTI, N448KA, N161LF, UR-VVL, EI-BXI
ASL Airlines (Ireland) Ltd   Dublin

EI-STL	Boeing 737-42C(SF)	24231	12.05.17

OY-JTL, N455KA, N301SC, VP-BTH, N60669, PH-BPD,
G-UKLC   ASL Airlines (Ireland) Ltd   Dublin

EI-STM	Boeing 737-4Z9(SF)	27094	03.03.17

OY-JTM, N837AC, UR-GAP, OE-LNI
ASL Airlines (Ireland) Ltd   Dublin

EI-STN	Boeing 737-4Q8(SF)	25106	06.04.17

OY-JTN, N773AS   ASL Airlines (Ireland) Ltd   Dublin

EI-STO	Boeing 737-43Q(SF)	28490	01.11.17

VT-SVA, T7-VXB, N237SC, VN-A189, PK-GWY, N490GE,
TC-IAF, B-18672   ASL Airlines (Ireland) Ltd   Dublin

EI-STP	Boeing 737-4Q8(SF)	26299	15.03.18

N134WF, EI-GAO, SP-ENB, HL7527, TC-JEK
ASL Airlines (Ireland) Ltd   Dublin

EI-SYM	Van's RV-7	72940	05.04.11

E Symes   Newcastle
Built by E Symes

EI-TAT	Bombardier CL-600-2B16 Challenger	5940	06.11.13

C-GVFI   Bandon Aircraft Leasing Ltd
Moscow-Domodedovo
Operated by AK Bars Aero

EI-TIM	Piper J-5A Cub Cruiser	5-36	01.02.08

N27151, NC27151   N Murphy & Partners   (Trim)

EI-TKI	Robinson R22 Beta	1195	22.08.91

G-OBIP   J McDaid   (Londonderry, Co Londonderry)
Henry Hugh scrapyard, Heather Road 03.16

EI-TON	Raj Hamsa X'Air 582(5)	718	09.02.06

G-CCCZ   T Merrigan   Birr
Built by M B Cooke as project BMAA/HB/200

EI-TVG	Boeing 737-7ZF BBJ	60406	30.06.16

LY-TVG   Hansel Jet Ireland Ltd   Vilnius

EI-UFO	Piper PA-22-150 Tri-Pacer	22-4942	12.02.94

G-BRZR, N7045D   W Treacy   (Trim)
Tail-wheel conversion; awaiting rebuild

EI-ULN	Boeing 737-73V	32426	30.01.19

HL8022, VT-JLG, (JY-JAT), G-EZKE
SASOF II (G) Aviation Ireland Ltd   Ulan Bator
Stored – due for delivery to Eznis Airways

EI-UNL	Boeing 777-312	28515	04.11.11
	9V-SYA Stecker Ltd Moscow-Vnukovo 'Sochi'		
	Operated by Rossiya Airlines		
EI-UNM	Boeing 777-312	28534	18.01.12
	9V-SYD VEBL-767-300 Ltd Moscow-Vnukovo		
	'Novosikirsk'		
	Operated by Rossiya Airlines		
EI-UNN	Boeing 777-312	28517	12.12.11
	9V-SYC Stecker Ltd Moscow-Vnukovo 'Moscow'		
	Operated by Rossiya Airlines		
EI-UNP	Boeing 777-312	28516	23.03.12
	9V-SYB VEBL-767-300 Ltd Moscow-Vnukovo		
	'Magadan'		
	Operated by Rossiya Airlines		
EI-UNR	Boeing 777-212ER	28523	11.10.10
	9V-SRE VEBL-767-300 Ltd Moscow-Domodedovo		
	Stored – for sale		
EI-VII	Van's RV-7	73112	13.02.09
	B Sheane Dublin Weston		
EI-VLN	Piper PA-18A-150 Super Cub	18-6797	17.10.07
	G-ASCU, VP-JBL D O'Mahoney Ballyboy		
EI-WAC	Piper PA-23-250 Aztec E	27-4683	26.05.95
	G-AZBK, N14077 Westair Aviation Ltd Shannon		
EI-WAT	Tecnam P.2002-JF Sierra	086	02.09.08
	Waterford Aero Club Ltd Waterford		
	Landing accident at Cork Airport 23.06.18		
EI-WFD	Tecnam P.2002-JF Sierra	080	15.05.08
	Waterford Aero Club Ltd Waterford		
EI-WFI	Bombardier CL-600-2B16 Challenger	5812	31.05.10
	C-FYUS Midwest Atlantic Ltd Shannon		
	'Wind Force One'		
	Operated by Westair Aviation		
EI-WIG	Best Off Skyranger 912(2)	SKR0504608	29.06.07
	K Lannery Limetree		
	Built by M Brereton		
EI-WLA	Boeing 777-3Q8ER	35783	23.06.17
	F-ONOU, N5573S AerCap Ireland Ltd		
	Rome-Fiumicino 'Roma'		
	Operated by Alitalia		
EI-WMN	Piper PA-23-250 Aztec F	27-7954063	12.10.00
	G-ZSFT, G-SALT, G-BGTH, N2551M, N9731N, N9559N		
	Westair Aviation Ltd Shannon		
EI-WOT	Currie Wot	xxxx	22.03.12
	G-CWOT D Doyle & Partners Limetree 'Jonah'		
	Built by D A Lord project PFA3019		
EI-WWI	Robinson R44 Raven II	11799	17.07.07
	Ourville Ltd (Baltinglass, Co Wicklow)		
EI-WXA	British Aerospace Avro 146-RJ85	E2310	30.09.09
	N503XJ, G-6-310 CityJet DAC Norwich 'Inis Oirr'		
	Stored		
EI-WXP	Raytheon Hawker 800XP	258382	09.11.07
	SE-DYE, N23451 Westair Aviation Ltd Shannon		
EI-XLC	Boeing 747-446	27100	11.05.11
	N919UN, JA8919 SB Leasing Ireland Ltd		
	Moscow-Vnukovo 'Krasnoyarsk'		
	Operated by Rossiya Airlines		
EI-XLD	Boeing 747-446	26360	03.05.11
	N914UN, JA8914 VEBL-767-300 Ltd		
	Moscow-Vnukovo 'Yuzhno Sakhalinsk'		
	Operated by Rossiya Airlines in 'Caring for Tigers together'		
	nose c/s		
EI-XLE	Boeing 747-446	26362	27.04.12
	N916UN, JA8916 SB Leasing Ireland Ltd		
	Moscow-Vnukovo 'Saint Petersburg'		
	Operated by Rossiya Airlines		
EI-XLF	Boeing 747-446	27645	29.07.11
	N921MM, JA8921, N747BA SB Leasing Ireland Ltd		
	Moscow-Vnukovo 'Nizhny Novgorod'		
	Operated by Rossiya Airlines		
EI-XLG	Boeing 747-446	29899	29.09.11
	N917UN, JA8917, N6009F SB Leasing Ireland Ltd		
	Moscow-Vnukovo 'Irkutsk'		
	Operated by Rossiya Airlines		

EI-XLH	Boeing 747-446	27650	04.11.11
	N918UN, JA8918 Pembroke Exchanges Ltd		
	Moscow-Vnukovo 'Kazan'		
	Operated by Rossiya Airlines		
EI-XLI	Boeing 747-446	27648	16.12.11
	N920UN, JA8920, N6005C Pembroke Exchanges Ltd		
	Moscow-Vnukovo 'Petrapavlovsk-Kamchatsky'		
	Operated by Rossiya Airlines		
EI-XLJ	Boeing 747-446	27646	11.05.12
	N922UN, JA8922 Richdale Investments Ltd		
	Moscow-Vnukovo 'Vladivostock'		
	Operated by Rossiya Airlines		
EI-XLK	Boeing 747-412	29950	19.07.11
	N747NB, 9V-SPM VEBL 767-300 Ltd Melbourne		
	Stored – for sale		
EI-XLL	Boeing 747-412	28031	24.08.11
	N747NP, 9V-SPN VEBL 767-300 Ltd Teruel		
	Stored – for sale		
EI-XLM	Boeing 747-412	28028	04.11.11
	N747WV, 9V-SPO Richdale Investments Ltd		
	Moscow-Vnukovo 'Khabarovsk'		
	Operated by Rossiya Airlines		
EI-XLN	Boeing 747-412	28029	27.06.12
	N747JV, 9V-SPP VEBL-767-300 Ltd Teruel		
	Stored – for sale		
EI-XLO	Boeing 747-412	28025	20.12.12
	N747KD, 9V-SPQ VEBL-767-300 Ltd Teruel		
	Stored – for sale		
EI-XLP	Boeing 777-312	28531	12.11.12
	9V-SYE VEBL-767-300 Ltd Moscow-Vnukovo		
	'Ekaterinburg'		
	Operated by Rossiya Airlines		
EI-YLG	Robin HR.200/120B	336	28.11.05
	G-BYLG The Leinster Aero Club Ltd Dublin Weston		
EI-ZEU	Cessna 525A CitationJet 2	525A-0202	25.10.17
	G-ZEUZ, SE-RKS, G-MROO, G-EEBJ		
	Airlink Airways Ltd Shannon		
EI-ZZZ	Bell 222	47061	28.04.08
	(EI-MED), N40EA, SE-HTN, G-DMAF, G-BLSZ, D-HCHS,		
	(D-HAAD) Dublin Pool & Juke Box Co Ltd		
	Celtic Heliport, Knocksedan		
EJ-ADMI	Gulfstream Aerospace Gulfstream G650ER 6171		10.12.18
	N2437, N671GA Gain Jet Ireland Ltd Shannon		
EJ-IOBN	Embraer ERJ-190-100ECJ	19000632	12.10.18
	N730MM, PR-LCW Gain Jet Ireland Ltd Shannon		
EJ-SAID	Bombardier BD-700-1A11 Global 5000 9486		xx.xx.19
	T7-STK, M-SAID, C-GMXH		
	Gain Jet Ireland Ltd Shannon		

REGISTRATIONS AWAITED 2019

EI-	AutoGyro Calidus	xxxx	17.05.16
	G-CGJD		
	Officially transferred from UK to Republic of Ireland		
	Assembled Rotorsport UK as c/n RSUK/CALS/004		
EI-	ICP MXP-740 Savannah VG Jabiru(1) 03-12-51-261		20.05.16
	G-CCSV		
	Officially transferred from UK to Republic of Ireland		
	Built by R D Wood as project BMAA/HB/362		
EI-	Montgomerie-Bensen B.8M	xxxx	27.07.16
	G-BSMG		
	Officially transferred from UK to Republic of Ireland		
	Built by A C Timperley as project PFA G/01-1170		
EI-	Ellipse Fuji/Pulma 2000	75015/UK001	20.01.17
	G-CGME		
	Officially transferred from UK to Republic of Ireland		
EI-	Flylight MotorFloater Fox 16T	MF006	20.01.17
	G-CGZL		
	Officially transferred from UK to Republic of Ireland		
EI-	Cyclone AX2000	7451	20.01.17
	G-MZMX		
	Officially transferred from UK to Republic of Ireland		

EI-	Zenair CH.701UL G-BZJP Officially transferred from UK to Republic of Ireland *Built by D Jerwood as project PFA 187-13579*	7-9115	18.05.17
EI-	Zenair CH.701UL G-CBMW Officially transferred from UK to Republic of Ireland *Built by C Long as project PFA 187-13788*	7-9259	23.06.17
EI-	Noble Hardman Snowbird Mk.IV G-MTXL Officially transferred from UK to Republic of Ireland	SB-006	05.09.17
EI-	Medway EclipseR G-CCZR Officially transferred from UK to Republic of Ireland	177/155	30.04.18
EI-	Zenair CH.701 STOL G-CCJB Officially transferred from UK to Republic of Ireland *Built by E G Brown as project PFA 187-13270*	7-3659	16.05.18
EI-	Air Création 582(1)/Kiss 400 G-CBRZ Officially transferred from UK to Republic of Ireland *Built by B Chantry as project BMAA/HB/226* *(Flylight kit FL015 wing s/n A02086-2080)*	T02052	11.02.19

EI-	Cessna 172S Skyhawk SP G-THYA, N610JA Officially transferred from UK to Republic of Ireland	172S10480	13.02.19
EI-	CASA 1-131E Jungmann Series 2000 G-BVPD, F-AZNG, Spanish AF E3B-482 Officially transferred from UK to Republic of Ireland	2086	19.02.19
EI-	Schleicher ASW 19B G-DEPE, BGA 2836-EPE, RAFGSA R18 Officially transferred from UK to Republic of Ireland	19335	25.02.19
EI-	Mainair Gemini Flash II G-MNYK Officially transferred from UK to Republic of Ireland	494-1086-4-W296	25.02.19
EI-	Thruster T600N 450 Sprint G-OASJ Officially transferred from UK to Republic of Ireland	0037-T600N-090	25.02.19

IRISH GLIDING AND SOARING ASSOCIATION REGISTER

The system was similar to the British Gliding Association and until 2007 the register was maintained by the Irish Gliding & Soaring Association. Originally this was kept by the Irish Aviation Club using the prefix 'IAC'. From 1960 until 1967 gliders were allocated with a number prefixed 'IGA'. The IGSA listing is updated from Air-Britain sources. In March 2007 responsibility for glider registration was taken over by the Irish Aviation Authority, and all active gliders were re-registered in the sequence from EI-GLA. Remaining aircraft are shown below.

No. / Code	Type	Constructor's No	Previous Identity	Date	Owner (Operator)	(Unconfirmed) Base
EI-100	SZD-12A Mucha 100A	494	OY-XAN	.95	J Finnan & M O'Reilly *Preserved at Cavan & Leitrim Railway 5.17*	Dromod
EI-102	Slingsby T.26 Kite 2	?	IGA 102 IAC 102	.54	Irish Air Corps Museum *Under restoration 6.17; reserved as EI-GMG*	Baldonnel
EI-118	EoN AP.8 Baby	EoN/B/001	BGA 608 RAFGSA 217, BGA 608, G-ALLU, BGA 608	73	D O'Reilly *Reserved as EI-GMK; under restoration 11.09* Perth, Western Australia	
EI-120	LET L-13 Blanik	175205	RAFGSA BGA 1730	.75	(Syndicate) *Stored 4.06; reserved as EI-GMM*	Gowran Grange
EI-123	Bölkow Phoebus C	840	D-0057	.78	Not known *Wreck stored 11.13*	Gowran Grange
EI-124 / 124	Grob G102 Astir CS 77 (Astir Standard)	1761		.80	Dublin Gliding Club *Stored 4.15*	Gowran Grange
EI-130	Scheibe L-Spatz	200	BGA 2199 D-4707	?	J J Sullivan *'White Cloud'; Reserved as EI-GMI*	Gowran Grange
EI-133 / 33	Schleicher K 8B	8557	D-8517 D-9367	.91	Dublin Gliding Club *Stored 5.10; reserved as EI-GLE*	Gowran Grange
EI-134 / 34	Schleicher ASW 15B	15249	D-1087	.91	J & C O'Brien *Reserved as EI-GLX*	Gowran Grange
EI-135	Slingsby T.38 Grasshopper *Wings from WZ756 or WZ768*	758	WZ762	.91	Irish Air Corps Museum *Wings from WZ756 or WZ768; stored as 'WZ762' 6.17*	Baldonnel
EI-139	Slingsby T.31B	902	BGA 3485 G-BOKG, XE789	.93	P Bedford *Preserved at Cavan & Leitrim Railway 6.18;* *reserved as EI-GMH*	Dromod
EI-140	SZD-12A Mucha 100A	491	HB-647	.93	D Mongey *Reserved as EI-GMJ*	Gowran Grange
EI-144	Scheibe SF 27A Zugvogel V	6049	(EI-142)	.94	R Staeps *Reserved as EI-GLY*	Gowran Grange
EI-157	Slingsby T.21B	1158	BGA 1465 RAFGSA 333, XN154	.02	C Sinclair *EI-GLZ not taken up; under restoration 2018*	Bellarena

AIRCRAFT TYPE INDEX (IRELAND)

Note: This Index covers only entries in that are currently on the Irish Civil Register.

AEROMERE
F.8L FALCO
  EI-BCJ

AERONCA AIRCRAFT CORPORATION –
see also **BELLANCA** and **CHAMPION**
65-TAC DEFENDER
  EI-AEI

7AC CHAMPION
  EI-BJC EI-DDD

7DC CHAMPION
  EI-BJB

11AC CHIEF
  EI-CCF EI-CRR

15AC SEDAN
  EI-BKC

AEROPRAKT
A-22
  EI-EHF

AEROPRO
EUROFOX
  EI-EWX EI-FMA EI-FNO

AÉROSPATIALE – ALENIA including
AVIONS TRANS REGIONAL
ATR.42 variants
  EI-CBK EI-EHH EI-FXA EI-FXB EI-FXC
  EI-FXD EI-FXE EI-GEV

ATR.72 variants
  EI-FAS EI-FAT EI-FAU EI-FAV EI-FAW EI-FAX
  EI-FCY EI-FCZ EI-FMJ EI-FMK EI-FNA
  EI-FSK EI-FSL EI-FSN EI-FSO EI-FXG EI-FXH
  EI-FXI EI-FXJ EI-FXK EI-GIW EI-GIX EI-REH
  EI-REI EI-REJ EI-REL EI-SLF EI-SLJ EI-SLP
  EI-SLS EI-SLT EI-SLU EI-SLV EI-SLW EI-SLX
  EI-SLY EI-SLZ EI-SOA EI-SOO EI-SOP

AGUSTA – see **LEONARDO HELICOPTERS**

AIR CRÉATION
KISS 400
  EI-DBO EI-DFX EI-DKE EI-DKU EI-ERI

IXESS (TANARG) 912
  EI-DRT EI-EHL

AIR & SPACE MANUFACTURING
18A Gyroplane
  EI-CNG

AIRBORNE WINDSPORTS
EDGE XT
  EI-EAK

AIRBUS SAS including **AIRBUS INDUSTRIE**
A300 variants
  EI-DGU EI-EXR EI-OZL EI-OZM

A319 variants
  EI-EPT EI-EYL EI-EYM EI-EZC EI-EZD
  EI-FVG EI-GFN EI-GFO EI-IMB EI-IMC
  EI-IMD EI-IME EI-IMF EI-IMG EI-IMH EI-IMI
  EI-IMJ EI-IML EI-IMM EI-IMN EI-IMO EI-IMP
  EI-IMR EI-IMS EI-IMT EI-IMU EI-IMV EI-IMW
  EI-IMX

A320 variants
  EI-CVA EI-CVB EI-CVC EI-DEA EI-DEB
  EI-DEC EI-DEE EI-DEF EI-DEG EI-DEH
  EI-DEI EI-DEJ EI-DEK EI-DEL EI-DEM
  EI-DEN EI-DEO EI-DEP EI-DER EI-DES

  EI-DFO EI-DSA EI-DSG EI-DSL EI-DSU
  EI-DSV EI-DSW EI-DSX EI-DSY EI-DSZ
  EI-DTA EI-DTB EI-DTD EI-DTE EI-DTF
  EI-DTG EI-DTH EI-DTI EI-DTJ EI-DTK EI-DTL
  EI-DTM EI-DTN EI-DTO EI-DVE EI-DVG
  EI-DVH EI-DVI EI-DVJ EI-DVK EI-DVL
  EI-DVM EI-DVN EI-EDP EI-EDS EI-EIA EI-EIB
  EI-EIC EI-EID EI-EIE EI-ERH EI-EUA EI-EYS
  EI-FBO EI-FNJ EI-GAL EI-GAM EI-GCC
  EI-GHE EI-GHF EI-GIB EI-GII EI-GKM EI-IKB
  EI-IKF EI-IKG EI-IKL EI-IKU EI-LIX EI-SIA
  EI-SIB EI-SIC EI-SID EI-SIE EI-SIF EI-SIG
  EI-SIH EI-SII

A321 variants
  EI-CPE EI-CPG EI-CPH EI-FSB EI-GIN EI-ITA
  EI-IXC EI-IXH EI-IXJ EI-IXV EI-IXZ EI-LIA

A330 variants
  EI-DAA EI-DDU EI-DIP EI-DIR EI-DUO
  EI-DUZ EI-EAV EI-EDY EI-EJG EI-EJH EI-EJI
  EI-EJJ EI-EJK EI-EJL EI-EJM EI-EJN EI-EJO
  EI-EJP EI-ELA EI-EWG EI-EWH EI-EWR
  EI-FBU EI-FNG EI-FNH EI-FNK EI-FNX
  EI-FSE EI-FSF EI-GAJ EI-GCF EI-GCU
  EI-GCZ EI-GEW EI-GEY EI-GFX EI-GGN
  EI-GGO EI-GGP EI-GGR EI-HEA EI-HEB
  EI-HED

AIRBUS HELICOPTERS including
AÉROSPATIALE, EUROCOPTER & EUROCOPTER DEUTSCHLAND
production
AS355N ECUREUIL 2
  EI-LOW

AS365N DAUPHIN 2
  EI-GJL

EC120 variants
  EI-FAB EI-MIK

EC135 variants
  EI-KEL ZJ-HLH

ALEXANDER SCHLEICHER
SEGELFLUGZEUGBAU GmbH – see under **SCHLEICHER**

ALPI AVIATION SRL
PIONEER 300
  EI-DUL

AMERICAN CHAMPION AIRCRAFT CORPORATION
BELLANCA 8KCAB SUPER DECATHLON
  EI-BIV

AMF MICROFLIGHT LTD
CHEVVRON
  EI-BVJ EI-CAU

ATEC v.o.s.
122 ZEPHYR 2000
  EI-CZA EI-DGV EI-GCT

AUSTER AIRCRAFT LTD including
TAYLORCRAFT AEROPLANES (ENGLAND) LTD
V J/1 AUTOCRAT
  EI-AEE EI-AGJ EI-AMK EI-AUM

AVIATIKA JOINT STOCK COMPANY
MAI-890
  EI-FEP EI-FEU

AVIONS PIERRE ROBIN including
ALPHA AVIATION MANUFACTURING LTD (R2160), APEX AIRCRAFT, CONSTRUCTIONS AÉRONAUTIQUES DE BOURGOGNE and **ROBIN AVIATION**
production – see under **ROBIN**

AVIONS TRANS REGIONAL – see
AÉROSPATIALE–ALENIA

AVTECH PTY LTD – see **JABIRU AIRCRAFT COMPANY PTY LTD**

A V ROE and CO LTD including **BAe** and
HAWKER SIDDELEY AVIATION design and production
643 CADET
  EI-ALP

BAE SYSTEMS (OPERATIONS) LTD
including **BRITISH AEROSPACE plc, BRITISH AEROSPACE (REGIONAL AIRCRAFT) Ltd, HANDLEY-PAGE** and **SCOTTISH AVIATION** production
146 including Avro variants
  EI-RJD EI-RJF EI-RJI EI-RJN EI-RJO EI-RJR
  EI-RJT EI-RJU EI-RJW EI-RJX EI-RJY EI-RJZ
  EI-WXA

BARNETT ROTORCRAFT COMPANY
JB4-2
  EI-DVO

BEAGLE AIRCRAFT LTD
B.121 PUP
  EI-ATJ

BEECH AIRCRAFT CORPORATION
including **HAWKER BEECHCRAFT CORPORATION & RAYTHEON AIRCRAFT COMPANY** production – see also **HAWKER**
55 and 58 BARON models
  EI-DUV

76 DUCHESS
  EI-BUN EI-EWC

BELL HELICOPTER TEXTRON CANADA INC including **AGUSTA BELL HELICOPTER** production
206A and 206B JETRANGER variants
  EI-CUS EI-ODD EI-PCI EI-PMI

222
  EI-DZN EI-ZZZ

505 JETRANGER X
  EI-GHW

BELLANCA AIRCRAFT CORPORATION –
see also **AERONCA** and **CHAMPION**
7GCAA
  EI-FMF

BENSEN AIRCRAFT CORPORATION
B.8 GYROPLANE
  EI-BCF EI-BSG EI-CVW EI-DDR

BEST OFF
SKY RANGER
  EI-DMB EI-ERL EI-FGU EI-FXV EI-FXW
  EI-GCP EI-GEN EI-WIG

BOEING AIRCRAFT CO including BOEING COMPANY

717-200 series
EI-EWI EI-EWJ EI-EXA EI-EXB EI-EXI EI-EXJ
EI-FBJ EI-FBL EI-FBM EI-FCB EI-FCU
EI-FGH EI-FGI

737-300 series
EI-CXN EI-CXR EI-ERP EI-FGX EI-STA

737-400 series
EI-CXK EI-DDY EI-DNM EI-GHA EI-GHB
EI-HAA EI-STJ EI-STK EI-STL EI-STM EI-STN
EI-STO EI-STP

737-700 series
EI-FFM EI-GCV EI-GFR EI-SEV EI-TVG
EI-ULN

737-800 series
EI-CSG EI-CSI EI-CXV EI-DAC EI-DAD
EI-DAE EI-DAF EI-DAG EI-DAH EI-DAI
EI-DAJ EI-DAK EI-DAL EI-DAM EI-DAN
EI-DAO EI-DAP EI-DAR EI-DAS EI-DCF
EI-DCG EI-DCH EI-DCI EI-DCJ EI-DCK
EI-DCL EI-DCM EI-DCN EI-DCO EI-DCP
EI-DCR EI-DCW EI-DCX EI-DCY EI-DCZ
EI-DHA EI-DHB EI-DHC EI-DHD EI-DHE
EI-DHF EI-DHG EI-DHH EI-DHN EI-DHO
EI-DHP EI-DHR EI-DHS EI-DHT EI-DHV
EI-DHW EI-DHX EI-DHY EI-DHZ EI-DLB
EI-DLC EI-DLD EI-DLE EI-DLF EI-DLG
EI-DLH EI-DLI EI-DLJ EI-DLK EI-DLN EI-DLO
EI-DLR EI-DLV EI-DLW EI-DLX EI-DLY
EI-DPB EI-DPC EI-DPD EI-DPF EI-DPG
EI-DPH EI-DPI EI-DPJ EI-DPK EI-DPL
EI-DPM EI-DPN EI-DPO EI-DPP EI-DPR
EI-DPT EI-DPV EI-DPW EI-DPX EI-DPY
EI-DPZ EI-DWA EI-DWB EI-DWC EI-DWD
EI-DWE EI-DWF EI-DWG EI-DWH EI-DWI
EI-DWJ EI-DWK EI-DWL EI-DWM EI-DWO
EI-DWP EI-DWR EI-DWS EI-DWT EI-DWV
EI-DWW EI-DWX EI-DWY EI-DWZ EI-DYA
EI-DYB EI-DYC EI-DYD EI-DYE EI-DYF
EI-DYL EI-DYM EI-DYN EI-DYO EI-DYP
EI-DYR EI-DYV EI-DYW EI-DYX EI-DYY
EI-DYZ EI-EBA EI-EBC EI-EBD EI-EBE
EI-EBF EI-EBG EI-EBH EI-EBI EI-EBK EI-EBL
EI-EBM EI-EBN EI-EBO EI-EBP EI-EBR
EI-EBS EI-EBV EI-EBW EI-EBX EI-EBY
EI-EBZ EI-ECL EI-ECM EI-EFC EI-EFD
EI-EFE EI-EFF EI-EFG EI-EFH EI-EFI EI-EFJ
EI-EFK EI-EFN EI-EFO EI-EFX EI-EFY EI-EFZ
EI-EGA EI-EGB EI-EGC EI-EGD EI-EKA
EI-EKB EI-EKC EI-EKD EI-EKE EI-EKF
EI-EKG EI-EKH EI-EKI EI-EKJ EI-EKK EI-EKL
EI-EKM EI-EKN EI-EKO EI-EKP EI-EKR
EI-EKS EI-EKT EI-EKV EI-EKW EI-EKX
EI-EKY EI-EKZ EI-EMA EI- EMB EI-EMC
EI-EMD EI-EME EI-EMF EI-EMH EI-EMI
EI-EMJ EI-EMK EI-EML EI-EMM EI-EMN
EI-EMO EI-EMP EI-EMR EI-ENA EI-ENB
EI-ENC EI-ENE EI-ENF EI-ENG EI-ENH
EI-ENI EI-ENJ EI-ENK EI-ENL EI-ENM
EI-ENN EI-ENO EI-ENP EI-ENR EI-ENS
EI-ENT EI-ENV EI-ENW EI-ENX EI-ENY
EI-EPA EI-EPB EI-EPC EI-EPD EI-EPE EI-EPF
EI-EPG EI-EPH EI-ESN EI-ESP EI-ESR
EI-ESS EI-EST EI-ESV EI-ESW EI-ESX
EI-ESY EI-ESZ EI-EVA EI-EVB EI-EVC EI-EVE
EI-EVF EI-EVG EI-EVH EI-EVI EI-EVJ EI-EVK
EI-EVL EI-EVM EI-EVN EI-EVO EI-EVP
EI-EVR EI-EVS EI-EVT EI-EVU EI-EVW EI-EVX
EI-EVY EI-EVZ EI-EXD EI-EXE EI-EXF EI-FCH
EI-FDS EI-FEG EI-FEH EI-FEI EI-FFW EI-FHA
EI-FHD EI-FHE EI-FHG EI-FHH EI-FHJ EI-FHK
EI-FHL EI-FHM EI-FHN EI-FHP EI-FHR
EI-FHS EI-FHT EI-FHU EI-FHV EI-FHW
EI-FHX EI-FHY EI- EI-FHZ EI-FIA EI-FIB
EI-FIC EI-FID EI-FIE EI-FIF EI-FIG EI-FIH
EI-FIJ EI-FIK EI-FIL EI-FIM EI-FIN EI-FIO
EI-FIP EI-FIR EI-FIS EI-FIT EI-FIV EI-FIW
EI-FIY EI-FIZ EI-FJA EI-FJB EI-FJD EI-FJE
EI-FJH EI-FJJ EI-FJK EI-FJL EI-FJM EI-FJN
EI-FJO EI-FJP EI-FJS EI-FJT EI-FJU EI-FJV
EI-FJW EI-FJX EI-FJY EI-FLM EI-FND

EI-FNU EI-FNW EI-FOA EI-FOB EI-FOC
EI-FOD EI-FOE EI-FOF EI-FOG EI-FOH
EI-FOI EI-FOJ EI-FOL EI-FOM EI-FON
EI-FOO EI-FOP EI-FOR EI-FOS EI-FOT
EI-FOV EI-FOW EI-FOY EI-FOZ EI-FRB
EI-FRC EI-FRD EI-FRE EI-FRF EI-FRG
EI-FRH EI-FRI EI-FRJ EI-FRK EI-FRL EI-FRM
EI-FRN EI-FRO EI-FRP EI-FRR EI- FRS
EI-FRT EI-FRV EI-FRW EI-FRX EI-FRY EI-FRZ
EI-FSJ EI-FTA EI-FTB EI-FTC EI-FTD EI-FTE
EI-FTF EI-FTG EI-FTH EI-FTJ EI-FTK EI-FTL
EI-FTM EI-FTN EI-FTO EI-FTP EI-FTR EI-FTS
EI-FTT EI-FTV EI-FTW EI-FTY EI-FTZ EI-FVH
EI-FVI EI-FVJ EI-FVK EI-FVL EI-FVM EI-FVN
EI-FVR EI-FVU EI-FVV EI-FVW EI-FVX EI-FVY
EI-FVZ EI-FZA EI-FZB EI-FZC EI-FZD EI-FZE
EI-FZF EI-FZG EI-FZH EI-FZI EI-FZJ EI-FZK
EI-FZL EI-FZM EI-FZN EI-FZO EI-FZP EI-FZR
EI-FZS EI-FZT EI-FZV EI-FZW EI-GAW
EI-GAX EI-GBB EI-GBF EI-GBG EI-GBI
EI-GDC EI-GDD EI-GDE EI-GDF EI-GDG
EI-GDH EI-GDI EI-GDK EI-GDM EI-GDN
EI-GDO EI-GDP EI-GDR EI-GDS EI-GDT
EI-GDV EI-GDW EI-GDX EI-GDY EI-GDZ
EI-GFP EI-GIM EI-GJA EI-GJB EI-GJC
EI-GJD EI-GJE EI-GJF EI-GJG EI-GJH EI-GJI
EI-GJJ EI-GJK EI-GJM EI-GJN EI-GJO
EI-GJP EI-GJS EI-GJT EI-GKX EI-GSG
EI-GSH EI-GSI EI-GSJ EI-GSK EI-GXG
EI-GXH EI-GXI EI-GXJ EI-GXK EI-GXL
EI-GXM EI-GXN EI-IRI EI-RUJ EI-RUK

737-900 series
EI-FMS

737-8 MAX
EI-FYA EI-FYB EI-FYC EI-FYD EI-FYE EI-FYF
EI-FYG EI-FYH EI-FYI EI-GFY EI-GGK
EI-GGL EI-HAT EI-HAV EI-HAW EI-MNG

747-400 series
EI-XLC EI-XLD EI-XLE EI-XLF EI-XLG EI-XLH
EI-XLI EI-XLJ EI-XLK EI-XLL EI-XLM EI-XLN
EI-XLO

757-200 series
EI-CJX EI-CJY EI-LBR EI-LBS EI-LBT

767-200 series
EI-CXZ

767-300 series
EI-DFS EI-FGN EI-GEP

777-200 series
EI-DBK EI-DBL EI-DBM EI-DDH EI-ISA
EI-ISB EI-ISD EI-ISE EI-UNR

777-300 series
EI-GES EI-GET EI-GEU EI-GFA EI-GFB
EI-UNL EI-UNM EI-UNN EI-UNP EI-WLA
EI-XLP

787-9
EI-NEO EI-NEU EI-NEW

BÖLKOW APPARATEBAU GmbH including MALMO and MBB production

PHOEBUS C
EI-GMD

BOMBARDIER INC

CL-600 CHALLENGER variants
EI-KWA EI-TAT EI-WFI

CANADAIR REGIONAL JET variants
EI-FPA EI-FPB EI-FPC EI-FPD EI-FPE EI-FPF
EI-FPG EI-FPH EI-FPI EI-FPJ EI-FPK EI-FPM
EI-FPN EI-FPO EI-FPP EI-FPR EI-FPS EI-FPT
EI-FPU EI-FPV EI-FPW EI-FPX EI-GEA
EI-GEB EI-GEC EI-GED EI-GEF EI-HBA

BD-700 GLOBAL variants
EI-ITN EJ-SAID

BRITTEN NORMAN LTD including PILATUS production

BN-2 ISLANDER variants
EI-AYN EI-BCE EI-CUW

BRM AERO

CITIUS
EI-FBX EI-FBY EI-FNC EI-GCG EI-GGE

LAND AFRICA
EI-DZS EI-ECG EI-EEH EI-EOH EI-ESC
EI-FBW EI-FGB EI-FLH EI-FLK EI-FMO

BRÜGGER

MB-2 COLIBRI
EI-EWZ

CAMERON BALLOONS LTD

65 variants
EI-BSN

69 variants
EI-EOB

77 variants
EI-CKJ

90 variants
EI-DGW EI-ECC EI-POP

105 variants
EI-FDD

CESSNA AIRCRAFT COMPANY including REIMS AVIATION SA production (F.prefix)

120
EI-AED EI-AEF

140
EI-AEM

150
EI-AII EI-AVM EI-BAT EI-CDV

A150 AEROBAT
EI-AUO

152
EI-BIB EI-BMN EI-CCM EI-DGX EI-EDB
EI-EMU

A152 AEROBAT
EI-BJM EI-EDC

172 SKYHAWK
EI-BCK EI-BPL EI-CFY EI-CLQ EI-COT
EI-CUJ EI-DDC EI-DDX EI-EAM EI-EAZ
EI-EYJ EI-FBC EI-GWY EI-ING EI-MCF
EI-MCG EI-NFW EI-OFM EI-OOR EI-SAC
EI-SKP EI-STT

172RG CUTLASS
EI-FII

R172K HAWK XP
EI-BJO EI-EZU

182 SKYLANE variants
EI-CAP EI-CDP EI-GSM

208 and 208B (GRAND) CARAVAN
EI-GHZ

210 CENTURION
EI-BUF EI-CAX EI-CGH

441 CONQUEST II
EI-DMG

525A CITATIONJET 2
EI-ZEU

750 CITATION X
EI-LEO

CFM METAL-FAX including CFM AIRCRAFT

STREAK SHADOW
EI-CHR EI-CZC EI-DXL EI-DXS

CHAMPION AIRCRAFT CORPORATION – see also AERONCA and BELLANCA

7ECA/7GCAA CITABRIA
EI-ANT EI-BYX

7EC TRAVELLER
EI-BHV

7FC TRI-TRAVELLER
  EI-BBE

COLT BALLOONS LTD
14A CLOUDHOPPER
  EI-DZB
21A CLOUDHOPPER
  EI-DZA

COMCO IKARUS GmbH
C.42
  EI-DXA EI-EDI EI-ELC EI-EOO EI-ERM
  EI-ETB EI-EWB EI-EWV EI-EYT EI-FDY
  EI-FGF EI-FGG EI-FLL EI-FLS EI-FLW EI-FNS
  EI-FST EI-GAH

CUBCRAFTERS INC
CC11-160
  EI-LSA

CURRIE
WOT
  EI-WOT

CYCLONE AIRSPORTS LTD
AX3/503
  EI-DXP

CZECH AIRCRAFT WORKS (CZAW)
SPORTCRUISER
  EI-EDJ EI-EMV EI-GCJ

DE HAVILLAND AIRCRAFT LTD
DH.82 TIGER MOTH
  EI-AHI EI-AWP
DH.84 DRAGON
  EI-ABI

DE HAVILLAND (CANADA) including BOMBARDIER INC and OGMA production
DHC-1 CHIPMUNK
  EI-AFZ EI-HFA EI-HFB EI-HFC

DENNEY AEROCRAFT COMPANY
KITFOX
  EI-FLO EI-MRB

DG FLUGZEUGBAU GmbH – see GLASER-DIRKS

DOMINATOR GYROPLANE
ULTRAWHITE
  EI-DZO EI-EZY EI-FLA

DRUINE
D.62B CONDOR
  EI-BCP EI-BDX

DUDEK
HADRON
  EI-PGA EI-PGB EI-PGI
NUCLEON
  EI-PGM
SYNTHESIS
  EI-PGH EI-PGL
UNIVERSAL
  EI-PGS

EIPPER AIRCRAFT INC
QUICKSILVER
  EI-BPP

ELA AVIACIÓN
ELA 07
  EI-DTT EI-EES EI-FEO EI-FSR

ELLIOTTS of NEWBURY
AP.5 OLYMPIA variants
  EI-GLP

EMBRAER
ERJ-170 variants
  EI-RDA EI-RDB EI-RDC EI-RDD EI-RDE
  EI-RDF EI-RDG EI-RDH EI-RDI EI-RDJ
  EI-RDK EI-RDL EI-RDM EI-RDN EI-RDO
ERJ-190 variants
  EI-FCT EI-FDJ EI-GAZ EI-GCA EI-GGA
  EI-GGB EI-GGC EI-GHJ EI-GHK EI-RNA
  EI-RNB EI-RNC EI-RND EI-RNE EJ-IOBN

ERCO including ALON and FORNEY production
ERCOUPE 415
  EI-CVL

EUROPA AVIATION
EUROPA
  EI-GHH

EVANS
VP-1
  EI-AYY EI-BRU
VP-2
  EI-BDL EI-BVT

EVEKTOR
EV-97 EUROSTAR variants
  EI-CXY EI-DFM EI-DKW EI-DRW EI-DUJ
  EI-EOU

FLIGHT DESIGN GmbH
CT2K
  EI-ERZ
CTSW
  EI-EOW

FLY MARKET
RELAX 25
  EI-PGO

GARDAN
GY80 Horizon
  EI-AYB

GLASER-DIRKS FLUGZEUGBAU GmbH
DG-200 and DG-202s
  EI-GLL
DG808
  EI-GMN

GLASFLUGEL
STANDARD LIBELLE 201
  EI-GMG

GROB-WERKE GMB & CO KG for GROB BURKHART GROB LUFT und RAUMFAHRT GmbH – see also SCHEMPP-HIRTH FLUGZEUGBAU
G115
  EI-CAC EI-CAD EI-CAE
G120TP-A
  EI-GPS

GRUMMAN AMERICAN AVIATION CORPORATION including AMERICAN-GENERAL AVIATION and GULFSTREAM AMERICAN CORPORATION production
GRUMMAN AA-5 TRAVELLER
  EI-FFV

GULFSTREAM AEROSPACE CORPORATION
GULSTREAM V-SP (GULFSTREAM 550)
  EI-EGO EI-LSY
GULFSTREAM VI (GULFSTREAM 650)
  EI-JSK EI-LSN EJ-ADMI

HAWKER SIDDELEY AVIATION including BRITISH AEROSPACE PLC, CORPORATE JETS LTD, DE HAVILLAND and RAYTHEON-HAWKER production
HAWKER 800XP/850XP
  EI-WXP

HUGHES TOOL CO and HUGHES HELICOPTERS INC including SCHWEIZER AIRCRAFT CORPORATION (269 wef 1986)
269
  EI-CZP

HUNT
PEGASUS XL
  EI-DBJ

ICP SRL
SAVANNAH
  EI-EPW EI-GEO EI-ICP

IIII (INZIATIVE INDUSTRIALI ITALIANE) SpA
SKY ARROW
  EI-CPX

ITV
BOXER
  EI-PGN EI-PGT

JABIRU AIRCRAFT COMPANY PTY LTD
JABIRU SP-430
  EI-EOF
JABIRU UL
  EI-FDO

JAVRON
PA-18
  EI-FNE

JODEL including CEA, SAN and WASSMER production – see also ROBIN
D9 BÉBÉ
  EI-BUC
D18
  EI-CKZ
D112
  EI-BSB EI-GFV
D120
  EI-CJS
DR1050
  EI-ARW EI-EPZ

JORA SPOL Sro
JORA
  EI-NVL

LAK including AB SPORTINE AVIAICIJA
LAK-17A
  EI-GLH

LEONARDO HELICOPTERS including AGUSTA SpA
A109 variants
  EI-IAL EI-MPC
AW119Ke
  EI-GHU

AW139
EI-GGS EI-LIM

AW169
EI-FMP EI-FNT EI-GGH EI-LID

LINDSTRAND BALLOONS LTD
LBL 90A
EI-CRB

LUSCOMBE AIRPLANE CORPORATION
8 SILVAIRE variants
EI-AEH EI-DJF

MAINAIR SPORTS LTD
BLADE
EI-DOW EI-DRH EI-ESD

GEMINI FLASH II
EI-EPJ

MERCURY
EI-CMU

AB MALMO FLYGINDUSTRI
MFI-9 JUNIOR
EI-AWR

MAULE AIRCRAFT CORPORATION
M(XT)-7 SUPER, STAR ROCKET and STARCRAFT models
EI-GER

MEDWAY MICROLIGHTS
ECLIPSE R
EI-ELL

HYBRED 44XLR
EI-EPI

MONNETT
SONERAI IIL
EI-BMU

MORANE-SAULNIER including GEMS, MORANE, SEEMS and SOCATA production
MS.880B RALLYE variants
EI-AYI EI-BJK EI-BNU EI-ETE

MS.892A RALLYE COMMODORE
EI-DMA

MS.893A RALLYE COMMODORE
EI-BUT

MS.893E RALLYE 180GT
EI-CEG

MS.894A RALLYE MINERVA 220
EI-AYT

OZONE POWER LTD
SPYDER 16
EI-PGK

PARAMANIA
FUSION 26
EI-PGP

REVOLUTION 2
EI-PGD

PEGASUS AVIATION including CYCLONE AIRSPORTS LTD
PEGASUS QUANTUM
EI-CNU EI-EPK EI-FSX

PEREIRA
OSPREY
EI-EEU

PHOENIX
LA-5 MAJOR
EI-CGF

PIEL AVIATION including ATELIERS AERONAUTIQUE ROSSEAU and SOCIÉTÉ SCINTEX production
CP.301 EMERAUDE
EI-CFG

CP.1310-C3 SUPER EMERAUDE
EI-DUH

PIPER AIRCRAFT CORPORATION including TAYLOR AIRCRAFT CO LTD and THE NEW PIPER AIRCRAFT INC production
J-3C CUB variants
EI-AET EI-AFE EI-AKM EI-BBV EI-BCM
EI-BCN EI-BEN EI-BIO EI-BSX EI-BYY
EI-CFO EI-COY EI-CPP

J-4E CUB COUPE
EI-GDJ

J-5A CUB CRUISER
EI-TIM

PA-12 SUPER CRUISER
EI-CFF EI-CFH EI-CMN

PA-16 CLIPPER
EI-AEL EI-EMT

PA-18 SUPER CUB variants
EI-ANY EI-BID EI-BIK EI-CIG EI-CKH EI-DTS
EI-ELM EI-VLN

PA-22-108 COLT
EI-AMI EI-BAV EI-EZX EI-FGW

PA-22-150 TRI-PACER
EI-GHI EI-UFO

PA-22-160 TRI-PACER
EI-EPP EI-ESF

PA-23-250 AZTEC variants
EI-WAC EI-WMN

PA-28-140 CHEROKEE (CRUISER)
EI-AOB EI-BSO EI-CGP

PA-28-161 (CHEROKEE) WARRIOR
EI-DJM EI-SKW

PA-28-180 CHEROKEE
EI-BDR EI-CIF

PA-28-181 (CHEROKEE) ARCHER
EI-EYI EI-KDH

PA-28R (CHEROKEE) ARROW variants
EI-EDR

PA-31 NAVAJO (& CHIEFTAIN) variants
EI-DIF

PA-34 SENECA variants
EI-BSL EI-CMT

PA-38 TOMAHAWK
EI-BVK

PIPISTREL DOO AJDOVSCINA
VIRUS
EI-FEJ EI-FSZ

SINUS
EI-DZF

PROGRESSIVE AERODYNE INC
SEAREY AMPHIBIAN
EI-SEA

PZL WARSZAWA-OKECIE SA
PZL-110 KOLIBER
EI-DOY EI-FDC

PZL-SWIDNIK
PW-5 SMYK
EI-GMI

QUAD CITY
CHALLENGER
EI-FDR

RAJ HAMSA
X'AIR variants
EI-CXC EI-DBI EI-DBV EI-DCA EI-DDJ
EI-DFY EI-DGG EI-DGH EI-DGJ EI-DGK
EI-DKK EI-DKT EI-DKY EI-DNR EI-DRL
EI-DRX EI-DXM EI-DXX EI-EAY EI-ECK
EI-ECP EI-ECZ EI-ELB EI-EOA EI-ETD
EI-ETV EI-FET EI-FEV EI-FFN EI-FLX EI-FVF
EI-KEV EI-TON

RAND-ROBINSON
KR-2
EI-BNL EI-BOV EI-EHM

RANS
S-6 COYOTE
EI-FAM EI-FSW EI-FTX

REALITY AIRCRAFT LTD
ESCAPADE
EI-DKZ

ROBIN
DR.400 and DR.500 variants
EI-CRG

HR.200/120B
EI-YLG

R.2160
EI-SKS EI-SKV

ROBINSON HELICOPTER CO INC
R22 variants
EI-DZK EI-EHG EI-GPT EI-GVM EI-TKI

R44 variants
EI-DVZ EI-DZM EI-JOR EI-LAD EI-MPW
EI-NJA EI-POK EI-WWI

ROKO AERO AS
NG4
EI-FXZ EI-MIR EI-RCA EI-ROK

ROTARY AIR FORCE INC
RAF 2000GTX-SE
EI-EAJ

ROTORWAY HELICOPTERS INTERNATIONAL
(SCORPION) EXEC
EI-CMW

RUTAN AIRCRAFT INC
LONG-EZ
EI-CMR EI-CPI

SCHEIBE-FLUGZEUGBAU GmbH including AVIALSA/ROCHETAU production
ZUGVOGEL III
EI-GLO

SCHEMPP-HIRTH FLUGZEUBAU GmbH including GROB production
DISCUS B
EI-GLT

SCHLEICHER
Ka 6 BR/CR RHÖNSEGLER
EI-GLG EI-GLM EI-GLU

Ka.6E
EI-GMO

K.8B
EI-GLF

ASK 13
  EI-GLD EI-GMF

ASK 16
  EI-AYR

ASW 17
  EI-GMB

ASW 18
  EI-GMC

ASW 19
  EI-GLV

ASK 21
  EI-GLA EI-GLB EI-GLZ

SIKORSKY AIRCRAFT
S-92A
  EI-ICA EI-ICD EI-ICG EI-ICR EI-ICS EI-ICU

SLINGSBY SAILPLANES LTD
T.31 MOTOR CADET
  EI-CJJ EI-CJT

SNCAN including AIA DE MAISON BLANCHE production
STAMPE SV-4C
  EI-BAJ

SOCATA – see also MORANE-SAULNIER
ST-10 DIPLOMATE
  EI-BUG

TB-9 TAMPICO
  EI-BMI EI-BSK EI-CRX

TBM-700 variants
  EI-LCM

SOCIÉTÉ NOUVELLE CENTRAIR
101A PEGASE
  EI-GLC

SOLAR WINGS LTD and SOLAR WINGS AVIATION LTD
PEGASUS XL-Q
  EI-DIA

PEGASUS XL-R
  EI-BSW EI-ERO EI-FMG

SOUTHDOWN SAILWINGS LTD
RAVEN
  EI-ERJ

SPRINT
  EI-DDP

SUKHOI
SUPERJET 100-95B
  EI-FWA EI-FWB EI-FWC EI-FWD EI-FWE EI-FWF

SWING FLUGSPORTGERÄTE GmbH
STING 2 PARAMOTOR
  EI-PGJ

TAKE OFF GmbH
MERLIN 1100
  EI-EOI

TAYLOR
JT.1 MONOPLANE
  EI-BKK

TAYLORCRAFT AIRCRAFT CORPORATION
BC-65
  EI-CES

TECNAM Srl
P.92 ECHO variants
  EI-DRU

P.2002 SIERRA
  EI-GIS EI-JPK EI-LFC EI-WAT EI-WFD

THRUSTER AIR SERVICES LTD including THRUSTER AIRCRAFT (UK) LTD
TST
  EI-CKI

T600
  EI-DKJ EI-DXV EI-EYW EI-FBZ

TL ULTRASPORTS
TL-3000 SIRIUS
  EI-FSA

URBAN AIR
UFM-10 SAMBA variants
  EI-DRM EI-DXT EI-DXZ EI-DZE EI-DZL
  EI-EHY EI-ESB EI-ETF EI-EXY EI-FAZ EI-FDF
  EI-FLI EI-JIM EI-MTZ

UFM-13 LAMBADA
  EI-DGA EI-DGP EI-DGT EI-DGY EI-DNV
  EI-EPY EI-FCA EI-GRA

VAN'S AIRCRAFT INC
RV-4
  EI-DIY

RV-6
  EI-EOC EI-EWY

RV-7
  EI-EEO EI-FAD EI-FEW EI-HUM EI-SYM
  EI-VII

RV-9
  EI-GIJ

VPM SNC and SRL including MAGNI GYRO
M-16 TANDEM TRAINER
  EI-FFZ EI-GIO

M-22 VOYAGER
  EI-EHK

M-24 ORION
  EI-FWC

WAG-AERO INC
CUBY SPORT TRAINER
  EI-GMH

WHITTAKER including AEROTECH INTERNATIONAL LTD
MW5 SORCERER
  EI-BUL EI-CAN EI-CTL

MW6 MERLIN
  EI-DMU

ZENAIR
CH.200/250 ZENITH variants
  EI-BVY EI-BYL

CH.601
  EI-DXN EI-ESE EI-FCI EI-GGX

CH.701 STOL
  EI-DOB EI-SMK

SECTION 5 – ISLE OF MAN

The Isle of Man is a self-governing British Crown Dependency and not part of the UK or the European Union. Their civil aircraft register came into existence on 1st May 2007. Over the past year, a number of aircraft have been reregistered. Exact dates of these changes are not recorded, so most have just month & year listed.

Aircraft that are listed as current are marked in **bold**. Those that both joined and departed the register in the period since the publication of the 2018 edition of this volume are displayed in roman (non-bold) text and indicated with a star (⋆).

Thanks go to Alan Johnson for his monthly updates and to all those that have provided additional information. Official details are up to late March 2019 via the Isle of Man authorities.

The type index cross-reference for aircraft on the Isle of Man register can be found on page 561.

Regn	Type / Previous identity / Owner/Cancellation details	C/n / Prob Base	Regn date
M-AAAA	Bombardier CL600-2B16 Challenger 605 N688JH, G-OTAG, (HB-JRI), N605AZ, C-GBYH Lee Fai International Ltd (Tortola, BVI)	5827	26.02.14
M-AAAL (2)	Gulfstream Aerospace Gulfstream VI *(Gulfstream 650)* N279GA ALM New Jet Ltd (Douglas, IOM)	6279	14.12.17
M-AAAM	Bombardier CL600-2B16 Challenger 604 OE-INJ, OE-IYA, N604PN, C-GLWZ Durstwell Ltd Tel Aviv, Israel	5435	23.05.16
M-AABG	Bombardier BD700-1A11 Global 5000 C-FGSU AB Air Holdings Riyadh, Saudi Arabia	9690	17.12.15
M-AAKV	Embraer EMB-135BJ Legacy PR-LBX AAK Company Ltd (Hamilton, Bermuda)	1451183	24.01.14
M-AATD	Bombardier BD700-1A10 Global 6000 M-IRAS, C-FNXK Unitrans IOM Ltd (Douglas, IOM)	9766	02.03.18
M-ABCC	Bombardier BD700-1A10 Global 6000 N562GX, (N14CK), N562GX, C-GUPL Global Aviation Partners LP Inc Oslo, Norway	9562	16.04.15
M-ABCD (3)	Gulfstream Aerospace Gulfstream V-SP M-ARDI, SE-RDZ, N923GA LGM Property Services Ltd To N550GP 14.12.18	5153	02.11.18
M-ABEC	Embraer EMB-135BJ Legacy 600 P4-MIV, PT-SZC Rozelda Investments Ltd (Tortola, BVI)	14501031	14.02.12
M-ABEF	Avions Transport Regional ATR72-202 D2-FLB, M-ABEF, CN-COC, F-WKVI, EI-REB, F-WQNH, F-WQOL, F-WQLM, G-BWTM, F-WWED Aircraft Solutions Lux V-B SARL (Luxembourg)	470	28.10.11
M-ABEU	Bombardier Learjet 45 VP-BSF, N5014F Aviation Leasing (IOM) Ltd London Stansted *Operated by Ryanair*	45-374	24.01.12
M-ABFD	Aerospatiale-Alenia ATR72-212A VT-KAB, F-WWEI KF Aero Chennai, India *DBR at Chennai 12.15*	728	19.04.12
M-ABFE	Aerospatiale-Alenia ATR72-212A VT-KAD, F-WWEK KF Aero Chennai, India *DBR at Chennai 12.15*	730	19.04.12
M-ABFI	Aerospatiale-Alenia ATR72-212A VT-DKA, F-WWES Plateau Aviation Ltd Chennai, India *DBR at Chennai 12.15*	718	01.05.12
M-ABGG	Bombardier CL600-2B16 Challenger 604 4X-CMZ, (N357AP), 4X-CMZ, N450DK, C-GLXH Bothwell Ltd (Tortola, BVI)	5450	06.06.13
M-ABGS	Bombardier CL600-2B16 Challenger 605 C-GURO Viking Travel Services Ltd Geneva, Switzerland	5932	18.11.13
M-ABGV	Bombardier Learjet 45 N589CH, C-FSDL, N5009V Aviation Leasing (IOM) Ltd London Stansted *Operated by Ryanair*	45-421	09.06.14

Regn	Type / Previous identity / Owner/Cancellation details	C/n / Prob Base	Regn date
M-ABJA	Bombardier Learjet 45 N849BA, N918BD, N5009T Aviation Leasing (IOM) Ltd London Stansted *Operated by Ryanair*	45-454	24.12.15
M-ABJL	Gulfstream Aerospace Gulfstream VI *(Gulfstream 650)* N698GD York Aviation Ltd (Douglas, IOM)	6198	01.09.16
M-ABJO	Eurocopter EC225LP Super Puma VH-WEV, G-NNCY Airbus Helicopters SAS Marignane, France *For Ukraine Air Force*	2768	30.08.16
M-ABJP	Eurocopter EC225LP Super Puma VH-WEX, G-CMJK, F-WWOY Dhoon Glen Aviation Ireland Ltd Marignane, France *For Ukraine Air Force*	2775	30.08.16
M-ABJR	Eurocopter EC225LP Super Puma 30.08.16 VH-WSO Dhoon Glen Aviation Ireland Ltd Marignane, France *For Ukraine Air Force*	2779	
M-ABJS	Eurocopter EC225LP Super Puma VH-TQU, G-YRKE Dhoon Glen Aviation Ireland Ltd Marignane, France *For Ukraine Air Force*	2827	30.08.16
M-ABJT	Eurocopter EC225LP Super Puma VH-TQV Dhoon Glen Aviation Ireland Ltd Marignane, France *For Ukraine Air Force*	2848	30.08.16
M-ABJU	Eurocopter EC225LP Super Puma VH-TQP, G-ITAV Dhoon Glen Aviation Ireland Ltd Marignane, France *For Ukraine Air Force*	2851	30.08.16
M-ABJV	Eurocopter EC225LP Super Puma VH-WGV Dhoon Glen Aviation Ireland Ltd Marignane, France *For Ukraine Air Force*	2794	30.08.16
M-ABJW	Eurocopter EC225LP Super Puma G-CHCJ Airbus Helicopters SAS Marignane, France *For Ukraine Air Force*	2745	30.08.16
M-ABKA	Eurocopter EC225LP Super Puma LN-OJC Airbus Helicopters SAS Marignane, France *For Ukraine Air Force*	2739	16.11.17
M-ABKC	Eurocopter EC225LP Super Puma LN-OJG Dhoon Glen Aviation Ireland Ltd Marignane, France *For Ukraine Air Force*	2747	16.11.17
M-ABKD	Eurocopter EC225LP Super Puma PR-CHX, G-CLAR, F-WJXL Airbus Helicopters SAS Marignane, France *For Ukraine Air Force*	2729	30.12.16
M-ABKE	Eurocopter EC225LP Super Puma PR-CHW, G-DRIT, F-WJXZ Airbus Helicopters SAS Marignane, France *For Ukraine Air Force*	2740	30.12.16

M

M (side tab)

M-ABKF	Eurocopter EC225LP Super Puma	2773	22.12.16
	PR-BGA, (PR-BGB), G-LCAS		
	Dhoon Glen Aviation Ireland Ltd Marignane, France		
	For Ukraine Air Force		
M-ABKG	Eurocopter EC225LP Super Puma	2798	22.12.16
	PR-BGH, C-GLIS		
	Dhoon Glen Aviation Ireland Ltd Marignane, France		
	For Ukraine Air Force		
M-ABKH	Eurocopter EC225LP Super Puma	2801	30.12.16
	PR-BGK, C-GMLI, F-WWOK		
	Dhoon Glen Aviation Ireland Ltd Marignane, France		
	For Ukraine Air Force		
M-ABKI	Eurocopter EC225LP Super Puma	2822	30.12.16
	PR-BGL, G-JSKN, F-WJXK		
	Dhoon Glen Aviation Ireland Ltd Marignane, France		
	For Ukraine Air Force		
M-ABKJ	Eurocopter EC225LP Super Puma	2708	30.12.16
	PR-YCL, (PR-CHV), LN-OHY, F-WWON		
	Airbus Helicopters SAS Marignane, France		
	For Ukraine Air Force		
M-ABKK	Eurocopter EC225LP Super Puma	2722	22.12.16
	PR-CHY, G-LJAM, F-WJXK		
	Airbus Helicopters SAS Marignane, France		
	For Ukraine Air Force		
M-ABKM	Avions Transport Regional ATR72-212A 699		29.09.16
	VT-APA, M-ABFC, VT-KAA, (7T-VVT), F-WWEV		
	Elix Assets 12 Ltd Francazal, France		
	Stored		
M-ABLE	Sikorsky S76D	761068	10.08.16
	N7668H Crowndale Aviation Ltd Attica, Greece		
M-ABLJ	Airbus A330-343	713	12.04.18
	B-6119, F-WWYT FDM 5		
	To 9M-XBD 19.10.18		
M-ABLK	Airbus A330-243	735	17.05.18
	B-6123, F-WWYA Aerotron Ltd Hong Kong		
M-ABLL	Airbus A330-343	791	21.11.18
	B-6129, F-WWKO GHY Aviation Lease 1739 Co Ltd		
	To HS-XTJ 08.01.19		
M-ABLM	Airbus A330-343	773	26.10.18
	B-6125, F-WWKF Yamasa Sangyo Co Ltd		
	To HS-XTH 14.12.18		
M-ABLN	Airbus A320-214	4379	30.08.18
	HC-CJM, F-WWIF Wells Fargo Trust Company		
	To VT-VTZ 06.09.18		
M-ABLO	Airbus A330-343	782	14.09.18
	B-6128, F-WWYV Saf Zhu Jiang		
	To 9M-XBE 22.11.18		
M-ABLR	Boeing 737-46J	27171	23.11.18
	OM-GTD, G-CIOE, VP-BQG, EI-DGL, SX-BMA, D-ABAE		
	Aerotron Ireland Ltd		
	To ZA-ALB 07.12.18		
M-ACPT	British Aerospace BAe 125 Series 1000B	259004	22.02.08
	VP-CPT, VR-CPT, G-5-779, G-LRBJ		
	Wari Holding Bournemouth		
	Stored		
M-ACRO	Eurocopter AS350B3 Ecureuil	4798	26.07.10
	N350E, N786AE F Aliani Gibraltar		
M-AERO	Dassault Falcon 2000LX	297	01.10.15
	F-WWMN Rirox Ltd Ronaldsway		
M-AFAJ	Dassault Falcon 900EX	200	15.04.10
	F-HBDA, F-WWFW		
	SG Equipment Finance (Zurich, Switzerland)		
M-AGIK	Dassault Falcon 900LX	274	01.07.14
	F-WWFA Amboy Overseas Ltd (Tortola, BVI)		
M-AGMA	Bombardier BD700-1A10 Global Express XRS 9347		02.10.17
	N101RE, HB-JFY, N115ZZ, C-FWGB		
	Magma Jet Management Ltd (Tortola, BVI)		
M-AGMF	Bombardier BD700-1A10 Global Express 9043		21.08.18
	D-AGMF, N904BR, PR-SIR, (N880NE), N416BB,		
	N416BD, N700ML, N700BU, C-GFKW		
	Unicorn Three AG (Wollerau, Switzerland)		
M-AHAA	Bombardier BD700-1A10 Global 6000 9525		xx.12.13
	'M-AHAR', M-AHAH, C-GSNB		
	AH Aviation Ltd (Tortola, BVI)		

M-AJOR (2)	Leonardo AW139	31771	22.06.17
	I-RAIN Major Aviation LLP Lyndhurst		
	Operated by Ineos		
M-AKAL (2)	Bombardier CL600-2B16 Challenger 604 5520		31.10.17
	2-NITE, VP-CST, VP-CBR, A6-MBH, VP-CBR,		
	N116BJ, XA-TVG, N520JR, C-GJTR, C-GLXQ		
	A & A Aviation Ltd Bournemouth		
M-AKAR	Sikorsky S-76C	760506	29.10.10
	VP-BNI, N7686S, TC-HRT, N728TP		
	Starspeed Ltd Blackbushe		
M-ALAY	Gulfstream Aerospace Gulfstream V-SP		
	(*Gulfstream 550*)	5391	18.12.12
	N591GA Credit Suisse AG (Zurich, Switzerland)		
M-ALCB	Pilatus PC-12/47E	1175	19.11.09
	HB-FSX M S Bartlett Bournemouth		
M-ALEN	Embraer EMB-135BJ Legacy 650	14501119	xx.01.13
	M-SAHA, PT-TKV ATT Aviation Ltd (Douglas, IOM)		
M-ALFA	Eurocopter MBB BK117C-2		
	(*Eurocopter EC145*)	9570	30.05.14
	G-JESP Starspeed Ltd Fairoaks		
M-ALIK (2)	Raytheon Hawker 4000	RC-76	30.04.18
	AP-RRR, N476HB		
	Golden Eagle Aviation Ltd Dubai, UAE		
M-ALTI	Bombardier CL600-2B16 Challenger 605 5733		11.09.14
	G-MACO, G-MACP, G-CGFF, G-OCSF, N533TS,		
	C-FPQW Hartsage International Ltd		
	Almaty, Kazakhstan		
M-ALUN	Hawker Siddeley BAe 125 Series 700A 257075		19.06.08
	N125XX, N124AR, N125TR, N125AM, (G-BHKF), G-5-13		
	Briarwood Products Ltd Bournemouth		
	Stored		
M-AMRM	Avions Transports Regional ATR72-212A 826		18.06.15
	D2-FLY, F-WKVD, F-WWEU		
	Fastjet Air Four Ltd (Ebene, Mauritius)		
M-ANGA	Embraer EMB-135BJ Legacy 600	14501086	06.01.12
	VQ-BLU, PT-SKJ Max Air Ltd (Kano, Nigeria)		
M-ANGO (2)	Bombardier BD700-1A11 Global 5000 9172		14.11.13
	N729KP, N729KF, C-FCTK		
	Waylawn Ltd (Tortola, BVI)		
M-ANNA	Bombardier CL600-2B16 Challenger 604 5375		08.07.15
	N352AP, XA-GRB, (D-ASTS), N604HP, C-GLXB		
	Generativity Ltd Dusseldorf, Germany		
M-ANTA	Bombardier CL600-2B19 Challenger 850 8094		10.11.09
	C-FUQX Miklos Services Corp (Tortola, BVI)		
M-ARDA	Embraer EMB-135BJ Legacy 600	14500948	20.12.16
	N124LS, PT-SCT MRH IOM Ltd (Douglas, IOM)		
M-ARDI (2)	Gulfstream Aerospace Gulfstream VI		
	(*Gulfstream 650*)	6337	15.11.18
	N637GA Comet Limited Partnership Inc Biggin Hill		
M-AREA	Raytheon Hawker 900XP	HA-0090	27.07.17
	VP-CFS, F-HGBY, N63890		
	Area Plus JV Ltd (Tortola, BVI)		
M-ARGO	Bombardier BD700-1A10 Global 6000 9554		30.09.14
	C-GUIY Sunburst Invest & Finance Inc		
	Moscow-Vnukovo		
M-ARIE (6)	Raytheon Hawker 850XP	258600	26.04.17
	M-GDRS (2), N908NR, N250XP, N61500		
	Guernsey PC-12 Ltd Guernsey		
M-ARKZ	Bombardier CL600-2B16 Challenger 605 5879		25.05.12
	C-GLNF Markz Jet Ltd (Tortola, BVI)		
M-ARRH	Bombardier BD100-1A10 Challenger 300 20400		19.06.13
	C-GVVF Treeforce Corp (Mahe, Seychelles)		
M-ARTY	Pilatus PC-12/47E	1114	31.03.09
	HB-FQN Crestron (UK) Ltd Fairoaks		
M-ARUB	Bombardier CL600-2B16 Challenger 650 6075		22.07.16
	C-GZQO Setfair Aviation Ltd Nice, France		
M-ARVA	Bombardier BD700-1A10 Global 6000 9809		17.04.18
	C-FVYA Newjourney Trading Ltd		
	Ben Gurion/Tel Aviv, Israel		
M-ARVY	Dassault Falcon 7X	216	20.12.13
	F-WWZW Almondine Ltd (Douglas, IOM)		

M-ASHI	Bombardier CL600-2B16 Challenger 605 5765		27.07.11
	VQ-BDG, C-FYTZ, N605FH, C-FUAU		
	Beckett Holding Ltd (Hamilton, Bermuda)		
M-ASIM	Bombardier CL600-2B16 Challenger 604 5598		02.07.18
	N959AM, M-DDDE, OE-IGJ, C-FDJN, C-GLWV		
	AIA Aviation Ltd (Tortola, BVI)		
M-ASRI	Bombardier BD700-1A10 Global Express 9165		06.02.10
	VP-BOS, C-FCSH		
	YYA Aviation Ltd (Hamilton, Bermuda)		
M-ATAK (2)	Gulfstream Aerospace Gulfstream VI		
	(Gulfstream 650)	6047	14.02.18
	VP-BJC, M-KSOI, M-KSSN, N647GD		
	STC Airliner Ltd Moscow-Vnukovo		
M-ATEX (2)	Dassault Falcon 8X	421	16.08.17
	F-WWQU Maritime Investment & Shipping		
	Company Ltd Geneva, Switzerland		
M-ATTI	Socata TBM-930	1127	23.08.16
	N930AR Vector Aircraft Leasing LP Inc (Douglas, IOM)		
	Operated by Attila Balogh		
M-AVIR	Bombardier BD700-1A10 Global 6000 9788		20.12.17
	C-FZDN, C-FUBH Anjet Co Ltd Moscow-Vnukovo		
M-AXIM	Cessna T206H Turbo Stationair 8	T20608513	24.07.08
	N357TR, N357TM C D B Cope Ronaldsway		
M-AYBE	IAI Gulfstream 280	2010	11.03.13
	N310GA, 4X-CVH Maybe Aviation Ltd (Ramsey, IOM)		
M-AZIA	Cessna 525C CitationJet CJ4	525C0009	03.07.13
	N100JS, N5254L Hunting Star Ltd (Douglas, IOM)		
M-BADU	Gulfstream Aerospace Gulfstream VI		
	(Gulfstream 650)	6083	16.12.14
	N683GD BH2 Aviation Ltd (Tortola, BVI)		
M-BAEP	Bombardier CL600-2B16 Challenger 605 5929		20.12.13
	C-GUKV Swift Cloud Aviation Services Ltd		
	(Douglas, IOM)		
M-BELL	Pilatus PC-12/47E	1223	15.03.18
	M-AMAN, HB-FQS B L Bell LP Inc (Douglas, IOM)		
M-BELR	Airbus A330-343	781	20.12.18
	B-6127, F-WWYT RIL Aviation No.2 Pty Ltd (Sydney, Australia)		
M-BEST	Cessna 750 Citation X	750-0277	30.06.10
	VP-CEG, UP-CS501, (OE-HEC), N52178		
	Lanara Ltd (Mahe, Republic of Seychelles)		
M-BETS	Rockwell Commander 695A	96034	21.04.11
	N700L, N508AB, (N24A), N508AB, (N9954S), C-GMMO,		
	N508AB, G-BWMP, N508AB, ZS-KZS, N9954S		
	Aldersey Aviation Ltd Gloucestershire		
M-BHBH	Gulfstream Aerospace Gulfstream VI		
	(Gulfstream 650)	6132	24.06.15
	N632GA Caldana Holding & Invest Ltd Nice, France		
M-BIGG (2)	Bombardier BD700-1A10 Global 5000 9597		16.05.16
	M-AGRI, C-GXAU		
	Harley Airlines Ltd (Douglas, IOM)		
M-BIRD (2)	Embraer EMB-135BJ Legacy 600	14500993	30.06.15
	A6-UGH, N912LX, PT-SKM Fly YH Ltd (Guernsey)		
M-BJEP	Gulfstream Aerospace Gulfstream V-SP		
	(Gulfstream 550)	5070	11.10.12
	HB-JEP, N870GA M-BJEP Ltd (Douglas IOM)		
M-BLGR	Airbus A330-343	777	04.02.19
	B-6126, F-WWKK RIL Aviation CEA No.1 Pty Ltd		
	Shanghai Pudong		
M-BLUE (2)	Bombardier BD700-1A10 Global 6000 9821		18.09.18
	C-FXRT Bluesky Aviation Group Ltd		
	Tel Aviv/Sde Dov, Israel		
M-BONO	Cessna 172N Skyhawk II	17270299	19.11.07
	G-BONO, C-GSMF, N738WS		
	J McCandless Ronaldsway		
M-BRAB	Diamond DA.42M Twin Star	42.MN057	26.01.18
	Bravura Group Of Companies Ltd (Tortola, BVI)		
M-BRAC	Diamond DA.42M Twin Star	42.MN058	26.01.18
	Bravura Group Of Companies Ltd (Tortola, BVI)		
M-CARA	Cessna 525 Citation M2	525-0859	14.01.15
	Anam Cara Aviation Ltd Oxford		
M-CCCP	Bombardier BD700-1A11 Global 5000 9418		19.08.11
	C-GGSU Heda Airlines Ltd (Douglas, IOM)		

M-CDBM	Beech B200GT Super King Air	BY-305	08.03.18
	N305BY BAE Systems Marine Ltd Farnborough		
M-CDJC	Beech B200GT Super King Air	BY-233	05.10.15
	N233KA BAE Systems Marine Ltd Walney Island		
M-CDMS	Beech B200GT Super King Air	BY-262	12.08.16
	N262BE BAE Systems Marine Ltd Farnborough		
M-CDZT	Beech B200 Super King Air	BB-1619	17.01.13
	G-CDZT, N240AJ, N719TA		
	BAE Systems Marine Ltd Walney Island		
M-CELT	Dassault Falcon 7X	110	01.04.11
	F-WWVM Cravant Ltd (Douglas, IOM)		
M-CHEM	Dassault Falcon 2000EX EASy	128	01.11.07
	N628SA, (VP-BOE), F-WWGS		
	Hampshire Aviation LLP Bournemouth		
	Operated by Ineos		
M-CICO	Dassault Falcon 50EX	345	11.11.10
	M-NICK, VP-BMP, F-WWHA BZ Air Ltd (London SW8)		
M-CIMO	Dassault Falcon 2000EX	113	30.09.11
	VP-CMI, F-WWMJ		
	Arirang Aviation IOM Ltd (Douglas, IOM)		
M-CITI	Bombardier BD700-1A11 Global 5000 9683		12.04.17
	N683JC, N402PM, C-FFGU		
	Global 9683 Ltd Stuttgart. Germany		
M-CITY	Cessna 525B Citationjet CJ3+	525B0557	21.09.18
	N5206T Iniala Jet Ltd Malta		
M-CKSB	Dassault Falcon 2000	6	14.09.16
	N954SC, N55EY, PR-WSM, N93GT, N93GH, F-WQBL,		
	F-GPAM, F-WWMD KAG Invest APS Biggin Hill		
M-CLAB	Bombardier BD100-1A10 Challenger 300 20271		29.01.10
	C-FYBO Shamrock Trading Ltd (Ramsey, IOM)		
M-CLHL	Bombardier CL600-2B16 Challenger 650 6130		21.12.18
	C-FAWU H C Luffy Inc Farnborough		
M-COOL	Cessna 510 Citation Mustang	510-0285	03.03.10
	Executive Aviation Ltd Guernsey		
M-CPRS	Embraer EMB-135BJ Legacy 600	14501160	21.01.16
	G-PPBA, M-PPBA, G-PPBA, PT-TCT		
	Puru Aviation Ltd (Douglas, IOM)		
M-CRAO	Beech B300 King Air 350	FL-515	06.08.13
	D-CRAO, N70155 Dr A Oetker (Bielefeld, Germany)		
M-CRDL	Gulfstream Aerospace Gulfstream IV-X		
	(Gulfstream 450)	4220	11.06.18
	M-DKVL, N920GA Samika Ltd (Tortola, BVI)		
M-CSMS	Bombardier Learjet 45	45-017	06.03.15
	D-CSMS, D-CESH, N417LJ, (D-CWER)		
	SMS Aviation Services SA (Tortola, BVI)		
M-CVGL	Bombardier BD700-1A11 Global 5000 9687		13.05.16
	C-FPQJ, C-FFVX		
	Aircraft Operations Ltd Birmingham		
M-DADA	Bombardier BD700-1A10 Global 6000 9482		28.03.13
	C-GMSU STC Aviation Services Ltd (Tortola, BVI)		
M-DADI	Dassault Falcon 900DX	622	29.11.10
	F-WWFO Club Premier Ltd (Tortola, BVI)		
M-DATA	Cessna 525 Citationjet	525-0347	19.12.18
	D-IARI, I-DAGF, N1133G, N5145P		
	Myworld Aero Ltd (San Gwann, Malta)		
M-DEND	Bombardier BD100-1A10 Challenger 300 20062		07.06.18
	N300MY, N888CN, C-GZER		
	Campino Ltd (Douglas, IOM)		
M-DMBP	Bombardier Learjet 40	2133	13.03.15
	PR-RNF, N49HM, N40079 Ven Air Southend		
M-DODO	Embraer EMB-545 Legacy 450	55010051	28.11.18
	PR-LBN Navajo SARL Le Bourget, France		
M-DRIL (2)	Pilatus PC-12/47E	1422	11.02.14
	G-DRIL, HB-FSV MFLT (Alpha) Ltd Bournemouth		
M-DSCL	Embraer EMB-135 Legacy	14500851	09.01.09
	OE-ISN, PT-SIO Legacy Aviation Ltd Jersey		
M-DSKY	Socata TBM930	1172	22.05.17
	F-WWRF Sterna Aviation Ltd (Santon, IOM)		
M-DSML	British Aerospace BAe 125 Series 800B 258037		31.10.14
	M-HDAM, 7O-ADC 4W-ACN, G-5-501, G-5-15		
	Corbally Group (Aviation) Ltd (Ullenhall, Henley-in-Arden)		

M

M-DSTZ Bombardier CL600-2B16 Challenger 650   6098   02.03.17
C-FAQB   Cameron Industries Consult Inc
Tel Aviv. Israel

M-DSUN (2) Bombardier BD700-1A10 Global 6000   9758   04.09.17
N758JF, N758WT, C-FMYX
Splendiferous Global Ltd   Beijing, China

M-DUBS (2) Dassault Falcon 900EX   256   30.07.18
G-YCKF, F-WWVD   Six Daughters Ltd   Oxford

M-EAGL Dassault Falcon 900EX   237   22.12.10
F-GZVA, F-WWFX   Faycroft Finance Corp   (Tortola, BVI)

M-EASY Bombardier Learjet 35A   341   15.05.13
OE-GPI, OE-GMS, P4-KIS, ZS-CEW, N259WJ,
XA-HOS, D-CARE, N3802G
PM Luftfahrzeugvermietung Gmbh & Co KG
(Vienna, Austria)

M-ECJI Dassault Falcon 10   161   08.09.11
G-ECJI, I-CREM, F-WWZK, I-CREM, N50SL, N30CN,
N230FJ, F-WZGM
ECJ Equity Partners Ltd   (Tortola, BVI)

M-EDZE Bombardier BD700-1A10 Global Express XRS   9097   18.06.18
M-ALSH, A6-HMA, N902MM, N908TE, N903TF, C-GIPD
WAB Air Ltd   (London, W14)

M-EGGA Beech 200 King Air   BB-1933   08.05.08
N3103L   Langley Aviation Ltd   Retford Gamston

M-ELAS IAI Gulfstream 280   2049   06.11.14
N249GA, 4X-CVJ
Aventurine Aviation Ltd   Paphos, Cyprus

M-ELON (2) Embraer EMB-505 Phenom 300   50500197   28.03.14
Sleepwell Aviation Ltd   Ronaldsway

M-ENTA Dassault Falcon 200   511   29.01.13
EC-JBH, F-WQBK, VT-TTA, (F-GNMF), F-OLET,
F-WGTF, F-OGSI, F-WWGR
Riviera Invest und Services SA   (Luxembourg)

M-ETAL Piaggio P.180 Avanti   1194   18.08.17
N191LW, N191SL   GFG Aviation Ltd   Gloucestershire

M-EVAN Bombardier BD100-1A10 Challenger 300   20096   28.03.11
G-MEGP, C-GPCZ, C-FHMI
Marcus Evans (Aviation) Ltd   (London W2)

M-EXPL Eurocopter AS355N Ecureuil 2   5667   24.05.10
N880RE, N5234E   Select Plant Hire Co Ltd   Southend

M-FAAF Dassault Falcon 7X   147   06.06.18
M-ORAD, M-ORAT, VP-CSX, N147FJ, F-WWHK
Swift New Jet Ltd
To N8HP 30.08.18

M-FALC (2) Dassault Falcon 7X   138   04.07.17
M-OMAN, F-WWUS   Premier Falcon Jet Ltd   Malta

M-FALZ Dassault Falcon 7X   224   01.10.14
F-WWHN   Pacelli Beteiligungs Gmbh & Company KG
Oberpfaffenhofen, Germany

M-FAST IAI Gulfstream 150   243   15.12.17
EC-KPJ, N443GA, 4X-WID
G-150 Aeronautics Ltd   (Tortola, BVI)

M-FINE Bombardier BD700-1A11 Global 5000   9594   28.06.14
C-GWKU   Noristevo Investments Ltd   (Tortola, BVI)

M-FISH Gulfstream Aerospace Gulfstream V   506   07.01.16
N33XE, N500GV, N158AF, N506GV
Osprey Wings SRO   Basle, Switzerland

M-FLCN Dassault Falcon 2000EX   075   01.03.17
F-GZLX, OO-GML, F-GUPH, F-WWGL
Omega Aviation Ltd   (Douglas, IOM)

M-FLIG Bombardier BD700-1A11 Global 5000   9639   20.03.19
M-KBSD, C-GZHO
Faraotis Holdings Ltd   Vienna, Austria

M-FLSN Agusta Westland AW139   31392   18.07.14
UR-CRG   Boutique Aviation Ltd   (Douglas, IOM)

M-FLYI (2) Cessna 525C CitationJet CJ4   525C0106   18.06.13
D-CCJS, (D-COJS), N5228J   M-FLYI LLP   Biggin Hill

M-FROG Raytheon RB390 Premier 1A   RB-165   10.02.10
N800FR, N7165X
SAM Sports & Marketing AG   (Switzerland)

M-FRZN (2) Bombardier CL600-2B16 Challenger 605   5920   26.06.13
C-GRZF   Iceland International Ltd   Hawarden

M-FUAD Gulfstream Aerospace Gulfstream V-SP
(Gulfstream 550)   5227   06.11.09
M-FPIA, N217GA
Future Pipe Aviation Ltd   (Georgetown, Cayman Islands)

M-GACB Dassault Falcon 10   22   16.04.10
VP-BBV, F-GJLL, N48JC, N44JC, N114FJ, F-WLCX
Valiant Aviation Ltd   Hamilton, Bermuda

M-GAGA Gulfstream Aerospace Gulfstream VI
(Gulfstream 650)   6173   21.06.16
N688JR, N673GD   Advance Global Developments Ltd
(Tortola, BVI)

M-GASG Gulfstream 150   299   16.04.12
N199GA, 4X-CVM   PIV Global Holding Ltd
(Nicosia, Cyprus)

M-GCAP Piaggio P.180 Avanti   1222   13.02.15
N539HC, (M-GCAP), N773RC
Greensill Capital (IOM) Ltd   Gloucestershire

M-GETS Pilatus PC-12/47E   1346   xx.09.15
M-WINT, HB-FSX   3FS Aviation Ltd   Fairoaks

M-GFGC Piaggio P.180 Avanti   1231   08.02.18
(D-IAII), B-8312, N179PA
Greensill Capital (IOM) Ltd   Gloucester

M-GGBL Dassault Falcon 7X   114   13.09.18
F-HKAR, 9H-MAK, G-UMKA, F-WWZO
Greensill Capital (IOM) Ltd   Gloucester

M-GLEX Bombardier BD700-1A10 Global Express   9139   03.06.11
VQ-BAM, OY-CVS, C-FYZP   Lyrkata SA   (Tortola, BVI)

M-GMKM Dassault Falcon 7X   183   18.03.14
VH-MQK, N183MK, F-WWZV   F7X Ltd   (Malta)

M-GOLF Reims/Cessna FR182RG Skylane RG   FR18200046   08.04.08
N409SA, N400SA, G-BJDI, N8062H
Etlee Ltd   Ronaldsway

M-GRAN Bombardier BD700-1A11 Global 5000   9324   23.08.10
G-GRAN, C-FUCY   Starflight Investments Ltd
(Georgetown, Cayman Islands)

M-GSIR Dassault Falcon 900DX   614   11.08.14
G-TAGK. VP-CHA, F-WWFS
Sublime Holdings Ltd   (Gerona, Italy)

M-GSKY Bombardier BD700-1A10 Global Express   9420   16.12.10
C-GGUG   Vadenzela Holdings   (Tortola, BVI)

M-GZOO IAI Gulfstream 200   224   16.05.09
G-GZOO, M-GZOO, N842GA, 4X-CVI
Multiflight Charter Services LLP   Leeds Bradford

M-HAWK (2) Bombardier BD700-1A10 Global 6000   9518   05.09.13
C-GRRI   Genetechma Finance Ltd
(Nicosia, Cyprus)

M-HELI Eurocopter EC155 B1   6898   08.12.10
Flambards Ltd   (Douglas, IOM)

M-HHHH Airbus A318-112CJ   4650   19.04.12
D-AUAG, F-WHUI, D-AUAG   Kutus Ltd   (Douglas, IOM)

M-HLAN Bombardier CL600-2B19 Challenger 850   8104   24.07.12
A6-JET, C-FXOK
Wonder Air International   (Tortola, BVI)

M-HOME Bombardier BD700-1A10 Global 6000   9577   30.09.14
C-GVRO   Symhony Master (IOM) Ltd   (Ramsey, IOM)

M-HSXP Raytheon Hawker 800XP   258645   11.08.11
HB-VOT, OY-AAA, N618AR, N733K, (N733L), N733K,
(N645XP), N733K, N645XP
HEWE Ltd   (Hamilton, Bermuda)

M-IABU Airbus A340-313   955   18.12.09
M-ABUS, F-WWJM   Klaret Aviation Ltd   Luxembourg

M-IAMI Dassault Falcon 7X   230   05.12.14
F-WWHQ   Delane Finance Ltd   (Belize City, Belize)

M-ICRO (3) Cessna 525C CitationJet CJ4   525C0257   04.01.18
N5233J   Pektron Group Ltd   Retford Gamston

M-IDAS Agusta A109E Power   11112   16.10.07
N555GS, N109LF   Benvarden Ltd   (Ballygawley, NI)

M-IFFY Cessna 510 Citation Mustang   510-0192   04.07.14
LX-FGC, N4107D   Xead Aviation Ltd   (Douglas, IOM)

M-IFLY Pilatus PC-12/47E   1022   23.06.08
HB-FRN   N J Vetch   Southampton

M-IGWT (2)	Bombardier BD700-1A10 Global 6000 9595 C-GWKZ Business Encore (IOM) Ltd (Castletown, IOM)		25.11.14
M-IKEY	Eurocopter AS365N3 Dauphin 2 6713 G-MRMJ Whirligig Ltd Letchmore Heath		07.01.15
M-ILAN	Embraer EMB-135BJ Legacy 650 14501192 OE-IIG, OE-LPV, PR-LEJ Artjet Ltd (Hamilton, Bermuda)		29.05.15
M-ILLA	Raytheon Beech 400XP RK-548 TC-NEU, N548XP Sunshine Aviation Ltd (Douglas, IOM)		30.03.17
M-ILTA	Dassault Falcon 900LX 306 F-WWFI Delta Technical Services Ltd Munich, Germany		30.05.17
M-INER (2)	Bombardier BD700-1A10 Global 6000 9708 C-FIEX ICC Aviation Ltd Fort Lauderdale, USA		23.02.17
M-INNI	Bombardier Learjet 60 60-348 N550DG, N226FX M-INNI Aviation Ltd (Douglas, IOM)		29.06.17
M-INOR (2)	Bell 429 57326 C-FULG Major Aviation LLP Lyndhurst *Operated by Ineos*		07.12.17
M-INSK	Gulfstream Aerospace Gulfstream VI *(Gulfstream 650)* 6096 N696GA Skyfort Aviation Ltd Moscow-Vnukovo		21.11.14
M-INTY	IAI Gulfstream 280 2086 N286GA, 4X-CVG Hampshire Aviation LLP Bournemouth *Operated by Ineos*		02.03.16
M-IPHS	Gulfstream Aerospace Gulfstream V-SP *(Gulfstream 550)* 5246 N846GA Islands Aviation Ltd Hamilton, Bermuda		29.12.09
M-IRNE	Raytheon Hawker 850XP 258778 N36578, OE-IPH, N36578 I.M. Aviation Ltd Birmingham		26.03.10
M-IRTH	Pilatus PC12/47E 1609 HB-FRB Wingmen Ltd (Douglas, IOM)		24.03.16
M-ISRA	Agusta A109E Power 11501 VH-NPY, N42-501 RAN, VH-NPY, I-POWR, I-RAIB Perfectway Services Ltd (Tortola, BVI)		19.03.19
M-ISTY	IAI Gulfstream 280 2085 N208GA, 4X-CVF Hampshire Aviation LLP Bournemouth *Operated by Ineos*		19.02.16
M-JACK	Beech B200GT Super King Air BY-94 N6394Z Jetstream Aviation Ltd (Ramsey, IOM)		14.12.09
M-JCBA	Sikorsky S-76C++ 760807 M-OMOO, N807A J C Bamford Excavators Ltd East Midlands		xx.08.12
M-JCBB	Gulfstream Aerospace Gulfstream VI *(Gulfstream 650)* 6049 N649GA J C Bamford Excavators Ltd East Midlands		17.01.14
M-JCBC	Sikorsky S-76C++ 760616 G-XJCB, N8093J J C Bamford Excavators Ltd East Midlands		31.01.14
M-JCCA	Embraer EMB-135BJ Legacy 14501182 PR-LBV Cana Assets Ltd (Tortola, BVI)		18.12.13
M-JETT	Dassault Falcon 200 490 N490SJ, PH-APV, N917JG, N917JC, HC-BVH, N200RT, (N208RT), N200RT, N95JT, N2TF, N806F, N14EN, N204FJ, F-WPUY Piraeus Leasing Chrimatodotikes Mishoseis Athens, Greece		10.12.08
M-JETZ	Dassault Falcon 2000EX 105 N994GP, F-WWGR Avtorita Holdings Ltd (Tortola, BVI)		30.09.11
M-JGVJ	Bombardier BD700-1A11 Global 5000 9623 C-GXZV Aquatic Ventures Holdings Ltd Douglas, IOM)		16.12.14
M-JJTL	Pilatus PC-12/47E 1126 HB-FQV JJTL Ltd (Ramsey, IOM)		18.12.09
M-JNJL	Bombardier BD700-1A10 Global Express 9046 N517TT, N1TS, N700BV, C-GFLS Global Thirteen Worldwide Resources Ltd (Tortola, BVI)		13.08.10
M-JSMN	Bombardier BD700-1A11 Global 5000 9216 N900LS, C-FIPN Jasmin Six Ltd (Douglas, IOM)		30.04.10
M-JSTA	Bombardier CL600-2B16 Challenger 604 5639 VP-BJA, C-FGYI, C-GLXB Jetsteff Aviation Ltd Hamilton, Bermuda		30.10.09
M-JSWB	Gulfstream Aerospace Gulfstream VI *(Gulfstream 650)* 6292 N292GA Treasure Depot Ltd Shanghai		03.03.18
M-KATE	Airbus A319-133X 4151 D-AVYB Sophar Property Holding (Tortola, BVI)		20.01.10
M-KBBG	Gulfstream Aerospace Gulfstream IV-X *(Gulfstream 450)* 4262 N462GA Golden Global Aviation Ltd (Tortola, BVI)		15.02.13
M-KELY	Embraer EMB-500 Phenom 100 50000040 PT-TFP Kelly Air Ltd (Douglas, IOM)		29.09.09
M-KGTS	Embraer EMB-505 Phenom 300 50500206 PR-PCD VTS Sp z.o.o (Gdansk, Poland)		27.03.14
M-KKCO	Gulfstream Aerospace Gulfstream IV-X *(Gulfstream 450)* 4306 N306GA Sadalsuud Ltd (Tortola, BVI)		11.07.14
M-KRAF	Cessna 550 Citation Bravo 550-0827 D-CCAB, N51042 Patagonia Assets Ltd (Tortola, BVI)		11.06.18
M-LANG	Dassault Falcon 900LX 245 B-8030, N777QG, F-WWFQ Longest Day International Ltd (Tortola, BVI)		14.12.15
M-LCFC (2)	Boeing 737-7EI (BBJ) 34683 B-LEX, N2121 Ceilo Del Rey Co Ltd (Douglas, IOM)		25.05.17
M-LEKT	Robin DR.400/180 Régent 1181 G-LEKT, D-EEKT T D Allan, P & J P Bromley Ronaldsway *Built by APEX Aircraft*		07.04.08
M-LENR	Beech B200GT King Air BY-135 N8105X BAE Systems Marine Ltd Walney Island		21.03.12
M-LILY	Bombardier CL600-2B19 Challenger 850 8108 C-GIVW Bright Loyal Ltd (George Town, Grand Cayman)		31.07.12
M-LION	Raytheon Hawker 900XP HA-0099 N60099 Lion Invest and Trade Ltd (Tortola, BVI)		21.05.09
M-LIZI	Eurocopter EC155 B1 Dauphin 6771 3A-MPG, F-WQDN Ledzone Investments Ltd (Tortola, BVI)		30.06.15
M-LJGI (2)	Dassault Falcon 7X 178 F-WWNF Ven Air (Dundalk, RoI)		24.05.13
M-LLIN	Bombardier BD700-1A10 Global 6000 9735 N283JA, C-FKSN Tian Yi Ltd (Tortola, BVI)		23.12.16
M-LLMW	Beech B300 Super King Air 350 FL-1080 N1080Q Trosa Ltd (Douglas, IOM)		06.01.17
M-LOLA	Bombardier BD700-1A10 Global Express 9287 HB-JGE, N169DT, C-FPGD TAG Aviation Services Ltd Farnborough		11.01.19
M-LOOK	Bombardier CL600-2B16 Challenger 604 5319 N27X, N5319, N2SA, N100SA, N14RU, N14R, N604KR, C-GLWT Kennington Ltd (Ramsey, IOM)		10.08.12
M-LUNA	Eurocopter MBB BK-117C-2 *(Eurocopter EC145)* 9242 P4-LNA Flambards Ltd (Douglas, IOM)		30.04.10
M-LVIA	Eurocopter AS365N3 Dauphin 2 6815 P4-LVA Flambards Ltd (Douglas, IOM)		24.02.10
M-LWSA	Bombardier BD700-1A10 Global Express 9092 N899WW, N799WW, N15FX, C-GIOK Lynx Aviation (IOM) Ltd (Douglas, IOM)		23.07.12
M-LWSG	Bombardier BD700-1A10 Global 6000 9583 N583JC, N116SF, C-GVXG Lynx Aircraft Ltd Stansted		08.06.17
M-MANX	Cessna 425 Conquest 425-0044 N425HS, N555BE, VH-PTH, N6774L Suas Investments Ltd Ronaldsway		16.08.07
M-MAVP	Bombardier BD700-1A10 Global 6000 9742 C-FLKC Sentonian Investments Ltd Moscow-Vnukovo		27.09.16
M-MAXX	Bombardier BD700-1A10 Global 6000 9678 N968DW, C-FFGZ Max Smart Developments Ltd Hong Kong		08.02.16

M

M-MBLY	Bombardier BD700-1A10 Global 6000 9776		27.10.17
	C-FPSF Asaj Holdings LLC Tel Aviv		
M-MDBD	Bombardier BD700-1A10 Global Express 9049		03.07.13
	N949GP, N471DG, C-GFLX		
	Cozuro Holdings Ltd (Douglas, IOM)		
M-MDMH (2)	Embraer EMB-550 Legacy 500 55000046		20.12.17
	N721EE, PR-LKF Herrenknecht Aviation Gmbh		
	Lahr, Germany		
M-MEVA	Cessna 560 Citation Ultra 560-0346		30.11.16
	N399AF, C-FNTM, C-GFCL, N346CC, N5269A		
	AVEM'R (Lamballe, France)		
M-MIKE (2)	Cessna 525C CitationJet CJ4 525C-0241		30.06.17
	N5245L Aviation By Westminster Ltd Oxford		
M-MJLD	Cessna 680A Citation Latitude 680A-0017		30.12.15
	N5262Z CCC Isle Of Man Ltd Wroclaw, Poland		
M-MNDG (2)	Gulfstream Aerospace Gulfstream V-SP		
	(Gulfstream 550) 5519		03.11.15
	N519GA Ovation Ltd Lagos, Nigeria		
M-MOON	Cessna 750 Citation X 750-0242		11.12.12
	9M-VAM, 9M-ATM, N1289G, N5194J		
	Lixoma Holdings Ltd (Limassol, Cyprus)		
M-MRBB	Bombardier Learjet 45 45-211		21.12.10
	N300AQ, N300AA, N50490, N50145		
	Boultbee Aviation 3 LLP Oxford		
M-MSGG (2)	Bombardier CL600-2B16 Challenger 605 5936		xx.08.14
	M-ABGU, C-GUSF Toyna Ltd (Douglas, IOM)		
M-MSVI	Cessna 525B CitationJet CJ3 525B0361		08.04.16
	N361EV, UR-DWL, N5263S JPM Ltd Biggin Hill		
M-MTOO	Bombardier BD100-1A10 Challenger 300 20050		15.08.13
	M-AKVI, A6-KNH, N350TG, C-FEPU		
	Nadremal Air Holdings ltd (Guernsey)		
M-MYNA	Bombardier BD700-1A10 Global 6000 9471		28.03.13
	C-GLFG Tibit Ltd (Tortola, BVI)		
M-NAME	Bombardier BD700-1A10 Global 6000 9706		19.04.16
	C-FIFK Blezir Aircraft Leasing (IOM) Ltd		
	Moscow Vnukovo		
M-NGNG	Gulfstream Aerospace Gulfstream VI		
	(Gulfstream 650) 6077		xx.01.15
	M-NNNN, N677GD		
	Infinity Sky Ltd Moscow-Vnukovo		
M-NGSN	Pilatus PC-12/47E 697		14.04.09
	OY-PPP, HB-FRA N Stolt-Nielsen Southampton		
M-NICE	Gulfstream Aerospace Gulfstream 200 246		01.08.11
	N146GA M-NICE Ltd (Douglas, IOM)		
M-NJSS	Embraer EMB-135BJ Legacy 145686		29.10.11
	P4-IVM, N686SG, PT-SAT		
	Saby Finance Ltd (Tortola, BVI)		
M-NLYY	Piper PA-42-1000 Cheyenne 400LS 42-5527010		26.01.10
	LN-LYY, SE-LYY, N105LV, N24KW, C-FHRV, N100AK,		
	N307CA Factory Leasing Ltd Guernsey		
M-NTOS	Cessna 525C CitationJet CJ4 525C0197		23.09.15
	N5244F Selementos Ltd Biggin Hill		
M-OBIL	Cessna 525C CitationJet CJ4 525C0132		29.10.13
	N50275 Popken Fashion Services Gmbh		
	(Rastede, Germany)		
M-OCNY	Bombardier BD100-1A10 Challenger 350 20581		29.10.15
	C-GOXU RH-Flugdienst Gmbh & Co KG		
	Frankfurt, Germany		
M-OCOM	Bombardier CL600-2B16 Challenger 604 5617		19.08.14
	G-OCOM, G-PRKR, C-FEYU, C-GKXB		
	Focus Holdings Ltd (Guernsey)		
M-ODEL	Gulfstream Aerospace Gulfstream IV-X		
	(Gulfstream 450) 4103		21.06.18
	VP-BTB, N603GA Hampshire Aviation LLP		
	Bournemouth		
	Operated by Ineos		
M-ODEM	Bombardier CL600-2B16 Challenger 605 5952		01.03.18
	N589MD, C-GWQL Parker Holdings Ltd Tel Aviv		
M-ODKZ	Dassault Falcon 900EX 086		27.08.09
	VP-BEZ, HB-IGX, N986EX, F-WWFC		
	Skylane LP (Douglas, IOM)		

M-OEPL (2)	Dassault Falcon 7X 163		13.07.17
	N163FJ, F-WWNB		
	Cloud Services Ltd (Douglas, IOM)		
M-OGUL	Agusta A109S Grand 22026		23.11.09
	F-GXKG, OY-HOO		
	Pure Leisure Air (North West) LLP Yealand, Redmayne		
M-OLEG	Embraer EMB-135BJ Legacy 14500991		21.08.09
	D-AAAI, (VP-COS), PT-SKL		
	Hermitage Air Ltd (Douglas, IOM)		
M-OLJM	Agusta Westland AW139 41008		18.07.14
	UR-CRB, 4O-HHH, N180AW		
	Boutique Aviation Ltd (Douglas, IOM)		
M-OLLY	Cessna 525 CitationJet CJ1 525-0544		13.07.12
	HB-VOG, OE-FUJ		
	EHRLE Gmbh (Illertissen, Germany)		
M-OLOT	Bombardier CL600-2B16 Challenger 604 5382		20.12.13
	N604HJ, C-GLXS I Annenskiy (Malta)		
M-OLTT	Pilatus PC-12/47E 1063		20.10.08
	HB-FRR One Luxury Travel LP Southampton		
M-ONDE	Eurocopter MBB BK-117C-2		
	(Eurocopter EC145) 9052		18.10.10
	P4-LGB (2), D-HMBE, D-HMBJ Lynx-Heli Ltd Jersey		
M-ONTE	Piaggio P180 Avanti II 1176		02.08.16
	LX-JFP Scotia Aviation Ltd (Douglas, IOM)		
M-ONTY (2)	Sikorsky S-76C 760696		20.10.08
	N2580E Trustair Ltd Euxton, Chorley		
M-OPHS	Gulfstream Aerospace Gulfstream V-SP 5572		10.12.18
	N572GA Islands Aviation Ltd		
	To LX-PHS 29.01.19		
M-ORIS	Embraer EMB-550 Legacy 500 55000056		07.11.17
	PR-LNK Legacy 500 Ltd Liverpool John Lennon		
	Operated by T J Morris Ltd		
M-ORZE	Eurocopter EC135 P2+ 0684		03.08.17
	SP-WWW, D-HAAD, N517JS, D-HECN		
	G650 Management Ltd (Douglas, IOM)		
M-OTOR (2)	Beech B200GT Super King Air BY-200		26.06.14
	N200BY Pektron Group Ltd (Derby)		
M-OUNT	Dassault Falcon 7X 175		03.05.17
	VQ-BTV, (M-LMAA), (M-ALAA), F-WWNA		
	Abelia Ltd (Hamilton, Bermuda)		
M-OUSE	Cessna 510 Citation Mustang 510-0340		04.10.10
	N4078H Mouse (IOM) Ltd (Douglas, IOM)		
M-OUTH	Diamond DA.42 Twin Star 42.AC082		25.11.11
	N482TS Sky Fly LP Inc (Douglas, IOM)		
M-OVIE	Gulfstream Aerospace Gulfstream VI		
	(Gulfstream 650) 6247		19.05.17
	N647GA Hampshire Aviation LLP		
	Bournemouth		
	Operated by Ineos		
M-PACF	Eurocopter EC135 P2+ 0895		28.06.10
	Starspeed Ltd Blackbushe		
M-PAPA	Airbus Helicopters EC130 T2 8273		12.07.17
	Papa Fly Ltd (Douglas, IOM)		
M-PCPC	Pilatus PC-12/45 648		xx.06.12
	M-YBUB, G-OLTT, HB-FSU		
	Treetops Aircraft LLP (Banstead)		
M-PHML	American General AG-5B Tiger 10141		19.12.07
	G-PHML, PH-MLB P H Davies Ronaldsway		
M-PIRA	Embraer EMB-135BJ Legacy 600 1451016		13.04.18
	OE-IMS, M-ESGR, D-ACBG, PT-SVD		
	ABA AG (Zug, Switzerland)		
M-PIRE	Piaggio P180 Avanti 1042		xx.06.14
	M-FRED, D-IXIE, HB-LTE		
	Northside Aviation PCC Ltd Exeter		
M-PLUS	Gulfstream Aerospace Gulfstream VI		
	(Gulfstream 650) 6113		04.03.15
	N613GD G650 Management Ltd Basle, Switzerland		
M-PMCN	Cessna 525A CitationJet CJ2 525A0067		12.10.16
	N525PM, N5141F		
	Continental Management Ltd Oxford		
M-POWR	Beech C90A King Air LJ-1229		02.08.11
	N94MG, D-IAAF, N422TW, N422RJ, N5547Y		
	Northside Aviation PCC Ltd (Douglas, IOM)		

M-PTGG	Dassault Falcon 8X	445	13.12.18
	F-WWVY Prime Galaxy International Ltd Singapore		
M-RBIG	Bombardier Learjet 45	45-280	05.02.16
	N145JP, CS-DTL, G-CDNK, N40079		
	Volantair LP Inc Belfast		
M-RBUS	Airbus A319-115X	3856	17.04.09
	D-AVWB Spread Eagle Ltd (Douglas, IOM)		
M-RCCG	Embraer EMB-135BJ Legacy 650	14501113	03.11.10
	PT-TKS Flight Holdings Ltd (Tortola, BVI)		
M-RCCH	Embraer EMB-135BJ Legacy 650	14501225	29.11.16
	PR-LKX Flight Holdings Ltd (Tortola, BVI)		
M-REEE	Dassault Falcon 7X	8	18.12.17
	N999BE, F-WWUE B C Ecclestone Biggin Hill		
M-RENT	Cessna 525 Citation M2	525-0864	27.03.17
	LX-FDJ, N4092E Sixt Air Gmbh Dusseldorf		
M-RFAP	Dassault Falcon 7X	165	03.04.18
	N165FJ, PR-YVL, (VP-CYL), F-WWZP		
	PPAR Enterprises Ltd (Douglas, IOM)		
M-RISE	Boeing 757-23N	27972	30.10.13
	N757LL, N516AT Talos Aviation Ltd (Tortola, BVI)		
M-RKAY	Raytheon RB390 Premier 1A	RB-88	06.05.11
	G-OMJC, N4488F SC Aviation Ltd Bournemouth		
M-RLIV	Bombardier CL600-2B16 Challenger 605	5731	28.03.08
	C-FPQT Mobyhold Ltd (London E1)		
M-RONE	Dassault Falcon 2000EX	028	14.05.11
	N4QG, (N28EX), N4QG, N2CC, F-GUFM, F-WWGC		
	Dunard Engineering Ltd (Tortola, BVI)		
M-RRRR (2)	Bombardier BD700-1A10 Global 6000 9704		17.11.16
	N161GF, C-FIFP		
	Prestige Investments Ltd Dubai, UAE		
M-RSKL	Bombardier BD700-1A10 Global Express XRS 9380		17.03.11
	C-FYOC Angel Aviation Ltd		
	(Georgetown, Cayman Islands)		
M-RTFS	Dassault Falcon 7X	207	25.04.16
	F-HGHF, F-WWHR		
	CIM Corporate Services Ltd Lagos, Nigeria		
M-RZDC	Gulfstream Aerospace Gulfstream V-SP		
	(Gulfstream 550)	5315	17.10.16
	G-GRZD, N835GA KRP Aviation Ltd (Dublin, RoI)		
M-SAAN	Embraer EMB-135BK Legacy 600	14501008	02.11.18
	TC-VSR, OE-IFF, S5-ABL, PT-SKY		
	Autolex Transport Ltd (Mahe, Seychelles)		
M-SAIL	Pilatus PC-12/47E	1154	14.09.09
	HB-FSH Sailfly Ltd Jersey		
M-SAMA	Bombardier BD700-1A10 Global 6000 9579		05.07.14
	C-GVRI Fanar Aviation Ltd Dubai, UAE		
M-SAPT (2)	Bombardier BD700-1A11 Global 5000 9668		30.06.15
	N968GX, C-FDUV		
	Sapetro Aviation Ltd Lagos, Nigeria		
M-SASS	IAI Gulfstream 200	233	xx.09.14
	M-SWAN (1), N533GA, 4X-CVF		
	Starex Ltd (Douglas, IOM)		
M-SAXY	Pilatus PC-12/45	508	27.01.17
	G-SAKS, M-ICKY, N508DL, (N118CD), ZS-KAL		
	Saxon Logistics Ltd Elstree		
M-SBUR	IAI Gulfstream 200	174	20.02.15
	N851SC, N148KB, B-8087, (PR-MMP), B-8097,		
	N674GA, 4X-CVH		
	Quinzol Ventures Ltd Moscow Vnukoko, Russia		
M-SCMG	Dassault Falcon 7X	96	25.11.10
	F-WWZU BlueSky International Management Ltd		
	(Tortola, BVI)		
M-SCOT	Dassault Falcon 7X	54	20.10.14
	F-HLIV, OY-JDE, F-WWVV		
	Arirang Aviation IOM Ltd Dhaka, Bangladesh		
M-SETT	Bombardier BD700-1A11 Global 5000 9782		06.09.17
	C-FRYO Lodgings 2020 LP Inc Tel Aviv		
M-SEVN	Bombardier CL600-2B16 Challenger 605 5962		27.06.14
	C-GXVJ M-SEVN Ltd (Tortola, BVI)		
M-SEXY	Embraer EMB-135BJ Legacy 650	14501221	27.01.16
	PR-LJQ Gefault Capital Ltd (Tortola, BVI)		

M-SFAM	McDonnell Douglas DC-9-87 (MD-87)	53042	22.03.12
	N870SG, HS-MSA, JA8373, N90126		
	Montavachi Ltd (Douglas, IOM)		
M-SFOZ (2)	Dassault Falcon 2000	121	17.04.15
	F-HFLX, OD-ONE, M-TANA, N78NT, VP-BNT,		
	(F-GDVA), F-ORAX, HZ-KSDA, F-WWVQ		
	Alaman For Jets Ltd Istanbul, Turkey		
M-SGCR	Cessna 550 Citation Bravo	550-0808	21.01.10
	YU-BSM, SE-DVZ, N1299B, N5216A		
	H Izterjave (Slovenia)		
M-SGJS	Bombardier BD100-1A10 Challenger 350 20588		02.10.15
	C-GOXZ Twenty 27(IOM) Ltd Delhi, India		
M-SHRM	AgustaWestland AW139	31716	01.07.16
	I-EASG Frozendale Ltd Stansted		
M-SIXT	Cessna 525C CitationJet CJ4	525C0188	09.10.15
	N225CJ, N51511 Sixt Air Gmbh (Pullach, Germany)		
M-SKSM	Bombardier BD700-1A11 Global 5000 9227		22.12.08
	M-LLGC, C-FJNZ IF Company Ltd (Belize City)		
M-SNER	Dassault Falcon 2000EX	95	09.02.11
	M-ROWL, N887CE, N168CE, F-WWGJ		
	Blue Cloud Ltd Bournemouth		
M-SOBM	Gulfstream Aerospace Gulfstream IV-X		
	(Gulfstream 450)	4303	29.09.17
	M-SOBR, N303GA		
	Sobha Aviation Ltd Dubai World Center		
M-SOLO	Airbus Helicopters MBB-BK117 D-2		
	(Airbus H145)	20251	29.03.19
	D-HCBQ Clear Skies Flights Ltd Jersey		
M-SPBM	Bombardier CL600-2B16 Challenger 605 5953		01.05.14
	C-GWQM G200 Ltd (Hamilton, Bermuda)		
M-SPEC (2)	Beech B300 King Air 350	FL-970	24.02.15
	N5070C Specsavers Corporate Aircraft Leasing Ltd		
	Guernsey		
M-SPEK	Beech B300 King Air 350	FL-959	24.02.15
	N5059U Specsavers Corporate Aircraft Leasing Ltd		
	Guernsey		
M-SPOR	Beech B200 King Air	BB-1557	03.09.10
	G-SPOR, N57TL, N57TS Oisan Aviation Ltd Southend		
M-SQAR	Gulfstream Aerospace Gulfstream V-SP		
	(Gulfstream 550)	5179	14.07.11
	VP-BZC, N979GA M Square Aviation Ltd		
	(Hamilton, Bermuda)		
M-SSYS	Cessna 525C CitationJet CJ4	525C0143	18.02.14
	N5045W Fimway Asset Holdings Ltd (Tortola, BVI)		
M-STAR (2)	Boeing 727-2X8	22687	15.10.11
	M-ETIS, N727LL, N721MF, N4532N, (N111MF)		
	Starling Aviation Ltd		
	(Georgetown, Cayman Islands)		
M-STRY	British Aerospace Avro 146-RJ70	E1267	07.08.15
	A6-LIW, A6-RJK, EI-CPL, 9H-ACP, G-6-267		
	B C Ecclestone Biggin Hill		
M-SUNY	Dassault Falcon 7X	143	06.07.18
	F-HMOE, VP-CSW, F-WWVX		
	Harmony Flight International Ltd (Tortola, BVI)		
M-SURE	Dassault Falcon 7X	155	06.09.17
	F-HPVE, OY-CLS, F-WWHD		
	Arirang Aviation IOM Ltd Seoul, Korea		
M-SVGN	Cessna 680 Citation Sovereign	680-0198	16.10.09
	G-SVGN, N51072		
	Eastpoint Resources Management Corp (Tortola, BVI)		
M-TAKE	Bombardier CL600-2B19 Challenger 850 8079		02.06.10
	C-FPSB, C-FMLQ		
	Caropan Company S.A. (Tortola, BVI)		
M-TBEA	Cessna 525A CitationJet CJ2	525A0191	28.02.17
	G-TBEA, N776LB Bealaw (Man) 8 Ltd Manchester		
M-TBUC	Dassault Falcon 2000LX	199	15.11.18
	M-FTHD, OE-HTO, F-WWGS		
	Blackthorn Aviation Ltd (Douglas, IOM)		
M-TECH	Bombardier BD100-1A10 Challenger 350 20621		27.04.16
	C-GOXB Primelock Investments Ltd Tel Aviv, Israel		

M

M

M-TELE	Gulfstream Aerospace Gulfstream IV		
	(*Gulfstream 400*)	1502	01.08.17
	N710EG, N710EC, N202GA		
	Arena Aviation Ltd Biggin Hill		
M-TFFS	Dassault Falcon 900LX	276	16.09.16
	B-8212, F-WWFF Astira Holdings Ltd (Douglas, IOM)		
M-THOR	Gulfstream Aerospace Gulfstream V	514	23.01.19
	N514GV, B-KDP, N256LK, N320K, N304K N777SW,		
	N514GA Argus Bahamas Ltd (Nassau, Bahamas)		
M-TINK (4)	Dassault Falcon 8X	450	27.03.19
	F-WWZN Velut Ltd (Douglas, IOM)		
M-TOPI	Bombardier CL600-2B16 Challenger 605 5780		13.07.09
	C-FUUW Gladiator Flight Ltd Gibraltar		
M-TRBS	Bombardier CL600-2B16 Challenger 605 5836		02.10.11
	N636XJ, C-GDSQ		
	Arrow Management Property Corp (Tortola, BVI)		
M-TSKW	Dassault Falcon 900C	202	30.06.14
	UR-CRD, VP-BMV, F-WWFF		
	Boutique Aviation Ltd (Douglas, IOM)		
M-TSRI (2)	Beech C90GTI King Air	LJ-2033	11.01.12
	N8133H Timpson Ltd (Manchester)		
M-TYRA	Bombardier BD700-1A11 Global 5000 9560		26.02.14
	C-GUPM KKCO Ltd (Douglas, IOM)		
M-ULTI	Bombardier BD700-1A10 Global Express XRS 9394		22.02.17
	VP-CBM, C-GCXE		
	Multibird Overseas Ltd (Tortola, BVI)		
M-UNIS	Bombardier BD700-1A10 Global Express 9371		10.12.10
	C-FYIH Lapwing Aviation Ltd Guernsey		
M-URRY	Raytheon Hawker 800XP	258311	29.01.18
	N225RP, N850J, N800RD, N804JT		
	Corporate Sealandair Ltd Bournemouth		
M-URUS	Boeing 737-7GC (BBJ)	34622	17.07.08
	P4-RUS, N357BJ Ingram Services Ltd (Tortola, BVI)		
M-USBA	Gulfstream Aerospace Gulfstream V	680	12.10.12
	N680GA, (OK-ONE), N680GA		
	Shukra Ltd (Hamilton, Bermuda)		
M-USIC	Gulfstream Aerospace Gulfstream V-SP		
	(*Gulfstream 550*)	5394	27.02.13
	N494GA Chem Aviation LLP Bournemouth		
	Operated by Ineos		
M-USIK	Gulfstream Aerospace Gulfstream VI		
	(*Gulfstream 650*)	6037	20.11.13
	N637GA OS Aviation Ltd Cairo, Egypt		
M-USTG (2)	Cessna 510 Citation Mustang	510-0089	08.12.09
	N63223 Mustang Aviation Ltd (Douglas, IOM)		
M-VGAL	Dassault Falcon 900EX	205	07.01.15
	VT-CAP, (M-TECH), F-WWFB Charter Air Ltd Oxford		
M-VITB	Gulfstream Aerospace Gulfstream VI		
	(*Gulfstream 650*)	6250	23.06.17
	N625G Talisman Aviation Ltd (Douglas, IOM)		
M-VITO	Raytheon Hawker 800XP	258512	28.09.12
	N501CT Beratex Group Ltd (Mahe, Seychelles)		
M-VRNY	Gulfstream Aerospace Gulfstream V-SP		
	(*Gulfstream 550*)	5225	07.07.09
	N325GA Mirtos Ltd (Tortola, BVI)		
M-WANG	Dassault Falcon 7X	272	29.06.16
	F-WWUJ Keystone International Co Ltd China		
M-WATJ	Beech B200GT Super King Air	BY-139	27.07.12
	N8019D M-WATJ LP Inc (Douglas, IOM)		
M-WIND (2)	Gulfstream Aerospace Gulfstream VI		
	(*Gulfstream 650*)	6080	08.08.14
	N7780, N608GA Nursam Invest SA (Tortola, BVI)		
M-WING (4)	Dassault Falcon 7X	215	11.08.16
	N715FJ, F-WWZN		
	Certeco Aviation Ltd Nice, France		
M-WONE	Gulfstream Aerospace Gulfstream IV-X		
	(*Gulfstream 450*)	4319	17.12.14
	N319GA Wone International Aviation Ltd		
	(Douglas, IOM)		

M-WRLD	Beech 58 Baron	TH-2001	07.03.18
	HB-GJO, N3231F		
	Myworld Aero Ltd (San Gwann, Malta)		
M-XHEC	Eurocopter EC155B	6600	27.09.10
	P4-HEC, LX-HEC, F-WQPX Catena Aviation Ltd		
	Lives on yacht 'Eclipse'		
M-YANG	Gulfstream Aerospace Gulfstream IV-X		
	(*Gulfstream 450*)	4260	20.02.14
	OE-IOK, N460GA DJM Holdings Ltd (Tortola, BVI)		
M-YBLS	Pilatus PC-12/45	176	03.01.13
	VP-BLS, N176BS, HB-FSL		
	Executors Of B L Schroder, c/o Withers LLP Fairoaks		
M-YBUS	Airbus A320-214CJ	6069	16.04.14
	F-WWDT STC Flight Ltd (Tortola, BVI)		
M-YFLY (3)	Pilatus PC-12/47E	1110	17.11.16
	C-GKRY, HB-FQJ Fly High Ltd (Douglas, IOM)		
M-YGIG	Gulfstream Aerospace Gulfstream VI		
	(*Gulfstream 650*)	6305	27.04.18
	N305GA AC Executive Aircraft (2017) Ltd Dublin, Rol		
M-YGJL	Bombardier BD700-1A10 Global Express 9033		08.09.17
	N600AK, C-GFAN Be Conseils SARL (Switzerland)		
M-YGLF	Gulfstream Aerospace Gulfstream VI		
	(*Gulfstream 650*)	6291	15.02.18
	N291GA Quantum Air Ltd Jersey		
M-YJET (2)	Dassault Falcon 7X	186	xx.02.15
	M-EDIA (2), F-WWHE		
	M-EDIA Aviation Ltd (Douglas, IOM)		
M-YKBO	Embraer EMB-135BJ Legacy	14501211	30.09.15
	PR-LHZ Transeurope Air Ltd (Douglas, IOM)		
M-YMCM	Bell 429	57107	10.09.13
	C-GTQT, (N4804D), C-GTQT, C-GLZQ		
	T J Morris Ltd Liverpool		
M-YNNS (2)	Gulfstream Aerospace Gulfstream VI		
	(*Gulfstream 650*)	6120	20.10.15
	9H-IKO, N620GD		
	Aviation One Ltd Abu Dhabi, UAE		
M-YOIL	Bombardier BD700-1A10 Global 6000 9637		07.03.16
	C-GZDS Shelf Support Shiphold Ltd (Nicosia, Cyprus)		
M-YRGL (2)	Avions Transport Regional ATR72-212A 733		21.05.13
	VT-DKJ, F-WWEN		
	AFIV Funding (Manx) Ltd (Douglas, IOM)		
M-YSAI	Bombardier BD700-1A11 Global 5000 9166		20.04.10
	N1990C, N166J, C-FCST		
	Capital Investment Worldwide Inc (Tortola, BVI)		
M-YSSF	Bombardier BD700-1A10 Global 6000 9521		14.08.15
	EI-SSF, C-GRTU Springtime Ltd (Douglas, IOM)		
M-YTAF	Beech B36TC Bonanza	EA-595	13.11.12
	ZS-TAF, N1836T FSB Aviation Ltd Lee On Solent		
M-YULI	Airbus A319-115CJ	5040	01.03.19
	VP-CAD, D-AVYK		
	Fourstars Trading Limited (Tortola, BVI)		
M-YVVF	Bombardier BD700-1A10 Global 6000 9590		27.10.14
	C-GWNY Lightstar Aviation Ltd Moscow-Vnukovo, Russia		
M-YWAY (2)	Gulfstream Aerospace Gulfstream IV-SP 1486		15.10.10
	VT-..., M-YWAY, N608PM, N486GA		
	Platinum Jets Co (Georgetown, Cayman Islands)		
M-ZELL	Cessna 208 Caravan	20800526	16.08.11
	N3036A, N52623		
	Ridler Verwaltungs und Vermittlungs GmbH		
	(Munich, Germany)		
M-ZJBT	Dassault Falcon 7X	97	18.12.15
	LX-MES, F-WWZX Thrive Star Global Ltd Beijing, PRC		
M-ZMDZ	Bombardier BD700-1A10 Global Express XRS 9409		24.07.17
	M-DSUN, 9H-ERO, S5-GMG, N368HK, C-GFKH		
	Zhong Jia Global Ltd (Tortola, BVI)		

AIRCRAFT TYPE INDEX (ISLE OF MAN)

Note: This Index covers only entries in that are currently on the Isle of Man Civil Register.

AÉROSPATIALE – see AIRBUS HELICOPTERS

AÉROSPATIALE – ALENIA including AVIONS TRANS REGIONAL
M-ABEF ABFD ABFE ABFI ABKM AMRM YRGL

AGUSTA – see LEONARDO HELICOPTERS

AIRBUS HELICOPTERS including AÉROSPATIALE, EUROCOPTER and EUROCOPTER DEUTSCHLAND production
AS350B3 ECUREUIL
M-ACRO

AS355N ECUREUIL 2
M-EXPL

AS365N DAUPHIN
M-IKEY LVIA

EC130
M-PAPA

EC135 variants
M-ORZE PACF

EC155
M-HELI LIZI XHEC

EC225
M-ABJO ABJP ABJR ABJS ABJT ABJU ABJV ABJW ABKA ABKC ABKD ABKE ABKF ABKG ABKH ABKI ABKJ ABKK

MBB BK-117C-2/D2 (EC145/H145)
M-ALFA LUNA ONDE SOLO

AIRBUS INDUSTRIE
A318 variants
M-HHHH

A319 variants
M-KATE RBUS YULI

A320 variants
M-YBUS

A330 variants
M-ABLK BELR BLGR

A340 variants
M-IABU

AMERICAN-GENERAL AVIATION
AG-5B TIGER
M-PHML

APEX AIRCRAFT
ROBIN DR400/180 REGENT
M-LEKT

AVIONS TRANS REGIONAL – see AÉROSPATIALE–ALENIA

BEECH AIRCRAFT CORPORATION including RAYTHEON AIRCRAFT COMPANY & HAWKER BEECHCRAFT production – see also HAWKER
36 BONANZA
M-YTAF

58 BARON
M-WRLD

90 KING AIR series
M-POWR TSRI

200 KING AIR series
M-CDBM CDJC CDMS CDZT EGGA JACK LENR OTOR SPOR WATJ

B300 KING AIR 350
M-CRAO LLMW SPEC SPEK

390 PREMIER IA
M-FROG

BELL HELICOPTERS
429
M-INOR YMCM

BOEING
727 variants
M-STAR

737 variants
M-LCFC URUS

757 variants
M-RISE

BOMBARDIER INC
BD100 CHALLENGER variants
M-ARRH CLAB DEND EVAN MTOO OCNY SGJS TECH

CL600 CHALLENGER variants
M-AAAA AAAM ABGG ABGS AKAL ALTI ANNA ANTA ARKZ ARUB ASHI ASIM BAEP CLHL DSTZ FRZN HLAN JSTA LILY LOOK MSGG OCOM ODEM OLOT RLIV SEVN SPBM TAKE TOPI TRBS

BD700 GLOBAL variants
M-AABG AATD ABCC AGMA AGMF AHAA ANGO ARGO ARVA ASRI AVIR BIGG BLUE CCCP CITI CVGL DADA DSUN EDZE FINE FLIG GLEX GRAN GSKY HAWK HOME IGWT INER JGVJ JNJL JSMN LLIN LOLA LWSA LWSG MAVP MAXX MBLY MDBD MYNA NAME RRRR RSKL SAMA SAPT SETT SKSM TYRA ULTI UNIS YGJL YOIL YSAI YSSF YVVF ZMDZ

BRITISH AEROSPACE PLC including HAWKER SIDDELEY AVIATION
HS 125 Series 700
M-ALUN

BAe 125 Series 800
M-DSML

BAe 125 Series 1000
M-ACPT

BAe 146 Series (Avro RJ)
M-STRY

CESSNA AIRCRAFT COMPANY including REIMS production
172N SKYHAWK
M-BONO

182RG SKYLANE RG
M-GOLF

206H TURBO STATIONAIR
M-AXIM

208 CARAVAN variants
M-ZELL

425 CONQUEST I
M-MANX

510 CITATION MUSTANG
M-COOL IFFY OUSE USTG

525 CITATIONJET variants
M-AZIA CARA CITY DATA FLYI ICRO MIKE MSVI NTOS OBIL OLLY PMCN RENT SIXT SSYS TBEA

550 CITATION variants
M-KRAF SGCR

560 CITATION ULTRA
M-MEVA

680 CITATION SOVEREIGN/LATITUDE
M-MJLD SVGN

750 CITATION X
M-BEST MOON

DASSAULT AVIATION
FALCON 7X
M-ARVY CELT FALC FALZ GGBL GMKM IAMI LJGI OEPL OUNT REEE RFAP RTFS SCMG SCOT SUNY SURE WANG WING YJET ZJBT

FALCON 8X
M-ATEX PTGG TINK

FALCON 10
M-ECJI GACB

FALCON 20
M-ENTA JETT

FALCON 50 variants
M-CICO

FALCON 900 variants
M-AFAJ AGIK DADI DUBS EAGL GSIR ILTA LANG ODKZ TFFS TSKW VGAL

FALCON 2000 variants
M-AERO CHEM CIMO CKSB FLCN JETZ RONE SFOZ SNER TBUC

DIAMOND AIRCRAFT INDUSTRIES GmbH
DA.42 TWIN STAR
M-BRAB BRAC OUTH

EMBRAER
EMB-135BJ LEGACY
M-AAKV ABEC ALEN ANGA ARDA BIRD CPRS DSCL ILAN JCCA NJSS OLEG PIRA RCCG RCCH SAAN SEXY YKBO

EMB-500/505 PHENOM 100/300
M-ELON KELY KGTS

EMB-545 LEGACY 450
M-DODO

EMB-550 LEGACY 500
M-MDMH ORIS

EUROCOPTER – see AIRBUS HELICOPTERS

GULFSTREAM AEROSPACE CORPORATION
GULFSTREAM 150 (IAI production)
M-FAST GASG

GULFSTREAM 200 (IAI GALAXY)
M-GZOO NICE SASS SBUR

GULFSTREAM 280
M-AYBE ELAS INTY ISTY

GULFSTREAM IV & IV-X (GULFSTREAM 400 & 450)
M-CRDL KBBG KKCO ODEL SOBM TELE WONE YANG YWAY

GULSTREAM V-SP (GULFSTREAM 550)
M-ALAY BJEP FISH FUAD IPHS MNDG RZDC SQAR THOR USBA USIC VRNY

GULFSTREAM VI (GULFSTREAM 650)
M-AAAL ABJL ARDI ATAK BADU BHBH GAGA INSK JCBB JSWB NGNG OVIE PLUS USIK VITB WIND YGIG YGLF YNNS

M

HAWKER including **HAWKER BEECHCRAFT & RAYTHEON** production – see also **BRITISH AEROSPACE PLC**

390 PREMIER 1A
    M-RKAY

400XP
    M-ILLA

800XP & 850XP
    M-ARIE HSXP IRNE URRY VITO

900XP
    M-AREA LION

4000 HORIZON
    M-ALIK

IAI CORPORATION – see **GULFSTREAM**

LEARJET INC including **BOMBARDIER AEROSPACE** production

LEARJET model 35
    M-EASY

LEARJET model 40
    M-DMBP

LEARJET model 45
    M-ABEU ABGV ABJA CSMS MRBB RBIG

LEARJET model 60
    M-INNI

LEONARDO HELICOPTERS including **AGUSTA SpA**

A109 variants
    M-IDAS ISRA OGUL

AW139
    M-AJOR FLSN OLJM SHRM

McDONNELL DOUGLAS

DC9-87 (MD87)
    M-SFAM

PIAGGIO AERO INDUSTRIES

P180 AVANTI
    M-ETAL GCAP GFGC ONTE PIRE

PILATUS AIRCRAFT LTD

PC.12 variants
    M-ALCB ARTY BELL DRIL GETS IFLY IRTH
    JJTL NGSN OLTT PCPC SAIL SAXY YBLS
    YFLY

PIPER AIRCRAFT CORPORATION

PA-42-1000 CHEYENNE 400LS
    M-NLYY

ROBIN – see **APEX**

ROCKWELL INTERNATIONAL CORPORATION

COMMANDER 695A
    M-BETS

SIKORSKY AIRCRAFT

S-76 variants
    M-ABLE AKAR JCBA JCBC ONTY

SOCATA

TBM-700 (TBM-850 & TBM-930)
    M-ATTI DSKY

M

SECTION 6 – GUERNSEY

Information is updated to 1st February 2019.

Aircraft that are listed as current are marked in **bold**. Those that both joined and departed the register in the period since the publication of the 2018 edition of this volume are displayed in roman (non-bold) text and indicated with a star (★).

The type index cross-reference for aircraft on the Guernsey and Jersey registers can be found on page 568.

Regn	Type Previous identity Owner/Cancellation details	C/n Prob Base	Regn date
2-ACED	Boeing 747-4EVERF B-2421 Ace Aviation III Ltd Tel Aviv, Israel	35169	13.04.18
2-ACSA	Boeing 737-8Q8 VP-CCF, TC-TJM, N282AG, C-GDGY, D-AXLF, C-GDGY, D-AXLF, C-GDGY, D-AXLF, G-XLAB, G-OJSW UMB Bank National Association Lourdes, France	28218	18.01.19
2-AERB★	Boeing 777-28E HL7597 Ballymoon Aircraft Solutions Ltd To UR-GOC 04.06.18	28686	01.02.18
2-AERC	Boeing 777-28EER EC-MIA, HL7500 AerCap Ireland Ltd Lourdes, France	28685	04.07.18
2-AKOP	Commander Aircraft Commander 114B 14663 N545DC Micressa Holding Ltd Guernsey		02.10.14
2-ALOU	Sud Aviation SE.3130 Alouette II G-CICS, XR379, (XJ379), F-WIEN Steven Atherton Crabtree Farm, Deighton	1583	20.10.17
2-ANLD	Piper PA-34-220T Seneca V SP-OTA, D-GOMB, N31328 David & Lynette Medcraft Blackbushe	3449325	10.02.17
2-ATLN★	Aérospatiale-Alenia ATR 42-500 XA-TLN, F-WWEC Elix Asset 5 Ltd To 9M- 21.01.19	564	14.05.18
2-ATRA	Aérospatiale-Alenia ATR 72-212A B-22823, F-WWEZ NAC Aviation 29 DAC Monchengladbach, Germany	1318	11.05.18
2-ATRB	Aérospatiale-Alenia ATR 72-212A B-22820, F-WWEU NAC Aviation 29 DAC Monchengladbach, Germany	1222	24.05.18
2-ATRC	Aérospatiale-Alenia ATR 72-212A B-22815, F-WWEV NAC Aviation 29 DAC Monchengladbach, Germany	1133	18.05.18
2-ATRD	Aérospatiale-Alenia ATR 72-212A B-22817, F-WWEJ NAC Aviation 29 DAC Monchengladbach, Germany	1145	29.05.18
2-ATRE	Aérospatiale-Alenia ATR 72-212A B-22818, F-WWEP NAC Aviation 29 DAC Monchengladbach, Germany	1198	29.05.18
2-ATRF	Aérospatiale-Alenia ATR 72-212A B-22821, F-WWEC NAC Aviation 29 DAC Monchengladbach, Germany	1251	18.05.18
2-ATRG	Aérospatiale-Alenia ATR 72-212A B-22822, F-WWEM NAC Aviation 29 DAC Monchengladbach, Germany	1261	24.05.18
2-ATRH★	Aérospatiale-Alenia ATR 72-212A HK-4828, N521NA, B-3022, F-WWED KA1 P/S Parted out 07.11.18	521	09.08.18
2-ATRI★	Aérospatiale-Alenia ATR 72-212A F-WTDC, HK-4863, N550NA, B-3026, F-WWLP KA1 P/S Parted out 26.10.18	552	08.08.18
2-ATRL	Aérospatiale-Alenia ATR 42-600 RP-C4205, F-WTDA, F-WWLN NAC Aviation 27 Ltd –	1210	04.10.18
2-AUER	Cirrus SF50 Vision Euro Aircraft Leasing Ltd –	0014	16.08.17
2-AVCO	Bombardier CL-600-2B19 Challenger 850 7625 N129WF, VP-CPP, C-GNBE, D-ACRP, I-ADJD, C-GJYW Avionco Ltd –		20.10.17
2-AWBN	Piper PA-30-160 Twin Comanche G-AWBN, N8517Y Bravo November Ltd Jersey	30-1472	18.06.16

Regn	Type Previous identity Owner/Cancellation details	C/n Prob Base	Regn date
2-AZFR	Cessna 401B N60FR, G-AZFR, N7981Q Robert Edgar Harding Wragg Guernsey	401B-0121	15.04.15
2-BASG	Boeing 737-73W BBJ VP-BOP, N449BJ Business Aviation Services Guernsey Ltd –	40117	18.09.17
2-BEST	Commander Aircraft Commander 114B 14636 G-HMBJ, N6036F David Best Guernsey		21.11.14
2-BHXG	Airbus A340-313 B-HXG, F-WWJC Aerfin Ltd Lourdes, France	208	15.06.17
2-BLUE	Bombardier CL-600-2B16 Challenger 601-3A 5129 VP-CRR, N129TF, (N603AГ), N129RH, C-GLXH Sable Air ApS Oxford		13.02.17
2-BOYS	Commander Aircraft Commander 114B 14609 N6024V Iain Barker Guernsey		02.05.14
2-BREM	MBB Bolkow BO.105DBS-5 G-EYNL, LN-OTJ, D-HDLR, EC-DSO, D-HDLR Wessex Aviation Ltd Biggin Hill	S.382	17.12.15
2-BYDF	Sikorsky S-76A+ G-BYDF, JA6615 Brecqhou Development Company Brecqhou	760364	30.06.14
2-CARQ★	Boeing 737-33R CC-ARQ, CX-OAB, UR-GAQ, SX-BLA, N964WP Aergo Trading Ltd To ZS- 05.09.18	28869	25.05.18
2-CAUL★	Bombardier DHC-8-402Q C9-AUL, LN-RDC, (SE-LRD), (OY-KCD), C-FDHW AeroCentury Corp Parted out 10.01.19	4019	16.01.18
2-CAUY	Bombardier DHC-8-402Q C9-AUY, G-ECOW, LN-RDF, (SE-LRF), C-FDHZ AeroCentury Corp Maastricht, Netherlands	4021	27.11.17
2-CAVL★	Boeing 737-36N CC-AVL, CX-OAA, UR-GAN, F-GRFC Aergo Trading Ltd To ZS- 05.09.18	28569	25.05.18
2-CETH★	Airbus A321-231 TC-ETH, TC-IEF, G-MIDH, D-AVZX AerCap Holdings NV To TC-OEB 29.03.18	0968	xx.02.18
2-CETJ★	Airbus A321-231 TC-ETJ, TC-IEG, G-MIDI, D-AVZA AerCap Holdings NV To TC-OEC 29.03.18	0974	xx.02.18
2-CFFV	Bombardier CL-600-2B19 CRJ-200ER 8050 JA207J, C-FFVJ Regional One Inc –		29.01.18
2-CFFX	Bombardier CL-600-2B19 CRJ-200ER 8059 JA208J Regional One Inc –		01.03.18
2-CFFZ	Bombardier CL-600-2B19 CRJ-200ER 8062 JA209J, C-FMNQ Regional One Inc Ljubljana, Slovenia		06.03.18
2-CFML	Bombardier CL-600-2B19 CRJ-200ER 7767 JA205J, C-FMLB Regional One Inc Ljubljana, Slovenia		04.10.17
2-CHEZ	Piper PA-28-161 Warrior II N123DU, G-BPDU, N5672V Fletcher Aviation Ltd Guernsey	28-7716195	24.07.14
2-CLEV	Cessna 525A CitationJet CJ2 N525DT, N132CJ, N5148N Clevewood Aviation Ltd –	525A0003	23.05.18
2-COOK	Piper PA-46-500TP Malibu Meridian N526AG William Cook Aviation –	4697562	19.09.18

2-CRBU★	Bombardier CL-600-2B16 Challenger 604 5481		17.07.18
	JY-GRP, M-AAAD, HZ-TFM, M-AAAD, JY-AAD,		
	N198DC, N481KW, C-GLYA Caribou Holdings Ltd		
	To N5481T 26.11.18		
2-CREW	Cessna 208B Grand Caravan 208B2148		05.09.17
	OO-PZG, F-HOBI, (D-FLYE) ASL NV –		
2-DARE	Pilatus PC-12/47E 1465		25.07.17
	N154WA, HB-FRK Brightling Services Ltd –		
2-DCBU	Aérospatiale-Alenia ATR 72-212A 755		20.04.17
	D4-CBU, F-WWEP		
	Elix Assets 14 Ltd Sonderborg, Denmark		
2-DEER	Boeing 787-8 BBJ 35309		04.08.16
	N28MS, N1006K Ocean Transportation Facility		
	Investment Ltd Hong Kong, PRC		
2-DITO	Piper PA-46-500TP Malibu Meridian 4697244		18.07.14
	N419GR, N219GR, N210MA, N3128S		
	Citavia BV Lelystad, Netherlands		
2-DLOO	Tecnam P.2006T MMA 097		12.06.18
	T7-NVH, OE-FMG White Arrow Associates Ltd –		
2-DOLU	Beech 58 Baron TH-1440		28.02.14
	G-BLKY Roger Allen Perrot Guernsey		
2-EACA	Aérospatiale-Alenia ATR 72-212A 527		27.06.17
	M-DMLM, B-22803, F-WWLC		
	Elix Assets 7 Ltd Sonderborg, Denmark		
2-EALA	Airbus A340-642 1040		08.05.18
	A6-EHL, F-WWCH		
	European Aviation Ltd Bournemouth		
2-EALB	Airbus A340-642 837		31.05.18
	A6-EHF, F-WWCB		
	European Aviation Ltd Bournemouth		
2-EALD	Airbus A340-642 870		12.09.18
	A6-EHH, F-WWCK		
	European Aviation Ltd Teruel, Spain		
2-EALF	Airbus A340-642 829		26.11.18
	A6-EHE, F-WWCG		
	European Aviation Ltd Teruel, Spain		
2-EALG	Airbus A340-541 783		24.09.18
	A6-EHD, F-WWTY		
	European Aviation Ltd Teruel, Spain		
2-EGJB	Cirrus SR22 4179		08.11.18
	N264MC – Guernsey		
2-ELIX★	Bombardier DHC-8-311 234		30.08.18
	N326EN, N386DC, D-BOBA, C-GDNG Elix Asset 2 Ltd		
	To 5Y- 08.10.18		
2-ELIX	Bombardier DHC-8-202 506		31.01.19
	N358PH, C-FWBB		
	Elix Assets 7 Ltd Toronto Pearson, Canada		
2-EPIC	Gulfstream Aerospace Gulfstream 650ER 6286		02.05.18
	N686GD Business Aviation Services Guernsey Ltd –		
2-ESKA	Boeing 737-301BDSF 23512		30.06.17
	N126WF, EC-LJI, OO-TNI, N94417, OO-TNI, N558AU,		
	N343US, N323P European Aviation Ltd Bournemouth		
2-EUNF	Boeing 767-3P6ER 26238		16.03.18
	EI-UNF, A4O-GT		
	Marey Aviation Ltd Shanghai Pudong, PRC		
2-FIEX	Airbus A340-642 933		25.01.18
	A6-EHJ, F-WWCF		
	European Aviation Ltd Bournemouth		
2-FIFI	Piper PA-46-500TP Malibu Meridian 4697090		11.06.15
	N46WK, SE-LTM, N189DB, N46WK, N5343C		
	Springhaven Ltd Jersey		
2-FINA★	Embraer ERJ-170-100LR 17000121		22.01.18
	HZ-AEE, PT-SDJ AerFin Ltd		
	Parted out 02.01.19		
2-FINB★	Embraer ERJ-170-100LR 17000108		21.03.18
	HZ-AEA, PT-SAQ AerFin Ltd		
	Parted out 03.12.18		
2-FINC	Embraer ERJ-170-100LR 17000123		07.02.18
	HZ-AEF, PT-SDM AerFin Ltd Naples, Italy		
2-FIND★	Embraer ERJ-170-100LR 17000114		07.02.18
	HZ-AEB, PT-SAZ AerFin Ltd		
	Parted out 03.12.18		

2-FINE★	Embraer ERJ-170-100LR 17000119		04.05.18
	HZ-AED, PT-SDG AerFin Ltd		
	Parted out 02.01.19		
2-FINF	Embraer ERJ-170-100LR 17000152		04.05.18
	HZ-AEL, PT-SEQ AerFin Ltd Norwich		
2-FING	Embraer ERJ-170-100LR 17000155		15.05.18
	HZ-AEM, PT-SES AerFin Ltd Norwich		
2-FINI	Embraer ERJ-170-100LR 17000142		05.06.18
	HZ-AEI, PT-SEG AerFin Ltd Norwich		
2-FINJ	Embraer ERJ-170-100LR 17000124		05.06.18
	HZ-AEG, PT-SDN AerFin Ltd Norwich		
2-FIXP	Airbus A340-642 1030		25.01.18
	A6-EHK, F-WWCX		
	European Aviation Ltd Bournemouth		
2-FLYE	Aérospatiale-Alenia ATR 42-320 378		24.05.17
	G-ISLJ, HR-AXN, N378NA, PJ-XLM, PH-XLM,		
	F-OHFE, F-WWLA Airtrails Leasing 1 GmbH –		
2-FLYT	Pilatus PC-12/47 802		25.01.19
	N425DK, N802EK, N802AF		
	Anatino Aviation Ltd (Isle of Man) –		
2-FLYY	Pilatus PC-12/47E 1658		27.10.16
	HB-FSY Mete Ozmerter –		
2-FPLF	Beech B350 Super King Air FL-744		14.07.16
	VQ-BNO, D-CCIS, N6444J		
	Miralty Holdings Ltd Guernsey		
2-GAFO	Agusta A109A II 7308		05.11.18
	2-LIFT, N30MD, N212AT, N109AG GFO Capital Ltd –		
2-GAZL★	Aérospatiale SA.341G Gazelle 1073		24.05.18
	G-EZEL, (F-GIVQ), I-ATOM, F-BXPG, G-BAZL		
	The Gazelle Squadron Display Team Ltd		
	To RA-	04.01.19	
2-GECB	Sikorsky S-76C++ 760691		11.04.17
	HS-HTT, C-FRSA, 9M-AIS, C-FRSA, N2582E		
	Wilmington Trust SP Services Ltd –		
2-GECC	Sikorsky S-76C++ 760693		11.04.17
	HS-HTL, 9M-AIP, C-FRSE, N2580P		
	Wilmington Trust SP Services Ltd –		
2-GECD	Sikorsky S-76C+ 760519		18.07.18
	PK-FUS, 9M-HLK, N101MM		
	GECAS Australia Pty Ltd –		
2-GEWQ★	Bombardier DHC-8-202 456		27.11.18
	5Y-WJF, N456YV, C-GFOD TCFI AL5 LLC		
	To N997MG 11.12.18		
2-GIAR	Bombardier CL-600-2B19 CRJ-200ER 7211		30.09.16
	N888AU, N624BR Rusline Aircraft Leasing Ltd –		
2-GJJA	Gulfstream Aerospace Gulfstream 650ER 6306		28.12.18
	N650ER, N306GA Gain Jet Ireland Ltd –		
2-GJSB	Aérospatiale-Alenia ATR 42-500 576		24.02.16
	A4O-AT, VT-ADN, A4O-AT, F-WWFP		
	Flair Aviation GmbH Monchengladbach, Germany		
2-GNSY	Commander Aircraft Commander 114B 14679		02.12.15
	N48CK, N850DW John Tostevin Guernsey		
2-GODS	Cirrus SR22T 1070		01.11.17
	2-GODD, N170TN Jetworx LtdMOxford		
2-GOLD	Piper PA-28-235 Cherokee F 28-7210009		26.10.18
	ZS-DAM – –		
2-GOLF	Cessna 525A CitationJet CJ2+ 525A0446		08.11.16
	N446TA, N446CJ, N2067E, N5068F MTEAM Ltd –		
2-GPIA	Aérospatiale-Alenia ATR 72-212A 706		21.01.19
	I-ADLK, F-WWEF GPFC Ireland Ltd Francazal, France		
2-GPIB	Aérospatiale-Alenia ATR 72-212A 707		21.01.19
	I-ADLW, F-WWEG GPFC Ireland Ltd Francazal, France		
2-GRND★	Agusta AW109SP Grand New 22237		xx.xx.18
	UR-GDF –		
	To G-GNMM 30.10.18		
2-GSYJ	Diamond DA.42 Twin Star 42.135		15.04.15
	G-GSYJ, OE-VPI Crosby Aviation Ltd Jersey		
2-GULF	Gulfstream Aerospace Gulfstream IVSP 1224		28.06.16
	2-TRAV, M-IVSP, C-GEIV, N124TS, N18TD, N18TM,		
	N454GA Travcorp Transportation Ltd		
	(Douglas, IOM)		

2-GZEH★	Airbus A319-111	2184		12.01.18
	G-EZEH, HB-JZF, G-EZEH, D-AVWO			
	SAP Meridian 7 LP			
	To G-EZEH 30.05.18			
2-GZEN★	Airbus A319-111	2245		12.02.18
	G-EZEN, HB-JZI, G-EZEN, D-AVYH			
	SAP Meridian 2245 LP			
	To G-EZEN 14.05.18			
2-HAUL	Boeing 737-3Y0QC	24255		19.12.16
	EI-CFQ, OY-JTH, OO-TNG, N255CF, G-STRB,			
	G-OBWX, SE-DUS, HB-IID, EI-CFQ, XA-RJP, G-MONL			
	European Aviation Ltd	Bournemouth		
2-HAWK	Sud Aviation SA.318C Alouette Astazou	2068		01.06.18
	HA-WKY, HA-RRY, A-68, OL-A68			
	Europlane Sales Ltd	Soper's Farm, Ashurst		
	For sale			
2-HELO	Agusta A109C	7630		08.04.16
	ZS-HJD, N502ZH, S7-NEL, G-ONEL, G-JBEK, VH-LUI,			
	M38-06	Helicopter (Seychelles) Ltd –		
2-HERM	Diamond DA.62 Twin Star	62.103		01.08.18
	– –			
2-HOVA	Agusta-Bell 206B-2 Jet Ranger II	8556		01.02.18
	G-PRFI, G-CPTS Topex Ltd Gloucestershire			
2-JACK	Piper PA-46-500TP Malibu Meridian	4697425		21.07.17
	2-RICH, M-OOSE, N6103Z Icaris Ventura SA –			
2-JBMF	Embraer EMB-500 Phenom 100	50000250		28.11.17
	N861CB, 4L-ALF, UR-ALB, PT-TJK JBFeggair ApS –			
2-JEFS	Piper PA-32R-301T Turbo Saratoga SP	3229003		08.12.16
	N9123X Jeff Barnett Gloucestershire			
2-JEZA	Eclipse EA500	000031		30.01.19
	N531EA Eclipse 2018 LLP –			
2-JFJC	Bombardier BD-700-1A10 Global Express	9094		01.12.16
	G-SENT, EC-KJH, A6-EJB, OY-GLA, ZS-DLJ, (ZS-DAJ),			
	C-GIOX Shanbeth Ltd Partnership Oxford			
2-JSEG	Eclipse EA500	000144		02.11.16
	N90NE, N545MA Truly Classic LP Inc Guernsey			
2-KOOL	Piper PA-28-181 Archer II	28-8690036		09.12.13
	G-JCAS, N9093N, (N170AV), N9648N			
	Charlie Alpha Ltd Jersey			
2-KYCM	Gulfstream Aerospace Gulfstream 650ER	6290		02.08.18
	N290GA Business Aviation Services Guernsey Ltd –			
2-LAND	Commander Aircraft Commander 114B	14662		07.09.15
	N6088Z, N6088F 88 Zulu Ltd Guernsey			
2-LCXO	British Aerospace Jetstream 3102	772		19.05.17
	G-LNKS, G-JURA, SE-LDH, OY-SVK, C-FAMJ,			
	G-31-772 Jonathan Ibbotson Oxford			
2-LFEA	Aérospatiale-Alenia ATR 42-500	621		24.11.16
	HK-4949, F-OIQB, F-WWLB, F-WWEE			
	Phoenix Aircraft Leasing PTE Ltd Francazal, France			
2-LIFE	Eclipse EA500	000023		18.12.15
	N223TE, N130DJ, (N223TE), N130DJ Briigitte Vonk –			
2-LIVE	Pilatus PC-12/47E	1486		14.06.17
	SP-NAP, HB-FSH Stammair Guernsey Guernsey			
2-LOLA	Beech A36 Bonanza	E-2116		27.09.18
	G-LOLA, N67501 Lima Alfa Ltd Guernsey			
2-LOUD	Sud Aviation SA.318C Alouette Astazou	2138		11.12.18
	HA-WKZ, A-79, OL-A79 – –			
2-LOVE	Beech A36 Bonanza	E-854		21.11.14
	D-EWUI, HB-EWU Jessica Noakes Guernsey			
2-MAPP	Cessna 421C Golden Eagle	421C0142		07.06.16
	N454BS MBA Aviation Ltd –			
2-MAPZ	Beech C90A King Air	LJ-1236		28.05.18
	UP-K9001, UN-K9001, OE-FMG, D-IPEL, N5598L			
	Zeusch Aviation BV Lelystad, Netherlands			
2-MATO	Bombardier CL-600-2B16 Challenger 601-3A	5114		19.10.15
	VP-BOA, VR-BOA, C-FOSK, C-GLYA			
	Volare Aviation Ltd Oxford			
2-META★	Bombardier DHC-8-311	340		16.11.18
	N343EN, OE-LLZ, N473AW, C-GLOT Elix 2 Asset 2 Ltd			
	To 5Y- 03.12.18			

2-MFID	Aérospatiale-Alenia ATR 72-212A	1178		07.09.18
	9M-FID, F-WWES			
	NAC Aviation 30 Ltd Sonderborg, Denmark			
2-MFIF	Aérospatiale-Alenia ATR 72-212A	1259		30.07.18
	9M-FIF, F-WWEK			
	NAC Aviation 29 DAC Monchengladbach, Germany			
2-MFIG	Aérospatiale-Alenia ATR 72-212A	1262		19.11.18
	9M-FIG, F-WWEN			
	NAC Aviation 30 Ltd Monchengladbach, Germany			
2-MIKE	Commander Aircraft Commander 114B	14676		17.04.14
	N6048B Michael Alfred Perry Guernsey			
2-MMTT	Boeing 727-76	19254		01.11.16
	M-FAHD, VP-BAB, N682G, N10XY, N8043B, VH-TJD,			
	(N8043B), VH-TJD Platinum Services Ltd Cotswold			
2-MMYD	Aérospatiale-Alenia ATR 72-212A	1107		20.00.18
	9M-MYD, F-WWED			
	NAC Aviation 30 Ltd Billund, Denmark			
2-MNBV★	Airbus A321-231	0915		xx.xx.18
	B-2371, D-AVZM China Aircraft Leasing Company			
	Parted out 28.11.18			
2-MOVE	Boeing 737-382QC	24364		23.02.17
	N596BC, OY-JTF, OK-GCG, F-GIXG, F-OGSX, CS-TIA			
	European Aviation Ltd Bournemouth			
2-MSCC★	Boeing 737-8H6	40145		xx.02.18
	9M-MSC ORIX Aviation			
	To N830BC 27.03.18			
2-MSDD★	Boeing 737-8H6	40146		26.03.18
	9M-MSD ORIX Aviation			
	To N832BC 19.04.18			
2-MSII	Boeing 737-8H6	40151		17.04.18
	9M-MSI SL Echo Ltd & Greip Leasing Co Inc			
	Marana, AZ			
2-MSJJ★	Boeing 737-8H6	40152		xx.02.18
	9M-MSJ ORIX Aviation			
	To N834BC 29.03.18			
2-MSTG	Cessna 510 Citation Mustang	510-0295		02.11.16
	N246RE, C-FSTX Mustang Sally Aviation Ltd –			
2-MUST	Cessna 510 Citation Mustang	510-0213		09.06.16
	N59LW William Francis McSweeney North Weald			
2-NICE	Bombardier CL-600-2B16 Challenger 604	5505		28.02.18
	N664D, G-OCSC, (D-ARTE), N655TS, VP-BHS, N505JD,			
	C-GLYK Beem Holdings Ltd –			
2-NNPK	Gulfstream Aerospace Gulfstream IV	1143		28.01.19
	N143PK, HZ-AFX, N410GA Jet Midwest Group LLC –			
2-NOOR	Commander Aircraft Commander 114B	14656		29.04.15
	G-NOOR, N142A As-Al Ltd Zell am See, Austria			
2-NOVA	Beech 95-B55 Baron	TC-1272		21.07.17
	F-HLEG, HB-GEC Novatrust Agency SRL Dunkeswell			
2-NYAW	Dassault Falcon 50	213		08.12.16
	N991LB, XA-RVV, N295FJ, F-WWHW H2M –			
2-OCST	Agusta-Bell 206B-3 Jet Ranger III	8694		29.10.15
	G-OCST, N39AH, VR-CDG, G-BMKM			
	Lift West Ltd Sparkford			
2-ODAY	Bombardier CL-600-2B16 Challenger 601-3A	5023		18.10.16
	2-JFJC, G-JFJC, D-AAMA, N623CW, N175ST, N601CJ,			
	EI-LJG, N608CC, (EI-BXN), N608CC, C-GLYO			
	Pixwood Ltd Partnership –			
2-OFUS	Cirrus SR22-GTS	1367		09.12.13
	N352CD Lawrence John Murray Guernsey			
2-OWLC	Piper PA-31 Turbo Navajo	31-679		09.06.16
	G-OWLC, G-AYFZ, N6771L			
	Channel Airways Ltd Guernsey			
2-PAOH	Airbus A330-203	811		12.10.18
	AP-BMI, 2-PAOH, PH-AOH, F-WWYH			
	Klaatu Aircraft Leasing Ltd Lourdes, France			
2-PAOK	Airbus A330-203	834		06.11.18
	AP-BMK, 2-PAOK, PH-AOK, F-WWKZ			
	Metal 2017-1 Leasing XV Ltd Istanbul, Turkey			
2-PCBS	Bombardier CL-600-2B16 Challenger 601-3A	5044		06.04.18
	VP-CBS, VP-CMC, VR-CMC, N901BM, I-NNUS,			
	C-FFBY, C-GLYK Volare Aviation Ltd Oxford			

2 and ZJ

2-PDPD	Agusta-Bell 206B-3 Jet Ranger III 8690		05.10.17
	G-PSHR, LN-OYE, G-PSHR, G-HSLB, F-GUJR,		
	SX-HEN, F-GRCY, I-ELEP Pink Time Ltd –		
2-PETE	Piper PA-32-300 Cherokee Six 32-7940242		29.12.17
	N2967N Peter Biggins Guernsey		
2-PJBA	Aérospatiale SA.341G Gazelle 1392		20.10.17
	HA-PJB, YU-PJB, G-BZLA, N2TV, N49534		
	Steven Atherton Crabtree Farm, Deighton		
2-PKSA	Aérospatiale-Alenia ATR 72-212A 1080		30.11.18
	PK-KSA, F-WWEQ		
	NAC Aviation 8 Ltd Seletar, Singapore		
2-PKSG	Aérospatiale-Alenia ATR 72-212A 1286		18.12.17
	PK-KSG, F-WWEP		
	NAC Aviation 8 Ltd Seletar, Singapore		
2-PKSU	Aérospatiale-Alenia ATR 72-212A 1108		30.11.18
	PK-KSU, F-WWEU		
	NAC Aviation 8 Ltd Seletar, Singapore		
2-PLAY	SOCATA TBM-700C1 302		09.12.13
	N700GY, D-FBFT N700 VB Ltd Guernsey		
2-POSH	Cessna 525B CitationJet CJ3 525B0156		21.12.17
	F-GVUJ, N5145V Danish Aircraft Management ApS –		
2-PROP	Beech 58 Baron TH-893		29.03.17
	N23659 Lawrence Moore Guernsey		
2-PSFI	Boeing 737-33A 23631		24.01.18
	G-CKTI, OY-JTA, N371FA, N172AW, (N3282R)		
	European Aviation Ltd Lasham		
2-RACE	Commander Aircraft Commander 114B 14603		02.10.14
	N6022C Michael Alfred Perry (Guernsey)		
	For Rebuild		
2-RBTS	Cessna 525B CitationJet CJ3+ 525B0537		29.03.18
	2-RBTS Ltd –		
2-RIOH	Navion H Rangemaster NAV-4-2548		26.05.15
	2-RICH, N2548T, (D-EINH)		
	Catherine Hayley Upchurch Dunkeswell		
2-RLAD	Embraer EMB-145LI 145755		09.07.15
	B-3061, PT-SNA Komiaviatrans Alverca, Portugal		
2-RLAS	Boeing 777-31H 29062		23.08.17
	A6-EMM SASOF III (B) Aviation Ireland DAC		
	Teruel, Spain		
2-RLAV	Airbus A340-541 694		22.02.18
	F-WXAA, A6-ERJ, F-WWTQ		
	Global Airways Ltd Lourdes, France		
2-RLAW	Airbus A340-541 611		09.04.18
	F-WHUF, A6-ERH, F-WWTY		
	Global Airways Ltd Lourdes, France		
2-RLAX	Airbus A330-223 943		23.08.18
	VN-A376, EI-ELI, EC-KUO, F-WWYM		
	UMB Bank National Association Lourdes, France		
2-RLAY	Airbus A330-223 962		22.10.18
	VN-A377, EI-ELJ, EC-KVS, F-WWYG		
	UMB Bank National Association Lourdes, France		
2-RLAZ	Airbus A330-203 819		12.11.18
	AP-BMJ, 2-PAOI, PH-AOI, F-WWYR		
	SASOF III (A14) Aviation Ireland DAC Istanbul, Turkey		
2-RLBA	Airbus A330-203 900		12.11.18
	AP-BML, 2-PAOL, PH-AOL, F-WWKP		
	SASOF IV (A3) Aviation Ireland DAC Lourdes, France		
2-RLBB	Boeing 737-7Q8 28210		05.10.18
	YL-PSF, OY-PSF, TF-JXG, TF-NBA, OY-MRS, EI-DZD,		
	5T-CLK, N801LF, LV-YYC, N801LF, HB-III, N5573P		
	SASOF IV (A3) Aviation Ireland DAC Chania, Greece		
2-RLBC	Airbus A340-541 520		07.11.18
	F-WHUJ, A6-ERD, F-WWTS		
	Global Airways Ltd Lourdes, France		
2-RLBD	Boeing 737-85F 30007		10.12.18
	LV-GWL, 9M-FFD, ZS-SJI, N1787B		
	UMB Bank National Association Francazal, France		
2-RLBG	Aérospatiale-Alenia ATR 42-500 643		22.11.18
	ZS-AFR, OH-ATB, F-WWLA		
	Metal 2017-1 Leasing XI Ltd –		
2-RNWL	Cessna 525 Citation M2 525-0980		29.03.18
	Norbert Blue Skies Ltd –		

2-ROCK	Cirrus SR22 1313		18.07.14
	N123DB Fletcher Aviation Ltd Guernsey		
2-ROBQ★	Airbus A320-251N 7918		xx.12.18
	PR-OBQ, F-WXAK, F-WWIH –		
	To PR-YYB 10.01.19		
2-ROBR★	Airbus A320-251N 8086		xx.12.18
	PR-OBR, F-WXAL, F-WWDH –		
	To PR-YYA 10.01.19		
2-RODS	Cessna 310Q 310Q0041		14.02.17
	N850KF, G-XLKF, G-BMMC, YU-BGY, N7541Q		
	Formalhaut Ltd Jersey		
2-ROKK	Saab 2000 2000-023		31.08.18
	G-CFLV, SE-023, LY-SBD, F-GTSD, D-ADSD, SE-023		
	Rockton Aviation AB Orebro, Sweden		
2-RORO	Cirrus SR22T 0701		01.08.18
	OK-OKP, N45AH Transport Safety Resolutions Ltd –		
2-ROSE	Airbus A320-232 2016		22.11.18
	SP-HAD, XU-710, SP-HAD, XU-710, P4-SAS,		
	SX-BVC, F-WWBS		
	Rockrose Aircraft Holding AB Francazal, France		
2-RPDA★	Aérospatiale-Alenia ATR 72-212A 1022		23.01.18
	PR-PDA, F-WWEW NAC Aviation 29 Ltd		
	To EC-NBG 14.12.18		
2-RPDC★	Aérospatiale-Alenia ATR 72-212A 1040		25.01.18
	PR-PDC, F-WWEC NAC Aviation 29 Ltd		
	To EC-NCC 16.01.19		
2-RPDI	Aérospatiale-Alenia ATR 72-212A 1059		16.04.18
	PR-PDI, F-WWED		
	NAC Aviation 27 Ltd Francazal, France		
2-SAIL	Agusta-Bell 206B-2 Jet Ranger II 8440		07.07.17
	G-OYST, G-JIMW, G-UNIK, G-TPPH, G-BCYP		
	Leo Ernest Vaughan Knifton Peldon		
2-SALA	Piper PA-32-300 Cherokee Six 32-7940106		13.04.16
	G-SALA, (G-BHEJ), N2184Z Sala Aviation Ltd Jersey		
2-SALE	Diamond DA.62 Twin Star 62.069		28.09.17
	Morson Group Ltd Gamston		
2-SEVN	Boeing 727-281A 21474		15.09.17
	N724YS, N240RC, HL7357, JA8355		
	TAG Aviation (Stansted) Ltd Lasham		
2-SEXY	Agusta A109E Power 11010		18.07.17
	ZS-RJD Volare Aviation Ltd Oxford		
2-SGSG	Boeing 737-7H6 BBJ 29274		16.05.18
	M53-01, 9M-BBJ, N6055X, N1785B, N1787B		
	Kuwait International Company –		
2-SLZK	Bombardier BD-700-1A10 Global Express XRS 9250		20.03.18
	M-BTAR, D-AKAZ, C-FMGK		
	Minsheng Jiatal Leasing Ltd –		
2-SMKM	Cirrus SR20 1662		18.03.16
	M-SMKM, G-SMKM, N50910 Keith Mallet Jersey		
2-SOAR	Sud Aviation SA.318C Alouette Astazou 2204		06.12.18
	HA-WKS, PK-DAD, N9707 – –		
2-STEV	Sud Aviation SE.3130 Alouette II 1388		03.07.18
	HA-IDL, 75+48, QW+233, OW+738, PA+139, PG+137,		
	F-WWEI –		
2-STRW	Boeing 757-2Q8 30045		17.04.18
	D4-CBP, N301AM		
	Wilmington Trust SP Services Ltd Goodyear, AZ		
2-SWKE	Aérospatiale-Alenia ATR 72-212A 767		01.05.17
	VT-CMA, M-IBAI, VT-KAN, F-WWEF		
	Elix Assets 12 Ltd –		
2-TAXI	Piper PA-34-200T Seneca II 34-8070003		16.11.16
	D-GAIR, N81008 Anton Murashov Guernsey		
2-TBGT	SOCATA TB-20 Trinidad GT 2027		13.03.18
	G-TBGT, F-OILF Leonard William Shepard –		
2-TBMI	SOCATA TBM-930 1182		13.06.17
	TBM Aviation Ltd Southend		
2-TGHA	Embraer EMB-145LI 14500848		02.12.15
	B-3050, PT-SOB Alphastream Ltd Alverca, Portugal		
2-TGHB	Embraer EMB-145LI 14500882		02.12.15
	B-3053, PT-SOC Alphastream Ltd Alverca, Portugal		
2-TGHC	Embraer EMB-145LI 14500839		17.12.15
	B-3049, PT-SOA Alphastream Ltd Alverca, Portugal		

2 and ZJ

Regn	Type / Previous identity	C/n	Regn date
2-TGHD	Embraer EMB-145LI	14500898	17.12.15
	B-3051, PT-SOD Alphastream Ltd Alverca, Portugal		
2-TGHE	Embraer EMB-145LI	14500928	05.04.16
	B-3056 Alphastream Ltd Alverca, Portugal		
2-TGHF	Embraer EMB-145LI	14500921	04.05.16
	B-3055 Alphastream Ltd Alverca, Portugal		
2-TGHG	Embraer EMB-145LI	14500932	29.09.16
	B-3057 Alphastream Ltd Alverca, Portugal		
2-TGHH	Embraer EMB-145LI	14500958	07.11.16
	B-3058 Alphastream Ltd Alverca, Portugal		
2-TGHI	Embraer EMB-145LI	14500949	07.11.16
	B-3058 Alphastream Ltd Alverca, Portugal		
2-TRAV	Gulfstream Aerospace Gulfstream G550 5452		28.05.16
	M-TRAV, N8JK, N352GA		
	Travcorp Air Transportation 2 Ltd (Douglas, IOM)		
2-TRVL	Bombardier CL-600-2B16 Challenger 650 6128		07.01.19
	C-FAQD Volare Aviation Guernsey Ltd –		
2-TSSA	Boeing 767-238ER	23896	13.06.18
	N2767, N772WD, VH-EAQ, N6009F Weststar Ltd –		
2-VAZV	Embraer EMB-135BJ Legacy	145516	14.12.18
	N976LR, PK-OME, PT-SAG Vivancon Holding Ltd –		
2-VSLJ★	Airbus A320-233	3570	07.06.18
	9V-SLJ, F-WWBD Crimson Sunbird Leasing 3570 DAC		
	To TC-ODC 11.09.18		
2-WESX	Westland Wessex HC.Mk.2	WA/624	07.08.18
	9G-AEL, 9G-BOB, G-HANA, XV729 – Biggin Hill		
2-WILD	Aérospatiale SA.342J Gazelle	1695	07.07.17
	D-HOPP Xavier de Tracy –		
2-WMAN	Aérospatiale SA.341G Gazelle	1277	20.10.17
	HA-LFJ, YU-MAN, G-WMAN, ZS-HUR, N4491L,		
	YV-54CP James Wightman –		
2-WOOD	Cessna 550 Citation Bravo	550-1042	28.04.17
	M-WOOD, G-OJMW, G-ORDB, N51869		
	Horizon Air LLP Gloucestershire		
2-WORK	Boeing 737-3L9	23718	23.03.17
	N127WF, OY-JTC, 9M-AAB, LZ-BOJ, N377PA,		
	N718CT, OO-CTX, N2371, PH-OZA, 9H-ADP,		
	PH-OZA, G-BOZA, PH-OZA, G-BOZA, OY-MMN		
	European Aviation Ltd Lasham		
2-XAJV★	Aérospatiale-Alenia ATR 72-212A	1229	07.05.18
	XY-AJV, F-WWED Billund Leasing XI Ltd		
	To PK- 20.12.18		
2-YULL	Piper PA-28R-201 Arrow	2844118	20.05.14
	OH-ARW, G-FROS, D-EGXC, N3117A		
	George Watkinson-Yull Guernsey		
2-ZERO	Cirrus SR22T	0189	07.02.18
	PH-PVR, N103NL Daniel Lee –		
2-ZEUZ	Beech C90A King Air	LJ-1164	26.10.18
	F-WTDE, N104AJ, ZS-MIL, N3079Z		
	Zeusch Aviation BV Lelystad, Netherlands		
2-ZOOM	Commander Aircraft Commander 114B 14635		21.09.16
	2-ADEL, N6095A Michael Aves Guernsey		
2-ZXCA★	Bombardier CL-600-2B19 CRJ-200PF 7452		xx.xx.18
	N452RH, JA201J, C-FMND –		
	To ES-LCA 19.07.18		

SECTION 7 – JERSEY

Information is updated to 16th June 2016.

The type index cross-reference for aircraft on the Guernsey and Jersey registers can be found on page 598.

Regn	Type / Previous identity	C/n	Regn date
	Owner/Cancellation details		Prob Base
ZJ-HLH	Eurocopter EC135 P2	0193	16.06.16
	ZK-HLH, N903CM Gama Aviation Ltd –		
ZJ-THC	Cessna 525C CitationJet 4	525C-0200	11.11.15
	N5135A Tower House Consultants Ltd Jersey		

AIRCRAFT TYPE INDEX (GUERNSEY and JERSEY)

Note: This Index covers only entries in that are currently on the Guernsey and Jersey Civil Registers.

**AÉROSPATIALE – ALENIA including
AVIONS TRANS REGIONAL**

ATR.42 variants
  2-ATRL 2-FLYE 2-GJSB 2-LFEA 2-RLBG

ATR.72 variants
  2-ATRA 2-ATRB 2-ATRC 2-ATRD 2-ATRE
  2-ATRF 2-ATRG 2-DCBU 2-EACA 2-GPIA
  2-GPIB 2-MFID 2-MFIF 2-MFIG 2-MMYD
  2-PKSA 2-PKSG 2-PKSU 2-RPDI 2-SWKE

**AGUSTA – see LEONARDO
HELICOPTERS**

**AIRBUS SAS including AIRBUS
INDUSTRIE**

A320 variants
  2-RAJB 2-ROSE 2-YVEM

A330 variants
  2-PAOH 2-PAOK 2-RLAX 2-RLAY 2-RLAZ
  2-RLBA

A340 variants
  2-BHXG 2-EALA 2-EALB 2-EALD 2-EALF
  2-EALG 2-FIEX 2-FIXP 2-RLAV 2-RLAW
  2-RLBC

**AIRBUS HELICOPTERS including
AÉROSPATIALE, EUROCOPTER
& EUROCOPTER DEUTSCHLAND
production**

EC135 variants
  ZJ-HLH

**BAE SYSTEMS (OPERATIONS) LTD
including BRITISH AEROSPACE plc,
BRITISH AEROSPACE (REGIONAL
AIRCRAFT) Ltd, HANDLEY-PAGE and
SCOTTISH AVIATION production**

JETSTREAM variants to Series 32
  2-LCXO

**BEECH AIRCRAFT CORPORATION
including HAWKER BEECHCRAFT
CORPORATION & RAYTHEON
AIRCRAFT COMPANY production**

36 BONANZA
  2-LOLA 2-LOVE

55 and 58 BARON models
  2-DOLU 2-NOVA 2-PROP

90 KING AIR
  2-MAPZ 2-ZEUZ

300 SUPER KING AIR models
  2-FPLF

**BELL HELICOPTER TEXTRON
CANADA INC including AGUSTA BELL
HELICOPTER production**

206A and 206B JETRANGER variants
  2-HOVA 2-OCST 2-PDPD 2-SAIL

**BOEING AIRCRAFT CO including
BOEING COMPANY**

727-100 series
  2-MMTT

727-200 series
  2-SEVN

737-300 series
  2-ESKA 2-HAUL 2-MOVE 2-PSFI 2-WORK

737-400 series
  2-VBAO

737-700 series
  2-BASG 2-RLBB 2-SGSG

737-800 series
  2-ACSA 2-MSII 2-RLBD

747-400 series
  2-ACED

757-200 series
  2-STRW

767-200 series
  2-TSSA

767-300 series
  2-EUNF

777-200 series
  2-AERC 2-MMRB 2-MMRH 2-MMRJ

777-300 series
  2-RLAS

787-8
  2-DEER

**BOMBARDIER INC see also LEARJET
INC**

CL-600 CHALLENGER variants
  2-BLUE 2-MATO 2-NICE 2-ODAY 2-PCBS
  2-TRVL

CANADAIR REGIONAL JET variants
  2-AVCO 2-CFFV 2-CFFX 2-CFFZ 2-CFML
  2-GIAR

BD-700 GLOBAL variants
  2-JFJC 2-SLZK

**CESSNA AIRCRAFT COMPANY including
REIMS AVIATION SA production (F.prefix)**

208 and 208B (GRAND) CARAVAN
  2-CREW

310
  2-RODS

401
  2-AZFR

421 GOLDEN EAGLE variants
  2-MAPP

510 CITATION MUSTANG
  2-MSTG 2-MUST

525 CITATION M2
  2-RNWL

525A CITATIONJET 2
  2-CLEV 2-GOLF

525B CITATIONJET 3
  2-POSH 2-RBTS

525C CITATIONJET 4
  ZJ-THC

*550, S550 CITATION BRAVO and 551 CITATION
II models*
  2-WOOD

CIRRUS DESIGN CORPORATION

SR20
  2-SMKM

SR22
  2-OFUS 2-ROCK

SR22T
  2-GODS 2-RORO 2-ZERO

SF50 VISION
  2-AUER

AVIONS MARCEL DASSAULT

FALCON 50
  2-NYAW

**DE HAVILLAND (CANADA) including
BOMBARDIER INC production**

DHC-8-202
  2-ELIX

DHC-8-402Q
  2-CAUY

**DIAMOND AIRCRAFT INDUSTRIES
GmbH**

DA.42 TWIN STAR
  2-GSYJ

DA.62 TWIN STAR
  2-HERM 2-SALE

ECLIPSE AVIATION CORPORATION

ECLIPSE 500
  2-JEZA 2-JSEG 2-LIFE

EMBRAER

EMB.500/505 PHENOM 100/300
  2-JBMF

EMB-145 variants
  2-RLAD 2-TGHA 2-TGHB 2-TGHC 2-TGHD
  2-TGHE 2-TGHF 2-TGHG 2-TGHH 2-TGHI
  2-VAZV

ERJ-170 variants
  2-FINC 2-FINF 2-FING 2-FINI 2-FINJ

**GULFSTREAM AEROSPACE
CORPORATION**

GULFSTREAM IV/IVSP (GULFSTREAM 300/450)
  2-GULF 2-NNPK

GULSTREAM V-SP (GULFSTREAM 550)
  2-TRAV

GULFSTREAM VI (GULFSTREAM 650)
  2-EPIC 2-GJJA 2-KYCM

**LEONARDO HELICOPTERS including
AGUSTA SpA**

A109 variants
  2-GAFO 2-HELO 2-SEXY

**MESSERSCHMITT-BÖLKOW-BLOHM
GmbH see also AIRBUS HELICOPTERS**

Bö 105D
  2-BREM

PILATUS AIRCRAFT LTD

PC.12 variants
  2-DARE 2-FLYT 2-FLYY 2-LIVE

**PIPER AIRCRAFT CORPORATION
including THE NEW PIPER AIRCRAFT
INC production**

PA-28-161 (CHEROKEE) WARRIOR
  2-CHEZ

PA-28-181 (CHEROKEE) ARCHER
  2-KOOL

PA-28-235 CHEROKEE
  2-GOLD

PA-28R (CHEROKEE) ARROW variants
  2-YULL

PA-30 TWIN COMANCHE
  2-AWBN

PA-31 NAVAJO (& CHIEFTAIN) variants
  2-OWLC

PA-32 CHEROKEE SIX variants
  2-PETE 2-SALA

PA-32R-301 SARATOGA variants
  2-JEFS

2 and ZJ

PA-34 SENECA variants
   2-ANLD 2-TAXI

PA-46 MALIBU variants
   2-COOK 2-DITO 2-FIFI 2-JACK

ROCKWELL INTERNATIONAL CORPORATION including **GULFSTREAM** and **COMMANDER AIRCRAFT COMPANY (114)** production

COMMANDER 112 and 114
   2-AKOP 2-BEST 2-BOYS 2-GNSY 2-LAND
   2-MIKE 2-NOOR 2-RACE 2-ZOOM

RYAN AERONAUTICAL CORPORATION

NAVION
   2-RIOH

SAAB

2000
   2-ROKK

SIKORSKY AIRCRAFT – see also **SUD-AVIATION**

S-58
   2-WESX

S-76 variants
   2-BYDF 2-GECB 2-GECC 2-GECD

SOCATA – see also **MORANE-SAULNIER**

TB-20 TRINIDAD
   2-TBGT

TBM-700 variants
   2-PLAY 2-TBMI

SUD-AVIATION including **AÉROSPATIALE, SOKO** and **WESTLAND HELICOPTERS** production

SE.313 and SA.318 ALOUETTE II
   2-ALOU 2-HAWK 2-LOUD 2-SOAR 2-STEV

SA.341 and SA.342 GAZELLE
   2-PJBA 2-WILD 2-WMAN

TECNAM Srl

P.2006T MMA
   2-DLOO

2 and ZJ

SECTION 8 – OVERSEAS REGISTERED AIRCRAFT

PART 1 – OVERSEAS CIVIL REGISTERED AIRCRAFT LOCATED IN THE BRITISH ISLES

Any aircraft not noted since January 2014 have been removed from this edition. If anyone can provide updates on their current status please notify paul.hewins@virgin.net.

As in previous editions, leased and stored airliners are omitted unless there is a reasonable likelihood that they will still be present when this reaches the reader. The numerous airliners at Cotswold, St Athan etc awaiting their turn in the scrapping queue have therefore been omitted. A star (★) in Part 1 denotes the registration no longer appears on the relevant country register.

This Section could not have been produced without the assistance of the following to whom due credit is acknowledged: Peter Budden, Mike Cain, Jim Brazier and Kevin Dupuy (Southend), Terry Dann, Dave Haines (Gloucestershire), South West Aviation Group, Martyn Steggalls (Crowfield) and Barrie Womersley plus the numerous contributors to the ABIX, Airfields, Civil Spotters and Helicopters mailing lists.

The type index cross-reference for aircraft in Part 1 of this section can be found on page 594.

Overseas

Regn	Type / Previous identity / Owner (Operator)	C/n (Unconfirmed Base)	Last noted
QATAR			
A7-HMD	Eurocopter EC155B1	6850	1.19
	F-WWOB Gulf Helicopters Ltd London Stansted		
CANADA			
C-FARA	Short SC.7 Skyvan Srs 3-100	SH1970	1.19
	HZ-ZAT, G-BHHT, (G-14-138)		
	Summit Air RAF Brize Norton		
C-FQIP	Lake LA-4-200 Buccaneer	679	2.19
	N1068L P J Molloy Elstree		
	Derelict		
C-FPSH	Dornier Do228-202	8071	1.19
	N253MC, N71FB, D-CEBA, (D-IECA)		
	8199400 Canada Inc RAF Brize Norton		
C-FRAH★	Laister-Kauffman TG-4A (*LK-10A*)	84	4.18
	CF-RAH, N49920, 42-53027 Gliding Heritage Centre		
	Lasham		
	static display		
C-GKOA	Short SC.7 Skyvan Srs 3-100	SH1905	11.18
	N52NS, C-GKOA, N8190U, (G-BMFS), PK-PSG, G-14-77		
	Summit Air RAF Brize Norton		
C-GWJO★	Boeing 737-2A3	20299	5.17
	HR-SHO, HR-TNR, CX-BHM, N1797B, N1787B		
	Newcastle Aviation Academy Newcastle Int'l		
	Instructional airframe		
PORTUGAL			
CS-ARI★	Robin HR.100-210 Safari	159	10.14
	F-BUHV Not known MoD St Athan		
	Stored – was to be G-CEGD		
GERMANY			
D-ASDB★	VFW-Fokker VFW-614	G-019	11.18
	OY-RRW D-ASDB, German AF 17+03		
	Lufthansa Resource Technical Training Cotswold		
	Instructional Airframe		
D-EAAW	Bölkow BÖ.209 Monsun 160RV	181	2.19
	Not known Farley Farm, Farley Chamberlayne		
D-EAMB	Bölkow BÖ.208C Junior	597	1.19
	OE-AMB, D-ECGE Not known (Compton Abbas)		
D-EAMZ	Fuji FA-200-160 Aero Subaru	165	7.16
	Not known Dunkeswell		
D-EARY	Piaggio FWP.149D	057	11.18
	(D-EIJR), HB-EVU, 90+43, SB+212, SC+402, AS+484		
	Not known North Weald *'Screaming Eagle'*		
D-EAWW	Piper PA-28R-201 Arrow III	28R-7837199	12.18
	N9469C Not known Oxford		
D-EBBV	Robin HR.100/285 Tiara	524	8.18
	G-BGWD, F-BXRF Not known Coventry		
D-EBIE	Mooney M.20K	25-0665	2.19
	N11620 Not known Biggin Hill		
D-EBLI★	Bölkow BÖ.207	223	5.18
	Not known Farley Farm, Farley Chamberlayne		
	Canx 9.14		
D-EBLO	Bölkow BO.207	224	6.18
	Not known Lane Farm, Builth Wells		
D-ECDU★	Cessna F172E	F172-0068	.17
	Not known (Fourdon, Aberdeenshire)		
	Fuselage stored as 'G-ASOK'; sold in Wales 2018		
D-ECFE	Oberlerchner JOB 15-150	058	11.18
	OE-CAO Not known Enstone		
	Stored dismantled		
D-EDNA	Bölkow BÖ.208C Junior	578	9.18
	C Hampson Dunkeswell		
D-EEAH	Bölkow BÖ.208C Junior	658	11.17
	(D-EJMH) S Buckingham MoD Boscombe Down		
D-EEPI★	Wassmer WA.54 Atlantic	151	4.14
	R Hunter Stapleford		
	Canx 8.14		
D-EFJG	Bölkow BÖ.209 Monsun 160RV	129	1.19
	R.Truesdale Navan, RoI		
D-EFQE	Bölkow BÖ.207	266	11.18
	J Webb Thruxton		
D-EFUC★	Cessna 172S	172S8003	10.16
	G-NEWI, N563ER Not known Bournemouth		
	Stored dismantled after accident 2.8.12; canx 1.16		
D-EGDC	Grumman AA-5B Tiger	AA5B-0728	10.18
	P.Millar Guernsey		
D-EGEU★	Piper PA-22-108 Colt	22-9055	4.15
	EL-AEU, 5N-AEH Not known Derby		
	Badly damaged by storms 27.10.02 Farley Farm,		
	Farley Chamberlayne		
D-EGHW	Bölkow BÖ.209 Monsun 150FV	170	11.18
	HB-UER, D-EAAJ N Wright Popham		
D-EGMC	CEA DR.253B Regent	155	8.18
	Not known Linley Hill, Beverley		
D-EGMT	Reims/Cessna F182Q	F18200057	4.18
	Not known Cumbernauld		

D-EHJL	Piaggio FWP.149	045	11.18
	90+31, AC+441, AS+441, GA+394, D-EGEW, GA+394		
	C A Tyers (*Windmill Aviation*) Spanhoe		
D-EHKY	Bölkow BÖ.207	272	9.14
	Not known Haverfordwest		
D-EHOP	Bölkow BÖ.207	206	6.18
	Not known Shenington		
D-EIAR★	CEA DR.250-160 Capitaine	98	1.19
	D G Holmann Leicester		
	Canx 1.16		
D-EIBR★	Piper PA-38-112 Tomahawk	38-81A0117	5.15
	N23137 Highland Aviation Inverness		
	Damaged landing Dornoch 3.11.12; for spares use		
D-EJLY	Cessna 182K Skylane	18257879	2.15
	N2679Q Not known Stoodleigh Barton Farm, Stoodleigh		
D-EKEU	Piper PA-46-350P Malibu Mirage	4636110	11.18
	OE-KEU, G-BXER J Lunt Blackpool		
D-EKHW	Piper PA-28RT-201T Turbo Arrow IV	28R-8031094	10.18
	Not known Hawarden		
D-EKJD★	Reims FR172J Rocket	FR17200582	5.17
	T Paravicni Bourn		
	Canx 8.11		
D-EKMY	Bölkow Bo.208C Junior	514	2.17
	G-ASAS, D-ENCY Not known Navan, Rol		
D-ELSR	Robin DR.400-180R Remo 180	2012	10.18
	Not known Wolverhampton Halfpenny Green		
D-EMER	Piper J-3C-85 Cub	13210	5.17
	HB-OCB Not known Kings Farm, Thurrock		
D-EMIM	Extra EA.300	03	9.18
	G-OHIM, D-EBTS Not known Headcorn		
D-ENTO	American General AG-5B Tiger	10166	2.19
	N1198T T Yarnold Elstree		
D-EOAJ	Piaggio FWP.149D	028	10.18
	90+18, AC+409, DE+394 Not known Goodwood		
D-EPPG	Piper PA-46-500TP Malibu Meridian	4697158	11.18
	N53667, (N117WT), N53667 Not known Lydd		
D-ETRE	Tecnam P2002-JF Sierra	003	8.18
	LX-TRE Not known Newcastle, Rol		
D-ETUR	Mudry CAP.10B	38	7.18
	I-AVAA, F-BUDH Not known Full Sutton		
D-EVFR	Cessna 150J	15070974	9.14
	N61337 P Reilly Ballyboy, Rol		
D-EXAD	Flight Design CTLSi	F-12-08-04	7.18
	(D-EOAE) Not known Jersey		
D-FBPS	Cessna 208B Grand Caravan	208B0494	1.19
	LV-YJC, N208BA, N1219G Not known Langar		
	Operated by British Parachute School		
D-FLOH	Cessna 208B Grand Caravan	208B0576	1.19
	N1041F Not known Langar		
	Operated by British Parachute School		
D-HACK	Agusta–Bell 47J-2A	2071	7.17
	5B-CAF, CR-1 Hields Aviation Sherburn in Elmet		
D-HCKV★	Agusta A109A-II	7345	1.19
	N109HC, N2GN Fire Dump Gloucestershire		
	Damaged near Newby Bridge, Cumbria 2.1.00;		
	hulk marked 'G-OPAS'		
D-HFCV	Robinson R.44 Raven I	1730	10.17
	EI-EXH V Nash PLS Sudbury		
D-IEDO	Dornier Do.28G92	4134	9.18
	HA-ACM, D-IDRD, 58+59 Wingglider Ltd Hibaldstow		
D-IFSB★	de Havilland Dove 6	04379	11.18
	D-CFSB, G-AMXR, N4280V		
	Aircraft Restoration Group Morgansfield Fishburn		
	Gate guard		
D-KADJ	Jonker JS3 Rapture	03-019	7.18
	R Cheetham (Husbands Bosworth) *'E1'*		
D-KAIB	Lange E1 Antares 18T	56T04	8.18
	W Inglis Bidford *'W'*		
	Reserved as BGA 5337/G-WWVV)		
D-KAIJ	Lange E1 Antares 18T	52T03	7.17
	J Inglis Husbands Bosworth *'895'*		
	Reserved as BGA 5334/G-CKSS		

D-KANH	Lange E1 Antares 18T	50T02	2.19
	N G G Hackett Husbands Bosworth *'X7'*		
	Reserved as BGA 5322/G-CKSF		
D-KBSO	HpH Glasflügel 304MS Shark	090-MS	8.18
	H Werner Camphill *'SO'*		
D-KBTR	Glaser-Dirks DG-500M	5E6M4	7.18
	F-CHJA, D-KGBE W Young & partners Pocklington		
D-KDLQ	Schempp-Hirth Duo Discus XLT	223	8.18
	A Thornhill Pocklington *'GB1'*		
D-KDPF	Schempp-Hirth Ventus 2cxaJ	J10/520	8.18
	D-4670 J Best Bicester *'P2'*		
D-KEWV	Schempp-Hirth Ventus-3T	020TS	7.18
	D Francis Bicester *'F2'*		
D-KGED	Stemme S-10V	14-016M	6.18
	(D-KDKS) HB-2185, D-KGCD Not known Lasham *'2L'*		
D-KIAH	Scheibe SF 25C Falke 2000	44456	10.18
	Recreational F/C Taghmon, Rol		
D-KJMH	Schempp-Hirth Ventus2cxa	25J/559	9.18
	D-4862 C Curtis Lasham *'V2'*		
D-KKVT	Schempp-Hirth Ventus 3T	024S	8.18
	P Jones Lasham *'3'*		
D-KLSU	Schempp-Hirth Ventus 2cxa FES	152	9.18
	D-5410 ? A Neofytou Lasham *'FA2'*		
	Reserved as BGA 5895 / G-CLSU		
D-KLTN	Schempp-Hirth Ventus-2cxa FES	153	8.17
	Not known Bicester *'MH'*		
	Reserved as BGA 5913 / G-CLTN		
D-KOOL	Schleicher ASH.25EB28	25258	1.19
	R May & partners Dunstable *'13'*		
D-KRUK	Stemme S6	16	4.15
	Not known Challock		
D-KTOF	Schempp-Hirth Discus 2c FES	3/178	7.18
	K Neave & C Smith Nympsfield *'921'*		
D-KXTC	Schempp-Hirth Ventus 2cxa	8J	7.18
	D-4760 D Hope (Husbands Bosworth) *'XTC'*		
D-KZEN	Lange E1 Antares	45E41	7.18
	I Baker Gransden Lodge		
D-MGWU	Greenwing ESpyder	0006	10.16
	Not known Darley Moor		
	Unmarked		
D-MHYU	Aveko VL-3i Evolution	132	1.19
	Not known Thurrock		
D-MSGE	Comco Ikarus C42	9902-6175	7.17
	Not known Kings Farm, Thurrock		
D-MYWE	Pipistrel Sinus	Not known	1.19
	Not known Goodwood		
D-0606	Lange E1 Antares 18T	46ST05	7.18
	T J Wills Bidford/New Zealand *'1'*		
D-1155★	Schleicher K.8B	8589	2.17
	Not known Shennington		
	Stored		
D-4818	Schempp-Hirth Mini-Nimbus HS7	13	7.18
	M Grosche Gransden Lodge		
D-9691	Rolladen-Schneider LS4-a	4347	5.18
	OH-691 B Manoiu Gransden Lodge *'KS'*		

SPAIN

EC-AIJ	Piper PA-18A-135 Super Cub	18-2479	5.18
	S Cleary Strathaven		
EC-CFA★	Boeing 727-256	20811	5.17
	N907RF, EC-CFA Not known Shannon, Rol		
	Rescue trainer		
EC-DDX★	Boeing 727-256A	21779	6.18
	National Aviation Academy		
	Robin Hood, Sheffield-Doncaster		
	Fuselage used as training aid		
EC-JZF	Robinson R22 Beta	2509	11.18
	G-RICE, N93MK HQ Aviation Denham		
	Spares use		

EC-XCM	Magni M-22 Voyager	'08102-2403'	9.18
	Not known London Colney		
EC-EP6★	ELA 07	03060940724	3.16
	Not known (Leith, Edinburgh)		

ESTONIA

ES-PJA	BAe Jetstream 3102	749	9.18
	G-NOSS, LN-FAZ, C-GJPU, (N839JS), G-31-749		
	Not known Cranfield		
	Stored		
ES-YLK★	Aero Vodochody L-29 Delfin	194521	3.16
	Estonian AF Not known Dolly's Grove , RoI		
	Stored		

FRANCE

F-BBSO★	Taylorcraft Auster 5	1792	2.15
	G-AMJM, TW452 D.J.Baker Carr Farm, Thorney, Newark		
	Dismantled frame		
F-BJDC★	Agusta-Bell 47G	052	2.16
	ALAT Europa Engineering Banks, Southport		
F-BMCY★	Potez 840	02	5.15
	N840HP F-BJSU, F-WJSU D Feather North Roe, Shetland		
	Damaged Sumburgh 29. 3.81; stored dismantled		
F-BMHM	Piper J-3C-65 Cub	11907	6.15
	Fr Military, 44-79611 M Kirk Haverfordwest		
F-BOXT	Piper PA-28-140 Cherokee	28-23133	7.18
	N9669W M Mendez Morgansfield Fishburn		
F-BXIL	Reims Cessna FTB.337GA	0034	11.13
	J-P Peeters Jenkinstown, RoI		
	Dismantled; for sale 1.18		
F-GAIF★	Wassmer WA.81 Pirana	804	5.17
	A Fourquemin Abbeyshrule, RoI		
	Canx 6.07		
F-GBVN	Robin DR.400/180 Regent	1408	2.19
	G Tvalashvili Bicester		
F-GCTU★	Piper PA-38-112 Tomahawk	38-80A0085	3.15
	N9694N Not known Sandford Holiday Park, Dorset		
	Stripped fuselage; scrapped by 2018?		
F-GDKJ	Robin DR.400/120 Petit Prince	1612	10.18
	W Cole Spilsted Farm, Sedlescombe		
F-GDQL★	SNCASE SE.313B Alouette II	1250	9.14
	F-MJBI Y Lagofun Breighton		
	Canx 4.13		
F-GFGH	SOCATA Rallye 235E Gabier	13337	8.18
	F-ODNQ I Watts Bagby		
F-GFOR	Robin ATL	42	9.18
	P Bird Haverfordwest		
F-GGBD	Piper PA-32R-301T Turbo Saratoga SP	32R-8129110	11.18
	N8442U M Crossley Duxford		
F-GIRL★	Aérospatiale AS355F Ecureuil II	5035	3.15
	Streetwise Safety Centre Bournemouth		
	Canx 5.96; marked as 'S-WISE'		
F-GITZ	American AG-5B Tiger	10140	2.19
	OO-MLA, PH-MLA Orion Aviation Turweston		
F-GKGN	Grumman-American AA-5B Tiger	AA5B-0089	6.18
	G-BGDN, N6147A B Moran Kilrush, RoI		
F-GKRO	Holste MH.1521C-1 Broussard	154	7.18
	AdlA M Babbage Damyns Hall, Upminster		
F-GOXD	Robin DR.400-180RP Remorquer	1817	10.17
	OO-CXD, HB-KBU, D-EAJD		
	G Richardson Little Staughton		
F-WREI★	Gardan GY-80 Horizon 180	242	8.17
	F-BREI Not known Enstone		
	Stored for spares; canx 12.15		
F-GRLX	Jodel D.140B	66	11.17
	G-ARLX J Shaw Perranporth		
F-GULY	Beech C90A King Air	LJ-1610	9.18
	OY-LSA, N44406 Victoria Group Holdings Exeter		
F-GXDB	Mudry CAP.232	33	6.18
	D Britten Fairoaks *'Diana'*		

F-HAUL	Xtremeair XA42	119	6.17
	The Fighter Collection Duxford		
F-HVAL	Mooney M.20J	24-0586	8.17
	R O'Connor Dublin Weston, RoI		
F-JTYB	Pipistrel Virus 912 SW 100	415 SWN 100	8.15
	G-MGAP Not known (Beccles)		
F-PURU	Dyn'Aéro MCR-01 Sportster	218	4.15
	M Frost (Dunkeswell)		
F-PYOY	Heintz Zenith 100	52	1.18
	Sold and left in open store at Southend by 8.18		
F-WUTH	Progressor Pou Gyrocopter	01	.17
	Not known Rathcash East, Gowran, RoI		
F-ZWWW	Eurocopter EC665P Tigre	PT-001	8.18
	Stratton Motors Long Stratton, Norfolk		
	Stored		
44ADC	Aeroprakt A20 Vista	Not known	.14
	Not known Ruskey, Convoy, RoI		
	Wreck stored		
59DFA	Atec 212 Solo	Not known	6.14
	Not known Headcorn		
79II	Raj Hamsa X'Air Hawk	Not known	7.17
	Not known Hanbury William, Worcs		
	Call sign F-JXEZ		
86AI	Aviasud Albatros	24	1.19
	A Witt North Coates		
	Stored		
95AGB	Aerostyle Breezer	UL129	7.17
	Not known Coventry		
	Callsign F-JAQF		

HUNGARY

HA-ACO	Dornier Do.28D-2 Skyservant	4335	9.18
	G-BWCN, 5N-AYE, D-ILID, 9V-BKL, D-ILID		
	Trener Kft Hibaldstow		
	Walter M-601 turbo conversion; operated Wingglider Ltd		
HA-ANG	Antonov An-2P	1G132-53	2.19
	A J Weeks Hinton in the Hedges		
HA-HIB	Dornier Do.28D-2 Skyservant	4328	10.18
	Kenya AF116, D-IAVO Wingglider Ltd Hibaldstow		
HA-JDH	Reims/Cessna F150M	F15000734	2.19
	D-ECLQ Not known Elstree		
HA-LFH	Aérospatiale SA.342J Gazelle	1775	9.18
	RP-C5131 S Atherton Crabtree Farm, Deighton		
HA-MKF	Antonov An-2	1G233-43	5.17
	OM-248, OM-UIN, OK-UIN Trener Kft Popham		
HA-NST	Sukhoi Su-26MZ	03-05	5.17
	Kobo-Coop 96 Kft Abbeyshrule, RoI		
HA-SMD	Yakovlev Yak-18T	13-35	10.18
	LZ-TCC Kobo-Coop 96 Kft Elstree		
HA-YAV	Yakovlev Yak-18T	22202047817	9.18
	RA-01153, DOSAAF, CCCP81559		
	Kobo-Coop 96 Kft Lower Wasing Farm, Brimpton		
HA-YAW	Sukhoi SU-29	74-05	7.18
	N229JD Not known White Waltham		
HA-YDF	Technoavia SMG-92 Finist	01-0005	4.17
	Trener Kft Hibaldstow		
	Operated by Wingglider Ltd		

SWITZERLAND

HB-CIU	Reims FR172J Rocket	FR17200437	8.17
	D-EJXX Bonanza Viaggi SA		
	Eddsfield, Octon Lodge Farm, Thwing		
	Operated by B Tiplady		
HB-PBF	Piper PA-28R-201 Cherokee Arrow III	28R-7737012	11.18
	N1764H Not known Dublin Weston, RoI		
HB-357★	Spalinger S.21H		8.18
	Gliding Heritage Centre Lasham		
	Static display		

SAUDI ARABIA

HZ-AB3 Boeing 727-2U5/W 22362 1.19
V8-BG1, V8-HM2, V8-HM1, V9-UB1, V8-HM1, JY-HNH
Al-Anwa Establishment Lasham
Stored

HZ-ARK Gulfstream Aerospace Gulfstream V-SP
(*Gulfstream 550*) 5074 2.19
N574GA Mawarid Ltd Farnborough

ITALY

I-DAVA★ McDonnell-Douglas DC-9-82 49215 7.18
ItAli Airlines Gatwick
Ground trainer; due for scrapping

I-EIXM★ Piper PA-18-135 Super Cub 18-3572 2.14
MM54-2372, 54-2372 Not known Kesgrave, Ipswich
In open store as 'EI-184'

I-IJMW Mooney M20J 24-1633 8.18
OO-JMW Not known Dunkeswell
Stored on trailer after wheels up landing 11.1.14

I-KILC Grob G 109 6108 11.18
D-KILC Not known Birr, RoI
For sale

I-6693 Pipistrel Sinus 912 Not known 9.18
Not known Headcorn

I-9753 ICP MXP-740 Savannah VG 07-05-51-603 5.14
Not known Haverfordwest

I-B946 Pipistrel Virus Not known 12.16
Not known Redhill

NORWAY

LN-GDA Brditschka HB-21 21013 3.15
PH-947, D-KIDU, HB-2046 Ståle Lien Shenington
To be G-CFBG

LN-LJE Piper PA-18-150 Super Cub 18-1883 2.19
N230JB, N2206A Not known Darley Moor

LUXEMBOURG

LX-ARS★ Grumman American AA-1B Trainer 0556 10.16
D-EHLD, (N1456R) Not known Bournemouth
Spares use

LITHUANIA

LY-AFO★ WSK-PZL Antonov An-2 1G211-42 3.16
LY-ADL, CCCP32683 Not known Dolly's Grove, RoI
Stored

LY-AWV★ PZL-104 Wilga 35A 21910918 4.18
02 Ukraine AF, DOSAAF R Kerr Newtownards

LY-UCB Aeroprakt A-22L2 449 3.16
UAB Senasis Medvegalis Conington

UNITED STATES

N1FD SOCATA TB-200 XL Tobago 1614 11.18
Siek Aviation Inc Fairoaks

N1FY★ Cessna 421C Golden Eagle 421C1067 10.16
N345TG LME Aviation Bournemouth
Operated by Estate Air; canx 9.13

N2CL Piper PA-28RT-201T Turbo Arrow IV 28R-8131054 2.19
N8333S, N9649N Southern Aircraft Consultancy Inc
Rochester
Operated by P Geldard

N2PD SOCATA TBM930 1141 2.19
N930ZD Highfield Aviation Nottingham City

N3HK Cessna 340 II 340-0538 1.19
G-VAUN, D-IOFW, N5148J
Southern Aircraft Consultancy Inc North Weald
Operated by A Barham

N4LV Beech A24R MC-86 11.18
International Air Services Rochester

N4ML Mooney M.20J 24-3400 2.19
Ross Aviation Leasing Oxford
Operated by B Morton

N5LL Piper PA-31 Navajo C 31-7812041 7.18
N27495 Southern Aircraft Consultancy Inc Shoreham

N5ZY SOCATA TB-20 Trinidad 468 1.19
G-TOAK, N83AV Optimus Fuga Pactum Ltd Henstridge

N7EY Piper PA-30 Twin Comanche 30-571 2.19
F-BNFH, F-OCDS, N7508Y
Charnwood Aviation Farley Farm, Farley Chamberlayne

N7NP Hughes 369HE 0260E 2.18
TJSSD Inc (PLS Hatfield, Doncaster)

N0MZ Piper PA-30 Twin Comanche B 30-1648 10.18
G-ORDO, N8485Y Southern Aircraft Consultancy Inc
Henstridge

N9AC Rockwell Commander 112TC-A 13304 4.14
G-JILL, (OO-HPB), G-JILL, N8070R, HB-NCW
Optimus Fuga Pactum Ltd Henstridge

N9FJ Aérospatiale AS.350B-2 Ecureuil 3148 2.19
Boultbee Aviation Redhill

N10CD Cirrus Design SR22T 0350 2.19
Southern Aircraft Consultancy Inc Lydd

N10GY★ Cessna 340A II 340A0114 .16
G-PUFN, N532KG, N532KC, N5477J
Checkflight Ltd Perranporth
Stored; canx 5.18

N10MC Cirrus Design SR22 1084 12.14
Southern Aircraft Consultancy Inc Henstridge

N11FV Cessna T303 Crusader T30300133 6.18
G-BXRI, HB-LNI, (N5143C) Auster Aviation Guernsey

N11MW Cirrus Design SR22T 1775 11.18
CRB Aviation Exeter

N11N Pitts S-1T 1051 2.19
International Air Services Henstridge

N12ZX Mooney M.20J 24-3227 2.19
S Ames Biggin Hill

N14EF Piper PA-46-350P Malibu 4622009 2.19
N91520 Altaclara Aviation Fairoaks
DLX conversion 145

N14MT Cessna TR182 Skylane RG R18201227 6.18
Southern Aircraft Consultancy Inc North Weald

N15NH Cessna 172RG Cutlass 172RG0115 5.17
D-EOCR, N6207R Southern Aircraft Consultancy Inc
Spilstead Farm, Seddlescombe

NC16S Beech D17S 6687 9.17
N9455H, Bu32870, FT466, (Bu23675), 44-67710
W M Charney Solent

N17UK Cirrus Design SR22 0200 9.18
N7UK Southern Aircraft Consultancy Inc Gloucestershire

N19CQ★ Hawker Siddeley Dominie T.1 25040 11.15
XS712 BAE Systems Aircraft Maintenance Academy
Humberside
Canx 7.18

N19CU★ Hawker Siddeley Dominie T.1 25048 6.18
XS728 Executive Jet Support DBA 19th Hole Inc
Cotswold
Stored; canx 1.15

N19DW Cirrus Design SR22T 1686 12.18
Hannah Aviation Liverpool John Lennon

N19EK★ Hawker Siddeley Dominie T.1 25076 8.16
XS737 Lufthansa Resource Technical Training
Cotswold
Canx 1.15

N19ET Liberty Aerospace XL-2 0091 6.17
E A Terris Wycombe Air Park

N19F Cessna 337A Super Skymaster 33700289 8.16
N6289F Southern Aircraft Consultancy Inc
Wadswick Manor Farm , Corsham
Robertson STOL conversion

Overseas

N19GL	Brantly B.2B	2004	5.16
	Eastern Stearman Inc Eaglescott		
N19UG★	Hawker Siddeley Dominie T.1	25050	9.18
	XS730 Lufthansa Resource Technical Training		
	Cotswold		
	Canx 1.15		
N19UK★	Hawker Siddeley Dominie T.1	25081	2.17
	XS739 BAE Systems Aircraft Maintenance Academy		
	Humberside		
	Canx 7.18		
N19XY★	Hawker Siddeley Dominie T.1	25055	2.15
	XS731 Flight Research Inc		
	Poulton Down Farm, Ogbourne St Andrew, Wilts		
	Fuselage stored; canx 1.15		
N20AG	SOCATA TB-20 Trinidad	2003	2.19
	N29KF Southern Aircraft Consultancy Inc North Weald		
N20TB	SOCATA TB-20 Trinidad GT	2008	2.19
	G-HOOD Southern Aircraft Consultancy Inc Blackbushe		
	Operated by C Ridout		
N20UK	Mooney M.20F Executive	22-1380	6.18
	N9155J, G-BDVU N Registration Service LLC Fenland		
N21GB	Cessna 310R II	310R1580	10.18
	G-BWYG, F-GBMY, (N1820E)		
	Southern Aircraft Consultancy Inc Biggin Hill		
N22CG	Cessna 441 Conquest II	441-0119	12.18
	Jubilee Airways Inc Prestwick		
	Operated by M.Klinge		
N22NN	Cessna 182P Skylane	18263497	2.19
	OE-DGU, N5717J Southern Aircraft Consultancy Inc		
	Haw Farm, Hampstead Norreys		
N22UB	Cessna 525C CitationJet CJ4	525C0182	1.19
	N5141T CJ4 FPL Inc Gloucestershire		
N22ZW	Bell 222	47031	9.18
	G-NOIR, G-OJLC, G-OSEB, G-BNDA, A4O-CG		
	Monster Aviation Manston Park		
N23KY	Cessna P210N Centurion	P21000447	2.19
	N731ER Southern Aircraft Consultancy Inc		
	Mayridge Farm, Englefield		
	Operated by Pacnet Europe		
N24KC	Zivko Edge 540A	0029A	11.18
	Southern Aircraft Consultancy Inc Oaksey Park		
N25AG★	Lockheed Jetstar Srs 2	5202	7.15
	3C-QRK, P4-CBG, VP-CBH, EC-FQX, EC-232, N20GB,		
	N333KN, N717X, N717, N5528L		
	Apple Camping Redberth		
	Fuselage as holiday home; canx 1.07		
N25PR	Piper PA-30-160 Twin Comanche B	30-1511	9.18
	G-AVPR, N8395Y International Air Services North Weald		
	Operated by M Hadley		
N25XL	Cessna 310Q II	310Q1076	4.18
	G-BBXL, EI-CLX, G-BBXL, (N1223G)		
	Southern Aircraft Consultancy Inc Sligo		
	Operated by M D Aviation		
N25XZ★	Cessna 182G	18255388	1.15
	HB-CST, OE-DDM, N2188R		
	Southern Aircraft Consultancy Inc North Weald		
	Canx 6.16		
N26RT	Beech F33A Bonanza	CE-1292	2.19
	G-RRRT, HB-KAM Optimus Fuga Pactum Ltd Henstridge		
N27BG	Cessna 340A	340A0656	8.17
	Traca Inc Cranfield		
	Operated by B Gregory		
N28SN	Cirrus Design SR22T	1729	2.19
	Aircraft Guaranty Corp Biggin Hill		
N30NW	Piper PA-30-160 Twin Comanche	30-312	8.16
	G-ASON, N7273Y AAT Inc Old Buckenham		
N30VT	Beech V35B Bonanza	D-9439	1.19
	Plane Fun Inc Weston, RoI		
	Operated by P Gorman		
N30WA	Cessna T303 Crusader	T30300143	8.18
	D-IRAS, PH-JAF, OY-BHC, SE-IHZ, (N5524C)		
	Ameri Air Support Inc Coventry		

N31GN★	Cessna 310R II	310R-1541	8.16
	N410RS, G-BTGN, N410RS, N5331C J A Keim Wick		
	Canx 9.12		
N31RB	Grumman-American AA-5B Tiger	AA5B-0156	2.19
	Tigre Ecossais Aviation Bournemouth		
N32LE	Piper PA-32-301T Turbo Saratoga SP	32R-8329016	2.18
	Southern Aircraft Consultancy Inc Conington		
	Operated by Light into Europe		
N32PL	Cessna 182Q	18267595	6.18
	P S Diette Biggin Hill		
N33NW	SOCATA TB-20 Trinidad	1073	8.18
	N666HM, OO-PDV, F-GLAC		
	Southern Aircraft Consultancy Inc Nottingham City		
	Operated by D Wheeler		
N35AL	Diamond DA 42 Twin Star	42.147	9.18
	OE-VPY Triple M Aviation Jersey		
N35SN	Beech 35-33 Debonair	CD-207	2.19
	D-EKOW Plane Fun Inc Bournemouth		
N37LW★	Piper PA-23-250 Aztec	27-134	1.14
	G-EEVA, G-ASND, N4800P		
	Newcastle Aviation Academy Newcastle Int'l		
	Canx 3.10		
N37US	Piper PA-34-200T Seneca II	34-8070111	6.18
	G-PLUS, N81406		
	Southern Aircraft Consultancy Inc Jersey		
	Operated by Skycabs		
N37VB	Cessna 421C	421C-0418	2.19
	EC-IFT, G-FWRP, N3919C		
	Lowndes Aviation Bournemouth		
N39CR	Piper PA-39 Twin Comanche C/R	39-4	2.19
	OY-RPM, OO-RPM, OY-RPM, D-GFHW, OE-FCG, N8845Y		
	Southern Aircraft Consultancy Inc Biggin Hill		
N39TA	Beech B24R Sierra 200	MC-230	11.18
	G-BBVJ Southern Aircraft Consultancy Inc		
	RAF Honington		
N40XR	Bombardier Learjet 40	45-2028	2.19
	Palace Aviation Bournemouth		
	Operated by Jet-Care International		
N42LJ	Cessna 525B CitationJet CJ3	525B0179	2.19
	HB-VTJ Whittlewood Aviation (US) Inc Oxford		
N43YP	Boeing-Stearman E75 Kaydet	75-6018	11.18
	Vintage Aeroplane Collection #2 Inc Enstone		
	As USN '443'; on rebuild		
N44EW	Aerotek Pitts Special S-1S	1-0058	9.18
	Extra Aircraft Inc Jersey		
N44NE	Cessna 414	414-0070	1.19
	G-DYNE, N8170Q J & G Aviation Nottingham City		
N45BN	Waco Classic YMF-5C	F5C-8-130	9.17
	Flylander Inc Solent		
N45KB	Cirrus Design SR22T	1800	1.19
	Sancerre Inc Leicester		
N50AG	Cirrus Vision SF.50	0054	12.18
	APG Aviation Biggin Hill		
N50AY	Rockwell Commander 114	14527	9.18
	HB-NCZ, G-BGTE, N5910N		
	International Air Services Rochester		
N51AH	Piper PA-32R-301 Saratoga SP	32R-8413017	8.18
	G-REAH, G-CELL, (G-BLRI), N4361D		
	Southern Aircraft Consultancy Inc PLS Welham Green		
	Operated by A Neal		
N51CK★	North American P-51D Mustang	122-31731	9.17
	44-64005 Skyfire Corp Sywell		
	For restoration as '464005'/E9-Z/Mary Mine; canx 3.18		
N51WF	Rockwell 690C Turbo Commander	11684	1.19
	N5936K Aviation Air Services Southend		
N52GM★	Taylor JT.1 Monoplane	51422	9.17
	N1GM Not known Sywell		
	Canx 6.11		
N53LG	Cirrus Design SR22T	0812	9.18
	N53LG Aviation Biggin Hill		
N53SB	Reims FR172H Rocket	FR172H0265	7.18
	G-CCSB, N53SB, G-CCSB, OO-RTC, F-BSHK		
	Southern Aircraft Consultancy Inc St Marys, Isles of Scilly		

N55BN	Beech 95-B55 Baron	TC-1572	1.19
	G-KCAS, G-KCEA, N2840W		
	Optimus Fuga Pactum Ltd Henstridge		
N55EU	Cessna P210N Turbo Centurion	P21000394	6.18
	C L Holdings LLC Elstree		
N55UK	Beech E55 Baron	TE-1128	2.19
	G-FLAK, N4771M Zoomair Inc Thruxton		
N56AH	Cirrus Design SR22	2781	1.19
	G-RBMS, N837SR 2781 Aviation Inc Exeter		
N56EK★	Piper PA-28-181 Archer II	2890145	9.16
	G-TNYA, D-EDFD, N649CT, N9203D		
	International Air Services Goodwood		
	Operated by Emile Al-Kirkhy; canx 4.17		
N58JA	Cessna 340	340-0521	2.19
	Rainbow Aviation Fairoaks		
N59SD	McDonnell Douglas MD.369E	0019E	2.19
	International Air Services (Faldingworth)		
N59VT	Beech K35 Bonanza	D-5897	8.16
	D-EMEF International Air Services		
	Carr Farm, Thorney, Newark		
	Operated by F Mumford		
N60GM	Cessna 421C Golden Eagle III	421C0828	9.18
	Southern Aircraft Consultancy Inc Isle Of Man		
N60GZ	Mooney M.20J	24-3035	1.15
	HB-DGZ ABL Aviation North Weald		
N60UK	Christen A-1C Husky	3006	4.17
	Southern Aircraft Consultancy Inc Carlisle		
N60VG	Bell 206L-3 Long Ranger	51494	11.18
	TVPX ARS Inc PLS Maynooth, RoI		
N61FD	SIAI – Marchetti SF.260C	719	1.18
	International Air Services North Weald		
	Operated by A Allan		
N61HB	Piper PA-34-220T Seneca V	3449217	5.17
	G-CBAA, N53445		
	HBC Aviation Inc Thurrock and Guernsey		
N61PS	Pitts S-2B	5230	12.18
	Kuki Inc Retford Gamston		
N63EN	Cessna 340	340-0063	1.19
	G-REEN, G-AZYR, N5893M		
	Echo November Inc North Weald		
N64EA	Agusta A109A II	7265	10.18
	G-DWAL, G-JODI, G-BVCJ, G-CLRL, G-EJCB		
	Eahot Inc Carters Barn, Huggate		
N64VB	Beech 58 Baron	TH-305	8.18
	N273TB Galv-Aero Flight Center Sleap		
N65JF	Piper PA-28-181 Archer II	28-7990140	1.19
	N2087C Southern Aircraft Consultancy Inc		
	Nottingham City		
	Operated by D Teece		
N65MJ	Beech 58P Baron	TJ-487	10.18
	Grange Aviation Dublin Weston, RoI		
N65PF	Piper PA-30 Twin Comanche B	30-1515	10.18
	G-AVUD, N8422Y		
	Southern Aircraft Consultancy Inc Stapleford		
N65TL	Cirrus Design SR22T	1747	2.19
	Les Chandons Two Inc White Waltham		
N66MS	Piper PA-28RT-201T Turbo Arrow IV	28R-8431021	10.18
	G-BRRJ, N4353T International Air Services		
	Wolverhampton Halfpenny Green		
	Operated by M Stower		
N67DP	Cirrus Design SR22-G3-GTS	2933	2.19
	Alexander James Aviation Turweston		
N67JK	Cessna P210N Turbo Centurion	P21000684	2.19
	DMW Aviation Fairoaks		
	Silver Eagle conversion		
N70AA	Beech 70 Queen Air	LB-35	8.18
	G-REXP, N70AA, G-KEAA, G-REXP, G-AYPC		
	Southern Aircraft Consultancy Inc Dunsfold		
N71CW	Cessna 180E	18051093	2.19
	N40SR, F-GMSR, F-BFVX, F-OBVX, N8693X		
	Southern Aircraft Consultancy Inc White Waltham		

N71UK	Cirrus Design SR22T	1002	2.19
	Southern Aircraft Consultancy Inc Liverpool John Lennon		
N71WZ	Piper PA-46-350P Malibu Mirage	4636275	2.19
	C-FLER Arlington Aviation Bournemouth		
N73BL	Piper PA-32R-301T Saratoga II	3257450	2.19
	Southern Aircraft Consultancy Inc Elstree		
N73GR	Piper PA-28-181 Archer III	2843586	8.17
	N586SE Southern Aircraft Consultancy Inc Kirknewton		
N74DC	Pitts S-2A Special	2228	9.18
	I-ALAT H J Seery Rush Green		
	Operated by D.Cockburn		
N74PM	Agusta A109C	7636	10.18
	D-HOFP, I-SEIN Ortac Inc (Whitegate)		
	Operated by Huktra UK Ltd		
N76CE	Christen Eagle II	GA0032	4.18
	International Air Services Morgansfield Fishburn		
N75TQ	Boeing Stearman B75N1(N2S-3)	75-1180	7.18
	G-BRSK, N5565N, USN 3403 Southern Aircraft Consultancy Inc		
	Priory Farm, Tibenham		
	USN marks as '3403/180'		
N76T	Beech G36 Bonanza	E-3901	2.19
	Seven Six Tango Inc Bournemouth		
N77YY	Piper PA-32R-301T Saratoga II TC	3257120	9.17
	G-LLYY, N4165C		
	Southern Aircraft Consultancy Inc North Weald		
N78DU	Beech G36 Bonanza	E-3897	12.16
	D A H Rogers Fairoaks		
N78GG	Beech F33A Bonanza	CE-699	12.18
	G-ENSI, D-ENSI		
	Southern Aircraft Consultancy Inc Blackbushe		
	Operated by G Garnett		
N78HB	Aviat A-1B Husky	2066	5.17
	N115BB, G-FOFF, N115BB		
	HBC Aviation Inc King's Farm, Thurrock		
	Operated by T Holding		
N78XP	Reims FR172K Hawk XP II	FR17200603	6.18
	G-BFFZ, F-WZDU		
	Southern Aircraft Consultancy Inc Bodmin		
N79EL	Beech 400A Beechjet	RK-214	2.19
	Edra Lauren Leasing Corporation East Midlands		
	For Sale 6.16		
N80AV	Cirrus Design SR22T	1549	9.18
	N80AG RB33 Inc East Midlands		
N80JN★	Mitsubishi MU-2J	626	9.15
	EC-GLU, OY-ATZ, SE-GHY, N476MA		
	Aircraft Guaranty Title Corp Waterford, RoI		
	Cancelled 6.07 by FAA: derelict		
N80MC	Mudry CAP.10B	221	10.16
	TJ Air Holdings Inc Kirkbride		
	Operated by P.Jackson		
N80N	Cessna T337G Super Skymaster	P3370197	4.17
	Southern Aircraft Consultancy Inc Wolverhampton		
N81AW	Piper PA-34-220T Seneca III	34-8133107	10.18
	Southern Aircraft Consultancy Inc East Midlands		
N81MG	Cessna P210N Pressurised Centurion	P21000476	7.18
	Stammair Inc Jersey		
	Silver Eagle conversion		
N83VK	Piper PA-32R-300 Cherokee Lance	32R-7780226	10.18
	Southern Aircraft Consultancy Inc Kings Farm, Thurrock		
N84VK	Piper PA-24-180 Comanche	24-1492	6.18
	D-EINS, N6382P N84VK Inc Tatenhill		
	Operated by L Darcy		
N85LB	Cessna 340A II	340A0486	2.19
	G-OPLB, G-FCHJ, G-BJLS, (N6315X)		
	Southern Aircraft Consultancy Inc Turweston		
	Operated by A Ruff		
N88EL	Raytheon RB390 Premier 1A	RB-157	11.18
	N6178X SCL Security Inc Biggin Hill		
N88NA	Piper PA-32R-301T Turbo Saratoga SP	32R-8529005	8.18
	G-PAPS, F-GELX, N4385D		
	Southern Aircraft Consultancy Inc Retford Gamston		
	Operated by Nicol Aviation; damaged by landing Baron		
	G-BYDY at Haydock Race Course 8.9.18		

Overseas

N88NL	Pitts S-2B	5147	10.16
	Simply Living LLC Tibenham		
N89GH	Cirrus Design SR22	1178	11.18
	Southern Aircraft Consultancy Inc Stapleford		
	Operated by K Cullum		
N89NB	Cirrus Design SR22-GTS	3680	10.18
	Strong Tower Services LLC Leeds		
N89SS	Bell 206B-2 JetRanger II	1010	4.18
	G-HMSS, ZS-HMS, C-GXOI, N58008		
	Aircraft Guaranty Corp Kilrush, RoI		
N90DJ	Reims/Cessna F182Q Skylane	F18200091	8.18
	D-EIIP Deejay Aviation Jersey		
N90PV	Cessna 310N	310N0054	5.16
	G-YHPV, N510PS, G-YHPV, N510PS, G-AWTA, EI-ATB,		
	N4154Q Southern Aircraft Consultancy Inc		
	Waterford, RoI		
	Operated by P Hayes & V Young		
N90YA	Cessna 425 Corsair	425-0090	12.18
	N90GA, G-BHNY, (N68476)		
	Southern Aircraft Consultancy Inc Donegal, RoI		
N91ME	SOCATA TB-20 Trinidad	2152	9.18
	International Air Services Guernsey		
N92RW	Beech F33A Bonanza	CE-972	3.16
	D M Lara City of Derry, Eglinton		
N94SA	Champion 7ECA Citabria	227	8.18
	OY-AUG, D-EFLO International Air Services Henstridge		
N95D	Piper PA-34-220T Seneca V	3449060	8.18
	N9506N Zeta Aviation Inc Guernsey		
N95GT	Cirrus Design SR22-GTS	1758	12.18
	N588CD Southern Aircraft Consultancy Inc Rochester		
	Operated by P Knowles		
N95TA	Piper PA-31 Turbo Navajo B	31-7300971	2.19
	N7576L Southern Aircraft Consultancy Inc Newcastle		
	Operated by A Jahanfar		
N95VB	Beech C90GTi King Air	LJ-2091	2.19
	N51091 Bank of Utah Sleap		
N96FL	Cirrus Design SR22-G3-GTSX	2899	10.18
	G-ETFL, N998CT Les Chardons Inc White Waltham		
N96JL	Cessna 421C Golden Eagle	421C-0627	8.18
	Aircraft Guaranty Corp Dunsfold		
N99ET	SOCATA TB-10 Tobago	226	7.18
	G-BJDG, F-BNGR		
	Southern Aircraft Consultancy Inc Andrewsfield		
N100JS	Dassault Falcon 2000LX	318	12.18
	F-WWMB TVPX ARS Inc Oxford		
	Operated by Jato Aviation		
N100RZ	Cirrus Design SR22T	0034	2.19
	International Air Services Blackbushe		
N100VA	Eclipse Aviation EA500	000138	11.18
	Victor Alpha Inc Jersey		
N100YY	Cirrus Design SR20	1183	2.19
	International Air Services Haverfordwest		
N101DW	Piper PA-32R-300 Cherokee Lance	32R-7680399	12.18
	Southern Aircraft Consultancy Inc Cranfield		
	Operated by N Webb		
N101VV	Cessna 172N	17272921	1.19
	N101VV, G-CKZK Southern Aircraft Consultancy Inc Biggin Hill		
N102CA	Aviat A-1B Husky	2272	2.18
	Southern Aircraft Consultancy Inc Wick, John O'Groats		
N104BP★	Vans RV-10	40688	6.15
	Phelan Aviation Limetree, RoI		
	Canx 9.18		
N105AN	Cessna 208B Grand Caravan	208B0956	9.18
	Cessna 2080660 Inc Hibaldstow		
N105SK	Reims Cessna F150L	1500877	2.18
	(EI-), N105SK, G-IAWE, EI-AWE		
	Aerospace Trust Management Sleap		
N109TF	Agusta A109A-II	7328	2.19
	VH-NWD, VH-DMR, (VH-MRS) Castle Air Inc Liskeard		
N109TK	Agusta A109C	7650	1.19
	N109TW, D-HCKM Botany Aviation Botany Bay, Chorley		

N111DT	Piper PA-24-180 Comanche	24-2260	7.18
	Southern Aircraft Consultancy Inc Leicester		
N111GW	American Champion 8KCAB	1123-2013	5.18
	Southern Aircraft Consultancy Inc Henstridge		
N111SC	Beech N35 Bonanza	D-6795	2.18
	G-ARZN, N215DM		
	International Air Services Glasgow Prestwick		
N112JA	Rockwell Commander 112TC-A	13182	7.17
	5Y-MBK Southern Aircraft Consultancy Inc		
	Top Farm, Croydon		
N112WM	Piper PA-32-300 Cherokee Six D	32-7140001	8.18
	G-AZTD, N8611N		
	Southern Aircraft Consultancy Inc Bagby		
N113AC	SOCATA TB-20 Trinidad GT	2121	7.18
	G-TTAC, F-OIMD, (N212GT)		
	Southern Aircraft Consultancy Inc Shoreham		
	Operated by P Holt		
N113BP	Piper PA-46-350P Malibu Mirage	4636363	1.19
	N3093B Southern Aircraft Consultancy Inc Wickenby		
	Operated by S Turley; DLX conversion 221		
N114AT	Commander Aircraft Commander 114B	14619	8.18
	Randle Aviation Coventry		
N114WG★	Westland WG.30	014	6.18
	Wessex Avn Biggin Hill		
	(Canx 3.13)		
N115MD	Commander Aircraft Commander 114TC	20039	8.18
	Southern Aircraft Consultancy Inc Fairoaks		
N116SB	Commander Aircraft Commander 114B	14678	2.19
	G-HPSB 114B Holding Inc Guernsey		
N116WG★	Westland WG-30-100	016	2.16
	(G-BLLG) Petrofax Training Services Montrose		
	Canx 8.13		
N117EA	Eclipse Aviation EA500	000104	10.18
	Cordite Inc Isle Of Man		
N119SX	Agusta A.119T Koala	14037	2.19
	N119JT, ZK-HIS, VH-PSR, N928KR, N48HH		
	Saxon Logistics Inc Elstree		
N120HH	Bell 407	53661	2.19
	407 Holding Inc Peldon, Colchester		
	Operated by Oyster Leasing Ltd		
N120MX	Cirrus Design SR20	2281	2.19
	Cirrus SR20 2281 Inc Retford Gamston		
N121EL★	Gates Learjet 25	25-010	10.06
	(N121GL), (N82UH), (N10BF), N102PS, N671WM,		
	N846HC, N846GA		
	Kingston University Roehampton, Surrey		
	Instructional airframe; current 12.16 on University website		
N121JF	Beech F33A Bonanza	CE-1578	2.19
	OO-PMK, F-GJGA, N81701		
	International Air Services Sleap		
N122MG	Cirrus Design SR22-GTS	1250	2.19
	122MG Inc Turweston		
N122ZT	Cirrus Design SR22-GTS	3828	10.18
	JDW Aviation Guernsey		
N123CA	Dornier Do.28A-1	3051	10.18
	G-ASUR, D-IBOM		
	International Air Services Shuttleworth (Old Warden)		
N123SA	Piper PA-18-150 Super Cub	18-1372	9.18
	French Army, 51-15372		
	Southern Aircraft Consultancy Inc Rougham		
	Operated by B Walsh; as US Army 15372		
N124CP★	Cirrus Design SR22-G3-GTSX Turbo	3040	11.18
	Southern Aircraft Consultancy Gloucestershire		
	Damaged fuselage for sale 11.15; canx 12.15		
N124PD	Hughes 369E	0502E	1.19
	N1604M Highfield Aviation Nottingham		
N129SC	Piper PA-32-300 Cherokee Six	32-7440057	1.19
	Manx Orthopaedic Services Isle Of Man		
N131CD	Cirrus Design SR20	1031	11.18
	Southern Aircraft Consultancy Inc Humberside		

N131MP Piper PA-31P Pressurised Navajo 31P-7400193 12.18
G-BWDE, G-HWKN, HB-LIR, D-IAIR, N7304L
N Registration Service LLC Sandtoft
Fuselage stored)

N132LE Piper PA-32-300 Cherokee Six 32-40038 8.18
G-AVFS Southern Aircraft Consultancy Inc
New Farm House, Great Oakley
Operated by Light into Europe

N138CM Piper PA-46-500TP Meridian M500 4697579 11.18
D-FIPA Hanys Aircraft Inc Fairoaks

N139LC Cirrus Design SR22T 1769 2.19
Amedeo Flight Ops Ltd Weston, RoI

N139PR Agusta Westland AW139 41273 7.17
N143EV Pista Acquisitions LLC Biggin Hill

N140NT Cessna 140A 16306 6.18
G-ANGK, N9675A Flight International Corp Goodwood

N141HT Cirrus Design SR22 Turbo 2219 2.19
Aircraft Guaranty Corp Gloucestershire

N141KJ Cirrus Design SR22T 0832 2.19
KJW Aircraft Inc Denham

N141WF Maule M-7-235 4036C 8.18
V5-KBW Southern Aircraft Consultancy Inc
Kings Farm, Thurrock

N142TW Beech 58 Baron TH-1841 7.18
Specialized Aircraft Services Inc Fairoaks

N145PC Reims FR172J Rocket FR17200383 8.18
Southern Aircraft Consultancy Inc Alderney

N145T★ Schleicher ASW 12 12011 8.16
G-AXZI, BGA1545 Not known Shenington *'X11'*
Stored; canx 6.12

N147DC Douglas C-47A-75-DL Dakota 19347 11.18
G-DAKS, TS423, '108841', 'KG374', 'G-AGHY', TS423,
42-100884 Aces High US Inc North Weald
As '2100884:L4' in US AF c/s

N147GT Cirrus Design SR22-G2 1069 2.19
147 Aviation Inc Blackpool

N147JT Cessna 172S Skyhawk 172S9978 9.18
G-LACI, N2310C
Southern Aircraft Consultancy Inc Andrewsfield

N147KB Cirrus Design SR22-GTS 1869 1.19
N112SR 1869 Holding Inc Biggin Hill
Operated by K Siggery

N147LD Cirrus Design SR22 0937 2.19
N23AM 1944 Holding Inc Blackbushe

N147LK Cirrus Design SR22-GTS 1687 2.19
N745CD N147LK Inc Blackbushe

N147VC Cirrus Design SR22 0689 1.19
0689 Holdings Inc Oxford

N150JC★ Beech A35 Bonanza D-2084 4.17
N8674A R M Hornblower Not known
Left Southend by road 4.17 unmarked on trailer; canx 6.12

N150SF Aérospatiale SA.341G Gazelle 1584 1.19
N158SF, N150SF, (N650SF), N150SF, N125ME, N90040
Southern Aircraft Consultancy Inc Nottingham City

N150ZZ Cirrus Design SR22-G3 2609 2.19
Middleton Cirrus GT3 Inc Leeds-Bradford Int'l

N151CG Cirrus Design SR22 0344 2.19
N151CG Inc Bembridge

N153H Bell 222B 47138 9.17
Yorkshire Helicopters USA Inc Coney Park, Leeds

N159AR Maule M4-180V 47013t 12.18
D Robertson Fledmyre Quarry, Forfar

N161FF Piper PA-28-161 Cherokee Warrior II 28-7716097 5.17
G-BYXU, EI-BXU, G-BNUP, N2282Q
Southern Aircraft Consultancy Inc Waterford, RoI
Operated by F McGovern & F O'Sullivan

N162AW Piper PA-18-150 Super Cub 18-8109082 2.19
Aircraft Guaranty Corp Elstree

N166MG Robinson R66 0694 2.19
M J Gallagher Denham

N170AZ Cessna 170A 19674 .16
HB-CAZ, N5720C Southern Aircraft Consultancy Inc
Nethershields Farm, Chapelton
Operated by A Gregori

N171WM Piper PA-23-250 Aztec C 27-3498 9.18
G-BXPS, G-AYLY, N6258Y
N Registration Service LLC Biggin Hill

N172AM Cessna 172M Skyhawk II 17264993 2.18
G-BXHG, N64057 Southern Aircraft Consultancy Inc
Coonagh, Co Limerick,RoI
Operated by PacNet Air

N177CK Eclipse Aviation EA500 000182 2.19
Southern Aircraft Consultancy Inc Retford Gamston

N177FH Cessna 177RG 177RG1034 8.18
Southern Aircraft Consultancy Inc Top Farm, Croydon

N177SA Reims Cessna F177RG Cardinal RG F177RG0171 11.18
F-GBFI Southern Aircraft Consultancy Inc Newcastle
Operated by Lord Stevens

N179JD Cirrus Design SR22T 1527 2.19
N179JD Inc Biggin Hill

N180BB Cessna 180K 18053103 12.18
Southern Aircraft Consultancy Inc
Colganstown, Baldonnel, RoI

N180FN Cessna 180K 18053201 7.18
Rivet Inc Great Massingham

N180HK Cessna 180K Skywagon II 18053191 10.18
N71763 China Pilot Inc Lydeway Field, Etchilhampton

N180LK Piper PA-28-180 Cherokee F 28-7105121 7.18
Boston Commercial Corporation Tatenhill

N181WW Beagle B.206 Series 1 B.018 12.18
G-BCJF, N181WW, G-BCJF, XS773
International Air Services Biggin Hill
Operated by G Nolan

N182GC Reims Cessna F182Q Skylane II F18200068 2.19
G-BFOD Southern Aircraft Consultancy Inc Lydd

N182K Cessna 182Q Skylane 18266882 11.18
Harland Aviation Garey, IOM
Peterson King Katami conversion

N183DH Bell 206B-3 Jet Ranger III 2410 8.18
G-WBHH, N5001N
Southern Aircraft Consultancy Inc Sywell

N184BK Bombardier BD-100 Challenger 300 20209 1.19
C-FSLR Latium 3 Inc Hawarden

N185RH Cessna A185A Skywagon 185-0413 1.19
M-BXRH, G-BXRH, HB-CRX, (N1613Z)
Optimus Fuga Pactum Ltd PLS St Marks, IOM

N187CP Piper PA-31T Cheyenne 31T-7920054 1.17
(N690CA), YV-187CP, N16RK, C-FBBO, N23406,
N799SW, N23406 A D Henson (London)

N187SA Piper PA-28R-200 Cherokee Arrow II 28R-7235139 5.18
G-BOJH, N2821T
Southern Aircraft Consultancy Inc City of Derry, Eglinton
'Knight of the Thistle'

N188B Hawker 850XP 258822 2.19
N915TB, N103AL, N822XP
Paramount Aviation IOM Inc London Stansted

N189SA Piper PA-31-325 Navajo C/R 31-7512045 2.19
G-BMGH, ZS-LEU, N8493, A2-CAT
Southern Aircraft Consultancy Inc Southend
Operated by J Jacques

N190L Beech G36 Bonanza E-3932 2.19
E-3932 Inc Gloucestershire

N195AM Piper PA-46R-350T Matrix 4692148 2.19
Southern Aircraft Consultancy Inc East Winch

N199MW Piper PA-32-300 Six 32-7940219 1.19
G-OTBY, N2932G Woftam Inc Jersey

N199ZZ Cirrus Design SR22-GTS-G 32542 1.19
November Zulu Ltd North Weald

N200GK Piper PA-28R-200 Cherokee Arrow II 28R-7335287 2.19
G-BBIA, N11C
Southern Aircraft Consultancy Inc Stapleford
Operated by G H Kilby

N200RE	Beech E90 King Air	LW-164	2.19
	Gray Aviation Sturgate		
N200ZK	Cessna 172H	17255678	7.17
	Southern Aircraft Consultancy Inc Andreas, IOM		
N201W★	Bell 47D-1	83	9.14
	48-0803 Southern Aircraft Consultancy Inc		
	Phoenix Farm, Lower Upham		
	Stored dismantled; canx 3.15		
N201YK	Mooney M.20J	24-0518	2.19
	FAA Registrations LLC Jersey		
	Operated by Mooney Aviators Ltd		
N202AA	Cessna 421C Golden Eagle	421C1015	12.18
	Simply Living Ltd Biggin Hill		
N203CD	Cirrus Design SR20-G2	1451	2.19
	Mustarrow Inc Liverpool-John Lennon		
N206HE	Bell 206B JetRanger	2880	9.18
	N316JP Southern Aircraft Consultancy Inc (Weymouth)		
N208AJ	Cessna 208B Grand Caravan	208B0711	10.18
	HP-1359APP Cessna 2080711 Inc		
	Bank End Farm, Cockerham		
N208AX	Cessna 208B Grand Caravan	208B0710	7.18
	HP-1358APP Cessna 2080710 Inc Beccles		
	Operated by UK Parachuting		
N208ER	Bell 206B Jet Ranger	4527	5.17
	Aircraft Guaranty Corp Kilrush, RoI		
N208UP	Cessna 208B Caravan I	208B-0637	1.18
	N208AD, TG-EAA, N1002Y		
	SAL Inc Shotton Colliery, Peterlee		
N209DW	Lancair Columbia LC41-550FG	41504	1.19
	White Columbia Inc Oxford		
N209SA	Piper PA-22-108 Colt	22-8448	5.17
	EI-AYS, G-ARKT Southern Aircraft Consultancy Inc		
	Abbeyshrule, RoI		
N210AD	Cessna 210G Centurion	21058835	10.18
	OE-DES Uniplane Inc Stapleford		
N210BE	Cessna P210N Pressurised Centurion II	P21000088	1.19
	G-VMDE, (N4717P)		
	Southern Aircraft Consultancy Inc Retford Gamston		
N210NM	Cessna 210K Centurion	21059255	6.16
	D-ECAL, N8255M		
	Southern Aircraft Consultancy Inc Milltown Pass, RoI		
N210SH	Cessna P210N Turbo Centurion	P21000739	11.18
	N6260W Twoten Inc Guernsey		
	Silver Eagle conversion		
N210UK	Cessna P210N Pressurized Centurion II P21000130		9.17
	G-PIIX, G-KATH, (N4898) Dueunozero Inc Sandtoft		
	Nosewheel collapsed landing Isle of Mull 31.5.17;		
	stored unmarked		
N212W	Hiller UH-12A	237	11.17
	51-4015 International Air Services		
	Crab Tree Farm, Deighton		
N214CL	Cirrus Design SR22	3830	2.19
	Birt Aviation Turweston		
N214DA	Mooney M.20R	29-0181	1.17
	H W Jordan Dunsfold		
N215BT	Cessna 208 Caravan 1	20800517	12.18
	Screenstar Inc Leeds East		
N215DS	Diamond DA 40 Star	40.829	11.18
	Southern Aircraft Consultancy Inc Bristol		
	Operated by T Dove		
N216GC	Piper PA-28R-200 Cherokee Arrow B 28R-7135151		2.19
	G-EVVA, G-BAZU, EI-AVH, N11C		
	Southern Aircraft Consultancy Inc Elstree		
	Operated by T Dove		
N216HK★	CGS Hawk II	AHT468R447	3.16
	see G-MWYP in SECTION 1 Castlerock, Co. Londonderry		
	C/n on plate H-CGS-490P		
N218SA	Piper PA-24-250 Comanche	24-1877	3.17
	G-OJOK, PH-DZE, D-EIEI, N6749P		
	International Air Services Breighton		
	Operated by Gojok Ltd; damaged 2017		
	at Mount Airey Farm, South Cave; stored		

N218U	Cessna 310Q	310Q0507	2.16
	N218Y, G-AZYM, N5893M, N4592L		
	Southern Aircraft Consultancy Inc		
	Bourne Park, Hurstbourne Tarrant		
N219DW	Cirrus Design SR22-G3-GTSX Turbo	3148	2.19
	Sunlit Beacon Inc Brighton City		
N219PM	Cirrus Design SR22-G3-GTSX Turbo	2756	1.19
	PMM Aviation Biggin Hill		
N220AD	Cirrus Design SR22 Turbo – X	3697	2.19
	Southern Aircraft Consultancy Inc Crosland Moor		
N220RJ	Cirrus Design SR22-GTS	1775	2.19
	CD Aero Fairoaks		
N222ED	Cirrus Design SR22-G2	1103	12.18
	Not known –sale reported Sherburn in Elmet		
N222SW	Cirrus Design SR22-G2	0977	2.19
	Staywhite Inc Fairoaks		
N223KB	Cirrus Design SR22T	1186	2.19
	PMJ Airplane Inc Leicester		
N224RC	Cirrus Design SR22-G3-GTS Turbo	2919	10.18
	N917PG Skywest Aviation (Dunkeswell)		
N225EE	Gulfstream V	563	6.18
	(N180CH), (N169PG), N169CA, N8CA, N463GA		
	Delaware Trust Co Farnborough		
	Operated by E Els		
N225RB	Cirrus Design SR22T	0010	2.19
	G-OOEX, N567UK 225 Romeo Lima Inc Redhill		
N228US	Diamond DA.42 Twin Star	42.347	8.14
	Aircraft Guaranty Corp Cardiff		
N234RG	Pilatus PC-12/45	520	3.18
	Delaware Trust Co George Best-Belfast City		
	Operated by Rotary Group		
N235PF	Piper PA-28-235 Cherokee Pathfinder 28-7410083		2.19
	OO-DDC International Air Services		
	Napps Field, Billericay		
	Operated by A Braybrooke		
N239AX	Dassault Falcon 900B	39	11.18
	N573J, N5733, N181BS, N1818S, (N900BF), N428FJ,		
	F-WWFF Bank of Utah Biggin Hill		
	Operated by Lord Foster		
N239KF	Beech B200GT	BY-239	12.17
	Bank of Utah Oxford		
N239MY	Hughes OH-6A	49-1132	9.18
	N910GD, 68-17172		
	Southern Aircraft Consultancy Inc Kilrush, RoI		
	As US Army '68-17172'		
N242CV	Diamond DA42NG Twinstar	42.N174	2.19
	Quality Bird Inc Warton		
N243SA	Piper PA-22-108 Colt	22-8376	6.18
	G-ARKR Optimus Fuga Pactum Ltd Henstridge		
N249SP	Cessna 210L Centurion	21060000	8.18
	4X-CGU Southern Aircraft Consultancy Inc North Weald		
N250CC	Piper PA-24-250 Comanche	24-1931	11.18
	N957JK, OE-DEU, N6798P		
	Aerodynamics Worldwide Isle Of Man		
N250DM★	Bell UH-1H Iroquois	5808	9.18
	66-16114 Bell Asset Management Inc Leeds East		
	Canx 11.14; stored		
N250MD	Piper PA-31 Turbo Navajo B	31-742	8.18
	D-ICHY, F-BTCK, N7222L		
	Southern Aircraft Consultancy Inc Southend		
N256PT	Beech G58 Baron	TH-2350	2.19
	Baron Aviation Elstree		
N257SA	Piper PA-32-300 Cherokee Six B	32-40755	2.19
	OY-PCF, OH-PCF International Air Services Henstridge		
	Operated by G Bridges		
N258HP	Cirrus Design SR22T	1544	10.18
	Cirrus SR22T 1544 Inc Cambridge		
N258RP	Beech 58 Baron	TH-1737	10.17
	G-BWRP, VR-BVB, N3217H Aradian Inc Guernsey		
N259SA	Reims Cessna F172G	F172-0278	1.19
	EI-BAO, G-ATNH International Air Services North Coates		
	On rebuild for Humberside Flying Club		

N260AP   SIAI-Marchetti F260D   839   9.16
Rother Aviation   Kirknewton

N260QB★ Pitts S-2S   3002   11.17
Western Aviation Leasing   Bodmin
Canx 1.18

N262DB   Cirrus Design SR22   2915   10.18
G-PHEW, N107CT   Dab Aviation   Sleap

N263MX   MX Technologies MX-2   3   11.18
Southern Aircraft Consultancy Inc
Shove Furlong Farm, Kingsley
Operated by Nigel Lamb

N266EA   Beech 58 Baron   TH-2031   2.19
B58 Aviation Inc   Fairoaks

N277CD   Cessna 210L Centurion   21059663   9.18
CE ICY, N1163Q   Not known   sale reported   Headcorn

N277SA★ Piper PA-28-140 Cherokee   28-21661   8.18
SE-EYG   C M McCoole   Newcastle, RoI
Canx 5.15

N278DB   Mooney M.20R   29-0301   12.18
Sienna Aviation   Biggin Hill

N278SA   Cessna 177RG Cardinal RG   177RG0571   4.18
OO-ALT, N2171Q   International Air Services   Gloucestershire
Operated by R Hodgkinson

N280CH★ Enstrom 280FX   2024   7.15
G-SOPP, G-OSAB, N86259   D Marrow   Carlingford, RoI
Damaged 19.7.15 near Carlingford; canx 1.18

N280SA   Maule MX-7-180 Star Rocket   11070C   7.18
G-BSKT   Southern Aircraft Consultancy Inc
Glenswinton Farm, Parton

N281A★ Aeronca 11AC   11AC-1364   9.18
Not known   Popham
Canx 2.94; stored for rebuild

N284WY   Aviat A1C-200 Husky   3284   9.17
Husky 3284 Inc   Sleap

N285AT   Cessna T303 Crusader   T30300005   11.18
G-CYLS, 9H-CYL, G-CYLS, N20736, G-BKXI,
N303CC, (N9355T)
Southern Aircraft Consultancy Inc   Brighton City

N297CJ   SNCASE SE.313B Alouette II   1847   11.17
F-GLPI, (FAP9214), 77+00
International Air Services   Crab Tree Farm, Deighton

N301GA   Cessna 180K Skywagon   18052490   5.18
G-BUPG, N52086
Southern Aircraft Consultancy Inc   Rendcomb

N302GP   Cessna 210E   21058682   6.18
Southern Aircraft Consultancy Inc
Newcastle, Co Wicklow, RoI

N302MC   Cessna T310Q   310Q0909   12.18
N310AP   Sleap

N304CS   Lockheed L-1011-500 Tristar   193V-1157   11.18
ZD948, G-BFCA, N48354   Tristar Air LLC   Bruntingthorpe
Stored

N305SE   Mooney M20K   25-0377   7.18
N231RH   Southern Aircraft Consultancy Inc   Stapleford

N308SF   Douglas C-47A Dakota   18984   7.18
N98BF, 18984 Marine, N45V, NC65384, 42-100521
Southern Aircraft Consultancy Inc   Coventry

N309CS   Lockheed L-1011-500 Tristar   193V-1165   11.18
ZD951, G-BFCD, ZD951, G-BFCD
Tristar Air LLC   Bruntingthorpe
Stored

N309LJ★ Learjet Inc Learjet 25   25-034   2.16
N309AJ, N19FN, N17AR, N3UC, N6GC, N242WT,
N954FA, N954GA   City of Bristol College   Bristol
Instructional airframe; canx 10.03

N310AJ   Cessna 310R II   310R1606   1.19
G-BIFA   International Air Services   Oxford
Operated by A Chesters)

N310RX   Cessna T310R II   310R1381   10.18
G-TROP, N4250C   Coppercrest Inc   Shoreham

N310UK   Cessna 310R II   310R0584   12.18
G-MPBI, F-GEBB, HB-LMD, N87473
International Air Services   Elstree
Operated by B.Davies

N310WT★ Cessna 310R II   310R1257   12.14
G-BGXK, N6070X   Southern Aircraft Consultancy Inc   (Perth)
Derelict – no marks; canx 6.10 – roaded out 11.12.14

N315P   Cessna 310Q   310Q0811   1.19
G-REDB, G-BBIC, N69600
International Air Services   Full Sutton
Operated by Red Baron Haulage Ltd

N321KL   Mooney M.20J (201)   24-1102   7.18
G-BPKL, N1008K   International Air Services   Stapleford
Operated by London Link Flying Ltd

N321W   Cirrus Design SR20-GTS   1727   2.19
Aircraft Guaranty Corp   Fairoaks

N322AH   Airbus Helicopters AS.350B3   8241   2.18
Wells Fargo Trust Co   Denham

N322JR   Cirrus Design SR22T   0374   2.19
Southern Aircraft Consultancy Inc   Coventry

N324JC   Cessna 500 Citation I   500-0324   8.18
N52TC, N324C, (N5324J)   FNEC Inc   Biggin Hill
Stored

N330DG   SIAI-Marchetti SF.260D   766   10.18
N401FD   Aerospace Trust Management   East Midlands
Operated by S Coulson

N330MG   Aérospatiale AS.350B Ecureuil   2516   8.18
J6-AAN   Southern Aircraft Consultancy Inc   Redhill

N333DE   Mooney M.20M TLS Bravo   27-0346   6.18
Aerotechnics Aviation   North Weald

N337UK   Reims Cessna F337G Skymaster   F33700084   12.18
G-BOWD, N337BC, G-BLSB, EI-BET, D-INAI, (N53697)
N Registration Service LLC   Sandtoft
Operated by D H Penny

N338CB★ Bell UH-1H Iroquois   5812   9.18
N312RB, 66-16118   Bell Asset Management Inc   Leeds East
Canx 6.17; stored

N340GJ   Cessna 340A   340A0637   2.19
Bee Bee Aviation   Elstree

N340SC★ Cessna 340   340-0363   8.17
IAE Ltd   Cranfield
Canx 8.13

N340SM   Aérospatiale SA.341G Gazelle   1509   12.18
G-CDJT, N401S   Southern Aircraft Consultancy Inc   (Derby)

N340YP   Cessna 340A II   340A0990   10.18
VR-CHR, G-OCAN, D-ICIC, (N3970C)   ILEA Inc   Biggin Hill

N345TB   SOCATA TB-20 Trinidad   1914   4.16
Monty 345TB LLC   Fenland

N346DW   Cessna 340A-II   340A0742   1.19
G-SAMM, N37TJ, N2671A
Southern Aircraft Consultancy Inc   Coventry
RAM conversion

N347DC   Cirrus Design SR22T   1104   8.18
N174MW   Cock Aviation   Leeds Bradford

N350DG   Lancair Columbia LC42-550FG   42074   9.18
Southern Aircraft Consultancy Inc   Coventry

N350NM   Piper PA-46-350P Malibu Mirage   4636659   2.19
SCH Aviation   Coventry

N350XT   Piper PA-46-350P Malibu M350   4636692   9.18
CMA Cirrus Inc   Cumbernauld

N351RH   Bell 206B Jet Ranger III   4663   5.15
Lough Ridge Inc   Kilrush, RoI

N355GW   Cessna 172S Skyhawk SP   172S9355   10.18
Southern Aircraft Consultancy Inc   Rochester

N355ZZ   Aerospatiale AS.355F1 Ecureuil 2   5027   5.18
G-DEUX, F-GIBI, D-HAST, F-ODNS
Southern Aircraft Consultancy Inc   Dungannon, Co Tyrone

N359DW   Piper PA-30 Twin Comanche   30-770   3.18
G-ATET, N230ET   L W Durrell   Jersey

N365RE   Cessna 340A   340A0459   2.19
Southern Aircraft Consultancy Inc   Elstree

N365TV	Agusta A109E Power	11732	9.18
	PR-HMK, (N965TA) Arena Aviation Group Biggin Hill		
N369AL	Cirrus Design SR20	1552	12.18
	Southern Aircraft Consultancy Inc Jersey		
N369AN	Cessna 182S Skylane	18280696	10.18
	N644WA, N58169 Air View Ltd Jersey		
N369E	McDonnell Douglas 369E	0474E	7.17
	TU-THV, N92MS, ZS-REO, F-GLQP, N1611B		
	Righ Inc Brighton City		
N369SY	McDonnell Douglas MD369E	0560E	2.19
	EAHOT Inc (Brighton City)		
N370AJ	SOCATA Rallye 150ST	2929	6.14
	EI-BHY P J Coyne Knock, RoI		
N370SA	Piper PA-23-250 Aztec F	27-8054005	11.18
	G-BKVN, N6959A		
	Southern Aircraft Consultancy Inc Guernsey		
	Operated by B Pugh		
N370WC	Piper PA32-300 Cherokee Six	32-7840196	9.18
	PH-SMD, N30156 CAS Llc Newcastle, RoI		
	Operated by P.Coyne		
N371WS	Pitts S-1S	1-0015	8.16
	Southern Aircraft Consultancy Inc Branscombe		
N374SR	Cirrus Design SR22 G3 Turbo	2734	2.19
	Mestrenca Inc Fairoaks		
N377C	SOCATA TB21 Trinidad TC	2222	2.19
	Southern Aircraft Consultancy Inc Cark		
N394SE	Piper PA46-350P Malibu Mirage	4636394	2.19
	N394SE Corp Upper Harford Farm, Bourton on the Water		
N395TC	Commander Aircraft Commander 114TC	20003	9.17
	AQZ Aviation Inc Solent		
N397CM	Cessna 510 Mustang	510-0397	1.19
	Aviation Services Inc Jersey		
N400HF	Lancair Columbia LC41-550FG	41577	1.19
	CB Air Inc Cotswold		
N400UK	Lancair Columbia LC41-550FG	41062	10.18
	International Air Services Sleap		
N400YY	Extra EA400	019	8.18
	Bas Aviation Bournemouth		
	Stored		
N401JN★	Cessna 401	401-0166	8.18
	G-ROAR, G-BZFL, G-AWSF, N4066Q		
	Not known – sale reported Coventry		
	Canx 5.15		
N405CS	Lockheed L-1011-500 Tristar	193V-1164	11.18
	ZD950, G-BFCC Tristar Air LLC Bruntingthorpe		
	Stored		
N411BC	Piper PA-28-181 Archer III	2843339	2.19
	Southern Aircraft Consultancy Inc Elstree		
	Operated by D Rogg		
N414MB	Pitts S-2A	2236	2.19
	Sunlit Beacon Inc Dunkeswell		
N418WS	Beech G58 Baron	TH-2254	6.17
	N254AV Milburn World Travel Services Two Inc		
	Wycombe Air Park		
N421CA★	Cessna 421C	421C0153	4.16
	Not known Full Sutton		
	Canx 2.07; stored fuselage		
N421EA★	Cessna 421C Golden Eagle	421C1079	10.16
	Nielaster Inc Ringwood		
	Canx 10.14; stored – for sale		
N424XC	Piper PA-34-220T Seneca	3448005	10.18
	A Jayousi Fowlmere		
N425DK	Cessna 425	425-0086	1.19
	N425DK Inc Fairoaks		
N425HB	Cessna 425	425-0073	1.19
	N45AC, N6845T Bank of Utah Sherburn in Elmet		
N425ST	Cessna 550 Citation II	550-0709	12.18
	VT-SGT, N709RS, N709VP, N85KC, N18RN, N12RN,		
	N709CC, N1203D		
	Aircraft Guaranty Corp Leeds/Bradford Int'l		
	Operated by Julian Storey		
N429JC	Bell 429	57021	2.19
	Adams Aviation Services Brighton City		
N437TH★	BAe Jetstream T3	667	3.16
	ZE441, G-31-667		
	Southern Aircraft Consultancy Inc Dunsfold		
	Canx 2.12; stored as 'HB-VEM'		
N437UH★	BAe Jetstream T3	647	3.17
	ZE438, G-31-647		
	Southern Aircraft Consultancy Inc Dunsfold		
	Canx 2.12; fuselage stored		
N440GC	Piper PA-44-180T Turbo Seminole	44-8107065	4.18
	G-GISO, D-GISO, N82112, N9602N N9DC LLC Coventry		
N442BJ	Reims Cessna F177RG Cardinal RG	F177RG0094	9.15
	F-BVBC Southern Aircraft Consultancy Inc Kirknewton		
N445KA	Robin R.2160	116	3.16
	G-SBMO CAS Llc Sligo, RoI		
N446SE	Piper PA-32R-301T Saratoga II	3257446	11.17
	PTS Aviation Liverpool-John Lennon		
N447FT	Conroy CL-44-O	16	2.19
	9G-LCA, RP-C8023, 9G-LCA, P4-GUP, 4K-GUP,		
	EI-BND, N447T H W Jordan Bournemouth		
	Stored unmarked		
N447NA	Beech F33C Bonanza	CJ-130	5.18
	G-BTHW, PH-BNA, N23787		
	Southern Aircraft Consultancy Inc North Weald		
N449C	Agusta A109S	22066	2.19
	C-FIIG Fawkes Inc Dublin		
N449TA	Piper PA-31 Turbo Navajo	31-480	2.19
	G-CCRY, F-BTMM, N449TA		
	Southern Aircraft Consultancy Inc Leicester		
N450AG	Hughes 369HM	1090202M	5.17
	RDAF H-202 International Air Services		
	(Faldingworth, Lincoln)		
	Operated by R Briggs		
N453BG	Reims Cessna F172K	F17200786	5.16
	OY-DRS, LN-LJY Eastern Stearman Inc Eaglescott		
N456TL	Reims Cessna FT337GP Super Skymaster	FP3370019	6.17
	SX-PBA, F-ODFY, F-BUDU CCC Aviation Coventry		
N457GM	McDonnell Douglas 369E	0603E	2.19
	N5282F Century Aviation Retford Gamston		
NX458BG★	de Havilland DHC.1 Chipmunk 22	C1/0508	4.17
	WG458 BG Chipmunks Inc Breighton		
	Canx 12.12; as 'WG458:2'		
N459PA	Piper PA-34-220T Seneca V	3449459	2.19
	Aircraft Guaranty Corp Isle Of Man		
N463RD	SOCATA TBM850	463	12.18
	Flanes Ltd Biggin Hill		
N464LB	Piper PA-46-350P Malibu Mirage	4622139	2.19
	N9220G Rio Aviation Fairoaks		
N464MA	Cessna 182S	18280822	7.18
	Southern Aircraft Consultancy Inc Swansea		
N466AB	Piper PA-46-500TP Malibu Meridian	4697105	2.19
	D-EVER, N429MM		
	Southern Aircraft Consultancy Inc Isle of Man		
N469WW	Diamond DA 42	42.AC074	11.18
	MX Jets Inc Little Hough Hall, Norton		
N470AC	Boeing 737-3L9	24570	2.19
	HZ-AMC, N570LL, 9M-AEE, B-2653, N2332Q, G-OABD,		
	9V-TRC, OY-MME		
	Southern Aircraft Consultancy Inc Bournemouth		
	Stored		
N473DC	Douglas C-47A Dakota III	19345	6.18
	N5831B, C-FKAZ, CF-KAZ, TS422, 42-100882		
	Dakota Heritage Inc East Kirkby		
	As '2100882/3X-P' in USAF c/s		
N475EL★	Boeing 737-53A	24754	2.19
	VP-BXN, G-GFFF, G-OBMZ, SE-DNC		
	Southern Aircraft Consultancy Inc Bournemouth		
	Canx 1.17; engine test bed marked 'EVRAMP'		
N477PM	Piper PA-31-310 Turbo Navajo B	31-7300956	1.19
	G-BBDS, N97RJ, G-SKKB, G-BBDS, N7565L		
	McPhar Aviation Gloucestershire		

Overseas

N479BC	Cirrus Design SR22T	1073	2.19
	N479BC Inc Denham		
N482CD	Cirrus Design SR22-GTS	1482	8.18
	Southern Aircraft Consultancy Inc Sleap		
N485ED	Piper PA-23-250 Aztec C	27-3864	9.16
	G-BAED, N6567Y		
	Southern Aircraft Consultancy Inc Guernsey		
N497XP	Raytheon Hawker 400XP	RK-497	2.19
	Aircraft Guaranty Corp East Midlands		
	Operated by V & P Midlands Ltd		
N498YY	Cessna 525 CitationJet	525-0498	2.19
	N5201J, N498YY, N5223K TVPX ARS Inc Dublin Weston		
N499AG★	Piper PA-30 Twin Comanche	30-1415	2.19
	F-GALF, G-AVJT, N8281Y		
	Not known – sale reported Bournemouth		
	Canx 5.15; dismantled in open store		
N499MS	Piper PA-28-181 Archer III	2843166	8.18
	G-EPJM, N41268 MS Aviation Jersey		
N500AV	Piper PA-24-260 Comanche C	24-4805	2.19
	OO-SAP Southern Aircraft Consultancy Inc Welshpool		
N500HL	Hughes 369HS	11-0288S	9.18
	N239MW, N113T, LV-RAJ, PA-34		
	Aircraft Guaranty Corp Kerry, RoI		
	Operated by P McGillicuddy		
N500SY	McDonnell Douglas MD.369E	0007E	6.17
	N5144Q Eastern Atlantic Helicopters Sales Brighton City		
	Operated by Hitachi Capital		
N500TY	McDonnell Douglas MD.369E	0086E	3.17
	C-GRVV Southern Aircraft Consultancy Inc PLS Somerton		
N500XV	Hughes 369D (*Hughes 500*)	120-0881D	4.17
	OO-LVK, OE-XBB, N190CA, N5293E, C-GHVK		
	Southern Aircraft Consultancy Inc Blackpool		
N503DW	Mudry CAP.10B	202	9.18
	International Air Services Headcorn		
	Operated by P Hamilton		
N504EA★	Eclipse EA500	EX500-109	7.18
	TWI Ltd Granta Park, Great Abington (*Displayed*)		
N505WC	Piper PA-32R-301 Saratoga II HP	3246034	8.18
	Aircraft Guaranty Corp White Waltham		
N506JA	Airbus Helicopters AS350B3	8021	12.18
	G-CIMA Bank of Utah Denham		
N507CS	Lockheed L-1011-500 Tristar	193V-1186	11.18
	ZE704, N508PA Tristar Air LLC Bruntingthorpe		
	Stored		
N508RA	Cirrus Design SR22	4458	2.19
	Woodford Aviation Stapleford		
N508XS	Bell 206B-2 JetRanger II	1957	6.14
	G-OMLS, N80367, G-OMLS, D-HAFN, N9909K		
	Southern Aircraft Consultancy Inc (Nottingham)		
	For sale 11.18		
N509MV	Beech B200 Super King Air	BB-877	10.18
	G-CFVO, N509MV, N711BU, N4CQ, N4C, N877AJ, N3837S		
	Southern Aircraft Consultancy Inc Bournemouth		
	Stored dismantled		
N510W	Bell 222B	47133	10.17
	N7040Z TVPX ARS Inc (PLS Cirencester)		
N511TE	Beech D55 Baron	TE-511	2.19
	Southern Aircraft Consultancy Inc Biggin Hill		
N513X★	Folland Gnat T.1	FL528	8.16
	XP513 Heritage Aircraft Trust North Weald		
	Canx 7.16		
N515CL	Cessna 182G Skylane	18255135	5.17
	G-NYZS, G-ASRR, (G-CBIL), EI-ATF, G-ASRR, N3735U		
	AAT Inc Old Buckenham		
N517FD	Piper PA-32R-301T Saratoga II TC	3257263	6.18
	Southern Aircraft Consultancy Inc Retford Gamston		
	Damaged undercarriage at Fair Isle, Shetland 16.5.18		
N518XL	Liberty Aerospace XL-2	0013	2.19
	Southern Aircraft Consultancy Inc Biggin Hill		
N519MC★	Piper PA-28-140 Cherokee Cruiser	28-7325519	5.16
	G-BBID R Lobell Elstree		
	Canx 10.17; derelict		
N520DS	Diamond DA.40 Star	40.620	2.19
	FSCK N520DS Inc White Waltham		
N520EA	McDonnell Douglas MD500N	LN062	5.18
	N128PD, N5209E		
	Eastern Atlantic Helicopters Brighton City		
N525DB	Reims Cessna F172H	F172-0484	6.18
	G-AWGR, N525DB, G-AWGR		
	International Air Services Mount Airey Farm, South Cave		
N525HA	Cessna 525 CitationJet	525-0081	12.18
	N181JT, N5090V		
	Southern Aircraft Consultancy Inc Guernsey		
	Operated by G de Rooy		
N531RM	Pitts S.2C	6018	8.14
	Southern Aircraft Consultancy Inc Redhill		
	Built Aviat		
N531TJ	Enstrom F280FX	2059	7.18
	HB-ZFS, G-MEYO, SX-HCN		
	Southern Aircraft Consultancy Inc Brighton City		
	Landing accident at Carrahane Strand, Co Derry 16.7.18		
N533DK	Eclipse EA500	000143	1.17
	Aircraft Guaranty Corp Oxford		
N533DL	Cessna 208 Caravan I	20800533	2.19
	Cessna 208533 Inc Gloucestershire		
N534MW	Cirrus Design SR22T	1534	1.19
	Alchemette Aviation Hawarden		
N535TK	Maule MXT-7-180	14025C	2.19
	Southern Aircraft Consultancy Inc Fenland		
N536K	Beech A36 Bonanza	E-3220	11.18
	Aircraft Guaranty Corp Oxford		
	Operated by Zaher Deir		
N540XS	MXR Technologies MXC	2	8.16
	Southern Aircraft Consultancy Inc		
	Shove Furlong Farm, Kingsley		
	Operated by Nigel Lamb – 'Team Breitling'		
N542AP	Dassault Falcon 2000EX	89	2.19
	M-SNAP, N642TA, M-XJOB, VP-CAM, F-WWGZ		
	Aviation Services the Second Inc Jersey		
N542CD	Cirrus Design SR22-GTS	1186	1.19
	1186 Holding Inc Biggin Hill		
N547MP	Honda HA-420 Hondajet	42000070	2.19
	N542MP, N230JL Aviation Services the Third Inc Jersey		
N551TT	Piper PA-32R-301T Saratoga II TC	3257026	10.18
	G-GOTO, N92965, G-GOTO, N92965		
	Southern Aircraft Consultancy Inc Blackbushe		
	Operated by M Tolbod		
N554CF	Beech E90 King Air	LW-66	5.17
	N3166W Southern Aircraft Consultancy Inc		
	Abbeyshrule, RoI		
N556L	Cirrus Design SR22	0132	2.19
	Blundy Aviation Leeds East		
N559C	Piper PA-34-220T Seneca V	3449238	2.19
	Chiswell Aviation Inc Guernsey		
N569JM	Cessna 414A	414A0125	8.18
	M-SMJJ, G-SMJJ, N2694H		
	Southern Aircraft Consultancy Inc Jersey		
N575DW	Luscombe 8E Silvaire	5216	11.18
	W T Chisholm Bournemouth		
	For sale		
N575GM	SOCATA TB-20 Trinidad	1872	1.19
	Wedd Aviation Cambridge		
N577AG★	Sud Est SE.313B Alouette II	1666	5.17
	HB-ZBE, (F-GPEP), OL-A23, F-WJDG		
	Not known Kilrush, RoI		
	Canx 10.14		
N581AF	Beech 58 Baron	TH-2063	5.18
	N581AF Inc Sleap		
N583CD	Cirrus Design SR22	1809	2.19
	International Air Services Haverfordwest		
N590CD	Cirrus Design SR22-G2	0957	12.18
	International Air Services Sherburn-in-Elmet		
N600LB	Cirrus Design SR22-GTS	1693	10.17
	G-LAWT, N401LX N600LB Inc Leeds/Bradford Int'l		

Overseas

N600PE	Beech G58 Baron Springair Inc Gloucestershire	TH-2404	1.19
N601AR★	Piper Aerostar 601P N3839H, F-GKCL, N3839H, G-RACE, N8083J The Fabric Factory Jersey *Canx 3.15*	61P-0569-7963247	5.16
N616CM	SOCATA TBM850 Kilo Aviation Liverpool John Lennon	540	11.18
N622RC	Cirrus Design SR22T Highwood Inc Bournemouth	1610	2.19
N623NP	Grumman G1159A Gulfstream III N723MM, N891MG, N802GA, N340, N303GA European Skybus Inc Bournemouth *Stored*	357	2.19
N642P	Piper PA-31 Turbo Navajo B N500UD, G-EEAC, G-SKKA, G-FOAL, G-RMAE, N7239L Corporate Air (Ireland) Inc Newtownards	31-761	1.19
N644BL	Beech B36TC Bonanza G-CIJP, D-EKPD, N15519 B Lord Fairoaks	EA-492	10.18
N644MW	Cirrus Design SR22T Cotswold Aviation Wellesbourne Mountford	1318	2.19
N648KM	Diamond DA.42 Twinstar Aerospace Trust Management Retford Gamston	42.316	2.19
N652P	Piper PA-18-150 Super Cub G-BTDX, N62595 Southern Aircraft Consultancy Inc Woodview, Co Armagh *Operated by K Troughton*	18-7809098	8.15
N656JM	Reims Cessna FR182 Skylane RGII G-BHEO S E Miserey Stapleford	FR1820049	1.19
N661KK	Piper PA-28-181 Archer II HB-PKN, N9104F Southern Aircraft Consultancy Inc Fairoaks	2890028	1.19
N662KK	Piper PA-18-150 Super Cub N45490, IDF/AF112 Southern Aircraft Consultancy Inc Fairoaks	18-8209023	6.18
N663CD	Cirrus Design SR22 Southern Aircraft Consultancy Sleap	1847	10.18
N663KK	Cirrus Design SR22-G3-GTS-Turbo Southern Aircraft Consultancy Inc Fairoaks	3064	2.19
N666GA	Gulfstream AA-5B Tiger Southern Aircraft Consultancy Inc Thruxton *Operated by B Evans*	AA5B-1136	9.18
N673SA	Piper PA-24-250 Comanche G-ARFH, N7087P Southern Aircraft Consultancy Inc Great Massingham *Undercarriage collapse at Firs Farm, Newbury 19.5.17*	24-2240	5.17
N678EM	Beech A36 Bonanza Aerospace Trust Management LLC Elstree	E-1285	1.19
N678J	Beech 58 Baron Optimus Fuga Pactum Ltd Lee-on-Solent	TH-821	10.18
N681EW	Reims/Cessna F182Q Skylane II G-BLEW, F-GAQD Southern Aircraft Consultancy Inc Henstridge	F18200039	10.18
N690CL	Rockwell 690A Turbo Commander N46663, N53RF, N57074 AAT Inc Old Buckenham	11153	8.18
N696PG	Cirrus Design SR22-GS N196PG Inc Bournemouth	3606	2.19
N697RB	Pitts S-1T Aerospace Trust Management Full Sutton	1042	10.18
N700EL	SOCATA TBM-700B N701AR Air Twinlite Inc Dolly's Grove,Dublin,RoI	209	2.19
N700KG	Bombardier Learjet 40XR N502JM, N5009T Florida Express Corp Southend *Operated by Kings Aviation*	45-2017	2.19
N703CS	Lockheed L-1011-500 Tristar ZE705, N509PA Tristar Air LLC Bruntingthorpe *Stored*	193V-1188	11.18
N705CS	Lockheed L-1011-500 Tristar ZD953, G-BFCF Tristar Air LLC Bruntingthorpe *Stored*	193V-1174	11.18
N707SN	Cirrus Vision SF50 Visionjet Inc Biggin Hill	0041	1.19

N707TJ	Boeing-Stearman A75N1 (N2S-1) Kaydet 75-950 N9PK, N50057, USN 3173 Merkel Air Rendcomb *Operated by V.S.E.Norman t/a AeroSupeBatics Wingwalking*		8.16
N707XJ	Cessna 177A Cardinal SE-FKO, (LN-FAK), (OY-AGM), N30579 Southern Aircraft Consultancy Inc Birr, RoI *Operated by D Corboy*	17701340	3.17
N709EL	Beech 400A Beechjet (N709EW), N709JB GAL Air Inc East Midlands *Operated by DFS Furniture*	RK-52	2.19
N715BC	Beech A36 Bonanza F-BXOZ N715BC Inc Denham	E-782	2.19
N717HS	Cirrus Design SR22T APG Aviation Elstree	1717	2.19
N719EL	Raytheon Hawker 400XP Edra Lauren Leasing Corp East Midlands *Operated by DFS Furniture*	RK-488	12.18
N720B	Bell 206L-1 LongRanger II G-DALE, G-HBUS Gentem Inc Dublin, RoI *Operated by Omega Air*	45452	1.16
N727CH	McDonnell Douglas 369E N1609B, D-HFMP EAHOT Inc Brighton City	0453E	2.19
N727EL★	Boeing 727-227F N481FE, N457BN Southern Aircraft Consultancy Inc Lasham *Canx 10.18; stored*	21463	11.18
N733UK	Boeing 737-3Q8 G-TOYD, G-EZYT, HB-IIE, N721LF, HB-IIE Southern Aircraft Consultancy Inc Bournemouth *Stored*	26307	2.19
N735CX	Cessna 182Q Skylane II Wilmington Trust Company West Horndon *Operated by B.Holmes; modified to Advanced Lift 260 STOL*	18265329	7.18
N735FL	Piper PA-28-140 Cherokee Optimus Fuga Pactum Ltd Henstridge	28-7225537	8.18
N747MM	Piper PA-28R-200 Cherokee Arrow II 28R-7335445 PH-MLP, N56489 Southern Aircraft Consultancy Inc Denham		2.19
N747YK	Cessna 310R II G-BTYK, N200VC, N5018J YK Inc Jersey	310R0138	12.18
N748AS	Cessna 182T Big Pond Hopper Inc (Fowle Hall Farm, Laddingford)	18283039	10.18
N750GF	Cessna 750 Citation X N52655 S'porter Air Inc Gloucestershire	750-0244	1.19
N752DS	Diamond DA 40 Star Coutale Inc Wycombe Air Park	40.752	10.18
N759AU	Cessna 182Q International Air Services Manchester Barton	18265846	1.19
N761JU	Cessna T210M Centurion Southern Aircraft Consultancy Inc Oaksey Park	21062300	11.18
N766AM	Aérospatiale AS.355N Ecureiuil 2 Beacon Aviation West Beacon Farm, Woodhouse Eaves	5601	1.19
N767CM	Beech A36 Bonanza G-ORSP, N56037 Southern Aircraft Consultancy Inc Leeds East	E-2723	5.18
N767GA	Cirrus Design SR22T Southern Sky Aviation Southampton	1745	2.19
N771SR	Cirrus Design SR22-GTS G3 Turbo Cirrus SR22 2771 Inc Denham	2771	1.19
N774E★	Dornier Do.28A-1 Not known Old Warden *Canx 9.14; stored*	3022	10.14
N775RG	Maule M5-210C Strata Rocket G-CBVW, A2-WNP, ZS-LVB Southern Aircraft Consultancy Inc Fife	6048C	10.16
N777MD	Piper PA-28RT-201T Turbo Arrow 28R-8131117 Southern Aircraft Consultancy Inc Thruxton		6.18
N780AC	Piper PA-30 Twin Comanche C G-TCOM, N555JC, N8810Y Southern Aircraft Consultancy Inc Jersey	30-1967	11.18
N781CD	Cirrus Design SR20-G2 Cirrus Charlie Delta Inc Leeds East	1423	2.19

N784F	Bell 206B-3 JetRanger III N16LT Southern Aircraft Consultancy Inc Oaksey Park	2508	12.18
N787CE	Piper PA-28-181 Archer III G-FORR, N4160Z, G-FORR, N4160Z Southern Aircraft Consultancy Inc Guernsey	2843336	11.18
N789MC ★	Cessna T310Q II G-LLMC, G-BKSB, VR-CEM, G-BKSB, HB-LMO, OE-FYL, (N69680) Aerospace Trust Management Coventry *Canx 3.18*	310Q0914	6.15
N789MD	Cessna 340A II G-LIZA, G-BMDM, ZS-KRH, N4620N N789MD Inc Oxford	340A1021	2.19
N790BH	Cirrus Design SR22-G3 N127PG IWG Aviation Norwich	2964	8.18
N799CD	Cirrus Design SR22-GTS GPA Inc Kilrush, RoI	1543	9.18
N799DS	Diamond Aircraft DA 40 Aircraft Guaranty Corp Blackbushe	40.799	1.19
N799JH	Piper PA-28RT-201T Turbo Arrow IV HB-PNE, PH-HJM, N8206B International Air Services North Weald *Operated by J Havers*	28R-8231051	12.18
N800HL	Bell 222 N800HH, N8140A, N37VA Yorkshire Helicopters USA Inc Coney Park, Leeds	47054	9.17
N800VM	Beech 76 Duchess G-BHGM Southern Aircraft Consultancy Inc Gloucestershire	ME-318	2.19
N800WK	Agusta A109A-II N500WK Nevada Aircraft Corp Henstridge	7341	12.16
N803SR	Cirrus Design SR22 Southern Aircraft Consultancy Inc Solent	1959	1.19
N808CA	Piper PA-32R-301 Saratoga II HP N808CA Inc Sandtoft	3246240	11.18
N808PC	de Havilland DHC-6-100 Twin Otter C-GDQY, YA-GAS MRC Aviation Lower Mountpleasant Farm, Chatteris	326	3.18
N808VT	Piper PA-28R-201 Cherokee Arrow III Southern Aircraft Consultancy Inc Denham	28R-7737051	2.19
N812AC	Beech A65-90 King Air N815K Southern Aircraft Consultancy Inc Newcastle, RoI	LJ-123	8.18
N821CC	Cirrus Design SR22 Cirrus N821CC Inc Cambridge	1427	2.19
N824US	Diamond DA.40 Star Strong Tower Services Wycombe Air Park	40.824	11.18
N829AA ★	Learjet 25B N25TK, N741F, N741E, N262JE Dublin Institute of Technology Dublin, RoI *Canx 4.13; instructional airframe*	25B-100	4.14
N834CD	Cirrus Design SR22 Southern Aircraft Consultancy Inc Seething	0168	6.18
N836TP	Beech A36TP Bonanza N6770M N836TP Inc Holt Farm, Melbury	E-2124	2.19
N840CD	Cirrus Design SR20-GTS Weston Flyers Dublin Weston, RoI	1535	1.19
N841WS	Gulfstream Aerospace Gulfstream IV (Gulfstream 450) N199GA Millburn World Travel Services Five Inc Farnborough *Operated by Walter Scott & Partners Ltd*	4099	2.19
N843TE	Eclipse Aviation EA500 Southern Aircraft Consultancy Inc Guernsey	00072	1.19
N844MS	Cirrus Design SR22T Not known – sale reported (Oxford) *Crashed on take off Sherburn 25.11.17*	0630	11.17
N850BG	SOCATA TBM700 Wren Aviation Oxford	367	2.19
N850NP	SOCATA TBM700N Aircraft Guaranty Corp Biggin Hill *Operated by Oyster Air*	431	10.18
N852CD	Cirrus Design SR22 Southern Aircraft Consultancy Inc Guernsey	0219	1.19
N866C	Cirrus Design SR22 Apus Aviation Fairoaks	0397	1.19
N866LP	Piper PA-46-350P Malibu Mirage N666LP, N92928 Southern Aircraft Consultancy Inc Swansea	4636130	2.19
N877SW	Agusta A109A-II N8772W, N877SW Southern Aircraft Consultancy Inc Biggin Hill	7283	6.18
N881AA ★	Beech RB390 Premier 1 OE-FRJ, N390BW, XA-TSN, N390P, N390TA Flight International Corp Dunsfold *Canx 4.18; stored*	RB-12	3.17
N882AA	Beech RB390 Premier 1 OE-FMC, N43HJ, (N111HH), N142HH Flight International Corp Lasham	RB-41	1.19
N882JH	Maule M.7-235B Southern Aircraft Consultancy Inc Gloucestershire *Operated by G Thomson)*	23056C	12.18
N888DM	Piper PA-30 Turbo Twin Comanche C N968BC, (N968P), N968PC International Air Services Enniskillen *Operated by D Keith*	30-1833	5.18
N899AE	Beech 99 C-FKCG, N218BH, N749A Beech 99 U23 Inc Dunkeswell *'The White Beech'*	U-23	3.17
N899AG	Beech 99 G-DLAB, N899AG, C-FYSJ, N209BH, N796A Beech 99 U73 Inc Dunkeswell *'The Starlight Express'*	U-73	1.19
N899DZ	Beech 99 C-GHVI, N17RX, N17RA Beech 99 U153 Inc Dunkeswell *'The Black Beech'*	U-153	1.19
N900PH	Piper PA-28R-180 Cherokee Arrow EC-BNY International Air Services Tatenhill *Operated by R Gardner*	28R-30302	7.18
N900TB ★	Piper PA-31P Pressurised Navajo C-GATP, N7343L Wings of Londi Inc Bournemouth *Canx 12.15; stored; Schaffer Turbo Comanchero conversion*	31P-7400227	2.19
N901B	Aerospatiale SA341G Gazelle International Air Services Crab Tree Farm, Deighton	1410	2.19
N902SR	Cirrus Design SR22-GTS Southern Aircraft Consultancy Inc Stapleford	2356	9.18
N907MM	Cirrus Design SR20 Upwind Inc Elstree	1270	2.19
N909PH	Piper PA-23-160 Apache D-GDCO, SE-EDG, D-GABA, N4369P International Air Services Mount Airey Farm, South Cave	23-1800	7.18
N910RW	SOCATA TBM910 Redwood 850 Inc Wycombe Air Park	1200	2.19
N911CS	Beech U-8F Seminole Orchtrans Inc Orchardleigh House, Buckland Dinham	LF-21	8.17
N911DN	Bell UH-1H Iroquois 67-17426 Yorkshire Helicopters USA Inc Coney Park, Leeds	9624	9.17
N915JM ★	Cessna 310Q G-IMLI, G-AZYK, N4182Q International Air Services Standalone Farm, Meppershall *Operated by R W Davies; canx 7.17 – for sale as spares*	310Q0491	3.17
N916CD	Cirrus Design SR22 Farnborough Aircraft Inc Redhill	0318	2.19
N916GS	Bell 206B JetRanger III I-MIAA, D-HEPI, N206TG, N1085V Flight International Corp Dunsfold	2916	6.15
N918DK	Enstrom F.28F N28HR W R Mott Woodside Farm, Elkington *Pod only – crashed at Twin Falls, ID 27.3.13*	755	7.18
N925CC	Cirrus Design SR22-G3-GTSX Turbo G-JOEB, N519PG Cirrus SR22 2992 Inc North Weald	2992	2.19
N928HW	Commander Aircraft Commander 114B 14672 Southern Aircraft Consultancy Inc Stapleford *Operated by F Parkes*		2.19
N928SK	Cirrus Design SR22T 0928 Aviation Inc Leeds/Bradford Int'l	0928	1.19

Overseas

N930SA	SOCATA TBM 930	1800	2.19
	Spectrum Medical Aviation Gloucestershire		
N930Z	Piper PA-46-350P Malibu Mirage	4622188	1.19
	D-ERBU, (D-ERUU), G-DODY Mirage 930 Corp Denham		
N936CT (1)★	Cirrus Design SR22–G3-GTS	3111	11.18
	G-OLCT, N948PG Southern Aircraft Consultancy Gloucestershire		
	Crashed at Cheltenham 6.6.13; fuselage stored		
N936CT (2)	Cirrus Design SR22T	0648	2.19
	Southern Aircraft Consultancy Denham		
N937BP	Mooney M.20J	24-3046	2.19
	G-OOOO, N205EE		
	Southern Aircraft Consultancy Inc Elstree		
N937DR	Cessna 172R	17280217	1.19
	Southern Aircraft Consultancy Inc Donegal, RoI		
	Operated by F Doherty		
N938AC	Cirrus Design SR22	4146	12.18
	Seascape Flyers Inc Newtownards		
N949AC	Cirrus Design SR22T	0833	9.18
	N947AC Inc Blackpool		
	Operated by A Chesworth		
N950AL★	Agusta A 109E	11628	10.14
	Castle Helicopters Trebrown, Liskeard		
	Canx 9.08; spares use		
N950M	Cessna 750 Citation X	750-0311	10.17
	G-OTEN, N51246 7500311 Inc Isle Of Man		
N955SH	Piper PA-46-350P Malibu Mirage	4636339	2.19
	N318ED, N5354K		
	Southern Aircraft Consultancy Cambridge		
	Operated by J Strutt; DLX conversion 206		
N957T	Piper PA-32R-301 Saratoga II HP	3246176	8.18
	Severn Valley Aviation Shobdon		
N967LV	Piper PA-32R-301T Saratoga II TC	3257481	1.19
	N967LV Inc Cranfield		
N971RJ	Piper PA-39 Twin Comanche C/R	39-111	11.18
	G-AZBC, N8951Y		
	Southern Aircraft Consultancy Inc Wycombe Air Park		
N980HB	Rockwell Commander 695	95006	6.18
	N171CT, N171CP, N4468F, YV-366CP, N9759S		
	HBC Aviation Inc Guernsey		
N982CD	Cirrus Design SR22-GTS	1853	2.19
	November CD Inc Denham		
N982NW	Maule MXT-7-180A	21046C	12.18
	International Air Services Isle Of Man		
	Operated by R Schreiber		
N986DT	Cirrus Design SR22T	1630	2.19
	Holroyd Aviation Cambridge		
N986JT	Cirrus Design SR22T	0937	1.19
	Juliet Tango Aviation Cambridge		
N988SR	Cirrus Design SR22-GT3	2038	2.19
	Aircraft Guaranty Corp Fairoaks		
N989PR	SOCATA TBM850	467	12.18
	Rory Fabio Inc Biggin Hill		
N992C	Lancair Legacy	L2K-312	6.18
	C D Baker North Weald		
N999F	Beech F33A Bonanza	CE-1282	2.16
	OO-OVB N T N Fox Systems Inc Newcastle Int'l		
N999MH	Cessna 195B	7168	9.18
	OH-CSE E Detiger Henstridge		
N999PD	Waco YMF-F5C	F5C108	1.19
	Airpark Aviators Coventry		
N999RL	Robinson R44 Raven II	10614	10.18
	G-CDEZ Heli Twinlite Dolly's Grove, Dublin, RoI		
N1033Y	Cessna 172S	172S10598	11.18
	M La Biche Ballyboy, RoI		
N1196R★	Raven S-40A Balloon (Hot Air)	S40A-141	6.16
	P Sweatman Coventry *'Froggy'*		
	Canx 6.12		
N1320S	Cessna 182P Skylane II	18264884	6.18
	International Air Services Haverfordwest		
	Peterson STOL conversion		

N1325M	Boeing Stearman E75(N2S-5) Kaydet	75-8484	8.16
	Eastern Stearman Inc Priory Farm, Tibenham		*Operated by*
	Blackbarn Aviation; spares use		
NC1328★	Fairchild F24R-46KS Argus	3310	5.17
	Eastern Stearman Inc Priory Farm, Tibenham		
	Operated by Blackbarn Aviation; frame only; canx 12.15		
N1350J	Rockwell Commander 112B	516	2.19
	Fish Associates Inc Tatenhill		
N1407J	Rockwell Commander 112A	407	1.19
	Blue Lake Aviation Inc Blackbushe		
N1424C	Cessna 182T Skylane	18281610	10.18
	Glendoe Inc Bowldown Farm, Tetbury		
N1502A	Piper PA-20 Pacer	20-686	1.19
	Southern Aircraft Consultancy Inc New Farm, Felton		
N1544M★	Boeing-Stearman E75N1 Kaydet	75-8059	1.15
	Not known Priory Farm, Tibenham		
	Canx 4.11; spares use		
N1551D	Cessna 190	7773	2.15
	Southern Aircraft Consultancy Inc White Waltham		
N1581D	Cessna 195	7864	1.19
	Spirit in the Sky Inc Dunkeswell		
	Overturned in forced landing 3.1.19 Honiton		
N1731B	Boeing A75N-1 Stearman	75-5716	5.18
	42-17553 Eastern Stearman Inc Compton Abbas		
	As '42-17553:716'		
N1909G	Cessna 310R II	310R1225	9.15
	G-TKPZ, G-BRAH, N1909G		
	Southern Aircraft Consultancy Inc Prestwick		
N2046Q★	Beech 56TC Baron	TG-10	4.16
	Satcom Distribution Glebe Farm, Stockton		
	Canx 4.13; stored unmarked		
N2086P	Piper PA-23 Apache	23-674	1.19
	N286GB, N2086P		
	Southern Aircraft Consultancy Inc Wellesbourne Mountford		
N2106V	Cessna 120	14627	8.18
	Southern Aircraft Consultancy Inc		
	Little Engeham Farm, Woodchurch		
	Operated by S Parsons		
N2121T	Gulfstream AA-5B Tiger	AA5B-1031	2.19
	J.Siebols Southend		
N2125K	Mooney M20M	27-0239	6.17
	Southern Aircraft Consultancy Inc Sturgate		
	Operated by D A Plange		
N2136E	Piper PA-28RT-201 Arrow IV	28R-7918002	12.18
	Southern Aircraft Consultancy Inc Sandtoft		
	Wheels up landing 22.7.17		
N2177G	Cessna 182A	51477	11.18
	Southern Aircraft Consultancy Inc Enstone		
N2231F	Cessna 182T Skylane	18281925	8.18
	Southern Aircraft Consultancy Inc Porth		
	Operated by D Paterson		
N2273Q	Piper PA-28-181 Cherokee Archer II	28-7790389	6.18
	Southern Aircraft Consultancy Inc		
	Wolverhampton Halfpenny Green		
N2299L	Beech F33A Bonanza	CE-677	9.18
	Optimus Fuga Pactum Ltd Perranporth		
N2366D	Cessna 170B	20518	2.19
	Southern Aircraft Consultancy Inc Turweston		
N2379C	Cessna R182 Skylane RG	R18200170	11.18
	West Country Aviation Inc (Bromsberrow)		
N2401Z	Piper PA-23-250 Aztec F	27-8054034	10.14
	Pan Maritime US Inc MoD St Athan		
N2445V	Cessna 182S Skylane	18280699	7.18
	N2445V Cessna Inc Low Park Farm, Ebbersdon		
N2530K	Cessna 180K	18052972	10.18
	International Air Services Tatenhill		
NC2612★	Stinson Junior R	8754	7.15
	A.L.Young Henstridge		
	Canx 10.11; stored		
N2652P	Piper PA-22-135 Tri Pacer	22-2992	8.16
	Aircraft Guaranty Corp (Cossan Point, Co Wesmeath, RoI)		

N2742Y	Hughes 369HS Southern Aircraft Consultancy Inc Staddon Heights, Plymouth *Operated by Hovercam*	62-0389S	6.16
N2844H	Erco 415D Ercoupe Southern Aircraft Consultancy Inc Spanhoe *Stored*	3469	11.18
N2923N	Piper PA-32-300 Cherokee Six Southern Aircraft Consultancy Inc Jersey	32-7940207	2.19
N2943D	Piper PA-28RT-201 Arrow IV G-BSLD, N2943D Southern Aircraft Consultancy Inc Liverpool John Lennon *Operated by A Eskander*	28R-7918231	11.18
N2989M	Piper PA-32-300 Six International Air Services Park Farm, Middleham *Operated by Mark Johnston Racing*	32-7840062	12.18
N3064B	Cessna 195B Southern Aircraft Consultancy Inc Audley End	7947	9.17
N3084F	Reims Cessna F150L D-ECGC MRC Aviation Crowfield	F1500670	2.19
N3084M	Beech B36TC Bonanza Simply Living LLC Elstree	EA-480	2.19
N3458V	Cessna 195 Eastern Stearman Inc Dunkeswell *As USAF '07159'; ground loop 23.4.17 & stored*	7159	5.17
N3544M	Piper PA-31-325 Navajo Southern Aircraft Consultancy Inc PLS Milton, Peterborough	31-8012005	2.19
N3549	de Havilland DH.82A Tiger Moth PG645 Southern Aircraft Consultancy Inc Retford Gamston	86554	2.19
N3586D	Piper PA-31-325 Navajo C/R L. W.Durrell Jersey	31-8012065	4.17
N3596T	Aero Commander 500 N359CT, N8437C, (N3821C) AAT Inc Old Buckenham	500-752	8.18
N3600X	Cirrus Design SR22T Southern Aircraft Consultancy Inc Perth	0491	2.19
N3777M	Bell 206L-3 Long Ranger Apple International Turweston	51485	5.15
N3864	Ryan Navion B International Air Services Earls Colne *Operated by Bulldog Aviation*	NAV-4-2285B	12.18
N3957S	Cessna 172E Southern Aircraft Consultancy Inc Felthorpe *Operated by M Powell*	17251157	8.18
N4037L	Hughes 369E G-RJCS, N4037L Southern Aircraft Consultancy Inc Not known	0589E	6.18
N4063V	Cessna 170 International Air Services Goodwood	18395	11.17
N4085E	Piper PA-18-150 Super Cub Grass Roots Flying Old Warden	18-7809059	10.18
N4117Y	Bellanca 7KCAB Citabria J L Morris Ballyboy, RoI	592-76	6.18
N4238C	Mudry CAP.10B Southern Aircraft Consultancy Inc Shuttleworth (Old Warden) *As '52' in Mexican AF c/s*	155	11.18
N4242C	Cessna 172C Skyhawk G-ARWO, N1487Y C A S LLC Newcastle, RoI *Operated by P Coyne*	49187	10.18
N4297A	Piper PA-39 Twin Comanche C/R G-AZBW, N8254Y Southern Aircraft Consultancy Inc Kirkwall *Operated by T Norman*	39-114	6.18
N4381Y	Beech 99 N216BH, N406UB, N406JB, N1034S Beech 99 U71 Inc Dunkeswell	U-71	2.19
N4422P	Piper PA-23-160 Geronimo Southern Aircraft Consultancy Inc Conington	23-1936	2.19
N4480W	Robinson R66 Sloane Helicopters North America Gloucestershire	0096	2.19

N4519U (1)	Head AX9-118 Balloon (Hot Air) P Sweatman Coventry *'Ground Hog'* *Stored – original envelope –replacement in use with Northern Light Balloon Expeditions*	184	6.16
NC4531H	Piper PA-15 Vagabond E A Terris Wycombe Air Park	15-305	6.17
N4575C★	Grumman G.21A Goose O J Kilkenny Dublin Weston *(Canx 4.13)*	B-120	5.17
N4596N	Boeing-Stearman E75 (PT-13D) Kaydet 75-5945 42-17782 Southern Aircraft Consultancy Inc Glenforsa, Isle of Mull *US Mail c/s*		4.18
N4698W	Rockwell RC112TCA Optimus Fuga Pactum Ltd Henstridge	13274	11.18
N4712V	Boeing Stearman PT-13D Kaydet 75-5094 42-16931 Southern Aircraft Consultancy Inc The Byre, Hardwick, Abergavenny *As 'W:104' in USAAC c/s*		7.16
N4728N	Cessna 182Q Southern Aircraft Consultancy Inc White Waltham	18267317	2.19
N4874W	Rockwell RC114 Southern Aircraft Consultancy Inc Stapleford	14204	12.18
N4956C	Ryan Navion International Air Services Earls Colne *Operated by G Spooner; as US Army '60344'*	NAV-4-344	8.18
N5023U★	Avian Magnum IX Balloon P Sweatman Coventry *Canx 12.98; stored*	169	6.16
N5039Q★	Aerospatiale/Alenia ATR42-300 UR-UTA, VP-BLP, D4-CBE, F-WWEA Not known Durham Tees Valley *Canx 1.14; fuselage as training aid*	382	3.18
N5043X	Cessna 172C G-BWJP, N1824Y International Air Services MoD St Athan *Converted to travelling simulator – for sale 10.18*	17249424	12.14
N5057V	Boeing-Stearman PT-13D Kaydet 75-5598 42-17435 Merkel Air Rendcomb *Operated by V.S.E.Norman as AeroSuperBatics Wingwalkers*		7.16
N5106Y	Hughes 369D (*Hughes 500*) Southern Aircraft Consultancy Inc Dublin Weston	81-1057D	5.17
N5190Y★	Government Aircraft Factory N22B Nomad N22B-26 VH-AUN Chatteris Aviation Lower Mountpleasant Farm, Chatteris (*Right undercarriage collapsed 9.5.09) (Canx 6.18)*		3.18
N5240H	Piper PA-16 Clipper Southern Aircraft Consultancy Inc Compton Abbas	16-44	11.18
N5257A	Cessna 182T Skylane Southern Aircraft Consultancy Inc White Waltham	18282181	2.19
N5264Q	MD Helicopters MD.369E Southern Aircraft Consultancy Inc Dungannon, RoI	0126E	8.15
N5308G	Cessna L-19A Bird Dog Southern Aircraft Consultancy Inc Sleap *As '0-16957'*	22829	7.18
N5315V	Hiller UH-12C Southern Aircraft Consultancy Inc Lower Upham *As US Army '779465'*	757	6.14
N5317V	Hiller UH-12C YV-E-FPK, N5317V Optimus Fuga Pactum Ltd Gloucestershire *On rebuild*	768	7.16
N5347V	Piper PA46-500TP Malibu Meridian 4697126 Shannon K Ferrand de Boissard de la Rigauderie Fairoaks		1.19
NC5427	Travel Air 4000 Southern Aircraft Consultancy Inc Henstridge *Operated by T Leaver*	516	10.17
N5428C	Cessna 170A Southern Aircraft Consultancy Inc Audley End *Operated by A Blatt*	19462	1.18
N5593Z	Piper PA-22-108 Colt Eastern Stearman Crowfield	22-9404	2.19

Overseas

Overseas

N5632R	Maule M-5-235C Lunar Rocket 7244C	11.18	

N5632R Maule M-5-235C Lunar Rocket 7244C 11.18
International Air Services Leicester/Old Warden
Operated by P Holloway

N5647S Maule M-5-235C Rocket 7345C 10.18
Southern Aircraft Consultancy Inc Sherburn-in-Elmet

N5730H Piper PA-16 Clipper 16-342 9.18
Southern Aircraft Consultancy Inc
Yeatsall Farm, Abbotts Bromley
Operated by J Bailey

N5834N★ Rockwell Commander 114 14383 11.18
Not known Cefn Mably
Canx 7.99; fuselage displayed in Farm Park

N5839P Piper PA-24-180 Comanche 24-920 1.19
Southern Aircraft Consultancy Inc Thruxton

N5880T★ Westland WG-30-100 009 5.18
G-17-31 Offshore Fire & Survival Training Centre Norwich
As 'G-DRNT'

N6010Y Commander Aircraft Commander 114B 14589 12.18
Southern Aircraft Consultancy Inc Biggin Hill
Operated by H Barrs

N6039X Commander Aircraft Commander 114B 14639 9.18
Little Beetle Inc Guernsey

N6081F Commander Aircraft Commander 114B 14681 2.19
Southern Aircraft Consultancy Inc Sleap
Operated by A Simpson

N6088F Commander Aircraft Commander 114TC 20043 2.19
N948PW AML Global Payments LLC Guernsey

N6130X Maule M6-235C Super Rocket 7497C 11.18
Southern Aircraft Consultancy Inc
Chattis Hill House, Stockbridge

N6298P Piper PA-24-250 Comanche 24-1278 2.19
Sky West Aviation Cotswold

N6302W★ Government Aircraft Factory N22B Nomad F-159 3.18
VH-HWB Chatteris Aviation Inc
Lower Mountpleasant Farm, Chatteris
Operated by London Parachute Centre, canx 5.18

N6438C Stinson L-5C Sentinel 1428 7.18
Eastern Stearman Inc Priory Farm, Tibenham
Operated by P Bennett and N Nice as '298177:R-8'

N6602Y Piper PA-28-140 Cherokee 28-21943 7.18
G-ATTG, N11C Southern Aircraft Consultancy Inc Seething

N6881E Cessna 175A 56381 5.18
International Air Services Rochester

N6920B Piper PA-34-220T Seneca III 34-8533025 10.15
Southern Aircraft Consultancy Inc Shipdham
Stored

N6954J Piper PA-32R-300 Cherokee Lance 32R-7680394 2.19
T P Hughston Coventry

N7021Z★ Robinson R66 0383 2.18
Delaware Trust Co Denham
Wreck stored – blown from luxury yacht in Baltic 4.9.17
canx 8.18

N7155N Cessna 182S 18280554 11.18
Southern Aircraft Consultancy Inc Jersey

N7180V Mooney M20E 21-0060 1.19
Flight International Corp Biggin Hill

N7205T★ Beech A36 Bonanza E-2182 9.17
Minster Enterprises Tatenhill
Damaged in force landing 30.8.13; canx 12.13

N7219L★ Beech B55 Baron TC-717 9.18
HB-GBX, OE-FDF, HB-GBX
Southern Aircraft Consultancy Inc (Elstree)
Canx 9.17; dismantled and left by road 9.18

N7223Y Beech 58 Baron TH-1456 2.19
Southern Aircraft Consultancy Inc Elstree

N7238X Piper PA-18-95 Super Cub 18-1629 10.18
G-BWUO, OO-MEU, OO-HNG, French Army, 51-15629
International Air Services Little Snoring
Operated by A W Myers

N7258 Cessna 172RG Cutlass II 172RG0508 5.18
Southern Aircraft Consultancy Inc Abbots Bromley

N7263S★ Cessna 150H 15067963 1.16
Cesna Inc Plaistows Farm, St Albans
Canx 11.14; stored

N7348P Piper PA-24-250 Comanche 24-2526 10.18
Southern Aircraft Consultancy Inc Netherthorpe
Operated by J.Bown

N7374A★ Cessna A150M Aerobat 135 A1500726 12.18
S Eustace Monewden
tail wheel conversion; canx 8.13 and stored

N7423V Mooney M.20E Chapparal 21-1163 2.19
International Air Services Thruxton
Operated by J Holme

N7456P Piper PA-24-250 Comanche 24-2646 12.18
Southern Aircraft Consultancy Inc Retford Gamston
Undercarriage collapsed landing 21.7.17

N7505B Schweizer 269C S1205 9.18
Silver Wings Inc Headcorn 'Otto'

N7508U★ Volmer VJ22 Sportsman 269 12.18
Not known Wickenby
Canx 1.75; stored dismantled

N7600E Bellanca 14-19-2 Cruisemaster 4102 1.15
Egmond Aircraft LLC Abbeyshrule, RoI
Stored

N7640F Piper PA-32R-300 Cherokee Lance 32R-7780069 2.19
ZS-OGX, N7640F
Southern Aircraft Consultancy Inc Coventry

N7832P Piper PA-24-250 Comanche 24-3052 6.18
Southern Aircraft Consultancy Inc RAF Benson

N7954J Piper PA-28R-200 Cherokee Arrow II 28R-7635125 8.18
HB-PAL, N7975C SCH Aviation Old Buckenham

N7976Y★ Piper PA-30 Twin Comanche B 30-1075 8.17
Southern Aircraft Consultancy Inc Henstridge
Damaged in forced landing Lymington 18.6.10; canx 5.11

N8004B Lake LA-4-200 1022 6.17
International Air Services Andrewsfield
Operated by R Morton

N8007K Piper PA-46-600TP M600 4698088 2.19
British European Aviation Sales Inc Wycombe Air Park

N8105Z Piper PA-28RT-201T Turbo Arrow IV 28R-8031007 10.18
Southern Aircraft Consultancy Inc Cark

NC8115 Travel Air D-4000 887 9.17
Southern Aircraft Consultancy Inc Turweston
On rebuild

N8153E Piper PA-28RT-201T Turbo Arrow IV 28R-8131185 7.18
N9561N, N84205 P B Payne RAF Mona
DBA Genesis Aircraft

N8163P Cirrus Design SR20 1391 2.19
Solent Aviation Solent

N8181Y Piper PA-30 Twin Comanche 30-1298 2.19
Southern Aircraft Consultancy Inc Coventry

N8205H★ Fisher Celebrity AVI001 9.18
I Pearson Newquay Cornwall
Canx 2.03; stored

N8220M Beech A36 Bonanza E-2795 11.18
T B Ellison Ltd PLS Wittering
Allison turbine conversion

N8225Y Cessna 177RG Cardinal RG 177RG1247 6.18
International Air Services Sleap
Operated by D J Knight Cardinal Group

N8241Z Piper PA-28-161 Warrior II 28-8316079 8.18
Pett Air Inc Henstridge

N8412B Piper PA-28RT-201T Turbo Arrow IV 28R-8131164 4.18
Plane Fun Inc Dublin Weston, RoI

N8523Y Piper PA-30 Twin Comanche 30-1684 1.19
Southern Aircraft Consultancy Inc Lydd
Operated by P Kelly

N8702K Cessna 340A 340A0623 7.18
Southern Aircraft Consultancy Inc Solent

N8818Y Piper PA-30 Twin Comanche 30-1976 10.18
Southern Aircraft Consultancy Inc Tibenham

N8829P Piper PA-24-260 Comanche 24-4285 10.18
International Air Services Avon Farm, Saltford

N8899W	Piper PA-28R-201T Turbo Arrow III	28R-7803046	1.19
	Southern Aircraft Consultancy Inc Dunkeswell		
N8968H	Ryan Navion	NAV-4-968	6.17
	Southern Aircraft Consultancy Inc Eaton Bray		
N8990F	Hughes 269C	64-0313	5.18
	Southern Aircraft Consultancy Inc Dublin Weston, RoI		
N9089Z★	North American TB-25N Mitchell	108-35186	10.18
	(G-BKXW), N9089Z, 44-30861		
	Aero Associates Inc (Wycombe Air Park)		
	Canx 2.17; left on low loader 13.10.18		
N9141Z	Piper PA-32R-301 Saratoga II SP	3213016	12.18
	Southern Aircraft Consultancy Inc Monewden		
	Operated by D Green		
N9381P	Piper PA-24-260 Comanche C	24-4882	6.18
	Chem Air Inc Guernsey		
N9405H	Beech D.17S	4803	8.16
	(D-EJVW), C-FJVW, N9405H, USN 33004		
	International Air Services Old Buckenham		
	Operated by G W Lynch		
N9422	Bell 206A JetRanger	605	5.15
	G-ONOW, G-AYMX		
	Southern Aircraft Consultancy Inc (Gateshead)		
	For sale 10.14		
N9425C	Cessna 180	31823	1.19
	Optimus Fuga Pactum Ltd White Waltham		
N9432B	Cessna 175	55232	1.19
	International Air Services Blackbushe		
N9576W★	Piper PA-28-140 Cherokee	28-23016	8.14
	E F Parks Chirk		
	Canx 5.13; dismantled		
N9616C	Christen A-1 Husky	1117	8.16
	Wyoming Services LLC Bodmin		
N9680Q	Cessna 172M	17265764	10.18
	Aircraft Guaranty Corp Jersey		
	Operated by Jersey Aero Club		
N9861M	Maule M.4-210C	1058C	9.18
	Southern Aircraft Consultancy Inc Rochester		
N10053	Boeing Stearman A75N1	75-4986	6.18
	XB-XIH Southern Aircraft Consultancy Inc Breighton		
	Operated by I Staines; as USN '286'		
N10522	Piper PA-46-350P Malibu Mirage	4636398	2.19
	N753TW Inc Leeds Bradford		
NC12467	Waco UEC	3620	11.18
	Southern Aircraft Consultancy Inc Enstone		
N13243	Cessna 172M	17262604	2.19
	N S Belew Denham		
N13253★	Cessna 172M Skyhawk	17262613	.16
	Anglia Aviation Inc Plaistows Farm, St Albans		
	Canx 9.12; stored		
NC17343	Ryan ST-A	458	7.17
	Little Beetle Inc Oaksey Park		
NC17615	Spartan 7W Executive	14	8.17
	Aircraft Preservation Inc Little Gransden		
	Operated by N Pickard		
NC17633	Spartan 7W Executive	21	9.17
	Aircraft Preservation Inc Little Gransden		
NC18028	Beech D17S	147	2.19
	P.H.McConnell Popham		
N19753	Cessna 172L	17260723	9.18
	Southern Aircraft Consultancy Inc Eastchurch		
N20249	Piper PA-28RT-201T Turbo Arrow IV	28R-7931117	9.18
	R M Cockrell Gloucestershire		
N21381★	Piper PA-34-200 Seneca	34-7350274	12.18
	F-BUTM, F-ETAL Tickton Inc Dunkeswell		
	Canx 12.12; derelict		
N23103	Cessna 150H	15068726	11.18
	International Air Services Elstree		
	Operated by G Rogers; for sale – dismantled		
N24730★	Piper PA-38-112 Tomahawk		12.17
	See G-BTIL – detail in SECTION 1 Eaglescott		

N28141	Bellanca 17-30A	80-30982	2.19
	Viking Air Cranfield		
	Operated by A Baker		
N28236	Grumman AA-5B Tiger	AA5B-0956	9.18
	R M Cathmoir Perth		
N29566	Piper PA-28RT-201 Arrow IV	28R-7918146	2.19
	D-EJLH International Air Services Denham		
	Operated by R Heath		
N30593	Cessna 210L Centurion	21059938	2.19
	Southern Aircraft Consultancy Inc Turweston		
N31008	Piper PA-32R-301 Saratoga IIHP	3246229	2.19
	China Saratoga Airline Elstree		
N32625★	Piper PA-34-200T Seneca II	34-7570039	1.16
	G-PALM, SE-LAN, N32625		
	(Fire Section) Guernsey		
	Canx 5.99		
N33870	Fairchild M62A (*PT-19-FA*) Cornell	T40-237	7.16
	G-BTNY, N33870, US Army		
	Aerospace Trust Management LLC Hardwick		
	Operated by P Earthey; as '02538' in US Army c/s		
N36362	Cessna 180 Skywagon	31691	6.18
	G-BHVZ, F-BHMU, N4739B		
	Southern Aircraft Consultancy Inc Radley Farm, Hungerford		
	(Operated by D Hunt)		
N36665	Beech A36 Bonanza	E-1696	10.18
	M Flynn Fairoaks		
N37379	Cessna 421C Golden Eagle	421C0654	8.18
	G-DJEA, TC-AAA, N37379, (N24BS), N37379		
	Aerospace Trust Management Wellesbourne Mountford		
N38273	Piper PA-28R-201 Cherokee Arrow III	28R-7737086	1.19
	Oakroyd Aviation Blackbushe		
	Operated by L.Slater		
N38763	Hiller UH-12B	497	7.18
	G-ATZB, 102 R Thai AF		
	International Air Services Mount Airey Farm, South Cave		
N38940	Boeing-Stearman A75N1 (*PT-17*) Kaydet	75-1822	7.18
	(G-BSNK), N38940, N55300, 41-8263		
	Eastern Stearman Inc Priory Farm, Tibenham		
	Operated by P Bennett; as '18263/822' in US Army c/s		
N41098★	Cessna 421B Golden Eagle	421B0448	6.15
	International Air Services Rye House Race Track, Thurrock		
	Fuselage, canx 9.17		
N41518	Piper PA-46-350P Malibu Mirage	4636302	2.19
	Southern Aircraft Consultancy Inc Fairoaks		
N44829	Robinson R66	0034	2.19
	Southern Aircraft Consultancy Inc Denham		
N44914	Douglas C-54D Skymaster	10630	11.18
	USN 56498, 42-72525		
	International Air Services North Weald		
	As '56498' in US Air Transport Command c/s		
N45507	Piper PA-18-150 Super Cub	18-8566	6.18
	IDF/AF024 Southern Aircraft Consultancy Inc Thruxton		
N46779	Piper J-3C-65 Cub	10573	6.17
	43-29282 Aerospace Trust Management LLC		
	Yeatsall Farm, Abbots Bromley		
	As USAAF '329282'		
N47494	Piper PA-28R-201 Cherokee Arrow III	28R-7737166	2.19
	Southern Aircraft Consultancy Inc Shobdon		
NC50238	Stinson V-77 Reliant	77-248	1.19
	Southern Aircraft Consultancy Inc Compton Abbas		
N54105	Cirrus Design SR22-G2	1139	10.18
	Gopub Aviation Leeds-Bradford Int'l		
N56200	Boeing-Stearman B75N1	75-7813	11.17
	3G Classic Aviation Inc Goodwood		
N56462	Maule M.6-235 Rocket	7409C	6.14
	Southern Aircraft Consultancy Inc East Winch		
N56643	Maule M.5-180C	8086C	8.18
	Southern Aircraft Consultancy Inc Brimpton		
	Operated by P.Ford		
N58283★	Sud Aviation SA.341G Gazelle	1015	10.18
	CF-CWN Gazelle Squadron Bourne Park		
	Canx 5.15; stored wfu		

N58342★	Hughes 269C	19-0759	10.17
	F-GBLI, N58342 R A Buis Headcorn		
	Canx 3.18; dismantled		
N60256★	Beech C35 Bonanza	D-3346	6.17
	OO-DOL, OO-JAN R.M.Hornblower White Waltham		
	Canx 6.17; stored		
N60526	Beech E55 Baron	TE-1159	2.19
	Southern Aircraft Consultancy Inc Elstree		
N61787	Piper J-3C-65 Cub	13624	9.15
	45-4884 International Air Servies Podington		
	As 330426/53-K/'Rosie the Rocketer'		
N61970	Piper PA-24-250 Comanche	24-3364	6.18
	OO-GOE, F-OCBM, 5R-MVA, N8198P, N10F		
	Southern Aircraft Consultancy Inc Netherthorpe		
	Operated by Nunn & Green		
N62658	Boeing Stearman A75N1 Kaydet	75-4270	9.18
	Aviator Flying Museum Thruxton		
	As USAAC '107'		
N63590	Boeing-Stearman N2S-3 Kaydet	75-7143	6.18
	USN 07539 Eastern Stearman Inc North Weald		
	Operated by I Stockwell; as '07539/143' in US Navy c/s		
N65200	Boeing-Stearman D75N1 Kaydet	75-3817	7.17
	FJ767 Eastern Stearman Inc Goodwood		
N66576★	Boeing-Stearman A75N1	75-2118	11.18
	Not known Enstone		
	Cx 10.12; frame for restoration		
N68427	Boeing-Stearman A75N1 (N2S-4) Kaydet	75-5000	5.18
	USN 55771 Eastern Stearman Inc Dunkeswell		
	Operated by as USN '55771/427'; for sale		
N69745	Stinson V-77 Reliant	77-64	6.18
	42-46703 Southern Aircraft Consultancy Inc Oaksey Park		
	As '42-46703'		
N74189	Boeing Stearman PT-17	75-717	8.18
	Merkel Air Rendcomb		
	Operated by AeroSuperBatics Wingwalkers		
N74677	Boeing-Stearman A75N1	75-7875	11.18
	Southern Aircraft Consultancy Inc Enstone		
	As USAAC '131'		
N75048	Piper PA-28-181 Cherokee Archer II	28-7690286	10.17
	Southern Aircraft Consultancy Inc St Mary's, Isles of Scilly		
	Operated by I Sibley		
N75822	Cessna 172N	17267979	1.19
	International Air Services Andrewsfield		
	Operated by C Brown		
N77072	Cessna 120	11526	9.17
	Condor Aviation Birchwood Lodge, Nth Duffield		
N80035	Pitts S-2A	2070	7.18
	Southern Aircraft Consultancy Inc Little Gransden		
N80364★	Cessna 500 Citation I	500-0299	6.18
	OY-TKI, N80364, (OY-EBD), N80364, PT-OZX, YV-940CP,		
	N5133K, ZS-MGH, N55AK, N66TR, N3JJ, HB-VEO,		
	N5299J Wells Fargo Bank Northwest NA		
	Robin Hood Doncaster Sheffield		
	Canx 9.17; stored		
N80533★	Cessna 172M Skyhawk	17266640	2.19
	Not known – sale reported Biggin Hill		
	Canx 9.18		
N81188	Piper PA-28-236 Dakota	28-8211026	7.18
	International Air Services Charlton Park, Malmesbury		
	Operated by Lord Suffolk & Lady Howard		
N89156	Cessna 140	8168	.15
	Edmond Aircraft LLC Belle Vue Farm, Yarnscombe		
N90011	MD Helicopters MD.902	900-00115	4.18
	Hirecopter Inc (Swettenham)		
	Operated by Heliace Ltd		
N93938	Erco 415C Ercoupe	1261	8.14
	P J Yocom (Panshanger)		
	Stored		
N97121★	Embraer EMB-110P1 Bandeirante	110.334	1.16
	PT-SDK Guernsey Airport Fire Service Guernsey		
	Canx 3.97; hulk only		

N99495	Erco 415C Ercoupe	2118	8.16
	G-BZNO, N99495		
	Southern Aircraft Consultancy Inc Solent		
	Stored		

AUSTRIA

OE-KDW	Prescott Pusher	025 ?	.16
	ModiFly Birchwood Lodge, North Duffield		
	Gate guard		
OE-XDT	Robinson R44 Clipper II	10498	11.18
	9H-EAT, SX-HTC Foxhill Holding Ltd Wycombe Air Park		

FINLAND

OH-SKA	Mudry CAP.232	30	7.18
	I-REBY, F-GRED Not known Dunkeswell		

CZECH REPUBLIC

OK-NNN	Zlin Z.526F Trener Master	1271	7.17
	SP-EMD Not known Goodwood		
OK-GUA 28	Urban Air UFM-10 Samba	21/10	6.16
	Not known Milltownpass, RoI		
OK-JUA 03	Urban Air Samba XXL	Not known	9.17
	Not known Cold Harbour Farm, Willingham		

BELGIUM

OO-GCO★	Grumman-American AA-5A Cheetah	AA5A-0526	1.14
	OO-HGB N Foden Broughton		
	Converted to flight simulator		
OO-MHB★	Piper PA-28-236 Dakota	28-8011143	10.17
	G-BMHB, D6-PAD, N81321, N9593N		
	Jungle Paradise Adventure Golf Course		
	Hunston, West Sussex		
OO-NSE	Airbus Helicopters H175 (EC.175B)	5007	2.19
	F-WJXF NHV Helicopters Aberdeen		
OO-NSF	Airbus Helicopters H175 (EC.175B)	5005	2.19
	F-WJXC NHV Helicopters Aberdeen		
OO-NSI	Airbus Helicopters H175 (EC.175B)	5010	2.19
	NHV Helicopters Aberdeen		
OO-NSN	Agusta Westland AW.139	31700	12.18
	NHV Helicopters Norwich		
OO-NSQ	Agusta Westland AW.139	41513	2.19
	N605SH NHV Helicopters Norwich		
OO-NSR	Airbus Helicopters H175 (EC.175B)	5033	2.19
	NHV Helicopters Aberdeen		
OO-RAB	Piper PA-38-112 Tomahawk	38-79A0569	4.18
	D-EKTS, N2313K Not known Little Staughton		
	Stored dismantled		
OO-STU	Diamond DA.40D Star	D4.350	2.19
	I-AEBS, (D-EEGU), I-AEBS, OE-VPU		
	Not known Bournemouth		
OO-TAQ★	BAe 146 Series 200QT	E-2078	8.18
	G-BNPJ, I-TNTC, G-BNPJ, G-5-078		
	Keen Max Development Exeter		
	Canx 4.13		

DENMARK

OY-AVW★	Piper PA-17 Vagabond	17-70	8.15
	D-EEMM, N4665H Not known Dunkeswell		
	Stored dismantled		
OY-DFD	Mooney M.20F Executive	670327	12.18
	N2968L P O'Donnell Denham		
OY-HSK	Eurocopter EC155B1 Dauphin 2	6660	6.18
	N155EW Dan Copter A/S Norwich		
OY-LGI	Bombardier BD-700-1A10 Global Express	9433	1.19
	C-GIOK Graff Global Aviation Luton		

Overseas

NETHERLANDS

PH-BIT	Reims/Cessna F172N Skyhawk II	F17201863	11.18
	New Flying PH-BIT Ltd Navan, RoI		
PH-MJC	Stidham HE Spezio DAL-1	162	4.18
	Not known Kilrush RoI		
PH-PIM	Cessna R172K Hawk XP	R1722376	6.18
	G-EPIM, PH-PIM, N736AQ		
	A H Creaser Old Manor Farm, Anwick		
PH-VBA	Aero Adventure Aventura II	012	5.17
	Not known Causeway, Co Londonderry		

PAPUA NEW GUINEA

P2-MFA	Cessna 172S	172S9018	11.18
	Missionary Aviation Fellowship (Scotland)		
	Trailer-mounted mobile fundraiser		

ARUBA

P4-GIU	BAe ARJ-85	E2349	2.19
	EI-RJL, OH-SAQ, EI-RJL, N524XJ, G-6-349		
	LaMiA Norwich		
	Stored		

RUSSIA

RA-01274	Yakovlev Yak-55	910103	6.18
	DOSAAF 03 Not known		
	Wolverhampton Halfpenny Green '03'		
RA-01611	Aero Vodochody L-29 Delfin	294699	4.18
	Not known Swansea		
	Displayed as 'G-STNR'		

PHILIPPINES

RP-C342★	Sud Aviation 342J Gazelle	1663	2.16
	Not known Crab Tree Farm, Deighton		

SWEDEN

SE-BOG	Boeing Stearman B75N1	75-7128	8.18
	N59085, USN 07524 V S Norman Rendcomb		
	Operated by AeroSuperBatics Wingwalkers		
SE-GVH	Piper PA-38-112 Tomahawk	38-78A0053	12.16
	Air Scouts White Waltham		
	Simulator		
SE-HXF	Rotorway Scorpion	SE-1	7.16
	J Water Earls Colne		
	Stored		
SE-IAM	Piper PA-28-161 Cherokee Warrior II	28-7816651	11.18
	Not known Hinton in the Hedges		
SE-IED	Cessna A185F Skywagon	18503320	5.17
	OH-COW, (SE-IED), N124JD, (N5075H)		
	Freefall Ireland Skydive Centre Abbeyshrule, RoI		
SE-IIV	Piper PA-24-260 Comanche C	24-4970	7.17
	HB-OHZ, N9462P Not known Netherthorpe		
SE-LHX	British Aerospace ATP	2020	7.18
	LX-WAN, SE-LHX, N851AW, G-WISS, N851AW, G-11-020		
	Save the ATP Trust Isle of Man		
	Stored		
SE-LPU★	British Aerospace ATP	2060	1.19
	LX-WAM, SE-LPU, LX-WAM, SE-LPU, (SE-LNZ),		
	G-OBWO, (EI-COS), G-11-060		
	West Atlantic Sweden Coventry		
	Canx 6.04; stored		
SE-MHC	BAe ATP	2007	1.19
	G-BTPA, EC-HGC, G-BTPA, EC-GYE, (N377AE), G-BTPA		
	West Atlantic Coventry		
	Stored		

SE-MHJ	BAe ATP	2024	1.19
	G-BUUR, EC-GUX, G-OEDJ, G-BUUR, CS-TGC, G-11-024		
	West Atlantic Coventry		
	Stored		

POLAND

SP-CHD★	PZL-101A Gawron	74134	2.14
	(T Wood) North Weald		
	Stored in container		
SP-HXA★	Augusta A109E	11630	10.14
	Castle Helicopters Trebrown, Liskeard		
	Crashed 20.11.09; spares use		
SP-KWN★	BAe Jetstream 3201	856	1.19
	LN-FAC, N856TE, N422AM, G-31-856		
	Cranfield Airport Fire Service Cranfield		
SP-YRL	Cub Crafters Carbon Cub	CCK-1865-1023	2.19
	Not known White Waltham		

TURKEY

TC-ALM★	Boeing 727-230	20431	12.17
	TC-IKO, TC-JUH, TC-ALB, N878UM, D-ABDI		
	Fire Services East Midlands		
	Used as trainer		
TC-NLB★	American AG-5B Tiger	10157	5.18
	PH-MLE, N11988 F & H Aircraft Ltd Dunkeswell		
	Stored dismantled		

SAN MARINO

T7-AMS	Pilatus PC-12/47	732	2.19
	HB-FXX, M-ZUMO, G-ZUMO, HB-FRQ		
	Acass Canada Ltd Bournemouth		
T7-ASH	Piper PA-46-350P Malibu Mirage	4622005	2.18
	D-EEEY, N9184V Flywatch Global Fairoaks		
	JetProp DLX conversion no 226		
T7-LSS	Agusta Westland AW.139	41265	12.18
	Skymedia AG Denham		
T7-NAV	Piper PA-31-350 Chieftain	31-7952110	2.19
	G-ONPA, N89PA, N35225 Not known Biggin Hill		

AUSTRALIA

VH-AHL★	Hawker Siddeley HS.748 Series 2/228	1606	2.19
	A10-606 Clewer Avn		
	Skylark Hotel & Conference Centre, Southend		
	In open store		
VH-AMQ★	Hawker Siddeley HS.748 Series 2/228	1603	2.19
	A10-603 Clewer Avn		
	Skylark Hotel & Conference Centre, Southend		
	'Wg Cdr Grant "Bing" Kelly'		
	In open store		

VIETNAM

VN-A190	Boeing 737-4H6	27383	9.14
	9M-MQJ Special Forces Support Group MoD St Athan		
	Fuselage as training aid		

BERMUDA (Current series)

VP-BCL	Bombardier CL-600-2C10 (*CRJ-700*)	10247	1.19
	N710TS, C-FHMG Global Jet Charters		
	Farnborough and Athens		
	Operated by Consolidated Contractors		
VP-BCT	Gulfstream G650	6169	2.19
	N669GD Rockfield Ltd Farnborough		
	Operated by P Green		
VP-BGX	Boeing 747-346	24156	11.18
	N741UN, JA8189, N6046P Transaero Buntingthorpe		
	Stored)		

Overseas

VP-BGY	Boeing 747-346	23640	11.18
	N743UN, JA8179, N6009F Transaero Buntingthorpe		
	Stored)		
VP-BLW	Gulfstream Aerospace Gulfstream V-SP		
	(Gulfstream 550)	5129	2.19
	N529GA Specialised Transportation Bermuda Ltd		
	Biggin Hill		
VP-BPW	Dassault Falcon 900EASy	225	2.19
	F-WWFK Service Aviation Jersey		
VP-BWR	Boeing 737-79T	29317	12.18
	N1787B Bel Air Ltd London Stansted		
VQ-BEB	Bombardier BD700-1A10 Global Express 9739		2.19
	C-FKRX Jetcapital Aviation Farnborough		
VQ-BHO	Piaggio P180 Avanti II	1156	11.18
	D-IPIA AMA Corporate Jet AG Manchester Int'l		
VQ-BLA	Gulfstream Aerospace Gulfstream V-SP		
	(Gulfstream 550)	5215	2.19
	N615GA International Jet Club Ltd Luton		
	Operated by Indo Aviation		

CAYMAN ISLANDS

VP-CFI★	British Aerospace HS125 Series 700B	257054	.16
	OD-BBF, OD-HHF, G-OURB, G-NCFR, RA-02802,		
	G-BVJY, C6-BET		
	ModiFly Birchwood Lodge, North Duffield		
	Converted to caravan		
VP-CGN	Gulfstream 650	6112	12.18
	N612GD Geniethree Ltd Luton		
VP-CMN★	Boeing 727-46	19282	1.19
	VR-CMN, VR-CLM, VR-CBE, N4245S, D-AHLQ, JA8325		
	Transatlantic Aviation Cotswold		
	Stored fuselage		
VP-CMO★	Boeing 727-212RE	21948	12.18
	N31TR, VR-COJ, N310AS, 9V-SGJ		
	Transatlantic Aviation Lasham		
	Stored		
VP-COM	Cessna 500 Citation I	500-318	2.19
	VR-COM, N944B, N518CC, N5318J		
	M O M Aircraft Services Ltd Southend		
VP-CZY★	Boeing 727-2P1A	21595	12.18
	N727MJ, A7-AAB Dunview Ltd Lasham		
	Stored		

BERMUDA (Old series)

VR-BEB★	British Aircraft Corporation One-Eleven 527FK BAC.226		2.19
	RP-C1181, PI-C1181 European Aviation Ltd Bournemouth		
	Fire Compound – all white with no marks		

INDIA

VT-EKT★	Westland 30 Series 100-60	035	5.18
	G-17-23 Wessex Aviation Biggin Hill		
VT-RAK	Bombardier BD100 Challenger 300	20174	8.18
	C-FOQR Not known Biggin Hill		

LATVIA

YL-LEU★	WSK-PZL Antonov An-2R	1G-165-45	8.18
	CCCP19731, SP-ZFP, CCCP19731		
	Hawarden Air Services Hawarden		
	As 'CCCP-19731" dismantled		
YL-LEV★	WSK-PZL Antonov An-2R	1G-148-29	8.18
	CCCP07268 Hawarden Air Services Hawarden		
	As 'CCCP07268'		
YL-LEW★	WSK-PZL Antonov An-2R	1G-182-28	8.18
	CCCP56471 Hawarden Air Services Hawarden		
	As 'CCCP56471'		
YL-LEX★	WSK-PZL Antonov An-2R	1G-187-58	8.18
	CCCP54949 Hawarden Air Services Hawarden		
	As 'CCCP54949'		

YL-LEY★	WSK-PZL Antonov An-2R	1G-173-11	8.18
	CCCP40784 Hawarden Air Services Hawarden		
	As 'CCCP40784'		
YL-LEZ★	WSK-PZL Antonov An-2R	1G-165-47	8.18
	CCCP19733 Hawarden Air Services Hawarden		
	As 'CCCP19733'		
YL-LFA★	WSK-PZL Antonov An-2R	1G-172-20	8.18
	CCCP40748 Hawarden Air Services Hawarden		
	As 'CCCP40748'		
YL-LFB★	WSK-PZL Antonov An-2R	1G-173-12	8.18
	CCCP40785 Hawarden Air Services Hawarden		
	As 'CCCP40785'		
YL-LFC★	WSK-PZL Antonov An-2R	1G-206-44	8.18
	CCCP17939 Hawarden Air Services Hawarden		
	As 'CCCP17939'		
YL-LFD★	WSK-PZL Antonov An-2R	1G-172-21	8.18
	CCCP40749 Hawarden Air Services Hawarden		
	As 'CCCP40749'		
YL-LHN★	Mil Mi-2	524006025	8.18
	CCCP20320 Hawarden Air Services Hawarden		
	As 'CCCP20320')		
YL-LHO★	Mil Mi-2	535025126	8.18
	CCCP20619 Hawarden Air Services Hawarden		
	As 'CCCP20619'		
YL-MIG★	Aviatika MAI-890	037	8.18
	Hawarden Air Services Hawarden *'37 yellow'*		
YL-PAF★	Aero Vodochody L-29 Delfin	591771	12.18
	Soviet AF 18 red Not known Hawarden		
	Stored dismantled		
YL-PAG★	Aero Vodochody L-29 Delfin	491273	1.18
	Soviet AF 51 red Not known Breighton		
	Gate guard		

SERBIA

YU-AON★	Boeing 737-3Q4	24208	4.16
	N181LF, S7-RGL, PT-TEF Not known Knock, RoI		
	Fuselage on dump as fire trainer		
YU-HES	Aérospatiale SA.342J Gazelle	1057	6.18
	F-GOSO, EC-EQU, C-GEJE, (N341NA), N9042U,		
	C-FGCE, CF-GCE Shuttle Air (Bell Bar, Hatfield)		
YU-HET	Aérospatiale SA.342J Gazelle	1204	8.18
	F-GFDG, TG-KOV		
	Martin Wood Helicopters d.o.o. Stapleford		
	Damaged during ground run 6.7.15		
YU-HEV	Aérospatiale SA.342J Gazelle	1393	5.18
	F-GCCZ (KAF-401)		
	Martin Wood Helicopters d.o.o. Hadleigh		
YU-HEY	Aérospatiale SA.341G Gazelle	1320	12.18
	F-GEHF, N905XX, N905X, N49508		
	Martin Wood Helicopters d.o.o. Crookfoot Farm, Elwick		
YU-HMC	Aérospatiale SA.341G Gazelle	1136	7.18
	G-KANE, G-GAZI, G-BKLU, N32PA, N341VH, N90957		
	Martin Wood Helicopters d.o.o		
YU-HOT	Aérospatiale SA.341G Gazelle	1390	8.18
	G-WCRD, F-GEHD, N6KT, N49527		
	Martin Wood Helicopters d.o.o. Stapleford		
YU-HPZ	Aérospatiale SA.342J Gazelle	1473	2.19
	G-TOPZ, F-GGTJ, C-GVWC, F-WXFX		
	Martin Wood Helicopters d.o.o. Stapleford		
YU-HWF	Aérospatiale SA.341G Gazelle 1	1407	8.16
	G-EHUP, F-GIJR, N869GT, N869, N49523		
	Martin Wood Helicopters d.o.o. Stapleford		

NEW ZEALAND

ZK-EVC★	Piper PA-38-112 Tomahawk	38-81A0019	5.17
	Not known Abbeyshrule RoI		
	Canx 4.14		
ZK-IGM	Eurocopter EC.130B4	3770	8.16
	F-WQDC North Shore Helicopters Ltd Redhill		
ZK-KAY	Pacific Aerospace PAC 750XL	107	8.18
	North West Parachute Centre Cark		

ZK-KCE	Pacific Aerospace PAC 750XL 185			2.19
	Hinton Skydiving Centre Ltd Hinton in the Hedges			
ZK-KNM	Pacific Aerospace PAC.750XL 194			10.18
	Oceania Aviatin Ltd Clonbullogue, RoI			
	Operated by Irish Parachute Club			

REPUBLIC of SOUTH AFRICA

ZS-DJI	Boeing 767-216ER 23624		12.18
	J2-KBE, ZS-DJI, N480JC, G-SJET, G-FJEC, N769BC,		
	TJ-AAC, N769BC, 5R-MFE, N151LF, PT-TAH,		
	CC-CJV, N4528Y Aeronexus Corp MoD St Athan		
	Stored		
ZS-ESG	SIAI-Marchetti S.205-18/R 364		9.18
	Not known Dunkeswell		
ZS-GAK	Jonker Sailplanes JS-1C Revelation 1C-057		6.14
	JS1-42 Partnership Lasham *'42'*		
	Operated by G Smith		
ZS-GBK	Jonker Sailplanes JS-1C Revelation 1C-059		4.17
	JS-VW Partnership Portmoak *'Z9'*		
	Operated by J Galloway		
ZS-GBL	Jonker Sailplanes JS-1C Revelation 1C-061		8.18
	JS1-XS Partnership Husbands Bosworth *'XS'*		
	Operated by R Browne		
ZS-GBM	Jonker Sailplanes JS1-C Revelation 1C-063		8.16
	D Rance Long Mynd *'TL'*		
ZS-GBR	Jonker Sailplanes JS-1C Revelation 1C-070		6.18
	JS1-ZB Partnership Lasham *'ZB'*		
	Operated by S Lapworth		
ZS-GCD	Jonker Sailplanes JS-1B Revelation 1B-012		8.18
	JS1-Nunn Partnership Lasham *'WZ'*		
	Operated by A Nunn		
ZS-GCE	Jonker Sailplanes JS-1B Revelation 1B-013		9.18
	JS1-Booth Husbands Bosworth *'B5'*		
	Operated by D Booth		
ZS-GCS	Jonker Sailplanes JS-1B Revelation 1B-006		8.18
	JS-1-ZS-GCS Partnership Lasham *'DZ'*		
	Operated by I MacArthur		
ZS-GEE	Jonker Sailplanes JS-1C Revelation 1C-040		8.18
	JS1-80 Partnership Nympsfield *'8Q'*		
	Operated by G Paul		

ZS-GEF	Jonker Sailplanes JS-1C Revelation 1C-041		8.18
	JS1-XZ Partnership Shobdon *'XZ'*		
	Operated by R Johnson		
ZS-GEG	Jonker Sailplanes JS-1C Revelation 1C-042		8.18
	JS1-HK Partnership Bicester *'N1'*		
	Operated by P Harvey		
ZS-GEH	Jonker Sailplanes JS-1C Revelation 1C-044		8.18
	JS1-RCII Partners Husbands Bosworth *'E1'*		
	Operated by R Cheetham		
ZS-GER	Jonker Sailplanes JS-1C Revelation 1C-053		8.18
	Tim Jenkinson Partnership (Husbands Bosworth) *'SB'*		
ZT-GAB	Jonker Sailplanes JS-3 Rapture 03-022		8.18
	I Evans Shobdon *'RZ'*		

NIGERIA

5N-JMA	Hawker 850XP 258658		2.18
	(ZS-ARK), N658XP Not known Hawarden		
	(Stored unmarked – scrapping commenced 2018)		
5N-MJA	Boeing 737-322 24360		8.18
	N354UA Arik Air Norwich *'Abubakar'*		
	Stored		

NIGER

5U-BAG	Boeing 737-2N9C 21499		12.18
	Republique du Niger Lasham		
	Stored		

GHANA

9G-ABS	Aermacchi AL.60B2 54/6234		3.16
	I-MACZ Not known Biggin Hill		
	Stored dismantled		
9G-ADI	Bölkow Bo105C S-180		9.17
	(PH-LBA), 9L-LBA, GS-AI/SLDF Not known Biggin Hill		

MALTA

9H-XYZ	Diamond DA.62 62.068		2.19
	Southern Aviation Holding Ltd Elstree		

PART 2 – OVERSEAS-REGISTERED ENTRIES REMOVED FROM PAGES 577-599 OF 2018 EDITION

Regn	Type / Reason for removal	C/n
GERMANY		
D-EADE	Maule MXT-7-180 / Returned to Germany by 2.18	14114C
D-EAGP	Xtreme Air XA-42 / No reports sine 3.13	103
D-EDQR	Robin DR.400/180R Remorqueur / To HB-KLC 8.18	1047
D-EFZC	SIAI-Marchetti S.208 / No reports since 8.13	2-18
D-EGCC	CEA DR.253B Régent / Returned to Germany by 6.18	178
D-EKNA	Mooney M.20F Executive / Returned to Germany by 3.18	670297
D-ELCH	Commander Aircraft 114B / To G-ELCH 1.19	14566
D-EMTK	Piper PA-28RT-201T Turbo Arrow IV / To G-VANU 7.18	28R-8131039
D-ENPC	Cessna F172H / Returned to Germany 13.11.18	F172-0600

Regn	Type / Reason for removal	C/n
D-ESIC	SIAI-Marchetti SF.260 / To G-RAZI 7.18	102
D-FLEX	SOCATA TBM-700C2 / To G-PTXC 11.18	321
D-FOXY	Cessna 208 Caravan I / To Switzerland by 10.18	20800303
D-GPEZ	Piper PA-30 Twin Comanche C / To G-PHIZ 2.19	30-1871
D-KIIJ	Schempp-Hirth Ventus 3T / To G-SIIO 2.19	3
D-3229	Scheibe Bergfalke II/55 / Listed in Section 9 – Museums	272
D-5410	Schempp-Hirth Ventus 2cxa / Cancelled 5.18. To D-KBPJ ?	116/513
SPAIN		
EC-KTC	Dornier Do.28D-2 Skyservant / Returned to Spain by 10.18	4125

Overseas

FRANCE

F-ANHO	Comper Swift No reports since 12.13	S33/4
F-GXHD	Robin ATL No reports since 4.13	110
65DAH	Pipistrel Alpha Trainer To G-RTEN 9.18 – correct French registration 67CAH	858AT912B

HUNGARY

HA-NAH	Technoavia SMG-92 Finist No reports since 8.13	00-003
HA-SHA	Boeing 737-505 To Cotswold for scrapping 15.8.18	24648
HA-WKS	Sud SA318C Alouette II To 2-SOAR 12.18	2204
HA-WKY	Sud SA318C Alouette II To 2-HAWK 6.18	2068
HA-WKZ	Sud SA318C Alouette II To 2-LOUD 12.18	2138
HA-YAC	Yakovlev Yak-18T To G-YACC 8.18	14-35
33-64	Urban Air UFM-13 Lambada To EI-GRA 12.18	86/13

UNITED STATES

N13FB	Bell 206B JetRanger Sold in Delaware, USA 5.18	118
N25KB	Piper PA-24-250 Comanche To M-…. 5.18	24-3034
N32HF	Piper PA-32RT-300 Lance II Sold in Ohio, USA 3.18	32R-7885186
N35KN	Cessna 401 No reports since 5.13	401-0082
N41FT	Piper PA-39 Twin Comanche C/R To Lyon Bron, France by 9.18	39-59
N60BM	Rockwell 690A Turbo Commander No reports since 10.13	11172
N69LP	Piper PA-61P Aerostar 601P To Germany by 9.17	61P-0541-230
N70VB	Ted Smith Aerostar 600A No reports since 6.13	60-0446-150
N80AG	Cirrus Design SR22T To N80AV 6.18	1549
N100MC	Piper PA-23-260 Apache G Scrapped 2018	23-1985
N101UK	Mooney M.20K To Germany by 9.17	25-0631
N107CB	Cirrus Design SR22-G3 GTS Turbo To Germany by 4.16	3244
N145DR	Piper PA-34-220T Seneca V To G-ULAG 9.18	3449240
N180EL	Cessna 180K Skywagon II To France by 8.16	18053121
N180WJ	Cessna 180K Skywagon To Italy by 11.18	180-52873
N181KA	Cessna 525B CitationJet CJ3 Sold in Texas, USA 7.18	525B0076
N183BM	Cirrus Design SR22 Sold in Germany 4.18	4080
N210EU	Cessna T210L Turbo Centurion To Netherlands by 5.18	21061152
N213CL	Cirrus Design SR22T To Saint Truiden, Belgium by 2.18	1410
N220T	Cessna P210N Turbo Centurion Returned to USA 7.18	P21000593
N238KA	Beech B200GT To G-NYCO 2.19	BY-238

N240LG	Dassault Falcon 900EX To N96LA 4.18	61
N264DB	Piper PA-46-310P Malibu Crashed in English Channel 21.1.19	46-8408037
N264MC	Cirrus Design SR22 To 2-EGJB 11.18	4179
N268ML	Piper PA-28-161 To G-CKZV 1.19	2842068
N272NR	Embraer 505 Phenom 300 To 2-NORN 1.19	50500272
N290PA	Beech C90 KingAir To Austria by 9.17	LJ-519
N310GG	Cessna 310R II To Germany by 11.17	310R1585
N322RJ	Beech 60 Duke To Germany by 5.18	P-322
N362EH	Bell 212 Restored as G-BIGB 9.18	30853
N389DF	Boeing 737-3M8 To scrapping Cotswold 2018	25017
N405FD	SIAI-Marchetti SF.260D Sold in Michelstadt, Germany 6.18	770
N414FZ	Cessna 414RAM Crashed near Enstone 26.6.18	414-0175
N456KF	Piper PA-46R-350T Matrix To Germany by 1.17	4692021
N473BJ	Cirrus Design SR22-G3-GTS Turbo To Germany by 4.18	3700
N480BB	Enstrom 480 To S5-… 12.18	5056
N480JB	Enstrom 480B No reports since 2.13	5108
N480W	Enstrom 480B Crashed 10.5.17 Fundes, Italy	5110
N500	Piper PA-31T Cheyenne II To Australia by 2018	31T-7920094
N500RK	Hughes 369HS To Czech Republic by 12.16	3-0502S
N518VS	Grumman AA-1B Trainer No reports since 11.13	AA1B-0399
N525DT	Cessna 525A CitatioJet CJ2 To 2-CLEV 5.18	525A0003
N531EA	Eclipse Aviation EA500 To 2-JEZA 1.19	000031
N550LD	Cessna 550 Citation II Dismantled 5.12.18 – to Cotswold for scrapping	550-0323
N573VE	Cirrus Design SR22-G2 To Netherlands by 4.18	1078
N600HV	McDonnell Douglas MD600N To 2-KILD 3.18	RN058
N666AW	Piper PA-31 Navajo C Cancelled 2.19. Not seen since 2015 – scrapped?	31-7612061
N666LS	Cirrus Design SR22T To Florida, USA 21.11.18	1001
N703JK	Beech 58 Baron Sold in Montana, USA 3.18	TH-1154
N709AM	SOCATA TB-21 Trinidad To France by 2.17	2101
N711TL	Piper PA-60 Aerostar 700P Sold in Germany 10.18	60-8423017
N726KM	North American AT-6G To Turkey 8.18	SA079
N731XB	Cessna P210N Pressurised Centurion II Sold in Texas, USA 10.18	P21000553
N790SR	Cirrus Design SR22-G3-GTS Turbo To Netherlands by 11.17	2859
N797EL	Boeing 737-505 Scrapped Bournemouth 9.18	25797
N820DL	Beech B200 Super King Air Sold in North Carolina, USA 8.18	BB-1820

N840PN	Rockwell 690C Turbo Commander To USA 6.18	11679
N871TM	Boeing 737-36N To 4L-AAK 7.18	28671
N900FZ	SOCATA TBM900 Sold in France 5.18	1108
N915C	Piper PA-46R-350T Malibu Matrix To Germany by 4.18	4692182
N918Y	Piper PA-30 Twin Comanche To Ukraine by 8.18	30-736
N980RJ	Cirrus Design SR22T To Germany by 9.18	0980
N3050S	Bell 407 Sold in Oregon, USA 4.18	53742
N4173T	Cessna 320D Skyknight Sold in 'Africa' 11.17	320D0073
N4599W	Rockwell Commander 112TC No reports since 3.13	13089
N6182G	Cessna 172N Skyhawk II To G-CWFT 7.18	17273576
N6554B	Tiger Aircraft AG.5B To Germany by 5.17	10251
N6601Y	Piper PA-23-250 Aztec C No reports since 9.13	27-3905
N7070A	Cessna S550 Citation II For sale in Florida, USA 10.18	S550-0068
N8862V	Bellanca 17-31ATC Turbo Super Viking To Netherlands by 8.18	31022
NC9048	TravelAir E4000 Returned to California, USA by 10.18	849
N9305M	Mooney M.20E No reports since 4.13	1238
N9325N	Piper PA-28R-200 Cherokee Arrow No reports since hard landing at Sibson 2.3.13	28R-35025
N20981	Cessna 172M To EW-.... 6.18	17263885
N21419	British Aircraft Corporation 167 Strikemaster Mk.81 EEP/JP/168 No reports since 11.13	
NC33543	Stinson V-77 Reliant Sold in Switzerland 12.18	77-373
N38945	Piper PA-32R-300 Cherokee Lance To France by 8.17	32R-7780490
N41702	Supermarine Spitfire XVIII No reports since 12.13	6S-676390
N47351	Cessna 152 No reports since 9.13	15283219
N49943	Boeing-Stearman A75N1 To G-IIYI 8.18	75-4645
N53517	Piper PA-46-350P Malibu Mirage To Germany by 2.18	4636330
N91384	Rockwell 690A Turbo Commander No reports since 6.13 – believed scrapped	11118
N97821	Mooney M.20J To Czech Republic by 6.18	24-1080

BELGIUM

OO-AJK	Nord 1203 Norecrin No reports since 1.13	261
OO-BAK	Enstrom F.28A No reports since 8.13	168
OO-SFA	Diamond DA 42 Twin Star To G-CTSU 5.18	42.340
OO-SFI	Diamond DA 42 Twin Star To G-CTSV 5.18	42.214

NETHERLANDS

PH-HEW	Robinson R44 Astro No reports since 8.13	0785
PH-ZVB	Piper PA-18-150 Super Cub To G-VCUB 3.17	18-7609021

GREECE

SX-HRK	Robinson R44 Clipper Returned to Greece 23.4.18	0633

SAN MARINO

T7-SCR	Cessna 525 CitationJet To Zurich, Switzerland by 9.17	525-0519

AUSTRALIA

'VH-FDT'	de Havilland DHA.3 Drover 2 No reports since 8.13	5014
VH-IXT *	Supermarine Spitfire IX No reports since 3.13	
VH-SCW	Ryan SCW145 Returned to Australia 2018	211

BERMUDA

VP-BAT	Boeing 747SP-21 Sold – to Kelowna 18.5.18	21648
VP-BGO	Bombardier CL-600-2B16 To N605CE 10.18	5851
VP-BZE	Dassault Falcon 7X Damaged by high winds on ground Luqa, Malta 27.12.17	14
VQ-BSK	Boeing 747-8ZV(BBJ) To TC-TRK 10.18	42096

CAYMAN ISLANDS

VP-CBS	Bombardier CL-600-2B16 To 2-PCBS 4.18	5044
VP-CIC	Bombardier CL-600-2B16 To N550NP 1.18	5011

SERBIA

YU-DLG	UTVA 66 No reports since 6.13	0812?
YU-HHS	Aérospatiale SA.341G Gazelle No reports since 9.13	1067

REPUBLIC of SOUTH AFRICA

ZS-APD	de Havilland DH.87B Hornet Moth No reports since 3.13	8163
ZS-GCG	Jonker Sailplanes JS-1B Revelation Sold in Germany 2017	1B-004
ZS-GCJ	Jonker Sailplanes JS-1B Revelation Sold in 2014	1B-019
ZS-ROY	de Havilland DH.87B Hornet Moth No reports since 3.13	8117
ZS-UKZ	Bellanca 14-13-3 Crusair No reports since 3.13	1633

NIGERIA

5N-MJB	Boeing 737-322 Scrapped Southend by 4.18	24454

GHANA

9G-AEL	Westland Wessex HC.2 To 2-WESX 8.18	WA/624

Overseas

AIRCRAFT TYPE INDEX (OVERSEAS)

Note: This Index covers only entries in that listed in Part 1 of this Section.

BRITISH AIRCRAFT CORPORATION (BAC)
ONE-ELEVEN
VP-BEB

CANADAIR
CL-44-0
N447FT

CESSNA AIRCRAFT COMPANY *including REIMS AVIATION SA production (F prefix)*
120
N9106W N770722

140
N140NT N881586

150
D-ELWH HA-SDH N-L033K N808H F-NYZ-L033
N291D3

AY150 AEROBAT
N7374A

170
N1704Z N2388D N4083W N5429C

172 SKYHAWK
D-EEGR D-EFEL N-L033K N147DT N1729AM
N9200ZK N2388SA N3335SW N453BRS N525DB
N837DP N1033Y N8857S N2442C N550-L33X
N9880DP N13243N 13233N 197533 N758822
N808333 F-RH B-TT P22 N4FA

172RG CUTLASS
N15NH N7238

R172K HAWK XP
N78X P-RH F-NM

REIMS FR172 ROCKET variants
D-ESKSD D-HB G-LUN 533 SBN 145RC

175 SKYLARK
N888-E N9433B

177 (RG) CARDINAL
N177FH N177SA N2788SA N442B N707XU
N8225Y

180 and SKYWAGON
N710GW N80BEB N18PR N180HK N8013SA
N2338K N9425C N888082

182 SKYLANE variants
D-EGMT D-EJLY N14MT N29N N825XZ
N83PL N900D N1825C N180K N889AN
N4894MA N51B3L N6836W N88EW N7358X
N74B0AS N7589AU N3849 N494C N817G
N2231F N23790 N2445V N472B N5857A
N713BN

185
N188 F-RH SE-IED

190 and 195 models
N9899MH N1851DN 158-LD N800G4B N9458W

206 and 208B (GRAND) CARAVAN
D-FBPRS D-FELGH N185AN N208AU N209AX
N208UF N92 SBT N533DRL

210 CENTURION
N23KY N33EU N870K N811MG N21040
N210BBE N9210SH N210UK N249SP
N977CSD N8202SP N7811U N308383

T303 CRUSADER
N11FV N80AVA N285AT

305 BIRD DOG
N53008S

310
N21GB N925XL N31CSN N90FW N9218U
N8029MC N31D4U N813DBX N310UK N310WTT
N315P N7147YK N789MC N91550W N1800RG

337 SUPER SKYMASTER
F-EBXL N18F N800N N337UK N458TL CO-EBYZ

340
N3HK N1051Y N27BRG N588A N83EN N831EB
N940GU N9405C N340Y F-N84B0W N885FRE
N7889MD N8702RK

CMS
HAWK
N9118HK

CHAMPION AIRCRAFT CORPORATION — see also BELLANCA
CITABRIA
N945A N4117Y

DECATHLON
N1113W

CHRISTEN INDUSTRIES INC *including AVIAT — see also PITTS*
A-1 HUSKY variants
N80UK N788HB N1025A N2894W Y N981RC

EAGLE
N780SE

CIRRUS DESIGN CORPORATION
SR20
N1009YY N120MX N131CSD N2082CSD N391W
N889AL N781CSD N84032D N907M W N81839P

SR22
N10MC N170UK N594A-H880P N892SH
N89NE N8863T N98FEL N1222TT N124GP
N141HTT N147G3T N174KEB N147UD N147UK
N147XC N180ZZ N151CS G-NN192ZZ N314SLL
N316BW N81979F N2024D N220BU N22EED
N2222SW N224HRC N3745F N4882CSD N808BRA
N542CSD N538-L N383CSD N500CSD N800LEB
N8838CSD N883KK N896RG N771SF N7908BH
N7999CSD N8003SF N821CC N8345CSD N883CSD
N8883C N9028SF N98 BSD N82832C N888CTT
N888A0 N8888SF N541C85

SR22T
N1082D N111MW N182W N283SN N445KEB
N331CS N98TL N71UK N882AW N102FEZ
N1981C N141KU N173JD N223KEB N223FBB
N288HP N322JF N382470RC N4789RC N534MW
N822BRC N804MW N717FHS N7876GA
N844MS N8882SK N888CTT N842AC N888DTT
N8882TT N8000XX

WISCONS SR550
N80AS N707SN

COMCO IKARUS GmbH
C-42
D-MSGE

COMMANDER AIRCRAFT COMPANY — see ROCKWELL

CUB CRAFTERS
CARBON CUB
SP-YRL

AVIONS MARCEL DASSAULT
FALCON 900 and 900EX models
N2389XX VP-BRW

FALCON 2000 and 2000EX models
N100US N5494P

DE HAVILLAND AIRCRAFT LTD
DH82 TIGER MOTH
N3549

DH104 DOVE
D-IFSB

DH125 — see HAWKER SIDDELEY

DE HAVILLAND (CANADA) *including BOMBARDIER INC and OGMA production*
DHC-1 CHIPMUNK
N458RG

DHC-2 BEAVER
C-GYY-JBR

DHC-6 TWIN OTTER
N808RC

DG FLUGZEUGBAU GmbH
DG808
D-KGMD

DIAMOND AIRCRAFT INDUSTRIES GmbH
DA40(XL) STAR
N21 BBS N820DS N782DS N788DS N824US
OO-STU

DA42 TWIN STAR
N85AL N288US N242GV N468W W N648KM

DA682
9H-XYZ

DORNIER
DO28 SKYSERVANT
D-HED D-HJA A-GOHJA-HB

DO289A
N128CA N774EE

DO228
C-FFRSH

DOUGLAS AIRCRAFT COMPANY INC
DC-3, C-47 DAKOTA and SKYTRAIN variants
N147DRC N8088SF N473DRC

DC-4
N44914

DC-9
I-EDAVA

DYN AÉRO SA
MCR-01
F-PRU-RU

ECLIPSE AVIATION CORPORATION
ECLIPSE 500
N100VA N117EA N77GK N504EA N338DK
N843TE

ERAVION OYY
PIK-20
SE-TXO

ELLA AVIACIÓN S.L.
ELLA-07
EC-EER6

Overseas

EMBRAER
110 BANDEIRANTE
  N97121

ENSTROM HELICOPTER CORPORATION
F28
  N918DK

280
  N280CH N531TJ

ERCO including ALON and FORNEY production
ERCOUPE 415
  N2844H N93938 N99495

EUROCOPTER – see also SUD-AVIATION
AS.350B ECUREUIL
  N9FJ N22AH N330MG N506JA N355ZZ

AS.355 TWIN SQUIRREL
  F-GIRL N766AM

EC130
  ZK-IGM

EC155
  A7-HMD OY-HSK

EC175
  OO-NSE OO-NSF OO-NSI OO-NSR

EC665
  F-ZWWW

EXTRA FLUGZEUGBAU GmbH
EA.300
  D-EMIM

EA.400
  N400YY

FAIRCHILD ENGINE and AIRPLANE
24 ARGUS
  NC1328

CORNELL
  N33870

FISHER FLYING PRODUCTS INC
CELEBRITY
  N8205H

FLIGHT DESIGN GmbH
CTLS
  D-EXAD

FOLLAND AIRCRAFT LTD
GNAT
  N513X

FUJI HEAVY INDUSTRIES LTD
FA.200
  D-EAMZ

GARDAN
GY80 Horizon
  F-WREI

GOVERNMENT AIRCRAFT FACTORY
N22 NOMAD
  N5190Y N6302W

GREENWING
ESPYDER
  D-MGWU

GROB-WERKE GMB & CO KG
G109
  I-KILC

GRUMMAN AIRCRAFT ENGINEERING
G.21 GOOSE
  N4575C

GRUMMAN AMERICAN AVIATION CORPORATION (1), AMERICAN GENERAL AVIATION (2) and GULFSTREAM AMERICAN CORPORATION (3) production
GRUMMAN AA-1B TRAINER (1)
  LX-ARS

GRUMMAN AA-5A CHEETAH (1)
  OO-GCO

GRUMMAN AA-5B TIGER (1)
  D-EGDC D-ENTO F-GKGN

GULFSTREAM AA-5B TIGER (3)
  N31RB N666GA N2121T N28236

AMERICAN GENERAL AG-5B TIGER (2)
  F-GITZ TC-NLB

GULFSTREAM AEROSPACE CORPORATION
GULFSTREAM III
  N623NP

GULFSTREAM IV and V variants
  HZ-ARK N225EE N841WS VP-BLW VQ-BLA

G650
  VP-BCT VP-CGN

HAWKER SIDDELEY AVIATION including BAe, CORPORATE JETS LTD, DE HAVILLAND and RAYTHEON-HAWKER production
HS.125
  N19CQ N19CU N19EK N19UG N19UK
  N19XY N188B N228TM VP-CFI 5N-JMA

HEAD BALLOONS INC
AX-9
  N4519U

HILLER HELICOPTERS INC
UH-12 (360)
  N212W N5315V N5317V N38763

HONDA
HA420
  N547MP

HUGHES TOOL CO and HUGHES HELICOPTERS INC including SCHWEIZER AIRCRAFT CORPORATION (269 wef 1986) and McDONNELL-DOUGLAS (369 wef 1983) production
269
  N7505B N8990F N58342

369
  N7NP N59SD N124PD N239MY N369HE
  N369SY N450AG N457GM N500HL N500SY
  N500TY N500XV N727CH N2742Y N4037L
  N5106Y N5264Q

ICP SRL
MXP740 SAVANNAH
  I-9753

JODEL including CEA, SAN and WASSMER production – see also ROBIN
D140
  F-GRLX

DR.250/160
  D-EIAR

DR253
  D-EGMC

JONKER SAILPLANES
JS-1 REVELATION
  ZS-GAK ZS-GBK ZS-GBL ZS-GBM ZS-GBR
  ZS-GCD ZS-GCE ZS-GCS ZS-GEE ZS-GEF
  ZS-GEG ZS-GEH ZS-GER

JS-3 RAPTURE
  D-KADJ ZT-GAB

LAKE AIRCRAFT CORPORATION INC
LA-4 BUCCANEER
  C-FQIP N8004B

LANG FLUGZEUGBAU
E1 ANTARES
  D-KAIB D-KAIJ D-KANH D-KZEN D-0606

LEARJET INC including BOMBARDIER AEROSPACE production
LEARJET Model 25
  N121EL N309LJ N829AA

LEARJET Model 40
  N40XR N700KG

LEARJET Model 45
  N66DN

LEONARDO HELICOPTERS including AGUSTA SpA
A109 variants
  D-HCKV N64EA N74PM N109TF N109TK
  N365TV N449C N800WK N877SW N950AL
  SP-HXA

A119
  N119SX

AW139
  N139PR OO-NSN OO-NSQ T7-LSS

LIBERTY AEROSPACE INC
XL-2
  N19ET N518XL

LOCKHEED AIRCRAFT CORPORATION including LOCKHEED-CALIFORNIA CO and CANADAIR production
JETSTAR
  N25AG

L-1011 TRISTAR
  N304CS N309CS N405CS N507CS N703CS
  N705CS

LUSCOMBE AIRPLANE CORPORATION
8 SILVAIRE
  N575DW

McDONNELL DOUGLAS HELICOPTER CO – see HUGHES and MD HELICOPTERS

AVIONS MAX HOLSTE
MH.1521 BROUSSARD
  F-GKRO

MAULE AIRCRAFT CORPORATION
M-4
  N159AR N9861M

M-5 LUNAR ROCKET
  N775RG N5632R N5647S N56643

M-6 SUPER ROCKET
  N6130X N56462

M(XT)-7 SUPER, STAR ROCKET and STARCRAFT models
  N141WF N280SA N535TK N882JH N982NW

MD HELICOPTERS INC
MD.520
  N520EA

MD.900
  N90011

MIL
Mil-2
  YL-LHN YL-LHO

MITSUBISHI
MU-2
  N80JN

MOONEY AIRCRAFT CORPORATION
M.20 and M.252 variants
  D-EBIE F-HVAL I-IJMW N4ML N12ZX N20UK
  N60GZ N201YK N214DA N278DB N305SE
  N321KL N333DF N937RP N2125K N7180V
  N7423V OY-DFD

MORANE-SAULNIER including GEMS, MORANE, SEEMS and SOCATA production
MS.880, MS.885, MS.887, MS.892 and MS.894 variants
  F-GFGH N370AJ

MORAVAN NARODNI PODNIK
ZLIN 526 TRENER MASTER
  OK-NNN

AVIONS MUDRY AND CIE including AKROTECH EUROPE and CONSTRUCTIONS AÉRONAUTIQUES DE BOURGOGNE
CAP.10
  D-ETUR N80MC N503DW N4238C

CAP.222, CAP.231 and CAP.232 variants
  F-GXDB OH-SKA

MXR TECHNOLOGIES
MXC and MX2
  N263MX N540XS

Neico
LANCAIR 360
  N250JF

LANCAIR LEGACY
  N992C

LANCAIR COLUMBIA variants
  N209DW N350DG N400HF N400UK

NORTH AMERICAN AVIATION INC including CAC, CCF, NOORDUYN AVIATION LTD and NORTH AMERICAN ROCKWELL production
B-25 MITCHELL
  N9089Z

P-51 MUSTANG
  N51CK

JOSEF Oberlerchner HOLZINDUSTRIE
JOB 15
  D-ECFE

Pacific AEROSPACE CORPORATION
PAC 750
  ZK-KAY ZK-KCE ZK-KNM

PIAGGIO AERO INDUSTRIES including FOCKE WULF production
P.149
  D-EARY D-EHJL D-EOAJ

P.180 AVANTI
  VQ-BHO

PILATUS AIRCRAFT LTD
PC.12
  N234RG T7-AMS

PIPER AIRCRAFT CORPORATION including TAYLOR AIRCRAFT CO LTD and THE NEW PIPER AIRCRAFT INC production
J-3C CUB (L-4 and O-59 versions)
  D-EMER F-BMHM N46779 N61787

PA-15 VAGABOND
  NC4531H

PA-16 CLIPPER
  N5240H N5730H

PA-17 VAGABOND
  OY-AVW

PA-18 SUPER CUB variants
  EC-AIJ I-EIXM LN-LJE N123SA N162AW
  N652P N662KK N4085E N7238X N45507

PA-20 PACER
  N1502A

PA-22-108 COLT
  D-EGEU N209SA N243SA N5593Z

PA-22 TRI-PACER
  N2652P

PA-23 APACHE variants,
  N909PH N2086P

PA-23-250 AZTEC variants
  N37LW N171WM N370SA N485ED N989Y
  N2401Z N4422P

PA-24 COMANCHE variants
  N84VK N111DT N218SA N250CC N500AV
  N673SA N5839P N6298P N7348P N7456P
  N7832P N8829P N9381P N61970 SE-IIV

PA-28-140 CHEROKEE (CRUISER)
  F-BOXT N277SA N519MC N735FL N6602Y
  N9576W

PA-28-161 (CHEROKEE) WARRIOR
  N161FF N8241Z SE-IAM

PA-28-180 CHEROKEE
  N180LK

PA-28-181 (CHEROKEE) ARCHER
  N56EK N65JF N73GR N411BC N499MS
  N661KK N787CE N2273Q N75048

PA-28-235 CHEROKEE
  N235PF

PA-28-236 DAKOTA
  N81188 OO-MHB

PA-28R (CHEROKEE) ARROW variants
  D-EAWW HB-PBF N187SA N200GK N216GC
  N747MM N808VT N900PH N7954J N38273
  N47494

PA-28RT ARROW variants
  D-EKHW N2CL N66MS N777MD N799JH
  N2136E N2943D N8105Z N8153E N8412B
  N8899W N20249 N29566

PA-30 TWIN COMANCHE – see also PA-39
  N7EY N8MZ N25PR N30NW N65PF N359DW
  N499AG N780AC N888DM N7976Y N8181Y
  N8523Y N8818Y

PA-31 NAVAJO (CHIEFTAIN) variants
  N5LL N95TA N131MP N189SA N250MD
  N449TA N477PM N642P N900TB N3544M
  N3586D T7-NAV

PA-31T CHEYENNE
  N187CP

PA-32 CHEROKEE SIX variants
  N112WM N129SC N132LE N199MW
  N257SA N370WC N2923N N2989M

PA-32R-300 (CHEROKEE) LANCE
  N83VK N101DW N6954J N7640F

PA-32R-301 SARATOGA variants
  F-GGBD N32LE N51AH N67SP N73BL
  N77YY N88NA N446SE N505WC N517FD
  N551TT N808CA N957T N987LV N9141Z
  N30614 N31008

PA-34 SENECA variants
  D-GACR N37US N61HB N81AW N95D
  N424XC N459PA N559C N6920B N21381
  N32625

PA-38 TOMAHAWK
  D-EIBR F-GCTU N24730 OO-RAS SE-GVH
  ZK-EVC

PA-39 TWIN COMANCHE C/R – see also PA-30
  N39CR N320MR N971RJ N4297A

PA-44-180 SEMINOLE
  N110GC

PA-46 MALIBU variants
  D-EKEU D-EPPG N14EF N71WZ N113BP
  N138CM N350NM N350XT N394SE N464LB
  N466AB N866LP N930Z N955SH N5347V
  N8007K N10522 N41518 T7-ASH

PA-46R MALIBU MATRIX
  N195AM

PIPISTREL DOO AJDOVSCINA
VIRUS
  F-JTYB I-B946

SINUS
  D-MYWE I-6693

PITTS AVIATION ENTERPRISES INC
S-1
  N11N N44EW N371WS N697RB

S-2
  N61PS N74DC N88NL N260QB N414MB
  N531RM N80035

AVIONS POTEZ
840
  F-BMCY

PROGRESSOR
POU GYRO
  F-WUTH

PZL WARSZAWA-OKECIE SA
PZL-101 GAWRON
  SP-CHD

PZL-104 WILGA
  LY-AWV

Raj HAMSA
X'AIR (FALCON and HAWK) variants
  79II

RAVEN INDUSTRIES
S.40
  N1196R

RAYTHEON AIRCRAFT COMPANY – see also HAWKER SIDDELEY AVIATION
RB390 PREMIER
  N88EL N881AA N882AA

AVIONS PIERRE ROBIN including CONSTRUCTIONS AÉRONAUTIQUES DE BOURGOGNE – see also JODEL
DR.400 and DR..500 variants
  D-ELSR F-GBVN F-GDKJ F-GOXD

HR.100
  CS-ARI D-EBBV

R.2160
  N445KA

ATL
  F-GFOR

ROBINSON HELICOPTER CO INC

R.22
EC-JZF

R.44 RAVEN I, II
D-HFCV N999RL OE-XDT

R.66
N166MG N4480W N7021Z N44829

ROCKWELL INTERNATIONAL CORPORATION including GULFSTREAM and COMMANDER AIRCRAFT COMPANY (114) production

500, 680, 685 and 690 COMMANDER variants
N51WF N690CL N980HB N3596T

COMMANDER 112 and 114
N9AC N14AF N50AY N112JA N114AT
N115MD N116SB N395TC N928HW N1350J
N1407J N4698W N4874W N5834N N6010Y
N6039X N6081F N6088F

ROTORWAY HELICOPTERS INTERNATIONAL

SCORPION
SE-HXF

RUSCHMEYER LUFTFAHRTTECHNIK GmbH

RUSHMEYER R90
N12AB

RYAN AERONAUTICAL CORPORATION

STA
N17343

NAVION
D-ECDL N3864 N4956C N8968H

SCHEIBE-FLUGZEUGBAU GmbH

SF-25 FALKE (inc SLINGSBY T.61)
D-KIAH

SCHEMPP-HIRTH FLUGZEUBAU GmbH

DISCUS
D-KDLQ

NIMBUS
D-4818

VENTUS
D-KDPF D-KEWV D-KJMH D-KKVT D-KLSU
D-KLTN D-KTOF D-KXTC

SHK
D-1538

ALEXANDER SCHLEICHER GmbH and CO

K.8B
D-1155

ASW 12
N145T

ASH.25
D-KOOL

SHORT BROTHERS LTD

SC.7 SKYVAN
C-FARA C-GKOA

SIAI-MARCHETTI SpA

S.205/208
ZS-ESG

SF.260
N61FD N260AP N330DG

SOCATA – see also MORANE-SAULNIER

TB-9 TAMPICO and TB-10 TOBAGO
N99ET

TB-20, TB-21 TRINIDAD and TB-200 TOBAGO GT/XL
N1FD N5ZY N20AG N20TB N33NW N91ME
N113AC N345TB N377C N575GM

TBM-700,TBM-850 and TBM-900
N2PD N181PC N463RD N616CM N700EL
N850BG N850NP N910RW N930SA N989PR

SPARTAN

7W EXECUTIVE
NC17615 NC17633

SPEZIO

DAL-1
PH-MJC

STEARMAN – see BOEING-STEARMAN

STEMME GmbH and Co KG

S.6
D-KRUK

S.10
D-KGED

STINSON AIRCRAFT CORPORATION

JUNIOR R
NC2612

L-5 SENTINEL
N6438C

RELIANT
NC50238 N69745

SUD-AVIATION including AÉROSPATIALE, SOKO and WESTLAND HELICOPTERS production

SE.313 and SE318 ALOUETTE II
F-GDQL N297CJ N577AG

SA.341 and SA.342 GAZELLE
HA-LFH N150SF N340SM N901B N58283
RP-C342 YU-HES YU-HET YU-HEV YU-HEY
YU-HMC YU-HOT YU-HPZ YU-HWF

SUKHOI

Su-26
HA-NST

Su-29
HA-YAW

TAYLOR

JT.1 MONOPLANE
N52GM

COSTRUZIONI AERONAUTICHE TECNAM Srl

P.2002 SIERRA
D-ETRE

SCF TECHNOAVIA

SMG-92 FINIST

HA-YDF

TRAVEL AIR

D-4000
NC5427 NC8115

URBAN AIR

UFM-10 SAMBA
OK-GUA 28 OK-JUA 03

VAN'S AIRCRAFT INC

RV-10
N104BP

VFW-FOKKER GmbH

VFW-614
D-ASDB

VOLMER

VJ22
N7508U

VPM SNC and SRL including MAGNI GYRO

M22 Voyager
EC-XCM

WACO AIRCRAFT CORPN

UEC
NC12467

YMF
N45BN N999PD

SOCIÉTÉ WASSMER

WA.54 ATLANTIC
D-EEPI

WA.81 PIRANA
F-GAIF

WESTLAND HELICOPTERS LTD

WG.30
N114WG N116WG N5880T VT-EKT

XTREME Air

XA-41/2
F-HAUL

YAKOVLEV including ACROSTAR, IAV-BACHAU, LET, NANCHANG, SPP and WSK production

Yak-18T
HA-SMD HA-YAV

Yak-55
RA-01274

ZENAIR

ZENITH 100
F-PYOY

ZIVKO AERONAUTICS INC

EDGE 540
N24KC

Overseas

SECTION 9 – MUSEUMS AND PRIVATE COLLECTIONS

Basic details are shown for all de-registered aircraft and gliders with previous British civil registered provenance – the full details of aircraft bearing British registrations can be found in SECTION 1 where the aircraft are marked with a superscript letter ([M]). These aircraft are held in Museums and other displayed public collections and are accessible for public viewing. Also included, for completeness, are a small number of exhibited overseas registered aircraft. The listing also includes replicas and full scale models (FSM), most of which are recorded on the expanded AHUK (formerly BAPC) Register now maintained by Lloyd Robinson, the Registrar of Airframes – full details are to be found in SECTION 3.

The collections are listed by county, with postal addresses and (where available) website addresses, followed by a short international section in country order. In this latter area, we only list those carrying British civil or military marks.

Updates this year are from Mike Cain, Howard Curtis, Lloyd Robinson, Benjamin Sadler, Barrie Womersley and all contributors to the 2018 & 2019 editions of *Air-Britain News*.

Regn	Type		C/n	Date
	Previous identity	Remarks		CofA Expy

ENGLAND

BEDFORDSHIRE
Richard Shuttleworth Trustees, Old Warden SG18 9EP
(shuttleworth.org)

Regn	Type		C/n	Date
	Previous identity	Remarks		CofA Expy
G-ARZB	Wallis WA-116 Series 1 Agile		B.203	
G-BFIP	Wallbro Monoplane 1909 replica		WA-1	
BGA 231[M]	Abbott-Baynes Scud II		215B	25.04.49
	G-ALOT Cancelled 10.01.64 as WFU	*Dismantled*		
	Built by Slingsby Sailplanes c08.35			
BGA 310[M]	Slingsby T.6 Kirby Kite		258B	
	VD218			
	Built by 02.37: rebuilt by M & T Maufe 1982: fuselage, port wing &			
	elevator of BGA 327 used in restoration			
BGA 580	EoN AP.7 Primary		EoN/P/003	06.05.49
	G-ALPS Cancelled 1955 as PWFU	*'AQQ'*		06.05.49
BGA 1999	Fauvel AV.36CR		133	xx.10.74
	RNGSA.xxx, F-CBSH			
	Built by Wassmer Aviation			
BAPC.008	Dixon Ornithopter reconstruction			
BAPC.038	Bristol Scout Type D replica			
BAPC.271	Messerschmitt Me 163B Komet fsm			
BAPC.337	Pilcher Bat Mk.3 replica			
BAPC.437	Lilienthal Kleiner 'Doppeldecker' reproduction			
BAPC.438	Lilienthal 'Normal Apparatus' reproduction			
BAPC.439	Lilienthal Type XI Glider reproduction			
BAPC.441	Pilcher Triplane reproduction			
BAPC.474	Philips British Matchless Flying Machine			

BERKSHIRE
British Balloon Museum & Library, Newbury (bbml.org.uk)
(Can be viewed on annual Inflation days @ Pidley, Huntingdon)

Regn	Type	C/n
G-ATGN	Thorn K-800 Coal Gas Balloon	2
G-ATXR	Abingdon Spherical Free HAB	AFB-1
G-AVTL	Brighton Ax7-65 HAB	01
G-AWCR	Piccard Ax6 HAB	6204
G-AWJB	Brighton MAB-65 HAB	MAB-3
G-AWMO	Omega O-84 HAB	01
G-AWOK	Sussex Gas Balloon	SARD.1
G-AXVU	Omega 84 HAB	09
G-AXXP	Bradshaw 76 (Ax7) HAB	RB.001
G-AYAJ	Cameron O-84 HAB	11
G-AYAL	Omega 56 HAB	10
G-AZBH	Cameron O-84 HAB	23
G-AZER	Cameron O-42 (Ax5) HAB	26
G-AZJI	Western O-65 HAB	007
G-AZOO	Western O-65 HAB	015
G-AZSP	Cameron O-84 HAB	43

Regn	Type	C/n
G-AZUV	Cameron O-65 HAB	41
G-AZUW	Cameron A-140 HAB	45
G-AZVT	Cameron O-84 HAB	40
G-AZXB	Cameron O-65	48
G-AZYL	Portslade Free HAB	MK 17
G-BAMK	Cameron D-96 HA Airship	72
G-BAVU	Cameron A-105 HAB	66
G-BAXF	Cameron O-77 HAB	74
G-BAXK	Thunder Ax7-77 HAB	0051
G-BBCK	Cameron O-77 HAB	76
G-BBFS	Vandem-Bemden K-460 Gas Balloon	75
G-BBLL	Cameron O-84 HAB	84
G-BBOX	Thunder Ax7-77 HAB	011
G-BBYU	Cameron O-56 HAB	96
G-BCAR	Thunder Ax7-77 HAB	019
G-BCFC	Cameron 0-65 HAB	116
G-BCFD	West Ax3-15 HAB	JW.1
G-BCFE	Byrne Odyssey 4000 MLB	AJB-2
G-BCGP	Gazebo Ax6-65 HAB	1
G-BDAC	Cameron 0-77 HAB	146
G-BDVG	Thunder Ax6-56A HAB	067
G-BDWO	Howes Ax6 HAB	RBH-2
G-BEEE	Thunder Ax6-56A HAB	070
G-BEPO	Cameron N-77 HAB	279
G-BEPZ	Cameron D-96 HA Airship	300
G-BETF	Cameron Champion 35 SS HAB	280
G-BETH	Thunder Ax6-56A HAB	113
G-BEVI (3)	Thunder Ax7-77A HAB	125
G-BFAB	Cameron N-56 HAB	297
G-BFLP	Amethyst Ax6-56	001
G-BFOZ	Thunder Ax6-56 Plug HAB	144
G-BGAS	Colting Ax8-105A HAB	001
G-BGOO	Colt Flame 56 Flame HAB	039
G-BGPF	Thunder Ax6-56Z HAB	206
G-BHHK	Cameron N-77 HAB	547
G-BHKN	Colt 14A Cloudhopper HAB	068
G-BHKR	Colt 14A Cloudhopper HAB	071
G-BHSN	Cameron N-56 HAB	595
G-BIAZ	Cameron AT-165 HAB	400
G-BIDV	Colt 17A Cloudhopper HAB	789
G-BIGF	Thunder Ax7-77 Bolt HAB	295
G-BIGT	Colt 77A HAB	078
G-BJXP	Colt 56B HAB	393
G-BKES	Cameron Bottle 57 SS HAB	846

G-BKJT	Cameron 0-65	148
G-BKMR	Thunder Ax3 Maxi Sky Chariot HAB	497
G-BKOR	Barnes 77 Firefly	F7-046
G-BLIO	Cameron R-42 Gas/HAB)	1015
G-BLWB	Thunder Ax6-56 Srs.1 HAB	645
G-BMEZ	Cameron DP-70 HA Airship	1130
G-BNHN	Colt Ariel Bottle SS HAB	1045
G-BOGL	Thunder Ax7-77 HAB	953
G-BOGR	Colt 180A HAB	1183
G-BOTL	Colt 42A SS HAB	466
G-BPKN	Colt AS-80 Mk.II HA Airship	1297
G-BPLD	Thunder & Colt AS-261 HA Airship	1380
G-BRZC	Cameron N-90 HAB	2227
G-BUBL	Thunder Ax8-105 HAB	1147
G-BUJW	Thunder Ax8-90 HAB	2208
G-BUUU	Cameron Bottle 77 SS HAB	2980
G-BVBX	Cameron N-90M HAB	3102
G-BVDS	Lindstrand LBL69A HAB	102
G-BVFY	Colt 210A HAB	2493
G-BVIO	Colt Flying Drinks Can SS HAB	2538
G-BVWH	Cameron N-90 Lightbulb SS HAB	3404
G-BWST	Sky 200-24 HAB	036
G-BXTJ	Cameron N-77 HAB	4332
G-CHUB	Colt Cylinder Two N-51 HAB	1720
G-EPDI	Cameron N-77 HAB	370
G-FTFT	Colt Financial Times 90 SS HAB	1163
G-FZZZ	Colt 56A HAB	507
G-HOME	Colt 77A HAB	032
G-HOUS	Colt 31A Air Chair HAB	099
G-ICES	Thunder Ax6-56 SP.1 HAB	283
G-IKEA	Cameron IKEA 120SS HAB	10562
G-JONO	Colt 77A HAB	1086
G-LCIO	Colt 240A HAB	1381
G-LOAG	Cameron N-77 HAB	359
G-OAAC	Airtour AH-77B	AH-010
G-OBUD	Colt 69A HAB	698
G-OFIZ	Cameron Can 80 SS HAB	2106
G-PARR	Colt Bottle 90 SS HAB	1953
G-PERR	Cameron Bottle 60 SS HAB	6994
G-PLUG	Colt 105A HAB	1958
G-PUBS	Colt Beer Glass 56 SS HAB	037
G-ZUMP	Cameron N-77 HAB	377
N4990T	Thunder Ax7-65B HAB	123
N12006	Raven S.50A HAB	111
	On loan from R Higbe 'Cheers'	
OY-BOW	Colting 77A HAB	77A-014
	SE-ZVB 'Circus'	

Beale Park Wildlife Park & Gardens, Lower Basildon, Pangbourne (bealepark.org.uk)
BAPC.242 Supermarine Spitfire VB replica

History of Wheels Museum, Longclose House, Common Road, Eton Wick, Windsor SL4 6QY (historyonwheels.co.uk)

G-CCUK	Agusta A109A II	7263

Museum of Berkshire Aviation, Woodley RG5 4UF (museumofberkshireaviation.co.uk)

G-AJJP	Fairey FB.2 Jet Gyrodyne	9420 & FB.2
G-AKKY	Miles M.14A Hawk Trainer 3	2078
G-APWA	Handley Page HPR.7 Dart Herald 100	149
G-MIOO	Miles M.100 Student	1008
TF-SHC	Miles M.25 Martinet TT.1	xxxx
	MS902, 251 Crashed 18.07.51	

BGA 589	EoN AP.7 Primary	EoN/P/012	28.03.49
	G-ALMN, BGA 589 Cancelled 12.03.51		
	As 'G-ALMN' & 'BGA589'		
BGA 1288	EoN 460-1	xxxx	'465'

BAPC.233 Broburn Wanderlust sailplane

BAPC.248 McBroom hang glider

BAPC.415 ML Aviation Sprite UAV

BRISTOL
Bristol City Museum & Art Gallery,Queen's Road, Clifton BS8 1RL (bristol-city.gov.uk/museums)

BAPC.040 Bristol Boxkite reconstruction   BOX 3 & BM.7281

M Shed, Princes Wharf, Wapping Road, Bristol BS1 4RN (bristolmuseums.org.uk)

G-AEHM	Mignet HM.14 Pou-du-Ciel	HJD1

Aerospace Bristol, Hayes Way, Patchway, Bristol BS34 5BZ (aerospacebristol.org)

G-ALBN	Bristol 173 Mk.1	12871
G-MBTH	Whittaker MW4	001
G-BOAF	BAC Concorde Type 1 Variant 102	216 & 100-016
N2138J	English Electric Canberra TT.18 EEA/R3/EA3/6640	
	WK126 S D Picatti As 'WK126:843'	
	Built by A V Roe & Co	
	On loan to Gloucestershire Aviation Collection	

BAPC.087 Bristol 30/46 Babe III reconstruction   1

BAPC.386 Bristol F.2B Fighter replica

BAPC.387 Bristol F.2B Fighter

BAPC.392 BAe Avro RJX-100

BAPC.496 Bristol F.2b Fighter reconstruction

Bristol Aero Collection Trust, Filton (bristolaero.org)

G-ALRX	Bristol 175 Britannia Series 101	12874

BUCKINGHAMSHIRE
Headquarters Air Command, RAF High Wycombe (raf.mod.uk/rafhighwycombe)

Gate Guards
BAPC.335 Supermarine Spitfire IIa fsm

BAPC.378 Hawker Hurricane I fsm

The Heritage Park, Pitstone Green Museum, Vicarage Road, Pitstone LU7 9EY (pitstonemuseum.co.uk)
BAPC.425 Avro Lancaster cockpit reproduction

Trenchard Museum and James McCudden Air Power Heritage Centre, RAF Halton (raf.mod.uk/rafhalton)

BGA.1143	Slingsby T.7 Cadet TX.1	xxxx	xx.08.63
	RAFGSA.273, RA905 As 'RA905'		14.03.00

BAPC.338 Halton Aero Club HAC.II Minus

CAMBRIDGESHIRE
American Air Museum, Duxford

G-BFYO	SPAD XIII replica	0035
G-BHDK	Boeing TB-29A-45-BN Superfortress	11225
G-BHUB	Douglas C-47A-85-DL Skytrain	19975
CF-EQS	Boeing-Stearman A75N1 Kaydet	
	(PT-17-BW)	75-1728
	41-8169 As '217786:25' in USAAF c/s	
	Composite including elements of 42-17786	
CF-KCG	Grumman TBM-3E Avenger	2066
	RCN 326, USN 69327 'Ginny'	
	As '46214:X-3' in USN c/s	
	Built by General Motors Co	
F-BDRS	Boeing B-17G-95-DL Flying Fortress	32376
	N68269, NL68269, 44-83735 'Mary Alice'	
	As '238133:IY-G' in USAAF c/s	
N47DD	Republic P47D-30-RA Thunderbolt	399-55731
	Peru AF FAP119, 45-49192 'Oregon's Britannia'	
	As '226413:UN-Z' in USAF c/s	
N7614C	North American TB-25J-30-NC Mitchell	108-37246
	44-31171 'Little Critter from the Moon'	
	As '34064:BU' in US Marines c/s	

Duxford Aviation Society (das.org.uk)

G-ALDG	Handley Page HP.81 Hermes IV	HP.81/8	
G-ALFU	de Havilland DH.104 Dove 6	04234	
G-ALWF	Vickers 701 Viscount	5	
G-ALZO (2)	Airspeed AS.57 Ambassador 2	5226	
G-ANTK	Avro 685 York C.1	xxxx	
G-AOVT	Bristol 175 Britannia 312	3427	
G-APDB	de Havilland DH.106 Comet 4	6403	
G-APWJ	Handley Page HPR.7 Dart Herald 201	158	
G-ASGC	Vickers Super VC-10 Series 1151	853	
G-AVFB	Hawker Siddeley HS.121 Trident 2E	2141	
G-AVMU	BAC One Eleven 510ED	BAC.148	
G-AXDN	BAC Concorde	01	

Imperial War Museum CB2 4QR (iwm.org.uk)

G-ACUU	Cierva C.30A (Avro 671)	726	
G-AFBS	Miles M.14A Hawk Trainer 3	539	
G-AHTW	Airspeed AS.40 Oxford 1	3083	
G-ALCK	Percival Proctor III	H.536	
G-AMDA	Avro 652A Anson 1	xxxx	
G-ASKC	de Havilland DH.98 Mosquito TT.35	xxxx	
G-BCYK	Avro (Canada) CF-100 Canuck Mk.IV	xxxx	
G-BESY	BAC 167 Strikemaster Mk.88A	xxxx	
G-LANC	Avro 683 Lancaster B.X	xxxx	
G-LIZY	Westland Lysander III	'504/39'	
G-USUK	Colt 2500A HAB	1100	
BAPC.057	Pilcher Hawk replica		
BAPC.090	Colditz Cock replica		
BAPC.093	Fieseler Fi 103 (V-1)		
BAPC.159	Yokosuka MXY-7 Ohka 11		
BAPC.198	Fieseler Fi 103 (V-1)		
BAPC.267	Hawker Hurricane fsm	Gate Guard	
BAPC.394	Supermarine Spitfire I fsm		
BAPC.396	Airspeed AS.58 Horsa II cockpit		
N66630	Schweizer TG-3A	63	
	42-52983 ?? As '252983' in USAAC c/s In store		
BAPC.255	North American P-51D Mustang fsm	In store	

Cambridge Bomber and Fighter Society, Little Gransden, Cambridge (cbfs.org.uk)

BAPC.362	Hawker Fury replica
BAPC.402	Hawker Hurricane I composite

CHESHIRE
RAF Burtonwood Heritage Centre, Burtonwood, Warrington (rafburtonwoodbase.org)

N31356	Douglas DC-4 1009	42914
	CF-TAW, EL-ADR, N6404	
	Forward fuselage only as '44-42914'	

Hooton Park Trust, Hooton Park (hootonparktrust,co.uk)

BGA.466	Slingsby T.8 Tutor	MHL/RT.7	xx.11.46
	Built by Martin Hearn Ltd		
BAPC.137	Sopwith Baby floatplane fsm		

The Aeroplane Collection, Hooton Park (theaeroplanecollection.org/tac)

G-EBZM	Avro 594A Avian IIIA	R3/CN/160
G-ADAH	de Havilland DH.89 Dragon Rapide	6278
G-AFIU	Parker CA.4 Parasol (Luton Minor).	CA-4
G-AHUI	Miles M.38 Messenger 2A	6335
G-AJEB	Auster J/1N Alpha	2325
'G-AKHZ'	Miles M.65 Gemini 7	6527
G-AOUO	de Havilland DHC-1 Chipmunk 22	C1/0179
G-APUD	Bensen B-7Mc	KHW.1
G-BFTZ	SOCATA MS.880B Rallye Club	1269
G-MJXE	Mainair Tri-Flyer 330/Hiway Demon 175	102-131082 & HS-001

BGA.473	Slingsby T.8 Tutor	MHL/RT.12	xx.10.47
	G-ALPU, BGA.473		xx.12.67
	Built by Martin Hearn Ltd On loan from J Howard		
BAPC.006	Roe Triplane Type I		
BAPC.012	Mignet HM.14 Pou-Du-Ciel replica		
BAPC.201	Mignet HM.14 Pou du Ciel replica		
BAPC.204	McBroom Cobra 88 hang glider		
BAPC.309	Fairey Gannet T.2		
BAPC.310	Miles Wings Gulp 100A hang glider		

Avro Heritage Museum, Chester Rd, Poynton, Woodford, Stockport SK7 1AG (avroheritagemuseum.co.uk)

G-AGPG	Avro C19 Series 2	1212
G-ORAL	Hawker Siddeley HS.748 Series 2A/334	1756
BAPC.328	Avro Type F Cabin replica	
BAPC.422	Avro 683 Lancaster composite cockpit	
BAPC.471	Avro 683 Lancaster cockpit reproduction	

CORNWALL
Cornwall At War Museum, Davidstow Moor, Camelford PL32 9YF (cornwallatwarmuseum.co.uk)

BAPC.345	Fieseler Fi.103 (FZG-76/V-1) fsm

Cornwall Aviation Heritage Centre, Newquay Cornwall Airport TR8 4JN (cornwallaviationhc.co.uk)

G-BEDV	Vickers 668 Varsity T.1	xxxx
G-BGKE	BAC One Eleven 539GL	BAC.263
G-BJBM	Monnett Sonerai I	xxxx
G-BTSC	Evans VP-2	xxxx
G-BWGN	Hawker Hunter T.8C	41H-670689
G-BWVI	Stern ST.80 Balade	xxxx
G-BZPB	Hawker Hunter GA.Mk.11	41H-670758
G-CCIS	Scheibe SF28A Tandem Falke	5791
G-CDSX	English Electric Canberra T.4	71367
G-CGUI	Clutton FRED Series II	xxxx
G-MNCV	Medway Hybred 44XL	26485/11
G-ULPS	Everett Gyroplane Series 1	007
BAPC.344	Fieseler Fi.103 (FZG-76/V-1) fsm	

Spitfire Corner, Newquay Cornwall Airport TR8 4EA (wallend.com)

BAPC.268	Supermarine Spitfire IX fsm

CUMBRIA
Cumbria's Museum of Military Life, Alma Block, The Castle, Carlisle, Cumbria, CA3 8UR (cumbriasmuseumofmilitarylife.org)

BAPC.435	WACO CG-4A Hadrian cockpit

Solway Aviation Museum, Carlisle Lake District Airport CA6 4NW (solway-aviation-museum.org.uk)

G-APLG	Auster J/5L Aiglet Trainer	3148
G-BDTT	Bede BD-5	3795
G-BJWY	Sikorsky S-55 (HRS.2) Whirlwind HAR.21	55289
G-BNNR	Cessna 152 II	15285146
G-BRHL	Montgomerie-Bensen B 8MR	xxxx
BAPC.231	Mignet HM.14 Pou-Du-Ciel	

Windermere Jetty – Museum of Boats, Stream and Stories, Rayrigg Road, Bowness, Windermere LA23 1BN (windermerejetty.org) (Under reconstruction 2019)

BGA 266	Slingsby T.1 Falcon 1 Waterglider	23.7A	29.05.36
	Stored		

DEVON
Cobbaton Combat Collection, Cobbaton, South Molton EX37 9RZ (cobbatoncombat.co.uk)

BAPC.351	Airspeed AS.58 Horsa II replica

DORSET
Bournemouth Aviation Museum, Bournemouth BH23 6BA (aviation-museum.co.uk)

G-BFZR	Gulfstream AA-5B Tiger	AA5B-097

G-BKRL	Chichester-Miles Leopard	0001
G-BWAF	Hawker Hunter F.58A	S41U/41H/698398
G-BWGS	BAC 145 Jet Provost T.5A	EEP/JP/974/XW63100
G-BZRE	Hunting Percival P.56 Provost T.1	PAC/F/0394
G-CEAH	Boeing 737-229	21135
G-DUSK	de Havilland DH.115 Vampire T.Mk.11	15596
G-SSLG	Avions Transport ATR.42-320	0019
G-TLET	Piper PA-28-161 Cadet	2841259

DURHAM
Historical Aviation Centre, Morgansfield, Fishburn
(Was under construction, to open 2018?)

| G-AMXR | de Havilland DH.104 Dove 6 | 04379 |
| G-BLKA | de Havilland DH.112 Venom FB.Mk.54 (FB.4) | 9960 |

Not confirmed

G-ARWU	Thruston Tawney Owl	TAN-11
BGA.1461	EoN AP.7 Primary	xxxxx
	(CDN) As 'CDN'	xx.05
xxxxx	Miles M.14 replica	
	Original aircraft built by mid 1980s but never completed	
	& finished as ground running restoration As un-allocated	
	'G-ADFZ'	

ESSEX
Boxted Airfield Historical Group (Museum), Boxted, Langham CO4 5NW
(boxted-airfield.com)

| G-BUDF | Rand-Robinson KR-2 | xxxxx |

North Weald Airfield Museum OM166AA
(northwealdairfieldmuseum.com)

Gate Guard
BAPC.369 Hawker Hurricane

Vulcan Restoration Trust, Southend Airport (avrovulcan.com)

| G-VJET | Avro 698 Vulcan B.2 | Set 44 |

Stow Maries Great War Aerodrome, Stow Maries (stowmaries.org.uk)

Hangar One
G-AWJD	Fokker E.III replica	PPS/FOK/6
G-AWBU	Morane-Saulnier Type N replica	PPS/REP/7
G-BPVE	Blériot Type XI 1909 replica	1
G-CIZO	Royal Aircraft Factory BE.2e replica	753

Hangar Two
| G-BMDB | Replica Plans SE.5A | xxxx |
BAPC.179 Sopwith Pup fsm
BAPC.407 de Havilland DH.2 fsm
BAPC.412 Gotha G.V cockpit reproduction
BAPC.413 Sopwith 1½ Strutter reproduction
BAPC.414 Sopwith F.1 Camel reproduction

Milton Hall Primary School, Salisbury Ave, Westcliffe-on-Sea SS0 7AU
(miltonhall.school.com)

| G-DWJM | Cessna 680 Citation III | 550-0296 |

GLOUCESTERSHIRE
Bristol Britannia XM496 Preservation Society, Cotswold (xm496.com)

| G-BDUP | Bristol 175 Britannia Series 253 | 13508 |

Jet Age Museum, Gloucestershire (jetagemuseum.btck.co.uk)

BAPC.072 Hawker Hurricane II fsm
BAPC.259 Gloster Gamecock replica
BAPC.331 Gloster E28/39 fsm
BAPC.363 Hawker Typhoon cockpit
BAPC.383 Airspeed AS.58 Horsa II cockpit replica

HAMPSHIRE
Farnborough Air Sciences Trust (FAST Museum), Trenchard House,
85 Farnborough Road, Farnborough GU14 6TF
(airsciences.org.uk)

| G-ARRM | Beagle B.206X | B.001 |
BAPC.391 Cody Type V Bi-Plane replica
| BAPC.531 | QinetiQ Zephyr 6 | 6-1 |

Sir Frank Whittle Memorial, Ively Roundabout, Farnborough GU14
BAPC.285 Gloster E.28/39 fsm

Prince's Mead Shopping Centre, Farnborough GU14 6YA
(princesmead.co.uk)
BAPC.208 Royal Aircraft Factory SE.5a replica

The Gliding Heritage Centre, Lasham, Alton GU34 5SS
(glidingheritage.org.uk)

G-AEKV	Kronfeld Drone	30	
G-ALJR	Abbott-Baynes Scud III	2	
G-ALRD	Scott Viking 1	6	
G-ALRU	EoN Baby	EoN/B/004	
BGA 162	Manuel Willow Wren	xxxx	xx.09.34
	'The Willow Wren' On loan from Brooklands Museum		
BGA 448	DFS Weihe	000348	xx.06.47
	G-ALJW As 'LJW' Donated by N Jaffrey		
	Built by Jacobs-Schweyer		
BGA 578	Grunau Baby IIB	G.3348	27.07.48
	G-ALSO (As 'AQN') 'Baby G'		30.04.15
	Built by Hawkridge Aircraft Ltd		
BGA 643	Slingsby T.15 Gull III	364A	xx.11.49
	TJ711 As 'ATH'		20.06.04
	Rebuilt by Hawkridge as Hawkridge Kittiwake		
	On loan from Brooklands Museum		
BGA 655	Zlin Z-24 Krajánek	101	xx.04.50
	G-ALMP, OK-8592 Donated by J Dredge		xx.04.78
BGA 685	Slingsby T.34A Sky	644	10.02.53
	G-644 As 'AVB'		17.04.18
BGA 759	Slingsby T.41 Skylark 2	1048	21.07.56
	As 'AYD'		29.07.17
BGA 815	Slingsby T.30B Prefect	1120	xx.01.58
	As 'BAN' Donated by Sir John Allison		
BGA 870	Slingsby T.43 Skylark 3b	1195	xx.04.59
	Donated by J Price		
BGA 962	EoN Olympia 2b	EON/O/124	xx.06.60
	As 'BGR' Donated by M Gagg		
BGA 1004	Slingsby T.43 Skylark 3F	1311	xx.07.61
	As 'BJK' Donated by R Page		
BGA 1183	Slingsby T.49B Capstan	1413	25.06.64
	As 'BRW'		24.04.18
BGA 1278	EoN Olympia 403	EoN/4/001	20.08.65
	RAFGSA 306, G-APEW As '403'		25.08.18
BGA 1365	Slingsby T.45 Swallow	1597	xx-07.67
	As 'BZM' Donated by F Webster		
BGA 1373	EoN Olympia 463	EON/S/046	xx.02.67
	As 'BZV' Donated by B Cooper		
BGA 1414	SZD-24-4A Foka 3	198	xx.07.67
	G-DCBP, CBP, OY-BXR		
	Donated by L Nicholson & G Sutton		
BGA 1698	Slingsby T.8 Tutor	SSK/FF477	26.04.72
	RAFGSA 183 As 'CPL' 'Mistress Tutor'		11.04.18
BGA 1778	Manuel Hawk	1	xx.11.72?
	Donated by T Coldwell		
BGA 1897	Yorkshire Sailplanes YS-53 Svereign	03	xx.07.74
	G-DCXV, CXV Donated by Y & H Stott and A & P Myers		
BGA 2146	Halford JSH Scorpion		001
	BGA 1666 '500'		
	Originally designed & Built by K Holmes as Holmes KH 1		
BGA 2267	München Mü-13D-3	005	14.06.77
	D-1327 Donated by G Moore		
BGA 2689	Schleicher Ka 3	5017	23.10.80
	D-9310 As 'EHB' Donated by L Hood		
BGA 2903	Oberlerchner Mg19A Steinadler	015	01.06.83
	OE-0324 As 'ERZ' Donated by Chris Wills Estate		
BGA 3148	Slingsby T.21B Sedbergh TX.1	MHL.017	12.05.85
	WB990 As '993'		22.07.18
BGA 3229	Slingsby T.31B Cadet TX.3	913	18.08.86
	XE800 As 'FFB'		30.06.18
BGA 3661	Hütter H17a	7	
	As 'FZT' Built J Lee		

BGA 3823	Slingsby T.45 Swallow	1386	16.05.93
	8801M, XS650 *As 'HBX' 'Sir Iain'*		19.07.18
BGA 3915	Vogtt Lo-100 Zwergreiher	02	xx.08.92
	D-6040 *As 'HFS' In use as flight simulator*		
BGA 3922	Abbott-Baynes Scud I replica	001	xx.xx.92
	As 'HFZ' On loan from Brooklands Museum		
BGA 4372	Slingsby T.38 Grasshopper TX.1	1262	08.06.98
	XP463 *As 'XP463' & 'JBA'*		09.09.15
	Assembled from components; p/i is starboard wing only		
BGA 5066	Grunau Baby IIB	5	16.08.03
	D-1932, D-6932 *As 'KFW' Donated by R Slade*		
BAPC.277	Mignet HM.14 Pou du Ciel replica	xxxx	
	'L'Autre Aviation' on tail		
BAPC.347	Colditz Cock replica	xxxx	
	On loan from South East Aircraft Services		
BAPC.405	Manuel Crested Wren	xxxx	
	As 'BGA178' – not the original BGA178		
	Donated by B Reed		
xxxx	Slingsby Grasshopper	xxxx	
	XA225 *Donated by I Pattingale In storage*		
xxxx	Laister-Kaufmann TG-4A		
	C-FRAH? *Unmarked fuselage Donated by D Ogle*		
xxxx	Weiss Olive replica		
	Built A Jarvis 2009 ⅝-scale radio controlled		
xxxx	Unidentified glider *As '597'*		

Museum of Army Flying, AAC Middle Wallop SO20 8DY (flying-museum.org.uk)

G-AKOW	Taylorcraft J Auster 5	1579
G-ARYD	Auster AOP.6	xxxx
G-AXKS	Westland-Bell 47G-4A	WA.723
G-CICN	Agusta-Bell 47G-3B1 Sioux AH.1	1540
G-CICP	de Havilland DHC-2 Beaver AL.1	1483
G-CICR	Auster AOP.9	B5/10/181
G-SARO	Saro Skeeter AOP.12	S2/5097
N33600	Cessna L-19A-CE Bird Dog	22303
	51-11989 *As '111989' in US Army c/s*	
BGA 285	Slingsby T.6 Kite 1	247A
	G-ALNH, BGA 285 *As 'G-285' in 1 GTS RAF c/s*	
BAPC.080	Airspeed AS.58 Horsa II	
BAPC.163	AFEE 10/42 Rotachute Rotabuggy replica	
BAPC.185	WACO CG-4A Hadrian Glider	
BAPC.261	General Aircraft Hotspur replica	
BAPC.416	ML Aviation Sprite UAV	
BAPC.417	Airspeed AS.** Horsa replica	
BAPC.418	Airspeed Horsa cockpit reproduction	

Sammy Miller Motorcycle Museum, Bashley Cross Road (B3055), New Milton BH25 5SZ (sammymiller.co.uk)

| G-EISO | SOCATA MS.892A Rallye Commodore 150 | 10563 |

Solent Sky, Southampton SO1 1FR (spitfireonline.co.uk)

G-ADWO	de Havilland DH.82A Tiger Moth	3455
G-ALZE	Britten-Norman BN-1F	1
G-APOI	Saunders-Roe Skeeter Srs.8	S2/5081
G-SWIF	Vickers Supermarine 552 Swift F.7	VA.9597
VH-BRC	Short S.24 Sandringham IV	SH.55C
	N158C, VP-LVE, N158C, VH-BRC, ZK-AMH, JM715	
	'Beachcomber' Ansett c/s	
	On loan from Science Museum	
BAPC.007	Southampton University Man Powered Aircraft (SUMPAC)	
BAPC.164	Wight Quadraplane Type 1 fsm	
BAPC.210	Avro 504J	
BAPC.215	Airwave hang glider	
BAPC.253	Mignet HM.14 Pou-Du-Ciel replica	

Winchester Science Centre, Telegraph Way, Winchester SO21 1HZ (winchestersciencecentre.org)

| BAPC.532 | QinetiQ Zephyr 6 | 6-2 |

HERTFORDSHIRE

de Havilland Aircraft Museum, Salisbury Hall, London Colney AL2 1BU (dehavillandmuseum.co.uk)

G-EBQP	de Havilland DH.53 Humming Bird	114
G-ABLM	Cierva C.24	710
G-ADOT	de Havilland DH.87B Hornet Moth	8027
G-AKDW	de Havilland DH.89A Dragon Rapide	6897
G-ANRX	de Havilland DH.82A Tiger Moth	3863
G-AOJT	de Havilland DH.106 Comet 1XB	06020
G-AOTI	de Havilland DH.114 Heron 2D	14107
G-AREA	de Havilland DH.104 Dove 8	04520
G-ARYC	de Havilland DH.125 Series 1	25003
G-AVFH	Hawker Siddeley HS.121 Trident 2E	2147
G-AWJV	de Havilland DH.98 Mosquito TT.35	xxxx
G-BBNC	de Havilland DHC-1 Chipmunk T.10	C1/0682
G-JEAO	British Aerospace BAe 146-100	E-1010
BAPC.186	de Havilland DH.82B Queen Bee	
BAPC.216	de Havilland DH.88 Comet fsm	
BAPC.232	Airspeed AS.51/58 Horsa I/II Glider	

ISLE OF MAN

Manx Aviation and Military Museum, Ronaldsway IM9 2AT

| G-BGYT | Embraer EMB-110P1 Bandeirante | 110-234 |
| G-WISS | British Aerospace ATP | 2020 |

KENT

Biggin Hill Heritage Ltd, Biggin Hill (bigginhillheritagehangar.co.uk)

| BAPC.476 | Supermarine Spitfire cockpit reproduction |

St George's RAF Chapel of Remembrance, Biggin Hill TN16 3BH (rafchapelbigginhill.com)

BAPC.273	Hawker Hurricane fsm
BAPC.431	Supermarine Spitfire fsm
BAPC.477	Hawker Hurricane fsm

The War & Peace Collection, The Old Rectory, 45 Sandwich Road, Ash, Canterbury CT3 2AF (warandpeace.uk.com)

BAPC.410	Supermarine Spitfire fsm
BAPC.411	Hawker Hurricane fsm
BAPC.473	Messerschmitt Bf.109x fsm

Dover Museum, Dover (dovermuseum.co.uk)

| BAPC.290 | Fieseler Fi.103 *(V-1)* fsm |

Battle of Britain Memorial, Capel Le Ferne, Folkestone

| BAPC.291 | Hawker Hurricane I fsm |
| BAPC.299 | Supermarine Spitfire I fsm |

Kent Battle of Britain Museum, Hawkinge CT18 7AG (kbobm.org)

G-BRDV	Viking Spitfire prototype replica	HD36/001
BAPC.036	Fieseler Fi 103 *(V-1)* fsm	
BAPC.063	Hawker Hurricane fsm	
BAPC.064	Hawker Hurricane fsm	
BAPC.065	Supermarine Spitfire fsm	
BAPC.066	Messerschmitt Bf109 fsm	
BAPC.067	Messerschmitt Bf109 fsm	
BAPC.069	Supermarine Spitfire fsm	
BAPC.074	Messerschmitt Bf109 fsm	
BAPC.133	Fokker Dr.1 fsm	
BAPC.168	de Havilland DH.60G Moth replica	
BAPC.272	Hawker Hurricane fsm	
BAPC.278	Hawker Hurricane fsm	
BAPC.281	Boulton Paul Defiant I fsm	
BAPC.297	Supermarine Spitfire replica	

Lashenden Air Warfare Museum, Headcorn TN27 9HX

| BAPC.091 | Fieseler Fi.103R-IV Reichenberg | 6/2080 |

RAF Manston History Museum, Manston Road, Ramsgate, Kent CT12 5DF (rafmanston.co.uk)

G-AJGJ	Auster 5	1147
G-BXVZ	WSK-PZL Mielec TS-11 Iskra	3H1625
G-SSWP	Short SD.3-30 Variant 100	SH.3030

The Spitfire & Hurricane Memorial Museum, The Airfield, Manston Road, Ramsgate CT12 5DF (spitfiremuseum.org.uk)

| G-BYOY | Canadair CL-30 Silver Star Mk.3 (*T-33AN*) | T33-231 |
| BAPC.465 Fieseler Fi.103 (FZG-76 / V-1) fsm |
| BAPC.466 Huntair Pathfinder 2 |
| BAPC.467 Nieuport 17 reproduction |
| BAPC.468 Sopwith 1½ Strutter reproduction |
| BAPC.469 Nieuport 17 reproduction |

Romney Marsh Wartime Collection incorporating Brenzett Aeronautical Museum Trust, Ivychurch Road, Brenzett, Romney Marsh, TN29 0EE (theromneymarsh.net/wartimecollection)

| G-APIT | Percival P.40 Prentice T.1 | PAC-016 |

LANCASHIRE

Fylde Coast Museum of Aviation and Aircraft Manufacturing, Blackpool

BAPC.223 Hawker Hurricane I fsm
BAPC.324 Supermarine Spitfire IX fsm
BAPC.325 Supermarine Spitfire fsm
BAPC.326 Supermarine Spitfire II fsm
BAPC.523 Supermarine Spitfire cockpit reproduction
BAPC.524 Morane-Saulnier MS.406 cockpit reproduction
BAPC.525 Messerschmitt Bf.109 cockpit reproduction

Bury Transport Museum, Bolton Street Station, Bury BL9 0EY (eastlancsrailway.org.uk)

BAPC.184 Supermarine Spitfire IX fsm

Bygone Times Antique Warehouse, Grove Mill, Eccleston, Chorley PF7 5PB

BAPC.176 Royal Aircraft Factory SE.5A scale model

LEICESTERSHIRE

Armourgeddon Miliitary Collection, Southfields Farm, Husbands Bosworth LE17 6NW (armourgeddon.co.uk)

| G-ARXH | Bell 47G | 40 |

British Aviation Heritage-Cold War Jets Collection, Bruntingthorpe (bruntingthorpeaviation.com)

G-CPDA	de Havilland DH.106 Comet 4C	6473
F-BTGV	Aero Spacelines 377SGT Super Guppy 201 N211AS *As '1'*	001
SX-OAD	Boeing 747-212B 9V-SQH *'Olympic Flame' & 'G-ASDA'*	21684

Charnwood Museum, Loughborough LE11 3QU

| G-AJRH | Auster J/1N Alpha | 2606 |

East Midlands Aeropark, East Midlands Airport

G-ANUW	de Havilland DH.104 Dove 6	04458
G-ASDL	Beagle A.61 Terrier 2	B.703
G-BAMH	Westland S-55 Whirlwind Series 3	WA.83
G-BBED	Socata MS.894A Rallye Minerva 220	12097
G-BEOZ	Armstrong-Whitworth AW.650 Argosy 101	6660
G-BHDD	Vickers 668 Varsity T.1	xxxx
(G-BLMC)	Avro 698 Vulcan B.2A	xxxx
G-FRJB	Aircraft Designs Sheriff SA-1	0001

Snibston Discovery Park, Coalville LE67 3LN (leics.gov.uk/snibston_museum) *(Closed 2015 – current status unknown)*

G-AFTN	Taylorcraft Plus C2	102
G-AGOH	Auster J/1 Autocrat	14425
G-AIJK	Auster V J/4 Archer	2067

Stanford Hall & Percy Pilcher Museum, Stanford Hall, Stanford LE17 6DH (stanfordhall.co.uk)

BAPC.045 Pilcher Hawk Glider reconstruction

Sir Frank Whittle Memorial A426, Lutterworth

BAPC.284 Gloster E.28/39 fsm

LINCOLNSHIRE

Battle of Britain Memorial Flight, RAF Coningsby LN4 4SY (bbmf@lincolnshire.gov.uk)

G-AISU	Vickers Supermarine 349 Spitfire LF.VB	CBAF.1061
G-AMAU	Hawker Hurricane IIc	xxxx
G-AWIJ	Vickers Supermarine 329 Spitfire IIA	CBAF.14

Lincolnshire Aviation Heritage Centre, East Kirkby PE23 4DE (lincsaviation.co.uk)

| G-ASXX | Avro 683 Lancaster B.VII | NX611 |
| BAPC.154 Druine D.31 Turbulent |
| BAPC.389 Heinkel He.111 recreation |
| BAPC.434 de Havilland DH.98 Mosquito composite reproduction |

RAF Elsham Wolds Memorial Garden & Memorial Room, Elsham Wolds (www.elshamwolds.org.uk/memorial-room)

BAPC.478 Supermarine Spitfire cockpit reproduction

Metheringham Airfield Visitor Centre, Westmoor Farm, Martin Moor LN4 3WF (metheringhamairfield.co.uk)

| G-AMHJ | Douglas C-47A-35-DL Dakota | 13468 |

Thorpe Camp Visitor Centre, Tattershall Thorpe LN4 4PL (thorpecamp.org)

BAPC.294 Fairchild Argus II replica
BAPC.367 Percival Mew Gull replica
BAPC.409 de Havilland DH.82a Tiger Moth composite

LONDON

The Bentley Priory Museum, Bentley Priory HA7 3FB (bentleypriory.org)

BAPC.218 Hawker Hurricane IIc fsm

Croydon Airport Visitor Centre, Croydon CR0 0SX (croydonairport.org.uk)

| G-ANUO | de Havilland DH.114 Heron 2D | 14062 |

Royal Air Force Museum, Hendon NW9 5LL (rafmuseum.org.uk)

Gate Guardians
BAPC.205 Hawker Hurricane IIc fsm
BAPC.206 Supermarine Spitfire IX fsm

Hangar 1
BAPC.341 Lockheed-Martin F-35 Lightning II fsm

Hangar 2
G-EBIC	Royal Aircraft Factory.SE.5A	688/2404	
G-EBJE	Avro 504K	927	
G-AETA	Caudron G.III	7487	
G-ATVP	Vickers FB.5 Gunbus replica	VAFA-01 & FB.5	
ZK-TVC	Royal Aircraft Factory RE.8 replica	2	*As 'A3930:B'*
ZK-TVD	Albatros Flugzeugwerke D.Va replica	0083	*As 'D7343:17'*
BAPC.107 Blériot Type XXVII
BAPC.165 Bristol F.2b Fighter
BAPC.181 Royal Aircraft Factory BE.2b replica
BAPC.400 Royal Aircraft Factory F.E.2b replica

Hangars 3 & 4
G-ABBB	Bristol 105A Bulldog IIA	7446	
G-ABMR	Hawker Hart	H.H-1	
G-AIXA	Taylorcraft Plus D	134	
G-ALSP	Bristol 171 Sycamore HR12	12900	
G-BEOX	Lockheed 414 Hudson IIIA (*A-29A-LO*)	414-6464	
G-FAAG	Armstrong-Whitworth R.33 Airship	R33	
G-OIOI	EH Industries EH-101 Heliliner	50008	
CF-BXO	Vickers-Supermarine 304 Stranraer RCAF 920 *As '920:QN' in RCAF c/s*	CV-209	
LN-BNM	Noorduyn AT-16-ND Harvard IIB 31-329, R.Danish AF, FE905, 42-12392 *As 'FE905' in RAF & RCAF c/s*	14-639	
SE-AZB	Cierva C.30A Autogiro (*Avro 671*) K4232 *As 'K4232'*	R3/CA.954	
BAPC.436 Bristol 152 Beaufort composite

Hangar 5

G-AITB	Airspeed AS.40 Oxford 1	xxxx
N51RT	North American F-51D Mustang	122-40949
	N555BM, YV-508CP, N555BM, N4409, N6319T,	
	RCAF9235, 44-74409	
	As '413317:VF-B' in 336FS-4th FG c/s 'The Duck'	
	On loan from R C Tullius	
N5237V	Boeing B-17G-95-DL Flying Fortress	32509
	(N6466D), N5237V, Bu.77233, 44-83868	
	As '44-83868:N' in 94th BG USAAF c/s	
N9115Z	North American TB-25N-20NC Mitchell	108-32641
	(8838M), 44-29366 As '34037' in USAAF c/s	
	'Hanover Street' & 'Catch 22'	
VH-ASM	Avro 652A Anson I	72960
	W2068 As 'W2068:68' in RAF c/s	

Royal Air Force, Northolt
Gate Guardians
BAPC.219 Hawker Hurricane I fsm

BAPC.221 Supermarine Spitfire LF.IX fsm

Science Museum, South Kensington, London SW7 2DD
(sciencemuseum.org.uk)
Flight Gallery

G-EBIB	Royal Aircraft Factory SE.5A	687/2404
G-AAAH	de Havilland DH.60G Moth	804
G-ACWP	Cierva C.30A (Avro 671)	728
G-ASSM	Hawker Siddeley HS.125 Series 1/522	25010
G-AWAW	Cessna F150F	F150-0037
G-AZPH	Pitts S.1S	S1S-001-C

BAPC.050 Roe Triplane Type I

BAPC.051 Vickers FB.27 Vimy IV   13

BAPC.053 Wright Flyer reconstruction

BAPC.054 JAP/Harding Monoplane

BAPC.055 Levasseur-Antoinette Developed Type VII Monoplane

BAPC.056 Fokker E.III

BAPC.062 Cody Type V Biplane

BAPC.124 Lilienthal Type XI glider replica

BAPC.199 Fieseler Fi 103 *(V-1)*

BGA 2091	Schempp-Hirth HS.4 Standard Cirrus	396	09.05.02
	AGA... As 'DFY'		

BAPC.429 Bleriot XI cockpit

BAPC.430 Army Balloon Factory Airship Beta II Gondola

Makers of the Modern World

G-LIOA	Lockheed 10A Electra	1037

Mathematics Gallery

G-AACN	Handley Page HP.39 Gugnunc	1

The Battle of Britain Bunker, Uxbridge (friendsof11group.co.uk)
BAPC.475 Hawker Hurricane I fsm

BAPC.499 Hawker Hurricane fsm

BAPC.500 Supermarine Spitfire fsm

MANCHESTER
Museum of Science & Industry, Liverpool Road, Manchester M3 4JP
(msimmanchester.org.uk)

G-EBZM	Avro 594A Avian IIIA	R3/CN/160
G-ABAA	Avro 504K	xxxx
G-ADAH	de Havilland DH.89 Dragon Rapide	6278
G-APUD	Bensen B-7Mc	1
G-AYTA	SOCATA MS.880B Rallye Club	1789
G-BLKU	Colt Flame 56 SS HAB	572
G-BYMT	Cyclone Airsports Pegasus Quantum 15-912	7549
G-CFTF	Roe Triplane replica	AH2-001
G-MJXE	Mainair Tri-Flyer 330/Hiway Demon 175 102-131082 & HS-001	

BGA 1156	EoN AP.10 460 Series 1	EoN/S/007	26.01.64
	BGA 2666, AGA.6, BGA 1156 As 'BQT'		18.04.97
	On loan from J.H.May		

BAPC.006 Roe Triplane Type I

BAPC.012 Mignet HM.14 Pou-Du-Ciel replica

BAPC.098 Yokosuka MXY-7 Ohka II

BAPC.175 Volmer VJ-23 Swingwing powered hang glider

BAPC.182 Wood Ornithopter

BAPC.251 Hiway Spectrum hang glider

BAPC.252 Flexiform Wing hang glider

BAPC.328 Avro Type F Cabin replica

BAPC.424 Manchester University/BAe Java UAV

BAPC.428 Cody Man-Lifting Kite reproduction

Runway Visitor Park, Manchester Airport

G-AWZK	Hawker Siddeley HS.121 Trident 3B Series 101	2312
G-BOAC	BAC Concorde Type 1 Variant 102	204 & 100-004
G-DMOA	McDonnell Douglas DC 10 30	18266
G-IRJX	BAE Systems Avro 146-RJX100	E3378

MERSEYSIDE
Aviation Archaeology Museum, Fort Perch Rock, Marine Promenade,
New Brighton, Wirral CH45 2JU (fortperchrock.org)
BAPC.352 Hawker Sea Hawk cockpit

Britannia Aircraft Preservation Trust (bristol-britannia.com)

G-ANCF	Bristol 175 Britannia Series 308F	12922

Wirral Aviation Society, Liverpool Crown Plaza Hotel, Liverpool-John
Lennon Airport (jetstream-club.org)

G-AMLZ	Percival P.50 Prince 6E	P 46
G-BEJD	Avro 748 Series 1/105	1543
G-JMAC	British Aerospace Jetstream Series 4100	41004
G-SEXY	American AA-1 Yankee	AA1-0442

BAPC.280 de Havilland DH.89 Dragon Rapide fsm

NORFOLK
City of Norwich Aviation Museum, Norwich International Airport
NR10 3JE

G-ASAT	Morane Saulnier MS.880B Rallye Club	178
G-ASKK	Handley Page HPR.7 Dart Herald 211	161
G-AWON	English Electric Lightning F.53	95291
G-AYMO	Piper PA-23-250 Aztec C	27-2995
G-BEBC	Westland WS-55 Whirlwind HAR.10	WA.371
G-BHMY	Fokker F.27 Friendship 600	10196
G-BTAZ	Evans VP-2	xxxx
G-OVNE	Cessna 401A	401A-0036

BAPC.433 Westland Whirlwind Mk.1 cockpit reproduction

Muckleburgh Collection, Weybourne (muckleburgh.co.uk)
BAPC.501 Northrop Shelduck D.1 composite

NORTHAMPTONSHIRE
'Carpetbagger' Aviation Museum, Harrington NN6 9PF
(harringtonmuseum.co.uk)

G-APWK	Westland S.51 Series 2 Widgeon	WA/H/152

NORTHUMBERLAND & TYNESIDE
North East Land Sea and Air Museum, Usworth, Sunderland SR5 3HZ
(nelsam.org.uk)

Outside Display

G-ARPO (2)	de Havilland DH.121 Trident 1C	2116
G-BCPK	Reims/Cessna F172M Skyhawk II	F17201194

Main Hangar

G-ALST	Bristol 171 Sycamore 3	12888
G-APTW	Westland S-51 Series 2 Widgeon	WA/H/150
G-AWRS	Avro 652A Anson C.19 Series 2	'33785'
G-AZLP	Vickers 813 Viscount	346
G-OGIL	Short SD.3-30 Var.100	SH.3068
G-SFTA	Westland SA.341G Gazelle 1	1039

BAPC.096 Brown Helicopter

BAPC.119 Bensen B.7 Gyroglider

BAPC.211 Mignet HM.14 Pou-Du-Ciel replica

Preserved

BAPC.419 Fieseler Fi.103 *(FZG-76/V-1)* fsm

BAPC.521 Hawker Hurricane I fsm composite

Admiralty S Hangar – Workshop

G-ANFU	Taylorcraft J Auster 5		1748	
BGA 2383	Carmam M100S Mésange	012		06.06.78
	F-CCSA As *'DUC'*			06.05.88

BAPC.472 Morane-Saulnier N reproduction

Inside Shipping Container

G-ARAD	Phoenix Luton LA-5A Major	PAL/1204
G-MBDL	Aero & Engineering Services Lone Ranger	109

BAPC.097 Luton LA.4 Minor

Stored in Bag
BAPC.228 Olympus hang glider

NOTTINGHAMSHIRE
Newark Air Museum, Winthorpe, Newark NG24 2NY (newarkairmuseum.co.uk)

Aircraft Hall 1

G-ALSW	Bristol 171 Sycamore 3	12891
G-APIY	Percival P.40 Prentice 1	PAC-075
G-APRT	Taylor JT.1 Monoplane	PFA 537
G-APVV	Mooney M.20A	1474
G-ASNY	Campbell-Bensen B.8M	RCA/203
G-AVVO	Avro 652A Anson 19 Series 2	34219
G-AYZJ	Westland WS-55 Whirlwind HAS.7	WA.263
G-BJAD	Clutton FRED Series II	CA.1
G-BKPY	SAAB 91B/2 Safir	91321
G-CCLT	Powerchute Kestrel	00443
G-MBBZ	Volmer VJ-24W	7
G-MBUE	MBA Tiger Cub 440	MBA-001
G-MBVE	Hiway Skytrike 160	TJD-01
G-MJCF	Maxair Hummer	SMC-01
G-MJDW	Eipper Quicksilver MXII	RI-01
G-TVII	Hawker Hunter T.7	41H-693834
VH-UTH	General Aircraft Monospar ST-12	ST12/36

BAPC.020 Lee-Richards Annular Biplane replica

BAPC.043 Mignet HM.14 Pou-Du-Ciel

BAPC.101 Mignet HM.14 Pou-Du-Ciel

BAPC.183 Zurowski ZP-1 Helicopter

'G-MAZY'	de Havilland DH 82A Tiger Moth	xxxx
	Fictitious marks – composite, mostly ex G-AMBB: port side sectioned	

Aircraft Hall 2

G-BKPG	Luscombe P3 Rattler Strike	003
G-MNRT	Midland Ultralights Sirocco 377GB	MU-016

External Display

G-AHRI	de Havilland DH.104 Dove 1B	04008
G-ANXB	de Havilland DH.114 Heron 1B	14048
G-APNJ	Cessna 310	35335
G-BFTZ	SOCATA MS.880B Rallye Club	1269

Unknown location
BAPC.330 Ward Gnome

BAPC.515 TASUMA Observer Concept UAV

BAPC.516 TASUMA Navigator CSV 30 UAV

BAPC.517 TASUMA Navigator CSV 30 UAV

BAPC.518 English Electric Canberra PR.9 cockpit

Wonderland Pleasure Park, Farnsfield, Mansfield NG22 8HZ (wonderlandpleasurepark.com)

BAPC.288 Hawker Hurricane fsm

OXFORDSHIRE
Royal Air Force Benson

BAPC.226 Supermarine Spitfire XI fsm

Royal Air Force Brize Norton

G-AMPO	Douglas C-47B-30DK Dakota 3	16437 & 33185

SHROPSHIRE
Royal Air Force Cosford Museum, Cosford TF11 8UP (rafmuseum.com)

Hangar 1

G-EBMB	Hawker Cygnet I	1
G-ACGL	Comper CLA.7 Swift	S33/6
G-AEEH	Mignet HM.14 Pou-Du-Ciel	EGD.1
'G-AFAP'	CASA 352L *(Junkers Ju 52/3m)* Spanish AF T2B-272 *Original 'British Airways Ltd, London' c/s Fictitious marks – not the original G-AFAP*	163
G-AIZE	Fairchild F.24W-41A Argus II *(UC-61A-FA)*	565
G-APAS	de Havilland DH.106 Comet 1A	06022

BAPC.094 Fieseler Fi 103 *(V-1)*

BAPC.333 Supermarine Spitfire II fsm

Hangar 3 – 'Warplanes'

G-APUP	Sopwith Pup replica	B.5292
G-BIDW	Sopwith 1½ Strutter replica	WA/5
G-BLWM	Bristol 20 M.1C replica	xxxx
G-USTV	Messerschmitt Bf.109G-2/Trop	10639
N6526D	North American P-51D-25NA Mustang 9133M, N6526D, RCAF 9289, 44-73415 As *'413573:B6-V'* in 361st FS-357th FG USAAC c/s) Composite	122-39874 *'Isabel III'*

BAPC.083 Kawasaki Ki-100-1b Army Type 5 Fighter 16336

BAPC.084 Mitsubishi Ki 46 III Dinah

BAPC.099 Yokosuka MXY-7 Ohka II

National Cold War Exhibition

G-AGNV	Avro 685 York C.1	1223
G-BRAM	Mikoyan MiG-21PF	xxxx

Michael Beetham Conservation Centre

G-AANJ (2)	Luft-Verkehrs Gesellschaft C.VI	4503

External Display

G-AOVF	Bristol 175 Britannia Series 312F	13237

Unknown location

VH-ALB	Vickers-Supermarine 228 Seagull V A2-4 As *'A2-4'*	xxxx

Wartime Aircraft Recovery Group Aviation Museum, Sleap (wargroup.homestead.com)

BAPC.148 Hawker Fury II fsm

SOMERSET
Fleet Air Arm Museum/FAAM Cobham Hall ($), RNAS Yeovilton BA22 8HT (fleetairarm.com)

Hall 1

G-AIZG	Vickers Supermarine 236 Walrus 1	6S/21840

BAPC.149 Short S.27 replica

Hall 2

G-AIBE	Fairey Fulmar 2	F.3707
G-ASTL	Fairey Firefly 1	F.5607
G-BMZF	WSK-Mielec LIM-2 *(MiG-15bis)*	1B-01420

Leading Edge

G-BSST	BAC Concorde 002	002

Cobham Hall

G-AOXG	de Havilland DH.82A Tiger Moth ($)	83805
G-APNV	Saunders-Roe P.531-1	S2/5268
G-AWYY	Slingsby T.57 Sopwith Camel F.1 replica	1701
G-AZAZ	Bensen B.8M ($)	RNEC.1
G-BEYB	Fairey Flycatcher replica	WA/3
G-BGWZ	Eclipse Super Eagle ($)	ESE.007
G-BIAU	Sopwith Pup replica	EMK 002

BAPC.058 Yokosuka MXY-7 Ohka II

BAPC.088 Fokker Dr.1 ⅝th scale model

BAPC.111 Sopwith Triplane fsm

BAPC.442 Sopwith Baby composite

The Helicopter Museum, Weston-super-Mare BS24 8PP
(helicoptermuseum.co.uk)
(& = Reserve Collection not on public display)

Gate Guard

G-BKGD	Westland WG.30 Series 100	002

Hangar

G-ACWM	Cierva C.30A (*Avro 671*)	715
G-ALSX	Bristol 171 Sycamore 3	12892
G-ANFH	Westland WS.55 Whirlwind Series 1 (&)	WA.15
G-ANJV	Westland WS-55 Whirlwind Series 3 (&)	WA.24
G-AODA	Westland WS-55 Whirlwind Series 3	WA.113
G-AOUJ	Fairey Ultralight Helicopter	F.9424
G-AOZE	Westland S.51 Series 2 Widgeon	WA/H/141
G-ARVN (2)	Servotec CR LTH1 Grasshopper 1 (&)	116.02.63
G-ASCT	Bensen B.7Mc (&)	DC.3
G-ASTP	Hiller UH-12C	1045
G-ATBZ	Westland WS-58 Wessex 60 Series 1 (&)	WA.461
G-ATFG	Brantly B.2B	448
G-AVKE	Gadfly HDW-1 (&)	HDW-1
G-AVNE	Westland WS-58 Wessex 60 Series 1	WA.561
G-AWRP	Servotec CR.LTH.1 Grasshopper II	GB.1
G-AXFM	Servotec CR.LTH.1 Grasshopper II (&)	GB.2
G-AXRA	Campbell Cricket	CA 321A
G-AYXT	Westland WS-55 Whirlwind HAS.7 (Series.2)	WA.167
G-AZAU	Servotec CR.LTH.1 Grasshopper II (&)	GB.3
G-AZYB	Bell 47H-1	1538
G-BAPS	Campbell Cougar Gyroplane	CA/6000
G-BGHF	Westland WG.30 Series 100-60	WA.001.P
G-BIGP	Bensen B.8M	xxxx
G-BKFF	Westland WG.30 Series.100 (&)	006
G-BODW	Bell 206B Jet Ranger II (&)	784
G-BRMA	Westland-Sikorsky S-51 Dragonfly HR.5	WA/H/50
G-BRMB	Bristol 192 Belvedere HC.1	13347
G-BVWL	Air & Space 18-A Gyroplane	18-63
G-BWCW	Barnett J4B-2	PFA G/14-1256
G-BXZN	Advanced Technologies CH1 ATI	00002
G-BYMP	Campbell Cricket Mk.1	0050
G-EHIL	EH Industries EH-101	50003
G-ELEC	Westland WG.30 Series 200	007
G-HAUL	Westland WG.30 Series 300	020
G-HEKY	McCulloch J.2	039
G-LYNX	Westland WG.13 Lynx 800	WA/102
G-OTED	Robinson R-22 HP	0209
G-PASA (1)	MBB BÖ.105D (&)	S.41
G-PASB	MBB BÖ.105D (&)	S.135
G-RWWW	Westland WS-55 Whirlwind HCC.12	WA/418
G-TIGE	Aérospatiale AS.332L Super Puma	2028
G-TPTR	Agusta-Bell 206B JetRanger II (&)	8587
G-WBAT	Julian Wombat Gyrocopter	CJ-001
D-HMQV	Bolkow Bö.102 Helitrainer	6216
	Development aircraft	
D-HOAY	Kamov Ka.26	7001309
	DDR-SPY, DM-SPY *As 'DDR-SPY'*	
D-HZYR	Bölkow Bö.105M	5100
	81+00 *As '81+00'*	
F-BTRP	Sud-Aviation SA.321F Super Frelon	01
	F-BMHC, F-BTRP, F-WKQC, F-OCZV, F-RAFR, F-OCMF,	
	F-BMHC, F-WMHC *As 'F-OCMF' in Olympic Airways c/s*	
	Converted from SA.321 c/n 116	
F-WGTZ	Liteco Heli Atlas	03
	Has boom of F-WGTX c/n 01	
F-WQAP	Aérospatiale SA365N Dauphin 2	6001
	F-WZJJ	

N6699D	Piasecki HUP-3 Retriever	51	
	RCN 622, USN 51-16622 *On loan as '622' in RCN c/s*		
SP-SAY	Mil Mi-2	529538125	
BGA.1759	Slingsby T.8 Tutor	xxxx	15.10.72
	RAFGSA 178		xx.07.77
BAPC.010	Hafner R-11 Revoplane		
BAPC.060	Murray M.1 Helicopter		
BAPC.128	Watkinson CG-4 Cyclogyroplane Man		
	Powered Gyroplane Mark IV		
BAPC.153	Westland WG-33 Mock-up		
BAPC.212	Bensen B.6 Gyrocopter (&)		
BAPC.213	Cranfield Vertigo Man Powered Helicopter (&)		
BAPC.264	Bensen B.8M		
BAPC.289	Gyro-Boat		
BAPC.444	Westland WG-25/WR-05 Mote remotely piloted Helicopter		
BAPC.445	Westland WG-25/WR-07 Wideye remotely piloted Helicopter		
BAPC.446	Westland WG-25/WR-06 Wisp remotely piloted Helicopter		
BAPC.447	Yamaha Motors remotely piloted Helicopter		
BAPC.450	Hawker Siddeley Harrier composite		
BAPC.451	Westland WG-25 Sharpeye mock up remotely piloted Helicopter7		

SUFFOLK
Bentwaters Cold War Museum, Rendlesham, Woodbridge IP12 2TW
(bcwm.org.uk)

G-BVYH	Hawker Hunter GA.11	HABL-003037

Norfolk & Suffolk Aviation Museum, Flixton, Bungay NR35 1NZ
(aviationmuseum.net)

Outside

N99163	North American T-28C Trojan	252-52	
	'N99153', Zaire AF FG-289, Congo AF FA-289, Bu.146289		
	'Makasi' Crashed Limoges, France 14.12.77		
	FAA quote c/n 226-93 Fuselage only as 'FG-289'		
	On loan from W R Montague		

Hangar 1

G-MTFK	Moult Trike/Flexiform Striker	DIM-01	
BGA.1461	Elliott AP.7 EoN Primary	xxxx	30.05.68
			29.05.69
BAPC.071	Supermarine Spitfire fsm		
BAPC.147	Bensen B.7 Gyroglider		
BAPC.364	Kiceniuk Icarus II		
BAPC.368	Supermarine 361 Spitfire LF.XVIe		
BAPC.372	Wasp Falcon 4 hang glider		
	No marks carried		
BAPC.374	Antonov C.12 hang glider		

Hangar 2

G-APUG	Phoenix Luton LA5 Major	PAL.1203	
G-ASRF	Gowland GWG.2 Jenny Wren	GWG.2	
G-AWSA	Avro 652A Anson C.19/2	'293483'	
G-BABY	Taylor JT.2 Titch	JRB-2	
G-CDFW	Lovegrove Sheffey Gyroplane	PCL129	
G-MJSU	MBA Tiger Cub 440	SO.75/1	
G-MJVI	Lee Rooster 1 Series 4	4	
N16676	Fairchild F.24CR-C8F Argus	3101	
	NC16676 *Civil Air Patrol c/s Fuselage only*		
	On loan from A Langendal		
BGA 2384	Grunau Baby III	xxxx	07.06.78
	BGA 2074, RAFGSA.374, D-9142 *As 'DUD'*		29.03.92
BGA 4002	Penrose Pegasus 2 replica	001	14.07.93
	HKJ (No marks carried)		15.09.98
	Built by J.M.Lee Suspended from rafters		
BGA 4757	Colditz Cock replica	SA3	xx.01.00
	JTA (No marks carried) *'Spirit of Colditz'*		20.02.00
	Built by Southdown Aero Services & J.M.Lee		
BAPC.115	Mignet HM.14 Pou-Du-Ciel replica		
BAPC.239	Fokker D.VIII ⅝th scale model		
BAPC.274	Boulton & Paul P.6 replica		

BAPC.303 Goldfinch Amphibian 161

BAPC.306 Lovegrove Autogyro Trainer

BAPC.358 Boulton Paul Overstrand cockpit replica

BAPC.375 Boeing-Stearman PT-27 Kaydet composite

BAPC.390 Felixstowe F.5 cockpit

On hangar wall
BGA.3833	Maupin Woodstock One	xxxx	07.10.92
	HCG *As 'HCG'*		23.03.11
	Built by R Harvey		

Not known
G-ARLP	Beagle A.61 Terrier 1	3724 (1)
G-BJZC	Thunder Ax7-65Z HAB	416
G-MBUD	Wheeler (Skycraft) Scout Mk.III/R/3	0432/R/3
G-MMWL	Eurowing Goldwing	SWA-09 & EW-91

Suffolk Aviation Heritage Museum, c/o former WT Station, Foxhall Road Heath, Kesgrave IP10 0AH (suffolkaviationheritage.org.uk/)

| G-KNOT | Hunting Percival P.84 Jet Provost T.3A | PAC/W/13893 |
| BAPC.017 | Woodhams Sprite | xxxx |

SURREY
Brooklands Museum, Brooklands, Weybridge KT13 0QN (brooklandsmuseum.com)

G-AEKV	Kronfeld Drone	30
G-AGRU	Vickers 657 Viking 1	112
G-APEP	Vickers 953C Vanguard Merchantman	719
G-APIM	Vickers 806 Viscount	412
G-ASIX	Vickers VC-10 Series 1103	820
G-ASYD	BAC One Eleven 475AM	BAC.053
G-BBDG	BAC Concorde Type 1 Variant 100	13523 & 100-02
G-BFCZ	Sopwith Camel F.1 replica	WA/2
G-BJHV	Voisin Scale replica	MPS-1
G-CHOI	White Monoplane 1912 Canard Pusher replica	1
G-HAWK	Hawker Siddeley HS.1182 Hawk 100	41H-4020010
G-LOTI	Blériot Type XI replica	xxxx
G-MJPB	Manuel Ladybird	WLM-14
G-ROEI	Avro Roe 1 Biplane replica	xxxx
G-VTOL	Hawker Siddeley Harrier T.52	B3/41H/735795
NX71MY	Vimy 19/94 Inc Vimy FB-27 replica	01
	'G-EAOU' As 'NX71MY' Built by L Kidby & P McMillan	

BGA 162	Manuel Willow Wren	xxxx	xx.09.34
	'The Willow Wren'		
	On loan to The Glider Heritage Centre, Lasham		
BGA 643	Slingsby T.15 Gull III	364A	xx.11.49
	TJ711 *As 'ATH'*		20.06.04
	On loan to The Glider Heritage Centre, Lasham		
BGA 3922	Abbott-Baynes Scud I replica	001	R
	As 'HFZ' On loan to The Glider Heritage Centre, Lasham)		

BAPC.029 Mignet HM.14 Pou-Du-Ciel replica

BAPC.114 Vickers Type 60 Viking IV reconstruction

BAPC.177 Avro 504K fsm

BAPC.187 Roe Type I Biplane reconstruction

BAPC.249 Hawker Fury I fsm

BAPC.250 Royal Aircraft Factory SE.5a replica

BAPC.256 Santos Dumont Type 20 Demoiselle reconstruction

BAPC.354 Sopwith Tabloid Floatplane replica

BAPC.420 Vickers FB.27A Vimy cockpit reproduction

BAPC.421 Vickers Wellington forward fuselage reproduction

Gatwick Aviation Museum, Charlwood RH6 0BT (gatwick-aviation-museum.co.uk)

G-BLID	de Havilland DH.112 Venom FB.50	815
G-GACA	Percival P.57 Sea Prince T.1	P57/58
G-JETH	Hawker Sea Hawk FGA.6	AW-6385
G-JETM	Gloster Meteor T.7	xxxx
G-VIXN	de Havilland DH.110 Sea Vixen FAW.2 (TT)	10145

SUSSEX
Shoreham Airport Historical Association, Brighton City BN43 5FF (thearchiveshoreham.co.uk)

BAPC.300 Piffard Hummingbird replica

BAPC.302 Mignet HM.14 Pou-Du-Ciel replica

Tangmere Military Aviation Museum, Tangmere PO20 6ES (tangmere-museum.org.uk)

| G-BZRD | de Havilland DH.115 Vampire T.11 | 15687 |

BAPC.214 Supermarine Spitfire prototype fsm

BAPC.241 Hawker Hurricane I fsm

BAPC.371 Westland Lysander fsm

TEES VALLEY
Thornaby Aerodrome Memorial Committee, A1045 Roundabout, Thornaby on Tees (stockton.gov.uk)

BAPC.301 Supermarine Spitfire Vb fsm

WARWICKSHIRE
Midland Air Museum, Coventry CV8 3AZ (midlandairmuseum.org.uk)

G-EBJG	Parnall Pixie III	xxxx
G-ABOI	Wheeler Slymph	AHW.1
G-AEGV	Mignet HM.14 Pou-Du-Ciel	EMAC.1
G-ALCU	de Havilland DH.104 Dove 2B	04022
G-AOKZ	Percival P.40 Prentice 1	PAC-238
G-APJJ (2)	Fairey Ultralight Helicopter	F.9428
G-APRL	Armstrong-Whitworth 650 Argosy Series 101	AW.6652
G-APWN	Westland WS-55 Whirlwind 3	WA.298
G-ARYB	de Havilland DH.125 Series 1	25002
G-ASWJ	Beagle B.206C Series 1	B.009
G-BRNM	Chichester-Miles Leopard	002
G-CHNX	Lockheed L188AF Electra	1068
(G-MJWH)	Chargus Vortex 120	xxxx
F-BGNR	Vickers 708 Viscount	35
	(OY-AFO), (OY-AFN), F-BGNR *Air Inter' c/s*	
N196B	North American F-86A-5-NA Sabre	151-43611
	48-0242 *As '8242:FU-242' in USAF c/s*	
BGA.538	Elliott AP.5 EoN Olympia 1	EoN/O/040	xx.07.47
	G-ALNE, BGA 538 *As 'ANW'*		
'BGA 804'	Slingsby Cadet TX.1	xxxx
	As 'BAA' & stored	

BAPC.009 Humber- Blériot Type XI replica

BAPC.032 Crossley Tom Thumb

BAPC.126 Rollason-Druine D.31 Turbulent

Wellesbourne Wartime Museum, Wellesbourne Mountford CV35 9EH

RA-01378	Yakovlev Yak-52	833004
	DOSAAF 14	
	Composite with c/n 833805, DOSAAF 134 which is now N54GT	

XM655 Maintenance and Preservation Society, Wellesbourne Mountford CV35 9EH

| G-VULC | Avro 698 Vulcan B.2A | xxxx |

WEST MIDLANDS
Tettenhall Transport Heritage Centre, Henwood Road, Wolverhampton WV6 8NY

G-MMFS	Micro Biplane Aviation:Tiger Club 440	SO.64
G-MVJM	Microflight Aircraft Spectrum	007
BAPC.194	Santos-Dumont Type 20 Demoiselle	PPS/DEM/1

BAPC.355 Slingsby T.7 Cadet

BAPC.432 Breen Hang Glider

BAPC.514 Miles M.25 Martinet cockpit composite

WILTSHIRE
Boscombe Down Aviation Collection, Old Sarum Airfield, Old Sarum, Salisbury SP4 6DZ (boscombedownaviationcollection.co.uk)

| G-ALYG | Taylorcraft J Auster 5D | 835 |
| G-BDCC | de Havilland DHC-1 Chipmunk 22 | C1/0258 |

G-BUEZ	Hawker Hunter F.6A	S4/U/3275	
BGA 1085	Slingsby T.21B	1355	xx.12.62
	9G-ABD As Sedbergh TX.1 'XN149'		
	Also carries '9G-ABD'		

BAPC.332 Royal Aircraft Factory BE.2b replica

BAPC.356 BAe Systems Phoenix UAV composite

BAPC.365 Northrop MQM-36 Shelduck D.1 UAV

BAPC.485 Government Aircraft Factory Jindivik Mk.103A

YORKSHIRE
Eden Camp Modern History Theme Museum, Malton YO17 6RT (edencamp.co.uk)

BAPC.230 Supermarine Spitfire fsm

BAPC.235 Fieseler Fi 103 (V-1) fsm

BAPC.236 Hawker Hurricane fsm

BAPC.399 Hawker Hurricane fsm

Fort Paull Armouries, Paull, Hedon HU12 8FP (fortpaull.com)

G-AOAI	Blackburn Beverley C.1	1002

BAPC.380 Blackburn Triplane replica

Museum & Art Gallery, Doncaster DN1 2AE (doncaster.gov.uk)

G-AEKR	Mignet HM.14 Pou-Du-Ciel	CAC.1

BAPC.275 Bensen B.7

South Yorkshire Aircraft Museum, Doncaster DN4 5EP (southyorkshireaircraft museum.org.uk)

Main Hangar

G-AHHX	Taylorcraft Plus D	173	
G-ALYB	Taylorcraft J Auster 5	1173	
G-ARYZ	Beagle A.109 Airedale	B.512	
G-AVAA	Cessna F150G	F150-0164	
G-DELB	Robinson R22 Beta	0799	
G-MJKP	Hiway Skystrike-Super Scorpion	PEB-01	
G-MMDK	Mainair Merlin/Striker	18116883	
G-MVNT	Aerotech MW-5(K) Sorcerer	5K-0008-02	
G-MYJX	Whittaker MW 8	xxxx	
G-OPFW	Hawker Siddeley HS.748 Series 2A/266	1714	
EI-JWM	Robinson R22 Beta	1386	21.11.92
	G-BSLB Cancelled 28.05.07 as destroyed		

BAPC.207 Austin Whippet fsm

BAPC.443 WACO CG-4A Hadrian cockpit reproduction

BAPC.484 Hawker Siddeley Harrier GR.1 composite

BGA 2036	Slingsby T.21B	630	xx.03.75
	RAFGSA 247, WB969		
BGA 2517	Slingsby T.30B Prefect TX.1	577	xx.06.79
	WE987 As 'WE987'		
BGA 3239	Slingsby T.31B	708	26.10.86
	WT913 As 'WT913'		21.07.96
	On loan from J.M.Brookes & Partners		

Outside Entrance to Hangar

G-APMY	Piper PA-23-160 Apache	23-1258

Outside

G-ARHX	de Havilland DH.104 Dove 8	04513
N4565L	Douglas DC-3-201A	2108
	(N3TV), LV-GYP, LV-PCV, N129H, N512, N51D, N80C, NC21744	

Building 19

G-ATXH	Handley Page HP.137 Jetstream 200	198
	Cockpit only	
G-AVHT	Beagle E.3	xxxx
G-AZCM	Beagle B.121 Pup Series.150	B121-155
G-BCLW	Grumman American AA1B Trainer	AA1B-0463
G-AVTT	Ercoupe 415D	4399
G-BRJC (1)	Cessna 120	12077

Building 21

G-ACBH	Blackburn B.2	4700/3
G-AEJZ	Mignet HM.14 Pou-Du-Ciel	TLC.1

BAPC.307 Blériot Type XI replica

Outside at rear

G-BAML	Bell 206B JetRanger	36
G-BECE	Aerospace Developments AD500	
	Series B.1 Airship (Hot Air)	

Workshop

G-BNNA	Stolp Starduster Too	1462

Main Storage Shed

G-MJPO	Eurowing Goldwing	018

Outside

G-BTYX	Cessna 140	11004

Stored

G-AOKO	Percival P.40 Prentice 1	PAC-234
G-RAYE	Piper PA-32-260 Cherokee Six	32-460

BAPC.061 Stewart Man-powered ornithopter

Not known

G-AHHP	Auster J1N Alpha	2019	
BGA3434	Schleicher K.8B		'FQD'

BAPC.533 Bensen B.8 Gyrocopter

BAPC.534 Hawker Typhoon 1B cockpit

BAPC.535 Hawker Typhoon 1B cockpit

BAPC.536 Hawker Tempest II cockpit

BAPC.537 Ford Flivver reproduction

Street Life Museum, High Street, Hull

BAPC.287 Blackburn Lincock fsm

St.Stephens Shopping Mall, Hull

BAPC.470 de Havilland DH.60G Gipsy Moth fsm	As 'G-AAAH' 'Jason'

Yorkshire Air Museum, Elvington YO41 4AU (yorkshireairmuseum.co.uk)

G-AJOZ	Fairchild 24W-41A Argus 1 (UC-61-FA)	347	
G-AMYJ	Douglas C-47B-25DK Dakota 6	15968 & 32716	
G-ASCD	Beagle A.61 Terrier 2	B.615	26.09.71
G-AWSV	Saro Skeeter AOP.12	S2/5107	
G-BKDT	Royal Aircraft Factory SE.5a replica	278	
G-BMYP	Fairey Gannet AEW.3	F.9461	
G-HNTR	Hawker Hunter T.7	HABL-003311	
G-KOOL	de Havilland DH.104 Sea Devon C.2/2	04220	
G-MJRA	Mainair Tri-Flyer 250/Hiway Demon	PRJM-01	
G-TFRB	Air Command 532 Elite Sport	0628	
G-YURO	Europa Aviation Europa	001	

BAPC.028 Wright Flyer fsm   FVAC.2

BAPC.041 Royal Aircraft Factory BE.2c replica

BAPC.042 Avro 504K fsm

BAPC.076 Mignet HM.14 Pou-Du-Ciel replica

BAPC.089 Cayley Glider fsm

BAPC.130 Blackburn (1911) Monoplane fsm

BAPC.157 WACO CG-4A Hadrian Glider

BAPC.240 Messerschmitt Bf.109G fsm

BAPC.254 Supermarine Spitfire 1 fsm

BAPC.265 Hawker Hurricane fsm

BAPC.449 Handley Page HP.61 Halifax B.III composite reconstruction

xxxx	Port Victoria P.V.8 Eastchurch Kitten replica xxxx
	As 'N540' Built by W Sneesby

CHANNEL ISLANDS
Oatlands Visitor Centre, St.Sampsons, Les Gigands, Guernsey GY2 4YT

G-JOEY	Fairey B-N BN-2A Mk.III-2 Trislander	1016

SCOTLAND
Grampian Transport Museum, Montgarrie Road, Alford, Aberdeen AB33 8AE (gtm.org.uk)

G-MNBG	Mainair Gemini Flash	347-585-3-W66

Dumfries & Galloway Aviation Museum, Tinwald Downs, Dumfries DG2 9PS (dumfriesaviationmuseum.com)

G-ALSS	Bristol 171 Sycamore 3	12887
G-AWZJ	Hawker Siddeley HS.121 Trident 3B Series 101	2311

Preserved

G-AZIL	Slingsby T61A Falke	1756		
G-AYFA	Scottish Aviation Twin Pioneer 3	538		
G-CESP	Rutan Cozy Mk.4	xxxx		
BAPC.270	de Havilland DH.60 Moth fsm			
BAPC.322	Handley Page Halifax III replica			
BAPC.370	Waco CG-4A replica			
BAPC.397	General Aircraft GAL.48 Hotspur II cockpit			
BAPC.503	Airspeed AS Horsa fuselage			

Edinburgh Airport
Gate Guardian
BAPC.227 Supermarine Spitfire IA fsm

Montrose Air Station Heritage Centre, Broomfield Industrial Estate, Montrose, Angus (rafmontrose.org.uk)

G-ADMW	Miles M.2H Hawk Major	177	
G-MMLM	MBA Tiger Cub 440	SO.172	
BAPC.059	Sopwith F1 Camel fsm		
BAPC.320	Supermarine Spitfire VB fsm		
BAPC.321	Royal Aircraft Factory BE.2c fsm		

Morayvia Sci-Tech Experience Project, North Rd, Kinloss IV36 3YA (morayvia.org.uk)

'G-AJOV'	Westland WS-51 Dragonfly HR.3 WP495 *BEA titles* *Fictitious marks – not the original G-AJOV*	WA/H/80	
G-ASVO	Handley Page HPR.7 Dart Herald 214	185	
G-MJSV	MBA Tiger Cub	SO.2/87	
HA-MKE	Antonov AN-2 UR-07714, 07714, CCCP-07714 Cancelled xx.xx.xx	1G158-34	16.08.96 28.02.01

Aircraft Preservation Society of Scotland, Congalton Gardens, East Lothian (www.apss.org.uk) *(Opening 2019?)*

G-BDIH	Jodel D.117	
G-BYBE	Jodel D.120A Paris-Nice	269
xxxx	Sopwith 1½ Strutter *Built J Maddocks – project PFA 335-14473; under construction 2019*	

National Museum of Flight Scotland, East Fortune EH39 5LF (nms.ac.uk/flight)

G-ABDW	de Havilland DH.80A Puss Moth	2051
G-ACYK	Spartan Cruiser III	101
G-AGBN	General Aircraft GAL.42 Cygnet 2	111
G-AHKY	Miles M.18 Series 2	4426
G-AMOG (2)	Vickers 701 Viscount	7
G-ANOV	de Havilland DH.104 Dove 6	04445
G-APHV	Avro 652A Anson C.19 Series 2	xxxx
G-ARCX	Gloster Meteor NF.14	AW.2163
G-ARSL	Beagle A.61 Terrier 2	2539
G-ASUG	Beech E18S-9700	BA-111
G-ATOY	Piper PA-24-260 Comanche B	24-4346
G-AVMO	BAC One Eleven 510ED	BAC.143
G-AVPC	Druine D.31 Turbulent	PFA 544
G-AXEH	Beagle Bulldog Series 125	B.125-001
G-BBBV	Handley Page HP.137 Jetstream	234
G-BBVF	Scottish Aviation Twin Pioneer 3	558
G-BCFN	Cameron O-65 HAB	109
G-BDFU	PMPS Dragonfly MPA Mk.1	01
G-BDIX	de Havilland DH.106 Comet 4C	6471
G-BDYG	Percival P.56 Provost T.1	PAC/F/056
G-BGXB	Piper PA-38-112 Tomahawk	38-79A1007
G-BIRW	Morane-Saulnier MS.505 Criquet	695/28
G-BOAA	BAC Concorde Type 1 Variant 102	206 & 100-006
G-BVWK	Air & Space 18-A Gyroplane	18-14
G-HEBZ	Fairey B-N BN-2A-26 Islander	823

G-JSSD	Handley Page HP.137 Jetstream 1	227		
G-MBJX	Hiway Skytrike I/Hiway Super Scorpion	MM-01		
G-MBPM	Eurowing Goldwing	EW-21		
G-MMLI	Mainair Tri-Flyer 250/Solar Wings Typhoon S	RPAT-01 & T484-423L		
G-SJEN	Comco Ikarus C42 FB80	0405-6602		
G-UNIV	Montgomerie-Parsons Two-Place Gyroplane	PFA G/08-1276		
VH-SNB	de Havilland DH.84A Dragon VH-ASK, A34-13	2002		
BGA 852	Slingsby T.8 Tutor TS291 *As 'TS291'*	xxxx	02.07.58 xx.12.66	
BGA 1014	Slingsby T.21B *As 'BJV' Stored*	556	30.04.81	
BAPC.049	Pilcher Hawk			
BAPC.085	Weir W-2			
BAPC.160	Chargus 18/50 hang glider			
BAPC.195	Birdman Sports Moonraker 77 hang glider			
BAPC.196	Southdown Sailwings Sigma 2m hang glider			
BAPC.197	Scotkites Cirrus III hang glider			
BAPC.245	Electraflyer Floater hang glider			
BAPC.246	Hiway Cloudbase hang glider			
BAPC.247	Albatros Flugzeugwerke ASG.21 hang glide			
BAPC.262	Catto CP-16			
BAPC.312	Airwave Magic Kiss hang glider			
BAPC.313	Firebird Sierra hang glider			
BAPC.314	Gold Marque Gyr hang glider			
BAPC.315	Bensen B.8 Gyroglider			
BAPC.317	Waco CG-4A Hadrian			
BAPC.480	Ferranti Slingsby T.68 Phoenix UAV			

National Museum of Scotland, Chambers Street, Edinburgh EH1 1JF (nms.ac.uk)

G-ACVA	Kay Gyroplane 33/1	1002	
G-AOEL	de Havilland DH.82A Tiger Moth	82537	
G-AXIG	Scottish Aviation Bulldog Series 100/104	BH120/002	
BGA 902	Slingsby T.12 Gull I *As 'BED' 'G-ALPHA'*	xxxx	15.05.59
BAPC.311	GEC-Marconi Phoenix UAV		

Riverside Museum, Glasgow Harbour G2 (glasgowmuseums.com)

BAPC.048 Pilcher Hawk replica
BAPC.316 Pilcher Bat Mk.2 replica
BAPC.336 Pilcher Bat Mk.2 replica

Scalloway Museum, Castle Street, Lerwick ZE 1 0TP (scallowaymuseum.org)

G-AMUW	Phoenix Luton LA-4A Minor	WP.1	

Merlin ERD Ltd, Merlin House, Necessity Brae, Cherrybank, Perth PH2 0PF

BAPC.220 Supermarine Spitfire IX fsm

WALES

Caernarfon Airworld Museum, Caernarfon, Gwynedd LL54 5TP (airworldmuseum.com)

G-ALTD	Bristol 171 Sycamore HR12	12898	
G-BNDW	de Havilland DH.82A Tiger Moth	3942	
BAPC.286	Mignet HM.14 Flea replica		

Store

G-BSMX	Bensen B.8MR	xxxx	
G-MBBB	Skycraft Scout II	0388W	
G-MBEP	American Aerolights Eagle 215B	2877	
BAPC.448	Bleriot XI reproduction		

National Waterfront Museum, Oystermouth Road, Maritime Quarter, Swansea SA1 3RD (museum.wales/swansea)

BAPC.047 Watkins CHW Monoplane

South Wales Aircraft Museum, MoD, St Athan (To open April 2019)

G-APXX	de Havilland DHA.3 Drover 2	5014		
G-BRFC	Percival P.57 Sea Prince T.1	P57-71		
G-BVGH	Hawker Hunter T.7	HABL-003360		
G-DACA	Percival P.57 Sea Prince T.1	P57/12		
G-KAEW	Fairey Gannet AEW.3	F9459		
G-OBLN	de Havilland DH.115 Vampire T.11			
G-RAFI	BAC P.84 Jet Provost T.4	PAC/W/17641		
G-SDEV	de Havilland DH.104 Sea Devon C.20	04472		
HZ-BIN	Hawker-Siddeley HS.125 Srs.1B/522	25106	18.11.66	

G-BOCB, G-OMCA, G-DJMJ, G-AWUF, 5N-ALY,
G-AWUF   Cancelled 22.02.95 as PWFU   16.10.90
Cockpit only; at South Wales Aircraft Museum

The Welsh Spitfire Museum, Bridge Street, Haverfordwest SA61 2AL

G-CFGA	Supermarine 502 Spitfire T.8	

NORTHERN IRELAND
Ulster Aviation Society, Gate 3, Maze Long Kesh, 94b Halftown Road, Lisburn BT27 5RF (ulsteraviationsociety.co.uk)

G-AJSN	Fairchild F.24W-41A Argus 2	849
G-BDBS	Short SD.3-30 UTT	SH.1935 & SH.3001
G-BEHX	Evans VP-2	V2 2338
G-BNZR	Clutton-Tabenor FRED Srs.II	xxxx
G-BTUC	Embraer EMB-312 Tucano	312007
G-CDUX	Piper PA-32-300 Cherokee Six	32-7340074
G-CJEN	Ferguson 1911 Monoplane	WM-001/2016
G-MBIV	Hiway Skytrike/Flexiform Sealande	EJPTQ-01
G-MBJV	Rotec Rally 2B	CJGW-01
G-MJWS	Eurowing Goldwing	EW-22
G-MZHM	TEAM Hi-Max 1700R	xxxx
G-RENT	Robinson R22 Beta	0758
G-TANK	Cameron N-90 HAB	3625
G-14-1	Short SB.4 Sherpa	SH.1604

G-36-1, G-14-1   Cancelled – WFU 05.66
Short & Harland Experimental & Research Aircraft Fuselage only

EI-BUO	Aero Composites Sea Hawker	80
N80BA	Pitts S-1A Special	648-4

Wreck only – crashed 11.07.99

BAPC.263 Chargus Cyclone
BAPC.266 Rogallo hang glider
BAPC.369 Supermarine Spitfire fsm
BAPC.403 Fieseler Fi.103 *(FZG-76/V-1)* fsm

Ulster Folk & Transport Museum, Cultra, Holywood BT18 0EU (nidex.com/uftm)

G-ACUX	Short S.16 Scion 1	S.776	
G-AJOC	Miles M.38 Messenger 2A	6370	
G-AKEL	Miles M.65 Gemini 1A	6484	
G-AKLW	Short SA.6 Sealand 1	SH.1571	
G-AOUR	de Havilland DH.82A Tiger Moth	86341	
G-ARTZ (1)	McCandless M.2	M2-1	
G-ATXX	McCandless M.4	M4-3	
G-BKMW	Short SD3-30-200 Sherpa	SH.3094	
BGA 470	Short Nimbus	S.1312	xx.xx .47
	'ALA' *Stored*		xx.08.75
EI-CNG	Air & Space 18A	18-75	
IAHC.6	Ferguson monoplane replica	xxxx	

Built by Capt J.Kelly Rogers 1974

IAHC.9	Ferguson monoplane replica	xxxx

Dismantled Built by L.Hannah 1980

REPUBLIC of IRELAND
Aviation Museum at Atlantic AirVenture, Link Road, Shannon, County Clare (atlanticairventure.com)

G-BTVV	Reims/Cessna F337G Super Skymaster	F33700058

G-DHUU	de Havilland DH.112 Venom FB.50 (FB.1)	749	
G-GFCD	Piper PA-34-220T Seneca III	34-8133073	
D-3229	Scheibe Bergfalke II/55	272	
EI-CIA	Socata MS-880B Rallye Club	1218	
EI-COZ	Piper PA28-140 Cherokee	28-26796	
xxxx	Bede BD5	xxxx	*Unregistered*
xxxx	Monerai Glider	xxxx	*Unregistered*

Meath Aero Museum, Ashbourne, County Meath

'EI-ABH'	HM.14 Pou-du-Ciel replica	1	
	Fuselage & rudder only		
G-AMDD	de Havilland DH.104 Dove 6	04292	
IGA.6	Slingsby T.8 Tutor	xxxx	xx.xx.56

IAC.6, VM65/

South East Aviation Enthusiasts Group c/o Cavan & Leitrim Railway, Dromod, Leitrim, County Leitrim

EI-BDM	Piper PA-23-250 Aztec D	27-4166	
EI-100	SZD-12A Mucha 100A	494	
EI-139	Slingsby T.31B	902	
G-ANIS	Taylorcraft Auster 5	1429	
G-AOGA	Miles M.75 Aries 1	75/1007	
G-AOIE	Douglas DC-7C	45115	
G-BJMM	Cremer MLB	717	
IAHC.1	Mignet HM.14 Pou-Du-Ciel replica	xxxx	
	'St Patrick' Stored		
BGA 1410	Grunau Baby III	xxxx	05.09.67
	RAFGSA 378, D-4676 *As 'CBK'*		xx.02.74
	Built by Sfg.Schaffin		
BGA 1424	Slingsby T.8 Tutor	SSK/FF27	xx.10.67
	RAFGSA 214 *As 'CBZ'*		xx.04.78

AUSTRALIA
Australian War Memorial, Canberra, Australian Capital Territory

G-EAQM	Airco DH.9	xxxx

National Museum of Australia, Canberra, Australian Capital Territory

G-AERD	Percival Type D Gull Six	D.65

Camden Museum of Aviation, Kogarah, New South Wales

G-AMWI	Bristol 171 Sycamore 4	13070

Darwin Aviation Museum, 557 Stuart Hwy, Winnellie, Northern Territory

G-AOFM	Auster J/5P Autocar	3178

Queensland Museum, South Brisbane, Queensland (qm.qld.gov.au)

G-EACQ	Avro 534 Baby	534/1
G-EBOV	Avro 581E Avian	5116
G-ABLK	Avro 616 Avian V	R3/CN/523

Hinkler Hall of Aviation, Bundaberg, Queensland (hinklerhallofaviation.com)

BAPC.509 Hinkler Ibis reproduction

Adelaide Airport, South Australia

G-EAOU	Vickers FB.27A Vimy IV	xxxx

Clyde North Aeronautical Preservation Group, Mount Waverley, Victoria

'G-ACSS'	de Havilland DH.88 Comet replica	xxxx
	As 'G-ACSP'	

Royal Australian Air Force Museum, Point Cook, Victoria (defence.gov.au/RAAF/raafmuseum)/

G-BYKV	Avro 504K replica	0015

BAPC.457 Supermarine Spitfire Mk.VIII fsm

RAAF Association Aviation Heritage Museum, Bull Creek, Western Australia (raafawa.org.au/wa/museum)

BAPC.507	Bristol 86A Tourer reproduction	As 'G-AUDK'
BAPC.508	Sopwith F.1 Camel reproduction	As M6394'

AUSTRIA
Austrian Aviation Museum, Bad Voslau, Nederosterreich (austrian-aviation-museum.com)

G-AGRW	Vickers 639 Viking 1	115

BARBADOS
Concorde Experience Museum, Grantley Adams International Airport, Seawell

G-BOAE	BAC Concorde Type 1 Variant 102	212 & 100-012

BELGIUM
Koninklijk Leger Museum-Musée Royal de l'Armée, Brussels (klm-mra.be)

G-ACGR	Percival Type D Gull Four IIA	D.29
G-AFJR	Tipsy Trainer 1	2
G-AFRV	Tipsy Trainer I	10
G-AKIS	Miles M.38 Messenger 2A	6725
G-AKNV	de Havilland DH.89A Dragon Rapide	6458
G-AMTP	de Havilland DH.82A Tiger Moth	84875
G-HAPR	Bristol 171 Sycamore HC.14	13387
BAPC.019	Bristol F2b Fighter fuselage frame	

Kokorico Night Club, N9, Eeklo-Gent in Zomergem

G-AZNA	Vickers 813 Viscount	350

Collection Henrad, Hamois-Mohiville

BGA 3439	Slingsby T.38 Grasshopper TX1	1263
	XP464 As 'BGA 3439'	

History of Ballooning, Sint-Niklaas

G-BKXX	Cameron V-65	1000
G-HLIX	Cameron Helix Oilcan 61SS HAB	1192
G-UMBO	Colt Jumbo SS HAB	747

CANADA
The Hangar Flight Museum, Calgary, Alberta (www.thehangarmuseum.ca)

BAPC.510	Sopwith Triplane reproduction	CP101

Alberta Aviation Museum, Edmonton, Alberta

BAPC.497	Cranwell CLA.4	As '4'
BAPC.506	Vickers Type 60 Viking IV ⅞ Scale Model	As 'G-CAEB'

Reynolds-Alberta Museum, Wetaskiwin, Alberta (machinemuseum.net)

BAPC.180 McCurdy Silver Dart reconstruction

Greenwood Military Aviation Museum, Greenwood, Kingston, Nova Scotia

BAPC.530 Supermarine Spitfire IX scale model
        Built by S Derrick; as 'BS306':AE-A'
        of 402 (City of Winnipeg) Sqn

National Air Force Museum of Canada, CFB Trenton, Astra, Ontario (airforcemuseum.ca)

BAPC.224 Supermarine Spitfire V fsm

Canada Aviation Museum, Rockcliffe, Ottawa, Ontario (casmuseum. techno-science.ca)

G-AANM (2)	Bristol F 2b Fighter composite	"67626"

CHILE
Museo Nacional de Aeronautica de Chile, Los Cerillos, Santiago

G-BPLT	Bristol 20 M.1C replica	AJD-1

DENMARK
Dansk Veteranflysamling, Stauning

G-AHKO	Taylorcraft Plus D	228

Stilling, Arhus

G-BNNI	Boeing 727-276 ADV	20950

EGYPT
Military Museum, Alexandria

G-AYBX	Campbell Cricket	CA/331

ESTONIA
Estonian Maritime Museum, Tallinn (meremuuseum.ee/en/estonian-maritime-museum/)

BAPC.502	Short 184 reproduction	As 'N9190':24'

FINLAND
Keski-Suomen Ilmailumuseo, Tikkakoski, Jyväskylä

GN-101	Folland Fo.141 Gnat F.1	FL-8
	G-39-6 As 'G-39-6'	

FRANCE (by Départements)
Musée de L'Automoiliste, Aire de Breguieres, Mougins, Cannes, 06 Alpes-Maritimes

(G-BLXI (1))	Blériot Type XI replica	EMK 010

Le Memorial de Caen, Esplanade Général Eisenhower, Caen, 14 Calvados, Normandy

BAPC.526 HawkerTyphoon reproduction
        As 'JP656:'BR-SW'

Musée des Ballons, Chateau de Balleroy, Balleroy, 14 Calvados

G-BKBR (2)	Cameron Chateau 84SS HAB	743
G-BKNN	Cameron Minar-E-Pakistan HAB	900
G-BLFE	Cameron Sphinx 72SS HAB	1011
G-BLRW	Cameron Elephant 77SS HAB	1074
G-BMUN	Cameron Harley 78SS HAB	1188
G-BMWN	Cameron Temple 80SS HAB	1211
G-BNFK	Cameron Egg 89SS HAB	1436
G-BNJU	Cameron Bust 80SS HAB	1324
G-BPOV	Cameron Magazine 90SS HAB	1890
G-BPSP	Cameron Ship 90SS HAB	1848
G-BRWZ	Cameron Macaw 90SS HAB	2206
G-TURK	Cameron Sultan 80SS HAB	1711

Ailes Anciennes Toulouse, Blagnac, Toulouse, 31 Haute-Garonne

G-ALWC	Douglas C-47A-25-DK Dakota	13590

Amicale Jean-Baptiste Salis, La Ferté-Alais, 91 Essonne

G-ANSG	de Havilland DH.82A Tiger Moth	85569

Musée de l'Air et de l'Espace, Le Bourget, 93 Seine-Saint-Denis, Paris (mae.org)

G-EBYY	Cierva C.8L Mk.2 (Avro 617)	xxxx

GERMANY
Luftwaffen Museum, Gatow, Berlin

G-HELI	Saro Skeeter AOP.12	S2/5110?

Sammler Und Hobbywelt Sammlung, Buseck

G-AYNP	Westland WS.55 Whirlwind HAR10	WA.71

Historische Flugzeug, Grossenhein

G-ANIX (2)	de Havilland DH.82 Tiger Moth	'84764'
G-ASZE	Beagle A.61 Terrier 2	B.636
G-BWRF	Morane-Saulnier MS.505 Criquet	73/1
G-BWRG	Mraz M.1D Sokol	304
G-BWRH	Blériot Type XI replica	001
G-BWRI	Mignet HM-19C Pou-du-Ciel replica	01

Luftfahrt Museum, Laatzen-Hannover, Hannover

G-FXIV	Supermarine 379 Spitfire FR.XIVc	xxxx

Flugausstellung Hermeskeil, Rhineland-Palatinate (flugaustellung.de)

G-AMXX	de Havilland DH.104 Dove 2A	04406
G-ARVF	Vickers VC-10-1101	808
G-BDIW	de Havilland DH.106 Comet 4C	6470
G-BKLZ	Vinten Wallis WA-116MC	UMA-01
BAPC.520	Aerospatiale/BAC Concorde scale model	As 'F-WTSA'

Luftfahrt Und Technik Museumpark, Merseburg Sud

G-DEVN	de Havilland DH.104 Devon C.2/2	04269

Auto und Technik Museum, Sinsheim (tecknik.museum.de)

G-ARUE (2)	de Havilland DH.104 Dove 7	04530

Albatros Flugmuseum, Stuttgart Airport, Stuttgart

G-AVHE	Vickers 812 Viscount	363

Deutsches Segelfligzeugmuseum, Wassererkuppe

BGA 3277	Lippisch Hols-der-Teufel replica	xxxx	xx.06.87
	FHQ As 'BGA 3277'		

HUNGARY
Kozlekedesi Muzeum, Budapest

G-BCPX	Szep HFC.125	AS.001

ITALY
Museo Dell'Araba Fenice, Reggio Nell'Emilia

G-BXDL	Hunting Percival P.84 Jet Provost T.3A	PAC/W/9286

Museo Piaggio, Pontedera, Pisa (museopiaggio.it)

'xxxx'	Wallis simulator	xxxx
	Marked as 'G-ARRT'	
	Built by Piaggio & Alpha Willis for 1967 film 'Dick Smart,	
	Agent 2.007' using Vespa 180 Super Sport scooter	

KINGDOM OF LESOTHO
Makoanyane Square, Kingsway, Maseru

BAPC.495	Supermarine Spitfire Vb fsm
	As 'L2016:RN-E' of RAF 72 Sqdn (Basutoland)

MALTA
Malta Aviation Museum Foundation, Ta'Qali

G-ANFW	de Havilland DH.82A Tiger Moth	85660

MALAYSIA
Muzium Tentera Udara Diraja Malaysia, Sungai Besi Airfield, Kuala Lumpur (malaysian-museums.org)

G-ANEJ	de Havilland DH.82A Tiger Moth	85592

NETHERLANDS
Luchtvaart Hobby Shop, Aalsmeerderburg

G-BPMP	Douglas C-47A-50-DL Dakota	10073

Steinadler Stegelflug, Amersfoort

BGA 3225	Slingsby T.21B Sedbergh TX1	583
	WB993 As 'BGA 3225'	

Rijksmuseum, Museumstraat 1, Amsterdam (rijksmuseum.nl)

G-EACN	BAT FK.23 Bantam	FK23/15

Zweeflvieggroep Hilversum, Hilversum

BGA 3181	Slingsby T.31B Cadet TX3	710
	WT 915 As 'BGA 3181'	
BGA 4228	Slingsby T.31B Cadet TX3	850
	XA308, (BGA 3249) As 'BGA 4228'	
BGA 4229	Slingsby T.38 Grasshopper TX1	765
	WZ769 As 'BGA 4229'	

Aviodrome Museum, Lelystad Airfield, Lelystad, Flevoland

G-AMCA	Douglas C-47B-30DK Dakota 3	16218 & 32966
G-BKRG	Beech C-45G-BH	AF-222
G-MAAC	Advanced Airship Corp ANR-1	01
BAPC.022	Mignet HM.14 Pou-Du-Ciel replica	
BAPC.105	Blériot Type XI replica	

Oorlogsmuseum, Overloon

G-DAKK	Douglas C-47A-35-DL Dakota	9798

Stitchting Historische Zweefvliegtuigen Venlo, Venlo, Breda

BGA 875	Slingsby T.21B	1205
	BGA 875, AGA 7 As 'BGA 875'	

NEW ZEALAND
Ashburton Aviation Museum, Ashburton (aviationmuseum.co.nz)

G-SHKK	Hughes 269A	111-0029

Jean Batten Memorial, Terminal Building, Auckland International Airport, Auckland

G-ADPR	Percival Type D Gull Six	D.55

Classic Flyers Museum, Tauranga Airport, Mount Maunganui

BAPC.527	Supermarine Spitfire Vc fsm
	As 'JK715':SN-A' of 485 Sqn
BAPC.528	Fairey Swordfish reproduction
	Built by Museum of Transport and Technology, Auckland;
	as 'DK791'

The Air Force Museum of New Zealand, RNZAF Wigram, Christchurch (airforcemuseum.co.nz)

G-AIKR	Airspeed AS.65 Consul	4338
G-BIAT	Sopwith Pup replica	001

Guy Menzies Memorial, Hari Hari, West Coast

BAPC.498	Avro 616 Avian IVA reproduction	As 'G-ABCF'

NORWAY
Forsvarsmuseet Flysamlingen, Gardemoen

G-ASCF	Beagle A.61 Terrier 2	B.617
G-BMEW	Lockheed 18-56 Lodestar (C-60A-5-LO)	18-2444

Warbirds of Norway, Kjeller

G-DHZZ	de Havilland DH.115 Vampire T55	990

OMAN
Sultanate of Oman Armed Forces Museum, Bait al Falaj Airfield, Muscat

G-BGSB	Hunting-Percival P.56 Provost T.1	PAC/F/057

REPUBLIC of SOUTH AFRICA
Classic Jets South Africa, Cape Town International Airport, Cape Town

G-FSIX	English Electric Lightning F.6	95116
G-LTNG	English Electric Lightning T.5	B1/95011
G-OPIB	English Electric Lightning F.6	95238

South African Air Force Museum, AFB Swartkop, Pretoria

G-EAML	Airco DH.6	xxxx
G-AITF	Airspeed AS.40 Oxford 1	xxxx

South African Air Force Museum, Port Elizabeth, Eastern Cape

BAPC.519	SupermarineSpitfire IX fsm
	Built R Tribelhorn; as 'JK769:AG-M'

SPAIN
Fundación Infante de Orleans, Cuatro Vientos, Madrid (fio.es)

G-EBXU	de Havilland DH.60X Moth	627
G-AEVZ	British Aircraft L.25c Swallow II	475
G-AFAX	British Aircraft Eagle 2	138

Museo de Aeronautica y Astronautica, Cuatro Vientos, Madrid (madrid.com/es/turismo)

G-ACYR	de Havilland DH.89 Dragon Rapide	6261

Fundacio Parc Aeronautic De Catalunya, Sabadell

G-APPN	de Havilland DH.82A Tiger Moth	83839

KINGDOM OF SAUDI ARABIA
Royal Saudi Air Force Museum (Saqer-Aljazirah Aviation Museum), Riyadh (sauditourism.sa)

BAPC.504	de Havilland DH.9
BAPC.505	WestlandWapiti reproduction

SWEDEN
Svedinos Bil Och Flygmuseum, Slöinge, Halmstad

G-ANSO	Gloster Meteor T.7	G5/1525

Flygvapenmuseum, Malmslätt, Linköping (flygvapenmuseum.se)

G-ANVU	de Havilland DH.104 Dove 1B	04082

SWITZERLAND
Vintage Aircraft Club, Basel

G-AIVG	Vickers 610 Viking 1B	220

Geneva-Cointrin, Geneva

G-ATTU	Piper PA-28-140 Cherokee	28-21987

Sammlung Poll, Ursy

BGA 1836	Pilatus B4-PC11	045	As 'BGA 1836'
BGA 2352	Pilatus B4-PC11AF	134	
	RAFGSA 718, RAFGSA 518		As 'BGA 2352'

SYRIA
Military Museum, Tekkiye Mosque, Damascus
(Removed – current status unknown)

G-AXVL	Campbell Cricket	CA/328

TURKEY
Rahmi M. Koc Museum, Istanbul

'G-AXNZ'	Pitts S-1C replica	
	Possibly ex BAPC134/'G-RKSF'/'G-CARS'?	
G-BWDR	Hunting Percival P.84 Jet Provost T.3A	PAC/W/660
G-MKVI	de Havilland DH.100 Vampire FB6	676

UNITED ARAB EMIRATES
Al Mahatta Museum, The Sharjah Aviation Museum, Sharjah

G-AJRE	Auster V J/1 Autocrat	2603
G-AMXA	de Havilland DH.106 Comet C.2R	06023
G-ARDE	de Havilland DH.104 Dove 6	04469
G-ARKU	de Havilland DH.114 Heron 2	14072
G-BSMF	Avro 652A Anson C.19	xxxx
N688EA	Douglas DC-3A-456 Skytrain	
	C-GCXE, Canada AF 12943, FZ 669, 42-92452	
	As 'G-AMZZ' in 'Gulf Aviation' c/s	

UNITED STATES
California

Planes of Fame Air Museum, Chino (planesoffame.org)

G-TWTD	CCF Hawker Sea Hurricane X	CCF/41H/8020
BAPC.110	Fokker D.VIIF fsm	
BAPC.136	Deperdussin 1913 Monoplane fsm	
BAPC.140	Curtiss 42A *(R3C2)* fsm	
BAPC.141	Macchi M.39 fsm	
BAPC.156	Supermarine S.6B fsm	
BAPC.493	Supermarine Spitfire fsm	

Western Aerospace Museum, Oakland (westernaerospacemuseum.org/

G-AKNP	Short S.45 Solent 3	S.1295

Aviation Museum of Santa Paula, Santa Paula (amszp.org/

G-AAMZ (2)	de Havilland DH.60G Moth	1293
G-AMLF	de Havilland DH.82A Tiger Moth	86572

**Travis Air Force Base Museum, Travis, Sacramento
(travis.af.mil/units/travisairmuseum.asp)**

G-MNXJ	Medway Half Pint	14/7886

Florida

Church Street Collection, Orlando

BAPC.139	Fokker Dr.1 Triplane fsm	*As '102/17'*

Fantasy of Flight, Polk City (fantasyofflight.com)

G-AHMJ	Cierva C.30A *(Avro 671)* (Rota I)	R3/CA/43
G-BCOH	Avro 683 Lancaster Mk.10 AR	277
G-BCWL	Westland Lysander IIIA	1244
G-BJHS	Short S.25 Sandringham	SH.55C
G-BWOL	Hawker Sea Fury FB.Mk.11	'61631'
G-CCVV	Supermarine 379 Spitfire FR.XIVe	6S/649186

Miami Auto Museum, 2000 NE 146 Street, Miami (dezercollection.com)

G-AWPY	Campbell-Bensen B.8M	CA.314
G-OBAY	Bell 206B JetRanger	276

Miami International, Terminal Concourse E

EI-ATP	Phoenix Luton LA-4A Minor	PAL 1124

Michigan

**World Heritage Air Museum, Coleman A. Young International Airport,
Detroit (worldheritageairmuseum.org)**

G-BWMF	Gloster Meteor T.7	G5/356460

Minnesota

Golden Wings Air Museum, Blaine (goldenwingsmuseum.com/)

G-AUFZ	Avro 594 Avian II	R3/AV/127	27.01.28
	To VH-UFZ 08.30 – subsequently NC7083		*As 'G-EBUG'*

New Mexico

**Anderson-Abruzzo International Balloon Museum Foundation, Balloon
Museum Drive NE, Albuquerque (cabq.gov/balloon) (incorporating
Soukup American International Balloon & Airship Museum)**

G-BIAZ	Cameron AT-165 (Helium/HAB)	400
G-ROZY	Cameron R-36 Gas.HAB	1141
G-UPPY	Cameron DP-80 Airship	2274
G-VIBA	Cameron DP-80 Airship	1729

New York

**Intrepid Air & Space Museum, Manhattan, New York
(intrepidmuseum.org/pages/concorde)**

G-BOAD	BAC Concorde Type 1 Variant 102	210 & 100-010

Rhinebeck Aerodrome Museum, Rhinebeck (oldrhinebeck.org)

G-ATXL	Avro 504K replica	HAC-1
xxxx	de Havilland DH.82A Tiger Moth	86556
	N3529, F-BGDH, PG647 *As 'G-ACDB'*	

Ohio

**National Museum of United States Air Force, Wright-Patterson Air Force
Base, Dayton (nationalmuseum.af.mil)**

G-MOSI	de Havilland DH.98 Mosquito TT.35	xxxx

Virginia

**Military Aviation Museum, 1341 Princess Anne Road, Virginia Beach
(militaryaviationmuseum.org)**

G-BKBB	Hawker Fury replica	WA/6

**National Air & Space Museum, Steven F.Udvar-Hazy Centre, Chantilly
(nasm.si.edu)**

G-AARO (2)	Arrow Sport A2-60	341
G-MURY	Robinson R44 Astro	0201

Washington

Olympic Flight Museum, Olympia (olympicflightmuseum.com)

G-AYHS	BAC 167 Strikemaster Mk.84	EEP/JP/1934

**Flying Heritage & Combat Armor Museum, Paine Field, 3407 109th Street
SW, Everett (flyingheritage.org)**

G-AWHB	CASA 2111D *(Heinkel 111H-16)*	049
G-KAMM	Hawker Hurricane IIC	CCF/R32207

**Historic Flight Foundation, Paine Field, 3407 109th Street SW, Everett
(historicflight.org/hf)**

G-AHXW	de Havilland DH.89A Dragon Rapide	6782

Museum of Flight, Boeing Field, Seattle (museumofflight.org)

G-BOAG	BAC Concorde Type 1 Variant 102	214 & 100-014

Wisconsin

**EAA AirVenture Museum, Witttman Field, Oshkosh
(http://museum.eaa.org/)**

G-ASKB	de Havilland DH.98 Mosquito TT.35	
G-HUNT	Hawker Hunter F.51	41H-680277

URUGUAY
Museo Aeronautico, San Gabriel, Montevideo

G-ANOW	de Havilland DHC-1 Chipmunk 21	C1/0972

SECTION 10 – DECODES & MISCELLANEOUS LISTINGS

PART 1 – OVERSEAS REGISTRATION PREFIX INDEX

The previous identity origins of many of the current UK and Irish registered aircraft are many and varied. Therefore, we include both current and historical lists of ICAO national country allocations so the reader can deduce, in brief, the aircraft's provenance.

CURRENT PREFIXES:

Prefix	Country	Commenced	Historical Prefix(es)
AP-	Pakistan	1947	
A2-	Botswana	1972	VQ-ZE -VQ-Z
A3-	Tonga	1971	VQ-F
A4O	Oman	1071	
A5-	Bhutan	1983	
A6-	United Arab Emirates-	1977	A6-
A7-	Qatar	1975	
A8-	Liberia	2003	LI-, EL-
A9C-	Bahrain	1977	
B-	China (Peoples' Republic of)	1975	XT
B-	China (Republic of)	1949	XT
B-H, -K, -L-	Hong Kong	1997	VR-H
B-M-	Macau	1999	CR-M
C-	Canada	1974	G-C, CF-
CC-	Chile	1929	
CN-	Morocco	1952	F-D
CP-	Bolivia	1954	CB
CS-	Portugal	1929	C-P
CU-	Cuba	1947	NM-
CX-	Uruguay	1929	
C2-	Nauru	1971	VH-
C3-	Andorra	1993	
C5-	Gambia	1978	VP-X
C6-	Bahamas	1975	VP-B
C9-	Mozambique	1975	CR-A, CR-B
D-	Germany	1929	
DQ-	Fiji	1971	VQ-F
D2-	Angola	1975	CR-L
D4-	Cape Verde Islands	1975	CR-C
D6-	Comoros	1975	F-O
EC-	Spain	1929	M-
EI-, EJ-	Ireland	1928	
EK-	Armenia	1991	CCCP-
EP-	Iran	1944	RV-
ER-	Moldova	1991	CCCP-
ES-	Estonia	1929	ES-, CCCP-
ET-	Ethiopia	1945	
EW-	Belarus	1991	CCCP-
EX-	Kyrgyzstan	1991	CCCP-
EY-	Tajiikstan	1991	CCCP-
EZ-	Turkmenistan	1993	CCCP-
E3-	Eritrea	1994	ET-
E5-	Cook Islands	2012	
E7-	Bosnia & Herzegovina	2009	YU-, T9-
F-	France	1919	
F-O	French Overseas Territories	1929	
G-	United Kingdom	1919	
HA-	Hungary	1935	H-M
HB-	Switzerland	1935	CH-
HC-	Ecuador	1929	
HH-	Haiti	1929	
HI-	Dominican Republic	1929	
HK-	Colombia	1946	C-
HL-	Korea (South)	1948	
HP-	Panama	1952	R-, RX-
HR-	Honduras	1961	XH-
HS-	Thailand	1929	H-S
HV-	Vatican state	1929	
HZ-	Saudi Arabia	1945	UH-
H4-	Solomon Islands	1978	VP-P
I-	Italy	1929	
JA-	Japan	1948	J-
JU-	Mongolia	1998	MT-, HMAY-
JY-	Jordan	1954	TJ- ,VQ-P
J2-	Djibouti	1977	F-O
J3-	Grenada	1974	VQ-G
J5-	Guinea Bissau	1979	CR-G
J6-	St. Lucia	1981	VQ-L
J7-	Dominica	1978	VP-L

Prefix	Country	Commenced	Historical Prefix(es)
J8-	St. Vincent	1979	VP-V
LN-	Norway	1931	N-
LQ-	Argentina (Government)	1932	
LV	Argentina	1932	R-
LX-	Luxembourg	1935	UL-
LY-	Lithuania	1936	LY-, RY-, CCCP-
LZ-	Bulgaria	1929	
M-	Isle of Man	2007	G-
N	United States	1921	
OB-	Peru	1940	OA-
OD-	Lebanon	1951	F-, LR-
OE-	Austria	1936	A-
OH-	Finland	1931	K-S
OK-	Czech Republic	1929	L-B
OM-	Slovakia	19xx	OK-
OO-	Belgium	1929	O-B
OY-	Denmark	1929	T-D
P-	Korea (North)	1953	
PH-	Netherlands	1929	H-N
PJ-	Netherlands Antilles	1929	
PK-	Indonesia	1929	
PP-	Brazil	1932	P-B
PR-	Brazil	1950	
PT-	Brazil	1950	
PU-	Brazil (ultralights)	1950	
PZ-	Suriname	1929	
P2-	Papua New Guinea	1974	VH-
P4-	Aruba	1986	PJ-
RA-	Russia	1991	RR-, CCCP-
RDPL-	Laos	1975	F-L, XW-
RP-	Philippines	1975	PI-
SE-	Sweden	1929	S-A
SP-	Poland	1929	P-P
ST-	Sudan	1959	SN-
SU-	Egypt	1931	
SU-Y	Palestine	1995	VQ-P (1930-48)
SX-	Greece	1929	
S2-	Bangladesh	1972	AP-
	(Formerly East Pakistan)		
S5-	Slovenia	1993	YU-, SL-
S7-	Seychelles	1976	VQ-S
S9-	Sao Tome	1977	CR-S
TC-	Turkey	1929	
TF-	Iceland	1937	
TG-	Guatemala	1948	LG-
TI-	Costa Rica	1927	
TJ-	Cameroon	1960	F-O, VR-N
TL-	Central African Republic	1961	F-O
TN-	Congo (Peoples' Republic of)	1960	F-O
TR-	Gabon	1960	F-O
TS-	Tunisia	1956	F-O
TT-	Chad	1960	F-O
TU-	Ivory Coast	1960	F-O
TY-	Benin	1960	F-O
TZ-	Mali	1960	F-O
T3-	Kiribati	1983	VP-P
T7-	San Marino	1997	
T8A-	Palau	2004	V6-
	(Formerly part of Micronesia)		
UK-	Uzbekistan	1991	CCCP-
UN-	Kazakhstan	1991	CCCP-
UP-	Kazakhstan	1991	CCCP-
UR-	Ukraine	1991	CCCP-
VH-	Australia	1929	G-AU
VN-	Vietnam	1975	F-VN, XV-
VP-A	Anguilla	1997	
VP-B	Bermuda	1997	VR-B
VP-C	Cayman Islands	1997	VR-C
VP-F	Falkland Islands	1929	

Prefix	Country	Commenced	Historical Prefix(es)
VP-G	Gibraltar	1997	VR-G
VP-LVA to VP-LZZ	British Virgin Islands	1971	
VP-M	Montserrat	2007	
VQ-B	Bermuda	2008	VP-B, VR-B
VQ-H	St. Helena	1929	
VQ-T	Turks and Caicos Islands	1980	VP-J
VT-	India	1930	G-IA, CR-I
V2-	Antigua	1981	VP-L, VP-A
V3-	Belize	1983	VP-H--
V4-	St.Kitts and Nevis	1983	VP-LKA-LLZ
V5-	Namibia	1990	ZS-
V6-	Micronesia	1990	
V7-	Marshall Islands	1991	MI-
V8-	Brunei	1984	VR-U-
XA-	Mexico (Commercial)	1929	X-
XB-	Mexico (Private)	1929	X-
XC-	Mexico (Government)	1929	X-
XT-	Burkina Faso (Formerly Upper Volta)	1984	F-O
XU-	Cambodia	1954	F-KH, KW-
XY-	Myanmar	1938	VT- (Formerly Burma)
YA-	Afghanistan	1929	
YI-	Iraq	1931	
YJ-	Vanuatu (Formerly New Hebrides)	1933	F-O or VP-P marks until 1980
YK-	Syria	1949	F-, SR-
YL-	Latvia	1929	YL-, CCCP
YN-	Nicaragua	1981	YN-, AN-
YR-	Romania	1936	CV-
YS-	El Salvador	1939	
YU-	Serbia (Formerly part of Yugoslavia until 1992, see also Montenegro now 4O- and Kosovo now Z6-)	1933	X-S, UN
YV-	Venezuela	1929	
Z-	Zimbabwe	1980	VP-W, VP-Y
ZA-	Albania	1946	
ZJ-	Jersey	2015	
ZK-, ZM-	New Zealand	1929	G-NZ
ZP-	Paraguay	1929	
ZS-, ZT-, ZU-	South Africa	1929	G-U
Z3-	Republic of North Macedonia	1992	YU-
Z6-	Kosovo	2011	YU- (ex Serbia)
Z8-	South Sudan	2012	ST-
2-	Guernsey	2013	
3A-	Monaco	1959	CZ, MC
3B-	Mauritius	1959	VQ-M

Prefix	Country	Commenced	Historical Prefix(es)
3C-	Equatorial Guinea	1970	EC-
3D-	Swaziland	1971	VQ-ZIA – ZLZ
3DC-	Swaziland	2012	3D-, VQ-ZIA – ZLZ
3X-	Guinea	1958	F-O
4K-	Azerbaijan	1991	CCCP-
4L-	Georgia	2000	RA-
4O-	Montenegro (Used YU- with Serbia 1992 until 2008)	2008	YU-
4R-	Sri Lanka	1954	VP-C, CY-
4X-	Israel	1948	
5A-	Libya	1959	I-
5B-	Cyprus	1960	VQ-C
5H-	Tanzania (Formerly Zanzibar (VP-Z) and Tanganyika VR-T)	1964	
5N-	Nigeria	1960	VR-N
5R-	Madagasgar	1960	F-O
5T-	Mauritania	1960	F-O
5U-	Niger	1960	F-O
5V-	Togo	1976	F-O
5W-	Western Samoa	1962	ZK-
5X-	Uganda	1962	VP-U
5Y-	Kenya	1963	VP-K
6O-	Somalia	1969	I-, 6OS-
6V-	Senegal	1960	F-O
6Y-	Jamaica	1964	VP-J
7O-	Yemen	1974	YE-, 4W-
7P-	Lesotho	1967	VQ-ZAA -ZDZ
7Q-	Malawi	1964	VP-Y
7T-	Algeria	1962	F-O
8P-	Barbados	1968	VQ-B
8Q-	Maldive Republic	1976	(VP-)
8R-	Guyana	1967	VP-G
9A-	Croatia	1991	YU-, RC-
9G-	Ghana	1957	VP-A
9H-	Malta	1968	VP-M
9J-	Zambia	1964	VP-Y
9K-	Kuwait	1960	K-
9L-	Sierra Leone	1961	VR-L
9M-	Malaysia	1963	VR-J, -O, -R, -S, -W
9N-	Nepal	1960	
9Q-, 9S-	Congo (Democratic Republic) (Formerly Belgian Congo and Zaïre)	1962	OO-C, 9O-
9U-	Burundi	1966	OO-C, BR-
9V-	Singapore	1966	VR-S, 9M-
9XR-	Rwanda	1966	OO-C
9Y-	Trinidad and Tobago	1965	VP-T

HISTORICAL PREFIXES:

Prefix	Country	Commenced	Historical Prefix(es)
A-	Austria	1929-1939	OE-
AN-	Nicaragua	1936-1981	YN-
BR-	Burundi	1962-1965	9U-
C-	Columbia	1929-1948	HK-
CB-	Bolivia	1929-1954	CP-
CCCP-	Soviet Union	1929-1991	RA- (Russia)
CF-	Canada	1929-1974	C
CH-	Switzerland	1929-1936	HB-
CR-A, -M	Mozambique	1929-1975	C9-
CR-B, -H	Mozambique	1971-1975	C9-
CR-C	Cape Verde Islands	1929-1975	D4-
CR-G	Portuguese Guinea (Guinea Bissau)	1929-1975	J5-
CR-I	Portuguese India	1929-1961	VT-
CR-L	Angola	1929-1975	D2-
CR-S	Sao Tome and Principe	1929-1977	S9-
CR-T	Timor	1929-1976	PK-
CV-	Romania	1929-1936	YR-
CY-	Ceylon	1948-1954	4R-
CZ-	Monaco	1929-1949	MC
DDR-	East Germany	1981-1990	D
DM-	East Germany	1955-1981	DDR-
EL-	Liberia	1952-2003	A8-.
ES-	Estonia	1929-1939	Merged into Soviet Union CCCP
EZ-	Saarland	1929-1933	SL-
F-D	French Morocco	1929-1952	CN-
F-KH	Cambodia	1953-1960	XU-
F-LA	Laos	1955-1959	XW-

Prefix	Country	Commenced	Historical Prefix(es)
F-O	Algeria	1929-1962	7T-
F-O	Benin	1929-1960	TY-
F-O	Cameroon	1929-1960	TJ-
F-O	Chad	1929-1960	TT-
F-O	Congo	1929-1960	TN-
F-O	Djibouti	1929-1977	J2-
F-O	Gabon	1929-1960	TR-
F-O	Guinea	1929-1958	3X-
F-O	Indo-China	1948-1950s	see Cambodia, Laos, Vietnam
F-O	Ivory Coast	1929-1960	TU-
F-O	Madagascar	1929-1960	5R-
F-O	Mali	1929-1960	TZ-
F-O	Mauritania	1929-1960	5T-
F-O	Niger	1929-1960	5U-
F-O	Senegal	1929-1960	6V-
F-O	Togo	1929-1976	5V-
F-O	Tunisia	1929-1956	TS-
F-O	Ubangi-Shari	1929-1960	TL-
F-O	Upper Volta	1929-1960	XT-
F-VN	French Indo-China	1949-1959	XV- Vietnam
FC-	Free French	1940-1944	F-
G-AU	Australia	1921-1928	VH-
G-C	Canada	1920-1928	CF-
G-IA	India	1919-1928	VT-
G-K	Kenya	1928-1928	VP-K
G-NZ	New Zealand	1921-1928	ZK-
G-U	Union of South Africa	1927-1928	ZS-
H-M	Hungary	19xx-1935	HA-

Prefix	Country	Commenced	Historical Prefix(es)
HMAY	Mongolia	19xx-1998	MT- (or JU-?)
H-S	Siam	1919-1929	HS-
J-	Japan	1929-1945	JA
JZ-	Dutch East Indies	1954-1963	PK-
K-	Kuwait	1967-1968	Interim – 9K
K-S	Finland	19xx-1931	OH-
KA-	Katanga	1961-1963	Unofficial – 9O
KW-	Cambodia	1954-1954	XU-
L-B	Czechoslovakia	1919-1929	OK-
LG	Guatemala	1936-1948	TG
LI-	Liberia	1929-1952	EL-, now A8-
LR-	Lebanon	1944-1954	OD-
LY-	Lithuania	1929-1939	Merged into Soviet Union CCCP-
M-	Spain	1929-1933	EC
MC-	Monaco	1949-1993	3A-
MT-	Mongolia	1948-1998	JU
N-	Norway	1919-1931	LN-
O-B	Belgium,	1919-1929	OO-
OA-	Peru	1929-1938	OB-
OO-C	Belgian Congo	1929-1960	9O-
OK-	Czechoslovakia	1929-1993	OK- (Czech Rep) OM- (Slovakia)
P-B	Brazil	1927-1932	PP-
P-P	Poland	1919-1929	SP-
PI-	Philippines	1945-1973	RP-
R-	Argentina (three digits)	1928-1937	LV-
R-	Argentina (four letters)	1927-1931	
R-	Panama (two digits)	1929-1943	RX-
RR	Russia	1922-1929	CCCP-
RV-	Persia (Iran)	1929-1944	EP-
RX-	Panama	1943-1952	HP-
RY-	Lithuania	1929-1939	Merged into Soviet Union CCCP-
S-A	Sweden	1929-1929	SE-.
SA-	Saudi Arabia	1946 1952	HZ-
SL-	Saarland	1953-1957	D-
SL-	Slovenia	1991-1991	Unofficial, to S5-.
SN-	Sudan	1929-1955	ST-
SR-	Syria	1946-1951	YK-.
T-D	Denmark	1919-1929	OY-.
TJ-	Transjordan	1946-1954	JY-
TS-	Saar Territory	1930-1931	Unofficial, to EZ-
T9-	Bosnia & Herzegovina	1992-2009	E7-
UL-	Luxembourg	1929-1935	LX-
UN-	Yugoslavia	1928-1933	YU-
VO-	Newfoundland	1934-1949	Merged into Canada CF-
VP-A	Gold Coast	1929-1957	9G- (Ghana)
VP-B	Bahamas	1929-1973	C6-
VP-C	Ceylon	1929-1948	CY-
VP-G	British Guiana	1929-1967	8R-
VP-H	British Honduras (Belize)	1947-1983	V3-
VP-J	Jamaica	1930-1962	6Y-(Jamaica) & VQ-T (Turks & Caicos Islands)
VP-K	Kenya	1929-1963	5Y-
VP-LAA to -LIZ	Leeward Is (Antigua)	1929-1981	V2-
VP-LKA to -LLZ	Leeward Is (St. Kitts, Nevis)	1929-1983	V4-
VP-LLA to -LLZ	Leeward Is (Anguilla)	1929-1997	VP-A
VP-LMA to -LMZ	Leeward Is (Dominica)	1929-1978	J7-
	(Montserrat)	1929-1997	VP-M

Prefix	Country	Commenced	Historical Prefix(es)
VP-LVA to -LZZ	Leeward Is (BVI)	1929-1997	VP-L
VP-M	Malta	1929-1968	9H-
VP-N	Nyasaland	1929-1953	VP-Y
VP-P	Western Pacific Islands	1929- 1978	H4- (Solomon Islands) &
		1929-1981	T3- (Kiribati)
VP-R	Northern Rhodesia	1929-1953	VP-Y (Central African Federation)
VP-S	Somaliland	1929-1960	6OS-
VP-T	Trinidad and Tobago	1931-1965	9Y-
VP-U	Uganda	1929-1962	5X-
VP-V	St. Vincent & Grenadines	1959-1979	J8-
VP-W	Wei-Hai-Wei (Shantung, China)	1929-1930	XT-
VP-W, VP-Y	(Southern) Rhodesia	1965-1980	Z- (Zimbabwe)
VP-X	The Gambia	1929-1945	C5-
VP-Y	Central African Federation	1953-1965	VP-W (Rhodesia), 7Q- (Malawi) & 9J- (Zambia)
VP-Z	Zanzibar	1929-1963	5H- (Tanzania)
VQ-B	Barbados	1952-1968	8P-
VQ-C	Cyprus	1952-1960	5B-
VQ-F	Fiji, Tonga and Friendly Isles	1929-1971	DQ- (Fiji), A3- (Tonga)
VQ-G	Grenada	1962-1974	J3-
VQ-L	St. Lucia	1965-1981	J6-
VQ-M	Mauritius	1929-1968	3B-
VQ-P	Palestine	1930-1948	either TJ- or 4X-
VQ-S	Seychelles	1929-1977	S7-
VQ-ZAA to -ZDZ	Basutoland	1929-1967	7P- (Lesotho)
VQ-ZEA to -ZHZ	Bechuanaland	1929-1968	A2- (Botswana)
VQ-ZIA to -ZLZ	Swaziland	1929-1975	3D-
VR-A	Aden	1939-1969	4W (Yemen)
VR-B	Bermuda	1931-1997	VP-B
VR-C	Cayman Islands	1968-1997	VP-C
VR-G	Gibraltar	1929-1997	VP-G
VR-H	Hong Kong	1929-1997	B-H
VR-J	Johore	1929-1957	9M-
VR-L	Sierra Leone	1929-1961	9L-
VR-N	British Cameroons	1929-1960	either TJ- or 5N
VR-O	Sabah (North Borneo)	1929-1963	9M-
VR-R	Malaya	1929-1959	9M-
VR-S	Singapore	1929-1963	9M-, then 9V- 1965
VR-T	Tanganyika	1930-1963	5H- (Tanzania)
VR-U	Brunei	1929-1984	V8-
VR-W	Sarawak	1929-1963	9M-
X-	Mexico	1929-1934	XA-, XB- & XC-.
X-S	Yugoslavia	1927-1928	UN-
XH-	Honduras	1929-1960	HR-
XT	China	1929-1949	B-
XV-	South Vietnam	1959-1975	VN-
XW-	Laos	1959-1975	RDPL-
YE-	Yemen	1955-1969	4W-
YL-	Latvia	1929-1939	Merged into Soviet Union CCCP-
YN-	Nicaragua	1929-1936	AN-
4W-	Yemen	1969-1990	Merged into 7O-
6OS	Somalia	1960-1969	6O-
9O-	Zaïre	1960-1966	9Q-

PART 2 – MILITARY SERIALS DECODE

In certain circumstances the Civil Aviation Authority may permit the operation of aircraft without the need to carry regulation size national registration letters. These conditions are referred to as 'exemptions'. The CAA issues Exemption Certificates to operators which are usually valid for two years. The basic requirements are that the owner undertakes to notify the CAA of the markings carried and may not fly overseas, without specific permission of the overseas country. In the case of aircraft wearing military marks the authority of the relevant department at the Ministry of Defence is required for UK markings whilst an equivalent establishment must sanction any overseas markings to be carried.

Below are current details of aircraft which are known to be wearing military and, in a very few cases, other markings. The information is compiled from members' observations and includes any AHUK (BAPC) and 'B' Conditions identities known to be located in the UK and Ireland. Some are known to wear incorrect serials as to their exemption, for example Harvard G-KAMY wears US Serial 285068, but has exemption to wear 8084. Those in **bold** are current on the register whilst the registrations marked with asterisk (*) do not currently have exemption to wears these marks. A number of serials are worn by two different aircraft of the same type, these are underlined to highlight this. Marks that are not currently being worn are shown in brackets. Full details of BAPC markings are carried in SECTION 3 and c/ns for the others can be found in their respective Sections. We should point out that some of the serials used are spurious. The Glider de-code can be found on page 499 of Section 2.

Serial	Code	Regn	Type
UNITED KINGDOM (RAF unless otherwise shown)			
2		G-LOTI	Bleriot XI replica
3		BAPC.354	Sopwith Tabloid Floatplane replica
4		G-EBNV	English Electric Wren
5		BAPC.351	Airspeed AS.58 Horsa II replica
6		**G-CAMM**	Hawker Cygnet replica
8		BAPC.238	Waxflatter Ornithopter replica
10		BAPC.328	Avro F Type Cabin replica
10		**G-BPVE***	Bleriot Type XI 1909 replica
12		**G-ARSG**	Roe Triplane IV replica
14		BAPC.006	Roe Triplane IV replica
20		BAPC.194	Santos Dumont Type 20 Demoiselle replica
168		G-BFDE	Sopwith Tabloid Scout replica (Royal Navy Air Service)
304		BAPC.062	Cody Type V Biplane (Royal Flying Corps)
453		BAPC.107	Bleriot Type XXVII replica
471		BAPC.321	Royal Aircraft Factory BE.2c replica
687		**G-AWYI**	RAF BE.2c Replica (Royal Flying Corps)
687		BAPC.181	Royal Aircraft Factory BE.2b replica (Royal Flying Corps)
1264		**G-FDHB**	Bristol Scout Model C replica (Royal Navy Air Service)
1881		BAPC.122	Avro 504K fsm
2345		G-ATVP	Vickers FB.5 Gunbus replica (Royal Flying Corps)
2783		BAPC.332	Royal Aircraft Factory BE.2c replica (Royal Flying Corps)
3066		G-AETA	Caudron G.III (RNAS)
5964		BAPC.112	AirCo DH.2 fsm (Royal Flying Corps)
5964		**G-BFVH**	AirCo DH.2 (Royal Flying Corps)
6232		BAPC.041	Royal Aircraft Factory BE.2c replica (Royal Flying Corps)
8151		BAPC.137	Sopwith Baby fsm
9828		BAPC.042	Avro 504K replica
9917		**G-EBKY**	Sopwith Pup (Royal Flying Corps)
10000		BAPC.041	Royal Aircraft Factory BE.2c replica (Royal Flying Corps)
A126		**G-CILI***	Rep. Nieuport 11 (Royal Flying Corps)
A213		BAPC.467	Nieuport 17 replica
A653		BAPC.179	Sopwith Pup fsm (Royal Flying Corps)
A1452		BAPC.234	Vickers FB.5 Gunbus replica
A1742		BAPC.038	Bristol Scout D fsm (Royal Flying Corps) Corps)

Serial	Code	Regn	Type
A2767		**G-CJZP**	Royal Aircraft Factory BE.2 replica (Royal Flying Corps)
A2943		**G-CJZO**	Royal Aircraft Factory BE.2 replica (Royal Flying Corps)
A3930	B	ZK-TVC	Royal Aircraft Factory RE8 replica
A4850		BAPC.176	Royal Aircraft Factory SE.5a replica (Royal Flying Corps)
A4850		**G-AVOU**	Royal Aircraft Factory SE.5a replica
A6526		BAPC.400	Royal Aircraft Factory FE.2b replica
A7228	7	BAPC.387	Bristol F.2b fighter replica
A7288		BAPC.386	Bristol F.2b fighter replica
A8226		G-BIDW	Sopwith 1½ Strutter replica (Royal Flying Corps)
A8274		BAPC.413	Sopwith 1½ Strutter Cockpit replica
B/415		BAPC.163	AFEE 10/42 Rotabuggy reconstruction
B595	W	**G-BUOD**	SE.5A replica (Royal Flying Corps)
B619		BAPC.468	Sopwith 1½ Strutter replica
B1807	A7	**G-EAVX***	Sopwith Pup (Royal Flying Corps) – intended marks
B4863		BAPC.113	Royal Aircraft Factory SE.5a fsm
B5577	II-W	BAPC.059	Sopwith F1 Camel replica (Royal Flying Corps)
B6401		G-AWYY	Sopwith F1 Camel replica (Royal Flying Corps)
B7270		G-BFCZ	Sopwith F1 Camel replica (Royal Flying Corps)
C1096		**G-ERFC**	Royal Aircraft Factory SE.5a (RFC)
C1904	Z	**G-PFAP**	Royal Aircraft Factory SE.5a (Currie Wot) (RFC)
C3009	B	**G-BFWD**	Royal Aircraft Factory SE.5a (Currie Wot) (RFC)
C3011	S	**G-SWOT**	Royal Aircraft Factory SE.5a (Currie Wot) (RFC)
C3988		BAPC.353	Sopwith 5F1 Dolphin composite
C4451		BAPC.210	Avro 504J replica (Royal Flying Corps)
C4912		BAPC.135	Bristol 20 M.1C fsm
C4918		**G-BWJM**	Bristol 20 M.1C Monoplane replica
C4994		G-BLWM	Bristol 20 M.1C Monoplane replica
C5430	V	**G-CCXG**	Royal Aircraft Factory SE.5a replica (Royal Flying Corps)
C9533	M	**G-BUWE**	Royal Aircraft Factory SE.5a replica (Royal Flying Corps)
D1851	X	**G-BZSC**	Sopwith F1 Camel replica
D276	A	BAPC.208	Royal Aircraft Factory SE.5a replica (Royal Flying Corps)
D6447		BAPC.385	Sopwith F.1 Camel replica
D7343	17	ZK-TVD	Albatros D.Va Replica

Serial	Code	Reg/BAPC	Type
D7889		BAPC.166	Bristol F.2b Fighter
D8096	D	**G-AEPH**	Bristol F.2b Fighter (Royal Air Force)
E373		BAPC.178	Avro 504K fsm
E449		G-EBJE	Avro 504K
E2466		BAPC.165	Bristol F.2b Fighter
E2977		**G-EBHB**	Avro 504K
E3273		**G-ADEV**	Avro 504K (Royal Air Force)
E6655	B	BAPC.348	Sopwith 7F.1 Snipe replica
E8894		**G-CDLI**	Airco DH.9
F-141	G	**G-SEVA**	Royal Aircraft Factory SE.5a replica (Royal Flying Corps)
F235	B	G-BMDB	Royal Aircraft Factory SE.5a replica (Royal Flying Corps)
F2211			Sopwith 1½ Strutter replica (under construction)
F2367	1-2	G-CKBB	The Vintage Aviator Sopwith F7 Snipe Replica
F-4L		BAPC.260	Mignet HM.280 replica
F50		BAPC.329	Mignet HM.14 Pou-du-Ciel
F904		**G-EBIA**	Royal Aircraft Factory SE.5a replica (Royal Flying Corps)
F938		G-EBIC	Royal Aircraft Factory SE.5a replica (Royal Flying Corps)
F-943		**G-BIHF**	Royal Aircraft Factory SE.5a replica (Royal Flying Corps)
F943		G-BKDT	Royal Aircraft Factory SE.5a replica (Royal Flying Corps)
F5447	N	**G-BKER**	Royal Aircraft Factory SE.5a replica (Royal Flying Corps)
F5459	Y	**G-INNY**	Royal Aircraft Factory SE.5a replica (Royal Flying Corps)
F5459		BAPC.142	Royal Aircraft Factory SE.5a fsm
F5475	A	BAPC.250	Royal Aircraft Factory SE.5a replica (Royal Flying Corps)
F8010	Z	**G-BDWJ**	Royal Aircraft Factory SE.5a replica (Royal Flying Corps)
F8614		G-AWAU	Vickers FB.27A Vimy replica
J-7326		**G-EBQP**	de Havilland DH.53 Humming Bird (Royal Air Force)
J7904		BAPC.259	Gloster Gamecock replica
J9941		G-ABMR	Hawker Hart II
K158		BAPC.207	Austin Whippet fsm
K1786		**G-AFTA**	Hawker Tomtit (Royal Air Force)
K1926		BAPC.362	Hawker Fury replica
K2048		**G-BZNW**	Hawker (Isaacs) Fury II
K2050		**G-ASCM**	Hawker (Isaacs) Fury II
K2059		G-PFAR*	Hawker (Isaacs) Fury II
K2060		G-BKZM*	Hawker (Isaacs) Fury II
K2065		**G-AYJY**	Hawker (Isaacs) Fury II
K2075		**G-BEER**	Hawker (Isaacs) Fury II
K2227		G-ABBB	Bristol Bulldog IIA
K-2567		**G-MOTH**	de Havilland DH.82A Tiger Moth
K2572		**G-AOZH**	de Havilland DH.82A Tiger Moth
K-2585		**G-ANKT**	de Havilland DH.82A Tiger Moth
K2587		**G-BJAP**	de Havilland DH.82A Tiger Moth
K3241		**G-AHSA**	Avro Tutor
K3661	562	**G-BURZ**	Hawker Nimrod I
K3731		**G-RODI**	Hawker (Isaacs) Fury
K4232		SE-AZB	Cierva C.30A
K-4259	71	**G-ANMO**	de Havilland DH.82A Tiger Moth
K4556	F	BAPC.358	Boulton-Paul Overstrand Cockpit replica
K5054		G-BRDV	Supermarine Spitfire Prototype replica
K5054		BAPC.190	Supermarine Spitfire IX fsm
K5054		BAPC.214	Supermarine Spitfire fsm
K5054		BAPC.297	Supermarine Spitfire replica
K5414	XV	**G-AENP**	Hawker Afghan Hind
K5414		BAPC.078	Hawker Hind
K5673		BAPC.249	Hawker Fury I replica
K5673		**G-BZAS**	Hawker (Isaacs) Fury I
K5674		**G-CBZP**	Hawker Fury I
K5682	6	**G-BBVO**	Hawker Nimrod (Isaacs Fury)
K7271		BAPC.148	Hawker Fury fsm
K7271		**G-CCKV**	Hawker (Isaacs) Fury I
K7985		**G-AMRK**	Gloster Gladiator I
K8203		**G-BTVE**	Hawker Demon I
K8303	D	**G-BWWN**	Hawker (Isaacs) Fury
K9998	QJ-K	BAPC.431	Supermarine Spitfire fsm
L1019	LO-S	BAPC.308	Supermarine Spitfire I fsm
L1035	SH-D	BAPC.500	Supermarine Spitfire fsm
L1067	XT-D	BAPC.227	Supermarine Spitfire I fsm
L1639		BAPC.402	Hawker Hurricane I composite
L1679	JX-G	BAPC.241	Hawker Hurricane 1 fsm
L1684		BAPC.219	Hawker Hurricane IIc fsm
L2016	RN-E	BAPC.495	Supermarine Spitfire Vb fsm
L2301		G-AIZG	Supermarine Walrus 1 (Royal Navy)
L6739	YP-Q	**G-BPIV**	Bristol Blenheim Mk I
L6906		G-AKKY	Miles M.14A Magister
L6906		BAPC.044	Miles M.14A Magister composite
L7005	PS-B	BAPC.281	Boulton-Paul Defiant I fsm
M6394		BAPC.508	Sopwith F.1 Camel replica
N500		**G-BWRA**	Sopwith Triplane replica
N500		BAPC.510	Sopwith Triplane replica
N548		BAPC.164	Wight Quadraplane Type 1 fsm
N1854		G-AIBE	Fairey Fulmar 2 (Royal Navy)
N2078		BAPC.442	Sopwith Baby composite
N2532	GZ-H	BAPC.272	Hawker Hurricane I fsm
N3200	QV	**G-CFGJ**	Supermarine Spitfire 1
N3289	DW-K	BAPC.065	Supermarine Spitfire fsm
N3310	AI-A	BAPC.393	Supermarine Spitfire fsm
N3313	KL-B	BAPC.069	Supermarine Spitfire fsm
N3317	BO-U	BAPC.071	Supermarine Spitfire replica
N3549		**N3549**	de Havilland DH.82A Tiger Moth
N3788		**G-AKPF**	Miles M.14A Hawk Trainer
N4877	MK-V	G-AMDA	Avro 652A Anson 1
N5137		G-BNDW	de Havilland DH.82A Tiger Moth
N5177		BAPC.452	Sopwith 1 ½ Strutter replica
N5182		G-APUP	Sopwith Pup replica (Royal Navy Air Service)
N5195		**G-ABOX***	Sopwith Pup (Royal Navy Air Service)
N5199		G-BZND	Sopwith Pup replica
N5492	B	BAPC.111	Sopwith Triplane fsm (Royal Navy Air Service)
N5903		**G-GLAD**	Gloster Gladiator II
N6161		**G-ELRT**	Sopwith Pup replica (Royal Navy Air Service)
N6290		**G-BOCK**	Sopwith Triplane replica (Royal Navy Air Service)
N6377		**G-BPOB**	Sopwith F1 Camel replica (Royal Flying Corps)
N6452		G-BIAU	Sopwith Pup replica (Royal Navy Air Service)
N-6466		**G-ANKZ**	de Havilland DH.82A Tiger Moth
N6537		**G-AOHY**	de Havilland DH.82A Tiger Moth
N6720	VX	**G-BYTN**	de Havilland DH.82A Tiger Moth
N-6797		**G-ANEH**	de Havilland DH.82A Tiger Moth
N6847		**G-APAL**	de Havilland DH.82A Tiger Moth
N6965	FL-J	**G-AJTW***	de Havilland DH.82A Tiger Moth
N9190		BAPC.502	Short 184 replica
N-9192		**G-DHZF**	de Havilland DH.82A Tiger Moth
N9328	69	**G-ALWS**	de Havilland DH.82A Tiger Moth

Serial	Code	Reg/BAPC	Type
N-9389		G-ANJA	de Havilland DH.82A Tiger Moth
N9503	39	G-ANFP	de Havilland DH.82A Tiger Moth
P641		BAPC.123	Vickers FB.5 Gunbus replica
P2725	TM-B	BAPC.068	Hawker Hurricane I fsm
P2793	SD-M	BAPC.236	Hawker Hurricane IIc fsm
P2793	SD-M	BAPC.399	Hawker Hurricane IIc fsm
P2902	DX-R	G-ROBT	Hawker Hurricane I
P2921	GZ-L	G-CHTK	Hawker Sea Hurricane
P2921	GZ-L	BAPC.273	Hawker Hurricane I fsm
P2921	GZ-L	BAPC.477	Hawker Hurricane fsm
P2954	WX-E	BAPC.267	Hawker Hurricane I fsm
P2970	US-X	BAPC.291	Hawker Hurricane I fsm
P3059	SD-N	BAPC.064	Hawker Hurricane I fsm
P3208	SD-T	BAPC.063	Hawker Hurricane I fsm
P3679	GZ-K	BAPC.278	Hawker Hurricane I fsm
P3700	RF-E	G-HURI	Hawker Hurricane IIB
P3717	SW-P	G-HITT	Hawker Hurricane I
P3854		BAPC.073	Hawker Hurricane I fsm
P3873	YO-H	BAPC.265	Hawker Hurricane I fsm
P3873	YO-H	BAPC.499	Hawker Hurricane I fsm
P3901	RF-E	BAPC.475	Hawker Hurricane I fsm
P6382	C	G-AJRS	Miles Magister
P7308	XR-D	G-AIST	Supermarine Spitfire 1A
P7350	XT-D	G-AWIJ	Supermarine Spitfire F.IIA
P7370	ZP-A	BAPC.410	Supermarine Spitfire II fsm
P7666	EB-Z	BAPC.335	Supermarine Spitfire IIa fsm
P7923	RN-N	BAPC.369	Supermarine Spitfire fsm
P8448	UM-D	BAPC.225	Supermarine Spitfire IX fsm
P9398	KL-B	G-CEPL	Super Marine Spitfire Mk.26
P9637	GR-B	G-RORB*	Super Marine Spitfire Mk.26
R4118	UP-W	G-HUPW	Hawker Hurricane I
R4229	GN-J	BAPC.334	Hawker Hurricane fsm
R4922		G-APAO	de Havilland DH.82A Tiger Moth
(R-4959)	59	G-ARAZ	de Havilland DH.82A Tiger Moth
R-5136		G-APAP	de Havilland DH.82A Tiger Moth
R-5172	FIJE	G-AOIS	de Havilland DH.82A Tiger Moth
R5868	PO-S	BAPC.471	Avro 683 Lancaster cockpit replica
R6690	PR-A	BAPC.254	Supermarine Spitfire fsm
R6775	YT-J	BAPC.299	Supermarine Spitfire fsm
S1287	5	G-BEYB	Fairey Flycatcher replica (FAA)
S1581	573	G-BWWK	Hawker Nimrod 1 (FAA)
S1595		BAPC.156	Supermarine S.6B fsm
S1615		G-BMEU*	Isaacs Fury II
T-5854		G-ANKK	de Havilland DH.82A Tiger Moth
T-5879	RUC-W	G-AXBW	de Havilland DH.82A Tiger Moth
T-6953		G-ANNI	de Havilland DH.82A Tiger Moth
T7109		G-AOIM	de Havilland DH.82A Tiger Moth
T7281		G-ARTL	de Havilland DH.82A Tiger Moth
T7290	14	G-ANNK	de Havilland DH.82A Tiger Moth
T7793		G-ANKV*	de Havilland DH.82A Tiger Moth
T7794		G-ASPV	de Havilland DH.82A Tiger Moth
T-7842		G-AMTF	de Havilland DH.82A Tiger Moth
T7909		G-ANON	de Havilland DH.82A Tiger Moth
T-7997		G-AHUF	de Havilland DH.82A Tiger Moth
T8191		G-BWMK	de Havilland DH.82A Tiger Moth
T9707		G-AKKR	Miles M.14A Hawk Trainer
T9738		G-AKAT	Miles M.14A Hawk Trainer
V3388		G-AHTW	Airspeed Oxford 1V
V6555	DT-A	BAPC.411	Hawker Hurricane fsm
V6799	SD-X	BAPC.072	Hawker Hurricane I fsm
V7313	US-F	BAPC.346	Hawker Hurricane fsm
V7467	LE-D	BAPC.223	Hawker Hurricane IIc fsm
V7467	LE-D	BAPC.288	Hawker Hurricane I fsm
V7467	LE-D	BAPC.378	Hawker Hurricane IIc fsm
V7497	SD-X	G-HRLI	Hawker Hurricane IB
V9312	LX-E	G-CCOM	Westland Lysander IIIA
V9367	MA-B	G-AZWT	Westland Lysander IIIA
V9673	MA-J	G-LIZY	Westland Lysander III
V9875	MA-J	BAPC.371	Westland Lysander fsm
W2068	68	VH-ASM	Avro 652A Anson I
W2718	AA5Y	G-WLRS*	Vickers Supermarine Walrus (Royal Navy) – intended marks
W3644	QV-J	BAPC.323	Supermarine Spitfire Vb fsm
W3850	PR-A	BAPC.304	Supermarine Spitfire Vb fsm
W4041/G		BAPC.331	Gloster E28/39 fsm
W5856	A2A	G-BMGC	Fairey Swordfish II
W9385	YG-L	G-ADND	de Havilland DH.87B Hornet Moth
X4178	EB-K	BAPC.394	Supermarine Spitfire I fsm
X4253	FY-N	BAPC.326	Supermarine Spitfire II fsm
X4650	KL-A	G-CGUK	Supermarine Spitfire I
X4683	EB-N	G-MUTS	Jurca MJ.100 Spitfire – intended marks
X4859	PQ-N	BAPC.319	Supermarine Spitfire fsm
X9407		G-AFFD	Percival Type Q Six – intended marks
Z2033	N/275	G-ASTL	Fairey Firefly TT.1
Z3427	XP-G	BAPC.205	Hawker Hurricane IIc fsm
Z7015	7-L	G-BKTH	Hawker Sea Hurricane IB (Royal Navy)
Z7197		G-AKZN	Percival Proctor III
AB196		G-CCGH	Super Marine Spitfire Mk.26
AB910	SH-F	G-AISU	Supermarine Spitfire LF.Vb
AD370	PJ-C	G-CHBW	Jurca MJ.10 Spitfire (scale replica Spitfire)
AG244		G-CBOE	Hawker Hurricane
AJ841		G-BJST	CCF Harvard 4
AP507	KX-P	G-ACWP	Cierva C.30A
AR501	NN-A	G-AWII	Supermarine Spitfire Vc
BB803	75	G-ADWJ	de Havilland DH.82A Tiger Moth
BB807		G-ADWO	de Havilland DH.82A Tiger Moth
BE505	XP-L	G-HHII	Hawker Hurricane X
BL735	BT-A	G-HABT	Super Marine Spitfire Mk.26
BL924	AZ-G	BAPC.242	Supermarine Spitfire fsm
(BL927)	JH-I	G-CGWI	Super Marine Spitfire Mk.26 (wears code only)
BM361	XR-C	BAPC.269	Supermarine Spitfire V fsm
BM481	YO-T	BAPC.301	Supermarine Spitfire Vb fsm
BM597	JH-C	G-MKVB	Supermarine Spitfire Vb
BN230	FT-A	BAPC.218	Hawker Hurricane IIc fsm
BR954	JP-A	BAPC.220	Supermarine Spitfire IX fsm
BS239	5R-E	BAPC.222	Supermarine Spitfire IX fsm
BS306	AE-A	BAPC.530	Supermarine Spitfire IX 2/3 Scale replica
BS435	FY-F	BAPC.324	Supermarine Spitfire IXc fsm
DD931		BAPC.436	Bristol 152 Beaufort composite
DE-208		G-AGYU	de Havilland DH.82A Tiger Moth
DE-470		G-ANMY	de Havilland DH.82A Tiger Moth
DE623		G-ANFI	de Havilland DH.82A Tiger Moth
DE673		G-ADNZ	de Havilland DH.82A Tiger Moth
DE971		G-OOSY	de Havilland DH.82A Tiger Moth
DE974		G-ANZZ	de Havilland DH.82A Tiger Moth
DE-992		G-AXXV	de Havilland DH.82A Tiger Moth
DF112		G-ANRM	de Havilland DH.82A Tiger Moth
DF-128	RCO-U	G-AOJJ	de Havilland DH.82A Tiger Moth
DK791		BAPC.528	Fairey Swordfish replica
EE602	DV-V	G-IBSY	Supermarine Spitfire Vc
EM720		G-AXAN	de Havilland DH.82A Tiger Moth
EM726	FY	G-ANDE	de Havilland DH.82A Tiger Moth
EM840		G-ANBY	de Havilland DH.82A Tiger Moth

Misc

Serial	Code	Registration	Type
EM973		**G-ALNA**	de Havilland DH.82A Tiger Moth – intended marks
EN130	FN-A	**G-ENAA**	Super Marine Spitfire Mk.26B
EN398		BAPC.190	Supermarine Spitfire IX fsm
EN398	JE-J/WO-A	BAPC.184	Supermarine Spitfire IX fsm
EN398		BAPC.377	Supermarine Spitfire IX fsm
EN961	SD-X	**G-CGIK**	Isaacs Spitfire
EP120	AE-A	**G-LFVB**	Supermarine Spitfire Vb
EP121	LO-D	BAPC.320	Supermarine Spitfire Vb fsm
EV771		BAPC.294	Fairchild F-24W Argus II replica
FE511		**G-CIUW**	Noorduyn AT-16 Harvard IIB
FE695	94	**G-BTXI**	North American Harvard IIB
FF788		**G-CTKL**	Noorduyn AT-16 Harvard IIB
FE905		LN-BNM	North American Harvard IIB
FH153	58	**G-BBHK**	Noorduyn AT-16-ND Harvard IIB (RCAF c/s)
FJ662		**G-CRNL**	Fairchild M-62 Cornell
FJ801		BAPC.375	Boeing Stearman PT-27 Kaydet composite
FR886		**G-BDMS**	Piper L-4J
FS628		G-AIZE	Fairchild Argus
FT391		**G-AZBN**	North American Harvard IIB
FZ626	YS-DH	G-AMPO	Douglas Dakota 3
HB612		G-AJSN	Fairchild Argus
HB737		**G-BCBH**	Fairchild Argus
HB751		**G-BCBL**	Fairchild Argus
HG691		**G-AIYR**	de Havilland DH.89A Dragon Rapide
HH268		BAPC.261	General Aircraft GAL48 Hotspur composite
HJ711		BAPC.434	de Havilland DH.98 Mosquito composite
HM580	KX-K	G-ACUU	Cierva C.30A
IR106		BAPC.360	Eurofighter Typhoon FGR.4 fsm
IR808		BAPC.361	Boeing-Vertol CH-47 Chinook HC.2 fsm
JG241	ZX-J	**G-SMSP**	Super Marine Spitfire Mk.26
JG891	T-B	**G-LFVC**	Supermarine Spitfire F Vc
JK715	SN-A	BAPC.527	Supermarine Spitfire Vc fsm
JK769	AGM	BAPC.519	Supermarine Spitfire IX fsm
JP656	BR-SW	BAPC.526	Hawker Typhoon replica
JV579	F	**G-RUMW**	Grumman FM-2 Wildcat (FAA)
KB889	NA-I	G-LANC	Avro Lancaster X
KD345	130	**G-FGID**	Vought FG-1D Corsair (Royal Navy)
KF183		**G-CORS**	Noorduyn AT-16 Harvard IIB
KF402	HT-Y	**G-TEXN**	North American T-6G-NT Texan
KG651		G-AMHJ	Douglas C47 Dakota
KH774	GA-S	**G-SHWN**	North American P51D Mustang
KJ351		BAPC.080	Airspeed AS.58 Horsa II composite
KK116		**G-AMPY**	Douglas C-47B Dakota 6
KK527		**G-RGUS**	Fairchild Argus
KN353		G-AMYJ	Douglas C47 Dakota
LB264		G-AIXA	Taylorcraft Plus D (Auster I)
LB294		G-AHWJ	Taylorcraft Plus D (Auster I)
LB323		**G-AHSD**	Taylorcraft Plus D (Auster I) (Army Air Corps)
LB352		**G-AHCR**	Taylorcraft Plus D (Auster I)
LB367		**G-AHGZ**	Taylorcraft Plus D (Auster I)
LB375		**G-AHGW***	Taylorcraft Plus D (Auster I)
LF786	R2-K	BAPC.186	de Havilland DH.82B Queen Bee composite
LF858		**G-BLUZ**	de Havilland DH.82 Queen Bee
LH291		BAPC.279	Airspeed AS51 Horsa I replica
LS326	L 2	G-AJVH	Fairey Swordfish II
LV907	NP-F	BAPC.449	Handley Page HP.61 Halifax B.III composite

Serial	Code	Registration	Type
LZ766		G-ALCK	Percival Proctor III
LZ842	EF-F	**G-CGZU***	Supermarine Spitfire IX
MAV467	R-O	BAPC.202	Supermarine Spitfire IX fsm
MH314	SZ-G	BAPC.221	Supermarine Spitfire IX fsm
MH415	FU-N	BAPC.209	Supermarine Spitfire V fsm
MH434	ZD-B	**G-ASJV**	Supermarine Spitfire IXB
MH486	FT-E	BAPC.206	Supermarine Spitfire IX fsm
MH526	LO-D	**G-CJWW**	Super Marine Spitfire Mk.26
MJ627	9G-Q	**G-BMSB**	Supermarine Spitfire IX
MJ772	NL-R	**G-AVAV***	Supermarine Spitfire LF.IX
MJ832	DN-Y	BAPC.229	Supermarine Spitfire IX fsm
MK356		BAPC.298	Supermarine Spitfire IX fsm
MK805	SH-B	BAPC.426	Supermarine Spitfire IX fsm
MK912	SH-L	**G-BRRA**	Supermarine Spitfire IX
ML135	YO-D	BAPC.513	Supermarine Spitfire fsm
ML296	DU-N	BAPC.538	Supermarine Spitfire fsm
ML380		BAPC.224	Supermarine Spitfire IX fsm
ML407	OU-V	**G-LFIX***	Supermarine Spitfire TR.9
MP425		G-AITB	Airspeed Oxford I
MT166		**G-BICD**	Auster 5
MT182		**G-AJDY**	Auster J/1N
MT197		**G-ANHS**	Auster 4
MT438		**G-AREI**	Auster III
MT818		**G-AIDN**	Supermarine Spitfire VIII
MV268	JE-J	**G-SPIT**	Supermarine Spitfire XIVe
MW763	HF	**G-TEMT***	Hawker Tempest II
NF314		BAPC.408	BAe Systems Phoenix UAV composite
NH341	DB-E	**G-CICK**	Supermarine Spitfire LFIXE
NJ633		**G-AKXP**	Auster 5
NJ673		**G-AOCR**	Auster 5
NJ689		**G-ALXZ**	Auster 5
NJ695		**G-AJXV**	Auster 4
NJ703		**G-AKPI**	Auster 5
NJ719		G-ANFU	Auster 5
NJ728		**G-AIKE**	Auster 5
NJ889		**G-AHLK**	Taylorcraft Plus D
NL750		**G-AOBH**	de Havilland DH.82A Tiger Moth
NM138	41	**G-ANEW**	de Havilland DH.82A Tiger Moth
NM181		**G-AZGZ**	de Havilland DH.82A Tiger Moth
NP763	H7-N	BAPC.449	Handley Page HP.61 Halifax B.III composite
NX534		**G-BUDL**	Taylorcraft E Auster III
NX611	LE-H/DX-F	**G-ASXX***	Avro Lancaster B.VII
PD685		BAPC.355	Slingsby T.7 Cadet
PG657		**G-AGPK**	de Havilland DH.82A Tiger Moth
PK651	B-RAO	BAPC.301	Supermarine Spitfire Vb fsm
PL256	L-TM	BAPC.325	Supermarine Spitfire fsm
PL279	ZF-Z	BAPC.268	Supermarine Spitfire IX fsm
PL788		**G-CIEN**	Super Marine Spitfire Mk.26
PL793		**G-CIXM**	Super Marine Spitfire Mk.26
PL904		BAPC.226	Supermarine Spitfire PR.XI fsm
PL965	R	**G-MKXI**	Supermarine Spitfire PR.XI
PL983		**G-PRXI**	Supermarine Spitfire PR.XI
PP972	II-5	**G-BUAR**	Supermarine Seafire III (Royal Navy)
PR478			Super Marine Spitfire Mk.26 (under construction)
PS853	C	**G-RRGN**	Supermarine Spitfire PR.XIX
PT462	SW-A	**G-CTIX**	Supermarine Spitfire IX
PT462	SW-A	BAPC.318	Supermarine Spitfire fsm
PT879		**G-PTIX***	Supermarine Spitfire IX
PV202	5R-H	**G-CCCA**	Supermarine Spitfire Tr.IX
PV303	ON-B	**G-CCJL**	Super Marine Spitfire Mk.26
PZ865	JX-E	G-AMAU	Hawker Hurricane IIc
RB142	DW-B	**G-CEFC**	Super Marine Spitfire Mk.26

RG333		**G-AIEK**	Miles Messenger
RG904	BT-K	BAPC.333	Supermarine Spitfire II fsm
RG907		BAPC.514	Miles M.25 Martinet composite
RK838	GE	BAPC.230	Supermarine Spitfire IX fsm
RK855	FT-C	**G-PIXY**	Super Marine Spitfire Mk.26
RM221		**G-ANXR**	Percival Proctor IV
RR232		**G-BRSF**	Supermarine Spitfire HF.IXc
RT486	PF-A	**G-AJGJ**	Auster 5
RT610		**G-AKWS**	Auster 5A
RW382	3W-P	**G-PBIX**	Supermarine Spitfire LF.XVIe
SM520	KJ-I	**G-ILDA**	Supermarine Spitfire HF.IX
SM845	R	**G-BUOS**	Supermarine Spitfire XVIIIe
SR661	P	**G-CBEL**	Hawker Fury (Royal Navy)
SX336	VL-105	**G-KASX**	Supermarine Seafire F.XVII (Royal Navy)
TA634	8K-K	G-AWJV	de Havilland DH.98 Mosquito TT.35
TA719		G-ASKC	de Havilland DH.98 Mosquito TT.35
TA805	FX-M	**G-PMNF**	Supermarine Spitfire IX
TB885	3W-V	**G-CKUE**	Supermarine Spitfire LF.XVI
TB885		BAPC.476	Supermarine Spitfire cockpit replica
TD248	CR-S	**G-OXVI**	Supermarine Spitfire LF.XVIe
TD248	8Q-T	BAPC.368	Supermarine 361 Spitfire LF.XVIe replica
TD314	FX-P	**G-CGYJ**	Supermarine Spitfire HF.IX
TE184	YN-B	**G-MXVI**	Supermarine Spitfire XVI
TJ343		**G-AJXC**	Auster 5
TJ398		BAPC.070	Auster AOP.5
TJ518		**G-AJIH**	Auster 5
TJ534		**G-AKSY**	Auster 5
TJ565		**G-AMVD**	Auster 5
TJ569		G-AKOW	Auster 5
TJ672	DT-S	**G-ANIJ**	Auster 5
TS798		G-AGNV	Avro 685 York C.1
TW439		**G-ANRP**	Auster 5
TW467		**G-ANIE**	Auster 5
TW501		**G-ALBJ**	Auster 5
TW511		**G-APAF**	Auster 5 (Army Air Corps)
TW519	ROA-V	**G-ANHX**	Auster 5
TW536	T-SV	**G-BNGE**	Auster AOP.6
TW591	N	**G-ARIH**	Auster AOP.6 (Army Air Corps)
TW641		**G-ATDN**	Auster AOP.6 (Army Air Corps)
TX176		**G-AHKX**	Avro 19
TX310		**G-AIDL**	de Havilland DH.89A Dragon Rapide 6
TZ164	OI-A	**G-ISAC**	Isaacs Spitfire
VF512	PF-M	**G-ARRX**	Auster AOP.6
VF516		**G-ASMZ**	Auster AOP.6
VF526	T	**G-ARXU**	Auster AOP.6 (Army Air Corps)
VF557	H	**G-ARHM**	Auster AOP.6 (Army Air Corps)
VF581	G	**G-ARSL**	Auster AOP.6 (Army Air Corps)
VL348		G-AVVO	Avro Anson C.19 Series 2
VL349	V7-Q	G-AWSA	Avro Anson C.19 Series 2
VM360		G-APHV	Avro Anson C.19 Series 2
VN799		G-CDSX	English Electric Canberra T.Mk.4 (Prototype)
VP955		**G-DVON**	de Havilland DH.104 Devon C.2/2
VP967		G-KOOL	de Havilland DH.104 Devon C.2/2
VP981		**G-DHDV**	de Havilland DH.104 Devon C.2/2
VR192		G-APIT	Percival Prentice T.1
VR249	FA-EL	G-APIY	Percival Prentice T.1
VR259	M	**G-APJB**	Percival Prentice T.1
VS618		G-AOLK	Percival Prentice T.1
VS623		G-AOKZ	Percival Prentice T.1
VV612		G-VENI	de Havilland DH.112 Venom FB.1

VW993		G-ASCD	Beagle A.61 Terrier 2 (Auster AOP.6)
VX113	36	**G-ARNO**	Auster AOP.6 (Army Air Corps)
VX281	120 VL	**G-RNHF**	Hawker Sea Fury T.20 (Royal Navy)
VX924		**G-NTVE**	Beagle A 61 Terrier 2 (Army Air Corps)
VX927		**G-ASYG**	Beagle A 61 Terrier 2 (Army Air Corps)
VZ345		**G-VZSF***	Hawker Sea Fury T.20 (Royal Navy)
VZ638		G-JETM	Gloster Meteor T.7 (RN and FRU)
VZ728		**G-AGOS**	Reid and Sigrist Trainer
WA577		G-ALST	Bristol Sycamore 3
WA638		**G-JWMA**	Gloster Meteor T.7
WB188		G-BZPC	Hawker Hunter GA.Mk.11 (all red c/s)
WB549		**G-BAPB***	de Havilland DHC-1 Chipmunk T.10
WB565	X	**G-PVET**	de Havilland DHC-1 Chipmunk T.10 (Army Air Corps)
WB569	R	**G-BYSJ**	de Havilland DHC-1 Chipmunk T.10
WB585	M	**G-AOSY**	de Havilland DHC-1 Chipmunk T.10
WB588	D	**G-AOTD**	de Havilland DHC-1 Chipmunk T.10
WB615	E	**G-BXIA**	de Havilland DHC-1 Chipmunk T.10 (Army Air Corps)
WB654	U	**G-BXGO**	de Havilland DHC-1 Chipmunk T.10 (Army Air Corps)
WB671	910	**G-BWTG**	de Havilland DHC-1 Chipmunk T.10 (Royal Navy)
WB697	95	**G-BXCT**	de Havilland DHC-1 Chipmunk T.10
WB702		**G-AOFE**	de Havilland DHC-1 Chipmunk T.10
WB703		**G-ARMC**	de Havilland DHC-1 Chipmunk T.10
WB711		**G-APPM**	de Havilland DHC-1 Chipmunk T.10
WB721		**G-CMNK***	de Havilland DHC-1 Chipmunk T.10
WB726	E	**G-AOSK**	de Havilland DHC-1 Chipmunk T.10
WB763	K	**G-BBMR**	de Havilland DHC-1 Chipmunk T.10
WD286		**G-BBND**	de Havilland DHC-1 Chipmunk T.10
WD292		**G-BCRX**	de Havilland DHC-1 Chipmunk T.10
WD310	B	**G-BWUN**	de Havilland DHC-1 Chipmunk T.10
WD331		**G-BXDH**	de Havilland DHC-1 Chipmunk T.10
WD363	5	**G-BCIH**	de Havilland DHC-1 Chipmunk T.10
WD373	12	**G-BXDI**	de Havilland DHC-1 Chipmunk T.10
WD390	68	**G-BWNK**	de Havilland DHC-1 Chipmunk T.10
WD413		**G-VROE**	Avro 652A Anson T.21
WE569		**G-ASAJ**	Beagle Terrier (Auster A.7) (Army Air Corps)
WE987		BGA2517	Slingsby T.30B Prefect
WF118		G-DACA	Percival P.57 Sea Prince T.1
WG308	8	**G-BYHL**	de Havilland DHC-1 Chipmunk T.10
WG316		**G-BCAH**	de Havilland DHC-1 Chipmunk T.10
WG321	G	**G-DHCC**	de Havilland DHC-1 Chipmunk T.10 (Army Air Corps)
WG322	H	**G-ARMF**	de Havilland DHC-1 Chipmunk T.10
WG348		**G-BBMV**	de Havilland DHC-1 Chipmunk T.10
WG350		**G-BPAL**	de Havilland DHC-1 Chipmunk T.10
WG407	67	**G-BWMX**	de Havilland DHC-1 Chipmunk T.10
WG422	16	**G-BFAX**	de Havilland DHC-1 Chipmunk T.10
WG458	2	N458BG	de Havilland DHC-1 Chipmunk T.10
WG465		**G-BCEY**	de Havilland DHC-1 Chipmunk T.10
WG472		**G-AOTY**	de Havilland DHC-1 Chipmunk T.10
WG599	161/R	**G-SEAF***	Hawker Sea Fury T20 (Royal Navy) – intended marks
WG655	GN/910	**G-INVN**	Hawker Sea Fury T20 (composite) (Royal Navy)
WG719		G-BRMA	Westland Dragonfly HR.5
WJ358		G-ARYD	Auster AOP.6 (Army Air Corps)
WJ368		**G-ASZX**	Beagle Terrier
WJ404		**G-ASOI**	Beagle Terrier
WJ945	21	G-BEDV	Vickers Varsity T.1
WK126	843	N2138J	English Electric Canberra TT.18

Misc

WK163		**G-CTTS**	English Electric Canberra B.2	WR421		G-DHTT	de Havilland DH.112 Venom FB.1
WK436		G-VENM	de Havilland Venom FB.50	WR470		G-DHVM	de Havilland DH.112 Venom FB.1
WK512	A	**G-BXIM**	de Havilland DHC-1 Chipmunk T.10 (Army Air Corps)	WR963	B-M	**G-SKTN***	Avro 696 Shackleton MR Mk2
				WT333		G-BVXC	English Electric Canberra B(I).8 (Royal Aircraft Est)
WK514		**G-BBMO**	de Havilland DHC-1 Chipmunk T.10				
WK517		**G-ULAS**	de Havilland DHC-1 Chipmunk T.10	WT722	878:VL	G-BWGN	Hawker Hunter T.8C (Royal Navy)
WK522		**G-BCOU**	de Havilland DHC-1 Chipmunk T.10	WT723	692:LM	**G-PRII**	Hawker Hunter PR.11 (Royal Navy)
WK549		**G-BTWF**	de Havilland DHC-1 Chipmunk T.10	WT933		G-ALSW	Bristol 171 Sycamore 3
WK558	DH	**G-ARMG**	de Havilland DHC-1 Chipmunk T.10	WV198	K	G-BJWY	Sikorsky Whirlwind HAR.21
WK577		**G-BCYM**	de Havilland DHC-1 Chipmunk T.10	WV256		G-BZPB	Hawker Hunter GA.Mk.11
WK585		**G-BZGA**	de Havilland DHC-1 Chipmunk T.10	WV318	D	**G-FFOX**	Hawker Hunter T.7B
WK586	V	**G-BXGX**	de Havilland DHC-1 Chipmunk T.10 (Army Air Corps)	WV322	Y	**G-BZSE**	Hawker Hunter T.11
				WV493	29:A-P	G-BDYG	Percival Provost T.1
WK590	69	**G-BWVZ**	de Havilland DHC-1 Chipmunk T.10	WV499	P-G	**G-BZRF***	Hunting Percival P.56 Provost T.1
WK609	93	**G-BXDN**	de Havilland DHC-1 Chipmunk T.10	WV514	CN	**G-BLIW**	Percival Provost T.51
WK611		**G-ARWB**	de Havilland DHC-1 Chipmunk T.10	WV740		**G-BNPH**	Hunting Percival Pembroke C.1
WK624		**G-BWHI**	de Havilland DHC-1 Chipmunk T.10	WV783		G-ALSP	Bristol 171 Sycamore 3
WK628		**G-BBMW**	de Havilland DHC-1 Chipmunk T.10	WW421	P-B	G-BZRE	Hunting Percival Provost T.1
WK630		**G-BXDG**	de Havilland DHC-1 Chipmunk T.10	WZ507	74	**G-VTII**	de Havilland DH.115 Vampire T.11
WK633	B	**G-BXEC***	de Havilland DHC-1 Chipmunk T.10	WZ584	K	G-BZRC	de Havilland DH.115 Vampire T.11
WK634	902	**G-CIGE**	de Havilland DHC-1 Chipmunk T.10	WZ662		**G-BKVK**	Auster AOP.9 (Army Air Corps)
WK635		**G-HFRH**	de Havilland DHC-1 Chipmunk 22(Royal Navy)	WZ679		**G-CIUX**	Auster AOP.9 (Army Air Corps) – intended marks
WK640		**G-CERD**	de Havilland DHC-1 Chipmunk 22	WZ706		**G-BURR**	Auster AOP.9 (Army Air Corps)
WK642		**EI-AFZ**	de Havilland DHC-1 Chipmunk 22	WZ711		G-AVHT	Auster AOP.9 (Army Air Corps)
WL419		**G-JSMA**	Gloster Meteor T7	WZ847	F	**G-CPMK**	de Havilland DHC-1 Chipmunk T.10
WL626	P	G-BHDD	Vickers Varsity T.1	WZ872	E	**G-BZGB**	de Havilland DHC-1 Chipmunk T.10
WM167		**G-LOSM**	Armstrong-Whitworth Meteor NF.11	WZ879	X	**G-BWUT**	de Havilland DHC-1 Chipmunk T.10
WP266		BAPC.423	EoN AP.5 Primary	WZ882	K	**G-BXGP**	de Havilland DHC-1 Chipmunk T.10 (Army Air Corps)
WP308	572	G-GACA	Hunting Percival P.57 Sea Prince T.1	XA880		G-BVXR	de Havilland DH.104 Devon C.2 (RAE)
WP321		**G-BRFC***	Hunting Percival P.57 Sea Prince T.1	XB259		G-AOAI	Blackburn Beverley C.1
				XD693	Z-Q	**G-AOBU***	Percival Jet Provost T.1
WP788		**G-BCHL**	de Havilland DHC-1 Chipmunk T.10	XE489		G-JETH	Armstrong-Whitworth Sea Hawk FGA.6
WP790	T	G-BBNC	de Havilland DHC-1 Chipmunk T.10				
WP795	901	**G-BVZZ**	de Havilland DHC-1 Chipmunk T.10 (Royal Navy)	XE665	876:VL	G-BWGM	Hawker Hunter T.8C (Royal Navy)
WP800	2	**G-BCXN**	de Havilland DHC-1 Chipmunk T.10	XE685	871:VL	**G-GAII**	Hawker Hunter T.8C (Royal Navy)
WP803		**G-HAPY**	de Havilland DHC-1 Chipmunk T.10	XE707	865	G-BVYH	Hawker Hunter GA.11 (Royal Navy)
WP805		**G-MAJR**	de Havilland DHC-1 Chipmunk T.10	XE856		G-DUSK	de Havilland DH.115 Vampire T.11
WP809	78	**G-BVTX**	de Havilland DHC-1 Chipmunk T.10 (Royal Navy)	XE956		**G-OBLN***	de Havilland DH.115 Vampire T.11
WP811		**G-BCKN**	de Havilland DHC-1 Chipmunk T.10	XF114		G-SWIF	Supermarine Swift
WP844		G-BWOX	de Havilland DHC-1 Chipmunk T.10	XF375	6	G-BUEZ	Hawker Hunter F.6A (ETPS)
WP848		**G-BFAW**	de Havilland DHC-1 Chipmunk T.10	XF597	AH	**G-BKFW**	Percival Provost T.1
WP860	6	**G-BXDA**	de Havilland DHC-1 Chipmunk T.10	XF603		**G-KAPW**	Percival Provost T.1
WP870	12	**G-BCOI**	de Havilland DHC-1 Chipmunk T.10	XF690		**G-MOOS**	Percival Provost T.1
WP896		**G-BWVY**	de Havilland DHC-1 Chipmunk T.10	XF785		G-ALBN	Bristol 173 Mk.1
WP901	B	**G-BWNT**	de Havilland DHC-1 Chipmunk T.10	XF836		**G-AWRY***	Percival Provost T.1
WP903		**G-BCGC**	de Havilland DHC-1 Chipmunk T.10 (Queens Flight)	XF994	873:VL	**G-CGHU***	Hawker Hunter T.8C (Royal Navy)
				XG160	U	G-BWAF	Hawker Hunter F.6A
WP925	C	**G-BXHA**	de Havilland DHC-1 Chipmunk T.10 (Army Air Corps)	XG452		G-BRMB	Bristol Belvedere HC.1
				XG588		G-BAMH	Westland S-55 Whirlwind
WP928	D	**G-BXGM**	de Havilland DHC-1 Chipmunk T.10 (Army Air Corps)	XH134		**G-OMHD**	English Electric Canberra PR.9
WP929		**G-BXCV**	de Havilland DHC-1 Chipmunk T.10	XH313	E	G-BZRD	de Havilland DH.115 Vampire T.11
WP930	J	**G-BXHF**	de Havilland DHC-1 Chipmunk T.10 (Army Air Corps)	XH558		G-VLCN	Avro Vulcan B.2
				XJ389		G-AJJP	Fairey Jet Gyrodyne
WP964		**G-HDAE**	de Havilland DHC-1 Chipmunk T.10 (Army Air Corps)	XJ729		**G-BVGE**	Westland Whirlwind HAR.10
				XK417		**G-AVXY***	Auster AOP.9
WP971		**G-ATHD**	de Havilland DHC-1 Chipmunk T.10	XK895	CU-19	G-SDEV	de Havilland DH.104 Sea Devon C.20 (Royal Navy)
WP973		**G-BCPU**	de Havilland DHC-1 Chipmunk T.10				
WP983	B	**G-BXNN**	de Havilland DHC-1 Chipmunk T.10 (Army Air Corps)	XK940		G-AYXT	Westland Whirlwind HAS.7
				XL426		**G-VJET***	Avro Vulcan B.2
WP984	H	**G-BWTO**	de Havilland DHC-1 Chipmunk T.10	XL500		**G-KAEW***	Fairey Gannet AEW.3 – intended marks
WR360	K	G-DHSS	de Havilland DH.112 Venom FB.1				
WR410		G-DHUU	de Havilland DH.112 Venom FB.1	XL502		G-BMYP	Fairey Gannet AEW.3 (Royal Navy)

Misc

XL571	V	G-HNTR	Hawker Hunter T.7 (Blue Diamonds c/s)		XT420	606	**G-CBUI**	Westland Wasp HAS.1 (Royal Navy)
XL573		**G-BVGH**	Hawker Hunter T.7		XT434	455	**G-CGGK***	Westland Wasp HAS.1 (Royal Navy)
XL602		**G-BWFT***	Hawker Hunter T.7		XT435	430	**G-RIMM**	Westland Wasp HAS.1 (Royal Navy)
XL714		**G-AOGR**	de Havilland DH.82A Tiger Moth		XT626		**G-CIBW**	Westland Scout AH.1 (Army Air Corps)
XL809		**G-BLIX**	Saro Skeeter AOP.12 (Army Air Corps)		XT630		G-BXRL	Westland Scout AH.1 (Army Air Corps)
XL812		G-SARO	Saro Skeeter AOP.12		XT787		**G-KAXT**	Westland Wasp HAS.1 (Royal Navy)
XL954		**G-BXES**	Percival Pembroke C.1		XT788	474	G-BMIR	Westland Wasp HAS.1 (Royal Navy)
XM365		G-BXBH	Hunting Jet Provost T.3A		XT793		G-BZPP	Westland Wasp HAS.1 (Royal Navy)
XM424	1FTS	**G-BWDS**	Hunting Jet Provost T.3A		XV130	R	G-BWJW	Westland Scout AH.1 (Army Air Corps)
XM479	54	**G-BVEZ**	Hunting Jet Provost T.3A		XV137		**G-CRUM**	Westland Scout AH.1 (Army Air Corps)
XM496		G-BDUP	Bristol 175 Britannia		XV138		**G-SASM**	Westland Scout AH.1 (Army Air Corps)
XM553		G-AWSV	Saro Skeeter AOP.12					
XM575		G-BLMC	Avro Vulcan B.2A		XV268		G-BVER	de Havilland DHC.2 Beaver (Army Air Corps)
XM655		G-VULC	Avro Vulcan B.2A		XV281		BAPC.484	British Aerospace Harrier composite
XM685	PO:513	G-AYZJ	Westland Whirlwind HAS.7					
XM697		G-NAAT	Folland Gnat		XW283		**G-CIMX**	Westland Scout AH.1 (Army Air Corps)
XM819		G-APXW	Lancashire Aircraft EP.9 (Army Air Corps)		XW289	73	G-JPVA	BAC Jet Provost T.5A
XN332	759	G-APNV	Saunders-Roe P.531-1		XW293	Z	**G-BWCS***	BAC Jet Provost T.5
XN351		G-BKSC	Saro Skeeter AOP12		XW324	U	**G-BWSG**	BAC Jet Provost T.5
XN441		**G-BGKT**	Auster AOP.9 (Army Air Corps)		XW325	E	**G-BWGF**	BAC Jet Provost T.5A
XN459		**G-BWOT**	Hunting Jet Provost T.3A		XW333		**G-BVTC**	BAC Jet Provost T.5A
XN629		G-KNOT	Hunting Jet Provost T.3A		XW354		**G-JPTV**	BAC Jet Provost T.5A (Poachers c/s)
XN637		**G-BKOU**	Hunting Percival P.84 Jet Provost T.3		XW422		**G-BWEB**	BAC Jet Provost T.5A
XP241		**G-CEHR**	Auster AOP.9 (Army Air Corps)		XW423	14	G-BWUW	BAC Jet Provost T.5A
XP254		**G-ASCC**	Auster AOP.11 (Army Air Corps)		XW433		**G-JPRO**	BAC Jet Provost T.5A (CFS)
XP279		G-BWKK	Auster AOP9		XW612		**G-KAXW**	Westland Scout AH.1 (Army Air Corps)
XP355	A	G-BEBC	Westland Whirlwind HAR.10		XW613		**G-BXRS**	Westland Scout AH.1 (Army Air Corps)
XP672	03	G-RAFI	Hunting Jet Provost T.4					
XP820		**G-CICP**	de Havilland DHC-2 Beaver AL.1 (Army Air Corps)		XW635		**G-AWSW**	Beagle Husky
XP883		G-BYNZ	Westland Scout AH.1 (Composite)		XW784	VL	**G-BBRN***	Mitchell-Procter Kittiwake (Royal Navy)
XP907		**G-SROE**	Westland Scout AH.1 (Army Air Corps)		XW851		**G-CIEY***	Westland SA.341 Gazelle AH.1
XP924	134	**G-CVIX**	de Havilland DH.110 Sea Vixen D.3 (Royal Navy)		XW858	C	**G-ONNE**	Westland SA.341 Gazelle HT.3
XR240		**G-BDFH**	Auster AOP.9 (Army Air Corps)		XW892		**G-CGJX***	Westland SA.341 Gazelle AH.1
XR241		**G-AXRR**	Auster AOP.9 (Army Air Corps)		XX110		BAPC.169	Sepecat Jaguar GR.1 fsm
XR244		**G-CICR**	Auster AOP.9 (Army Air Corps)		XX227		BAPC.152	BAe Hawk T.1A fsm
XR246		**G-AZBU**	Auster AOP.9 (RAE Radio Flight)		XX308		BAPC.171	BAe Hawk T.1 fsm
XR267		**G-BJXR**	Auster AOP.9 (Army Air Corps)		XX386		**G-KEMH***	Westland SA.341D Gazelle AH.1
XR442		G-HRON	de Havilland DH114 Heron 2B		XX406	P	G-CBSH	Westland SA.341D Gazelle HT.3
XR486		G-RWWW	Westland Whirlwind HCC.12 (Queens Flight)		XX436	CU-39	**G-ZZLE**	Westland SA.341C Gazelle HT.2 (Royal Navy)
XR537		G-NATY	Folland Gnat T.1		XX467	86	G-TVII	Hawker Hunter T.7 (TWU)
XR538	01	**G-RORI**	Folland Gnat T.1 (Training c/s)		XX475		G-AWVJ	Handley Page 137 Jetstream 1
XR595	M	**G-BWHU**	Westland Scout AH.1 (Army Air Corps)		XX513	10	**G-KKKK**	Scottish Aviation Bulldog
XR673		**G-BXLO**	Hunting Jet Provost T.4		XX515	4	**G-CBBC**	Scottish Aviation Bulldog
XR724		G-BTSY	English Electric Lightning F.6		XX518	S	**G-UDOG**	Scottish Aviation Bulldog
XR944		**G-ATTB**	Wallis WA.116		XX521	H	**G-CBEH**	Scottish Aviation Bulldog
XR992		**G-MOUR**	Folland Gnat T.1 (Yellowjacks c/s)		XX522	06	**G-DAWG**	Scottish Aviation Bulldog
XR993		G-BVPP	Folland Gnat T.1 (Red Arrows c/s)		XX524	04	**G-DDOG**	Scottish Aviation Bulldog
XS104		**G-FRCE***	Folland Gnat T.1		XX528	D	**G-BZON**	Scottish Aviation Bulldog
XS235		G-CPDA	de Havilland DH.106 Comet 4C		XX534	B	**G-EDAV**	Scottish Aviation Bulldog
XS587		G-VIXN	de Havilland DH.110 Sea Vixen FAW.2 (Royal Navy)		XX537	C	**G-CBCB**	Scottish Aviation Bulldog
XS921	BA	BAPC.357	BAC Lightning F.6 fsm		XX538	O	**G-TDOG**	Scottish Aviation Bulldog
XT005		BAPC.365	Northrop MQM-36 Shelduck SD-1 UAV replica		XX546	03	**G-WINI**	Scottish Aviation Bulldog
					XX549	6	**G-CBID**	Scottish Aviation Bulldog
XT131		**G-CICN**	Westland Sioux AH.1 (Army Air Corps)		XX550	Z	**G-CBBL**	Scottish Aviation Bulldog
					XX551	E	**G-BZDP**	Scottish Aviation Bulldog
XT223		**G-XTUN**	Westland Sioux AH.1 (Army Air Corps)		XX561	7	**G-BZEP**	Scottish Aviation Bulldog
					XX611	7	**G-CBDK**	Scottish Aviation Bulldog

XX612	A:03	G-BZXC	Scottish Aviation Bulldog
XX614	1	**G-GGRR**	Scottish Aviation Bulldog
XX619	T	**G-CBBW**	Scottish Aviation Bulldog
XX621	H	**G-CBEF**	Scottish Aviation Bulldog
XX622	B	**G-CBGX**	Scottish Aviation Bulldog
XX624	E	**G-KDOG**	Scottish Aviation Bulldog
XX625	45	**G-UWAS**	Scottish Aviation Bulldog
XX626	W:02	**G-CDVV**	Scottish Aviation Bulldog
XX628	9	**G-CBFU**	Scottish Aviation Bulldog
XX629		**G-BZXZ**	Scottish Aviation Bulldog
XX630	25	**G-SIJW**	Scottish Aviation Bulldog
XX631	W	**G-BZXS**	Scottish Aviation Bulldog
XX636	Y	**G-CBFP**	Scottish Aviation Bulldog
XX638		**G-DOGG**	Scottish Aviation Bulldog
XX667	16	**G-BZFN**	Scottish Aviation Bulldog
XX668	I	**G-CBAN**	Scottish Aviation Bulldog
XX692	A	**G-BZMH***	Scottish Aviation Bulldog
XX693	07	**G-BZML**	Scottish Aviation Bulldog
XX694	E	**G-CBBS**	Scottish Aviation Bulldog
XX695	3	**G-CBBT**	Scottish Aviation Bulldog
XX698	9	**G-BZME**	Scottish Aviation Bulldog
XX700	17	**G-CBEK**	Scottish Aviation Bulldog
XX702		**G-CBCR**	Scottish Aviation Bulldog
(XX704)		**G-BCUV**	Scottish Aviation Bulldog
XX707	4	G-CBDS	Scottish Aviation Bulldog
XX725	GU	BAPC.150	Sepecat Jaguar GR.1 fsm
XX824		BAPC.151	Sepecat Jaguar GR.1A fsm
XX885		**G-HHAA**	Hawker Siddeley Buccaneer S.2B
XZ321	D	**G-CDNS***	Westland SA.341 Gazelle AH.1 (Army Air Corps)
XZ329	J	**G-BZYD**	Westland SA.341 Gazelle AH.1 (Army Air Corps)
XZ345	T	G-SFTA	Westland SA.341G Gazelle 1 (Army Air Corps)
XZ597		**G-SKNG***	Westland Sea King HAR3
XZ933		**G-CGJZ**	Westland SA.341C Gazelle HT3
XZ934	U	**G-CBSI**	Westland SA.341C Gazelle HT.2 (Royal Navy)
XZ995	3G	G-CBGK	British Aerospace Harrier GR3
ZA556	Z	BAPC.155	Panavia Tornado GR.1 fsm
ZA630		**G-BUGL***	Slingsby T.61F Venture T.2
ZA634	C	**G-BUHA**	Slingsby T.61F Venture T.2
ZA652		**G-BUDC**	Slingsby T.61F Venture T.2
ZA656		**G-BTWC**	Slingsby T.61F Venture T.2
ZA730		**G-FUKM***	Westland SA.314G Gazelle AH.1
ZB500		G-LYNX	Westland Lynx 800 (Army Air Corps)
ZB627	A	**G-CBSK**	Westland SA.314G Gazelle HT.3
ZB647	40	**G-CBSF***	Westland SA.314G Gazelle HT.2
ZB682		**G-CIEX***	Westland Gazelle AH.1
ZH139	01	BAPC.191	BAe Harrier GR.5 replica
ZH763		G-BGKE	BAC One Eleven 539GL (ETPS)
ZZ194		**G-HHAC**	Hawker Hunter F.58
8449M		G-ASWJ	Beagle B.206
	AR-B	**G-SOCT***	Yakovlev Yak-52

"B" Conditions markings

G-17-3	G-AVNE	Westland Wessex 60
G-29-1	G-APRJ	Avro Lincoln B.2 (Fuselage only)
U-0247	G-AGOY	Miles M.38 Messenger – intended marks
W-2	BAPC.085	Weir W-2 Helicopter
X-25	BAPC.274	Boulton-Paul P.6 replica

Other markings

SR-XP020	**G-BZUG**	TLAC RL7A XP Sherwood Ranger

OTHER ARMED FORCES

AUSTRALIA

A2-4		VH-ALB	Supermarine Seagull
A11-301	931	**G-ARKG**	Auster J5G Cirrus Autocar
A16-199	SF-R	G-BEOX	Lockheed Hudson IIIA
A17-48	48	**G-BPHR**	DH.82A Tiger Moth
A17-376		**G-ANJI***	DH.82A Tiger Moth
A58-492		BAPC.457	Supermarine Spitfire VIII fsm
A92-466		BAPC.485	Government Aircraft Factory Jindivik Mk.103A composite

BELGIUM

66	BAPC.019	Bristol F2b Fighter (fuselage frame)

BURKINA FASO

BF8431	31	**G-NRRA**	SIAI-Marchetti SF.260W

CANADA

622		N6699D	Piasecki HUP-3 Retreiver (RCN)
671		**G-BNZC**	de Havilland DHC-1 Chipmunk
920	Q-N	CF-BXO	Supermarine Stranraer
3091		**G-CPPM**	North American Harvard II
3349		**G-BYNF**	North American NA-64 Yale I
5084		**G-FCTK**	de Havilland DH.82C Tiger Moth – intended marks
16693	693	**G-BLPG**	Auster J/1N (AOP.6 c/s)
18393		G-BCYK	Avro Canada CF.100 Canuck IV
FE992	ER-992	**G-BDAM**	North American Harvard II

PEOPLES' REPUBLIC OF CHINA

68 Red		**G-BVVG**	Nanchang CJ-6A (Chinese AF)
72 White		**G-CGFS***	Nanchang CJ-6A (Chinese AF)
61367	37	**G-CGHB***	Nanchang CJ-6A (Chinese AF)

FINLAND

HC-465	**G-BYDL***	Hawker Hurricane – intended marks

FRANCE

7		**G-NORD**	SNCAC NC.854 (Armée de l'Air)
7		**G-BMZX**	SPAD replica (Wolf W.II)
10		**G-BPVE***	Bleriot 1909 Type XI Replica
19		BAPC.136	Deperdussin 1913 Monoplane fsm
54	AOM	**G-CGWR**	SNCAC NC.856A (Armée de l'Air)
78		**G-BIZK**	Nord 3202 (Air Force)
82 X881	8	**G-CCVH**	Curtiss H75A-1
143		**G-MSAL**	Morane-Saulnier MS.733 (Aéronavale)
154	315-SM	F-GKRO	Max Holste Broussard
156		**G-NIFE***	Stampe SV-4A (Air Force)
164		BAPC.106	Bleriot Type XI replica
208	IR	**G-YYYY**	Max Holste Broussard
(255)	5-ML	**G-CIGH**	Max Holste Broussard
351	HY-22	**G-MOSA**	Morane Saulnier MS.317 (Navy)
354		**G-BZNK**	Morane Saulnier MS.315E (Air Force)
5191		BAPC.472	Morane-Saulnier N replica
24541	BMG	**G-JDOG**	Cessna O-1E Bird Dog (ALAT)
54513	1	G-BFYO	SPAD XIII replica
181391	AN-R	**G-BHOM**	Piper L-18C Super Cub (ALAT)
18-5395	CDG	**G-CUBJ**	Piper L-18C Super Cub (ALAT)
MS.824		**G-AWBU***	Morane-Saulnier N replica (Air Force)
N856		**G-CDWE***	SNCAC NC.856A (Armée de l'Air)
N1977	8	**G-BWMJ**	Nieuport Scout 17/23 replica (French AF)
XC		**G-BSYO**	Piper L-4B-PI (Armée de l'Air)

GERMANY

1		**G-WULF**	WAR FW190 scale replica
2+1	7334	**G-SYFW**	WAR FW190 scale replica
4+1		**G-BSLX**	WAR FW190 scale replica
– + 9		**G-CCFW**	WAR FW190 scale replica
6 (Yellow)		BAPC.376	Messerschmitt Bf.109E-4 fsm
7 (Yellow)		**G-AWHM**	Hispano HA.1112-MIL Buchon
9 (White)		**G-AWHH**	Hispano HA.1112-MIL Buchon
10 (Yellow)		**G-AWHK***	Hispano HA.1112-MIL Buchon
11 (Red)		**G-AWHC**	Hispano HA.1112-MIL Buchon
14		BAPC.067	Messerschmitt Bf.109G fsm
14 (White)	3579	**G-CIPB**	Messerschmitt Bf.109
14 (yellow)		**G-ETME**	Nord 1002 Pingouin
102/17		BAPC.088	Fokker Dr.1 ⅝th scale model (German Army Air Service)
105/15		**G-UDET**	Fokker E-III replica (German Army Air Service)
107/15		**G-AVJO***	Fokker E-III replica (German Army Air Service)
102/17		BAPC.139	Fokker Dr.1 Triplane fsm
152/17		**G-BVGZ**	Fokker Dr.1 Triplane replica (German Army Air Service)
210/16		BAPC.056	Fokker E-III replica (German Army Air Service)
403/17		**G-CDXR**	Fokker Dr.1 Triplane replica (German Army Air Service)
416/15		**G-GSAL**	Fokker E-III replica (German Army Air Service)
422/15		**G-FOKR**	Fokker E-III replica (German Army Air Service)
425/17		BAPC.133	Fokker Dr.1 Triplane fsm (German Army Air Service)
425/17	1729	**G-DREI**	Fokker Dr.1 Triplane replica (German Army Air Service)
477/17		**G-FOKK**	Fokker Dr.1 Triplane replica (German Army Air Service)
480	6	BAPC.066	Messerschmitt Bf.109G fsm
556/17		**G-CFHY**	Fokker Dr.1 Triplane replica (German Army Air Service)
694		BAPC.239	Fokker D.VIII ⅝th scale model
1801/18		**G-BNPV**	Bowers Fly Baby (German Army Air Service)
1803/18		**G-BUYU**	Bowers Fly Baby (German Army Air Service)
4477	GD+EG	**G-RETA**	CASA 1131E Jungmann Series 2000
5128/18		BAPC.110	Fokker D.VIIF fsm
6357	6	BAPC.074	Messerschmitt Bf.109G fsm
7198/18		G-AANJ	LVG C.VI
10639	6 (Black)	G-USTV	Messerschmitt Bf.109G-2
15919	1	BAPC.240	Messerschmitt Bf.109G-6 fsm
191454		BAPC.271	Messerschmitt Me 163B Komet fsm
442795		BAPC.199	Fieseler Fi 103 (V-1)
D.2263		**G-WAHT***	The Vintage Aviator Albatros DVA. Replica
E33/15		**G-CHAW**	Fokker E-III replica (German Army Air Service)
E37/15		**G-CGJF**	Fokker E-III replica (German Army Air Service)
81+00		D-HZYR	MBB Bo105
99+18		**G-ONAA**	North American OV-10B Bronco (German AF)
	6G+ED	**G-BZOB**	Slepcev Storch
	BF+070	**G-CHYN**	CCF Harvard 4
	BG+KM	**G-ASTG**	Messerschmitt Bf.108 (Nord 1002)
	BU+CC	**G-BUCC**	CASA 1131E Jungmann
	CG+EV	**G-CGEV**	Heliopolis Gomhouria Mk6
	CX+HI	**G-CDJU**	CASA 1131E Jungmann
	DG+BE	**G-BHPL**	CASA 1131E Jungmann

FI+S		G-BIRW	Morane-Saulnier MS.505 Criquet
KG+GB		**G-BHSL***	CASA 1131E Jungmann
LG+01		**G-CIJV**	CASA 131 Jungmeister
NJ+C11		**G-ATBG**	Messerschmitt Bf.108 (Nord 1002)
NM+AA		**G-BZJV**	CASA 1131E Jungmann
S4+A07		**G-BWHP**	CASA 1131E Jungmann
TP+WX		**G-TPWX**	Heliopolis Gomhouria Mk6

HONG KONG

HKG-5		**G-BULL**	Scottish Aviation Bulldog
HKG-6		**G-BPCL**	Scottish Aviation Bulldog
HKG-11		**G-BYRY**	Slingsby T.67M-200 Firefly
HKG-13		**G-BXKW**	Slingsby T.67M-200 Firefly

HUNGARY

503		G-BRAM	MiG 21PF

INDIA

E-296		**G-SLYR***	Hindustan Aircraft Gnat

IRELAND

168		**EI-HFA**	de Havilland DHC-1 Chipmunk T.10
169		**EI-HFB**	de Havilland DHC-1 Chipmunk T.10
170		**EI-HFC**	de Havilland DHC-1 Chipmunk T.10

ITALY

mm51-15302	EI-51	**G-BJTP**	Piper L-18C Super Cub
mm52-2392	EI-69	**G-HELN**	Piper PA-18-95 Super Cub
mm53211	ZI-4	BAPC.079	Fiat G.46-4B
mm54-2372	EI-184	I-EIXM	Piper PA-18-95 Super Cub
mm6976	85-16	**G-CBLS***	Fiat CR42

JAPAN

5439		BAPC.084	Mitsubishi Ki 46 Dinah III
10461		BAPC.099	Yokosuka MXY-7 Ohka II
15-1585		BAPC.058	Yokosuka MXY-7 Ohka II
16336		BAPC.083	Kawasaki Ki 100-1b Army Fighter
997		BAPC.098	Yokosuka MXY-7 Ohka II

MEXICO

52		**N4238C**	Mudry CAP.10B (Air Force)

NETHERLANDS

174	K	**G-BEPV**	Fokker S.11 Instructor (Navy)
BI-005		**G-BUVN**	CASA 1131E Jungmann
F-15		**G-BIYU**	Fokker S.11 Instructor
K-123		G-EACN	BAT FK.23 Bantam
N-294		**G-KAXF**	Hawker Hunter F.6A
N-321		**G-BWGL**	Hawker Hunter T.8C
R-55 (52-2466)		**G-BLMI***	Piper L-18C Super Cub (Air Force)
R-151 (54-2441)		**G-BIYR**	Piper L-21B Super Cub
R-156		**G-ROVE**	Piper L-21B Super Cub (Air Force)
R-167		**G-LION**	Piper L-21B Super Cub (Air Force)

NEW ZEALAND

NZ3909		**G-KANZ***	Westland Wasp HAS.1

NORTH KOREA

No marks		G-BMZF	MiG-15

NORTH VIETNAM

1211		**G-MIGG***	PZL LIM-5 (Mig 17)

NORWAY

56321		G-BKPY	Saab Safir

OMAN

Misc

| 417 | | G-RSAF | BAC 167 Strikemaster Mk.82A |
| 425 | | G-SOAF | BAC 167 Strikemaster Mk.82A |

POLAND

| 1018 | | G-ISKA | WSK PZL Mielec TS-11 Iskra |

PORTUGAL

1350		G-CGAO	de Havilland DHC-1 Chipmunk
1365		G-DHPM	de Havilland DHC-1 Chipmunk
1367		G-UANO	de Havilland DHC-1 Chipmunk
1373		G-CBJG	de Havilland DHC-1 Chipmunk
1377		G-BARS	de Havilland DHC-1 Chipmunk
1747		G-BGPB	CCF Harvard 4
3303		G-CBGL	Max Holste MH.1521M Broussard

RUSSIA

(unmarked)		G-BTUB	Yakovlev Yak C-11 (Soviet AF)
00 (White)		G-OLEG	Yakovlev Yak-3
03 (Blue)		RA-01274	Yakovlev Yak-55 (DOSAAF)
03 (White)		G-CEIB	Yakovlev Yak-18 (Soviet AF)
07 (Yellow)		G-BMJY	Yakovlev Yak-18 (Soviet AF)
1 (White)		G-BZMY	Yakovlev Yak C-11 (Soviet AF)
3 (Red)		G-BAYV	SNCAN Nord 1101 Noralpha
9 (White)		G-OYAK	Yakovlev Yak-11 (Soviet AF)
10 (Red)		G-YAKE	Yakovlev Yak-52 (Soviet AF)
18		G-BTZB	Yakovlev Yak-52 (Soviet AF)
20		G-YAAK	Yakovlev Yak-50 (Soviet AF)
21 (White)		G-CDBJ	Yakovlev Yak-3 (Russian AF c/s)
(23)		G-YKSO	Yakovlev Yak-50 (Soviet AF)
26 (Grey)		G-BVXK	Yakovlev Yak-52 (DOSAAF)
27 (Red)		G-YAKX	Yakovlev Yak-52 (DOSAAF)
28 (Yellow)		G-BSSY	Polikarpov PO-2 (Soviet AF)
33 (White)		G-YAKH	Yakovlev Yak-52 (Soviet AF)
33 (Red)		G-YAKZ	Yakovlev Yak-50 (Soviet AF)
37 (Yellow)		YL-MIG	Aviatika MAI-890 (DOSAAF)
43 (Blue)		G-BWSV	Yakovlev Yak-52 (DOSAAF)
49 (Red)		G-YAKU	Yakovlev Yak-50 (Soviet AF)
50 (Grey)		G-CBRW	Yakovlev Yak-52 (DOSAAF)
51 (Red)		LY-PAG	Aero L29 Delfin
52 (Yellow)		G-BWVR*	Yakovlev Yak-52
52 (White)		G-FLSH	Yakovlev Yak-52
52 (White)		G-CCJK	Yakovlev Yak-52 (DOSAAF)
61 (Red)		G-YAKM	Yakovlev Yak-50 (Soviet AF)
66 (Red)		G-YAKN	Yakovlev Yak-52 (Soviet AF)
86		G-YAKC	Yakovlev Yak-52 (Soviet AF)
100		G-YAKI*	Yakovlev Yak-52
100 (White)		G-CGXG	Yakovlev Yak-3M (Soviet AF)
125 (Black)		G-JMGP*	Aero L39 Albatros

SAUDI ARABIA

| 1133 | | G-BESY | BAC 167 Strikemaster Mk.88A |
| 53-686 | | G-AWON | English Electric Lightning F.53 |

SINGAPORE

| 311 | | G-MXPH | BAC 167 Strikemaster Mk.80A |

SOUTH AFRICA

| 92 | | G-BYCX* | Westland Wasp |

SOUTH ARABIA (South Yemen)

| 104 | | G-PROV | Hunting Percival P.84 Jet Provost T.52A (T.4) |

SPAIN

| E3B-153 | 781-75 | G-BPTS | CASA 1131 Jungmann |
| E3B-494 | 81-47 | G-CDLC | CASA 1131 Jungmann |

| E3B-599 | 791-31 | G-CGTX | CASA 1131 Jungmann |
| | 35-23 | G-RPAX | CASA 1131 Jungmann |

SRI LANKA

| CT180 | | G-BXZB | Nanchang CJ-6A |
| (CT190) | | G-CGFS | Nanchang CJ-6A |

SWITZERLAND

A-23		G-BYIJ	CASA 1131E Jungmann
A-44		G-CIUE	CASA 1131E Jungmann
A-57		G-BECT	CASA 1131E Jungmann
A-125		G-BLKZ	Pilatus P.2
A-806		G-BTLL	Pilatus P.3
C-552		G-DORN	EKW C-3605
J-1573		G-VICI	de Havilland DH.112 Venom FB.50
J-1605		G-BLID	de Havilland DH.112 Venom FB.50
J-1790		G-BLKA	de Havilland DH.112 Venom FB.54
U-80	RV	G-BUKK	Bücker Bü.133 Jungmeister
U-95		G-BVGP	Bücker Bü.133 Jungmeister
U-99		G-AXMT*	Bücker Bü.133 Jungmeister
V-54		G-BVSD	SE.3130 Alouette II

UNITED STATES

001		G-BYPY	Ryan ST3-KR (Army)
3		BAPC.140	Curtiss R3C2 (42A) fsm
10		BAPC.464	North American P-51D Mustang fsm
14		G-ISDN	Boeing Stearman Kaydet (Army)
26		G-BAVO	Boeing Stearman Kaydet (Army Air Corps)
27	VS-932	G-BRVG	North American SNJ-7 Texan (Navy)
27		G-AGYY	Ryan PT-21 (Army Air Corps)
28		G-CKSR	Boeing Stearman Kaydet
31		G-KAYD	Boeing Stearman Kaydet
43		G-CIPE	Boeing Stearman A75N1 (USAAC)
43	SC	G-AZSC	North American AT-16 Texan (Army Air Force)
44		G-DINS	Boeing Stearman Kaydet (Army Air Corps)
72	JF	G-DHHF	North American AT-6D Harvard (Marines)
104	W	N4712V	Boeing Stearman PT-13D Kaydet (Army Air Corps)
107		N62658	Boeing Stearman Kaydet
112		G-BSWC	Boeing Stearman Kaydet (Army Air Corps)
118		G-BSDS	Boeing Stearman Kaydet (Army Air Corps)
131		N74677	Boeing Stearman Kaydet (Army Air Corps)
286		N10053	Boeing Stearman Kaydet (Navy)
309		G-IIIG	Boeing Stearman Kaydet (Army)
317		G-CIJN	Boeing Stearman Kaydet (Army Air Force)
379		G-ILLE	Boeing Stearman Kaydet (Army Air Corps)
441		G-BTFG	Boeing Stearman Kaydet (Navy)
443		N43YP	Boeing Stearman Kaydet (Navy)
560		G-HUEY*	Bell UH-1H (Army Air Corps)
624	D-39	EI-GMH	Piper L-4 (Wag-Aero Cuby) (Army Air Corps)
669		G-CCXA	Boeing Stearman A75N1 (Army Air Corps)
671	VN2S-5	G-CGPY	Boeing Stearman A75N1 (Navy)
699		G-CCXB	Boeing Stearman A75N1 (Army Air Corps)
854		G-BTBH	Ryan PT-22 (Army Air Corps)
897	E	G-BJEV	Aeronca Chief (Navy)

Serial	Code	Reg	Type
1102	102	G-AZLE	Boeing Stearman Kaydet (Navy)
1164		G-BKGL	Beech C-45 (Army)
1270		G-CDJB*	Vans RV4
2610	408	G-FRDM	Boeing Stearman Kaydet
3397	174	G-OBEE	Boeing Stearman A75N-1 (Navy)
3403	180	N75TQ	Boeing Stearman (N2S-3) (Navy)
3583	44-D	G-FINT	Piper L-4B
3681		G-AXGP	Piper L-4J (USAAF)
3789	466	G-PTBA	Boeing Stearman A75N1 (USAAC)
3914		G-BHZU	Piper J-3C-65 Cub (USAAF)
4406	12	G-ONAF	Naval Aircraft Factory N3N-3 (Navy)
4826	582	G-CJIN	Boeing Stearman A75N1 (Navy)
6136	205	G-BRUJ	Boeing Stearman Kaydet (Navy)
8084		G-KAMY	North American AT.6D (Army Air Force) – See Editorial
8242	FU-242	N196B	North American F-86A Sabre (Air Force)
01532		BAPC.336	Northrop F-5E Tiger II fsm
02538		N33870	Fairchild PT-19 Cornell (Army Air Corps)
07159		N3458V	Cessna 195 (Air Force)
07539	143	N63590	Boeing Stearman Kaydet (Navy)
14863		G-BGOR	North American AT-6D Texan (Army Air Force)
15372		N123SA	Piper L4 (US Army)
16037		G-BSFD	Piper J-3C-65 Cub (Army)
18263	822	N38940	Boeing Stearman Kaydet (Army Air Corps)
24550	GP	G-PDOG	Cessna O-1E Bird Dog (Air Force)
24582		G-VDOG	Cessna L-1E Bird Dog (Army)
26359	32	G-BNXM	Piper L-21B (Navy)
28521	TA-521	G-TVIJ	North American T-6J Harvard (Air Force)
28562	TA-562	G-BSBG	North American Harvard IV
31145	G-26	G-BBLH	Piper L-4B (Army)
31952		G-BRPR	Aeronca L-3C Grasshopper (Army)
34037		N9115Z	North American B-25J Mitchell
34064	BU	N7614C	North American B-25J Mitchell (Marines)
36922	WD-Y	G-CMPC	Titan T-51 Mustang (Army Air Force)
43517	227	G-NZSS	Boeing Stearman Kaydet (Army Air Corps)
46214	X-3	CF-KCG	Grumman TBM-3E Avenger (Navy)
51970	V	G-TXAN	North American Harvard III (Navy)
55771	427	N68427	Boeing Stearman Kaydet (Navy)
56498		N44914	Douglas C-54D Skymaster
60344		N4956C	Ryan Navion (Army)
74013		G-BNRR*	Cessna 172
80105	19	G-CCBN	Replica SE5A (US Air Service)
82127		G-APNJ	Cessna U-3A
85061	7F 061	G-CHIA	North American Harvard III (Navy)
86690	F-2	G-KINL*	Grumman FM2 Wildcat (Navy)
111836	JZ-6	G-TSIX	North American AT-6C Texan (Navy)
111989		N33600	Cessna L-19A Bird Dog (Army)
115042	TA-042	G-BGHU	North American T-6G Texan (Air Force)
115227		G-BKRA	North American T-6G Texan (Navy)
115373	A-373	G-AYPM	Piper L-21A Super Cub (Army)
115684	849	G-BKVM	Piper L-21A Super Cub (Army)
117415	TR-415	G-BYOY	Lockheed T33 Shooting Star
121714	201B	G-RUMM	Grumman F8F-2P Bearcat (Navy)
124485	DF-A	G-BEDF	Boeing B-17G Flying Fortress (Army Air Force)
126922	H 503	G-RADR	Douglas AD-4NA Skyraider (Navy)
217786	25	CF-EQS	Boeing Stearman Kaydet (Army Air Force)
226413	ZU-N	N47DD	Republic P-47D Thunderbolt (Army Air Force)
236657	D-72	G-BGSJ	Piper L-4A-PI (Army Air Corps)
238133	O	F-BDRS	Boeing B-17G Flying Fortress (Army Air Force)
238410	A-44	G-BHPK	Piper L-4A (Army Air Corps)
241079		BAPC.370	Waco CG-4A Hadrian replica
243809		BAPC.185	Waco CG-4A Hadrian composite
252983		N66630	Schweizer TG-3A (Army Air Corps)
285068		G-KAMY	North American AT.6D (Army Air Force) – Official exemption is to wear 8084
298177	R-8	N6438C	Stinson L-5C Sentinel
313048		G-TDJN	North American AT-6D Harvard III
314887		G-AJPI	Fairchild UC-61 Forwarder (Army Air Force)
315509	W7-S	G-BHUB	Douglas C-47A Dakota (Army Air Force)
319764		BAPC.157	Waco CG-4A Hadrian composite
329282		N46779	Piper J-3C-65 Cub (Army Air Force)
329405	A-23	G-BCOB	Piper L-4H (Army Air Corps)
329417		G-BDHK	Piper L-4A (Army Air Corps)
329471	F-44	G-BGXA	Piper L-4H (Army Air Corps)
329601	D-44	G-AXHR	Piper L-4H (Army Air Corps)
329707	S-44	G-BFBY	Piper L-4H (Army Air Force)
329854	R-44	G-BMKC	Piper L-4H (Army Air Corps)
329934	B-72	G-BCPH	Piper L-4H (Army Air Corps)
330238	A-24	G-LIVH	Piper L-4H (Army Air Corps)
330244	C-46	G-CGIY	Piper J-3C-65 Cub (Army Air Corps)
330314		G-BAET	Piper L-4H (Army Air Corps)
330372		G-AISX	Piper L-4H (Army Air Force)
330426	K/53	N61787	Piper J-3C-65 Cub
330485	C-44	G-AJES	Piper L-4H (Army Air Corps)
379994	J-52	G-BPUR	Piper J-3L-65 Cub
413317	VF-B	N51RT	North American P-51D Mustang (Army Air Corps)
413573	B6-V	N6526D	North American P-51D Mustang (Army Air Corps)
413926	E2-S	G-CGOI	Stewart S51 Mustang (Army Air Force)
414419	LH-F	G-MSTG	North American P-51D Mustang (Army Air Force)
414673	LH-I	G-BDWM	Bonsall DB-1 Mustang (Army Air Force)
414907	CY-S	G-DHYS	Titan T-51 Mustang
433915		G-PBYA	Consolidated PBY-5A Catalina (Army Air Force)
436021		G-BWEZ	Piper L-4 (Army Air Corps)
441968	VF-E	G-FION	Titan T51 Mustang
454467	J-44	G-BILI	Piper L-4J (Army Air Corps)
454537	J-04	G-BFDL	Piper L-4J (Army Air Corps)
454630	LI-7	G-BDOL	Piper L-4J (Army Air Corps)
461748	Y	G-BHDK	Boeing B-29A Superfortress (Air Force)
463209	WZ-S	BAPC.255	North American P-51D Mustang fsm (Army Air Corps)
464005	E9-Z	N51CK	North American P-51D Mustang
472216	HO-M	G-BIXL	North American P-51D Mustang (Army Air Corps)
472218	WZ-I	G-MUZY	Titan T-51 Mustang (Army Air Corps)
474008	VF-R	G-PSIR	Jurca M.77 Gnatsum (Army Air Corps)
479651		EI-CFO	Piper L-4H (Army Air Corps)
479712	8-R	G-AHIP	Piper L-4H (Army Air Corps)
479744	49-M	G-BGPD	Piper L-4H (Army Air Corps)
479766	63-D	G-BKHG	Piper L-4H (Army Air Corps)
479897	JD	G-BOXJ	Piper L-4H (Army Air Corps)

Misc

479878	MF-D	**G-BEUI**	Piper L-4H (Army Air Corps)
480015	M-44	**G-AKIB**	Piper L-4H (Army Air Corps)
480133	B-44	**G-BDCD**	Piper L-4J (Army Air Corps)
480173	H-57	**G-RRSR**	Piper L-4J (Army Air Corps)
480321	H-44	**G-FRAN**	Piper L-4J (Army Air Corps)
480361	H-47	**EI-BIO**	Piper L-4J (Army Air Corps)
480480	E-44	**G-BECN**	Piper L-4J (Army Air Corps)
480636	A-58	**G-AXHP**	Piper L-4J (Army Air Corps)
480723	E5-J	**G-BFZB**	Piper L-4J (Air Force)
480752	E-39	**G-BCXJ**	Piper L-4J (Army Air Corps)
480762		**EI-BBV**	Piper L-4J (Army Air Corps)
481273		**G-CJWE**	North American T-6 Harvard
493209	ANG	**G-DDMV**	North American T-6G Texan (California Air Nat.Guard)
517692	LT-692	**G-TROY**	North American T-28A Trojan
549192	F4-J	**G-THUN**	Republic P47D Thunderbolt
779465		**N5315V**	Hiller UH12 (Army)
2100882	P-3X	**N473DC**	Douglas C-47A Dakota III (Air Force)
2100884	L4	**N147DC**	Douglas C-47A-75-DL Dakota (Air Force)
2106638	E9-R	**G-CIFD**	Titan T51 Mustang (Army Air Force)
0-16957		**N5308G**	Cessna L-19A Bird Dog
18-2001		**G-BIZV**	Piper L-18C Super Cub (Army)
146-11083	5	**G-BNAI**	SPAD replica (Wolf W.II) (Army Air Corps)
3-1923		**G-BRHP**	Aeronca L-3C-AE (Army Air Corps)
39-160	160/10AB	**G-CIIO**	Curtiss P40 Warhawk (Army Air Corps)
41-33275	CE	**G-BICE**	North American AT-6C Texan (Army Air Corps)
42-5772		**G-BSXT**	Piper J-5A (Army Air Corps)
42-38384		**G-BHVV**	Piper J-3C-65 Cub (Marines)
42-17553	716	**N1731B**	Boeing A75N-1 Stearman
42-46703		**N69745**	Stinson V77 (Royal Navy)
42-78044		**G-BRXL**	Aeronca L-3F (Army)
42-84555	EP-H	**G-ELMH**	North American AT-6D Harvard (Army Air Corps)
43-35943		**G-BKRN***	Beech D.18S
44-14251	WZ-I	**G-TFSI**	North American TP-51 Mustang (Army Air Corps)
44-42914		**N31356**	Douglas DC-4-1009 (Air Force)

44-63684		**G-CKVJ**	Titan T51 Mustang
44-79609	S-44	**G-BHXY**	Piper L-4H (Army Air Force)
44-79649	69-K	**G-AIIH**	Piper L-4H (Marine Corps)
44-79790	J-44	**G-BJAY**	Piper L-4H
44-83868	N	**N5237V**	Boeing B-17G Flying Fortress (Army Air Force)
47-797	A-797	**G-BFAF**	Aeronca L-16A (Army)
5-624KT		**G-BPKT**	Piper J/5A Cub Cruiser (Navy – Airship Squadron 32)
51-15555		**G-OSPS**	Piper L-18C Super Cub (Army)
51-15319	A-319	**G-FUZZ**	Piper L-18C Super Cub (Army)
54-2445	A-445	**G-OTAN**	Piper L-21B Super Cub (Army)
54-2447		**G-SCUB**	Piper L-21B Super Cub (Army)
66-374	EO	**G-BAGT**	Helio Super Courier (Air Force)
68-17172		**N239MY**	Hughes OH-6
69-16011		**G-OHGA**	Hughes OH-6A (Army)
72-21509	129	**G-UHIH**	Bell UH-1H Iroquois (Army)
75-4826	27	**G-CJYK**	Boeing Stearman A75N-1
108-1601	H	**G-CFGE**	Stinson 108-1 (USAAF)
AS.22.296		**G-BLXT**	Eberhard SE5 Rep (US Army Air Service)
C1661-TA		**EI-AEI**	Aeronca 65TAC Defender (Air Force)
	A3-3	**G-SIJJ**	North American P-51D Mustang
	CY G	**G-TSIM**	Titan T-51 Mustang (Army Air Force)
	E-44	**G-ECMK***	Piper PA18-150
	FG 289	**N99153**	North American T-28C Trojan
	PA50	**G-CIXJ**	Curtiss P-36C (USAAC)
	X-17	**G-CGZP**	Curtiss P-40F Kittyhawk (Air Force)

YUGOSLAVIA

30140	140	**G-RADA***	Soko P-2 Kraguj
(30146)	146	**G-BSXD**	Soko P-2 Kraguj
30149	149	**G-SOKO**	Soko P-2 Kraguj

UNATTRIBUTED

5	BAPC.141	Macchi M.39 fsm
2292	BAPC.138	Hansa-Brandenburg W.29 fsm
LHS-1	BAPC.147	Bensen B.7 Gyroglider
PCL-132	BAPC.440	Lovegrove Rota-Glida GyroGlider
PCL-129	BAPC.306	Lovegrove Discord Autogyro

Misc

PART 3 – 'B CONDITIONS' MARKINGS

Air Navigation Order (ANO2016) promulgates the specific circumstances under which aerospace manufacturers can pursue the conduct of aircraft trials without the need for valid Certificates of Airworthiness. ANO2016 establishes both 'A' and 'B' conditions but we are only concerned here with the latter requirements which stipulate the use of identity marks as approved by the CAA for the purposes of 'B Conditions' flight.

In brief, under 'B Conditions' an aircraft must fly only for the purpose of:

(a) experimenting with or testing the aircraft (including any engines installed thereon) or any equipment installed or carried in the aircraft;
(b) enabling it to qualify for the issue of a certificate of airworthiness or the validation thereof or the approval of a modification of the aircraft or the issue of apermit to fly;
(c) demonstrating and displaying the aircraft, any engines installed thereon or any equipment installed or carried in the aircraft with a view to the sale thereofor of other similar aircraft, engines or equipment;
(d) demonstrating and displaying the aircraft to employees of the operator;
(e) the giving of flying training to or the testing of flight crew employed by the operator or the training or testing of other persons employed by the operator; or
(f) proceeding to or from a place at which any experiment, inspection, repair, modification, maintenance, approval, test or weighing of the aircraft, the installation of equipment in the aircraft, demonstration, display or training is to take place or at which installation of furnishings in, or the painting of, the aircraft is to be undertaken.
(g) proceeding to or from a place at which the installation of furnishings in, or the painting of the aircraft is to be undertaken.

The flight must be operated by a person approved by the CAA for the purposes of these Conditions and subject to any additional conditions which may be specified in such an approval. If not registered in the United Kingdom the aircraft must be marked in a manner approved by the CAA for the purposes of these Conditions. The aircraft must carry such flight crew as may be necessary to ensure the safety of the aircraft. No person can act as pilot in command of the aircraft except a person approved for the purpose by the CAA.

Prompted by the SBAC a radically new system was introduced in 1948. In essence, this remains in existence today. Whilst deemed 'current' many Companies included have long since merged or ceased to trade and so, by coincidence, the table below encscapsulates in miniature the absorbing changes within the UK aircraft industry which have occurred during the period 1948 to date. The same can also be said for the original series covering the period from 1929 to 1948.

CURRENT SERIES

Prefix	Company	Period	Issued	Remarks
G-1-	Sir W G Armstrong-Whitworth Aircraft Ltd	1948-1967	01.01.48	Cancelled
G-1-	Rolls-Royce Ltd (Bristol Engines Division)	1949-19xx	09.04.69	Cancelled
G-2-	Blackburn Aircraft Ltd	1949-1967	01.01.48	Cancelled
G-3-	Boulton Paul Aircraft Ltd	1948-1973	01.01.48	Cancelled 31.12.73
G-03	BAE Systems (Operating) Ltd	19xx-		Cancelled
G-4-	Portsmouth Aviation Ltd	1948-1949	01.01.48	Cancelled 23.05.49
G-4-	Miles Aviation and Transport (R & D) Ltd	1969-19xx	01.05.69	Cancelled
G-04	BAe Systems (Operating) Ltd	19xx-		Cancelledt
G-5-	The de Havilland Aircraft Co Ltd *(became Raytheon Services Ltd)*	1948-	01.01.48	Cancelled
G-6-	Fairey Aviation Ltd	1948-1969	01.01.48	Cancelled 17.01.69
G-7-	Gloster Aircraft Ltd	1948-1961	01.01.48	Cancelled
G-7-	Slingsby Sailplanes Ltd *(became Slingsby Aviation Ltd)*	1971-	21.10.71	Cancelled
G-8-	Handley Page Ltd	1948-1970	01.01.48	Cancelled 28.02.70
G-08	BAE Systems (Operating) Ltd	19xx-		Current
G-9-	Hawker Aircraft Ltd *(became British Aerospace Defence Ltd)*	1948-1996	10.01.48	Cancelled
G-10-	Reid and Sigrist Ltd	1948-1953	01.01.48	Cancelled 01.04.53
G-11-	A.V.Roe and Co. Ltd *(became BAe Systems (Operations) Ltd)*	1948-	01.01.48	Cancelled
G-12-	Saunders-Roe Ltd	1948-1967	01.01.48	Cancelled 09.06.67
G-13-	Not allocated			
G-14-	Short Brothers and Harland Ltd *(became Short Brothers plc)*	1948-	01.01.48	Cancelled
G-15-	Vickers Armstrong Ltd, Supermarine Division	1948-1968	01.01.48	Cancelled 17.10.68
G-16-	Vickers Armstrong Ltd, Weybridge Division *(became British Aerospace Airbus Ltd)*	1948-1999	01.01.48	Cancelled
G-17-	Westland Aircraft Ltd *(became AgustaWestland Helicopters)*	1948-	01.01.48	Current
G-18-	The Bristol Aeroplane Co.Ltd	1948-1975	01.01.48	Cancelled 31.07.75
G-19-	Heston Aircraft Ltd	1948-1960	01.01.48	Cancelled 04.02.60
G-20-	General Aircraft Ltd	1948-1949	01.01.48	Cancelled 23.05.49
G-21-	Miles Aircraft Ltd (H P Reading Ltd)	1948-1963	01.01.48	Cancelled 11.02.63
G-22-	de Havilland Aircraft Co Ltd, Airspeed Division	1948-1952	01.01.48	Cancelled 23.05.52
G-23-	Percival Aircraft Ltd	1948-1966	01.01.48	Cancelled 31.05.66
G-24-	Cunliffe-Owen Aircraft Ltd	1948-1949	01.01.48	Cancelled 23.05.49
G-25-	Auster Aircraft Ltd	1948-1962	01.01.48	Cancelled
G-26-	Slingsby Sailplanes Ltd	1948-1949	01.01.48	Cancelled 19.12.49
G-27-	English Electric Co Ltd Aircraft Division *(became British Aerospace Military Aircraft Division Ltd)*	1948-1991	01.01.48	Cancelled

G-28-	British European Airways Corporation (Helicopters) (became Brintel Helicopters Ltd)	1948-	01.01.48	Cancelled
G-29-	D Napier and Son Ltd	1948-1962	01.01.48	Cancelled 09.11.62
G-30-	Pest Control Ltd	1952-1957	01.01.48	Cancelled 04.03.57
G-31-	Scottish Aviation Ltd (became BAe Systems (Operations) Ltd)	1948-	01.01.48	Cancelled
G-32-	Cierva Autogiro Co. Ltd	1948-1951	01.01.48	Cancelled 09.03.51
G-33-	Flight Refuelling Ltd	Not known		
G-34-	Chrislea Aircraft Ltd	1948-1952	01.01.48	Cancelled
G-35-	F.G.Miles Ltd (became Beagle Aircraft Ltd)	1951-1970	09.08.54	Cancelled 29.06.70
G-36-	College of Aeronautics (became Cranfield University)	1954-	09.08.54	Current
G-37-	Rolls-Royce Ltd	1954-1971	09.08.54	Cancelled 17.09.71
G-38-	de Havilland Propellers Ltd (became Hawker Siddeley Dynamics)	1954-1975	09.08.54	Cancelled 22.10.75
G-39-	Folland Aircraft Ltd	1954-1965	09.08.54	Cancelled.02.04.65
G-40-	Wiltshire School of Flying Ltd	Not known		Not taken up
G-41-	Aviation Traders (Engineering) Ltd	1956-1976	03.10.56	Cancelled 27.02.76
G-42-	Armstrong Siddeley Motors Ltd	1956-1959	13.11.56	Cancelled 28.08.59
G-43-	Edgar Percival Aircraft Ltd	1956-1959	21.11.56	Cancelled 26.06.59
G-44-	Agricultural Aviation Ltd	1959-1959	17.04.59	Cancelled 14.12.59
G-45-	Bristol Siddeley Engines Ltd	1959-1969	27.05.59	Cancelled 08.04.69
G-46-	Saunders-Roe Ltd, Helicopter Division	1959-1962	15.06.59	Cancelled 03.05.62
G-47-	Lancashire Aircraft Co. Ltd	1960-19xx	08.02.60	Cancelled
G-48-	Westland Aircraft Ltd, Bristol Division	1960-1969	07.07.60	Cancelled 28.02.69
G-49-	F.G.Miles Engineering Ltd	1965-1969	23.07.65	Cancelled c.1969
G-50-	Alvis Ltd	1967-1975	16.02.67	Cancelled
G-51-	Britten-Norman Ltd (became BN Group Ltd)	1967-	20.09.67	Current
G-52-	Marshall of Cambridge (Engineering) Ltd (became Marshall Aerospace & Defence Group)	1968-	18.01.68	Current
G-53-	Norman Aeroplane Co. Ltd	1977-19xx	23.05.77	Cancelled
G-54-	Cameron Balloons Ltd	197x-	Not known	Cancelled
G-55-	W.Vinten Ltd	19xx-19xx	Not known	Cancelled
G-56-	Edgley Aircraft Ltd	19xx-19xx	Not known	Cancelled
G-57-	Airship Industries (UK) Ltd	19xx-19xx	Not known	Cancelled
G-58-	ARV Aviation (became Island Aircraft)	19xx-19xx	Not known	Cancelled
G-59-	Mainair Sports Ltd	19xx	07.05	Cancelle
G-60-	FR Aviation Ltd	19xx-	Not known	Cancelled)
G-61-	Aviation Enterprises Ltd	19xx-	Not known	Cancelled
G-62-	Curtiss and Green Ltd	19xx-19xx	Not known	Cancelled
G-63-	Thunder and Colt Balloons Ltd	1994-19xx	c.1994	Cancelled
G-64-	Brooklands Aerospace Group plc	19xx-19xx	Not known	Cancelled
G-65-	Solar Wings Aviation Ltd	19xx-1995	Not known	Cancelled
G-66-	Aerial Arts Ltd	19xx-19xx	Not known	Cancelled
G-67-	Atlantic Aerengineering Ltd (became Tenencia Limited)	19xx	Not known	Current
G-68-	Medway Microlights Ltd (became Mr G Draper)	19xx	Not known	Current
G-69-	Cyclone Airsports Ltd (formerly Aerial Arts)	19xx	07.05	Cancelled
G-70-	FLS Aerospace (Lovaux) Ltd	19xx	1997	Cancelled
G-71-	FR Aviation Ltd	19xx	Not known	Current
G-72-	Lindstrand Balloons Ltd	19xx	Not known	Cancelled
G-73-	Aviation (Scotland) Ltd	19xx	1995	Cancelled
G-74-	Fleaplanes UK Ltd	19xx	2001	Cancelled
G-75-	Chichester Miles Consultants Ltd	19xx	Not known	Cancelled
G-76-	Police Aviation Services Ltd	19xx	Not known	Current
G-77-	Thruster Air Services Ltd	19xx	Not known	Current
G-78-	Bristow Helicopters Ltd	19xx	Not known	Current
G-79-	McAlpine Helicopters Ltd (became Airbus Helicopters)	19xx	Not known	Current
G-80-	British Microlight Aircraft Association	19xx	Not known	Current
G-81-	Cooper Aerial Services Ltd	19xx	Not known	Cancelled
G-82-	European Helicopters Ltd	19xx	1999	Cancelled
G-83-	Mann Aviation Group (Engineering) Ltd	19xx	Not known	Cancelled
G-84-	Intora-Firebird plc	19xx	Not known	Cancelled
G-85-	CFM Aircraft Ltd	19xx	2004	Cancelled
G-86-	Advanced Technologies Group Ltd	19xx	Not known	Cancelled
G-87-	CHC Scotia Ltd	19xx	Not known	Cancelled
G-88-	Air Hanson Engineering	19xx	Not known	Cancelled
G-89-	Cosmik Aviation Ltd	19xx	Not known	Current
G-90-	Not known			
G-91-	Bella Aviation	2004-2005		Cancelled
G-92-	Not known			
G-93-	P&M Aviation Ltd	2005		Cancelled
G-94-	Rotorsport UK Ltd	2006		Cancelled

ORIGINAL SERIES

Prefix	Company	Period	Issued	Remarks
A	The Sir W G Armstrong Whitworth Aircraft Ltd	1929-1948	23.12.29	
B	Blackburn Aeroplane and Motor Co.Ltd	1929-1948	23.12.29	
C	Boulton and Paul Ltd	1929-1948	23.12.29	
D	Bristol Aeroplane Co.	Not taken up		
D	Cunliffe Owen Aircraft Ltd	Not taken up		
D	Portmouth Aviation Ltd	1947-1948	1947	
E	de Havilland Aircraft Co Ltd	1929-1948	23.12.29	
F	The Fairey Aviation Co Ltd	1929-1948	23.12.29	
G	Gloster Aircraft Ltd	1929-1948	23.12.29	
H	Handley Page Ltd	1929-1948	23.12.29	
I	H G Hawker Engineering Co Ltd	1929-1948	23.12.29	
J	George Parnall and Co *(became Parnall Aircraft Ltd)*	1929-1946	23.12.29	Cancelled 1946
J	Reid and Sigrist Ltd	1947-1948	1947	
K	A V Roe and Co Ltd	1929-1948	23.12.29	
L	Saunders-Roe Ltd	1929-1948	23.12.29	
M	Short Bros (Rochester & Bedford) Ltd	1929-1948	23.12.29	
N	Supermarine Aviation Works (Vickers) Ltd	1929-1948	23.12.29	
O	Vickers (Aviation) Ltd	1929-1948	23.12.29	
P	Westland Aircraft Works	1929-1948	23.12.29	
R	The Bristol Aeroplane Co.Ltd	1929-1948	23.12.29	
S	Spartan Aircraft Ltd	1930-1936	30.08.30	Cancelled 29.02.36
S	Heston Aircraft Ltd	1936-1948	15.05.36	
S	Comper Aircraft Co. Ltd	Not taken up		
T	General Aircraft Ltd	1933-1948	08.05.33	
U	Phillips & Powis Aircraft Ltd	1934-1948	05.02.34	
V	Airspeed (1934) Ltd	1934-1948	27.06.34	
W	G & J Weir Ltd	1933-1948	08.05.33	Cancelled 1946
X	Percival Aircraft Ltd	1936-1948	21.01.36	
Y	The British Aircraft Manufacturing Co.Ltd	1936-1938	1936	Cancelled 1938
Y	Cunliffe Owen Aircraft Ltd	1940-1948	28.10.40	
Z	Taylorcraft Aeroplanes (England) Ltd	1946-1948	12.01.46	
AA	Believed not allocated			
AB	Slingsby Sailplanes Ltd	1947-1948	1947	

PART 4 & PART 5 Notes:

(a)	Details at SECTION 3 and SECTION 9
(b)	Details at SECTION 9
(c)	Details at SECTION 1
(d)	Details at SECTION 8

Misc

PART 4 – FICTITIOUS MARKINGS

Registration	Type	Remarks	Location
'K-158'	Austin Whippet replica	See BAPC.207 – (a)	Doncaster
'EI-ABH'	Mignet HM.14 Pou-du-Ciel replica	(b)	Meath, RoI
'EVRAMP'	Boeing 737-53A	See N375EL – (d)	Bournemouth
'F-OCMF'	Sud SA.321F Super Frelon	See F-BTRP – (b)	Weston-super-Mare
'G-EASQ'	Bristol 30/46 Babe III replica	See BAPC.087 – (a)	Filton
'G-EBED'	Vickers 60 Viking IV replica	See BAPC.114 – (a)	Brooklands
'G-EBUG'	Avro 594 Avian II	See G-AUFZ – (b)	Blaine, Minnesota
'G-EBVO'	Blackburn Lincock fsm	See BAPC.287 – (a)	Hull
'G-EGCK'	Mignet HM.14 Pou-du-Ciel replica	See BAPC.286 – (a)	Caernarfon
'G-AAAH'	de Havilland DH.60G Gipsy Moth replica	See BAPC.270 – (a)	Tinwald Downs
'G-AAAH'	de Havilland DH.60G Gipsy Moth replica	See BAPC.168 – (a)	Hawkinge
'G-AAAH'	de Havilland DH.60G Gipsy Moth replica	See BAPC.470 – (a)	Hull – Paragon Station
'G-AACA'	Avro 504K replica	See BAPC.177 – (a)	Brooklands
'G-ABCF'	Avro 616 Avian IVA replica	See BAPC.498 – (a)	New Zealand
'G-ABUL'	de Havilland DH.82A Tiger Moth	See G-AOXG – (c)	RNAS Yeovilton
'G-ACSS'	de Havilland DH.88 Comet replica	See BAPC.216 – (a)	Kings Langley
'G-ACSS'	de Havilland DH.88 Comet replica	(b)	Mount Waverley, Victoria
'G-ACSS'	de Havilland DH.88 Comet ⅞th scale model	See BAPC.257 – (a)	Sywell
'G-ADGV'	de Havilland DH.82A Tiger Moth	See G-AMLF – (c)	Santa Paula, California
'G-ADRG'	Mignet HM.14 Pou-du-Ciel replica	See BAPC.077 – (a)	Not known
'G-ADRX'	Mignet HM.14 Pou-du-Ciel replica	See BAPC.231 – (a)	Crosby On Eden
'G-ADRY'	Mignet HM.14 Pou-du-Ciel replica	See BAPC.029 – (a)	Brooklands
'G-ADRZ'	Mignet HM.14 Pou-du-Ciel replica	See BAPC.481 – (a)	Masham
'G-ADVU'	Mignet HM.14 Pou-du-Ciel replica	See BAPC.211 – (a)	Usworth
'G-ADYV'	Mignet HM.14 Pou-du-Ciel replica	See BAPC.243 – (a)	Backbarrow, Ulverston
'G-ADZW'	Mignet HM.14 Pou-du-Ciel replica	See BAPC.253 – (a)	Southampton
'G-AEFG'	Mignet HM.14 Pou-du-Ciel replica	See BAPC.075 – (a)	Yorkshire
'G-AEJZ'	Mignet HM.14 Pou-du-Ciel replica	See BAPC.120 – (a)	Doncaster
'G-AEKR'	Mignet HM.14 Pou-du-Ciel replica	See BAPC.121 – (a)	Doncaster
'G-AEOF'	Mignet HM.14 Pou-du-Ciel replica	See BAPC.022 – (a)	Lelystad
'G-AEXF'	Percival E.2H Mew Gull replica	See BAPC.366 – (a)	Hendon
'G-AEXF'	Percival E.2H Mew Gull replica	See BAPC.367 – (a)	Tattershall Thorpe
'G-AFAP'	CASA 352L	(b)	RAF Cosford
'G-AFFI'	Mignet HM.14 Pou-du-Ciel replica	See BAPC.076 – (a)	Elvington
'G-AFUG'	Luton LA.4 Minor	See BAPC.097 – (a)	Usworth
'G-AGIH'	Lockheed 18-56 Lodestar	See G-BMEW – (c)	Gardemon, Norway
'G-AJCL'	de Havilland DH.89 Dragon Rapide replica	See BAPC.280 – (a)	Liverpool
'G-AJOV'	Westland WS.51 Dragonfly HR.3	(b)	RAF Cosford
'G-AJOZ'	Fairchild 24W-41A Argus 1	(b)	Elvington
'G-AJPR'	de Havilland DH.104 Dove 6	See G-ARDE – (c)	Sharjah, UAE
'G-ALVD'	de Havilland DH.104 Dove 2B	See G-ALCU – (c)	Coventry
'G-AMZZ'	Douglas C-47A-DK Dakota	See N688EA – (b)	Sharjah, UAE
'G-ANNN'	de Havilland DH.82A Tiger Moth composite	See BAPC.409 – (a)	Tattershall Thorpe
'G-AOXL'	de Havilland DH.114 Heron 2D	See G-ANUO – (c)	Croydon
'G-AUDK'	Bristol 86A Tourer replica	See BAPC.507 – (a)	Perth, Australia
'G-AXEH'	Scottish Aerospace Bulldog	See G-CCOA – (c)	Sandown
'G-AXNZ'	Pitts S-2A Special	See BAPC.134 – (a)	Istanbul
'G-BGEI'	Oldfield Baby Lakes	See G-BGLS – (c)	Kettering
'G-CAEB'	Vickers Type 60 Viking IV ½ Scale replica	See BAPC.508 – (a)	Alberta, Canada
'G-CDBS'	MBB Bö.105D	See G-BCXO – (c)	Land's End
'G-DHEA'	HS 125 Series 3B/RA	See G-OHEA – (c)	Cranfield
'G-FIRE'	Piper PA-28-161 Warrior II	See G-BYKR – (c) [see also G-FIRE (b) Palm Springs, CA]	Oxford
'G-MAZY'	de Havilland DH.82A Tiger Moth	'Maisie', Composite, mostly ex-G-AMBB [T6801]	Newark
'G-OBWB'	Embraer EMB.110P2 Bandeirante	See G-OBPL – (c)	Abridge
'G-OPAS'	Agusta A109A-II	See D-HCKV – (d)	Gloucestershire
'G-OTAA'	Robin HR.200-120B Club	See G-MFLC – (c)	Leeds-Bradford Int'l
'G-RAFM'	Robinson R22 Beta	See G-OTHL – (c)	Hendon
'K-HALL'	Schweizer 269D (Schweizer 333)	See G-TAMA – (c)	Keltham
'N1GM'	Taylor JT1 Monoplane	See N52GM – (d)	Sywell
'N64EA'	Agusta A109A II	See G-CCUK – (c)	Windsor
'N247CK'	Piper PA-31 Navajo C	See G-BLFZ – (c)	White Waltham
'N247CK'	Bombardier CL-600-1A11 Challenger 600S	See G-NREG – (c)	White Waltham
'VH-FDT'	de Havilland DHA.3 Drover 2	(d)	MoD St Athan
'GO-CSE'	Gulfstream AA-5B Tiger	(b)	Bournemouth

PART 5 – NO EXTERNAL MARKINGS

These are listed by Type to ease identification.

Registration	Type	Comments		Registration	Type	Comments
G-EROE	Avro 504K Rep	(c)		G-CJEN	Fergusson 1911	(c)
G-AANI	Blackburn Monoplane	(c)		G-BAAF	Manning-Flanders MF.1	(c)
G-AANG	Bleriot XI	(c)		G-CFTF	Roe Triplane Replica	(c)
G-ASPP	Bristol Boxkite	(c)		G-BFIP	Wallbro Monoplane	(c)
G-AANH	Deperdussin Monoplane	(c)		G-BTUB	Yakolev Yak 18	(c)
G-EBNV	English Electric Wren	(c)				

NOTES

NOTES

NOTES

NOTES

NOTES

NOTES

NOTES

NOTES

NOTES